HANDLING THE DWI CASE IN NEW YORK

2016-2017 EDITION
Issued in October 2016

By

PETER GERSTENZANG, ESQ.

ERIC H. SILLS, ESQ.

THOMSON REUTERS®

For Customer Assistance Call 1-800-328-4880

Mat #41742304

ISBN # 978-0-314-84050-9

INTRODUCTION TO THE 2016-2017 EDITION

Handling the DWI Case in New York is a practical resource for prosecutors, defense attorneys, judges, and law enforcement officers. Updated annually, it provides guidance through evolving laws by analyzing the latest DWI legislation and groundbreaking cases. It discusses important legal principles relevant to local criminal court practice and includes practice-oriented insights, effective negotiation tactics and strategies, in-depth explanations, and extensive trial preparation materials.

New features and recent developments in the 2016-2017 Edition include:

- New § 1:7, When can a police officer stop a person suspected of being the victim of a crime?
- New § 2:15, Admissibility of statement of unavailable witness who claimed to have been the operator of the vehicle
- New § 2:16, Sufficiency of evidence of operation before Grand Jury
- New § 2:17, Effect of witness' inability to identify defendant at trial
- New § 6:20, Permissibility of playing video of field sobriety tests where officer who administered tests is unavailable
- New § 11:98, DWI conviction dismissed/reduced on appeal due to insufficient evidence
- New § 12:29, Fetus not "person" for purposes of manslaughter charge
- A completely rewritten Chapter 27, *Miranda* Warnings
- New § 41:30, VTL § 1194(2)(f) claim is waived by guilty plea
- New § 42:21, Inability of breath test operator to identify defendant as person tested
- New § 44:20, Prosecutor's improper comments regarding defendant's medical history results in reversal
- New § 55:29, Court of Appeals to decide the lawfulness of the new regulations

RELATED PRODUCTS

WEST'S McKINNEY'S FORMS

Civil Practice Law and Rules

Uniform Commercial Code

Business Corporation Law

Matrimonial and Family Law

Real Property Practice

Estates and Surrogate Practice

Criminal Procedure Law

Not-For-Profit Corporation Law

Tax Practice and Procedure

Local Government Forms

Selected Consolidated Law Forms

McKinney's Consolidated Laws of New York Annotated

West's New York Legal Update

New York Digest

New York Law Finder

Thomson Reuters® thanks you for subscribing to this product. Should you have any questions regarding this product please contact Customer Service at 1-800-328-4880 or by fax at 1-800-340-9378. If you would like to inquire about related publications or place an order, please contact us at 1-800-344-5009.

 THOMSON REUTERS®   Thomson Reuters
610 Opperman Drive
Eagan, MN 55123

legalsolutions.thomsonreuters.com

WEST'S NEW YORK PRACTICE SERIES

WEST'S NEW YORK PRACTICE SERIES

Vol. 1 Walker, et al., New York Limited Liability Companies and Partnerships: A Guide to Law and Practice

Vols. 2-4 Haig, et al., Commercial Litigation in New York State Courts

Vol. 5 Barker and Alexander, Evidence in New York State and Federal Courts

Vol. 6 Greenberg, Marcus, et al., New York Criminal Law

Vol. 7 Marks, et al., New York Pretrial Criminal Procedure

Vol. 8 Davies, Stecich, Gold, et al., New York Civil Appellate Practice

Vol. 9 Ginsberg, Weinberg, et al., Environmental Law and Regulation in New York

Vol. 10 Sobie, et al., New York Family Court Practice

Vols. 11-12 Scheinkman, et al., New York Law of Domestic Relations

Vol. 13 Taber, et al., Employment Litigation in New York

Vols. 14-16 Kreindler, Rodriguez, et al., New York Law of Torts

Vols. 17-19 Field and Moskin, et al., New York and Delaware Business Entities: Choice, Formation, Operation, Financing and Acquisitions

Vols. 20-25 Ostertag, Benson, et al., General Practice in New York

Vol. 26 Borchers and Markell, et al. New York State Administrative Procedure and Practice

Vol. A Borges, et al., Enforcing Judgments and Collecting Debts in New York

Vols. B-C   Bensel, Frank, McKeon, et al., Personal Injury Practice in New York

Vols. D-E   Preminger, et al., Trusts and Estates Practice in New York

Vols. F-G   Finkelstein and Ferrara, Landlord and Tenant Practice in New York

---

New York Practice 2d
David D. Siegel

Handling the DWI Case in New York
Peter Gerstenzang

PAMPHLETS

New York Civil Practice Law and Rules

New York Sentence Charts

Westlaw®

WESTCheck® and WESTMATE®

West CD-ROM Libraries™

To order any of these New York practice tools, call your West Group Representative or 1-800-328-9352.

NEED RESEARCH HELP?

If you have research questions concerning Westlaw or West Group Publications, call West Group's Reference Attorneys at 1-800-733-2889.

PREFACE

The purpose of this book is to provide a complete reference to the statutes, case law and administrative rules and regulations pertaining to handling a DWI case in New York State. The book is narrowly focused on New York State with references to other state and Federal cases included only when relevant to New York State practice. The intent of the book is to provide a specific guide to lawyers, judges and prosecutors engaged in handling DWI cases.

In writing the book, we have sought and received the help of many attorneys, judges, police officers and Department of Motor Vehicles' personnel. While the faults and deficiencies are ours, much of the credit for the book belongs to people within the Criminal Justice System who handle DWI cases on a daily basis.

Our thanks to Neal W. Schoen, Esq., Ida L. Traschen, Esq., and Christine M. Legorius, Esq. of the Department of Motor Vehicles' Counsel's Office. Their willingness to respond to our questions and provide advice and counsel is greatly appreciated.

Finally, our deepest appreciation to Joan Dugan, the administrator of our office, counselor and friend.

PETER GERSTENZANG
ERIC H. SILLS

DEDICATION

This edition of the book is dedicated to my beloved wife, Karen. For over 40 years, Karen has been at my side helping me deal with every obstacle and accomplish every goal. When the first edition of this book was written, she coped with our four small children on her own in order to give me the space and time to write this book while dealing with a busy practice. In addition to being an excellent lawyer, Karen is an accomplished gardener, cook, and photographer. She is adept at dealing with almost every manual skill except golf. Carpentry, plumbing, electrical work, as well as minor surgery are among her many skills. She is the love of my life, my best friend, and my esteemed colleague. It is with great pride, love, and affection that I dedicate this issue of the book to Karen Gerstenzang.

ABOUT THE AUTHORS

PETER GERSTENZANG is the senior partner in the Albany, New York law firm of Gerstenzang, Sills, Davis, Cohn & Gerstenzang. He is a well known criminal defense lawyer with a practice that ranges from Long Island to Buffalo, and throughout Upstate New York. His practice is focused on the defense of Driving While Intoxicated cases and Vehicular Crimes.

Mr. Gerstenzang commenced his legal career as a prosecutor for the United States Army in the Republic of Vietnam. From 1972 to 1975, he was an Assistant District Attorney for the County of Albany. For 12 years, he taught at the New York State Police Academy in their DWI Breathalyzer training program and was certified as a Breath Test operator.

In addition to trying DWI and Vehicular Crimes cases, he serves on the faculty of the Office of Court Administration Judges Training Program, and lectures for the New York State Bar Association, as well as numerous defense and law enforcement organizations. He is Co-Chairman of the New York State Bar Association's Committee on Traffic Safety. He also serves on the Board of Regents of the National College for DUI Defense, Inc.

ERIC H. SILLS is a criminal defense attorney in Albany, New York, whose practice focuses on DWI defense. He is a partner in the law firm of Gerstenzang, Sills, Davis, Cohn & Gerstenzang. Previously, Eric served as a law clerk to retired United States Magistrate Judge Ralph W. Smith, Jr. of the United States District Court for the Northern District of New York.

Eric is a 1992 graduate of Boston College Law School, where he served as a Production Editor on the Boston College Environmental Affairs Law Review. He is a member of the Committee on Character and Fitness for the Third Judicial District, NACDL's DUI Committee, and lectures for the New York State Bar Association and other organizations.

Peter and Eric are both Board Certified as specialists in DUI Defense Law by the National College for DUI Defense (NCDD). The NCDD is the only organization accredited by the American Bar Association to certify attorney specialists in DUI law.[1] There are currently only three attorneys in New York State who are

---

[1] The NCDD is not affiliated with any governmental authority. Certification is not a requirement for the practice of law in the State of New York and does not necessarily indicate greater competence than other attorneys experienced in this field of law. See Rules of Prof. Con., Rule 7.4(c)(1); Code of Prof. Resp., DR 2-105(C)(1).

Board Certified by the NCDD. The third is Edward L. Fiandach of Rochester.

THOMSON REUTERS PROVIEW™

LIST OF ABBREVIATIONS

The following abbreviations and acronyms are used in the text for frequently cited terms, statutes and authorities:

ADA	Assistant District Attorney
AIR	Alcoholic/Drug Influence Report
AUO	Aggravated Unlicensed Operation
BAC	Blood Alcohol Concentration
CDL	Commercial Driver's License
CNS	Central Nervous System
CPL	Criminal Procedure Law
CPLR	Civil Practice Law and Rules
CR.L.RPTR.	Criminal Law Reporter
D.A./DA	District Attorney
DDP	Drinking Driver Program
DEA	Drug Enforcement Administration
DOH	Department of Health
DMV	Department of Motor Vehicles
DRE	Drug Recognition Expert
DWAI	Driving While Ability Impaired
DWI	Driving While Intoxicated
EMT	Emergency Medical Technician
FAUO	Facilitating Aggravated Unlicensed Operation
FOIL	Freedom of Information Law
HGN	Horizontal Gaze Nystagmus
IDE	Intoxicated Drivers Examination
IDTU	Intoxicated Driver Testing Unit
NHTSA	National Highway Traffic Safety Administration
OCA	Office of Court Administration
NYCRR	Official Compilation of Rules & Regulations of the State of New York
PCP	Phencyclidine
PL	Penal Law
U.T.T.	Uniform Traffic Ticket
VDF	Voluntary Disclosure Form
VTL	Vehicle and Traffic Law

Summary of Contents

Table of Contents

PART I.   STOP AND ARREST

CHAPTER 1. ISSUES FROM THE STOP TO THE ARREST

CHAPTER 2.   OPERATION

CHAPTER 3. PUBLIC HIGHWAYS, PRIVATE ROADS, AND PARKING LOTS

CHAPTER 4. WARRANTLESS ARRESTS IN THE HOME

CHAPTER 5. SOBRIETY CHECKPOINTS

PART II.   FIELD SOBRIETY TESTS

CHAPTER 6.   FIELD SOBRIETY TESTS

CHAPTER 7.   ALCO-SENSOR—THE BREATH SCREENING TEST

CHAPTER 8. GAZE NYSTAGMUS

PART III.   OFFENSES

CHAPTER 9. DWI FELONIES

CHAPTER 10. DRIVING WHILE ABILITY IMPAIRED BY DRUGS

CHAPTER 11. VTL § 1192 ISSUES

CHAPTER 12. VEHICULAR CRIMES

CHAPTER 13. AGGRAVATED UNLICENSED OPERATION OF A MOTOR VEHICLE (AUO)

CHAPTER 15. UNDERAGE OFFENDERS

PART IV. ACCUSATORY INSTRUMENTS

CHAPTER 16. LOCAL CRIMINAL COURT ACCUSATORY INSTRUMENTS

CHAPTER 17. SUPPORTING DEPOSITIONS

PART V.   PLEA BARGAINING

CHAPTER 18.   LOCAL CRIMINAL COURT PRACTICE: PRACTICAL ASPECTS

CHAPTER 19.   PLEA BARGAINING

PART VI.   PRETRIAL MATTERS

CHAPTER 20. DISCOVERY IN CRIMINAL CASES

CHAPTER 21. *BRADY* MATERIAL

CHAPTER 22. *SANDOVAL* ISSUES: ADMISSION OF PRIOR CONVICTIONS AT TRIAL

CHAPTER 23. DOUBLE JEOPARDY

CHAPTER 24. PRETRIAL MOTIONS

PART VII. STATEMENTS

CHAPTER 25. STATEMENTS

CHAPTER 26. CPL § 710.30 NOTICE ISSUES

CHAPTER 27. *MIRANDA* WARNINGS

CHAPTER 28. *ROSARIO* MATERIAL

PART VIII.   CHEMICAL TESTS

CHAPTER 29.   BREATH TESTING

CHAPTER 30.   ADDITIONAL CHEMICAL TEST

CHAPTER 31.   TWO-HOUR RULE

CHAPTER 32. THE BLOOD-BREATH CONVERSION RATIO

CHAPTER 33. PRESERVATION OF BREATHALYZER AMPOULES

CHAPTER 34. DUTY OF POLICE TO CONDUCT INTOXICATION-RELATED TESTS AND TO PRESERVE BLOOD/BREATH SAMPLES

CHAPTER 35. RADIO FREQUENCY INTERFERENCE

CHAPTER 39. EXTRAPOLATION

CHAPTER 40. COMPULSORY CHEMICAL TEST

PART X.   TEST REFUSALS

CHAPTER 41. TEST REFUSALS

PART XI.   EVIDENCE ISSUES

CHAPTER 42.   BREATH TEST FOUNDATION

CHAPTER 43. ADMISSIBILITY OF DOCUMENTS

CHAPTER 44. PHYSICIAN-PATIENT PRIVILEGE

PART XII. PENALTIES AND CONSEQUENCES

CHAPTER 45. SUSPENSION PENDING PROSECUTION

CHAPTER 46. PENALTIES FOR VTL § 1192 OFFENSES

CHAPTER 47. SURCHARGES AND CRIME VICTIM ASSISTANCE FEES

CHAPTER 48. IGNITION INTERLOCK DEVICE PROGRAM

CHAPTER 49. THE 20-DAY ORDER

CHAPTER 50. THE DRINKING DRIVER PROGRAM

CHAPTER 51. CERTIFICATE OF RELIEF FROM DISABILITIES

CHAPTER 52. SEAL AND RETURN ORDERS: CLEARING THE RECORD

CHAPTER 53. TIMELINESS OF PROSECUTIONS AND SPEEDY TRIAL

CHAPTER 54.   MANDATORY ALCOHOL/SUBSTANCE ABUSE TREATMENT

CHAPTER 55.   NEW DMV REGULATIONS AFFECTING REPEAT DWI OFFENDERS

APPENDICES

Part I

STOP AND ARREST

Chapter 1

Issues from the Stop to the Arrest

KeyCite®: Cases and other legal materials listed in KeyCite Scope can be researched through the KeyCite service on Westlaw®. Use KeyCite to check citations for form, parallel references, prior and later history, and comprehensive citator information, including citations to other decisions and secondary materials.

---

§ 1:1   In general

The typical arrest for Driving While Intoxicated (hereinafter DWI) commences with a motorist attracting the attention of the police by driving erratically or otherwise violating some provision of the Vehicle and Traffic Law (hereinafter VTL). Once the motorist is pulled over, the police will invariably observe common indicia of intoxication (*e.g.*, the odor of an alcoholic beverage, glassy/bloodshot eyes, flushed face, impaired speech, impaired motor coordination, etc.). The motorist will then generally be requested to submit to a variety of field sobriety tests and/or a breath screening test, following which he or she will be placed under arrest.

This chapter addresses a variety of common issues that arise in connection with DWI arrests.

§ 1:2 When can a police officer approach a parked vehicle?

The approach of a parked vehicle by a police officer is governed by the same rules that govern police-civilian street encounters. Such approaches are governed by *People v. Hollman*, 79 N.Y.2d 181, 581 N.Y.S.2d 619, 590 N.E.2d 204 (1992), and *People v. De Bour*, 40 N.Y.2d 210, 386 N.Y.S.2d 375, 352 N.E.2d 562 (1976). *See also People v. Moore*, 6 N.Y.3d 496, 498–99, 814 N.Y.S.2d 567, 568, 847 N.E.2d 1141 (2006); *People v. Ocasio*, 85 N.Y.2d 982, 984, 629 N.Y.S.2d 161, 162, 652 N.E.2d 907 (1995) ("approach of a parked car may be undertaken for an objective, credible reason"). In both *Hollman* and *DeBour*, the Court of Appeals identified 4 levels of police-civilian street encounters—(1) a request for information, (2) a common-law right of inquiry, (3) a forcible stop/detention, and (4) an arrest.

Pursuant to a *DeBour* level 1 request for information:

> [P]olice officers have fairly broad authority to approach individuals and ask questions relating to identity or destination, provided that the officers do not act on whim or caprice and have an articulable reason not necessarily related to criminality for making the approach. *DeBour* also stands for the proposition that the brevity of the encounter and the absence of harassment or intimidation will be relevant in determining whether a police-initiated encounter is a mere request for information. * * *
>
> [W]e emphasize that a request for information is a general, nonthreatening encounter in which an individual is approached for an articulable reason and asked briefly about his or her identity, destination, or reason for being in the area. If the individual is carrying something that would appear to a trained police officer to be unusual, the police officer can ask about that object.

Hollman, 79 N.Y.2d at 190, 191, 581 N.Y.S.2d at 624–25.

By contrast:

> Once the police officer's questions become extended and accusatory and the officer's inquiry focuses on the possible criminality of the

person approached, this is not a simple request for information. Where the person approached from the content of the officer's questions might reasonably believe that he or she is suspected of some wrongdoing, the officer is no longer merely asking for information. The encounter has become a common-law inquiry that must be supported by founded suspicion that criminality is afoot. No matter how calm the tone of [police] officers may be, or how polite their phrasing, a request to search a bag is intrusive and intimidating and would cause reasonable people to believe that they were suspected of criminal conduct. These factors take the encounter past a simple request for information.

79 N.Y.2d at 191–92, 581 N.Y.S.2d at 625. Stated another way:

Once the officer asks more pointed questions that would lead the person approached reasonably to believe that he or she is suspected of some wrongdoing and is the focus of the officer's investigation, the officer is no longer merely seeking information. This has become a common-law inquiry that must be supported by a founded suspicion that criminality is afoot.

79 N.Y.2d at 185, 581 N.Y.S.2d at 621.

The distinction between a *DeBour* level 1 request for information and a *DeBour* level 2 common-law right of inquiry:

[R]ests on the content of the questions, the number of questions asked, and the degree to which the language and nature of the questions transform the encounter from a merely unsettling one to an intimidating one. We do not purport to set out a bright line test for distinguishing between a request for information and a common-law inquiry. These determinations can only be made on a case-by-case basis.

79 N.Y.2d at 192, 581 N.Y.S.2d at 625.

Applying these principles to the facts of the companion case of *People v. Saunders*, the Court of Appeals held that where the police officer only had enough information to support a *DeBour* level 1 request for information, it was improper for the officer to have requested permission to search the defendant's bag. 79 N.Y.2d at 194, 581 N.Y.S.2d at 626 ("[Officer] Canale crossed the line, however, when he asked to search the defendant's bag. The defendant's behavior, while it may have provided the officer with adequate basis for an approach and for a few general, nonaccusatory questions, was certainly not so suspicious as to warrant the further intrusion of a request to rummage through the defendant's luggage. Because the defendant's consent was a product of the improper police inquiry, the Appellate Division was in error when it found that the defendant had in fact consented to the search of his bag"). *See also Matter of Antoine W.*, 79 N.Y.2d 888, 889–90, 581 N.Y.S.2d 648, 648, 590 N.E.2d 233, 233 (1992) ("Although the police had an 'objective credible reason' for approaching the defendant, the pointed questioning regarding the ownership of the bag and consent to search it was improper because it was not based on a founded suspicion of criminal activity"); *People v. Irizarry*, 79 N.Y.2d 890, 581 N.Y.S.2d 649, 590 N.E.2d 234 (1992) (same).

In *People v. Harrison*, 57 N.Y.2d 470, 478, 457 N.Y.S.2d 199, 204, 443 N.E.2d 447 (1982), the Court of Appeals agreed that:

> [T]he defendants' use of a dirty rental car in the City of New York did not establish reasonable suspicion that they were involved in criminal conduct. Contrary to the dissenter's view it is not common knowledge that ordinarily rental cars are relatively clean and well maintained. Rental companies may rent their cars in that condition but their customers are not always so fastidious. The cars are often rented to individual customers for weeks or months at a time and it is not always possible, even for concerned customers, to maintain the cars in their original condition, particularly in large metropolitan areas.

The Court further agreed that the officers' demand that the vehicle's occupants remain in the vehicle was illegal absent reasonable suspicion that criminal activity was afoot. 57 N.Y.2d at 476, 457 N.Y.S.2d at 202–03 ("Confining the occupants to the car, even temporarily, is at least equivalent to a stop. A temporary stop is . . . a limited seizure of the person which at least requires reasonable suspicion.") (citations omitted). *See also People v. Cantor*, 36 N.Y.2d 106, 112–13, 365 N.Y.S.2d 509, 516, 324 N.E.2d 872 (1975) ("Reasonable suspicion is the quantum of knowledge sufficient to induce an ordinarily prudent and cautious man under the circumstances to believe criminal activity is at hand."); *People v. Sobotker*, 43 N.Y.2d 559, 564, 402 N.Y.S.2d 993, 996, 373 N.E.2d 1218 (1978) ("Mere 'hunch' or 'gut reaction' will not do."); *People v. Pizzo*, 144 A.D.2d 930, 534 N.Y.S.2d 249 (4th Dep't 1988).

In *People v. McIntosh*, 96 N.Y.2d 521, 525, 730 N.Y.S.2d 265, 267, 755 N.E.2d 329 (2001), the Court of Appeals noted that "[a]lthough police officers have 'fairly broad authority' to approach and pose questions, they may not do so on mere 'whim or caprice'; the request must be based on 'an articulable reason not necessarily related to criminality.'" (Citations omitted). Critically, the *McIntosh* Court pointed out that:

> We have never held that a police encounter was justified by anything so general as knowledge that an entire city is a known source of drugs. Even a discrete area of a city identified as a high crime area has not, by itself, been sufficient justification for informational requests . . . .

96 N.Y.2d at 526, 730 N.Y.S.2d at 267.

The *McIntosh* Court made clear, several times, that in order to satisfy *Hollman* and *DeBour*, the police need an "objective, credible reason" to approach an individual to request information *in addition to* the mere fact that the person is in a "high crime" or "high drug" area. 96 N.Y.2d at 525, 730 N.Y.S.2d at 267; 96 N.Y.2d at 526, 730 N.Y.S.2d at 268; 96 N.Y.2d at 527, 730 N.Y.S.2d at 268; 96 N.Y.2d at 527, 730 N.Y.S.2d at 269. In this regard, the Court distinguished cases in which it had previously upheld requests for information, noting that in each such case the police had observed objective, credible suspicious activity above and beyond the mere fact that the defendant was located in a high crime or high drug area:

> The events in all of these cases occurred in vicinities classified by police as "drug-prone" or with a high incidence of crime. Notably, we did not base our holdings on this factor alone. In determining the legality of an encounter under *DeBour* and *Hollman*, it has been crucial whether a nexus to conduct existed, that is, whether the police were aware of or observed conduct which provided a particularized reason to request information. The fact that an encounter occurred in a high crime vicinity, without more, has not passed *DeBour* and *Hollman* scrutiny.

96 N.Y.2d at 526–27, 730 N.Y.S.2d at 268. *See also In re Michael F.*, 84 A.D.3d 468, 923 N.Y.S.2d 61 (1st Dep't 2011); *People v. Miles*, 82 A.D.3d 1010, 918 N.Y.S.2d 594 (2d Dep't 2011); *People v. Mobley*, 48 A.D.3d 374, 853 N.Y.S.2d 31 (1st Dep't 2008); *People v. Rutledge*, 21 A.D.3d 1125, 804 N.Y.S.2d 321 (2d Dep't 2005); *People v. Chism*, 194 A.D.2d 351, 598 N.Y.S.2d 481 (1st Dep't 1993); *People v. Morrison*, 161 A.D.2d 608, 555 N.Y.S.2d 183 (2d Dep't 1990); *People v. Medda*, 28 Misc. 3d 1239(A), 2010 WL 3703269 (Nassau Co. Dist. Ct. 2010); *People v. Powell*, 16 Misc. 3d 1115(A), 847 N.Y.S.2d 898 (Nassau Co. Dist. Ct. 2007); *People v. Rosenbluth*, 4 Misc. 3d 1025(A), 798 N.Y.S.2d 347 (Suffolk Co. Dist. Ct. 2004); *People v. McMaster*, 3 Misc. 3d 1107(A), 787 N.Y.S.2d 680 (Webster Just. Ct. 2004).

§ 1:3 When can a police officer approach a vehicle that is stopped but not parked?

This issue was addressed in *People v. Ocasio*, 85 N.Y.2d 982, 629 N.Y.S.2d 161, 652 N.E.2d 907 (1995). In *Ocasio*, two police officers walked up to the defendant's vehicle—which was stopped at a red light—tapped on the window, displayed badges, and asked the defendant for identification. The Court of Appeals laid out the factors to be considered in determining whether such a "stop" is permissible:

> Determination whether a seizure occurred here—where the car was neither parked nor moving—requires the fact finder to apply a settled standard: whether a reasonable person would have believed, under the circumstances, that the officer's conduct was a significant limitation on his or her freedom. That involves consideration of all

the facts—for example, was there a chase; were lights, sirens or a loudspeaker used; was the officer's gun drawn, was the individual prevented from moving; how many verbal commands were given; what was the content and tone of the commands; how many officers were involved; where did the encounter take place.

85 N.Y.2d at 984, 629 N.Y.S.2d at 162 (citation omitted).

Considering these factors, the Court held that:

While there may be instances in which approach of a car at a stoplight constitutes a seizure, the courts below, having considered the relevant factors, found no seizure. We cannot say, as a matter of law, that this determination was wrong.

85 N.Y.2d at 984–85, 629 N.Y.S.2d at 162.

In *People v. Thomas*, 19 A.D.3d 32, 33, 792 N.Y.S.2d 472, 477 (1st Dep't 2005), the Appellate Division, First Department, held that "police officers are entitled to conduct a level I inquiry of a person at the wheel of a stationary car that is blocking a fire hydrant." The Court further held that "[i]n concluding that the officer is justified in asking to see the license, we are influenced by the consideration that a person who stops a car alongside a fire hydrant plainly invites, and should reasonably expect, an interaction with law enforcement. We also conclude that a police approach to a person in a car that is already stopped does not constitute a level III 'forcible stop and detention', even if the police stop their vehicle in a position that incidentally blocks the civilian vehicle's path." 19 A.D.3d at __, 792 N.Y.S.2d at 474 (citation omitted). *See also People v. Grady*, 272 A.D.2d 952, 708 N.Y.S.2d 765 (4th Dep't 2000). *Cf. People v. Kojac*, 176 Misc. 2d 187, 671 N.Y.S.2d 949 (N.Y. Co. Sup. Ct. 1998) (approach of stopped car illegal where approach was based on nothing more than a "hunch").

§ 1:4   Police jurisdiction to stop

Where a police officer observes an offense committed within the geographical area of the officer's employment, *see* CPL § 140.50(1), the officer may pursue and serve an appearance ticket upon the offender "anywhere in the county in which the designated offense was allegedly committed or in any adjoining county." CPL § 150.40(3). In addition:

A police officer may, for the purpose of serving an appearance ticket upon a person, follow him in continuous close pursuit, commencing either in the county in which the alleged offense was committed or in an adjoining county, in and through any county of the state, and may serve such appearance ticket upon him in any county in which he overtakes him.

CPL § 150.40(4).

If such a traffic stop evolves into an arrest for DWI, the arrest would likely be upheld. *See People v. Leitch*, 178 A.D.2d 864, 577 N.Y.S.2d 725 (3d Dep't 1991). In *Leitch*, a village police officer:

> [W]itnessed a vehicle driven by defendant inside the Village limits following too closely behind another vehicle as it headed out of the Village. The officer turned his vehicle around and began following defendant's car outside the Village limits. The officer observed that defendant failed twice to signal turns, failed to reduce his speed at an intersection and made a wide turn into the oncoming lane of traffic. Upon pulling over defendant's vehicle and asking to see his license and registration, the officer noticed a strong odor of alcohol emanating from the car. Defendant, whose eyes were glassy and bloodshot, admitted that he had no driver's license. After defendant performed poorly on various sobriety tests and an alco-sensor breath test administered by the officer, he was arrested for drunk driving.

178 A.D.2d at 864, 577 N.Y.S.2d at 725–26. Relying on CPL § 140.10, the Appellate Division, Third Department, held that defendant's arrest was legal.

By contrast, if the initial conduct which attracted the officer's attention in *Leitch* had occurred outside of the geographical area of the officer's employment, the vehicle stop would have been illegal. In this regard, it is well settled that:

> Although CPL 140.10(3) grants law enforcement officers the power to arrest a person without a warrant anywhere in the state for a crime they have probable cause to believe he committed, *the power to stop and question a person on reasonable suspicion of criminal activity is specifically limited by statute to the geographical area of the officer's employment* (CPL 140.50[1]).

Brewster v. City of New York, 111 A.D.2d 892, 893, 490 N.Y.S.2d 601, 602 (2d Dep't 1985) (emphasis added) (citation omitted). *See also* CPL § 140.50(1); *People v. Wolf*, 166 Misc. 2d 372, 636 N.Y.S.2d 570 (App. Term, 2d Dep't 1995); *People v. Graham*, 192 Misc. 2d 528, 531-532, 748 N.Y.S.2d 203, 206 (Erie Co. Sup. Ct. 2002), order aff'd, 1 A.D.3d 1066, 767 N.Y.S.2d 383 (4th Dep't 2003) ("the Amherst police officer herein, restricted by the clear and unambiguous language of CPL § 140.10-2(a), exceeded his authority herein from the moment he illuminated the lights on his marked patrol vehicle for the purpose of stopping the defendant for petty offenses outside the Town of Amherst, his 'bailiwick' "); *People v. Edmonds*, 157 Misc. 2d 966, 599 N.Y.S.2d 441 (Dutchess Co. Ct. 1993). *Cf. People v. Nenni*, 269 A.D.2d 785, 704 N.Y.S.2d 405 (4th Dep't 2000) (*Brewster* and CPL § 140.50(1) inapplicable where police officer had probable cause to arrest defendant at time of stop); *People v. Nesbitt*, 1 A.D.3d 889, 889-890, 767 N.Y.S.2d 187, 188 (4th Dep't 2003) (stop of defendant by village police officer *inside* village for traffic infractions he observed defendant commit *outside* village limits was lawful where the officer's observations of defendant's erratic driving outside of village "gave rise to reasonable suspicion that defendant was driving while intoxicated within the Village").

CPL § 140.50(1) provides, in pertinent part, that:

[A] police officer may stop a person in a public place located *within the geographical area of such officer's employment* when he reasonably suspects that such person is committing, has committed or is about to commit either (a) a felony[,] or (b) a misdemeanor defined in the penal law, and may demand of him his name, address and an explanation of his conduct.

(Emphasis added). In addition:

A county, city, town or village, as the case may be, constitutes the "geographical area of employment" of any police officer employed as such by an agency of such political subdivision or by an authority which functions only in such political subdivision.

CPL § 1.20(34-a)(b).

Since most DWI cases emanate from police observation of traffic infractions, CPL § 140.50(1) and *Brewster* should be asserted where the officer is improperly operating outside of his or her geographical area of employment.

In *People v. Van Buren*, 4 N.Y.3d 640, 644, 797 N.Y.S.2d 802, 803, 830 N.E.2d 1130, 35 Envtl. L. Rep. 20098, 18 A.L.R.6th 865 (2005), the Court of Appeals held that "the New York City Department of Environmental Protection (DEP) Water Supply Police are authorized to enforce traffic laws within the city watershed." "This authority includes enforcing the Vehicle and Traffic Law, violations of which necessarily create a danger to the driver of an automobile, passengers and other members of the public." 4 N.Y.3d at 648, 797 N.Y.S.2d at 806.

By contrast, in *People v. Williams*, 4 N.Y.3d 535, 538–39, 797 N.Y.S.2d 35, 37, 829 N.E.2d 1203 (2005), the same Court held that a Housing Authority peace officer who acts (a) outside of the geographical jurisdiction of his employment, (b) under color of law, and (c) "with all the accouterments of official authority" cannot make a valid traffic stop/citizen's arrest.

§ 1:5 When can a police officer stop a moving vehicle?

"[T]he right to stop a moving vehicle is distinct from the right to approach the occupants of a parked vehicle." *People v. Spencer*, 84 N.Y.2d 749, 753, 622 N.Y.S.2d 483, 486, 646 N.E.2d 785 (1995). In this regard, a vehicle stop by the police is a *DeBour* level 3 seizure. *See, e.g., People v. Ocasio*, 85 N.Y.2d 982, 984, 629 N.Y.S.2d 161, 162, 652 N.E.2d 907 (1995); *Spencer*, 84 N.Y.2d at 753, 622 N.Y.S.2d at 485–86; *People v. May*, 81 N.Y.2d 725, 727, 593 N.Y.S.2d 760, 761–62, 609 N.E.2d 113 (1992); *People v. Sobot-*

ker, 43 N.Y.2d 559, 563–64, 402 N.Y.S.2d 993, 995–96, 373 N.E.2d
1218 (1978). *Cf. People v. Johnson*, 194 A.D.2d 870, 599 N.Y.S.2d
162 (3d Dep't 1993); *People v. Holstein*, 154 A.D.2d 905, 545
N.Y.S.2d 865 (4th Dep't 1989). So is a gunpoint stop by the police.
See, e.g., People v. Moore, 6 N.Y.3d 496, 499, 814 N.Y.S.2d 567,
569, 847 N.E.2d 1141 (2006); *People v. Allende*, 39 N.Y.2d 474,
384 N.Y.S.2d 416, 348 N.E.2d 891 (1976).

While a *DeBour* level 3 seizure requires "reasonable suspicion
that a particular person has committed, is committing or is about
to commit a felony or misdemeanor," *People v. De Bour*, 40 N.Y.2d
210, 223, 386 N.Y.S.2d 375, 385, 352 N.E.2d 562 (1976); *see also
People v. Cantor*, 36 N.Y.2d 106, 112–13, 365 N.Y.S.2d 509, 516,
324 N.E.2d 872 (1975), in the context of vehicle stops the Court
of Appeals has relaxed this standard to include probable cause to
believe that a motorist has committed a traffic infraction. *See
People v. Robinson*, 97 N.Y.2d 341, 354, 741 N.Y.S.2d 147, 155,
767 N.E.2d 638 (2001) ("the decision to stop a vehicle is reasonable where the police have probable cause to believe that a traffic
infraction has occurred"). *See also People v. Guthrie*, 25 N.Y.3d
130, 133, 8 N.Y.S.3d 237, 240, 30 N.E.3d 880 (2015); *Sobotker*,
supra, 43 N.Y.2d at 563, 402 N.Y.S.2d at 996; *People v. Ingle*, 36
N.Y.2d 413, 414, 369 N.Y.S.2d 67, 69, 330 N.E.2d 39 (1975).

Notably, however, the term "probable cause" as used in *Robinson*
is akin to *DeBour* level 3 "reasonable suspicion" as opposed to
DeBour level 4 "probable cause to arrest." In this regard, in *Ingle*,
supra, the Court of Appeals made clear that:

> A single automobile traveling on a public highway may be stopped
> . . . when a police officer reasonably suspects a violation of the Ve-
> hicle and Traffic Law. Absent reasonable suspicion of a vehicle
> violation, a "routine traffic check" to determine whether or not a ve-
> hicle is being operated in compliance with the Vehicle and Traffic
> Law is permissible only when conducted according to nonarbitrary,
> nondiscriminatory, uniform procedures for detecting violations. It
> should be emphasized that, in the context of a motor vehicle inspec-
> tion "stop", the degree of suspicion required to justify the stop is
> minimal. *Nothing like probable cause as that term is used in the
> criminal law is required.* * * *
>
> Thus, an arbitrary stop of a single automobile for a purportedly
> "routine traffic check" is impermissible unless the police officer rea-
> sonably suspects a violation of the Vehicle and Traffic Law. * * *
>
> [I]n Pennsylvania an approach quite similar to that taken here was
> followed. *The position there taken, however, took the form of requir-
> ing as a basis for a "routine" traffic stop what was characterized as
> probable cause, but which may be no different than the reasonable
> suspicion suggested earlier as the basis for a "routine" traffic stop.*

It should be emphasized that the factual basis required to support a stop for a "routine traffic check" is minimal. An actual violation of the Vehicle and Traffic Law need not be detectable. For example, an automobile in a general state of dilapidation might properly arouse suspicion of equipment violations. All that is required is that the stop be not the product of mere whim, caprice, or idle curiosity. It is enough if the stop is based upon "specific and articulable facts which, taken together with rational inferences from those facts, reasonably warrant [the] intrusion."

36 N.Y.2d at 414–15, 419, 420, 369 N.Y.S.2d at 69, 74, 74–75 (emphases added) (citations omitted). *See also Sobotker*, 43 N.Y.2d at 563, 402 N.Y.S.2d at 996 ("our repeated decisions make abundantly clear that, absent at least a reasonable suspicion that its occupants had been, are then, or are about to be, engaged in conduct in violation of law, the stopping of an automobile by the police constitutes an impermissible seizure").

Robinson is somewhat difficult to reconcile with *Sobotker* and *Ingle*. In this regard, the *Robinson* Court stated that "[t]his Court has always evaluated the validity of a traffic stop based on probable cause that a driver has committed a traffic violation." 97 N.Y.2d at 350, 741 N.Y.S.2d at 152. However, *Sobotker* and *Ingle* clearly indicate that "reasonable suspicion" has always been the relevant legal standard. On the other hand, there probably isn't a meaningful distinction between "reasonable suspicion" to believe that a person has committed a traffic infraction and "probable cause" to believe that he or she did so. *See Ingle*, 36 N.Y.2d at 420, 369 N.Y.S.2d at 74 ("what was characterized as probable cause . . . may be no different than the reasonable suspicion suggested earlier as the basis for a 'routine' traffic stop"). *Cf. Deveines v. New York State Dept. of Motor Vehicles Appeals Bd.*, 136 A.D.3d 1383, __, 25 N.Y.S.3d 760, 761 (4th Dep't 2016) (" '[s]ince *Ingle*,. . . the Court of Appeals has made it "abundantly clear" . . . that "police stops of automobiles in this State are legal only pursuant to routine, nonpretextual traffic checks to enforce traffic regulations or when there exists at least a reasonable suspicion that the driver or occupants of the vehicle have committed, are committing, or are about to commit a crime" . . . [,] or where the police have "probable cause to believe that the driver . . . has committed a traffic violation" ' ") (citation omitted).

The bottom line is this: the police can lawfully stop a vehicle whenever they (a) have probable cause to believe that the driver has committed a traffic infraction, (b) observe an equipment violation, (c) have reasonable suspicion that criminal activity is afoot, or (d) are properly administering a valid checkpoint. *See* §§ 5:1 et seq., *infra*.

§ 1:6   When can a police officer "stop" a parked vehicle?

A police officer can "stop" a parked vehicle by, for example, using the officer's patrol car to prevent the parked vehicle from leaving a parking space, activating the police car's emergency lights and shining a light into the vehicle. In *Stewart v. Fiala*, 129 A.D.3d 852, __, 12 N.Y.S.3d 138, 138 (2d Dep't 2015), the Appellate Division, Second Department, held that such a stop was illegal under the following circumstances:

> On December 17, 2011, at 1:22 a.m., a police officer was patrolling West Boston Post Road in Mamaroneck as part of his assignment to a driving-while-intoxicated detail, when he observed a parked motor vehicle in the parking lot of a gym. The vehicle was parked in a marked space, with the front end of the vehicle facing a fence, while the back end was facing the lot. The lights of the vehicle were on, and its engine was running. It was the only vehicle in the lot. Although the gym was closed, the officer knew that patrons of the adjacent restaurant, which was open, parked their vehicles in the gym's lot. The officer pulled his vehicle perpendicular to the rear of the parked vehicle, activated the emergency lights, and shined a light from his vehicle into the parked vehicle.

§ 1:7   When can a police officer stop a person suspected of being the victim of a crime?

In *People v. Coronado*, 139 A.D.3d 452, __, 30 N.Y.S.3d 628, 629 (1st Dep't 2016):

> Two police officers testified that they saw defendant sitting in the driver's seat of a car, while he and a man standing outside the car but inside the driver's open door were pushing and pulling each other. The police also heard yelling but could not understand what the men were saying. After defendant got out of the car, the two men walked together toward a nearby bar. The officers indicated that they suspected that the other man had been committing a crime against defendant, such as robbery, and had coerced him to walk away from the car. However, there is no testimony indicating that the officers believed that defendant was a perpetrator of a crime until after one of the officers forcibly stopped him, by grabbing him by the shoulder to stop him from moving away, and the police then observed signs that he was intoxicated, such as bloodshot, watery eyes and an odor of alcohol on his breath.

Under these circumstances, the Court held that:

> The officers' reasonable belief that defendant might have been a crime victim "authorized the police to ask [him] questions . . . and to follow [him] while attempting to engage him—but not to seize him in order to do so." * * *
>
> Because proof of defendant's intoxication depended on the fruits of the unlawful stop, we dismiss the accusatory instrument.

Id. at __, __, 30 N.Y.S.3d at 629, 630 (citation omitted).

§ 1:8   When can a police officer ask the occupants of a lawfully stopped vehicle if they possess weapons?

In *People v. Garcia*, 20 N.Y.3d 317, 319-20, 959 N.Y.S.2d 464, 465, 983 N.E.2d 259 (2012), the Court of Appeals held as follows:

> On this appeal, we must determine whether a police officer may, without founded suspicion for the inquiry, ask the occupants of a lawfully stopped vehicle if they possess any weapons. We answer in the negative and, in so holding, necessarily conclude that the graduated framework set forth in *People v. De Bour* and *People v. Hollman* for evaluating the constitutionality of police-initiated encounters with private citizens applies with equal force to traffic stops.

(Citations omitted). *See also id.* at 324, 959 N.Y.S.2d at 468 ("Whether the individual questioned is a pedestrian or an occupant of a vehicle, a police officer who asks a private citizen if he or she is in possession of a weapon must have founded suspicion that criminality is afoot").

Critically, the *Garcia* Court made clear that this rule also applies to more general questions such as "Is there anything in the car I should know about?" *Id.* at 323 n.*, 959 N.Y.S.2d at 468 n.*.

§ 1:9   Standard for stop differs from standard for arrest

It is well settled that an entirely different legal standard applies to the *stop* of a motor vehicle for a traffic infraction (*i.e.*, reasonable suspicion) than applies to the *arrest* of an occupant of the vehicle for a crime (*i.e.*, probable cause). As is noted in the previous section, a vehicle stop by the police is a *DeBour* level 3 seizure requiring reasonable suspicion. By contrast, an arrest for a crime such as DWI is a *DeBour* level 4 seizure requiring probable cause. *See, e.g., People v. Moore*, 32 N.Y.2d 67, 70, 343 N.Y.S.2d 107, 111, 295 N.E.2d 780 (1973) ("the standard of reasonable suspicion to stop is lower than the standard of probable cause for an arrest"); *People v. Martinez*, 80 N.Y.2d 444, 447, 591 N.Y.S.2d 823, 824, 606 N.E.2d 951 (1992); *People v. Sobotker*, 43 N.Y.2d 559, 402 N.Y.S.2d 993, 373 N.E.2d 1218 (1978); *People v. Ingle*, 36 N.Y.2d 413, 369 N.Y.S.2d 67, 330 N.E.2d 39 (1975); *People v. Hollman*, 79 N.Y.2d 181, 581 N.Y.S.2d 619, 590 N.E.2d 204 (1992); *People v. De Bour*, 40 N.Y.2d 210, 386 N.Y.S.2d 375, 352 N.E.2d 562 (1976). *See also People v. Sarfaty*, 291 A.D.2d 889, 889-890, 736 N.Y.S.2d 817, 818 (4th Dep't 2002); *People v. Pistone*, 284 A.D.2d 415, __, 727 N.Y.S.2d 439, 440 (2d Dep't 2001); *People v. Swanston*, 277 A.D.2d 600, __, 716 N.Y.S.2d 118, 121 (3d Dep't 2000); *People v. Sawinski*, 246 A.D.2d 689, __, 667 N.Y.S.2d 472, 473 (3d Dep't 1998); *People v. May*, 191 A.D.2d 1011, __, 595 N.Y.S.2d 165, 166 (4th Dep't 1993); *People v. Barnum*, 175 A.D.2d 332, __, 572 N.Y.S.2d 88, 89 (3d Dep't 1991); *People v.*

Dunlap, 163 A.D.2d 814, __, 558 N.Y.S.2d 347, 348 (4th Dep't 1990).

§ 1:10   Can the police issue tickets for unobserved traffic infractions?

Pursuant to CPL § 140.10(1)(a), a police officer can only make a warrantless arrest for a traffic infraction when the officer has reasonable cause to believe that such infraction *was committed in his or her presence. See* § 1:11, *infra.* This raises the question of whether a police officer can validly issue a ticket for an unobserved traffic infraction.

In *People v. Boback*, 23 N.Y.2d 189, 191–92, 295 N.Y.S.2d 912, 914, 243 N.E.2d 135 (1968), the Court of Appeals held that "the use of the Simplified Traffic Information is authorized where the information is signed by an officer whose knowledge of the facts is based upon information and belief." *See also* 23 N.Y.2d at 194, 295 N.Y.S.2d at 917 ("It is . . . evident that neither the language nor the legislative history of the Simplified Traffic Information statute limits the use of the information to those cases where the officer making the information has some personal knowledge of the violation."); *Farkas v. State*, 96 Misc. 2d 784, __, 409 N.Y.S.2d 696, 698–99 (Ct. of Claims 1978); 1987 N.Y. Op. Atty. Gen. (Informal Opinion No. 87–78). *Cf. People v. Genovese*, 156 Misc. 2d 569, 593 N.Y.S.2d 925 (Mendon Just. Ct. 1992) (reaching opposite conclusion).

The authors would like to thank Deputy James Di Mele of the Ulster County Sheriff's Office, who brought to our attention convincing authority supporting the position that police officers can issue STIs for unobserved traffic infractions.

It should be noted that issuance of a traffic ticket is not an arrest. *See, e.g., People v. Marsh*, 20 N.Y.2d 98, 100, 281 N.Y.S.2d 789, 791, 228 N.E.2d 783 (1967); *People v. McMillan*, 112 Misc. 2d 901, 902, 447 N.Y.S.2d 626, 628 (Monroe Co. Ct. 1982); *Farkas, supra; Coville v. Bennett*, 57 Misc. 2d 838, 839, 293 N.Y.S.2d 685, 687 (Ontario Co. Sup. Ct. 1968).

§ 1:11   Can the police arrest a person for a mere traffic infraction?

The statutory authority for making a warrantless arrest is set forth in CPL Article 140. In the field of DWI law, the primary authority for a warrantless arrest comes from CPL § 140.10. CPL § 140.10 provides, in pertinent part:

§ 140.10. Arrest without a warrant; by police officer; when and where authorized.

1. Subject to the provisions of subdivision two, a police officer may arrest a person for:

(a) Any offense when he or she has reasonable cause to believe that such person has committed such offense in his or her presence; and

(b) A crime when he or she has reasonable cause to believe that such person has committed such crime, whether in his or her presence or otherwise.

2. A police officer may arrest a person for a petty offense, pursuant to subdivision one, only when:

(a) Such offense was committed or believed by him or her to have been committed within the geographical area of such police officer's employment or within [100] yards of such geographical area; and

(b) Such arrest is made in the county in which such offense was committed or believed to have been committed or in an adjoining county; except that the police officer may follow such person in continuous close pursuit, commencing either in the county in which the offense was or is believed to have been committed or in an adjoining county, in and through any county of the state, and may arrest him or her in any county in which he or she apprehends him or her.

3. A police officer may arrest a person for a crime, pursuant to subdivision one, whether or not such crime was committed within the geographical area of such police officer's employment, and he or she may make such arrest within the state, regardless of the situs of the commission of the crime. In addition, he or she may, if necessary, pursue such person outside the state and may arrest him or her in any state the laws of which contain provisions equivalent to those of section 140.55.

CPL § 140.10(1)-(3).

For purposes of CPL § 140.10, a traffic infraction is an offense. *See, e.g.*, VTL § 155 ("For purposes of arrest without a warrant, pursuant to [CPL Article 140], a traffic infraction shall be deemed an offense."); PL § 10.00(2) (" 'Traffic infraction' means any offense defined as 'traffic infraction' by [VTL § 155]."); CPL § 1.20(39) (" 'Petty offense' means a violation or a traffic infraction.").

Although it is clear that a police officer has the authority to arrest a person for a mere traffic infraction (committed in his or her presence), *see, e.g.*, CPL § 140.10(1)(a); *Atwater v. City of Lago Vista*, 532 U.S. 318, 354, 121 S. Ct. 1536, 1557, 149 L. Ed. 2d 549 (2001) ("If an officer has probable cause to believe that an individual has committed even a very minor criminal offense in his presence, he may, without violating the Fourth Amendment, arrest the offender."), it is equally clear that doing so is both uncommon and disfavored. *See, e.g.*, *People v. Marsh*, 20 N.Y.2d 98, 100,

281 N.Y.S.2d 789, 791, 228 N.E.2d 783 (1967); *People v. Cooper*, 38 A.D.3d 678, __, 833 N.Y.S.2d 118, 120 (2d Dep't 2007); *People v. Bulgin*, 29 Misc. 3d 286, __, 908 N.Y.S.2d 817, 827 (Bronx Co. Sup. Ct. 2010); Preiser, Practice Commentaries, McKinney's Cons. Laws of N.Y., Book 11A, CPL § 140.10. *See generally People v. Howell*, 49 N.Y.2d 778, 426 N.Y.S.2d 477, 403 N.E.2d 182 (1980); *People v. Troiano*, 35 N.Y.2d 476, 363 N.Y.S.2d 943, 323 N.E.2d 183 (1974).

Indeed, the whole purpose of permitting uniform traffic tickets, *see* VTL § 207, and appearance tickets, *see* CPL Article 150, is to avoid full-blown arrests/detentions for relatively minor offenses.

§ 1:12 Can the police arrest a person for an unobserved DWAI?

Pursuant to CPL § 140.10(1)(a), a police officer can only make a warrantless arrest for a traffic infraction when the officer has reasonable cause to believe that such infraction was committed in his or her presence. *See* previous section. Since DWAI, in violation of VTL § 1192(1), is generally a traffic infraction, *see* VTL § 1193(1)(a), it would appear that a police officer could not arrest a person for DWAI unless the officer had personally observed the person operate the vehicle. In this regard, however, VTL § 1194(1)(a) provides that:

> 1. Arrest and field testing. (a) Arrest. Notwithstanding the provisions of [CPL § 140.10], a police officer may, without a warrant, arrest a person, in case of a violation of [VTL § 1192(1)], if such violation is coupled with an accident or collision in which such person is involved, which in fact has been committed, though not in the police officer's presence, when the officer has reasonable cause to believe that the violation was committed by such person.

§ 1:13 When can a police officer pursue a fleeing person?

In *People v. Holmes*, 81 N.Y.2d 1056, 601 N.Y.S.2d 459, 619 N.E.2d 396 (1993), the Court of Appeals addressed the issue of when a police officer can lawfully pursue a person who responds to a valid *DeBour* request for information by fleeing. In this regard, the Court held that:

> Flight alone, however, or even in conjunction with equivocal circumstances that might justify a police request for information, is insufficient to justify pursuit because an individual has a right "to be let alone" and refuse to respond to police inquiry. * * *

> While the police may have had an objective credible reason to approach defendant to request information—having observed him in a "known narcotics location" with an unidentified bulge in the pocket of his jacket—those circumstances, taken together with defendant's flight, could not justify the significantly greater intrusion of police

pursuit. Defendant was merely observed in the daytime, talking with a group of men on a New York City street. Given the unfortunate reality of crime in today's society, many areas of New York City, at one time or another, have probably been described by the police as "high crime neighborhoods" or "narcotics-prone locations." Moreover, a bulging jacket pocket is hardly indicative of criminality. As we have recognized, a pocket bulge, unlike a waistband bulge, "could be caused by any number of innocuous objects."

If these circumstances could combine with flight to justify pursuit, then in essence the right to inquire would be tantamount to the right to seize, and there would, in fact, be no right "to be let alone." That is not, nor should it be, the law.

81 N.Y.2d at 1058, 601 N.Y.S.2d at 461 (citations omitted). *See also People v. May*, 81 N.Y.2d 725, 593 N.Y.S.2d 760, 609 N.E.2d 113 (1992) (police cannot stop vehicle based solely upon fact that vehicle was parked on a desolate street in a high crime area and the driver slowly pulled away when the police approached).

§ 1:14   When is a vehicle stop improper?

Since the police can lawfully stop a vehicle whenever they have probable cause to believe that the driver has committed a traffic infraction—no matter how minor—there is little need to provide a comprehensive list of cases holding that a vehicle stop was lawful. By contrast, since there are comparatively few cases holding that a vehicle stop was improper, a comprehensive list of such cases is useful.

Vehicle stops have been found to be improper under the following circumstances:

1. Where the stop was nothing more than a "routine traffic check." *Delaware v. Prouse*, 440 U.S. 648, 99 S. Ct. 1391, 59 L. Ed. 2d 660 (1979); *People v. Simone*, 39 N.Y.2d 818, 385 N.Y.S.2d 765, 351 N.E.2d 432 (1976); *People v. Ingle*, 36 N.Y.2d 413, 369 N.Y.S.2d 67, 330 N.E.2d 39 (1975); *People v. Mason*, 69 A.D.2d 769, 415 N.Y.S.2d 31 (1st Dep't 1979); *People v. Mestey*, 61 A.D.2d 447, 402 N.Y.S.2d 577 (1st Dep't 1978); *People v. Conroy*, 51 A.D.2d 1007, 380 N.Y.S.2d 766 (2d Dep't 1976); *People v. Deacy*, 140 Misc. 2d 232, 530 N.Y.S.2d 753 (Nassau Co. Dist. Ct. 1988);

2. Where there was a lack of probable cause to believe that the defendant committed a traffic infraction. *People v. Chilton*, 69 N.Y.2d 928, 516 N.Y.S.2d 633, 509 N.E.2d 327 (1987); *People v. Mandato*, 195 Misc. 2d 636, 760 N.Y.S.2d 809 (App. Term, 2d Dep't 2003);

3. Where the stop was based solely upon the fact that the vehicle was parked on a desolate street in a high crime area

and the driver slowly pulled away when the police approached. *People v. May*, 81 N.Y.2d 725, 593 N.Y.S.2d 760, 609 N.E.2d 113 (1992);

4. Where the stop was based upon the officer's opinion that the occupants of the vehicle looked "suspicious," the vehicle or its occupants "seemed out of place," or the officer sensed that "something was not right." *People v. Lopez*, 75 A.D.3d 610, 905 N.Y.S.2d 647 (2d Dep't 2010); *People v. Hoglen*, 162 A.D.2d 1036, 557 N.Y.S.2d 817 (4th Dep't 1990); *People v. Murray*, 48 A.D.2d 907, 370 N.Y.S.2d 10 (2d Dep't 1975); *People v. Deer*, 39 Misc. 3d 677, 960 N.Y.S.2d 891 (St. Lawrence Co. Ct. 2013); *People v. Mejia*, 133 Misc. 2d 755, 507 N.Y.S.2d 957 (Bronx Co. Sup. Ct. 1986); *Blanchfield v. State*, 104 Misc. 2d 21, 427 N.Y.S.2d 682 (Ct. Cl. 1980);

5. Where the purpose of the stop was to request information of the driver concerning the whereabouts of a criminal suspect or if he knew anything about a recent crime. *People v. Spencer*, 84 N.Y.2d 749, 622 N.Y.S.2d 483, 646 N.E.2d 785 (1995); *People v. Taylor*, 31 A.D.3d 1141, 817 N.Y.S.2d 816 (4th Dep't 2006); *People v. Washburn*, 309 A.D.2d 1270, 765 N.Y.S.2d 76 (4th Dep't 2003); *People v. McMaster*, 3 Misc. 3d 1107(A), 787 N.Y.S.2d 680 (Webster Just. Ct. 2004). *Cf. Illinois v. Lidster*, 540 U.S. 419, 124 S. Ct. 885, 157 L. Ed. 2d 843 (2004); *People v. John BB.*, 56 N.Y.2d 482, 453 N.Y.S.2d 158, 438 N.E.2d 864 (1982);

6. Where the stop was based upon the officer's "hunch" that a crime was about to be committed. *People v. Sobotker*, 43 N.Y.2d 559, 402 N.Y.S.2d 993, 373 N.E.2d 1218 (1978); *People v. Farrell*, 90 A.D.2d 396, 457 N.Y.S.2d 260 (1st Dep't 1982), order aff'd, 59 N.Y.2d 686, 463 N.Y.S.2d 416, 450 N.E.2d 222 (1983);

7. Where the stop was based upon the officer's "hunch" that a crime had recently been attempted/committed. *People v. Peterson*, 266 A.D.2d 738, 698 N.Y.S.2d 777 (3d Dep't 1999); *People v. Sunley*, 171 A.D.2d 1063, 568 N.Y.S.2d 994 (4th Dep't 1991); *People v. Cascio*, 63 A.D.2d 183, 407 N.Y.S.2d 703 (2d Dep't 1978); *People v. Gutierrez*, 8 Misc. 3d 1012(A), 801 N.Y.S.2d 780 (Nassau Co. Dist. Ct. 2005);

8. Where the stop was based upon the officer's "hunch" that the defendant—who the police were looking for—was the driver of the car. *People v. Lindsey*, 13 A.D.3d 651, 787 N.Y.S.2d 385 (2d Dep't 2004);

9. Where the stop was " '[d]ue to the rash of crimes in the immediate area.' " *People v. McMaster*, 3 Misc. 3d 1107(A), 787 N.Y.S.2d 680 (Webster Just. Ct. 2004), at *1;

10. Where the stop was made pursuant to an invalid checkpoint. *See* §§ 5:1 et seq., *infra*;

11. Where the stop was due to the defendant's purported evasion of a sobriety checkpoint. *People v. Bigger*, 2 Misc. 3d 937, 771 N.Y.S.2d 826 (Webster Just. Ct. 2004); *People v. Rocket*, 156 Misc. 2d 641, 594 N.Y.S.2d 568 (Pleasant Valley Just. Ct. 1992). *Cf. People v. Chaffee*, 183 A.D.2d 208, 590 N.Y.S.2d 625 (4th Dep't 1992);

12. Where the stop was based upon a mistake of law (*i.e.*, where the officer's belief that the defendant had committed a VTL infraction was based on an erroneous interpretation of the law). *See* § 1:15, *infra*;

13. Where the stop was an invalid anonymous tip stop. *See* § 1:16, *infra*;

14. Where the testimony of the arresting officer(s) at a suppression hearing was not credible. *People v. Anokye*, 88 A.D.3d 736, 930 N.Y.S.2d 485 (2d Dep't 2011); *People v. Lewis*, 195 A.D.2d 523, 600 N.Y.S.2d 272 (2d Dep't 1993); *People v. Akwa*, 151 Misc. 2d 106, 573 N.Y.S.2d 216 (Kings Co. Sup. Ct. 1991); *People v. Jones*, 125 Misc. 2d 91, 477 N.Y.S.2d 975 (N.Y. Co. Sup. Ct. 1984); *People v. Ananaba*, 25 Misc. 3d 1242(A), 906 N.Y.S.2d 781 (Queens Co. Sup. Ct. 2009); *People v. Aquiar*, 2003 WL 21739071 (Westchester Co. Ct. 2003);

15. Where the police lacked reasonable suspicion that criminal activity was afoot. *People v. Layou*, 71 A.D.3d 1382, 897 N.Y.S.2d 325 (4th Dep't 2010); *People v. Solano*, 46 A.D.3d 1223, 848 N.Y.S.2d 431 (3d Dep't 2007); *People v. Brown*, 112 A.D.2d 945, 492 N.Y.S.2d 625 (2d Dep't 1985), opinion amended on other grounds, 114 A.D.2d 417, 494 N.Y.S.2d 333 (2d Dep't 1985); *People v. Spicer*, 105 A.D.2d 1100, 482 N.Y.S.2d 169 (4th Dep't 1984); *People v. Corcoran*, 89 A.D.2d 696, 453 N.Y.S.2d 877 (3d Dep't 1982); *People v. La Borde*, 66 A.D.2d 803, 410 N.Y.S.2d 886 (2d Dep't 1978);

16. Where the stop was based upon a claim that the vehicle was observed driving erratically almost an hour earlier. *People v. Royko*, 201 A.D.2d 863, 607 N.Y.S.2d 515 (4th Dep't 1994);

17. Where the stop was based upon the fact that the defendant was driving slowly, had an out-of-State license plate, or appeared to be lost. *People v. Joe*, 63 A.D.2d 737, 405 N.Y.S.2d 295 (2d Dep't 1978). *See also People v. Conroy*, 51 A.D.2d 1007, 380 N.Y.S.2d 766 (2d Dep't 1976); *People v. Bergers*, 50 A.D.2d 764, 377 N.Y.S.2d 67 (1st Dep't 1975);

18. Where the description of the vehicle/person the police were looking for was too vague. *People v. Tindal*, 231 A.D.2d 404, __, 646 N.Y.S.2d 814, 814 (1st Dep't 1996) ("absent some additional information identifying the vehicle involved in the alleged crime beyond its make and color or

distinguishing the driver from other young black males with a commonly worn haircut, the information available to the officers fell far short of that required to justify a stop of defendant's vehicle 24 hours after receipt of this general, limited information provided by the complainant");

19. Where the stop was based upon a vague police radio transmission. *People v. Nicodemus*, 247 A.D.2d 833, __, 669 N.Y.S.2d 98, 99 (4th Dep't 1998) ("The dispatch did not give a description of the robbers and did not mention a vehicle. It stated only that two males, one of whom wore a mask, had left the scene on foot."); *People v. Crump*, 217 A.D.2d 902, 629 N.Y.S.2d 602 (4th Dep't 1995) (a "dark-colored vehicle"—possibly a Cadillac—was seen speeding from a specified area); *People v. Scheu*, 177 Misc. 2d 922, 677 N.Y.S.2d 904 (Nassau Co. Dist. Ct. 1998) (a "part of a partial plate" of a "dark Ford");

20. Where the vehicle that was stopped did not sufficiently match the description of the vehicle that the officer was theoretically looking for. *People v. Brooks*, 266 A.D.2d 864, 697 N.Y.S.2d 804 (4th Dep't 1999);

21. Where the vehicle was stopped a second time, by a second set of officers, based upon their opinion that the first set of officers had conducted an inadequate search (even though they were apparently correct). *People v. Major*, 263 A.D.2d 360, 693 N.Y.S.2d 30 (1st Dep't 1999);

22. Where the stop was based upon the defendant's failure to signal a right turn upon leaving a parking lot. *Byer v. Jackson*, 241 A.D.2d 943, 661 N.Y.S.2d 336 (4th Dep't 1997); *People v. Silvers*, 195 Misc. 2d 739, 761 N.Y.S.2d 472 (Mount Vernon City Ct. 2003); *People v. Mazzola*, 12 Misc. 3d 1165(A), 819 N.Y.S.2d 212 (Suffolk Co. Dist. Ct. 2006);

23. Where the stop was based upon the fact that the defendant was leaving the parking lot of a closed group home shortly after midnight. *People v. Stock*, 57 A.D.3d 1424, 871 N.Y.S.2d 545 (4th Dep't 2008);

24. Where the defendant was driving through the parking lot of a closed car dealership—where crimes had recently been committed—at approximately 1:00 AM. *Byer v. Jackson*, 241 A.D.2d 943, 661 N.Y.S.2d 336 (4th Dep't 1997). *See also People v. Buttitta*, 27 Misc. 3d 1204(A), 910 N.Y.S.2d 407 (Pendleton Just. Ct. 2010) (similar facts);

25. Where the stop was based upon a claim that the defendant's vehicle had insufficient plate lamps, but there was insufficient proof supporting this claim at a probable cause hearing. *People v. Lang*, 30 Misc. 3d 1224(A), 926 N.Y.S.2d 346 (Webster Just. Ct. 2011);

26. Where the stop was based upon an air freshener hanging from the defendant's rearview mirror that did not violate VTL § 375(30). *People v. O'Hare*, 73 A.D.3d 812, 900 N.Y.S.2d 400 (2d Dep't 2010);

27. Where the stop was based upon the fact that one of the defendant's passengers was hanging out of the vehicle's window apparently making a remark to a person on a nearby sidewalk. *People v. Henry*, 159 A.D.2d 990, 552 N.Y.S.2d 749 (4th Dep't 1990);

28. Where the stop was based upon the defendant's vehicle weaving within its own lane. *People v. Culcross*, 184 Misc. 2d 67, 706 N.Y.S.2d 605 (Monroe Co. Ct. 2000) (defendant's vehicle "swerved" within its lane twice and the front tire "struck" the center dotted line once); *People v. Teall*, 32 Misc. 3d 1223(A), 936 N.Y.S.2d 60 (Rochester City Court 2011); *People v. Lochan*, 23 Misc. 3d 1106(A), 885 N.Y.S.2d 712 (N.Y. City Crim. Ct. 2009);

29. Where the defendant was stopped solely because his right front tire traveled partially onto the fog line 3 or 4 times. *People v. Davis*, 58 A.D.3d 896, 870 N.Y.S.2d 602 (3d Dep't 2009);

30. Where the stop was based upon the fact that the defendant briefly crossed the fog line. *People v. Schoonmaker*, 44 Misc. 3d 1201(A), 2014 WL 2863707 (Red Hook N.Y. Just. Ct. 2014); *People v. Luster*, 35 Misc. 3d 735, 946 N.Y.S.2d 407 (Suffolk Co. Dist. Ct. 2012); *People v. Bordeau*, 21 Misc. 3d 1121(A), 873 N.Y.S.2d 513 (Essex Co. Ct. 2008); *People v. Fisher*, 20 Misc. 3d 1136(A), 867 N.Y.S.2d 377 (Wappinger Just. Ct. 2008). *Cf. People v. Wohlers*, 138 A.D.2d 957, —, 526 N.Y.S.2d 290 (4th Dep't 1988) ("the court's finding that defendant's vehicle 'strayed slightly to the right of the driving lane' established a valid basis for the stop. Such conduct is a violation of Vehicle and Traffic Law § 1128(a), which requires drivers to remain in lane");

31. Where the stop was based upon an alleged "high beams" violation, but the defendant's conduct did not actually hinder or hamper the officer's ability to operate his vehicle. *People v. Allen*, 89 A.D.3d 742, 932 N.Y.S.2d 142 (2d Dep't 2011), leave to appeal granted, 18 N.Y.3d 888, 939 N.Y.S.2d 758, 963 N.E.2d 135 (2012); *People v. Rose*, 67 A.D.3d 1447, 889 N.Y.S.2d 789 (4th Dep't 2009); *People v. Garlock*, 29 Misc. 3d 1223(A), 920 N.Y.S.2d 243 (Lockport Just. Ct. 2010);

32. Where the stop was based upon the fact that the defendant floored the gas pedal of his vehicle and squealed the tires, "leaving rubber." *People v. Simmons*, 58 A.D.2d 524, 395 N.Y.S.2d 188 (1st Dep't 1977);

33. Where the stop was based upon the fact that the defendant caused his moving vehicle to "fishtail." *McDonell v. New York State Dept. of Motor Vehicles*, 77 A.D.3d 1379, 908 N.Y.S.2d 507 (4th Dep't 2010);

34. Where the stop was based upon the fact that the defendant, who had been stopped at a red light, did not start until the light had turned from green to yellow. *People v. Martinez*, 31 Misc. 3d 201, 915 N.Y.S.2d 819 (Nassau Co. Dist. Ct. 2011);

35. Where the stop was based upon the fact that the defendant was driving below the posted speed limit. *People v. Beeney*, 181 Misc. 2d 201, 694 N.Y.S.2d 583 (Monroe Co. Ct. 1999);

36. Where the defendant technically committed an offense, but did so as the result of an involuntary act. PL § 15.10; *People v. Marzulli*, 76 Misc. 2d 971, 351 N.Y.S.2d 775 (App. Term, 2d & 11th Jud. Dist. 1973) (per curiam); *People v. Soe*, 9 Misc. 3d 1069, 805 N.Y.S.2d 262 (Valley Stream Just. Ct. 2005); *People v. Shaughnessy*, 66 Misc. 2d 19, 319 N.Y.S.2d 626 (Nassau Co. Dist. Ct. 1971);

37. Where a plainclothes police officer in his own private vehicle stopped defendant's vehicle and approached with gun drawn based upon the fact that the officer saw burning pieces of paper thrown from defendant's vehicle. *People v. Steg*, 51 A.D.2d 810, 380 N.Y.S.2d 270 (2d Dep't 1976);

38. Where the stop was based upon the fact that the defendant's car had a broken rear vent window. *People v. Elam*, 179 A.D.2d 229, 584 N.Y.S.2d 780 (1st Dep't 1992);

39. Where the stop was based upon an alleged cell phone violation that the Court found did not violate VTL § 1225-c. *People v. Abdul-Akim*, 27 Misc. 3d 1220(A), 910 N.Y.S.2d 764 (Kings Co. Sup. Ct. 2010); and

40. Where the stop was based upon suspicion that the defendant was driving while intoxicated. *People v. Ball*, 132 A.D.3d 1286, 17 N.Y.S.3d 358 (4th Dep't 2015).

In *People v. Rice*, 11 Misc. 3d 539, ___, 810 N.Y.S.2d 306, 311–12 (N.Y. Co. Sup. Ct. 2006), the Court held that VTL § 1163 "does not require signaling when a lane change can be made in complete safety without such signal." The Appellate Division, First Department, reversed, holding that "[i]n view of the clear language of the statute, coupled with its unequivocal legislative history, we can only conclude that the hearing court erred when it determined that VTL 1163 does not require a signal, in all instances, when changing a lane." 44 A.D.3d at ___, 841 N.Y.S.2d at 76. In so holding, the Court reasoned that:

VTL 1163(d) unequivocally requires that a turn signal *"shall be used* to indicate an intention to . . . change lanes" (emphasis added). While the legislature's employment of mandatory language, such as "shall" or "must," is not, by itself, conclusive, "such a word of command is ordinarily construed as peremptory in the absence of circumstances suggesting a contrary legislative intent." Here, not only is there an absence of any contrary intent, but the absence of any such qualification or limitation is consistent with the wording of section 1163(a), which imposes a duty to signal a lane change under all circumstances. Indeed, if a duty to signal a lane change existed only under certain circumstances, as found by the hearing court, then a harmonizing reference to such a limitation would have been included in section 1163(d).

44 A.D.3d at __, 841 N.Y.S.2d at 75 (citations omitted). *See also People v. Tamburrino*, 26 Misc. 3d 930, 892 N.Y.S.2d 852 (Saratoga Springs N.Y. City Ct. 2009); *People v. James*, 17 Misc. 3d 623, 842 N.Y.S.2d 859 (N.Y. City Crim. Ct. 2007); *People v. Martinez-Lopez*, 16 Misc. 3d 298, 834 N.Y.S.2d 852 (Nassau Co. Dist. Ct. 2007).

§ 1:15 Mistake of law stop

In *Byer v. Jackson*, 241 A.D.2d 943, 661 N.Y.S.2d 336 (4th Dep't 1997), the petitioner's car was stopped by the police "after he turned right out of a parking lot without using his turn signal," which led to the petitioner being arrested for, among other things, DWI. 241 A.D.2d at __, 661 N.Y.S.2d at 337. The petitioner thereafter refused to submit to a chemical test. A chemical test refusal hearing was held by DMV, following which the petitioner's driver's license was revoked.

On appeal, DMV conceded "that petitioner did not violate Vehicle and Traffic Law § 1163(a), the underlying predicate for the stop, because the statute does not require a motorist to signal a turn from a private driveway," but nonetheless contended "that the officer's good faith belief that there was a violation of the Vehicle and Traffic Law, coupled with the surrounding circumstances, provided reasonable suspicion of criminality to justify the stop." 241 A.D.2d at __, 661 N.Y.S.2d at 337–38. The Appellate Division, Fourth Department, disagreed, holding that "[w]here the officer's belief is based on an erroneous interpretation of law, the stop is illegal at the outset and any further actions by the police as a direct result of the stop are illegal." 241 A.D.2d at __, 661 N.Y.S.2d at 338.

Subsequent to *Byer*, numerous Courts have held that "mistake of law" stops are illegal, requiring the suppression of any evidence obtained as a direct result thereof. *See, e.g., McDonell v. New York State Dept. of Motor Vehicles*, 77 A.D.3d 1379, __, 908 N.Y.S.2d 507, 508 (4th Dep't 2010) (causing a moving vehicle to "fishtail" does not violate VTL § 1162, "which [only] prohibits unsafely moving a stopped, standing or parked vehicle"); *People* *v. Rose*, 67 A.D.3d 1447, __, 889 N.Y.S.2d 789, 791 (4th Dep't 2009) (the mere flashing of high beams does not violate VTL § 375(3); rather, the high beams must interfere with the driver of an approaching vehicle); *People v. Garlock*, 29 Misc. 3d 1223(A), 920 N.Y.S.2d 243 (Lockport Just. Ct. 2010) (same); *People v. Smith*, 67 A.D.3d 1392, __, 887 N.Y.S.2d 883 (4th Dep't 2009) ("We conclude that County Court properly suppressed the evidence on the ground that the police officer made a mistake of law in stopping defendant's vehicle, which had in fact performed a legal pass on the right pursuant to Vehicle and Traffic Law § 1123(a)(1) and (2)."); *People v. MacKenzie*, 61 A.D.3d 703, __, 875 N.Y.S.2d 908 (2d Dep't 2009) ("the stop of the defendant's vehicle was unlawful, because reasonable suspicion to believe that he had violated Vehicle and Traffic Law § 375(2)(a) (1) was lacking"); *People v. Smith*, 1 A.D.3d 965, __, 767 N.Y.S.2d 327, 328 (4th Dep't 2003) ("The lack of a license plate on a vehicle generally will justify a stop of the vehicle for violation of Vehicle and Traffic Law § 402. Here, however, upon stopping defendant's vehicle, the officer observed that it had a Florida rear license plate and realized that no front plate was required.") (citations omitted); *People v. Silvers*, 195 Misc. 2d 739, __, 761 N.Y.S.2d 472 (Mount Vernon City Ct. 2003) ("nothing in [VTL § 1163(b)] requires a motorist to signal a turn when exiting a parking lot"); *People v. Mazzola*, 12 Misc. 3d 1165(A), 819 N.Y.S.2d 212 (Suffolk Co. Dist. Ct. 2006) (defendant's failure to signal right turn out of parking lot did not violate VTL § 1163(d)); *People v. Yendo*, 30 Misc. 3d 135(A), 924 N.Y.S.2d 311 (App. Term, 9th & 10th Jud. Dist. 2011), at *1 ("Vehicle and Traffic Law § 1201(a) does not prohibit a motorist from stopping a vehicle within 'a business or residence district.' . . . [T]he trooper acknowledged that the spot where he had observed defendant's car stopped was 'a residential or business district.' ").

In *People v. Guthrie*, 25 N.Y.3d 130, 132, 8 N.Y.S.3d 237, 239, 30 N.E.3d 880 (2015), the Court of Appeals partially abrogated the mistake of law doctrine, holding that as long as "the officer's mistake about the law is reasonable, the stop is constitutional." In so holding, the Court reasoned that "the relevant question before us is not whether the officer acted in good faith, but whether his belief that a traffic violation had occurred was objectively reasonable. Recently, in *Heien v. North Carolina*, the Supreme Court of the United States clarified that the Fourth Amendment tolerates objectively reasonable mistakes supporting such a belief, whether they are mistakes of fact or mistakes of law." *Id.* at 134, 8 N.Y.S.3d at 240-41 (citations and footnote omitted).

Critically, in the footnote omitted from the above quote, the *Guthrie* Court stated:

This distinction is significant in that a mistake of law that is merely made in "good faith" will not validate a traffic stop; rather, unless the mistake is objectively reasonable, any evidence gained from the stop—whether based on a mistake of law or a mistake of fact—must be suppressed. Thus, contrary to the dissent's suggestion, our holding in this case does not represent a limitation on the rule set forth in *People v. Bigelow* that there is no good faith exception to the exclusionary rule.

Id. at 134, 8 N.Y.S.3d at 240 (citation omitted). *See also id.* at 139, 8 N.Y.S.3d at 244-45 ("As the Supreme Court explained, the requirement that the mistake be objectively reasonable prevents officers from 'gain[ing] [any] Fourth Amendment advantage through a sloppy study of the laws [they are] duty-bound to enforce'") (citation omitted).

Thus, *Guthrie* clearly does not stand for the proposition that all mistake of law stops are now valid. It merely stands for the proposition that "objectively reasonable" mistake of law stops are valid. *See generally People v. Abrucci-Kohan*, __ Misc. 3d __, __ N.Y.S.3d __, 2016 WL 1174766 (Monroe N.Y. J. Ct. 2016).

§ 1:16 Anonymous tip stops

In *Florida v. J.L.*, 529 U.S. 266, 268, 120 S. Ct. 1375, 1377, 146 L. Ed. 2d 254 (2000), the United States Supreme Court held that an anonymous tip that a person is carrying a gun, without more, is insufficient to justify a police officer's stop and frisk of the person. In so holding, the Court reasoned as follows:

The anonymous call concerning J.L. provided no predictive information and therefore left the police without means to test the informant's knowledge or credibility. That the allegation about the gun turned out to be correct does not suggest that the officers, prior to the frisks, had a reasonable basis for suspecting J.L. of engaging in unlawful conduct: The reasonableness of official suspicion must be measured by what the officers knew before they conducted their search. All the police had to go on in this case was the bare report of an unknown, unaccountable informant who neither explained how he knew about the gun nor supplied any basis for believing he had inside information about J.L. * * *

Florida contends that the tip was reliable because its description of the suspect's visible attributes proved accurate: There really was a young black male wearing a plaid shirt at the bus stop. The United States as *amicus curiae* makes a similar argument, proposing that a stop and frisk should be permitted "when (1) an anonymous tip provides a description of a particular person at a particular location illegally carrying a concealed firearm, (2) police promptly verify the pertinent details of the tip except the existence of the firearm, and (3) there are no factors that cast doubt on the reliability of the tip . . . ." These contentions misapprehend the reliability needed for a tip to justify a *Terry* stop.

An accurate description of a subject's readily observable location and appearance is of course reliable in this limited sense: It will help the police correctly identify the person whom the tipster means to accuse. Such a tip, however, does not show that the tipster has knowledge of concealed criminal activity. *The reasonable suspicion here at issue requires that a tip be reliable in its assertion of illegality, not just in its tendency to identify a determinate person.*

529 U.S. at 271–72, 120 S.Ct. at 1379 (emphasis added) (citations omitted). Notably, the *J.L.* Court declined the government's request that it create a "firearm exception" to the anonymous tip rules on the ground that firearms are dangerous. 529 U.S. at 272–73, 120 S.Ct. at 1379–80.

In *People v. Moore*, 6 N.Y.3d 496, 814 N.Y.S.2d 567, 847 N.E.2d 1141 (2006), the Court of Appeals discussed the requirements for a valid anonymous tip stop in light of both *J.L.* and the Court's own post-*J.L.* decision in *People v. William "II"*, 98 N.Y.2d 93, 745 N.Y.S.2d 792, 772 N.E.2d 1150 (2002):

An anonymous tip cannot provide reasonable suspicion to justify a seizure, except where that tip contains predictive information— such as information suggestive of criminal behavior—so that the police can test the reliability of the tip (*see Florida v. J.L.*; *[People v.] William II*). Indeed, in *J.L.*, a unanimous United States Supreme Court held that an anonymous tip regarding a young Black male standing at a particular bus stop, wearing a plaid shirt and carrying a gun, was insufficient to provide the requisite reasonable suspicion to authorize a stop and frisk of the defendant.

The State argued in *J.L.* that the tip was sufficient to justify the police intrusion because the defendant matched the detailed description provided by the tipster. The Supreme Court held, however, that reasonable suspicion "requires that a tip be reliable in its assertion of illegality, not just in its tendency to identify a determinate person." The Court further explained that an anonymous tip could demonstrate the tipster's reliability and thus provide reasonable suspicion of criminal activity only if it predicted actions subsequently engaged in by the suspect. * * *

[T]he anonymous tip triggered only the police officers' common-law right of inquiry. This right authorized the police to ask questions of defendant—and to follow defendant while attempting to engage him—but not to seize him in order to do so. Thus, defendant remained free to continue about his business without risk of forcible detention. * * *

Under our settled DeBour jurisprudence, to elevate the right of inquiry to the right to forcibly stop and detain, the police must obtain additional information or make additional observations of suspicious conduct sufficient to provide reasonable suspicion of criminal behavior. * * *

> [T]he Court's decision today is wholly in line with our precedent: a forcible stop requires reasonable suspicion that the suspect has committed a crime, not merely the founded suspicion—triggering the officers' common-law right of inquiry—present here.

6 N.Y.3d at 499, 500, 500–01, 501, 814 N.Y.S.2d at 569, 570 (emphasis added) (citations omitted). *See also People v. William "II"*, 98 N.Y.2d 93, 99, 745 N.Y.S.2d 792, 794–95, 772 N.E.2d 1150 (2002) (*"[a] tipster's reliability would be demonstrated only if the suspect subsequently engaged in actions, preferably suggestive of concealed criminal activity, which the anonymous tip predicted in detail*. . . . [R]easonable suspicion 'requires that a tip be reliable in its assertion of illegality, not just in its tendency to identify a determinate person'") (emphasis added) (citations omitted); *People v. Sampson*, 68 A.D.3d 1455, 891 N.Y.S.2d 518 (3d Dep't 2009); *People v. Hoffman*, 224 A.D.2d 853, __, 638 N.Y.S.2d 203, 205 (3d Dep't 1996) ("An anonymous telephone tip must be viewed with undiluted suspicion, as it is a notoriously weak and unreliable source of information."); *People v. Letts*, 180 A.D.2d 931, 580 N.Y.S.2d 525 (3d Dep't 1992); *People v. Vega*, 178 A.D.2d 1018, 578 N.Y.S.2d 342 (4th Dep't 1991); *People v. Burpee*, 175 A.D.2d 585, 572 N.Y.S.2d 250 (4th Dep't 1991); *People v. Clark*, 133 A.D.2d 955, 520 N.Y.S.2d 668 (3d Dep't 1987).

In *People v. Rance*, 227 A.D.2d 936, __, 644 N.Y.S.2d 447 (4th Dep't 1996), a "police officer received a radio dispatch that an anonymous informant had reported that an intoxicated woman was leaving a business establishment . . . and was entering the driver's seat of a red Oldsmobile with a particular license plate number." The officer arrived at that location within minutes and observed the car backing out of a space in the parking lot. The officer blocked the car's path with his police car, and approached the defendant to request her license and registration. Only *after* stopping the defendant's vehicle did the officer observe indicia of intoxication and elicit an incriminating admission from the defendant, which led to her arrest for DWI and AUO 1st. In a memorandum decision, the Appellate Division, Fourth Department, held that:

> The information in the radio dispatch provided reasonable suspicion to believe that defendant had committed or was about to commit a crime, thereby justifying a stop of the vehicle. Police action may be based upon information from an anonymous source where, as here, it relates to "matters gravely affecting personal or public safety."

227 A.D.2d at __, 644 N.Y.S.2d at 447 (citations omitted).

It is the authors' opinion that *Rance* has been effectively overruled by *J.L.*, *Moore*, and/or *William II*. At the outset, the *Rance* Court's claim that "[t]he information in the radio dispatch

provided reasonable suspicion to believe that defendant had committed or was about to commit a crime, thereby justifying a stop
of the vehicle" was expressly rejected by *J.L.*, *Moore*, and *William
II*. Specifically, these cases make clear that an anonymous tip
must "be reliable in its assertion of illegality, not just in its tendency to identify a determinate person," and that the tip must
accurately predict (*i.e.*, be corroborated by) behavior indicative of
criminality. *See also People v. Braun*, 299 A.D.2d 246, __, 750
N.Y.S.2d 58, 58–59 (1st Dep't 2002) ("we are constrained to reverse by recent precedent authoritatively holding that an anonymous tip alleging that a described person has engaged in criminal activity, unless corroborated so as to render it 'reliable in its
assertion of illegality, not just in its tendency to identify a
determinate person,' does not create reasonable suspicion sufficient to justify a stop and frisk") (citation omitted). *See generally People v. Elwell*, 50 N.Y.2d 231, 234–35, 428 N.Y.S.2d 655,
657, 406 N.E.2d 471 (1980) ("We affirm the Appellate Division's
holding that for police observation to constitute the verification
that will establish probable cause and permit a warrantless
search or arrest predicated upon data from an informer who has
not revealed the basis for his knowledge, it is not enough that a
number, even a large number, of details of noncriminal activity
supplied by the informer be confirmed. Probable cause for such
an arrest or search will have been demonstrated only when there
has been confirmation of sufficient details suggestive of or directly
related to the criminal activity informed about to make reasonable the conclusion that the informer has not simply passed along
rumor, or is not involved (whether purposefully or as a dupe) in
an effort to 'frame' the person informed against.").

Since the police observed no illegal conduct by Rance prior to
stopping her, the stop clearly violated *J.L.*, *Moore*, and *William
II*. *See generally Harris v. Com.*, 276 Va. 689, 696, 698, 668 S.E.2d
141, 146, 147 (Va. 2008) ("An anonymous tip need not include
predictive information when an informant reports readily observable criminal actions. However, the crime of driving while
intoxicated is not readily observable unless the suspected driver
operates his or her vehicle in some fashion objectively indicating
that the driver is intoxicated; such conduct must be observed
before an investigatory stop is justified. * * * Therefore, we hold
that Officer Picard's observations, when considered together with
the anonymous tip, were not sufficient to create a reasonable
suspicion of criminal activity, and that, therefore, Harris was
stopped in violation of his rights under the Fourth Amendment.")
(citation omitted). *Cf. People v. Wright*, 98 N.Y.2d 657, 746
N.Y.S.2d 273, 773 N.E.2d 1011 (2002) (anonymous tip of reckless
driving irrelevant in light of Trooper's own observations of traffic
infraction); *People v. Pealer*, 89 A.D.3d 1504, 933 N.Y.S.2d 473

(4th Dep't 2011), leave to appeal granted, 18 N.Y.3d 961, 944 N.Y.S.2d 489, 967 N.E.2d 714 (2012) (anonymous tip of intoxicated driver irrelevant in light of officer's own observations of traffic infraction); *People v. Walters*, 213 A.D.2d 810, 623 N.Y.S.2d 396 (3d Dep't 1995) (anonymous tip of erratic driving corroborated by Trooper's own observations of same).

J.L., *Moore*, and *William II* further make clear that an uncorroborated anonymous tip only gives the police authority to engage in a *DeBour* level 2 common-law right of inquiry—*not* a *DeBour* level 3 seizure. *See also People v. Russ*, 61 N.Y.2d 693, 694–95, 472 N.Y.S.2d 601, 460 N.E.2d 1086 (1984) ("Finding defendant in a car meeting the description and the specific location indicated by the informant provided reasonable suspicion that a crime had occurred or was about to occur and warranted the officer's request that she step out of the car for inquiry. It did not, however, justify the frisk. . . . A frisk requires reliable knowledge of facts providing reasonable basis for suspecting that the individual to be subjected to that intrusion is armed and may be dangerous.") (citations omitted).

As is noted in § 1:5, *supra*, a vehicle stop by the police is a *DeBour* level 3 seizure. *See, e.g., People v. Ocasio*, 85 N.Y.2d 982, 984, 629 N.Y.S.2d 161, 162, 652 N.E.2d 907 (1995); *People v. Spencer*, 84 N.Y.2d 749, 753, 622 N.Y.S.2d 483, 485–86, 646 N.E.2d 785 (1995); *People v. May*, 81 N.Y.2d 725, 727, 593 N.Y.S.2d 760, 761–62, 609 N.E.2d 113 (1992); *People v. Sobotker*, 43 N.Y.2d 559, 563–64, 402 N.Y.S.2d 993, 995–96, 373 N.E.2d 1218 (1978). Indeed, in *William II* the Court of Appeals applied *J.L.* to a vehicle stop. *See* 98 N.Y.2d at 99, 745 N.Y.S.2d at 795 ("the only basis for reasonable suspicion advanced before the suppression court for stopping the vehicle in which defendant was a passenger was that he matched the physical description provided by an anonymous tipster. Without more, the tip could not provide reasonable suspicion to stop the car") (footnote omitted).

Further undermining the continued validity of *Rance* is the *Rance* Court's statement that "[p]olice action may be based upon information from an anonymous source where, as here, it relates to 'matters gravely affecting personal or public safety.' " 227 A.D.2d at __, 644 N.Y.S.2d at 447 (quoting *People v. Taggart*, 20 N.Y.2d 335, 283 N.Y.S.2d 1, 229 N.E.2d 581 (1967). However, it is clear that *Taggart* (*i.e.*, the case cited by the *Rance* Court in support of its apparent creation of a "DWI exception" to the normal anonymous tip rules) was overruled by *J.L.* Indeed, the facts of *Taggart* are *strikingly* similar to the facts of *J.L.—yet the Supreme Court reached the exact opposite conclusion of that reached by the Taggart Court.*

The facts of *Taggart* are as follows:

The detective, Richard Delaney, was the only witness at the hearing on the motion to suppress. He testified that on the day of the arrest he received an anonymous telephone call at the police station informing him that "there was a male, white youth on the corner of 135th and Jamaica Avenue * * * (who) had a loaded 32 calibre [sic] revolver in his left hand jacket pocket". The caller also stated that the youth was "eighteen", had "blue eyes, blond hair" and was wearing "white chino-type pants".

Delaney then proceeded to that location and observed from across the street an individual who "matched perfectly" the description given to Delaney by the informer. The youth (defendant) "was standing in the middle of a group of children that had just finished bowling". Thereupon, Delaney crossed the street, "took him (defendant) by the arm and put him against the wall and took the revolver out of his left-hand jacket pocket". Delaney did not notice any bulge in the defendant's pocket prior to the search as the weapon "was inside the lining of the jacket".

20 N.Y.2d at 4, 283 N.Y.S.2d at 337–38.

The facts of *J.L.* are as follows:

On October 13, 1995, an anonymous caller reported to the Miami-Dade Police that a young black male standing at a particular bus stop and wearing a plaid shirt was carrying a gun. So far as the record reveals, there is no audio recording of the tip, and nothing is known about the informant. Sometime after the police received the tip—the record does not say how long—two officers were instructed to respond. They arrived at the bus stop about six minutes later and saw three black males "just hanging out [there]." One of the three, respondent J.L., was wearing a plaid shirt. Apart from the tip, the officers had no reason to suspect any of the three of illegal conduct. The officers did not see a firearm, and J.L. made no threatening or otherwise unusual movements. One of the officers approached J.L., told him to put his hands up on the bus stop, frisked him, and seized a gun from J.L.'s pocket.

529 U.S. at 268, 120 S.Ct. at 1377 (citations omitted).

It is clear that *Taggart* and *J.L.* are factually indistinguishable, and thus *Taggart* is no longer good law. To make matters worse, *Taggart* created the very "firearm exception" to the normal anonymous tip rules that was expressly rejected by *J.L. See J.L.*, 529 U.S. at 272, 120 S.Ct. at 1379–80 ("an automatic firearm exception to our established reliability analysis would rove too far. Such an exception would enable any person seeking to harass another to set in motion an intrusive, embarrassing police search of the targeted person simply by placing an anonymous call falsely reporting the target's unlawful carriage of a gun. *Nor could one securely confine such an exception to allegations involving firearms*") (emphasis added). Thus, *J.L.* not only clearly overruled *Taggart*, but also foresaw—and disapproved of—what the *Rance* Court did (which was to expand a "firearm exception" to include a "DWI exception").

Simply stated, since the *Rance* Court's reasoning has been expressly rejected by higher Courts in more recent cases, it is fair to say that *Rance* is no longer good law. The same Court's post-*J.L.* decision in *People v. Jeffery*, 2 A.D.3d 1271, 769 N.Y.S.2d 675 (4th Dep't 2003), seems to literally defy *J.L.* and *William II*. In any event, *Jeffery* seems hard to reconcile with the Court of Appeals' subsequent decision in *Moore, supra*.

Notably, the *Taggart* Court stated that:

It is recognized . . . that using anonymous information as a basis for intrusive police action is highly dangerous. To limit its use to exigent circumstances the police action must relate to matters gravely affecting personal or public safety or irreparable harm to property of extraordinary value. As noted earlier, it should not extend to all contraband or criminal violations. And, of course, the credibility of the police in claiming anonymous information should be subject to the most careful and critical scrutiny, unless abuse should merit or lead to still greater restrictions on police actions. Moreover, the police should be required to make contemporaneous or reasonably prompt detailed records of any such communications which should be subject to inspection and examination on a suppression hearing on the issue of credibility. It would be unfortunate if the people must be subject to the mercy of the criminal because of the limited and non-lethal risks arising from the conduct of the anonymous informer or from the conduct of police too gullible or too crafty.

20 N.Y.2d at 9, 283 N.Y.S.2d at 343.

In *Navarette v. California*, ___ U.S. ___, ___, 134 S. Ct. 1683, 1686, 188 L. Ed. 2d 680 (2014), the Supreme Court held as follows:

After a 911 caller reported that a vehicle had run her off the road, a police officer located the vehicle she identified during the call and executed a traffic stop. We hold that the stop complied with the Fourth Amendment because, under the totality of the circumstances, the officer had reasonable suspicion that the driver was intoxicated.

It remains to be seen whether the Court of Appeals will follow *Navarette*, as it has previously made clear that "[t]his Court, as a matter of State constitutional law, adheres to the *Aguilar/Spinelli* test and has expressly rejected the less protective 'totality of the circumstances' standard which the United States Supreme Court adopted in *Illinois v. Gates* in lieu of *Aguilar/Spinelli*." *People v. DiFalco*, 80 N.Y.2d 693, 697 n.1, 594 N.Y.S.2d 679, 681 n.1, 610 N.E.2d 352 (1993) (citation omitted).

The Court had the opportunity to decide this issue in *People v. Argyris*, 24 N.Y.3d 1138, 3 N.Y.S.3d 711, 27 N.E.3d 425 (2014), cert. denied, 135 S. Ct. 2902 (2015) and petition for certiorari filed (U.S. May 7, 2015). In *Argyris*, the Court addressed the validity of two separate vehicle stops involving anonymous 911 calls. However, the Court sidestepped the issue of which test should be applied, holding that:

> Regardless of whether we apply a totality of the circumstances test or the *Aguilar-Spinelli* standard, there is record support for the lower courts' findings that the stops were lawful in *People v. Argyris* and *People v. DiSalvo.* The police had reasonable suspicion to stop defendants' vehicle based on the contents of a 911 call from an anonymous individual and the confirmatory observations of the police. Specifically, because sufficient information in the record supports the lower courts' determination that the tip was reliable under the totality of the circumstances, satisfied the two-pronged *Aguilar-Spinelli* test for the reliability of hearsay tips in this particular context and contained sufficient information about defendants' unlawful possession of a weapon to create reasonable suspicion, the lawfulness of the stop of defendants' vehicle is beyond further review. Furthermore, under these circumstances, the absence of predictive information in the tip was not fatal to its reliability. On this record, the lower courts did not err in concluding that the police's other actions were lawful.

> In *People v. Johnson*, whether evaluated in light of the totality of the circumstances or under the *Aguilar-Spinelli* framework, the reliability of the tip was not established. The caller's cursory allegation that the driver of the car was either sick or intoxicated, without more, did not supply the sheriff's deputy who stopped the car with reasonable suspicion that defendant was driving while intoxicated. Although the deputy observed defendant commit a minor traffic infraction, this did not authorize the vehicle stop because he was outside his geographical jurisdiction at the time of the infraction, and defendant's actions in committing the violation did not elevate the deputy's suspicion sufficiently to justify the stop of defendant's car. The issue of whether suppression should be denied on the theory that the deputy's violation of the statutory limits on his jurisdiction does not warrant suppression is not before us.

Id. at 1140-41, 3 N.Y.S.3d at 712 (citations omitted).

§ 1:17   Stops based on tips from "known informant" or "identified citizen"

There is a critical distinction between a tip received from an anonymous tipster and a tip received from a "known informant" or an "identified citizen." The former "must be viewed with undiluted suspicion, as it is a notoriously weak and unreliable source of information." *People v. Hoffman*, 224 A.D.2d 853, —, 638 N.Y.S.2d 203, 205 (3d Dep't 1996). *See also* previous section. By contrast, "[a]n identified citizen informant is presumed to be personally reliable." *People v. Parris*, 83 N.Y.2d 342, 350, 610 N.Y.S.2d 464, 468, 632 N.E.2d 870 (1994). *See also People v. Hetrick*, 80 N.Y.2d 344, 349, 590 N.Y.S.2d 183, 185, 604 N.E.2d 732 (1992) ("because Katy was an identified citizen informant, and not an unnamed informant, there was a 'built-in' basis for crediting her reliability"); *People v. Cantre*, 65 N.Y.2d 790, 493 N.Y.S.2d 127, 482 N.E.2d 923 (1985); *People v. Hicks*, 38 N.Y.2d 90, 94, 378 N.Y.S.2d 660, 664–65, 341 N.E.2d 227 (1975).

Tips received from a known informant or an identified citizen are nonetheless subject to the so-called *Aguilar/Spinelli* test. *See, e.g.*, *People v. DiFalco*, 80 N.Y.2d 693, 696, 594 N.Y.S.2d 679, 680, 610 N.E.2d 352 (1993); *Hetrick*, 80 N.Y.2d at 348, 590 N.Y.S.2d at 185. In this regard, it should be noted that New York adheres to the *Aguilar/Spinelli* test despite a change in federal law. *See, e.g.*, *People v. Edwards*, 95 N.Y.2d 486, 495 n.5, 719 N.Y.S.2d 202, 207 n.5, 741 N.E.2d 876 (2000); *DiFalco*, 80 N.Y.2d at 696 n.1, 594 N.Y.S.2d at 680 n.1; *Hetrick*, 80 N.Y.2d at 348, 590 N.Y.S.2d at 185; *People v. Griminger*, 71 N.Y.2d 635, 637, 529 N.Y.S.2d 55, 55–56, 524 N.E.2d 409 (1988).

The *Aguilar/Spinelli* test provides that:

> [B]efore probable cause based on hearsay is found it must appear . . . that the informant has some basis of knowledge for the information he transmitted to the police and that the information is reliable. The basis of the informant's knowledge must be demonstrated because the information related by an informant, even a reliable one, is of little probative value if he does not have knowledge of the events he describes. Conversely, no matter how solid his basis of knowledge, the information will not support a finding of probable cause unless it is reliable. Since police officers may not arrest a person on mere suspicion or rumor, they likewise may not arrest a suspect on the basis of an informant's tip, perhaps born of suspicion or rumor or intentional fabrication.

People v. Johnson, 66 N.Y.2d 398, 402–03, 497 N.Y.S.2d 618, 621, 488 N.E.2d 439 (1985) (citations omitted). *See also People v. Ketcham*, 93 N.Y.2d 416, 420, 690 N.Y.S.2d 874, 877, 712 N.E.2d 1238 (1999); *People v. Bigelow*, 66 N.Y.2d 417, 497 N.Y.S.2d 630, 488 N.E.2d 451 (1985); *People v. Rodriguez*, 52 N.Y.2d 483, 438 N.Y.S.2d 754, 420 N.E.2d 946 (1981).

"[I]n the ordinary case where a police officer has obtained evidence from a third person providing probable cause, the defendant has the opportunity to question the officer about the third person's identity, relationship to the crime, basis of knowledge, past relationship to the police and criminal history. The defendant is thus able to raise any appropriate question about the officer's testimony to the suppression court." *Edwards*, 95 N.Y.2d at 491, 719 N.Y.S.2d at 205.

In *People v. Washington*, 50 A.D.3d 1539, __, 856 N.Y.S.2d 783, 784 (4th Dep't 2008), the Appellate Division, Fourth Department, held that "[t]he police officer had reasonable suspicion for the initial stop of the vehicle based upon information from an identified citizen informant that the driver of the vehicle was drinking

alcohol and driving erratically." *See also People v. Kirkey*, 17
A.D.3d 1149, __, 793 N.Y.S.2d 856, 857 (4th Dep't 2005) ("The police had the requisite reasonable suspicion to stop the vehicle
driven by defendant based on information provided by an identified citizen informant, and that information was corroborated by
the personal observations of the officer who stopped the vehicle.")
(citation omitted); *People v. Hoffman*, 283 A.D.2d 928, __, 725
N.Y.S.2d 494, 496 (4th Dep't 2001) ("the police had reasonable
suspicion to stop his vehicle based on information from an identified citizen informant concerning a hit-and-run accident. The
identified citizen informant was presumed to be reliable and his
basis of knowledge was his observation of the offense").

§ 1:18   Pretext stops

"A pretext stop has generally been defined as a police officer's
use of a traffic infraction as a subterfuge to stop a motor vehicle
in order to investigate the driver or occupant about an unrelated
matter." *People v. Robinson*, 271 A.D.2d 17, __, 711 N.Y.S.2d 384,
386 (1st Dep't 2000), order aff'd, 97 N.Y.2d 341, 741 N.Y.S.2d
147, 767 N.E.2d 638 (2001). Although the terms "pretext stop"
and "illegal stop" had tended to be synonymous, in *Whren v. U.S.*,
517 U.S. 806, 116 S. Ct. 1769, 135 L. Ed. 2d 89 (1996), the United
States Supreme Court held that a police officer's underlying
intent or motivation is irrelevant for 4th Amendment purposes.
Thus, as long as a police officer possesses a legal basis to stop a
vehicle for a traffic violation, the defendant cannot argue that the
traffic violation was used as a mere pretext to investigate an unrelated crime. In other words, in determining whether the 4th
Amendment has been violated, Courts must apply a standard of
objective reasonableness, without regard to the underlying intent
or motivation of the officer.

In *People v. Robinson*, 97 N.Y.2d 341, 741 N.Y.S.2d 147, 767
N.E.2d 638 (2001), a sharply divided Court of Appeals held that
pretext stops are now legal in New York as well:

> The issue here is whether a police officer who has probable cause to
> believe a driver has committed a traffic infraction violates article I,
> § 12 of the New York State Constitution when the officer, whose
> primary motivation is to conduct another investigation, stops the
> vehicle. We conclude that there is no violation, and we adopt *Whren
> v. United States* as a matter of state law. * * *
>
> We hold that where a police officer has probable cause to believe
> that the driver of an automobile has committed a traffic violation, a
> stop does not violate article I, § 12 of the New York State
> Constitution. In making that determination of probable cause, nei-
> ther the primary motivation of the officer nor a determination of
> what a reasonable traffic officer would have done under the circum-
> stances is relevant. * * *

Because the Vehicle and Traffic Law provides an objective grid upon which to measure probable cause, a stop based on that standard is not arbitrary in the context of constitutional search and seizure jurisprudence.

97 N.Y.2d at 346, 349, 355, 741 N.Y.S.2d at 149, 151, 155 (citation omitted). *See also People v. Wright*, 98 N.Y.2d 657, 746 N.Y.S.2d 273, 773 N.E.2d 1011 (2002); *People v. Pealer*, 20 N.Y.3d 447, 457 n.2, 962 N.Y.S.2d 592, 598 n.2, 985 N.E.2d 903 (2013), petition for cert. filed (U.S. May 16, 2013).

Nonetheless, the *Robinson* Court did note that:

To be sure, the story does not end when the police stop a vehicle for a traffic infraction. Our holding in this case addresses only the initial police action upon which the vehicular stop was predicated. The scope, duration and intensity of the seizure, as well as any search made by the police subsequent to that stop, remain subject to the strictures of article I, § 12, and judicial review.

97 N.Y.2d at 353, 741 N.Y.S.2d at 154.

§ 1:19   Checkpoint stops

This topic is covered at length in §§ 5:1 et seq., *infra*.

§ 1:20   Mistaken arrests

In *People v. Jennings*, 54 N.Y.2d 518, 520, 446 N.Y.S.2d 229, 230, 430 N.E.2d 1282 (1981), the Court of Appeals held that:

An arrest is invalid when the arresting officer acts upon information in criminal justice system records which, though correct when put into the records, no longer applies and which, through fault of the system, has been retained in its records after it became inapplicable. Accordingly, an arrest made in reliance upon the computerized criminal record file of defendant, which showed as outstanding a parole violation warrant which had in fact been executed nine months before and vacated four months before the arrest, is made without probable cause.

See also People v. Watson, 100 A.D.2d 452, 474 N.Y.S.2d 978 (2d Dep't 1984) (rejected on other grounds by, State v. Phillips, 194 W. Va. 569, 461 S.E.2d 75 (1995)); *People v. Lent*, 92 A.D.2d 941, 460 N.Y.S.2d 369 (2d Dep't 1983).

Notably, the *Jennings* Court "expressly reject[ed] the People's contention that Officer Enright's 'good faith' reliance upon the parole warrant 'hit' renders the exclusionary rule inapplicable," reasoning that:

An assessment of probable cause turns on what was reasonably and objectively in the mind of law enforcement authorities. It does not turn on such subjective considerations as the absence of malice against a suspect, the lack of intent to violate constitutional rights, or any other variation of what has been referred to in another context as the "white heart and empty head" standard. The good faith of the enforcement authorities cannot validate an arrest based upon a warrant which had been vacated four months before and had been executed nine months before the arrest was made.

54 N.Y.2d at 523, 446 N.Y.S.2d at 232 (citations omitted). *Cf. Herring v. U.S.*, 555 U.S. 135, 129 S. Ct. 695, 172 L. Ed. 2d 496 (2009).

It should be noted that *Herring* utilized the "good faith" exception to the 4th Amendment exclusionary rule created by *U.S. v. Leon*, 468 U.S. 897, 104 S. Ct. 3405, 82 L. Ed. 2d 677 (1984). This exception to the exclusionary rule was expressly rejected by the Court of Appeals on State Constitutional law grounds in *People v. Bigelow*, 66 N.Y.2d 417, 497 N.Y.S.2d 630, 488 N.E.2d 451 (1985).

§ 1:21 Warrantless arrests in the home

This topic is covered at length in §§ 4:1 et seq., *infra*.

§ 1:22 Out-of-state stops and arrests

Pursuant to CPL § 140.10(3), a police officer may only pursue a person out-of-state to arrest the person for a crime. By contrast, where the arrest is for a petty offense, the officer can "follow such person in continuous close pursuit, commencing either in the county in which the offense was or is believed to have been committed or in an adjoining county, in and through any county of the state, and may arrest him or her in any county in which he or she apprehends him or her." CPL § 140.10(2)(b).

In the context of a DWI case, the defendant is literally never arrested for DWI based upon his or driving. Rather, the defendant is typically stopped for a traffic infraction that evolves into an arrest for DWI. Thus, where a motorist is pursued out-of-state for a traffic infraction which ultimately leads to an out-of-state arrest for DWI, the issue arises as to whether the arrest is lawful. In *People v. Lane*, 144 Misc. 2d 953, 550 N.Y.S.2d 529 (App. Term, 9th and 10th Jud. Dist. 1989), the Court reversed the defendant's conviction of DWI under these circumstances. In so holding, the Court reasoned that:

In the instant case, the record indicates that a deputy sheriff pursued defendant into Connecticut only for driving to the left of the pavement markings (Vehicle and Traffic Law § 1126[a]), a mere traffic infraction. The testimony is clear that he made no judgment or opinion as to whether defendant was intoxicated until after the completion of performance tests, all of which were done in Connecticut. Hence, the subject arrest violated CPL 140.10(3) because the deputy was not pursuing a person outside the state who he had probable cause to believe committed a crime. " 'Crime' means a misdemeanor or a felony" (Penal Law § 10.00[6]). It does not mean a petty offense which is defined as ". . . a violation or a traffic infraction" (CPL 1.20[39]). * * *

Clearly, in the absence of the evidence unlawfully obtained, the court below could not have found defendant guilty beyond a reasonable doubt of driving while intoxicated pursuant to Vehicle and Traffic Law section 1192.

144 Misc. 2d at __, 550 N.Y.S.2d at 530–31.

§ 1:23 Authority of out-of-state police officers to make arrests in New York

In *People v. LaFontaine*, 92 N.Y.2d 470, 682 N.Y.S.2d 671, 705 N.E.2d 663 (1998), the Court of Appeals made clear that, although "[o]ut-of-State police officers may be authorized to make arrests in New York, [they may] generally only [do so] when they are in hot pursuit." 92 N.Y.2d at 475, 682 N.Y.S.2d at 674. *See also* CPL § 140.55. In so holding, the Court reversed the Appellate Division, First Department, decision reported at 235 A.D.2d 93, 664 N.Y.S.2d 587 (1st Dep't 1997).

§ 1:24 Even where initial stop is lawful, continued detention may not be

Even where the initial stop is lawful, the defendant's continued detention can be unlawful where the police immediately discover that the reason for the stop was invalid. *See, e.g., People v. Smith*, 1 A.D.3d 965, __, 767 N.Y.S.2d 327, 328 (4th Dep't 2003) ("The lack of a license plate on a vehicle generally will justify a stop of the vehicle for violation of Vehicle and Traffic Law § 402. Here, however, upon stopping defendant's vehicle, the officer observed that it had a Florida rear license plate and realized that no front plate was required.") (citations omitted); *People v. Mowatt*, 176 Misc. 2d 919, __, 674 N.Y.S.2d 585, 586–87 (N.Y. City Crim. Ct. 1998) ("The initial stop of the defendant was justified based upon the fact that his car did not have front or rear license plates . . . . [However, h]aving seen the temporary license [affixed to the vehicle's rear window], P.O. Hibbert no longer had any reasonable suspicion that the defendant was violating any law or traffic regulation. There was, therefore, no longer any legal basis to further detain the defendant.").

§ 1:25 Length of traffic stop must be reasonable

In *People v. Banks*, 85 N.Y.2d 558, 562, 626 N.Y.S.2d 986, 988, 650 N.E.2d 833 (1995), the Court of Appeals held that a lawful

stop turned into an illegal detention under the following
circumstances:

> For a traffic stop to pass constitutional muster, the officer's action
> in stopping the vehicle must be justified at its inception and the
> seizure must be reasonably related in scope, including its length, to
> the circumstances which justified the detention in the first instance.
> While the stop was justified in the instant case, the length and cir-
> cumstances of the detention were not. Consequently, the evidence
> ultimately seized must be suppressed.
>
> Trooper Cuprill's observations of Jones' seat belt violation justified
> the initial stop of Jones and defendant in the vehicle. However,
> once Cuprill's license and stolen vehicle radio check came back neg-
> ative and he prepared the traffic tickets for the seat belt violations,
> the initial justification for seizing and detaining defendant and
> Jones was exhausted. The Trooper nevertheless retained their li-
> censes, effectively forcing them to remain at the scene while he
> awaited the appearance of the backup Trooper he had requested.
> This continued involuntary detention of defendant and Jones and
> their vehicle constituted a seizure in violation of their constitutional
> rights, unless circumstances coming to Cuprill's attention following
> the initial stop furnished him with reasonable suspicion that they
> were engaged in criminal activity. Contrary to the holdings of the
> courts below, defendant's nervousness and the innocuous discrepan-
> cies in his and Jones' answers to the Trooper's questions regarding
> the origin, destination and timing of their trip did not alone, as a
> matter of law, provide a basis for reasonable suspicion of criminality.

(Citations omitted). *See also People v. Milaski*, 62 N.Y.2d 147,
156, 476 N.Y.S.2d 104, 108, 464 N.E.2d 472 (1984) ("The two different reasons given by defendant for his presence in the parking
area, although at variance, along with defendant's nervousness
and other inconsistencies in his statements, provided no indication of criminality on his part which would have justified further
detention"); *People v. May*, 52 A.D.3d 147, 861 N.Y.S.2d 276 (1st
Dep't 2008); *People v. Barreras*, 253 A.D.2d 369, 677 N.Y.S.2d
526 (1st Dep't 1998); *People v. Turriago*, 219 A.D.2d 383, 644
N.Y.S.2d 178 (1st Dep't 1996), aff'd as modified and remanded,
90 N.Y.2d 77, 659 N.Y.S.2d 183, 681 N.E.2d 350 (1997); *People v.
Pizzo*, 144 A.D.2d 930, 534 N.Y.S.2d 249 (4th Dep't 1988). *See
generally People v. Major*, 263 A.D.2d 360, 693 N.Y.S.2d 30 (1st
Dep't 1999); *People v. Chann*, 221 A.D.2d 155, __, 633 N.Y.S.2d
150 (1st Dep't 1995) ("During a traffic stop, defendant made a
hand motion as if to place an object in the back seat. This did not
provide sufficient basis to search the vehicle."); *People v. Antelmi*,
196 A.D.2d 658, __, 601 N.Y.S.2d 634, 635 (2d Dep't 1993) ("the
record supports the hearing court's finding that the vehicle in
which the defendant was a passenger was properly stopped by
the police for a traffic violation. However, the police thereafter
forcibly detained and searched the defendant when he attempted

to leave. We find that this conduct exceeded that which is permissible during a normal traffic stop, as there was no showing of a reasonable suspicion on the part of the police that the defendant was committing, had committed, or was about to commit a crime.") (citations omitted).

§ 1:26 When can the police request a person's driver's license and registration?

Whenever a person has been lawfully stopped for a traffic infraction, the police can validly request to see the person's driver's license and registration (and related information). *See, e.g.,* *People v. Ellis*, 62 N.Y.2d 393, 396, 477 N.Y.S.2d 106, 107, 465 N.E.2d 826 (1984) ("The police officers, observing a traffic infraction, properly followed and stopped defendant and asked him for his driver's license and the rental agreement for the car."); *People v. Graham*, 54 A.D.3d 1056, __, 865 N.Y.S.2d 259, 262 (2d Dep't 2008) ("the officer's observation of traffic infractions justified the initial stop and gave him 'the right to ask questions relating to the defendant's destination, to request that he produce his license and registration, and to ask him to stand by momentarily pending further investigation' ") (citation omitted); *People v. Leiva*, 33 A.D.3d 1021, __, 823 N.Y.S.2d 494, 495–96 (2d Dep't 2006); *People v. Derrell*, 26 Misc. 3d 697, __, 889 N.Y.S.2d 905, 913 (N.Y. Co. Sup. Ct. 2009).

Indeed, anyone approached pursuant to a valid *DeBour* level 1 request for information (involving a motor vehicle) can be asked to produce his or her driver's license. *See People v. Thomas*, 19 A.D.3d 32, __, 792 N.Y.S.2d 472, 480 (1st Dep't 2005) ("it is well established by prior case law that a police officer, in directing a level I request for information to an occupant of an already-stationary vehicle, is entitled to ask such a person—whether the driver or a passenger—for documentary identification, such as a driver's license").

In *People v. Hale*, 75 A.D.2d 606, __, 426 N.Y.S.2d 827, 828 (2d Dep't 1980), the Appellate Division, Second Department, rejected the defendant's claim "that the police had no right, where there had been no accident, to require production of an insurance identification card after defendant had already produced a valid license and registration." In so holding, the Court reasoned that "[a] New York motorist is required to carry an insurance identification card whenever operating a motor vehicle and to produce it upon request of any police officer, and this duty is not negated by the production of a valid license and registration. The purpose of this requirement is to insure that the highways of the State are utilized by insured vehicles." 75 A.D.2d at __, 426 N.Y.S.2d at 828 (citations omitted).

§ 1:27   What if the person doesn't produce driver's license and registration?

A person who either fails or refuses to produce his or her driver's license and registration following a proper request therefor will generally be arrested. The reason why is simple: a person who does not have proper identification cannot be issued a traffic ticket. *See, e.g., People v. Ellis*, 62 N.Y.2d 393, 396, 477 N.Y.S.2d 106, 107–08, 465 N.E.2d 826 (1984) ("Once it became evident that defendant could not be issued a summons on the spot because of his inability to produce any identification, the officers were warranted in arresting him to remove him to the police station and in frisking him before doing so."); *People v. Copeland*, 39 N.Y.2d 986, 986–87, 387 N.Y.S.2d 234, 234, 355 N.E.2d 288, 288 (1976) (same); *U.S. v. Barber*, 839 F. Supp. 193, 200–01 (W.D. N.Y. 1993); *People v. Cooper*, 38 A.D.3d 678, __, 833 N.Y.S.2d 118, 120 (2d Dep't 2007); *People v. Mezon*, 228 A.D.2d 621, 644 N.Y.S.2d 763 (2d Dep't 1996); *People v. Clark*, 227 A.D.2d 983, __, 643 N.Y.S.2d 836, 836-37 (4th Dep't 1996); *People v. Miller*, 149 A.D.2d 538, __, 539 N.Y.S.2d 809, 812 (2d Dep't 1989); *People v. Bohn*, 91 Misc. 2d 132, __, 397 N.Y.S.2d 514, 515 (App. Term, 9th & 10th Jud. Dist. 1977) (per curiam) ("The failure or refusal of a motorist to exhibit a license or registration when properly requested is not a violation that falls within the scope of section 1102. We note that where an operator of a motor vehicle fails to exhibit the required documents he may be charged with being an unlicensed operator or operating an unregistered vehicle. Moreover, if he fails or refuses to sufficiently identify himself, the operator may also be arrested."); *People v. Alston*, 9 Misc. 3d 1046, __, 805 N.Y.S.2d 258, 261 (N.Y. City Crim. Ct. 2005) (although "refusal to comply with a request for documentation [justifies arrest, it] is not an independently unlawful act that amounts to obstruction of governmental administration"). *See generally People v. Branigan*, 67 N.Y.2d 860, 501 N.Y.S.2d 655, 492 N.E.2d 783 (1986).

It should be noted that the failure to produce a validly requested driver's license, registration, or insurance card (a) violates the VTL, and (b) is presumptive evidence that the driver/vehicle is not validly licensed/registered/insured. *See, e.g.*, VTL §§ 507(2), 401(4), 312(1)(b) & 319(3); *Branigan*, 67 N.Y.2d at 862, 501 N.Y.S.2d at 656; *Cooper*, 38 A.D.3d at __, 833 N.Y.S.2d at 120.

§ 1:28   When can a police officer demand that the driver exit the vehicle?

"In *Pennsylvania v. Mimms*, the United States Supreme Court held that the inherent and inordinate risk of danger confronting an officer as he approaches the driver of an automobile that has been stopped for a traffic infraction justifies the minimal additional intrusion of ordering the driver out of the car." *People v. McLaurin*, 70 N.Y.2d 779, 781, 521 N.Y.S.2d 218, 219, 515 N.E.2d 904 (1987) (citation omitted). *See also People v. Garcia*, 20 N.Y.3d 317, 321-22, 959 N.Y.S.2d 464, 466, 983 N.E.2d 259 (2012); *People v. Robinson*, 74 N.Y.2d 773, 774, 545 N.Y.S.2d 90, 90, 543 N.E.2d 733, 733 (1989); *People v. Livigni*, 88 A.D.2d 386, 453 N.Y.S.2d 708 (2d Dep't 1982), order aff'd, 58 N.Y.2d 894, 460 N.Y.S.2d 530, 447 N.E.2d 78 (1983).

In *People v. Tittensor*, 244 A.D.2d 784, 666 N.Y.S.2d 267 (3d Dep't 1997), the Appellate Division, Third Department, held that the defendant was properly requested to exit his vehicle and perform field sobriety tests after (1) the officer observed the defendant commit a violation of the VTL, (2) the defendant failed to produce a driver's license at the officer's request, (3) the officer observed several indicia of intoxication (*i.e.*, glassy eyes, slurred speech and strong odor of alcohol), and (4) the defendant admitted consuming 4 rum and coke drinks.

In *People v. McCarthy*, 135 A.D.2d 1113, 523 N.Y.S.2d 291 (4th Dep't 1987), the Appellate Division, Fourth Department, reversed the County Court's finding that the defendant was improperly requested to exit his vehicle. The Court's memorandum decision held as follows:

> After a hearing, County Court dismissed the indictment charging defendant with driving while intoxicated. The court wrote that the arresting officer stopped defendant's car for an equipment violation at 3:00 A.M. and, other than that, there was no evidence of any moving violation. Without making any other findings, the court concluded, "On these facts we find there was no probable cause to require the defendant to exit his vehicle, retire to the back of the police vehicle and submit to a roadside sensor test." The arresting officer was the only witness who testified at the hearing. His testimony reveals that, after stopping the car, he talked to defendant, who was sitting in his car, and noticed that defendant's eyes were bloodshot, that his speech was slurred, and that there was a strong odor of alcohol coming from the car. Based on those facts, we conclude that the officer had probable cause to believe that defendant had been driving his automobile while at least his ability was impaired by the consumption of alcohol (Vehicle & Traffic Law § 1192[1]). The fact that the stop was based only on the officer's observation of an equipment violation does not preclude a finding that, after the lawful stop, the officer had reason to believe that defendant was guilty of driving while intoxicated or, at least, driving while his ability had been impaired by the consumption of alcohol.

135 A.D.2d at __, 523 N.Y.S.2d at 291.

What if the stop was for a reason other than a traffic infraction (*e.g.*, a sobriety checkpoint)? In *People v. Scott*, 63 N.Y.2d 518, 522, 483 N.Y.S.2d 649, 650, 473 N.E.2d 1 (1984), the Court of Appeals held that:

A roadblock established pursuant to a written directive of the County Sheriff for the purpose of detecting and deterring driving while intoxicated or while impaired, *and as to which operating personnel are prohibited from administering sobriety tests unless they observe listed criteria, indicative of intoxication, which give substantial cause to believe that the operator is intoxicated*, is constitutionally permissible, notwithstanding that the location of the roadblock is moved several times during the three- to four-hour period of operation, and notwithstanding that legislative initiatives have also played a part in reducing the incidence of driving while intoxicated in recent years.

(Emphasis added). *See also People v. Rios*, 27 Misc. 3d 963, —, 898 N.Y.S.2d 797, 803 (Kings Co. Sup. Ct. 2010) ("Normally, a police officer can direct a motorist to exit a vehicle as part of a routine traffic stop. However, as noted above, this case does not involve the stop of a moving vehicle; the police directed an individual to exit a vehicle that was stationary and parked alongside a curb. Under these circumstances, without reasonable suspicion, it is improper for the police to direct occupants out of a car."); *People v. Harris*, 173 Misc. 2d 49, —, 660 N.Y.S.2d 792, 795 (Monroe Co. Sup. Ct. 1997) ("because there was no traffic violation, and because there was no reasonable suspicion of criminal activity, Sergeant Giaconia lacked the authority to order the defendant and his passengers out of the defendant's vehicle. As a result, he was not lawfully in the position to observe the handgun") (footnote omitted).

§ 1:29   When can a police officer demand that passengers exit the vehicle?

In *People v. Robinson*, 74 N.Y.2d 773, 774–75, 545 N.Y.S.2d 90, 90–91, 543 N.E.2d 733 (1989), the Court of Appeals held as follows:

The Fourth Amendment of the United States Constitution is not violated when a driver is directed to step out briefly from a lawfully stopped and detained vehicle because the inherent and inordinate danger to investigating police officers in completing their authorized official responsibilities in such circumstances justifies that precautionary action. The United States Supreme Court has reiterated that out of a concern for safety, "officers may, consistent with the Fourth Amendment, exercise their discretion to require a driver who commits a traffic violation to exit the vehicle *even though they lack any particularized reason for believing the driver possesses a weapon.*"

Defendant was a passenger in a car which unquestionably was lawfully stopped by two officers because it made an unsignalled right
turn from the left lane of a New York City street across the flow of
right-lane traffic cutting off another car and motorist one and a half
car lengths behind it in the right lane. After pulling the car over,
the officers approached one on each side. While one officer spoke
with the driver about the traffic infraction, the other directed the
defendant passenger to step out onto the sidewalk. With the passenger door open, the butt of a loaded .357 magnum handgun was
plainly visible protruding from beneath the seat. The gun was
seized and defendant was arrested. A postarrest search disclosed
an additional six rounds of ammunition in defendant's pocket.

We conclude, as to defendant's Federal constitutional argument,
the only one preserved in this case, that precautionary police
conduct directed at a passenger in a lawfully stopped vehicle is
equally authorized, within Federal constitutional guideposts, as
that applied to a driver. Inasmuch as the risks in these police/
civilian vehicle encounters are the same whether the occupant is a
driver or a passenger, "police may order persons out of an
automobile during a stop for a traffic violation." Brief and uniform
precautionary procedures of this kind are not per se unreasonable
and unconstitutional.

(Citations omitted). *See also People v. Garcia*, 20 N.Y.3d 317,
321-22, 959 N.Y.S.2d 464, 466, 983 N.E.2d 259 (2012); *People v.
Mundo*, 99 N.Y.2d 55, 750 N.Y.S.2d 837, 780 N.E.2d 522 (2002);
People v. McLaurin, 70 N.Y.2d 779, 521 N.Y.S.2d 218, 515 N.E.2d
904 (1987); *People v. Livigni*, 88 A.D.2d 386, 453 N.Y.S.2d 708
(2d Dep't 1982), order aff'd, 58 N.Y.2d 894, 460 N.Y.S.2d 530, 447
N.E.2d 78 (1983).

§ 1:30 "Reasonable cause" and "probable cause" are synonymous

The CPL uses the phrase "reasonable cause" in lieu of the
phrase "probable cause." *See, e.g.*, CPL § 70.10(2). However, it is
well settled that "[r]easonable cause means probable cause." *People
v. Maldonado*, 86 N.Y.2d 631, 635, 635 N.Y.S.2d 155, 158, 658
N.E.2d 1028 (1995). *See also People v. Johnson*, 66 N.Y.2d 398,
402 n.2, 497 N.Y.S.2d 618, 621 n.2, 488 N.E.2d 439 (1985).

§ 1:31 Probable cause to arrest in a VTL § 1192 case

CPL § 70.10(2) provides, in pertinent part, that:

"Reasonable cause to believe that a person has committed an offense" exists when evidence or information which appears reliable
discloses facts or circumstances which are collectively of such weight
and persuasiveness as to convince a person of ordinary intelligence,
judgment and experience that it is reasonably likely that such offense was committed and that such person committed it.

As the previous section demonstrates, although the CPL uses the phrase "reasonable cause" in lieu of the phrase "probable cause," it is well settled that "[r]easonable cause means probable cause." *People v. Maldonado*, 86 N.Y.2d 631, 635, 635 N.Y.S.2d 155, 158, 658 N.E.2d 1028 (1995). *See also People v. Johnson*, 66 N.Y.2d 398, 402 n.2, 497 N.Y.S.2d 618, 621 n.2, 488 N.E.2d 439 (1985). The Court of Appeals has consistently made clear that:

> In passing on whether there was probable cause for an arrest, . . . the basis for such a belief must not only be reasonable, but it must appear to be at least more probable than not that a crime has taken place and that the one arrested is its perpetrator, for conduct equally compatible with guilt or innocence will not suffice.

People v. Carrasquillo, 54 N.Y.2d 248, 254, 445 N.Y.S.2d 97, 100, 429 N.E.2d 775 (1981). *See also People v. Vandover*, 20 N.Y.3d 235, 237, 958 N.Y.S.2d 83, 84, 981 N.E.2d 784 (2012) (same); *People v. De Bour*, 40 N.Y.2d 210, 216, 386 N.Y.S.2d 375, 380, 352 N.E.2d 562 (1976) ("We have frequently rejected the notion that behavior which is susceptible of innocent as well as culpable interpretation, will constitute probable cause.").

Interestingly, the Court of Appeals had never addressed the issue of what constitutes probable cause to arrest in a VTL § 1192 case until it decided *Vandover, supra,* in 2013. In *Vandover*, the Court held that "[t]he standard to be followed is that it is more probable than not that defendant is actually impaired." 20 N.Y.3d at 239, 958 N.Y.S.2d at 85. *Vandover* makes clear that probable cause is not established in a VTL § 1192 case where there is proof that the defendant consumed alcohol (or drugs) but no proof of actual impairment.

Applying the "more probable than not that defendant is actually impaired" standard to the facts of the case, the Court of Appeals affirmed the Appellate Term's determination that there was a lack of probable cause under the following circumstances:

> On October 1, 2008, defendant appeared in Justice Court on an unrelated traffic ticket. While at the courthouse, defendant spoke with an Officer James who noticed that she had glassy, bloodshot eyes, an odor of alcohol on her breath and seemed lethargic. Concerned that defendant may well be intoxicated and intending to drive a vehicle, Officer James informed Officer Barry of his observations. Both officers proceeded to follow defendant to the parking lot where they observed her getting into her automobile and moving in reverse for approximately two feet as she exited the parking spot. Officer Barry stopped defendant. Upon her exiting the vehicle, Officer Barry administered a field sobriety test. Officer James had gone to the nearby police headquarters to retrieve a portable breath analyzer and did not observe the full field sobriety test given by Officer Barry. When Officer James returned with the equipment, he noticed, for the first time a young child in the back seat of the car

without a seatbelt. Officer Barry also performed the portable breath test on defendant, which recorded a positive result. Defendant made statements, prior to her arrest, to the effect that she "had gotten off work at 8:00 [a.m.]" and "ha[d] a couple of drinks," but those were consumed several hours prior and that she was not currently under the influence of alcohol. * * *

Defendant moved to suppress her statements and other evidence obtained and a probable cause hearing was held at which Officer James and a Sergeant Metzger, who had come upon the scene, testified. Officer Barry, who administered the field sobriety test and the portable breathalyzer test, however, did not testify. Justice Court found the officers' testimony to be credible but that Sergeant Metzger's testimony was generally cumulative of Officer James' testimony. However, Sergeant Metzger did testify that the positive reading of the portable breath analyzer, in this instance, was as consistent with an alcohol content below the statutory level of impairment as with a blood alcohol level above the limit. Justice Court noted Officer Barry's absence and stated that "without [his] testimony there is insufficient testimony in the record necessary for a finding that the arrest on any of the charges was based upon probable cause." Justice Court, citing the testimony of Officer James, that defendant had glassy bloodshot eyes, breath that smelled of alcohol and a generally fatigued demeanor, found that this was insufficient to establish probable cause to arrest defendant and accordingly dismissed the charges. The Appellate Term affirmed the dismissal.

Id. at 237-38, 958 N.Y.S.2d at 84-85 (citation omitted).

Although courts find a lack of probable cause to arrest in DWI cases on a somewhat regular basis, such decisions are almost never published. Since virtually every published decision has held that probable cause to arrest (as opposed to probable cause to stop) existed, there is little need to provide a comprehensive list of cases holding that a DWI arrest was lawful.

Other than proof that it is more likely than not that the defendant was actually impaired, the key to a probable cause determination is that the People's proof must be credible. *See, e.g.,* *People v. Berrios,* 28 N.Y.2d 361, 369, 321 N.Y.S.2d 884, 890, 270 N.E.2d 709 (1971) ("Where the Judge at the suppression hearing determines that the testimony of the police officer is unworthy of belief, he should conclude that the People have not met their burden of coming forward with sufficient evidence and grant the motion to suppress."); 28 N.Y.2d at 368, 321 N.Y.S.2d at 889 ("we are not oblivious to the problem that there is always a possibility that a witness will perjure himself. Indeed, this is why credibility is usually a crucial issue whenever facts are in dispute and courts have traditionally addressed themselves to the resolution of this basic question as a part of the fact-finding process"); *People v. Clough,* 70 A.D.3d 474, __, 895 N.Y.S.2d 52, 52–53 (1st Dep't

2010) ("the People have the burden of going forward to show the legality of the police conduct in the first instance, and that burden cannot be met by testimony that the hearing court finds incredible") (citation omitted); *People v. Farrell*, 89 A.D.2d 987, __, 454 N.Y.S.2d 306, 308 (2d Dep't 1982) ("It is well settled that witnesses must be adjudged by their demeanor as well as their testimony and that the trial judge, who saw and heard the witnesses, is in a much better position to judge their testimony than an appellate court.").

Simply stated, anyone can take the witness stand and rattle off a list of indicia of impairment (*e.g.*, odor of an alcoholic beverage, glassy/bloodshot eyes, slurred speech, impaired motor coordination, failure of field sobriety tests, etc.). The mere claim that these things were observed does not make it so. Indeed, the authors find that, where they exist, videos of a defendant's arrest for DWI often depict a very different series of events than what is portrayed in the arresting officer's paperwork and/or testimony. For example, in *Fermin-Perea v. Swarts*, 95 A.D.3d 439, __, 943 N.Y.S.2d 96, 98–99 (1st Dep't 2012), which dealt with a motorist's appeal of a DMV chemical test refusal revocation:

> The arresting officer's refusal report, admitted in evidence at the hearing, indicates that upon stopping petitioner because he was speeding, following too closely, and changing lanes without signaling, the officer observed that petitioner was unsteady on his feet, had bloodshot eyes, slurred speech and "a strong odor of alcoholic beverage on [his] breath." However, the field sobriety test, administered approximately 25 minutes later, a video of which was admitted in evidence at the hearing, establishes that petitioner was not impaired or intoxicated. Specifically, the video demonstrates that over the course of four minutes, petitioner was subjected to standardized field sobriety testing and at all times clearly communicated with the arresting officer, never slurred his speech, never demonstrated an inability to comprehend what he was being asked, and followed all of the officer's commands. Petitioner successfully completed the three tests he was asked to perform; thus never exhibiting any signs of impairment or intoxication.

> Certainly, the contents of the arresting officer's refusal report, standing alone, establish reasonable grounds for the arrest under the Vehicle and Traffic Law. However, where, as here, a field sobriety test conducted less than 30 minutes after the officer's initial observations, convincingly establishes that petitioner was not impaired or intoxicated, respondent's determination that there existed reasonable grounds to believe that petitioner was intoxicated has no rational basis and is not inferable from the record. . . . Here, the field sobriety test, conducted shortly after petitioner was operating his motor vehicle, which failed to establish that petitioner was intoxicated or otherwise impaired, leads us to conclude that respondent's determination is not supported by substantial evidence.

The dissent ignores the threshold issue here, namely, that refusal to submit to a chemical test only results in revocation of an operator's driver's license if there are reasonable grounds to believe that the operator was driving while under the influence of drugs or alcohol and more specifically, insofar as relevant here, while intoxicated or impaired. Here, while the officer's initial observations are indeed indicative of intoxication or at the very least, impairment, the results of the field sobriety test administered thereafter—a more objective measure of intoxication—necessarily precludes any conclusion that petitioner was operating his vehicle while intoxicated or impaired. Any conclusion to the contrary simply disregards the applicable burden which, as the dissent points out, requires less than a preponderance of the evidence, demanding only that "a given inference is reasonable and plausible." Even under this diminished standard of proof, it is simply unreasonable and uninferable that petitioner was intoxicated or impaired while operating his motor vehicle and yet, 25 minutes later he successfully and without any difficulty passed a field sobriety test.

(Citations omitted).

It seems clear that after reviewing the video, the majority in *Fermin-Perea* believed that the arresting officer's Report of Refusal was not credible.

§ 1:32   A valid arrest is a prerequisite to a lawful request to submit to a chemical test

VTL § 1194(2)(a) provides, in pertinent part:

2. Chemical tests. (a) When authorized. Any person who operates a motor vehicle in this state shall be deemed to have given consent to a chemical test of one or more of the following: breath, blood, urine, or saliva, for the purpose of determining the alcoholic and/or drug content of the blood provided that such test is administered by or at the direction of a police officer with respect to a chemical test of breath, urine or saliva or, with respect to a chemical test of blood, at the direction of a police officer:

(1) having reasonable grounds to believe such person to have been operating in violation of any subdivision of [VTL § 1192] and within two hours after such person has been placed under arrest for any such violation; or . . .

(2) within two hours after a breath [screening] test, as provided in [VTL § 1194(1)(b)], indicates that alcohol has been consumed by such person and in accordance with the rules and regulations established by the police force of which the officer is a member. . . .

For underage offenders being requested to submit to a chemical test pursuant to the Zero Tolerance laws, *see* § 15:30, *infra*.

As VTL § 1194(2)(a) makes clear, either a lawful VTL § 1192 arrest, or a positive result from a lawfully requested breath

screening test, is a prerequisite to a valid request that a DWI
suspect submit to a chemical test. *See, e.g., People v. Moselle*, 57
N.Y.2d 97, 107, 454 N.Y.S.2d 292, 296, 439 N.E.2d 1235 (1982);
Gagliardi v. Department of Motor Vehicles, 144 A.D.2d 882, __,
535 N.Y.S.2d 203, 204 (3d Dep't 1988) ("In order for the testing
strictures of Vehicle and Traffic Law § 1194 to come into play,
there must have been a lawful arrest for driving while
intoxicated."); *People v. Stisi*, 93 A.D.2d 951, __, 463 N.Y.S.2d 73,
74 (3d Dep't 1983); *June v. Tofany*, 34 A.D.2d 732, __, 311
N.Y.S.2d 782, 783 (4th Dep't 1970); *Burns v. Hults*, 20 A.D.2d
752, __, 247 N.Y.S.2d 311, 312 (4th Dep't 1964); *Leonard v. Melton*,
58 A.D.2d 669, __, 395 N.Y.S.2d 526, 527 (3d Dep't 1977) (proof
that DWI suspect operated vehicle is necessary prerequisite to
valid request to submit to chemical test pursuant to VTL § 1194).
See also Welsh v. Wisconsin, 466 U.S. 740, 744, 104 S. Ct. 2091,
2095, 80 L. Ed. 2d 732 (1984) ("It is not disputed by the parties
that an arrestee's refusal to take a breath test would be reasonable, and therefore operating privileges could not be revoked, if
the underlying arrest was not lawful. Indeed, state law has consistently provided that a valid arrest is a necessary prerequisite
to the imposition of a breath test.").

§ 1:33   Probable cause can generally consist of reliable
hearsay

CPL § 70.10(2) provides that:

"Reasonable cause to believe that a person has committed an offense" exists when evidence or information which appears reliable
discloses facts or circumstances which are collectively of such weight
and persuasiveness as to convince a person of ordinary intelligence,
judgment and experience that it is reasonably likely that such offense was committed and that such person committed it. *Except as
otherwise provided in this chapter, such apparently reliable evidence
may include or consist of hearsay.*

(Emphasis added). *See also* CPL § 710.60(4) (at a suppression
hearing, "hearsay evidence is admissible to establish any material fact").

Critically, however, probable cause cannot be established based
solely upon hearsay evidence. In this regard, in *People v. Randall*,
135 A.D.2d 915, __, 522 N.Y.S.2d 314, 315 (3d Dep't 1987):

At the [suppression] hearing the People failed to produce any of the
officers involved in the original street encounter with defendant to
testify as to probable cause. The only evidence of the officers' probable cause to detain defendant on the street was the hearsay
testimony of Sergeant Angel. As the Court of Appeals has held,
probable cause cannot be established solely upon hearsay evidence.

See also People v. Gonzalez, 80 N.Y.2d 883, 587 N.Y.S.2d 607,

600 N.E.2d 238 (1992); *People v. Havelka*, 45 N.Y.2d 636, 641, 412 N.Y.S.2d 345, 347, 384 N.E.2d 1269 (1978).

In *Gonzalez, supra*:

The issue [was] whether the hearsay testimony of Detective Grossman, the People's sole witness at the suppression hearing, was sufficient, standing alone, to meet the People's burden of showing that defendant voluntarily went to the police precinct where he allegedly made the inculpatory statements.

Detective Grossman testified at the suppression hearing that the three detectives present when defendant was taken from his house told him that defendant voluntarily accompanied them to the precinct. Defendant's wife, however, testified that although her husband was not arrested, the detectives said to him that if he did not come to the precinct voluntarily, he would be forced to do so. The People did not produce any of the three detectives. Nor did the People give any indication that the three detectives were unavailable or offer any reason for not producing at least one of them. The Appellate Division, with one Justice dissenting, affirmed Supreme Court's denial of defendant's suppression motion, holding that it was up to the hearing court to determine the weight and credibility of Detective Grossman's hearsay testimony.

We agree with the dissent at the Appellate Division that the People did not meet their burden of showing that defendant freely consented to go to the precinct. Although Detective Grossman's hearsay testimony was admissible (CPL 710.60[4]), it did not supply the necessary proof of consent. That Grossman, who had no personal knowledge of the relevant facts, testified truthfully as to what the detectives told him has no bearing on the pertinent issue of whether the other detectives' statements were true. Thus, the finding of the hearing court that Grossman was credible is irrelevant. * * *

The hearing evidence presented substantial questions concerning the legality of the non-testifying detectives' conduct. There is no basis for attributing reliability to the hearsay information related by Grossman or for assuming its truth. Thus, because the People produced no witness with firsthand knowledge of the police conduct in dispute, their proof was insufficient to meet their burden of showing that defendant's consent was voluntary.

80 N.Y.2d at 884–85, 587 N.Y.S.2d at 607–08 (citations omitted).

In *People v. Moses*, 32 A.D.3d 866, __, 823 N.Y.S.2d 409, 410–11 (2d Dep't 2006):

At a combined *Dunaway/Wade* hearing, the prosecution presented only the testimony of the arresting officer, who stated that he received a radio communication regarding a robbery in progress and responded to the complainant's location. After speaking with the complainant, the officer received a second radio communication indicating that there was a person stopped in the vicinity of a nearby intersection. The officer then drove the complainant to that location, where the officer and the complainant observed the defendant leaning against an unmarked police car between two plainclothes police officers wearing "NYPD" jackets. The complainant identified the defendant as the man who broke into her home, and he was placed under arrest. The prosecution did not call either of the plainclothes officers to testify at the hearing regarding the circumstances by which the defendant came to be in their company near the intersection.

(Citations omitted).

Under these circumstances, the Appellate Division, Second Department, held as follows:

At a suppression hearing, the prosecution has the initial burden of going forward with evidence to demonstrate the legality of the police conduct in the first instance. The prosecution in this case failed to present any evidence to establish that the defendant was lawfully stopped and detained before the complainant made her identification. In this regard, the original radio communication regarding a robbery in progress, assuming that it was heard by the plainclothes police officers, was insufficient by itself to provide the officers with a legal basis for stopping the defendant. Similarly, the vague and equivocal hearsay testimony of the arresting officer concerning a statement made by one of the plainclothes officers was inadequate to demonstrate that the defendant's presence at the scene was lawfully obtained. Accordingly, the prosecution failed to satisfy its burden of establishing the legality of the police conduct which led to the identification of the defendant, and the pretrial identification should have been suppressed.

32 A.D.3d at __, 823 N.Y.S.2d at 411 (citations omitted).

§ 1:34   Fellow officer rule

In *People v. Ketcham*, 93 N.Y.2d 416, 419–21, 690 N.Y.S.2d 874, 877–78, 712 N.E.2d 1238 (1999), the Court of Appeals set forth a concise summary of the "fellow officer rule":

Under the fellow officer rule, a police officer can make a lawful arrest even without personal knowledge sufficient to establish probable cause, so long as the officer is acting " 'upon the direction of or as a result of communication with' " a fellow officer or another police agency in possession of information sufficient to constitute probable cause for the arrest. Information received from another police officer is presumptively reliable. Where, however, an arrest is challenged by a motion to suppress, the prosecution bears the burden of establishing that the officer imparting the information had probable cause to act.

The People may, of course, establish probable cause for a warrantless arrest with hearsay information that satisfies *Aguilar-Spinelli*. To meet that two-part test, the prosecution must demonstrate the reliability of the hearsay informant and the basis of the informant's knowledge. In other words, there must be evidence that the informant is generally trustworthy and that the information imparted was "obtained in a reliable way"—that it constitutes more than unsubstantiated rumor, unfounded accusation or conclusory characterization. An unsubstantiated hearsay communication— even when transmitted by a fellow officer—will not satisfy the People's burden.

Where, however, the People demonstrate—through direct or circumstantial evidence—how a reliable hearsay informant acquired the information, both prongs of *Aguilar-Spinelli* may be satisfied. When, for example, the hearsay informant is a police officer who imparts to fellow officers information gathered while personally participating in or observing an undercover drug transaction, there is little doubt as to the reliability of the informant or the basis of knowledge (*see, e.g., People v. Petralia* [officer made lawful arrest on the basis of radio communication from undercover officer who had purchased heroin and then relayed information describing suspect and suspect's car]; *People v. Maldonado* [probable cause established based on transmission by primary undercover who engaged in a hand-to-hand drug transaction with a suspect, stating "positive buy," followed by description of individual]; *People v. Washington* [undercover officer charged with observing primary undercover transmitted "positive observation," a phrase commonly used to indicate exchange of drugs for money, and arresting officer understood those words to mean that the transmitting officer had personally witnessed a drug transaction]).

The prosecution may satisfy its burden even with "double hearsay," or "hearsay-upon-hearsay," so long as both prongs of *Aguilar-Spinelli* are met at every link in the hearsay chain. As such, police officers may rely on hearsay information derived from a trustworthy informant who did not personally observe a defendant's criminal activity, but came by that information in a reliable, albeit indirect, way. Where, however, there is no evidence indicating how the informant obtained the information passed from one officer to another, there is nothing by which to measure the trustworthiness of that information (*People v. Parris* [police officer's conclusory characterization of informant as an "eyewitness" did not satisfy basis of knowledge requirement where there was no further evidence indicating how the informant obtained description of the suspected burglar]).

(Citations omitted). *See also People v. Landy,* 59 N.Y.2d 369, 465 N.Y.S.2d 857, 452 N.E.2d 1185 (1983).

It has been held that the fellow officer rule applies to auxiliary police officers, *see People v. Rosario,* 78 N.Y.2d 583, 578 N.Y.S.2d 454, 585 N.E.2d 766 (1991), as well as to out-of-State law enforcement officers. *See People v. Lypka,* 36 N.Y.2d 210, 366 N.Y.S.2d 622, 326 N.E.2d 294 (1975).

§ 1:35   Probable cause must exist at time of arrest

In determining whether probable cause existed for a defendant's arrest, observations made, or evidence obtained, *subsequent to* the arrest (such as incriminating statements, the results of a chemical test, etc.) cannot be considered. *See, e.g.*, *People v. McCarthy*, 14 N.Y.2d 206, 209, 250 N.Y.S.2d 290, 292, 199 N.E.2d 382 (1964) (per curiam); *People v. O'Neill*, 11 N.Y.2d 148, 153, 227 N.Y.S.2d 416, 419, 182 N.E.2d 95 (1962); *People v. Loria*, 10 N.Y.2d 368, 373, 223 N.Y.S.2d 462, 467, 179 N.E.2d 478 (1961) (overruled in part on other grounds by, People v. McQueen, 18 N.Y.2d 337, 274 N.Y.S.2d 886, 221 N.E.2d 550 (1966)); *People v. Oquendo*, 221 A.D.2d 223, __, 633 N.Y.S.2d 492, 493 (1st Dep't 1995); *People v. Feingold*, 106 A.D.2d 583, __, 482 N.Y.S.2d 857, 859 (2d Dep't 1984); *People v. Bruno*, 45 A.D.2d 1025, __, 358 N.Y.S.2d 183, 184 (2d Dep't 1974); *People v. Garafolo*, 44 A.D.2d 86, __, 353 N.Y.S.2d 500, 502 (2d Dep't 1974).

Similarly, "[t]he police may not justify a stop by a subsequently acquired suspicion resulting from the stop. This reasoning is the same which refuses to validate a search by what it produces." *People v. De Bour*, 40 N.Y.2d 210, 215–16, 386 N.Y.S.2d 375, 380, 352 N.E.2d 562 (1976). *See also People v. Sobotker*, 43 N.Y.2d 559, 565, 402 N.Y.S.2d 993, 996–97, 373 N.E.2d 1218 (1978) ("Subsequent events did indeed demonstrate that the officers' hunch may well have been correct. But a search may not be justified by its avails alone. Constitutionally protected rights are not to be dispensed with in this case solely because the results of the improper search and seizure uncovered the fact that one or all of the persons who were its targets were armed with a deadly weapon. Almost any series of indiscriminate seizures is bound to produce some instances of criminality that might otherwise have gone undetected or unprevented. But were hindsight alone to furnish the governing criteria, a vital constitutional safeguard of our personal security would soon be gone.").

§ 1:36   When is a probable cause hearing required?

A warrantless arrest is presumptively illegal. *See, e.g.*, *Broughton v. State*, 37 N.Y.2d 451, 458, 373 N.Y.S.2d 87, 94, 335 N.E.2d 310 (1975) ("Whenever there has been an arrest and imprisonment without a warrant, the officer has acted extrajudicially and the presumption arises that such an arrest and imprisonment are unlawful."); *People v. Chaney*, 253 A.D.2d 562, __, 686 N.Y.S.2d 871, 873 (3d Dep't 1998) ("When the validity of a warrantless arrest is challenged, the presumption of probable cause disappears and the People bear the burden of coming forward with evidence showing that it was supported by probable cause.").

In addition, "all evidence obtained by searches and seizures in violation of the Constitution is, by that same authority, inadmissible in a state court." *Mapp v. Ohio*, 367 U.S. 643, 655, 81 S. Ct. 1684, 1691, 6 L. Ed. 2d 1081, 86 Ohio L. Abs. 513, 84 A.L.R.2d 933 (1961). *See also Dunaway v. New York*, 442 U.S. 200, 99 S. Ct. 2248, 60 L. Ed. 2d 824 (1979); *Brown v. Illinois*, 422 U.S. 590, 95 S. Ct. 2254, 45 L. Ed. 2d 416 (1975). In this regard, obtaining a breath or blood sample from a DWI suspect for alcohol and/or drug analysis constitutes a "search" and "seizure" within the meaning of the 4th Amendment. *See, e.g., Skinner v. Railway Labor Executives' Ass'n*, 489 U.S. 602, 616–17, 109 S. Ct. 1402, 1413, 103 L. Ed. 2d 639, 4 I.E.R. Cas. (BNA) 224, 130 L.R.R.M. (BNA) 2857, 13 O.S.H. Cas. (BNA) 2065, 49 Empl. Prac. Dec. (CCH) P 38791, 111 Lab. Cas. (CCH) P 11001, 1989 O.S.H. Dec. (CCH) P 28476 (1989); *Schmerber v. California*, 384 U.S. 757, 767, 86 S. Ct. 1826, 1834, 16 L. Ed. 2d 908 (1966); *People v. Kates*, 53 N.Y.2d 591, 594–95, 444 N.Y.S.2d 446, 448, 428 N.E.2d 852 (1981).

In *Brown v. Illinois*, *supra*, the defendant "was arrested without probable cause and without a warrant. He was given, in full, the warnings prescribed by *Miranda v. Arizona*. Thereafter, while in custody, he made two inculpatory statements. The issue [was] whether evidence of those statements was properly admitted, or should have been excluded, in petitioner's subsequent trial for murder in state court. Expressed another way, the issue [was] whether the statements were to be excluded as the fruit of the illegal arrest, or were admissible because the giving of the *Miranda* warnings sufficiently attenuated the taint of the arrest." 422 U.S. at 591–92, 95 S.Ct. at 2256 (citation omitted). In other words, the issue in *Brown* was whether statements that were voluntarily made under the 5th Amendment were admissible at trial if the statements were the fruits of an illegal arrest without probable cause.

The United States Supreme Court held that:

The exclusionary rule, . . . when utilized to effectuate the Fourth Amendment, serves interests and policies that are distinct from those it serves under the Fifth. It is directed at all unlawful searches and seizures, and not merely those that happen to produce incriminating material or testimony as fruits. In short, exclusion of a confession made without *Miranda* warnings might be regarded as necessary to effectuate the Fifth Amendment, but it would not be sufficient fully to protect the Fourth. *Miranda* warnings, and the exclusion of a confession made without them, do not alone sufficiently deter a Fourth Amendment violation.

Thus, even if the statements in this case were found to be voluntary under the Fifth Amendment, the Fourth Amendment issue

remains. In order for the causal chain, between the illegal arrest
and the statements made subsequent thereto, to be broken, *Wong
Sun* requires not merely that the statement meet the Fifth Amendment standard of voluntariness but that it be "sufficiently an act of
free will to purge the primary taint." *Wong Sun* thus mandates
consideration of a statement's admissibility in light of the distinct
policies and interests of the Fourth Amendment.

If *Miranda* warnings, by themselves, were held to attenuate the
taint of an unconstitutional arrest, regardless of how wanton and
purposeful the Fourth Amendment violation, the effect of the
exclusionary rule would be substantially diluted. Arrests made
without warrant or without probable cause, for questioning or
"investigation," would be encouraged by the knowledge that evidence derived therefrom could well be made admissible at trial by
the simple expedient of giving *Miranda* warnings. Any incentive to
avoid Fourth Amendment violations would be eviscerated by making the warnings, in effect, a "cure-all," and the constitutional
guarantee against unlawful searches and seizures could be said to
be reduced to "a form of words."

422 U.S. at 601–03, 95 S.Ct. at 2260–61 (citations and footnotes
omitted).

Brown is not a model of clarity, and it apparently confused the
Appellate Division, Fourth Department, in *People v. Dunaway*,
61 A.D.2d 299, 402 N.Y.S.2d 490 (4th Dep't 1978) (as the United
States Supreme Court reversed it in *Dunaway v. New York*, 442
U.S. 200, 99 S. Ct. 2248, 60 L. Ed. 2d 824 (1979)). In *Dunaway*,
the Supreme Court held that:

[D]etention for custodial interrogation—regardless of its label—
intrudes so severely on interests protected by the Fourth Amendment as necessarily to trigger the traditional safeguards against illegal arrest. We accordingly hold that the Rochester police violated
the Fourth and Fourteenth Amendments when, without probable
cause, they seized petitioner and transported him to the police station for interrogation.

442 U.S. at 216, 99 S.Ct. at 2258. This is where the so-called
Dunaway hearing (a.k.a. probable cause hearing) comes from.

Since virtually every DWI arrest is warrantless—and thus
presumptively unconstitutional—it would seem that probable
cause hearings would be available for the asking. However, this
is not the case. *See, e.g., People v. Gruden*, 42 N.Y.2d 214, 217,
397 N.Y.S.2d 704, 706, 366 N.E.2d 794 (1977) ("Generally hearings are not available merely for the asking."). Rather, CPL
§ 710.60 sets forth the procedure governing suppression motions.
Critically, however, if the defendant's motion papers are sufficient, then the Court literally *must* grant a *Dunaway* (*i.e.*, probable cause) and/or a *Mapp* (*i.e.*, suppression) hearing. *See infra*.

The defendant's motion papers are sufficient when they (a) challenge the lawfulness of the defendant's arrest, and (b) assert sworn allegations of fact in support of such claim that raise a factual dispute on a material point. *See* CPL § 710.60(3), (4). In this regard, it is well settled that an attorney's affirmation signed by defense counsel is sufficient to satisfy the pleading requirements of CPL § 710.60 (*i.e.*, an affidavit of the defendant is not required). *See, e.g.*, CPL § 710.60(1) ("Such allegations may be based upon personal knowledge of the deponent or upon information and belief, provided that in the latter event the sources of such information and the grounds of such belief are stated."); *People v. Mendoza*, 82 N.Y.2d 415, 425, 604 N.Y.S.2d 922, 926, 624 N.E.2d 1017 (1993); *People v. Mabeus*, 47 A.D.3d 1073, __, 850 N.Y.S.2d 664, 666 (3d Dep't 2008); *People v. Lopez*, 263 A.D.2d 434, __, 695 N.Y.S.2d 76, 77 (1st Dep't 1999); *People v. Marquez*, 246 A.D.2d 330, __, 667 N.Y.S.2d 359, 360 (1st Dep't 1998); *People v. Ayarde*, 220 A.D.2d 519, __, 632 N.Y.S.2d 174, 175 (2d Dep't 1995); *People v. Bailey*, 218 A.D.2d 569, __, 630 N.Y.S.2d 499, 500 (1st Dep't 1995); *People v. Vasquez*, 200 A.D.2d 344, __, 613 N.Y.S.2d 595, 596 (1st Dep't 1994); *People v. Foster*, 197 A.D.2d 411, __, 602 N.Y.S.2d 395 (1st Dep't 1993); *People v. Aponte*, 193 A.D.2d 529, __, 598 N.Y.S.2d 937 (1st Dep't 1993); *People v. Moore*, 186 A.D.2d 591, __, 588 N.Y.S.2d 388, 389 (2d Dep't 1992); *People v. Rodriguez*, 185 A.D.2d 802, __, 586 N.Y.S.2d 968, 968–69 (1st Dep't 1992); *People v. Miller*, 162 A.D.2d 248, __, 556 N.Y.S.2d 607 (1st Dep't 1990); *People v. Huggins*, 162 A.D.2d 129, __, 556 N.Y.S.2d 75, 75–76 (1st Dep't 1990); *People v. Marte*, 149 A.D.2d 335, __, 539 N.Y.S.2d 912, 913 (1st Dep't 1989); *People v. Lee*, 130 A.D.2d 400, __, 515 N.Y.S.2d 260, 262 (1st Dep't 1987); *People v. Patterson*, 129 A.D.2d 527, __, 514 N.Y.S.2d 378, 379 (1st Dep't 1987); *People v. Marshall*, 122 A.D.2d 283, __, 504 N.Y.S.2d 782, 783 (2d Dep't 1986); *People v. Sutton*, 91 A.D.2d 522, __, 456 N.Y.S.2d 771, 772 (1st Dep't 1982).

The Court of Appeals has made clear that:

> A trial court is *required* to grant a hearing if the defendant "raise[s] a factual dispute on a material point which must be resolved before the court can decide the legal issue" of whether evidence was obtained in a constitutionally permissible manner.

People v. Burton, 6 N.Y.3d 584, 587, 815 N.Y.S.2d 7, 9, 848 N.E.2d 454 (2006) (emphasis added) (citation omitted). *See also* CPL § 710.60(3), (4); *People v. Mendoza*, 82 N.Y.2d 415, 426, 604 N.Y.S.2d 922, 926, 624 N.E.2d 1017 (1993); *People v. Gruden*, 42 N.Y.2d 214, 215, 397 N.Y.S.2d 704, 705, 366 N.E.2d 794 (1977); *People v. Bennett*, 240 A.D.2d 292, __, 659 N.Y.S.2d 260, 261 (1st Dep't 1997) ("It is not necessary that a moving defendant raise an issue of fact as to every factual allegation put forth by the prosecution in order for a hearing to be ordered.").

Nonetheless, many prosecutors oppose the granting of a *Dunaway/Mapp* hearing in literally every single case, reflexively asserting that the defendant has failed to allege sufficient facts to entitle him/her to a hearing regardless of the facts alleged in the defendant's motion papers. In this regard, the People typically cite cases such as *People v. Roberto H. (Anonymous)*, 67 A.D.2d 549, 416 N.Y.S.2d 305 (2d Dep't 1979), in which the defendant failed to allege a single fact in support of his motion to suppress.

A review of *Roberto H.* demonstrates that defense counsel's affirmation in that case was patently inadequate to justify a suppression hearing. Specifically, as the *Roberto H.* Court noted:

With regard to the remaining portions of the motion to suppress, defense counsel submitted a supporting affirmation alleging:

"That your affirmant has been served with a notice, a copy of which is annexed hereto, by the District Attorney's office that testimony will be offered at the trial of this matter identifying the defendant as the perpetrator of the within crimes.

"That your affirmant submits that should it appear that the identification herein was made under circumstances highly suggestive, unfair and prejudicial to the defendant, so as to deny him due process of law in violation of the 'FOURTH', 'FIFTH', 'SIXTH' and 'FOURTEENTH' Amendments to the United States Constitution, that evidence should be suppressed from the trial of this matter and your affirmant requests a hearing to determine that issue.

* * * * * *

"That upon information and belief, upon the date of his arrest an illegal and unlawful search was conducted by arresting law enforcement officials.

"That the District Attorney has failed to disclose the exact facts and circumstances surrounding the search and it is your affirmant's belief that contraband which is the subject of the within indictment was obtained therefrom.

"That your affirmant respectfully submits that if it should appear that the search conducted was an unreasonable search and seizure in violation of defendant's 'FOURTH', 'FIFTH' and 'FOURTEENTH' Amendment Rights of the United States Constitution, the contraband obtained therefrom should be suppressed from use upon the trial of this matter and your affirmant requests a hearing to determine that issue."

It is abundantly clear from these excerpts, which comprise the sum and substance of the allegations in support of the motion, that

defendant failed to comply with the requirements of CPL 710.60.
The affirmation fails to allege any facts whatever, let alone facts in
support of the grounds for the motion.

67 A.D.2d at __, 416 N.Y.S.2d at 306–07 (emphasis added).

Simply stated, there was literally not one single fact alleged by
the attorney in *Roberto H.* that either (a) dealt with any of the
specific facts of the case, and/or (b) stated a ground for
suppression.

Another case that is frequently misapplied by the People is
People v. Gruden, 42 N.Y.2d 214, 397 N.Y.S.2d 704, 366 N.E.2d
794 (1977). In *Gruden, the defendants* brought speedy trial motions pursuant to CPL § 30.30. The defendants' motion papers alleged sufficient facts which, if undisputed, would require that the
motions be summarily *granted* without a hearing. "The People
did not dispute the facts alleged in the defendants' motion papers.
Instead they consented to a hearing." 42 N.Y.2d at 215, 397
N.Y.S.2d at 705. The People claimed that the relevant statute
should be construed "so as to preclude the court from summarily
granting the motion to dismiss unless the facts are expressly
conceded by the People to be true, arguing that a failure on the
part of the People to controvert is not necessarily to be deemed a
concession under the statute." 42 N.Y.2d at 216, 397 N.Y.S.2d at
705.

In other words, in *Gruden,* the People claimed that they were
entitled to an evidentiary hearing on every speedy trial motion
even if none of the defendants' factual allegations were in dispute.
The specific holding in *Gruden* was as follows: "Generally hearings are not available merely for the asking. We therefore hold
that the court may summarily grant a motion to dismiss unless
the papers submitted *by the prosecutor* show that there is a
factual dispute which must be resolved at a hearing." 42 N.Y.2d
at 217, 397 N.Y.S.2d at 706 (emphasis added). *See also* 42 N.Y.2d
at 216, 397 N.Y.S.2d at 706 ("Obviously it is not the statutory
language but *the prosecution's* interpretation of it which is
unusual. Normally what is not disputed is deemed to be conceded.
Generally a party *opposing* a motion cannot arbitrarily demand a
hearing to conduct a fishing expedition.") (emphases added).
Simply stated, *Gruden* dealt with the sufficiency of the People's
responding papers (*not* the defendant's motion papers); and, as in
Roberto H., not one single fact was alleged in the relevant papers.

A fair reading of *Gruden* is that if the defendant's motion
papers do not dispute any of the material factual allegations surrounding the stop, arrest, detention, search, etc., then the
defendant should not expect a suppression hearing to be granted.
On the other hand, if the defendant's motion papers do raise a
"factual dispute on a material point," then a suppression hearing

must be granted. In other words, where the defendant contests material factual assertions raised by the People, a hearing is required as a matter of law (*i.e.*, discretion plays no part in the analysis).

Where material facts are in dispute, the Court is called upon to assess credibility—which cannot be done in the absence of a hearing involving live witnesses and the opportunity for cross-examination. In this regard, the People frequently quote the "hearings are not available merely for the asking" line in *Gruden* out of context. *Gruden* makes clear that a party generally cannot demand a hearing without putting forth any facts whatsoever in support of its position. By contrast, *Gruden* clearly does not stand for the proposition that Courts should scour defense motions looking for any excuse to deny a suppression hearing. Indeed, the Court of Appeals has indicated that even where the defendant's motion papers are deficient, a Court should both (a) seriously consider granting the defendant a requested suppression hearing as a matter of discretion, *see Mendoza*, 82 N.Y.2d at 429–30, 604 N.Y.S.2d at 928–29, and (b) grant the defendant "the opportunity to seek leave to cure the defect, often a simple matter." 82 N.Y.2d at 430, 604 N.Y.S.2d at 929. *See also People v. Bonilla*, 82 N.Y.2d 825, 827, 604 N.Y.S.2d 937, 938, 624 N.E.2d 1032 (1993) (same).

Notably, CPL § 710.60(6) requires that "[r]egardless of whether a hearing [i]s conducted, the court, upon determining the motion, must set forth on the record its findings of fact, its conclusions of law and the reasons for its determination." *See also Bonilla*, 82 N.Y.2d at 827–28, 604 N.Y.S.2d at 938. Where material facts are disputed, a Court cannot fairly and impartially make the "findings of fact" required by CPL § 710.60(6) without holding a hearing, because:

> The question of probable cause is a mixed question of law and fact. Determination of the facts and circumstances bearing on the issue, which hinges primarily on questions of witness credibility, is a question of fact. However, it is a question of law whether the facts found to exist are sufficient to constitute probable cause.

People v. Morales, 42 N.Y.2d 129, 134, 397 N.Y.S.2d 587, 590, 366 N.E.2d 248 (1977). More specifically, in *People v. Oden*, 36 N.Y.2d 382, 384, 368 N.Y.S.2d 508, 511, 329 N.E.2d 188 (1975), the Court of Appeals held that:

> Probable cause exists if the facts and circumstances known to the arresting officer warrant a prudent man in believing that the offense has been committed. The question of probable cause is a mixed question of law and fact: the truth and existence of the facts and circumstances bearing on the issue being a question of fact, and the determination of whether the facts and circumstances found to exist and to be true constitute probable cause being a question of law. If the facts and circumstances adduced as proof of probable cause

are controverted so that conflicting evidence is to be weighed, if different persons might reasonably draw opposing inferences therefrom, or if the credibility of witnesses is to be passed upon, issues as to the existence or truth of those facts and circumstances are to be passed upon as a question of fact; however, when the facts and circumstances are undisputed, when only one inference can reasonably be drawn therefrom and when there is no problem as to credibility, or when certain facts and circumstances have been found to exist, the issue as to whether they amount to probable cause is a question of law.

(Citations omitted).

In the absence of a hearing, the "facts" alleged in the parties' motion papers are merely *allegations of fact*—they do not constitute evidence. "While it may turn out that [the defendant's claims are not] borne out by the facts ultimately found, the existence of sworn allegations supporting . . . viable legal arguments mandates that a hearing be held." *People v. Marshall*, 122 A.D.2d 283, __, 504 N.Y.S.2d 782, 783 (2d Dep't 1986).

The Court of Appeals has expressly rejected a prosecution claim that the "defendant must offer an innocent explanation for his conduct." *People v. Hightower*, 85 N.Y.2d 988, 990, 629 N.Y.S.2d 164, 166, 652 N.E.2d 910 (1995). *See also People v. Bailey*, 218 A.D.2d 569, __, 630 N.Y.S.2d 499, 501 (1st Dep't 1995) (same); *People v. Lopez*, 263 A.D.2d 434, __, 695 N.Y.S.2d 76, 77 (1st Dep't 1999) (defendant "need not prove his entire case in the motion papers").

Rather, the standard to be used in deciding whether the defendant's motion papers raise a factual dispute on a material point was set forth by the Court of Appeals in *Mendoza*: "We conclude that the sufficiency of defendant's factual allegations should be evaluated by (1) the face of the pleadings, (2) assessed in conjunction with the context of the motion, and (3) defendant's access to information." 82 N.Y.2d at 426, 604 N.Y.S.2d at 926. *See also People v. Jones*, 95 N.Y.2d 721, 723 N.Y.S.2d 761, 746 N.E.2d 1053 (2001). In this regard, *Mendoza* makes clear that "[i]t would be unreasonable to construe the CPL to require precise factual averments when, in parallel circumstances, defendant . . . does not have access to or awareness of the facts necessary to support suppression." 82 N.Y.2d at 429, 604 N.Y.S.2d at 928.

In *People v. Vasquez*, 200 A.D.2d 344, 613 N.Y.S.2d 595 (1st Dep't 1994), the Appellate Division, First Department, stated that:

[I]t should be stressed that whether or not the defendant knew he had done something illegal was not the relevant issue in determining whether there had been an unreasonable search and seizure; it was rather whether the *police* knew a sufficient amount about any transgressions by the defendant to render their intrusion upon him legal. Plainly, the defendant was not obliged globally to assert his innocence of all wrongdoing as a condition of maintaining his motion to suppress. All that he was obliged to do was to raise an issue as to the legality of the arrest, and to do that no more could reasonably have been required than that he cast into question, to the extent possible given the nature of the factual context and the information made available to him, whether the arresting officers' knowledge of any wrongdoing by him was sufficient to constitute probable cause. * * *

As *Mendoza* implicitly recognizes, and as is in any case obvious, it was not the Legislature's intention in enacting CPL § 710.60 to create an insuperable barrier to the assertion of possibly meritorious suppression claims.

200 A.D.2d at __-__, 613 N.Y.S.2d at 597–98.

Even if the defendant's factual allegations are deficient, the Court of Appeals has indicated a preference that a suppression hearing be granted where the defendant claims that the People's evidence was unlawfully obtained. In this regard, the *Mendoza* Court stated that, in addition to the three traditional factors used to decide the sufficiency of a defendant's motion papers, a fourth factor—"(4) Court's Discretion to Conduct a Hearing"— comes into play. *See* 82 N.Y.2d at 429, 604 N.Y.S.2d at 928.

In explaining why it is preferable for a Court to conduct suppression hearings where the defendant claims that evidence was unlawfully obtained, the *Mendoza* Court stated:

The CPL does not mandate summary denial of defendant's motion even if the factual allegations are deficient (*see*, CPL 710.60[3] ["The court *may* summarily deny the motion"] [emphasis added]). If the court orders a *Huntley* . . . hearing, and defendant's *Mapp* motion is grounded in the same facts involving the same police witnesses, the court may deem it appropriate in the exercise of discretion to consider the *Mapp* motion despite a perceived pleading deficiency. Indeed, considerations of judicial economy militate in favor of this procedure; an appellate court might conclude that summary denial of the *Mapp* motion was improper, requiring the parties and witnesses to reassemble for a new hearing, often months or years later.

82 N.Y.2d at 429–30, 604 N.Y.S.2d at 928–29. *See also People v. Higgins*, 124 A.D.3d 929, __, 1 N.Y.S.3d 424, 428-29 (3d Dep't 2015) ("we wholly reject the People's contention that County Court erred in granting defendant's request for a *Mapp/Dunaway* hearing. Although a defendant seeking a suppression hearing must make sworn factual allegations supporting his or her motion, CPL 710.60 'does not mandate summary denial of defendant's motion even if the factual allegations are deficient.' Here, the People had consented to a *Huntley* hearing 'grounded in the

same facts involving the same police witnesses.' Principles of judicial economy clearly weighed in favor of conducting any related suppression hearings, and we cannot find any error in so proceeding") (citations omitted).

In keeping with this stated preference that suppression hearings be granted where the defendant's motion papers are minimally sufficient, appellate courts in New York "have frequently criticized the practice of summarily denying suppression motions without a hearing where defendant sets forth a minimally sufficient showing to warrant a hearing on the suppression issue," *People v. Harris*, 160 A.D.2d 515, __, 554 N.Y.S.2d 170, 171 (1st Dep't 1990), and routinely hold appeals in abeyance and order that improperly denied suppression hearings be conducted. *See, e.g., People v. Hightower*, 85 N.Y.2d 988, 629 N.Y.S.2d 164, 652 N.E.2d 910 (1995); *People v. Mendoza*, 82 N.Y.2d 415, 604 N.Y.S.2d 922, 624 N.E.2d 1017 (1993); *People v. Jones*, 73 A.D.3d 662, 901 N.Y.S.2d 274 (1st Dep't 2010); *People v. Acosta*, 66 A.D.3d 792, 887 N.Y.S.2d 187 (2d Dep't 2009); *People v. Frank*, 65 A.D.3d 461, 884 N.Y.S.2d 718 (1st Dep't 2009); *People v. Trotter*, 54 A.D.3d 1065, 863 N.Y.S.2d 924 (2d Dep't 2008); *People v. Otero*, 51 A.D.3d 553, 858 N.Y.S.2d 157 (1st Dep't 2008); *People v. Mabeus*, 47 A.D.3d 1073, 850 N.Y.S.2d 664 (3d Dep't 2008); *People v. Joyner*, 46 A.D.3d 473, 848 N.Y.S.2d 146 (1st Dep't 2007); *People v. Bacon*, 6 A.D.3d 241, 774 N.Y.S.2d 332 (1st Dep't 2004); *People v. Phillips*, 4 A.D.3d 233, 771 N.Y.S.2d 658 (1st Dep't 2004); *People v. Muhammed*, 290 A.D.2d 248, 736 N.Y.S.2d 19 (1st Dep't 2002); *People v. Mathison*, 282 A.D.2d 283, 722 N.Y.S.2d 872 (1st Dep't 2001); *People v. Butler*, 280 A.D.2d 399, 720 N.Y.S.2d 788 (1st Dep't 2001); *People v. Lopez*, 263 A.D.2d 434, 695 N.Y.S.2d 76 (1st Dep't 1999); *People v. Nenni*, 261 A.D.2d 900, 689 N.Y.S.2d 912 (4th Dep't 1999); *People v. Wright*, 256 A.D.2d 106, 682 N.Y.S.2d 154 (1st Dep't 1998); *People v. Face*, 247 A.D.2d 336, 669 N.Y.S.2d 289 (1st Dep't 1998); *People v. Lewis*, 247 A.D.2d 227, 668 N.Y.S.2d 356 (1st Dep't 1998); *People v. Marquez*, 246 A.D.2d 330, 667 N.Y.S.2d 359 (1st Dep't 1998); *People v. Perrilla*, 240 A.D.2d 313, 660 N.Y.S.2d 113 (1st Dep't 1997); *People v. Bennett*, 240 A.D.2d 292, 659 N.Y.S.2d 260 (1st Dep't 1997); *People v. Sanchez*, 236 A.D.2d 243, 653 N.Y.S.2d 563 (1st Dep't 1997); *People v. Ayarde*, 220 A.D.2d 519, 632 N.Y.S.2d 174 (2d Dep't 1995); *People v. Bailey*, 218 A.D.2d 569, 630 N.Y.S.2d 499 (1st Dep't 1995); *People v. Youngblood*, 210 A.D.2d 948, 621 N.Y.S.2d 265 (4th Dep't 1994); *People v. Holmes*, 206 A.D.2d 604, 614 N.Y.S.2d 474 (3d Dep't 1994); *People v. Vasquez*, 200 A.D.2d 344, 613 N.Y.S.2d 595 (1st Dep't 1994); *People v. Altruz*, 198 A.D.2d 423, 604 N.Y.S.2d 134 (2d Dep't 1993); *People v. Foster*, 197 A.D.2d 411, 602 N.Y.S.2d 395 (1st Dep't 1993); *People v. Aponte*, 193 A.D.2d 529, 598 N.Y.S.2d 937

(1st Dep't 1993); *People v. Cole*, 187 A.D.2d 873, 590 N.Y.S.2d
542 (3d Dep't 1992); *People v. Moore*, 186 A.D.2d 591, 588
N.Y.S.2d 388 (2d Dep't 1992); *People v. Rodriguez*, 185 A.D.2d
802, 586 N.Y.S.2d 968 (1st Dep't 1992); *People v. Davis*, 169
A.D.2d 379, 564 N.Y.S.2d 320 (1st Dep't 1991); *People v. Miller*,
162 A.D.2d 248, 556 N.Y.S.2d 607 (1st Dep't 1990); *People v.
Huggins*, 162 A.D.2d 129, 556 N.Y.S.2d 75 (1st Dep't 1990); *People
v. Harris*, 160 A.D.2d 515, 554 N.Y.S.2d 170 (1st Dep't 1990);
People v. Zarate, 160 A.D.2d 466, 554 N.Y.S.2d 137 (1st Dep't
1990); *People v. Whiten*, 151 A.D.2d 708, 543 N.Y.S.2d 944 (2d
Dep't 1989); *People v. Alvarez*, 151 A.D.2d 684, 543 N.Y.S.2d 935
(2d Dep't 1989); *People v. Marte*, 149 A.D.2d 335, 539 N.Y.S.2d
912 (1st Dep't 1989); *People v. Estrada*, 147 A.D.2d 407, 538
N.Y.S.2d 5 (1st Dep't 1989); *People v. Lee*, 130 A.D.2d 400, 515
N.Y.S.2d 260 (1st Dep't 1987); *People v. Patterson*, 129 A.D.2d
527, 514 N.Y.S.2d 378 (1st Dep't 1987); *People v. Marshall*, 122
A.D.2d 283, 504 N.Y.S.2d 782 (2d Dep't 1986); *People v. Sutton*,
91 A.D.2d 522, 456 N.Y.S.2d 771 (1st Dep't 1982); *People v.
Calhoun*, 73 A.D.2d 972, 424 N.Y.S.2d 247 (2d Dep't 1980); *People
v. Carter*, 72 A.D.2d 963, 422 N.Y.S.2d 258 (4th Dep't 1979);
People v. Carrasquillo, 70 A.D.2d 842, 418 N.Y.S.2d 3 (1st Dep't
1979); *People v. Werner*, 55 A.D.2d 317, 390 N.Y.S.2d 711 (4th
Dep't 1977).

The Appellate Division, First Department's decision in *People
v. Estrada*, 147 A.D.2d 407, __, 538 N.Y.S.2d 5, 5–6 (1st Dep't
1989), is illustrative:

> Defendant made a pretrial motion to suppress his confession, claim-
> ing that it was the product of an illegal arrest. In his motion papers,
> defendant alleged that prior to his arrest he had not been observed
> with any contraband or acting in a suspicious manner. He claimed,
> therefore, that there had not been probable cause for his arrest. As
> the People now concede, and as is in any case evident, defendant's
> allegations were sufficient to require that a *Dunaway* hearing be
> held. Justice Rothwax, however, summarily denied the defendant's
> *Dunaway* motion without a hearing. Although the summary denial
> may have appeared efficient at the time, its ultimate consequence
> will be unnecessarily to delay the adjudication of defendant's case.
> If this were an isolated case it would not merit comment but we
> have on at least six previous occasions had to hold appeals in abey-
> ance and remand for hearings upon suppression motions inap-
> propriately denied by the same judge.

(Citations omitted). Notably, following the remand the New York
County Supreme Court "granted defendant-appellant's motion to
suppress on the District Attorney's concession that it was unable
to proceed. The prosecution concede[d] that without this confession it [was] unable to sustain its burden of proof. In view of this
concession the indictment [was] dismissed." *People v. Estrada*,
152 A.D.2d 499, __, 544 N.Y.S.2d 475 (1st Dep't 1989).

In *People v. Misuis*, 47 N.Y.2d 979, 981, 419 N.Y.S.2d 961, 962–63, 393 N.E.2d 1034 (1979), the Court of Appeals made clear that:

> Clearly, statements obtained by exploitation of unlawful police conduct or detention must be suppressed, for their use in evidence under such circumstance violates the Fourth Amendment (*Dunaway v. New York*, __ U.S. __, 99 S.Ct. 2248, 60 L.Ed.2d 824). It is therefore "incumbent upon the suppression court to permit an inquiry into the propriety of the police conduct." Unless the People establish that the police had probable cause to arrest or detain a suspect, and unless the defendant is accorded an opportunity to delve fully into the circumstances attendant upon his arrest or detention, his motion to suppress should be granted.

(Quoting *People v. Wise*, 46 N.Y.2d 321, 329, 413 N.Y.S.2d 334, 339, 385 N.E.2d 1262, 14 A.L.R.4th 666 (1978) (footnote omitted). *See also People v. Chaney*, 253 A.D.2d 562, __, 686 N.Y.S.2d 871, 873 (3d Dep't 1998); *People v. Sanchez*, 236 A.D.2d 243, __, 653 N.Y.S.2d 563, 564–65 (1st Dep't 1997). *See generally People v. Gonzalez*, 71 A.D.2d 775, __, 419 N.Y.S.2d 322, 323–24 (3d Dep't 1979).

In *Misuis*, the Court of Appeals reversed the Appellate Division, vacated the defendant's guilty plea, and remitted the case for a probable cause hearing where:

> At the hearing on defendant's motion to suppress [various] admissions, his counsel repeatedly attempted to interrogate the two officers in an effort to discover whether the police had probable cause to make the arrest. His avowed intention was to show that the detention was unlawful and thus any statements made as a result of the claimed unlawful arrest and detention tainted any admissions. However, at the insistent urging of the prosecutor the court refused to permit that inquiry and permitted only questions concerning the voluntariness of the statements themselves.

47 N.Y.2d at 980, 419 N.Y.S.2d at 962.

The same conclusion was reached in *People v. Whitaker*, 79 A.D.2d 668, __, 433 N.Y.S.2d 849, 850 (2d Dep't 1980):

> As the People concede, the suppression court erred in severely limiting the defendant's cross-examination of the sole arresting officer who testified, with respect to the issue of whether there was probable cause to arrest defendant. It is well-settled that on a motion to suppress a defendant's postarrest statements, the suppression court is required to permit the defendant to "delve fully into the circumstances attendant upon his arrest", for "[a] statement, voluntary under Fifth Amendment standards, will nevertheless be suppressed if it has been obtained through the exploitation of an illegal arrest."

(Citations omitted). *See also People v. Lopez*, 56 A.D.3d 280, 867 N.Y.S.2d 83 (1st Dep't 2008); *People v. Roberts*, 81 A.D.2d 674,

441 N.Y.S.2d 408 (2d Dep't 1981); *People v. King*, 79 A.D.2d 1033, 437 N.Y.S.2d 931 (2d Dep't 1981); *People v. Specks*, 77 A.D.2d 669, 430 N.Y.S.2d 157 (2d Dep't 1980). *See generally People v. Williamson*, 79 N.Y.2d 799, 800, 580 N.Y.S.2d 170, 171, 588 N.E.2d 68 (1991) ("We agree that it was error to restrict cross-examination under these circumstances . . . . Unlike the Appellate Division, however, we conclude that the error requires a reversal.") (citation omitted); *People v. Garriga*, 189 A.D.2d 236, __, 596 N.Y.S.2d 25, 29 (1st Dep't 1993) ("We also find reversible error in the excessive constraints placed upon defense counsel in cross-examination of the People's witnesses both at the *Mapp* hearing and at trial.").

Practically speaking, probable cause hearings are granted routinely as a matter of judicial and prosecutorial economy. In the authors' experience, many prosecutors are willing to stipulate to a so-called *Huntley/Dunaway/Mapp* hearing. Such hearings tend to resolve most of the issues that would arise at trial, and give both sides a preview of the case (which generally results in a pretrial disposition). Thus, pretrial hearings are often a very efficient use of scarce judicial resources.

Another factor warrants consideration. Many people accused of DWI have no prior experience with the criminal justice system. They expect to be treated fairly and impartially by both the People and the Court. When the People vehemently oppose the granting of a probable cause hearing, and the Court finds that an arrest was lawful based solely on a police officer's hearsay accusations, the defendant is often left with the perception that the system is biased and unfair, which undermines respect for the rule of law.

§ 1:37 Standing

In response to a defense motion to suppress, the People frequently claim that the defendant has failed to allege facts establishing his or her standing to pursue the motion. Such claims are generally frivolous when made in connection with DWI cases. In this regard, the doctrine of standing typically applies to cases where a search of *someone else's* property yields evidence that the People seek to use against the defendant. The doctrine is all but inapplicable to a typical DWI case, where the primary thing searched and seized is the defendant's person (including a sample of the defendant's breath and/or blood).

It is well settled that a defendant has a legitimate expectation of privacy in, and thus standing to contest, a search of his or her own "person" by the police. *See, e.g., People v. Burton*, 6 N.Y.3d 584, 588, 815 N.Y.S.2d 7, 10, 848 N.E.2d 454 (2006) ("Under the Fourth Amendment to the United States Constitution, individuals possess a legitimate expectation of privacy with regard to their persons."); *People v. Wesley*, 73 N.Y.2d 351, 361, 540 N.Y.S.2d 757, 763, 538 N.E.2d 76 (1989) (in case of search of defendant's person, "there plainly is standing"); *People v. Moore*, 186 A.D.2d 591, __, 588 N.Y.S.2d 388, 389–90 (2d Dep't 1992) ("the defendant clearly had standing to contest the search of his person"); *People v. Marte*, 149 A.D.2d 335, __, 539 N.Y.S.2d 912, 913 (1st Dep't 1989) ("There is no question that defendant had standing to challenge the legitimacy of the search and seizure of evidence from his person."); *People v. Lee*, 130 A.D.2d 400, __, 515 N.Y.S.2d 260, 262 (1st Dep't 1987) ("since it was clear that defendant's person had been subjected to a search and seizure, no proprietary interest need be asserted").

Similarly, where the defendant is the driver of a vehicle stopped by the police, he or she has standing to challenge the lawfulness of the stop—*even if the vehicle is stolen. See People v. May*, 81 N.Y.2d 725, 727, 593 N.Y.S.2d 760, 761, 609 N.E.2d 113 (1992).

§ 1:38 Proving the basis to stop at a suppression hearing

It is axiomatic that the People's burden of proof at a probable cause hearing is less onerous than their burden of proof at trial. In this regard, in *People v. Saylor*, 166 A.D.2d 899, __, 560 N.Y.S.2d 560, 561 (4th Dep't 1990), the Appellate Division, Fourth Department, held that:

> The issue at the hearing was not whether defendant was speeding, but whether the police officer had reasonable suspicion to believe that defendant was speeding. Although the officer did not testify in detail about his training, the court was entitled to assume, for purposes of this hearing, that a police officer with over a year's experience can visually estimate the speed of a moving vehicle. Moreover, the radar unit clocked defendant's speed at 54 miles per hour, adding additional support to the officer's estimate. Although at trial it would be necessary for the People to establish that the radar unit was in proper working order, the suppression court properly concluded that such detailed proof was not required at a probable cause hearing.

(Citation omitted). *See also People v. Robinson*, 97 N.Y.2d 341, 354, 741 N.Y.S.2d 147, 155, 767 N.E.2d 638 (2001) ("the decision to stop a vehicle is reasonable where the police have probable cause to believe that a traffic infraction has occurred"); 97 N.Y.2d at 350, 741 N.Y.S.2d at 152 ("This Court has always evaluated the validity of a traffic stop based on probable cause that a driver has committed a traffic violation."); *People v. Guthrie*, 25 N.Y.3d 130, 133, 8 N.Y.S.3d 237, 240, 30 N.E.3d 880 (2015).

§ 1:39 Prosecution generally only has one chance to prove probable cause

Where the People fail to call a necessary witness or witnesses at a pretrial hearing, and/or fail to prove a necessary piece of evidence at the hearing, it is generally improper for a Court to reopen the proof to allow the People to "cure" the defect. Stated another way, Courts traditionally refrain from giving the People a "second bite at the apple" in such circumstances. *See, e.g., People v. Kevin W.*, 22 N.Y.3d 287, 289, 295, 980 N.Y.S.2d 873, 873, 877-78, 3 N.E.3d 1121 (2013); *People v. Havelka*, 45 N.Y.2d 636, 643, 412 N.Y.S.2d 345, 348–49, 384 N.E.2d 1269 (1978); *People v. Bryant*, 37 N.Y.2d 208, 211, 371 N.Y.S.2d 881, 884, 333 N.E.2d 161 (1975) (per curiam); *People v. Knapp*, 57 N.Y.2d 161, 175, 455 N.Y.S.2d 539, 544, 441 N.E.2d 1057 (1982); *People v. Dodt*, 61 N.Y.2d 408, 418, 474 N.Y.S.2d 441, 447, 462 N.E.2d 1159 (1984).

An exception to this rule exists where "the People were 'deprived of an opportunity to fully present all the available evidence * * * because the hearing court made an incorrect ruling.'" *People v. Serrano*, 93 N.Y.2d 73, 79, 688 N.Y.S.2d 90, 94, 710 N.E.2d 655 (1999) (citation omitted). *See also People v. Crandall*, 69 N.Y.2d 459, 464, 515 N.Y.S.2d 745, 747, 508 N.E.2d 657 (1987) (" 'the People should not be deprived of one full opportunity to present evidence of the dispositive issues involved at the suppression hearing. If an error of law is committed by the hearing court which directly causes the People to fail to offer potentially critical evidence a rehearing should be ordered so that the evidence may be presented' ") (citation omitted); *Havelka*, 45 N.Y.2d at 643, 412 N.Y.S.2d at 348 (same).

§ 1:40   Where trial testimony conflicts with testimony at suppression hearing, defendant should move to reopen hearing

In *People v. Badia*, 130 A.D.3d 744, 14 N.Y.S.3d 73 (2d Dep't 2015), a pre-trial suppression hearing was held, following which the defendant's blood test results were found to be admissible. On appeal, "the defendant relie[d] on portions of the trial record in support of his contention that the blood test results should have been suppressed." *Id.* at ___, 14 N.Y.S.3d at 74. The Appellate Division, Second Department, held that:

> [T]his Court is precluded from reviewing trial testimony in determining whether the hearing court acted properly. The propriety of the hearing court's ruling must be determined only in light of the evidence that was before that court. Since the defendant did not seek to reopen the hearing based on the trial testimony, or move for a mistrial, the question of whether the trooper's trial testimony undermined the hearing court's determination is not properly before this Court.

Id. at ___, 14 N.Y.S.3d at 74-75 (citations omitted).

§ 1:41 When can a police officer search the interior of a vehicle during a stop for a traffic infraction?

In *People v. Class*, 67 N.Y.2d 431, 503 N.Y.S.2d 313, 494 N.E.2d 444 (1986) (per curiam), after the U.S. Supreme Court held that the *Federal* Constitution was not violated, *see New York v. Class*, 475 U.S. 106, 106 S. Ct. 960, 89 L. Ed. 2d 81 (1986), the Court of Appeals reconsidered the case under the *State* Constitution and held that a "police 'officer's nonconsensual entry into [defendant's] automobile to determine the vehicle identification number violates the . . . State Constitution[ ] where it is based solely on a stop for a traffic infraction.' " 67 N.Y.2d at 432–33, 503 N.Y.S.2d at 314 (citation omitted). Similarly, in *People v. Torres*, 74 N.Y.2d 224, 226, 229–30, 544 N.Y.S.2d 796, 797, 800, 543 N.E.2d 61 (1989), the Court of Appeals held as follows:

> A police officer acting on reasonable suspicion that criminal activity is afoot and on an articulable basis to fear for his own safety may intrude upon the person or personal effects of the suspect only to the extent that is actually necessary to protect himself from harm while he conducts the inquiry authorized by CPL 140.50(1). In *People v. Lindsay*, we left open the question whether under article I, § 12 of our State Constitution such an intrusion may extend to items within the passenger compartment of the suspects' vehicle solely on the theory that "if the suspect is not placed under arrest, he will be permitted to reenter his automobile, and will then have access to any weapons inside." Having been squarely presented with the issue by the parties' submissions on this appeal, we now answer that question in the negative and hold that, despite the Supreme Court's approval of such intrusions in *Michigan v. Long*, our more protective State constitutional provisions prohibit them under the circumstances presented here (N.Y. Const. Art. I, § 12).
> * * *

> A police officer's entry into a citizen's automobile and his inspection of personal effects located within are significant encroachments upon that citizen's privacy interests. Under our own long-standing precedent, such intrusions must be both justified in their inception and reasonably related in scope and intensity to the circumstances which rendered their initiation permissible.

(Citations omitted). *Cf. People v. Carvey*, 89 N.Y.2d 707, 709, 657 N.Y.S.2d 879, 880, 680 N.E.2d 150 (1997) ("We agree with the courts below that the police action here was proper. Defendant was wearing an article uniquely indicative of his present readiness to use an available firearm—a bulletproof vest. This salient fact, when coupled with the police observation of defendant furtively placing something beneath his seat, warranted the conclusion that a weapon located in the vehicle presented an actual and specific threat to the officers' safety. In these particular circumstances, the officers could lawfully reach into the vehicle, even after removing the driver and passengers.").

§ 1:42 Search of vehicle incident to lawful arrest for traffic infraction

In *People v. Marsh*, 20 N.Y.2d 98, 100, 281 N.Y.S.2d 789, 791, 228 N.E.2d 783 (1967), the Court of Appeals made clear that:

> There is no question, and the entire court agrees, that a police officer is not authorized to conduct a search every time he stops a motorist for speeding or some other ordinary traffic infraction. It is urged, however, that the officer is empowered to conduct a search, as incident to a lawful arrest, when the defendant is taken into custody for a traffic violation on a warrant of arrest, following his failure to appear in court pursuant to the summons initially issued. We find no basis for making such a distinction, concluding as we do that it not only would offend against the legislative design for the treatment of traffic offenders but would also exceed constitutional limits on search and seizure.

See also 20 N.Y.2d at 101, 281 N.Y.S.2d at 792 ("Although, as a general rule, when an individual is lawfully arrested, the police officer may conduct a contemporaneous search of his person 'for weapons or for the fruits of or implements used to commit the crime', we do not believe that the Legislature intended the rule to cover arrests for traffic violations. It is obvious that, except in the most rare of instances, there can be no 'fruits' or 'implements' of such infractions and the search, to be upheld, would have to be justified as one for weapons. However, there is something incongruous about treating traffic offenders as noncriminals, on the one hand, and subjecting them, on the other, to the indignity of a search for weapons.") (citation omitted); *People v. Erwin*, 42 N.Y.2d 1064, 1065, 399 N.Y.S.2d 637, 638, 369 N.E.2d 1170 (1977) ("Although there may have been reasonable cause to effectuate an arrest for a traffic infraction, no such arrest was made and indeed, Officer Bennett testified that he did not even intend to issue a summons, but was merely 'going to give him a warning'. There being no arrest the subsequent search of defendant's person and his automobile can be justified only if independent reasonable cause existed."); *People v. Adams*, 32 N.Y.2d 451, 455, 346 N.Y.S.2d 229, 232, 299 N.E.2d 653 (1973) ("We hold in this case that a violation of [former] section 422 of the Vehicle and Traffic Law, without more, will not sustain [the warrantless] search" of the defendant's person, followed by a search incident to his arrest for such charge (even though the charge was a misdemeanor).). *Cf. People v. Troiano*, 35 N.Y.2d 476, 478, 363 N.Y.S.2d 943, 945, 323 N.E.2d 183 (1974) ("so long as an arrest is lawful, the consequent exposure to search is inevitable. If the unnecessarily intrusive personal search is to be restricted, the cure must be by limiting the right to arrest or to take into custody."). *See generally Knowles v. Iowa*, 525 U.S. 113, 119 S. Ct. 484, 142 L. Ed. 2d 492 (1998) (police cannot, consistent with the 4th

Amendment, conduct a full search of motorist's car where motorist is stopped for speeding and issued citation in lieu of arrest).

§ 1:43   Search of defendant's person incident to arrest

In *People v. Reid*, 24 N.Y.3d 615, 2 N.Y.S.3d 409, 26 N.E.3d 237 (2014), although probable cause existed to arrest the defendant for DWI, the officer had no intention of placing the defendant under arrest. Nonetheless, the officer "asked defendant to step out of the car and patted him down. In the course of doing so, he found a switchblade knife in defendant's pocket. Defendant was then arrested." *Id.* at 618, 2 N.Y.S.3d at 410. "The People ma[d]e no claim that the pat down in this case was justified either by reasonable suspicion that defendant presented a danger to the officer or by probable cause to believe contraband would be discovered. The only justification the People offer[ed] for the search [was] that it was incident to a lawful arrest, and exempt for that reason from the general rule that searches require a warrant." *Id.* at 618, 2 N.Y.S.3d at 411.

Under these circumstances, the Court of Appeals held as follows:

> It is not disputed that, before conducting the search, [the officer] could lawfully have arrested defendant for driving while intoxicated. And it is clear that the search was not unlawful solely because it preceded the arrest, since the two events were substantially contemporaneous. Nor is it decisive that the police chose to predicate the arrest on the possession of a weapon, rather than on driving while intoxicated. The problem is that, as [the officer] testified, but for the search there would have been no arrest at all.

> Where that is true, to say that the search was incident to the arrest does not make sense. It is irrelevant that, because probable cause existed, there *could* have been an arrest without a search. A search must be incident to an actual arrest, not just to probable cause that might have led to an arrest, but did not. * * *

> The incident to arrest exception is a "bright-line rule" that does not depend on whether there is a threat of harm to the officer or destruction of evidence in a particular case—but the rule is inapplicable to cases that fall, as does this one, outside the bright line. * * *

> [T]he "search incident to arrest" doctrine, by its nature, requires proof that, at the time of the search, an arrest has already occurred or is about to occur. Where no arrest has yet taken place, the officer must have intended to make one if the "search incident" exception is to be applied.

Id. at 618-19, 619, 620, 2 N.Y.S.3d at 411, 412 (citations omitted).

See also People v. Mangum, 125 A.D.3d 401, 3 N.Y.S.3d 332 (1st Dep't 2015).

§ 1:44   Search of vehicle incident to lawful DWI arrest

One of the exceptions to the Fourth Amendment's warrant requirement is a search incident to a lawful arrest. *See, e.g., Weeks v. U.S.*, 232 U.S. 383, 392, 34 S. Ct. 341, 344, 58 L. Ed. 652 (1914). In *Chimel v. California*, 395 U.S. 752, 763, 89 S. Ct. 2034, 2040, 23 L. Ed. 2d 685 (1969), the Supreme Court held that the scope of such a search is limited to:

> [A] search of the arrestee's person and the area "within his immediate control"—construing that phrase to mean the area from within which he might gain possession of a weapon or destructible evidence.

> There is no comparable justification, however, for routinely searching any room other than that in which an arrest occurs—or, for that matter, for searching through all the desk drawers or other closed or concealed areas in that room itself. Such searches, in the absence of well-recognized exceptions, may be made only under the authority of a search warrant.

In *New York v. Belton*, 453 U.S. 454, 460–61, 101 S. Ct. 2860, 2864, 69 L. Ed. 2d 768 (1981), the Court applied *Chimel* to a situation where the arrested person was the occupant of a motor vehicle, and held that:

> [W]hen a policeman has made a lawful custodial arrest of the occupant of an automobile, he may, as a contemporaneous incident of that arrest, search the passenger compartment of that automobile.

> It follows from this conclusion that the police may also examine the contents of any containers found within the passenger compartment, for if the passenger compartment is within reach of the arrestee, so also will containers in it be within his reach. Such a container may, of course, be searched whether it is open or closed, since the justification for the search is not that the arrestee has no privacy interest in the container, but that the lawful custodial arrest justifies the infringement of any privacy interest the arrestee may have.

(Citations and footnotes omitted). The *Belton* Court defined the term "container" as:

> [A]ny object capable of holding another object. It thus includes closed or open glove compartments, consoles, or other receptacles located anywhere within the passenger compartment, as well as luggage, boxes, bags, clothing, and the like. *Our holding encompasses only the interior of the passenger compartment of an automobile and does not encompass the trunk.*

453 U.S. at 460 n.4, 101 S.Ct. at 2864 n.4 (emphasis added).

In *Arizona v. Gant*, 556 U.S. 332, 349, 129 S. Ct. 1710, 1722–23, 173 L. Ed. 2d 485, 47 A.L.R. Fed. 2d 657 (2009), the Supreme Court concluded that a broad reading of *Belton* had resulted in countless unconstitutional searches in the 28 years since *Belton* was decided. In this regard, the Court stated that:

Although we have recognized that a motorist's privacy interest in his vehicle is less substantial than in his home, the former interest is nevertheless important and deserving of constitutional protection. It is particularly significant that *Belton* searches authorize police officers to search not just the passenger compartment but every purse, briefcase, or other container within that space. A rule that gives police the power to conduct such a search whenever an individual is caught committing a traffic offense, when there is no basis for believing evidence of the offense might be found in the vehicle, creates a serious and recurring threat to the privacy of countless individuals. Indeed, the character of that threat implicates the central concern underlying the Fourth Amendment—the concern about giving police officers unbridled discretion to rummage at will among a person's private effects. * * *

Construing *Belton* broadly to allow vehicle searches incident to any arrest would serve no purpose except to provide a police entitlement, and it is anathema to the Fourth Amendment to permit a warrantless search on that basis. * * *

Although it appears that the State's reading of *Belton* has been widely taught in police academies and that law enforcement officers have relied on the rule in conducting vehicle searches during the past 28 years, many of these searches were not justified by the reasons underlying the *Chimel* exception. Countless individuals guilty of nothing more serious than a traffic violation have had their constitutional right to the security of their private effects violated as a result. . . . If it is clear that a practice is unlawful, individuals' interest in its discontinuance clearly outweighs any law enforcement "entitlement" to its persistence. * * *

The experience of the 28 years since we decided *Belton* has shown that the generalization underpinning the broad reading of that decision is unfounded. We now know that articles inside the passenger compartment are rarely "within 'the area into which an arrestee might reach,' " and blind adherence to *Belton*'s faulty assumption would authorize myriad unconstitutional searches. The doctrine of *stare decisis* does not require us to approve routine constitutional violations.

556 U.S. at 345, 347, 349, 350–51, 129 S.Ct. at 1720, 1721, 1722–23, 1723 (citations and footnote omitted).

Accordingly, the *Gant* Court held that:

Police may search a vehicle incident to a recent occupant's arrest only if the arrestee is within reaching distance of the passenger compartment at the time of the search or it is reasonable to believe the vehicle contains evidence of the offense of arrest. When these justifications are absent, a search of an arrestee's vehicle will be unreasonable unless police obtain a warrant or show that another exception to the warrant requirement applies.

556 U.S. at 351, 129 S.Ct. at 1723–24. *See also* 556 U.S. at 335, 129 S.Ct. at 1714 ("we hold that *Belton* does not authorize a vehicle search incident to a recent occupant's arrest after the arrestee has been secured and cannot access the interior of the vehicle"); 556 U.S. at 335, 129 S.Ct. at 1714 ("we also conclude that circumstances unique to the automobile context justify a search incident to arrest when it is reasonable to believe that evidence of the offense of arrest might be found in the vehicle"); 556 U.S. at 343, 129 S.Ct. at 1719 ("we . . . hold that the *Chimel* rationale authorizes police to search a vehicle incident to a recent occupant's arrest only when the arrestee is unsecured and within reaching distance of the passenger compartment at the time of the search"); 556 U.S. at 343, 129 S.Ct. at 1719 ("Although it does not follow from *Chimel*, we also conclude that circumstances unique to the vehicle context justify a search incident to a lawful arrest when it is 'reasonable to believe evidence relevant to the crime of arrest might be found in the vehicle.' In many cases, as when a recent occupant is arrested for a traffic violation, there will be no reasonable basis to believe the vehicle contains relevant evidence.") (citation omitted). *Compare People v. Belton*, 55 N.Y.2d 49, 55, 447 N.Y.S.2d 873, 876, 432 N.E.2d 745 (1982) ("we hold, that where police have validly arrested an occupant of an automobile, and they have reason to believe that the car may contain evidence related to the crime for which the occupant was arrested or that a weapon may be discovered or a means of escape thwarted, they may contemporaneously search the passenger compartment, including any containers found therein"); *Wyoming v. Houghton*, 526 U.S. 295, 307, 119 S. Ct. 1297, 1304, 143 L. Ed. 2d 408 (1999) ("We hold that police officers with probable cause to search a car may inspect passengers' belongings found in the car that are capable of concealing the object of the search.").

In assessing *Gant*'s applicability to DWI cases, two issues immediately come to mind. First, will the courts create a "DWI exception" to *Gant*, concluding that it is *always* reasonable to believe that relevant evidence (*e.g.*, open containers of alcohol) might be found in the vehicle of a person arrested for DWI? Second, if such a search-incident-to-arrest is permissible, will its scope be limited to locations where it is likely that relevant evidence might be found; or rather will a full-blown *Belton* search of every container in the vehicle be authorized?

Regardless, a critical aspect of *Gant* is the Court's comment that even where a search-incident-to-arrest would be improper, a warrantless vehicle search can nonetheless be conducted where "another exception to the warrant requirement applies." In DWI cases, such a search can generally be conducted pursuant to the "inventory search" exception to the warrant requirement. *See, e.g., Florida v. Wells*, 495 U.S. 1, 110 S. Ct. 1632, 109 L. Ed. 2d 1 (1990); *Colorado v. Bertine*, 479 U.S. 367, 107 S. Ct. 738, 93 L. Ed. 2d 739 (1987). *See also Maryland v. Dyson*, 527 U.S. 465, 119 S. Ct. 2013, 144 L. Ed. 2d 442 (1999) (discussing the "automobile exception" to the warrant requirement). An inventory search is easier to challenge, however, as such a search must be conducted pursuant to "standardized criteria" or an "established routine" limiting the "latitude" and "discretion" of the officer(s) conducting it, and "must not be a ruse for a general rummaging in order to discover incriminating evidence." *Wells*, 495 U.S. at 4, 110 S.Ct. at 1635.

In *People v. Johnson*, 1 N.Y.3d 252, 771 N.Y.S.2d 64, 803 N.E.2d 385 (2003), the Court of Appeals found an inventory search to be invalid where, *inter alia*:

> [T]he evidence adduced at the [suppression] hearing was clearly insufficient to satisfy the prosecutor's initial burden of establishing a valid inventory search. Although the officer testified that he knew of the general objectives of an inventory search, and declared that his search of the glove compartment box fulfilled those objectives, the People offered no evidence to establish the existence of any *departmental policy* regarding inventory searches. Even assuming such a policy existed, the People failed to produce evidence demonstrating either that the procedure itself was "rationally designed to meet the objectives that justify inventory searches in the first place," or that this particular officer conducted this search properly and in compliance with *established procedures*.

1 N.Y.3d at 256, 771 N.Y.S.2d at 66–67 (emphases added) (citation omitted). *See also People v. Gomez*, 13 N.Y.3d 6, 884 N.Y.S.2d 339, 912 N.E.2d 555 (2009); *People v. Galak*, 80 N.Y.2d 715, 719, 594 N.Y.S.2d 689, 692, 610 N.E.2d 362 (1993); *People v. Francisco*, 63 A.D.3d 1554, 880 N.Y.S.2d 806 (4th Dep't 2009); *People v. Elpenord*, 24 A.D.3d 465, 806 N.Y.S.2d 675 (2d Dep't 2005).

More recently, in *People v. Padilla*, 21 N.Y.3d 268, 272-73, 970 N.Y.S.2d 486, 488-89, 992 N.E.2d 414 (2013), petition for cert. filed, 82 U.S.L.W. 3095 (U.S. Aug. 5, 2013), the Court of Appeals held that:

> Our jurisprudence in this area is clear. Following a lawful arrest of a driver of a vehicle that is required to be impounded, the police may conduct an inventory search of the vehicle. The search is "designed to properly catalogue the contents of the item searched." However, an inventory search must not be "a ruse for a general rummaging in order to discover incriminating evidence." To guard against this danger, the search must be conducted pursuant to an

established procedure "clearly limiting the conduct of individual officers that assures that the searches are carried out consistently and reasonably." "While incriminating evidence may be a consequence of an inventory search, it should not be its purpose." The People bear the burden of demonstrating the validity of the inventory search.

Here the People proffered written guidelines, the officer's testimony regarding his search of the vehicle, and the resulting list of items retained. Although defendant takes issue with the officer's removal of the speakers by arguing that such action was a ruse designed to search for drugs, the officer's testimony that it was police protocol to remove any owner-installed equipment, was accepted by the hearing court and we perceive no grounds upon which to overturn that determination. Thus, the People met their burden of establishing that the search was in accordance with procedure and resulted in a meaningful inventory list.

The fact that the officer did not follow the written police procedure when he gave some of the contents of the vehicle to defendant's sister without itemizing that property, did not invalidate the search. Notably, it was defendant himself who called his sister to come to the precinct to retrieve his property. The primary objectives of the search—to preserve the property of defendant, to protect the police from a claim of lost property and to protect the police and others from dangerous instruments—were met when the officer complied with defendant's request and gave the items to his sister and then prepared a list of the other items retained by the police.

Finally, it is clear the officer's intention for the search was to inventory the items in the vehicle. It was reasonable for the officer to check in the seat panels that were askew as part of his inventory. The fact that the officer knew that contraband is often hidden by criminals in the panels did not invalidate the entire search.

(Citations omitted).

In *People v. Walker*, 20 N.Y.3d 122, 124, 957 N.Y.S.2d 272, 273, 980 N.E.2d 937 (2012), the Court of Appeals held as follows:

Having decided to arrest defendant for driving with a revoked license, a police officer also decided to impound the car he was driving. The officer did not inquire whether defendant's passenger, who was not the registered owner of the car, was licensed and authorized to drive it. We hold that such an inquiry was not constitutionally required. We also hold that the officer's search of the car after he decided to impound it was a valid inventory search.

In so holding, the Court reasoned as follows:

When the driver of a vehicle is arrested, the police may impound the car, and conduct an inventory search, where they act pursuant to "reasonable police regulations relating to inventory procedures administered in good faith." Here, the trooper testified that it is state police procedure to "tow the vehicle" if the operator's license "is either suspended or revoked" and the registered owner is not present. We hold this to be a reasonable procedure, at least as applied to this case, where no facts were brought to the trooper's attention to show that impounding would be unnecessary.

Neither defendant nor his girlfriend asked the trooper if the girlfriend could drive the car, or told him that she had a driver's license and the owner's permission to drive it. The trooper was not required, as a matter of constitutional law, to raise the question, or to initiate a phone call to the owner. To impose such a requirement on police in such situations would not only create an administrative burden, but would involve them in making (and the courts in reviewing) difficult decisions in borderline cases. If a person present claims to have the owner's permission to drive, must the police take her word for it? If the owner is called and does not answer immediately, must police wait for a call back? It is reasonable for the police to institute clear and easy-to-follow procedures that avoid such questions.

Id. at 125, 957 N.Y.S.2d at 273-74 (citation omitted).

Regarding the inventory search itself, the Court found that:

We have held that, even where a vehicle has been lawfully impounded, the inventory search itself must be conducted pursuant to "an established procedure" that is related "to the governmental interests it is intended to promote" and that provides "appropriate safeguards against police abuse." Defendant argues that the inventory search in this case failed to meet this requirement. We reject the argument.

Defendant's argument focuses on several alleged deficiencies in the proof relating to the inventory search: the written policy that governed the search was never produced; the state trooper's description of the policy was very vague; and the descriptions of the returned property on the inventory form—"MISC ITEMS" and "PAPERWORK"—would be of limited usefulness in the event the car's owner claimed that some of her property was missing. These criticisms are not without force. Certainly, it would be better for a prosecutor seeking to prove the existence of a written policy to put a copy of the policy into evidence. On the other hand, defense counsel could have demanded that the policy be produced to help her cross-examine the trooper. She did not do so.

When a car has been lawfully impounded, the reasonable expectation of the person who was driving it that its contents will remain private is significantly diminished. In such a case, the driver presumably expects the police to find whatever is in the car. *Galak, Johnson* and *Gomez* establish that this does not give the police carte blanche to conduct any search they want and call it an "inventory search." The police must follow a reasonable procedure, and must prepare a "meaningful inventory list." But it would serve little purpose for courts to micromanage the procedures used to search properly impounded cars. The United States Supreme Court implicitly recognized as much in *Bertine* by upholding as constitutionally valid a search producing what a trial court had found to be a "somewhat slipshod" inventory. The inventory here, while not a model, was sufficient to meet the constitutional minimum.

Id. at 126-27, 957 N.Y.S.2d at 275-76 (citations omitted).

In *People v. Wells*, 21 N.Y.3d 716, 977 N.Y.S.2d 712, 999 N.E.2d 1157 (2013), the Court of Appeals held that the defendant's guilty plea was invalid where it was induced by the trial court's erroneous ruling upholding an improper inventory search.

§ 1:45   Use of GPS device to track suspect's movements

In *People v. Weaver*, 12 N.Y.3d 433, 447, 882 N.Y.S.2d 357, 365, 909 N.E.2d 1195 (2009), the Court of Appeals held that "[u]nder our State Constitution, in the absence of exigent circumstances, the installation and use of a GPS device to monitor an individual's whereabouts requires a warrant supported by probable cause." *See also U.S. v. Jones*, 132 S. Ct. 945, 181 L. Ed. 2d 911 (2012) (attachment of GPS tracking device to vehicle and use of such device to monitor vehicle's movements on public streets is search within meaning of 4th Amendment). The *Weaver* Court reasoned as follows:

Here, we are not presented with the use of a mere beeper to facilitate visual surveillance during a single trip. GPS is a vastly different and exponentially more sophisticated and powerful technology that is easily and cheaply deployed and has virtually unlimited and remarkably precise tracking capability. With the addition of new GPS satellites, the technology is rapidly improving so that any person or object, such as a car, may be tracked with uncanny accuracy to virtually any interior or exterior location, at any time and regardless of atmospheric conditions. Constant, relentless tracking of anything is now not merely possible but entirely practicable, indeed much more practicable than the surveillance conducted in *Knotts*. GPS is not a mere enhancement of human sensory capacity, it facilitates a new technological perception of the world in which the situation of any object may be followed and exhaustively recorded over, in most cases, a practically unlimited period. The potential for a similar capture of information or "seeing" by law enforcement would require, at a minimum, millions of additional police officers and cameras on every street lamp.

That such a surrogate technological deployment is not—particularly when placed at the unsupervised discretion of agents of the state "engaged in the often competitive enterprise of ferreting out crime"—compatible with any reasonable notion of personal privacy or ordered liberty would appear to us obvious. One need only consider what the police may learn, practically effortlessly, from planting a single device. The whole of a person's progress through the world, into both public and private spatial spheres, can be charted and recorded over lengthy periods possibly limited only by the need to change the transmitting unit's batteries. Disclosed in the data retrieved from the transmitting unit, nearly instantaneously with the press of a button on the highly portable receiving unit, will be trips the indisputably private nature of which takes little imagination to conjure: trips to the psychiatrist, the plastic surgeon, the abortion clinic, the AIDS treatment center, the strip club, the criminal defense attorney, the by-the-hour motel, the union meeting, the mosque, synagogue or church, the gay bar and on and on. What the technology yields and records with breathtaking quality and quantity is a highly detailed profile, not simply of where we go, but by easy inference, of our associations—political, religious, amicable and amorous, to name only a few—and of the pattern of our professional and avocational pursuits. When multiple GPS devices are utilized, even more precisely resolved inferences about our activities are possible. Also, with GPS becoming an increasingly routine feature in cars and cell phones, it will be possible to tell from the technology with ever increasing precision who we are and are not with, when we are and are not with them, and what we do and do not carry on our persons—to mention just a few of the highly feasible empirical configurations.

12 N.Y.3d at 441–42, 882 N.Y.S.2d at 361–62 (citation omitted).

§ 1:46   Lawfulness of canine sniff of automobile

In *People v. Devone*, 15 N.Y.3d 106, 110, 905 N.Y.S.2d 101, 102, 931 N.E.2d 70 (2010), the Court of Appeals held both (a) that "a canine sniff of the exterior of a lawfully stopped vehicle constitutes a search under article I, § 12 of our State Constitution," and (b) that, to be lawful, such search requires "founded suspicion that criminal activity is afoot." In so holding, the Court reasoned as follows:

> [W]hether a canine sniff constitutes a search is necessarily dependent upon whether it constitutes an intrusion into a place where a person has a reasonable expectation of privacy. One clearly has a greater expectation of privacy in one's home than in an automobile, but that does not render the latter interest undeserving of constitutional protection. There is a legitimate, albeit reduced, expectation of privacy in an automobile. But that expectation is greater than the significantly reduced expectation of privacy one has in luggage turned over to a common carrier. We therefore hold that a canine sniff of the exterior of an automobile constitutes a search under article I, § 12.

> In both of these cases the Appellate Division properly concluded that the officers' "founded suspicion" that criminality was afoot provided sufficient grounds for the search. While the more demanding "reasonable suspicion" standard applies to a canine sniff outside the door of one's residence, there is a "diminished expectation of

privacy attributed to individuals and their property when traveling in an automobile." It follows that law enforcement need only meet a lesser standard before conducting a canine sniff of the exterior of a lawfully stopped vehicle. Given that diminished expectation of privacy, coupled with the fact that canine sniffs are far less intrusive than the search of a residence and provide "significant utility to law enforcement authorities," application of the founded suspicion standard in these cases is appropriate.

15 N.Y.3d at 113, 905 N.Y.S.2d at 104–05 (citations omitted).

§ 1:47 Lawfulness of stop based on automated license plate scanning device

In *People v. Davila*, 27 Misc. 3d 921, 901 N.Y.S.2d 787 (Bronx Co. Sup. Ct. 2010), the Court addressed the lawfulness of a vehicle stop based on information obtained via an automated license plate scanning device. In *Davila*, the Court held a lengthy suppression hearing at which the NYPD procedures regarding "plate reader" stops were spelled out in considerable detail. According to the hearing testimony:

In 2007, the NYPD issued departmental guidelines for the "use, maintenance and accountability," of plate readers (NYPD Operations Order No. 33). The guidelines set forth a [2]-step process to ensure the reliability of plate reader information. First, before operating the device, officers are required to update the plate reader's database by downloading the hot list issued within the last [24] hours. Second, if the plate reader alarm sounds, before "initiating any law enforcement action", an officer must consult the NYSPIN database to check whether the plate reader information is accurate.

27 Misc. 3d at ___, 901 N.Y.S.2d at 789 (citation omitted).

Although the police officers in *Davila* failed to follow either of the steps in the Department's guidelines (*i.e.*, they failed to either update the plate reader's database within the past 24 hours or consult the NYSPIN database to confirm that the plate reader's information was accurate), the Court upheld the lawfulness of the stop. 27 Misc. 3d at ___, 901 N.Y.S.2d at 791.

Chapter 2

Operation

Research References

Westlaw Databases

Charges to the Jury and Requests to Charge in Criminal Case in New
  York (CTJNY)
Drinking/Driving Litigation (2d ed.) (DRNKDRIVING)
Handling Drunk Driving Cases (2d ed.) (HDRUNKDR)
New York Vehicle and Traffic Law 2d (NYVEH)

Treatises and Practice Aids

New York Charges to the Jury §§ 47:1 to 47:7
Nichols and Whited, Drinking/Driving Litigation: Criminal and Civil
  §§ 2:1 to 2:13 (2d ed.)
Fiandach, Handling Drunk Driving Cases §§ 1:19 to 1:20 (2d ed.)
Rose, New York Vehicle and Traffic Law 2d §§ 2:1 to 2:3

> **KeyCite®:** Cases and other legal materials listed in KeyCite Scope can be researched through the KeyCite service on Westlaw®. Use KeyCite to check citations for form, parallel references, prior and later history, and comprehensive citator information, including citations to other decisions and secondary materials.

§ 2:1 In general

Research References

West's Key Number Digest, Automobiles ⊙1

Two of the essential elements of a VTL § 1192 charge are that the defendant "operate" a "motor vehicle." In a typical traffic stop, operation is generally observed by the police. However, the issue can be of critical significance where, among other things, there is an accident and no operation is observed, the defendant is found sleeping or unconscious behind the wheel, and/or there are several passengers in the vehicle.

§ 2:2 What is a "motor vehicle"?

Research References

West's Key Number Digest, Automobiles ⊙1

The definition of what constitutes a "motor vehicle" is found in VTL § 125, which provides in pertinent part:

> Every vehicle operated or driven upon a public highway which is propelled by any power other than muscular power, except (a) electrically-driven mobility assistance devices operated or driven by a person with a disability, (a-1) electric personal assistive mobility devices operated outside a city with a population of one million or more, (b) vehicles which run only upon rails or tracks, (c) snowmobiles as defined in [VTL Article 47], and (d) all terrain vehicles as defined in [VTL Article 48-B].

See also VTL § 159 (definition of "vehicle"); VTL § 2281 (definition of "all terrain vehicle" (ATV)); VTL § 2229 (snowmobile *not* "motor vehicle"); *People v. Canute*, 8 A.D.3d 1125, __, 778 N.Y.S.2d 247, 248 (4th Dep't 2004) (lawn tractor is a "motor vehicle" within "broad definition" of VTL § 125); *People v. Szymanski*, 63 Misc. 2d 40, 311 N.Y.S.2d 120 (N.Y. City Crim. Ct. 1970) (horse-drawn stage coach not a "motor vehicle" for purposes of VTL § 1192).

VTL § 125 appears to exempt ATVs from the definition of "motor vehicle," and thus from the scope of VTL § 1192. However, VTL § 2404(5) expressly provides that, for purposes of VTL Title VII (which encompasses VTL § 1192), "an ATV shall be a motor vehicle and the provisions of such title shall be applicable to

ATVs." Accordingly, a person operating an ATV on a public highway *can* be charged with violating VTL § 1192.

By contrast, a person operating a snowmobile on a public highway *cannot* be charged with violating VTL § 1192. However, he or she *can* be charged with Snowmobiling While Intoxicated, Snowmobiling While Ability Impaired, or Snowmobiling While Ability Impaired by Drugs. *See* PRHPL § 25.24; PRHPL § 25.03(3).

In *People v. Lopez*, 144 Misc. 2d 325, 544 N.Y.S.2d 410 (N.Y. Co. Sup. Ct. 1989), the court addressed the issue of "whether a vehicle which may have been incapable of being operated under motorized power was a motor vehicle at such time" or, more specifically, "[i]s an automobile without a battery a 'motor vehicle' within the meaning of Vehicle and Traffic Law § 125?" Holding that it was, the court reasoned that:

> If the test as to whether an automobile is a "motor vehicle" is dependent on whether it is operable at the moment to be considered, then for example, one could disconnect the engine connection and then "drive" a car down an Adirondack mountain road while inebriated, without fear of being charged with driving while intoxicated. It seems the appropriate conclusion is that an automobile and all other ordinary motorized vehicles are "motor vehicles" regardless of whether technically capable of being motor driven, and that only a limited class of vehicles which are *ordinarily* muscle powered, should be exempted.

144 Misc. 2d at __, 544 N.Y.S.2d at 411.

By contrast, in *People v. Madden*, 26 Misc. 3d 1203(A), 906 N.Y.S.2d 782, *3 (Rye City N.Y. City Ct. 2009), the Court dismissed an Aggravated DWI charge where:

> Defendant was clearly not able to start her vehicle from the "inside", but required an outside mechanism to make use of the vehicle's own "mechanical or electrical agency . . . (to) set (her car) in motion . . . ." That is, the car itself was inoperable and defendant required the outside battery pack to attempt to start it. Further, the car was parked within a designated parking area and defendant made no statements indicating that she had been driving the car in her obviously intoxicated state. Therefore, there was no corroboration of operation.

§ 2:3   What constitutes "operation" of a motor vehicle?

Research References

West's Key Number Digest, Automobiles ⚖316, 332

The Office of Court Administration Pattern Criminal Jury Instructions defines operation as follows:

To OPERATE a motor vehicle means to drive it.

[NOTE: Add the following if there is an issue as to operation:

A person also OPERATES a motor vehicle when such person is sitting behind the wheel of a motor vehicle for the purpose of placing it in operation, and when the motor vehicle is moving, or even if it is not moving, the engine is running.]

CJI (NY) (2d ed.) VTL 1192, at 1002–03 (footnote omitted). A former version of this instruction reads as follows:

[NOTE: If "operation" is placed in issue, add:

"Operation" of a motor vehicle is established upon proof beyond a reasonable doubt that the defendant had recently driven the vehicle or by such proof that he was seated at the wheel, with the motor running and with a present intention of placing the vehicle in operation.]

3 CJI (NY) V. & T.L. § 1192(1), (2), & (3), at 2306.

In *People v. Prescott*, 95 N.Y.2d 655, 662, 722 N.Y.S.2d 778, 782 (2001), the court of appeals stated that:

Our courts have long recognized that the definition of operation is broader than that of driving and that " '[a] person operates a motor vehicle within the meaning of [the statute] when, in the vehicle, he intentionally does any act or makes use of any mechanical or electrical agency which alone or in sequence will set in motion the motive power of the vehicle.' " Thus, criminal liability under section 1192 can attach to conduct 'dangerously close' to driving, as long as that conduct occurs upon locations covered by the statute.

(Citation and footnote omitted). *See also People v. Alamo*, 34 N.Y.2d 453, 458, 358 N.Y.S.2d 375, 379 (1974); *People v. Marriott*, 37 A.D.2d 868, __, 325 N.Y.S.2d 177, 178 (3d Dep't 1971); *People v. Beyer*, 21 A.D.3d 592, __, 799 N.Y.S.2d 620, 622–23 (3d Dep't 2005); *People v. Cunningham*, 274 A.D.2d 484, 711 N.Y.S.2d 909 (2d Dep't 2000); *People v. Page*, 266 A.D.2d 733, 698 N.Y.S.2d 774 (3d Dep't 1999); *People v. Totman*, 208 A.D.2d 970, 617 N.Y.S.2d 234 (3d Dep't 1994); *People v. Thornton*, 130 A.D.2d 78, 517 N.Y.S.2d 807 (3d Dep't 1987); *People v. David "W,"* 83 A.D.2d 690, 442 N.Y.S.2d 278 (3d Dep't 1981); *People v. Collins*, 70 A.D.2d 986, 417 N.Y.S.2d 819 (3d Dep't 1979); *Matter of Tomasello v. Tofany*, 32 A.D.2d 962, 303 N.Y.S.2d 22 (2d Dep't 1969); *Matter of Prudhomme v. Hults*, 27 A.D.2d 234, 278 N.Y.S.2d 67 (3d Dep't 1967); *People v. Moore*, 196 Misc. 2d 120, 761 N.Y.S.2d 431 (App. Term, 2d Dep't 2002); *People v. Khan*, 182 Misc. 2d 83, 697 N.Y.S.2d 457 (App. Term, 2d Dep't 1997); *People v. Rose*, 8 Misc. 3d 184, __, 794 N.Y.S.2d 630, 632 (Nassau Co. Dist. Ct. 2005); *People v. Navarrette*, 7 Misc. 3d 623, 790 N.Y.S.2d 835 (City Crim. Ct. 2005). *See generally People v. Crombleholme*, 8 A.D.3d 1068, __, 778 N.Y.S.2d 256, 258 (4th Dep't 2004) (although defendant was *passenger* in vehicle, "[d]efendant's actions in grabbing the steering wheel and controlling the direction of the vehicle fall within the definition of operation of a motor vehicle, which is broad in scope").

Generally speaking, the pattern jury instructions clearly state the law in this area. *See People v. Dunning*, 305 A.D.2d 1074, —, 759 N.Y.S.2d 416, 417 (4th Dep't 2003) (Appellate Division, Fourth Department, approved "operation" charge which apparently utilized "CJI2d (N.Y.)"). Nonetheless, issues can arise, especially when there has been an accident or the defendant is found asleep in the vehicle. In *People v. Khan*, 168 Misc. 2d 192, —, 638 N.Y.S.2d 858, 863 to 64 (N.Y. City Crim. Ct. 1995), *rev'd*, 182 Misc. 2d 83, 697 N.Y.S.2d 457 (App. Term, 2d Dep't 1997), the court set forth a comprehensive analysis of the law in this area.

In *People v. Hurley*, 86 Misc. 2d 601, —, 383 N.Y.S.2d 177, 181 (Onondaga Co. Ct. 1976), the Onondaga County Court, sitting as an appellate court, found that the trial court committed reversible error where:

> [T]he court defined the word "operate" after having been requested to do so by the jury, and stated:
>
> > "So in my opinion, the fact that his wheels are stopped, that he's there on the highway, the engine is running, perhaps slumped over the seat or sleeping, whether he is intoxicated or not, he is operating a motor vehicle."
>
> Although the court upon exception to this portion of the charge attempted to correct this by stating, "Let me put it this way, it has been held," instead of "in my opinion," this court believes that reversible error was committed when the court interjected its opinion on the facts. It might be noted that five minutes after such charge, the jury returned with the verdict and in the context of this record it appears that the issue of operating was the key fact to be resolved by the jury.

§ 2:4   Operation requires intent to move the vehicle

Research References

West's Key Number Digest, Automobiles ⬡316, 332

It is well-settled that, for purposes of VTL § 1192, the concept of "operation" requires the intent to move the vehicle. *See, e.g., People v. O'Connor*, 159 Misc. 2d 1072, —, 607 N.Y.S.2d 856, 857 (Nassau Co. Dist. Ct. 1994) (DWI charge dismissed where "defendant was seated behind the wheel of the vehicle with the motor running only for the purpose of helping the owner start the vehicle and without any intention of driving same"); *People v. Dymond*, 158 Misc. 2d 677, —, 601 N.Y.S.2d 1001, 1002 (Greene Co. Ct. 1993) ("case law establishes that the definition of 'operates' does include a mental state, namely, the intention to move the vehicle"); *People v. Marriott*, 37 A.D.2d 868, __, 325 N.Y.S.2d 177, 178 (3d Dep't 1971) ("a person operates a motor vehicle when he begins to use the mechanism of the automobile for the purpose of putting the automobile in motion even though he does not move it"); *Matter of Prudhomme v. Hults*, 27 A.D.2d 234, 278 N.Y.S.2d 67 (3d Dep't 1967) (same). *Cf. People v. Khan*, 182 Misc. 2d 83, 697 N.Y.S.2d 457 (App. Term, 2d Dep't 1997); *People v. Membrino*, 181 Misc. 2d 796, 695 N.Y.S.2d 865 (N.Y. City Crim. Ct. 1999).

In *People v. Edwards*, 158 Misc. 2d 615, __, 601 N.Y.S.2d 539, 540 (Oswego City Ct. 1993), the stipulated facts were that the defendant "was behind the steering wheel of the vehicle for the distinct purpose of sleeping off his intoxicated condition," and that "while he was sitting behind the wheel and asleep his foot came in contact with the clutch pedal which caused the car to roll backwards into another vehicle." Under these circumstances, the court held that:

> [W]here an individual engages in conduct that was unintentional or at least could not be proved by direct testimony to be intentional, it is the opinion of this Court that it would be impossible to determine that the person behind the wheel was guilty, beyond a reasonable doubt of operating a motor vehicle in violation of section 1192. For that reason the charges of violation of section 1192(2) and 1192(3) are dismissed.

158 Misc. 2d at __, 601 N.Y.S.2d at 540. *See also People v. Marzulli*, 76 Misc. 2d 971, __, 351 N.Y.S.2d 775, 776 (App. Term, 2d & 11th Jud. Dist. 1973) (per curiam) (no operation where "the movement of the car was unintentionally caused by this defendant who was seated in the passenger seat at the time of the accident").

In *People v. DeSantis*, 5/21/90 N.Y.L.J., at 32, col. 4 (App. Term, 9th & 10th Jud. Dist. 1990), the Appellate Term affirmed the trial court's finding that "the defendant did not start the motor 'for the purpose of putting the automobile into motion' (*Matter of Prudhomme v. Hults*, 27 A.D.2d 234; *People v. Marriott*, 37 A.D.2d 868)" where the police:

> [F]ound defendant slumped over the wheel of a vehicle which had its lights on and motor running. The car was legally parked in the "Station Plaza" of the City of Rye and . . . bore a Connecticut license plate. When the officers were unable to rouse the defendant, they determined that he was intoxicated and arrested him.
>
> The defendant did not dispute the fact that he was intoxicated or that the motor of his vehicle was running. However, he explained that he had driven to Station Plaza from Stamford that morning and had taken the train to New York City. He left his place of

employment at about 3:10 p.m. and thereafter had dinner and some drinks with "a bunch of guys." He returned to Rye at about 12 or 12:05 am., aware that he was unable to drive. He stated that he intended to find alternate means of returning home and started the motor of the vehicle solely to turn on the heater in an effort to keep warm. He thereafter fell asleep.

In *People v. Moore*, 186 Misc. 2d 614, 720 N.Y.S.2d 898 (Suffolk Co. Dist. Ct. 2000), the defendant's defense was that he, like the defendant in *DeSantis*, turned the engine of his motor vehicle on for the sole purpose of using the heater to stay warm; and that he had no intention of moving the vehicle. In response to the defendant's motion in limine seeking a jury instruction which departed from the standard CJI pattern instructions on the issue of operation, *see* previous section, the Court held:

> While this court will not adopt the proposed substitute to the standard instructions, this Court will enlarge the standard instructions if, in this court's opinion, the trial evidence would warrant such enlargement. If during the course of trial, the facts uncovered would permit a reasonable inference that the actions of the defendant could have been for some purpose other than placing the automobile in motion, the Jury should be instructed that in order to conclude that the defendant was guilty of the charge, it must first conclude that the defendant specifically intended to operate the vehicle, that is, to place the vehicle in motion.

186 Misc. 2d at ___, 720 N.Y.S.2d at 900.

§ 2:5   Where intent to operate in dispute, defendant entitled to grand jury instruction on this issue

Research References

West's Key Number Digest, Automobiles ⊙⇒316, 332

In *People v. Dymond*, 158 Misc. 2d 677, 601 N.Y.S.2d 1001 (Greene Co. Ct. 1993), the court dismissed an indictment because of the prosecution's failure to instruct the grand jury on the element of intent to operate. In *Dymond*, defendant was found intoxicated in a parked vehicle with the engine running. Defendant testified before the grand jury that his sole reason for starting the vehicle was to use the heater. Nonetheless, "the A.D.A. erroneously instructed [the grand jury] that 'keys in the ignition and engine running' was as a matter of law 'operation' within the meaning of the statute." 158 Misc. 2d at ___, 601 N.Y.S.2d at 1003.

§ 2:6   Operation and intoxication must be simultaneous

Research References

West's Key Number Digest, Automobiles ⊙⇒316, 332

In a DWI case, operation and intoxication must occur simultaneously. *See, e.g., People v. Mertz*, 68 N.Y.2d 136, 139, 506 N.Y.S.2d 290, 291 (1986) ("A violation of Vehicle and Traffic Law § 1192(2) is not established unless the trier of fact finds that *while* operating a motor vehicle defendant had a blood alcohol content (BAC) of .10 of 1% or more") (emphasis added); *People v. Schools*, 122 A.D.2d 502, __, 505 N.Y.S.2d 462, 463 (3d Dep't 1986) ("The sine qua non for conviction is the operation of a vehicle simultaneously with intoxication"); *People v. Strauss*, 260 A.D. 880, __, 22 N.Y.S.2d 880, 881 (2d Dep't 1940) ("intoxication and operation must be simultaneous or there is no crime"); *People v. Hust*, 74 Misc. 2d 887, __, 346 N.Y.S.2d 303, 307 (Broome Co. Ct. 1973). *See generally People v. Spencer*, 289 A.D.2d 877, __, 736 N.Y.S.2d 428, 431 (3d Dep't 2001); *People v. Saplin*, 122 A.D.2d 498, __, 505 N.Y.S.2d 460, 461 (3d Dep't 1986); *People v. Matthews*, 11 A.D.2d 784, 205 N.Y.S.2d 26 (2d Dep't 1960); *People v. Hemleb*, 4 A.D.2d 878, 166 N.Y.S.2d 837 (2d Dep't 1957).

§ 2:7   Accusatory instrument charging defendant with DWI must properly allege that defendant operated the vehicle

Research References

West's Key Number Digest, Automobiles ⚬332, 351.1

To be sufficient, an accusatory instrument charging a defendant with DWI must, inter alia, provide reasonable cause to believe both:

(a) That the defendant operated the vehicle. *See, e.g., People v. Key*, 45 N.Y.2d 111, 116, 408 N.Y.S.2d 16, 19 (1978) ("In this case, there was no allegation that defendant was operating his automobile or even that the engine was running, an allegation necessary to establish commission of the crime. Hence, as both courts below have held, the information was insufficient"); *People v. Key*, 87 Misc. 2d 262, __, 391 N.Y.S.2d 781, 785 (App. Term, 9th & 10th Jud. Dist. 1976) ("In the instant matter, the supporting deposition fails to set forth any facts from which it could reasonably be inferred that the defendant was 'operating' the vehicle, a prerequisite to a conviction of violating [VTL §] 1192(2)"), *aff'd*, 45 N.Y.2d 111, 408 N.Y.S.2d 16 (1978); and

(b) That the defendant operated the vehicle while in an intoxicated condition. *See People v. Hust*, 74 Misc. 2d 887, __, 346 N.Y.S.2d 303, 307 (Broome Co. Ct. 1973) ("The 'allegations of fact' within the meaning of CPL § 100.25(2) must refer not only to the driving, but also to the intoxication since in any driving while intoxicated case there are two elements to be proven: (1) that the defendant was driving the vehicle in question and (2) that the defendant was intoxicated while so driving"). *See also* previous section.

§ 2:8 Corroboration of admission of operation

Research References

West's Key Number Digest, Automobiles ⊙355(1), 355(6)

CPL § 60.50 provides that "[a] person may not be convicted of any offense solely upon evidence of a confession or admission made by him without additional proof that the offense charged has been committed." In *People v. Booden*, 69 N.Y.2d 185, 513 N.Y.S.2d 87 (1987), the Court of Appeals held that CPL § 60.50:

> [D]oes not require corroboration of confessions or admissions in every detail, but only "some proof, of whatever weight," that the offense charged has in fact been committed by someone. Its purpose is to avoid the possibility that a crime may be confessed when, in fact, no crime has been committed. The requirements of the rule are not rigorous and sufficient corroboration exists when the confession is "supported" by independent evidence of the corpus delicti. The necessary additional evidence may be found in the presence of defendant at the scene of the crime, his guilty appearance afterward, or other circumstances supporting an inference of guilt.

69 N.Y.2d at 187, 513 N.Y.S.2d at 89 (citations omitted). Applying the foregoing to the facts of the case, the court found that:

> There was sufficient corroborative evidence in this case that the offense of driving while impaired had been committed on the evening in question. The vehicle owned by defendant's father was found in a ditch, facing in the wrong direction of travel; the pavement of the highway was dry, negativing suggestions of an accidental skid; defendant and his companions were standing next to the vehicle when the investigating officer arrived and, when defendant and his companions were asked who had been driving the vehicle, defendant volunteered to answer the question and produced his identification, indicating by his conduct that he was the driver. The officer noticed that defendant exhibited outward signs of intoxication and his breath smelled of alcohol.

69 N.Y.2d at 187–88, 513 N.Y.S.2d at 89. *See also People v. Tatro*, 245 A.D.2d 1040, 667 N.Y.S.2d 560 (4th Dep't 1997); *People v. Kestler*, 201 A.D.2d 955, 607 N.Y.S.2d 823 (4th Dep't 1994); *People v. Cook*, 191 A.D.2d 993, 595 N.Y.S.2d 163 (4th Dep't 1993); *People v. Hennigan*, 135 A.D.2d 1082, 523 N.Y.S.2d 302 (4th Dep't 1987); *Matter of Van Tassell v. New York State Comm'r of Motor Vehicles*, 46 A.D.2d 984, 362 N.Y.S.2d 281 (3d Dep't 1974) (corroboration requirement lower at refusal hearing than at criminal trial). *Cf. People v. Matthews*, 11 A.D.2d 784, __, 205 N.Y.S.2d 26, 27 (2d Dep't 1960) ("Except for defendant's alleged admission, made while intoxicated, that he had been driving the motor vehicle, there is no proof in the record that he was the one who, while intoxicated, operated the vehicle. In the absence of additional proof the conviction may not stand"); *People v. Hemleb*, 4 A.D.2d 878, __, 166 N.Y.S.2d 837, 838 (2d Dep't 1957) (same).

Judge Bellacosa filed a dissenting opinion in *Booden*, stating that:

> [T]he publicly and statutorily induced campaigns for rigorous enforcement of drunk driving offenses, laudable as they are, require a proportionate and judicious neutralization against excessive zeal at the expense of the rights of those affected with potentially serious criminal and even felony prosecutions and records. I am confident that law enforcement officials will be able to enforce properly not only the new and more serious drunk driving laws but also can concomitantly safeguard the procedural rights of all citizens affected by all these laws.

69 N.Y.2d at 189, 513 N.Y.S.2d at 90 (Bellacosa, J., dissenting).

§ 2:9   Applicability of CPL § 60.50 to misdemeanor informations

Research References

West's Key Number Digest, Criminal Law ☞409(6.1)

In *People v. Suber*, 19 N.Y.3d 247, 946 N.Y.S.2d 552, 969 N.E.2d 770 (2012), the Court of Appeals held that the "confession corroboration rule" of CPL § 60.50 is inapplicable to misdemeanor informations. In light of this holding, cases such as *People v. Miedema*, 24 Misc. 3d 132(A), 899 N.Y.S.2d 62 (App. Term, 9th & 10th Jud. Dist. 2009), *People v. Morales*, 35 Misc. 3d 558, 939 N.Y.S.2d 824 (N.Y. City Crim. Ct. 2012), *People v. Walker*, 21 Misc. 3d 748, 865 N.Y.S.2d 530 (N.Y. City Crim. Ct. 2008), *People v. Pappas*, 163 Misc. 2d 1029, 623 N.Y.S.2d 83 (N.Y. City Crim. Ct. 1994), *People v. Mauro*, 147 Misc. 2d 381, 555 N.Y.S.2d 533 (N.Y. City Crim. Ct. 1990), *People v. Kaminiski*, 143 Misc. 2d 1089, 542 N.Y.S.2d 923 (N.Y. City Crim. Ct. 1989), and *People v. Alvarez*, 141 Misc. 2d 686, 534 N.Y.S.2d 90 (N.Y. City Crim. Ct. 1988), should no longer be followed.

§ 2:10   Operation can be proven by circumstantial evidence

Research References

West's Key Number Digest, Automobiles ☞351.1

The element of operation can be proven by circumstantial evidence (*i.e.*, there need not be direct, eyewitness testimony that the defendant operated the vehicle). *See, e.g., People v. Booden*, 69 N.Y.2d 185, 513 N.Y.S.2d 87 (1987); *People v. Blake*, 5 N.Y.2d 118, 180 N.Y.S.2d 775 (1958); *People v. Spencer*, 289 A.D.2d 877, 736 N.Y.S.2d 428 (3d Dep't 2001); *People v. Thompson*, 217 A.D.2d 929, 629 N.Y.S.2d 893 (4th Dep't 1995); *People v. Saplin*, 122 A.D.2d 498, 505 N.Y.S.2d 460 (3d Dep't 1986); *People v. Collins*,

70 A.D.2d 986, 417 N.Y.S.2d 819 (3d Dep't 1979); *People v. Williams*, 161 Misc. 2d 523, 614 N.Y.S.2d 711 (N.Y. City Crim. Ct. 1994).

§ 2:11 Operation at command of police officer

Research References

West's Key Number Digest, Automobiles ⬤351.1; Criminal Law ⬤37(1), 38

In *People v. Asche*, 175 Misc. 2d 639, __, 669 N.Y.S.2d 788, 790 (Nassau Co. Dist. Ct. 1998), the court held that DWI charges would be dismissed in the interest of justice where "a probably-intoxicated defendant who otherwise had no intention of driving in that condition, . . . operated a motor vehicle for a short distance at the direct command of a police officer."

Similarly, in *People v. Donovan*, 53 Misc. 2d 687, 279 N.Y.S.2d 404 (Scarsdale Ct. of Special Sessions 1967), the Court held that the People were "estopped to prosecute this defendant" for DWAI where the defendant had been found sleeping in the driveway of a private residence and only drove because the police woke her up and said "Lady, you're on private property; you can't stay here; you'll have to leave."

By contrast, in *People v. Kaeppel*, 74 Misc. 2d 220, 342 N.Y.S.2d 882 (Suffolk Co. Dist. Ct. 1973), the court held that the defense of entrapment was not available to the defendant where, among other things, there was conflicting testimony as to whether the police had commanded him to drive and, in any event, he had clearly driven the vehicle prior to the police arriving.

§ 2:12 Operation to stop out-of-control vehicle

In *People v. Rodriguez*, 72 A.D.3d 238, __, 895 N.Y.S.2d 58, 59-60 (1st Dep't 2010), "[t]he prosecution's theory of th[e] case is that defendant entered a delivery truck, without authorization and while intoxicated, and caused it to strike vehicles and pedestrians in the intersection below. Defendant, however, alleges that he entered the vehicle only after it was already in motion, rolling downhill and, without starting the engine, unsuccessfully attempted to stop it. No witness actually saw defendant enter the vehicle, which was poorly maintained and grossly overloaded." Under these circumstances, the Appellate Division, First Department, concluded that "[s]ince there is a reasonable view of the evidence that defendant unlawfully entered and operated the vehicle while intoxicated in an attempt to avoid injury while confronting a situation not of his making, he was entitled to a justification charge, and Supreme Court's unexplained omission to so instruct the jury constitutes reversible error." 72 A.D.3d at __, 895 N.Y.S.2d at 60.

The Court of Appeals reversed, reasoning as follows:

Addressing the most serious felonies of which defendant was convicted—manslaughter in the second degree and assault in the second degree—we conclude that there was no reasonable view of the evidence that would have supported a justification charge relative to either of those crimes. Penal Law § 35.05(2) is often referred to as the "choice-of-evils" defense, and properly so. To be entitled to such a charge there must be two "evils." And here, even under defendant's scenario, there was no "evil" on his part. According to defendant, he was not committing any offense when he jumped into a runaway vehicle to prevent it doing harm to others. So, as to the most serious charges, a justification charge was clearly unwarranted.

Supreme Court erred, however, in refusing to give a justification charge relative to the counts of operating a motor vehicle while intoxicated. If defendant elected to operate a motor vehicle, here the truck, while under the influence of alcohol, in an attempt to prevent injury, he faced the choice of two evils: drive while intoxicated or risk a runaway truck causing injury. Therefore, Supreme Court should have granted defendant's request for a justification charge with respect to the operating a motor vehicle while intoxicated counts. However, any error was harmless as evidenced by the jury's conviction of defendant of the second-degree manslaughter and assault counts. To find defendant guilty of those charges, the jury was required to conclude, beyond a reasonable doubt, that defendant caused the truck's movement, i.e., that it was not moving before he entered it. Because the jury concluded that it was defendant who caused the truck to move, and not, as defendant contended, that the truck was already moving, the jury never would have considered his "choice-of-evils" defense on the charge of driving while intoxicated. As a result, the error of not giving the justification charge with respect to the vehicular manslaughter and vehicular assault counts, which include as an element the operation of a motor vehicle while intoxicated, was harmless, and defendant is not entitled to a new trial to correct the error.

People v. Rodriguez, 16 N.Y.3d 341, 345-46, 921 N.Y.S.2d 628, 630-31, 946 N.E.2d 726 (2011) (citation omitted). *See generally People v. Torres*, 125 A.D.3d 1481, __, 3 N.Y.S.3d 851, 853 (4th Dep't 2015), leave to appeal denied, 25 N.Y.3d 1172, 15 N.Y.S.3d 304, 36 N.E.3d 107 (2015) ("Even assuming, arguendo, that defendant was initially justified within the meaning of Penal Law § 35.05(2) in driving while intoxicated to escape an imminent threat of physical injury, we cannot conclude that the jury improperly weighed the evidence in determining that defendant was not justified in continuing to operate the vehicle for several miles, with no evidence that he was being pursued").

§ 2:13   Operation of boat

Research References

West's Key Number Digest, Shipping ⚖17

In *People v. Briggs*, 148 Misc. 2d 935, __, 562 N.Y.S.2d 8, 12 (Nassau Co. Dist. Ct. 1990), a Boating While Intoxicated case, the court held that:

> It is not sufficient evidence of "operation" to merely establish that a defendant was in charge of a vessel that was underway. If, as here, there is no evidence that the vessel was capable of navigation by use of its engines, then there must be evidence that he or she could have controlled the vessel through some other mechanical capability of the vessel.

§ 2:14   Admissibility of prior driving record to prove vehicle operation

In *People v. Reichel*, 110 A.D.3d 1356, 975 N.Y.S.2d 470 (3d Dep't 2013), leave to appeal denied, 22 N.Y.3d 1090, 981 N.Y.S.2d 675, 4 N.E.3d 977 (2014), the defendant was convicted of Manslaughter 2nd as a result of a motor vehicle accident. The primary issue in the case was whether the operator of the vehicle at the time of the accident was the defendant or rather the victim (who was the defendant's pregnant girlfriend). In this regard, the Appellate Division, Third Department, held, *inter alia*, that:

> Supreme Court [did not abuse] its discretion in refusing to allow defendant to introduce evidence of the victim's prior traffic infractions and accidents, which, defendant contends, would have provided the jury with an alternative explanation for the accident, to wit, that it was the victim, not defendant, who was driving the Mitsubishi at the time of the accident. The flaw in defendant's argument on this point is that the victim's allegedly poor driving history simply is not probative of whether she was a passenger in or the driver of the Mitsubishi on the night in question, no more so than defendant's driving history—which included two prior convictions for driving while intoxicated and six prior convictions for aggravated unlicensed operation of a motor vehicle—would be probative of whether he was a passenger in or the operator of the vehicle.

Id. at __, 975 N.Y.S.2d at 475 (citations omitted).

§ 2:15   Admissibility of statement of unavailable witness who claimed to have been the operator of the vehicle

In *People v. Soto*, 26 N.Y.3d 455, 23 N.Y.S.3d 632, 44 N.E.3d 930 (2015), the Court of Appeals affirmed the reversal of the defendant's DWI conviction on the ground that the trial court improperly precluded the defense from introducing into evidence the signed statement of a woman who claimed she, rather than the defendant, had been the operator of the vehicle at the time of the accident. In so holding, the Court reasoned as follows:

> The declaration-against-interest exception to the hearsay rule "flows from the fact that a person ordinarily does not reveal facts that are

contrary to his own interest" unless those facts are true. A statement qualifies as a declaration against interest if four elements are met: (1) the declarant is unavailable to testify as a witness; (2) when the statement was made, the declarant was aware that it was adverse to his or her penal interest; (3) the declarant has competent knowledge of the facts underlying the statement; and (4) supporting circumstances independent of the statement itself attest to its trustworthiness and reliability.

Here, the first and third factors are not in dispute. Hunt was unavailable to testify because she had invoked her Fifth Amendment right to remain silent, and the People refused to grant her immunity, despite defense requests. The third factor was met because Hunt would have had direct knowledge as to whether she was driving the vehicle at the time of the accident. . . .

As the Appellate Division appropriately concluded, the second factor was satisfied. Seconds after she made the statement to the defense investigator, Hunt asked if she could get into trouble and asked for an attorney. Only the most constricted reading of the contemporaneity requirement could support excluding Hunt's statement.

The trial court failed to apply the proper standard when it ruled that the statement was not sufficiently against Hunt's penal interest. We have never held, as the trial court concluded, that the declaration-against-interest exception is limited to serious penal consequences. * * *

The fourth factor was also satisfied because Lamar Larson's testimony corroborated Hunt's statement. . . . Statements offered against the defendant are "subjected to even more exacting standards" and are admissible only when "the interest compromised is of sufficient magnitude or consequence to the declarant to all but rule out any motive to falsify."

By contrast, declarations that exculpate the defendant, as here, are subject to a more lenient standard. In such circumstances, a defendant need not show that the penal consequences to the declarant were of such magnitude that they "all but rule out any motive to falsify." Rather, "[s]upportive evidence is sufficient if it establishes a reasonable possibility that the statement might be true." . . . In addition, it is irrelevant whether the court believes the statement to be true: "[i]f the proponent of the statement is able to establish this possibility of trustworthiness, it is the function of the jury alone to determine whether the declaration is sufficient to create reasonable doubt of guilt."

Id. at 460-62, 23 N.Y.S.3d at 635-37 (citations omitted).

§ 2:16   Sufficiency of evidence of operation before grand jury

In *People v. Wisey*, 133 A.D.3d 799, —, 21 N.Y.S.3d 111, 113

(2d Dep't 2015), the Appellate Division, Second Department, held that County Court should not have dismissed an indictment charging defendant with DWI under the following circumstances:

> Here, the evidence presented to the grand jury, when viewed in the light most favorable to the People, was legally sufficient to establish the charge of driving while intoxicated. The arresting officer testified that when he responded to the subject scene, he observed a Hummer vehicle tipped over on its side, with telephone poles, trees, and light poles knocked over. The defendant was standing outside the vehicle and there were no other vehicles or persons in the vicinity. The defendant, who had cuts and bruises, smelled of alcohol, had bloodshot and glassy eyes, and was staggering on his feet. He informed the officer that he was "just in an accident." The owner of the vehicle testified that he had given the defendant, and only the defendant, permission to operate the vehicle on the night in question. Contrary to the County Court's conclusion, based on this testimony, and the inferences that logically flow therefrom, the grand jury could have reasonably inferred that the defendant had been operating the vehicle on the date in question. Since the grand jury could have rationally drawn such an inference, the fact that the evidence presented is susceptible to other inferences is irrelevant. Accordingly, the County Court erred in granting the defendant's application to dismiss the indictment, made on the ground that the evidence presented to the grand jury was legally insufficient.

(Citations omitted).

§2:17 Effect of witness' inability to identify defendant at trial

In *People v. Foose*, 132 A.D.3d 1236, __, 16 N.Y.S.3d 875, 876-77 (4th Dep't 2015), leave to appeal denied, 26 N.Y.3d 1145, 32 N.Y.S.3d 59, 51 N.E.3d 570 (2016):

> Defendant contends that the evidence [was] legally insufficient to establish that he was the operator of the vehicle because the witness was unable to identify him in court, and her testimony was incredible or unreliable as a matter of law. We reject that contention. The witness testified that she was outside at night when she heard a crash and observed that a vehicle had collided with a parked vehicle. The witness called 911, and watched the driver exit the vehicle, wander around the street, and get into arguments with other people. When the police arrived, she pointed out the driver, and a police officer testified that she arrested defendant. The witness's inability to identify defendant in court does not render her testimony regarding her observations and identification of the driver after the accident " 'manifestly untrue, physically impossible, contrary to experience, or self-contradictory.' " The witness testified that, although she did not see the driver very well because of the dimly-lit street, she did not think that there was any chance that she pointed out the wrong person to the police inasmuch as she lost track of the person for only a second or two, and the person was

wearing the same shirt as the one who exited the vehicle. In addition, the officer testified that defendant was standing near the vehicle when she arrived at the scene.

(Citations omitted).

Chapter 3

Public Highways, Private Roads, and Parking Lots

Research References

Westlaw Databases
Handling Drunk Driving Cases (2d ed.) (HDRUNKDR)
New York Vehicle and Traffic Law 2d (NYVEH)

Treatises and Practice Aids
Fiandach, Handling Drunk Driving Cases §§ 1:21, 1:22 (2d ed.)
Rose, New York Vehicle and Traffic Law 2d §§ 2:1 to 2:3

> **KeyCite®:** Cases and other legal materials listed in KeyCite Scope can be
> researched through the KeyCite service on Westlaw®. Use KeyCite to check
> citations for form, parallel references, prior and later history, and comprehen-
> sive citator information, including citations to other decisions and secondary
> materials.

§ 3:1   In general

Research References
West's Key Number Digest, Automobiles ⚷13

Whether or not a person is guilty of DWI, AUO, Reckless Driving, etc. is oftentimes dependent upon the status of the "roadway"
where the vehicle operation takes place. For purposes of VTL
§ 1192, operation must occur on a roadway listed in VTL
§ 1192(7). For purposes of AUO or Reckless Driving, operation
must occur on a "public highway." For purposes of most violations covered by VTL Title VII (which encompasses VTL §§ 1100
to 1277), operation must occur on a roadway listed in VTL § 1100.
For purposes of penal law violations (*e.g.*, vehicular crimes), the

statutes apply regardless of the location of the driving. *See People v. Harris*, 81 N.Y.2d 850, 597 N.Y.S.2d 620 (1993).

§ 3:2   Roadways upon which VTL § 1192 applies

Research References

West's Key Number Digest, Automobiles ⊙13, 332

VTL § 1100(a) provides that "[t]he provisions of [VTL Title VII] apply upon public highways, private roads open to public motor vehicle traffic and any other parking lot, *except where a different place is specifically referred to in a given section.*" (Emphasis added). VTL § 1192 is part of VTL Title VII.

However, VTL § 1192(7) provides an exception of the type referred to in VTL § 1100(a). VTL § 1192(7) expressly lists the types of "roadways" upon which the provisions of VTL § 1192 apply:

> Where applicable. The provisions of this section shall apply upon public highways, private roads open to motor vehicle traffic and any other parking lot. For the purposes of this section "parking lot" shall mean any area or areas of private property, including a driveway, near or contiguous to and provided in connection with premises and used as a means of access to and egress from a public highway to such premises and having a capacity for the parking of four or more motor vehicles. The provisions of this section shall not apply to any area or areas of private property comprising all or part of property on which is situated a one or two family residence.

VTL § 134 defines the term "public highway" as "[a]ny highway, road, street, avenue, alley, public place, public driveway or any other public way."

VTL § 118 defines the term "highway" as "[t]he entire width between the boundary lines of every way publicly maintained when any part thereof is open to the use of the public for purposes of vehicular travel."

VTL § 133 defines the term "private road" as "[e]very way or place in private ownership and used for vehicular travel by the owner and those having express or implied permission from the owner, but not by other persons."

The definition of the term "parking lot" in VTL § 1192(7) differs from that in VTL § 129-b, which defines a "parking lot" as:

> Any area or areas of private property near or contiguous to and provided in connection with premises having one or more *stores or business establishments*, and used by the public as a means of access to and egress from such *stores and business establishments* and for the parking of motor vehicles of customers and patrons of such *stores and business establishments*.

(Emphases added).

In fact, the current version of VTL § 1192(7) was designed to legislatively overrule cases which had applied the VTL § 129-b "store or business establishment" test to determine whether a parking lot is a "parking lot" for purposes of VTL § 1192, *see, e.g.*, *People v. Williams*, 66 N.Y.2d 659, 495 N.Y.S.2d 964 (1985); *People v. McDonnell*, 27 Misc. 3d 56, 901 N.Y.S.2d 451 (App. Term, 9th & 10th Jud. Dist. 2010); *People v. Copeland*, 132 Misc. 2d 990, 506 N.Y.S.2d 249 (Suffolk Co. Dist. Ct. 1986), replacing that test with a "capacity for the parking of four or more motor vehicles" test.

In *People v. Hampton*, 176 Misc. 2d 405, 673 N.Y.S.2d 485 (Suffolk Co. Dist. Ct. 1997), the defendant was charged with DWI in the parking lot of a funeral home. It was undisputed that, at the time of the incident, (a) the defendant was in the funeral home parking lot, (b) the lot provided parking capacity for more than four vehicles, and (c) the lot was private property. The court held that the parking lot fell within the ambit of both VTL § 1192(7) and VTL § 129-b, regardless of the fact that the funeral home was closed at the time. *See also People v. Tornatore*, 125 Misc. 2d 400, 479 N.Y.S.2d 462 (Nassau Co. Dist. Ct. 1984) (parking lot of White Castle restaurant clearly falls within ambit of VTL § 1192(7)).

In *People v. Beyer*, 21 A.D.3d 592, __, 799 N.Y.S.2d 620, 622 (3d Dep't 2005), the Appellate Division, Third Department, held that a ditch adjoining a public highway is part of the highway for purposes of VTL § 1192(7). In so holding, the court reasoned that:

> The Vehicle and Traffic Law broadly defines a public highway as "[a]ny highway, road, street, avenue, alley, public place, public driveway or any other public way" (Vehicle and Traffic Law § 134). Although not further defined in the Vehicle and Traffic Law, under the Highway Law the term highway is "deemed to include necessary sluices, drains, ditches" and similar accouterments (Highway Law § 2[4]).

21 A.D.3d at __, 799 N.Y.S.2d at 622.

In *People v. Haszinger*, 149 Misc. 2d 856, __, 567 N.Y.S.2d 575, 576 (Nassau Co. Dist. Ct. 1991), the court, relying on VTL § 1100(a) rather than VTL § 1192(7), held that "the grass adjoining an exit ramp falls within the definition of public highway" for purposes of VTL § 1192. In so holding, the Court reasoned that:

> [T]his court finds that the area adjoining a public highway where cars can readily pull off, be it grass, dirt, gravel or paved, is part of the public highway, and falls within the bounds of its definition for purposes of Vehicle and Traffic Law violations. It would defy logic to permit motorists to drive on an area adjoining the road with total disregard of the Vehicle and Traffic law.

149 Misc. 2d at __, 567 N.Y.S.2d at 576–77.

However, the validity of *Haszinger* is questionable in light of the Court of Appeals' subsequent decision in *People v. Harris*, 81 N.Y.2d 850, 852, 597 N.Y.S.2d 620, 622 (1993), which makes clear that liability under VTL § 1192 is limited to operation on roadways listed in VTL § 1192(7). *See also* § 3:7, *infra*; *People v. Prescott*, 95 N.Y.2d 655, 722 N.Y.S.2d 778 (2001).

In any event, the real issue is not whether the defendant's vehicle ultimately came to rest in a location outside of the scope of VTL § 1192(7), but rather whether the People can prove, circumstantially, that the defendant recently operated the vehicle on a roadway listed in VTL § 1192(7). For example, in *Craig v. Swarts*, 68 A.D.3d 1407, ___, 891 N.Y.S.2d 204 (3d Dep't 2009), the Appellate Division, Third Department, held that:

> In view of petitioner's admissions to [Trooper] LeBarron and the discovery of petitioner's vehicle in a field adjacent to Friends Point Road North, it was entirely reasonable for LeBarron to infer, under the totality of the circumstances presented, that petitioner was driving on that road at the time of the accident. As to the legal status of Friends Point Road North, while there was no direct testimony on this point, LeBarron stated that this road is located in the vicinity of State Route 9N and that there were numerous residences in the area where petitioner's accident occurred. Additionally, a letter from the local highway superintendent indicating that "[t]he roads in Friends Point Association . . . are private roads, including but not limited to Friends Point Drive, Friends Point Drive North and South," and an accompanying photograph, give rise to the inference that the road in question is open to motor vehicle traffic and, hence, falls within the purview of Vehicle and Traffic Law § 1192(7).

See also People v. Thompson, 217 A.D.2d 929, 629 N.Y.S.2d 893 (4th Dep't 1995). *See generally People v. Blake*, 5 N.Y.2d 118, 180 N.Y.S.2d 775 (1958); *People v. Collins*, 70 A.D.2d 986, ___, 417 N.Y.S.2d 819, 821 (3d Dep't 1979).

In *People v. Murphy*, 169 Misc. 2d 357, 649 N.Y.S.2d 962 (App. Term, 2d Dep't 1996), the defendant was observed driving erratically in a ShopRite Plaza parking lot. The police approached defendant, and determined that he was intoxicated. Defendant was thereafter charged with, among other things, violating VTL §§ 1192(2)/(3). Town court granted defendant's motion to dismiss the charges based on its reading of VTL § 1640-a(2), which grants local governments authority to enact ordinances regulating traffic in certain parking lots. On appeal, the Appellate Term, Second Department, reversed, holding that VTL § 1640-a(2) grants local governments *additional*, rather than *exclusive*, authority in this area, and thus does not preempt VTL § 1192(7) and/or VTL § 1100(a).

§3:3 Proof that parking lot constitutes "parking lot" as defined in VTL §1192(7) is element of VTL §1192 charge

Research References

West's Key Number Digest, Automobiles ☞13; Criminal Law ☞86

Proof that a parking lot constitutes a "parking lot" as defined in VTL §1192(7) is an element of a VTL §1192 charge. *See People v. Whipple*, 97 N.Y.2d 1, 7, 734 N.Y.S.2d 549, 552 (2001). In *Whipple*, the Court of Appeals addressed the following issue:

> [W]hether, when the People rest without evidence establishing an element of an offense [*i.e.*, the capacity of the parking lot that the defendant committed DWI in], and the defendant moves for a trial order of dismissal on that basis, the trial court can permit the People to reopen their case and cure the omission. We conclude that reopening is permissible where the missing element is simple to prove and not seriously contested, and reopening the case does not unduly prejudice the defense. Because this rule did not, as a matter of law, preclude the trial court's decision to let the People present limited additional evidence, we reverse the Appellate Division order and remit the matter to the Appellate Division for consideration of the facts.

97 N.Y.2d at 3, 734 N.Y.S.2d at 549–50. In so holding, the court reasoned that:

> In this case, . . . the People simply forgot a technically necessary element: the number of spaces in the parking lot. This element was simple to prove, and uncontested . . .
>
> The motion for a trial order of dismissal gave the People notice of the technical omission, and the issue now is whether, *as a matter of law*, a trial court may never permit the People to act on such notice—a sort of "gotcha" principle of law.

97 N.Y.2d at 7, 734 N.Y.S.2d at 552 (emphasis added).

The court made clear, however, that a trial court is not required to allow the People to reopen their case to cure the omission:

> Leave to reopen remains, of course, a precarious dispensation upon which counsel rely at their peril. Courts, which have abundant discretion to deny such leave even to defendants, have at least the same latitude to deny such motions when brought by the People. We hold only that in the narrow circumstances where, as here, the missing element is simple to prove and not seriously contested, and reopening the case does not unduly prejudice the defense, a court may, in its discretion, grant a motion to reopen.

97 N.Y.2d at 8, 734 N.Y.S.2d at 553 (citations omitted). *See generally People v. Thompson*, 217 A.D.2d 929, 629 N.Y.S.2d 893 (4th Dep't 1995) (County court erred in permitting People to

amend DWI indictment at close of People's case to allege that operation took place in parking lot as opposed to on highway).

In *People v. De France*, 265 A.D.2d 837, __, 696 N.Y.S.2d 740, 740 (4th Dep't 1999), which involved this issue in the context of a plea allocution, the Appellate Division, Fourth Department, stated in dicta that:

> [W]e reject the contention of defendant that his plea allocution was insufficient because it failed to establish that the parking lot in which he was operating a motor vehicle falls within the parameters of Vehicle and Traffic Law § 1192(7). Defendant acknowledged during the plea allocution that he operated a motor vehicle in the parking lot of an apartment complex while he was intoxicated (*see*, Vehicle and Traffic Law § 1192[7]).

Whipple, *Thompson*, and *De France* make clear that the defense must properly make and preserve an objection in this regard. *See also People v. Swan*, 248 A.D.2d 1010, 670 N.Y.S.2d 155 (4th Dep't 1998) (same issue as in *Thompson* rejected by same court on ground that defendant failed to object to the amendment, and thus failed to preserve claim).

In *People v. Marotti*, 20 Misc. 3d 16, 862 N.Y.S.2d 712 (App. Term, 9th & 10th Jud. Dist. 2008), the Court addressed the facial sufficiency of an accusatory instrument charging the defendant with common law DWI where there were no factual allegations addressing the size of the parking lot. In this regard, the Court held:

> The accusatory instrument alleging driving while intoxicated in violation of Vehicle and Traffic Law § 1192(3) is facially sufficient. The information alleged that defendant committed the offense in a "parking lot" at a specified location. Vehicle and Traffic Law § 1192(3) does not set forth the locations where driving while intoxicated is prohibited. Vehicle and Traffic Law § 1192(7) applies the sanction, inter alia, to parking lots, with exclusions for small lots and those on private property otherwise occupied by a one-or two-family residence. An allegation that the offense occurred in a "parking lot" suffices to allege that the offense occurred in a place in which the intoxicated operation of a motor vehicle is subject to the penal sanction. Although the relevant definitions of a parking lot explicitly exclude certain classes of locations, the exclusions involved herein need not be pleaded. "Legislative intent to create an exception has generally been found when the language of exclusion is contained entirely within a Penal Law provision . . . [However, where t]he exclusionary language . . . does not provide a complete definition of the class of cases that the Legislature intended to remove from the ambit of [the offense] . . . the [exclusion] operates as a proviso that the accused may raise in defense of the charge rather than an exception that must be pleaded by the People in the accusatory instrument." Here, the exclusions for

certain types of parking lots are not part of the provision defining the offense, *i.e.*, Vehicle and Traffic Law § 1192(3), and thus are merely provisos that need not be pleaded. Given the specificity with which the instrument alleged the location of the offense's commission, defendant was placed on ample notice of the time, place and manner in which the offense was committed.

20 Misc. 3d at ___, 862 N.Y.S.2d at 714–15 (citations omitted).

In the authors' opinion, the reasoning of *Marotti* is flawed. *Marotti* held that the size of a parking lot is "a proviso that the accused may raise in defense of the charge rather than an exception that must be pleaded by the People in the accusatory instrument." However, as is noted above, the Court of Appeals has made clear that proof that a parking lot constitutes a "parking lot" as defined in VTL § 1192(7) is an element of a VTL § 1192 charge that must be affirmatively proven by the People. *See People v. Whipple*, 97 N.Y.2d 1, 7, 734 N.Y.S.2d 549, 552, 760 N.E.2d 337 (2001). Thus, it clearly is *not* an affirmative defense that must be raised and proven by the defendant. *See generally People v. Rodriguez*, 68 N.Y.2d 674, 505 N.Y.S.2d 593, 496 N.E.2d 682 (1986), for the reasons stated in the dissenting opinion below.

In addition, *Marotti* held that VTL § 1192(7) *excludes* certain types of parking lots—as opposed to *includes* them—despite the fact that VTL § 1192(7) clearly defines the roadways upon which VTL § 1192 is applicable (as opposed to the roadways upon which it is inapplicable). Indeed, VTL § 1192(7) is entitled "Where applicable."

Furthermore, with regard to the "exception" versus "proviso" distinction, *see People v. Santana*, 7 N.Y.3d 234, 236–37, 818 N.Y.S.2d 842, 842–43, 851 N.E.2d 1193 (2006), it is arguable that the issue of the size of the parking lot is neither an exception nor a proviso. Notably, the text of VTL § 1192(3) does not specify where it is illegal to drive while intoxicated. Rather, it merely provides that "[n]o person shall operate a motor vehicle while in an intoxicated condition." Thus, VTL § 1192(7) is clearly part of the statute defining the offense. In this regard, even if the "exception" versus "proviso" distinction is applicable, the issue of the size of the parking lot is clearly an exception contained within the statute as opposed to a proviso contained external thereto.

§ 3:4   Roadways upon which AUO statute applies

Research References

West's Key Number Digest, Automobiles ⚷13, 322, 332

The AUO statute (*i.e.*, VTL § 511) is part of Title V, *not* Title VII, of the VTL. As such, VTL § 1100(a) is inapplicable. In addition, VTL § 511 by its express terms is only applicable to driving on a "public highway." As such, a person caught driving in a parking lot with a suspended or revoked license cannot validly be charged with AUO. *See People v. Stewart*, 92 A.D.3d 1146, —, 940 N.Y.S.2d 178, 180 (3d Dep't 2012); *People v. Mills*, 45 A.D.3d 1348, —, 845 N.Y.S.2d 597, 598 (4th Dep't 2007). *See also* VTL § 512 (driving with suspended or revoked registration).

In *People v. Hopper*, 165 Misc. 2d 694, 629 N.Y.S.2d 943 (Dewitt Just. Ct. 1995), the Court concluded that:

> [T]he New York State Legislature, amended Section 1192 of the Vehicle and Traffic Law by adding Subdivision (5), now renumbered Subdivision (7). (*See*, L. 1990, ch.173, § 62.)

> In the above section of the Vehicle and Traffic Law the Legislature directly addressed the situation concerning driving while intoxicated in a parking lot.

> Conversely, the New York State Legislature, in its infinite wisdom, and for good or for ill, has not chosen to amend the statutes concerning Suspended Registration and Aggravated Unlicensed Operation of a Motor Vehicle.

> It is the decision of this Court that the motion to dismiss the charges against the Defendant consisting of violations of Sections 512 Suspended registration; 511(1)(a) Aggravated Unlicensed Operation of a motor vehicle, third degree; 511(2)(a)(i) Aggravated Unlicensed Operation of a motor vehicle is hereby granted and those charges are dismissed.

165 Misc. 2d at —, 629 N.Y.S.2d at 945.

In *People v. Brazill*, 1/4/99 NYLJ 28, (col. 3), the Nassau County Court reached the same conclusion, holding that "the parking lot of the Waldbaum's Shopping Center in the City of Long Beach is [not] a public highway for purposes of a [VTL §] 511.3 charge." In so holding, the court reasoned that:

> By failing to expand the public highway definition to include 'parking lots' for purposes of V.T.L. Section 511, the Legislature has provided a person operating a motor vehicle with a suspended license—whether it is suspended for failing to answer a single ticket or for multiple DWI convictions—with a technical loophole through which he or she may wiggle off the hook of criminal liability should he or she be so fortunate as to be caught driving in a parking lot. Even in this age of supermalls and vast parking fields, the Legislature has, in effect, said to those who decide to take the wheel even while their licenses are suspended that they may drive with impunity, so long as they stay in the 'lot'.

See generally People v. Thew, 44 N.Y.2d 681, 405 N.Y.S.2d 433 (1978); *People v. Kenyon*, 85 A.D.2d 916, 446 N.Y.S.2d 783 (4th

Dep't 1981); *People v. Conzo*, 100 Misc. 2d 143, 418 N.Y.S.2d 750 (Suffolk Co. Sup. Ct. 1979).

§ 3:5 Roadways upon which reckless driving statute applies

Research References

West's Key Number Digest, Automobiles ⊙13, 330

VTL § 1100(a) provides that "[t]he provisions of [VTL Title VII] apply upon public highways, private roads open to public motor vehicle traffic and any other parking lot, *except where a different place is specifically referred to in a given section*." (Emphasis added). The reckless driving statute (*i.e.*, VTL § 1212) is part of VTL Title VII. However, VTL § 1212 by its express terms appears to be only applicable to driving on a "public highway." *Cf. People v. Miller*, 196 Misc. 2d 591, __, 764 N.Y.S.2d 498, 500 (Sand Lake Just. Ct. 2003) (Court reaches opposite conclusion, but does not address applicability of VTL § 1100(a) to VTL § 1212).

As such, a person caught driving recklessly in a parking lot cannot validly be charged with reckless driving. *See People v. Tracey*, 6 Misc. 2d 681, 167 N.Y.S.2d 320 (Niagara Co. Ct. 1957) (Reckless Driving statute inapplicable to driving in privately owned parking area of plaza containing several stores). Notably, the *Tracey* Court, just like several of the other cases cited in this Chapter, commented that "it might be advisable to call to the attention of the Legislature the desirability of amending the Chapter to cover situations such as the instant one." 6 Misc. 2d at __, 167 N.Y.S.2d at 322. *See generally People v. Wormuth*, 108 Misc. 2d 652, 438 N.Y.S.2d 455 (Saratoga Co. Ct. 1981) (VTL § 1227(1) inapplicable in public parking lot of Grand Union shopping center, as statute by its express terms only applies to conduct "upon the public highways"); *People v. Moore*, 196 Misc. 2d 340, 765 N.Y.S.2d 218 (Cayuga Heights Just. Ct. 2002) (VTL § 1225-c (use of mobile telephones) inapplicable in parking lot of privately owned shopping center, as statute by its express terms only applies to conduct "upon a public highway").

§ 3:6 Roadways upon which VTL Title VII applies

Research References

West's Key Number Digest, Automobiles ⊙344

VTL Title VII encompasses VTL Articles 23 through 34-B (*i.e.*, VTL §§ 1100 to 1277). VTL § 1100(a) provides that "[t]he provisions of this title apply upon public highways, private roads open to public motor vehicle traffic and any other parking lot, *except*

where a different place is specifically referred to in a given section."
(Emphasis added).

VTL § 134 defines the term "public highway" as "[a]ny highway,
road, street, avenue, alley, public place, public driveway or any
other public way."

VTL § 118 defines the term "highway" as "[t]he entire width
between the boundary lines of every way publicly maintained
when any part thereof is open to the use of the public for purposes
of vehicular travel."

VTL § 133 defines the term "private road" as "[e]very way or
place in private ownership and used for vehicular travel by the
owner and those having express or implied permission from the
owner, but not by other persons."

VTL § 129-b defines the term "parking lot" as:

> Any area or areas of private property near or contiguous to and
> provided in connection with premises having one or more stores or
> business establishments, and used by the public as a means of ac-
> cess to and egress from such stores and business establishments
> and for the parking of motor vehicles of customers and patrons of
> such stores and business establishments.

It is important to note that VTL § 129-b uses a "store or business establishment" test to determine whether a parking lot is a
"parking lot" for purposes of VTL Title VII generally, whereas
VTL § 1192(7) uses a "capacity for the parking of four or more
motor vehicles" test to determine whether a parking lot is a "parking lot" for purposes of VTL § 1192. *See* § 3:2, *supra*.

As such, the reasoning of cases such as *People v. Williams*, 66
N.Y.2d 659, 495 N.Y.S.2d 964 (1985), and *People v. Copeland*,
132 Misc. 2d 990, 506 N.Y.S.2d 249 (Suffolk Co. Dist. Ct. 1986),
while no longer valid in the DWI context, is still valid in
determining whether a parking lot is a "parking lot" in non-DWI
cases. *See also Stevens v. Calspan-Corp.*, 292 A.D.2d 809, 739
N.Y.S.2d 792 (4th Dep't 2002) (VTL § 1210(a) inapplicable where
vehicle not kept in "parking lot" as defined in VTL § 129-b); *Surace
v. Kersten*, 278 A.D.2d 226, 717 N.Y.S.2d 283 (2d Dep't 2000)
(private parking area of condominium development not "parking
lot" for purposes of VTL § 1210(a)); *Koenig v. Price*, 200 A.D.2d
559, 606 N.Y.S.2d 310 (2d Dep't 1994) (private driveway not
"parking lot" for purposes of VTL § 1210(a)).

VTL § 1100(b) provides that:

> The provisions of this title relating to obedience to stop signs, flash-
> ing signals, yield signs, traffic-control signals and other traffic-
> control devices, and to one-way, stopping, standing, parking and
> turning regulations shall apply to a parking lot only when the
> legislative body of any city, village or town has adopted a local law,
> ordinance, rule or regulation ordering such signs, signals, devices,
> or regulations.

In *People v. Murphy*, 169 Misc. 2d 357, 649 N.Y.S.2d 962 (App. Term, 2d Dep't 1996), the defendant was observed driving erratically in a ShopRite Plaza parking lot. The police approached defendant, and determined that he was intoxicated. Defendant was thereafter charged with violating VTL §§ 1192(2)/(3) (DWI), 1162 (Unsafe Start), and 1211(a) (Unsafe Backing). The Appellate Term, Second Department, held that VTL § 1100(b) was inapplicable to the charges against the defendant, as this section by its express terms only applies to offenses related to "stop signs, flashing signals, yield signs, traffic-control signals and other traffic-control devices, and to one-way, stopping, standing, parking and turning regulations."

§ 3:7 Locations upon which penal law statutes apply

Research References

West's Key Number Digest, Automobiles ⊕13, 332

In *People v. Harris*, 81 N.Y.2d 850, 597 N.Y.S.2d 620 (1993), the defendant was convicted of, among other things, Vehicular Manslaughter in the 2nd Degree, in violation of Penal Law § 125.12, after a passenger in the vehicle he was driving (while intoxicated) died. Defendant argued that, since the driving at issue took place in a farmer's field, he did not operate the vehicle on a roadway encompassed by VTL § 1192(7), and thus that he did not violate VTL § 1192.

Since a violation of VTL § 1192(2), (3) or (4) is an element of Vehicular Manslaughter, defendant claimed that he was improperly convicted thereof. The Court of Appeals disagreed, reasoning that:

> With the understanding that penal laws have different purposes than vehicle and traffic laws, we conclude the vehicular manslaughter statute applies to any person causing a death by driving under the influence of alcohol or drugs, *regardless of location*, even though there could be no separate punishment for such driving under Vehicle and Traffic Law § 1192 where the driving did not occur on public roads or other areas defined in that section.

81 N.Y.2d at 852, 597 N.Y.S.2d at 622 (emphasis added).

Chapter 4

Warrantless Arrests in the Home

KeyCite®: Cases and other legal materials listed in KeyCite Scope can be researched through the KeyCite service on Westlaw®. Use KeyCite to check citations for form, parallel references, prior and later history, and comprehensive citator information, including citations to other decisions and secondary materials.

---

§ 4:1   In general

The Supreme Court has made clear that "the 'physical entry of the home is the chief evil against which the wording of the Fourth Amendment is directed.'" *Payton v. New York*, 445 U.S. 573, 585, 100 S. Ct. 1371, 1379, 63 L. Ed. 2d 639 (1980) (citation omitted).

> To be arrested in the home involves not only the invasion attendant to all arrests but also an invasion of the sanctity of the home. This is simply too substantial an invasion to allow without a warrant, at least in the absence of exigent circumstances, even when it is accomplished under statutory authority and when probable cause is clearly present.

445 U.S. at 588–89, 100 S.Ct. at 1381 (citation omitted). *See also New York v. Harris*, 495 U.S. 14, 17, 110 S. Ct. 1640, 1643, 109 L. Ed. 2d 13 (1990) ("*Payton* itself emphasized that our holding in that case stemmed from the 'overriding respect for the sanctity of the home that has been embedded in our traditions since the origins of the Republic'") (citation omitted); *People v. Knapp*, 52 N.Y.2d 689, 694, 439 N.Y.S.2d 871, 874, 422 N.E.2d 531 (1981)

("our Constitutions accord special protection to a person's expectation of privacy in his own home. To further insulate this right, subject only to carefully drawn and narrow exceptions, a warrantless search of an individual's home is per se unreasonable and hence unconstitutional. Further, to militate against any rationalizing away of these protections, the burden of proving the existence of sufficiently exceptional circumstances is placed squarely on the shoulders of the government") (citations omitted).

Based on this respect for the sanctity of the home, "[i]t is a 'basic principle of Fourth Amendment law' that searches and seizures inside a home without a warrant are presumptively unreasonable." *Payton*, 445 U.S. at 586, 100 S.Ct. at 1380. *See also Brigham City, Utah v. Stuart*, 547 U.S. 398, 403, 126 S. Ct. 1943, 1947, 164 L. Ed. 2d 650 (2006) (same); *Welsh v. Wisconsin*, 466 U.S. 740, 749, 104 S. Ct. 2091, 2097, 80 L. Ed. 2d 732 (1984) (same); *People v. McBride*, 14 N.Y.3d 440, 445, 902 N.Y.S.2d 830, 833, 928 N.E.2d 1027 (2010), petition for cert. filed (U.S. July 26, 2010) (same); *People v. Molnar*, 98 N.Y.2d 328, 331, 746 N.Y.S.2d 673, 674–75, 774 N.E.2d 738 (2002) (same).

This chapter deals with issues pertaining to warrantless arrests in the home, with a focus on such arrests in DWI cases.

§ 4:2   Standing to challenge warrantless arrest in home

It is well settled that "[o]ne seeking standing to assert a violation of his Fourth Amendment rights must demonstrate a legitimate expectation of privacy." *People v. Ortiz*, 83 N.Y.2d 840, 842, 611 N.Y.S.2d 500, 501, 633 N.E.2d 1104 (1994). Of course, a person has a legitimate expectation of privacy in his or her own home. *People v. Mercado*, 68 N.Y.2d 874, 876, 508 N.Y.S.2d 419, 421, 501 N.E.2d 27 (1986). In addition, "[o]ne may have an expectation of privacy in premises not one's own, e.g., an overnight guest or a familial or other socially recognized relationship." *Ortiz*, 83 N.Y.2d at 842, 611 N.Y.S.2d at 501 (citation omitted). In this regard:

> The number of times a person stays in a particular place, the length and nature of the stay, the indicia of connectedness and privacy, like change of clothes or sharing expenses or household burdens, are all factors which may alone or in combination with other factors support a reasonable expectation of privacy which is protected by the Fourth Amendment. The burden of demonstrating the factors and their reasonableness to support the legal conclusion is on the defendant.

People v. Rodriguez, 69 N.Y.2d 159, 163, 513 N.Y.S.2d 75, 78, 505 N.E.2d 586 (1987) (citations omitted).

In *People v. Mason*, 248 A.D.2d 751, 669 N.Y.S.2d 712, 714 (3d Dep't 1998), the Appellate Division, Third Department, held that:

County Court erred in its determination that defendant lacked standing to assert a *Payton* challenge based upon its finding that defendant had no reasonable expectation of privacy in Rubio's home. In light of the sworn statements by defendant that he frequently stayed at Rubio's home and kept extra clothes there and Rubio's uncontroverted testimony that defendant was an overnight guest at her home at least four days a week, there was sufficient evidence to establish his standing to assert a *Payton* violation.

(Citations omitted). *See also People v. Couluris*, 148 Misc. 2d 984, 562 N.Y.S.2d 345 (Suffolk Co. Dist. Ct. 1990) (standing to challenge warrantless arrest existed where defendant was renting the garage/apartment in question as his residence).

§ 4:3 Exception to warrant requirement—Exigent circumstances

In *Payton v. New York*, 445 U.S. 573, 590, 100 S. Ct. 1371, 1382, 63 L. Ed. 2d 639 (1980), the Supreme Court held that "the Fourth Amendment has drawn a firm line at the entrance to the house. Absent exigent circumstances, that threshold may not reasonably be crossed without a warrant." *See also Brigham City, Utah v. Stuart*, 547 U.S. 398, 403, 126 S. Ct. 1943, 1947, 164 L. Ed. 2d 650 (2006) (" '[W]arrants are generally required to search a person's home or his person unless "the exigencies of the situation" make the needs of law enforcement so compelling that the warrantless search is objectively reasonable under the Fourth Amendment' ") (citation omitted).

In determining whether "exigent circumstances" exist, Courts traditionally consider the following factors:

(1) the gravity or violent nature of the offense with which the suspect is to be charged; (2) whether the suspect is reasonably believed to be armed; (3) a clear showing of probable cause . . . to believe that the suspect committed the crime; (4) strong reason to believe that the suspect is in the premises being entered; (5) a likelihood that the suspect will escape if not swiftly apprehended; and (6) the peaceful circumstances of the entry.

People v. McBride, 14 N.Y.3d 440, 446, 902 N.Y.S.2d 830, 834, 928 N.E.2d 1027 (2010), petition for cert. filed (U.S. July 26, 2010). *See also People v. Mason*, 248 A.D.2d 751, 669 N.Y.S.2d 712, 715 (3d Dep't 1998) (same); *People v. Cruz*, 149 A.D.2d 151, 545 N.Y.S.2d 561, 566 (1st Dep't 1989) (same).

"We agree that these factors will appropriately assist a suppression court in its analysis of whether exigent circumstances are present, but are mindful that this list is illustrative and 'not to be viewed as definitive or exhaustive.' Indeed, the ultimate inquiry a suppression court must make is 'whether in light of all the facts of the particular case there was an urgent need that justifies a warrantless entry.' " *People v. McBride*, 14 N.Y.3d 440, 446, 902 N.Y.S.2d 830, 834, 928 N.E.2d 1027 (2010) (citations omitted).

§ 4:4   *Welsh v. Wisconsin*

In *Welsh v. Wisconsin*, 466 U.S. 740, 104 S. Ct. 2091, 80 L. Ed. 2d 732 (1984), the Supreme Court issued a rare ruling upholding the rights of a drunk driver. In *Welsh*, the defendant, who was driving erratically, ultimately drove his car off the road and into an open field. This occurred shortly before 9:00 PM. A civilian witness who observed the defendant's driving used his truck to block the defendant from driving back onto the road, and asked a passerby to call the police. Before the police arrived, however, the defendant fled the scene on foot, walked home, went upstairs to his bedroom, stripped naked and went to sleep. The police located the defendant's home (by checking the registration of the abandoned car), and proceeded thereto, arriving at approximately 9:00 PM. Without obtaining a warrant, the police entered the home, went upstairs, woke the defendant up, and arrested him for DWI.

The *Welsh* Court started with the premise that:

> Prior decisions of this Court . . . have emphasized that exceptions to the warrant requirement are "few in number and carefully delineated," and that the police bear a heavy burden when attempting to demonstrate an urgent need that might justify warrantless searches or arrests. Indeed, the Court has recognized only a few such emergency conditions, see, e.g., *United States v. Santana* (hot pursuit of a fleeing felon); *Warden v. Hayden* (same); *Schmerber v. California* (destruction of evidence); *Michigan v. Tyler* (ongoing fire), and has actually applied only the "hot pursuit" doctrine to arrests in the home.

466 U.S. at 749–50, 104 S.Ct. at 2097–98 (citations omitted).

In holding that the warrantless nighttime entry into the defendant's home violated the 4th Amendment, the *Welsh* Court found that, "in the circumstances presented by this case, there were no exigent circumstances sufficient to justify a warrantless home entry." 466 U.S. at 749 n.11, 104 S.Ct. at 2097 n.11. A "circumstance" that the *Welsh* Court found to be important was the fact that "[t]he State of Wisconsin has chosen to classify the first offense for driving while intoxicated as a noncriminal, civil forfeiture offense for which no imprisonment is possible." 466 U.S. at 754, 104 S.Ct. at 2100. In this regard, the Court held that "an important factor to be considered when determining whether any exigency exists is the gravity of the underlying offense for which the arrest is being made." 466 U.S. at 753, 104 S.Ct. at 2099. The Court also found that:

The State attempts to justify the arrest by relying on the hot-pursuit doctrine, on the threat to public safety, and on the need to preserve evidence of the petitioner's blood-alcohol level. On the facts of this case, however, the claim of hot pursuit is unconvincing because there was no immediate or continuous pursuit of the petitioner from the scene of a crime. Moreover, because the petitioner had already arrived home, and had abandoned his car at the scene of the accident, there was little remaining threat to the public safety. Hence, the only potential emergency claimed by the State was the need to ascertain the petitioner's blood-alcohol level.

466 U.S. at 753, 104 S.Ct. at 2099. The "need to ascertain the petitioner's blood-alcohol level" was found to be insufficient to overcome the 4th Amendment concerns involved. 466 U.S. at 754, 104 S.Ct. at 2100.

Notably, the Court pointed out that "[o]ur decision in *Payton*, allowing warrantless home arrests upon a showing of probable cause and exigent circumstances, was also expressly limited to felony arrests." 466 U.S. at 749 n.11, 104 S.Ct. at 2097 n.11. *See also* 466 U.S. at 750 n.12, 104 S.Ct. at 2098 n.12 ("Even the dissenters in *Payton*, although believing that warrantless home arrests are not prohibited by the Fourth Amendment, recognized the importance of the felony limitation on such arrests"). Thus, the *Welsh* Court seemed to clearly indicate that a warrantless arrest in the home should be limited to cases where the police are investigating a felony. *See generally People v. Cruz*, 149 A.D.2d 151, 545 N.Y.S.2d 561, 564 (1st Dep't 1989) ("A warrantless governmental intrusion into the privacy of a home is, with limited exceptions, prohibited by constitutional limitations. At a minimum, there must be probable cause to believe that the suspect sought therein has committed a felony.") (citations omitted).

§ 4:5 Applying *Welsh*

In *Brigham City, Utah v. Stuart*, 547 U.S. 398, 400, 126 S. Ct. 1943, 1946, 164 L. Ed. 2d 650 (2006), the Supreme Court addressed the issue of "whether police may enter a home without a warrant when they have an objectively reasonable basis for believing that an occupant is seriously injured or imminently threatened with such injury." In holding that such entry is permissible, the Court reasoned that:

One exigency obviating the requirement of a warrant is the need to assist persons who are seriously injured or threatened with such injury. " 'The need to protect or preserve life or avoid serious injury is justification for what would be otherwise illegal absent an exigency or emergency.' " Accordingly, law enforcement officers may enter a home without a warrant to render emergency assistance to an injured occupant or to protect an occupant from imminent injury.

547 U.S. at 403, 126 S.Ct. at 1947 (citations omitted).

Two other aspects of *Brigham City* are noteworthy. First, in keeping with a theme that the Supreme Court has been developing, *see Whren v. U.S.*, 517 U.S. 806, 116 S. Ct. 1769, 135 L. Ed. 2d 89 (1996), the Court held that "[t]he officer's subjective motivation [in entering the home] is irrelevant." 547 U.S. at 404, 126 S.Ct. at 1948. Second, the Court found *Welsh* to be distinguishable:

> Respondents further contend that their conduct was not serious enough to justify the officers' intrusion into the home. They rely on *Welsh v. Wisconsin*, in which we held that "an important factor to be considered when determining whether any exigency exists is the gravity of the underlying offense for which the arrest is being made." This contention, too, is misplaced. *Welsh* involved a warrantless entry by officers to arrest a suspect for driving while intoxicated. There, the "only potential emergency" confronting the officers was the need to preserve evidence (i.e., the suspect's blood-alcohol level)—an exigency that we held insufficient under the circumstances to justify entry into the suspect's home. Here, the officers were confronted with ongoing violence occurring within the home. *Welsh* did not address such a situation.

547 U.S. at 405, 126 S.Ct. at 1948–49 (citations omitted).

In *People v. Fallucchi*, 22 Misc. 3d 253, 865 N.Y.S.2d 874, 876 (Yates Co. Ct. 2008), a warrantless arrest of the defendant in his home was found to have violated the Fourth Amendment where, at the defendant's *Huntley*/probable cause hearing, "no proof was presented showing how the officers knew to go to the defendant's residence." Specifically, although there had been a report of a " 'possible intoxicated male operating a black Jeep Cherokee leaving the Lake Street Plaza heading towards the main exit,' " *People v. Fallucchi*, 865 N.Y.S.2d at 875, the proof at the hearing failed to link the black Jeep Cherokee to the defendant. *People v. Fallucchi*, 865 N.Y.S.2d at 876–77.

In *People v. Mason*, 248 A.D.2d 751, 669 N.Y.S.2d 712, 715–16 (3d Dep't 1998), the Appellate Division, Third Department, upheld a warrantless entry/arrest in a home where, among other things:

> [T]here was a very clear showing of probable cause that defendant committed the [violent felony] of burglary in the second degree. The Deputies had strong reason to believe that defendant was in the house. They had checked around the house and observed that the footprints led into but not away from it. Finally, the Deputies entered peacefully through the open back door and immediately announced their presence. Added to the forgoing circumstances, we also find that defendant's flight from the police and forced predawn entry into the dwelling raised a reasonable inference that his presence inside posed a danger to any occupants.

In our view, the record demonstrates the presence of probable cause and exigent circumstances sufficient to overcome the presumption of unreasonableness which attached to the Deputies' warrantless home entry.

In *People v. Stockman*, 159 Misc. 2d 730, 606 N.Y.S.2d 864 (Amherst Just. Ct. 1993), a State Trooper attempted to stop the defendant for a variety of traffic infractions. The defendant refused to pull over. Instead, he drove home, opened his garage door electronically, and pulled into his garage. The Trooper entered the garage on foot as the garage door was closing, tapped on the driver's window, and asked for the defendant's license and registration. The defendant responded " 'you're in my garage.' " 159 Misc. 2d at __, 606 N.Y.S.2d at 865. In finding the Trooper's warrantless entry into the garage to be illegal, the Court reasoned that:

Anything that Trooper Baker may have observed in the defendant's garage while the overhead door was up and while the officer was outside would be admissible because there is no expectation of privacy from view in such a circumstance, but an "up" door on a garage used in connection with a dwelling is not an invitation to enter. The raising and lowering of the door is a necessity for garaging a vehicle and storing other personal property as well as for personal ingress or egress.

When a dwelling door opens it may be possible for one to look into the dwelling without violation of the Fourth Amendment, but certainly no one can argue that if a householder opens the outer door to his house, to enter or exit, that such opening is an abandonment of the right to be free from physical invasion into the dwelling.

We therefore rule that absent exigent circumstances Officer Baker had no right to enter the garage. * * *

The egregious driving by defendant was not sufficient without more, to create probable cause for arrest for Driving While Intoxicated. The defendant did drive erratically, which conduct constituted Vehicle and Traffic Law infractions which permitted a "stop" of the vehicle on the public highway. However, conduct which only constitutes traffic infractions under the Vehicle and Traffic Law does not permit a warrantless entry.

159 Misc. 2d at __, __, 606 N.Y.S.2d at 866, 866–67 (citation omitted).

A similar result was reached in *People v. Couluris*, 148 Misc. 2d 984, 562 N.Y.S.2d 345 (Suffolk Co. Dist. Ct. 1990). In *Couluris*, the Court held that:

[T]he testimony at the hearing reveals that the only indicia of the defendant's intoxication which the police observed prior to the entry into the garage/apartment was that the defendant failed to stop at a stop sign; that an accident almost ensued; and that the defendant fled and failed to yield to the officers. There was no testimony to establish that the defendant was weaving; that he straddled a lane; or that he staggered upon exiting his vehicle. In the court's opinion the defendant's conduct, while certainly sufficient to permit the police to arrest him for traffic violations, did not afford the police probable cause to arrest for Driving While Intoxicated. Hence, the analysis of whether exigent circumstances existed must be based not upon the serious offense of Driving While Intoxicated, but rather on the relatively minor traffic infractions involved. When judged in this light the court is constrained to conclude that exigent circumstances were not present.

148 Misc. 2d at __, 562 N.Y.S.2d at 346.

In *Stark v. New York State Dept. of Motor Vehicles*, 104 A.D.2d 194, 483 N.Y.S.2d 824, 826 (3d Dep't 1984), judgment aff'd, 65 N.Y.2d 720, 492 N.Y.S.2d 8, 481 N.E.2d 548 (1985), the Appellate Division, Third Department addressed a case involving "factual circumstances strikingly similar" to those in *Welsh*. Nonetheless, the Court reached the opposite conclusion of *Welsh* (*i.e.*, the Court found that the warrantless arrest of the defendant in his home was legal). In reaching this result, the Court found that:

The instant case is readily distinguishable from *Welsh* in which the Supreme Court noted that the penalty imposed by a State for a particular offense was "the best indication of the state's interest in precipitating an arrest." New York classifies a first offense for driving while intoxicated as a misdemeanor. . . . This classification is reflective of the State's profound and grave concern to remove the incapacitated driver from the State's highways. By invalidating the arrest in *Welsh*, the Supreme Court did not intend to suggest that deterrence of drunk driving was not a matter of major concern to the States. Indeed, the Supreme Court has clearly recognized the compelling State interest in highway safety. Given this State's strong interest in protecting the public and in preventing the tragic consequences of drunk driving, we conclude that a warrantless home arrest of an intoxicated driver may be made where exigent circumstances exist.

Here, the arrest was justified as a continuation of the uninterrupted pursuit of petitioner and a measure designed to prevent the destruction of evidence by timely ascertaining petitioner's blood alcohol level. To ensure an accurate measurement, the chemical test for intoxication must be administered within two hours after the driver has been arrested. This fact, coupled with the possibility that a suspect could consume additional alcohol upon arriving at his home, makes immediate action by an arresting officer imperative. We also note that the deputies in the instant case gained peaceful entry into petitioner's home. Considering all these factors, we conclude that the arrest was lawful and that the determination to revoke petitioner's license is supported by substantial evidence in the record.

104 A.D.2d at __-__, 483 N.Y.S.2d at 826–27 (citations omitted).

Thus, the *Stark* Court distinguished *Welsh* on the grounds that (1) New York treats a first offense DWI more severely than Wisconsin does, (2) there was "hot pursuit," (3) the officers gained peaceful entry into the home, and (4) the "two-hour rule" (*see* §§ 31:1 et seq., *infra*) requires that a chemical test be administered within two hours of a DWI suspect's arrest.

The Court of Appeals' affirmance in *Stark* focused on only two of these issues: "that there was an uninterrupted pursuit of petitioner by the police and that the intrusion into his home was necessary to enable them to attempt to ascertain petitioner's blood alcohol level within the two-hour time limit prescribed by Vehicle and Traffic Law § 1194." 65 N.Y.2d at 722, 492 N.Y.S.2d at 9.

While the doctrines of "hot pursuit" and "third-party consent" (*i.e.*, reasons (2) and (3) above) may support the outcome in *Stark*, it is the authors' opinion that reasons (1) and (4) above do not. With regard to reason (1), as is noted in the previous section, both *Welsh* and *Payton* clearly indicate that warrantless, nonconsensual home entries should be limited to arrests for felonies. Thus, regardless of whether New York considers DWI a "serious" offense, a first offense is only a misdemeanor (and DWAI is only a traffic infraction).

With regard to reason (4), the two-hour rule commences from the time of arrest, not from the time that driving ceases. *See* VTL § 1194(2)(a). As a result, a delay in making the arrest is irrelevant for purposes of VTL § 1194. In addition, as the dissent in *Stark* pointed out, compulsory chemical tests require a Court order; and the delay in obtaining such an order is not prohibitive. Furthermore, the two-hour rule was eviscerated by the Court of Appeals' post-*Stark* decision in *People v. Atkins*, 85 N.Y.2d 1007, 630 N.Y.S.2d 965, 654 N.E.2d 1213 (1995). Accordingly, this rationale for upholding a warrantless intrusion into a home to make a routine arrest for misdemeanor DWI is no longer valid (assuming it ever was).

In *People v. Odenweller*, 137 A.D.2d 15, 527 N.Y.S.2d 127 (3d Dep't 1988), another pre-*Atkins* case, the Appellate Division, Third Department, again relied on the two-hour rule to justify a warrantless home entry in a DWI case. Relying heavily on *Stark*, the Court again distinguished *Welsh* on the ground that New York treats a first offense DWI more severely than Wisconsin does. Nonetheless, apparently reluctant to create a blanket DWI exception to the warrant requirement, the Court held as follows:

> The fact that important evidence was being lost and that this State has a strong interest in removing intoxicated drivers from its highways are not, by themselves, sufficient reason to justify this

warrantless arrest. We emphasize that in cases such as this the court must, as County Court did, carefully scrutinize the specific facts and circumstances. There is no per se rule authorizing warrantless arrests of suspected intoxicated drivers in their homes. Here, all the following factors, viewed cumulatively, are significant. Andrews' entry into defendant's residence was made during daylight hours. The manner of the entry was peaceful. [Trooper] Andrews merely stepped through a door which had been opened by defendant's grandson, who was temporarily residing at the premises and who knew that Andrews was seeking to speak to defendant. Andrews was immediately confronted by defendant as she took a step into the residence; she did not wander throughout the house seeking defendant. It is also significant that, as previously discussed, there was strong evidence that the crime of driving while intoxicated, as well as other crimes, had been committed. Further, Andrews' pursuit, while unable to fit within the legal definition of "hot pursuit," was nevertheless, as noted by County Court, at least "luke warm." It covered in a matter of minutes a direct line from the eyewitnesses to the vehicle's passenger to defendant. If Andrews had left defendant's residence in order to obtain a warrant, a situation would have existed whereby defendant could have entered her car, yet another time creating a grave danger to the public. All these factors, together with the seriousness of the crime and the loss of evidence which was occurring, lead to the conclusion that County Court's decision not to suppress the result of the blood alcohol test was correct.

137 A.D.2d at __, 527 N.Y.S.2d at 130 (emphasis added) (citations omitted). The dissent in *Odenweller* validly pointed out that *Stark* can only be harmonized with *Welsh* where there is actual "hot pursuit." 137 A.D.2d at __ n.1, 527 N.Y.S.2d at 130 n.1. "To be in hot pursuit means that some sort of a chase is taking place." 137 A.D.2d at __, 527 N.Y.S.2d at 131. And the "pursuit" in *Odenweller* was precisely the type of pursuit that the *Welsh* Court found did not constitute hot pursuit.

In *People v. Cavanaugh*, 264 A.D.2d 903, 695 N.Y.S.2d 625, 626 (3d Dep't 1999), the Third Department held that "the relevant facts and circumstances in this case are indistinguishable from those in *People v. Odenweller*" despite the fact that the relevant facts and circumstances were clearly distinguishable from those in *Odenweller*. For example, in *Cavanaugh*, there was not even a "luke warm" pursuit, and the police not only entered the defendant's home uninvited—they were repeatedly ordered to leave. Simply stated, while the Third Department commented, both in *Odenweller* and in *Cavanaugh*, that "the holding in *Odenweller* does not establish a per se rule authorizing warrantless arrests of suspected intoxicated drivers in their homes," 264 A.D.2d at __, 695 N.Y.S.2d at 626, it has apparently never found such an arrest to be improper.

A troubling aspect of *Stark*, *Odenweller*, and *Cavanaugh* is the fact that in these types of cases the police are almost never entering the home to arrest the defendant for DWI. Rather, they are entering the home to investigate a DWI (since, at the time of the home entry, they generally have little or no evidence that the defendant is intoxicated as opposed to impaired by drugs (licit or illicit), sick, tired, injured, distracted, etc.). In other words, the sanctity of the home is violated in many such cases not to make an immediate arrest for DWI, but rather to fish for evidence of DWI.

Realistically speaking, the police would not be able to obtain a valid warrant to arrest the defendant for DWI in most of these situations based on the evidence available to them before they entered the home. As such, claims that exigent circumstances exist because the defendant's body is eliminating alcohol are generally flawed—as the police have no valid reason to believe that the defendant had been drinking. As the Court noted in *People v. Stockman*, supra, "egregious driving by defendant [i]s not sufficient without more, to create probable cause for arrest for Driving While Intoxicated. The defendant did drive erratically, which conduct constituted Vehicle and Traffic Law infractions which permitted a 'stop' of the vehicle on the public highway. However, conduct which only constitutes traffic infractions under the Vehicle and Traffic Law does not permit a warrantless entry." 159 Misc. 2d at ___, 606 N.Y.S.2d at 866–67 (citation omitted).

§ 4:6 Admissibility of evidence obtained as the fruit of a *Payton* violation

Is evidence obtained as the fruit of a *Payton* violation required to be suppressed? The answer is—it depends. The Court of Appeals discussed relevant factors to consider in *People v. Borges*, 69 N.Y.2d 1031, 1033, 517 N.Y.S.2d 914, 916, 511 N.E.2d 58 (1987):

When a defendant challenges the admission of evidence obtained by a consensual search, claiming the consent was the product of an illegal arrest, the burden rests on the People to demonstrate that the consent was "acquired by means sufficiently distinguishable from the arrest to be purged of the illegality." Although the voluntariness of the consent is an important factor in the court's determination of attenuation, it is not dispositive. Rather, consideration must be given to a variety of factors, including but not limited to the temporal proximity of the consent to the arrest, the presence or absence of intervening circumstances, whether the police purpose underlying the illegality was to obtain the consent or the fruits of the search, whether the consent was volunteered or requested, whether the defendant was aware he could decline to consent, and particularly, the purpose and flagrancy of the official misconduct. Of course, the relevant factors will vary from case to case and each case must be individually considered on the particular facts and circumstances presented and the determination made with due regard for the purposes sought to be served by the exclusionary rule.

(Citations omitted).

Subsequent to *Borges*, the Supreme Court addressed the issue of incriminating statements obtained following a *Payton* violation. *See New York v. Harris*, 495 U.S. 14, 110 S. Ct. 1640, 109 L. Ed. 2d 13 (1990). In *Harris*, the Supreme Court ruled that:

Because the officers had probable cause to arrest Harris for a crime, Harris was not unlawfully in custody when he was removed to the station house, given *Miranda* warnings, and allowed to talk. For Fourth Amendment purposes, the legal issue is the same as it would be had the police arrested Harris on his doorstep, illegally entered his home to search for evidence, and later interrogated Harris at the station house. Similarly, if the police had made a warrantless entry into Harris' home, not found him there, but arrested him on the street when he returned, a later statement made by him after proper warnings would no doubt be admissible. * * *

To put the matter another way, suppressing the statement taken outside the house would not serve the purpose of the rule that made Harris' in-house arrest illegal. The warrant requirement for an arrest in the home is imposed to protect the home, and anything incriminating the police gathered from arresting Harris in his home, rather than elsewhere, has been excluded, as it should have been; the purpose of the rule has thereby been vindicated. * * *

We hold that, where the police have probable cause to arrest a suspect, the exclusionary rule does not bar the State's use of a statement made by the defendant outside of his home, even though the statement is taken after an arrest made in the home in violation of *Payton*.

495 U.S. at 18, 20, 21, 110 S.Ct. at 1643, 1644, 1644–45.

On remand, the Court of Appeals found that *Harris* does not adequately protect the rights of New York citizens, and held that the New York State Constitution provides more protection than the federal Constitution on this issue:

Inasmuch as the Supreme Court ruled against defendant on his Federal claim, we are now obliged to consider on remand the other claim he advanced, whether the State Constitution requires suppression of the station house statement. We conclude that the Supreme Court's rule does not adequately protect the search and seizure rights of citizens of New York. Accordingly, we hold that our State Constitution requires that statements obtained from an accused following a *Payton* violation must be suppressed unless the taint resulting from the violation has been attenuated.

People v. Harris, 77 N.Y.2d 434, 437, 568 N.Y.S.2d 702, 703–04, 570 N.E.2d 1051 (1991) (footnote omitted). In so holding, the Court reasoned as follows:

[A]lthough attenuation may not be necessary to deter *Payton* violations under Federal law or in the Nation generally, the Supreme Court's rule is not adequate to protect New York citizens from *Payton* violations because of our right to counsel rule.

The safeguards guaranteed by this State's Right to Counsel Clause are unique. By constitutional and statutory interpretation, we have established a protective body of law in this area resting on concerns of due process, self-incrimination and the right to counsel provisions of the State Constitution which is substantially greater than that recognized by other State jurisdictions and "far more expansive than the Federal counterpart." The Court has described the New York rule as a "cherished principle," rooted in this State's prerevolutionary constitutional law and developed "independent of its Federal counterpart." The "highest degree of [judicial] vigilance" is required to "safeguard" it. Manifestly, protection of the right to counsel has become a matter of singular concern in New York and it is appropriate that we consider the effect of *Payton* violations upon it.

The different views expressed by the Supreme Court and this Court in the case before us illustrate the distinctive Federal and State right to counsel rules and the concerns they engender. Under both Federal and State law, the right to counsel attaches once criminal proceedings have commenced. Under the Federal rule, however, criminal proceedings do not necessarily start when an arrest warrant is issued. Police may interrogate a suspect in the absence of a lawyer without violating his or her right to counsel even though the arrest is made pursuant to a warrant. But in New York, criminal proceedings must be instituted before the police can obtain a warrant. Our Criminal Procedure Law provides that an arrest warrant may not issue until an "accusatory instrument" has been filed. Thus, in New York once an arrest warrant is authorized, criminal proceedings have begun, the indelible right to counsel attaches and police may not question a suspect in the absence of an attorney.
* * *

In New York, . . . police are prohibited from questioning a suspect after an arrest pursuant to a warrant unless counsel is present. They have every reason to violate *Payton*, therefore, because doing so enables them to circumvent the accused's indelible right to counsel. Indeed, the evidence indicated that the police were motivated by just such considerations in this case. . . . If the police had entered the apartment pursuant to a warrant, they could not have questioned defendant in the absence of counsel. They should not enjoy greater latitude simply because they neglected to obtain a warrant, as *Payton* requires, and entered the apartment illegally. It is this interplay between the right to counsel rules established by New York law and the State's search and seizure provisions which provides a compelling reason for deviating from the Supreme Court's determination in this case. We adhere to our earlier decision, therefore, and hold that statements obtained from an accused

119

following an arrest made in violation of *Payton* are not admissible under the State Constitution if they are a product of the illegality.

77 N.Y.2d at 439–40, 568 N.Y.S.2d at 705–06 (citations omitted).

§ 4:7   Exception to warrant requirement—Consent

In *Schneckloth v. Bustamonte*, 412 U.S. 218, 219, 93 S. Ct. 2041, 2043–44, 36 L. Ed. 2d 854 (1973), the Supreme Court made clear that "one of the specifically established exceptions to the requirements of both a warrant and probable cause is a search that is conducted pursuant to consent." The question in *Schneckloth* was "what must the prosecution prove to demonstrate that a consent was 'voluntarily' given." 412 U.S. at 223, 93 S.Ct. at 2045. The Court concluded that:

> [T]he question whether a consent to a search was in fact 'voluntary' or was the product of duress or coercion, express or implied, is a question of fact to be determined from the totality of all the circumstances. While knowledge of the right to refuse consent is one factor to be taken into account, the government need not establish such knowledge as the sine qua non of an effective consent. As with police questioning, two competing concerns must be accommodated in determining the meaning of a 'voluntary' consent — the legitimate need for such searches and the equally important requirement of assuring the absence of coercion. * * *

> But the Fourth and Fourteenth Amendments require that a consent not be coerced, by explicit or implicit means, by implied threat or covert force. For, no matter how subtly the coercion was applied, the resulting 'consent' would be no more than a pretext for the unjustified police intrusion against which the Fourth Amendment is directed.

412 U.S. at 227, 228, 93 S.Ct. at 2047–48, 2048.

The specific holding in *Schneckloth* was as follows:

> Our decision today is a narrow one. We hold only that when the subject of a search is not in custody and the State attempts to justify a search on the basis of his consent, the Fourth and Fourteenth Amendments require that it demonstrate that the consent was in fact voluntarily given, and not the result of duress or coercion, express or implied. Voluntariness is a question of fact to be determined from all the circumstances, and while the subject's knowledge of a right to refuse is a factor to be taken into account, the prosecution is not required to demonstrate such knowledge as a prerequisite to establishing a voluntary consent.

412 U.S. at 248–49, 93 S.Ct. at 2059.

The seminal New York case on this issue is *People v. Gonzalez*, 39 N.Y.2d 122, 383 N.Y.S.2d 215, 347 N.E.2d 575 (1976). In *Gonzalez*, the Court of Appeals addressed the issue of whether "defendants' written consents to search their apartment were involuntary as a matter of law." 39 N.Y.2d at 124, 383 N.Y.S.2d at 216. In concluding that they were, the Court reasoned as follows:

> Consent to search, a relinquishment of constitutional protection under both the Federal and State Constitutions against unjustified official intrusion, must be a free and unconstrained choice. Official coercion, even if deviously subtle, nullifies apparent consent. Whether consent has been voluntarily given or is only a yielding to overbearing official pressure must be determined from the circumstances. * * *

> One of the limited exceptions to the warrant requirement and, indeed, to the requirement of probable cause, is voluntary consent to the search. In the instant case, the People concede that the legality of the search of the Gonzalez apartments turns entirely upon the validity of either of the Gonzalez' consents. . . . Of course, the People also recognize that theirs is the heavy burden of proving the voluntariness of the purported consents.

> Consent to search is voluntary when it is a true act of the will, an unequivocal product of an essentially free and unconstrained choice. Voluntariness is incompatible with official coercion, actual or implicit, overt or subtle. As the Supreme Court stated in *Bumper v. North Carolina*, "Where there is coercion there cannot be consent."

> No one circumstance is determinative of the voluntariness of consent. Whether consent has been voluntarily given or is only a yielding to overbearing official pressure must be determined from the circumstances.

> An important, although not dispositive, factor in determining the voluntariness of an apparent consent is whether the consenter is in custody or under arrest, and the circumstances surrounding the custody or arrest. True, custody or arrest alone does not necessarily preclude voluntariness. Custody, or, more compellingly, the immediate events of an arrest, especially a resisted arrest, do, however, engender an atmosphere of authority ordinarily contradictory of a capacity to exercise a free and unconstrained will.

> This is especially true when the individual in custody or under arrest is confronted by a large number of police agents. Moreover, the fact that a defendant was handcuffed has been considered a significant factor in determining whether his apparent consent was but a capitulation to authority. Submission to authority is not consent. * * *

> Another factor to be considered in determining the voluntariness of an apparent consent is the background of the consenter. * * *

> Another factor to be considered is whether the consenter has been,

previously to the giving of the consents, or for that matter even later, evasive or un-co-operative with the law enforcement authorities. * * *

A final factor is whether a defendant was advised of his right to refuse to consent. Such advice is not mandatory. Failure to advise, however, may be considered in determining whether a consent was voluntary.

39 N.Y.2d at 124, 127–29, 129, 130, 383 N.Y.S.2d at 217, 219–20, 220, 221 (citations omitted).

§ 4:8   Third party consent to warrantless entry

In *U.S. v. Matlock*, 415 U.S. 164, 171, 94 S. Ct. 988, 993, 39 L. Ed. 2d 242 (1974), the Supreme Court held that "when the prosecution seeks to justify a warrantless search by proof of voluntary consent, it is not limited to proof that consent was given by the defendant, but may show that permission to search was obtained from a third party who possessed common authority over or other sufficient relationship to the premises or effects sought to be inspected." In this regard:

> Common authority is, of course, not to be implied from the mere property interest a third party has in the property. The authority which justifies the third-party consent does not rest upon the law of property, with its attendant historical and legal refinements, see *Chapman v. United States*, 365 U.S. 610, 81 S.Ct. 776, 5 L.Ed.2d 828 (1961) (landlord could not validly consent to the search of a house he had rented to another), *Stoner v. California*, 376 U.S. 483, 84 S.Ct. 889, 11 L.Ed.2d 856 (1964) (night hotel clerk could not validly consent to search of customer's room) but rests rather on mutual use of the property by persons generally having joint access or control for most purposes, so that it is reasonable to recognize that any of the coinhabitants has the right to permit the inspection in his own right and that the others have assumed the risk that one of their number might permit the common area to be searched.

415 U.S. at 171 n.7, 94 S.Ct. at 993 n.7 (citations omitted).

In *Illinois v. Rodriguez*, 497 U.S. 177, 179, 110 S. Ct. 2793, 2796, 111 L. Ed. 2d 148 (1990), the Supreme Court addressed "an issue we expressly reserved in *Matlock*: Whether a warrantless entry is valid when based upon the consent of a third party whom the police, at the time of the entry, reasonably believe to possess common authority over the premises, but who in fact does not" have such authority. (Citation omitted). In holding that the entry would be valid, the Court reasoned that:

> [W]hat we hold today does not suggest that law enforcement officers may always accept a person's invitation to enter premises. Even when the invitation is accompanied by an explicit assertion that the person lives there, the surrounding circumstances could

conceivably be such that a reasonable person would doubt its truth and not act upon it without further inquiry. As with other factual determinations bearing upon search and seizure, determination of consent to enter must "be judged against an objective standard: would the facts available to the officer at the moment . . . 'warrant a man of reasonable caution in the belief' " that the consenting party had authority over the premises? If not, then warrantless entry without further inquiry is unlawful unless authority actually exists. But if so, the search is valid.

497 U.S. at 188–89, 110 S.Ct. at 2801 (citation omitted).

In *People v. Gonzalez*, 88 N.Y.2d 289, 296, 644 N.Y.S.2d 673, 676, 667 N.E.2d 323 (1996), the Court of Appeals, relying on *Matlock* and *Rodriguez*, held that a third party's consent to a "general search" of an apartment did not permit the police to search "defendant's zipped closed duffel bag secreted under the mattress of his bed."

§ 4:9   Validity of warrantless arrest at threshold of home

There is a critical difference between a warrantless entry/arrest inside of a home and a warrantless inquiry/arrest at the threshold thereto. *See, e.g., Payton v. New York*, 445 U.S. 573, 590, 100 S. Ct. 1371, 1382, 63 L. Ed. 2d 639 (1980) ("the Fourth Amendment has drawn a firm line at the entrance to the house. Absent exigent circumstances, that threshold may not reasonably be crossed without a warrant"). In *People v. Kozlowski*, 69 N.Y.2d 761, 513 N.Y.S.2d 101, 505 N.E.2d 611 (1987), a police officer was investigating a one-car accident. The officer's investigation led him to the defendant's residence.

Investigating the report, the officer walked up the driveway and onto an open-ended porch. He opened the screen door in order to knock on the front door and knocked loudly, and defendant (identified as the driver) came to the door. Defendant (described by the officer as having a strong odor of alcohol on his breath, glassy, bloodshot eyes, slurred speech and unsteady gait) told the officer that he had been drinking, that he had lost control of his car and hit the fences and pole, that he had left the scene and would pay for any damage caused. The officer then arrested defendant for driving while intoxicated and leaving the scene of a property damage accident. The officer apparently entered the house in the course of the arrest.

69 N.Y.2d at 762, 513 N.Y.S.2d at 102.

In upholding the lawfulness of the arrest, the Court of Appeals held that *Payton v. New York*, 445 U.S. 573, 100 S. Ct. 1371, 63 L. Ed. 2d 639 (1980), was inapplicable. Specifically, the Court held that:

Payton precludes the introduction of evidence obtained as the result

of a warrantless, nonconsensual entry into a suspect's home in order to make an arrest. Here, however, the incriminating evidence
was not the product of an illegal arrest; rather, it was obtained in
the course of the officer's investigation and before any arrest. Nor
were defendant's constitutional rights violated when the officer
investigating the reported traffic incident entered upon defendant's
property, knocked on the front door, and asked questions which
defendant chose to answer. The police officer reached defendant's
front door by the means defendant had made available for public
access to his house, and did not intrude into any area in which
defendant had a legitimate expectation of privacy. Absent evidence
of intent to exclude the public, the entryway to a person's house offers implied permission to approach and knock on the front door.
Thus, where (as here) the police utilized an unobstructed access to
defendant's home for the purpose of making inquiry, no warrant
was required by the State or Federal Constitution.

69 N.Y.2d at 762–63, 513 N.Y.S.2d at 102 (citations omitted). *See
also U.S. v. Santana*, 427 U.S. 38, 43, 96 S. Ct. 2406, 2410, 49 L.
Ed. 2d 300 (1976) ("a suspect may not defeat an arrest which has
been set in motion in a public place, and is therefore proper under
Watson, by the expedient of escaping to a private place"); *People
v. Skinner*, 284 A.D.2d 906, __, 726 N.Y.S.2d 193, 194 (4th Dep't
2001) (same); *People v. Minley*, 68 N.Y.2d 952, 953, 510 N.Y.S.2d
87, 88, 502 N.E.2d 1002 (1986) ("Neither the letter nor the spirit
of the *Payton* rule was violated here, where the police approached
defendant's home, saw defendant, whom they did not know, peek-
ing through a window and directed him to come out").

By contrast, in *People v. Levan*, 62 N.Y.2d 139, 142–43, 476
N.Y.S.2d 101, 102, 464 N.E.2d 469 (1984), the Court of Appeals
found a warrantless home entry to be improper under the following circumstances:

On May 2, 1979, an eyewitness identified Levan as the person who
shot Keeler. The police went to defendant's home, located on the
second floor of an apartment building, on several occasions during
the following week but did not find him there. Instructions were
left with someone in the building to contact the police when
defendant returned. On May 9, 1979 the police received a telephone
call informing them that the defendant was at home, and two cars
containing six policemen proceeded to defendant's apartment. At no
time during the week since defendant was identified did the police
attempt to obtain either an arrest warrant or a search warrant, although it is undisputed that they had probable cause to do so.

When the police arrived at the defendant's apartment building, two
officers proceeded to the second floor and secreted themselves at
points in the hallway near the entrance to defendant's apartment.
They then observed a woman (one of defendant's neighbors) approach defendant's apartment carrying a pot of food, ring the
doorbell, and knock on defendant's door. When defendant opened

his door, the officers saw him and, with guns drawn, bypassed the woman, entered the apartment and arrested defendant inside.

In holding the entry to be illegal, the Court noted that "[i]t is clear that in this case defendant was arrested in his apartment and that the police forcibly entered without a warrant and without consent. The fact that the police may have been able to see defendant when he opened his door in response to his neighbor's knock does not affect the constitutional prohibition against such entry." 62 N.Y.2d at 144–45, 476 N.Y.S.2d at 103.

§ 4:10   Validity of warrantless search of probationer's home

In *Griffin v. Wisconsin*, 483 U.S. 868, 107 S. Ct. 3164, 97 L. Ed. 2d 709 (1987), the Supreme Court addressed the validity of a warrantless search of the home of a person who is on probation. In holding that the search in question was valid, the Court reasoned that:

> A probationer's home, like anyone else's, is protected by the Fourth Amendment's requirement that searches be "reasonable." Although we usually require that a search be undertaken only pursuant to a warrant (and thus supported by probable cause, as the Constitution says warrants must be), *see, e.g., Payton v. New York*, we have permitted exceptions when "special needs, beyond the normal need for law enforcement, make the warrant and probable-cause requirement impracticable." Thus, we have held that government employers and supervisors may conduct warrantless, work-related searches of employees' desks and offices without probable cause, *O'Connor v. Ortega*, and that school officials may conduct warrantless searches of some student property, also without probable cause, *New Jersey v. T.L.O.* We have also held, for similar reasons, that in certain circumstances government investigators conducting searches pursuant to a regulatory scheme need not adhere to the usual warrant or probable-cause requirements as long as their searches meet "reasonable legislative or administrative standards."
>
> A State's operation of a probation system, like its operation of a school, government office or prison, or its supervision of a regulated industry, likewise presents "special needs" beyond normal law enforcement that may justify departures from the usual warrant and probable-cause requirements.

483 U.S. at 873–74, 107 S.Ct. at 3168 (citations omitted).

The Court further found that "the special needs of Wisconsin's probation system make the warrant requirement impracticable and justify replacement of the standard of probable cause by 'reasonable grounds.'" 483 U.S. at 875–76, 107 S.Ct. at 3169–70.

The Court of Appeals applied *Griffin* in *People v. Hale*, 93 N.Y.2d 454, 692 N.Y.S.2d 649, 714 N.E.2d 861 (1999). In *Hale*, the defendant was on felony probation for striking and killing a swimmer with a boat that he operated while impaired. "As a condition of probation in connection with a negotiated plea and sentence, defendant consented in writing to provisions permitting his probation officer to search his person, his vehicle, and his 'place of abode' for illegal drugs and narcotic implements, during the period of probation." 93 N.Y.2d at 457, 692 N.Y.S.2d at 650. The specific condition of probation at issue, which the defendant had expressly agreed to, provided as follows:

That you permit search of your vehicle and place of abode where such place of abode is legally under your control, and seizure of any narcotic implements and/or illegal drugs found, such search to be conducted by a Probation Officer or a Probation Officer and his agent.

93 N.Y.2d at 458, 692 N.Y.S.2d at 650.

In upholding the validity of this condition of probation, the Court reasoned as follows:

We begin with the premise that a probationer's home is protected by the constitutional requirement that searches be reasonable. It all comes down to what is "reasonable" under the circumstances, bearing in mind that the reasonableness of a search is measured by, among other things, the relative privacy expectation and entitlement of the person to be searched. For example, a defendant on probation does not stand in the same constitutional shoes as someone entirely free of judicial supervision and control. At one extreme, a person who has just been lawfully placed under arrest for armed robbery has an expectation of privacy vastly inferior to a law-abiding citizen who is enjoying a quiet evening at home. A defendant on probation is at neither extreme of the constitutional spectrum. * * *

In the case before us the search was not conducted pursuant to a State regulation but under a provision which, we hold, carries as much if not more constitutional weight: a court-ordered probationary condition, based on a negotiated sentence, and the written, counseled consent of the probationer. * * *

In reviewing the thrust of the probationary sentence before us, we conclude readily that the court concentrated on the statutory goal that the conditions be fundamentally rehabilitative, and imposed them accordingly. The condition in dispute was calculatedly included among the terms of probation because all parties were ostensibly seeking the same objective: that defendant refrain from abusing drugs. In addition to the standard conditions set forth under Penal Law § 65.10(2)(a) through (k) the court individualized defendant's probationary plan to comport with the nature of the original conviction and what it considered appropriate to further defendant's rehabilitative prospects, given his background, history, and proclivities. Among the additional conditions, the court ordered defendant to perform community service, to undergo drug testing when directed by the Probation Department, and to enter a drug treatment facility, if warranted. Defendant, represented by counsel, signed both the standard and the additional terms, attesting that he understood them and would abide by them.

These conditions are not punitive or misdirected. Considering that the program was designed to keep defendant free of drugs, one way to encourage him to do so was to hold out the possibility that he would be checked up on, and stood to be incarcerated if he betrayed the terms of his negotiated probationary status. The additional conditions were individually tailored in relation to the offense, and were reasonably related to defendant's rehabilitation. * * *

Defendant contends that his consent may not be based on his having signed the conditions of probation, and that any such consent was the product of coercion. We disagree with this contention to the extent that defendant claims that his consent is invalid as a matter of law. In order to obtain the benefits of a favorable sentence, defendant negotiated an agreement that assured his avoidance of a prison term. He had no "right" to a sentence of probation and he sought the probation sentence, along with its obligations and its obvious benefits, as a far more desirable disposition than the potential alternative.

93 N.Y.2d at 459, 460, 461–62, 463, 692 N.Y.S.2d at 651, 652, 653, 654 (citations and footnote omitted).

In a footnote, the Court noted that "[c]onsidering that the case before us is based upon a consent provision we do not undertake to decide whether, when and to what extent a sentencing court may unilaterally impose search conditions in a sentence of probation." 93 N.Y.2d at 460 n.4, 692 N.Y.S.2d at 652 n.4.

Chapter 5

Sobriety Checkpoints

Research References

Westlaw Databases

Drinking/Driving Litigation (DRNKDRIVING)
Handling a Criminal Case in New York (HCCNY)
Search and Seizure (SEARCHSZR)

Treatises and Practice Aids

Nichols and Whited, Drinking/Driving Litigation: Criminal and Civil §§ 4:3 to 4:6 (2d ed.)
Muldoon, Handling a Criminal Case in New York §§ 9:67, 9:68
LaFave, 6 Search and Seizure § 9.7 (4th ed.)

Law Reviews and Other Periodicals

Brown, Sobriety Checkpoints: Statutory Guidelines to Clear the Roadblocks to Constitutionality, 40 Wash. U. J. Urb. & Contemp. L. 141 (Fall, 1991)
Craig, Constitutional Law-The United States Supreme Court Upholds the Use of Sobriety Checkpoints-Michigan Department of State Police v. Sitz, 110 S. Ct. 2481 (1990), 25 Suffolk U. L. Rev. 230 (Spring, 1991)
English, Sobriety Checkpoints Under State Constitutions: What Has Happened to Sitz?, 59 U. Pitt. L. Rev. 453 (Winter, 1998)
Kenney, Constitutionality of Sobriety Checkpoints, Other Holdings, 45-MAY Res Gestae 34 (May, 2002)
Piepmeier, Practical Problems of Sobriety Checkpoints, 1992-MAR Army Law. 15 (March, 1992)
Reynolds, The Use of Sobriety Checkpoints to Combat Drunk Drivers: Knowing When to Say When State v. Welch, 54 Mo. L. Rev. 485 (Spring, 1989)
Sheldon, Sobriety Checkpoints, the Rational-Basis Test, and the Law Court, 8 Me. B.J. 80 (March, 1993)

Soble, Clearing the Roadblocks to Sobriety Checkpoints, 21 U. Mich. J. L. Ref. 489 (Spring, 1988)

KeyCite®: Cases and other legal materials listed in KeyCite Scope can be researched through the KeyCite service on Westlaw®. Use KeyCite to check citations for form, parallel references, prior and later history, and comprehensive citator information, including citations to other decisions and secondary materials.

---

§ 5:1 In general

Research References

West's Key Number Digest, Arrest ☞63.5(6); Automobiles ☞349(9)

Sobriety checkpoints are a source of both legal and political concern. The emphasis on DWI enforcement has resulted in the widespread use of sobriety checkpoints in various locations throughout New York State. From a law enforcement perspective, the sobriety checkpoint requires the assignment of more personnel than the number of arrests resulting therefrom would appear to justify. With the exception of New York City, very few intoxicated drivers are apprehended as a result of stopping hundreds of cars. The primary benefit derived from this procedure is the deterrence of potential violators. In New York City, where the volume of traffic renders traditional patrol methods far less effective than in upstate New York, the checkpoint has been a valuable tool for both enforcement and deterrence.

It is well-settled that stopping an automobile and detaining its occupants constitutes a "seizure" for purposes of the Fourth and 14th Amendments to the U.S. Constitution. *Delaware v. Prouse*, 440 U.S. 648, 653, 99 S. Ct. 1391, 1396, 59 L. Ed. 2d 660 (1979). In *Prouse*, the Supreme Court held that "random spot checks" of automobiles violate the Fourth and 14th Amendments, reasoning that "[t]his kind of standardless and unconstrained discretion is the evil the Court has discerned when in previous cases it has insisted that the discretion of the official in the field be circumscribed, at least to some extent." *Prouse*, 440 U.S. at 661, 99 S.Ct. at 1400. In so holding, however, the Court noted that:

> This holding does not preclude the . . . States from developing methods for spot checks that involve less intrusion or that do not involve the unconstrained exercise of discretion. *Questioning of all oncoming traffic at roadblock-type stops is one possible alternative.* We hold only that persons in automobiles on public roadways may not for that reason alone have their travel and privacy interfered with at the unbridled discretion of police officers.

Prouse, 440 U.S. at 663, 99 S.Ct. at 1402 (emphasis added) (footnote omitted).

Thereafter, in *Michigan Dept. of State Police v. Sitz*, 496 U.S. 444, 110 S. Ct. 2481, 110 L. Ed. 2d 412 (1990), the court expressly held that a state's use of highway sobriety checkpoints does not, in and of itself, violate the Fourth and 14th Amendments. However, the Court made clear that it was addressing "only the initial stop of each motorist passing through a checkpoint and the associated preliminary questioning and observation by checkpoint officers. Detention of particular motorists for more extensive field sobriety testing may require satisfaction of an individualized suspicion standard." *Sitz*, 496 U.S. at 450–51, 110 S.Ct. at 2485.

§ 5:2   New York law—*People v. Scott*

Research References

West's Key Number Digest, Arrest ☞63.5(6); Automobiles ☞349(9)

People v. Scott, 63 N.Y.2d 518, 483 N.Y.S.2d 649, 473 N.E.2d 1 (1984), defines the law in this state with regard to sobriety checkpoints. In *Scott*, the court of appeals held that:

> A roadblock established pursuant to a written directive of the County Sheriff for the purpose of detecting and deterring driving while intoxicated or while impaired, and as to which operating personnel are prohibited from administering sobriety tests unless they observe listed criteria, indicative of intoxication, which give substantial cause to believe that the operator is intoxicated, is constitutionally permissible, notwithstanding that the location of the roadblock is moved several times during the three- to four-hour period of operation, and notwithstanding that legislative initiatives have also played a part in reducing the incidence of driving while intoxicated in recent years.

Scott, 63 N.Y.2d at 522, 483 N.Y.S.2d at 650.

In so holding, the *Scott* Court made clear that, to be constitutional, a sobriety checkpoint (1) may not "intrude to an impermissible degree upon the privacy of motorists approaching the checkpoint," (2) must be "maintained in accordance with a uniform procedure which afford[s] little discretion to operating personnel," and (3) must utilize "adequate precautions as to safety, lighting and fair warning of the existence of the checkpoint." *Scott*, 63 N.Y.2d at 526, 483 N.Y.S.2d at 652.

In *In re Muhammad F.*, 94 N.Y.2d 136, 700 N.Y.S.2d 77, 722 N.E.2d 45 (1999), the court of appeals reaffirmed and reemphasized the fact that "limiting the discretion of officers in the field" is of "decisive" significance in determining whether a checkpoint-type vehicle stop is Constitutional. *See Matter of Muhammad F.* 94 N.Y.2d at 144, 700 N.Y.S.2d at 81.

§ 5:3 Applying *Scott*

Research References

West's Key Number Digest, Arrest ☞63.5(6); Automobiles ☞349(9)

In *People v. Richmond*, 174 Misc. 2d 40, 662 N.Y.S.2d 998, 1000 (Monroe County Ct. 1997), the court held that "*Scott* . . . contemplates that the plan [pursuant to which a sobriety checkpoint is carried out] be established pursuant to a directive issued by the chief law enforcement official—the person most directly accountable to the people or their elected representatives." In addition, the court noted that although *Scott* did not explicitly hold that the plan must be in writing, "it did hold that there had to be a plan for officers to follow and by which personnel's actions could be objectively measured." *Richmond*, 174 Misc. 2d at __, 662 N.Y.S.2d at 1000. "*Scott* further contemplates that the people operating the roadblock will not act with unlimited discretion but rather will act pursuant to a 'listed criteria' of the plan. Limiting discretion of individual officers thus lessening the likelihood of arbitrary law enforcement is a well-recognized constitutional imperative." *Richmond*, 174 Misc. 2d at __, 662 N.Y.S.2d at 1000 (citation omitted). Applying these principles to the case before it, the *Richmond* court found that:

> [T]he record fails to reveal any proof of any plan promulgated by the Chief of Police. What directives were shown to exist, came from an officer to other personnel and were, in any event, bereft of explicit and neutral limitations on the conduct of operating personnel. Thus . . ., the roadblock failed to adhere to the requirements established in *Scott*.

Richmond, 174 Misc. 2d at __, 662 N.Y.S.2d at 1000–01.

In *People v. Smith*, 170 Misc. 2d 486, 649 N.Y.S.2d 313 (N.Y. City Crim. Ct. 1996), a checkpoint stop was found to be invalid where there were no written guidelines issued to the officers administering the checkpoint and:

> [T]he manner in which this checkpoint was operated failed to meet even the most basic requirements established by the Court of Appeals. Here there was no uniform, nonarbitrary plan. Instead, it was explicitly left to the discretion of the individual officers to determine which trucks to stop and how to effectuate the stops. The only "guideline" issued was an oral instruction to stop as many trucks as possible. This left it entirely to Officer Little and other officers to decide which trucks and how many trucks to stop. Moreover, there were no visible manifestations that a checkpoint was in effect at the Holland Tunnel. The officers would simply order a truck to pull over, as they did in the defendant's case.

Smith, 170 Misc. 2d at __, 649 N.Y.S.2d at 315.

Similarly, in *People v. Holley*, 157 Misc. 2d 402, 596 N.Y.S.2d

1016 (N.Y. City Crim. Ct. 1993), a DWI checkpoint stop was held to be unconstitutional where the testimony at the suppression hearing:

> [F]ailed to establish that there were any procedures in effect to limit the discretion of the individual officers operating the roadblock. No evidence was provided to show that the checkpoint was set up according to any written procedure or plan. . . . [The testimony] also provided no information as to who determined the location and layout of the checkpoint. . . . Furthermore, the record contains no evidence to establish that a supervisor reviewed the layout of the checkpoint. . . . No evidence was presented as to what Officer Fleury said to motorists when they pulled up to the roadblock. . . . The record was also bereft of any evidence that the police had any signs or other safety devices in place to alert motorists that they were approaching a checkpoint. No testimony was presented to show that the police had any flares or cones on the road, any special lighting or any police cars stationed in plain view of oncoming traffic. . . . Furthermore, . . . no proof was presented to show that the checkpoint location was chosen by supervisory personnel or that the placement of this roadblock was part of an overall police department plan.

Holley, 157 Misc. 2d at __, 596 N.Y.S.2d at 1020–21 (citation omitted).

In *People v. Collura*, 160 Misc. 2d 831, 610 N.Y.S.2d 1018 (N.Y. City Crim. Ct. 1994), the court upheld the constitutionality of a sobriety checkpoint where:

> [T]he testimony established that the checkpoint was operated in a consistent, non-arbitrary manner. All drivers who approached the checkpoint were questioned. No testimony was elicited to suggest that the individual officers had any authority to let some drivers pass through without stopping them. Furthermore, a supervisor was present to insure that the officers followed the required procedure.
>
> In addition, both the location and the layout of the checkpoint were determined by the supervisor and not by the individual officers. . . . No testimony was presented to show that any of the officers had the authority to revise the layout, alter the checkpoint procedure or to move the roadblock during the evening. Rather, the basic structure of the roadblock was determined by Sergeant Soto, whose involvement provided the necessary check on the discretion of the individual officers.

Collura, 160 Misc. 2d at __, 610 N.Y.S.2d at 1019–20. Notably, the *Collura* decision distinguished *Holley*, (a decision written by the same Judge), on the ground that, in *Holley*, *supra*, there was inadequate testimony with regard to the supervisor's role in overseeing the checkpoint.

In *People v. Restrepo*, 7/9/93 N.Y.L.J. 25 (col. 2) (N.Y. City

Crim. Ct.), the court granted the defendant's motion to suppress his Breathalyzer result where he was stopped at a sobriety checkpoint administered as follows:

> [T]he checkpoint was arranged so that traffic cones funnelled the oncoming vehicular traffic into one lane. The area was illuminated by flashing lights and the high beams of a police car's headlights. As vehicles approached the checkpoint, they were randomly stopped by the police. There was no systematic program directing the police officers to stop any particular type of car, whether by model, number or otherwise. Vehicles merely passed the police officer at approximately 5–10 miles per hour and would be arbitrarily stopped if, in the subjective opinion of the police officer, he believed the operator to be intoxicated.

§ 5:4   Checkpoint guidelines

Research References

West's Key Number Digest, Arrest ☞63.5(6); Automobiles ☞349(9)

Despite the fact that the sobriety checkpoints upheld in *Michigan Dept. of State Police v. Sitz*, 496 U.S. 444, 110 S. Ct. 2481, 110 L. Ed. 2d 412 (1990) and *People v. Scott*, 63 N.Y.2d 518, 483 N.Y.S.2d 649, 473 N.E.2d 1 (1984) involved the use of detailed written checkpoint guidelines limiting the discretion of officers in the field, a troubling number of lower courts in New York have found, without adequate explanation, that written checkpoint guidelines are unnecessary. *See, e.g., People v. Serrano*, 233 A.D.2d 170, 650 N.Y.S.2d 95 (1st Dep't 1996) (written guidelines not necessarily required for "stolen car" roadblock); *People v. Herbert*, 172 Misc. 2d 377, 661 N.Y.S.2d 434, 435 (App. Term, 1st Dep't 1997) (per curiam) (Court upheld a "stolen car" checkpoint where the only instruction given to the officers running the checkpoint was "to 'random[ly]' pull over every third vehicle at East 15th Street near the FDR Drive to check for stolen cars, with logistics providing the only limitation"); *People v. Dongarra*, 24 Misc. 3d 469, __, 875 N.Y.S.2d 869, 871 (Chautauqua Co. Ct. 2009) ("Even though they are present in the current case, the lack of written guidelines does not invalidate a sobriety checkpoint"); *People v. Hill*, 166 Misc. 2d 148, 631 N.Y.S.2d 988, 989 (Monroe County Ct. 1995) ("[a]lthough the court of appeals has never spoken directly to this issue, a review of the record on appeal in Scott compels the conclusion that a specific written directive for each checkpoint is not necessary"); *People v. Diplan*, 180 Misc. 2d 294, 688 N.Y.S.2d 436 (N.Y. City Crim. Ct. 1999) (written guidelines not required for sobriety checkpoint); *People v. Snead*, 160 Misc. 2d 466, 609 N.Y.S.2d 520 (Nassau Co. Dist. Ct. 1994) (same); *People v. Collura*, 160 Misc. 2d 831, 610 N.Y.S.2d 1018, 1019 (N.Y. City Crim. Ct. 1994) ("[a]lthough a written plan would be one way to meet [the *Scott*] uniformity requirement, it is not the only way"). *Cf. People v. Richmond*, 174 Misc. 2d 40, 662 N.Y.S.2d 998 (Monroe County Ct. 1997) (*Scott* requires that there be a plan for officers to follow and by which police action can be objectively measured); *People v. Holley*, 157 Misc. 2d 402, 596 N.Y.S.2d 1016, 1020 (N.Y. City Crim. Ct. 1993) ("[t]he existence of . . . written guidelines was one of the critical factors in the *Scott* decision").

However, all of these decisions predate the court of appeals' decisions in both *In re Muhammad F.*, 94 N.Y.2d 136, 700 N.Y.S.2d 77, 722 N.E.2d 45 (1999), and *People v. Johnson*, 1 N.Y.3d 252, 771 N.Y.S.2d 64, 803 N.E.2d 385 (2003)—both of which appear to mandate that written directives containing "listed criteria" limiting the discretion of officers in the field are a Constitutional requirement. For example, in *Muhammad F.*, the court stated that "suspicionless stops of vehicles to conduct sobriety checks at checkpoints *under written guidelines* are constitutional, even if the location of the roadblock regularly changes." 94 N.Y.2d at 145, 700 N.Y.S.2d at 81 (emphasis added). *See also Matter of Muhammad F.*, 94 N.Y.2d at 145, 700 N.Y.S.2d at 82 ("there was no question in *Sitz* that the discretion of officers in the field was adequately circumscribed, because the checkpoint was operated according to 'guidelines setting forth procedures governing checkpoint operations, site selection, and publicity' ") (citation omitted); *Matter of Muhammad F.*, 94 N.Y.2d at 147–48, 700 N.Y.S.2d at 83–84:

> [T]he records in these cases contain no showing that the Task Force had attempted to mitigate the constitutional infirmity of "standardless and unconstrained discretion" of "the official in the field" other than the vague and purely conclusory testimony that the officers had *verbal instructions* to stop taxis "in a set basis and not just arbitrarily." For example, had the Police Department produced evidence of *particularized guidelines* with "listed criteria" that "established procedures for site selection, lighting and signs; avoidance of discrimination by stopping all vehicles, or every second, third or fourth vehicle; [and] location of screening areas," then we would have some assurance that the stops were "being maintained in accordance with a uniform procedure which afforded little discretion to operating personnel." Since the officers here were not even required to make a written record of stops that had taken place, in conducting our "post-stop judicial review" we are relegated to the self-verifying evidence from the officers whose conduct is being challenged to determine whether they were using uniform and nondiscriminatory procedures.

(Emphases added) (citations omitted).

While *Johnson, supra*, dealt with inventory searches, the legal requirements of such searches are strikingly similar to those of checkpoint stops. *See, e.g.*, 1 N.Y.3d at 256, 771 N.Y.S.2d at 66 ("an inventory search should be conducted pursuant to 'an established procedure clearly limiting the conduct of individual officers . . .' The procedure must be standardized so as to 'limit the discretion of the officer in the field' "); *People v. Galak*, 80 N.Y.2d 715, 719, 594 N.Y.S.2d 689, 692, 610 N.E.2d 362 (1993) ("it is an established procedure clearly limiting the conduct of individual officers that assures that the searches are carried out consistently and reasonably"); *People v. Robinson*, 97 N.Y.2d 341, 354, 741 N.Y.S.2d 147, 154, 767 N.E.2d 638 (2001) ("[i]n inventory cases, an officer who has impounded a vehicle following a valid arrest can inventory the contents only pursuant to *established guidelines* to identify and protect the owner's property") (emphasis added). *See also People v. Padilla*, 21 N.Y.3d 268, 970 N.Y.S.2d 486, 992 N.E.2d 414 (2013), petition for cert. filed, 82 U.S.L.W. 3095 (U.S. Aug. 5, 2013) (inventory search upheld where "the People proffered written guidelines, the officer's testimony regarding his search of the vehicle, and the resulting list of items retained"); *People v. Walker*, 20 N.Y.3d 122, 127, 957 N.Y.S.2d 272, 275, 980 N.E.2d 937 (2012) ("Certainly, it would be better for a prosecutor seeking to prove the existence of a written policy to put a copy of the policy into evidence. On the other hand, defense counsel could have demanded that the policy be produced to help her cross-examine the trooper. She did not do so").

In *Johnson*, the court of appeals found an inventory search to be invalid where, inter alia:

> [T]he evidence adduced at the [suppression] hearing was clearly insufficient to satisfy the prosecutor's initial burden of establishing a valid inventory search. Although the officer testified that he knew of the general objectives of an inventory search, and declared that his search of the glove compartment box fulfilled those objectives, the People offered no evidence to establish the existence of any *departmental policy* regarding inventory searches. Even assuming such a policy existed, the People failed to produce evidence demonstrating either that the procedure itself was "rationally designed to meet the objectives that justify inventory searches in the first place," or that this particular officer conducted this search properly and in compliance with *established procedures*.

1 N.Y.3d at 256, 771 N.Y.S.2d at 66–67 (emphases added) (citation omitted). *See also People v. Gomez*, 13 N.Y.3d 6, 884 N.Y.S.2d 339, 912 N.E.2d 555 (2009); *People v. Francisco*, 63 A.D.3d 1554, 880 N.Y.S.2d 806 (4th Dep't 2009); *People v. Elpenord*, 24 A.D.3d 465, 806 N.Y.S.2d 675 (2d Dep't 2005).

Following *Muhammad F., supra*, at least one court has ruled that written checkpoint guidelines are a Constitutional necessity. *See People v. Velit*, 2002 WL 334690 (N.Y. City Crim. Ct. 2002).

Where they exist, written checkpoint guidelines are generally drafted in an attempt to conform with the requirements of the court of appeals' decision in *Scott*.

In *People v. Sears*, 2 Misc. 3d 447, 769 N.Y.S.2d 708 (Webster J. Ct. 2003), the court held both (a) that the law does not "require the chief of police to establish the specific site of a sobriety checkpoint at any given time," *Sears*, 2 Misc. 3d at __, 769 N.Y.S.2d at 710, and (b) that "[n]o prior empirical evidence of alcohol related arrests or accidents at a particular site is required before that site can be used for a sobriety checkpoint." *Sears*, 2 Misc. 3d at __, 769 N.Y.S.2d at 711.

§ 5:5 Checkpoint evasion

Research References

West's Key Number Digest, Arrest ☞63.5(6); Automobiles ☞349(9)

In *People v. Chaffee*, 183 A.D.2d 208, 590 N.Y.S.2d 625, 626 (4th Dep't 1992), the Appellate Division, Fourth Department, held that "a police officer, who is participating in a sobriety checkpoint, may lawfully stop a vehicle which makes a legal turn into a parking lot in an apparent attempt to avoid that roadblock." However, although the defendant's turn into the parking lot was lawful, the facts of the case made clear that he was attempting to evade the checkpoint.

On the other hand, in *People v. Rocket*, 156 Misc. 2d 641, 594 N.Y.S.2d 568 (Pleasant J. Ct. 1992), the court held that:

> While there are a number of cases which suggest that the avoidance of a checkpoint is in fact an articulable reason for a stop, it appears that the prevailing view and that more consistent with the articulations made by the U.S. Supreme Court is that the mere making of a U-turn or a turnoff to avoid a DWI checkpoint is not, in and of itself, sufficient basis for a stop.

Rocket, 156 Misc. 2d at __, 594 N.Y.S.2d at 570 (citations omitted). However, the court did state that "[t]his is not to suggest that drivers have carte blanc [sic] to avoid DWI checkpoints in all circumstances." *Rocket*, 156 Misc. 2d at __, 594 N.Y.S.2d at 570.

In *People v. Bigger*, 2 Misc. 3d 937, 771 N.Y.S.2d 826, 831 (Webster J. Ct. 2004), the court found a stop for suspected checkpoint evasion to be invalid. In so holding, the court found it significant that (a) no written guidelines or other procedures were in place addressing the issue of checkpoint evasion (leaving the issues of whether and how to pursue suspected checkpoint evaders to the discretion of the officers at the scene), and (b) the officer who made the stop "was not part of the sobriety checkpoint detail" (and thus "[h]e must have an independent articulable reason to stop an individual vehicle").

It is noteworthy that, in *People v. Scott*, 63 N.Y.2d 518, 483 N.Y.S.2d 649, 473 N.E.2d 1 (1984), "two patrol cars were stationed in the area [of the checkpoint] *to follow and observe for possible violations* any vehicle that avoided the roadblock by making a U-turn." *Scott*, 63 N.Y.2d at 524, 483 N.Y.S.2d at 651 (emphasis added). In other words, a U-turn would not, in and of itself, have been a sufficient basis for a stop.

In *People v. Horeth*, 7/13/99 N.Y.L.J. 33 (col. 6), the Watertown City Court granted defendant's motion to suppress the evidence of her intoxication in a "checkpoint evasion" case. In *Horeth*, the court determined that the sobriety checkpoint at issue was set up in a manner and at a location in which a person seeking to avoid the checkpoint would be forced to make an "illegal" turn, which the police then used as a pretext to stop the vehicle to investigate the driver for DWI.

§ 5:6   Checkpoint stops noncustodial for *Miranda* purposes

Research References

West's Key Number Digest, Arrest ⚿63.5(6); Automobiles ⚿349(9)

In *People v. Christopher S.*, 126 Misc. 2d 594, 483 N.Y.S.2d 609 (N.Y. City Crim. Ct. 1984), the court held that admissions obtained from a defendant stopped at a checkpoint are subject to the same analysis as any other routine traffic stop. *See Berkemer v. McCarty*, 468 U.S. 420, 104 S. Ct. 3138, 82 L. Ed. 2d 317 (1984) (the roadside questioning of a motorist detained pursuant to a traffic stop does not constitute custodial interrogation for purposes of the doctrine enunciated in *Miranda v. Arizona*). Accordingly, "[t]here was no need for the officer to inform the defendant of his *Miranda* rights." *Christopher S.*, 126 Misc. 2d at —, 483 N.Y.S.2d at 611.

§ 5:7   Supreme Court decision dramatically affects checkpoint law—*Indianapolis v. Edmond*

Research References

West's Key Number Digest, Arrest ⚿63.5(6); Automobiles ⚿349(9)

Checkpoint stops—which are not based upon any individualized suspicion—are a distinctly un-American concept. In this regard, in *City of Indianapolis v. Edmond*, 531 U.S. 32, 121 S. Ct. 447, 148 L. Ed. 2d 333 (2000), the Supreme Court made clear that checkpoint-type vehicle stops are *presumptively unconstitutional*—subject to certain limited exceptions (such as sobriety checkpoints and Border Patrol checkpoints). *See also Illinois v. Lidster*, 540 U.S. 419, 426, 124 S. Ct. 885, 890, 157 L. Ed. 2d 843 (2004).

Specifically, the *Edmond* court held that "a checkpoint program whose primary purpose [is] to detect evidence of ordinary criminal wrongdoing," 531 U.S. at 38, 121 S.Ct. at 452, violates the Fourth Amendment. *Edmond*, 531 U.S. at 42–44, 121 S.Ct. at 454–55. If this were not the case:

> [T]here would be little check on the ability of the authorities to construct roadblocks for almost any conceivable law enforcement purpose. Without drawing the line at roadblocks designed primarily to serve the general interest in crime control, the Fourth Amendment would do little to prevent such intrusions from becoming a routine part of American life.

Edmond, 531 U.S. at 42, 121 S.Ct. at 454.

Thus, *Edmond* establishes an important new threshold requirement in checkpoint cases: The People must affirmatively prove, at a pretrial hearing and through an appropriate witness (or witnesses), that the "primary purpose" of the checkpoint was not merely to "serve the general interest in crime control" or to "detect evidence of ordinary criminal wrongdoing." *Edmond*, 531 U.S. at 38, 42, 44, 47–48, 121 S.Ct. at 452, 454, 455, 457. *See also People v. Jackson*, 99 N.Y.2d 125, 131–32, 752 N.Y.S.2d 271, 275, 782 N.E.2d 67 (2002).

Critically, *Edmond* makes clear that the People cannot satisfy their burden of proving the "primary purpose" of a checkpoint simply by calling it a "sobriety checkpoint." *Edmond*, 531 U.S. at 46, 121 S.Ct. at 457. Rather, the People must prove that the *stated* primary purpose of the checkpoint was, in fact, its *actual* primary purpose. Otherwise, "law enforcement authorities would be able to establish checkpoints for virtually any purpose so long as they also included a license or sobriety check." *Edmond*, 531 U.S. at 46, 121 S.Ct. at 457. "For this reason, [a court must] examine the available evidence to determine the primary purpose of the checkpoint program." *Edmond*, 531 U.S. at 46, 121 S.Ct. at 457.

In this regard, *Edmond* clearly indicates that, for purposes of proving the primary purpose of a checkpoint program, the testimony of a high ranking (*i.e.*, policy making) police official is required. *See Edmond*, 531 U.S. at 48, 121 S.Ct. at 457 ("we caution that the [primary] purpose inquiry . . . is to be conducted only at the programmatic level and is not an invitation to probe the minds of individual officers acting at the scene").

To prove that the primary purpose of a particular checkpoint was truly DWI-related, the "available evidence" should include testimony from a high-ranking police official responsible for establishing the operation and parameters of the checkpoint at a "programmatic level." It should also include documentary proof (such as statistics regarding the number of vehicles stopped, the average length of a stop, the number of vehicles pulled over for further scrutiny, the number of tickets issued, the number of arrests made, what the arrests were for, the types of evidence seized, the number of designated drivers observed, copies of literature handed out at the checkpoint, etc.).

Notably, the record in *Michigan Dept. of State Police v. Sitz*, 496 U.S. 444, 110 S. Ct. 2481, 110 L. Ed. 2d 412 (1990), contained proof regarding, inter alia, the duration of the checkpoint, how many vehicles passed through it, the average delay for each vehicle, the number of drivers detained for field sobriety testing, and the number of arrests. *Sitz*, 496 U.S. at 448, 110 S.Ct. at 2484. A critical issue in this regard appears to be whether the police *created* sufficient empirical data in connection with a checkpoint— *not* whether such empirical data demonstrates that the checkpoint was, in fact, effective. The reason is that, where suspicionless vehicle stops are concerned, appellate courts want to be able to judge police conduct based upon some proof other than "the self-verifying evidence from the officers whose conduct is being challenged." *In re Muhammad F.*, 94 N.Y.2d 136, 148, 700 N.Y.S.2d 77, 83–84, 722 N.E.2d 45 (1999).

While this is burdensome, it must be kept in mind (a) that checkpoint stops are presumptively unconstitutional, and (b) that the Supreme Court does not want such stops to become "a routine part of American life." In this regard, the *Edmond* court expressly "recognize[d] the challenges inherent in a [primary] purpose inquiry," but nonetheless found such inquiry necessary "as a means of sifting abusive governmental conduct from that which is lawful." 531 U.S. at 46–47, 121 S.Ct. at 457.

§ 5:8 Applying *Edmond*

Research References

West's Key Number Digest, Arrest ☞63.5(6); Automobiles ☞349(9)

The court of appeals applied *Edmond* in *People v. Jackson*, 99 N.Y.2d 125, 752 N.Y.S.2d 271, 782 N.E.2d 67 (2002). In *Jackson*, the court made clear that "[u]nder the holding in *City of Indianapolis*, the People have the burden of establishing that the primary *programmatic* objective (not the subjective intent of the participating officers) for initiating a suspicionless vehicle stop procedure was not merely to further general crime control." *Jackson*, 99 N.Y.2d at 131–32, 752 N.Y.S.2d at 275. The *Jackson* court thereafter concluded that "the roadblock stop of defendant's vehicle contravened the Fourth Amendment under the teaching of *City of Indianapolis v. Edmond*." *Jackson*, 99 N.Y.2d at 132, 752 N.Y.S.2d at 275.

In *People v. Trotter*, 28 A.D.3d 165, 810 N.Y.S.2d 610 (4th Dep't 2006), leave to appeal denied, 6 N.Y.3d 839, 814 N.Y.S.2d 87, 847

N.E.2d 384 (2006), the Appellate Division, Fourth Department, applying *Edmond*, affirmed the lower court's dismissal of the indictment on the ground that the checkpoint in question failed the "primary purpose" test. In so holding, the court noted that there was no other constitutional infirmity in the administration of the checkpoint. *Trotter*, 28 A.D.3d at __, 810 N.Y.S.2d at 614. In other words, the checkpoint would have satisfied *Scott*, *supra*. *See also People v. Pope*, 190 Misc. 2d 508, 738 N.Y.S.2d 543 (Bronx Co. Sup 2002), order aff'd, 303 A.D.3d 307, 755 N.Y.S.2d 843 (1st Dep't 2003) (checkpoint illegal under *Edmond*). *See generally Casalino Interior Demolition Corp. v. Martinez*, 29 A.D.3d 691, 814 N.Y.S.2d 720, 721–22 (2d Dep't 2006) (insufficient proof was submitted at DMV hearing to demonstrate that officers administering temporary weigh station were in fact stopping trucks in nondiscriminatory manner).

By contrast, in *People v. Dugan*, 57 A.D.3d 300, 869 N.Y.S.2d 57 (1st Dep't 2008), leave to appeal denied, 11 N.Y.3d 924, 874 N.Y.S.2d 9, 902 N.E.2d 443 (2009), the Appellate Division, First Department, upheld a checkpoint where:

> The police testimony satisfied the elements of a valid checkpoint stop. The testimony established that the primary purpose of the checkpoint was roadway safety and enforcement of vehicular laws and regulations rather than general crime control, that the checkpoint was effective in advancing those interests, and that the degree of intrusion on drivers' liberty and privacy interests was minimal. Furthermore, one of the officers testified that he kept a written record of the checkpoint stops that had taken place.

(Citations omitted).

In *People v. Cabrera*, 13 Misc. 3d 1205(A), 2006 WL 2572061, *2 (N.Y. City Crim. Ct. 2006), the Court cogently summarized the current state of the law in this area:

> In *Scott*, and more recently in *Matter of Muhammad F.* and *People v. Jackson*, the Court of Appeals discussed the constitutional requirements applicable to so-called police roadblocks or checkpoints. The guidelines more recently discussed in *Jackson* reflect the United States Supreme Court's own exhaustive review of the subject in *City of Indianapolis v. Edmond*, which built upon that Court's earlier decision in *Brown v. Texas*.
>
> All of these cases proceed from the initial premise that checkpoint stops come before the Court bearing a legal stigma of ostensibly violating the Fourth Amendment proscription against warrantless and suspicionless stops. In order to remove that stigma, the People bear the burden of proving at a suppression hearing that the particular checkpoint in question was conducted in a non-discretionary manner; that is, the officers actually conducting the checkpoint did so under rigid protocols formally set out by their superiors and that

the officers did not exercise individual discretion as to which cars to stop or what questions to ask. Additionally, however, in *Indianapolis v. Edmond*, supra, the United States Supreme Court made clear that the People's proof must also establish an articulable public safety concern that in the first instance justified utilization of a checkpoint at the particular chosen location. As the Court in *Jackson* put it, "the People have the burden of establishing that the primary programmatic objective (not the subjective intent of the officers) for initiating a suspicionless vehicle stop procedure was not merely to further general crime control."

(Citations omitted).

Similarly, in *People v. Perez-Correoso*, 48 Misc. 3d 839, __, 11 N.Y.S.3d 405, 412 (N.Y. City Crim. Ct. 2015), the Court stated that:

Federal and New York State precedents indicate that where evidence is recovered during a checkpoint stop, the People bear the burden of establishing: (1) that the primary purpose of the checkpoint was to address a legitimate law enforcement objective; (2) that the checkpoint was established at the programmatic level; (3) that the checkpoint was an effective means of meeting that objective; (4) that the checkpoint was administered in accordance with a uniform procedure which embodied "explicit, neutral limitations on the conduct of [the] individual officers involved"; (5) that the procedures employed at the checkpoint "did not intrude to an impermissible degree upon the privacy of motorists approaching the checkpoint"; and (6) that the checkpoint "provided adequate precautions as to safety, lighting and fair warning of the existence of the checkpoint's operation."

(Citations omitted). The Court went on to hold that these requirements were not satisfied.

§ 5:9   Necessity of pretrial hearing

In light of the fact that checkpoint stops are presumptively unconstitutional, *see, e.g., City of Indianapolis v. Edmond*, 531 U.S. 32, 121 S. Ct. 447, 148 L. Ed. 2d 333 (2000), and in light of the fact that the People are required to establish the validity of a checkpoint, *see, e.g., People v. Jackson*, 99 N.Y.2d 125, 131-32, 752 N.Y.S.2d 271, 275, 782 N.E.2d 67 (2002), it would seem that a pretrial hearing addressing this issue is literally required upon the defendant's mere claim that he or she was stopped at an illegal checkpoint. *See, e.g., U.S. v. Ramirez-Gonzalez*, 87 F.3d 712 (5th Cir. 1996) (district court was required to hold full evidentiary hearing to determine primary purpose of and need for checkpoint). Indeed, such a hearing was held in virtually every single published case which has addressed the issue of the lawfulness of a particular checkpoint.

Nonetheless, in *People v. Haskins*, 86 A.D.3d 794, 928 N.Y.S.2d

374 (3d Dep't 2011), leave to appeal denied, 17 N.Y.3d 903, 933 N.Y.S.2d 658, 957 N.E.2d 1162 (2011), the Appellate Division, Third Department, treated a suppression motion in a checkpoint case as if it were no different from any other suppression motion (*i.e.*, the Court held that the motion could be summarily denied without a hearing if the defendant's motion papers do not contain sufficient sworn factual allegations supporting the defendant's position). Notably, however, *Haskins* fails to address Supreme Court and Court of Appeals precedent which makes clear that a hearing is required where the defendant challenges the lawfulness of a checkpoint. *See, e.g., Edmond, supra; Jackson, supra.*

In any event, as the Court of Appeals made clear in *People v. Mendoza*, 82 N.Y.2d 415, 604 N.Y.S.2d 922, 624 N.E.2d 1017 (1993), the sufficiency of the factual allegations in a defendant's motion papers must be assessed in the context of, *inter alia*, the "defendant's access to information." 82 N.Y.2d at 426, 604 N.Y.S.2d at 926. In this regard, how could a defendant possibly be in a position to know whether the checkpoint that he or she was stopped at was established, set up and/or administered in compliance with, among other cases, *Edmond, Michigan Dept. of State Police v. Sitz*, 496 U.S. 444, 110 S. Ct. 2481, 110 L. Ed. 2d 412 (1990), and/or *People v. Scott*, 63 N.Y.2d 518, 483 N.Y.S.2d 649, 473 N.E.2d 1 (1984)? In other words, checkpoints present a situation where the defendant is unlikely to ever have sufficient access to information to meet the pleading requirements of CPL § 710.60(3)(b)—yet lack of access to information is a factor that the *Mendoza* Court expressly mandated must be taken into account. *Cf. People v. Edwards*, 95 N.Y.2d 486, 496, 719 N.Y.S.2d 202, 208, 741 N.E.2d 876 (2000) ("contrary to the Appellate Division, defendant was not required to make any threshold showing in order to be entitled to a *Darden* hearing. Obviously, it would be difficult, if not impossible, for a defendant to present evidence that a confidential informant did not exist or was unreliable. It was error for the Appellate Division to place a burden on defendant that he could not reasonably have been expected to meet") (citations omitted).

In addition, the *Edmond* Court expressly "recognize[d] the challenges inherent in a [primary] purpose inquiry," but nonetheless found that such an inquiry is necessary "as a means of sifting abusive governmental conduct from that which is lawful." 531 U.S. at 46-47, 121 S.Ct. at 457. This language clearly implies that a suppression hearing is literally required in checkpoint cases (*i.e.*, how can a Court conduct a "primary purpose inquiry" and "sift[] abusive governmental conduct from that which is lawful" without holding an evidentiary hearing?).

Similarly, the *Sitz* Court made clear that the police must compile "empirical data" which can be examined to determine a checkpoint's "effectiveness." 496 U.S. at 453-55, 110 S.Ct. at 2487-88. *See also In re Muhammad F.*, 94 N.Y.2d 136, 145, 146-47, 700 N.Y.S.2d 77, 81-82, 82-83, 722 N.E.2d 45 (1999). This is both (a) another Constitutional requirement that must be established by the People, and (b) information that the defendant would not have access to.

Part II

FIELD SOBRIETY TESTS

Chapter 6

Field Sobriety Tests

Research References

Westlaw Databases

Drinking/Driving Litigation: Criminal and Civil (2d ed.) (DRNKDRIVING)
Handling Drunk Driving Cases (2d ed.) (HDRUNKDR)
New York Vehicle and Traffic Law 2d (NYVEH)

Treatises and Practice Aids

Nichols and Whited, Drinking/Driving Litigation: Criminal and Civil §§ 17:1 to 17:19 (2d ed.)

Fiandach, Handling Drunk Driving Cases §§ 7:1 to 7:32 (2d ed.)
Rose, New York Vehicle and Traffic Law 2d § 35:21.50

KeyCite®: Cases and other legal materials listed in KeyCite Scope can be researched through the KeyCite service on Westlaw®. Use KeyCite to check citations for form, parallel references, prior and later history, and comprehensive citator information, including citations to other decisions and secondary materials.

---

§ 6:1 Nature of tests

Research References

West's Key Number Digest, Automobiles ☞411

In determining whether there is reasonable cause to believe that a person is driving while intoxicated, many police departments use "field sobriety tests." A suspect is requested to step from his vehicle and engage in a number of physical acts which are designed to test the person's coordination for the purpose of determining intoxication. The finger-to-nose, one-leg stand, walk-and-turn, finger count, alphabet, Romberg, and numerous other tests have become a common part of DWI arrest procedure. Motorists are generally cooperative and rarely refuse to participate in these tests.

§ 6:2 Validity and relevancy of tests

Research References

West's Key Number Digest, Automobiles ☞422.1, 424, 425

It is interesting to note that the issue of the validity and relevancy of field sobriety tests is rarely raised. Attorneys closely cross-examine the administration of the tests and their clients' performance. The validity of the tests as an indicator of intoxication, and the subjectivity of the judgment of the police officer, are far less commonly challenged.

In *People v. Frank L. Bevis, Jr.*, County Court, Broome County, (trial verdict on 6/28/96), County Court Judge Patrick H. Mathews gave the following charge to the jury:

In this case, the People offered testimony regarding, so called, field sobriety tests, on the issue of intoxication. I caution you there is no established scientific reliability regarding the degree to which, if any, these tests can in any particular case accurately determine whether an individual is under the influence of alcohol and, if so, to what extent. Intoxication has a legal definition as it relates to the crime of driving while intoxicated. The legal definition refers to the degree to which alcohol consumption has affected the physical and mental abilities of the driver as they relate to operating an automobile. To the extent the field sobriety tests, considering all the circumstances that might affect their performance, may or may not, in your opinion, reveal impaired ability in such things as coordination, reaction time, and mental functioning, they are a relevant factor to consider in determining the issue of intoxication. In this regard, however, I caution you there are a multitude of factors which might affect one's ability to perform any particular field sobriety test. You should consider these various factors in determining how much weight, if any, to give to the defendant's performance of field sobriety tests. Regarding the officer's opinion regarding the degree of the defendant's intoxication, you are free to accept or reject his opinion, for only the jury may ultimately determine the facts in this case. In evaluating the officer's opinion you should give it such weight as you believe it deserves based on your determination as to whether the facts he based his opinion on were fully established to your satisfaction; and all of the other evidence in this case.

In *People v. DiNonno*, 171 Misc. 2d 335, 659 N.Y.S.2d 390 (App. Term, 2d Dep't 1997), the court held that field sobriety tests:

[A]re not truly scientific in nature. Rather, they are based upon the indisputable fact that intoxication affects physical coordination and mental acuity and they are designed to enhance the ability of the officer who administers them to detect "unstable responses." Although their evaluation is necessarily to some extent subjective, so too are any of the ordinary indicia of intoxication and therefore this fact does not serve to preclude admissibility. Since the tests are not scientific in nature, proof of their acceptance in the scientific community is not required.

171 Misc. 2d at 335, 659 N.Y.S.2d at 390 (citation omitted). *See also People v. DeRojas*, 196 Misc. 2d 171, __ 763 N.Y.S.2d 386, 388 (App. Term, 2d Dep't 2003).

§ 6:3 Refusal to participate in field sobriety tests does not violate VTL

Research References

West's Key Number Digest, Automobiles ⚷413

A driver does not have to participate in field sobriety tests. Although a driver is deemed to have given consent to a "chemical test" for the purpose of determining intoxication pursuant to VTL § 1194(2), field sobriety tests are not chemical tests. Further, one of the bases for obtaining a chemical test is the existence of reasonable grounds to believe that the suspect driver has operated in violation of VTL § 1192. Field sobriety tests are used to develop those reasonable grounds. However, although there is no common law, nor statutory requirement to perform field sobriety tests; similarly, there is no statutory, nor common law prohibition against the introduction into evidence of a refusal to perform these tests. The prosecutor may attempt to introduce the refusal to perform these tests into evidence.

In *People v. Sheridan*, 192 A.D.2d 1057, 596 N.Y.S.2d 245 (4th Dep't 1993), the Appellate Division, Fourth Department, held that since "[t]here is no statutory or other requirement for the establishment of rules regulating field sobriety tests," the police are not required to inform a defendant that he or she has a right to refuse to perform such tests. 192 A.D.2d at 1059, 596 N.Y.S.2d at 245 to 46.

§ 6:4   Refusal to perform field sobriety tests as evidence

Research References

West's Key Number Digest, Automobiles ⊙➞413

Although a defendant is not obligated to perform field sobriety tests, *see* § 6:3, *supra*, the refusal to perform such tests may be admissible against him or her at trial. In *People v. Berg*, 92 N.Y.2d 701, 685 N.Y.S.2d 906 (1999), the Court of Appeals held that "evidence of defendant's refusal to submit to certain field sobriety tests [is] admissible in the absence of *Miranda* warnings . . . because the refusal was not compelled within the meaning of the Self-Incrimination Clause." 92 N.Y.2d at 703, 685 N.Y.S.2d at 907. On the other hand, the court noted that "the inference of intoxication arising from failure to complete the tests successfully 'is far stronger than that arising from a refusal to take the test.'" 92 N.Y.2d at 706, 685 N.Y.S.2d at 909 (citation omitted).

Similarly, in *People v. Powell*, 95 A.D.2d 783, ___, 463 N.Y.S.2d 473, 476 (2d Dep't 1983), the court held that:

> It is true that the admission into evidence of defendant's refusal to submit to the sobriety test here cannot be deemed a violation of his Federal or State privilege against self-incrimination on the basis that it was coerced . . . . There is no constitutional violation in so using defendant's refusal even if defendant was not specifically warned that it could be used against him at trial . . .

> [However,] though *admissible*, the defendant's refusal to submit to co-ordination tests in this case on the ground that they would be painful because of his war wounds was nevertheless of *limited probative value* in proving circumstantially that defendant would have failed the tests.

Notably, the *Powell* Court made clear that "'[t]his court has always recognized the ambiguity of evidence of flight and insisted that the jury be closely instructed as to its weakness as an indication of guilt of the crime charged' (*People v. Yazum*, 13 N.Y.2d 302, 304, 246 N.Y.S.2d 626, 196 N.E.2d 263)." 95 A.D.2d at 786, 463 N.Y.S.2d at 476.

§ 6:5   Description of tests

Research References

West's Key Number Digest, Automobiles ⊙➞422.1

After pulling a vehicle over, the officer will ask the driver to step out of the vehicle in order to perform field sobriety tests. The determination of intoxication, however, starts well before this. Initially, the officer will evaluate the odor of the driver's breath, condition of eyes, color of face, demeanor, dexterity, speech, and clothing. Although alcohol, itself, does not have an odor, the police are taught to sense the odor of alcoholic beverage coming from the vehicle. Because alcohol dilates the blood vessels, the eyes are examined to determine if they are bloodshot. Similarly, the face tends to flush as a result of dilation of the blood vessels.

As for demeanor, the officer is trained to note any changes in the driver's attitude. Although a request for the driver's license and registration is routine in most traffic stops, this provides the officer an opportunity to observe the driver's coordination and dexterity. The clarity and coherence of one's speech is affected by alcohol. Finally, police are trained to observe the driver's clothing. Although these initial observations may provide sufficient suspicion for arrest, the field sobriety tests are most often relied upon.

§ 6:6 The "standardized" field sobriety tests

Research References

West's Key Number Digest, Automobiles ⊸411

In recent years, there has been a national attempt to standardize the field sobriety tests used by police officers across the country. This effort has been spearheaded by the National Highway Traffic Safety Administration which has sponsored training throughout the country in the performance of these standardized field sobriety tests (SFST). The manual, "DWI Detection and Standardized Field Sobriety Testing" is the training manual used to provide this training.

The manual can be obtained from the National Technical Information Services at 5285 Port Royal Road, Springfield, Virginia 22161. The telephone number is (703) 487-4650. At seminars, I have been given the telephone number: 1-800-553-6847. The cost of the Teacher's Manual is $120; and $98 for the Student Manual. I have found little or no use for the Teacher's Manual, but the Student Manual has been invaluable in conducting cross-examinations.

The manual sets forth the protocol of three standardized field sobriety tests which have been recommended based upon research conducted for the National Highway Traffic Safety Administration by Dr. Marcelline Burns and Herbert Moskowitz. This research is set forth in "Psychophysical Tests for DWI"; June 1977 NHTSA Report No. DOT HS-HO2 424 (available from

National Technical Information Service, Springfield, Virginia 22161). The initial report was followed up with another report entitled "Development and Field Test of Psychophysical Tests for DWI Arrests," March 1981, NHTSA Report No. DOT HS-805 864 (available from NTIS, Springfield, Virginia 22161). This report was authored by V. Tharp, Dr. Marcelline Burns, and Herbert Moskowitz. An overview of these reports and their objective are set forth in Chapter VIII of the aforementioned student manual.

The result of this research was recognition and validation of three standardized field sobriety tests. These are horizontal gaze nystagmus, the walk-and-turn test, and the one-leg stand test. Insofar as other tests are concerned, the manual refers to the "alphabet test," "the countdown," which consists of counting backwards and the "finger count," which consists of having the defendant touch the tip of his or her thumb, in turn, to the tip of each finger on the same hand while simultaneously counting up—one, two, three, four; then reversing direction on the fingers while simultaneously counting down—four, three, two, one. Insofar as these tests are concerned, the manual states:

> These techniques are not as reliable as the standardized field sobriety tests but they can still be useful for obtaining evidence of impairment. These techniques should not replace the SFST.

SFST Manual, VI-4.

§ 6:7   The "validated" tests

Research References

West's Key Number Digest, Automobiles ⚍411

Horizontal Gaze Nystagmus, Walk-and-Turn and One-Leg Stand

We now consider the three tests validated by the government sponsored studies: horizontal gaze nystagmus, (hereinafter HGN), the walk-and-turn; and the one-leg stand:

> The three standardized tests were found to be highly reliable in identifying subjects whose BACs were 0.10 or more. Considered independently, the nystagmus test was 77% accurate, the Walk-and-Turn, 68% accurate, and the One-Leg Stand, 65% accurate. However, Horizontal Gaze Nystagmus used in combination with Walk-and-Turn, was 80% accurate.

SFST Manual, VIII-11.

At the outset, it is interesting to note two important things. First, even when these tests are perfectly performed, there is ample room for error. If the combination of tests is 80% accurate, it is also 20% inaccurate.

Secondly, these tests do not speak to "intoxication," they speak to the blood alcohol concentration of 0.10%. Since these tests are not performed with calibrated instruments and, since, the percentage range for error is unacceptable insofar as the determination of blood alcohol concentrations are concerned, conclusions based upon a defendant's performance of these tests should be objected to as inadmissible.

Standardized Field Sobriety Tests Must Be Administered Precisely as Taught

The SFSTs are as much a police competency test as they are a field sobriety test. The validity of the tests depends upon their being administered in exactly the manner set forth in the manual. Validation of the tests is completely dependent upon this precision in their administration:

> But it is also necessary to emphasize one final and major point. This validation applies *ONLY* **WHEN THE TESTS ARE ADMINISTERED IN THE PRESCRIBED, STANDARDIZED MANNER; AND** *ONLY* **WHEN THE STANDARDIZED CLUES ARE USED TO ASSESS THE SUSPECT'S PERFORMANCE; AND** *ONLY* **WHEN THE STANDARDIZED CRITERIA ARE EMPLOYED TO INTERPRET THAT PERFORMANCE.**
>
> **IF ANY ONE OF THE STANDARDIZED FIELD SOBRIETY TEST ELEMENTS IS CHANGED, THE VALIDITY IS COMPROMISED**.

SFST Manual, VIII-12.

§ 6:8 The horizontal gaze nystagmus test

Research References
West's Key Number Digest, Automobiles ⚬━411

§§ 8:1 et seq. provide a detailed description of this field sobriety test as well as the law pertaining to it.

§ 6:9 The walk-and-turn test

Research References
West's Key Number Digest, Automobiles ⚬━411

The walk-and-turn test is a field sobriety test based on the concept of divided attention, which requires the individual to divide his attention among mental tasks and physical tasks.

Essentially, the test requires a person to assume a heel to toe position placing their right heel against their left toe. The initial instructions call for the person to stand in that position while they receive instructions in regard to the performance of the test. They must stand there with their arms down at their side and must wait for the police officer to finish his or her instructions before they commence the test. After the person being tested is placed in this heel to toe position, they are given the following instructions:

- When I tell you to start, take nine heel-to-toe steps down the line, turn around, and take nine heel-to-toe steps back up the line. (Demonstrate 2 or 3 heel-to-toe steps.)
- When you turn, keep the front foot on the line, and turn by taking a series of small steps with the other foot, like this. (Demonstrate.)
- While you are walking, keep your arms at your sides, watch your feet at all times, and count your steps out loud.
- Once you start walking, don't stop until you have completed the test.
- Do you understand the instructions? (Make sure suspect understands.)
- Begin, and count your first step from the heel-to-toe position as "One." SFST Manual, VIII-19.

The test interpretation portion of the manual lists behaviors which are most likely to be observed in someone with a 0.10 or more blood alcohol concentration. These behaviors are:

A. Cannot keep balance while listening to the instructions. (Manual states that this clue should not be recorded unless the defendant fails to maintain the heel to toe position throughout the instructions. The clue should not be recorded if the suspect merely sways or uses his or her arms to balance, but maintains the heel to toe position.)

B. Starts before the instructions are finished.

C. Stops while walking to steady self.

D. Does not touch heel-to-toe.

E. Steps off the line.

F. Uses arms to balance.

G. Improper turn.

H. Incorrect number of steps. SFST Manual, VIII-20.

The officer is taught that:

If the suspect exhibits two or more distinct clues on this test or fails to complete it, classify the suspect's BAC as above 0.10. Using this criterion, you will be able to correctly classify about 68% of your suspects.

SFST Manual, VIII-21.

Test Conditions

The manual requires that the walk-and-turn test be performed on a designated straight line. My clients never seem to get the opportunity to perform this test on a real line. They are constantly being asked to walk along an imaginary line. The officer never specifies whether it is my client's imagination, or the officer's which governs. Inevitably, the client is graded off for stepping off the imaginary line. The fact that this manual requires a *visible* line is very helpful.

The manual states that:

Some people have difficulty with balance even when sober. The test criteria for Walk-and-Turn is not necessarily valid for suspects 65 years of age or older, persons with injuries to their legs, or persons with inner ear disorders. Individuals wearing heels more than 2 inches high should be given the opportunity to remove their shoes. Individuals who cannot see out of one eye may also have trouble with this test because of poor depth perception.

SFST Manual, VIII-21.

According to the Bureau for Municipal Police Manual, the individual is to walk heel-to-toe along a straight line, turn around in a prescribed fashion, and return in the same manner. The officer is only to conduct this test if there is a reasonably level and smooth surface and a visible straight line present. If there is not a straight line available, the officer may draw one on the pavement with chalk, or, to provide another "simple" field sobriety test, have the suspect draw the line.

Prior to having the defendant perform the test, the officer is required to determine if the defendant has any handicaps which would prevent proper performance of the test. Next, the individual is instructed to place her left foot on the line, and place her right foot ahead of the left, in heel-to-toe position. The subject is then instructed to place her arms down at her sides, and to maintain that position until the officer has completed instructions. According to the manual, this stance is not difficult for a sober person in reasonably good physical condition to maintain.

Next, the suspect is instructed to take nine heel-to-toe steps along the line, turn on the line, and return nine heel-to-toe steps, counting each step out loud. With regard to the turning procedure, after completion of the ninth step, the defendant is asked to keep her front foot on the line, and turn by taking several small steps with the other foot. Finally, the subject is instructed to watch her feet at all times, keeping her arms to her side, and continue walking without stopping until the test is completed.

The officers are trained to look for eight clues. The first two clues occur during the instruction stage. The officer observes whether the individual can maintain her balance and whether she starts too soon. With regard to the balance, the defendant fails only if her feet break apart.

While the individual is walking, the following four clues are checked. First, if the individual stops while walking, misses heel-to-toe, steps off the line, and/or uses her arms to balance, the officer is to note it. With regard to a heel-to-toe miss, a gap of at least one-half inch is required. Similarly, the driver must move an arm six inches or more from the side to fail the arms-at-side test.

With regard to the turn, the officer looks to determine if the individual staggers, stumbles, falls, or turns in any way other than instructed. Next, the driver must take the requested number of steps. Interestingly, an individual who takes the correct number of steps, but errs in the verbal count, has not failed this portion of the test. Finally, the officer records "can't do test at all" if the suspect steps off the line three or more times, falls, or crosses her legs and is unable to move.

If the person exhibits at least two out of the possible eight clues, the BMP Manual instructs that the implication is that she has a 0.10 or higher BAC. If the person exhibits zero or one clue, the implication is that she has a BAC less than .10. Using these guidelines, this test is considered 68% reliable.

§ 6:10   The one-leg stand test

Research References

West's Key Number Digest, Automobiles ⊙411, 422.1

This test requires the suspect to stand on one leg and count in accordance with the instructions of the officer. The suspect is told initially to stand with their feet together and their arms down at their sides and to listen to the instructions. They are told not to start to perform the test until told to do so. The following instructions are then given to the suspect:

- When I tell you to start, raise one leg, either leg, approximately six inches off the ground, toes pointed out. (Demonstrate one leg stance.)
- You must keep both legs straight, arms at your side.
- While holding that position, count out loud for thirty seconds in the following manner: "one thousand and one, one thousand and two, until told to stop." (Demonstrate a count as follows: "one thousand and one, one thousand and two, etc." Officer should not look at his foot when conducting the demonstration—OFFICER SAFETY.)
- Keep your arms at your sides at all times and keep watching the raised foot.
- Do you understand? (Make sure suspect indicates misunderstanding.)
- Go ahead and perform the test. (Officer should always time the 30 seconds. Test should be discontinued after 30 seconds.)

• Observe the suspect from at least 3 feet away. If the suspect puts the foot down, give instructions to pick the foot up again and continue counting from the point at which the foot touched the ground. If the suspect counts very slowly, terminate the test after 30 seconds. If the suspect is counting quickly, have the suspect continue counting until told to stop. SFST Manual, VIII-23.

The officer is to look for the following clues:

A. *The suspect sways while balancing.* This refers to side-to-side or back-and-forth motion while the suspect maintains the one-leg stand position.

B. *Uses arms for balance.* Suspect moves arms 6 or more inches from the side of the body in order to keep balance.

C. *Hopping.* Suspect is able to keep one foot off the ground, but resorts to hopping in order to maintain balance.

D. *Puts foot down.* The suspect is not able to maintain the one-leg stand position, putting the foot down one or more times during the 30-second count.

Note: If suspect cannot do test or puts foot down three or more times, record as if all four clues were observed. Consideration should be given to terminating the test if the suspect cannot safely complete it.

Remember that time is critical in this test. Research has shown that a person with a BAC above 0.10 can maintain balance for up to 25 seconds, but seldom as long as 30.

If an individual shows two or more clues or fails to complete the One-Leg Stand, there is a good chance the BAC is above 0.10. Using that criterion, you will correctly classify about 65% of the people you test as to whether their BAC's are above or below 0.10.

Observe the suspect from at least 3 feet away, and remain as motionless as possible during the test so as not to interfere. If the suspect puts the foot down, give instructions to pick the foot up again and continue counting from the point at which the foot touched the ground. If the suspect counts very slowly, terminate the test after 30 seconds. If the suspect is counting quickly, have the suspect continue counting until 30 seconds have elapsed. SFST Manual, VIII-24.

The manual requires that the test be administered on a reasonably level and smooth surface with adequate lighting to provide the suspect with a visual frame of reference. The manual cautions that some people have difficulty with the one-leg stand even when sober. It states that the test criterion is not necessarily valid for people 65 years of age or older, or 50 pounds or more overweight. In addition, people with injuries to their legs, or inner ear disorders, may have difficulty with the test. Again, individuals having heels more than two inches high are to be given the opportunity to remove their shoes. SFST Manual, VIII-25.

With the one-leg stand, the State Police are to instruct the suspect to stand erect, feet together, arms at side, and to raise his or her foot forward approximately six to 12 inches off the ground without bending the leg at the knee. The driver then counts a certain number of seconds without putting her foot down.

In addition to the foregoing instructions, the BMP Manual requires the individual to keep the toes on her raised foot pointed down, raise the foot six inches, count out loud for 30 seconds, and to watch the raised foot at all times.

While the New York State Police Manual merely instructs the officer to describe whether the individual was sure, wobbling, needs support, and/or falling, the BMP Manual sets forth four "clues" for this test. The first clue is swaying. Swaying is defined as a very distinct, very noticeable side-to-side or front-to-back movement of the elevated foot or the suspect's body. Slight tremors of the foot or body are not considered swaying. Next, a movement of the arms six inches or more from the side is a clue. The third clue is hopping. Lastly, if the individual puts her foot down prior to 30 seconds, this clue is noted. However, because some suspects count slowly, the individual's placing the foot down after 30 seconds is not a clue. Where the person exhibits at least two of the four possible clues, the implication is that the individual has a BAC of .10 or more. Where the person exhibits zero or one clue, the implication is that the BAC is below 0.10%. Using these factors, this test is deemed 65% reliable.

§ 6:11   The "non"-standardized field sobriety tests—The Romberg test

Research References

West's Key Number Digest, Automobiles ☞411, 422.1

The Romberg test is used to determine balance. The New York State Police are trained to have the suspect stand at "attention" position, heels and toes together, arms at side, head tilted back and eyes closed for approximately 10 seconds. The officer looks for excessive body sway. As with most of these tests, the acceptable amount of body sway is subjective.

Pursuant to the Impaired Driver Recognition Program conducted by the Bureau of Municipal Police (BMP) of the Division of Criminal Justice Services, the officer asks the driver to stand with feet together and hands down at sides. The driver is told to listen to the instructions and not to begin until the officer says so. He is then instructed to close his eyes, tilt his head slightly back, and estimate 30 seconds. When the individual believes 30 seconds has passed, the individual is to open his eyes and say, "Now." While conducting the test, the officer checks his watch and moves about to determine if the subject sways from side to side, forward and back, or circular. A time period of 25 to 35 seconds is considered passing. If the subject fails to open his eyes within 90 seconds, the test is stopped.

§ 6:12 The finger-to-nose test

Research References

West's Key Number Digest, Automobiles ☞411, 422.1

With the finger-to-nose test, the State Police Manual and BMP Manual state that the suspect is instructed to stand erect with feet together, eyes closed, arms stretched out to the side at shoulder height, with the index finger of each hand extended. Then, the suspect is instructed to touch the tip of her nose with the tip of her finger by swinging the arm in at the elbow. The process is then repeated for the other hand. The officer may alter the test by requesting the individual to bring her arms up from her side.

The BMP Manual instructs the officer to observe whether the subject actually touches the tip of her finger to the tip of her nose, brings her arms down immediately; and follows directions as to which hand to use. The New York State Police Manual instructs the officer to determine if the driver followed instructions and, whether the individual, when attempting the test, was sure, uncertain, and/or missed.

§ 6:13 The alphabet test

Research References

West's Key Number Digest, Automobiles ☞411, 422.1

The alphabet test may come in various forms. The New York State Police are trained to ask the driver to repeat aloud the alphabet from A to Z. Often, this test is modified with the subject instructed to start with a letter other than A and/or stopping with a letter other than Z.

The Municipal Police are instructed to ask the person if she knows the alphabet. Upon receiving an affirmative answer, the individual is asked to recite the alphabet out loud, starting with the letter the officer picks. After the individual stops or misses letters, the officer asks her, "Are you done?" The officer is taught to make a note of the type of speech the individual has.

§ 6:14 Mitigation

Research References

West's Key Number Digest, Automobiles ☞411, 422.1

While the prosecutor will point out the specific aspects of the test that the defendant failed, defense counsel can focus in on the areas of the test which the driver performed satisfactorily. For example, while the driver may not have touched the tip of her nose while performing the finger-to-nose test, the driver may have stood erect with feet together, kept eyes closed at all times, stretched her arms out to the side at shoulder height, extended the index finger of each hand, and properly swung her arm in at the elbow. The driver's failure to touch the exact tip of her nose may appear less severe in view of her satisfactory completion of the remainder of the test. Further, defense counsel may point out, where applicable, that the defendant was commanded to perform these tests on a graded, rocky side of a busy highway, while neighbors were driving by, police car lights flashing, and in the general state of fear one experiences when being pulled over by a uniformed police officer in a marked police car.

§ 6:15   Field sobriety tests and the Fifth Amendment

Research References

West's Key Number Digest, Automobiles ⚬➞411

The Fifth Amendment of the United States Constitution provides that no person "shall be compelled in any criminal case to be a witness against himself." It is well-settled that, in the absence of *Miranda* warnings, or an exception thereto, a court must suppress any verbal statements of a defendant that are both (1) communicative or testimonial in nature, and (2) elicited during custodial interrogation. *See Pennsylvania v. Muniz*, 496 U.S. 582, 590, 110 S.Ct. 2638, 2644 (1990).

§ 6:16   Is the defendant in custody?

Research References

West's Key Number Digest, Automobiles ⚬➞411

In many cases it will be clear that the defendant is in custody at the time that he or she is requested to submit to field sobriety tests. For example, the defendant in *Muniz* was asked to perform such tests both at a roadside stop and later after he was arrested and transported back to the police station. On the other hand, in *Berkemer v. McCarty*, 468 U.S. 420, 104 S.Ct. 3138 (1984), the Supreme Court made clear that, although the protections of *Miranda* apply to misdemeanor traffic offenses, persons detained during "ordinary" or "routine" traffic stops are not "in custody" for purposes of *Miranda*. *See also Pennsylvania v. Bruder*, 488 U.S. 9, 109 S.Ct. 205 (1988).

However, in both *Berkemer* and *Bruder* the court made clear that it "did not announce an absolute rule for all motorist detentions, observing that lower courts must be vigilant that police do not 'delay formally arresting detained motorists, and . . . subject them to sustained and intimidating interrogation at the scene of their initial detention.' " *Bruder*, 488 U.S. at 10 n.1, 109 S.Ct. at 207 n.1 (quoting *Berkemer*). In other words, "[i]f a motorist who has been detained pursuant to a traffic stop thereafter is subjected to treatment that renders him 'in custody' for practical purposes, he will be entitled to the full panoply of protections prescribed by *Miranda*." *Berkemer,* 468 U.S. at 440, 104 S.Ct. at 3150.

§ 6:17 Is the defendant subjected to custodial interrogation?

Research References

West's Key Number Digest, Automobiles ⚷411

The United States Supreme Court has made clear that the critical issue in determining whether a defendant was subjected to custodial interrogation is whether, while in custody, he or she was asked any questions, or given any instructions, that were "likely to be perceived as calling for [a] verbal response." *Muniz*, 496 U.S. at 603, 110 S.Ct. at 2651. "Thus, custodial interrogation for purposes of *Miranda* includes both express questioning and words or actions that . . . the officer knows or reasonably should know are likely to 'have . . . the force of a question on the accused,' and therefore be reasonably likely to elicit an incriminating response." 496 U.S. at 601, 110 S.Ct. at 2650 (citation omitted). This is true regardless of whether the verbal response is itself "testimonial or communicative" in nature. *See* 496 U.S. at 603 n.17, 110 S.Ct. at 2651 n.17.

Thus, a request that a DWI suspect who is in police custody (a) count during the "walk-and-turn" and "one-leg stand" field sobriety tests, or (b) perform the "alphabet" field sobriety test, constitutes custodial interrogation. *See* 496 U.S. at 603 n.17, 110 S.Ct. at 2651 n.17 ("Muniz's counting at the officer's request qualifies as a response to custodial interrogation"); *Bruder*, 488 U.S. at 11 n.3, 109 S.Ct. at 207 n.3 ("We thus do not reach the issue whether recitation of the alphabet *in response to custodial questioning* is testimonial and hence inadmissible under *Miranda v. Arizona*") (emphasis added).

Similarly, asking a DWI suspect who is in police custody the question "Do you know what the date was of your sixth birthday?" constitutes custodial interrogation. *Muniz*, 496 U.S. at 598–99, 110 S.Ct. at 2649. Indeed, the Supreme Court has made clear that, where a defendant is in police custody, even pedigree questions constitute custodial interrogation. 496 U.S. at 601, 110 S.Ct. at 2650 ("We disagree with the Commonwealth's contention that Officer Hosterman's first seven questions regarding Muniz's name, address, height, weight, eye color, date of birth, and current age do not qualify as custodial interrogation").

By contrast, in *People v. Berg*, 92 N.Y.2d 701, 685 N.Y.S.2d 906 (1999), the Court of Appeals held that "evidence of defendant's *refusal* to submit to certain field sobriety tests [is] admissible in the absence of *Miranda* warnings . . . because the refusal was not compelled within the meaning of the Self-Incrimination Clause." 92 N.Y.2d at 703, 685 N.Y.S.2d at 907 (emphasis added). Stated another way, the court held that "defendant's refusal to perform the field sobriety tests was not compelled, and therefore was not the product of custodial interrogation." 92 N.Y.2d at 704, 685 N.Y.S.2d at 908. *See also People v. Powell*, 95 A.D.2d 783, ___, 463 N.Y.S.2d 473, 476 (2d Dep't 1983).

§ 6:18 Are defendant's responses to field sobriety tests "testimonial or communicative" in nature?

Research References

West's Key Number Digest, Automobiles ⬤411

In *Schmerber v. California*, 384 U.S. 757, 761, 86 S.Ct. 1826, 1830 (1966), the supreme court held that the Fifth Amendment protects a defendant only from being compelled to either testify against himself or herself "or otherwise provide the State with evidence of a testimonial or communicative nature." *See also People v. Hager*, 69 N.Y.2d 141, 142, 512 N.Y.S.2d 794, 795 (1987) ("Evidence is 'testimonial or communicative' when it reveals a person's subjective knowledge or thought processes"). In *Pennsylvania v. Bruder*, 488 U.S. 9, 11 n.3, 109 S.Ct. 205, 207 n.3 (1988), the court expressly left unanswered the question of whether a person's response to the alphabet field sobriety test is "testimonial."

Two years later, in *Pennsylvania v. Muniz*, 496 U.S. 582, 110 S.Ct. 2638 (1990) the court addressed the issue of "whether various incriminating utterances of a drunken-driving suspect, made while performing a series of sobriety tests, constitute testimonial responses. . . ." 496 U.S. at 584, 110 S.Ct. at 2641. The court stated that " 'in order to be testimonial, an accused's communication must itself, explicitly or implicitly, relate a factual assertion or disclose information.' " 496 U.S. at 594, 110 S.Ct. at 2646 (quoting *Doe v. United States*, 487 U.S. 201, 210, 108 S.Ct. 2341, 2347 (1988)).

"Whenever a suspect is asked for a response requiring him to communicate an express or implied assertion of fact or belief, the suspect confronts the 'trilemma' of truth, falsity, or silence, and hence the response (whether based on truth or falsity) contains a testimonial component." 496 U.S. at 597, 110 S.Ct. at 2648 (footnote omitted).

> Whatever else it may include, therefore, the definition of "testimonial" evidence articulated in *Doe* must encompass all responses to questions that, if asked of a sworn suspect during a criminal trial, could place the suspect in the "cruel trilemma." This conclusion is consistent with our recognition in *Doe* that *"[t]he vast majority of verbal statements thus will be testimonial"* because *"[t]here are very few instances in which a verbal statement, either oral or written, will not convey information or assert facts."*

496 U.S. at 596–97, 110 S.Ct. at 2648 (emphasis added) (citation omitted).

Under this definition, the court held that Muniz's response to the question "Do you know what the date was of your sixth birthday?" was testimonial:

> When Officer Hosterman asked Muniz if he knew the date of his sixth birthday and Muniz, for whatever reason, could not remember or calculate that date, he was confronted with the trilemma . . . Muniz was left with the choice of incriminating himself by admitting that he did not then know the date of his sixth birthday, or answering untruthfully by reporting a date that he did not then believe to be accurate (an incorrect guess would be incriminating as well as untruthful). The content of his truthful answer supported an inference that his mental faculties were impaired, because his assertion (he did not know the date of his sixth birthday) was different from the assertion (he knew the date was (correct date)) that the trier of fact might reasonably have expected a lucid person to provide. Hence, the incriminating inference of impaired mental faculties stemmed, not just from the fact that Muniz slurred his response, but also from a testimonial aspect of that response.

496 U.S. at 598–99, 110 S.Ct. at 2649.

Thus, *Muniz* makes clear that responses to questions designed to demonstrate a lack of "lucid thinking" are testimonial in nature, precisely because they convey information with regard to a person's subjective thought processes. Nonetheless, the court expressly left open the question of whether a request that a person "count aloud from one to nine while performing the 'walk-and-turn' test and that he count aloud from one to 30 while balancing during the 'one-leg stand' test" calls for a "testimonial" response. 496 U.S. at 603 n.17, 110 S.Ct. at 2651 n.17.

However, in *People v. Berg*, 92 N.Y.2d 701, 685 N.Y.S.2d 906 (1999), the Court of Appeals stated, in dicta, that:

> Reciting the alphabet and counting are not testimonial or communicative because these acts do not require a person to reveal

knowledge of facts relating to the offense or to share thoughts and beliefs with the government. Instead, these tests attempt to determine whether alcohol has impaired the reflexive process by which the alphabet and numbers are recalled from memory and spoken.

92 N.Y.2d at 705, 685 N.Y.S.2d at 909. *See also People v. Hasenflue*, 252 A.D.2d 829, __, 675 N.Y.S.2d 464, 466 (3d Dep't 1998); *People v. Turner*, 234 A.D.2d 704, __, 651 N.Y.S.2d 655, 657 (3d Dep't 1996).

Similarly, *Miranda* warnings are not required to be given to a DWI suspect prior to the administration of physical performance tests:

> Physical performance tests do not reveal a person's subjective knowledge or thought processes but, rather, exhibit a person's degree of physical coordination for observation by police officers. The defendant's responses to those tests in this case indicated he had imbibed alcohol, not because the tests revealed defendant's thoughts, but because his body's responses differed from those of a sober person (*see People v. Boudreau*, 115 A.D.2d 652, 654, 496 N.Y.S.2d 489). We conclude, therefore, the *Miranda* warnings were not required to be given to defendant prior to the administration of the performance tests.

People v. Hager, 69 N.Y.2d 141, 142, 512 N.Y.S.2d 794, 795 (1987). *See also People v. Berg*, 92 N.Y.2d 701, 703, 705, 685 N.Y.S.2d 906, 907, 908–09 (1999); *People v. Jacquin*, 71 N.Y.2d 825, 826, 527 N.Y.S.2d 728, 729 (1988) ("Performance tests need not be preceded by *Miranda* warnings and, generally an audio/visual tape of such tests, including any colloquy between the test-giver and the defendant *not constituting custodial interrogation*, is admissible") (emphasis added); *People v. Dougal*, 266 A.D.2d 574, __, 698 N.Y.S.2d 66, 69 (3d Dep't 1999); *People v. Villeneuve*, 232 A.D.2d 892, __, 649 N.Y.S.2d 80, 83 (3d Dep't 1996). *See generally Muniz*, 496 U.S. at 592, 110 S.Ct. at 2645 ("Under *Schmerber* and its progeny, . . . any slurring of speech and other evidence of lack of muscular coordination revealed by Muniz's responses to Officer Hosterman's direct questions constitute nontestimonial components of those responses").

Berg does expressly leave open one question in this regard— "While the *results* of the field sobriety tests defendant was asked to perform are not testimonial or communicative, we do not in this case address whether defendant's *refusal* to perform the tests was also nontestimonial." 92 N.Y.2d at 705, 685 N.Y.S.2d at 909.

§ 6:19 Constitutionality of NYPD's policy of only offering field sobriety tests to English-speaking DWI suspects

The New York City Police Department apparently has a policy of only offering field sobriety tests to English-speaking DWI suspects. The policy has been challenged on both Equal Protection and Due Process grounds. In *People v. Salazar*, 112 A.D.3d 5, __, 973 N.Y.S.2d 140, 141-142 (1st Dep't 2013), leave to appeal denied, 22 N.Y.3d 1090, 981 N.Y.S.2d 676, 4 N.E.3d 978 (2014), the Appellate Division, First Department, held that "the failure of the police to administer a physical coordination test to a non-English speaking defendant of Hispanic origin arrested for driving while intoxicated [does not] violate equal protection [or] due process [even though] such tests are routinely administered to English-speaking defendants."

Salazar resolved a conflict amongst the lower Courts. *Compare People v. Perez*, 27 Misc. 3d 880, 898 N.Y.S.2d 402 (Bronx Co. Sup. Ct. 2010), *People v. Burnet*, 24 Misc. 3d 292, 882 N.Y.S.2d 835 (Bronx Co. Sup. Ct. 2009), and *People v. Perez*, 27 Misc. 3d 880, 898 N.Y.S.2d 402 (Bronx Co. Sup. Ct. 2010) (holding policy Constitutional), *with People v. Garcia-Cepero*, 22 Misc. 3d 490, 874 N.Y.S.2d 689 (Bronx Co. Sup. Ct. 2008), and *People v. Molina*, 25 Misc. 3d 362, 887 N.Y.S.2d 784 (Bronx Co. Sup. Ct. 2009) (holding policy unconstitutional).

§ 6:20 Permissibility of playing video of field sobriety tests where officer who administered tests is unavailable

In *People v. Scullion*, 137 A.D.3d 645, __, 29 N.Y.S.3d 24, 25 (1st Dep't 2016), leave to appeal denied, 27 N.Y.3d 1139, 2016 WL 3768027 (2016), the Appellate Division, First Department, held as follows:

> The court properly exercised its discretion in admitting a videotape of defendant performing coordination tests. Although the police officer who administered the tests did not testify, the videotape was authenticated by the arresting officer, who was a witness to the recorded events. Since no testimony was elicited regarding the conclusion to be drawn from the tests, or what the person administering the tests looked for in determining whether or not the arrestee was intoxicated, the reliability of the tests and whether the officer utilized the proper protocols in administering the tests were not in issue. Instead, the video was admitted solely to show how defendant appeared on the night of his arrest.

(Citation omitted).

Chapter 7

Alco-Sensor—The Breath Screening Test

Research References

Westlaw Databases

Handling Drunk Driving Cases (2d ed.) (HDRUNKDR)
Intoxication Test Evidence (2d ed.) (INTOX)

Treatises and Practice Aids

Fiandach, Handling Drunk Driving Cases §§ 7:26, 7:31 (2d ed.)
Fitzgerald, Intoxication Test Evidence §§ 54:1 to 54:48 (2d ed.)

§ 7:1 In general

Research References

West's Key Number Digest, Automobiles ☞411

In the field of New York DWI law, the phrase "breath test" refers to a preliminary test of a DWI suspect's breath for the presence or absence of alcohol using a preliminary breath screening device (commonly referred to as a PBT). By contrast, the phrase "chemical test" is the term used to describe a test of the alcoholic and/or drug content of a DWI suspect's blood using an instrument other than a PBT. In other words, BAC tests conducted utilizing breath testing instruments, such as the Breathalyzer, DataMaster, Intoxilyzer, Alcotest, etc., are referred to as "chemical tests," *not* "breath tests."

The most common type of breath screening test is an Alco-Sensor test. An Alco-Sensor is a portable, pocket-sized device that many police officers keep in their cars while on patrol. It is generally used to help establish probable cause for a DWI arrest and/or to rule out the use of alcohol in a suspected DWAI Drugs case. The Alco-Sensor test is usually the last "field test" administered to the suspect at the scene prior to his or her arrest.

Although breath screening devices generate numerical test results, the devices have typically not been considered sufficiently accurate or reliable for such results to be admissible at trial. *See* § 7:8, infra. Essentially, breath screening devices have been found to be reliable for determining the presence or absence of alcohol in a person's breath, but not for determining the person's actual blood alcohol concentration. *See, e.g.*, Carrieri, Practice Commentaries, McKinney's Cons. Laws of N.Y., Book 62A, VTL § 1194, at 91 ("Th[e] screening or breath test machine is used as a pass/fail test and is basically reliable for the determination of some presence of alcohol in a person's blood but not the actual percentage or concentration"); *People v. Jones*, 10 Misc. 3d 413, __, 805 N.Y.S.2d 807, 809 (Dutchess Co. Ct. 2005), aff'd, 50 A.D.3d 1058, 856 N.Y.S.2d 225 (2d Dep't 2008). As a result, breath screening devices are used as the name implies: to screen a DWI suspect's breath to determine whether he or she has consumed alcohol.

§ 7:2 Statutory authority for breath screening tests

Research References

West's Key Number Digest, Automobiles ☞412

As is noted in the previous section, in the field of New York DWI law, the phrase "breath test" refers to a breath screening test conducted in the "field" using a device such as an Alco-Sensor—not to a "chemical test" of the suspect's breath conducted at the police station utilizing a breath testing instrument such as the Breathalyzer, DataMaster, Intoxilyzer, Alcotest, etc. The statutory authorization for breath screening tests is found in VTL § 1194(1)(b) (formerly VTL § 1193-a), which provides as follows:

(b) Field testing. Every person operating a motor vehicle which has been involved in an accident or which is operated in violation of any of the provisions of [the VTL] shall, at the request of a police officer, submit to a breath test to be administered by the police officer. If such test indicates that such operator has consumed alcohol, the police officer may request such operator to submit to a chemical test in the manner set forth in [VTL § 1194(2)].

VTL § 1194(1)(b) makes clear that a person is under no obligation to submit to a breath screening test unless he or she has either (a) operated a motor vehicle which has been involved in an accident, or (b) operated a motor vehicle in violation of any of the provisions of the VTL. Thus, for example, a motorist found sleeping in a lawfully parked vehicle is under no obligation to submit to a breath screening test.

§ 7:3 Use of breath screening test as a probable cause substitute

Research References

West's Key Number Digest, Automobiles ⊘411

VTL § 1194(2) governs the field of chemical testing. Pursuant to this statute, either a lawful VTL § 1192 arrest or a positive result from a lawfully requested breath screening test is a prerequisite to a valid request that a DWI suspect submit to a chemical test (if the suspect is 21 years of age or older). In this regard, VTL § 1194(2)(a) provides, in pertinent part:

2. Chemical tests. (a) When authorized. Any person who operates a motor vehicle in this state shall be deemed to have given consent to a chemical test of one or more of the following: breath, blood, urine, or saliva, for the purpose of determining the alcoholic and/or drug content of the blood provided that such test is administered by or at the direction of a police officer with respect to a chemical test of breath, urine or saliva or, with respect to a chemical test of blood, at the direction of a police officer:

(1) having reasonable grounds to believe such person to have been operating in violation of any subdivision of [VTL § 1192] and within two hours after such person has been placed under arrest for any such violation; or . . .

(2) *within two hours after a breath test, as provided in [VTL § 1194(1)(b)], indicates that alcohol has been consumed by such person* and in accordance with the rules and regulations established by the police force of which the officer is a member.

(Emphasis added).

Thus, pursuant to a plain reading of this statute, a positive breath screening test can be used to request that a DWI suspect submit to a chemical test even in the absence of probable cause to believe that the suspect violated VTL § 1192. However, courts have expressed serious reservations as to the constitutionality of the statute if it were applied in this manner. *See* § 7:6, *infra*. In practice, breath screening tests are used to *help establish* probable cause for a DWI suspect's arrest, not as a probable cause substitute (so this issue rarely arises).

§ 7:4 Duty of police to conduct breath screening test

Research References

West's Key Number Digest, Automobiles ☞411

In *Arizona v. Youngblood*, 488 U.S. 51, 58, 109 S.Ct. 333, 337 (1988), the Supreme Court held that "unless a criminal defendant can show bad faith on the part of the police, failure to preserve potentially useful evidence does not constitute a denial of due process of law." In so holding, the Court reasoned that:

If the [lower] court meant . . . that the Due Process Clause is violated when the police fail to use a particular investigatory tool, we strongly disagree. *The situation here is no different than a prosecution for drunken driving that rests on police observation alone; the defendant is free to argue to the finder of fact that a breathalyzer test might have been exculpatory, but the police do not have a constitutional duty to perform any particular tests.*

488 U.S. at 58 to 59, 109 S.Ct. at 338 (emphasis added).

In *People v. Winchell*, 250 A.D.2d 942, __, 673 N.Y.S.2d 474, 476 (3d Dep't 1998), "[d]efendant contend[ed] that police investigators were obligated to preserve evidence which might have been useful to his [intoxication] defense and that their failure to perform an alco-sensor, breathalyzer or blood sample test hindered such efforts, thereby denying him due process of law." In rejecting defendant's claim, the Appellate Division, Third Department, found it to be:

Critically important . . . that defendant was not arrested for any intoxication-related offense, thereby relieving any investigative obligation to scientifically determine his blood alcohol content. Under the requisite "bad faith" analysis, no denial of due process can be predicated upon a failure of police agencies to acquire evidence deemed unnecessary to their prosecution.

250 A.D.2d at __, 673 N.Y.S.2d at 476.

§ 7:5 The Alco-Sensor test and the Fifth Amendment

Research References

West's Key Number Digest, Automobiles ☞411, 412

The Fifth Amendment to the United States Constitution provides that no person "shall be compelled in any criminal case to be a witness against himself." In *Schmerber v. California*, 384 U.S. 757, 761, 86 S.Ct. 1826, 1830 (1966), the Supreme Court held that the Fifth Amendment protects a defendant "only from being compelled to testify against himself, or otherwise provide the State with evidence of a testimonial or communicative nature," as opposed to "real or physical" evidence. *See also People v. Kates*, 53 N.Y.2d 591, 594, 444 N.Y.S.2d 446, 448 (1981); *People v. Thomas*, 46 N.Y.2d 100, 106, 412 N.Y.S.2d 845, 848 (1978); *People v. Craft*, 28 N.Y.2d 274, 276, 321 N.Y.S.2d 566, 568 (1971).

In this regard, a DWI suspect's breath sample does not constitute "evidence of a testimonial or communicative nature," and thus, the Alco-Sensor test does not implicate the *Fifth Amendment*. *People v. Brockum*, 88 A.D.2d 697, __, 451 N.Y.S.2d 326, 327 (3d Dep't 1982). *See also People v. Johnson*, 134 Misc. 2d 474, __, 511 N.Y.S.2d 773, 774 (N.Y. City Crim. Ct. 1987); *People v. Pecora*, 123 Misc. 2d 259, __, 473 N.Y.S.2d 320, 321–22 (Wappinger Just. Ct. 1984); *People v. Graser*, 90 Misc. 2d 219, __, 393 N.Y.S.2d 1009, 1014 (Amherst Just. Ct. 1977). *Cf. People v. Hamza*, 109 Misc. 2d 1055, __, 441 N.Y.S.2d 579, 581 (Gates Just. Ct. 1981); *People v. Delaney*, 83 Misc. 2d 576, __, 373 N.Y.S.2d 477, 480 (Nassau Co. Dist. Ct. 1975).

§ 7:6 The Alco-Sensor test and the Fourth Amendment

Research References

West's Key Number Digest, Automobiles ☞411, 412

Obtaining a breath sample from a DWI suspect for alcohol analysis constitutes a "search" within the meaning of the Fourth Amendment. *See Skinner v. Railway Labor Executives' Ass'n*, 489 U.S. 602, 616–17, 109 S.Ct. 1402, 1413 (1989). *See also Schmerber v. California*, 384 U.S. 757, 767, 86 S.Ct. 1826, 1834 (1966); *People v. Johnson*, 134 Misc. 2d 474, __, 511 N.Y.S.2d 773, 774 (N.Y. City Crim. Ct. 1987); *People v. McMillan*, 112 Misc. 2d 901, __, 447 N.Y.S.2d 626, 629 (Monroe Co. Ct. 1982). As such, submission to an Alco-Sensor test cannot lawfully be required in the absence of probable cause. *See People v. Pecora*, 123 Misc. 2d 259,

__, 473 N.Y.S.2d 320, 322 (Wappinger Just. Ct. 1984). *See generally People v. Kates*, 53 N.Y.2d 591, 594–95, 444 N.Y.S.2d 446, 448 (1981); *People v. Brockum*, 88 A.D.2d 697, __, 451 N.Y.S.2d 326, 327 (3d Dep't 1982).

Thus, ironically, although the People generally attempt to use the Alco-Sensor test to help *establish* probable cause for a DWI suspect's arrest, it is arguable that probable cause must already exist before an Alco-Sensor test can lawfully be requested. In this regard, in *People v. Brockum*, 88 A.D.2d 697, __, 451 N.Y.S.2d 326, 327 (3d Dep't 1982), the defendant claimed "that the [Alco-Sensor] testing of his breath in the absence of probable cause to believe that his ability to drive was impaired by alcohol constituted an unreasonable search violative of the Fourth Amendment." 88 A.D.2d at __, 451 N.Y.S.2d at 327. In rejecting the defendant's claim, the Appellate Division, Third Department, held that:

> The record amply demonstrates that the police officer had reasonable grounds to suspect defendant's intoxication. The vehicle swerved into the opposite lane forcing the police car off the road and was pursued for about one mile by the police car with flashing lights before stopping. These actions constituted sufficient factors from which the officer could reasonably infer that defendant was driving while under the influence of alcohol. At the very minimum, the stop was justified. Once stopped, defendant exhibited watery and bloodshot eyes, emanated an odor of alcohol from both his person and vehicle, and admitted that he had a long day at work and had a few beers. *In these prevailing circumstances, there was further probable cause for the officer to believe defendant to be driving under the influence of alcohol justifying the breath test.*

88 A.D.2d at __, 451 N.Y.S.2d at 327 (emphasis added) (citations omitted). *See also People v. Rosario*, 136 Misc. 2d 445, __, 518 N.Y.S.2d 906, 911 (N.Y. City Crim. Ct. 1987).

Thus, the *Brockum* court sidestepped the Fourth Amendment issue raised by the defendant (*i.e.*, that an Alco-Sensor test administered in the absence of probable cause constitutes an unreasonable search), by finding that probable cause *already existed* at the time that the Alco-Sensor test was administered to the defendant.

In *People v. Pecora*, 123 Misc. 2d 259, __, 473 N.Y.S.2d 320, 322 (Wappinger Just. Ct. 1984), the court held that:

> Just as the mere presence of a defective tire does not automatically give rise to an inference of a driver's intoxication, mere speeding does not automatically create a suspicion that a driver has been driving while intoxicated. In this case, the officer articulated no other indicia of Defendant's intoxication. * * *

Had the facts herein even suggested that probable cause existed for the breath test, we would not have to consider the constitutionality of Vehicle & Traffic Law 1193-a [currently VTL § 1194(1)(b)]. However, since that statute authorizes a search even in the absence of probable or reasonable cause, we must hold it to be unconstitutional as applied.

(Citation omitted).

Similarly, in *People v. Graser*, 90 Misc. 2d 219, __-__, 393 N.Y.S.2d 1009, 1014 to 15 (Amherst Just. Ct. 1977), the court held that:

Sec. 1193-a authorizes the police officer to demand a sample of breath after a violation of any provision of the Vehicle and Traffic Law.

Suppose a motorist is stopped for a violation of sec. 375-35c (defective tire) or 306b (no inspection certificate) and is arrested, can the demand for a breath sample be considered a search and seizure incident to a lawful arrest? . . .

If the officer after stopping the defendant, has reasonable cause to believe that the defendant has committed the crime of driving while intoxicated, he can arrest him, and make a search and seizure of the defendant's breath after arresting him, by demanding a sample of the breath by means of a breath screening test. It would be a search and seizure, incident to a lawful arrest, and not constitutionally proscribed.

If the police officer demands the motorist give him a breath sample before arresting him, but after having probable cause to make the arrest, such search and seizure also would not be proscribed merely because the police officer is searching for evidence of a particular crime, committed—to wit driving while intoxicated.

However, if the police officer has no probable cause to make the arrest for driving while intoxicated, he may "in appropriate circumstances and in an appropriate manner approach a person for purposes of investigating possible criminal behavior even though there is no probable cause to make an arrest," *Terry v. Ohio*, supra. There, however, has to be "reasonable suspicion."

The mere violation of the defective tire, or lack of an inspection certificate, would not in this court's opinion give rise to the necessary suspicion required by *Terry v. Ohio*, supra.

By virtue of the same reasoning, the mere happening of an accident does not of itself give rise to probable cause, or even suspicion of commission of the crime of driving while intoxicated. * * *

This court believes that in certain circumstances, the defendant's compulsory submitting to the breath screening test, under penalty of a traffic infraction for refusal, would constitute a violation of his constitutional rights; while in other circumstances it would not.

Therefore, this court does not believe that sec. 1193-a is unconstitutional on its face, but would be unconstitutional if applied in certain factual situations.

(Citations omitted).

§ 7:7   Alco-Sensor test constitutes a "scientific test or experiment" for purposes of CPL § 240.20(1)(c)

Research References

West's Key Number Digest, Automobiles ⊙411, 422.1

People v. Vargulik, 130 A.D.2d 530, 515 N.Y.S.2d 111 (2d Dep't 1987), makes clear that an Alco-Sensor test constitutes a "scientific test or experiment" for purposes of CPL § 240.20(1)(c). Thus, the results thereof, the most recent inspection, calibration, and repair records with regard thereto, etc. are discoverable. *Cf. People v. Mondon*, 129 Misc. 2d 13, __, 492 N.Y.S.2d 344, 347 (N.Y. Co. Sup. Ct. 1985) ("despite widespread judicial reluctance to admit polygraph results in evidence in criminal cases, the polygraph examination qualifies as a 'scientific test or experiment', at least for purposes of pretrial discovery (CPL 240.20[1][c])").

§ 7:8   Admissibility of Alco-Sensor test evidence at trial

Research References

West's Key Number Digest, Automobiles ⊙426

Evidence concerning the administration of an Alco-Sensor test, as well as evidence of the actual Alco-Sensor test results, is clearly inadmissible at trial. *See People v. Thomas*, 121 A.D.2d 73, __, 509 N.Y.S.2d 668, 671 (4th Dep't 1986), order *aff'd*, 70 N.Y.2d 823, 523 N.Y.S.2d 437 (1987). *See also People v. MacDonald*, 227 A.D.2d 672, __, 641 N.Y.S.2d 749, 751 (3d Dep't), order *aff'd*, 89 N.Y.2d 908, 653 N.Y.S.2d 267 (1996); *People v. O'Reilly*, 16 Misc. 3d 775, __, 842 N.Y.S.2d 292, 297 (Suffolk Co. Dist. Ct. 2007); *People v. Gray*, 190 Misc. 2d 40, __, 736 N.Y.S.2d 856, 860 (Kings Co. Sup. Ct. 2002); *People v. Ottino*, 178 Misc. 2d 416, __, 679 N.Y.S.2d 271, 273 (Sullivan Co. Ct. 1998). *Thomas* is the seminal case in this area. It provides, in pertinent part:

The Alco-Sensor testimony was clearly not admissible to show intoxication. It is well settled that "[t]here must be a sufficient showing of reliability of the test results before scientific evidence may be introduced." "[S]cientific evidence will only be admitted at trial if the procedure and results are generally accepted as reliable in the scientific community." Thus, the Alco-Sensor evidence should have been excluded because as it was presented to the jury it served as proof of intoxication and the People failed to lay a proper foundation showing its reliability for this purpose . . . Moreover, cases from other jurisdictions hold that the Alco-Sensor test is not reliable evidence of intoxication. * * *

In our view, evidence regarding the Alco-Sensor test had no place in the trial and the objection to its admission should have been sustained. The jury should not have been given the opportunity "to use the screening test result to corroborate the evidential test result."

121 A.D.2d at __, __, 509 N.Y.S.2d at 671, 673 (citations omitted).

Aside from the judicially recognized *un*reliability of the Alco-Sensor test, there is an equally important reason why Alco-Sensor test results are inadmissible at trial. In order for a breath test result to be admissible, a proper foundation must be laid. Such a foundation requires, inter alia, proof that the testing device was (a) properly calibrated and otherwise in proper working order, (b) properly administered, and (c) administered in accordance with both VTL § 1194 and the applicable Department of Health rules and regulations pertaining to breath testing. *See, e.g.*, VTL § 1194(1)(b); VTL § 1194(4)(c); 10 NYCRR § 59.5; *People v. Campbell*, 73 N.Y.2d 481, 484, 541 N.Y.S.2d 756, 757 (1989); *People v. Freeland*, 68 N.Y.2d 699, 700, 506 N.Y.S.2d 306, 307 (1986); *People v. Mertz*, 68 N.Y.2d 136, 148, 506 N.Y.S.2d 290, 296–97 (1986); *People v. Todd*, 38 N.Y.2d 755, 381 N.Y.S.2d 50 (1975); *People v. Robinson*, 53 A.D.3d 63, __, 860 N.Y.S.2d 159, 165 (2d Dep't 2008); *People v. Hampe*, 181 A.D.2d 238, __ n.1, 585 N.Y.S.2d 861, 862 n.1 (3d Dep't 1992); *Matter of Constantine v. Leto*, 157 A.D.2d 376, __, 557 N.Y.S.2d 611, 613 (3d Dep't 1990), aff'd for the reasons stated in the opinion below, 77 N.Y.2d 975, 571 N.Y.S.2d 906 (1991); *People v. Donaldson*, 36 A.D.2d 37, 319 N.Y.S.2d 172 (4th Dep't 1971); *People v. Meikrantz*, 77 Misc. 2d 892, 351 N.Y.S.2d 549 (Broome Co. Ct. 1974).

In this regard, most police departments do not calibrate their Alco-Sensors at regular intervals like they do with their chemical testing instruments, *see People v. Delaney*, 83 Misc. 2d 576, __, 373 N.Y.S.2d 477, 478 (Nassau Co. Dist. Ct. 1975), nor do they keep proper and adequate records of Alco-Sensor maintenance and calibration. In addition, the police do not prepare an operational check list in conjunction with Alco-Sensor tests. Furthermore, a reference standard (*i.e.*, simulator) test using a certified simulator solution is not run before or after a subject's Alco-Sensor test, in violation of 10 NYCRR § 59.5(d). Moreover, the subject is rarely observed "for at least 15 minutes prior to the collection of the breath sample," in violation of both 10 NYCRR § 59.5(b) and the manufacturer's instruction manual.

Simply stated, the procedures required to lay a proper foundation for the admission of breath test results into evidence are rarely, if ever, followed in connection with Alco-Sensor testing. Accordingly, even assuming an Alco-Sensor device is theoretically capable of producing an accurate reading, a defendant's Alco-Sensor test results would be inadmissible at trial.

Recently, several trial courts in New York City have found that Alco-Sensor test results are potentially admissible at trial. *See People v. Santiago*, 47 Misc. 3d 195, 4 N.Y.S.3d 829 (Bronx Co. Sup. Ct. 2014); *People v. Ginther*, 42 Misc. 3d 664, 976 N.Y.S.2d 368 (Richmond Co. Sup. Ct. 2013); *People v. Aliaj*, 36 Misc. 3d 682, 946 N.Y.S.2d 430 (N.Y. Co. Sup. Ct. 2012); *People v. Hargobind*, 34 Misc. 3d 1237(A), 2012 WL 762897 (N.Y. City Crim. Ct. 2012); *People v. Jones*, 33 Misc. 3d 181, 927 N.Y.S.2d 586 (N.Y. City Crim. Ct. 2011). *See also People v. Turner*, 47 Misc. 3d 100, 10 N.Y.S.3d 794 (App. Term, 1st Dep't 2015), leave to appeal denied, 25 N.Y.3d 1208, 2015 WL 4876319 (2015). Aside from the fact that this is by far the minority position, it is the authors' opinion that these decisions are erroneous. In this regard, regardless of whether a particular Alco-Sensor device is listed in the Department of Health Rules and Regulations, *see* 10 NYCRR § 59.4(b), these devices, among other things, (a) are not, as a matter of law, chemical tests, (b) are not administered in the manner required by 10 NYCRR § 59.5(d), and (c) are neither maintained nor administered in the manner required by case law addressing the admissibility of BAC readings.

It seems obvious that the results of a less reliable machine administered in a less reliable manner under less reliable conditions cannot be admitted into evidence with a lesser evidentiary foundation than is required for the admission of chemical test results using machines such as the DataMaster, Intoxilyzer, Alcotest, etc. Any such radical change in the longstanding law of this State would have to come from the Legislature. *See, e.g., People v. Santana*, 31 Misc. 3d 1232(A), 930 N.Y.S.2d 176 (N.Y. City Crim. Ct. 2011), at *2 ("To admit evidence of a portable breath test in a case in chief would be to circumvent the law. For the People to be able to rely on a portable alcohol breath test conducted at the scene in the field to prove their case in chief there must be a different statutory scheme than that in existence."); *People v. Reed*, 5 Misc. 3d 1032(A), 799 N.Y.S.2d 163 (Bronx Co. Sup. Ct. 2004), at *7 ("The position urged by the People does violence to th[e] statutory scheme and is contrary to the weight of judicial authority construing VTL 1194. Clearly, the Legislature intended to differentiate between preliminary tests done at the scene of the crime and those conducted back at the station house. The obvious rationale for this distinction is that the conditions surrounding a field test do not give the same assurance of reliability and accuracy as those in a controlled environment.").

Notably, subsequent to *Aliaj, Hargobind,* and *Jones,* the Appellate Division, Third Department, decided *People v. Kulk,* 103 A.D.3d 1038, 962 N.Y.S.2d 408 (3d Dep't 2013), which reaffirmed the longstanding rule that Alco-Sensors are not scientifically accepted as being reliable. Specifically, the *Kulk* Court held as follows:

> We reject defendant's claim that County Court should have admitted into evidence the results of an alco-sensor preliminary breath test that allegedly measured his BAC at only .06. Although the alco-sensor test may be used to establish probable cause for an arrest, it is not admissible to establish intoxication, as its reliability for this purpose is not generally accepted in the scientific community. We are not persuaded that a test that is not deemed sufficiently reliable to measure and thus establish a level of intoxication should be admissible to establish the lack of such level of intoxication. Defendant failed to preserve his related claim that the alco-sensor results should have been admitted for the limited purpose of showing that the breathalyzer machine—which obtained a higher BAC reading—may not have been functioning correctly. In any event, in the absence of any showing that the test is scientifically accepted as reliable for this purpose, no modification in the interest of justice is warranted.

Id. at __, 962 N.Y.S.2d at 411 (citations omitted).

More recently, the Appellate Division, Second Department, has reiterated that "[g]enerally, the result of a PBT, such as an Alco-sensor, 'is not admissible to establish intoxication, as its reliability for this purpose is not generally accepted in the scientific community.' " *People v. Krut,* 133 A.D.3d 781, __, 21 N.Y.S.3d 106, 110 (2d Dep't 2015), leave to appeal denied, 27 N.Y.3d 1001, 2016 WL 2889519 (2016) (citation omitted). *See also People v. Palencia,* 130 A.D.3d 1072, __, 15 N.Y.S.3d 89, 91 (2d Dep't 2015), leave to appeal granted, 26 N.Y.3d 1044, 22 N.Y.S.3d 174, 43 N.E.3d 384 (2015) and appeal dismissed, 27 N.Y.3d 1111, 36 N.Y.S.3d 88, 55 N.E.3d 1061 (2016) (same). *Palencia* makes clear that this is the case despite the fact that various PBT devices appear on the "Conforming Products List of Evidential Breath Measurement Devices" set forth at 10 NYCRR § 59.4(b). *See Palencia,* 130 A.D.3d at __, 15 N.Y.S.3d at 91. *See also Krut,* 133 A.D.3d at __, 21 N.Y.S.3d at 110-11 ("The court told the jury that the PBT was a 'generally accepted instrument in determining blood alcohol content,' and that no scientific expert was necessary. This was error"). *See generally People v. George,* 48 Misc. 3d 676, __, 10 N.Y.S.3d 851, 854 (N.Y. City Crim. Ct. 2015) ("Until a contrary ruling is pronounced by the Appellate Division, Second Department, by another Appellate Division or the Court of Appeals, we are constrained by *People v. Kulk*"). In light of this line of precedent, the continued admission of PBT results by certain lower courts in the First Department is, to say the least, troubling.

On the other hand, defense counsel can "open the door" to the admission of evidence concerning the administration of an Alco-Sensor test if he or she attempts to mislead the jury by making a false argument with regard to the Alco-Sensor. In this regard, in *People v. Seavy*, 16 A.D.3d 1130, ___, 791 N.Y.S.2d 249, 250 (4th Dep't 2005):

> Defendant contend[ed] that County Court erred in admitting the result of an alco-sensor test in evidence. The prosecutor did not question the Sheriff's Deputy on direct examination about the alco-sensor test that was given to defendant. On cross-examination, defense counsel asked the Deputy if he administered an alco-sensor test to defendant, and the Deputy replied that he did. Defense counsel then established that defendant's wife wanted to know the result of that test, but the Deputy would not show it to her. On redirect, the prosecutor asked the Deputy if defendant passed or failed the test, and he answered that the defendant failed the test. The prosecutor then asked what would indicate a failed test, and the Deputy answered, a "point 10 percentile blood alcohol concentration or higher." During summation, defense counsel argued that the Deputy did not show defendant or his wife the result of the alco-sensor test because defendant had actually passed it, while in her summation the prosecutor commented on the Deputy's testimony that defendant actually failed the alco-sensor test.

Under these circumstances, the Appellate Division, Fourth Department, held that:

> [D]efendant opened the door to that testimony and comment during summation. "[O]therwise inadmissible evidence may become admissible where the adverse party has 'opened the door' to it by offering evidence, or making an argument based on the evidence, which might otherwise mislead the factfinder." In questioning the Deputy about the alco-sensor test, defense counsel was attempting to mislead the jury by creating the impression that defendant actually passed the test, and thus it was proper for the prosecutor to question the Deputy about the result of that test.

16 A.D.3d at ___, 791 N.Y.S.2d at 250 (citations omitted). *See also People v. Martin*, 100 A.D.3d 930, 953 N.Y.S.2d 893 (2d Dep't 2012). *See generally People v. Vines*, 51 A.D.3d 827, 859 N.Y.S.2d 661 (2d Dep't 2008).

§ 7:9   Erroneous admission of evidence concerning Alco-Sensor test at trial subject to harmless error analysis

Research References

West's Key Number Digest, Automobiles ⚷426

Although evidence concerning the administration of an Alco-Sensor test is inadmissible at trial, *see* previous section, the erroneous admission of such evidence is subject to harmless error analysis. *See People v. Thomas*, 121 A.D.2d 73, __, 509 N.Y.S.2d 668, 673 (4th Dep't 1986), order *aff'd*, 70 N.Y.2d 823, 523 N.Y.S.2d 437 (1987); *People v. Schwartz*, 12 A.D.3d 210, 783 N.Y.S.2d 806 (1st Dep't 2004); *People v. Brockum*, 88 A.D.2d 697, __, 451 N.Y.S.2d 326, 328 (3d Dep't 1982). Accordingly, defense counsel should file a motion in limine to preclude such evidence, in order to minimize the risk that such evidence will be elicited by the People at trial (either intentionally or inadvertently). *See People v. Gray*, 190 Misc. 2d 40, __, 736 N.Y.S.2d 856, 860 (Kings Co. Sup. Ct. 2002) (Court granted defendant's motion in limine to preclude the results of the defendant's Alco-Sensor test at trial on the ground that an Alco-Sensor test is not reliable evidence of intoxication).

Notably, the *Thomas* court found that the erroneous admission of evidence concerning the administration of an Alco-Sensor test to the defendant was *not* harmless. 121 A.D.2d at __, 509 N.Y.S.2d at 673. *Cf. Brockum*, 88 A.D.2d at __, 451 N.Y.S.2d at 328.

In *People v. Cannella*, N.Y.L.J., 4/12/94, p. 25, Col. 3 (Nassau Co. Ct. 1994), the court granted a mistrial when, "[d]uring presentation of the People's case, the arresting officer testified that he administered, and received a positive result from a preliminary breath test." The court held that, under the circumstances presented, a curative instruction was insufficient to ensure the defendant a fair trial. As such, the defendant's request for a mistrial was granted.

The defendant must properly preserve an objection to the erroneous admission of Alco-Sensor test evidence at trial, or an appellate court may refuse to consider the claim. *See People v. Reding*, 167 A.D.2d 716, __, 564 N.Y.S.2d 489, 490 (3d Dep't 1990). *See generally People v. Smith*, 126 A.D.2d 863, __, 511 N.Y.S.2d 421, 422 (3d Dep't 1987).

§ 7:10 Defense counsel should file motion in limine to preclude Alco-Sensor test results at trial

Research References

West's Key Number Digest, Automobiles ☞411

A motion in limine to preclude the People from introducing the results of an Alco-Sensor test at trial is appropriate. *See People v. Gray*, 190 Misc. 2d 40, __, 736 N.Y.S.2d 856, 860 (Kings Co. Sup. Ct. 2002) (Court granted defendant's motion in limine to preclude the results of the defendant's Alco-Sensor test at trial on the ground that an Alco-Sensor test is not reliable evidence of intoxication). *See also People v. Thomas*, 121 A.D.2d 73, 509 N.Y.S.2d 668 (4th Dep't 1986), order *aff'd*, 70 N.Y.2d 823, 523 N.Y.S.2d 437 (1987).

In *Thomas*, the Appellate Division, Fourth Department, made clear both (a) that the courts of this state and of other states "hold that the Alco-Sensor test is not reliable evidence of intoxication," 121 A.D.2d at __, 509 N.Y.S.2d at 671, and (b) that "evidence regarding the Alco-Sensor test had no place in the trial and the objection to its admission should have been sustained. The jury should not have been given the opportunity 'to use the screening test result to corroborate the evidential test result.'" 121 A.D.2d at __, 509 N.Y.S.2d at 673 (citation omitted). *See also People v. MacDonald*, 227 A.D.2d 672, __, 641 N.Y.S.2d 749, 751 (3d Dep't), order *aff'd*, 89 N.Y.2d 908, 653 N.Y.S.2d 267 (1996).

§ 7:11 Refusal to submit to Alco-Sensor test—Generally

Research References
West's Key Number Digest, Automobiles ⚯413

VTL § 1194(1)(b) makes clear that a motorist is under no obligation to submit to a breath screening test unless he or she has either (a) been involved in an accident, or (b) committed a VTL violation. In addition, since obtaining a breath sample from a motorist for alcohol analysis constitutes a "search" within the meaning of the Fourth Amendment, *see Skinner v. Railway Labor Executives' Ass'n*, 489 U.S. 602, 616–17, 109 S.Ct. 1402, 1413 (1989); *see also Schmerber v. California*, 384 U.S. 757, 767, 86 S.Ct. 1826, 1834 (1966); *People v. Johnson*, 134 Misc. 2d 474, __, 511 N.Y.S.2d 773, 774 (N.Y. City Crim. Ct. 1987); *People v. McMillan*, 112 Misc. 2d 901, __, 447 N.Y.S.2d 626, 629 (Monroe Co. Ct. 1982), submission to such a search cannot lawfully be required in the absence of probable cause. *See People v. Pecora*, 123 Misc. 2d 259, __, 473 N.Y.S.2d 320, 322 (Wappinger Just. Ct. 1984). *See also People v. Kates*, 53 N.Y.2d 591, 594–95, 444 N.Y.S.2d 446, 448 (1981); *People v. Brockum*, 88 A.D.2d 697, __, 451 N.Y.S.2d 326, 327 (3d Dep't 1982). As such, absent a proper factual predicate for a police officer to request that a motorist submit to a breath screening test, a refusal to submit thereto does not violate VTL § 1194(1)(b).

§ 7:12 Refusal to submit to Alco-Sensor test is a traffic infraction

Research References
West's Key Number Digest, Automobiles ⚯413

The refusal to submit to a validly requested Alco-Sensor test is a traffic infraction. *See* VTL § 1194(1)(b); VTL § 1800(a); *People v. Leontiev*, 38 Misc. 3d 716, __, 956 N.Y.S.2d 832, 837-38 (Nassau Co. Dist. Ct. 2012); *People v. Pecora*, 123 Misc. 2d 259, __, 473 N.Y.S.2d 320, 323 (Wappinger Just. Ct. 1984); *People v. Steves*, 117 Misc. 2d 841, __, 459 N.Y.S.2d 402, 403 (Webster Just. Ct. 1983); *People v. Hamza*, 109 Misc. 2d 1055, __, 441 N.Y.S.2d 579, 581 (Gates Just. Ct. 1981); *People v. Graser*, 90 Misc. 2d 219, __, 393 N.Y.S.2d 1009, 1014 (Amherst Just. Ct. 1977). *See generally People v. Cunningham*, 95 N.Y.2d 909, 910, 717 N.Y.S.2d 68, 68 (2000), as amended nunc pro tunc, 95 N.Y.2d 949, 722 N.Y.S.2d 466, 745 N.E.2d 385 (2000).

Punishment for such traffic infraction is set forth in VTL § 1800(b). There are no driver's license consequences associated with a refusal to submit to an Alco-Sensor test.

Notably, there is precedent in the Appellate Term holding that VTL § 1194(1)(b) is *not* a legally cognizable offense. *See, e.g., People v. Sorhaindo*, 42 Misc. 3d 140(A), 986 N.Y.S.2d 867 (App. Term, 9th & 10th Jud. Dist. 2014).

§ 7:13 Refusal to submit to Alco-Sensor test— Admissibility at trial

Research References

West's Key Number Digest, Automobiles ⊙413

In perhaps the only published decision dealing directly with the issue of the admissibility of an Alco-Sensor test *refusal* at trial, the court held that an Alco-Sensor test refusal, like an Alco-Sensor test result, is inadmissible. *See People v. Ottino*, 178 Misc. 2d 416, __, 679 N.Y.S.2d 271, 273 (Sullivan Co. Ct. 1998). In so holding, the court reasoned that:

> Since the results of the alco-sensor field test are not admissible to prove intoxication at trial, the refusal to take that field test must also be inadmissible . . .
>
> Thus, to allow the jury to hear the evidence of an alco-sensor test refusal would in effect make admissible that evidence which is clearly inadmissible.

178 Misc. 2d at __, 679 N.Y.S.2d at 273.

Although *People v. MacDonald*, 89 N.Y.2d 908, 653 N.Y.S.2d 267 (1996) appears at first glance to hold otherwise, *MacDonald* is readily distinguishable from *Ottino*. In *MacDonald*, the evidence at issue was not evidence of the defendant's refusal to submit to an Alco-Sensor test, but rather "testimony regarding defendant's [conduct in] attempt[ing] to avoid giving an adequate breath sample for alco-sensor testing." 89 N.Y.2d at 910, 653

N.Y.S.2d at 268. *See also People v. MacDonald*, 227 A.D.2d 672, —, 641 N.Y.S.2d 749, 751 (3d Dep't) ("the testimony introduced by the People regarding the test was to show defendant's consciousness of guilt in refusing to comply with the procedures and pretending to blow into the straw. *Under these circumstances*, we find the testimony regarding the attempt to give defendant the alco-sensor test permissible, particularly in light of the court's limiting instructions to the jury on this point") (emphasis added), *aff'd*, 89 N.Y.2d 908, 653 N.Y.S.2d 267 (1996).

§ 7:14 Admissibility of Alco-Sensor test evidence at pretrial hearing

Research References

West's Key Number Digest, Automobiles ⚖︎426

People v. Thomas, 121 A.D.2d 73, —, 509 N.Y.S.2d 668, 671 (4th Dep't 1986), *aff'd*, 70 N.Y.2d 823, 523 N.Y.S.2d 437 (1987) is widely cited for the proposition that "breath screening devices have won acceptance as being sufficiently reliable to establish probable cause for an arrest." *See also Matter of Smith v. Commissioner of Motor Vehicles*, 103 A.D.2d 865, —, 478 N.Y.S.2d 103, 104 (3d Dep't 1984); *People v. Ottino*, 178 Misc. 2d 416, —, 679 N.Y.S.2d 271, 273 (Sullivan Co. Ct. 1998).

Notably, however, this statement in *Thomas* is dicta. It is also somewhat inaccurate. First of all, both *Thomas* and *Ottino* cite *Smith* in support of their position. However, *Smith*, which addressed the sufficiency of the evidence at a DMV chemical test refusal hearing, merely stated that "[t]he arresting officer acquired probable cause to believe that petitioner had violated the provisions of section 1192 of the Vehicle and Traffic Law from *his personal observation of petitioner's conduct and appearance, as well as* from the result of the alco-sensor test." 103 A.D.2d at —, 478 N.Y.S.2d at 104 (emphasis added).

In other words, even if an Alco-Sensor test can be used to *help establish* probable cause for a DWI suspect's arrest, it cannot, in and of itself, establish probable cause for such arrest. In this regard, even where admissible at a pretrial hearing, Alco-Sensor test results are only appropriately expressed as "positive" or "negative" for the presence of alcohol—they cannot appropriately be expressed as a numerical BAC percentage. This is particularly true in light of the fact that most police departments, among other things, (a) do not calibrate their Alco-Sensors at regular intervals, (b) do not keep proper and adequate records of Alco-Sensor maintenance and calibration, and (c) do not run a reference standard (*i.e.*, simulator) test in conjunction with the subject's Alco-Sensor test. In addition, most police officers administer Alco-Sensor tests within 15 minutes of first observing the suspect, in violation of both 10 NYCRR § 59.5(b) and the manufacturer's instruction manual.

Stated another way, *Thomas* and *Smith* merely stand for the proposition that a properly functioning, properly administered Alco-Sensor test can help establish probable cause for the arrest of a DWI suspect. By contrast, neither *Thomas, Smith,* nor any other case can be read to hold that the results of an *improperly functioning, improperly administered* Alco-Sensor test has any evidentiary value whatsoever. Indeed, the whole concept of an evidentiary foundation is that the party offering the results of a scientific test into evidence must prove, inter alia, (a) that the testing device was in proper working order, and (b) that the test was properly administered. *See, e.g., People v. Campbell,* 73 N.Y.2d 481, 484, 541 N.Y.S.2d 756, 757 (1989); *People v. Mertz,* 68 N.Y.2d 136, 148, 506 N.Y.S.2d 290, 296–97 (1986); *People v. Hampe,* 181 A.D.2d 238, __ n.1, 585 N.Y.S.2d 861, 862 n.1 (3d Dep't 1992); *Matter of Constantine v. Leto,* 157 A.D.2d 376, __, 557 N.Y.S.2d 611, 613 (3d Dep't 1990), aff'd for the reasons stated in the opinion below, 77 N.Y.2d 975, 571 N.Y.S.2d 906 (1991).

§ 7:15   Admissibility of Alco-Sensor test evidence at violation of probation hearing

Research References

West's Key Number Digest, Automobiles ☞426

In a logical extension of the principle that "breath screening devices have won acceptance as being sufficiently reliable to establish probable cause for an arrest," *People v. Thomas,* 121 A.D.2d 73, __, 509 N.Y.S.2d 668, 671 (4th Dep't 1986), *aff'd,* 70 N.Y.2d 823, 523 N.Y.S.2d 437 (1987), the Dutchess County Court held that the results of an Alco-Sensor test both (a) are admissible at a violation of probation (VOP) hearing, and (b) established that the defendant had consumed alcohol in violation of the orders and conditions of his probation. *People v. Jones,* 10 Misc. 3d 413, __, 805 N.Y.S.2d 807, 810 (Dutchess Co. Ct. 2005) aff'd, 50 A.D.3d 1058, 856 N.Y.S.2d 225 (2d Dep't 2008).

In so holding, the court noted that the burden of proof at a VOP hearing is merely "a preponderance of the evidence," 10 Misc. 3d at __, 805 N.Y.S.2d at 809, and that "[t]he only issue to be determined is *whether* the defendant consumed alcohol—*not* how much." 10 Misc. 3d at __, 805 N.Y.S.2d at 810 (emphases added).

§ 7:16 Arresting officer's false testimony at Grand Jury that no Alco-Sensor test was administered to defendant found not to require dismissal of indictment

Research References

West's Key Number Digest, Automobiles ⌘411

In *People v. Spencer*, 289 A.D.2d 877, 736 N.Y.S.2d 428 (3d Dep't 2001), it came to light at a *Huntley* hearing that the arresting officer had administered an Alco-Sensor test to the defendant shortly after the defendant had exited his vehicle; yet (at the direction of the People) the officer testified at the grand jury that no such test had been administered. As a result, county court dismissed the indictment on the ground that "the integrity of the Grand Jury proceeding had been impaired by the perjured testimony of the arresting officer." 289 A.D.2d at __, 736 N.Y.S.2d at 429.

The Appellate Division, Third Department, reversed. While stating that "we do not excuse what happened here," the court concluded that the officer's testimony "lacked the potential to prejudice the Grand Jury's ultimate decision since the remaining evidence was sufficient to sustain the indictment." 289 A.D.2d at __, 736 N.Y.S.2d at 430.

Chapter 8

Gaze Nystagmus

Research References

Westlaw Databases

Drinking/Driving Litigation (2d ed.) (DRNKDRIVING)
Handling Drunk Driving Cases (2d ed.) (HDRUNKDR)
New York Vehicle and Traffic Law 2d (NYVEH)

Treatises and Practice Aids

Nichols and Whited, Drinking/Driving Litigation: Criminal and Civil
   §§ 15:10 to 17:1 (2d ed.)
Fiandach, Handling Drunk Driving Cases §§ 7:10, 7:12 (2d ed.)
Rose, New York Vehicle and Traffic Law 2d § 35:21.50

Law Reviews and Other Periodicals

Pariser, In Vino Veritas: The Truth About Blood Alcohol Presumptions
   in State Drunk Driving Law, 64 N.Y.U. L. Rev. 141 (April, 1989)

KeyCite®: Cases and other legal materials listed in KeyCite Scope can be
researched through the KeyCite service on Westlaw®. Use KeyCite to check
citations for form, parallel references, prior and later history, and comprehensive citator information, including citations to other decisions and secondary
materials.

---

§ 8:1   In general

Research References

West's Key Number Digest, Automobiles ☞411, 422.1

The United States Department of Transportation, National
Highway Traffic Safety Administration, DWI Detection and Stan-
dardized Field Sobriety Testing Student Manual (the NHTSA
Manual) defines "nystagmus" as follows:

> Nystagmus is the involuntary jerking of the eyes, occurring as the
> eyes gaze toward the side. Also, nystagmus is [a] natural, normal
> phenomenon. Alcohol and certain other drugs do not cause this phe-
> nomenon; they merely exaggerate or magnify it.

NHTSA Manual, at VIII-12.

There are numerous types (and causes) of nystagmus. However, for purposes of field sobriety testing in DWI and DWAI drugs cases, law enforcement primarily focuses on a type of nystagmus called "horizontal gaze nystagmus," commonly referred to as "HGN." According to the NHTSA Manual:

> *Horizontal* Gaze Nystagmus occurs as the eyes move to the side. It is the observation of the eyes for *horizontal* gaze nystagmus that provides the first and most valid test in the standardized field sobriety testing battery. Although this type of nystagmus is most accurate for determining alcohol influence, its presence may also indicate use of PCP, certain inhalants and other central nervous system depressants.

NHTSA Manual, at VIII-13.

The HGN test attempts to use the phenomenon of horizontal gaze nystagmus to help identify drivers who are either intoxicated and/or impaired by drugs.

§ 8:2　The "standardized" elements of the HGN test

Research References

West's Key Number Digest, Automobiles ⟜411, 422.1

The HGN test is one of the so-called "standardized field sobriety tests" (SFSTs). *See* §§ 6:1 et seq., *supra.*

The tests are "standardized" in the sense that:
- they are always administered in the same way;
- the officer administering the tests always looks for a specific set of clues on each test; and,
- the officer always assesses a suspect's performance relative to a specific criterion for each test.

NHTSA Manual, at VIII-7.

The "standardized" elements of the HGN test are:
(1) Standardized Administrative Procedures
- Hold the stimulus 12–15 inches in front of the suspect's nose.
- Keep the tip of the stimulus slightly above the suspect's eyes.
- Always move the stimulus smoothly.
- Always check for all three clues in both eyes, starting with [the] suspect's left eye.
- Check the clues in this sequence: lack of smooth pursuit; distinct nystagmus at maximum deviation; onset of nystagmus prior to 45 degrees.
- Always check for each clue at least *twice* in each eye.
(2) Standardized Clues
- Lack of smooth pursuit.

- Distinct nystagmus at maximum deviation.
- Onset of nystagmus prior to 45 degrees.

No other "clues" are recognized by the NHTSA as valid indicators of horizontal gaze nystagmus. In particular, the NHTSA does not support the allegation that onset angle can reliably be used to estimate BAC, and considers any such estimation to be misuse of the horizontal gaze nystagmus test.

(3) Standardized Criterion

The maximum number of clues of horizontal gaze nystagmus that a suspect can exhibit is *six*. That would occur when all three clues are observed in both eyes. If a suspect exhibits four or more clues, it should be considered evidence that the suspect's BAC is above 0.10. (New information indicates that HGN may be present in suspects under the influence of certain other drugs).

NHTSA Manual, at VIII-7-VIII-8.

§ 8:3   Proper procedures for administering the HGN test

Research References

West's Key Number Digest, Automobiles ☞411, 422.1

The NHTSA Manual, which is the standard reference in this field, provides as follows:

Procedures of Horizontal Gaze Nystagmus Testing: The Three Clues

As explained earlier, nystagmus means a jerking of the eyes. There are a number of different kinds of nystagmus. The test you will use at roadside is a test of "horizontal gaze nystagmus"—the nystagmus that occurs when the eyes move to the side. Many eyes will show some jerking if moved far enough to the side. Under the influence of alcohol and certain other drugs, three signs often will be observed:

1. *The suspect cannot follow a slowly moving stimulus smoothly with the eyes*; instead, the eyes can be observed to jerk or "bounce" as they move left and right in pursuit of a smoothly moving object, such as a pencil or penlight.

2. When you have the suspect move their eyes as far to the side as possible, *distinct nystagmus will be evident when the eye is held at maximum deviation for approximately four seconds*; some people exhibit slight jerking of the eye at maximum deviation, even when sober, but when under the influence of alcohol, the jerking is likely to be very pronounced, and easily observable.

3. The more intoxicated a person becomes, the less the eyes have to move toward the side before jerking begins. Usually when a person's BAC is above 0.10, *the jerking will begin before the eye has moved 45 degrees to the side*.

Estimating a 45-Degree Angle

Because the 45-degree angle is a key factor in assessing a suspect's degree of alcohol influence, it is important to know how to estimate that angle.

For practice, a 45-degree template can be prepared by making a 15'-square cardboard and connecting its opposite corners with a diagonal line.

To use this device, hold it up so that the person's nose is above the diagonal line. Be certain that one edge of the template is centered on the nose and perpendicular to (or, at right angles to) the face. Have the person you are examining follow a penlight or some other object until [the] suspect is looking down the 45-degree diagonal. Note the position of the eye. With practice, you should be able to recognize this angle without using the template.

Specific Procedures

Begin by asking "are you wearing contact lenses," make a note whether or not the suspect wears contacts before starting the test.

If the suspect is wearing eyeglasses, have them removed.

Give the suspect the following instructions from a position of interrogation (FOR OFFICER SAFETY KEEP YOUR WEAPON AWAY FROM THE SUSPECT):
- "I am going to check your eyes."
- "Keep your head still and follow this stimulus with your eyes only."
- "Keep focusing on this stimulus until I tell you to stop."

Position the stimulus approximately 12–15 inches from the suspect's nose and slightly above eye level. Check the suspect's eyes for the ability to track together. Move the stimulus smoothly across the suspect's entire field of vision. Check to see if the eyes track the stimulus together or one lags behind the other. If the eyes don't track together it could indicate a possible medical disorder, injury, or blindness.

Next, check to see that both pupils are equal in size. If they are not, this may indicate a head injury.

Check the suspect's left eye by moving the stimulus to your right. Move the stimulus smoothly, at a speed that requires about two seconds to bring the suspect's eye as far to the side as it can go. While moving the stimulus, look at the suspect's eye and determine whether it is *able to pursue smoothly*. Now, move the stimulus all the way to the left, back across [the] suspect's face checking if the right eye pursues smoothly. Movement of the stimulus should take approximately two seconds out and two seconds back for each eye. Repeat the procedure.

After you have checked both eyes for lack of smooth pursuit, check the eyes for *distinct nystagmus at maximum deviation* beginning with the suspect's left eye. Simply move the object to the suspect's left side until the eye has gone as far to the side as possible. Usually, no white will be showing in the corner of the eye at maximum deviation. Hold the eye at that position for approximately four seconds, and observe the eye for distinct nystagmus. Move the stimulus all the way across the suspect's face to check the right eye holding that position for approximately four seconds. Repeat the procedure.

After checking the eyes at maximum deviation, check for onset of nystagmus prior to 45 degrees. Start moving the stimulus towards the right (suspect's left eye) at a speed that would take about four seconds for the stimulus to reach the edge of the suspect's shoulder. Watch the eye carefully for any sign of jerking. When you see it, stop and verify that the jerking continues. Now, move the stimulus to the left (suspect's right eye) at a speed that would take about four seconds for the stimulus to reach the edge of the suspect's shoulder. Watch the eye carefully for any sign of jerking. When you see it, stop and verify that the jerking continues. Repeat the procedure. NOTE: It is important to use the full four seconds when checking for onset of nystagmus. If you move the stimulus too fast, you may go past the point of onset or miss it altogether.

If the suspect's eyes start jerking before they reach 45 degrees, check to see that some white of the eye is still showing on the side closest to the ear. If no white of the eye is showing, you either have taken the eye too far to the side (that is more than 45 degrees) or the person has unusual eyes that will not deviate very far to the side.

NOTE: Nystagmus may be due to causes other than alcohol. These other causes include seizure medications, PCP, inhalants, barbiturates and other depressants. A large disparity between the performance of the right and left eye may indicate a medical condition.

Test Interpretation

You should look for three clues of nystagmus in each eye.
1. The eye cannot follow a moving object smoothly.
2. Nystagmus is distinct when the eye is at maximum deviation.
3. The angle of onset of nystagmus is prior to 45 degrees.

If you observe four or more clues, it is likely that the suspect's BAC is above 0.10. Using this criterion you will be able to classify correctly about 77% of your suspects with respect to whether they are above 0.10. That probability was determined during laboratory and field testing and helps you weigh the various field sobriety tests in this battery as you make your arrest decision. * * *

Horizontal . . . Gaze Nystagmus can be observed directly and does not require special equipment. You will need something for the suspect to follow with the eyes, but this can be as simple as the tip of your index finger, penlight, or pen. The stimulus used should be held slightly above eye level, so that the eyes are wide open when they look directly at it. It should be held about 12–15 inches in front of the nose for ease of focus.

NHTSA Manual, at VIII-14-VIII-18.

§ 8:4   Case law

Research References

West's Key Number Digest, Automobiles ☞411, 422.1

Unlike other field sobriety tests such as the walk-and-turn test and the one-leg stand, which simply test a person's motor coordination and ability to think and speak clearly, the HGN test deals with involuntary physiological movements of the eye and how such movements *may* be affected by the consumption of alcohol and/or drugs. As such, the HGN test is considered "scientific" in nature, placing it within the ambit of *Frye v. United States*, 293 F. 1013 (D.C. Cir. 1923). *See also People v. Wernick*, 89 N.Y.2d 111, 651 N.Y.S.2d 392 (1996); *People v. Wesley*, 83 N.Y.2d 417, 611 N.Y.S.2d 97 (1994); *People v. Middleton*, 54 N.Y.2d 42, 444 N.Y.S.2d 581 (1981).

The appellate courts of this state have made clear both (a) that "the courts of our State have not conclusively determined that HGN is generally accepted as reliable," *People v. Heidelmark*, 214 A.D.2d 767, __, 624 N.Y.S.2d 656, 658 (3d Dep't 1995), and (b) that a trial court commits error "in allowing testimony concerning the HGN field sobriety test without a proper foundation as to its scientific acceptance or reliability." 214 A.D.2d at __, 624 N.Y.S.2d at 658. *See also People v. Erickson*, 156 A.D.2d 760, __, 549 N.Y.S.2d 182, 184 (3d Dep't 1989) ("County Court acted improperly in allowing testimony at trial concerning the field sobriety test known as 'Horizontal Gaze Nystagmus' without a proper foundation as to its scientific acceptance or reliability. . . ."); *People v. Torrey*, 144 A.D.2d 865, __, 534 N.Y.S.2d 807, 809 (3d Dep't 1988) (same); *People v. Saputo,* No. 87-211 (App. Term, 9th & 10th Jud. Dists. 4/14/88). *See generally Romano v. Stanley*, 90 N.Y.2d 444, 661 N.Y.S.2d 589 (1997).

In *People v. Quinn*, 153 Misc. 2d 139, 580 N.Y.S.2d 818 (Suffolk Co. Dist. Ct. 1991), *rev'd on other grounds*, 158 Misc. 2d 1015, 607 N.Y.S.2d 534 (App. Term, 9th & 10th Jud. Dists. 1993), the court held a *Frye* hearing to determine, inter alia, whether the HGN test individually, and/or the so-called Drug Recognition Expert (DRE) protocol as a whole, satisfies the requirements of

Frye. In this regard, the People called nine witnesses, some from as far away as California. At the conclusion of the hearing, the court held that "the People have successfully established that both the HGN test and the DRE protocol meet the standards enunciated by *Frye* and *Middleton*." 153 Misc. 2d at __, 580 N.Y.S.2d at 826.

Notably, however, *Quinn* involved the use of the HGN test in the context of a DWAI drugs case, specifically in the context of the DRE protocol. In other words, HGN was discussed in the context of a case in which alcohol was not even alleged to be present. In fact, the defendant's BAC in *Quinn* was 0.00. 153 Misc. 2d at __, 580 N.Y.S.2d at 819. Thus, the relationship between alcohol and HGN was not at issue in *Quinn*. Furthermore, the "defendant was unable to focus her attention on the stimulus, [and thus] no nystagmus of any sort was observable." 153 Misc. 2d at __, 580 N.Y.S.2d at 820.

In addition, in *Heidelmark, supra*, the Appellate Division, Third Department, eviscerated *Quinn* with the following statement— "The People's reliance upon *People v. Quinn*, 153 Misc. 2d 139, 580 N.Y.S.2d 818, *revd.* 158 Misc. 2d 1015, 607 N.Y.S.2d 534 to support their contention that HGN has been upheld as scientifically reliable was reversed, with the Appellate Term refusing to directly address that issue." 214 A.D.2d at __, 624 N.Y.S.2d at 658.

Nonetheless, a disturbing trend is emerging in New York with regard to the HGN test. Specifically, various courts are holding so-called *Frye* hearings on the issue of the scientific acceptance and reliability of the HGN test, and are holding that the HGN test satisfies the *Frye* standard, despite shockingly little expert witness testimony presented at the hearings. *See, e.g., People v. Miley*, 12/6/2002 NYLJ 30, col. 6 (Nassau Co. Ct. 2002); *People v. Prue*, 2001 WL 1729710 (Franklin Co. Ct. 2001), *aff'd*, 8 A.D.3d 894, 779 N.Y.S.2d 271 (3d Dep't 2004); *People v. Vanderlofske*, 186 Misc. 2d 182, 717 N.Y.S.2d 450 (Greene Co. Ct. 2000); *People v. Shirley*, Indictment No. 99-739 (Broome Co. Ct. 2000); *People v. Tomeny*, Docket No. 99-29384 (Ithaca City Ct. 1999). *Cf. State v. Doriguzzi*, 334 N.J. Super. 530, 540, 760 A.2d 336, 342 (N.J. Super. Ct. App. Div. 2000) ("While it may very well be that HGN testing can meet the *Frye* test, we believe that the case which decides the issue for all other cases in New Jersey should be grounded in sufficient expert testimony to assure defendants and the State alike that a conviction for driving under the influence, when based in part on HGN testing, is a conviction grounded in reliable scientific data. The consequences of a drunk driving conviction are severe and may include incarceration.").

Notably, the courts in *Miley, Prue, Vanderlofske,* and *Tomeny* apparently heard from the same "expert" witness who, despite alarmingly little expertise or background with regard to the issue of HGN as it pertains to alcohol and/or drug consumption, goes from court to court lauding the virtues of the HGN test. Simply stated, if the *Frye* standard were applied in such a loose manner in other contexts, evidence such as polygraph test results would become admissible following a brief hearing involving a single biased witness called by the prosecution.

Moreover, in *People v. Gallup*, 302 A.D.2d 681, __, 755 N.Y.S.2d 498, 501–02 (3d Dep't 2003), the Appellate Division, Third Department, indicated, in dicta, its willingness to grant *Frye* acceptance to the HGN test *despite the fact that a Frye* hearing was not even held in the court below:

> Defendant's contention that the People's failure at trial to establish a proper scientific foundation for the HGN test requires a new trial is unpreserved, as defendant did not request a *Frye* hearing or object to the testimony concerning the administration or results of this test. While this Court in years past has found error in allowing testimony concerning HGN field sobriety tests without a proper foundation as to its scientific acceptance or reliability, albeit harmless error, subsequent decisions predating the trial in this case in which *Frye* hearings were held have determined that HGN tests are generally accepted within the scientific community as a reliable indicator of intoxication. Thus, if defendant had raised the issue at trial, County Court could have declined to hold a *Frye* hearing and taken judicial notice of the reliability of the HGN procedure and could have, instead, conducted only a foundational inquiry into whether the accepted techniques were actually employed in this case and the tester's qualifications.

(Citations and footnote omitted). *See also People v. Tetrault*, 53 A.D.3d 558, __, 861 N.Y.S.2d 408, 409–10 (2d Dep't 2008); *People v. Hammond*, 35 A.D.3d 905, __, 827 N.Y.S.2d 298, 299–300 (3d Dep't 2006), leave to appeal denied, 8 N.Y.3d 946, 836 N.Y.S.2d 556, 868 N.E.2d 239 (2007); *People v. Grune*, 12 A.D.3d 944, __, 785 N.Y.S.2d 178, 179 (3d Dep't 2004).

In any event, the apparent trend toward *Frye* acceptance of the HGN test by no means guarantees that the results of this test are admissible at trial. As with chemical test results, a proper foundation for admission of the results of the HGN test requires, inter alia, proof that the test was properly administered by a qualified person. In this regard, the *Vanderlofske* court held that:

> [T]he People are permitted to attempt to lay an evidentiary foundation at trial for HGN evidence as relevant to defendant. To do so, the People must prove that [the officer administering the test] was trained in the administration of the HGN field sobriety test and that his administration of such test to defendant . . ., as well as his scoring/ assessment of the results of such testing, was in accordance with the accepted techniques/ procedures.

Should the People lay the proper foundation to allow the admission into evidence of defendant's HGN field sobriety test results, the weight to be accorded such results is to be determined by the jury, the finder of fact.

The Court will not rule on the People's request that it determine whether the aforementioned proper foundation may be laid by the testimony of the trooper alone or whether expert testimony is necessary.

186 Misc. 2d at ___, 717 N.Y.S.2d at 454.

The court in *Shirley*, *supra*, went even further:

At the conclusion of [the *Frye*] hearing the Court ruled that as a general principle HGN evidence is admissible in terms of its scientific reliability. As the Court noted in its ruling at the hearing, a defendant should and does have a right to a pretrial hearing on the admissibility of such evidence in any given case where by sworn allegation of fact, he or she creates a question of fact as to whether such evidence should be admissible as a matter of law. That is, notwithstanding the scientific reliability of HGN evidence in theory, since the testimony adduced at the *Frye* hearing clearly established that if the HGN testing was not done by a properly and sufficiently trained officer, or if it was done under improper conditions, the results of such HGN testing are invalid, the defendant must be afforded an opportunity to assert such grounds before trial.

See also Miley, *supra*, ("This Court therefore concludes that the People may introduce the HGN test and its results, provided the test was properly administered").

Part III

OFFENSES

Chapter 9

DWI Felonies

§ 9:28   Vince's Law

Research References

Westlaw Databases

Drinking/Driving Litigation (2d ed.) (DRNKDRIVING)
Handling Drunk Driving Cases (2d ed.) (HDRUNKDR)
New York Vehicle and Traffic Law 2d (NYVEH)

Treatises and Practice Aids

Nichols and Whited, Drinking/Driving Litigation: Criminal and Civil
    § 2:2 (2d ed.)
Fiandach, Handling Drunk Driving Cases §§ 6:4, 31:4, 31:14 (2d ed.)
Rose, New York Vehicle and Traffic Law 2d § 35:6

KeyCite®: Cases and other legal materials listed in KeyCite Scope can be
researched through the KeyCite service on Westlaw®. Use KeyCite to check
citations for form, parallel references, prior and later history, and comprehensive citator information, including citations to other decisions and secondary
materials.

---

§ 9:1   In general

Research References

West's Key Number Digest, Automobiles ☞324, 332

If the defendant has prior drinking and driving convictions and
one of these is for DWI, and the conviction was obtained within
10 years of his present arrest, defense counsel must consider the
very real possibility of an indictment. If there is no predicate
DWI conviction, counsel will still have a very difficult time obtaining a satisfactory plea bargain. In the absence of a predicate DWI
conviction (*i.e.*, prior convictions for DWAI), most district attorneys' offices will require a plea of guilty to the outstanding
misdemeanor charge and counsel will probably be arguing
whether his client will be suffering a straight revocation, or be
placed on three years' probation, a condition of which being that
he not operate a motor vehicle or apply for a driver's license for
that period of time.

If the defendant does have a predicate DWI conviction, local
custom will govern and counsel should ascertain at the earliest
possible time what the position of the district attorney and the
county court is in regard to felony DWI cases. Split sentences
consisting of a short period of incarceration combined with probation are not uncommon. The imposition of five years' probation
with the condition that the defendant not operate a motor vehicle
or apply for a license while he is on probation is, also, not
unusual.

§ 9:2 Probation prohibition of relicensure

Research References

West's Key Number Digest, Automobiles ⌖324, 332

In some instances, a court will place a defendant on probation, but will permit him to obtain a driver's license and operate a motor vehicle. Instead of imposing its own restrictions, the court will leave the relicensure of the defendant up to the Department of Motor Vehicles. VTL § 1193(2)(e)(5) prohibits the Commissioner of Motor Vehicles from issuing a driver's license to a defendant who has been sentenced to probation with a condition that he not operate a motor vehicle, nor apply for a driver's license during the period of probation.

Since most courts do impose some kind of restrictions on a defendant's driving, the DMV has adopted a policy of refusing to relicense individuals on probation for DWI unless the defendant submits proof that no such restriction has been imposed. This proof consists of a form to be filled out by the probation officer. A copy of a letter dated June 10, 1985, from the Department of Motor Vehicles setting forth this policy is set forth at Appendix 4.

Where a person's license is either revoked, or she is prohibited from applying for a license as a condition of probation, VTL § 1193(2)(e)(6) provides that such a defendant may, within 45 days prior to the expiration of her probation, and/or minimum period of revocation (whichever expires last) apply for restoration of her driving privileges. The purpose of this procedure is to allow sufficient time to process the defendant's application in order that she reobtain her privileges at the time authorized.

§ 9:3 Prior convictions as predicates for felony treatment

Research References

West's Key Number Digest, Automobiles ⌖324, 332

Where a person operates a motor vehicle in violation of VTL § 1192(2), (3), or (4), and has a prior conviction of VTL § 1192(2), (3), or (4), within the preceding 10 years, the pending charge shall be a Class E felony. VTL § 1193(1)(c)(i). Upon conviction of this Class E felony, the defendant shall be punished by a fine of not less than $1,000, nor more than $5,000, and/or by a period of imprisonment as provided by the penal law, to wit: a maximum sentence of $1^{1}/_{3}$ to four years.

Where the defendant has *two* or more prior convictions of VTL § 1192(2), (3), or (4) within the preceding 10 years, the pending charge shall be a Class D felony. Upon conviction of this Class D felony, the defendant shall be punished by a fine of not less than $2,000, nor more than $10,000, and/or by a period of imprisonment as provided by the penal law, to wit: a maximum sentence of 2⅓ to seven years imprisonment.

In *People v. Witthuhn*, 172 Misc. 2d 749, 658 N.Y.S.2d 830 (Nassau Co. Ct. 1997), the court rejected the defendant's claim that, in enacting VTL § 1193(1)(c)(ii), "the Legislature intended to elevate a repeat DWI offense to a class D felony only if one of a defendant's prior DWI convictions was for a class E felony," finding that the language of the statute is "clear, plain and unambiguous on its face." 172 Misc. 2d at 749, 750, 658 N.Y.S.2d at 830, 831. *See also People v. Homero*, 172 Misc. 2d 99, 656 N.Y.S.2d 843 (Nassau Co. Sup. Ct. 1997) (same).

In *People v. Maldonado*, 173 Misc. 2d 612, 661 N.Y.S.2d 937 (Nassau Co. Sup. Ct. 1997), the defendant was charged with two *separate* instances of DWI which took place approximately three months apart. He thereafter pled guilty to two separate counts of DWI on the same date, and was sentenced with regard to both convictions on the same date. When he was subsequently charged with a *third* instance of DWI, the defendant claimed "that because he pled guilty and was sentenced on the same date for the two prior DWI convictions he cannot be properly charged as a class 'D' felon." 173 Misc. 2d at 613, 661 N.Y.S.2d at 938. The court disagreed, holding that the defendant "is liable for a class D felony even though his prior sentences happened to be imposed on the same date." 173 Misc. 2d at 616, 661 N.Y.S.2d at 940.

In addition, the court held that VTL § 1193(1)(c)(ii) does not violate the Ex Post Facto Clause of the U.S. Constitution. In so holding, the Court reasoned that "elevating DWI to a class D felony based on two prior DWI convictions is not imposing an additional penalty upon the earlier DWI convictions. Rather it is merely stiffening the penalties for the latest DWI offense based upon the defendant's repetitive conduct." 173 Misc. 2d at 618, 661 N.Y.S.2d at 941.

In *People v. Lancaster*, 260 A.D.2d 660, 688 N.Y.S.2d 711 (3d Dep't 1999), the defendant, who pled guilty to misdemeanor DWI, claimed on appeal that "County Court erred by accepting his plea without advising him that a subsequent conviction of the crime of driving while intoxicated would constitute a felony." 260 A.D.2d at ___, 688 N.Y.S.2d at 712. On appeal, the Appellate Division, Third Department, stated that "[i]t is abundantly clear that the fact that a defendant is subject to enhanced criminal treatment for an offense that he or she may commit in the future is a collateral consequence of the plea, about which a defendant need not be advised." 260 A.D.2d at ___, 688 N.Y.S.2d at 712.

In addition to a prior conviction for DWI occurring within 10 years of a present charge of DWI, a defendant can be indicted for felony DWI if they have predicate convictions for vehicular assault in the first or second degree as defined in Penal Law §§ 120.03 and 120.04, or vehicular manslaughter in the first or second degree, as defined by Penal Law §§ 125.12 and 125.13, within the preceding 10-year period.

In addition, VTL § 1193(1)(d)(4) defines commercial alcohol felonies. Unlike conventional DWAIs, a conviction for VTL § 1192(1) while operating a commercial vehicle is a misdemeanor and can be a predicate for repeat offenses occurring within 10 years. Similarly, it can serve as a predicate for violations of VTL § 1192(2) and (3) when the defendant is charged with *commercial* vehicle operation.

Where a defendant operates a motor vehicle in violation of § 1192(6) (commercial DWI), and has prior convictions for *two* or more violations of subdivisions (1), (2), (3), (4), or (6) of VTL § 1192, one of which was a misdemeanor, within the preceding *five* years, the pending charge shall be a Class E felony. VTL § 1193(1)(d)(4)(i). Upon conviction of this Class E felony, the defendant shall be punished by a fine of not less than $1,000, nor more than $5,000, and/or by a period of imprisonment as provided by the penal law, to wit: a maximum sentence of $1^1/_3$ to four years.

Where the defendant is charged with a violation of VTL § 1192(1), (2), (3), or (4) arising out of the operation of a school bus, special vehicle, or commercial vehicle and has *three* or more prior convictions for the same conduct, one of which was a misdemeanor, within the preceding five years, the pending charge shall be a Class D felony. VTL § 1193(1)(d)(4)(ii). Upon conviction of this Class D felony, the defendant shall be punished by a fine of not less than $2,000 nor more than $10,000, and/or by a period of imprisonment as provided by the penal law, to wit: a maximum sentence of $2^1/_3$ to seven years.

§ 9:4   Proving the underlying conviction

Research References

West's Key Number Digest, Automobiles ⚖324

The procedure for proving the underlying conviction in a vehicular crimes prosecution is somewhat challenging. On the face of it, the defendant either admits the validity of the underlying conviction, or the prosecutor must submit independent proof of it. The challenge arises out of having to meet both the statutory and case law requirements. If a defendant elects to admit the underlying conviction, this admission must be obtained in accordance with the requirements of CPL § 200.60.

CPL § 200.60(3)(a) provides that where a defendant has admitted a previous conviction, which has raised an offense of lower grade to higher grade and becomes an element of the higher grade offense, "no evidence in support thereof may be adduced by the people, and the court must submit the case to the jury without reference thereto, and as if the fact of such previous conviction were not an element of the offense." In felony DWI cases, however, the Third Department has held that although it is the better practice not to inform the jury that the DWI charges were felonies, it is not reversible error to do so. *See People v. Koponen*, 129 A.D.2d 838, 513 N.Y.S.2d 851 (3d Dep't 1987). The statute only prohibits the submission of evidence concerning the admitted conviction, and does not direct the court to refrain from reading the indictment in full to the jury or otherwise characterizing the crime as a felony. 513 N.Y.S.2d at 853.

CPL § 200.60 is inapplicable where the charged crime is of no higher grade than the prior enumerated conviction(s), and where limiting instructions are given to the jury as to the limited purposes for which evidence of the prior crime(s) could be considered. *See People v. Poje*, 129 A.D.2d 744, 514 N.Y.S.2d 504 (2d Dep't 1987) (statute inapplicable where both charged and predicate offenses were misdemeanors).

CPL § 200.60 is violated where the defendant is not arraigned upon a "special information" alleging a previous DWI conviction, and under these circumstances, is denied the opportunity to contest the validity of the predicate conviction. The defendant may only be tried on misdemeanor charges. *See People v. Hegedus*, 146 A.D.2d 586, 536 N.Y.S.2d 508 (2d Dep't 1989) (DWI felony counts for which defendant was convicted reduced to misdemeanors where defendant was not arraigned on Special Information). *Cf. People v. Yunga*, 122 A.D.3d 951, __, 997 N.Y.S.2d 470, 471 (2d Dep't 2014), leave to appeal denied, 25 N.Y.3d 993, 10 N.Y.S.3d 536, 32 N.E.3d 973 (2015) ("The defendant additionally claims that the People failed to file a special information pursuant to CPL 200.60, charging that he had previously been convicted of driving while intoxicated. However, that nonjurisdictional procedural defect was forfeited by the defendant's plea of guilty").

The option to admit the underlying conviction pursuant to CPL § 200.60 is mandatory. It is the defendant's choice and not the prosecutor's.

A felony DWI defendant must be given an opportunity to admit, outside of the jury's presence, the element that raised his crime to felony in grade, without the risk that the prior conviction will come out before the jury. In *People v. Cooper*, 78 N.Y.2d 476, 577 N.Y.S.2d 202 (1991), the Court of Appeals addressed this situation and held:

That opportunity could have been afforded by a special information charging him with the prior conviction, the revocation of his license, and knowledge of the conviction and revocation. If defendant chose to admit those facts, no mention of them was necessary before the jury. If defendant denied all or any of those facts, the People could have proceeded with their proof as the statute provides.

78 N.Y.2d at 483, 577 N.Y.S.2d at 205.

Failure to follow the *Cooper* procedure is manifestly prejudicial to a defendant because it shows him to be a repeat offender before the jury, and limiting instructions cannot suffice to remove the resulting prejudice. 78 N.Y.2d at 484.

Where the county court and the prosecutor comment upon the defendant's prior conviction in the presence of the jury, a new trial is warranted. In *People v. Johnson*, 209 A.D.2d 1013, 620 N.Y.S.2d 21 (4th Dep't 1994), the court stated:

The failure to follow the procedure mandated by CPL 200.60 "was manifestly prejudicial to defendant because it showed him before the jury to be a repeat offender" (*People v. Sawyer*, 188 A.D.2d 939, 940, 592 N.Y.S.2d 92). Although the Court instructed the jury that the prior conviction should not be considered on the issue whether defendant was operating a vehicle while intoxicated, "such limiting instructions cannot be relied upon to eliminate the likelihood of prejudice resulting from a jury's knowledge that the defendant is a repeat offender" (*People v. Cooper*, 78 N.Y.2d 476, 484, 577 N.Y.S.2d 202, 206, 583 N.E.2d 915, 919).

People v. Johnson, 620 N.Y.S.2d at 22. *See also People v. Sawyer*, 188 A.D.2d 939, 592 N.Y.S.2d 92 (3d Dep't 1992); *People v. Brockway*, 202 A.D.2d 1015, 609 N.Y.S.2d 481 (4th Dep't 1994) (no infirmity in prosecutor's later amendment of special information transferring from indictment to special information all facts to be established through proof of prior conviction).

In *People v. Mason*, 248 A.D.2d 751, 669 N.Y.S.2d 712 (3d Dep't 1998), the defendant, who was charged with felony DWI and AUO, admitted, pursuant to CPL § 200.60, that he had a prior alcohol conviction and the resultant license revocation within the past 10 years. Nonetheless, at trial the People elicited the fact of the revocation from the arresting officer. The defendant's motion for a mistrial was denied, but the court gave the jury a curative instruction. The defendant was convicted of both charges. On appeal, the Appellate Division, Third Department, held that:

County Court committed reversible error by providing the curative instruction instead of granting defendant's motion for a mistrial. Revelation of the conviction-related fact of defendant's previous license revocation rendered the special information and arraignment procedure of CPL 200.60 "an empty gesture." The court's limiting instruction was insufficient to eliminate the likelihood of prejudice to defendant. Therefore, a new trial is necessary.

248 A.D.2d at 752–53, 669 N.Y.S.2d at 714 (citation omitted).

A court need only advise a defendant of his option to admit or deny a prior DWI, and need not inform him that he may controvert the constitutionality of the prior offense. *People v. Cagle*, 158 A.D.2d 931, 551 N.Y.S.2d 95 (4th Dep't 1990).

If the defendant chooses not to admit the underlying conviction, the People have the burden of proving this element. In the past, the submission of a certificate of conviction was deemed sufficient proof of this element. The certificate of conviction, however, does not establish that the defendant named in the certificate is the same defendant being presently prosecuted. The People have the burden of proving that the defendant on trial is the same person who was the subject of the certificate of conviction.

In *People v. Vollick*, 148 A.D.2d 950, 539 N.Y.S.2d 187 (4th Dep't 1989), order *aff'd*, 75 N.Y.2d 877, 554 N.Y.S.2d 473 (1990), the People introduced into evidence a certificate certifying that a judgment of conviction was entered in the Town of Gates Court on September 26, 1978, convicting Gary H. Vollick of the offense of DWI. No other evidence was offered to show that the defendant was the same person named in the certificate of conviction. At the close of the People's proof, the defendant moved to dismiss the information on the ground that a certificate of conviction, standing alone, was insufficient to establish that the defendant had previously been convicted of a DWI. The court denied the motion and the defendant was found guilty.

On appeal, the Appellate Division, Fourth Department reversed, concluding:

> The evidence was legally insufficient to establish that defendant committed a felony. When defendant chose to remain mute at his arraignment on the special information, the burden fell to the People to prove defendant's prior conviction as an element of the offense charged. (*See*, CPL 200.60[3][b]; *cf.*, CPL 400.15, 400.16, 400.20, 400.21 [where uncontroverted allegations are deemed to be admitted]). To meet their burden, the People relied solely upon the facts recited in the certificate of conviction. CPL 60.60(1) provides that a certificate of conviction "constitutes presumptive evidence of the facts stated in such certificate." While the certificate here states that Gary H. Vollick was previously convicted, it does not otherwise state any facts demonstrating that the person named in the certificate is the defendant (*cf.*, CPL 60.60[2] [presumptive evidence rule governing reports of official fingerprint records]). The certificate proves only that a person by the same name as defendant was previously convicted. We conclude, therefore, that the evidence fails to establish that defendant's violation of Vehicle and Traffic Law § 1192(2) and (3) constituted felonies.

People v. Vollick, 539 N.Y.S.2d at 188. The Court of Appeals affirmed for the reasons stated in the memorandum of the Appellate Division.

Vollick concerned proof of a prior DWI at *trial*. A similar issue, which was addressed by the Court of Appeals several years later, was whether a certificate of conviction was sufficient proof before a *grand jury* to establish prima facie evidence of the prior conviction. In other words, since a grand jury does not require proof beyond a reasonable doubt, but, rather, merely prima facie evidence of each element of the crime, the issue was whether the certificate of conviction would suffice to establish the prior conviction before a grand jury.

In *People v. Van Buren*, 82 N.Y.2d 878, 609 N.Y.S.2d 170 (1993), the prosecutor submitted to the grand jury a certificate of conviction indicating that within the last 10 years a Robert L. Van Buren had been convicted of DWI in Genesee County. No further evidence regarding the identity of the previously convicted individual was presented. The defendant moved to dismiss or reduce the felony count, claiming there was insufficient prima facie proof before the grand jury to establish the predicate conviction. The county court granted the motion and reduced the felony charge to a misdemeanor. On the People's appeal, the Appellate Division reversed and reinstated the DWI felony count.

The Court of Appeals concluded there was insufficient proof before the grand jury to establish the prior conviction.

> That a person named Robert L. Van Buren was convicted of driving while intoxicated within the preceding 10-year period even in the same county did not constitute prima facie proof that the defendant was the same person previously convicted of DWI within the last 10 years. The certificate of conviction standing alone without some further, connecting evidence tending to show that defendant was the same Robert L. Van Buren named in the certificate, was insufficient to "establish every element of [the] offense charged" (CPL 70.10(1); *cf. People v. Vollick*, 148 A.D.2d 950, 539 N.Y.S.2d 187, order *aff'd* 75 N.Y.2d 877, 554 N.Y.S.2d 473, 553 N.E.2d 1021).

People v. Van Buren, 609 N.Y.S.2d at 171.

If the certificate of conviction is insufficient to prove the presence of a prior conviction, what evidence would be sufficient to establish the prior conviction? In *People v. Rattelade*, 226 A.D.2d 1107, 642 N.Y.S.2d 1 (4th Dep't 1996), the grand jury was presented with the certificate of conviction which indicated that an individual by the defendant's name was previously convicted of DWI within the last 10 years. Also before the grand jury were the Breathalyzer test record and a DMV driver's abstract. Each of the above documents included the defendant's date of birth. The court concluded that the documentation before the grand jury provided sufficient connecting evidence tending to show that the defendant was the same person who had been previously convicted of DWI.

In *People v. O'Bannard*, N.Y.L.J., 5/20/94, p.25, Col.2 (Sup. Ct. Queens Co.), an inspection of the grand jury minutes indicated that in addition to the oral testimony of the witnesses, the People introduced a chemical test analysis document, signed and certified by a police officer, which included the defendant's name, address, place of test, etc. The address listed was 113-*17* Sutphin Blvd., Jamaica, New York.

The second document submitted was the certificate of conviction, which contained the defendant's name, address, date of birth, the date of arrest, docket number 6Q020269, the arraignment charges, the court, and the disposition of the case. In this document, the address listed was 113-*13* Sutphin Blvd., Queens, N.Y.

The Court concluded that the similarity of the two addresses, together with the defendant's unusual name "is enough evidence linking the present defendant with the person who pled guilty within the last 10 years . . . [T]he court is satisfied that it is 'reasonably likely' that we are dealing with the same Clyde O'Bannard."

In *People v. Dugan*, 188 A.D.2d 927, 592 N.Y.S.2d 117 (3d Dep't 1992), in addition to producing the certificate of conviction, the People called the defense attorney who had represented an individual with the same name as the defendant in the prior matter. The attorney testified that he represented an individual with the same name on a DWI charge and that such an individual had the same birth date as the defendant. The Appellate Division, Third Department, found that based on this information, a jury could reasonably infer that the individual convicted in the prior matter and the present defendant were one and the same.

Similarly, in *People v. Wenstley*, 152 A.D.2d 1000, 544 N.Y.S.2d 96 (4th Dep't 1989), the city court judge who accepted the defendant's plea and imposed sentence thereon, produced his original notes and testified that the defendant had pled guilty to DWI and had been sentenced on that plea. The court found this evidence, even in the absence of the certificate of conviction, sufficient to prove the defendant's prior conviction. Note that this case was decided prior to *Vollick* and *Van Buren*.

In *People v. Jones*, 177 A.D.2d 1000, 578 N.Y.S.2d 20 (4th Dep't 1991), the People relied on the transcripts from the earlier trial regarding the defendant's date of birth, together with a certificate of conviction, to establish the defendant's identity. The Appellate Division, Fourth Department, found this evidence insufficient in view of the fact that there was a discrepancy in the birth date information. The certificate of conviction contained a birth date of January 23, 1966, whereas the defendant in the present case told the arresting officer that he was born on January

23, 1969. Given the lack of identifying information, the court found the proof insufficient to establish the prior conviction.

With regard to a grand jury proceeding, in addition to introducing sufficient evidence to establish the prior conviction, the People must also instruct the jury as to the requirements necessary to justify indictment for a felony DWI. VTL § 1193(1)(c) explains that it is a felony for a person to operate a vehicle in violation of VTL § 1192(2), (3), or (4) after having been convicted of one of the following offenses within the preceding 10 years: VTL § 1192(2), (3), or (4); vehicular assault (Penal Law §§ 120.03 or 120.04); or, vehicular manslaughter (Penal Law §§ 125.12 or 125.13). In *People v. Keller*, 214 A.D.2d 825, 625 N.Y.S.2d 325 (3d Dep't 1995), the court dismissed a felony DWI count based upon the People's failure to do so.

> [F]or although proof of defendant's prior convictions had been placed in evidence, it does not appear from the record that the grand jury was furnished with any legal instructions as to the findings necessary to justify indictment for the higher grade offense. This significant omission could have resulted in prejudice to defendant.

People v. Keller, 625 N.Y.S.2d at 326–27.

§ 9:5   Challenging the predicate conviction

Research References

West's Key Number Digest, Automobiles ⚷324

A previous conviction obtained in violation of the United States Constitution cannot be "counted" in determining whether a defendant is a predicate and/or persistent felony offender. *See* CPL § 400.20(6); CPL § 400.21(7)(b). In this regard, the CPL provides a legislatively created procedure for challenging the constitutionality of felony convictions sought to be used to enhance a defendant's *sentence*. *See* CPL § 400.20; CPL § 400.21. By contrast, no such statutory authority exists permitting a defendant to challenge the constitutionality of a prior conviction sought to be used to enhance a current *charge* (*e.g.*, a prior DWI conviction sought to be used to elevate a current DWI charge from a misdemeanor to a felony, and/or from a class E felony to a class D felony).

In *People v. Knack*, 72 N.Y.2d 825, 530 N.Y.S.2d 541 (1988), *aff'g* 128 A.D.2d 307, 516 N.Y.S.2d 465 (2d Dep't 1987), the Court of Appeals refused to judicially create such a procedure. *See also People v. DeJesus*, 122 Misc. 2d 190, 471 N.Y.S.2d 195 (N.Y. Co. Sup. Ct. 1983). Pursuant to *Knack*, a defendant cannot file a motion in limine, a motion to suppress, or a motion to controvert a special information challenging the constitutionality of a prior, aggravating DWI conviction *within the context of a pending crim-*

inal action. See also People v. Brown, 160 A.D.2d 1037, __, 553 N.Y.S.2d 875, 877 (3d Dep't 1990) (validity of prior conviction is question of law for court, *not* question of fact for jury).

Several lower court decisions reaching the opposite conclusion should thus be disregarded. *See, e.g., People v. Ryan*, 127 Misc. 2d 138, 485 N.Y.S.2d 933 (Westchester Co. Ct. 1985), judgment aff'd, 161 A.D.2d 677, 558 N.Y.S.2d 838 (2d Dep't 1990); *People v. Solomon*, 113 Misc. 2d 790, 449 N.Y.S.2d 875 (Kings Co. Sup. Ct. 1982); *People v. Sirianni*, 109 Misc. 2d 781, 440 N.Y.S.2d 988 (Cattaraugus Co. Ct. 1981), order *rev'd*, 89 A.D.2d 775, 453 N.Y.S.2d 485 (4th Dep't 1982); *People v. Dorn*, 105 Misc. 2d 244, 431 N.Y.S.2d 974 (Oneida Co. Ct. 1980). *See generally People v. Knickerbocker*, 136 A.D.2d 769, __, 523 N.Y.S.2d 227, 228 (3d Dep't 1988) ("A misdemeanor conviction which was obtained when the defendant was not represented by counsel or had not intelligently waived counsel cannot be used as the basis to enhance a subsequent crime from a misdemeanor to a felony"). Notably, *Ryan, Solomon, Sirianni, Dorn* and *Knickerbocker* all rely on *Baldasar v. Illinois*, 446 U.S. 222, 100 S.Ct. 1585 (1980), which was overruled by *Nichols v. United States*, 511 U.S. 738, 114 S.Ct. 1921 (1994).

In any event, the rationale of the *Knack* Court was that a judicially created procedure permitting a constitutional challenge to a prior DWI conviction within the context of a pending DWI case is unnecessary, "since there already exist several procedural vehicles for challenging the constitutional propriety of guilty pleas under the facts presented here (*cf., People v. Lopez*, 71 N.Y.2d 662, 529 N.Y.S.2d 465, 525 N.E.2d 5)." *Knack,* 72 N.Y.2d at 827, 530 N.Y.S.2d at 542. For example, the defendant could have challenged the constitutionality of the prior conviction by utilizing one (or more) of the following procedures:

(a) A motion to withdraw the plea. *See* CPL § 220.60(3);

(b) A direct appeal from the judgment of conviction; and/or

(c) A motion to vacate the judgment of conviction (*i.e.*, a coram nobis application). *See* CPL § 440.10.

In *People v. Grubstein*, a defendant charged with felony DWI in 2010 moved to vacate his predicate misdemeanor DWI conviction, which took place in 2008, on the ground that the Town Justice had let him plead guilty *pro se* and without a proper waiver of his right to counsel. Town Court granted the motion. The Appellate Term reversed on the ground that the defendant had not filed a direct appeal of the predicate conviction. 2012 WL 6554673 (App. Term, 9th & 10th Jud. Dist. 2012). The Court of Appeals granted leave and reversed the Appellate Term, holding that "a defendant who asserts that he was deprived of his right to counsel when he pleaded guilty pro se is not barred from raising that claim in a motion under CPL 440.10 by his failure to raise it on direct appeal." 24 N.Y.3d 500, 501-02, 2 N.Y.S.3d 1, 1 (2015). On remand, the Appellate Term considered Town Court's order on the merits, and affirmed. 2015 WL 3369828 (App. Term, 9th & 10th Jud. Dist. 2015).

§ 9:6 Vacating prior conviction

Research References

West's Key Number Digest, Automobiles ⊙~324

Vacatur of the predicate conviction, even if occurring after conviction for felony DWI based on predicate, requires reduction of the convicted felony counts to misdemeanors. *See People v. Frieary*, 144 A.D.2d 382, 533 N.Y.S.2d 935 (2d Dep't 1988).

A CPL Article 440 motion to vacate a judgment of conviction must be made in the court in which the judgment was entered. *See Pirro v. Cirigliano*, 226 A.D.2d 465, 641 N.Y.S.2d 324 (2d Dep't 1996), judgment aff'd, 88 N.Y.2d 1033, 651 N.Y.S.2d 11, 673 N.E.2d 1238 (1996).

§ 9:7 Effect of out-of-state DWI convictions

Research References

West's Key Number Digest, Automobiles ⊙~324, 332

Prior to November 1, 2006, VTL § 1192(8) provided that, for purposes of determining the consequences of a violation of VTL § 1192, a prior out-of-state conviction for operating a motor vehicle while under the influence of alcohol or drugs was deemed to be a prior conviction of DWAI in violation of VTL § 1192(1). Effective November 1, 2006, VTL § 1192(8) provides as follows:

Effect of prior out-of-state conviction. A prior out-of-state conviction for operating a motor vehicle while under the influence of alcohol or drugs shall be deemed to be a prior conviction of a violation of this section for purposes of determining penalties imposed under this section or for purposes of any administrative action required to be taken pursuant to [VTL § 1193(2)]; provided, however, that such conduct, had it occurred in this state, would have constituted a misdemeanor or felony violation of any of the provisions of [VTL § 1192]. Provided, however, that if such conduct, had it occurred in this state, would have constituted a violation of any provisions of [VTL § 1192] which are not misdemeanor or felony offenses, then such conduct shall be deemed to be a prior conviction of a violation of [VTL § 1192(1)] for purposes of determining penalties imposed under this section or for purposes of any administrative action required to be taken pursuant to [VTL § 1193(2)].

Thus, a prior out-of-state DWI conviction can now potentially be used as a predicate conviction for a felony DWI charge.

Critically, however, the enabling portion of this change to VTL § 1192(8) expressly provides that it only applies to out-of-state convictions that occurred on or after November 1, 2006. *See also People v. Ballman*, 15 N.Y.3d 68, 70, 904 N.Y.S.2d 361, 362, 930 N.E.2d 282, ___ (2010) ("This appeal raises the issue whether Vehicle and Traffic Law § 1192(8) allows an out-of-state conviction occurring prior to November 1, 2006 to be considered for purposes of elevating a charge of driving while intoxicated from a misdemeanor to a felony. We hold that it does not.").

§ 9:8   Grand jury notification and action

Research References

West's Key Number Digest, Automobiles ☞332; Grand Jury ☞35, 36.1

CPL § 190.50(5)(a) requires the district attorney to inform a defendant who has been charged with a felony in a local criminal court of his intent to submit the case to a grand jury. A defendant has a right to testify before the grand jury and this requirement of notification is imposed in order to accord the defendant an opportunity to exercise this right.

The statute, however, refers to "a defendant who has been arraigned in a local criminal court upon a currently undisposed of felony complaint." In many instances, a felony DWI case will commence with the filing of a misdemeanor complaint rather than a felony complaint. The reason for this is that the police may not be aware of the defendant's prior conviction at the time of his arrest, or they may simply wish to avoid the additional paperwork associated with a felony. Since a large number of defendants charged with a felony DWI are allowed to plead to a misdemeanor in local criminal court, their reasoning is valid. In such cases, the People are not required to serve notice of their intent to submit the case to the grand jury because the defendant has not, in fact, been charged with a felony in local criminal court.

When the People do serve a notice pursuant to CPL § 190.50(5)(a), of their intent to submit a case to the grand jury, the burden shifts to the defendant to serve the People with a written notice making a request to testify and providing an address to which communications may be sent.

The request to testify must be unequivocal. In *People v. Leggio*, 133 Misc. 2d 320, 507 N.Y.S.2d 131 (N.Y. Co. Sup. Ct. 1986), the defense responded to a notice from the People saying, "Please take notice that the defendant Phillip Leggio reserves his right to testify upon notice to this office of presentment of evidence against Mr. Leggio before the aforesaid grand jury." The People presented the case to the grand jury without making any provision for the defendant to testify. In denying the defendant's subsequent motion to dismiss the indictment, Judge Irving Lang held that:

> [I]n order to effectuate that right, the defendant must activate it in an affirmative manner by making an unqualified, specific request to come before the grand jury and testify . . . "Reserving" one's right to testify, as Leggio did, and "requesting" to appear before the grand jury, as the statute requires, are not synonymous. Since defendant's letter did not constitute a request to testify within the meaning of the statute, the prosecutor had no obligation to notify Leggio to appear before the grand jury.

507 N.Y.S.2d at 133.

> Where a putative defendant exercises his right to testify on his own behalf before the grand jury, the defendant must be given an opportunity to give his version of events prior to being examined by the prosecutor. See, People v. Miller, 144 A.D.2d 94, 537 N.Y.S.2d 318 (3d Dep't 1989). An indictment will be dismissed where a prosecutor continually interrupts the defendant and fails to give him the opportunity to continue his narrative testimony.

537 N.Y.S.2d at 320.

In a grand jury proceeding, it is not necessary for an expert witness to appear in person. Rather, in order to avoid needless delay and time consumption, CPL § 190.30(2) permits the introduction of certified reports of experts as an alternative to live testimony. See People v. Washington, 228 A.D.2d 23, 652 N.Y.S.2d 750 (2d Dep't 1997).

In the event the defendant is indicted on a misdemeanor, the filing of the charges in a superior court divests the local criminal court of jurisdiction. See CPL § 170.20. However, pursuant to the N.Y. Constitution, Article VI, § 19(b), a county court has the authority to transfer the matter back to the lower court or to any court having jurisdiction, other than the supreme court, even over the People's objection. See Matter of Clute v. McGill, 229 A.D.2d 70, 655 N.Y.S.2d 201 (3d Dep't 1997).

A prosecutor may not, without court order, reopen a case before the grand jury or after a vote has been taken. See, e.g., People v. Wilkins, 68 N.Y.2d 269, 508 N.Y.S.2d 893 (1986). See also CPL § 190.75(3).

§ 9:9   Waiver of indictment

Research References

West's Key Number Digest, Automobiles ⚷324, 332

A defendant may waive indictment and consent to be prose-

cuted by a superior court information when: (1) a local criminal
court has held the defendant for the action of a grand jury; (2)
the defendant is not charged with a Class A felony; and (3) the
district attorney consents to the waiver. CPL § 195.10(1).

§ 9:10   Defendant charged with misdemeanor DWI may not waive indictment

Research References

West's Key Number Digest, Automobiles ⚷324, 332

A defendant charged with a misdemeanor DWI cannot waive
indictment and plead to a superior court information charging
him with a felony. CPL § 195.10(1)(a) requires that the matter be
held for grand jury action before the defendant may waive
indictment. A defendant can only be ordered held for the action
of a grand jury following waiver of a hearing on a *felony* complaint (*see* CPL § 180.30(1)); or upon a finding made at the conclusion of a hearing on a *felony* complaint that there is reasonable
cause to believe that the defendant committed a crime (*see* CPL
§ 180.70(1)).

In *People v. Chamberlain*, 221 A.D.2d 869, 634 N.Y.S.2d 249
(3d Dep't 1995), the court found that because the defendant was
originally charged with a misdemeanor, the matter could not be
held for grand jury action. Thus, his waiver was ineffective and
the superior court information on which he was prosecuted was
jurisdictionally defective. As a consequence, the defendant's
conviction was a nullity.

§ 9:11   Second felony offenders

Research References

West's Key Number Digest, Automobiles ⚷324, 332

Sentencing as a "second felony offender" is governed by Penal
Law (PL) § 70.06. This section provides, in pertinent part, that
"[a] second felony offender is a person . . . who stands convicted
of a felony defined in this chapter, . . . after having previously
been subjected to one or more predicate felony convictions . . ."
PL § 70.06(1)(a).

The express language of PL § 70.06, as well as the case law
interpreting it, makes clear that a defendant is not eligible for
second felony offender status unless the present felony conviction
is for a PL offense. Thus, a defendant presently convicted of a
felony under the Vehicle and Traffic Law (such as felony DWI,
felony AUO or felony leaving the scene of an accident) *cannot* be
sentenced as a second felony offender. *See, e.g., People v. Attea*,
269 A.D.2d 829, 703 N.Y.S.2d 804 (4th Dep't 2000); *People v.*

Givens, 268 A.D.2d 240, __, 701 N.Y.S.2d 352, 353–54 (1st Dep't 2000); *People v. Cammarata*, 216 A.D.2d 965, 629 N.Y.S.2d 716 (4th Dep't 1995); *People v. Clearwater*, 98 A.D.2d 912, 470 N.Y.S.2d 934 (3d Dep't 1983); *People v. Morris*, 86 A.D.2d 763, 448 N.Y.S.2d 82 (4th Dep't 1982); *People v. Smith*, 58 A.D.2d 635, 396 N.Y.S.2d 31 (2d Dep't 1977).

By contrast, where the present felony conviction is for a PL offense, a prior non-PL felony conviction (such as felony DWI, felony AUO, or felony leaving the scene of an accident) *can* serve as a predicate felony conviction for purposes of PL § 70.06. *See, e.g.*, *People v. Shannon*, 89 N.Y.2d 1000, 657 N.Y.S.2d 394 (1997); *People v. Butts*, 127 A.D.2d 777, 512 N.Y.S.2d 172 (2d Dep't 1987); *People v. Clearwater*, 98 A.D.2d 912, 470 N.Y.S.2d 934 (3d Dep't 1983).

This distinction does not violate the Equal Protection Clause, nor is it otherwise unconstitutional. *See, e.g.*, *Dillard v. LaVallee*, 559 F.2d 873 (2d Cir.1977); *People v. Shannon*, 89 N.Y.2d 1000, 657 N.Y.S.2d 394 (1997); *People v. Eastman*, 181 A.D.2d 1050, 582 N.Y.S.2d 586 (4th Dep't 1992); *People v. Clearwater*, 98 A.D.2d 912, 470 N.Y.S.2d 934 (3d Dep't 1983).

Where a defendant is illegally sentenced as a second felony offender, the issue (a) cannot be waived, and (b) can be raised on appeal regardless of whether it is properly preserved. *See, e.g.*, *People v. Attea*, 269 A.D.2d 829, 703 N.Y.S.2d 804 (4th Dep't 2000); *People v. Cammarata*, 216 A.D.2d 965, 629 N.Y.S.2d 716 (4th Dep't 1995).

§ 9:12 Persistent felony offender

Research References

West's Key Number Digest, Automobiles ⟜324, 332

Insofar as persistent felony offenders are concerned, Penal Law § 70.10 makes no distinction as to whether the present felony conviction arises out of the VTL, Penal Law, or any other statute. Accordingly, persistent felony offender status has been upheld when applied to a defendant convicted of multiple charges of DWI. *See People v. Daggett*, 88 A.D.3d 1296, __, 930 N.Y.S.2d 745, 748 (4th Dep't 2011), leave to appeal denied, 18 N.Y.3d 956, 944 N.Y.S.2d 485, 967 N.E.2d 710 (2012); *People v. Bowers*, 201 A.D.2d 830, 608 N.Y.S.2d 347 (3d Dep't 1994); *People v. Turner*, 234 A.D.2d 704, 651 N.Y.S.2d 655 (3d Dep't 1996). Of course, there must be sufficient proof that the defendant is the same person convicted of the prior felony offenses. *People v. Radcliffe*, 204 A.D.2d 1035, 612 N.Y.S.2d 534 (4th Dep't 1994).

A persistent felony offender is a person who stands convicted of a felony after having previously been convicted of two or more felonies. To constitute a previous felony conviction, a sentence in *excess* of one-year imprisonment must have been imposed. PL § 70.10(1)(b)(i). A prior conviction for which defendant had received a sentence of exactly one year, and no days in excess, was not considered a prior "felony" for persistent felony offender purposes. *People v. Melero*, 182 A.D.2d 839, 582 N.Y.S.2d 795 (2d Dep't 1992). In *People v. Roman*, 176 A.D.2d 568, 574 N.Y.S.2d 742 (1st Dep't 1991), the court concluded that a sentence of imprisonment of one year and one day was properly considered a predicate felony conviction for persistent felony offender treatment. Where a person was sentenced to drug rehabilitation for a maximum period of 60 months, the sentence was considered a "term of imprisonment" in excess of one year and it was not error to sentence the defendant as a persistent felony offender. *See also People v. Johnson*, 107 A.D.2d 763, 484 N.Y.S.2d 129 (2d Dep't 1985). Similarly, in *People v. Knapp*, 113 A.D.2d 154, 495 N.Y.S.2d 985 (3d Dep't 1985), the defendant was sentenced to a five-year probationary term which he subsequently violated. The court resentenced the defendant to a reformatory term of zero to four years. This reformatory sentence was found to be a sufficient predicate to sentence the defendant as a persistent felony offender.

In addition to the requirement that the sentence of imprisonment for the prior convictions be in excess of one year, the defendant must have been imprisoned for such prior convictions prior to the commission of the present felony. Penal Law § 70.10(1)(b)(ii).

Where a defendant meets the criteria for persistent felony offender treatment and the court "is of the opinion that the history and character of the defendant and the nature and circumstances of his criminal conduct indicate that extended incarceration and life-time supervision will best serve the public interest," the court *may* impose the sentence of imprisonment authorized for a Class A-1 felony, to wit, a minimum of 15 years to life. *See* Penal Law § 70.10(2).

In light of the severity of the persistent felony offender sentence, the statute "should be utilized only in the most extreme cases." *People v. Wright*, 104 Misc. 2d 911, 919, 429 N.Y.S.2d 993, 999 (S.Ct. N.Y. Co. 1980). *See also People v. Bowers*, 153 Misc. 2d 422, __, 581 N.Y.S.2d 575, 577 (Essex Co. Ct. 1992), judgment aff'd, 201 A.D.2d 830, 608 N.Y.S.2d 347 (3d Dep't 1994) ("enhanced sentencing must be approached with the greatest caution insofar as it is applied to the DWI defendant"), aff'd, 201 A.D.2d 830, 608 N.Y.S.2d 347 (3d Dep't 1994).

In *People v. Donhauser*, 255 A.D.2d 933, __, 683 N.Y.S.2d 357, 358 (4th Dep't 1998), as amended on reargument, (Dec. 31, 1998),

the Appellate Division, Fourth Department, modified a 15 years
to life sentence for felony DWI and AUO 1st to an indeterminate
sentence of 1¹/₃ to 4 years "[a]s a matter of discretion in the interest of justice." In so doing, the Court noted that "had defendant's
offense been committed after October 31, 1996, it could have been
punishable as a class D felony (*see*, Vehicle and Traffic Law
§ 1193[1][c][ii], added by L.1996, ch. 652)." *People v. Donhauser*,
683 N.Y.S.2d at 358. Similarly, in *People v. Beckwith*, 309 A.D.2d
1253, 767 N.Y.S.2d 713 (4th Dep't 2003), the same Court reduced
a 16 years to life sentence for class D felony DWI to 2 1/3 to 7
years "[a]s a matter of discretion in the interest of justice."

By contrast, in *People v. Travis*, 67 A.D.3d 1034, __, 890
N.Y.S.2d 552, 554 (2d Dep't 2009), leave to appeal denied, 14
N.Y.3d 845, 901 N.Y.S.2d 151, 927 N.E.2d 572 (2010), the Appellate Division, Second Department, upheld a sentence of 15 years
to life for defendant's convictions of felony DWI and AUO 1st,
reasoning as follows:

> In our view, the imposition of the enhanced sentence in the instant
> case corresponds to defendant's long and unwavering criminal
> history. A sentence of 15 years to life for a persistent felony of-
> fender convicted of operating a motor vehicle while under the influ-
> ence of alcohol or drugs in violation of Vehicle and Traffic Law
> § 1192(3) [driving while intoxicated] and aggravated unlicensed
> operation of a vehicle in the first degree has previously been upheld
> (*see People v. Turner*, 234 A.D.2d 704, 651 N.Y.S.2d 655; *People v.
> Bowers*, 201 A.D.2d 830, 608 N.Y.S.2d 347). Here, the County Court
> noted the defendant's extensive criminal background. In the 23
> years prior to sentencing, the defendant had been arrested and
> convicted of eight previous charges of operating a motor vehicle
> while under the influence of alcohol or drugs in violation of Vehicle
> and Traffic Law § 1192(3) [driving while intoxicated], six of which
> were felonies. Based upon the defendant's continued drinking and
> his continued failure to refrain from mixing alcohol and the privi-
> lege of driving an automobile, we find no reason to disturb the
> County Court's treatment of the defendant as a persistent felony
> offender. The sentence imposed was not excessive.

Notably, the defendants in *Travis*, *Turner* and *Bowers* not only
had extensive histories of committing DWI, but they also committed AUO 1st in connection with the offense for which they were
sentenced as persistent felony offenders. In other words, these
defendants not only refused to stop drinking and driving—they
continued to commit DWI while their driver's licenses were
revoked for DWI.

In *People v. Licausi*, 122 A.D.3d 771, __, 996 N.Y.S.2d 188, 190
(2d Dep't 2014), leave to appeal denied, 25 N.Y.3d 1166, 15
N.Y.S.3d 298, 36 N.E.3d 101 (2015), the defendant was convicted
of Aggravated Vehicular Homicide, Manslaughter 2nd, Unlawful
Fleeing a Police Officer 1st, DWAI Drugs, Reckless Driving and

numerous traffic infractions. The defendant was sentenced, as a persistent felony offender, to 25-years-to-life. On appeal, "as a matter of discretion in the interest of justice," the Appellate Division, Second Department, reduced the sentence to 18-years-to-life. *Id.* at __, 996 N.Y.S.2d at 189.

§ 9:13 Felony forfeiture of defendant's vehicle

Research References

West's Key Number Digest, Automobiles ⬥324, 332; Forfeitures ⬥3 to 5

In *Holtzman v. Bailey*, 132 Misc. 2d 25, 503 N.Y.S.2d 473 (Kings Co. Ct. 1986), the Kings County District Attorney moved for the forfeiture of the defendant's vehicle based upon the defendant having been convicted of felony DWI. In granting the motion, Judge Gerald Adler cited CPLR 1311, which provides for the forfeiture of the proceeds of a crime "or an instrumentality of a crime" where the defendant is convicted of a felony.

CPLR 1310(4) defines "instrumentality of a crime" as:

[A]ny property, other than real property and any buildings, fixtures, appurtenances, and improvements thereon, whose use contributes directly and materially to the commission of a crime defined in subdivisions 5 and 6 hereof.

CPLR 1310(5) defines "post-conviction forfeiture crime" as:

[A]ny felony defined in the Penal Law or any other chapter of the consolidated laws of the State.

Based upon these sections, Judge Adler entered an order directing the forfeiture of the defendant's 1984 Pontiac, or in the alternative, a money judgment in the sum of $11,125. Obviously, this rather innovative approach to the CPLR has substantially increased the cost of DWI in Brooklyn. *See also Dillon v. Castelli*, 132 Misc. 2d 1077, 506 N.Y.S.2d 418 (Nassau Co. Ct. 1986) (DWI defendant's vehicle subject to forfeiture).

§ 9:14 Forfeiture imposed though not referenced in plea bargain

Research References

West's Key Number Digest, Automobiles ⬥324, 332; Forfeitures ⬥3 to 5

CPLR 1311 is the statutory authority for forfeiture of the instrumentality of a felony. In *District Attorney of Kings County v. Roman*, 141 A.D.2d 601, 529 N.Y.S.2d 522 (2d Dep't 1988), the People applied for forfeiture of the defendant's vehicle which had been used in the commission of a felony.

The trial court had denied the People's motion in the interests of justice. The court found that the defendant had entered a plea of guilty based upon his good faith reliance on the district attorney's expressed and implied promises, which completely omitted any reference to the possible forfeiture of the defendant's vehicle. *People v. Roman*, 136 Misc. 2d 876, 519 N.Y.S.2d 463 (Kings Co. 1987), decision *rev'd*, 141 A.D.2d 601, 529 N.Y.S.2d 522 (1988).

Upon appeal, the Appellate Division reversed, and stated that:

> Promises which are not placed on the record are not enforceable (see, People v. Hood, 62 N.Y.2d 863, 477 N.Y.S.2d 621, 466 N.E.2d 161). Moreover, since the forfeiture action is a collateral consequence of the defendant's guilty plea, there was no requirement that the defendant be informed that the District Attorney would attempt to gain possession of the automobile (*see*, CPLR 1311(1); *People v. Mitchell*, 121 A.D.2d 403, 502 N.Y.S.2d 805).

District Attorney of Kings County v. Roman, 141 A.D.2d 601, 529 N.Y.S.2d 522 (2d Dep't 1988).

In the *Matter of Property Clerk of New York City Police Department v. Ferris*, 77 N.Y.2d 428, 568 N.Y.S.2d 577 (1991), the respondent's vehicle was seized as a result of the respondent's arrest for a drug charge. Ultimately, the respondent pled guilty to disorderly conduct and paid a fine. At the time of the plea, the prosecutor agreed to the release of the respondent's vehicle and subsequently indicated to the petitioner that the People had no further need of the vehicle. Despite this notification, a forfeiture proceeding was initiated.

In reversing the dismissal of the forfeiture petition, the Court of Appeals held that the prosecutor lacked authority to promise that the seized car would be returned as part of a plea bargain:

> In this case, assuming the prosecutor had promised to return the property rather than having stated the intention merely to certify that the evidence was no longer needed, he could not waive petitioner's claim. The Property Clerk is a separate and independent agency and has no discretion under the Code to recognize respondent as a "lawful claimant entitled to . . . such . . . property." . . . The court could not intervene and compel it to do so without statutory authorization.

568 N.Y.S.2d at 580 (citation omitted).

§ 9:15 Forfeiture denied where vehicle transferred prior to commencement of proceeding

Research References
West's Key Number Digest, Forfeitures ⊜3 to 5

Absent fraudulent transfer to avoid forfeiture, one Nassau

County court denied the district attorney the right to recover the value of the defendant's automobile in a civil forfeiture proceeding as an instrumentality of the crime of DWI. Here, the defendant had transferred his interest in the car prior to the commencement of the forfeiture proceeding. The district attorney sought to recover the value of the transferred automobile in disregard of the fact that the defendant no longer possessed any interest in the property at issue. In denying the motion, the court concluded:

> Plaintiff has submitted evidentiary proof that the defendant did not own the vehicle at the time the action was commenced. Plaintiff has also shown that the defendant did not fraudulently transfer his interest to avoid forfeiture or to promote his own gain. Under these facts, the court will not grant a money judgment for the value of the vehicle.

Dillon v. Hawthorne, 139 Misc. 2d 33, 526 N.Y.S.2d 733, 736 (Nassau Co. Ct. 1988).

§ 9:16   Charge to the jury—Intoxication defined

Research References
West's Key Number Digest, Automobiles ☞357(1), 357(6)

In *People v. Cruz*, 48 N.Y.2d 419, 423 N.Y.S.2d 625 (1979), the Court of Appeals defined the distinction between DWAI and DWI. They held that a person is impaired when the voluntary consumption of alcohol has:

> [A]ctually impaired, to any extent, the physical and mental abilities which he is expected to possess in order to operate a vehicle as a reasonable and prudent driver.

423 N.Y.S.2d at 628.

In contrast, the Court of Appeals held that intoxication is a greater degree of impairment which is reached when:

> [T]he driver has voluntarily consumed alcohol to the extent that he is incapable of employing the physical and mental abilities which he is expected to possess in order to operate a vehicle as a reasonable and prudent driver.

People v. Cruz, 48 N.Y.2d 419, 423 N.Y.S.2d 625, 629 (1979).

Despite this holding, trial courts are still using sample definitions which define impaired as voluntarily consuming alcohol to such an extent as to "diminish or reduce" their ability to operate the motor vehicle even in the slightest degree. In *People v. Stack*, 140 A.D.2d 389, 527 N.Y.S.2d 569 (2d Dep't 1988), the court held that this charge was reversible error in light of the fact that the proof of intoxication in the case was not overwhelming. The reversal was entered despite the fact that the defendant had failed to object to the charge as given during the course of the trial.

In *People v. Ardila*, 85 N.Y.2d 846, 623 N.Y.S.2d 847 (1995), the Court affirmed a jury instruction which defined "intoxication" as meaning the voluntary consumption of alcohol to the point where the individual's ability to drive safely is impaired to a substantial extent. This instruction had been objected to by defense counsel as being at variance with the standards set forth in *People v. Cruz*, 48 N.Y.2d 419, 423 N.Y.S.2d 625 (1979). In rejecting this challenge, the Court held:

> Contrary to defendant's contention, there is no meaningful semantic difference between being so inebriated that one's "ability to drive safely is impaired to a substantial extent"-the formula used by the trial court here-and being so inebriated that one is "incapable of employing the physical and mental abilities which [one] is expected to possess in order to operate a vehicle as a reasonable and prudent driver"-the formula used by this Court in People v. Cruz (48 N.Y.2d 419, 428, 423 N.Y.S.2d 625, 629, 399 N.E.3d 513). While the term "incapable" may connote absolute inability in the abstract, it loses that unconditional quality when it is used in conjunction with a relative concept like operating a vehicle in a "reasonable and prudent" manner (*see*, 48 N.Y.2d 419, 428, 423 N.Y.S.2d 625, 629, 399 N.E.3d 513; *see also*, *Matter of Johnston*, 75 N.Y.2d 403, 554 N.Y.S.2d 88, 553 N.E.2d 566).

People v. Ardila, 623 N.Y.S.2d at 847–48.

In *People v. Cunningham*, 95 N.Y.2d 909, 717 N.Y.S.2d 68 (2000), as amended nunc pro tunc, 95 N.Y.2d 949, 722 N.Y.S.2d 466, 745 N.E.2d 385 (2000), the trial court convicted the defendant of common law DWI following a bench trial. However, "the Trial Judge applied a definition of intoxication which improperly lowered the prosecution's burden of proof." 95 N.Y.2d at 910, 717 N.Y.S.2d at 68. When this issue was raised via a motion to set aside the verdict, the court reconsidered the evidence using the correct legal standard, and again found the defendant guilty of DWI. On appeal, the Court of Appeals reversed, holding that:

> The Court's reconsideration of its verdict under a different standard constituted a factual determination that "comes too late and exceeds the scope of [the court's] authority." To allow the second verdict to stand would permit the Trial Judge to engage in postverdict fact finding that would not be possible in a jury trial, thereby according "less finality to the verdict of a Trial Judge when sitting as [the trier of fact] than to a jury verdict."

95 N.Y.2d at 910, 717 N.Y.S.2d at 68 (citations omitted).

In *People v. Boice*, 89 A.D.2d 33, 455 N.Y.S.2d 859 (3d Dep't

1982), the jury charge for DWAI stated that a person's ability to operate a motor vehicle is impaired when "he has voluntarily consumed alcohol to such an extent as to diminish or reduce his ability to operate said motor vehicle, even in the slightest degree." Although this issue had not been preserved for appellate review, the court concluded that there may be merit to defendant's position.

> [S]ince the instructions given to the jury indicated that defendant would be guilty of the lesser included offense if his consumption of alcohol had even the slightest affect on *his* physical or mental abilities to operate his vehicle and did not judge defendant's abilities against the objective standard expected of the *average* driver.

People v. Boice, 455 N.Y.S.2d at 861.

§ 9:17   Intoxication—The factual determination

Research References

West's Key Number Digest, Automobiles ☞356(1), 356(6)

Generally, it is the finder of fact who determines whether the evidence establishes beyond a reasonable doubt that a defendant has:

> [V]oluntarily consumed alcohol to the extent that he is incapable of employing the physical and mental abilities which he is expected to possess in order to operate a vehicle as a reasonable and prudent driver.

People v. Cruz, 48 N.Y.2d 419, 423 N.Y.S.2d 625, 629 (1979).

That determination, however, is subject to appellate review. In *People v. Hagmann*, 175 A.D.2d 502, 572 N.Y.S.2d 952 (3d Dep't 1991), the defendant testified that he had had a full dinner before leaving with his date to attend a party. He had taken one or two puffs from a pipe containing marijuana on his way to the party. After arriving at the party, he drank two 12-ounce bottles of beer and two bar glasses of beer. Prior to leaving the party, he also drank "two fireball shots." A fireball was defined as 40-proof alcohol served in a three-quarter ounce shot glass. This consumption occurred between 9:15 PM and 1:30 AM. Subsequently, the defendant was involved in a fatal accident.

In reversing the defendant's conviction for DWI, the court provided guidance in regard to the factual determination of intoxication:

The common-law prohibition against driving while one's ability is impaired and driving while intoxicated both require a finding that "the driver has voluntarily consumed alcohol to the extent that he is incapable of employing the physical and mental abilities which he is expected to possess in order to operate a vehicle as a reasonable and prudent driver." * * * However, "[d]riving while intoxicated is a more serious offense * * * and thus involves a greater degree of impairment" (citation omitted). The Court of Appeals also stated in *People v. Cruz* (*supra*) that:

[T]he Legislature [has] recognized that the average person can consume a certain amount of alcohol without impairing his ability to operate a motor vehicle as he should. Otherwise the Legislature would not have provided that proof of .05 of 1% or less of blood alcohol content is prima facie evidence that the driver was not impaired or intoxicated . . . And the Legislature also recognized that some individuals may be able to consume greater amounts of alcohol without being impaired, as would the average driver . . . Thus the impairment statute, by simply providing prima facie standards, takes into account the "subjective" tolerance of individuals in determining the ability to drive possessed by a defendant at the time of arrest (48 N.Y.2d at 426, 423 N.Y.S.2d 625, 399 N.E.2d 513 (citations omitted)).

Considering the foregoing, it appears that in the instant record there is insufficient evidence to warrant the conclusion that defendant's consumption of alcohol caused him to be incapable of operating a vehicle as a reasonable and prudent driver. There is no testimony that any of his physical or mental abilities were impaired before impact to a degree sufficient to render him intoxicated. No chemical test results showing defendant's blood alcohol content were introduced into evidence. The only evidence of any actual impairment was that of a nurse who testified that, when brought into the hospital on a stretcher wearing a neck brace and hooked up to an intravenous needle, she observed that defendant had a number of abrasions, his eyes looked dazed and his speech was slow. The nurse detected an odor of alcohol on his breath but felt that he did not appear highly intoxicated. The evidence of speed and of driving over the center line of the roadway is equivocal in the circumstances of this case on the issue of the degree of impairment and not sufficient to warrant a finding of intoxication.

People v. Hagmann, 572 N.Y.S.2d at 953–54.

In *Senn v. Scudieri*, 165 A.D.2d 346, 567 N.Y.S.2d 665 (1st Dep't 1991), the court held that the fact that a person had consumed alcoholic beverages over a lengthy period of time and had slurred speech was insufficient to support a conclusion that the person was intoxicated.

In contrast, in *People v. Monk*, 177 A.D.2d 602, 576 N.Y.S.2d 172 (2d Dep't 1991), the court affirmed a conviction for DWAI based upon the testimony that the defendant staggered when he walked, had an impaired sense of balance, had slurred speech, bloodshot eyes, and an odor of alcohol on his breath. In addition, the defendant admitted that he had consumed "a few drinks."

In *People v. Lizzio*, 178 A.D.2d 741, 577 N.Y.S.2d 178 (3d Dep't 1991), the court set forth what is, perhaps, the minimum standard requisite to sustain a conviction for DWAI. In *Lizzio*, the evidence established that the defendant had been drinking and that she had struck the back of another vehicle in an area where there was little traffic. There was testimony to the effect that her eyes were bloodshot, her speech was slurred, and that she smelled of the odor of an alcoholic beverage. Two police officers testified that, in their opinion, the defendant was intoxicated. An ambulance volunteer testified that she felt that the defendant had been drinking.

Absent the aberrant driving and the opinions of intoxication, it is doubtful whether the court would have affirmed the conviction. The physical symptoms, in and of themselves, would not appear sufficient to sustain the conviction.

§ 9:18   DWAI as lesser included offense of DWI

Research References
West's Key Number Digest, Indictment and Information ⌖189(1), 189(8)

CPL § 1.20(37) defines "lesser included offense" as follows:

When it is impossible to commit a particular crime without concomitantly committing, by the same conduct, another offense of lesser grade or degree, the latter is, with respect to the former, a "lesser included offense." In any case in which it is legally possible to attempt to commit a crime, an attempt to commit such crime constitutes a lesser included offense with respect thereto.

CPL § 300.50 provides, in pertinent part, that:
  1. In submitting a count of an indictment to the jury, the court in its discretion may, in addition to submitting the greatest offense which it is required to submit, submit in the alternative any lesser included offense if there is a reasonable view of the evidence which would support a finding that the defendant committed such lesser offense but did not commit the greater. If there is no reasonable view of the evidence which would support such a finding, the court may not submit such lesser offense. Any error respecting such submission, however, is waived by the defendant unless he objects thereto before the jury retires to deliberate.
  2. If the court is authorized by subdivision one to submit a lesser included offense and is requested by either party to do so, it must do so. In the absence of such a request, the court's failure to submit such offense does not constitute error. *See also* CPL § 360.50(1), (2).

DWAI, in violation of VTL § 1192(1), is a lesser included offense of common law DWI, in violation of VTL § 1192(3). *See People v. Brown*, 53 N.Y.2d 979, 981, 441 N.Y.S.2d 662, 663 (1981); *People v. Hoag*, 51 N.Y.2d 632, 634, 435 N.Y.S.2d 698, 698

(1981). By contrast, DWAI is *not* a lesser included offense of *per se* DWI (*i.e.*, driving with a BAC of .10% or more), in violation of VTL § 1192(2). *See Brown*, 53 N.Y.2d at 981, 441 N.Y.S.2d at 663 ("A driver need not be impaired to be convicted under subdivision 2 of section 1192, and therefore driving while impaired is not a lesser included offense of that crime").

In *Hoag*, the Court of Appeals held that:

> [A] Trial Judge, who declines to submit DWAI as a lesser included offense to DWI on the ground that there is no reasonable view of the evidence that would support a finding that defendant committed the lesser charge makes a ruling on the law rather than in the exercise of discretion. In such a case, there being a reasonable view of the evidence to support submission of DWAI, defendant's DWI conviction must be reversed and a new trial ordered.

51 N.Y.2d at 634, 435 N.Y.S.2d at 698. In so holding, the Court reasoned that:

> To entitle defendant to a DWAI charge the evidence need not establish that she acted as a "normal, sober person," but only that she had not been rendered incapable by alcoholic beverage of employing the physical or mental abilities needed to operate a car, even though her abilities to do so were to some degree impaired. The standard by which that determination is to be made was succinctly stated in People v. Henderson, 41 N.Y.2d 233, 236, 391 N.Y.S.2d 563, 359 N.E.2d 1357: *"The court's appraisal of the persuasiveness of the evidence indicating guilt of the higher count is irrelevant; the question simply is whether on any reasonable view of the evidence it is possible for the trier of the facts to acquit the defendant on the higher count * * * and still find him guilty on the lesser one."*

51 N.Y.2d at 636, 435 N.Y.S.2d at 700 (emphasis added) (citation omitted). *See generally People v. Maharaj*, 89 N.Y.2d 997, 999, 657 N.Y.S.2d 392, 393 (1997) (In DWI case involving bench trial, "[d]efendant was entitled to the court's consideration of the lesser included offense under the common-law count as he requested, and the court's misapprehension [of the applicable law] and failure to do so constitutes reversible error"); *People v. Weinert*, 178 Misc. 2d 675, __, 683 N.Y.S.2d 690, 691 (App. Term, 2d Dep't 1998) (trial court's failure to include lesser included offense of DWAI on verdict sheet provided to jury constituted reversible error).

If the jury is unable to agree on a verdict with regard to the greater offense (*i.e.*, DWI), and asks the court if it can proceed to consider the lesser included offense (*i.e.*, DWAI), the proper response from the court is to instruct the jury "to consider the lesser included offense only upon reaching a unanimous verdict of not guilty of the greater." *People v. Boettcher*, 69 N.Y.2d 174, 183, 513 N.Y.S.2d 83, 87 (1987).

It should be noted that misdemeanor DWAI is not a lesser

included offense of misdemeanor DWI. *See People v. Harris*, 23 Misc. 3d 250, —, 870 N.Y.S.2d 859, 865 (Monroe Co. Ct. 2008); *People v. Jamison*, 170 Misc. 2d 974, —, 652 N.Y.S.2d 495, 496 (Rochester City Ct. 1996).

§ 9:19   No mandatory fine for felony DWI

Research References

West's Key Number Digest, Automobiles ⛬332

A defendant who is convicted of DWI as a class E felony is subject to "a fine of not less than one thousand dollars nor more than five thousand dollars *or . . .* a period of imprisonment as provided in the penal law, *or . . .* both such fine and imprisonment." VTL § 1193(1)(c)(i) (emphases added).

A defendant who is convicted of DWI as a class D felony is subject to "a fine of not less than two thousand dollars nor more than ten thousand dollars *or . . .* a period of imprisonment as provided in the penal law, *or . . .* both such fine and imprisonment." VTL § 1193(1)(c)(ii) (emphases added).

Accordingly, there is no mandatory fine with regard to a felony DWI. This fact was recognized by the court in *People v. Moore*, 212 A.D.2d 1062, 623 N.Y.S.2d 42 (4th Dep't 1995). In *Moore*, the Appellate Division, Fourth Department, vacated a felony DWI sentence on the ground that "County Court's statement that there was a mandatory minimum fine was based upon a misapprehension that the court did not have discretion in sentencing," 212 A.D.2d at 1062, 623 N.Y.S.2d at 43, and that such misapprehension was "a departure from the 'essential nature' of the right to be sentenced as provided by law." 212 A.D.2d at 1062, 623 N.Y.S.2d at 43 (citation omitted). *See also People v. Thomas*, 245 A.D.2d 1136, 667 N.Y.S.2d 536 (4th Dep't 1997) (same).

§ 9:20   Felony complaint cannot be orally reduced to misdemeanor complaint

Research References

West's Key Number Digest, Automobiles ⛬324

In *People v. Grune*, 175 Misc. 2d 281, 281–82, 670 N.Y.S.2d 300, 300 (App. Term, 2d Dep't 1997), the court held that "[e]ven though the defendant expressly consented to an oral reduction of the felony complaint, such a reduction was invalid and the defect nonwaivable." *See also People v. Jones*, 151 Misc. 2d 582, 584, 582 N.Y.S.2d 325, 326 (App. Term, 2d & 11th Jud. Dist. 1991).

§ 9:21 Duty of prosecutor to present *Brady* material to grand jury

Research References

West's Key Number Digest, Automobiles ⊙⃫324, 332

It is the duty of the prosecution to both properly instruct the indicting grand jury on the law and to bring before the grand jury relevant exculpatory evidence. *See People v. Lancaster*, 69 N.Y.2d 20, 511 N.Y.S.2d 559 (1986); *People v. Valles*, 62 N.Y.2d 36, 476 N.Y.S.2d 50 (1984).

In *People v. Livingston*, 175 Misc. 2d 322, 668 N.Y.S.2d 443 (Broome Co. Ct. 1997), the court dismissed an indictment charging the defendant with DWI where the People failed to show the grand jury a videotape of the defendant performing various field sobriety tests. Although the officers' grand jury testimony described the defendant as failing the tests, the court held that "any objective review of the videotape clearly indicates that the defendant's performance of those tests was far from failing." 175 Misc. 2d at 323, 668 N.Y.S.2d at 444. As such, the videotape constituted exculpatory evidence that should have been presented to the grand jury.

In *People v. Stanton*, 241 A.D.2d 687, __, 660 N.Y.S.2d 169, 170 (3d Dep't 1997), the Appellate Division, Third Department, affirmed the dismissal of a DWI indictment where (a) the defendant testified before the grand jury that he did not operate the vehicle, and indicated that the person who did "was in the courthouse and presumably available to testify before the Grand Jury," (b) a grand juror asked the ADA if that person was going to testify, and (c) the ADA responded that " '[w]ho comes in front of the grand jury and gives testimony is in the prosecutor's discretion.' " "The ADA's advice was clearly erroneous in view of CPL 190.50(3), which authorizes the Grand Jury to call witnesses who it believes possess relevant knowledge or information." 241 A.D.2d at __, 660 N.Y.S.2d at 170.

Similarly, in *People v. Butterfield*, 267 A.D.2d 870, __, 702 N.Y.S.2d 140, 141 (3d Dep't 1999), the Appellate Division, Third Department, reversed the defendant's conviction of DWI and AUO 1st, and dismissed the indictment, in an "appeal present-[ing] a question of first impression relating to the timeliness of a defense request pursuant to CPL § 190.50(6) that the Grand Jury hear the testimony of a witness designated by defendant." In *Butterfield*, the court held that "a defense request pursuant to CPL 190.50 is timely if delivered or communicated to the prosecutor at *any* time prior to the presentment of the case to the Grand Jury." 267 A.D.2d at __, 702 N.Y.S.2d at 143 (emphasis added).

In this regard, the Court of Appeals has repeatedly made clear that:

Prosecutors occupy a dual role as advocates and as public officers and, as such, they are charged with the duty not only to seek convictions but also to see that justice is done. In their role as public officers, they must deal fairly with the accused and be candid with the courts.

People v. Steadman, 82 N.Y.2d 1, 7, 603 N.Y.S.2d 382, 384 (1993). *See also People v. Pelchat*, 62 N.Y.2d 97, 105, 476 N.Y.S.2d 79, 83 (1984).

§ 9:22   Seizure and retention of vehicle at direction of DA's office

Research References

West's Key Number Digest, Automobiles ⚲324, 332

In *Montecalvo v. Columbia County*, 180 Misc. 2d 995, 695 N.Y.S.2d 235 (Columbia Co. Sup. Ct. 1999), order rev'd on other grounds, 274 A.D.2d 868, 711 N.Y.S.2d 849 (3d Dep't 2000), the court invalidated the seizure and retention of petitioner's pickup truck at the direction of the Columbia County DA's Office. The DA's Office claimed that the truck both (a) was the instrumentality of a crime (*i.e.*, DWI and AUO), and (b) may be needed as evidence in the criminal case against the driver (who was *not* the lessee of the truck). In so holding, the court reasoned that:

> Unless and until the New York State Legislature proclaims that all vehicles driven by allegedly drunk drives [sic] constitute *contraband* subject to seizure, this Court will not interfere with what is perhaps the most precious and fundamental of all rights, the right to possess personal property unfettered by governmental interference. The unlawful confiscation and retention of Petitioner's Vehicle, under the veil of needing the same as evidence against [the driver], is arbitrary and capricious, and without sound reasoning. Respondent has deprived Petitioner of her property without due process of law in violation of both the Fourteenth Amendment of the U.S. Constitution and Article I, Section 6 of the New York State Constitution.

180 Misc. 2d at __, 695 N.Y.S.2d at 237–38. In addition, the court ordered the county to pay all costs associated with the towing and storage of the truck. 180 Misc. 2d at __, 695 N.Y.S.2d at 238.

§ 9:23   NYC seizure and forfeiture policy upheld

Research References

West's Key Number Digest, Automobiles ⚲332; Forfeitures ⚲3 to 5

In *Grinberg v. Safir*, 266 A.D.2d 43, 698 N.Y.S.2d 218 (1st Dep't 1999), *aff'g* 181 Misc. 2d 444, 694 N.Y.S.2d 316 (N.Y. Co. Sup. Ct. 1999), the Appellate Division, First Department, rejected the petitioner's challenge, on numerous grounds, to the New York

City policy pursuant to which the City, utilizing § 14-140 of the Administrative Code of the City of New York, can seize and seek forfeiture of vehicles operated by individuals arrested for DWI.

However, the United States Court of Appeals for the Second Circuit subsequently held that:

[W]e find that the Due Process Clause requires that claimants be given an early opportunity to test the probable validity of further deprivation, including probable cause for the initial seizure. * * *

As a remedy, we order that claimants be given a prompt post-seizure retention hearing, with adequate notice, for motor vehicles seized as instrumentalities of crime pursuant to N.Y.C.Code § 14-140(b). * * *

Although we decline to dictate a specific form for the prompt retention hearing, we hold that, at a minimum, the hearing must enable claimants to test the probable validity of continued deprivation of their vehicles, including the City's probable cause for the initial warrantless seizure. In the absence of either probable cause for the seizure or post-seizure evidence supporting the probable validity of continued deprivation, an owner's vehicle would have to be released during the pendency of the criminal and civil proceedings. * * *

In conclusion, we hold that promptly after their vehicles are seized under N.Y.C.Code § 14-140 as alleged instrumentalities of crime, plaintiffs must be given an opportunity to test the probable validity of the City's deprivation of their vehicles *pendente lite*, including probable cause for the initial warrantless seizure.

Krimstock v. Kelly, 306 F.3d 40, 68, 68–69, 69, 70 (2d Cir. 2002) (footnote omitted). *See also County of Nassau v. Canavan*, 1 N.Y.3d 134, 144–45, 770 N.Y.S.2d 277, 286 (2003); *Property Clerk of Police Dept. of City of New York v. Harris*, 9 N.Y.3d 237, 239-40, 848 N.Y.S.2d 588, 590, 878 N.E.2d 1004 (2007) (pursuant to *Krimstock* and *Canavan*, "due process requires that an innocent co-owner be given an opportunity to demonstrate that his or her present possessory interest in a seized vehicle outweighs the City's interest in continuing impoundment") (footnote omitted). *See generally People v. Ramroop*, 50 Misc. 3d 1090, 27 N.Y.S.3d 811 (N.Y. City Crim. Ct. 2016).

In *Property Clerk, New York City Police Dep't v. Lee*, 183 Misc. 2d 360, 702 N.Y.S.2d 792 (N.Y. Co. Sup. Ct. 2000), the court held that a finance company which held a security interest in a vehicle that the City sought to forfeit pursuant to this policy could intervene in the forfeiture action to protect its rights.

§ 9:24 Nassau County seizure and forfeiture policy found to be unconstitutional

Research References

West's Key Number Digest, Automobiles ⚎332; Forfeitures ⚎3 to 5

In *County of Nassau v. Canavan*, 1 N.Y.3d 134, 138, 770 N.Y.S.2d 277, 281 (2003), the Court of Appeals held that the portion of the Nassau County Administrative Code being utilized to seize and forfeit vehicles operated by individuals arrested for DWI "did not satisfy constitutional requirements." Specifically, the ordinance at issue (a) permits vehicle forfeiture for *any* offense—including minor traffic infractions—which "risks violation of the Excessive Fines Clause" and "enhanc[es] the opportunity for disproportionate enforcement," 1 N.Y.3d at 141, 770 N.Y.S.2d at 283, and (b) fails to "limit forfeitures to vehicles not subject to a defense of innocent ownership." 1 N.Y.3d at 143, 770 N.Y.S.2d at 285.

By contrast, the *Canavan* Court pointed out that "when implemented pursuant to a carefully drafted statute, civil forfeiture of automobiles can be an extremely effective tool in the battle against drunk driving," 1 N.Y.3d at 138, 770 N.Y.S.2d at 281, and that "[g]iven the gravity of the crime of drunk driving, it is difficult to imagine that forfeiture of an automobile for such a crime could ever be excessive." 1 N.Y.3d at 140, 770 N.Y.S.2d at 283.

§ 9:25 *Attempted* DWI is *not* a legally cognizable offense

Research References

West's Key Number Digest, Automobiles ⚎332

Penal Law § 110.00 provides that "[a] person is guilty of an attempt to commit a crime when, with intent to commit a crime, he engages in conduct which tends to effect the commission of such crime." In terms of punishment, an attempt to commit a crime is generally punished one level lower than the crime itself. *See* PL § 110.05.

In *People v. Prescott*, 263 A.D.2d 254, 704 N.Y.S.2d 410 (4th Dep't 2000), order rev'd, 95 N.Y.2d 655, 722 N.Y.S.2d 778, 745 N.E.2d 1000 (2001), the Appellate Division, Fourth Department, *temporarily* created the crime of attempted DWI. On appeal, however, the Court of Appeals reversed, holding that attempted DWI is *not* a legally cognizable offense. *People v. Prescott*, 95 N.Y.2d 655, 722 N.Y.S.2d 778 (2001).

Ironically, although attempted DWI is not an appropriate *charge*, it apparently can be a valid *plea bargain. See People v. Foster*, 19 N.Y.2d 150, 278 N.Y.S.2d 603 (1967) (plea of guilty to nonexistent crime not invalid where defendant sought, and freely and knowingly accepted, such plea as part of a plea bargain struck for defendant's benefit). *See also People v. Francis*, 38 N.Y.2d 150, 155, 379 N.Y.S.2d 21, 26 (1975) ("a plea may be to a hypothetical crime"); *People v. Keizer*, 100 N.Y.2d 114, 118 n.2, 760 N.Y.S.2d 720, 723 n.2 (2003) (same); Donnino, Practice Commentary, McKinney's Cons. Laws of N.Y., Book 39, Penal Law § 110.00, at 85 ("Though there may not logically be an attempt to commit a particular substantive crime, a bargained-for guilt plea to such an attempt struck for the defendant's benefit may not be set aside on appeal").

One reason why a defendant might find a plea bargain to attempted DWI to be advantageous is that "license sanctions could not be administered because it is not apparent under the Vehicle and Traffic Law what period of revocation or suspension should be imposed upon someone who commits 'attempted' driving while intoxicated." *Prescott*, 95 N.Y.2d at 662 n.7, 722 N.Y.S.2d at 782 n.7.

§ 9:26   Conviction of felony DWI results in disbarment

In New York, conviction of a felony results in an attorney's automatic disbarment. *See* Judiciary Law § 90(4). This includes felony DWI. *See, e.g., In re Sullivan*, 140 A.D.3d 1391, 32 N.Y.S.3d 748 (3d Dep't 2016) (per curiam); *In re Dawson*, 133 A.D.3d 1083, 20 N.Y.S.3d 216 (3d Dep't 2015) (per curiam); *Matter of McGee*, 77 A.D.3d 376, 908 N.Y.S.2d 346 (2d Dep't 2010) (per curiam); *Matter of Bailey*, 57 A.D.3d 1529, 869 N.Y.S.2d 352 (4th Dep't 2008); *Matter of Woods*, 56 A.D.3d 184, 867 N.Y.S.2d 45 (1st Dep't 2008) (per curiam); *Matter of Shmaruk*, 29 A.D.3d 138, 812 N.Y.S.2d 623 (2d Dep't 2006) (per curiam); *Matter of Baxter*, 231 A.D.2d 964, 647 N.Y.S.2d 592 (4th Dep't 1996). *Cf. Matter of Johnston*, 75 N.Y.2d 403, 554 N.Y.S.2d 88, 553 N.E.2d 566 (1990) (felony of 1st degree involuntary manslaughter in Texas not sufficiently analogous to vehicular manslaughter in New York to constitute "felony" for purposes of automatic disbarment).

Critically, the automatic disbarment rule applies even where the parties anticipate that the felony conviction will be vacated and reduced to a misdemeanor if the defendant successfully completes interim probation. *See In re Tendler*, 131 A.D.3d 1301, ___, 16 N.Y.S.3d 185, 185 (3d Dep't 2015) (per curiam) ("While an attorney's disbarment upon a plea of guilty to a felony is automatic, the fact that her plea agreement contemplates the subsequent withdrawal of her felony guilty plea upon successful completion of a period of interim probation, leaving only a plea to a misdemeanor offense, would not serve to automatically restore her to the bar—to attain said relief, she must make a motion for reinstatement").

By contrast, misdemeanor DWI convictions have generally led to a letter of admonition, a letter of caution or public censure, depending upon the circumstances of the case. *See, e.g., In re Bratton*, 141 A.D.3d 182, 33 N.Y.S.3d 743 (2d Dep't 2016) (per curiam); *In re Ackerman*, 136 A.D.3d 115, 21 N.Y.S.3d 629 (2d Dep't 2015) (per curiam); *In re Grossman*, 132 A.D.3d 216, 16 N.Y.S.3d 259 (2d Dep't 2015) (per curiam); *In re Antomattei*, 96 A.D.3d 136, 945 N.Y.S.2d 31 (1st Dep't 2012) (per curiam); *Matter of Piken*, 86 A.D.3d 143, 924 N.Y.S.2d 527 (2d Dep't 2011) (per curiam); *Shmaruk, supra; Matter of Gross*, 34 A.D.3d 23, 824 N.Y.S.2d 825 (4th Dep't 2006) (per curiam); *Matter of Brody*, 23 A.D.3d 94, 803 N.Y.S.2d 605 (2d Dep't 2005) (per curiam); *Matter of Shichman*, 20 A.D.3d 111, 796 N.Y.S.2d 369 (2d Dep't 2005) (per curiam); *Matter of Bach*, 20 A.D.3d 114, 796 N.Y.S.2d 382 (2d Dep't 2005) (per curiam); *Matter of Zalesak*, 17 A.D.3d 66, 793 N.Y.S.2d 439 (2d Dep't 2005) (per curiam); *Matter of McCarthy*, 11 A.D.3d 162, 782 N.Y.S.2d 766 (2d Dep't 2004) (per curiam); *Matter of O'Brien*, 309 A.D.2d 184, 765 N.Y.S.2d 71 (2d Dep't 2003) (per curiam); *Matter of Wynne*, 283 A.D.2d 55, 726 N.Y.S.2d 111 (2d Dep't 2001) (per curiam); *Matter of Valentine*, 224 A.D.2d 70, 647 N.Y.S.2d 802 (2d Dep't 1996) (per curiam). *Cf. Matter of LaPenta*, 67 A.D.3d 117, 885 N.Y.S.2d 294 (2d Dep't 2009) (per curiam); *Matter of Kinne*, 17 A.D.3d 16, 794 N.Y.S.2d 757 (4th Dep't 2005) (per curiam). In this regard, the *Gross* Court ruled as follows:

> The Grievance Committee filed a petition charging respondent with misconduct arising from his two convictions of driving while intoxicated as a misdemeanor. Respondent filed an answer admitting the material allegations of the petition and raising, in mitigation, his alcoholism.

> We conclude that respondent violated the following Disciplinary Rules of the Code of Professional Responsibility:
> DR 1-102(A)(3) (22 NYCRR 1200.3[a][3])—engaging in illegal conduct that adversely reflects on his honesty, trustworthiness or fitness as a lawyer; and

> DR 1-102(A)(5) (22 NYCRR 1200.3[a][5])—engaging in conduct that is prejudicial to the administration of justice.

> Additionally, by failing to report his first conviction of driving while intoxicated to this Court, respondent violated Judiciary Law § 90(4)(c).

> We have considered, in mitigation, respondent's admitted alcoholism for which he is currently in treatment. Additionally, we note that respondent has an otherwise unblemished record and that his

misconduct was unrelated to his practice of law. Accordingly, after consideration of all of the factors in this matter, we conclude that respondent should be censured on condition that he agrees to continue in treatment for his alcoholism for a period of 24 months. In the event that respondent fails to continue in treatment or commits additional misconduct during that period, the Grievance Committee shall immediately apply for an order returning the proceeding to this Court for imposition of appropriate discipline.

34 A.D.3d at __, 824 N.Y.S.2d at 825-26.

§ 9:27   Felony DWI sentence reduced as unduly harsh and severe

In *People v. Becker*, 71 A.D.3d 1372, 894 N.Y.S.2d 926 (4th Dep't 2010), the defendant was convicted, following a bench trial, of DWI as a class E felony. County Court sentenced the defendant to one to three years in State prison. On appeal, the Appellate Division, Fourth Department, held that "the sentence imposed is unduly harsh and severe. Thus, as a matter of discretion in the interest of justice, we modify the judgment by reducing the sentence imposed for driving while intoxicated as a class E felony to time served, a five-year period of probation and a fine of $1,000." *Id.* at __, 894 N.Y.S.2d at 926 (citation omitted).

§ 9:28   Vince's Law

Effective November 1, 2014, a defendant who is charged with DWI, Aggravated DWI, DWAI Drugs or DWAI Combined Influence after having been convicted of a violation of VTL § 1192(2), (2-a), (3), (4) or (4-a) (or of Vehicular Assault in the 1st or 2nd degree, Vehicular Manslaughter in the 1st or 2nd degree, Aggravated Vehicular Assault or Aggravated Vehicular Homicide) three or more times within the preceding 15 years can be charged with a class D felony. VTL § 1193(1)(c)(ii-a). This law is known as Vince's Law. The consequences for a violation of Vince's Law are set forth in § 46:14, *infra*.

The only difference between Vince's Law and the pre-existing class D felony DWI law (*i.e.*, VTL § 1193(1)(c)(ii)), is that VTL § 1193(1)(c)(ii) requires two prior convictions within the preceding 10 years, whereas Vince's Law requires three or more prior convictions within the preceding 15 years. In other words, the look-back period in Vince's Law increases to 15 years—but the minimum number of predicate convictions increases to three or more.

Chapter 10

Driving While Ability Impaired by Drugs

Research References

Westlaw Databases

Drinking/Driving Litigation: Criminal and Civil (2d ed.)
(DRNKDRIVING)
Handling Drunk Driving Cases (2d ed.) (HDRUNKDR)
New York Vehicle and Traffic Law 2d (NYVEH)

Treatises and Practice Aids

Nichols and Whited, Drinking/Driving Litigation: Criminal and Civil
§ 17:18 (2d ed.)
Fiandach, Handling Drunk Driving Cases § 2:3 (2d ed.)
Rose, New York Vehicle and Traffic Law 2d § 35:21.50

KeyCite®: Cases and other legal materials listed in KeyCite Scope can be
researched through the KeyCite service on Westlaw®. Use KeyCite to check
citations for form, parallel references, prior and later history, and comprehensive citator information, including citations to other decisions and secondary
materials.

---

§ 10:1 Generally

Research References

West's Key Number Digest, Automobiles ⚭332

Driving while under the influence of drugs is a violation of
§ 1192(4) of the VTL. With the exception of the specification of
drugs as the substance at issue, this section has wording similar
to driving while ability impaired by alcohol in violation of VTL
§ 1192(1).

> No person shall operate a motor vehicle while the person's ability to
> operate such a motor vehicle is impaired by the use of a drug as
> defined in this chapter.

VTL § 1192(4). The words "as defined in this chapter" refer to
VTL § 114-a which defines a drug as follows:

> The term "drug" when used in this chapter, means and includes
> any substance listed in section thirty-three hundred six of the pub-
> lic health law.

VTL § 114-a.

Section 3306 of the Public Health Law establishes five
schedules of controlled substances and lists those substances.
While the list is extensive, its effect is to restrict the application
of the statute to the listed substances. Those persons operating a

motor vehicle under the influence of substances not set forth in the schedule do not come within the purview of this statute. *See People v. Mercurio*, N.Y.L.J., 8/30/93, p. 25, Col. 5 (Suffolk Co. Ct.).

In contrast, the California Vehicle Code section 312 defines a drug as:

The term "drug" means any substance or combination of substances, other than alcohol, which could so affect the nervous system, brain, or muscles of a person as to impair, to an appreciable degree, his ability to drive a vehicle in the manner that an ordinary prudent and cautious man, in full possession of his faculties, using reasonable care, would drive a similar vehicle under like conditions.

There is no generic statute in New York State which prohibits the impaired operation of a motor vehicle. The statutory framework is specific to the substance at issue. The People must specifically charge the defendant with the statutes pertaining to alcohol, or those pertaining to drugs, or both. In *People v. Bayer*, 132 A.D.2d 920, 518 N.Y.S.2d 475 (4th Dep't 1987), the court articulated the rule as follows:

Vehicle and Traffic Law § 1192, entitled "Operating a motor vehicle while under the influence of alcohol or drugs," contains three subdivisions relating to alcohol (subds. [1], [2], [3]) and one relating to drugs (subds. [4]). Subdivision (3) prohibits operation of a motor vehicle while defendant "is in an intoxicated condition", but does not refer to a substance creating the condition. It is clear as a matter of law, however, that the subdivision is intended to apply only to intoxication caused by alcohol. That conclusion is buttressed by examining Vehicle and Traffic Law § 1196(1) which permits conviction of a violation of subdivision (1), (2) or (3) of Vehicle and Traffic Law § 1192, notwithstanding that the charge laid before the court alleged a violation of subdivision (2) or (3), but does not permit conviction of a violation of subdivision (4). Additionally, while a violation of either subdivision (3) or (4) of Vehicle and Traffic Law § 1192 is a misdemeanor, the elements of the two crimes differ. Proof that defendant was in an intoxicated condition is essential to a prosecution under subdivision (3), but is not required under subdivision (4).

People v. Bayer, 132 A.D.2d 920, 518 N.Y.S.2d 475, 476–77 (1987). *See also People v. Grinberg*, 4 Misc. 3d 670, 781 N.Y.S.2d 584 (N.Y. City Crim. Ct. 2004); *People v. Wiley*, 59 Misc. 2d 519, 299 N.Y.S.2d 704 (Nassau Co. Dist. Ct. 1969); *People v. Cheperuk*, 64 Misc. 2d 498, 315 N.Y.S.2d 203 (Nassau Co. Ct. 1970).

§ 10:2 Elements of proof

Research References

West's Key Number Digest, Automobiles ☞332, 355(6)

In *People v. Kahn*, 160 Misc. 2d 594, 610 N.Y.S.2d 701 (Nassau Co. Dist. Ct. 1994), Judge Mahon set forth the elements of proof.

> In order for the People to prove the defendant guilty beyond a reasonable doubt they must prove the following elements of the crime:
>   1) The defendant ingested a drug.
>   2) The drug ingested by the defendant is one proscribed by Public Health Law section 3306. *See* VTL 114-a.
>   3) After ingesting the drug, the defendant operated a motor vehicle. *See* VTL section 125.
>   4) While operating this motor vehicle the defendant's ability to operate the motor vehicle was impaired by the ingestion of the drug.

610 N.Y.S.2d at 703. *See also People v. Felicia*, 52 Misc. 3d 212, __, 27 N.Y.S.3d 841, 846 (N.Y. City Crim. Ct. 2016) (same); *People v. Rose*, 8 Misc. 3d 184, __, 794 N.Y.S.2d 630, 631 (Nassau Co. Dist. Ct. 2005) ("A driving while impaired by drugs prosecution requires that the individual's impairment be shown to have been caused by a drug specifically listed in the Public Health Law").

Here, the court found the defendant not guilty based upon the fact that the People failed to prove that the defendant suffered impairment, to any extent, of his physical or mental abilities which he was expected to possess as a reasonable and prudent driver. 610 N.Y.S.2d at 703–04. *Cf. People v. Crandall*, 255 A.D.2d 617, 681 N.Y.S.2d 99 (3d Dep't 1998).

When charging a jury, one of the most common references is the New York Office of Court Administration's Criminal Jury Instructions. In defining the charge of driving a motor vehicle while ability impaired by drugs, the Office of Court Administration (OCA) parallels the definition of impairment by alcohol and sets forth the following charge:

> In order to drive safely, a driver is expected at all times to be able to think clearly and act carefully. If, by reason of the consumption of drugs, a driver loses to any extent control of his mental faculties and his physical responses, our law considers that he has operated his vehicle while under the influence of a drug or drugs.
>
> The key words in that law are "to any extent."
>
> According to the law, a person's ability to drive safely is impaired by the use of drugs when, by voluntarily consuming drugs, he has actually impaired, to any extent, the physical and mental abilities which he is expected to possess in order to operate his vehicle as a reasonable and prudent driver. The law does not require proof that such ability to operate his vehicle has been substantially affected. The proof need only show that such ability to drive safely has been affected "to any extent."

New York Criminal Jury Instructions, Vol. 3, VTL § 1192(4), pg. 2318S.

While both DWI (alcohol) and DWAI (drugs) are class A misdemeanors, the standards of proof are quite different. The People's
burden in proving DWAI (drugs) is lower than that for intoxication by alcohol. The standard for drugs is identical to that of
DWAI (alcohol). Specifically, the People's burden in a drug case is
impairment, *to any* extent, of the physical and mental abilities a
person is expected to possess in order to operate his vehicle as a
reasonable and prudent driver. The standard for DWI (alcohol)
is:

> [A] greater *degree* of impairment which is reached when the driver
> has voluntarily consumed alcohol to the extent that he is *incapable*
> *of employing the physical and mental abilities which he is expected*
> *to possess in order to operate a vehicle as a reasonable and prudent*
> *driver.*

People v. Cruz, 48 N.Y.2d 419, 427, 423 N.Y.S.2d 625, 628 (1979)
(emphases added).

§ 10:3 Probable cause to arrest

Research References

West's Key Number Digest, Automobiles ☞332

In *People v. Shapiro*, 141 A.D.2d 577, 529 N.Y.S.2d 186 (2d
Dep't 1988), the Appellate Division, Second Department, upheld
the hearing court's finding of probable cause where the evidence
indicated erratic driving, dilated pupils, fidgety behavior, presence of white powder, and colloquy with the defendant which
indicated that he was not ill or under the influence of prescription medication:

> We agree with the hearing court's conclusion that there was prob-
> able cause for the arrest of the defendant and that the seizure of
> physical evidence from the defendant's car was proper. The evi-
> dence adduced at the hearing established that the two arresting of-
> ficers observed the defendant driving at erratic speeds as well as
> swerving across a double yellow line. Upon pulling the defendant's
> vehicle over, the officers further observed that the defendant's
> pupils were dilated, his hair was "disheveled," his clothing was
> "mussed" and his behavior was "fidgety" and "jumpy." At the same
> time, Officer Casetelli observed a vial containing white powder on
> the front seat of defendant's car. After engaging in conversation
> with the defendant and ascertaining that he was not ill, or under
> the influence of prescription medication, the officers concluded that
> the defendant's behavior bore the characteristic manifestations of
> cocaine influence and thus arrested him for driving while his ability
> was impaired by the use of drugs.

People v. Shapiro, 529 N.Y.S.2d at 187.

In *People v. Kaminski*, 151 Misc. 2d 664, 573 N.Y.S.2d 394
(Rhinebeck Just. Ct. 1991), the following evidence was sufficient
to establish probable cause to arrest for VTL § 1994(4):

Upon approaching the vehicle, one of the officers reported smelling the odor of marijuana emanating from the cab. The senior officer conducted four field tests generally associated with developing probable cause to make an arrest under Vehicle and Traffic Law 1192. He testified that the defendant failed all or portions of several of these tests, that the defendant displayed several of the traditional signs of impairment, namely slow speech, bloodshot eyes as well as the odor of marijuana. In addition, the defendant admitted to the officer that he had a "joint" before entering the bridge toll plaza.

People v. Kaminski, 573 N.Y.S.2d at 395.

§ 10:4   Quantifying drug impairment

Research References

West's Key Number Digest, Automobiles ⬦332, 422.1

The major distinction between alcohol and drug cases is that there is an acknowledged correlation between blood alcohol concentrations and impaired driving. Most states have recognized .08 as the blood alcohol concentration correlating to intoxication. A blood alcohol concentration can be determined by analysis of breath, blood, or urine. Drugs are far more subjective, and there are no numerical standards associating so many nanograms of a drug with a level of impairment or intoxication. In this regard, *People v. Rossi*, 163 A.D.2d 660, 558 N.Y.S.2d 698 (3d Dep't 1990) is somewhat of an anomaly. Here, the Appellate Division affirmed vehicular crimes convictions on the ground, in part, that the amount of drugs detected in the motorist's blood was sufficient to support imposition of criminal liability:

Defendant also argues that the amount of drugs detected was insufficient to warrant criminal liability. There was testimony from a forensic toxicologist that the amount of drugs detected in defendant's blood, totaling 46 nanograms per milliliter of methamphetamine and 13 nanograms per milliliter of amphetamine, was sufficient to affect driving ability detrimentally. That the amount of drugs in defendant's blood was detected by the private laboratory rather than the State Police Laboratory is of no moment considering that the State Police only test for at least 100 nanograms per milliliter and the applicable statute proscribes any impairment of the ability to drive (cf., *People v. Scallero*, 122 A.D.2d 350, 352, 504 N.Y.S.2d 318), which can be evidenced not only by alcohol or drug presence in blood but by descriptions of the driver's conduct (122 A.D.2d 350, 352, 504 N.Y.S.2d 318). Considering the testimony by the forensic toxicologist concerning the effect of the drugs and by the police officers and others concerning defendant's conduct and driving, we do not believe that defendant was improperly convicted based on an insufficient amount of drugs.

558 N.Y.S.2d at 700.

In *People v. Prowse*, 60 A.D.3d 703, __, 875 N.Y.S.2d 121, 122

(2d Dep't 2009), the Appellate Division, Second Department, held that:

> The County Court properly admitted into evidence at trial the opinion testimony of a forensic toxicologist with respect to the effect that a certain amount of cocaine would have on a person's ability to operate a motor vehicle, and as to whether the level of cocaine present in a person's body would be higher four hours before a blood sample was drawn. The forensic toxicologist's testimony regarding her qualifications and experience provided a sufficient foundation for her subsequent opinion testimony. The County Court was not required to formally declare or certify the forensic toxicologist to be an expert witness.

(Citations omitted).

In *People v. Clark*, 309 A.D.2d 1076, ___, 766 N.Y.S.2d 710, 711 (3d Dep't 2003), the Appellate Division, Third Department, found that there was legally sufficient evidence to support the defendant's conviction of DWAI drugs where:

> The evidence is that while on routine parole in the City of Schenectady, Schenectady County on the night of November 17, 2000, two police officers observed a vehicle approaching them without its headlights on. As they watched, it turned into an intersecting street, pulled to the curb and defendant exited the vehicle. He approached the police car, but when the officers started to exit the car, defendant ran. In the ensuing chase and capture, one of the officers used pepper spray to help subdue defendant. A glassine envelope containing a white substance was found in defendant's car and a glass pipe of the type used to smoke crack cocaine was found on defendant's person. As a result, State Trooper Joseph Germano, a certified drug recognition expert, was called and he performed a standardized 12-step evaluation process. He testified that, in his opinion, defendant's ability to operate his vehicle was impaired by the use of crack cocaine. Of note, during the 12-step process, defendant admitted to having smoked crack cocaine earlier that evening.

The mere presence of a metabolite in a person's body at the time of arrest, coupled with observations of impairment, was found insufficient to establish driving while ability impaired by drugs. In *People v. Kahn*, 160 Misc. 2d 594, 610 N.Y.S.2d 701 (Nassau Co. Dist. Ct. 1994), Police Officer Read testified that he observed the defendant's vehicle weaving and, at one point, leaving the paved portion of the roadway. After stopping the defendant's vehicle, the defendant staggered and swayed, exhibited bloodshot and glassy eyes, slurred speech, and had difficulty producing documents requested by the officer. Officer Read testified that he detected a slight odor of an alcoholic beverage on the defendant's breath. Police Officer Fox testified to similar observations and, in addition, stated that the defendant had indicated that he had taken a medication known as Ciprin. A laboratory analysis of the defendant's urine revealed the presence of benzodiazapine.

The defendant testified that he had recently returned from a 10-day business trip in South Africa, which subjected him twice to a nine-hour difference in time zones. He also testified that he used Dalmane, a prescription medication used to induce sleep, also known as flurazepam. He testified that he had last taken the drug approximately 48 hours before his arrest.

The defendant's expert witness testified that the clinical effect of Dalmane lasts only eight to 10 hours. Thereafter, the person could expect to awaken and function normally. Further, the witness testified that, after Dalmane is ingested, the human body metabolizes the drug into a substance known as benzodiazapine. This metabolite remains detectable in the human blood stream up to 14 days after ingestion. A urine test, such as the one administered to the defendant, can only establish the presence of flurazepam in the human body, not the quantity.

The court concluded that the People failed to establish that the defendant drove while his ability was impaired by drugs.

> In the absence of a blood test given to the defendant near the time of his arrest, the quantity of the drug flurazepam in the defendant's body while operating his motor vehicle is unknown. In view of the expert testimony, . . . it cannot be said that the mere presence of the metabolite, benzodiazapine, in the defendant's body at the time of his arrest, coupled with the observations of the defendant's behavior . . . establishes beyond a reasonable doubt the defendant's impaired ability to drive on the night in question. To find criminal culpability upon the stricter standard of mere presence of a proscribed drug in the defendant's body, coupled with observations of the defendant's behavior, would, on these facts, fly in the face of generally accepted scientific fact within our medical community and, in our view, impermissibly strain the meaning of the statute.

People v. Kahn, 610 N.Y.S.2d at 704. *See also People v. Mercurio*, N.Y.L.J., 8/30/93, p. 25, Col. 5 (Suffolk Co. Ct.) (mere presence of metabolites in blood insufficient to prove controlled substance actually impaired the ability of defendant to drive).

§ 10:5   Statute is not unconstitutionally vague

Research References

West's Key Number Digest, Automobiles ⟜332

In *People v. Percz*, 100 Misc. 2d 1018, 420 N.Y.S.2d 477 (Suffolk Co. Dist. Ct. 1979), the defendant argued that VTL § 1192(4) is unconstitutionally vague in that it contains no definition of the term "impaired." The court upheld the statute, concluding that the statute is sufficiently clear so as to warn a person of ordinary intelligence that the conduct contemplated is forbidden.

§ 10:6 Must impairment be voluntary?

Research References

West's Key Number Digest, Criminal Law ☞38

The OCA jury charge requires only a finding that the drugs at issue had been voluntarily consumed. Some of the case law, however, seems to require that the impairment resulting from the consumption be voluntary. In *People v. Koch*, 250 A.D. 623, 294 N.Y.S. 987 (2d Dep't 1937), the defendant had taken a drug known as luminol for the purpose of relieving headaches arising from a fractured skull. The drug had been prescribed by a physician. The defendant, inadvertently, took an overdose which had an intoxicating effect upon him. In reversing and dismissing a conviction for DWI under the statute in existence at that time, the court stated:

> The statute contemplates only voluntary intoxication resulting from imbibing alcoholic liquors or the voluntary taking in to the system of other intoxicating agents; and not the condition from which the appellant was suffering, induced by the drug.

People v. Koch, 294 N.Y.S. at 989.

Citing *People v. Koch, the Appellate Term in People v. Van Tuyl*, 79 Misc. 2d 262, 359 N.Y.S.2d 958 (App. Term, 9th & 10th Jud. Dist. 1974), held:

> The quality of evidence remains virtually the same in charges of intoxication or impairment. The People must prove that by reason of the impairment the defendant was incapable of operating the motor vehicle in a prudent and cautious manner (cf. People v. Weaver, 188 App. Div. 395, 177 N.Y.S. 71; People v. Bevilacqua, 12 Misc. 2d 558, 170 N.Y.S.2d 423; People v. Davis, 270 Cal.App.2d 197, 75 Cal. Rptr. 627) and that the impairment was *voluntarily induced* (People v. Koch, 250 App. Div. 623, 294 N.Y.S. 987, *supra*).

359 N.Y.S.2d at 963–64 (emphasis added).

In *People v. Van Tuyl*, the proof indicated that the defendant had been taking butazolidin alka as prescribed by a physician for an arthritic condition of his spine and knees. The defendant had been advised to take two pills daily, but had not been advised regarding potential adverse side effects. Expert testimony indicated that approximately 40% of the patients using butazolidin had severe orientation problems including "confusional state, lethargy, vertigo, unsteadiness afoot, blurred vision and possibly even slurred speech." 359 N.Y.S.2d at 960.

Prior to the accident which led to his arrest, the defendant had attended a cocktail party and had had two drinks consisting of scotch and soda. Charged initially with DWI in violation of VTL § 1192(3), the defendant was convicted of a violation of VTL

§ 1192(1), DWAI. The testimony at trial was that the defendant weighed 220 pounds. An expert witness for the defense testified that the defendant could not have been intoxicated from the two drinks he consumed.

In reversing and dismissing the information, the Court noted that the proof indicated that impairment was induced by the drug butazolidin. In addition, the Court observed that there was a failure of proof in regard to voluntary impairment, and that butazolidin was not a scheduled drug under VTL § 114-a. Finally, the defendant was convicted of DWAI in violation of VTL § 1192(1). Inasmuch as VTL § 1192(1) was not a lesser included offense of VTL § 1192(4), the conviction could not stand. 359 N.Y.S.2d at 964.

In *People v. Calcasola*, 80 Misc. 2d 429, 364 N.Y.S.2d 301 (App. Term, 9th & 10th Jud. Dist. 1975), the Court distinguished *People v. Van Tuyl*, and affirmed a conviction of a defendant who had been adjudicated impaired by virtue of an overdose of methadone. Judge Gagliardi, who wrote the majority opinion in *People v. Van Tuyl*, dissented in *Calcasola* on the ground that the proof failed to establish that the defendant had been advised not to operate a motor vehicle while using methadone, and the consumption of the drug was in accordance with a physician's advice and, therefore, any resultant impairment or intoxication was involuntary.

The majority, seemingly, retreated from the position taken in *People v. Van Tuyl*, and noted that the conviction in *Van Tuyl* was for a violation of VTL § 1192(1), impairment by alcohol. Since the proof in *People v. Van Tuyl* indicated that the impairment in issue was the result of the use of a drug, the Court distinguished *Van Tuyl* on the basis that the defendant was convicted under a statute that was not applicable to drugs. The majority affirmed the conviction in *People v. Calcasola*, holding that the fact that the defendant was legally participating in the methadone maintenance program did not excuse his operation of a motor vehicle while impaired by methadone. 364 N.Y.S.2d at 302–03.

§ 10:7 Absence of alcohol held not relevant to drug prosecution

Research References

West's Key Number Digest, Automobiles ⚷354

Since the legislative framework is specific for alcohol or drugs, evidence of the absence of alcohol in a drug prosecution would seem to be most pertinent. In *People v. Salino*, 139 Misc. 2d 386, 527 N.Y.S.2d 169 (N.Y. City Crim. Ct. 1988), the court held to the contrary. Here, the People attempted to introduce the results of a Breathalyzer test indicating a 0.00 reading. In suppressing this test result, the court held:

> The .00% reading of the breathalyzer exam regarding defendant's blood alcohol content is indicative of nothing else other than, at the time of defendant's arrest, no alcohol was present in his blood. This court is unable to see the relevancy of permitting such blood test results into evidence to show that defendant was impaired by drugs. It has no probative worth; additionally, it is neither rational nor logical to allow such results into evidence. To do so would offend due process, concomitantly, the basic rules of circumstantial evidence, and permit an inference on an inference which is impermissible.

527 N.Y.S.2d at 171.

§ 10:8 Drug evaluation and classification

Research References

West's Key Number Digest, Automobiles ⚷332

Over the last several years, the Los Angeles Police Department has developed a series of clinical and psycho-physical examinations. These procedures are designed to enable trained police officers to determine whether a suspect is under the influence of drugs and, furthermore, what category of drugs he has been using. In the 1980s, the Los Angeles Police Department developed a series of clinical and psychophysical examinations. These procedures were designed to enable trained police officers to determine whether a subject was under the influence of drugs and furthermore, what category of drugs he had been using. While the program began in Los Angeles, it has expanded throughout the country. In New York, the New York City Police, the Nassau County Police, Bureau for Municipal Police, and New York State Police have been actively involved in the training of police officers in these procedures.

The program and procedures are controversial in that their end product is the expression of an opinion by the drug recognition expert (DRE) as to the use by a defendant of a particular category of drugs. Given the almost limitless possibilities of human physiology and the potential physical and mental effects of various legal and illegal substances, to say nothing of the possibilities arising out of polydrug use, the admissibility of an opinion by a drug recognition expert is questionable.

In *People v. Quinn*, 153 Misc. 2d 139, 580 N.Y.S.2d 818 (Suffolk Co. Dist. Ct. 1991), *rev'd on unrelated grounds* 158 Misc. 2d 1015, 607 N.Y.S.2d 534 (1993), Judge Dounias conducted a hearing pursuant to *Frye v. United States*, 293 Fed. 1013 (D.C. Cir. 1923) and *People v. Middleton*, 54 N.Y.2d 42, 444 N.Y.S.2d 581 (1981). After hearing extensive testimony, the court held that both horizontal gaze nystagmus and the DRE protocol met the standards enunciated by *Frye* and *Middleton*. 580 N.Y.S.2d at 826.

Following Judge Dounias' grant of judicial recognition, the case proceeded to trial before District Court Judge Ira P. Block. Judge Block noted that there was no testimony elicited at the trial; rather the parties stipulated as to what the testimony would be if the witnesses were called and submitted the test and results as previously received in evidence at the hearing before Judge Dounias. In entering the verdict of guilty, the judge noted:

> [I]n the within case we had a confession by the defendant, a voluntary submission to a blood test which revealed that the defendant had cocaine in her blood stream, observations of erratic operation of a motor vehicle by two police officers, attempts by the defendant to conceal materials within the car, drugs found in the vehicle and on the person of the defendant . . . were any or all of these not present would this change the effect of this case? We do not pass upon that since that is not before us. Would there be any different effect if any or all of these elements were not present . . . this is another question which does not have to be addressed at this time.

People v. Quinn, N.Y.L.J., 2/11/92, at p. 25–26, Col. 5.

In *People v. Villeneuve*, 232 A.D.2d 892, 649 N.Y.S.2d 80 (3d Dep't 1996), the Appellate Division, Third Department, rejected the defendant's challenge to the admissibility of Officer Murphy's testimony as a DRE, stating that:

> Murphy testified about his training, the tests given defendant, the process of metabolization of drugs by the body and specifically the metabolism of cocaine by this defendant. We reject defendant's challenge. The attack on Murphy's expertise was not supported by any evidence. Defendant's conclusary [sic] allegations as to Murphy's limitations as an expert fail to make out a ground for exclusion of his testimony.

232 A.D.2d at __, 649 N.Y.S.2d at 83.

§ 10:9   DRE training

Research References

West's Key Number Digest, Automobiles ⚖423

The approved training is a three-phase process. The initial phase is not specific to drug recognition, rather it is the NHTSA-approved standardized field sobriety test program. This is used to detect alcohol impaired motorists as well as the drugged defendant.

Phase I of the drug recognition training consists of a two-day (16-hour) preschool. Phase II is a seven-day (56-hour) classroom program. The two-day preschool defines the term "drug" as it is used in the DRE program and also familiarizes students with the techniques of the drug evaluation process. Phase II provides detailed instruction in the techniques of drug evaluation examination as well as physiology. Students are required to pass a comprehensive written examination before proceeding to Phase III, which consists of field certification.

The field certification portion of the training begins upon completion of the classroom training and is conducted periodically over a period of 60 to 90 days. Students work under the direction of certified instructors and evaluate persons suspected of being impaired by drugs other than alcohol. Students are required to participate and document the results of at least 12 drug evaluations and complete a comprehensive examination. Upon successful completion of the examination and the evaluations, a student is certified as a drug recognition expert. The DRE, Winter 1993, Vol. 5, Issue 1, (Phoenix City Prosecutor's Office, Phoenix, Arizona).

DREs are trained in performing the drug recognition evaluation, and distinguishing between seven broad categories of drug groups. The categories have been developed based upon shared symptomatology. The seven categories are:

1) Central nervous system depressants;
2) Central nervous system stimulants;
3) Hallucinogens;
4) Phencyclidine;
5) Narcotic analgesics;
6) Inhalants; and
7) Cannabis.

Much of the training concerns breaking drugs down into these seven categories and discussing their symptomology and the physical manifestations that people exhibit when they are under the influence of these substances. There is also a great deal of training in regard to the effects of combinations of the illegal drugs or polydrug usage.

§ 10:10   Drug classifications: central nervous system depressants

Research References

West's Key Number Digest, Automobiles ⬩332, 411, 422.1

Central nervous system depressants are defined by the DRE training materials as substances that slow down the operation of the central nervous system which consists of the brain, brain stem, and spinal cord. They can slow down the user's reactions and cause him or her to process information more slowly. They relieve anxiety and tension and have a sedative effect. In high enough doses they have the effect of general anesthesia and can induce coma and death. *See* Preliminary Training For Drug Evaluation And Classification, Administrators Guide, HS172A R4/88, pgs. I-4 to I-5.

Included within this classification are alcohol, valium, Xanax, and various other tranquilizers and sedatives.

Central Nervous System Stimulants

Central nervous system stimulants speed up the operation of the central nervous system and the bodily functions controlled by the central nervous system. They can cause the user to become hyperactive, talkative, and to have rapid and repetitive speech patterns. The stimulants increase heart rate, blood pressure, and body temperature. They induce emotional reactions of excitement, restlessness, and irritability. They can also induce unstable beating of the heart (cardiac arrhythmia), seizures, and death. *See* Preliminary Training for Drug Evaluation And Classification, Administrators Guide, HS172A R4/88, page I-6.

Central nervous system stimulants include such commonly abused drugs as cocaine and amphetamines.

Hallucinogens

In addition to causing hallucinations, hallucinogens can distort perception so that the user's perceptions of real stimuli are distorted. What they see, hear, and smell are different from the objective reality of what is present. Rather than speeding up or slowing down the central nervous system, "hallucinogens cause the nervous system to send strange or false signals to the brain." Preliminary Training for Drug Evaluation And Classification, Administrators Guide, HS172A R4/88 at pg. I-7.

They "produce sights, sounds and odors that aren't real; induce a temporary condition very much like psychosis or insanity; and can create a 'mixing' of sensory modalities, so that the user 'hears colors', 'sees music', 'tastes sounds', etc." Preliminary Training for Drug Evaluation And Classification, Administrators Guide, HS172A R4/88 at pg. I-7.

Included among hallucinogens are LSD and Peyote.

Disassociative Anesthetics

While similar to hallucinogens, disassociative anesthetics are given its own category because of the various kinds of impairment they create. PCP or phencyclidine is the primary disassociative anesthetic that is commonly abused. It is a synthetic drug and does not occur naturally. People under the influence of PCP can exhibit a combination of symptoms associated with hallucinogens, stimulants, and depressants. Preliminary Training for Drug Evaluation And Classification, Administrators Guide, HS172A R4/88 at I-7.

Like central nervous system depressants, PCP depresses brain wave activity, causing a slow down in thought, reaction time, and verbal responses. It is similar to central nervous system stimulants in that it causes increases in heart rate, blood pressure, adrenalin production, and body temperature and causes muscles to become rigid.

It is akin to hallucinogens in that it distorts or "scrambles" signals received by the brain. PCP distorts sight, hearing, taste, smell, and touch. Perceptions of time and space may be affected, and the user can become paranoid, feel isolated, and depressed. The user may develop a strong fear of and preoccupation with death, and may become unpredictably violent. Preliminary Training for Drug Evaluation And Classification, Administrators Guide, HS172A R4/88 at I-8.

Narcotic Analgesics

The drugs in this category tend to reduce a person's reaction to pain. They produce euphoria, drowsiness, apathy, lessened physical activity, and sometimes impaired vision. Persons under the influence may appear as being semiconscious, or what is commonly referred to as "on the nod." In high enough doses, narcotic analgesics can produce coma, respiratory failure, and death. Preliminary Training for Drug Evaluation And Classification, Administrators Guide, HS172A R4/88 at I-9 to I-10.

Narcotic analgesics include heroin, morphine, and codeine.

Inhalants

Inhalants are defined by the DRE training materials as fumes of volatile substances. Common among these are gasoline, oil, base paints, glue, aerosol cans, varnish remover, cleaning fluid, and nitrous oxide. Symptoms vary with the inhalant used and the effects can vary from the stuporous and passive to irritable, violent, and dangerous. Preliminary Training for Drug Evaluation And Classification, Administrators Guide, HS172A R4/88 at pg. I-10 to I-11.

Cannabis

Cannabis includes all forms and products derived from the Cannabis Sativa plant. The active ingredient in cannabis products is the substance known as "Delta-9 Tetrahydrocannabinol," or "THC." Its most common form is marijuana. Marijuana is neither a central nervous system depressant nor a central nervous system stimulant. Its effects are to interfere with the attention process and produce a distortion of the user's perception of time. Its symptoms include an increased heart beat and reddening of the eyes. Preliminary Training for Drug Evaluation And Classification, Administrators Guide, HS172A R4/88 at pg. I-11.

§ 10:11 Evaluation procedures

Research References
West's Key Number Digest, Automobiles ⬥422.1

There are basically eight procedures that are used to evaluate a defendant for the purpose of determining whether and/or what group of drugs the defendant has been using. The evaluation is extensive and consumes a fair amount of time during which the DRE is performing procedures that are akin to those done by a nurse or a physician. It should be noted that the claimed rate of accuracy for these evaluations is very high. It should also be noted that over the course of the evaluation, a high percentage of defendants will voluntarily disclose the specifics as to their drug usage.

Drug recognition evaluations are, at present, not done on the road. Rather, they are a postarrest procedure which is followed once the defendant has been taken into custody and brought to the police station. The defendant is already under arrest, and the drug recognition expert (DRE) is not, generally, present at the time of arrest. The issue of probable cause is, therefore, of great interest particularly where the arrest is for driving while under the influence of drugs in the first instance.

One of the great problems associated with enforcement in this area is the difficulty in developing probable cause. With alcohol, there is the odor of alcoholic beverage and commonly recognized signs of intoxication which have been traditionally used to justify the arrest of DWI defendants. With drugs, the physical manifestations vary with the drug and personality of the defendant. The fact that DREs are available back at the station once the arrest is made is of little assistance to the officer on the scene if she is unable to develop the probable cause she needs to justify her arrest.

While the DRE program is a response to the increasing number of drugged drivers, it cannot be effective unless it is combined with training for police officers on the street. Since the DREs do not become involved until after the arrest, they will have little to do unless valid arrests are being made. Once the arrest is made, the DRE is called to the station and the evaluation process begins.

§ 10:12 Breath alcohol test

Research References
West's Key Number Digest, Automobiles ⬥411, 422.1

The first part of the drug recognition evaluation is a breath alcohol test. In New York State, the most common possibilities are the Alco-Sensor, BAC DataMaster, Intoxilyzer, and Alcotest 7110.

In a DWI prosecution, the Alco-Sensor would be inadmissible at trial. *People v. Thomas*, 121 A.D.2d 73, 509 N.Y.S.2d 668 (4th Dep't 1986), order *aff'd*, 70 N.Y.2d 823, 523 N.Y.S.2d 437 (1987). In a DWI prosecution, breath test devices, other than the Breathalyzer, are subject to challenge particularly where judicial recognition has not been granted in the jurisdiction in which the test result is being offered into evidence. Even a Breathalyzer result requires a fairly extensive foundation consisting of the testimony and documentation set forth in §§ 42:1 et seq.

In a DWAI (drug) case, the primary purpose in performing the breath alcohol test is to obtain a negative result indicating that alcohol is not a cause or contributing factor to the impaired condition of the defendant. The inference is that if you are not under the influence of alcohol and you are impaired, the cause of that impairment lies elsewhere and may be drug-related.

While that is the inference, Judge Sparks of the New York City Criminal Court has held that a negative breath alcohol test is not relevant, and, therefore, not admissible in a driving while under the influence of drugs case. *People v. Salino*, 139 Misc. 2d 386, 527 N.Y.S.2d 169 (1988). In *Salino*, the defendant obtained a 0.00% reading on a Breathalyzer. The People attempted to offer this result into evidence as part of their proof of driving while under the influence of drugs. The Court, citing *Richardson on Evidence*, held that the result was inadmissible in that it was an inference based upon an inference. 527 N.Y.S.2d at 171.

§ 10:13   Interview of arresting officer

Research References

West's Key Number Digest, Automobiles ☞349(14.1), 411, 414

The next component of the evaluation is the interview of the arresting officer. While any testimony from the DRE in regard to statements obtained from the arresting officer constitutes hearsay, the fact that he interviewed the arresting officer should be admissible. Insofar as the observations of the arresting officer are concerned, they would normally be elicited directly from the arresting officer, and he or she would, normally, testify prior to the DRE.

§ 10:14   Preliminary examination

Research References

West's Key Number Digest, Automobiles ☞349(14.1), 414, 422.1

The preliminary examination consists of a series of questions asked of the defendant by the DRE. The questions are designed to elicit information from the defendant in regard to his physical condition, use of medication, and consumption of food and beverage. In addition, the defendant is asked the time of day to determine whether or not he or she is oriented as to time. The questions are all obtained from the drug evaluation form (*See* Appendix 5) and the defendant's answers are placed on that form.

§ 10:15   Eye examination

Research References
West's Key Number Digest, Automobiles ⊙⇒349(14.1), 411, 422.1

Eye Movements—Gaze Nystagmus & Convergence

This portion of the examination consists of a series of tests during which the evaluator determines whether the defendant's eyes move smoothly or with a jerking motion in response to a stimulus. The tests are referred to as *horizontal gaze nystagmus, vertical gaze nystagmus*, and *convergence*. In addition to the discussion immediately below, *see* §§ 8:1 et seq. for more material on horizontal gaze nystagmus and vertical gaze nystagmus.

§ 10:16   Horizontal gaze nystagmus

Research References
West's Key Number Digest, Automobiles ⊙⇒411, 422.1

The horizontal gaze nystagmus portion consists of three distinct tests of both eyes. The first is called "smooth pursuit."

Smooth Pursuit

The smooth pursuit portion of the test is performed by moving an object, usually a pen, from a point near the defendant's nose outward towards the side of the defendant's face. The defendant is asked to follow the movement of the pen with his eyes and to do so without moving his head. The DRE starts with the left eye and observes whether or not the eye moves smoothly or with a jerking motion. A "normal" eye will move smoothly in a manner similar to a marble moving over a hard surface. If the defendant is under the influence of alcohol and/or certain drugs, a nystagmus may be observed. Nystagmus refers to a jerking motion which is similar to rolling a marble over sandpaper. The eye does not proceed smoothly, but moves with an apparent jerking motion. After the left eye is tested, the test is performed on the right eye.

Maximum Deviation

The second part of the horizontal gaze nystagmus test is called maximum deviation. On this part of the test, the defendant is asked to follow the stimulus, which is moved to the side of his face. The defendant's left pupil is directed to the corner of the eye and the stimulus is held stationary for a period of approximately four seconds. While the eye is in this position, it is observed for nystagmus. Again, the presence of nystagmus may indicate that the defendant is under the influence of alcohol or certain drugs. This process is repeated with the right eye.

Onset of Jerkiness

The third part of the horizontal gaze nystagmus test is called angle of onset. The purpose of the test is to determine the angle with the nose at which the eye commences to jerk. A test is performed by placing the pen about 15 inches from the defendant's nose and by slowly moving the pen toward the outer corner of his eye. The DRE starts with the left eye and watches it closely for the first sign of jerking. If she observes any jerking, the DRE stops moving the pen and holds it steady. The DRE makes sure that the eye is jerking. If it is not, the DRE is required to start the procedure over again by moving the pen further towards the outer portion of the eye and observing for the "onset" of jerking. Once the DRE determines the point of onset, he estimates the angle of this point with the defendant's nose.

Vertical Gaze Nystagmus

The fourth part of the eye examination tests for vertical nystagmus. Here, the defendant again is asked to follow the movement of a pen. Instead of being held up and down, the pen is held sideways and the defendant is asked to keep his eyes on the middle of the pen. The pen is then moved up and the defendant's eyes are moved up to maximum elevation and held for a minimum of four seconds. This test is almost identical to the maximum deviation portion of the horizontal gaze nystagmus test, except the movement is vertical.

Lack of Convergence

The fifth part of the eye test is designed to observe how the defendant's eyes converge. The pen is held about 15 inches in front of the defendant's face with the tip pointing at his nose. The defendant is directed to hold his head still and follow the pen with his eyes. The pen is moved in a slow circle until the technician performing the test observes that the defendant is tracking the pen. The pen is then moved in slowly and steadily towards the bridge of the defendant's nose. The defendant's eyes are then observed to determine whether they move together and converge at the bridge of the defendant's nose.

§ 10:17 Pupil reaction

Research References

West's Key Number Digest, Automobiles ⊙411, 422.1

Pupil reaction consists of a series of tests which are designed to determine the effect of various conditions on the size of the defendant's pupils. The DRE has an eye gauge which contains circles representing different sizes of pupils. These dark circles have diameters ranging from 1.0 millimeters to 9.0 millimeters in half-millimeter increments. The eye gauge is held up alongside the defendant's eyes and the gauge is moved up and down until the technician locates the circle closest in size to the defendant's pupil.

Initially, the eye gauge is used during the preliminary examination to determine whether the defendant's pupils are of equal size. Later on, the eye gauge is used under various lighting conditions for the purpose of determining the size of the pupils. The first part of the examination consists of determining the size of the defendant's pupils under normal or room light conditions.

Dark Room Examination

After determining the size of the defendant's pupils under room light, the defendant is taken into a room which is almost completely dark. The DRE and the defendant wait for 90 seconds to allow their eyes to adjust to the dark. The DRE then takes a penlight and covers the tip of the penlight with his finger or thumb so that there is only a reddish glow and no white light emerges. The glowing tip of the penlight is then moved to the vicinity of the defendant's left eye until the DRE can see the pupil separate and apart from the colored portion of the eye or the iris. The eye gauge is then brought up alongside the defendant's left eye, and the circle nearest in size to the pupil as it appears in the dark room is estimated and noted. The procedure is then repeated with the defendant's right eye.

Indirect Light

The pupil size is then estimated in indirect light. Indirect light is obtained by the DRE uncovering the tip of the penlight and shining it across the defendant's left eye so that the light just barely eliminates the shadow from the bridge of his nose. The DRE is careful not to shine the light directly into the defendant's eyes, but rather across them. Again, both eyes are gauged, and the estimated pupil size noted.

Direct Light

In the direct light portion of the evaluation, the tip of the penlight is uncovered and is shone directly into the defendant's eyes. Each eye is done in turn, and an estimation of the pupil size obtained.

§ 10:18   Psycho-physical tests

Research References

West's Key Number Digest, Automobiles ⚖411, 422.1

Four psycho-physical or field sobriety tests are administered as part of the drug recognition evaluation. The purpose of the tests is to determine the defendant's physical coordination as well as his ability to understand and follow instructions. The presumption is that a defendant who does not listen or follow instructions, or exhibits a lack of balance and coordination, may be under the influence of a drug.

Romberg Balance Test

The first test performed is the Romberg balance test. This involves the technician asking the defendant to stand erect with his feet together and his arms down to his sides. He is told to stay in this position while being given instructions in regard to the performance of the test. He is observed to see if he follows that instruction, or whether he starts the test prior to being told to begin.

The defendant is told that when he is told to *"begin"* he is to tilt his head back slightly and close his eyes. He is told to maintain that position for what he deems to be 30 seconds. The DRE compares this period of time with a watch for the purpose of determining whether the defendant's internal clock is functioning. In addition, the DRE looks for swaying, tremors, and other physical symptoms.

Walk and Turn Test

The second test is the walk and turn test. In this test, the defendant is asked to walk heel-to-toe along a line for nine steps, turn around, and walk back nine steps. He is told to watch his feet, and to count off the steps out loud. Again, he is observed to see whether he follows the instructions and whether he begins when he is directed to *"begin,"* as opposed to beginning on his own. He is observed to see whether he keeps his balance, steps off the line, raises his arms while walking, walks heel-to-toe, stops walking, takes the wrong number of steps, turns improperly, has body tremors, exhibits muscle tension, or makes any statements or sounds.

One Leg Stand

The third test is the one leg stand. Here the defendant is told to stand with his feet together, his arms down at his sides, and to raise his left foot in a stiff leg manner approximately six inches off the ground and count to 30. The test is then repeated with the right leg.

The DRE looks for swaying, hopping, body tremors, muscle tension, and whether or not the defendant puts his foot down during the test.

Finger to Nose Test

The final psycho-physical test is the finger to nose test. As with all these tests, the defendant is observed for the purpose of seeing whether he follows the instructions given. Here, he is told to put his feet together, stand straight and extend his arms towards the instructor, and to make a fist with each hand. The defendant is then told to extend the index finger from each hand and to bring his arms back down to his sides with the index fingers extended. He is further instructed that when he is told to *"begin,"* he is to tilt his head back slightly and close his eyes. He is then told that he is to bring the tip of the index finger up to the tip of his nose, and that upon touching his nose he is to return his arm to his side. He is then told that he will be instructed as to which hand to use by the evaluator who will say the word "right" or "left." He is told to tilt his head back and close his eyes and keep them closed until he is told to open them.

The DRE notes where on his or her face the defendant's fingertips touch, any swaying, body tremors, eyelid tremors, muscle tension, and/or any other statements or sounds made by the defendant.

These four psycho-physical tests may or may not be videotaped. In New York City, the New York City Police Department asks the defendant if he or she is willing to perform these tests and have them videotaped. The New York City Police Department does not videotape any other portion of the evaluation.

§ 10:19 Vital signs

Research References

West's Key Number Digest, Automobiles ☜411, 422.1

Part of the evaluation consists of a check of the defendant's pulse, blood pressure, and temperature. This is performed by the DRE using a blood pressure cuff and thermometer. The pulse is taken three times during the evaluation. The first during the preliminary examination, the second at the time that the blood pressure and temperature are taken, and the third following the examination of the defendant's arms for drug injection sites.

Interestingly, the Oregon Court of Appeals has held that a person's pulse is private and not subject to examination absent a warrant or a constitutionally recognized exception to the warrant requirement. In *State v. Stowers*, 136 Or. App. 448, 902 P.2d 117 (1995), upon being stopped for a traffic infraction, the officer suspected that the defendant might be under the influence of drugs. After asking the defendant to exit the vehicle, the officer placed his fingers on the defendant's neck and took the defendant's carotid pulse. The court concluded that the taking of the defendant's pulse revealed aspects of the defendant's physical and psychological condition that were not otherwise observable to the public. The court held that a person's pulse is private and is not subject to examination absent a warrant or a constitutionally recognized exception to the warrant requirement.

§ 10:20   Drug administration sites

Research References

West's Key Number Digest, Automobiles ☜422.1

Nasal and Oral Examination

Prior to leaving the dark room, the DRE will shine his penlight into the defendant's nose and mouth. The purpose of this is to check for signs of drug use. Certain drugs will leave a residue around the mouth and nose. The DRE may observe signs of redness and irritation in the defendant's nose and mouth, or even blistering. There may be an absence of nasal hair. Frequently, the DRE will detect distinctive odors in the vicinity of the defendant's mouth and nose caused by the use of various drugs.

Arm and Neck Examination

The arm and neck examination consists of checking the defendant's arms and neck to see if there are needle marks and to determine whether his muscles are rigid, "normal," or relaxed. The DRE runs his hands over the defendant's arms and neck feeling for bumps that would indicate needle marks. Any bumps that are located are examined using a lighted magnifying glass which helps the DRE determine whether or not the bump is a needle mark.

§ 10:21   Urine sample

Research References

West's Key Number Digest, Automobiles ☜411, 422.1

Finally, the DRE obtains a blood or urine sample from the defendant for submission to a laboratory.

§ 10:22   Drug symptom chart

Research References

West's Key Number Digest, Automobiles ☜332, 411

While the physiology associated with various drugs is far too extensive for this chapter, a copy of the drug symptom chart commonly used by police departments is set forth at Appendix 6.

§ 10:23 Drug Influence Evaluation form

Research References

West's Key Number Digest, Automobiles ⬥332

A copy of the Drug Influence Evaluation form which is completed by the drug recognition expert is set forth at Appendix 5.

§ 10:24 Trial guide

Research References

West's Key Number Digest, Automobiles ⬥332

A copy of a trial guide setting forth a suggested direct examination, which was developed for the New York City Police Department and the district attorneys of the five boroughs of the City of New York, is set forth at Appendix 7.

§ 10:25 Person convicted of DWAI drugs not eligible for conditional license

Research References

West's Key Number Digest, Automobiles ⬥332

A person who is convicted of DWAI drugs is not eligible for a conditional license, but may be eligible for a restricted use license. *See* N.Y. Comp. Codes R. & Regs. tit. 15, § 134.7(a)(10); § 50:18, *infra*.

§ 10:26 Plea bargain limitations

Research References

West's Key Number Digest, Automobiles ⬥332

VTL § 1192(10)(a)(i) provides that:

In any case wherein the charge laid before the court alleges a violation of [VTL § 1192(2), (3), (4) or (4-a)], any plea of guilty thereafter entered in satisfaction of such charge must include at least a plea of guilty to the violation of the provisions of one of the subdivisions of [VTL § 1192], other than [VTL § 1192(5) or (6)], and no other disposition by plea of guilty to any other charge in satisfaction of such charge shall be authorized; provided, however, if the district attorney, upon reviewing the available evidence, determines that the charge of a violation of [VTL § 1192] is not warranted, such district attorney may consent, and the court may allow a disposition by plea of guilty to another charge in satisfaction of such charge; provided, however, in all such cases, the court shall set forth upon the record the basis for such disposition.

In other words, where a defendant is charged with DWAI drugs, any plea bargain must generally contain at least a plea to DWAI alcohol.

In *People v. Lehman*, 183 Misc. 2d 97, 702 N.Y.S.2d 551 (Watertown City Ct. 2000), the court denied the People's motion to amend/reduce a charge of VTL § 1192(4) (*i.e.*, DWAI drugs), to VTL § 1192(1) (*i.e.*, DWAI alcohol), where there was no evidence that the defendant's impairment was in any way caused by alcohol.

However, the Court of Appeals has made clear that:

[A] plea may be to . . . a crime for which the facts alleged to underlie the original charge would not be appropriate.

A plea is a bargain struck by a defendant and a prosecutor who may both be in doubt about the outcome of a trial. Only the events of time, place, and, if applicable, victim, need be the same for the crime pleaded as for the one charged.

People v. Francis, 38 N.Y.2d 150, 155, 379 N.Y.S.2d 21, 26 (1975) (citations omitted). *See also People v. Clairborne*, 29 N.Y.2d 950, __, 329 N.Y.S.2d 580, 581 (1972) ("A bargained guilty plea to a lesser crime makes unnecessary a factual basis for the particular crime confessed"); *People v. Adams*, 57 N.Y.2d 1035, 1038, 457 N.Y.S.2d 783, 784–85 (1982) (same).

§ 10:27 Sufficiency of accusatory instrument charging defendant with DWAI drugs

Research References

West's Key Number Digest, Automobiles ☞332

"A driving while impaired by drugs prosecution requires that the individual's impairment be shown to have been caused by a drug specifically listed in the *Public Health Law*." *People v. Rose*, 8 Misc. 3d 184, __, 794 N.Y.S.2d 630, 631 (Nassau Co. Dist. Ct. 2005). *See also People v. Grinberg*, 4 Misc. 3d 670, __ n.1, 781 N.Y.S.2d 584, 586 n.1 (N.Y. City Crim. Ct. 2004). In this regard, the *Rose* court found that an accusatory instrument to a DWAI drugs charge is not necessarily required to include a chemical test result or an admission by the defendant of using a specific drug in order to provide "reasonable cause" to believe that the defendant committed the offense. 8 Misc. 3d at __, 794 N.Y.S.2d at 635.

Rather, "[t]he written record of an opinion of a DRE can, and

in the instant case does, provide 'reasonable cause' for believing
that the defendant committed the offense charged." 8 Misc. 3d at
__, 794 N.Y.S.2d at 635. On the other hand, in the absence of a
chemical test result or an admission by the defendant, "the failure to have referred to, summarized, or annexed the drug influence evaluation to the supporting deposition renders the accusatory instrument dismissible." 8 Misc. 3d at __, 794 N.Y.S.2d at
635. *See also People v. Jackson*, 32 Misc. 3d 139(A), 936 N.Y.S.2d
60 (App. Term, 9th & 10th Jud. Dist. 2011) ("The supporting deposition in the instant case fails to provide reasonable cause to
believe that defendant was impaired by the use of any of the substances set forth in Public Health Law § 3306 (*see* CPL 100.25[2]).
Consequently, the accusatory instrument charging defendant
with driving while ability impaired by drugs (Vehicle and Traffic
Law § 1192[4]) is jurisdictionally defective and must be dismissed"); *People v. Matozzo*, 47 Misc. 3d 1212(A), 2015 WL
1786184 (Nassau Co. Dist. Ct. 2015) (same).

Similarly, in *People v. Hill*, 16 Misc. 3d 176, __, 834 N.Y.S.2d
840, 845 (N.Y. City Crim. Ct. 2007), the Court held that:

> [W]here testimony of a drug recognition expert is available or the
> testimony of a lesser expert is combined with an admission or other
> physical evidence, a laboratory test is not required for conversion of
> a complaint to an information in cases where the defendant is
> charged with driving while impaired under VTL § 1192(4).

See also People v. Felicia, 52 Misc. 3d 212, 27 N.Y.S.3d 841 (N.Y.
City Crim. Ct. 2016).

§ 10:28   Level of impairment required by VTL § 1192(4) is same as for VTL § 1192(1)

In *People v. Cruz*, 48 N.Y.2d 419, 426–27, 423 N.Y.S.2d 625,
628, 399 N.E.2d 513 (1979), the Court of Appeals defined the
degree of impairment required to be "impaired" within the meaning of VTL § 1192(1):

> In sum the prohibition against driving while the ability to do so is
> impaired by alcohol (Vehicle and Traffic Law, § 1192, subd. 1) is not
> a vague and indefinite concept as the defendant contends. It is
> evident from the statutory language and scheme that the question
> in each case is whether, by voluntarily consuming alcohol, this par-
> ticular defendant has actually impaired, to any extent, the physical
> and mental abilities which he is expected to possess in order to
> operate a vehicle as a reasonable and prudent driver.

The *Cruz* Court further defined the degree of impairment
required to be "intoxicated" within the meaning of VTL § 1192(3):

> In sum, intoxication is a greater degree of impairment which is
> reached when the driver has voluntarily consumed alcohol to the

extent that he is incapable of employing the physical and mental abilities which he is expected to possess in order to operate a vehicle as a reasonable and prudent driver.

48 N.Y.2d at 428, 423 N.Y.S.2d at 629.

In *People v. Shakemma*, 19 Misc. 3d 771, 855 N.Y.S.2d 871 (Suffolk Co. Dist. Ct. 2008), the defendant was charged with DWAI Drugs in violation of VTL § 1192(4). The Court noted that being impaired by alcohol is a traffic infraction, not a misdemeanor; and thus held that, since DWAI Drugs is a misdemeanor, "VTL 1192(4) must be interpreted to mean that where marijuana is present the impairment must be *substantial*." 19 Misc. 3d at __, 855 N.Y.S.2d at 873 (emphasis added). However, the Appellate Term reversed, holding that:

> As the statutory prohibitions with respect to operating a motor vehicle while ability impaired by alcohol (Vehicle and Traffic Law § 1192[1]) and while ability impaired by drugs (Vehicle and Traffic Law § 1192[4]) are identical as to the degree of impairment constituting the offense, the People were required to establish only that there was probable cause to infer that defendant's ability to operate a motor vehicle was impaired "to any extent."

People v. Davis, 23 Misc. 3d 30, __, 879 N.Y.S.2d 268, 269 (App. Term, 9th & 10th Jud. Dist. 2009) (citation omitted). Notably, in the trial court the defendant's name was listed as Davis I. Shakemma, but on appeal the defendant's name was listed as Shakeema I. Davis. *See also People v. Bayer*, 132 A.D.2d 920, __, 518 N.Y.S.2d 475, 477 (4th Dep't 1987) ("while a violation of either subdivision (3) or (4) of Vehicle and Traffic Law § 1192 is a misdemeanor, the elements of the two crimes differ. Proof that defendant was in an intoxicated condition is essential to a prosecution under subdivision (3), but is not required under subdivision (4)").

§ 10:29 Defendant under the influence of drugs cannot be charged with common law DWI in violation of VTL § 1192(3)

In *People v. Litto*, 8 N.Y.3d 692, 840 N.Y.S.2d 736 (2007), the defendant was accused of driving while impaired by a drug not listed in Public Health Law § 3306. Accordingly, he could not be charged with VTL § 1192(4). However, the People charged the defendant with violating VTL § 1192(3), claiming that New York's common law DWI statute is not limited to intoxication caused by alcohol, but rather applies to intoxication caused by any substance, including drugs.

Rejecting this argument, the Court of Appeals held that "[b]ased on the language, history and scheme of the statute, we conclude that the Legislature here intended to use 'intoxication' to refer to a disordered state of mind caused by alcohol, not by drugs." 8 N.Y.3d at 694, 840 N.Y.S.2d at 737. *See also People v. Farmer*, 36 N.Y.2d 386, 390, 369 N.Y.S.2d 44, 45, 330 N.E.2d 22 (1979) ("subdivisions 1, 2 and 3 of section 1192 proscribe separable offenses based upon the degree of impairment caused by alcohol ingestion"); *People v. Bayer*, 132 A.D.2d 920, __, 518 N.Y.S.2d 475, 476 (4th Dep't 1987) (VTL § 1192(3) "prohibits operation of a motor vehicle while defendant 'is in an intoxicated condition', but does not refer to a substance creating the condition. It is clear as a matter of law, however, that the subdivision is intended to apply only to intoxication caused by alcohol").

§ 10:30   DWAI combined influence of drugs or alcohol and drugs

VTL § 1192(4-a) makes it a crime for a person to operate a motor vehicle while his or her ability to do so is impaired by a combination of either: (a) 2 or more drugs, or (b) alcohol and a drug or drugs. In this regard, VTL § 1192(4-a) provides as follows:

4-a. Driving while ability impaired by the combined influence of drugs or of alcohol and any drug or drugs. No person shall operate a motor vehicle while the person's ability to operate such motor vehicle is impaired by the combined influence of drugs or of alcohol and any drug or drugs.

Notably, unlike DWAI drugs, in violation of VTL § 1192(4)—which expressly limits the drugs applicable thereto to "a drug as defined in this chapter"—VTL § 1192(4-a) contains no such limitation. However, VTL § 114-a provides that "[t]he term 'drug' when used in this chapter, means and includes any substance listed in [Public Health Law § 3306]." *See People v. Primiano*, 16 Misc. 3d 1023, 843 N.Y.S.2d 799, 801 (Sullivan Co. Ct. 2007).

In *People v. Schell*, 18 Misc. 3d 972, 849 N.Y.S.2d 882, 884 (N.Y. City Crim. Ct. 2008), the Court held that "the People are correct in reasoning that the offense with which the defendant is charged, VTL § 192 subd. 4-a, contemplates chemicals beyond those listed in Public Health Law § 3306." Notably, the *Schell* Court did not cite any case law, legislative history or rule of statutory construction in support of its position. In the authors' opinion, the Court's conclusion in *Schell* is clearly erroneous.

Since VTL § 114-a expressly defines the term "drug" as meaning any substance listed in Public Health Law § 3306 whenever such term is used in the VTL, there is no need for either VTL § 1192(4) or VTL § 1192(4-a) to cross-reference VTL § 114-a in order to have this definition apply. Rather, if the Legislature had intended to use a different definition of the term "drug" for purposes of VTL § 1192(4-a), it would have been required to expressly say so. This conclusion is literally compelled by VTL § 100, which provides as follows:

Definition of words and phrases. The following words and phrases when used in this chapter shall, for the purpose of this chapter, have the meanings respectively ascribed to them in this article except where another definition is specifically provided in any title, article or section for application in such title, article or section.

In *People v. Gonzalez*, 90 A.D.3d 1668, 935 N.Y.S.2d 826 (4th Dep't 2011), the defendant was convicted of both DWI and DWAI Drugs. On appeal, he claimed that the convictions should be reversed on the ground that he was in actuality guilty of—but not charged with—DWAI Combined Influence. The Appellate Division, Fourth Department, affirmed the convictions, holding that "the evidence presented at trial is sufficient to establish that he was separately impaired by alcohol and by drugs." 90 A.D.3d at __, 935 N.Y.S.2d at 827.

§ 10:31   Penalties for conviction of VTL 1192(4-a)

The penalties for a conviction of VTL § 1192(4-a) are the same as the penalties for a conviction of VTL § 1192(2), (3) or (4). *See* VTL § 1193(1)(b); VTL § 1193(2)(b)(2); VTL § 1193(2)(b)(3). *See also* §§ 46:1 et seq., infra.

§ 10:32   DWAI drugs conviction reversed for improper cross-examination of defendant's doctor

In *People v. Dimiceli*, 27 Misc. 3d 84, 902 N.Y.S.2d 774 (App. Term, 9th & 10th Jud. Dist. 2010), the defendant was convicted of DWAI drugs and resisting Arrest. The drugs in question were prescribed medications. The Appellate Term reversed the defendant's convictions in the interest of justice based upon the following excerpt of the prosecutor's cross-examination of the defendant's doctor:

[THE PROSECUTOR:] * * * [Y]ou found out . . . that the defendant was arrested for this crime, correct?

[THE DOCTOR:] Uh-huh. Yes.

[THE PROSECUTOR:] And when you received word of that, that he was accused of being medicated while driving—

[THE DOCTOR:] Yes.

[THE PROSECUTOR:] —you ordered an end to all narcotic pain medicine, correct?

[THE DOCTOR:] Could I just refer to my notes?

[THE PROSECUTOR:] Of course.

[THE DOCTOR:] (Perusing.) Because I can't order a sudden end, because then they go into withdrawal, I probably recommended later on that he be detoxed. Here we go, yes, sorry. 4-27-05; gave tapering schedule of meds, but suggest patient be detoxed.

[THE PROSECUTOR:] You followed that up with a letter to Pain Management Services recommending a detox, correct?

[THE DOCTOR:] I followed it up with—it is back here somewhere. It wasn't the Pain Management Services, ultimately it went to South Oaks, if I remember correctly.

[THE PROSECUTOR:] For a detox program in South Oaks.

And that would be to rid all pain medicine from the body, correct?

[THE DOCTOR:] Correct.

[THE PROSECUTOR:] And then attend a treatment program because of that, correct?

[THE DOCTOR:] Correct.

[THE PROSECUTOR:] And because you got word of the defendant's arrest, you didn't prescribe any more pain medicine for approximately 10 months, correct?

[THE DOCTOR:] Correct.

There was no evidence that the doctor's decision to taper off defendant's medications, and his recommendation that defendant undergo "detox," were based on any information other than the fact that defendant had been charged with driving while ability impaired in the instant case. The doctor's choice of a course of treatment thus had no probative value with respect to defendant's actual condition before, during, or even after the incident. Because it was not relevant to any issue in the case, the course-of-treatment testimony should not have been admitted.

Furthermore, the testimony was highly prejudicial to defendant. It conveyed the impression that defendant's own doctor believed that he had been overmedicating at the time of the incident. It also conveyed the impression that the doctor believed that defendant was a prescription medication abuser in need of "detox." Particularly in light of the fact that the jury specifically requested the doctor's "detox statement" during its deliberations, we are of the opinion that the testimony was so prejudicial that it deprived defendant of a fair trial. Accordingly, we reverse the judgments of conviction as a matter of discretion in the interest of justice, and remit the matter to the District Court for a new trial.

27 Misc. 3d at __, 902 N.Y.S.2d at 775-76 (citations omitted).

§ 10:33 Significance of odor of burnt marijuana

In *People v. Chestnut*, 43 A.D.2d 260, __, 351 N.Y.S.2d 26, 27 (3d Dep't 1974), order aff'd, 36 N.Y.2d 971, 373 N.Y.S.2d 564, 335 N.E.2d 865 (1975), the Appellate Division, Third Department, held that "the smell of marihuana smoke, with nothing more, can be sufficient to provide police officers with probable cause to search an automobile and its occupants." Notably, however, the Court made clear that:

[I]t is critical to the outcome of this case that we are here concerned with an automobile, which is stopped on the highway and readily movable, whose occupants have been alerted, and whose contents "may never be found again if a warrant must be obtained." Equally important is the experience and training of the police officers involved. Here, both Troopers Carmody and Standish had extensive training with marihuana, formally at the State Police Academy in Albany and informally at their local substation. Each, likewise, had smelled marihuana smoke and was familiar with its distinctive odor.

People v. Chestnut, 351 N.Y.S.2d at 28-29 (citations omitted).

In *People v. Hanson*, 5 Misc. 3d 67, __, 785 N.Y.S.2d 825, 827 (App. Term, 9th & 10th Jud. Dist. 2004), the Court applied *Chestnut* as follows:

It is well settled that the smell of marijuana alone is sufficient to provide trained and experienced police officers in the area of narcotics probable cause to search a vehicle and its occupants. For a hearing court to make a finding that an officer had probable cause to conduct a search, the officer's expertise, training or experience with respect to knowledge of the smell of burnt marijuana must be adequately developed in the record. As we are bound by the court's return, the hearing court properly determined that the troopers lacked probable cause to search the defendant since there was no testimony regarding their training or experience in identifying the smell of burnt marijuana. Thus, the search of the defendant and the subsequent search of the automobile were not justified, and the marijuana was properly suppressed by the hearing court. In addition, the silver clip containing contraband, the pills, the statements made by the defendant after the illegal search and arrest, and the results of the field sobriety and chemical tests were also properly suppressed under the fruit of the poisonous tree doctrine.

(Citations omitted).

Chapter 11

VTL § 1192 Issues

KeyCite®: Cases and other legal materials listed in KeyCite Scope can be researched through the KeyCite service on Westlaw®. Use KeyCite to check citations for form, parallel references, prior and later history, and comprehensive citator information, including citations to other decisions and secondary materials.

---

§ 11:1   In general

Despite the fact that VTL § 1192 has the generic title "Operating a motor vehicle while under the influence of alcohol or drugs," New York does not have a charge entitled Operating Under the Influence (a.k.a. OUI). Rather, New York characterizes the relevant offenses as:

(a) Driving while ability impaired (a.k.a. "DWAI"). *See* VTL § 1192(1);

(b) Driving while intoxicated; per se (a.k.a. "per se DWI"). *See* VTL § 1192(2);

(c) Driving while intoxicated (a.k.a. "common law DWI"). *See* VTL § 1192(3);

(d) Aggravated driving while intoxicated (a.k.a. "Aggravated DWI"). *See* VTL § 1192(2-a);

(e) Driving while ability impaired by drugs (a.k.a. "DWAI Drugs"). *See* VTL § 1192(4); and

(f) Driving while ability impaired by the combined influence of drugs or of alcohol and any drug or drugs (a.k.a. "DWAI Combined Influence"). *See* VTL § 1192(4-a).

This chapter addresses various issues pertinent to VTL §§ 1192(1), (2), (2-a) and (3) charges. Issues pertinent to VTL §§ 1192(4) and (4-a) charges are addressed in §§ 10:1 et seq., *supra*. Issues pertinent to VTL §§ 1192(5) and (6) charges are addressed in §§ 14:1 et seq., *infra*.

§ 11:2   It is not illegal to drink and drive

Unless a person is under 21 years of age, the mere act of driving after consuming alcohol is not illegal in New York. In this regard, in *People v. Cruz*, 48 N.Y.2d 419, 426, 423 N.Y.S.2d 625, 628, 399 N.E.2d 513 (1979), the Court of Appeals made clear that:

That is not to say, of course, that every person who drinks before driving violates the law. On the contrary the Legislature recognized that the average person can consume a certain amount of alcohol without impairing his ability to operate a motor vehicle as he should. Otherwise the Legislature would not have provided that proof of .05 of 1% or less of blood alcohol content is prima facie evidence that the driver was not impaired or intoxicated (Vehicle and Traffic Law, § 1195, subd. 2, par. (a)). Of course some persons may find their driving faculties impaired by the least consumption of alcohol and, therefore, would be guilty of driving while impaired while others would not. And the Legislature also recognized that some individuals may be able to consume greater amounts of alcohol without being impaired, as would the average driver (Vehicle and Traffic Law, § 1195, subd. 2, par. (c)). Thus the impairment statute, by simply providing prima facie standards, takes into account the "subjective" tolerance of individuals in determining the ability to drive possessed by a defendant at the time of arrest. But in determining whether that ability is less than he *should* possess, the statute necessarily contemplates the use of the objective standard expected of the average driver.

(Citation omitted). *See also People v. Hagmann*, 175 A.D.2d 502, —, 572 N.Y.S.2d 952, 954 (3d Dep't 1991) (same).

§ 11:3   Legislative history of VTL § 1192

In *People v. Mertz*, 68 N.Y.2d 136, 142, 506 N.Y.S.2d 290, 293, 497 N.E.2d 657 (1986), the Court of Appeals endorsed the recitation of the Legislative history of VTL § 1192 contained in *People v. Schmidt*, 124 Misc. 2d 102, 478 N.Y.S.2d 482 (City Crim. Ct. 1984). In this regard, the *Schmidt* Court wrote:

Traffic deaths in the United States exceed 50,000 annually. Of the fatalities on the nation's highways, approximately one-half of the fatalities are alcohol related. The Supreme Court has observed that "[t]he increasing slaughter on our highways . . . now reaches astounding figures only heard of on the battlefield." Specifically, in New York State alone, there were 1,947 fatal accidents in 1982. Alcohol was an apparent contributing factor in 785 of those deaths.

The Legislature's response to this growing problem has been to increase the penalties for operating a motor vehicle while under the influence of alcohol and to make convictions easier to obtain.

Driving while intoxicated was first classified as an offense in the laws of New York in 1910. Convictions under that statute were based solely on the defendant's conduct and demeanor at the time of arrest. The statute did not define "intoxication" or "operation of a motor vehicle." Its focus was on punishment; a first offense was treated as a misdemeanor and the second as a felony. The Appellate Division, in 1910, interpreted the prohibition against driving while intoxicated to mean "that one shall not be affected by alcoholic beverages to such an extent as to impair his judgment or his ability to operate an automobile."

The next statutory modification came in 1926 when a new felony was created—causing serious bodily injury to another while driving in an intoxicated condition. This was followed in 1929, by the repeal of the 1910 statute and the enactment of Section 70(5). The felony/misdemeanor distinction was retained and the major difference between the two provisions involved license suspension and revocation. Under the earlier statute, suspension and revocation were discretionary, whereas the later statute mandated revocation if the driver was convicted of driving while intoxicated.

In 1939, the National Safety Council Committee on tests for intoxication reported on the relationship between blood alcohol content and intoxication. The Committee established three "zones of influence"—(1) any person having up to .05 percent of alcohol in the blood was considered not to be under the influence of alcohol; (2) any person having .05 percent and less than .15 percent of alcohol in the blood was considered to be possibly under the influence of alcohol; (3) any person having .15 percent or more of alcohol in the blood was presumed to be under the influence of alcohol. The American Medical Association officially adopted this classification scheme.

In 1941[,] the New York Legislature allowed test results indicating blood alcohol content (hereinafter, BAC) to be admitted at trial. It was at this point in the evolution of the drunk driving statute that the Legislature attempted to define intoxication in scientific, mathematical terms. Specifically, a finding that a driver had .05 of one percent or less by weight of alcohol in his blood was admissible as prima facie evidence of no intoxication. A test result indicating more than .05 but less than .15 of one percent BAC was considered relevant evidence of intoxication. A BAC of .15 or above was deemed prima facie evidence of intoxication.

In the post-war period, the incidence of motor vehicle accidents and fatalities received national attention. The existence of blood alcohol evidentiary provisions and license revocation penalties did not serve as an adequate deterrent. In 1953, the New York State Joint Legislative Committee on Motor Vehicle Problems took the position that observational testimony of the indicia of intoxication was inaccurate and unpersuasive before a jury. The scientific blood alcohol content test was viewed as producing a more reliable type of evidence. Thus, in July, 1953, apparently acting on this assumption, Sec. 71-a of the New York Vehicle and Traffic Law was passed by the Legislature. This provision stated that any person driving a vehicle in New York State *implicitly consents* to a BAC test, administered at the direction of an officer who has reasonable grounds to suspect that the driver is intoxicated. If the driver refused to submit to such test, the Commissioner of Motor Vehicles was obligated to revoke the driver's license or permit.

Shortly after its enactment, Sec. 71-a was successfully challenged on due process grounds. The constitutional infirmity was two-fold: (1) the statute did not require a valid arrest as a basis for the officer's demand that the driver submit to a BAC test; and (2) a license could be revoked without a hearing. The Legislature responded, in 1954, by amending Sec. 71-a to provide the following: (1) the police officer needed reasonable grounds to *believe* (as opposed to reasonable grounds to suspect) that the driver was intoxicated; (2) an arrest had to precede the request to submit to the chemical test; and (3) the accused had to be granted an opportunity to be heard before revocation of a license or permit.

Despite the new laws, the problems increased and the concerns of the Legislature were more pronounced. Under the auspices of the Temporary State Commission on Coordination of State Activities the Vehicle and Traffic Law was recodified. The evidentiary weight to be given BAC measurements remained unchanged. Soon after the new VTL took effect, the American Medical Association, in November of 1960, adopted a policy that .10 percent should be considered prima facie evidence of being under the influence of alcohol.

Within the first year of its enactment, the New York Legislature added a new classification of proscribed conduct to VTL Section 1192—the traffic infraction of driving while impaired. Blood alcohol content of .10 of one percent was deemed evidence of impairment. Originally, impairment could *only* be established by scientific proof showing a specific blood alcohol content. This requirement was subsequently eliminated.FN13

FN13. In 1963, the Legislature focused upon the problem of minors (defined as persons under the age of 21) who drink and drive. Section 1192 was amended to provide that a BAC of more than .05 was prima facie evidence of impairment for a minor driver. BAC of .15 or more continued to be prima facie evidence of intoxication for minor and adult drivers.

In 1966, Section 1192 was revised to state that a driver who operates a motor vehicle while his ability is impaired by the use of drugs is guilty of a misdemeanor.

In 1970, the Legislature undertook a major revision of Section 1192 and enacted the general format in effect today. The proscription against driving while ability was impaired by alcohol remained a traffic infraction. Operation of a motor vehicle while in an intoxicated condition was classified as a misdemeanor. The evidentiary significance of BAC levels (contained in a new section—Section 1195) was as follows:

.05 BAC or less—prima facie evidence of no impairment, and no intoxication;

more than .05 and less than .10—prima facie evidence of no intoxication; relevant evidence of impairment;

.05 or more for driver under 21—prima facie impairment (repealed);

.10 or more—prima facie evidence of impairment; relevant evidence of intoxication.

Finally, and most importantly, the 1970 Legislature enacted an absolute liability provision. It substituted the former presumption of intoxication with the *per se* crime of driving with a certain percentage of alcohol in the blood. Specifically, the 1970 statute stated that it was a misdemeanor to drive with a BAC of .15. That provision was the direct forerunner of the present Section 1192(2).

In 1971, the Legislature lowered the prima facie standards for intoxication and impairment. Replacing the .15 BAC level, it established .12 of one percent by weight of alcohol in the blood as the baseline standard of intoxication.FN17 The Legislature also lowered the BAC levels admissible as evidence of intoxication or impairment:

more than .05 and less than .08—prima facie evidence of no intoxication; relevant evidence of impairment;

.08 or more—prima facie evidence of impairment; relevant evidence of intoxication.

FN17. In addition, separate BAC levels for minor drivers were eliminated.

Aware of the view advocated by the National Highway Safety Bureau, and adopted by an increasing number of states, that the liability level of blood alcohol content should be still lower, the New York Legislature finally acquiesced in 1972. Sec. 1192(2) was revised to its present form, which establishes a *per se* crime if a person operates a motor vehicle with a blood alcohol content of .10. In addition, the BAC levels admissible as evidence of impairment and intoxication were simultaneously modified:

.05 or less—prima facie evidence that the operator is not impaired or intoxicated;

more than .07 but less than .10—prima facie evidence that the driver is not intoxicated; prima facie evidence of impairment.

In 1974, a final provision was enacted stating that more than .05 of one percent, but not more than .07 of one percent, BAC is prima facie evidence of no intoxication, but is relevant evidence of impairment. These are the quantitative standards in effect today.

The statutory development set forth above reveals a gradual but deliberate attempt on the part of the Legislature to fortify the effectiveness of the drunk driving laws. The culmination of this effort—the enactment of a .10 *per se* liability standard—reflects a determination that when a defendant drives with that amount of alcohol in his blood, the question of guilt need not be defined by his subjective behavior and condition. Rather, what is required is that the People prove, by objective, scientific criteria that at the time defendant was driving, his BAC was .10 percent.

People v. Schmidt, 478 N.Y.S.2d at 483–87 (citations and footnotes omitted).

In 2001, the Court of Appeals updated the legislative history of New York's DWI laws:

In the early 1980's, drunk driving became a dominant social issue. Drunk drivers were the leading cause of highway deaths in New York. In response, the Legislature enacted a series of reforms and in 1988 consolidated and recodified pertinent provisions into a single article. Article 31 emerged as a tightly and carefully integrated statute the sole purpose of which is to address drunk driving.FN3

FN3. Under article 31, the offenses and penalties are systematically interwoven with police procedures and rehabilitative programs. Section 1192 defines the offenses and section 1193 sets forth the sanctions (both criminal and administrative). Section 1194 details arrest and field test guidelines for section 1192 violations including the administration of chemical tests and penalties for driver refusals of testing. Section 1195 prescribes the circumstances when and how chemical test evidence is to be admitted. Section 1196 establishes an alcohol and drug rehabilitation program and sets forth eligibility criteria in the context of section 1192 violations. Section 1196 also creates a "conditional license" for program participants that affords limited and essential driving privileges to a holder. The section also authorizes, with some restrictions, termination of the license suspension or revocation after completion of the program. Finally, section 1197 authorizes counties to establish their own driving while intoxicated prevention programs.

The penalties for section 1192 violations are specific; each offense is accorded its own criminal punishment. Violations incurred during the operation of special motor vehicles are subject to different penalties. Section 1193 classifies each section 1192 violation and correlates penalties to the specific degree of the violation. The penalties for multiple section 1192 violations increase with each violation that occurs over a specific period of time. Unlike the Penal Law, section 1193 mandates minimum fines where a fine is imposed.

In addition to criminal penalties, section 1193 further imposes mandatory minimum periods for license suspension or revocation. These sanctions, like the criminal penalties, are correlated to the specific nature and degree of the section 1192 violation.

The Legislature placed great significance on the enforcement of specific statutory penalties for drunk driving. The statute provides that sentences for special vehicle offenses must be imposed despite contrary provisions in the Penal Law. Moreover, a sentencing court is prohibited from imposing an unconditional discharge for a section 1192 violation, and conditional discharges or probation sentences must be accompanied by a fine. When a person is convicted of a felony under the Vehicle and Traffic Law where a minimum fine has been established, the sentencing court is authorized to impose the minimum notwithstanding the fines schedule established for Penal Law felonies. Thus, the Legislature has made it clear that the courts must look to section 1193 for the appropriate penalties and sentencing options for drunk driving offenses.

People v. Prescott, 95 N.Y.2d 655, 659–61, 722 N.Y.S.2d 778, 780–82, 745 N.E.2d 1000 (2001) (citations and footnotes omitted). *See also People v. Litto*, 8 N.Y.3d 692, 840 N.Y.S.2d 736, 872 N.E.2d 848 (2007).

There have been numerous amendments to the DWI laws since 2001. For example, on July 1, 2003, New York became a ".08" State. That is, the threshold BAC currently deemed to constitute legal intoxication was lowered from .10% to .08%. *See* VTL § 1192(2). In a conforming amendment, VTL § 1195(2) was amended to change the probative values to be accorded BAC readings under .08%.

In 2006, the Legislature enacted major, sweeping changes to New York's DWI laws. For example, the Legislature:

1. Created the crime of Aggravated DWI (*i.e.*, driving with a BAC of .18% or more). *See* VTL § 1192(2-a);
2. Created the crime of DWAI Combined Influence. *See* VTL § 1192(4-a);
3. Created a new category of AUO 1st. *See* VTL § 511(3)(a)(iii);
4. Made many more people subject to prosecution for Vehicular Assault 1st and Vehicular Manslaughter 1st. *See* PL §§ 120.04 and 125.13;
5. Increased the penalties for refusal to submit to a chemical test. *See* VTL § 1194(2)(d);
6. Increased the plea bargaining restrictions applicable to DWI cases. *See* VTL § 1192(10);
7. Created "permanent" driver's license revocations for certain repeat offenders. *See* VTL § 1193(2)(b)(12);
8. Required alcohol/substance abuse screening and/or treatment in virtually every VTL § 1192 case. *See* VTL § 1198-a; and

9. Amended VTL § 1192(8) to permit certain out-of-state DWI convictions to be used as predicates to raise the level of a subsequent in-state DWI to a felony.

In 2007, the Legislature created the crimes of Aggravated Vehicular Assault and Aggravated Vehicular Homicide. *See* PL §§ 120.04-a and 125.14.

In 2009, the Legislature enacted "Leandra's Law," which (a) makes it a felony to commit DWI, DWAI Drugs or DWAI Combined Influence with a child under the age of 16 in the vehicle, and (b) requires everyone who is sentenced on or after August 15, 2010, for a conviction of DWI or Aggravated DWI (committed on or after November 18, 2009) to install an ignition interlock device in any vehicle that they own or operate (with the exception of certain employer-owned vehicles) for at least six months. *See* VTL §§ 1192(2-a)(b) and 1198.

§ 11:4   What are the primary DWI statutes?

The primary DWI-related statutes are contained in VTL Article 31, which is comprised of VTL §§ 1192 to 1199. VTL § 1192 defines offenses such as DWAI, per se DWI, common law DWI, Aggravated DWI, DWAI Drugs, DWI Combined Influence, and DWI in commercial motor vehicles. It also, *inter alia*, sets forth the roadways upon which VTL § 1192 applies; the effect of a prior out-of-state DWI/DUI conviction; the effect of a prior Zero Tolerance law adjudication; and various plea bargain limitations applicable to DWI-related charges.

VTL § 1192-a is the so-called Zero-Tolerance law applicable to underage drinking drivers.

VTL § 1193 sets forth the criminal and civil penalties, including driver's license sanctions, that apply to convictions for VTL § 1192 offenses (as well as to convictions for out-of-state DWI/DUI offenses committed by NY licensees). It also, *inter alia*, addresses issues such as suspension pending prosecution; the effect of successful DDP completion on certain driver's license revocation periods; and re-application for a driver's license following revocation.

VTL § 1194 addresses breath screening tests, chemical tests, and chemical test refusals. It also, *inter alia*, sets forth the procedures for DMV chemical test refusal hearings; the consequences of a chemical test refusal; the effect of successful DDP completion on a chemical test refusal revocation; the defendant's right to an independent chemical test; and the procedures applicable to compulsory chemical tests. VTL § 1194 further requires the Department of Health ("DOH") to promulgate rules and regulations pertaining to chemical testing (the relevant regulations are contained in 10 NYCRR Part 59).

VTL § 1194-a sets forth the procedures applicable to Zero Tolerance law hearings, as well as the civil consequences of a Zero Tolerance law adjudication.

VTL § 1195 addresses the admissibility and probative value of a chemical test result administered pursuant to VTL § 1194.

VTL § 1196 creates and regulates the Drinking Driver Program (DDP) and conditional driver's licenses. In particular, it establishes eligibility for the DDP and/or for a conditional license; sets forth the scope of a conditional license; sets forth the consequences of driving in violation of the scope of a conditional license; and sets forth the effect of successful DDP completion on the reinstatement of full driving privileges.

VTL § 1197 provides the authority for counties to establish a Special Traffic Options Program for Driving While Intoxicated (a.k.a. STOP-DWI), and addresses issues such as Program organization, approval and audit, required reports, and the functions of the county STOP-DWI coordinator.

VTL § 1198 addresses ignition interlock devices (IIDs), including issues such as the scope of the IID program; who is required to install and maintain an IID; proof of compliance with the IID requirement; cost, installation and maintenance of IIDs; applicability of IID requirement to employer-owned vehicles; and penalties for circumvention of IID or violation of IID requirement. VTL § 1198 further requires the DOH and the Office of Probation and Correctional Alternatives (OPCA) to promulgate rules and regulations pertaining to IIDs (the relevant DOH regulations are contained in 10 NYCRR Part 59; the relevant OPCA regulations are contained in 9 NYCRR Part 358).

VTL § 1198-a establishes "special procedures" regarding mandatory alcohol/substance abuse screening and/or treatment that are applicable to most VTL § 1192 cases.

VTL § 1199 establishes Driver Responsibility Assessments, which are, in effect, additional fines imposed on defendants convicted of alcohol- and drug-related driving offenses above and beyond the mandatory fines, surcharges and fees associated with such convictions.

§ 11:5   What is "common law DWI"?

VTL § 1192(3) is commonly referred to as "common law DWI." In essence, it means to drive drunk. No proof of the defendant's BAC is required to sustain a charge of common law DWI. In fact, an argument can be made that the defendant's BAC is irrelevant to a common law DWI charge. In this regard, VTL § 1195 provides that certain BACs constitute evidence of impairment—but provides no guidance as to the probative value of a BAC of .08% or more. This is presumably because having a BAC of .08% or more is itself a form of DWI. See VTL § 1192(2).

Defendants who refuse to submit to a chemical test are typically charged with common law DWI. Indeed, it is almost unheard of for a defendant who refuses to submit to a chemical test to only be charged with DWAI.

Common law DWI is based upon whether the defendant's driving, appearance, demeanor, manner of speech, motor coordination, performance on field sobriety tests, etc. establish that he or she was intoxicated. Not all of the symptoms of intoxication must be present; nor is erratic driving a requirement. Rather, the totality of the circumstances must lead to the conclusion that the defendant "voluntarily consumed alcohol to the extent that he is incapable of employing the physical and mental abilities which he is expected to possess in order to operate a vehicle as a reasonable and prudent driver." *People v. Cruz*, 48 N.Y.2d 419, 428, 423 N.Y.S.2d 625, 629, 399 N.E.2d 513 (1979).

New York's test for intoxication is objective as opposed to subjective. *See, e.g., Matter of Johnston*, 75 N.Y.2d 403, 409, 554 N.Y.S.2d 88, 91, 553 N.E.2d 566 (1990). Accordingly, to sustain a charge of common law DWI the defendant must actually appear intoxicated. Thus, if a particular defendant has a higher tolerance for alcohol than the average person, that subjective tolerance benefits him or her with respect to a common law DWI charge. *See, e.g., Cruz*, 48 N.Y.2d at 426, 423 N.Y.S.2d at 628; *People v. Hagmann*, 175 A.D.2d 502, __, 572 N.Y.S.2d 952, 954 (3d Dep't 1991).

§ 11:6   What is "common law DWI"?—VTL § 1192(3) only applies to intoxication caused by alcohol

Unlike VTL §§ 1192(1), (2), (2-a), (4) and (4-a)—VTL § 1192(3) does not expressly mandate that the defendant's intoxication be caused by any particular substance. Nonetheless, the Court of Appeals has made clear that the phrase "driving while intoxicated," as used in VTL § 1192(3), means driving while intoxicated by alcohol. *See People v. Litto*, 8 N.Y.3d 692, 840 N.Y.S.2d 736, 872 N.E.2d 848 (2007). Specifically, the *Litto* Court held that:

> Over the last 97 years, the Legislature has crafted and repeatedly refined statutes with the goal of removing from the road those who drive while intoxicated. This appeal centers on the phrase "driving while intoxicated" in Vehicle and Traffic Law § 1192(3). Based on the language, history and scheme of the statute, we conclude that the Legislature here intended to use "intoxication" to refer to a disordered state of mind caused by alcohol, not by drugs.

People v. Litto, 8 N.Y.3d at 693–94, 840 N.Y.S.2d at 736–37. *See also People v. Farmer*, 36 N.Y.2d 386, 390, 369 N.Y.S.2d 44, 45, 330 N.E.2d 22 (1975) ("subdivisions 1, 2 and 3 of section 1192 proscribe separable offenses based upon the degree of impairment caused by alcohol ingestion"); *People v. Bayer*, 132 A.D.2d 920, __, 518 N.Y.S.2d 475, 476 (4th Dep't 1987) (VTL § 1192 "[s]ubdivision (3) prohibits operation of a motor vehicle while defendant 'is in an intoxicated condition', but does not refer to a substance creating the condition. It is clear as a matter of law, however, that the subdivision is intended to apply only to intoxication caused by alcohol"). *See generally People v. Cruz*, 48 N.Y.2d 419, 428, 423 N.Y.S.2d 625, 629, 399 N.E.2d 513 (1979) (for purposes of VTL § 1192(3), "intoxication is a greater degree of impairment which is reached when the driver has voluntarily consumed alcohol to the extent that he is incapable of employing the physical and mental abilities which he is expected to possess in order to operate a vehicle as a reasonable and prudent driver").

In *People v. Tracey*, 25 Misc. 3d 849, 885 N.Y.S.2d 559 (Livingston Co. Ct. 2009), the Court confronted the issue of whether ethylene glycol (*i.e.*, anti-freeze) constitutes "alcohol" for purposes of VTL § 1192(3). Concluding that it does not, the Court reasoned as follows:

> This court must now determine whether the consumption of alcohol refers to ethyl alcohol or any substance chemically defined as an alcohol. * * *

> This court could find no reported case directly on point. However, the language used and history recited by the Court of Appeals in *Litto* was highly instructive on the issue before this court. * * *

> The term "intoxication" is now defined using the phrase "consumed alcohol" in place of "imbibed enough liquor." But, "alcohol" has virtually the same meaning as "liquor" did in 1919. While "alcohol" is not defined in the Vehicle and Traffic Law (as "liquor" was not in 1910), the legislature has defined it in the Alcoholic Beverage Control Law. " 'Alcohol' means ethyl alcohol, hydrated oxide of ethyl or spirit of wine." "Alcoholic beverages" are defined as spirits, wine, liquor, beer, cider and every liquid containing alcohol and capable of being consumed by a human being.

> Therefore, the conclusion is inescapable that "intoxication" meant in 1910 and still means today intoxication by the consumption of alcoholic beverages. Alcoholic beverages meaning spirits, wine, liquor, beer, cider and every liquid containing alcohol and capable of being consumed by a human being. In other words, ethyl alcohol. Ethyl alcohol is also known as ethanol or drinking alcohol. * * *

> Ethylene glycol, while technically defined as an alcohol, is not an alcoholic beverage. It is not manufactured for human consumption and it is hazardous to human health. * * *

> Therefore, to be charged with driving while intoxicated, a defendant

must be "intoxicated" by the consumption of alcohol, more specifically an alcoholic beverage.

A defendant may not be charged with driving while intoxicated based upon the presence of *ethylene glycol*.

25 Misc. 3d at __, __, __, __, 885 N.Y.S.2d at 560, 561, 562, 563 (citations omitted).

§ 11:7 Attempted DWI is not a legally cognizable offense

Penal Law § 110.00 provides that "[a] person is guilty of an attempt to commit a crime when, with intent to commit a crime, he engages in conduct which tends to effect the commission of such crime." In terms of punishment, an attempt to commit a crime is generally punished one level lower than the crime itself. *See* PL § 110.05.

In *People v. Prescott*, 263 A.D.2d 254, 704 N.Y.S.2d 410 (4th Dep't 2000), the Appellate Division, Fourth Department, temporarily created the crime of attempted DWI. On appeal, however, the Court of Appeals reversed, holding that attempted DWI is *not* a legally cognizable offense. *People v. Prescott*, 95 N.Y.2d 655, 722 N.Y.S.2d 778, 745 N.E.2d 1000 (2001).

Interestingly, however, although attempted DWI is not an appropriate *charge*, it apparently can be a valid *plea bargain*. *See People v. Foster*, 19 N.Y.2d 150, 278 N.Y.S.2d 603, 225 N.E.2d 200 (1967) (plea of guilty to nonexistent crime not invalid where defendant sought, and freely and knowingly accepted, such plea as part of a plea bargain struck for defendant's benefit). *See also People v. Johnson*, 23 N.Y.3d 973, 975, 989 N.Y.S.2d 680, 681, 12 N.E.3d 1109, 1109 (2014) ("Where a defendant enters a negotiated plea to a lesser crime than one with which he is charged, no factual basis for the plea is required. Indeed, under such circumstances defendants can even plead guilty to crimes that do not exist.") (citations omitted); *People v. Francis*, 38 N.Y.2d 150, 155, 379 N.Y.S.2d 21, 26, 341 N.E.2d 540 (1975) ("a plea may be to a hypothetical crime"); *People v. Keizer*, 100 N.Y.2d 114, 118 n.2, 760 N.Y.S.2d 720, 723 n.2, 790 N.E.2d 1149 (2003) (same); *People v. Clairborne*, 29 N.Y.2d 950, 951, 329 N.Y.S.2d 580, 581, 280 N.E.2d 366 (1972) ("A bargained guilty plea to a lesser crime makes unnecessary a factual basis for the particular crime confessed."); Donnino, Practice Commentary, McKinney's Cons. Laws of N.Y., Book 39, Penal Law § 110.00, at 85 ("Though there may not logically be an attempt to commit a particular substantive crime, a bargained-for guilt plea to such an attempt struck for the defendant's benefit may not be set aside on appeal").

One reason why a defendant might find a plea bargain to attempted DWI to be advantageous is that "license sanctions could not be administered because it is not apparent under the Vehicle and Traffic Law what period of revocation or suspension should be imposed upon someone who commits 'attempted' driving while intoxicated." *Prescott*, 95 N.Y.2d at 662 n.7, 722 N.Y.S.2d at 782 n.7.

§ 11:8   Can driving while intoxicated ever be "justified"?

In *People v. Maher*, 79 N.Y.2d 978, 980, 584 N.Y.S.2d 421, 421–22, 594 N.E.2d 915 (1992):

> At 4:20 on a Saturday morning, after consuming alcohol, defendant was involved in a minor traffic accident on a New York City street. According to defendant, the driver of the second vehicle became belligerent when defendant attempted to exchange license and insurance information with him and the driver reached into the back seat of his car. Believing that the driver was about to produce a weapon, defendant returned to his own car and fled the scene. A short distance from the first accident defendant struck and killed a pedestrian.

The defendant claimed that he was justified in his actions based upon the perceived threat to his safety. The trial court agreed to instruct the jury with a justification defense, *see* PL § 35.05(2), with regard to the "leaving the scene of an accident" charge, but refused to do so with regard to the DWI and vehicular crimes charges. The defendant was acquitted of the leaving the scene charge based upon the justification theory, but was convicted of DWAI and Criminally Negligent Homicide.

The Court of Appeals reversed the convictions, holding that the defendant was entitled to the justification instruction with regard to all of the charges:

> If on any reasonable view of the evidence, the jury might have decided that defendant's actions were justified, the failure to charge the defense constitutes reversible error. It is not for the trial court to hypothesize other reasonable alternatives to the course of action chosen by the defendant. By giving the charge to the jury on the leaving the scene charge, the Judge concluded that one reasonable view of the evidence justified that conduct. Defendant argues, and we agree, that under these circumstances he was entitled to have the jury determine if the manner in which he fled the scene was also justified. That no weapon was observed does not act to bar the charge, but rather is one element of the circumstances that gave rise to the conduct.
>
> Finally, there was no testimony that the emergency had ceased. Defendant stated only that he no longer observed the car following him and that he had started to reduce his speed. It was for the jury to determine whether the threat of harm that the defendant perceived had ceased to exist and if so whether defendant had sufficient time to react prior to the crash.

People v. Maher, 79 N.Y.2d at 982, 584 N.Y.S.2d at 423 (citation omitted).

In *People v. Asche*, 175 Misc. 2d 639, __, 669 N.Y.S.2d 788, 790 (Nassau Co. Dist. Ct. 1998), the Court held that DWI charges would be dismissed in the interest of justice where "a probably-intoxicated defendant who otherwise had no intention of driving in that condition, . . . operated a motor vehicle for a short distance at the direct command of a police officer."

Similarly, in *People v. Donovan*, 53 Misc. 2d 687, 279 N.Y.S.2d 404 (Scarsdale Ct. of Special Sessions 1967), the Court held that the People were "estopped to prosecute this defendant" for DWAI where the defendant had been found sleeping in the driveway of a private residence and only drove because the police woke her up and said "Lady, you're on private property; you can't stay here; you'll have to leave."

By contrast, in *People v. Kaeppel*, 74 Misc. 2d 220, 342 N.Y.S.2d 882 (Suffolk Co. Dist. Ct. 1973), the Court held that the defense of entrapment was not available to the defendant where, among other things, there was conflicting testimony as to whether the police had commanded him to drive and, in any event, he had clearly driven the vehicle prior to the police arriving.

§ 11:9   What is "per se DWI"?

VTL § 1192(2) is commonly referred to as "per se DWI." Per se DWI is the converse of common law DWI. *See* § 11:5, *supra*. The charge is called "per se" because it makes it illegal for a person to drive with a BAC of .08% or more regardless of whether such BAC rendered the person "intoxicated." *See, e.g., People v. Farmer*, 36 N.Y.2d 386, 393, 369 N.Y.S.2d 44, 47, 330 N.E.2d 22 (1975) (Fuchsberg, J., concurring) ("Obviously, it is possible for a defendant to have had the quantity of alcohol in his blood required for conviction under subdivision 2 and yet not be found to be in an intoxicated condition under subdivision 3. Likewise, he could be found to be in an intoxicated condition though the level of the weight of alcohol in his blood fell below the '.[08] of one per centum' statutory level"); *People v. Miller*, 199 A.D.2d 692, __, 605 N.Y.S.2d 160, 163 (3d Dep't 1993) ("§ 1192(2) is based upon a defendant's blood alcohol content while § 1192(3) is based upon the manner a defendant operated his vehicle and his condition"); *People v. Blowers*, 79 Misc. 2d 462, __, 360 N.Y.S.2d 369, 373 (Rensselaer Co. Ct. 1974) (VTL § 1192(2) "prohibits the operation of a motor vehicle while the operator has .[08] of one percentum or more by weight of alcohol in his blood and that is unrelated to whether or not the operator was in fact intoxicated"). Thus, if a particular defendant has a higher tolerance for alcohol than the average person, that subjective tolerance is no defense with respect to a per se DWI charge.

On the other hand, the term per se DWI can be misleading, because the defendant's BAC is never determined while the defendant is driving (and thus the defendant's chemical test result is only circumstantial proof of his or her BAC at the time of operation). In this regard, the Court of Appeals has made clear that "in this State a positive breathalyzer test establishes only a prima facie case and is not per se evidence of guilt, thus allowing defendant to argue, for example, that his blood alcohol content was lower when he was driving than when the test was given." *People v. Alvarez*, 70 N.Y.2d 375, 380, 521 N.Y.S.2d 212, 214, 515 N.E.2d 898 (1987).

The Court of Appeals addressed this issue more specifically in *People v. Mertz*, 68 N.Y.2d 136, 139, 506 N.Y.S.2d 290, 291, 497 N.E.2d 657 (1986):

> A violation of Vehicle and Traffic Law § 1192(2) is not established unless the trier of fact finds that *while* operating a motor vehicle defendant had a blood alcohol content (BAC) of .[08] of 1% or more. Evidence that a breathalyzer test administered within two hours of arrest showed defendant to have such a BAC is sufficient to establish prima facie a violation of the subdivision. It is, however, error not to permit defendant's attorney to argue on the basis of evidence, whether through cross-examination of the People's witnesses or testimony of defendant's witnesses, expert or other, from which it could be found that defendant's BAC at the time of vehicle operation was less than .[08]%, that if the jury so found defendant was not guilty of violating the subdivision.

(Emphasis added). The *Mertz* Court further made clear that:

> [T]he BAC count shown within two hours after arrest is strong but not conclusive evidence of the BAC during operation . . . . We conclude, therefore, that proof of a breathalyzer reading of [.08] or more within two hours after arrest establishes prima facie a violation of Vehicle and Traffic Law § 1192(2) which, together with evidence of one or more of defendant's deportment, speech, stability and the odor of his or her breath, is sufficient to sustain a conviction, absent evidence, expert or other and by whichever party produced, from which the trier of fact could conclude that defendant's BAC at the time of vehicle operation was less than [.08].

People v. Mertz, 68 N.Y.2d at 146, 506 N.Y.S.2d at 295. *See also People v. Mertz*, 68 N.Y.2d at 143–44, 506 N.Y.S.2d at 294 (it is a "scientifically accepted fact that a .[08] reading within two hours after operation does not establish a .[08] reading while operating").

§ 11:10   Reversal of VTL § 1192(2) conviction generally requires reversal of VTL § 1192(1)/(3) conviction(s)

In *People v. Gower*, 42 N.Y.2d 117, 122, 397 N.Y.S.2d 368, 371,

366 N.E.2d 69 (1977), the Court of Appeals reversed the defendant's VTL § 1192(2) conviction, and also held that:

> It is not possible . . . to determine that the erroneous admission of the breathalyzer results did not also infect the convictions for violation of subdivisions 1 and 3 of section 1192.

> Accordingly, in each case the order of County Court . . . should be reversed, and the same remitted for a new trial.

Similarly, in *People v. English*, 103 A.D.2d 979, __, 480 N.Y.S.2d 56, 58 (3d Dep't 1984), the Appellate Division, Third Department, held that "[a] chemical test result is highly probative evidence and it is impossible to assess the effect of such evidence on the jury as opposed to the weight given to the other evidence. Therefore, the conviction on the [VTL § 1192(3)] count should also be reversed." (Citation omitted). *See also People v. Corley*, 124 A.D.2d 390, __, 507 N.Y.S.2d 491, 493 (3d Dep't 1986) (same); *People v. Griesbeck*, 17 A.D.3d 717, __, 793 N.Y.S.2d 227, 228 (3d Dep't 2005); *People v. Baker*, 51 A.D.3d 1047, __, 856 N.Y.S.2d 707, 709–10 (3d Dep't 2008); *People v. Borst*, 49 Misc. 3d 63, __, 20 N.Y.S.3d 838, 841 (App. Term, 9th & 10th Jud. Dist. 2015). *Cf. People v. Grune*, 12 A.D.3d 944, 785 N.Y.S.2d 178 (3d Dep't 2004).

§ 11:11   What is "Aggravated DWI"?

VTL § 1192(2-a) is commonly referred to as "Aggravated DWI." There are two types of Aggravated DWI. The first type, per se Aggravated DWI, makes it illegal to operate a motor vehicle with a BAC of .18% or more. *See* VTL § 1192(2-a)(a). Although the name Aggravated DWI implies that the defendant is highly intoxicated, it is not an element of this crime that the defendant's high BAC actually rendered him or her "intoxicated."

The second type of Aggravated DWI makes it illegal to violate VTL §§ 1192(2), (3), (4) or (4-a) with a child under the age of 16 in the vehicle. *See* VTL § 1192(2-a)(b). This offense is known as "Leandra's Law"—in memory of a child killed by a drunk driver. A Leandra's Law violation is a felony, even for a first offense. *See* VTL § 1193(1)(c)(i)(B).

§ 11:12   High BAC is not synonymous with intoxication

The Court of Appeals has made clear that "it is well known that the effects of alcohol consumption 'may differ greatly from person to person' and that tolerance for alcohol is subject to wide individual variation. Thus, even where it can be established, a high blood alcohol count in the person served may not provide a sound basis for drawing inferences about the individual's appearance or demeanor." *Romano v. Stanley*, 90 N.Y.2d 444, 450–51, 661 N.Y.S.2d 589, 592, 684 N.E.2d 19 (1997) (citations and footnote omitted).

§ 11:13   What is "felony DWI"?

A defendant who is charged with DWI, Aggravated DWI, DWAI Drugs or DWAI Combined Influence after having been convicted of a violation of VTL §§ 1192(2), (2-a), (3), (4) or (4-a) (or of Vehicular Assault in the 1st or 2nd degree, Vehicular Manslaughter in the 1st or 2nd degree, Aggravated Vehicular Assault or Aggravated Vehicular Homicide) within the preceding 10 years can be charged with a class E felony. VTL § 1193(1)(c)(i).

A defendant who is charged with DWI, Aggravated DWI, DWAI Drugs or DWAI Combined Influence after having been convicted of a violation of VTL §§ 1192(2), (2-a), (3), (4) or (4-a) (or of Vehicular Assault in the 1st or 2nd degree, Vehicular Manslaughter in the 1st or 2nd degree, Aggravated Vehicular Assault or Aggravated Vehicular Homicide) *twice* within the preceding 10 years can be charged with a class D felony. VTL § 1193(1)(c)(ii).

Effective November 1, 2014, a defendant who is charged with DWI, Aggravated DWI, DWAI Drugs or DWAI Combined Influence after having been convicted of a violation of VTL § 1192(2), (2-a), (3), (4) or (4-a) (or of Vehicular Assault in the 1st or 2nd degree, Vehicular Manslaughter in the 1st or 2nd degree, Aggravated Vehicular Assault or Aggravated Vehicular Homicide) three or more times within the preceding 15 years can be charged with a class D felony. VTL § 1193(1)(c)(ii-a).

This topic is covered at length in §§ 9:1 et seq., *supra*.

§ 11:14   What is "felony DWI"?—Effect of out-of-state convictions

Prior to November 1, 2006, VTL § 1192(8) provided that, for purposes of determining the consequences of a violation of VTL § 1192, a prior out-of-state conviction for operating a motor vehicle while under the influence of alcohol or drugs was deemed to be a prior conviction of DWAI in violation of VTL § 1192(1). *See also People v. Pardee*, 202 Misc. 238, 117 N.Y.S.2d 515 (Westchester Co. Ct. 1952), order aff'd, 282 A.D. 735, 122 N.Y.S.2d 902 (2d Dep't); order aff'd, 306 N.Y. 660, 116 N.E.2d 495 (1953); *People v. Gagne*, 127 Misc. 2d 327, 485 N.Y.S.2d 938 (Ontario Co. Ct. 1985). Effective November 1, 2006, VTL § 1192(8) now provides as follows:

> Effect of prior out-of-state conviction. A prior out-of-state conviction for operating a motor vehicle while under the influence of alcohol or drugs shall be deemed to be a prior conviction of a violation of this

section for purposes of determining penalties imposed under this section or for purposes of any administrative action required to be taken pursuant to [VTL § 1193(2)]; provided, however, that such conduct, had it occurred in this state, would have constituted a misdemeanor or felony violation of any of the provisions of [VTL § 1192]. Provided, however, that if such conduct, had it occurred in this state, would have constituted a violation of any provisions of [VTL § 1192] which are not misdemeanor or felony offenses, then such conduct shall be deemed to be a prior conviction of a violation of [VTL § 1192(1)] for purposes of determining penalties imposed under this section or for purposes of any administrative action required to be taken pursuant to [VTL § 1193(2)].

As a result, a prior out-of-state DWI conviction can now potentially be used as a predicate conviction for a felony DWI charge.

Critically, however, the enabling portion of this amendment to VTL § 1192(8) expressly provides that the new law only applies to out-of-state convictions that occurred on or after November 1, 2006. *See also People v. Ballman*, 15 N.Y.3d 68, 70, 904 N.Y.S.2d 361, 362, 930 N.E.2d 282 (2010) ("This appeal raises the issue whether Vehicle and Traffic Law § 1192(8) allows an out-of-state conviction occurring prior to November 1, 2006 to be considered for purposes of elevating a charge of driving while intoxicated from a misdemeanor to a felony. We hold that it does not").

§ 11:15   What is "felony DWI"?—Proving a predicate DWI conviction

A defendant who commits DWI within 10 years of a prior DWI conviction or convictions can be charged with felony DWI. *See* VTL § 1193(1)(c). In this regard, if the People indict the defendant for felony DWI, they must properly prove the defendant's predicate DWI conviction(s) before the Grand Jury. In *People v. Van Buren*, 82 N.Y.2d 878, 879–80, 609 N.Y.S.2d 170, 170, 631 N.E.2d 112 (1993):

The only evidence submitted by the prosecutor to the Grand Jury as prima facie proof of defendant's prior conviction was a certificate of conviction for driving while intoxicated (DWI), indicating that within the last 10 years a Robert L. Van Buren had been convicted in Genesee County for a DWI violation under Vehicle and Traffic Law § 1192. No additional evidence as to the identity of the previously convicted individual was presented.

The Court of Appeals held that:

To make a prima facie showing that the offense of felony DWI (Vehicle and Traffic Law § 1192[3]; § 1193[1][c]) has been committed, sufficient proof must be adduced before the Grand Jury to establish that the person charged has a prior conviction for driving while intoxicated or alcohol-impaired within the last 10 years. That a person named Robert L. Van Buren was convicted of driving while intoxicated within the preceding 10-year period even in the same county did not constitute prima facie proof that defendant was the person previously convicted of DWI within the last 10 years. The certificate of conviction standing alone, without some further, connecting evidence tending to show that defendant was the same Robert L. Van Buren named in the certificate, was insufficient to "establish every element of [the] offense charged."

People v. Van Buren, 82 N.Y.2d at 880–81, 609 N.Y.S.2d at 171 (citation omitted).

In *People v. Smith*, 258 A.D.2d 245, 697 N.Y.S.2d 783 (4th Dep't 1999), the Appellate Division, Fourth Department, affirmed the reduction of a class D felony DWI to a class E felony DWI where the copy of the defendant's DMV abstract that was presented to the Grand Jury was not properly certified and/or authenticated.

§ 11:16   What is "felony DWI"?—Challenging a predicate DWI conviction

A previous conviction obtained in violation of the United States Constitution cannot be "counted" in determining whether a defendant is a predicate and/or persistent felony offender. *See* CPL § 400.20(6); CPL § 400.21(7)(b). In this regard, the CPL provides a legislatively created procedure for challenging the constitutionality of felony convictions sought to be used to enhance a defendant's *sentence*. *See* CPL § 400.20; CPL § 400.21. By contrast, no such statutory authority exists permitting a defendant to challenge the constitutionality of a prior conviction sought to be used to enhance a current *charge*.

In *People v. Knack*, 72 N.Y.2d 825, 530 N.Y.S.2d 541, 526 N.E.2d 32 (1988), aff'g 128 A.D.2d 307, 516 N.Y.S.2d 465 (2d Dep't 1987) the Court of Appeals refused to judicially create such a procedure. *See also People v. DeJesus*, 122 Misc. 2d 190, 471 N.Y.S.2d 195 (N.Y. Co. Sup. Ct. 1983). Pursuant to *Knack*, a defendant cannot file a motion *in limine*, a motion to suppress, or a motion to controvert a special information challenging the constitutionality of a prior, aggravating DWI conviction *within the context of a pending criminal action. See also People v. Brown*, 160 A.D.2d 1037, __, 553 N.Y.S.2d 875, 877 (3d Dep't 1990) (validity of prior conviction is question of law for Court, *not* question of fact for jury).

Several lower Court decisions reaching the opposite conclusion should thus be disregarded. *See, e.g., People v. Ryan*, 127 Misc. 2d 138, 485 N.Y.S.2d 933 (Westchester Co. Ct. 1985), judgment aff'd, 161 A.D.2d 677, 558 N.Y.S.2d 838 (2d Dep't 1990); *People v.*

King Solomon, 113 Misc. 2d 790, 449 N.Y.S.2d 875 (Kings Co. Sup. Ct. 1982); *People v. Sirianni*, 109 Misc. 2d 781, 440 N.Y.S.2d 988 (Cattaraugus Co. Ct. 1981), order rev'd, 89 A.D.2d 775, 453 N.Y.S.2d 485 (4th Dep't 1982); *People v. Dorn*, 105 Misc. 2d 244, 431 N.Y.S.2d 974 (Oneida Co. Ct. 1980). *See generally People v. Knickerbocker*, 136 A.D.2d 769, __, 523 N.Y.S.2d 227, 228 (3d Dep't 1988) ("A misdemeanor conviction which was obtained when the defendant was not represented by counsel or had not intelligently waived counsel cannot be used as the basis to enhance a subsequent crime from a misdemeanor to a felony"). Notably, *Ryan*, *Solomon*, *Sirianni*, *Dorn* and *Knickerbocker* all rely on *Baldasar v. Illinois*, 446 U.S. 222, 100 S. Ct. 1585, 64 L. Ed. 2d 169 (1980), which was overruled by *Nichols v. U.S.*, 511 U.S. 738, 114 S. Ct. 1921, 128 L. Ed. 2d 745 (1994).

In any event, the rationale of the *Knack* Court was that a judicially created procedure permitting a constitutional challenge to a prior DWI conviction within the context of a pending DWI case is unnecessary, "since there already exist several procedural vehicles for challenging the constitutional propriety of guilty pleas under the facts presented here." *Knack*, 72 N.Y.2d at 827, 530 N.Y.S.2d at 542. For example, the defendant could have challenged the constitutionality of the prior conviction by utilizing one (or more) of the following procedures:

   (a) A motion to withdraw the plea. *See* CPL § 220.60(3);

   (b) A direct appeal from the judgment of conviction; and/or

   (c) A motion to vacate the judgment of conviction (*i.e.*, a *coram nobis* application). *See* CPL § 440.10.

In *People v. Grubstein*, a defendant charged with felony DWI in 2010 moved to vacate his predicate misdemeanor DWI conviction, which took place in 2008, on the ground that the Town Justice had let him plead guilty *pro se* and without a proper waiver of his right to counsel. Town Court granted the motion. The Appellate Term reversed on the ground that the defendant had not filed a direct appeal of the predicate conviction. 2012 WL 6554673 (App. Term, 9th & 10th Jud. Dist. 2012). The Court of Appeals granted leave and reversed the Appellate Term, holding that "a defendant who asserts that he was deprived of his right to counsel when he pleaded guilty pro se is not barred from raising that claim in a motion under CPL 440.10 by his failure to raise it on direct appeal." 24 N.Y.3d 500, 501-02, 2 N.Y.S.3d 1, 1 (2015). On remand, the Appellate Term considered Town Court's order on the merits, and affirmed. 2015 WL 3369828 (App. Term, 9th & 10th Jud. Dist. 2015).

In *People v. Pozzi*, 117 A.D.3d 1325, __, 986 N.Y.S.2d 669, 669 (3d Dep't 2014), the Appellate Division, Third Department, held that:

Defendant's challenges to his underlying 2009 conviction, including that he received the ineffective assistance of counsel and that the police lacked probable cause to arrest him, cannot be raised on an appeal from the judgment resentencing him following a revocation of his probation.

See also People v. Whitlock, 114 A.D.3d 970, 980 N.Y.S.2d 831 (2d Dep't 2014) (same).

§ 11:17   What are the elements of DWI?

Surprisingly, there does not appear to be a single published case that sets forth a comprehensive list of the elements of a DWI charge. The elements of common law DWI, in violation of VTL § 1192(3), are:

1. Identification;
2. Operation;
3. Motor vehicle;
4. Roadway listed in VTL § 1192(7);
5. While (i.e., operation and intoxication must be simultaneous); and
6. Intoxicated by alcohol.

Technically, there is another element (i.e., the defendant's consumption of alcohol must be "voluntary"). See § 11:22, infra. However, "[c]ases of involuntary intoxication are virtually nonexistent." People v. Van Tuyl, 79 Misc. 2d 262, __, 359 N.Y.S.2d 958, 961 (App. Term, 9th & 10th Jud. Dist. 1974).

The elements of most other VTL § 1192 offenses, such as DWAI, per se DWI, Aggravated DWI, DWAI Drugs, etc. differ from the elements of common law DWI only with respect to element "6" above. Thus, for example, the elements of DWAI, in violation of VTL § 1192(1), are:

1. Identification;
2. Operation;
3. Motor vehicle;
4. Roadway listed in VTL § 1192(7);
5. While; and
6. Impaired by alcohol.

§ 11:18   What are the elements of DWI?—Reasonable cause to arrest defendant is not an element of DWI

In People v. Thomas, 70 N.Y.2d 823, 825, 523 N.Y.S.2d 437, 438, 517 N.E.2d 1323 (1987), aff'g 121 A.D.2d 73, 509 N.Y.S.2d 668 (4th Dep't 1986) the Court of Appeals held that:

We agree with the Appellate Division that the trial court erred in admitting evidence, over defendant's objection, that he was arrested "based on the results" of an Alco-Sensor test. The stated purpose of this proof was to permit the prosecution to establish that the arresting officer had "reasonable grounds" to give defendant a breathalyzer test. The evidence should have been excluded as irrelevant since reasonable cause is not an element of the crime charged (*see*, Vehicle and Traffic Law § 1192[2]).

§ 11:19 What are the elements of DWI?—Erratic driving is not an element of DWI

A defendant can, of course, drive erratically without being intoxicated. Conversely, it is possible for a defendant to drive while intoxicated without driving erratically. *See, e.g., People v. Krause*, 71 A.D.3d 1506, __, 896 N.Y.S.2d 755, 756 (4th Dep't 2010), leave to appeal denied, 15 N.Y.3d 752, 906 N.Y.S.2d 825, 933 N.E.2d 224 (2010) ("Contrary to defendant's contention with respect to the conviction of DWI, there is no requirement that an officer observe a defendant driving improperly to support such a conviction"); *People v. Shank*, 26 A.D.3d 812, __, 808 N.Y.S.2d 533, 535 (4th Dep't 2006) ("Contrary to the contention of defendant, the fact that the officer had not observed anything improper in the manner in which defendant drove his vehicle was merely one factor for the trier of fact to consider in determining whether defendant was intoxicated and did not preclude the trier of fact from finding that defendant was guilty of driving while intoxicated").

§ 11:20 What does it mean to be "intoxicated"?

The Court of Appeals defined what it means to be "intoxicated" in *People v. Cruz*, 48 N.Y.2d 419, 428, 423 N.Y.S.2d 625, 629, 399 N.E.2d 513 (1979):

> In sum, intoxication is a greater degree of impairment which is reached when the driver has voluntarily consumed alcohol to the extent that he is incapable of employing the physical and mental abilities which he is expected to possess in order to operate a vehicle as a reasonable and prudent driver.

See also People v. Hagmann, 175 A.D.2d 502, __, 572 N.Y.S.2d 952, 953–54 (3d Dep't 1991); *People v. Stack*, 140 A.D.2d 389, __, 527 N.Y.S.2d 569, 570–71 (2d Dep't 1988); *People v. Ottomanelli*, 107 A.D.2d 212, __, 486 N.Y.S.2d 748, 752 (2d Dep't 1985).

In other words, a person is not "intoxicated" for purposes of VTL § 1192(3) unless he is *highly* impaired (*i.e.*, "drunk"). In this regard, in *Ottomanelli*, the Appellate Division, Second Department, expressly considered the issue of "the proper legal standard for determining if the accused was driving while intoxicated within the meaning of Vehicle and Traffic Law § 1192(3)." 107

A.D.2d at __, 486 N.Y.S.2d at 749. The Court found that *Cruz* imposes a "total incapacity test":

> Before a defendant may be convicted of driving while intoxicated, under the *Cruz* definition of intoxication, the accused's voluntary consumption of alcohol must have rendered him *incapable* of performing the physical or mental acts required to operate a motor vehicle as a reasonable and prudent driver.

People v. Ottomanelli, 486 N.Y.S.2d at 752.

The Court of Appeals reiterated the "total incapacity test" standard in *Matter of Johnston*, 75 N.Y.2d 403, 409, 554 N.Y.S.2d 88, 91, 553 N.E.2d 566 (1990). *See also People v. Ardila*, 85 N.Y.2d 846, 847, 623 N.Y.S.2d 847, 847, 647 N.E.2d 1355 (1995) (*Cruz* test is semantically the same as "being so inebriated that one's 'ability to drive safely is impaired to a substantial extent' ").

§ 11:21 What does it mean to be "intoxicated"?—*Cruz* imposes an objective standard in determining whether a person was intoxicated

In *People v. Cruz*, 48 N.Y.2d 419, 426, 423 N.Y.S.2d 625, 628, 399 N.E.2d 513 (1979), the Court of Appeals held that VTL §§ 1192(1) and 1192(3) require the use of an objective, as opposed to a subjective, standard in determining whether a person was intoxicated. *See also Matter of Johnston*, 75 N.Y.2d 403, 409, 554 N.Y.S.2d 88, 91, 553 N.E.2d 566 (1990) ("The New York test . . . is objective and measures the actor's ability to employ physical and mental faculties against that of a reasonable prudent driver"). *See generally Romano v. Stanley*, 90 N.Y.2d 444, 450–51, 661 N.Y.S.2d 589, 592, 684 N.E.2d 19 (1997) ("it is well known that the effects of alcohol consumption 'may differ greatly from person to person' and that tolerance for alcohol is subject to wide individual variation") (citation omitted).

Thus, if a particular defendant has a higher tolerance for alcohol than the average person, that subjective tolerance benefits him or her with respect to a VTL §§ 1192(1) or 1192(3) charge, and *vice versa*. By contrast, a high tolerance for alcohol is not helpful with respect to a VTL §§ 1192(2) or 1192(2-a) charge—as a person's tolerance for alcohol does not affect his or her BAC.

§ 11:22 What does it mean to be "intoxicated"?— Intoxication must be voluntary

In *People v. Koch*, 250 A.D. 623, __, 294 N.Y.S. 987, 989 (2d Dep't 1937), the Appellate Division, Second Department, held that "[t]he statute contemplates only voluntary intoxication." The Court of Appeals reiterated this requirement in its landmark decision in *People v. Cruz*, 48 N.Y.2d 419, 428, 423 N.Y.S.2d 625,

629, 399 N.E.2d 513 (1979) ("intoxication is a greater degree of impairment which is reached when the driver has *voluntarily* consumed alcohol to the extent that he is incapable of employing the physical and mental abilities which he is expected to possess in order to operate a vehicle as a reasonable and prudent driver") (emphasis added).

However, "[c]ases of involuntary intoxication are virtually nonexistent." *People v. Van Tuyl*, 79 Misc. 2d 262, __, 359 N.Y.S.2d 958, 961 (App. Term, 9th & 10th Jud. Dist. 1974). In this regard, Courts have rejected the claim that the defendant's intoxication was involuntary because the defendant is a chronic alcoholic. *See People v. Starowicz*, 207 A.D.2d 994, __, 617 N.Y.S.2d 100, 101 (4th Dep't 1994) ("Defendant's drinking was not involuntary in the sense intended by the Penal Law merely because it was the result of chronic alcoholism or post-traumatic stress disorder"); *People v. Williams*, 186 A.D.2d 770, __, 589 N.Y.S.2d 70, 71 (2d Dep't 1992) ("Contrary to the defendant's contention, alcoholism does not render an alcoholic's intoxication involuntary so as to relieve him from liability for the reckless acts committed while he is intoxicated"). *See generally People v. Wells*, 53 A.D.3d 181, __, 862 N.Y.S.2d 20, 21 (1st Dep't 2008); *People v. Berkley*, 152 A.D.2d 788, 543 N.Y.S.2d 568 (3d Dep't 1989); *People v. Wondolowski*, 116 A.D.2d 959, 498 N.Y.S.2d 528 (3d Dep't 1986).

§ 11:23 What does it mean to be "intoxicated"?—A person can be intoxicated with a BAC below .08%, and can have a BAC above .08% without being intoxicated

It is well settled that a person can be intoxicated with a BAC below .08%, and can have a BAC above .08% without being intoxicated. *See, e.g., People v. Farmer*, 36 N.Y.2d 386, 393, 369 N.Y.S.2d 44, 47, 330 N.E.2d 22 (1975) (Fuchsberg, J., concurring) ("Obviously, it is possible for a defendant to have had the quantity of alcohol in his blood required for conviction under subdivision 2 and yet not be found to be in an intoxicated condition under subdivision 3. Likewise, he could be found to be in an intoxicated condition though the level of the weight of alcohol in his blood fell below the '.[08] of one per centum' statutory level"); *People v. Miller*, 199 A.D.2d 692, __, 605 N.Y.S.2d 160, 163 (3d Dep't 1993) ("§ 1192(2) is based upon a defendant's blood alcohol content while § 1192(3) is based upon the manner a defendant operated his vehicle and his condition"); *People v. Blowers*, 79 Misc. 2d 462, __, 360 N.Y.S.2d 369, 373 (Rensselaer Co. Ct. 1974) (VTL § 1192(2) "prohibits the operation of a motor vehicle while the operator has .[08] of one percentum or more by weight of alcohol in his blood and that is unrelated to whether or not the operator was in fact intoxicated"). *See generally People v. Blair*, 98 N.Y.2d 722, 749 N.Y.S.2d 809, 779 N.E.2d 748 (2002) (chemical test result below "legal limit" does not preclude VTL § 1192(3) charge); *People v. Lawrence*, 53 A.D.2d 705, ___, 384 N.Y.S.2d 37, 38 (3d Dep't 1976) ("the results of the breathalyzer test showing less than .05 of 1% by weight of alcohol in the blood do not establish conclusively that the defendant was innocent of the charge of driving while intoxicated. It is merely prima facie evidence that defendant's ability was not impaired and that he was not intoxicated").

In this regard, case law makes clear that jury verdicts convicting a defendant of VTL § 1192(2) yet acquitting him or her of VTL § 1192(3), and *vice versa*, are neither inconsistent nor repugnant (because being "intoxicated" and having an elevated BAC are distinct concepts). *See, e.g., People v. Brown*, 53 N.Y.2d 979, 441 N.Y.S.2d 662, 424 N.E.2d 549 (1981); *People v. Lawson*, 191 A.D.2d 514, 594 N.Y.S.2d 346 (2d Dep't 1993); *People v. Mascolo*, 175 A.D.2d 812, 572 N.Y.S.2d 937 (2d Dep't 1991); *People v. Carvalho*, 174 A.D.2d 687, 571 N.Y.S.2d 332 (2d Dep't 1991); *People v. VanCasselle*, 115 A.D.2d 255, 496 N.Y.S.2d 172 (4th Dep't 1985); *People v. Collins*, 92 A.D.2d 740, 461 N.Y.S.2d 90 (4th Dep't 1983). *See generally People v. Loughlin*, 76 N.Y.2d 804, 559 N.Y.S.2d 962, 559 N.E.2d 656 (1990) (jury's verdicts acquitting defendant of Vehicular Manslaughter yet convicting him of Vehicular Assault were inconsistent/repugnant—as these charges share the essential element of intoxication).

§ 11:24 Intoxication alone does not constitute criminal negligence

It has long been the law of this State that:

> Proof of intoxication alone is not enough to sustain a conviction of criminal negligence. The People must also prove that the defendant's intoxication affected his physical and mental capacity to the extent that it caused him to operate his vehicle in a culpably reckless manner.

People v. Bast, 19 N.Y.2d 813, 815, 280 N.Y.S.2d 149, 150, 227 N.E.2d 47 (1967). *See also Matter of Johnston*, 75 N.Y.2d 403, 409–10, 554 N.Y.S.2d 88, 91, 553 N.E.2d 566 (1990) (same).

Notably, it appears that the use of the phrase "criminal negligence" in *Bast* refers not to the *mens rea* of criminal negligence, but rather to the crime currently denominated Criminally Negligent Homicide. *See* PL § 125.10. In this regard, the statute at issue in *Bast* (*i.e.*, PL § 1053-a), a predecessor statute to PL § 125.10, provided:

> § 1053-a. Criminal negligence in operation of vehicle resulting in

death. A person who operates or drives any vehicle of any kind in a reckless or culpably negligent manner, whereby a human being is killed, is guilty of criminal negligence in the operation of a vehicle resulting in death.

Taken in this context, the above quote from *Bast* probably should have read as follows:

Proof of intoxication alone is not enough to sustain a conviction of the crime of criminal negligence in the operation of a vehicle resulting in death. The People must also prove that the defendant's intoxication affected his physical and mental capacity to the extent that it caused him to operate his vehicle in a reckless or culpably negligent manner.

Indeed, the *Bast* Court went on to say: "The evidence adduced by the People failed to establish that defendant drove at an excessive rate of speed or that his intoxication caused him to strike the decedent." 19 N.Y.2d at 815, 280 N.Y.S.2d at 150. Simply stated, it appears that, as a result of *Bast*, the issue of "criminal negligence" has long been confused with the issue of "causation." However, the 2005 amendments to the Vehicular Assault/ Vehicular Manslaughter statutes, which removed the *mens rea* requirement therefrom (except where AUO is an element of the offense), rendered this issue moot.

§ 11:25 Opinion of intoxication can be rendered by layman

In *People v. Cruz*, 48 N.Y.2d 419, 428, 423 N.Y.S.2d 625, 629, 399 N.E.2d 513 (1979), the Court of Appeals held that "the concept of intoxication does not require expert opinion. A layman, including the defendant and those charged with administering the law, should be able to determine whether the defendant's consumption of alcohol has rendered him incapable of operating a motor vehicle as he should." *See also People v. Cronin*, 60 N.Y.2d 430, 433, 470 N.Y.S.2d 110, 112, 458 N.E.2d 351 (1983) ("While jurors might be familiar with the effects of alcohol on one's mental state, the combined impact of a case of beer, several marihuana cigarettes and 5 to 10 Valium tablets on a person's ability to act purposefully cannot be said as a matter of law to be within the ken of the typical juror."); *People v. Kehn*, 109 A.D.2d 912, __, 486 N.Y.S.2d 380, 383 (3d Dep't 1985) ("jurors have been recognized as being 'familiar with the effects of alcohol on one's mental state' ") (citation omitted).

§ 11:26 What does it mean to be "impaired"?

The Court of Appeals defined what it means to be "impaired" in *People v. Cruz*, 48 N.Y.2d 419, 427, 423 N.Y.S.2d 625, 628, 399 N.E.2d 513 (1979):

[T]he question in each case is whether, by voluntarily consuming alcohol, this particular defendant has actually impaired, to any extent, the physical and mental abilities which he is expected to possess in order to operate a vehicle as a reasonable and prudent driver.

There are three critical issues to note here. First, the defendant's physical and mental abilities are only required to be impaired *to any extent*. Second, the defendant's consumption of alcohol is required to have *actually impaired* his or her physical and mental abilities. Third, while the *Cruz* definition of impairment appears to be quite simple for the prosecution to meet, the *Cruz* Court noted that:

> That is not to say, of course, that every person who drinks before driving violates the law. On the contrary the Legislature recognized that the average person can consume a certain amount of alcohol without impairing his ability to operate a motor vehicle as he should. Otherwise the Legislature would not have provided that proof of .05 of 1% or less of blood alcohol content is prima facie evidence that the driver was not impaired or intoxicated (Vehicle and Traffic Law, § 1195, subd. 2, par. (a)). Of course some persons may find their driving faculties impaired by the least consumption of alcohol and, therefore, would be guilty of driving while impaired while others would not. And the Legislature also recognized that some individuals may be able to consume greater amounts of alcohol without being impaired, as would the average driver (Vehicle and Traffic Law, § 1195, subd. 2, par. (c)). Thus the impairment statute, by simply providing prima facie standards, takes into account the "subjective" tolerance of individuals in determining the ability to drive possessed by a defendant at the time of arrest. But in determining whether that ability is less than he *should* possess, the statute necessarily contemplates the use of the objective standard expected of the average driver.

People v. Cruz, 48 N.Y.2d at 426, 423 N.Y.S.2d at 628 (citation omitted).

§ 11:27 Significance of an odor of alcoholic beverage, or lack thereof

"The odor of alcohol simply is evidence that the defendant had consumed an alcoholic beverage." *People v. Koch*, 135 Misc. 2d 352, __, 515 N.Y.S.2d 405, 407 (Rochester City Ct. 1987). *See also People v. Alberto*, 22 Misc. 3d 786, __, 877 N.Y.S.2d 628, 632 (Suffolk Co. Dist. Ct. 2008) ("The trooper's remaining observation of the odor of alcohol on the defendant's breath raised a possibility that the defendant may have consumed alcohol, but was not sufficient, in itself, to provide the trooper with probable cause to arrest the defendant for Driving While Intoxicated"); *People v. Butts*, 21 Misc. 2d 799, __, 201 N.Y.S.2d 926, 932 (Poughkeepsie City Ct. 1960) (" 'The test for odor of liquor on the breath is unsatisfactory for the breath odor observed is really the flavoring matter of the liquor and the strength of the odor depends not only on the amount of the alcohol consumed, but also on the particular beverage which happened to have been used' ") (citation omitted); *People, on Complaint of Mulrean v. Fox*, 256 A.D. 578, ___, 10 N.Y.S.2d 694, 696 (1st Dep't 1939) ("The odor of liquor on the defendant's breath was not proof of intoxication, . . . for it was entirely consistent with the defendant's explanation to the officer and with his testimony at the trial, that 'he had a couple of beers' "). *See generally Coleman v. New York City Transit Authority*, 37 N.Y.2d 137, 144, 371 N.Y.S.2d 663, 669, 332 N.E.2d 850 (1975) ("The evidence of alcoholic breath and the three drinks is not in itself proof of intoxication"); *Senn v. Scudieri*, 165 A.D.2d 346, ___, 567 N.Y.S.2d 665, 668 (1st Dep't 1991) ("Evidence that a person has consumed alcohol, and has the odor of alcohol on his or her breath, is not conclusive proof of intoxication").

In *DeMichele v. Department of Motor Vehicles of New York State*, 136 A.D.3d 629, ___, 24 N.Y.S.3d 402, 402-03 (2d Dep't 2016), the Appellate Division, Second Department, annulled a refusal revocation, with costs, under the following circumstances:

> In August 2012, while riding his motorcycle in Westchester County, the petitioner lost control and crashed; no other vehicles or individuals were involved in the accident. The petitioner alleges that the accident happened when a coyote struck his motorcycle. As a result of the accident, the petitioner was injured and transferred by ambulance to a nearby hospital. Approximately two hours later, while he was still at the hospital, the petitioner was questioned by a New York State Trooper, who asked if he had consumed alcohol prior to the crash. The petitioner denied such consumption. Nevertheless, according to the Trooper's later filed "Report of Refusal to Submit to Chemical Test" (hereinafter the report), the Trooper detected a "strong odor of alcoholic beverage emanating from [the petitioner's] breath" during their conversation. The petitioner was then arrested for driving while intoxicated in violation of Vehicle and Traffic Law § 1192(3), and subsequently warned that, pursuant to Vehicle and Traffic Law § 1194, a refusal to submit to a chemical test would result in immediate suspension of his driver license. The petitioner declined to submit to the test.

> Following an administrative hearing, at which the petitioner testified and the Trooper did not appear, but the report was admitted into evidence, the petitioner was found to have violated Vehicle and Traffic Law § 1194, and his license was revoked. This determination was affirmed after an administrative appeal to the New York State Department of Motor Vehicles Administrative Appeals Board. The petitioner then commenced this CPLR article 78 proceeding to review the determination, contending that the determination was not supported by substantial evidence. The Supreme Court transferred the matter to this Court pursuant to CPLR 7804(g).

"To annul an administrative determination made after a hearing directed by law at which evidence is taken, a court must conclude that the record lacks substantial evidence to support the determination." Review of the record in this matter demonstrates that the finding of the Administrative Law Judge is not supported by substantial evidence.

As a prerequisite to the chemical test, the Trooper had to have reasonable grounds to believe that the petitioner was operating his motorcycle while under the influence of alcohol. Reasonable grounds are to be determined on the basis of the totality of the circumstances. Here, the Trooper did not witness the circumstances leading to the accident or the accident itself, and his report states that no field sobriety tests were conducted at the scene. Other than the statement in the report that there was a strong odor of alcoholic beverage on the petitioner's breath, there was no evidence that would suggest the petitioner operated his vehicle in an intoxicated state. Accordingly, the totality of circumstances did not warrant the determination that the petitioner violated Vehicle and Traffic Law § 1194 by refusing to submit to a chemical test and to revoke the petitioner's driver license.

(Citations omitted).

In other words, while the odor of an alcoholic beverage constitutes evidence that a person has been drinking, it does not distinguish between a person who recently took a sip of alcohol, a person who had a couple of drinks, and a person who is intoxicated. Furthermore, it does not provide any guidance as to the actual effect of the alcohol on a particular individual.

Indeed, the odor of an alcoholic beverage is of such limited probativeness in a DWI case that even the *absence* of such an odor has been found to be of limited significance. *See, e.g., People v. Farrell*, 89 A.D.2d 987, __, 454 N.Y.S.2d 306, 307 (2d Dep't 1982) ("Since it is possible to produce intoxicating beverages which can be imbibed without leaving any odor[,] the absence of an odor of alcohol would not necessarily negate a finding of reasonable cause for defendant's arrest . . . . The mere absence of an odor of alcohol is insufficient to minimize the arresting officer's other observations as established by the record before us"); *People v. Alfaro*, 179 Misc. 2d 589, __, 686 N.Y.S.2d 638, 639 (Greenburgh Just. Ct. 1999). *Cf. People v. Khuns*, 191 Misc. 2d 655, __, 746 N.Y.S.2d 230, 232 (Greece Just. Ct. 2001) ("Although the record demonstrates that the defendant was driving erratically and failed the field sobriety tests, without proof of the presence of alcohol, the court must conclude that the People have not met their burden. Proof that an arresting officer in some manner detected an odor of an alcoholic beverage during his investigation is an essential element to support a finding of probable cause for a driving while intoxicated arrest. Absent such proof, the defendant's failure to properly perform the field sobriety tests, her physical appearance and condition, or the fact that she operated a motor vehicle in violation of the vehicle and traffic laws, can reasonably be attributed to causes other than intoxication") (citations omitted); *People v. Vedder*, 43 Misc. 3d 1234(A), 2014 WL 2696622, *2 (Amsterdam City N.Y. City Ct. 2014) ("The facts possessed by Deputy Liggett were that he observed the defendant leave Imperial Lanes and eventually fail to keep right, that he did not stop his vehicle immediately after Deputy Liggett turned on his emergency lights, that his eyes were glassy and bloodshot, and his speech seemed a little slurred. Absent any testimony that Deputy Liggett smelled an odor of alcohol from either the defendant's vehicle or his breath there were no reasonable grounds to believe that the defendant was operating a motor vehicle in violation of VTL § 1192 and no authority existed to require the defendant to exit his motor vehicle.").

§ 11:28 What constitutes probable cause to arrest in a VTL § 1192 case?

CPL § 70.10(2) provides, in pertinent part, that:

> "Reasonable cause to believe that a person has committed an offense" exists when evidence or information which appears reliable discloses facts or circumstances which are collectively of such weight and persuasiveness as to convince a person of ordinary intelligence, judgment and experience that it is reasonably likely that such offense was committed and that such person committed it.

Although the CPL uses the phrase "reasonable cause," it is well settled that "[r]easonable cause means probable cause." *People v. Maldonado*, 86 N.Y.2d 631, 635, 635 N.Y.S.2d 155, 158, 658 N.E.2d 1028 (1995). *See also People v. Johnson*, 66 N.Y.2d 398, 402 n.2, 497 N.Y.S.2d 618, 621 n.2, 488 N.E.2d 439 (1985). The Court of Appeals has consistently made clear that:

> In passing on whether there was probable cause for an arrest, . . . the basis for such a belief must not only be reasonable, but it must appear to be at least more probable than not that a crime has taken place and that the one arrested is its perpetrator, for conduct equally compatible with guilt or innocence will not suffice.

People v. Carrasquillo, 54 N.Y.2d 248, 254, 445 N.Y.S.2d 97, 100, 429 N.E.2d 775 (1981). *See also People v. Vandover*, 20 N.Y.3d 235, 237, 958 N.Y.S.2d 83, 84, 981 N.E.2d 784 (2012) (same); *People v. De Bour*, 40 N.Y.2d 210, 216, 386 N.Y.S.2d 375, 380, 352 N.E.2d 562 (1976) ("We have frequently rejected the notion that behavior which is susceptible of innocent as well as culpable interpretation, will constitute probable cause").

Interestingly, the Court of Appeals had never addressed the issue of what constitutes probable cause to arrest in a VTL § 1192 case until it decided *Vandover, supra,* in 2013. In *Vandover,* the Court held that "[t]he standard to be followed is that it is more probable than not that defendant is actually impaired." 20 N.Y.3d at 239, 958 N.Y.S.2d at 85. *See also* § 1:30, *supra.*

§ 11:29 What constitutes "operation" of a motor vehicle?

The Office of Court Administration Pattern Criminal Jury Instructions define operation as follows:

To OPERATE a motor vehicle means to drive it.

[NOTE: Add the following if there is an issue as to operation:

A person also OPERATES a motor vehicle when such person is sitting behind the wheel of a motor vehicle for the purpose of placing it in operation, and when the motor vehicle is moving, or even if it is not moving, the engine is running.]

CJI(NY) (2d ed.) VTL 1192, at 1002 to 03 (footnote omitted). A former version of this instruction reads as follows:

[NOTE: If "operation" is placed in issue, add:

"Operation" of a motor vehicle is established upon proof beyond a reasonable doubt that the defendant had recently driven the vehicle or by such proof that he was seated at the wheel, with the motor running and with a present intention of placing the vehicle in operation.]

3 CJI(NY) V. & T.L. § 1192(1), (2), & (3), at 2306.

In *People v. Prescott,* 95 N.Y.2d 655, 662, 722 N.Y.S.2d 778, 782, 745 N.E.2d 1000 (2001), the Court of Appeals stated that:

Our courts have long recognized that the definition of operation is broader than that of driving and that " '[a] person operates a motor vehicle within the meaning of [the statute] when, in the vehicle, he intentionally does any act or makes use of any mechanical or electrical agency which alone or in sequence will set in motion the motive power of the vehicle.' " Thus, criminal liability under section 1192 can attach to conduct 'dangerously close' to driving, as long as that conduct occurs upon locations covered by the statute.

(Citations and footnote omitted). *See also People v. Alamo,* 34 N.Y.2d 453, 458, 358 N.Y.S.2d 375, 379, 315 N.E.2d 446, 70 A.L.R.3d 1193 (1974); *People v. Marriott,* 37 A.D.2d 868, __, 325 N.Y.S.2d 177, 178 (3d Dep't 1971).

This topic is covered at length in §§ 2:1 et seq., *supra.*

§ 11:30 Operation and intoxication must be simultaneous

Although often overlooked, in a DWI case the defendant's

operation of a motor vehicle and his or her intoxication must occur simultaneously (*i.e.*, the crime is driving *while* intoxicated). *See, e.g., People v. Mertz*, 68 N.Y.2d 136, 139, 506 N.Y.S.2d 290, 291, 497 N.E.2d 657 (1986) ("A violation of Vehicle and Traffic Law § 1192(2) is not established unless the trier of fact finds that *while* operating a motor vehicle defendant had a blood alcohol content (BAC) of .[08] of 1% or more") (emphasis added); *People v. Schools*, 122 A.D.2d 502, __, 505 N.Y.S.2d 462, 463 (3d Dep't 1986) ("The *sine qua non* for conviction is the operation of a vehicle simultaneously with intoxication"); *People v. Strauss*, 260 A.D. 880, __, 22 N.Y.S.2d 880, 881 (2d Dep't 1940) ("intoxication and operation must be simultaneous or there is no crime"); *People v. Hust*, 74 Misc. 2d 887, __, 346 N.Y.S.2d 303, 307 (Broome Co. Ct. 1973). *See generally People v. Spencer*, 289 A.D.2d 877, __, 736 N.Y.S.2d 428, 431 (3d Dep't 2001); *People v. Saplin*, 122 A.D.2d 498, __, 505 N.Y.S.2d 460, 461 (3d Dep't 1986); *People v. Matthews*, 11 A.D.2d 784, 205 N.Y.S.2d 26 (2d Dep't 1960); *People v. Hemleb*, 4 A.D.2d 878, 166 N.Y.S.2d 837 (2d Dep't 1957).

§ 11:31   Defense must be allowed to argue that defendant's BAC was less than .08% at time of operation

In *People v. Mertz*, 68 N.Y.2d 136, 139, 506 N.Y.S.2d 290, 291, 497 N.E.2d 657 (1986), the Court of Appeals held that:

> A violation of Vehicle and Traffic Law § 1192(2) is not established unless the trier of fact finds that while operating a motor vehicle defendant had a blood alcohol content (BAC) of .[08] of 1% or more . . . . It is . . . error not to permit defendant's attorney to argue on the basis of evidence, whether through cross-examination of the People's witnesses or testimony of defendant's witnesses, expert or other, from which it could be found that defendant's BAC at the time of vehicle operation was less than .[08]%, that if the jury so found defendant was not guilty of violating the subdivision.

See also id. at 146–47, 506 N.Y.S.2d at 295–96 ("When . . . such evidence has been presented, defendant must be permitted to argue its significance to the jury. Because he was foreclosed from doing so and because the court's ruling during defendant's attorney's summation and its instructions at the close of the case were in conflict on this issue, there must be a reversal").

§ 11:32   Operation must occur on a roadway covered by VTL § 1192(7)

VTL § 1100(a) provides that "[t]he provisions of [VTL Title VII] apply upon public highways, private roads open to public motor vehicle traffic and any other parking lot, *except where a different place is specifically referred to in a given section*." (Emphasis added). VTL § 1192 is part of VTL Title VII. However, VTL § 1192(7) provides an exception of the type referred to in VTL § 1100(a). Specifically, VTL § 1192(7) expressly lists the types of roadways upon which the provisions of VTL § 1192 apply:

> Where applicable. The provisions of this section shall apply upon public highways, private roads open to motor vehicle traffic and any other parking lot. For the purposes of this section "parking lot" shall mean any area or areas of private property, including a driveway, near or contiguous to and provided in connection with premises and used as a means of access to and egress from a public highway to such premises and having a capacity for the parking of four or more motor vehicles. The provisions of this section shall not apply to any area or areas of private property comprising all or part of property on which is situated a one or two family residence.

The current definition of the term "parking lot" in VTL § 1192(7) was designed to legislatively overrule cases which had applied the VTL § 129-b "store or business establishment" test to determine whether a parking lot is a "parking lot" for purposes of VTL § 1192, *see, e.g., People v. Williams*, 66 N.Y.2d 659, 495 N.Y.S.2d 964, 486 N.E.2d 822 (1985); *People v. McDonnell*, 27 Misc. 3d 56, 901 N.Y.S.2d 451 (App. Term, 9th & 10th Jud. Dist. 2010); *People v. Copeland*, 132 Misc. 2d 990, 506 N.Y.S.2d 249 (Suffolk Co. Dist. Ct. 1986), replacing that test with a "capacity for the parking of four or more motor vehicles" test.

Proof that a parking lot constitutes a "parking lot" as defined in VTL § 1192(7) is an element of a VTL § 1192 charge. *See People v. Whipple*, 97 N.Y.2d 1, 7, 734 N.Y.S.2d 549, 552, 760 N.E.2d 337 (2001).

This topic is covered at length in §§ 3:1 et seq., *supra*.

§ 11:33   Operation must occur on a roadway covered by VTL § 1192(7)—Unless a Penal Law charge is involved

In *People v. Harris*, 81 N.Y.2d 850, 597 N.Y.S.2d 620, 613 N.E.2d 526 (1993), the defendant was convicted of, among other things, Vehicular Manslaughter in the 2nd Degree, in violation of Penal Law § 125.12, after a passenger in the vehicle he was driving (while intoxicated) died. Defendant argued that, since the driving at issue took place in a farmer's field, he did not operate the vehicle on a roadway encompassed by VTL § 1192(7), and thus that he did not violate VTL § 1192.

Since, on the date of the offense, a violation of VTL § 1192(2), (3) or (4) was an element of Vehicular Manslaughter, defendant claimed that he was improperly convicted thereof. The Court of Appeals disagreed, reasoning that:

With the understanding that penal laws have different purposes than vehicle and traffic laws, we conclude the vehicular manslaughter statute applies to any person causing a death by driving under the influence of alcohol or drugs, *regardless of location*, even though there could be no separate punishment for such driving under Vehicle and Traffic Law § 1192 where the driving did not occur on public roads or other areas defined in that section.

Id. at 852, 597 N.Y.S.2d at 622 (emphasis added).

§ 11:34 Corroboration of admission of operation

CPL § 60.50 provides that "[a] person may not be convicted of any offense solely upon evidence of a confession or admission made by him without additional proof that the offense charged has been committed." In *People v. Booden*, 69 N.Y.2d 185, 513 N.Y.S.2d 87, 505 N.E.2d 598 (1987), the Court of Appeals held that CPL § 60.50:

[D]oes not require corroboration of confessions or admissions in every detail, but only "some proof, of whatever weight", that the offense charged has in fact been committed by someone. Its purpose is to avoid the possibility that a crime may be confessed when, in fact, no crime has been committed. The requirements of the rule are not rigorous and sufficient corroboration exists when the confession is "supported" by independent evidence of the corpus delicti. The necessary additional evidence may be found in the presence of defendant at the scene of the crime, his guilty appearance afterward, or other circumstances supporting an inference of guilt.

Id. at 187, 513 N.Y.S.2d at 89 (citations omitted). Applying the foregoing to the facts of the case, the Court found that:

There was sufficient corroborative evidence in this case that the offense of driving while impaired had been committed on the evening in question. The vehicle owned by defendant's father was found in a ditch, facing in the wrong direction of travel; the pavement of the highway was dry, negativing suggestions of an accidental skid; defendant and his companions were standing next to the vehicle when the investigating officer arrived and, when defendant and his companions were asked who had been driving the vehicle, defendant volunteered to answer the question and produced his identification, indicating by his conduct that he was the driver. The officer noticed that defendant exhibited outward signs of intoxication and his breath smelled of alcohol.

Id. at 187–88, 513 N.Y.S.2d at 89. *See also People v. Tatro*, 245 A.D.2d 1040, 667 N.Y.S.2d 560 (4th Dep't 1997); *People v. Kestler*, 201 A.D.2d 955, 607 N.Y.S.2d 823 (4th Dep't 1994); *People v. Cook*, 191 A.D.2d 993, 595 N.Y.S.2d 163 (4th Dep't 1993); *People v. Hennigan*, 135 A.D.2d 1082, 523 N.Y.S.2d 302 (4th Dep't 1987); *Van Tassell v. New York State Com'r of Motor Vehicles*, 46 A.D.2d 984, 362 N.Y.S.2d 281 (3d Dep't 1974) (corroboration requirement lower at refusal hearing than at criminal trial). *Cf. People v. Matthews*, 11 A.D.2d 784, __, 205 N.Y.S.2d 26, 27 (2d Dep't 1960)

("Except for defendant's alleged admission, made while intoxicated, that he had been driving the motor vehicle, there is no proof in the record that he was the one who, while intoxicated, operated the vehicle. In the absence of additional proof the conviction may not stand"); *People v. Hemleb*, 4 A.D.2d 878, __, 166 N.Y.S.2d 837, 838 (2d Dep't 1957) (same).

Judge Bellacosa filed a dissenting opinion in *Booden*, stating that:

> [T]he publicly and statutorily induced campaigns for rigorous enforcement of drunk driving offenses, laudable as they are, require a proportionate and judicious neutralization against excessive zeal at the expense of the rights of those affected with potentially serious criminal and even felony prosecutions and records. I am confident that law enforcement officials will be able to enforce properly not only the new and more serious drunk driving laws but also can concomitantly safeguard the procedural rights of all citizens affected by all these laws.

69 N.Y.2d at 189, 513 N.Y.S.2d at 90 (Bellacosa, J., dissenting).

§ 11:35   DWI is a "continuing crime"

"A continuing crime is one 'that by its nature may be committed either by one act or by multiple acts and readily permits characterization as a continuing offense over a period of time.'" *People v. Shack*, 86 N.Y.2d 529, 540, 634 N.Y.S.2d 660, 667, 658 N.E.2d 706 (1995) (citation omitted). DWI is a continuing crime. *People v. Miller*, 163 A.D.2d 627, __, 558 N.Y.S.2d 269, 270 (3d Dep't 1990). *See also People v. Tuszynski*, 57 A.D.3d 1380, __, 871 N.Y.S.2d 542, 542 (4th Dep't 2008) ("We agree with defendant that the sentences of two consecutive terms of imprisonment of $1\frac{1}{3}$ to 4 years are illegal on the ground that his operation of a motor vehicle while intoxicated consisted of a single, continuous act").

§ 11:36   DWI is a "strict liability" offense

DWI has been referred to as a "strict liability" offense, in that there is no traditional *mens rea* component. While the defendant's intoxication must be "voluntary," *see* § 11:22, *supra*, and the defendant must "intend" to operate the vehicle, *see* § 2:4, *supra*, the defendant does not need to otherwise act "intentionally," "knowingly," "recklessly," or with "criminal negligence." *See* PL § 15.05.

Thus, for example, there is no requirement that the defendant intend to get drunk, or that the defendant have knowledge that his or her BAC is above the legal limit. Similarly, the defendant is not required to drive recklessly to be guilty of DWI. All that is required is that the defendant operate a motor vehicle while intoxicated on a roadway covered by VTL § 1192(7).

§ 11:37 DWAI as a lesser included offense of common law DWI

It is well settled that DWAI, in violation of VTL § 1192(1), is a lesser included offense of common law DWI, in violation of VTL § 1192(3). *See, e.g., People v. Litto*, 8 N.Y.3d 692, 705–06, 840 N.Y.S.2d 736, 744–45, 872 N.E.2d 848 (2007); *People v. Green*, 96 N.Y.2d 195, 197–98, 726 N.Y.S.2d 357, 359, 750 N.E.2d 59 (2001); *People v. Brown*, 53 N.Y.2d 979, 981, 441 N.Y.S.2d 662, 663, 424 N.E.2d 549 (1981); *People v. Hoag*, 51 N.Y.2d 632, 634, 435 N.Y.S.2d 698, 698, 416 N.E.2d 1033 (1981); *People v. Cruz*, 48 N.Y.2d 419, 428, 423 N.Y.S.2d 625, 629, 399 N.E.2d 513 (1979).

In fact, in *Green*, the Court of Appeals held that an accusatory "instrument charging driving while intoxicated also, by operation of law, charge[s] the offense of driving while impaired." 96 N.Y.2d at 199, 726 N.Y.S.2d at 361.

§ 11:38 DWAI as a lesser included offense of per se DWI

It has been held that DWAI, in violation of VTL § 1192(1), is *not* a lesser included offense of per se DWI, in violation of VTL § 1192(2). *See, e.g., People v. Brown*, 53 N.Y.2d 979, 981, 441 N.Y.S.2d 662, 663, 424 N.E.2d 549 (1981); *People v. Maharaj*, 89 N.Y.2d 997, 998–99, 657 N.Y.S.2d 392, 393, 679 N.E.2d 631 (1997); *People v. Poole*, 41 A.D.3d 867, __, 841 N.Y.S.2d 588, 589 (2d Dep't 2007); *People v. Abel*, 166 A.D.2d 841, __, 563 N.Y.S.2d 531, 533 (3d Dep't 1990). The reason why is spelled out in *Brown*:

> A lesser included offense is one which must by definition be concomitantly committed in the commission of the greater offense (CPL 1.20, subd. 37). Here that was not true, since driving while ability is impaired pertains to the driver's motor coordination, while the charge on which defendant was convicted pertains only to blood alcohol level without regard to the effect which that alcohol may have on the driver. A driver need not be impaired to be convicted under subdivision 2 of section 1192, and therefore driving while impaired is not a lesser included offense of that crime.

53 N.Y.2d at 981, 441 N.Y.S.2d at 663 (citation omitted).

On the other hand, the Court of Appeals has more recently stated that:

> Subdivision 1 is a lesser-included offense of subdivisions 2 and 3. Subdivisions 2 and 2-a require a showing of a specific amount of blood alcohol content to result in a per se criminal violation, whereas subdivision 3—"in an intoxicated condition"—allows for a circumstantial showing of inability to operate a motor vehicle while

under the influence of alcohol. Confirming this scheme, subdivision
9 explicitly permits a conviction under subdivision 1, 2 or 3 even
when the charge alleges a violation of either subdivision 2 or 3.

People v. Litto, 8 N.Y.3d 692, 705–06, 840 N.Y.S.2d 736, 744–45,
872 N.E.2d 848 (2007). *See also* next section.

§ 11:39   DWAI as a lesser included offense of per se DWI—
What about VTL § 1192(9)?

VTL § 1192(9) (formerly VTL § 1196(1)) provides as follows:

Conviction of a different charge. A driver may be convicted of a
violation of subdivision one, two or three of this section, notwithstanding that the charge laid before the court alleged a violation of
subdivision two or three of this section, and regardless of whether
or not such conviction is based on a plea of guilty.

In other words, VTL § 1192(9) expressly provides that a person
charged with VTL § 1192(2) can be convicted of VTL § 1192(1)—
either by plea of guilty or after trial. Doesn't that clearly make
DWAI a codified lesser included offense of per se DWI? While the
Appellate Division, Third Department, answered this question in
the negative in *People v. Sawinski*, 148 A.D.2d 888, __, 539
N.Y.S.2d 522, 523–24 (3d Dep't 1989), the Court of Appeals appeared to reach the opposite conclusion in *People v. Litto*, 8
N.Y.3d 692, 705–06, 840 N.Y.S.2d 736, 744–45, 872 N.E.2d 848
(2007). *See* previous section. *See also People v. Green*, 96 N.Y.2d
195, 198, 726 N.Y.S.2d 357, 359, 750 N.E.2d 59 (2001); *People v.
Farmer*, 36 N.Y.2d 386, 390, 369 N.Y.S.2d 44, 45, 330 N.E.2d 22
(1975).

In addition, since VTL § 1195(2) correlates BACs with impairment (*e.g.*, a BAC of .05% or less constitutes legal sobriety; a
BAC of .06% constitutes relevant evidence of impairment; a BAC
of .07% constitutes *prima facie* evidence of impairment), it is
clear that the Legislature does not view per se DWI and DWAI
as being completely separate and distinct from one another.

Simply stated, while DWAI may not be a lesser included offense of per se DWI in the traditional sense, a strong argument
can be made, in light of *Litto*, that the Legislature has made it a
codified lesser included offense. In this regard, the Court of Appeals' decision in *Litto* is clearly not reconcilable with its decision
in *People v. Brown*, 53 N.Y.2d 979, 981, 441 N.Y.S.2d 662, 663,
424 N.E.2d 549 (1981), on this issue. Rather, *Litto* appears to
agree with the Appellate Division majority in *Brown*. *See People
v. Brown*, 73 A.D.2d 112, 426 N.Y.S.2d 128 (3d Dep't 1980).

* * * * * * * * * *

VTL § 1192(9) raises another vexing issue. If a person refused
to submit to a chemical test, how can he or she be proven guilty

beyond a reasonable doubt of violating VTL § 1192(2)—which requires proof of ".08 of one per centum or more by weight of alcohol in the person's blood as shown by chemical analysis of such person's blood, breath, urine or saliva, made pursuant to the provisions of section eleven hundred ninety-four of this article"? Simply stated, regardless of what VTL § 1192(9) says, in the absence of a chemical test there cannot be a valid conviction of VTL § 1192(2). *See People v. Freeman*, 46 A.D.3d 1375, __, 848 N.Y.S.2d 800, 802 (4th Dep't 2007) ("a conviction of driving while intoxicated per se must be proved by chemical analysis (*see* Vehicle and Traffic Law § 1192[2])").

§ 11:40 Refusal to charge DWAI as a lesser included offense can be reversible error

In *People v. Hoag*, 51 N.Y.2d 632, 634, 435 N.Y.S.2d 698, 698, 416 N.E.2d 1033 (1981), the Court of Appeals held that:

> [A] Trial Judge, who declines to submit DWAI as a lesser included offense to DWI on the ground that there is no reasonable view of the evidence that would support a finding that defendant committed the lesser charge makes a ruling on the law rather than in the exercise of discretion. In such a case, there being a reasonable view of the evidence to support submission of DWAI, defendant's DWI conviction must be reversed and a new trial ordered.

51 N.Y.2d at 634, 435 N.Y.S.2d at 698. In so holding, the Court reasoned that:

> To entitle defendant to a DWAI charge the evidence need not establish that she acted as a "normal, sober person," but only that she had not been rendered incapable by alcoholic beverage of employing the physical or mental abilities needed to operate a car, even though her abilities to do so were to some degree impaired. The standard by which that determination is to be made was succinctly stated in *People v. Henderson*, 41 N.Y.2d 233, 236, 391 N.Y.S.2d 563, 359 N.E.2d 1357: "The court's appraisal of the persuasiveness of the evidence indicating guilt of the higher count is irrelevant; the question simply is whether on any reasonable view of the evidence it is possible for the trier of the facts to acquit the defendant on the higher count * * * and still find him guilty on the lesser one."

Id. at 636, 435 N.Y.S.2d at 700 (citation omitted). *See also People v. Carota*, 93 A.D.3d 1072, __, 941 N.Y.S.2d 302, 306-07 (3d Dep't 2012). *See generally People v. Maharaj*, 89 N.Y.2d 997, 999, 657 N.Y.S.2d 392, 393, 679 N.E.2d 631 (1997) (In DWI case involving bench trial, "[d]efendant was entitled to the court's consideration of the lesser included offense under the common-law count as he requested, and the court's misapprehension [of the applicable law] and failure to do so constitutes reversible error"); *People v. Yost*, 50 A.D.2d 577, __, 374 N.Y.S.2d 704, 707 (2d Dep't 1975) ("There was also error in refusing defendant's request to charge

the lesser included offense of operating a vehicle while impaired");
People v. Weinert, 178 Misc. 2d 675, __, 683 N.Y.S.2d 690, 691
(App. Term, 2d Dep't 1998) (trial court's failure to include lesser
included offense of DWAI on verdict sheet provided to jury constituted reversible error).

If the jury is unable to agree on a verdict with regard to the
greater offense (*i.e.*, DWI), and asks the Court if it can proceed to
consider the lesser included offense (*i.e.*, DWAI), the proper response from the Court is to instruct the jury "to consider the
lesser included offense only upon reaching a unanimous verdict
of not guilty of the greater." *People v. Boettcher*, 69 N.Y.2d 174,
183, 513 N.Y.S.2d 83, 87, 505 N.E.2d 594 (1987).

§ 11:41 Misdemeanor DWAI as a lesser included offense of DWI

A defendant who is charged with DWAI after having been
convicted of 2 or more violations of any subdivision of VTL § 1192
within the preceding 10 years can be charged with *misdemeanor
DWAI*. *See* VTL § 1193(1)(a). Misdemeanor DWAI is not a lesser
included offense of misdemeanor DWI. *See People v. Harris*, 23
Misc. 3d 250, __, 870 N.Y.S.2d 859, 865 (Monroe Co. Ct. 2008);
People v. Jamison, 170 Misc. 2d 974, __, 652 N.Y.S.2d 495, 496
(Rochester City Ct. 1996).

On the other hand, misdemeanor DWAI is a lesser included offense of class D felony DWI, which also requires 2 prior VTL
§ 1192 convictions within the preceding 10 years. *See* VTL
§ 1193(1)(c)(ii).

§ 11:42 Reckless driving as a lesser included offense of DWI

Reckless driving, in violation of VTL § 1212, is not a lesser
included offense of DWI. *See People v. Crandall*, 39 A.D.3d 1077,
832 N.Y.S.2d 828 (3d Dep't 2007); *People v. Darling*, 50 A.D.2d
1038, __, 377 N.Y.S.2d 718, 721 (3d Dep't 1975). *See also People
v. Starowicz*, 207 A.D.2d 994, __, 617 N.Y.S.2d 100, 101 (4th
Dep't 1994) ("One can drive recklessly without being intoxicated
and, as the jury apparently found, one can drive while intoxicated
without being reckless"); *People v. Byrne*, 65 Misc. 2d 174, __, 317
N.Y.S.2d 242, 243 (App. Term, 2d Dep't 1970) (per curiam).

§ 11:43 Speeding as a lesser included offense of DWI

In *Blumberg v. Lennon*, 44 A.D.2d 769, 354 N.Y.S.2d 261 (4th
Dep't 1974), a Village Justice allowed the defendant to plead
guilty—without the People's consent—to speeding, in violation of
VTL § 1180(a), in satisfaction of a charge of DWI, in violation of

VTL § 1192(2). Aside from finding that this was clearly improper, the Appellate Division, Fourth Department, also made clear that speeding is not a lesser included offense of DWI. *Blumberg v. Lennon*, 354 N.Y.S.2d at 263.

§ 11:44   What is a "chemical test"?

In the field of New York DWI law, the phrase "breath test" refers to a preliminary test of a DWI suspect's breath for the presence of alcohol using a preliminary breath screening device such as an Alco-Sensor (a.k.a. a "PBT"). *See* §§ 7:1 et seq., *supra*. By contrast, the phrase "chemical test" is the term used to describe a test of the alcoholic and/or drug content of a DWI suspect's blood using an instrument other than a PBT.

In other words, BAC tests conducted utilizing breath testing instruments such as the Breathalyzer, DataMaster, Intoxilyzer, Alcotest, etc. are generally referred to as "chemical tests," *not* "breath tests." Similarly, the phrase "refusal to submit to a chemical test" refers to a DWI suspect's refusal to submit to such a test—*not* to the refusal to submit to a breath screening test in violation of VTL § 1194(1)(b).

A chemical test is usually performed both (a) at a police station, and (b) *after* the suspect has been placed under arrest for DWI. By contrast, a breath test is usually performed both (a) at the scene of a traffic stop, and (b) *before* the suspect has been placed under arrest for DWI.

In *People v. Jones*, 118 Misc. 2d 687, __, 461 N.Y.S.2d 962, 966 (Albany Co. Ct. 1983), the Court rejected the defendant's claim that modern infrared breath testing devices do not constitute "chemical tests" because, unlike the old Breathalyzers, no chemical reaction takes place.

§ 11:45   Breath test result constitutes suppressible evidence

By its terms, CPL § 710.20(1) only authorizes the suppression of "tangible property obtained by means of an unlawful search and seizure." Prosecutor's occasionally seize upon this language and claim that a DWI defendant's breath test result is not suppressible, *even if it was illegally obtained*, because such evidence does not constitute "tangible property."

However, the United States Supreme Court has made clear both (a) that "*all* evidence obtained by searches and seizures in violation of the Constitution is, by that same authority, inadmissible in a state court," *Mapp v. Ohio*, 367 U.S. 643, 655, 81 S. Ct. 1684, 1691, 6 L. Ed. 2d 1081, 86 Ohio L. Abs. 513, 84 A.L.R.2d 933 (1961) (emphasis added), and (b) that obtaining a breath sample from a DWI suspect for alcohol analysis constitutes a "search" within the meaning of the 4th Amendment. *Skinner v. Railway Labor Executives' Ass'n*, 489 U.S. 602, 616–17, 109 S. Ct. 1402, 1413, 103 L. Ed. 2d 639, 4 I.E.R. Cas. (BNA) 224, 130 L.R.R.M. (BNA) 2857, 13 O.S.H. Cas. (BNA) 2065, 49 Empl. Prac. Dec. (CCH) P 38791, 111 Lab. Cas. (CCH) P 11001, 1989 O.S.H. Dec. (CCH) P 28476 (1989) ("Subjecting a person to a breathalyzer test, which generally requires the production of alveolar or "deep lung" breath for chemical analysis, implicates similar concerns about bodily integrity and, like the blood-alcohol test we considered in *Schmerber*, should also be deemed a search") (citation omitted). *See also Dunaway v. New York*, 442 U.S. 200, 99 S. Ct. 2248, 60 L. Ed. 2d 824 (1979); *Brown v. Illinois*, 422 U.S. 590, 95 S. Ct. 2254, 45 L. Ed. 2d 416 (1975); *People v. Johnson*, 134 Misc. 2d 474, __, 511 N.Y.S.2d 773, 774–75 (N.Y. City Crim. Ct. 1987) ("the Court holds that a breathalyzer test result is evidence as contemplated by *Mapp v. Ohio*, and CPL Section 710.60. It is, in fact, significant evidence and may not be proferred [sic] if it is the result of an illegal search"); *People v. Thomas*, 164 Misc. 2d 721, __, 626 N.Y.S.2d 405, 407–08 (N.Y. City Crim. Ct. 1995) ("The doctrine of the 'fruit of the poisonous tree' . . . is not limited to suppression of physical tangible evidence but applies as well to evidence which flows from the illegal seizure and search, such as verbal statements, identifications, tests performed upon the defendant, and testimony at trial as to matters observed during the unlawful intrusion").

In addition, in *People v. Ayala*, 89 N.Y.2d 874, 653 N.Y.S.2d 92, 675 N.E.2d 846 (1996), the Court of Appeals made clear that CPL § 710.20(5) is applicable to consented-to breath tests as well as to compulsory blood tests.

§ 11:46   Admissibility of chemical test result obtained despite refusal

In the field of chemical testing and chemical test refusals, there is a clear (and critical) distinction between a DWI suspect's constitutional rights and his or her statutory rights. Thus, for example, while a DWI suspect has no *constitutional* right to refuse to submit to a chemical test, *see, e.g., South Dakota v. Neville*, 459 U.S. 553, 560 n.10, 103 S. Ct. 916, 921 n.10, 74 L. Ed. 2d 748 (1983); *Schmerber v. California*, 384 U.S. 757, 86 S. Ct. 1826, 16 L. Ed. 2d 908 (1966); *People v. Smith*, 18 N.Y.3d 544, 548, 942 N.Y.S.2d 426, 429, 965 N.E.2d 928 (2012); *People v. Shaw*, 72 N.Y.2d 1032, 1033, 534 N.Y.S.2d 929, 930, 531 N.E.2d 650 (1988); *People v. Kates*, 53 N.Y.2d 591, 594–95, 444 N.Y.S.2d 446, 448, 428 N.E.2d 852 (1981); *People v. Thomas*, 46 N.Y.2d 100, 106, 412 N.Y.S.2d 845, 848, 385 N.E.2d 584 (1978), he or she nonetheless has a well recognized *statutory* right to do so. *See, e.g., Smith*,

18 N.Y.3d at 548, 942 N.Y.S.2d at 429; *Shaw*, 72 N.Y.2d at 1034, 534 N.Y.S.2d at 930; *People v. Daniel*, 84 A.D.2d 916, __, 446 N.Y.S.2d 658, 659 (4th Dep't 1981), order aff'd, 57 N.Y.2d 97, 454 N.Y.S.2d 292, 439 N.E.2d 1235 (1982); *People v. Wolter*, 83 A.D.2d 187, __, 444 N.Y.S.2d 331, 333 (4th Dep't 1981), order aff'd, sub nom. People v. Moselle, 57 N.Y.2d 97, 454 N.Y.S.2d 292, 439 N.E.2d 1235 (1982); *People v. Haitz*, 65 A.D.2d 172, __, 411 N.Y.S.2d 57, 60 (4th Dep't 1978).

In this regard, VTL § 1194(2)(b)(1) provides that, unless a Court Order has been granted pursuant to VTL § 1194(3), if a DWI suspect has refused to submit to a chemical test *"the test shall not be given* and a written report of such refusal shall be immediately made by the police officer before whom such refusal was made." (Emphasis added). *See also* VTL § 1194(3)(b) ("Upon refusal by any person to submit to a chemical test or any portion thereof as described above, *the test shall not be given* unless a police officer or a district attorney . . . requests and obtains a court order to compel [the test]") (emphasis added).

In *People v. Moselle*, 57 N.Y.2d 97, 454 N.Y.S.2d 292, 439 N.E.2d 1235 (1982), the Court of Appeals:

(a) Made clear that VTL § "1194 has pre-empted the administration of chemical tests for determining alcoholic blood content with respect to violations under [VTL §] 1192." *Id.* at 109, 454 N.Y.S.2d at 297; and

(b) Held that "[a]bsent a manifestation of a defendant's consent thereto, blood samples taken without a court order other than in conformity with the provisions of subdivisions 1 and 2 of section 1194 of the Vehicle and Traffic Law are inadmissible in prosecutions for operating a motor vehicle while under the influence of alcohol under section 1192 of that law. Beyond that, blood samples taken without a defendant's consent are inadmissible in prosecutions under the Penal Law unless taken pursuant to an authorizing court order." *Id.* at 101, 454 N.Y.S.2d at 293.

See also People v. Smith, 18 N.Y.3d 544, 549 n.2, 942 N.Y.S.2d 426, 429 n.2, 965 N.E.2d 928 (2012) ("If the motorist declines to consent, the police may not administer the test unless authorized to do so by court order (*see* Vehicle and Traffic Law § 1194[3])."); *People v. Kates*, 53 N.Y.2d 591, 596, 444 N.Y.S.2d 446, 448, 428 N.E.2d 852 (1981) ("the Legislature . . . provide[d] that the police must request the driver's consent, advise him of the consequences of refusal *and honor his wishes if he decides to refuse*") (emphasis added); *People v. Thomas*, 46 N.Y.2d 100, 108, 412 N.Y.S.2d 845, 850, 385 N.E.2d 584 (1978) ("Under the procedure prescribed by section 1194 of the Vehicle and Traffic Law a driver who has initially declined to take one of the described chemical tests is to be informed of the consequences of such refusal. If he thereafter persists in a refusal *the test is not to be given* (§ 1194, subd. 2); the choice is the driver's") (emphasis added).

Clearly, according to VTL §§ 1194(2)(b)(1), 1194(3)(b), *Moselle*, *Smith, Kates,* and *Thomas*, where a DWI suspect is requested to submit to a chemical test, declines, is read refusal warnings, and thereafter persists in his or her refusal, *"the test shall not be given"* (absent a Court Order pursuant to VTL § 1194(3)). *See also Mackey v. Montrym*, 443 U.S. 1, 5, 99 S. Ct. 2612, 2614, 61 L. Ed. 2d 321 (1979) ("The statute leaves an officer no discretion once a breath-analysis test has been refused: 'If the person arrested refuses to submit to such test or analysis, . . . the police officer before whom such refusal was made *shall immediately* prepare a written report of such refusal' "). Accordingly, a test result obtained under such circumstances should be inadmissible—not because it violates the Constitution—but rather because it violates the statutory scheme of VTL § 1194.

Nonetheless, in *People v. Stisi*, 93 A.D.2d 951, __, 463 N.Y.S.2d 73, 74–75 (3d Dep't 1983), the Appellate Division, Third Department, held:

> Defendant interprets section 1194 (subd. 2) of the Vehicle and Traffic Law to mandate that once a defendant refuses to submit to a chemical test after being fully apprised of the consequences of such refusal, all further requests and prompting by the police for defendant to reconsider and submit must immediately cease and the chemical test not be given . . . . Defendant's suggested literal interpretation of the subject statutory provision is misplaced and without merit . . . .

> Section 1194 of the Vehicle and Traffic Law does not, either expressly or by implication, foreclose the police from resuming discussion with a defendant and renewing their request that he submit to a chemical test.

Notably, the *Stisi* Court failed to cite *Kates* and/or *Thomas*, both of which appear to support the defendant's "suggested literal interpretation" of VTL § 1194(2).

Although *People v. Cragg*, 71 N.Y.2d 926, 528 N.Y.S.2d 807, 524 N.E.2d 128 (1988), appears at first glance to reach the same conclusion as the *Stisi* Court, in actuality it does not. In *Cragg*, "[d]efendant contend[ed] that the police violated Vehicle and Traffic Law § 1194(2) by administering a breathalyzer test despite defendant's initial refusal to submit to the test, and by informing him of certain consequences—not specifically prescribed by the statute—of such refusal." In rejecting defendant's claims, the Court of Appeals held:

> Contrary to defendant's assertion, the statute is not violated by an arresting officer informing a person as to the consequences of his

choice to take or not take a breathalyzer test. Thus, it cannot be said, *in the circumstances of this case*, that by informing defendant that his refusal to submit to the test would result in his arraignment before a Magistrate and the posting of bail, the officer violated the provisions of the Vehicle and Traffic Law.

71 N.Y.2d at 927, 528 N.Y.S.2d at 807–08 (emphasis added).

However, the wording of the *Cragg* decision indicates that defendant's "initial refusal" to submit to the test preceded the refusal warnings—requiring that defendant be informed of the consequences of a refusal and given a chance to change his mind. *See Thomas*, 46 N.Y.2d at 108, 412 N.Y.S.2d at 850 ("Under the procedure prescribed by section 1194 of the Vehicle and Traffic Law a driver who has initially declined to take one of the described chemical tests is to be informed of the consequences of such refusal. If he thereafter persists in a refusal the test is not to be given (§ 1194, subd. 2); the choice is the driver's"). Thus, the procedure followed in *Cragg* did not constitute an attempt to persuade the defendant to change his mind after a valid, persistent refusal had occurred. Rather, it is an example of the statute being implemented exactly as envisioned by the Legislature and the Court of Appeals. The position that *Cragg* was not intended to change settled law in this area is supported by the fact that *Cragg* (a) is a memorandum decision, (b) did not cite *Stisi*, and (c) did not cite *Moselle*, *Kates*, and/or *Thomas*.

§ 11:47   Breath test foundation—Generally

Assuming that the breath test device in question is included on the Department of Health's list of accepted breath test instruments, *see* § 11:51, *infra*, a proper foundation for the admission of a breath test result at trial requires proof (a) that the device was properly calibrated and otherwise in proper working order, (b) that any chemicals used in conducting the test were of the proper kind and mixed in the proper proportions, and (c) that the test was properly administered. *See, e.g., People v. Boscic*, 15 N.Y.3d 494, 497, 912 N.Y.S.2d 556, 558, 938 N.E.2d 989 (2010); *Constantine v. Leto*, 157 A.D.2d 376, __, 557 N.Y.S.2d 611, 613 (3d Dep't 1990), aff'd for the reasons stated in the opinion below,order aff'd, 77 N.Y.2d 975, 571 N.Y.S.2d 906, 575 N.E.2d 392 (1991); *People v. Campbell*, 73 N.Y.2d 481, 484, 541 N.Y.S.2d 756, 757, 539 N.E.2d 584 (1989); *People v. Alvarez*, 70 N.Y.2d 375, 380, 521 N.Y.S.2d 212, 214, 515 N.E.2d 898 (1987); *People v. Freeland*, 68 N.Y.2d 699, 700, 506 N.Y.S.2d 306, 307, 497 N.E.2d 673 (1986); *People v. Mertz*, 68 N.Y.2d 136, 148, 506 N.Y.S.2d 290, 296–97, 497 N.E.2d 657 (1986); *People v. Gower*, 42 N.Y.2d 117, 121–22, 397 N.Y.S.2d 368, 370–71, 366 N.E.2d 69 (1977); *People v. Todd*, 38 N.Y.2d 755, 381 N.Y.S.2d 50, 343 N.E.2d 767

(1975); *People v. Robinson*, 53 A.D.3d 63, __, 860 N.Y.S.2d 159, 165 (2d Dep't 2008); *People v. Hampe*, 181 A.D.2d 238, __ n.1, 585 N.Y.S.2d 861, 862 n.1 (3d Dep't 1992); *People v. Donaldson*, 36 A.D.2d 37, 319 N.Y.S.2d 172 (4th Dep't 1971); *People v. Meikrantz*, 77 Misc. 2d 892, 351 N.Y.S.2d 549 (Broome Co. Ct. 1974).

This topic is covered at length in §§ 42:1 et seq., *infra*.

§ 11:48   Timeliness of instrument calibration

In *People v. Todd*, 79 Misc. 2d 630, __, 360 N.Y.S.2d 754, 759 (Delaware Co. Ct. 1974), the breath test machine used to test the defendant's breath "had not been calibrated for more than six months." County Court found that:

> By analogy in speeding cases, there is a requirement that speedometers of police vehicles be calibrated at least once every six months and it would appear that the same standard should apply to the breathalyzer machine and any similar type of evidence which is used in a criminal prosecution and may deprive a citizen of his right to operate a motor vehicle in this state.

Id. at __, 360 N.Y.S.2d at 759. On appeal, the Court of Appeals held that "[t]he People failed to establish that the breathalyzer apparatus had been timely calibrated; hence, the results of the breath test were inadmissible. It was incumbent upon the District Attorney to show that the machine was in proper working order." *People v. Todd*, 38 N.Y.2d 755, 756, 381 N.Y.S.2d 50, 50, 343 N.E.2d 767 (1975).

Based upon the above, it had been generally accepted that *Todd* created a "six-month rule" pursuant to which a breath test result obtained from a machine that had not been calibrated for more than six months is inadmissible. In this regard, in *People v. Mickle*, 187 Misc. 2d 718, __, 724 N.Y.S.2d 570, 573 (Canaan Just. Ct. 2001), the Court stated:

> [M]any courts view *People v. Todd* as a clear and controlling authority for support of the proposition of a "six-month rule." This court agrees and finds it to be dispositive here. The rule may be modified at some point by a higher court; however, this court sees no lower court rulings that have been confirmed or overruled by the Court of Appeals. In the absence of such pronouncement, six months is the rule of *Todd*.

(Citation omitted).

The pronouncement that the *Mickle* Court was seeking has come. *See People v. Boscic*, 15 N.Y.3d 494, 912 N.Y.S.2d 556, 938 N.E.2d 989 (2010). In *Boscic*, the Court of Appeals held as follows:

> In this case, we consider whether our decision in *People v. Todd* adopted a standard requiring that breath-alcohol detection devices

must be calibrated at least every six months in order for the test results to be admissible at trial. We hold that there is no per se, six-month rule and that the People must instead lay a foundation demonstrating that the particular device used was in proper working order when the test was administered.

Id. at 496, 912 N.Y.S.2d at 557 (citation omitted). In so holding, the Court reasoned as follows:

Defendant claims that *People v. Todd* established a six-month calibration requirement . . . . Although *Todd* is susceptible to such an interpretation, we do not read it in such a rigid manner. * * *

Todd did not explicitly articulate a six-month standard or allude to a specific calibration time frame.

We have not relied on a six-month, bright-line rule in subsequent cases that dealt with the foundation requirements for breath-alcohol evidence. Rather than applying a specific temporal limitation, our post-*Todd* decisions have repeatedly emphasized that the applicable principle is whether the detection instrument was in "proper working order" at the time a test was administered. The Third and Fourth Departments have interpreted our precedent similarly and rejected the notion that it is impossible for a breath-alcohol device to function properly simply because it has not been calibrated for six months. We concur with that view and therefore hold that such evidence is admissible if the People demonstrate that the machine was in proper working order at the time it issued the test results in question.

Todd was decided almost 35 years ago and in the ensuing decades, scientific knowledge has advanced dramatically, leading to significant technological changes in breath-alcohol detection devices. The scientific methods incorporated in modern-day breath testing instruments are substantially different from the earlier generations of these devices . . . . More recent technology relies on infrared absorption spectrometry. This technology—which is used in the BAC DataMaster—calculates blood-alcohol concentration by passing infrared light through a chamber holding the breath sample to gauge the absorption rate of "infrared radiation at specific wavelengths." Given the technological advances that have occurred and will continue to evolve, paired with the proliferation of available breath-alcohol detection devices approved for use by the New York State Department of Health (DOH) (*see* 10 NYCRR 59.4), we do not believe that a court-imposed calibration timing rule for all current technologies would be helpful in achieving the primary objective, which is to provide the factfinder a basis to determine whether the particular instrument used produced reliable results in a specific instance. Even if we had articulated a bright-line calibration rule more than three decades ago, the changes in scientific testing methods would have provided reason to revisit it.

It further bears noting that both parties to this litigation recognize that DOH has been charged by the Legislature to evaluate and approve specific models of breath-alcohol testing machines (*see* Vehicle and Traffic Law § 1194[4][c]). In its regulatory capacity, DOH has determined that such instruments must be calibrated "at a frequency as recommended by the device manufacturer" *but not less than once a year*. The promulgation of these regulations will . . . provide courts with information regarding recommended calibration intervals, *not to exceed one year*, when assessing the adequacy of foundation requirements for the admissibility of breath-alcohol test results.

Id. at 497–500, 912 N.Y.S.2d at 558–59 (emphases added) (citations and footnote omitted).

In light of the last portion of this quote from *Boscic*, it can now be persuasively argued that there exists a "one-year rule" for breath test instrument calibration.

The *Boscic* Court also noted that:

Our conclusion does not mean that appropriate and adequate calibration procedures can be disregarded by law enforcement. Rather, the admissibility of breath-alcohol analysis results remains premised on the People's ability to demonstrate, among other requirements, that the device was in "proper working order" when it was used to test an accused. And nothing prevents an accused from seeking to introduce relevant evidence that may affect other foundational issues or the weight that should be given to results generated by a particular device, as defendant attempted during his trial.

Id. at 500, 912 N.Y.S.2d at 560 (citation omitted).

§ 11:49   Admissibility of calibration records

In *People v. Mertz*, 68 N.Y.2d 136, 147–48, 506 N.Y.S.2d 290, 296, 497 N.E.2d 657 (1986), the Court of Appeals held that:

Admission of the breathalyzer logs over objection that it had not been shown that the entries were made at the time of the acts recorded in them or within a reasonable time thereafter was also error. CPLR 4518(a) expressly requires such foundation evidence. * * *

[In addition,] admissibility under [CPLR § 4518(c)] is governed by the same standards as the general business record exception in subdivision (a). Thus, a certificate made under CPLR 4518(c) which does not set forth that the entries in the certified record were made at the time of the events they record or within a reasonable time thereafter is not admissible under that subdivision. * * *

While the scientific reliability of breathalyzers in general is no longer open to question, there must still be either proper foundation testimony under CPLR 4518(a) or a proper CPLR 4518(c) certificate to establish that the particular instrument used to test a defendant's BAC and the ampoules used with it had been tested within a reasonable period in relation to defendant's test and found to be properly calibrated and in working order.

(Citations omitted). *See generally People v. Freeland*, 68 N.Y.2d 699, 506 N.Y.S.2d 306, 497 N.E.2d 673 (1986); *People v. Gower*, 42 N.Y.2d 117, 121, 397 N.Y.S.2d 368, 370, 366 N.E.2d 69 (1977) ("It would seem that the requirements of CPLR 4518 could very easily be met and thus its benefits be realized by the prosecution").

§ 11:50 The arresting officer can also be the breath test operator (*i.e.*, no "witness" to the test is required)

In *People v. Evers*, 68 N.Y.2d 658, 659, 505 N.Y.S.2d 68, 69, 496 N.E.2d 227 (1986), the Court of Appeals held that:

Vehicle and Traffic Law § 1194(1) [currently VTL § 1194(2)(a)], which requires chemical testing of a motor vehicle operator's breath, blood, urine or saliva to be administered "at the direction of" a police officer, does not preclude the police officer who determines that testing is warranted from administering the test as well. Where the test is given by an officer trained to administer it and no unusual circumstances have been shown, corroboration of the results is not required.

§ 11:51 Necessity of expert witness testimony as part of chemical test foundation

"In criminal matters the scientific reliability and accuracy of a machine measuring blood alcohol content for forensic purposes must be established before such test results may be admitted in evidence." *People v. Campbell*, 73 N.Y.2d 481, 485, 541 N.Y.S.2d 756, 758, 539 N.E.2d 584 (1989). With respect to breath testing, the inclusion of a particular testing device on the Department of Health's list of accepted breath test instruments, *see* 10 NYCRR § 59.4, satisfies this requirement. *See, e.g., People v. Robinson*, 53 A.D.3d 63, __, 860 N.Y.S.2d 159, 165 (2d Dep't 2008) ("the Intoxilyzer, manufactured by CMI, Inc., appears on the list of approved breath-testing instruments compiled by the New York State Department of Health, and the machine is thus presumed reliable"); *People v. Hampe*, 181 A.D.2d 238, __, 585 N.Y.S.2d 861, 862–63 (3d Dep't 1992) ("the general acceptance of the reliability and accuracy of the test results of the BAC Verifier, sufficient to dispense with the foundational evidence thereof through expert testimony, was established by reason of the specific inclusion of the BAC Verifier in the list of breath-testing instruments approved by DOH in regulations promulgated pursuant to Vehicle and Traffic Law § 1194(4)(c)").

On the other hand, since there is no corresponding list of approved blood test instruments, the results of such tests are inadmissible absent expert witness testimony. *See Campbell. See also People v. Dean*, 74 N.Y.2d 643, 644, 542 N.Y.S.2d 512, 512, 540 N.E.2d 707 (1989) ("We agree with defendant, for the reasons stated in *People v. Campbell*, 73 N.Y.2d 481, 541 N.Y.S.2d 756, 539 N.E.2d 584 (1989) [decided herewith], that County Court properly reversed defendant's conviction for violating Vehicle and Traffic Law § 1192(3)").

§ 11:52 Significance of failure to follow police department's chemical test rules and regulations

VTL § 1194(2)(a) provides, in pertinent part, that:

Any person who operates a motor vehicle in this state shall be deemed to have given consent to a chemical test of one or more of the following: breath, blood, urine, or saliva, for the purpose of determining the alcoholic and/or drug content of the blood provided that such test is administered by or at the direction of a police officer with respect to a chemical test of breath, urine or saliva or, with respect to a chemical test of blood, at the direction of a police officer: * * *

(2) within two hours after a breath test, as provided in [VTL § 1194(1)(b)], indicates that alcohol has been consumed by such person and *in accordance with the rules and regulations established by the police force of which the officer is a member*.

(Emphasis added).

In response to this statute, many police departments have enacted rules and regulations pertaining to chemical testing. This raises the following issues: (1) is proof of compliance with such rules and regulations required; and (2) if not, what is the significance of a failure to comply with the applicable police department rules and regulations?

The Court of Appeals resolved the first issue in *People v. Monahan*, 25 N.Y.2d 378, 306 N.Y.S.2d 453, 254 N.E.2d 758 (1969). In *Monahan*, the defendant was convicted of violating VTL § 1192(2). On appeal, County Court reversed on the ground that "the People had failed to prove by competent evidence the content of, and police compliance with[,] the police 'rules and regulations'" pursuant to VTL § 1194(1) (currently VTL § 1194(2)(a)(2)). *Id.* at 380, 306 N.Y.S.2d at 453–54. The Court of Appeals reversed, reasoning as follows:

We have concluded that the evidence was not necessary to the People's case and, in consequence, that the reversal was in error. The intent of the statute seems to be twofold, first, to provide that the police officer, and not the accused, shall determine which of the several permitted forms of test shall be employed, and, second, to assure that the accused, whose implied consent, although revocable, is under the compulsion of the statute, will receive fair treatment in the selection and administering of the testing procedure, this pursuant to rules and regulations and not according to a police officer's *ad hoc* determination in the particular case. It follows that proof of the existent regulations is unnecessary in cases such as this, in which there is presented no substantial question with respect to the validity of the consent or the propriety of the particular form of test selected to be given. The provision for rules and regulations does not bear upon the substantive results of the test, for their reliability is determinable in accordance with medical and scientific standards generally and not according to regulations promulgated by one "police force" or another.

Id. at 380, 306 N.Y.S.2d at 454.

The *Monahan* Court further stated that:

In dealing with medical evidence or scientific proof generally, a foundation does, of course, have to be laid. The blood tested must be identified as that taken from defendant within the prescribed period and it must be shown that the tests were properly and accurately made, pursuant to proper and accepted scientific and technological standards. If, as here, the taking, handling and testing of the blood are items unassailably proven as to reliability, it would then appear irrelevant what the departmental rules contained or whether they were complied with. It could not well be argued that substandard regulations would qualify the report of a scientifically inadequate test or exclude proof of a test meeting otherwise recognized standards.

Id. at 381, 306 N.Y.S.2d at 454–55. *See also People v. Fogerty*, 18 N.Y.2d 664, 666, 273 N.Y.S.2d 343, 344, 219 N.E.2d 801 (1966) ("The failure to file, in a public office, rules governing the [taking of blood] tests does not affect the admissibility in evidence of the results of the tests if found by the court to be intrinsically accurate and reliable").

* * * * * * * * * *

With regard to the second issue, in *People v. Williams*, 62 N.Y.2d 765, 767, 477 N.Y.S.2d 315, 316, 465 N.E.2d 1251 (1984), the Court of Appeals held that "it was error on the part of the trial court . . . to instruct the jury in effect that they could ignore the failure of the police to have administered the breathalyzer test in accordance with the rules and regulations of the Tioga County Sheriff's Department (Vehicle and Traffic Law, § 1194)."

In sum, *Monahan* makes clear that the failure of the police to follow the applicable police department rules and regulations does not affect the admissibility of the defendant's chemical test result, but *Williams* makes clear that the defense can argue that an officer's failure to follow his or her department's rules and regulations affects the weight to be afforded to such result.

Notably, in *Constantine v. Leto*, 157 A.D.2d 376, __, 557
N.Y.S.2d 611, 613 (3d Dep't 1990), aff'd for the reasons stated in
the opinion below, order aff'd, 77 N.Y.2d 975, 571 N.Y.S.2d 906,
575 N.E.2d 392 (1991), the Court, citing *Williams*, made clear
that a police agency's chemical test rules and regulations are
discoverable. *Cf. Dzialak v. Hults*, 19 N.Y.2d 805, 806, 279
N.Y.S.2d 964, 964, 226 N.E.2d 698 (1967) (rules and regulations
not discoverable for purposes of DMV chemical test refusal
hearing).

§ 11:53   Preservation of sample of defendant's breath for independent testing is not required

Both the United States Supreme Court and the New York State
Court of Appeals have expressly held that, where a breath alcohol
test is utilized, preservation of a sample of the defendant's breath
for independent testing is *not* required under either the Federal
or State Constitutions. *See, e.g., California v. Trombetta*, 467
U.S. 479, 104 S. Ct. 2528, 81 L. Ed. 2d 413 (1984); *People v. Alvarez*,
70 N.Y.2d 375, 381, 521 N.Y.S.2d 212, 215, 515 N.E.2d 898 (1987)
("as a matter of State constitutional law the police are not
required to obtain and preserve a second breath sample for later
use by the accused"). *See also* §§ 34:1 et seq., *infra*.

§ 11:54   Chain of custody of blood sample

In *People v. Malone*, 14 N.Y.2d 8, 247 N.Y.S.2d 641, 197 N.E.2d
189 (1964), the chain of custody of the defendant's blood sample
was at issue on appeal. The proof at trial was as follows:

> The doctor who took the blood sample testified that he asked the
> nurse to furnish him with a nonalcoholic solution with which to
> sterilize defendant's arm. Although he could not swear that she did
> so, he assumed that she did since he was not conscious of an
> alcoholic odor when the solution was used by him. The sample was
> then placed in a vial, sealed and placed in a container for mailing.
> A State Trooper took the container home with him when he went
> off duty, locking it in a strongbox to which he alone had a key. The
> next day, the sample was mailed to the State Police Laboratory in
> Albany by certified mail. At the laboratory, the sample was tested
> by a college graduate, a major in chemistry with two years' gradu-
> ate work in biochemistry, employed by the State as a chemist for
> some ten years.

Id. at 10, 247 N.Y.S.2d at 642–43.

Under these circumstances, the Court of Appeals held that:

> We think that, since a proper chain of identification linking the
> defendant with the unadulterated fluid which was examined by a
> qualified person was established, the results of the blood test were
> competent evidence and thereby properly admitted into evidence by
> the trial court. * * *

Since there was ample proof that the liquid tested at the laboratory was the same as that taken from the arm of the defendant, it was not necessary to conduct an additional test to ascertain whether the sample was blood as suggested by the County Court. Moreover the doctor's testimony was sufficiently positive to allow the jury to find that a nonalcoholic preparation was used. The State Trooper's testimony indicates that the specimen was not accessible to persons not called as witnesses, hence there was no possibility that it had been tampered with.

Id. at 10, 11, 247 N.Y.S.2d at 642, 643.

By contrast, in *Amaro v. City of New York*, 40 N.Y.2d 30, 35, 386 N.Y.S.2d 19, 22, 351 N.E.2d 665 (1976), the Court of Appeals held that there was insufficient proof of the chain of custody of a blood sample under the following circumstances:

Here the doctor who drew the sample gave it to a fire department chauffeur whose name he could not recall and who was not produced at trial. Moreover, the sample was given to the chauffeur on Saturday evening and not delivered until Monday morning, "at the earliest", leaving over 36 hours of custody completely unaccounted for. No testimony was adduced to indicate who received the sample at the laboratory, its condition on receipt, the size of the vial containing the specimen, whether it was refrigerated during the long weekend, how the vial was labeled or identified, or the quantity or condition of its contents upon arrival. Hence, there can be no reasonable assurance of the unchanged condition of the blood sample. Nonetheless, it is argued that there is no indication that the sample was tampered with while it was in the chauffeur's possession and that it ought to be admitted for that reason. This claim, of course, begs the question for the driver was never produced and could not be examined regarding his care and custody of the sample.

§ 11:55 There is no constitutional right to refuse to submit to a chemical test

"[A] person suspected of drunk driving has no constitutional right to refuse to take a blood-alcohol test." *South Dakota v. Neville*, 459 U.S. 553, 560 n.10, 103 S. Ct. 916, 921 n.10, 74 L. Ed. 2d 748 (1983). *See also id.* at 565, 103 S.Ct. at 923 ("Respondent's right to refuse the blood-alcohol test . . . is simply a matter of grace bestowed by the . . . legislature"); *People v. Smith*, 18 N.Y.3d 544, 548, 942 N.Y.S.2d 426, 429, 965 N.E.2d 928 (2012); *People v. Thomas*, 46 N.Y.2d 100, 106, 412 N.Y.S.2d 845, 848, 385 N.E.2d 584 (1978) ("inasmuch as a defendant can constitutionally be compelled to take such a test, he has no constitutional right not to take one"); *id.* at 109, 412 N.Y.S.2d at 850 ("defendant had no constitutional privilege or statutory right to refuse to take the test; hence comment on his refusal represents no infringement of privilege or right"); *People v. Shaw*, 72 N.Y.2d 1032, 1033, 534 N.Y.S.2d 929, 930, 531 N.E.2d 650 (1988); *People v. Haitz*, 65

A.D.2d 172, __, 411 N.Y.S.2d 57, 60 (4th Dep't 1978) ("The admission of defendant's refusal is not a penalty exacted for his exercise of a constitutional right, for he has no constitutional privilege to refuse to take the test"). There are, however, three exceptions to this general rule:

> Taking a driver's blood for alcohol analysis does not . . . involve an unreasonable search under the Fourth Amendment when there is [1] probable cause, [2] exigent circumstances and [3] a reasonable examination procedure. So long as these requirements are met . . . the test may be performed absent defendant's consent and indeed over his objection without violating his Fourth Amendment rights.

People v. Kates, 53 N.Y.2d 591, 594–95, 444 N.Y.S.2d 446, 448, 428 N.E.2d 852 (1981) (citation omitted). *See also Schmerber v. California*, 384 U.S. 757, 86 S. Ct. 1826, 16 L. Ed. 2d 908 (1966); *Missouri v. McNeely*, 133 S. Ct. 1552, 185 L. Ed. 2d 696 (2013).

Test refusals are covered at length in §§ 41:1 et seq., *infra*.

§ 11:56   Chemical tests and the 4th Amendment

Obtaining a blood sample from a DWI suspect for alcohol/drug analysis constitutes a "search and seizure" within the meaning of the 4th Amendment. *See Missouri v. McNeely*, 133 S. Ct. 1552, 1558, 185 L. Ed. 2d 696 (2013); *Schmerber v. California*, 384 U.S. 757, 767, 86 S. Ct. 1826, 1834, 16 L. Ed. 2d 908 (1966); *People v. Kates*, 53 N.Y.2d 591, 594–95, 444 N.Y.S.2d 446, 448, 428 N.E.2d 852 (1981). Similarly, obtaining a breath sample from a DWI suspect for alcohol analysis constitutes a 4th Amendment "search." *See Skinner v. Railway Labor Executives' Ass'n*, 489 U.S. 602, 616–17, 109 S. Ct. 1402, 1413, 103 L. Ed. 2d 639, 4 I.E.R. Cas. (BNA) 224, 130 L.R.R.M. (BNA) 2857, 13 O.S.H. Cas. (BNA) 2065, 49 Empl. Prac. Dec. (CCH) P 38791, 111 Lab. Cas. (CCH) P 11001, 1989 O.S.H. Dec. (CCH) P 28476 (1989).

In addition, a lawful VTL § 1192 arrest is a prerequisite to a valid request that a DWI suspect submit to a chemical test. *See, e.g., People v. Daniger*, 227 A.D.2d 846, __, 642 N.Y.S.2d 732, 733–34 (3d Dep't 1996) (probable cause to arrest defendant for DWI is predicate for request to submit to chemical test); *Gagliardi v. Department of Motor Vehicles*, 144 A.D.2d 882, __, 535 N.Y.S.2d 203, 204 (3d Dep't 1988) ("In order for the testing strictures of Vehicle and Traffic Law § 1194 to come into play, there must have been a lawful arrest for driving while intoxicated"); *June v. Tofany*, 34 A.D.2d 732, __, 311 N.Y.S.2d 782, 783 (4th Dep't 1970) ("a prerequisite to a valid request to submit to a chemical test for alcoholic content of the blood under . . . section 1194 of the Vehicle and Traffic Law is that there be a valid arrest"). *See also Welsh v. Wisconsin*, 466 U.S. 740, 744, 104 S. Ct. 2091, 2095, 80 L. Ed. 2d 732 (1984) ("It is not disputed by the parties that an arrestee's refusal to take a breath test would be reasonable, and therefore operating privileges could not be revoked, if the underlying arrest was not lawful. Indeed, state law has consistently provided that a valid arrest is a necessary prerequisite to the imposition of a breath test").

In *Birchfield v. North Dakota*, 136 S. Ct. 2160, 2184-85, 195 L. Ed. 2d 560 (2016), the Supreme Court held that:

> [T]he Fourth Amendment permits warrantless breath tests incident to arrests for drunk driving. The impact of breath tests on privacy is slight, and the need for BAC testing is great.
>
> We reach a different conclusion with respect to blood tests. Blood tests are significantly more intrusive, and their reasonableness must be judged in light of the availability of the less invasive alternative of a breath test. Respondents have offered no satisfactory justification for demanding the more intrusive alternative without a warrant. * * *
>
> It is true that a blood test, unlike a breath test, may be administered to a person who is unconscious (perhaps as a result of a crash) or who is unable to do what is needed to take a breath test due to profound intoxication or injuries. But we have no reason to believe that such situations are common in drunk-driving arrests, and when they arise, the police may apply for a warrant if need be. * * *
>
> Because breath tests are significantly less intrusive than blood tests and in most cases amply serve law enforcement interests, we conclude that a breath test, but not a blood test, may be administered as a search incident to a lawful arrest for drunk driving. As in all cases involving reasonable searches incident to arrest, a warrant is not needed in this situation.

See also id. at 2185 n.8 ("today's decision provides very clear guidance that the Fourth Amendment allows warrantless breath tests, but as a general rule does not allow warrantless blood draws, incident to a lawful drunk-driving arrest").

> Having concluded that the search incident to arrest doctrine does not justify the warrantless taking of a blood sample, we must address respondents' alternative argument that such tests are justified based on the driver's legally implied consent to submit to them. * * * Our prior opinions have referred approvingly to the general concept of implied-consent laws that impose civil penalties and evidentiary consequences on motorists who refuse to comply. Petitioners do not question the constitutionality of those laws, and nothing we say here should be read to cast doubt on them.
>
> It is another matter, however, for a State not only to insist upon an intrusive blood test, but also to impose criminal penalties on the refusal to submit to such a test. There must be a limit to the conse-

quences to which motorists may be deemed to have consented by virtue of a decision to drive on public roads. * * *

[W]e conclude that motorists cannot be deemed to have consented to submit to a blood test on pain of committing a criminal offense.

Id. at 2185-86 (citations omitted).

§ 11:57 *Miranda* warnings need not precede request to submit to chemical test

In *South Dakota v. Neville*, 459 U.S. 553, 564 n.15, 103 S. Ct. 916, 923 n.15, 74 L. Ed. 2d 748 (1983), the Supreme Court held that "[i]n the context of an arrest for driving while intoxicated, a police inquiry of whether the suspect will take a blood-alcohol test is not an interrogation within the meaning of *Miranda*." *See also South Dakota v. Neville*, 459 U.S. at 564, 103 S.Ct. at 923 ("We hold . . . that a refusal to take a blood-alcohol test, after a police officer has lawfully requested it, is not an act coerced by the officer, and thus is not protected by the privilege against self-incrimination"); *People v. Berg*, 92 N.Y.2d 701, 703, 685 N.Y.S.2d 906, 907, 708 N.E.2d 979 (1999) ("It is . . . settled that *Miranda* warnings are not required in order to admit the results of chemical analysis tests, or a defendant's refusal to take such tests"); *People v. Kates*, 53 N.Y.2d 591, 594, 444 N.Y.S.2d 446, 448, 428 N.E.2d 852 (1981) ("Taking a driver's blood for alcohol analysis does not call for testimonial compulsion prohibited by the Fifth Amendment"); *People v. Thomas*, 46 N.Y.2d 100, 103, 412 N.Y.S.2d 845, 846, 385 N.E.2d 584 (1978); *People v. Craft*, 28 N.Y.2d 274, 321 N.Y.S.2d 566, 270 N.E.2d 297 (1971); *People v. Boudreau*, 115 A.D.2d 652, __, 496 N.Y.S.2d 489, 491 (2d Dep't 1985); *Hoffman v. Melton*, 81 A.D.2d 709, __, 439 N.Y.S.2d 449, 450–51 (3d Dep't 1981); *People v. Haitz*, 65 A.D.2d 172, __, 411 N.Y.S.2d 57, 60 (4th Dep't 1978); *People v. Dillin*, 150 Misc. 2d 311, __, 567 N.Y.S.2d 991, 992 (N.Y. City Crim. Ct. 1991).

§ 11:58 *Miranda* warnings need not precede most field sobriety tests

In *Schmerber v. California*, 384 U.S. 757, 761, 86 S. Ct. 1826, 1830, 16 L. Ed. 2d 908 (1966), the Supreme Court held that the Fifth Amendment protects a defendant only from being compelled to either testify against himself or herself "or otherwise provide the State with evidence of a testimonial or communicative nature." *See also People v. Hager*, 69 N.Y.2d 141, 142, 512 N.Y.S.2d 794, 795, 505 N.E.2d 237 (1987) ("Evidence is 'testimonial or communicative' when it reveals a person's subjective knowledge or thought processes").

In *Pennsylvania v. Muniz*, 496 U.S. 582, 110 S. Ct. 2638, 110

L. Ed. 2d 528 (1990), the Court addressed the issue of "whether various incriminating utterances of a drunken-driving suspect, made while performing a series of sobriety tests, constitute testimonial responses to custodial interrogation for purposes of the Self-Incrimination Clause of the Fifth Amendment." 496 U.S. at 584, 110 S.Ct. at 2641. The defendant in *Muniz* was asked to perform various tests both at a roadside stop and later after he was arrested and transported back to the police station.

The Supreme Court held that Muniz's response to the question "Do you know what the date was of your sixth birthday?" was testimonial:

> When Officer Hosterman asked Muniz if he knew the date of his sixth birthday and Muniz, for whatever reason, could not remember or calculate that date, . . . Muniz was left with the choice of incriminating himself by admitting that he did not then know the date of his sixth birthday, or answering untruthfully by reporting a date that he did not then believe to be accurate (an incorrect guess would be incriminating as well as untruthful). The content of his truthful answer supported an inference that his mental faculties were impaired, because his assertion (he did not know the date of his sixth birthday) was different from the assertion (he knew the date was (correct date)) that the trier of fact might reasonably have expected a lucid person to provide. Hence, the incriminating inference of impaired mental faculties stemmed, not just from the fact that Muniz slurred his response, but also from a testimonial aspect of that response.

Id. at 598–99, 110 S.Ct. at 2649.

By contrast, the results of physical performance tests are not testimonial. As a result, they do not implicate the 5th Amendment, and thus need not be preceded by *Miranda* warnings. *See, e.g., Pennsylvania v. Muniz*, 496 U.S. at 592, 110 S.Ct. at 2645 ("Under *Schmerber* and its progeny, . . . any slurring of speech and other evidence of lack of muscular coordination revealed by Muniz's responses to Officer Hosterman's direct questions constitute nontestimonial components of those responses"); *People v. Berg*, 92 N.Y.2d 701, 703, 685 N.Y.S.2d 906, 907, 708 N.E.2d 979 (1999) ("It is settled that *Miranda* warnings are not required to allow the results of field sobriety tests into evidence"); *People v. Berg*, 92 N.Y.2d at 705, 685 N.Y.S.2d at 908–09 ("Results of field sobriety tests such as the horizontal gaze nystagmus, walk and turn and one-leg stand are not deemed testimonial or communicative because they 'do not reveal a person's subjective knowledge or thought processes but, rather, exhibit a person's degree of physical coordination for observation by police officers.' Responses to such tests incriminate an intoxicated suspect 'not because the tests [reveal] defendant's thoughts, but because [defendant's] body's responses [differ] from those of a sober person.' Thus, the results of such tests may be introduced despite the failure of the police to administer *Miranda* warnings") (citations omitted); *People v. Jacquin*, 71 N.Y.2d 825, 826, 527 N.Y.S.2d 728, 729, 522 N.E.2d 1026 (1988) ("Performance tests need not be preceded by *Miranda* warnings and, generally an audio/visual tape of such tests, including any colloquy between the test-giver and the defendant not constituting custodial interrogation, is admissible"); *People v. Hager*, 69 N.Y.2d 141, 142, 512 N.Y.S.2d 794, 795, 505 N.E.2d 237 (1987).

Regardless of whether the results of sobriety tests are testimonial or not, where such tests are performed in the "field" the defendant is generally not yet in custody—which is a further reason why *Miranda* warnings would not be required. *See, e.g., Pennsylvania v. Bruder*, 488 U.S. 9, 10–11, 109 S. Ct. 205, 206–07, 102 L. Ed. 2d 172 (1988); *Berkemer v. McCarty*, 468 U.S. 420, 440, 104 S. Ct. 3138, 3150, 82 L. Ed. 2d 317 (1984) ("The . . . noncoercive aspect of ordinary traffic stops prompts us to hold that persons temporarily detained pursuant to such stops are not 'in custody' for the purposes of *Miranda*"). *See also People v. Bennett*, 70 N.Y.2d 891, 893–94, 524 N.Y.S.2d 378, 380, 519 N.E.2d 289 (1987); *People v. Hasenflue*, 252 A.D.2d 829, __, 675 N.Y.S.2d 464, 466 (3d Dep't 1998); *People v. McGreal*, 190 A.D.2d 869, __, 593 N.Y.S.2d 868, 869 (2d Dep't 1993); *People v. Hampe*, 181 A.D.2d 238, __, 585 N.Y.S.2d 861, 863 (3d Dep't 1992); *People v. McAleavey*, 159 A.D.2d 646, __, 553 N.Y.S.2d 38, 38–39 (2d Dep't 1990); *People v. Mathis*, 136 A.D.2d 746, __, 523 N.Y.S.2d 915, 916 (2d Dep't 1988); *People v. Brown*, 104 A.D.2d 696, __, 480 N.Y.S.2d 578, 579 (3d Dep't 1984). *Cf. People v. Norton*, 135 A.D.2d 984, 522 N.Y.S.2d 958 (3d Dep't 1987); *People v. Benson*, 114 A.D.2d 506, __, 494 N.Y.S.2d 727, 728 (2d Dep't 1985).

§ 11:59   Chemical tests and the right to counsel

In *People v. Smith*, 18 N.Y.3d 544, 549-50, 942 N.Y.S.2d 426, 429-30, 965 N.E.2d 928 (2012), the Court of Appeals summarized the law in this area:

Vehicle and Traffic Law § 1194 does not address whether a motorist has a right to consult with a lawyer prior to determining whether to consent to chemical testing. However, if the motorist is arrested for driving while intoxicated or a related offense, this Court has recognized a limited right to counsel associated with the criminal proceeding. In *People v. Gursey*, we held that if a defendant arrested for driving while under the influence of alcohol asks to contact an attorney before responding to a request to take a chemical test, the police "may not, without justification, prevent access between the criminal accused and his lawyer, available in person or by immediate telephone communication, if such access does not interfere unduly with the matter at hand." If such a request is made, and it is feasible for the police to allow defendant to attempt to reach counsel without unduly delaying administration of the chemical test, a defendant should be afforded such an opportunity. As we explained in *Gursey*, the right to seek the advice of counsel— typically by telephone—could be accommodated in a matter of minutes and in most circumstances would not substantially interfere with the investigative procedure. That being said, we made clear that there is no absolute right to refuse to take the test until an attorney is actually consulted, nor can a defendant use a request for legal consultation to significantly postpone testing. "If the lawyer is not physically present and cannot be reached promptly by telephone or otherwise," a defendant who has asked to consult with an attorney can be required to make a decision without the benefit of counsel's advice on the question. Where there has been a violation of the limited right to counsel recognized in *Gursey*, any resulting evidence may be suppressed at the subsequent criminal trial.

(Citations omitted). *See also People v. Shaw*, 72 N.Y.2d 1032, 1033-34, 534 N.Y.S.2d 929, 930, 531 N.E.2d 650 (1988); *People v. Gursey*, 22 N.Y.2d 224, 292 N.Y.S.2d 416, 239 N.E.2d 351 (1968).

The reason why the right to counsel is more limited in this regard than it is in other contexts is because, where chemical testing is concerned, the right to counsel comes from the Due Process Clause rather than from the 6th Amendment.

Nonetheless, in *People v. Washington*, 23 N.Y.3d 228, 989 N.Y.S.2d 670, 12 N.E.3d 1099 (2014), the Court of Appeals affirmed the suppression of a chemical test result where the defendant consented to the test but, unbeknownst to the defendant, an attorney had contacted the police department on the defendant's behalf prior to the administration of the test and demanded that no test be given. In so holding, the Court reasoned as follows:

> In our view, the statutory right to legal consultation applies when an attorney contacts the police before a chemical test for alcohol is performed and the police must alert the subject to the presence of counsel, whether the contact is made in person or telephonically. *Gursey* contemplated that a lawyer retained to represent a DWI arrestee can directly communicate with the police, reasoning that "law enforcement officials may not, without justification, prevent access between the criminal accused and [the] lawyer, available in person or by immediate telephone communication, if such access does not interfere unduly." The fact that defendant consented to the breathalyzer about the same time that the attorney was communicating with the police is not dispositive since defendant, after conferring with counsel, could have revoked her consent prior to administration of the test. The police therefore must advise the accused that a lawyer has made contact on the accused's behalf. Once so informed, the accused may choose to consult with counsel or forgo that option and proceed with the chemical test.

In this case, when the attorney telephoned the police to intervene on defendant's behalf, the police should have informed defendant of this development since breathalyzer testing had not yet begun. Defendant could then have decided if she wished to discuss her situation with counsel. Since the police officers here made no effort to advise defendant about the lawyer's communication and the People did not demonstrate that a notification of this nature would have been unreasonable under the circumstances, we hold that the chemical test was administered in violation of the statutorily-based *Gursey* right to counsel. Consequently, the courts below correctly concluded that defendant is entitled to suppression of the test results.

Id. at 233-34, 989 N.Y.S.2d at 674 (citations and footnote omitted).

§ 11:60   Defendant's right to additional chemical test

VTL § 1194(4)(b) (formerly VTL § 1194[8]) provides:

(b) Right to additional test. The person tested shall be permitted to choose a physician to administer a chemical test in addition to the one administered at the direction of the police officer.

This right is statutory (*i.e.*, not constitutional) in nature. *People v. Finnegan*, 85 N.Y.2d 53, 59, 623 N.Y.S.2d 546, 549, 647 N.E.2d 758 (1995). *See also People v. Alvarez*, 70 N.Y.2d 375, 381, 521 N.Y.S.2d 212, 215, 515 N.E.2d 898 (1987).

In *Finnegan*, the Court of Appeals held that:

The simple, straightforward declaration of Vehicle and Traffic Law § 1194(4)(b) is that defendants are entitled to their own additional chemical test. The statute is starkly silent as to any implementary duties imposed on the law enforcement personnel as to notice or to direct assistance in obtaining an independent chemical test . . . . The statutory right is the defendant's and so is the responsibility to take advantage of it.

We hold, therefore, that law enforcement personnel are not required to arrange for an independent test or to transport defendant to a place or person where the test may be performed. Of course, the police should not impede arrested individuals from exerting or accomplishing their statutory prerogative. The authorities should even assist persons in custody with appropriate advice and communication means, e.g., a telephone call opportunity. On the other hand, we have settled the general question that the police have no affirmative duty to gather or help gather evidence for an accused.

85 N.Y.2d at 58, 623 N.Y.S.2d at 548–49 (citations omitted).

This topic is covered at length in §§ 30:1 et seq., *infra*.

§ 11:61   Unconscious defendant need not be formally arrested for purposes of implied consent law

New York's implied consent law provides, in pertinent part, that:

Any person who operates a motor vehicle in this state shall be deemed to have given consent to a chemical test of one or more of the following: breath, blood, urine, or saliva, for the purpose of determining the alcoholic and/or drug content of the blood provided that such test is administered by or at the direction of a police officer with respect to a chemical test of breath, urine or saliva or, with respect to a chemical test of blood, at the direction of a police officer:

(1) having reasonable grounds to believe such person to have been operating in violation of any subdivision of [VTL § 1192] of this article and within two hours *after such person has been placed under arrest* for any such violation.

VTL § 1194(2)(a)(1) (emphasis added).

In *People v. Goodell*, 79 N.Y.2d 869, 581 N.Y.S.2d 157, 589 N.E.2d 380 (1992), the defendant was unconscious at the time the police arrived at the accident scene, and remained so at all relevant times. He claimed that his blood test result should have been suppressed on the ground that VTL § 1194(2)(a)(1) requires an actual, formal arrest—yet he was never formally arrested. In rejecting this claim, the Court of Appeals held as follows:

[A] formal arrest would have been an empty gesture in defendant's case, since defendant was unconscious when the police first arrived at the scene of the accident and he remained comatose for approximately two more weeks. Under these circumstances, we decline to hold that the police officer's failure formally to announce defendant's arrest was alone sufficient to vitiate his Vehicle and Traffic Law § 1194(2)(a)(1) authority to direct the administration of a chemical blood alcohol test (*cf., People v. Almond*, 151 A.D.2d 820, 542 N.Y.S.2d 59 [blood test taken pursuant to Vehicle and Traffic Law § 1194(1) (now § 1194[2][a][1]) suppressed where police found defendant in a conscious state but, without formally placing him under arrest, waited until subsequent medical treatment rendered him unconscious before administering test]).

Id. at 871, 581 N.Y.S.2d at 158.

§ 11:62   "Two-hour rule" inapplicable where defendant expressly and voluntarily consents to test

Virtually everyone involved in the field of DWI law is familiar with the so-called two-hour rule, which "provides that a chemical test must generally be administered within two hours of either the time of arrest for a violation of VTL § 1192 or the time of a positive breath screening test, whichever is later." *People v. Morris*, 8 Misc. 3d 360, ___, 793 N.Y.S.2d 754, 758 (N.Y. City Crim. Ct. 2005). *See also* VTL § 1194(2)(a).

Less well known is the fact that, in *People v. Atkins*, 85 N.Y.2d 1007, 1009, 630 N.Y.S.2d 965, 966, 654 N.E.2d 1213 (1995), the

Court of Appeals all but eliminated the rule, holding that "the two-hour limitation contained in Vehicle and Traffic Law § 1194(2)(a) has no application here where, as found by Appellate Term, defendant expressly and voluntarily consented to administration of the blood test." *See also People v. Ward*, 307 N.Y. 73, 76, 120 N.E.2d 211 (1954). In so holding, the *Atkins* Court stated both:

(a) That the two-hour rule does not apply to "the additional test which the driver must be permitted to have administered by a physician of his or her choosing under [VTL] section 1194(4)(b)." 85 N.Y.2d at 1009, 630 N.Y.S.2d at 966. *See also People v. Smith*, 18 N.Y.3d 544, 548 n.1, 942 N.Y.S.2d 426, 428 n.1, 965 N.E.2d 928 (2012); *People v. Finnegan*, 85 N.Y.2d 53, 59, 623 N.Y.S.2d 546, 549, 647 N.E.2d 758 (1995); and

(b) That there is no two-hour "time limit for court-ordered chemical testing under [VTL] section 1194(3)." 85 N.Y.2d at 1009, 630 N.Y.S.2d at 966. *See also People v. Smith*, 18 N.Y.3d 544, 548 n.1, 942 N.Y.S.2d 426, 428 n.1, 965 N.E.2d 928 (2012); *People v. McGrath*, 135 A.D.2d 60, 524 N.Y.S.2d 214 (2d Dep't), aff'd for the reasons stated in the opinion below, order aff'd, 73 N.Y.2d 826, 537 N.Y.S.2d 480, 534 N.E.2d 318 (1988).

This topic is covered at length in §§ 31:1 et seq., *infra*.

§ 11:63   Constitutionality of VTL §§ 1192(1), (2) and (3)

In *People v. Cruz*, 48 N.Y.2d 419, 422, 423 N.Y.S.2d 625, 626, 399 N.E.2d 513 (1979), the Court of Appeals addressed the issue of "whether subdivision 1 of section 1192 of the Vehicle and Traffic Law, which prohibits driving while the ability to operate a motor vehicle 'is impaired by the consumption of alcohol', and subdivision 3, which prohibits driving 'while * * * in an intoxicated condition', are unconstitutionally vague in a case where the driver has refused to submit to any scientific test for determining the amount of alcohol he has consumed." The lower courts in *Cruz* "held that the statutory terms, impaired and intoxicated, were too vague and indefinite to satisfy due process requirements when applied to cases where no chemical test results were available." 48 N.Y.2d at 423, 423 N.Y.S.2d at 626.

The Court of Appeals reversed, holding that "subdivisions 1 and 3 of section 1192 of the Vehicle and Traffic Law are not unconstitutionally vague or indefinite when applied to a case where an analysis of the driver's blood alcohol content is unavailable." 48 N.Y.2d at 428, 423 N.Y.S.2d at 630. *See also People v. Khan*, 291 A.D.2d 898, __, 737 N.Y.S.2d 738, 739 (4th Dep't 2002); *People v. Stack*, 140 A.D.2d 389, __, 527 N.Y.S.2d 569, 570 (2d Dep't 1988).

VTL § 1192(2) has also been found to be constitutional. *See, e.g.*, *People v. Golley*, 195 A.D.2d 713, 601 N.Y.S.2d 871 (3d Dep't 1993); *People v. Mascolo*, 175 A.D.2d 812, __, 572 N.Y.S.2d 937, 938 (2d Dep't 1991); *People v. Perez*, 73 A.D.2d 677, 423 N.Y.S.2d 220 (2d Dep't 1979); *People v. Lebron*, 130 Misc. 2d 831, __, 501 N.Y.S.2d 975, 976–77 (App. Term, 1st Dep't 1986); *People v. Schmidt*, 124 Misc. 2d 102, 478 N.Y.S.2d 482 (City Crim. Ct. 1984).

§ 11:64 Constitutionality of VTL § 1192(4)

In *People v. Rossi*, 163 A.D.2d 660, __, 558 N.Y.S.2d 698, 700–01 (3d Dep't 1990), the Appellate Division, Third Department, held that VTL § 1192(4) is constitutional. *See also People v. Percz*, 100 Misc. 2d 1018, 420 N.Y.S.2d 477 (Suffolk Co. Dist. Ct. 1979). *See generally People v. Primiano*, 16 Misc. 3d 1023, 843 N.Y.S.2d 799 (Sullivan Co. Ct. 2007) (addressing potential challenge to VTL § 1192(4-a)).

§ 11:65 Constitutionality of VTL § 1192(9)

VTL § 1192(9) (formerly VTL § 1196(1)) provides as follows:

Conviction of a different charge. A driver may be convicted of a violation of subdivision one, two or three of this section, notwithstanding that the charge laid before the court alleged a violation of subdivision two or three of this section, and regardless of whether or not such conviction is based on a plea of guilty.

In *People v. Farmer*, 36 N.Y.2d 386, 390, 369 N.Y.S.2d 44, 45, 330 N.E.2d 22 (1975), the Court of Appeals held that this statute is constitutional. *See generally People v. Clapper*, 123 A.D.2d 484, __, 506 N.Y.S.2d 494, 496 (3d Dep't 1986) ("The Legislature has specifically provided that a defendant may be convicted of violating subdivisions 1, 2 or 3 even if only charged with violating subdivisions 2 or 3 of Vehicle and Traffic Law § 1192"); *People v. Crandall*, 199 A.D.2d 867, __, 606 N.Y.S.2d 357, 358 (3d Dep't 1993) (same); *People v. Ebner*, 195 A.D.2d 1006, __, 600 N.Y.S.2d 569, 570 (4th Dep't 1993) (same).

§ 11:66 Constitutionality of VTL § 1193(1)(c)

VTL § 1193(1)(c) (formerly VTL § 1192(5)), permits the charging of felony DWI where the defendant has been convicted of DWI one or more times within the previous 10 years. Such enhancement of a subsequent offense is constitutional. *See, e.g.*, *People v. Butler*, 96 A.D.2d 140, 468 N.Y.S.2d 274 (4th Dep't 1983); *People v. Maldonado*, 173 Misc. 2d 612, __, 661 N.Y.S.2d 937, 940–41 (Nassau Co. Sup. Ct. 1997). *See generally Nichols v. U.S.*, 511 U.S. 738, 747, 114 S. Ct. 1921, 1927, 128 L. Ed. 2d 745 (1994) (enhancement statutes have repeatedly been upheld).

§ 11:67   Constitutionality of VTL § 1193(2)(b)(3)

VTL § 1193(2)(b)(3) addresses the length of the minimum driver's license revocation for repeat DWI offenders. In *People v. Demperio*, 86 N.Y.2d 549, 551, 634 N.Y.S.2d 672, 673, 658 N.E.2d 718 (1995) (per curiam), "[d]efendant argued, and both Town Court and County Court agreed, that Vehicle and Traffic Law § 1193(2)(b)(3) is unconstitutionally vague in that it does not inform violators that they must make a new application in order to have a revoked license reinstated." In reversing the lower courts, the Court of Appeals held as follows:

> The word "revoke"—meaning to annul, void or cancel—is commonly understood as having a core element of permanence. Moreover, any possible doubt as to the meaning of the word as used in Vehicle and Traffic Law § 1193(2)(b)(3) would be laid to rest by the immediately following paragraph (not cited in the opinion of either lower court):
>
> "(c) Reissuance of licenses; restrictions. (1) Except as otherwise provided in this paragraph, where a license is revoked pursuant to paragraph (b) of this subdivision, no new license shall be issued after the expiration of the minimum period specified in such paragraph, except in the discretion of the commissioner."
>
> This statute alone gave defendant reason to know that upon revocation of his license, a new license application was required.

Id. at 551–52, 634 N.Y.S.2d at 673 (footnote omitted).

In a footnote, the Court pointed out that DMV "sends the following written notices (form C-40) to persons whose drivers' licenses have been suspended or revoked because of alcohol-related offenses: 'If your license was revoked, you must apply to the Department of Motor Vehicles for a new license.'" *Id.* at 552 n.*, 634 N.Y.S.2d at 673 n.*.

§ 11:68   Constitutionality of VTL § 1194(2)(b)(3)

At arraignment in a chemical test refusal case, the Court is required to temporarily suspend the defendant's driving privileges pending the outcome of a DMV refusal hearing. *See* VTL § 1194(2)(b)(3) ("For persons placed under arrest for a violation of any subdivision of [VTL § 1192], the license or permit to drive and any non-resident operating privilege shall, upon the basis of such written report, be temporarily suspended by the court without notice pending the determination of a hearing as provided in [VTL § 1194(2)(c)]"). *See also* 15 NYCRR § 139.3(a).

In *Application of Ventura*, 108 Misc. 2d 281, 437 N.Y.S.2d 538 (Monroe Co. Sup. Ct. 1981), the Court held that this procedure does not violate the Due Process Clause. *See generally Mackey v. Montrym*, 443 U.S. 1, 99 S. Ct. 2612, 61 L. Ed. 2d 321 (1979).

§ 11:69 Constitutionality of VTL § 1194(2)(c)

The provisions of VTL § 1194 pertaining to chemical testing and chemical test refusals were formerly contained in VTL § 71-a. In *Schutt v. MacDuff*, 205 Misc. 43, 127 N.Y.S.2d 116 (Orange Co. Sup. Ct. 1954), the Orange County Supreme Court found the chemical test refusal revocation portion of the statute to be unconstitutional "because of the failure to contain a provision limiting its application to a case where there has been a lawful arrest and in that there is no provision entitling the licensee to an ultimate hearing upon an adequate record before the final taking away of his license." 205 Misc. at __, 127 N.Y.S.2d at 128. As a result of *MacDuff*, the statute was amended to require, *inter alia*, a lawful arrest and a meaningful Due Process hearing before a driver's license can be revoked for a chemical test refusal. *See* VTL § 1194(2)(c).

While the current procedure has never explicitly been found to be constitutional, the Court of Appeals' decision in *Gray v. Adduci*, 73 N.Y.2d 741, 536 N.Y.S.2d 40, 532 N.E.2d 1268 (1988), makes clear that any challenge to the constitutionality of the statute would fail.

§ 11:70 Constitutionality of VTL § 1194(2)(f)

VTL § 1194(2)(f) (formerly VTL § 1194(4)) provides that:

> Evidence of a refusal to submit to [a] chemical test or any portion thereof shall be admissible in any trial, proceeding or hearing based upon a violation of the provisions of [VTL § 1192] but only upon a showing that the person was given sufficient warning, in clear and unequivocal language, of the effect of such refusal and that the person persisted in the refusal.

In *People v. Thomas*, 46 N.Y.2d 100, 103, 412 N.Y.S.2d 845, 846, 385 N.E.2d 584 (1978), the Court of Appeals held that this statute is constitutional, and that it "does not violate the defendant's privilege against self incrimination under either the Federal or the State Constitution." *See also* 46 N.Y.2d at 110, 412 N.Y.S.2d at 851 ("We conclude that the evidence of defendant's persistent refusal to take the test was properly admitted, that the jury was correctly charged that it could consider such evidence, and that [VTL § 1194(4)] is not violative of a defendant's rights under either [the] Federal or New York State Constitution").

§ 11:71 Constitutionality of implied consent law

New York's implied consent law provides, in pertinent part, that:

> Any person who operates a motor vehicle in this state shall be

deemed to have given consent to a chemical test of one or more of the following: breath, blood, urine, or saliva, for the purpose of determining the alcoholic and/or drug content of the blood provided that such test is administered by or at the direction of a police officer with respect to a chemical test of breath, urine or saliva or, with respect to a chemical test of blood, at the direction of a police officer:

> (1) having reasonable grounds to believe such person to have been operating in violation of any subdivision of [VTL § 1192] of this article and within two hours after such person has been placed under arrest for any such violation; . . . [or]

> (2) within two hours after a breath test, as provided in [VTL § 1194(1)(b)], indicates that alcohol has been consumed by such person and in accordance with the rules and regulations established by the police force of which the officer is a member.

VTL § 1194(2)(a).

In *People v. Kates*, 53 N.Y.2d 591, 594–96, 444 N.Y.S.2d 446, 448–49, 428 N.E.2d 852 (1981), the Court of Appeals held that this statute is constitutional. *See generally People v. Thomas*, 46 N.Y.2d 100, 110, 412 N.Y.S.2d 845, 851, 385 N.E.2d 584 (1978) ("the admissibility of refusal evidence may also be viewed as a permissible condition reasonably attached to the grant of permission to operate a motor vehicle on the highways of the State").

§ 11:72   Constitutionality of prompt suspension law

In *Pringle v. Wolfe*, 88 N.Y.2d 426, 646 N.Y.S.2d 82, 668 N.E.2d 1376 (1996), the Court of Appeals declared VTL § 1193(2)(e)(7) to be constitutional. In so holding, the Court summed up the due process issue as follows:

> In sum, though the private interest affected by the prompt suspension law is substantial, the severity of the license suspension is mitigated by its temporary duration, the availability of a conditional license and hardship relief, and the significant protection of a presuspension judicial hearing, which militates heavily in favor of the statute's constitutionality. Further weighing against the driver's interest in maintaining his license are the slight risk of an erroneous deprivation and the overriding State interest in "the prompt removal of a safety hazard" from its streets. Based on the foregoing, we hold that the prompt suspension law affords the driver all the process that is constitutionally due.

Id. at 435, 646 N.Y.S.2d at 87–88 (citations omitted).

This topic is covered at length in §§ 45:1 et seq., *infra*.

§ 11:73   Constitutionality of compulsory chemical tests

New York has two statutes which authorize a Court to order a compulsory chemical test prior to the filing of an accusatory instrument against the defendant. *See* VTL § 1194(3); CPL § 690.10. Both statutes have been found to be constitutional. *See People v. Elysee*, 12 N.Y.3d 100, 105, 876 N.Y.S.2d 677, 679–80, 904 N.E.2d 813 (2009) ("chemical tests can . . . be compelled by court order under Vehicle and Traffic Law § 1194(3) when, among other circumstances, 'a person other than the operator was killed or suffered serious physical injury . . .; and such person operated the vehicle in violation of any subdivision of section eleven hundred ninety-two of this article . . . and . . . has been placed under lawful arrest; and . . . has refused to submit to a chemical test . . . or is unable to give consent to such a test' ") (internal quotation marks omitted); *Matter of Abe A.*, 56 N.Y.2d 288, 291, 452 N.Y.S.2d 6, 7, 437 N.E.2d 265 (1982) ("we hold a court order to obtain a blood sample of a suspect may issue provided the People establish (1) probable cause to believe the suspect has committed the crime, (2) a 'clear indication' that relevant material evidence will be found, and (3) the method used to secure it is safe and reliable. In addition, the issuing court must weigh the seriousness of the crime, the importance of the evidence to the investigation and the unavailability of less intrusive means of obtaining it, on the one hand, against concern for the suspect's constitutional right to be free from bodily intrusion on the other. Only if this stringent standard is met, as we conclude it was here, may the intrusion be sustained"). *See also* § 11:83, *infra*.

In this regard, the Court of Appeals has made clear that:

> Taking a driver's blood for alcohol analysis does not . . . involve an unreasonable search under the Fourth Amendment when there is [1] probable cause, [2] exigent circumstances and [3] a reasonable examination procedure. So long as these requirements are met . . . the test may be performed absent defendant's consent and indeed over his objection without violating his Fourth Amendment rights.

People v. Kates, 53 N.Y.2d 591, 594–95, 444 N.Y.S.2d 446, 448, 428 N.E.2d 852 (1981) (citation omitted). *See also Schmerber v. California*, 384 U.S. 757, 86 S. Ct. 1826, 16 L. Ed. 2d 908 (1966); *Missouri v. McNeely*, 133 S. Ct. 1552, 1558, 185 L. Ed. 2d 696 (2013).

This topic is covered at length in §§ 40:1 et seq., *infra*.

§ 11:74 Constitutionality of pretext stops to hunt for drunk drivers

Where a police officer has probable cause to believe that a motorist has committed a traffic infraction, it is permissible for the officer to use such infraction as a pretext to stop the motorist in order to ascertain whether he or she is intoxicated. *See, e.g., People v. Wright*, 98 N.Y.2d 657, 658-59, 746 N.Y.S.2d 273,

273-74, 773 N.E.2d 1011 (2002); *People v. Robinson*, 97 N.Y.2d 341, 349, 741 N.Y.S.2d 147, 151, 767 N.E.2d 638 (2001) ("We hold that where a police officer has probable cause to believe that the driver of an automobile has committed a traffic violation, a stop does not violate article I, § 12 of the New York State Constitution. In making that determination of probable cause, neither the primary motivation of the officer nor a determination of what a reasonable traffic officer would have done under the circumstances is relevant"). *See generally People v. Pealer*, 20 N.Y.3d 447, 457 n.2, 962 N.Y.S.2d 592, 598 n.2, 985 N.E.2d 903 (2013), petition for cert. filed (U.S. May 16, 2013).

On the other hand, the *Robinson* Court made clear that:

> To be sure, the story does not end when the police stop a vehicle for a traffic infraction. Our holding in this case addresses only the initial police action upon which the vehicular stop was predicated. The scope, duration and intensity of the seizure, as well as any search made by the police subsequent to that stop, remain subject to the strictures of article I, § 12, and judicial review.

97 N.Y.2d at 353, 741 N.Y.S.2d at 154.

§ 11:75 Constitutionality of DWI checkpoints

A properly administered DWI checkpoint is constitutional. *See, e.g., Michigan Dept. of State Police v. Sitz*, 496 U.S. 444, 110 S. Ct. 2481, 110 L. Ed. 2d 412 (1990); *People v. Scott*, 63 N.Y.2d 518, 483 N.Y.S.2d 649, 473 N.E.2d 1 (1984). In *Scott*, the Court of Appeals held that:

> A roadblock established pursuant to a written directive of the County Sheriff for the purpose of detecting and deterring driving while intoxicated or while impaired, and as to which operating personnel are prohibited from administering sobriety tests unless they observe listed criteria, indicative of intoxication, which give substantial cause to believe that the operator is intoxicated, is constitutionally permissible, notwithstanding that the location of the roadblock is moved several times during the three- to four-hour period of operation, and notwithstanding that legislative initiatives have also played a part in reducing the incidence of driving while intoxicated in recent years.

63 N.Y.2d at 522, 483 N.Y.S.2d at 650.

In so holding, the *Scott* Court made clear that, to be constitutional, a sobriety checkpoint (1) may not "intrude to an impermissible degree upon the privacy of motorists approaching the checkpoint," (2) must be "maintained in accordance with a uniform procedure which afford[s] little discretion to operating personnel," and (3) must utilize "adequate precautions as to safety, lighting and fair warning of the existence of the checkpoint." 63 N.Y.2d at 526, 483 N.Y.S.2d at 652.

This topic is covered at length in §§ 5:1 et seq., *supra*.

§ 11:76 Constitutionality of vehicle seizure/forfeiture laws

As long as sufficient Due Process protections are in place, the seizure and subsequent forfeiture of a drunk driver's vehicle is permissible. *See, e.g., County of Nassau v. Canavan*, 1 N.Y.3d 134, 138, 770 N.Y.S.2d 277, 281, 802 N.E.2d 616 (2003) ("when implemented pursuant to a carefully drafted statute, civil forfeiture of automobiles can be an extremely effective tool in the battle against drunk driving . . . . Driving while intoxicated poses a grave risk of injury or death to innocent motorists and pedestrians. Nevertheless, . . . we conclude that the ordinance adopted by Nassau County did not satisfy constitutional requirements").

Where a vehicle is seized pending a forfeiture proceeding, the defendant must be provided with a prompt, meaningful Due Process hearing. 1 N.Y.3d at 144–45, 770 N.Y.S.2d at 286 ("due process requires that a prompt post-seizure retention hearing before a neutral magistrate be afforded, with adequate notice, to all defendants whose cars are seized and held for possible forfeiture. At such a hearing, the County must establish that probable cause existed for the defendant's initial warrantless arrest, that it is likely to succeed on the merits of the forfeiture action, and that retention is necessary to preserve the vehicle from destruction or sale during the pendency of the proceeding"). *See also Krimstock v. Kelly*, 306 F.3d 40 (2d Cir. 2002); *Property Clerk of Police Dept. of City of New York v. Harris*, 9 N.Y.3d 237, 239–40, 848 N.Y.S.2d 588, 590, 878 N.E.2d 1004 (2007) (pursuant to *Krimstock* and *Canavan*, "due process requires that an innocent co-owner be given an opportunity to demonstrate that his or her present possessory interest in a seized vehicle outweighs the City's interest in continuing impoundment") (footnote omitted). *See generally People v. Ramroop*, 50 Misc. 3d 1090, 27 N.Y.S.3d 811 (N.Y. City Crim. Ct. 2016).

Notably, where the People choose to impound a defendant's vehicle during the pendency of the case, the defendant is not responsible for storage fees. *See, e.g., Catti v. W.E. Bryant's, Inc.*, 107 A.D.2d 865, __, 484 N.Y.S.2d 307, 308 (3d Dep't 1985) ("Although the District Attorney has the power to impound plaintiff's tractor pending investigation to preserve possible evidence, such authority does not impose upon plaintiff the cost of said impoundment and investigatory work. Indeed, defendant has presented no authority to support such an argument") (citation omitted); *Kane v. Caprara*, 182 Misc. 2d 572, 699 N.Y.S.2d 275 (Schenectady City Ct. 1999).

§ 11:77　Court cannot impose "scarlet letter" penalty

In *People v. Letterlough*, 86 N.Y.2d 259, 261, 631 N.Y.S.2d 105, 106, 655 N.E.2d 146 (1995) the sentencing Court imposed a condition of probation that, if the defendant regained his driving privileges, he would have to affix a fluorescent sign stating "CONVICTED DWI" to the license plates of any vehicle that he operated. The Court of Appeals reversed, holding that "the condition is not reasonably related to defendant's rehabilitation, and, more generally, because, in the absence of more specific legislation, such a condition is outside the authority of the court to impose." In addition, the Court noted that "[t]he distraction occasioned by special judicially ordered 'scarlet letter' plates and the reactions of other motorists upon seeing them also poses a potential safety threat." *Id.* at 268, 631 N.Y.S.2d at 110. *See also Bursac v. Suozzi*, 22 Misc. 3d 328, 868 N.Y.S.2d 470, 37 Media L. Rep. (BNA) 1109 (Nassau Co. Sup. Ct. 2008) (Court granted DWI defendant's petition seeking a permanent injunction enjoining and restraining County Executive from posting petitioner's name, picture and identifying information on "Wall of Shame" Internet website and directing the removal of same).

Similarly, a condition of probation that the defendant must attend A.A. meetings, which are religious in nature, without offering a choice of other alcohol treatment providers has been held to violate the Establishment Clause of the First Amendment. *See Warner v. Orange County Dept. of Probation*, 115 F.3d 1068 (2d Cir. 1997).

§ 11:78　Conviction of both VTL §§ 1192(2) and 1192(3) does not violate Double Jeopardy

In *People v. Carvalho*, 174 A.D.2d 687, __, 571 N.Y.S.2d 332, 333 (2d Dep't 1991), "[t]he defendant contend[ed] that the indictment charging him with violating Vehicle and Traffic Law §§ 1192(2) and 1192(3) violated the constitutional prohibition against double jeopardy." In rejecting this claim, the Appellate Division, Second Department, held that:

It is clear that subdivisions 2 and 3 of Vehicle and Traffic Law § 1192 were intended to be separate crimes, neither mutually inclusive nor mutually exclusive. To suggest that the People should be compelled to elect between the two counts at any stage of the criminal proceedings would run counter to the intention of the Legislature which has determined that the social evil in question—driving while intoxicated—warrants separate offenses.

174 A.D.2d at __, 571 N.Y.S.2d at 333. *See also People v. Rudd*, 41 A.D.2d 875, __, 343 N.Y.S.2d 17, 19 (3d Dep't 1973); *People v. McDonough*, 39 A.D.2d 188, __, 333 N.Y.S.2d 128, 129 (3d Dep't 1972).

§ 11:79 Prosecution for DWI following chemical test refusal revocation by DMV does not violate Double Jeopardy

The prosecution of a defendant for a violation of VTL § 1192 following a chemical test refusal revocation arising out of the same incident does not violate the Double Jeopardy Clause. *Brennan v. Kmiotek*, 233 A.D.2d 870, 649 N.Y.S.2d 611 (4th Dep't 1996). *See also Barnes v. Tofany*, 27 N.Y.2d 74, 77, 313 N.Y.S.2d 690, 693, 261 N.E.2d 617 (1970) ("We hold that the 'double punishment' feature of our Vehicle and Traffic statute—one criminal and the other administrative—is lawful"); *People v. Frank*, 166 Misc. 2d 277, 631 N.Y.S.2d 1014 (City Crim. Ct. 1995).

§ 11:80 Prosecution for DWI following suspension pending prosecution does not violate Double Jeopardy

The prosecution of a defendant for DWI following the suspension of his or her driver's license pending prosecution does not violate the Double Jeopardy Clause. *See People v. Haishun*, 238 A.D.2d 521, 656 N.Y.S.2d 660 (2d Dep't 1997); *People v. Roach*, 226 A.D.2d 55, 649 N.Y.S.2d 607 (4th Dep't 1996); *Smith v. County Court of Essex County*, 224 A.D.2d 89, 649 N.Y.S.2d 507 (3d Dep't 1996); *People v. Malone*, 175 Misc. 2d 893, 673 N.Y.S.2d 809 (App. Term, 2d Dep't 1997); *People v. Busby*, 175 Misc. 2d 509, 670 N.Y.S.2d 960 (App. Term, 2d Dep't 1997); *People v. Steele*, 172 Misc. 2d 860, 661 N.Y.S.2d 908 (App. Term, 2d Dep't 1997); *People v. Uzquaino*, 172 Misc. 2d 388, 661 N.Y.S.2d 438 (App. Term, 2d Dep't 1997); *People v. Conrad*, 169 Misc. 2d 1066, 654 N.Y.S.2d 226 (App. Term, 2d Dep't 1996). *See generally People v. Demetsenare*, 243 A.D.2d 777, __, 663 N.Y.S.2d 299, 303 (3d Dep't 1997) ("We reject defendant's contention that double jeopardy forecloses his conviction based on a prior suspension of his license pursuant to Vehicle and Traffic Law § 510(3) for the same events").

Courts have similarly rejected the argument that the prompt suspension law violates the Equal Protection Clause. *See Roach*, 226 A.D.2d at __, 649 N.Y.S.2d at 610; *People v. Condarco*, 166 Misc. 2d 470, 633 N.Y.S.2d 930 (City Crim. Ct. 1995); *People v. Boulton*, 164 Misc. 2d 604, 625 N.Y.S.2d 428 (Troy City Ct. 1995).

§ 11:81 Double Jeopardy effect of dismissal for prosecutor's failure to give sufficient opening statement

In *People v. Kurtz*, 51 N.Y.2d 380, 434 N.Y.S.2d 200, 414 N.E.2d 699 (1980), the prosecutor gave a legally insufficient opening statement at trial, in violation of CPL § 260.30(3), which resulted in the dismissal of DWI and speeding charges against the defendant. The primary issue in the case was whether re-trial was barred by the Double Jeopardy Clause. The Court of Appeals held that re-trial was not barred, reasoning as follows:

> [T]he doctrine [of Double Jeopardy] distinguishes between trial orders terminating the trial in the defendant's favor prior to any determination of guilt or innocence and those orders which terminate the trial based on evidentiary insufficiency. Because a dismissal based on insufficient evidence is tantamount to an acquittal, reprosecution is precluded in the latter category of cases. Retrial of cases falling within the former category of dismissals, however, is permissible because "the defendant, by deliberately choosing to seek termination of the proceeding against him on a basis unrelated to factual guilt or innocence of the offense of which he is accused, suffers no injury cognizable under the Double Jeopardy Clause."
>
> In the case before us, the trial court dismissed the action on defendant's motion solely because of the insufficiency of the prosecutor's opening statement. As mentioned earlier, this dismissal was not premised on any evidentiary determination that the People were not entitled to a conviction or that the prosecutor had acted in bad faith by deliberately delivering an incomplete opening in order to terminate the trial over defendant's objection. Rather, dismissal here was the result of the trial court's misconception of the requirements of CPL 260.30 (subd. 3) and occurred without any evaluation on the trial court's part as to the factual elements of the offenses with which defendant was charged. Inasmuch as this dismissal . . . in no sense resembles an acquittal of the defendant and indeed appears functionally indistinguishable from the declaration of a mistrial, retrial of defendant is prohibited neither by the double jeopardy clauses of the State and Federal Constitutions nor by the statutory double jeopardy provisions.

51 N.Y.2d at 386–87, 434 N.Y.S.2d at 204–05 (citations and footnote omitted).

Notably, the *Kurtz* Court disapproved of the manner in which the trial court handled the defendant's motion to dismiss for failure of the People to give a sufficient opening statement, and set forth guidelines as to how trial courts should address such motions in the future:

> In this case, . . . the only deficiency in the opening statement was that it did not adequately amplify the charges against defendant and the facts to be proven in support thereof. Moreover, before dismissing the information, the Trial Judge not only failed to inform the prosecutor of the nature of the defect in his opening, but denied him the opportunity to correct this deficiency before permitting the trial to go forward. As County Court concluded, such action was an abuse of discretion, contrary to law.

The better practice concerning such motions directed at the adequacy of the prosecutor's opening statement would be that a motion should be made immediately after the prosecutor has completed his opening to the jury. The trial court should then inform the prosecutor of the nature of the defect, if any, and afford him an opportunity to rectify it. If the prosecutor is unable to do so, then the motion to dismiss the accusatory instrument must be granted. Under no circumstances should the court allow the trial to proceed without first ruling on the motion . . . . [I]t was the belated disposition of the motion which has created the difficulty in this case, a problem which should be avoided in all other cases.

51 N.Y.2d at 385–86, 434 N.Y.S.2d at 203–04 (citation omitted). *See also People v. Baltes*, 75 A.D.3d 656, __, 904 N.Y.S.2d 554, 558 (3d Dep't 2010), leave to appeal denied, 15 N.Y.3d 918, 913 N.Y.S.2d 645, 939 N.E.2d 811 (2010); *Lacerva v. Dwyer*, 177 A.D.2d 747, 575 N.Y.S.2d 984 (3d Dep't 1991).

§ 11:82 Imposition of punitive damages in civil case arising out of DWI-related accident does not violate Double Jeopardy

In *Wittman v. Gilson*, 70 N.Y.2d 970, 971–72, 525 N.Y.S.2d 795, 796, 520 N.E.2d 514 (1988):

Plaintiff's daughter died from injuries suffered in a head-on collision between the car she was driving and a vehicle driven by defendant while intoxicated. Defendant was charged with criminally negligent homicide and pleaded guilty. Shortly thereafter, plaintiff, administratrix of her daughter's estate, commenced this action seeking compensatory damages for wrongful death and for conscious pain and suffering of her decedent. Punitive damages were also sought. The trial court directed a verdict as to civil liability and the jury returned a verdict in the amount of $2,853 for wrongful death, $4,500 for conscious pain and suffering, and $45,000 in punitive damages.

On appeal, defendant argue[d] that punitive damages following a criminal conviction arising out of the same drunk driving incident should not be imposed as a matter of policy as implicated by the constitutional prohibition against double jeopardy.

The Court of Appeals disagreed, holding as follows:

[W]hile punitive damages and criminal sanctions share a common purpose of punishing misconduct, there are also significant distinctions between the two. Unlike the sanction imposed on behalf of all the people of the State in a criminal case, punitive damages in a civil case context afford the injured party a personal monetary recovery over and above compensatory loss. The procedures and standards of proof are also, of course, very different. Additionally, a civil verdict directing payment of punitive damages does not carry the same heavy societal stigma stamped by a criminal conviction no matter what sentence is imposed.

Whittman v. Gilson, 70 N.Y.2d at 972, 525 N.Y.S.2d at 796.

§ 11:83   Admissibility of Alco-Sensor test evidence at trial

Evidence concerning the administration of an Alco-Sensor test, as well as evidence of the actual Alco-Sensor test results, is clearly inadmissible at trial. *See People v. Thomas*, 121 A.D.2d 73, __, 509 N.Y.S.2d 668, 671 (4th Dep't 1986), order aff'd, 70 N.Y.2d 823, 523 N.Y.S.2d 437, 517 N.E.2d 1323 (1987). *See also People v. MacDonald*, 227 A.D.2d 672, __, 641 N.Y.S.2d 749, 751 (3d Dep't), order aff'd, 89 N.Y.2d 908, 653 N.Y.S.2d 267, 675 N.E.2d 1219 (1996). *Thomas* is the seminal case in this area. It provides, in pertinent part:

> The Alco-Sensor testimony was clearly not admissible to show intoxication. It is well settled that "[t]here must be a sufficient showing of reliability of the test results before scientific evidence may be introduced." "[S]cientific evidence will only be admitted at trial if the procedure and results are generally accepted as reliable in the scientific community." Thus, the Alco-Sensor evidence should have been excluded because as it was presented to the jury it served as proof of intoxication and the People failed to lay a proper foundation showing its reliability for this purpose . . . . Moreover, cases from other jurisdictions hold that the Alco-Sensor test is not reliable evidence of intoxication. * * *
>
> In our view, evidence regarding the Alco-Sensor test had no place in the trial and the objection to its admission should have been sustained. The jury should not have been given the opportunity "to use the screening test result to corroborate the evidential test result."

121 A.D.2d at __, __, 509 N.Y.S.2d at 671, 673 (citations omitted). *See also People v. Santana*, 31 Misc. 3d 1232(A), 2011 WL 2119503 (N.Y. City Crim. Ct. 2011); *People v. Gray*, 190 Misc. 2d 40, __, 736 N.Y.S.2d 856, 860 (Kings Co. Sup. Ct. 2002).

This topic is covered at length in §§ 7:1 et seq., *supra.*

§ 11:84   Admissibility of chemical test result obtained pursuant to CPL § 690.10 search warrant

In *People v. Moselle*, 57 N.Y.2d 97, 101, 454 N.Y.S.2d 292, 293, 439 N.E.2d 1235 (1982), the Court of Appeals held that:

> Absent a manifestation of a defendant's consent thereto, blood samples taken without a court order other than in conformity with the provisions of subdivisions 1 and 2 of section 1194 of the Vehicle and Traffic Law are inadmissible in prosecutions for operating a motor vehicle while under the influence of alcohol under section 1192 of that law. Beyond that, blood samples taken without a defendant's consent are inadmissible in prosecutions under the Penal Law unless taken pursuant to an authorizing court order.

In *People v. Casadei*, 66 N.Y.2d 846, 847, 498 N.Y.S.2d 357, 358, 489 N.E.2d 244 (1985):

Defendant was involved in a two-car accident in which the driver of the other vehicle was fatally injured. Subsequently charged in an eight-count indictment with manslaughter in the second degree, criminally negligent homicide, driving while intoxicated, and other violations of the Vehicle and Traffic Law, he sought to suppress the results of a chemical blood test administered without his consent pursuant to a search warrant (CPL 690.10).

Relying on *Moselle*, the defendant claimed that VTL § 1194 was the exclusive means of obtaining a blood sample for violations of Vehicle and Traffic Law § 1192. The Court of Appeals held that:

Although two of the three prosecutions in *Moselle* involved Penal Law violations in addition to Vehicle and Traffic Law violations, there was not in those cases, as there is here, a court order based on probable cause, authorizing the taking of a blood sample. It is clear that a search warrant may validly be issued to obtain a blood sample, in the event of a violation of the Penal Law, and, in such circumstances, we decline to extend *Moselle* to require separate resort to Vehicle and Traffic Law § 1194 to sustain Vehicle and Traffic Law offenses which are part of the same indictment. Moreover, the Legislature has amended Vehicle and Traffic Law § 1194 (L. 1983, ch. 481) to overrule *Moselle* on its facts.

66 N.Y.2d at 848, 498 N.Y.S.2d at 358 (citation omitted). *See also People v. Ladd*, 89 N.Y.2d 893, 896, 653 N.Y.S.2d 259, 261, 675 N.E.2d 1211 (1996).

§ 11:85   Admissibility of evidence of defendant's reputation for sobriety

In *People v. Nester*, 275 N.Y. 628, 628–29, 11 N.E.2d 790 (1937) (per curiam), the defendant claimed that the trial court improperly excluded evidence of his reputation for sobriety. In a 4-3 decision, the Court of Appeals affirmed the defendant's conviction of DWI.

In *People v. O'Brien*, 77 A.D.3d 1445, __, 908 N.Y.S.2d 787, 788 (4th Dep't 2010), leave to appeal denied, 15 N.Y.3d 923, 913 N.Y.S.2d 649, 939 N.E.2d 815 (2010), the Appellate Division, Fourth Department, held that:

Although defendant preserved for our review his further contention that the court erred in precluding him from calling [two sitting] judges as character witnesses to testify concerning his reputation for "sobriety," we conclude that defendant's contention lacks merit inasmuch as the probative value of such testimony was "substantially outweighed by the danger that it [would] unfairly prejudice the [prosecution] or mislead the jury."

(Citation omitted).

§ 11:86 Sufficiency of "check box" Supporting Deposition/ DWI Bill of Particulars

In *People v. Hohmeyer*, 70 N.Y.2d 41, 517 N.Y.S.2d 448, 510 N.E.2d 317 (1987), the Court of Appeals upheld the use of the "check box" format Supporting Deposition/DWI Bill of Particulars commonly used in DWI cases in much of the State. An example of such a supporting deposition is set forth at Appendix 14.

Supporting depositions are covered at length in §§ 17:1 et seq., *infra*.

§ 11:87 Court must advise defendant of direct consequences of plea

Prior to accepting a guilty plea from a defendant, the Court is required to advise the defendant of "direct" consequences of the plea—but is *not* required to advise the defendant of "collateral" consequences thereof. *See, e.g., People v. Cornell*, 16 N.Y.3d 801, 921 N.Y.S.2d 641, 946 N.E.2d 740 (2011); *People v. Harnett*, 16 N.Y.3d 200, 205, 920 N.Y.S.2d 246, 248, 945 N.E.2d 439 (2011); *People v. Gravino*, 14 N.Y.3d 546, 553, 902 N.Y.S.2d 851, 855, 928 N.E.2d 1048 (2010); *People v. Catu*, 4 N.Y.3d 242, 244, 792 N.Y.S.2d 887, 888, 825 N.E.2d 1081 (2005); *People v. Ford*, 86 N.Y.2d 397, 403, 633 N.Y.S.2d 270, 272, 657 N.E.2d 265 (1995).

In *Harnett*, the Court of Appeals summarized the law in this area:

> Our cases have drawn a line between the direct and collateral consequences of a plea. The importance of the distinction is that a trial court "*must* advise a defendant of the direct consequences." A court's failure to comply with that obligation "requires reversal" because harmless error analysis is inapposite. * * *
>
> Direct consequences, as we explained in *Ford*, are those that have "a definite, immediate and largely automatic effect on defendant's punishment." Consequences that are "peculiar to the individual's personal circumstances and . . . not within the control of the court system" have been held to be collateral. The direct consequences of a plea—those whose omission from a plea colloquy makes the plea per se invalid—are essentially the core components of a defendant's sentence: a term of probation or imprisonment, a term of post-release supervision, a fine. Our cases have identified no others.

16 N.Y.3d at 205, 920 N.Y.S.2d at 248–49 (citations omitted).

In this regard, the *Harnett* Court held that "failing to warn a defendant who pleads guilty to a sex offense that he may be subject to the Sex Offender Management and Treatment Act (SOMTA)" is a collateral consequence of the plea. *Id.* at 206, 920

N.Y.S.2d at 249. *See also Gravino*, 14 N.Y.3d at 550, 902 N.Y.S.2d at 852 ("We hold that because they are collateral rather than direct consequences of a guilty plea, Sex Offender Registration Act (SORA) registration and the terms and conditions of probation are not subjects that a trial court must address at the plea hearing. Put another way, a trial court's neglect to mention SORA or identify potential stipulations of probation during the plea colloquy does not undermine the knowing, voluntary and intelligent nature of a defendant's guilty plea").

In *Catu*, the defendant accepted a plea bargain pursuant to which he would be sentenced to a three-year determinate prison sentence and a $1,000 fine. The Court of Appeals vacated the plea on the ground that the Court failed to advise the defendant that, as a second felony offender, his sentence would include a mandatory period of five years' post-release supervision. 4 N.Y.3d at 244, 792 N.Y.S.2d at 887.

In *Ford*, the Court of Appeals held that neither Trial Judges nor defense counsel are required to advise a defendant of the possible deportation consequences of his or her plea. 86 N.Y.2d at 401, 633 N.Y.S.2d at 271–72. Critically, while the *Ford* Court held that defense counsel's failure to advise the defendant of such consequences did not constitute ineffective assistance, *id.* at 404–05, 633 N.Y.S.2d at 273–74, the U.S. Supreme Court reached the opposite conclusion in *Padilla v. Kentucky*, __ U.S. __, __, 130 S. Ct. 1473, 1486, 176 L. Ed. 2d 284 (2010):

> It is our responsibility under the Constitution to ensure that no criminal defendant—whether a citizen or not—is left to the "mercies of incompetent counsel." To satisfy this responsibility, we now hold that counsel must inform her client whether his plea carries a risk of deportation. Our longstanding Sixth Amendment precedents, the seriousness of deportation as a consequence of a criminal plea, and the concomitant impact of deportation on families living lawfully in this country demand no less.

(Citation omitted).

Another aspect of *Ford* has been called into question. Specifically, the *Ford* Court commented in *dicta* that:

> Illustrations of collateral consequences are loss of the right to vote or travel abroad, loss of civil service employment, *loss of a driver's license*, loss of the right to possess firearms or an undesirable discharge from the Armed Services. The failure to warn of such collateral consequences will not warrant vacating a plea because they are peculiar to the individual and generally result from the actions taken by agencies the court does not control.

86 N.Y.2d at 403, 633 N.Y.S.2d at 272–73 (emphasis added) (citations omitted).

In support of its claim that the loss of a driver's license is a collateral consequence, the *Ford* Court cited *Moore v. Hinton*, 513 F.2d 781 (5th Cir. 1975), a federal class action lawsuit challenging the manner in which DWI cases were being handled in Tuscaloosa, Alabama. Critically, however, the *Moore* Court pointed out that:

> *Of crucial importance here . . . is the fact that the Alabama Department of Public Safety, not the court, deprives the defendant of his license,* acting under authority of 36 Ala.Code § 68. The court merely accepts the defendant's plea, and sentences him to a fine and/or imprisonment. The Department of Public Safety then institutes a separate proceeding for suspension of his license; this suspension is not, therefore, punishment imposed by the court as a result of the guilty plea, but a collateral consequence of the defendant's conviction.

513 F.2d at 782 (emphasis added).

In stark contrast to the situation addressed in *Moore*, a definite, immediate and mandatory component of every DWI-related sentence in New York is that *the Court* is required to suspend or revoke the defendant's driver's license. *See* VTL § 1193(2)(d)(1). In this regard, in *People v. Castellini*, 24 Misc. 3d 66, __, 884 N.Y.S.2d 550, 551 (App. Term, 1st Dep't 2009), the Appellate Term vacated the defendant's guilty plea to DWAI where the trial court misinformed the defendant with regard to the length of the mandatory driver's license revocation she would receive, reasoning as follows:

> In order for a guilty plea to be entered knowingly, intelligently and voluntarily, a defendant must be advised of the direct consequences of the plea. Although there is no mandatory catechism, a minimum requirement for a valid plea is that the defendant understands the direct penal consequences. Here, the plea minutes show that the court misinformed defendant of the nature and duration of the requisite driver's license sanction, erroneously stating that the sentence would include a 90-day license suspension, when in fact the mandatory sanction was a one-year license revocation. While in some jurisdictions the loss of a driver's license "result[s] from the actions taken by agencies the court does not control," and thus is considered a collateral consequence (*People v. Ford*, 86 N.Y.2d at 403, 633 N.Y.S.2d 270, 657 N.E.2d 265, citing *Moore v. Hinton*, 513 F.2d 781 [5th Cir.1975]), the license sanction here involved constituted punishment directly imposed by the court as a result of defendant's guilty plea (*see* Vehicle and Traffic Law § 1193[2][a], [b]), and was thus a direct consequence of the plea. The court's error is not subject to harmless error analysis, and renders the plea invalid.

(Citations omitted). *Cf. People v. Trathen*, 121 A.D.3d 1594, 993 N.Y.S.2d 426 (4th Dep't 2014).

In *People v. Lancaster*, 260 A.D.2d 660, __, 688 N.Y.S.2d 711,

712 (3d Dep't 1999), the Appellate Division, Third Department, held that a Court sentencing a defendant for DWI is not required to advise him or her "that a subsequent conviction of the crime of driving while intoxicated would constitute a felony[, as] [i]t is abundantly clear that the fact that a defendant is subject to enhanced criminal treatment for an offense that he or she may commit in the future is a collateral consequence of the plea, about which a defendant need not be advised." In this regard, "[a] second D.W.I. conviction leading to felony sanctions can be avoided simply by not drinking and driving." *People v. Butler*, 96 A.D.2d 140, __, 468 N.Y.S.2d 274, 277 (4th Dep't 1983).

In *People v. Smith*, 136 A.D.3d 1107, __, 25 N.Y.S.3d 395, 396 (3d Dep't 2016), leave to appeal denied, 27 N.Y.3d 1075, 2016 WL 3403005 (2016), the Appellate Division, Third Department, held that the length of time that the defendant would be required to remain in "alcohol or substance abuse treatment" as part of a judicial diversion program was a collateral consequence of the defendant's plea.

§ 11:88   People cannot comment on defendant's failure to advise them that someone else drove the vehicle

In *People v. Petersen*, 4 N.Y.2d 992, 993–94, 177 N.Y.S.2d 510, 511, 152 N.E.2d 532 (1958) (per curiam), the Court of Appeals held, in full, as follows:

> Prejudicial error was committed by the trial court in allowing the prosecution to exploit the fact that defendant had not told the police, the Judge, the District Attorney and the Grand Jury that he was not driving his car at the time he was so charged, but that it had been driven by someone else. Defendant was under no duty to speak when in the custody of the authorities, and his failure to do so cannot be the basis of an inference of guilt on his part.

> The further references to this subject in the prosecutor's summation aggravated the error, which error was not cured by the instruction of the trial court properly stating the applicable law.

(Citations omitted).

§ 11:89   Where defendant indicted for misdemeanor DWI, superior court can transfer case back to local court

The People occasionally indict a defendant for misdemeanor DWI. Such a procedure, which is highly unusual, certainly has the appearance of forum shopping. In *Clute v. McGill*, 229 A.D.2d 70, __, 655 N.Y.S.2d 201, 203 (3d Dep't 1997), the Appellate Division, Third Department, noted that Article VI, § 19(b) of the New York State Constitution permits a superior court to transfer

indicted misdemeanors to any local criminal court having jurisdiction over the subject matter of the case; and recognized the
superior court's right to effectuate such a transfer in order to
prevent the People from gaining an unfair advantage not only
over defendants, but also over neutral magistrates. In this regard,
the *Clute* Court held that:

> [W]hile the People have a clear legal right to present misdemeanor
> charges to a Grand Jury in order to prosecute crimes by indictment
> "in a superior court" (CPL 170.20[2]), if the indictment returned
> does not charge a felony County Court has the constitutional
> authority to transfer the matter to any Justice Court having
> jurisdiction.

229 A.D.2d at __, 655 N.Y.S.2d at 203.

§ 11:90 Defendant indicted for misdemeanor DWI entitled to 12-person jury

Article VI, § 18(a) of the New York State Constitution provides
that "crimes prosecuted by indictment shall be tried by a jury
composed of twelve persons, unless a jury trial has been waived
as provided in section two of article one of this constitution." In
this regard, in *People v. Dean*, 80 A.D.2d 695, __, 436 N.Y.S.2d
455, 456–57 (3d Dep't 1981), the Appellate Division, Third
Department, made clear that a defendant indicted for misdemeanor DWI is constitutionally entitled to a 12-person jury. *See
also People v. Warren*, 145 A.D.2d 966, __, 536 N.Y.S.2d 337, 338
(4th Dep't 1988); *People v. Griffin*, 142 Misc. 2d 41, __, 536
N.Y.S.2d 386, 387–88 (Monroe Co. Sup. Ct. 1988).

§ 11:91 Court conducting bench trial cannot reconsider its verdict after the fact

In *People v. Cunningham*, 95 N.Y.2d 909, 717 N.Y.S.2d 68, 740
N.E.2d 213 (2000), as amended nunc pro tunc, 95 N.Y.2d 949,
722 N.Y.S.2d 466, 745 N.E.2d 385 (2000), the trial court convicted
the defendant of common law DWI following a bench trial.
However, "the Trial Judge applied a definition of intoxication
which improperly lowered the prosecution's burden of proof." *Id.*
at 910, 717 N.Y.S.2d at 68. When this issue was raised via a motion to set aside the verdict, the Court reconsidered the evidence
using the correct legal standard, and again found the defendant
guilty of DWI. On appeal, the Court of Appeals reversed, holding
that:

> The Court's reconsideration of its verdict under a different stan-
> dard constituted a factual determination that "comes too late and
> exceeds the scope of [the court's] authority." To allow the second
> verdict to stand would permit the Trial Judge to engage in

postverdict fact finding that would not be possible in a jury trial, thereby according "less finality to the verdict of a Trial Judge when sitting as [the trier of fact] than to a jury verdict."

95 N.Y.2d at 910, 717 N.Y.S.2d at 68 (citations omitted). *See also People v. Maharaj*, 89 N.Y.2d 997, 657 N.Y.S.2d 392, 679 N.E.2d 631 (1997) (DWI conviction reversed because Trial Judge utilized incorrect legal standard in convicting defendant following bench trial).

§ 11:92   Police officer who arrests person for DWI is responsible for such person's safety

In *Thomas v. State*, 46 N.Y.2d 1043, 1044, 416 N.Y.S.2d 546, 547, 389 N.E.2d 1068 (1979), the Court of Appeals held that "a police officer who arrests an intoxicated driver assumes the duty of exercising the care reasonably required in the circumstances to assure the safety of a person in that condition."

§ 11:93   Insurer's liability to motorist for injuries caused by driving in violation of VTL § 1192

Insurance Law § 5103(b)(2) provides that:

(b) An insurer may exclude from coverage required by subsection (a) hereof a person who: * * *

(2) Is injured as a result of operating a motor vehicle while in an intoxicated condition or while his ability to operate such vehicle is impaired by the use of a drug within the meaning of [VTL § 1192]; provided, however, that an insurer shall not exclude such person from coverage with respect to necessary emergency health services rendered in a general hospital, as defined in [Public Health Law § 2801(10)], including ambulance services attendant thereto and related medical screening. Notwithstanding any other law, where the covered person is found to have violated [VTL § 1192], the insurer has a cause of action for the amount of first party benefits paid or payable on behalf of such covered person against such covered person.

See also Fafinski v. Reliance Ins. Co., 65 N.Y.2d 990, 992, 494 N.Y.S.2d 92, 93, 484 N.E.2d 121 (1985) (conviction under VTL § 1192 not required for Ins. Law § 5103(b)(2) to apply).

§ 11:94   Applicability of "moral certainty" standard to DWI cases

Where the People's case is based *entirely* on circumstantial evidence, the defendant is entitled to a "circumstantial evidence charge" pursuant to which the jury is instructed that the defendant's guilt must be proven to a "moral certainty." *See, e.g.*,

People v. Barnes, 50 N.Y.2d 375, 379–80, 429 N.Y.S.2d 178, 180, 406 N.E.2d 1071 (1980) ("While it is the oft-quoted rule in criminal cases which depend entirely upon circumstantial evidence that " 'the facts from which the inference of the defendant's guilt is drawn must be established with certainty—they must be inconsistent with his innocence and must exclude to a moral certainty every other reasonable hypothesis,'" this legal standard does not apply to a situation where, as here, both direct and circumstantial evidence are employed to demonstrate a defendant's culpability") (citations omitted). *See generally People v. Miller*, 194 A.D.2d 230, __, 607 N.Y.S.2d 507, 508 (4th Dep't 1993) ("trial judges are advised to avoid using 'moral certainty' language in their instructions except in circumstantial evidence cases where the words are appropriate. Trial judges are further advised to adhere to the charge set forth in 1 CJI(NY) 6.20 in order to help curb the recurring problems that arise in instructing a jury on reasonable doubt") (citations omitted).

In a DWI case, most of the evidence against the defendant is circumstantial in nature. For example, observations of the condition of the defendant's eyes and face, the odor of the defendant's breath, the manner of the defendant's speech, the defendant's performance on field sobriety tests, admissions of consuming alcohol in the recent past, etc., clearly constitute circumstantial—as opposed to direct—evidence regarding the issue of whether the defendant was intoxicated at the time that he or she operated the vehicle. *See, e.g., U.S. v. Horn*, 185 F. Supp. 2d 530, 533, 58 Fed. R. Evid. Serv. 357 (D. Md. 2002) ("A police officer trained and qualified to perform SFSTs may testify with respect to his or her observations of a subject's performance of these tests, if properly administered, to include the observation of nystagmus, and these observations are admissible as circumstantial evidence that the defendant was driving while intoxicated or under the influence"); *U.S. v. Horn*, 185 F. Supp. 2d at 560–61 ("The results of properly administered WAT, OLS and HGN SFSTs may be admitted into evidence in a DWI/DUI case only as circumstantial evidence of intoxication or impairment but not as direct evidence of specific BAC").

Simply stated, a person can exhibit most, if not all, indicators commonly associated with intoxication without having consumed any alcohol whatsoever. For example, the person could be sick, tired, nervous, embarrassed, injured, uncoordinated, mentally ill, diabetic or epileptic; and/or could have a speech impediment, allergies, other medical conditions, etc. *See, e.g., People v. Butts*, 21 Misc. 2d 799, 201 N.Y.S.2d 926 (Poughkeepsie City Ct. 1960).

In addition, since a chemical test is never administered simultaneously with the defendant's operation of the vehicle, a chemical test result clearly constitutes circumstantial evidence of the defendant's BAC at the time of operation. *See People v. Fisher*, 9 Misc. 3d 1121(A), __, 862 N.Y.S.2d 809, 2005 WL 2780686 at *17 (Rochester City Ct. 2005).

Nonetheless, most of these types of evidence have been found to constitute direct evidence. *See, e.g., People v. Coker*, 121 A.D.3d 1305, __, 995 N.Y.S.2d 288, 291 (3d Dep't 2014), leave to appeal denied, 26 N.Y.3d 927 (2015) ("Jacqueway's testimony that immediately following the crash defendant admitted to having consumed approximately 'nine drinks,' together with police testimony regarding defendant's condition and demeanor, constituted direct evidence of the element of intoxication"); *People v. Crandall*, 287 A.D.2d 881, __, 731 N.Y.S.2d 553, 555 (3d Dep't 2001) ("we reject defendant's contention that County Court erred when it refused to charge the jury that the facts giving rise to defendant's guilt had to satisfy the 'moral certainty' standard. Defendant's admission that he had consumed four beers, together with police testimony regarding defendant's condition and demeanor and the eyewitness testimony regarding his erratic driving, constituted direct evidence of his impaired ability to operate his vehicle. Inasmuch as both direct and circumstantial evidence were present, defendant was not entitled to a circumstantial evidence charge") (citations omitted); *People v. Merrick*, 188 A.D.2d 764, __, 591 N.Y.S.2d 564, 565–66 (3d Dep't 1992); *People v. Heidorf*, 186 A.D.2d 915, __, 589 N.Y.S.2d 628, 629 (3d Dep't 1992); *People v. Abel*, 166 A.D.2d 841, __, 563 N.Y.S.2d 531, 532 (3d Dep't 1990); *People v. Green*, 174 A.D.2d 511, __, 571 N.Y.S.2d 290, 291 (1st Dep't 1991); *People v. Becht*, 163 A.D.2d 811, __, 558 N.Y.S.2d 342, 343 (4th Dep't 1990); *People v. Scallero*, 122 A.D.2d 350, __, 504 N.Y.S.2d 318, 319–20 (3d Dep't 1986).

Regardless, one type of evidence that is clearly direct in nature is eyewitness testimony from a witness who actually observed the defendant operate the vehicle on a roadway covered by VTL § 1192(7). Thus, the only situation where a circumstantial evidence charge would potentially be applicable in a DWI case is a situation where the defendant (a) was not observed operating the vehicle, *and* (b) did not admit to operating the vehicle (*i.e.*, a case in which the evidence of operation is entirely circumstantial in nature). *See, e.g., People v. Wells*, 186 A.D.2d 867, 588 N.Y.S.2d 938 (3d Dep't 1992); *People v. White*, 173 A.D.2d 897, 569 N.Y.S.2d 816 (3d Dep't 1991); *People v. Saplin*, 122 A.D.2d 498, 505 N.Y.S.2d 460 (3d Dep't 1986); *People v. Collins*, 70 A.D.2d 986, 417 N.Y.S.2d 819 (3d Dep't 1979). *See generally People v. Blake*, 5 N.Y.2d 118, 180 N.Y.S.2d 775, 154 N.E.2d 818 (1958); *People v. Eckert*, 2 N.Y.2d 126, 157 N.Y.S.2d 551, 138 N.E.2d 794 (1956); *People v. Barnes*, 137 A.D.3d 1571, 27 N.Y.S.3d 745 (4th Dep't 2016), leave to appeal denied, 27 N.Y.3d 1128, 2016 WL 3766853 (2016).

§ 11:95   Effect of VTL § 1192 conviction on pistol permit

A conviction of DWAI, in violation of VTL § 1192(1), as a first offense and with no aggravating factors (*e.g.*, committing the offense with a loaded weapon in the vehicle), does not provide grounds for a pistol permit to be revoked—but can result in a suspension thereof. *See, e.g., Matter of Boersma v. Erie County Pistol Permit Dept.*, 233 A.D.2d 938, ___, 649 N.Y.S.2d 879, 879 (4th Dep't Nov. 8, 1996) ("The record establishes and respondent Supreme Court Justice concedes that the sole reason that petitioner's pistol permit was revoked was petitioner's conviction of driving while ability impaired in violation of Vehicle and Traffic Law § 1192(1). Under the circumstances of this case, we conclude that the appropriate penalty is to suspend petitioner's pistol permit for six months commencing September 26, 1995"); *Matter of Klein v. Police Com'r of City of New York*, 99 Misc. 2d 186, 415 N.Y.S.2d 735 (N.Y. Co. Sup. Ct. 1979).

By contrast, a conviction of DWI, or a conviction of DWAI with aggravating factors, can result in the revocation of a pistol permit. For example, in *Matter of Biggerstaff v. Drago*, 65 A.D.3d 728, ___, 883 N.Y.S.2d 657, 657 (3d Dep't 2009), the Appellate Division, Third Department, affirmed the revocation of a pistol permit where "petitioner had an extremely high blood alcohol content at the time of his arrest and pleaded guilty to aggravated driving while intoxicated which, as respondent concluded, called his judgment and character into question."

In *Matter of Broadus v. City of New York Police Dept. (License Div.)*, 62 A.D.3d 527, ___, 878 N.Y.S.2d 738, 739 (1st Dep't 2009), the Appellate Division, First Department, held that:

> The finding that petitioner lacks the good moral character required to possess a pistol license (Penal Law § 400.00[1][b]) is rationally supported by evidence of petitioner's arrest under Vehicle and Traffic Law § 1192 for driving while intoxicated, possession of a loaded firearm when arrested, refusal to take a breathalyzer test in violation of Vehicle and Traffic Law § 1194, subsequent conviction under Vehicle and Traffic Law § 1192(1) for driving while his ability to drive was impaired by alcohol, failure to immediately notify respondent of his arrest in violation of 38 RCNY 5-30(a) and (d), and failure to immediately voucher his second firearm in violation of 38 RCNY 5-30(f).

The same Court affirmed the revocation of a pistol permit in *Matter of Papaioannou v. Kelly*, 14 A.D.3d 459, ___, 788 N.Y.S.2d 378, 379 (1st Dep't 2005), where:

> In this matter, respondent's determination was based upon: petitioner's October 2000 arrest for driving while ability impaired by alcohol (Vehicle and Traffic Law § 1192[1]), which arrest cast doubt on his character and fitness to possess a firearm; petitioner's

failure to promptly report his arrest to the License Division; his failure to report his change of address to the License Division in a timely manner; the fact that he transported his handguns to an address other than that designated on his license without permission from the agency; and his failure to cooperate with respondent's investigation of his arrest.

See also Matter of DiMonda v. Bristol, 219 A.D.2d 830, —, 631 N.Y.S.2d 968, 969 (4th Dep't 1995) ("We reject the contention that respondent acted arbitrarily and capriciously in denying petitioner's application for a pistol permit . . . . The failure of petitioner to report on his application a prior arrest for driving while intoxicated provided a sufficient basis to deny the application"); *Matter of Przybylowicz v. White*, 115 A.D.2d 939, —, 496 N.Y.S.2d 832, 832 (3d Dep't 1985) ("Petitioner's two convictions for driving while ability impaired and testimony from neighbors as to petitioner's proclivity for drinking were sufficient to support the decision" to deny his application for a pistol permit).

§ 11:96   Effect of VTL § 1192 conviction on law license

In New York, conviction of a felony results in an attorney's automatic disbarment. *See* Judiciary Law § 90(4). This includes felony DWI. *See, e.g., In re Sullivan*, 140 A.D.3d 1391, 32 N.Y.S.3d 748 (3d Dep't 2016) (per curiam); *In re Dawson*, 133 A.D.3d 1083, 20 N.Y.S.3d 216 (3d Dep't 2015) (per curiam); *Matter of McGee*, 77 A.D.3d 376, 908 N.Y.S.2d 346 (2d Dep't 2010) (per curiam); *Matter of Bailey*, 57 A.D.3d 1529, 869 N.Y.S.2d 352 (4th Dep't 2008); *Matter of Woods*, 56 A.D.3d 184, 867 N.Y.S.2d 45 (1st Dep't 2008) (per curiam); *Matter of Shmaruk*, 29 A.D.3d 138, 812 N.Y.S.2d 623 (2d Dep't 2006) (per curiam); *Matter of Baxter*, 231 A.D.2d 964, 647 N.Y.S.2d 592 (4th Dep't 1996). *Cf. Matter of Johnston*, 75 N.Y.2d 403, 554 N.Y.S.2d 88, 553 N.E.2d 566 (1990) (felony of 1st degree involuntary manslaughter in Texas not sufficiently analogous to vehicular manslaughter in New York to constitute "felony" for purposes of automatic disbarment).

Critically, the automatic disbarment rule applies even where the parties anticipate that the felony conviction will be vacated and reduced to a misdemeanor if the defendant successfully completes interim probation. *See In re Tendler*, 131 A.D.3d 1301, —, 16 N.Y.S.3d 185, 185 (3d Dep't 2015) (per curiam) ("While an attorney's disbarment upon a plea of guilty to a felony is automatic, the fact that her plea agreement contemplates the subsequent withdrawal of her felony guilty plea upon successful completion of a period of interim probation, leaving only a plea to a misdemeanor offense, would not serve to automatically restore her to the bar—to attain said relief, she must make a motion for reinstatement").

By contrast, misdemeanor DWI convictions have generally led

to a letter of admonition, a letter of caution or public censure, depending upon the circumstances of the case. *See, e.g.*, *In re Bratton*, 141 A.D.3d 182, 33 N.Y.S.3d 743 (2d Dep't 2016) (per curiam); *In re Ackerman*, 136 A.D.3d 115, 21 N.Y.S.3d 629 (2d Dep't 2015) (per curiam); *In re Grossman*, 132 A.D.3d 216, 16 N.Y.S.3d 259 (2d Dep't 2015) (per curiam); *Matter of Antomattei*, 96 A.D.3d 136, 945 N.Y.S.2d 31 (1st Dep't 2012) (per curiam); *In re Piken*, 86 A.D.3d 143, 924 N.Y.S.2d 527 (2d Dep't 2011) (per curiam); *Shmaruk, supra*; *Matter of Gross*, 34 A.D.3d 23, 824 N.Y.S.2d 825 (4th Dep't 2006) (per curiam); *Matter of Brody*, 23 A.D.3d 94, 803 N.Y.S.2d 605 (2d Dep't 2005) (per curiam); *Matter of Shichman*, 20 A.D.3d 111, 796 N.Y.S.2d 369 (2d Dep't 2005) (per curiam); *Matter of Bach*, 20 A.D.3d 114, 796 N.Y.S.2d 382 (2d Dep't 2005) (per curiam); *Matter of Zalesak*, 17 A.D.3d 66, 793 N.Y.S.2d 439 (2d Dep't 2005) (per curiam); *Matter of McCarthy*, 11 A.D.3d 162, 782 N.Y.S.2d 766 (2d Dep't 2004) (per curiam); *Matter of O'Brien*, 309 A.D.2d 184, 765 N.Y.S.2d 71 (2d Dep't 2003) (per curiam); *Matter of Goldstein*, 285 A.D.2d 187, 728 N.Y.S.2d 758 (2d Dep't 2001) (per curiam); *Matter of Wynne*, 283 A.D.2d 55, 726 N.Y.S.2d 111 (2d Dep't 2001) (per curiam); *Matter of Valentine*, 224 A.D.2d 70, 647 N.Y.S.2d 802 (2d Dep't 1996) (per curiam). *See also In re Barry*, 129 A.D.3d 57, 6 N.Y.S.3d 528 (4th Dep't 2015) (per curiam). *Cf. Matter of LaPenta*, 67 A.D.3d 117, 885 N.Y.S.2d 294 (2d Dep't 2009) (per curiam); *Matter of Kinne*, 17 A.D.3d 16, 794 N.Y.S.2d 757 (4th Dep't 2005) (per curiam). In this regard, the *Gross* Court ruled as follows:

> The Grievance Committee filed a petition charging respondent with misconduct arising from his two convictions of driving while intoxicated as a misdemeanor. Respondent filed an answer admitting the material allegations of the petition and raising, in mitigation, his alcoholism.

> We conclude that respondent violated the following Disciplinary Rules of the Code of Professional Responsibility:
>> DR 1-102(A)(3) (22 NYCRR 1200.3[a][3])—engaging in illegal conduct that adversely reflects on his honesty, trustworthiness or fitness as a lawyer; and

>> DR 1-102(A)(5) (22 NYCRR 1200.3[a][5])—engaging in conduct that is prejudicial to the administration of justice.

> Additionally, by failing to report his first conviction of driving while intoxicated to this Court, respondent violated Judiciary Law § 90(4)(c).

> We have considered, in mitigation, respondent's admitted alcoholism for which he is currently in treatment. Additionally, we note

that respondent has an otherwise unblemished record and that his misconduct was unrelated to his practice of law. Accordingly, after consideration of all of the factors in this matter, we conclude that respondent should be censured on condition that he agrees to continue in treatment for his alcoholism for a period of 24 months. In the event that respondent fails to continue in treatment or commits additional misconduct during that period, the Grievance Committee shall immediately apply for an order returning the proceeding to this Court for imposition of appropriate discipline.

34 A.D.3d at __, 824 N.Y.S.2d at 825–26.

§ 11:97   Arraigning Judge as witness for prosecution

In felony DWI cases, it is not uncommon for the defendant to be brought before a local criminal court Judge for arraignment shortly after his or her arrest. Putting aside the issue of whether it is appropriate to arraign an intoxicated person without counsel, the issue has arisen as to whether the arraigning Judge can subsequently be called as a witness to the defendant's alleged intoxication.

In *People v. Rossback*, 243 A.D.2d 919, __, 663 N.Y.S.2d 409, 409-10 (3d Dep't 1997), the Appellate Division, Third Department, held that:

> While certain courts have found no error in the admission of the testimony of the arraigning justice at a defendant's trial for driving while intoxicated, we need not decide this issue here since County Court granted defense counsel's objection and refused to allow the Justice who arraigned defendant to testify concerning his observations of defendant during the arraignment. Contrary to defendant's claim, no negative inferences could be drawn from the Justice's testimony inasmuch as he was immediately excused as a witness out of the presence of the jury before he made any statements regarding defendant's demeanor. Moreover, to the extent that the prosecutor made improper remarks regarding anticipated testimony of the Justice which was never received, we find this error harmless in light of the overwhelming evidence adduced at the trial of defendant's guilt.

(Citations omitted).

In *People v. Ireland*, 175 A.D.2d 139, __, 572 N.Y.S.2d 29, 30-31 (2d Dep't 1991), the Appellate Division, Second Department, held that:

> The trial court properly permitted the People to call as a rebuttal witness the Town Justice who arraigned the defendant one hour after his arrest. The witness's testimony served to contradict the defendant's claim that, while he had refused the request of the arresting officers to submit to sobriety tests, he had offered to do so in the presence of the judge. Moreover, the Justice's opinion as to the defendant's sobriety was properly received to rebut the defendant's

testimony that he had not consumed alcoholic beverages on the date in question. The defense advanced a theory that the arrest was the result of a personal vendetta by the local police department, and thereby attempted to undermine the veracity of the arresting officers' opinions as to the defendant's intoxication elicited on the People's case-in-chief. Accordingly, the rebuttal testimony of the Town Justice was highly relevant to this issue and was properly admitted. Even if this testimony were not technically of a rebuttal nature, the court properly exercised the discretion afforded it by CPL 260.30(7) to allow the presentation of evidence which is more properly a part of the direct case in the interest of justice.

See also People v. Jones, 158 A.D.2d 911, 551 N.Y.S.2d 78 (4th Dep't 1990) ("The trial court did not err in admitting testimony from a town justice regarding defendant's intoxication. Even if there were error it would be harmless because there is overwhelming evidence of defendant's guilt and there is no significant probability that the jury would have acquitted defendant had it not been for that testimony.").

§ 11:98   DWI conviction dismissed/reduced on appeal due to insufficient evidence

In *People v. Grennon*, 36 Misc. 3d 33, __, 949 N.Y.S.2d 566, 568 (App. Term, 9th & 10th Jud. Dist. 2011), the Appellate Term dismissed the defendant's common law DWI conviction under the following circumstances:

> The evidence adduced as to the state of defendant's intoxication was that he operated his vehicle at an excessive rate of speed, exhibited glassy eyes, had an odor of an alcoholic beverage, and admitted having consumed beer some time earlier. The arresting officer observed no other indicia of actual impairment of motor coordination and conducted no field sobriety tests, and while another trooper apparently conducted such tests, the People elicited no testimony with respect to them. Although speeding might be taken to reveal a diminishment of the "mental abilities which [a person] is expected to possess in order to operate a vehicle as a reasonable and prudent driver," absent any other evidence tending to prove defendant's inability physically to operate his vehicle as a reasonable and prudent person, the proof of speeding is too equivocal to be given significant weight as to defendant's state of intoxication.

> Where, as here, a conviction of common law driving while intoxicated is involved, unlike a conviction for driving while intoxicated per se, "a high blood alcohol count," while supporting an inference of "some evidence of intoxication," does not, standing alone, provide a sufficient basis to infer a state of intoxication, beyond a reasonable doubt, where there are insufficient additional indicia that the alcohol actually diminished a person's ability to operate a motor vehicle in a reasonable and prudent fashion to the degree consistent with intoxication. Accordingly, the conviction of common law driv-

ing while intoxicated is reversed, the accusatory instrument dismissed, and the fine, if paid, remitted.

(Citations omitted).

In *People v. St. John*, 6 Misc. 3d 127(A), *1, 800 N.Y.S.2d 354, *1 (App. Term, 9th & 10th Jud. Dist. 2004), the Court held that:

The evidence adduced at trial was insufficient to warrant the finding that defendant's consumption of half a glass of beer caused her to be incapable of operating her vehicle as a reasonably prudent driver. There was no testimony that any of her physical or mental abilities were impaired before the impact to a degree sufficient to render her intoxicated. No field sobriety test results were introduced into evidence and the only evidence of any actual impairment was the testimony of the police officers and emergency medical technician that they detected the odor of alcohol on defendant's breath, that she had glassy bloodshot eyes and her speech was slurred. However, the evidence established that defendant's nose was broken and bleeding as a result of the accident, and required seven stitches, that she had been crying and was able to comprehend the instructions of the police and the emergency medical technician. Furthermore, the officers testified they were able to understand her speech, that the defendant had no trouble walking, did not stumble and needed no assistance in exiting her vehicle. Under the circumstances, the verdict was against the weight of the evidence

See also People v. Belakh, 21 Misc. 3d 136(A), 873 N.Y.S.2d 513 (App. Term, 2d & 11th Jud. Dist. 2008); *People v. Wenz*, 12 Misc. 3d 134(A), 820 N.Y.S.2d 845 (App. Term, 9th & 10th Jud. Dist. 2006).

In *People v. Elithorpe*, 50 Misc. 3d 1077, __, 21 N.Y.S.3d 848, 852 (Monroe Co. Ct. 2015), a common law DWI conviction was reduced to DWAI on appeal under the following circumstances:

Here, defendant admitted to consuming two beers at dinner; however, the testimony did not establish at what time he had dinner, and in any event, that admission alone would not support a finding of intoxication. He had an odor of alcohol, however, that would not have been unexpected nor was it inconsistent with the two beers he admitted consuming. He had watery eyes, but the Deputy conceded that such could have been the result of the very cold weather that evening. Defendant passed [3] of [5] field sobriety tests administered, and on the "walk and turn" test, which he failed, the defendant did not lose his balance and completed most of the walk portion successfully. While defendant lost control of his vehicle, it is clear that the road was snow and ice-covered, and as noted above there is little or no evidence that he was speeding or operating his vehicle in an unsafe manner, the deputy's "professional opinion" notwithstanding, unsupported as it was by some degree of scientific or technical knowledge. A blood alcohol test was received into evidence and showed that the defendant's BAC was .14; however, the trial court acquitted on the charge based on that finding, and so this Court gives no weight to that evidence as it relates to whether the defendant was incapable of operating his vehicle. Finally, while the defendant was issued a ticket for Driving While Intoxicated, no testimony was elicited as to whether the Deputy formed an opinion that the defendant was intoxicated.

The Court considers in its discretion the lesser-included offense of Driving While Ability Impaired, Vehicle and Traffic Law § 1192(1). A person's ability to operate a motor vehicle is impaired by the consumption of alcohol "when that person's consumption of alcohol has actually impaired, to any extent, the physical and mental abilities which such person is expected to possess in order to operate a vehicle as a reasonable and prudent driver."

Although the defense did not request the charge, the Court finds that a reasonable view of the evidence would support a conviction for that charge, and upon its independent review of the evidence, the Court finds that the evidence establishes, beyond a reasonable doubt, the defendant's guilt of the lesser-included offense.

(Citations omitted).

Chapter 12

Vehicular Crimes

Research References

Westlaw Databases

Charges to the Jury and Requests to Charge in Criminal Case in New York (CTJNY)

Handling Drunk Driving Cases (2d ed.) (HDRUNKDR)

New York Vehicle and Traffic Law 2d (NYVEH)

Treatises and Practice Aids

New York Charges to the Jury §§ 41:1 to 41:19.50

Fiandach, Handling Drunk Driving Cases §§ 3:1 to 3:13 (2d ed.)

Rose, New York Vehicle and Traffic Law 2d §§ 30:1 to 30:8

Law Reviews and Other Periodicals

Kamins, 2007 Criminal Law Legislation, 80-FEB N.Y. St. B.J. 35 (February, 2008)

KeyCite®: Cases and other legal materials listed in KeyCite Scope can be researched through the KeyCite service on Westlaw®. Use KeyCite to check citations for form, parallel references, prior and later history, and comprehensive citator information, including citations to other decisions and secondary materials.

---

§ 12:1 In general

Research References

West's Key Number Digest, Automobiles ⚖324, 332

Significant changes to the vehicular crimes statutes have radically altered the legal landscape pertaining to these offenses. In the past, much of the litigation in vehicular crimes cases focused on whether, despite the defendant's intoxication, his/her conduct rose to the level of criminal negligence or recklessness. In this regard, it has long been the law of this state that:

> Proof of intoxication alone is not enough to sustain a conviction of criminal negligence. The People must also prove that the defendant's intoxication affected his physical and mental capacity to the extent that it caused him to operate his vehicle in a culpably reckless manner.

People v. Bast, 19 N.Y.2d 813, 815, 280 N.Y.S.2d 149, 150 (1967). *See also Matter of Johnston*, 75 N.Y.2d 403, 409–10, 554 N.Y.S.2d 88, 91 (1990) (same).

In 2005, the legislature removed the mens rea element from the vehicular assault/vehicular manslaughter laws (except where AUO is an element of the offense). As such, the large body of case law addressing the issue of whether the defendant acted with criminal negligence has in all likelihood been rendered moot.

§ 12:2 Vehicular crimes—Legislative preemption

Research References

West's Key Number Digest, Automobiles ⚖324, 332

The authors have long argued that, in enacting the vehicular assault and vehicular manslaughter statutes, the legislature had made its intent clear, and that prosecutorial attempts to "overcharge" a defendant by making use of the generic assault and manslaughter statutes in vehicular crimes cases were improper.

In particular, prior to the changes to the vehicular crimes laws which removed the element of criminal negligence therefrom, it was common for the People to indict the defendant for both vehicular manslaughter 2nd, a class D felony, as well as generic manslaughter 2nd, a class C felony; and/or to indict the defendant for both vehicular assault 2nd, a class E felony, as well as generic assault 2nd, a class D violent felony. In this regard, although generic assault/manslaughter charges are less applicable to the facts of a vehicular crime case, they subject the defendant to a substantially longer prison sentence.

To make matters worse, generic assault/manslaughter charges are potentially far easier to prove than vehicular assault/ vehicular manslaughter charges. The reason is that a person cannot be found guilty of vehicular assault/vehicular manslaughter (in an alcohol-related accident case) unless he/she has been proven guilty of DWI—as DWI is an element of the crime(s). By contrast, acquittal of DWI is *not* a bar to a conviction of generic assault/ manslaughter—as DWI is *not* an element of the crime(s). Accordingly, a defendant who was ultimately acquitted of DWI but found guilty of DWAI:

> (a) Would be acquitted of vehicular manslaughter (a class D felony requiring a mental state of criminal negligence), but could nonetheless be convicted of generic manslaughter (a class C felony requiring a mental state of recklessness); and/or
>
> (b) Would be acquitted of vehicular assault (a class E felony requiring a mental state of criminal negligence), but could nonetheless be convicted of generic assault (a class D violent felony requiring a mental state of recklessness).

"This is an unreasonable and unjust result and could not have been intended by the *Legislature.*" *People v. Snow*, 138 A.D.2d 217, __, 530 N.Y.S.2d 913, 915 (4th Dep't 1988), *aff'd for the reasons stated in the opinion below*, 74 N.Y.2d 671, 543 N.Y.S.2d 385 (1989). *See also People v. Belizaire*, 234 A.D.2d 467, __, 651 N.Y.S.2d 574, 574–75 (2d Dep't 1996) (same).

In addition, there is a well-settled rule of statutory construction which provides that:

> **A special statute which is in conflict with a general act covering the same subject matter controls the case and repeals the general statute insofar as the special act applies**.
>
> A special act which is in conflict with a general statute covering the same subject matter controls the case, and the general law is repealed insofar as the special act applies. This rule is applicable to a situation where a general law conflicts with a particular law . . . In other words, a special statute prevails over a general statute . . .
>
> Any other conclusion would destroy the effect of all special acts on subjects covered by general legislation. A repeal of this kind, however, is more in the nature of the creation of an exception to the general rule, than an abrogation of any part of the general law. The general law retains its force, but an exception is made for the particular case, and the special statute is deemed to have modified the general statute pro tanto.
>
> A prior general statute yields to a later specific or special statute.

McKinney's Cons. Laws of N.Y., Book 1, Statutes § 397, at 574 to 77 (footnotes omitted). *See also* McKinney's Cons. Laws of N.Y., Book 1, Statutes § 144 ("Statutes will not be construed as to render them ineffective"); Statutes § 271(e) ("Penal statutes are not extended to doubtful situations").

In this regard, it is noteworthy that the vehicular assault/ vehicular manslaughter statutes were enacted long after the generic assault/manslaughter statutes. We thus argued that, if a defendant could be charged with generic assault/manslaughter in a vehicular crime case, then the vehicular assault/vehicular manslaughter statutes, which both (a) were enacted subsequent to the generic assault/manslaughter statutes, and (b) were specifically enacted to *enhance* the penalties faced by intoxicated drivers who caused injury/death—were all but irrelevant.

We further argued that, if the legislature intended to punish intoxicated drivers who cause death as class C felons, it would have classified vehicular manslaughter 2nd as a class C felony; and that, if the legislature intended to punish intoxicated drivers who cause serious physical injury as class D felons, it would have classified vehicular assault 2nd as a class D felony. Having chosen to classify vehicular manslaughter 2nd as a class D felony, and to classify vehicular assault 2nd as a class E felony, the legislature must be presumed to have made a conscious, well-reasoned decision—which decision cannot be overridden by utilizing generic statutes to nullify the specific statutes enacted to cover the precise conduct at issue.

This interpretation of the law is bolstered by the Court of Appeals' decision in *People v. Prescott*, 95 N.Y.2d 655, 722 N.Y.S.2d 778 (2001). *Prescott* made clear that the Legislature has given significant thought to the topics of DWI, AUO, and vehicular crimes, and has enacted "tightly and carefully integrated" statutes covering these offenses; and that, as a result, creative attempts to expand criminal liability under the DWI, AUO, and vehicular crimes laws are inappropriate—*even if such interpretation of the laws would otherwise be valid. See also Snow, supra*; *People v. Rivera*, 16 N.Y.3d 654, 926 N.Y.S.2d 16, 949 N.E.2d 964 (2011) (defendant whose driver's license is revoked for DWI and who commits a new DWI while on a conditional license cannot be prosecuted for the felony of AUO 1st, in violation of VTL § 511(3), but rather can only be prosecuted for the traffic infraction of VTL § 1196(7)(f)); *People v. Litto*, 8 N.Y.3d 692, 840 N.Y.S.2d 736, 872 N.E.2d 848 (2007) (the term "intoxicated" in VTL § 1192(3) only applies to intoxication caused by alcohol—not, as the People claimed, to intoxication caused by *any* substance).

Significant 2005, 2006, 2007, and 2009 amendments to the vehicular assault/vehicular manslaughter statutes, *see infra*, have further clarified the legislature's intent in this area—and clearly demonstrate that the legislature is constantly monitoring and tinkering with this area of the law. Thus, any future resort to the generic assault/manslaughter statutes in vehicular crimes cases would appear to be both unnecessary and inappropriate.

That said, the Court of Appeals has upheld Depraved Indifference Murder charges in DWI cases where the facts of the case justify such a charge. *See People v. Heidgen*, 22 N.Y.3d 259, 980 N.Y.S.2d 320, 3 N.E.3d 657 (2013). In *Heidgen*, the Court of Appeals held as follows:

> Defendants in these three appeals challenge their convictions of depraved indifference murder. Each defendant drove in an outrageously reckless manner while intoxicated by alcohol or drugs and caused the death of at least one other person. Defendants maintain that the evidence was not legally sufficient to support their convictions—specifically, that there was insufficient proof that they had the requisite mental state of depraved indifference. Although intoxicated driving cases that present circumstances evincing a depraved indifference to human life are likely to be few and far between, we find that the evidence in each of these unusually egregious cases was legally sufficient to support the convictions.

Id. at 267, 980 N.Y.S.2d at 322-23. *Cf. People v. Valencia*, 14 N.Y.3d 927, 927-28, 906 N.Y.S.2d 515, 515, 932 N.E.2d 871 (2010) ("There is insufficient evidence to support a conviction for depraved indifference assault. The trial evidence established only that defendant was extremely intoxicated and did not establish that he acted with the culpable mental state of depraved indifference.").

Notably, the *Heidgen* Court stated:

These cases demonstrate that cases involving a depraved indifference to human life are highly fact-specific and dependent upon the individual defendant's particular mental state—a factor that may be extremely difficult to establish. Indeed, intoxicated driving cases in general, although clearly examples of dangerous behavior, are not thought of as "quintessential" cases of depraved indifference— such as,

> firing into a crowd; driving an automobile along a crowded sidewalk at high speed; opening the lion's cage at the zoo; placing a time bomb in a public place; poisoning a well from which people are accustomed to draw water; opening a drawbridge as a train is about to pass over it and dropping stones from an overpass onto a busy highway.

Recognizing that "it is important that law enforcement and prosecutors have the tools necessary to properly charge and convict [those] who have committed a DWI resulting in personal injury or death," the legislature has enacted the aggravated vehicular homicide and assault statutes (Penal Law §§ 125.14, 120.04-a), which provide for enhanced punishment of those individuals who cause death or serious physical injury while operating a motor vehicle while intoxicated, when, for example, the individual has a blood alcohol content of at least .18. These statutes, however, do not foreclose the possibility of prosecution for depraved indifference murder where egregious circumstances warrant that charge, as they do here.

Id. at 276-77, 980 N.Y.S.2d at 329 (citations omitted).

The dissent in *Heidgen* persuasively argued that:

Of course, Heidgen's and McPherson's drunkenness does not excuse what they did. They were unforgivably reckless in getting on the highway at all in the condition they were in, and the consequences of their recklessness were horrible. They were unquestionably guilty of manslaughter in the second degree, a class C felony punishable by up to 15 years in prison, and under today's statutes they would also be guilty of aggravated vehicular homicide, a class B felony punishable by up to 25 years. But it is clear, and the majority implicitly recognizes, that unless these two defendants knew they were driving the wrong way they were not guilty of depraved indifference murder. In the absence of such knowledge, their conduct does not show "depraved indifference to human life" . . . .

The majority decides that the jury could have found that Heidgen and McPherson "knew they were driving on the wrong side of the parkway and proceeded regardless." I agree that, if that happened, these defendants could be found guilty of depraved indifference murder; and perhaps it did happen—but I do not see how a rational jury could find beyond a reasonable doubt that it did. Anyone who knowingly drives the wrong way on a divided highway must either have chosen a bizarre way of committing suicide or else be prey to some grandiose illusion that all the other cars will get out of his way. These records contain no more than hints that either Heidgen or McPherson was in such an extraordinary state of mind. * * *

As to both Heidgen and McPherson, the majority suggests that the very fact that they did drive the wrong way for miles, ignoring many signs and other events that should have alerted them, supports an inference that they knew what they were doing. To me, it supports more strongly the inference that—as blood tests proved— they were very drunk. Ignoring warnings that would alert a sober person is what drunk people do. I do not doubt that, as the majority says, a drunk person is not biologically incapable of perceiving and reacting to his surroundings, but anyone who has ever met one knows that they often fail to do so.

I find the Heidgen and McPherson cases to be indistinguishable from *People v. Valencia*, another case involving a drunken wrong-way driver. The majority distinguishes *Valencia* on the ground that there was, in that case, a finding of fact that defendant was oblivious to the risks he was running. But our memorandum in *Valencia* does not rely on, or even mention, that finding; it says the evidence was "insufficient" to support a finding of depraved indifference. If it was insufficient there, it is insufficient here.

There is, of course, one conspicuous difference between these two cases and *Valencia*: Valencia did not kill anyone. The conviction we reversed in *Valencia* was for depraved indifference assault. In these cases, three people died, one of them a young child. Heidgen and McPherson are at fault for these deaths, and deserve severe punishment. But they are not—or at least, were not proved to be— murderers. They did not kill their victims intentionally, and— drawing all reasonable inferences in favor of the People—there is no more than a possibility that they did so with depraved indifference to human life. Their convictions should be reduced to manslaughter in the second degree.

Id. at 281-84, 980 N.Y.S.2d at 333-35 (citations omitted) (Smith, J., dissenting). *See also id.* at 285-86, 980 N.Y.S.2d at 335-36 (Read, J., dissenting).

Notably, shortly after it decided *Heidgen*, the Court of Appeals reduced a Depraved Indifference Murder conviction to Manslaughter 2nd where:

Here, defendant sought to mitigate the consequences of his reckless driving because he "actively attempt[ed] to avoid hitting other vehicles" by swerving, conduct which establishes a lack of depraved indifference. Although defendant drove on the wrong side of the road, this conduct was episodic and part of his effort to avoid other vehicles while evading the police. This conscious avoidance of risk is the antithesis of a complete disregard for the safety of others. Defendant was unquestionably reckless, but he was not depravedly indifferent as we have defined and interpreted that state of mind. Unlike our dissenting colleagues, we conclude that, given this evidence, a rational jury could not have reasonably found depraved indifference beyond a reasonable doubt. * * *

Unlike the defendants in *Heidgen*, defendant never tracked or followed the movements of any driver, nor did he purposefully impede another driver's efforts to avoid a collision. Defendant drove in the wrong lane for brief periods of time in order to pass other cars, not as part of a deadly game. He immediately returned to the proper lane once clear of congestion in order to avoid hitting other vehicles. Eyewitness testimony established that he repeatedly tried to avoid collisions while evading capture by the police. Although defendant swerved around cars and across lanes of traffic, he did so both to speed his flight and to avoid crashing into other vehicles or pedestrians. * * *

If we accepted the People's argument, depraved indifference murder could arguably be charged in every case where a defendant killed someone during a high-speed police chase. By its nature, a high-speed chase endangers pedestrians and other drivers and carries the potential for grave injuries and fatalities. Defendants who take part in high-speed chases violate accepted rules of the road and drive in what is generally considered a reckless manner. Yet, not every vehicular police chase resulting in death will take place under circumstances evincing the defendant's depraved indifference. Cases of depraved indifference murder "are highly fact-specific and dependent upon the individual defendant's particular mental state—a factor that may be extremely difficult to establish." Where, as here, there is no additional evidence evincing a fleeing defendant's wanton disregard for the risk that the defendant's reckless flight from police poses to others, a charge for depraved indifference murder should not be submitted to the jury.

People v. Maldonado, 2014 WL 2931529 (N.Y. 2014) (citations omitted). *See also People v. Jakobson*, 119 A.D.3d 815, 990 N.Y.S.2d 88 (2d Dep't 2014).

§ 12:3   Vehicular assault—Generally

Research References

West's Key Number Digest, Automobiles ⊙347

Vehicular assault is the name given to a series of penal law felonies, initially enacted in 1983, which specifically address the issue of how to punish intoxicated and drug-impaired drivers who cause "serious physical injury" to others.

[T]he 1983 enactment of the vehicular assault and manslaughter statutes (L. 1983, ch. 298) was prompted by legislative concern with injury and death caused by intoxicated drivers. When serious physical injury is caused the crime is vehicular assault; when death is caused the crime is vehicular manslaughter (*see*, 1983 New York State Legislative Annual, at 134). While first-degree assault is a class C felony (Penal Law § 120.10), vehicular manslaughter, at the time of the defendant's conviction, was only a class D felony (Penal

Law § 125.12). In 1985, the legislature amended the vehicular manslaughter provision by adding a higher degree of the crime (class C felony if the defendant is driving with a suspended or revoked license) (Penal Law § 125.13, added by L. 1985, ch. 507), and similarly amended the vehicular assault provisions (Penal Law § 120.04, added by L. 1985, ch. 507).

People v. Snow, 138 A.D.2d 217, __, 530 N.Y.S.2d 913, 914 (4th Dep't 1988), *aff'd for the reasons stated in the opinion below*, 74 N.Y.2d 671, 543 N.Y.S.2d 385 (1989). *See also* 138 A.D.2d at __, 530 N.Y.S.2d at 916 ("While we recognize that injuries and death caused by intoxicated drivers are of significant concern, the Legislature has adequately responded by establishing increased penalties under the Vehicle and Traffic Law and by adding vehicular assault and vehicular manslaughter provisions to the Penal Law"); *People v. Belizaire*, 234 A.D.2d 467, __, 651 N.Y.S.2d 574, 574–75 (2d Dep't 1996).

Effective June 8, 2005, the Legislature performed major surgery on the core element of the crimes of vehicular assault in the second degree and vehicular manslaughter in the second degree [Penal Law §§ 120.03 and 125.12]. L.2005, c. 39. . . .

The major change in the second-degree crimes was to repeal the requirement that the offender act with "criminal negligence" in causing the serious physical injury (vehicular assault) or death (vehicular manslaughter).

Donnino, Practice Commentary, McKinney's Cons. Laws of N.Y., Book 39, Penal Law § 125.00, at 120.

In 2006, new laws were enacted increasing the penalties for vehicular assault and vehicular manslaughter in situations where the defendant (a) commits the offense in conjunction with aggravated DWI, (b) has a prior VTL § 1192 conviction (or an analogous out-of-state conviction) within the past 10 years, (c) seriously injures or kills more than one other person, or (d) has previously been convicted of vehicular assault or vehicular manslaughter.

In 2007, new laws were enacted increasing the level of the offenses even further where the defendant commits them in conjunction with reckless driving, in violation of VTL § 1212.

In 2009, new laws were enacted increasing the penalties for Vehicular Assault and Vehicular Manslaughter in situations where the victim was a passenger in the vehicle who was under the age of 16.

§ 12:4 Serious physical injury

Research References

West's Key Number Digest, Automobiles ⚷332

The vehicular assault statutes require that the victim(s) suffer "serious physical injury." In this regard, the term "serious physical injury" is a term of art which is defined in the Penal Law as:

> [P]hysical injury which creates a substantial risk of death, or which causes death or serious and protracted disfigurement, protracted impairment of health or protracted loss or impairment of the function of any bodily organ.

PL § 10.00(10). *Cf.* PL § 10.00(9) (" 'Physical injury' means impairment of physical condition or substantial pain").

To qualify as a "serious physical injury" for penal law purposes, an injury must be far more severe than what a layperson would consider "serious" as that term is commonly used. Simply stated, to satisfy the PL § 10.00(10) definition, an injury must generally be life-threatening (or even cause death), seriously disfiguring, or result in the loss of, or prolonged loss of use of, a bodily organ. In this regard, in *People v. Stewart*, 18 N.Y.3d 831, 832-33, 939 N.Y.S.2d 273, 273-74, 962 N.E.2d 764 (2011), the Court of Appeals held as follows:

> While the assault upon which defendant's conviction is based was serious, involving numerous blows with a sharp instrument, the resulting injuries were described in their most acute aspect by the treating emergency room physician as "superficial"; no organ damage or injury to muscle tissue was radiologically evident. Three of the victim's four wounds required only gauze dressing. And, while the remaining six-to-seven-centimeter wound on the victim's inner forearm was sutured, the victim spent just one day in the hospital without follow-up medical care, apart from the removal of his stitches. These injuries were not shown to be objectively "distressing or objectionable" so as to justify the conclusion that they constituted "serious . . . disfigurement" qualifying as a serious physical injury predicate for first degree assault under Penal Law § 120.10(1) and § 10.00(10).

> Nor was serious physical injury proved upon the alternative ground set forth in the same Penal Law provisions, that the victim suffered "protracted impairment of health." It is true that the victim complained of daily pain attributable to his healing scars, but there was no basis for the jury reasonably to conclude that these sensations, discomfiting as they may have been, were indicative of or causally related to any protracted health impairment. There was, as noted, no medical evidence of an injury even potentially giving rise to extended health impairment. And, while we do not exclude the possibility that pain may itself be disabling and result in protracted impairment of health, there was no evidence that the pain complained of by the present victim was so severe as to have had that effect; the victim did not, for example, testify as to his pain's severity or his need to resort to palliative measures. We note in this connection that the governing definitional statute, Penal Law § 10.00(10), provides that, apart from an injury that is protract-

edly health impairing, "serious physical injury" alternatively may be "physical injury which creates a substantial risk of death, or which causes death or serious and protracted disfigurement . . . [or] protracted loss or impairment of the function of any bodily organ." It would not have been consistent with the Legislature's evident intent in this enumeration, rigorously to require verifiable proof of serious and consequential injury, to have included in it what would amount to a catchall option for complaints of persisting discomfort unconnected to ascertainable health impairment.

(Citation omitted).

Injuries such as broken bones, serious lacerations, etc.—which presumably constitute "serious" physical injuries in common parlance—do not satisfy this standard. *See, e.g., Stewart, supra; People v. Daniels*, 97 A.D.3d 845, 847, 948 N.Y.S.2d 431, 433-434 (3d Dep't 2012), leave to appeal denied, 20 N.Y.3d 931, 957 N.Y.S.2d 691, 981 N.E.2d 288 (2012) ("Although stabbed in the head (not penetrating the skull) and suffering a concussion, together with residual headaches, victim B acknowledged that she was no longer experiencing headaches some six months later at the time of the trial. She stated that the only continuing physical problem she had was a 'kind of sore [knee] every once in a while,' but she was able to resume playing soccer and the medical evidence regarding her knee failed to establish a serious physical injury within the meaning of the statute."); *People v. Nimmons*, 95 A.D.3d 1360, __, 945 N.Y.S.2d 358, 359 (2d Dep't 2012) ("The People sought to satisfy the element of serious physical injury by demonstrating that the gunshot wound sustained by the victim 'create[d] a substantial risk of death' (Penal Law § 10.00[10]). The People, however, failed to present any evidence that would support such a finding. They presented the testimony of an emergency medical technician (hereinafter the EMT), who described the 'potential consequences' of gunshot wounds to the chest. The EMT, however, did not testify as to whether the gunshot wound inflicted here did, in fact, create a substantial risk of death to this victim."); *People v. Sudol*, 89 A.D.3d 499, __, 932 N.Y.S.2d 49, 51 (1st Dep't 2011) ("The evidence was insufficient to establish that the victim suffered serious physical injury (*see* Penal Law § 10.00[10]) as a result of the attack. The fracture to the orbital socket of the victim's eye was surgically repaired and the victim suffered no lasting ill effects beyond an occasional twitching of his eye."); *People v. Felipe*, 79 A.D.3d 1454, 913 N.Y.S.2d 398 (3d Dep't 2010); *People v. Ham*, 67 A.D.3d 1038, __, 889 N.Y.S.2d 110, 112 (3d Dep't 2009) ("Although the victim testified that he suffered intense pain as a result of the gunshot, his hospital records indicate that he experienced only a 'small amount of associated bleeding' with the one-centimeter exit and entrance wounds on his left thigh, denied any loss of consciousness, and was stable upon examination at the hospital. Moreover, his X rays were unremarkable and his condition was deemed 'satisfactory' when he checked himself out of the hospital 'against medical advice.' Indeed, the victim's aunt testified that she was aware that he 'walked out of the hospital after the shooting' ''); *People v. Pittman*, 33 A.D.3d 1118, 823 N.Y.S.2d 256 (3d Dep't 2006); *People v. Gray*, 30 A.D.3d 771, 816 N.Y.S.2d 609 (3d Dep't 2006); *People v. Sleasman*, 24 A.D.3d 1041, 805 N.Y.S.2d 736 (3d Dep't 2005); *People v. Phillip*, 279 A.D.2d 802, 718 N.Y.S.2d 727 (3d Dep't 2001) (fracture of assault victim's left mandible causing, inter alia, loss of work for six-eight weeks, inability to eat solid foods for two months, long-term pain, etc. not "serious physical injury" within meaning of PL § 10.00(10)); *People v. Horton*, 9 A.D.3d 503, 780 N.Y.S.2d 654 (3d Dep't 2004); *People v. Snyder*, 294 A.D.2d 381, 741 N.Y.S.2d 892 (2d Dep't 2002); *People v. White*, 283 A.D.2d 964, 725 N.Y.S.2d 499 (4th Dep't 2001); *People v. Castillo*, 199 A.D.2d 276, 604 N.Y.S.2d 220 (2d Dep't 1993); *People v. Robles*, 173 A.D.2d 337, 569 N.Y.S.2d 704 (1st Dep't 1991); *People v. Birmingham*, 168 A.D.2d 503, 562 N.Y.S.2d 746 (2d Dep't 1990); *People v. Santos*, 161 A.D.2d 816, 556 N.Y.S.2d 376 (2d Dep't 1990); *People v. Rucker*, 94 A.D.2d 948, 464 N.Y.S.2d 73 (4th Dep't 1983). *See also People v. Jornov*, 65 A.D.3d 363, __, 881 N.Y.S.2d 776, 779-80 (4th Dep't 2009).

In *People v. Tucker*, 91 A.D.3d 1030, __, 936 N.Y.S.2d 386, 387-88 (3d Dep't 2012), the Appellate Division, Third Department, held that:

> The evidence was legally insufficient to prove that the victim suffered a serious physical injury. * * * The victim suffered eight stab wounds. Although they all bled, at least seven of them were described by doctors as superficial. The most serious wound was approximately four inches long and 2½ inches deep and transected the victim's rectus abdominis muscle, but the bleeding was stopped with a few sutures. At the hospital, the victim was alert, never lost consciousness, was not in shock, no internal organs were punctured, his blood loss was not massive and his vital signs were essentially normal throughout his time in the hospital. The treating emergency room physician testified that the wounds collectively "could[] have caused substantial risk of death," but he did not further explain that opinion or state that the wounds actually did create such a substantial risk. The surgeon who sutured the wounds testified that it was "possible" that the victim's collective wounds would have been fatal if the injuries had all gone untreated. But he also testified that had the most serious wound and the nearest wound to it been left untreated, they probably would not have been fatal. Considering the victim's actual injuries, rather than mere possibilities or what could have happened, the evidence was insufficient to establish that the victim's injuries created a substantial risk of death.

The other categories of serious physical injury were also not established. The victim displayed his chest scars to the jury, and he also had scars on his back, but the record does not contain any pictures or descriptions of what the jury saw so as to prove that these scars constitute serious or protracted disfigurement. The victim testified that he took pain medication for a few weeks and continued to feel some pain thereafter, but that he was completely pain free about 2½ months after the incident. He testified that his injuries have affected his ability to throw a ball and swing a baseball bat, but he did not elaborate on these effects and he still intended to try out for his college baseball team. No medical evidence was submitted to link his diminished baseball skills to his injuries, as opposed to his reduced ability to practice after receiving his injuries. There was no proof of protracted impairment of health or function of bodily organs. Thus, the People failed to prove that the victim suffered a serious physical injury.

(Citations omitted).

Where scarring is concerned, Courts had sometimes found that relatively minor scars fell within the definition of "serious and protracted disfigurement" for purposes of PL § 10.00(10). However, the Court of Appeals has now made clear that more than minor, unobtrusive scarring is required. In this regard, in *People v. McKinnon*, 15 N.Y.3d 311, 910 N.Y.S.2d 767, 937 N.E.2d 524 (2010), the Court of Appeals held as follows:

A person is "seriously" disfigured when a reasonable observer would find her altered appearance distressing or objectionable. The standard is an objective one, but we do not imply that the only relevant factor is the nature of the injury; the injury must be viewed in context, considering its location on the body and any relevant aspects of the victim's overall physical appearance. To apply the standard to this case, we examine what the evidence shows about the marks that defendant created by biting the victim's inner forearm.

The record contains a picture of the bite marks, taken on the day of the crime. It shows two ovals with reddish discoloration, one located at and above the midpoint between the wrist and the elbow, the other closer to, but still several inches above, the wrist. According to hospital records, one bite mark measured 3.5 by 3 centimeters, the other 3 by 3 centimeters. Police officers who saw the victim's injuries on the day she suffered them described them as "severe" and "deep." Hospital records show that the victim's flesh was torn but that there was no "exudation" (oozing of fluid from blood vessels). The wounds did not require any stitches. The victim was told to follow up with a plastic surgeon for "optimal" cosmetic results, but there is no evidence that she did so.

There is no later photograph of the wounds, and the record as to what they looked like after they had time to heal is not precise. The victim displayed her arm to the jury at trial, but there is no

contemporaneous description of what the jury saw. Later in the
trial, both counsel described the wounds briefly: the prosecutor
referred to "two large brown bite wounds," the defense lawyer to
"scars, little black and blues right now."

This limited record is not sufficient to support a finding of serious
disfigurement. It shows no more than that the victim had two scars
of moderate size on her inner forearm. This is certainly a disfigurement, but no basis appears in the record for finding it a serious one,
as we have defined the term. The mere existence of such scars,
considering their location, would not make the victim's appearance
distressing or objectionable to a reasonable person observing her.
The case might be different if there were something unusually
disturbing about the scars, but if there was the prosecution failed
to make a record of it, in the form of either a photograph or a
detailed description. We decline the prosecution's invitation to infer,
in effect, that whatever the jury saw must have supported its
verdict; a court reviewing the sufficiency of the evidence cannot rely
on facts of which no record is made. A contemporaneous photograph
or description is not necessary in every case where a victim's wound
is shown to a jury—but it is necessary where, as here, there is no
other evidence in the record supporting an inference that what the
jury saw amounted to serious disfigurement.

15 N.Y.3d at 315-16, 910 N.Y.S.2d at 769-70.

Indeed, case law addressing whether an injury even constitutes
a mere "physical injury" within the meaning of PL § 10.00(9)
demonstrates that trial courts should be vigilant in ensuring that
the statutory requirements are met. *See, e.g., People v. Jiminez*,
55 N.Y.2d 895, 896, 449 N.Y.S.2d 22, 22 (1982) ("Testimony that
the victim suffered a one centimeter cut above her lip, without
more, was not adequate to prove that the victim suffered either
'substantial pain' or 'impairment of a physical condition'") (citation omitted); *People v. McDowell*, 28 N.Y.2d 373, 375, 321
N.Y.S.2d 894, 895 (1971) ("In this case the incidental reference to
a blackened eye without any development of its appearance,
seriousness, accompanying swelling, or suggestion of pain was
insufficient" to satisfy PL § 10.00[9]); *People v. Zalevsky*, 82
A.D.3d 1136, __, 918 N.Y.S.2d 790, 792 (2d Dep't 2011) (insufficient proof of "physical injury" where victim testified that
defendant kicked him in the leg, he was "bruised up a little bit"
at the location of the kick, the pain was "minor", he did not seek
any medical treatment or miss any work, and there was no
testimony as to the duration or severity of the pain).

In *Matter of Philip A.*, 49 N.Y.2d 198, 424 N.Y.S.2d 418 (1980),
the Court of Appeals provided guidelines for defining "substantial
pain":

Pain is, of course, a subjective matter. Thus, touching the skin of a
person who has suffered third degree burns will cause exquisite

pain, while the forceful striking of a gymnast in the solar plexus may cause him no discomfort at all. Yet it is clear from the inclusion of the word "substantial" in the Penal Law definition that the Legislature did not intend a wholly subjective criterion to govern. This is so both because it abjured the Model Penal Code's definition, and because the Revisors' notes state that "petty slaps, shoves, kicks and the like delivered out of hostility, meanness and similar motives" are not within the definition.

Thus, while the question whether the "substantial pain" necessary to establish assault in the third degree has been proved is generally a question for the trier of fact, who in reaching his or its conclusion can consider, among other factors, the subjective reaction of the person claimed to have been assaulted, there is an objective level, suggested by the Revisors' notes, below which the question is one of law, and the charge should be dismissed.

Here we have nothing more than evidence that complainant was hit, that it caused him pain, the degree of which was not spelled out, caused him to cry and caused a red mark. All of that is consistent with "petty slaps" and, therefore, was insufficient to establish "substantial pain" beyond a reasonable doubt.

49 N.Y.2d at 200, 424 N.Y.S.2d at 419–20 (citations omitted).

§ 12:5 Vehicular assault 2nd

Research References

West's Key Number Digest, Automobiles ⬤332

Effective November 1, 2006, PL § 120.03 provides that:

A person is guilty of vehicular assault in the second degree when he or she causes serious physical injury to another person, and either:

(1) operates a motor vehicle in violation of [VTL § 1192(2), (3), (4) or (4-a)] or operates a vessel or public vessel in violation of [Navigation Law § 49-a(2)(b), (c), (d) or (e)], and as a result of such intoxication or impairment by the use of a drug, or by the combined influence of drugs or of alcohol and any drug or drugs, operates such motor vehicle, vessel or public vessel in a manner that causes such serious physical injury to such other person, or

(2) operates a motor vehicle with a [GVWR] of more than [18,000] pounds which contains flammable gas, radioactive materials or explosives in violation of [VTL § 1192(1)], and such flammable gas, radioactive materials or explosives is the cause of such serious physical injury, and as a result of such impairment by the use of alcohol, operates such motor vehicle in a manner that causes such serious physical injury to such other person, or

(3) operates a snowmobile in violation of [PRHPL
§ 25.24(1)(b), (c) or (d)] or operates an all terrain vehicle as
defined in [VTL § 2281(1)(a)] and in violation of [VTL § 1192(2),
(3), (4) or (4-a)], and as a result of such intoxication or impairment by the use of a drug, or by the combined influence of
drugs or of alcohol and any drug or drugs, operates such
snowmobile or all terrain vehicle in a manner that causes such
serious physical injury to such other person.

If it is established that the person operating such motor vehicle, vessel, public vessel, snowmobile or all terrain vehicle caused
such serious physical injury while unlawfully intoxicated or
impaired by the use of alcohol or a drug, then there shall be a rebuttable presumption that, as a result of such intoxication or
impairment by the use of alcohol or a drug, or by the combined
influence of drugs or of alcohol and any drug or drugs, such
person operated the motor vehicle, vessel, public vessel, snowmobile or all terrain vehicle in a manner that caused such serious
physical injury, as required by this section.

Vehicular assault in the second degree is a class E felony.

§ 12:6   Vehicular assault 1st

Research References
West's Key Number Digest, Automobiles ⊙332

Vehicular assault 2nd is a class E felony. *See* PL § 120.03.
Vehicular assault 1st is a class D felony. *See* PL § 120.04. Prior
to various amendments which started in 2005, the only difference
between vehicular assault 2nd and vehicular assault 1st was the
added element of AUO 1st. *See* VTL § 511(3). In other words, a
person who committed vehicular assault 2nd in conjunction with
AUO 1st committed vehicular assault 1st. Now, many more
people are subject to being charged with this offense.

Effective December 18, 2009, PL § 120.04 provides that:

A person is guilty of vehicular assault in the first degree when he
or she commits the crime of [Vehicular Assault 2nd] as defined in
[PL § 120.03], and either:

(1) commits such crime while operating a motor vehicle while
such person has .18 of one per centum or more by weight of
alcohol in such person's blood as shown by chemical analysis of
such person's blood, breath, urine or saliva made pursuant to the
provisions of [VTL § 1194];

(2) commits such crime while knowing or having reason to know
that: (a) his or her license or his or her privilege of operating a
motor vehicle in another state or his or her privilege of obtaining
a license to operate a motor vehicle in another state is suspended

or revoked and such suspension or revocation is based upon a conviction in such other state for an offense which would, if committed in this state, constitute a violation of any of the provisions of [VTL § 1192]; or (b) his or her license or his or her privilege of operating a motor vehicle in the state or his or her privilege of obtaining a license issued by [DMV] is suspended or revoked and such suspension or revocation is based upon either a refusal to submit to a chemical test pursuant to [VTL § 1194] or following a conviction for a violation of any of the provisions of [VTL § 1192];

(3) has previously been convicted of violating any of the provisions of [VTL § 1192] within the preceding [10] years, provided that, for the purposes of this subdivision, a conviction in any other state or jurisdiction for an offense which, if committed in this state, would constitute a violation of [VTL § 1192], shall be treated as a violation of such law;

(4) causes serious physical injury to more than [1] other person;

(5) has previously been convicted of violating any provision of this article or [PL Article 125] involving the operation of a motor vehicle, or was convicted in any other state or jurisdiction of an offense involving the operation of a motor vehicle which, if committed in this state, would constitute a violation of this article or [PL Article 125]; or

(6) commits such crime while operating a motor vehicle while a child who is [15] years of age or less is a passenger in such motor vehicle and causes serious physical injury to such child.

If it is established that the person operating such motor vehicle caused such serious physical injury or injuries while unlawfully intoxicated or impaired by the use of alcohol or a drug, or by the combined influence of drugs or of alcohol and any drug or drugs, then there shall be a rebuttable presumption that, as a result of such intoxication or impairment by the use of alcohol or a drug, or by the combined influence of drugs or of alcohol and any drug or drugs, such person operated the motor vehicle in a manner that caused such serious physical injury or injuries, as required by this section and [PL § 120.03].

Vehicular assault in the first degree is a class D felony.

§ 12:7   Aggravated vehicular assault

Research References

West's Key Number Digest, Automobiles ⊙⟶332

Effective November 1, 2007, the new offense of aggravated vehicular assault came into existence. *See* PL § 120.04-a. Aggravated vehicular assault is, in essence, vehicular assault 1st committed in conjunction with reckless driving. In this regard, PL § 120.04-a currently provides that:

A person is guilty of aggravated vehicular assault when he or she engages in reckless driving as defined by [VTL § 1212], and commits the crime of [Vehicular Assault 2nd] as defined in [PL § 120.03], and either:

(1) commits such crimes while operating a motor vehicle while such person has .18 of one per centum or more by weight of alcohol in such person's blood as shown by chemical analysis of such person's blood, breath, urine or saliva made pursuant to the provisions of [VTL § 1194];

(2) commits such crimes while knowing or having reason to know that: (a) his or her license or his or her privilege of operating a motor vehicle in another state or his or her privilege of obtaining a license to operate a motor vehicle in another state is suspended or revoked and such suspension or revocation is based upon a conviction in such other state for an offense which would, if committed in this state, constitute a violation of any of the provisions of [VTL § 1192]; or (b) his or her license or his or her privilege of operating a motor vehicle in this state or his or her privilege of obtaining a license issued by [DMV] is suspended or revoked and such suspension or revocation is based upon either a refusal to submit to a chemical test pursuant to [VTL § 1194] or following a conviction for a violation of any of the provisions of [VTL § 1192];

(3) has previously been convicted of violating any of the provisions of [VTL § 1192] within the preceding [10] years, provided that, for the purposes of this subdivision, a conviction in any other state or jurisdiction for an offense which, if committed in this state, would constitute a violation of [VTL § 1192], shall be treated as a violation of such law;

(4) causes serious physical injury to more than [1] other person;

(5) has previously been convicted of violating any provision of this article or [PL Article 125] involving the operation of a motor vehicle, or was convicted in any other state or jurisdiction of an offense involving the operation of a motor vehicle which, if committed in this state, would constitute a violation of this article or [PL Article 125]; or

(6) commits such crime while operating a motor vehicle while a child who is [15] years of age or less is a passenger in such motor vehicle and causes serious physical injury to such child.

If it is established that the person operating such motor vehicle caused such serious physical injury or injuries while unlawfully intoxicated or impaired by the use of alcohol or a drug, or by the combined influence of drugs or of alcohol and any drug or drugs, then there shall be a rebuttable presumption that, as a result of such intoxication or impairment by the use of alcohol or a drug, or by the combined influence of drugs or of alcohol and any drug or drugs, such person operated the motor vehicle in a manner that caused such serious physical injury or injuries, as required by this section and [PL § 120.03].

Aggravated vehicular assault is a class C felony.

§ 12:8   Vehicular manslaughter—Generally

Research References

West's Key Number Digest, Automobiles ⛐344

Vehicular manslaughter is the name given to a series of penal law felonies, initially enacted in 1983, which specifically address the issue of how to punish intoxicated and drug-impaired drivers who cause the death of others.

> [T]he 1983 enactment of the vehicular assault and manslaughter statutes (L. 1983, ch. 298) was prompted by legislative concern with injury and death caused by intoxicated drivers. When serious physical injury is caused the crime is vehicular assault; when death is caused the crime is vehicular manslaughter (*see*, 1983 New York State Legislative Annual, at 134). While first degree assault is a class C felony (Penal Law § 120.10), vehicular manslaughter, at the time of defendant's conviction, was only a class D felony (Penal Law § 125.12). In 1985, the Legislature amended the vehicular manslaughter provision by adding a higher degree of the crime (class C felony if the defendant is driving with a suspended or revoked license) (Penal Law § 125.13, added by L. 1985, ch. 507), and similarly amended the vehicular assault provisions (Penal Law § 120.04, added by L. 1985, ch. 507).

People v. Snow, 138 A.D.2d 217, __, 530 N.Y.S.2d 913, 914 (4th Dep't 1988), *aff'd for the reasons stated in the opinion below*, 74 N.Y.2d 671, 543 N.Y.S.2d 385 (1989). *See also* 138 A.D.2d at __, 530 N.Y.S.2d at 916 ("While we recognize that injuries and death caused by intoxicated drivers are of significant concern, the Legislature has adequately responded by establishing increased penalties under the Vehicle and Traffic Law and by adding vehicular assault and vehicular manslaughter provisions to the Penal Law"); *People v. Belizaire*, 234 A.D.2d 467, __, 651 N.Y.S.2d 574, 574–75 (2d Dep't 1996).

> Effective June 8, 2005, the Legislature performed major surgery on the core element of the crimes of vehicular assault in the second degree and vehicular manslaughter in the second degree [Penal Law §§ 120.03 and 125.12]. L.2005, c. 39. . . .

The major change in the second-degree crimes was to repeal the requirement that the offender act with "criminal negligence" in causing the serious physical injury (vehicular assault) or death (vehicular manslaughter).

Donnino, Practice Commentary, McKinney's Cons. Laws of N.Y., Book 39, Penal Law § 125.00, at 120.

In 2006, new laws were enacted increasing the penalties for vehicular assault and vehicular manslaughter in situations where the defendant (a) commits the offense in conjunction with aggravated DWI, (b) has a prior VTL § 1192 conviction (or an analogous out-of-state conviction) within the past 10 years, (c) seriously injures or kills more than one other person, or (d) has previously been convicted of vehicular assault or vehicular manslaughter.

In 2007, new laws were enacted increasing the level of the offenses even further where the defendant commits them in conjunction with reckless driving, in violation of VTL § 1212.

In 2009, new laws were enacted increasing the penalties for Vehicular Assault and Vehicular Manslaughter in situations where the victim was a passenger in the vehicle who was under the age of 16.

§ 12:9 Vehicular manslaughter 2nd

Research References

West's Key Number Digest, Automobiles ⟜344

Effective November 1, 2006, PL § 125.12 provides that:

A person is guilty of vehicular manslaughter in the second degree when he or she causes the death of another person, and either:

(1) operates a motor vehicle in violation of [VTL § 1192(2), (3), (4) or (4-a)] or operates a vessel or public vessel in violation of [Navigation Law § 49-a(2)(b), (c), (d) or (e)], and as a result of such intoxication or impairment by the use of a drug, or by the combined influence of drugs or of alcohol and any drug or drugs, operates such motor vehicle, vessel or public vessel in a manner that causes the death of such other person, or

(2) operates a motor vehicle with a [GVWR] of more than [18,000] pounds which contains flammable gas, radioactive materials or explosives in violation of [VTL § 1192(1)], and such flammable gas, radioactive materials or explosives is the cause of such death, and as a result of such impairment by the use of alcohol, operates such motor vehicle in a manner that causes the death of such other person, or

(3) operates a snowmobile in violation of [PRHPL § 25.24(1)(b),

(c) or (d)] or operates an all terrain vehicle as defined in [VTL § 2281(1)(a)] in violation of [VTL § 1192(2), (3), (4) or (4-a)], and as a result of such intoxication or impairment by the use of a drug, or by the combined influence of drugs or of alcohol and any drug or drugs, operates such snowmobile or all terrain vehicle in a manner that causes the death of such other person.

If it is established that the person operating such motor vehicle, vessel, public vessel, snowmobile or all terrain vehicle caused such death while unlawfully intoxicated or impaired by the use of alcohol or a drug, then there shall be a rebuttable presumption that, as a result of such intoxication or impairment by the use of alcohol or a drug, or by the combined influence of drugs or of alcohol and any drug or drugs, such person operated the motor vehicle, vessel, public vessel, snowmobile or all terrain vehicle in a manner that caused such death, as required by this section.

Vehicular manslaughter in the second degree is a class D felony.

§ 12:10 Vehicular manslaughter 1st

Research References

West's Key Number Digest, Automobiles ⊘344

Vehicular manslaughter 2nd is a class D felony. *See* PL § 125.12. Vehicular manslaughter 1st is a class C felony. *See* PL § 125.13. Prior to various amendments which started in 2005, the only difference between vehicular manslaughter 2nd and vehicular manslaughter 1st was the added element of AUO 1st. *See* VTL § 511(3). In other words, a person who committed vehicular manslaughter 2nd in conjunction with AUO 1st committed vehicular manslaughter 1st. Now, many more people are subject to being charged with this offense.

Effective December 18, 2009, PL § 125.13 provides that:

A person is guilty of vehicular manslaughter in the first degree when he or she commits the crime of [Vehicular Manslaughter 2nd] as defined in [PL § 125.12], and either:

(1) commits such crime while operating a motor vehicle while such person has .18 of one per centum or more by weight of alcohol in such person's blood as shown by chemical analysis of such person's blood, breath, urine or saliva made pursuant to the provisions of [VTL § 1194];

(2) commits such crime while knowing or having reason to know that: (a) his or her license or his or her privilege of operating a motor vehicle in another state or his or her privilege of obtaining a license to operate a motor vehicle in another state is suspended or revoked and such suspension or revocation is based upon a

conviction in such other state for an offense which would, if committed in this state, constitute a violation of any of the provisions of [VTL § 1192]; or (b) his or her license or his or her privilege of operating a motor vehicle in the state or his or her privilege of obtaining a license issued by [DMV] is suspended or revoked and such suspension or revocation is based upon either a refusal to submit to a chemical test pursuant to [VTL § 1194] or following a conviction for a violation of any of the provisions of [VTL § 1192];

(3) has previously been convicted of violating any of the provisions of [VTL § 1192] within the preceding [10] years, provided that, for the purposes of this subdivision, a conviction in any other state or jurisdiction for an offense which, if committed in this state, would constitute a violation of [VTL § 1192], shall be treated as a violation of such law;

(4) causes the death of more than [1] other person;

(5) has previously been convicted of violating any provision of this article or [PL Article 120] involving the operation of a motor vehicle, or was convicted in any other state or jurisdiction of an offense involving the operation of a motor vehicle which, if committed in this state, would constitute a violation of this article or [PL Article 120]; or

(6) commits such crime while operating a motor vehicle while a child who is [15] years of age or less is a passenger in such motor vehicle and causes the death of such child.

If it is established that the person operating such motor vehicle caused such death or deaths while unlawfully intoxicated or impaired by the use of alcohol or a drug, or by the combined influence of drugs or of alcohol and any drug or drugs, then there shall be a rebuttable presumption that, as a result of such intoxication or impairment by the use of alcohol or a drug, or by the combined influence of drugs or of alcohol and any drug or drugs, such person operated the motor vehicle in a manner that caused such death or deaths, as required by this section and [PL § 125.12].

Vehicular manslaughter in the first degree is a class C felony.

§ 12:11   Aggravated vehicular homicide

Research References

West's Key Number Digest, Automobiles ⊙─342.1

Effective November 1, 2007, the new offense of aggravated vehicular homicide came into existence. *See* PL § 125.14. Aggravated vehicular homicide is, in essence, vehicular manslaughter 1st committed in conjunction with reckless driving. In this regard, PL § 125.14 currently provides that:

A person is guilty of aggravated vehicular homicide when he or she engages in reckless driving as defined by [VTL § 1212], and commits the crime of [Vehicular Manslaughter 2nd] as defined in [PL § 125.12], and either:

(1) commits such crimes while operating a motor vehicle while such person has .18 of one per centum or more by weight of alcohol in such person's blood as shown by chemical analysis of such person's blood, breath, urine or saliva made pursuant to the provisions of [VTL § 1194];

(2) commits such crimes while knowing or having reason to know that: (a) his or her license or his or her privilege of operating a motor vehicle in another state or his or her privilege of obtaining a license to operate a motor vehicle in another state is suspended or revoked and such suspension or revocation is based upon a conviction in such other state for an offense which would, if committed in this state, constitute a violation of any of the provisions of [VTL § 1192]; or (b) his or her license or his or her privilege of operating a motor vehicle in this state or his or her privilege of obtaining a license issued by [DMV] is suspended or revoked and such suspension or revocation is based upon either a refusal to submit to a chemical test pursuant to [VTL § 1194] or following a conviction for a violation of any of the provisions of [VTL § 1192];

(3) has previously been convicted of violating any of the provisions of [VTL § 1192] within the preceding [10] years, provided that, for the purposes of this subdivision, a conviction in any other state or jurisdiction for an offense which, if committed in this state, would constitute a violation of [VTL § 1192], shall be treated as a violation of such law;

(4) causes the death of more than [1] other person;

(5) causes the death of [1] person and the serious physical injury of at least [1] other person;

(6) has previously been convicted of violating any provision of this article or [PL Article 120] involving the operation of a motor vehicle, or was convicted in any other state or jurisdiction of an offense involving the operation of a motor vehicle which, if committed in this state, would constitute a violation of this article or [PL Article 120]; or

(7) commits such crime while operating a motor vehicle while a child who is [15] years of age or less is a passenger in such motor vehicle and causes the death of such child.

If it is established that the person operating such motor vehicle caused such death or deaths while unlawfully intoxicated or impaired by the use of alcohol or a drug, or by the combined influence of drugs or of alcohol and any drug or drugs, then there shall be a rebuttable presumption that, as a result of such intoxication or impairment by the use of alcohol or a drug, or by the combined influence of drugs or of alcohol and any drug or drugs, such person operated the motor vehicle in a manner that caused such death or deaths, as required by this section and [PL § 125.12].

Aggravated vehicular homicide is a class B felony.

In *People v. Goldblatt*, 98 A.D.3d 817, 950 N.Y.S.2d 210 (3d Dep't 2012), leave to appeal denied, 20 N.Y.3d 932, 957 N.Y.S.2d 692, 981 N.E.2d 289 (2012), the Appellate Division, Third Department, reversed the defendant's conviction of Aggravated Vehicular Homicide on the ground that the trial court improperly instructed the jury regarding the Reckless Driving element of the offense. Specifically:

> County Court erred by failing to instruct the jury that its analysis of the reckless driving element of aggravated vehicular homicide should focus on whether defendant's manner of operating the vehicle violated the statutory language of Vehicle and Traffic Law § 1212 without regard to defendant's intoxication. . . . A significant part of defendant's defense to the top charge in the indictment was premised upon his argument that intoxication should not be used as part of two separate elements in the same crime, i.e., for the intoxication element of vehicular manslaughter and also to show reckless driving. Defense counsel made such an argument before the jury in summation. When the prosecutor made a statement in summation indicating that the jury should consider intoxication as part of reckless driving, defense counsel objected. County Court did not rule on the objection, but stated that it would "explain it all to the jury." * * *
>
> Defendant argues and the concurring opinion agrees that the jury should have been instructed that it could not consider evidence of defendant's intoxication to prove the reckless driving element of aggravated vehicular manslaughter. In that regard, there is no doubt that the jury should have been instructed that intoxication, absent more, does not establish reckless driving. However, it does not follow that evidence of an individual's intoxication and how that condition may have affected his or her ability to perceive and react to risks commonly encountered while operating a motor vehicle on a public highway is not relevant or admissible to establish that the motor vehicle was being operated recklessly when it was involved in a fatal accident.
>
> Since the jury was not properly instructed as to what was required to find that defendant was recklessly driving his automobile when

involved in this fatal accident, his conviction for aggravated vehicular homicide must be reversed and the matter remitted for a new trial on that charge.

Id. at 821-22, 950 N.Y.S.2d at 214-15, 215-16 (footnote omitted).

In *People v. Hoffman*, 130 A.D.3d 1152, __, 13 N.Y.S.3d 619, 624 (3d Dep't 2015), the Appellate Division, Third Department, found that the Reckless Driving element of Aggravated Vehicular Homicide was satisfied where:

Two of defendant's friends testified that they were with defendant during the hours before the accident and that defendant was intoxicated after drinking steadily from approximately 6:00 p.m. on June 27, 2012 until the time he left the victim's house at approximately 12:45 a.m. on June 28, 2012, and that he smoked marihuana at least two times during that time. When defendant left the victim's house, the victim followed him because he was "not okay to drive." Borghi testified that defendant's car drove toward him "at a high rate of speed" and across the double-yellow line approximately two feet into his lane. Borghi watched as defendant's car "went screeching by [him]," then he saw the tires lose traction and the car flip. The evidence also showed that defendant's blood alcohol content was 0.057% approximately 6 1/2 hours after the accident and his blood tested positive for marihuana. There was expert testimony that, given defendant's weight and the type of alcohol consumed, defendant's blood alcohol content would have been between 0.125% and 0.226% at the time of the accident. Viewing the evidence in the light most favorable to the People, the cumulative evidence that defendant became intoxicated, drove at a high rate of speed, crossed the center line and lost control of the car was sufficient to permit the jury to conclude that defendant drove in reckless disregard of the consequences.

(Citation omitted).

§ 12:12 Causation

Research References

West's Key Number Digest, Automobiles ⊘342.1

Although the vehicular assault/vehicular manslaughter statutes, are now "strict liability" in nature—in that the mens rea element has been removed (except where AUO is an element of the offense)—the People are still required to prove that the defendant's conduct "caused" the victim's serious physical injury/death. *See, e.g., People v. Kibbe*, 35 N.Y.2d 407, 412, 362 N.Y.S.2d 848, 851 (1974) ("defendants should not be found guilty unless their conduct 'was a cause of death sufficiently direct as to meet the requirements of the *criminal*, and not the *tort*, law'") (citation omitted); 35 N.Y.2d at 413, 362 N.Y.S.2d at 852 ("We subscribe to the requirement that the defendants' actions must be *a sufficiently direct cause* of the ensuing death before there can be any imposition of criminal liability"); *People v. Bast*, 19 N.Y.2d 813, 815, 280 N.Y.S.2d 149, 150 (1967) ("Proof of intoxication alone is not enough to sustain a conviction of criminal negligence. The People must also prove that the defendant's intoxication affected his physical and mental capacity to the extent that it caused him to operate his vehicle in a culpably reckless manner"); *People v. Mojica*, 62 A.D.3d 100, __, 874 N.Y.S.2d 195, 203 (2d Dep't 2009) ("if a driver's operation of a vehicle cannot be deemed a proximate cause of the subject accident, then the rebuttable presumption would not arise"); *People v. Carley*, 248 A.D.2d 548, 669 N.Y.S.2d 870 (2d Dep't 1998) (even though evidence before grand jury proved that defendant was both intoxicated *and* speeding, vehicular manslaughter/vehicular assault charges nonetheless dismissed on ground that evidence failed to establish that defendant's conduct "caused" the victims' deaths/injuries); *People v. Phippen*, 232 A.D.2d 790, __, 649 N.Y.S.2d 191, 192 (3d Dep't 1996) ("Causation, like the other ingredients of the crimes at issue . . . is 'an essential element which the People must prove beyond a reasonable doubt.' It requires that '"the defendant's actions must be *a sufficiently direct cause* of the ensuing death"'; a '"merely probable connection between [the act] and death will * * * require acquittal * * *"'") (citations omitted); 232 A.D.2d at __, 649 N.Y.S.2d at 193 ("There being a lack of proof of a causal connection between defendant's conduct and the accident, the evidence is insufficient to convict defendant of either manslaughter in the second degree or criminally negligent homicide"); *People v. Donohue*, 229 A.D.2d 396, __, 645 N.Y.S.2d 60, 62 (2d Dep't 1996) ("the People's burden is to prove beyond a reasonable doubt that the [defendant's] intoxication was *causally related* to the deceased's demise") (emphasis added); *People v. Holt*, 109 A.D.2d 174, __, 491 N.Y.S.2d 526, 528 (4th Dep't 1985) ("An essential element of the crime is that the alleged criminally negligent conduct '*causes* the death of another person'") (emphasis added) (citation omitted); 109 A.D.2d at __, 491 N.Y.S.2d at 529 ("Defendant should not be found guilty of homicide unless his conduct 'was a cause of death sufficiently direct as to meet the requirements of the *criminal*, and not the *tort*, law'") (citation omitted).

In this regard, in *People v. DaCosta*, 6 N.Y.3d 181, 184, 811 N.Y.S.2d 308, 310, 844 N.E.2d 762 (2006), the Court of Appeals held that:

> To be held criminally responsible for a homicide, a defendant's conduct must actually contribute to the victim's death by "set[ting] in motion" the events that result in the killing. Liability will attach even if the defendant's conduct is not the sole cause of death if the actions were a " 'sufficiently direct cause of the ensuing death.' " More than an " 'obscure or merely probable connection' " between

the conduct and result is required. Rather, an act "qualifies as a sufficiently direct cause when the ultimate harm should have been reasonably foreseen."

(Citations omitted).

In *People v. Stickler*, 97 A.D.3d 854, 948 N.Y.S.2d 696 (3d Dep't 2012), leave to appeal denied, 20 N.Y.3d 989, 958 N.Y.S.2d 704, 982 N.E.2d 624 (2012), the defendant was found guilty, following a bench trial conducted on stipulated facts, of Vehicular Manslaughter 2nd. On appeal, the Appellate Division, Third Department, reversed the conviction, holding that:

> County Court . . . erred by treating the statutory presumption as mandatory, rather than permissive, and therefore did not make the necessary finding of guilt beyond a reasonable doubt. Specifically, the court concluded that the presumption mandates a finding of guilt whenever "the defendant is intoxicated and death occurs," thereby "reliev[ing] the People from proving that the defendant . . . operated the vehicle in a manner which was a sufficiently direct cause of death." Inasmuch as the factfinder was evidently unaware that it remained free to reject the inference set forth in the presumption (CJI2d[NY] Penal Law § 125.12), and did not determine whether defendant, in fact, operated the vehicle in a manner that caused the victim's death and did so as a result of unlawful intoxication—elements necessary to sustain a finding of guilt—we must remit this matter for trial or other appropriate disposition on the vehicular manslaughter charge.

Id. at __, 948 N.Y.S.2d at 700-01 (citation omitted).

In *People v. Ryan*, 42 Misc. 3d 643, 980 N.Y.S.2d 246 (Nassau Co. Sup. Ct. 2013), the defendant allegedly caused an accident on the Long Island Expressway while driving while intoxicated. Five to 10 later, a responding police officer was struck and killed by a different motorist who was driving near the accident scene. The issue was whether the defendant, by setting in motion this chain of events, could be charged with causing the death of the police officer. The Court held as follows:

> Although it has been held that a person whose actions result in a victim's presence on a major highway should reasonably foresee that a victim could be struck and killed by a vehicle, a determination must be made to ascertain that the third party driver's operation of his automobile was not an intervening cause, sufficient to relieve the defendant of criminal liability for the directly foreseeable consequences of his actions.
>
> Based upon the evidence presented to the Grand Jury, the Court finds that the third party driver grossly deviated from the standard of care a reasonable person would have observed under the circumstances. The operator bypassed stopped traffic proceeding into the accident scene at a speed of at least 40 mph. He engaged in

rubbernecking causing him to fail to see the officer directly in front of him. He failed to take evasive action. He closed his eyes just prior to impact only applying his brakes one second before striking the police officer. Moreover his was the only vehicle traveling in the HOV lane.

The Court also holds that the foregoing evidence viewed in the light most favorable to the People which, if unexplained and uncontradicted, would not warrant a conviction by a petit jury, as the evidence establishes that the third party driver's operation of his motor vehicle constitutes an intervening cause sufficient to relieve the defendant RYAN of criminal culpability in the tragic death of Officer Olivieri. In this case the death of Officer Olivieri is solely attributable to the driver of the Escalade, and not at all induced by the defendant RYAN.

Id. at __, 980 N.Y.S.2d at 251 (citation and footnote omitted).

§ 12:13   Challenges to the new vehicular assault/vehicular manslaughter laws

Research References

West's Key Number Digest, Automobiles ☞342.1, 344

An issue with regard to the new vehicular assault/vehicular manslaughter laws is that they appear to include a "rebuttable presumption" that the defendant "caused" the serious physical injury/death to the victim(s). However, such presumption only comes into effect once "it is established that the [defendant] caused such serious physical injury [or death] while unlawfully intoxicated or impaired by the use of alcohol or a drug [or a combination thereof]." *See* PL §§ 120.03, 120.04, 120.04-a, 125.12, 125.13, 125.14. As such, the presumption appears to be a presumption in name only.

In any event, to avoid the danger of impermissibly shifting the burden of proof to the defendant, "[i]n criminal cases in New York, presumptions are permissive, which means that the jury may, but need not, accept the inference supported by the presumption." Prince, Richardson on Evidence (11th Ed. 1995), at § 3-105. In this regard, "the jury must receive careful instruction on the use it may make of the specific 'presumption.'" Prince, Richardson on Evidence (11th Ed. 1995), at § 3-105.

In *People v. Baker*, 14 Misc. 3d 629, 826 N.Y.S.2d 550 (Essex Co. Ct. 2006), the court found the 2005 amendments to PL § 125.12 to be constitutional.

In *People v. Mojica*, 62 A.D.3d 100, 874 N.Y.S.2d 195 (2d Dep't 2009), the Appellate Division, Second Department, upheld the Constitutionality of PL § 120.03, including the rebuttable presumption contained therein. In so holding, however, the Court noted that:

The statute provides, in pertinent part, that the rebuttable presumption that the defendant's intoxication caused the subject accident arises only "[i]f it is established that the person operating such motor vehicle . . . . caused such serious injury while unlawfully intoxicated or impaired by the use of alcohol or a drug." *Thus, if a driver's operation of a vehicle cannot be deemed a proximate cause of the subject accident, then the rebuttable presumption would not arise.* We further note that, even if the defendant is correct that the statute would deny due process to hypothetical defendants who may have been DWI in violation of Vehicle and Traffic Law § 1192 but did not cause the accident, we do not reach that issue, as the defendant may not assert a due process challenge contending that the statute is vague as applied to the conduct of others.

62 A.D.3d at ___, 874 N.Y.S.2d at 203 (emphasis added).

In rejecting the defendant's claim that the statute is void for vagueness, the *Mojica* Court stated:

In essence, the statute prohibits operating a vehicle in a manner that causes serious physical injury and while intoxicated and/or impaired by drugs in violation of Vehicle and Traffic Law § 1192(2), (3), (4) or (4-a). We find that the language conveys sufficiently definite warning as to the proscribed conduct "when measured by common understanding and practices." Specifically, the phrase "as a result of such intoxication" would be understood to mean that "by virtue of" or "flowing from" a driver's voluntary consumption of alcohol "to the extent that he is incapable of employing the physical and mental abilities which he is expected to possess in order to operate a vehicle as a reasonable and prudent driver[,]" serious physical injury occurs. Similarly, the statute provides clear guidelines to law enforcement personnel; a person may be arrested for violating Penal Law § 120.03 based upon probable cause to believe that the defendant was DWI and in doing so, operated a vehicle in a manner that caused serious physical injury.

62 A.D.3d at ___, 874 N.Y.S.2d at 204–05 (citations omitted).

Similarly, in *People v. Stickler*, 97 A.D.3d 854, ___, 948 N.Y.S.2d 696, 700 (3d Dep't 2012), leave to appeal denied, 20 N.Y.3d 989, 958 N.Y.S.2d 704, 982 N.E.2d 624 (2012), the Appellate Division, Third Department, held that:

Contrary to defendant's argument that the statute improperly relieves the People from proving that the charged conduct was a sufficiently direct cause of death, the statutory terms expressly provide that the rebuttable presumption arises only "[i]f it is established that the person operating such motor vehicle . . . . *caused such death* while unlawfully intoxicated" (Penal Law § 125.12 [emphasis added]). Thus, as the Second Department has explained, "if a driver's operation of a vehicle cannot be deemed [the] cause of the subject accident, then the rebuttable presumption would not arise." Defendant's challenges to the statute are undermined by his failure to distinguish between the separate elements of causation to which the statute refers. The People must establish that a defendant, in operating a vehicle while unlawfully intoxicated, caused the victim's death; only then may the jury draw an inference regarding the second element of causation—that it was the driver's intoxication that caused him or her to operate the vehicle in a dangerous manner.

In our view, the rebuttable presumption does not render the statute vague inasmuch as "it contains sufficient standards to afford a reasonable degree of certainty so that a person of ordinary intelligence is not forced to guess at its meaning, and to safeguard against arbitrary enforcement." Moreover, according deference to the Legislature's judgment, "there is a fair and rational connection" between the fact that a defendant caused death or serious physical injury by operating a vehicle while impaired by alcohol and the presumption that it was the alcohol impairment that caused the defendant to operate the vehicle in a dangerous manner.

(Citations omitted).

§ 12:14 Limitation on roadways to which VTL § 1192 is applicable does not apply to vehicular crimes statutes

Research References

West's Key Number Digest, Automobiles ⬬324

VTL § 1192(7) expressly lists the types of "roadways" upon which the provisions of VTL § 1192 apply:

Where applicable. The provisions of this section shall apply upon public highways, private roads open to motor vehicle traffic and any other parking lot. For the purposes of this section "parking lot" shall mean any area or areas of private property, including a driveway, near or contiguous to and provided in connection with premises and used as a means of access to and egress from a public highway to such premises and having a capacity for the parking of four or more motor vehicles. The provisions of this section shall not apply to any area or areas of private property comprising all or part of property on which is situated a one or two family residence.

In *People v. Harris*, 81 N.Y.2d 850, 597 N.Y.S.2d 620 (1993), the defendant was convicted of, among other things, vehicular manslaughter 2nd, in violation of PL § 125.12, after a passenger in the vehicle he was driving (while intoxicated) died. The defendant argued that, since the driving at issue took place in a farmer's field, he did not operate the vehicle on a roadway encompassed by VTL § 1192(7), and thus that he did not violate VTL § 1192.

Since, in *Harris*, a violation of certain sections of VTL § 1192 was a required element of the vehicular manslaughter charge, the defendant claimed that he was improperly convicted thereof. The Court of Appeals disagreed, reasoning that:

With the understanding that penal laws have different purposes than vehicle and traffic laws, we conclude the vehicular manslaughter statute applies to any person causing a death by driving under the influence of alcohol or drugs, *regardless of location*, even though there could be no separate punishment for such driving under Vehicle and Traffic Law § 1192 where the driving did not occur on public roads or other areas defined in that section.

81 N.Y.2d at 852, 597 N.Y.S.2d at 622 (emphasis added).

§ 12:15 Criminally negligent homicide

Research References

West's Key Number Digest, Automobiles ☞342.1

PL § 125.10 provides that:

A person is guilty of criminally negligent homicide when, with criminal negligence, he causes the death of another person.

Criminally negligent homicide is a class E felony.

This statute is not unconstitutionally vague. *See People v. Kealey*, 33 N.Y.2d 897, 352 N.Y.S.2d 449, 307 N.E.2d 564 (1973).

In light of the 2005, 2006, and 2007 changes to the vehicular manslaughter statutes, it appears that there is little reason to resort to a charge of criminally negligent homicide in a DWI case. At the outset, vehicular manslaughter has become an offense that no longer requires a mens rea. In this regard, criminally negligent homicide is no longer a lesser included offense of vehicular manslaughter.

Moreover, where a person drives while intoxicated and causes the death of another person, such act would constitute vehicular manslaughter 2nd, a class D felony, but would not, without more, constitute criminally negligent homicide, a class E felony. *See People v. Bast*, 19 N.Y.2d 813, 815, 280 N.Y.S.2d 149, 150 (1967) ("Proof of intoxication alone is not enough to sustain a conviction of criminal negligence. The People must also prove that the defendant's intoxication affected his physical and mental capacity to the extent that it caused him to operate his vehicle in a culpably reckless manner").

Thus, in a typical vehicular homicide case, a charge of criminally negligent homicide is now superfluous, and may only serve to inject an irrelevant issue (*i.e.*, whether the defendant acted with criminal negligence) into the case. *See also* § 12:2, *supra*.

In *People v. McGrantham*, 12 N.Y.3d 892, 893-94, 885 N.Y.S.2d 244, 913 N.E.2d 936 (2009), the Court of Appeals dismissed the count of an indictment charging the defendant with Criminally Negligent Homicide where:

There was evidence before the grand jury that, in the early morning hours of March 29, 2006, defendant was driving eastbound on Cropsey Avenue in Brooklyn and intended to enter the westbound lanes of the Belt Parkway. Defendant, who was sober and had not been speeding, missed the entrance ramp and mistakenly drove onto the exit ramp for westbound traffic. Attempting to correct his mistake, defendant slowly made a U-turn across the three westbound lanes of traffic. He had almost completed the turn when a westbound motorcycle struck his driver's side door. The 20-year-old operator of the motorcycle was killed.

Viewing the evidence in the light most favorable to the People, defendant's motion seeking to dismiss the count of the indictment charging him with criminally negligent homicide must be granted. Defendant's decision to make a U-turn across three lanes of traffic to extricate himself from a precarious situation was not wise, but it does not rise to the level of moral blameworthiness required to sustain a charge of criminally negligent homicide.

The Court of Appeals has shown a clear hesitation to uphold a Criminally Negligent Homicide charge where a sober driver merely commits a traffic infraction that results in death—unless the driver, in addition, engages in "risk-creating" behavior. *See McGrantham*, supra. *See also People v. Cabrera*, 10 N.Y.3d 370, 377, 858 N.Y.S.2d 74, 78, 887 N.E.2d 1132 (2008). In *Cabrera*, the Court of Appeals held that "[f]or a 17 year old to badly misgauge his ability to handle road conditions is not the kind of seriously condemnatory behavior that the Legislature envisioned when it defined "criminal negligence," even though the consequences here were fatal. This crash resulted from noncriminal failure to perceive risk; it was not the result of criminal risk creation." 10 N.Y.3d at 378, 858 N.Y.S.2d at 79-80. In so holding, the Court set forth a concise history of its prior rulings in this regard:

We have examined section 15.05(4) in detail on numerous occasions, most recently in *People v. Conway*. * * *

Cabrera protests that excessive speed is never enough to make out a case of criminally negligent homicide, citing *People v. Bearden*, and *People v. Eckert*, two decades-old cases decided under Penal Law § 1053-a, a predecessor statute to Penal Law § 125.10. While Cabrera reads *Bearden* and *Eckert* as, in effect, establishing a per se rule, our more recent cases take a slightly different tack.

In 1990, for example, we decided two companion cases involving criminally negligent homicide arising out of automobile accidents: *People v. Boutin*, and *People v. Paul V.S.* In *Boutin*, we reversed a conviction for criminally negligent homicide where the defendant-traveling near, and possibly under, the speed limit—struck a marked police car stopped in the right—hand travel lane of Interstate 87 on a rainy, foggy night. In *Paul V.S.*, decided in a memorandum the same day as *Boutin*, we affirmed a conviction for criminally negligent homicide where the defendant was traveling 90 miles per hour in a 55 miles per hour "radar zone," accelerated after being warned by his passenger to slow down, continued past a line of cars that had been stopped by police, and ultimately struck and killed a state trooper attempting to direct him off the highway.

When discussing our precedents in *Boutin*, we observed that the common thread was the "creation," rather than the "non-perception," of risk. *Boutin* implicated noncriminal "risk non-perception" because the defendant had simply "fail[ed] to see the vehicle stopped in the lane ahead of him[,] result[ing] in the fatal accident." This was to be distinguished from cases where there was "criminally culpable risk-creating conduct—e.g., dangerous speeding, racing, failure to obey traffic signals, or any other misconduct that created or contributed to a 'substantial and unjustifiable' risk of death."

In short, it takes some additional affirmative act by the defendant to transform "speeding" into "dangerous speeding"; conduct by which the defendant exhibits the kind of "serious[ly] blameworth[y]" carelessness whose "seriousness would be apparent to anyone who shares the community's general sense of right and wrong." Thus, in the cases where we have considered the evidence sufficient to establish criminally negligent homicide, the defendant has engaged in some other "risk-creating" behavior in addition to driving faster than the posted speed limit (*compare People v. Haney* [defendant was speeding on city street and failed to stop at red light before killing pedestrian crossing street with green light in her favor]; *People v. Soto* [defendant, who was speeding and drag racing on city street, struck and killed driver stopped at red light]; *People v. Ricardo B.* [defendant was drag racing at between 70 and 90 miles per hour on a busy metropolitan street, ran a red light and struck vehicle crossing intersection with light in its favor]; *People v. Loughlin* [intoxicated defendant was speeding on obstructed street under construction in residential neighborhood in Queens]; *People v. Maher* [intoxicated defendant drove at speeds of 50 to 100 miles per hour in 35 miles per hour zone in Manhattan, disobeying several traffic signals]; *People v. Harris* ["defendant, while legally intoxicated, drove his motor vehicle in the dark of night from a public highway into an unfamiliar farmer's field, accelerated at times to a speed approximating 50 miles per hour, intermittently operated the vehicle without headlights, and suddenly and forcefully drove through a hedgerow of small trees and shrubs, not knowing what obstacles and dangers lurked on the other side"]; *People v. Ladd* [intoxicated defendant driving on wrong side of a foggy road at 4:30 a.m.], *with People v. Perry*, [no criminal negligence present where defendant was driving approximately 80 miles per hour in a 55 miles per hour zone "on a rural road, on a dark night," struck a utility pole, and killed two passengers; defendant's "conduct . . . d(id) not constitute a gross deviation from the ordinary standard of care held by those who share the community's general sense of right and wrong"]).

The question on this appeal is therefore whether, when viewed in the light most favorable to the People, the evidence adduced at trial showed that Cabrera's conduct constituted "not only a failure to perceive a risk of death, but also some serious blameworthiness in the conduct that caused it." Measured by this standard, the evidence falls short.

There was testimony and forensic evidence that Cabrera, a young and inexperienced but sober driver, entered a tricky downhill curve, the site of other accidents, at a rate of speed well in excess of the posted warning sign. This behavior is certainly negligent, and unquestionably "blameworthy." But our decisions have uniformly looked for some kind of morally blameworthy component to excessive speed in determining criminal negligence; for example, consciously accelerating in the presence of an obvious risk (*see Paul V.S.*). No such morally blameworthy behavior could be inferred from the testimony in this case.

10 N.Y.3d at 376-78, 858 N.Y.S.2d at 77-79 (citations omitted).

In *People v. Caban*, 14 N.Y.3d 369, 372, 901 N.Y.S.2d 566, 567, 927 N.E.2d 1050 (2010), "[d]efendant, while backing her car, hit and killed a pedestrian. At the time of that event, defendant's license to drive had been suspended, because of an earlier incident with some noticeable similarities to the later, fatal one. Defendant was convicted of criminally negligent homicide, after a trial in which the trial court admitted into evidence the fact of her license suspension." In holding that this evidence was properly admitted, the Court reasoned that:

This was not the first time defendant had backed a car carelessly. Three months earlier . . . 2002, her car was illegally parked at a bus stop, and a police officer began to write a ticket. Arriving at her car, defendant sought to escape the parking ticket by jumping into the car and backing away quickly—going, according to the People's description, into a busy intersection in the vicinity of a school at 8:30 in the morning. Her escape was thwarted when a bus blocked her path, and she received four summonses, including one for unsafe backing and one for failing to yield to pedestrians in a crosswalk. Her license to drive was suspended as a result. * * *

[T]he jury in this case had to consider not only whether defendant failed to perceive "a substantial and unjustifiable risk" that her careless driving would kill someone, but also whether that failure was "a gross deviation from the standard of care that a reasonable person would observe in the situation." In other words, the jury not only had to decide whether defendant was at fault, but also had to consider how much she was at fault. The license suspension was relevant to this question, because a jury could find that it proved defendant to be more negligent than the other evidence showed her to be.

A jury could find that it is unreasonable to back up quickly into a crosswalk, without checking carefully to be sure that no one is in the way; but that it is even more unreasonable to do so when the State has forbidden the driver from driving at all. A jury could find that the license suspension should, if it did not keep defendant off the road, at least have prompted her to pay more attention to safety while she was driving, and that in failing to do so she deviated grossly from what a reasonable person would have done.

14 N.Y.3d at 372, 374, 901 N.Y.S.2d at 567, 568.

Notably, the *Caban* Court addressed the issue of whether evidence of a license suspension would always be admissible in a case involving criminally negligent homicide:

While a license suspension is, as a general proposition, relevant to the issue of criminal negligence, that does not mean evidence of a suspension is admissible whenever criminal negligence is in issue. Evidence, though relevant, may be excluded where "its probative value is substantially outweighed by the danger that it will unfairly prejudice the other side or mislead the jury." That danger is not present here. Defendant would have a better argument for exclusion if her license had been suspended, for example, for failure to pay parking tickets. But it was not. It was suspended for conduct frighteningly similar to the conduct that caused Francesca Maytin's death—backing unsafely into a crosswalk. If the jury inferred from the license suspension that defendant should have known that it was unsafe for her to drive, the jury was not misled.

The admission of the license suspension, to the extent it informed the jury about defendant's earlier misbehavior, did not violate the familiar rule that a defendant's uncharged crimes or bad acts are generally inadmissible when they serve only to show the defendant's criminal propensity. When the issue is criminal negligence, a prior similar act for which defendant has been punished shows more than propensity; a defendant who is repeatedly negligent in the same way may be found to be unable or unwilling to learn from her mistakes—and thus to be guilty not just of deviation, but of "gross deviation," from reasonable care. The prior conduct is thus directly relevant to the extent of defendant's negligence in the case on trial—to her mens rea.

14 N.Y.3d at 374-75, 901 N.Y.S.2d at 568-69 (citations omitted). *See also People v. Simmons*, 31 A.D.3d 1143, 817 N.Y.S.2d 817 (4th Dep't 2006).

In *People v. Rooney*, 57 N.Y.2d 822, 823, 455 N.Y.S.2d 595, 596, 441 N.E.2d 1113 (1982), the Court of Appeals held that a defendant can properly be convicted of Criminally Negligent Homicide despite being acquitted of Driving While Intoxicated. In so holding, the Court reasoned that:

Not every fact mentioned in an indictment is essential to establish

the defendant's guilt of the crime charged, and thus it is not necessary in every case that the People prove all acts alleged in the
indictment when the remaining acts alleged are sufficient to sustain
a conviction. In this case the jury could find that the defendant was
criminally negligent when he drove the vehicle on the wrong side of
the road while speeding even though he may not have been
intoxicated at the time.

§ 12:16   Aggravated criminally negligent homicide

PL § 125.11 provides that:

A person is guilty of aggravated criminally negligent homicide
when, with criminal negligence, he or she causes the death of a police officer or peace officer where such officer was in the course of
performing his or her official duties and the defendant knew or reasonably should have known that such victim was a police officer or
peace officer.

Aggravated criminally negligent homicide is a class C felony.

In *People v. Carncross*, 14 N.Y.3d 319, 901 N.Y.S.2d 112 (2010),
the defendant appealed his convictions of Aggravated Criminally
Negligent Homicide and Reckless Driving, which convictions
arose out of an incident in which a State Trooper died after losing control of his vehicle and crashing into a tree while pursuing
a motorcycle driven by defendant, who was speeding. In affirming the convictions, the Court of Appeals, held that:

In *People v. DaCosta*, we explained the law regarding causation in
this context:

To be held criminally responsible for a homicide, a defendant's
conduct must actually contribute to the victim's death by setting
in motion the events that result in the killing. Liability will attach even if the defendant's conduct is not the sole cause of death
if the actions were a sufficiently direct cause of the ensuing death.
More than an obscure or merely probable connection between the
conduct and result is required. Rather, an act qualifies as a sufficiently direct cause when the ultimate harm should have been
reasonably foreseen.

In that case, we held that the evidence was legally sufficient with
respect to causation where a police officer, while chasing the fleeing
defendant across a busy expressway, was struck and killed by a
vehicle. Similarly, in *People v. Matos*, evidence of causation was
legally sufficient where a police officer fell down an air shaft to his
death in the course of pursuing the fleeing defendant up a ladder
and across a roof. These cases establish that where a defendant's
flight naturally induces a police officer to engage in pursuit, and
the officer is killed in the course of that pursuit, the causation element of the crime will be satisfied.

Defendant argues that the trooper was negligent by excessively speeding and losing control of his vehicle and violated State Police pursuit policy and Vehicle and Traffic Law § 1104, and that these acts were intervening and unforeseeable causative circumstances. However, it is plain that had defendant not fled, the trooper would not have engaged in the high-speed chase that resulted in his death. Additionally, contrary to defendant's contention, there is no requirement that a defendant's vehicle actually make contact with the trooper's vehicle in order for the causation element to be satisfied. Rather, the essential inquiry is whether defendant's conduct was a sufficiently direct cause of the trooper's death, a question we answer in the affirmative. There can be no doubt that defendant's conduct set in motion the events that led to the trooper's death, and it was reasonably foreseeable that a fatal accident would occur as a result of defendant leading the trooper on a high-speed pursuit. Accordingly, the evidence was legally sufficient to establish a causal connection between defendant's conduct and the trooper's death.

14 N.Y.3d at 325-26, 901 N.Y.S.2d at 115 (citations omitted).

§ 12:17 Manslaughter 2nd

Research References

West's Key Number Digest, Automobiles ☞344

PL § 125.15 provides, in pertinent part, that:

A person is guilty of manslaughter in the second degree when:
  1. He recklessly causes the death of another person; . . .

Manslaughter in the second degree is a class C felony.

As with criminally negligent homicide, in light of the 2005, 2006, and 2007 changes to the vehicular manslaughter statutes, it appears that there is little reason to resort to a charge of manslaughter 2nd in a DWI case. At the outset, vehicular manslaughter has become an offense that no longer requires a mens rea.

In addition, in light of the modifications to the class D felony of vehicular manslaughter 2nd and to the class C felony of vehicular manslaughter 1st, see PL §§ 125.12, 125.13, and in further light of the creation of the class B felony of aggravated vehicular homicide, see PL § 125.14, it is now beyond dispute that the legislature has clearly and expressly defined the situations in which it wants a vehicular homicide to be treated as a class C felony.

Thus, in a typical vehicular homicide case, a charge of manslaughter 2nd is now superfluous, and may only serve to inject an irrelevant issue (*i.e.*, whether the defendant acted recklessly) into the case. *See also* § 12:2, *supra*. *People v. Briskin*, 125 A.D.3d 1113, 3 N.Y.S.3d 200 (3d Dep't 2015), leave to appeal denied, 25 N.Y.3d 1069, 12 N.Y.S.3d 621, 34 N.E.3d 372 (2015), presents a situation where a Manslaughter 2nd charge was not superfluous in a DWI-related homicide case—as the defendant's recklessness was more apparent than her intoxication. In this regard, the *Briskin* Court held as follows:

[T]he fact that defendant was acquitted of driving while intoxicated does not preclude a finding that her conduct on the night in question was reckless, nor does her acquittal in this regard undermine her conviction of manslaughter in the second degree. Intoxication is not an element of manslaughter in the second degree. Moreover, there was ample evidence before the jury that defendant was impaired by the consumption of alcohol on the night in question—indeed, the jury convicted defendant of driving while ability impaired—and such impairment, coupled with defendant's admitted conduct in attempting to retrieve her GPS unit and the overall manner in which she operated her motor vehicle on the night in question, established the recklessness necessary to sustain her conviction of manslaughter in the second degree.

Id. at 1119, 3 N.Y.S.3d at 206 (citations omitted).

§ 12:18   Assault 1st

Research References

West's Key Number Digest, Automobiles ⚖347

PL § 120.10 provides, in pertinent part, that:

A person is guilty of assault in the first degree when: . . .

> 3. Under circumstances evincing a depraved indifference to human life, he recklessly engages in conduct which creates a grave risk of death to another person, and thereby causes serious physical injury to another person; or

> 4. In the course of and in furtherance of the commission or attempted commission of a felony . . ., he, or another participant if there be any, causes serious physical injury to a person other than one of the participants.

Assault in the first degree is a class B felony.

In *People v. Valencia*, 58 A.D.3d 879, __, 873 N.Y.S.2d 97, 98 (2d Dep't 2009), order aff'd, 14 N.Y.3d 927, 906 N.Y.S.2d 515, 932 N.E.2d 871 (2010), the Appellate Division, Second Department, held that the defendant's voluntary act of getting extremely intoxicated knowing that he would subsequently be driving home did not constitute "depraved indifference to human life":

We agree with the defendant that the evidence at trial, viewed in the light most favorable to the prosecution, was legally insufficient to establish that he acted with the culpable mental state of depraved indifference to human life at the time he collided with the complainants' vehicles and, thus, did not support his conviction of assault in the first degree (*see* Penal Law § 120.10[3]). In this regard, we find unpersuasive the prosecution's contention that the mens rea component of depraved indifference assault may be satisfied by considering the defendant's state of mind at a point much earlier in time than the accident, when the defendant allegedly made a conscious decision to consume an excessive amount of alcohol with the awareness that he subsequently would be operating a motor vehicle. . . . [W]e conclude that the defendant's state of mind at the time he consumed the alcohol was too temporally remote from his operation of the vehicle to support a conviction for depraved indifference assault in this case. We find unpersuasive our dissenting colleague's reliance upon dicta to the contrary set forth in the majority opinion in People v. Wells, 53 A.D.3d 181, 862 N.Y.S.2d 20 (1st Dep't 2008), leave to appeal denied, 11 N.Y.3d 858, 872 N.Y.S.2d 81, 900 N.E.2d 564 (2008).

(Citations omitted). *See also People v. Fountain*, 44 A.D.2d 685, ___, 353 N.Y.S.2d 813, 814 (2d Dep't 1974) ("Although the People proved that while defendant was in an intoxicated condition he drove through an intersection in violation of a traffic signal and thus acted recklessly, the People failed to prove that defendant's reckless conduct occurred under circumstances evincing a depraved indifference to human life.").

The Second Department's decision in *Valencia* directly conflicts with the First Department's decision in *People v. Wells*, 53 A.D.3d 181, ___, 862 N.Y.S.2d 20, 29 (1st Dep't 2008), leave to appeal denied, 11 N.Y.3d 858, 872 N.Y.S.2d 81, 900 N.E.2d 564 (2008), which found that:

[D]efendant's mental state at the time of the collision, as attested by numerous witnesses, is not dispositive; rather, culpability is appropriately assessed at the time defendant made the conscious decision to embark on a course of conduct that inevitably resulted in his operation of a motor vehicle while in a state of extreme intoxication.

The Court of Appeals sided with the Second Department, affirming *Valencia* in a brief memorandum decision:

The order of the Appellate Division, insofar as appealed from, should be affirmed. There is insufficient evidence to support a conviction for depraved indifference assault. The trial evidence established only that defendant was extremely intoxicated and did not establish that he acted with the culpable mental state of depraved indifference.

People v. Valencia, 14 N.Y.3d 927, 927-928, 906 N.Y.S.2d 515, 515, 932 N.E.2d 871 (2010).

Less clear is whether the Court of Appeals would disagree with the *Wells* Court's statement that:

Operation of a vehicle weighing in excess of two tons at a high rate of speed on city streets while highly intoxicated is the very epitome of depraved indifference to human life, culpably equivalent to "shooting into a crowd, placing a time bomb in a public place, or opening the door of the lion's cage at the zoo." It demonstrates "an utter disregard for the value of human life—a willingness to act not because one intends harm, but because one simply doesn't care whether grievous harm results or not."

53 A.D.3d at _, 862 N.Y.S.2d at 28 (citations omitted).

In *People v. Snow*, 138 A.D.2d 217, __, 530 N.Y.S.2d 913, 913 (4th Dep't 1988), *aff'd for the reasons stated in the opinion below*, 74 N.Y.2d 671, 543 N.Y.S.2d 385 (1989), the court held that felony DWI cannot "serve as the predicate for conviction of assault in the first degree under Penal Law § 120.14[4]." *See also* 138 A.D.2d at __, 530 N.Y.S.2d at 914 ("Defendant argues that DWI should not be considered a felony for purposes of this statute. We agree"). In so holding, the Court reasoned that:

[T]he 1983 enactment of the vehicular assault and manslaughter statutes (L. 1983, ch. 298) was prompted by legislative concern with injury and death caused by intoxicated drivers. When serious physical injury is caused the crime is vehicular assault; when death is caused the crime is vehicular manslaughter (*see*, 1983 New York State Legislative Annual, at 134). While first degree assault is a class C felony (Penal Law § 120.10), vehicular manslaughter, at the time of defendant's conviction, was only a class D felony (Penal Law § 125.12). In 1985, the Legislature amended the vehicular manslaughter provision by adding a higher degree of the crime (class C felony if the defendant is driving with a suspended or revoked license) (Penal Law § 125.13, added by L. 1985, ch. 507), and similarly amended the vehicular assault provisions (Penal Law § 120.04, added by L. 1985, ch. 507).

On the facts of this case, defendant could have been found guilty only of second degree vehicular assault, a class E felony (Penal Law § 120.03), because the victim of the incident suffered serious physical injury. Had the victim died, defendant could have been convicted of second degree vehicular manslaughter, a class D felony (Penal Law § 125.12). Defendant, however, was convicted of first degree assault under Penal Law § 120.10(4), a class C felony, a more serious crime than could have been charged if the victim had died. This is an unreasonable and unjust result and could not have been intended by the Legislature.

138 A.D.2d at __, 530 N.Y.S.2d at 914–15.

In sum, the statutory scheme relating to assault and vehicular offenses, as well as the history of the felony assault doctrine, compels the conclusion that felony DWI may not serve as the basis for a conviction of first degree assault. While we recognize that injuries and death caused by intoxicated drivers are of significant concern, the Legislature has adequately responded by establishing increased penalties under the Vehicle and Traffic Law and by adding vehicular assault and vehicular manslaughter provisions to the Penal Law. For reasons of policy, logic and legislative history, however, the application of the first degree felony assault statute should not be extended to felony DWI.

138 A.D.2d at __, 530 N.Y.S.2d at 916.

In *People v. Belizaire*, 234 A.D.2d 467, 651 N.Y.S.2d 574 (2d Dep't 1996), the People again tried to make improper use of PL § 120.10(4)—this time attempting to use AUO 1st as the underlying felony for purposes of an assault 1st charge. The Appellate Division, Second Department, following *Snow*, held that "[t]he interpretation of the Penal Law advocated by the People would lead to an unjust and unreasonable result." 234 A.D.2d at __, 651 N.Y.S.2d at 575.

Similarly, in *People v. Rucinski*, 24 A.D.3d 1171, __, 808 N.Y.S.2d 511, 513 (4th Dep't 2005), the Appellate Division, Fourth Department, held that "a felony DWI may not serve as the underlying felony for assault in the second degree."

§ 12:19 Inconsistent counts must be submitted to jury in the alternative

Research References

West's Key Number Digest, Automobiles ☞324, 332

A common, and significant, error in vehicular crimes trials is that the defendant winds up convicted of two or more crimes that have different mental states (*e.g.*, manslaughter 2nd and criminally negligent homicide)—which is legally impossible. *See, e.g., People v. Gallagher*, 69 N.Y.2d 525, 531, 516 N.Y.S.2d 174, 176 (1987) ("The accused by definition cannot be found to have had more than one of the mental states on the kaleidoscope of culpable mental states, and the trier of fact must determine which one is applicable").

Thus, where an indictment contains two inconsistent counts, and the trial court submits both counts to the jury, "it must do so in the alternative; it may not permit the jury to find the defendant guilty of both." 69 N.Y.2d at 530, 516 N.Y.S.2d at 176. *See also* CPL §§ 300.30(5), 300.40(5).

In *People v. Spurling*, 199 A.D.2d 624, 604 N.Y.S.2d 997 (3d Dep't 1993), the defendant was convicted, following a jury trial, of both manslaughter 2nd and vehicular manslaughter 2nd. On appeal, the Appellate Division, Third Department, reversed the convictions and ordered a new trial, holding that:

> There is merit . . . to defendant's . . . argument that County Court erred in denying her request that the crimes of manslaughter in the second degree (Penal Law § 125.15[1]) (and its lesser included offenses) and vehicular manslaughter in the second degree (Penal Law § 125.12[1]) (along with its lesser included offenses) be submitted to the jury in the alternative (*see*, CPL 300.40[5]) . . . . The two counts require different mental states (*recklessness*—a person is aware of and consciously disregards a substantial risk of death;

criminal negligence—a person culpably fails to perceive the substantial and unjustifiable risk of death), so that "guilt of one necessarily negates guilt of the other."

199 A.D.2d at ___, 604 N.Y.S.2d at 998 (citations omitted).

Similarly, in *People v. Extale*, 42 A.D.3d 897, 839 N.Y.S.2d 402 (4th Dep't 2007), the defendant was convicted, following a jury trial, of both Assault 1st and Vehicular Assault 1st. On appeal, the Appellate Division, Fourth Department, reversed the convictions and ordered a new trial, holding that:

> Counts are inconsistent "when guilt of the offense charged in one necessarily negates guilt of the offense charged in the other" (CPL 300.30[5]). Here, the court should have submitted the counts to the jury in the alternative and instructed the jury that it could find defendant guilty of only one of the counts (*see* CPL 300.40[5]). Assault in the first degree requires a finding that defendant acted intentionally (*see* Penal Law § 120.10[1]), while vehicular assault in the first degree requires a finding that defendant was criminally negligent (*see* § 120.04). Thus, in failing to instruct the jury to consider the counts in the alternative, the court thereby erred in permitting the jury to find defendant guilty of crimes requiring different mental states. It cannot be said that defendant simultaneously intended to cause serious physical injury to the police officer while failing to perceive a substantial and unjustifiable risk of serious injury to the police officer.

42 A.D.3d at ___, 839 N.Y.S.2d at 403 (citation omitted).

It should be noted that 2005 amendments to the Vehicular Assault/Vehicular Manslaughter statutes removed the *mens rea* element therefrom—and thus the issue in *Spurling* and *Extale* will no longer arise.

§ 12:20 Conviction of higher level offense mandates dismissal of lesser included offense(s)

Research References

West's Key Number Digest, Automobiles ⚖324, 332

Another common error in vehicular crimes trials is that the defendant winds up convicted of lesser included offenses (*e.g.*, vehicular assault 2nd and DWI). In submitting such charges to the jury, CPL § 300.40(3)(b) provides, in pertinent part, that:

> With respect to inclusory concurrent counts, the court must submit the greatest or inclusive count and may or must, under circumstances prescribed in [CPL § 300.50], also submit, but in the alternative only, one or more of the lesser included counts. A verdict of guilty upon the greatest count submitted is deemed a dismissal of every lesser count submitted, but not an acquittal thereon. A verdict of guilty upon a lesser count is deemed an acquittal upon every greater count submitted.

See also CPL § 300.30(4).

In *People v. Grove*, 272 A.D.2d 480, __, 708 N.Y.S.2d 329, 330 (2d Dep't 2000), the Appellate Division, Second Department, held that "the defendant's convictions of criminally negligent homicide and driving while intoxicated should have been dismissed as lesser included offenses of vehicular manslaughter in the second degree (*see*, CPL 300.40[3][b])." *See also People v. Bank*, 129 A.D.3d 1445, __, 12 N.Y.S.3d 673, 677 (4th Dep't 2015), leave to appeal granted, 26 N.Y.3d 925 (2015) ("as the People correctly concede, counts four, five and seven must be dismissed as lesser inclusory counts of count three, vehicular manslaughter in the first degree. . . . Because it is impossible to commit the crime of vehicular manslaughter in the first degree under Penal Law § 125.13(4), without concomitantly committing the crime of vehicular manslaughter in the second degree under Penal Law § 125.12, or without concomitantly committing the crime of, inter alia, driving while ability impaired by drugs under Vehicle and Traffic Law § 1192(4), the latter two crimes are inclusory concurrent counts of the former crime"); *People v. Davis*, 112 A.D.3d 959, __, 977 N.Y.S.2d 87, 89 (2d Dep't 2013), leave to appeal denied, 22 N.Y.3d 1155, 984 N.Y.S.2d 639, 7 N.E.3d 1127 (2014) ("As the People correctly concede, the convictions of driving while intoxicated in violation of subdivisions (2) and (3) of Vehicle and Traffic Law § 1192 must be dismissed as inclusory concurrent counts of vehicular manslaughter in the second degree."); *People v. Bain*, 85 A.D.3d 1193, __, 926 N.Y.S.2d 301, 302 (2d Dep't 2011), leave to appeal denied, 17 N.Y.3d 902, 933 N.Y.S.2d 657, 957 N.E.2d 1161 (2011) ("As the People correctly concede, the defendant's conviction of vehicular manslaughter in the second degree requires dismissal of the lesser inclusory concurrent count of driving while intoxicated per se."); *People v. Peryea*, 68 A.D.3d 1144, __, 889 N.Y.S.2d 741, 743 (3d Dep't 2009), leave to appeal denied, 14 N.Y.3d 804, 899 N.Y.S.2d 138, 925 N.E.2d 942 (2010) ("The People concede that both driving while intoxicated counts (Vehicle and Traffic Law § 1192[2], [3]) must be dismissed as lesser inclusory concurrent counts in light of defendant's conviction for vehicular manslaughter in the second degree."); *People v. Osborne*, 60 A.D.3d 1310, __, 875 N.Y.S.2d 396, 397 (4th Dep't 2009); *People v. Smith*, 162 A.D.2d 999, __, 557 N.Y.S.2d 789, 789 (4th Dep't 1990) (DWI convictions dismissed, and sentences imposed thereon vacated, on ground that such charges "are inclusory concurrent counts of the count of vehicular assault in the second degree (*see*, CPL 300.40[3][b])"); *People v. Eccleston*, 161 A.D.2d 1184, __, 556 N.Y.S.2d 182, 183 (4th Dep't 1990). *Cf. People v. Joseph*, 75 A.D.3d 1080, __, 903 N.Y.S.2d 651, 654 (4th Dep't 2010), leave to appeal denied, 15 N.Y.3d 853, 909 N.Y.S.2d 30, 935 N.E.2d 822 (2010) ("Because it is possible to commit aggravated vehicular assault without concomitantly, by the same conduct, driving in a condition impaired by the combined influence of drugs or of alcohol and any drug or drugs, the latter is not a lesser included count of the former.").

In *People v. Hoffman*, 130 A.D.3d 1152, __, 13 N.Y.S.3d 619, 622-23 (3d Dep't 2015), the Appellate Division, Third Department, held that:

> Counts 2, 5 and 8 of the indictment charged defendant with vehicular manslaughter in the first degree pursuant to Penal Law § 125.13(3), which requires proof that defendant (1) committed the crime of vehicular manslaughter in the second degree and (2) had been convicted within the preceding 10 years of violating Vehicle and Traffic Law § 1192. Counts 1, 4 and 7 of the indictment charged defendant with aggravated vehicular homicide pursuant to Penal Law § 125.14(3), which requires proof that defendant (1) committed the crime of vehicular manslaughter in the second degree, (2) engaged in reckless driving and (3) had previously been convicted of a Vehicle and Traffic Law § 1192 violation within the preceding 10 years. As relevant here, a person is guilty of vehicular manslaughter in the second degree when he or she operates a motor vehicle in violation of Vehicle and Traffic Law § 1192(2), (3) or (4-a) thereby causing the death of another person.
>
> In our view, these charges were predicated upon the same statutory provisions (*see* Penal Law §§ 125.13[3]; 125.14[3]), act and victim, differing only in the nature of defendant's impairment. In this regard, defendant was alleged to have been driving while per se intoxicated (counts 1 and 2), in an intoxicated condition (counts 4 and 5) and impaired by a combination of drugs or alcohol and drugs (counts 7 and 8) (*see* Vehicle and Traffic Law § 1192[2], [3], [4-a]). The essential elements of both crimes do not address the specific manner in which defendant was impaired; rather, they include only a single offense of some form of impaired driving as defined within Penal Law § 125.12(1). Accordingly, counts 4 and 7 should have been dismissed as multiplicitous of count 1, and counts 5 and 8 must be dismissed as multiplicitous of count 2.

(Citations omitted).

§ 12:21   Marking UTTs in cases involving serious physical injury or death

Research References

West's Key Number Digest, Automobiles ⚎324

At least since *Corbin v. Hillery*, 74 N.Y.2d 279, 545 N.Y.S.2d 71 (1989), *aff'd sub nom. Grady v. Corbin*, 495 U.S. 508, 110 S.Ct. 2084 (1990), there has been legitimate concern that a defendant involved in a vehicular crime will be undercharged by the police, and will plead guilty to a lesser offense in local criminal court—

thereby precluding further prosecution on double jeopardy grounds.

In *Corbin*, the defendant was involved in a DWI-related fatal motor vehicle accident. He was served with two uniform traffic tickets (UTTs), charging him with DWI and failure to keep right. The return date on the tickets was changed to a non-ADA night. The ADA covering the court was "inexplicably unaware" that the case involved a fatality, and thus he "did not alert the court to the seriousness of the incident." 74 N.Y.2d at 283, 545 N.Y.S.2d at 73.

The defendant appeared with counsel on the return date, and pled guilty to both charges. Sentencing was adjourned for the purpose of obtaining the People's sentencing recommendation. On the sentencing date, an ADA unfamiliar with the case did not request a further adjournment. As a result, the court, unaware of the severity of the offense, imposed a sentence consistent with a run-of-the-mill DWI. 74 N.Y.2d at 284, 545 N.Y.S.2d at 73.

The People subsequently charged the defendant with, inter alia, manslaughter 2nd and vehicular manslaughter 2nd. The case was litigated all the way up to the U.S. Supreme Court, which agreed with the Court of Appeals that further prosecution of such charges was barred by the Double Jeopardy Clause of the Fifth Amendment. 74 N.Y.2d at 291, 545 N.Y.S.2d at 78.

In order to avoid such a result in the future, CPL § 170.10(8) provides that:

Notwithstanding any other provision of law to the contrary, a local criminal court may not, at arraignment or within [30] days of arraignment on a simplified traffic information charging a violation of [VTL § 1192(2), (2-a), (3), (4) or (4-a)] and upon which a notation has been made pursuant to [VTL § 1192(12)], accept a plea of guilty to a violation of any subdivision of [VTL § 1192], nor to any other traffic infraction arising out of the same incident, nor to any other traffic infraction, violation or misdemeanor where the court is aware that such offense was charged pursuant to an accident involving death or serious physical injury, except upon written consent of the district attorney.

Similarly, VTL § 1192(12) provides that:

Driving while intoxicated or while ability impaired by drugs—serious physical injury or death. In every case where a person is charged with a violation of [VTL § 1192(2), (2-a), (3), (4) or (4-a)], the law enforcement officer alleging such charge shall make a clear notation in the "Description of Violation" section of a simplified traffic information if, arising out of the same incident, someone other than the person charged was killed or suffered serious physical injury as defined in [PL § 10.00]; such notation shall be in the form of a "D" if someone other than the person charged was killed and such notation shall be in the form of a "S.P.I." if someone other than the person charged suffered serious physical injury; provided, however, that the failure to make such notation shall in no way affect a charge for a violation of subdivision [VTL § 1192(2), (2-a), (3), (4) or (4-a)].

Furthermore, VTL § 603-b provides that:

In addition to the requirements of [VTL § 603] and [VTL § 1192(12)], in every case where a law enforcement officer is required to report pursuant to [VTL § 603] and a person is charged with a violation of this chapter arising out of such accident, the law enforcement officer alleging such charge shall make a clear notation in the "Description of Violation" section of a simplified traffic information, or in an area provided on a summons and complaint pursuant to [VTL § 226(1)], if, arising out of the same accident, someone other than the person charged was killed or suffered serious physical injury as defined in [PL § 10.00]; such notation shall be in the form of a "D" if someone other than the person charged was killed and such notation shall be in the form of a "S.P.I." if someone other than the person charged suffered serious physical injury; provided however, that the failure to make such notation shall in no way affect a charge for a violation of this chapter.

§ 12:22   Endangering the welfare of a child

Research References

West's Key Number Digest, Automobiles ⚷324

If a person driving with a child in the vehicle is arrested for DWI, the police invariably also charge him or her with endangering the welfare of a child. In this regard, Penal Law § 260.10(1) provides, in pertinent part, that "[a] person is guilty of endangering the welfare of a child when . . . [h]e knowingly acts in a manner likely to be injurious to the physical, mental or moral welfare of a child less than [17] years old."

In *People v. Chase*, 186 Misc. 2d 487, 720 N.Y.S.2d 707 (App. Term, 2d Dep't 2000), the court rejected the notion that a person driving in violation of VTL § 1192 with a child in the vehicle is automatically guilty of endangering the welfare of the child. In *Chase*, the defendant was convicted of DWAI, two other traffic infractions, and endangering the welfare of a child. In reversing the endangering conviction, the court noted, among other things, that:

Absent from the record is the required evidence to show how unsafe, if at all, the shoulder was at the subject location. Nor does it appear that there was evidence of defendant speeding or swerving in a manner perilous to the infant passenger. It does appear that the infant had been restrained in a car seat in the rear of defendant's car by her mother, defendant's friend. Under the circumstances, it was not established beyond a reasonable doubt that defendant acted "knowingly" or that his conduct was "likely" to be injurious to the child.

In so holding, we neither condone defendant's conduct nor wish to imply that whenever a defendant commits only a traffic infraction while a child is in his vehicle, he should be deemed not guilty, per se, of endangering the welfare of a child (Penal Law § 260.10). The evidence in a given case might evince conduct so egregious as to establish the requisite knowledge and a true likelihood of injury which is not "speculative." In the case at bar, however, these elements were not sufficiently proven.

186 Misc. 2d at __, 720 N.Y.S.2d at 709 (citation omitted). *Cf. People v. D'Ambrosia*, 192 Misc. 2d 560, 746 N.Y.S.2d 556 (Brighton Just. Ct. 2002) (allegations that defendant drove 19 MPH over the speed limit and with an alleged BAC of 0.18%, on a "heavily residential" road, with his four-year-old son in the vehicle, are sufficient to support a charge of endangering the welfare of a child); *People v. Lowe*, 47 Misc. 3d 843, __, 1 N.Y.S.3d 756, 760 (N.Y. City Crim. Ct. 2015) ("driving while intoxicated with a child in the car constitutes Endangering the Welfare of a Child").

In light of the 2009 enactment of Leandra's Law—which makes it a felony to commit DWI, DWAI Drugs or DWAI Combined Influence with a child under the age of 16 in the vehicle, *see* VTL § 1192(2-a)(b)—resort to the Endangering the Welfare of a Child statute in DWI cases should be rare.

§ 12:23 Leaving the scene of a property damage accident without reporting

Research References

West's Key Number Digest, Automobiles ⌖336

VTL § 600(1) addresses the issue of leaving the scene of a property damage accident without reporting. In this regard, VTL § 600(1)(a) provides that:

Any person operating a motor vehicle who, knowing or having cause to know that damage has been caused to the real property or to the personal property, not including animals, of another, due to an incident involving the motor vehicle operated by such person shall, before leaving the place where the damage occurred, stop, exhibit his or her license and insurance identification card for such vehicle, when such card is required pursuant to [VTL Articles 6 and 8], and give his or her name, residence, including street and number, insurance carrier and insurance identification information including but not limited to the number and effective dates of said individual's insurance policy, and license number to the party sustaining the damage, or in case the person sustaining the damage is not present at the place where the damage occurred then he or she shall report the same as soon as physically able to the nearest police station, or judicial officer.

Violation of VTL § 600(1)(a) is a traffic infraction punishable by:

1. A fine of up to $250;
2. Up to 15 days in jail; or
3. Both.

VTL § 600(1).

In *People v. Flynn*, 79 N.Y.2d 879, 881-82, 581 N.Y.S.2d 160, 161, 589 N.E.2d 383 (1992), the Court of Appeals reversed the defendant's conviction of violating VTL § 600(1)(a) where "the court instructed the jury that the People need only prove that defendant did not report the accident at the scene. By instructing the jury in this manner, the court deprived it of the opportunity to pass upon whether complainant had fled the scene of the accident before defendant had an opportunity to exchange information with him and whether defendant had actually attempted to report the accident to the police from his home."

In *People v. Marotti*, 20 Misc. 3d 16, __, 862 N.Y.S.2d 712, 714 (App. Term, 9th & 10th Jud. Dist. 2008), the Court addressed the facial sufficiency of an accusatory instrument charging the defendant with leaving the scene of a property damage accident without reporting, and held that:

> The accusatory instrument charging defendant with leaving the scene of an incident without reporting (Vehicle and Traffic Law § 600[1]) is defective on its face. "The primary purpose of section 600 of the Vehicle and Traffic Law is to prevent the evasion of civil liability by a motorist who may be liable for negligently causing damage by his leaving the scene of the accident." The gravamen of the offense is that a person "who, knowing or having cause to know that damage has been caused to the real property or to the personal property . . . of another, . . . leav[es] the place where the damage occurred" without producing the required documentation or reporting the incident to the police (Vehicle and Traffic Law 600[1][a]). Absent damage to the property of another of which a person knows or has reason to know, no violation is committed by the mere departure from an accident scene. The accusatory instrument alleged merely that an accident had occurred which resulted in damage, without facts sufficient to identify the property damaged or to establish that the property was owned by another and that defendant knew or had reason to know of such damage. Knowledge, of course, may be proved circumstantially, but there must be an assertion of evidentiary facts with respect to the damage upon which an inference of knowledge may be based. Accordingly, the judgment of conviction of leaving the scene of an incident in violation of Vehicle and Traffic Law § 600(1)(a) is reversed, the accusatory instrument dismissed, and the $250 fine, if paid, remitted.

(Citations omitted).

In *People v. Wenceslao*, 69 Misc. 2d 160, 329 N.Y.S.2d 391, 392 (N.Y. City Crim. Ct. 1972), the Court held that:

When the owner of a motor vehicle was near but not in the vehicle and another person operated the vehicle and caused it to collide with and damage a parked vehicle, and the owner of the first vehicle saw this and thereupon immediately entered his vehicle, took over its operation and drove it and the operator who caused the accident away from the scene of the accident, and neither complied with the reporting and exchange of information provisions of Section 600 of the Vehicle & Traffic Law, . . . both [are] guilty of leaving the scene of the accident without giving the information or reporting the accident as required by Section 600 of the Vehicle and Traffic Law.

§ 12:24 Leaving the scene of a personal injury accident without reporting

Research References

West's Key Number Digest, Automobiles ☞336

VTL § 600(2) addresses the issue of leaving the scene of a personal injury accident without reporting. In this regard, VTL § 600(2)(a) provides that:

Any person operating a motor vehicle who, knowing or having cause to know that personal injury has been caused to another person, due to an incident involving the motor vehicle operated by such person shall, before leaving the place where the said personal injury occurred, stop, exhibit his or her license and insurance identification card for such vehicle, when such card is required pursuant to [VTL Articles 6 and 8], and give his or her name, residence, including street and street number, insurance carrier and insurance identification information including but not limited to the number and effective dates of said individual's insurance policy and license number, to the injured party, if practical, and also to a police officer, or in the event that no police officer is in the vicinity of the place of said injury, then, he or she shall report said incident as soon as physically able to the nearest police station or judicial officer.

The level of the offense of leaving the scene of a personal injury accident without reporting, as well as the punishment therefor, depends on certain factors:

If the violation of VTL § 600(2)(a) consists solely of "the failure of an operator to exhibit his or her license and insurance identification card for the vehicle or exchange the information required in such paragraph" *as a first offense*, the offense is a class B misdemeanor punishable by:

    1. A fine of between $250 and $500; and

    2. Any other penalties provided by law. VTL § 600(2)(c).

Any subsequent such violation is a class A misdemeanor punishable by:

    1. A fine of between $500 and $1,000; and

2. Any other penalties provided by law. VTL § 600(2)(c).

If the violation of VTL § 600(2)(a) is "other than for the mere failure of an operator to exhibit his or her license and insurance identification card for such vehicle or exchange the information required in such paragraph" *as a first offense*, the offense is a class A misdemeanor punishable by:
1. A fine of between $500 and $1,000; and
2. Any other penalties provided by law. VTL § 600(2)(c).

"Any such violation committed by a person after such person has previously been convicted of such a violation" is a class E felony punishable by:
1. A fine of between $1,000 and $2,500; and
2. Any other penalties provided by law. VTL § 600(2)(c).

If the violation of VTL § 600(2)(a) is "other than for the mere failure of an operator to exhibit his or her license and insurance identification card for such vehicle or exchange the information required in such paragraph," and the personal injury involved is a "serious physical injury" as defined in PL § 10.00, the offense is a class E felony punishable by:
1. A fine of between $1,000 and $5,000; and
2. Any other penalties provided by law. VTL § 600(2)(c)(i).

If the violation of VTL § 600(2)(a) is "other than for the mere failure of an operator to exhibit his or her license and insurance identification card for such vehicle or exchange the information required in such paragraph," and the personal injury involved results in death, the offense is a class D felony punishable by:
1. A fine of between $2,000 and $5,000; and
2. Any other penalties provided by law. VTL § 600(2)(c)(ii).

In *People v. Samuel*, 29 N.Y.2d 252, 327 N.Y.S.2d 321, 277 N.E.2d 381 (1971), the Court of Appeals held both: (a) that VTL § 600 is Constitutional, and (b) that the statute does not violate motorists' Fifth Amendment rights.

VTL § 600(2) " 'does not require the People to establish that the defendant acted with any culpable mental state as to [the element of] leaving the scene of the accident.' " *People v. Toussaint*, 40 A.D.3d 1017, __, 837 N.Y.S.2d 218, 219-20 (2d Dep't 2007) (citation omitted). *See also People v. Useo*, 156 A.D.2d 739, 549 N.Y.S.2d 490, 491-92 (2d Dep't 1989); *People v. Castanheira*, 16 Misc. 3d 751, __, 842 N.Y.S.2d 287, 291 (White Plains City Ct. 2007), judgment aff'd, 21 Misc. 3d 146(A), 875 N.Y.S.2d 822 (App. Term 2008). *Cf. Peresluha v. City of New York*, 60 A.D.2d 226, __, 400 N.Y.S.2d 818, 820 (1st Dep't 1977) (VTL § 600 "requires knowledge on the part of the offender that damage has been caused to either a person or property").

In *People v. Mullady*, 178 A.D.2d 614, 577 N.Y.S.2d 491, 491-2

(2d Dep't 1991), the Appellate Division, Second Department, held that:

> [W]e find, as a matter of law, that [the defendant] could not be found guilty of leaving the scene of an incident without reporting based solely upon his failure to identify himself as the driver. Although requiring such information would not be violative of the defendant's Fifth Amendment right against self-incrimination, Vehicle and Traffic Law § 600(2)(a) places no affirmative obligation upon a driver of a motor vehicle to identify himself as the driver. Therefore, a person involved in a motor vehicle accident who provides all of the statutorily-mandated information to police at the scene, but who maintains that he was not an operator of a vehicle involved, is not subject to prosecution for leaving the scene of an incident without reporting.

(Citations omitted).

In *Matter of Greene v. Melton*, 54 A.D.2d 1060, ___, 388 N.Y.S.2d 714, 715 (3d Dep't 1976), the Appellate Division, Third Department, reversed the revocation of petitioner's driver's license for violating VTL § 600, holding that:

> With no one at the scene of the accident to whom he could report, and with the only visible damage being a few guard rails, and with petitioner being "dazed and shaken," we hold that under the facts and circumstances of the case a two and one half hour delay in reporting the accident did not constitute a violation of the statute. A person must have a reasonable time within which to report an accident bearing in mind the prevailing circumstances. The section in question is obviously designed to prohibit negligent drivers from evading civil or criminal consequences by leaving the scene before their identity may be established. No such situation exists in the instant case. The petitioner driver acted within a reasonable time and reported the accident to the Sheriff and thus did not violate the statute in question.

In *People v. Hatcher*, 181 Misc. 2d 622, ___, 694 N.Y.S.2d 602, 603 (N.Y. City Crim. Ct. 1999), the Court addressed the facial sufficiency of an accusatory instrument charging the defendant with leaving the scene of a personal injury accident without reporting, and held that:

> [T]he complaint neither describes the nature or extent of the purported injuries to the passenger's leg nor contains any allegations concerning the severity or aftermath of the incident. As a consequence, it is unclear from the pleading whether the unnamed rider simply re-boarded defendant's scooter and departed the scene without so much as a whimper or, instead, was left at the curb writhing in pain. Moreover, the complaint does not allege that the defendant turned to face the passenger at any point during the incident, or was otherwise in a position to observe the purported injury that had occurred. Instead, the complaint states only the bald conclusion that defendant's unnamed passenger had "injure[d]

his leg." That conclusory statement provides no basis upon which it can be inferred that defendant knew or had cause to know that his passenger had been injured. Accordingly, the complaint is defective and must be dismissed.

It should be noted that the necessary injury for purposes of VTL § 600(2)(a) is personal injury—*not* physical injury (as defined in PL § 10.00[9]). *See People v. Bogomolsky*, 14 Misc. 3d 26, __, 829 N.Y.S.2d 803, 804 (App. Term, 2d & 11th Jud. Dist. 2006); *People v. Lovero*, 7 Misc. 3d 575, 788 N.Y.S.2d 585, 586-87 (Nassau Co. Dist. Ct. 2005).

In *People v. Navarrette*, 7 Misc. 3d 623, 790 N.Y.S.2d 835 (City Crim. Ct. 2005), the Court held that the concept of vehicle "operation" is narrower for purposes of VTL § 600 than it is for purposes of VTL § 1192. In so holding, the Court reasoned that:

> The People contend that the same broad meaning of operation applicable to the driving while intoxicated provisions of the Vehicle and Traffic Law ought to apply to leaving the scene of an incident charges, but that ignores an important distinction between the two crimes. * * *
>
> Vehicle and Traffic Law § 600(2)(a) triggers the obligation to report an incident only when the incident and its proximate injuries arise out of the actual operation of the motor vehicle. Section 600(2)(a) ties the reporting requirement to injuries that occur "due to an incident involving the motor vehicle operated by such person," and therefore an accident that involves the motor vehicle but does not involve its operation is simply not contemplated by the statute. In this regard, a carelessly parked car that causes an injury to a motorist or pedestrian would not seem to involve the reporting requirements of Vehicle and Traffic Law § 600(2)(a), even if the person who parked the car was present at the time. Nor would the requirements be implicated if personal injury occurs while luggage is removed from the roof of a parked car, or during the opening of its hood or trunk, or when it is undergoing repairs on a public street.
>
> Here, the defendant had ceased operating the motor vehicle well before the incident involving the bicyclist and the car door occurred. The fact that defendant may have carelessly opened the car door in the process of leaving the car does not satisfy the operation element. Indeed, if defendant had caused the injury by carelessly opening the door just before he was about to operate the car, the People would be hard pressed to claim that the operation element had been satisfied.

7 Misc. 3d at __, 790 N.Y.S.2d at 836-37. *See also People v. Marzulli*, 76 Misc. 2d 971, __, 351 N.Y.S.2d 775, 776 (App. Term, 2d & 11th Jud. Dist. 1973) (per curiam).

It is critical to note that a sentence for leaving the scene of a personal injury accident can be imposed consecutively to a sentence for a crime related to the underlying accident (*e.g.*, vehicular assault/vehicular manslaughter). *See, e.g., People v. Chambers*, 257 A.D.2d 418, __, 683 N.Y.S.2d 238, 239 (1st Dep't 1999) ("We reject defendant's contention that the court was required to impose concurrent sentences for defendant's convictions for vehicular assault in the second degree (Penal Law § 120.03) and leaving the scene of an incident without reporting (Vehicle and Traffic Law § 600)"); *People v. Isaac*, 224 A.D.2d 993, 637 N.Y.S.2d 827 (4th Dep't 1996) ("The contention of defendant that the court erred in imposing consecutive sentences for his convictions of vehicular manslaughter in the second degree and leaving the scene of an accident is without merit"). In this regard, it should be noted that the Court of Appeals' decision in *People v. Catone*, 65 N.Y.2d 1003, 494 N.Y.S.2d 97, 484 N.E.2d 126 (1985), was legislatively overruled by a subsequent amendment to VTL § 600.

In *People v. Markidis*, 142 A.D.2d 990, 991, 531 N.Y.S.2d 153, 154 (4th Dep't 1988), the Appellate Division, Fourth Department, held that where the personal injury at issue was death, misdemeanor leaving the scene is not a lesser included offense of felony leaving the scene—since "there is [no] reasonable view of the evidence in th[is] particular case that would support a finding that defendant committed the lesser offense but not the greater."

In *People v. Saporita*, 132 A.D.2d 713, __, 518 N.Y.S.2d 625, 628-29 (2d Dep't 1987), the Appellate Division, Second Department, held that:

> [W]e note that *Saporita* was illegally sentenced to a term of imprisonment of one year for having committed the crime of leaving the scene of an accident without reporting as a misdemeanor, since that crime, absent any proof that *Saporita* committed the same crime in the past, is a class B, not a class A misdemeanor, and carries a maximum term of imprisonment of three months (Vehicle and Traffic Law § 600[2][b]; Penal Law § 70.15).

See also People v. Fox, 99 A.D.2d 553, 471 N.Y.S.2d 642 (2d Dep't 1984) (defendant was illegally sentenced to one to three years for leaving the scene because offense was class B misdemeanor when committed).

In *People v. Santangelo*, 134 Misc. 2d 615, __, 512 N.Y.S.2d 288, 288 (Kings Co. Sup. Ct. 1986), the Court held "that the jury [would] be charged that a motor vehicle operator need not remain at the scene of an accident if a person under similar circumstances reasonably believes a belligerent crowd may cause him bodily harm."

In *People v. Slocum*, 112 A.D.2d 641, 492 N.Y.S.2d 159 (3d Dep't 1985), the Appellate Division, Third Department, held that where a passenger in the defendant's vehicle intentionally opens the door and jumps out, this is an "accident" within the meaning of VTL § 600.

In *People v. Petterson*, 103 A.D.2d 811, __, 477 N.Y.S.2d 691, 692 (2d Dep't 1984), the Appellate Division, Second Department, held that "the mere occurrence of an injury to another person is sufficient to trigger the statutory provisions [of VTL § 600], irrespective of whether the motorist is at fault."

Interestingly, in *People v. Lewis*, 162 Misc. 2d 954, __, 618 N.Y.S.2d 737, 742 (N.Y. City Crim. Ct. 1994), the Court held that "a passenger, who aids a driver in leaving the scene of an accident, may be found guilty of violating a hit-and-run statute as an accomplice."

§ 12:25 Unlawful fleeing a police officer

Research References

West's Key Number Digest, Automobiles ⬥324, 332

Following the death of a state trooper during a high-speed chase, the legislature enacted three statutes addressing the issue of how to punish motorists who fail to stop for the police. The level of the offense of unlawful fleeing a police officer rises with the seriousness of the harm resulting from such conduct. In this regard, PL § 270.25 provides that:

> A person is guilty of unlawful fleeing a police officer in a motor vehicle in the third degree when, knowing that he or she has been directed to stop his or her motor vehicle by a uniformed police officer or a marked police vehicle by the activation of either the lights or the lights and siren of such vehicle, he or she thereafter attempts to flee such officer or such vehicle by driving at speeds which equal or exceed [25 MPH] above the speed limit or engaging in reckless driving as defined by [VTL § 1212].

Unlawful fleeing a police officer in a motor vehicle in the third degree is a class A misdemeanor.

Where "serious physical injury" results, PL § 270.30 provides that:

> A person is guilty of unlawful fleeing a police officer in a motor vehicle in the second degree when he or she commits the offense of [Unlawful Fleeing a Police Officer 3rd], as defined in [PL § 270.25], and as a result of such conduct a police officer or a third person suffers serious physical injury.

Unlawful fleeing a police officer in a motor vehicle in the second degree is a class E felony.

Where "death" results, PL § 270.35 provides that:

> A person is guilty of unlawful fleeing a police officer in a motor vehicle in the first degree when he or she commits the offense of

[Unlawful Fleeing a Police Officer 3rd], as defined in [PL § 270.25], and as a result of such conduct a police officer or a third person is killed.

Unlawful fleeing a police officer in a motor vehicle in the first degree is a class D felony.

§ 12:26 Reckless driving

Research References

West's Key Number Digest, Automobiles ⚷330

In light of new statutes which make reckless driving an element thereof, there will likely be renewed interest in what exactly constitutes the crime of reckless driving. At the outset, VTL § 1212 provides that:

> Reckless driving shall mean driving or using any motor vehicle, motorcycle or any other vehicle propelled by any power other than muscular power or any appliance or accessory thereof in a manner which unreasonably interferes with the free and proper use of the public highway, or unreasonably endangers users of the public highway. Reckless driving is prohibited. Every person violating this provision shall be guilty of a misdemeanor.

A former, but similarly worded, version of this statute was held to be constitutional in *People v. Grogan*, 260 N.Y. 138 (1932). Notably, however, the *Grogan* Court provided some guidance in how to interpret the statute in order to avoid it being declared unconstitutionally vague. At the outset, *Grogan* held that " 'reckless driving' calls for evidence showing something more than mere negligence." 260 N.Y. at 143. "Mere speed in itself in excess of that allowed by the Highway Law is not alone sufficient." 260 N.Y. at 144. "Reckless driving, therefore, standing by itself means the running or operation of an automobile under such circumstances as to show a reckless disregard of the consequences." 260 N.Y. at 144. *See also Matter of Sheridan v. Fletcher*, 270 A.D 29, —, 58 N.Y.S.2d 466, 469 (3d Dep't 1945).

Subsequent case law appears to have judicially added the mens rea of "recklessness," *see* PL § 15.05(3), to the crime of Reckless Driving. *See, e.g., People v. Boice*, 89 A.D.2d 333, —, 455 N.Y.S.2d 859, 860 (3d Dep't 1982); *People v. Lamphear*, 35 A.D.2d 305, —, 316 N.Y.S.2d 113, 115 (3d Dep't 1970). However, in *People v. McGrantham*, 12 N.Y.3d 892, 893-94, 885 N.Y.S.2d 244, 244-45, 913 N.E.2d 936 (2009), the Court of Appeals muddied the waters by holding, in a memorandum decision, that evidence that was legally insufficient to sustain a charge of Criminally Negligent Homicide was sufficient to support a charge of Reckless Driving. *See also People v. Badke*, 21 Misc. 3d 471, —, 865 N.Y.S.2d 488, 494 (Suffolk Co. Ct. 2008) ("The Court notes as to Reckless Driving that, despite the name of the charge, 'the culpable mental state of recklessness, as set forth in Penal Law § 15.05(3), is not an "element" of the offense of reckless driving' ") (citation omitted); *People v. Ackroyd*, 144 Misc. 2d 149, __, 543 N.Y.S.2d 848, 850-51 (Albany Co. Sup. Ct. 1989) (same).

In *People v. Hoffman*, 130 A.D.3d 1152, __, 13 N.Y.S.3d 619, 623 (3d Dep't 2015), the Appellate Division, Third Department, utilized the *Grogan* definition, holding that:

> "[R]eckless driving 'calls for evidence showing something more than mere negligence,' " and reckless driving has been defined as operating a vehicle "under such circumstances as to show a reckless disregard of the consequences."

(Citations omitted). *See also People v. Earley*, 121 A.D.3d 1192, __, 994 N.Y.S.2d 443, 445 (3d Dep't 2014), leave to appeal denied, 25 N.Y.3d 1200, 2015 WL 4875883 (2015) (" 'Determining whether conduct rises to the level of unreasonable interference or endangerment such that it constitutes the requisite recklessness involves the presence of additional aggravating acts or circumstances beyond a single violation of a rule of the road' ") (citation omitted).

§ 12:27   Victim's failure to wear seat belt not a defense to a Vehicular Assault/Vehicular Manslaughter charge

Unlike in a civil negligence case, the victim's contributory negligence is not a defense in a criminal case. *See People v. Grogan*, 260 N.Y. 138, 149, 183 N.E. 273, 86 A.L.R. 1266 (1932) ("in criminal offenses there is no such thing as contributing negligence"). In this regard, in *People v. Mojica*, 62 A.D.3d 100, __, 874 N.Y.S.2d 195, 205–06 (2d Dep't 2009), the Appellate Division, Second Department, held as follows:

> We further note that it was not error to bar the defense from contending that Officer Poluzzi's failure to wear a seat belt was an intervening cause of his serious physical injuries. The defendant's contention on this point was pure speculation, as defense counsel conceded that it had no expert witness available who could quantify or specify which of Officer Poluzzi's injuries would have been mitigated had he worn his seat belt. In any event, Officer Poluzzi, as an operator of an authorized emergency vehicle, was exempt from the requirement that he wear a seat belt. Further, even if no exemption applied, and the victim were a lay person, the mere necessity of drafting a statute such as Vehicle and Traffic Law § 1229-c(3), which generally requires drivers to wear seat belts, and imposing fines for its violation, compels the conclusion that it is reasonably foreseeable that a driver of another vehicle might not be wearing a seat belt, and that as a result, a broadside collision would produce serious physical injuries. Put differently, it cannot be stated

that Officer Poluzzi's conduct in electing not to wear his seat belt "constituted such a departure from driving norms as to be unforeseeable, i.e., beyond the mere negligence of the other motorists, sufficient to negate the defendant's responsibility in causing the accident." Moreover, although the issue of foreseeability is generally one for the fact-finder, under these circumstances, the court properly decided the issue as a matter of law.

(Citations omitted).

§ 12:28 DWI is not properly classified as a "violent crime"

Vehicular crimes involving DWI (*e.g.*, Vehicular Assault and Vehicular Manslaughter) are not defined as "violent felonies" in the Penal Law. *See* PL § 70.02(1). This is consistent with the U.S. Supreme Court's holdings in both *Leocal v. Ashcroft*, 543 U.S. 1, 125 S. Ct. 377, 160 L. Ed. 2d 271 (2004), and *Begay v. U.S.*, 553 U.S. 137, 128 S. Ct. 1581, 170 L. Ed. 2d 490 (2008).

In *Leocal*, the Court held that driving under the influence of alcohol and causing serious bodily injury is not a "crime of violence" under 18 U.S.C. 16, and thus is not an "aggravated felony" under the Immigration and Nationality Act. 543 U.S. at 3-4, 125 S.Ct. at 379. In so holding, the Court reasoned that:

In construing both parts of 16, we cannot forget that we ultimately are determining the meaning of the term "crime of violence." The ordinary meaning of this term, combined with 16's emphasis on the use of physical force against another person (or the risk of having to use such force in committing a crime), suggests a category of violent, active crimes that cannot be said naturally to include DUI offenses. Interpreting § 16 to encompass accidental or negligent conduct would blur the distinction between the "violent" crimes Congress sought to distinguish for heightened punishment and other crimes. * * *

This case does not present us with the question whether a state or federal offense that requires proof of the reckless use of force against a person or property of another qualifies as a crime of violence under 18 U.S.C.A. § 16. DUI statutes such as Florida's do not require any mental state with respect to the use of force against another person, thus reaching individuals who were negligent or less. Drunk driving is a nationwide problem, as evidenced by the efforts of legislatures to prohibit such conduct and impose appropriate penalties. But this fact does not warrant our shoehorning it into statutory sections where it does not fit.

543 U.S. at 11, 13, 125 S.Ct. at 383, 384 (citations omitted).

In *Begay*, the Court held that driving under the influence of alcohol is not a "violent felony" for purposes of the Armed Career Criminal Act. 553 U.S. at 139, 128 S.Ct. at 1583. In so holding, the Court reasoned that:

In our view, DUI differs from the example crimes [listed in the statute]—burglary, arson, extortion, and crimes involving the use of explosives—in at least one pertinent, and important, respect. The listed crimes all typically involve purposeful, "violent," and "aggressive" conduct. * * *

By way of contrast, statutes that forbid driving under the influence, such as the statute before us, typically do not insist on purposeful, violent, and aggressive conduct; rather, they are, or are most nearly comparable to, crimes that impose strict liability, criminalizing conduct in respect to which the offender need not have had any criminal intent at all. * * *

The distinction we make does not minimize the seriousness of the risks attached to driving under the influence. . . . [W]e hold only that, for purposes of the particular statutory provision before us, a prior record of DUI, a strict liability crime, differs from a prior record of violent and aggressive crimes committed intentionally such as arson, burglary, extortion, or crimes involving the use of explosives. The latter are associated with a likelihood of future violent, aggressive, and purposeful "armed career criminal" behavior in a way that the former are not.

We consequently conclude that New Mexico's crime of "driving under the influence" falls outside the scope of the Armed Career Criminal Act's clause (ii) "violent felony" definition.

553 U.S. at 144-45, 147-48, 128 S.Ct. at 1586-87, 1588.

§ 12:29   Fetus not "person" for purposes of manslaughter charge

In *People v. Jorgensen*, 26 N.Y.3d 85, 19 N.Y.S.3d 814, 41 N.E.3d 778 (2015), the Court of Appeals held that a fetus is not a "person" for purposes of a Manslaughter charge. Specifically:

The sole issue that we reach on this appeal, however, is whether a woman can be convicted of manslaughter for reckless conduct that she engaged in while pregnant that caused injury to the fetus *in utero* where the child was born alive but died as a result of that injury days later. We hold that it is evident from the statutory scheme that the legislature, in enacting Penal Law §§ 125.05(1) and 125.15(1), did not intend to hold pregnant women criminally responsible for conduct with respect to themselves and their unborn fetuses unless such conduct is done intentionally.

The issue is strictly one of statutory interpretation. As relevant here, "[a] person is guilty of manslaughter in the second degree when . . . [h]e [or she] recklessly causes the death of another person." Penal Law § 125.05(1) provides that, when referring to the victim of a homicide, a person is "a human being who has been born and is alive." The question is, did the legislature, through its enactment of the two statutory provisions, intend to hold pregnant women criminally responsible for engaging in reckless conduct against themselves and their unborn fetuses, such that they should be subject to criminal liability for prenatal conduct that results in postnatal death? Under the current statutory scheme, the answer to this question is no.

Id. at 89-90, 19 N.Y.S.3d at 815-16 (citations and footnote omitted).

Chapter 13

Aggravated Unlicensed Operation of a Motor Vehicle (AUO)

§ 13:1   In general

One of the most common crimes in New York is Aggravated Unlicensed Operation of a Motor Vehicle (a.k.a. AUO). AUO comes in 3 degrees: AUO 3rd (a misdemeanor), *see* VTL § 511(1); AUO 2nd (a more serious misdemeanor), *see* VTL § 511(2); and AUO 1st (a class E felony). *See* VTL § 511(3). Unlicensed Operation, a traffic infraction, *see* VTL § 509(1), is a lesser included offense of AUO. *See* § 13:10, *infra*. DWI-related AUO is an aggravating factor that raises the felony class level of various vehicular crimes. *See, e.g.*, PL § 120.04(2); PL § 120.04-a(2); PL § 125.13(2); PL § 125.14(2).

This chapter addresses a variety of common issues that arise in connection with AUO charges.

§ 13:2   AUO 3rd—Generally

The lowest level of AUO is AUO 3rd. In this regard, VTL § 511(1)(a) provides as follows:

1. Aggravated unlicensed operation of a motor vehicle in the third degree.

(a) A person is guilty of the offense of [AUO 3rd] when such person operates a motor vehicle upon a public highway while knowing or having reason to know that such person's license or privilege of operating such motor vehicle in this state or privilege of obtaining a license to operate such motor vehicle issued by the commissioner is suspended, revoked or otherwise withdrawn by the commissioner.

AUO 3rd is an unclassified misdemeanor. VTL § 511(1)(b).

§ 13:3   Proof that defendant "knew or had reason to know" license was suspended or revoked is essential element of AUO

"[A]ggravated unlicensed operation has a mens rea element. To be convicted, a defendant must know or have reason to know that his driving privileges have been revoked, suspended or otherwise withdrawn by the Commissioner of Motor Vehicles." *People v. Pacer*, 6 N.Y.3d 504, 508, 814 N.Y.S.2d 575, 576–77, 847 N.E.2d 1149 (2006). *See also* VTL § 511(1)(a).

In *People v. Crandall*, 199 A.D.2d 867, __, 606 N.Y.S.2d 357, 359 (3d Dep't 1993), the Appellate Division, Third Department, held that:

The record indicates that the prosecution sustained its burden of proving beyond a reasonable doubt that defendant operated a motor vehicle while knowing or having reason to know that his license was revoked in violation of [VTL] § 511(3)(a). The Chief Clerk of the Schenectady City Court testified that defendant had signed an acknowledgment of the order of suspension or revocation. Defendant identified his signature on the order and testified that he believed that a stay on his prior conviction permitted him to drive. However, the order of stay provided that "jail along with any fine imposed, [should] be stayed pending the termination of the appeal taken." This evidence permitted a fact-finder to conclude beyond a reasonable doubt that defendant knew that his license was revoked.

In *People v. Strauss*, 136 A.D.3d 1340, __, 23 N.Y.S.3d 924, 924-25 (4th Dep't 2016), the Appellate Division, Fourth Department, held that:

The Court of Appeals has held that "[t]he felony offense of first-degree [AUO] has a mens rea element," which derives from the basic definition of AUO pursuant to Vehicle and Traffic Law § 511(1)(a). "To be convicted, a defendant must know or have reason to know that his [or her] driving privileges have been revoked, suspended or otherwise withdrawn by the Commissioner of Motor Vehicles." Based on the statutory language and interpretation thereof by the Court of Appeals, and consistent with the pattern Criminal Jury Instructions, we conclude that the People were not required to prove that defendant knew or had reason to know that his driving privileges had been revoked, suspended, or otherwise withdrawn *as a result of a prior conviction.*

(Emphasis added) (citations omitted).

§ 13:4 Applicability of *Crawford v. Washington* to AUO cases

Prior to the United States Supreme Court's landmark Confrontation Clause decision in *Crawford v. Washington*, 541 U.S. 36, 124 S. Ct. 1354, 158 L. Ed. 2d 177, 63 Fed. R. Evid. Serv. 1077 (2004), the defendant's knowledge of the fact that his or her driver's license was suspended or revoked was often proven at trial, pursuant to VTL § 214, by the introduction into evidence of:

[A] document titled "Affidavit of Regularity/Proof of Mailing" from a Department of Motor Vehicles official, purporting to explain the Department's ordinary mailing procedures for revocation notices. The affidavit contained a statement, on the official's "information and belief," that the ordinary procedures described in the affidavit had been followed in defendant's case.

People v. Pacer, 6 N.Y.3d 504, 509, 814 N.Y.S.2d 575, 577, 847 N.E.2d 1149 (2006). *See also People v. Darrisaw*, 66 A.D.3d 1427, 886 N.Y.S.2d 315 (4th Dep't 2009); *People v. Wolters*, 41 A.D.3d 518, 838 N.Y.S.2d 117 (2d Dep't 2007); *People v. Capellan*, 6 Misc. 3d 809, __, 791 N.Y.S.2d 315, 316 (N.Y. City Crim. Ct. 2004).

In this regard, VTL § 214 affidavits were allowed to substitute for the live testimony of a DMV employee. However, in *Pacer*, *supra*, the Court of Appeals held that this procedure violates *Crawford*. *See Pacer*, 6 N.Y.3d at 507, 814 N.Y.S.2d at 576.

In *People v. Abelo*, 79 A.D.3d 668, __, 914 N.Y.S.2d 54, 56 (1st Dep't 2010), the People attempted to satisfy *Pacer* by calling a DMV employee as a witness. However, the employee who was called was not employed by DMV at the time of the suspensions in question, nor was she familiar with the DMV procedures in effect at the time. Under these circumstances, the Appellate Division, First Department, held that:

> [T]he only basis for admitting the required notice of suspension was the testimony of a witness who was not qualified to testify concerning procedures in use at the time that the notice was sent. Admitting such evidence contravenes the rationale of *People v. Pacer*, *supra*. A witness who on cross-examination denies knowing what procedures were used at the time of mailing does not satisfy the obligation to produce a witness who can be adequately cross-examined concerning notice to defendant. In essence, the notice of suspension was admitted without foundation, and under the facts of this case its admission constituted reversible error.

Id. at __, 914 N.Y.S.2d at 56 (citation omitted). *Cf. People v. Morales*, 273 A.D.2d 102, __, 709 N.Y.S.2d 544, 545 (1st Dep't 2000) ("The court properly exercised its discretion in permitting expert testimony as to records and procedures of the Department of Motor Vehicles, since this subject was beyond the knowledge of the average juror and the testimony did not usurp the functions of the jury").

In *People v. Rayford*, 80 A.D.3d 780, __, 916 N.Y.S.2d 603, 605 (2d Dep't 2011), the Appellate Division, First Department, stated that "[t]he defendant correctly contends that the admission of a certain document as proof that a 'Notice of Suspension' of his driver's license had been mailed to him constituted testimonial hearsay and, thus, violated his right of confrontation."

In *People v. Baker*, 14 Misc. 3d 23, __, 829 N.Y.S.2d 806, 807 (App. Term, 9th & 10th Jud. Dist. 2006), the Appellate Term found that, irrespective of *Pacer*, the purported "Affidavit of Regularity/Proof of Mailing" was undated and was not notarized. As such, the document was "not an affidavit despite its title." *Id.* at __, 829 N.Y.S.2d at 807.

In *People v. Brown*, 31 Misc. 3d 794, __, 919 N.Y.S.2d 324, 326 (Rochester City N.Y. City Ct. 2011), the Court found that DMV's Mailing Record for Notice of Suspension or Revocation form, which is a substitute for a VTL § 214 Affidavit of Regularity/Proof of Mailing, was an "attempt by the Department of Motor Vehicles to skirt the holding in *People v. Pacer*." (Citation omitted). As such, the Court dismissed the simplified traffic information charging the defendant with AUO 2nd on the ground that there was no valid allegation that the defendant "knew or had reason to know" that his driver's license was suspended. *See generally People v. Parson*, 143 Misc. 2d 592, 541 N.Y.S.2d 321 (Rochester City N.Y. City Ct. 1989).

By contrast, a properly certified copy of the defendant's DMV driving abstract apparently can be admitted into evidence without violating *Crawford. See, e.g., People v. Strauss*, 136 A.D.3d 1340, __, 23 N.Y.S.3d 924, 924 (4th Dep't 2016); *People v. Smith*, 118 A.D.3d 920, __, 988 N.Y.S.2d 233, 235 (2d Dep't 2014); *People v. Stewart*, 68 A.D.3d 1438, __, 892 N.Y.S.2d 570, 573 (3d Dep't 2009); *People v. Carney*, 41 A.D.3d 1239, __, 838 N.Y.S.2d 316, 317 (4th Dep't 2007). *See generally People v. Wray*, 183 Misc. 2d 444, 704 N.Y.S.2d 787 (Kings Co. Sup. Ct. 2000) (DMV documents admissible under business records exception to hearsay rule); *People v. Michaels*, 174 Misc. 2d 982, 667 N.Y.S.2d 646 (N.Y. City Crim. Ct. 1997) (properly authenticated DMV abstract is admissible). *Cf. People v. Maldonado*, 42 Misc. 3d 81, __, 981 N.Y.S.2d 241, 245 (App. Term, 2d, 11th & 13th Jud. Dist. 2013) (two counts of AUO 2nd and one count of AUO 3rd dismissed where DCJS printout purportedly supporting charges was not properly certified/authenticated); *People v. Watson*, 167 Misc. 2d 441, 634 N.Y.S.2d 634 (N.Y. City Crim. Ct. 1995) (AUO 2nd charge dismissed at trial on ground that defendant's DMV driving abstract was not properly certified/authenticated). Critically, however, although a DMV driving abstract can demonstrate whether a person's driver's license was suspended or revoked on a particular date, it is unclear whether a DMV driving abstract, standing alone, can prove beyond a reasonable doubt that the person "knew or had reason to know" of such suspension/revocation.

In *People v. Jarocha*, 66 A.D.3d 1384, __, 885 N.Y.S.2d 803, 803 (4th Dep't 2009), the Appellate Division, Fourth Department, found that "the People presented the order of suspension and revocation with defendant's signature and thus established that defendant knew or had reason to know that his license had been revoked."

In *People v. Maldonado*, 44 A.D.3d 793, __, 843 N.Y.S.2d 415, 416–17 (2d Dep't 2007), Appellate Division, Second Department, held that:

> The Supreme Court properly found, based upon a preponderance of the evidence, that the defendant violated a condition of his probation by knowingly operating a motor vehicle with a suspended license. Contrary to the defendant's contention, the admission of a certified copy of his New York State Department of Motor Vehicles driver abstract (hereinafter the DMV abstract) did not implicate

the Confrontation Clause under the Sixth Amendment of the United States Constitution, because a probation revocation hearing is not a criminal prosecution. In addition, the DMV abstract was properly admitted under the business records exception to the hearsay rule.

(Citations omitted).

§ 13:5 Effect of failure to notify DMV of address change

VTL § 505(5) provides that:

5. Change of address. It shall be the duty of every licensee to notify the commissioner in writing of any change of residence of such licensee within [10] days after such change occurs and to make a notation of such change of residence on such license in the place provided by the commissioner.

In *People v. Kirksey*, 186 Misc. 2d 514, 718 N.Y.S.2d 583 (Ithaca City N.Y. City Ct. 2000), the defendant—who was charged with AUO 3rd—(a) failed to notify DMV of his change of address from New York City to Ithaca, (b) apparently did not receive a suspension notice that DMV mailed to his former address, and (c) claimed that since he never received the suspension notice he did not "know or have reason to know" that his license was suspended. The Court held that the defendant was estopped from claiming improper service of the suspension notice due to his failure to comply with VTL § 505(5). *See generally People v. Suarez*, 167 Misc. 2d 189, __, 638 N.Y.S.2d 1020, 1022 (Valley Stream Just. Ct. 1996) (same rule applied to claim that supporting deposition was improperly served).

§ 13:6 Incriminating admission regarding knowledge of license suspension/revocation must be included in People's CPL § 710.30 notice

In *People v. Calise*, 167 Misc. 2d 277, 639 N.Y.S.2d 671 (N.Y. City Crim. Ct. 1996), no CPL § 710.30 notice was given. However, the accusatory instrument provided, in pertinent part:

Deponent is further informed by informant that informant's basis for believing that the defendant knew or had reason to know that his/her license was suspended or revoked is as follows: The defendant was unable to produce a valid license. The defendant stated, in sum and substance, that he/she did not have a driver's license. The defendant stated, in sum and substance that he/she knew his/her driver's license was suspended or revoked.

Id. at __, 639 N.Y.S.2d at 672.

The Court rejected the People's claim that the contents of the accusatory instrument gave the defendant actual notice of the People's intent to use the statements at trial despite the lack of CPL § 710.30 notice. In so holding, the Court noted that "[t]he

clear language of the statute imposes on the People the obligation not only to inform the defendant of the statements but also
of their intent to use them at trial." *Id.* at __, 639 N.Y.S.2d at
672.

In *People v. Boyles*, 210 A.D.2d 732, 621 N.Y.S.2d 118 (3d Dep't
1994), a DWI/AUO 1st case, the defendant was served with two
CPL § 710.30 notices: the first at the time of his arrest; the second
following his indictment and arraignment in County Court. The
second CPL § 710.30 notice omitted a significant statement that
was contained in the first. On appeal, the Appellate Division,
Third Department, held as follows:

> Because we are remitting this case for a new trial, we also address
> defendant's contention that County Court erred when it admitted
> into evidence his statement that he was coming from Shoprite and
> was on his way to Fallsburg because he was not given proper notice
> pursuant to CPL 710.30. That statement is significant because the
> officers apparently knew that Shoprite closed some two hours
> earlier. The People served two CPL 710.30 notices on defendant;
> one personally at the time he was arrested and brought before the
> Monticello Justice Court and a second within 15 days of the ar-
> raignment in County Court. Only the earlier notice contained
> defendant's statement that he was coming from Shoprite . . . .
> Because the CPL 710.30 notice served at that arraignment in
> County Court failed to apprise defendant of the People's intention
> to use his statement that he was coming from Shoprite against him
> at the trial in that court, that statement should have been
> suppressed. Defendant was entitled to rely upon the contents of the
> subsequent CPL 710.30 notice to determine whether to move for
> suppression of any evidence specified therein before trial in County
> Court.

Id. at __, 621 N.Y.S.2d at 120.

§ 13:7   License suspension/revocation does not automatically terminate

Defendants charged with AUO often claim that they thought
that their license suspension/revocation had automatically
terminated at the conclusion of the minimum suspension/
revocation period. However, VTL § 503(2)(j) makes clear that a
driver's license suspension does not terminate until a suspension
termination fee is paid; and VTL §§ 510(5), 510(6), 1193(2)(c)(1)
and 1194(2)(d)(1) make clear that an application for relicensure
is required after a period of license revocation.

Accordingly, it is no defense to an AUO charge that the
defendant thought that the suspension/revocation of his or her
driver's license automatically terminated at the expiration of the
minimum suspension/revocation period. *See, e.g., People v.
Demperio*, 86 N.Y.2d 549, 552, 634 N.Y.S.2d 672, 673, 658 N.E.2d

718 (1995) (per curiam) (VTL § 1193(2)(c) provides a defendant with "reason to know that upon revocation of his license, a new license application [is] required"); *People v. Campbell*, 36 A.D.3d 1016, __, 827 N.Y.S.2d 768, 768–69 (3d Dep't 2007) ("[VTL] § 511(3) and [VTL] § 503(2)(j), when read together, 'put defendant on notice that the [AUO] statute encompasses a suspension that continued in effect based upon a failure to pay the termination of suspension fee' ") (citation omitted); *People v. Cleveland*, 238 A.D.2d 897, __, 660 N.Y.S.2d 771, 772 (4th Dep't 1997) (same); *People v. Fisher*, 165 Misc. 2d 650, 630 N.Y.S.2d 188 (Nassau Co. Dist. Ct. 1995) (same); *People v. Bell*, 163 Misc. 2d 432, __, 620 N.Y.S.2d 923, 926 (Clarkstown Just. Ct. 1994). *Cf. People v. Root*, 267 A.D.2d 1103, 701 N.Y.S.2d 227 (4th Dep't 1999) (under former rule, a license suspension did automatically terminate by operation of law at the conclusion of the suspension period).

§ 13:8 Reading a DMV driving abstract

An essential skill for handling VTL cases is the ability to read and interpret a DMV driving abstract. To assist in this regard, DMV created a mock driving abstract along with an explanation of the symbols and words used therein. A copy of this document is set forth as Appendix 10.

§ 13:9 Admissibility of passenger's driving record to attempt to prove that passenger—Rather than defendant—Operated vehicle

In *People v. Reichel*, 110 A.D.3d 1356, 975 N.Y.S.2d 470 (3d Dep't 2013), leave to appeal denied, 22 N.Y.3d 1090, 981 N.Y.S.2d 675, 4 N.E.3d 977 (2014), the defendant was convicted of Manslaughter 2nd as a result of a motor vehicle accident. The primary issue in the case was whether the operator of the vehicle at the time of the accident was the defendant or rather the victim (who was the defendant's pregnant girlfriend). In this regard, the Appellate Division, Third Department, held, *inter alia*, that:

> Supreme Court [did not abuse] its discretion in refusing to allow defendant to introduce evidence of the victim's prior traffic infractions and accidents, which, defendant contends, would have provided the jury with an alternative explanation for the accident, to wit, that it was the victim, not defendant, who was driving the Mitsubishi at the time of the accident. The flaw in defendant's argument on this point is that the victim's allegedly poor driving history simply is not probative of whether she was a passenger in or the driver of the Mitsubishi on the night in question, no more so than defendant's driving history—which included two prior convictions for [DWI] and [6] prior convictions for [AUO]—would be probative of whether he was a passenger in or the operator of the vehicle.

Id. at __, 975 N.Y.S.2d at 475 (citations omitted).

§ 13:10 Unlicensed operation is a lesser included offense of AUO

"Defendants who drive without a license but who neither know nor have reason to know that their driving privileges have been terminated commit a violation ([VTL] § 509[1])." *People v. Pacer*, 6 N.Y.3d 504, 508, 814 N.Y.S.2d 575, 577, 847 N.E.2d 1149 (2006). A trial court's failure to charge unlicensed operation, in violation of VTL § 509(1), as a lesser included offense of AUO where there is a reasonable view of the evidence which would support such a finding constitutes reversible error. *Id.* at 513, 814 N.Y.S.2d at 580. *See also People v. Gribben*, 164 A.D.2d 944, 560 N.Y.S.2d 52 (2d Dep't 1990). *See generally People v. Wolters*, 41 A.D.3d 518, __, 838 N.Y.S.2d 117, 117–18 (2d Dep't 2007) ("We note that if the Supreme Court, upon retrial, submits to the jury the lesser-included offense of unlawfully operating or driving a motor vehicle on a public highway, that count must be submitted in the alternative (*see* CPL 300.40[3][b], 300.50)"). *Cf. People v. Kulk*, 103 A.D.3d 1038, __, 962 N.Y.S.2d 408, 411 (3d Dep't 2013), leave to appeal denied, 22 N.Y.3d 956, 977 N.Y.S.2d 187, 999 N.E.2d 552 (2013) (under circumstances of case, failure to charge AUO 2nd as lesser included offense of AUO 1st was not reversible error); *People v. Taylor*, 246 A.D.2d 610, __, 667 N.Y.S.2d 299, 299–300 (2d Dep't 1998) ("On the facts of this case, no reasonable view of the evidence would have permitted the jury to conclude that the defendant committed the lesser offense but did not commit the greater"); *People v. Peters*, 188 A.D.2d 1037, 592 N.Y.S.2d 1004 (4th Dep't 1992) (same).

In *People v. Osborne*, 60 A.D.3d 1310, __, 875 N.Y.S.2d 396, 397 (4th Dep't 2009), the Appellate Division, Fourth Department, held that:

> The People correctly concede that . . . count 11, charging defendant with unlicensed operation of a motor vehicle, is a lesser inclusory concurrent count of count 6, charging defendant with [AUO]. Thus, [count 11] must be dismissed as a matter of law.

In *People v. Alshoaibi*, 273 A.D.2d 871, __, 711 N.Y.S.2d 646, 648 (4th Dep't 2000):

> Defendant contend[ed] that the court erred in refusing to charge unlicensed operation of a motor vehicle ([VTL] § 509[1]) as a lesser included offense of [AUO 1st] ([VTL] § 511[3][a]). That contention is foreclosed by the jury's verdict finding him guilty of [AUO 1st] and the jury's implicit rejection of the charged lesser-included offenses of [AUO] in the [2nd] and [3rd] degrees.

§ 13:11 Roadways upon which AUO statute applies

VTL § 1100(a) provides that "[t]he provisions of [VTL Title VII] apply upon public highways, private roads open to public motor vehicle traffic and any other parking lot, except where a different place is specifically referred to in a given section." VTL § 511 is part of Title V—*not* Title VII—of the VTL. In addition, VTL § 511 by its express terms only applies to operation "upon a public highway." As such, a person caught driving in a parking lot with a suspended or revoked driver's license cannot validly be charged with AUO. *See People v. Stewart*, 92 A.D.3d 1146, __, 940 N.Y.S.2d 178, 180 (3d Dep't 2012); *People v. Mills*, 45 A.D.3d 1348, __, 845 N.Y.S.2d 597, 598 (4th Dep't 2007). *See also* VTL § 512 (driving with suspended or revoked registration).

In *People v. Hopper*, 165 Misc. 2d 694, __, 629 N.Y.S.2d 943, 945 (Dewitt Just. Ct. 1995), the Court concluded that:

[T]he New York State Legislature, amended Section 1192 of the [VTL] by adding . . . Subdivision (7).

In the above section of the [VTL] the Legislature directly addressed the situation concerning driving while intoxicated in a parking lot.

Conversely, the New York State Legislature, in its infinite wisdom, and for good or for ill, has not chosen to amend the statutes concerning Suspended Registration and [AUO].

It is the decision of this Court that the motion to dismiss the charges against the Defendant consisting of violations of Sections 512 Suspended registration; 511(1)(a) [AUO 3rd]; 511(2)(a)(i) [AUO 2nd] is hereby granted and those charges are dismissed.

(Citation omitted). *See generally People v. Thew*, 44 N.Y.2d 681, 405 N.Y.S.2d 433, 376 N.E.2d 906 (1978); *People v. Kenyon*, 85 A.D.2d 916, 446 N.Y.S.2d 783 (4th Dep't 1981); *People v. Conzo*, 100 Misc. 2d 143, 418 N.Y.S.2d 750 (Suffolk Co. Sup. Ct. 1979); *People v. Robillard*, 2002 WL 377027 (Cayuga Co. N.Y. County Ct. 2002).

§ 13:12   AUO is a "continuing crime"

"A continuing crime is one 'that by its nature may be committed either by one act or by multiple acts and readily permits characterization as a continuing offense over a period of time.'" *People v. Shack*, 86 N.Y.2d 529, 540, 634 N.Y.S.2d 660, 667, 658 N.E.2d 706 (1995) (citation omitted). AUO is a continuing crime. *People v. Miller*, 163 A.D.2d 627, __, 558 N.Y.S.2d 269, 270 (3d Dep't 1990). As such, a defendant may only be prosecuted once for a single incident of AUO—even if, in so doing, he or she operated the vehicle in more than one jurisdiction. *See, e.g., Johnson v. Morgenthau*, 69 N.Y.2d 148, 512 N.Y.S.2d 797, 505 N.E.2d 240 (1987).

§ 13:13 *Attempted* AUO is not a legally cognizable offense

Penal Law § 110.00 provides that "[a] person is guilty of an attempt to commit a crime when, with intent to commit a crime, he engages in conduct which tends to effect the commission of such crime." In terms of punishment, an attempt to commit a crime is generally punished one level lower than the crime itself. *See* PL § 110.05.

In *People v. Prescott*, 263 A.D.2d 254, 704 N.Y.S.2d 410 (4th Dep't 2000), the Appellate Division, Fourth Department, *temporarily* created the crime of attempted AUO. On appeal, however, the Court of Appeals reversed, holding that attempted AUO is *not* a legally cognizable offense. *People v. Prescott*, 95 N.Y.2d 655, 722 N.Y.S.2d 778, 745 N.E.2d 1000 (2001).

Interestingly, however, although attempted AUO is not an appropriate *charge*, it can be a valid *plea bargain*. *See People v. Foster*, 19 N.Y.2d 150, 278 N.Y.S.2d 603, 225 N.E.2d 200 (1967) (plea of guilty to nonexistent crime not invalid where defendant sought, and freely and knowingly accepted, such plea as part of a plea bargain struck for his benefit). *See also People v. Johnson*, 23 N.Y.3d 973, 975, 989 N.Y.S.2d 680, 681, 12 N.E.3d 1109 (2014) ("Where a defendant enters a negotiated plea to a lesser crime than one with which he is charged, no factual basis for the plea is required. Indeed, under such circumstances defendants can even plead guilty to crimes that do not exist") (citations omitted); *People v. Francis*, 38 N.Y.2d 150, 155, 379 N.Y.S.2d 21, 26, 341 N.E.2d 540 (1975) ("a plea may be to a hypothetical crime"); *People v. Keizer*, 100 N.Y.2d 114, 118 n.2, 760 N.Y.S.2d 720, 723 n.2, 790 N.E.2d 1149 (2003) (same); *People v. Clairborne*, 29 N.Y.2d 950, 951, 329 N.Y.S.2d 580, 581, 280 N.E.2d 366 (1972) ("A bargained guilty plea to a lesser crime makes unnecessary a factual basis for the particular crime confessed"); Donnino, Practice Commentary, McKinney's Cons. Laws of N.Y., Book 39, Penal Law § 110.00 ("Although there may not be a separately prosecutable crime of attempt to commit a particular substantive crime, a bargained-for guilt plea to such an attempt, as a lesser crime than the one charged in the accusatory instrument, which is struck for the benefit of the defendant, may bind the defendant").

§ 13:14 AUO 3rd—Sentence

When a person is convicted of AUO 3rd, the sentence of the Court must be:

1. A fine of between $200 and $500, up to 30 days in jail, or both. VTL § 511(1)(b);
2. Effective July 1, 2008, a mandatory surcharge of $55. VTL § 1809(1)(c);
3. Effective August 1, 2008, an additional surcharge of $20 (ef-

fective July 26, 2013, this amount is $28). VTL § 1809-e(1)(a);

4. A crime victim assistance fee of $5. VTL § 1809(1)(c); and

5. If the case is in either a Town or Village Court, an additional $5 surcharge. VTL § 1809(9).

In other words, if the case is in a Town or Village Court, the mandatory surcharge for most VTL offenses is $93; otherwise, the mandatory surcharge for most VTL offenses is $88.

In *People v. Edenholm*, 9 A.D.3d 892, __, 779 N.Y.S.2d 688, 689 (4th Dep't 2004), the Appellate Division, Fourth Department, held that a 90-day jail sentence for AUO 3rd was illegal. *See also People v. Laurino*, 205 A.D.2d 556, 613 N.Y.S.2d 206 (2d Dep't 1994).

* * * * * * * * * *

When a person is convicted of committing AUO 3rd in a vehicle with a GVWR of more than 18,000 pounds, the sentence of the Court must be:

1. A fine of between $500 and $1,500, up to 30 days in jail, or both. VTL § 511(1)(c);

2. Effective July 1, 2008, a mandatory surcharge of $55. VTL § 1809(1)(c);

3. Effective August 1, 2008, an additional surcharge of $20 (effective July 26, 2013, this amount is $28). VTL § 1809-e(1)(a);

4. A crime victim assistance fee of $5. VTL § 1809(1)(c); and

5. If the case is in either a Town or Village Court, an additional $5 surcharge. VTL § 1809(9).

In other words, if the case is in a Town or Village Court, the mandatory surcharge is $93; otherwise, the mandatory surcharge is $88.

§ 13:15   Sentence for AUO 3rd not required to include fine

A sentence for AUO 3rd is not required to include a fine. *See, e.g.*, VTL § 511(1)(b); *People v. Kropp*, 49 A.D.3d 1339, 854 N.Y.S.2d 273 (4th Dep't 2008). Where the sentencing Court misapprehends the law and refers to the fine as mandatory (in a case where the defendant is also sentenced to jail), the sentence will be vacated and the case remanded for resentencing. *See Kropp*, 49 A.D.3d at __, 854 N.Y.S.2d at 273–74.

§ 13:16   Sentence for AUO can be more lenient where license suspension was for support arrears or overdue taxes

VTL § 511(7) provides an exception to the mandatory sentencing provisions of VTL §§ 511(1)(b) and 511(2)(b) in cases where the defendant's driver's license was suspended due to support arrears or past-due tax liabilities and the defendant has adequately addressed the issue. In this regard, VTL § 511(7) provides as follows:

> Exceptions. When a person is convicted of a violation of [VTL § 511(1) or (2)], and the suspension was issued pursuant to (a) [VTL § 510(4-e)] due to a support arrears, or (b) [VTL § 510(4-f)] due to past-due tax liabilities, the mandatory penalties set forth in [VTL § 511(1) or (2)] shall not be applicable if, on or before the return date or subsequent adjourned date, such person presents proof that such support arrears or past-due tax liabilities have been satisfied as shown by certified check, notice issued by the court ordering the suspension, or notice from a support collection unit or department of taxation and finance as applicable. The sentencing court shall take the satisfaction of arrears or the payment of the past-due tax liabilities into account when imposing a sentence for any such conviction. For licenses suspended for non-payment of past-due tax liabilities, the court shall also take into consideration proof, in the form of a notice from the department of taxation and finance, that such person has made payment arrangements that are satisfactory to the commissioner of taxation and finance.

§ 13:17 Successful DDP completion does not terminate sentence for AUO

VTL § 1196(4) provides, in pertinent part, that:

> Notwithstanding any contrary provisions of this chapter, satisfactory participation in and completion of [the Drinking Driver Program] shall result in the termination of any sentence of imprisonment that may have been imposed by reason of a conviction [of, or youthful offender adjudication for, alcohol or drug-related traffic offenses]; provided, however, that nothing contained in this section shall delay the commencement of such sentence.

In *People ex rel. Paganini v. Jablonsky*, 79 N.Y.2d 586, 584 N.Y.S.2d 415, 594 N.E.2d 909 (1992), the defendant was convicted of DWI and AUO 2nd arising out of the same incident. The defendant was sentenced to a year in jail for the DWI charge and 180 days in jail for the AUO charge. While his appeal was pending, however:

> Paganini enrolled in and completed a [VTL] § 1196 certified alcohol rehabilitation program. He subsequently petitioned Supreme Court, Nassau County, for a writ of habeas corpus alleging that, pursuant to [VTL] § 1196(4), both of his jail sentences should terminate upon completion of the program. That court sustained the writ and directed petitioner's immediate release from custody. The Appellate Division reversed and dismissed the habeas corpus proceeding, concluding that the sentence termination provisions in [VTL] § 1196(4), as interpreted and implemented by the regulations of the

Commissioner of Motor Vehicles, were not applicable to his sentence for [AUO 2nd]. That sentence is the only matter before us inasmuch as Paganini's sentence for his [DWI] conviction was properly terminated under [VTL] § 1196(4) upon his successful completion of the rehabilitation program.

Id. at 589, 584 N.Y.S.2d at 415–16 (citation omitted).

The defendant argued that AUO 2nd, in violation of VTL § 511(2)(a)(ii), is an "alcohol or drug-related traffic offense" within the meaning of VTL § 1196(4). The Court of Appeals disagreed. In so holding, the Court reasoned that:

The goal of [VTL] § 1196 rehabilitation programs is to induce drivers with alcohol or drug problems to obtain professional help, thus reducing threats to the public safety from persons who disregard the dangers of driving with diminished capacities due to intoxication and impairment. The statute and the implementing regulation, by targeting and limiting eligibility to participate in the programs, foster that goal. They reflect a rational policy choice not to extend the termination-of-sentence incentive to [VTL] offenders who knowingly drive without a license—the core element of the [VTL] § 511(2) offense at issue in this case—because that would not directly foster the particular goals of [VTL] § 1196 rehabilitation and education programs. That Paganini's unlicensed driving conviction may be traced back to a suspension, which was based on his prior refusal to take a chemical test and a prior [DWAI] conviction, therefore does not qualify him for the termination-of-sentence remedy.

Id. at 590, 584 N.Y.S.2d at 416 (citation omitted).

§ 13:18   Court can consider pending AUO charge in sentencing defendant for DWI

In *People v. Rawleigh*, 89 A.D.3d 1483, __, 932 N.Y.S.2d 660, 662–63 (4th Dep't 2011), leave to appeal denied, 18 N.Y.3d 961, 944 N.Y.S.2d 490, 967 N.E.2d 715 (2012), the Appellate Division, Fourth Department, held that "County Court did not err in considering defendant's arrests for [AUO] in sentencing him despite the fact that those charges were still pending. The court suspended defendant's license during the pendency of the trial, and defendant did not deny that he drove without a license in contravention of the court's order." (Citations omitted).

§ 13:19   Attorney suspended from practice of law for 6 months for AUO 3rd conviction

In *In re Semel-DeFeo*, 78 A.D.3d 82, 906 N.Y.S.2d 914 (2d Dep't 2010) (per curiam), an attorney was suspended from the practice of law for 6 months for an AUO 3rd conviction. Notably, although this was the attorney's only criminal conviction:

[T]he record evinces the respondent's pattern of contempt and disregard for the Traffic Violations Division of the Department of Motor Vehicles by virtue of his numerous license suspensions for failing to answer summonses and pay fines. Despite his misdemeanor conviction, the respondent continued to drive with a suspended license. While the respondent's underlying actions do not directly impact on his practice of law, the repetitive nature of such conduct reflects an overall disrespect for the law.

Id. at __, 906 N.Y.S.2d at 915. *Cf. In re DelCol*, 23 A.D.3d 7, 802 N.Y.S.2d 188 (2d Dep't 2005) (per curiam) (attorney censured for DWI and AUO convictions, as well as for failure to report same); *In re Plante*, 7 A.D.3d 98, 776 N.Y.S.2d 817 (2d Dep't 2004) (per curiam) (attorney censured for DWI and AUO convictions); *In re Goldstein*, 285 A.D.2d 187, 728 N.Y.S.2d 758 (2d Dep't 2001) (per curiam) (attorney censured for DWI, AUO and Reckless Driving convictions).

§ 13:20 AUO 2nd—Generally

The middle level of AUO is AUO 2nd. In this regard, VTL § 511(2)(a) provides as follows:

> 2. Aggravated unlicensed operation of a motor vehicle in the second degree. (a) A person is guilty of the offense of [AUO 2nd] when such person commits the offense of [AUO 3rd]; and
>
> (i)   has previously been convicted of an offense that consists of or includes the elements comprising the offense committed within the immediately preceding [18] months; or
>
> (ii) the suspension or revocation is based upon a refusal to submit to a chemical test pursuant to [VTL § 1194], a finding of driving after having consumed alcohol in violation of [VTL § 1192-a] or upon a conviction for a violation of any of the provisions of [VTL § 1192]; or
>
> (iii) the suspension was a mandatory suspension pending prosecution of a charge of a violation of [VTL § 1192] ordered pursuant to [VTL § 1193(2)(e)] or other similar statute; or
>
> (iv) such person has in effect [3] or more suspensions, imposed on at least [3] separate dates, for failure to answer, appear or pay a fine, pursuant to [VTL § 226(3) or VTL § 510(4-a)].

AUO 2nd is an unclassified misdemeanor. VTL § 511(2)(b).

§ 13:21 Proof that defendant "knew or had reason to know" license was suspended on 3 or more separate dates not required in connection with VTL § 511(2)(a)(iv) charge

AUO 2nd, in violation of VTL § 511(2)(a)(iv), requires that the defendant have in effect 3 or more suspensions imposed on at least 3 separate dates. In *People v. Abelo*, 79 A.D.3d 668, 914 N.Y.S.2d 54 (1st Dep't 2010), the defendant contended that, in connection with a VTL § 511(2)(a)(iv) charge, the People are required to prove that he "knew or had reason to know" that he was driving with 3 outstanding suspensions. The Appellate Division, First Department, summarily rejected the claim, holding that "the statute only requires knowledge or reason to know of [1] such suspension, not of [3] suspensions." *Id.* at __, 914 N.Y.S.2d at 56. *See also People v. Pabon*, 167 Misc. 2d 214, 640 N.Y.S.2d 421 (N.Y. City Crim. Ct. 1995) (same).

§ 13:22 AUO 2nd—Sentence

When a person is convicted of AUO 2nd pursuant to VTL § 511(2)(a)(i) (*i.e.*, the AUO is enhanced because the person has a prior AUO conviction within the past 18 months), the sentence of the Court must be:

1. A fine of not less than $500, *and* either (a) up to 180 days in jail, (b) where appropriate, a sentence of probation as provided in VTL § 511(6), or (c) a "split sentence" of jail and probation. VTL § 511(2)(b);
2. Effective July 1, 2008, a mandatory surcharge of $55. VTL § 1809(1)(c);
3. Effective August 1, 2008, an additional surcharge of $20 (effective July 26, 2013, this amount is $28). VTL § 1809-e(1)(a);
4. A crime victim assistance fee of $5. VTL § 1809(1)(c); and
5. If the case is in either a Town or Village Court, an additional $5 surcharge. VTL § 1809(9).

In other words, if the case is in a Town or Village Court, the mandatory surcharge is $93; otherwise, the mandatory surcharge is $88.

The AUO 2nd statute does not provide for a maximum fine. However, in *People v. Jimerson*, 13 A.D.3d 1140, __, 788 N.Y.S.2d 526, 527 (4th Dep't 2004), the Appellate Division, Fourth Department, stated that the maximum fine for AUO 2nd is $1,000. *See generally* PL § 80.05(1) (the maximum fine for most class A misdemeanors is $1,000).

In *People v. Borush*, 39 A.D.3d 890, __, 834 N.Y.S.2d 340, 341 (3d Dep't 2007), the Appellate Division, Third Department, held that an 8-month jail sentence for AUO 2nd was illegal. *See also People v. Greene*, 195 A.D.2d 1079, 602 N.Y.S.2d 581 (4th Dep't 1993) (360-day jail sentence for AUO 2nd was illegal). *See generally People v. Head*, 145 Misc. 2d 984, 554 N.Y.S.2d 751 (App. Term, 9th & 10th Jud. Dist. 1990).

* * * * * * * * * *

When a person is convicted of AUO 2nd pursuant to VTL

§ 511(2)(a)(ii), (iii) or (iv) (*i.e.*, the AUO is enhanced because the underlying suspension/revocation is DWI-related or the person has in effect 3 or more suspensions imposed on at least 3 separate dates), the sentence of the Court must be:

1. A fine of between $500 and $1,000, *and* either (a) between 7 and 180 days in jail, (b) where appropriate, a sentence of probation as provided in VTL § 511(6), or (c) a "split sentence" of jail and probation. VTL § 511(2)(b);

2. Effective July 1, 2008, a mandatory surcharge of $55. VTL § 1809(1)(c);

3. Effective August 1, 2008, an additional surcharge of $20 (effective July 26, 2013, this amount is $28). VTL § 1809-e(1)(a);

4. A crime victim assistance fee of $5. VTL § 1809(1)(c); and

5. If the case is in either a Town or Village Court, an additional $5 surcharge. VTL § 1809(9).

In other words, if the case is in a Town or Village Court, the mandatory surcharge is $93; otherwise, the mandatory surcharge is $88.

§ 13:23   Sentence for AUO 2nd must include fine and either jail or probation

A sentence for AUO 2nd must include a fine and either jail or probation. *See, e.g.*, VTL § 511(2)(b); *People v. Jimerson*, 13 A.D.3d 1140, —, 788 N.Y.S.2d 526, 527 (4th Dep't 2004).

§ 13:24   AUO 1st—Generally

The highest level of AUO is AUO 1st. In this regard, VTL § 511(3)(a) provides as follows:

3. Aggravated unlicensed operation of a motor vehicle in the first degree. (a) A person is guilty of the offense of [AUO 1st] when such person:

    (i)   commits the offense of [AUO 2nd] as provided in [VTL § 511(2)(a)(ii), (iii) or (iv)] and is operating a motor vehicle while under the influence of alcohol or a drug in violation of [VTL § 1192(1), (2), (2-a), (3), (4), (4-a) or (5)]; or

    (ii)   commits the offense of [AUO 3rd] as defined in [VTL § 511(1)]; and is operating a motor vehicle while such person has in effect [10] or more suspensions, imposed on at least [10] separate dates for failure to answer, appear or pay a fine, pursuant to [VTL § 226(3) or VTL § 510(4-a)]; or

    (iii)   commits the offense of [AUO 3rd] as defined in [VTL § 511(1)]; and is operating a motor vehicle while under permanent revocation as set forth in [VTL § 1193(2)(b)(12)]; or

    (iv)   operates a motor vehicle upon a public highway while holding a conditional license issued pursuant to [VTL § 1196(7)(a)] while under the influence of alcohol or a drug in violation of [VTL § 1192(1), (2), (2-a), (3), (4), (4-a) or (5)].

AUO 1st is a class E felony. VTL § 511(3)(b).

It is important to note that VTL § 511(3)(a)(i) and VTL § 511(3)(a)(iv) do not require proof that the defendant was intoxicated. Rather, proof that the defendant was merely impaired is sufficient. *See, e.g., People v. Tuszynski*, 120 A.D.3d 1568, __, 993 N.Y.S.2d 402, 403 (4th Dep't 2014), leave to appeal denied, 25 N.Y.3d 954, 7 N.Y.S.3d 283, 30 N.E.3d 174 (2015).

§ 13:25 CPL § 200.60 applies to felony AUO

An element of AUO is that the defendant "knew or had reason to know" that his or her driving privileges were suspended or revoked. *See* VTL § 511(1)(a). In the felony AUO (*i.e.*, AUO 1st) context, the suspension/revocation often resulted from a DWI-related conviction and/or chemical test refusal revocation. In such a situation, the DWI-related suspension/revocation (a) raises the grade of the offense from a misdemeanor to a felony, and (b) is an element of the charge.

As a result, the People and the Court must utilize the procedure set forth in CPL § 200.60. *See People v. Cooper*, 78 N.Y.2d 476, 478, 577 N.Y.S.2d 202, 203, 583 N.E.2d 915 (1991) ("When a defendant's prior conviction raises the grade of an offense, and thus becomes an element of the higher grade offense, the Criminal Procedure Law—reflecting a concern for potential prejudice and unfairness to the defendant in putting earlier convictions before the jury—specifies a procedure for alleging and proving the prior convictions (CPL 200.60)"). This statute provides, in pertinent part, that:

A previous conviction that "raises an offense of lower grade to one of higher grade and thereby becomes an element of the latter" may not be referred to in the indictment (CPL 200.60[1]). Instead, it must be charged by special information filed at the same time as the indictment (CPL 200.60[2]). An arraignment must be held on the special information outside the jury's presence. If a defendant admits a previous conviction, "that element of the offense * * * is deemed established, no evidence in support thereof may be adduced by the people, and the court must submit the case to the jury without reference thereto and as if the fact of such previous conviction were not an element of the offense." (CPL 200.60[3][a]). If, however, the defendant denies the previous conviction or remains silent, the People may prove that element before the jury as part of their case (CPL 200.60[3][b]).

Id. at 481–82, 577 N.Y.S.2d at 205.

Construed literally, CPL § 200.60 only applies to a defendant's previous *convictions*, *not* to "conviction-related facts"—such as a prior DWI-related license revocation—that necessarily reveal the prior DWI conviction to the jury. Faced with this situation in *Cooper*, the Court of Appeals held that the spirit and purpose of CPL § 200.60 requires that the statute be applied not only to previous convictions, but also to relevant "conviction-related facts":

> In a situation such as the one before us—where pleading and proving knowledge of a prior conviction necessarily reveals the conviction—the protection afforded by CPL 200.60 can be effectuated only by reading the statute to require resort to the special information procedure for all of the conviction-related facts that constitute the enhancing element.

> Proper application of CPL 200.60 required that defendant be given an opportunity to admit—outside the jury's presence—the element that raised his crime in grade. That opportunity could have been afforded by a special information charging him with the prior conviction, the revocation of his license, and knowledge of the conviction and revocation. If defendant chose to admit those facts, no mention of them was necessary before the jury. If defendant denied all or any of those facts, the People could have proceeded with their proof, as the statute provides.

Id. at 482–83, 577 N.Y.S.2d at 205.

Although *Cooper* involved a charge of Vehicular Manslaughter, its rationale also applies to felony AUO. *See, e.g., People v. Burgess*, 89 A.D.3d 1100, 933 N.Y.S.2d 715 (2d Dep't 2011); *People v. Anderson*, 89 A.D.3d 1161, 932 N.Y.S.2d 561 (3d Dep't 2011); *People v. Flanagan*, 247 A.D.2d 899, 668 N.Y.S.2d 528 (4th Dep't 1998); *People v. Boyles*, 210 A.D.2d 732, 621 N.Y.S.2d 118 (3d Dep't 1994); *People v. Brockway*, 202 A.D.2d 1015, 609 N.Y.S.2d 481 (4th Dep't 1994); *People v. Williams*, 197 A.D.2d 721, 602 N.Y.S.2d 912 (2d Dep't 1993); *People v. Sawyer*, 188 A.D.2d 939, 592 N.Y.S.2d 92 (3d Dep't 1992). *See generally People v. Cleophus*, 81 A.D.3d 844, 916 N.Y.S.2d 624 (2d Dep't 2011) (defense counsel's mishandling of CPL § 200.60 issue constituted ineffective assistance of counsel); *People v. Miller*, 142 A.D.2d 760, 530 N.Y.S.2d 866 (3d Dep't 1988).

When the *Cooper*/CPL § 200.60 procedure is utilized in an AUO 1st case, if the defendant concedes the predicate DWI-related suspension/revocation, then a conviction of either DWI or DWAI would also result in a conviction of AUO 1st. In this regard, the People and the defense can enter into a stipulation whereby the jury would "automatically" find the defendant guilty of AUO 1st if it finds the defendant guilty of either DWI or DWAI. *See, e.g.,*

People v. Swan, 277 A.D.2d 1033, 716 N.Y.S.2d 194 (4th Dep't 2000); *People v. Donhauser*, 255 A.D.2d 933, 683 N.Y.S.2d 357 (4th Dep't 1998), as amended on reargument, (Dec. 31, 1998); *People v. Tatro*, 245 A.D.2d 1040, 667 N.Y.S.2d 560 (4th Dep't 1997); *People v. Nedoroscik*, 178 A.D.2d 684, 577 N.Y.S.2d 157 (3d Dep't 1991).

A chemical test refusal revocation is also a "conviction-related fact" for purposes of *Cooper* and CPL § 200.60. *See, e.g., People v. Alshoaibi*, 273 A.D.2d 871, 711 N.Y.S.2d 646 (4th Dep't 2000); *People v. Orlen*, 170 Misc. 2d 737, 651 N.Y.S.2d 860 (Nassau Co. Ct.1996).

In *People v. Mason*, 248 A.D.2d 751, __, 669 N.Y.S.2d 712, 714 (3d Dep't 1998), the Appellate Division, Third Department, reversed the defendant's DWI and AUO 1st convictions where:

> Revelation of the conviction-related fact of defendant's previous license revocation rendered the special information and arraignment procedure of CPL 200.60 "an empty gesture." The court's limiting instruction was insufficient to eliminate the likelihood of prejudice to defendant. Therefore, a new trial is necessary.

(Citations omitted).

§ 13:26 CPL § 400.40 does not apply to felony AUO

In *People v. Worley*, 43 A.D.3d 571, __, 840 N.Y.S.2d 489, 490 (3d Dep't 2007), the Appellate Division, Third Department, held that:

> [D]efendant contends, with regard to his conviction for [AUO], that the People were required to file proof of the previous suspension of his driving privileges pursuant to CPL 400.40. We disagree. That statutory provision prescribes the procedure for determining prior convictions for the enhancement of sentence where a defendant has been convicted of an unclassified misdemeanor or a traffic violation. Inasmuch as defendant here was convicted of a class E felony, the cited statutory provision is inapplicable.

(Citation omitted).

§ 13:27 AUO 2nd is a lesser included offense of AUO 1st

In *People v. Sikorski*, 280 A.D.2d 414, __, 721 N.Y.S.2d 48, 49 (1st Dep't 2001), the Appellate Division, First Department, reduced defendant's conviction of AUO 1st to AUO 2nd where:

> [T]he People failed to establish that defendant committed the crime of [AUO 1st], which requires proof that defendant operated a vehicle with 10 or more license suspensions in effect ([VTL] § 511[3][a][ii]). In this regard, the abstract of defendant's driving record that was introduced into evidence by the People was not properly certified as required by CPLR 4540(b).

The evidence was, however, sufficient to sustain a conviction for the lesser included offense of [AUO 2nd], which requires proof that defendant had [3] or more suspensions in effect (*see*, [VTL] § 511[2][a][iv]). We note that this charge was supported by the admission of [8] notices of suspension and defendant has not challenged the admissibility of this evidence on appeal.

(Citation omitted).

In *People v. Whipple*, 276 A.D.2d 827, 714 N.Y.S.2d 374 (3d Dep't 2000), the Appellate Division, Third Department, reduced defendant's conviction of AUO 1st to AUO 2nd where the jury convicted the defendant of AUO 1st but was deadlocked on the associated DWI and DWAI charges.

§ 13:28   *Conviction* of VTL § 1192 is not an element of AUO 1st

While a *violation* of VTL § 1192 is an essential element of an AUO 1st charge (pursuant to VTL § 511(3)(a)(i)), a *conviction* of VTL § 1192 is not. *People v. Keller*, 252 A.D.2d 817, __, 675 N.Y.S.2d 441, 442 (3d Dep't 1998). In *Keller*:

[D]efendant was convicted by a jury of [AUO 1st], [DWAI], failure to keep right and unlicensed operation of a motor vehicle, all as a result of his operation of a motor vehicle on January 1, 1994. The convictions were appealed and were upheld by this court, with the exception of the conviction for [DWAI] which was reversed due to an inordinate delay in sentencing.

Id. at __, 675 N.Y.S.2d at 442.

On appeal, the defendant claimed that the reversal of the DWAI conviction required the reduction of his AUO 1st conviction to AUO 2nd—as a violation of VTL § 1192 is an element of the AUO 1st charge. Rejecting the argument, the Appellate Division, Third Department, held that:

To find defendant guilty of the crime of [AUO 1st], the jury was required, as pertinent to this appeal, to find that defendant was operating a motor vehicle while under the influence of alcohol in violation of [VTL] § 1192(1), (2), (3), (4) or (5). There is no question that the jury found defendant guilty of, *inter alia*, the infraction of [DWAI] in violation of [VTL] § 1192(1) since this was their verdict on count one of the indictment. The mere fact that, due to an apparent oversight, sentencing for the conviction of [DWAI] was not imposed does not negate the jury's finding that on the day in question defendant was operating a motor vehicle while his ability was impaired due to the consumption of alcohol. Since a conviction under [VTL] § 1192 is not an element of [AUO 1st] and all of the elements necessary to convict defendant of this charge were presented to the jury, we find that their verdict should not be disturbed.

Id. at —, 675 N.Y.S.2d at 442 (citation omitted). *Cf. People v. Miner*, 261 A.D.2d 420, 689 N.Y.S.2d 233 (2d Dep't 1999) (jury's verdict convicting defendant of AUO 1st but acquitting him of DWI and DWAI was repugnant, since essential element of AUO 1st is that defendant was driving in violation of VTL § 1192(1), (2), (3), (4) or (5)).

§ 13:29   AUO 1st cannot serve as underlying felony for Assault 1st charge

In *People v. Belizaire*, 234 A.D.2d 467, —, 651 N.Y.S.2d 574, 574–75 (2d Dep't 1996), the Appellate Division, Second Department, held that "[AUO 1st] may not serve as the underlying felony for [Assault 1st] . . . . The interpretation of the Penal Law advocated by the People would lead to an unjust and unreasonable result."

§ 13:30   VTL § 511(3) is not unconstitutionally vague

VTL § 511(3), the AUO 1st statute, has been challenged as being unconstitutionally vague. Such challenges have been unsuccessful. *See People v. Campbell*, 36 A.D.3d 1016, 827 N.Y.S.2d 768 (3d Dep't 2007); *People v. Cleveland*, 238 A.D.2d 897, 660 N.Y.S.2d 771 (4th Dep't 1997).

§ 13:31   VTL § 511(3) is not an *ex post facto* law

In *People v. Guszack*, 237 A.D.2d 715, 654 N.Y.S.2d 845 (3d Dep't 1997), the Appellate Division, Third Department, rejected the defendant's claim that VTL § 511(3)(a) constitutes an *ex post facto* law. In so holding, the Court reasoned that:

> Because the enactment of [VTL] § 511(3)(a) provided defendant with fair warning that, upon his commission of an alcohol-related vehicular offense, he would be subjected to enhanced criminal liability as the result of the continued revocation of his driver's license, the statutory scheme suffers no constitutional infirmity.

Id. at —, 654 N.Y.S.2d at 845–46. *See also People v. Cintron*, 163 Misc. 2d 881, —, 622 N.Y.S.2d 662, 663 (Kings Co. Sup. Ct. 1995) ("the punishment to be imposed herein would not be punishment for earlier license suspensions but only a stiffened penalty for the present crime because it is a repetitive one. Moreover, defendant was given fair warning by the amendment to section 511 of the [VTL] that his continued operation of a motor vehicle while his license suspensions were in effect would be regarded as felonious conduct") (citations omitted).

§ 13:32   Conviction of both DWAI and AUO 1st does not violate Double Jeopardy

In *People v. Khan*, 291 A.D.2d 898, __, 737 N.Y.S.2d 738, 739 (4th Dep't 2002), the Appellate Division, Fourth Department, held that:

> We reject the contention of defendant that his conviction of both DWAI and AUO in the first degree violates the constitutional prohi-bition against double jeopardy. Although in this case commission of DWAI is an element of AUO in the first degree and therefore does not "require[ ] proof of an additional fact which [AUO in the first degree] does not," here both charges are contained within a single indictment and were disposed of by a single plea, and Penal Law § 70.25(2) requires that the sentences upon conviction of both counts be concurrent. Double jeopardy therefore is not implicated.

(Citations omitted).

§ 13:33   AUO 1st—Sentence

When a person is convicted of AUO 1st, the sentence of the Court must be:

1. A fine of between $500 and $5,000, *and* either (a) up to 4 years in state prison, (b) where appropriate and a term of imprisonment is not required by the Penal Law, a sentence of probation as provided in VTL § 511(6), or (c) a "split sentence" of jail and probation. VTL § 511(3)(b);
2. Effective July 1, 2008, a mandatory surcharge of $55. VTL § 1809(1)(c);
3. Effective August 1, 2008, an additional surcharge of $20 (ef-fective July 26, 2013, this amount is $28). VTL § 1809-e(1)(a); and
4. A crime victim assistance fee of $5. VTL § 1809(1)(c).

In other words, the mandatory surcharge is $88.

§ 13:34   Sentence for AUO 1st must include fine and either jail or probation

A sentence for AUO 1st must include a fine and either jail or probation. *See, e.g.*, VTL § 511(3)(b); *People v. Duquette*, 100 A.D.3d 1105, __ n.2, 952 N.Y.S.2d 909, 910 n.2 (3d Dep't 2012); *People v. Rodriguez*, 164 Misc. 2d 974, 627 N.Y.S.2d 254 (Kings Co. Sup. Ct. 1995).

In *People v. Faulcon*, 109 A.D.3d 1021, __, 971 N.Y.S.2d 356, 357 (3d Dep't 2013):

> County Court promised defendant that his sentence would not include a fine, but such sentence would have been illegal. The legal sentence that County Court imposed [which included a fine] was in-

consistent with that promise. Although defendant failed to preserve this issue by moving to withdraw the plea or vacate the judgment of conviction, the sentence must nevertheless "be vacated, and the matter remitted . . . to afford . . . defendant the opportunity to accept the sentence that was actually imposed, or permit him to withdraw his plea of guilty."

(Citations omitted). *See also People v. Ryan*, 83 A.D.3d 1128, __, 920 N.Y.S.2d 806, 809 (3d Dep't 2011); *People v. Eron*, 79 A.D.3d 1774, __, 914 N.Y.S.2d 849, 851 (4th Dep't 2010); *People v. Barber*, 31 A.D.3d 1145, __, 818 N.Y.S.2d 391, 391–92 (4th Dep't 2006).

In *People v. Jenkins*, 94 A.D.3d 1474, 942 N.Y.S.2d 397 (4th Dep't 2012), the defendant pled guilty to felony DWI and AUO 1st. The sentencing court "advised defendant that it could sentence him to a term of incarceration of up to [4] years or to probation, but it did not indicate to defendant that it was required to impose either a fine, or a term of incarceration, or both." *Id.* at __, 942 N.Y.S.2d at 397. The Appellate Division, Fourth Department, held that "inasmuch as the court failed to advise defendant that he must either be fined, or incarcerated or both, we conclude that the plea was not knowingly, voluntarily and intelligently entered. We therefore reverse the judgment and vacate the plea, and we remit the matter to County Court for further proceedings on the superior court information." *Id.* at __, 942 N.Y.S.2d at 397–98.

§ 13:35 Consecutive sentences in AUO cases

Penal Law § 70.25(2) provides that:

When more than one sentence of imprisonment is imposed on a person for two or more offenses committed through a single act or omission, or through an act or omission which in itself constituted one of the offenses and also was a material element of the other, the sentences . . . must run concurrently.

In *People v. Goldstein*, 12 N.Y.3d 295, 300, 879 N.Y.S.2d 814, 817, 907 N.E.2d 692 (2009), the Court of Appeals held that "the conduct underlying the count alleging [AUO] was distinct from that involved in the ensuing reckless endangerment offenses and thus permitted a consecutive sentence." *See also People v. Goddeau*, 43 A.D.3d 491, 840 N.Y.S.2d 244 (3d Dep't 2007).

In *People v. Clemens*, 177 A.D.2d 1053, __, 578 N.Y.S.2d 296, 296 (4th Dep't 1991), the Appellate Division, Fourth Department, held that "[t]he trial court erred in ordering that the sentence imposed on defendant's conviction for [DWI] be served consecutively to the sentence of [AUO 1st]," (citation omitted), and modified defendant's sentences to run concurrently. *See also People v. Milo*, 235 A.D.2d 552, 654 N.Y.S.2d 146 (2d Dep't 1997) (same); *People v. Magistro*, 156 A.D.2d 1029, 550 N.Y.S.2d 875 (4th Dep't

1989) (same); *People v. Khan*, 291 A.D.2d 898, 737 N.Y.S.2d 738 (4th Dep't 2002) (PL § 70.25(2) requires concurrent sentences where defendant convicted of AUO 1st and DWAI).

In *People v. Richburg*, 287 A.D.2d 790, —, 731 N.Y.S.2d 256, 258 (3d Dep't 2001), the Appellate Division, Third Department, stated that sentences imposed for felony DWI and AUO 1st could run consecutively without running afoul of PL § 70.25(2). Critically, however, in *People v. De Maio*, 304 A.D.2d 988, —, 760 N.Y.S.2d 558, 559 (3d Dep't 2003), the Court clarified its position in *Richburg*:

> Although there are numerous factual circumstances that can comprise both the crimes of [AUO 1st] (*see* [VTL] § 511[3][a][i], [ii]) and felony [DWI] (*see* [VTL] § 1193[1][c][i], [ii]), it is apparent that [DWI] can constitute a material element of [AUO 1st]. It was thus incumbent upon the People to show either that defendant's felony [DWI] was not, in fact, a material element of his [AUO 1st] (*see e.g.* [VTL] § 511[3][a][ii] [authorizing such charge based upon nonalcohol-related elements]) or that the two offenses were based upon separate and distinct acts. Here, the indictment alleges defendant's driving while under the influence as an element of the charge of [AUO 1st]. Both the offenses to which defendant eventually pleaded guilty are alleged in the indictment to have occurred on the same date, place and time. The plea allocution confirms such facts and, indeed, further reveals that the same prior offenses provided the basis for both the previous revocation of defendant's license and the elevation of the [DWI] to felony status. It is thus clear that defendant's felony [DWI] charge was a material element of his [AUO 1st] and the People failed to show that the two offenses arose from separate and distinct acts.
>
> The People's reliance upon *People v. Richburg*, with no concomitant case-specific factual analysis, is misplaced. *Richburg should not be construed as holding that felony [DWI] and [AUO 1st] cannot fall within the parameters of Penal Law § 70.25(2). To the contrary, since felony [DWI] can constitute a material element of [AUO 1st], the People bear the burden when advocating consecutive sentences of showing identifiable separate acts sustaining such sentences.* The People failed to make such a showing in this case and, therefore, the sentences must be modified to run concurrently.

(Emphasis added) (citation and footnote omitted).

Shortly after *DeMaio* was decided, the Third Department upheld consecutive sentences in a felony DWAI Drugs/AUO 1st case where the defendant's only challenge to such sentence was that it was harsh and excessive. *See People v. Clark*, 309 A.D.2d 1076, 766 N.Y.S.2d 710 (3d Dep't 2003). Thus, it is critical that defense counsel in a felony DWI/AUO 1st case expressly object to consecutive sentences on the specific ground that such sentences violate PL § 70.25(2).

In *People v. Borush*, 39 A.D.3d 890, 834 N.Y.S.2d 340 (3d Dep't 2007), the Third Department, citing *DeMaio*, invalidated consecutive sentences for a VOP involving charges of *misdemeanor* DWI and AUO 2nd. In so holding, the Court stated that "[b]ecause the act of driving a motor vehicle while intoxicated and while suspended was a single act, concurrent sentences should have been imposed." *Id.* at ___, 834 N.Y.S.2d 341. Notably, however, the *DeMaio* Court had noted that "[t]he common element of merely operating a motor vehicle is not a *material* element" in combined DWI/AUO cases. 304 A.D.2d at ___ n.1, 760 N.Y.S.2d at 559 n.1. Thus, consecutive sentences *are* permissible where the defendant is convicted of misdemeanor DWI and misdemeanor AUO arising out of the same act. *See People v. Skarczewski*, 287 N.Y. 826, 41 N.E.2d 99 (1942). It should be noted, however, that the combined sentences cannot exceed one year. *See* PL § 70.25(3) ("Where consecutive definite sentences of imprisonment are not prohibited by [PL § 70.25(2)] and are imposed on a person for offenses which were committed as parts of a single incident or transaction, the aggregate of the terms of such sentences shall not exceed one year"). *See also People v. Furber*, 169 A.D.2d 841, ___, 565 N.Y.S.2d 210, 211 (2d Dep't 1991) (same).

§ 13:36   AUO convictions and "second felony offender" sentencing

Sentencing as a "second felony offender" is governed by PL § 70.06. This section provides, in pertinent part, that "[a] second felony offender is a person . . . who stands convicted of a felony defined in this chapter, . . . after having previously been subjected to one or more predicate felony convictions." PL § 70.06(1)(a).

The express language of PL § 70.06, as well as the case law interpreting it, make clear that a defendant is not eligible for second felony offender status unless the present felony conviction is for a PL offense. Thus, a defendant presently convicted of a felony under the VTL (such as AUO 1st) cannot be sentenced as a second felony offender. *See, e.g., People v. Cammarata*, 216 A.D.2d 965, ___, 629 N.Y.S.2d 716, 716 (4th Dep't 1995) ("The People concede . . . that defendant was illegally sentenced as a second felony offender on his conviction of [AUO 1st] ([VTL] § 511[3][a]) and felony [DWI] ([VTL] § 1192[3]; § 1193[1][c]) because sentencing as a second felony offender applies only to Penal Law violations").

§ 13:37   Violation of conditional license as AUO

When a person's driver's license is suspended or revoked in connection with a VTL § 1192 violation, the person may be eligible for a conditional driver's license. Where such license is granted by DMV, although the person's license status is technically "suspended" or " revoked," he or she will nonetheless possess a license that is valid for certain purposes. *See* VTL § 1196(7)(a). This raises the question: What is the appropriate charge where a person operates a motor vehicle in violation of a conditional license?

Prior to the enactment of VTL § 1196(7)(f), an issue existed as to whether a person driving outside of the parameters of a conditional license committed AUO, a misdemeanor, or rather merely committed the traffic infraction of driving in violation of a licensing restriction, in violation of VTL § 509(3). In *People v. Tousley*, 86 Misc. 2d 1059, 383 N.Y.S.2d 996 (Yates Co. Ct. 1976), the Court held that the appropriate charge under the circumstances is the traffic infraction. In so holding, the Court commented that if the Legislature "intended that these specially considered drivers should be guilty of a misdemeanor for driving other than to and from work, school or class, at work or during the specific 3 hours on the weekend, . . . then the legislature should have said so." *Id.* at __, 383 N.Y.S.2d at 998. It never did. Thus, pursuant to the doctrine of legislative acquiescence, which provides that "[w]here the practical construction of a statute is well known, the Legislature is charged with knowledge and its failure to interfere indicates acquiescence," *Engle v. Talarico*, 33 N.Y.2d 237, 242, 351 N.Y.S.2d 677, 680–81, 306 N.E.2d 796 (1973), this issue should have been put to rest.

However, 12 years later, in *People v. Sabin*, 139 Misc. 2d 641, 528 N.Y.S.2d 288 (Westchester Co. Ct. 1988) (rejected by, People v. Buckley, 13 Misc. 3d 910, 821 N.Y.S.2d 859 (County Ct. 2006)), the Court expressly disagreed with *Tousley*, and held that the defendant could validly be charged with AUO. This time, the Legislature did not acquiesce. Rather, in 1989, subsequent to *Sabin*, the Legislature enacted VTL § 1196(7)(f), which expressly provides, in pertinent part:

> It shall be a traffic infraction for the holder of a conditional license or privilege to operate a motor vehicle upon a public highway for any use other than those authorized pursuant to [VTL § 1196(7)(a)].

VTL § 1196(7)(f) clearly legislatively overrules *Sabin*. In addition, published decisions decided subsequent to the enactment of VTL § 1196(7)(f) have consistently agreed with *Tousley* (and either disagreed with or distinguished *Sabin*). *See, e.g., People v. Buckley*, 13 Misc. 3d 910, 821 N.Y.S.2d 859 (Sullivan Co. Ct. 2006) (AUO 1st charge dismissed where defendant possessed valid pre-conviction conditional license at time of new DWI charge); *People v. Greco*, 151 Misc. 2d 859, __, 583 N.Y.S.2d 714, 715 (App. Term, 9th & 10th Jud. Dist. 1992) ("It is the opinion of this Court that a person holding a restricted use license, has a license and may not be charged as if he is operating the motor vehicle with a revoked or suspended license").

In *People v. Rivera*, 16 N.Y.3d 654, 655–56, 926 N.Y.S.2d 16, 17, 949 N.E.2d 964 (2011), the Court of Appeals (temporarily) resolved this issue, holding as follows: "a driver whose license has been revoked, but who has received a conditional license and failed to comply with its conditions, may be prosecuted only for the traffic infraction of driving for a use not authorized by his license, not for the crime of driving while his license is revoked."

Effective November 1, 2013, however, *Rivera* was partially legislatively overruled. In this regard, newly enacted VTL § 511(3)(a)(iv) provides that a person commits the felony of AUO 1st when the person "operates a motor vehicle upon a public highway while holding a conditional license issued pursuant to [VTL § 1196(7)(a)] while under the influence of alcohol or a drug in violation of [VTL § 1192(1), (2), (2-a), (3), (4), (4-a) or (5)]." The title of this new offense (*i.e.*, AUO 1st) is a misnomer—as a person who commits this offense is not unlicensed (and is thus not committing AUO). Perhaps this offense should be a new category of Aggravated DWI (akin to Leandra's Law) or a new category of felony DWI.

Regardless, *Rivera* still applies to cases that fall below the level of AUO 1st. In other words, a person who drives in violation of the conditions of a valid conditional license—but not in a manner constituting AUO 1st—"may be prosecuted only for the traffic infraction of driving for a use not authorized by his license." *Rivera*, 16 N.Y.3d at 655–56, 926 N.Y.S.2d at 17.

§ 13:38   Can a person commit AUO on a lawn tractor?

In *People v. Canute*, 8 A.D.3d 1125, __, 778 N.Y.S.2d 247, 248–49 (4th Dep't 2004), the Appellate Division, Fourth Department, held both:

(a) that a lawn tractor is a "motor vehicle" within the "broad definition" of VTL § 125; and

(b) "that [VTL] § 511(3)(a), when read in conjunction with sections 125 and 509(1), placed defendant on notice that the statute prohibiting [AUO] encompasses the operation of a lawn tractor on a public highway."

It is the authors' opinion that the dissent in *Canute* makes more sense (particularly in light of the Court of Appeals' subsequent decision in *People v. Rivera*, 16 N.Y.3d 654, 926 N.Y.S.2d 16, 949 N.E.2d 964 (2011)):

Even assuming, arguendo, that a lawn tractor constitutes a motor vehicle within the meaning of [VTL] § 125, we conclude that defendant cannot be convicted of [AUO 1st] pursuant to [VTL] § 511(3)(a) because a license is not required to operate a lawn tractor in this State. In order to establish that defendant committed the crime of [AUO 1st], the People must prove, inter alia, that he was operating a motor vehicle "while knowing or having reason to know that [his] license or privilege of operating such motor vehicle . . . [has been] suspended, revoked or otherwise withdrawn" (§ 511[1][a]). As County Court properly noted, the crime at issue requires both operation of a motor vehicle and knowledge, or reason to know, that the license to operate "such motor vehicle" has been suspended or revoked. Because no license is required to operate the vehicle at issue, defendant cannot have committed the crime of [AUO 1st].

8 A.D.3d at __, 778 N.Y.S.2d at 249.

§ 13:39   Can the police stop a car for suspicion of AUO?

In *People v. Pate*, 52 A.D.3d 1118, __, 860 N.Y.S.2d 318, 318–19 (3d Dep't 2008):

In November 2005, a police officer encountered defendant in the course of a domestic disturbance call. After concluding that the situation was under control and checking to make sure that defendant did not have any outstanding warrants, the officer advised defendant to leave the premises. Defendant drove away. The officer then ran a check of defendant's license and determined that it was suspended. As a result, the officer filed an information alleging [AUO 3rd], leading to an arrest warrant being issued for defendant.

About six weeks later, the same officer recognized that a radio transmission concerned the vehicle which defendant had previously been driving. The officer responded to the area, pulled the vehicle over, requested defendant's identification and arrested him. During a search of defendant incident to the arrest, the officer discovered crack cocaine.

The Appellate Division, Third Department, held that "[t]he arresting officer knew that, six weeks prior to the stop at issue, defendant had driven the same vehicle while his driver's license was suspended. This knowledge gave the officer reasonable cause to stop the vehicle." *Id.* at __, 860 N.Y.S.2d at 31.

Similarly, in *People v. Haynes*, 35 A.D.3d 1212, __, 825 N.Y.S.2d 627, 628 (4th Dep't 2006), the Appellate Division, Fourth Department, held that:

The police officer who stopped the vehicle was aware that defendant had recently been ticketed for unlicensed operation of a motor vehicle, and that knowledge gave the officer the requisite level of suspicion to justify the stop of defendant's vehicle. While a computer check would have confirmed the status of defendant's license, we cannot conclude under the circumstances of this case that a computer check was necessary inasmuch as the ticket for unlicensed operation of a motor vehicle was issued close in time to the stop of defendant's vehicle.

(Citations omitted). *See generally People v. Reed*, 45 A.D.3d 1333, 844 N.Y.S.2d 809 (4th Dep't 2007); *People v. Eason*, 283 A.D.2d 655, __, 725 N.Y.S.2d 84, 84 (2d Dep't 2001) ("The stop was validly based on the police officer's concededly correct knowledge that the registration for the vehicle had been suspended"); *People v. Clark*, 227 A.D.2d 983, __, 643 N.Y.S.2d 836, 836 (4th Dep't 1996) ("The officer knew defendant and knew that his driver's license had been revoked. Furthermore, before stopping defendant's vehicle, the officer confirmed by a computer check that defendant's driver's license had been revoked. Therefore, the officer had reasonable suspicion that defendant was committing [AUO]"); *People v. Riggio*, 202 A.D.2d 609, __, 609 N.Y.S.2d 257, 258 (2d Dep't 1994) ("the police officer testified that several days earlier he had run a check on the defendant's license after seeing the defendant behind the wheel of a parked car. In this manner, the police officer learned that the defendant, who the officer had arrested for [DWI] on a prior occasion, did not have a valid license. Therefore, at the time he stopped the defendant, the police officer had a reasonable suspicion that the defendant was operating his vehicle without a valid license"); *People v. Beckwith*, 163 A.D.2d 863, 558 N.Y.S.2d 394 (4th Dep't 1990).

§ 13:40   Suppressibility of DMV records as "fruit of the poisonous tree"

For many years, the lower Courts had reached differing conclusions with regard to the issue of whether a person's DMV records are suppressible under the "fruit of the poisonous tree" doctrine. In *People v. Tolentino*, 14 N.Y.3d 382, 900 N.Y.S.2d 708, 926 N.E.2d 1212 (2010), the Court of Appeals held that they are not. Specifically, the Court held that "a defendant may not invoke the fruit-of-the-poisonous-tree doctrine when the only link between improper police activity and the disputed evidence is that the police learned the defendant's name." *Id.* at 388, 900 N.Y.S.2d at 712. In so holding, the Court reasoned that:

> In *INS v. Lopez-Mendoza*, the Supreme Court held that the " 'body' or identity of a defendant . . . in a criminal or civil proceeding is never itself suppressible as a fruit of an unlawful arrest, even if it is conceded that an unlawful arrest, search, or interrogation occurred." A contrary holding would "permit[ ] a defendant to hide who he is [and] would undermine the administration of the criminal justice system." Accordingly, defendant does not argue that his name or identity would be subject to suppression as a fruit of the allegedly unlawful stop. Rather, he claims that the preexisting DMV records are subject to suppression because without the al-

leged illegality, the police would not have learned his name and would not have been able to access these records.

Federal circuit courts addressing this issue in the context of those suspected of illegally residing in the country have held that, when the police stop or seize a defendant, learn his or her name, and use that name to check preexisting government immigration files, the records are not subject to suppression. * * *

The facts here are analogous. The officers learned defendant's identity when they stopped his car; that knowledge permitted the police to run a computer check that led to the retrieval of defendant's DMV records. Under the rationale of *Lopez-Mendoza* and the above federal circuit court decisions, defendant's DMV records were therefore not suppressible as the fruit of the purportedly illegal stop. In short, "there is no sanction . . . when an illegal arrest only leads to discovery of the man's identity and that merely leads to the official file or other independent evidence."

While not forming an independent basis for this outcome, the result is further supported by the nature of the records at issue, which were public records already in the possession of authorities.

Id. at 384–85, 385–86, 900 N.Y.S.2d at 710, 710–11 (citations omitted).

§ 13:41 AUO—Defense

VTL § 511(4) provides that:

In any prosecution under [VTL § 511] or [VTL § 511-a], it is a defense that the person operating the motor vehicle has at the time of the offense a license issued by a foreign country, state, territory or federal district, which license is valid for operation in this state in accordance with the provisions of [VTL § 250].

§ 13:42 AUO—*Not* a defense

Where a person's New York driving privileges are suspended or revoked, it is no defense to an AUO charge that the person possesses a valid out-of-state or out-of-country driver's license. In this regard, VTL § 250(2) provides, in pertinent part, that:

The exemption granted in this subdivision shall not apply to persons whose privilege of operating a motor vehicle in this state, or whose former license to drive in this state, has been suspended or revoked, until such suspension or revocation has been terminated or privilege of operating a motor vehicle restored.

§ 13:43 AUO—Plea bargain limitations

Similar to VTL § 1192(10), which contains various plea bargaining limitations in DWI cases, VTL § 511(5) places a plea bargaining limitation on AUO charges. Specifically, VTL § 511(5) provides:

5. Limitation on pleas. Where an accusatory instrument charges a violation of [VTL § 511], any plea of guilty entered in satisfaction of such charge must include at least a plea of guilty of one of the offenses defined by this section and no other disposition by plea of guilty to any other charge in satisfaction of such charge shall be authorized; provided, however, that if the district attorney upon reviewing the available evidence determines that the charge of a violation of this section is not warranted, he may set forth upon the record the basis for such determination and consent to a disposition by plea of guilty to another charge in satisfaction of such charge, and the court may accept such plea.

In the authors' experience, in stark contrast with the plea bargaining limitations in VTL § 1192(10), the plea bargaining limitation in VTL § 511(5) is largely ignored. In this regard, AUO charges are commonly plea bargained to the traffic infractions of Unlicensed Operation, in violation of VTL § 509(1), or Facilitating Aggravated Unlicensed Operation in the 3rd Degree, in violation of VTL § 511-a(1). The likely reason why is that, unlike VTL § 1192(10)(a)(i)—which generally allows a DWI charge to be plea bargained to the traffic infraction of DWAI—VTL § 511(5) generally prohibits an AUO charge from being reduced to a non-criminal offense. Many people consider this to be a legislative oversight, as AUO 3rd was originally classified as a traffic infraction. Thus, when VTL § 511(5) was enacted it was similar to VTL § 1192(10)(a)(i).

§ 13:44   AUO—Sentence of probation

VTL § 511(6) provides an alternative to incarceration as a penalty for AUO. In this regard, VTL § 511(6) provides:

6. Sentence of probation. In any case where a sentence of probation is authorized by [VTL § 511], the court may in its discretion impose such sentence, provided however, if the court is of the opinion that a program of alcohol or drug treatment may be effective in assisting in prevention of future offenses of a similar nature upon imposing such sentence, the court shall require as a condition of the sentence that the defendant participate in such a program.

§ 13:45   AUO—Accusatory instrument sufficient

In *People v. Maldonado*, 42 Misc. 3d 81, __, 981 N.Y.S.2d 241, 244 (App. Term, 2d, 11th & 13th Jud. Dist. 2013), the Appellate Term held that an accusatory instrument charging the defendant with AUO 2nd and AUO 3rd was facially sufficient where:

The deponent police officer alleged in the accusatory instrument that, upon his search of the official, computerized records of the DMV, he had discovered that the records indicate that defendant's driving privilege had been suspended/revoked on July 19, 2008 as a result of defendant's failure to answer or appear in response to a traffic summons; that all such summonses contain the warning that "if you don't answer this ticket by mail within 15 days your license will be suspended"; and that the "Department of Motor Vehicles mails a notice of suspension to any such person at their last known address."

In *People v. Sanago*, 35 Misc. 3d 143(A), 953 N.Y.S.2d 552 (App. Term, 11th & 13th Jud. Dist. 2012), leave to appeal denied, 19 N.Y.3d 1000, 951 N.Y.S.2d 477, 975 N.E.2d 923 (2012), the Appellate Term held that an accusatory instrument charging the defendant with AUO 2nd was facially sufficient where:

In his supporting deposition, the arresting officer alleged that he believed that defendant had reason to know that his license had been suspended based upon the officer's search of the official, computerized records of the Department of Motor Vehicles, which indicated that defendant's license had been suspended at the time of the instant offense on December 27, 2009 as a result of defendant's failure to answer a summons, and that all such summonses feature a warning that "if you do not answer this ticket by mail within fifteen (15) days, your license will be suspended. The suspension occurs automatically (by computer) within four (4) weeks of the defendant's failure to answer." The arresting officer further alleged that, during the traffic stop, defendant was unable to produce a valid driver's license. Also supporting an inference that defendant was aware of the suspension of his license was a certified copy of defendant's driving abstract, which was attached to the supporting deposition and listed a 2008 suspension of defendant's license.

In *People v. Michtavy*, 32 Misc. 3d 133(A), 936 N.Y.S.2d 60 (App. Term, 2d, 11th & 13th Jud. Dist. 2011):

The sole issue raised on appeal is whether the information set forth sufficient factual allegations of the alleged offense [of AUO 3rd]. Contrary to defendant's contention, the information did not need to establish that defendant knew how the Department of Motor Vehicles would effectuate the suspension of his license by computer, only that defendant "knew or had reason to know" that his license was suspended at the time of the incident. The supporting deposition stated that defendant was aware that he had received a prior traffic summons, that he knew that he had failed to answer that traffic summons, and that all such summonses have printed on them that "if you do not answer this ticket by mail within fifteen (15) days, your *license will be suspended*" (emphasis added). Since defendant knew that he did not answer the earlier traffic summons, he "had reason to know" that his license was suspended at the time of the incident involved herein.

(Citations omitted).

In *People v. Crawley*, 32 Misc. 3d 131(A), 930 N.Y.S.2d 176 (App. Term, 1st Jud. Dist. 2011), leave to appeal denied, 19 N.Y.3d 863, 947 N.Y.S.2d 412, 970 N.E.2d 435 (2012) (per curiam), the Appellate Term held that an accusatory instrument charging the defendant with AUO 3rd was facially sufficient where:

> The underlying misdemeanor complaint alleged that, at a specified time and location, defendant was operating a motor vehicle; that a computer check of records of the Department of Motor Vehicles revealed that her license had been suspended for failure to pay assessments for prior traffic violations; that [6] points were charged against her driving record during a period of 18 months; and that a notice was sent to defendant's last known address directing her to pay the minimum assessment amount. These factual allegations were sufficient, for pleading purposes, to establish reasonable cause to believe that defendant was driving "while knowing or having reason to know" that her license was suspended.

See also People v. Mayes, 19 Misc. 3d 48, 858 N.Y.S.2d 856 (App. Term, 9th & 10th Jud. Dist. 2008); People v. Quarles, 168 Misc. 2d 638, 639 N.Y.S.2d 661 (Rochester City N.Y. City Ct. 1996); People v. Rodriguez, 165 Misc. 2d 684, 630 N.Y.S.2d 205 (N.Y. City Crim. Ct. 1995); People v. Gabriel, 164 Misc. 2d 473, 625 N.Y.S.2d 433 (N.Y. City Crim. Ct. 1995); People v. Howell, 158 Misc. 2d 653, 601 N.Y.S.2d 778 (N.Y. City Crim. Ct. 1993).

In People v. Brothers, 123 A.D.3d 1240, ___, 999 N.Y.S.2d 225, 225-26 (3d Dep't 2014), the Appellate Division, Third Department, held as follows:

> [W]e disagree with defendant's contention that the SCI was jurisdictionally defective. Specifically, defendant argues that the SCI failed to allege all material elements of [AUO 1st] because the People did not state that the crime occurred on a public highway. While this claim survives defendant's guilty plea and appeal waiver, no defect exists when the SCI incorporates elements by specific reference to the crime's relevant statutory authority, because such incorporation "constitute[s] allegations of all the elements of the crime," while also giving the defendant "fair notice of the charges made against him [or her]." Here, although the SCI failed to state that the road on which defendant was driving was a public highway, it specifically referenced Vehicle and Traffic Law § 511(3)(a) and, as such, sufficiently incorporated all of the specific elements of the crime.

(Citations omitted).

§ 13:46   Facial sufficiency of simplified traffic information charging AUO in NYC

In People v. Fernandez, 20 N.Y.3d 44, 46, 956 N.Y.S.2d 443, 444, 980 N.E.2d 491 (2012), the Court of Appeals held that:

> [T]he accusatory instrument was a facially sufficient simplified traffic information, although it was titled "Complaint/Information," and contained factual information. For the reasons set forth below, we hold that the accusatory instrument was sufficient to serve as a

simplified traffic information because it was substantially in the form prescribed by the Commissioner of Motor Vehicles.

See also id. at 50, 956 N.Y.S.2d at 447 (in the case of simplified traffic informations, the title of the accusatory instrument "cannot be dispositive when it is the legislature's intention that no single part of the form be dispositive . . . . [T]he Commissioner of Motor Vehicles does not require a simplified traffic information to have any title at all (*see* 15 NYCRR 122.2). It would be illogical, then, to find that the title of the form governs over its substance").

Notably, *Fernandez* may only apply to cases in New York City and other cities having a population of one million or more. *See id.* at 51, 956 N.Y.S.2d at 447 ("Defendant also argues this is not a facially sufficient simplified traffic information since the form used in this case does not comply with 15 NYCRR part 91, promulgated pursuant to [VTL] § 207, which authorizes the Commissioner of Motor Vehicles to prescribe the form of a uniform summons and complaint in traffic violation cases. However, neither [VTL] § 207 nor 15 NYCRR part 91 apply to simplified traffic informations in New York City").

In addition, the *Fernandez* Court concluded with the following comment:

> Although we hold that according to the technical specifications of the regulations, [NYPD] Procedure No. 209-11 substantially complies with 15 NYCRR 122.2, and is therefore sufficient as a simplified traffic information, a new more carefully drawn form would better service the city and the public. The present form is confusing and hardly "simplified." It would seem clear that, at the very least, a simplified traffic information used in New York City should be titled "simplified traffic information" and should not include any space for factual allegations.

Id. at 53, 956 N.Y.S.2d at 449.

§ 13:47   AUO—Accusatory instrument insufficient

In *People v. Brown*, 31 Misc. 3d 794, __, 919 N.Y.S.2d 324, 326 (Rochester City N.Y. City Ct. 2011), the Court found that DMV's Mailing Record for Notice of Suspension or Revocation form, which is a substitute for a VTL § 214 Affidavit of Regularity/ Proof of Mailing, was an "attempt by the Department of Motor Vehicles to skirt the holding in *People v. Pacer*." (Citation omitted). As such, the Court dismissed the simplified traffic information charging the defendant with AUO 2nd on the ground that there was no valid allegation that the defendant "knew or had reason to know" that his driver's license was suspended.

In *People v. Acevedo*, 27 Misc. 3d 889, __, 897 N.Y.S.2d 899, 903 (N.Y. City Crim. Ct. 2010), the Court held that:

Here, the Complaint specifically alleges that Defendant's license was suspended for failure to pay a driver's responsibility assessment, and that Defendant was instructed to pay the minimum amount in [30] days or less by a notice sent to his last known address or his license would be suspended by the DMV. Defendant's license was not suspended for failure to answer a traffic summons, but rather for his alleged failure to answer a notice sent by the DMV. Yet the People failed to provide a copy of this notice, or an affidavit from an employee of the DMV setting forth the DMV's procedure for issuing and mailing such notices. As with defendant Gonzalez in *Brown, supra*, the only allegation supporting the element that Defendant had knowledge of his license being suspended is Police Officer Checa's "belief" based upon a computer check of DMV records. Because this allegation is based on facts of which Officer Checa has no personal knowledge, we find that the count of [AUO] has been insufficiently alleged. Defendant's motion to dismiss this count is accordingly granted.

See also People v. J.T., 13 Misc. 3d 1212(A), 824 N.Y.S.2d 757 (N.Y. City Crim. Ct. 2006); *People v. Pierre*, 157 Misc. 2d 812, 599 N.Y.S.2d 412 (N.Y. City Crim. Ct. 1993).

In *People v. Lesnak*, 165 Misc. 2d 706, __, 630 N.Y.S.2d 459, 461 (Suffolk Co. Dist. Ct. 1995), the Court held as follows:

The court rules, then, that the deposition supporting a simplified traffic information, to the extent it is based on information and belief, must contain a statement of the source of that information and belief if it is to be sufficient on its face.

In docket number 3346496, containing the [VTL] § 511(1)(a) charge, the complainant officer has not specified the source of his information that the license of defendant was suspended. Docket number 3405443 contains the [VTL] § 511(2)(a)(iv) charge, [AUO 2nd], based on more than [3] suspensions imposed on [3] different dates. The complainant officer does not provide the source of his knowledge about the suspensions. The court finds docket numbers 3346496 and 3405443, containing charges of the violation of [VTL] §§ 511(1)(a) and 511(2)(a)(iv) are insufficient for their failure to contain a statement of the source of the information and belief on which they are partially based. The motion to dismiss them is granted.

See also People v. Dumas, 42 Misc. 3d 265, __, 974 N.Y.S.2d 921, 924 (Buffalo City N.Y. City Ct. 2013). *See generally People v. Kouyate*, 159 Misc. 2d 179, 603 N.Y.S.2d 374 (N.Y. City Crim. Ct. 1993).

§ 13:48 AUO—Evidence before Grand Jury insufficient

In *People v. Williams*, 12 Misc. 3d 824, 819 N.Y.S.2d 423 (Kings Co. Sup. Ct. 2006), the defendant was indicted for, *inter alia*, AUO 1st, AUO 2nd and AUO 3rd. The allegation before the

Grand Jury was that, on the date of his arrest, the defendant's driver's license was suspended pending prosecution for a violation of VTL § 1192. Apparently, however, although the defendant's driver's license was definitely suspended and/or revoked, it was *not* suspended pending prosecution for a violation of VTL § 1192. Accordingly, the Court dismissed the AUO 1st and AUO 2nd charges. *Id.* at __, 819 N.Y.S.2d at 425.

In *People v. Carlsons*, 171 Misc. 2d 943, __, 656 N.Y.S.2d 116, 118 (Nassau Co. Sup. Ct. 1997), the Court held that:

> This Court now holds based upon the language of Section 214 of the [VTL], that in order to establish a legally sufficient case of [AUO], the People must offer evidence that defendant was driving and also submit to the grand jury a certified copy of defendant's Abstract of Driving Record together with an affidavit from a responsible DMV employee based on the employee's personal knowledge, setting forth the procedure utilized for the issuance and mailing of the notice of suspension to the driver whose license was suspended.

Cf. People v. Keller, 214 A.D.2d 825, __, 625 N.Y.S.2d 325, 326 (3d Dep't 1995) ("Inasmuch as defendant's guilt with respect to two of the crimes with which he had been charged—felony DWI and [AUO]—was predicated upon, among other things, his having been previously convicted of certain offenses, the certificate of conviction and Department of Motor Vehicles abstract, which constituted evidence of those prior convictions, were quite properly put before the Grand Jury") (citations omitted).

§ 13:49 AUO—Proof at trial insufficient

In *People v. Francis*, 114 A.D.3d 699, __, 979 N.Y.S.2d 687, 688–89 (2d Dep't 2014), leave to appeal denied (N.Y. July 24, 2014), the Appellate Division, Second Department, held that:

> Viewing the evidence in the light most favorable to the prosecution, the Supreme Court correctly determined that it was legally insufficient to establish the defendant's guilt of [AUO 3rd] pursuant to [VTL] § 511(1)(a) . . . . In order to support a conviction of [AUO 3rd], the People must establish that the defendant knew or had reason to know that his or her driving privilege had been revoked, suspended, or otherwise withdrawn by the Commissioner of Motor Vehicles. Here, the evidence was legally insufficient to prove that the defendant knew or had reason to know that her license had been suspended.
>
> The testimony on behalf of the People, given by an employee from the Kings County office of the New York State Department of Motor Vehicles (hereinafter the DMV), revealed that the employee had no personal knowledge of the procedures utilized by the Albany DMV office, which handled the mailing of the notices of impending and actual suspension of the defendant's license. Consequently, the

People failed to present sufficient proof regarding the standard practice and procedure of the Albany DMV office that were designed to ensure that the suspension orders were properly addressed and mailed, did not establish that the suspension orders were mailed to the defendant, and, thus, failed to prove that the defendant knew, or had reason to know, that her license had been suspended.

(Citation omitted). *See also People v. Outram*, 22 Misc. 3d 131(A), 880 N.Y.S.2d 875 (App. Term, 2d, 11th & 13th Jud. Dist. 2009).

§ 13:50 When is an AUO verdict repugnant?

In *People v. Whipple*, 276 A.D.2d 827, ___, 714 N.Y.S.2d 374, 376 (3d Dep't 2000), the Appellate Division, Third Department, held that the defendant's conviction of AUO 1st was repugnant "given the fact that the jury was deadlocked on the crimes of [DWI] and [DWAI]." In so holding, the Court reasoned that:

[B]ecause the record reveals that the jury could not reach an agreement on [DWI] *or* [DWAI] and was therefore deadlocked on an essential element of [AUO 1st], the verdict on this count was repugnant. We thus modify the judgment by reducing defendant's conviction under count three to the lesser included offense of [AUO 2nd] (*see generally*, CPL 470.15[2][a]).

Id. at ___, 714 N.Y.S.2d at 376 (citation omitted). *Cf. People v. Morgan*, 219 A.D.2d 759, ___, 631 N.Y.S.2d 449, 450 (3d Dep't 1995) (similar verdict affirmed where "[t]he nature of the deadlock remained unexplored and the jury was discharged without objection").

In *People v. Miner*, 261 A.D.2d 420, 689 N.Y.S.2d 233 (2d Dep't 1999), the Appellate Division, Second Department, held that the jury's verdict convicting the defendant of AUO 1st but acquitting him of DWI and DWAI was repugnant, since an essential element of AUO 1st is that the defendant was driving in violation of VTL § 1192(1), (2), (3), (4) or (5). Accordingly, the Court reversed the defendant's conviction of AUO 1st, but affirmed his conviction of AUO 2nd. *Cf. People v. Keller*, 252 A.D.2d 817, 675 N.Y.S.2d 441 (3d Dep't 1998) (AUO 1st conviction survives reversal of DWAI conviction due to an inordinate delay in sentencing).

§ 13:51 Amendment of indictment during trial to change theory of prosecution of AUO 1st charge improper

In *People v. Allen*, 158 A.D.2d 932, ___, 551 N.Y.S.2d 96, 97 (4th Dep't 1990), the Appellate Division, Fourth Department, held that:

The court erred in permitting the People to amend the second count of the indictment during trial. The amendment changed the theory of prosecution on the charge of [AUO 1st]. Accordingly, defendant's conviction on that count should be reversed and the count dismissed.

(Citations omitted). *Cf. People v. Crandall*, 199 A.D.2d 867, __, 606 N.Y.S.2d 357, 358 (3d Dep't 1993) ("we hold that the amendment did not change the theory of the prosecution's case nor did it otherwise tend to prejudice defendant on the merits").

§ 13:52   AUO plea vacated where plea allocution deficient

In *People v. Ham*, 265 A.D.2d 674, __, 697 N.Y.S.2d 359, 360 (3d Dep't 1999):

> A review of the plea allocution reveals that defendant responded to County Court's inquiry as to whether he had a valid driver's license by replying that he had a Pennsylvania license and that at the time of this incident he thought, based upon the paperwork he received, that his driving privileges in New York had been reinstated. Defendant also stated that he did not learn otherwise until later.

(Footnote omitted). The Appellate Division, Third Department, held that:

> Although defendant did not move to withdraw his plea or make a postallocution motion, the People concede that this issue falls within the narrow exception to the preservation requirement. Our review of the record confirms defendant's contention that the plea allocution was deficient with respect to this count in that defendant's statement negated that—at the time of this offense—he knew or had reason to know that his license in this State was suspended or revoked. Accordingly, defendant's plea to this count must be vacated and the matter remitted to County Court.

Id. at __, 697 N.Y.S.2d at 360 (citations omitted).

In *People v. Reed*, 1 Misc. 3d 44, __, 768 N.Y.S.2d 541, 542 (App. Term, 2d & 11th Jud. Dist. 2003), the Appellate Term vacated a guilty plea where:

> The plea and sentencing transcript reveals that defense counsel informed the court below that some of defendant's driver's license suspensions "were in his brother's name", after which the court made no further inquiry. Considering the fact that defendant was charged with [AUO] based on said suspensions, we find that counsel's incongruous statement clearly required further inquiry by the court inasmuch as it casts a significant doubt upon defendant's guilt or otherwise calls into question the voluntariness of the plea. Moreover, the transcript reveals that defendant only said two words, "No" and "Yes", during his entire plea. Although the court was not required to make a factual inquiry, the record must demonstrate that defendant's plea was made knowingly and voluntarily, and the transcript herein fails to indicate the foregoing or that he intentionally relinquished or abandoned any right or privilege, and a waiver cannot be presumed from a silent record.

(Citations omitted).

§ 13:53   AUO and *Sandoval*

In *People v. Black*, 77 A.D.3d 966, __, 911 N.Y.S.2d 78, 79 (2d Dep't 2010), the Appellate Division, Second Department, held that:

> The County Court properly ruled that the People could question the defendant on cross-examination, if he were to testify at trial, concerning his prior convictions for operating a motor vehicle while under the influence of alcohol and [AUO], by allowing the People to solely inquire if the defendant had ever been convicted of a felony or a misdemeanor.

See also § 13:25, *supra.*

In a case not involving driving, the Appellate Division, Third Department, held that:

> Defendant also claims that County Court abused its discretion by permitting the People to cross-examine her—had she chosen to testify—concerning the circumstances that led to her being previously convicted of [DWI] and [AUO 3rd]. These convictions, as well as the underlying acts, are indicative of defendant's willingness to place her individual interest ahead of that of society and were relevant on the issue of her credibility as a witness.

People v. Stevens, 65 A.D.3d 759, __, 884 N.Y.S.2d 283, 287 (3d Dep't 2009). *See also People v. Pomales*, 49 A.D.3d 962, 853 N.Y.S.2d 407 (3d Dep't 2008).

§ 13:54   Where person arrested for AUO, police can impound vehicle and conduct inventory search

Where a person is arrested for AUO, the police can impound the person's vehicle and conduct an inventory search thereof (at least where there is no licensed driver immediately available). *See, e.g., People v. Washington*, 50 A.D.3d 1539, __, 856 N.Y.S.2d 783, 785 (4th Dep't 2008); *People v. Cochran*, 22 A.D.3d 677, 804 N.Y.S.2d 346 (2d Dep't 2005); *People v. Figueroa*, 6 A.D.3d 720, 776 N.Y.S.2d 574 (2d Dep't 2004); *People v. Rhodes*, 206 A.D.2d 710, 614 N.Y.S.2d 641 (3d Dep't 1994).

However, the inventory search must be properly conducted/ proven or any evidence obtained pursuant thereto will be suppressed. *See, e.g., People v. Johnson*, 1 N.Y.3d 252, 771 N.Y.S.2d 64, 803 N.E.2d 385 (2003); *People v. Leonard*, 119 A.D.3d 1237, 991 N.Y.S.2d 159 (3d Dep't 2014); *People v. Wright*, 285 A.D.2d 984, 730 N.Y.S.2d 388 (4th Dep't 2001); *People v. Lloyd*, 167 A.D.2d 856, 562 N.Y.S.2d 257 (4th Dep't 1990).

§ 13:55   Seizure and redemption of unlawfully operated vehicles

VTL § 511-b sets forth a very specific set of procedures for the

seizure and redemption of unlawfully operated vehicles. In this
regard, VTL § 511-b(1) provides that:

> Upon making an arrest or upon issuing a summons or an appear-
> ance ticket for the crime of [AUO 1st or AUO 2nd] committed in his
> presence, an officer shall remove or arrange for the removal of the
> vehicle to a garage, automobile pound, or other place of safety where
> it shall remain impounded, subject to the provisions of this section
> if: (a) the operator is the registered owner of the vehicle or the vehi-
> cle is not properly registered; or (b) proof of financial security is not
> produced; or (c) where a person other than the operator is the
> registered owner and, such person or another properly licensed and
> authorized to possess and operate the vehicle is not present. The
> vehicle shall be entered into the New York statewide police infor-
> mation network as an impounded vehicle and the impounding po-
> lice department shall promptly notify the owner and the local
> authority that the vehicle has been impounded.

The remaining subdivisions of VTL § 511-b set forth the
procedures for obtaining the release of vehicles seized pursuant
to VTL § 511-b(1). Notably, VTL § 511-b only applies if, *inter
alia*:

(a) The defendant is arrested/ticketed for AUO 1st or AUO
    2nd (*i.e.*, the statute does not apply to AUO 3rd). *See* VTL
    § 511-b(1); *People v. Miles*, 3 Misc. 3d 566, __ n.1, 774
    N.Y.S.2d 647, 650 n.1 (Rochester City N.Y. City Ct. 2003);
    and

(b) The offense was committed in the officer's presence. *See*
    VTL § 511-b(1).

§ 13:56 Forfeiture of vehicles used in the commission of AUO 1st

VTL § 511-c sets forth a very intricate and complicated set of
procedures for the forfeiture of vehicles used in the commission of
felony AUO. Notably, the decision to seek forfeiture under VTL
§ 511-c is discretionary—not mandatory. *See* VTL § 511-c(2).

Chapter 14

Commercial Drivers and Special Vehicles

KeyCite®: Cases and other legal materials listed in KeyCite Scope can be researched through the KeyCite service on Westlaw®. Use KeyCite to check citations for form, parallel references, prior and later history, and comprehensive citator information, including citations to other decisions and secondary materials.

---

§ 14:1   In general

Prior to September 30, 2005, most of the DWI-related statutes pertinent to commercial drivers were only applicable if the defendant was operating a commercial motor vehicle at the time of the offense—which was a relatively rare occurrence. However, critical changes to the laws took effect on September 30, 2005. As of that date, the critical issue is no longer whether the defendant was operating a commercial motor vehicle, but rather whether the defendant possesses a commercial driver's license (CDL).

Under the new laws, VTL § 1192 convictions, chemical test refusals, and certain other offenses have a dramatic impact on a CDL *regardless of the type of motor vehicle that the CDL holder was operating in connection with the offense*. In addition, the traffic infraction of leaving the scene of a property damage accident in violation of VTL § 600(1) is now treated as seriously as VTL § 1192 offenses when committed by the holder of a CDL.

It is essential that defense attorneys representing CDL holders become familiar with the rules regarding "permanent" CDL revocation for repeat offenders. *See* §§ 14:11 to 14:13, *infra*. This issue is one of the most serious—and least understood—in the field of DWI law.

This chapter addresses important issues faced by CDL holders, as well as by those who operate commercial or so-called "special vehicles." It should be noted that there is some overlap between commercial and special vehicles. For example, certain vehicles that are denominated "special vehicles" in VTL § 1193(1)(d) (*e.g.*, school buses and certain vehicles transporting hazardous materials) are commercial motor vehicles requiring a CDL.

§ 14:2   What is a "CDL"?

The term "commercial driver's license" or "CDL" is defined as:

> A class A or B driver's license or a class C driver's license which bears an H, P or X endorsement, which licenses contain the legend commercial driving license or CDL thereon and which is issued in accordance with the commercial motor vehicle safety act of 1986, public law 99-570, title XII, and this article which authorizes a person to operate a commercial motor vehicle.

VTL § 501-a(1). *See also* VTL § 501(2).

§ 14:3   What is a "commercial motor vehicle"?

The term "commercial motor vehicle" is defined in two places in the VTL—and thus it can have different meanings in different contexts. For purposes of VTL Article 19 (*i.e.*, VTL §§ 501 to 09), VTL Article 20 (*i.e.*, VTL §§ 510 to 17) and VTL Article 31 (*i.e.*, VTL §§ 1192 to 99), the term "commercial motor vehicle" is defined as "[a] motor vehicle or combination of vehicles designed or used to transport passengers or property," and which:

1. Has a GVWR of more than 26,000 pounds;
2. Has a GCWR of more than 26,000 pounds, including any towed unit with a GVWR of more than 10,000 pounds;
3. Is designed or used to transport 15 or more passengers, in addition to the driver;
4. Is defined as a "bus" in VTL § 509-a(1); or
5. Is of any size—other than a farm vehicle operated within 150 miles of the operator's farm—used in the transportation of "hazardous materials."

VTL § 501-a(4)(a)(i) to (v). *See also Barnes v. Board of Co-op Educ. Servs. of Nassau County*, 172 Misc. 2d 402, —, 656 N.Y.S.2d 839, 840 (Nassau Co. Sup. Ct. 1997).

For purposes of VTL Article 19-B (*i.e.*, VTL §§ 509-p-509-y), the term "commercial motor vehicle" is defined as a motor vehicle or combination of vehicles having a GCWR of more than 10,000 pounds used in commerce to transport property, including a tow truck with a GVWR of at least 8,600 pounds. VTL § 509-p(1).

Some of the terms used in VTL § 501-a are terms of art which are defined by the statute. For example:

1. The term "gross vehicle weight rating" or "GVWR" is defined as:

   The weight of a vehicle consisting of the unladen weight and the maximum carrying capacity recommended by the manufacturer of such vehicle. The GVWR of a combination of vehicles (commonly referred to as the "Gross Combination Weight Rating" or GCWR) is the GVWR of the power unit plus the GVWR of each vehicle in the combination.
   VTL § 501-a(2). *See also* VTL § 509-p(2).

2. The term "hazardous materials" is defined as:

   Any material that has been designated as hazardous under 49 U.S.C. 5103 and is required to be placarded under subpart F of 49 CFR part 172 or any quantity of a material listed as a select agent or toxin in 42 CFR part 73.
   VTL § 501-a(3).

3. The term "farm vehicle" is defined as:

   A vehicle having a GVWR of not more than [26,000] pounds which is controlled and operated by a farmer, is used to transport agricultural products, farm machinery, farm supplies or all of the aforementioned to or from the farm and is not used in the operations of a common or contract motor carrier and, such a vehicle having a GVWR of more than [26,000] pounds while being used within [150] miles of the person's farm.
   VTL § 501-a(7).

§ 14:4   What is *not* a commercial motor vehicle?

The following vehicles are excluded from the definition of "commercial motor vehicle":

1. A personal use vehicle, a farm vehicle, or a combination of such vehicles;
2. Any motor vehicle or combination of motor vehicles operated by a "member of the armed forces" for military purposes;
3. A police or fire vehicle, or a vehicle during its use in an "emergency operation," as defined in VTL § 114-b, owned and identified as being owned by the state or a political subdivision thereof;
4. An "ambulance service" as defined in Public Health Law § 3001(2), or a "voluntary ambulance service" as defined in Public Health Law § 3001(3), used to provide "emergency medical service" as defined in Public Health Law § 3001; or
5. A vehicle or combination of vehicles which is designed and

primarily used for purposes other than the transportation of persons or property and which is operated on a public highway only occasionally for the purpose of being transported to a construction or off-highway site at which its primary purpose is to be performed (except as may otherwise be specifically provided by DMV regulations).

VTL § 501-a(4)(b)(i) to (iv).

Some of the terms used in VTL § 501-a are terms of art which are defined by the statute. For example:

1. The term "personal use vehicle" is defined as:

A vehicle constructed or altered to be used for recreational purposes which is exclusively used to transport family members and/or personal possessions of such family members for non-business recreational purposes by the operator, or a rental truck which is exclusively used to transport personal possessions of the person who has rented the truck for non-business purposes.

VTL § 501-a(8).

2. The term "farm vehicle" is defined as:

A vehicle having a GVWR of not more than [26,000] pounds which is controlled and operated by a farmer, is used to transport agricultural products, farm machinery, farm supplies or all of the aforementioned to or from the farm and is not used in the operations of a common or contract motor carrier and, such a vehicle having a GVWR of more than [26,000] pounds while being used within [150] miles of the person's farm.

VTL § 501-a(7).

3. The term "member of the armed forces":

[S]hall include active duty military personnel; members of the reserve components of the armed forces; members of the national guard on active duty, including personnel on full time active guard duty, personnel on part-time national guard training, and national guard military technicians (civilians who are required to wear military uniforms); and active duty United States coast guard personnel. The term shall not include United States reserve technicians.

VTL § 501-a(4)(b).

§ 14:5 A commercial motor vehicle can only be operated by a person possessing a full, unrestricted CDL

Effective September 30, 2005, DMV will no longer grant or recognize any type of limited, restricted or conditional driver's license or driving privileges in connection with the operation of commercial motor vehicles. Accordingly, a hardship privilege, a preconviction conditional license, a conditional license and/or a restricted use license can no longer be used to operate a commercial motor vehicle—*even if the motorist is granted a certificate of relief from disabilities issued pursuant to* Correction Law Article 23. *See* VTL § 1193(2)(e)(7)(e); VTL § 1193(2)(e)(7)(d); VTL § 1196(7)(g); VTL § 530(5). *See also* 15 NYCRR § 134.9(c); 15 NYCRR § 134.18(a); 15 NYCRR § 135.9(b).

Prior to September 30, 2005, if a CDL holder obtained a certificate of relief from disabilities relieving him or her from the application of VTL § 1196(7)(g), DMV would have issued the holder a conditional license valid for the operation of a commercial motor vehicle. Similarly, if a CDL holder obtained a certificate of relief from disabilities relieving him or her from the application of VTL § 530(5), DMV would have issued the holder a restricted use license valid for the operation of a commercial motor vehicle.

§ 14:6 Length of CDL revocation for VTL § 1192 offenses committed in a non-commercial vehicle

A VTL § 1192 offense committed by a CDL holder is only considered to be a "first offense" if the holder has *never* previously been convicted of any of the following offenses:

1. Refusing to submit to a chemical test in violation of VTL § 1194 (although a chemical test refusal is not an "offense," and does not result in a "conviction," it is referred to as such herein for the sake of convenience); *see also* VTL § 109-c; § 14:42, *infra*;
2. Any violation of VTL § 1192;
3. Any violation of VTL § 600(1) or (2); or
4. Any felony involving the use of a motor vehicle.

VTL § 1193(2)(e)(3)(b). *See also* VTL § 1194(2)(d)(1)(c); VTL § 510-a(2)(c); VTL § 510(6)(d).

In other words, the way the statute reads, if a CDL holder has *ever* been convicted of any of the above offenses—*in any type of vehicle*—the holder is considered a "repeat offender" for CDL revocation purposes. Thus, the mere fact that a CDL holder (a) has no prior VTL § 1192 convictions, and/or (b) has never been convicted of a VTL § 1192 offense while operating a commercial motor vehicle, does not mean that the holder is a "first offender" for CDL revocation purposes. This is critical because the CDL revocation for a repeat offender is a "permanent" revocation. *See* §§ 14:11 to 14:13, *infra*.

That said, DMV counsel's office has advised the authors that DMV only counts the above-referenced "priors" towards permanent CDL revocation if such "prior" would have counted towards permanent CDL revocation prior to September 30, 2005.

Where a CDL holder is convicted as a first offender of violating any subdivision of VTL § 1192 (or an analogous out-of-state offense) in a non-commercial vehicle, his or her CDL will be revoked for at least 1 year. VTL § 1193(2)(b)(5)(i). However, the non-CDL portion of the person's driver's license will be suspended/revoked in the same manner that it would be if the person was a non-CDL holder. In this regard, *see* §§ 46:1 et seq., *infra*.

Thus, DMV will generally allow the defendant to obtain a regular, non-commercial conditional license or regular driver's license (if he or she is otherwise eligible therefor). *See* § 14:10, *infra*.

§ 14:7   CDL holders and chemical test refusals

A chemical test refusal committed by a CDL holder is only considered to be a "first offense" if the holder has *never* previously been convicted of any of the following offenses:

1. Refusing to submit to a chemical test in violation of VTL § 1194;
2. Any violation of VTL § 1192;
3. Any violation of VTL § 600(1) or (2); or
4. Any felony involving the use of a motor vehicle.

VTL § 1194(2)(d)(1)(c).

In other words, the way the statute reads, if a CDL holder has *ever* been convicted of any of the above offenses—*in any type of vehicle*—the holder is considered a "repeat offender" for CDL revocation purposes. Thus, the mere fact that a CDL holder (a) has no prior chemical test refusal convictions, and/or (b) has never previously been convicted of a chemical test refusal while operating a commercial motor vehicle, does *not* mean that the holder is a "first offender" for CDL revocation purposes. This is critical because the CDL revocation for a repeat offender is a "permanent" revocation. *See* §§ 14:11 to 14:13, *infra*.

That said, DMV counsel's office has advised the authors that DMV only counts the above-referenced "priors" towards permanent CDL revocation if such "prior" would have counted towards permanent CDL revocation prior to September 30, 2005.

A CDL holder who refuses to submit to a chemical test in violation of VTL § 1194 as a first offender is subject to the following civil sanctions:

1. Mandatory revocation of the person's CDL for at least 18 months (at least 3 years if the person was operating a commercial motor vehicle transporting hazardous materials). VTL § 1194(2)(d)(1)(c); and
2. A civil penalty in the amount of $500 ($550 if the person was operating a commercial motor vehicle). VTL § 1194(2)(d)(2).

A CDL holder who is found to have refused to submit to a

chemical test in violation of VTL § 1194 as a repeat offender is subject to the following civil sanctions:

1. "Permanent" disqualification from operating a commercial motor vehicle. VTL § 1194(2)(d)(1)(c); and

2. A civil penalty in the amount of $750. VTL § 1194(2)(d)(2).

If the person was operating a non-commercial vehicle in connection with the chemical test refusal, the non-CDL portion of the person's driver's license will be revoked in the same manner that it would be if he or she was a non-CDL holder. In this regard, *see* §§ 41:1 et seq., *infra*.

Thus, DMV will generally allow the person to obtain a regular, non-commercial conditional license or regular driver's license (if he or she is otherwise eligible therefor). *See* § 14:10, *infra*.

§ 14:8 Periods of license revocation are *minimum* periods

Where a driver's license is revoked pursuant to VTL § 1193(2)(b), "no new license shall be issued after the expiration of the minimum period specified in such paragraph, except in the discretion of the commissioner." VTL § 1193(2)(c).

In *People v. Demperio*, 86 N.Y.2d 549, 552, 634 N.Y.S.2d 672, 673, 658 N.E.2d 718 (1995), the Court of Appeals held that this statute provides a defendant with "reason to know that upon revocation of his license, a new license application [is] required."

§ 14:9 Successful DDP completion does *not* terminate CDL revocation

Ordinarily, upon successful completion of the Drinking Driver Program (DDP), "a participant may apply to the commissioner . . . for the termination of the suspension or revocation order issued as a result of the participant's conviction which caused the participation in such course." VTL § 1196(5). In other words, successful DDP completion generally allows the defendant to apply for reinstatement of his or her full driving privileges.

VTL § 1193(2)(b)(9) expressly exempts CDL holders from this rule:

Effect of rehabilitation program. No period of revocation arising out of [VTL § 1193(2)(b)(4), (5), (6) or (7)] may be set aside by the commissioner for the reason that such person was a participant in the alcohol and drug rehabilitation program set forth in [VTL § 1196].

See also VTL § 1196(5); VTL § 1194(2)(d)(3); 15 NYCRR § 134.10(b).

On the other hand, where the conviction leading to the CDL revocation was committed in a non-commercial vehicle, successful

DDP completion will generally allow the defendant to apply for reinstatement of regular, non-commercial driving privileges (unless the revocation was for a chemical test refusal, or the defendant was under 21 years of age at the time of the offense, or there is some other disqualification). In this regard, 15 NYCRR § 136.2(a) provides that:

> If the licensee holds a [CDL] and a conviction results in the revocation of both the commercial and non-commercial portion of his or her driver's license, the commercial portion of the driver's license shall be automatically restored after the minimum [1]-year revocation period is served, if the non-commercial portion of the license has been restored as the result of either completion of the [DDP] or approval for re-licensure pursuant to this Part.

See also § 14:10, infra.

§ 14:10   Where a CDL is suspended or revoked pursuant to VTL §§ 510-a, 1193 or 1194, DMV will generally allow the holder to obtain a regular, noncommercial driver's license (if he or she is otherwise eligible therefor)

Where a defendant's CDL is suspended or revoked pursuant to VTL §§ 510-a, 1193 or 1194, DMV will generally allow the defendant to obtain a regular, non-commercial conditional license or regular driver's license (if he or she is otherwise eligible therefor). In this regard, VTL § 510-a(5) provides that:

> Any revocation or suspension of a [CDL] issued pursuant to this section shall be applicable only to that portion of the holder's driver's license or privilege which permits the operation of commercial motor vehicles, and the commissioner shall immediately issue a license, other than a [CDL], to such person, provided that such person is otherwise eligible to receive such license and further provided that issuing a license to such person does not create a substantial traffic safety hazard.

See also VTL § 510-a(8)(b).

Similarly, VTL § 1193(2)(b)(11) provides that:

> Where revocation is mandatory pursuant to [VTL § 1193(2)(b)(5)] for a conviction of a violation of [VTL § 1192(5)], such revocation shall be issued only by the commissioner and shall be applicable only to that portion of the holder's driver's license or privilege which permits the operation of commercial motor vehicles, and the commissioner shall immediately issue a license, other than a [CDL], to such person provided that such person is otherwise eligible to receive such license and further provided that issuing a license to such person does not create a substantial traffic safety hazard.

With regard to CDL revocations under VTL §§ 1193 and 1194, the same rule generally applies. Thus, for example, a CDL holder convicted of a first offense DWAI or DWI committed in a non-commercial vehicle can obtain a class D conditional license (if he or she is otherwise eligible therefor). The authority for this procedure cannot be found either in the VTL or in DMV regulations (*i.e.*, Title 15 of the NYCRR). Rather, it is an internal DMV policy based on the logic of the above-quoted statutes and fundamental fairness.

It should be noted, however, that if the defendant is convicted of a violation of VTL § 1192—other than a violation of VTL § 1192(5) (and perhaps VTL § 1192(1))—*while operating a commercial motor vehicle*, DMV will *not* grant the defendant a class D conditional license during the revocation period. The rationale for this policy comes from 15 NYCRR § 134.7(a)(8), which prohibits the issuance of a conditional license where the offense was committed in a "special vehicle."

§ 14:11 "Permanent" CDL revocation—Generally

For non-CDL holders, the general rule is that DWI-related offenses have, at most, a 10-year window within which they affect:

    (a) The level of a new offense;

    (b) The length of a driver's license revocation; and/or

    (c) The defendant's eligibility for a conditional license.

See, e.g., VTL § 1193(1)(a); VTL § 1193(1)(c); VTL § 1193(2)(b)(3); 15 NYCRR § 134.7(a)(11). *Cf.* VTL § 1193(2)(c).

This rule does *not* apply to CDL holders. DWI-related (and certain other) offenses committed by CDL holders:

    (a) Stay on the holder's DMV record "forever." *See* § 14:14, *infra*;

    (b) Result in a 10-year "permanent" CDL revocation if the holder is convicted of a second offense. *See* § 14:12, *infra*; and

    (c) Result in a permanent, lifetime CDL revocation for a third offense. *See* § 14:13, *infra*;

even if none of the offenses were committed in a commercial motor vehicle.

The relevant offenses that can lead to a "permanent" CDL revocation are:

    1. Refusing to submit to a chemical test in violation of VTL § 1194;

    2. Any violation of VTL § 1192;

    3. Any violation of VTL § 600(1) or (2);

    4. Any felony involving the use of a motor vehicle;

    5. Operating a commercial motor vehicle when, as a result of prior violations committed while operating a commercial

motor vehicle, the driver's CDL is revoked, suspended, or canceled, or the driver is disqualified from operating a commercial motor vehicle; and/or

6. Causing a fatality through the negligent operation of a commercial motor vehicle, including, but not limited to, the crimes of vehicular manslaughter or criminally negligent homicide.

§ 14:12   10-year "permanent" CDL revocation

The way the relevant statutes read, upon a second conviction of any of the offenses listed in the previous section (not arising out of the same incident) *at any point in a CDL holder's lifetime*, the holder faces "permanent" CDL revocation—regardless of whether the first conviction was obtained prior to the September 30, 2005 changes to the laws affecting CDL holders, and regardless of whether the first conviction was obtained prior to the time that the defendant obtained a CDL. However, DMV counsel's office has advised the authors that DMV only counts a "prior" towards permanent CDL revocation if such "prior" would have counted towards permanent CDL revocation prior to September 30, 2005.

Notably, the term "permanent" does not necessarily mean *permanent* for second offenders. Rather, it means a minimum of 10 years. In this regard, four separate statutes address the issue of a 10-year "permanent" CDL revocation for second offenders:

1. VTL § 1193(2)(e)(3)(b);
2. VTL § 1194(2)(d)(1)(c);
3. VTL § 510-a(2)(c); and
4. VTL § 510(6)(d).

1. VTL § 1193(2)(e)(3)(b)

VTL § 1193(2)(e)(3)(b) deals with the reinstatement of a CDL where the holder's second offense is a VTL § 1192 conviction. This section provides that DMV can waive a "permanent" CDL revocation where:

1. At least 10 years have elapsed from such sentence;
2. During such 10-year period, the person has not been convicted of any of the following offenses:
   (a) Refusing to submit to a chemical test in violation of VTL § 1194;
   (b) Any violation of VTL § 1192;
   (c) Any violation of VTL § 600(1) or (2); or
   (d) Any felony involving the use of a motor vehicle;
3. The person provides acceptable documentation to DMV that he or she is not in need of alcohol or drug treatment, or has

satisfactorily completed a prescribed course of such treatment; and

4. After such documentation is accepted, the person is granted a certificate of relief from disabilities pursuant to Correction Law § 701 by the Court in which such person was last penalized.

2. VTL § 1194(2)(d)(1)(c)

VTL § 1194(2)(d)(1)(c) deals with the reinstatement of a CDL where the holder's second offense is a chemical test refusal. This section provides that DMV can waive a "permanent" CDL revocation where:

1. At least 10 years have elapsed from the commencement of the revocation;
2. During such 10-year period, the person has not been convicted of any of the following offenses:
   (a) Refusing to submit to a chemical test in violation of VTL § 1194;
   (b) Any violation of VTL § 1192;
   (c) Any violation of VTL § 600(1) or (2); or
   (d) Any felony involving the use of a motor vehicle;
3. The person provides acceptable documentation to DMV that he or she is not in need of alcohol or drug treatment, or has satisfactorily completed a prescribed course of such treatment; and
4. After such documentation is accepted, the person is granted a certificate of relief from disabilities pursuant to Correction Law § 701 by the Court in which such person was last penalized.

3. VTL § 510-a(2)(c)

VTL § 510-a provides additional offenses that can lead to a "permanent" CDL revocation in addition to the offenses listed in VTL § 1193(2)(e)(3)(b) and VTL § 1194(2)(d)(1)(c). Specifically, conviction of the following offenses can lead to a "permanent" CDL revocation under VTL § 510-a (whether committed in New York or out-of-state):

1. A felony involving the use of a motor vehicle;
2. A felony involving the manufacturing, distributing or dispensing of a "drug," as defined in VTL § 114-a, or possession of any such drug with intent to manufacture, distribute or dispense such drug in which a motor vehicle was used;
3. A violation of VTL § 600(1) or (2);
4. Operating a commercial motor vehicle when, as a result of prior violations committed while operating a commercial motor vehicle, the driver's CDL is revoked, suspended, or

canceled, or the driver is disqualified from operating a commercial motor vehicle; and/or

5. Causing a fatality through the negligent operation of a commercial motor vehicle, including, but not limited to, the crimes of vehicular manslaughter or criminally negligent homicide.

VTL § 510-a(2)(c) deals with the reinstatement of a CDL where the holder's second offense is for a violation listed in paragraphs "1," "4" or "5" above. This section provides that DMV can waive a "permanent" CDL revocation where:

1. At least 10 years have elapsed from such sentence;
2. During such 10-year period, the person has not been convicted of any of the following offenses:
   (a) Refusing to submit to a chemical test in violation of VTL § 1194;
   (b) Any violation of VTL § 1192;
   (c) Any violation of VTL § 600(1) or (2);
   (d) Any felony involving the use of a motor vehicle;
   (e) Operating a commercial motor vehicle when, as a result of prior violations committed while operating a commercial motor vehicle, the driver's CDL is revoked, suspended, or canceled, or the driver is disqualified from operating a commercial motor vehicle; or
   (f) Causing a fatality through the negligent operation of a commercial motor vehicle, including, but not limited to, the crimes of vehicular manslaughter or criminally negligent homicide;
3. If any of the grounds upon which the permanent CDL revocation is based involved a chemical test refusal or a VTL § 1192 conviction, that the person provides acceptable documentation to DMV that he or she has voluntarily enrolled in and successfully completed an appropriate rehabilitation program; and
4. After such documentation, if required, is accepted, the person is granted a certificate of relief from disabilities pursuant to Correction Law § 701 by the Court in which such person was last penalized.

4. VTL § 510(6)(d)

VTL § 510(6)(d) deals with the reinstatement of a CDL where the holder's second offense is a conviction of violating VTL § 600(2), VTL § 392 or a local law or ordinance making it unlawful to leave the scene of an accident without reporting. This section provides that DMV can waive a "permanent" CDL revocation where:

1. At least 10 years have elapsed from such sentence;
2. During such 10-year period, the person has not been convicted of any of the following offenses:
   (a) Refusing to submit to a chemical test in violation of VTL § 1194;
   (b) Any violation of VTL § 1192;
   (c) Any violation of VTL § 600(1) or (2); or
   (d) Any felony involving the use of a motor vehicle;
3. If any of the grounds upon which the permanent CDL revocation is based involved a chemical test refusal or a VTL § 1192 conviction, that the person provides acceptable documentation to DMV that he or she has voluntarily enrolled in and successfully completed an appropriate rehabilitation program; and
4. After such documentation, if required, is accepted, the person is granted a certificate of relief from disabilities pursuant to Correction Law § 701 by the Court in which such person was last penalized.

Prior to September 30, 2005, "permanent" CDL revocations were relatively rare—as both of the offenses in question were required to have been committed while operating a commercial motor vehicle. However, the law no longer distinguishes between convictions obtained while operating a commercial motor vehicle and those obtained while operating a passenger car, a pickup truck, an SUV, a motorcycle, an ATV, or even a riding lawnmower. In other words, the critical issue is no longer whether the defendant was operating a commercial motor vehicle, but rather whether the defendant possesses a CDL.

Notably, however, DMV counsel's office has advised the authors that DMV only counts a "prior" towards permanent CDL revocation if such "prior" would have counted towards permanent CDL revocation prior to September 30, 2005. On the other hand, eligible prior convictions accrued before the new laws took effect will count if a new offense is committed.

§ 14:13   Truly permanent CDL revocation

A CDL holder who is convicted of three of the following offenses (not arising out of the same incident)—*at any point during the CDL holder's lifetime*—will receive a truly permanent, lifetime CDL revocation:

1. Refusing to submit to a chemical test in violation of VTL § 1194;
2. Any violation of VTL § 1192;
3. Any violation of VTL § 600(1) or (2);
4. Any felony involving the use of a motor vehicle;

5. Operating a commercial motor vehicle when, as a result of prior violations committed while operating a commercial motor vehicle, the driver's CDL is revoked, suspended, or canceled, or the driver is disqualified from operating a commercial motor vehicle; and/or

6. Causing a fatality through the negligent operation of a commercial motor vehicle, including, but not limited to, the crimes of vehicular manslaughter or criminally negligent homicide.

See VTL § 510(6)(e); VTL § 510-a(2)(d); VTL § 1193(2)(e)(3)(c); VTL § 1194(2)(d)(1)(d).

Prior to September 30, 2005, this was an extremely rare occurrence—as all three of the offenses in question were required to have been committed while operating a commercial motor vehicle. There could be little dispute that a CDL holder who has been convicted 3 separate times of operating a commercial motor vehicle in violation of VTL § 1192 should be prohibited from ever operating a commercial motor vehicle again. However, the law no longer distinguishes between convictions obtained while operating a commercial motor vehicle and those obtained while operating a passenger car, a pickup truck, an SUV, a motorcycle, an ATV, or even a riding lawnmower. In other words, the critical issue is no longer whether the defendant was operating a commercial motor vehicle, but rather whether the defendant possesses a CDL.

Notably, however, DMV counsel's office has advised the authors that DMV only counts a "prior" towards permanent CDL revocation if such "prior" would have counted towards permanent CDL revocation prior to September 30, 2005. On the other hand, eligible, prior convictions accrued before the new laws took effect will count if a new offense is committed.

In addition, conviction of (a) a felony involving the manufacturing, distributing or dispensing of a "drug," as defined in VTL § 114-a, or (b) the possession of any such drug with intent to manufacture, distribute or dispense such drug, in which a motor vehicle was used, will also result in a truly permanent, lifetime CDL revocation—even for a first offense. VTL § 510-a(2)(e).

§ 14:14   DMV will retain records that can lead to permanent CDL revocation for 55 years

VTL § 201 addresses the issue of how long DMV is required to retain various records. VTL § 201(1)(i)(ii)(A) mandates that records of convictions and of license suspensions/revocations that can lead to permanent CDL revocation, *see* §§ 14:11 to 14:13, *supra*, must be retained for 55 years.

Specifically, VTL § 201(1)(i)(ii)(A)(1) provides that DMV cannot destroy, for 55 years, any "conviction certificates and closed suspension and revocation orders" obtained by a CDL holder—regardless of the type of motor vehicle operated by the CDL holder at the time of the offense—where the conviction, suspension, or revocation relates to:

1. Refusing to submit to a chemical test in violation of VTL § 1194;
2. Any violation of VTL § 1192(2), (3), (4), (5) or (6);
3. Any violation of VTL § 600(1) or (2);
4. Any felony involving the use of a motor vehicle;
5. Operating a commercial motor vehicle when, as a result of prior violations committed while operating a commercial motor vehicle, the driver's CDL is suspended or revoked; or
6. Causing a fatality through the negligent operation of a commercial motor vehicle, including, but not limited to, the crimes of vehicular manslaughter and criminally negligent homicide as set forth in Penal Law Article 125.

Where the conviction, suspension or revocation relates to "violating an out of service order as provided for in the rules and regulations of [DOT] while operating a commercial motor vehicle," the retention period is 15 years. VTL § 201(1)(i)(ii)(A)(2).

Where the conviction, suspension, or revocation relates to any conviction "arising out of the use of a motor vehicle in the commission of a felony involving manufacturing, distributing, or dispensing a controlled substance," the retention period is forever. VTL § 201(1)(i)(ii)(B).

§ 14:15 Non-DWI-related grounds for suspension/revocation of a CDL—Generally

The sections that follow address the suspension/revocation of a CDL for various reasons other than for violations of VTL §§ 1192 and 1194.

§ 14:16 "Serious traffic violations" applicable to CDLs

Certain VTL offenses committed while operating a commercial motor vehicle are classified as "serious traffic violations." *See* VTL § 510-a(4). Conviction of two or more "serious traffic violations," in separate incidents, during any three-year period (whether in New York or elsewhere), will result in a CDL suspension. VTL § 510-a(3)(a), (b). *See also* § 14:18, *infra*.

Pursuant to VTL § 510-a(4), the following offenses constitute "serious traffic violations" if committed in a commercial motor vehicle:

1. Excessive speeding (which is defined as 15 or more MPH over the speed limit);

2. Reckless driving;
3. Improper or erratic lane change;
4. Following too closely;
5. Any moving violation committed in connection with a fatal accident;
6. Operation of a commercial motor vehicle without first obtaining a CDL;
7. Operation of a commercial motor vehicle by a person who possesses a valid CDL but does not have it in his or her actual possession; and
8. Operation of a commercial motor vehicle without the proper class of CDL, and/or without the proper endorsement for either the specific vehicle being operated or the passengers/cargo being transported.

VTL § 510-a(4)(a)(i) to (viii).

§ 14:17 Dismissal of certain "serious traffic violations"

With regard to "serious traffic violations" "6," "7" and "8" in the previous section—which deal with defendants who operate commercial motor vehicles (a) without possessing a CDL, (b) without having their CDL in their possession, and/or (c) with the wrong class of CDL—VTL § 510-a(4-a) provides that:

> The court shall dismiss any charge of operating a commercial motor vehicle without a [CDL] in the driver's possession if, between the date the driver is charged with such violation and the appearance date for such violation, the driver supplies the court with proof that he or she held a valid [CDL] on the date of such violation. Such driver must also supply such proof to the law enforcement authority that issued the citation, prior to such driver's appearance in court.

§ 14:18 Non-DWI-related grounds for *suspension* of a CDL

VTL § 510-a(3) provides for the suspension of a CDL as a result of various convictions. The suspension periods are as follows:

1. 60 days—where the defendant is convicted, during any 3-year period, of 2 "serious traffic violations," as defined in VTL § 510-a(4), in separate incidents (whether in New York or elsewhere);
2. 120 days—where the defendant is convicted, during any 3-year period, of 3 "serious traffic violations," as defined in VTL § 510-a(4), in separate incidents (whether in New York or elsewhere). Such suspension takes effect consecutive to any other suspension in effect pursuant to VTL § 510-a(3);
3. 60 days—where the defendant is convicted of a violation of VTL § 1180(g), and either:
   (a) the speed upon which the conviction was based was more than 20 MPH over the speed limit; or

      (b) the speed upon which the conviction was based was more than 10 MPH over the speed limit, and the vehicle was either:

          (i)   in violation of any rule or regulation involving an out-of-service defect relating to its brakes, steering, and/or couplings; or

          (ii) transporting flammable gas, radioactive materials or explosives;

4. 90 days—where the defendant is found to have operated a commercial motor vehicle designed or used to transport property, as defined in VTL § 501-a(4)(a)(i) & (ii), in violation of an out-of-service order (whether in New York or elsewhere);

5. 1 year—where, during any 10-year period, the defendant is found to have committed 2 such violations, not arising out of the same incident (whether in New York or elsewhere);

6. 3 years—where, during any 10-year period, the defendant is found to have committed 3 or more such violations, not arising out of the same incident (whether in New York or elsewhere);

7. 180 days—where the defendant is found to have operated a commercial motor vehicle designed or used to transport passengers or property, as defined in VTL § 501-a(4)(a)(iii) & (iv), in violation of an out-of-service order, while transporting hazardous materials or passengers (whether in New York or elsewhere);

8. 3 years—where, during any 10-year period, the defendant is found to have committed 2 or more such violations, not arising out of the same incident (whether in New York or elsewhere);

9. 60 days—where the defendant is convicted of a violation of VTL § 1171 or VTL § 1176 (or an analogous out-of-state offense);

10. 120 days—where, during any 3-year period, the defendant is convicted of a 2nd such violation (or an analogous out-of-state offense); and

11. 1 year—where, during any 3-year period, the defendant is convicted of a 3rd such violation (or an analogous out-of-state offense).

VTL § 510-a(3)(a) to (e).

§ 14:19 Non-DWI-related grounds for *revocation* of a CDL

A CDL will be revoked by DMV whenever the holder is convicted in New York or elsewhere of:

(a) A felony involving the use of a motor vehicle;

(b) A felony involving the manufacturing, distributing or

dispensing of a "drug," as defined in VTL § 114-a, or possession of any such drug with intent to manufacture, distribute or dispense such drug in which a motor vehicle was used;

(c) A violation of VTL § 600(1) or (2);

(d) Operating a commercial motor vehicle when, as a result of prior violations committed while operating a commercial motor vehicle, the driver's CDL is revoked, suspended, or canceled, or the driver is disqualified from operating a commercial motor vehicle; or

(e) Causing a fatality through the negligent operation of a commercial motor vehicle, including, but not limited to, the crimes of vehicular manslaughter or criminally negligent homicide.

VTL § 510-a(1). *See also* VTL § 510(2)(a)(iii).

Where a CDL is revoked pursuant to paragraph (a), (d) or (e) above *as a first offense*, the mandatory CDL revocation is for a period of at least 1 year (at least 3 years if the person was operating a commercial motor vehicle transporting hazardous materials). VTL § 510-a(2)(a), (b).

If the defendant is a "repeat offender," the revocation is "permanent." VTL § 510-a(2)(a), (b). *See also* §§ 14:11 to 14:13, *infra*.

In addition, where a CDL is revoked pursuant to paragraph (b) above, even as a first offense, "such revocation shall be permanent and may not be waived by the commissioner under any circumstances." VTL § 510-a(2)(e).

VTL § 510-a does not appear to address the length of a CDL revocation for a conviction involving paragraph (c) above. However, VTL § 510(6) makes clear that the revocation is for a period of at least one year (at least three years if the person was operating a commercial motor vehicle transporting hazardous materials)—at least where the conviction was for VTL § 600(2). VTL § 510(6)(b), (c).

§ 14:20   What happens if a VTL § 510-a offense is committed by a person who does not possess a CDL?

VTL § 510-a deals with the suspension/revocation of a CDL. What happens if a person who does not possess a CDL commits an offense that would require the suspension or revocation of the person's CDL if he or she had one?

The answer is set forth in VTL § 510-a(6), which provides as follows:

Application of section to persons not holding a [CDL]. Whenever a person who is not the holder of a [CDL] issued by the commissioner is convicted of a violation which would require the mandatory revocation or suspension of a [CDL] pursuant to this section, the privilege of such person to operate a commercial motor vehicle and/or to obtain a [CDL] issued by the commissioner will be suspended or revoked for the same periods of time and subject to the same conditions provided in this section which would be applicable to the holder of a [CDL].

"*[I]n addition*, the driver's license or privilege of operating a motor vehicle by such person shall be suspended or revoked for the same periods of time for which the privilege of operating a commercial motor vehicle or the privilege to obtain a [CDL] are suspended or revoked." VTL § 510-a(6). (emphasis added).

§ 14:21   VTL § 510-a does not preclude other permissible CDL suspensions/revocations from being imposed

VTL § 510-a(7) provides that:

Other revocation or suspension action not prohibited. The provisions of [VTL § 510-a] shall not be construed to prevent any person who has the authority to suspend or revoke a license to drive or privilege of operating pursuant to [VTL § 510] from exercising any such authority based upon a conviction for which suspension or revocation of a [CDL] by the commissioner is mandated.

§ 14:22   VTL § 1192 offenses committed in commercial motor vehicles—Generally

For obvious reasons, the government does not want people who operate commercial motor vehicles to do so with even low BACs— even if the operator would not be considered impaired or intoxicated in the traditional sense. In this regard, VTL § 1192 contains two subdivisions—*i.e.*, VTL §§ 1192(5) and 1192(6)— which lower the "legal limit" for drivers operating commercial motor vehicles.

VTL § 1192(5) makes it a traffic infraction to operate a commercial motor vehicle with a BAC of between .04% and .06%— regardless of whether the driver is actually impaired. VTL § 1192(6) lowers the threshold for *per se* DWI from .08% to .07% where a commercial motor vehicle is involved. These subdivisions are discussed in the sections that follow.

It should be noted that VTL §§ 1192(5) and 1192(6) merely add to the number of offenses applicable to commercial drivers—they do not preempt them. Thus, the operator of a commercial motor vehicle can also be charged with violating VTL §§ 1192(1), (2), (2-a), (3), (4), and/or (4-a) in an appropriate case.

§ 14:23   VTL § 1192(5)—Commercial motor vehicles: Per se—level I

VTL § 1192(5) prohibits the operation of a commercial motor

vehicle with a BAC between .04% and .06%. Specifically, VTL § 1192(5) provides:

> Commercial motor vehicles: per se—level I. Notwithstanding the provisions of [VTL § 1195], no person shall operate a commercial motor vehicle while such person has .04 of one per centum or more but not more than .06 of one per centum by weight of alcohol in the person's blood as shown by chemical analysis of such person's blood, breath, urine or saliva, made pursuant to the provisions of [VTL § 1194].

§ 14:24   VTL § 1192(5) does not preclude a charge of DWAI or VTL § 1192-a where appropriate

VTL § 1192(5) is not the exclusive means of prosecuting a person who operates a commercial motor vehicle with a low BAC. Such drivers can also, where appropriate, be charged with DWAI in violation of VTL § 1192(1), or, if the person's BAC is between .02% and .03% (and he or she is under 21 years of age), with a violation of the Zero Tolerance law in violation of VTL § 1192-a. In this regard, VTL § 1192(5) provides that:

> [N]othing contained in this subdivision shall prohibit the imposition of a charge of a violation of [VTL § 1192(1)], or of [VTL § 1192-a] where a person under the age of [21] operates a commercial motor vehicle where a chemical analysis of such person's blood, breath, urine, or saliva, made pursuant to the provisions of [VTL § 1194], indicates that such operator has .02 of one per centum or more but less than .04 of one per centum by weight of alcohol in such operator's blood.

Thus, while the Zero Tolerance law applies to BACs up to .07%, *see* VTL § 1192-a, it cannot be charged in lieu of VTL § 1192(1) or (5) where the defendant operates a commercial motor vehicle with a BAC of .04% or more. *See also* VTL § 1192-a ("[e]xcept as otherwise provided in [VTL § 1192(5)], this section shall not apply to a person who operates a commercial motor vehicle").

Note that a violation of VTL § 1192(1) committed in a commercial motor vehicle is a higher level offense than a violation of VTL § 1192(5). In this regard, a violation of VTL § 1192(1) committed in a commercial motor vehicle is a misdemeanor, whereas a violation of VTL § 1192(5) is a traffic infraction. VTL § 1193(1)(d)(2). In addition, a violation of VTL § 1192(1) committed in a commercial motor vehicle can be a felony, and/or can be used as a predicate for a felony; whereas a violation of VTL § 1192(5) cannot. *See* VTL § 1193(1)(d)(4).

§ 14:25   VTL § 1192(6)—Commercial motor vehicles: Per se—level II

VTL § 1192(6) prohibits the operation of a commercial motor vehicle with a BAC of .07%. Specifically, VTL § 1192(6) provides:

Notwithstanding the provisions of [VTL § 1195], no person shall operate a commercial motor vehicle while such person has more than .06 of one per centum but less than .08 of one per centum by weight of alcohol in the person's blood as shown by chemical analysis of such person's blood, breath, urine or saliva, made pursuant to the provisions of [VTL § 1194].

Notably, since the Department of Health Rules and Regulations mandate that BACs be reported only to the second decimal place, *see* § 37:2, *infra*, VTL § 1192(6) is only applicable to a BAC of *exactly* .07% (as .07 is the only 2-decimal-place number greater than .06 and less than .08).

§ 14:26 VTL § 1192(6) does not preclude a charge of DWAI where appropriate

VTL § 1192(6) is not the exclusive means of prosecuting a person who operates a commercial motor vehicle with a BAC of .07%. Such drivers can also, where appropriate, be charged with DWAI in violation of VTL § 1192(1). In this regard, VTL § 1192(6) provides that "nothing contained in this subdivision shall prohibit the imposition of a charge of a violation of [VTL § 1192(1)]."

§ 14:27 VTL §§ 1192(5) and 1192(6) only apply to operators of commercial motor vehicles

"No person other than an operator of a commercial motor vehicle may be charged with or convicted of a violation of [VTL § 1192(5) or (6)]." VTL § 1192(11). *See also* VTL § 1192(10)(a)(i).

§ 14:28 Plea bargain limitation applicable to commercial drivers

VTL § 1192(10) sets forth various plea bargain limitations applicable to VTL § 1192 cases. With respect to commercial drivers, VTL § 1192(10)(b) provides that:

In any case wherein the charge laid before the court alleges a violation of [VTL § 1192(1) or (6)] while operating a commercial motor vehicle, any plea of guilty thereafter entered in satisfaction of such charge must include at least a plea of guilty to the violation of the provisions of one of the subdivisions of [VTL § 1192] and no other disposition by plea of guilty to any other charge in satisfaction of such charge shall be authorized; provided, however, if the district attorney upon reviewing the available evidence determines that the charge of a violation of [VTL § 1192] is not warranted, he may consent, and the court may allow, a disposition by plea of guilty to another charge [in] satisfaction of such charge.

§ 14:29 Applicability of certificate of relief from disabilities to commercial drivers

Prior to September 30, 2005, VTL § 1196(7)(g) provided that

"[a]ny conditional license or privilege issued to a person convicted of a violation of any subdivision of [VTL § 1192] shall not be valid for the operation of any commercial motor vehicle." However, if a commercial driver obtained a certificate of relief from disabilities relieving him or her from the application of VTL § 1196(7)(g), DMV would issue the driver a conditional license valid for the operation of a commercial motor vehicle.

Effective September 30, 2005, VTL § 1196(7)(g) now provides that the prohibition against using a conditional license for the operation of a commercial motor vehicle applies "[n]otwithstanding anything to the contrary contained in a certificate of relief from disabilities issued pursuant to [Correction Law Article 23]."

A similar amendment was made to VTL § 530(5), which now prohibits DMV from issuing a restricted use license valid for the operation of a commercial motor vehicle notwithstanding anything to the contrary contained in a certificate of relief from disabilities.

§ 14:30   Penalties for first VTL § 1192 offense committed in a commercial motor vehicle

For CDL purposes, a VTL § 1192 offense is only considered a first offense if the defendant has *never* previously been convicted of:

(a) Refusing to submit to a chemical test in violation of VTL § 1194;

(b) Any violation of VTL § 1192;

(c) Any violation of VTL § 600(1) or (2); or

(d) Any felony involving the use of a motor vehicle.

VTL § 1193(2)(e)(3)(b). *See also* § 14:6, § 14:12, *supra*.

Violating VTL § 1192(5) is a traffic infraction punishable as provided in VTL § 1193(1)(a). VTL § 1193(1)(d)(2). In other words, the criminal penalties for a violation of VTL § 1192(5) are the same as those for DWAI in violation of VTL § 1192(1). *See* §§ 46:3 to 46:5, *infra*.

By contrast, the licensing consequences for a violation of VTL § 1192(5) are *not* the same as those for DWAI in violation of VTL § 1192(1). Rather, the defendant's CDL will be revoked for at least 1 year (at least 3 years if the violation was committed while operating a commercial motor vehicle transporting hazardous materials). VTL § 1193(2)(b)(5)(i), (ii). Note that:

Where revocation is mandatory pursuant to [VTL § 1193(2)(b)(5)] for a conviction of a violation of [VTL § 1192(5)], such revocation shall be issued only by the commissioner and shall be applicable only to that portion of the holder's driver's license or privilege which permits the operation of commercial motor vehicles, and the commissioner shall immediately issue a license, other than a [CDL], to such person provided that such person is otherwise eligible to receive such license and further provided that issuing a license to such person does not create a substantial traffic safety hazard.

VTL § 1193(2)(b)(11).

In addition, the defendant will be subject to all of the other usual consequences of a VTL § 1192 conviction. *See* §§ 46:1 et seq., *infra*.

Violating VTL § 1192(1), (2), (3), (4), (4-a) or (6) while operating a commercial motor vehicle, or any motor vehicle registered or registerable under Schedule F of VTL § 401(7) (*e.g.*, vehicles such as snow plows, road sweepers, road building machines, earth movers, etc.), is a misdemeanor. VTL § 1193(1)(d)(2). Note that DWAI in violation of VTL § 1192(1) is a misdemeanor under VTL § 1193(1)(d)(2).

A defendant who is convicted of VTL § 1192(6) as a first offense is subject to the following consequences:

1. A fine of between $500 and $1,500, up to 180 days in jail, or both. VTL § 1193(1)(d)(2);
2. A period of probation of three years. PL § 65.00(3)(d);
3. Mandatory revocation of his or her driver's license for at least one year (at least three years if the violation was committed while operating a commercial motor vehicle transporting hazardous materials). VTL § 1193(2)(b)(5)(i), (ii); and
4. Discretionary revocation of his or her registration for at least one year (at least three years if the violation was committed while operating a commercial motor vehicle transporting hazardous materials). VTL § 1193(2)(b)(5)(i), (ii).

In addition, the defendant will be subject to all of the other usual consequences of a VTL § 1192 conviction. *See* §§ 46:1 et seq., *infra*.

A defendant who is convicted of VTL § 1192(1), (2), (3), (4) or (4-a) as a first offense is subject to the following consequences:

1. A fine of between $500 and $1,500, up to one year in jail, or both. VTL § 1193(1)(d)(2); PL § 55.10(2)(b); PL § 70.15(1);
2. A period of probation of three years. PL § 65.00(3)(d);
3. Mandatory revocation of his or her driver's license for at least one year (at least three years if the violation was committed while operating a commercial motor vehicle transporting hazardous materials). VTL § 1193(2)(b)(5)(i), (ii); and
4. Discretionary revocation of his or her registration for at least one year (at least three years if the violation was committed while operating a commercial motor vehicle transporting hazardous materials). VTL § 1193(2)(b)(5)(i), (ii).

In addition, the defendant will be subject to all of the other usual consequences of a VTL § 1192 conviction. *See* §§ 46:1 et seq., *infra*.

Committing Aggravated DWI in violation of VTL § 1192(2-a) while operating a commercial motor vehicle, or any motor vehicle registered or registerable under Schedule F of VTL § 401(7), is a class E felony. VTL § 1193(1)(d)(2). A defendant who is convicted of this offense as a first offense is subject to the following consequences:

1. A fine of between $1,000 and $5,000, up to four years in state prison, or both. VTL § 1193(1)(d)(2); PL § 70.00(2)(e);

2. A period of probation of five years. PL § 65.00(3)(a)(i);

3. Mandatory revocation of his or her driver's license for at least one year (at least three years if the violation was committed while operating a commercial motor vehicle transporting hazardous materials). VTL § 1193(2)(b)(5)(i), (ii); and

4. Discretionary revocation of his or her registration for at least one year (at least three years if the violation was committed while operating a commercial motor vehicle transporting hazardous materials). VTL § 1193(2)(b)(5)(i), (ii).

In addition, the defendant will be subject to all of the other usual consequences of a VTL § 1192(2-a) conviction. *See* §§ 46:1 et seq., *infra*.

§ 14:31   Penalties for first VTL § 1192 offense committed in a vehicle with a GVWR greater than 18,000 pounds transporting hazardous materials

For CDL purposes, a VTL § 1192 offense is only considered a first offense if the defendant has *never* previously been convicted of:

(a) Refusing to submit to a chemical test in violation of VTL § 1194;

(b) Any violation of VTL § 1192;

(c) Any violation of VTL § 600(1) or (2); or

(d) Any felony involving the use of a motor vehicle.

VTL § 1193(2)(e)(3)(b). *See also* §§ 14:6, 14:12, *supra*.

Committing DWAI in violation of VTL § 1192(1) while operating a motor vehicle with a GVWR of more than 18,000 pounds which contains flammable gas, radioactive materials or explosives is a misdemeanor. VTL § 1193(1)(d)(3). A defendant who is convicted of this offense as a first offense is subject to the following consequences:

1. A fine of between $500 and $1,500, up to one year in jail, or both. VTL § 1193(1)(d)(3); PL § 55.10(2)(b); PL § 70.15(1);

2. A period of probation of three years. PL § 65.00(3)(d);
3. Mandatory revocation of his or her driver's license for at least three years. VTL § 1193(2)(b)(5)(ii); and
4. Discretionary revocation of his or her registration for at least three years. VTL § 1193(2)(b)(5)(ii).

In addition, the defendant will be "permanently" disqualified from operating a motor vehicle with a GVWR of more than 18,000 pounds which contains flammable gas, radioactive materials or explosives. VTL § 1193(2)(e)(3)(a). However, DMV can waive such "permanent" disqualification where:

1. At least five years have elapsed from such sentence;
2. During such five-year period, the person has not violated any of the provisions of VTL § 1192 or any alcohol-or drug-related traffic offense in New York or elsewhere;
3. The person provides acceptable documentation to DMV that he or she is not in need of alcohol or drug treatment, or has satisfactorily completed a prescribed course of such treatment; and
4. After such documentation is accepted, the person is granted a certificate of relief from disabilities pursuant to Correction Law § 701 by the Court in which such person was last penalized.

VTL § 1193(2)(e)(3)(a)(i) to (iii).

Furthermore, the defendant will be subject to all of the other usual consequences of a VTL § 1192 conviction. *See* §§ 46:1 et seq., *infra*.

Violating VTL § 1192(2), (3), (4) or (4-a) while operating a motor vehicle with a GVWR of more than 18,000 pounds which contains flammable gas, radioactive materials or explosives is a class E felony. VTL § 1193(1)(d)(5). A defendant who is convicted of any of these offenses as a first offense is subject to the following consequences:

1. A fine of between $1,000 and $5,000, up to four years in state prison, or both. VTL § 1193(1)(d)(5); PL § 70.00(2)(e); PL § 80.00(1)(a);
2. A period of probation of five years. PL § 65.00(3)(a)(i);
3. Mandatory revocation of his or her driver's license for at least three years. VTL § 1193(2)(b)(5)(ii); and
4. Discretionary revocation of his or her registration for at least three years. VTL § 1193(2)(b)(5)(ii).

In addition, the defendant will be subject to all of the other usual consequences of a VTL § 1192 conviction. *See* §§ 46:1 et seq., *infra*.

Note that "a conviction for such violation shall not be considered a predicate felony pursuant to [Penal Law § 70.06], or a previous felony conviction pursuant to [Penal Law § 70.10]." VTL § 1193(1)(d)(5).

Committing Aggravated DWI in violation of VTL § 1192(2-a) while operating a motor vehicle with a GVWR of more than 18,000 pounds which contains flammable gas, radioactive materials or explosives is a class D felony. VTL § 1193(1)(d)(5). A defendant who is convicted of this offense as a first offense is subject to the following consequences:

1. A fine of between $2,000 and $10,000, up to 7 years in state prison, or both. VTL § 1193(1)(d)(5); PL § 70.00(2)(d);
2. A period of probation of 5 years. PL § 65.00(3)(a)(i);
3. Mandatory revocation of his or her driver's license for at least 3 years. VTL § 1193(2)(b)(5)(ii); and
4. Discretionary revocation of his or her registration for at least 3 years. VTL § 1193(2)(b)(5)(ii).

In addition, the defendant will be subject to all of the other usual consequences of a VTL § 1192(2-a) conviction. *See* §§ 46:1 et seq., *infra*.

Note that "a conviction for such violation shall not be considered a predicate felony pursuant to [Penal Law § 70.06], or a previous felony conviction pursuant to [Penal Law § 70.10]." VTL § 1193(1)(d)(5).

§ 14:32   Commercial motor vehicles—Repeat offense

Violating VTL § 1192(6) after having been convicted within the preceding 5 years of violating VTL § 1192(1), (2), (2-a), (3), (4), (4-a), or (6) is a misdemeanor which subjects the defendant to the following consequences:

1. A fine of between $500 and $1,500, up to one year in jail, or both. VTL § 1193(1)(d)(2); PL § 55.10(2)(b); PL § 70.15(1);
2. A period of probation of three years. PL § 65.00(3)(d);
3. Mandatory revocation of his or her driver's license for at least one year (at least three years if the violation was committed while operating a commercial motor vehicle transporting hazardous materials). VTL § 1193(2)(b)(5)(i), (ii); and
4. "Permanent" disqualification from operating a commercial motor vehicle. *See* §§ 14:11 to 14:13, *supra*.

In addition, the defendant will be subject to all of the other usual consequences of a VTL § 1192 conviction. *See* §§ 46:1 et seq., *infra*.

A defendant who violates VTL § 1192(1), (2), (2-a), (3), (4), or (4-a) while operating a commercial motor vehicle, or any motor vehicle registered or registerable under Schedule F of VTL § 401(7), after having been convicted within the preceding 10 years of violating VTL § 1192(1), (2), (2-a), (3), (4), or (4-a) while:

(a) Operating a taxicab carrying a passenger for compensation;

(b) Operating a livery carrying a passenger for compensation;

(c) Operating a truck with a GVWR of more than 18,000 pounds but not more than 26,000 pounds which is *not* a commercial motor vehicle;

(d) Operating a school bus carrying at least one student passenger;

(e) Operating a commercial motor vehicle, or any motor vehicle registered or registerable under Schedule F of VTL § 401(7); or

(f) Operating a motor vehicle with a GVWR of more than 18,000 pounds which contains flammable gas, radioactive materials or explosives;

can be charged with a class E felony, and is subject to the following consequences:

1. A fine of between $1,000 and $5,000, up to four years in state prison, or both. VTL § 1193(1)(d)(4)(i); PL § 70.00(2)(e);

2. A period of probation of five years. PL § 65.00(3)(a)(i);

3. Mandatory revocation of his or her driver's license for at least one year (at least three years if the violation was committed while operating a school bus or a commercial motor vehicle transporting hazardous materials). VTL §§ 1193(2)(b)(4-a)(B), 1193(2)(b)(5); and

4. "Permanent" disqualification from operating a commercial motor vehicle. VTL § 1193(1)(d)(4)(i); VTL § 1193(2)(e)(3). *See* §§ 14:11 to 14:13, *supra*.

The defendant can also be charged with any other applicable felony for any acts arising out of the same incident. VTL § 1193(1)(d)(7).

A defendant who violates VTL § 1192(6) after having been convicted of two or more violations of VTL § 1192(1), (2), (2-a), (3), (4), (4-a), or (6) within the preceding five years is subject to the same consequences. VTL § 1193(1)(d)(4)(i).

In addition, the defendant will be subject to all of the other usual consequences of a VTL § 1192 conviction. *See* §§ 46:1 et seq., *infra*.

A defendant who violates VTL § 1192(1), (2), (2-a), (3), (4) or (4-a) while operating a commercial motor vehicle, or any motor vehicle registered or registerable under Schedule F of VTL § 401(7), after having been convicted twice within the preceding 10 years of violating VTL § 1192(1), (2), (2-a), (3), (4), or (4-a) while:

(a) Operating a taxicab carrying a passenger for compensation;

(b) Operating a livery carrying a passenger for compensation;

(c) Operating a truck with a GVWR of more than 18,000 pounds but not more than 26,000 pounds which is *not* a commercial motor vehicle;

(d) Operating a school bus carrying at least one student passenger;

(e) Operating a commercial motor vehicle, or any motor vehicle registered or registerable under Schedule F of VTL § 401(7); or

(f) Operating a motor vehicle with a GVWR of more than 18,000 pounds which contains flammable gas, radioactive materials or explosives;

can be charged with a class D felony, and is subject to the following consequences:

1. A fine of between $2,000 and $10,000, up to seven years in state prison, or both. VTL § 1193(1)(d)(4)(ii); PL § 70.00(2)(d);

2. A period of probation of five years. PL § 65.00(3)(a)(i);

3. Mandatory revocation of his or her driver's license for at least one year (at least three years if the violation was committed while operating a school bus or a commercial motor vehicle transporting hazardous materials). VTL §§ 1193(2)(b)(4-a)(B), 1193(2)(b)(5); and

4. "Permanent" disqualification from operating a commercial motor vehicle. VTL § 1193(1)(d)(4)(ii); VTL § 1193(2)(e)(3). *See* §§ 14:11 to 14:13, *supra*.

The defendant can also be charged with any other applicable felony for any acts arising out of the same incident. VTL § 1193(1)(d)(7).

A defendant who violates VTL § 1192(6) after having been convicted of three or more violations of VTL § 1192(1), (2), (2-a), (3), (4), (4-a) or (6) within the preceding five years is subject to the same consequences. VTL § 1193(1)(d)(4)(ii).

In addition, the defendant will be subject to all of the other usual consequences of a VTL § 1192 conviction. *See* §§ 46:1 et seq., *infra*.

Note that a violation of VTL § 1192(5) is excluded from the list of offenses that can serve as a predicate for a felony charge under VTL § 1193(1)(d)(4). *See also* VTL § 1193(1)(c).

§ 14:33   Miscellaneous issues related to commercial motor vehicles and CDLs—Generally

The sections that follow address various miscellaneous issues related to commercial motor vehicles and CDLs.

§ 14:34 Unlicensed operation of a commercial motor vehicle

VTL § 509(7) provides that "[n]o person shall operate a commercial motor vehicle without being in possession of the appropriate license for the motor vehicle being operated." In addition, VTL § 509(1-a) provides that "[w]henever a license is required to operate a commercial motor vehicle, no person shall operate a commercial motor vehicle without the proper endorsements for the specific vehicle being operated or for the passengers or type of cargo being transported."

A violation of VTL § 509(7) is a traffic infraction punishable by a fine of not more than $75. VTL § 509(11). A violation of VTL § 509(1-a) is a traffic infraction punishable by a fine of between $75 and $300, up to 15 days in jail, or both. VTL § 509(11).

§ 14:35 AUO in vehicle with a GVWR greater than 18,000 pounds

A person is guilty of Aggravated Unlicensed Operation of a Motor Vehicle in the Third Degree (AUO 3rd), "when such person operates a motor vehicle upon a public highway while knowing or having reason to know that such person's license or privilege of operating such motor vehicle in this state or privilege of obtaining a license to operate such motor vehicle issued by the commissioner is suspended, revoked or otherwise withdrawn by the commissioner." VTL § 511(1)(a).

If the defendant is convicted of AUO 3rd with respect to the operation of a motor vehicle with a GVWR of more than 18,000 pounds, the sentence of the Court must be: a fine of between $500 and $1,500, up to 30 days in jail, or both. VTL § 511(1)(c).

§ 14:36 Vehicular assault/vehicular manslaughter provisions applicable to certain commercial motor vehicles

Vehicular Assault 2nd generally requires that the defendant drive while intoxicated or while impaired by drugs in connection with the offense. *See* PL § 120.03. *See also* § 12:5, *supra*. However, PL § 120.03(2) provides that the offense is also committed where the defendant:

> [O]perates a motor vehicle with a [GVWR] of more than [18,000] pounds which contains flammable gas, radioactive materials or explosives in violation of [VTL § 1192(1)], and such flammable gas, radioactive materials or explosives is the cause of such serious physical injury, and as a result of such impairment by the use of alcohol, operates such motor vehicle in a manner that causes such serious physical injury to such other person.

Similarly, Vehicular Manslaughter 2nd generally requires that the defendant drive while intoxicated or while impaired by drugs in connection with the offense. *See* PL § 125.12. *See also* § 12:9, *supra*. However, PL § 125.12(2) provides that the offense is also committed where the defendant:

> [O]perates a motor vehicle with a [GVWR] of more than [18,000] pounds which contains flammable gas, radioactive materials or explosives in violation of [VTL § 1192(1)], and such flammable gas, radioactive materials or explosives is the cause of such death, and as a result of such impairment by the use of alcohol, operates such motor vehicle in a manner that causes the death of such other person.

§ 14:37 Operating large commercial motor vehicle on wet road while speeding and impaired by alcohol constitutes criminal negligence

In *People v. Kricfalusi*, 291 A.D.2d 907, ___, 738 N.Y.S.2d 270, 271 (4th Dep't 2002), the defendant appealed his conviction of Assault 3rd. The Appellate Division, Fourth Department, held that the "proof that defendant was operating a large commercial vehicle on a wet road in excess of the posted speed limit while his ability to operate the vehicle was impaired by alcohol [was] sufficient to establish that defendant acted with criminal negligence."

§ 14:38 Where element of offense requires operation of a commercial motor vehicle, failure to allege that vehicle in question was a commercial motor vehicle renders accusatory instrument facially insufficient

In *People v. Hoffman Floor Covering Corp.*, 179 Misc. 2d 656, ___, 686 N.Y.S.2d 651, 652 (N.Y. City Crim. Ct. 1999), the Court held that:

> It is well settled that a valid and sufficient accusatory instrument is a non-waivable jurisdictional prerequisite to criminal prosecution. Here the universal summons alleges only that defendant's driver was operating a "vehicle" without the requisite tax stamp. By its terms, Title 11, Chapter 8 of the New York City Administrative Code imposes a tax on commercial vehicles and motor vehicles for the transportation of passengers other than medallion taxicabs. By failing to allege that the subject vehicle was of a type specified by the ordinance, the universal summons omitted an essential element of the violation and was therefore facially insufficient.

(Citation omitted).

§ 14:39 Where CDL is a job requirement, failure to maintain a valid CDL precludes collection of unemployment insurance benefits

In *In re Geer*, 255 A.D.2d 676, ___, 679 N.Y.S.2d 457, 457 (3d Dep't 1998), the Appellate Division, Third Department, held that:

> Claimant was terminated from his employment as a special motor equipment operator when the employer learned that the commercial driver's license that claimant was required to maintain as a condition of his employment had expired several years earlier. The Unemployment Insurance Appeal Board ruled that claimant was disqualified from receiving unemployment insurance benefits because he voluntarily left his employment without good cause. We affirm.
>
> The record reveals that claimant failed to take appropriate measures to renew his commercial driver's license so as to comply with the employer's legitimate licensing requirement. Since claimant voluntarily engaged in conduct which rendered him ineligible for continued work and left the employer with no choice but to terminate his employment, we find substantial evidence to support the Board's conclusion that claimant provoked his discharge and thereby voluntarily left his employment without good cause.

See also In re Decker, 27 A.D.3d 821, 809 N.Y.S.2d 476 (3d Dep't 2006) (same result where CDL was suspended for failure to pay traffic fines); *Claim of Killorin*, 232 A.D.2d 696, 648 N.Y.S.2d 182 (3d Dep't 1996) (same result where CDL was revoked for DWI); *Claim of Kinnicutt*, 226 A.D.2d 870, 640 N.Y.S.2d 663 (3d Dep't 1996) (same).

§ 14:40 Restrictions on use of radar/laser detector in certain vehicles

VTL § 1180 addresses speeding violations. VTL § 1180(g)(i) provides that:

> No person who uses a radar or laser detector in a vehicle with a [GVWR] of more than [18,000] pounds, or a commercial motor vehicle with a [GVWR] of more than [10,000] pounds, shall drive at a speed in excess of [55 MPH] or, if a maximum speed limit other than [55 MPH] . . . has been established, at a speed in excess of such speed limit.

With regard to the issue of establishing that the defendant was "using" such radar/laser detector, VTL § 1180(g)(i) provides that:

> The presence in any such vehicle of either: (1) a radar or laser detector connected to a power source and in an operable condition; or (2) a concealed radar or laser detector where a part of such detector is securely affixed to some part of the vehicle outside of the cab, in a manner which renders the detector not readily observable, is

presumptive evidence of its use by any person operating such vehicle.

However, either of these presumptions "shall be rebutted by any credible and reliable evidence which tends to show that such radar or laser detector was not in use." VTL § 1180(g)(i).

Finally, VTL § 1180(g)(ii) provides that "[t]he provisions of this section shall not be construed as authorizing the seizure or forfeiture of a radar or laser detector, unless otherwise provided by law."

§ 14:41   The term "conviction" has a special definition as pertains to CDL holders

For most purposes, the term "conviction" is defined in CPL § 1.20(13), which defines a conviction as "the entry of a plea of guilty to, or a verdict of guilty upon, an accusatory instrument other than a felony complaint, or to one or more counts of such instrument." VTL § 109-c provides an additional definition of the term "conviction" pertinent to CDL holders:

> Any conviction as defined in [CPL § 1.20(13)]; provided, however, where a conviction or administrative finding in this state or another state results in a mandatory sanction against a [CDL], as set forth in [VTL §§ 510, 510-a, 1192 and 1194], conviction shall also mean an unvacated adjudication of guilt, or a determination that a person has violated or failed to comply with the law in a court of original jurisdiction or by an authorized administrative tribunal, an unvacated forfeiture of bail or collateral deposited to secure the person's appearance in court, a plea of guilty or nolo contendere accepted by the court, the payment of a fine or court cost, or violation of a condition of release without bail, regardless of whether or not the penalty is rebated, suspended, or probated.

§ 14:42   Duty of CDL holder to notify employer and/or DMV of convictions, suspensions, revocations, etc.

VTL § 514-a imposes an affirmative obligation on CDL holders to notify their employers and/or to notify DMV of convictions for any moving violation, and of any CDL suspension, revocation, cancellation and/or disqualification that they accrue. For CDL holders who drive for a New York employer, VTL § 514-a(1) provides that:

> Each person who operates a commercial motor vehicle for a New York state employer who is convicted of violating within or outside of this state, *in any type of motor vehicle*, a state or local law relating to motor vehicle traffic control (other than a parking violation), shall notify his/her current employer of such conviction.

(Emphasis added).

In addition, VTL § 514-a(2) provides that:

Each person who operates a commercial motor vehicle for a New York state employer who has a driver's license suspended, revoked, or canceled by the commissioner or by the appropriate authorities of any other state, District of Columbia or Canadian province, or who loses the right to operate a commercial motor vehicle in any state or jurisdiction for any period, or who is disqualified from operating a commercial motor vehicle for any period, shall notify his/her current employer of such suspension, revocation, cancellation, lost privilege, or disqualification.

For CDL holders who drive for an out-of-state employer, or who are self-employed, VTL § 514-a(1) provides that:

Any person who holds a [CDL] issued by the commissioner who does not operate a commercial motor vehicle for a New York state employer or who operates a commercial motor vehicle while self-employed who is convicted in any other state, the District of Columbia or a Canadian province of violating any law relating to motor vehicle traffic control (other than a parking violation) while operating a commercial motor vehicle shall notify the commissioner of such conviction.

The notification required by VTL § 514-a(1) "must be made within [30] days after the date that the person has been convicted except that if a person is a bus driver as defined in [VTL § 509-a], such notification must be made within [5] days after the date the person has been convicted as required by [VTL § 509-i]." VTL § 514-a(1). The required content of the notification is as follows:

The above notification must be made in writing and contain the following information:
  (a) driver's full name;
  (b) driver's license number;
  (c) date of conviction;
  (d) the specific criminal or other offense(s), serious traffic violation(s) of state or local law relating to motor vehicle traffic control, for which the person was convicted and any suspension, revocation, cancellation of any driving privileges or disqualification from operating a commercial motor vehicle which resulted from such conviction(s);
  (e) indication whether the violation was in a commercial motor vehicle;
  (f) location of offense;
  (g) court or tribunal in which the conviction occurred; and
  (h) driver's signature.

VTL § 514-a(1).

When DMV receives information relating to a conviction, suspension, revocation, cancellation or disqualification pertaining to a CDL holder, "the commissioner shall take action as may be required and may take action as may be permitted by [the VTL] based upon such conviction or notice." VTL § 514-b.

§ 14:43   Cheating on CDL exam can lead to suspension of driver's license by DMV independent of any criminal conviction flowing from the offense

In *Brady v. Department of Motor Vehicles*, 98 N.Y.2d 625, 626, 748 N.Y.S.2d 889, 889, 778 N.E.2d 539 (2002):

> The Department of Motor Vehicles (DMV) charged petitioner with violating Vehicle and Traffic Law § 392, which provides that "[a]ny person * * * who shall deceive * * * in connection with any examination * * * shall be guilty of a misdemeanor." Following a hearing, an Administrative Law Judge (ALJ) found that petitioner committed such deception in connection with the written portion of a Commercial Driver's License test when, contrary to DMV's test procedures and explicit directions, he left the testing area with the test materials, giving rise to a risk of their illegal use. The ALJ found this constituted "cheating" and "attempt[ing] to gain an unfair advantage," and suspended petitioner's driver's license for 60 days.

Although the Court of Appeals affirmed on procedural grounds, it stated that:

> With some exceptions, drivers' licenses may be suspended or revoked for any violation of the Vehicle and Traffic Law, and "a court conviction shall not be necessary to sustain a revocation or suspension." Indeed, petitioner was not convicted of violating section 392 or of any other crime. Rather, in an administrative proceeding, the ALJ found that petitioner had engaged in deception in connection with the Commercial Driver's License test, violating Vehicle and Traffic Law § 392 and thus establishing the predicate for the administrative act of suspending his license.

98 N.Y.2d at 626, 748 N.Y.S.2d at 890 (citation omitted).

§ 14:44   Special vehicles—Generally

The sections that follow deal with issues facing drivers of so-called "special vehicles."

§ 14:45   What is a "special vehicle"?

The term "special vehicle" refers to a vehicle typically used to carry passengers for hire such as a bus, a school bus, a taxicab, a livery, etc. It also applies to a tow truck and to a truck with a GVWR of more than 18,000 pounds but not more than 26,000 pounds which is *not* a commercial motor vehicle. Some of these terms are defined in the VTL:

1. "Bus" is defined as "[e]very motor vehicle having a seating

capacity of [15] or more passengers in addition to the driver and used for the transportation of persons." VTL § 104. *See also* VTL § 509-a(1);

2. "School bus" is defined as "[e]very motor vehicle owned by a public or governmental agency or private school and operated for the transportation of pupils, children of pupils, teachers and other persons acting in a supervisory capacity, to or from school or school activities or privately owned and operated for compensation for the transportation of pupils, children of pupils, teachers and other persons acting in a supervisory capacity to or from school or school activities." VTL § 142;

3. "Taxicab" is defined as "[e]very motor vehicle, other than a bus, used in the business of transporting passengers for compensation, and operated in such business under a license or permit issued by a local authority. However, it shall not include vehicles which are rented or leased without a driver." VTL § 148-a;

4. "Livery" is defined as "[e]very motor vehicle, other than a taxicab or a bus, used in the business of transporting passengers for compensation. However, it shall not include vehicles which are rented or leased without a driver." VTL § 121-e; and

5. "Tow truck" is defined as "[a] motor vehicle that tows or carries a disabled, illegally parked or abandoned motor vehicle or a motor vehicle involved in an accident." VTL § 148-b.

Some "special vehicles" listed in VTL § 1193 are commercial motor vehicles requiring a CDL. Taxicabs and livery vehicles can be operated with a class E driver's license—which is *not* a CDL. However, a school bus is a commercial motor vehicle requiring a CDL, as is a tow truck with a GVWR of at least 8,600 pounds. Accordingly, there is a degree of overlap in the VTL between commercial and special vehicles—particularly in light of the September 30, 2005, changes to the laws affecting CDL holders.

§ 14:46 Buses other than school buses—License sanctions

VTL § 509-c provides for various disqualifications from operating buses other than school buses. As the list is lengthy, this section focuses on DWI-related disqualifications. It should be noted that since a bus is a commercial motor vehicle requiring a CDL, *see* VTL § 501-(a)(4); VTL § 509-a(1), the September 30, 2005 changes to the laws affecting CDL holders, *see* §§ 14:1, 14:5, 14:11 to 14:13, 14:29, *supra*, likely render various provisions of VTL § 509-c redundant and/or obsolete.

VTL § 509-c(2)(g) provides for a bus disqualification "for the period that such person's license is revoked or suspended for violat-

ing [VTL § 1192 (or an analogous out-of-state offense)]. Such
disqualification shall be for not less than [6] months."

A person is subject to a five-year disqualification from operating a bus (commencing from the date of his or her last conviction)
where the person has been convicted of:

1. A violation of any subdivision of VTL § 1192 (or an analogous out-of-state offense) committed while the person was
operating a bus;

2. A violation of any subdivision of VTL § 1192 (or an analogous out-of-state offense) twice within a 10-year period;

3. Leaving the scene of an accident which resulted in personal
injury or death in violation of VTL § 600(2) (or an analogous
out-of-state offense);

4. A violation of PL § 120.04, 120.04-a, 125.13 or 125.14; or

5. AUO 1st in violation of VTL § 511(3).

VTL § 509-c(2)(b), (2)(c).

A person is subject to a one-year disqualification from operating a bus:

[I]f that person accumulates [9] or more points on his or her driving
record for acts occurring during an [18] month period, provided,
however, that the disqualification shall terminate if the person has
reduced the points to less than [9] through the successful completion of a motor vehicle accident prevention course.

VTL § 509-c(2)(d).

§ 14:47 Penalties for first VTL § 1192 offense committed in a school bus carrying at least 1 student passenger

At the outset, it must be noted that a school bus is a commercial motor vehicle requiring a CDL, see VTL § 501-(a)(4); VTL
§ 509-a(1), and that, for CDL purposes, a VTL § 1192 offense is
only considered a first offense if the defendant has *never* previously been convicted of:

(a) Refusing to submit to a chemical test in violation of VTL
§ 1194;

(b) Any violation of VTL § 1192;

(c) Any violation of VTL § 600(1) or (2); or

(d) Any felony involving the use of a motor vehicle.

VTL § 1193(2)(e)(3)(b). *See also* § 14:6, § 14:12, *supra*.

Committing DWAI in violation of VTL § 1192(1) while operating a school bus carrying at least one student passenger is a
misdemeanor. VTL § 1193(1)(d)(1-a). A defendant who is convicted
of this offense as a first offense is subject to the following
consequences:

1. A fine of between $500 and $1,500, up to one year in jail, or both. VTL § 1193(1)(d)(1-a); PL § 55.10(2)(b); PL § 70.15(1);
2. A period of probation of three years. PL § 65.00(3)(d); and
3. Mandatory revocation of his or her driver's license for at least one year. VTL § 1193(2)(b)(4-a)(A). *See also* § 14:48, *infra*.

In addition, the defendant will be subject to all of the other usual consequences of a VTL § 1192 conviction. *See* §§ 46:1 et seq., *infra*.

Violating VTL § 1192(2), (3), (4) or (4-a) while operating a school bus carrying at least 1 student passenger is a class E felony. VTL § 1193(1)(d)(4-a). A defendant who is convicted of any of these offenses as a first offense is subject to the following consequences:

1. A fine of between $1,000 and $5,000, up to four years in state prison, or both. VTL § 1193(1)(d)(4-a); PL § 70.00(2)(e);
2. A period of probation of five years. PL § 65.00(3)(a)(i); and
3. Mandatory revocation of his or her driver's license for at least one year. VTL § 1193(2)(b)(4-a)(A). *See also* § 14:48, *infra*.

In addition, the defendant will be subject to all of the other usual consequences of a VTL § 1192 conviction. *See* §§ 46:1 et seq., *infra*.

Committing Aggravated DWI in violation of VTL § 1192(2-a) while operating a school bus carrying at least one student passenger is a class D felony. VTL § 1193(1)(d)(4-a). A defendant who is convicted of this offense as a first offense is subject to the following consequences:

1. A fine of between $2,000 and $10,000, up to seven years in state prison, or both. VTL § 1193(1)(d)(4-a); PL § 70.00(2)(d);
2. A period of probation of five years. PL § 65.00(3)(a)(i); and
3. Mandatory revocation of his or her driver's license for at least one year. VTL § 1193(2)(b)(4-a)(A). *See also* § 14:48, *infra*.

In addition, the defendant will be subject to all of the other usual consequences of a VTL § 1192(2-a) conviction. *See* §§ 46:1 et seq., *infra*.

§ 14:48 School buses—Additional license sanctions

VTL § 1193(2)(b)(4-a) addresses the licensing consequences of VTL § 1192 offenses committed while operating a school bus. It should be noted, however, that since a school bus is a commercial motor vehicle requiring a CDL, *see* VTL § 501-(a)(4); VTL § 509-

a(1), the September 30, 2005 changes to the laws affecting CDL holders, *see* §§ 14:1, 14:5, 14:11 to 14:13, 14:29, *supra*, likely render VTL § 1193(2)(b)(4-a) redundant and/or obsolete.

VTL § 509-cc also provides for various disqualifications from operating a school bus. As the list is lengthy, this section focuses on DWI-related disqualifications.

VTL § 509-cc(2)(h) provides for a school bus disqualification "for the period that such person's license is revoked or suspended for violating [VTL § 1192 (or an analogous out-of-state offense)]. Such disqualification shall be for not less than [6] months."

A person is subject to a "permanent" disqualification from operating a school bus where the person has been convicted of, *inter alia*, PL §§ 125.10, 125.12, 125.15, an analogous out-of-state offense, or an attempt to commit any such offense. *See* VTL §§ 509-cc(2)(a), (2)(b), (4)(a), (4)(b). However, DMV can waive such "permanent" disqualification where:

1. At least five years have elapsed since the person was discharged or released from a sentence of imprisonment imposed for a conviction of such offense;
2. The person has been granted a certificate of relief from disabilities pursuant to Correction Law § 701;
3. Where the certificate of relief is issued by a Court for a conviction which occurred in New York, it must be issued by the court having jurisdiction over the conviction; and
4. Such certificate must specifically indicate that the Court granting it "has considered the bearing, if any, the criminal offense or offenses for which the person was convicted will have on the applicant's fitness or ability to operate a bus transporting school children."

VTL §§ 509-cc(2)(a), (2)(b). *See also People v. Martin*, 196 Misc. 2d 583, 764 N.Y.S.2d 546, 181 Ed. Law Rep. 225 (Yates Co. Ct. 2003). VTL § 509-cc(2)(b) authorizes earlier reinstatement, in DMV's discretion, where the conviction is for an offense listed in VTL § 509-cc(4)(b).

A person is subject to a five-year disqualification from operating a school bus (commencing from the date of his or her last conviction) where the person has been convicted of:

1. PL §§ 120.03, 120.04, 120.04-a, 120.05, 120.10, 120.25, 125.13, 125.14, an analogous out-of-state offense, or an attempt to commit any such offense, within the preceding five years;
2. A violation of any subdivision of VTL § 1192 (or an analogous out-of-state offense) committed while the person was operating a bus;
3. A violation of any subdivision of VTL § 1192 (or an analogous out-of-state offense) twice within a 10-year period;

4. Leaving the scene of an accident which resulted in personal injury or death in violation of VTL § 600(2) (or an analogous out-of-state offense);

5. A violation of PL § 120.04, 120.04-a, 125.13 or 125.14; or

6. AUO 1st in violation of VTL § 511(3).

VTL § 509-cc(2)(c), (2)(d).

If the conviction is for a violation listed in paragraph "1" above:

Such disqualification shall be waived provided that the applicant has been granted a certificate of relief from disabilities as provided for in [Correction Law § 701]. When the certificate is issued by a court for a conviction which occurred in this state, it shall only be issued by the court having jurisdiction over such conviction. Such certificate shall specifically indicate that the authority granting such certificate has considered the bearing, if any, the criminal offense or offenses for which the person was convicted will have on the applicant's fitness or ability to operate a bus transporting school children, prior to granting such a certificate.

VTL § 509-cc(2)(c)(i).

A person is subject to a one-year disqualification from operating a school bus:

[I]f that person accumulates [9] or more points on his or her driving record for acts occurring during an [18] month period, provided, however, that the disqualification shall terminate if the person has reduced the points to less than [9] through the successful completion of a motor vehicle accident prevention course.

VTL § 509-cc(2)(e).

§ 14:49 DMV will not revoke the registration of a school bus driven in violation of VTL § 1192

"Notwithstanding the provisions of the opening paragraph of [VTL § 1193(2)(b)], the commissioner shall not revoke the registration of a school bus driven in violation of [VTL § 1192]." VTL § 1193(2)(b)(4-a)(C).

§ 14:50 Bus drivers cannot possess or consume alcohol or drugs while on duty or consume alcohol or drugs within 6 hours beforehand

VTL § 509-l provides as follows:

1. No person shall:

(a) consume a drug, controlled substance or an intoxicating liquor, regardless of its alcoholic content, or be under the influence of an intoxicating liquor or drug, within [6] hours before going on duty or operating, or having physical control of a bus, or

(b) consume a drug, controlled substance or an intoxicating liquor, regardless of its alcoholic content while on duty, or operating, or in physical control of a bus, or

(c) possess a drug, controlled substance or an intoxicating liquor, regardless of its alcoholic content while on duty, operating or in physical control of a bus. However, this paragraph does not apply to possession of a drug, controlled substance or an intoxicating liquor which is transported as part of a shipment or personal effects of a passenger or to alcoholic beverages which are in sealed containers.

2. No motor carrier shall require or permit a driver to:

(a) violate any provision of [VTL § 509-l(1)]; or

(b) be on duty or operate a bus if, by such person's general appearance or by such person's conduct or by other substantiating evidence, such person appears to have consumed a drug, controlled substance or an intoxicating liquor within the preceding [6] hours.

See also Northland Transp. Inc. v. Jackson, 271 A.D.2d 846, 706 N.Y.S.2d 501 (3d Dep't 2000).

§ 14:51   Penalties for first VTL § 1192 offense committed in certain special vehicles

Violating VTL § 1192(1), (2), (3), (4) or (4-a) while:

(a) Operating a taxicab carrying a passenger for compensation;

(b) Operating a livery carrying a passenger for compensation; or

(c) Operating a truck with a GVWR of more than 18,000 pounds but not more than 26,000 pounds which is *not* a commercial motor vehicle;

is a misdemeanor. VTL § 1193(1)(d)(1). Note that DWAI in violation of VTL § 1192(1) is a misdemeanor under VTL § 1193(1)(d)(1). *See People v. Padro*, 132 A.D.3d 485, 17 N.Y.S.3d 641 (1st Dep't 2015). A defendant who is convicted of any of these offenses as a first offense is subject to the following consequences:

1. A fine of between $500 and $1,500, up to one year in jail, or both. VTL § 1193(1)(d)(1); PL § 55.10(2)(b); PL § 70.15(1);

2. A period of probation of three years. PL § 65.00(3)(d);

3. Mandatory revocation of his or her driver's license for at least one year. VTL § 1193(2)(b)(4); and

4. Discretionary revocation of his or her registration for at least one year. VTL § 1193(2)(b)(4).

In addition, the defendant will be subject to all of the other usual consequences of a VTL § 1192 conviction. *See* §§ 46:1 et seq., *infra*. Note that unless the conviction is for VTL § 1192(1), the defendant is *not* eligible for a conditional license. *See* 15 NYCRR § 134.7(a)(8).

Committing Aggravated DWI in violation of VTL § 1192(2-a) while:

(a) Operating a taxicab carrying a passenger for compensation;

(b) Operating a livery carrying a passenger for compensation; or

(c) Operating a truck with a GVWR of more than 18,000 pounds but not more than 26,000 pounds which is *not* a commercial motor vehicle;

is a class E felony. VTL § 1193(1)(d)(1). A defendant who is convicted of this offense as a first offense is subject to the following consequences:

1. A fine of between $1,000 and $5,000, up to four years in state prison, or both. VTL § 1193(1)(d)(1); PL § 70.00(2)(e);

2. A period of probation of five years. PL § 65.00(3)(a)(i);

3. Mandatory revocation of his or her driver's license for at least one year. VTL § 1193(2)(b)(4); and

4. Discretionary revocation of his or her registration for at least one year. VTL § 1193(2)(b)(4).

In addition, the defendant will be subject to all of the other usual consequences of a VTL § 1192(2-a) conviction. *See* §§ 46:1 et seq., *infra*. Note that the defendant is *not* eligible for a conditional license. *See* 15 NYCRR § 134.7(a)(8).

§ 14:52 Special vehicles—Repeat offense

A defendant who violates VTL § 1192(1), (2), (2-a), (3), (4), or (4-a) while:

(a) Operating a taxicab carrying a passenger for compensation;

(b) Operating a livery carrying a passenger for compensation; or

(c) Operating a truck with a GVWR of more than 18,000 pounds but not more than 26,000 pounds which is *not* a commercial motor vehicle;

after having been convicted within the preceding 10 years of violating VTL § 1192(1), (2), (2-a), (3), (4), or (4-a) while:

(a) Operating a taxicab carrying a passenger for compensation;

(b) Operating a livery carrying a passenger for compensation;

(c) Operating a truck with a GVWR of more than 18,000 pounds but not more than 26,000 pounds which is *not* a commercial motor vehicle;

(d) Operating a school bus carrying at least one student passenger;

(e) Operating a commercial motor vehicle, or any motor vehicle registered or registerable under Schedule F of VTL § 401(7); or

   (f) Operating a motor vehicle with a GVWR of more than 18,000 pounds which contains flammable gas, radioactive materials or explosives;

can be charged with a class E felony, and is subject to the following consequences:

1. A fine of between $1,000 and $5,000, up to four years in state prison, or both. VTL § 1193(1)(d)(4)(i); PL § 70.00(2)(e);
2. A period of probation of five years. PL § 65.00(3)(a)(i);
3. Mandatory revocation of his or her driver's license for at least one year. VTL § 1193(2)(b)(4);
4. Discretionary revocation of his or her registration for at least one year. VTL § 1193(2)(b)(4); and
5. "Permanent" disqualification from operating a commercial motor vehicle (even if the defendant does not have a CDL). VTL § 1193(1)(d)(4)(i); VTL § 1193(2)(e)(3). *See* §§ 14:11 to 14:13, *supra.*

The defendant can also be charged with any other applicable felony for any acts arising out of the same incident. VTL § 1193(1)(d)(7).

In addition, the defendant will be subject to all of the other usual consequences of a VTL § 1192 conviction. *See* §§ 46:1 et seq., *infra*.

A defendant who violates VTL § 1192(1), (2), (2-a), (3), (4), or (4-a) while:

   (a) Operating a taxicab carrying a passenger for compensation;
   (b) Operating a livery carrying a passenger for compensation; or
   (c) Operating a truck with a GVWR of more than 18,000 pounds but not more than 26,000 pounds which is *not* a commercial motor vehicle;

after having been convicted twice within the preceding 10 years of violating VTL § 1192(1), (2), (2-a), (3), (4), or (4-a) while:

   (a) Operating a taxicab carrying a passenger for compensation;
   (b) Operating a livery carrying a passenger for compensation;
   (c) Operating a truck with a GVWR of more than 18,000 pounds but not more than 26,000 pounds which is *not* a commercial motor vehicle;
   (d) Operating a school bus carrying at least one student passenger;
   (e) Operating a commercial motor vehicle, or any motor vehicle registered or registerable under Schedule F of VTL § 401(7); or
   (f) Operating a motor vehicle with a GVWR of more than 18,000 pounds which contains flammable gas, radioactive materials or explosives;

can be charged with a class D felony, and is subject to the following consequences:

1. A fine of between $2,000 and $10,000, up to seven years in state prison, or both. VTL § 1193(1)(d)(4)(ii); PL § 70.00(2)(d);
2. A period of probation of five years. PL § 65.00(3)(a)(i);
3. Mandatory revocation of his or her driver's license for at least one year. VTL § 1193(2)(b)(4);
4. Discretionary revocation of his or her registration for at least one year. VTL § 1193(2)(b)(4); and
5. "Permanent" disqualification from operating a commercial motor vehicle (even if the defendant does not have a CDL). VTL § 1193(1)(d)(4)(ii); VTL § 1193(2)(e)(3). *See* §§ 14:11 to 14:13, *supra*.

The defendant can also be charged with any other applicable felony for any acts arising out of the same incident. VTL § 1193(1)(d)(7).

In addition, the defendant will be subject to all of the other usual consequences of a VTL § 1192 conviction. *See* §§ 46:1 et seq., *infra*.

§ 14:53 Commercial/special vehicles penalties apply regardless of contrary provisions in other laws

The sentences required to be imposed by VTL § 1193(1)(d)(1), (1-a), (2), (3), (4), (4-a), or (5) "shall be imposed notwithstanding any contrary provision of [the VTL] or the penal law." VTL § 1193(1)(d)(6).

§ 14:54 Commercial/special vehicles statute does not preclude other relevant felonies from being charged if appropriate

VTL § 1193(1)(d)(7) provides that nothing contained in VTL § 1193(1)(d) "shall prohibit the imposition of a charge of any other felony set forth in this or any other provision of law for any acts arising out of the same incident."

§ 14:55 Applicability of preconviction conditional license to taxicabs

A preconviction conditional license "shall not be valid for the operation of a commercial motor vehicle or a taxicab." 15 NYCRR § 134.18(a).

§ 14:56 Applicability of regular, post-conviction conditional license to taxicabs

VTL § 1196(7)(g) provides that:

Notwithstanding anything to the contrary contained in a certificate of relief from disabilities issued pursuant to [Correction Law Article 23], any conditional license or privilege issued to a person convicted of a violation of any subdivision of [VTL § 1192] shall not be valid for the operation of any commercial motor vehicle. *In addition, no such conditional license or privilege shall be valid for the operation of a taxicab as defined in this chapter.*

(Emphasis added). *See also* 15 NYCRR § 134.9(c).

Critically, when VTL § 1196(7)(g) was amended effective September 30, 2005, the language in the first sentence thereof (which prohibits DMV from issuing a conditional license valid for the operation of a commercial motor vehicle notwithstanding anything to the contrary contained in a certificate of relief from disabilities) was *not* incorporated into the second sentence (which pertains to taxicabs).

As a result, if a taxicab driver obtains a certificate of relief from disabilities relieving him or her from the application of VTL § 1196(7)(g), DMV will still issue the driver a conditional license valid for the operation of a taxicab (if he or she is otherwise eligible therefor).

In this regard, this procedure will not override 15 NYCRR § 134.7(a)(8), which precludes the issuance of a conditional license where the underlying VTL § 1192 conviction leading to the revocation of the defendant's driver's license was committed while the defendant was:

(a) Operating a taxicab carrying a passenger for compensation;

(b) Operating a livery carrying a passenger for compensation; or

(c) Operating a truck with a GVWR of more than 18,000 pounds but not more than 26,000 pounds which is *not* a commercial motor vehicle;

unless the conviction was for DWAI in violation of VTL § 1192(1). *See* 15 NYCRR § 134.7(a)(8). *See also* VTL § 1196(7)(a).

§ 14:57 Applicability of conditional license to other special vehicles

As is noted in the previous section, the driver of a special vehicle is ineligible for a conditional license where the underlying VTL § 1192 conviction leading to the revocation of his or her driver's license was committed while such person was:

(a) Operating a taxicab carrying a passenger for compensation;

(b) Operating a livery carrying a passenger for compensation; or

(c) Operating a truck with a GVWR of more than 18,000 pounds but not more than 26,000 pounds which is *not* a commercial motor vehicle;

unless the conviction was for DWAI in violation of VTL § 1192(1). *See* 15 NYCRR § 134.7(a)(8). *See also* VTL § 1196(7)(a).

In addition, a conditional license cannot be used to operate either a bus or a school bus where the holder is disqualified from operating such bus pursuant to VTL § 509-c or VTL § 509-cc. *See* 15 NYCRR §§ 6.27(b), 6.28(b). *See also* VTL § 1196(7)(g); 15 NYCRR § 134.9(c).

Although VTL § 1196(7)(g) and 15 NYCRR § 134.9(c) do not reference any special vehicles other than taxicabs, a certificate of relief from disabilities may be required to obtain a conditional license valid for the operation of certain special vehicles.

§ 14:58 Successful DDP completion does *not* terminate certain "special vehicle" license revocations

Ordinarily, upon successful completion of the Drinking Driver Program (DDP), "a participant may apply to the commissioner . . . for the termination of the suspension or revocation order issued as a result of the participant's conviction which caused the participation in such course." VTL § 1196(5). In other words, successful DDP completion generally allows the defendant to apply for reinstatement of his or her full driving privileges.

VTL § 1193(2)(b)(9) expressly exempts certain "special vehicle" drivers from this rule:

> Effect of rehabilitation program. No period of revocation arising out of [VTL § 1193(2)(b)(4), (5), (6) or (7)] may be set aside by the commissioner for the reason that such person was a participant in the alcohol and drug rehabilitation program set forth in [VTL § 1196].

See also VTL § 1196(5); VTL § 1194(2)(d)(3); 15 NYCRR § 134.10(b).

Specifically, successful DDP completion will *not* terminate a license revocation where the underlying offense was committed while the defendant was:

(a) Operating a taxicab carrying a passenger for compensation;
(b) Operating a livery carrying a passenger for compensation; or
(c) Operating a truck with a GVWR of more than 18,000 pounds but not more than 26,000 pounds which is *not* a commercial motor vehicle.

See VTL § 1193(2)(b)(4); VTL § 1193(1)(d)(1).

§ 14:59 Applicability of restricted use license to special vehicles

VTL Article 21-A "provides for the issuance of a restricted use license to a person whose driver's license has been suspended or revoked pursuant to section 318 or 510 of the Vehicle and Traffic Law." 15 NYCRR § 135.1(a). VTL § 530(5) addresses the use of a restricted use license to operate special vehicles:

> A restricted use license or privilege shall be valid for the operation of any motor vehicle, *except a commercial motor vehicle or a vehicle for hire as a taxicab, livery, coach, limousine, van or wheelchair accessible van or tow truck as defined in this chapter* subject to the conditions set forth herein, which the holder would otherwise be entitled to operate had his drivers license or privilege not been suspended or revoked. Notwithstanding anything to the contrary in a certificate of relief from disabilities issued pursuant to [Correction Law Article 23], a restricted use license shall not be valid for the operation of a commercial motor vehicle.

(Emphasis added). *See also* 15 NYCRR § 135.9(b) ("[a]ny restricted license . . . shall be limited to the operation of vehicles which are not commercial motor vehicles as defined in [VTL § 501-a] or which are not for-hire vehicles as set forth in [VTL § 530]").

In addition, a restricted use license cannot be used to operate either a bus or a school bus where the holder is disqualified from operating such bus pursuant to VTL § 509-c or VTL § 509-cc. *See* 15 NYCRR §§ 6.27(b), 6.28(b). *See also* VTL § 530(5); 15 NYCRR § 135.9(b).

Critically, when VTL § 530(5) was amended effective September 30, 2005, the language in the second sentence thereof (which prohibits DMV from issuing a restricted use license valid for the operation of a commercial motor vehicle notwithstanding anything to the contrary contained in a certificate of relief from disabilities) was *not* incorporated into the first sentence (which pertains to vehicles for hire as a taxicab, livery, coach, limousine, van, wheelchair accessible van, or tow truck).

As a result, if the driver of one of these vehicles obtains a certificate of relief from disabilities relieving him or her from the application of VTL § 530(5), DMV will still issue the driver a restricted use license valid for the operation of such vehicle (if he or she is otherwise eligible therefor, and if such vehicle can lawfully be operated without a CDL).

§ 14:60   Unlicensed operation of certain special vehicles

VTL § 509(2) provides that "[w]henever a license is required to operate a motor vehicle, no person shall operate a motor vehicle unless he is the holder of a class of license which is valid for the operation of such vehicle."

A violation of VTL § 509(2) involving the operation for hire of any vehicle as a taxicab, "livery" as defined in VTL § 121-e, coach, limousine, van, wheelchair accessible van or tow truck without the appropriate license therefor is a traffic infraction punishable by a fine of between $225 and $450. VTL § 509(12).

A second such offense within 5 years is a traffic infraction punishable by a fine of between $375 and $750. VTL § 509(12).

A third or subsequent such offense within 10 years is a traffic infraction punishable by a fine of between $750 and $1,500. VTL § 509(12).

Chapter 15

Underage Offenders

Research References

Westlaw Databases

Handling a Criminal Case in New York (HCCNY)
Handling Drunk Driving Cases (2d ed.) (HDRUNKDR)
Intoxication Test Evidence (2d ed.) (INTOX)
New York Driving While Intoxicated Defense Forms (NYDWIFM)
New York Vehicle and Traffic Law 2d (NYVEH)

Treatises and Practice Aids

Muldoon, Handling a Criminal Case in New York §§ 20:64 to 20:89
Fiandach, Handling Drunk Driving Cases § 1:30 (2d ed.)
Fitzgerald, Intoxication Test Evidence § 36:4 (2d ed.)
Rose, New York Vehicle and Traffic Law 2d §§ 35:30.50 to 35:30.70

Forms

Taheri and Orr, NY DWI Defense Forms § 1:8

Law Reviews and Other Periodicals

Treuthart, Lowering The Bar: Rethinking Underage Drinking, 9 N.Y.U. J. Legis. & Pub. Pol'y 303 (2006)

KeyCite®: Cases and other legal materials listed in KeyCite Scope can be researched through the KeyCite service on Westlaw®. Use KeyCite to check citations for form, parallel references, prior and later history, and comprehensive citator information, including citations to other decisions and secondary materials.

---

§ 15:1   In general

Research References

West's Key Number Digest, Automobiles ⟜332

In the context of New York DWI law, an "underage offender" is a person under 21 years of age. By contrast, a "youthful offender" is a person at least 16 years of age and under 19 years of age. *See* CPL § 720.10(1). As a general rule, the laws pertaining to, and the consequences of, alcohol-and drug-related driving offenses are identical for motorists over and under 21, with two major exceptions: (1) certain statutes such as VTL § 1192-a and VTL § 1194-a (*i.e.*, the "Zero Tolerance" laws) only apply to underage offenders, and (2) license suspension/revocation periods are generally longer for underage offenders. This chapter focuses on situations in which underage offenders are treated differently than offenders over the age of 21.

§ 15:2   Whether person is "under 21" is determined by person's age on date of offense

Research References

West's Key Number Digest, Automobiles ⊙⟳332

In determining whether a person is under 21 years of age for purposes of the underage offender laws, the person's age is determined based upon his or her age on the date of the commission of the offense—*not* his or her age on the date of conviction. Thus, it is possible for a person well over the age of 21 to be punished as an underage offender (if the offense was committed when the person was under 21).

§ 15:3   Junior learner's permits and driver's licenses

Research References

West's Key Number Digest, Automobiles ⊙⟳138, 332

A class D license is a regular, noncommercial driver's license. VTL § 501(2)(a)(iv). A class DJ license is a "junior" driver's license. VTL § 501(2)(a)(vi). A class M license is a motorcycle driver's license. VTL § 501(2)(a)(vii). A class MJ license is a "junior" motorcycle driver's license. VTL § 501(2)(a)(viii).

A person between 16 and 18 years of age can apply for a junior learner's permit/driver's license. VTL § 502(2)(d); VTL § 502(3). VTL § 501(5) places various restrictions on the use of class DJ and class MJ learner's permits. VTL § 501(3) places various restrictions on the use of class DJ and class MJ driver's licenses. VTL § 501-b places various additional restrictions on the use of class DJ and class MJ permits/licenses.

The holder of a class DJ or class MJ learner's permit is not eligible to obtain a class DJ or class MJ driver's license unless, inter alia, at least six months have elapsed since the issuance of such permit (excluding any time period during which the permit was suspended or revoked). VTL § 501-b(1)(d). *See also* VTL § 503-a(2). However, if the holder of a class DJ or class MJ learner's permit passes a road test pursuant to VTL § 502(4)(b) less than six months after acquiring such permit, he or she will be issued a "limited class DJ or MJ license." VTL § 503-a(1). VTL § 503-a places certain restrictions on the use of limited class DJ or MJ licenses. Use of a limited class DJ or MJ license for a purpose other than those authorized by VTL § 503-a(1) is a traffic infraction. VTL § 503-a(6).

"A limited class DJ or MJ license issued pursuant to [VTL § 503-a] shall automatically become a class DJ or MJ license after such limited class DJ or MJ license, singly or in combination with the class DJ or MJ learner's permit, has been valid for [6] months." VTL § 503-a(2). However, "[a]ny time period during which such license or learner's permit has been suspended or revoked shall not be counted in determining such period of validity." VTL § 503-a(2). *See also* VTL § 501-b(1)(d).

A class DJ or class MJ driver's license can be converted to a class D or class M driver's license if the holder is at least 17 years of age and has, inter alia, successfully completed an approved high school or college driver education course. VTL § 502(2)(c). *See also* 15 NYCRR § 2.5. At age 18, a valid class DJ or class MJ driver's license automatically converts to a class D or class M driver's license. VTL § 501(2)(a)(vi); VTL § 501(2)(a)(viii).

§ 15:4   Suspension/revocation of junior learner's permits and driver's licenses

Research References

West's Key Number Digest, Automobiles ⊙144.1(1), 144.1(1.11)

VTL § 510-c provides for the suspension or revocation of junior learner's permits and driver's licenses for certain violations. A class DJ or class MJ learner's permit will be suspended for 60 days:

(i) upon a conviction or finding of a serious traffic violation as defined in [VTL § 510-c(4)], committed while the holder had a class DJ or class MJ learner's permit; or

(ii) upon the *second* conviction or finding of such holder of a violation of any other provision of [the VTL] or any other law, ordinance, order, rule, or regulation relating to traffic [*i.e.*, any *moving* violation], committed while such holder had such learner's permit. VTL § 510-c(1)(a) (emphasis added).

A class DJ or class MJ learner's permit will be *revoked* for 60 days "upon the conviction or finding of the holder of a violation or violations, committed within [6] months after the restoration of a class DJ or class MJ learner's permit suspended pursuant to

[VTL § 510-c(1)(a)], which convictions or findings would result in the suspension of such permit pursuant to [VTL § 510-c(1)(a)]." VTL § 510-c(1)(b).

A class DJ or class MJ driver's license or limited class DJ or class MJ license will be suspended for 60 days:

(i) upon a conviction or finding of a serious traffic violation as defined in [VTL § 510-c(4)], committed while the holder had such license; or

(ii) upon the *second* conviction or finding of the holder of a violation of any other provision of [the VTL] or any other law, ordinance, order, rule, or regulation relating to traffic [*i.e.*, any *moving* violation], committed while such holder had such license. VTL § 510-c(2)(a) (emphasis added).

A class DJ or class MJ driver's license or a limited class DJ or class MJ license will be revoked for 60 days "upon the conviction or finding of the holder of a violation or violations, committed within [6] months either after the restoration of such driver's license suspended pursuant to [VTL § 510-c(2)(a)] or after the restoration of a learner's permit suspended or revoked pursuant to [VTL § 510-c(1)], which convictions or findings would result in the suspension of such license pursuant to [VTL § 510-c(2)(a)]." VTL § 510-c(2)(b).

A driver's license that has been restored following a suspension of a class DJ or class MJ driver's license or a limited class DJ or class MJ license pursuant to VTL § 510-c(2) will be revoked for 60 days "upon the conviction or finding, within [6] months of such restoration, of any violation or violations which would result in the suspension of a class DJ or class MJ driver's license or a limited class DJ or class MJ license pursuant to [VTL § 510-c(2)(a)]." VTL § 510-c(3).

For purposes of VTL § 510-c, the term "serious traffic violation" means operating a motor vehicle in violation of any of the following provisions of the VTL:

1. VTL Articles 25 and 26 (*i.e.*, VTL §§ 1120 to 1131 and 1140 to 1146-A);

2. VTL § 600(1) (leaving the scene of an incident without reporting);

3. VTL § 601 (leaving the scene of injury to certain animals without reporting);

4. VTL § 1111 (traffic-control signals);

5. VTL § 1170 (obedience to signal indicating approach of train);

6. VTL § 1172 (stop signs and yield signs);

7. VTL § 1174 (passing school bus);

8. VTL § 1180(a), (b), (c), (d) and (f) (speeding)—provided that the violation involved 10 or more MPH over the speed limit;

9. VTL § 1182 (speed contests/races);

10. VTL § 1229-c(3-a) (safety seats and seat belts)—for violations involving the use of safety seats or seat belts by a child under the age of 16; and

11. VTL § 1212 (reckless driving).

§ 15:5 Probationary driver's licenses

Research References

West's Key Number Digest, Automobiles ⊱136, 138

With limited exceptions, "[a]ny driver's license, other than a class DJ and class MJ license or limited class DJ and MJ license, shall be considered probationary until the expiration of [6] months following the date of issuance thereof, and thereafter as provided in [VTL § 510-b]." VTL § 501(4).

§ 15:6 Suspension/revocation of probationary driver's licenses

Research References

West's Key Number Digest, Automobiles ⊱144.1(1)

VTL § 510-b provides for the suspension or revocation of probationary driver's licenses for certain violations committed during the probationary period. A probationary license will be suspended for 60 days "upon the first conviction of the licensee of a violation, committed during the probationary period," of:

1. VTL § 1129 (following too closely);

2. VTL § 1180 (speeding) or any ordinance or regulation limiting the speed of motor vehicles and motorcycles;

3. VTL § 1182 (speed contests/races);

4. VTL § 1192(1) (DWAI); or

5. VTL § 1212 (reckless driving). VTL § 510-b(1)(i).

A probationary license will also be suspended for 60 days "upon the *second* conviction of the licensee of a violation, committed during the aforesaid probationary period, of any other provision of [the VTL] or of any other law, ordinance, order, rule, or regulation relating to traffic [*i.e.*, any *moving* violation]." VTL § 510-b(1)(ii) (emphasis added).

Where a probationary license "is restored or issued to a person who has had his last valid license suspended or revoked pursuant to" VTL § 510-b, such license will be probationary for an additional six months following the date of restoration or issuance thereof. VTL § 510-b(3).

If, within six months of the restoration of a probationary license, the probationary licensee is convicted of any offense which "would result in the suspension of a probationary license pursuant to [VTL § 510-b(1)]," such probationary license will be revoked. VTL § 510-b(2).

Finally, VTL § 510-b(4) provides that:

The provisions of [VTL § 510(1), (5), (6) and (7)] shall apply to any suspension or revocation under [VTL § 510-b]. However, the provisions of [VTL § 510-b] shall not operate to prevent a mandatory revocation or suspension for a greater period of time under [VTL § 510(2)] or [VTL § 1193]; nor shall the provisions of [VTL § 510-b] prevent revocation or suspension under [VTL § 510(2) and (3)] based upon [2] or more violations, including the same violation which was the basis for suspension or revocation under [VTL § 510-b].

§ 15:7   VTL §§ 1192-a and 1194-a—The Zero Tolerance laws

Research References
West's Key Number Digest, Automobiles ⚖144.1(1.11), 332

VTL § 1192-a provides, in pertinent part:

Operating a motor vehicle after having consumed alcohol; under the age of [21]; per se

No person under the age of [21] shall operate a motor vehicle after having consumed alcohol as defined in this section. For purposes of this section, a person under the age of [21] is deemed to have consumed alcohol only if such person has 0.02 of 1% or more but not more than 0.07 of 1% by weight of alcohol in the person's blood [i.e., between 0.02% and 0.07%], as shown by chemical analysis of such person's blood, breath, urine, or saliva, made pursuant to the provisions of [VTL § 1194].

VTL § 1194-a sets forth the procedures applicable to a violation of VTL § 1192-a, as well as the procedures applicable to a Zero Tolerance law chemical test refusal.

VTL § 1192-a was created to send a message to underage drivers that if they merely drink and drive they will lose their driver's licenses *regardless of whether they are actually impaired to any extent* (*i.e.*, New York has "zero tolerance" for underage drinking and driving). In this regard, since the intent of the Zero Tolerance laws was to deter underage drinking and driving without inordinately punishing the underage drinking driver, and since a person who drives in violation of VTL § 1192-a may not be at all impaired by the consumption of alcohol, the statute makes clear that it is civil, not criminal, in nature. *See* VTL § 1192-a ("Notwithstanding any provision of law to the contrary, a finding that a person under the age of [21] operated a motor vehicle after having consumed alcohol in violation of this section is not a judgment of conviction for a crime or any other offense"). *See also* VTL § 1194-a(2) (a person found guilty of a Zero Tolerance law violation is not subject to a fine, but rather to a "civil penalty").

§ 15:8 Alleged violation of Zero Tolerance laws adjudicated at DMV—Not in court

Research References

West's Key Number Digest, Automobiles ☞144.1(1.11), 332

Consistent with the fact that a Zero Tolerance law violation is civil, not criminal, in nature, *see* previous section, the adjudication of an alleged violation of the Zero Tolerance laws takes place at DMV, *not* in a local criminal court. *See* VTL § 1192-a ("Any person who operates a motor vehicle in violation of this section, and who is not charged with a violation of any subdivision of [VTL § 1192] arising out of the same incident shall be referred to [DMV] for action in accordance with the provisions of [VTL § 1194-a]").

§ 15:9 Person cannot be charged with Zero Tolerance law violation if charged with violating VTL § 1192

Research References

West's Key Number Digest, Automobiles ☞144.1(1.11), 332

VTL § 1192-a expressly provides that "[a]ny person who operates a motor vehicle in violation of this section, *and who is not charged with a violation of any subdivision of [VTL § 1192] arising out of the same incident* shall be referred to [DMV] for action in accordance with the provisions of [VTL § 1194-a]." (Emphasis added). *See also* VTL § 1194-a(1)(a); VTL § 1194-a(1)(b). Thus, a person cannot be charged with violating VTL § 1192-a if he or she is charged with a violation of VTL § 1192 arising out of the same incident.

Similarly, a person cannot be charged with violating VTL § 1192-a in a criminal Court. Rather, such "charge" must be filed with DMV. In this regard, in *People v. Pesantes*, 10 Misc. 3d 676, __–__, 809 N.Y.S.2d 859, 860–61 (N.Y. City Crim. Ct. 2005), the Court held that:

> While defendant correctly argues that the information fails to establish the necessary elements of Vehicle and Traffic Law § 1192-a, the charge is also subject to dismissal for a more fundamental reason, i.e., Vehicle and Traffic Law § 1192-a is a non-criminal offense which is adjudicated exclusively before a Department of Motor Vehicles hearing officer. * * *
>
> While the New York City Criminal Court generally has jurisdiction to hear, try and determine misdemeanors and all offenses of a grade less than misdemeanor, the Legislature has explicitly limited the adjudication of Vehicle and Traffic Law § 1192-a offenses to the Department of Motor Vehicles. Accordingly, this Court is without jurisdiction to hear, try and determine this charge.

§ 15:10 Person can be *convicted* of Zero Tolerance law violation if charged with violating VTL § 1192

Research References

West's Key Number Digest, Automobiles ⬤—144.1(1.11), 332

Although a person cannot be *charged* with violating VTL § 1192-a if he or she is charged with a violation of VTL § 1192 arising out of the same incident, *see* previous section, a person can be *convicted* of violating VTL § 1192-a even if he or she is charged with a violation of VTL § 1192(1). *See* VTL § 1192(10)(a)(iii), (c). *See also* § 15:11, *infra*; *People v. Pesantes*, 10 Misc. 3d 676, __, 809 N.Y.S.2d 859, 861 (N.Y. City Crim. Ct. 2005).

In addition, VTL § 1192(10)(a)(i) provides that if a person is charged with violating VTL § 1192(2), (3), (4), or (4-a) and "the district attorney, upon reviewing the available evidence, determines that the charge of a violation of [VTL § 1192] is not warranted, such district attorney may consent, and the court may allow a disposition by plea of guilty to another charge in satisfaction of such charge." Since, in such a case, a plea outside of VTL § 1192 is authorized, a plea to a violation of VTL § 1192-a is permissible (as long as the defendant was under 21 years of age on the date of the offense) even if the original charge consisted of a violation of VTL § 1192(2), (3), (4), and/or (4-a).

Indeed, an argument can be made that VTL § 1192-a is a lesser included offense of VTL §§ 1192(1) and (3). In this regard, CPL § 1.20(37) defines "lesser included offense" as follows:

When it is impossible to commit a particular crime without concomitantly committing, by the same conduct, another offense of lesser grade or degree, the latter is, with respect to the former, a "lesser included offense." In any case in which it is legally possible to attempt to commit a crime, an attempt to commit such crime constitutes a lesser included offense with respect thereto.

CPL § 300.50 provides, in pertinent part, that:

1. In submitting a count of an indictment to the jury, the court in its discretion may, in addition to submitting the greatest offense which it is required to submit, submit in the alternative any lesser included offense if there is a reasonable view of the evidence which would support a finding that the defendant committed such lesser offense but did not commit the greater. If there is no reasonable view of the evidence which would support such a finding, the court may not submit such lesser offense. Any error respecting such submission, however, is waived by the defendant unless he objects thereto before the jury retires to deliberate.

2. If the court is authorized by subdivision one to submit a

lesser included offense and is requested by either party to do so, it must do so. In the absence of such a request, the court's failure to submit such offense does not constitute error. *See also* CPL § 360.50(1), (2); §§ 9:1 et seq., *supra*.

§ 15:11 Plea bargain limitations applicable to underage offenders

Research References

West's Key Number Digest, Automobiles ⊕332

VTL § 1192(10) sets forth certain plea bargain limitations applicable to VTL § 1192 cases. With respect to underage offenders, VTL § 1192(10)(a)(iii) provides, in pertinent part, that:

> In any case wherein the charge laid before the court alleges a violation of [VTL § 1192(1)] and the operator was under the age of [21] at the time of such violation, any plea of guilty thereafter entered in satisfaction of such charge must include at least a plea of guilty to the violation of [VTL § 1192(1)]; provided, however, such charge may instead be satisfied as provided in [VTL § 1192(10)(c)].

VTL § 1192(10)(a)(iii) further provides that:

> [I]f the district attorney, upon reviewing the available evidence, determines that the charge of a violation of [VTL § 1192(1)] is not warranted, such district attorney may consent, and the court may allow a disposition by plea of guilty to another charge in satisfaction of such charge; provided, however, in all such cases, the court shall set forth upon the record the basis for such disposition.

VTL § 1192(10)(b) sets forth plea bargain limitations where the defendant was charged with VTL § 1192(1) or (6) while operating a commercial motor vehicle.

VTL § 1192(10)(c) provides that:

> (c) Except as provided in [VTL § 1192(10)(b)], in any case wherein the charge laid before the court alleges a violation of [VTL § 1192(1)] by a person who was under the age of [21] at the time of commission of the offense, the court, with the consent of both parties, may allow the satisfaction of such charge by the defendant's agreement to be subject to action by [DMV] pursuant to [VTL § 1194-a]. In any such case, the defendant shall waive the right to a hearing under [VTL § 1194-a] and such waiver shall have the same force and effect as a finding of a violation of [VTL § 1192-a] entered after a hearing conducted pursuant to [VTL § 1194-a]. The defendant shall execute such waiver in open court, and, if represented by counsel, in the presence of his attorney, on a form to be provided by [DMV], which shall be forwarded by the court to [DMV] within [96] hours.

VTL § 1192(10)(c) further provides that:

> To be valid, such form shall, at a minimum, contain clear and

conspicuous language advising the defendant that a duly executed waiver: (i) has the same force and effect as a guilty finding following a hearing pursuant to [VTL § 1194-a]; (ii) shall subject the defendant to the imposition of sanctions pursuant to [VTL § 1194-a]; and (iii) may subject the defendant to increased sanctions upon a subsequent violation of [VTL § 1192] or [VTL § 1192-a].

"Upon receipt of a duly executed waiver pursuant to this paragraph, [DMV] shall take such administrative action and impose such sanctions as may be required by [VTL § 1194-a]." VTL § 1192(10)(c).

§ 15:12   Sealing of records in Zero Tolerance law case

Research References

West's Key Number Digest, Records ☞3, 15, 22

VTL § 201(1)(k) provides, in pertinent part, that the Commissioner may destroy:

> [A]ny records, including any reproductions or electronically created images of such records and including any records received by the commissioner from a court pursuant to [VTL § 1192(10)(c)] or [Navigation Law § 49-b], relating to a finding of a violation of [VTL § 1192-a] or a waiver of the right to a hearing under [VTL § 1194-a] or a finding of a refusal following a hearing conducted pursuant to [VTL § 1194-a(3)] or a finding of a violation of [Navigation Law § 49-b] or a waiver of the right to a hearing or a finding of refusal following a hearing conducted pursuant to [Navigation Law § 49-b], after remaining on file for [3] years after such finding or entry of such waiver or refusal or until the person that is found to have violated such section reaches the age of [21], whichever is the greater period of time.

At such time:

> [T]he entirety of the proceedings concerning the violation or alleged violation of [VTL § 1192-a] or [Navigation Law § 49-b], from the initial stop and detention of the operator to the entering of a finding and imposition of sanctions pursuant to any subdivision of [VTL § 1194-a] or of [Navigation Law § 49-b] shall be deemed a nullity, and the operator shall be restored, in contemplation of law, to the status he occupied before the initial stop and prosecution.

VTL § 201(1)(k). It is critical to note that, *upon the expiration of the retention period set forth in VTL § 201(1)(k), all records in a Zero Tolerance law case "shall be deemed destroyed as a matter of law for all purposes" whether or not such records are actually destroyed.* VTL § 201(5) (emphasis added).

In addition, CPL § 160.55(5) provides, in pertinent part, that:
  (b) Where a person under the age of [21] is referred by the

police to [DMV] for action pursuant to [VTL § 1192-a or VTL § 1194-a], or [Navigation Law § 49-b] and a finding in favor of the motorist or operator is rendered, the commissioner of [DMV] shall, as soon as practicable, but not later than [3] years from the date of commission of the offense or when such person reaches the age of [21], whichever is the greater period of time, notify the commissioner of [DCJS] and the heads of all appropriate police departments and other law enforcement agencies that such finding in favor of the motorist or operator was rendered. Upon receipt of such notification, the commissioner of [DCJS] and the heads of such police departments and other law enforcement agencies shall take the actions required by [CPL § 160.50(1)(a), (b) and (c)].

(c) Where a person under the age of [21] is referred by the police to [DMV] for action pursuant to [VTL § 1192-a or VTL § 1194-a], or [Navigation Law § 49-b], and no notification is received by the commissioner of [DCJS] and the heads of all appropriate police departments and other law enforcement agencies pursuant to [CPL § 160.55(5)(b)], such commissioner of [DCJS] and such heads of police departments and other law enforcement agencies shall, after [3] years from the date of commission of the offense or when the person reaches the age of [21], whichever is the greater period of time, take the actions required by [CPL § 160.50(1)(a), (b) and (c)]. CPL § 160.55(5)(b), (c).

§ 15:13 Sealing of records where VTL § 1192 charge reduced to violation of VTL § 1192-a

Research References

West's Key Number Digest, Criminal Law ☞1226(5)

Where a VTL § 1192 charge is reduced to a violation of VTL § 1192-a, CPL § 160.55(5)(a) provides:

When a criminal action or proceeding is terminated against a person by the entry of a waiver of a hearing pursuant to [VTL § 1192(10)(c)] or [Navigation Law § 49-b], the record of the criminal action shall be sealed in accordance with [CPL § 160.55(5)]. Upon the entry of such waiver, the court or the clerk of the court shall immediately notify the commissioner of [DCJS] and the heads of all appropriate police departments and other law enforcement agencies that a waiver has been entered and that the record of the action shall be sealed when the person reaches the age of [21] or [3] years from the date of commission of the offense, whichever is the greater period of time. At the expiration of such period, the commissioner of [DCJS] and the heads of all appropriate police departments and other law enforcement agencies shall take the actions required by [CPL § 160.50(1)(a), (b) and (c)].

§ 15:14   Zero Tolerance law generally inapplicable to operator of commercial motor vehicle

Research References
West's Key Number Digest, Automobiles ⊂⇒332

VTL § 1192-a expressly provides that "[e]xcept as otherwise provided in [VTL § 1192(5)], this section shall not apply to a person who operates a commercial motor vehicle." VTL § 1192(5) provides that:

> Commercial motor vehicles: per se—level I. Notwithstanding the provisions of [VTL § 1195], no person shall operate a commercial motor vehicle while such person has .04 of one per centum or more but not more than .06 of one per centum by weight of alcohol in the person's blood as shown by chemical analysis of such person's blood, breath, urine or saliva, made pursuant to the provisions of [VTL § 1194].

VTL § 1192(5) further provides that:

> [N]othing contained in this subdivision shall prohibit the imposition of a charge of a violation of [VTL § 1192(1)], or of [VTL § 1192-a] where a person under the age of [21] operates a commercial motor vehicle where a chemical analysis of such person's blood, breath, urine, or saliva, made pursuant to the provisions of [VTL § 1194], indicates that such operator has .02 of one per centum or more but less than .04 of one per centum by weight of alcohol in such operator's blood.

In other words, an underage offender who operates a commercial motor vehicle with a BAC of 0.02% or 0.03%—which is below the threshold required to be charged with violating VTL § 1192(5)—can nonetheless be charged with violating VTL § 1192-a or VTL § 1192(1).

§ 15:15   Underage offenders—First offense

Research References
West's Key Number Digest, Automobiles ⊂⇒144.1(1.11), 332

Where a person under the age of 21 is found guilty of a violation of VTL § 1192-a, his or her driver's license will be *suspended*, and his or her registration may be suspended, for a period of six months. VTL § 1193(2)(a)(2). He or she will also be liable for a civil penalty in the amount of $125. VTL § 1194-a(2). *See also* § 15:50, *infra*. The person will most likely be eligible for the Drinking Driver Program and a conditional license. *See* §§ 50:1 et seq., *infra*.

Where a defendant under the age of 21 is convicted of, or adjudicated a youthful offender for, a violation of any subdivision of VTL § 1192, his or her driver's license will be *revoked*, and his or her registration may be revoked, for a period of at least one year. VTL § 1193(2)(b)(6). He or she will otherwise be subject to the same consequences as a person 21 years of age or older. *See* §§ 46:1 et seq., *infra*.

In this situation, the defendant will most likely be eligible for the Drinking Driver Program and a conditional license. However, successful completion of the Drinking Driver Program will *not* result in full restoration of the defendant's driving privileges prior to the expiration of the minimum revocation period. VTL § 1193(2)(b)(9). *See also* § 15:25, *infra*; §§ 50:1 et seq., *infra*.

§ 15:16 Underage offenders—Second offense

Research References

West's Key Number Digest, Automobiles ⭐144.1(1.11), 332

Where a person under the age of 21 is either (a) found guilty of a violation of VTL § 1192-a, or (b) convicted of, or adjudicated a youthful offender for, a violation of any subdivision of VTL § 1192, and the person has previously been either (a) found guilty of a violation of VTL § 1192-a, or (b) convicted of, or adjudicated a youthful offender for, a violation of any subdivision of VTL § 1192 *not arising out of the same incident*, his or her driver's license will be revoked, and his or her registration may be revoked, for a period of at least one year or until the person reaches the age of 21, *whichever is longer*. VTL § 1193(2)(b)(7). In addition, the person will *not* be eligible for either the Drinking Driver Program or a conditional license. *See* §§ 50:1 et seq., *infra*.

If the second conviction is for a violation of VTL § 1192-a, the person will also be liable for a civil penalty in the amount of $125. VTL § 1194-a(2). *See also* § 15:50, *infra*. If the second conviction is for a violation of VTL § 1192, the person will otherwise be subject to the same consequences as a person 21 years of age or older. *See* §§ 46:1 et seq., *infra*.

§ 15:17 Underage offenders—Chemical test refusal revocation

Research References

West's Key Number Digest, Automobiles ⭐144.1(1.11), 332

A person under the age of 21 who is found to have refused to submit to a chemical test, in violation of either VTL § 1194(2)(c) or VTL § 1194-a(3), will have his or her driver's license, permit, or nonresident operating privilege revoked for at least one year. VTL § 1194(2)(d)(1)(b).

A person under the age of 21 who is found to have refused to

submit to a chemical test, in violation of either VTL § 1194(2)(c)
or VTL § 1194-a(3), and who "has a prior finding, conviction or
youthful offender adjudication resulting from a violation of [VTL
§ 1192] or [VTL § 1192-a], *not arising from the same incident*,"
will have his or her driver's license, permit, or nonresident operating privilege revoked for at least one year or until the person
reaches the age of 21, *whichever is longer*. VTL § 1194(2)(d)(1)(b)
(emphasis added). *See also* §§ 41:1 et seq., *infra*.

§ 15:18   Effect of prior Zero Tolerance law adjudication

Research References

West's Key Number Digest, Automobiles ☞144.1(1.11), 332

For purposes of determining the length of a license suspension
or revocation to be imposed for a subsequent offense/refusal committed after a person has been found guilty of a violation of VTL
§ 1192-a, the effect of the prior Zero Tolerance law adjudication is
the same as a conviction of DWAI in violation of VTL § 1192(1),
*provided that the subsequent offense is committed during the
retention period set forth in VTL § 201(1)(k)*. VTL § 1192(8-a).
VTL § 201(1)(k) provides, in pertinent part, that the Commissioner may destroy:

> [A]ny records, including any reproductions or electronically created
> images of such records and including any records received by the
> commissioner from a court pursuant to [VTL § 1192(10)(c)] or
> [Navigation Law § 49-b], relating to a finding of a violation of [VTL
> § 1192-a] or a waiver of the right to a hearing under [VTL § 1194-a]
> or a finding of a refusal following a hearing conducted pursuant to
> [VTL § 1194-a(3)] or a finding of a violation of [Navigation Law
> § 49-b] or a waiver of the right to a hearing or a finding of refusal
> following a hearing conducted pursuant to [Navigation Law § 49-b],
> after remaining on file for [3] years after such finding or entry of
> such waiver or refusal or until the person that is found to have
> violated such section reaches the age of [21], whichever is the
> greater period of time.

In other words, if a subsequent offense/refusal is committed after the retention period set forth in VTL § 201(1)(k) has expired,
a prior violation of VTL § 1192-a will have no effect on the length
of the suspension/revocation for the new offense/ refusal.

§ 15:19   Effect of prior Zero Tolerance law chemical test
refusal adjudication

Research References

West's Key Number Digest, Automobiles ☞144.1(1.11), 332

VTL § 1194(2)(d)(1)(a) provides, in pertinent part, that:

> [A] prior finding that a person under the age of [21] has refused to

submit to a chemical test pursuant to [VTL § 1194-a(3)] shall have the same effect as a prior finding of a refusal pursuant to [VTL § 1194(2)(d)] solely for the purpose of determining the length of any license suspension or revocation required to be imposed under any provision of this article, provided that the subsequent offense or refusal is committed or occurred prior to the expiration of the retention period for such prior refusal as set forth in [VTL § 201(1)(k)].

The pertinent portion of VTL § 201(1)(k) is set forth in the previous section.

In other words, if a subsequent offense/refusal is committed after the retention period set forth in VTL § 201(1)(k) has expired, a prior Zero Tolerance law chemical test refusal will have no effect on the length of the suspension/revocation for the new offense/refusal.

§ 15:20 Out-of-state convictions

Research References
West's Key Number Digest, Automobiles ⊙⇒332

Prior to November 1, 2006, VTL § 1192(8) provided that, for purposes of determining the consequences of a violation of VTL § 1192, a prior out-of-state conviction for operating a motor vehicle while under the influence of alcohol or drugs was deemed to be a prior conviction of DWAI in violation of VTL § 1192(1). Effective November 1, 2006, VTL § 1192(8) provides as follows:

Effect of prior out-of-state conviction. A prior out-of-state conviction for operating a motor vehicle while under the influence of alcohol or drugs shall be deemed to be a prior conviction of a violation of this section for purposes of determining penalties imposed under this section or for purposes of any administrative action required to be taken pursuant to [VTL § 1193(2)]; provided, however, that such conduct, had it occurred in this state, would have constituted a misdemeanor or felony violation of any of the provisions of [VTL § 1192]. Provided, however, that if such conduct, had it occurred in this state, would have constituted a violation of any provisions of [VTL § 1192] which are not misdemeanor or felony offenses, then such conduct shall be deemed to be a prior conviction of a violation of [VTL § 1192(1)] for purposes of determining penalties imposed under this section or for purposes of any administrative action required to be taken pursuant to [VTL § 1193(2)].

Thus, a prior out-of-state DWI conviction can now potentially be used as a predicate conviction for a felony DWI charge.

Critically, however, the enabling portion of this change to VTL § 1192(8) expressly provides that it only applies to out-of-state convictions that occurred on or after November 1, 2006. *See also People v. Ballman*, 15 N.Y.3d 68, 70, 904 N.Y.S.2d 361, 362, 930 N.E.2d 282, ___ (2010) ("This appeal raises the issue whether Vehicle and Traffic Law § 1192(8) allows an out-of-state conviction occurring prior to November 1, 2006 to be considered for purposes of elevating a charge of driving while intoxicated from a misdemeanor to a felony. We hold that it does not").

In addition, where a New York licensee under the age of 21 is convicted of operating a motor vehicle while under the influence of alcohol in another State, his or her driver's license will be revoked, and his or her registration may be revoked, for at least:

(a) one year, if the licensee is a "first offender." VTL § 1193(2)(b)(6); VTL § 1193(2)(b)(8); or

(b) one year or until age 21, *whichever is longer*, if the licensee is a "repeat offender." VTL § 1193(2)(b)(7); VTL § 1193(2)(b)(8).

§ 15:21 Court must notify parent or guardian of certain minors of VTL charges

Research References

West's Key Number Digest, Automobiles ⬥332

VTL § 1193(2)(e)(7)(f) provides that the court must promptly notify the parent or guardian of a person under the age of 18 (if the minor lives with such parent or guardian) where the minor was charged with a violation of VTL § 1192(1), (2), and/or (3):

> Notice of charges to parent or guardian. Notwithstanding the provisions of [VTL § 1807(2)], upon the first scheduled appearance of any person under [18] years of age who resides within the household of his or her parent or guardian upon a charge of a violation of [VTL § 1192(1), (2), and/or (3)], the local criminal court before which such first appearance is scheduled shall forthwith transmit written notice of such appearance or failure to make such appearance to the parent or guardian of such minor person.

In a situation where the minor pleads guilty by mail or at arraignment, VTL § 1193(2)(e)(7)(f) provides that "transmittal of notice of his or her conviction as provided in [VTL § 514] shall be sufficient and the notice required by this paragraph need not be given."

VTL § 1193(2)(e)(7)(f) further provides "that the failure of a local criminal court to transmit the notice required by this paragraph shall in no manner affect the validity of a conviction subsequently obtained."

VTL § 1193(2)(e)(7)(f) is somewhat redundant, as VTL § 1807(2) provides identical rules for virtually all moving violations:

> Upon the arraignment of any person under [18] years of age who resides within the household of his parent or guardian upon a charge of a violation of the [VTL] or other law or ordinance relating to the operation of motor vehicles or motor cycles, except a violation

relating to parking, stopping or standing, the local criminal court which arraigns him shall forthwith transmit written notice of such arraignment to the parent or guardian of such minor person.

VTL § 1807(2).

In a situation where the minor pleads guilty by mail or at arraignment, VTL § 1807(2) provides that "transmittal of notice of his conviction as provided in [VTL § 514] shall be sufficient and the notice of arraignment hereunder need not be given."

VTL § 1807(2) further provides "that the failure of a local criminal court to transmit such notice of arraignment shall in no manner affect the validity of a conviction subsequently obtained."

§ 15:22   Underage offenders and the Drinking Driver Program

Research References

West's Key Number Digest, Automobiles ☞136, 138, 144.1(1)

A conditional license allows a person to drive, among other places, to, from and during work, and to and from school, during the time period that the person's driving privileges are suspended or revoked as a result of an alcohol-related traffic offense. *See* VTL § 1196(7); 15 NYCRR § 134.9(b). *See also* §§ 50:1 et seq., *infra*. To be eligible for a conditional license, a person must, among other things, participate in the so-called Drinking Driver Program (DDP).

However, eligibility for the DDP requires an alcohol-or drug-related conviction or a Zero Tolerance adjudication. In this regard, VTL § 1196(4) provides, in pertinent part, that:

> *Participation in the [DDP] shall be limited to those persons convicted of alcohol or drug-related traffic offenses or persons who have been adjudicated youthful offenders for alcohol or drug-related traffic offenses, or persons found to have been operating a motor vehicle after having consumed alcohol in violation of [VTL § 1192-a],* who choose to participate and who satisfy the criteria and meet the requirements for participation as established by [VTL § 1196] and the regulations promulgated thereunder.

(Emphasis added). *See also* 15 NYCRR § 134.2.

In addition, eligibility for the DDP is limited to individuals who, inter alia, have neither (a) participated in the DDP within the preceding five years, nor (b) been convicted of a violation of any subdivision of VTL § 1192 within the preceding five years. *See* VTL § 1196(4); 15 NYCRR § 134.2; §§ 50:1 et seq., *infra*. Thus, it will be extremely rare for an underage offender to be eligible for the DDP more than once.

First offense underage offenders, whether convicted of, or

adjudicated a youthful offender for, a violation of any subdivision of VTL § 1192, or found guilty of a violation of VTL § 1192-a, will generally be eligible for both the DDP and a conditional license (or, if convicted of DWAI Drugs, for a restricted use license). *See* §§ 50:1 et seq., *infra*.

§ 15:23   Chemical test refusals and the DDP

Research References

West's Key Number Digest, Automobiles ⚖144.1(1.20)

As the previous section demonstrates, eligibility for the DDP requires an alcohol-or drug-related conviction or a VTL § 1192-a adjudication. Thus, a person who refuses to submit to a chemical test and whose driving privileges are revoked by DMV as a result thereof (and who is otherwise eligible for a conditional license), will not be able to obtain a conditional license unless and until the person obtains a VTL § 1192 conviction or a VTL § 1192-a adjudication. As a result, many people who lose their chemical test refusal hearings (and who need to drive to earn a living or to obtain an education) are virtually forced to accept a DWAI or DWI plea in criminal court in order to obtain a conditional license. This seemingly unfair restriction on conditional license eligibility has been found to be constitutional. *See Matter of Miller v. Tofany*, 88 Misc. 2d 247, __–__, 387 N.Y.S.2d 342, 345–46 (Broome Co. Sup. Ct. 1975).

§ 15:24   Zero Tolerance law chemical test refusals and the DDP

Research References

West's Key Number Digest, Automobiles ⚖144.1(1.20)

As § 15:22 demonstrates, eligibility for the DDP requires an alcohol-or drug-related driving conviction or a VTL § 1192-a adjudication. In the usual chemical test refusal case, the defendant is charged with both a chemical test refusal as well as a violation of VTL § 1192(1) or (3). As a result, if the defendant loses his or her DMV chemical test refusal hearing, he or she can obtain a conditional license (if otherwise eligible) by pleading guilty to DWAI or DWI in criminal court.

By contrast, an underage offender charged with a Zero Tolerance law chemical test refusal will not, by definition, be charged with a violation of either VTL § 1192 or VTL § 1192-a in conjunction therewith, since:

    (a) A person cannot be charged with a Zero Tolerance law violation and a violation of any subdivision of VTL § 1192 arising out of the same incident; and

(b) A person cannot be charged with a Zero Tolerance law chemical test refusal and a violation of VTL § 1192-a arising out of the same incident (as VTL § 1192-a requires a chemical test result).

Thus, an underage offender who is found guilty of a Zero Tolerance law chemical test refusal will be ineligible for a conditional license.

Such a situation will likely be extremely rare, however, as drivers who refuse to submit to chemical tests are almost always charged with common law DWI in violation of VTL § 1192(3). In other words, if an underage offender (who would have qualified for a charge of VTL § 1192-a if he or she took the chemical test) refuses to submit to a chemical test, he or she will generally, *at a minimum*, be charged with a violation of VTL § 1192(1) in criminal court—not merely with a Zero Tolerance law chemical test refusal.

§ 15:25 Successful DDP completion does not permit early termination of VTL § 1192 revocation for underage offenders

Research References
West's Key Number Digest, Automobiles ⊕144.1(1)

Ordinarily, upon successful completion of the DDP, "a participant may apply to the commissioner . . . for the termination of the suspension or revocation order issued as a result of the participant's conviction which caused the participation in such course." VTL § 1196(5). In other words, successful DDP completion generally allows the defendant to apply for reinstatement of his or her full driving privileges.

However, VTL § 1193(2)(b)(9) expressly exempts underage offenders revoked for a violation of VTL § 1192 from this rule:

Effect of rehabilitation program. No period of revocation arising out of [VTL § 1193(2)(b)(4), (5), (6) or (7)] may be set aside by the commissioner for the reason that such person was a participant in the alcohol and drug rehabilitation program set forth in [VTL § 1196].

In addition, VTL § 1194(2)(d)(3) expressly exempts *any* offender revoked for a chemical test refusal from this rule:

Effect of rehabilitation program. No period of revocation arising out of [VTL § 1194] may be set aside by the commissioner for the reason that such person was a participant in the alcohol and drug rehabilitation program set forth in [VTL § 1196].

See also VTL § 1196(5); 15 NYCRR § 134.10(b); 15 NYCRR § 136.3(a).

Nonetheless, DMV will allow the person to continue to use his or her conditional license pending the expiration of the revocation period (provided that the person does not violate any of the conditions of the conditional license). *See generally* VTL § 1196(7)(e), (f); 15 NYCRR § 134.9(d)(1). In addition:

> [I]f any such person's conditional license is revoked and such person has completed a rehabilitation program as provided for in [15 NYCRR § 134.10], time served shall be credited toward the remaining portion of the revocation period, calculated from the effective date of the order of revocation which resulted in the issuance of the conditional license, to the date of the violation which resulted in the revocation of the conditional license.

15 NYCRR § 134.9(d)(2).

§ 15:26 Successful DDP completion *does* permit early termination of VTL § 1192-a suspension

Research References

West's Key Number Digest, Automobiles ⚷144.1(1)

As the previous section demonstrates, the relevant statutes prohibit an underage offender whose driver's license is revoked for a violation of VTL § 1192 from reaping the benefit of early license reinstatement provided by VTL § 1196(5). The same rule was apparently intended to apply to underage offenders whose driver's licenses are suspended for 6 months for a violation of VTL § 1192-a. However, when the Zero Tolerance laws were enacted no provision analogous to VTL § 1193(2)(b)(9) was included, and no amendment was made to VTL § 1196(5).

As a result, successful completion of the DDP *does* allow an underage offender suspended for a violation of VTL § 1192-a to apply for early reinstatement of his or her full driving privileges (which would have the effect of shortening the suspension/conditional license time from six months to approximately two months).

§ 15:27 Suspension pending prosecution—Special rules applicable to underage offenders

Research References

West's Key Number Digest, Automobiles ⚷144.1(1)

In addition to the usual suspension pending prosecution laws, *see* §§ 45:1 et seq., *infra*, VTL § 1193(2)(e)(7)(a-1) applies to drivers under 18 years of age who do not yet possess a full class D or class M driver's license. A class D license is a regular, noncommercial driver's license. A class M license is a motorcycle driver's license. VTL § 1193(2)(e)(7)(a-1) provides:

A court shall suspend a class DJ or MJ learner's permit or a class DJ or MJ driver's license, pending prosecution, of any person who has been charged with a violation of [VTL § 1192(1), (2) and/or (3)].

The "J" designation pertains to a junior learner's permit or junior driver's license. A person between 16 and 18 years of age can apply for a junior permit/license. A class DJ or MJ driver's license can be converted to a class D or M driver's license if the holder is at least 17 years of age and has, among other things, successfully completed an approved high school or college driver education course. *See* 15 NYCRR § 2.5. At age 18, a valid class DJ or MJ driver's license automatically converts to a class D or M driver's license.

Notably, unlike the prompt suspension law for class D or M driver's license holders, VTL § 1193(2)(e)(7)(a-1) applies not only where the defendant is charged with VTL § 1192(2) and/or (3), but also where he or she is charged with VTL § 1192(1) (*i.e.*, DWAI). In addition, unlike the prompt suspension law for class D or M driver's license holders, no chemical test result is required. Thus, VTL § 1193(2)(e)(7)(a-1) can be applied to chemical test refusal cases and to cases where the chemical test results are not yet available.

VTL § 1193(2)(e)(7)(b) provides that "the suspension occurring under [VTL § 1193(2)(e)(7)(a-1)] shall occur immediately after the holder's first appearance before the court on the charge which shall, whenever possible, be the next regularly scheduled session of the court after the arrest or at the conclusion of all proceedings required for the arraignment."

In terms of due process, in order to impose a suspension under VTL § 1193(2)(e)(7)(1-a), the court must make two findings. First, the court "must find that the accusatory instrument conforms to the requirements of [CPL §] 100.40." VTL § 1193(2)(e)(7)(b). CPL § 100.40 sets forth the facial sufficiency requirements for local criminal court accusatory instruments. Second, the court must find that "there exists reasonable cause to believe either that":

(a) the holder operated a motor vehicle while such holder had 0.08 of one percent or more by weight of alcohol in his or her blood as was shown by chemical analysis of such person's blood, breath, urine, or saliva, made pursuant to the provisions of [VTL § 1194]; or

(b) *the person was the holder of a class DJ or MJ learner's permit or a class DJ or MJ driver's license and operated a motor vehicle while such holder was in violation of [VTL § 1192(1), (2) and/or (3)].* VTL § 1193(2)(e)(7)(b) (emphasis added).

If such *tentative* findings are made, the statute provides that "the holder shall be entitled to an opportunity to make a statement regarding these two issues and to present evidence tending to rebut the court's findings." VTL § 1193(2)(e)(7)(b). In addition, the additional procedural due process requirements set forth in the Court of Appeals' decision in *Pringle v. Wolfe*, 88 N.Y.2d 426, 646 N.Y.S.2d 82 (1996), apply. *See* § 45:3, *infra*.

§ 15:28 Suspension pending prosecution is *not* applicable to Zero Tolerance laws

Research References

West's Key Number Digest, Automobiles ⊗144.1(1)

VTL § 1194-a(1)(b) provides that "[u]nless otherwise provided by law, the license or permit to drive or any non-resident operating privilege of such person shall *not* be suspended or revoked prior to the scheduled date for [a Zero Tolerance law] hearing." (Emphasis added).

Similarly, in a Zero Tolerance law chemical test refusal case there is no prehearing license suspension. *See* § 15:55, *infra*.

§ 15:29 Zero Tolerance laws—Generally

Research References

West's Key Number Digest, Automobiles ⊗144.1(1.11), 332

For purposes of the sections that follow, the phrase "Zero Tolerance law" refers to VTL § 1192-a, the phrase "Zero Tolerance laws" refers to VTL §§ 1192-a and 1194-a, and the phrase "Zero Tolerance refusal" refers to a Zero Tolerance law chemical test refusal.

§ 15:30 Zero Tolerance laws—Who can lawfully be requested to submit to a chemical test?

Research References

West's Key Number Digest, Automobiles ⊗144.1(1.11), 332

Where a police officer has reasonable grounds to believe that a person under the age of 21 has been operating a motor vehicle in violation of VTL § 1192, VTL § 1194(2)(a)(1) and (2) sets forth the circumstances pursuant to which such person can properly be requested to submit to a chemical test.

Where a police officer does *not* have reasonable grounds to believe that a person under the age of 21 has been operating a motor vehicle in violation of VTL § 1192, but nonetheless has reasonable grounds to believe that the person has been operating a motor vehicle after having consumed alcohol in violation of VTL § 1192-a (*i.e.*, where a police officer has reasonable grounds to believe that a minor has been drinking, but is neither impaired nor intoxicated), VTL § 1194(2)(a) provides, in pertinent part:

2. Chemical tests. (a) When authorized. Any person who operates a motor vehicle in this state shall be deemed to have given consent to a chemical test of one or more of the following: breath, blood, urine, or saliva, for the purpose of determining the alcoholic and/or drug content of the blood provided that such test is administered by or at the direction of a police officer with respect to a chemical test of breath, urine, or saliva or, with respect to a chemical test of blood, at the direction of a police officer:

    (1) . . . having reasonable grounds to believe such person to have been operating in violation of [VTL § 1192-a] and within two hours after the stop of such person for any such violation, * * *

    (3) for the purposes of [VTL § 1194(2)(a)], "reasonable grounds" to believe that a person has been operating a motor vehicle after having consumed alcohol in violation of [VTL § 1192-a] shall be determined by viewing the totality of circumstances surrounding the incident which, when taken together, indicate that the operator was driving in violation of such subdivision. Such circumstances may include any visible or behavioral indication of alcohol consumption by the operator, the existence of an open container containing or having contained an alcoholic beverage in or around the vehicle driven by the operator, or any other evidence surrounding the circumstances of the incident which indicates that the operator has been operating a motor vehicle after having consumed alcohol at the time of the incident.

VTL § 1194(2)(a)(1), (3).

In such a situation, the motorist cannot be arrested, but "may be temporarily detained by the police solely for the purpose of requesting or administering [a] chemical test." VTL § 1194(2)(a)(4). *See also* § 15:31, *infra.*

§ 15:31   Minor suspected of violating Zero Tolerance law cannot be arrested

Research References

West's Key Number Digest, Automobiles ⊙⟶332

Where a police officer does not have reasonable grounds to believe that a person under the age of 21 has been operating a motor vehicle in violation of VTL § 1192, but nonetheless has reasonable grounds to believe that the person has been operating a motor vehicle after having consumed alcohol in violation of VTL § 1192-a (*i.e.*, where a police officer has reasonable grounds to believe that a minor has been drinking, but is neither impaired nor intoxicated), VTL § 1194(2)(a)(4) provides that:

[N]otwithstanding any other provision of law to the contrary, no person under the age of [21] shall be arrested for an alleged violation of [VTL § 1192-a]. However, a person under the age of [21] for whom a chemical test is authorized pursuant to [VTL § 1194(2)(a)] may be temporarily detained by the police solely for the purpose of requesting or administering such chemical test whenever arrest without a warrant for a petty offense would be authorized in accordance with the provisions of [CPL § 140.10] or [VTL § 1194(1)(a)].

§ 15:32 Zero Tolerance law—Procedure where chemical test result is obtained

Research References

West's Key Number Digest, Automobiles ☞144.2(.5), 332

Where a chemical test result between 0.02% and 0.07% is obtained and the underage offender will be charged with violating VTL § 1192-a (and will *not* be charged with violating any subdivision of VTL § 1192 arising out of the same incident):

> [T]he police officer who administered the test shall forward a report of the results of such test to [DMV] within [24] hours of the time when such results are available in a manner prescribed by the commissioner, and the operator shall be given a hearing notice as provided in [VTL § 1194-a(1-a)], to appear before a hearing officer in the county where the chemical test was administered, or in an adjoining county under such circumstances as prescribed by the commissioner, on a date to be established in accordance with a schedule promulgated by the commissioner.

VTL § 1194-a(1)(a). Note that in such a case the underage offender will *not* be brought or sent to Court. Rather, everything will be handled at DMV.

§ 15:33 Zero Tolerance law—Chemical test result report—Verification

Research References

West's Key Number Digest, Automobiles ☞144.2(.5), 332

Where a chemical test result between 0.02% and 0.07% is obtained and the underage offender will be charged with violating VTL § 1192-a, "the police officer who administered the test shall forward a report of the results of such test to [DMV] within [24] hours of the time when such results are available." VTL § 1194-a(1)(a). "The report of the police officer shall be verified by having the report sworn to, or by affixing to such report a form notice that false statements made therein are punishable as a class A misdemeanor pursuant to [PL § 210.45] and such form notice together with the subscription of the deponent shall constitute verification of the report." VTL § 1194-a(1)(a).

§ 15:34 Zero Tolerance law hearings—Generally

Research References

West's Key Number Digest, Automobiles ☞144.2(.5), 332

VTL § 1194-a(1)(b) provides for a Due Process hearing prior to the imposition of sanctions for a violation of VTL § 1192-a:

Every person under the age of [21] who is alleged to have operated a motor vehicle after having consumed alcohol as set forth in [VTL § 1192-a], and who is not charged with violating any subdivision of [VTL § 1192] arising out of the same incident, is entitled to a hearing before a hearing officer in accordance with the provisions of [VTL § 1194-a].

§ 15:35   Zero Tolerance law hearing—Waiver of right to hearing

Research References

West's Key Number Digest, Automobiles ☞144.2(.5), 332

VTL § 1194-a(1)(c) provides that:

Any person may waive the right to a hearing under [VTL § 1194-a(1)], in a form and manner prescribed by the commissioner, and may enter an admission of guilt, in person or by mail, to the charge of operating a motor vehicle in violation of [VTL § 1192-a]. Such admission of guilt shall have the same force and effect as a finding of guilt entered following a hearing conducted pursuant to [VTL § 1194-a(1)].

See also 15 NYCRR § 127.7(f)(7).

§ 15:36   Zero Tolerance law hearing—Hearing notice

Research References

West's Key Number Digest, Automobiles ☞144.2(.5), 332

VTL § 1194-a(1-a) sets forth the requirements for a Zero Tolerance law hearing notice:

Hearing notice. The hearing notice issued to an operator pursuant to [VTL § 1194-a(1)] shall be in a form as prescribed by the commissioner. In addition to containing information concerning the time, date, and location of the hearing, and such other information as the commissioner deems appropriate, such hearing notice shall also contain the following information: the date, time, and place of the offense charged; the procedures for requesting an adjournment of a scheduled hearing as provided in [VTL § 1194-a], the operator's right to a hearing conducted pursuant to [VTL § 1194-a] and the right to waive such hearing and plead guilty, either in person or by mail, to the offense charged.

§ 15:37   Zero Tolerance law hearing—Time of hearing

Research References

West's Key Number Digest, Automobiles ☞144.2(.5), 332

A Zero Tolerance law hearing:

[S]hall occur within [30] days of, but not less than [48] hours from, the date that the chemical test was administered, provided, however, where the commissioner determines, based upon the availability of hearing officers and the anticipated volume of hearings at a particular location, that the scheduling of such hearing within [30] days would impair the timely scheduling or conducting of other hearings pursuant to this chapter, such hearing shall be scheduled at the next hearing date for such particular location.

VTL § 1194-a(1)(a).

§ 15:38   Zero Tolerance law hearing—Prehearing discovery

Research References

West's Key Number Digest, Automobiles ⌾144.2(.5), 332

In sharp contrast with the rules of discovery applicable to a VTL § 1192 prosecution, in a Zero Tolerance law case the motorist must be provided with the discovery set forth in CPL § 240.20(1)(c) and (k), *without a demand therefor*, at the time that the motorist is provided with the hearing notice:

When providing the operator with [the] hearing notice, the police officer shall also give to the operator, and shall, prior to the commencement of the hearing, provide to [DMV], copies of the following reports, documents and materials: any written report or document, or portion thereof, concerning a physical examination, a scientific test or experiment, including the most recent record of inspection, or calibration or repair of machines or instruments utilized to perform such scientific tests or experiments and the certification certificate, if any, held by the operator of the machine or instrument, which tests or examinations were made by or at the request or direction of a public servant engaged in law enforcement activity.

VTL § 1194-a(1)(a).

§ 15:39   Zero Tolerance law hearing—Failure of motorist to appear at hearing

Research References

West's Key Number Digest, Automobiles ⌾144.2(.5), 332

VTL § 1194-a(1)(c) provides that:

Unless an adjournment of the hearing date has been granted, upon the operator's failure to appear for a scheduled hearing, the commissioner shall suspend the license or permit to drive or non-resident operating privilege until the operator petitions the commissioner and a rescheduled hearing is conducted, provided, however, the commissioner shall restore such person's license or permit to drive or non-resident operating privilege if such rescheduled hearing is adjourned at the request of a person other than the operator.

See also 15 NYCRR § 127.7(f)(6).

Critically, "[i]f the respondent fails to appear at a hearing, the hearing shall be rescheduled and no testimony shall be taken in the respondent's absence." 15 NYCRR § 127.7(f)(8). *Cf.* 15 NYCRR § 127.9(b). *In other words, if the motorist fails to appear for (or to waive) a Zero Tolerance law hearing, the motorist's driving privileges will be suspended indefinitely until he or she petitions DMV and a rescheduled hearing is conducted (or a hearing waiver is received by DMV).*

§ 15:40 Zero Tolerance law hearing—Failure of police officer to appear at hearing

Research References

West's Key Number Digest, Automobiles ⊂⇒144.2(.5), 332

If the arresting officer fails to appear at a DMV chemical test refusal hearing on the first scheduled hearing date, the hearing will be adjourned. 15 NYCRR § 127.9(c). By contrast, "[i]f a police officer does not appear for a [Zero Tolerance law] hearing, the hearing officer shall have the authority to dismiss the charge." VTL § 1194-a(1)(c). *See also* 15 NYCRR § 127.7(f)(7).

§ 15:41 Zero Tolerance law hearing—Requests for adjournments

Research References

West's Key Number Digest, Automobiles ⊂⇒144.2(.5), 332

VTL § 1194-a(1)(c) provides that:

Requests for adjournments shall be made and determined in accordance with regulations promulgated by the commissioner. If such a request by the operator for an adjournment is granted, the commissioner shall notify the operator of the rescheduled hearing, which shall be scheduled for the next hearing date. If a second or subsequent request by the operator for an adjournment is granted, the operator's license or permit to drive or non-resident operating privilege may be suspended pending the hearing at the time such adjournment is granted; provided, however, that the records of [DMV] or the evidence already admitted furnishes reasonable grounds to believe such suspension is necessary to prevent continuing violations or a substantial traffic safety hazard; and provided further, that such hearing shall be scheduled for the next hearing date.

The relevant DMV regulations are found at 15 NYCRR § 127.7(f)(1) to (5):

Adjournments of hearings held under [VTL § 1194-a]. (1) Adjournments of hearings may only be granted by the hearing officer responsible for the particular hearing, by a supervisor of such hearing officer or by the Safety Hearing Bureau.

(2) It is [DMV's] general policy to grant a request for adjournment for good cause if such request is received at least [7] days prior to the scheduled date of hearing and if no prior requests for adjournment have been made. Notwithstanding this policy, requests for adjournments made more than [7] days prior to hearing may be denied by the hearing officer, or supervisor of the hearing office[r] or by the Safety Hearing Bureau. Grounds for such a denial include, but are not limited to, such a request being a second or subsequent request for adjournment, or where there is reason to believe such request is merely an attempt to delay the holding of a hearing, or where an adjournment will significantly affect the availability of other witnesses scheduled to testify.

(3) Any motorist or designated representative requesting an adjournment should obtain the name and title of the person granting such request. This information will be required in the event of any dispute as to whether an adjournment was in fact granted. Any request which is not specifically granted shall be deemed denied.

(4) Requests for adjournments within [7] days of a scheduled hearing must be made directly to the hearing officer. Such requests will generally not be granted, unless the initial hearing was scheduled less than [7] days from the date on which respondent was first notified of the hearing by the police officer.

(5) A temporary suspension of a license, permit or privilege may be imposed at the time a second or subsequent adjournment requested by the respondent is granted provided that the records of [DMV] or the evidence already admitted furnishes reasonable grounds to believe such suspension is necessary to prevent continuing violations or a substantial traffic safety hazard.

§ 15:42   Zero Tolerance law hearing—Rights of motorist

Research References

West's Key Number Digest, Automobiles ⊂⊃144.2(.5), 332

VTL § 1194-a(1)(b)(ii) affords the motorist the following rights at a Zero Tolerance law hearing:

(a) The right to be present at the hearing;

(b) The right to be represented by attorney, or in the hearing officer's discretion, by any other person the operator chooses;

(c) The right to receive and review discovery materials as provided in VTL § 1194-a(1);

(d) The right not to testify;

(e) The right to present evidence and witnesses in his own behalf;

(f) The right to cross-examine adverse witnesses; and

(g) The right to appeal from an adverse determination in accordance with VTL Article 3-A.

See generally State Administrative Procedure Act (SAPA).

While the motorist may be permitted to be represented by a nonattorney, "[a]ny person representing the operator must conform to the standards of conduct required of attorneys appearing before state courts, and failure to conform to these standards will be grounds for declining to permit his continued appearance in the hearing." VTL § 1194-a(1)(b)(ii).

§ 15:43   Zero Tolerance law hearing—Hearing procedures

Research References

West's Key Number Digest, Automobiles ⊕144.2(.5), 332

VTL § 1194-a(1)(b)(iii) provides that Zero Tolerance law hearings are to be conducted in accordance with both (a) VTL § 1194-a(1), and (b) the provisions applicable to the adjudication of traffic infractions pursuant to the following provisions of 15 NYCRR Part 124:

    1. 15 NYCRR § 124.1(b) regarding the opening statement;

    2. 15 NYCRR § 124.2(b) regarding the rights to representation and to remain silent; and

    3. 15 NYCRR § 124.4(a) to (e) regarding the conduct of the hearing, procedure, and recusal.

"[H]owever, . . . nothing contained in [VTL § 1194-a(1)(b)(iii)] shall be deemed to preclude a hearing officer from changing the order of a hearing conducted pursuant to [VTL § 1194-a(1)] as justice may require and for good cause shown." VTL § 1194-a(1)(b)(iii).

See also 15 NYCRR § 127.5(e).

15 NYCRR § 124.1(b) provides that *the ALJ* must make an "opening statement" informing motorists (a) of the rights set forth in § 15:42, *supra*, and (b) of hearing and adjournment procedures, including (i) the order in which the hearing will be conducted, and (ii) that the police officer bears the burden of proving the motorist's guilt by clear and convincing evidence.

15 NYCRR § 124.2(b) reiterates the rights to representation and to remain silent set forth in § 15:42, *supra*. It also provides that *"[n]o negative inference will be drawn from the exercise of the motorist's right not to testify."* (Emphasis added).

15 NYCRR § 124.4 provides that:

    (a) The administrative law judge will call the police officer, the motorist, and the attorney or other representative, if any, to the dais. After the charge is read, the police officer will testify. The burden of proving the charge rests with the police officer, who has the obligation to present evidence which is sufficient to establish each material element of the charge by clear and convincing evidence. Other testimony in support of the charge may then be given.

(b) *The administrative law judge may question the police officer for the purpose of clarifying evidence already presented; leading questions addressed to material elements of the charge which have been omitted from the police officer's testimony may not be asked.*

(c) After the people's case has been presented, the motorist may then testify on his or her own behalf and call witnesses. Any person who testifies may be examined by the administrative law judge and cross-examined by the adverse party. All testimony shall be given under oath or affirmation. The administrative law judge may exclude any witness, except the motorist or police officer, during the testimony of another person. Documentary evidence may be introduced by any party.

(d) When the administrative law judge has received all of the evidence, the police officer and motorist or his or her representative may make a closing statement. The administrative law judge will then consider all the evidence in the record and announce whether or not the charge has been sustained by clear and convincing evidence.

(e) The motorist may request recusal of a presiding administrative law judge. The request and the reason for it must be stated to the presiding administrative law judge at the commencement of the hearing or as soon after the beginning as the motorist receives information which forms the basis for such request. An administrative law judge's denial of a request for recusal is appealable provided a hearing determination is subsequently made which is appealable by the requestor to the Traffic Violations Appeals Board pursuant to [VTL Article 2-A]. (Emphasis added).

§ 15:44   Zero Tolerance law hearing—Rules of evidence

Research References

West's Key Number Digest, Automobiles ☞144.2(.5), 332

VTL § 1194-a(1)(b)(iv) provides that the rules governing the receipt of evidence in a court of law shall not apply in a Zero Tolerance law hearing except as follows:

(1) On the merits of the charge, and whether or not a party objects, the hearing officer shall exclude from consideration the following:

(a) A privileged communication;

(b) Evidence which, for constitutional reasons, would not be admissible in a court of law;

(c) Evidence of prior misconduct, incompetency or illness (except where such evidence would be admissible in a court of law); and

(d) Evidence which is irrelevant or immaterial; and

(2) No negative inference shall be drawn from the operator's exercising the right not to testify. *See also* 15 NYCRR § 124.5 (same).

§ 15:45   Zero Tolerance law hearing—Issues to be determined at hearing

Research References

West's Key Number Digest, Automobiles ⬳144.2(.5), 332

VTL § 1194-a(1)(b)(i) provides that a Zero Tolerance law hearing shall be limited to the following issues:

(1) Did such person operate the motor vehicle;

(2) Was a valid request to submit to a chemical test made by the police officer in accordance with the provisions of VTL § 1194;

(3) Was such person less than 21 years of age at the time of operation of the motor vehicle;

(4) Was the chemical test properly administered in accordance with the provisions of VTL § 1194;

(5) Did the test find that such person had driven after having consumed alcohol as defined in VTL § 1192-a; and

(6) Did the police officer make a lawful stop of such person.

§ 15:46   Zero Tolerance law hearing—Burden of proof

Research References

West's Key Number Digest, Automobiles ⬳144.2(.5), 332

At a Zero Tolerance law hearing, "[t]he burden of proof shall be on the police officer to prove each of the[] issues [set forth in the previous section] by clear and convincing evidence." VTL § 1194-a(1)(b)(i).

§ 15:47   Zero Tolerance law hearing—DMV action where evidence establishes all six issues at hearing

Research References

West's Key Number Digest, Automobiles ⬳144.2(.5), 332

"If, after such hearing, the hearing officer, acting on behalf of the commissioner, finds all of the issues set forth in [VTL § 1194-a(1)] in the affirmative, the hearing officer shall suspend or revoke the license or permit to drive or non-resident operating privilege of such person in accordance with the time periods set forth in [VTL § 1193(2)]." VTL § 1194-a(1)(b)(v). *See also* §§ 15:15 and 15:16, *supra*.

§ 15:48   Zero Tolerance law hearing—DMV action where evidence fails to establish all six issues at hearing

Research References

West's Key Number Digest, Automobiles ⬤─144.2(.5), 332

"If, after such hearing, the hearing officer, acting on behalf of the commissioner, finds any of said issues in the negative, the hearing officer must find that the operator did not drive after having consumed alcohol." VTL § 1194-a(1)(b)(v).

§ 15:49   Zero Tolerance law hearing—Right to appeal adverse decision

Research References

West's Key Number Digest, Automobiles ⬤─144.2(.5), 332

"A person who has had a license or permit to drive or nonresident operating privilege suspended or revoked pursuant to the provisions of [VTL § 1194-a] may appeal the finding of the hearing officer in accordance with the provisions of [VTL Article 3-A (*i.e.*, VTL §§ 260 to 63)]." VTL § 1194-a(1)(b)(vi). *See also* § 41:68, *infra*.

§ 15:50   Zero Tolerance laws—Civil penalty

Research References

West's Key Number Digest, Automobiles ⬤─144.2(.5), 332

A person who is found guilty of either (a) a violation of the Zero Tolerance law, or (b) a Zero Tolerance law chemical test refusal, is not only subject to the suspension or revocation of his or her driver's license, permit to drive, or nonresident operating privilege—the person "shall also be liable for a civil penalty in the amount of [$125]." VTL § 1194-a(2).

In addition, where the person's license or operating privilege has been *suspended* for a violation of VTL § 1192-a, the person must also pay a suspension termination fee of $100 before his or her driving privileges will be reinstated. VTL § 503(2)(j).

Similarly, where the person's license has been *revoked* for a violation of VTL § 1192-a, the person must also pay a reapplication fee of $100 (unless the person has been issued a conditional or restricted use license). VTL § 503(2)(h). If the person has an out-of-state license, the reapplication fee is $25. VTL § 503(2)(i).

§ 15:51   Zero Tolerance refusals—Procedure upon detention—Zero Tolerance Report of Refusal

Research References

West's Key Number Digest, Automobiles ⬤─144.2(.5), 332

Where a person has been lawfully detained for a suspected violation of VTL § 1192-a, VTL § 1194(2)(b)(1) provides, in pertinent part:

> Report of Refusal. (1) If: (A) such person having been placed under arrest; or (B) after a breath [screening] test indicates the presence of alcohol in the person's system; or *(C) with regard to a person under the age of [21], there are reasonable grounds to believe that such person has been operating a motor vehicle after having consumed alcohol in violation of [VTL § 1192-a]*; and having thereafter been requested to submit to such chemical test and having been informed that the person's license or permit to drive and any non-resident operating privilege [a] shall be immediately suspended and subsequently revoked, or, [b] *for operators under the age of [21] for whom there are reasonable grounds to believe that such operator has been operating a motor vehicle after having consumed alcohol in violation of [VTL § 1192-a], shall be revoked* for refusal to submit to such chemical test or any portion thereof, whether or not the person is found guilty of the charge for which such person is arrested *or detained*, refuses to submit to such chemical test or any portion thereof, unless a court order has been granted pursuant to [VTL § 1194(3)], the test shall not be given and a written report of such refusal shall be immediately made by the police officer before whom such refusal was made.

(Emphases added).

§ 15:52   Zero Tolerance Report of Refusal—Verification

Research References

West's Key Number Digest, Automobiles ☞144.2(.5), 332

A Zero Tolerance Report of Refusal "may be verified by having the report sworn to, or by affixing to such report a form notice that false statements made therein are punishable as a class A misdemeanor pursuant to [PL § 210.45] and such form notice together with the subscription of the deponent shall constitute a verification of the report." VTL § 1194(2)(b)(1).

§ 15:53   Zero Tolerance Report of Refusal—Contents

Research References

West's Key Number Digest, Automobiles ☞144.2(.5), 332

The officer's Zero Tolerance Report of Refusal must "set forth reasonable grounds to believe [1] . . . such detained person under the age of [21] had been driving in violation of . . . [VTL § 1192-a], [2] that said person had refused to submit to such chemical test, and [3] that no chemical test was administered pursuant to the requirements of [VTL § 1194(3)]." VTL § 1194(2)(b)(2).

§ 15:54   Zero Tolerance Report of Refusal—To whom is it submitted?

Research References

West's Key Number Digest, Automobiles ☞144.2(.5), 332

[I]n the case of a person under the age of [21], for whom a test was authorized pursuant to the provisions of [VTL § 1194(2)(a)(2) or (3)], and who has not been placed under arrest for a violation of any of the provisions of [VTL § 1192], [the officer's Zero Tolerance Report of Refusal] shall be forwarded to the commissioner within [48] hours in a manner to be prescribed by the commissioner, and all subsequent proceedings with regard to refusal to submit to such chemical test by such person shall be as set forth in [VTL § 1194-a(3)].

VTL § 1194(2)(b)(2).

§ 15:55   Zero Tolerance refusals—There is no prehearing license suspension

Research References

West's Key Number Digest, Automobiles ☞144.2(.5), 332

At arraignment in a "regular" DWI chemical test refusal case, the court is required to temporarily suspend the defendant's driving privileges pending the outcome of a DMV refusal hearing. *See* VTL § 1194(2)(b)(3) ("For persons placed under arrest for a violation of any subdivision of [VTL § 1192], the license or permit to drive and any non-resident operating privilege shall, upon the basis of such written report, be temporarily suspended by the court without notice pending the determination of a hearing as provided in [VTL § 1194(2)(c)]"). *See also* 15 NYCRR § 139.3(a).

By contrast, in a Zero Tolerance refusal case there is no prehearing license suspension (nor is there an arrest and/or an arraignment).

§ 15:56   Zero Tolerance refusal hearings—Generally

Research References

West's Key Number Digest, Automobiles ☞144.2(.5), 332

VTL § 1194-a(3)(a) provides for a Due Process hearing prior to the imposition of sanctions for a Zero Tolerance law chemical test refusal:

Any person under the age of [21] who is suspected of operating a motor vehicle after having consumed alcohol in violation of [VTL § 1192-a], and who is not charged with violating any subdivision of [VTL § 1192] arising out of the same incident, and who has been

requested to submit to a chemical test pursuant to [VTL
§ 1194(2)(a)] and after having been informed that his license or
permit to drive and any non-resident operating privilege shall be
revoked for refusal to submit to such chemical test or any portion
thereof, whether or not there is a finding of driving after having
consumed alcohol, and such person refuses to submit to such chemical test or any portion thereof, shall be entitled to a hearing in accordance with a schedule promulgated by the commissioner.

§ 15:57   Zero Tolerance refusal hearing—Waiver of right to hearing

Research References

West's Key Number Digest, Automobiles ☞144.2(.5), 332

VTL § 1194-a(3)(b) provides that "[a]ny person may waive the
right to a hearing under this subdivision." *See also* 15 NYCRR
§ 127.7(f)(7).

§ 15:58   Zero Tolerance refusals—Police officer must provide motorist with waiver form and notice of refusal hearing date

Research References

West's Key Number Digest, Automobiles ☞144.2(.5), 332

VTL § 1194(2)(b)(4) provides that:

The . . . police officer, in the case of a person under the age of [21]
alleged to be driving after having consumed alcohol, shall provide
such person with a scheduled hearing date, a waiver form, and
such other information as may be required by the commissioner. If
a hearing, as provided for in . . . [VTL § 1194-a(3)], is waived by
such person, the commissioner shall immediately revoke the license,
permit, or non-resident operating privilege, as of the date of receipt
of such waiver in accordance with the provisions of [VTL
§ 1194(2)(d)].

§ 15:59   Zero Tolerance refusal hearing—Time of hearing

Research References

West's Key Number Digest, Automobiles ☞144.2(.5), 332

A Zero Tolerance law chemical test refusal hearing:

[S]hall occur within [30] days of, but not less than [48] hours from,
the date of such refusal, provided, however, where the commissioner determines, based upon the availability of hearing officers
and the anticipated volume of hearings at a particular location,
that the scheduling of such hearing within [30] days would impair
the timely scheduling or conducting of other hearings pursuant to
this chapter, such hearing shall be scheduled at the next hearing
date for such particular location.

§ 15:60   Zero Tolerance refusal hearing—Failure of motorist to appear at hearing

Research References

West's Key Number Digest, Automobiles ⊙144.2(.5), 332

VTL § 1194-a(3)(b) provides that:

Unless an adjournment of the hearing date has been granted, upon the operator's failure to appear for a scheduled hearing, the commissioner shall suspend the license or permit to drive or non-resident operating privilege until the operator petitions the commissioner and a rescheduled hearing is conducted, provided, however, the commissioner shall restore such person's license or permit to drive or non-resident operating privilege if such rescheduled hearing is adjourned at the request of a person other than the operator.

See also 15 NYCRR § 127.7(f)(6).

Critically, "[i]f the respondent fails to appear at a hearing, the hearing shall be rescheduled and no testimony shall be taken in the respondent's absence." 15 NYCRR § 127.7(f)(8). *Cf.* 15 NYCRR § 127.9(b). *In other words, if the motorist fails to appear for (or to waive) a Zero Tolerance refusal hearing, the motorist's driving privileges will be suspended indefinitely until he or she petitions DMV and a rescheduled hearing is conducted (or a hearing waiver is received by DMV).*

§ 15:61   Zero Tolerance refusal hearing—Failure of police officer to appear at hearing

Research References

West's Key Number Digest, Automobiles ⊙144.2(.5), 332

If the arresting officer fails to appear at a "regular" DMV chemical test refusal hearing on the first scheduled hearing date, the hearing will be adjourned. 15 NYCRR § 127.9(c). By contrast, "[i]f a police officer does not appear for a [Zero Tolerance refusal] hearing, the hearing officer shall have the authority to dismiss the charge." VTL § 1194-a(3)(b). *See also* 15 NYCRR § 127.7(f)(7).

§ 15:62   Zero Tolerance refusal hearing—Requests for adjournments

Research References

West's Key Number Digest, Automobiles ⊙144.2(.5), 332

VTL § 1194-a(3)(b) provides that:

Requests for adjournments shall be made and determined in accordance with regulations promulgated by the commissioner. If such a request by the operator for an adjournment is granted, the commissioner shall notify the operator of the rescheduled hearing, which shall be scheduled for the next hearing date. If a second or subsequent request by the operator for an adjournment is granted, the operator's license or permit to drive or non-resident operating privilege may be suspended pending the hearing at the time such adjournment is granted; provided, however, that the records of [DMV] or the evidence already admitted furnishes reasonable grounds to believe such suspension is necessary to prevent continuing violations or a substantial traffic safety hazard; and provided further, that such hearing shall be scheduled for the next hearing date.

The relevant DMV regulations are found at 15 NYCRR § 127.7(f)(1) to (5):

Adjournments of hearings held under [VTL § 1194-a]. (1) Adjournments of hearings may only be granted by the hearing officer responsible for the particular hearing, by a supervisor of such hearing officer or by the Safety Hearing Bureau.

(2) It is [DMV's] general policy to grant a request for adjournment for good cause if such request is received at least [7] days prior to the scheduled date of hearing and if no prior requests for adjournment have been made. Notwithstanding this policy, requests for adjournments made more than [7] days prior to hearing may be denied by the hearing officer, or supervisor of the hearing office[r] or by the Safety Hearing Bureau. Grounds for such a denial include, but are not limited to, such a request being a second or subsequent request for adjournment, or where there is reason to believe such request is merely an attempt to delay the holding of a hearing, or where an adjournment will significantly affect the availability of other witnesses scheduled to testify.

(3) Any motorist or designated representative requesting an adjournment should obtain the name and title of the person granting such request. This information will be required in the event of any dispute as to whether an adjournment was in fact granted. Any request which is not specifically granted shall be deemed denied.

(4) Requests for adjournments within [7] days of a scheduled hearing must be made directly to the hearing officer. Such requests will generally not be granted, unless the initial hearing was scheduled less than [7] days from the date on which respondent was first notified of the hearing by the police officer.

(5) A temporary suspension of a license, permit or privilege may be imposed at the time a second or subsequent adjournment requested by the respondent is granted provided that the records of [DMV] or the evidence already admitted furnishes reasonable grounds to believe such suspension is necessary to prevent continuing violations or a substantial traffic safety hazard.

§ 15:63   Zero Tolerance refusal hearing—Issues to be determined at hearing

Research References

West's Key Number Digest, Automobiles ⚖144.2(.5), 332

VTL § 1194-a(3)(c) provides that a Zero Tolerance refusal hearing shall be limited to the following issues:

(1) Was a valid request to submit to a chemical test made by the police officer in accordance with the provisions of VTL § 1194;

(2) Was such person given sufficient warning, in clear or unequivocal language, prior to such refusal that such refusal to submit to such chemical test or any portion thereof, would result in the revocation of such person's license or permit to drive or nonresident operating privilege, whether or not such person is found to have operated a motor vehicle after having consumed alcohol;

(3) Did such person refuse to submit to such chemical test or any portion thereof;

(4) Did such person operate the motor vehicle;

(5) Was such person less than 21 years of age at the time of operation of the motor vehicle; and

(6) Did the police officer make a lawful stop of such person.

§ 15:64   Zero Tolerance refusal hearing—DMV action where evidence establishes all six issues at hearing

Research References

West's Key Number Digest, Automobiles ⚖144.2(.5), 332

"If, after such hearing, the hearing officer, acting on behalf of the commissioner, finds all of the issues in the affirmative, such hearing officer shall immediately revoke the license or permit to drive or any non-resident operating privilege in accordance with the provisions of [VTL § 1194(2)(d)]." VTL § 1194-a(3)(c). *See also* § 15:17, *supra*.

§ 15:65   Zero Tolerance refusal hearing—DMV action where evidence fails to establish all six issues at hearing

Research References

West's Key Number Digest, Automobiles ⚖144.2(.5), 332

"If, after such hearing, the hearing officer, acting on behalf of the commissioner, finds on any [1] said issue in the negative, the hearing officer shall not revoke the operator's license or permit to drive or non-resident operating privilege and shall immediately terminate any outstanding suspension of the operator's license, permit to drive or non-resident operating privilege arising from such refusal." VTL § 1194-a(3)(c).

§ 15:66 Zero Tolerance refusal hearing—Right to appeal adverse decision

Research References

West's Key Number Digest, Automobiles ⟋144.2(.5), 332

"A person who has had a license or permit to drive or non-resident operating privilege suspended or revoked pursuant to the provisions of [VTL § 1194-a] may appeal the findings of the hearing officer in accordance with the provisions of [VTL Article 3-A (*i.e.*, VTL §§ 260 to 63)]. VTL § 1194-a(3)(c). *See also* § 41:68, *infra*.

§ 15:67 Underage offenders and AUO

Research References

West's Key Number Digest, Automobiles ⟋326

Aggravated Unlicensed Operation of a Motor Vehicle (AUO) is a multistage offense, in that a person who commits AUO 2nd also, by definition, commits AUO 3rd; and a person who commits AUO 1st also, by definition, commits AUO 2nd. *See* VTL §§ 511(1)(a); 511(2)(a); 511(3)(a). Thus, an analysis of the elements of AUO 1st requires an analysis of the elements of AUO 2nd and AUO 3rd as well.

The elements of AUO 3rd are:

1. Operation;
2. motor vehicle;
3. public highway;
4. The defendant's driver's license or privilege to drive in New York is suspended, revoked, or otherwise withdrawn by DMV; and
5. The defendant knew or had reason to know that his or her driver's license or privilege to drive in New York had been suspended, revoked, or otherwise withdrawn by DMV. VTL § 511(1)(a).

The elements of AUO 2nd are:

1. AUO 3rd; and
2. Any of the following four additional elements:

   (a) A previous AUO conviction within the preceding 18 months; or

   (b) The underlying suspension/revocation resulted from (i) a chemical test refusal in violation of VTL § 1194, (ii) *a viola-*

tion of VTL § 1192-a (*i.e.*, the Zero Tolerance law), or (iii) a conviction of a violation of any of the provisions of VTL § 1192; or

(c) The underlying suspension was a suspension pending prosecution of a pending DWI charge; or

(d) The defendant had in effect three or more scofflaw suspensions imposed on at least three separate dates. VTL § 511(2)(a).

Notably, VTL § 511(2)(a)(ii) does not make reference to a Zero Tolerance law chemical test refusal revocation. Thus, while a VTL § 1192-a suspension/revocation elevates the crime of AUO 3rd to AUO 2nd, a Zero Tolerance law chemical test refusal revocation does not.

The elements of AUO 1st are:

1. AUO 2nd (involving aggravating element (b), (c), or (d) above); and

2. Either of the following two additional elements:

(a) DWAI, DWI or DWAI-Drugs in violation of VTL § 1192(1), (2), (3), (4), or (5); or

(b) The defendant had in effect 10 or more scofflaw suspensions imposed on at least 10 separate dates. VTL § 511(3)(a).

Since VTL § 511(3)(a)(i) does not make reference to VTL § 1192-a and/or VTL § 1194-a, an underage offender charged with a Zero Tolerance law violation cannot be charged with AUO 1st. *See also* §§ 13:1 et seq., *supra*.

§ 15:68 Youthful offenders—License suspension/ revocation applies

Research References

West's Key Number Digest, Automobiles ⬤⤳144.1(1)

Although "[a] youthful offender adjudication is not a judgment of conviction for a crime or any other offense," CPL § 720.35(1), where such adjudication results from a "conviction" of a violation of VTL § 1192, the license suspension/revocation which would normally arise from such conviction is still applicable. In this regard, VTL § 1193(2)(e)(4) provides:

Youthful offenders. Where a youth is determined to be a youthful offender, following a conviction of a violation of [VTL § 1192] for which a license suspension or revocation is mandatory, the court shall impose such suspension or revocation as is otherwise required upon conviction and, further, shall notify the commissioner of said suspension or revocation and its finding that said violator is granted youthful offender status as is required pursuant to [VTL § 513].

In such a case, the license suspension/revocation will appear on the person's DMV abstract, but the underlying "conviction" will not. In addition, VTL § 201(7) provides that:

> Where a judge or magistrate reports a license suspension or revocation to the commissioner, following a youthful offender determination, as is required by [VTL § 513], the commissioner shall not make available the finding of the court of youthful offender status to any person, or public or private agency.

§ 15:69 Youthful offenders—Mandatory surcharge applicable

Research References

West's Key Number Digest, Automobiles ⊙144.1(1)

In the past, the mandatory surcharge provisions of the law only applied where the defendant had been "convicted" of a crime or an offense. *See* VTL § 1809(1); VTL § 1809-c(1); PL § 60.35(1). In this regard, since "[a] youthful offender adjudication is not a judgment of conviction for a crime or any other offense," CPL § 720.35(1), a court could not properly impose a surcharge or crime victim assistance fee where a defendant was adjudicated a youthful offender. *See, e.g., People v. Floyd J.,* 61 N.Y.2d 895, 474 N.Y.S.2d 476 (1984); *People v. Michael "M",* 161 A.D.2d 911, 557 N.Y.S.2d 177 (3d Dep't 1990); *People v. Spencer,* 138 A.D.2d 976, 526 N.Y.S.2d 414 (4th Dep't 1988); *People v. Huertas,* 127 A.D.2d 475, 511 N.Y.S.2d 621 (1st Dep't 1987); *People v. Bain,* 126 A.D.2d 985, 511 N.Y.S.2d 801 (4th Dep't 1987).

However, effective February 16, 2005, VTL § 1809(10) and PL § 60.35(10) legislatively overruled these cases by expressly making mandatory surcharges and crime victim assistance fees applicable to youthful offender adjudications.

§ 15:70 Youthful offender adjudication cannot be used as predicate conviction for felony DWI charge

Research References

West's Key Number Digest, Automobiles ⊙332

A defendant who is charged with DWI or DWAI Drugs after having been "convicted" of a violation of VTL § 1192(2), (3), or (4) (or of Vehicular Assault in the 1st or 2nd degree or Vehicular Manslaughter in the 1st or 2nd degree) within the preceding 10 years can be charged with a class E felony. *See* VTL § 1193(1)(c)(i).

A defendant who is charged with DWI or DWAI Drugs after having been "convicted" of a violation of VTL § 1192(2), (3), or (4) (or of Vehicular Assault in the 1st or 2nd degree or Vehicular Manslaughter in the 1st or 2nd degree) *twice* within the preceding 10 years can be charged with a class D felony. *See* VTL § 1193(1)(c)(ii).

However, since "[a] youthful offender adjudication is not a judgment of conviction for a crime or any other offense," CPL § 720.35(1), a youthful offender adjudication cannot be used as a predicate conviction for a felony DWI charge. *See generally People v. Kuey*, 83 N.Y.2d 278, 283, 609 N.Y.S.2d 568, 570 (1994) ("Under New York law, . . . a felony conviction of a person given youthful offender status may not be used as a predicate for enhanced sentencing"); *People v. Lane*, 60 N.Y.2d 748, 751, 469 N.Y.S.2d 663, 665 (1983) ("a youthful offender adjudication may not be counted as a conviction for purposes of second offender status (see CPL 720.35, subd. 1)").

§ 15:71   Youthful offender adjudication cannot be used as predicate conviction for lifetime license revocation

Research References

West's Key Number Digest, Automobiles ⊘—144.1(1)

VTL § 1193(2)(c) provides for a lifetime license revocation "where a person has been twice *convicted* of a violation of [VTL § 1192(3), (4), or (4-a)] or of driving while intoxicated or of driving while ability is impaired by the use of a drug or of driving while ability is impaired by the combined influence of drugs or of alcohol and any drug or drugs where physical injury, as defined in [PL § 10.00], has resulted from such offense in each instance." (Emphasis added).

However, since "[a] youthful offender adjudication is not a judgment of conviction for a crime or any other offense," CPL § 720.35(1), a youthful offender adjudication cannot be used as a predicate conviction for such lifetime license revocation.

§ 15:72   Use of youthful offender or juvenile delinquency adjudication for impeachment purposes

Research References

West's Key Number Digest, Witnesses ⊘—337(8)

"It is . . . impermissible to use a youthful offender or juvenile delinquency adjudication as an impeachment weapon, because 'these adjudications are not convictions of a crime.' Nevertheless, the cross-examiner may bring out 'the illegal or immoral acts underlying such adjudications.' " *People v. Gray*, 84 N.Y.2d 709, 712, 622 N.Y.S.2d 223, 224 (1995) (citations omitted). *See also People v. Greer*, 42 N.Y.2d 170, 176, 397 N.Y.S.2d 613, 617 (1977) (same).

Part IV

ACCUSATORY INSTRUMENTS

Chapter 16

Local Criminal Court Accusatory Instruments

Research References

Westlaw Databases

Handling a Criminal Case in New York (HCCNY)

Treatises and Practice Aids

Muldoon, Handling a Criminal Case in New York §§ 3:1 to 3:114

KeyCite®: Cases and other legal materials listed in KeyCite Scope can be researched through the KeyCite service on Westlaw®. Use KeyCite to check citations for form, parallel references, prior and later history, and comprehensive citator information, including citations to other decisions and secondary materials.

---

§ 16:1   In general

Research References

West's Key Number Digest, Automobiles ⚖351.1

There are five different types of local criminal court accusatory instruments:
   (1) an information (a.k.a. a long form information);
   (2) a simplified information;
   (3) a prosecutor's information;
   (4) a misdemeanor complaint; and
   (5) a felony complaint.
This chapter defines each type of local criminal court accusatory instrument, sets forth the form, content, and sufficiency requirements thereof, and addresses common issues which arise with regard thereto.

§ 16:2   Commencement of action in local criminal court

Research References

West's Key Number Digest, Indictment and Information ⚖1, 4, 5, 41(2)

The commencement of an action in a local criminal court is governed by N.Y. Crim. Proc. Law § 100.05, which provides as follows:

> A criminal action is commenced by the filing of an accusatory instrument with a criminal court, and if more than one such instrument is filed in the course of the same criminal action, such action commences when the first of such instruments is filed. The only way in which a criminal action can be commenced in a superior court is by the filing therewith by a grand jury of an indictment against a defendant who has never been held by a local criminal court for the action of such grand jury with respect to any charge contained in such indictment. Otherwise, a criminal action can be commenced only in a local criminal court, by the filing therewith of a local criminal court accusatory instrument, namely:
>   (1) an information; or
>   (2) a simplified information; or
>   (3) a prosecutor's information; or
>   (4) a misdemeanor complaint; or
>   (5) a felony complaint.

See also N.Y. Crim. Proc. Law § 1.20(16) ("A criminal action . . . commences with the filing of an accusatory instrument against a defendant in a criminal court . . . ."); N.Y. Crim. Proc. Law § 1.20(17) ("A criminal action is commenced by the filing of an accusatory instrument against a defendant in a criminal court, and, if more than one accusatory instrument is filed in the course of the action, it commences when the first of such instruments is filed").

§ 16:3   Simplified information—Defined

Research References

West's Key Number Digest, Automobiles ☞351.1; Indictment and Information ☞45

There are three different types of simplified informations:
    (1) simplified traffic informations;
    (2) simplified parks informations; and
    (3) simplified environmental conservation informations.
Such accusatory instruments are defined as follows:

    (a) A "simplified traffic information" is a written accusation by a police officer or other public servant authorized by law to issue same, filed with a local criminal court, which charges a person with the commission of one or more traffic infractions and/or misdemeanors relating to traffic, and which, being in a brief or simplified form prescribed by the commissioner of motor vehicles, designates the offense or offenses charged but contains no factual allegations of an evidentiary nature supporting such charge or charges. It serves as a basis for commencement of a criminal action for such traffic offenses, alternative to the charging thereof by a regular information, and, under circumstances prescribed in [N.Y. Crim. Proc. Law §] 100.25, it may serve, either in whole or in part, as a basis for prosecution of such charges.

    (b) A "simplified parks information" is a written accusation by a police officer or other public servant authorized by law to issue same, filed with a local criminal court, which charges a person with the commission of one or more offenses, other than a felony, for which a uniform simplified parks information may be issued pursuant to the parks and recreation law and navigation law, and which being in a brief or simplified form prescribed by the commissioner of parks and recreation, designates the offense or offenses charged but contains no factual allegations of an evidentiary nature supporting such charge or charges. It serves as a basis for commencement of a criminal action for such offenses, alternative to the charging thereof by a regular information, and, under circumstances prescribed in [N.Y. Crim. Proc. Law §] 100.25, it may serve, either in whole or in part, as a basis for prosecution of such charges.

(c) A "simplified environmental conservation information" is a written accusation by a police officer or other public servant authorized by law to issue same, filed with a local criminal court, which charges a person with the commission of one or more offenses, other than a felony, for which a uniform simplified environmental conservation information may be issued pursuant to the environmental conservation law, and which being in a brief or simplified form prescribed by the commissioner of environmental conservation, designates the offense or offenses charged but contains no factual allegations of an evidentiary nature supporting such charge or charges. It serves as a basis for commencement of a criminal action for such offenses, alternative to the charging thereof by a regular information, and, under circumstances prescribed in [N.Y. Crim. Proc. Law §] 100.25, it may serve, either in whole or in part, as a basis for prosecution of such charges.

N.Y. Crim. Proc. Law § 100.10(2). *See also* N.Y. Crim. Proc. Law § 1.20(5).

N.Y. Crim. Proc. Law § 100.10(2) makes clear that a simplified traffic information can only be issued by "a police officer or other public servant authorized by law to issue same." *See also People v. Shapiro*, 61 N.Y.2d 880, 882, 474 N.Y.S.2d 470, 462 N.E.2d 1188 (1984) ("In view of the fact that the village constabulary was not lawfully constituted, the constable in this case had no authority to issue a uniform traffic information (CPL 100.10, subd. 2, par. [a]") (citation omitted); *People v. Wolf*, 166 Misc. 2d 372, 636 N.Y.S.2d 570 (App. Term 1995).

§ 16:4 Simplified information—Form and content

Research References

West's Key Number Digest, Automobiles ⬥351.1; Indictment and Information ⬥47

"A simplified information must be substantially in the form prescribed by the commissioner of motor vehicles, the commissioner of parks and recreation, or the commissioner of environmental conservation, as the case may be." N.Y. Crim. Proc. Law § 100.25(1). *See also* N.Y. Veh. & Traf. Law § 207; *People v. Nuccio*, 78 N.Y.2d 102, 104, 571 N.Y.S.2d 693, 694, 575 N.E.2d 111 (1991); *People v. Vierno*, 159 Misc. 2d 770, 606 N.Y.S.2d 557 (City Crim. Ct. 1993). The required form for simplified traffic informations is set forth at 15 NYCRR Part 91.

"The simplified information is a statutory creation designed to provide an uncomplicated form for handling the large volume of traffic infractions and petty offenses for which it is principally used. It need not provide on its face reasonable cause to believe defendant has committed the offense." *Nuccio*, 78 N.Y.2d at 104, 571 N.Y.S.2d at 694. *See also People v. Key*, 45 N.Y.2d 111, 115–16, 408 N.Y.S.2d 16, 19, 379 N.E.2d 1147 (1978).

However, "[a] defendant charged by a simplified information is, upon a timely request, entitled as a matter of right to have filed with the court and served upon him, or if he is represented by an attorney, upon his attorney, a supporting deposition of the complainant police officer or public servant, containing allegations of fact, based either upon personal knowledge or upon information and belief, providing reasonable cause to believe that the defendant committed the offense or offenses charged." N.Y. Crim. Proc. Law § 100.25(2). *See also* Ch 17 (Supporting Depositions), infra; *Nuccio*, 78 N.Y.2d at 104, 571 N.Y.S.2d at 694, ("If a timely request for a supporting deposition is made, the failure to supply one renders the simplified information insufficient on its face (CPL 100.40[2]) and subjects it to dismissal upon motion (CPL 170.35[1][a]; 170.30[1][a])"); *Key*, 45 N.Y.2d at 116, 408 N.Y.S.2d at 19; *People v. Koenig*, 31 Misc. 3d 827, __, 919 N.Y.S.2d 319, 320 (Sullivan Co. Ct. 2011).

In *People v. Fernandez*, 20 N.Y.3d 44, 46, 956 N.Y.S.2d 443, 444, 980 N.E.2d 491 (2012), the Court of Appeals held that:

> [T]he accusatory instrument was a facially sufficient simplified traffic information, although it was titled "Complaint/Information," and contained factual information. For the reasons set forth below, we hold that the accusatory instrument was sufficient to serve as a simplified traffic information because it was substantially in the form prescribed by the Commissioner of Motor Vehicles.

§ 16:5 Simplified information—Sufficiency on face

Research References

West's Key Number Digest, Automobiles ⚷351.1

The facial sufficiency requirements of a simplified information are set forth in N.Y. Crim. Proc. Law § 100.40(2):

> A simplified information is sufficient on its face when, as provided by [CPL § 100.25(1)], it substantially conforms to the requirements therefor prescribed by or pursuant to law; provided that when the filing of a supporting deposition is ordered by the court pursuant to [CPL § 100.25(2)], a failure of the complainant police officer or public servant to comply with such order within the time provided by [CPL § 100.25(2)] renders the simplified information insufficient on its face.

See also §§ 17:1 et seq., *infra*.

In *People v. Key*, 45 N.Y.2d 111, 115–16, 408 N.Y.S.2d 16, 19, 379 N.E.2d 1147 (1978), the Court of Appeals restated this rule:

> A simplified traffic information, to be sufficient on its face, need

only comply with the requirements of the Commissioner of Motor Vehicles; it need not provide on its face reasonable cause to believe defendant committed the offense charged (CPL 100.25, 100.40, subd. 2). But if defendant requests a supporting deposition, to which he has a statutory right, it must provide reasonable cause (CPL 100.25, subd. 2). The People's tender of such a deposition voluntarily, rather than waiting for defendant's request, should not obviate the need for the deposition to provide reasonable cause.

See also People v. Nuccio, 78 N.Y.2d 102, 104, 571 N.Y.S.2d 693, 694, 575 N.E.2d 111 (1991) ("The simplified information is a statutory creation designed to provide an uncomplicated form for handling the large volume of traffic infractions and petty offenses for which it is principally used. It need not provide on its face reasonable cause to believe defendant has committed the offense").

In *People v. Bize*, 30 Misc. 3d 68, 918 N.Y.S.2d 696 (App. Term, 9th & 10th Jud. Dist. 2010), the defendant challenged the sufficiency of a simplified traffic information on the ground that it failed to allege that the offense took place in the State of New York. In rejecting the defendant's argument, the Appellate Term held that:

> In this case, the simplified traffic information is an E-ticket, the form of which is specifically authorized by the Commissioner of Motor Vehicles (15 NYCRR 91.21). It adequately designates the offense as Vehicle and Traffic Law § 1180(b), "speed viol exceed 55 MPH," and indicates that defendant traveled 113 miles per hour in a 55 miles per hour zone. While not explicitly stating that the occurrence took place in New York State, the facts contained in the instrument—including the road, highway, location code, town and county—clearly establish that the occurrence transpired in the State of New York. Therefore, the instrument is facially sufficient.
>
> We note that a supporting deposition was furnished to defendant upon his request, in which the ticketing officer specifically stated that the violations had occurred in "the County of Suffolk, NY."

918 N.Y.S.2d at 697 (citation omitted).

§ 16:6 Simplified information can be based entirely upon information and belief

Research References

West's Key Number Digest, Automobiles ⟜351.1

In *People v. Boback*, 23 N.Y.2d 189, 194, 295 N.Y.S.2d 912, 917, 243 N.E.2d 135 (1968), the Court of Appeals held that "the use of the Simplified Traffic Information is authorized where the information is signed by an officer whose knowledge of the facts is based upon information and belief." *See also People v. Boback*,

23 N.Y.2d 189, 295 N.Y.S.2d 912, 243 N.E.2d 135 (1968) ("It is
. . . evident that neither the language nor the legislative history
of the Simplified Traffic Information statute limits the use of the
information to those cases where the officer making the information has some personal knowledge of the violation"); *Farkas v.
State*, 96 Misc. 2d 784, 787–88, 409 N.Y.S.2d 696, 698–99 (Ct. Cl.
1978); 1987 N.Y. Op. Atty. Gen. (Informal Opinion No. 87–78).
Cf. People v. Genovese, 156 Misc. 2d 569, 593 N.Y.S.2d 925 (J. Ct.
1992) (reaching opposite conclusion).

Notably, however, Boback made clear that "[t]he Constitution
does require that the defendant be informed of the nature of the
charge and the circumstances under which he is alleged to have
violated the law. But the bill of particulars, which the defendants
could have had upon demand, fulfills this function." 23 N.Y.2d at
195, 295 N.Y.S.2d at 917 (1968).

§ 16:7   Uniform traffic ticket cannot be used to charge parking, stopping or standing violations

Research References

West's Key Number Digest, Automobiles ☞351.1

Both the VTL and the DMV regulations promulgated pursuant
thereto prohibit the issuance of a UTT for parking, stopping or
standing violations. *See* N.Y. Veh. & Traf. Law § 207(1); 15
NYCRR § 91.4(b).

§ 16:8   Information—Defined

Research References

West's Key Number Digest, Automobiles ☞351.1

"An 'information' is a verified written accusation by a person,
filed with a local criminal court, charging one or more other
persons with the commission of one or more offenses, none of
which is a felony. It may serve as a basis both for the commencement of a criminal action and for the prosecution thereof in a local criminal court." N.Y. Crim. Proc. Law § 100.10(1). *See also*
N.Y. Crim. Proc. Law § 1.20(4).

§ 16:9   Information—Sufficiency on face

Research References

West's Key Number Digest, Automobiles ☞351.1

The facial sufficiency requirements of an information are set
forth in N.Y. Crim. Proc. Law § 100.40(1):

An information, or a count thereof, is sufficient on its face when:

(a) It substantially conforms to the requirements prescribed in [N.Y. Crim. Proc. Law §] 100.15; and

(b) The allegations of the factual part of the information, together with those of any supporting depositions which may accompany it, provide reasonable cause to believe that the defendant committed the offense charged in the accusatory part of the information; and

(c) Non-hearsay allegations of the factual part of the information and/or of any supporting depositions establish, if true, every element of the offense charged and the defendant's commission thereof.

In *People v. Alejandro*, 70 N.Y.2d 133, 517 N.Y.S.2d 927, 511 N.E.2d 71 (1987), the Court of Appeals set forth the facial sufficiency requirements for an information, and held that an insufficient information constitutes a nonwaivable jurisdictional defect. The defendant in Alejandro was charged, in an information, with resisting arrest in violation of N.Y. Penal Law § 205.30. The information contained the following factual allegations:

> The above-named defendant intentionally prevented or attempted to prevent a peace officer or police officer from effecting an authorized arrest of himself [sic] or another person. To wit: On 1/4/84 at approx. 1035 hrs. at Nimitz Ave., Brentwood, N.Y. Defendant did intentionally resist a lawful arrest of herself by pulling her arms away, kicking your deponent with her high heels, slapping your deponent, attempting to bite same, putting her 1974 Pontiac sedan into reverse while deponent was attempting to remove her from the vehicle, knocking your deponent to the ground.

70 N.Y.2d at 136 n. 1, 517 N.Y.S.2d at 929 n. 1. The Court of Appeals held that:

> This misdemeanor information for resisting arrest was unquestionably insufficient on its face (CPL 100.40[1][c]). The Penal Law defines resisting arrest as intentionally preventing or attempting to prevent a police officer "from effecting an *authorized* arrest" (Penal Law § 205.30 [emphasis added]). It is an essential element of the crime of resisting arrest that the arrest be authorized and, absent proof that the arresting officer had a warrant or probable cause to arrest defendant for commission of some offense, a conviction cannot stand. Thus, to comply with the statute, the factual part of the information for resisting arrest must contain "[n]on-hearsay allegations [which would] establish, if true" (CPL 100.40[1][c]) that the underlying arrest was authorized. These essential allegations are omitted from the information here. The factual portion pertains only to defendant's actions in resisting the arrest.

People v. Alejandro, 70 N.Y.2d 133, 135–136, 517 N.Y.S.2d 927, 928–929, 511 N.E.2d 71 (1987) (citations omitted).

In ruling that this defect is jurisdictional in nature, the Court reasoned that:

> We conclude that an information which fails to contain nonhearsay allegations establishing "if true, every element of the offense charged and the defendant's commission thereof" (CPL 100.40[1][c]) is fatally defective. This conclusion is compelled by the natural and obvious meaning of CPL 100.40(1)(c) and CPL 100.15(3) which establish a specific requirement applicable to informations beyond what is required for the sufficiency of other accusatory instruments and by the evident legislative purpose behind such special requirement, as revealed in an analysis of the pertinent statutes and the relevant legislative history. * * *

> The "reasonable cause" requirement for a finding of facial sufficiency (subd. [b]) is applicable not only to informations but to the other local criminal court accusatory instruments, simplified informations (CPL 100.40[2]) and misdemeanor and felony complaints (CPL 100.40[4]; 100.15[3]). . . . The "prima facie case" requirement—that the factual part establish every element of the offense charged (subd. [c])—applies, however, to informations alone. * * *

> The reason for requiring the additional showing of a prima facie case for an information lies in the unique function that an information serves under the statutory scheme established by the Criminal Procedure Law. An information is often the instrument upon which the defendant is prosecuted for a misdemeanor or a petty offense. Unlike a felony complaint (CPL 180.10), it is not followed by a preliminary hearing and a Grand Jury proceeding. Thus, the People need not, at any time prior to trial, present actual evidence demonstrating a prima facie case, as with an indictment following a felony complaint.

70 N.Y.2d at 136–38, 517 N.Y.S.2d at 929–30 (citation omitted). *See also People v. Jones*, 9 N.Y.3d 259, 261-62, 848 N.Y.S.2d 600, 602, 878 N.E.2d 1016 (2007).

N.Y. Crim. Proc. Law § 100.40(1)(c) itself contains 2 requirements: (1) that the factual allegations of the information "establish, if true, every element of the offense charged and the defendant's commission thereof," and (2) "those allegations must be 'non-hearsay.'" *People v. Casey*, 95 N.Y.2d 354, 362, 717 N.Y.S.2d 88, 92, 740 N.E.2d 233 (2000). The "non-hearsay requirement is met so long as the allegation would be admissible under some hearsay rule exception." 95 N.Y.2d at 361, 717 N.Y.S.2d at 91. An example is an intoxicated defendant's admission to operating the vehicle. 95 N.Y.2d at 364, 717 N.Y.S.2d at 94.

In *Casey,* the Court of Appeals re-examined its decision in *Alejandro* and held that the failure of an information to allege facts establishing every element of the offense charged and the defendant's commission thereof is still considered a non-waivable jurisdictional defect; however, "hearsay pleading defects in the factual portion of a local criminal court information must be preserved in order to be reviewable as a matter of law on appeal." 95 N.Y.2d at 367, 717 N.Y.S.2d at 96. *See also* 95 N.Y.2d at 362, 717 N.Y.S.2d at 92.

To be sufficient, "an information must set forth the required nonhearsay evidentiary allegations within 'the four corners of the instrument itself' or in annexed supporting depositions." *People v. Thomas*, 4 N.Y.3d 143, 146, 791 N.Y.S.2d 68, 70, 824 N.E.2d 499 (2005). *See also People v. Bottari*, 31 Misc. 3d 90, __, 924 N.Y.S.2d 733, 735-36 (App. Term, 9th & 10th Jud. Dist. 2010).

§ 16:10 Applicability of *Alejandro* to simplified informations and misdemeanor complaints

Research References

West's Key Number Digest, Automobiles ⊗351.1

The different types of local criminal court accusatory instruments have different requirements for facial sufficiency. *See* N.Y. Crim. Proc. Law § 100.40(1) (facial sufficiency requirements for an "information"); N.Y. Crim. Proc. Law § 100.40(2) (facial sufficiency requirements for a "simplified information"); N.Y. Crim. Proc. Law § 100.40(3) (facial sufficiency requirements for a "prosecutor's information"); N.Y. Crim. Proc. Law § 100.40(4) (facial sufficiency requirements for a "misdemeanor complaint").

Since an "information" is the only local criminal court accusatory instrument that requires "non-hearsay allegations of fact" which would "establish, if true, every element of the offense charged and the defendant's commission thereof," *see* N.Y. Crim. Proc. Law § 100.40(1)(c), a regular, long form information appears to be the only local criminal court accusatory instrument to which the *prima facie case* requirement of *People v. Alejandro*, 70 N.Y.2d 133, 517 N.Y.S.2d 927, 511 N.E.2d 71 (1987), applies. *See, e.g., People v. DeRojas*, 180 Misc. 2d 690, 691, 693 N.Y.S.2d 404, 405 (App. Term 1999); *People v. Quarles*, 168 Misc. 2d 638, 642–43, 639 N.Y.S.2d 661, 664–65 (City Ct. 1996); *People v. Gindi*, 166 Misc. 2d 672, 680, 630 N.Y.S.2d 863, 869 (City Crim. Ct. 1995); *People v. Curtis*, 166 Misc. 2d 753, 755, 634 N.Y.S.2d 981, 982 (J. Ct. 1995) ("This court holds that the rule of *People v. Alejandro, supra*, does not require that a simplified traffic information be dismissed for failure to meet the standards of a long form information"); *People v. Kaid*, 165 Misc. 2d 489, 495, 629 N.Y.S.2d 617, 621 (City Crim. Ct. 1995); *People v. Howell*, 158 Misc. 2d 653, 655, 601 N.Y.S.2d 778, 780 (City Crim. Ct. 1993);

People v. Campbell, 141 Misc. 2d 470, 474–75, 533 N.Y.S.2d 666, 669–70 (City Crim. Ct. 1988). *See generally People v. Nuccio*, 78 N.Y.2d 102, 571 N.Y.S.2d 693, 575 N.E.2d 111 (1991); *People v. Hohmeyer*, 70 N.Y.2d 41, 517 N.Y.S.2d 448, 510 N.E.2d 317 (1987); *People v. Key*, 45 N.Y.2d 111, 408 N.Y.S.2d 16, 379 N.E.2d 1147 (1978); *People v. DeRojas*, 196 Misc. 2d 171, 763 N.Y.S.2d 386, 387–88 (App. Term 2003).

However, at least two reported decisions have held that *Alejandro* applies to simplified traffic informations charging a misdemeanor. *See People v. Krenzer*, 180 Misc. 2d 757, 690 N.Y.S.2d 838 (City Ct. 1999); *People v. Smith*, 163 Misc. 2d 353, 363, 621 N.Y.S.2d 449, 456 (J. Ct. 1994) ("this court holds that where a defendant is charged by a simplified information with one or more misdemeanor offenses and the defendant timely requests a supporting deposition, or one is voluntarily provided by the People . . ., the factual allegations of the supporting deposition or depositions . . . must contain nonhearsay allegations of fact which establish, if true, a prima facie case against the defendant"). *See also People v. Scott*, 176 Misc. 2d 393, 396–97, 671 N.Y.S.2d 961, 963–64 (City Ct. 1998) (applying *Alejandro* to misdemeanor complaint).

Regardless of whether *Alejandro* is applicable, "the deposition supporting a simplified traffic information, to the extent it is based on information and belief, must contain a statement of the source of that information and belief if it is to be sufficient on its face." *People v. Lesnak*, 165 Misc. 2d 706, 709, 630 N.Y.S.2d 459, 461 (Dist. Ct. 1995). *See also People v. Dumas*, 42 Misc. 3d 265, —, 974 N.Y.S.2d 921, 924 (Buffalo City N.Y. City Ct. 2013); *People v. Noblett*, 172 Misc. 2d 826, 829, 660 N.Y.S.2d 517, 519–20 (County Ct. 1997); *Quarles*, 168 Misc.at 647, 639 N.Y.S.2d at 668; *People v. Born*, 166 Misc. 2d 757, 761, 634 N.Y.S.2d 915, 917–18 (J. Ct. 1995); *People v. Smith*, 163 Misc. 2d 353, 363–64, 621 N.Y.S.2d 449, 456–57 (J. Ct. 1994); *People v. Moretti*, 142 Misc. 2d 331, 332, 537 N.Y.S.2d 735, 736 (Yonkers City Ct. 1988). *See generally People v. Hawkins*, 50 Misc. 3d 907, 21 N.Y.S.3d 859 (Ossining J. Ct. 2015); *People v. Scott*, 176 Misc. 2d 393, 397, 671 N.Y.S.2d 961, 964 (City Ct. 1998) (applying this rule to misdemeanor complaint); *People v. Pleva*, 96 Misc. 2d 1020, 410 N.Y.S.2d 261 (Dist. Ct. 1978) (same).

§ 16:11 Prosecutor's information—Defined

Research References

West's Key Number Digest, Automobiles ⬥351.1

A "prosecutor's information" is a written accusation by a district attorney, filed with a local criminal court, either (a) at the direction of a grand jury pursuant to [CPL §] 190.70, or (b) at the direction of a local criminal court pursuant to [CPL §] 180.50 or 180.70, or (c) at the district attorney's own instance pursuant to [CPL § 100.50(2)], or (d) at the direction of a superior court pursuant to [CPL § 210.20(1-a)], charging one or more persons with the commission of one or more offenses, none of which is a felony. It serves as a basis for the prosecution of a criminal action, but it commences a criminal action only where it results from a grand jury direction issued in a case not previously commenced in a local criminal court.

N.Y. Crim. Proc. Law § 100.10(3). *See also* N.Y. Crim. Proc. Law § 1.20(6).

§ 16:12 Prosecutor's information—Form and content

Research References

West's Key Number Digest, Automobiles ☞351.1; Indictment and Information ☞47

A prosecutor's information must contain the name of the local criminal court with which it is filed and the title of the action, and must be subscribed by the district attorney by whom it is filed. Otherwise it should be in the form prescribed for an indictment, pursuant to [[CPL §] 200.50, and must, in one or more counts, allege the offense or offenses charged and a plain and concise statement of the conduct constituting each such offense. The rules prescribed in [CPL §§] 200.20 and 200.40 governing joinder of different offenses and defendants in a single indictment are also applicable to a prosecutor's information.

N.Y. Crim. Proc. Law § 100.35.

§ 16:13 Prosecutor's information—Sufficiency on face

Research References

West's Key Number Digest, Automobiles ☞351.1; Indictment and Information ☞54

"A prosecutor's information, or a count thereof, is sufficient on its face when it substantially conforms to the requirements prescribed in [N.Y. Crim. Proc. Law §] 100.35." N.Y. Crim. Proc. Law § 100.40(3). *See generally People v. Thomas*, 4 N.Y.3d 143, 146, 791 N.Y.S.2d 68, 70, 824 N.E.2d 499 (2005).

§ 16:14 Misdemeanor complaint—Defined

Research References

West's Key Number Digest, Automobiles ☞351.1; Indictment and Information ☞54

"A 'misdemeanor complaint' is a verified written accusation by a person, filed with a local criminal court, charging one or more other persons with the commission of one or more offenses, at least one of which is a misdemeanor and none of which is a felony. It serves as a basis for the commencement of a criminal action, but it may serve as a basis for prosecution thereof only where a defendant has waived prosecution by information pursuant to [CPL § 170.65(3)]." N.Y. Crim. Proc. Law § 100.10(4). *See also* N.Y. Crim. Proc. Law § 1.20(7); *People v. Keizer*, 100 N.Y.2d 114, 117–18, 760 N.Y.S.2d 720, 722, 790 N.E.2d 1149 (2003).

> The misdemeanor complaint . . . serves merely as the basis for commencement of a criminal action, permitting court arraignment and temporary control over the defendant's person where there is as yet no prima facie case. However, it is not designed for prosecution purposes and a defendant is not required to plead to a misdemeanor complaint and cannot be tried thereon unless he consents. (CPL 170.65, subds. 1, 3.) By statute, a defendant has the right to be prosecuted by information. (CPL 100.10, subd. 1; 170.65, subd. 1.) The right is substantial and takes into account a fundamental difference between these accusatory instruments—i. e., that a misdemeanor complaint may rest on hearsay allegations while an information may not. (CPL 100.40, subds. 1, 4.)

People v. Weinberg, 34 N.Y.2d 429, 431, 358 N.Y.S.2d 357, 359, 315 N.E.2d 434 (1974).

§ 16:15   Misdemeanor complaint—Sufficiency on face

Research References
West's Key Number Digest, Automobiles ☞351.1; Indictment and Information ☞54

The facial sufficiency requirements of a misdemeanor complaint are set forth in N.Y. Crim. Proc. Law § 100.40(4):

> A misdemeanor complaint or a felony complaint, or a count thereof, is sufficient on its face when:
>
> (a) It substantially conforms to the requirements prescribed in [N.Y. Crim. Proc. Law §] 100.15; and
>
> (b) The allegations of the factual part of such accusatory instrument and/or any supporting depositions which may accompany it, provide reasonable cause to believe that the defendant committed the offense charged in the accusatory part of such instrument.

§ 16:16   Replacement of misdemeanor complaint by information and waiver of right to be prosecuted by information

Research References
West's Key Number Digest, Automobiles ☞351.1

N.Y. Crim. Proc. Law § 100.50(3) provides that "[a] misdemeanor complaint must or may be replaced and superseded by an information pursuant to the provisions of [N.Y. Crim. Proc. Law §] 170.65." N.Y. Crim. Proc. Law § 170.65 provides that:

(1) A defendant against whom a misdemeanor complaint is pending is not required to enter a plea thereto. For purposes of prosecution, such instrument must, except as provided in [N.Y. Crim. Proc. Law § 170.65(3)], be replaced by an information, and the defendant must be arraigned thereon. If the misdemeanor complaint is supplemented by a supporting deposition and such instruments taken together satisfy the requirements for a valid information, such misdemeanor complaint is deemed to have been converted to and to constitute a replacing information.

(2) An information which replaces a misdemeanor complaint need not charge the same offense or offenses, but at least one count thereof must charge the commission by the defendant of an offense based upon conduct which was the subject of the misdemeanor complaint. In addition, the information may, subject to the rules of joinder, charge any other offense which the factual allegations thereof or of any supporting depositions accompanying it are legally sufficient to support, even though such offense is not based upon conduct which was the subject of the misdemeanor complaint.

(3) A defendant who has been arraigned upon a misdemeanor complaint may waive prosecution by information and consent to be prosecuted upon the misdemeanor complaint. In such case, the defendant must be required, either upon the date of the waiver or subsequent thereto, to enter a plea to the misdemeanor complaint.

"Unless [the defendant] specifically waives prosecution by information (N.Y. Crim. Proc. Law 170.65[3]) the misdemeanor complaint must be replaced by an information which meets the requirement for facial sufficiency (N.Y. Crim. Proc. Law 100.40[1][c]; 100.15[3]; 170.35) and the defendant must be prosecuted thereon." *People v. Alejandro*, 70 N.Y.2d 133, 138 n.2, 517 N.Y.S.2d 927, 930 n.2, 511 N.E.2d 71 (1987).

The mere waiver, by defense counsel, of a formal reading of the charges at arraignment does *not* constitute a knowing and intelligent waiver of the right to be prosecuted by information. *See, e.g., People v. Casey*, 95 N.Y.2d 354, 359, 717 N.Y.S.2d 88, 90, 740 N.E.2d 233 (2000); *People v. Weinberg*, 34 N.Y.2d 429, 431, 358 N.Y.S.2d 357, 359, 315 N.E.2d 434 (1974). *Cf. People v. Dumay*, 23 N.Y.3d 518, 522-23, 992 N.Y.S.2d 672, 675, 16 N.E.3d 1150 (2014) ("Defense counsel replied 'So waive' in open court, in defendant's presence, and in response to Criminal Court's direct inquiry as to whether defendant waived prosecution by information. This statement communicated, in no uncertain terms, defendant's choice to waive his right.").

People v. Connor, 63 N.Y.2d 11, 479 N.Y.S.2d 197, 468 N.E.2d 35 (1984), is not to the contrary. In *Connor*, the Court merely held that various conduct by the defendant and his attorney, *throughout the entire course of the case,* "must be deemed in the circumstances of this case to have constituted a waiver of prosecution by information and a consent to prosecution on the misdemeanor complaint." 63 N.Y.2d at 14, 479 N.Y.S.2d at 198. Notably, the Court found that the conduct of defense counsel throughout the case constituted a tactical ploy that should be neither rewarded nor tolerated. 63 N.Y.2d at 16, 479 N.Y.S.2d at 199. By contrast, the Court clearly stated that defense counsel's conduct in waiving a formal reading of the defendant's rights and charges "did not, of course, by itself constitute a waiver of the procedural right to be tried on information." 63 N.Y.2d at 14 n.*, 479 N.Y.S.2d at 198 n.*.

§ 16:17   Felony complaint—Defined

Research References

West's Key Number Digest, Automobiles ☞351.1; Indictment and Information ☞54

"A 'felony complaint' is a verified written accusation by a person, filed with a local criminal court, charging one or more other persons with the commission of one or more felonies. It serves as a basis for the commencement of a criminal action, but not as a basis for prosecution thereof." N.Y. Crim. Proc. Law § 100.10(5). *See also* N.Y. Crim. Proc. Law § 1.20(8).

§ 16:18   Information, misdemeanor complaint and felony complaint—Form and content

Research References

West's Key Number Digest, Automobiles ☞351.1; Indictment and Information ☞47

The form and content requirements of informations, misdemeanor complaints and felony complaints are set forth in N.Y. Crim. Proc. Law § 100.15, which provides, in pertinent part, as follows:

(1) An information, a misdemeanor complaint and a felony complaint must each specify the name of the court with which it is filed and the title of the action, and must be subscribed and verified by a person known as the "complainant." The complainant may be any person having knowledge, whether personal or upon information and belief, of the commission of the offense or offenses charged. Each instrument must contain an accusatory part and a factual part. The complainant's verification of the instrument is deemed to apply only to the factual part thereof and not to the accusatory part.

(2) The accusatory part of each such instrument must designate the offense or offenses charged. As in the case of an indictment, and subject to the rules of joinder applicable to indictments, two or more offenses may be charged in separate counts. Also as in the case of an indictment, such instrument may charge two or more defendants provided that all such defendants are jointly charged with every offense alleged therein.

(3) The factual part of such instrument must contain a statement of the complainant alleging facts of an evidentiary character supporting or tending to support the charges. Where more than one offense is charged, the factual part should consist of a single factual account applicable to all the counts of the accusatory part. The factual allegations may be based either upon personal knowledge of the complainant or upon information and belief. Nothing contained in this section, however, limits or affects the requirement, prescribed in [N.Y. Crim. Proc. Law § 100.40(1)], that in order for an information or a count thereof to be sufficient on its face, every element of the offense charged and the defendant's commission thereof must be supported by non-hearsay allegations of such information and/or any supporting depositions.

In *People v. Casey*, 95 N.Y.2d 354, 717 N.Y.S.2d 88, 740 N.E.2d 233 (2000), an accusatory instrument that would have qualified as a misdemeanor complaint was nonetheless denominated an information. In this regard, the Court of Appeals noted that:

> [A]s the Appellate Term acknowledged, the accusatory instrument here was denominated, and purported to be, a misdemeanor information with a supporting deposition, not a misdemeanor complaint. That the instrument would have *qualified* as a misdemeanor complaint did not make it one. . . . [T]he accusatory instrument here was in fact a local criminal court information, and not a misdemeanor complaint.

95 N.Y.2d at 359, 717 N.Y.S.2d at 90. *Cf. People v. Fernandez*, 20 N.Y.3d 44, 50, 956 N.Y.S.2d 443, 447, 980 N.E.2d 491 (2012) (in the case of simplified traffic informations, "title then cannot be dispositive when it is the legislature's intention that no single part of the form be dispositive. . . . [T]he Commissioner of Motor Vehicles does not require a simplified traffic information to have any title at all (*see* 15 NYCRR 122.2). It would be illogical, then, to find that the title of the form governs over its substance"); *People v. Dumay*, 23 N.Y.3d 518, 523, 992 N.Y.S.2d 672, 675, 16 N.E.3d 1150 (2014); *People v. Ferro*, 22 Misc. 3d 7, 871 N.Y.S.2d 814 (App. Term, 9th & 10th Jud. Dist. 2008). *See generally People v. Towey*, 52 Misc. 3d 471, 28 N.Y.S.3d 838 (Nassau Co. Dist. Ct. 2016).

Notably, the *Fernandez* Court concluded with the following comment:

Although we hold that according to the technical specifications of the regulations, [NYPD] Procedure No. 209-11 substantially complies with 15 NYCRR 122.2, and is therefore sufficient as a simplified traffic information, a new more carefully drawn form would better service the city and the public. The present form is confusing and hardly "simplified." It would seem clear that, at the very least, a simplified traffic information used in New York City should be titled "simplified traffic information" and should not include any space for factual allegations.

20 N.Y.3d at 53, 956 N.Y.S.2d at 449.

§ 16:19 Information, misdemeanor complaint, felony complaint and supporting deposition— Verification

Research References

West's Key Number Digest, Automobiles ☞351.1; Indictment and Information ☞52(.5)

N.Y. Crim. Proc. Law §§ 100.15 and 100.20 require that informations, misdemeanor complaints, felony complaints and supporting depositions be "subscribed and verified." N.Y. Crim. Proc. Law § 100.30 sets forth the permissible methods of verification:

(1) An information, a misdemeanor complaint, a felony complaint, a supporting deposition, and proof of service of a supporting deposition may be verified in any of the following manners:

(a) Such instrument may be sworn to before the court with which it is filed.

(b) Such instrument may be sworn to before a desk officer in charge at a police station or police headquarters or any of his superior officers.

(c) Where such instrument is filed by any public servant following the issuance and service of an appearance ticket, and where by express provision of law another designated public servant is authorized to administer the oath with respect to such instrument, it may be sworn to before such public servant.

(d) Such instrument may bear a form notice that false statements made therein are punishable as a class A misdemeanor pursuant to [N.Y. Penal Law § 210.45], and such form notice together with the subscription of the deponent constitute a verification of the instrument.

(e) Such instrument may be sworn to before a notary public.

(2) an instrument specified in [N.Y. Crim. Proc. Law § 100.30(1)] may be verified in any manner prescribed therein unless in a particular case the court expressly directs verifica-

tion in a particular manner prescribed in [N.Y. Crim. Proc. Law § 100.30(1)].

An accusatory instrument which is not verified pursuant to N.Y. Crim. Proc. Law § 100.30 is invalid. *Matter of Shirley v. Schulman*, 78 N.Y.2d 915, 917, 573 N.Y.S.2d 456, 457, 577 N.E.2d 1048 (1991). *See also People v. Roslyn Sephardic Center*, 17 Misc. 3d 74, __, 847 N.Y.S.2d 332, 333-34 (App. Term, 9th & 10th Jud. Dist. 2007) ("While each of the purported supporting depositions annexed to each of the accusatory instruments filed in this case by Officers Trotto and Lamb stated in the preprinted portion thereof that they were 'duly sworn,' in fact they were not verified by using any of the prescribed methods of verification in accordance with CPL 100.30. Accordingly, they are not valid supporting depositions, and the allegations contained therein cannot be relied upon when determining whether the informations are legally sufficient"); *People v. Gabbay*, 175 Misc. 2d 421, 670 N.Y.S.2d 962, 963 (App. Term 1997) (parking violation summonses which "only provide the statement 'Affirmed under the penalty of perjury' followed by the date and signature of the officer" were not verified pursuant to CPL 100.30, and thus "the summonses were not valid as accusatory instruments"). *See generally People v. Lopez*, 170 Misc. 2d 278, 281, 648 N.Y.S.2d 231, 234 (City Crim. Ct. 1996).

In *People v. Holmes*, 93 N.Y.2d 889, 891, 689 N.Y.S.2d 687, 688, 711 N.E.2d 965 (1999), the Court of Appeals held that compliance with N.Y. Crim. Proc. Law § 100.30(1)(b) does not require that the complainant actually "raise his hand and orally recite an oath. It was sufficient for him to read and sign the instrument in front of the [desk] officer, appreciating the significance of his actions."

In *People v. Ryan*, 185 Misc. 2d 477, 713 N.Y.S.2d 447 (Dist. Ct. 2000), the Court dismissed an information charging the defendant with DWI where, although the information purported to be signed before a desk officer in compliance with CPL 100.30(1)(b), it came to light that the arresting officer had signed the information in a separate room from where the desk sergeant was located. Accordingly, since the information was not sworn to "in front of" or "before" the desk officer, the Court held that it was "not properly verified in accordance with [the] statute and must be dismissed." 185 Misc. 2d at 480, 713 N.Y.S.2d at 449.

In *People v. Coldiron*, 77 Misc. 2d 102, 355 N.Y.S.2d 518 (Yonkers Ct. of Spec. Sess. 1974), the Court held that an information charging the defendant with DWI was defective where it purportedly complied with CPL § 100.30(1)(d), but the arresting officer's signature appeared above the form notice warning the officer that false statements made therein are punishable as a class A misdemeanor pursuant to PL § 210.45. On appeal, however, the Appellate Term reversed, holding that:

> In our opinion, the failure to place above deponent's signature the form notice advising deponent of his criminal liability, pursuant to Penal Law 210.45, did not render the verification of the information defective. While the information must be subscribed, this merely requires that deponent's signature be at the conclusion of the statement being verified but does not require such signature to also follow the form notice. Concededly, it would be better practice to have the form notice immediately beneath the statement being verified and directly above deponent's signature so as to forcefully call the criminal penalty for making false statements to deponent's attention. However, the placing of the notice below deponent's signature, as done on the New York State Police form used as an information here, is sufficient to constitute a verification pursuant to CPL 100.30, subd. 1(d).

People v. Coldiron, 79 Misc. 2d 338, 360 N.Y.S.2d 788, 788–89 (App. Term 1974) (citation omitted). *Cf. People v. Lennox*, 94 Misc. 2d 730, 405 N.Y.S.2d 581 (Greenburgh Just. Ct. 1978) (simplified traffic informations were defective where the officer's signature appeared above, as opposed to below, the phrase "affirmed under penalty of perjury").

§ 16:20   Information, prosecutor's information and misdemeanor complaint—Severance and consolidation

Research References

West's Key Number Digest, Automobiles ⬅351.1

"Where appropriate, the provisions of [CPL §§] 200.20 and 200.40, governing severance of counts of an indictment and severance of defendants for trial purposes, and governing consolidation of indictments for trial purposes, apply to informations, to prosecutor's informations and to misdemeanor complaints." N.Y. Crim. Proc. Law § 100.45(1).

§ 16:21   Amendment of informations and prosecutor's informations

Research References

West's Key Number Digest, Automobiles ⬅351.1

The amendment of local criminal court accusatory instruments is governed by N.Y. Crim. Proc. Law § 100.45. N.Y. Crim. Proc. Law § 100.45(3) provides that:

> At any time before the entry of a plea of guilty to or the commencement of a trial of an information, the court may, upon application of

the people and with notice to the defendant and opportunity to be heard, order the amendment of the accusatory part of such information by addition of a count charging an offense supported by the allegations of the factual part of such information and/or any supporting depositions which may accompany it. In such case, the defendant must be accorded any reasonable adjournment necessitated by the amendment.

In *People v. Harper*, 37 N.Y.2d 96, 98, 371 N.Y.S.2d 467, 468–69, 332 N.E.2d 336 (1975), the Court of Appeals held that "if there is to be an amendment of an accusatory instrument within the scope of CPL 100.45 (subd. 3), Consol.Laws, c. 11-A there must be strict compliance with the prescriptions of that section." *See also People v. Warren*, 17 Misc. 3d 27, __, 844 N.Y.S.2d 563, 564 (App. Term, 2d & 11th Jud. Dist. 2007).

In *People v. Easton*, 307 N.Y. 336, 338, 121 N.E.2d 357 (1954), the information charged the defendant with committing DWI "on December 17, *1953*, instead of December 17, *1952*." Due to this "obvious typographical error in the information," the defendant was accused of committing the offense on "a date not yet come." *Id.* Under these circumstances, the Court of Appeals held that the information could be amended to correct the date. *Id.*

N.Y. Crim. Proc. Law § 100.45(2) provides that "[t]he provisions of [CPL §] 200.70 governing amendment of indictments apply to prosecutor's informations." *See also People v. Warren*, 17 Misc. 3d 27, __, 844 N.Y.S.2d 563, 564 (App. Term, 2d 2007), leave to appeal denied, 9 N.Y.3d 993, 848 N.Y.S.2d 611, 878 N.E.2d 1027 (11th Jud. Dist. 2007).

§ 16:22 Amendment of simplified informations and misdemeanor complaints

Research References

West's Key Number Digest, Automobiles ☞351.1

The Court of Appeals has made clear that "if there is to be an amendment of an accusatory instrument within the scope of CPL 100.45 (subd. 3), Consol.Laws, c. 11-A there must be strict compliance with the prescriptions of that section." *People v. Harper*, 37 N.Y.2d 96, 98, 371 N.Y.S.2d 467, 468–69, 332 N.E.2d 336 (1975). Since N.Y. Crim. Proc. Law § 100.45(3), by its express terms, only permits the amendment of informations and prosecutor's informations, it does not permit the amendment of either:

(a) Simplified informations. *See People v. Gingello*, 181 Misc. 2d 163, 167, 694 N.Y.S.2d 579, 583 (City Ct. 1999) (abrogated on other grounds by, People v. Blair, 98 N.Y.2d 722, 749 N.Y.S.2d 809, 779 N.E.2d 748 (2002)); *People v. Engeman*, 135 Misc. 2d 228, 230, 514 N.Y.S.2d 588, 589 (City Ct. 1987). *Cf. People v. Kreismann*, 162 Misc. 2d 726, 619 N.Y.S.2d 253 (J.

Ct. 1994) (minor typographical error in simplified traffic information is amendable irregularity). *See generally People v. Almendarez*, 24 Misc. 3d 649, __, 876 N.Y.S.2d 861, 862 (Nassau Co.
Dist. Ct. 2009) ("The issue before the Court is whether the
Prosecutor may maintain a criminal proceeding via simplified
information against a defendant who has assumed the identity
of another individual. The follow-up question is whether a
prosecutor may amend a simplified information to change the
name of the defendant. The answer to both question in the circumstances of this case must be no"). *Cf. People v. Iqbal*, 31
Misc. 3d 94, __, 926 N.Y.S.2d 256, 258, (App. Term, 9th & 10th
Jud. Dist. 2011) (*Almendarez* should not be followed); or

(b) Misdemeanor complaints. *See People v. McDonald*, 179
Misc. 2d 479, 480, 689 N.Y.S.2d 600, 602 (City Crim. Ct. 1999).

§ 16:23   Information, prosecutor's information and misdemeanor complaint—Bill of particulars

Research References

West's Key Number Digest, Automobiles ☞351.1

N.Y. Crim. Proc. Law § 100.45(4) provides that "[t]he provisions of [CPL §] 200.95, governing bills of particulars with respect to indictments, apply to informations, to misdemeanor
complaints and to prosecutor's informations." Thus, "[a] defendant
is not entitled to a bill of particulars when the underlying accusatory instrument is a simplified information (see CPL 100.45(4))."
People v. Malone, 166 Misc. 2d 54, 55, 631 N.Y.S.2d 223 (Dist. Ct.
1995). *See also Turck*, 178 Misc. 2d 892, 893, 681 N.Y.S.2d 454,
455 (Sand Lake J. Ct. 1998); *People v. McGettrick*, 139 Misc. 2d
403, 404, 528 N.Y.S.2d 758 (City Ct. 1988); *People v. Cohen*, 131
Misc. 2d 898, 899, 502 N.Y.S.2d 123, 124 (City Ct. 1986).

Where the accusatory instrument is a long form information,
the rules governing bills of particulars apply regardless of
whether the defendant is charged with a misdemeanor or a
violation. *People v. Turck*, 178 Misc. 2d 892, 893, 681 N.Y.S.2d
454, 455–56 (J. Ct. 1998). *See also People v. All State Properties,
LLC*, 29 Misc. 3d 201, __, 907 N.Y.S.2d 549, 553 (Hempstead
Just. Ct. 2010).

Bills of particulars are addressed in detail in §§ 20:1 et seq.,
24:1 et seq., *infra*.

§ 16:24   Bill of particulars cannot cure a deficient information

Research References

West's Key Number Digest, Automobiles ☞351.1

"Because an information must, for jurisdictional purposes,

contain nonhearsay factual allegations sufficient to establish a prima facie case, a prosecutor's hearsay statements, set forth in a bill of particulars, cannot supply necessary factual allegations to cure a deficient information." *People v. Alejandro*, 70 N.Y.2d 133, 138, 517 N.Y.S.2d 927, 930, 511 N.E.2d 71 (1987).

§ 16:25   Superseding informations and prosecutor's informations

Research References

West's Key Number Digest, Automobiles ☜351.1

The superseding of informations and prosecutor's informations is governed by N.Y. Crim. Proc. Law § 100.50, which provides as follows:

1. If at any time before entry of a plea of guilty to or commencement of a trial of an information or a prosecutor's information, another information or, as the case may be, another prosecutor's information is filed with the same local criminal court charging the defendant with an offense charged in the first instrument, the first such instrument is, with respect to such offense, superseded by the second and, upon the defendant's arraignment upon the latter, the count of the first instrument charging such offense must be dismissed by the court. The first instrument is not, however, superseded with respect to any count contained therein which charges an offense not charged in the second instrument.

2. At any time before entry of a plea of guilty to or commencement of a trial of an information, the district attorney may file with the local criminal court a prosecutor's information charging any offenses supported, pursuant to the standards prescribed in [N.Y. Crim. Proc. Law § 100.40(1)], by the allegations of the factual part of the original information and/or any supporting depositions which may accompany it. In such case, the original information is superseded by the prosecutor's information and, upon the defendant's arraignment upon the latter, is deemed dismissed.

3. A misdemeanor complaint must or may be replaced and superseded by an information pursuant to the provisions of [N.Y. Crim. Proc. Law §] 170.65.

In *People v. Thomas*, 4 N.Y.3d 143, 145, 791 N.Y.S.2d 68, 69, 824 N.E.2d 499 (2005), the Court of Appeals held that, consistent with CPL 100.50, "the People may file a new information that alleges additional facts or charges offenses that were not included in a previously filed information but stem from the same criminal transaction." In so holding, the Court reasoned that:

Subdivision (1) of CPL 100.50 authorizes the People to file "another

information" prior to the "entry of a plea of guilty to or commencement of a trial of an information" (CPL 100.50[1]; *see also* CPL
100.05). Significantly, the statute imposes no restrictions on the
type of crimes that may be included in a new information. Since a
new crime may be charged, the statute necessarily implies that new
facts may be alleged in support of any additional offenses (see CPL
100.40[1][c]). Notably, nothing in subdivision (2) of CPL 100.50
restricts the People's ability to provide additional factual detail in a
new information.

4 N.Y.3d at 147, 791 N.Y.S.2d at 71.

Nonetheless, "a prosecutor's information is jurisdictionally
defective if the original information it supersedes and any supporting depositions do not contain adequate factual allegations.
To be adequate, the allegations must establish, if true, every element of the crime charged and the defendant's commission of
each." *People v. Inserra*, 4 N.Y.3d 30, 32, 790 N.Y.S.2d 72, 73, 823
N.E.2d 437 (2004). *See also People v. English*, 189 Misc. 2d 230,
731 N.Y.S.2d 350, 353 (City Crim. Ct. 2001).

It has been held that, pursuant to N.Y. Crim. Proc. Law
§ 100.50(1), "it 'is proper to file a superseding information in response to a defense motion to dismiss the original instrument for
insufficiency.' " *People v. McDonald*, 179 Misc. 2d 479, 481, 689
N.Y.S.2d 600, 602 (City Crim. Ct. 1999) (quoting *People v. Cibro
Oceana Terminal Corp.*, 148 Misc. 2d 149, 151, 559 N.Y.S.2d 782,
784 (City Crim. Ct. 1990)).

In addition, while "CPL 100.50(1) provides that upon the filing
of a subsequent information, the first instrument is 'superseded
by the second and, upon the defendant's arraignment upon the
latter, the count of the first instrument charging such offense
must be dismissed by the court,' " this rule does not apply where
the "defendant was never arraigned on the succeeding
information." *People v. Bowman*, 84 N.Y.2d 923, 924–25, 620
N.Y.S.2d 810, 644 N.E.2d 1366 (1994). *See also People v. Gutir-
rez*, 184 Misc. 2d 60, 61, 706 N.Y.S.2d 609, 610 (J. Ct. 2000).

A misdemeanor complaint cannot be superseded by another
misdemeanor complaint. *People v. Torres*, 151 Misc. 2d 682, 573
N.Y.S.2d 255 (City Crim. Ct. 1991). *See also People v. Hussein*,
177 Misc. 2d 139, 677 N.Y.S.2d 653, 658 (City Crim. Ct. 1998)
("to effectively supersede a [misdemeanor] complaint, the People
must convert at the time they intend to supersede").

§ 16:26 Simplified information may not be superseded

Research References
West's Key Number Digest, Automobiles ⊚351.1

Similar to N.Y. Crim. Proc. Law § 100.45 (which, by its express terms, only permits the amendment of informations and prosecutor's informations), N.Y. Crim. Proc. Law § 100.50, by its express terms, only permits the supersedure of informations, prosecutor's informations and misdemeanor complaints. Thus, it does not permit the supersedure of simplified informations. *See, e.g., People v. Baron,* 107 Misc. 2d 59, 59–60, 438 N.Y.S.2d 425, 426–27 (App. Term 1980); *People v. Flood,* 25 Misc. 3d 843, __, 885 N.Y.S.2d 190, 192 (Nassau Co. Dist. Ct. 2009) ("What the people continue to fail to recognize is that a simplified traffic information is not an accusatory instrument that can be superceded, therefore, [CPL § 100.50(2)] is not applicable"); *People v. Finch,* 19 Misc. 3d 840, __, 854 N.Y.S.2d 885, 888 (Nassau Co. Dist. Ct. 2008); *People v. Quarles,* 168 Misc. 2d 638, 646, 639 N.Y.S.2d 661, 667 (City Ct. 1996); *People v. Kaid,* 165 Misc. 2d 489, 492, 629 N.Y.S.2d 617, 619 (City Crim. Ct. 1995); *People v. Pregent,* 142 Misc. 2d 344, 345, 537 N.Y.S.2d 424 (City Ct. 1988); *People v. Origlia,* 138 Misc. 2d 286, 524 N.Y.S.2d 163 (City Ct. 1988).

However, "[a]lthough the People cannot supersede a simplified information with a long form information, if a simplified information is dismissed due to facial insufficiency, the People may refile the charges using a long form information." *People v. Quarles,* 168 Misc. 2d 638, at 647 n.7, 639 N.Y.S.2d 661, 668 n.7 (City Ct. 1996). *See also People v. Nuccio,* 78 N.Y.2d 102, 104, 571 N.Y.S.2d 693, 694, 575 N.E.2d 111 (1991); *People v. Holden,* 990 N.Y.S.2d 409 (Canandaigua City Ct. 2014); *People v. Brady,* 196 Misc. 2d 993, 768 N.Y.S.2d 157, 161 (Dist. Ct. 2003); *People v. Green,* 192 Misc. 2d 296, 298, 745 N.Y.S.2d 656, 658 (Dist. Ct. 2002) ("although the Court of Appeals ruled in *People v. Nuccio (supra)* that the People are at liberty to commence a new prosecution by long form information even where a simplified traffic information has been dismissed for failure to provide a supporting deposition, I conclude they cannot cure the defect in a simplified information prosecution by making use of supersedure pursuant to CPL 100.50"); *People v. Rossi,* 154 Misc. 2d 616, 620, 587 N.Y.S.2d 511, 515 (J. Ct. 1992).

In *People v. Koenig,* 31 Misc. 3d 827, __, 919 N.Y.S.2d 319, 320 (Sullivan Co. Ct. 2011), the People failed to serve the defendant with a supporting deposition despite his timely request therefor. The defendant filed a written motion to dismiss. In response, the arresting officer filed a long form information with the Justice Court. Finding numerous errors in how Justice Court handled the case, County Court held, *inter alia,* that:

> [T]he Village Justice mistakenly allowed the Village Police Officer to file a long form information with the Justice Court while an accusatory instrument (the simplified information) was still pending based upon *People v. Nuccio,* 78 N.Y.2d 102, 571 N.Y.S.2d 693, 575 N.E.2d 111 (1991).

People v. Nuccio, supra stands for the proposition that a defendant may be prosecuted in a local criminal court by a sufficient long form information *after* a prior simplified information, charging the same offense(s), has been dismissed for failure to supply a timely supporting deposition required by CPL 100.25(2).

The fact that a police officer may file a long form information after a simplified information has been dismissed for failure to serve a timely supporting deposition is not a basis to deny a defendant's properly made motion to dismiss the simplified information.

Lastly, the Village Justice served a Notice of Appearance on the defendant for March 25, 2010 as a pretext to lure the defendant to the Village of Liberty so the Village Police Officer could effectuate personal service of the illegally filed long form information. The Village Justice, after service, and presumably arraignment, of the long form information, denied defendant his right to an adjournment to obtain an attorney. Defendant was immediately forced to participate in a non-jury trial. The interest of justice is not served by allowing such behavior on the part of the Village Judge.

919 N.Y.S.2d at 320-21.

§ 16:27   Waivability of requirement that accusatory instrument be valid and sufficient

Research References

West's Key Number Digest, Automobiles ⚖351.1

As a general rule, "[a] valid and sufficient accusatory instrument is a nonwaivable jurisdictional prerequisite to a criminal prosecution." *People v. Harper*, 37 N.Y.2d 96, 99, 371 N.Y.S.2d 467, 469, 332 N.E.2d 336 (1975). *See also People v. Dumay*, 23 N.Y.3d 518, 2014 WL 2515692 (2014); *People v. Dreyden*, 15 N.Y.3d 100, 103, 905 N.Y.S.2d 542, 543, 931 N.E.2d 526 (2010); *People v. Alejandro*, 70 N.Y.2d 133, 135, 517 N.Y.S.2d 927, 928, 511 N.E.2d 71 (1987); *People v. Hall*, 48 N.Y.2d 927, 425 N.Y.S.2d 56, 57, 401 N.E.2d 179 (1979); *People v. Case*, 42 N.Y.2d 98, 99, 396 N.Y.S.2d 841, 842, 365 N.E.2d 872, 87 A.L.R.3d 77 (1977); *People v. Noblett*, 172 Misc. 2d 826, 830, 660 N.Y.S.2d 517, 520 (County Ct. 1997); *People v. Gingello*, 181 Misc. 2d 163, 164, 694 N.Y.S.2d 579, 580 (City Ct. 1999) (abrogated on other grounds by, People v. Blair, 98 N.Y.2d 722, 749 N.Y.S.2d 809, 779 N.E.2d 748 (2002)); *People v. Hoffman Floor Covering Corp.*, 179 Misc. 2d 656, 686 N.Y.S.2d 651 (City Crim. Ct. 1999). In this regard, "[a]n objection to the substantive sufficiency of the information, such as one that it does not state a crime, as distinguished from an objection to the form of the instrument, is not waived by a plea of guilty." *People v. Case*, 42 N.Y.2d 98, at 100, 396 N.Y.S.2d 841, 842, 365 N.E.2d 872, 87 A.L.R.3d 77 (1977).

Nonetheless, there are exceptions to this rule. For example, in *People v. Key*, 45 N.Y.2d 111, 408 N.Y.S.2d 16, 379 N.E.2d 1147 (1978), the Court of Appeals held that a legally insufficient supporting deposition to a simplified traffic information in a DWI case is a waivable defect:

In this case, there was no allegation that defendant was operating his automobile or even that the engine was running, an allegation necessary to establish commission of the crime. Hence, as both courts below have held, the information was insufficient. * * *

[However], there should be no question that the defect in this information was, in fact waivable. Even if, despite the CPL provisions, there be some defects in accusatory instruments that may never be waived, the defect in this case is not of that class. Since a simplified traffic information can proceed to trial without any supporting deposition at all, and hence without any facts providing reasonable cause, it is unacceptable that absence of a factual allegation in the deposition is nonwaivable.

45 N.Y.2d at 116–17, 408 N.Y.S.2d at 19.

To avoid waiver, *Key* made clear that a motion to dismiss for lack of a sufficient supporting deposition, like all other pretrial motions, must be made in accordance with N.Y. Crim. Proc. Law § 255.20(1). *People v. Key*, 45 N.Y.2d 111, 116, 408 N.Y.S.2d 16, 19, 379 N.E.2d 1147 (1978). *See also People v. Dean*, 74 N.Y.2d 643, 542 N.Y.S.2d 512, 540 N.E.2d 707 (1989); *People v. Fattizzi*, 98 Misc. 2d 288, 413 N.Y.S.2d 804 (App. Term 1978); *People v. Rose*, 8 Misc. 3d 184, 794 N.Y.S.2d 630, 635 (Dist. Ct. 2005); *People v. Sirkin*, 146 Misc. 2d 1030, 553 N.Y.S.2d 593 (J. Ct. 1990). *See generally People v. Nuccio*, 78 N.Y.2d 102, 104, 571 N.Y.S.2d 693, 694, 575 N.E.2d 111 (1991). In other words, a motion to dismiss for lack of a sufficient supporting deposition should, among other things, be made:

(a) In writing. *See* N.Y. Crim. Proc. Law §§ 170.45 & 210.45(1). *Cf. People v. Jennings*, 69 N.Y.2d 103, 113, 512 N.Y.S.2d 652, 656, 504 N.E.2d 1079 (1986) (by failing to insist upon conformity with the procedural requirements of N.Y. Crim. Proc. Law § 210.45(1), the People waived their right to written notice under the statute);

(b) Upon reasonable notice to the People. *See* N.Y. Crim. Proc. Law §§ 170.45 & 210.45(1); and

(c) With certain exceptions, within 45 days after arraignment (or within such additional time as the Court may fix upon application of the defendant). *See* N.Y. Crim. Proc. Law §§ 255.10(1)(b) & 255.20(1).

People v. Casey, 95 N.Y.2d 354, 362, 717 N.Y.S.2d 88, 92, 740 N.E.2d 233 (2000), the Court of Appeals created another waivable defect: "Now squarely confronted with the issue whether a hearsay pleading violation of CPL 100.40(1)(c) is jurisdictional and non-waivable, we conclude that it is not." *See also Casey*, 95 N.Y.2d at 367, 717 N.Y.S.2d at 96 ("we conclude that hearsay pleading defects in the factual portion of a local criminal court information must be preserved in order to be reviewable as a matter of law on appeal").

Similarly, in *People v. Keizer*, 100 N.Y.2d 114, 121, 760 N.Y.S.2d 720, 724, 790 N.E.2d 1149 (2003), the Court of Appeals held "that a purported hearsay defect in an accusatory instrument is nonjurisdictional and, thus, forfeited by a guilty plea." In so holding, the Court commented that "[a] guilty plea . . . generally marks the end of a criminal case, not a gateway to further litigation." 100 N.Y.2d at 118, 760 N.Y.S.2d at 722.

§ 16:28 Latent vs. facially apparent defects

Research References

West's Key Number Digest, Automobiles ⚬351.1

The Court of Appeals has ruled that where a hearsay pleading defect is latent—as opposed to facially apparent—dismissal is not required, as a motion to dismiss is only permitted to address *facial* insufficiency. *See People v. Casey*, 95 N.Y.2d 354, 361, 717 N.Y.S.2d 88, 91, 740 N.E.2d 233 (2000) ("Whether the allegation of an element of an offense is hearsay, rendering the information defective, is to be determined on a facial reading of the accusatory instrument"); *Matter of Edward B.*, 80 N.Y.2d 458, 461, 591 N.Y.S.2d 962, 606 N.E.2d 1353 (1992) (dismissal of juvenile delinquency petition not required "when the hearsay character of the facts alleged in the supporting deposition is not facially apparent but is discovered at some point in the course of the proceeding"); *Edward B.*, 80 N.Y.2d at 464, 591 N.Y.S.2d at 964 ("CPL 100.40 concerns the 'facial sufficiency' of local criminal court accusatory instruments"); *People v. DeLeon*, 157 Misc. 2d 62, 66, 595 N.Y.S.2d 909, 912 (City Crim. Ct. 1993) ("this court holds that the latent deficiency in the accusatory instrument revealed during the trial does not provide grounds for mandatory dismissal under C.P.L. § 100.40"). *Cf. Matter of Rodney J.*, 83 N.Y.2d 503, 507, 611 N.Y.S.2d 485, 487, 633 N.E.2d 1089 (1994) (defect facially apparent—Court distinguishes *Edward B.* on this ground).

Nonetheless, the *Edward B.* Court noted that "practices such as occurred here, where the young complainant was permitted to sign a supporting deposition *under oath* despite the fact that she had never read or been read its exact contents, are not to be endorsed or condoned." 80 N.Y.2d 458 at 465 n.2, 591 N.Y.S.2d at 965 n.2.

In any event, "[i]t is well-settled law that where an information is used as the basis for the issuance of a warrant of arrest or subpoenas, it is insufficient if it rests on information and belief without a statement of the sources of the information and grounds of the belief." *People v. James*, 4 N.Y.2d 482, 485, 176 N.Y.S.2d 323, 325, 151 N.E.2d 877 (1958). *See also People v. Jeffries*, 19 N.Y.2d 564, 281 N.Y.S.2d 67, 227 N.E.2d 870 (1967); *People v. Pleva*, 96 Misc. 2d 1020, 410 N.Y.S.2d 261 (Dist. Ct. 1978) (applying this rule to misdemeanor complaint).

Similarly, "the deposition supporting a simplified traffic information, to the extent it is based on information and belief, must contain a statement of the source of that information and belief if it is to be sufficient on its face." *People v. Lesnak*, 165 Misc. 2d 706, 709, 630 N.Y.S.2d 459, 461 (Dist. Ct. 1995). *See also People v. Dumas*, 42 Misc. 3d 265, ___, 974 N.Y.S.2d 921, 924 (Buffalo City N.Y. City Ct. 2013); *People v. Noblett*, 172 Misc. 2d 826, 828–29, 660 N.Y.S.2d 517, 519–20 (County Ct. 1997); *People v. Quarles*, 168 Misc. 2d 638, 647, 639 N.Y.S.2d 661, 668 (City Ct. 1996); *People v. Born*, 166 Misc. 2d 757, 759–60, 634 N.Y.S.2d 915, 917–18 (J. Ct. 1995); *People v. Smith*, 163 Misc. 2d 353, 363–64, 621 N.Y.S.2d 449, 456–57 (J. Ct. 1994); *People v. Moretti*, 142 Misc. 2d 331, 332, 537 N.Y.S.2d 735, 736 (City Ct. 1988). *See generally People v. Scott*, 176 Misc. 2d 393, 397, 671 N.Y.S.2d 961, 964 (City Ct. 1998) (applying this rule to misdemeanor complaint); *People v. Pleva*, 96 Misc. 2d 1020, 410 N.Y.S.2d 261 (Dist. Ct. 1978) (same).

§ 16:29 Where defendant appears without counsel, Court is obligated to scrutinize accusatory instrument for facial sufficiency

Research References

West's Key Number Digest, Automobiles ☞351.1

N.Y. Crim. Proc. Law § 170.10 sets forth the procedure for arraigning a defendant upon a local criminal court accusatory instrument (other than a felony complaint). The official Practice Commentaries thereto provide, in pertinent part, that:

The statutory procedure . . . omits an essential first step that should be the responsibility of the court whenever the defendant appears without counsel and there has been no warrant of arrest. This is scrutiny of the accusatory instrument for legal sufficiency. The reason for immediate initial appraisal of that instrument is of course that it is the basis of the court's jurisdiction; and, accordingly, if the instrument is not legally sufficient, the court has no authority at all to proceed with the arraignment. It must dismiss the instrument and discharge the defendant (see Practice Commentary for CPL § 100.15; see also CPL §§ 140.45, 150.50[2]).

Preiser, Practice Commentaries, McKinney's Cons. Laws of N.Y., Book 11A, CPL § 170.10, at 12. *See also People v. Machado*, 182 Misc. 2d 194, 698 N.Y.S.2d 416 (City Crim. Ct. 1999).

§ 16:30   Sufficiency of informations—Specific cases

Research References

West's Key Number Digest, Automobiles ☞351.1

In *People v. Alejandro*, 70 N.Y.2d 133, 134–36, 517 N.Y.S.2d 927, 928–29, 511 N.E.2d 71 (1987):

Defendant was charged with resisting arrest (Penal Law § 205.30), tried before a jury and convicted on the basis of a misdemeanor information which set forth no factual allegations establishing that the police officer was effecting an authorized arrest. The information was insufficient on its face because it lacked the necessary nonhearsay allegations which would establish, "if true, every element of the offense charged and the defendant's commission thereof" (CPL 100.40[1][c]); 100.15[3]). We hold that this omission constituted a jurisdictional defect which was not waived by defendant's failure to raise the issue until after completion of the trial. * * *

This misdemeanor information for resisting arrest was unquestionably insufficient on its face (CPL 100.40[1][c]). The Penal Law defines resisting arrest as intentionally preventing or attempting to prevent a police officer "from effecting an *authorized* arrest" (Penal Law § 205.30 [emphasis added]). It is an essential element of the crime of resisting arrest that the arrest be authorized and, absent proof that the arresting officer had a warrant or probable cause to arrest defendant for commission of some offense, a conviction cannot stand. Thus, to comply with the statute, the factual part of the information for resisting arrest must contain "[n]on-hearsay allegations [which would] establish, if true" (CPL 100.40[1][c]) that the underlying arrest was authorized. These essential allegations are omitted from the information here. The factual portion pertains only to defendant's actions in resisting the arrest.

(Citations omitted).

In *People v. McNamara*, 78 N.Y.2d 626, 629, 578 N.Y.S.2d 476, 478, 585 N.E.2d 788 (1991), the Court held that "the informations charging respondents with public lewdness were facially defective because they failed to establish the statutory element that respondents' acts were committed in a 'public place' (Penal Law § 245.00[a])."

In *People v. Tarka*, 75 N.Y.2d 996, 997, 557 N.Y.S.2d 266, 556 N.E.2d 1073 (1990), the Court held that "[i]nasmuch as the information charging defendant with disorderly conduct fails to allege the essential element of either intent or recklessness (see, Penal

Law § 240.20[3]), as the People concede, the information is
jurisdictionally defective and must be dismissed."

In *People v. Dumas*, 68 N.Y.2d 729, 731, 506 N.Y.S.2d 319, 320,
497 N.E.2d 686 (1986), the Court held that:

> We agree with the Criminal Court that the misdemeanor complaints
> are facially insufficient. * * *
>
> In each case the complaint contains a conclusory statement that
> the defendant sold marihuana, but in neither case is this supported
> by evidentiary facts showing the basis for the conclusion that the
> substance sold was actually marihuana. There is, for instance, no
> allegation that the police officer is an expert in identifying
> marihuana, nor any allegation that the defendant represented the
> substance as being marihuana. Neither are any additional facts
> provided by the supporting depositions in which the undercover po-
> lice officer merely adopts the statements alleged in the complaints.

(Citation omitted).

In Matter of Jahron S., 79 N.Y.2d 632, 634, 584 N.Y.S.2d 748,
749, 595 N.E.2d 823 (1992), the Court held that a Family Court
petition (which is analogous to an information) charging appellant with possession of crack cocaine, taken together with its supporting deposition, was legally insufficient "in the absence of a
laboratory report identifying the substance seized as cocaine." In
so holding, the Court stated that:

> It is certainly implicit in our holding in Matter of David T. *(supra)*
> that the prima facie standard applicable to informations applies
> equally to Family Court petitions. Today, we make clear that
> because both informations and petitions are the ultimate instru-
> ments of prosecution and because both are required, in identical
> language, to contain nonhearsay allegations that establish, if true,
> every element of the offense charged and the accused's commission
> of the offense, that a prima facie case standard is applicable to
> both. . . .
>
> This does not entirely resolve the present case, however. The ques-
> tion that remains is whether Officer Henry's statement that based
> on his experience with illicit narcotics, the substance seized from
> appellant appeared to be crack cocaine, was sufficient to meet this
> prima facie case requirement. We conclude that it was not.
>
> In People v. Dumas, 68 N.Y.2d 729, 506 N.Y.S.2d 319, 497 N.E.2d
> 686 (1986), this Court held that a misdemeanor complaint contain-
> ing a conclusory statement that the defendant sold marihuana, but
> unsupported by evidentiary facts showing the basis for this conclu-
> sion, was legally insufficient. We suggested in dicta, however, that
> an allegation that the police officer was an expert in identifying
> marihuana might have rendered the complaint legally sufficient.
> The presentment agency has seized upon our language in Dumas

and argues that such an allegation was contained in the supporting deposition here, and that the petition should be deemed legally sufficient as a result.

Dumas differs from the present case in one key respect, however. As noted above, that case involved a misdemeanor complaint, and the factual part of a misdemeanor complaint must simply establish "reasonable cause" to believe that the defendant committed the crime charged (CPL 100.40[4][b]). Thus, a much lower standard is applicable when determining the legal sufficiency of complaints, which, unlike informations and petitions, do not serve as the sole instrument of prosecution and adjudication. Our language in Dumas does not, therefore, resolve the case now before us.

Appellants urge us to hold that a laboratory report is always necessary in order to establish a prima facie case of cocaine possession. There is no need to establish a per se rule. We leave open the possibility that a deposition based on personal knowledge and expertness may, in now unforeseen circumstances, qualify as sufficient evidence to establish a prima facie case of drug possession because of the nature of the crime, or its elements, or the special knowledge of the affiant. In this case, however, the deposition was insufficient to satisfy the prima facie case standard.

79 N.Y.2d 632 at 639–40, 584 N.Y.S.2d at 753.

In *People v. Swamp*, 84 N.Y.2d 725, 728, 622 N.Y.S.2d 472, 473, 646 N.E.2d 774 (1995), the Court held that, for purposes of assessing the legal sufficiency of an indictment charging the defendant with possession of cocaine, legally sufficient evidence can be established by "the results of a preliminary field test [a.k.a. a NIK field test or a Scott-Reagent field test] indicating the presence of cocaine"; in other words, the People were *not* required to provide the Grand Jury with "the results of a formal laboratory analysis." In so holding, the Court reasoned, *inter alia*, that "in a drug-related prosecution, the People's case is legally sufficient if the evidence provides a 'reliable basis' for inferring the presence of a controlled substance. More than conclusory assertions that the defendant possessed a drug are required at the Grand Jury stage." 84 N.Y.2d at 730, 622 N.Y.S.2d at 474 (citation omitted).

Critically, however, the Court noted that "[p]roof beyond a reasonable doubt was not required at this stage. Contrary to the warning of the dissent, therefore, we do not hold that a defendant may be proven guilty beyond a reasonable doubt based solely on the results of a NIK field test, and we do not shift the ultimate burden of persuasion to defendant." 84 N.Y.2d at 733, 622 N.Y.S.2d at 476. *See also In re Angel A.*, 92 N.Y.2d 430, 434, 681 N.Y.S.2d 787, 789, 704 N.E.2d 554 (1998) (the reasoning of Swamp applies to juvenile delinquency petitions); *People v. Jason F.*, 181 Misc. 2d 653, 694 N.Y.S.2d 908 (J. Ct. 1999).

Matter of Rodney J., 83 N.Y.2d 503, 507, 611 N.Y.S.2d 485, 487, 633 N.E.2d 1089 (1994), the Court held that a juvenile delinquency petition charging respondent with criminal possession of a weapon was legally insufficient in that "the petition and its supporting documents in the instant case were jurisdictionally defective on their face insofar as they failed to contain a nonhearsay allegation of the weapon's operability."

In *People v. Inserra*, 4 N.Y.3d 30, 32, 790 N.Y.S.2d 72, 823 N.E.2d 437 (2004), the Court held that, in assessing the sufficiency of an information charging the defendant with criminal contempt of an order of protection, "a defendant's name on the signature line of an order of protection adequately supports an allegation that the defendant knew of the order's contents."

In *People v. Henderson*, 92 N.Y.2d 677, 681, 685 N.Y.S.2d 409, 411, 708 N.E.2d 165 (1999), the Court held that "[u]nder these circumstances, allegations of substantial pain, swelling and contusions, following kicks, must be deemed sufficient to constitute 'physical injury' to support a facially valid local criminal court information. We hold, therefore that the factual allegations contained in the accusatory instrument are sufficient to make out a prima facie case of assault in the third degree."

In *People v. Miles*, 64 N.Y.2d 731, 732, 485 N.Y.S.2d 747, 748, 475 N.E.2d 118 (1984), the Court held an information charging the defendant with issuing a bad check, in violation of N.Y. Penal Law § 190.05(1), to be jurisdictionally sufficient where it, *inter alia*, "sets forth sufficient evidentiary facts by alleging that defendant knew of his insufficient funds and intended or believed payment would be refused."

In *People v. Hall*, 48 N.Y.2d 927, 927–28, 425 N.Y.S.2d 56, 57, 401 N.E.2d 179 (1979):

> [T]he information charging harassment recited only that defendant, who it also alleges indicated that his desire was that the complainant leave the defendant's premises, "did strike, shove and otherwise subject [the complainant] to physical contact and threatened * * * physical harm." It failed to specify an essential element of the crime, which is that the acts be done "with intent to harass, annoy or alarm" (Penal Law, § 240.25). Absent such an allegation, the acts complained of did not constitute criminal conduct and, hence, defendant's conviction was jurisdictionally defective.

In *People v. Case*, 42 N.Y.2d 98, 99, 396 N.Y.S.2d 841, 842, 365 N.E.2d 872, 87 A.L.R.3d 77 (1977), the Court held that "[a] CB radio message from one motor vehicle operator to another as to the highway location of a radar speed checkpoint does not constitute the crime of obstructing governmental administration. To say that there is a Smokey takin' pictures up the road does not subject the speaker to a year's imprisonment." In so holding, the Court reasoned that:

Significantly, the statute [*i.e.,* [N.Y. Penal Law § 195.05] has been uniformly interpreted to the effect that mere words alone do not constitute "physical force or interference" such as to support the charge of obstructing governmental administration. * * *

Under the express provisions of the statute, the interference would have to be, in part at least, physical in nature. The line is so drawn. To interpret and apply section 195.05, as suggested by the prosecution, would mean that there would be no outer limits to the statute. Under such a notion, the imparting of information as to location of the radar speed checkpoint would be penally condemned without physical interference and irrespective of whether the recipients of the messages were violating or were about to violate the law. A casual meeting of two travelers at a rest stop along a thoroughfare followed by a casual remark by one that a radar setup had been seen, with nothing more, would be enough to mark the author of the remark as a criminal.

People v. Case, 42 N.Y.2d 98, 102–03, 396 N.Y.S.2d 841, 843–44, 365 N.E.2d 872, 87 A.L.R.3d 77 (1977).

In *People v. Key,* 45 N.Y.2d 111, 116, 408 N.Y.S.2d 16, 19, 379 N.E.2d 1147 (1978), the Court held that the supporting deposition to a simplified traffic information in a DWI case was legally insufficient where "there was no allegation that defendant was operating his automobile or even that the engine was running, an allegation necessary to establish commission of the crime. Hence, as both courts below have held, the information was insufficient."

In *People v. Moore,* 5 N.Y.3d 725, 727, 800 N.Y.S.2d 49, 51, 833 N.E.2d 192 (2005), the Court held that:

Since the information and supporting deposition here fail to allege facts establishing that the campus building defendant entered into was in any way "fenced or otherwise enclosed in a manner designed to exclude intruders" (Penal Law § 140.10[a])—a required element of the crime—it was insufficient to establish criminal trespass in the third degree (*see* CPL 100.15[3]; 100.40[1][c]). Thus, the information was properly dismissed as facially insufficient.

In *People v. Dreyden,* 15 N.Y.3d 100, 103, 905 N.Y.S.2d 542, 544, 931 N.E.2d 526 (2010), the Court held that a misdemeanor complaint which claimed that the defendant possessed a gravity knife, but which failed to contain any factual allegations establishing the basis for the arresting officer's conclusion that the knife in question was a "gravity knife" as defined by the statute, was jurisdictionally defective. In so holding, the Court reasoned that:

A conclusory statement that an object recovered from a defendant is a gravity knife does not alone meet the reasonable cause requirement. An arresting officer should, at the very least, explain briefly, with reference to his training and experience, how he or she formed the belief that the object observed in defendant's possession was a gravity knife. Here, the accusatory instrument contained no factual basis for the officer's conclusion that the knife was a gravity knife, as opposed to a pocket knife, craft knife or other type of knife that does not fit the definition of a per se weapon as defined in Penal Law article 265.

15 N.Y.3d at 104, 905 N.Y.S.2d at 544.

In *People v. Jones*, 9 N.Y.3d 259, 260-61, 848 N.Y.S.2d 600, 601, 878 N.E.2d 1016 (2007), the information charging the defendant with Disorderly Conduct provided, in pertinent part:

(a) That "on June 12, 2004, at approximately 2:01 A.M., on 42nd Street and Seventh Avenue 'defendant, with intent to cause public inconvenience, annoyance and alarm and recklessly creating a risk thereof, obstructed vehicular and pedestrian traffic' ";

(b) That a police officer "observed defendant along with a number of other individuals standing around at the above location, to wit a public sidewalk, not moving, and that as a result of defendants' [sic] behavior, numerous pedestrians in the area had to walk around defendants [sic] . . ."; and

(c) That "[D]eponent directed defendant to move and defendant refused and as deponent attempted to stop defendant, defendant did run."

The Court of Appeals held that:

To meet the jurisdictional requisite to prosecute defendant for disorderly conduct under Penal Law § 240.20(5), the People were obliged to set forth a prima facie case that defendant "with intent to cause public inconvenience, annoyance or alarm, or recklessly creating a risk thereof . . . obstruct[ed] vehicular or pedestrian traffic."

The allegations in the information do not meet this burden. Nothing in the information indicates how defendant, when he stood in the middle of a sidewalk at 2:01 A.M., had the intent to or recklessly created a risk of causing "public inconvenience, annoyance or alarm." The conduct sought to be deterred under the statute is "considerably more serious than the apparently innocent" conduct of defendant here. Something more than a mere inconvenience of pedestrians is required to support the charge. Otherwise, any person who happens to stop on a sidewalk—whether to greet another, to seek directions or simply to regain one's bearings—would be subject to prosecution under this statute.

Thus, as the information fails to set forth a prima facie case of disorderly conduct under Penal Law § 240.20(5), the accusatory instrument is jurisdictionally defective and must be dismissed.

9 N.Y.3d at 262-63, 848 N.Y.S.2d at 602-03 (citations and footnote omitted).

In *People v. South*, 29 Misc. 3d 92, __, 912 N.Y.S.2d 837, 841 (App. Term, 9th & 10th Jud. Dist. 2010), the Court that accusatory instruments charging the defendant with Endangering the Welfare of a Child were insufficient where:

> The factual portion of the accusatory instruments involved herein merely alleged that defendant was guilty of endangering the welfare of her two children because she drove her vehicle, while she was "in an intoxicated condition," with her two minor children in the vehicle. The accusatory instruments were bare of any facts from which one could conclude that defendant was intoxicated and, as a result, endangered the welfare of her children by driving the motor vehicle. While the accusatory instruments referred to an Intoxilyzer 5000 evidence card as a basis to establish that defendant's blood alcohol content was above the legal limit, they did not set forth defendant's blood alcohol content, and a sworn copy of said card was not included in the record. Therefore, since the factual allegations of the accusatory instruments were too conclusory, they were jurisdictionally defective.

Similarly, in *People v. Bottari*, 31 Misc. 3d 90, __-__, 924 N.Y.S.2d 733, 735-36 (App. Term, 9th & 10th Jud. Dist. 2011), the Court held that:

> The factual portion of the information herein alleged that defendant was guilty of endangering the welfare of her child because she drove her motor vehicle, while she was "in an intoxicated state," with her child in the vehicle. These factual allegations were too conclusory and failed to meet the requirements of CPL 100.15(3) and 100.40(4)(b) that the information "alleg[e] facts of an evidentiary character" demonstrating "reasonable cause" to believe the defendant committed the crime charged in that they did not include any facts from which one could conclude that defendant was intoxicated and, thus, endangered the welfare of her child by operating the vehicle. In assessing the facial sufficiency of the information, we do not take into consideration the allegations set forth in the informations charging defendant with driving while intoxicated per se or driving while intoxicated, since "an information must set forth the required nonhearsay evidentiary allegations within the four corners of the instrument itself or in annexed supporting depositions." Consequently, the information charging defendant with endangering the welfare of a child is jurisdictionally defective and must be dismissed.

(Citations omitted).

Another Endangering the Welfare of a Child charge was dismissed for facial insufficiency where:

> Neither the factual part of the original Information nor the complainant's supporting deposition set forth the complainant's age or date of birth. While the People have annexed a copy of a Domes-

tic Incident Report to the original Information which lists the complainant's date of birth and her age as fourteen (14) year [sic] old, this document is unsworn and fails to disclose the source of this information.

Having failed to provide any "non-hearsay allegations to establish the child's age," the count charging Endangering the Welfare of a Child is dismissed.

People v. Taylor, 23 Misc. 3d 361, __, 877 N.Y.S.2d 837, 841 (Nassau Co. Dist. Ct. 2009) (citations omitted). *See also People v. Mercado*, 184 Misc. 2d 40, 705 N.Y.S.2d 889 (City Crim. Ct. 2000).

§ 16:31 Required contents of accusatory instrument charging violation of VTL § 1192(3)

Research References

West's Key Number Digest, Automobiles ☞351.1; Indictment and Information ☞1, 4, 35

An accusatory instrument charging a defendant with violating N.Y. Veh. & Traf. Law § 1192(3) (*i.e.,* common law DWI) must, *inter alia,* provide reasonable cause to believe:

(a) That the defendant operated the vehicle. *See, e.g., People v. Key*, 45 N.Y.2d 111, 116, 408 N.Y.S.2d 16, 19, 379 N.E.2d 1147 (1978) ("In this case, there was no allegation that defendant was operating his automobile or even that the engine was running, an allegation necessary to establish commission of the crime. Hence, as both courts below have held, the information was insufficient"); *People v. Key*, 87 Misc. 2d 262, 266, 391 N.Y.S.2d 781, 785 (App. Term 1976), judgment aff'd, 45 N.Y.2d 111, 408 N.Y.S.2d 16, 379 N.E.2d 1147 (1978) ("In the instant matter, the supporting deposition fails to set forth any facts from which it could reasonably be inferred that the defendant was 'operating' the vehicle, a prerequisite to a conviction of violating [VTL §] 1192(2)");

(b) That the defendant was intoxicated. *See, e.g., People v. Hust*, 74 Misc. 2d 887, 890, 346 N.Y.S.2d 303, 307 (County Ct. 1973) ("The 'allegations of fact' within the meaning of CPL § 100.25(2) must refer not only to the driving, but also to the intoxication since in any driving while intoxicated case there are two elements to be proven: (1) that the defendant was driving the vehicle in question and (2) that the defendant was intoxicated while so driving"); and

(c) That the operation and the intoxication occurred simultaneously. *See, e.g., People v. Mertz*, 68 N.Y.2d 136, 139, 506 N.Y.S.2d 290, 291, 497 N.E.2d 657 (1986) ("A violation of Vehicle and Traffic Law § 1192(2) is not established unless the trier of fact finds that *while* operating a motor vehicle defendant

had a blood alcohol content (BAC) of .10 of 1% or more.")
(emphasis added); *People v. Schools*, 122 A.D.2d 502, 503, 505
N.Y.S.2d 462, 463 (3d Dep't 1986) ("The *sine qua non* for conviction is the operation of a vehicle simultaneously with intoxication"); *People v. Strauss*, 260 A.D. 880, 881, 22 N.Y.S.2d 880,
881 (2d Dep't 1940) ("intoxication and operation must be simultaneous or there is no crime"); *Hust, supra. See generally People
v. Spencer*, 289 A.D.2d 877, 879, 736 N.Y.S.2d 428, 431 (3d
Dep't 2001); *People v. Saplin*, 122 A.D.2d 498, 499, 505
N.Y.S.2d 460, 461 (3d Dep't 1986); *People v. Matthews*, 11
A.D.2d 784, 205 N.Y.S.2d 26 (2d Dep't 1960); *People v. Hemleb*,
4 A.D.2d 878, 166 N.Y.S.2d 837 (2d Dep't 1957).

In *People v. Fiumara*, 116 A.D.3d 421, —, 982 N.Y.S.2d 482,
483 (1st Dep't 2014), leave to appeal denied (N.Y. July 21, 2014),
the Appellate Division, First Department, held that:

> The accusatory instrument was not jurisdictionally defective. Giv-
> ing the misdemeanor information "a fair and not overly restrictive
> or technical reading," we find "as a matter of common sense and
> reasonable pleading" that it was legally sufficient to charge
> defendant with violating [VTL] § 1192(3). The arresting officer al-
> leged that defendant operated a motor vehicle, that he had
> bloodshot, watery eyes, slurred speech, and a strong odor of alcohol
> on his breath, that he was unsteady on his feet, and that he admit-
> ted to the officer that he had been drinking, but refused to submit
> to a breath test. There was no requirement that the information
> also contain an allegation of erratic driving.

(Citations omitted).

§ 16:32 Required contents of accusatory instrument charging violation of VTL § 1192(2)

Research References

West's Key Number Digest, Automobiles ⚮351.1; Indictment and Information ⚮1, 4, 35

In *People v. Lopez*, 170 Misc. 2d 278, 280, 648 N.Y.S.2d 231,
233 (City Crim. Ct. 1996), the Court held that:

> [A]n accusatory instrument charging V.T.L. § 1192.2 (operating a
> motor vehicle while under the influence of alcohol with .10% or
> more blood alcohol level) must be supported by a chemical test
> analysis certificate which is both verified by the individual who
> administered the test in compliance with C.P.L. § 100.30 and which
> indicates defendant's blood alcohol level. The absence of either of
> these factors renders the instrument jurisdictionally defective.

In so holding, the court reasoned that:

> Corroboration or non-hearsay allegations which support a charge of
> V.T.L. § 1192.2, must take the form of a blood alcohol test result

verified by the individual who administered the test. An individual's blood alcohol level is an element of the offense and its omission from the instant chemical test analysis renders that portion of the accusatory instrument charging a violation of V.T.L. § 1192.2 jurisdictionally defective.

People v. Lopez, 170 Misc. 2d 278, 280, 648 N.Y.S.2d 231, 233–34 (City Crim. Ct. 1996). *See also People v. Richberg*, 125 Misc. 2d 975, 979, 481 N.Y.S.2d 237, 240 (City Crim. Ct. 1984). *See generally People v. Mertz*, 68 N.Y.2d 136, 139, 506 N.Y.S.2d 290, 291, 497 N.E.2d 657 (1986) ("A violation of Vehicle and Traffic Law § 1192(2) is not established unless the trier of fact finds that *while* operating a motor vehicle defendant had a blood alcohol content (BAC) of .10 of 1% or more.") (emphasis added).

In *People v. Hernandez*, 46 Misc. 3d 151(A), 9 N.Y.S.3d 594 (App. Term, 1st Dep't 2015) (per curiam), the Court held that:

> Contrary to defendant's claim, the accusatory instrument was not required to allege that the chemical analysis of his breath was made within two hours of his arrest, in accordance with Vehicle and Traffic Law § 1194, or with his consent, as such factors are "solely for the purpose of qualifying the results of the test for admission into evidence," rather than elements of the underlying aggravated driving while intoxicated charge that the People must plead and prove.

(Citations omitted).

§ 16:33 Required contents of accusatory instrument charging misdemeanor DWAI

Research References

West's Key Number Digest, Automobiles ⚷351.1; Indictment and Information ⚷1, 4, 35

In *People v. Powlowski*, 172 Misc. 2d 240, 242, 658 N.Y.S.2d 558, 560 (City Ct. 1997), the Court held that where the People seek to charge a defendant with DWAI as a misdemeanor under N.Y. Veh. & Traf. Law § 1193(1)(a), the defendant's prior convictions "become an element of the higher level offense," and thus "must be pled in the accusatory instrument." *See also People v. Jamison*, 170 Misc. 2d 974, 652 N.Y.S.2d 495 (City Ct. 1996).

Thus, to be sufficient, the accusatory instrument in such a situation must allege facts providing reasonable cause to believe that the defendant has "two or more convictions for a violation of any subdivision of [VTL § 1192] within the preceding ten years." *Powlowski*, 172 Misc. 2d 240, 241, 658 N.Y.S.2d 558, 562–63 (Rochester City Ct. 1997). *See also People v. Peacock*, 193 Misc. 2d 672, 674, 751 N.Y.S.2d 676, 677 (App. Term 2002).

§ 16:34 Required contents of accusatory instrument charging DWI-related "recklessness" or "criminal negligence"

Research References

West's Key Number Digest, Automobiles ☞351.1; Indictment and Information ☞1, 4, 35

Where a defendant is charged with DWI in connection with a motor vehicle accident involving either "physical injury," *see* N.Y. Penal Law § 10.00(9), or property damage greater than $250, the People sometimes charge the defendant with additional crimes such as Assault 3rd, *see* N.Y. Penal Law § 120.00(2), (3), or Criminal Mischief 4th. *See* N.Y. Penal Law § 145.00(3). In this regard, however, the Court of Appeals has both held and reiterated that "[p]roof of intoxication alone is not enough to sustain a conviction of criminal negligence. The People must also prove that the defendant's intoxication affected his physical and mental capacity to the extent that it caused him to operate his vehicle in a culpably reckless manner." *People v. Bast*, 19 N.Y.2d 813, 815, 280 N.Y.S.2d 149, 150, 227 N.E.2d 47 (1967). *See also Matter of Johnston*, 75 N.Y.2d 403, 409–10, 554 N.Y.S.2d 88, 91, 553 N.E.2d 566 (1990) (same).

People v. Figueroa, 164 Misc. 2d 814, 625 N.Y.S.2d 839 (City Crim. Ct. 1995), addressed the facial sufficiency of an information charging the defendant with Assault 3rd in connection with a DWI-related motor vehicle accident. In this regard, the Court held that:

> The factual allegation that the defendant was driving under the influence of alcohol when she rear ended another vehicle is insufficient, without more, to support the charge that the defendant acted "recklessly" pursuant to PL § 120.00(2) or with "criminal negligence" pursuant to PL § 120.00(3) for facial sufficiency purposes. * * *
>
> In the present case, the defendant has not been apprised of what conduct, on her part, constitutes either reckless assault or criminally negligent assault. The allegation, if true, that defendant was driving under the influence of alcohol when she rear ended another vehicle would not make her culpable *per se* under either PL § 120.00(2) or PL § 120.00(3) without any allegations related to how the accident occurred or whether the defendant was driving in an erratic, reckless or negligent manner. Even if the act of defendant's driving her vehicle under the influence of alcohol constitutes a gross deviation from the required standard of care, there are insufficient allegations in the information which would show that the accident resulted from defendant's alleged "recklessness" or "criminal negligence" in violation of PL § 120.00(2) or PL § 120.00(3).

Accordingly, defendant's motion to dismiss the two counts of assault, PL § 120.00(2) and PL § 120.00(3), is granted. People v. Figueroa, 164 Misc. 2d 814, at 818–19, 625 N.Y.S.2d 839, at 842–43 (City Crim. Ct. 1995) (citations omitted). *See generally* People v. Carley, 248 A.D.2d 548, 669 N.Y.S.2d 870 (2d Dep't 1998) (even though evidence before Grand Jury proved that defendant was both intoxicated *and* speeding, Vehicular Manslaughter/Vehicular Assault charges nonetheless dismissed on ground that evidence failed to establish that defendant's conduct "caused" the victims' deaths/ injuries).

§ 16:35 Information charging common law DWI charges DWAI by operation of law

Research References

West's Key Number Digest, Automobiles ☞351.1; Indictment and Information ☞35

In *People v. Green*, 96 N.Y.2d 195, 726 N.Y.S.2d 357, 750 N.E.2d 59 (2001):

Defendant was arrested and charged in a misdemeanor information with driving while intoxicated. At trial before the Justice Court for the Town of East Hampton, the court also charged the jury on the lesser-included offense of driving while impaired. The jury acquitted defendant of driving while intoxicated but failed to reach a verdict on the lesser charge. The court then declared a mistrial as to that charge. * * *

The question before us is whether a new accusatory instrument was necessary to commence defendant's retrial on the lesser-included charge of driving while impaired (Vehicle and Traffic Law § 1192[1]), on which the first jury hung. We hold that it was not.

96 N.Y.2d at 196–98, 726 N.Y.S.2d at 359. In so holding, the Court reasoned that:

Vehicle and Traffic Law § 1192(9) specifically permits a conviction of driving while impaired on an instrument charging driving while intoxicated. Thus, the original instrument charging driving while intoxicated also, by operation of law, charged the offense of driving while impaired. No new accusatory instrument was required. * * *

[S]ince misdemeanor charges may be brought on a prosecutor's information, no purpose would be served by requiring the prosecutor to file a new information before proceeding to retrial on a lesser-included offense. Notably, the People had the right, at any time, to convert the original information charging driving while intoxicated to a new information charging driving while impaired, since the allegations in the original instrument were sufficient to support the lesser driving while impaired charge. Thus, mandating a new information prior to retrial would do nothing more than require the prosecutor to file another piece of paper.

96 N.Y.2d at 199–200, 726 N.Y.S.2d at 361. *Cf. People v. Ligon*, 188 Misc. 2d 477, 729 N.Y.S.2d 849 (Dist. Ct. 2001).

§ 16:36 People's right to appeal dismissal for facial insufficiency

Research References

West's Key Number Digest, Automobiles ☞351.1

"No appeal lies from a determination made in a criminal proceeding unless specifically provided for by statute." *People v. Hernandez*, 98 N.Y.2d 8, 10, 743 N.Y.S.2d 778, 770 N.E.2d 566 (2002). In this regard, "CPL 450.20(1) only authorizes an appeal from an order dismissing an accusatory instrument if the order was entered 'pursuant to [CPL §] 170.30, 170.50, or 210.20'. In contrast, the Legislature has not provided the People with any right of appeal from CPL 140.45 dismissals." 98 N.Y.2d at 10, 743 N.Y.S.2d at 778.

§ 16:37 Applicability of CPL § 60.50 to misdemeanor informations

Research References

West's Key Number Digest, Automobiles ☞351.1

In *People v. Suber*, 19 N.Y.3d 247, 946 N.Y.S.2d 552, 969 N.E.2d 770 (2012), the Court of Appeals held that the "confession corroboration rule" of CPL § 60.50 is inapplicable to misdemeanor informations. In light of this holding, cases such as *People v. Miedema*, 24 Misc. 3d 132(A), 899 N.Y.S.2d 62 (App. Term, 9th & 10th Jud. Dist. 2009), *People v. Morales*, 35 Misc. 3d 558, 939 N.Y.S.2d 824 (N.Y. City Crim. Ct. 2012), *People v. Walker*, 21 Misc. 3d 748, 865 N.Y.S.2d 530 (N.Y. City Crim. Ct. 2008), *People v. Pappas*, 163 Misc. 2d 1029, 623 N.Y.S.2d 83 (N.Y. City Crim. Ct. 1994), *People v. Mauro*, 147 Misc. 2d 381, 555 N.Y.S.2d 533 (N.Y. City Crim. Ct. 1990), *People v. Kaminiski*, 143 Misc. 2d 1089, 542 N.Y.S.2d 923 (N.Y. City Crim. Ct. 1989), and *People v. Alvarez*, 141 Misc. 2d 686, 534 N.Y.S.2d 90 (N.Y. City Crim. Ct. 1988), should no longer be followed.

§ 16:38 Appearance tickets

Research References

West's Key Number Digest, Automobiles ☞351.1

N.Y. Crim. Proc. Law § 150.10(1) provides, in pertinent part, that "[a]n appearance ticket [a.k.a. a desk appearance ticket (DAT) or a uniform traffic ticket (UTT)] is a written notice issued and subscribed by a police officer or other public servant authorized . . . to issue the same, directing a designated person to appear in a designated local criminal court at a designated future time in connection with his alleged commission of a designated offense." *See also* N.Y. Crim. Proc. Law § 1.20(26). An appearance ticket is commonly referred to as an "invitation to appear."

> *An appearance ticket serves solely as a notice to appear: it does not commence a criminal action. The only document that can commence a criminal action is an accusatory instrument; and an appearance ticket is not an accusatory instrument.* (See CPL § 1.20 subds. 1 to 8, 17). That document is to be filed by the issuer with a criminal court prior to the date specified in the ticket for defendant's appearance at court for arraignment. * * *

> Subdivision two was inserted in 1996 to reflect the procedural distinction between ordinary appearance tickets and the uniform traffic summons or ticket (see Vehicle & Traffic Law, § 207). In that situation the accusatory instrument is prepared at the same time as the ticket by filling out different parts of a carbonized multi-part form. One part is served upon the person summoned to appear (*e.g.*, the operator of the vehicle) and another part will be filed with a local criminal court. The part served upon the motorist is an appearance ticket and the part filed with the court is an accusatory instrument; to wit, a simplified information. (see CPL § 100.25 and Practice Commentary thereon).

Preiser, Practice Commentaries, McKinney's Cons. Laws of N.Y., Book 11A, CPL § 150.10, at 563–4 (emphasis added). *See also People v. Tyler*, 1 N.Y.3d 493, 494, 776 N.Y.S.2d 199, 200, 808 N.E.2d 334 (2004); *People v. Gindi*, 166 Misc. 2d 672, 674, 630 N.Y.S.2d 863, 865 (City Crim. Ct. 1995); *People v. Genovese*, 156 Misc. 2d 569, 570–71, 593 N.Y.S.2d 925, 926–27 (J. Ct. 1992) ("the yellow copy of the Simplified Traffic Information is an appearance ticket as defined by Criminal Procedure Law § 150.10"); *People v. Solomon*, 124 Misc. 2d 33, 34, 475 N.Y.S.2d 749, 750 (Dist. Ct. 1984) (rejected by, People v. Pregent, 142 Misc. 2d 344, 537 N.Y.S.2d 424 (City Ct. 1988)) (same); *Farkas v. State*, 96 Misc. 2d 784, 787 n.2, 409 N.Y.S.2d 696, 698 n.2 (Ct. Cl. 1978) ("'Appearance tickets' includes, by definition, 'uniform traffic tickets'. (See CPL 150.10.)").

In *People v. Stirrup*, 91 N.Y.2d 434, 439, 671 N.Y.S.2d 433, 436, 694 N.E.2d 434 (1998), the Court of Appeals held that:

> Once a defendant appears in response to a DAT, the criminal action is *deemed* commenced for ready-trial purposes. For all other purposes, including acquisition of jurisdiction over a defendant, the general rule applies—the action does not commence until the filing of the accusatory instrument. A court therefore may not arraign a defendant who voluntarily answers a DAT, where no accusatory instrument has been filed; nor may a court issue a warrant of ar-

rest to secure the presence of a defendant to answer the DAT, in the absence of an accusatory instrument.

(Citations omitted).

In *People v. Dillin*, 148 Misc. 2d 311, 313, 560 N.Y.S.2d 940, 942 (City Crim. Ct. 1990), the Court held that "where, as here, a defendant's appearance in court is obtained by the issuance of an appearance ticket, the People may file and defendant may be prosecuted on an accusatory instrument which is sufficient under CPL § 100.40 charging any offense based on the conduct for which the defendant was arrested and the People are not limited to charging the offenses specified in the appearance ticket."

"When an appearance ticket as defined in [CPL § 150.10(1)] is issued to a person in conjunction with an offense charged in a simplified information, said appearance ticket shall contain the language, set forth in [CPL § 100.25(4)], notifying the defendant of his right to receive a supporting deposition." N.Y. Crim. Proc. Law § 150.10(2).

§ 16:39   Parking summons constitutes an appearance ticket but not an accusatory instrument

Research References

West's Key Number Digest, Automobiles ⊕351.1

A parking summons has been found to constitute a valid appearance ticket but *not* a valid accusatory instrument. As such, "its filing does not give a criminal court jurisdiction over the defendant." *People v. Weinberg*, 146 Misc. 2d 441, 558 N.Y.S.2d 439 (App. Term 1990). *See also People v. Horner*, 176 Misc. 2d 93, 94, 673 N.Y.S.2d 811, 812 (App. Term 1998); *People v. Gabbay*, 175 Misc. 2d 421, 422, 670 N.Y.S.2d 962, 963 (App. Term 1997); *People v. Gilberg*, 166 Misc. 2d 772, 637 N.Y.S.2d 917 (App. Term 1995). *But see People v. Wienclaw*, 183 Misc. 2d 727, 704 N.Y.S.2d 445 (J. Ct. 2000) (finding particular parking summons at issue to constitute a valid accusatory instrument).

§ 16:40   Effect of failure to file accusatory instrument prior to return date of appearance ticket

Research References

West's Key Number Digest, Automobiles ⊕351.1

N.Y. Crim. Proc. Law § 150.50(1) requires that "[a] police officer or other public servant who has issued and served an appearance ticket *must*, at or before the time such appearance ticket is returnable, file or cause to be filed with the local criminal court in which it is returnable a local criminal court accusatory instrument charging the person named in such appearance ticket with the offense specified therein." (Emphasis added). The official Practice Commentaries thereto provide that N.Y. Crim. Proc. Law § 150.50(1):

> [R]equires the filing of an accusatory instrument with the court at or before the time the appearance ticket is returnable. *Prior to the filing of that instrument the court has no jurisdiction to take any action with respect to the charge or the individual upon whom the ticket was served* (see Practice Commentary for CPL § 150.10).

Preiser, Practice Commentaries, McKinney's Cons. Laws of N.Y., Book 11A, CPL § 150.50, at 581 (emphasis added).

While the CPL mandates the filing of the accusatory instrument at or before the time that the appearance ticket is returnable, it does not address the issue of the consequence of a failure to do so. Accordingly, what remedy is available to a defendant who appears in Court on the return date specified in the appearance ticket only to be informed that no accusatory instrument has been filed?

The Courts have reached differing conclusions in this regard. It has been stated that the defendant has no remedy, in that "there is no provision which furnishes a sanction for the failure to abide by the dictates of CPL § 150.50[1]." *People v. Fysekis*, 164 Misc. 2d 627, 630, 625 N.Y.S.2d 861, 865 (City Crim. Ct. 1995).

Nonetheless, it has been held that the appropriate remedy is dismissal since, in the absence of a timely filed accusatory instrument, the appearance ticket is rendered a nullity, and the Court can neither (a) arraign the defendant (which is required for the court to acquire *in personam* jurisdiction over him or her), nor (b) grant an adjournment or compel the defendant's future appearance in court. *See People v. Consolidated Edison Co.*, 161 Misc. 2d 907, 913–14, 615 N.Y.S.2d 978, 982–83 (City Crim. Ct. 1994); *People v. Consolidated Edison Co.*, 159 Misc. 2d 354, 604 N.Y.S.2d 482 (City Crim. Ct. 1993). *See also People v. Lowry*, 184 Misc. 2d 306, 708 N.Y.S.2d 811 (App. Term 2000); *People v. Horner*, 176 Misc. 2d 93, 94, 673 N.Y.S.2d 811, 812 (App. Term 1998); *People v. Gabbay*, 175 Misc. 2d 421, 423, 670 N.Y.S.2d 962, 963 (App. Term 1997).

This remedy is particularly appropriate where the accusatory instrument is a simplified information, as neither a summons nor a warrant of arrest can be issued to secure the defendant's future appearance for arraignment where the accusatory instrument is a simplified information. *See, e.g.*, N.Y. Crim. Proc. Law § 130.10(1); Preiser, Practice Commentaries, McKinney's Cons. Laws of N.Y., Book 11A, CPL § 130.10, at 534. ("Local criminal courts have discretion to issue a summons upon commencement of a criminal action there through filing of a facially sufficient local criminal court accusatory instrument that establishes reasonable cause for the arrest (see CPL § 120.20). *This does not include a simplified information.*") (emphasis added); N.Y. Crim. Proc. Law § 120.20(1); Preiser, Practice Commentaries, McKinney's Cons. Laws of N.Y., Book 11A, CPL § 120.20, at 485 ("The simplified traffic information is specifically excluded by subdivision one as an instrument that can be the basis of an arrest warrant"); Preiser, Practice Commentaries, McKinney's Cons. Laws of N.Y., Book 11A, CPL § 150.10, at 564 ("A simplified information cannot however be the basis for a summons or a warrant of arrest"); Preiser, Practice Commentaries, McKinney's Cons. Laws of N.Y., Book 11A, CPL § 100.25, at 366 ("Since a simplified information does not establish reasonable cause, it cannot serve as the basis for a warrant of arrest. If defendant does not appear, an information would [have to] be filed to obtain a warrant of arrest or a summons.").

Other Courts have found that the most appropriate remedy is "to invoke CPL 30.30, the speedy trial statute." *People v. D'Alessio*, 134 Misc. 2d 1005, 1010, 513 N.Y.S.2d 906, 909 (City Crim. Ct. 1986). *See also People v. Hausch*, 187 Misc. 2d 202, 204, 721 N.Y.S.2d 745, 746 (J. Ct. 2001); *People v. Giusti*, 176 Misc. 2d 377, 382, 673 N.Y.S.2d 824, 827 (City Crim. Ct. 1998); *People v. Brisotti*, 167 Misc. 2d 688, 635 N.Y.S.2d 442 (City Crim. Ct. 1995), aff'd, 169 Misc. 2d 672, 652 N.Y.S.2d 206 (App. Term 1996); *People v. Weaver*, 166 Misc. 2d 488, 634 N.Y.S.2d 968 (City Crim. Ct. 1995); *People v. Han*, 166 Misc. 2d 246, 249, 632 N.Y.S.2d 748, 750 (City Crim. Ct. 1995); *People v. Consolidated Edison Co. of New York, Inc.*, 153 Misc. 2d 595, 598, 582 N.Y.S.2d 614, 617 (City Crim. Ct. 1992). *See generally People v. Stirrup*, 91 N.Y.2d 434, 439, 671 N.Y.S.2d 433, 436, 694 N.E.2d 434 (1998) ("Once a defendant appears in response to a DAT, the criminal action is *deemed* commenced for ready-trial purposes").

However, this remedy would appear to be inappropriate where the only charges against the defendant are traffic infractions, as N.Y. Crim. Proc. Law § 30.30 does not apply to traffic infractions. *See, e.g., People v. Taylor*, 189 Misc. 2d 313, 314, 731 N.Y.S.2d 324, 325 (App. Term 2001); *People v. Gonzalez*, 168 Misc. 2d 136, 645 N.Y.S.2d 978 (App. Term 1996) (per curiam); *People v. Zagorsky*, 73 Misc. 2d 420, 422–24, 341 N.Y.S.2d 791, 793–95 (County Ct. 1973); *People v. Pilewski*, 173 Misc. 2d 800, 803, 660 N.Y.S.2d 525, 527 (J. Ct. 1997); *People v. Faison*, 171 Misc. 2d 68, 72, 662 N.Y.S.2d 973, 975 (City Crim. Ct. 1996); *People v. Fisher*, 167 Misc. 2d 850, 852–53, 635 N.Y.S.2d 1002, 1003–04 (City Crim. Ct. 1995); *People v. Henry*, 166 Misc. 2d 824, 826, 634 N.Y.S.2d 983, 985 (City Crim. Ct. 1995); *People v. Vancol*, 166 Misc. 2d 93, 96, 631 N.Y.S.2d 996, 998 (J. Ct. 1995); *People v. Howell*, 158 Misc. 2d 653, 654 n.1, 601 N.Y.S.2d 778, 779 n.1

(City Crim. Ct. 1993); *People v. Blake*, 154 Misc. 2d 660, 662 n.2, 585 N.Y.S.2d 993, 994 n.2 (City Crim. Ct. 1992); *People v. Fiacco*, 146 Misc. 2d 330, 331, 549 N.Y.S.2d 901, 902 (City Ct. 1989); *People v. Matute*, 141 Misc. 2d 988, 989, 535 N.Y.S.2d 524 (City Crim. Ct. 1988); *People v. Wise*, 141 Misc. 2d 409, 410–11, 532 N.Y.S.2d 833, 834–35 (Dist. Ct. 1988); *People v. Michalek*, 138 Misc. 2d 1, 2, 521 N.Y.S.2d 609, 610 (City Crim. Ct. 1987) (rejected by, People v. Pregent, 142 Misc. 2d 344, 537 N.Y.S.2d 424 (City Ct. 1988)); *People v. Solomon*, 124 Misc. 2d 33, 34, 475 N.Y.S.2d 749, 750 (Dist. Ct. 1984) (rejected by, People v. Pregent, 142 Misc. 2d 344, 537 N.Y.S.2d 424 (City Ct. 1988)). *See also* Preiser, Practice Commentaries, McKinney's Cons. Laws of N.Y., Book 11A, CPL § 30.30, at 168–69. *But see People v. Pregent*, 142 Misc. 2d 344, 346, 537 N.Y.S.2d 424, 425 (City Ct. 1988) (N.Y. Crim. Proc. Law § 30.30 applies to DWAI charge).

It has also been suggested that the charges could, in appropriate circumstances, be dismissed in the interest of justice. *See, e.g., People v. Hausch*, 187 Misc. 2d 202, 203, 721 N.Y.S.2d 745, 746 (J. Ct. 2001); *People v. Consolidated Edison Co. of New York, Inc.*, 153 Misc. 2d 595, 598–99, 582 N.Y.S.2d 614, 617 (City Crim. Ct. 1992).

Finally, one Court found that the appropriate remedy is to "release" the defendant and return any bail that had been posted. *People v. Rodriguez*, 90 Misc. 2d 356, 394 N.Y.S.2d 542 (J. Ct. 1977).

§ 16:41 Effect of failure of court to be in session on return date of simplified information

Research References

West's Key Number Digest, Automobiles ⊙351.1

Where a defendant has been issued a Uniform Traffic Ticket (*i.e.*, a UTT) and the Court is not in session at the time such UTT is returnable, (a) jurisdiction over the defendant is not acquired, (b) there can be no proper adjournment, and thus (c) the charges should be dismissed (albeit without prejudice). *See Shapiro v. MacAffer*, 99 Misc. 2d 694, 416 N.Y.S.2d 955 (Sup 1979); *Abbott v. Rose*, 40 Misc. 2d 64, 242 N.Y.S.2d 773 (Sup 1963).

Critically in this regard, if the Court is not in session on the return date of the appearance ticket, the defendant cannot be arraigned. As a result, the Court can neither (a) exercise control over the defendant's person with respect to the accusatory instrument, nor (b) set the course of further proceedings in the action. *See* N.Y. Crim. Proc. Law § 1.20(9) (" 'Arraignment' means the occasion upon which a defendant against whom an accusatory instrument has been filed appears before the court in which the criminal action is pending for the purpose of having such court acquire and exercise control over his person with respect to such accusatory instrument and of setting the course of further proceedings in the action."). *See also People v. Mitchell*, 235 A.D.2d 834, 835, 652 N.Y.S.2d 827, 828 (3d Dep't 1997) ("Absent arraignment, County Court never acquired the requisite control of defendant's person with respect to the accusatory instrument . . ., and was therefore precluded from 'setting the course of further proceedings in the action' (CPL 1.20[9]).").

People v. Fatsis, 180 Misc. 2d 172, 688 N.Y.S.2d 378 (J. Ct. 1999), reached a contrary result, it is the authors' opinion that *Fatsis* was incorrectly decided. At the outset, *Fatsis* cites no case law which supports its position. In addition, the precise reasoning of *Fatsis* was expressly considered—and rejected—by the Court in *Matter of Shapiro v. MacAffer, supra*; yet *Fatsis* failed to even cite, let alone refute, this well established case. Furthermore, the statutes cited by the *Fatsis* Court in support of its position (*i.e.*, N.Y. Veh. & Traf. Law § 207 and N.Y. Crim. Proc. Law §§ 100.25, 100.10(2)(a) and 150.10) appear to be inapposite. Moreover, the *Fatsis* Court failed to address the critical and fundamental distinction between *in personam* jurisdiction and subject matter jurisdiction, relying solely upon the latter—even though the issue presented dealt primarily with the former.

Finally, *Fatsis* asserts that "[u]pon the filing of a uniform traffic information the court has the jurisdiction to issue process and warrants." 180 Misc. 2d at 173, 688 N.Y.S.2d at 379. However, this assertion is incorrect, as neither a summons nor a warrant of arrest can be issued where the accusatory instrument is a simplified information. *See, e.g.*, N.Y. Crim. Proc. Law § 130.10(1); Preiser, Practice Commentaries, McKinney's Cons. Laws of N.Y., Book 11A, CPL § 130.10, at 534 ("Local criminal courts have discretion to issue a summons upon commencement of a criminal action there through filing of a facially sufficient local criminal court accusatory instrument that establishes reasonable cause for the arrest (see CPL § 120.20). *This does not include a simplified information.*"); N.Y. Crim. Proc. Law § 120.20(1); Preiser, Practice Commentaries, McKinney's Cons. Laws of N.Y., Book 11A, CPL § 120.20, at 485 ("The simplified traffic information is specifically excluded by subdivision one as an instrument that can be the basis of an arrest warrant."); Preiser, Practice Commentaries, McKinney's Cons. Laws of N.Y., Book 11A, CPL § 150.10, at 564 ("A simplified information cannot however be the basis for a summons or a warrant of arrest."); Preiser, Practice Commentaries, McKinney's Cons. Laws of N.Y., Book 11A, CPL § 100.25, at 366 ("Since a simplified information does not establish reasonable cause, it cannot serve as the basis for a warrant of arrest. If defendant does not appear, an information would [have to] be filed to obtain a warrant of arrest or a summons.").

§ 16:42 Superior court information cannot replace simplified information

In *People v. Chamberlain*, 221 A.D.2d 869, 634 N.Y.S.2d 249 (3d Dep't 1995), the defendant committed DWAI Drugs within 10 years of a prior DWI conviction—making the new charge a felony. *See* VTL § 1193(1)(c). However, the arresting officer only charged the defendant with misdemeanor DWAI Drugs, and did not file a felony complaint. The defendant thereafter signed a waiver of indictment and pled guilty in County Court to a superior court information (SCI) charging him with felony DWAI Drugs. On appeal, the Appellate Division, Third Department, reversed the conviction, reasoning as follows:

Under CPL 195.10, a defendant may only waive indictment and consent to be prosecuted by a superior court information where he or she has been "held * * * for the action of a grand jury." A defendant can only be ordered held for the action of a Grand Jury (1) following waiver of a hearing on a *felony* complaint, or (2) upon a finding made at the conclusion of a hearing on a *felony* complaint that there is reasonable cause to believe that the defendant committed a felony. Here, defendant was originally charged with only . . . a misdemeanor and not a felony. Thus, at the time defendant waived indictment and consented to be prosecuted on a superior court information, he was not being held for Grand Jury action with respect to the offense charged in the superior court information. His waiver was, therefore, ineffective and the superior court information on which he was prosecuted was jurisdictionally defective. As a consequence, defendant's conviction is a nullity.

221 A.D.2d at __, 634 N.Y.S.2d at 250 (citations omitted).

Chapter 17

Supporting Depositions

§ 17:24   Denial of motion to dismiss simplified traffic
          information for failure to provide timely supporting
          deposition not reviewable in collateral proceeding
§ 17:25   Re-use of supporting deposition to DWI charge where
          original charge is dismissed and re-filed

Research References

Westlaw Databases
Handling a Criminal Case in New York (HCCNY)

Treatises and Practice Aids
Muldoon, Handling a Criminal Case in New York §§ 3:44, 3:73, 3:74, 3:76, 3:111, 3:114

KeyCite®: Cases and other legal materials listed in KeyCite Scope can be researched through the KeyCite service on Westlaw®. Use KeyCite to check citations for form, parallel references, prior and later history, and comprehensive citator information, including citations to other decisions and secondary materials.

---

§ 17:1   In general

Research References

West's Key Number Digest, Automobiles ☞351.1; Indictment and Information ☞52(.5)

CPL § 100.25 is the primary statute pertaining to supporting depositions. In analyzing case law applying CPL § 100.25, the practitioner must remember that this statute has been amended several times. Accordingly, a case which appears at first glance to persuasively interpret the statute (*e.g.*, *People v. Perry*, 87 N.Y.2d 353, 639 N.Y.S.2d 307 (1996)) may be legislatively overruled (or at least rendered irrelevant). Similarly, several appellate level decisions have implicitly (and in some instances explicitly) overruled lower court decisions in this area.

§ 17:2   Supporting deposition defined

Research References

West's Key Number Digest, Automobiles ☞351.1; Indictment and Information ☞52(4)

A supporting deposition is a written instrument accompanying or filed in connection with an information, a simplified information, a misdemeanor complaint or a felony complaint, subscribed and verified by a person other than the complainant of such accusatory instrument, and containing factual allegations of an evidentiary character, based either upon personal knowledge or upon information and belief, which supplement those of the accusatory instrument and support or tend to support the charge or charges contained therein.

CPL § 100.20. The official Practice Commentaries to CPL § 100.20 state that:

> A supporting deposition is an affidavit filed with a local criminal court accusatory instrument (other than a "prosecutor's information") setting forth additional facts of an evidentiary nature sworn to by a person other than the "complainant." The facts may be alleged on personal knowledge or on information and belief. The primary purpose of the deposition is to supplement the accusatory instrument and it is read together with that instrument when determining either reasonable cause or the legal sufficiency of the instrument.

Preiser, Practice Commentaries, McKinney's Cons. Laws of N.Y., Book 11A, CPL § 100.20, at 361.

A close look at CPL § 100.20 reveals an apparent drafting error—the statute requires that a supporting deposition be "subscribed and verified *by a person other than the complainant of [the underlying] accusatory instrument*" (emphasis added). In *People v. Quinn*, 100 Misc. 2d 582, 419 N.Y.S.2d 811 (Cohoes Police Ct. 1979), the court rejected the defendant's argument that this language requires that the supporting deposition be subscribed and verified by a person other than the complainant police officer.

§ 17:3 Supporting deposition must be verified

Research References
West's Key Number Digest, Automobiles ☞351.1; Indictment and Information ☞52(4)

CPL § 100.20 requires that a supporting deposition be "subscribed and verified." CPL § 100.30 provides that:

1. An information, a misdemeanor complaint, a felony complaint, *a supporting deposition, and proof of service of a supporting deposition* may be verified in any of the following manners:

(a) Such instrument may be sworn to before the court with which it is filed.

(b) Such instrument may be sworn to before a desk officer in charge at a police station or police headquarters or any of his superior officers.

(c) Where such instrument is filed by any public servant following the issuance and service of an appearance ticket, and where by express provision of law another designated public servant is authorized to administer the oath with respect to such instrument, it may be sworn to before such public servant.

(d) Such instrument may bear a form notice that false statements made therein are punishable as a class A misdemeanor pursuant to [PL § 210.45], and such form notice together with the subscription of the deponent constitute a verification of the instrument.

(e) Such instrument may be sworn to before a notary public.

2. An instrument specified in [CPL § 100.30(1)] may be verified in any manner prescribed therein unless in a particular case the court expressly directs verification in a particular manner prescribed in [CPL § 100.30(1)]. (Emphasis added).

An unsigned supporting deposition is defective, and such defect cannot be cured by providing a new, signed supporting deposition after the statutory time limit has expired. *People v. Holden*, 44 Misc. 3d 736, 990 N.Y.S.2d 409 (Canandaigua City Ct. 2014).

§ 17:4 Defendant's right to supporting deposition

Research References

West's Key Number Digest, Automobiles ⟳351.1; Indictment and Information ⟳52(1)

"A defendant charged by a simplified information is, upon a timely request, entitled as a matter of right to have filed with the court and served upon him, or if he is represented by an attorney, upon his attorney, a supporting deposition of the complainant police officer or public servant." CPL § 100.25(2). *See also People v. Nuccio*, 78 N.Y.2d 102, 104, 571 N.Y.S.2d 693, 694 (1991). Where a timely request therefor is made, a supporting deposition must be provided "within [30] days of the date [that the defendant's] request is received by the court, or at least [5] days before trial, whichever is earlier." CPL § 100.25(2). *See also People v. Titus*, 178 Misc. 2d 687, __, 682 N.Y.S.2d 521, 522 (App. Term, 2d Dep't 1998); *People v. Green*, 192 Misc. 2d 296, __, 745 N.Y.S.2d 656, 658 (Nassau Co. Dist. Ct. 2002); *People v. Ryan*, 179 Misc. 2d 670, __, 685 N.Y.S.2d 891, 893 (Suffolk Co. Dist. Ct. 1999). *See generally People v. DeFeo*, 77 Misc. 2d 523, __, 355 N.Y.S.2d 905, 906 (App. Term, 2d Dep't 1974) ("it would be improper to grant an adjournment for the purpose of preparing a supporting deposition"); *People v. Aucello*, 146 Misc. 2d 417, __-__, 558 N.Y.S.2d 436, 437–38 (App. Term, 9th & 10th Jud. Dist. 1990) (same); *People v. Hust*, 74 Misc. 2d 887, __, 346 N.Y.S.2d 303, 306 (Broome Co. Ct. 1973) (same); *People v. Zagorsky*, 73 Misc. 2d 420, __, 341 N.Y.S.2d 791, 796 (Broome Co. Ct. 1973) (same).

The People sometimes take the curious position that "based on the contents of the simplified traffic information(s) themselves, . . . there was no right or requirement of a supporting deposition." *People v. Titus*, 178 Misc. 2d 687, __, 682 N.Y.S.2d 521, 522 (App. Term, 2d Dep't 1998). *See also People v. Ryan*, 179

Misc. 2d 670, __-__, 685 N.Y.S.2d 891, 892–93 (Suffolk Co. Dist. Ct. 1999); *People v. Pivovonsky*, 165 Misc. 2d 1021, __-__, 630 N.Y.S.2d 1007, 1007–08 (Suffolk Co. Dist. Ct. 1995); *People v. Mercurio*, 93 Misc. 2d 1126, __, 404 N.Y.S.2d 252, 253 (Nassau Co. Dist. Ct. 1978).

Although *People v. Schuttinger*, 143 Misc. 2d 1032, 542 N.Y.S.2d 927 (Suffolk Co. Dist. Ct. 1989), supports such a claim, *Titus* expressly overrules *Schuttinger* in this regard. *See Titus*, 178 Misc. 2d at __, 682 N.Y.S.2d at 523. *See also People v. Shapiro*, 61 N.Y.2d 880, 882, 474 N.Y.S.2d 470, 470 (1984). Simply stated, this position has been flatly rejected by the courts, and any such claim in the future could appropriately be characterized as frivolous.

§ 17:5 Request for supporting deposition must be timely

Research References
West's Key Number Digest, Automobiles ⊙351.1

As a general rule:

To be timely, . . . a request [for a supporting deposition] must, except as otherwise provided [in [CPL §§ 100.25(2) & (3)], be made before entry of a plea of guilty to the charge specified and before commencement of a trial thereon, but not later than [30] days after the date the defendant is directed to appear in court as such date appears upon the simplified information and upon the appearance ticket issued pursuant thereto. If the defendant's request is mailed to the court, the request must be mailed within such [30] day period.

CPL § 100.25(2).

There are two statutory exceptions to this general rule. The first exception is that:

Notwithstanding any provision to the contrary, where a defendant is issued an appearance ticket in conjunction with the offense charged in the simplified information and the appearance ticket fails to conform with the requirements of [CPL § 150.10(2)], a request [for a supporting deposition] is timely when made not later than [30] days after (a) entry of the defendant's plea of not guilty when he or she has been arraigned in person, or (b) written notice to the defendant of his or her right to receive a supporting deposition when a plea of not guilty has been submitted by mail.

CPL § 100.25(2). *See also* CPL § 100.25(4); § 17:9, *infra. Accord People v. DiGioia*, 98 Misc. 2d 359, 413 N.Y.S.2d 825 (App. Term, 9th & 10th Jud. Dist. 1978).

The second exception is that:

When at least one of the offenses charged in a simplified information is a misdemeanor, the court may, upon motion of the defendant, for good cause shown and consistent with the interest of justice, permit the defendant to request a supporting deposition beyond the [30] day request period set forth in [CPL § 100.25(2)] provided, however, that no motion may be brought under this subdivision after [90] days has elapsed from the date the defendant is directed to appear in court as such date appears upon the simplified information and upon the appearance ticket issued pursuant thereto.

CPL § 100.25(3). *See People v. Holden*, 44 Misc. 3d 736, 990 N.Y.S.2d 409 (Canandaigua City Ct. 2014).

Where a request for a supporting deposition is untimely (or no request is made), the otherwise absolute right to a supporting deposition is waived. *See, e.g., People v. Nuccio*, 78 N.Y.2d 102, 104, 571 N.Y.S.2d 693, 694 (1991); *People v. Curtis*, 166 Misc. 2d 753, __, 634 N.Y.S.2d 981, 981–82 (Perinton Just. Ct. 1995); *People v. DeLuca*, 166 Misc. 2d 313, __, 633 N.Y.S.2d 249, 251 (Yonkers City Ct. 1995); *People v. Malone*, 166 Misc. 2d 54, __-__, 631 N.Y.S.2d 223, 223–24 (Suffolk Co. Dist. Ct. 1995); *People v. Sperling*, 165 Misc. 2d 1024, __, 631 N.Y.S.2d 221, 222 (Suffolk Co. Dist. Ct. 1995); *People v. Smith*, 163 Misc. 2d 353, __, 621 N.Y.S.2d 449, 456 (Perinton Just. Ct. 1994); *People v. Rossi*, 154 Misc. 2d 616, __, 587 N.Y.S.2d 511, 514 (Muttontown Just. Ct. 1992).

In *People v. Scherbner*, 21 Misc. 3d 251, 863 N.Y.S.2d 352 (Muttontown Just. Ct. 2008), the Court held that the defendant's request for a supporting deposition was untimely, but nonetheless found that "in the interest of justice, the Court exercises its jurisdiction and discretion to require that the People now supply the equivalent of a supporting deposition to the defendant within 30 days of receipt of this Order, failing which this case will be dismissed." 863 N.Y.S.2d at 358.

§ 17:6   Request for supporting deposition can be made prior to arraignment

Research References

West's Key Number Digest, Automobiles ⊕351.1

CPL § 100.25(2) was amended subsequent to the Court of Appeals' decision in *People v. Perry*, 87 N.Y.2d 353, 639 N.Y.S.2d 307 (1996), which had the effect of legislatively overruling *Perry*. Specifically, "CPL 100.25(2) formerly 'expressly provide[d] that a defendant is only entitled to a supporting deposition after he has been "arraigned upon a simplified information." ' After *Perry* was decided, the Legislature amended the statute to replace 'arraigned upon' with 'charged by.' " *People v. Tyler*, 1 N.Y.3d 493, 496 n.3, 776 N.Y.S.2d 199, 201 n.3 (2004) (citation omitted).

In *Tyler*, the Court of Appeals held that the present version of "CPL 100.25(2) does not force a defendant to wait until arraignment to request a supporting deposition. The statute provides that a defendant may request one when *'charged* by a simplified information,' and defendant was 'charged' when he was ticketed." 1 N.Y.3d at 495–96, 776 N.Y.S.2d at 201 (footnote omitted). *See also* 1 N.Y.3d at 496, 776 N.Y.S.2d at 201 ("In short, while a defendant cannot ask for a supporting deposition later than 30 days after the return date on the appearance ticket, nothing in CPL 100.25 or elsewhere prohibits a request prior to this return date so long as the defendant has not pleaded guilty and trial has not started"); *People v. Guerrerio*, 181 Misc. 2d 517, __, 694 N.Y.S.2d 619, 619 (North Hills Just. Ct. 1999) (even "in the absence of a valid arraignment, a defendant's mail request for a supporting deposition sent prior to the return date that the defendant is directed to appear in Court, is timely and valid and triggers a response by the People"); 181 Misc. 2d at __, 694 N.Y.S.2d at 621 ("The new language of CPL § 100.25 . . . articulates a defendant's right to receive a supporting deposition, so long as defendant's request is made during the period between the date when the defendant is *charged* with the offense and 30 days after the return date stated on the face of the appearance ticket. This right to receive a supporting deposition is not dependent on defendant first being arraigned where the required statutory language is imprinted on the appearance ticket").

In light of *Tyler*, *People v. Ney*, 191 Misc. 2d 185, 742 N.Y.S.2d 506 (Ithaca City Ct. 2002), should be considered overruled.

§ 17:7 Request for supporting deposition can be made by fax

In *People v. Smith*, 195 Misc. 2d 41, 757 N.Y.S.2d 217 (Webster Just. Ct. 2002), the Court held that a request for a supporting deposition cannot be made via fax. However, in *People v. Zappula*, 41 Misc. 3d 226, __, 970 N.Y.S.2d 440, 442-44 (Muttontown Just. Ct. 2013), the Court strongly disagreed with *Smith*, reasoning as follows:

> One case, *People v. Smith*, held, almost a decade ago, that a faxed request does not start the 30 day period for providing a supporting deposition because allowing such a mode of request "imposes too severe a burden on the court's employees, who would have to scrutinize each piece of paper faxed to it" and, in contrast to daytime mail deliveries, faxes "are received at the court office at all hours of day and night." With due respect, the Court finds that case and its reasoning out of date, unpersuasive, and contrary to the policy of the statute.

> The statute simply requires *receipt* of a request, i.e. "within thirty

days of the date such request is received by the court," without say-ing how receipt must be attained. The general purpose of requiring that a request be received before an obligation arises is to assure that the putative obligor knows of the request and therefore should attend to the obligation it triggers. Here, the "court" admittedly "received" the fax request no later than May 28th (when the clerk checked the court fax machine upon opening the court office) and thus saw the request then. Strictly applying the words of the stat-ute, therefore, the court was aware of the obligation to provide a supporting deposition on May 28th, two days before the court received the mailed copy of the previously-faxed request.

A veritable revolution in communication has occurred during the past decade. Faxing of communications and even formal notices has become commonplace, and is consistent with modern modes of communication. Email and fax communication have become standard. Indeed, they are so commonplace that persons and enti-ties (including some courts) now often insist on such a mode of com-munication for its speed and reliability, and since confirmation of receipt is available in one's email and fax machine. * * *

Acceptance of faxing CPL § 100.25 requests is reflected in recent case law. Thus, without questioning the sufficiency of a fax request, recent cases involving failures to serve timely supporting deposi-tions have passed on the merits of that issue even though the requests had been made by fax or fax followed by mailing.

In today's world, allowing and accepting fax requests does not ap-pear to impose an undue burden on the court or its employees. Pre-sumably, one who makes a fax telephone number available to the general public intends to receive communications by fax; indeed, such a person has invited that to occur. If one wishes not to receive or to have to check for a fax at any particular time (e.g. at night), he/she can either turn off the fax machine during that period (preventing receipt) or specify that faxes during that period will not be accepted and will be deemed received only during other specified times.

No evidence has been presented to support the suggestion in *Smith* that one is more careful about checking mail than receipts on one's fax machine. Regardless of that suggestion, however, it is not un-reasonable to expect and require the clerk of a court with a fax machine to look in both places to see what has been sent; and recent case [law] supports that conclusion. * * *

Smith also appears to be contrary to the salutary policy of the stat-ute, as more recently recognized, at least implicitly, by the Court of Appeals in *People v. Tyler*. * * *

For these reasons, the Court concludes that a request for a support-ing deposition made by fax to the court is sufficient under CPL

§ 100.25 and starts the 30 day period within which such a supporting deposition must be provided.

(Citations and footnotes omitted).

§ 17:8 Request for supporting deposition need not be served upon District Attorney

Research References

West's Key Number Digest, Automobiles ☞351.1

A request for a supporting deposition does not have to be served upon the District Attorney's Office to be valid. *See, e.g., People v. Thumser*, 148 Misc. 2d 472, __, 567 N.Y.S.2d 571, 572 (App. Term, 9th & 10th Jud. Dist. 1990) ("This court has previously indicated that CPL 100.25 does not require service of a request for a supporting deposition upon the District Attorney but rather places the responsibility upon the court to forward the request. We now hold that a letter request directed to the clerk of the court is sufficient to trigger the requirements of CPL 100.25") (citations omitted); *People v. Furst*, 1 Misc. 3d 654, __, 765 N.Y.S.2d 753, 754 (White Plains City Ct. 2003) ("The prosecution's contention that the defendant should be required to serve a separate request for a supporting deposition has been expressly rejected by the Appellate Term"); *People v. Rossi*, 154 Misc. 2d 616, __, 587 N.Y.S.2d 511, 514 (Muttontown Just. Ct. 1992) ("The proper party to be served with the request for a supporting deposition is the Clerk of the Court, not the prosecuting attorney"); *People v. Branchinelli*, 146 Misc. 2d 73, __, 545 N.Y.S.2d 914, 916 (Nassau Co. Dist. Ct. 1989) ("Defendant is not required to notify the District Attorney of his request for the supporting deposition nor is he required to make a formal application to the court").

In this regard, the Appellate Term's decision in *Thumser* should be construed as overruling *People v. Schlosser*, 129 Misc. 2d 690, 493 N.Y.S.2d 750 (Nassau Co. Dist. Ct. 1985).

§ 17:9 Procedure where appearance ticket used in conjunction with simplified information

Research References

West's Key Number Digest, Automobiles ☞351.1

Notwithstanding any provision of law to the contrary, where a person is charged by a simplified information and is served with an appearance ticket as defined in [CPL §] 150.10, such appearance ticket shall contain the following language: "NOTICE: YOU ARE ENTITLED TO RECEIVE A SUPPORTING DEPOSITION FURTHER EXPLAINING THE CHARGES PROVIDED YOU REQUEST SUCH SUPPORTING DEPOSITION WITHIN THIRTY DAYS

FROM THE DATE YOU ARE DIRECTED TO APPEAR IN COURT
AS SET FORTH ON THIS APPEARANCE TICKET. DO YOU
REQUEST A SUPPORTING DEPOSITION? [ ] Yes [ ] No"

CPL § 100.25(4). *See also* CPL § 150.10(2). *Accord People v.
DiGioia*, 98 Misc. 2d 359, 413 N.Y.S.2d 825 (App. Term, 9th &
10th Jud. Dist. 1978).

In this regard, it is noteworthy that a Uniform Traffic Ticket
(UTT) is not the same thing as, and is not identical to, a simplified traffic information:

> [T]he accusatory instrument is prepared at the same time as the
> ticket by filling out different parts of a carbonized multi-part form.
> One part is served upon the person summoned to appear (*e.g.*, the
> operator of the vehicle) and another part will be filed with a local
> criminal court. The part served upon the motorist is an appearance
> ticket and the part filed with the court is an accusatory instrument;
> to wit, a simplified information (see CPL § 100.25 and Practice
> Commentary thereon).

Preiser, Practice Commentaries, McKinney's Cons. Laws of N.Y.,
Book 11A, CPL § 150.10, at 564. *See also* 15 NYCRR §§ 91.7(a),
(b); 91.11(a). In other words, a UTT is merely an "appearance
ticket" pursuant to CPL § 150.10, *see People v. Tyler*, 1 N.Y.3d
493, 494, 776 N.Y.S.2d 199, 200 (2004), whereas a simplified traffic information is an "accusatory instrument" pursuant to CPL
§ 100.10(2)(a).

§ 17:10 Procedure upon timely request for supporting deposition

Research References

West's Key Number Digest, Automobiles ☞351.1

> Upon [a timely request for a supporting deposition], the court must
> order the complainant police officer or public servant to serve a
> copy of such supporting deposition upon the defendant or [if the
> defendant is represented by an attorney, upon] his attorney, within
> [30] days of the date such request is received by the court, or at
> least [5] days before trial, whichever is earlier, and to file such sup-
> porting deposition with the court together with proof of service
> thereof.

CPL § 100.25(2).

"[W]hen the filing of a supporting deposition is ordered by the
court pursuant to [CPL § 100.25(2)], a failure of the complainant
police officer or public servant to comply with such order within
the time provided by [CPL § 100.25(2)] renders the simplified information insufficient on its face." CPL § 100.40(2). *See also People
v. Nuccio*, 78 N.Y.2d 102, 104, 571 N.Y.S.2d 693, 694 (1991).

In *People v. Titus*, 178 Misc. 2d 687, 682 N.Y.S.2d 521 (App.
Term, 2d Dep't 1998), the Appellate Term, Second Department,

rejected the People's claim that the 30-day period within which they must serve a supporting deposition upon the defendant does not begin to run until the date on which the court orders a supporting deposition to be served. Rather, a supporting deposition must be served upon the defendant within 30 days of the date that the defendant's request therefore is *received by the court*, or at least five days before trial, whichever is earlier. In so holding, the court reasoned that:

> The weight of case law also supports an interpretation of CPL 100.25(2) and 100.40(2) that requires the defendant to do no more than file a timely, written request with the court to become entitled to a supporting deposition as of right. * * *

> We are of the view that to require the defendant . . . to take any such further and unprescribed steps to receive his supporting deposition could work to "defeat the very purpose of the statute, disregard the interests of judicial economy and, in many cases, render the defense of traffic matters impracticable."

178 Misc. 2d at __, 682 N.Y.S.2d at 522 (citation omitted). *See also People v. Thumser*, 148 Misc. 2d 472, __, 567 N.Y.S.2d 571, 572 (App. Term, 9th & 10th Jud. Dist. 1990) ("We now hold that a letter request [for a supporting deposition] directed to the clerk of the court is sufficient to trigger the requirements of CPL 100.25"); *People v. Furst*, 1 Misc. 3d 654, __, 765 N.Y.S.2d 753, 754 (White Plains City Ct. 2003) ("Dismissal based upon the noncompliance with CPL § 100.25 is required when the complainant police officer is never ordered by the court to serve a supporting deposition"); *People v. Brady*, 196 Misc. 2d 993, __, 768 N.Y.S.2d 157, 162 (Nassau Co. Dist. Ct. 2003) ("The plain language of CPL 100.25(2) and CPL 100.40(2), as well as controlling appellate authority, establish that the designated 30-day period for supplying supporting deposition[s] runs, not from the date of the order directing compliance with a defendant's demand, but from the date the demand is received by the court") (citations omitted); *People v. Ryan*, 179 Misc. 2d 670, __, 685 N.Y.S.2d 891, 893 (Suffolk Co. Dist. Ct. 1999) ("Furnishing a supporting deposition in response to a request that has been timely filed with the court is an absolute requirement, regardless of the contents of the simplified information itself, and regardless of whether the court has issued an order. If the deposition is not served, dismissal is mandated").

In *Brady*, *supra*, the court further held that the 30-day time limit in CPL § 100.25(2) applies "only to *service* of the supporting depositions"—not to the requirement that the supporting depositions be filed with the court. 196 Misc. 2d at __, 768 N.Y.S.2d at 162. In this regard, "so long as the act of filing occurs within a reasonable time, service of supporting depositions within the 30-day period specified in CPL 100.25(2) is sufficient." 196 Misc. 2d at ___, 768 N.Y.S.2d at 162–63.

§ 17:11   If defendant represented by attorney, supporting deposition should be served on attorney

Research References

West's Key Number Digest, Automobiles ⏪351.1

If the defendant is represented by an attorney, the supporting deposition should be served on the attorney. *See* CPL § 100.25(2). *See also People v. Furst*, 1 Misc. 3d 654, ___, 765 N.Y.S.2d 753, 755 (White Plains City Ct. 2003); *People v. Suarez*, 167 Misc. 2d 189, ___, 638 N.Y.S.2d 1020, 1021 (Valley Stream Just. Ct. 1996); *People v. Rossi*, 154 Misc. 2d 616, ___, 587 N.Y.S.2d 511, 513 (Muttontown Just. Ct. 1992); *People v. Scherbner*, 21 Misc. 3d 251, ___, 863 N.Y.S.2d 352, 355 (Muttontown Just. Ct. 2008).

In *People v. Brady*, 196 Misc. 2d 993, ___, 768 N.Y.S.2d 157, 161–62 (Nassau Co. Dist. Ct. 2003), the court agreed with *Suarez* and *Rossi* but found that the defendant was nonetheless estopped from raising such a claim where her attorney had neither made a formal appearance in the case, nor "[m]ore importantly, . . . endorse[d] the demand for supporting depositions with counsel's name, address and telephone number." Under these circumstances, "defendant cannot now be heard to complain that the arresting state trooper served the supporting depositions at the only address available to him." 196 Misc. 2d at ___, 768 N.Y.S.2d at 162.

§ 17:12   Remedy for failure to supply supporting deposition is dismissal

Research References

West's Key Number Digest, Automobiles ⏪351.1; Indictment and Information ⏪144

"If a timely request for a supporting deposition is made, the failure to supply one renders the simplified information insufficient on its face (CPL 100.40[2]) and subjects it to dismissal upon motion (CPL 170.35[1][a]; 170.30[1][a])." *People v. Nuccio*, 78 N.Y.2d 102, 104, 571 N.Y.S.2d 693, 694 (1991). However, the dismissal is without prejudice, and thus "prosecution can be renewed on a facially sufficient information following such a dismissal." 78 N.Y.2d at 104, 571 N.Y.S.2d at 694. *See also People v. Holden*, 44 Misc. 3d 736, ___, 990 N.Y.S.2d 409, 412 (Canandaigua City Ct. 2014). "Nor is double jeopardy a bar to the refiling of the charges against defendant." 78 N.Y.2d at 105, 571

N.Y.S.2d at 695. *See also People v. Key*, 45 N.Y.2d 111, 117, 408 N.Y.S.2d 16, 19 (1978); *People v. Koenig*, 31 Misc. 3d 827, 919 N.Y.S.2d 319 (Sullivan Co. Ct. 2011).

Nonetheless, at least one appellate level court has held, subsequent to *Nuccio*, that absent "special circumstances" it is an abuse of discretion for a court to allow the refiling of a simplified information following dismissal for failure to supply a supporting deposition. *People v. Rosenfeld*, 163 Misc. 2d 982, 626 N.Y.S.2d 352 (App. Term, 9th & 10th Jud. Dist. 1994). The court's rationale was that "[s]uch actions, in this court's opinion, defeat the very purpose of the CPL, disregard the interests of judicial economy and, often times, render the defense of traffic matters impracticable." 163 Misc. 2d 982 at __, 626 N.Y.S.2d at 352. *See also People v. Aucello*, 146 Misc. 2d 417, __, 558 N.Y.S.2d 436, 438 (App. Term, 9th & 10th Jud. Dist. 1990) (same).

In this regard, *Aucello* expressly (a) overruled both *People v. Spiegelman*, 142 Misc. 2d 617, 537 N.Y.S.2d 964 (Kensington Just. Ct. 1989), and *People v. Hartmann*, 123 Misc. 2d 553, 473 N.Y.S.2d 935 (White Plains City Ct. 1984), to the extent that they conflict therewith, and (b) disapproved of various "dicta" in *People v. Jeck-Tisch*, 133 Misc. 2d 1090, 509 N.Y.S.2d 463 (White Plains City Ct. 1986). *See Aucello*, 146 Misc. 2d at __, 558 N.Y.S.2d at 438.

§ 17:13 Motion to dismiss—Procedure

Research References

West's Key Number Digest, Automobiles ☞351.1; Indictment and Information ☞144

Technically, a motion to dismiss for lack of a sufficient supporting deposition, like all other pretrial motions, should be made in accordance with CPL § 255.20(1). *People v. Dean*, 74 N.Y.2d 643, 644, 542 N.Y.S.2d 512, 512 (1989); *People v. Key*, 45 N.Y.2d 111, 116, 408 N.Y.S.2d 16, 19 (1978). *See also People v. Fattizzi*, 98 Misc. 2d 288, 413 N.Y.S.2d 804 (App. Term, 9th & 10th Jud. Dist. 1978); *People v. Rose*, 8 Misc. 3d 184, __, 794 N.Y.S.2d 630, 635 (Nassau Co. Dist. Ct. 2005); *People v. Sirkin*, 146 Misc. 2d 1030, 553 N.Y.S.2d 593 (Arcadia Just. Ct. 1990). *See generally People v. Nuccio*, 78 N.Y.2d 102, 104, 571 N.Y.S.2d 693, 694 (1991); CPL §§ 255.10(1)(b), 255.20, 100.40(2), 170.30(1)(a), 170.30(1)(f), 170.30(2), 170.30(3), 170.35(1)(a), 170.45 and 210.45. In other words, a motion to dismiss for lack of a sufficient supporting deposition should, among other things, be made:

(a) In writing. *See* CPL §§ 170.45 & 210.45(1);

(b) Upon reasonable notice to the People. *See* CPL §§ 170.45 & 210.45(1); and

(c) With certain exceptions, within 45 days after arraignment (or within such additional time as the Court may fix upon application of the defendant). *See* CPL §§ 255.10(1)(b) & 255.20(1).

However, the writing and reasonable notice requirements appear to be waivable. *See People v. Jennings*, 69 N.Y.2d 103, 113, 512 N.Y.S.2d 652, 656 (1986) (by failing to insist upon conformity with the procedural requirements of CPL § 210.45(1), the People waived their right to written notice under the statute). *See also People v. Mezon*, 80 N.Y.2d 155, 157, 589 N.Y.S.2d 838, 839 (1992); *People v. Singleton*, 42 N.Y.2d 466, 470–71, 398 N.Y.S.2d 871, 874 (1977).

In addition, presumably recognizing that strict adherence to these requirements would oftentimes "defeat the very purpose of the statute, disregard the interests of judicial economy and, in many cases, render the defense of traffic matters impracticable," *see, e.g., People v. Titus*, 178 Misc. 2d 687, __, 682 N.Y.S.2d 521, 522 (App. Term, 2d Dep't 1998); *People v. Rosenfeld*, 163 Misc. 2d 982, __, 626 N.Y.S.2d 352, 352 (App. Term, 9th & 10th Jud. Dist. 1994); *People v. Aucello*, 146 Misc. 2d 417, __, 558 N.Y.S.2d 436, 438 (App. Term, 9th & 10th Jud. Dist. 1990), many courts summarily dismiss simplified informations in response to an oral motion (or the court's own motion) where the People have failed to provide a properly requested supporting deposition.

An excellent example of how strict adherence to formal rules of procedure in traffic infraction cases can "defeat the very purpose of the statute, disregard the interests of judicial economy and, in many cases, render the defense of traffic matters impracticable," is found in *People v. Furst*, 1 Misc. 3d 654, 765 N.Y.S.2d 753 (White Plains City Ct. 2003). *See generally People v. Maran*, 174 Misc. 2d 327, 666 N.Y.S.2d 870 (App. Term, 2d Dep't 1997).

§ 17:14 Required contents of supporting deposition— Generally

Research References

West's Key Number Digest, Automobiles ☞351.1

"A valid and sufficient accusatory instrument is a nonwaivable jurisdictional prerequisite to a criminal prosecution." *People v. Harper*, 37 N.Y.2d 96, 99, 371 N.Y.S.2d 467, 469 (1975). *See also People v. Noblett*, 172 Misc. 2d 826, __, 660 N.Y.S.2d 517, 520 (Monroe Co. Ct. 1997); *People v. Gingello*, 181 Misc. 2d 163, __, 694 N.Y.S.2d 579, 580 (Rochester City Ct. 1999) (abrogated on other grounds by, People v. Blair, 98 N.Y.2d 722, 749 N.Y.S.2d 809, 779 N.E.2d 748 (2002)). To be sufficient, a supporting deposition must, inter alia, "contain[ ] allegations of fact, based either upon personal knowledge or upon information and belief, providing reasonable cause to believe that the defendant committed the offense or offenses charged." CPL § 100.25(2). *See also* CPL § 100.20; CPL § 70.10(2).

In *People v. Hohmeyer*, 70 N.Y.2d 41, 517 N.Y.S.2d 448 (1987), the Court of Appeals upheld the "check sheet of multiple choice information" supporting deposition commonly used in DWI cases. An example of such a supporting deposition is set forth at Appendix 14. In so holding, the court found that the "check sheet" format used by the police satisfied the requirements that:

> A supporting deposition must be a "written instrument," "subscribed and verified," and "containing factual allegations of an evidentiary character * * * which supplement those of the accusatory instrument and support or tend to support the charge or charges contained therein" (CPL 100.20). In addition, CPL 100.25(2) mandates that the supporting deposition contain "allegations of fact * * * providing reasonable cause to believe that the defendant committed the offense or offenses charged."

70 N.Y.2d at 43, 517 N.Y.S.2d at 450. *See generally People v. Key*, 45 N.Y.2d 111, 408 N.Y.S.2d 16 (1978); *Gingello*, 181 Misc. 2d at __, 694 N.Y.S.2d at 581; *People v. Lesnak*, 165 Misc. 2d 706, __, 630 N.Y.S.2d 459, 460 (Suffolk Co. Dist. Ct. 1995).

In *People v. Ellis*, __ Misc. 3d __, __, 34 N.Y.S.3d 880, 881 (Albany N.Y. City Ct. 2016), the issue before the Court was "whether the failure of the People to check the box designating the document as a 'Supporting Deposition', and only checking the box designating the document as a 'DWI Bill of Particulars', precludes its function as a supporting deposition." The Court held that:

> [T]he failure of the subscribing officer to check the box designating the document in question as a supporting deposition does not preclude its function as a supporting deposition to the accusatory instrument filed in this case. The document meets the requirements set forth in Criminal Procedure Law Section 100.20, and thus the failure to check the box labeling the document as a supporting deposition constitutes a ministerial error.

Id. at *2.

Critically, however, the Supporting Deposition/DWI Bill of Particulars form "may be insufficient to act as a supporting deposition for any traffic violations accompanying the DWI arrest." *People v. Fox*, 47 Misc. 3d 245, __, 2 N.Y.S.3d 755, 755 (Canandaigua City Ct. 2014). In *Fox*:

> Here, the supporting deposition was clearly intended to serve as a supporting deposition for only the DWI charge. The DWI supporting deposition form states in the pre-printed opening paragraph "The above 'defendant' is charged . . . with operating a motor vehi-

cle under the influence of alcohol and/or drugs contrary to section 1192 of the Vehicle and Traffic Law." Two pre-printed boxes on the upper right are labeled "supporting deposition" and "DWI bill of particulars." It is clearly a form intended for use specifically with violations of VTL § 1192.

The DWI supporting deposition references the two traffic violations:

(1) in paragraph 2—the illegal turn signal is indicated as the reason for the stop;

(2) in paragraph 4(c)—the evidence at the scene of the arrest includes an open container of an alcoholic beverage; and

(3) paragraph 7—the statutory sections for both charges are listed under "other VTL violations."

These bits of information are not enough to provide reasonable cause to believe that Mr. Fox made an illegal turn and had an open container of alcohol in his car on the date in question.

Id. at __, 2 N.Y.S.3d at 756 (citation omitted).

"In order to be considered adequate, a supporting deposition must set forth facts in a plain and concise manner which provide a reasonable cause to believe that the defendant committed every necessary element of the offense charged. Furthermore, because a supporting deposition is so vital to the defendant in traffic infraction cases, the failure to provide an adequate one cannot be looked upon as a mere technical defect." *People v. Hust*, 74 Misc. 2d 887, __, 346 N.Y.S.2d 303, 307 (Broome Co. Ct. 1973). *See also People v. Baron*, 107 Misc. 2d 59, __, 438 N.Y.S.2d 425, 426 (App. Term, 9th & 10th Jud. Dist. 1980); *People v. Key*, 87 Misc. 2d 262, __, 391 N.Y.S.2d 781, 785 (App. Term, 9th & 10th Jud. Dist. 1976), *judgment aff'd*, 45 N.Y.2d 111, 408 N.Y.S.2d 16 (1978); *People v. Brooks*, 38 Misc. 3d 946, __, 957 N.Y.S.2d 626, 627-28 (Muttontown Just. Ct. 2013); *People v. Rothman*, 193 Misc. 2d 247, __, 750 N.Y.S.2d 441, 442 (Hunter Just. Ct. 2002); *People v. Chittaranjans*, 185 Misc. 2d 871, __, 714 N.Y.S.2d 650, 651–52 (Nassau Co. Dist. Ct. 2000); *People v. Powlowski*, 172 Misc. 2d 240, __, 658 N.Y.S.2d 558, 562 (Rochester City Ct. 1997); *People v. Born*, 166 Misc. 2d 757, __, 634 N.Y.S.2d 915, 916 (Perinton Just. Ct. 1995).

In addition, "the deposition supporting a simplified traffic information, to the extent it is based on information and belief, must contain a statement of the source of that information and belief if it is to be sufficient on its face." *Lesnak*, 165 Misc. 2d at __, 630 N.Y.S.2d at 461. *See also People v. Colburn*, 48 Misc. 3d 971, __, 8 N.Y.S.3d 898, 900 (Webster J. Ct. 2015); *People v. Dumas*,

42 Misc. 3d 265, —, 974 N.Y.S.2d 921, 924 (Buffalo City N.Y. City Ct. 2013); *Noblett*, 172 Misc. 2d at —, 660 N.Y.S.2d at 519–20; *People v. Quarles*, 168 Misc. 2d 638, —, 639 N.Y.S.2d 661, 668 (Rochester City Ct. 1996); *Born*, 166 Misc. 2d at —, 634 N.Y.S.2d at 917–18; *People v. Smith*, 163 Misc. 2d 353, —, 621 N.Y.S.2d 449, 456–57 (Perinton Just. Ct. 1994); *People v. Moretti*, 142 Misc. 2d 331, —, 537 N.Y.S.2d 735, 736 (Yonkers City Ct. 1988).

Furthermore, where a statute contains an exception, a supporting deposition claiming a violation of the statute must allege that the exception is inapplicable. *See, e.g., People v. Deming*, 80 Misc. 2d 53, 362 N.Y.S.2d 804 (Albany Co. Ct. 1974) (this rule applies to VTL § 1120(a)); *People v. Dailey*, 69 Misc. 2d 691, 330 N.Y.S.2d 899 (Saratoga Co. Ct. 1972); *People v. Bailey*, 60 Misc. 2d 283, 302 N.Y.S.2d 874 (Fulton Co. Ct. 1969) (this rule applies to VTL § 1120(a)). *See generally People v. Kohut*, 30 N.Y.2d 183, 187, 331 N.Y.S.2d 416, 420 (1972); *People v. Smith*, 299 N.Y. 707 (1949), *aff'g* 192 Misc. 965, 83 N.Y.S.2d 181 (Suffolk Co. Ct. 1948); *People v. Hogabone*, 278 A.D.2d 525, —, 716 N.Y.S.2d 836, 837 (3d Dep't 2000); *People v. Bingham*, 263 A.D.2d 611, —, 692 N.Y.S.2d 823, 824 (3d Dep't 1999); *People v. Krathaus*, 181 Misc. 2d 378, 693 N.Y.S.2d 872 (Cattaraugus Co. Ct. 1999). *Cf. People v. Gill*, — Misc. 3d —, — N.Y.S.2d —, 2012 WL 2331976 (App. Term, 9th & 10th Jud. Dist. 2012) (this rule does *not* apply to VTL § 1120(a)).

In *Noblett, supra*, the court commented that:

This court well recognizes and appreciates the need for safety on our highways and the difficulty in enforcing traffic laws on busy, speedy interstate highways; this court understands the difficulties involved in trying these cases in local courts where the defendants tend to be strangers to the court while the troopers are familiar participants in the proceedings. Even such a learned and respected judge as in the instant case may be affected by the press of business on his busy calendar and the "same-old-song" familiarity of another contested speeding ticket case. It is just such circumstances that yield an occasional oversight by a trial court. Appellate courts, with the benefit of hindsight and the time for deliberation, sometimes see important issues that are not readily apparent at time of trial during hectic court dockets. Nevertheless, the requirements of the Criminal Procedure Law are designed to make sure that the court has jurisdiction and to accurately describe the nature of the probable cause that exists to arrest a person without a warrant. These requirements were not met here and good-faith beliefs and best efforts are not a substitute for the requirements of the law.

172 Misc. 2d at —, 660 N.Y.S.2d at 520.

In *People v. Bollag*, 42 Misc. 3d 149(A), 986 N.Y.S.2d 866, *1 (App. Term, 9th & 10th Jud. Dist. 2014), the Appellate Term reversed the defendant's conviction of violating VTL § 1110(a) where:

In the case at bar, the simplified traffic information and supporting deposition fail to set forth any facts from which it could reasonably be inferred that defendant failed to obey a specific sign, signal, marking, or device (*see* [VTL] § 153), since the complaining officer neither identified the type of traffic control device defendant failed to obey nor detailed defendant's actions from which it could be reasonably inferred that he had violated [VTL] § 1110. The supporting deposition set forth little more than the conclusory assertion that defendant had violated [VTL] § 1110 by his failure to obey an unspecified traffic control device. In view of the foregoing, the simplified traffic information is jurisdictionally defective.

In *People v. Colburn*, 48 Misc. 3d 971, __, 8 N.Y.S.3d 898, 899 (Webster J. Ct. 2015), the Court found a supporting deposition to a VTL § 1111(d)(1) charge to be insufficient where it provided as follows:

"That on or about 08:52 A.M. on the 14th day of January, 2015, the above named defendant . . . did operate a 2014 Nissan Color Grey, bearing State of New York registration plate number GRG 8779, in a southerly direction on Holt Road, that being a public highway of the Town of Webster, County of Monroe, State of New York. Further, that at said time and place, your defendant's vehicle did pass a steady circular red signal at Route 104 east access road without stopping causing a four car accident.

The forgoing factual allegations are based upon oral admissions of the defendant and the witnesses on scene of the accident."

With regard to the required contents of a supporting deposition to a speeding charge, *see, e.g., People v. Cohen*, 131 Misc. 2d 898, __, 502 N.Y.S.2d 123, 124 (Yonkers N.Y. City Ct. 1986) (supporting deposition to speeding charge defective for failure to specify whether officer's "determination of excessive speed is based on personal observation or by a mechanical means or a technical device"); *People v. Gutterson*, 93 Misc. 2d 1105, __, 403 N.Y.S.2d 998, 1000 (Lattingtown J. Ct. 1978) ("If a speed detection device was employed to clock defendant's speed, he should be apprised of the manufacturer and model name and number of said device in the bill of particulars"); *People v. Marchhart*, 49 Misc. 3d 345, __, 12 N.Y.S.3d 871, 873-74 (Muttontown J. Ct. 2015) ("where a supporting deposition identifies radar or laser as a means of measuring the speed of a defendant's vehicle, the failure of such supporting deposition to designate the model, make, year or type of such radar or laser does not render such supporting deposition legally insufficient"). *See generally People v. Chess*, 149 Misc. 2d 430, 565 N.Y.S.2d 416 (Kensington J. Ct. 1991) (Court held that failure to disclose use of radar to determine defendant's speed did not render accusatory instrument insufficient, but it nonetheless precluded the People from offering any evidence concerning the use of any speed measuring device as a result of such failure).

§ 17:15 Voluntarily provided supporting deposition must satisfy requirements of CPL § 100.25

Research References

West's Key Number Digest, Automobiles ⚷351.1

A supporting deposition that is voluntarily provided by the People within the time period for the defendant to make a proper demand therefor in effect "moots" the defendant's right to demand the same, and "[t]hus, the People, in supplying the deposition, must satisfy the minimum requirements as set forth in CPL 100.25." *People v. Key*, 87 Misc. 2d 262, __, 391 N.Y.S.2d 781, 785 (App. Term, 9th & 10th Jud. Dist. 1976), judgment aff'd, 45 N.Y.2d 111, 408 N.Y.S.2d 16 (1978). *See also People v. Key*, 45 N.Y.2d 111, 116, 408 N.Y.S.2d 16, 19 (1978) ("The People's tender of such a deposition voluntarily, rather than waiting for defendant's request, should not obviate the need for the deposition to provide reasonable cause"); *People v. Chittaranjans*, 185 Misc. 2d 871, __, 714 N.Y.S.2d 650, 651 (Nassau Co. Dist. Ct. 2000).

§ 17:16 Required contents of supporting deposition to DWI charge

Research References

West's Key Number Digest, Automobiles ⚷351.1

The supporting deposition to a DWI charge must, inter alia, provide reasonable cause to believe:

(a) That the defendant operated the vehicle. *See, e.g., People v. Key*, 45 N.Y.2d 111, 116, 408 N.Y.S.2d 16, 19 (1978) ("In this case, there was no allegation that defendant was operating his automobile or even that the engine was running, an allegation necessary to establish commission of the crime. Hence, as both courts below have held, the information was insufficient"); *People v. Key*, 87 Misc. 2d 262, __, 391 N.Y.S.2d 781, 785 (App. Term, 9th & 10th Jud. Dist. 1976), judgment aff'd, 45 N.Y.2d 111, 408 N.Y.S.2d 16, 379 N.E.2d 1147 (1978) ("In the instant matter, the supporting deposition fails to set forth any facts from which it could reasonably be inferred that the defendant was 'operating' the vehicle, a prerequisite to a conviction of violating [VTL §] 1192(2)"), *aff'd*, 45 N.Y.2d 111, 408 N.Y.S.2d 16 (1978);

(b) That the defendant was intoxicated. *See, e.g., People v. Hust*, 74 Misc. 2d 887, __, 346 N.Y.S.2d 303, 307 (Broome Co. Ct. 1973) ("The 'allegations of fact' within the meaning of CPL § 100.25(2) must refer not only to the driving, but also to the intoxication since in any driving while intoxicated case there are two elements to be proven: (1) that the defendant was driving the vehicle in question and (2) that the defendant was intoxicated while so driving"); and

(c) That the operation and the intoxication occurred simultaneously. *See, e.g., People v. Mertz*, 68 N.Y.2d 136, 139, 506 N.Y.S.2d 290, 291 (1986) ("A violation of Vehicle and Traffic Law § 1192(2) is not established unless the trier of fact finds that *while* operating a motor vehicle defendant had a blood alcohol content (BAC) of [.08] of 1% or more") (emphasis added); *People v. Schools*, 122 A.D.2d 502, __, 505 N.Y.S.2d 462, 463 (3d Dep't 1986) ("The *sine qua non* for conviction is the operation of a vehicle simultaneously with intoxication"); *People v. Strauss*, 260 A.D. 880, __, 22 N.Y.S.2d 880, 881 (2d Dep't 1940) ("intoxication and operation must be simultaneous or there is no crime"); *Hust, supra. See generally People v. Spencer*, 289 A.D.2d 877, __, 736 N.Y.S.2d 428, 431 (3d Dep't 2001); *People v. Saplin*, 122 A.D.2d 498, __, 505 N.Y.S.2d 460, 461 (3d Dep't 1986); *People v. Matthews*, 11 A.D.2d 784, 205 N.Y.S.2d 26 (2d Dep't 1960); *People v. Hemleb*, 4 A.D.2d 878, 166 N.Y.S.2d 837 (2d Dep't 1957).

§ 17:17 Required contents of supporting deposition to common law DWI charge where defendant's chemical test result less than 0.08%

Research References

West's Key Number Digest, Automobiles ⊕351.1

Occasionally, the prosecution will charge a defendant with common law DWI (*i.e.*, VTL § 1192(3)) despite the fact that the defendant submitted to a chemical test which produced a BAC reading of less than 0.08%. In such a case, the defendant is charged with driving while *intoxicated* despite the fact that the Legislature has determined that the defendant's BAC constitutes prima facie evidence that he or she was *not* intoxicated. *See* VTL § 1195(2).

Although such a charge is legally possible, *see, e.g., People v. Lawrence*, 53 A.D.2d 705, 384 N.Y.S.2d 37 (3d Dep't 1976), the accusatory instrument in such a situation must do more than follow the "check sheet" format of the standard DWI supporting deposition, as most of the factors on the standard form deposition (*i.e.*, odor of alcoholic beverage, glassy eyes, impaired speech, impaired motor coordination, admission of alcohol consumption, etc.), are consistent not only with intoxication, but also with impairment. *See, e.g., People v. Gingello*, 181 Misc. 2d 163, __, 694 N.Y.S.2d 579, 582 (Rochester City Ct. 1999) (abrogated on other grounds by, People v. Blair, 98 N.Y.2d 722, 749 N.Y.S.2d 809, 779 N.E.2d 748 (2002)).

Accordingly, to be sufficient, the supporting deposition to a common law DWI charge involving a BAC of less than 0.08%

must allege *additional* factual allegations, above and beyond the boilerplate on the form, which overcome the statutory presumption that the defendant was *not* intoxicated. *See Gingello*, 181 Misc. 2d at __, 694 N.Y.S.2d at 582; *People v. Coutard*, 115 Misc. 2d 630, __-__, 454 N.Y.S.2d 639, 643–45 (Nassau Co. Dist. Ct. 1982). *Cf. People v. Gristina*, 186 Misc. 2d 877, 721 N.Y.S.2d 491 (N.Y. City Crim. Ct. 2001).

In *Coutard*, the court held that "[i]n order to overcome the statutory presumption accorded the operator of a motor vehicle by VTL Section 1195, the arresting [officer] must submit a deposition of substantially greater proportion, depth and detail than submitted in [this] case." 115 Misc. 2d at __, 454 N.Y.S.2d at 644. In so holding, the court reasoned that *"[i]t would appear to this Court that before a proper charge for the misdemeanor crime of Driving While Intoxicated can be sufficiently laid in [the] face of a blood alcohol content reading of less than [.08]%, a police officer must be able to provide something more than the usual supporting deposition."* 115 Misc. 2d at __, 454 N.Y.S.2d at 644–45 (emphasis added).

People v. Blair, 98 N.Y.2d 722, 749 N.Y.S.2d 809 (2002), is not to the contrary. In *Blair*, the defendant was charged with violating VTL § 1192(3) despite the fact that, "[45] minutes after he was stopped for a traffic infraction, defendant took a breathalyzer test indicating that he had a .08% blood alcohol level." 98 N.Y.2d at 723, 749 N.Y.S.2d at 810. At the time *Blair* was decided, VTL § 1192(2) prohibited driving with a BAC of 0.10% or more. The Court of Appeals held that:

> The accusatory instrument's supporting documentation contains factual allegations sufficient to establish reasonable cause that defendant violated Vehicle and Traffic Law § 1192(3). Defendant drove without head or tail lights; upon stopping defendant's vehicle, the arresting officer observed defendant had glassy eyes and impaired speech and motor coordination, smelled of alcohol and failed four field sobriety tests, including a "Finger Count Test" in which he was unable to "count his fingers correctly or in order"; and defendant admitted that he drank five to six beers prior to driving and should not have been operating his vehicle. The People were thus entitled to an opportunity to rebut the section 1195(2)(c) presumption at trial.

98 N.Y.2d at 724, 749 N.Y.S.2d at 810. *See also People v. McConnell*, 11 Misc. 3d 57, __-__, 812 N.Y.S.2d 742, 744–45 (App. Term, 9th & 10th Jud. Dist. 2006).

§ 17:18 Required contents of supporting deposition to charge of misdemeanor DWAI

Research References

West's Key Number Digest, Automobiles ⊙351.1

In *People v. Powlowski*, 172 Misc. 2d 240, __, 658 N.Y.S.2d 558, 560 (Rochester City Ct. 1997), the court held that where the People seek to charge a defendant with DWAI as a misdemeanor under VTL § 1193(1)(a), the defendant's prior convictions "become an element of the higher level offense," and thus "must be pled in the accusatory instrument." *See also People v. Jamison*, 170 Misc. 2d 974, 652 N.Y.S.2d 495 (Rochester City Ct. 1996).

Thus, to be sufficient, the supporting deposition in such a situation must allege facts providing reasonable cause to believe that the defendant has "two or more convictions for a violation of any subdivision of [VTL § 1192] within the preceding ten years." *Powlowski*, 172 Misc. 2d at __, 658 N.Y.S.2d at 562–63.

§ 17:19 Supporting deposition to DWI charge need not be "certified"

Research References

West's Key Number Digest, Automobiles ☞351.1

For purposes of suspension pending prosecution in a DWI case, a "court may not order suspension of the [defendant's driver's] license unless it has in its possession the results of the chemical test, and . . . *these results must be presented to the court in certified, documented form (see,* CPLR 4518[c])." *Pringle v. Wolfe*, 88 N.Y.2d 426, 432, 646 N.Y.S.2d 82, 85–86 (1996) (emphasis added). *See* § 45:3, *infra*.

In *People v. DeRojas*, 180 Misc. 2d 690, __, 693 N.Y.S.2d 404, 405 (App. Term, 2d Dep't 1999), *rev'g* People v. DeRojas, 176 Misc. 2d 887, 673 N.Y.S.2d 889 (Nassau Co. Dist. Ct. 1998), the Appellate Term, Second Department, held that a "supporting deposition need not be 'certified' for purposes of arraignment, or in order to be facially sufficient pursuant to CPL 100.25." In so holding, the court reasoned that the above-quoted requirement in *Pringle* "relates solely to a suspension hearing held pursuant to [VTL §] 1193(2)(e)(7)(b) and has no bearing on the facial sufficiency of the supporting deposition." 180 Misc. 2d at __, 693 N.Y.S.2d at 405.

§ 17:20 Requirement that DMV "DALL" form attached to, and made part of, supporting deposition be "certified"

Research References

West's Key Number Digest, Automobiles ☞351.1

In *People v. Krenzer*, 180 Misc. 2d 757, 690 N.Y.S.2d 838 (Rochester City Ct. 1999), the court held that a charge of operating with a suspended registration, in violation of VTL § 512, was facially sufficient. In so holding, the court upheld the use of an *uncertified* "NYS DMV DALL form" (which is similar to an uncertified DMV abstract), which was attached to, and made a part of, the officer's supporting deposition, *despite the fact that*:

> The court notes that the "form" referred to in the supporting deposition is no more than a computer generated print-out from the officer's mobile data terminal. It is uncertain and there is nothing to permit the court to determine either the origin of the document or whether it is an official New York State DMV form.

180 Misc. 2d at __, 690 N.Y.S.2d at 841.

However, the continued validity of *Krenzer* is questionable in light of the Appellate Division, Fourth Department's subsequent decision in *People v. Smith*, 258 A.D.2d 245, 697 N.Y.S.2d 783 (4th Dep't 1999) (class D felony DWI found to have been properly reduced to class E felony where defendant's DMV abstract presented to grand jury was not properly certified and/or authenticated).

§ 17:21 Right to *renew* claim of insufficiency in supporting deposition waived by guilty plea

Research References

West's Key Number Digest, Automobiles ⊸351.1

In *People v. Beattie*, 80 N.Y.2d 840, 587 N.Y.S.2d 585 (1992), after town court rejected the defendant's claim that the supporting deposition provided to him pursuant to CPL § 100.25(2) was factually insufficient, the defendant pled guilty to VTL § 1192(2). County court reversed the defendant's conviction, holding both (a) that the supporting deposition was factually insufficient, and (b) that this constituted a nonwaivable jurisdictional defect.

In reversing county court, the Court of Appeals ruled that although "it is clear that a defendant who pleads guilty does not waive the right to argue than an accusatory instrument is jurisdictionally defective," a guilty plea, among other things, " 'effects a forfeiture of the right to *renew* many arguments made before the plea' [such as] a claimed deficiency in a jurisdictionally sufficient accusatory instrument." 80 N.Y.2d at 842, 587 N.Y.S.2d at 586–87 (emphasis added) (citation omitted).

§ 17:22 Supporting depositions not applicable to traffic infractions governed by VTL Article 2-A

Research References

West's Key Number Digest, Automobiles ⊸351.1

VTL Article 2-A (*i.e.*, VTL §§ 225 to 28) provides an alternate means of adjudicating traffic infractions in both (a) cities with populations of 200,000 or more, and (b) part of Suffolk County. In cases governed by VTL Article 2-A, the supporting deposition provisions of the CPL are inapplicable. *See, e.g., Matter of Stamos v. Appeals Bd. of N.Y. State Dep't of Motor Vehicles*, 309 A.D.2d 572, __, 765 N.Y.S.2d 342, 343 (1st Dep't 2003); *Matter of Steiger v. Wozniak*, 72 A.D.2d 944, 422 N.Y.S.2d 228 (4th Dep't 1979); *Matter of Sulli v. Appeals Bd. of Admin. Adjudication Bureau*, 55 A.D.2d 457, __, 390 N.Y.S.2d 758, 760 (4th Dep't 1977); *Matter of Wahl v. Jackson*, 276 A.D.2d 797, 715 N.Y.S.2d 160 (2d Dep't 2000).

§ 17:23   Supporting depositions not applicable to parking violation summonses

Research References

West's Key Number Digest, Automobiles ⚷351.1

The supporting deposition provisions of the CPL are inapplicable to parking violation summonses. *See, e.g., People v. Wienclaw*, 183 Misc. 2d 727, __, 704 N.Y.S.2d 445, 448 (Valley Stream Just. Ct. 2000); *People v. Pilewski*, 173 Misc. 2d 800, __, 660 N.Y.S.2d 525, 527 (Great Neck Just. Ct. 1997); *People v. Crist Trucking*, 113 Misc. 2d 136, __, 448 N.Y.S.2d 344, 345 (Mount Vernon City Ct. 1980). *See generally* VTL Article 2-B.

§ 17:24   Denial of motion to dismiss simplified traffic information for failure to provide timely supporting deposition not reviewable in collateral proceeding

Research References

West's Key Number Digest, Automobiles ⚷351.1

The denial of a motion to dismiss a simplified traffic information for failure to provide the defendant with a timely supporting deposition, *see People v. Nuccio*, 78 N.Y.2d 102, 104, 571 N.Y.S.2d 693, 694 (1991), "is not reviewable in a collateral proceeding." *Matter of Strax v. New York State Dep't of Motor Vehicles*, 8 A.D.3d 396, __, 777 N.Y.S.2d 709, 709 (2d Dep't 2004).

§ 17:25   Re-use of supporting deposition to DWI charge where original charge is dismissed and re-filed

In *People v. Cordeiro*, 24 Misc. 3d 526, 876 N.Y.S.2d 636 (Webster Just. Ct. 2009), the defendant was charged with DWI via simplified traffic informations supplemented by a form DWI supporting deposition. The DWI charges were dismissed on the ground that the DWI supporting deposition was facially insufficient. *See People v. Cordeiro*, 18 Misc. 3d 1135(A), 859 N.Y.S.2d 897 (Table) (Webster Just. Ct. 2008). The People re-filed the DWI charges via new simplified traffic informations supplemented, in part, by the original, facially insufficient DWI supporting deposition. The Court held that the original supporting deposition could not be re-used in this manner, reasoning as follows:

> Criminal Procedure Law 160.50(1) requires that when a case is resolved in favor of a defendant, the record of said action must be sealed, unless otherwise directed by the court. No such previous direction has been made by this court relative to said original charges. . . . The same charges that are currently before the court were dismissed against the defendant for insufficiency as set out in this court's aforementioned written decision. Thus pursuant to C.P.L. 160.50(1) & (3) the previous case was decided in favor of the defendant, which required that the entire record of that previous action be sealed. The sealing of said record would not allow the supporting deposition issued in support of the original simplified traffic informations to be used in support of the simplified traffic informations filed in the subsequent action. This would render the re-filed simplified traffic informations charging the defendant with both Common Law Driving While Intoxicated, V.T.L. 1192(3) and Aggravated Driving While Intoxicated V.T.L. 1192(2-a) insufficient, requiring their dismissal . . . unless a supporting deposition, dated after the date the of previous dismissal, attesting to some of the alleged indicia of intoxication of the defendant was re-filed as well.

Cordeiro, 24 Misc. 3d at __, 876 N.Y.S.2d at 637-38.

Part V

PLEA BARGAINING

Chapter 18

Local Criminal Court Practice: Practical Aspects

Research References

Westlaw Databases
Handling Drunk Driving Cases (2d ed.) (HDRUNKDR)

Treatises and Practice Aids
Fiandach, Handling Drunk Driving Cases § 20:10 (2d ed.)

KeyCite®: Cases and other legal materials listed in KeyCite Scope can be researched through the KeyCite service on Westlaw®. Use KeyCite to check citations for form, parallel references, prior and later history, and comprehensive citator information, including citations to other decisions and secondary materials.

Leona Helmsley. Ollie North. Manuel Noriega. They have never been my clients.

Kastigar motions. Mandamus petitions. United States Supreme Court stays. They have never graced my word processor.

But, I too, represent people in trouble. Shoemakers, truckers, accountants, Uncle Fred or Niece Mary, charged with misdemeanors, petty offenses, traffic violations, and drunken driving. It is an art, never learned on Wall Street or discussed in the New York Times. It is my work and, if it is or may become yours, I have a few observations and words of advice to offer.

First, keep the environment in perspective. Local criminal courts face a legion of cases. The system survives through plea bargaining. Litigation is not encouraged.

A local criminal court practitioner handles a large number of cases with the same people over a long period of time. Reputation and relationships with the other players in the courthouse are your most valuable tools.

Most agreements in this courthouse are oral. Honesty is important, and deceit—no matter how minor—can have long-term consequences. A lawyer who cannot trust and be trusted will suffer.

Courtesy ranks second only to integrity among the vital tools of this trade. Everyone plays a role in the local criminal court. The us-against-them mentality that may serve the anti-trust litigator will hurt a local defense lawyer and his clients. For the most part, at the local court, everyone is simply trying to do a job. Everyone is in it together.

The personalities and eccentricities of the actors influence every case. A defense attorney who does not perceive the needs, problems, and priorities of the people who share the cases will miss opportunities to work out advantageous resolutions or will suffer in other ways.

§ 18:1   The prosecutor

Research References

West's Key Number Digest, Criminal Law ☞273.1(2)

Prosecutors are center stage. In *some* ways, they are the unwilling partners of the defense attorneys. The partnership is often rocky, filled with anger, loud exchanges, and distrust. But it need not be that way.

The defense attorney who has been a prosecutor understands that prosecutors view themselves as protectors of the innocent, champions of law enforcement, and problem solvers. Prosecutors use a tough demeanor to move cases. They consider their cases valid unless shown otherwise. But prosecutors do not want unjust results. They want dispositions. They rarely have time for personal involvement or animosity.

Prosecutors also realize that most defendants enter the system because of personal problems—alcoholism, drug addiction, mental illness, ignorance, poverty, and the like. While maintaining their scowls and barks, prosecutors spend a great deal of time referring defendants to various social service agencies. Although they are not social workers, prosecutors often properly use the coercion of a criminal charge to force people to confront their problems.

The prosecutor's expressions of anger and impatience are the product of caseload pressure, or they are tactical ploys. Attorneys, especially those who primarily handle civil cases, are too quick to take offense and hold grudges. Attorneys in civil courts work more or less on an equal footing. No such parity exists in a criminal case, and equality before the Bench exists primarily in principle.

Your demeanor helps determine the attitude of the prosecutor. The defense attorney who treats every prosecutor as an adversary will find an adversary in every case. Litigation maneuvers and posturing simply hurt your ability to negotiate favorable dispositions.

The art of negotiation is knowing what the other side wants. Prosecutors and defense attorneys do not want the same things. Few prosecutors are interested in trying cases in local criminal courts. They do so when defense attorneys do not accept the offered plea bargain. Prosecutors' and defense attorneys' criteria for striking a bargain differ.

Empathetic defense attorneys care a great deal about their clients' hardships. But only the foolish attorney believes that the description of such problems will be determinative in striking a deal. Trying to generate empathy in a prosecutor frequently is futile and counterproductive.

The inexperienced defense attorney begins the long and sad tale: The client is a sober citizen who normally does not drink and drive, but the client had been fighting with his wife, who was having an affair. He went to the local gin mill and had a few.

The rustling sounds that interrupt the monologue are the prosecutor going through mail, waiting for the lawyer to finish. The prosecutor knows that once past the marital problem, the attorney will explain the client's need to drive to support the children of the impending broken home.

Are prosecutors born without hearts? No. But they have heard it all before. And they make decisions based on different criteria. Equitable arguments can help only if they distinguish a case from the norm. Most defendants need a license to work. Most support themselves and others. Unless someone held a gun to a defendant's head and forced him to drink and drive, the reason for the offense matters little.

§ 18:2   Negotiating dispositions

Research References

West's Key Number Digest, Criminal Law ☞273.1(2)

To negotiate effectively, the defense attorney's presentation must address the criteria that matter to the prosecutor. In fact, most prosecutors would not listen to a narrative about an unfaithful spouse without interrupting. The prosecutor usually will try to focus the defense attorney on those facts that might make a difference.

Prosecutors care about the defendant's prior record. They want to know if damage was done. Was there an accident or injury? The prosecutor will focus, as well, on the strength of his case. Was there a timely chemical result? Is there proof of operation?

In civil cases, each side tries to obtain the best possible disposition. In criminal cases, the prosecutor is charged with following office policy and doing justice. Justice is frequently what the prosecutor thinks is fair.

Yet the fairness goal occasionally will cause a prosecutor to protect a defendant from an attorney who is trying to plead guilty to defective charges. Prosecutors sometimes point out defects and consent to motions to *dismiss*.

Some time ago, I was defending a DWI charge where the defendant was found drunk and unconscious at the scene of an accident. The defendant owned the car, but had no recollection of driving it. During a pretrial hearing, it became apparent that a key prosecution witness was lying and may well have been the driver of the car. Instead of attempting to bolster the fallacious testimony, the assistant district attorney interrupted my cross-examination to suggest a more fruitful area of impeachment. The case ended with a joint motion to dismiss.

If negotiations come to a stalemate, make a counter-offer to the prosecutor by devising an alternative disposition. The options are limited only by your imagination and the prosecutor's office policy.

Consider, for example, the college student, with no prior record, who parked illegally. After leaving a party at which he had a few too many, the student discovers that his car has been towed. The student hops the fence at the tow yard. He borrows someone else's car to create an exit by driving through the fence. The student then liberates his car.

To negotiate a plea, examine the case from the prosecutor's perspective. Both the tow truck owner and the owner of the neighboring car got hurt. The defendant avoided tow fees by helping himself. The police and the court also have relevant interests.

The prosecutor initially will offer a plea to a misdemeanor in satisfaction of the felony—a short jail sentence, probation with restitution and/or a fine.

You should seek to avoid a criminal record, jail, and probation. First, limit or neutralize any pressure from the victims by having your client make immediate restitution.

Next, work out a program of community service to present to the court and the prosecutor. By stressing the need to avoid a criminal record and incarceration, and by providing a viable alternative, you will improve the chances of obtaining a favorable plea.

Not all local criminal court cases can be settled. Office policy may preclude a prosecutor from offering a deal that the defendant can accept. In such instances, protracted argument is a waste of time. If the case must be tried, save your argument for the jury.

Although the goal changes on the march to trial, the smart practitioner's attitude will remain the same. The inexperienced lawyer will substitute discourteous and insulting behavior for advocacy, believing that the defense is the champion of liberty and due process while the prosecution is the tyrannical enemy.

The opponents reciprocate. The lawyers engage in contests matching wits, fighting skirmishes with gusto. Such conduct is self-indulgent, unprofessional, and reprehensible. Advocacy requires lawyers to do those things, consistent with ethics, that advance the interests of the clients. Antagonizing an opponent rarely benefits the client.

Play smart. If taking offense will help the cause, take offense. If ignoring obnoxious behavior is in the client's interest, ignore the behavior. Offend whomever you please after you leave the office.

§ 18:3 Motion practice

Research References

West's Key Number Digest, Criminal Law ⟜273.1(2)

Although you would never know it from lawyer shows on television, pretrial motions and discovery demands are the opening guns even in these cases. Litigation begins, not with drama but with paper.

Although the filing of paper is tolerated in felony cases, prosecutors view motions in local criminal court with disfavor. Most prosecutors's offices are inadequately staffed. Superior court cases take priority, and prosecutors assigned to local criminal courts have little support.

In civil litigation, both sides usually are funded by private entities. In criminal cases, the prosecution is publicly funded. Paper practice is a luxury.

In civil cases, mutual discovery is expected, encouraged, and required. Judges do not want to try cases that lingered because the parties never learned the facts. The expectations differ in a routine misdemeanor case. Motions often are answered here by law students clerking part-time. On occasion, the prosecution will respond with whatever is in the word processor. A pleading may even oppose or consent to relief that was not requested. Prosecutors assume that defense pleadings also are word processor packages. They are often correct.

Defense attorneys who truly need discovery should ask for what they need and explain why they need it. Do not expend credibility seeking something you do not need and cannot get.

Few prosecutors in local criminal court are interested in hiding evidence. Often, however, the prosecutor does not possess the requested material and may not even know that it exists. The prosecutor's major objection to discovery is the time and trouble involved in getting the discovery for you.

If you truly need specific items for the defense, help yourself and your client by making a narrow and focused demand. A cooperative approach will often be more effective than an adversarial one. You can often do best by submitting a proposed order resolving discovery issues. The prosecutor will welcome the chance to save time by negotiating the order rather than responding to motions.

Once the order is approved by the court, the prosecutor can give a copy to the police and ask them to obtain the material ordered. By saving the prosecutor's time, you may get everything you need.

A working relationship has other benefits. Although the case could not be settled at the outset, a relationship of mutual cooperation opens new opportunities to reach agreement on the entire matter.

At the outset, prosecutors frequently have little information about a particular case. Motion practice occasionally forces a prosecutor to learn the facts of the case. If the prosecutor has discretion to dispose of weak cases, a defense attorney may be able to use information gleaned from discovery to persuade the prosecutor to reduce or dismiss the charge. That practice is known as trying the case in the prosecutor's office.

It is risky. Revealing weaknesses in the government's case may simply help the prosecutor prepare a better case. You also lose the chance to surprise the prosecution at trial. But if you proceed carefully, you may score a major victory without trial. Prosecutors do not want to be blindsided or lose at trial. Most will not expend time on a flawed prosecution. A major advantage of taking this risk is that it builds trust. Most prosecutors are sensitive to your risk as well as their own.

§ 18:4 The pretrial hearings

Research References

West's Key Number Digest, Criminal Law ☞273.1(2)

The pretrial hearing usually is the last chance to resolve the case before trial. The hearing often is a mini-trial in which both sides get to see the case. Hearings also give clients a preview of the testimony and force them to confront the possibility of a conviction.

The pretrial hearing also is an opportunity for the defense to gain discovery and prepare for trial. It fixes the testimony of some of the prosecution's witnesses. For that reason, prosecutors call only those witnesses whose testimony is necessary to satisfy the judge. However, nothing prevents you, as the defense attorney, from calling other relevant prosecution witnesses. For example, it is a rare case in which there is only one police witness. At most pretrial hearings, however, the People rarely call more than the minimum witnesses needed to meet their burden. This usually translates into the arresting officer. You, however, can call that officer's partner and any other police officers who have information relevant to the issue at hand.

In one jurisdiction, the police seem to have a "know nothing rule" requiring that only the arresting officer recollect the facts of the case. This is designed to prevent defense attorneys from obtaining conflicting testimony. Accordingly, a pretrial hearing can be used to eliminate potential police witnesses by establishing a lack of recall. Absent your subpoena, this testimonial lobotomy would not be discovered until trial.

Approach trial as a good doctor approaches surgery: do it when nothing else works. No one can control or predict the result. If you practice in other courts, do not be lulled into strategic mistakes. Local criminal courts do not necessarily apply the rules of evidence or procedure. Because prosecutors in local criminal court have little time to prepare and virtually no support, they may run into problems of proof. Be alert to such opportunities.

Prepare an initial strategy. But be ready to shift gears. The prosecution might fail, for example, to establish a necessary element of the offense. Avoid establishing the missing piece on cross-examination. In local criminal court, less may often be more.

§ 18:5 The judge

Research References

West's Key Number Digest, Criminal Law ⊜273.1(2)

Judges make up the second most important group of participants in the local courts. The vast majority of these courts are staffed by lay judges who work long hours for little money. These judges are proud of the civic duty they perform.

For most judges, the desire to do a good job is exceeded only by the fear of doing a bad one. Judges are visible, vulnerable, and relatively defenseless. The power of the Bench extends over lawyers and litigants; it provides no protection from public criticism.

The currency of public office is respect, honor and prestige. Some lawyers assume that because these are "lower" courts, they may treat the judges with less regard that those who preside in superior court. Defense lawyers who fail to treat the judge with respect serve their clients poorly.

Judges view themselves as protectors of the society they serve. They often feel responsible when people suffer from the actions of defendants who have previously been before them. That is particularly true in DWI cases. When a serious accident happens, judges scan the newspaper hoping the name of the defendant is not familiar.

In New York, most local criminal courts are staffed by lay judges. Although they are not attorneys, they do receive basic training, and most try hard to do the job well. I recall a two-day jury trial before a part-time judge whose full-time job was clerking in a grocery store. Prior to the trial, she prepared extensively. She did an admirable job. The conviction withstood my appeal. In retrospect, a less dedicated jurist would have been preferable.

In proposing a plea agreement, parties must satisfy the judge's sense of responsibility. Because most prosecutors have a working knowledge of what the judge wants or will accept, it is rare for a judge to disapprove of a negotiated disposition.

Judges also share the prosecutors' aversion to paper. Most local criminal court judges have vast dockets, with cases involving small claims, environmental conservation offenses, municipal ordinances, leash law regulations, traffic offenses, and criminal cases of every kind. It is impossible for any judge to be competent and current in all these areas.

These judges have little time to read pleadings and even less time to research questions of law. Some judges will avoid lengthy consideration of complex or technical issues by resolving doubt in favor of the prosecution. If you can, negotiate a proposed order with the prosecutor. When negotiation fails, you must convince the judge that the defense is correct. Bring copies of the relevant cases to court. Highlight or underline the relevant portions of each opinion.

A defense lawyer who battles with the judge will lose. Any short-term victory will be offset by the long-term damage to your reputation. Judges talk to other judges and tend to see things from the fellow judge's perspective.

Do not express emotions that could harm the client. Use emotion only as a tool to help the client's case. Expressing annoyance or irritation with the court will very likely hurt the case.

On the other hand, everyone respects a lawyer who shows self-discipline and restraint. Even the most arbitrary judges may reconsider their decision if combative attorneys do not force them to become more resolute. The polite and persistent attorney will often change minds over the course of a case.

§ 18:6 Court personnel

Research References

West's Key Number Digest, Criminal Law ☞273.1(2)

Although judges wear the robes and lawyers carry the brief-cases, law clerks, court clerks, and secretaries run the court. A lawyer who speaks to the clerk is, in effect, speaking to the judge. The information conveyed by the court personnel shapes the judge's impression. The clerks control both the calendar and access to the judge. They can influence the disposition of a case.

Every lawyer has scheduling conflicts. Every lawyer will need adjournments. Some will get them. Court personnel will help resolve conflicts for those attorneys whom the clerks respect. They will have a great deal more trouble finding solutions for attorneys who are discourteous or disreputable.

Seek an adjournment only when you really need it. The judges, prosecutors, and clerks know those lawyers who seek adjournments solely to delay. These lawyers have a difficult time obtaining even necessary extensions. By not seeking specious adjournments, you reduce the chance of having the request denied.

§ 18:7 Clients

Research References

West's Key Number Digest, Criminal Law ☞273.1(2)

Clients make up the last but perhaps most important group of players in the local criminal court. The most talented lawyer will starve without clients. Referrals are critical to building a local criminal practice. Each client is connected to other potential clients. When people get into trouble, they consult friends, relatives, and acquaintances who have been in trouble.

Few people can judge the quality of a professional's work. Listen to people describe their doctors, builders, or teachers. People are impressed by factors related to the quality of the work. Because clients cannot judge your work, they judge what they can.

I have a good dentist, but I know nothing about teeth. My dentist is warm and friendly and explains what is going on with my teeth and what to expect. Because I understand, I am comfortable with the dentist and my condition.

People similarly judge their lawyers by the personal contact and the results of their case. A criminal charge is more frightening than a dental problem. A good lawyer dispels fear by explaining the law. The clearer the explanation, the better the attorney.

The initial interview is your opportunity to assess the client's situation and explain it in simple terms. In first aid, the first goal is to stop the bleeding. In criminal law, the first goal is to control the fear with information and attorney contact. Clients need to know that attorneys care about them and their case. They need to feel secure about their lawyers.

Many lawyers feel harassed by clients's constant phone calls. They do not return the calls, or they wait a day or two before calling back. Clients respond by making more phone calls. Phone tag results in an irritated lawyer and a dissatisfied client. Unhappy clients refer no one.

Encourage the client to call with any questions. Return all phone calls promptly. Call clients at night and on weekends when you are likely to be working anyway. The clients will appreciate your concern. Clients believe lawyers spend weekends on the golf course. There is nothing more gratifying, therefore, than a client's reaction to a telephone call on a Sunday evening.

My phone number is listed, and I encourage my clients to call me at home. I would, of course, dislike receiving many calls at home. But I have learned that the more secure the client, the fewer the phone calls. By assuring clients that help is available at all times, you will reduce the number of phone calls you receive.

Clients also feel more secure when they receive written work product. Send the client all motions and correspondence. Law is the practice of abstractions. There is no laying on of hands or surgery. Unless the case is tried, the client sees little of the actual effort. It is important, therefore, that the client see what can be seen.

Send clients copies of the pleadings and ask for comments. Giving the client homework will also reduce the number of phone calls. Clients will not call when they have not done their homework.

Carefully screen out problem clients. They come in many varieties. Avoid the attorney without a degree. These clients refuse to stay on their side of the desk. They want to run the case. They want to save money by doing part of the work. But they will share none of the blame.

In most cases, also avoid shoppers. Shoppers like to hire a lawyer the way they buy a car. They rarely are happy with the service or the bill. Barterers are always a temptation. Sometimes the cash poor client can help the lawyer in some way. But the practice is risky and should be avoided.

The worst clients, and the ones to be avoided in all cases, are the influence peddlers. They bowl with the chief of police, go to church with the judge, and know everyone on the jury. They need a lawyer simply to stand next to them in court. Influence peddlers tell their attorney that the disposition will be arranged by the prosecutor, who is a third cousin, and the judge, who is godfather to their children. The attorney will be paid a pro forma fee to cover travel time to and from court. After receiving the small retainer from the influence peddler, you will almost always learn that the prosecutor and judge do, in fact, know the client. And they think he belongs in jail. When instinct tells you something is wrong, it is.

To be happy and successful, you have to be efficient. Backlog hurts a practice and a career. The overworked attorney is not receptive to new clients. A new case becomes a burden, not an exciting challenge. Law becomes less fun.

§ 18:8 Fees

Make sure you are paid fairly. Competent representation requires adequate compensation. There is no substitute for money. You cannot do good work if you are resentful.

The local criminal defense attorney should be paid in full, in advance. Fees in local court are small enough to make advance payment reasonable. Clients rarely will complain about having to pay a reasonable fee for professional service.

The fact that law is a profession, not a business, does not excuse attorneys from applying sound principles of commerce. Law offices run on money. One of the great advantages of local criminal court practice is that the fees are predictable. Retainers constituting the entire fee can be set and collected before you begin work.

Use a retainer agreement. Write the retainer agreement in simple language. Have clients read the agreement and ask questions before they sign it. Do not accept the case until the retainer has been paid. Keep proper time records and request additional funds if you exceed the retainer.

Some clients will request payment terms. Explain that you cannot handle such arrangements. Recommend that the client borrow the money from a friend or relative. If the client's friends are not willing to extend credit, you certainly should not do so.

Contrary to popular belief, there is little shopping in criminal defense work. There are few successful cut-rate lawyers. The real competition lies in the quality of services. How a lawyer treats clients and what results a lawyer obtains are more important than how much the lawyer charges. People believe that they get what they pay for. They do not value a cheap deal when they are in trouble.

Many of this country's most proficient attorneys are provided to their clients without cost. They will tell you, however, that even when the results are outstanding, there is frequently little appreciation. Experience indicates that cutting fees is not appreciated. And cutting the time and effort that a lawyer puts into a case is never appreciated.

Regardless of the ideals of our profession, the quality of services is affected by the funds available. The number of cases necessary to sustain a cut-rate practice affects the quality of work. When a lawyer cuts corners on time, it shows up in the manner in which the lawyer interviews clients, returns phone calls, and handles the case. Lawyers tend to become brusque and intemperate as they find themselves working long hours for little money. Clients quickly become disillusioned by discourtesy and unresponsiveness. Inevitably, the practice suffers.

Lawyers who are paid adequately and in advance have time to provide excellent service. Being a lawyer is fun when you have time to do it well.

Clients are most willing to pay you when the need is greatest. In criminal work, the need is greatest at the beginning of the case. Clients will be more reluctant to pay you after work begins.

There is a long stretch from the payment of the initial retainer to the conclusion of the case. If that interval is filled with competence, compassion, and a decent result, the client will consider the money well spent.

§ 18:9 Night jury trials

One of the interesting facets of local criminal court practice in upstate New York is the concept of the "night jury trial." In the past, it was not unheard of for a Town Court jury trial to commence at 7 or 8 PM and conclude the following morning. Not surprisingly, this procedure was challenged on Constitutional grounds. In *People v. Hurley*, 86 Misc. 2d 601, 383 N.Y.S.2d 177 (Onondaga Co. Ct. 1976), the defendant was convicted of violating VTL § 1192(2) following an all-night jury trial. "[T]he trial started at 9:00 P.M. on June 19, 1975, and a verdict was returned at 6:05 A.M. the following morning. During the trial there were two recesses of six and seven minutes respectively, the last being at 12:05 A.M. on June 20, 1975. The court began its charge to the jury on the law at 4:10 A.M. and the verdict was received at 6:05 A.M." 383 N.Y.S.2d at 178. On appeal, the Onondaga County Court reversed the defendant's conviction, reasoning as follows:

> The issue of the night jury trial is most certainly the most troublesome issue presented upon this appeal. Our judicial system is historic and noble, but yet like many other systems of our day it is based on precedent and habit, oftentimes structured to accom-

modate times long since past. The evolution of the nighttime trials arose out of the necessity of small municipalities having to employ part-time judges who after fulfilling their daily duties at their various occupations, would then converge on the town hall or local meeting place and ascend to the bench to hear and decide the controversies of the local town's people, as well as preside over criminal trials of crimes committed within the town. Thus to the present day, most town justices are part-time employees of the local municipalities of our State, who preside over the various town courts at night. However, as a result of the rapid expansion of our suburban areas, a tremendous increase in those courts' caseloads has occurred, especially in the drinking-driving area. In conjunction with this increase in caseload, more and more jury trials are being conducted and out of the necessities of the system, for the most part, the trials must be conducted at night when the judge and jurors are available. * * *

While this court cannot say that all-night jury trials are per se violative of a defendant's right to a fair trial, it is of the opinion that certain night jury trials by virtue of their very length and time of the night presented are. In a criminal trial a jury by virtue of the very nature of the proceedings must consider all the facts presented to it by both the people, and the defendant, and be further able to consider those facts determined upon, in light of the charge given to it by the court relative to the legal principles of law, and apply that law to the facts of the case before it, to ultimately determine the guilt or innocence of the defendant. This court is of the opinion that this task cannot properly be performed by a jury made up of people who have been awake the whole day of the trial and who must then remain awake throughout the evening and throughout the night until the early morning hours of the next day.

Additionally it must be extremely difficult for the judge, the prosecutor and the defense attorney to properly perform each of their several functions as the strain of the hours build up. Most importantly the witness to the event must be able to be mentally alert enough to be able to recall all the facts within their knowledge that bares on the defendant's guilt or innocence. This obligation most certainly is hindered by one whose mind has been dulled by the work of the day and the expectation that the following day's labor will have to be performed with little or no sleep.

This court frequently asks jurors in trials before it to draw on their everyday experiences in deciding issues presented to it, and so must an appellate court in light of the record presented to it, and in so doing this court is of the opinion that the jurors in the instant case could not properly consider the guilt or innocence of this defendant after an all-night trial as disclosed in this record on appeal. The times involved in the instant case must certainly support the position of the defendant-appellant and his attorney's observation upon the oral argument of this appeal, wherein he indicated that the jurors appeared quite tired to him during the early morning hours.

The public as well as a defendant is entitled to the assurance that there will be a fair trial, and when an appellate court concludes from the record before it that such was not possible that conviction cannot stand unimpeached.

383 N.Y.S.2d at 179, 180. *See also People v. Passero*, 78 Misc. 2d 548, 357 N.Y.S.2d 677 (Monroe Co. Ct. 1974); *People on Complaint of Hanna v. Murphy*, 42 Misc. 2d 413, 248 N.Y.S.2d 363 (Westchester Co. Ct. 1964); *People v. Rodgers*, 205 Misc. 1106, 131 N.Y.S.2d 622 (Schenectady Co. Ct. 1954).

As a result of decisions such as these, it is no longer common for night jury trials to continue past midnight.

Chapter 19

Plea Bargaining

Research References

Westlaw Databases

Complete Manual of Criminal Forms (3d ed.) (CMCRF)

Constitutional Rights of the Accused (3d ed.) (CONRTACC)
Criminal Procedure (2d ed.) (CRIMPROC)
Handling a Criminal Case in New York (HCCNY)
Handling Drunk Driving Cases (2d ed.) (HDRUNKDR)

Treatises and Practice Aids

Cook, Constitutional Rights of the Accused § 16:4 (3d ed.)
LaFave, Israel, and King, Criminal Procedure § 21.1(a)
Muldoon, Handling a Criminal Case in New York § 17:70
Fiandach, Handling Drunk Driving Cases § 32:5 (2d ed.)

Forms

Bailey and Fishman, Complete Manual of Criminal Forms § 48:11 (3d ed.)

KeyCite®: Cases and other legal materials listed in KeyCite Scope can be researched through the KeyCite service on Westlaw®. Use KeyCite to check citations for form, parallel references, prior and later history, and comprehensive citator information, including citations to other decisions and secondary materials.

---

§ 19:1 Negotiating with the ADA—A typical approach

Research References

West's Key Number Digest, Criminal Law ⚖268

You have been retained by a client to represent him in regard to a charge of DWI. After an extensive interview in which you ascertain the facts of his case as well as his personal background, you call the district attorney's office and are routed to an assistant district attorney (hereinafter referred to as an ADA) whom you start to advise of your client's situation.

The ADA interrupts you in midsentence and asks you where your client was arrested and what he was charged with. Although you deem this interruption discourteous, you answer the question and resume your discourse concerning your client's personal qualities and standing in the community. You are again interrupted and asked if your client has any prior convictions. Although you are somewhat put off by the impatient tone of your adversary, you tolerate his lack of decorum because your client's interests are at stake. Before you are halfway into the facts surrounding the arrest of your client and the essential details which make up the foundation for your arguments in regard to the law, the ADA interrupts you again, offers you a disposition, and attempts to terminate the conversation.

§ 19:2 What to tell the ADA

Research References

West's Key Number Digest, Criminal Law ⚖268

The intemperate and abrupt ADA discussed above is merely reacting to the approach adopted by the attorney in presenting his case. The attorney knows what he wants to impart, but is uninformed as to the information the ADA needs to evaluate the case. First, you should provide the ADA with: 1) your client's name, the charge, and the court in which the case is pending; 2) the test result, and 3) your client's prior record, if you know it. These are the items that enable a prosecutor to grasp the case and discuss it intelligently.

Many offices assign ADAs to specific courts. Accordingly, the first thing the ADA wants to know is whether the case is his or some other prosecutor's. Upon hearing your client's name, he will start checking to see if he has a police report in regard to your case. The charge, test result, and prior record are critical for his evaluation and formulation of a proposed disposition. Attempting to discuss the case without giving the ADA this basic information is a waste of time. In the prosecutor's mind, you assume the position of a client in your office who insists on detailing a lengthy narrative without giving you any idea of whether the case concerns a matrimonial, contract, criminal charge, etc. Only attorneys blessed with unusual patience are willing to sit and hear a detailed narrative without first determining the area of law in which the matter lies.

§ 19:3 The prosecutor's perspective

Research References

West's Key Number Digest, Criminal Law ☞268

An ADA is not an adversary in the same sense as an opponent in a civil case. The ADA has a quasi-judicial responsibility which gives him a broader perspective than that encompassed by the traditional adversarial role. In the private sector, an attorney's negotiating position is determined by the strength of his case. In the public sector, an ADA's negotiating position is determined more by equitable considerations than the legal or factual strength of his case. An ADA seeks what he perceives as being a fair and just result. Although his perception of equity is subject to challenge, his motivation is rarely questioned. An ADA deals with a large volume of local criminal court cases. Accordingly, it is imperative that each file be swiftly evaluated and disposed of expeditiously. In order to accomplish this, most prosecutors utilize informal criteria to arrive at an acceptable plea bargain.

§ 19:4 Prosecutorial criteria

Research References

West's Key Number Digest, Criminal Law ☞268

The primary factors which an ADA considers in arriving at a proposed disposition are:

(1) *The charge and the facts upon which it is based*. As a general rule, the more common the charge, the more likely the existence of a policy in regard to a negotiated disposition. For example, first offense DWI charges are normally subject to being reduced to DWAI. If the facts involve a personal injury accident, however, the ADA may not be willing to consent to such a reduction. Property damage may also affect the disposition of the case.

(2) *The defendant's age*. As set forth in §§ 15:1 et seq. "Underage Offenders," age is a critical factor in determining the effect of a conviction on a defendant's license. It is also a major factor in determining a plea bargain. A relatively young defendant with a prior record may cause an ADA to hesitate in negotiating a disposition.

(3) *The defendant's prior record*. In virtually every criminal case, the defendant's prior record is one of the most critical (if not the most critical) considerations in arriving at a negotiated disposition. This record will be checked through the Department of Motor Vehicles as well as the Division of Criminal Justice Services. In DWI cases, most courts and district attorney's offices have policies which are predicated upon your client's prior record of alcohol-related convictions. In addition to convictions, the ADA will consider any prior arrests. In plea bargaining, arrests are often given the same weight as convictions. It is important, therefore, that you delve into the details of your client's prior record and be able to explain the circumstances surrounding any prior charges.

(4) *Chemical test result*. Many district attorney's offices emphasize the significance of a chemical test result and will not agree to the reduction of a DWI charge where the chemical test result exceeds a specified concentration. Such counties will adhere to this policy even though the defendant has no prior record and would, otherwise, be granted a reduction of the charge.

(5) *Circumstances of the arrest*. The politics of the criminal justice system dictate that courts and ADAs be responsive to the law enforcement community. The police can have a definite influence on the disposition of a case. The strength of this influence varies from community to community and is affected by both the nature of the case and the defendant. Generally, the client who is polite to the police is easier to defend than one who is not.

(5) In misdemeanor cases, the police will advise the ADA if they were given a "hard time." Conversely, a police officer's indication that your client was "no problem" will often tip the

balance in your favor in a close situation. Generally, ADAs are responsive to police who have been harassed by defendants. Accordingly, it is important to interview your client closely as to whether there were any problems at the time of the arrest. If your client tells you that the police gave him a hard time, the chances are that the feeling was mutual and you may have a tougher case than would otherwise be apparent from the facts.

(6) *Office policy*. When a prosecutor tells you that his office has a policy in regard to a particular charge, you should find out how firm the policy is, and whether there are exceptions for which you might qualify. Because of the publicity and emphasis accorded DWI enforcement, prosecutorial policy has become increasingly rigid. Reduction of DWI cases to speed or other traffic offenses is rare.

(7) *Factual, legal, and equitable considerations*. The listing of the facts and legal considerations at the bottom of a list of prosecutorial criteria is probably surprising. In virtually every other legal proceeding, the facts and law would be listed as the primary consideration with all others following thereafter. In the criminal justice system, however, ADAs are rarely acquainted with the factual or legal insufficiency of a criminal case pending in local criminal court. Serious felonies are the exception to this rule because of the police practice of calling in the district attorney at the beginning of the case. In local court misdemeanors, however, the ADA usually knows nothing of the case until well after the arrest. At best, she will have an arrest summary detailing the charge and a statement of the underlying facts. At worst, all she will have is a copy of the information.

Consequently, the determination of legal and factual problems is a defense role. The volume of cases requires an ADA to operate on the presumption that there are no factual or legal problems. In a very real sense, the prosecutor relies upon her adversary to apprise her of the existence of any such issues. Once apprised, the prosecutor will then check with the police to see whether they confirm the defense assertions.

If the facts or law of your case merit a disposition other than that specified by a prosecutor's policy, it is incumbent upon you to make this fact clear to the ADA and to do so in a manner which is meaningful to her. Bear in mind that your phone call to the ADA will frequently be the first time that she has heard of this arrest. If your claim to distinction is based upon equity, you are probably better off discussing this with the ADA on the telephone.

If your assertion is legal in nature, it might be to your advantage to reduce it to writing in order to allow the ADA an opportunity to review your argument. Legal arguments in criminal cases are predicated upon facts which you obtain from an inherently unreliable source: your client. Prosecutors rely on police reports which are only slightly more reliable. It is not unusual for both attorneys to wind up at trial and discover that they are litigating two different cases. Most criminal cases are determined by which side has the most accurate facts, rather than which is more conversant with the law.

§ 19:5 Specific plea bargains—The first offender

Research References

West's Key Number Digest, Criminal Law ☞268

Until recently, a first-time offender walking into your office could be presented with a fairly straightforward scenario of how their case might be resolved. Typically, you could obtain a reduction of the misdemeanor DWI charge to the violation of driving while ability impaired (hereinafter referred to as DWAI) with a fine of not less than $300, nor more than $500, together with the state-mandated surcharge. Upon entry of that plea, the court would issue a 20-day order allowing the client to continue his or her driving privileges while the client's paperwork was processed by the Department of Motor Vehicles (hereinafter referred to as the DMV). Once the client obtained a conditional license application in the mail from the DMV, the client would proceed to the local district office, pay the fee for the conditional license, and register for the Drinking Driver Program (hereinafter referred to as DDP).

Upon entering the DDP, your client would pay a fee for their participation in that program. At the completion of that program, their full license is restored. Recent developments in prosecutorial policy, as well as DMV procedures, however, present some complications in this common scenario.

It is now critical to ascertain from your client what their breath test result, if any, was. This will establish what the plea bargaining parameters are with the district attorney's office. By way of example, the Columbia County District Attorney has a policy of not reducing any DWI case wherein the breath test result is 0.13 blood alcohol content or higher. To discourage breath test refusals, that office refuses to plea bargain any case in which there is a test refusal. In either case, the offer will be a plea to the misdemeanor DWI charge with a fine of not less than $500 nor more than $1,000, and a state-mandated surcharge. The client's license is subject to a six-month revocation, but the conditional license is available and successful completion of the Drinking Driver Program will terminate the revocation arising out of a conviction for DWI. A test refusal revocation, however, will not be terminated by DDP completion.

The DDP may refer your client for alcohol evaluation and, if deemed appropriate, alcohol treatment. Pursuant to VTL § 1196(1), your client can be required to participate in such alcohol treatment for a period of up to eight months. In the event that the officials administering the program recommend additional treatment, your client may be required to stay in that program until satisfactory completion.

From the above brief example, it is critical to know the particular DA's policy as well as those of the DDP and DMV. While the policies of the DMV are rather consistent, it is difficult to generalize with regard to the DA's offices, because each office has a different standard. As stated above, the Columbia County District Attorney has a 0.13 or above policy; the Greene County District Attorney has a 0.20 or above policy, while Ulster County has a 0.15 cutoff. Many counties have no policy and the first-time offender can obtain an offer of DWAI regardless of the client's test result. You must know the policy in your area in order to avoid surprise and embarrassment when you appear in court.

If your client does not fall within the policy exceptions of the local DA, the first-time offender will be offered a plea to the violation of DWAI resulting in a 90-day suspension of his license. A fine in the range of $300 to $500 will be imposed, and the client will be eligible for a conditional license if he participates in the DDP. In most cases, the client can choose to attend or not attend the DDP. In the event the client chooses to forgo the DDP, his license will be returned to him automatically at the end of the 90-day suspension period upon payment of a suspension termination fee. *See* VTL § 503(2)(j).

Two further cautionary notes. While it is indeed rare, in addition to the suspension of the license, VTL § 1193(2) also provides for a permissive suspension of your client's motor vehicle registration for the same period of time. Further, should your client's insurance company learn of his conviction for either operating while intoxicated or impaired, his policy is subject to cancellation on that basis and he will be placed in "the assigned risk pool" for at least 36 months. *See* Ins. Law § 3425.

§ 19:6   The second offender

Research References

West's Key Number Digest, Criminal Law ☞271

Many district attorneys are reluctant to reduce a misdemeanor DWI charge where your client has been convicted of a DWAI in the preceding 10 years.

For most individuals, a second offense will often result in an offer to plea to the charge. Where your client is convicted of the misdemeanor DWI, there will be a revocation of her license for a minimum of six months. Additionally, the fine will be anywhere between a minimum of $500 and a maximum of $1,000, and a surcharge. While unlikely, your client can be imprisoned for up to one year in jail, or placed on three-year probation.

The questions most asked by clients with a second alcohol-related arrest are regarding their eligibility for a conditional license. On a second offense, a motorist is eligible to participate in the DDP and obtain a conditional license if more than five years have elapsed from the date of the client's last participation in the DDP to the date of the new arrest. If your client did not attend the DDP after their last conviction, then the five year period is determined from the date of conviction to the new arrest. If eligible for a conditional license, the client will have the conditional license until the expiration of the period of revocation; or successful completion of the DDP and any referral, whichever is longer. *See* Section 136.9 of Title 15 of the NYCRR (attached as Appendix 15).

If your client is not eligible for the DDP, her license will be revoked for at least six months. The client will be required by the DMV to obtain an independent alcohol evaluation and treatment before an application for a license is accepted. Section 136.4(a)(2) of Title 15 of the NYCRR requires the Department to deny any application for a license if there is insufficient evidence of alcohol rehabilitative effort. No application will be accepted unless it is accompanied by an alcohol and drug abuse rehabilitative program summary showing successful completion of treatment. A copy of a sample alcohol drug abuse rehabilitative program summary is attached hereto as Appendix 16.

If eligible for a conditional license, your client will have the conditional license until the revocation period is served. Successful completion of the DDP and any referral will not terminate the revocation of a second offender as it does for a first offender.

§ 19:7 Multiple offenders

Research References

West's Key Number Digest, Criminal Law ⚯270

When representing the multiple offender, the chief objective is a disposition which does not include jail. In the event your client has a prior misdemeanor DWI conviction within the preceding 10 years, and the new offense is a violation of § 1192(2), (3), or (4), they are chargeable with a class E felony. The maximum sentence for this felony is $1\frac{1}{3}$ to four years in jail, or a fine of $1,000 to $5,000, or both such fine and imprisonment.

Until recently, most third-time offenders with a DWI conviction within the preceding 10 years would be offered a plea to a misdemeanor DWI with a fine and probation. Again, it is important to know the district attorney's policy for the third-time offender. Absent a policy, here more than in any other case, the particular facts surrounding the arrest will be of utmost importance in negotiating a disposition. If the facts involve a personal injury or property damage accident, this will adversely affect the outcome. If it is a standard vehicle and traffic stop with no accident, chances of a disposition without incarceration are enhanced.

The chemical test result is significant. The lower the test result, the better your chances for a favorable result. Unlike the first or second offender, a refusal to submit to a chemical test may benefit your client. Most prosecutors loath trials where there has been a chemical test refusal absent the additional charge of felony AUO.

Before you work out any disposition, it is imperative that you obtain your client's lifetime driving record from the Department of Motor Vehicles. Presently, it is necessary to file a Freedom of Information Law request to obtain that record. Defendants with multiple convictions are subject to the Department of Motor Vehicles' regulations which call for lifetime revocations in some cases. *See* Chapter 55, *infra*.

Where your client is not eligible for the DDP and serves the applicable minimum period, he must provide evidence of alcohol evaluation and/or treatment prior to relicensure. This must be obtained by your client from a recognized alcohol treatment provider. You must ascertain if the alcohol counseling agency is one which DMV will recognize. The DMV requires:

> (4) *Rehabilitative Effort. Rehabilitative effort* shall consist of referral of an individual with a history of abuse of alcohol or drugs to any agency certified by the office of Alcoholism and Substance Abuse and/or agents authorized by professional license or professional certification, such as that granted by a Board of Examiners of the State Education Department, for evaluation of the extent of alcohol and/or drug use and satisfactory participation in any treatment recommended by such agency, and/or evidence of abstinence from, or controlled use of alcohol and/or drugs for a period of time sufficient to indicate that such person no longer constitutes a danger to other users of the highway.

15 NYCRR § 136(1)(b)(4).

If the agency does not meet the above criteria, the DMV will not accept their evaluation and/or treatment of your client. It is the policy of the DMV to prescreen and approve treatment agencies. If the treatment agency selected by your client has not been preapproved, this will significantly delay the processing of his application.

You should maintain a list of local alcohol counseling agencies in your area and know their reputations. By examining your client's prior history, you can predict if he is a likely candidate for referral. The agencies in your area have established reputations. Apprising your client of that reputation will greatly assist him in making the appropriate choice.

VTL § 1193(1)(c) now elevates a misdemeanor DWI to a felony where there has been a conviction of vehicular assault in the second or first degree, or a conviction of vehicular manslaughter in the second or first degree within the preceding 10 years. You can no longer plead your client to any one of these charges in full satisfaction of an indictment and prevent a subsequent misdemeanor DWI arrest from being elevated to a felony.

§ 19:8   Probationary sentences

Research References

West's Key Number Digest, Criminal Law ⬤268

VTL § 1193(2)(e)(5) provides:

Probation. When a license to operate a motor vehicle has been revoked pursuant to this chapter, and the holder has been sentenced to a period of probation pursuant to section 65.00 of the penal law for a violation of any provision of this chapter, or any other provision of the laws of this state, and a condition of such probation is that the holder thereof not operate a motor vehicle or not apply for a license to operate a motor vehicle during the period of such condition of probation, the commissioner may not restore such license until the period of the condition of probation has expired.

It is generally a condition of probation in a DWI case that your client not own or operate a motor vehicle. Absent a precisely worded plea bargain agreement excluding or limiting that condition, your client will be without a license while on probation. Where possible, this provision should be deleted or limited.

A goal of both the court and the prosecution is to require your client to obtain alcohol counseling. Since that counseling is mandated by the DMV as well, an effective means of limiting these probation conditions is to have your client voluntarily undergo alcohol counseling. You should advise the prosecutor and the court that DMV will not accept an application for a new license until provided with proof of alcohol rehabilitation. Once the court and prosecutor are aware of this regulation, they will often be willing to delete, or at least limit that condition of probation.

§ 19:9 Conditioning dismissal on execution of civil release

Research References

West's Key Number Digest, Criminal Law ☞268

In the past, ADAs were uncomfortable with requiring the execution of a release as a condition for the dismissal of a marginal case. The reason for this discomfort was the perception that they were trespassing onto the civil realm and that their actions were contrary to public policy.

Cowles v. Brownell, 73 N.Y.2d 382, 540 N.Y.S.2d 973 (1989), reinforces this perception. Here, the Court of Appeals held that a release, given by a plaintiff as a condition for the People's consent to the dismissal of criminal harassment charges, should not be enforced. At the outset, it should be clear that this ruling is case-specific and is not a general declaration of the invalidity of civil releases obtained in consideration of the dismissal of criminal charges. The refusal of the majority to broaden the application of its holding is the subject of Judge Titone's concurring opinion which agrees with the result, but would expand the parameters of the ruling beyond this specific case.

Facts

On July 20, 1984, Stephen Cowles was arrested by the Amsterdam Police. He alleged that one of the officers, Thomas Brownell, arrested him without cause and beat him without provocation. Mr. Cowles was charged with counts of harassment which were ultimately dismissed based upon Mr. Cowles releasing the city and the arresting officers from all civil claims arising out of the incident. Following the dismissal, Mr. Cowles brought suit against Officer Brownell for malicious prosecution, false arrest, assault, and battery.

Legal Background

The defendant police officer's motion to dismiss the civil suit on the grounds of the release was opposed by Mr. Cowles on the ground that the release was unenforceable. Mr. Cowles argued that the district attorney was aware that Officer Brownell had been involved in many similar instances leading to civil suits and that the district attorney made a practice of demanding releases in those cases. The supreme court dismissed the complaint and was reversed by the Appellate Division, which remitted the case for further proceedings on the grounds that summary judgment had been improperly granted.

At the resultant hearing, Mr. Cowles' attorney testified that the prosecutor had consistently indicated that the criminal charges were unfounded and that the city had been repeatedly sued because of the defendant police officer's conduct. In contrast, the ADA testified that he believed the criminal charges to be valid, but had entered into the agreement in order to avoid the threat of civil suit. Finding that the agreement had been voluntarily entered into, the supreme court, once again, dismissed the complaint. This holding was affirmed by the Appellate Division on the grounds that Mr. Cowles was fully aware of the rights he was waiving and the benefit he was receiving.

Court of Appeals

In reversing the Appellate Division, the Court of Appeals distinguished this situation from that of a normal plea bargain. In a plea bargain, both the People and the defendant benefit; and the agreement is in the public interest "not only because of economy, but also because a wrongdoer is punished with speed and certainty." 540 N.Y.S.2d at 975.

In contrast, the Court found that the agreement in *Cowles* benefited the defendant, but placed the integrity of the criminal justice system at issue.

> The same cannot be said of the agreement in this case. Insofar as the integrity of the criminal justice system was concerned—the paramount interest here—on this record there was no benefit, only a loss. Assuming plaintiff to have been guilty of the criminal charges leveled against him (as the prosecutor maintains) the People's interest in seeing a wrongdoer punished has not been vindicated. Assuming him to have been innocent (as he maintains), or the case against him to have been unprovable, the prosecutor was under an ethical obligation to drop the charges without exacting any price for doing so.

73 N.Y.2d 382, 540 N.Y.S.2d 973.

The Court found not only that there was no benefit, but that the agreement was detrimental to the public confidence in the criminal justice system.

> There is no public interest to be advanced by enforcing the agreement here. Rather, the agreement may be viewed as undermining the legitimate interests of the criminal justice system solely to protect against the possibility of civil liability; it surely does not foster public confidence that the justice system operates evenhandedly.

> Insulation from civil liability is not the duty of the prosecutor. The prosecutor's obligation is to represent the people and to that end, to exercise independent judgment in deciding to prosecute or refrain from prosecution. This obligation cannot be fulfilled when the prosecutor undertakes also to represent a police officer for reasons divorced from any criminal justice concern. To enforce a release-dismissal agreement under these circumstances is simply to encourage violation of the prosecutor's obligation.

73 N.Y.2d 382, 540 N.Y.S.2d 973.

In his concurring opinion, Judge Titone advocates expanding the parameter of the Court's holding from a case-specific ruling to a general rule declaring release/dismissal agreements unenforceable. He cites several potential problems arising out of this practice:

> First, as noted by the United States Court of Appeals and acknowledged by the Supreme Court majority in *Rumery*, such agreements " 'tempt prosecutors to trump up charges in reaction to a defendant's (civil) claims, suppress evidence of police misconduct, and leave unremedied deprivations of constitutional rights' " (480 U.S. at 394, 107 S.Ct. at 1193, *supra,* quoting 778 F.2d 66, 69 (1st Cir.)). Second, the availability of such agreements creates a troublesome conflict of interest for prosecutors, who are called upon to balance the private concerns of witnesses and public servants against the legitimate concerns of their primary client, the People of the State of New York, in the enforcement of the criminal laws (*see* 480 U.S. at 412–414, 107 S.Ct. at 1202–03 (Stevens, J., dissenting)). Third, they give rise to a serious risk that the societal interest in the prosecution of meritorious criminal charges will be compromised in an effort to protect local law enforcement personnel from the embarrassment and expense that attends civil litigation (*see* 480 U.S. at 400, 107 S.Ct. at 1196 (O'Connor, J., concurring)). Finally, by providing potential private litigants with a powerful incentive to forgo arguably meritorious claims, these release/dismissal arrangements interfere with an important mechanism for vindicating individual rights and holding public servants accountable, much "to the detriment . . . of society as a whole" (480 U.S. at 400, 107 S.Ct. at 1196).

540 N.Y.S.2d at 976.

As matters presently stand, the release/dismissal agreement is still a viable option. Any such agreement, however, must have its basis clearly set forth on the record. The reasons must be "genuine, compelling and legitimately related to the prosecutorial function." 540 N.Y.S.2d at 975. Otherwise, it will not "overcome the strong policy consideration disfavoring enforcement of such agreements." 540 N.Y.S.2d at 975.

In *People v. Grune*, 278 A.D.2d 668, 717 N.Y.S.2d 750 (3d Dep't 2000), the defendant was charged with class D felony DWI. The defendant was offered a plea bargain allowing him to plead guilty to class E felony DWI, together with a recommended sentence of 10 months in jail (instead of 12 months), conditioned upon his waiver of his right to appeal as well as his withdrawal of a notice of claim that he had filed against the County. The defendant appealed, claiming that the requirement that he withdraw his civil claim rendered the plea/sentence illegal. The Appellate Division, Third Department, held as follows:

> There is arguable merit to defendant's contention that the People

exceeded their authority in requiring him to waive his right to seek civil damages in exchange for a diminished jail sentence. It does not necessarily follow, however, that his waiver of appeal or judgment of conviction should be vacated as a result. To the contrary, the appropriate remedy for the impermissible extraction of a criminal defendant's release of a civil claim is to deny enforcement of the release when and if it is asserted by way of defense in a civil action. Within the context of the present criminal action, the release worked only to defendant's advantage: by giving it, he obtained a two-month reduction in the bargained-for jail sentence. To the extent that the release is unenforceable, an issue which we need not decide, he will have received a preferential sentence in exchange for illusory consideration. Obviously, his release did not induce his plea of guilty or waiver of appeal. Because defendant has raised no valid issue concerning the voluntariness of his plea of guilty or his waiver of appeal, they should be enforced.

(Citations omitted).

§ 19:10 Plea bargain *can* be conditioned upon waiver of right to appeal

Research References
West's Key Number Digest, Criminal Law ☞273.4(1)

In *People v. Seaberg*, 74 N.Y.2d 1, 543 N.Y.S.2d 968 (1989), the Court of Appeals considered a case where the defendant had been convicted after trial, but was spared a lengthy prison sentence on condition that he complete a rehabilitation program. If he failed to complete the program, he was to be sentenced to one year in jail. As part of this negotiated sentence, the defendant agreed to waive his right to appeal.

The defendant's subsequent appeal to the Appellate Division was dismissed. 139 A.D.2d 53, 530 N.Y.S.2d 278 (1988). In affirming the dismissal of the appeal, the Court held that such waivers are consistent with public policy:

We conclude that the public interest concerns underlying plea bargains generally are served by enforcing waivers of the right to appeal. Indeed, such waivers advance that interest, for the State's legitimate interest in finality extends to the sentence itself and to holding defendants to bargains they have made. While a defendant always retains the right to challenge the legality of the sentence or the voluntariness of the plea (*see, People v. Francabandera*, 33 N.Y.2d 429, 434, n. 2, 354 N.Y.S.2d 609, 310 N.E.2d 292, *supra*), the negotiating process serves little purpose if the terms of "a carefully orchestrated bargain" can subsequently be challenged (*see People v. Prescott*, 66 N.Y.2d 216, 220, 495 N.Y.S.2d 955, 486 N.E.2d 813, *supra*). Moreover, the People need not particularize "some legitimate State interest" to justify conditioning a plea bargain on defendant's waiver of the right to appeal (*see People v. Ventura*, 139 A.D.2d 196, 203, 531 N.Y.S.2d 526). The validity of the waiver is supported by the interests supporting plea bargains generally. Accordingly, we find no public policy precluding defendants from waiving their rights to appeal as a condition of the plea and sentence bargains. . . .

543 N.Y.S.2d at 972.

In *People v. Johnson*, 14 N.Y.3d 483, 903 N.Y.S.2d 299, 929 N.E.2d 361 (2010), the Court of Appeals held that:

> Because the court did not advise defendant that it was reserving approval of the negotiated disposition until it reviewed the presentencing report or other pertinent information, defendant could not have knowingly and intelligently waived his right to appeal the court's decision not to abide by the original promise of youthful offender treatment and a prison sentence of 1 1/3 to 4 years. Supreme Court's subsequent decision to modify the material terms affecting sentencing therefore vitiated defendant's knowing and intelligent entry of the waiver of appeal. Consequently, once the decision to impose the more severe sentence was announced, it was incumbent on the court to elicit defendant's continuing consent to waive his right to appeal. However, there was no need for the judge to reallocute defendant on his decision to plead guilty because his choice not to withdraw his plea effectively reaffirmed his knowing and intelligent consent to concede guilt. Since defendant was not asked if he further agreed to waive his right to pursue an appeal regarding the modified terms of his sentence, he is not foreclosed from requesting appellate review of the propriety of the denial of youthful offender treatment or the severity of the imposed sentence.

§ 19:11 Defendant may not be penalized for asserting right to trial

Research References

West's Key Number Digest, Criminal Law ⚖268

In *People v. Patterson*, 106 A.D.2d 520, 483 N.Y.S.2d 55 (2d Dep't 1984), the court considered a case in which the trial court had increased the defendant's punishment because the defendant had asserted his right to trial. While the Appellate Division held that plea bargaining was an acknowledged part of the criminal justice system, and that such bargaining might encourage a guilty plea by offering a reduced potential sentence, this did not justify the imposition of a greater sentence solely on the basis of the defendant's assertion of his right to trial:

> Once a defendant has been convicted after trial, the sentence to be imposed can reflect the sentencing principles appropriate to the individual case, for the leverages involved in the plea-bargaining process are gone. Therefore, the fact that a sentence imposed after trial is greater than that offered during a plea negotiation is no indication that the defendant is being punished for asserting his right to proceed to trial. A person may not, of course, be punished

for doing what the law allows him to do. . . . If a defendant refuses to plead guilty and goes to trial, retaliation or vindictiveness may play no role in sentencing following a conviction. . . . Rather, the conventional concerns involved in sentencing, which include the considerations of deterrence, rehabilitation, retribution, and isolation, must be the only factors weighed when sentence is imposed. . . . In this case, the record establishes that in imposing sentence, the trial court impermissibly increased defendant's punishment solely for asserting his right to a trial. Based upon our independent review of the proper factors to be considered, we have reduced the sentence to one which satisfies the acceptable objectives of sentencing.

483 N.Y.S.2d at 57 (citations omitted). *See also People v. Brown*, 157 A.D.2d 790, 550 N.Y.S.2d 389 (2d Dep't 1990) (court found no evidence in record to indicate defendant was punished for exercising right to trial).

§ 19:12   Prosecution can validly indict defendant if misdemeanor plea offer is rejected

The Court of Appeals has made clear that the People can validly indict a defendant for felony DWI where the defendant rejects a plea bargain offer of misdemeanor DWI. *See People v. Jacquin*, 71 N.Y.2d 825, 827, 527 N.Y.S.2d 728, 729, 522 N.E.2d 1026 (1988) ("We have considered defendant's remaining argument—that the prosecutor was vindictive in indicting him for a felony after negotiations for a plea to a misdemeanor charge of driving while intoxicated failed—and find no merit to it.").

§ 19:13   Plea bargain may not be obtained via threat of incarceration

Research References

West's Key Number Digest, Criminal Law ☞268

In *People v. Beverly*, 139 A.D.2d 971, 528 N.Y.S.2d 450 (4th Dep't 1988), the court reversed and remitted a conviction obtained as a result of the trial court's promise of incarceration if the case went to trial. The defendant was told by the lower court that "if we have to go to trial and work" the judge would probably sentence him to $3^1/_2$ to seven years, the maximum sentence "on top of" the sentence for another crime. 528 N.Y.S.2d at 450. Citing *People v. Glasper*, 14 N.Y.2d 893, 252 N.Y.S.2d 92, 200 N.E.2d 776 (1964), and *People v. Hollis*, 74 A.D.2d 585, 424 N.Y.S.2d 483 (1980), the Appellate Division held that the statement by the trial court "constituted coercion" which rendered the guilty plea involuntary, and mandated reversal of the conviction. 528 N.Y.S.2d at 450. *See also People v. Fisher*, 70 A.D.3d 114, 890 N.Y.S.2d 477 (1st Dep't 2009).

§ 19:14   Court policy of not accepting plea bargains on eve of trial improper

In *People v. Compton*, 157 A.D.2d 903, 550 N.Y.S.2d 148 (3d Dep't 1990), the defendant sought to accept a plea bargain which had been previously offered.

> When defendant attempted to plead in accordance with this arrangement, County Court refused to accept the plea on the ground that the case was already set for trial and that it was the court's "policy" not to accept a negotiated plea on the eve of trial. The court further stated that, pursuant to this policy, the only acceptable guilty plea would be one to the top count of the indictment. Although defense counsel objected on the ground that he had never been informed by the court of its policy of imposing time limits for accepting plea offers, the court adhered to its refusal to accept the negotiated plea.

550 N.Y.S.2d at 149.

On appeal, the Appellate Division, Third Department, held that:

> We cannot endorse a court's general policy of not permitting plea bargains based on circumstances unrelated to the particular defendant and the proposed bargain at issue. Moreover, the record appears to support defendant's contention that he was given no prior notice of the court's policy of terminating all outstanding plea offers once the case was ready for trial.

550 N.Y.S.2d at 149-50 (citation omitted).

§ 19:15   Court policy of not accepting plea bargains in DWI cases improper

In *People v. Glendenning*, 127 Misc. 2d 880, 487 N.Y.S.2d 952 (Westchester Co. Sup. Ct. 1985), a Justice of the Scarsdale Village Court had an announced policy of not accepting plea bargains in DWI cases. The defendant's motion to remove the case to another Court was granted. In this regard, the Westchester County Supreme Court held not only that Village Court's policy was improper, but also that such policy violated various provisions of the Code of Judicial Conduct. In so holding, the Court reasoned:

> The policy of rejecting pleas in Driving While Intoxicated cases is an improper exercise of judicial discretion. The categorical rejection of certain types of pleas is by its nature an impermissible infringement on the prosecutorial function. It is not within the Court's inherent power to instruct the prosecutor regarding his plea bargaining posture. An established policy has precisely this effect. It renders prosecutorial discretion with regard to the type of plea involved meaningless[,] thus forcing the prosecutor to revise his procedures to conform with the Court's wishes. An announced policy also runs contrary to the purposes of plea bargaining. A legitimate

goal of a prosecutor's charging decision is to avoid the stigma of a particular conviction to a particular defendant. The prosecutor, it should be noted, is in the best position to determine whether resources should be devoted to trials of drunk driving cases or elsewhere. A blanket policy of rejecting these pleas obviates both the need for prosecutorial discretion and the goal of individualized sentences and justice.

Moreover, notwithstanding the importance of keeping drunk drivers off the road, the legislature has not deemed it appropriate to prevent plea bargaining in Driving While Intoxicated cases. The reason for this is obvious. The legislature has deemed it undesirable and not in the public's best interests to impose across-the-board restrictions on plea bargaining. * * *

Thus, by forbidding plea bargaining in Driving While Intoxicated cases, then, the Court is not only interfering with the function of the prosecutor but is also invading the province of the legislature.

The announced policy of the Local Court Judge also runs afoul of the *Code of Judicial Conduct* adopted by the New York State Bar Association effective March 3, 1973.

487 N.Y.S.2d at 954-55 (citation omitted).

§ 19:16   Plea bargain cannot waive appeal of illegal sentence

Research References

West's Key Number Digest, Criminal Law ☞268

In *Agoney v. Feinberg*, 132 A.D.2d 829, 517 N.Y.S.2d 834, 836 (3d Dep't 1987), the court stated that any plea bargain is conditioned upon it being lawful and appropriate. In this case, restitution ordered by the court was not authorized and could not be validated by the plea bargain. *See also People v. West*, 80 A.D.2d 680, 436 N.Y.S.2d 424 (3d Dep't 1981); *People v. Bourne*, 139 A.D.2d 210, 531 N.Y.S.2d 899 (1st Dep't 1988) (rejected by, People v. Smith, 142 A.D.2d 195, 535 N.Y.S.2d 732 (2d Dep't 1988)) (waiver of right to appeal does not preclude interest of justice review by Appellate Division of plea-bargained sentence, as such review of sentence is not waivable).

§ 19:17   Court is limited in its power to correct erroneous plea bargain

Research References

West's Key Number Digest, Criminal Law ☞268

It is a well-settled legal principle that after sentence has commenced, a court which has accepted a plea in violation of the

CPL may not vacate the illegal plea and reinstate the original charges. In *Kisloff v. Covington*, 73 N.Y.2d 445, 541 N.Y.S.2d 737, 539 N.E.2d 565 (1989), the defendant brought an Article 78 proceeding to prohibit the supreme court from vacating the defendant's erroneous conviction and sentence. The defendant had entered a plea of guilty to what the parties believed to be the felony of attempted grand larceny, third degree. The defendant was sentenced to 1½ to three years pursuant thereto. At the time of the commission of the crime, however, attempted grand larceny, third degree, was a class A misdemeanor. After commencement of sentence, the error was discovered and the defendant was returned to court for the purpose of vacating his conviction, repleading, and being resentenced in accordance with the plea bargain. Upon the defendant's rejection of this procedure, the supreme court vacated his conviction and set the matter down for trial.

The defendant commenced an Article 78 proceeding, seeking prohibition of further prosecution on the felony charge and to have his original plea reinstated and to be resentenced on the misdemeanor conviction. The Appellate Division granted the application and the People appealed.

In affirming the Appellate Division, the Court of Appeals stated:

> Additionally, we have held recently that a court which has accepted a plea in violation of the Criminal Procedure Law may not vacate the illegal plea and reinstate the original charges after sentence has commenced (*Matter of Campbell v. Pesce*, 60 N.Y.2d, at 167, 60 N.Y.2d 165, 468 N.Y.S.2d 865, 456 N.E.2d 806, *supra*). In doing so, however, we recognized and reaffirmed a court's power, within the statutory framework, to correct its own error in connection with accepting a plea or imposing sentence. We have recognized such power in instances where the record demonstrates that the Judge merely misspoke, in imposing sentence (*People v. Wright*, 56 N.Y.2d 613, 614, 450 N.Y.S.2d 473, 435 N.E.2d 1088; *People v. Minaya*, 54 N.Y.2d 360, 364, 445 N.Y.S.2d 690, 429 N.E.2d 1161, cert. denied 455 U.S. 1024, 102 S.Ct. 1725, 72 L.Ed.2d 144) or it is clear from the record that a patent clerical error has been made in imposing sentence (*People ex rel. Hirschberg v. Orange County Ct.*, 271 N.Y. 151, 156, 2 N.E.2d 521). We noted in *Matter of Campbell v. Pesce*, however, that "[i]n no instance have we recognized a court's inherent power to vacate a plea and sentence over defendant's objection where the error goes beyond mere clerical error apparent on the face of the record and where the proceeding has been terminated by the entry of judgment" (60 N.Y.2d at 169, 60 N.Y.2d 165, 468 N.Y.S.2d 865, 456 N.E.2d 806, *supra*; *cf.*, *People v. Bartley*, 47 N.Y.2d 965, 419 N.Y.S.2d 956, 393 N.E.2d 1029, *supra* (illegally accepted plea vacated on court's inherent power prior to imposition of sentence)).

541 N.Y.S.2d at 740.

The Court noted that the plea bargain at issue was illegal in both the entry of the plea and the sentence imposed. Once the sentence was imposed and judgment entered, the plea could not be disturbed on the basis of its mistaken entry. Absent the defendant's consent to do otherwise, the only remedy was the imposition of a new sentence consistent with the defendant's conviction for a misdemeanor. 541 N.Y.S.2d at 741. *See also People v. Antis*, 147 Misc. 2d 513, 558 N.Y.S.2d 455 (Fulton Co. Ct. 1990) (absent motion by the People, court has no inherent power to restore case to calendar that has been adjourned in contemplation of dismissal).

In *Cummings v. Koppell*, 212 A.D.2d 11, 627 N.Y.S.2d 480 (3d Dep't 1995), the court articulated an exception to the principle that after sentence has commenced, a court which has accepted a plea in violation of the CPL may not vacate the illegal plea and reinstate the original charges. Here, the illegal plea was entered in a court that was wholly without jurisdiction over the subject matter of the action. Specifically, a local criminal court accepted a plea to a misdemeanor in full satisfaction of an indictment which charged the defendant with a class B violent felony. Noting that the jurisdiction of a local criminal court is automatically divested by action of a grand jury, the Appellate Division, Third Department, concluded that the local criminal court's acceptance of the plea agreement "transcended mere illegality."

> Petitioner's illegal pleas were entered in a court that was wholly without jurisdiction over the subject matter of the action.

Cummings v. Koppell, 627 N.Y.S.2d at 482. As such, the pleas and resulting convictions were a nullity and did not constitute a previous prosecution for double jeopardy purposes, nor did it constitute a bar to the court vacating the illegal plea and reinstating the original charges.

§ 19:18 Failure to specify fine as part of plea bargain results in waiver

Research References

West's Key Number Digest, Criminal Law ⛐268

In *People v. Youngs*, 156 A.D.2d 885, 550 N.Y.S.2d 106 (3d Dep't 1989), the defendant was charged with two counts of felony DWI. At the time, VTL § 1192(5) provided for a mandatory fine. Pursuant to a plea agreement, the defendant was to be sentenced to one to three years' imprisonment with no fines. However, the sentencing court imposed the prison sentence, together with the then-mandatory fine.

On appeal, the Appellate Division, Third Department, held (a) that the defendant was entitled to specific performance of his plea bargain, and (b) that county court should have informed the defendant that the plea bargain could not be kept, and afforded the defendant an opportunity to withdraw his plea. 156 A.D.2d at 886, 550 N.Y.S.2d at 107. *See also People v. Rockwell*, 137 A.D.3d 1586, __, 27 N.Y.S.3d 754, 756 (4th Dep't 2016); *People v. Legette*, 131 A.D.3d 546, __, 14 N.Y.S.3d 697, 698 (2d Dep't 2015); *People v. Barber*, 31 A.D.3d 1145, __, 818 N.Y.S.2d 391, 392 (4th Dep't 2006); *People v. Cote*, 265 A.D.2d 681, 697 N.Y.S.2d 184 (3d Dep't 1999) (fine imposed at sentencing vacated where it was not part of plea bargain or plea allocution); *People v. Fulton*, 238 A.D.2d 439, 657 N.Y.S.2d 348 (2d Dep't 1997).

The same rule applies to restitution. *See, e.g., People v. Sirico*, 135 A.D.3d 19, __, 18 N.Y.S.3d 430, 436-37 (2d Dep't 2015), leave to appeal denied, 27 N.Y.3d 1075, 2016 WL 3402992 (2016); *Legette, supra.*

§ 19:19   Off-the-record plea bargain agreement not entitled to judicial recognition

Research References

West's Key Number Digest, Criminal Law ⟐268

An off-the-record promise made in the course of plea bargaining is not entitled to judicial recognition. In *People v. Curdgel*, 83 N.Y.2d 862, 611 N.Y.S.2d 827, 634 N.E.2d 199 (1994), the Court stated:

> In order to promote certainty and openness in the plea negotiation process, we generally withhold judicial recognition from plea bargains not submitted for judicial approval (*People v. Danny G.*, 61 N.Y.2d 169, 173, 473 N.Y.S.2d 131, 461 N.E.2d 268).

People v. Curdgel, 611 N.Y.S.2d at 828. *See also People v. Huertas*, 85 N.Y.2d 898, 626 N.Y.S.2d 750, 650 N.E.2d 408 (1995); *Matter of Benjamin v. Kuriansky*, 55 N.Y.2d 116, 447 N.Y.S.2d 905, 432 N.E.2d 777 (1982).

§ 19:20   Plea bargain limitations

Research References

West's Key Number Digest, Criminal Law ⟐268

VTL § 1192(10) contains various plea bargaining limitations which are applicable where a person is charged with certain violations of VTL § 1192. In this regard, VTL § 1192(10) provides:

> Plea bargain limitations. (a)(i) In any case wherein the charge laid before the court alleges a violation of [VTL § 1192(2), (3), (4) or (4-a)], any plea of guilty thereafter entered in satisfaction of such charge must include at least a plea of guilty to the violation of the

provisions of one of the subdivisions of [VTL § 1192], other than
[VTL § 1192(5) or (6)], and no other disposition by plea of guilty to
any other charge in satisfaction of such charge shall be authorized;
provided, however, if the district attorney, upon reviewing the available evidence, determines that the charge of a violation of [VTL
§ 1192] is not warranted, such district attorney may consent, and
the court may allow a disposition by plea of guilty to another charge
in satisfaction of such charge; provided, however, in all such cases,
the court shall set forth upon the record the basis for such
disposition.

(ii) In any case wherein the charge laid before the court alleges a
violation of [VTL § 1192(2), (3), (4) or (4-a)], no plea of guilty to
[VTL § 1192(1)] shall be accepted by the court unless such plea
includes as a condition thereof the requirement that the defendant
attend and complete the [DDP], including any assessment and
treatment required thereby; provided, however, that such requirement may be waived by the court upon application of the district
attorney or the defendant demonstrating that the defendant, as a
condition of the plea, has been required to enter into and complete
an alcohol or drug treatment program prescribed pursuant to an
alcohol or substance abuse screening or assessment conducted
pursuant to [VTL § 1198-a] or for other good cause shown. The
provisions of this subparagraph shall apply, notwithstanding any
bars to participation in the [DDP]; provided, however, that nothing in this paragraph shall authorize the issuance of a conditional
license unless otherwise authorized by law.

(iii) In any case wherein the charge laid before the court alleges a
violation of [VTL § 1192(1)] and the operator was under the age
of [21] at the time of such violation, any plea of guilty thereafter
entered in satisfaction of such charge must include at least a plea
of guilty to the violation of [VTL § 1192(1)]; provided, however,
such charge may instead be satisfied as provided in [VTL
§ 1192(10)(c)], and, provided further that, if the district attorney,
upon reviewing the available evidence, determines that the
charge of a violation of [VTL § 1192(1)] is not warranted, such
district attorney may consent, and the court may allow a disposition by plea of guilty to another charge in satisfaction of such
charge; provided, however, in all such cases, the court shall set
forth upon the record the basis for such disposition.

(b) In any case wherein the charge laid before the court alleges a
violation of [VTL § 1192(1) or (6)] while operating a commercial motor vehicle, any plea of guilty thereafter entered in satisfaction of
such charge must include at least a plea of guilty to the violation of
the provisions of one of the subdivisions of [VTL § 1192] and no
other disposition by plea of guilty to any other charge in satisfaction of such charge shall be authorized; provided, however, if the
district attorney upon reviewing the available evidence determines
that the charge of a violation of [VTL § 1192] is not warranted, he

may consent, and the court may allow, a disposition by plea of guilty to another charge i[n] satisfaction of such charge.

(c) Except as provided in [VTL § 1192(10)(b)], in any case wherein the charge laid before the court alleges a violation of [VTL § 1192(1)] by a person who was under the age of [21] at the time of commission of the offense, the court, with the consent of both parties, may allow the satisfaction of such charge by the defendant's agreement to be subject to action by [DMV] pursuant to [VTL § 1194-a]. In any such case, the defendant shall waive the right to a hearing under [VTL § 1194-a] and such waiver shall have the same force and effect as a finding of a violation of [VTL § 1192-a] entered after a hearing conducted pursuant to [VTL § 1194-a]. The defendant shall execute such waiver in open court, and, if represented by counsel, in the presence of his attorney, on a form to be provided by [DMV], which shall be forwarded by the court to [DMV] within [96] hours. To be valid, such form shall, at a minimum, contain clear and conspicuous language advising the defendant that a duly executed waiver: (i) has the same force and effect as a guilty finding following a hearing pursuant to [VTL § 1194-a]; (ii) shall subject the defendant to the imposition of sanctions pursuant to [VTL § 1194-a]; and (iii) may subject the defendant to increased sanctions upon a subsequent violation of [VTL § 1192] or [VTL § 1192-a]. Upon receipt of a duly executed waiver pursuant to this paragraph, [DMV] shall take such administrative action and impose such sanctions as may be required by [VTL § 1194-a].

(d) In any case wherein the charge laid before the court alleges a violation of [VTL § 1192(2-a)], any plea of guilty thereafter entered in satisfaction of such charge must include at least a plea of guilty to the violation of the provisions of [VTL § 1192(2), (2-a) or (3)], and no other disposition by plea of guilty to any other charge in satisfaction of such charge shall be authorized; provided, however, if the district attorney, upon reviewing the available evidence, determines that the charge of a violation of [VTL § 1192] is not warranted, such district attorney may consent and the court may allow a disposition by plea of guilty to another charge in satisfaction of such charge, provided, however, in all such cases, the court shall set forth upon the record the basis for such disposition. Provided, further, however, that no such plea shall be accepted by the court unless such plea includes as a condition thereof the requirement that the defendant attend and complete the [DDP], including any assessment and treatment required thereby; provided, however, that such requirement may be waived by the court upon application of the district attorney or the defendant demonstrating that the defendant, as a condition of the plea, has been required to enter into and complete an alcohol or drug treatment program prescribed pursuant to an alcohol or substance abuse screening or assessment conducted pursuant to [VTL § 1198-a] or for other good cause shown. The provisions of this paragraph shall apply, notwithstanding any bars to participation in the [DDP]; provided, however, that nothing in this paragraph shall authorize the issuance of a conditional license unless otherwise authorized by law.

In *People v. Lehman*, 183 Misc. 2d 97, 702 N.Y.S.2d 551 (Watertown City Ct. 2000), the court denied the People's motion to amend/reduce a charge of VTL § 1192(4) (*i.e.*, DWAI drugs), to VTL § 1192(1) (*i.e.*, DWAI alcohol), where there was no evidence that the defendant's impairment was in any way caused by alcohol.

However, the Court of Appeals has made clear that:

[A] plea may be to . . . a crime for which the facts alleged to underlie the original charge would not be appropriate.

A plea is a bargain struck by a defendant and a prosecutor who may both be in doubt about the outcome of a trial. Only the events of time, place, and, if applicable, victim, need be the same for the crime pleaded as for the one charged.

People v. Francis, 38 N.Y.2d 150, 155, 379 N.Y.S.2d 21, 26 (1975) (citations omitted). *See also People v. Clairborne*, 29 N.Y.2d 950, —, 329 N.Y.S.2d 580, 581 (1972) ("A bargained guilty plea to a lesser crime makes unnecessary a factual basis for the particular crime confessed"); *People v. Adams*, 57 N.Y.2d 1035, 1038, 457 N.Y.S.2d 783, 784–85 (1982) (same).

§ 19:21 Waiver of test refusal not allowed

Research References

West's Key Number Digest, Criminal Law ⌇268

VTL § 1194(2)(b) specifies that a report of refusal must be forwarded to the Commissioner of Motor Vehicles "and such transmittal may not be waived even with the consent of all the parties." This legislation was enacted to discourage a practice of neutralizing the refusal as part of the plea bargain by the simple expedient of not submitting the report of refusal to the Commissioner of Motor Vehicles.

§ 19:22 Plea bargaining restrictions applicable to indictment are inapplicable to felony complaint

Research References

West's Key Number Digest, Criminal Law ⌇268

In *People v. McLaurin*, 260 A.D.2d 944, 690 N.Y.S.2d 289 (3d Dep't 1999), the Appellate Division, Third Department, held that the plea bargaining restrictions contained in CPL § 220.10:

[E]xpressly apply "to pleas which may be entered to an indictment" (CPL 220.10). An indictment serves as the basis for prosecution of a criminal action; a felony complaint is not encompassed by the term indictment (*see* CPL 200.10). We agree with County Court that the plea-bargaining restrictions contained in CPL 220.10 are not triggered by the filing of a felony complaint.

260 A.D.2d at __, 690 N.Y.S.2d at 291.

§ 19:23 Court cannot offer defendant a plea bargain without the consent of the people

People v. Christensen, 77 A.D.3d 174, 906 N.Y.S.2d 301 (2d Dep't 2010), resolved a power struggle that arose between the State Police and various local criminal courts when the State Police adopted a policy of refusing to plea bargain traffic tickets. Various Town Justices found the State Police policy to be unfair, and were offering defendants plea bargains similar to those being offered to defendants who were ticketed by other police agencies appearing before the Court. The Appellate Division, Second Department, held that:

> Many district attorneys of counties in New York State, when faced with inadequate resources, have lawfully delegated their authority to prosecute Vehicle and Traffic Law (hereinafter VTL) cases to the police agencies which issue the tickets for those offenses. One such police agency, the Division of New York State Police (hereinafter the Division), adheres to a policy against plea bargaining. On this appeal, we are asked to consider whether a trial court may, in the interest of justice, accept a defendant's plea of guilty to a lesser-included offense over the objection of the People in a case prosecuted by the Division. We conclude that, while we are sympathetic to the burden imposed on the courts by any blanket policy against plea bargaining a certain class of offenses, the trial courts are without authority to offer a defendant a plea to a reduced charge without the consent of the People. We also conclude that a district attorney may properly delegate authority to the Division to represent the People in a CPLR article 78 proceeding to challenge a trial court's acceptance of a plea of guilty over the People's objection in a case prosecuted by the Division.

77 A.D.3d at __, 906 N.Y.S.2d at 303.

§ 19:24 Attorney's misrepresentations regarding client's prior DWI history results in nine-month suspension from practice

In *In re Bybel*, 121 A.D.3d 286, __, 991 N.Y.S.2d 502, 505 (4th Dep't 2014) (per curiam), a defense attorney was found to have made "a series of calculated misrepresentations" on behalf of a client facing DWI charges in two separate Courts. In imposing an appropriate sanction, the Appellate Division, Fourth Department, found that:

> We have considered, in determining an appropriate sanction, that

respondent has previously received four letters of caution and that the misconduct at issue involved a series of calculated misrepresentations. Accordingly, after consideration of all of the factors in this matter, we conclude that respondent should be suspended for a period of nine months, and until further order of the Court.

Id. at __, 991 N.Y.S.2d at 505.

Part VI

PRETRIAL MATTERS

Chapter 20

Discovery in Criminal Cases

Research References

Westlaw Databases

Complete Crim Forms (CMCRF)
Criminal Procedure (2d ed.) (CRIMPROC)
Handling Drunk Driving Cases (HDRUNKDR)
New York Vehicle and Traffic Law 2d (NYVEH)

Treatises and Practice Aids

LaFave, Israel and King, Criminal Procedure §§ 20.3(a) to 20.3(n), 20.5(g)
Muldoon, Handling a Criminal Case in New York §§ 8:6 to 8:14, 8:27 to 8:33, 8:89, 8:99 to 8:103, 8:109 to 8:135, 8:146 to 8:160
Fiandach, Handling Drunk Driving Cases §§ 21:1 to 21:11 (2d ed.)
Rose, New York Vehicle and Traffic Law 2d § 35:31

Forms

Bailey and Fishman, Complete Manual of Criminal Forms §§ 14:10, 14:11, 15:8 to 15:10, 17:10 to 17:16, 20:9, 23:24 (3d ed.)

Law Reviews and Other Periodicals

Roberts, Too Little, Too Late: Ineffective Assistance of Counsel, The Duty to Investigate, and Pretrial Discovery in Criminal Cases, 31 Fordham Urb. L.J. 1097 (May, 2004)

KeyCite®: Cases and other legal materials listed in KeyCite Scope can be researched through the KeyCite service on Westlaw®. Use KeyCite to check citations for form, parallel references, prior and later history, and comprehensive citator information, including citations to other decisions and secondary materials.

---

§ 20:1 In general

Research References

West's Key Number Digest, Criminal Law ⬅627.5(1)

In New York, "the Legislature has prescribed a detailed discovery regimen . . . embodied in article 240 of the Criminal Procedure Law. Items not enumerated in article 240 are not discoverable as a matter of right unless constitutionally or otherwise specially mandated." *People v. Colavito*, 87 N.Y.2d 423, 427, 639 N.Y.S.2d 996, 999 (1996) (citations omitted). This chapter addresses criminal discovery in New York in general, paying particular attention to discovery issues pertinent to DWI cases.

§ 20:2 Right to discovery in criminal cases—Generally

Research References

West's Key Number Digest, Criminal Law ⬅627.5(1)

The Court of Appeals has made various somewhat contradictory pronouncements on the scope of a criminal defendant's right to discovery in New York, and has steadfastly avoided setting forth comprehensive lists of what items are, or are not, discoverable. As a result, both the prosecution *and* the defense can find good quotes from the high Court supporting their respective positions.

For example, in *Matter of Miller v. Schwartz*, 72 N.Y.2d 869, 870, 532 N.Y.S.2d 354, 355 (1988), which involved a speeding charge which was adjudicated administratively, the Court stated that "It is settled . . . that there is no general constitutional right to discovery in criminal cases or administrative proceedings. Such matters are regulated by statute or rule and since petitioner had no statutory or regulatory right to pretrial discovery here, his request was properly denied." (Citations omitted). *See also Matter of Heisler v. Hynes*, 42 N.Y.2d 250, 253, 397 N.Y.S.2d 727, 730 (1977) ("prosecutors have no general right to discovery in criminal cases under our State law").

By contrast, the Court has also made clear that CPL Article 240:

[E]vinces a legislative determination that the trial of a criminal charge should not be a sporting event where each side remains ignorant of facts in the hands of the adversary until events unfold at trial. Broader pretrial discovery enables the defendant to make a more informed plea decision, minimizes the tactical and often unfair advantage to one side, and increases to some degree the opportunity for an accurate determination of guilt or innocence. In short, pretrial discovery by the defense and prosecution contributes substantially to the fair and effective administration of justice.

People v. Copicotto, 50 N.Y.2d 222, 226, 428 N.Y.S.2d 649, 652 (1980) (citation omitted). *See also People v. DaGata*, 86 N.Y.2d 40, 45, 629 N.Y.S.2d 186, 189 (1995) (New York has a "philosophy of broad pretrial disclosure"); *People v. Contreras*, 12 N.Y.3d 268, 272, 879 N.Y.S.2d 369, 372, 907 N.E.2d 282 (2009) ("Prosecutors and trial judges invite trouble when they push the rules of disclosure to their limit").

§ 20:3   Demand to produce—Defined

Research References

West's Key Number Digest, Criminal Law ☞627.8(3)

" 'Demand to produce' means a written notice served by and on a party to a criminal action, without leave of the court, demanding to inspect property pursuant to [CPL Article 240] and giving reasonable notice of the time at which the demanding party wishes to inspect the property designated." CPL § 240.10(1). CPL §§ 240.10(1) and 240.20(1) limit the scope of discovery thereunder to "property," which is defined in § 20:10, *infra*.

§ 20:4   Demand to produce should be as specific as possible

Research References

West's Key Number Digest, Criminal Law ☞627.8(3)

In theory, a defendant's demand to produce can be as simple as a letter to the district attorney requesting disclosure of all property discoverable pursuant to CPL Article 240. A slightly more detailed demand to produce would request disclosure of all property discoverable pursuant to CPL § 240.20(1)(a) to (k), and would quote the statutory language.

While such demands might be considered competent, they do not adequately protect the defendant's rights—at least not in a DWI case. The reasons for this are twofold. First, when it comes to discovery, especially in a DWI case, an ADA might not be aware that a specific item exists, or that it is discoverable, without being placed on specific notice that such item is sought.

For example, *Matter of Constantine v. Leto*, 157 A.D.2d 376, —, 557 N.Y.S.2d 611, 613 (3d Dep't 1990), *aff'd for the reasons stated in the opinion below*, 77 N.Y.2d 975, 571 N.Y.S.2d 906 (1991), makes clear that the police agency's chemical test rules and regulations are discoverable. Many ADAs are unaware of this, and thus will not disclose such information absent a specific request therefor (which request should cite *Leto*).

Similarly, a general request, pursuant to CPL § 240.20(1)(d), for "any photograph or drawing relating to the criminal action," is likely to trigger the response "none known to exist." By contrast, a specific request for a copy of the defendant's arrest photograph (*i.e.*, mug shot)—which request cites *People v. Shcherenkov*, 21 A.D.3d 651, 799 N.Y.S.2d 663 (3d Dep't 2005), *People v. Dudley*, 268 A.D.2d 442, 703 N.Y.S.2d 489 (2d Dep't 2000), *People v. Halikias*, 106 A.D.2d 811, 484 N.Y.S.2d 182 (3d Dep't 1984), *People v. Cobb*, 104 A.D.2d 656, —, 480 N.Y.S.2d 33, 36 (2d Dep't 1984), and *People v. Morrison*, 148 Misc. 2d 61, —, 559 N.Y.S.2d 1013, 1019 (N.Y. City Crim. Ct. 1990), will almost certainly lead to disclosure thereof.

Second, and critically important, where the People fail to disclose exculpatory material, the Court of Appeals has established a significantly lower standard for reversal on appeal where the undisclosed material was sought by the defendant in a specific, as opposed to a general, discovery request. *See People v. Vilardi*, 76 N.Y.2d 67, 556 N.Y.S.2d 518 (1990). In *Vilardi*, the Court of Appeals stated, among other things, that:

> This court has . . . found the prosecution's failure to turn over specifically requested evidence to be "seldom, if ever, excusable" and to verge on prosecutorial misconduct. * * *

> We agree with the Appellate Division that a showing of a "reasonable *possibility*" that the failure to disclose the exculpatory [material] contributed to the verdict remains the appropriate standard to measure materiality, where the prosecutor was made aware by a specific discovery request that defendant considered the material important to the defense. * * *

> Where the defense itself has provided specific notice of its interest in particular material, heightened rather than lessened prosecutorial care is appropriate.

> The "reasonable possibility" standard applied by the Appellate Division—essentially a reformulation of the "seldom if ever excusable" rule—is a clear rule that properly encourages compliance with these obligations, and we therefore conclude that as a matter of State

constitutional law it is preferable to *Bagley* [*i.e.*, *United States v. Bagley*, 473 U.S. 667, 105 S.Ct. 3375 (1985)].

76 N.Y.2d at 74, 77, 556 N.Y.S.2d at 521, 523 (emphasis added). By contrast, where the undisclosed material was sought by the defendant in a general discovery request (or was not requested at all), the standard for reversal on appeal is whether there is a "reasonable *probability*" that the failure to disclose the exculpatory material contributed to the verdict.

Accordingly, a defendant's demand to produce should be as specific as possible.

§ 20:5 Demand to produce should request preservation of *Rosario* and discoverable material

Research References

West's Key Number Digest, Criminal Law ☞627.8(3)

It is well settled that, in addition to the duty to *produce Rosario* and discoverable material, the People have an affirmative duty to *preserve* such material as well. *See, e.g., People v. Joseph*, 86 N.Y.2d 565, 570–71, 635 N.Y.S.2d 123, 126 (1995); *People v. Wallace*, 76 N.Y.2d 953, 955, 563 N.Y.S.2d 722, 723 (1990); *People v. Martinez*, 71 N.Y.2d 937, 940, 528 N.Y.S.2d 813, 815 (1988); *People v. Kelly*, 62 N.Y.2d 516, 520, 478 N.Y.S.2d 834, 836 (1984). *See also People v. Watkins*, 189 A.D.2d 623, ___, 592 N.Y.S.2d 347, 348 (1st Dep't 1993) (duty to preserve *Rosario* material lasts "until all appeals have been exhausted, and a Police Department policy of destroying evidence does not excuse the People from making *Rosario* material available on retrial"). In *Martinez*, the Court of Appeals held that:

> [I]t is no answer to a demand to produce that the material has been lost or destroyed. If the People fail to exercise care to preserve it and defendant is prejudiced by their mistake, the court must impose an appropriate sanction. The determination of what is appropriate is committed to the trial court's sound discretion, and while the degree of prosecutorial fault may be considered, the court's attention should focus primarily on the overriding need to eliminate prejudice to the defendant.

71 N.Y.2d at 940, 528 N.Y.S.2d at 815. Similarly, in *Wallace*, the Court held that:

> Where the People fail to exercise due care in preserving *Rosario* material, and defendant is prejudiced thereby, "the [trial] court *must* impose an appropriate sanction." Although the trial court had discretion to determine the specific sanction to be imposed, it was an abuse of discretion to decline to impose any sanction where, as here, defendant was prejudiced.

76 N.Y.2d at 955, 563 N.Y.S.2d at 723 (citations omitted). *See*

also People v. Minihan, 180 Misc. 2d 776, 695 N.Y.S.2d 238 (App. Term, 2d Dep't 1999).

Unfortunately, however, police agencies often engage in the so-called "routine destruction" of *Rosario* material—particularly 911 and other police tape recordings. *See, e.g., People v. Boyd*, 254 A.D.2d 740, __, 679 N.Y.S.2d 768, 769–70 (4th Dep't 1998); *People v. Morris*, 231 A.D.2d 911, __, 647 N.Y.S.2d 893, 893–94 (4th Dep't 1996); *People v. Thomas*, 226 A.D.2d 1071, __, 642 N.Y.S.2d 749, 751 (4th Dep't 1996); *People v. Cortez*, 149 Misc. 2d 886, __-__, 564 N.Y.S.2d 963, 966–68 (N.Y. City Crim. Ct. 1990). Although such a practice would seem to be inexcusable and unacceptable, the courts have been forced to "excuse" such behavior, largely due to the sheer prevalence of the problem.

Nonetheless, where *Rosario* material is destroyed despite a timely and specific request by the defense that it be preserved, the degree of prosecutorial fault is significantly greater, and it is generally an abuse of discretion for the trial court to fail to impose a sanction therefor on the People. *See, e.g., People v. Jackson*, 271 A.D.2d 455, __, 707 N.Y.S.2d 128, .129 (2d Dep't 2000) ("Where the tape of a 911 call is not preserved and the defendant is prejudiced thereby, the court must impose an appropriate sanction and the failure to do so requires reversal"); *People v. Burch*, 247 A.D.2d 546, __, 669 N.Y.S.2d 299, 300 (2d Dep't 1998) (same); *People v. Huynh*, 232 A.D.2d 655, __, 649 N.Y.S.2d 160, 161 (2d Dep't 1996) (same); *People v. Parker*, 157 A.D.2d 519, __, 549 N.Y.S.2d 710, 711–12 (1st Dep't 1990) (same); *People v. Nesbitt*, 230 A.D.2d 755, 646 N.Y.S.2d 522 (2d Dep't 1996) (it was abuse of discretion, and prejudicial error, for trial court to deny defendant's request for adverse inference charge where audiotapes unavailable).

By contrast, in *People v. Morris*, 231 A.D.2d 911, __, 647 N.Y.S.2d 893, 893–94 (4th Dep't 1996), the Appellate Division, Fourth Department, held that:

> Contrary to defendant's contention, the routine destruction of the 911 tapes did not warrant sanctions. Although those tapes constituted *Rosario* material that the People had an obligation to turn over to defendant upon proper demand, **the record does not disclose that any demand was made for discovery of those tapes pursuant to either** CPL 240.20 **or** 240.44. **In the absence of a timely demand, the routine destruction of 911 tapes will not be viewed as a lack of due diligence**.

(Emphasis added) (citation omitted).

Similarly, in *People v. Thomas*, 226 A.D.2d 1071, __, 642 N.Y.S.2d 749, 751 (4th Dep't 1996), the same court held that:

> By failing to request sanctions as a result of the failure of the People

to preserve a 911 tape, defendant failed to preserve for review his present contention that the court erred in failing to impose sanctions. In any event, sanctions were not warranted. In Erie County, 911 tapes are preserved for a 90-day period and are then taped over. **In the absence of a timely request by a defendant that a 911 tape be preserved, its routine destruction will not be viewed as a lack of due diligence**.

(Emphasis added) (citation omitted). *See also People v. Hyde*, 172 A.D.2d 305, __, 568 N.Y.S.2d 388, 389 (1st Dep't 1991).

Accordingly, it is critical that a defendant's demand to produce (which is served within 30 days of arraignment) expressly request that the People take appropriate action, make appropriate requests and inquiries, etc. to ascertain the location of, and to ensure the preservation of, any so-called *Rosario* material (*i.e.*, any written or recorded statement made by a person whom the People intend to call as a witness at any pretrial hearing and/or at trial) and other discoverable material. In addition, the demand should list, in as much detail as possible, specific documents, notes, tape recordings, etc. that the defense believes may exist. *See generally People v. Vilardi*, 76 N.Y.2d 67, 74, 556 N.Y.S.2d 518, 521 (1990) ("This court has . . . found the prosecution's failure to turn over specifically requested evidence to be 'seldom, if ever, excusable' and to verge on prosecutorial misconduct").

§ 20:6 Demand to produce should request that discovery pursuant to CPL §§ 240.43 and 240.44 be disclosed to the defendant at the appropriate times

Research References

West's Key Number Digest, Criminal Law ⟐627.8(3)

Discovery pursuant to CPL §§ 240.43 and 240.44 is only available to the defendant "upon request." *See* §§ 20:77 and 20:80, *infra*. Accordingly, absent a timely request therefor, the defendant will be found to have waived his or her right to such discovery.

However, if such request is made in the defendant's demand to produce, defense counsel will have preserved the issue early on in the case—and will be protected even if he or she forgets to reiterate the request orally later on (*e.g.*, during a pretrial hearing). In addition, a written request for such information in a demand to produce is likely to be more specific, and will provide the People with more time to locate such information.

Accordingly, the defendant's demand to produce should expressly request that the People:

(a) Disclose to the defendant, at the appropriate time, all specific instances of the defendant's prior uncharged criminal, vicious, or immoral conduct of which the People have knowledge and which the People intend to use at trial for purposes of impeaching the credibility of the defendant. *See* CPL § 240.43. *See also People v. Ventimiglia*, 52 N.Y.2d 350, 438 N.Y.S.2d 261 (1981);

(b) Take appropriate action, make appropriate requests and inquiries, etc. to ascertain the location of, and to ensure the preservation of, any so-called *Rosario* material (*i.e.*, any written or recorded statement made by a person whom the People intend to call as a witness at any pretrial hearing and/or at trial), and to disclose such information to the defendant at the appropriate times. *See* CPL § 240.44(1); CPL § 240.45(1)(a); *People v. Rosario*, 9 N.Y.2d 286, 213 N.Y.S.2d 448 (1961); *People v. Malinsky*, 15 N.Y.2d 86, 262 N.Y.S.2d 65 (1965);

(c) Take appropriate action, make appropriate requests and inquiries, etc. to ascertain the existence of any judgment(s) of conviction of any person the People intend to call as a witness at any pretrial hearing and/or at trial, and to disclose such information to the defendant at the appropriate times. *See* CPL § 240.44(2); CPL § 240.45(1)(b); and

(d) Take appropriate action, make appropriate requests and inquiries, etc. to ascertain the existence of any pending criminal action against any person the People intend to call as a witness at any pretrial hearing and/or at trial, and to disclose such information to the defendant at the appropriate times. *See* CPL § 240.44(3); CPL § 240.45(1)(c).

§ 20:7   Demand to produce—Time for service thereof

Research References

West's Key Number Digest, Criminal Law ☞627.8(3)

CPL § 240.80(1) provides that:

> A demand to produce shall be made within [30] days after arraignment and before the commencement of trial. If the defendant is not represented by counsel, and has requested an adjournment to obtain counsel or to have counsel assigned, the [30]-day period shall commence, for purposes of a demand by the defendant, on the date counsel initially appears on his behalf. However, the court may direct compliance with a demand to produce that, for good cause shown, could not have been made within the time specified.

"The requirement of a written demand for discovery contained in CPL § 240.20 can be waived by the failure of the People to object to variance of the procedure or by the offer of the People to comply with the statute *sua sponte*." *People v. Smith*, 169 Misc. 2d 258, __, 646 N.Y.S.2d 228, 231 (Onondaga Co. Sup. Ct. 1996).

§ 20:8   Demand to produce—Time for compliance therewith

Research References

West's Key Number Digest, Criminal Law ⚖627.8(3)

"Absent a refusal to comply with a demand to produce, compliance with such demand shall be made within [15] days of the service of the demand or as soon thereafter as practicable." CPL § 240.80(3).

§ 20:9   Demand to produce—Refusal to comply therewith

Research References

West's Key Number Digest, Criminal Law ⚖627.8(3)

CPL § 240.35 provides that:

Notwithstanding the provisions of [CPL §§] 240.20 and 240.30, the prosecutor or the defendant, as the case may be, may refuse to disclose any information which he reasonably believes is not discoverable by a demand to produce, pursuant to [CPL §] 240.20 or [CPL §] 240.30 as the case may be, or for which he reasonably believes a protective order would be warranted. **Such refusal shall be made in a writing, which shall set forth the grounds of such belief as fully as possible, consistent with the objective of the refusal**. The writing shall be served upon the demanding party and a copy shall be filed with the court.

(Emphasis added).

"A refusal to comply with a demand to produce shall be made within [15] days of the service of the demand to produce, but for good cause may be made thereafter." CPL § 240.80(2).

§ 20:10   CPL § 240.20(1)(a) to (k)—Discovery available to defendant upon demand

Research References

West's Key Number Digest, Criminal Law ⚖627.8(3)

CPL § 240.20(1) provides that, "[e]xcept to the extent protected by court order, upon a demand to produce by a defendant against whom an indictment, superior court information, prosecutor's information, information, or simplified information charging a misdemeanor is pending, the prosecutor shall disclose to the defendant and make available for inspection, photographing, copying or testing, the . . . *property*" (emphasis added) enumerated in CPL § 240.20(1)(a) to (k).

For purposes of CPL Article 240, " '[p]roperty' means any existing tangible personal or real property, *including but not limited to*, books, records, reports, memoranda, papers, photographs, tapes or other electronic recordings, articles of clothing, fingerprints, blood samples, fingernail scrapings or handwriting specimens, but excluding attorneys' work product." CPL § 240.10(3) (emphasis added).

The term "property" expressly excludes "attorneys' work product," which is defined as "property to the extent that it contains the opinions, theories or conclusions of the prosecutor, defense counsel or members of their legal staffs." CPL § 240.10(2). "In criminal proceedings, CPL 240.10(2) extends the exemption only 'to the extent that [the material] contains the opinions, theories or conclusions of the prosecutor, defense counsel or members of their legal staffs.'" *People v. Banch*, 80 N.Y.2d 610, 620, 593 N.Y.S.2d 491, 497 (1992). *See also* § 28:4, *infra*.

The phrase "'[a]t the trial' means as part of the people's or the defendant's direct case." CPL § 240.10(4).

Subdivisions (a) to (k) of CPL § 240.20(1) are discussed individually in the sections that follow.

§ 20:11   CPL § 240.20(1)(a)—Statements of the defendant— Generally

Research References

West's Key Number Digest, Criminal Law ⚓627.7(2)

CPL § 240.20(1)(a) provides for the disclosure of:

Any written, recorded or oral statement of the defendant, and of a co-defendant to be tried jointly, made, other than in the course of the criminal transaction, to a public servant engaged in law enforcement activity or to a person then acting under his direction or in cooperation with him.

In this regard, "[i]t is beyond dispute that a defendant's own statements to police are highly material and relevant to a criminal prosecution. It is for this reason that such statements are *always* discoverable, even when the People do not intend to offer them at trial." *People v. Combest*, 4 N.Y.3d 341, 347, 795 N.Y.S.2d 481, 485 (2005) (emphasis added). *See also People v. Fields*, 258 A.D.2d 809, __, 687 N.Y.S.2d 184, 186 (3d Dep't 1999) ("CPL § 240.20(1)(a) . . . . is not limited to statements intended to be offered by the People 'at trial', i.e., statements offered as part of the People's direct case (*see*, CPL § 240.10[4])"); *People v. Crider*, 301 A.D.2d 612, __, 756 N.Y.S.2d 223, 225 (2d Dep't 2003) (pursuant to CPL § 240.20(1)(a), "the People shall provide the defendant with notice of *any* of his statements they are aware of, whether or not they intend to use them for *any* purpose, including but not limited to rebuttal") (emphases added); *People v. Wyssling*, 82 Misc. 2d 708, 372 N.Y.S.2d 142 (Suffolk Co. Ct. 1975); *People v.*

Bennett, 75 Misc. 2d 1040, __-__, 349 N.Y.S.2d 506, 519–20 (Erie Co. Sup. Ct. 1973). Thus, any argument by the People that they need only disclose statements to which CPL § 710.30 applies is without merit. *See Combest*, 4 N.Y.3d at 347, 795 N.Y.S.2d at 485; *Fields*, 258 A.D.2d at __, 687 N.Y.S.2d at 185; *People v. Hall*, 181 A.D.2d 1008, 581 N.Y.S.2d 951 (4th Dep't 1992).

"Generally, an accused's '[s]tatements made to civilian witnesses are not discoverable.'" *People v. Mitchell*, 289 A.D.2d 776, __, 734 N.Y.S.2d 353, 357 (3d Dep't 2001) (citation omitted). *See also People v. Swart*, 273 A.D.2d 503, __, 709 N.Y.S.2d 653, 655 (3d Dep't 2000); *People v. Rivera*, 210 A.D.2d 178, __, 620 N.Y.S.2d 365, 366 (1st Dep't 1994); *People v. Simmons*, 173 A.D.2d 875, __, 571 N.Y.S.2d 80, 80–81 (2d Dep't 1991); *People v. Hall*, 133 A.D.2d 845, 520 N.Y.S.2d 409 (2d Dep't 1987).

In *People v. Seeley*, 179 Misc. 2d 42, __, 683 N.Y.S.2d 795, 803 (Kings Co. Sup. Ct. 1998), the court stated that it "agrees with the People's contention that the legislative purpose behind CPL 240.20(1)(a) was to allow the discovery of defendant's statements made about the *present* criminal act." (Emphasis added). *See also People v. D'Amico*, 136 Misc. 2d 16, __-__, 517 N.Y.S.2d 881, 883–85 (Oneida Co. Ct. 1987), *aff'd*, 148 A.D.2d 982, 538 N.Y.S.2d 965 (4th Dep't 1989).

In addition, "CPL 240.20(1)(a) specifically limits a defendant's statutory right of discovery to statements 'other than [those made] in the course of the criminal transaction.'" *People v. McCaskell*, 217 A.D.2d 527, __, 630 N.Y.S.2d 66, 68 (1st Dep't 1995). *See also People v. McLean*, 128 A.D.3d 1094, __, 10 N.Y.S.3d 277, 281 (2d Dep't 2015), leave to appeal denied, 27 N.Y.3d 1071, 2016 WL 3388313 (2016); *People v. Wells*, 133 A.D.2d 385, __, 519 N.Y.S.2d 553, 554 (2d Dep't 1987).

§ 20:12 Pedigree information

Research References

West's Key Number Digest, Criminal Law ☞627.7(1)

It has been "held" that "pedigree information is neither *Rosario* nor *Brady* material, and is not discoverable as a statement." *People v. Daniels*, 254 A.D.2d 54, __, 681 N.Y.S.2d 483, 483 (1st Dep't 1998). *See also People v. Andrews*, 236 A.D.2d 735, __, 654 N.Y.S.2d 838, 840 (3d Dep't 1997); *People v. Fortunato*, 161 A.D.2d 455, __, 555 N.Y.S.2d 366, 367 (1st Dep't 1990).

However, *Daniels* merely cites *Fortunato* in support of its position; *Andrews* merely cites *Fortunato* and footnote 1 of *People v. Berkowitz*, 50 N.Y.2d 333, 428 N.Y.S.2d 927 (1980), in support of its position; and *Fortunato* merely cites footnote 1 of *Berkowitz* in support of its position. In other words, all of the cases, which "hold" that pedigree information is not discoverable as a statement, rely on footnote 1 of *Berkowitz* in support of their position.

However, footnote 1 of *Berkowitz* merely states, without explanation, that pedigree information need not be included in the People's CPL § 710.30 notice—which is an entirely separate and distinct issue from whether such information is discoverable as a statement of the defendant pursuant to CPL § 240.20(1)(a). In fact, the Court of Appeals recently made clear that "[i]t is beyond dispute that a defendant's own statements to police are highly material and relevant to a criminal prosecution. It is for this reason that such statements are *always* discoverable, even when the People do not intend to offer them at trial." *People v. Combest*, 4 N.Y.3d 341, 347, 795 N.Y.S.2d 481, 485 (2005) (emphasis added). *See also People v. Fields*, 258 A.D.2d 809, __, 687 N.Y.S.2d 184, 185 (3d Dep't 1999); *People v. Hall*, 181 A.D.2d 1008, 581 N.Y.S.2d 951 (4th Dep't 1992).

Moreover, although there exists a so-called "pedigree question exception" to the *Miranda* warning requirement, it is nonetheless well settled that " 'routine booking questions' constitute custodial interrogation." *People v. Rodney*, 85 N.Y.2d 289, 293, 624 N.Y.S.2d 95, 97 (1995). *See also Pennsylvania v. Muniz*, 496 U.S. 582, 601, 110 S. Ct. 2638, 2650 (1990) ("We disagree with the Commonwealth's contention that Officer Hosterman's first seven questions regarding Muniz's name, address, height, weight, eye color, date of birth, and current age do not qualify as custodial interrogation").

In that it is clear that pedigree information constitutes statements of the defendant elicited by the police through custodial interrogation, a strong argument can be made that such statements are discoverable pursuant to CPL § 240.20(1)(a) regardless of whether they can be suppressed as involuntary.

§ 20:13 Failure of People to disclose defendant's statements in their CPL § 710.30 notice cannot be cured by discovery

Research References

West's Key Number Digest, Criminal Law ⊚394.6(1), 627.7(2)

CPL § 710.30 provides, with certain exceptions, that whenever the People intend to offer at trial evidence of a statement made by the defendant to a public servant, they must serve upon the defendant a notice of such intention, specifying the evidence intended to be offered, within 15 days after arraignment. *See* CPL § 710.30(1); CPL § 710.30(2). To be sufficient, CPL § 710.30 notice must "inform defendant of the time and place the oral or written statements were made and of the sum and substance of those statements. Full copies of the statements need not be supplied but they must be described sufficiently so that the defendant can intelligently identify them." *People v. Lopez*, 84 N.Y.2d 425, 428, 618 N.Y.S.2d 879, 881 (1994) (citations omitted). *See also People v. Utley*, 77 Misc. 2d 86, __, 353 N.Y.S.2d 301, 313 (Nassau Co. Ct. 1974).

If the People fail to comply with the requirements of CPL § 710.30, the remedy is preclusion. *See* CPL § 710.30(3); *Lopez*, 84 N.Y.2d at 428, 618 N.Y.S.2d at 882. Lack of prejudice to the defendant is irrelevant. *Lopez*, 84 N.Y.2d at 428, 618 N.Y.S.2d at 882. *"Nor can the inadequacy of the notice be cured by discovery."* 84 N.Y.2d at 428, 618 N.Y.S.2d at 882 (emphasis added). *See also People v. Phillips*, 183 A.D.2d 856, 584 N.Y.S.2d 83 (2d Dep't 1992).

§ 20:14   CPL § 240.20(1)(b)—Defendant's grand jury testimony

Research References

West's Key Number Digest, Criminal Law ☞627.9(4)

CPL § 240.20(1)(b) provides for the disclosure of "[a]ny transcript of testimony relating to the criminal action or proceeding pending against the defendant, given by the defendant, or by a co-defendant to be tried jointly, before any grand jury."

§ 20:15   CPL § 240.20(1)(c)—Documents concerning physical or mental examinations, or scientific tests or experiments—Generally

Research References

West's Key Number Digest, Criminal Law ☞627.6(2)

CPL § 240.20(1)(c) provides for the disclosure of:

Any written report or document, or portion thereof, concerning a physical or mental examination, or scientific test or experiment, relating to the criminal action or proceeding which was made by, or at the request or direction of a public servant engaged in law enforcement activity, or which was made by a person whom the prosecutor intends to call as a witness at trial, or which the people intend to introduce at trial.

In *People v. DaGata*, 86 N.Y.2d 40, 41, 44, 629 N.Y.S.2d 186, 187, 189 (1995), the Court of Appeals held that 10 pages of notes used by the FBI in preparation of, and related to, a one-page DNA testing report were discoverable pursuant to CPL § 240.20(1)(c) (*i.e.*, the notes were CPL § 240.20(1)(c) material regardless of whether they also constituted *Rosario* material or *Brady* material), and that the People were required to provide these notes upon the defendant's request even though the notes were not in the People's possession. *See also People v. Scott*, 216 A.D.2d 592, __, 628 N.Y.S.2d 965, 967 (2d Dep't 1995) ("scratch report" entitled "HOMICIDE BUREAU INFORMATION SHEET" was discoverable pursuant to both CPL § 240.20(1)(c) and *Brady*), *aff'd*, 88 N.Y.2d 869, 644 N.Y.S.2d 912 (1996).

In *People v. Slowe*, 125 Misc. 2d 591, 479 N.Y.S.2d 962 (Tompkins Co. Ct. 1984), a pre-*DaGata* case, the court reached a similar conclusion. In *Slowe*, the defendant sought disclosure, pursuant to CPL § 240.20(1)(c), of "laboratory notes made by the State Police Crime Laboratory serologist who processed a 'rape kit' consisting of specimens and body samples taken from the victim for analysis." 125 Misc. 2d at __, 479 N.Y.S.2d at 963. The court held that:

> [T]he people should disclose any laboratory notes or checklists formalized by protocol or routine as an integral element of a final report, including notes, calculations, impressions or similar matter routinely made in the course of scientific testing. However, the court also concludes that any other notations, made only as personal aids in computation or experimentation, need not be disclosed under the language and intent of CPL § 240.20(1)(c).

125 Misc. 2d at __, 479 N.Y.S.2d at 963. *See also People v. Palumbo*, 162 Misc. 2d 650, __, 618 N.Y.S.2d 197, 200 (Kings Co. Sup. Ct. 1994).

In *People v. Cubero*, 181 Misc. 2d 431, __, 695 N.Y.S.2d 271, 273 (Kings Co. Sup. Ct. 1999), the court held that "[t]he statements and reports reviewed by the People's expert in formulating his written report concerning defendant's mental examination are precisely the kinds of material that must be turned over to the defense upon request."

§ 20:16 Alco-Sensor breath screening test constitutes a "scientific test or experiment" for purposes of CPL § 240.20(1)(c)

Research References

West's Key Number Digest, Criminal Law ⚖627.6(2)

People v. Vargulik, 130 A.D.2d 530, 515 N.Y.S.2d 111 (2d Dep't 1987), makes clear that an Alco-Sensor breath screening test constitutes a "scientific test or experiment" for purposes of CPL § 240.20(1)(c). Thus, the results thereof, and the most recent inspection, calibration and repair records with regard thereto, are discoverable—even though the results of an Alco-Sensor test are inadmissible at trial. *See* §§ 7:1 et seq., *supra*. *See generally People v. Mondon*, 129 Misc. 2d 13, __, 492 N.Y.S.2d 344, 347 (N.Y. Co. Sup. Ct. 1985) ("despite widespread judicial reluctance to admit polygraph results in evidence in criminal cases, the polygraph examination qualifies as a 'scientific test or experiment', at least for purposes of pretrial discovery (CPL § 240.20[1][c])").

§ 20:17 DWI Investigative Notes, Alcoholic Influence Report (A.I.R.), Physical Condition Report, and similar forms

Research References
West's Key Number Digest, Criminal Law ⬦627.5(1)

Police officers in DWI cases frequently take notes with regard to the defendant's performance on field sobriety tests, as well as the defendant's responses to standardized questions, on forms or note cards entitled DWI Investigative Notes, Alcoholic Influence Report (A.I.R.), Physical Condition Report, etc. While many prosecutors claim that such notes constitute *Rosario* material and thus do not have to be turned over until a pretrial hearing, *see* CPL § 240.44(1), or at trial, *see* CPL § 240.45(1)(a), the portions of these notes pertaining to the defendant's statements, as well as to the defendant's performance on field sobriety tests, is in fact discoverable pursuant to CPL § 240.20. *People v. Lawrence*, 74 Misc. 2d 1019, __, 346 N.Y.S.2d 330, 333 (Suffolk Co. Dist. Ct. 1973). *See also People v. DiLorenzo*, 134 Misc. 2d 1000, __, 513 N.Y.S.2d 938, 940 (Nassau Co. Ct. 1987).

This is especially apparent with regard to the horizontal gaze nystagmus (HGN) test, which is considered "scientific" in nature within the ambit of *Frye v. United States*, 293 F. 1013 (D.C. Cir. 1923), *see, e.g., People v. Gallup*, 302 A.D.2d 681, __, 755 N.Y.S.2d 498, 501 (3d Dep't 2003); *People v. Heidelmark*, 214 A.D.2d 767, __, 624 N.Y.S.2d 656, 658 (3d Dep't 1995); *People v. Erickson*, 156 A.D.2d 760, __, 549 N.Y.S.2d 182, 184 (3d Dep't 1989); *People v. Torrey*, 144 A.D.2d 865, __, 534 N.Y.S.2d 807, 809 (3d Dep't 1988); §§ 8:1 et seq., *supra*, and thus clearly constitutes a "scientific test or experiment" for purposes of CPL § 240.20(1)(c).

§ 20:18 Accident investigation/reconstruction reports

Research References
West's Key Number Digest, Criminal Law ⬦627.6(4)

Accident investigation/reconstruction reports are discoverable pursuant to CPL § 240.20(1)(c). *See People v. Hess*, 140 A.D.2d 895, __, 528 N.Y.S.2d 921, 922 (3d Dep't 1988); *People v. Reynolds*, 193 Misc. 2d 697, __, 749 N.Y.S.2d 687, 693 (Essex Co. Ct. 2002) ("The People are required to disclose reports of their accident reconstruction expert and any written report or document concerning any crush tests performed on the vehicles involved in the accident in this case. [CPL § 240.20(1)(c)]"), *aff'd on other grounds*, 307 A.D.2d 391, 762 N.Y.S.2d 683 (3d Dep't 2003); *People v. Morrison*, 148 Misc. 2d 61, __, 559 N.Y.S.2d 1013, 1019 (N.Y. City Crim. Ct. 1990) ("the Accident and Aided Report is obtainable pursuant to CPL 240.20(1)(c)"); *People v. Delaney*, 125 Misc. 2d 928, __-__, 481 N.Y.S.2d 229, 230–32 (Suffolk Co. Ct. 1984) (where the People's accident reconstruction expert purposely did not reduce his findings to writing [presumably to circumvent the discovery statute], the expert's grand jury testimony is discoverable pursuant to CPL § 240.20(1)(c)). *Cf. People v. Murray*, 147 A.D.2d 925, 537 N.Y.S.2d 399 (4th Dep't 1989) (where "blood splatter" expert witness did not prepare a written report, there was no discoverable report to furnish to defense); *People v. Thompson*, 25 Misc. 3d 1065, __, 885 N.Y.S.2d 897, 899 (Ulster Co. Ct. 2009) (Court declines to follow *Delaney*, *supra*).

§ 20:19 Autopsy reports

Research References

West's Key Number Digest, Criminal Law ☞627.6(4)

"The final written autopsy report is obtainable by the defense, on demand pursuant to CPL 240.20[1][c], which is part of the general discovery statute in criminal cases." *People v. Washington*, 196 A.D.2d 346, __ n.4, 612 N.Y.S.2d 586, 589 n.4 (2d Dep't 1994). *See also People v. Solomon*, 160 Misc. 2d 945, __, 612 N.Y.S.2d 779, 780 (Kings Co. Sup. Ct. 1994) (autopsy report "is a discoverable scientific report, CPL 240.20(1)(c), and is *Rosario* material if the Medical Examiner who prepared the report testifies at trial"); *People v. France*, 159 Misc. 2d 869, __, 608 N.Y.S.2d 1006, 1008 (Kings Co. Sup. Ct. 1994); *People v. Reynolds*, 193 Misc. 2d 697, __, 749 N.Y.S.2d 687, 695–96 (Essex Co. Ct. 2002), *aff'd on other grounds*, 307 A.D.2d 391, 762 N.Y.S.2d 683 (3d Dep't 2003).

§ 20:20 Victim's medical/hospital records

Research References

West's Key Number Digest, Criminal Law ☞627.6(3)

The victim's medical/hospital records are discoverable pursuant to CPL § 240.20(1)(c). *See People v. Reynolds*, 193 Misc. 2d 697, __, 749 N.Y.S.2d 687, 695–96 (Essex Co. Ct. 2002), *aff'd on other grounds*, 307 A.D.2d 391, 762 N.Y.S.2d 683 (3d Dep't 2003). *See also People v. Bugayong*, 182 A.D.2d 450, __, 582 N.Y.S.2d 175, 176 (1st Dep't 1992).

§ 20:21 Ballistics reports

Research References

West's Key Number Digest, Criminal Law ☞627.6(4)

Ballistics reports are discoverable pursuant to CPL § 240.20(1)(c). *People v. Eleby*, 137 A.D.2d 708, __, 525 N.Y.S.2d 51, 52 (2d Dep't 1988); *People v. Pilotti*, 127 A.D.2d 23, __, 511 N.Y.S.2d 248, 250 (1st Dep't 1987).

§ 20:22 Polygraph tests

Research References

West's Key Number Digest, Criminal Law ☞627.6(3)

"[D]espite widespread judicial reluctance to admit polygraph results in evidence in criminal cases, the polygraph examination qualifies as a 'scientific test or experiment', at least for purposes of pretrial discovery (CPL 240.20[1][c])." *People v. Mondon*, 129 Misc. 2d 13, __, 492 N.Y.S.2d 344, 347 (N.Y. Co. Sup. Ct. 1985). The *Mondon* court further stated that:

> Because the statute explicitly directs the disclosure of reports, or parts thereof, of scientific tests or experiments made in connection with a case, and not just those that will be introduced in evidence, the inadmissibility of polygraph findings at trial does not exclude them from the law's *pretrial* ambit.
>
> Furthermore, the use of the word "any" in the statute in connection with these written reports or documents, obviously encompasses any and all such items, including both the full body of the documents or reports, as well as the results and findings.
>
> Nor does there appear any discernible legislative intent to limit even the ordinarily broad meaning of the term "scientific test." Instead, the statute goes beyond the realm of established and definitive procedures by including within its scope not only written reports and documentation of scientific "tests," but also of scientific "experiments."
>
> Moreover, with respect to the contents of the written reports or documentation of such scientific tests or experiments, the mandates of this discovery statute do not distinguish between information secured from a prospective People's witness or from a person whom the prosecutor has no ultimate intention of calling as a witness. Parenthetically, it should also be noted that the portion of a polygraph report, which contains the statements—even in question and answer form—of a person who will testify for the prosecution at trial, constitutes *Rosario* material and should be discoverable on that ground alone (see CPL 240.45).

In addition, where polygraph results are favorable to a defendant's cause, there appears a further legal basis for a turnover of such information to the defense; namely, that it falls within the spirit, if not the letter, of *Brady v. Maryland*.

Accordingly, law, logic and simple fairness dictate that whenever a prosecutor takes the time and makes the effort to order a polygraph of a possible witness, the defendant is entitled to a complete report of the examination.

129 Misc. 2d at __, 492 N.Y.S.2d at 347 (citations omitted).

§ 20:23   Scientific testing protocol/methodology

Research References

West's Key Number Digest, Criminal Law ☞627.6(2)

The testing protocol or methodology used by a laboratory in connection with a scientific test is not discoverable pursuant to CPL § 240.20(1)(c) (although it could be the proper subject of a subpoena duces tecum upon a showing of relevance and materiality). *See People v. Hough*, 297 A.D.2d 575, __, 747 N.Y.S.2d 168, 169 (1st Dep't 2002); *People v. Kelly*, 288 A.D.2d 695, __, 732 N.Y.S.2d 484, 485–86 (3d Dep't 2001).

§ 20:24   Police training manuals

Research References

West's Key Number Digest, Criminal Law ☞627.6(2)

Several courts have held that police training manuals pertaining to topics such as standardized field sobriety testing and/or the operation of chemical testing or speed detecting devices are neither discoverable nor subject to a defense subpoena duces tecum—in the absence of a sufficient factual predicate justifying such disclosure. *See, e.g., Matter of Constantine v. Leto*, 157 A.D.2d 376, 557 N.Y.S.2d 611 (3d Dep't 1990), *aff'd for the reasons stated in the opinion below*, 77 N.Y.2d 975, 571 N.Y.S.2d 906 (1991); *Matter of Suffolk County Police Dep't v. Gorman*, 202 A.D.2d 438, __, 608 N.Y.S.2d 532, 533 (2d Dep't 1994); *Matter of Constantine v. Solomon*, 194 A.D.2d 538, __, 598 N.Y.S.2d 316, 317 (2d Dep't 1993). *See generally Matter of Shay v. Mullen*, 215 A.D.2d 935, 626 N.Y.S.2d 580 (3d Dep't 1995). *Cf. People v. Drake*, 152 Misc. 2d 441, __, 576 N.Y.S.2d 774, 776 (Nassau Co. Dist. Ct. 1991) ("this Court finds the operator's training manual for the Intoxilyzer and related materials to be properly discoverable"). *See also* § 20:100, *infra*.

§ 20:25   CPL § 240.20(1)(d)—Photographs and drawings relating to the criminal action—Generally

Research References

West's Key Number Digest, Criminal Law ⚖627.6(2)

CPL § 240.20(1)(d) provides for the disclosure of:

Any photograph or drawing relating to the criminal action or proceeding which was made or completed by a public servant engaged in law enforcement activity, or which was made by a person whom the prosecutor intends to call as a witness at trial, or which the people intend to introduce at trial.

"All images taken in the course of an incident must be preserved." *People v. Cannon*, 191 Misc. 2d 136, __, 743 N.Y.S.2d 224, 229 (Kings Co. Sup. Ct. 2002).

Photographs of a crime scene are clearly discoverable pursuant to CPL § 240.20(1)(d). *See People v. Collins*, 288 A.D.2d 860, 732 N.Y.S.2d 188 (4th Dep't 2001).

People v. Rios-Liberato, 50 Misc. 3d 737, __, 22 N.Y.S.3d 326, 329 (N.Y. City Crim. Ct. 2015) ("The Court has considered that the complainant's knowledge that the un-redacted photographs were released to the defense might be embarrassing or emotionally painful for her. However, this risk is 'outweighed by the defendant's 6th Amendment right of confrontation as well as his right pursuant to *Brady v. Maryland* to receive evidence which is material to guilt or innocence' ") (citation omitted).

§ 20:26   Defendant's arrest photograph (*i.e.*, mug shot)

Research References

West's Key Number Digest, Criminal Law ⚖627.6(2)

The defendant's mug shot is discoverable pursuant to CPL § 240.20(1)(d). *See People v. Shcherenkov*, 21 A.D.3d 651, 799 N.Y.S.2d 663 (3d Dep't 2005); *People v. Dudley*, 268 A.D.2d 442, 703 N.Y.S.2d 489 (2d Dep't 2000); *People v. Halikias*, 106 A.D.2d 811, 484 N.Y.S.2d 182 (3d Dep't 1984); *People v. Cobb*, 104 A.D.2d 656, __, 480 N.Y.S.2d 33, 36 (2d Dep't 1984); *People v. Morrison*, 148 Misc. 2d 61, __, 559 N.Y.S.2d 1013, 1019 (N.Y. City Crim. Ct. 1990). In *Dudley*, the Appellate Division, Second Department, held that "[t]he trial court erred in failing to sanction the People for their failure to provide the defendant with his arrest photograph (*see*, CPL 240.20[1][d]). The failure to provide the photograph prejudiced the defendant and warrants reversal." 268 A.D.2d at __, 703 N.Y.S.2d at 489.

In *People v. Peters*, 135 A.D.2d 841, __, 522 N.Y.S.2d 944, 945 (2d Dep't 1987), the Appellate Division, Second Department, held that "the defendant's contention that the admission of his arrest photograph violated his Fifth Amendment right against self-incrimination is without merit. The photograph is not testimonial in nature and, thus, did not violate his Fifth Amendment rights."

§ 20:27 Videotapes of the defendant made by the police

Research References

West's Key Number Digest, Criminal Law ⊕627.6(1)

Videotapes of the defendant made by the police are discoverable. *See, e.g.*, CPL § 240.20(1)(d); CPL § 240.20(1)(g); *People v. Marr*, 177 A.D.2d 964, 577 N.Y.S.2d 1008 (4th Dep't 1991); *People v. Karns*, 130 Misc. 2d 247, 495 N.Y.S.2d 890 (Rochester City Ct. 1985).

In *Marr*, the police erased a videotape which had contained discoverable evidence pertaining to, among other things, the defendant's alleged unsuccessful attempts to submit to a Breathalyzer test. Following a hearing, the county court "imposed a sanction precluding the People from introducing any evidence of defendant's alleged refusal to submit to the breathalyzer test." 177 A.D.2d at __, 577 N.Y.S.2d at 1009.

On appeal, the Appellate Division, Fourth Department, held that "County Court properly exercised its discretion in fashioning an appropriate sanction. Although an adverse inference charge may also have been appropriate, in our view, the court did not abuse its discretion in precluding the prosecution from introducing evidence at trial of defendant's alleged refusal to submit to the breathalyzer test as its sole sanction for the prosecution's failure to preserve the videotape." 177 A.D.2d at __, 577 N.Y.S.2d at 1009 (citations omitted). *See also People v. Litarov*, 188 Misc. 2d 234, __, 727 N.Y.S.2d 293, 297 (N.Y. City Crim. Ct. 2001) (under circumstances presented, adverse inference charge appropriate sanction for People's loss of videotape of defendant's chemical test refusal).

§ 20:28 CPL § 240.20(1)(e)—Photographs of stolen property

Research References

West's Key Number Digest, Criminal Law ⊕627.6(1)

Penal Law (PL) § 450.10 deals with the disposal of stolen property. CPL § 240.20(1)(e) provides for the disclosure of:

> Any photograph, photocopy or other reproduction made by or at the direction of a police officer, peace officer or prosecutor of any property prior to its release pursuant to the provisions of [PL § 450.10], irrespective of whether the people intend to introduce at trial the property or the photograph, photocopy or other reproduction.

§ 20:29   CPL § 240.20(1)(f)—Other property obtained from the defendant—Generally

Research References

West's Key Number Digest, Criminal Law ☞627.6(1)

CPL § 240.20(1)(f) provides for the disclosure of "[a]ny other property obtained from the defendant, or a co-defendant to be tried jointly." It should be noted that CPL § 240.20(1)(f) only applies to "property obtained *from* a defendant. The section does not apply to a defendant's property obtained from a source other than the defendant." *People v. Ordine*, 177 A.D.2d 734, __, 575 N.Y.S.2d 977, 978 (3d Dep't 1991). *See also People v. De May*, 213 A.D.2d 1022, 624 N.Y.S.2d 495 (4th Dep't 1995); *People v. McKay*, 101 A.D.2d 960, __, 479 N.Y.S.2d 87, 89 (3d Dep't 1984).

In *People v. John*, 288 A.D.2d 848, __, 732 N.Y.S.2d 505, 507 (4th Dep't 2001), the Appellate Division, Fourth Department, held that "the vehicle allegedly driven by defendant was discoverable as 'property obtained from the defendant' (CPL 240.20[1][f])." *See also People v. Brown*, 104 Misc. 2d 157, __, 427 N.Y.S.2d 722, 725–26 (N.Y. City Crim. Ct. 1980).

In *People v. Naran*, 119 A.D.3d 615, __, 987 N.Y.S.2d 891, 891-92 (2d Dep't 2014), the Appellate Division, Second Department, held that:

> The trial court erred in denying the defendant's motion to compel the People to provide the defendant with the opportunity to inspect the laptop computer that was seized from his home and for an adjournment of the trial, in order to permit the defense to examine that computer. The defendant was entitled to inspect the laptop computer, pursuant to CPL 240.20(1)(f), and the defendant made a timely demand to inspect the laptop computer.

(Citations omitted).

§ 20:30   Blood samples

Research References

West's Key Number Digest, Criminal Law ☞627.6(1)

CPL § 240.20(1)(f) provides that, upon a demand to produce of a defendant, the People must disclose to the defendant, and make available for inspection and testing, any "property" obtained from the defendant. In this regard, CPL § 240.10(3) expressly provides that "blood samples" constitute "property." Thus, if the defendant's blood is withdrawn for chemical testing, the People are required to preserve a sample thereof, and to make a portion of such sample available to the defendant for independent testing. *See People v. Karpeles*, 146 Misc. 2d 53, 549 N.Y.S.2d 903 (N.Y. City Crim. Ct. 1989); *People v. North*, 96 Misc. 2d 637, 409

N.Y.S.2d 482 (Amherst Just. Ct. 1978). *See generally People v. White*, 40 N.Y.2d 797, 390 N.Y.S.2d 405 (1976).

In *Karpeles*, the court stated, inter alia, that:

> Since testimony of blood alcohol content is invariably dispositive in drunk driving cases, independent testing by a defense expert is imperative if the defense is to have a fair opportunity to confront the toxicologist and the findings . . . Finally, as a matter of public policy, it is fundamentally unfair to deny someone reasonable access to fluid specimens taken from one's own body, sought to be used by an adversary and likely to be outcome-determinative.

146 Misc. 2d at __, 549 N.Y.S.2d at 909.

The *inadvertent* failure of the People to preserve the defendant's blood sample for independent testing by the defense does not render the defendant's blood test results inadmissible at trial. *See People v. Briggs*, 81 A.D.2d 1017, __, 440 N.Y.S.2d 143, 144–45 (4th Dep't 1981); *People v. Swanda*, 87 A.D.2d 940, __, 451 N.Y.S.2d 240, 241 (3d Dep't 1982).

However, the trial court *must* impose a sanction on the People for such failure to preserve. *See People v. Scalzo*, 178 A.D.2d 444, 574 N.Y.S.2d 782 (2d Dep't 1991). In *Scalzo*, the Appellate Division, Second Department, reversed the defendant's convictions of, inter alia, vehicular manslaughter 2nd and vehicular assault 2nd:

> [B]ecause of the trial court's failure to impose even the most minimal sanctions on the People for their failure to preserve the defendant's blood sample. In fashioning an "appropriate" response to the prosecutor's failure to preserve evidence (*see*, CPL 240.70[1]), the overriding concern must be to eliminate any prejudice to the defendant while protecting the interests of society. The fact that the People lose evidence through inadvertence does not excuse the loss. In the instant case, the court's instruction which suggested that the failure to preserve the sample was of "no consequence" clearly did not even attempt to eliminate the prejudice caused the defendant. We consider this failure particularly grave under the instant set of circumstances where the chemical test performed on the sample of the defendant's blood yielded a blood alcohol content that was below the statutory level of intoxication.

178 A.D.2d at __, 574 N.Y.S.2d at 784 (citations omitted).

§ 20:31 Breath samples

Research References

West's Key Number Digest, Criminal Law ⟐627.6(1)

Both the United States Supreme Court and the New York State Court of Appeals have expressly held that, where a breath alcohol test is utilized, preservation of a sample of the defendant's breath for independent testing is *not* required under either the federal or state constitutions. *See, e.g., California v. Trombetta*, 467 U.S. 479, 104 S.Ct. 2528 (1984); *People v. Alvarez*, 70 N.Y.2d 375, 521 N.Y.S.2d 212 (1987).

In *Trombetta*, the Supreme Court addressed the issue of "whether the Due Process Clause requires law enforcement agencies to preserve breath samples of suspected drunken drivers in order for the results of breath-analysis tests to be admissible in criminal prosecutions," 467 U.S. at 481, 104 S.Ct. at 2530, and concluded that "the Due Process Clause of the Fourteenth Amendment does not require that law enforcement agencies preserve breath samples in order to introduce the results of breath-analysis tests at trial." 467 U.S. at 491, 104 S.Ct. at 2535.

Notably, unlike in New York, DWI suspects in California have the right to choose the type of BAC test that they will submit to (*i.e.*, blood, breath or urine). *See* 467 U.S. at 482 n.2, 104 S.Ct. at 2530 n.2. In addition, where the suspect chooses a breath test, the test results are inadmissible in court unless, among other things, two separate breath samples are tested and the results register within 0.02 of each other. *See* 467 U.S. at 481, 104 S.Ct. at 2530. *See generally People v. Shepherd*, 130 Misc. 2d 284, __, 496 N.Y.S.2d 205, 207 (Monroe Co. Ct. 1985) ("California's testing methods provide for a safeguard by requiring two samples and, in effect, two tests of a suspect's breath. Since New York has no such statutory or administrative requirement, a suspect is effectively powerless to conduct a cross-check of his own breath"), *rev'd on other grounds*, 68 N.Y.2d 841, 508 N.Y.S.2d 173 (1986).

In a footnote, the *Trombetta* Court stated that "State courts and legislatures, of course, remain free to adopt more rigorous safeguards governing the admissibility of scientific evidence than those imposed by the Federal Constitution." 467 U.S. at 491 n.12, 104 S.Ct. at 2535 n.12. The New York State Court of Appeals addressed this issue in *People v. Alvarez*, 70 N.Y.2d 375, 381, 521 N.Y.S.2d 212, 215 (1987), and held that "as a matter of State constitutional law the police are not required to obtain and preserve a second breath sample for later use by the accused."

In so holding, the Court reasoned that, although "there can be no doubt in New York that the fairness of a criminal proceeding is of particular State concern, and New York historically has provided various protections in this area above the Federal constitutional minimum," 70 N.Y.2d at 379, 521 N.Y.S.2d at 214, "[t]he Supreme Court's analysis and result in *Trombetta* . . . are consonant with New York State law and interests and, we believe, they are analytically correct and provide a fair and proper rule under our State Constitution." 70 N.Y.2d at 379–80, 521 N.Y.S.2d at 214. *See also People v. Merrick*, 188 A.D.2d 764, __, 591 N.Y.S.2d 564, 566–67 (3d Dep't 1992).

The *Alvarez* Court also noted, among other things, that the police are not required "to affirmatively gather evidence for the accused," 70 N.Y.2d at 381, 521 N.Y.S.2d at 215, and that "the Legislature has provided that a defendant has a statutory right to have a personal physician administer an additional chemical test." 70 N.Y.2d at 381, 521 N.Y.S.2d at 215. *See also* VTL § 1194(4)(b) (formerly VTL § 1194[8]); *People v. DiLorenzo*, 134 Misc. 2d 1000, __, 513 N.Y.S.2d 938, 939 (Nassau Co. Ct. 1987); §§ 30:1 et seq., *infra*.

§ 20:32   Fingerprints

Research References

West's Key Number Digest, Criminal Law ⬤⟶627.6(1)

CPL § 240.20(1)(f) provides for the disclosure of "property" obtained from the defendant. In this regard, CPL § 240.10(3) expressly provides that "fingerprints" constitute "property." As such, the defendant's fingerprints are discoverable pursuant to CPL § 240.20(1)(f).

In addition, fingerprint reports are discoverable pursuant to CPL § 240.20(1)(c). *See People v. Lyons*, 150 A.D.2d 804, __, 542 N.Y.S.2d 40, 41 (2d Dep't 1989); *People v. Germeo*, 188 A.D.2d 1027, __, 592 N.Y.S.2d 191, 192 (4th Dep't 1992).

§ 20:33   Body of the victim in a homicide case

Research References

West's Key Number Digest, Criminal Law ⬤⟶627.5(1)

"[T]he body of the victim in a homicide case is not listed among the discoverable items the prosecution must produce upon demand by a defendant (*see,* CPL 240.20[1])." *People v. Rose*, 122 A.D.2d 484, __, 505 N.Y.S.2d 244, 246 (3d Dep't 1986).

§ 20:34   CPL § 240.20(1)(g)—Tapes and electronic recordings that the People intend to introduce at trial

Research References

West's Key Number Digest, Criminal Law ⬤⟶627.6(1)

CPL § 240.20(1)(g) provides for the disclosure of "[a]ny tapes or other electronic recordings which the prosecutor intends to introduce at trial, irrespective of whether such recording was made during the course of the criminal transaction."

§ 20:35   CPL § 240.20(1)(h)—*Brady* material—Generally

Research References

West's Key Number Digest, Criminal Law ⬤⟶627.6(1)

CPL § 240.20(1)(h) provides for the disclosure of "[a]nything required to be disclosed, prior to trial, to the defendant by the prosecutor, pursuant to the constitution of this state or of the United States." In other words, CPL § 240.20(1)(h) codifies the right to disclosure required by *Brady v. Maryland*, 373 U.S. 83, 83 S.Ct. 1194 (1963), and its progeny. *See* §§ 21:1 et seq., *infra*.

In *People v. Morgan*, 178 Misc. 2d 595, __, 682 N.Y.S.2d 533, 538 (Fulton Co. Ct. 1998), the court held that "evidence bearing on the intoxication of Defendant on the night in question, whatever form it may take, constitutes potential *Brady* material," and directed the People "to review all the evidence in their possession, and in the possession of any related law enforcement entities, and disclose to Defendant any evidence that is *Brady* material."

§ 20:36   Search warrants and supporting documents

Research References

West's Key Number Digest, Criminal Law ⬥627.6(2)

Subject to a protective order, search warrants and the documents submitted in support thereof are discoverable pursuant to CPL § 240.20(1)(h). *See, e.g., People v. Chahine*, 150 Misc. 2d 242, 568 N.Y.S.2d 526 (N.Y. City Crim. Ct. 1991); *People v. Velez*, 147 Misc. 2d 865, 556 N.Y.S.2d 818 (N.Y. Co. Sup. Ct. 1990); *People v. Seychel*, 136 Misc. 2d 310, 518 N.Y.S.2d 754 (N.Y. Co. Sup. Ct. 1987); *People v. Brown*, 104 Misc. 2d 157, __, 427 N.Y.S.2d 722, 726 (N.Y. City Crim. Ct. 1980) ("Clearly, the existence of a search warrant and the supporting affidavits for same is a fact of constitutional dimension").

§ 20:37   CPL § 240.20(1)(h) does not alter the time frame for the disclosure of *Brady* material

Research References

West's Key Number Digest, Criminal Law ⬥627.6(1)

CPL § 240.80(3) provides that, absent a refusal to comply with a defendant's demand to produce, compliance with such demand must be made within 15 days of the service thereof, or as soon thereafter as practicable. However, as a general rule, *Brady* material need only be provided to the defense in time for the defendant to have a "meaningful opportunity" to use it at trial. In this regard, *Matter of Sacket v. Bartlett*, 241 A.D.2d 97, __, 671 N.Y.S.2d 156, 159 (3d Dep't 1998), holds that "CPL 240.20(1)(h) may not be utilized as a vehicle for directing earlier discovery than is otherwise mandated."

§ 20:38 CPL § 240.20(1)(i)—Date, time, and place of offense charged and of defendant's arrest

Research References

West's Key Number Digest, Criminal Law ⟨Key⟩627.6(1)

CPL § 240.20(1)(i) provides for the disclosure of "[t]he approximate date, time and place of the offense charged and of defendant's arrest."

§ 20:39 CPL § 240.20(1)(j)—Offenses involving computers

Research References

West's Key Number Digest, Criminal Law ⟨Key⟩627.6(1)

Penal Law (PL) Article 156 deals with offenses involving computers. CPL § 240.20(1)(j) provides for the disclosure of "[i]n any prosecution under [PL §] 156.05 or 156.10, the time, place and manner of notice given pursuant to [PL § 156.00(6)]."

§ 20:40 CPL § 240.20(1)(k)—Documents pertaining to chemical test in a DWI case

Research References

West's Key Number Digest, Criminal Law ⟨Key⟩627.6(2)

Discovery of documents pertaining to a chemical test in a DWI case is governed by statute, case law, and the Constitution. The starting point is CPL § 240.20(1)(k), which provides for the disclosure of the following:

> In any prosecution commenced in a manner set forth in this subdivision alleging a violation of the vehicle and traffic law, in addition to any material required to be disclosed pursuant to this article, any other provision of law, or the constitution of this state or of the United States, any written report or document, or portion thereof, concerning a physical examination, a scientific test or experiment, including the most recent record of inspection, or calibration or repair of machines or instruments utilized to perform such scientific tests or experiments and the certification certificate, if any, held by the operator of the machine or instrument, which tests or examinations were made by or at the request or direction of a public servant engaged in law enforcement activity or which was made by a person whom the prosecutor intends to call as a witness at trial, or which the people intend to introduce at trial.

The official Practice Commentaries to CPL § 240.20 provide, in pertinent part, that:

> The purpose of paragraph (k) is to make it clear that the material described therein is discoverable on demand in prosecution of a Vehicle and Traffic Law misdemeanor. Although reported opinions

had not expressed any doubt about the fact that this material generally fell within the ambit of paragraph (c) (*see e.g.*, *People v. Briggs*, 136 Misc. 2d 687, 519 N.Y.S.2d 294 [Town Ct. Monroe Co.] and cases cited therein), the State Magistrates' Association (which requested the legislation) expressed the need for clarification. Apparently the problem involved the scope of discovery of records of inspection, repair and operation of machines and equipment utilized for scientific tests. This is the only issue mentioned in the sponsor's memorandum which, after acknowledging the general sufficiency of paragraph (c), alleges "[m]any courts are not granting discovery . . . without statutory mandate," and then states that "[t]he experience record of the operator of any such machine or equipment and, of course, the name of the operator is needed to determine the proficiency of the machine operator to determine blood and alcohol readings."

Preiser, Practice Commentaries, McKinney's Cons. Laws of N.Y., Book 11A, CPL § 240.20, at 342. *See also People v. Karpeles*, 146 Misc. 2d 53, __ n.1, 549 N.Y.S.2d 903, 905 n.1 (N.Y. City Crim. Ct. 1989) ("The new paragraph (k) is redundant and unnecessary, duplicating the intent and express wording of the pre-existing statute [*i.e.*, [CPL § 240.20(1)(c)]. It was apparently adopted to clarify the right to discovery on demand, in the face of resistance in some local courts. *See* Preiser, Supp. Practice Comm. to C.P.L. sec. 240.20(1)(k) (McKinney ed., 1990; Cumulative supp. at 141)").

Many prosecutors claim that only the items expressly listed in CPL § 240.20(1)(k) are discoverable. Such a claim is patently false. Critically in this regard, CPL § 240.20(1)(k) expressly states that the listed items are discoverable "*in addition to* any material required to be disclosed pursuant to this article, any other provision of law, or the constitution of this state or of the United States." (Emphasis added).

In addition, the listed items are but examples of what must be provided—they do not constitute a comprehensive list of all discoverable material. In this regard, the legislature expressly placed the word "*including*" immediately prior to listing particular discoverable items in CPL § 240.20(1)(k) (emphasis added). Furthermore, both CPL § 240.20(1)(c) and CPL § 240.20(1)(k) mandate disclosure of "*any* written report or document, *or portion thereof*" (emphases added), concerning scientific tests and experiments, etc.

Indeed, case law has recognized the right to discovery in DWI cases of various documents not expressly listed in CPL § 240.20. *See, e.g.*, *Matter of Constantine v. Leto*, 157 A.D.2d 376, __, 557 N.Y.S.2d 611, 613 (3d Dep't 1990) ("records indicating that a machine was not operating properly are discoverable, as are the State Police rules and regulations and the checklist and calibration records") (citations omitted), *aff'd for the reasons stated in the opinion below*, 77 N.Y.2d 975, 571 N.Y.S.2d 906 (1991); *People v. Crandall*, 228 A.D.2d 794, __, 644 N.Y.S.2d 817, 818 (3d Dep't 1996) ("documents relating to ampoule analysis and simulator solution analysis"); *People v. Erickson*, 156 A.D.2d 760, __, 549 N.Y.S.2d 182, 183 (3d Dep't 1989) ("breathalyzer operator's permit and the weekly test record"); *People v. Torre*, 48 Misc. 3d 745, __, 11 N.Y.S.3d 445, 451 (Nassau Co. Dist. Ct. 2015); *People v. Brown*, 48 Misc. 3d 582, 9 N.Y.S.3d 830 (N.Y. City Crim. Ct. 2015); *People v. Ramrup*, 47 Misc. 3d 1223(A), 2015 WL 3385133 (Bronx Co. Sup. Ct. 2015); *People v. Ramrup*, 51 Misc. 3d 393, 26 N.Y.S.3d 417 (Bronx Co. Sup. Ct. 2016); *People v. DiLorenzo*, 134 Misc. 2d 1000, __, 513 N.Y.S.2d 938, 940–41 (Nassau Co. Ct. 1987) (Court lists several specific documents subject to disclosure). *See also People v. Alvarez*, 70 N.Y.2d 375, 380, 521 N.Y.S.2d 212, 214 (1987) ("defendant may not be denied discovery which prevents him from challenging the reliability and accuracy of the machine"); *People v. Corley*, 124 A.D.2d 390, 507 N.Y.S.2d 491 (3d Dep't 1986) (same); *People v. English*, 103 A.D.2d 979, 480 N.Y.S.2d 56 (3d Dep't 1984) (same). *See generally People v. DaGata*, 86 N.Y.2d 40, 629 N.Y.S.2d 186 (1995) (10 pages of FBI notes related to a one-page DNA testing report are discoverable pursuant to CPL § 240.20(1)(c), and prosecution was required to provide these notes upon defendant's request, even though they were not in its possession).

Notably, the above analysis of what is discoverable in a DWI case has been expressly endorsed, almost verbatim, by the Appellate Division, Second Department. *See People v. Robinson*, 53 A.D.3d 63, __-__, 860 N.Y.S.2d 159, 162–64 (2d Dep't 2008), leave to appeal denied, 11 N.Y.3d 857, 872 N.Y.S.2d 80, 900 N.E.2d 563 (2008). In *Robinson*, the Second Department addressed the issue of "whether the computer source code governing the operation of a breathalyzer machine is subject to disclosure as a written document within the meaning of CPL 240.20(1)(c) and/or as a document concerning a scientific test or calibration of an instrument utilized to perform a scientific test within the meaning of CPL 240.20(1)(k)." 53 A.D.3d at __, 860 N.Y.S.2d at 161. "Source codes are the computer instructions followed by a computing device in processing information." 53 A.D.3d at __, 860 N.Y.S.2d at 161. The *Robinson* Court held:

(a) "Since a computer source code is a species of 'text' that must be written onto a computer chip, and 'concerns' scientific tests of the particular machine to which it relates, it is, contrary to the People's contention, a written document within the meaning of CPL 240.20(1)(c)." 53 A.D.3d at __, 860 N.Y.S.2d at 163;

(b) "Since the computer source code of the Intoxilyzer constitutes a document 'concerning' inspection, repair, and calibration of the relevant machinery, it is included in the definition of discoverable material within [CPL § 240.20(1)(k)]." 53 A.D.3d at ___, 860 N.Y.S.2d at 164; and

(c) "Similarly, the computer source code for the Intoxilyzer is a written instrument within the meaning of the Penal Law, a conclusion which supports our interpretation of the CPL." 53 A.D.3d at ___, 860 N.Y.S.2d at 164.

Nonetheless, having found that the computer source code of the Intoxilyzer clearly constitutes discoverable material within the meaning of both the CPL and the Penal Law, the *Robinson* Court went on to hold that "the People were not required to make available the Intoxilyzer's source code because the People never possessed it, actually or constructively. The People did not have control over the program simply because it was installed in the EPROM. The Intoxilyzer source code was not the property of the State, since it was owned and copyrighted by its manufacturer, CMI, Inc., a Kentucky corporation, and is a trade secret of CMI, Inc." 53 A.D.3d at ___, 860 N.Y.S.2d at 167 (citations omitted). *See also* 53 A.D.3d at ___, 860 N.Y.S.2d at 161. *See generally People v. Cialino*, 14 Misc. 3d 999, 831 N.Y.S.2d 680 (N.Y. City Crim. Ct. 2007).

Relying on the case law and principles set forth in the preceding paragraphs, in *People v. Torre*, 48 Misc. 3d 745, ___, 11 N.Y.S.3d 445, 451 (Nassau Co. Dist. Ct. 2015), the Court ordered the People to:

[D]isclose to the Defendant and make available for inspection, photographing, copying or testing the following items, if not otherwise provided:

1. All documents, records and reports relating to the preparation of Simulator Solution Lot Number 13320, including, but not limited to the applicable chromatograms;

2. All documents, records and reports relating to the testing of Simulator Solution Lot Number 13320, between the dates of February 4, 2014 and April 1, 2014, inclusive, including, but not limited to, the applicable chromatograms; [and]

3. All documents, records and reports relating to the repair, maintenance, inspection and/or calibration of the Intoxilyzer 5000, Serial Number 68-013839 and Simulator Serial Number 3046, between the dates of February 4, 2014 and April 1, 2014, inclusive.

In so holding, the Court reasoned as follows:

While recognizing that the documents the Defendant seeks go directly to the calibration, maintenance, repair, testing and operation of the instrument used to test the Defendant's breath, the People take the position that the Defendant is only entitled to records pertaining to the Defendant's breath test itself. The People take the position that because the documents sought might only go to "foundational matter[s] the People do not generally disclose this information." The People seem to take the position that the Defendant is required to simply accept the People's conclusory "foundational" paperwork, thereby paving the way for the admission of the test results, without challenge, withholding from the Defendant the notes and memoranda created when the simulator solution was created and tested and when the instrument itself was calibrated, maintained, tested and/or repaired. While the People give voice to "[f]airness [being] the ultimate goal of and rationale behind the Criminal Justice System[,]" they appear to overlook a bedrock principle of our adversarial system, "that the best judge of the value of evidence to a defendant's case is the single-minded devotion of counsel for the accused." * * *

[T]he People's insistence that CPL § 240.20(1)(c) and (k) are limited to discovery of documents relating exclusively to the Defendant's breath test itself is misguided. Focusing on that part of CPL § 240.20(1)(k) which provides for the discovery of documents relating to "a scientific test or experiment," the People overlook that the statute mandates the People provide, upon demand, "any written report or document, or portion thereof, concerning the most recent record of inspection, or calibration or repair of machines or instruments utilized to perform such scientific tests or experiments." Clearly, the nature of the documents sought by the Defendant "concern" the "inspection or calibration or repair" of the instrument used to conduct a "scientific test" upon the Defendant's breath. As the People concede, the proper preparation of the simulator solution and the proper maintenance, repair, calibration and operation of the instrument used to conduct the chemical test of the Defendant's breath being foundational to the admission of the results of that breath test, one cannot separate the two, and the Defendant is entitled to the discovery of all written reports and documents concerning both. * * *

The Defendant is not to be limited to the conclusory reports regarding the maintenance, repair, testing, preparation and calibration of the simulator solution and breath test instrument used in this case, but is entitled to all back-up documentation related thereto.

Id. at __, __, __, 11 N.Y.S.3d at 447, 448-49, 450 (citations omitted). *See also People v. Brown*, 48 Misc. 3d 582, 9 N.Y.S.3d 830 (N.Y. City Crim. Ct. 2015); *People v. Ramrup*, 47 Misc. 3d 1223(A), 2015 WL 3385133 (Bronx Co. Sup. Ct. 2015); *People v. Ramrup*, 51 Misc. 3d 393, 26 N.Y.S.3d 417 (Bronx Co. Sup. Ct. 2016).

It has also been held that the defendant is entitled to CPL § 240.20 discovery of "all documentary evidence that the People intend to introduce . . . to establish the foundation for the breathalyzer test results." *People v. Amidon*, 102 Misc. 2d 850, __, 427 N.Y.S.2d 727, 728 (Geneva City Ct. 1980).

In *People v. Briggs*, 136 Misc. 2d 687, 519 N.Y.S.2d 294 (Brighton Just. Ct. 1987), the People took the position that the certification and calibration documents pertaining to the Breathalyzer machine were not within their control. The court rejected the People's claim, calling it "ludicrous." 136 Misc. 2d at __, 519 N.Y.S.2d at 294.

Notably, VTL § 1194(4)(c) requires that the Department of Health issue and file rules and regulations approving satisfactory breath testing techniques; and the relevant Department of Health regulations require, among other things, that "[p]roper and adequate records of methods and procedures, analyses, and results shall be maintained by each agency or laboratory using breath analysis instruments, including but not limited to operational check list, calibration test records, and certifications for standards and ampoules." 10 NYCRR § 59.5(f).

Finally, records indicating that a chemical test device was not operating properly constitute *Brady* material. *See Brady v. Maryland*, 373 U.S. 83, 83 S.Ct. 1194 (1963). In this regard, the CPL, the New York State Court of Appeals, and the United States Supreme Court all make clear that:

> The mandate of *Brady* extends beyond any particular prosecutor's actual knowledge. **Furthermore, "the individual prosecutor has a duty to learn of any favorable evidence known to the others acting on the government's behalf in the case, including the police."** The People therefore were not relieved of their obligation to turn over *Brady* material by the trial prosecutor's failure to discover that the police were in possession of exculpatory information.

People v. Wright, 86 N.Y.2d 591, 598, 635 N.Y.S.2d 136, 139 (1995) (quoting *Kyles v. Whitley*, 514 U.S. 419, __, 115 S. Ct. 1555, 1567) (emphasis added) (citation omitted). *See also* CPL § 240.20(2) ("The prosecutor shall make a diligent, good faith effort to ascertain the existence of demanded property and to cause such property to be made available for discovery where it exists but is not within the prosecutor's possession, custody or control").

Simply stated, the People have a clear legal and ethical obligation to conduct an actual investigation into whether any information exists indicating that the chemical test device was not operating properly, and to disclose any such information to the defense. *See, e.g., People v. White*, 990 N.Y.S.2d 403, 408-09 (N.Y. City Crim. Ct. 2014) ("the People have a continuing *Brady* obligation to conduct an actual investigation into whether any information exists indicating that the chemical test device was not operating properly, and to disclose any of this information to the defense. This duty includes review of the most recent maintenance records to see if they contain repair information") (citation omitted).

In this regard, the *White* Court cited *People v. Ariosa*, 172 Misc. 2d 312, __, 660 N.Y.S.2d 255, 257 (Monroe Co. Ct. 1997), which stated that:

> None of the specific provisions of [CPL] § 240.70 would sufficiently sanction the People for this gross failure to fulfill their discovery, *Rosario* and *Brady* obligations. Accordingly, this Court finds that the appropriate sanction would be one that would send a message to the People that their review of discoverable materials requested by the defense and their response to those requests has to be more than just a boilerplate, cursory review and response. It must be a pro-active, vigorous attempt to respond to the requests made by defense counsel or to seek protective orders in circumstances they feel are inappropriate for discovery. The consequences to a defendant for the People's failure to turn over materials are severe indeed. Accordingly, the sanctions for failing to disclose such materials must also send a clear message.

§ 20:41   Documents pertaining to radar/laser speed detection device

Research References

West's Key Number Digest, Criminal Law ☞627.6(2)

Radar and laser speed detection devices are considered to be scientific in nature. *See, e.g.*, *People v. Knight*, 72 N.Y.2d 481, 534 N.Y.S.2d 353 (1988) ("moving" radar); *People v. Dusing*, 5 N.Y.2d 126, 181 N.Y.S.2d 493 (1959) (radar); *People v. Magri*, 3 N.Y.2d 562, 170 N.Y.S.2d 335 (1958) (radar); *People v. Clemens*, 168 Misc. 2d 56, 642 N.Y.S.2d 760 (Chatham Just. Ct. 1995) (laser); *People v. Depass*, 165 Misc. 2d 217, 629 N.Y.S.2d 367 (Roslyn Harbor Just. Ct. 1995) (laser). *See generally People v. Olsen*, 22 N.Y.2d 230, 292 N.Y.S.2d 420 (1968); *People v. Correia*, 140 Misc. 2d 813, 531 N.Y.S.2d 998 (Muttontown Just. Ct. 1988). As such, they constitute "scientific tests or experiments" for purposes of CPL §§ 240.20(1)(c) and 240.20(1)(k). *But see People v. Guagnini*, 143 Misc. 2d 676, __, 541 N.Y.S.2d 907, 908 (Kensington Just. Ct. 1989) (Court reached opposite conclusion in dicta).

Nonetheless, since discovery pursuant to CPL § 240.20 is only available to "a defendant against whom an indictment, superior court information, prosecutor's information, information, or simplified information *charging a misdemeanor* is pending," CPL § 240.20(1) (emphasis added), CPL § 240.20 discovery is not available to a defendant where the *sole* accusatory instrument is a simplified information *charging a traffic infraction. See, e.g., People v. Malone*, 166 Misc. 2d 54, __, 631 N.Y.S.2d 223, 224 (Suffolk Co. Dist. Ct. 1995); *People v. Chess*, 149 Misc. 2d 430, __, 565 N.Y.S.2d 416, 418 (Kensington Just. Ct. 1991); *Guagnini*, 143 Misc. 2d at __, 541 N.Y.S.2d at 908; *People v. McGettrick*, 139 Misc. 2d 403, __, 528 N.Y.S.2d 758, 759 (Hudson City Ct. 1988);

People v. Cohen, 131 Misc. 2d 898, __, 502 N.Y.S.2d 123, 124 (Yonkers City Ct. 1986). *See generally People v. Ross*, 110 Misc. 2d 818, 442 N.Y.S.2d 848 (Glens Falls City Ct. 1981).

Accordingly, maintenance, calibration, and similar documents pertaining to a radar/laser speed detection device are generally not discoverable pursuant to CPL § 240.20 in speeding prosecutions. *But see People v. Russo*, 149 A.D.2d 255, __, 545 N.Y.S.2d 211, 212 (2d Dep't 1989) ("A defendant charged with a violation of Vehicle and Traffic Law § 1180(b) is entitled to the issuance of a properly worded judicial subpoena duces tecum under CPLR 2307 requiring the production of relevant records at the hearing before the Traffic Violations Bureau").

However, if the defendant is either (a) charged with speeding in an information (or an indictment), or (b) charged with speeding in a simplified information, *and* is also charged with one or more misdemeanors (or felonies), he or she is entitled to full CPL § 240.20 discovery with regard to any radar/laser speed detection device used to determine his or her alleged speed (including the operator's certification card).

§ 20:42   Defendant's chemical test results

Research References

West's Key Number Digest, Criminal Law ⊕627.6(2)

VTL § 1194(2) regulates chemical testing. VTL § 1194(2)(g) states that "[u]pon the request of the person who was tested, the results of such test shall be made available to such person." *See also* CPL § 240.20(1)(c); CPL § 240.20(1)(k).

§ 20:43   Report of refusal to submit to chemical test

Research References

West's Key Number Digest, Criminal Law ⊕627.6(2)

Where a DWI defendant refuses to submit to a chemical test, or any portion thereof, to determine the alcoholic and/or drug content of his or her blood, "unless a court order has been granted pursuant to [VTL § 1194(3)], the test shall not be given and *a written report of such refusal shall be immediately made by the police officer before whom such refusal was made*." VTL § 1194(2)(b)(1) (emphasis added). *See also* §§ 41:1 et seq., *infra*. Such a report (a.k.a. a Report of Refusal to Submit to Chemical Test) constitutes a written report or document concerning a physical examination and/or a scientific test or experiment relating to the criminal action. As such, it is discoverable pursuant to CPL §§ 240.20(1)(c) and 240.20(1)(k) (and is not merely *Rosario* material).

A defendant's refusal to submit to a chemical test is also discoverable pursuant to CPL § 240.20(1)(a), which provides for the disclosure of "[a]ny written, recorded or oral statement of the defendant . . . made, other than in the course of the criminal transaction, to a public servant engaged in law enforcement activity or to a person then acting under his direction or in cooperation with him."

§ 20:44 Accusatory instruments

Research References

West's Key Number Digest, Criminal Law ☞627.6(2)

CPL § 170.10(2) provides that, at arraignment on a local criminal court accusatory instrument, the court "must furnish [the defendant] with a copy of the accusatory instrument." In this regard, it is noteworthy that a uniform traffic ticket (UTT) is not the same thing as, and is not identical to, a simplified traffic information:

> [T]he accusatory instrument is prepared at the same time as the ticket by filling out different parts of a carbonized multi-part form. One part is served upon the person summoned to appear (*e.g.*, the operator of the vehicle) and another part will be filed with a local criminal court. The part served upon the motorist is an appearance ticket and the part filed with the court is an accusatory instrument; to wit, a simplified information (see CPL § 100.25 and Practice Commentary thereon).

Preiser, Practice Commentaries, McKinney's Cons. Laws of N.Y., Book 11A, CPL § 150.10, at 564. *See also* 15 NYCRR §§ 91.7(a), (b); 91.11(a). In other words, a UTT is merely an "appearance ticket" pursuant to CPL § 150.10, *see People v. Tyler*, 1 N.Y.3d 493, 494, 776 N.Y.S.2d 199, 200 (2004), whereas a simplified traffic information is an "accusatory instrument" pursuant to CPL § 100.10(2)(a).

CPL § 210.15(1) provides that, at arraignment on an indictment, "the district attorney must cause [the defendant] to be furnished with a copy of the indictment."

§ 20:45 Defendant's "rap sheet"

Research References

West's Key Number Digest, Criminal Law ☞627.6(1)

CPL Article 160 provides that, upon the taking of a defendant's fingerprints:
    (a) The police must forward two copies thereof to the Division of Criminal Justice Services (DCJS);
    (b) The DCJS must thereafter search its records for informa-

tion concerning the defendant's prior record, if any, and transmit a report thereof (*i.e.*, a "rap sheet") to the forwarding police officer or agency;

(c) The recipient police officer or agency must thereafter transmit the defendant's rap sheet to both the district attorney and the court; and

(d) The court must thereafter furnish a copy of the defendant's rap sheet to defense counsel.

See CPL §§ 160.10, 160.20, 160.30 & 160.40. *See also Matter of Legal Aid Soc'y of Suffolk County v. Mallon*, 47 A.D.2d 646, 364 N.Y.S.2d 17 (2d Dep't 1975); *People v. Morrison*, 148 Misc. 2d 61, —, 559 N.Y.S.2d 1013, 1019 (N.Y. City Crim. Ct. 1990). *See generally* CPL § 530.20(2)(b)(ii).

§ 20:46   Inventory search guidelines

In *People v. Walker*, 20 N.Y.3d 122, 126-27, 957 N.Y.S.2d 272, 275, 980 N.E.2d 937 (2012), the defendant challenged the results of an inventory search on several grounds, one of which was that "the written policy that governed the search was never produced." In rejecting the defendant's claims, the Court of Appeals stated that:

> Certainly, it would be better for a prosecutor seeking to prove the existence of a written policy to put a copy of the policy into evidence. On the other hand, defense counsel could have demanded that the policy be produced to help her cross-examine the trooper. She did not do so.

Id. at 127, 957 N.Y.S.2d at 275. *Walker* makes clear that a police department's written inventory search guidelines are discoverable. By analogy, it would seem that a police department's written DWI checkpoint guidelines are also discoverable.

§ 20:47   Names and addresses of witnesses

Research References

West's Key Number Digest, Criminal Law ☞627.6(1)

"[G]enerally a defendant is not entitled to pretrial disclosure of the identity of a prosecution witness." *Matter of Molea v. Marasco*, 64 N.Y.2d 718, 723, 485 N.Y.S.2d 738, 742 (1984) (Simons, J., dissenting). *See also People v. Estrada*, 1 A.D.3d 928, —, 767 N.Y.S.2d 552, 554 (4th Dep't 2003) (there is no statutory basis to compel disclosure of the addresses and telephone numbers of potential prosecution witnesses); *People v. Izquierdo*, 292 A.D.2d 247, —, 739 N.Y.S.2d 78, 79 (1st Dep't 2002). *But see People v. Andre W.*, 44 N.Y.2d 179, 186 & n.*, 404 N.Y.S.2d 578, 582 & n.* (1978) (identity of witness may be discoverable if witness might possess exculpatory information).

In *People v. Miller*, 106 A.D.2d 787, __, 484 N.Y.S.2d 183, 184 (3d Dep't 1984), the Appellate Division, Third Department, ruled that:

> [CPL] article 240 does not entitle a defendant to pretrial disclosure of prospective witnesses as a matter of right. This is not to suggest that a trial court is precluded from granting such disclosure. To be entitled to relief, however, a defendant must first demonstrate a material need for such information and the reasonableness of the request.

(Citations omitted). *See also People v. Contento*, 146 A.D.2d 959, __, 537 N.Y.S.2d 88, 90 (3d Dep't 1989); *People v. Bianco*, 169 Misc. 2d 127, 642 N.Y.S.2d 815 (N.Y. City Crim. Ct. 1996).

Regardless, "[n]otwithstanding any other provision of [CPL Article 240], the personal residence address of a police officer or correction officer shall not be required to be disclosed except pursuant to an order issued by a court following a finding of good cause." CPL § 240.50(4).

§ 20:48 Breathalyzer ampoules

Research References

West's Key Number Digest, Criminal Law ☞627.6(1)

Unlike newer, infrared breath testing instruments (such as the DataMaster, Intoxilyzer, Alcotest 7110 MK III, etc.), Breathalyzers utilize a chemical solution which comes in vacuum-sealed glass tubes. These tubes, together with the chemical solution contained therein, are commonly referred to as "ampoules." If the chemicals contained in the ampoule solution are not of the proper kind and mixed in the proper proportions, a Breathalyzer test result will not be accurate.

Although fairness would seem to dictate that the defense be provided, upon request, with a sample of the ampoule solution for independent testing, case law makes clear that no such right exists. *See, e.g., People v. Farrell*, 58 N.Y.2d 637, 458 N.Y.S.2d 514 (1982); *People v. DiLorenzo*, 134 Misc. 2d 1000, __, 513 N.Y.S.2d 938, 940 (Nassau Co. Ct. 1987); *People v. Torres*, 125 Misc. 2d 78, __, 478 N.Y.S.2d 771, 776 (N.Y. City Crim. Ct. 1984); *People v. Molina*, 121 Misc. 2d 483, 468 N.Y.S.2d 551 (N.Y. City Crim. Ct. 1983), *rev'd on other grounds*, 128 Misc. 2d 638, 494 N.Y.S.2d 606 (App. Term, 1st Dep't 1985); *People v. Santiago*, 116 Misc. 2d 340, 455 N.Y.S.2d 511 (N.Y. Co. Sup. Ct. 1982); *People v. LePree*, 105 Misc. 2d 1066, 430 N.Y.S.2d 778 (Rochester City Ct. 1980). *Cf. People v. Richter*, 102 Misc. 2d 285, 423 N.Y.S.2d 610 (Nassau Co. Dist. Ct. 1979).

By contrast, *the defendant does have "the option of examining another ampoule from the same batch along with the procedures required to authenticate the test results.*" Farrell, 58 N.Y.2d at 638, 458 N.Y.S.2d at 515 (emphasis added). *See also DiLorenzo*, 134 Misc. 2d at __, 513 N.Y.S.2d at 940.

§ 20:49 Discovery upon request pursuant to CPL § 240.20 is mandatory

Research References

West's Key Number Digest, Criminal Law ⚬627.5(1)

In *People v. DaGata*, 86 N.Y.2d 40, 44, 629 N.Y.S.2d 186, 189 (1995), the Court of Appeals stated that CPL "section 240.20 is generally construed as a mandatory directive, compelling the People to provide the items when sought by the defendant." *See also* CPL § 240.20(2) ("The prosecutor shall make a diligent, good faith effort to ascertain the existence of demanded property and to cause such property to be made available for discovery where it exists but is not within the prosecutor's possession, custody or control"); *People v. Jenkins*, 98 N.Y.2d 280, 284, 746 N.Y.S.2d 651, 654 (2002) ("Section 240.20 requires the People to furnish the items when sought by the defendant"); *People v. Corley*, 124 A.D.2d 390, __, 507 N.Y.S.2d 491, 493 (3d Dep't 1986) ("defendant's failure to move pursuant to CPL 240.40 to compel the People to produce this documentation did not constitute a waiver of his right to this information"); *People v. Smith*, 169 Misc. 2d 258, __, 646 N.Y.S.2d 228, 231 (Onondaga Co. Sup. Ct. 1996) ("There is no responsibility imposed by statute upon defense counsel").

In addition, the People are not permitted to assess the value of discoverable material to the defendant and unilaterally declare that such material is not exculpatory. Rather, the Court of Appeals has "often repeated that the best judge of the value of evidence to a defendant's case is 'the single-minded devotion of counsel for the accused.'" *DaGata*, 86 N.Y.2d at 45, 629 N.Y.S.2d at 189 (citation omitted).

§ 20:50 Accusatory instruments to which discovery pursuant to CPL § 240.20 is applicable

Research References

West's Key Number Digest, Criminal Law ⚬627.5(1)

By its express terms, discovery pursuant to CPL § 240.20 is only available "upon a demand to produce by a defendant against whom an indictment, superior court information, prosecutor's information, information, or simplified information *charging a misdemeanor* is pending." CPL § 240.20(1) (emphasis added). Accordingly, CPL § 240.20 discovery is not available to a defendant where the *sole* accusatory instrument is either:

(a) A misdemeanor or felony complaint. *See, e.g., Matter of Hynes v. Cirigliano*, 180 A.D.2d 659, __, 579 N.Y.S.2d 171, 171–72 (2d Dep't 1992); *People v. Hale*, 167 Misc. 2d 872, __, 638 N.Y.S.2d 886, 888 (Kings Co. Sup. Ct. 1996); *Matter of Faulkner v. Carney*, 166 Misc. 2d 886, __, 635 N.Y.S.2d 1019, 1021 (Schenectady Co. Sup. Ct. 1995); *People v. Woodson*, 165 Misc. 2d 784, __, 630 N.Y.S.2d 670, 673 (Queens Co. Sup. Ct. 1995); *People v. Arturo*, 122 Misc. 2d 1058, __, 472 N.Y.S.2d 998, 1003 (N.Y. City Crim. Ct. 1984); *People v. Delgado*, 110 Misc. 2d 492, __, 442 N.Y.S.2d 748, 750 (N.Y. City Crim. Ct. 1981); *People v. Webb*, 105 Misc. 2d 660, __, 432 N.Y.S.2d 826, 827 (N.Y. City Crim. Ct. 1980); or

(b) A simplified information *charging a traffic infraction or a violation. See, e.g., People v. Malone*, 166 Misc. 2d 54, __, 631 N.Y.S.2d 223, 224 (Suffolk Co. Dist. Ct. 1995); *People v. Chess*, 149 Misc. 2d 430, __, 565 N.Y.S.2d 416, 418 (Kensington Just. Ct. 1991); *People v. Guagnini*, 143 Misc. 2d 676, __, 541 N.Y.S.2d 907, 908 (Kensington Just. Ct. 1989); *People v. McGettrick*, 139 Misc. 2d 403, __, 528 N.Y.S.2d 758, 759 (Hudson City Ct. 1988); *People v. Cohen*, 131 Misc. 2d 898, __, 502 N.Y.S.2d 123, 124 (Yonkers City Ct. 1986). *See generally People v. Ross*, 110 Misc. 2d 818, 442 N.Y.S.2d 848 (Glens Falls City Ct. 1981).

In *McGettrick*, the court stated:

In 1983 the Legislature added the words, "simplified information charging a misdemeanor" to the list of pending accusatory instruments in [CPL §§ 240.20, 240.30 and [240.40]. Clearly, then, discovery is not authorized where the accusatory instrument is a simplified information charging a traffic infraction as in the instant case. Presumably the intent of the Legislature in enacting the 1983 amendment was to make it clear that discovery was available in Driving While Intoxicated cases. Although this was accomplished, no provision was made for those cases where the defendant is charged initially with Driving While Ability Impaired. This apparent Legislative oversight is unfortunate, since a defendant charged with Driving While Ability Impaired must confront the same evidence that a Driving While Intoxicated defendant must face. It seems fundamentally unfair to deny the Driving While Ability Impaired defendant the same discovery rights a Driving While Intoxicated defendant possesses. Nevertheless, the statute provides no authority for the court to order discovery, and accordingly, the motion for discovery is denied. However, since the District Attorney has consented to discovery of some items contained in defendant's motion, the court will bind the People to disclose such materials.

139 Misc. 2d at __, 528 N.Y.S.2d at 759 (citation omitted).

Nonetheless, the Court of Appeals has made clear that, in addition to the discovery provided for in CPL Article 240, other material or information can be discoverable as a matter of right based upon "overarching imperatives premised on *constitutional rights and fundamental fairness.*" *People v. Colavito*, 87 N.Y.2d 423, 426–27, 639 N.Y.S.2d 996, 999 (1996) (emphasis added). *See also* 87 N.Y.2d at 427, 639 N.Y.S.2d at 999 ("Voluntary inspection of [evidence not expressly covered by the CPL] may be prudent . . ., and ought in any event to be encouraged to help prevent delays and potential prejudice").

In *People v. Russo*, 149 A.D.2d 255, __, 545 N.Y.S.2d 211, 212 (2d Dep't 1989), the Appellate Division, Second Department, held that "[a] defendant charged with a violation of Vehicle and Traffic Law § 1180(b) is entitled to the issuance of a properly worded judicial subpoena duces tecum under CPLR 2307 requiring the production of relevant records at the hearing before the Traffic Violations Bureau." The *Russo* court distinguished *Matter of Miller v. Schwartz*, 72 N.Y.2d 869, 532 N.Y.S.2d 354 (1988), on the ground that:

> In *Miller*, the Court of Appeals was concerned solely with the discovery phase of the case and based its determination on the ground that the petitioner therein was not entitled to such pretrial discovery . . .
>
> Pretrial discovery is not sought here. Rather, the defendant has sought a subpoena duces tecum, to which he plainly has a statutory right under CPLR 2307, for the mere production at the hearing itself, not beforehand, of the very item upon which the People rely in bringing the instant charges of speeding . . .
>
> Accordingly, if the People rely upon radar evidence to establish the alleged excessive speed of the defendant's vehicle, then the defendant will be entitled to receive those records, if any, which document the maintenance and testing of the radar device.

149 A.D.2d at __-__, 545 N.Y.S.2d at 215–16.

It should be noted that discovery pursuant to CPL § 240.20 is available in cases charging violations if the accusatory instrument is an indictment, a superior court information, a prosecutor's information, and/or an information. *See, e.g., People v. Turck*, 178 Misc. 2d 892, __, 681 N.Y.S.2d 454, 455-56 (Sand Lake Just. Ct. 1998); *People v. All State Properties, LLC*, 29 Misc. 3d 201, __, 907 N.Y.S.2d 549, 552-53 (Hempstead Just. Ct. 2010).

§ 20:51   CPL § 240.30—Discovery available to People upon demand

Research References

West's Key Number Digest, Criminal Law ⊙⇒627.5(1)

CPL § 240.30 governs the People's right to discovery upon demand from the defendant. It provides as follows:

1. Except to the extent protected by court order, upon a demand to produce by the prosecutor, a defendant against whom an indictment, superior court information, prosecutor's information, information, or simplified information charging a misdemeanor is pending shall disclose and make available for inspection, photographing, copying or testing, subject to constitutional limitations:

(a) any written report or document, or portion thereof, concerning a physical or mental examination, or scientific test, experiment, or comparisons, made by or at the request or direction of, the defendant, if the defendant intends to introduce such report or document at trial, or if the defendant has filed a notice of intent to proffer psychiatric evidence and such report or document relates thereto, or if such report or document was made by a person, other than defendant, whom defendant intends to call as a witness at trial; and

(b) any photograph, drawing, tape or other electronic recording which the defendant intends to introduce at trial.

2. The defense shall make a diligent good faith effort to make such property available for discovery where it exists but the property is not within its possession, custody or control, provided, that the defendant shall not be required to obtain by subpoena duces tecum demanded material that the prosecutor may thereby obtain.

In *People v. O'Brien*, 140 A.D.3d 1325, __, 32 N.Y.S.3d 741, 744 (3d Dep't 2016), the Appellate Division, Third Department, held that "the outright preclusion of [defendant's proffered medical] evidence was an abuse of discretion" "[s]ince a less drastic remedy was readily available."

§ 20:52 Discovery pursuant to CPL §§ 240.20 and 240.30 need only be "disclosed" and "made available" to opposing party

Research References
West's Key Number Digest, Criminal Law ☞627.5(1)

To comply with their disclosure obligations under CPL § 240.20, the People need only (a) "disclose" discoverable material to the defendant, and (b) "make [such material] available for inspection, photographing, copying or testing." CPL § 240.20(1). *See also People v. Caussade*, 162 A.D.2d 4, __, 560 N.Y.S.2d 648, 653 (2d Dep't 1990); *People v. Cole*, 90 A.D.2d 27, __, 457 N.Y.S.2d 589, 590 (3d Dep't 1982). In other words, the law does not require the People to actually deliver a copy of CPL § 240.20 discovery to the defendant. *See generally* CPL § 240.30 (the same rule applies to discovery upon demand of the People).

In addition, CPL § 240.70(3) provides that "[a] fee for copies of records required to be disclosed may be charged. Such fee shall not exceed [25] cents per photocopy not in excess of [9] inches by [14] inches, or the actual cost of reproducing any other record, except when a different fee is otherwise prescribed by law."

§ 20:53   Duty to disclose discoverable material is a continuing duty

Research References

West's Key Number Digest, Criminal Law ☞627.5(1)

CPL § 240.60 provides that:

If, after complying with the provisions of [CPL Article 240] or an order pursuant thereto, a party finds, either before or during trial, additional material subject to discovery or covered by such order, he shall promptly comply with the demand or order, refuse to comply with the demand where refusal is authorized, or apply for a protective order.

§ 20:54   Motion to compel discovery—Procedure for filing

Research References

West's Key Number Digest, Criminal Law ☞627.8(3)

CPL § 240.90 provides the procedure for filing a motion to compel discovery:

1. A motion by a prosecutor for discovery shall be made within [45] days after arraignment, but for good cause shown may be made at any time before commencement of trial.

2. A motion by a defendant for discovery shall be made as prescribed in [CPL § 255.20].

3. Where the interests of justice so require, the court may permit a party to a motion for an order of discovery or a protective order, or other affected person, to submit papers or to testify ex parte or in camera. Any such papers and transcript of such testimony shall be sealed, but shall constitute a part of the record on appeal.

§ 20:55   Motion to compel discovery—By the defendant

Research References

West's Key Number Digest, Criminal Law ☞627.8(3)

Motions by the defendant to compel discovery are governed by CPL § 240.40(1), which provides, in pertinent part, that:

Upon motion of a defendant against whom an indictment, superior court information, prosecutor's information, information, or simplified information charging a misdemeanor is pending, the court in which such accusatory instrument is pending:

(a) must order discovery as to any material not disclosed upon a demand pursuant to [CPL §] 240.20, if it finds that the prosecutor's refusal to disclose such material is not justified;

(b) must, unless it is satisfied that the people have shown good cause why such an order should not be issued, order discovery or any other order authorized by [CPL § 240.70(1)] as to any material not disclosed upon demand pursuant to [CPL §] 240.20 where the prosecutor has failed to serve a timely written refusal pursuant to [CPL §] 240.35; and

(c) may order discovery with respect to any other property, which the people intend to introduce at the trial, upon a showing by the defendant that discovery with respect to such property is material to the preparation of his defense, and that the request is reasonable.

Notably, CPL § 240.40(1)(c) expressly permits a court, in certain circumstances, to compel discovery of property *not* listed in CPL § 240.20. *People v. Colavito*, 87 N.Y.2d 423, 427, 639 N.Y.S.2d 996, 999 (1996) ("in the sound exercise of responsible discretion, the trial court may order early prosecutorial disclosure under certain defined circumstances (*see*, CPL 240.40[1][c])"). It also makes clear that, if disclosure pursuant thereto is ordered, "the court shall, upon motion of the people showing such to be material to the preparation of their case and that the request is reasonable, condition its order of discovery by further directing discovery by the people of property, of the same kind or character as that authorized to be inspected by the defendant, which he intends to introduce at the trial." CPL § 240.40(1)(c).

The official Practice Commentaries to CPL § 240.40 provide, in pertinent part, that:

Subdivision one serves two functions: (1) paragraphs (a) and (b) provide a vehicle for court enforcement of defendant disclosure demands where there is no justifiable reason for the People's refusal, or the People did not serve a timely written refusal and are unable to show good cause for failure to disclose material covered by § 240.20; and (2) paragraph (c) authorizes court orders for defendant's discovery of unspecified evidence material to defendant's defense—*i.e.*, such as is deemed within defendant's constitutional right of access to evidence.

Preiser, Practice Commentaries, McKinney's Cons. Laws of N.Y., Book 11A, CPL § 240.40, at 416.

"An order pursuant to [CPL § 240.40] may be denied, limited or conditioned as provided in [CPL §] 240.50." CPL § 240.40(3).

§ 20:56   Motion to compel discovery—By the People

Research References

West's Key Number Digest, Criminal Law ⬠627.8(3)

Motions by the People to compel discovery are governed by CPL § 240.40(2), which provides as follows:

Upon motion of the prosecutor, and subject to constitutional limitation, the court in which an indictment, superior court information, prosecutor's information, information, or simplified information charging a misdemeanor is pending:

(a) must order discovery as to any property not disclosed upon a demand pursuant to [CPL §] 240.30, if it finds that the defendant's refusal to disclose such material is not justified; and

(b) may order the defendant to provide non-testimonial evidence. Such order may, among other things, require the defendant to:

(i) Appear in a line-up;

(ii) Speak for identification by witness or potential witness;

(iii) Be fingerprinted;

(iv) Pose for photographs not involving reenactment of an event;

(v) Permit the taking of samples of blood, hair or other materials from his body in a manner not involving an unreasonable intrusion thereof or a risk of serious physical injury thereto;

(vi) Provide specimens of his handwriting;

(vii) Submit to a reasonable physical or medical inspection of his body.

This subdivision shall not be construed to limit, expand, or otherwise affect the issuance of a similar court order, as may be authorized by law, before the filing of an accusatory instrument consistent with such rights as the defendant may derive from the constitution of this state or of the United States. This section shall not be construed to limit or otherwise affect the administration of a chemical test where otherwise authorized pursuant to [VTL § 1194-a (currently VTL § 1194[3])].

See generally People v. Moselle, 57 N.Y.2d 97, 106–10, 454 N.Y.S.2d 292, 295–97 (1982).

"An order pursuant to [CPL § 240.40] may be denied, limited or conditioned as provided in [CPL §] 240.50." CPL § 240.40(3).

In *Matter of Abe A.*, 56 N.Y.2d 288, 291, 452 N.Y.S.2d 6, 7 (1982), the Court of Appeals held that:

> [A] court order to obtain a blood sample of a suspect may issue provided the People establish (1) probable cause to believe the suspect has committed the crime, (2) a "clear indication" that relevant material evidence will be found, and (3) the method used to secure it is safe and reliable. In addition, the issuing court must weigh the seriousness of the crime, the importance of the evidence to the investigation and the unavailability of less intrusive means of obtaining it, on the one hand, against concern for the suspect's constitutional right to be free from bodily intrusion on the other. Only if this stringent standard is met, as we conclude it was here, may the intrusion be sustained.

In so holding, the Court stated, inter alia, that "the method by which the authorized intrusion is to be accomplished must be safe, reliable and impose no more physical discomfort than is reasonably necessary. **When, as here, the body is to be invaded, the procedure should be carried out by a qualified physician in accordance with accepted medical standards.**" 56 N.Y.2d at 297–98, 452 N.Y.S.2d at 11 (emphasis added) (citations omitted). *See generally Schmerber v. California*, 384 U.S. 757, 771–72, 86 S.Ct. 1826, 1836 (1966).

In *People v. Afrika*, 13 A.D.3d 1218, __, 787 N.Y.S.2d 774, 776-77 (4th Dep't 2004), the Appellate Division, Fourth Department, reiterated the rule that a Court-ordered blood test must be supported by probable cause:

> We note at the outset that we reject the contention of the People that they could obtain a sample of defendant's blood without a showing of probable cause. Although CPL 240.40(2)(b)(v) does not explicitly require a showing of probable cause, that section is "subject to constitutional limitation" (240.40 [2]). In *Matter of Abe A.*, the Court of Appeals determined that probable cause must be shown before obtaining a blood sample from a defendant in order to safeguard his or her Fourth Amendment rights. Thus, CPL 240.40 does not vitiate the requirement that the People must establish probable cause before obtaining an order authorizing them to obtain a blood sample from a defendant.

(Citation omitted).

§ 20:57 Failure to comply with court-ordered discovery can result in preclusion

Research References

West's Key Number Digest, Criminal Law ⚖627.8(6)

While courts often impose seemingly minimal sanctions on the People for the loss of, destruction of, or delay in providing discoverable material, they are far less forgiving when the People fail to comply with court-ordered discovery—which frequently results in preclusion. *See, e.g., Matter of Santucci v. Rotker*, 110 A.D.2d 842, __, 488 N.Y.S.2d 244, 245 (2d Dep't 1985); *People v. Smith*, 169 Misc. 2d 258, __, 646 N.Y.S.2d 228, 231 (Onondaga Co. Sup. Ct. 1996). *See generally People v. Fields*, 258 A.D.2d 809, __, 687 N.Y.S.2d 184, 186 (3d Dep't 1999); *People v. Ariosa*, 172 Misc. 2d 312, __, 660 N.Y.S.2d 255, 257 (Monroe Co. Ct. 1997) (appropriate remedy for People's "gross failure to fulfill their discovery, *Rosario* and *Brady* obligations" was dismissal); *People v. Cortez*, 149 Misc. 2d 886, 564 N.Y.S.2d 963 (N.Y. City Crim. Ct. 1990) (appropriate remedy for erasure of subpoenaed police communication tapes was dismissal).

§ 20:58 Where court orders discovery in excess of that authorized by CPL Article 240, writ of prohibition will lie

Research References

West's Key Number Digest, Criminal Law ⬅627.5(1)

"During the course of a criminal action, it is not within the authorized powers of the courts to compel disclosure which is not provided for in CPL article 240, and attempts to do so generally warrant issuance of a writ of prohibition." *Matter of Pittari v. Pirro*, 258 A.D.2d 202, __, 696 N.Y.S.2d 167, 171 (2d Dep't 1999) (citations omitted). *See also Matter of Sacket v. Bartlett*, 241 A.D.2d 97, __, 671 N.Y.S.2d 156, 159 (3d Dep't 1998); *Matter of Pirro v. LaCava*, 230 A.D.2d 909, __, 646 N.Y.S.2d 866, 867 (2d Dep't 1996).

§ 20:59 Bill of particulars—Defined

Research References

West's Key Number Digest, Criminal Law ⬅627.6(2)

[A] "[b]ill of particulars" is a written statement by the prosecutor specifying, as required by [CPL § 200.95], items of factual information which are not recited in the indictment and which pertain to the offense charged and including the substance of each defendant's conduct encompassed by the charge which the people intend to prove at trial on their direct case, and whether the people intend to prove that the defendant acted as principal or accomplice or both, and the items of factual information which are not recited in a special forfeiture information or prosecutor's forfeiture information containing one or more forfeiture counts and which pertain to the substance of each defendant's conduct giving rise to the forfeiture claim, the approximate value of the property for which forfeiture is sought, the nature and extent of the defendant's interest in such property, and the extent of the defendant's gain, if any, from the offense charged. However, the prosecutor shall not be required to include in the bill of particulars matters of evidence relating to how the people intend to prove the elements of the offense charged or how the people intend to prove any item of factual information included in the bill of particulars.

CPL § 200.95(1)(a).

CPL § 100.45(4) provides that "[t]he provisions of [CPL § 200.95], governing bills of particulars with respect to indictments, apply to informations, to misdemeanor complaints and to prosecutor's informations." As such, "[a] defendant is not entitled to a bill of particulars when the underlying accusatory instrument is a simplified information (*see* CPL 100.45(4))." *People v. Malone*, 166 Misc. 2d 54, __, 631 N.Y.S.2d 223, 223 (Suffolk Co. Dist. Ct. 1995). *See also People v. Rose*, 8 Misc. 3d 184, __, 794 N.Y.S.2d 630, 633 (Nassau Co. Dist. Ct. 2005); *People v. Turck*, 178 Misc. 2d 892, __, 681 N.Y.S.2d 454, 455 (Sand Lake Just. Ct. 1998); *People v. McGettrick*, 139 Misc. 2d 403, __, 528 N.Y.S.2d 758, 758 (Hudson City Ct. 1988); *People v. Cohen*, 131 Misc. 2d 898, __, 502 N.Y.S.2d 123, 124 (Yonkers City Ct. 1986).

Where the accusatory instrument is a long-form information, the rules governing bills of particulars apply regardless of whether the defendant is charged with a misdemeanor or a violation. *Turck*, 178 Misc. 2d at __, 681 N.Y.S.2d at 455–56. *See also People v. All State Properties, LLC*, 29 Misc. 3d 201, __, 907 N.Y.S.2d 549, 553 (Hempstead Just. Ct. 2010).

§ 20:60 Request for a bill of particulars—Defined

Research References
West's Key Number Digest, Criminal Law ⚖627.6(2)

"[A] '[r]equest for a bill of particulars' is a written request served by defendant upon the people, without leave of the court, requesting a bill of particulars, specifying the items of factual information desired, and alleging that defendant cannot adequately prepare or conduct his defense without the information requested." CPL § 200.95(1)(b).

The Court of Appeals has indicated that the failure to include an allegation "that defendant cannot adequately prepare or conduct his defense without the information requested" in a request for a bill of particulars is not a fatal defect. *See People v. Villani*, 59 N.Y.2d 781, 783–84, 464 N.Y.S.2d 726, 727 (1983).

§ 20:61 Bill of particulars is not a discovery device

Research References
West's Key Number Digest, Criminal Law ⚖627.6(2)

"A bill of particulars serves to clarify the pleading; it is not a discovery device." *People v. Davis*, 41 N.Y.2d 678, 680, 394 N.Y.S.2d 865, 867 (1977). Nonetheless:

> A word of caution is in order. It is beyond cavil that a defendant has a basic and fundamental right to be informed of the charges against him so that he will be able to prepare a defense. Hence the courts must exercise careful surveillance to ensure that a defendant is not deprived of this right by an overzealous prosecutor attempting to protect his case or his witnesses. Any effort to leave a defendant in ignorance of the substance of the accusation until the time of trial must be firmly rebuffed. This is especially so where the indictment itself provides a paucity of information. In such cases, **the court must be vigilant in safeguarding the defendant's rights to a bill of particulars and to effective discovery**. Should the prosecutor decide to use an indictment which, although technically sufficient, does not adequately allow a defendant to properly prepare for trial, he may well run afoul of the defendant's right to be informed of the accusations against him.

People v. Iannone, 45 N.Y.2d 589, 599, 412 N.Y.S.2d 110, 117 (1978) (emphasis added).

§ 20:62   Accusatory instruments to which bill of particulars is applicable

Research References
West's Key Number Digest, Criminal Law ⚖627.6(2)

CPL § 100.45(4) provides that "[t]he provisions of [CPL § 200.95], governing bills of particulars with respect to indictments, apply to informations, to misdemeanor complaints and to prosecutor's informations." Thus, "[a] defendant is not entitled to a bill of particulars when the underlying accusatory instrument is a simplified information (*see* CPL 100.45(4))." *People v. Malone*, 166 Misc. 2d 54, __, 631 N.Y.S.2d 223, 223 (Suffolk Co. Dist. Ct. 1995). *See also People v. Rose*, 8 Misc. 3d 184, __, 794 N.Y.S.2d 630, 633 (Nassau Co. Dist. Ct. 2005); *People v. Turck*, 178 Misc. 2d 892, __, 681 N.Y.S.2d 454, 455 (Sand Lake Just. Ct. 1998); *People v. McGettrick*, 139 Misc. 2d 403, __, 528 N.Y.S.2d 758, 758 (Hudson City Ct. 1988); *People v. Cohen*, 131 Misc. 2d 898, __, 502 N.Y.S.2d 123, 124 (Yonkers City Ct. 1986).

Where the accusatory instrument is a long-form information, the rules governing bills of particulars apply regardless of whether the defendant is charged with a misdemeanor or a violation. *Turck*, 178 Misc. 2d at __, 681 N.Y.S.2d at 455–56. *See also People v. All State Properties, LLC*, 29 Misc. 3d 201, __, 907 N.Y.S.2d 549, 553 (Hempstead Just. Ct. 2010).

§ 20:63 Bill of particulars cannot cure a deficient information

Research References

West's Key Number Digest, Criminal Law ⚷627.6(2)

"Because an information must, for jurisdictional purposes, contain nonhearsay factual allegations sufficient to establish a prima facie case, a prosecutor's hearsay statements, set forth in a bill of particulars, cannot supply necessary factual allegations to cure a deficient information." *People v. Alejandro*, 70 N.Y.2d 133, 138, 517 N.Y.S.2d 927, 930 (1987).

§ 20:64 Bill of particulars—Timeliness of request therefor

Research References

West's Key Number Digest, Criminal Law ⚷627.8(2)

CPL § 200.95(3) provides that:

A request for a bill of particulars shall be timely if made within [30] days after arraignment and before the commencement of trial. If the defendant is not represented by counsel, and has requested an adjournment to obtain counsel or to have counsel assigned, the [30] day period shall commence, for the purposes of a request for a bill of particulars by the defendant, on the date counsel initially appears on his behalf. However, the court may direct compliance with a request for a bill of particulars that, for good cause shown, could not have been made within the time specified.

§ 20:65 Bill of particulars—Time for compliance therewith

Research References

West's Key Number Digest, Criminal Law ⚷627.8(2)

CPL § 200.95(2) provides that:

Upon a timely request for a bill of particulars by a defendant against whom an indictment is pending, the prosecutor shall within [15] days of the service of the request or as soon thereafter as is practicable, serve upon the defendant or his attorney, and file with the court, the bill of particulars, except to the extent the prosecutor shall have refused to comply with the request pursuant to [CPL § 200.95(4)].

§ 20:66 Bill of particulars—Refusal to comply therewith

Research References

West's Key Number Digest, Criminal Law ⚷627.6(2)

CPL § 200.95(4) provides that:

The prosecutor may refuse to comply with the request for a bill of particulars or any portion of the request for a bill of particulars to the extent he reasonably believes that the item of factual information requested is not authorized to be included in a bill of particulars, or that such information is not necessary to enable the defendant adequately to prepare or conduct his defense, or that a protective order would be warranted or that the demand is untimely. **Such refusal shall be made in a writing, which shall set forth the grounds of such belief as fully as possible, consistent with the reason for the refusal**. Within [15] days of the request or as soon thereafter as practicable, the refusal shall be served upon the defendant and a copy shall be filed with the court.

(Emphasis added).

§ 20:67   Bill of particulars—Amendment

Research References

West's Key Number Digest, Criminal Law ☜627.6(2)

CPL § 200.95(8) provides that:

At any time before commencement of trial, the prosecutor may, without leave of the court, serve upon defendant and file with the court an amended bill of particulars. At any time during trial, upon application of the prosecutor and with notice to the defendant and an opportunity for him to be heard, the court must, upon finding that no undue prejudice will accrue to defendant and that the prosecutor has acted in good faith, permit the prosecutor to amend the bill of particulars. Upon any amendment of the bill of particulars, the court must, upon application of defendant, order an adjournment of the proceedings or any other action it deems appropriate which may, by reason of the amendment, be necessary to accord the defendant an adequate opportunity to defend.

§ 20:68   Court-ordered bill of particulars—Generally

Research References

West's Key Number Digest, Criminal Law ☜627.6(2)

CPL § 200.95(5) provides that:

Where a prosecutor has timely served a written refusal pursuant to [CPL § 200.95(4)] and upon motion, made in writing, of a defendant, who has made a request for a bill of particulars and whose request has not been complied with in whole or in part, the court must, to the extent a protective order is not warranted, order the prosecutor to comply with the request if it is satisfied that the items of factual information requested are authorized to be included in a bill of particulars, and that such information is necessary to enable the defendant adequately to prepare or conduct his defense and, if the request was untimely, a finding of good cause for the delay. Where a prosecutor has not timely served a written refusal pursuant to [CPL § 200.95(4)] the court must, unless it is satisfied that the people have shown good cause why such an order should not be issued, issue an order requiring the prosecutor to comply or providing for any other order authorized by [CPL § 240.70(1)].

§ 20:69 Court-ordered bill of particulars—Motion procedure

Research References

West's Key Number Digest, Criminal Law ☜627.6(2)

CPL § 200.95(6) provides that:

A motion for a bill of particulars shall be made as prescribed in [CPL §] 255.20. Upon an order granting a motion pursuant to this section, the prosecutor must file with the court a bill of particulars, reciting every item of information designated in the order, and serve a copy thereof upon the defendant. Pending such filing and service, the proceedings are stayed.

§ 20:70 Bill of particulars in criminal negligence case

Research References

West's Key Number Digest, Criminal Law ☜627.6(2)

In *People v. Fitzgerald*, 45 N.Y.2d 574, 580, 412 N.Y.S.2d 102, 105 (1978), the Court of Appeals held that:

[A] person accused of causing death or injury by acting with "criminal negligence" is entitled to know specifically what conduct on his part involved a "substantial and unjustifiable risk" of death or injury and "a gross deviation" from the standard of reasonable care. That information, however, may be provided by a bill of particulars which is designed to insure that the defendant is supplied with sufficient information to properly prepare his defense.

(Citation omitted). It should be noted that the second sentence quoted above is inapplicable to long-form informations, as "a prosecutor's hearsay statements, set forth in a bill of particulars, cannot supply necessary factual allegations to cure a deficient information." *People v. Alejandro*, 70 N.Y.2d 133, 138, 517 N.Y.S.2d 927, 930 (1987).

§ 20:71 Delay in providing bill of particulars generally does not affect People's readiness for trial

Research References

West's Key Number Digest, Criminal Law ☜627.6(2)

As a general rule, the People's delay in providing a bill of particulars does not affect their readiness for trial for purposes of CPL § 30.30. *See People v. Cole*, 90 A.D.2d 27, __, 457 N.Y.S.2d 589, 590–91 (3d Dep't 1982).

§ 20:72 Protective orders—Generally

Research References

West's Key Number Digest, Criminal Law ☞627.5(1)

CPL § 240.50(1) provides that:

The court in which the criminal action is pending may, upon motion of either party, or of any affected person, or upon determination of a motion of either party for an order of discovery, or upon its
own initiative, issue a protective order denying, limiting, conditioning, delaying or regulating discovery pursuant to [CPL Article 240]
for good cause, including constitutional limitations, danger to the
integrity of physical evidence or a substantial risk of physical harm,
intimidation, economic reprisal, bribery or unjustified annoyance or
embarrassment to any person or an adverse effect upon the legitimate needs of law enforcement, including the protection of the
confidentiality of informants, or any other factor or set of factors
which outweighs the usefulness of the discovery.

The same rule applies to bills of particulars. *See* CPL
§ 200.95(7)(a).

§ 20:73 Protective order can require that discovery be kept in exclusive possession of attorney for discovering party

Research References

West's Key Number Digest, Criminal Law ☞627.5(1)

CPL § 240.50(2) provides that:

An order limiting, conditioning, delaying or regulating discovery
may, among other things, require that any material copied or
derived therefrom be maintained in the exclusive possession of the
attorney for the discovering party and be used for the exclusive
purpose of preparing for the defense or prosecution of the criminal
action.

The same rule applies to bills of particulars. *See* CPL
§ 200.95(7)(b).

§ 20:74 Motion for protective order suspends discovery

Research References

West's Key Number Digest, Criminal Law ☞627.8(3)

CPL § 240.50(3) provides that "[a] motion for a protective order
shall suspend discovery of the particular matter in dispute."

§ 20:75 Protection of personal residence addresses of police and correction officers

Research References

West's Key Number Digest, Criminal Law ☞627.5(1)

CPL § 240.50(4) provides that "[n]otwithstanding any other provision of [CPL Article 240], the personal residence address of a police officer or correction officer shall not be required to be disclosed except pursuant to an order issued by a court following a finding of good cause."

§ 20:76 CPL § 240.43—Discovery of prior uncharged criminal, vicious, or immoral conduct of the defendant—Generally

Research References

West's Key Number Digest, Criminal Law ☞627.5(1)

CPL § 240.43 provides that "the prosecutor shall notify the defendant of all specific instances of a defendant's prior uncharged criminal, vicious or immoral conduct of which the prosecutor has knowledge and which the prosecutor intends to use at trial for purposes of impeaching the credibility of the defendant."

In *People v. Dokes*, 79 N.Y.2d 656, 661 n.3, 584 N.Y.S.2d 761, 764 n.3 (1992), the Court of Appeals noted that:

> In *People v. Matthews*, 68 N.Y.2d 118, 121–122, 506 N.Y.S.2d 149, 497 N.E.2d 287) we held that the defendant bears the burden of bringing to the court's attention those prior bad acts about which he seeks to preclude cross-examination by the People. The 1987 enactment of CPL 240.43 modified that holding to the extent of permitting the defendant to require the prosecution to notify him of any *uncharged* bad acts that it intends to use at trial for impeachment purposes.

See also People v. Ventimiglia, 52 N.Y.2d 350, 438 N.Y.S.2d 261 (1981).

§ 20:77 Discovery pursuant to CPL § 240.43 is only available upon request

Research References

West's Key Number Digest, Criminal Law ☞627.8(3)

CPL § 240.43 makes clear that discovery thereunder is only available "[u]pon a request by a defendant." Accordingly, absent a request therefor, the defendant will be found to have waived his or her right to discovery pursuant to CPL § 240.43. *See People v. Woods*, 185 A.D.2d 687, __, 586 N.Y.S.2d 62, 63 (4th Dep't 1992).

§ 20:78 Time for disclosure of CPL § 240.43 discovery

Research References

West's Key Number Digest, Criminal Law ☞627.8(2)

CPL § 240.43 provides that notification by the People pursuant thereto:

[S]hall be made immediately prior to the commencement of jury selection, except that the court may, in its discretion, order such notification and make its determination as to the admissibility for impeachment purposes of such conduct within a period of three days, excluding Saturdays, Sundays and holidays, prior to the commencement of jury selection.

§ 20:79   CPL § 240.44—Discovery upon pretrial hearing of prior statements and criminal history of witnesses—Generally

Research References

West's Key Number Digest, Criminal Law ☞627.5(1)

CPL § 240.44 provides for the following discovery at a pretrial hearing:

Subject to a protective order, at a pretrial hearing held in a criminal court at which a witness is called to testify, each party, at the conclusion of the direct examination of each of its witnesses, shall, upon request of the other party, make available to that party to the extent not previously disclosed:

1. Any written or recorded statement, including any testimony before a grand jury, made by such witness other than the defendant which relates to the subject matter of the witness's testimony.

2. A record of a judgment of conviction of such witness other than the defendant if the record of conviction is known by the prosecutor or defendant, as the case may be, to exist.

3. The existence of any pending criminal action against such witness other than the defendant if the pending criminal action is known by the prosecutor or defendant, as the case may be, to exist.

The official Practice Commentaries to CPL § 240.44 provide, in pertinent part, that:

Subdivision one of this section simply codifies the proposition—previously made unmistakably clear by the Court of Appeals—that the exchange of *Rosario* material is required at any pretrial hearing. *People v. Malinsky*, 15 N.Y.2d 86, 262 N.Y.S.2d 65, 209 N.E.2d 694 (1965) . . .

Subdivisions two and three furnish the defendant as a matter of legislative policy with ammunition for impeachment cross-examination of the People's witnesses. Subdivision three is especially valuable, as it opens the door to exploration of whether any promise of leniency has been given in return for favorable testimony.

Preiser, Practice Commentaries, McKinney's Cons. Laws of N.Y., Book 11A, CPL § 240.44, at 446. *See also People v. Banch*, 80 N.Y.2d 610, 615, 593 N.Y.S.2d 491, 494 (1992). *See generally People v. McPhee*, 161 Misc. 2d 660, 614 N.Y.S.2d 884 (Queens Co. Sup. Ct. 1994) (CPL § 240.44, by its express and unambiguous terms, applies to *any* pretrial hearing—such as competency hearing); *People v. Diggs*, 140 Misc. 2d 794, 531 N.Y.S.2d 723 (Nassau Co. Dist. Ct. 1988) (CPL § 240.44 applies to CPL § 180.60 preliminary hearing).

The issue of *Rosario* material is discussed at length in §§ 28:1 et seq., *infra*.

§ 20:80   Discovery pursuant to CPL § 240.44 is only available upon request

Research References

West's Key Number Digest, Criminal Law ☞627.8(3)

CPL § 240.44 makes clear that discovery thereunder is only available "*upon request* of the other party." (Emphasis added). *See generally People v. Zephir*, 226 A.D.2d 408, __, 640 N.Y.S.2d 584, 585 (2d Dep't 1996); *People v. Duprey*, 174 A.D.2d 835, __, 571 N.Y.S.2d 137, 138 (3d Dep't 1991). Accordingly, absent a timely request therefor, a party will be found to have waived its right to pretrial hearing discovery pursuant to CPL § 240.44.

§ 20:81   Time for disclosure of CPL § 240.44 discovery

Research References

West's Key Number Digest, Criminal Law ☞627.8(2)

Although the disclosure of pretrial hearing discovery pursuant to CPL § 240.44 typically takes place prior to the commencement of the hearing, the statute states that a party can make such disclosure "at the conclusion of the direct examination of each of its witnesses." Even though such belated disclosure often results in a significant waste of scarce judicial resources (since counsel must be afforded adequate time to review the material), it appears that courts are powerless to order a party to make earlier disclosure. *See, e.g., Matter of Pittari v. Pirro*, 258 A.D.2d 202, __, 696 N.Y.S.2d 167, 171 (2d Dep't 1999); *People v. Zephir*, 226 A.D.2d 408, __, 640 N.Y.S.2d 584, 585 (2d Dep't 1996); *Matter of Catterson v. Rohl*, 202 A.D.2d 420, __, 608 N.Y.S.2d 696, 699 (2d Dep't 1994).

§ 20:82   Remedy for CPL § 240.44 violation is a "reopened" hearing

Research References

West's Key Number Digest, Criminal Law ☞627.5(1)

In *People v. Banch*, 80 N.Y.2d 610, 618, 593 N.Y.S.2d 491, 496 (1992), the Court of Appeals held that "a defendant is entitled to a new hearing as a remedy for a pretrial *Rosario* violation, without inquiry into prejudice." In so holding, the *Banch* Court made clear that the trial court cannot simply review the *Rosario* material and determine its value to the defense, as " 'a judge's impartial determination as to what portions [of *Rosario* material] may be useful to the defense, is no substitute for the single-minded devotion of counsel for the accused,' " and " 'there is no way, short of speculation, of determining how it might have been used or how its denial to counsel might have damaged defendant's case.' " 80 N.Y.2d at 618, 593 N.Y.S.2d at 496 (citations omitted). In addition, the Court noted "that the remedy for a pretrial *Rosario* violation is not automatic reversal of the conviction but a new hearing. Retrial is necessary only if, after that hearing, the motion court concludes that defendant should prevail." 80 N.Y.2d at 619, 593 N.Y.S.2d at 496.

In *People v. Feerick*, 93 N.Y.2d 433, 451, 692 N.Y.S.2d 638, 647 (1999), the Court of Appeals reaffirmed its holding in *Banch*, but held that "[a]lthough *Banch* states a 'new' hearing should be granted," and "[a]lthough some *Rosario* violations may require or lead to . . . a 'full blown' hearing," under the circumstances presented the rationale of *Rosario* only required (a) that the pretrial hearing be "reopened" to the extent necessary to explore the contents of the *Rosario* documents, and (b) that a "new" ruling be issued by the hearing court.

CPL § 240.75 partially affects the *Banch/Feerick* rule. Specifically, CPL § 240.75 provides that:

> The failure of the prosecutor or any agent of the prosecutor to disclose statements that are required to be disclosed under [CPL § 240.44(1)] . . . shall not constitute grounds for any court to order a new pre-trial hearing or set aside a conviction, or reverse, modify or vacate a judgment of conviction in the absence of a showing by the defendant that there is a reasonable possibility that the nondisclosure materially contributed to the result of the trial or other proceeding; *provided, however, that nothing in this section shall affect or limit any right the defendant may have to a re-opened pretrial hearing when such statements were disclosed before the close of evidence at trial.*

(Emphasis added).

In other words, if a pretrial hearing *Rosario* violation is disclosed *prior to* the close of evidence at trial, *Banch* and *Feerick* still apply. By contrast, if the disclosure occurs *after* the close of evidence at trial, CPL § 240.75 provides that the pretrial hearing will not be reopened "in the absence of a showing by the defendant that there is a reasonable possibility that the nondisclosure materially contributed to the result of the trial or other proceeding." *See also* §§ 28:1 et seq., *infra*.

§ 20:83 CPL § 240.45(1)—Discovery upon trial by the defendant of prior statements and criminal history of witnesses

Research References

West's Key Number Digest, Criminal Law ☞627.5(1)

CPL § 240.45(1) provides for the following discovery at trial:

After the jury has been sworn and before the prosecutor's opening address, or in the case of a single judge trial after commencement and before submission of evidence, the prosecutor shall, subject to a protective order, make available to the defendant:

(a) Any written or recorded statement, including any testimony before a grand jury and an examination videotaped pursuant to [CPL § 190.32], made by a person whom the prosecutor intends to call as a witness at trial, and which relates to the subject matter of the witness's testimony;

(b) A record of judgment of conviction of a witness the people intend to call at trial if the record of conviction is known by the prosecutor to exist;

(c) The existence of any pending criminal action against a witness the people intend to call at trial, if the pending criminal action is known by the prosecutor to exist.

The provisions of paragraphs (b) and (c) of this subdivision shall not be construed to require the prosecutor to fingerprint a witness or otherwise cause the division of criminal justice services or other law enforcement agency or court to issue a report concerning a witness.

Subdivision (1)(a) merely codifies the rule of *People v. Rosario*, 9 N.Y.2d 286, 213 N.Y.S.2d 448 (1961). The issue of *Rosario* material is discussed at length in §§ 28:1 et seq., *infra*.

"Paragraphs (b) and (c) of subdivision one furnish the defendant as a matter of legislative policy with ammunition for impeachment cross-examination of the People's witnesses. Paragraph (c) is especially valuable, as it opens the door to exploration of whether any promise of leniency has been given in return for favorable testimony." Preiser, Practice Commentaries, McKinney's Cons. Laws of N.Y., Book 11A, CPL § 240.45, at 9–10.

It should be noted that CPL 240.45(1)(b) "only requires that a prosecutor disclose a record of a judgment of conviction of a prosecution witness 'if the record of conviction is known by the prosecutor to exist.'" *People v. Ingraham*, 274 A.D.2d 828, __, 711 N.Y.S.2d 863, 865 (3d Dep't 2000) (citation omitted). *See also People v. Clark*, 228 A.D.2d 326, __, 644 N.Y.S.2d 236, 237 (1st Dep't 1996). *Cf. Matter of Williams v. Erie County District Attorney*, 255 A.D.2d 863, __, 682 N.Y.S.2d 316, 318 (4th Dep't 1998) ("the disclosure of criminal history records by a District Attorney is required, provided such records are limited to criminal convictions and pending criminal actions of witnesses called by the People in a criminal trial").

"[A]djournments in contemplation of dismissal [ACODs or ACDs] . . . are not *convictions* . . . but instead are considered *pending charges* to be disclosed pursuant to CPL 240.45(1)(c)." *People v. Clark*, 194 A.D.2d 868, __ n.2, 598 N.Y.S.2d 847, 849 n.2 (3d Dep't 1993) (emphases added). *See also People v. Benjamin*, 147 Misc. 2d 617, __, 558 N.Y.S.2d 825, 827 (N.Y. City Crim. Ct. 1990).

A youthful offender adjudication is not a judgment of conviction for purposes of CPL § 240.45(1)(b), but a defendant is "entitled, for purposes of impeachment, to cross-examine that witness with respect to the acts underlying his youthful offender adjudication." *People v. Fyffe*, 249 A.D.2d 938, __, 672 N.Y.S.2d 552, 553 (4th Dep't 1998).

A juvenile delinquency adjudication is not a criminal conviction for purposes of CPL § 240.45(1)(b), but it may constitute *Brady* material. *People v. Bennett*, 273 A.D.2d 914, __, 709 N.Y.S.2d 773, 774 (4th Dep't 2000).

It is unclear whether a disorderly conduct conviction must be disclosed pursuant to CPL § 240.45(1)(b); however, if such conviction comes to light, defense counsel is entitled to pursue the matter on cross-examination. *See People v. Osborne*, 91 N.Y.2d 827, 828, 666 N.Y.S.2d 556, 556 (1997); *People v. Bennett*, 273 A.D.2d 914, __, 709 N.Y.S.2d 773, 774 (4th Dep't 2000).

In *People v. Buckley*, 131 Misc. 2d 744, __, 501 N.Y.S.2d 554, 557 (Monroe Co. Sup. Ct. 1986), the court expressly rejected the final paragraph of CPL § 240.45(1) (which provides that the People are not required to cause the DCJS to issue an NYSIS report (*i.e.*, a "rap sheet") with regard to their witnesses). In this regard, the court found, inter alia, that an NYSIS report which reveals that a prosecution witness has a prior criminal conviction, and/or a pending criminal charge, constitutes *Brady* material. 131 Misc. 2d at __, 501 N.Y.S.2d at 555. *See also People v. Bazemore*, 272 A.D.2d 64, 707 N.Y.S.2d 831 (1st Dep't 2000). *Cf. People v. Graham*, 289 A.D.2d 417, 734 N.Y.S.2d 243 (2d Dep't 2001).

§ 20:84 CPL § 240.45(2)—Discovery upon trial by the People of prior statements and criminal history of witnesses

Research References

West's Key Number Digest, Criminal Law ⟾627.5(1)

CPL § 240.45(2) provides for the following discovery at trial:

After presentation of the people's direct case and before the presentation of the defendant's direct case, the defendant shall, subject to a protective order, make available to the prosecutor:

(a) any written or recorded statement made by a person other than the defendant whom the defendant intends to call as a witness at the trial, and which relates to the subject matter of the witness's testimony;

(b) a record of judgment of conviction of a witness, other than the defendant, the defendant intends to call at trial if the record of conviction is known by the defendant to exist;

(c) the existence of any pending criminal action against a witness, other than the defendant, the defendant intends to call at trial, if the pending criminal action is known by the defendant to exist.

§ 20:85 Discovery pursuant to CPL § 240.45 is mandatory

Research References

West's Key Number Digest, Criminal Law ⟾627.5(1)

CPL § 240.45 makes clear that discovery thereunder is mandatory—*i.e.*, no request by the other side need be made to invoke the right to such discovery. *See, e.g., People v. King*, 241 A.D.2d 329, __, 659 N.Y.S.2d 469, 470 (1st Dep't 1997).

§ 20:86 Time for disclosure of CPL § 240.45 discovery

Research References

West's Key Number Digest, Criminal Law ⟾627.8(2)

Although the disclosure of trial discovery pursuant to CPL § 240.45 typically takes place prior to trial, CPL § 240.45(1) states that the People can make such disclosure "[a]fter the jury has been sworn and before the prosecutor's opening address, or in the case of a single judge trial after commencement and before submission of evidence." In addition, CPL § 240.45(2) provides that the defense can make its disclosure thereunder "[a]fter presentation of the people's direct case and before the presentation of the defendant's direct case."

Even though such belated disclosure often results in a significant waste of scarce judicial resources (since counsel must be afforded adequate time to review the material), it appears that courts are powerless to order a party to make earlier disclosure. *See, e.g., Matter of Pittari v. Pirro*, 258 A.D.2d 202, __, 696 N.Y.S.2d 167, 171 (2d Dep't 1999); *Matter of Catterson v. Rohl*, 202 A.D.2d 420, __-__, 608 N.Y.S.2d 696, 698–99 (2d Dep't 1994). In *Rohl*, the Appellate Division, Second Department, held that:

> The statute is clear on its face that a prosecutor is not obligated to provide a defendant with copies of witnesses' statements until such time as trial has commenced, and there is no provision contained in the statute which would give the court authority to vary that statutory time frame. Indeed, CPL 240.40 sets forth the limited circumstances under which the court is authorized to direct discovery.

202 A.D.2d at __, 608 N.Y.S.2d at 698–99.

§ 20:87 Remedy for CPL § 240.45 violation

Research References

West's Key Number Digest, Criminal Law ☞627.5(1)

With certain limited exceptions, *People v. Ranghelle*, 69 N.Y.2d 56, 511 N.Y.S.2d 580 (1986), and its progeny had created a "per se" reversal rule where the defendant had been deprived of *Rosario* material at trial. CPL § 240.75 legislatively abrogates the "per se" reversal rule of *Ranghelle*. This statute provides, in pertinent part:

> The failure of the prosecutor or any agent of the prosecutor to disclose statements that are required to be disclosed under . . . [CPL § 240.45(1)(a)] shall not constitute grounds for any court to . . . set aside a conviction, or reverse, modify or vacate a judgment of conviction in the absence of a showing by the defendant that there is a reasonable possibility that the non-disclosure materially contributed to the result of the trial or other proceeding; provided, however, that nothing in this section shall affect or limit any right the defendant may have to a re-opened pre-trial hearing when such statements were disclosed before the close of evidence at trial.

In *People v. Sorbello*, 285 A.D.2d 88, 729 N.Y.S.2d 747 (2d Dep't 2001), the Appellate Division, Second Department, analyzed CPL § 240.75, and held that CPL § 240.75 applies retroactively "to all cases in prosecution or appeal as of its effective date" of February 1, 2001.

The burden of proof placed on the defendant by CPL § 240.75 (*i.e.*, "that there is a reasonable possibility that the non-disclosure materially contributed to the result of the trial or other proceeding"), merely codifies the "prejudice" standard previously established by the Court of Appeals in the *Rosario* context. *See, e.g., People v. Machado*, 90 N.Y.2d 187, 188–89, 193, 659 N.Y.S.2d

242, 243, 245 (1997); *People v. Jackson*, 78 N.Y.2d 638, 649, 578 N.Y.S.2d 483, 490 (1991). In this regard, the Court of Appeals has noted that:

> The "reasonable possibility" test is, after all, "perhaps the most demanding test yet formulated" for harmless error analysis. And we have recognized that the "reasonable possibility" test "properly encourages compliance" with the People's *Brady* obligations. That should be no less true with respect to the People's *Rosario* obligations.

Machado, 90 N.Y.2d at 193, 659 N.Y.S.2d at 245–46 (citations omitted).

Cases applying this standard to *Rosario* violations include *People v. Potter*, 254 A.D.2d 831, __, 681 N.Y.S.2d 704, 705 (4th Dep't 1998); *People v. Wahad*, 204 A.D.2d 156, __, 612 N.Y.S.2d 14, 15 (1st Dep't 1994); *People v. Ramos*, 201 A.D.2d 78, 614 N.Y.S.2d 977 (1st Dep't 1994); *People v. Alvarado*, 201 A.D.2d 486, __, 607 N.Y.S.2d 399, 400 (2d Dep't 1994); *People v. Nikollaj*, 155 Misc. 2d 642, __-__, 589 N.Y.S.2d 1013, 1017–18 (Bronx Co. Sup. Ct. 1992). *See also* §§ 28:1 et seq., *infra*.

§ 20:88 CPL §§ 240.44 and 240.45 discovery must be copied and delivered to opposing party

Research References

West's Key Number Digest, Criminal Law ⚮627.6(1)

To comply with the obligation to disclose *Rosario* material under CPL §§ 240.44 and 240.45, as well as *People v. Rosario*, 9 N.Y.2d 286, 213 N.Y.S.2d 448 (1961), and *People v. Malinsky*, 15 N.Y.2d 86, 262 N.Y.S.2d 65 (1965), a party must actually "deliver a copy" of such material to the opposing party. *See People v. Caussade*, 162 A.D.2d 4, __, 560 N.Y.S.2d 648, 653 (2d Dep't 1990).

§ 20:89 People's obligation to "gather" evidence for defendant

Research References

West's Key Number Digest, Criminal Law ⚮627.5(1)

People v. Alvarez, 70 N.Y.2d 375, 381, 521 N.Y.S.2d 212, 215 (1987), dealt with a defense claim that the police are required to affirmatively "obtain and preserve a second breath sample for later use by the accused." In holding that no such requirement exists, the Court of Appeals stated that the police are not required "to affirmatively gather evidence for the accused," 70 N.Y.2d at 381, 521 N.Y.S.2d at 215. Taken in context, this language in *Alvarez* merely stands for the proposition that the police need not affirmatively assist the defense in obtaining and preserving evidence that would not otherwise exist.

By contrast, it does not alter the requirement that the People locate and "gather" discoverable documents in their possession and in the possession of the police. *See, e.g.*, CPL § 240.20(2) ("The prosecutor shall make a diligent, good faith effort to ascertain the existence of demanded property and to cause such property to be made available for discovery where it exists but is not within the prosecutor's possession, custody or control; provided, that the prosecutor shall not be required to obtain by subpoena duces tecum demanded material which the defendant may thereby obtain"). *Cf. People v. Wright*, 225 A.D.2d 430, __-__, 639 N.Y.S.2d 361, 363–64 (1st Dep't 1996).

In this regard, in *People v. Ariosa*, 172 Misc. 2d 312, __, 660 N.Y.S.2d 255, 257 (Monroe Co. Ct. 1997), the court stated:

> None of the specific provisions of [CPL] § 240.70 would sufficiently sanction the People for this gross failure to fulfill their discovery, *Rosario* and *Brady* obligations. Accordingly, this Court finds that the appropriate sanction would be one that would send a message to the People that their review of discoverable materials requested by the defense and their response to those requests has to be more than just a boilerplate, cursory review and response. It must be a pro-active, vigorous attempt to respond to the requests made by defense counsel or to seek protective orders in circumstances they feel are inappropriate for discovery. The consequences to a defendant for the People's failure to turn over materials are severe indeed. Accordingly, the sanctions for failing to disclose such materials must also send a clear message.

§ 20:90   Sanctions for failure to comply with CPL Article 240

Research References

West's Key Number Digest, Criminal Law ☞627.8(1)

CPL § 240.70(1) provides that:

> If, during the course of discovery proceedings, the court finds that a party has failed to comply with any of the provisions of [CPL Article 240], the court may order such party to permit discovery of the property not previously disclosed, grant a continuance, issue a protective order, prohibit the introduction of certain evidence or the calling of certain witnesses or take any other appropriate action.

An order precluding the admission of evidence pursuant to CPL § 240.70(1) is not appealable. *People v. Myers*, 226 A.D.2d 557, __, 641 N.Y.S.2d 333, 334 (2d Dep't 1996).

§ 20:91   Loss or destruction of discoverable material requires sanction

Research References

West's Key Number Digest, Criminal Law ☞627.8(1)

In *People v. Martinez*, 71 N.Y.2d 937, 940, 528 N.Y.S.2d 813, 815 (1988), the Court of Appeals held that:

> [I]t is no answer to a demand to produce that the material has been lost or destroyed. If the People fail to exercise care to preserve it and defendant is prejudiced by their mistake, the court must impose an appropriate sanction. The determination of what is appropriate is committed to the trial court's sound discretion, and while the degree of prosecutorial fault may be considered, the court's attention should focus primarily on the overriding need to eliminate prejudice to the defendant.

See also People v. Jenkins, 98 N.Y.2d 280, 284, 746 N.Y.S.2d 651, 654 (2002).

Similarly, in *People v. Kelly*, 62 N.Y.2d 516, 478 N.Y.S.2d 834 (1984), the Court of Appeals held that:

> A necessary corollary of the duty to disclose is the obligation to preserve evidence until a request for disclosure is made. Any other rule would facilitate evasion of the disclosure requirements. Accordingly, where discoverable evidence gathered by the prosecution or its agent is lost, the People have a heavy burden of establishing that diligent, good-faith efforts were made to prevent the loss. Otherwise, sanctions will be imposed. * * *
>
> Although the choice of "appropriate" action is committed to the sound discretion of the trial court, as a general matter the drastic remedy of dismissal should not be invoked where less severe measures can rectify the harm done by the loss of evidence.

62 N.Y.2d at 520, 521, 478 N.Y.S.2d at 836, 837 (citations omitted).

In *People v. Torres*, 190 A.D.2d 52, __, 597 N.Y.S.2d 492, 494 (3d Dep't 1993), the Appellate Division, Third Department, made clear that "[i]t is now axiomatic that where the People are in possession of discoverable material, they are duty bound to preserve such evidence and, in the event such evidence is lost or destroyed, sanctions will be imposed." (Citation omitted). In *Torres*, an audiotape was "deliberately destroyed by personnel of the [Police] Department" and, if the events on the tape corroborated defendant's version of events, "it would have severely undercut the People's case." 190 A.D.2d at __, 597 N.Y.S.2d at 495. Under such circumstances, the Court held that "the only appropriate sanction is the preclusion of all testimony relating to that encounter." 190 A.D.2d at __, 597 N.Y.S.2d at 495. *See generally People v. Gomez-Kadawid*, 66 A.D.3d 1124, __, 888 N.Y.S.2d 621, 623 (3d Dep't 2009) ("reversal is required due to the People's failure to preserve a critical piece of evidence"); *People v. Miller*, 156 Misc. 2d 824, 594 N.Y.S.2d 978 (Queens Co. Sup. Ct. 1993) (loss of "rape kit").

§ 20:92   Effect of failure to call particular witness or to introduce disclosed material at trial

Research References

West's Key Number Digest, Criminal Law ☞627.8(1)

CPL § 240.70(2) provides that:

The failure of the prosecution to call as a witness a person specified in [CPL § 240.20(1)] or of any party to introduce disclosed material at the trial shall not, *by itself*, constitute grounds for any sanction or for adverse comment thereupon by any party in summation to the jury or at any other point.

(Emphasis added). "This does not preclude circumstances where such action or comment may be appropriate for reasons relating to fair advocacy." Preiser, Practice Commentaries, McKinney's Cons. Laws of N.Y., Book 11A, CPL § 240.70, at 81.

§ 20:93   Delay in production of discoverable material generally requires continuance

Research References

West's Key Number Digest, Criminal Law ☞627.8(1)

Where the People fail to provide the defense with discoverable material pertaining to, inter alia, a scientific test (such as a chemical test in a DWI case) until immediately prior to, or during, trial, the court generally must offer the defense a continuance to review the material and/or consult with a potential expert witness. *See, e.g., People v. Crandall*, 228 A.D.2d 794, —, 644 N.Y.S.2d 817, 818 (3d Dep't 1996) ("It is abundantly clear that where materials of the type we are dealing with here are not produced until the day of trial, it is reversible error for the trial court to admit such into evidence without granting a continuance in order to permit defendant's examination thereof"); *People v. Corley*, 124 A.D.2d 390, —, 507 N.Y.S.2d 491, 493 (3d Dep't 1986) ("defendant's failure to move pursuant to CPL 240.40 to compel the People to produce this documentation did not constitute a waiver of his right to this information"). *See generally People v. Sullivan*, 261 A.D.2d 652, —, 691 N.Y.S.2d 581, 582 (3d Dep't 1999); *People v. Heidelmark*, 214 A.D.2d 767, —, 624 N.Y.S.2d 656, 657 (3d Dep't 1995); *People v. Erickson*, 156 A.D.2d 760, 549 N.Y.S.2d 182 (3d Dep't 1989); *People v. Hess*, 140 A.D.2d 895, —, 528 N.Y.S.2d 921, 922–23 (3d Dep't 1988); *People v. English*, 103 A.D.2d 979, 480 N.Y.S.2d 56 (3d Dep't 1984).

§ 20:94   Delay in complying with CPL § 240.20 generally does not affect People's readiness for trial

Research References

West's Key Number Digest, Criminal Law ☞627.8(1)

As a general rule, the People's delay in complying with CPL § 240.20 does not affect their readiness for trial for purposes of CPL § 30.30. The rationale is that CPL § 240.70 is "the section of law specifically designed to impose sanctions for such failure." *People v. Caussade*, 162 A.D.2d 4, __, 560 N.Y.S.2d 648, 653 (2d Dep't 1990). *See also People v. Anderson*, 66 N.Y.2d 529, __, 498 N.Y.S.2d 119, 128 (1985); *People v. Cole*, 90 A.D.2d 27, __, 457 N.Y.S.2d 589, 590 (3d Dep't 1982).

By contrast, where a formal laboratory test result is required for the People to present a prima facie case at trial, the People cannot validly declare that they are ready for trial if the lab test has not been performed. *See People v. Hyndman*, 194 Misc. 2d 335, 753 N.Y.S.2d 811 (Schenectady Co. Ct. 2002); *People v. Blunt*, 189 Misc. 2d 471, 732 N.Y.S.2d 852 (Albany Co. Sup. Ct. 2001).

§ 20:95 Delay in complying with CPL §§ 240.44 or 240.45 generally does not affect People's readiness for trial

Research References
West's Key Number Digest, Criminal Law ⬮627.8(1)

As a general rule, the People's delay in complying with CPL §§ 240.44 or 240.45 does not affect their readiness for trial for purposes of CPL § 30.30. *See, e.g., People v. Anderson*, 66 N.Y.2d 529, __, 498 N.Y.S.2d 119, 124 (1985); *People v. Langhorn*, 141 Misc. 2d 612, 533 N.Y.S.2d 820 (N.Y. City Crim. Ct. 1988).

§ 20:96 Reversal for delay in complying with CPL § 240.20

Research References
West's Key Number Digest, Criminal Law ⬮627.8(1)

"The People's delay in complying with the provisions of CPL 240.20 constitutes reversible error . . . only when the delay substantially prejudices defendant." *People v. Watson*, 213 A.D.2d 996, __, 624 N.Y.S.2d 710, 712 (4th Dep't 1995). *See also People v. Herrera*, 136 A.D.2d 567, __, 523 N.Y.S.2d 562, 563–64 (2d Dep't 1988). Such prejudice was found not to exist in *People v. Alves*, 1 A.D.3d 938, 767 N.Y.S.2d 754 (4th Dep't 2003). In *Alves*, "the People inadvertently disclosed the calibration log for a breathalyzer instrument that was not used in connection with defendant's arrest. At trial, however, the People introduced the calibration log for the correct breathalyzer instrument." 1 A.D.3d at __, 767 N.Y.S.2d at 754. Holding that neither preclusion nor reversal for the late disclosure was required, the Appellate Division, Fourth Department, reasoned that:

While the People concededly delayed in disclosing the certificates of calibration for the correct breathalyzer instrument, that delay did not deny defendant the ability to prepare an adequate defense, and nothing contained in the log would have "proved useful to the defense" or might have resulted in a different verdict. Thus, . . . the delay in disclosing the proper records did not "deprive defendant of his legitimate challenge to the reliability of the breathalyzer" instrument.

1 A.D.3d at ___, 767 N.Y.S.2d at 754–55 (citations omitted).

§ 20:97   Reversal for delay in complying with CPL § 240.45

Research References

West's Key Number Digest, Criminal Law ☞627.8(1)

A delay in turning over *Rosario* material will require reversal if the defendant is substantially prejudiced by the delay. *See People v. Banch*, 80 N.Y.2d 610, 617, 593 N.Y.S.2d 491, 495 (1992); *People v. Martinez*, 71 N.Y.2d 937, 940, 528 N.Y.S.2d 813, 815 (1988); *People v. Ranghelle*, 69 N.Y.2d 56, 63, 511 N.Y.S.2d 580, 585 (1986); *People v. Perez*, 65 N.Y.2d 154, 159, 490 N.Y.S.2d 747, 750 (1985). In this regard, the Court of Appeals has stated that:

Although a delay, particularly an inadvertent one, will generally not adversely affect the defendant's rights, delay in a particular case may cause substantial prejudice to the defense. An attorney preparing for cross-examination must not only decide what questions to ask, but what questions to avoid asking. The fairness concept embodied in the *Rosario* rule cannot be said to have been satisfied when pretrial statements revealing a potential trap for the cross-examiner are furnished to defense counsel only after the trap has sprung.

Perez, 65 N.Y.2d at 160, 490 N.Y.S.2d at 750. *See also People v. Goins*, 73 N.Y.2d 989, 540 N.Y.S.2d 994 (1989) (delayed production of police officer's "daily activity report" required reversal); *People v. Thompson*, 71 N.Y.2d 918, 528 N.Y.S.2d 532 (1988) (delayed production of arresting officer's memo book entry substantially prejudiced defendant).

In *People v. Mackey*, 249 A.D.2d 329, ___, 670 N.Y.S.2d 879, 880 (2d Dep't 1998), the Appellate Division, Second Department, held that:

The defendant's conviction must be reversed . . . because he was substantially prejudiced by the People's failure to provide certain *Rosario* material related to a critical aspect of the complainant's testimony until after she had been cross-examined. As a result of the People's delay in providing the material—a record book maintained by the complainant which was in the People's control—

damaging testimony was unwittingly elicited during her cross-examination. * * *

Rosario material must be provided at a time when it meaningfully can be used to prepare cross-examination. "The fairness concept embodied in the *Rosario* rule cannot be said to have been satisfied when pretrial statements revealing a potential trap for the cross-examiner are furnished to defense counsel only after the trap has sprung."

(Citation omitted). *See also People v. Jarrells*, 190 A.D.2d 120, 597 N.Y.S.2d 305 (1st Dep't 1993) (prosecutor's failure to turn over "voucher" prepared by arresting officer substantially prejudiced defendant). *See generally People v. King*, 241 A.D.2d 329, 659 N.Y.S.2d 469 (1st Dep't 1997); *People v. Rutter*, 202 A.D.2d 123, 616 N.Y.S.2d 598 (1st Dep't 1994).

§ 20:98   Discovery pursuant to CPL §§ 240.43, 240.44, and 240.45, as well as *Brady v. Maryland* and its progeny, is applicable to traffic infractions

Research References

West's Key Number Digest, Criminal Law ⚖627.8(1)

A defendant charged by simplified information with a traffic infraction is entitled to discovery pursuant to CPL §§ 240.43, 240.44, and 240.45, as well as *Brady v. Maryland*, 373 U.S. 83, 83 S.Ct. 1194 (1963), and its progeny. The reasons for this are simple. At the outset, while CPL § 240.20, by its clear and express terms, does not apply to simplified informations charging traffic infractions, *see* § 20:50, *supra*, CPL §§ 240.43, 240.44, and 240.45, as well as *Brady v. Maryland* and its progeny, contain no such limitation.

In addition, the Court of Appeals has repeatedly held that, for most purposes, "traffic infractions [are] to be treated as misdemeanors as far as the procedure for their prosecution [is] concerned." *Squadrito v. Griebsch*, 1 N.Y.2d 471, 477, 154 N.Y.S.2d 37, 42 (1956). *See also People v. Byron*, 17 N.Y.2d 64, 66, 268 N.Y.S.2d 24, 26 (1966) ("The prosecution in this case was for a 'traffic infraction,' not a crime, but such a prosecution is penal in nature and the rules of criminal law are generally applicable"); *People v. Lewis*, 13 N.Y.2d 180, 182, 245 N.Y.S.2d 1, 3 (1963) (" 'This conviction was not for a crime but for a so-called "traffic infraction." However, there are applicable to such prosecutions the rules of the criminal law' ") (citations omitted); *People v. Firth*, 3 N.Y.2d 472, 474, 168 N.Y.S.2d 949, 950 (1957) (same); *People v. Hildebrandt*, 308 N.Y. 397, 399–400 (1955). *See generally People v. Phinney*, 22 N.Y.2d 288, 290, 292 N.Y.S.2d 632, 634 (1968) ("a speeding conviction may have serious implications, including fine, imprisonment and possible suspension of a driver's license. Consequently, at least in the absence of any undue administrative hardships, we have generally held that such prosecutions are governed by the rules of the criminal law").

Furthermore, this well-settled rule is codified in VTL § 155, which expressly provides, inter alia, that traffic infractions "*shall be deemed misdemeanors and all provisions of law relating to misdemeanors except as provided in [VTL § 1805] and except as herein otherwise expressly provided shall apply* except that no jury trial shall be allowed for traffic infractions." (Emphasis added).

§ 20:99   Subpoena duces tecum cannot be used to circumvent discovery statutes

Research References

West's Key Number Digest, Criminal Law ⚭627.5(4)

[A] subpoena duces tecum may not be used to circumvent the discovery provisions of CPL 240.20 and 240.40, "to ascertain the existence of evidence" or "to fish for impeaching material." Rather, its purpose is "to compel the production of specific documents that are relevant and material to facts at issue in a pending judicial proceeding." A showing that certain documents carry a potential for establishing relevant evidence is insufficient; instead, a defendant must put forth "some factual predicate" which would make it reasonably likely that documentary information will bear relevant and exculpatory evidence.

Matter of Constantine v. Leto, 157 A.D.2d 376, __, 557 N.Y.S.2d 611, 613 (3d Dep't 1990) (citations omitted), *aff'd for the reasons stated in the opinion below*, 77 N.Y.2d 975, 571 N.Y.S.2d 906 (1991). *See also Matter of Pirro v. LaCava*, 230 A.D.2d 909, __, 646 N.Y.S.2d 866, 867 (2d Dep't 1996); *Matter of Suffolk County Police Dep't v. Gorman*, 202 A.D.2d 438, __, 608 N.Y.S.2d 532, 533 (2d Dep't 1994); *Matter of Constantine v. Solomon*, 194 A.D.2d 538, __, 598 N.Y.S.2d 316, 317 (2d Dep't 1993); *Matter of DeCrosta v. State Police Lab.*, 182 A.D.2d 930, 581 N.Y.S.2d 938 (3d Dep't 1992); *People v. DiLorenzo*, 134 Misc. 2d 1000, 513 N.Y.S.2d 938 (Nassau Co. Ct. 1987). *See generally People v. Morrison*, 148 Misc. 2d 61, __, 559 N.Y.S.2d 1013, 1019 (N.Y. City Crim. Ct. 1990) ("where material is discoverable under Article 240 it may not independently be obtained by a defendant by subpoena even if it is evidentiary, unless due process requires that a defendant have that material earlier than provided under the discovery statute"). *Cf. People v. Russo*, 149 A.D.2d 255, __, 545 N.Y.S.2d 211, 212 (2d Dep't 1989) ("A defendant charged with a violation of Vehicle and Traffic Law § 1180(b) is entitled to the issuance of a properly worded judicial subpoena duces tecum under CPLR

2307 requiring the production of relevant records at the hearing before the Traffic Violations Bureau").

In *County of Nassau Police Dep't v. Judge*, 237 A.D.2d 354, 654 N.Y.S.2d 174 (2d Dep't 1997), the respondent was arrested by a Nassau County highway patrol officer on the Long Island Expressway and charged with, among other things, DWI. As part of his defense, the respondent served a subpoena duces tecum on the County of Nassau Police Department seeking the production of "internal police directives and orders which, he claimed, established a quota system with regard to the making of arrests for DWI, inter alia, on the Long Island Expressway." 237 A.D.2d at __, 654 N.Y.S.2d at 175.

On appeal, the Appellate Division, Second Department, quashed the subpoena, relying primarily on *Leto*, *supra*. In so holding, the court found that the respondent (a) "has failed to demonstrate that the requested materials are relevant and material to facts at issue in the pending criminal proceeding against him," and (b) "has not established the existence of a factual predicate which would make it reasonably likely that 'documentary information will bear relevant and exculpatory evidence.'" 237 A.D.2d at __, 654 N.Y.S.2d at 175. *See generally People v. Burnette*, 160 Misc. 2d 1005, 612 N.Y.S.2d 774 (N.Y. Co. Sup. Ct. 1994).

In *People v. Van Dyne*, 175 Misc. 2d 558, 669 N.Y.S.2d 199 (Monroe Co. Ct. 1998), the defense counsel moved to be relieved from the notice requirements applicable to judicial subpoenas duces tecum, *see* CPL § 610.20(3); CPLR § 2307, and thus for permission to seek such relief ex parte. The court contrasted the notice requirements with a defendant's right to prepare a defense without alerting the prosecution of its strategy, and held that:

> The Court would . . . grant the motion allowing the opportunity for the defendant to present ex parte an application for judicial subpoenas and will rule on each application determining whether notice to the adverse party will be required consistent with the law and defendant's due process right to a fair opportunity to prepare a defense.

175 Misc. 2d at __, 669 N.Y.S.2d at 201.

In *People v. Nesci*, 178 Misc. 2d 685, 683 N.Y.S.2d 375 (App. Term, 2d Dep't 1998), the Appellate Term, Second Department, held that the New York State Police could not appeal from "[a]n order determining a motion to quash a subpoena issued in the course of the prosecution of a criminal action," as no direct appellate review of such an order is authorized.

It is critical to distinguish the power to issue a subpoena duces tecum (which is quite limited) from the power to issue a subpoena ad testificandum (which is virtually unlimited). The law on this issue is well settled: "Since the court should not anticipate potential lines of questioning, the power to issue a subpoena *ad testificandum* is absolute and unlimited." *Ocean-Clear, Inc. v. Continental Casualty Co.*, 94 A.D.2d 717, 719 (2d Dep't 1983). *See also Matter of Hirshfield v. Craig*, 239 N.Y. 98, 117–18 (1924); *23/23 Communications Corp. v. General Motors Corp.*, 172 Misc. 2d 821, 824 (N.Y. Co. Sup. Ct. 1997); *People v. Slochowsky*, 116 Misc. 2d 1069, 1072 (Kings Co. Sup. Ct. 1982); *Matter of Marius v. Leonard La Monica, Inc.*, 115 Misc. 2d 12, 13 (N.Y. Co. Sup. Ct. 1982).

§ 20:100   FOIL requests—Generally

Research References

West's Key Number Digest, Criminal Law ⚖627.8(3)

In New York, Freedom of Information Law (FOIL) requests are governed by Article 6 of the Public Officers Law. In *Matter of Gould v. New York City Police Dep't*, 89 N.Y.2d 267, 653 N.Y.S.2d 54 (1996), the Court of Appeals reiterated the following well-settled principles applicable to FOIL requests:

> To promote open government and public accountability, the FOIL imposes a broad duty on government to make its records available to the public. Moreover, access to government records does not depend on the purpose for which the records are sought . . .

> All government records are thus presumptively open for public inspection and copying unless they fall within one of the enumerated exemptions of Public Officers Law § 87(2). To ensure maximum access to government documents, the "exemptions are to be narrowly construed, with the burden resting on the agency to demonstrate that the requested material indeed qualifies for exemption." As this Court has stated, "[o]nly where the material requested falls squarely within the ambit of one of these statutory exemptions may disclosure be withheld."

> In keeping with these settled principles, blanket exemptions for particular types of documents are inimical to FOIL's policy of open government. Instead, to invoke one of the exemptions of section 87(2), the agency must articulate "particularized and specific justification" for not disclosing requested documents.

89 N.Y.2d at 274–75, 653 N.Y.S.2d at 57 (citations omitted). *See also Matter of Russo v. Nassau County Community College*, 81 N.Y.2d 690, 603 N.Y.S.2d 294 (1993); *Matter of Fink v. Lefkowitz*, 47 N.Y.2d 567, 419 N.Y.S.2d 467 (1979).

Public Officers Law § 87(2)(g) (the "intra-agency materials" exemption) provides that an:

> [A]gency may deny access to records or portions thereof that . . . are inter-agency or intra-agency materials which are not:

i. statistical or factual tabulations or data;

ii. instructions to staff that affect the public;

iii. final agency policy or determinations; or

iv. external audits, including but not limited to audits performed by the comptroller and the federal government . . .

See also Gould, 89 N.Y.2d at 276, 653 N.Y.S.2d at 58.

In *Gould*, the Court of Appeals held that, "under a plain reading of section 87(2)(g), the exemption for intra-agency material does not apply as long as the material falls within any one of the provision's four enumerated exceptions." 89 N.Y.2d at 276, 653 N.Y.S.2d at 58. The Court has also made clear that this exemption only applies to " 'deliberative material,' i.e., communications exchanged for discussion purposes not constituting final policy decisions." *Russo*, 81 N.Y.2d at 699, 603 N.Y.S.2d at 298.

Thus, police complaint follow-up reports are not entitled to blanket exemption from FOIL disclosure under the intra-agency materials exemption. *Gould*, 89 N.Y.2d at 276–77, 653 N.Y.S.2d at 58–59. In addition, various course materials taught at a public college have been held to constitute "final agency policy or determinations" for purposes of this exemption. *See Russo*, 81 N.Y.2d at 699–700, 603 N.Y.S.2d at 298. In so holding, the *Russo* Court reasoned that:

> Respondents contend that the classroom environment in which the films are used is one of "deliberation"—not "final determinations." We disagree with respondents' characterizations of the items. Recognizing that the College has used them in the course for years, there is no valid reason to hold that the items used do not constitute "final agency policy or determinations." Although respondents argue that the classroom environment is one of "deliberation," that in itself does not alter the status of the items used in the classroom. Respondents have not shown that the items petitioner seeks rest "squarely within the ambit of one of [the] statutory exemptions," thereby justifying respondents' refusal to disclose them to petitioner.

81 N.Y.2d at 699–700, 603 N.Y.S.2d at 298 (quoting *Fink*, 47 N.Y.2d at 571, 419 N.Y.S.2d at 471).

Public Officers Law § 87(2)(e) (the "law enforcement" exemption) provides that an:

> [A]gency may deny access to records or portions thereof that . . . are compiled for law enforcement purposes and which, if disclosed, would:
>
> i. interfere with law enforcement investigations or judicial proceedings;

ii. deprive a person of a right to a fair trial or impartial adjudication;

iii. identify a confidential source or disclose confidential information relating to a criminal investigation; or

iv. reveal criminal investigative techniques or procedures, *except routine techniques and procedures.*

(Emphasis added).

It should be noted that, under both the plain language of Public Officers Law § 87(2)(e)(iv), as well as the clear mandate of the Court of Appeals in *Fink, supra,* the appropriate inquiry is not whether disclosure would reveal criminal investigative techniques or procedures, but rather whether disclosure would reveal *nonroutine* criminal investigative techniques or procedures. *See* Public Officers Law § 87(2)(e)(iv); *Fink,* 47 N.Y.2d at 571–72, 419 N.Y.S.2d at 471. In this regard, the Court has made clear that "[i]ndicative, but not necessarily dispositive, of whether investigative techniques are nonroutine is whether disclosure of those procedures would give rise to a *substantial likelihood* that violators could evade detection by deliberately tailoring their conduct in anticipation of avenues of inquiry to be pursued by agency personnel." *Fink,* 47 N.Y.2d at 572, 419 N.Y.S.2d at 471 (emphasis added).

In *Matter of Sills v. New York State Div. of State Police,* 248 A.D.2d 920, 669 N.Y.S.2d 990 (3d Dep't 1998), the petitioner (one of the authors of this book) filed a FOIL request seeking portions of a State Police training manual pertaining to Trooper Michelle Smith's training with regard to standardized field sobriety testing. The State Police denied the request, invoking, inter alia, subdivisions (i) and (iv) of Public Officers Law § 87(2)(e). In other words, the State Police asserted that the requested records were secret, and that their disclosure would (a) interfere with its investigations, and (b) reveal nonroutine criminal investigative techniques or procedures.

However, when the petitioner filed an Article 78 proceeding challenging the applicability of the claimed exemptions, the State Police claimed that "when copies of the requested documents were sought for in camera inspection in connection with this proceeding, it was learned for the first time that the documents were not maintained by respondents." 248 A.D.2d at __, 669 N.Y.S.2d at 990. When the petitioner pointed out that Trooper Smith had testified (in the DWI case which led to the FOIL request) that she still possessed the copy of the manual provided to her during her training at the State Police Academy, the respondents claimed, for the first time, that the manual at issue was in fact not a State Police record after all; rather, the manual becomes the personal property of each individual trooper upon his or her graduation from the State Police Academy.

Nonetheless, the Appellate Division, Third Department, found "the record to adequately establish that copies of the requested manuals are no longer maintained by respondents, thus rendering the FOIL controversy concerning such documents moot." 248 A.D.2d at __, 669 N.Y.S.2d at 991.

§ 20:101   FOIL request cannot be used to circumvent discovery statutes

Research References

West's Key Number Digest, Criminal Law ⟐627.8(3)

As a general rule, a FOIL request, like a subpoena duces tecum, cannot be used to circumvent the discovery provisions of CPL Article 240. *See, e.g., Matter of Pittari v. Pirro*, 258 A.D.2d 202, __, 696 N.Y.S.2d 167, 171 (2d Dep't 1999); *Matter of Legal Aid Soc'y v. New York City Police Dep't*, 274 A.D.2d 207, __, 713 N.Y.S.2d 3, 7–8 (1st Dep't 2000). *Cf. Matter of Moore v. Santucci*, 151 A.D.2d 677, __, 543 N.Y.S.2d 103, 106 (2d Dep't 1989) ("The mere fact that disclosure was available to the applicant through some other discovery device, such as . . . under CPL article 240 in a criminal proceeding, does not ipso facto preclude FOIL relief, if warranted").

§ 20:102   Intoxilyzer 5000 manual subject to FOIL request

In *Matter of Lockwood v. Suffolk County Police Dept.*, 42 A.D.3d 538, __, 839 N.Y.S.2d 808, 809 (2d Dep't 2007), the Appellate Division, Second Department, held that:

> The Supreme Court providently exercised its discretion in directing that the "Operating Manual" of the Intoxilyzer Model 5000 alcohol detection machine, manufactured by CMI, Inc., be made available for inspection, but not copying, at the offices of the Suffolk County Police Department at a time mutually convenient to the parties. Under the circumstances of this case, the Supreme Court properly balanced the competing rights of the petitioner under the Freedom of Information Law (Public Officers Law article 6) and the obligations of the Suffolk County Police Department to CMI, Inc., the nonparty copyright holder of the manual.

§ 20:103   First Department issues landmark ruling affecting access to maintenance and calibration records for all Intoxilyzers used by the NYPD

The law firm of Perlmutter & McGuinness, P.C. (formerly the Law Offices of Adam D. Perlmutter, P.C.) waged a years-long

FOIL battle seeking the maintenance and calibration records for all of the Intoxilyzer devices used by the NYPD. In *Matter of Law Offices of Adam D. Perlmutter, P.C. v. New York City Police Dept.*, 123 A.D.3d 500, 999 N.Y.S.2d 26 (1st Dep't 2014), the Appellate Division, First Department, held as follows:

> Petitioner seeks all calibration and maintenance records for all Intoxilyzer machines owned or maintained by respondent New York City Police Department since January 2008. Contrary to respondents' contention, the records sought are not exempt from FOIL on the ground that they "are compiled for law enforcement purposes and . . ., if disclosed, would . . . interfere with law enforcement investigations or judicial proceedings." Respondents' conclusive assertions that such records are often requested in DWI cases involving Intoxilyzer test results, and that thousands of such cases are pending in New York City, do not meet the burden of "identify[ing] . . . the generic risks posed by disclosure of these categories of documents."
>
> Respondents' argument that the records sought "are specifically exempted from disclosure by state . . . statute" is not properly before us, since that exemption to FOIL was not cited by respondents at the administrative level. Were we to review it, we would reject it on the merits, since the statute cited by respondents does not exempt the records from disclosure.

Id. at ___, 999 N.Y.S.2d at 26-27 (citations omitted).

This somewhat innocuous looking decision has resulted in the NYPD disclosing to Mr. Perlmutter's office all of the maintenance and calibration records for all of the Intoxilyzer machines owned or maintained by the NYPD since January of 2008—and in Mr. Perlmutter's office making such records publicly available on its website. *See* newyorklegaldefense.com/dwi-records.

Chapter 21

Brady Material

Research References

Westlaw Databases

Complete Manual of Criminal Forms (3d ed.) (CMCRF)
Handling a Criminal Case in New York (HCCNY)

Treatises and Practice Aids

Muldoon, Handling a Criminal Case in New York §§ 8:15 to 8:25, 8:144,
8:145

Forms

Bailey and Fishman, Complete Manual of Criminal Forms § 18:12 (3d
ed.)

Law Reviews and Other Periodicals

Deal, Brady Materiality Before Trial: The Scope of the Duty to Disclose
and the Right to a Trial by Jury, 82 N.Y.U. L. Rev. 1780 (December,
2007)
Harris, Two Constitutional Wrongs do not Make a Right: Double
Jeopardy and Prosecutorial Misconduct Under the Brady Doctrine, 28

Cardozo L. Rev. 931 (November, 2006)

KeyCite®: Cases and other legal materials listed in KeyCite Scope can be
researched through the KeyCite service on Westlaw®. Use KeyCite to check
citations for form, parallel references, prior and later history, and comprehensive citator information, including citations to other decisions and secondary
materials.

---

§ 21:1 Exculpatory material—The federal standard

Research References

West's Key Number Digest, Criminal Law ⟐1990

Brady v. Maryland, 373 U.S. 83, 83 S.Ct. 1194, 10 L.Ed.2d 215
(1963), requires the prosecution to turn over any exculpatory evidence in its possession to the defense. This Supreme Court decision has been statutorily incorporated into CPL § 240.20(1)(h)
which states that upon demand to produce by a defendant, the
People must disclose:

> Anything required to be disclosed, prior to trial, to the defendant by
> the prosecutor, pursuant to the constitution of this state or of the
> United States.

Brady material should be specifically identified within the
defendant's motion. A simple recitation of the statute is usually
ignored by the prosecution or, at best, generates a reply that the
People possess no exculpatory material, or that such material
will be made available as soon as the People are aware of its
existence. Unfortunately, the People will frequently ignore
specific requests as well, but at least specification places the
defense in a far better position to appeal any constitutional deprivation should such material surface during the course of the
proceeding.

The defense is entitled to disclosure of favorable or exculpatory
evidence which is material to the defendant's guilt or the mitiga-
tion of his punishment, and regardless of whether such exculpatory evidence would be admissible in the defendant's behalf at
trial ". . . or in obtaining further evidence." *Giles v. Maryland*,
386 U.S. 66, 74, 87 S.Ct. 793, 797, 17 L.Ed.2d 737 (1967). The evidence need not be competent evidence nor admissible at trial.
United States v. Gleason, 265 F.Supp. 880, 886 (S.D.N.Y. 1967).
The right to disclosure under *Brady* includes the right to pretrial discovery by the defense. *See United States ex rel. Drew v.
Myers*, 327 F.2d 174 (3d Cir. 1964), *cert. den.* 379 U.S. 847, 85
S.Ct. 88, 13 L.Ed.2d 52 (1964); *United States v. Ahmad*, 53 F.R.D.
186, 193–94 (M.D.Pa. 1971); *United States v. Partin*, 320 F.Supp.
275, 284–85 (E.D.La. 1970); *United States v. Ladd*, 48 F.R.D. 266
(D.Alaska 1969); *United States v. Gleason*, 265 F.Supp. 880,

884–85 (S.D.N.Y. 1967); *United States v. Morrison*, 43 F.R.D. 516, 520 (N.D.Ill. 1967); A.B.A. Standards For Criminal Justice: Prosecution Function and Defense Function (3d ed. 1993), Standard 3-3.11.

After *Brady* was decided, there was some doubt as to whether a specific request for the exculpatory evidence was an indispensable element of a *Brady* claim. *See Comment Brady v. Maryland and the Prosecutor's Duty to Disclose,* 40 U.Chi.L.Rev. 112, 115–17 (1972). In *United States v. Agurs*, 427 U.S. 97, 96 S.Ct. 2392, 49 L.Ed.2d 342 (1976), the United States Supreme Court created a two-tiered framework for courts to determine if favorable evidence was "material," such that the failure to disclose it required a new trial. Under the *Agurs* standard, evidence which was specifically requested by the defense was "material" if it "might have affected the outcome of the trial." 427 U.S. at 104, 96 S.Ct. at 2398. However, where there was either no defense request or only a general *Brady* request, undisclosed exculpatory evidence was "material" only if it created a reasonable doubt that did not otherwise exist. 427 U.S. at 112, 96 S.Ct. at 2402.

In *Agurs*, the Supreme Court stated that a lesser burden on the defendant making a "specific request" was appropriate since the prosecutor is on notice that there is particular evidence the defense does not have and believes to be important. As the Court noted, "[w]hen the prosecutor receives a specific and relevant request, the failure to make any response is seldom, if ever, excusable." 427 U.S. at 106, 96 S.Ct. at 2399.

Nine years after its decision in *Agurs*, a divided Supreme Court in *United States v. Bagley*, 473 U.S. 667, 105 S.Ct. 3375, 87 L.Ed.2d 481 (1985), abandoned the two-tiered approach it had carved out in *Agurs*, replacing it with a single standard applicable in all cases. Not surprisingly, the Court adopted the same test it had formulated one year earlier in *Strickland v. Washington*, 466 U.S. 668, 104 S.Ct. 2052, 80 L.Ed.2d 674 (1984), for determining ineffective assistance of counsel claims—a test which had eviscerated ineffective assistance of counsel claims based on federal constitutional law. The Court in *Bagley* held that undisclosed evidence is "material" if there is a "reasonable probability" that, had the evidence been disclosed at trial, it would have altered the outcome of the trial. A reasonable probability is "a probability sufficient to undermine confidence in the outcome." *Bagley*, 473 U.S. at 682, 105 S.Ct. at 3383. The Court reasoned that this standard was "sufficiently flexible" to cover both the "specific request" and "no request/general request" cases.

Justice Blackmun observed that a prosecutor's failure to respond to a specific request not only deprives the defense of the exculpatory evidence, but also may have the effect of misleading the defense to conclude that the particular evidence does not exist. Relying on this misrepresentation, defense counsel might abandon defense or trial strategies that he might have pursued. However, Justice Blackmun concluded that under the *Strickland* formulation, any adverse consequences could be taken into consideration by a reviewing court in the totality of the circumstances, and no separate standard was necessary.

> This possibility of impairment does not necessitate a different standard of materiality, however, for under the *Strickland* formulation the reviewing court may consider directly any adverse effect that the prosecutor's failure to respond might have had on the preparation or presentation of the defendant's case. The reviewing court should assess the possibility that such effect might have occurred in light of the totality of the circumstances and with an awareness of the difficulty of reconstructing in a post-trial proceeding the course that the defense and the trial would have taken had the defense not been misled by the prosecutor's incomplete response.

473 U.S. at 683, 105 S.Ct. at 3383–84.

Rather than giving more serious consideration to specific requests based upon the greater degree of notice provided to the prosecutor, and out of reasons of fairness, the *Bagley* Court summarily discarded such considerations in favor of a single standard, which in some undefined measure may or may not include adverse consequences in the specific request context. *See Note Specific Requests and the Prosecutorial Duty to Disclose Evidence: The Impact of United States v. Bagley*, 1986 Duke L.J. 892.

From a former federal standard of "seldom, if ever, excusable," under *Agurs*, the prosecution's failure to turn over specifically requested evidence, will now "seldom, if ever," be sanctioned by an order of a new trial.

§ 21:2 The state standard

The New York Court of Appeals in 1990 refused to adopt *Bagley* as a matter of state law. In *People v. Vilardi*, 76 N.Y.2d 67, 556 N.Y.S.2d 518, 555 N.E.2d 915 (1990), the Court of Appeals affirmed the Second Department's reversal of an arson, reckless endangerment, and conspiracy conviction on the ground that the People failed to disclose a report prepared by its explosives expert that had been specifically requested by the defendant in his discovery motion.

In *Vilardi*, the defendant allegedly planted several pipe bombs; one beneath a pizzeria which did not explode; and another beneath a nearby laundromat which did.

Among the prosecution witnesses was a bomb squad member, who had inspected the basement of the laundromat the day after the pipe bomb explosion. In his report, he stated that after a thorough inspection, he observed no evidence of an explosion, but requested that the case be kept open. After reinspection of the premises a year later, the witness concluded that there had been an explosion.

Before the defendant's trial, defense counsel made a pretrial request for all reports "by ballistics, firearm and explosive experts" concerning the laundromat explosion. He was sent 12 reports, but not the initial report by the bomb squad witness in which he had indicated that there had been no explosion. At trial, the bomb squad witness was not questioned about the first report, and no effort was made to establish that the People had failed to prove that there was an explosion, which was an element of the top arson charge. The defense was limited to an attack upon the credibility of the police informant. The defendant was convicted.

In preparing for the appeal, the defendant's appellate counsel discovered the undisclosed explosives report, and made a motion to vacate pursuant to CPL § 440.10, arguing both that there was a failure to disclose *Brady* material and that trial counsel was ineffective. In response, the People argued that the conviction should not be vacated since the evidence of the defendant's guilt was overwhelming.

The trial court denied the CPL Art. 440 motion. The Appellate Division reversed the conviction on *Brady* grounds, and vacated the first-degree arson conviction, distinguishing the case from cases in which no specific request had been made. The Appellate Division held that the prosecution had violated the defendant's constitutional right to be informed of exculpatory information known to the State. Further, the court concluded that reversal was required since there was a "reasonable possibility" that the undisclosed material contributed to the defendant's conviction. *People v. Vilardi*, 150 A.D.2d 819, 820, 542 N.Y.S.2d 238, 239 (2d Dep't 1989).

On appeal to the Court of Appeals, the People argued that the standard used by the Appellate Division was erroneous, claiming that the single standard enunciated by the United States Supreme Court in *United States v. Bagley* should have been used. 76 N.Y.2d at 72, 556 N.Y.S.2d at 520. In *Bagley*, the Supreme Court held that the failure to disclose favorable evidence was constitutional error only if the evidence is material in the sense that there is a *"reasonable probability"* that, had the evidence been disclosed to the defense, the result of the proceeding would have been different. 473 U.S. at 678, 105 S.Ct. at 3381, 3383 (emphasis added). The Appellate Division, the People argued, improperly used a *"reasonable possibility"* standard, which favored the defendant. 76 N.Y.2d at 72, 556 N.Y.S.2d at 520.

The Court of Appeals declined to accept the *Bagley* standard as a matter of state law and affirmed the Appellate Division's reversal of the arson conviction.

> In accordance with our long-standing State concerns in cases involving failure to disclose material specifically requested by a defendant, we have described the standard as one premised on *Agurs*, and that has been understood and cited again and again as the governing standard throughout the State . . .
>
> We decline to abandon these accepted principles in order to conform to the lesser protections of *Bagley*.
>
> We agree with the Appellate Division that a showing of a "reasonable possibility" that the failure to disclose the exculpatory report contributed to the verdict remains the appropriate standard to measure materiality, where the prosecutor was made aware by a specific discovery request that defendant considered the material important to the defense.

People v. Vilardi, 556 N.Y.S.2d at 522–24. *See also People v. Bond*, 95 N.Y.2d 840, 713 N.Y.S.2d 514 (2000).

Where the defense does not make a request for specific *Brady* material, the standard to measure materiality is heightened to a showing of a "reasonable probability" that the failure to disclose the exculpatory material contributed to the verdict.

§ 21:3   Request for "all evidence favorable to the defense" is not a "specific" *Brady* request

Research References

West's Key Number Digest, Criminal Law ⚖1990, 2007

In *People v. Gutkaiss*, 206 A.D.2d 628, 614 N.Y.S.2d 599 (3d Dep't 1994), the defendant made a pretrial *Brady* request for "all evidence favorable to the defense." A few days before trial, the People turned over a letter from the victim's doctor indicating that the victim was suffering from hallucinations. The defendant alleged that the tardy response to the defendant's request for *Brady* material was ground for reversal. The court concluded:

> First, assuming the letter is *Brady* material, because defendant did not make a specific *Brady* request for medical reports, reversal is not mandated due to defendant's failure to establish that, had the letter been disclosed sooner, there is a reasonable probability that the result of the trial would have been different . . . Second, defendant had a meaningful opportunity to use the purportedly exculpatory information in his defense . . .

People v. Gutkaiss, 614 N.Y.S.2d at 601 (citations omitted).

§ 21:4   Implied specific request

Research References

West's Key Number Digest, Criminal Law ⚖2006

In *People v. Ramos*, N.Y.L.J., 1/29/90, p. 26, Col. 1 (Bronx Co. Sup. Ct.), Judge Sheindlin set the defendant's conviction aside where the People failed to reveal the existence of a prosecution witness's criminal record. Here, the prosecution discovered a witness, Adolfo Guzman, after the trial had commenced. Although Guzman informed the prosecutor that he had never been arrested, the prosecutor ordered a record check to confirm it. As a result of Guzman's representation, neither side questioned Guzman about any prior record. Following the defendant's conviction, the prosecutor disclosed that the record check revealed that the witness had two prior misdemeanor weapons convictions.

The defense moved to set the verdict aside on the ground that the People had violated CPL § 240.45(1)(b) in failing to make the witness's criminal record available to the defense. In opposition, the People argued that the defense had made no specific requests for the record and, alternatively, the impeachment evidence was not material to the outcome of the trial.

In granting the motion, Judge Sheindlin set forth the following analysis:

> The principle that evidence exculpatory in nature and in the possession of the prosecution must be made accessible to the defendant, (*Brady v. Maryland*, 373 U.S. 83, 86–88, 83 S.Ct. 1194, 119–97, 10 L.Ed.2d 215 (1963)) also applies to evidence which impeaches the credibility of a People's witness (*Giglio v. United States*, 405 U.S. 150, 154–55, 92 S.Ct. 763, 766, 31 L.Ed.2d 104 (1972); *People v. Cwikla*, 46 N.Y.2d 434, 441, 414 N.Y.S.2d 102, 105, 386 N.E.2d 1070 (1979); *People v. Howard*, 127 A.D.2d 109, 113, 513 N.Y.S.2d 973, 976 (1st Dept. 1987)). A witness's criminal conviction record is evidence which must be disclosed under *Brady* principles. (*People v. Santiago*, 138 A.D.2d 327, 327, 526 N.Y.S.2d 456 (1st Dept. 1988)).

> In *United States v. Agurs*, (427 U.S. 97, 96 S.Ct. 2392, 49 L.Ed.2d 342 (1976)), the United States Supreme Court noted that the *Brady* rule applied in "three quite different situations." (*United States v. Agurs*, *supra* at 103). Hence, three (3) distinct classes of violations were set forth. A class I violation involves the use by the prosecution of testimony that the prosecutor knew, or should have known, was perjurious. Such a conviction is fundamentally unfair, and must be set aside, if there is any reasonable likelihood that the false testimony could have affected the judgment of the jury. Hence, materiality is a factor in this class of violation. A class II violation occurs when exculpatory evidence is not disclosed pursuant to a specific relevant request. (*Brady v. Maryland*, 373 U.S. at 86–88; *People v. Smith*, 63 N.Y.2d 41, 66–67, 479 N.Y.S.2d 706, 717–18, 468 N.E.2d 879 (1984); *People v. Cwikla*, 46 N.Y.2d 434, 441, 414 N.Y.S.2d 102, 105, 386 N.E.2d 1070 (1979)). When a prosecutor fails to disclose *Brady* material in response to such a particularized specific request, "the failure to make any response is seldom, if ever, excusable" and hence, reversal is required. (*United States v.*

Agurs, 427 U.S. at 106; *People v. Brown*, 67 N.Y.2d 555, 559, 505 N.Y.S.2d 574, 575, 496 N.E.2d 663 (1986), cert. denied, 479 U.S. 1093, 107 S.Ct. 1307, 94 L.Ed.2d 161 (1987); *People v. Cwikla*, 46 N.Y.2d at 441). Materiality of the non-disclosed evidence is not a factor. The class III violations involve cases where there is either no defense request at all, or a generalized request (i.e., "produce *Brady* material"). Under such circumstances, reversal is required only if the omitted evidence was material, that is, if "there is a reasonable probability that, had the evidence been disclosed to the defense, the result of the proceeding would have been different." (*People v. Chin*, 67 N.Y.2d 22, 33, 499 N.Y.S.2d 638, 646, 490 N.E.2d 505 (1986)).

In the case at bar, difficulty arises in determining which *Agurs* formulation to apply. Certainly, this case does not involve a class I situation, since the witness informed the prosecutor that he had no criminal record. Indeed, the prosecutor's good faith is not questioned here, since the prosecutor, with commendable candor, informed this Court and defense counsel immediately upon discovery of the prior convictions. Nor does this case fall squarely within the class II category, since defense counsel made no specific request for the omitted material. In light of the prosecutor's specific representation that the witness did not have a prior record, it would be fundamentally unfair to place this case into the class III situation.

Accordingly, a fourth category must be established to encompass the circumstances presented. Specifically, this Court holds that when a prosecutor makes an affirmative specific representation as to specific *Brady* material, a defense attorney is not required to make a particularized request for that material. A specific request for that material will, instead, be implied. To require defense counsel to utter a request for specific material, the existence of which has already been denied, in order to trigger the class II standard, is placing form over substance.

People v. Ramos, N.Y.L.J., 1/29/90, p. 26, Col. 1 (Bronx Co. Sup. Ct.). The court, applying the "seldom, if ever, excusable" standard applicable to specific *Brady* requests, granted the defendant's motion to set aside the verdict and ordered a new trial.

§ 21:5   Evidence need not be in prosecutor's possession

Research References
West's Key Number Digest, Criminal Law ☞2003

The prosecutor's lack of personal knowledge of *Brady* material is not a justification for their failure to turn over *Brady* material to the defense. In *People v. Wright*, 86 N.Y.2d 591, 635 N.Y.S.2d 136, 658 N.E.2d 1009, (1995), the Court stated:

The People's reliance in their opposition papers on the trial prosecutor's lack of personal knowledge regarding any instances in which [the victim] had operated as an informant is unavailing. The mandate of *Brady* extends beyond any particular prosecutor's actual knowledge (see, e.g. *Giglio v. United States*, 405 U.S. 150 [nondisclosure of promise made to witness by another prosecutor in trial prosecutor's office, which promise was not known to trial prosecutor]). Furthermore, "the individual prosecutor has a duty to learn of any favorable evidence known to the others acting on the government's behalf in this case, including the police." (*Kyles v. Whitley*, 115 S.Ct. 1555, 1567. The People therefore were not relieved of their obligation to turn over *Brady* material by the trial prosecutor's failure to discover that the police were in possession of exculpatory information see, *People v. Simmons*, 36 N.Y.2d 126, 132 [(negligent, as well as deliberate, nondisclosure may deny due process)].

People v. Wright, *supra*.

Similarly, in *People v. Jackson*, 154 Misc. 2d 718, 593 N.Y.S.2d 410 (Kings Co. Sup. Ct. 1992), *order aff'd*, 198 A.D.2d 301, 603 N.Y.S.2d 558 (2d Dep't 1993), the defendant's arson conviction was reversed and vacated on the ground that a governmental investigatory agency failed to deliver exculpatory material notwithstanding the fact that the prosecutor was unaware of the existence of such evidence.

Because fairness of the trial is the major focus of *Brady*, information possessed by investigative agencies of the government and unknown to the prosecutor, will still result in a violation of defendant's due process rights . . .

Two theories have been espoused why a vacatur of a conviction is necessary where the prosecutor does not know of the information but a governmental investigatory agency does possess the information.

The first theory is that all governmental investigatory agencies are arms of the Prosecutor. Therefore, one arm of the prosecution team is in possession of and responsible for all the other functioning parts of the team . . .

The second theory is that the "Government" has the *Brady* duty and not only the Prosecutor. There is an independent duty on the part of each investigatory agency to disclose exculpatory material irrespective of the Prosecutor's knowledge . . .

New York seems to adopt the approach that governmental investigatory agencies have an independent *Brady* duty of disclosure. In *People v. Russo*, 109 A.D.2d 855, 856, 486 N.Y.S.2d 769, the court said:

. . . the police have a duty to disclose exculpatory material in their control, failure to so disclose will constitute reversible error if such evidence is material to defense and likely to have changed the jury's verdict . . .

The form that the exculpatory material takes is irrelevant. Whether something is oral or written, if it tends to disprove defendant's guilt or proves defendant's innocence, justice is served if it is disclosed to defendant, and society gains by having a fair trial.

593 N.Y.S.2d at 417–18 (citations omitted). *See also People v. Benard*, 163 Misc. 2d 176, 620 N.Y.S.2d 242 (N.Y. Co. Sup. Ct. 1994) (prosecution charged with constructive possession and control of material). *But see People v. Muniz*, 215 A.D.2d 881, 627 N.Y.S.2d 115 (3d Dep't 1995) (no *Brady* violation where prosecutor does not know of *Brady* material until after plea entered).

§ 21:6   Not necessary for *Brady* material to be reduced to writing

Research References

West's Key Number Digest, Criminal Law ☞1990

In *People v. Murray*, 147 A.D.2d 925, 537 N.Y.S.2d 399 (4th Dep't 1989), the court affirmed the trial court's admission of the prosecution's expert witness's testimony concerning blood splatter even though defense counsel was not furnished with a written report in regard to that testimony. The court held that since the witness did not prepare a written report setting forth his opinion concerning the blood splatter patterns found on the defendant's clothes, there was no such report to furnish and, accordingly, the People had not been derelict in regard to their obligations pursuant to CPL § 240.20. 537 N.Y.S.2d at 399.

However, if such testimony or report was exculpatory in nature, the prosecutor would have had an obligation to disclose the information pursuant to the *Brady* doctrine. Further, the form that the exculpatory material takes is irrelevant. In *People v. Jackson*, 154 Misc. 2d 718, 593 N.Y.S.2d 410 (Kings Co. Sup. Ct. 1992), *aff'd*, 198 A.D.2d 301, 603 N.Y.S.2d 558 (2d Dep't 1993), the court held:

Whether something is oral or written, if it tends to disprove defendant's guilt or proves defendant's innocence, justice is served if it is disclosed to defendant, and society gains by having a fair trial.

Defendant's due process right does not depend upon whether the government decides to place exonerating information on a paper or keeps it in the mind of an investigatory agent. Nothing is gained, nor is society's interest in a fair trial fostered by the failure of investigatory agencies to write down exculpatory information.

People v. Jackson, 593 N.Y.S.2d at 418.

§ 21:7 Preservation of evidence

Research References

West's Key Number Digest, Criminal Law ☞1990

In *People v. Alvarez*, 70 N.Y.2d 375, 521 N.Y.S.2d 212, 515 N.E.2d 898 (1987), the Court of Appeals adopted the reasoning of *California v. Trombetta*, 467 U.S. 479, 104 S.Ct. 2528, 81 L.Ed.2d 413 (1984), and held that the People were not required to preserve a sample of the defendant's breath following the administration of a chemical breath test. 521 N.Y.S.2d at 213. In *Trombetta*, the United States Supreme Court held that the duty to preserve was limited to:

> [E]vidence that is either material to the guilt of the defendant or relevant to the punishment to be imposed.

467 U.S. at 485, 104 S.Ct. at 2532. The Court defined constitutional materiality as follows:

> Whatever duty the Constitution imposes on the States to preserve evidence, that duty must be limited to evidence that might be expected to play a significant role in the suspect's defense. To meet this standard of constitutional materiality, evidence must both possess an exculpatory value that was apparent before the evidence was destroyed, and be of such a nature that the defendant would be unable to obtain comparable evidence by other reasonably available means. Neither of these conditions is met on the facts of this case.

467 U.S. at 488, 104 S.Ct. at 2534 (citations omitted). *See* §§ 34:1 et seq., "Preservation of a Breath Sample."

In *People v. Alvarez*, 70 N.Y.2d 375, 521 N.Y.S.2d 212, 515 N.E.2d 898 (1987), the defendant, upon being arrested for DWI, moved to suppress the Breathalyzer results on the ground that the police failed to take and preserve a breath sample for later use by the defendant. The hearing court held that the taking and preservation of a second breath sample, a "simple and accurate" procedure, was required under the due process clause of the State constitution. The appellate term reversed and denied the defendant's suppression motion. On appeal to the Court of Appeals, the Court affirmed the appellate term's orders denying the defendant's motion to suppress, concluding:

> The Supreme Court's analysis and result in *Trombetta*, however, are consonant with New York State law and interests and, we believe, they are analytically correct and provide a fair and proper rule under our State Constitution.

521 N.Y.S.2d at 214.

Alvarez and *Trombetta* dealt with evidence that had an apparent exculpatory value. Where the evidence is merely potentially exculpatory, a different standard is applied.

In *Arizona v. Youngblood*, 488 U.S. 51, 109 S.Ct. 333, 102 L.Ed.2d 281 (1988), Justice Rehnquist, writing for the majority, held that the failure of the police to preserve potentially useful evidence does not constitute denial of due process, absent a showing of bad faith on the part of the police. The distinction here is between evidence that is apparently exculpatory versus evidence that is potentially exculpatory. In this case, the defendant was accused of sexual abuse and sodomy of a 10-year-old boy. Although the treating physician used a "sexual assault kit" to collect evidence of the attack, the police failed to properly preserve semen samples for subsequent testing. Expert testimony indicated that such testing could have exonerated the defendant.

The United States Supreme Court set forth the standard to be applied to *potentially* exculpatory evidence:

> The Due Process Clause of the Fourteenth Amendment, as interpreted in *Brady*, makes the good or bad faith of the State irrelevant when the State fails to disclose to the defendant material exculpatory evidence. But we think the Due Process Clause requires a different result when we deal with the failure of the State to preserve evidentiary material of which no more can be said than that it could have been subjected to tests, the results of which might have exonerated the defendant. Part of the reason for the difference in treatment is found in the observation made by the Court in *Trombetta, supra*, 467 U.S., at 486, 104 S.Ct., at 2532, that "[w]henever potentially exculpatory evidence is permanently lost, courts face the treacherous task of divining the import of materials whose contents are unknown and, very often, disputed." Part of it stems from our unwillingness to read the "fundamental fairness" requirement of the Due Process Clause, *see Lisenba v. California*, 314 U.S. 219, 236, 62 S.Ct. 280, 289, 86 L.Ed. 166 (1941), as imposing on the police an undifferentiated and absolute duty to retain and to preserve all material that might be of conceivable evidentiary significance in a particular prosecution. We think that requiring a defendant to show bad faith on the part of the police both limits the extent of the police's obligation to preserve evidence to reasonable bounds and confines it to that class of cases where the interests of justice most clearly require it, *i.e.*, those cases in which the police themselves by their conduct indicate that the evidence could form a basis for exonerating the defendant. We therefore hold that unless a criminal defendant can show bad faith on the part of the police, failure to preserve potentially useful evidence does not constitute a denial of due process of law.

Arizona v. Youngblood, 488 U.S. at 57–58, 109 S.Ct. at 337. *See also People v. Bridges*, 184 A.D.2d 1042, 584 N.Y.S.2d 360 (4th Dep't 1992); *People v. Bradshaw*, 172 A.D.2d 328, 568 N.Y.S.2d 401 (1st Dep't 1991); *People v. Scattareggia*, 152 A.D.2d 679, 543 N.Y.S.2d 742 (2d Dep't 1989).

§ 21:8   Losing names of witnesses

Research References

West's Key Number Digest, Criminal Law ⟶1999

Where the police lose the names of witnesses prior to turning them over to the prosecution, and there is no showing that those witnesses would provide exculpatory testimony, the prosecutorial failure to preserve and turn over such names does not constitute reversible error.

> There is no per se constitutional right of an accused to access to evidence once in the hands of law enforcement authorities . . . The record does not even suggest, let alone establish, that the troopers' loss of identifying information as to these witnesses was anything but inadvertent. Moreover, the misplacement of this information did not render that source of potential evidence totally beyond reach of defendant, who could have sought to locate the witnesses through his own investigative resources once put on notice, months before the trial, that their names and addresses were not in the prosecution's files . . .

People v. Thornton, 130 A.D.2d 78, 517 N.Y.S.2d 807, 809 (3d Dep't 1987) (citations omitted).

However, where the statement of a witness is exculpatory, and the People withhold such evidence on the ground that they deem it to be unreliable, such action is deemed reversible error even where the evidence presented against the defendants was strong.

> At the very least, the defendants in this case, who were evidently unaware that this witness had given such exculpatory information, were "deprived of the opportunity to make an informed decision regarding the trial strategy that would have been in [their] best interest to pursue." (*People v. Smith*, 127 A.D.2d 864, 866, 512 N.Y.S.2d 244.)

People v. Robinson, 133 A.D.2d 859, 520 N.Y.S.2d 415, 416 (2d Dep't 1987).

§ 21:9   Evidence used to impeach

Research References

West's Key Number Digest, Criminal Law ⟶1999

The right to exculpatory evidence extends to evidence which impeaches the credibility of the People's witnesses. *See Giglio v. United States*, 405 U.S. 150, 154–55, 92 S.Ct. 763, 766, 31 L.Ed.2d 104; *People v. Cwikla*, 46 N.Y.2d 434, 386 N.E.2d 1070, 414 N.Y.S.2d 102 (1979); *Dabbs v. Vergari*, 149 Misc. 2d 844, 570 N.Y.S.2d 765 (Westchester Co. Sup. Ct. 1990). Such evidence falls within the *Brady* doctrine, since it consists of information ". . . favorable to the accused either as direct or impeaching evidence." *Williams v. Dutton*, 400 F.2d 797, 800 (5th Cir. 1968). *See also United States v. Keogh*, 391 F.2d 138 (2d Cir. 1968), *on remand* 289 F.Supp. 265 (S.D.N.Y.1968), *aff'd* 417 F.2d 885 (2d Cir. 1969) (disclosure of financial report which may have impeached government witness); *Guerrero v. Beto*, 384 F.2d 886 (5th Cir. 1967) (fact that eyewitness to crime initially failed to identify defendant at lineup); *Powell v. Wiman*, 287 F.2d 275 (5th Cir. 1961) (mental instability on part of key prosecution witness).

The fact that impeaching testimony is available under the *Brady* doctrine was further recognized by the Supreme Court in *Giles v. Maryland*, 386 U.S. 66, 87 S.Ct. 793, 17 L.Ed.2d 737 (1967), wherein evidence of prior unchastity and mental condition of the complaining witness was held to be discoverable.

In *People v. Velez*, 118 A.D.2d 116, 504 N.Y.S.2d 404 (1986), the Appellate Division, First Department, reversed the defendant's conviction and ordered a new trial where the People failed to disclose that their key witness believed that the defendant had robbed the witness's wife two weeks before the trial. It was not until after the witness had completed his testimony and left the court that the defense was apprised of this belief. Efforts to locate the witness for recall to the stand were fruitless.

Even though the defense failed to move for a mistrial on this basis, the court ordered a new trial in the interest of justice. The court observed that the People had produced a strong case against the defendant. The compelling character of the case, however, depended almost entirely upon the jury's acceptance of this key witness.

> Therefore, the jury was entitled to hear any evidence which would assist them in a valid assessment of this witness' credibility. We are satisfied that fairness to the defendant required that he be permitted to submit evidence of Gonzalez' possible overriding animosity against him and to show that this witness' testimony might have been motivated, or at least strongly affected by, a strong desire either for vengeance or to protect his wife from possible further harm. Potential bias of that magnitude cannot be viewed as a "collateral" matter . . .

People v. Velez, 504 N.Y.S.2d at 406–07 (citations omitted). *See also People v. Andre W.*, 44 N.Y.2d 179, 404 N.Y.S.2d 578, 375 N.E.2d 758; *People v. Rivera*, 119 A.D.2d 517, 501 N.Y.S.2d 38 (1st Dep't 1986) (requiring People to turn over names of witnesses where testimony is material to guilt, innocence, or punishment).

§ 21:10   People's promises to witnesses

Research References

West's Key Number Digest, Criminal Law ⊕1991, 1992

In *People v. Novoa*, 70 N.Y.2d 490, 522 N.Y.S.2d 504, 517 N.E.2d 219 (1987), Judge Kaye confronted a common problem in the prosecutorial determination of what is and isn't *Brady* material. Here, a witness to a homicide agreed to testify for the People. At the time, the witness was the subject of an unrelated narcotics prosecution. In exchange for her testimony, the prosecutor agreed to recommend a lenient sentence with regard to her pending charges.

At the defendant's trial, the witness testified that she had received no promises from the People in exchange for her cooperation. On summation, the prosecutor addressed the issue of the witness's credibility saying:

> There's no reason for Anita to come to the defense of Maria Rodriguez unless what she heard and saw actually happened . . . . Anita is a very strong, intelligent, forthright woman. Yes, she has been indicted for a crime . . . . She also told you she wasn't promised anything, ladies and gentlemen. Anita did not have to be promised anything. I submit she's a woman who will stand or fall on her own merits.

People v. Novoa, 522 N.Y.S.2d at 506. Subsequently, the trial assistant denied knowing of any agreement, but acknowledged having told the witness:

> I was making no promises in exchange for her testimony. I stated that if I were ever asked by anyone in the Special Prosecutor's Office I would tell them that she cooperated.

People v. Novoa, 522 N.Y.S.2d at 507.

In reversing the defendant's conviction, Judge Kaye addressed the People's obligation in regard to disclosure of this kind of *Brady* material:

> This duty of candor and disclosure is no less applicable when the evidence is relevant only to the issue of credibility . . . Thus, it is now firmly established that the "existence of an agreement between the prosecution and a witness, made to induce the testimony of the witness, is evidence which must be disclosed under *Brady* principles." . . . . As a further incident of defendant's right to a fair trial, a prosecutor has an obligation to correct misstatements by a witness concerning the nature of a promise . . . A prosecutor may not sit by silently while her witness testifies falsely that she did not receive any promise in return for testimony . . . If a witness mischaracterizes or falsely denies a promise, the prosecutor must "by immediate statement of his own or by further appropriate examination . . . forthrightly [expose] the lie, so that the court and jury [will know] that the witness had reason to expect lenient treatment for 'continued . . . co-operation' . . . [I]f [a lie] is in any way relevant to the case, the district attorney has the responsibility and duty to correct what he knows to be false and elicit the truth."

It is not the form of a promise, or any label the parties may affix to it, that triggers the prosecutor's duty of disclosure . . . Rather, the obligation arises from the fact that the prosecutor and the witness have reached an understanding in which the witness's cooperation has been exchanged for some quid pro quo on the part of the prosecutor. Once such an understanding has been reached, it is for the jury to determine how much value to assign it in terms of assessing the witness's credibility.

People v. Novoa, 522 N.Y.S.2d at 508 (citations omitted). *See also People v. Wright*, 86 N.Y.2d 591, 635 N.Y.S.2d 136, 658 N.E.2d 1009 (1995) (People's failure to inform the defendant that the complainant had previously operated as an informant for a local police department violated due process); *People v. Lewis*, 174 A.D.2d 294, 580 N.Y.S.2d 6 (1st Dep't 1992) (reversal where witness lied about leniency agreement and agreement never communicated to defense).

The Court of Appeals again addressed this issue in *People v. Steadman*, 82 N.Y.2d 1, 603 N.Y.S.2d 382, 623 N.E.2d 509 (1993). Here, the defendant sought pretrial disclosure of any promises of leniency made to Tony Malloy, the prosecution's principle witness. Although the prosecution revealed some arrangements made with Malloy, the prosecution failed to advise the defense that ADA Dan McCarthy, the trial assistant's superior, had, in fact, negotiated an agreement with Malloy's attorney that Malloy would not go to prison on three pending felony charges if he testified against the defendant. Further, Malloy himself was not made aware of the plea agreement. Thus, during cross-examination, when defense counsel inquired as to whether any promises had been made, Malloy answered no.

Subsequently, the defense attorney learned that promises of leniency had been made to Malloy's attorney, Latimer. The defendant subpoenaed Latimer, who testified that agreements had been negotiated but refused to disclose what, if anything, he told Malloy about the agreement, asserting the attorney-client privilege. Latimer further testified that when he met with the trial assistants and Malloy to prepare Malloy's trial testimony, the trial assistants instructed Malloy that if he were asked about promises of leniency, he was to respond that no promises had been made to him. The defendant moved to dismiss the indictment on the ground that the promise of leniency constituted *Brady* material which should have been disclosed before trial. The trial court ruled that although a *Brady* violation had occurred, a new trial was not necessary in view of the fact that the agreement was made known to the defense in time for use at trial.

On appeal to the Court of Appeals, the People argued that since Malloy was never informed of the agreement, it could not have influenced his testimony or affected his credibility.

Judge Simons, writing for the Court of Appeals, initially noted that no prosecutor had made a full disclosure to any court regarding the details of the agreement.

Thus, the People's argument that Malloy's credibility was not affected by the agreement requires that we accept the assertions of Malloy and the trial assistants that they did not know of McCarthy's promises. Even if Malloy were ignorant of the agreement or its details, however, the scheme employed by the District Attorney's office . . . cannot be condoned.

603 N.Y.S.2d at 384. The Court denounced the DA's tactics:

In a studied effort, McCarthy sought to "shield" the trial assistants and Malloy from knowledge of the agreement. He sought to arrange negotiations so that only he and attorney Latimer knew of the promises and he urged Latimer not to divulge them to his client. Moreover, after the defendants learned of the agreement and subpoenaed Latimer to testify, they were blocked from determining whether Latimer had advised his client of the agreement by Latimer's invocation of the attorney-client privilege. McCarthy's scheme effectively foreclosed any meaningful inquiry into Malloy's knowledge and whether promises of leniency affected his testimony. Moreover, it placed the trial assistants in the position of not only advising Malloy to testify that no promises of leniency had been made to him when they had been, either directly or indirectly, but also, because the trial preparation took place in his presence, of compromising Latimer's ethical position and implicating him in the scheme to mislead the court and the defendants.

In the final analysis, however, it does not matter whether the trial assistants were genuinely unaware of the arrangement or not. A prosecutor's obligation to correct false testimony given by prosecution witnesses and to disclose *Brady* material are duties exercised by individual prosecutors and shared by the prosecutor's office as a whole. Promises made to a defendant by one prosecutor are generally binding on others in the criminal law enforcement system and certainly promises made by a superior are binding on subordinates in the same office. More importantly, the trial assistants here were chargeable with knowledge of McCarthy's promises to Malloy's attorney. After Malloy had testified that no deal for leniency had been struck, the trial assistants, as representatives of their office, had the responsibility of clarifying the record by disclosing all the details of what had actually transpired between their office and Malloy and his attorney. They could not profess ignorance of the arrangement and rely on Latimer's successful invocation of the attorney-client privilege to conceal the facts about the arrangement between Latimer and McCarthy. If the trial assistants had no personal knowledge of the agreement and could not advise the court and the jury about it, then they were required to produce McCarthy or someone else who could. The one thing they could not do was sit silently by and leave the issue in doubt . . . .

People v. Steadman, 603 N.Y.S.2d at 385 (citations omitted). The

Court of Appeals ruled that the error was not harmless and ordered new trials. *See also People v. Benjamin*, 147 Misc. 2d 617, 558 N.Y.S.2d 825 (Queens Co. Crim. Ct. 1990) (failure to disclose adjournment in contemplation of dismissal [ACOD] not *Brady* violation where witness recalled to testify as to ACOD).

§ 21:11   Exculpatory reports

Research References

West's Key Number Digest, Criminal Law ⊸627.8(6), 1992

In *People v. Vilardi*, 76 N.Y.2d 67, 556 N.Y.S.2d 518, 555 N.E.2d 915 (1990), the Court of Appeals affirmed the Second Department's reversal of an arson, reckless endangerment, and conspiracy conviction on the ground that the People failed to disclose a report prepared by its explosives expert that had been specifically sought by the defendant in his discovery request.

In spite of defense counsel's pretrial request for all reports "by ballistics, firearm and explosive experts" concerning the laundromat explosion, counsel received 12 reports, but not the initial exculpatory report.

In preparing for the defendant's appeal, appellate counsel discovered the undisclosed explosives report and made a motion to vacate pursuant to CPL § 440.10. He argued that there was a failure to disclose *Brady* material.

The Appellate Division reversed the conviction on *Brady* grounds and vacated the first-degree arson conviction, distinguishing the case from cases in which no specific request had been made. The Appellate Division held that the undisclosed report was exculpatory and that the prosecution had violated the defendant's constitutional right to be informed of exculpatory information known to the State. The Appellate Division, finding that there was a reasonable possibility that the undisclosed material contributed to the defendant's conviction, ordered a new trial.

The Court of Appeals affirmed the Appellate Division's reversal of the arson conviction, holding that the possibility that the undisclosed evidence might have led to a trial strategy that resulted in a different outcome required reversal. 76 N.Y.2d at 78, 556 N.Y.S.2d at 524.

§ 21:12   Hospital reports

Research References

West's Key Number Digest, Criminal Law ⊸1994, 1997

Hospital records which are exculpatory in nature and in the possession of the People are *Brady* material. In *People v. Davis*,

81 N.Y.2d 281, 598 N.Y.S.2d 156, 614 N.E.2d 719 (1993), the complainant was attacked by 10 men between 3:30 AM and 4:00 AM on November 4, 1987. One week later, the complainant returned to the location of the attack and identified four men, the defendant, Hunter, Sweeper, and Johnson, as the attackers.

Hunter's indictment was dismissed based upon hospital records in the possession of the DA which indicated that Hunter had been in the emergency room from midnight to 6:00 AM on the night of the attack. Subsequently, the defendant requested from the DA all of Hunter's hospital records. The People refused, claiming that Hunter's medical records were not relevant to the identification of the defendant. At trial, although the prosecutor stipulated that Hunter had been admitted into the emergency room at midnight, the DA argued that there was no evidence Hunter had not left at any time during the night. The defendant was found guilty of robbery and assault. The Appellate Division affirmed the conviction, concluding that had the hospital records been disclosed to defense counsel, it is unlikely that a different result would have been reached.

On appeal to the Court of Appeals, the Court initially noted that if Hunter had not responded to his name being called by the emergency room doctor, an "N/A" would have been noted on the records. No such indication appeared on Hunter's records. The Court concluded:

> Hunter's hospital records and the hospital policy concerning "N/A" notations are "evidence favorable to an accused" within the scope of the *Brady* exculpatory material rule (*Brady v. Maryland*, 373 U.S., at 87, 83 S.Ct., at 1197, supra; *see also People v. Vilardi*, 76 N.Y.2d 67, 556 N.Y.S.2d 518, 555 N.E.2d 915), because to the extent [the complainant] misidentified Hunter, the likelihood of misidentification of defendant is affected.

People v. Davis, 598 N.Y.S.2d at 159.

§ 21:13 *Brady* material does not encompass public report

Research References

West's Key Number Digest, Criminal Law ⚷1990

In *People v. Sperber*, N.Y.L.J., 3/23/89, pg. 27, Col. 3, *reversed on other grounds*, 177 A.D.2d 725, 577 N.Y.S.2d 94 (2d Dep't 1991), Judge West of the Westchester County Court held that the Report of the Auditor General of the Commonwealth of Pennsylvania, pertaining to Breathalyzer ampoules and simulator solution, was not *Brady* material.

Here, Jonathan Gradess, Esq., Director of the New York State Defenders Association, mailed copies of the Auditor General's Report to the office of the district attorney. The report questioned the reliability of a certain lot of ampoules. The district attorney failed to deliver this document to the defense as part of the *Brady* material. Defense counsel requested a dismissal of the indictment based upon the alleged *Brady* violation. The motion was denied and the defendant convicted.

In denying the motion, Judge West held:

> In this case, we had a published report from out-of-state which was available to the public and not within the exclusive control of the People. The obligation of the People to disclose evidence mainly involves matters which are within the domain and control of the prosecutor's office [*United States v. Iverson*, 648 F.2d 737 (1981)]. The report of the Auditor General of the Commonwealth of Pennsylvania did not deal with lot number 0217, the ampoules used in this case. Thus, the information contained was not directly "adverse to the position" of the People. In addition, this authority was not from a controlling jurisdiction and, therefore, there was no violation of the Code of Professional Responsibility Section DR7-106(1). In addition, it is stated in the defendant's affirmation that the defense counsel first became aware of the existence of this report the evening before this trial commenced. Clearly, evidence which the defendant has knowledge of is not considered to be *Brady* material [*People v. Murphy*, 109 A.D.2d 895, 487 N.Y.S.2d 89 (1985); *People v. Fein*, 18 N.Y.2d 162, 272 N.Y.S.2d 753, 219 N.E.2d 274 (1966)]. In any event, the defense attorney was able to obtain a copy of this report on January 7, 1989 and was further allowed to litigate the issue of reliability at some length in the course of this trial. Accordingly, this Court finds that there was no violation of the mandates of *Brady v. Maryland*, and, thereby, denies the defendant's motion to set aside the verdict based upon that allegation.

People v. Sperber, N.Y.L.J., 3/23/89, at pg. 27.

§ 21:14   Timely disclosure

Research References

West's Key Number Digest, Criminal Law ⚷2007

Although the *Brady* rule does not require that disclosure of exculpatory material be made at any particular point in the proceedings, it must be disclosed in time for the defense to use it effectively. In *People v. Bolling*, 157 A.D.2d 733, 550 N.Y.S.2d 27 (2d Dep't 1990), the lab report at issue was provided to the defense during the cross-examination of the complainant, the People's first witness. The Second Department concluded that the defense was provided an ample opportunity to utilize the report. *See also People v. Subervi*, 178 A.D.2d 669, 578 N.Y.S.2d 227 (2d Dep't 1991).

In *People v. Roberts*, 203 A.D.2d 600, 611 N.Y.S.2d 214 (2d Dep't 1994), the prosecution provided defense counsel, on the eve of trial, with a statement from a second eyewitness to the crime. The statement was taken from the eyewitness on the same day as the shooting, approximately one year prior to its disclosure. Defense counsel moved to dismiss the indictment, contending that he had been unable to locate the witness or conduct an adequate investigation because of the late disclosure. Although the trial court denied the defendant's motion, the court permitted defense counsel to read the statement into evidence. On appeal, the Appellate Division, Second Department, concluded:

> There is no doubt that the People violated the principles of *Brady v. Maryland*, 373 U.S. 83, 83 S.Ct. 1194, 10 L.Ed.2d 215 by waiting until the eve of trial to disclose the content of [the witness'] statement . . . Although disclosure of such material evidence need not be made at any particular point in the proceedings, they must be turned over to the defendant in time for it to be used effectively . . .
>
> In our view the delay in disclosing Chapman's statement deprived the defendant of a fair opportunity to locate the witness and conduct an adequate investigation of the facts she recounted to the prosecution . . . Further, we find a reasonable possibility that the delay in disclosure of [the witness'] statement affected the outcome of the trial . . . and even though the defendant did not properly preserve this issue for appellate review, we conclude that a new trial should be ordered in the interests of justice.

People v. Roberts, 611 N.Y.S.2d at 215–16 (citations omitted).

§ 21:15 Judicial sanctions

Research References

West's Key Number Digest, Criminal Law ⚖2008

If the defendant requests specific *Brady* material and the People fail to deliver such material, the defendant is entitled to a new trial upon demonstrating that there is a "reasonable possibility" that had the material been disclosed, the results of the trial might have been different. *People v. Davis*, 81 N.Y.2d 281, 598 N.Y.S.2d 156, 614 N.E.2d 719 (1993); *People v. Vilardi*, 76 N.Y.2d 67, 556 N.Y.S.2d 518, 555 N.E.2d 915 (1990).

Where the defendant fails to make a request for *Brady* material, or merely makes a general request, the standard is higher. The defendant must demonstrate that there is a "reasonable probability" that had the evidence been disclosed to the defense, the result of the trial would have been different. *People v. Vilardi*, 556 N.Y.S.2d at 520.

Where the People fail to "preserve" exculpatory evidence, the breach of this duty will rarely result in dismissal of the case. In *People v. Kelly*, 62 N.Y.2d 516, 467 N.E.2d 498, 478 N.Y.S.2d 834

(1984), the Court of Appeals reversed a dismissal granted by the
Criminal Court of the City of New York, which was based on the
People's failure to preserve critical evidence. Although the Court
of Appeals agreed that the People were bound to preserve the evidence in question, they held that prosecutorial fault was just one
consideration in determining a remedy. Elimination of prejudice
was the overriding concern to be addressed and methods other
than dismissal should be considered. The Court cited various possibilities such as the reduction of a drug sale charge to one of
possession where tape recordings of the sale had been erased
(*People v. Saddy*, 84 A.D.2d 175, 445 N.Y.S.2d 601 (2d Dep't
1981)), preclusion of witness testimony where minutes of prior
testimony had been lost, (*People v. Lunney*, 84 Misc. 2d 1090, 378
N.Y.S.2d 559 (N.Y. Co. Sup. Ct. 1975)), a reconstruction hearing,
(*People v. Hicks*, 85 Misc. 2d 649, 381 N.Y.S.2d 794 (N.Y. City
Crim. Ct. 1976)), and a turnover of all remaining minutes and records of witnesses' statements, (*People v. Aviles*, 89 Misc. 2d 1,
391 N.Y.S.2d 303 (N.Y. Co. Sup. Ct. 1977)). The Court concluded:

> Although the choice of "appropriate" action is committed to the
> sound discretion of the trial court, as a general matter the drastic
> remedy of dismissal should not be invoked where less severe
> measures can rectify the harm done by the loss of evidence. Since
> such measures were clearly available here, the court abused its
> discretion in dismissing the charges.

People v. Kelly, 62 N.Y.2d at 521, 478 N.Y.S.2d at 836. *See also
People v. Vargulik*, 130 A.D.2d 530, 515 N.Y.S.2d 111 (2d Dep't
1987) (reversing trial court's suppression of chemical test in
vehicular manslaughter prosecution; suppression of blood test
result because of prosecutorial failure to turn over report of Alco-
Sensor breath screening test result deemed abuse of discretion).

In *People v. Marr*, 177 A.D.2d 964, 577 N.Y.S.2d 1008 (4th
Dep't 1991), upon being arrested for DWI, the defendant was
brought to the police station where he was videotaped. The
videotape was erased prior to trial. Following a hearing, the trial
court concluded that dismissal was not warranted in these
circumstances. Rather, the court precluded the People from
introducing evidence of the defendant's refusal to submit to the
Breathalyzer. On appeal, the Fourth Department concluded:

> The court did not abuse its discretion in precluding the prosecution
> from introducing evidence at trial of defendant's alleged refusal to
> submit to the Breathalyzer test as its sole sanction for the prosec-
> ution's failure to preserve the videotape.

People v. Marr, 577 N.Y.S.2d at 1009.

The rule enunciated in *Kelly* not only applies to cases where
the People fail to preserve *Brady* material, but also where the

People fail to disclose *Brady* material in a timely manner. For example, in *People v. Beam*, 161 A.D.2d 1153, 556 N.Y.S.2d 181 (4th Dep't 1990), the People neglected to turn over *Brady* material until the commencement of trial. Defense counsel requested an adjournment so that he could review the *Brady* material. On appeal, the defendant argued that the granting of an adjournment was an insufficient sanction to impose for the *Brady* violation. The Fourth Department, citing *Kelly*, ruled that dismissal or preclusion of testimony is too harsh a sanction "where less severe measures can rectify the harm done." 577 N.Y.S.2d at 1009. Here, the Court stated that an adjournment was the proper procedure. *See also People v. Lussier*, 205 A.D.2d 910, 613 N.Y.S.2d 466 (3d Dep't 1994).

§ 21:16 *Brady* violation survives guilty plea

Research References

West's Key Number Digest, Criminal Law ☞1990

In *People v. Day*, 150 A.D.2d 595, 541 N.Y.S.2d 463 (2d Dep't 1989), the court concluded that the defendant's guilty plea waived his appellate claim that the prosecutor failed to turn over *Brady* material prior to the plea. The Second Department said the items not produced by the prosecutor went:

> [T]o the issue of factual guilt, which, while appropriate for litigation at a trial, are [sic] waived by a plea of guilty.

150 A.D.2d at __, 541 N.Y.S.2d at 467.

However, the Appellate Division, Third Department, concluded that a claim of a *Brady* violation is not waived by a plea of guilty. In *People v. Armer*, 119 A.D.2d 930, 501 N.Y.S.2d 203 (3d Dep't 1986), the Third Department held that a defendant must be provided an opportunity to withdraw his guilty plea if the prosecutor fails to disclose exculpatory material and if there is a reasonable probability that the defendant would not have pled guilty had the material been disclosed.

In *People v. Benard*, 163 Misc. 2d 176, 620 N.Y.S.2d 242 (N.Y. Co. Sup. Ct. 1994), the defendant was charged with criminal possession of a controlled substance in the first degree. The prosecutor and defense counsel entered into a plea agreement where the defendant would plead guilty to criminal possession of a controlled substance in the third degree with a promise that he would receive a sentence of one to three years. Thereafter, prior to sentence, the defendant moved to withdraw his plea. The defendant alleged that subsequent to his plea, defense counsel learned that the arresting officer had been sanctioned for misconduct. The defendant asserted that had he known that the arresting officer was the subject of an ongoing investigation, he would have rejected the plea offer. The court concluded:

> [I]f a prosecutor has failed to disclose exculpatory material required to be disclosed to a defendant, a defendant who pleads guilty may have his/her plea set aside if the court determines that the information would have materially affected defendant's decision to plead guilty. Materiality in this context is a showing that there is a reasonable probability that had the exculpatory material been disclosed as required, defendant's attorney would have recommended against a plea or defendant, notwithstanding counsel's advice, would have insisted on proceeding to trial. In order to determine whether a basis exists for a defendant here to withdraw his plea, the court must determine first whether a violation of defendant's right to disclosure of exculpatory material has occurred, and only if that question is determined in the affirmative, must the court further determine whether there is a reasonable probability that had such information been disclosed, it would have been material to defendant's and counsel's decision to enter a plea of guilty.

People v. Benard, 620 N.Y.S.2d at 245. *See also Miller v. Angliker*, 848 F.2d 1312 (2d Cir.), *cert. den.* 488 U.S. 890, 109 S.Ct. 224, 102 L.Ed.2d 214 (1988).

§ 21:17 Duty of prosecutor to present *Brady* material to grand jury

Research References

West's Key Number Digest, Criminal Law ⟜2003

It is the duty of the prosecution to both properly instruct the indicting grand jury on the law and bring before the grand jury relevant exculpatory evidence. *See People v. Lancaster*, 69 N.Y.2d 20, 511 N.Y.S.2d 559, 503 N.E.2d 990 (1986), *cert. denied*, 480 U.S. 922, 107 S.Ct. 1383, 94 L.Ed.2d 697 (1987); *People v. Valles*, 62 N.Y.2d 36, 476 N.Y.S.2d 50, 464 N.E.2d 418 (1984).

In *People v. Livingston*, 175 Misc. 2d 322, 668 N.Y.S.2d 443 (Broome Co. Ct. 1997), the court dismissed an indictment charging the defendant with DWI where the People failed to show the grand jury a videotape of the defendant performing various field sobriety tests. Although the officers' grand jury testimony described the defendant as failing the tests, the court held that "any objective review of the videotape clearly indicates that the defendant's performance of those tests was far from failing." 175 Misc. 2d at 324, 668 N.Y.S.2d at 444. As such, the videotape constituted exculpatory evidence that should have been presented to the grand jury.

§ 21:18 Unavailability of prosecution witness

If the People are aware that the complaining witness has died, are they obligated to notify the defense of this fact? More specifically, if the People are aware that the complaining witness has died and do not notify the defense of this fact, but instead negotiate a plea bargain with the defense that the defendant clearly would not have accepted if he/she knew that the complaining witness was permanently unavailable—is the defendant entitled to withdraw his/her guilty plea under Due Process and/or *Brady* principles? The answer is "no." *See People v. Jones*, 44 N.Y.2d 76, 404 N.Y.S.2d 85, 375 N.E.2d 41 (1978).

In *Jones*, the Court of Appeals held that "defendant was not denied due process when the District Attorney's office did not disclose during plea negotiations that it had received information that the complaining witness had died." 44 N.Y.2d at 78, 44 N.Y.2d at 86. In so holding, the Court reasoned as follows:

> The circumstance that the testimony of the complaining witness was no longer available to the prosecution was not evidence at all. Further, to the extent that proof of the fact of the death of this witness might have been admissible on trial, it would not have constituted exculpatory evidence—i.e., evidence favorable to an accused where the evidence is material either to guilt or to punishment. Accordingly, it does not fall within the doctrine enunciated by the Supreme Court of the United States in *Brady v. Maryland*. . . . Rather, . . . the death of Rodriguez would merely have been one of the factors—though a most significant factor—to be weighed by defendant in reaching his decision whether, as a matter of tactics in light of the strength of the People's case against him, to interpose a negotiated plea of guilty.

> The question remains as to the extent of the prosecution's obligation to disclose information in its possession which, as here, is highly material to the practical, tactical considerations which attend a determination to plead guilty, but not to the legal issue of guilt itself. Analytically the issue is not whether this defendant was entitled to evidence in the possession of the prosecution; the question before us on this appeal is whether the pretrial conduct of the prosecutor in the course of plea negotiation was such as to constitute a denial of due process to defendant in the circumstances disclosed in this record. * * *

> [N]otwithstanding that the responsibilities of a prosecutor for fairness and open-dealing are of a higher magnitude than those of a private litigant, no prosecutor is obliged to share his appraisal of the weaknesses of his own case (as opposed to specific exculpatory evidence) with defense counsel. . . . At the other extreme it is equally clear that the courts will allow a defendant to withdraw a guilty plea when the prosecution has either coerced him by threats or persuaded him by affirmative deceit to enter a guilty plea. * * *

It may be of more than passing interest that the formal statements of the professional responsibilities of prosecutors to make disclosure appear to address only the obligation to disclose exculpatory evidence. None touches on disclosure of tactical data. * * *

Turning then to the present case, we hold that there was no obligation on the part of the prosecutor to reveal to defense counsel that Rodriguez had died, prior to acceptance of defendant's plea of guilty. Defendant does not protest his innocence; on the contrary he testified to the factual basis for the charge to which he pleaded. While the prosecutor failed to inform defense counsel of Rodriguez' death, there is no claim of affirmative misrepresentation. And, it is critical, the failure to disclose did not involve exculpatory evidence.

44 N.Y.2d at 79-82, 404 N.Y.S.2d at 87-89 (citations and footnote omitted). *Jones* appears to be directly adverse to certain *dicta* in *People v. Perez*, 193 Misc. 2d 169, __, 749 N.Y.S.2d 850, 852 (Westbury Just. Ct. 2002), indicating that there would be a duty to disclose the complaining witness' unavailability in traffic infraction cases.

It should be noted that the *Jones* Court left open the possibility that Due Process might be violated:

[W]here in the course of plea negotiation a particular defendant staunchly and plausibly maintains his innocence but states explicitly and creditably that as a matter of balanced judgment in the light of the apparent strength of the People's proof he wishes to interpose a negotiated plea to reduced charges to avoid the risk of a more severe sentence likely to attend conviction after trial; failure of the prosecutor to reveal the death of a critical complaining witness might then call for a vacatur of the plea. Silence in such circumstances might arguably be held to be so subversive of the criminal justice process as to offend due process.

44 N.Y.2d at 81-82, 404 N.Y.S.2d at 88.

Chapter 22

Sandoval Issues: Admission of Prior Convictions at Trial

Research References

Westlaw Databases

Charges to the Jury and Requests to Charge in Criminal Case in New York (CTJNY)

Handling a Criminal Case in New York (HCCNY)

Treatises and Practice Aids

New York Charges to the Jury §§ 6:19 to 6:24

Muldoon, Handling a Criminal Case in New York § 6:92

KeyCite®: Cases and other legal materials listed in KeyCite Scope can be researched through the KeyCite service on Westlaw®. Use KeyCite to check citations for form, parallel references, prior and later history, and comprehensive citator information, including citations to other decisions and secondary materials.

---

§ 22:1   Prior convictions—Generally

Research References

West's Key Number Digest, Witnesses ⚷337(7), 337(31)

People v. Sandoval, 34 N.Y.2d 371, 357 N.Y.S.2d 849, 314

N.E.2d 413 (1974), entitles the defense to a pretrial hearing to determine what prior convictions and/or prior bad acts the prosecution will be allowed to use to impeach the defendant should he elect to take the stand. This hearing usually consists of an informal pretrial conference in which the court hears argument and renders a determination in regard to the individual convictions and/or prior bad acts. It is incumbent upon the defense, however, to make a "*Sandoval*" motion in order that this determination be had prior to trial.

§ 22:2   Prior convictions—Procedure

Research References

West's Key Number Digest, Criminal Law ⚖369.1; Witnesses ⚖337(31)

CPL § 60.40 governs the use of prior convictions in a criminal trial. It allows the prosecution to impeach a defendant by inquiring as to a previous conviction for a specified offense. If the defendant answers in the negative or in an equivocal manner, the People may independently prove such conviction.

Procedurally, the DA is required to provide the defense with the defendant's prior record. The burden is on the defense, however, to inform the court of the prior convictions it wishes suppressed and to convince the court of their prejudicial effect.

> In each case the defendant shall inform the court of prior convictions and misconduct which might unfairly affect him as a witness in his own behalf. The trial court in its discretion and in the interests of justice shall then determine whether and to what extent the particular defendant has met his burden, and it is his, of demonstrating that the prejudicial effect of the admission of evidence thereof for impeachment purposes would so far outweigh the probative worth of such evidence on the issue of credibility as to warrant its exclusion.

People v. Sandoval, 357 N.Y.S.2d at 856.

Where the People intend to cross-examine the defendant and/or examine another witness in regard to prior crimes of the defendant which the People are introducing as part of their direct case, the burden falls upon the People to ask for a ruling from the court out of the presence of the jury before attempting to introduce such evidence. This inquiry by the People should be made prior to trial, just before the trial begins, or just before the witness testifies, depending upon the circumstances of the particular case. In any event, it should be made prior to the elicitation of the testimony in the courtroom. *See People v. Ventimiglia*, 52 N.Y.2d 350, 438 N.Y.S.2d 261, 420 N.E.2d 59 (1981). The distinction here is not between prior convictions, and "other crimes," rather it is whether the evidence is being used to impeach the defendant, or as proof in support of the People's direct case.

Where the defense neglects to raise the issue of a prior unrelated crime as part of its *Sandoval* motion and the defendant takes the stand, the People may impeach the defendant by inquiring in regard to this unrelated criminal act. In *People v. Matthews*, 68 N.Y.2d 118, 506 N.Y.S.2d 149, 497 N.E.2d 287 (1986), the Court of Appeals affirmed the conviction of a defendant where the prosecutor had cross-examined him in such regard. 506 N.Y.S.2d at 151.

Here, the People asked the defendant if he had committed a bank robbery in Atlanta, Georgia, while he was awaiting trial of the instant case. The defense objection was sustained, but the motion for a mistrial was denied. In response to the defense's motion, the People noted that the defense was aware of the other charges, but had not moved with respect to them during the *Sandoval* hearing.

In affirming the conviction, the Court of Appeals held that whereas the defendant cannot anticipate what the People will attempt to prove on their direct case, the decision to testify is within his control and he should anticipate cross-examination regarding prior criminal or immoral acts. It is up to him to prevent prejudice by moving to prohibit or limit questioning on these matters before he takes the stand. 506 N.Y.S.2d at 151. *See also People v. Booker*, 145 A.D.2d 564, 536 N.Y.S.2d 118 (2d Dep't 1988).

In *People v. Mandigo*, 176 A.D.2d 386, 574 N.Y.S.2d 92 (3d Dep't 1991), the Court held that the defendant was denied effective assistance of counsel due to counsel's failure to make a *Sandoval* motion, where the defendant was the only source of defense testimony, and where counsel erroneously believed that the prosecutor was required to seek judicial approval prior to cross examining the defendant about the prior conviction. 574 N.Y.S.2d at 93.

§ 22:3 Prior convictions—*Sandoval* criteria

Research References

West's Key Number Digest, Witnesses ⚯227(27), 337(7), 337(25), 337(28)

Although there are no hard and fast rules utilized by courts in determining "*Sandoval*" motions, there are some general criteria which are normally considered:

(a) *Whether the crimes were remote in time from the present charges.*

There is no specific time period specified in the Criminal Procedure Law. Remoteness will depend on the particular circumstances of any given case. Twelve-year-old convictions were allowed after a *Sandoval* hearing, where they demonstrated the defendant's willingness to place his self-interest ahead of principle or the interests of society. *People v. Dupree*, 157 A.D.2d 847, 550 N.Y.S.2d 735 (2d Dep't 1990).

Generally, most courts use 10 years as a rule of thumb. This is probably derived from Rule 609 of the Federal Rules of Evidence which precludes the introduction of evidence of a conviction for impeachment purposes if more than 10 years has elapsed since the date of the conviction or since the release of the witness from the confinement imposed from that conviction, whichever is the later date.

The Appellate Division, Third Department, ruled in *People v. Miller*, 217 A.D.2d 810, 630 N.Y.S.2d 99 (3d Dep't 1995), that the trial court did not abuse its discretion in permitting the People to inquire into three of the defendant's prior convictions which were over 10 years old. Citing *People v. Walker*, 83 N.Y.2d 455, 611 N.Y.S.2d 118, 633 N.E.2d 472, the court stated that there was no per se rules requiring preclusion because of the age, nature, and number of a defendant's prior crimes.

(b) *Whether the prior crime or misconduct was based upon an addiction or uncontrollable habit.*

Since the purpose of the cross-examination is to impugn the credibility of the defendant, crimes arising out of addiction or compulsion are of less probative value for the purpose of establishing a lack of in-court veracity. Accordingly, their value lies more in prejudicing the jury against the defendant. This is improper and the courts will generally not allow impeachment under such circumstances. Fed. R. Evid. 609(b).

Similarly, the courts will not allow the cross-examination of a defendant in regard to violent misconduct if such was spontaneous or impulsive in nature. In *People v. English*, 75 A.D.2d 981, 429 N.Y.S.2d 98 (4th Dep't 1980), the court upheld the trial court's ruling excluding evidence of the defendant's prior crimes of violence, but permitting evidence of his attempted possession of stolen goods in a burglary.

The corollary of the court's reluctance to allow impeachment for the purpose of prejudicing a jury is where the prior crimes or misconduct involves individual dishonesty. Since veracity is the issue under consideration, such crimes or misconduct will usually be allowed into evidence for the purpose of impeaching the defendant. As stated in *People v. Sandoval*, the purpose of a cross-examination is to impeach credibility and to demonstrate the defendant's "determination to further self-interest at the expense of society or in derogation of the interests of others . . . " *People v. Sandoval*, 357 N.Y.S.2d at 855. Consequently, prior convictions for perjury, theft, fraud, bribery, acts of deceit, cheating, and breach of trust will almost always be allowed into evidence.

(c) *Whether the crimes and conduct at issue are similar to that with which the defendant is presently charged.*

Again, the purpose of impeachment is not to convince the jury of the defendant's guilt, but to establish his lack of truthfulness. Accordingly, the prosecution would not normally be allowed to utilize a prior conviction for DWI to impeach a defendant charged with that crime. If the defense does not admit the existence of a prior DWI misdemeanor in a felony prosecution, the People would be allowed as part of their direct proof to establish the prior conviction as an element of the felony charge. Generally, the defense admits the underlying conviction, and the People are precluded from using the prior conviction for purposes of impeachment.

In *People v. McAleavey*, 133 Misc. 2d 987, 509 N.Y.S.2d 278 (1986), *affd.* 159 A.D.2d 646, 553 N.Y.S.2d 38 (2d Dep't 1990), the Suffolk County Court reached a contrary result and held that evidence of a defendant's prior DWI convictions was admissible to impeach the defendant if he testified. 509 N.Y.S.2d at 282. Here, the court observed that the credibility of the defendant and the arresting officer were crucial to the question of guilt or innocence since the defendant claimed that his son was operating the vehicle, and the arresting officer testified that the defendant was alone in the vehicle at the time in question. The court stated:

> In the opinion of this court, the violation of the laws prohibiting the operation of a motor vehicle upon a public highway while under the influence of alcohol clearly evinces a marked willingness on the part of the perpetrator to consider his own self interests paramount to those of society.

509 N.Y.S.2d at 282. *See also People v. Perry*, 221 A.D.2d 736, 633 N.Y.S.2d 848 (3d Dep't 1995) (similarity of prior convictions to charged crime does not necessarily preclude inquiry).

In *People v. Cooke*, 101 A.D.2d 983, 477 N.Y.S.2d 730 (3d Dep't 1984), the Appellate Division, Third Department, reversed a conviction for sodomy in the first degree because of the trial court's ruling that the People could cross-examine the defendant on a 1978 rape conviction and on a nine-year-old conviction for petty larceny and criminal trespass. Insofar as the petty larceny and criminal trespass convictions were concerned, the court held that they were too remote in time. 477 N.Y.S.2d at 732. Allowance of the use of the rape conviction was held to be erroneous because of the possibility that the cross-examination would go beyond the issue of credibility and influence the jury to find the defendant guilty of the instant crime based upon his conviction of a prior, similar offense. 477 N.Y.S.2d at 732.

In *People v. Dickman*, 42 N.Y.2d 294, 397 N.Y.S.2d 754, 366 N.E.2d 843 (1977), the Court of Appeals reversed a town court conviction for reckless driving where the lower court allowed a district attorney to impeach the defendant with a prior two-year-old reckless driving conviction. In that same decision, the Court of Appeals held it was error to allow cross-examination into prior violations of improper turn and unsafe driving.

Insofar as traffic violations are concerned, VTL § 155 prohibits their use for impeachment purposes.

> A traffic infraction is not a crime . . . and shall not affect or impair the credibility as a witness or otherwise of any person convicted thereof.

VTL § 155.

However, in *People v. Beavers*, 173 A.D.2d 348, 569 N.Y.S.2d 718 (1st Dep't 1991), the First Department made it clear that this did not preclude the use at trial for impeachment purposes of numerous unpaid parking tickets. In *Beavers*, the defendant had accumulated 44 unpaid parking tickets in two years. Although acknowledging the prohibitions of VTL § 155, the court held:

> [T]he statute does not preclude inquiry into the consistent failure to pay fines imposed on traffic tickets. Defendant's pattern of failing to pay the parking tickets was relevant to a determination of her credibility, particularly her willingness to place her own interests above those of society.

569 N.Y.S.2d at 718. The court nevertheless considered the possibility that its holding was erroneous by holding that the error, if any, "paled into harmlessness" given the overwhelming evidence of guilt. 569 N.Y.S.2d at 718–19.

The thrust of all of these cases is that the court must balance the danger that the jury might regard the commission of a prior similar offense as proof of the commission of the present charge, rather than as legitimate proof of the defendant's propensity to violate the law to further his own interests which is material proof as to his lack of credibility.

(d) *Sandoval* compromise: In certain situations, a court may be reluctant to allow the People to use a specific conviction because its nature might be prejudicial to the defense. Instead of precluding the People altogether, a court may compromise and allow the People to establish the existence of a conviction without specifying its nature. In *People v. Bermudez*, 98 Misc. 2d 704, 414 N.Y.S.2d 645 (N.Y. Co. 1979), the People wished to impeach a defendant charged with robbery through use of prior convictions which included robbery. The Court allowed the district attorney to establish the fact of the existence of the prior convictions, but did not allow the People to specify what they were for. *See also People v. Lotz*, 145 A.D.2d 900, 536 N.Y.S.2d 281 (4th Dep't 1988); *People v. Davis*, 168 A.D.2d 218, 562 N.Y.S.2d 104 (1st Dep't 1990) (even 11 prior convictions permissible with *Sandoval* "compromise").

(e) Finally, the court will consider the age of the defendant at the time the prior misconduct or conviction occurred. Generally, youthful offender adjudications may not be brought out at trial. However, the Court may, in its discretion, allow questions in regard to the underlying acts which led to the adjudication. *See People v. Sanza*, 37 A.D.2d 632, 323 N.Y.S.2d 632 (2d Dep't 1971).

§ 22:4 Prior uncharged criminal, vicious, or immoral conduct

Research References

West's Key Number Digest, Witnesses ⚎227(27), 337(7), 337(25), 337(28)

The Criminal Procedure Law requires the People to inform the defense, upon request, of any specific instances of uncharged conduct which the People know of, and intend to use at trial for the purpose of impeachment. CPL § 240.43.

In *People v. Vargas*, 88 N.Y.2d 856, 644 N.Y.S.2d 484 (1996), the Court of Appeals reiterated that "[e]vidence of uncharged crimes and offenses is 'inadmissible if offered for no purpose other than to raise an inference that a defendant is of a criminal disposition and, therefore, likely to have committed the crime charged.'" 88 N.Y.2d at 858, 644 N.Y.S.2d at 485 (citation omitted).

§ 22:5 Violation of *Sandoval* ruling

Research References

West's Key Number Digest, Criminal Law ⚎1170.5(1)

A defendant has the right to rely on the court's ruling when he takes the witness stand. He can expect that the court will not permit cross-examination on matters precluded by the ruling. *See People v. Aponte*, 168 A.D.2d 274, 562 N.Y.S.2d 503 (1st Dep't. 1990).

In *People v. Butchino*, 141 A.D.2d 986, 530 N.Y.S.2d 642 (3d Dep't 1988), the court ruled that the People could inquire into the date, court and level of the defendant's prior convictions, but not into the specific acts. At trial, however, the prosecutor asked the defendant about the specific acts. The court, finding that the prosecutor had violated its *Sandoval* ruling, denied the defendant's motion to dismiss on the grounds that the defendant did not object until the conclusion of that day's testimony after the jury had been excused. The appellate court reversed, stating:

This is the only logical result since the name of the crime itself would greatly prejudice defendant, and county court tailored its ruling to avoid such prejudice by limiting the use of the prior conviction to impeach defendant's credibility. Since the violation of the *Sandoval* ruling was highly prejudicial, a reversal is warranted.

530 N.Y.S.2d at 644.

§ 22:6   Failure to assert *Sandoval* deemed waiver

Research References

West's Key Number Digest, Criminal Law ☞1044.1(4)

In *People v. Matthews*, 68 N.Y.2d 118, 506 N.Y.S.2d 149, 497 N.E.2d 287 (1986), the Court reminded the practicing bar that a failure to assert and specify crimes constitutes a waiver of any objection to impeachment of the defendant at trial using such crimes. Here, the defendant testified in a robbery prosecution and was cross-examined as to an out-of-state robbery. While the defendant had filed a *Sandoval* motion, he had omitted a charge of bank robbery that had been filed in Georgia but had not been adjudicated. In fact, the charge had been dismissed pending the determination of the New York indictment. The prosecutor had been advised by the federal authorities, and the information had been passed on to defense counsel.

In affirming the defendant's conviction, the Court held that the burden of asserting the defendant's rights lay with the defense, and although the charge had been dismissed, it was not a final dismissal on the merits. Accordingly, the underlying act was a proper subject for inquiry by the prosecutor on cross-examination. The failure to include this charge in the *Sandoval* motion constituted a waiver of the defendant's right to an advance ruling, and deprived him of the claim of prejudice arising out of the fact that the question was asked at trial. 506 N.Y.S.2d at 151.

Similarly, in *People v. Booker*, 145 A.D.2d 564, 536 N.Y.S.2d 118 (2d Dep't 1988), the court held that it was proper for the People to inquire into certain prior convictions which had been omitted from the defendant's original *Sandoval* application. The court rebuffed the defendant's assertion that the People were obligated to disclose their intention to use these convictions at the time of the *Sandoval* hearing. 536 N.Y.S.2d at 119.

§ 22:7   Procedural issues: failure of court to rule

Research References

West's Key Number Digest, Witnesses ☞337(31)

People v. Oglesby, 137 A.D.2d 840, 525 N.Y.S.2d 304 (2d Dep't 1988), is a classic presentation of the conundrum posed by a judge sitting as both finder of fact and adjudicator of the law in a bench trial. Here, the defendant requested a *Sandoval* ruling in regard to prior convictions. The judge refused to make such a rul-

ing on the ground that the court felt that it would unduly prejudice him to review the defendant's criminal history. The court
directed the prosecution to examine the record and to perform
the court's role of balancing which materials to allow and which
to exclude.

On appeal, the Appellate Division reversed, holding that the
defendant was entitled to the ruling in order that he might make
an informed choice as to whether or not to testify. Insofar as the
court's concern as to being prejudiced, or compromised, by having
reviewed the defendant's criminal record, the Appellate Division
observed that the law considered a judge capable of distinguishing the prejudicial aspects of a defendant's prior record from
those crimes which bear on his credibility. *See also People v.
Moreno*, 70 N.Y.2d 403, 521 N.Y.S.2d 663, 516 N.E.2d 200 (1987);
People v. Brown, 24 N.Y.2d 168, 299 N.Y.S.2d 190, 247 N.E.2d
153 (1969); *People v. Cortese*, 136 A.D.2d 724, 524 N.Y.S.2d 62
(2d Dep't 1988).

Splitting with Second Department, the Third Department has
held that a judge in a bench trial need not hold a *Sandoval*
hearing. *People v. Stevenson*, 163 A.D.2d 854, 558 N.Y.S.2d 383
(4th Dep't 1990). The court in *Stevenson* reasoned:

> Although a jury may tend to conclude, despite limiting instructions,
> that a defendant who has committed previous crimes is more likely
> to have committed the crime charged . . . the judge in a nonjury
> trial will not have that tendency.

163 A.D.2d at __, 558 N.Y.S.2d at 383 (citations omitted).

The same judge who presided at pretrial hearings may also
preside at a bench trial even though the pretrial hearing
concerned evidence which was held inadmissible at trial. *See
People v. Davenport*, 173 A.D.2d 633, 570 N.Y.S.2d 219 (2d Dep't
1991); *People v. Burch*, 142 A.D.2d 586, 530 N.Y.S.2d 241 (2d
Dep't 1988).

Finally, the court may not refuse to make a *Sandoval* ruling
based upon the defendant's failure to commit to testifying. *See
People v. Aponte*, 168 A.D.2d 274, 562 N.Y.S.2d 503 (1st Dep't
1990).

§ 22:8 Error to change *Sandoval* ruling after defendant takes stand

Research References
West's Key Number Digest, Criminal Law ☞1170.5(1); Witnesses
☞337(7)

In *People v. Powe*, 146 A.D.2d 718, 537 N.Y.S.2d 208 (2d Dep't
1989), the defendant was on trial for assault. Prior to the

defendant taking the stand, the court ruled that he could be questioned about his previous assault conviction. Subsequently, the court altered its ruling and limited the People's inquiry to simply whether the defendant had been convicted of a crime. Upon the defendant taking the stand, the court reinterpreted its original *Sandoval* ruling as meaning that the defendant could be asked about the nature of his prior conviction, whereupon the People established that the misdemeanor of which the defendant had been previously convicted was, in fact, assault.

In reversing the conviction, the Appellate Division held:

"The policy underlying *Sandoval* was that the accused has the right to make an informed choice concerning the important determination as to whether he should take the stand." . . . Here, the defendant was denied that right when, after making what he believed to be an informed judgment and taking the stand, the court effectively changed the ruling upon which the defendant had relied. The court's ruling, coming after the defendant had already taken the stand, denied the defendant a fair trial.

537 N.Y.S.2d at 209 (citations omitted).

In *People v. Owens*, 203 A.D.2d 106, 610 N.Y.S.2d 485 (1st Dep't 1994), the *Sandoval* ruling restricted inquiry into a prior burglary conviction and the underlying facts. The prosecution, however, went beyond the scope of the ruling by cross-examining the defendant about charges which arose as a result of stolen credit cards and marijuana found on his person at the time of his prior burglary arrest. Reversing the conviction, the First Department held that after the trial court had made its *Sandoval* ruling, the defendant was entitled to rely upon it when he took the witness stand. By allowing the prosecutor to stray beyond the *Sandoval* ruling, the court deprived the defendant of his right to make an informed decision about whether to testify. *See also People v. Hemingway*, 179 A.D.2d 898, 579 N.Y.S.2d 185 (3d Dep't 1992) (trial court improperly permitted cross-examination on pending indictment contrary to *Sandoval* ruling); *People v. Aponte*, 168 A.D.2d 274, 562 N.Y.S.2d 503 (1st Dep't 1990).

In *People v. Wright*, 260 A.D.2d 935, ___, 690 N.Y.S.2d 286, 287 (3d Dep't 1999), the Appellate Division, Third Department, held that "the People's violation of County Court's *Sandoval* ruling and County Court's subsequent erroneous modification of that ruling deprived defendant of a fair trial, requiring reversal."

§ 22:9   Pending criminal charges

Research References

West's Key Number Digest, Witnesses ⊙═337(30)

While particular circumstances may permit a prosecutor to use pending unrelated criminal charges to impeach the defendant's credibility, the defendant's choice to testify does not, by itself, effect a waiver of the privilege against self-incrimination as to pending unrelated charges.

In *People v. Betts*, 70 N.Y.2d 289, 520 N.Y.S.2d 370, 514 N.E.2d 865 (1987), the trial court ruled that if the defendant testified, the People would be permitted to inquire into a pending burglary charge, and that the defendant would not be permitted to exercise his Fifth Amendment right not to incriminate oneself. In reversing the conviction, the Court of Appeals held:

> "While an accused, unlike an ordinary witness, has an option whether to testify at all, exacting such a [sweeping] waiver as the price of taking the stand leaves little of the right to testify on one's own behalf" . . .

> This rule will not, on the other hand, preclude prosecutors from inquiry into pending criminal charges if a defendant, in taking the stand, makes assertions that open the door and render those charges relevant for contradiction and response.

520 N.Y.S.2d at 373 (citation omitted). *See also People v. Hemingway*, 179 A.D.2d 898, 579 N.Y.S.2d 185 (3d Dep't 1992) (trial court improperly permitted cross-examination on pending indictment after disallowing questioning in *Sandoval* hearing); *People v. Chambers*, 184 A.D.2d 716, 585 N.Y.S.2d 84 (2d Dep't 1992) (inquiry of conviction pending appeal prohibited).

§ 22:10 Use of youthful offender adjudications

Research References
West's Key Number Digest, Witnesses ⬥337(30)

Although a youthful offender adjudication may not be used for impeachment purposes because these adjudications are not convictions of a crime, the prosecution may be permitted to cross-examine the defendant as to the illegal act which constituted the basis for the adjudication. *See People v. Wallis*, 147 A.D.2d 821, 537 N.Y.S.2d 910 (3d Dep't 1989); *People v. Ashley*, 145 A.D.2d 782, 535 N.Y.S.2d 763 (3d Dep't 1988).

In *People v. Gray*, 84 N.Y.2d 709, 622 N.Y.S.2d 223, 646 N.E.2d 444 (1995), the defendant had been previously convicted of a felony in Maryland when he was 15 years old which, had it occurred in New York, would have resulted in a juvenile delinquency adjudication. The defendant moved to preclude exploration of the conviction on cross-examination. The Court of Appeals declined to adopt a per se rule automatically excluding any and all foreign criminal convictions involving acts that, if committed in New York, would result in youthful offender or juvenile delinquency treatment. The decision to permit such cross-examination rests in the discretion of the trial court.

§ 22:11 Use of charges adjourned in contemplation of dismissal

Research References

West's Key Number Digest, Witnesses ⊕337(30)

In *People v. Fenti*, 106 A.D.2d 912, 912–13, 483 N.Y.S.2d 495, 495 (4th Dep't 1984), the Appellate Division, Fourth Department, held that "[t]he prosecutor erred in asking defendant whether he was convicted of criminal possession of a controlled substance in 1975 because he knew or should have known . . . that the charge was adjourned in contemplation of dismissal and, therefore, dismissed by operation of law."

> By contrast, in *People v. Hall*, 243 A.D.2d 651, 663 N.Y.S.2d 245 (2d Dep't 1997), the Appellate Division, Second Department, found "no error in the [trial] court's Sandoval ruling permitting the People to question the defendant about two prior arrests which were adjourned on [sic] contemplation of dismissal (*see People v. Hightower*, 163 A.D.2d 489, 559 N.Y.S.2d 671; *People v. Magee*, 126 A.D.2d 573, 510 N.Y.S.2d 690)." 243 A.D.2d at 651, 663 N.Y.S.2d at 246.

However, neither *Hightower* nor *Magee*, cited by the *Hall* court, support this holding. Rather, both of these cases held that "as we have noted previously, inquiry into the underlying facts of charges dismissed in satisfaction of a defendant's *plea of guilty to other charges* is permissible." *Hightower*, 163 A.D.2d at 489, 559 N.Y.S.2d at 671 (emphasis added); *Magee*, 126 A.D.2d at 574, 510 N.Y.S.2d at 691 (emphasis added). Unlike the situation presented in both *Hightower* and *Magee*, a defendant whose case is adjourned in contemplation of dismissal has not pled guilty to anything. Furthermore, upon expiration of the statutory time period, charges adjourned in contemplation of dismissal are dismissed by operation of law and should be sealed pursuant to CPL § 160.50. *See* §§ 52:1 et seq., *infra*.

§ 22:12 Defendant's presence at *Sandoval* hearing

Research References

West's Key Number Digest, Criminal Law ⊕636(3)

In *People v. Dokes*, 79 N.Y.2d 656, 584 N.Y.S.2d 761, 595 N.E.2d 836 (1992), the Court of Appeals held that a defendant has a right to be present during a *Sandoval* hearing, except when such presence would be "superfluous." A violation of this right ordinarily requires reversal of a conviction even in the absence of an objection. 584 N.Y.S.2d at 765. *See also People v. Beasley*, 80 N.Y.2d 981, 592 N.Y.S.2d 644, 607 N.E.2d 791 (1992). This ruling was held by the Court of Appeals to apply retroactively. *People v. Favor*, 82 N.Y.2d 254, 604 N.Y.S.2d 494, 624 N.E.2d 631 (1993).

§ 22:13 When would defendant's presence be superfluous?

Research References

West's Key Number Digest, Criminal Law ⊙636(3)

The *Dokes* Court did not define "superfluous" for purposes of determining under what circumstances a defendant's presence might not be required at a *Sandoval* hearing. This issue was addressed by the Court of Appeals in *People v. Odiat*, 82 N.Y.2d 872, 609 N.Y.S.2d 166, 631 N.E.2d 108 (1993). In *Odiat*, where the defendant was charged with robbery and assault, the record was ambiguous as to his presence at the *Sandoval* hearing. During the *Sandoval* hearing, both the defense counsel and the prosecutor expressed some unfamiliarity with the actual facts of those cases. The trial court ruled that if the defendant testified, the People could bring out the fact that the defendant had been convicted of two unspecified misdemeanors and a felony attempted drug sale, but not about the underlying facts of that felony conviction. 609 N.Y.S.2d at 167.

At trial, the defendant testified at length about his prior drug dealings. After conviction, the defendant appealed, claiming that he was deprived of his right to be present during the *Sandoval* hearing. The Appellate Division affirmed holding that the defendant's presence would have been "superfluous" at the hearing in view of the defendant's lengthy testimony concerning his prior drug dealings.

Remitting the case for a reconstruction hearing on the issue of whether the defendant indeed was absent during the *Sandoval* hearing, the Court of Appeals, when determining whether the defendant's presence would be superfluous, considered: (1) whether the prosecutor or defense counsel was able to fully apprise the court of the underlying acts of the defendant's prior convictions; (2) whether the outcome of the hearing was wholly favorable to the defendant [*see also People v. Favor*, 82 N.Y.2d 254, 604 N.Y.S.2d 494, 624 N.E.2d 631 (1993)], and (3) whether the defendant, given the surrounding circumstances, might have made a meaningful contribution to the colloquy. *Odiat*, 609 N.Y.S.2d at 167.

Even though a defendant's testimony at trial encompasses an admission of the prior bad acts precluded by the *Sandoval* ruling, a superfluousness ruling is not proper, where other prior convictions, inconsistent with the defendant's position at trial, are still utilized against him. 609 N.Y.S.2d at 167.

In *People v. Michalek*, 82 N.Y.2d 906, 609 N.Y.S.2d 172, 631 N.E.2d 114 (1994), the Court of Appeals reaffirmed the importance of the *Sandoval* ruling being "wholly favorable" to the defendant before it would tolerate the defendant's absence therein. In *Michalek*, upon the defendant's claim that he was not present at the two *Sandoval* hearings, the Second Department ruled that the defendant's presence would have been superfluous in view of the trial court's determination that the People would be permitted to question the defendant concerning a prior felony conviction, without permitting exploration of the underlying facts.

In remitting the case to the trial court for a determination of whether the defendant was actually absent at the hearing, the Court of Appeals stated:

> Since it cannot be ascertained from the record whether the defendant was present for either stage of the *Sandoval* hearing, *and because the outcomes of both stages were "not wholly favorable" to defendant* . . ., the case must be remitted to Supreme Court for a reconstruction hearing to determine whether defendant was present during both stages of the hearing.

609 N.Y.S.2d at 173 (citation omitted and emphasis supplied).

A failure of the court to conduct the *Sandoval* hearing in the defendant's presence may be cured by a reading of the minutes of the hearing in the defendant's presence, and giving the defendant an opportunity to consult with counsel and raise any objections with regard to any *Sandoval* issues. *See People v. Lamour*, 189 A.D.2d 825, 592 N.Y.S.2d 451 (2d Dep't 1993).

However, in *People v. Kirkland*, 188 A.D.2d 1083, 592 N.Y.S.2d 188 (4th Dep't 1992), a trial court's mere recitation of the *Sandoval* ruling in the defendant's presence violated his state and federal constitutional rights to be present at all material stages of trial where the defendant was absent during the *Sandoval* hearing.

§ 22:14 Presence may be waived

Research References

West's Key Number Digest, Criminal Law ☞636(3)

In *People v. Peterson*, 151 A.D.2d 512, 542 N.Y.S.2d 301 (2d Dep't 1989), the defendant appealed on the ground that he was denied due process when the trial court held a *Sandoval* hearing without him being present. In rebuffing this challenge, the Appellate Division held:

A criminal defendant's constitutional and statutory right to be present during all material portions of the trial of an indictment . . . may be waived, either expressly or impliedly, providing that the waiver was knowing, voluntary and intelligent . . . In the instant case, defense counsel expressly waived his client's presence at the beginning of the pre-trial conference which encompassed the hearing, and participated in the hearing in the absence of the defendant without objection. Moreover, neither the defendant nor his attorney raised an objection or moved to reopen the hearing at any point in time subsequent thereto. Under such circumstances, it cannot be said that the defendant's rights were prejudiced by his absence from the *Sandoval* hearing . . .

542 N.Y.S.2d at 301–302 (citations omitted).

However, the Fourth Department held, in *People v. Brockenshire*, 197 A.D.2d 921, 602 N.Y.S.2d 459 (4th Dep't 1993), that defense counsel's consent to the defendant's absence from the *Sandoval* hearing did not permit an inference that the defendant knowingly, voluntarily, and intelligently relinquished his right to be present. Defense counsel neither informed the court what the defendant had been told concerning the nature of his right to be present, nor did the court make an express finding that the defendant had waived his right to be present.

The precedential value of the *Peterson* decision is further weakened by *People v. Gebrosky*, 80 N.Y.2d 995, 592 N.Y.S.2d 650, 607 N.E.2d 797 (1992), where the Court of Appeals held that the defendant's deprivation of his right to be present at the *Sandoval* hearing was reviewable despite the defendant's failure to object at trial. 592 N.Y.S.2d at 651. *See also People v. Beasley*, 80 N.Y.2d 981, 592 N.Y.S.2d 644, 607 N.E.2d 791 (1992).

§ 22:15 *Sandoval* severance

Research References

West's Key Number Digest, Criminal Law ☞622.6(1), 622.7(1)

What happens when codefendants are on trial with competing theories of the case which requires one defendant to impeach the credibility of the other? Does the court's preclusion of the use of certain prior convictions in a *Sandoval* ruling apply to a codefendant? In *People v. McGee*, 68 N.Y.2d 328, 508 N.Y.S.2d 927, 501 N.E.2d 576 (1986), the Court of Appeals held that a codefendant's right of cross-examination could not be limited by the Court's *Sandoval* ruling. A court's pretrial ruling pertaining to *Sandoval* is applicable to the prosecution only. Thus, the Court's *Sandoval* ruling will not be binding on a codefendant who is entitled to a full opportunity to cross-examine the defendant regarding all prior bad acts. Where this problem arises, the appropriate remedy is a motion for severance pursuant to CPL § 200.40.

Potential difficulties in a joint trial arising from the parties' opposing theories of defense may be averted. The remedy is a timely motion for severance pursuant to CPL § 200.40 so that the court, mindful that *Sandoval* does not apply, may determine whether the rights of either defendant will likely be prejudiced in a joint trial. In a similar case, the court properly held that it "could not limit the right of either defense attorney to examine his client's codefendant regarding prior criminal or immoral acts" (*People v. Rodriguez*, 91 A.D.2d 591, 592, 457 N.Y.S.2d 268 [1st Dept.1982]) and that severance should be granted where a significant possibility exists that each defense will prejudice the other. If good cause is shown why the joint trial will prejudice substantial rights of the codefendants, failure to sever may amount to an abuse of discretion (*see People v. La Belle*, 18 N.Y.2d 405, 276 N.Y.S.2d 105, 222 N.E.2d 727 [1966]).

People v. McGee, 508 N.Y.S.2d at 930. *See also People v. Medley*, N.Y.L.J., 12/2/96, p.33, Col.2 (Queens Co. Sup. Ct.).

Chapter 23

Double Jeopardy

§ 23:1   In general

New York "law contains extraordinarily broad proscriptions against multiple prosecutions of the same defendant for the same crime or for different crimes based on the same transaction." *People v. Berkowitz*, 50 N.Y.2d 333, 345–46, 428 N.Y.S.2d 927, 934, 406 N.E.2d 783 (1980).

[D]ouble jeopardy implicates the very power of the State to prosecute a particular defendant for a particular crime and serves as an important check on the potential power of the State to intimidate its citizenry. The constitutional prohibition against double jeopardy is fundamental not only to the process of criminal justice, but to our system of government itself. It is, moreover, a doctrine with obvious jurisdictional overtones.

People v. Michael, 48 N.Y.2d 1, 7, 420 N.Y.S.2d 371, 373, 394 N.E.2d 1134 (1979) (per curiam).

"[T]he evil to which the double jeopardy clause is addressed occurs when a defendant is brought into court to defend against a criminal charge for the second time and is again subjected to the attendant expense, personal anxiety and social opprobrium." *People v. Mayo*, 48 N.Y.2d 245, 250, 422 N.Y.S.2d 361, 364, 397 N.E.2d 1166 (1979).

In New York, Double Jeopardy protections come from several sources:

1. The 5th Amendment to the United States Constitution, which provides that "[n]o person shall . . . be subject for the same offence to be twice put in jeopardy of life or limb";
2. Article 1, § 6 of the New York State Constitution, which provides that "[n]o person shall be subject to be twice put in jeopardy for the same offense"; and
3. Statutes. *See, e.g.*, CPL Article 40 ("Exemption from prosecution by reason of previous prosecution"); PL § 70.25 ("Concurrent and consecutive terms of imprisonment"); PL § 70.30 ("Calculation of terms of imprisonment"); PL § 70.35 ("Merger of certain definite and indeterminate or determinate sentences"); PL § 80.15 (Fines for multiple offenses other than VTL offenses).

This chapter addresses issues pertaining to Double Jeopardy, with a focus on Double Jeopardy issues in DWI cases.

§ 23:2　Double Jeopardy Clause of the 5th Amendment— Generally

The Double Jeopardy Clause of the Fifth Amendment of the United States Constitution states that no person shall "be subject for the same offence to be twice put in jeopardy of life or limb." The United States Supreme Court has interpreted this language to provide three distinct protections: "(1) the right to be free from a second trial following an acquittal for the same crime; (2) the right to be free from a second trial following a conviction for the same offense; and (3) the right not to be punished more than once for the same crime."

People v. Cintron, 22 N.Y.3d 757, 760, 986 N.Y.S.2d 386, 387–88, 9 N.E.3d 881 (2014) (citations omitted). *See also People v. Williams*, 14 N.Y.3d 198, 214, 899 N.Y.S.2d 76, 85, 925 N.E.2d 878 (2010); *People v. Biggs*, 1 N.Y.3d 225, 228–29, 771 N.Y.S.2d 49, 51, 803 N.E.2d 370 (2003); *People v. Gonzalez*, 99 N.Y.2d 76, 82, 751 N.Y.S.2d 830, 832, 781 N.E.2d 894 (2002); *People v. Prescott*, 66 N.Y.2d 216, 221, 495 N.Y.S.2d 955, 958, 486 N.E.2d 813 (1985).

"The underlying idea" is, in the familiar words of Justice Black, "deeply ingrained in at least the Anglo-American system of jurisprudence"; namely,

> that the State with all its resources and power should not be allowed to make repeated attempts to convict an individual for an alleged offense, thereby subjecting him to embarrassment, expense and ordeal and compelling him to live in a continuing state of anxiety and insecurity, as well as enhancing the possibility that even though innocent he may be found guilty.

Matter of Suarez v. Byrne, 10 N.Y.3d 523, 531–32, 860 N.Y.S.2d 439, 445, 890 N.E.2d 201 (2008) (citation omitted).

§ 23:3　Violation of Double Jeopardy Clause not subject to harmless error analysis

In *People v. Mayo*, 48 N.Y.2d 245, 252–53, 422 N.Y.S.2d 361, 366, 397 N.E.2d 1166 (1979), the Court of Appeals held as follows:

[W]e eschew the "harmless error" approach adopted by the Appellate Division and instead base our holding on the fundamental principles inherent in the double jeopardy clause itself. It has been observed that "(t)he guarantee against double jeopardy is significantly different from (other) procedural guarantees * * * While this guarantee, like the others, is a constitutional right of the criminal defendant, its practical result is to prevent a trial from taking place at all, rather than to prescribe procedural rules that govern the conduct of the trial." When a defendant is brought to trial in violation of his rights under the double jeopardy clause of the Fifth Amendment, the very power of the court to try him is implicated. Thus, while a double jeopardy claim may be waivable under certain limited circumstances, it cannot be gainsaid that, absent such a waiver, a trial held in violation of the double jeopardy clause must be deemed to be a nullity having no legal effect. Any less exacting standard would contravene the clear purpose of the double jeopardy clause, to deprive the State of the power to subject a citizen to the risk of trial after he has been exonerated of the charges against him.

(Citations omitted).

§ 23:4 Federal and State Constitutional Double Jeopardy protections are apparently the same

The Court of Appeals has stated that "[t]he Double Jeopardy Clauses in the State and Federal Constitutions are nearly identically worded, and we have never suggested that state constitutional double jeopardy protection differs from its federal counterpart." *Matter of Suarez v. Byrne*, 10 N.Y.3d 523, 534, 860 N.Y.S.2d 439, 447, 890 N.E.2d 201 (2008). *See also People v. Latham*, 83 N.Y.2d 233, 239, 609 N.Y.S.2d 141, 144, 631 N.E.2d 83 (1994) ("Defendant does not claim that he is entitled to greater protection under the State constitutional double jeopardy prohibition").

§ 23:5 Statutory Double Jeopardy protection is much broader than protection provided by the Constitution

"The Legislature . . . has enacted statutory double jeopardy provisions offering broader protection than the Federal Constitution requires (*see* CPL art. 40)." *Matter of Suarez v. Byrne*, 10 N.Y.3d 523, 534, 860 N.Y.S.2d 439, 447, 890 N.E.2d 201 (2008) (citation omitted). *See also People v. Goodman*, 69 N.Y.2d 32, 40, 511 N.Y.S.2d 565, 570–71, 503 N.E.2d 996 (1986) ("our statutes extend[] double jeopardy protection well beyond constitutional requirements"); *People v. Prescott*, 66 N.Y.2d 216, 219, 495 N.Y.S.2d 955, 956–57, 486 N.E.2d 813 (1985) ("In 1970, the New York State Legislature expanded the protection against double jeopardy found in the 5th Amendment of the United States Constitution by enacting CPL article 40 which contains additional grounds for prohibiting multiple prosecution of offenses. CPL 40.20, the section before us on this appeal, prohibits separate prosecutions for 'two offenses based upon the same act or criminal transaction', unless one of six exceptions is met").

§ 23:6 Double Jeopardy claim can be brought via Article 78 proceeding

Where the defendant raises a Double Jeopardy claim in the trial court and loses, the defendant can file an Article 78 proceeding seeking a writ of prohibition preventing a retrial. *See, e.g.,*

Matter of Davis v. Brown, 87 N.Y.2d 626, 641 N.Y.S.2d 819, 664 N.E.2d 884 (1996); *Matter of Randall v. Rothwax*, 78 N.Y.2d 494, 577 N.Y.S.2d 211, 583 N.E.2d 924 (1991); *Matter of Schmidt v. Roberts*, 74 N.Y.2d 513, 549 N.Y.S.2d 633, 548 N.E.2d 1284 (1989); *Matter of Corbin v. Hillery*, 74 N.Y.2d 279, 285 n.3, 545 N.Y.S.2d 71, 74 n.3, 543 N.E.2d 714 (1989), judgment aff'd, 495 U.S. 508, 110 S. Ct. 2084, 109 L. Ed. 2d 548 (1990) (overruled by, U.S. v. Dixon, 509 U.S. 688, 113 S. Ct. 2849, 125 L. Ed. 2d 556 (1993)) ("Of course, prohibition lies to restrain violations of both statutory and constitutional double jeopardy rights"), *aff'd sub nom. Grady v. Corbin*, 495 U.S. 508, 110 S. Ct. 2084, 109 L. Ed. 2d 548 (1990) (overruled by, U.S. v. Dixon, 509 U.S. 688, 113 S. Ct. 2849, 125 L. Ed. 2d 556 (1993)); *Matter of Kisloff v. Covington*, 73 N.Y.2d 445, 448–49, 541 N.Y.S.2d 737, 739, 539 N.E.2d 565 (1989); *Matter of Kaplan v. Ritter*, 71 N.Y.2d 222, 525 N.Y.S.2d 1, 519 N.E.2d 802 (1987); *Matter of Johnson v. Morgenthau*, 69 N.Y.2d 148, 150, 512 N.Y.S.2d 797, 798, 505 N.E.2d 240 (1987); *Matter of Rush v. Mordue*, 68 N.Y.2d 348, 509 N.Y.S.2d 493, 502 N.E.2d 170 (1986); *People v. Prescott*, 66 N.Y.2d 216, 220, 495 N.Y.S.2d 955, 957, 486 N.E.2d 813 (1985) ("an article 78 proceeding [is available] to prohibit the People from prosecuting a case that violates statutory, as well as constitutional, double jeopardy principles"); *Matter of Enright v. Siedlecki*, 59 N.Y.2d 195, 198 n.1, 464 N.Y.S.2d 418, 420 n.1, 451 N.E.2d 176 (1983); *People v. Michael*, 48 N.Y.2d 1, 7, 420 N.Y.S.2d 371, 373, 394 N.E.2d 1134 (1979) (per curiam); *Matter of Abraham v. Justices of New York Supreme Court of Bronx County*, 37 N.Y.2d 560, 376 N.Y.S.2d 79, 338 N.E.2d 597 (1975); *Matter of Di Lorenzo v. Murtagh*, 36 N.Y.2d 306, 309, 367 N.Y.S.2d 761, 763, 327 N.E.2d 805 (1975); *Matter of Scranton v. Supreme Court of State of New York*, 36 N.Y.2d 704, 366 N.Y.S.2d 417, 325 N.E.2d 876 (1975).

Where the defendant has previously litigated a Double Jeopardy claim in an Article 78 proceeding, the doctrine of *res judicata* bars the defendant from relitigating the claim on direct appeal from an ensuing conviction. *People v. Di Raffaele*, 55 N.Y.2d 234, 243, 448 N.Y.S.2d 448, 452, 433 N.E.2d 513 (1982).

§ 23:7   CPL § 40.10—Definitions pertinent to CPL Article 40

CPL § 40.10 provides, in full, as follows:

§ 40.10. Previous prosecution; definitions of terms

The following definitions are applicable to this article:

1. "Offense." An "offense" is committed whenever any conduct is performed which violates a statutory provision defining an offense; and when the same conduct or criminal transaction violates

[2] or more such statutory provisions each such violation constitutes a separate and distinct offense. The same conduct or criminal transaction also establishes separate and distinct offenses when, though violating only [1] statutory provision, it results in death, injury, loss or other consequences to [2] or more victims, and such result is an element of the offense as defined. In such case, as many offenses are committed as there are victims.

2. "Criminal transaction" means conduct which establishes at least [1] offense, and which is comprised of [2] or more or a group of acts either (a) so closely related and connected in point of time and circumstance of commission as to constitute a single criminal incident, or (b) so closely related in criminal purpose or objective as to constitute elements or integral parts of a single criminal venture.

§ 23:8   CPL § 40.20—New York's primary Double Jeopardy statute

CPL § 40.20(1) codifies the Constitutional prohibition against Double Jeopardy: "A person may not be twice prosecuted for the same offense." This statute "provides, at most, no more double jeopardy protection than the Constitutions do." *Matter of Polito v. Walsh*, 8 N.Y.3d 683, 690, 840 N.Y.S.2d 1, 5, 871 N.E.2d 537 (2007).

CPL § 40.20(2) is far broader. "Under CPL 40.20(2), a subsequent prosecution for offenses involving the 'same criminal . . . transaction,' as defined by CPL 40.10(2), violates the statutory bar against double jeopardy unless an exception applies." *People v. Lynch*, 25 N.Y.3d 331, 334, 12 N.Y.S.3d 590, 34 N.E.3d 341 (2015). Specifically, CPL § 40.20(2) provides, in pertinent part:

2. A person may not be separately prosecuted for [2] offenses based upon the same act or criminal transaction unless:

(a) The offenses as defined have substantially different elements and the acts establishing [1] offense are in the main clearly distinguishable from those establishing the other; or

(b) Each of the offenses as defined contains an element which is not an element of the other, *and* the statutory provisions defining such offenses are designed to prevent very different kinds of harm or evil; or

(c) [1] of such offenses consists of criminal possession of contraband matter and the other offense is one involving the use of such contraband matter, other than a sale thereof; or

(d) [1] of the offenses is assault or some other offense resulting in physical injury to a person, and the other offense is one of homicide based upon the death of such person from the same physical injury, *and* such death occurs after a prosecution for the assault or other non-homicide offense; or

(e) Each offense involves death, injury, loss or other consequence to a different victim; or

(f) [1] of the offenses consists of a violation of a statutory provision of another jurisdiction, which offense has been prosecuted in such other jurisdiction and has there been terminated by a court order expressly founded upon insufficiency of evidence to establish some element of such offense which is not an element of the other offense, defined by the laws of this state; or

(g) The present prosecution is for a consummated result offense, as defined in [CPL § 20.10(3)], which occurred in this state and the offense was the result of a conspiracy, facilitation or solicitation prosecuted in another state.

(Emphases added).

§ 23:9   VTL § 1800(d) supersedes CPL § 40.20 in vehicular assault/homicide cases

VTL § 1800(d) provides that "[a] conviction of violation of any provision of this chapter shall not be a bar to a prosecution for an assault or for a homicide committed by any person in operating a motor vehicle or motorcycle." This statute does not supersede the Constitution. *See Matter of Corbin v. Hillery*, 74 N.Y.2d 279, 288, 545 N.Y.S.2d 71, 76, 543 N.E.2d 714 (1989), judgment aff'd, 495 U.S. 508, 110 S. Ct. 2084, 109 L. Ed. 2d 548 (1990) (overruled by, U.S. v. Dixon, 509 U.S. 688, 113 S. Ct. 2849, 125 L. Ed. 2d 556 (1993)). However:

> Because this is a specific statute obviously enacted for a special purpose, it must be deemed to take precedence over the more general rules for successive prosecutions that are contained in CPL article 40. Thus, Vehicle and Traffic Law § 1800(d) supersedes CPL 40.20 and, to the extent that it does not conflict with constitutional double jeopardy principles, it permits successive prosecution for homicide and assault charges, notwithstanding a prior prosecution for traffic offenses arising out of the same incident.

Id. at 288, 545 N.Y.S.2d at 76 (citations omitted).

§ 23:10   Applicability of the "dual sovereignty" doctrine in New York

"[U]nder the so-called 'dual sovereignty' doctrine, the Double Jeopardy Clause of the United States Constitution does not prohibit successive federal and state prosecutions for the same conduct." *Matter of Polito v. Walsh*, 8 N.Y.3d 683, 686, 840 N.Y.S.2d 1, 2, 871 N.E.2d 537 (2007). However, the "dual sovereignty" doctrine is generally inapplicable in New York. *See,*

e.g., CPL § 40.20(2); *Polito*, 8 N.Y.3d at 690, 840 N.Y.S.2d at 5;
People v. Bryant, 92 N.Y.2d 216, 226, 677 N.Y.S.2d 286, 288, 699
N.E.2d 910 (1998) ("CPL 40.20, New York's statutory double jeopardy provision, generally prohibits successive prosecutions for
two offenses based on a single act or criminal transaction"); *People
v. Rivera*, 60 N.Y.2d 110, 114, 468 N.Y.S.2d 601, 604, 456 N.E.2d
492 (1983); *People v. Abbamonte*, 43 N.Y.2d 74, 81, 400 N.Y.S.2d
766, 769, 371 N.E.2d 485 (1977) ("Under CPL 40.20, not only is
the 'dual sovereignties' doctrine ignored, but double jeopardy
protection is extended, generally, to offenses arising out of a common event"); *id.* at 81–82, 400 N.Y.S.2d at 769 ("Restated, absent
the statutory exceptions, no matter the number of statutory offenses technically violated, or the number of jurisdictions
involved, an accused is not to suffer repeated prosecution for the
same general conduct"); *Matter of Abraham v. Justices of New
York Supreme Court of Bronx County*, 37 N.Y.2d 560, 376
N.Y.S.2d 79, 338 N.E.2d 597 (1975).

The *Polito* court made clear that:

> New York does indeed have relatively broad statutory protection
> against double jeopardy, and our statutory law does reject, in large
> part, the dual sovereignty doctrine. To the extent our protections go
> beyond those afforded by the State or Federal Constitution,
> however, they are to be found in CPL 40.20(2), not CPL 40.20(1).
> CPL 40.20(1) provides, at most, no more double jeopardy protection
> than the Constitutions do.

8 N.Y.3d at 690, 840 N.Y.S.2d at 5.

In *Bryant*, *supra*, the Court of Appeals held as follows:

> The primary issue on this appeal requires us to decide whether,
> under New York's statutory double jeopardy provision (CPL 40.20),
> the prosecution of certain offenses contained in a State indictment
> is barred by the prior prosecution of a Federal indictment where,
> concededly, both prosecutions are based upon a single criminal
> transaction. For the reasons that follow, we conclude that the three
> challenged State offenses fall within the exception set forth in
> paragraph (b) of CPL 40.20(2) and, thus, the sequential State pros-
> ecution was lawful.

92 N.Y.2d at 224, 677 N.Y.S.2d at 287. *See also People v. Mono*,
197 A.D.2d 909, __, 602 N.Y.S.2d 266, 267 (4th Dep't 1993) ("The
prosecution of the burglary charge in Jefferson County was not
barred by the separate prosecution in Oneida County of the motor vehicle charges because the burglary and the motor vehicle
offenses were not committed as part of the same criminal
transaction"). *Cf. Matter of Booth v. Clary*, 83 N.Y.2d 675, 680,
613 N.Y.S.2d 110, 113, 635 N.E.2d 279 (1994) ("in the absence of
any statutory exclusion under New York's CPL article 40, a court-
martial tribunal is a court within the meaning of CPL 40.30(1),

and the prior prosecutions in each case bar the appellant District Attorney from proceeding under the indictments for the identical crimes as violations of New York's Penal Law"); *Matter of Schmidt on Behalf of McNell v. Roberts*, 74 N.Y.2d 513, 519, 549 N.Y.S.2d 633, 636, 548 N.E.2d 1284 (1989) ("we conclude that the Federal and State prosecutions are based on the same criminal transaction and that prosecution of the State indictment is barred unless one or more of the exceptions specified in paragraphs (a) through (h) of CPL 40.20(2) is applicable"); *Matter of Wiley v. Altman*, 52 N.Y.2d 410, 438 N.Y.S.2d 490, 420 N.E.2d 371 (1981); *People v. Vera*, 47 N.Y.2d 825, 826, 418 N.Y.S.2d 575, 576, 392 N.E.2d 562 (1979) ("the defendant's conviction in Federal court for conspiracy to distribute cocaine precludes subsequent prosecution in this State for the sale which concededly was part of the conspiracy" even though "the State and Federal indictments were the result of completely separate and independent investigations and . . . the Federal authorities were not informed of the sale which formed the basis of the State indictment").

§ 23:11 Applicability of Double Jeopardy to "continuing" crimes

"A continuing crime is one 'that by its nature may be committed either by one act or by multiple acts and readily permits characterization as a continuing offense over a period of time.'" *People v. Shack*, 86 N.Y.2d 529, 540, 634 N.Y.S.2d 660, 667, 658 N.E.2d 706 (1995) (citation omitted). Double Jeopardy principles prohibit the People from prosecuting a person in two different counties for a continuing crime. *See, e.g., People v. Okafore*, 72 N.Y.2d 81, 83, 531 N.Y.S.2d 762, 762–63, 527 N.E.2d 245, 80 A.L.R.4th 615 (1988); *Matter of Johnson v. Morgenthau*, 69 N.Y.2d 148, 149, 512 N.Y.S.2d 797, 798, 505 N.E.2d 240 (1987) ("This appeal questions whether petitioner can be twice prosecuted because of his unlawful possession of a weapon at different times and places during the six days he possessed it. We hold that unlawful possession is a continuing offense and that constitutional double jeopardy principles preclude the second prosecution"); *id.* at 151, 512 N.Y.S.2d at 799 (" '[t]he Double Jeopardy Clause is not such a fragile guarantee that prosecutors can avoid its limitations by the simple expedient of dividing a single crime into a series of temporal or spatial units' ") (citation omitted).

DWI is a continuing crime. *People v. Miller*, 163 A.D.2d 627, __, 558 N.Y.S.2d 269, 270 (3d Dep't 1990). *See also People v. Tuszynski*, 57 A.D.3d 1380, __, 871 N.Y.S.2d 542, 542 (4th Dep't 2008) ("We agree with defendant that the sentences of two consecutive terms of imprisonment of 1 1/3 to 4 years are illegal on the ground that his operation of a motor vehicle while intoxicated consisted of a single, continuous act"). *Cf. People v. Keindl*, 68 N.Y.2d 410, 420–21, 509 N.Y.S.2d 790, 795, 502 N.E.2d 577 (1986) ("Although the 'continuing crime' theory may be appropriately applied in the proper case, it has no applicability here as to the crimes of sodomy and sexual abuse of which this defendant has been convicted. Sodomy and sexual abuse, as those crimes are defined in the Penal Law, punish the performance of a single act").

§ 23:12   "Delayed death" exception to CPL § 40.20

Sometimes a defendant is convicted of a crime involving causing injury to a victim—but the victim subsequently dies. The issue arises as to whether the defendant can be charged with a new, more serious crime due to this significant change in circumstances. The answer is generally yes. *See, e.g.*, CPL § 40.20(2)(d); *People v. Latham*, 83 N.Y.2d 233, 609 N.Y.S.2d 141, 631 N.E.2d 83 (1994); *People v. Rivera*, 60 N.Y.2d 110, 468 N.Y.S.2d 601, 456 N.E.2d 492 (1983). *Cf. People v. Jacob*, 161 Misc. 2d 768, 615 N.Y.S.2d 601 (Sup 1994) (People's motion to resubmit denied).

§ 23:13   "Different victim" exception to CPL § 40.20

CPL § 40.20(2)(e) provides that "[a] person may not be separately prosecuted for two offenses based upon the same act or criminal transaction unless: * * * [e]ach offense involves death, injury, loss or other consequence to a different victim." The "different victim" exception:

[I]s available [to the People] only where each of the offenses in the separate prosecutions involves one or more specific, individually identifiable victims. Accordingly, where, as here, the accuseds have previously been tried and convicted on Federal conspiracy, racketeering and fraud charges, all of which were based on a bribery scheme having no specifically identifiable victims, the "different victim" exception of CPL 40.20(2)(e) cannot be invoked to justify a separate prosecution for State larceny and securities fraud arising from the same bribery scheme. * * *

Prior cases in which the "different victim" exception was successfully invoked have all involved successive prosecutions for offenses that arose from the same transaction but caused loss or injury to separate, individually identifiable persons or entities. * * *

In instances where, because of either the nature of the offense or the nature of the specific criminal acts charged, identification of a specific victim is not feasible, separate prosecution may be justified only if the conditions in one of the other statutory exceptions, such as CPL 40.20(2)(b), are fully satisfied.

Matter of Kaplan v. Ritter, 71 N.Y.2d 222, 224, 228, 230, 525 N.Y.S.2d 1, 1–2, 4, 5, 519 N.E.2d 802 (1987).

§ 23:14 CPL § 40.30—What constitutes a "previous prosecution" for purposes of CPL § 40.20?

CPL § 40.30 provides as follows:

§ 40.30. Previous prosecution; what constitutes

1. Except as otherwise provided in this section, a person "is prosecuted" for an offense, within the meaning of section 40.20, when he is charged therewith by an accusatory instrument filed in a court of this state or of any jurisdiction within the United States, and when the action either:

(a) Terminates in a conviction upon a plea of guilty; or

(b) Proceeds to the trial stage and a jury has been impaneled and sworn or, in the case of a trial by the court without a jury, a witness is sworn.

2. Despite the occurrence of proceedings specified in subdivision one, a person is not deemed to have been prosecuted for an offense, within the meaning of section 40.20, when:

(a) Such prosecution occurred in a court which lacked jurisdiction over the defendant or the offense; or

(b) Such prosecution was for a lesser offense than could have been charged under the facts of the case, and the prosecution was procured by the defendant, without the knowledge of the appropriate prosecutor, for the purpose of avoiding prosecution for a greater offense.

3. Despite the occurrence of proceedings specified in subdivision one, if such proceedings are subsequently nullified by a court order which restores the action to its pre-pleading status or which directs a new trial of the same accusatory instrument, the nullified proceedings do not bar further prosecution of such offense under the same accusatory instrument.

4. Despite the occurrence of proceedings specified in subdivision one, if such proceedings are subsequently nullified by a court order which dismisses the accusatory instrument but authorizes the people to obtain a new accusatory instrument charging the same offense or an offense based upon the same conduct, the nullified proceedings do not bar further prosecution of such offense under any new accusatory instrument obtained pursuant to such court order or authorization.

§ 23:15 CPL § 40.40—When is separate prosecution of "joinable" offenses barred?

CPL § 40.40 provides as follows:

§ 40.40. Separate prosecution of jointly prosecutable offenses; when barred

1. Where [2] or more offenses are joinable in a single accusatory instrument against a person by reason of being based upon the same criminal transaction, pursuant to [CPL § 200.20(2)(a)], such person may not, under circumstances prescribed in this section, be separately prosecuted for such offenses even though such separate prosecutions are not otherwise barred by any other section of this article.

2. When (a) one of two or more joinable offenses of the kind specified in subdivision one is charged in an accusatory instrument, and (b) another is not charged therein, or in any other accusatory instrument filed in the same court, despite possession by the people of evidence legally sufficient to support a conviction of the defendant for such uncharged offense, and (c) either a trial of the existing accusatory instrument is commenced or the action thereon is disposed of by a plea of guilty, any subsequent prosecution for the uncharged offense is thereby barred.

3. When (a) two or more of such offenses are charged in separate accusatory instruments filed in the same court, and (b) an application by the defendant for consolidation thereof for trial purposes, pursuant to [CPL § 200.20(5)] or [CPL §] 100.45, is improperly denied, the commencement of a trial of one such accusatory instrument bars any subsequent prosecution upon any of the other accusatory instruments with respect to any such offense.

It has been held that "pursuant to CPL 40.40, 'the prohibition against separate prosecution of jointly prosecutable offenses applies *only* if the defendant has requested consolidation thereof for trial purposes and the request is denied.'" *People v. Madden*, 49 A.D.3d 1264, __, 856 N.Y.S.2d 344, 345 (4th Dep't 2008) (citation omitted). *See also Matter of Wiley v. Altman*, 52 N.Y.2d 410, 415, 438 N.Y.S.2d 490, 493, 420 N.E.2d 371 (1981); *People v. Dean*, 56 A.D.2d 242, __, 392 N.Y.S.2d 134, 138 (4th Dep't 1977), judgment aff'd, 45 N.Y.2d 651, 412 N.Y.S.2d 353, 384 N.E.2d 1277 (1978).

§ 23:16 When are two offenses "the same" for Double Jeopardy purposes?

"In order to determine whether two different statutory offenses are the same for purposes of constitutional double jeopardy, we apply the Supreme Court's *Blockburger* or 'same elements' test. Under *Blockburger*, two offenses are the same unless each requires proof of a fact the other does not." *Matter of Suarez v. Byrne*, 10 N.Y.3d 523, 532, 860 N.Y.S.2d 439, 446, 890 N.E.2d 201 (2008) (citations omitted). *See also People v. Wood*, 95 N.Y.2d 509, 513, 719 N.Y.S.2d 639, 642, 742 N.E.2d 114 (2000) ("The test focuses on 'the proof necessary to prove the statutory elements of each offense charged against the defendant, not on the actual evidence to be presented at trial' ") (citation omitted); *People v. Prescott*, 66 N.Y.2d 216, 221, 495 N.Y.S.2d 955, 958, 486 N.E.2d 813 (1985) ("The test for determining whether two offenses are the same within the meaning of the double jeopardy clause is whether two distinct statutory provisions each requires proof of a fact that the other does not").

> The Double Jeopardy Clause precludes consecutive prosecutions for greater and lesser included offenses where, "the lesser offense . . . requires no proof beyond that which is required for conviction of the greater." "The applicable rule is that, where the same act or transaction constitutes a violation of two distinct statutory provisions, the test to be applied to determine whether there are two offenses or only one is whether each provision requires proof of an additional fact which the other does not."

People v. Biggs, 1 N.Y.3d 225, 230, 771 N.Y.S.2d 49, 52, 803 N.E.2d 370 (2003) (citations omitted). *See also Wood*, 95 N.Y.2d at 514, 719 N.Y.S.2d at 643 ("under *Blockburger*, a lesser included offense is the 'same' as a greater offense and, thus, the successive prosecution and cumulative punishment for a greater offense after conviction for a lesser included offense is barred by the Double Jeopardy Clause"); *Matter of Johnson v. Morgenthau*, 69 N.Y.2d 148, 152, 512 N.Y.S.2d 797, 800, 505 N.E.2d 240 (1987) ("Possessing a firearm at one's home or place of business constitutes criminal possession of a weapon in the [4th] degree, a lesser included offense of criminal possession of a weapon in the [3rd] degree, and constitutes the same crime for double jeopardy purposes") (citation omitted). *Cf. People v. Luongo*, 47 N.Y.2d 418, 430, 418 N.Y.S.2d 365, 370, 391 N.E.2d 1341 (1979) ("As an additional ground for reversal, defendant maintains that principles of both statutory and constitutional double jeopardy precluded his trial in Nassau County in connection with charges arising out of the same plan which was the predicate for his prior Suffolk County convictions. The flaw in these arguments lies in the fact that each larceny was an independent criminal transaction which can be prosecuted independently").

§ 23:17 When does jeopardy attach?

In a jury trial, "jeopardy attaches when a jury is impaneled and sworn (*see* CPL 40.30[1][b])." *Matter of Rivera v. Firetog*, 11 N.Y.3d 501, 506, 872 N.Y.S.2d 401, 404, 900 N.E.2d 952 (2008). *See also People v. Baptiste*, 72 N.Y.2d 356, 359, 533 N.Y.S.2d 853, 855, 530 N.E.2d 377 (1988); *People v. Ferguson*, 67 N.Y.2d 383, 388, 502 N.Y.S.2d 972, 975, 494 N.E.2d 77 (1986); *Matter of Lockett v. Juviler*, 65 N.Y.2d 182, 187, 490 N.Y.S.2d 764, 768, 480 N.E.2d 378 (1985) ("Jeopardy cannot be said to have attached

until the accused has been subjected to the risk of conviction");
id. at 187, 490 N.Y.S.2d at 768 ("As the Supreme Court has noted:
'an accused must suffer jeopardy before he can suffer double jeopardy'") (citation omitted); *Matter of Scranton v. Supreme Court of
State of New York*, 36 N.Y.2d 704, 706, 366 N.Y.S.2d 417, 418,
325 N.E.2d 876 (1975) ("The petitioner was not placed in jeopardy despite the fact that three jurors had been sworn before a
mistrial was declared"); *People v. Moyer*, 292 A.D.2d 793, __, 738
N.Y.S.2d 810, 812 (4th Dep't 2002) ("Jeopardy never attached at
the first trial because 'the entire jury had not been impaneled
and sworn at the time of the declaration of the mistrial'") (citation omitted); *People v. Clearwater*, 269 A.D.2d 462, 702 N.Y.S.2d
921 (2d Dep't 2000) (same).

In a non-jury trial, jeopardy attaches when the case "[p]roceeds
to the trial stage and . . . a witness is sworn." CPL § 40.30(1)(b).

§ 23:18   Applicability of Double Jeopardy to legal
sufficiency of accusatory instruments

To be legally sufficient, an accusatory instrument must, among
other things, provide the defendant "with sufficient notice of the
charged crime to satisfy the demands of due process and double
jeopardy." *People v. Dreyden*, 15 N.Y.3d 100, 103, 905 N.Y.S.2d
542, 544, 931 N.E.2d 526 (2010). *See also People v. Dumay*, 23
N.Y.3d 518, 524, 992 N.Y.S.2d 672, 676, 16 N.E.3d 1150 (2014);
People v. Kasse, 22 N.Y.3d 1142, 1143, 984 N.Y.S.2d 287, 287, 7
N.E.3d 500 (2014); *People v. Kalin*, 12 N.Y.3d 225, 231–32, 878
N.Y.S.2d 653, 657, 906 N.E.2d 381 (2009); *People v. Sedlock*, 8
N.Y.3d 535, 538, 838 N.Y.S.2d 14, 16, 869 N.E.2d 14 (2007); *People
v. Casey*, 95 N.Y.2d 354, 363, 717 N.Y.S.2d 88, 93, 740 N.E.2d
233 (2000); *People v. Shack*, 86 N.Y.2d 529, 540, 634 N.Y.S.2d
660, 667, 658 N.E.2d 706 (1995); *People v. Davis*, 72 N.Y.2d 32,
38, 530 N.Y.S.2d 529, 532, 526 N.E.2d 20 (1988). In this regard:

> An indictment serves three important purposes. "First and
> foremost, an indictment * * * provid[es] the defendant with fair
> notice of the accusations against him, so that he will be able to
> prepare a defense." Second, the indictment prevents the prosecutor
> from usurping the powers of the Grand Jury by ensuring that the
> crime for which defendant is tried is the same crime for which he
> was indicted, "rather than some alternative seized upon by the
> prosecution in light of subsequently discovered evidence." Finally,
> an indictment prevents later retrials for the same offense in
> contravention of the constitutional prohibition against double
> jeopardy.

People v. Grega, 72 N.Y.2d 489, 495–96, 534 N.Y.S.2d 647, 650,
531 N.E.2d 279 (1988) (citations omitted). *See also People v. Davis*,
72 N.Y.2d 32, 38, 530 N.Y.S.2d 529, 532, 526 N.E.2d 20 (1988);
People v. Charles, 61 N.Y.2d 321, 326–27, 473 N.Y.S.2d 941, 943,

462 N.E.2d 118 (1984); *People v. Morris*, 61 N.Y.2d 290, 293, 473 N.Y.S.2d 769, 771, 461 N.E.2d 1256 (1984); *People v. Spann*, 56 N.Y.2d 469, 472, 452 N.Y.S.2d 869, 870, 438 N.E.2d 402 (1982); *People v. Iannone*, 45 N.Y.2d 589, 595, 412 N.Y.S.2d 110, 114, 384 N.E.2d 656 (1978).

§ 23:19 Indictment cannot contain duplicitous counts

In *People v. Bauman*, 12 N.Y.3d 152, 154–55, 878 N.Y.S.2d 235, 236, 905 N.E.2d 1164 (2009), the Court of Appeals held that:

CPL 200.30(1) provides that "[e]ach count of an indictment may charge one offense only." As this Court explained in *People v. Keindl*, "acts which separately and individually make out distinct crimes must be charged in separate and distinct counts, and where one count alleges the commission of a particular offense occurring repeatedly during a designated period of time, that count encompasses more than one offense and is duplicitous." Compliance with CPL 200.30(1) is essential because "[t]he prohibition against duplicity furthers not only the functions of notice to a defendant and of assurance against double jeopardy, but also ensures the reliability of the unanimous verdict."

(Citations omitted). *See also People v. Alonzo*, 16 N.Y.3d 267, 269, 920 N.Y.S.2d 302, 303, 945 N.E.2d 495 (2011); *People v. Wells*, 7 N.Y.3d 51, 56 n.2, 817 N.Y.S.2d 590, 593 n.2, 850 N.E.2d 637 (2006); *People v. Davis*, 72 N.Y.2d 32, 38, 530 N.Y.S.2d 529, 532, 526 N.E.2d 20 (1988); *People v. Keindl*, 68 N.Y.2d 410, 416, 509 N.Y.S.2d 790, 792, 502 N.E.2d 577 (1986).

§ 23:20 Misdemeanor information charging common law DWI charges DWAI by operation of law

In *People v. Green*, 96 N.Y.2d 195, 196–97, 197–98, 726 N.Y.S.2d 357, 359, 750 N.E.2d 59 (2001):

Defendant was arrested and charged in a misdemeanor information with driving while intoxicated. At trial before the Justice Court for the Town of East Hampton, the court also charged the jury on the lesser-included offense of driving while impaired. The jury acquitted defendant of driving while intoxicated but failed to reach a verdict on the lesser charge. The court then declared a mistrial as to that charge. * * *

The question before us is whether a new accusatory instrument was necessary to commence defendant's retrial on the lesser-included charge of driving while impaired (Vehicle and Traffic Law § 1192[1]), on which the first jury hung. We hold that it was not.

In so holding, the Court found that this procedure did not violate the Double Jeopardy Clause. *See also Matter of Case v. Sedita*, 128 A.D.3d 1328, 8 N.Y.S.3d 744 (4th Dep't 2015). *Cf.*

People v. Gonzalez, 61 N.Y.2d 633, 471 N.Y.S.2d 847, 459 N.E.2d 1285 (1983); *People v. Mayo*, 48 N.Y.2d 245, 422 N.Y.S.2d 361, 397 N.E.2d 1166 (1979).

§ 23:21 What is an "acquittal" for Double Jeopardy purposes?

In *Matter of Pastrana v. Baker*, 55 N.Y.2d 315, 317, 449 N.Y.S.2d 461, 462, 434 N.E.2d 697 (1982), the Court of Appeals held as follows:

> Reprosecution on a charge is not barred by the constitutional protection against double jeopardy when the earlier "acquittal" was based on an erroneous legal ruling not involving any review of the facts. The retrial of a lesser count, on which the jury deadlocked, is not prohibited when, after discharging the jury and without adjudication on the facts, the Judge ordered an acquittal in the mistaken belief that the jury's acquittal on the greater count required the same result on the lesser.

In so holding, the Court made clear that "[a]lthough the term 'acquit' evokes the concept of a determination based on factual grounds, the mere use of that word will not preclude a reviewing court from ascertaining the true nature of the decree in light of all the circumstances. A new trial may be held if the dismissal or acquittal does not amount to an adjudication on the facts, even if jeopardy has attached." *Id.* at 319, 449 N.Y.S.2d at 463 (citation omitted).

§ 23:22 Jury required to acquit defendant of more serious count(s) before considering lesser offense(s)

New York utilizes an "acquit-first" jury instruction procedure, *see, e.g.*, CPL §§ 300.40(3)(b); 300.50(1); 300.50(4); 360.50, pursuant to which:

> [A] jury must deliberate on charges in decreasing order of culpability, unanimously acquitting on the more serious crime before considering any lesser included offense. Where there are inconsistent counts, the jury must acquit of the greater counts before considering any lesser included count, and must cease deliberations upon finding the defendant guilty of one of the crimes submitted. In endorsing the "acquit-first" approach, we sought to minimize compromise verdicts, and took into account the effect on double jeopardy.

Matter of Suarez v. Byrne, 10 N.Y.3d 523, 534, 860 N.Y.S.2d 439, 447, 890 N.E.2d 201 (2008) (citations omitted). *See also People v. Boettcher*, 69 N.Y.2d 174, 183, 513 N.Y.S.2d 83, 87, 505 N.E.2d 594 (1987); *People v. Helliger*, 96 N.Y.2d 462, 466, 729 N.Y.S.2d 654, 656, 754 N.E.2d 756 (2001) (per curiam).

Nonetheless, the defendant is sometimes convicted of a lesser included offense (or of an offense that is reversed or dismissed on appeal)—leaving open the question of whether the defendant can be retried for the greater offense (or for an offense that the jury did not expressly render a verdict on).

In *People v. Gause*, 19 N.Y.3d 390, 392, 394, 948 N.Y.S.2d 211, 212, 213, 971 N.E.2d 341 (2012), the Court of Appeals held as follows:

> In this case, where the defendant's conviction for depraved indifference murder was reversed on appeal, the issue before this Court is whether, in accord with the principles of double jeopardy, defendant was impliedly acquitted of intentional murder when the jury was instructed to consider intentional murder and depraved indifference murder in the alternative, but that it could return a verdict on only one of the offenses. Because the first jury had a full opportunity to return a verdict on both inconsistent charges, defendant was impliedly acquitted of the other count when the jury convicted defendant of the depraved indifference murder and his second trial for intentional murder twice placed defendant in jeopardy for the same offense. * * *

> Defendant contends now, as he did below, that double jeopardy barred the retrial of the intentional murder charge even though the jury verdict had not specifically indicated an acquittal on that count. We agree. Because the first jury had before it counts of depraved indifference murder and intentional murder—inconsistent counts—and it reached a guilty verdict on one, that determination necessarily acquitted defendant of the other crime and, therefore, double jeopardy barred the People from reprosecuting defendant for it.

In *Helliger, supra:*

> [T]he jury delivered [a] note stating it was in agreement on one of the counts [of the indictment] but deadlocked on the other three. The People, objecting to a "partial verdict" under these circumstances, . . . asked the court to apply the *Boettcher* "acquit-first" rule, emphasizing (correctly) that under the court's ruling, the People would be barred from retrying defendant on the higher charges. The trial court persisted in its refusal, stating that the *Boettcher* decision created a process "out of whole cloth" that was at odds with the statutory scheme. He added that *Boettcher*, which he apparently regarded as dictum, is "not a direct holding applicable to me." Indeed, he acknowledged that he may "stick out by being the only Judge" who does not follow it. At one point the Judge noted that he had "written much of the CPL and the Penal Law for thirteen years between 1979 and 1992." Ultimately, the jury stated it had not reached a verdict on the murder and manslaughter charges, but found defendant guilty of criminally negligent homicide.

96 N.Y.2d at 464–65, 729 N.Y.S.2d at 655.

Under these circumstances, the Court of Appeals held that

"[t]he Appellate Division correctly concluded that the trial court's improper refusal to follow *Boettcher* marks the end of the case. * * * We are unwilling to upset established precedent in order to cure a refusal to recognize a case that our trial courts have appropriately applied for 14 years." *Id.* at 466, 467, 729 N.Y.S.2d at 656, 657. *See also People v. Fuller*, 96 N.Y.2d 881, 883–84, 730 N.Y.S.2d 773, 774, 756 N.E.2d 61 (2001) ("By operation of law, defendant was deemed acquitted of second degree assault when the jury failed to reach a verdict as to that count, but found him guilty of the lesser included offense of third degree assault . . . . His retrial was thus prohibited under settled principles of double jeopardy") (footnote omitted). *Cf. People v. McFadden*, 20 N.Y.3d 260, 959 N.Y.S.2d 108, 982 N.E.2d 1241 (2012); *People v. Echevarria*, 6 N.Y.3d 89, 809 N.Y.S.2d 509, 843 N.E.2d 149 (2005).

§ 23:23 Implicit acquittals

For purposes of Double Jeopardy, "[a]n acquittal may be implicit." *Matter of Suarez v. Byrne*, 10 N.Y.3d 523, 532, 860 N.Y.S.2d 439, 445, 890 N.E.2d 201 (2008). However, "[t]he implied acquittal bar to reprosecution presupposes that the first jury 'was given a full opportunity to return a verdict' on the particular charge that the prosecutor seeks to advance in the second trial." *Id.* at 532, 860 N.Y.S.2d at 445 (citation omitted).

Where a defendant pleads to one count of an indictment in satisfaction of all counts thereof, but the plea is subsequently properly vacated because it was illegal, there is no Double Jeopardy bar to restoring *all* counts of the indictment. *See People v. Bartley*, 47 N.Y.2d 965, 419 N.Y.S.2d 956, 393 N.E.2d 1029 (1979). In this regard, the *Bartley* court held as follows:

> Realistically the plea bargain must be considered as a nonseverable entity, and accordingly the bargain in its entirety was a total nullity as to all [6] counts of the indictment . . . . The court thereupon properly vacated the plea of guilty as to the [1] count and reinstated the not guilty pleas as to all [6] counts. * * *

> Our Legislature had power to provide that acceptance of a plea in satisfaction did not constitute an acquittal of the "satisfied" counts. CPL 40.30 (subd. 3) so provides and is controlling . . . . Retrial under the original indictment was accordingly not barred by statute.

> Nor has there been any violation of defendants' constitutional right not to be twice put in jeopardy. Neither the satisfaction of the [5] remaining counts on the initial acceptance of the plea of guilty to the [1] count nor the vacatur of the guilty plea to that count was the equivalent of an acquittal based on an adjudication as to the factual elements of the charge.

Id. at 966–67, 419 N.Y.S.2d at 956–57 (citations omitted). *See also People v. Charles*, 78 N.Y.2d 1044, 1047, 576 N.Y.S.2d 81, 83, 581 N.E.2d 1336 (1991) ("where a jury is not given an opportunity to return a verdict as to some of the offenses charged, its failure to do so cannot be construed as an acquittal barring retrial").

§ 23:24 Unreported verdict does not count for Double Jeopardy purposes

Occasionally a jury will indicate on a verdict sheet that the defendant was found not guilty, yet for some reason the actual verdict differs from the verdict sheet. In this regard, it is well settled that an unreported verdict does not count for Double Jeopardy purposes. *See, e.g., People v. Khalek*, 91 N.Y.2d 838, 840, 666 N.Y.S.2d 1020, 1021, 689 N.E.2d 914 (1997) ("Because the jury's unreported verdict was not announced in court, recorded in the minutes, or accepted by the court, it does not constitute a final verdict for double jeopardy purposes").

§ 23:25 Trial orders of dismissal

In *Matter of Holtzman v. Goldman*, 71 N.Y.2d 564, 571, 528 N.Y.S.2d 21, 25, 523 N.E.2d 297 (1988), the Court of Appeals pointed out that:

> When the Criminal Procedure Law was enacted, the Legislature, for the first time, attempted to authorize the People to appeal trial orders of dismissal. That attempt failed when we held that such appeals were barred by double jeopardy concerns. In response, the Legislature amended the statute to limit the appealability of trial orders of dismissal to instances where double jeopardy does not proscribe further review.

(Citations omitted). *See also People v. Consolazio*, 40 N.Y.2d 446, 451, 387 N.Y.S.2d 62, 64, 354 N.E.2d 801 (1976) ("we agree with defendant that under principles of double jeopardy as enunciated by the United States Supreme Court the People were barred from appealing to the Appellate Division from the trial order dismissing certain counts of defendant's indictment"). *See generally People v. Casiel*, 41 N.Y.2d 945, 394 N.Y.S.2d 630, 363 N.E.2d 354 (1977); *People v. Brown*, 40 N.Y.2d 381, 382, 391, 386 N.Y.S.2d 848, 849, 855, 353 N.E.2d 811 (1976) ("We now hold that CPL 450.20 (subd. 2) providing that the People may appeal a trial order of dismissal entered pursuant to CPL 290.10 is unconstitutional as violative of the right not to be placed twice in jeopardy for the same offense * * * except in the instance where disposition of the motion is reserved until after the jury verdict has been returned"); *id.* at 393, 386 N.Y.S.2d at 856 ("The inescapable rule which the Supreme Court has fashioned . . . is that the double jeopardy clause precludes the People from appealing a trial court's order dismissing an indictment where retrial of the defendant, or indeed any supplemental fact finding, might result from appellate reversal of the order sought to be appealed"); *id.* at 394, 386 N.Y.S.2d at 857 ("In exercising his responsible discretion in deciding whether to grant a motion for a trial order of dismissal, the Trial Judge must now be aware that the consequence of granting such a motion prior to the return of the jury verdict will be to foreclose appeal by the prosecution").

§ 23:26 Dismissal due to insufficient evidence is tantamount to acquittal

"It is settled that dismissal of a count due to insufficient evidence is tantamount to an acquittal for purposes of double jeopardy and protects a defendant against additional prosecution for such count." *People v. Biggs*, 1 N.Y.3d 225, 229, 771 N.Y.S.2d 49, 51–52, 803 N.E.2d 370 (2003). *See also Matter of Holtzman v. Goldman*, 71 N.Y.2d 564, 570 n.2, 528 N.Y.S.2d 21, 25 n.2, 523 N.E.2d 297 (1988); *People v. Sailor*, 65 N.Y.2d 224, 230, 491 N.Y.S.2d 112, 117, 480 N.E.2d 701 (1985) ("a defendant may not be retried if the reversal of his conviction is based on an appellate finding of insufficient evidence to convict"); *People v. Kurtz*, 51 N.Y.2d 380, 386, 434 N.Y.S.2d 200, 204, 414 N.E.2d 699 (1980); *People v. Mayo*, 48 N.Y.2d 245, 248 n.1, 249, 422 N.Y.S.2d 361, 363 n.1, 397 N.E.2d 1166 (1979); *People v. Snyder*, 110 A.D.2d 296, __, 494 N.Y.S.2d 481, 482–83 (3d Dep't 1985) ("the reversal of the conviction for violation of Vehicle and Traffic Law § 1192(2) was founded upon legal insufficiency. Accordingly, dismissal of that count of the indictment founded solely on such evidence was mandated by CPL 470.20(2) and, of course, defendant could not be retried on such count because of well-established principles of double jeopardy").

§ 23:27 Can defendant be prosecuted on count of indictment dismissed for legal insufficiency if dismissed count is reinstated on appeal?

In *People v. Moquin*, 77 N.Y.2d 449, 568 N.Y.S.2d 710, 570 N.E.2d 1059 (1991), the defendant was charged with murder, manslaughter and 6 other charges in connection with a DWI-related automobile accident. County Court dismissed the murder charge for legal insufficiency. Thereafter, over the People's objection, County Court accepted the defendant's plea of guilty to the remaining counts of the indictment. After the defendant had begun to serve her sentence, the Appellate Division reinstated the murder charge. County Court again dismissed the murder charge, this time on Double Jeopardy grounds. On appeal, the Court of Appeals held as follows:

The initial—and most critical—question in this appeal is whether the trial court had authority to vacate the previously imposed plea and sentence at the People's request. Absent such authority, the judgment entered upon defendant's plea could not be reopened.

An examination of the Criminal Procedure Law reveals no statutory source of authority to undo the judgment in these circumstances. CPL 440.10(1)(a) authorizes the court to entertain postjudgment motions by *defendants* to vacate on the ground that the court lacked jurisdiction, and CPL 440.40 provides for postjudgment motions by the People to set aside legally invalid *sentences*; however, there is no provision which confers the power to set aside a *plea* at the People's behest.

Nor does the law recognize any *inherent* judicial authority to vacate the plea and restore the action to the prepleading stage under the facts presented here. We have previously held that the trial courts' "inherent" authority may be used to vacate an illegally accepted plea *before* sentence is imposed and, in the absence of a specific constitutional impediment, to vacate a final criminal judgment on grounds of fraud or misrepresentation. Additionally, although CPL 430.10 prohibits a court from altering a sentence once its "term or period * * * has commenced," we have held that the court's " 'inherent power to correct [its] records [in] relat[ion] to mistakes, or errors, which may be termed clerical' " extends to correcting sentencing errors where the court merely misspoke or a patent clerical mistake has been made. However, as our recent case law makes clear, the limited "inherent authority" to vacate a plea after imposition of sentence may not be utilized to remedy a substantive legal error in the acceptance of the plea, at least after the defendant has begun serving his sentence. * * *

[O]nce the sentence has been imposed and the defendant has begun to serve it, a guilty plea is *final* and not subject to defeasance upon a trial court's determination of prior legal error made on a postjudgment motion by the People.

Id. at 452, 454–55, 568 N.Y.S.2d at 712, 714 (citations omitted). *See also People v. Donnelly*, 176 A.D.2d 404, 574 N.Y.S.2d 111 (3d Dep't 1991).

§ 23:28   Defendant's "subjective belief" that Double Jeopardy prevented further prosecution is irrelevant

In *People v. Latham*, 83 N.Y.2d 233, 239, 609 N.Y.S.2d 141, 144, 631 N.E.2d 83 (1994), the Court of Appeals held that "[n]either defendant's asserted belief that his plea would end all criminal exposure stemming from his conduct nor the fact that [the victim's] death was reasonably foreseeable at the time of plea can prevent as a matter of double jeopardy a subsequent prosecution for murder in the second degree. New York does not adhere to a subjective double jeopardy rule."

§ 23:29 Mistrial exception to Double Jeopardy

As a general principle, the People are entitled to only one opportunity to compel a defendant to stand trial because the "defendant possesses a 'valued right' to have his trial completed by a particular tribunal on the first presentation of the evidence."

Nevertheless, if the merits of the charges have not been resolved, the right to have a trial completed by a specific tribunal "may be subordinate to the public interest in seeing that a criminal prosecution proceed to verdict." In the oft-quoted words of Justice Story, the court may exercise its power to declare a mistrial when, "taking all the circumstances into consideration, there is a manifest necessity for the act." The classic example of charges that may be retried after the termination of a trial without the defendant's consent occurs when the trial court discharges a genuinely deadlocked jury. To justify a mistrial on deadlock grounds, it must be "clear that the jury is hopelessly deadlocked and that there is no reasonable probability it can agree."

Matter of Rivera v. Firetog, 11 N.Y.3d 501, 506, 872 N.Y.S.2d 401, 404, 900 N.E.2d 952 (2008) (citations omitted). *See also Matter of Suarez v. Byrne*, 10 N.Y.3d 523, 534, 860 N.Y.S.2d 439, 447, 890 N.E.2d 201 (2008); *Matter of Plummer v. Rothwax*, 63 N.Y.2d 243, 249–50, 481 N.Y.S.2d 657, 662, 471 N.E.2d 429 (1984); *People v. Michael*, 48 N.Y.2d 1, 10, 420 N.Y.S.2d 371, 375, 394 N.E.2d 1134 (1979) (per curiam) ("A defendant's right to have his fate determined as expeditiously as possible and by the first jury to which the case is presented is a basic one, and may not be set aside without strong reason").

"Nor is there a double jeopardy bar to retrial when a mistrial is granted because of 'manifest necessity' or with defendant's consent." *Suarez*, 10 N.Y.3d at 534, 860 N.Y.S.2d at 447. *See also Matter of Randall v. Rothwax*, 78 N.Y.2d 494, 498, 577 N.Y.S.2d 211, 213, 583 N.E.2d 924 (1991); *People v. Catten*, 69 N.Y.2d 547, 554, 516 N.Y.S.2d 186, 189, 508 N.E.2d 920 (1987); *People v. Ferguson*, 67 N.Y.2d 383, 388, 502 N.Y.S.2d 972, 975, 494 N.E.2d 77 (1986); *People v. Michael*, 48 N.Y.2d 1, 9, 420 N.Y.S.2d 371, 375, 394 N.E.2d 1134 (1979) (per curiam) ("Where a court declares a mistrial without obtaining the defendant's consent the double jeopardy provisions of both our State Constitution and the Federal Constitution prohibit retrial for the same crime unless 'there is a manifest necessity for (the mistrial), or the ends of public justice would otherwise be defeated.' These principles have to some extent been codified in CPL 280.10 (subd. 3), which allows a court to declare a mistrial on its own motion only 'when it is physically impossible to proceed with the trial in conformity with law' ") (citations omitted). Cf. *Matter of Zeigler v. Morgenthau*, 64 N.Y.2d 932, 488 N.Y.S.2d 633, 477 N.E.2d 1087 (1985) ("manifest necessity" found not to exist; Double Jeopardy barred reprosecution); *Michael*, 48 N.Y.2d at 9, 420 N.Y.S.2d at 375 ("a mistrial founded solely upon the convenience of the court and the jury is certainly not manifestly necessary").

With regard to the efforts that the trial court is required to undertake to determine whether a mistrial should be granted, the Court of Appeals has "repeatedly stressed that no per se rules or mechanical formulas apply to mistrial determinations, and we decline to create one in this case." *Firetog*, 11 N.Y.3d at 509, 872 N.Y.S.2d at 406–07 (citations omitted). *See also Matter of Owen v. Stroebel*, 65 N.Y.2d 658, 491 N.Y.S.2d 611, 481 N.E.2d 243 (1985).

In *Suarez, supra*, the Court of Appeals held that the defendant "may be retried for first-degree manslaughter—a count submitted to but not considered by the jury in his first trial—after his acquittal of intentional murder and our reversal of his conviction for depraved indifference murder on the ground of legal insufficiency." 10 N.Y.3d at 525, 860 N.Y.S.2d at 440–41.

In *Matter of Green v. County Court of Tompkins County*, 61 A.D.2d 1098, __, 403 N.Y.S.2d 560, 561 (3d Dep't 1978), a DWI-related homicide case, the defendant "was acquitted of the manslaughter and driving while intoxicated charges. The jury, however, was unable to reach an agreement as to the criminally negligent homicide count and a mistrial was declared thereon." The Appellate Division, Third Department, held that retrying the defendant on the Criminally Negligent Homicide charge did not violate Double Jeopardy.

§ 23:30 Exception to mistrial exception to Double Jeopardy

A defendant cannot always be retried following a mistrial. *See, e.g., People v. Baptiste*, 72 N.Y.2d 356, 533 N.Y.S.2d 853, 530 N.E.2d 377 (1988). In this regard, the *Baptiste* court made clear that:

> The determination of a Trial Judge that deadlock has occurred and that a mistrial is necessary involves the exercise of discretion. The trial court's judgment is entitled to great deference by reviewing courts for it is best situated to take all the circumstances of the particular proceeding into account and determine whether a mistrial is in fact required. Nevertheless, Trial Judges are not free to act without restraint. The defendant's right to obtain a verdict from the first jury selected should not be foreclosed unless it is clear that the jury is hopelessly deadlocked and that there is no reasonable probability it can agree. In the words of Justice Story, the court's power to declare a mistrial must be exercised with the "greatest

caution, under urgent circumstances, and for very plain and obvious causes"; the authority to discharge the jury is limited to those situations where, "taking all the circumstances into consideration, there is a manifest necessity for the act."

The record in this case does not demonstrate a manifest necessity for terminating defendant's trial. * * *

There is, of course, no mechanical formula for determining the necessity for a new trial and no minimum time a jury must deliberate before a mistrial is considered. These jurors, however, had little opportunity to decide this case. Although the trial had been relatively short, [9] witnesses had been sworn and there were serious discrepancies in their versions of the underlying incident. In an effort to resolve these discrepancies, the jury had requested the court to read back testimony several times and was in the process of considering some of this testimony when the mistrial occurred. There is no support in the record for the court's determination that the jury had found the problem insoluble or believed itself hopelessly deadlocked and in the absence of such evidence, the trial court abused its discretion in declaring a mistrial, as a matter of law.

Id. at 360–61, 361–62, 533 N.Y.S.2d at 856, 857 (citations omitted). *See also Matter of Plummer v. Rothwax*, 63 N.Y.2d 243, 251, 481 N.Y.S.2d 657, 662, 471 N.E.2d 429 (1984) ("Those factors, which should be considered by the trial court before exercising discretion, include the length and complexity of the trial, the length of the deliberations, the extent and nature of the communications between the court and the jury, and the potential effects of requiring further deliberation").

§ 23:31   People's right to retry defendant following mistrial or reversal caused by prosecutorial misconduct

In *Matter of Gorghan v. DeAngelis*, 7 N.Y.3d 470, 473–74, 824 N.Y.S.2d 202, 204–05, 857 N.E.2d 523 (2006), the Court of Appeals set forth the law regarding the People's right to retry a defendant following a reversal or a mistrial caused by prosecutorial misconduct:

At its essence, the Double Jeopardy Clause protects criminal defendants from multiple prosecutions for the same offense. This protection includes the valued, though not absolute, right to proceed to verdict before the empaneled jury. Thus, ordinarily, when a defendant obtains a verdict or chooses to prevent one by successfully seeking a mistrial, double-jeopardy principles are not implicated.

An exception to this rule exists, however, in instances where a prosecutor has engaged in prejudicial misconduct deliberately intended to provoke a mistrial motion. In such circumstances, the prosecutor has effectively eviscerated the defendant's right to complete the trial before the empaneled jury and thus double jeopardy may bar retrial even though the defendant's own successful mistrial motion prevented the verdict. * * *

We hold that this well-established but narrow exception is equally applicable to reversals on appeal when a trial court has erroneously denied a defendant's mistrial motion. As we noted in *Adames*, "[t]he corrective action for prosecutorial trial misconduct should ordinarily not vary whether a verdict is nullified by a trial court or by an appellate court." The misconduct is the same, the prejudice to the defendant is the same and the result should therefore be the same. Indeed, to differentiate between granted mistrial motions and reversals on appeal would create an anomalous result. Defendants who suffer both prejudicial prosecutorial misconduct intended to cause a mistrial and erroneous denial of a mistrial motion would never be entitled to double-jeopardy protection, whereas defendants subjected only to prosecutorial misconduct resulting in the grant of a mistrial would be entitled to that protection.

Here, although the prosecutor's conduct was deplorable, it was—as found by the Appellate Division—motivated by an intent to secure a conviction, not to provoke a mistrial motion. Thus, petitioner is entitled only to the ordinary remedy for harmful trial misconduct—a new, fair trial—and not dismissal of the indictment.

(Citations omitted). *See also People v. Adames*, 83 N.Y.2d 89, 607 N.Y.S.2d 919, 629 N.E.2d 391 (1993).

In *Matter of Davis v. Brown*, 87 N.Y.2d 626, 641 N.Y.S.2d 819, 664 N.E.2d 884 (1996), the prosecution twice elicited evidence at trial that had been specifically precluded. The first time this happened the defendant requested a mistrial. The second time the defendant again requested a mistrial—but this time made clear that he was only requesting a mistrial if the mistrial would be granted with prejudice. The Court of Appeals held as follows:

This case requires us to decide whether a criminal defendant may specifically limit a motion to one for a mistrial with prejudice—one based on the ground that the prosecution engaged in misconduct intended to provoke a mistrial, with its attendant retrial bar. We conclude that a defendant should be permitted to so delimit a mistrial motion and be given the opportunity to withdraw it if the total relief requested will not be granted. * * *

[W]e conclude that petitioner apprised the court, before it granted the mistrial without prejudice, that petitioner's motion was specifically limited to a motion for a mistrial with prejudice. In the absence of petitioner's unequivocal acquiescence to a mistrial without prejudice, the court lacked petitioner's consent to the discharge of the first jury and his retrial is therefore barred by the constitutional prohibition against double jeopardy.

Id. at 630–31, 631, 641 N.Y.S.2d at 821, 822.

In so holding, the Court reasoned as follows:

A cornerstone of the double jeopardy protection is the defendant's right, in the event of prosecutorial or judicial error warranting a mistrial, to choose whether to request a new trial before an untainted jury or to continue to defend the case before the already empaneled jury. Recognizing the importance of the defendant's right to have the case completed before the first jury, we have held that the defendant is free to withdraw a motion for a mistrial at any time before its grant and to continue before the already empaneled jury.

It follows that when a mistrial is granted over the defendant's objection or without the defendant's consent, double jeopardy will, as a general rule, bar retrial. However, the right to have one's case decided by the first empaneled jury is not absolute, and a mistrial granted as the product of manifest necessity will not bar a retrial. There is no claim of manifest necessity in this case.

Conversely, when the defendant requests or consents to a mistrial, double jeopardy typically erects no barrier to a retrial. There is one situation, however, in which retrial will be barred even though the defendant requests, and thereby consents to, a mistrial—when the prosecution deliberately provokes a mistrial. When the prosecution fears the case is headed toward acquittal and intentionally causes a mistrial, the calculated result of this prosecutorial misconduct is to deprive the defendant of the right to have the case completed before the first jury. In such a case, a second trial of the defendant would constitute an impermissible second bite at the apple for the prosecution, in direct violation of the letter and spirit of both the State and Federal Double Jeopardy Clauses' prohibitions against repeated prosecution.

Id. at 630, 641 N.Y.S.2d at 821 (citations omitted).

It is important to recognize that a specifically limited motion for a mistrial with prejudice will impose no greater burden on the trial courts than an unqualified mistrial motion. Whenever the court agrees that the prosecution has engaged in prejudicial misconduct deliberately intended to cause a mistrial, then a mistrial should be granted and retrial will be barred. On the other hand, if the court believes the prosecution has acted entirely properly, or simply that the prosecution's conduct, albeit improper, was not intended to provoke a mistrial, the court should deny the defendant's motion for a mistrial with prejudice and the trial will continue apace.

The People would have us adopt a rule whereby the defendant would in effect be penalized when the prosecution's misconduct, though not rising to the level of misconduct intended to cause a mistrial, nevertheless would warrant the grant of a mistrial. Such a rule, requiring the defendant to surrender the first jury and proceed before a new jury because the level of deliberateness of prosecutorial misconduct was misperceived, would unnecessarily erode the defendant's valued right to have the first empaneled jury determine the case.

The better rule, and the one more in keeping with double jeopardy jurisprudence, is that the defendant may challenge questionable prosecutorial conduct based on the specifically limited theory that the prosecution intended to provoke a mistrial, while reserving the right to have the case determined by the first jury in the event the court rejects the defendant's argument.

Id. at 631, 641 N.Y.S.2d at 822 (citations omitted).

§ 23:32 "Manifest necessity"

As the previous sections demonstrate, Double Jeopardy does not bar a retrial when a mistrial is granted because of "manifest necessity." In determining whether manifest necessity exists:

The Trial Judge's discretion is not without limits, however. The reasons underlying the grant of a mistrial may not be illusory; rather, in order fully to protect the defendant's right to trial by a particular tribunal they must be necessitous, actual and substantial. Thus, if the Judge acts so abruptly as not to permit consideration of the alternatives or otherwise acts irrationally or irresponsibly or solely for convenience of the court and jury or other similar abuse of discretion, retrial will be barred.

The Trial Judge's grant of a mistrial will be subjected to strict scrutiny when the basis for doing so is the unavailability of critical prosecution evidence, for the People are not entitled to a mistrial merely to gain " "'a more favorable opportunity to convict.'" " On the other hand, "the trial judge's evaluation of the likelihood that the impartiality of one or more jurors may have been affected by * * * improper comment" will be accorded "the highest degree of respect." . . . "The decision whether a mistrial is necessary because of juror bias [is] often based on subtle indications of discontent, not always apparent on the cold face of the record presented to an appellate court. Hence * * * a Trial Judge is entrusted with considerable discretion in making such determinations, for it is the Trial Judge, better than any other, who can detect the ambience of partiality."

Matter of Enright v. Siedlecki, 59 N.Y.2d 195, 200–01, 464 N.Y.S.2d 418, 422, 451 N.E.2d 176 (1983) (citations omitted). *See also* CPL § 280.10.

Manifest necessity for the declaration of a mistrial in a criminal case exists when after opening statements referring to a confession have been made, the prosecutor discovers a *Miranda* warnings statement indicating that defendant had requested counsel and the confession is, after a hearing, suppressed. Manifest necessity likewise exists when an essential defense witness becomes unavailable; the Trial Judge is not limited by defendant's attorney's request for a continuance rather than a mistrial and in passing upon the continuance request may take into account an appeal to sympathy by defense counsel during *voir dire* even though the Trial Judge denied the prosecution's motion for mistrial made during *voir dire*.

Siedlecki, 59 N.Y.2d at 197, 464 N.Y.S.2d at 420. *See also People v. Tinsley*, 58 N.Y.2d 990, 461 N.Y.S.2d 1005, 448 N.E.2d 790 (1983) (manifest necessity found to exist where sequestered juror disappeared overnight in the middle of deliberations without notifying anyone); *Matter of Hall v. Potoker*, 49 N.Y.2d 501, 427 N.Y.S.2d 211, 403 N.E.2d 1210 (1980) (manifest necessity found to exist due to the unavailability of a key prosecution witness which resulted from an unforeseeable contingency not within the People's control); *People v. Paquette*, 31 N.Y.2d 379, 339 N.Y.S.2d 959, 292 N.E.2d 17 (1972) (manifest necessity found to exist where mistrial was caused by defendant's conduct in threatening witnesses). Cf. *Matter of Zeigler v. Morgenthau*, 64 N.Y.2d 932, 488 N.Y.S.2d 633, 477 N.E.2d 1087 (1985) (manifest necessity found not to exist; Double Jeopardy barred reprosecution); *People v. Michael*, 48 N.Y.2d 1, 9, 420 N.Y.S.2d 371, 375, 394 N.E.2d 1134 (1979) (per curiam) ("a mistrial founded solely upon the convenience of the court and the jury is certainly not manifestly necessary"); *Matter of Ferlito v. Judges of County Court, Suffolk County*, 31 N.Y.2d 416, 340 N.Y.S.2d 635, 292 N.E.2d 779 (1972) (manifest necessity found not to exist).

§ 23:33 Where defendant consents to mistrial there is no Double Jeopardy violation

In *Matter of Gorman v. Rice*, 24 N.Y.3d 1032, 1034, 998 N.Y.S.2d 141, 142, 22 N.E.3d 1009 (2014), a DWI case:

[D]efense counsel announced, outside the presence of the jury, that he intended to file a complaint against the judge for alleged pro-prosecution rulings. The judge stated, "I'm declaring a mistrial based on the threats of counsel to file a complaint against me. I'll be back in five minutes." When the judge returned, he noted that "[b]efore we broke, I declared a mistrial. I reviewed the record, and it is clear that defense counsel said that my conduct verged on needing a complaint being filed. That being said, I am unable to preside over this trial." The judge then remarked to defense counsel, "I'm assuming . . . that you agree that . . . I should not be able to preside over this trial," to which defense counsel responded, "Yes, sir." The court continued that "on consent, I'm going to declare a mistrial." Defense counsel then objected that he was "not consenting to a mistrial."

Further discussion ensued among the court and the parties, and the prosecutor suggested that the trial be adjourned to the following week to give everyone "a chance to cool down" so that "[m]aybe [they could] continue the trial." The judge responded, "Well, I think . . . [it] is really up to the defendant and [defense counsel]."

The defense was given the choice, and chose to "go with the mistrial." The defendant thereafter sought to preclude a retrial on Double Jeopardy grounds. The Court of Appeals held that, having consented to the mistrial before the jury was discharged, the defendant's Double Jeopardy claim was without merit. *Id.* at 1036, 998 N.Y.S.2d at 143–44. *See also People v. Catten*, 69 N.Y.2d 547, 554, 516 N.Y.S.2d 186, 190, 508 N.E.2d 920 (1987) ("by moving for a mistrial, retrial generally is not barred, regardless of whether there was manifest necessity for the mistrial"); *People v. Ferguson*, 67 N.Y.2d 383, 386, 502 N.Y.S.2d 972, 974, 494 N.E.2d 77 (1986) ("The issues on this appeal are whether defendant's lawyer consented to the mistrial, and whether a lawyer has the authority to do so where the defendant is not present and was not consulted. We answer both of these questions affirmatively"); *id.* at 390 n.*, 502 N.Y.S.2d at 977 n.* ("It would seem preferable, of course, for the lawyer to consult with the client, in court, before making such a decision. We are limited here, however, to the constitutional issue, and we hold only that for purposes of double jeopardy there was consent to the mistrial"). *See generally People v. Rodriquez*, 39 N.Y.2d 976, 978, 387 N.Y.S.2d 110, 111, 354 N.E.2d 850 (1976) ("Since no order of mistrial had been entered and the jury had not been discharged, the trial court's purported declaration of a mistrial obviously was a statement of intention rather than a completed act, despite its declarative form. It was rescinded almost immediately. Hence, there is no basis for the assertion of double jeopardy").

§ 23:34 Double Jeopardy claim can be relinquished by defendant's conduct

"[A] defendant can, by his or her conduct, relinquish a double jeopardy claim." *People v. McFadden*, 20 N.Y.3d 260, 264, 959 N.Y.S.2d 108, 110, 982 N.E.2d 1241 (2012). In *McFadden*, the Court of Appeals held that "defense counsel failed to object to the improper jury instruction and affirmatively requested a mistrial after the court specifically stated that defendant faced retrial on the top two counts. Having charted his own course by opting for a mistrial and a retrial on the remaining counts, defendant cannot now claim that his retrial is barred." *Id.* at 264, 959 N.Y.S.2d at 110. *See also People v. Catten*, 69 N.Y.2d 547, 554, 516 N.Y.S.2d 186, 190, 508 N.E.2d 920 (1987) ("by moving for a mistrial, retrial generally is not barred, regardless of whether there was manifest necessity for the mistrial"). *See generally Matter of Marte v. Berkman*, 16 N.Y.3d 874, 925 N.Y.S.2d 388, 949 N.E.2d 479 (2011) (defendants impliedly consented to mistrial after jury submitted note stating that it had reached a verdict on two counts and that it was deadlocked on others); *People v. Echevarria*, 6 N.Y.3d 89, 809 N.Y.S.2d 509, 843 N.E.2d 149 (2005) (defendant forfeited claim that partial verdict finding him guilty of Murder 2nd had to be deemed acquittal of Murder 1st charge); *Matter of Harris v. Justices of Supreme Court, Kings County*, 44 N.Y.2d 874, 875, 407 N.Y.S.2d 478, 479, 378 N.E.2d 1048 (1978) ("before the mistrial was declared petitioner had not expressly objected and the court could reasonably have concluded that his attorney was willing to see the trial aborted since he stated that he stood on the record which was replete with his own requests for a mistrial").

§ 23:35 Right to withdraw motion for mistrial

Whether to allow a defendant to withdraw his mistrial application after it has been granted is a matter committed to the discretion of the trial court. This, of course, is to be distinguished from the motion not yet ruled upon, which a party may withdraw, provided nothing has occurred to prejudice the opposing party.

People v. Catten, 69 N.Y.2d 547, 555, 516 N.Y.S.2d 186, 190, 508 N.E.2d 920 (1987) (citation omitted).

§ 23:36 Reversal on appeal exception to Double Jeopardy

"A defendant who succeeds in having a conviction reversed on appeal may be retried for the same offense without contravening double jeopardy principles." *Matter of Suarez v. Byrne*, 10 N.Y.3d 523, 532, 860 N.Y.S.2d 439, 446, 890 N.E.2d 201 (2008).

§ 23:37 Exception to reversal on appeal exception to Double Jeopardy

Although "[a] defendant who succeeds in having a conviction reversed on appeal may be retried for the same offense without contravening double jeopardy principles," *Matter of Suarez v. Byrne*, 10 N.Y.3d 523, 532, 860 N.Y.S.2d 439, 446, 890 N.E.2d 201 (2008), " "'the Double Jeopardy Clause precludes a second trial once the reviewing court has found the evidence legally insufficient.'" " *Id.* at 533, 860 N.Y.S.2d at 446 (citations omitted). *See also People v. Sailor*, 65 N.Y.2d 224, 230, 491 N.Y.S.2d 112, 117, 480 N.E.2d 701 (1985) ("a defendant may not be retried if the reversal of his conviction is based on an appellate finding of insufficient evidence to convict").

§ 23:38 Legality of vacating plea that was accepted in violation of the CPL

In *Matter of Campbell v. Pesce*, 60 N.Y.2d 165, 167, 468 N.Y.S.2d 865, 866, 456 N.E.2d 806 (1983), the Court of Appeals held that "[a]fter sentence has commenced, a court which has accepted a plea in violation of the Criminal Procedure Law may not vacate the illegal plea and reinstate the original charges." *Cf. People v. Bartley*, 47 N.Y.2d 965, 419 N.Y.S.2d 956, 393 N.E.2d 1029 (1979) (opposite result reached where error was discovered prior to sentencing).

§ 23:39 Legality of vacating plea where parties thought defendant had pled to felony but offense was in fact only misdemeanor

In *Matter of Kisloff v. Covington*, 73 N.Y.2d 445, 541 N.Y.S.2d 737, 539 N.E.2d 565 (1989), the defendant entered into a plea bargain where the defense, the prosecution and the Court all believed that the crime that the defendant pled guilty to was a class E felony. As it turned out, however, the crime was only a misdemeanor. When the defendant insisted on being sentenced as a misdemeanor offender—which was not the intent of the plea bargain—"the court vacated the plea and set the matter down for trial on the indictment." *Id.* at 448, 541 N.Y.S.2d at 739. The Court of Appeals held as follows:

> In the case at bar, it appears that both the agreed to plea and sentence were illegal: the plea, because defendant, a predicate felon, was permitted to plead to what in fact was a misdemeanor offense in full satisfaction of the indictment in violation of CPL 220.10(5)(c) and the sentence, because Supreme Court directed that defendant serve felony time for this misdemeanor plea. Once defendant's sentence was imposed and judgment was entered, however, his plea could not be disturbed based upon the parties' mutual mistake since no statutory basis existed for setting aside such a plea and courts have no "inherent power to vacate a plea and sentence over defendant's objection where the error goes beyond mere clerical error apparent on the face of the record and where the proceeding has terminated by the entry of judgment." And while defendant's sentence was assailable for illegality pursuant to the CPL, the proper curative course in the absence of defendant's consent to do otherwise, was to impose a new sentence consistent as a matter of law with defendant's misdemeanor plea.

> In sum, because no statutory or other basis existed for Supreme Court's vacatur of the judgment of conviction, the court acted in excess of its power. Additionally, any further criminal proceedings on the original charges are barred by petitioner's constitutional right not to be twice put in jeopardy.

Id. at 452, 541 N.Y.S.2d at 741–42 (citations omitted).

§ 23:40 Legality of resentencing defendant whose sentence was affected by a clerical or ministerial error

In *People v. Gammon*, 19 N.Y.3d 893, 950 N.Y.S.2d 65, 973 N.E.2d 160 (2012), a misdemeanor DWI case, the defendant was sentenced to 60 days in jail and 3 years' probation. When the defendant subsequently violated the terms of his probation, the Court sentenced him to 60 *additional* days in jail and terminated his probation. Due to a clerical error/misunderstanding, the jail released the defendant on the same day that the new sentence commenced (erroneously crediting the defendant with time served for his original 60-day sentence). "Days after learning of defendant's release, the District Court resentenced him to '120 days in jail which is an additional 60 days to the 60 days sentence that he already served.'" *Id.* at 895, 950 N.Y.S.2d at 66. The defendant claimed that the resentencing violated CPL § 430.10 and Double Jeopardy. On appeal, the Court of Appeals held that:

> It is well established that courts have the "inherent power to correct their records, where the correction relates to mistakes, or errors, which may be termed clerical in their nature, or where it is made in order to conform the record to the truth." Consequently, we have recognized that courts can exercise this authority "in circumstances where it clearly appears that a mistake or error occurred at the time a sentence was imposed." It is evident, on this record, that District Court intended to impose an "additional 60 days incarceration" for the violation of probation. Its failure to specify that this was a successive term of imprisonment created the type of ambiguity a court has the inherent authority to clarify. * * *

> Nor did the resentencing violate defendant's constitutional right against double jeopardy. In *People v. Williams*, 14 N.Y.3d 198, 899 N.Y.S.2d 76 (2010), we held that once defendants had satisfied their original judgments by completing their sentences and been released from incarceration at the termination of their sentences, a reasonable expectation of finality had attached and double jeopardy prevented imposition of postrelease supervision (PRS) at resentencing. The defendants in *Williams* served out their terms of imprisonment, and the sentencing judges unambiguously did not pronounce PRS, whereas here, defendant received an ambiguous sentence and did not serve out the original sentence imposed, as reasonably understood by all the parties.

Id. at 895–96, 950 N.Y.S.2d at 66–67 (citations omitted). *See generally People v. Carter*, 63 N.Y.2d 530, 533, 483 N.Y.S.2d 654, 655–56, 473 N.E.2d 6 (1984) ("A Trial Judge who has rendered a guilty verdict after a nonjury trial has neither inherent power nor statutory authority to reconsider his factual determination. Although he may correct clerical or ministerial errors, he is without authority to reassess the facts and change a guilty verdict to not guilty").

In *People v. Minaya*, 54 N.Y.2d 360, 362, 445 N.Y.S.2d 690, 691, 429 N.E.2d 1161 (1981), the Court of Appeals held that "a court which mistakenly sentenced a defendant to [3] years, instead of [8] years as agreed at the time of plea, could correct its error a few months later without violating either the statutory prohibition against changing sentences (CPL 430.10) or the defendant's constitutional rights under the double jeopardy clause." On the other hand, "[o]f course a court cannot, in the guise of correcting an error, change or amend a sentence which is not defective." *Id.* at 364, 445 N.Y.S.2d at 692.

§ 23:41 Legality of resentencing defendant whose sentence was illegal

"In 1998, as part of Jenna's Law, the Legislature adopted Penal Law § 70.45, which directs that postrelease supervision [PRS] is a mandatory component of all determinate prison sentences." *People v. Williams*, 14 N.Y.3d 198, 206, 899 N.Y.S.2d 76, 79, 925 N.E.2d 878 (2010). Nonetheless, Courts repeatedly fail to mention this requirement at sentencing—which has led to a substantial amount of litigation.

In *People v. Catu*, 4 N.Y.3d 242, 243, 792 N.Y.S.2d 887, 887, 825 N.E.2d 1081 (2005), the Court of Appeals held that the sentencing court's "failure to advise defendant of a direct consequence of his conviction [*i.e.*, that defendant was required to be sentenced to 5 years of PRS] requires that his plea be vacated." *See also People v. Boyd*, 12 N.Y.3d 390, 880 N.Y.S.2d 908, 908 N.E.2d 898 (2009); *People v. Hill*, 9 N.Y.3d 189, 849 N.Y.S.2d 13, 879 N.E.2d 152 (2007); *People v. Louree*, 8 N.Y.3d 541, 838 N.Y.S.2d 18, 869 N.E.2d 18 (2007); *People v. Van Deusen*, 7 N.Y.3d 744, 819 N.Y.S.2d 854, 853 N.E.2d 223 (2006).

The failure of a sentencing court to impose mandatory PRS cannot be administratively corrected by either (a) the Department of Correctional Services, *see Matter of Garner v. New York State Dept. of Correctional Services*, 10 N.Y.3d 358, 362, 859 N.Y.S.2d 590, 592–93, 889 N.E.2d 467 (2008), or (b) a Court Clerk. *See People v. Sparber*, 10 N.Y.3d 457, 470–71, 859 N.Y.S.2d 582, 588, 889 N.E.2d 459 (2008). The *Sparber* court found that "the failure to pronounce the required sentence amounts only to a procedural error, akin to a misstatement or clerical error, which the sentencing court could easily remedy." *Id.* at 472, 859 N.Y.S.2d at 589. "[S]triking the PRS terms would leave defendants with a windfall that greatly exceeds any harm that they have purportedly suffered." *Id.* at 469, 859 N.Y.S.2d at 587. However, "[t]he sole remedy for a procedural error such as this is to vacate the sentence and remit for a resentencing hearing so that the trial judge can make the required pronouncement." *Id.* at 471, 859 N.Y.S.2d at 588.

All of this led to *People v. Williams*, 14 N.Y.3d 198, 899 N.Y.S.2d 76, 925 N.E.2d 878 (2010). The *Williams* court held that:

As a general principle, a sentence cannot be changed once a defendant begins to serve it; however, this applies only if the "sentence is in accordance with law" (CPL 430.10). Our precedent has long recognized that courts have the inherent authority to correct illegal sentences. Because PRS is a mandatory component of a sentence for a crime punishable by a determinate prison term (*see* Penal Law § 70.45[1]), there is no dispute that defendants' original sentences that omitted the imposition of terms of PRS were illegal. * * *

Defendants next challenge the imposition of PRS as a violation of the Double Jeopardy Clause of the Federal Constitution because the resentencing proceedings occurred after they were released from prison after completing their terms of imprisonment. * * *

We . . . conclude that, after release from prison, a legitimate expectation in the finality of a sentence arises and the Double Jeopardy Clause prevents reformation to attach a PRS component to the original completed sentence . . . . Since criminal defendants are charged with knowledge of the relevant laws that apply to them, they are presumed to be aware that a determinate prison sentence without a term of PRS is illegal and, thus, may be corrected by the sentencing court at some point in the future. So long as an illegal sentence is subject to correction, a defendant cannot claim a legitimate expectation that the originally-imposed, improper sentence is final for all purposes.

Yet, there must be a temporal limitation on a court's ability to resentence a defendant since criminal courts do not have perpetual jurisdiction over all persons who were once sentenced for criminal acts. Even where a defendant's sentence is illegal, there is a legitimate expectation of finality once the initial sentence has been served and the direct appeal has been completed (or the time to appeal has expired). In these situations, the sentences are beyond the court's authority and an additional term of PRS may not be imposed. With the caveats we have identified, in a case where PRS was not formally pronounced by the sentencing court pursuant to CPL 380.20, we hold that the Double Jeopardy Clause prohibits a court from resentencing the defendant to the mandatory term of PRS after the defendant has served the determinate term of imprisonment and has been released from confinement by DOCS. * * *

To summarize, once a defendant is released from custody and returns to the community after serving the period of incarceration that was ordered by the sentencing court, and the time to appeal the sentence has expired or the appeal has been finally determined, there is a legitimate expectation that the sentence, although illegal under the Penal Law, is final and the Double Jeopardy Clause prevents a court from modifying the sentence to include a period of postrelease supervision.

Id. at 212, 214, 217, 219–20, 899 N.Y.S.2d at 84, 85, 87–88, 89 (citations omitted). *See also People v. Velez*, 19 N.Y.3d 642, 951 N.Y.S.2d 461, 975 N.E.2d 907 (2012); *People v. Jordan*, 15 N.Y.3d 727, 905 N.Y.S.2d 797, 931 N.E.2d 1053 (2010); *People v. Williams*, 14 N.Y.3d 924, 905 N.Y.S.2d 555, 931 N.E.2d 539 (2010); *People v. Hassell*, 14 N.Y.3d 925, 905 N.Y.S.2d 555, 931 N.E.2d 539 (2010). *See generally People v. Williams*, 87 N.Y.2d 1014, 1015, 643 N.Y.S.2d 469, 470, 666 N.E.2d 174 (1996) ("the trial court had the inherent power to correct an illegal sentence").

In *People v. Lingle*, 16 N.Y.3d 621, 630, 926 N.Y.S.2d 4, 7, 949 N.E.2d 952 (2011), the Court of Appeals declined to extend *Williams* to cases where the defendants had "served 'significant' or 'substantial' portions of their originally-imposed sentences before resentencing." *See also id.* at 630–31, 926 N.Y.S.2d at 8 ("The defendants in *Williams* and the cases decided along with it had all completed their sentences (including any discharge on conditional release) before being resentenced. By contrast, the six defendants in these cases had not yet completed their originally-imposed sentences of imprisonment when they were resentenced to add PRS"). *See also People v. Brinson*, 21 N.Y.3d 490, 496, 972 N.Y.S.2d 182, 186, 995 N.E.2d 144 (2013) ("As we stated in *Williams* and *Lingle*, a legitimate expectation of finality turns on the completion of a sentence. Where multiple sentences are properly aggregated into a single sentence, that expectation arises upon completion of that sentence . . . . Until such time, resentencing for purposes of correcting their illegal determinate sentences does not run afoul of the Double Jeopardy Clause and the prohibition against 'multiple punishments' ").

In *People v. Cintron*, 22 N.Y.3d 757, 759, 986 N.Y.S.2d 386, 387, 9 N.E.3d 881 (2014), the Court of Appeals held that "an appellate court [can] correct a defendant's illegal sentence on direct appeal by imposing a term of postrelease supervision (PRS) after the defendant has completed the illegal sentence." The *Cintron* court distinguished *Williams* on the ground that Mr. Cintron "has served his sentence, but the direct appeal of that sentence is not over; it presently is before us. Consequently defendant has not acquired a legitimate expectation of finality in his sentence." *Id.* at 760–61, 986 N.Y.S.2d at 388.

§ 23:42 Constitutional Double Jeopardy claim is generally not subject to the preservation requirement

"Constitutional double jeopardy violations generally constitute mode of proceedings errors" that fall within an exception to the preservation requirement. *People v. Williams*, 14 N.Y.3d 198, 220, 899 N.Y.S.2d 76, 90, 925 N.E.2d 878 (2010). *See also People v. Hanley*, 20 N.Y.3d 601, 604–05 & n.2, 964 N.Y.S.2d 491, 493 n.2, 987 N.E.2d 268 (2013); *People v. Biggs*, 1 N.Y.3d 225, 231, 771 N.Y.S.2d 49, 53, 803 N.E.2d 370 (2003); *People v. Gonzalez*, 99 N.Y.2d 76, 82–83, 751 N.Y.S.2d 830, 833, 781 N.E.2d 894 (2002); *People v. Fuller*, 96 N.Y.2d 881, 883–84, 730 N.Y.S.2d 773, 774, 756 N.E.2d 61 (2001); *People v. Ahmed*, 66 N.Y.2d 307, 310, 496 N.Y.S.2d 984, 985, 487 N.E.2d 894 (1985); *People v. Michael*, 48 N.Y.2d 1, 6–7, 420 N.Y.S.2d 371, 373, 394 N.E.2d 1134 (1979); *People v. Michael*, 48 N.Y.2d 1, 420 N.Y.S.2d 371, 394 N.E.2d 1134 (1979) (per curiam).

§ 23:43　Statutory Double Jeopardy claim is subject to the preservation requirement

A statutory Double Jeopardy claim cannot be raised on appeal unless it is properly preserved. *See, e.g., People v. Hanley*, 20 N.Y.3d 601, 604–05 & n.2, 964 N.Y.S.2d 491, 493 & n.2, 987 N.E.2d 268 (2013); *People v. Biggs*, 1 N.Y.3d 225, 231, 771 N.Y.S.2d 49, 53, 803 N.E.2d 370 (2003). *See generally People v. Gonzalez*, 99 N.Y.2d 76, 82–83, 751 N.Y.S.2d 830, 833, 781 N.E.2d 894 (2002) (Constitutional Double Jeopardy claim that multiple punishments for the same offense were illegal was a statutory interpretation question that must be properly preserved); *People v. Dodson*, 48 N.Y.2d 36, 38, 421 N.Y.S.2d 47, 47, 396 N.E.2d 194 (1979) (per curiam) ("A statutory claim that one may not be separately prosecuted for two offenses based on the same act or criminal transaction, as distinguished from a constitutional double jeopardy claim, must be duly preserved if there is to be appellate review").

§ 23:44　Constitutional Double Jeopardy claim survives guilty plea

A claim that one's Constitutional Double Jeopardy rights were violated can be raised on appeal despite a guilty plea. *See, e.g., People v. Parilla*, 8 N.Y.3d 654, 659, 838 N.Y.S.2d 824, 827, 870 N.E.2d 142 (2007); *People v. Konieczny*, 2 N.Y.3d 569, 573, 780 N.Y.S.2d 546, 548, 813 N.E.2d 626 (2004); *People v. Hansen*, 95 N.Y.2d 227, 230–31, 715 N.Y.S.2d 369, 372, 738 N.E.2d 773 (2000); *People v. Prescott*, 66 N.Y.2d 216, 218, 495 N.Y.S.2d 955, 956, 486 N.E.2d 813 (1985); *People v. Taylor*, 65 N.Y.2d 1, 5, 489 N.Y.S.2d 152, 154–55, 478 N.E.2d 755 (1985); *People v. Dodson*, 48 N.Y.2d 36, 39, 421 N.Y.S.2d 47, 48, 396 N.E.2d 194 (1979) (per curiam); *People v. Menna*, 38 N.Y.2d 850, 382 N.Y.S.2d 56, 345 N.E.2d 599 (1976).

§ 23:45   Statutory Double Jeopardy claim does not survive guilty plea

A claim that one's statutory Double Jeopardy rights were violated is forfeited by a guilty plea. *See, e.g., People v. Konieczny*, 2 N.Y.3d 569, 574, 780 N.Y.S.2d 546, 550, 813 N.E.2d 626 (2004); *People v. Okafore*, 72 N.Y.2d 81, 85 n.1, 531 N.Y.S.2d 762, 764 n.1, 527 N.E.2d 245, 80 A.L.R.4th 615 (1988); *People v. Prescott*, 66 N.Y.2d 216, 219, 495 N.Y.S.2d 955, 957, 486 N.E.2d 813 (1985) ("a guilty plea results in forfeiture of a defendant's 40.20 claim even though the claim has been presented to the court prior to the plea").

§ 23:46   Constitutional Double Jeopardy claim can be waived if waiver is knowing, voluntary and intelligent

Although a Constitutional Double Jeopardy claim does not have to be preserved, it can be validly waived. In this regard, in *People v. Muniz*, 91 N.Y.2d 570, 573–74, 673 N.Y.S.2d 358, 360–61, 696 N.E.2d 182 (1998), the Court of Appeals held that:

> A criminal defendant's waiver of the right to appeal, obtained as a condition of a sentence or plea bargain, will be upheld if it is voluntary, knowing and intelligent, and implicates no larger societal interest or important public policy concern. As long as those conditions are satisfied, the scope of the waiver of the right to appeal can be fully comprehensive, and is enforceable consistent with the actual intent underlying its execution.

> We have, however, previously identified certain defects in the proceedings leading to a conviction which are unwaivable as part of a plea bargain. This narrow class of appellate claims, grounded in the integrity of our criminal justice system and "the reality of fairness in the process," implicate either an infirmity in the waiver itself or a public policy consideration that transcends the individual concerns of a particular defendant to obtain appellate review.

> In *People v. Allen*, we determined that a claim of constitutional double jeopardy falls outside of that class of nonwaivable claims and, if all the other conditions for a valid waiver are satisfied, a double jeopardy claim may be expressly waivable through a condition to a sentence or plea bargain. We noted specifically in *Allen* that none of the societal interests which justify the narrow exceptions "to the general rule that an accused may waive any right he or she enjoys as part of a plea bargain" are present in a claim of double jeopardy. Thus, while a claim of constitutional double jeopardy ordinarily is not waived by a counseled guilty plea and may be raised for the first time on appeal, where, as a condition of the plea to lesser charges, a defendant validly waived his right to appeal, including any claim of double jeopardy, such a bargained-for waiver is effective and enforceable.

(Citations omitted). *See also People v. Allen*, 86 N.Y.2d 599, 635 N.Y.S.2d 139, 658 N.E.2d 1012 (1995); *People v. Coppa*, 45 N.Y.2d 244, 248, 408 N.Y.S.2d 365, 367, 380 N.E.2d 195 (1978).

§ 23:47   PL § 70.25(2), which prohibits consecutive sentencing in certain situations, embodies Double Jeopardy principles

Penal Law § 70.25(2) provides that:

When more than one sentence of imprisonment is imposed on a person for two or more offenses committed through a single act or omission, or through an act or omission which in itself constituted one of the offenses and also was a material element of the other, the sentences, except if one or more of such sentences is for a violation of section 270.20 of this chapter, must run concurrently.

See also People ex rel. Maurer v. Jackson, 2 N.Y.2d 259, 264, 159 N.Y.S.2d 203, 206, 140 N.E.2d 282 (1957) ("It is . . . not open to dispute that if there were merely a single inseparable act violative of more than one statute, or if there were an act which itself violated one statute and was a material element of the violation of another, there would have to be single punishment").

In *People v. Ramirez*, 89 N.Y.2d 444, 451 n.5, 654 N.Y.S.2d 998, 1001 n.5, 677 N.E.2d 722 (1996), the Court of Appeals made clear that:

This Court has noted that the constitutional prohibition against double jeopardy "is embodied in, if not * * * extended by" Penal Law § 70.25(2). Section 70.25(2) does not prohibit convictions of multiple offenses containing overlapping elements. Rather, the statute prohibits double punishment for an act or omission which violates more than one section of the law and is accordingly punishable in different ways.

(Citation omitted).

In *People v. Catone*, 65 N.Y.2d 1003, 494 N.Y.S.2d 97, 484 N.E.2d 126 (1985), the defendant drove into and killed a teenage girl as she was crossing the road. After briefly reducing his speed, the defendant sped off. The defendant was subsequently convicted of Manslaughter in the Second Degree and felony Leaving the Scene of an Accident, and sentenced to consecutive terms of imprisonment. On appeal, the Court of Appeals found that "[t]he relevant law and facts of this case demonstrate that the offense of manslaughter in the second degree was a material element of the offense of felony leaving the scene without reporting." *Id.* at 1005, 494 N.Y.S.2d at 98. Accordingly, the Court modified defendant's sentences to run concurrently.

In so holding, the Court noted that "it appears anomalous that the crime of leaving the scene of an accident should be essentially unpunished under these circumstances," and invited the Legislature to "reexamine" the language of VTL § 600. *Id.* at 1005, 494 N.Y.S.2d at 98. In 1986, the Legislature followed this suggestion and amended VTL § 600 to permit consecutive sentences for similar crimes in the future. *See, e.g., People v. Chambers*, 257 A.D.2d 418, 683 N.Y.S.2d 238 (1st Dep't 1999); *People v. Isaac*, 224 A.D.2d 993, —, 637 N.Y.S.2d 827, 829 (4th Dep't 1996); *People v. Levy*, 157 Misc. 2d 941, 599 N.Y.S.2d 898 (Sup 1993).

In *People v. Backus*, 56 A.D.3d 1119, —, 867 N.Y.S.2d 290, 291 (4th Dep't 2008), rev'd in part, vacated in part, 14 N.Y.3d 876, 903 N.Y.S.2d 333, 929 N.E.2d 396 (2010), the Appellate Division, Fourth Department, held that "[a]s defendant correctly contends, the offense of driving while intoxicated is a material element of the offense of vehicular assault in the second degree and thus the sentence is illegal insofar as County Court imposed consecutive sentences."

In *People v. Clemens*, 177 A.D.2d 1053, —, 578 N.Y.S.2d 296, 296 (4th Dep't 1991), the Appellate Division, Fourth Department, held that "[t]he trial court erred in ordering that the sentence imposed on defendant's conviction for driving while intoxicated be served consecutively to the sentence of aggravated unlicensed operation of a motor vehicle in the first degree" (citation omitted), and modified defendant's sentences to run concurrently. *See also People v. Milo*, 235 A.D.2d 552, 654 N.Y.S.2d 146 (2d Dep't 1997) (same); *People v. Magistro*, 156 A.D.2d 1029, 550 N.Y.S.2d 875 (4th Dep't 1989) (same).

In *People v. Richburg*, 287 A.D.2d 790, —, 731 N.Y.S.2d 256, 258 (3d Dep't 2001), the Appellate Division, Third Department, stated that sentences imposed for felony DWI and AUO 1st could run consecutively without violating PL § 70.25(2). Critically, however, in *People v. De Maio*, 304 A.D.2d 988, —, 760 N.Y.S.2d 558, 559 (3d Dep't 2003), the Court clarified its position in *Richburg*:

> Although there are numerous factual circumstances that can comprise both the crimes of [AUO 1st] and felony [DWI], it is apparent that [DWI] can constitute a material element of [AUO 1st]. It was thus incumbent upon the People to show either that defendant's felony [DWI] was not, in fact, a material element of his [AUO 1st] or that the two offenses were based upon separate and distinct acts. Here, the indictment alleges defendant's driving while under the influence as an element of the charge of [AUO 1st]. Both the offenses to which defendant eventually pleaded guilty are alleged in the indictment to have occurred on the same date, place and time. The plea allocution confirms such facts and, indeed, further reveals that the same prior offenses provided the basis for both the previous revocation of defendant's license and the elevation of the [DWI] to felony status. It is thus clear that defendant's felony [DWI] charge was a material element of his [AUO 1st] and the

People failed to show that the two offenses arose from separate and distinct acts.

> The People's reliance upon *People v. Richburg*, with no concomitant case-specific factual analysis, is misplaced. *Richburg* should not be construed as holding that felony [DWI] and [AUO 1st] cannot fall within the parameters of Penal Law § 70.25(2). To the contrary, since felony [DWI] can constitute a material element of [AUO 1st], the People bear the burden when advocating consecutive sentences of showing identifiable separate acts sustaining such sentences. The People failed to make such a showing in this case and, therefore, the sentences must be modified to run concurrently.

(Citations and footnote omitted). *See also People v. Khan*, 291 A.D.2d 898, 737 N.Y.S.2d 738 (4th Dep't 2002) (PL § 70.25(2) requires concurrent sentences where defendant convicted of AUO 1st and DWAI); *People v. Fleenor*, 162 A.D.2d 832, 557 N.Y.S.2d 735 (3d Dep't 1990) (concurrent sentences required where defendant convicted of criminally negligent homicide and DWAI); *People v. Coleman*, 138 A.D.2d 963, 526 N.Y.S.2d 296 (4th Dep't 1988) (concurrent sentences required where defendant convicted of criminally negligent homicide and DWI).

Shortly after *DeMaio* was decided, the Third Department upheld consecutive sentences in a felony DWAI Drugs/AUO 1st case where the defendant's only challenge to such sentence was that it was harsh and excessive. *See People v. Clark*, 309 A.D.2d 1076, 766 N.Y.S.2d 710 (3d Dep't 2003). Thus, it is critical that defense counsel in a felony DWI/AUO 1st case expressly object to consecutive sentences on the specific ground that such sentences violate PL § 70.25(2).

In this regard, where the issue was preserved, the Third Department invalidated consecutive sentences imposed upon the defendant for a VOP involving charges of misdemeanor DWI and AUO 2nd. *See People v. Borush*, 39 A.D.3d 890, 834 N.Y.S.2d 340 (3d Dep't 2007). In so holding, the Court stated that "[b]ecause the act of driving a motor vehicle while intoxicated and while suspended was a single act, concurrent sentences should have been imposed." *Id.* at __, 834 N.Y.S.2d 341. *Cf. People v. Skarczewski*, 287 N.Y. 826, 41 N.E.2d 99 (1942) (per curiam).

In *People v. Goldstein*, 12 N.Y.3d 295, 300, 879 N.Y.S.2d 814, 817, 907 N.E.2d 692 (2009), the Court of Appeals stated that "it is clear . . . that the conduct underlying the count alleging aggravated unlicensed operation of a motor vehicle was distinct from that involved in the ensuing reckless endangerment offenses and thus permitted a consecutive sentence."

In *People v. Crane*, 129 A.D.3d 741, __, 8 N.Y.S.3d 924, __ (2d Dep't 2015), the Appellate Division, Second Department, held that:

Contrary to the defendant's contention, the imposition of a consecutive term of imprisonment for his conviction of unauthorized use of a vehicle in the first degree (Penal Law § 165.08) was not illegal. Although the defendant's conviction of unauthorized use of a vehicle in the first degree, and his convictions of aggravated [DWI] and two counts of [DWI] arose out of a single, extended transaction, the plea colloquy establishes that the convictions of the unauthorized use of a vehicle offense and the above-mentioned driving while intoxicated offenses arose out of separate acts.

(Citations omitted).

§ 23:48   Applicability of Double Jeopardy to defendant who testifies before Grand Jury

In *Matter of Rush v. Mordue*, 68 N.Y.2d 348, 350–51, 509 N.Y.S.2d 493, 495, 502 N.E.2d 170 (1986), the Court of Appeals held as follows:

Where a witness is called before a Grand Jury and, without having executed a waiver of immunity, gives testimony concerning the truthfulness of a prior sworn statement and disavows that prior statement as having been false when given, transactional immunity resulting from the compelled testimony is acquired with respect to that prior statement, and the witness may not thereafter be prosecuted for perjury based upon the inconsistency between the prior sworn statement and the Grand Jury testimony. Where such prosecution is threatened, a writ of prohibition under CPLR article 78 will lie to raise the claim of immunity and interdict the prosecution.

§ 23:49   Applicability of Double Jeopardy to local criminal court accusatory instruments dismissed for facial insufficiency

In *People v. Nuccio*, 78 N.Y.2d 102, 105–06, 571 N.Y.S.2d 693, 695, 575 N.E.2d 111 (1991), the Court of Appeals held as follows:

[T]he former Code of Criminal Procedure contained various provisions in which the Legislature expressly barred reprosecution of both felony and misdemeanor charges following a dismissal. When the Criminal Procedure Law replaced the Code in 1970, however, the Legislature chose to treat dismissals of indictments separate from dismissal of informations and misdemeanor complaints. When it did so, the provisions of the Code prohibiting reprosecution were transferred to CPL 210.20(4), a section dealing exclusively with the dismissal of an indictment without the enactment of a similar provision prohibiting the reprosecution of charges contained in a dismissed information.

The Legislature undoubtedly was aware of prior restraints on reprosecution when it enacted the Criminal Procedure Law because it expressly addressed dismissals based on legal insufficiency with respect to indictments in section 210.20(4). Nevertheless, it failed to include a similar bar for informations dismissed on those same grounds pursuant to CPL 170.30(1)(a). We conclude, therefore, that the different treatment accorded indictments and informations in the statute manifests the Legislature's intention to permit reprosecution for nonfelony charges when the information is dismissed for legal insufficiency.

Nor is double jeopardy a bar to the refiling of the charges against defendant since "reprosecution is permitted whenever a dismissal has been granted on motion by defendant, so long as the dismissal does not constitute an adjudication on the facts going to guilt or innocence." Here, the simplified information was dismissed for legal insufficiency and thus reprosecution for the same charges was proper absent some statutory bar.

(Citations omitted). *See also People v. Key*, 45 N.Y.2d 111, 115, 408 N.Y.S.2d 16, 18, 379 N.E.2d 1147 (1978) ("when a dismissal on motion by defendant, even after a jury has been sworn, is based only on the legal insufficiency of the information, retrial is forbidden neither by the double jeopardy clauses of the State and Federal Constitutions nor by the statutory double jeopardy provisions"); *Matter of Sena v. Zittell*, 81 A.D.2d 245, __, 440 N.Y.S.2d 377, 378 (3d Dep't 1981) ("petitioner is not in danger of being twice jeopardized for the same offense for reprosecution is tolerated whenever a dismissal has been granted on the defendant's motion, if the dismissal did not constitute an adjudication on the facts going to guilt or innocence. And this rule applies even if the dismissal occurs after jeopardy has attached"); *id.* at __, 440 N.Y.S.2d at 378 ("A trial on the merits of whether petitioner was innocent or guilty of the driving while intoxicated charges never occurred here. The dismissal of these charges was prompted by a technicality, a [3]-hour discrepancy between the time alleged in the accusatory instruments and the actual time the purported crimes were committed. Inasmuch as double jeopardy offers no impediment to reprosecution of petitioner on those very same charges, prosecution of him for reckless endangerment, a different charge, also is not barred") (citation omitted). *See generally People v. Morgan*, 90 Misc. 2d 416, 395 N.Y.S.2d 363 (Suffolk Co. Sup. Ct. 1977).

The *Key* court concluded its decision as follows:

One final comment is merited. If trial courts in cases like this one were, whenever practicable, only to reserve decision until after trial has been completed and determinations of fact made, much difficulty would be avoided. Of course, if the motion had been made and decided, as it should have been, before trial, no problem would have arisen. But, once trial has started, decision on a belated motion might well be delayed until after jury verdict or decision on the facts. If defendant were to be acquitted, that would be the end of the matter; if convicted, appeal of the ruling, and, if appropriate, retrial or reinstatement of the verdict or decision would be permissible on any view of double jeopardy doctrine. It is the premature dismissal that has caused the trouble in this case, and that should be avoidable in most other cases.

Key, 45 N.Y.2d at 120, 408 N.Y.S.2d at 22.

§ 23:50 Applicability of Double Jeopardy to repeat felony offender statutes

Repeat felony offender statutes do not violate Double Jeopardy. *See, e.g., People v. Hunt*, 162 A.D.2d 782, __, 557 N.Y.S.2d 694, 695 (3d Dep't 1990), order aff'd, 78 N.Y.2d 932, 574 N.Y.S.2d 178, 579 N.E.2d 208 (1991) ("In a case involving this State's second and persistent felony offender statutes, the Court of Appeals held 'that the protections embodied in the double jeopardy clauses of the Federal and State Constitutions do not apply to these enhanced sentencing proceedings' ") (citation omitted), *aff'd for the reasons stated in the opinion below*, 78 N.Y.2d 932, 574 N.Y.S.2d 178 (1991); *People v. Sailor*, 65 N.Y.2d 224, 226–27, 491 N.Y.S.2d 112, 115, 480 N.E.2d 701 (1985); *People v. Parker*, 41 N.Y.2d 21, 25 n.5, 390 N.Y.S.2d 837, 840 n.5, 359 N.E.2d 348 (1976). *See generally Nichols v. U.S.*, 511 U.S. 738, 747, 114 S. Ct. 1921, 1927, 128 L. Ed. 2d 745 (1994) (enhancement statutes have repeatedly been upheld).

Similarly, VTL § 1193(1)(c) (formerly VTL § 1192(5)), permits the charging of felony DWI where the defendant has been convicted of DWI one or more times within the previous 10 years. Such enhancement of a subsequent offense is constitutional. *See, e.g., People v. Butler*, 96 A.D.2d 140, 468 N.Y.S.2d 274 (4th Dep't 1983); *People v. Maldonado*, 173 Misc. 2d 612, __, 661 N.Y.S.2d 937, 940–41 (Nassau Co. Sup. Ct. 1997).

§ 23:51 Applicability of Double Jeopardy where Court imposes more severe sentence following reversal and retrial

"[I]mposition of a more severe sentence on retrial following the reversal of a conviction does not violate double jeopardy." *People v. Sailor*, 65 N.Y.2d 224, 230, 491 N.Y.S.2d 112, 117, 480 N.E.2d 701 (1985). *See also North Carolina v. Pearce*, 395 U.S. 711, 723, 89 S. Ct. 2072, 2079, 23 L. Ed. 2d 656 (1969) (overruled by, *Alabama v. Smith*, 490 U.S. 794, 109 S. Ct. 2201, 104 L. Ed. 2d 865 (1989)) ("We hold . . . that neither the double jeopardy provision nor the Equal Protection Clause imposes an absolute bar to a more severe sentence upon reconviction. A trial judge is not constitutionally precluded, in other words, from imposing a new sentence, whether greater or less than the original sentence, in the light of events subsequent to the first trial that may have thrown new light upon the defendant's 'life, health, habits, conduct, and mental and moral propensities' ") (citation omitted).

Nonetheless, "vindictiveness against a defendant for having successfully attacked his first conviction must play no part in the sentence he receives after a new trial." *Pearce*, 395 U.S. at 725, 89 S. Ct. at 2080. "In order to assure the absence of such a motivation, we have concluded that whenever a judge imposes a more severe sentence upon a defendant after a new trial, the reasons for his doing so must affirmatively appear. Those reasons must be based upon objective information concerning identifiable conduct on the part of the defendant occurring after the time of the original sentencing proceeding. And the factual data upon which the increased sentence is based must be made part of the record, so that the constitutional legitimacy of the increased sentence may be fully reviewed on appeal." *Id.* at 726, 89 S. Ct. at 2081.

In addition, "the constitutional guarantee against multiple punishments for the same offense absolutely requires that punishment already exacted must be fully 'credited' in imposing sentence upon a new conviction for the same offense." *Id.* at 718–19, 89 S. Ct. at 2077 (footnote omitted). "[T]he same rule would be equally applicable where a fine had been actually paid upon the first conviction. Any new fine imposed upon reconviction would have to be decreased by the amount previously paid." *Id.* at 718 n.12, 89 S. Ct. at 2077 n.12.

§ 23:52   Applicability of Double Jeopardy where Judge instructs jury to reconsider improper "verdict"

In *People v. Salemmo*, 38 N.Y.2d 357, 359, 379 N.Y.S.2d 809, 810, 342 N.E.2d 579 (1976):

> The trial court submitted . . . [3] counts to the jury, directing them either to find the defendant guilty of only [1] of the counts, or not guilty of any of the [3] counts. * * *

> The jury reported a verdict of guilty of the first [2] counts of the indictment and not guilty of the third count. After a bench conference with both counsel, the trial court stated that the verdict, as reported by the foreman, was not in accordance with the court's instructions and directed the jurors, after giving them additional instructions, to reconsider their verdict. Thereafter, the jury returned a verdict finding the defendant not guilty of the first [2] counts of the indictment and guilty of the third count—criminal possession of a dangerous drug in the third degree.

Rejecting the defendant's Double Jeopardy claim, the Court of Appeals held that:

> [A] verdict reported by the jury is not final unless properly recorded and accepted by the court. Here, as stated before, the verdict reported was not in accordance with the court's instructions and,

therefore, was not accepted by the court. Since the defendant had a "weighty" right to be judged by the jury impaneled to determine his innocence or guilt, double jeopardy did not attach where the same jury reconsiders its defective or inconsistent verdict. Rather than constituting a new and second jeopardy, the reconsideration of a defective or inconsistent verdict was part of the process by which the defendant's first jeopardy was resolved.

Id. at 361–62, 379 N.Y.S.2d at 813 (citations omitted).

§ 23:53 Applicability of Double Jeopardy to contempt proceedings

In *People v. Sweat*, 24 N.Y.3d 348, 350, 998 N.Y.S.2d 688, 690, 23 N.E.3d 955 (2014), the Court of Appeals held that:

[W]here a court subjects a defendant to conditional imprisonment in an attempt to compel defendant to testify, and does not otherwise adjudicate defendant to be in criminal contempt or impose punishment that is criminal in nature, double jeopardy will not bar a subsequent prosecution for contempt under the Penal Law.

In so holding, the Court reasoned as follows:

This appeal illustrates the confusion attendant to the proper legal characterization of a contempt determination under our Judiciary Law. That confusion is compounded when, as in the case before us, a defendant is also prosecuted for criminal contempt under the Penal Law . . . . The courts and the parties here struggled with whether the contempt determination was more appropriately labeled "civil" or "criminal." As we discuss below, for purposes of a double jeopardy analysis, labels are not dispositive; what matters is the "character and purpose" of the actions of the court imposing contempt. As explained by the United States Supreme Court, "[t]he test may be stated as: what does the court primarily seek to accomplish by imposing sentence?" (*Shillitani v. United States*). * * *

The test for determining whether contempt is of the type that constitutes punishment in a constitutional sense is well articulated in *Shillitani*, and its companion case, *Pappadio v. United States*. * * *

Where a defendant is held in contempt for the remedial purpose of compelling compliance, imprisonment continues until such time as the contemnor acquiesces or is no longer able to do so. Once the contemnor agrees, there is no remedial purpose to be served by continued confinement. Contemnors, therefore, hold "the keys of their prison in their own pockets."

In contrast, where a contemnor is sentenced to imprisonment for a definite period which cannot be affected—that is, ended—by the contemnor's compliance with the law, then the contempt is not remedial but punitive. As the Supreme Court has stated, "[i]f the sentence is limited to imprisonment for a definite period, the defendant is furnished no key, and [the defendant] cannot shorten the term by promising not to repeat the offense."

Id. at 353, 356, 357, 998 N.Y.S.2d at 692, 694, 695 (citations omitted). *See also People v. Colombo*, 31 N.Y.2d 947, 341 N.Y.S.2d 97, 293 N.E.2d 247 (1972).

§ 23:54 Applicability of Double Jeopardy to prison disciplinary proceedings

In *People v. Vasquez*, 89 N.Y.2d 521, 525, 655 N.Y.S.2d 870, 871–72, 678 N.E.2d 482 (1997), the Court of Appeals held that:

> The primary issue in each of these appeals is whether the Double Jeopardy Clauses of the State and Federal Constitutions bar the criminal prosecution of an inmate who has previously been the subject of internal prison disciplinary sanction. We conclude that the disciplinary sanctions imposed do not constitute "criminal punishment" triggering double jeopardy protections. Thus, the claims that the criminal prosecutions were barred under double jeopardy principles were correctly rejected.

See also id. at 533, 655 N.Y.S.2d at 877 ("Assuming without deciding that, under rare circumstances, a prison disciplinary sentence might be so harsh and extreme as to invoke double jeopardy protections, that is not the case here"); *People v. Hart*, 93 N.Y.2d 825, 826, 687 N.Y.S.2d 617, 617–18, 710 N.E.2d 263 (1999) ("The indeterminate sentence of 3½ to 7 years defendant received upon his conviction for escape in the first degree, in addition to the Department of Correctional Services' disciplinary sanction of 15 years' confinement in a Special Housing Unit for the same conduct, does not violate the Double Jeopardy Clauses of either the Federal or State Constitution") (citations omitted); *Matter of Escobar v. Roberts*, 29 N.Y.2d 594, 324 N.Y.S.2d 318, 272 N.E.2d 898 (1971).

§ 23:55 Applicability of Double Jeopardy to juvenile proceedings

In *Matter of Tony M.*, 44 N.Y.2d 899, 900, 407 N.Y.S.2d 634, 635, 379 N.E.2d 162 (1978), the Court of Appeals held that "[i]t is now settled that double jeopardy is applicable in juvenile proceedings. That bar precludes appellate review of factual determinations which have been resolved in the accused's favor by the original trier of facts." (Citation omitted).

§ 23:56 Applicability of Double Jeopardy to child neglect proceedings

Double Jeopardy does not bar criminal prosecution following a child neglect proceeding. *See People v. Roselle*, 84 N.Y.2d 350,

618 N.Y.S.2d 753, 643 N.E.2d 72 (1994). *See also id.* at 355, 618 N.Y.S.2d at 755 ("We begin by reiterating that the 'separate and civil' nature of an article 10 proceeding is indelibly clear from its provisions").

§ 23:57 Applicability of Double Jeopardy to civil punitive damages arising out of DWI homicide

In *Wittman v. Gilson*, 70 N.Y.2d 970, 972, 525 N.Y.S.2d 795, 796, 520 N.E.2d 514 (1988), the Court of Appeals ruled as follows:

> [D]efendant argues that punitive damages [in a civil case] following a criminal conviction arising out of the same drunk driving incident should not be imposed as a matter of policy as implicated by the constitutional prohibition against double jeopardy. The quasi-criminal punitive aspect of exemplary damages has presented a concern that safeguards against successive or multiple prosecutions, available to a criminal defendant, should also be extended to defendants civilly exposed to punitive damages.

> We are not persuaded to adopt that view in this case because, while punitive damages and criminal sanctions share a common purpose of punishing misconduct, there are also significant distinctions between the two. Unlike the sanction imposed on behalf of all the people of the State in a criminal case, punitive damages in a civil case context afford the injured party a personal monetary recovery over and above compensatory loss. The procedures and standards of proof are also, of course, very different. Additionally, a civil verdict directing payment of punitive damages does not carry the same heavy societal stigma stamped by a criminal conviction no matter what sentence is imposed.

§ 23:58 Applicability of collateral estoppel to criminal cases

The doctrine of collateral estoppel, or issue preclusion, operates in a criminal prosecution to bar relitigation of issues necessarily resolved in defendant's favor at an earlier trial. Underlying the doctrine are concerns for conserving the time and resources of courts and litigants, as well as fairness to the defendant. Defendant, having once been acquitted by a jury, should not at a subsequent trial be subjected to the burden of meeting issues that were already necessarily decided in his favor. By the same token, where the People have had a full and fair opportunity to contest issues, but have failed, it would be inequitable and harassive to again permit the prosecution to establish these same matters, as if the first trial had never taken place.

Collateral estoppel may implicate constitutional double jeopardy considerations as, for example, where the People seek to relitigate issues resolved against them in a prior prosecution arising from the same offense . . . . Thus, even where a defendant is being tried for an offense unrelated to the one for which he was earlier prosecuted, collateral estoppel may preclude relitigation of factual issues previously resolved in his favor.

People v. Acevedo, 69 N.Y.2d 478, 484–85, 515 N.Y.S.2d 753, 758, 508 N.E.2d 665 (1987) (citations omitted).

In *People v. Goodman*, 69 N.Y.2d 32, 38, 511 N.Y.S.2d 565, 569, 503 N.E.2d 996 (1986), the Court of Appeals held that:

Before collateral estoppel may be applied in a subsequent criminal case, there must be an identity of parties and issues and a prior proceeding resulting in a final and valid judgment in which the party opposing the estoppel had a "full and fair opportunity" to litigate.

Estoppel is asserted customarily in situations involving an acquittal followed by subsequent charges arising from the same incident. It may also apply, however, to a mixed verdict in a single prosecution which acquits defendant of some counts of a multiple count indictment and convicts him of others.

(Citations omitted). *See also People v. Sailor*, 65 N.Y.2d 224, 228, 491 N.Y.S.2d 112, 116, 480 N.E.2d 701 (1985) ("Collateral estoppel principles, as they exist independent of the prohibition against double jeopardy, apply to criminal as well as civil actions, but because of the different interests involved, they are applied with greater flexibility in criminal matters than in civil litigation"); *People v. Plevy*, 52 N.Y.2d 58, 64–65, 436 N.Y.S.2d 224, 227–28, 417 N.E.2d 518 (1980); *People v. Berkowitz*, 50 N.Y.2d 333, 344–45, 428 N.Y.S.2d 927, 933, 406 N.E.2d 783 (1980); *People ex rel. Dowdy v. Smith*, 48 N.Y.2d 477, 479–80, 423 N.Y.S.2d 862, 863, 399 N.E.2d 894 (1979) ("A prior acquittal based on the defense of entrapment in a criminal proceeding collaterally estops the Board of Parole from revoking parole on the basis of the transactions proved and admitted in the criminal action"); *Matter of McGrath v. Gold*, 36 N.Y.2d 406, 411–12, 369 N.Y.S.2d 62, 65–66, 330 N.E.2d 35 (1975).

§ 23:59 Guilty plea to misdemeanor in local court as bar to prosecution for more serious charge in superior court

Occasionally, charges such as DWI that could have been charged as felonies are inadvertently charged as misdemeanors. In such situations the defendant may attempt to take advantage of the oversight by pleading guilty to the misdemeanor charge(s) and then claiming that Double Jeopardy bars prosecution on the felony charge(s). Where the defense handles this opportunity ethically and competently, this strategy will generally be successful. *See, e.g., People v. Antonelli*, 250 A.D.2d 999, __, 673 N.Y.S.2d 479, 481 (3d Dep't 1998) ("Defendant's decision to plead guilty to the crime of driving while intoxicated as a misdemeanor, and to reap the benefits of the arresting officer's failure to file a felony charge, did not amount to procurement of the misdemeanor charge, especially given the lack of evidence that defendant induced the officer to file the lesser charge or made affirmative misrepresentations to City Court"); *People v. Snyder*, 99 A.D.2d 83, __, 471 N.Y.S.2d 430, 432 (4th Dep't 1984) ("Arguably, in this case defendant chose to enter his plea at a time when he was aware that his prior DWI convictions would serve to elevate his present offense to a felony. This knowledge, however, cannot be equated to conduct on his part 'to bring about' or 'initiate' the charging of the misdemeanor offense by an accusatory instrument. The record does not establish that defendant made any misrepresentation to the arresting officer or did anything to induce that officer to charge him with the misdemeanor offense only. No affirmative duty was imposed upon the defendant to advise the police regarding his past record. There is no hint of any misrepresentation by either the defendant or his counsel at the time the plea was entered. The District Attorney's lack of knowledge of defendant's plea is immaterial"); *People v. Sherk*, 154 Misc. 2d 120, 584 N.Y.S.2d 266 (Lackawanna City Ct. 1992); *People v. Hale*, 119 Misc. 2d 499, 463 N.Y.S.2d 669 (Oneida Co. Ct. 1983). *But see People v. Barkin*, 49 N.Y.2d 901, 428 N.Y.S.2d 192, 405 N.E.2d 674 (1980) (local court not required to accept defendant's attempt to plead guilty to misdemeanor in order to avoid felony); *People v. Wystozaly*, 80 A.D.3d 894, 914 N.Y.S.2d 426 (3d Dep't 2011) (factual issue as to whether Town Court had accepted defendant's plea to misdemeanor DWI before offer was withdrawn resolved in People's favor).

By contrast, where the defense fails to handle this opportunity properly this strategy will be unsuccessful. *See, e.g.*, CPL § 40.30(2)(b) ("a person is not deemed to have been prosecuted for an offense, within the meaning of section 40.20, when * * * [s]uch prosecution was for a lesser offense than could have been charged under the facts of the case, and the prosecution was procured by the defendant, without the knowledge of the appropriate prosecutor, for the purpose of avoiding prosecution for a greater offense"); *Matter of Cosnett v. Daley*, 27 A.D.3d 1145, 811 N.Y.S.2d 837 (4th Dep't 2006) (Court found that defendant "procured" his plea to misdemeanor DWI and Failure To Keep Right, and thus Double Jeopardy did not bar subsequent prosecution for Assault 2nd and Vehicular Assault 2nd); *People v. Butler*, 96 A.D.2d 140, __, 468 N.Y.S.2d 274, 277 (4th Dep't 1983) ("Defendant's attempted plea by mail [to misdemeanor DWI] was a nullity and, therefore, jeopardy did not attach prior to the indictment"); *People v. Dishaw*, 54 A.D.2d 1122, __, 388 N.Y.S.2d 795, 795 (4th Dep't 1976) ("at the time of the acceptance of defendant's plea of guilty [to misdemeanor DWI], his attorney made affirmative [mis]representations to the assistant district attorney in Traffic Court that the plea had been specifically authorized by a senior assistant district attorney and the representations were relied upon by the assistant. This procurement of a prosecution on a lesser charge does not bar defendant's subsequent indictment and prosecution for the felony offense and the court properly held that the misdemeanor conviction must be deemed a nullity") (citation omitted). *See generally People v. Kurtz*, 129 Misc. 2d 1098, __, 495 N.Y.S.2d 608, 611 (St. Lawrence Co. Ct. 1985) ("since a felony information was filed in Justice Court, . . . said court was without jurisdiction to accept a plea or to reduce the charge without the consent of the District Attorney and its action in doing so was a nullity").

Perhaps the most famous case involving this situation is *Matter of Corbin v. Hillery*, 74 N.Y.2d 279, 545 N.Y.S.2d 71, 543 N.E.2d 714 (1989), judgment aff'd, 495 U.S. 508, 110 S. Ct. 2084, 109 L. Ed. 2d 548 (1990) (overruled by, U.S. v. Dixon, 509 U.S. 688, 113 S. Ct. 2849, 125 L. Ed. 2d 556 (1993)). In *Grady*, the defendant was involved in a DWI-related fatal motor vehicle accident. The defendant was served with UTTs charging him with DWI and Failure to Keep Right. The return date on the tickets was changed to a non-ADA night. The ADA covering the Court was "inexplicably unaware" that the case involved a fatality, and thus he "did not alert the court to the seriousness of the incident." 74 N.Y.2d at 283, 545 N.Y.S.2d at 73. The defendant appeared with counsel on the return date and pled guilty to both charges. Sentencing was adjourned for purposes of obtaining the People's sentencing recommendation. On the sentencing date, an ADA unfamiliar with the case did not request a further adjournment. As a result, the Court, unaware of the severity of the offense, imposed a sentence consistent with a run-of-the-mill DWI. *Id.* at 284, 545 N.Y.S.2d at 73.

The People subsequently charged the defendant with, *inter alia*, Manslaughter 2nd and Vehicular Manslaughter 2nd. The case was litigated all the way up to the U.S. Supreme Court, which agreed with the Court of Appeals that further prosecution of such charges was barred by the Double Jeopardy Clause. *Id.* at 291, 545 N.Y.S.2d at 78. *See also* Grady, 495 U.S. at 510, 110 S.Ct. at 2087 ("We hold that the Double Jeopardy Clause bars a subsequent prosecution if, to establish an essential element of an offense charged in that prosecution, the government will prove conduct that constitutes an offense for which the defendant has already been prosecuted"). *See also People v. Claud*, 76 N.Y.2d 951, 952, 563 N.Y.S.2d 720, 721, 565 N.E.2d 469 (1990); *People v. Claud*, 181 A.D.2d 830, 581 N.Y.S.2d 387 (2d Dep't 1992); *People v. Thompson*, 136 Misc. 2d 740, 519 N.Y.S.2d 320 (Yates Co. Ct. 1987).

In order to avoid such a result in the future, CPL § 170.10(8) provides that:

> Notwithstanding any other provision of law to the contrary, a local criminal court may not, at arraignment or within [30] days of arraignment on a simplified traffic information charging a violation of [VTL § 1192(2), (2-a), (3), (4) or (4-a)] and upon which a notation has been made pursuant to [VTL § 1192(12)], accept a plea of guilty to a violation of any subdivision of [VTL § 1192], nor to any other traffic infraction arising out of the same incident, nor to any other traffic infraction, violation or misdemeanor where the court is aware that such offense was charged pursuant to an accident involving death or serious physical injury, except upon written consent of the district attorney.

See also VTL § 603-b (where "serious physical injury" involved, VTL charges required to be marked with "S.P.I."; where death involved, VTL charges required to be marked with "D"); VTL § 1192(12) (same); VTL § 1800(d) ("A conviction of violation of any provision of this chapter shall not be a bar to a prosecution for an assault or for a homicide committed by any person in operating a motor vehicle or motorcycle").

Notably, *Grady*, *supra*, was overruled in *U.S. v. Dixon*, 509 U.S. 688, 113 S. Ct. 2849, 125 L. Ed. 2d 556 (1993). The *Dixon* Court noted that "[w]e recently held in *Grady* that in addition to passing the *Blockburger* test, a subsequent prosecution must satisfy a 'same-conduct' test to avoid the double jeopardy bar.' " *Id.* at 697, 113 S.Ct. at 2856. Finding this new test unworkable, the Court held that:

> Having encountered today yet another situation in which the pre-*Grady* understanding of the Double Jeopardy Clause allows a second trial, though the "same-conduct" test would not, we think it time to acknowledge what is now, three years after *Grady*, compellingly clear: the case was a mistake. We do not lightly reconsider a precedent, but, because *Grady* contradicted an "unbroken line of decisions," contained "less than accurate" historical analysis, and has produced "confusion," we do so here. Although *stare decisis* is the "preferred course" in constitutional adjudication, "when governing decisions are unworkable or are badly reasoned, 'this Court has never felt constrained to follow precedent.' " We would mock *stare decisis* and only add chaos to our double jeopardy jurisprudence by pretending that *Grady* survives when it does not. We therefore accept the Government's invitation to overrule *Grady*.

Id. at 711–12, 113 S.Ct. at 2864 (citations and footnote omitted).

In *People v. Brancoccio*, 83 N.Y.2d 638, 639, 612 N.Y.S.2d 353, 354, 634 N.E.2d 954 (1994):

> The issue here is whether CPL 170.20(2)(a), which authorizes divestiture of jurisdiction from the local criminal court where an

indictment "results" in a superior court prior to the entry of a plea
on the accusatory instrument in criminal court, requires filing for
operative effect. We hold that, for purposes of removing jurisdiction
from the criminal court, filing is not required.

See also id. at 641, 612 N.Y.S.2d at 355 ("We agree with the Appellate Division that Criminal Court was divested of jurisdiction
pursuant to CPL 170.20 when, on December 4, 1989, the Assistant District Attorney requested an adjournment to present the
case to the Grand Jury and an indictment resulted prior to the
December 8 plea. Thus, there was no double jeopardy").

§ 23:60   Double Jeopardy effect of pleading guilty to underlying traffic infraction(s) in attempt to avoid DWI charge(s) arising out of same incident

Defendants charged with DWI are generally also charged with
one or more so-called underlying traffic infractions that formed
the basis for the initial stop of the defendant's vehicle. The
underlying traffic infractions are sometimes filed in a different
Court than the DWI charge(s). Attempts by defendants to plead
guilty to the lesser charge(s) and invoke Double Jeopardy regarding the DWI charge(s) have generally failed. *See, e.g., People v.
Madden*, 49 A.D.3d 1264, 856 N.Y.S.2d 344 (4th Dep't 2008);
People v. Lindsly, 99 A.D.2d 99, __, 472 N.Y.S.2d 115, 116 (2d
Dep't 1984) ("On the facts of this case," "the defendant's plea of
guilty in a village Justice Court to leaving the scene of an ac-
cident [does not bar] the prosecution of an indictment charging
two felony counts of operating a motor vehicle while under the
influence of alcohol which arises out of the same incident"); *People
v. Roopnarine*, 11 Misc. 3d 416, 809 N.Y.S.2d 862 (Nassau Co.
Dist. Ct. 2006); *People v. Ferguson*, 162 Misc. 2d 187, 616
N.Y.S.2d 440 (Newburgh Just. Ct. 1994); *People v. Foster*, 133
Misc. 2d 427, 507 N.Y.S.2d 119 (Nassau Co. Ct. 1986); *Matter of
Serignese v. Henry*, 101 Misc. 2d 982, 424 N.Y.S.2d 810 (Suffolk
Co. Sup. Ct. 1978).

The *Roopnarine* Court summarized the issue as follows:

The principle at play, both in the *Serignese* line of cases and the
Lindsly line of cases, is that, at least where the charges against a
defendant are not so inextricably intertwined that the double jeopardy principle of the United States Constitution is implicated, or
even so connected as to constitute a single criminal transaction
under the New York statutory scheme, a defendant may not
insulate himself from prosecution on a more serious charge
contemporaneously pending, whether in the same court or in a different court, of which he is aware, by silently pleading to a lesser
one without making known his desire to have that charge heard
together with the more serious one, and thus giving the People and
the court an opportunity to consciously address the issue.

11 Misc. 3d at __, 809 N.Y.S.2d at 866–67.

§ 23:61 DMV Traffic Violations Bureau ("TVB") is not a "court" for Double Jeopardy purposes

In *People v. Serrano*, 46 Misc. 3d 960, __, 996 N.Y.S.2d 884, 891 (Bronx Co. Sup. Ct. 2014), the Court rejected the defendant's claim "that the TVB is 'a court of this state' for purposes of double jeopardy."

§ 23:62 Double Jeopardy effect of bifurcating DWI charge from AUO charge

In *People v. Dulmage*, 86 A.D.2d 756, __, 448 N.Y.S.2d 71, 71–72 (4th Dep't 1982):

A single indictment charged defendant in count one with [felony] driving while intoxicated and in count two with operating a motor vehicle while his license was revoked. After the direct testimony of the first witness, the trial court, concerned that the proof on count two (the underlying revocation was based on a plea of guilty to refusal to take a breathalyzer test) would affect the jury's consideration of count one, bifurcated the trial over defendant's objection. In this unusual procedure, the court permitted the trial to go forward on count one only. The jury found defendant guilty of the lesser included charge of driving while ability impaired. The next day the court permitted a further trial on count two before the same trial jurors. There were new openings, additional proof and summations, and another charge to the jury. The jury found defendant guilty as charged on that count.

The conviction on count two is reversed and that count of the indictment dismissed because with respect to that charge defendant was exposed to double jeopardy. Jeopardy had clearly attached in the first trial before the court "withdrew" the second charge. Defendant was then subjected to a second trial on that charge before a jury which had already found him guilty on a charge arising from the same incident. The procedure was not compelled by "manifest necessity"—indeed, on the second trial the certificate of conviction underlying the license revocation was redacted to omit any reference to the predicate refusal to take the breathalyzer test.

(Citations omitted).

§ 23:63 Double Jeopardy effect of dismissal for prosecutor's failure to give sufficient opening statement

In *People v. Kurtz*, 51 N.Y.2d 380, 434 N.Y.S.2d 200, 414 N.E.2d 699 (1980), the prosecutor gave a legally insufficient opening statement at trial, in violation of CPL § 260.30(3), which resulted in the dismissal of DWI and speeding charges against the defendant. The primary issue in the case was whether retrial was barred by the Double Jeopardy Clause. The Court of Appeals held that retrial was not barred, reasoning as follows:

> [T]he doctrine [of Double Jeopardy] distinguishes between trial orders terminating the trial in the defendant's favor prior to any determination of guilt or innocence and those orders which terminate the trial based on evidentiary insufficiency. Because a dismissal based on insufficient evidence is tantamount to an acquittal, reprosecution is precluded in the latter category of cases. Retrial of cases falling within the former category of dismissals, however, is permissible because "the defendant, by deliberately choosing to seek termination of the proceeding against him on a basis unrelated to factual guilt or innocence of the offense of which he is accused, suffers no injury cognizable under the Double Jeopardy Clause."
>
> In the case before us, the trial court dismissed the action on defendant's motion solely because of the insufficiency of the prosecutor's opening statement. As mentioned earlier, this dismissal was not premised on any evidentiary determination that the People were not entitled to a conviction or that the prosecutor had acted in bad faith by deliberately delivering an incomplete opening in order to terminate the trial over defendant's objection. Rather, dismissal here was the result of the trial court's misconception of the requirements of CPL 260.30 (subd. 3) and occurred without any evaluation on the trial court's part as to the factual elements of the offenses with which defendant was charged. Inasmuch as this dismissal . . . in no sense resembles an acquittal of the defendant and indeed appears functionally indistinguishable from the declaration of a mistrial, retrial of defendant is prohibited neither by the double jeopardy clauses of the State and Federal Constitutions nor by the statutory double jeopardy provisions.

Id. at 386–87, 434 N.Y.S.2d at 204–05 (citations and footnote omitted).

Notably, the *Kurtz* court disapproved of the manner in which the trial court handled the defendant's motion to dismiss, and set forth guidelines as to how trial courts should address such motions in the future:

> In this case, . . . the only deficiency in the opening statement was that it did not adequately amplify the charges against defendant and the facts to be proven in support thereof. Moreover, before dismissing the information, the Trial Judge not only failed to inform the prosecutor of the nature of the defect in his opening, but denied him the opportunity to correct this deficiency before permitting the trial to go forward. As County Court concluded, such action was an abuse of discretion, contrary to law.
>
> The better practice concerning such motions directed at the adequacy of the prosecutor's opening statement would be that a motion

should be made immediately after the prosecutor has completed his opening to the jury. The trial court should then inform the prosecutor of the nature of the defect, if any, and afford him an opportunity to rectify it. If the prosecutor is unable to do so, then the motion to dismiss the accusatory instrument must be granted. Under no circumstances should the court allow the trial to proceed without first ruling on the motion . . . . [I]t was the belated disposition of the motion which has created the difficulty in this case, a problem which should be avoided in all other cases.

Id. at 385–86, 434 N.Y.S.2d at 203–04 (citation omitted). *See also People v. Baltes*, 75 A.D.3d 656, __, 904 N.Y.S.2d 554, 558 (3d Dep't 2010); *Matter of Lacerva v. Dwyer*, 177 A.D.2d 747, 575 N.Y.S.2d 984 (3d Dep't 1991).

§ 23:64 Double Jeopardy effect of violation of probation proceeding

"It may simply be stated that the Double Jeopardy Clause is not implicated when a sentence of probation is revoked and a term of imprisonment imposed." *People v. Johnson*, 159 A.D.2d 725, __, 553 N.Y.S.2d 206, 207 (2d Dep't 1990). *See also People v. Pollak*, 130 A.D.2d 908, __, 516 N.Y.S.2d 509, 511 (3d Dep't 1987) ("The violation of probation proceeding did not constitute a prosecution within the meaning of CPL 40.20(1)"); *People v. Gilmore*, 63 A.D.2d 45, __, 407 N.Y.S.2d 48, 49 (2d Dep't 1978) ("The question involved on this appeal is whether the defendant, when found guilty of violation of probation, was entitled to jail time credit for the time he was out on the street on probation. We hold that he was not"). *See generally Matter of Maisonet v. Merola*, 69 N.Y.2d 965, 516 N.Y.S.2d 646, 509 N.E.2d 341 (1987).

§ 23:65 Double Jeopardy effect of parole revocation hearing

In *People v. Fagan*, 66 N.Y.2d 815, 816, 498 N.Y.S.2d 335, 335, 489 N.E.2d 222 (1985), the Court of Appeals held as follows:

The courts below properly found that the dismissal, at the conclusion of a final parole revocation hearing of charges lodged against the defendant, did not bar a later prosecution of criminal charges based on the same acts. Collateral estoppel is a flexible doctrine, not to be applied automatically just because its formal prerequisites are met. Strong policy considerations militate against giving issues determined in prior litigation preclusive effect in a criminal case, and indeed we have never done so. The correct determination of guilt or innocence is paramount in criminal cases, and the People's incentive to litigate in a felony prosecution would presumably be stronger than in a parole revocation proceeding.

(Citations omitted).

§ 23:66 Double Jeopardy effect of favorable plea procured by fraud

In *Matter of Lockett v. Juviler*, 65 N.Y.2d 182, 490 N.Y.S.2d 764, 480 N.E.2d 378 (1985), the defendant fraudulently obtained a plea of "not responsible by reason of mental disease or defect" pursuant to CPL § 220.15. When the fraud was discovered, the prosecutor moved to vacate the plea. The Court of Appeals held as follows:

Courts traditionally have inherent power to vacate orders and judgments obtained by fraud or misrepresentation. . . . This power, it should be noted, does not extend to intrinsic fraud, such as perjury at trial, which for policy reasons has been held not to invalidate a judgment. However, the power does extend to a plea obtained by fraud and misrepresentation. * * *

Jeopardy cannot be said to have attached until the accused has been subjected to the risk of conviction. In the case now before us, the petitioner never faced that risk during the plea proceedings. Under the statute governing this special plea, there were only two options available to the court. First, the court could accept the plea, thus terminating the criminal proceedings and initiating the civil commitment proceedings. Second, the court could reject the petitioner's plea offer and permit the criminal proceedings to continue in the normal course. In no event could the court make a binding factual finding of the defendant's guilt. Therefore, the trial court correctly held that the double jeopardy clause does not preclude restoration of the criminal charges because jeopardy had not attached when the special plea was accepted. As the Supreme Court has noted: "an accused must suffer jeopardy before he can suffer double jeopardy."

Id. at 186–87, 490 N.Y.S.2d at 767–68 (citations omitted).

§ 23:67 Conviction of both VTL § 1192(2) and VTL § 1192(3) does not violate Double Jeopardy

In *People v. Carvalho*, 174 A.D.2d 687, __, 571 N.Y.S.2d 332, 333 (2d Dep't 1991), "[t]he defendant contend[ed] that the indictment charging him with violating Vehicle and Traffic Law §§ 1192(2) and 1192(3) violated the constitutional prohibition against double jeopardy." In rejecting this claim, the Appellate Division, Second Department, held that:

It is clear that subdivisions 2 and 3 of Vehicle and Traffic Law § 1192 were intended to be separate crimes, neither mutually inclusive nor mutually exclusive. To suggest that the People should be compelled to elect between the two counts at any stage of the criminal proceedings would run counter to the intention of the Legislature which has determined that the social evil in question— driving while intoxicated—warrants separate offenses.

Id. at __, 571 N.Y.S.2d at 333. *See also People v. Rudd*, 41 A.D.2d 875, __, 343 N.Y.S.2d 17, 19 (3d Dep't 1973); *People v. McDonough*, 39 A.D.2d 188, __, 333 N.Y.S.2d 128, 129 (3d Dep't 1972).

§ 23:68   Conviction of both DWAI and AUO 1st does not violate Double Jeopardy

In *People v. Khan*, 291 A.D.2d 898, __, 737 N.Y.S.2d 738, 739 (4th Dep't 2002), the Appellate Division, Fourth Department, held that:

> We reject the contention of defendant that his conviction of both DWAI and AUO in the first degree violates the constitutional prohibition against double jeopardy. Although in this case commission of DWAI is an element of AUO in the first degree and therefore does not "require[] proof of an additional fact which [AUO in the first degree] does not," here both charges are contained within a single indictment and were disposed of by a single plea, and Penal Law § 70.25(2) requires that the sentences upon conviction of both counts be concurrent. Double jeopardy therefore is not implicated.

(Citations omitted).

§ 23:69   PL § 60.21 does not violate Double Jeopardy

PL § 60.21 provides that whenever a person is sentenced to imprisonment for a conviction of VTL § 1192(2), (2-a) or (3), the Court is also required to both (a) sentence the person to either probation or a conditional discharge, and (b) order the person to install an ignition interlock device. Such period of probation or conditional discharge is required to run *consecutively* to any period of imprisonment, and to commence immediately upon the person's release from imprisonment. Specifically, PL § 60.21 provides that:

> Notwithstanding [PL § 60.01(2)(d)], when a person is to be sentenced upon a conviction for a violation of [VTL § 1192(2), (2-a) or (3)], the court may sentence such person to a period of imprisonment authorized by [PL Article 70] and shall sentence such person to a period of probation or conditional discharge in accordance with the provisions of [PL § 65.00] and shall order the installation and maintenance of a functioning ignition interlock device. Such period of probation or conditional discharge shall run consecutively to any period of imprisonment and shall commence immediately upon such person's release from imprisonment.

This statute does not violate Double Jeopardy. *See, e.g., People v. Barkley*, 113 A.D.3d 1002, __, 978 N.Y.S.2d 920 (3d Dep't 2014); *People v. Brainard*, 111 A.D.3d 1162, 975 N.Y.S.2d 498, 499–500 (3d Dep't 2013); *People v. Marvin*, 108 A.D.3d 1109, 967 N.Y.S.2d 897 (4th Dep't 2013).

§ 23:70 Civil vehicle forfeiture following VTL § 1192 conviction does not violate Double Jeopardy

In *Nassau County v. Bigler*, 1 Misc. 3d 910(A), 781 N.Y.S.2d 626, 2001 WL 34378415, *1, *8 (Nassau Co. Sup. Ct. 2001), the Court held as follows:

This is a case brought under plaintiff Nassau County's Administrative Code . . . for forfeiture of defendant's Toyota automobile. It was seized upon her arrest for driving while intoxicated on June 24, 1999. * * *

The contention defendant next advances is not supported by any argument or authority; she simply states that because the County's civil case is dependent on the outcome of the criminal case, her right to be free of Double Jeopardy has been violated. Civil forfeiture cases do not implicate this constitutional protection provided they are not so harsh and extreme as to constitute criminal sanctions.

See generally Matter of Grinberg v. Safir, 181 Misc. 2d 444, __, 694 N.Y.S.2d 316, 321–22 (N.Y. Co. Sup. Ct. 1999), aff'd, 266 A.D.2d 43, 698 N.Y.S.2d 218 (1st Dep't 1999).

§ 23:71 Driver's license suspensions/revocations do not violate Double Jeopardy

It is well settled that the suspension or revocation of a driver's license separate and apart from an associated criminal charge or traffic infraction does not violate Double Jeopardy. *See, e.g., Matter of Barnes v. Tofany*, 27 N.Y.2d 74, 77, 313 N.Y.S.2d 690, 693, 261 N.E.2d 617 (1970) ("We hold that the 'double punishment' feature of our Vehicle and Traffic statute—one criminal and the other administrative—is lawful"); *Matter of Smith v. County Court of Essex County*, 224 A.D.2d 89, __, 649 N.Y.S.2d 507, 509 (3d Dep't 1996). *See also* §§ 23:72 and 23:73, *infra*.

§ 23:72 Suspension pending prosecution does not violate Double Jeopardy

The prosecution of a defendant for DWI following the suspension of his or her driver's license pending prosecution does not violate Double Jeopardy. *See, e.g., People v. Haishun*, 238 A.D.2d 521, 656 N.Y.S.2d 660 (2d Dep't 1997); *People v. Roach*, 226 A.D.2d 55, 649 N.Y.S.2d 607 (4th Dep't 1996); *Matter of Smith v. County Court of Essex County*, 224 A.D.2d 89, 649 N.Y.S.2d 507 (3d Dep't 1996). *See also People v. Demetsenare*, 243 A.D.2d 777, __, 663 N.Y.S.2d 299, 303 (3d Dep't 1997); *People v. DeRojas*, 196 Misc. 2d 171, 763 N.Y.S.2d 386 (App. Term, 2d Dep't 2003); *People v. Malone*, 175 Misc. 2d 893, 673 N.Y.S.2d 809 (App. Term, 2d Dep't 1997); *People v. Busby*, 175 Misc. 2d 509, 670 N.Y.S.2d 960

(App. Term, 2d Dep't 1997); *People v. Steele*, 172 Misc. 2d 860, 661 N.Y.S.2d 908 (App. Term, 2d Dep't 1997); *People v. Uzquaino*, 172 Misc. 2d 388, 661 N.Y.S.2d 438 (App. Term, 2d Dep't 1997); *People v. Conrad*, 169 Misc. 2d 1066, 654 N.Y.S.2d 226 (App. Term, 2d Dep't 1996).

§ 23:73   Chemical test refusal sanctions do not violate Double Jeopardy

The prosecution of a defendant for a violation of VTL § 1192 following a DMV chemical test refusal revocation does not violate Double Jeopardy. *Matter of Brennan v. Kmiotek*, 233 A.D.2d 870, 649 N.Y.S.2d 611 (4th Dep't 1996). *See also People v. Frank*, 166 Misc. 2d 277, ___, 631 N.Y.S.2d 1014, 1018 (N.Y. City Crim. Ct. 1995) ("the initial suspension after a refusal is not imposed at a proceeding separate from the criminal prosecution. To the contrary, while the initial suspension is based upon the written report made by a police officer before whom the refusal was made, the suspension is imposed by the criminal court").

Similarly, the Double Jeopardy Clause is not violated where a DMV license revocation proceeding is commenced despite the motorist's previous acquittal in a criminal case stemming from the same conduct. *Matter of Giudice v. Adduci*, 176 A.D.2d 1175, ___, 575 N.Y.S.2d 611, 612 (3d Dep't 1991).

Chapter 24

Pretrial Motions

Research References

Westlaw Databases

Criminal Procedure (2d ed.) (CRIMPROC)
Handling a Criminal Case in New York (HCCNY)
Handling Drunk Driving Cases (2d ed.) (HDRUNKDR)
New York Vehicle and Traffic Law 2d (NYVEH)

Treatises and Practice Aids

LaFave, Israel and King, Criminal Procedure § 10.1(a) (2d ed.)
Muldoon, Handling a Criminal Case in New York §§ 7:7, 7:8, 7:19
Fiandach, Handling Drunk Driving Cases §§ 23:1 to 23:4 (2d ed.)
Rose, New York Vehicle and Traffic Law 2d § 35:33

KeyCite®: Cases and other legal materials listed in KeyCite Scope can be researched through the KeyCite service on Westlaw®. Use KeyCite to check citations for form, parallel references, prior and later history, and comprehensive citator information, including citations to other decisions and secondary materials.

---

§ 24:1 In general

Research References

West's Key Number Digest, Criminal Law ⊙═632(3.1)

In New York, pretrial motions are governed primarily by CPL Article 255. However, numerous additional pretrial motions have been judicially recognized and/or created over the years. This chapter addresses pretrial motions in general, paying particular attention to such motions pertinent to DWI cases.

§ 24:2 Pretrial motion—Defined

Research References

West's Key Number Digest, Criminal Law ⊙═632(3.1)

In the context of a criminal case, the phrase "pre-trial motion" is a term of art which is defined in CPL § 255.10(1):

"Pre-trial motion" as used in [CPL Article 255] means any motion by a defendant which seeks an order of the court:

(a) dismissing or reducing an indictment pursuant to article 210 or removing an action to the family court pursuant to section 210.43; or

(b) dismissing an information, prosecutor's information, simplified information or misdemeanor complaint pursuant to article 170; or

(c) granting discovery pursuant to article 240; or

(d) granting a bill of particulars pursuant to sections 100.45 or 200.90 [*sic*—should read 200.95]; or

(e) removing the action pursuant to sections 170.15, 230.20 or 230.30; or

(f) suppressing the use at trial of any evidence pursuant to article 710; or

(g) granting separate trials pursuant to article 100 or 200.

The phrase "pre-trial motion" (a.k.a. "omnibus pre-trial motion" or "omnibus motion") does not encompass *any and all* pretrial motions. Rather, a "pre-trial motion" is only required to contain pretrial motions brought pursuant to the specific CPL sections and articles listed in CPL § 255.10(1). Any other pretrial motion, whether it seeks the suppression of evidence and/or an evidentiary ruling from the court, is commonly referred to as a "motion in *limine*"—*not* a "pre-trial motion."

It is critical to note that motions in limine are not required to be included in the defendant's omnibus pretrial motion, and thus are not governed by the 45-day time limit of CPL § 255.20(1). *See* § 24:4, *infra*. On the other hand, there is no rule prohibiting most motions in limine from being included in the omnibus motion.

§ 24:3   Legislative intent behind CPL Article 255

Research References

West's Key Number Digest, Criminal Law ⊙═632(3.1)

In 1974, the legislature enacted CPL Article 255, "the omnibus pre-trial motion provisions which sought to impose order and speed on pre-trial motion practice by requiring the defendant to make substantially all pre-trial motions at one time, on one set of papers before one Judge, within 45 days after arraignment." *People v. O'Doherty*, 70 N.Y.2d 479, 488, 522 N.Y.S.2d 498, 503 (1987). *See also People v. Lawrence*, 64 N.Y.2d 200, 204–05, 485 N.Y.S.2d 233, 236 (1984) ("The Legislature's purpose in enacting CPL 255.20 was to regulate pre-trial proceedings by requiring a single omnibus motion to be made promptly after arraignment and thus to avoid the proliferation experienced under prior procedure in which a defendant could bombard the courts and Judges with dilatory tactics continuing right up to the eve of trial"); Preiser, Practice Commentaries, McKinney's Cons. Laws of N.Y., Book 11A, CPL § 255.10, at 143.

§ 24:4 Pretrial motions—Time for filing

Research References

West's Key Number Digest, Criminal Law ⬮632(3.1)

CPL § 255.20(1) sets forth the general rule that:

> [W]hether the defendant is represented by counsel or elects to proceed pro se, all pre-trial motions shall be served or filed within [45] days after arraignment and before commencement of trial, or within such additional time as the court may fix upon application of the defendant made prior to entry of judgment.

See also CPL § 100.45; CPL § 170.30(2); CPL § 200.95(6); CPL § 210.20(2); CPL § 240.90(2); CPL § 710.40(1).

However, "[i]f the defendant is not represented by counsel and has requested an adjournment to obtain counsel or to have counsel assigned, such [45] day period shall commence on the date counsel initially appears on defendant's behalf." CPL § 255.20(1).

With certain exceptions discussed below, "[a]ny other pre-trial motion made after the [45] day period *may* be summarily denied." CPL § 255.20(3) (emphasis added).

"The time restrictions fixed by CPL 255.20 are not casual. Rather, the deadlines imposed by the statute rest on " 'the strong public policy to further orderly trial procedures and preserve scarce trial resources.' " Plainly, the Legislature intended that a potentially dispositive motion that could be made by a defendant at the outset of a prosecution should not be delayed until after an unfavorable verdict." *People v. Davidson*, 98 N.Y.2d 738, 739, 751 N.Y.S.2d 161, 162 (2002) (citations omitted).

§ 24:5 Court lacks authority to shorten time period in which to make pretrial motions

Research References

West's Key Number Digest, Criminal Law ⬮632(3.1)

In *Matter of Veloz v. Rothwax*, 65 N.Y.2d 902, 903, 493 N.Y.S.2d 452, 452 (1985), the Court of Appeals made clear that:

> CPL 255.20(1) prescribes a minimum, fixed time period of 45 days in which a defendant may make pre-trial motions. This provision carefully balances considerations of judicial economy with defendant's need for adequate time in which to prepare and make pre-trial motions. A trial court may not, *sua sponte*, alter this statutory time period. Thus, we agree with the Appellate Division that respondent lacked the authority to shorten the statutory time period in which to make pre-trial motions.

(Citations omitted).

§ 24:6 Exceptions to the 45-day rule of CPL § 255.20(1)

Research References

West's Key Number Digest, Criminal Law ⚖═632(3.1)

There are several exceptions to the general rule, set forth in CPL § 255.20(1), that all pretrial motions must be served within 45 days after arraignment. At the outset, the 45-day rule only applies "[e]xcept as otherwise expressly provided by law." CPL § 255.20(1). In addition, "[i]f the defendant is not represented by counsel and has requested an adjournment to obtain counsel or to have counsel assigned, such [45] day period shall commence on the date counsel initially appears on defendant's behalf." CPL § 255.20(1).

Furthermore, "[i]n an action in which an eavesdropping warrant and application have been furnished pursuant to [CPL § 700.70] or a notice of intention to introduce evidence has been served pursuant to [CPL § 710.30], such period shall be extended until [45] days after the last date of such service." CPL § 255.20(1).

Moreover, CPL § 255.20(3) provides both:

(a) That "[n]otwithstanding the provisions of [CPL § 255.20(1) and CPL § 255.20(2)], the court must entertain and decide on its merits, at anytime before the end of the trial, any appropriate pre-trial motion based upon grounds of which the defendant could not, with due diligence, have been previously aware, or which, for other good cause, could not reasonably have been raised within the period specified in [CPL § 255.20(1)] or included within the single set of motion papers as required by [CPL § 255.20(2)]"; and

(b) That "the court, in the interest of justice, and for good cause shown, may, in its discretion, at any time before sentence, entertain and dispose of the motion on the merits."
See also CPL § 170.30(3); CPL § 210.20(3); CPL § 710.40(2); § 24:7, *infra*.

§ 24:7 Motions to dismiss on speedy trial grounds are exempt from the 45-day rule of CPL § 255.20(1)

Research References

West's Key Number Digest, Criminal Law ⚖═632(3.1)

A motion to dismiss on speedy trial grounds is exempt from the 45-day rule of CPL § 255.20(1). *People v. Lawrence*, 64 N.Y.2d 200, 205, 485 N.Y.S.2d 233, 236 (1984). Such a motion "may be made at any time before commencement of trial or entry of a plea of guilty." 64 N.Y.2d at 205, 485 N.Y.S.2d at 236. *See also* CPL § 170.30(2); CPL § 210.20(2).

§ 24:8 Pretrial motions—Procedure

Research References

West's Key Number Digest, Criminal Law ☞632(3.1)

CPL § 255.20(2) sets forth the general rule that:

> All pre-trial motions, with supporting affidavits, affirmations, exhibits and memoranda of law, whenever practicable, shall be included within the same set of motion papers, and shall be made returnable on the same date, unless the defendant shows that it would be prejudicial to the defense were a single judge to consider all the pre-trial motions.

See also CPL § 100.45; CPL § 170.30(3) ("Upon the motion, a defendant who is in a position adequately to raise more than one ground in support thereof should raise every such ground upon which he intends to challenge the accusatory instrument"); CPL § 170.45; CPL § 200.95(6); CPL § 210.20(3) ("Upon the motion, a defendant who is in a position adequately to raise more than one ground in support thereof should raise every such ground upon which he intends to challenge the indictment"); CPL § 240.90(2); CPL § 710.40(1).

However, "[w]here one motion seeks to provide the basis for making another motion, it shall be deemed impracticable to include both motions in the same set of motion papers pursuant to this subdivision." CPL § 255.20(2).

§ 24:9 Applicability of CPLR to pretrial motions in criminal cases

Research References

West's Key Number Digest, Criminal Law ☞632(3.1)

Pretrial motion practice in criminal cases is clearly governed by the CPL, and *not* by the CPLR. *See, e.g., People v. Crisp*, 268 A.D.2d 247, 700 N.Y.S.2d 693 (1st Dep't 2000) (Court noted "the Court of Appeals' practice of interpreting CPL provisions in accordance with the CPL's statutory scheme and without resort to the CPLR"); *People v. Holden*, 260 A.D.2d 233, __, 689 N.Y.S.2d 40, 41 (1st Dep't 1999) ("The time set forth in CPLR 2214(b) for answering a motion was not applicable"); *People v. Silva*, 122 A.D.2d 750, __, 506 N.Y.S.2d 55, 56 (1st Dep't 1986) ("the CPLR has no application to criminal actions and proceedings (see CPL 1.10)"); *People v. Manupelli*, 22 Misc. 3d 67, 877 N.Y.S.2d 599 (App. Term, 9th & 10th Jud. Dist. 2008); *People v. Zappula*, 41 Misc. 3d 226, __, 970 N.Y.S.2d 440, 442 (Muttontown Just. Ct. 2013) ("This proceeding is brought and will be conducted under the Criminal Procedure Law"); *People v. Ekinici*, 191 Misc. 2d 510, __, 743 N.Y.S.2d 651, 654 (Kings Co. Sup. Ct. 2002) ("Generally, the Civil Practice Law and Rules (CPLR) are inapplicable to criminal matters"); *People v. Fulton*, 162 Misc. 2d 360, __ & n.3, 616 N.Y.S.2d 881, 883 & n.3 (Monroe Co. Sup. Ct. 1994); *Matter of Tucker*, 145 Misc. 2d 1011, __, 549 N.Y.S.2d 350, 352–53 (Bronx Co. Sup. Ct. 1989) ("Absent specific legislative direction, proceedings under the CPL are governed solely by that statute (CPL 1.10[1])"); *People v. Kyriazas*, 2002 WL 31972172 (Westchester Co. Sup. Ct. 2002) ("where the CPL is silent on a given issue, the Court's research has revealed a number of miscellaneous decisions which have permitted the CPLR to be applied in a criminal action. Unfortunately . . ., this line of miscellaneous cases is plainly at odds with a more authoritative line of Appellate cases which expressly hold that the CPLR simply has no application to criminal cases") (citations omitted). *See generally People v. Knobel*, 94 N.Y.2d 226, 230, 701 N.Y.S.2d 695, 697–98 (1999) (Court of Appeals refused to analogize civil tolling provision of CPLR § 207 in interpreting CPL § 30.10(4)(a)(i)); UJCA § 2001(2) ("Unless otherwise specifically prescribed, the practice and procedure in the court shall be governed by the criminal procedure law"); 22 NYCRR § 200.21 ("Procedure in each local criminal court shall be as provided by the Criminal Procedure Law and such local court rules as may be adopted in compliance with Part 9 of the Rules of the Chief Judge").

In *People v. Wienclaw*, 183 Misc. 2d 727, __, 704 N.Y.S.2d 445, 447 (Valley Stream Just. Ct. 2000), the court took what it acknowledged was an "unprecedented step," deciding that "in general motion practice, this court should follow the time frame under CPLR 2214," as "there is no timetable for filing and return of papers in the C.P.L." At the outset, the assertions of the *Wienclaw* court are inaccurate. The CPL does, in fact, address the procedure and timetable for motion practice in criminal cases. For example, CPL § 255.20(1) provides that all pretrial motions generally must be served within 45 days after arraignment; CPL § 255.20(2) provides that all pretrial motions generally must (a) be included within the same set of motion papers, and (b) be made returnable on the same date; CPL §§ 170.45, 210.45(1), and 710.60(1) provide that motions to dismiss and to suppress evidence must be made in writing and upon reasonable notice to the People; and CPL §§ 170.45, 210.45(2) and 710.60(1) provide that the People *may* file an answer thereto.

In any event, *Wienclaw* contradicts the authorities cited above and stands in direct conflict with *Holden*, *supra*, which held that "[t]he time set forth in CPLR 2214(b) for answering a motion was not applicable" in a criminal case. 260 A.D.2d at __, 689 N.Y.S.2d at 41.

§ 24:10 Motion to dismiss for lack of a sufficient supporting deposition

Research References

West's Key Number Digest, Criminal Law ⚷632(3.1)

Technically, a motion to dismiss for lack of a sufficient supporting deposition, like all other pretrial motions, should be made in accordance with CPL § 255.20(1). *People v. Dean*, 74 N.Y.2d 643, 644, 542 N.Y.S.2d 512, 512 (1989); *People v. Key*, 45 N.Y.2d 111, 116, 408 N.Y.S.2d 16, 19 (1978). *See also People v. Fattizzi*, 98 Misc. 2d 288, 413 N.Y.S.2d 804 (App. Term, 9th & 10th Jud. Dist. 1978); *People v. Rose*, 8 Misc. 3d 184, __, 794 N.Y.S.2d 630, 635 (Nassau Co. Dist. Ct. 2005); *People v. Sirkin*, 146 Misc. 2d 1030, 553 N.Y.S.2d 593 (Arcadia Just. Ct. 1990). In other words, a motion to dismiss for lack of a sufficient supporting deposition should, among other things, be made:

(a) In writing. *See* CPL §§ 170.45 & 210.45(1);

(b) Upon reasonable notice to the People. *See* CPL §§ 170.45 & 210.45(1); and

(c) With certain exceptions, within 45 days after arraignment (or within such additional time as the court may fix upon application of the defendant). *See* CPL §§ 255.10(1)(b) & 255.20(1).

However, the writing and reasonable notice requirements appear to be waivable. *See People v. Jennings*, 69 N.Y.2d 103, 113, 512 N.Y.S.2d 652, 656 (1986) (by failing to insist upon conformity with the procedural requirements of CPL § 210.45(1), the People waived their right to written notice under the statute). *See also People v. Mezon*, 80 N.Y.2d 155, 157, 589 N.Y.S.2d 838, 839 (1992); *People v. Singleton*, 42 N.Y.2d 466, 470–71, 398 N.Y.S.2d 871, 874 (1977). In addition, presumably recognizing that strict adherence to these requirements would oftentimes "defeat the very purpose of the statute, disregard the interests of judicial economy and, in many cases, render the defense of traffic matters impracticable," *see, e.g., People v. Titus*, 178 Misc. 2d 687, __, 682 N.Y.S.2d 521, 522 (App. Term, 2d Dep't 1998); *People v. Rosenfeld*, 163 Misc. 2d 982, __, 626 N.Y.S.2d 352, 352 (App. Term, 9th & 10th Jud. Dist. 1994); *People v. Aucello*, 146 Misc. 2d 417, __, 558 N.Y.S.2d 436, 438 (App. Term, 9th & 10th Jud. Dist. 1990), many courts summarily dismiss simplified informations in response to an oral motion (or the court's own motion) where the People have failed to provide a properly requested supporting deposition.

§ 24:11   People can waive requirement that pretrial motion be made in writing and upon reasonable notice to the People

Research References

West's Key Number Digest, Criminal Law ⊸632(3.1)

The requirement that a pretrial motion be made in writing and upon reasonable notice to the People can be waived. *See, e.g.*, *People v. Mezon*, 80 N.Y.2d 155, 157, 589 N.Y.S.2d 838, 839 (1992) (People can waive their right to insist that motion to suppress evidence be made "in writing and upon reasonable notice to the people" in conformity with CPL § 710.60(1)); *People v. Jennings*, 69 N.Y.2d 103, 113, 512 N.Y.S.2d 652, 656 (1986) (by failing to insist upon conformity with the procedural requirements of CPL § 210.45(1), the People waived their right to written notice under the statute); *People v. Singleton*, 42 N.Y.2d 466, 470–71, 398 N.Y.S.2d 871, 874 (1977).

§ 24:12   Failure to make timely motion to dismiss can result in waiver of issue

Research References

West's Key Number Digest, Criminal Law ⊸632(3.1)

As a general rule, "[a] valid and sufficient accusatory instrument is a nonwaivable jurisdictional prerequisite to a criminal prosecution." *People v. Harper*, 37 N.Y.2d 96, 99, 371 N.Y.S.2d 467, 469 (1975). *See also People v. Alejandro*, 70 N.Y.2d 133, 135, 517 N.Y.S.2d 927, 928 (1987); *People v. Hall*, 48 N.Y.2d 927, 927, 425 N.Y.S.2d 56, 57 (1979); *People v. Case*, 42 N.Y.2d 98, 99, 396 N.Y.S.2d 841, 842 (1977); *People v. Noblett*, 172 Misc. 2d 826, __, 660 N.Y.S.2d 517, 520 (Monroe Co. Ct. 1997); *People v. Gingello*, 181 Misc. 2d 163, __, 694 N.Y.S.2d 579, 580 (Rochester City Ct. 1999) (abrogated on other grounds by, People v. Blair, 98 N.Y.2d 722, 749 N.Y.S.2d 809, 779 N.E.2d 748 (2002)). In this regard, "[a]n objection to the substantive sufficiency of the information, such as one that it does not state a crime, as distinguished from an objection to the form of the instrument, is not waived by a plea of guilty." *Case*, 42 N.Y.2d at 100, 396 N.Y.S.2d at 842.

However, the failure to preserve the issue by making a timely motion to dismiss can result in a waiver thereof. *See, e.g.*, *People v. Davidson*, 98 N.Y.2d 738, 739–40, 751 N.Y.S.2d 161, 162 (2002); *People v. Casey*, 95 N.Y.2d 354, 367, 717 N.Y.S.2d 88, 96 (2000) ("we conclude that hearsay pleading defects in the factual portion of a local criminal court information must be preserved in order to be reviewable as a matter of law on appeal"); *People v. Dean*, 74 N.Y.2d 643, 542 N.Y.S.2d 512 (1989); *People v. Iannelli*, 69

N.Y.2d 684, 512 N.Y.S.2d 16 (1986); *People v. Iannone*, 45 N.Y.2d 589, 600, 412 N.Y.S.2d 110, 117 (1978); *People v. Key*, 45 N.Y.2d 111, 116–17, 408 N.Y.S.2d 16, 19 (1978).

§ 24:13 Breath test result constitutes suppressible evidence

Research References

West's Key Number Digest, Criminal Law ⬤632(3.1)

By its terms, CPL § 710.20(1) only authorizes the suppression of "tangible property obtained by means of an unlawful search and seizure." Occasionally, an overzealous prosecutor will seize upon this language and claim that a DWI defendant's breath test result is not suppressible, *even if it was illegally obtained*, because such evidence does not constitute "tangible property."

However, the United States Supreme Court has made clear both (a) that "*all evidence* obtained by searches and seizures in violation of the Constitution is, by that same authority, inadmissible in a state court," *Mapp v. Ohio*, 367 U.S. 643, 655, 81 S.Ct. 1684, 1691 (1961) (emphasis added), and (b) that obtaining a breath sample from a DWI suspect for alcohol analysis constitutes a "search" within the meaning of the Fourth Amendment. *Skinner v. Railway Labor Executives' Ass'n*, 489 U.S. 602, 616–17, 109 S.Ct. 1402, 1413 (1989). *See also People v. Johnson*, 134 Misc. 2d 474, __, 511 N.Y.S.2d 773, 774–75 (N.Y. City Crim. Ct. 1987) ("the Court holds that a breathalyzer test result is evidence as contemplated by *Mapp v. Ohio*, (supra) and CPL Section 710.60. It is, in fact, significant evidence and may not be proferred [sic] if it is the result of an illegal search"); *People v. Thomas*, 164 Misc. 2d 721, __, 626 N.Y.S.2d 405, 407–08 (N.Y. City Crim. Ct. 1995) ("The doctrine of the 'fruit of the poisonous tree' . . . is not limited to suppression of physical tangible evidence but applies as well to evidence which flows from the illegal seizure and search, such as verbal statements, identifications, tests performed upon the defendant, and testimony at trial as to matters observed during the unlawful intrusion").

§ 24:14 Motion to suppress compulsory chemical test

Research References

West's Key Number Digest, Criminal Law ⬤632(3.1)

CPL § 710.20 sets forth the grounds upon which a defendant can make a pretrial motion to suppress evidence. CPL § 710.20(5) authorizes the suppression of "a chemical test of the defendant's blood administered in violation of the provisions of [VTL § 1194(3)], [Navigation Law § 49-a(8)], [PRHPL § 25.24(7)], or any other applicable law." *See also* VTL § 1195(3).

§24:15 Motion to suppress consented-to breath test pursuant to CPL §710.20(5)

Research References

West's Key Number Digest, Criminal Law ⊶632(3.1)

Prior to the Court of Appeals' decision in *People v. Ayala*, 89 N.Y.2d 874, 653 N.Y.S.2d 92 (1996), it was unclear whether CPL §710.20(5), *see* previous section, is applicable to consented-to breath tests, as the statutes enumerated therein—*i.e.*, VTL §1194(3), Navigation Law §49-a(8), and PRHPL §25.24(7)—deal with the administration of compulsory chemical tests of a defendant's blood.

On the one hand, see *People v. Nania*, 177 A.D.2d 1015, __, 578 N.Y.S.2d 34, 35 (4th Dep't 1991); *People v. Singh*, 144 Misc. 2d 402, __, 542 N.Y.S.2d 1018, 1023 (N.Y. City Crim. Ct. 1989); *People v. Amores*, 143 Misc. 2d 527, __, 541 N.Y.S.2d 695, 698 (N.Y. City Crim. Ct. 1989); *People v. Hicks*, 134 Misc. 2d 594, __, 511 N.Y.S.2d 1003, 1004 (Perinton Just. Ct. 1987); *People v. Tyree*, 75 Misc. 2d 912, __, 349 N.Y.S.2d 580, 581 (Mount Vernon City Ct. 1973).

On the other hand, see *People v. Colon*, 180 A.D.2d 876, __, 580 N.Y.S.2d 95, 97 (3d Dep't 1992); *People v. Sherwood*, 160 A.D.2d 1203, __, 555 N.Y.S.2d 464, 466 (3d Dep't 1990); *People v. Nieves*, 143 Misc. 2d 734, __, 541 N.Y.S.2d 1008, 1012–13 (N.Y. City Crim. Ct. 1989); *People v. Pantaleo*, 141 Misc. 2d 251, 536 N.Y.S.2d 369 (N.Y. City Crim. Ct. 1988); *People v. Batista*, 128 Misc. 2d 1054, 491 N.Y.S.2d 966 (N.Y. City Crim. Ct. 1985) (abrogated on other grounds by, People v. Finnegan, 85 N.Y.2d 53, 623 N.Y.S.2d 546, 647 N.E.2d 758 (1995)).

All of the above-cited cases were decided prior to the Court of Appeals' decision in *Ayala*. In *Ayala*, *supra*, the trial court suppressed the results of a consented-to Breathalyzer test due to the fact that the test was administered more than two hours after the defendant's arrest. The People appealed.

The Appellate Term dismissed the People's appeal on the ground that an as-of-right appeal pursuant to CPL §450.20(8) requires that the order suppressing evidence be entered pursuant to CPL §710.20. *See People v. Laing*, 79 N.Y.2d 166, 581 N.Y.S.2d 149 (1992). In other words, the Appellate Term found (a) that CPL §710.20(5) is inapplicable to consented-to breath tests, (b) that the trial court's suppression order was thus not entered pursuant to CPL §710.20, and therefore (c) that the People could not appeal pursuant to CPL §450.20(8). *See People v. Cardenas*, 165 Misc. 2d 587, __, 632 N.Y.S.2d 937, 938 (App. Term, 1st Dep't 1995) (per curiam) (reaching same conclusion).

The Court of Appeals reversed, holding that CPL §710.20(5)

"permits suppression not only of court-ordered chemical tests, but also tests administered pursuant to '*any other applicable law.*'" *People v. Ayala*, 89 N.Y.2d 874, 875, 653 N.Y.S.2d 92, 93 (1996) (emphasis added). In so holding, the court made clear that the "any other applicable law" language in CPL § 710.20(5) encompasses consented-to breath tests, which are governed by VTL § 1194(2). Thus, *Ayala* clearly resolves the issue of whether consented-to breath tests are suppressible pursuant to CPL § 710.20(5).

§ 24:16   Motion in limine to suppress consented-to breath test

Research References

West's Key Number Digest, Criminal Law ☞632(4)

Regardless of whether CPL § 710.20(5) is applicable to consented-to breath tests, *see* previous section, an extensive body of case law has made clear that consented-to chemical tests can be challenged via a motion in limine where the defendant raises a substantial question as to whether the People will be able to lay the necessary foundation for admissibility of the defendant's chemical test results at trial. *See, e.g., People v. Krebs*, 195 A.D.2d 696, —, 600 N.Y.S.2d 317, 318 (3d Dep't 1993) ("County Court erred in summarily denying defense counsel's motion to suppress the breathalyzer test results"); *People v. Colon*, 180 A.D.2d 876, —, 580 N.Y.S.2d 95, 97 (3d Dep't 1992) ("the breathalyzer test results should not have been admitted into evidence without holding a fact-finding hearing"); *People v. Serrano*, 142 Misc. 2d 1087, —, 539 N.Y.S.2d 845, 846 (N.Y. City Crim. Ct. 1989) ("the Court ordered a pretrial evidentiary hearing to be held, modelled to some extent on CPL § 710.60, but mindful that this was not strictly a statutory or constitutional suppression hearing. It was one designed to make an *in limine* evidentiary ruling as a matter of law"); *People v. Pantaleo*, 141 Misc. 2d 251, —, 536 N.Y.S.2d 369, 373 (N.Y. City Crim. Ct. 1988) ("Issues of fact on a question necessary to establish the proper foundation for admissibility of the breathalyzer can only be resolved by a fact-finding hearing"); *People v. Mickle*, 187 Misc. 2d 718, 724 N.Y.S.2d 570 (Canaan Just. Ct. 2001); *People v. Iwasiw*, 167 Misc. 2d 1013, —, 641 N.Y.S.2d 521, 523 (Penfield Just. Ct. 1996).

"Moreover, because of the potential for prejudice to defendant if the issue was litigated during trial in the jury's presence, only thereafter to be found inadmissible, we believe that hearings of this sort should properly occur prior to trial." *Colon*, 180 A.D.2d at —, 580 N.Y.S.2d at 97. *See also Pantaleo*, 141 Misc. 2d at —, 536 N.Y.S.2d at 373 ("as a practical matter a pre-trial hearing is necessary. To select a jury and commence the trial only to later

determine that the charge (VTL § 1192[2]) would ultimately fall
for failure to establish a necessary element would be a wasteful
use of limited judicial resources"). *See generally People v. Ventimiglia*, 52 N.Y.2d 350, 362, 438 N.Y.S.2d 261, 265 (1981) ("There
is . . . a greater probability of error, and consequent waste of
scarce judicial resources, when evidentiary rulings are made during trial [rather] than in the more relaxed atmosphere of an inquiry out of the presence of the jury").

§ 24:17   Motion to suppress blood test results

Research References

West's Key Number Digest, Criminal Law ☞632(3.1)

   In blood test cases, the defendant can move for pretrial suppression of his or her blood test results on the ground that the
blood was withdrawn in violation of VTL § 1194(4)(a)(1). *See, e.g.,
People v. Moser*, 70 N.Y.2d 476, 522 N.Y.S.2d 497 (1987); *People
v. Miller*, 17 A.D.3d 708, 793 N.Y.S.2d 231 (3d Dep't 2005); *People
v. Reynolds*, 307 A.D.2d 391, 762 N.Y.S.2d 683 (3d Dep't 2003),
aff'g 193 Misc. 2d 697, 749 N.Y.S.2d 687 (Essex Co. Ct. 2002);
People v. Olmstead, 233 A.D.2d 837, 649 N.Y.S.2d 624 (4th Dep't
1996); *People v. Ebner*, 195 A.D.2d 1006, 600 N.Y.S.2d 569 (4th
Dep't 1993); *People v. Gertz*, 189 Misc. 2d 315, 731 N.Y.S.2d 326
(App. Term, 2d Dep't 2001); *People v. Ellis*, 190 Misc. 2d 98, 737
N.Y.S.2d 232 (Cattaraugus Co. Ct. 2001), *aff'd*, 309 A.D.2d 1314,
765 N.Y.S.2d 313 (4th Dep't 2003); *People v. Pickard*, 180 Misc.
2d 942, 691 N.Y.S.2d 884 (Chautauqua Co. Sup. Ct. 1999). *See
generally People v. Moselle*, 57 N.Y.2d 97, 104, 454 N.Y.S.2d 292,
294 (1982).

§ 24:18   Motion to suppress chemical test refusal

Research References

West's Key Number Digest, Criminal Law ☞632(3.1)

   The courts of this state have long recognized the need for a
pretrial suppression hearing on the issue of the admissibility of a
defendant's alleged refusal to submit to a chemical test. *See, e.g.,
People v. Boone*, 71 A.D.2d 859, __, 419 N.Y.S.2d 187, 187 (2d
Dep't 1979) ("the denial, without a hearing, of defendant's motion
to suppress his alleged refusal to submit to a chemical test" constituted reversible error); *People v. Smith*, 18 N.Y.3d 544, 547,
942 N.Y.S.2d 426, 428, 965 N.E.2d 928 (2012) (issue of admissibility of alleged chemical test refusal was addressed at pretrial
hearing); 18 N.Y.3d at 551, 942 N.Y.S.2d at 430 ("whether
defendant's words or actions amounted to a refusal often constitutes a mixed question of law and fact that requires the court to

view defendant's actions in light of all the surrounding circumstances and draw permissible inferences from equivocal words or conduct"); *People v. Popko*, 33 Misc. 3d 277, __, 930 N.Y.S.2d 782, 784 (N.Y. City Crim. Ct. 2011) (Court held "combined *Ingle* and refusal hearing."); *People v. Brito*, 26 Misc. 3d 1097, 892 N.Y.S.2d 752 (Bronx Co. Sup. Ct. 2010); *People v. Rodriguez*, 26 Misc. 3d 238, 891 N.Y.S.2d 246 (Bronx Co. Sup. Ct. 2009); *People v. O'Reilly*, 16 Misc. 3d 775, __, 842 N.Y.S.2d 292, 294 (Suffolk Co. Dist. Ct. 2007) (Court held "a *Dunaway/Huntley/Mapp* and refusal hearing."); *People v. Davis*, 8 Misc. 3d 158, __, 797 N.Y.S.2d 258, 259 (Bronx Co. Sup. Ct. 2005) ("pre-trial 'refusal hearings' have become common in New York criminal practice"); *People v. Lynch*, 195 Misc. 2d 814, __, 762 N.Y.S.2d 474, 476 (N.Y. City Crim. Ct. 2003) ("the determination of the admissibility of a refusal to submit to a chemical test is best addressed at a hearing held prior to commencement of trial"); *People v. An*, 193 Misc. 2d 301, __, 748 N.Y.S.2d 854, 855 (N.Y. City Crim. Ct. 2002) (Court held *Dunaway*-"Refusal" hearing); *People v. Burtula*, 192 Misc. 2d 597, __, 747 N.Y.S.2d 692, 693 (Nassau County Dist. Ct. 2002) ("Whether this request is labeled one for 'suppression' or for a pre-trial determination into the admissibility of evidence, there exists a sufficient body of case law establishing that a defendant is entitled to such a hearing"); *People v. Dejac*, 187 Misc. 2d 287, __, 721 N.Y.S.2d 492, 493 (Monroe County Supreme Ct. 2001) (Court held "combined probable cause/*Huntley* and chemical test refusal hearing"); *People v. Robles*, 180 Misc. 2d 512, __, 691 N.Y.S.2d 697, 699 (N.Y. City Crim. Ct. 1999) ("It has become common practice for defendants to request and for the courts to conduct pre-trial hearings on the issue of the admissibility of a defendant's refusal to consent to a chemical test"); *People v. Coludro*, 166 Misc. 2d 662, 634 N.Y.S.2d 964 (N.Y. City Crim. Ct. 1995); *People v. Pagan*, 165 Misc. 2d 255, 629 N.Y.S.2d 656 (N.Y. City Crim. Ct. 1995); *People v. Camagos*, 160 Misc. 2d 880, 611 N.Y.S.2d 426 (N.Y. City Crim. Ct. 1993); *People v. McGorman*, 159 Misc. 2d 736, 606 N.Y.S.2d 566 (N.Y. County Supreme Ct. 1993); *People v. Ferrara*, 158 Misc. 2d 671, 602 N.Y.S.2d 86 (N.Y. City Crim. Ct. 1993); *People v. Rosado*, 158 Misc. 2d 50, 600 N.Y.S.2d 624 (N.Y. City Crim. Ct. 1993); *People v. Martin*, 143 Misc. 2d 341, __, 540 N.Y.S.2d 412, 416 (Newark Just. Ct. 1989) ("This Court thus holds that a defendant is entitled to a separate pre-trial hearing to determine whether his refusal to take a breathalyzer [sic] test should be submitted to the jury"); *People v. Walsh*, 139 Misc. 2d 161, 527 N.Y.S.2d 349 (Nassau County Dist. Ct. 1988); *People v. Cruz*, 134 Misc. 2d 115, 509 N.Y.S.2d 1002 (N.Y. City Crim. Ct. 1986); *People v. Delia*, 105 Misc. 2d 483, 432 N.Y.S.2d 321 (Onondaga County Ct. 1980); *People v. Hougland*, 79 Misc. 2d 868, 361 N.Y.S.2d 827 (Suffolk County Dist. Ct. 1974).

Cf. People v. Carota, 93 A.D.3d 1072, __, 941 N.Y.S.2d 302, 307 (3d Dep't 2012); *People v. Kinney*, 66 A.D.3d 1238, 888 N.Y.S.2d 260 (3d Dep't 2009) (hearing held after both parties had rested but before case was submitted to jury).

The rationale for such a hearing was set forth by the Court in *Cruz, supra*:

> A hearing held during trial, or a ruling made during the course of the trial, has little practical value to a defendant. Absent pre-trial suppression, the prosecutor is entitled to discuss the refusal to submit to the breathalyzer test with the jury in his opening statement. Once the jury is made aware of this evidence, the damage is done regardless of whether the prosecution is permitted to introduce that evidence at trial. A ruling made during trial excluding that evidence may thus be futile. Nor would curative instructions warning the jury not to consider the evidence eliminate the tremendous prejudicial effect. Therefore the ruling must be made pre-trial.

134 Misc. 2d at __, 509 N.Y.S.2d at 1004. *See also Burtula*, 192 Misc. 2d at __, 747 N.Y.S.2d at 693–94.

§ 24:19 Motion to preclude Alco-Sensor test results at trial

Research References

West's Key Number Digest, Criminal Law ⬅632(3.1)

A motion in limine to preclude the People from introducing the results of an Alco-Sensor breath screening test is appropriate. *See People v. Gray*, 190 Misc. 2d 40, __, 736 N.Y.S.2d 856, 860 (Kings Co. Sup. Ct. 2002) (Court granted defendant's motion in limine to preclude the results of the defendant's Alco-Sensor test at trial on the ground that an Alco-Sensor test is not reliable evidence of intoxication). *See also People v. Thomas*, 121 A.D.2d 73, 509 N.Y.S.2d 668 (4th Dep't 1986), *order aff'd*, 70 N.Y.2d 823, 523 N.Y.S.2d 437 (1987).

In *Thomas*, the Appellate Division, Fourth Department, made clear both (a) that the courts of this state and of other states "hold that the Alco-Sensor test is not reliable evidence of intoxication," 121 A.D.2d at __, 509 N.Y.S.2d at 671, and (b) that "evidence regarding the Alco-Sensor test had no place in the trial and the objection to its admission should have been sustained. The jury should not have been given the opportunity 'to use the screening test result to corroborate the evidential test result.'" 121 A.D.2d at __, 509 N.Y.S.2d at 673 (citation omitted).

§ 24:20 Motion to depart from standard CJI pattern jury instructions

Research References

West's Key Number Digest, Criminal Law ⬅632(3.1)

In *People v. Moore*, 186 Misc. 2d 614, 720 N.Y.S.2d 898 (Suffolk Co. Dist. Ct. 2000), the defendant was charged with DWI. His defense was that he turned on the engine of his motor vehicle for the sole purpose of using the heater to stay warm; and that he had no intention of moving the vehicle. In response to the defendant's motion in limine seeking a jury instruction which departed from the standard CJI pattern instructions on the issue of operation, *see* § 2:3, *supra*, the court held that:

> While this court will not adopt the proposed substitute to the standard instructions, this Court will enlarge the standard instructions if, in this court's opinion, the trial evidence would warrant such enlargement. If during the course of trial, the facts uncovered would permit a reasonable inference that the actions of the defendant could have been for some purpose other than placing the automobile in motion, the Jury should be instructed that in order to conclude that the defendant was guilty of the charge, it must first conclude that the defendant specifically intended to operate the vehicle, that is, to place the vehicle in motion.

186 Misc. 2d at __, 720 N.Y.S.2d at 900.

§ 24:21 Motion to suppress predicate conviction in felony DWI case

Research References

West's Key Number Digest, Criminal Law ⊙=632(3.1)

A previous conviction obtained in violation of the United States Constitution cannot be "counted" in determining whether a defendant is a predicate and/or a persistent felony offender. *See* CPL § 400.20(6); CPL § 400.21(7)(b). In this regard, the CPL provides a legislatively created procedure for challenging the constitutionality of felony convictions sought to be used to enhance a defendant's *sentence*. *See* CPL § 400.20; CPL § 400.21. By contrast, no such statutory authority exists permitting a defendant to challenge the constitutionality of a prior conviction which the People have used to raise the level of a current charge (*e.g.*, a prior DWI conviction used to elevate a current DWI charge from a misdemeanor to a felony, and/or from a class E felony to a class D felony).

In *People v. Knack*, 72 N.Y.2d 825, 530 N.Y.S.2d 541 (1988), *aff'g* 128 A.D.2d 307, 516 N.Y.S.2d 465 (2d Dep't 1987), the Court of Appeals refused to judicially create such a procedure. *See also People v. DeJesus*, 122 Misc. 2d 190, 471 N.Y.S.2d 195 (N.Y. Co. Sup. Ct. 1983). Pursuant to *Knack*, a defendant cannot file a motion in limine, a motion to suppress, or a motion to controvert a special information challenging the constitutionality of a prior, aggravating DWI conviction *within the context of a pending criminal action. See also People v. Brown*, 160 A.D.2d 1037, __, 553

N.Y.S.2d 875, 877 (3d Dep't 1990) (validity of prior conviction is question of law for court, *not* question of fact for jury).

Several lower court decisions reaching the opposite conclusion should thus be disregarded. *See, e.g., People v. Ryan*, 127 Misc. 2d 138, 485 N.Y.S.2d 933 (Westchester Co. Ct. 1985), judgment aff'd, 161 A.D.2d 677, 558 N.Y.S.2d 838 (2d Dep't 1990); *People v. Solomon*, 113 Misc. 2d 790, 449 N.Y.S.2d 875 (Kings Co. Sup. Ct. 1982); *People v. Sirianni*, 109 Misc. 2d 781, 440 N.Y.S.2d 988 (Cattaraugus Co. Ct. 1981), *order rev'd*, 89 A.D.2d 775, 453 N.Y.S.2d 485 (4th Dep't 1982); *People v. Dorn*, 105 Misc. 2d 244, 431 N.Y.S.2d 974 (Oneida Co. Ct. 1980). *See generally People v. Knickerbocker*, 136 A.D.2d 769, __, 523 N.Y.S.2d 227, 228 (3d Dep't 1988) ("A misdemeanor conviction which was obtained when the defendant was not represented by counsel or had not intelligently waived counsel cannot be used as the basis to enhance a subsequent crime from a misdemeanor to a felony"). Notably, *Ryan, Solomon, Sirianni, Dorn* and *Knickerbocker* all rely on *Baldasar v. Illinois*, 446 U.S. 222, 100 S.Ct. 1585 (1980), which was overruled by Nichols v. United States, 511 U.S. 738, 114 S.Ct. 1921 (1994).

In any event, the rationale of the *Knack* Court was that a judicially created procedure permitting a constitutional challenge to a prior DWI conviction within the context of a pending DWI case is unnecessary, "since there already exist several procedural vehicles for challenging the constitutional propriety of guilty pleas under the facts presented here (*cf., People v. Lopez*, 71 N.Y.2d 662, 529 N.Y.S.2d 465, 525 N.E.2d 5)." *Knack*, 72 N.Y.2d at 827, 530 N.Y.S.2d at 542. For example, the defendant could have challenged the constitutionality of the prior conviction by utilizing one (or more) of the following procedures:

(a) A motion to withdraw the plea. *See* CPL § 220.60(3);

(b) A direct appeal from the judgment of conviction; and/or

(c) A motion to vacate the judgment of conviction (*i.e.*, a coram nobis application). *See* CPL § 440.10.

In *People v. Grubstein*, a defendant charged with felony DWI in 2010 moved to vacate his predicate misdemeanor DWI conviction, which took place in 2008, on the ground that the Town Justice had let him plead guilty *pro se* and without a proper waiver of his right to counsel. Town Court granted the motion. The Appellate Term reversed on the ground that the defendant had not filed a direct appeal of the predicate conviction. 2012 WL 6554678 (App. Term, 9th & 10th Jud. Dist. 2012). The Court of Appeals granted leave and reversed the Appellate Term, holding that "a defendant who asserts that he was deprived of his right to counsel when he pleaded guilty pro se is not barred from raising that claim in a motion under CPL 440.10 by his failure to raise it on direct appeal." 24 N.Y.3d 500, 501-02, 2 N.Y.S.3d 1, 1 (2015). On remand, the Appellate Term considered Town Court's order on the merits, and affirmed. 2015 WL 3369828 (App. Term, 9th & 10th Jud. Dist. 2015).

§ 24:22   Motion to reduce DWI charge

Research References

West's Key Number Digest, Criminal Law ⚖632(3.1)

CPL § 210.20(1-a) provides for the reduction of a pending charge to a lower level (*i.e.*, to a lesser included offense) where "the evidence before the grand jury was not legally sufficient to establish the commission by the defendant of the offense charged . . ., but was legally sufficient to establish the commission of a lesser included offense."

In *People v. Van Buren*, 82 N.Y.2d 878, 609 N.Y.S.2d 170 (1993), the Court of Appeals found that the county court properly reduced the level of the defendant's DWI charge from a felony to a misdemeanor on the ground that there was insufficient evidence before the grand jury of the defendant's alleged predicate DWI conviction. Specifically, the court held that:

> To make a prima facie showing that the offense of felony DWI (Vehicle and Traffic Law § 1192[3]; § 1193[1][c]) has been committed, sufficient proof must be adduced before the Grand Jury to establish that the person charged has a prior conviction for driving while intoxicated or alcohol-impaired within the last 10 years. That a person named Robert L. Van Buren was convicted of driving while intoxicated within the preceding 10-year period even in the same county did not constitute prima facie proof that defendant was the person previously convicted of DWI within the last 10 years. The certificate of conviction standing alone, without some further, connecting evidence tending to show that defendant was the same Robert L. Van Buren named in the certificate, was insufficient to "establish every element of [the] offense charged."

82 N.Y.2d at 880–81, 609 N.Y.S.2d at 171 (citation omitted).

Similarly, in *People v. Smith*, 258 A.D.2d 245, 697 N.Y.S.2d 783 (4th Dep't 1999), the Appellate Division, Fourth Department, affirmed the reduction of a class D felony DWI to a class E felony DWI where the defendant's DMV abstract presented to the grand jury was not properly certified and/or authenticated.

In addition, both the Court of Appeals and the Appellate Division, Third Department, have made clear that:

> * * * the Legislature [has] recognized that the average person can consume a certain amount of alcohol without impairing his ability to operate a motor vehicle as he should. Otherwise the Legislature would not have provided that proof of .05 of 1% or less of blood

alcohol content is prima facie evidence that the driver was not impaired or intoxicated * * *. And the Legislature also recognized that some individuals may be able to consume greater amounts of alcohol without being impaired, as would the average driver * * *. Thus the impairment statute, by simply providing prima facie standards, takes into account the 'subjective' tolerance of individuals in determining the ability to drive possessed by a defendant at the time of arrest.

People v. Hagmann, 175 A.D.2d 502, __, 572 N.Y.S.2d 952, 954 (3d Dep't 1991) (quoting *People v. Cruz*, 48 N.Y.2d 419, 426, 423 N.Y.S.2d 625, 628 (1979)).

In other words, the evidence before the grand jury can be legally insufficient to establish the commission by the defendant of the offense of common law DWI (*i.e.*, VTL § 1192(3)), as opposed to the lesser included offense of DWAI (*i.e.*, VTL § 1192(1)).

§ 24:23 Motion to delete reference in indictment to class level of felony DWI charge

Research References
West's Key Number Digest, Criminal Law ☞632(3.1)

In a felony DWI case, the defendant should consider moving to delete the phrases "a class D felony" and/or "a class E felony" from the indictment (if such phrases are included therein). While the use of the phrase "as a felony" in an indictment is expressly authorized by CPL § 200.60(1), *see People v. Woodrow*, 212 A.D.2d 834, __, 622 N.Y.S.2d 351, 352 (3d Dep't 1995); *People v. Koponen*, 129 A.D.2d 838, __, 513 N.Y.S.2d 851, 853 (3d Dep't 1987), the use of the phrase "a class D felony" and/or "a class E felony" would appear to violate both the letter and the spirit of CPL § 200.60. *See generally People v. Cooper*, 78 N.Y.2d 476, 577 N.Y.S.2d 202 (1991).

In this regard, reference to the "class D" and/or "class E" nature of the charges both (a) unfairly highlights the fact that there are varying levels of felonies, and (b) implies that the defendant is being charged with a higher-level felony than if just the phrase "as a felony" were being used. Notably, the *Koponen* court stated that:

It may have been the better practice for County Court to have omitted any reference to the crimes charged as felonies and thus to have obviated any conceivable risk of prejudice rising from the possibility of independent awareness by jurors that such status was predicated upon a prior conviction.

129 A.D.2d at __, 513 N.Y.S.2d at 852–53.

§ 24:24   Pretrial motions—Referral to judicial hearing officer

Research References

West's Key Number Digest, Criminal Law ⊖632(3.1)

CPL § 255.20(4) provides that:

Any pre-trial motion, whether made before or after expiration of the period specified in [CPL § 255.20(1)], may be referred by the court to a judicial hearing officer ["JHO"] who shall entertain it in the same manner as a court. In the discharge of this responsibility, the [JHO] shall have the same powers as a judge of the court making the assignment, except that the [JHO] shall not determine the motion but shall file a report with the court setting forth findings of fact and conclusions of law. The rules of evidence shall be applicable at any hearing conducted hereunder by a [JHO]. A transcript of any testimony taken, together with the exhibits or copies thereof, shall be filed with the report. The court shall determine the motion on the motion papers, affidavits and other documents submitted by the parties thereto, the record of the hearing before the [JHO], and the [JHO's] report.

In *People v. Scalza*, 76 N.Y.2d 604, 610, 562 N.Y.S.2d 14, 17 (1990), the Court of Appeals held that CPL § 255.20(4) is constitutional *on its face*. However, the Court left undecided the issue of whether a defendant can challenge the constitutionality of the statute *as applied* to his or her particular case. 76 N.Y.2d at 610, 562 N.Y.S.2d at 17.

§ 24:25   Effect of People's refusal to go forward at court-ordered pretrial suppression hearing

Research References

West's Key Number Digest, Criminal Law ⊖632(3.1)

Where the People refuse to go forward at a court-ordered pretrial suppression hearing, the court has two options:

(a) Grant the defendant's motion to suppress. *See People v. Berrios*, 28 N.Y.2d 361, 367, 321 N.Y.S.2d 884, 889 (1971) (People have the burden of *"going forward"* at suppression hearing); *People v. Hartley*, 188 Misc. 2d 70, 726 N.Y.S.2d 540 (Albany Co. Ct. 2001) (defendant's breath test result suppressed due to People's failure to participate in court-ordered *Ayala* hearing); *People v. Henderson*, 149 Misc. 2d 852, 566 N.Y.S.2d 1016 (Kings Co. Sup. Ct. 1991) (defendant's motion to suppress granted due to People's failure to put forth evidence at *Mapp/Dunaway* hearing); and/or

(b) Hold the People in contempt. *See* Judiciary Law § 750;

UJCA § 210; *Matter of Brostoff v. Berkman*, 79 N.Y.2d 938, 582 N.Y.S.2d 989 (1992); *Matter of Balter v. Regan*, 63 N.Y.2d 630, 479 N.Y.S.2d 506 (1984).

The Court of Appeals' decisions in *Balter* and *Brostoff* make clear that the People's conduct in refusing to go forward at a suppression hearing is simply not acceptable. In *Balter*, the trial court ordered the petitioner, an assistant public defender, to proceed to trial representing a criminal defendant despite a conflict of interest. The petitioner refused to proceed and was held in contempt. The petitioner filed an Article 78 petition challenging the trial court's contempt ruling. In affirming the dismissal of the petition, the Court of Appeals held that:

> Notwithstanding petitioner's good-faith belief that the court's order raised [a] conflict of interest, we agree with the Appellate Division that the court's order was not thereby rendered unlawful. However misguided and erroneous the court's order may have been, petitioner was not free to disregard it and decide for himself the manner in which to proceed. The prejudice sought to be avoided by petitioner was not irreparable; indeed, . . . any prejudice could have been remedied through the appellate process.

63 N.Y.2d at 631, 479 N.Y.S.2d at 507.

Similarly, in *Brostoff* the Court of Appeals affirmed the trial court's holding of an assistant district attorney in contempt for willfully disobeying a lawful court order. In so holding, the court reaffirmed its statement in *Balter* that " '[h]owever misguided and erroneous the court's order may have been, petitioner was not free to disregard it and decide for himself the manner in which to proceed.' " *Brostoff*, 79 N.Y.2d at 940, 582 N.Y.S.2d at 990 (quoting *Balter*). *See also Matter of Brostoff v. Berkman*, 170 A.D.2d 364, __, 566 N.Y.S.2d 927, 928 (1st Dep't 1991), judgment aff'd, 79 N.Y.2d 938, 582 N.Y.S.2d 989, 591 N.E.2d 1175 (1992) ("Certainly, the presiding judge, not an assistant district attorney, possesses the authority to govern the functioning of the court"), aff'd, 79 N.Y.2d 938, 582 N.Y.S.2d 989 (1992).

In *People v. Hartley*, 188 Misc. 2d 70, 726 N.Y.S.2d 540 (Albany Co. Ct. 2001), the town court granted the defendant's motion for an *Ayala* hearing. *See* § 24:15, *supra*. The People refused to participate in the hearing, claiming that there is no such thing as an *Ayala* hearing, and/or that the defendant failed to allege sufficient facts to justify the granting of the hearing. As a result of the People's failure to participate in the hearing, the town court suppressed the defendant's breath test result.

On appeal, the county court held that "[t]he People's refusal to go forward with the pretrial suppression hearing ordered by the Town Court constrains this Court to affirm the Town Court's suppression of the results of the Breathalyzer test." 188 Misc. 2d at __, 726 N.Y.S.2d at 541. In so holding, the court reasoned that:

As succinctly stated by the Court of Appeals: ". . . however misguided and erroneous the court's order may have been, [the assistant district attorney] was not free to disregard it and decide for [herself] the manner in which to proceed." (*Matter of Brostoff v. Berkman*, 79 N.Y.2d 938, 940, 582 N.Y.S.2d 989, 591 N.E.2d 1175 [1992], citing *Matter of Balter v. Regan*, 63 N.Y.2d 630, 479 N.Y.S.2d 506, 468 N.E.2d 688 [1984]). * * *

Once the pre-trial suppression hearing was ordered by the Town Court, the People were obligated to proceed.

There is a critical distinction in the law between an *unlawful* court order and an *erroneous* court order. That an appellate court might later determine that a lower court's order was erroneous clearly does *not* give a litigant in the lower court the right to disobey or disregard such order. If the People were permitted to refuse to go forward in this lawfully ordered hearing, then the People could refuse to go forward in *any* court ordered pre-trial suppression hearing which they felt had been improperly granted. Fundamental to our legal system is the principle that neither the People nor any other litigant possesses a veto power over lawful court orders. Simply stated, the People's refusal to offer evidence at, or participate in, the pre-trial suppression hearing ordered by the Town Court mandates the affirmance of the Town Court's suppression order resulting therefrom. Based upon the foregoing, the Town Court's suppression of the Breathalyzer results must be and the same is hereby affirmed.

188 Misc. 2d at __-__, 726 N.Y.S.2d at 541–42.

§ 24:26 Appealability of suppression order

Research References

West's Key Number Digest, Criminal Law ☜632(3.1)

CPL § 710.70(2) provides that "[a]n order finally denying a motion to suppress evidence may be reviewed upon an appeal from an ensuing judgment of conviction notwithstanding the fact that such judgment is entered upon a plea of guilty." Thus, a defendant's guilty plea does not constitute a waiver of his or her right to appeal an order finally denying a suppression motion.

Nonetheless, the Court of Appeals has made clear that "a defendant's general waiver of the right to appeal, as part of a negotiated plea agreement, [can] encompass[] an attempted appeal concerning an adverse suppression ruling, notwithstanding the statutory provision authorizing an appeal of such ruling following entry of a guilty plea (CPL 710.20[2])." *People v. Kemp*, 94 N.Y.2d 831, 833, 703 N.Y.S.2d 59, 60 (1999).

§ 24:27 Motion to dismiss in interest of justice

Motions to dismiss in the interest of justice are governed by

CPL § 170.40. In *People v. Haugh*, 26 Misc. 3d 1029, —, 894 N.Y.S.2d 359, 361 (Henrietta Just. Ct. 2009), the Court dismissed DWI charges in the interest of justice where:

> Prior to the offenses charged in this matter, the Defendant endured a series of misfortunes through no fault of her own. On December 1, 2007, the Defendant's husband was shot to death while hunting in the Southern Tier of New York State. Shortly thereafter, in February of 2008, the Defendant suffered a miscarriage of her deceased husband's baby. During the Spring of 2008, a criminal investigation was conducted regarding the death of the Defendant's husband, whereby it was determined that his death was the result of a homicide. In June of 2008, the Defendant's step-son, whom the Defendant had helped raise for more than four (4) years, was removed from the Defendant's household due to the child's misconduct. In March of 2009, the suspect accused of killing the Defendant's husband was acquitted of homicide. The acquittal resulted in the Defendant losing all faith in the criminal justice system, and even in God.

> The following month, April of 2009, the Defendant was arrested for DWI, which was her first offense, and her first and only contact with the criminal justice system. Since the time of her arrest, the Defendant has ceased drinking alcohol, and she has become reacquainted with her faith and church, both of which discourage even moderate use of alcohol.

§ 24:28 People's right to withdraw charge

In *People v. Extale*, 18 N.Y.3d 690, 692, 943 N.Y.S.2d 801, 802, 967 N.E.2d 179 (2012), the Court of Appeals held that:

> [A] prosecutor does not have the unilateral power to dismiss a count of a grand jury indictment over a defendant's objection. Whether such a count should be dismissed at the prosecutor's request is an issue to be decided by the court in its discretion.

In so holding, the Court reasoned that:

> Usually, of course, a defendant is happy to have a charge against him dismissed, and it is the People who oppose dismissal. But a role reversal can occur when a defendant, not optimistic about the likelihood of acquittal, wants the jury to have a chance to compromise or exercise mercy by convicting him of a lesser crime. This line of thinking often leads defendants to request submission of a lesser included offense, in addition to the offense charged in the indictment, and the defendant is entitled to have such an offense submitted "if there is a reasonable view of the evidence which would support a finding that the defendant committed such lesser offense but did not commit the greater."

> Here, the crime that defendant wanted the jury to consider, and the People did not, was not a lesser included offense, but one of the offenses for which defendant was indicted. The People argue that

they have discretion to withdraw such a count. We disagree: the discretion is the trial court's, not the People's. * * *

That does not mean that the count *had* to be submitted to the jury if defendant wanted it to be, but the issue was one for the trial court's discretion, not the prosecutor's. The People could have moved for dismissal in the interest of justice under CPL 210.40(3), or the court could have exercised its discretion under CPL 300.40(6)(a) to withdraw a count from the jury when "[t]he people consent that it not be submitted." And it may be that the court has inherent power to dismiss a count with the consent of the People even in situations to which neither CPL 210.40(3) nor 300.40(6)(a) applies; that is an issue not before us, on which we express no opinion. Nor need we address a situation in which the prosecutor wants to dismiss a count of an accusatory instrument that did not originate with a grand jury. We hold only that in a case like this the prosecutor is not empowered to dismiss a count without court approval.

Of course it is possible that, if County Court had understood itself to have discretion in this case, it would have exercised that discretion in the prosecutor's favor and dismissed the first degree vehicular assault count. We cannot know that, however: the trial judge made quite clear that he was deferring to the prosecutor's choice, not making a choice of his own. Nor can we be sure that the dismissal of the vehicular assault count did not affect the jury's verdict. We have recognized that, "as a practical matter," the opportunity to convict a defendant of a less serious charge "may affect a jury's deliberations." Here, the jury might have chosen to convict defendant on the withdrawn count, first degree vehicular assault, rather than the second degree assault charge on which it did convict him. If it had made that choice, that would have benefitted defendant, because, while both these crimes are class D felonies, second degree assault is defined as a violent felony while first degree vehicular assault is not. Defendant is therefore entitled to have his conviction set aside.

18 N.Y.3d at 693-94, 695-96, 943 N.Y.S.2d at 802-03, 804 (citations omitted). *See also Donnaruma v. Carter*, __ Misc. 3d __, 969 N.Y.S.2d 755 (Albany Co. Sup. Ct. 2013); *People v. Donnaruma*, 39 Misc. 3d 1056, 963 N.Y.S.2d 848 (Albany City Ct. 2013); *People v. Rossi*, 39 Misc. 3d 496, 960 N.Y.S.2d 616 (Stuyvesant Just. Ct. 2013); *People v. Beckman*, 38 Misc. 3d 878, 957 N.Y.S.2d 830 (Columbia Co. Ct. 2012).

Part VII

STATEMENTS

Chapter 25

Statements

Research References

Westlaw Databases

Handling a Criminal Case in New York (HCCNY)

Law of Confessions (2d ed.) (LAWCONFESS)

Treatises and Practice Aids
Muldoon, Handling a Criminal Case in New York §§ 9:130 to 9:136, 9:194, 9:285
Nissman and Hagen, Law of Confessions § 8:10 (2d ed.)

KeyCite®: Cases and other legal materials listed in KeyCite Scope can be researched through the KeyCite service on Westlaw®. Use KeyCite to check citations for form, parallel references, prior and later history, and comprehensive citator information, including citations to other decisions and secondary materials.

---

§ 25:1 Involuntary statements

Research References
West's Key Number Digest, Criminal Law ⚖=412.1(1)

It is well settled that an involuntary statement is inadmissible against an accused. *Blackburn v. Alabama*, 361 U.S. 199, 207, 80 S.Ct. 274, 280 (1960); *People v. Anderson*, 42 N.Y.2d 35, 396 N.Y.S.2d 625 (1977). This principle is based upon the privilege against self-incrimination and the Due Process clause. In New York, this rule is also codified in CPL § 60.45 which states:

1. Evidence of a written or oral confession, admission, or other statement made by a defendant with respect to his participation or lack of participation in the offense charged, may not be received in evidence against him in a criminal proceeding if such statement was involuntarily made.

2. A confession, admission or other statement is "involuntary made" by a defendant when it is obtained from him:

(a) By any person by the use or threatened use of physical force upon the defendant or another person, or by means of any other improper conduct or undue pressure which impaired the defendant's physical or mental condition to the extent of undermining his ability to make a choice whether or not to make a statement; or

(b) By a public servant engaged in law enforcement activity or by a person then acting under his direction or in cooperation with him:

(i) by means of any promise or statement of fact, which promise or statement creates a substantial risk that the defendant might falsely incriminate himself; or

(ii) in violation of such rights as a defendant may derive from the constitution of this state or of the United States.

It is not necessary for the statement to be made to a police officer or public official in order for the statement to be deemed involuntary where the statement was obtained *by use or threatened use of physical force*, or under the other circumstances set forth in CPL § 60.45(2)(a). In such situation, a statement may be involuntary even if made to a private person. *See People v. Pagan*, 211 A.D.2d 532, 622 N.Y.S.2d 9 (1st Dep't 1995); *People v. Grillo*, 176 A.D.2d 346, 574 N.Y.S.2d 583 (2d Dep't 1991); CPL § 60.45(2)(a); § 25:3 for further discussion. However, statements obtained by a private person by means of *any promise or statement of fact* are admissible even though the same statements might not be admissible if obtained by a public servant. *See* CPL § 60.45(2)(b)(i); *People v. Price*, 224 A.D.2d 1014, 637 N.Y.S.2d 536 (4th Dep't 1996).

The defendant is entitled to a pretrial hearing and judicial determination as to whether his statements were voluntary before the statements may be admitted at trial. *People v. Huntley*, 15 N.Y.2d 72, 255 N.Y.S.2d 838 (1965); *People v. Chennault*, 20 N.Y.2d 518, 285 N.Y.S.2d 289 (1967); *People v. Grillo*, 176 A.D.2d 346, 574 N.Y.S.2d 583 (2d Dep't 1991). To obtain a *Huntley* hearing to determine the voluntariness of the statement, the defendant must merely allege that his statement was involuntary. *People v. Weaver*, 49 N.Y.2d 1012, 429 N.Y.S.2d 399 (1980); *People v. Knights*, 124 A.D.2d 935, 508 N.Y.S.2d 679 (3d Dep't 1986).

In *People v. Huntley*, 15 N.Y.2d 72, 255 N.Y.S.2d 838 (1965), the Court concluded that it is the People's burden to establish, beyond a reasonable doubt, that a statement was voluntarily made. *See also People v. Jin Cheng Lin*, 26 N.Y.3d 701, 719, 27 N.Y.S.3d 439, 451, 47 N.E.3d 718 (2016) ("It is the People's 'heavy burden' 'to prove beyond a reasonable doubt that statements of a defendant they intend to rely upon at trial are voluntary' ") (citations omitted); *People v. Witherspoon*, 66 N.Y.2d 973, 498 N.Y.S.2d 789 (1985); *People v. Rosa*, 65 N.Y.2d 380, 492 N.Y.S.2d 542 (1985).

The terms involuntary and coerced "are not simple to define." *People v. Anderson*, 42 N.Y.2d 35, 396 N.Y.S.2d 625, 627 (1977). The court must look at the totality of the circumstances to determine if the statement was given voluntarily. *See Arizona v. Fulminante*, 499 U.S. 279, 111 S.Ct. 1246 (1991); *People v. Hamelinck*, 222 A.D.2d 1024, 635 N.Y.S.2d 916 (4th Dep't 1995) (officers' assurance that defendant would be permitted to go home after giving his statement did not render statement involuntary).

In *People v. Turkenich*, 137 A.D.2d 363, 529 N.Y.S.2d 385 (2d Dep't 1988), the Court concluded that a defendant who does not have the capacity to comprehend *Miranda* warnings also lacks capacity to understand the nature and consequences of his statements to the police and, thus, such statements are "involuntary."

In *People v. Hernandez*, 19 Misc. 3d 527, __, 854 N.Y.S.2d 282,

290 (Albany Co. Sup. Ct. 2008), the Court held that a police officer's promise to the defendant that their conversation would be "off the record" rendered the defendant's subsequent statements involuntary.

§ 25:2 Involuntary statements resulting from mental condition/intoxication

Research References

West's Key Number Digest, Criminal Law ⚖412.1(1)

In *Colorado v. Connelly*, 479 U.S. 157, 107 S.Ct. 515 (1986), the Supreme Court concluded that coercive police activity is a necessary predicate to a finding of involuntariness under the Due Process clause. Notwithstanding a person's mental state, there must be coercive police activity. Here, the defendant, responding to voices from God, approached a police officer to inform him that he wanted to confess to a murder. Upon being taken into custody, the defendant provided inculpatory statements. Although the trial court found that the police exercised no coercion in securing the defendant's confession, they suppressed the confession, finding it to be "involuntary." The Colorado Supreme Court affirmed, concluding that the statements were not "the product of a rational intellect and a free will."

The United States Supreme Court reversed and found:

> [W]hile mental condition is surely relevant to an individual's susceptibility to police coercion, mere examination of the confessant's state of mind can never conclude that due process inquiry.

Colorado v. Connelly, 479 U.S. at 165, 107 S.Ct. at 521.

> We hold that coercive police activity is a necessary predicate to the finding that a confession is not "voluntary" within the meaning of the due process clause of the Fourteenth Amendment.

Colorado v. Connelly, 479 U.S. at 167, 107 S.Ct. at 522. Thus, with regard to the federal Constitution, the defendant's mental condition alone is insufficient for a finding that the statement was involuntary pursuant to the Due Process clause.

In contrast, the New York Court of Appeals, in *People v. Schompert*, 19 N.Y.2d 300, 279 N.Y.S.2d 515, 519 (1967), has held:

> [T]hat in the instance of self-induced intoxication the problem is really one of trustworthiness rather than of coercion or unfairness which will bar even truthful statements.

In *Schompert*, the Court addressed the issue of whether a defendant's severe alcoholism and intoxication at the time he made inculpatory statements to the police rendered his confession involuntary. Here, the police did not engage in coercion or any other unfair methods. Upon stating that the standard is whether the confession is reliable, the Court proceeded to discuss the factors to consider.

> Lack of awareness or understanding alone might be sufficient to exclude a confession in the rare case where it clearly appears that at the time of the confession, the confessant was so intoxicated as to lack mental capacity, that is, he was unable to appreciate the nature and consequences of his statements. This, no doubt, is the 'mania' referred to in the older cases.

> Another factor is whether content of the statement was accurate; and accuracy may be tested by subsequent events.

> The general rule applicable to confessions obtained from persons under intoxication has been well stated to the effect that "proof that the accused was intoxicated at the time he confessed his guilt of crime will not, without more, bar the reception of the confession in evidence. But if it is shown that the accused was intoxicated to the degree of mania, or of being unable to understand the meaning of his statements, then the confession is inadmissible."

People v. Schompert, 279 N.Y.S.2d at 518–19. *See also People v. Johnson*, 81 A.D.3d 745, __, 916 N.Y.S.2d 510, 510 (2d Dep't 2011) ("It is well settled that intoxication alone is insufficient to render a waiver of *Miranda* rights invalid and a resultant statement involuntary. The evidence was insufficient to establish that the defendant was intoxicated 'to a degree of mania or of being unable to understand the meaning of his statement so as to render his statement involuntary' ") (citations omitted).

The criteria that is applied to statements made by one who is intoxicated are applicable to statements made by one who is mentally ill. *See People v. Adams*, 26 N.Y.2d 129, 137, 309 N.Y.S.2d 145, 150 (1970).

§ 25:3 Involuntary statements made to private individual

Research References

West's Key Number Digest, Criminal Law ⊜412.1(1)

While the United States Constitution does not mandate suppression of an involuntary confession made to a private party, *Colorado v. Connelly*, *supra*, it has long been the law in New York that a defendant's involuntary statement, whether obtained by the police or a private individual, may not be used against him or her where the statement was obtained by use or threatened use of physical force, or under the other circumstances set forth in CPL § 60.45(2)(a). *See People v. Pagan*, 211 A.D.2d 532, 622 N.Y.S.2d 9 (1st Dep't 1995); *People v. Grillo*, 176 A.D.2d 346, 574 N.Y.S.2d 583 (2d Dep't 1991); *People v. Sorbo*, 170 Misc. 2d 390, 649 N.Y.S.2d 318 (N.Y. Co. Sup. Ct. 1996).

In *People v. Sorbo, supra*, the Court explained that the defendant is entitled to a hearing on the issue whenever he has reasonable cause to believe that an involuntary statement made to a private party may be offered against him.

> Defendant has a right to move to suppress an involuntarily made statement whenever he or she has "reasonable cause to believe that such statement may be offered against him." The right to a motion, hearing and ruling is not contingent upon receipt of notice under CPL § 710.30(1)(a). The notice provision is limited solely to situations where the People intend to offer a statement made to a public servant. On the other hand, CPL § 710.20 affords the right to suppression when a defendant reasonably fears use of an involuntary statement against him even in the absence of notice or police involvement.

People v. Sorbo, supra.

Not only are the statements suppressible, the fruits of the involuntarily obtained statements must also be suppressed.

> The second salient feature of CPL § 710.20 is the explicit directive in subdivision (4) requiring suppression of the derivative evidence, or "fruits" of an involuntarily obtained statement. Subdivision 3 speaks of an involuntarily made statement "within the meaning of § 60.45." It does not limit itself to an illegally obtained statement made to a public servant . . . The fruits of an involuntary statement as defined in CPL § 60.45(2)(a), which includes statements obtained by private parties, are inadmissable by the plain language of CPL § 710.20(4).

People v. Sorbo, supra.

With regard to the procedure at the hearing, the Court set forth the following:

> At the hearing, the People will have the initial burden of going forward and the statements made by the defendant will necessarily be elicited. Once a hearing has begun, "the court has a duty to permit a full exposition of all the familiar elements that bear on the question of the voluntary nature of the defendant's statement" and "no meaningful exploration of this issue can be had without any reference to the substance and content of the statement attributed to the defendant." *People v. David*, 44 A.D.2d 548, 353 N.Y.S.2d 764, 766 (1st Dep't 1974). In *David*, the court held that "it is crystal clear that without any regard to the discovery rights of a defendant, his counsel is entitled to cross-examine the interrogating officer with respect to the questions that were asked and the responses made thereto." . . . It would be unfair and a waste of judicial resources to conduct a hearing without requiring the People to disclose the defendant's statements in advance.

People v. Sorbo, supra.

§ 25:4 Involuntary statements may not be used to impeach

Research References

West's Key Number Digest, Criminal Law ⚷412.1(1)

An involuntary statement is inherently unreliable and, thus, may not be used in the People's direct case or to impeach the defendant.

> [A] statement actually coerced from a defendant is inadmissible for all purposes (*Mincey v. Arizona*, 437 U.S. 385, 399, 98 S.Ct. 2408, 2417, 57 L.Ed.2d 290). By contrast, a defendant's statement, voluntarily made but obtained in violation of *Miranda v. Arizona*, 384 U.S. 436, 86 S.Ct. 1602, 16 L.Ed.2d 694, is inadmissible on the prosecution's direct case, but may nevertheless be used for impeachment where "the trustworthiness of the evidence satisfies the legal standard" (*Harris v. New York*, 401 U.S. 222, 224, 91 S.Ct. 643, 645, 28 L.Ed.2d 1, affirming 25 N.Y.2d 175, 303 N.Y.S.2d 71, 250 N.E.2d 349; *see also, People v. Washington*, 51 N.Y.2d 214, 433 N.Y.S.2d 745, 413 N.E.2d 1159).

People v. Hults, 76 N.Y.2d 190, 197, 557 N.Y.S.2d 270, 274 (1990). *See* § 26:19.

§ 25:5 *Huntley* hearing mandatory even if statement used solely for impeachment purposes

Research References

West's Key Number Digest, Criminal Law ⚷414

Since a statement that is involuntary may not be used in the People's case-in-chief or for impeachment purposes, a *Huntley* hearing is required whenever the defendant claims that his statement was involuntary. In *People v. Clemons*, 166 A.D.2d 363, 561 N.Y.S.2d 425 (1st Dep't 1990), the DA opposed the *Huntley* hearing on the ground that he only intended to use the statement for impeachment purposes. The Court ruled that the defendant was entitled to a *Huntley* hearing to determine the voluntariness of the statement.

§ 25:6 Applicability of harmless error doctrine

Research References

West's Key Number Digest, Criminal Law ⚷1169.12

In *Arizona v. Fulminante*, 499 U.S. 279, 111 S.Ct. 1246 (1991), the United States Supreme Court ruled that the harmless error doctrine was applicable to erroneously admitted involuntary statements. In *Fulminante*, the Supreme Court abandoned its long-held rule that a defendant in a criminal case was deprived of due process of law if his conviction was founded, in whole or in part, upon an involuntary confession, without regard for the truth or falsity of the confession, and even though there was ample evidence to support the conviction.

§ 25:7   Language barrier results in suppression

Research References

West's Key Number Digest, Criminal Law ⚏412(4)

The defendant must understand the language used by an accuser for an admission to be received in evidence. In *People v. Lourido*, 70 N.Y.2d 428, 522 N.Y.S.2d 98 (1987), the Court of Appeals held that a defendant's response of a "high shrug of the shoulders" to an accusation made by a police officer in English should not have been admitted into evidence, and was reversible error where the accusation was made in a language he did not understand. This error was compounded by the prosecutor's summation comment on the shrug as being indicative of the defendant's guilt. *See also People v. Niedzwiecki*, 127 Misc. 2d 919, 487 N.Y.S.2d 694 (N.Y. City Crim. Ct. 1985).

§ 25:8   Use of defendant's prearrest silence

Research References

West's Key Number Digest, Criminal Law ⚏407(1)

In *People v. De George*, 73 N.Y.2d 614, 543 N.Y.S.2d 11 (1989), the Court of Appeals held that a defendant's prearrest silence may not "generally" be used to impeach the defendant's testimony on cross-examination, or as direct evidence on the People's case as proof of the defendant's mental state. Here, the defendant was involved in a confrontation which escalated to a struggle and ultimately, a gunshot wound to the victim. The defendant admitted to accidentally shooting the victim while trying to strike the victim on the head with a gun.

Upon the approach of the police, the defendant made no response to the officer's general inquiries, or to subsequent specific inquiries in regard to who had shot the victim, or who had the gun. This silence was introduced in the People's direct case as evidence of depraved indifference in support of the charge of assault first (*i.e.*, recklessly engaging in conduct under circumstances evincing a depraved indifference to human life which created a grave risk of death to another person and thereby causes serious physical injury to another person in violation of Penal Law § 120.10[3]).

In ordering a new trial, the Court held that neither prearrest silence nor pretrial silence is generally admissible, either as direct evidence, or for purposes of impeachment on cross-examination. *See People v. Conyers*, 49 N.Y.2d 174, 424 N.Y.S.2d 402 (1980) (*Conyers I*), remanded by the United States Supreme Court for further consideration, 449 U.S. 809, 101 S.Ct. 56 (1980); *People v. Conyers II*, 52 N.Y.2d 454, 438 N.Y.S.2d 741 (1981).

> Silence in these circumstances is ambiguous because an innocent person may have many reasons for not speaking. Among those identified are a person's "awareness that he is under no obligation to speak or to the natural caution that arises from his knowledge that anything he says might later be used against him at trial" (*Conyers II*, 52 N.Y.2d at 458, 438 N.Y.S.2d 741, 420 N.E.2d 933), a belief that efforts at exoneration would be futile under the circumstances (*People v. Dawson*, 50 N.Y.2d 311, 322, 428 N.Y.S.2d 914, 406 N.E.2d 771), or because of explicit instructions not to speak from an attorney (*see, People v. Conrow*, 200 N.Y. 356, 367–369, 93 N.E. 943; *Fisch*, N.Y.Evid. 792 [2d Ed. 1977]). Moreover, there are individuals who mistrust law enforcement officials and refuse to speak to them not because they are guilty of some crime, but rather because "they are simply fearful of coming into contact with those whom they regard as antagonists" (*People v. Conyers*, 52 N.Y.2d 454, 458, 438 N.Y.S.2d 741, 420 N.E.2d 933, *supra*). In most cases, it is impossible to conclude that a failure to speak is more consistent with guilt than with innocence.

> Moreover, despite its lack of probative value, the evidence undoubtedly affects the witness' credibility. Jurors, who may not be sensitive to the wide variety of alternative explanations for a defendant's pretrial silence, may assign much more weight to it than is warranted and, thus, the evidence may create a substantial risk of prejudice.

People v. De George, 543 N.Y.S.2d at 13 (citations omitted).

The word "generally" is used because the Court did contemplate limited circumstances in which evidence of silence may be used to impeach a defendant's credibility. The Court cited *People v. Rothschild*, 35 N.Y.2d 355, 361 N.Y.S.2d 901 (1974), where a police officer, charged with larceny, testified that he had been engaged in a police undercover operation and had not been attempting to obtain money illegally. The cross-examination, concerning his silence at the time of his arrest, was affirmed by the Court of Appeals because the surrounding circumstances gave this evidence a highly probative value. In light of the officer's obligation to inform his superiors of undercover activities, the officer's silence, in the face of direct accusations by fellow officers, was deemed significant evidence of guilt. *See also People v. Savage*, 50 N.Y.2d 673, 431 N.Y.S.2d 382 (1980); *People v. Durden*, 211 A.D.2d 568, 621 N.Y.S.2d 611 (1st Dep't 1995).

In *People v. Hollis*, 215 A.D.2d 777, 627 N.Y.S.2d 415 (2d Dep't 1995), a police officer testified that after the defendant made certain statements, the defendant then indicated that he did not want to speak to the police anymore. The defendant argued that the admission of this testimony constituted an impermissible use of his postarrest silence. Although the court agreed with the defendant that the admission of such testimony was error, the court denied the defendant's request for a mistrial in view of the fact that the defendant rejected the court's offer to issue a curative instruction to the jury.

In *People v. Davis*, 61 N.Y.2d 202, 473 N.Y.S.2d 146 (1984), two police officers were summoned to an apartment building to investigate the report of a person with a gun. Upon exiting the building, the defendant ran. At trial, the police testified that during the chase they ordered the defendant to stop. One officer testified that, after arresting the defendant, the defendant stated, "I should have killed you when I had the chance." The defendant testified that he did not know the men chasing him were police officers, but, rather, thought they were persons out to get him. The prosecutor asked, without objection, if he spoke to the officers at the time of the arrest. The defendant testified that he said nothing.

During summation, defense counsel argued that while the defendant may have cursed at the officers, he did not do or say what the officers attributed to him upon his arrest.

The prosecutor stated on summation:

> When I asked him, "did you say anything at all" he said, "I didn't say anything to them." Is that how someone who is the innocent, the innocent victim, is that how he reacts? Wouldn't he have said something more consistent with his position? Would he have really stood there and said nothing while handcuffs are being put on him?

People v. Davis, 473 N.Y.S.2d at 147.

The trial court sustained the defense counsel's objections to these comments. Upon defense counsel's motion for a mistrial, the prosecutor suggested that a curative instruction be given to the jury. Defense counsel objected to such an instruction and none was given. The Appellate Division affirmed the conviction.

The defendant argued on appeal that it was error for the prosecutor to use postarrest silence for impeachment purposes on summation. The Court of Appeals affirmed the conviction, finding that the defendant himself placed the issue of his postarrest silence in question by testifying that he said nothing to the police officers at his arrest, thereby disputing the officer's testimony.

> This is not a case, like *Conyers*, where the prosecution tried to use evidence of the fact of a defendant's post-arrest silence against him by contending that such silence itself renders a later exculpatory version of events incredible. Here the defendant testified as to his

post-arrest silence, contradicting the prosecution witnesses, and the prosecutor attacked the veracity of defendant's testimony upon summation. In such a situation, the prosecutor's statements on summation about whether defendant was or was not silent at the time of his arrest concerned a key issue of fact.

Given these circumstances, the mistrial demanded by defendant was in no event required.

People v. Davis, 473 N.Y.S.2d at 148.

When the omission of exculpatory facts from a defendant's previous statements is used for impeachment purposes on cross-examination, the defendant must be provided with certain protection. In *People v. Spinelli*, 214 A.D.2d 135, 631 N.Y.S.2d 863 (2d Dep't 1995), the court held:

The court is required, upon the defendant's request, to advise the jury that he was under no obligation to speak, and the defendant must be provided an opportunity to explain the omissions, either through his answers to the prosecutor's questions or through questioning by defense counsel on redirect examination.

People v. Spinelli, 631 N.Y.S.2d at 868. Finding that the trial court failed to provide such protection, the conviction was reversed.

Where the defendant remains silent in the presence of his attorney, who is providing inculpatory statements to the police, cautionary instructions are required to guard against the adverse inference that such silence constituted corroboration of his attorney's statements. In *People v. Cassas*, 84 N.Y.2d 718, 622 N.Y.S.2d 228 (1995), the defendant and his attorney visited the police precinct, at which the defendant's attorney stated, "I brought my client in to surrender. I believe he shot his wife. You'll find the gun in the room. It will have my client's prints on it." The Supreme Court denied the defendant's motion to suppress the statements, concluding that the attorney was acting as the defendant's agent at the time the statements were made and, thus, the statements were binding on the defendant. The Appellate Division affirmed.

The Court of Appeals reversed, finding, inter alia, that the trial court improperly refused to instruct the jury that no adverse inference could be drawn from the defendant's silence at the time that the statements were made. Although the Court of Appeals found that this case did not implicate the defendant's absolute right to remain silent in the face of accusatory statements or questions by law enforcement officials, the trial court was required to guard against the adverse inference that the defendant's silence might be used as evidence against the defendant.

The due process considerations articulated in *Conyers* are not applicable where the People seek to use the prior silence of a defense witness, who was not involved in the crime, to impeach that witness's testimony at trial. In *People v. Dawson*, 50 N.Y.2d 311, 428 N.Y.S.2d 914 (1980), the court explained that whereas a defendant's silence is not probative on the issue of innocence/guilt in light of the defendant's right to remain silent, there is nothing inherently improper about cross-examining a defense witness concerning her failure to come forward with exculpatory information at an earlier date. Assuming a proper foundation has been laid, the People may attempt to impeach the defense witness's credibility by cross-examining her about her prior failure to come forward. The proper foundation may be laid by demonstrating that the witness was aware of the nature of the charges pending against the defendant, had reason to recognize that she possessed exculpatory information; had a reasonable motive to provide such information; and was familiar with the means to make such information available to law enforcement authorities. *People v. Dawson*, 428 N.Y.S.2d at 921.

§ 25:9 Use of guilty plea as evidence

Research References

West's Key Number Digest, Criminal Law ⊗274(1)

In *Kercheval v. United States*, 274 U.S. 220, 47 S.Ct. 582 (1927), the Supreme Court ruled, based upon nonconstitutional grounds, that where a defendant is permitted to withdraw his guilty plea, it may not later be used against him at a subsequent criminal trial.

Two years prior to *Kercheval*, the New York Court of Appeals decided *People v. Steinmetz*, 240 N.Y. 411 (1925), concluding that evidence of the defendant's withdrawn guilty plea was admissible at a subsequent trial. It was not until 1961 that the New York Court of Appeals adopted the ruling of *Kercheval*, and held that a guilty plea that is later withdrawn "is out of the case forever and for all purposes." *People v. Spitaleri*, 9 N.Y.2d 168, 212 N.Y.S.2d 53 (1961).

In *People v. Moore*, 66 N.Y.2d 1028, 499 N.Y.S.2d 393 (1985), it was made clear that a guilty plea, once withdrawn, may not be used at a subsequent criminal proceeding for any purpose.

> This rule, which applies both to the fact of the plea and the contents of the plea allocution, prohibits the use of such material, either on the People's direct case (*People v. Spitaleri*, *supra*) or for impeachment purposes should the defendant take the stand.

People v. Moore, 499 N.Y.S.2d at 394 (citations omitted).

However, the *Moore* Court distinguished the facts from those found in *People v. Evans*, 58 N.Y.2d 14, 457 N.Y.S.2d 757 (1982), where it was held that the use of the preplea statement would not be unfair to the defendant given that the People bargained for such statement in their plea agreement. In *Evans*, the prosecutor agreed to a plea bargain, provided that the defendant gave a complete statement of the crimes committed and testified at the codefendant's trial. The defendant agreed, and acknowledged that the statements would be completely voluntary. Thereafter, the defendant, in the presence of his attorney, provided a complete account of the crimes for which he was charged. Later that day, the defendant pled guilty pursuant to the plea agreement. The conviction was later reversed for unrelated reasons, and the People sought to use the preplea statement at the defendant's subsequent trial. The Court of Appeals concluded:

> [N]either defendant nor his attorney expressed as a condition of the plea that statements made pursuant thereto could be withdrawn upon a successful appeal of his motion to suppress statements made at the time of his arrest. The record is entirely devoid of any such condition to the plea bargain. Defendant, therefore, by agreeing to enter an unconditional plea when it would have been a simple task to include such a limiting condition as part of that plea, assumed the risk that the challenged evidence might be used against him if he succeeded on his appeal to have his original station house confession suppressed.

People v. Evans, 457 N.Y.S.2d at 761.

Subsequently, in *People v. Moore*, the Court of Appeals explained the distinction as follows:

> *People v. Evans*, 58 N.Y.2d 14, 457 N.Y.S.2d 757, 444 N.E.2d 7, is not to the contrary. There, the defendant had been allowed to plead to a lesser charge on condition that he give the District Attorney a sworn statement describing the crime in detail and testify at his accomplice's trial. The conviction upon the guilty plea was reversed for unrelated reasons, and the People sought to use at trial the preplea statement and the defendant's subsequent testimony at his accomplice's trial. We held that under those circumstances allowing the use of the preplea statement and subsequent testimony would not be unfair to the defendant whereas precluding their use would be unfair to the People since that was the very material that the People had bargained for in the plea agreement. The same considerations do not apply to the plea itself or to admissions made during the plea allocution since the subsequent use of those statements should the plea later be withdrawn is not something the People have bargained for and would be decidedly unfair to the defendant.

People v. Moore, 499 N.Y.S.2d at 394.

The Court of Appeals extended the *Evans* rationale in *People v. Curdgel*, 83 N.Y.2d 862, 611 N.Y.S.2d 827 (1994). Here, in exchange for a sentence of 1 1/2 to three years' imprisonment, the defendant agreed to testify before a grand jury about the crime and "cooperate fully" in the prosecution of his accomplices. Soon after testifying before the grand jury, the defendant made public statements that he had lied to the grand jury, apologizing to his accomplices. As a result, the People refused to honor the plea agreement and the defendant was subsequently convicted.

On appeal, the defendant argued that he was entitled to specific performance of the plea agreement, and, in the alternative, that the People could not use his grand jury testimony against him at his own trial. The Appellate Division affirmed the conviction.

The Court of Appeals, after initially noting that the defendant was not entitled to specific performance, addressed the issue of whether the People were entitled to use the defendant's grand jury testimony against him at his own trial.

> We declined in *People v. Evans*, 58 N.Y.2d 14, 457 N.Y.S.2d 757, 444 N.E.2d 7, to extend the *Spitaleri* doctrine to preclude use of statements induced by a plea promise. As in defendant's case, the Evans defendant offered to testify against his accomplices with the assistance of counsel and set no conditions on the subsequent use of his testimony.

> Defendant's grand jury testimony, like the testimony of Evans defendant, was induced by the plea agreement. In addition, the People bargained for use of defendant's testimony in the prosecution of his accomplices. The People could not compel defendant's testimony in service of those prosecutions once they voided the agreement, but they could use the testimony he had already given in any manner they saw fit, as this was a counseled, foreseeable use of his testimony, and a benefit that should not be "retroactively vitiated" (*Evans*, 58 N.Y.2d at 24, 457 N.Y.S.2d 757, 444 N.E.2d 7).

People v. Curdgel, 611 N.Y.S.2d at 828–29.

In *People v. Latham*, 90 N.Y.2d 795, 666 N.Y.S.2d 557 (1997), the defendant pled guilty to attempted murder following a violent assault on his victim. As part of the plea allocution, the defendant made various factual admissions. The defendant's victim subsequently died as a result of her injuries, and the defendant was thereafter charged with murder. At the ensuing trial, the People introduced factual admissions the defendant made as a part of his attempted murder plea allocution.

On appeal, the Court of Appeals held that, "[b]ecause the plea is presumed voluntary, there was no bar to the People's use of the plea allocution at defendant's murder trial. The Fifth Amendment only precludes the use of statements obtained under legal compulsion." 90 N.Y.2d at 799, 666 N.Y.S.2d at 558–59. On the other hand, "[i]f defendant had successfully moved to withdraw or to set aside the plea to attempted murder as involuntary, the allocution could not have been used against defendant in the later trial." 90 N.Y.2d at 798–99, 666 N.Y.S.2d at 558.

§ 25:10   Use of defense attorney's statements against defendant

Research References
West's Key Number Digest, Criminal Law ⚷410

Statements made by a defense attorney concerning the circumstances surrounding the offense charged may be admissible against the defendant. In *People v. Rivera*, 58 A.D.2d 147, 396 N.Y.S.2d 26 (1st Dep't 1977), *aff'd on opinion below* 45 N.Y.2d 989, 413 N.Y.S.2d 146 (1978), the defense attorney submitted an affidavit specifically indicating that he had spoken to the defendant, who admitted that he had a marked $20 bill in his pocket, but had obtained it from giving change to a person who was involved in a drug transaction. At trial, the defendant denied being in possession of the $20 bill. The Appellate Division upheld the use of the attorney's affidavit for *impeachment* purposes, concluding that:

> [T]he attorney was plainly acting within the scope of his authority, and probably with express authority, in making and filing the affidavit.

People v. Rivera, 396 N.Y.S.2d at 28.

However, the use of an attorney's statement against the defendant in the prosecutor's *case-in-chief* was held to be error where there was no evidence that the defendant specifically waived the attorney-client privilege.

In *People v. Cassas*, 84 N.Y.2d 718, 622 N.Y.S.2d 228 (1995), the defense attorney, standing next to the defendant, entered the police precinct and stated, "I brought my client in to surrender. I believe he shot his wife. You'll find the gun in the room. It will have my client's prints on it." The trial court denied the defendant's motion to suppress the statement made by the attorney, concluding that the defense attorney, as the defendant's agent, was authorized to speak about the subject matter within the scope of the parties' agency relationship. The Appellate Division affirmed.

On appeal to the Court of Appeals, the Court distinguished the facts from *Rivera*.

> Here, the attorney's statement was oral and made out of court, to a third party. Moreover, there is nothing to suggest the attorney had authority to speak on behalf of his client. There was testimony from the attorney at the hearing that contradicted even the making of this statement. Further, the statement here was used in the prosec-

ution's case in chief against the defendant, as contrasted to *Rivera*, where the attorney explicitly stated that the defendant had informed him of the facts which were contained in the written affidavit, filed in open court, and used for impeachment purposes.

Significantly and key to the disposition of the instant case, the admissions would violate the attorney-client privilege because there is no evidentiary record support for a finding of waiver of the privilege by defendant.

The fact that the attorney is the agent of the client-principle, does not alone equate to a waiver of this privilege. The specific authorization must come from defendant-principle to attorney-agent to constitute a waiver of the attorney-client privilege. [The defense attorney] was not called as a witness at trial, and no evidence was presented as to the full and detailed scope of the parties' relationship in the relevant context of the issue at hand.

People v. Cassas, 622 N.Y.S.2d at 229–30 (citations omitted).

§ 25:11   Corroboration of admission or confession required

Research References
West's Key Number Digest, Criminal Law ☞406(5)

Frequently, police do not observe the defendant's operation of a motor vehicle and must rely on the defendant's admission of operation in order to sustain a conviction. The classic situation is that of the accident in which police have no direct observation of the operation of the vehicles or vehicle involved. CPL § 60.50 states:

A person may not be convicted of any offense solely upon evidence of a confession or admission made by him without additional proof that the offense charged has been committed.

Heretofore, police confronting an unwitnessed, one-car accident were hard-pressed to overcome the requirement of CPL § 60.50. The Court of Appeals has eased this burden by interpreting CPL § 60.50 to require only slight evidence that the crime alleged has occurred. The Court held:

The section does not require corroboration of confessions or admissions in every detail, but only "some proof, of whatever weight," that the offense charged has in fact been committed by someone . . . Its purpose is to avoid the possibility that a crime may be confessed when, in fact, no crime has been committed. The requirements of the rule are not rigorous and sufficient corroboration exists when the confession is "supported" by independent evidence of the corpus delicti . . . . The necessary additional evidence may be found in the presence of defendant at the scene of the crime, his guilty appearance afterwards, or other circumstances supporting an inference of guilt.

People v. Booden, 69 N.Y.2d 185, 513 N.Y.S.2d 87, 89 (1987) (citations omitted).

Here, the Court found sufficient corroborative evidence in the following facts: (1) the vehicle was found in a ditch facing in the wrong direction; (2) the pavement of the highway was dry, negating any suggestion of an accidental skid; (3) the defendant and his companions were standing next to the vehicle when the investigating officer arrived, and (4) the vehicle was registered to the defendant's father.

Citing *Booden*, the Appellate Division, Fourth Department, has held that the defendant's admissions were deemed corroborated by the fact that he was observed walking unsteadily in the roadway approximately 200 feet away from his automobile which had been involved in an accident. Additionally, there was a single trail of footprints leading from the car to the place where the defendant was observed walking, his hands were bloodied, and he exhibited the classic signs of intoxication. *People v. Hennigan*, 135 A.D.2d 1082, 523 N.Y.S.2d 302 (4th Dep't 1987).

In *People v. Cook*, 191 A.D.2d 993, 595 N.Y.S.2d 163 (4th Dep't 1993), the Court held that the defendant's DWI admissions were sufficiently corroborated by evidence that: (1) his car had struck guardrails on both sides of the roadway before coming to rest against one of them; (2) the defendant was the only person in the car at the time of the accident; (3) he admitted having been in an accident and having had six or seven beers earlier that evening; (4) he exhibited all the classic signs of intoxication, and (5) he failed a field sobriety test that a deputy administered.

However, in *People v. Kocowitz*, N.Y.L.J., 3/19/93, p. 23 (Kings Co. Crim. Ct.), the Court dismissed a DWI charge where the People's original and first superseding informations were devoid of any indicia of corroboration, and a second superseding information was untimely filed. *See also People v. Green*, N.Y.L.J., 8/18/94, p. 26, Col. 1 (Kings Co. Crim. Ct.); § 2:4 *supra*.

§ 25:12   Applicability of CPL § 60.50 to misdemeanor informations

Research References

West's Key Number Digest, Criminal Law ⚖406(5)

In *People v. Suber*, 19 N.Y.3d 247, 946 N.Y.S.2d 552, 969 N.E.2d 770 (2012), the Court of Appeals held that the "confession corroboration rule" of CPL § 60.50 is inapplicable to misdemeanor informations. In light of this holding, cases such as *People v. Miedema*, 24 Misc. 3d 132(A), 899 N.Y.S.2d 62 (App. Term, 9th &

10th Jud. Dist. 2009), *People v. Morales*, 35 Misc. 3d 558, 939 N.Y.S.2d 824 (N.Y. City Crim. Ct. 2012), *People v. Walker*, 21 Misc. 3d 748, 865 N.Y.S.2d 530 (N.Y. City Crim. Ct. 2008), *People v. Pappas*, 163 Misc. 2d 1029, 623 N.Y.S.2d 83 (N.Y. City Crim. Ct. 1994), *People v. Mauro*, 147 Misc. 2d 381, 555 N.Y.S.2d 533 (N.Y. City Crim. Ct. 1990), *People v. Kaminiski*, 143 Misc. 2d 1089, 542 N.Y.S.2d 923 (N.Y. City Crim. Ct. 1989), and *People v. Alvarez*, 141 Misc. 2d 686, 534 N.Y.S.2d 90 (N.Y. City Crim. Ct. 1988), should no longer be followed.

§ 25:13 Impeachment of own witness's statement

Research References
West's Key Number Digest, Criminal Law ⬛321

CPL § 60.35 provides:

1. When, upon examination by the party who called him, a witness in a criminal proceeding gives testimony upon a material issue of the case which tends to disprove the position of such party, such party may introduce evidence that such witness has previously made either a written statement signed by him or an oral statement under oath contradictory to such testimony.

Notably, the prior contradictory statement may be introduced only for the purpose of impeachment, and not as evidence in chief.

Before one may impeach his/her own witness, the witness must give testimony upon a material issue which "tends to disprove" the position of such party. In *People v. Andre*, 185 A.D.2d 276, 585 N.Y.S.2d 792 (2d Dep't 1992), the defendant was being retried for murder and criminal possession of a weapon. At the first trial, the People's witness implicated the defendant as the shooter. On retrial, the witness testified that he did not hear the argument or witness the shooting. The trial court, over objection, permitted the People to impeach the witness by asking him in detail about his testimony at the first trial.

Because the witness's testimony did not "affirmatively damage" the People's case, the Second Department concluded that it was error to permit the People to impeach their own witness.

"The testimony sought to be impeached must, however, 'affirmatively damage' the People's position, and may not simply constitute a mere failure to recollect" (*People v. Comer*, 146 A.D.2d 794, 795, 537 N.Y.S.2d 272, quoting *People v. Magee*, 128 A.D.2d 811, 513 N.Y.S.2d 514; *see also, People v. Fitzpatrick*, 40 N.Y.2d 44, 386 N.Y.S.2d 28, 351 N.E.2d 675). In the instant case, the witness's testimony did not "affirmatively damage" the People's case; he never specifically denied that the defendant was involved in the shooting or claimed that the defendant was not present during the incident (*cf.*, *People v. Broomfield*, 163 A.D.2d 403, 558 N.Y.S.2d 126; *People v. Mercado*, 162 A.D.2d 722, 557 N.Y.S.2d 123). Rather, he merely testified that he did not witness the shooting or argument. Accordingly, the court should not have permitted the People to impeach this witness by his prior trial testimony (*see*, *People v. Rios*, 166 A.D.2d 616, 560 N.Y.S.2d 901; *People v. Comer*, *supra*; *People v. Smith*, 104 A.D.2d 160, 481 N.Y.S.2d 879; *People v. Dann*, 100 A.D.2d 909, 912, 474 N.Y.S.2d 566).

People v. Andre, 585 N.Y.S.2d at 793.

CPL § 60.35(2) requires the court to instruct the jury that the statement is being introduced to impeach the testimony of the witness, and not as evidence. In *People v. Patterson*, 203 A.D.2d 597, 611 N.Y.S.2d 217 (2d Dep't 1994), the Second Department held that the trial court's failure to provide such limiting instruction was prejudicial error.

§ 25:14 Prior inconsistent statements used to impeach have no independent evidentiary value

Research References

West's Key Number Digest, Criminal Law ⊸412(4)

In *People v. Hall*, 208 A.D.2d 1044, 617 N.Y.S.2d 579 (3d Dep't 1994), a witness, who had given a statement to the police, subsequently provided inconsistent testimony at trial. During summation, the prosecutor argued that the jury could believe the defendant's trial testimony or the statements the witness provided to the police. The Third Department ruled that it was improper for the prosecutor to instruct the jury that they could consider the witness's prior statement as evidence.

Prior inconsistent statements used for purposes of testimonial impeachment have no substantial or independent evidentiary value (*see People v. Freeman*, 9 N.Y.2d 600, 605, 217 N.Y.S.2d 5, 176 N.E.2d 39; *People v. Blanchard*, 177 A.D.2d 854, 856, 577 N.Y.S.2d 322, lv. den. 79 N.Y.2d 918, 582 N.Y.S.2d 78, 590 N.E.2d 1206), and it was error for the prosecutor to ask the jury to choose between [the witness'] out of court statement and her trial testimony.

People v. Hall, 617 N.Y.S.2d at 581.

§ 25:15 Unsigned statement not admissible in evidence

In *People v. Lee*, 159 A.D.2d 238, 552 N.Y.S.2d 218 (1st Dep't 1990), following the defendant's arrest, the police officer questioned the defendant at the precinct, and wrote down the conversation on a piece of paper, which was later transposed into his memo book. The photocopies of these papers were introduced into evidence at trial. The Appellate Court ruled:

It was error to allow a purported confession into evidence where it is handwritten by a law enforcement official, never signed or orally acknowledged by the defendant nor read to or by him (*People v. Mc-Cargo*, 144 A.D.2d 496, 534 N.Y.S.2d 195).

As pertinent here, although the statement may be used to refresh the recollection of the witness as to any admission made by defendant, it may not be admitted into evidence (*People v. Duffy*, 23 A.D.2d 699, 258 N.Y.S.2d 209).

People v. Lee, 552 N.Y.S.2d at 219. *See also, People v. Coleman*, 199 A.D.2d 330, 605 N.Y.S.2d 105 (2d Dep't 1993).

§ 25:16   Notarized statement qualifies as oath

Written notarized statements by the defendant which include the statement that the defendant read the statements and that they are "true, factual and voluntarily given," were considered statements under oath, notwithstanding the fact that the statement did not indicate whether the defendant had been sworn. *See Collins v. AA Trucking Renting Corp.*, 209 A.D.2d 363, 618 N.Y.S.2d 801 (1st Dep't 1994).

§ 25:17   Third-party's presence waives attorney-client privilege

Research References

West's Key Number Digest, Witnesses ⊙⇒206

In *People v. Osorio*, 75 N.Y.2d 80, 550 N.Y.S.2d 612 (1989), the Court of Appeals held that the presence of a codefendant, acting as an interpreter, negated any claim to attorney-client privilege. Here, the defendant, Osorio, had acted as an interpreter in regard to a conversation had between his codefendant, Pena, and Pena's attorney. At trial, Pena's counsel objected to defendant Osorio's attempt to testify in regard to statements made by Pena during that conference. The trial court sustained this objection and defendant Osorio was subsequently convicted.

On appeal, the Court of Appeals reversed the conviction, holding that the trial court should not have precluded Osorio from testifying on the ground of attorney-client privilege.

Generally, communications made between a defendant and counsel in the known presence of a third party are not privileged . . . An exception exists for statements made by a client to the attorney's employees or in their presence because clients have a reasonable expectation that such statements will be used solely for their benefit and remain confidential . . . Similarly, communications made to counsel through a hired interpreter, or one serving as an agent of either attorney or client to facilitate communication, generally will be privileged . . .

The scope of the privilege is not defined by the third parties' employment or function, however, it depends on whether the client had a reasonable expectation of confidentiality under the circumstances . . .

In this case neither Pena nor the People established that defendant was an agent of Pena or his counsel, or that the relationship between the codefendants was otherwise such that Pena had a reasonable expectation that statements made in defendant's presence would remain confidential . . . Any inference that Pena expected his remarks to be confidential is overcome by the fact that defendant was not planning a common defense with Pena and, therefore, had an adversarial relationship to him.

It was Pena's responsibility to establish facts sufficient to support the privilege and he failed to do so. Accordingly, the claim of privilege should not have been sustained and defendant should have been permitted to disclose Pena's statements if the evidence was otherwise admissible.

People v. Osorio, 550 N.Y.S.2d at 614–15 (citations omitted).

§ 25:18   Right of defendant to have both inculpatory and exculpatory statements presented to jury

Research References

West's Key Number Digest, Criminal Law ⊙396(2)

Where part of a defendant's statement has been received into evidence, the defendant may introduce any other part of the statement made by him which tends to modify or clarify the original statement. In *People v. Rodriguez*, 188 A.D.2d 566, 591 N.Y.S.2d 463 (2d Dep't 1992), the investigating officer testified regarding inculpatory statements made by the defendant. The court denied defense counsel's request to introduce a videotape containing the defendant's exculpatory statements which were made at or about the same time as the inculpatory statements. The Appellate Court reversed, holding that the defendant was entitled to have "the inculpatory and exculpatory portions of a statement introduced into evidence."

Where part of a conversation or writing has been received into evidence as an admission, the party against whom it is offered has the right to prove any other statement made by him at the same time which tends to modify or destroy the effect of the admission.

People v. Rodriguez, 591 N.Y.S.2d at 464. The court's denial of the introduction of the videotape deprived the defendant of a fair trial.

The inculpatory and the exculpatory statements must have been made at or about the same time period. In *People v. Armstrong*,

210 A.D.2d 182, 621 N.Y.S.2d 21 (1st Dep't 1994), the court allowed the introduction of inculpatory statements made by the
defendant, but denied the defendant the opportunity to introduce
exculpatory statements which were made approximately 50
minutes after the inculpatory statements had been made. The
court distinguished *Rodriguez*, finding that *Rodriguez* concerned
a relatively brief interval between the inculpatory statement and
the exculpatory videotaped statement. Here, there was no such
"continuous interrogation."

In *People v. Anderson*, 256 A.D.2d 413, 682 N.Y.S.2d 231 (2d
Dep't 1998), the Appellate Division, Second Department, reversed
the defendant's conviction where:

> At trial, the prosecutor brought out only the inculpatory portion of
> the [defendant's] statement and succeeded in blocking the defen-
> dant's attempt to bring out the remaining, exculpatory portion. The
> court erred in allowing the prosecution to do so.

> During summations, the prosecutor exploited the ruling and capital-
> ized upon it by arguing improperly to the jury . . . Because the
> prosecutor misled the jury by pointing to the absence of evidence
> that he knew existed, reversal is warranted.

256 A.D.2d at __, 682 N.Y.S.2d at 231–32 (citations omitted).

§ 25:19 Court of Appeals holds defendant's surrender of illegally possessed handgun in compliance with court order to be privileged under Fifth Amendment

Research References

West's Key Number Digest, Criminal Law ⊙393(1)

In *People v. Havrish*, 8 N.Y.3d 389, 834 N.Y.S.2d 681 (2007),
the defendant was ordered by the Delhi Town Court, in connection with various charges pending against him, to " 'surrender
any and all firearms owned or possessed.' " 8 N.Y.3d at 391, 834
N.Y.S.2d at 683. When the defendant, in complying with this order, led the police to, an unlicensed handgun, he was charged
with criminal possession of a weapon in the fourth degree.

Holding that this scenario implicated the Fifth Amendment—
not merely the Fourth Amendment (as argued by the People)—
the Court of Appeals applied the two-prong "act of production"
test set forth by the Supreme Court in Fisher v. United States,
425 U.S. 391, 96 S.Ct. 1569 (1976). In this regard, the Court
found that the defendant's compelled act of production was both
(a) sufficiently testimonial, and (b) incriminating.

Finding both prongs of the "act of production" doctrine to have
been satisfied, the Court held that the "defendant's surrender of

the unlicensed handgun was privileged under the Fifth Amendment and suppression of the evidence was therefore warranted in the weapon possession prosecution." 8 N.Y.3d at 397, 834 N.Y.S.2d at 687.

§ 25:20   Use of statements on booking video

It is increasingly common for booking videos to exist which record lengthy conversations between the police and an arrestee. Such videos are particularly important in DWI cases, as they can either bolster or undermine a police officer's claims that the defendant had impaired speech and/or impaired motor coordination. Since a wide variety of conversations can be captured on such videos, including conversations as to prior DWI arrests, invocation of the right to counsel, etc., it is important that defense counsel make a motion for redaction of inadmissible material.

In *People v. Johnson*, 70 A.D.3d 1188, 896 N.Y.S.2d 199 (3d Dep't 2010), the Appellate Division, Third Department, reversed the defendant's DWI conviction and granted him a new trial—even though no objection had been made—where County Court improperly allowed a portion of the defendant's booking video into evidence. Specifically:

> "It is axiomatic that a defendant's invocation of his [or her] right to counsel during custodial interrogation may not be used against him [or her] by the People as part of their case-in-chief." Here, County Court allowed the People to enter into evidence as part of their direct case a videotape of the booking process pertaining to defendant. At the time of the events portrayed in that videotape, defendant was clearly in custody, having been arrested and given his *Miranda* and DWI warnings. On the videotape, defendant invoked both his right to remain silent and his right to counsel. While County Court gave appropriate curative instructions with respect to defendant's invocation of his right to remain silent, it gave no such instruction as to the invocation of his right to counsel. Under the circumstances here, we are unable to conclude "that there is no reasonable possibility that the evidence of defendant's invocation of his right to counsel contributed to his conviction." Moreover, even though defendant did not object to the admission of the videotape, "we cannot ignore the potential for prejudice."

70 A.D.3d at _, 896 N.Y.S.2d at 202-03 (citations omitted).

In *People v. Anderson*, 150 Misc. 2d 339, 568 N.Y.S.2d 306 (Nassau Co. Dist. Ct. 1991), the Court suppressed all of the statements on the defendant's booking video on the ground that the police violated the defendant's right to counsel. However, the Court ruled that "since defendant's movements are not considered to be testimonial, the video portion of the tape shall not be suppressed." *Id.* at __, 568 N.Y.S.2d at 309.

In *People v. Higgins*, 124 A.D.3d 929, —, 1 N.Y.S.3d 424, 428-30 (3d Dep't 2015), the Appellate Division, Third Department, addressed this issue with substantially more specificity:

The People further contend that County Court erred in suppressing all of defendant's statements during the booking process as well as the video depicting them. The court found that defendant had invoked his right to counsel when he stated at the outset of the booking process—specifically at 3:23 a.m.—that he wanted to speak to his attorney before he would sign anything. A defendant's request for an attorney will invoke his or her indelible right to counsel if the request is unequivocal, an inquiry which "is a mixed question of law and fact that must be determined with reference to the circumstances surrounding the request including the defendant's demeanor, manner of expression and the particular words found to have been used by the defendant." Generally, remarks that are subject to numerous objective interpretations or a defendant's mere "suggestion that counsel might be desired . . . will not suffice." Here, considering the circumstances existing at the time of the statement, defendant's request to speak to his attorney *before signing anything* was prospective, as he had not been asked to sign anything. An objective officer could interpret the statement as merely a forewarning of a possible, contingent desire to confer with counsel rather than an unequivocal statement of defendant's present desire to do so. Accordingly, defendant's statement at 3:23 a.m. did not suffice to invoke his right to counsel.

However, defendant's statement at 3:41 a.m., requesting that he be allowed to call his attorney, was sufficiently unequivocal to invoke his right to counsel. The officers agreed to allow defendant to contact his attorney, but never provided him with the means to do so. Thus, any testimonial statements that were elicited from defendant after this point were properly subject to suppression. The People argue, however, that County Court's order was not limited to testimonial statements, but also improperly suppressed defendant's responses to pedigree questions, spontaneous declarations, physical appearance and refusal to submit to chemical testing.

Initially, although a defendant's responses to routine booking questions that are "reasonably related to . . . administrative concerns" are not subject to suppression, neither the parties' arguments nor the video discloses any such pedigree questions or responses following defendant's valid invocation of his right to counsel at 3:41 a.m. As for spontaneous declarations, it is established law that, even after the right to counsel has attached, a defendant's statements are not subject to suppression if they were "not the result of inducement, provocation, encouragement or acquiescence, no matter how subtly employed." It is well established that the police bear no obligation "to silence a chatterbox." "The test is not whether defendant, through hindsight, claims that the police intended to provoke an incriminating response; rather, County Court, using an objective standard, must determine whether defendant's statement can be said to have been triggered by police conduct that should reasonably have been anticipated to evoke a statement from defendant."

With a few exceptions, the video reveals that defendant's statements in the period preceding the reading of his *Miranda* rights were made without any triggering words or conduct by the police. As the officers played no role in soliciting them, these statements constitute spontaneous declarations and should not have been subject to suppression. However, at three points following defendant's successful invocation of his right to counsel, officers asked him questions that should reasonably have been anticipated to elicit responses. The first such exchange occurred between 03:47:49 a.m. and 03:48:10 a.m., when defendant responded after an officer asked him what he thought would occur as a result of refusing a chemical test. The second occurred between 03:50:01 a.m. and 03:50:09 a.m., when defendant confirmed his last drinking location in response to a question by one of the officers. The third occurred between 04:01:05 a.m. and 04:06:23 a.m., when an officer asked defendant several questions about chemical testing and the events of the evening. Defendant's responses to these inquiries cannot be said to be spontaneous. Thus, his statements during these three time periods and the corresponding portions of the video were properly suppressed.

As to portions of the video in which defendant was not speaking, evidence obtained from a defendant following invocation of the right to counsel is subject to suppression where it constitutes "a communicative act that disclose[s] the contents of defendant's mind." Generally, a defendant's physical characteristics and appearance are not considered to be communicative in nature. Here, portions of the video in which defendant is silent show only his physical condition and appearance and do not disclose any communicative statements made after he had invoked his right to counsel. Whether any of these video segments may ultimately be deemed admissible at trial depends on other considerations not presented here, but there is no basis for their suppression as communicative statements.

Finally, as to defendant's refusals to submit to chemical tests, we note the legal distinction between admitting evidence of the test refusals and admitting defendant's accompanying statements and/or the video depictions of such statements. An individual suspected of driving while intoxicated is allowed a limited right to counsel for the purpose of deciding whether to submit to a chemical test. To invoke this limited right, a suspect must make "a specific request for an attorney vis-à-vis this decision." When defendant requested counsel at 3:41 a.m., he had been read two chemical test warnings and had refused to submit both times. The third warning and refusal followed defendant's request for counsel. Upon review, and considering both the timing and the phrasing of defendant's request, it does not appear that he was seeking advice relative to the testing, but, instead, was asserting his right to counsel in a broad and general manner. As defendant's invocation of his right to counsel lacked the requisite specificity, the fact that he refused to submit to chemical testing on each occasion is admissible. However, this rule does not alter the protections afforded by law relative to his statements or the video depiction of same, as set forth above, after he invoked his right to counsel.

(Citations omitted).

In *People v. Tomlin*, 130 A.D.3d 1455, —, 12 N.Y.S.3d 740, 742 (4th Dep't 2015), the Appellate Division, Fourth Department, held as follows:

Defendant further contends that the court erred in permitting the prosecutor to play portions of the booking video for the jury because the booking video was not included in the People's CPL 710.30 notice. We reject that contention, inasmuch as the portions of the booking video played for the jury showed defendant's physical condition, and they contained questions and answers about defendant's pedigree information as well as spontaneous statements by defendant not in response to any questions or interrogation.

§ 25:21 Prosecutor's improper implication that defendant fabricated his trial testimony requires reversal

In *People v. Vielman*, 31 A.D.3d 674, 818 N.Y.S.2d 291 (2d Dep't 2006), the Appellate Division, Second Department, reversed the defendant's convictions of burglary and bail jumping where the prosecutor's summation improperly implied that the defendant had fabricated his trial testimony. Specifically:

When the defendant was arrested for burglary, he made an exculpatory statement to the police. At the suppression hearing, he testified in conformity with that statement and, at trial, his testimony was consistent with his earlier accounts. Nevertheless, the prosecutor, in summation, implied that he had fabricated his trial testimony after hearing the prosecution witnesses testify when [s]he stated: "[the defendant has] been able to sit here and listen to everybody else testify, right? So that he could tell you his story to fit what's already in evidence. No other person has been able to do that. No other person is allowed to do something like that."

The prosecutor knew that her argument here rested on a false premise. Her argument was a blatant attempt to mislead the jury, and thus violated her responsibilities and the trust placed in her as a prosecutor.

818 N.Y.S.2d at 292.

§ 25:22 Use of statement made to EMT

In *People v. Jones*, 169 A.D.2d 986, —, 565 N.Y.S.2d 262, 264-65 (3d Dep't 1991), the Appellate Division, Third Department, held that statements made by the defendant to an ambulance worker were not suppressible. In so holding, the Court reasoned that:

[D]efendant made statements to an ambulance worker while being treated. Defendant contends that the statements are inadmissible in that they were never offered at the *Huntley* hearing. We disagree. The District Attorney was under no obligation to inform defendant about admissions made to a private person who is not a police agent. A private person may acquire information to be used in a criminal investigation even where police would be constitutionally restrained. Further, there is no evidence in the record from which it could be inferred that the ambulance worker was a police agent. The statements were voluntarily made and were thus admissible.

565 N.Y.S.2d 262, 264-65 (citations omitted).

Similarly, in *People v. Esmail*, 260 A.D.2d 396, ___, 688 N.Y.S.2d 186, 188 (2d Dep't 1999), the Appellate Division, Second Department, held that:

Contrary to the defendant's contention, the testimony at the hearing did not establish that the emergency medical service workers were acting as agents of the police. Accordingly, suppression of the defendant's statement to the EMS workers was properly denied.

(Citations omitted).

§ 25:23   Statements overheard by the police

Where the police do not elicit, but rather merely overhear, a conversation between the defendant and a third person such as an attorney or a nurse, such statements are admissible (as long as the police acted in good faith). The Court of Appeals addressed this issue in *People v. Harris*, 57 N.Y.2d 335, 342-43, 456 N.Y.S.2d 694, 696-97, 442 N.E.2d 1205, 8 Media L. Rep. (BNA) 2532 (1982):

[S]tatements made by a defendant who has invoked the right to counsel may nevertheless be admissible at trial if they were made spontaneously. In order for such statements to be characterized as spontaneous, it must "be shown that they were in no way the product of an 'interrogation environment', the result of 'express questioning or its functional equivalent.' "

On the record before us, it is clear that no questioning of Mrs. Harris occurred after she invoked her right to counsel. The statement was neither induced, provoked nor encouraged by the actions of the police officers, who had been entirely solicitous of Mrs. Harris's request to speak with a lawyer and had scrupulously honored her rights in this regard. There is nothing in the record to indicate that Officer Tamilio endeavored, by subtle maneuvering or otherwise, to overhear Mrs. Harris's conversation with her attorney. Indeed, the record reflects that this officer, having assisted Mrs. Harris to the telephone, was backing out of the room when he inadvertently overheard the statement. It appears, therefore, that the officer had no opportunity to remove himself from earshot before Mrs. Harris made the damaging statement. Thus, we are not presented with a situation in which the police have failed to respect a defendant's right to consult privately with an attorney. Under the circumstances of this case, we conclude that no violation of defendant's right to counsel occurred.

Although we hold today that a statement properly characterized as spontaneous is no less so simply because it was made to an attorney, a further aspect of the admissibility of such statements should be considered. Given that the communication received in evidence was made to an attorney, the attorney-client privilege is implicated, in addition to the right to counsel. This privilege protects those communications made by a defendant to an attorney that are intended to be confidential. It cannot be said, on the facts of this case, that Mrs. Harris, in speaking over the telephone to a lawyer in the known presence of both a police officer and the house manager's husband, intended this communication to be confidential. Generally, communications made in the presence of third parties, whose presence is known to the defendant, are not privileged from disclosure. We see no reason to depart from this general rule simply because one of those parties present was a police officer, who, as has been noted, did nothing to purposely overhear the conversation or conceal his presence from defendant. Thus, we conclude that defendant's attorney-client privilege was not violated by the officer's testimony regarding this communication and that the testimony was properly admitted by the trial court.

(Citations and footnotes omitted). *See also People v. Jones*, 169 A.D.2d 986, __, 565 N.Y.S.2d 262, 265 (3d Dep't 1991) ("The record indicates that the officer was standing by while defendant was being treated and overheard defendant's unsolicited and incriminatory statement made to the nurse. Such statement is admissible"); *People v. Cascio*, 79 A.D.3d 1809, __, 914 N.Y.S.2d 490, 492 (4th Dep't 2010), leave to appeal denied, 16 N.Y.3d 893, 926 N.Y.S.2d 29, 949 N.E.2d 977 (2011); *People v. Bolarinwa*, 258 A.D.2d 827, __, 687 N.Y.S.2d 442, 446 (3d Dep't 1999); *People v. Robertson*, 149 A.D.2d 442, __, 539 N.Y.S.2d 785, 786 (2d Dep't 1989); *People v. Borcsok*, 107 A.D.2d 42, __, 485 N.Y.S.2d 766, 767-68 (2d Dep't 1985). *Cf. People v. Grimaldi*, 52 N.Y.2d 611, 617, 439 N.Y.S.2d 833, 836, 422 N.E.2d 493 (1981) ("In the present circumstances, the statements overheard by the officer were indeed the result of the illegal questioning"); *People v. Jackson*, 202 A.D.2d 689, __, 609 N.Y.S.2d 320, 321-22 (2d Dep't 1994) (defendant's statements suppressed where police intentionally overheard and tape recorded them); *People v. Moss*, 179 A.D.2d 271, __, 583 N.Y.S.2d 699, 700 (4th Dep't 1992) ("Defendant is entitled to a new trial, however, because the court erred in denying the motion to suppress the telephone conversation between defendant and his brother, which was surreptitiously overheard by a police officer while defendant was being treated in the hospital emergency room"); *People v. Sanders*, 169 Misc. 2d 813, __-__, 646 N.Y.S.2d 955, 958-61 (Bronx Co. Sup. Ct. 1996).

In *People v. Aponte*, 151 Misc. 2d 981, ___, 574 N.Y.S.2d 131, 131 (N.Y. City Crim. Ct. 1991), the Court held as follows:

It is a standard part of the booking procedure for the New York City police to arrange for an arrestee to make a phone call. It is apparently a further part of standard police procedure to monitor that phone call for security reasons. Our Court of Appeals has repeatedly expressed "special solicitude" for the right to counsel and a defendant's right against self-incrimination as contained in § 6 of Article 1 of the New York Constitution. Consequently, this Court holds that when a police officer arranges a phone call for a defendant who has previously invoked his right to counsel and to remain silent, the police must inform the defendant that his phone call will be monitored and any statement he makes can be used against him. In the absence of such warnings, any statement overheard by routine police monitoring must be suppressed.

(Citations omitted).

Chapter 26

CPL § 710.30 Notice Issues

KeyCite®: Cases and other legal materials listed in KeyCite Scope can be researched through the KeyCite service on Westlaw®. Use KeyCite to check citations for form, parallel references, prior and later history, and comprehensive citator information, including citations to other decisions and secondary materials.

---

§ 26:1   In general

CPL § 710.30 provides, with certain exceptions, that whenever the People intend to offer evidence at trial of a statement made by the defendant to a public servant, they must, within 15 days after arraignment, serve the defendant with notice of such intent, specifying the statement(s) intended to be offered. For purposes of this chapter, such notice is referred to as "710.30 notice."

CPL § 710.30 also requires that the People provide 710.30 notice of an intent to offer testimony at trial by a witness who has previously identified the defendant in connection with the offense (*e.g.*, in a police-arranged identification procedure). This second type of 710.30 notice is rarely pertinent in DWI cases. Accordingly, this chapter focuses on statements made by the defendant to a public servant.

§ 26:2   CPL § 710.30—The statute

CPL § 710.30 provides, in full, as follows:

§ 710.30. Motion to suppress evidence; notice to defendant of intention to offer evidence

1. Whenever the people intend to offer at a trial (a) evidence of a statement made by a defendant to a public servant, which statement if involuntarily made would render the evidence thereof suppressible upon motion pursuant to [CPL § 710.20(3)], or (b) testimony regarding an observation of the defendant either at the time or place of the commission of the offense or upon some other occasion relevant to the case, to be given by a witness who has previously identified him as such, they must serve upon the defendant a notice of such intention, specifying the evidence intended to be offered.

2. Such notice must be served within [15] days after arraignment and before trial, and upon such service the defendant must be accorded reasonable opportunity to move before trial, pursuant to [CPL § 710.40(1)], to suppress the specified evidence. For good cause shown, however, the court may permit the people to serve such notice, thereafter and in such case it must accord the defendant reasonable opportunity thereafter to make a suppression motion.

3. In the absence of service of notice upon a defendant as prescribed in this section, no evidence of a kind specified in subdivision one may be received against him upon trial unless he has, despite the lack of such notice, moved to suppress such evidence and such motion has been denied and the evidence thereby rendered admissible as prescribed in [CPL § 710.70(2)].

§ 26:3   History and purpose of CPL § 710.30

With respect to CPL § 710.30(1)(a) (*i.e.*, statements of the defendant to a public servant):

> [T]he purpose of CPL 710.30 is to inform a defendant that the People intend to offer evidence of a statement to a public officer at trial so that a timely motion to suppress the evidence may be made. The defendant may challenge the statement upon three grounds: that it was (1) elicited by threat of physical force or other improper conduct or undue pressure; (2) induced by a promise or statement made to defendant which created a substantial risk of false self-incrimination; or (3) obtained in violation of defendant's constitutional rights (*see*, CPL 60.45[2]).

People v. Rodney, 85 N.Y.2d 289, 291–92, 624 N.Y.S.2d 95, 97, 648 N.E.2d 471 (1995) (citations omitted). *See also People v. Greer*, 42 N.Y.2d 170, 178, 397 N.Y.S.2d 613, 619, 366 N.E.2d 273 (1977) ("The obvious purpose of the statute is to afford a defendant adequate time in preparing his case in respect to the voluntariness of a confession or admission."). *See generally People v. O'Doherty*,

70 N.Y.2d 479, 484, 522 N.Y.S.2d 498, 501, 517 N.E.2d 213 (1987) ("CPL 710.30, insofar as it concerns confessions or admissions by a defendant, finds its origins in *Jackson v. Denno*, 378 U.S. 368, 84 S.Ct. 1774, 12 L.Ed.2d 908, in which the United States Supreme Court held that [confessions or admissions by a defendant] may not be considered by the jury which is to adjudicate guilt or innocence unless there has first been a determination by a separate fact finder, following an evidentiary hearing, that such statements were made voluntarily.").

The Court of Appeals has also stated that:

The stated preference for pretrial notice of the People's intention to use a defendant's statements as evidence against him implements the purpose of the statute. That purpose, it has been repeatedly said, is to give a defendant adequate time to prepare his case for questioning the voluntariness of a confession or an admission. The statutory procedure permits an orderly hearing and determination of the issue of the fact and voluntariness of statements before trial, thereby preventing the interruption of trial to challenge initially the admission into evidence of the statements.

Moreover, pretrial notice affords defense counsel an opportunity, prior to trial, to investigate the circumstances of the alleged fact and voluntariness of the purported statements and prepare the defense accordingly. Although a defendant may often be aware of prior statements or even the likelihood that the prosecution will offer his prior statements as evidence against him at trial, there is a reasonable probability of his unawareness in some instances, or even a greater probability of his counsel's unawareness. Thus, independent of considerations of challenging the voluntariness of his statements, considerations of fair play demand that a possibly unaware defendant be apprised before trial of any incriminating statements intended to be offered against him.

People v. Briggs, 38 N.Y.2d 319, 322–23, 379 N.Y.S.2d 779, 782, 342 N.E.2d 557 (1975) (citations omitted).

In *O'Doherty, supra*, the Court of Appeals addressed the purpose of the "15-day" and "good cause" requirements of the statute:

The 15-day rule was approved only five months after our decision in *Briggs*, but there is no hint of disapproval in the amendment or the relevant legislative history. More importantly, however, we believe that the goals of the statute would not be well served by the dilution or disregard of the good cause requirement.

Although CPL 710.30 retains as its central purpose that of providing a defendant with the opportunity to obtain a pretrial ruling on the admissibility of statements to be used against him, the 1976 amendment was designed to serve an ancillary goal—the orderly, swift and efficient determination of pretrial motions. The impetus for the amendment was the enactment of article 255 of the Criminal Procedure Law, the omnibus pretrial motion provisions which sought to impose order and speed on pretrial motion practice by requiring the defendant to make substantially all pretrial motions at one time, on one set of papers before one Judge, within 45 days after arraignment. Until the 1976 amendment, however, these goals were compromised by the prosecutor's ability under CPL 710.30 to serve a notice on defendant at any time before trial, which triggered the defendant's right to make an additional pretrial motion, requiring a hearing and resulting in additional delay. It was to alleviate this problem that the 1976 amendments to CPL 710.30, requiring notice to defendant within 15 days after arraignment, along with conforming changes to CPL 255.20 and CPL 700.70, were proposed.

Thus, not only considerations of fairness to the defendant, but also concerns for the efficient conduct of criminal prosecutions underlie the Legislature's directive. The exclusionary sanction for failure to comply contained in CPL 710.30(3) reflects a judgment that the loss of the use of the evidence is an acceptable price to pay to achieve the desired goals. Although the People complain that the price is too high and the requirements of the statute burdensome, we cannot dilute or disregard the requirements in an effort to avoid exacting the price without trespassing on the Legislature's domain and undermining the purposes of the statute.

70 N.Y.2d at 488–89, 522 N.Y.S.2d at 503–04 (citations omitted).

* * * * * * * * * *

With respect to CPL § 710.30(1)(b) (*i.e.*, witness identifications):

The Legislature enacted CPL 710.30 to give a defendant the opportunity, before trial, to test the admissibility of any identification testimony the People intend to offer. The main concern motivating the statute was the possibility, recognized in three Supreme Court decisions, that pretrial identification procedures could be so suggestive or misleading as to compromise a defendant's constitutional right to due process of law. The danger sought to be avoided is, and always has been, the risk of convicting the innocent through tainted identification procedures.

People v. Gee, 99 N.Y.2d 158, 161–62, 753 N.Y.S.2d 19, 21–22, 782 N.E.2d 1155 (2002) (citations and footnotes omitted). *See also People v. Laing*, 79 N.Y.2d 166, 170, 581 N.Y.S.2d 149, 150–51, 589 N.E.2d 372 (1992); *People v. Newball*, 76 N.Y.2d 587, 590–91, 561 N.Y.S.2d 898, 900, 563 N.E.2d 269 (1990) ("CPL 710.30 constitutes a legislative attempt to deal effectively with the reality that not all police-arranged identifications are free from unconstitutional taint. By requiring that notice be given, the statute acts to ensure that a defendant is given the opportunity, prior to trial, to test the reliability of the identification testimony that the People plan to offer against him.") (citation omitted); *People v. White*, 73 N.Y.2d 468, 474, 541 N.Y.S.2d 749, 752, 539 N.E.2d 577 (1989); *People v. Gissendanner*, 48 N.Y.2d 543, 552, 423 N.Y.S.2d 893, 899, 399 N.E.2d 924 (1979) ("The statute was apparently a legislative response to the problem of suggestive and misleading pretrial identification procedures treated by the Supreme Court in *Gilbert v. California, United States v. Wade*, and *Stovall v. Denno*. The focus of those decisions was on in-court identifications predicated on earlier police-arranged confrontations between a defendant and an eyewitness, typically involving the use of lineups, showups or photographs, for the purpose of establishing the identity of the criminal actor.") (citations omitted).

§ 26:4   CPL § 710.30 notice requirement is strictly construed

It has been repeatedly held that the CPL § 710.30 notice requirement is to be strictly construed. *See, e.g., People v. Showers*, 200 A.D.2d 864, __, 606 N.Y.S.2d 816, 817 (3d Dep't 1994); *People v. Phillips*, 183 A.D.2d 856, __, 584 N.Y.S.2d 83, 85 (2d Dep't 1992); *People v. Riley-James*, 168 A.D.2d 740, __, 563 N.Y.S.2d 894, 896 (3d Dep't 1990); *People v. Centeno*, 168 Misc. 2d 172, __, 637 N.Y.S.2d 254, 257 (N.Y. Co. Sup. Ct. 1995).

In this regard, in *People v. O'Doherty*, 70 N.Y.2d 479, 486, 522 N.Y.S.2d 498, 502, 517 N.E.2d 213 (1987), the Court of Appeals expressly rejected the People's claim that since the penalty for failure to comply with the 15-day rule of CPL § 710.30 is preclusion, the standard for making a showing of "good cause" for late notice should be relaxed. *See also People v. Briggs*, 38 N.Y.2d 319, 323–24, 379 N.Y.S.2d 779, 783, 342 N.E.2d 557 (1975) (absent a showing of "good cause" for late notice, "a failure to give the required notice before trial mandates exclusion of those statements. To hold otherwise would be to condone and encourage noncompliance in the prosecutor's office and to undermine the salutary purposes of the statute") (citations omitted).

§ 26:5   Failure to comply with CPL § 710.30 is not a trivial matter

The Court of Appeals has made clear that the failure of the People to comply with CPL § 710.30 is a not a trivial matter:

> The issue is not a trivial or merely technical one. Prior statements, especially oral ones, to a police officer, are accorded high credibility by fact finders, jury or Judges. Whether in fact they were made, whether they were voluntary, and the precise form which they took may be crucial to the determination of innocence or guilt. To deprive

defendants in criminal matters unnecessarily of an advance opportunity to investigate the facts and circumstances is neither fair nor conducive to establishing the truth through the adversary process with the assistance of counsel. A cavalier treatment of the statute's requirements frustrates its ends.

People v. Briggs, 38 N.Y.2d 319, 324, 379 N.Y.S.2d 779, 784, 342 N.E.2d 557 (1975).

§ 26:6   CPL § 710.30 only applies to evidence that the People intend to offer "at trial"

By its express terms, CPL § 710.30 only applies to evidence that the People intend to offer at trial. In *People v. Grajales*, 8 N.Y.3d 861, 832 N.Y.S.2d 466, 864 N.E.2d 596 (2007), the victim of a robbery identified the defendant both at an "on-the-street point-out" and at a station house photographic array. The People's 710.30 notice referenced the point-out identification, but did not reference the photographic array identification. The Court of Appeals held as follows:

> The People acknowledge that the customary and better practice is to give defendant notice of all prior police-arranged identifications made by a witness from whom they intend to elicit in-court identification testimony. CPL 710.30(1)(b), however, only mandates preclusion in the absence of timely notice "specifying" the pretrial identification evidence "intended to be offered" at trial. Because evidence of a witness's pretrial photographic identification of an accused is not admissible in the prosecution's case-in-chief, the People could not intend to offer it at trial, and therefore the CPL 710.30(1)(b) notice in this case was adequate.

> While the dissent puts forward sound policy reasons to support notice of photographic arrays, we are unwilling to read the statute more expansively than the Legislature has chosen to write it, especially when the remedy is preclusion.

8 N.Y.3d at 862, 832 N.Y.S.2d at 467 (citations omitted). *See also People v. Jones*, 10 Misc. 3d 413, __, 805 N.Y.S.2d 807, 809 (Dutchess Co. Ct. 2005), aff'd, 50 A.D.3d 1058, 856 N.Y.S.2d 225 (2d Dep't 2008) (CPL § 710.30 inapplicable to violation of probation hearing); *People v. Smith*, 149 Misc. 2d 998, __, 567 N.Y.S.2d 577, 580 (Kings Co. Sup. Ct. 1991) ("The fact that a witness made a photographic identification is not admissible as evidence in N.Y. Thus, the People cannot intend to offer the previous photo identification in evidence.") (citations omitted).

§ 26:7   710.30 notice generally must be served within 15 days of arraignment

CPL § 710.30(2) provides that, absent good cause, "[s]uch notice must be served within [15] days after arraignment and before trial." *See also People v. Chase*, 85 N.Y.2d 493, 500, 626 N.Y.S.2d 721, 724, 650 N.E.2d 379 (1995); *People v. Lopez*, 84 N.Y.2d 425, 428, 618 N.Y.S.2d 879, 881, 643 N.E.2d 501 (1994) ("the statute requires that whenever the People intend to offer evidence of defendant's statements to a public officer or testimony of observations of defendant, they must serve notice of such evidence on defendant within 15 days of arraignment and before trial"). The reason for the 15-day rule is as follows:

> When CPL 710.30 was first enacted it contained no timeliness requirement and the courts experienced considerable delay by prosecutors. Accordingly, the Legislature amended the statute to establish a narrow 15-day time requirement to facilitate "the orderly, swift and efficient determination of pretrial motions." Permitting the People to rely on defendant's eventual receipt of the information through discovery would undermine the statutory scheme and negate the legislative directive embodied in the amended statute.

Lopez, 84 N.Y.2d at 429, 618 N.Y.S.2d at 882 (citation omitted). *See also People v. Laing*, 79 N.Y.2d 166, 170, 581 N.Y.S.2d 149, 151, 589 N.E.2d 372 (1992) ("A 1976 amendment to CPL 710.30 pinpointed the time for serving notice from "before trial" to "within fifteen days after arraignment and before trial." This change, along with conforming changes to the omnibus pretrial motion provisions, was designed to further another goal of CPL 710.30—"the orderly, swift and efficient determination of pretrial motions." This Court has recognized that "[the exclusionary sanction for failure to comply contained in CPL 710.30(3) reflects a [legislative] judgment that the loss of the use of the evidence is an acceptable price to pay to achieve the desired goals.") (citations omitted).

In *People v. Godoy*, 180 Misc. 2d 771, 698 N.Y.S.2d 390 (City Crim. Ct. 1999), the Court pointed out that "service" does not require "filing"; nor does it require actual "receipt" by the defendant. Thus, for example, where a 710.30 notice is mailed to a valid address, the People are not responsible for a Post Office error.

§ 26:8 When does the 15-day time period begin?

For purposes of CPL § 710.30(2), the date of arraignment is not counted. Thus, the 15-day time period for serving a 710.30 notice begins the day after the defendant's arraignment. *See People v. Morales*, 159 Misc. 2d 745, 610 N.Y.S.2d 720 (N.Y. City Crim. Ct. 1994).

In addition, where the defendant is arraigned on a new or superceding accusatory instrument, the 15-day time period starts over—unless the new accusatory instrument is filed as a mere pretext for the filing of the 710.30 notice. *See, e.g., People v. Littlejohn,* 184 A.D.2d 790, __, 585 N.Y.S.2d 495, 496 (2d Dep't 1992); *People v. Davis,* 163 Misc. 2d 947, __, 623 N.Y.S.2d 92, 93–94 (N.Y. City Crim. Ct. 1995); *People v. Lopez,* 159 Misc. 2d 264, 603 N.Y.S.2d 948 (N.Y. City Crim. Ct. 1993); *People v. Alcindor,* 157 Misc. 2d 725, 598 N.Y.S.2d 449 (N.Y. City Crim. Ct. 1993); *People v. Haines,* 139 Misc. 2d 762, __, 528 N.Y.S.2d 475, 477 (N.Y. City Crim. Ct. 1988) ("CPL 710.30 refers to notice being served 'within 15 days after arraignment'; not arraignment on a specific accusatory instrument nor arraignment on the accusatory instrument that commenced the criminal action.").

Notably, however, when the defendant is arraigned on a new accusatory instrument his or her right to file pretrial motions starts over as well. *See Littlejohn,* 184 A.D.2d at __, 585 N.Y.S.2d at 496 ("It is clear that following arraignment on the second indictment the defendant is permitted to, and in this case did, file new pretrial motions pursuant to CPL 255.20."); *Davis,* 163 Misc. 2d at __, 623 N.Y.S.2d at 94; *Lopez,* 159 Misc. 2d at __, 603 N.Y.S.2d at 950; *Alcindor,* 157 Misc. 2d at __, 598 N.Y.S.2d at 451.

§ 26:9   710.30 notice can be served prior to arraignment

710.30 notice can be served prior to arraignment. *See, e.g., People v. Berisha,* 12 Misc. 3d 344, __, 816 N.Y.S.2d 830, 831 (N.Y. City Crim. Ct. 2006); *People v. Alcindor,* 157 Misc. 2d 725, __, 598 N.Y.S.2d 449, 452 (N.Y. City Crim. Ct. 1993); *People v. Hilton,* 147 Misc. 2d 200, __, 555 N.Y.S.2d 550, 553 (Queens Co. Sup. Ct. 1990). In this regard, in *People v. Korang,* 160 Misc. 2d 604, __, 610 N.Y.S.2d 730, 731 (Queens Co. Sup. Ct. 1994), the Court held that:

> In the opinion of the court, the People have satisfied the mandates of CPL 710.30, which requires notice to "be served within fifteen days after arraignment and before trial". The court notes that while the *deadline* for service is fifteen days after the defendant's Supreme Court arraignment, there is no requirement that service be made *only* during that fifteen-day period, and not before. Such an interpretation of the statute would be strained and illogical, for service of the 710.30 notice at an earlier time, such as at the Criminal Court arraignment, is more advantageous to a defendant, who will be better equipped to make an informed and meaningful decision with respect to such matters as testifying before the Grand Jury or accepting a plea offer.

§ 26:10   If the defendant is represented by an attorney, 710.30 notice should be served on the attorney

If the defendant is represented by an attorney, the People's

710.30 notice should be served on the attorney. In this regard, in *People v. Brown*, 168 Misc. 2d 923, __, 646 N.Y.S.2d 241, 243–44 (Rochester City Ct. 1996), the Court held that:

> There can be no question that when a party is represented by counsel in a pending action, papers to be served on the party must be served not upon the party directly, but upon the party's attorney, in the absence of a law, court order, or agreement providing otherwise (CPLR 2103[b]; Code of Professional Responsibility DR 7-104[A][1] [22 NYCRR 1200.35(a)(1)].
>
> It is equally clear that where a defendant in a criminal matter is represented, law enforcement officials may not communicate directly with the defendant relating to the subject of that representation in defense counsel's absence.
>
> Only where a party has not appeared by counsel or the party's attorney cannot be served is service of papers in a pending action on a party permitted (*see*, CPLR 2103[c]). In light of the above, once counsel has appeared for a defendant in a criminal proceeding, the requirement of CPL § 710.30(1) that the People serve their notice of intention to introduce evidence upon "the defendant" must be read to require that such service be made not on defendant personally, but on defense counsel. Any other construction would sanction a procedure which is contrary to clearly expressed legislative intent, well-settled case law, and the plain language of Disciplinary Rule 7-104 of the Code of Professional Responsibility (22 NYCRR 1200.35).
>
> In this case, defendant appeared with counsel at arraignment. Thereafter, the People were required to serve any notices, including their CPL § 710.30 notice, not on the defendant personally, but on defense counsel. The People concede that this was not done. Thus, service of the People's CPL § 710.30 notice on defendant personally did not satisfy the People's notice obligation under CPL Article 710.

(Citations omitted). *See also People v. Sears*, 195 Misc. 2d 266, __, 757 N.Y.S.2d 836, 838 (Webster Just. Ct. 2003) ("It is certainly well established that once an attorney appears in a criminal matter on behalf of a defendant the prosecution cannot communicate directly with a defendant. Nor could the prosecution deal directly with a defendant, once they have been put on notice that the defendant is represented by an attorney."); *People v. Godoy*, 180 Misc. 2d 771, __, 698 N.Y.S.2d 390, 392 (N.Y. City Crim. Ct. 1999).

§ 26:11 When can the People serve late 710.30 notice?

Although 710.30 notice must generally be served within 15 days after arraignment, *see* § 26:7, *supra*, CPL § 710.30(2) provides that "[f]or good cause shown, however, the court may permit the people to serve such notice, thereafter." *See also People v. Chase*, 85 N.Y.2d 493, 500, 626 N.Y.S.2d 721, 724, 650 N.E.2d 379 (1995) ("Late notice may be given only upon good cause."); *People v. O'Doherty*, 70 N.Y.2d 479, 487, 522 N.Y.S.2d 498, 503, 517 N.E.2d 213 (1987) ("the court may permit service of an untimely notice 'only upon a showing of good cause' ") (citation omitted); *People v. Greer*, 42 N.Y.2d 170, 179, 397 N.Y.S.2d 613, 619, 366 N.E.2d 273 (1977) ("Only upon a showing of good cause may the court permit service of the notice during trial with a reasonable opportunity to make a suppression motion during trial (CPL 710.30[2]) and, if good cause is not shown, a failure to give the required notice of intention before trial mandates exclusion of the statement or statements."); *People v. Briggs*, 38 N.Y.2d 319, 322, 379 N.Y.S.2d 779, 781–82, 342 N.E.2d 557 (1975) (same).

§ 26:12   What constitutes "good cause" for late notice?

The Court of Appeals has made clear that, for purposes of CPL § 710.30(2), "good cause" for late 710.30 notice should only be found in "unusual circumstances." *See People v. O'Doherty*, 70 N.Y.2d 479, 486, 522 N.Y.S.2d 498, 502, 517 N.E.2d 213 (1987); *People v. Briggs*, 38 N.Y.2d 319, 324, 379 N.Y.S.2d 779, 783, 342 N.E.2d 557 (1975). *See also People v. Showers*, 200 A.D.2d 864, __, 606 N.Y.S.2d 816, 817 (3d Dep't 1994); *People v. Riley-James*, 168 A.D.2d 740, __, 563 N.Y.S.2d 894, 896 (3d Dep't 1990); *People v. Socia*, 150 Misc. 2d 518, __, 568 N.Y.S.2d 864, 866 (Bronx Co. Sup. Ct. 1991).

In *People v. Michel*, 56 N.Y.2d 1014, 453 N.Y.S.2d 639, 439 N.E.2d 355 (1982), the Court of Appeals found that "good cause" existed where the defendant had actual notice not only of the existence of the statement in question, but also of the People's intent to use the statement against him at trial. Specifically, the *Michel* Court held as follows:

Defendant contends that the prosecution was required to serve statutory notice of its intention to introduce his written confession into evidence at trial (CPL 710.30). The statute, however, expressly permits the trial court to dispense with the notice requirement "[f]or good cause shown" (CPL 710.30[2]). Here the confession itself was negotiated, drafted, and signed by both the defendant and his attorney and specifically stated that it was "going to be used in court". Moreover it was clear to the defense that the confession was an integral part of the agreement ultimately concluded and that a default on defendant's part would result in prosecution and use of the confession. Under these circumstances we cannot say that the trial court erred as a matter of law in finding that the defense had actual notice of the prosecution's intent to introduce the confession at trial and, therefore, good cause for dispensing with the statutory notice requirement.

56 N.Y.2d at 1015, 453 N.Y.S.2d at 640.

It is critical to note that the "actual notice" rule of *Michel* only applies to situations where the defendant has actual notice of the People's intent to use the statement at issue—not to situations where the defendant merely has actual notice that he or she made the statement. *See, e.g., People v. Phillips*, 183 A.D.2d 856, 584 N.Y.S.2d 83 (2d Dep't 1992); *People v. Heller*, 180 Misc. 2d 160, __, 689 N.Y.S.2d 327, 334 (N.Y. City Crim. Ct. 1998); *People v. Brown*, 168 Misc. 2d 923, __, 646 N.Y.S.2d 241, 244 (Rochester City Ct. 1996); *People v. Calise*, 167 Misc. 2d 277, __, 639 N.Y.S.2d 671, 672 (N.Y. City Crim. Ct. 1996); *People v. Centeno*, 168 Misc. 2d 172, __, 637 N.Y.S.2d 254, 258 (N.Y. Co. Sup. Ct. 1995) ("merely providing the defendant with a copy of a statement, without also stating the intent to utilize that particular statement at trial is not sufficient; the defendant must be informed of both the intent to utilize each statement at trial, the statement's substance, and information to identify when and where the statement was made"); *People v. Holley*, 157 Misc. 2d 402, __, 596 N.Y.S.2d 1016, 1018 (N.Y. City Crim. Ct. 1993) ("The service of the IDE on defense counsel at the arraignment was not sufficient to comply with the notice requirements of CPL § 710.30"); 157 Misc. 2d at __, 596 N.Y.S.2d at 1018 ("The crucial question is not whether defendant knew about the existence of the statement, but rather whether he knew that the People intended to introduce the statement on their direct case at trial. Since the People had not included the IDE statements in their 710.30 notice, defense counsel in the instant case had every right to assume that the People did not plan to use these statements on their direct case. Counsel therefore had no reason to include these statements in his pretrial motion to suppress."); *People v. Wright*, 127 Misc. 2d 885, __ n.*, 487 N.Y.S.2d 688, 692 n.* (Nassau Co. Ct. 1985) ("The fact that the defendant may be aware of a number of other statements he made to public officials is irrelevant. It is for the People to tell defendant which statements they intend to offer at the trial. It is not every statement the defendant makes that the People intend to offer at the trial. It is their obligation to be specific, so that when defendant requests a *Huntley* hearing, the request can be directed at those statements the People intend to offer at the trial, notice of which is the very essence of CPL 710.30.").

If this were not the case, then the exception would swallow the rule (as the defendant theoretically has actual notice of every statement that he or she has ever made). *See generally People v. Boyles*, 210 A.D.2d 732, __, 621 N.Y.S.2d 118, 120 (3d Dep't 1994) (defendant entitled to rely on contents of second, subsequent 710.30 notice that omitted statement contained in first notice); *Holley*, 157 Misc. 2d at __, 596 N.Y.S.2d at 1018–19 ("If the

People's argument in the instant case were adopted, they would have little incentive to see that their statement notice was complete. Rather, the People could simply provide defense counsel with copies of the police reports and memo books and then determine at a later date whether there were any statements in those documents that had not been included in the original notice.").

The above-quoted language in *Holley* would appear to be directly applicable to a 710.30 notice that attaches a video thereto but makes no attempt to summarize the statements of the defendant allegedly contained in the video that the People intend to use at trial.

§ 26:13   What does *not* constitute "good cause" for late notice?

The Court of Appeals has made clear that there are two things that, as a matter of law, do not constitute "good cause" for late 710.30 notice: (1) office failure within the prosecutor's office, and (2) office failure between the police department and the prosecutor's office. In this regard, in *People v. Briggs*, 38 N.Y.2d 319, 324, 379 N.Y.S.2d 779, 783–84, 342 N.E.2d 557 (1975), the Court of Appeals held that:

> The People, alleging only a "lack of continuity" in the prosecutor's office, have not shown good cause for their failure to give defendant the required notice before trial. In fact, it is questionable whether the prosecutor has shown any cause, good or bad. The term "lack of continuity" evidently referred, as the trial court seemed to believe, to the trial prosecutor's lack of knowledge whether any pretrial notice had been served by his office. The record gives no further information, and the briefs do no better. Lack of continuity or other office failure does not constitute the "unusual circumstances" contemplated by the statute. Instead, the People's failure to give notice, because of lack of continuity in the prosecutor's office, is but another example of an absence of orderly office procedure. While this failure may be due, in some part, to a heavy workload in the prosecutor's office, a failure is not excusable. As the court stated in *Santobello v. New York*, a case involving a lack of continuity in the same prosecutor's office, "The staff lawyers in a prosecutor's office have the burden of 'letting the left hand know what the right hand is doing.' "
>
> The issue is not a trivial or merely technical one. Prior statements, especially oral ones, to a police officer, are accorded high credibility by fact finders, jury or Judges. Whether in fact they were made, whether they were voluntary, and the precise form which they took may be crucial to the determination of innocence or guilt. To deprive defendants in criminal matters unnecessarily of an advance opportunity to investigate the facts and circumstances is neither fair nor conducive to establishing the truth through the adversary pro-

cess with the assistance of counsel. A cavalier treatment of the statute's requirements frustrates its ends.

(Citations omitted).

Similarly, in *People v. Spruill*, 47 N.Y.2d 869, 870–71, 419 N.Y.S.2d 69, 70, 392 N.E.2d 1252 (1979), the Court of Appeals held that:

> The court erred in admitting the defendant's confession at trial. The People concededly had not given the defendant pretrial notice as required by statute (CPL 710.30) nor, in our view, did they establish "good cause" for filing a late notice. We have previously held that "[l]ack of continuity or other office failure" within the prosecutor's office does not provide an adequate excuse. The excuse offered in this case that the police officer had not informed the prosecutor of the confession prior to trial is no different in principle. Under similar circumstances we have noted that "[k]nowledge on the part of the police department would, of course, be imputed to the District Attorney's office. A defendant ought not be penalized because of any inadequacy of internal communication within the law enforcement establishment."

(Citations omitted).

In *People v. O'Doherty*, 70 N.Y.2d 479, 485–86, 522 N.Y.S.2d 498, 502, 517 N.E.2d 213 (1987), the Court of Appeals, comparing the facts of the case to those in *Briggs* and *Spruill*, held that:

> We agree with defendant that the People's excuse should fare no better in this case, where the police officer who had knowledge of the statement did not inform the prosecutor in time to comply with the requirements of the statute. * * *
>
> There may be instances where, given the time, place and context of the defendant's statement to a police officer and an attenuated connection between that officer and the prosecutor, the untimely disclosure of the statement to the prosecutor would present the "unusual circumstances" to which the good cause requirement is addressed. There are no such circumstances here.

§ 26:14 What if the statement/identification does not arise until after arraignment?

CPL § 710.30 fails to address the situation where a statement and/or identification does not arise until after the defendant has been arraigned. The Court addressed this issue in *People v. G.*, 158 Misc. 2d 893, —, 602 N.Y.S.2d 512, 518 (Kings Co. Sup. Ct. 1993):

> [A]pplying the 15-day deadline to post-arraignment identifications or statements would add little to "the orderly, swift and efficient determination of pretrial motions" or fairness to the defendant. Weighed against that marginal gain is the enormous mandatory

sanction of absolute preclusion of evidence when the notice is untimely. Here, that would have required preclusion of two identifications for serious alleged crimes, including A-I felonies, regardless of the absence of any suggestivity in the identification procedures, prejudice to the defendant, or delay in the proceedings. . . . But in the case of post-arraignment evidence, the loss would be an arbitrary price to pay for no significant benefit. Such a result would be "plainly at odds with the policy of the legislation as a whole."

If the 15-day time limit for notice does not apply to post-arraignment identifications and statements, what is the time limit? The answer is in the normal discovery rules covering the prosecution's continuing duty to disclose newly discovered evidence "promptly." If those disclosures are not made within an appropriate time, the court may in its discretion impose sanctions. The same procedures and requirements apply for evidence obtained after arraignment but within the 15-day period as apply for evidence obtained after the 15 days. No special problem is presented in either case, and the court can readily apply the normal discovery rules.

(Citations omitted). *See also People v. Coleman*, 12 Misc. 3d 712, __, 819 N.Y.S.2d 407, 412 (Bronx Co. Sup. Ct. 2006) ("It is this court's opinion that C.P.L. § 710.30 applies to this instant case . . . even where the identification procedure took place approximately a year after arrest and arraignment. Obviously, the fifteen day statutory notice provision is inapplicable, however, the purpose, reasons and intent of the legislature in enacting C.P.L. § 710.30 compels this court to conclude that section 710.30 imposes a *continuing obligation* upon the People to *promptly* notify the accused of any post-arraignment identification procedure and failure to comply with this obligation mandates the court to preclude the in-court identification testimony of the potential witness.").

§ 26:15   Required contents of 710.30 notice

To be sufficient, 710.30 notice must:

[I]nform defendant of the time and place the oral or written statements were made and of the sum and substance of those statements. Full copies of the statements need not be supplied but they must be described sufficiently so that the defendant can intelligently identify them. Similarly, the People were also required to inform defendant of the time, place and manner in which the identification was made.

People v. Lopez, 84 N.Y.2d 425, 428, 618 N.Y.S.2d 879, 881, 643 N.E.2d 501 (1994) (citations omitted). *See also People v. Bennett*, 56 N.Y.2d 837, 839, 453 N.Y.S.2d 164, 165, 438 N.E.2d 870 (1982); *People v. Centeno*, 168 Misc. 2d 172, __, 637 N.Y.S.2d 254, 258 (N.Y. Co. Sup. Ct. 1995) ("merely providing the defendant with a copy of a statement, without also stating the intent to utilize that particular statement at trial is not sufficient; the defendant must be informed of both the intent to utilize each statement at trial, the statement's substance, and information to identify when and where the statement was made"); *People v. Olds*, 140 Misc. 2d 458, __, 531 N.Y.S.2d 479, 481 (Bronx Co. Sup. Ct. 1988) ("Mere notice of the statement, without recitation of its sum and substance, is inadequate."); *People v. Feliciano*, 139 Misc. 2d 247, 527 N.Y.S.2d 964 (N.Y. City Crim. Ct. 1988) (same); *People v. Utley*, 77 Misc. 2d 86, __, 353 N.Y.S.2d 301, 313 (Nassau Co. Ct. 1974).

In *Lopez*, *supra*, the 710.30 notice at issue:

[W]as a printed form, listing various types of evidence and containing appropriate boxes before each so the prosecutor could indicate the type to be offered at trial. The prosecutor had placed an "x" within the boxes which appeared before "[a]n oral statement made to a public servant," "[a] written statement made to a public servant" and "[i]dentification of the defendant * * * by a witness who has previously identified the defendant" at a "[l]ineup." The form provided no further information about the evidence, and no documents were attached.

84 N.Y.2d at 427, 618 N.Y.S.2d at 881.

The Court of Appeals affirmed the Appellate Division's finding that "the notice required of the People by CPL 710.30(1) was inadequate, [and thus] the People should have been precluded from offering evidence of defendant's oral and written statements to police and of his pretrial identification." 84 N.Y.2d at 426, 618 N.Y.S.2d at 880. In so holding, the Court reasoned that:

Manifestly, a defendant cannot challenge that of which he lacks knowledge; thus the statute requires that the notice "[specify] the evidence intended to be offered" (CPL 710.30[1]). The notice served by the People in this case informed Lopez that the People intended to offer oral and written statements and identification evidence but failed to specify the evidence as the statute commands.

84 N.Y.2d at 428, 618 N.Y.S.2d at 881.

§ 26:16 Inadequate 710.30 notice cannot be cured by discovery

In *People v. Lopez*, 84 N.Y.2d 425, 428, 618 N.Y.S.2d 879, 882, 643 N.E.2d 501 (1994), the Court of Appeals made clear that an inadequate 710.30 notice cannot be cured by discovery. In this regard, the Court reasoned as follows:

The Legislature has enacted a statutory scheme that purposefully distinguishes between pretrial motion practice and discovery. The provisions of CPL 710.30 are clearly related to defendant's preparation of pretrial motions, not his subsequent ability to defend himself at trial. Although there will be some degree of overlap between the information provided by the 710.30 notice and the People's response to defendant's discovery demands, the timing provisions of the statutes are correlated to their underlying purposes. Thus, defendant must receive a 710.30 notice within 15 days of his arraignment (CPL 710.30[2]); he need not make his discovery demands until 30 days after his arraignment, and the People's response is not due until 15 days after service of defendant's demands (*see*, CPL 240.80).

When CPL 710.30 was first enacted it contained no timeliness requirement and the courts experienced considerable delay by prosecutors. Accordingly, the Legislature amended the statute to establish a narrow 15-day time requirement to facilitate "the orderly, swift and efficient determination of pretrial motions." Permitting the People to rely on defendant's eventual receipt of the information through discovery would undermine the statutory scheme and negate the legislative directive embodied in the amended statute.

84 N.Y.2d at 428–29, 618 N.Y.S.2d at 882 (citations omitted). *See also People v. Phillips*, 183 A.D.2d 856, 584 N.Y.S.2d 83 (2d Dep't 1992); *People v. Utria*, 165 Misc. 2d 54, __, 626 N.Y.S.2d 948, 950–51 (N.Y. City Crim. Ct. 1995).

§ 26:17 Lack of prejudice to the defendant is irrelevant

If the People fail to comply with the requirements of CPL § 710.30, the remedy is preclusion. *See* CPL § 710.30(3); *People v. Lopez*, 84 N.Y.2d 425, 428, 618 N.Y.S.2d 879, 882, 643 N.E.2d 501 (1994). Lack of prejudice to the defendant is irrelevant. 84 N.Y.2d at 428, 618 N.Y.S.2d at 881–82. In this regard, the *Lopez* Court held that "[i]t is irrelevant that the People's failure to satisfy the requirements of 710.30 did not prejudice defendant. The statutory remedy for the People's failure to comply with the statute is preclusion; prejudice plays no part in the analysis." 84 N.Y.2d at 428, 618 N.Y.S.2d at 881–82. *See also People v. O'Doherty*, 70 N.Y.2d 479, 481, 522 N.Y.S.2d 498, 499, 517 N.E.2d 213 (1987) ("Lack of prejudice to the defendant resulting from the delay does not obviate the need for the People to meet the statutory requirement of good cause before they may be permitted to serve a late notice."); *People v. McMullin*, 70 N.Y.2d 855, 856, 523 N.Y.S.2d 455, 456, 517 N.E.2d 1341 (1987); *People v. Briggs*, 38 N.Y.2d 319, 322, 379 N.Y.S.2d 779, 782, 342 N.E.2d 557 (1975); 38 N.Y.2d at 323–24, 379 N.Y.S.2d at 783 ("If . . . no good cause is shown, a failure to give the required notice before trial mandates exclusion of those statements. To hold otherwise would be to condone and encourage noncompliance in the prosecutor's office and to undermine the salutary purposes of the statute.") (citations omitted). *See generally People v. Boughton*, 70 N.Y.2d 854, 855, 523 N.Y.S.2d 454, 455, 517 N.E.2d 1340 (1987) (where the People withdraw their 710.30 notice, they cannot change their mind after the 15-day time period has run).

§ 26:18   Prejudice to the defendant *is* relevant

The Court of Appeals has made clear that even where "good cause" for delay in serving 710.30 notice is demonstrated, late notice should nonetheless not be allowed where the defendant is prejudiced by the delay. In this regard, in *People v. O'Doherty*, 70 N.Y.2d 479, 487, 522 N.Y.S.2d 498, 503, 517 N.E.2d 213 (1987), the Court of Appeals held that:

> The language which triggers the People's opportunity to serve a late notice—"[f]or good cause shown * * * the court may permit the people to serve such notice"—was unaffected by the 1976 amendment and thus remains an "unqualifie[d] command" that the court may permit service of an untimely notice "only upon a showing of good cause." Such a showing is, therefore, indispensable. Only if that threshold is crossed may the court move on to considerations of prejudice to the defendant, and only then because the existence of prejudice may preclude granting the relief sought by the People, notwithstanding their showing of good cause.

(Citation omitted).

§ 26:19   To what statements does CPL § 710.30 apply?

In *People v. Chase*, 85 N.Y.2d 493, 499–500, 626 N.Y.S.2d 721, 724, 650 N.E.2d 379 (1995), the Court of Appeals stated that:

> CPL 710.30(1)(a) . . . provides that the People must give notice to the defendant whenever they "intend to offer at a trial * * * evidence of a statement made by a defendant to a public servant" which would be suppressible if involuntarily made. An involuntary statement includes one that has been physically or psychologically coerced, obtained by a promise or statement that creates a risk of falsely incriminating oneself or obtained by the failure to give *Miranda* warnings (CPL 60.45).

Thus, pursuant to the express terms of CPL § 710.30, 710.30 notice need only be given with regard to statements that would be suppressible if involuntarily made. This raises an interesting question: Do statements that are spontaneously made by the defendant have to be noticed pursuant to CPL § 710.30? The *Chase* Court made clear that such statements should nonetheless be noticed. The reason why is simple: *"It is for the court and not the parties to determine whether a statement is truly voluntary or is one in which the actions of the police are the functional equivalent of interrogation causing the statement to be made."* 85 N.Y.2d at 500, 626 N.Y.S.2d at 724 (emphasis added). *See also People v.*

Brown, 140 A.D.2d 266, __, 528 N.Y.S.2d 565, 568 (1st Dep't 1988) ("Whether or not a particular statement is suppressible is a matter which must be resolved by the court, not the prosecution.").

The only exception to this rule is "where 'there is no question of voluntariness.'" *Chase*, 85 N.Y.2d at 500, 626 N.Y.S.2d at 724 (citation omitted). *See also People v. Greer*, 42 N.Y.2d 170, 178, 397 N.Y.S.2d 613, 619, 366 N.E.2d 273 (1977) (same). In this regard, the *Chase* Court concluded that:

> Since the statement here was made to a law enforcement official and the defendant had the right to have a court review the circumstances under which the statement was given and to determine its voluntariness, including whether it was truly spontaneous or the functional equivalent of interrogation, defendant was entitled to notice under CPL 710.30(1)(a). Both prior courts determined that the first statement was voluntary and there is evidence in the record to support that determination. The first statement, made in the police car, should have been precluded because of the lack of CPL 710.30(1)(a) notice.

85 N.Y.2d at 500, 626 N.Y.S.2d at 724–25 (citations omitted).

Chase appears to call into question a line of lower court cases which have held that so-called *res gestae* statements of the defendant do not have to be noticed pursuant to CPL § 710.30 on the ground that they are voluntary *per se*. *See, e.g., People v. McCaskell*, 217 A.D.2d 527, __, 630 N.Y.S.2d 66, 68 (1st Dep't 1995); *People v. Copes*, 200 A.D.2d 680, __, 606 N.Y.S.2d 751, 752 (2d Dep't 1994); *People v. Wells*, 133 A.D.2d 385, __, 519 N.Y.S.2d 553, 554 (2d Dep't 1987); *People v. McFadden*, 126 A.D.2d 970, 511 N.Y.S.2d 745 (4th Dep't 1987). In this regard, the rationale of these cases is that there is no question as to the voluntariness of a *res gestae* statement; whereas *Chase* makes clear that such a determination is for the Court—not the People—to make.

§ 26:20   710.30 notice only applies to statements made to public servants and their agents

By its express terms, CPL § 710.30(1)(a) only applies to "statement[s] made by a defendant to a public servant." "Public servant" is defined in PL § 10.00(15) as:

> (a) any public officer or employee of the state or of any political subdivision thereof or of any governmental instrumentality within the state, or (b) any person exercising the functions of any such public officer or employee. The term public servant includes a person who has been elected or designated to become a public servant.

Accordingly, "[a] defendant is not entitled to notice with respect to statements made to a prosecution witness where that witness was a civilian and was neither a public servant nor acting as an agent of law enforcement authorities." *People v. Paredes*, 166 A.D.2d 677, __, 561 N.Y.S.2d 267, 268 (2d Dep't 1990). *See also People v. Wilhelm*, 34 A.D.3d 40, __, 822 N.Y.S.2d 786, 790 (3d Dep't 2006); *People v. Williams*, 21 A.D.3d 1401, __, 801 N.Y.S.2d 659, 661 (4th Dep't 2005); *People v. Jones*, 292 A.D.2d 792, 738 N.Y.S.2d 790 (4th Dep't 2002); *People v. Abdul*, 279 A.D.2d 298, __, 720 N.Y.S.2d 5, 6 (1st Dep't 2001) ("The court properly denied defendant's motion for preclusion, made on the ground of lack of notice pursuant to CPL 710.30(1)(a), of his statement to Emergency Medical Services (EMS) personnel in which he declined medical treatment. There is no evidence that the EMS workers acted as police agents."); *People v. Quinto*, 245 A.D.2d 121, __, 666 N.Y.S.2d 146, 147 (1st Dep't 1997) ("Since the security officers were private citizens, . . . the People were not obliged to provide defendant with notice of their intention to introduce such statements at trial (CPL 710.30[1][a]). The record establishes that these private citizens, who had no Special Police Officer status, were not agents of law enforcement."); *People v. Boswell*, 193 A.D.2d 690, __, 598 N.Y.S.2d 34, 35 (2d Dep't 1993); *People v. Rivera*, 173 A.D.2d 360, __, 570 N.Y.S.2d 5, 6 (1st Dep't 1991); *People v. Velez*, 168 A.D.2d 207, __, 562 N.Y.S.2d 91, 92 (1st Dep't 1990); *People v. Bell*, 161 A.D.2d 772, __, 556 N.Y.S.2d 118, 119 (2d Dep't 1990); *People v. Stewart*, 160 A.D.2d 966, __, 554 N.Y.S.2d 687, 688 (2d Dep't 1990); *People v. Duffy*, 124 A.D.2d 258, __, 508 N.Y.S.2d 267, 269 (3d Dep't 1986); *People v. Rodriguez*, 114 A.D.2d 525, __, 494 N.Y.S.2d 426, 427 (2d Dep't 1985). *See generally People v. Miranda*, 23 N.Y.2d 439, 448, 297 N.Y.S.2d 532, 538, 245 N.E.2d 194 (1969) ("We do not . . . interpret the legislative intent [of the predecessor statute to CPL § 710.30] as requiring the District Attorney to notify defendants of admissions made to private parties who were not police agents.").

In *Wilhelm*, *supra*, the Appellate Division, Third Department, held that "the [CPS] caseworkers' conduct was 'so pervaded by governmental involvement' that it constituted state action." 34 A.D.3d at __, 822 N.Y.S.2d at 792 (citation omitted). In this regard, the Court reasoned that:

Despite the CPS caseworkers' insistence that their investigation was separate, and that their interview of defendant and cooperation with the District Attorney's office were undertaken solely pursuant to the dictates of the Social Services Law and Family Ct. Act, we note that no Family Court proceeding was ever initiated or even contemplated as of the date of the interview. Moreover, as noted above, the CPS caseworkers were part of a multidisciplinary team with the common purpose of "enhanc[ing] the prosecutor[ial] process" in criminal proceedings such as this one. While the police and District Attorney may not have expressly requested that the CPS caseworkers interview defendant—a request that was unnecessary in light of the statutory mandates that the interview be performed in any event and that the CPS caseworkers cooperate with the District Attorney's office regarding the case—the supervising caseworker was aware, prior to interviewing defendant in detail about the crimes charged herein, that she would be testifying for the prosecution before a grand jury.

Furthermore, notwithstanding the caseworkers' denial of any understanding that they would communicate incriminating statements obtained from defendant to the prosecution or that they even remained in contact with the prosecution after the interview, the People concede that the caseworkers had a duty to cooperate by sharing information when asked. * * *

Thus, while social workers are generally not considered to be agents of the police, we are satisfied that the CPS caseworkers involved here had a "cooperative working arrangement" with and were acting as agents of the police and prosecutor in interviewing defendant and relaying her incriminating statements.

34 A.D.3d at __, 822 N.Y.S.2d at 792–93 (citations omitted). *See also People v. Whitmore*, 12 A.D.3d 845, __, 785 N.Y.S.2d 140, 142 (3d Dep't 2004) ("This Court has previously stated that 'social workers are generally not agents of the police,' although they may be considered agents under certain circumstances.") (citation omitted); *People v. Batista*, 277 A.D.2d 141, __, 717 N.Y.S.2d 113, 114 (1st Dep't 2000).

§ 26:21 Every statement made by the defendant to a public servant is discoverable regardless of whether the People intend to offer the statement at trial

There is a common misconception that the People are only required to advise the defense of statements made by the defendant that are subject to the 710.30 notice requirement. Such belief is clearly misplaced. In this regard, CPL § 240.20(1)(a) provides for the disclosure of:

Any written, recorded or oral statement of the defendant, and of a co-defendant to be tried jointly, made, other than in the course of the criminal transaction, to a public servant engaged in law enforcement activity or to a person then acting under his direction or in cooperation with him.

In this regard, "[i]t is beyond dispute that a defendant's own statements to police are highly material and relevant to a criminal prosecution. It is for this reason that such statements are *always* discoverable, even when the People do not intend to offer them at trial." *People v. Combest*, 4 N.Y.3d 341, 347, 795 N.Y.S.2d 481, 485, 828 N.E.2d 583, 33 Media L. Rep. (BNA) 1666 (2005) (emphasis added). *See also People v. Fields*, 258 A.D.2d 809, __,

687 N.Y.S.2d 184, 186 (3d Dep't 1999) ("CPL 240.20(1)(a) . . . is not limited to statements intended to be offered by the People 'at trial', i.e., statements offered as part of the People's direct case (*see*, CPL 240.10[4]).") ; *People v. Crider*, 301 A.D.2d 612, __, 756 N.Y.S.2d 223, 225 (2d Dep't 2003) (pursuant to CPL § 240.20(1)(a), "the People shall provide the defendant with notice of *any* of his statements they are aware of, whether or not they intend to use them for any purpose, including but not limited to rebuttal") (emphasis added); *People v. Wyssling*, 82 Misc. 2d 708, __-__, 372 N.Y.S.2d 142, 145-46 (Suffolk Co. Ct. 1975); *People v. Bennett*, 75 Misc. 2d 1040, __-__, 349 N.Y.S.2d 506, 519-20 (Erie Co. Sup. Ct. 1973).

Thus, any argument by the People that they need only disclose statements to which CPL § 710.30 applies is without merit. *See Combest*, 4 N.Y.3d at 347, 795 N.Y.S.2d at 485; *Fields*, 258 A.D.2d at __, 687 N.Y.S.2d at 185; *People v. Hall*, 181 A.D.2d 1008, 581 N.Y.S.2d 951 (4th Dep't 1992).

§ 26:22   Knowledge that statement exists is not the same as knowledge that the People intend to use it at trial

In the field of CPL § 710.30 law, there is a critical distinction between providing the defendant with notice that a statement was made and providing the defendant with notice that the People intend to use the statement at trial. Thus, for example, 710.30 notice violations cannot be cured by discovery. *See, e.g., People v. Lopez*, 84 N.Y.2d 425, 428, 618 N.Y.S.2d 879, 882, 643 N.E.2d 501 (1994); *People v. Phillips*, 183 A.D.2d 856, 584 N.Y.S.2d 83 (2d Dep't 1992). In *Phillips*, the Appellate Division, Second Department, made clear that advising the defendant of the existence of a statement is not a substitute for 710.30 notice:

On the date of the defendant's arraignment, he was served with a Voluntary Disclosure Form (hereinafter VDF) which contained the following declaration:

"*PLEASE TAKE NOTICE*, that, pursuant to CPL 240.20(1)(a), statements in the form noted below were made by the defendant" (emphasis in original).

Thereafter, the VDF provided space to enter five different types of statements: "Written", "Stenographic", "Audio tape", "Video tape" and "Oral". Only the space for "Video tape" contained an entry. The substance of the videotaped statement was then summarized. There followed the additional declaration:

"*PLEASE TAKE FURTHER NOTICE*, that, pursuant to CPL 710.30(1)(a), the People intend to offer evidence of the above statement(s) of the defendant(s) on the People's direct case at the trial of this action, except for the statements specified above in paragraph(s) __" (emphasis in original).

Also annexed to the VDF were copies of several police reports, including a copy of a page from the arresting officer's memo book reporting that, prior to the videotape statement, the defendant made the oral statement, "I raped [the complainant], I'm guilty".

Over two months after the defendant's arraignment, the People served a second VDF in which they indicated that they intended to offer at trial both the videotape and the oral statement contained in the memo book. This second notice was apparently served in response to the defendant's omnibus motion in which he moved to suppress the videotape, but did not mention the memo book entry. At the *Huntley* hearing, the defendant moved to preclude the memo book statement solely on the ground that he had not been given timely notice pursuant to CPL 710.30. The hearing court denied the motion to preclude, holding that the initial VDF, which was served on the date of arraignment, contained the statement and thus constituted notice of the existence of the statement. The statement was subsequently admitted at the trial. That was error. * * *

A review of the first VDF demonstrates that the People only specified their intent to offer the videotape at trial. Although the memo book entry annexed to the VDF informed the defendant of the existence of the oral statement, the VDF did not notify him that the People intended to offer that statement on their direct case. Therefore, the notice contained in the initial VDF was ineffective with respect to the oral statement.

183 A.D.2d at __-__, 584 N.Y.S.2d at 84–85.

In *People v. Calise*, 167 Misc. 2d 277, 639 N.Y.S.2d 671 (N.Y. City Crim. Ct. 1996), the Court rejected the People's claim that the inclusion of certain statements of the defendant in the accusatory instrument gave the defendant actual notice of the People's intent to use the statements at trial despite the lack of 710.30 notice. In so holding, the Court noted that "[t]he clear language of the statute imposes on the People the obligation not only to inform the defendant of the statements but also of their intent to use them at trial." 167 Misc. 2d at __, 639 N.Y.S.2d at 672. *See also People v. Heller*, 180 Misc. 2d 160, __, 689 N.Y.S.2d 327, 334 (N.Y. City Crim. Ct. 1998) ("Inclusion of defendant's statements in the accusatory instrument affords defendant notice of the statements, but not notice of the People's intention to offer the statements at trial."); *People v. Centeno*, 168 Misc. 2d 172, __, 637 N.Y.S.2d 254, 258 (N.Y. Co. Sup. Ct. 1995) ("merely providing the defendant with a copy of a statement, without also stating the intent to utilize that particular statement at trial is not sufficient; the defendant must be informed of both the intent to utilize each statement at trial, the statement's substance, and information to identify when and where the statement was made").

§ 26:23 Responses to pedigree questions are exempt from CPL § 710.30

In *People v. Rodney*, 85 N.Y.2d 289, 624 N.Y.S.2d 95, 648 N.E.2d 471 (1995), the Court of Appeals held that the defendant's answers to so-called "routine booking" or "pedigree" questions do not have to be noticed pursuant to CPL § 710.30. The Court's rationale was that:

> Because responses to routine booking questions—pedigree questions, as we have referred to them—are not suppressible even when obtained in violation of *Miranda*, defendant lacks a constitutional basis upon which to challenge the voluntariness of his statement and where there is no question of voluntariness, the People are not required to serve defendant with notice. Because routine administrative questioning by the police presumptively avoids any grounds for challenging the voluntariness of statements given in response to those questions, notice of such statements is not required.

85 N.Y.2d at 293, 624 N.Y.S.2d at 97–98 (citations omitted). *See also People v. Berkowitz*, 50 N.Y.2d 333, 338 n.1, 428 N.Y.S.2d 927, 929 n.1, 406 N.E.2d 783 (1980).

Nonetheless, while not suppressible, pedigree statements appear to be discoverable pursuant to CPL § 240.20(1)(a). *See* § 26:21, *supra. See also* § 20:12, *supra.*

The question remains: What is a pedigree question? Pedigree questions are questions such as "what is your name, address, height, weight, eye color, date of birth, current age," etc. *See Pennsylvania v. Muniz*, 496 U.S. 582, 601, 110 S. Ct. 2638, 2650, 110 L. Ed. 2d 528 (1990). To qualify as pedigree questions, questions must be "limited in scope to those necessary for processing a defendant or providing for his physical needs." *People v. Hester*, 161 A.D.2d 665, ___, 556 N.Y.S.2d 97, 98 (2d Dep't 1990). *See also Rodney*, 85 N.Y.2d at 292, 624 N.Y.S.2d at 97 (pedigree questions are questions " 'reasonably related to the police's administrative concerns' ") (quoting *Muniz*). *See also* §§ 27:1 et seq., *infra*. In this regard, the *Rodney* Court made clear that:

> [T]he People may not rely on the pedigree exception if the questions, though facially appropriate, are likely to elicit incriminating admissions because of the circumstances of the particular case. Such questions fall outside the pedigree exceptions. Thus, the mere claim by the People that an admission was made in response to a question posed solely as an administrative concern does not automatically qualify that admission for the pedigree exception to *Miranda* or exempt the People from the necessity of supplying a CPL 710.30 notice.

85 N.Y.2d at 293, 624 N.Y.S.2d at 98 (citations omitted).

Applying these principles to the case before it, the *Rodney* Court held that:

In this case, the inquiry about defendant's employment status comes within the exception. The arresting officer's question was part of a routine booking form and was reasonably related to such administrative concerns as assignment of counsel, setting of bail, and the arraigning court's determination whether to release defendant on his own recognizance. Accordingly, we find no error in the People's failure to give notice of their intent to offer evidence of defendant's statement that he was "in sales." Although the question about defendant's occupation is arguably related to the conduct for which defendant had been arrested, it was not a disguised attempt at investigatory interrogation, and was not reasonably likely to elicit an incriminating response from defendant. Indeed, the incriminating nature of defendant's response arose from his apparent attempt to be humorous, and though the answer was incriminating, preclusion of the evidence is not required because the pedigree exception excuses the absence of CPL 710.30 notice.

85 N.Y.2d at 294, 624 N.Y.S.2d at 98 (citation omitted).

§ 26:24 Applicability of CPL § 710.30 to chemical test refusals

It would seem that a DWI defendant's alleged refusal to submit to a chemical test is a statement that should be included in the People's 710.30 notice. Indeed, the standardized Supporting Deposition/DWI Bill of Particulars form used in much of the State contains check box entries entitled "would not take a chemical test" in the 710.30 notice portion of the form. Nonetheless, in *People v. Peeso*, 266 A.D.2d 716, __, 699 N.Y.S.2d 136, 138 (3d Dep't 1999), the Appellate Division, Third Department, stated— arguably in *dicta*—that:

We . . . reject the contention that the absence of notice pursuant to CPL 710.30 precluded the People's offer of evidence concerning defendant's test refusal (*see*, Vehicle and Traffic Law § 1194[2][f]). It is settled law that because there is no compulsion on a defendant to refuse to submit to the chemical test provided for in Vehicle and Traffic Law § 1194(2), the defendant "ha[s] no constitutional privilege or statutory right to refuse to take the test." Therefore, defendant's refusal, although constituting communicative or testimonial evidence, could not "[c]onsist[ ] of a record or potential testimony reciting or describing a statement of [ ] defendant involuntarily made, within the meaning of [CPL] 60.45" (CPL 710.20[3]) or thereby implicate the notice requirement of CPL 710.30(1)(a).

(Citations omitted). *Cf. People v. Burtula*, 192 Misc. 2d 597, __, 747 N.Y.S.2d 692, 694 (Nassau Co. Dist. Ct. 2002).

Regardless, it would be a rare case in which the People would fail to notify the defendant of their intent to use a refusal to submit to a chemical test against him or her at trial; and such refusal is clearly discoverable pursuant to CPL §§ 240.20(1)(a), (c) and/or (k). In addition, the defendant can move to suppress such refusal on various grounds unrelated to voluntariness. For example, a chemical test refusal, like a chemical test result, can be suppressed:

(a) As the fruit of an illegal stop. *See, e.g., Byer v. Jackson,* 241 A.D.2d 943, 661 N.Y.S.2d 336 (4th Dep't 1997); *McDonell v. New York State Dept. of Motor Vehicles,* 77 A.D.3d 1379, 908 N.Y.S.2d 507 (4th Dep't 2010);

(b) As the fruit of an illegal arrest. *See, e.g., Dunaway v. New York,* 442 U.S. 200, 99 S. Ct. 2248, 60 L. Ed. 2d 824 (1979); *Brown v. Illinois,* 422 U.S. 590, 95 S. Ct. 2254, 45 L. Ed. 2d 416 (1975); *Mapp v. Ohio,* 367 U.S. 643, 81 S. Ct. 1684, 6 L. Ed. 2d 1081, 86 Ohio L. Abs. 513, 84 A.L.R.2d 933 (1961). *See generally Welsh v. Wisconsin,* 466 U.S. 740, 744, 104 S. Ct. 2091, 2095, 80 L. Ed. 2d 732 (1984);

(c) If it is obtained in violation of the right to counsel. *See, e.g., People v. Washington,* 23 N.Y.3d 228, 989 N.Y.S.2d 670, 12 N.E.3d 1099 (2014); *People v. Smith,* 18 N.Y.3d 544, 550, 942 N.Y.S.2d 426, 430, 965 N.E.2d 928 (2012); *People v. Shaw,* 72 N.Y.2d 1032, 534 N.Y.S.2d 929, 531 N.E.2d 650 (1988); *People v. Gursey,* 22 N.Y.2d 224, 292 N.Y.S.2d 416, 239 N.E.2d 351 (1968); and/or

(d) If it is obtained in violation of VTL § 1194. *See, e.g.,* VTL § 1194(2)(f); *People v. Boone,* 71 A.D.2d 859, 419 N.Y.S.2d 187 (2d Dep't 1979).

See also § 20:42, *supra;* § 41:33, *infra.*

§ 26:25 Applicability of CPL § 710.30 to statements overheard by the police

Where the defendant utters a statement that is merely overheard by the police, 710.30 notice is not required (because the statement is not made to a public servant). *See, e.g., People v. Umana,* 76 A.D.3d 1111, __, 908 N.Y.S.2d 244, 246 (2d Dep't 2010), leave to appeal denied, 15 N.Y.3d 924, 913 N.Y.S.2d 651, 939 N.E.2d 817 (2010) ("Notice was not required because the defendant's statement in Spanish was made in response to a question posed by one of his coworkers at the time of arrest, and was merely overheard by a law enforcement official who, unbeknownst to the defendant, also spoke Spanish."); *People v. Cole,* 24 A.D.3d 1021, __, 807 N.Y.S.2d 166, 171 (3d Dep't 2005); *People v. Murphy,* 163 A.D.2d 425, __, 558 N.Y.S.2d 140, 141 (2d Dep't 1990); *People v. Stewart,* 160 A.D.2d 966, __, 554 N.Y.S.2d 687, 688 (2d Dep't 1990).

Nonetheless, where the overheard statement was made to the defendant's attorney, the statement may be suppressible pursuant to the attorney-client privilege. In this regard, in *People v. Boone,* 51 A.D.2d 25, __, 379 N.Y.S.2d 181, 184 (3d Dep't 1976):

Defendant . . . objected to the admission of a statement which was made to his attorney on the telephone and overheard by the police. While the statement is not within the technical notice provisions of CPL 710.30, since it was not made to a public servant, defendant contends that admission of the statement would be a violation of the attorney-client privilege. If defendant voluntarily made the statement with full knowledge of the officers' presence and no attempt to prevent them from hearing, no privilege would attach. However, if defendant sought and was deprived of the opportunity for a private conversation with his attorney, then a question as to deprivation of counsel is raised. In view of the necessity of a hearing on the voluntariness of defendant's third statement, the circumstances of the statement to his attorney should also be disclosed.

(Citations omitted).

§ 26:26   Applicability of CPL § 710.30 to statements made to off-duty police officer

In *People v. Miller*, 142 A.D.2d 760, __, 530 N.Y.S.2d 866, 868 (3d Dep't 1988), the Appellate Division, Third Department, held that:

Defendant's admission to [off-duty part-time Schuyler County Deputy Sheriff Kenneth] Switzer was "made by a defendant to a public servant" (CPL 710.30[1]) and, therefore, the statutory notice was required to be given within 15 days after arraignment (CPL 710.30[2]). The People failed to establish good cause for the failure to give timely notice. Accordingly, the reception of the statement into evidence was statutorily barred (CPL 710.30[3]). Although there was evidence that Switzer was only on limited duty in the Schuyler County Sheriff's office, there is nothing in the record which would lead to any conclusion other than that, when he spoke to defendant, he was a duly appointed Deputy Sheriff. As such, he clearly met the broad statutory definition of a public servant, which includes, *inter alia*, not only "any public officer or employee of the state or of any political subdivision thereof or of any governmental instrumentality", but also any person "who has been * * * designated to *become* a public servant" (Penal Law § 10.00[15] [emphasis supplied]). Obviously, under this definition, the status of Switzer as a public servant was not removed because he was not officially on duty when the statement was made nor in the county where he was employed. Indeed, as a Deputy Sheriff, Switzer was a "police officer" (CPL 1.20[34][b]) and, as such, could have arrested defendant in Tompkins County without a warrant for the crime of driving while intoxicated (CPL 140.10[1][b]).

142 A.D.2d at __, 530 N.Y.S.2d at 868. *Cf. People v. Socia*, 150 Misc. 2d 518, __, 568 N.Y.S.2d 864, 865–66 (Bronx Co. Sup. Ct. 1991); *People v. Ridley*, 65 Misc. 2d 547, __, 318 N.Y.S.2d 331, 336 (Tompkins Co. Ct. 1971) (no notice required where "[n]o police inquiry was made, no custodial atmosphere prevailed, Wil-

liams merely being an employee of Cornell University Safety Division, who was off-duty, off campus, in his own private car, not in uniform and without any police jurisdiction at the scene whatsoever and who was in no way working at that time for any police agency").

§ 26:27   710.30 notice inapplicable to conduct not amounting to a statement

CPL § 710.30(1)(a) applies to evidence of a "statement" made by the defendant. In *People v. Peters*, 43 A.D.2d 599, —, 348 N.Y.S.2d 786, 788 (3d Dep't 1973), the Appellate Division, Second Department, held that:

> Section 710.30 imposes a notice requirement when the prosecution intends to offer at a trial "a statement" made by the defendant. Here, the testimony involved concerned the defendant's physical act of delivering the keys to the car to an officer. While concededly conduct may, under some circumstances, amount to an admission, we cannot construe section 710.30 as requiring notice that proof is intended to be offered of such a physical act as is here involved. As noted, there is no assertion made that delivery of the keys was in any way involuntary and defendant cannot possibly claim that such testimony came as a surprise, which is a main reason behind the enactment of section 710.30.

See also People v. Morales, 248 A.D.2d 731, —, 670 N.Y.S.2d 591, 591–92 (2d Dep't 1998).

§ 26:28   Applicability of CPL § 710.30 to pretrial hearings

In *People v. Aldrich-O'Shea*, 6 Misc. 3d 35, 789 N.Y.S.2d 804 (App. Term, 9th & 10th Jud. Dist. 2004), a DWI case, the People failed to provide the defendant with CPL § 710.30 notice with regard to the defendant's statements admitting that she had operated the vehicle. Following a probable cause hearing, the Village Court (a) held that such failure would result in the defendant's admissions being "suppressed," and (b) dismissed the accusatory instrument on the ground that without such admissions the People would be unable to prove the issue of operation. On appeal, the Appellate Term held as follows:

> While we leave undisturbed the court's determination to preclude the statements at trial, said determination provided no basis to exclude the evidence from its probable cause review or to dismiss the accusatory instrument. Because suppression hearings are not part of a trial, a court may consider precluded statements in a suppression motion determination, for example, whether the People had probable cause to arrest. Accordingly, we remand the matter to the court below for a determination de novo of the suppression motion.

We also agree that the accusatory instrument should not have been dismissed. A preclusion order based on a CPL 710.30 violation affects only the evidence's use "upon trial." Whether, absent the precluded proof, there remains sufficient evidence to prosecute the charge is a matter for the People to determine.

6 Misc. 3d at ___, 789 N.Y.S.2d at 805–06 (citations omitted).

§ 26:29   Subsequent 710.30 notice supercedes prior notice

In *People v. Boyles*, 210 A.D.2d 732, 621 N.Y.S.2d 118 (3d Dep't 1994), a DWI/AUO 1st case, the defendant was served with two 710.30 notices: the first at the time of his arrest; the second following his indictment and arraignment in County Court. The second 710.30 notice omitted a significant statement that was contained in the first. On appeal, the Appellate Division, Third Department, held as follows:

Because we are remitting this case for a new trial, we also address defendant's contention that County Court erred when it admitted into evidence his statement that he was coming from Shoprite and was on his way to Fallsburg because he was not given proper notice pursuant to CPL 710.30. That statement is significant because the officers apparently knew that Shoprite closed some two hours earlier. The People served two CPL 710.30 notices on defendant; one personally at the time he was arrested and brought before the Monticello Justice Court and a second within 15 days of the arraignment in County Court. Only the earlier notice contained defendant's statement that he was coming from Shoprite. . . . Because the CPL 710.30 notice served at that arraignment in County Court failed to apprise defendant of the People's intention to use his statement that he was coming from Shoprite against him at the trial in that court, that statement should have been suppressed. Defendant was entitled to rely upon the contents of the subsequent CPL 710.30 notice to determine whether to move for suppression of any evidence specified therein before trial in County Court.

210 A.D.2d at ___, 621 N.Y.S.2d at 120.

By contrast, "the People are not required under CPL 710.30 to re-serve a properly served statement notice after filing a superceding complaint." *People v. Berisha*, 12 Misc. 3d 344, ___, 816 N.Y.S.2d 830, 831 (N.Y. City Crim. Ct. 2006). In *Berisha*:

Neither side denies that the People served and filed a statement notice pursuant to CPL 710.30 within 15-days of Defendant's arraignment on the initial complaint. The statement of Defendant appearing with the notice has not changed. Defendant's argument is based on the fact that the People did not re-serve such notice after filing a superceding complaint. The court finds this argument to be without merit.

12 Misc. 3d at ___, 816 N.Y.S.2d at 831.

§ 26:30 Amendment of 710.30 notice

People v. Centeno, 168 Misc. 2d 172, —, 637 N,Y.S.2d 254, 258 (N.Y. Co. Sup. Ct. 1995), nicely summarizes the law in this area:

> Where the notice is otherwise correct and not misleading, minor mistakes can be corrected by amending the notice, even after the notice period has run. (*People v. Canute*, 190 A.D.2d 745, 593 N.Y.S.2d 539 [2d Dep't 1993] [notice that identification was a showup could be amended to correctly state that it was a lineup]; *People v. Ocasio*, 183 A.D.2d 921, 922–23, 584 N.Y.S.2d 156 [2d Dep't 1992] [identification notice giving name of wrong witness could be amended to identify the correct witness].) It is only when the notice is so erroneous as to mislead the defendant into understanding that the noticed identification procedure or statement was an entirely different procedure or statement than the one that the People actually seek to utilize that the errors cannot be corrected by amendment. (*See People v. Greene*, 163 Misc. 2d 187, 620 N.Y.S.2d 232 [Sup. Ct. Kings Co. 1994] [notice that identification took place at wrong time and place could not be cured by amendment because it was so defective as to constitute notice of an entirely different identification procedure].)

Cases decided subsequent to *Centeno* follow the same reasoning. For example, in *People v. Pannell*, 287 A.D.2d 659, —, 731 N.Y.S.2d 750, 751 (2d Dep't 2001), the Appellate Division, Second Department, held that:

> Contrary to the defendant's contention, the hearing court properly permitted the People to amend their CPL 710.30 notice to correct an error regarding the name of one of the witnesses who identified the defendant at a showup. The primary purpose of a CPL 710.30 notice is to alert the defendant "to the possibility that evidence identifying him as the person who committed the crime may be constitutionally tainted and subject to a motion to suppress." Here, the People gave the defense timely notice that the defendant had been identified at a showup by two witnesses, which enabled the defendant to move to suppress the prospective identification testimony. Moreover, the defendant was granted a *Wade* hearing which explored the issue of whether the showup identifications were impermissibly suggestive. Under these circumstances, the notice given to the defense satisfied the intent of the statute.

(Citations omitted).

In addition, in *People v. Moore*, 178 Misc. 2d 163, 682 N.Y.S.2d 798 (Westchester Co. Ct. 1998), a multi-defendant case, the People's 710.30 notice erroneously stated that a statement made by the defendant, Roosevelt Payne, was made by a woman named Juanita Jackson. The People served an amended 710.30 notice correcting this error. The Court held that:

> An amendment to a CPL 710.30 notice of statement is permissible where, as here, the amendment and the original timely served no-

tice are identical, except to the extent that the amendment seeks to change that which is readily apparent to the defendant from a mere reading of the statement; here, that the statement is one alleged to have been made by him.

178 Misc. 2d at __, 682 N.Y.S.2d at 800.

§ 26:31 Consequence of People's failure to attach proper statement to their 710.30 notice

In *People v. Sian*, 167 A.D.2d 435, __, 561 N.Y.S.2d 791, 792 (2d Dep't 1990), the Appellate Division, Second Department, held that:

Contrary to the People's contention, the defendant's motion to preclude his inculpatory statement was properly granted. While the defendant received a timely *Huntley* notice which provided that the prosecution would offer a statement taken from him on the date of his arrest, the People concede that a copy of another, unrelated confession taken from the defendant on the same date was appended thereto. Only after the 15-day period for giving notice (*see*, CPL 710.30[2]) had expired, was the defendant served with a copy of the statement pertaining to the indictment in this case. Inasmuch as the wrong inculpatory statement was attached to the *Huntley* notice, and that notice did not otherwise convey the sum and substance of the statement which the prosecution intended to use in this case, the People failed to comply with the requirements of CPL 710.30. Moreover, while the correct statement was eventually served upon the defendant, the People failed to demonstrate the existence of "good cause" (CPL 710.30[2]) for the untimely service, as their proffered explanation amounted to nothing more than office failure.

In contrast to the above situation (*i.e.*, where the People attached the wrong 710.30 notice), it has been held that where the People's 710.30 notice refers to an attachment, but the "attachment" is not attached, it is incumbent upon defense counsel to bring this issue to the People's attention. *See, e.g., People v. Kelly*, 200 A.D.2d 440, __, 607 N.Y.S.2d 240, 241 (1st Dep't 1994); *People v. Black*, 177 A.D.2d 1040, __, 578 N.Y.S.2d 53, 53–54 (4th Dep't 1991); *People v. Manzi*, 162 A.D.2d 955, __, 558 N.Y.S.2d 337, 338 (4th Dep't 1990).

§ 26:32 Redaction of 710.30 notice can be reversible error

In *People v. Charles*, 78 N.Y.2d 1044, 1046, 576 N.Y.S.2d 81, 82–83, 581 N.E.2d 1336 (1991), the Court of Appeals reversed the Appellate Division and ordered a new trial where:

Defendant was tried jointly with another on three drug charges arising from the possession of cocaine and marihuana. At the *Huntley* hearing, one of the arresting officers testified to a joint statement made by the two defendants immediately before he arrested them in the basement of an apartment house. The officer stated that "both said the [marijuana] bag was theirs and that they have been selling marijuana out the back door of the location through the peephole for a man named Oswald" and that "they were getting high." Inasmuch as the admissions were inadmissible against the codefendant for failure to serve notice under CPL 710.30, the court redacted them to omit any reference to the codefendant. The changes included substituting singular pronouns for plurals. Thus, at trial, the officer was permitted to testify that the defendant made the entire statement.

Before the evidence was received, the People had to establish that the statement was made by defendant and that it could be effectively redacted for the jury without prejudice to him. They failed to sustain that burden. The police officer testified at the *Huntley* hearing that he was unable to ascertain which admissions, if any, were attributed to defendant because "both [suspects] spoke at the same time." Inasmuch as no other evidence was offered to establish the speaker, the People have failed to meet their burden and should not have been allowed to offer this evidence against defendant at trial. For the same reason it was impossible for the court to effectively redact the statement without prejudice to defendant. By changing the pronouns and permitting the officer to testify at trial that defendant made the entire statement, the jury was led to believe that all of the admissions had been made by defendant when in fact the People had not established that he made any of them.

(Citations omitted).

§ 26:33   When is a *Huntley* hearing required?

CPL § 710.60(3)(b) "expressly provides that the absence of factual basis does not permit denial of a motion to suppress a statement claimed to have been involuntarily made to a law enforcement official." *People v. Weaver*, 49 N.Y.2d 1012, 1013, 429 N.Y.S.2d 399, 399, 406 N.E.2d 1335, 1336 (1980). "Thus, . . . there *must* be a hearing whenever defendant claims his statement was involuntary no matter what facts he puts forth in support of that claim." 49 N.Y.2d at 1013, 429 N.Y.S.2d at 399. *See also People v. Jones*, 95 N.Y.2d 721, 725 n.2, 723 N.Y.S.2d 761, 764 n.2, 746 N.E.2d 1053 (2001); *People v. Mendoza*, 82 N.Y.2d 415, 421–22, 604 N.Y.S.2d 922, 924, 624 N.E.2d 1017 (1993).

On the other hand, CPL § 710.60(2)(b) "provides that the court must summarily grant a motion to suppress if '[t]he people stipulate that the evidence * * * will not be offered in evidence *in any criminal action or proceeding* against defendant.' " *People v. White*, 73 N.Y.2d 468, 475–76, 541 N.Y.S.2d 749, 753, 539 N.E.2d 577 (1989) (citation omitted). In *White*, the Court of Appeals noted that "[t]he Criminal Procedure Law does not define the term 'stipulation' and no authority has been cited interpreting that term as used in the statute." 73 N.Y.2d at 476, 541 N.Y.S.2d at 753. In this regard, the Court held that "[we accept the definition, recently stated by one court, that a stipulation is "'[an agreement, admission, or concession made in a judicial proceeding by the parties thereto or their attorneys, in respect of some matter incident to the proceeding, for the purpose, ordinarily, of avoiding delay, trouble and expense.'" " 73 N.Y.2d at 476, 541 N.Y.S.2d at 753 (citations omitted).

In *White*, prior to the defendant's *first* trial the People stated that a *Huntley* hearing was unnecessary because the People did not intend to use the defendant's statements. Applying the above definition to the facts of the case, the Court of Appeals found that this statement constituted a stipulation precluding the People from offering the statements at the defendant's *second* trial. 73 N.Y.2d at 476, 541 N.Y.S.2d at 753. *See generally People v. Boughton*, 70 N.Y.2d 854, 855, 523 N.Y.S.2d 454, 455, 517 N.E.2d 1340 (1987) (where the People withdraw their 710.30 notice, they cannot change their mind after the 15-day time period has run).

§ 26:34   Scope of a *Huntley* hearing

The Court of Appeals made clear in *People v. Misuis*, 47 N.Y.2d 979, 981, 419 N.Y.S.2d 961, 962–63, 393 N.E.2d 1034 (1979), that:

> Clearly, statements obtained by exploitation of unlawful police conduct or detention must be suppressed, for their use in evidence under such circumstance violates the Fourth Amendment (*Dunaway v. New York*, — U.S. —, 99 S.Ct. 2248, 60 L.Ed.2d 824). It is therefore "incumbent upon the suppression court to permit an inquiry into the propriety of the police conduct." Unless the People establish that the police had probable cause to arrest or detain a suspect, and unless the defendant is accorded an opportunity to delve fully into the circumstances attendant upon his arrest or detention, his motion to suppress should be granted.

(Quoting *People v. Wise*, 46 N.Y.2d 321, 329, 413 N.Y.S.2d 334, 339, 385 N.E.2d 1262, 14 A.L.R.4th 666 (1978)) (footnote omitted). *See also People v. Chaney*, 253 A.D.2d 562, —, 686 N.Y.S.2d 871, 873 (3d Dep't 1998); *People v. Sanchez*, 236 A.D.2d 243, —, 653 N.Y.S.2d 563, 564–65 (1st Dep't 1997).

In *Misuis*, the Court of Appeals reversed the Appellate Division, vacated the defendant's guilty plea, and remitted the case for a probable cause hearing where:

> At the hearing on defendant's motion to suppress [various] admissions, his counsel repeatedly attempted to interrogate the two officers in an effort to discover whether the police had probable cause to make the arrest. His avowed intention was to show that the

detention was unlawful and thus any statements made as a result of the claimed unlawful arrest and detention tainted any admissions. However, at the insistent urging of the prosecutor the court refused to permit that inquiry and permitted only questions concerning the voluntariness of the statements themselves.

47 N.Y.2d at 980, 419 N.Y.S.2d at 962.

The same conclusion was reached in *People v. Whitaker*, 79 A.D.2d 668, __, 433 N.Y.S.2d 849, 850 (2d Dep't 1980):

> As the People concede, the suppression court erred in severely limit-ing the defendant's cross-examination of the sole arresting officer who testified, with respect to the issue of whether there was prob-able cause to arrest defendant. It is well-settled that on a motion to suppress a defendant's postarrest statements, the suppression court is required to permit the defendant to "delve fully into the circum-stances attendant upon his arrest", for "[a] statement, voluntary under Fifth Amendment standards, will nevertheless be suppressed if it has been obtained through the exploitation of an illegal arrest."

(Citations omitted). *See also People v. Lopez*, 56 A.D.3d 280, 867 N.Y.S.2d 83 (1st Dep't 2008); *People v. Roberts*, 81 A.D.2d 674, 441 N.Y.S.2d 408 (2d Dep't 1981); *People v. King*, 79 A.D.2d 1033, 437 N.Y.S.2d 931 (2d Dep't 1981); *People v. Specks*, 77 A.D.2d 669, 430 N.Y.S.2d 157 (2d Dep't 1980). *See generally People v. Gonzalez*, 71 A.D.2d 775, __, 419 N.Y.S.2d 322, 323–24 (3d Dep't 1979).

§ 26:35 When is a *Wade* hearing required?

In *People v. Boyer*, 6 N.Y.3d 427, 813 N.Y.S.2d 31, 846 N.E.2d 461 (2006), the Court of Appeals summarized the law as it pertains to when a *Wade* hearing is required:

> The People ask us to extend the "confirmatory identification" excep-tion derived from *People v. Wharton*, 74 N.Y.2d 921, 550 N.Y.S.2d 260, 549 N.E.2d 462 [1989] to situations where a police officer's initial encounter with a suspect and subsequent identification of that suspect are temporally related, such that the two might be considered part of a single police procedure. To do so, however, would run afoul of CPL 710.30. Moreover, such an exception would eliminate the protections offered by a *Wade* hearing even when the initial police viewing—albeit part of a single police procedure—was fleeting, unreliable and susceptible of misidentification. * * *
>
> *The Applicable Law*
>
> CPL 710.30 could not be clearer. The Legislature has prescribed that, within 15 days of arraignment, the prosecution must serve upon the defendant notice of its intention to introduce at trial "testimony regarding an observation of the defendant either at the time or place of the commission of the offense or upon some other occasion relevant to the case, to be given by a witness who has previously identified him as such" (CPL 710.30[1][b]). Upon the ser-

vice of notice, "the defendant must be accorded reasonable opportunity to move before trial, pursuant to subdivision one of section 710.40, to suppress" the identification (CPL 710.30[2]). If notice is not given, the prosecution will be precluded from introducing such evidence at trial, unless (1) it is permitted to serve a late notice for good cause shown, or (2) the defendant has moved to suppress the identification testimony and the motion is denied (*see* CPL 710.30[2], [3]). Neither of these exceptions is relevant here.

CPL 710.30 underscores and facilitates the defendant's right, prior to trial, to test the reliability of any out-of-court identifications that the People intend to introduce. The statutory scheme ensures that the identifications are not the product of undue suggestiveness, and lessens the possibility of misidentification. The statutory mandate is plain and the procedure simple: the People serve notice, the defendant moves to suppress and the court holds a *Wade* hearing to consider the suppression motion. A court may summarily deny a suppression motion without a hearing only if "[t]he motion papers do not allege a ground constituting [a] legal basis for the motion" (CPL 710.60[3][a]). Thus, once the People serve notice that they intend to introduce identification testimony, the defendant may choose to respond with a motion to suppress that testimony and, so long as the motion alleges undue suggestiveness, the defendant is generally entitled to a *Wade* hearing.

We have recognized, however, two instances when, as a matter of law, the identification at issue could not be the product of undue suggestiveness. Under such circumstances, the defendant is not entitled to a *Wade* hearing and thus the People are not obligated to provide notice pursuant to CPL 710.30(1)(b). This so-called "confirmatory identification" exception carries significant consequences and is therefore limited to the scenarios set forth in *People v. Wharton* and *People v. Rodriguez*, where there is no risk of misidentification. As we noted in *Rodriguez*, a court may summarily deny a *Wade* hearing (and hence no CPL 710.30 notice would be required) where the court concludes that, as a matter of law, the identifying, civilian witness knew the "defendant so well that no amount of police suggestiveness could possibly taint the identification."

Here, we are concerned only with the *Wharton* scenario. In *Wharton*, an experienced undercover officer observed the defendant face-to-face during a planned buy-and-bust operation. The officer then radioed his backup team with a description of the defendant, who was immediately arrested. As planned, within five minutes of the arrest, the purchasing officer drove past the defendant specifically for the purpose of identifying him, and then again identified him a few hours later at the police station.

Under such circumstances, we held that the defendant was not entitled to a *Wade* hearing (and thus would not be entitled to CPL 710.30 notice) to test the officer's identification. * * *

[T]he quality of the officer's initial viewing must be a critical factor in any *Wharton*-type analysis. The risk of undue suggestiveness is obviated only when the identifying officer's observation of the defendant is so clear that the identification could not be mistaken. When there is a risk that the quality of the initial observation has eroded over time, we have consistently held that police identifications do not enjoy any exemption from the statutory notice and hearing requirements.

6 N.Y.3d at 429, 431–33, 813 N.Y.S.2d at 31–32, 33–34 (citations omitted). *See also People v. Dixon*, 85 N.Y.2d 218, 623 N.Y.S.2d 813, 647 N.E.2d 1321 (1995); *People v. Rodriguez*, 79 N.Y.2d 445, 583 N.Y.S.2d 814, 593 N.E.2d 268 (1992); *People v. Newball*, 76 N.Y.2d 587, 561 N.Y.S.2d 898, 563 N.E.2d 269 (1990).

In *Rodriguez*, *supra*, the Court of Appeals held that:

The People bear the burden in any instance they claim that a citizen identification procedure was "merely confirmatory." The unusual treatment accorded such identifications—no CPL 710.30 notice or *Wade* hearing is necessary—requires that the exception be narrowly confined to situations where " 'suggestiveness' is not a concern." Thus, the People must show that the protagonists are known to one another, or where (as here) there is no mutual relationship, that the witness knows defendant so well as to be impervious to police suggestion.

Contrary to the People's argument, prior familiarity should not be resolved at trial in the first instance. The Legislature mandates *pretrial* resolution of the admissibility of identification testimony where it is alleged that an improper procedure occurred (*see*, CPL 710.20[6] 710.60). Moreover, when the defendant's theory at trial is mistaken identity, the exploration of prior familiarity on cross-examination may actually bolster the People's case.

79 N.Y.2d at 452, 583 N.Y.S.2d at 818–19 (citation omitted). *See also People v. White*, 73 N.Y.2d 468, 473, 541 N.Y.S.2d 749, 751, 539 N.E.2d 577 (1989) (CPL § 710.30 does not apply to judicially supervised identifications which occur when the defendant is represented by counsel); *People v. Gissendanner*, 48 N.Y.2d 543, 552, 423 N.Y.S.2d 893, 899 (1979) ("In cases in which the defendant's identity is not in issue, or those in which the protagonists are known to one another, 'suggestiveness' is not a concern and, hence, the statute does not come into play.").

In *People v. Coker*, 121 A.D.3d 1305, __, 995 N.Y.S.2d 288, 290-91 (3d Dep't 2014), leave to appeal denied, 26 N.Y.3d 927 (2015), the Appellate Division, Third Department, held that:

[T]he People were [not] required to provide notice pursuant to CPL

710.30 regarding their intent to offer identification testimony at trial. The evidence at the preclusion hearing established that, when police arrived at the scene, Jacqueway—without any prompting by police—pointed to defendant and stated to police that "[h]e's right there on the sidewalk." As this identification of defendant occurred spontaneously without any police involvement, CPL 710.30 notice of such identification was not required.

§ 26:36   When is a pre-*Wade* hearing required?

As the previous section demonstrates, a *Wade* hearing is not required where the identification procedure at issue is merely "confirmatory." Ironically, however, a hearing is often required to determine whether the identification procedure was truly confirmatory (*i.e.*, the determination whether the identification procedure was truly confirmatory is for the Court—not the People—to make). In this regard, in *People v. Williamson*, 79 N.Y.2d 799, 801, 580 N.Y.S.2d 170, 171, 588 N.E.2d 68 (1991), the Court of Appeals held that:

> The case must be remitted for a hearing to determine whether a *Wade* hearing is required. If, after that pre-*Wade* hearing, the court concludes that a *Wade* hearing is not required, the judgment should be amended to reflect that determination and the judgment of conviction and sentence treated as affirmed. If, after the pre-*Wade* hearing, the nisi prius court determines that a *Wade* hearing is required, a *Wade* hearing should be held and further proceedings, including a new trial, should be carried out as circumstances may warrant.

Similarly, in *People v. Rodriguez*, 79 N.Y.2d 445, 453, 583 N.Y.S.2d 814, 820, 593 N.E.2d 268 (1992), the Court of Appeals held that:

> [T]he case should be remitted to Supreme Court for a hearing to determine whether the identification procedure was confirmatory. If, after that hearing, the court concludes that the People have not sustained their burden, a *Wade* hearing should be held and further proceedings, including a new trial, should be had as the circumstances may warrant.

See generally People v. Ross, 160 Misc. 2d 1, 603 N.Y.S.2d 652 (Bronx Co. Sup. Ct. 1993) (non-eyewitness can testify at pre-*Wade* hearing to establish victim's prior familiarity with defendant for purposes of invoking confirmatory identification exception to CPL § 710.30(1)(b)).

§ 26:37   Defendant waives 710.30 notice claim by moving to suppress rather than preclude

Where the People fail to comply with the requirements of CPL § 710.30, the remedy is preclusion—*unless* the defendant moves to suppress, rather than preclude, and the motion to suppress is denied. In this regard, CPL § 710.30(3) provides that:

In the absence of service of notice upon a defendant as prescribed in this section, no evidence of a kind specified in [CPL § 710.30(1)] may be received against [the defendant] upon trial unless he has, despite the lack of such notice, moved to suppress such evidence and such motion has been denied and the evidence thereby rendered admissible as prescribed in [CPL § 710.70(2)].

It is critical to note that the waiver provision contained in CPL § 710.30(3) applies even if the defendant had initially moved to preclude and the motion was improperly denied—prompting the defendant to subsequently move to suppress. In this regard, in *People v. Kirkland*, 89 N.Y.2d 903, 904–05, 653 N.Y.S.2d 256, 257, 675 N.E.2d 1208 (1996), the Court of Appeals held that:

When the People intend to offer identification testimony from a witness, a notice of intent must be served upon the defendant specifying the evidence which the People intend to offer (CPL 710.30). The notice requirement is excused when a defendant moves for suppression of the identification testimony (CPL 710.30[3]). Since the defendant here moved to suppress the identification testimony and received a full hearing on the fairness of the identification procedure, any alleged deficiency in the notice provided by the People was irrelevant.

(Citations omitted). *See also People v. Merrill*, 87 N.Y.2d 948, 641 N.Y.S.2d 587, 664 N.E.2d 498 (1996); *People v. Newball*, 76 N.Y.2d 587, 590, 561 N.Y.S.2d 898, 900, 563 N.E.2d 269 (1990). Notably, the Appellate Division majority in *Merrill*, relying on *People v. Bernier*, 73 N.Y.2d 1006, 541 N.Y.S.2d 760, 539 N.E.2d 588 (1989), held that "[a] defendant who initially moves to preclude and loses does not waive his right to preclusion by later participating in a Wade hearing." 212 A.D.2d 987, ___, 624 N.Y.S.2d 702, 702 (4th Dep't 1995). This holding seems to be a correct application of *Bernier*. Nonetheless, the Court of Appeals reversed, with no opinion, for the reasons stated in the dissenting opinion at the Appellate Division.

Kirkland and *Merrill* are difficult to reconcile with *Bernier*. In *Bernier*:

Defense counsel learned during trial jury selection that a person with respect to whom no CPL 710.30(1) pretrial notice had been given would be called as the prosecution's main identifying witness. He then made a motion to preclude the testimony based on lack of notice and surprise. Inasmuch as the People failed to present or establish any excuse for not giving the required notice, the court should have granted the preclusion motion and suppressed the identification testimony. Instead, it denied the motion on condition that the prosecution make available the officers who investigated the robberies. After speaking with an officer, defense counsel stated on the record that he had "no idea based on the information I have whether [Gedeon the unnoticed witness] made any kind of out-of-court identification and if he did *maybe* we need a *Wade* Hearing with respect to that. *I have no idea.*" (Emphasis added.) When the prosecutor then acknowledged that an out-of-court identification had been made, the court ordered a *Wade* hearing.

73 N.Y.2d at 1007–08, 541 N.Y.S.2d at 761 (citations omitted).

The Court of Appeals held that the Appellate Division correctly reversed the defendant's conviction. In this regard, the Court rejected the People's claim that "defendant . . . waived the preclusion protection pursuant to the exception of CPL 710.30(3) by making a suppression motion or participating in a suppression hearing," holding that "[t]he waiver exception cannot become operative in a case such as this when the defendant clearly moved initially to preclude and lost." 73 N.Y.2d at 1008, 541 N.Y.S.2d at 761. The *Bernier* Court further held that defense counsel, who merely acquiesced in the *Wade* hearing ordered by the trial court, "made no suppression motion qualifying under CPL 710.30(3)." 73 N.Y.2d at 1008, 541 N.Y.S.2d at 761.

In light of *Kirkland* and *Merrill*, where the defendant believes that his or her motion to preclude has been improperly denied, a strategy decision has to be made as to whether to preserve this issue for appeal or rather to waive the issue by moving to suppress the evidence. *See, e.g., People v. Lopez*, 84 N.Y.2d 425, 427, 618 N.Y.S.2d 879, 881, 643 N.E.2d 501 (1994) ("Electing to preserve for appellate review his claim that the notice was insufficient, defendant did not seek suppression and no *Huntley* or *Wade* hearings were held."); *People v. O'Doherty*, 70 N.Y.2d 479, 483, 522 N.Y.S.2d 498, 500, 517 N.E.2d 213 (1987) ("Supreme Court . . ., over defendant's objection, held a *Huntley* hearing."); *People v. Amparo*, 73 N.Y.2d 728, 729, 535 N.Y.S.2d 588, 589, 532 N.E.2d 94 (1988) ("The exception contained in CPL 710.30(3)—where a defendant has 'moved to suppress such evidence and such motion has been denied and the evidence thereby rendered admissible'—is inapplicable here. Defense counsel did not make a motion for suppression of the oral statement on the ground that it was in substance inadmissible at trial . . . . Rather, defense counsel moved only for preclusion of the oral statement on account of late notice, which does not fall within the exception contained in CPL 710.30(3).").

In this regard, it is critical to note that a motion by the defendant to suppress "any and all" statements on the ground of involuntariness—together with participation in a *Huntley* hearing—constitutes a waiver of the preclusion issue. *See, e.g., People v. Sturiale*, 262 A.D.2d 1003, __, 693 N.Y.S.2d 374, 375 (4th Dep't 1999) ("defendant sought suppression of 'any and all' statements made by him. Because the oral statements were the very subject of the suppression hearing, the sufficiency of the CPL 710.30 notice was irrelevant"). *Cf. People v. St. Martine*, 160 A.D.2d 35, —, 559 N.Y.S.2d 697, 700–01 (1st Dep't 1990) ("Defendant, in the instant matter, did not, by seeking to suppress any and all statements, in effect waive his right to object to the admission of statements of which he was at the time of the motion still unacquainted."); *People v. Holley*, 157 Misc. 2d 402, —, 596 N.Y.S.2d 1016, 1018 (N.Y. City Crim. Ct. 1993) ("this court finds that the request to suppress 'any and all statements' covered only those statements for which notice had been given and not every statement contained in the police paperwork served at the arraignment"); *People v. Utria*, 165 Misc. 2d 54, —, 626 N.Y.S.2d 948, 952 (N.Y. City Crim. Ct. 1995) ("the defendant does not waive the right to seek and obtain preclusion when he moves to suppress 'all statements', since he does not waive his right to object to the admission of statements of which he was unaware at the time of the motion"); *People v. Wright*, 127 Misc. 2d 885, — n.*, 487 N.Y.S.2d 688, 691-92 n.* (Nassau Co. Ct. 1985):

> When defendant moved for "a *Huntley* hearing," he must have been addressing the statement contained in the CPL 710.30 notice, for that is the only one of which he had formal notice the People intended to offer.

> The fact that the defendant may be aware of a number of other statements he made to public officials is irrelevant. It is for the People to tell defendant which statements they intend to offer at the trial. It is not every statement the defendant makes that the People intend to offer at the trial. It is their obligation to be specific, so that when defendant requests a *Huntley* hearing, the request can be directed at those statements the People intend to offer at the trial, notice of which is the very essence of CPL 710.30.

It should also be kept in mind that the 710.30 notice issue will be waived by a guilty plea. *See* § 26:40, *infra*.

§ 26:38   Use of non-noticed statement to impeach defendant's testimony

CPL § 710.30 notice only applies to statements that the People intend to use against the defendant during their case-in-chief. *See, e.g., People v. Goodson*, 57 N.Y.2d 828, 829–30, 455 N.Y.S.2d 757, 758, 442 N.E.2d 54 (1982). Accordingly, 710.30 notice does not apply to statements used to impeach the defendant if the defendant chooses to testify. *See, e.g., People v. Ashley*, 15 Misc. 3d 80, —, 836 N.Y.S.2d 758, 759 (App. Term, 9th & 10th Jud. Dist. 2007).

Nonetheless, since the defendant is entitled to discovery of *every* statement he or she made to a public servant, regardless of whether the People intend to offer the statement(s) during their direct case, *see, e.g.*, § 26:21, *supra*, CPL § 240.20(1)(a); *People v. Fields*, 258 A.D.2d 809, 687 N.Y.S.2d 184 (3d Dep't 1999), this rule should not lead to surprise. In *Fields, supra*, the Appellate Division, Third Department, reversed the defendant's conviction and remanded for a new trial where the trial court failed to preclude certain statements made by the defendant that were not disclosed by the People pursuant to either the defendant's demand to produce and/or the trial court's discovery order. In this regard, the Court held that discovery pursuant to CPL § 240.20(1)(a) "is not limited to statements intended to be offered by the People 'at trial', i.e., statements offered as part of the People's direct case (*see*, CPL 240.10[4])." 258 A.D.2d at __, 687 N.Y.S.2d at 186. In so holding, the Court expressly rejected the People's claim that they need only disclose statements to which CPL § 710.30 applies. 258 A.D.2d at __, 687 N.Y.S.2d at 185.

§ 26:39 Defendant can "open the door" to the admission of a non-noticed statement

In *People v. Goodson*, 57 N.Y.2d 828, 829–30, 455 N.Y.S.2d 757, 758, 442 N.E.2d 54 (1982), the defendant "opened the door" to the admission of a non-noticed statement under the following circumstances:

> Defendant contends that it was error to admit the testimony of Officer McCartney that when defendant was arrested he stated "that he was there, but he didn't rob the old lady", inasmuch as no reference had been made to this statement in the prosecutor's notice under CPL 710.30. That section, unlike an all-embracing demand in a demand for a bill of particulars, requires disclosure only of statements which the People "intend to offer at a trial". The quoted statement of defendant did not fall into that category, and there was, therefore, no violation of the statutory prescription. It was only after defense counsel on cross-examination of Officer McCartney, a third-party witness for the People, inquired as to whether there ever came a time when defendant "denied his involvement in this" and the witness responded in the affirmative that on redirect the prosecutor, questioning the witness as to the exact words that defendant used, elicited the testimony now challenged. The trial court correctly ruled that defense counsel had opened the door to its admission.

See also People v. Merlino, 145 A.D.2d 654, 536 N.Y.S.2d 170 (2d Dep't 1988).

§ 26:40 710.30 notice claim is waived by guilty plea

"Although a guilty plea does not extinguish every claim on appeal, only a limited number of claims survive a valid waiver. These are either jurisdictional matters, such as an insufficient accusatory instrument, or rights of a constitutional dimension that 'go to the very heart of the process (such as the constitutional speedy trial right, the protection against double jeopardy or a defendant's competency to stand trial).' " *People v. Parilla*, 8 N.Y.3d 654, 659, 838 N.Y.S.2d 824, 827, 870 N.E.2d 142 (2007) (citation omitted).

710.30 notice claims do not fall within the category of claims that survive a valid guilty plea. 8 N.Y.3d at 659, 838 N.Y.S.2d at 827. *See also People v. Hansen*, 95 N.Y.2d 227, 231 n.3, 715 N.Y.S.2d 369, 372 n.3, 738 N.E.2d 773 (2000); *People v. Taylor*, 65 N.Y.2d 1, 489 N.Y.S.2d 152, 478 N.E.2d 755 (1985).

§ 26:41   Failure to give 710.30 notice is subject to harmless error analysis

The Court of Appeals has made clear that the failure to provide the defendant with 710.30 notice is subject to harmless error analysis where the evidence of the defendant's guilt is overwhelming. *See, e.g., People v. Rivera*, 9 N.Y.3d 904, 843 N.Y.S.2d 532, 875 N.E.2d 24 (2007); *People v. Oliver*, 34 N.Y.2d 859, 359 N.Y.S.2d 112, 316 N.E.2d 578 (1974). Nonetheless, in *People v. Amparo*, 73 N.Y.2d 728, 729, 535 N.Y.S.2d 588, 589, 532 N.E.2d 94 (1988), the Court of Appeals held that:

> The error in admitting defendant's oral statement cannot be viewed as harmless. That statement was the only one made by him establishing his prior connection to the burglarized premises, and it might well have contributed to the jury's verdict. Indeed, after the case was submitted, the jury requested a read-back of that very testimony.

See also People v. McMullin, 70 N.Y.2d 855, 857, 523 N.Y.S.2d 455, 456, 517 N.E.2d 1341 (1987) ("under the circumstances of this case the error was not harmless. Here defendant was convicted of burglary in the second degree, and the erroneously admitted in-court identifications were the only direct evidence placing him inside the victims' home").

§ 26:42   People cannot appeal preclusion order issued pursuant to CPL § 710.30

Unlike the defendant, the People's right to appeal in a criminal case is quite limited. The People can only appeal Court orders that are issued pursuant to statutes listed in CPL § 450.20. Thus, for example, CPL § 450.20(8) provides that the People can appeal "[a]n order suppressing evidence, entered before trial pursuant to [CPL §] 710.20; provided that the people file a statement in the appellate court pursuant to [CPL §] 450.50."

A preclusion order issued pursuant to CPL § 710.30 is not listed in CPL § 450.20. Accordingly, the People cannot appeal from such an order. *See People v. Laing*, 79 N.Y.2d 166, 581 N.Y.S.2d 149, 589 N.E.2d 372 (1992). The *Laing* Court reasoned as follows:

> CPL article 450 governs appealability of orders in criminal proceedings. CPL 450.20 delineates the instances in which the People may appeal as of right to an intermediate appellate court. Significantly absent is any authorization for a People's appeal from an order precluding evidence pursuant to CPL 710.30. It is fundamental that in the absence of a statute expressly authorizing a criminal appeal, there is no right to appeal. This principle recognizes the Legislature's policy prerogative "to limit appellate proliferation in criminal matters."

> The People contend, nevertheless, that CPL 450.20(8) should be interpreted to authorize a People's appeal from a CPL 710.30 preclusion order by, in effect, melding CPL 710.30 with CPL 710.20 suppression orders, for which an appeal is explicitly allowed. CPL 450.20(8) authorizes a People's appeal from "[a]n order suppressing evidence, entered before trial pursuant to section *710.20.*" (Emphasis added.) Section 710.20 allows a defendant to move to suppress evidence on several grounds, including improper pretrial identification procedures (CPL 710.20[6]), but *not* including failure to provide timely notice as required by CPL 710.30. * * *

> The words and numerical references and incorporations in CPL 450.20 could not be plainer—the Legislature left CPL 710.30 preclusion orders out of the People's appeal authorization section.

> The People, and *amici curiae* who favor the People's view of the issue, argue that CPL 450.20(8) should be interpreted "broadly" to permit appeal of any trial order which results in the unavailability of evidence, including those for CPL 710.30 notice violations. They urge that appellate courts should, for the limited purpose of CPL 450.20(8) appealability, treat CPL 710.30 preclusion orders as if they were CPL 710.20 suppression orders inasmuch as failure to give timely notice provides an additional ground for, in effect, seeking suppression of such evidence. Their argument concludes that the list of grounds for suppression contained in CPL 710.20 is not meant to be all-inclusive.

> The argument cannot be sustained. * * *

> The People's appeal to policy-driven judicial rewriting of the legislation would require us to read CPL 710.30 into CPL 710.20 and 450.20(8) and, thus, to create a right to appeal out of thin air. The Legislature, for whatever reason, simply did not include the words and statutory numbers in its very detailed enactments. While the People and their *amici* are correct that the omission leaves them out of appeals court, " 'any arguments for a change in the practice, however persuasive, must be addressed to the legislature.' "

79 N.Y.2d at 151–52, 581 N.Y.S.2d at 170–72 (citations omitted).

Chapter 27

Miranda Warnings

KeyCite®: Cases and other legal materials listed in KeyCite Scope can be researched through the KeyCite service on Westlaw®. Use KeyCite to check citations for form, parallel references, prior and later history, and comprehensive citator information, including citations to other decisions and secondary materials.

---

§ 27:1   In general

In *Miranda v. Arizona*, 384 U.S. 436, 86 S. Ct. 1602, 16 L. Ed. 2d 694, 10 A.L.R.3d 974 (1966), the Supreme Court held that the:

[P]rotection of the privilege against self-incrimination during pre-trial questioning requires application of special "procedural safeguards." "Prior to any questioning, the person must be warned that he has a right to remain silent, that any statement he does make may be used as evidence against him, and that he has a right to the presence of an attorney, either retained or appointed." Unless a suspect "voluntarily, knowingly and intelligently" waives these rights, any incriminating responses to questioning may not be introduced into evidence in the prosecution's case in chief in a subsequent criminal proceeding.

Pennsylvania v. Muniz, 496 U.S. 582, 589, 110 S. Ct. 2638, 2644, 110 L. Ed. 2d 528 (1990) (citations omitted). *See also Michigan v. Tucker*, 417 U.S. 433, 443-44, 94 S. Ct. 2357, 2363-64, 41 L. Ed. 2d 182 (1974) (same).

"In the wake of [*Miranda*], Congress enacted 18 U.S.C. § 3501, which in essence laid down a rule that the admissibility of such statements should turn only on whether or not they were voluntarily made." *Dickerson v. U.S.*, 530 U.S. 428, 432, 120 S. Ct. 2326, 2329, 147 L. Ed. 2d 405 (2000). *Dickerson* held that "*Miranda,* being a constitutional decision of this Court, may not be in effect overruled by an Act of Congress, and we decline to overrule *Miranda* ourselves. We therefore hold that *Miranda* and its progeny in this Court govern the admissibility of statements made during custodial interrogation in both state and federal courts." *Id.* at 432, 120 S.Ct. at 2329-30.

This chapter addresses *Miranda* and related right to counsel issues, paying particular attention to issues pertinent to DWI cases.

§ 27:2 When is a statement involuntary?

In *People v. Chase*, 85 N.Y.2d 493, 500, 626 N.Y.S.2d 721, 724, 650 N.E.2d 379 (1995), the Court of Appeals stated that "[a]n involuntary statement includes one that has been physically or psychologically coerced, obtained by a promise or statement that creates a risk of falsely incriminating oneself or obtained by the failure to give *Miranda* warnings (CPL 60.45)." *See also People v. Rodney*, 85 N.Y.2d 289, 292, 624 N.Y.S.2d 95, 97, 648 N.E.2d 471 (1995) (same). The *Chase* Court made clear that "[i]t is for the court and not the parties to determine whether a statement is truly voluntary or is one in which the actions of the police are the functional equivalent of interrogation causing the statement to be made." 85 N.Y.2d at 500, 626 N.Y.S.2d at 724. *See also People v. Brown*, 140 A.D.2d 266, __, 528 N.Y.S.2d 565, 568 (1st Dep't 1988) ("Whether or not a particular statement is suppressible is a matter which must be resolved by the court, not the prosecution"). The only exception to this rule is "where 'there is no question of voluntariness.' " *Chase,* 85 N.Y.2d at 500, 626

N.Y.S.2d at 724 (citation omitted). *See also People v. Greer*, 42 N.Y.2d 170, 178, 397 N.Y.S.2d 613, 619, 366 N.E.2d 273 (1977) (same).

"Of course, 'coercive police activity is a necessary predicate to the finding that a confession is not "voluntary" within the meaning of the Due Process Clause of the Fourteenth Amendment.' " *People v. Mateo*, 2 N.Y.3d 383, 413-14, 779 N.Y.S.2d 399, 417, 811 N.E.2d 1053 (2004) (citation omitted).

§ 27:3 *Miranda* warnings—Generally

"In *Miranda v. Arizona,* the Supreme Court held that 'the prosecution may not use statements, whether exculpatory or inculpatory, stemming from custodial interrogation of the defendant unless it demonstrates the use of procedural safeguards effective to secure the privilege against self-incrimination.' The court defined custodial interrogation as 'questioning initiated by law enforcement officers after a person has been taken into custody or otherwise deprived of his freedom of action in any significant way.' " *People v. Jones*, 47 N.Y.2d 528, 532, 419 N.Y.S.2d 447, 449, 393 N.E.2d 443 (1979) (citation omitted). *See also People v. Harris*, 48 N.Y.2d 208, 215, 422 N.Y.S.2d 43, 45, 397 N.E.2d 733 (1979) ("It is now well settled that unless a police officer administers *Miranda* warnings to a suspect in his custody, any statement elicited from the suspect cannot be admitted against him in a subsequent criminal trial").

> Both the State and Federal Constitutions guarantee that individuals shall not "be compelled in any criminal case to be a witness against" themselves. In *Miranda v. Arizona,* the United States Supreme Court held that the privilege against self-incrimination protects individuals from "informal compulsion exerted by law-enforcement officers during in-custody questioning" as well as from legal compulsion to testify in court. In order to preserve this right, the Court prescribed "procedural safeguards effective to secure the privilege against self-incrimination" in the form of the now-familiar *Miranda* warnings.

People v. Berg, 92 N.Y.2d 701, 704, 685 N.Y.S.2d 906, 908, 708 N.E.2d 979 (1999) (citations omitted). *Miranda* provides that:

> An individual taken into custody by law enforcement authorities for questioning "must be adequately and effectively apprised of his rights" safeguarded by the Fifth Amendment privilege against self-incrimination. First, the authorities must inform a suspect in "clear and unequivocal terms" of the right to remain silent. Second, they must make a suspect "aware not only of the privilege, but also of the consequences of forgoing it" by explaining that "anything" he says during the interrogation "can and will be used against [him] in court." "[T]o assure that [this] right to choose between silence and speech remains unfettered throughout the interrogation process," the authorities must also explain to the suspect that he has a right

to the presence of an attorney. And finally, so that the right to an attorney is not "hollow," the authorities must also advise the suspect "that if he is indigent a lawyer will be appointed to represent him."

These four warnings are an "absolute prerequisite to interrogation." Further,

> [t]he Fifth Amendment privilege is so fundamental to our system of constitutional rule and the expedient of giving an adequate warning as to the availability of the privilege so simple, [a court does] not pause to inquire in individual cases whether the defendant was aware of his rights *without* a warning being given.

In sum, absent a "full and effective warning of [these] rights" and a knowing, intelligent and voluntary waiver, statements made by a suspect during custodial interrogation must be suppressed.

Although *Miranda*'s bright-line rule was controversial at first, it "has become embedded in routine police practice to the point where the warnings have become part of our national culture." Prior to the *Miranda* decision, courts looked at every confession individually for voluntariness, using a totality-of-the-circumstances test grounded in notions of due process. This due process test took into consideration "the totality of all the surrounding circumstances— both the characteristics of the accused and the details of the interrogation."

While the prosecution still must prove voluntariness of a confession, "*Miranda* changed the focus of much of the inquiry." Indeed, "giving the warnings and getting a waiver has generally produced a virtual ticket of admissibility . . . ."

Since *Miranda* was handed down, the Supreme Court has declined to return to the totality-of-the-circumstances test of voluntariness, or to allow the government to meet its burden without demonstrating compliance with the *Miranda* procedure. In *Dickerson,* the Court rejected a congressional attempt to revive the former totality-of-the-circumstances test, holding that *Miranda* is "constitutionally based" and reaffirming that it governs the admissibility of statements in federal and state courts.

People v. Dunbar, 24 N.Y.3d 304, 313-15, 998 N.Y.S.2d 679, 684-85, 23 N.E.3d 946 (2014), cert. denied, 135 S. Ct. 2051, 191 L. Ed. 2d 971 (2015) and cert. denied, 135 S. Ct. 2052, 191 L. Ed. 2d 971 (2015) (citations omitted). *See also Dickerson v. U.S.*, 530 U.S. 428, 120 S. Ct. 2326, 147 L. Ed. 2d 405 (2000); *People v. Ramos*, 99 N.Y.2d 27, 35, 750 N.Y.S.2d 821, 826, 780 N.E.2d 506 (2002) ("A person who is arrested, brought into police custody and interrogated must first be given *Miranda* warnings. If, during the course of custodial police interrogation, the person chooses to remain silent or otherwise invokes the right to counsel, all interrogation must cease") (citation omitted).

> *Miranda v. Arizona* requires not only that before interrogation can begin a suspect must be advised concerning his right to remain silent and of his right to counsel, but also that, "If the individual indicates in any manner, at any time prior to or during questioning, that he wishes to remain silent, the interrogation must cease." Moreover, the rule being designed to counteract the coercive pressure of the custodial setting, a suspect's right to remain silent, once invoked, must be "scrupulously honored." He may not within a short period thereafter and without a fresh set of warnings be importuned to speak about the same suspected crime, but a statement volunteered or spontaneously made will not be suppressible unless it is about the same crime and results from express questioning or its functional equivalent under circumstances which do not include fresh warnings and do not scrupulously honor the suspect's right to cut off questioning.

People v. Ferro, 63 N.Y.2d 316, 322, 482 N.Y.S.2d 237, 240, 472 N.E.2d 13 (1984) (citations and footnote omitted). *See generally People v. Ferrara*, 158 Misc. 2d 671, —, 602 N.Y.S.2d 86, 88 (N.Y. City Crim. Ct. 1993) ("In this case, after the defendant refused to answer questions, his refusal was not 'scrupulously honored' ").

§ 27:4 Applicability of *Miranda* to *Terry* stops

In *People v. Morales*, 65 N.Y.2d 997, 998, 494 N.Y.S.2d 95, 95, 484 N.E.2d 124 (1985), the Court of Appeals held that:

> Criminal Term erred in holding that a person who is frisked is thereafter in custody as a matter of law for the purpose of administration of *Miranda* warnings. There is a clear distinction between a stop and frisk inquiry and a forcible seizure which curtails a person's freedom of action to the degree associated with a formal arrest. Thus, questioning after a frisk, without more, does not constitute custodial interrogation.

(Citations omitted). *See also People v. Bennett*, 70 N.Y.2d 891, 894, 524 N.Y.S.2d 378, 380, 519 N.E.2d 289 (1987) ("When a seizure of a person remains at the stop and frisk inquiry level and does not constitute a restraint on his or her freedom of movement of the degree associated with a formal arrest, *Miranda* warnings need not be given prior to questioning"); *Kwok T. v. Mauriello (In Matter of Kwok T.)*, 43 N.Y.2d 213, 218, 401 N.Y.S.2d 52, 55, 371 N.E.2d 814 (1977) ("routine police investigation of suspicious conduct on the street generally does not entail a significant deprivation of freedom which would require *Miranda* warnings"); *People v. Huffman*, 41 N.Y.2d 29, 390 N.Y.S.2d 843, 359 N.E.2d 353 (1976). *See generally Berkemer v. McCarty*, 468 U.S. 420, 440, 104 S. Ct. 3138, 3150, 82 L. Ed. 2d 317 (1984) ("The comparatively nonthreatening character of detentions of this sort explains the absence of any suggestion in our opinions that *Terry* stops are subject to the dictates of *Miranda*").

§ 27:5 Applicability of *Miranda* to routine traffic stops

The *Miranda* Court stated that "[b]y custodial interrogation, we mean questioning initiated by law enforcement officers after a person has been taken into custody *or otherwise deprived of his freedom of action in any significant way.*" *Miranda v. Arizona*, 384 U.S. 436, 444, 86 S. Ct. 1602, 1612, 16 L. Ed. 2d 694, 10 A.L.R.3d 974 (1966) (emphasis added). It would seem that a routine traffic stop—particularly one that progresses to the point where the motorist is required to exit and remain outside of his or her vehicle—falls into the latter category. Nonetheless, in *Berkemer v. McCarty*, 468 U.S. 420, 440, 104 S. Ct. 3138, 3150, 82 L. Ed. 2d 317 (1984), the Supreme Court held that "[t]he . . . noncoercive aspect of ordinary traffic stops prompts us to hold that persons temporarily detained pursuant to such stops are not 'in custody' for the purposes of *Miranda.*" The Court reasoned that "the usual traffic stop is more analogous to a so-called '*Terry* stop' than to a formal arrest." *Id.* at 439, 104 S.Ct. at 3150.

> Typically, this means that the officer may ask the detainee a moderate number of questions to determine his identity and to try to obtain information confirming or dispelling the officer's suspicions. But the detainee is not obliged to respond. And, unless the detainee's answers provide the officer with probable cause to arrest him, he must then be released. The comparatively nonthreatening character of detentions of this sort explains the absence of any suggestion in our opinions that *Terry* stops are subject to the dictates of *Miranda.*

Id. at 439-40, 104 S.Ct. at 3150 (footnotes omitted). *See also Pennsylvania v. Bruder*, 488 U.S. 9, 109 S. Ct. 205, 102 L. Ed. 2d 172 (1988) (per curiam).

However, it should be noted that *Berkemer* "did not announce an absolute rule for all motorist detentions, observing that lower courts must be vigilant that police do not 'delay formally arresting detained motorists, and . . . subject them to sustained and intimidating interrogation at the scene of their initial detention.'" *Bruder,* 488 U.S. at 10 n.1, 109 S.Ct. at 207 n.1 (quoting *Berkemer*). In other words, "[i]f a motorist who has been detained pursuant to a traffic stop thereafter is subjected to treatment that renders him 'in custody' for practical purposes, he will be entitled to the full panoply of protections prescribed by *Miranda.*" *Berkemer,* 468 U.S. at 440, 104 S.Ct. at 3150. *See, e.g., People v. Austin*, 128 Misc. 2d 923, 491 N.Y.S.2d 982 (Cattaraugus County Ct. 1985).

In *People v. Christopher S.*, 126 Misc. 2d 594, 483 N.Y.S.2d 609 (N.Y. City Crim. Ct. 1984), the Court held that admissions obtained from a defendant stopped at a checkpoint are subject to the same analysis as any other routine traffic stop.

§ 27:6   Applicability of *Miranda* to routine accident investigation

"*Miranda* warnings are not required where police officers are investigating traffic accidents, since the investigation has not reached the custodial stage." *People v. Aia*, 105 A.D.2d 592, __, 482 N.Y.S.2d 56, 57 (3d Dep't 1984). *See also People v. Bennett*, 70 N.Y.2d 891, 524 N.Y.S.2d 378, 519 N.E.2d 289 (1987); *People v. Carbonaro*, 134 A.D.3d 1543, __, 23 N.Y.S.3d 525, 529 (4th Dep't 2015), leave to appeal denied, 27 N.Y.3d 994, 2016 WL 2888591 (2016) ("Inasmuch as it is common knowledge that the police prepare reports with respect to motor vehicle accidents even where no criminal conduct is suspected, we conclude that a reasonable, innocent person in defendant's position at the hospital would not have felt that he or she was in custody when asked questions about the accident by the deputy"); *People v. Shelton*, 111 A.D.3d 1334, __, 974 N.Y.S.2d 224, 227 (4th Dep't 2013), leave to appeal denied, 23 N.Y.3d 1025, 992 N.Y.S.2d 808, 16 N.E.3d 1288 (2014); *People v. Steinhilber*, 48 A.D.3d 958, __, 852 N.Y.S.2d 437, 439 (3d Dep't 2008); *People v. Miller*, 21 A.D.3d 1146, __, 800 N.Y.S.2d 782, 783 (3d Dep't 2005); *People v. Atwood*, 2 A.D.3d 1331, __, 768 N.Y.S.2d 918, 919 (4th Dep't 2003); *People v. DeBlase*, 142 A.D.2d 926, __, 530 N.Y.S.2d 352, 353 (4th Dep't 1988); *People v. Hennigan*, 135 A.D.2d 1082, __, 523 N.Y.S.2d 302, 302 (4th Dep't 1987); *People v. Palmiere*, 124 A.D.2d 1016, 508 N.Y.S.2d 775 (4th Dep't 1986); *People v. Brown*, 104 A.D.2d 696, __, 480 N.Y.S.2d 578, 579 (3d Dep't 1984); *People v. McMillan*, 112 Misc. 2d 901, __, 447 N.Y.S.2d 626, 628 (Monroe Co. Sup. Ct. 1982).

§ 27:7   Applicability of *Miranda* to non-felony offenses

In *Berkemer v. McCarty*, 468 U.S. 420, 434, 104 S. Ct. 3138, 3147, 82 L. Ed. 2d 317 (1984), the Supreme Court held that "a person subjected to custodial interrogation is entitled to the benefit of the procedural safeguards enunciated in *Miranda,* regardless of the nature or severity of the offense of which he is suspected or for which he was arrested." (Footnote omitted).

Although an issue technically exists as to whether a person charged solely with a traffic infraction is entitled to *Miranda* warnings, *see People v. Phinney*, 22 N.Y.2d 288, 290-91, 292 N.Y.S.2d 632, 634, 239 N.E.2d 515 (1968) ("at least in the absence of any undue administrative hardships, we have generally held that [speeding] prosecutions are governed by the rules of the criminal law. Whether or not this includes the right to a warning under *Miranda* is, however, a question which we need not decide in the present case") (citations omitted), since motorists charged solely with traffic infractions are rarely taken into custody or interrogated within the meaning of *Miranda* this issue is somewhat academic.

§ 27:8 Applicability of *Miranda* to field sobriety tests

In *Schmerber v. California*, 384 U.S. 757, 761, 86 S. Ct. 1826, 1830, 16 L. Ed. 2d 908 (1966), the Supreme Court held that the 5th Amendment protects a defendant only from being compelled to either testify against himself or herself "or otherwise provide the State with evidence of a testimonial or communicative nature." "For evidence to be testimonial or communicative, it 'must itself, explicitly or implicitly, relate a factual assertion or disclose information.'" *People v. Berg*, 92 N.Y.2d 701, 704, 685 N.Y.S.2d 906, 908, 708 N.E.2d 979 (1999) (citation omitted). *See also People v. Hager*, 69 N.Y.2d 141, 142, 512 N.Y.S.2d 794, 795, 505 N.E.2d 237 (1987) (per curiam) ("Evidence is 'testimonial or communicative' when it reveals a person's subjective knowledge or thought processes").

In *Pennsylvania v. Muniz*, 496 U.S. 582, 584, 110 S. Ct. 2638, 2641, 110 L. Ed. 2d 528 (1990), the Supreme Court addressed the issue of "whether various incriminating utterances of a drunken-driving suspect, made while performing a series of sobriety tests, constitute testimonial responses to custodial interrogation for purposes of the Self-Incrimination Clause of the Fifth Amendment." The defendant in *Muniz* had been asked to perform various sobriety tests both pre-arrest at the roadside and post-arrest at the police station.

The Court held that the results of physical performance tests are not testimonial. As a result, they do not implicate the 5th Amendment and need not be preceded by *Miranda* warnings. 496 U.S. at 592, 110 S.Ct. at 2645 ("Under *Schmerber* and its progeny, . . . any slurring of speech and other evidence of lack of muscular coordination revealed by Muniz's responses to Officer Hosterman's direct questions constitute nontestimonial components of those responses"). *See also Berg,* 92 N.Y.2d at 703, 685 N.Y.S.2d at 907 ("It is settled that *Miranda* warnings are not required to allow the results of field sobriety tests into evidence"); *id.* at 705, 685 N.Y.S.2d at 908-09 ("Results of field sobriety tests such as the horizontal gaze nystagmus, walk and turn and one-leg stand are not deemed testimonial or communicative because they 'do not reveal a person's subjective knowledge or thought processes but, rather, exhibit a person's degree of physical coordination for observation by police officers.' Responses to such tests incriminate an intoxicated suspect 'not because the tests [reveal] defendant's thoughts, but because [defendant's] body's responses [differ] from those of a sober person.' Thus, the results of such tests may be introduced despite the failure of the police to administer *Miranda* warnings") (citations omitted); *People v. Jacquin*, 71 N.Y.2d 825, 826, 527 N.Y.S.2d 728, 729, 522 N.E.2d 1026 (1988) ("Performance tests need not be preceded by *Miranda* warnings and, generally an audio/visual tape of such tests, including any colloquy between the test-giver and the defendant not constituting custodial interrogation, is admissible"); *Hager,* 69 N.Y.2d at 142, 512 N.Y.S.2d at 795.

Similarly, "[r]eciting the alphabet and counting are not testimonial or communicative because these acts do not require a person to reveal knowledge of facts relating to the offense or to share thoughts and beliefs with the government. Instead, these tests attempt to determine whether alcohol has impaired the reflexive process by which the alphabet and numbers are recalled from memory and spoken." *Berg,* 92 N.Y.2d at 705, 685 N.Y.S.2d at 909. *Berg* further held that "evidence of defendant's refusal to submit to certain field sobriety tests [is] admissible in the absence of *Miranda* warnings . . . because the refusal was not compelled within the meaning of the Self-Incrimination Clause." *Id.* at 703, 685 N.Y.S.2d at 907. The Court noted, however, that "the inference of intoxication arising from failure to complete the tests successfully 'is far stronger than that arising from a refusal to take the test.'" *Id.* at 706, 685 N.Y.S.2d at 909 (citation omitted). *See also People v. Powell*, 95 A.D.2d 783, __, 463 N.Y.S.2d 473, 476 (2d Dep't 1983).

By contrast, the *Muniz* Court held that the defendant's response to the question "Do you know what the date was of your sixth birthday?" *was* testimonial:

> When Officer Hosterman asked Muniz if he knew the date of his sixth birthday and Muniz, for whatever reason, could not remember or calculate that date, . . . Muniz was left with the choice of incriminating himself by admitting that he did not then know the date of his sixth birthday, or answering untruthfully by reporting a date that he did not then believe to be accurate (an incorrect guess would be incriminating as well as untruthful). The content of his truthful answer supported an inference that his mental faculties were impaired, because his assertion (he did not know the date of his sixth birthday) was different from the assertion (he knew the date was (correct date)) that the trier of fact might reasonably have expected a lucid person to provide. Hence, the incriminating inference of impaired mental faculties stemmed, not just from the fact that Muniz slurred his response, but also from a testimonial aspect of that response.

496 U.S. at 598-99, 110 S.Ct. at 2649.

Regardless of whether the results of sobriety tests are testimonial, where such tests are performed pre-arrest at the roadside (*i.e.,* in the "field") the defendant is generally not yet in custody—which is a further reason why *Miranda* warnings would not be required. *See, e.g., Pennsylvania v. Bruder*, 488 U.S. 9, 10-11, 109 S. Ct. 205, 206-07, 102 L. Ed. 2d 172 (1988) (per curiam); *Berkemer v. McCarty*, 468 U.S. 420, 440, 104 S. Ct. 3138, 3150, 82 L. Ed. 2d 317 (1984) ("The . . . noncoercive aspect of ordinary traffic stops prompts us to hold that persons temporarily detained pursuant to such stops are not 'in custody' for the purposes of *Miranda*"). *See also People v. Bennett*, 70 N.Y.2d 891, 893-94, 524 N.Y.S.2d 378, 380, 519 N.E.2d 289 (1987); *People v. Archer*, 137 A.D.3d 449, __, 25 N.Y.S.3d 873, 873 (1st Dep't 2016), leave to appeal denied, 27 N.Y.3d 1128, 2016 WL 3766825 (2016); *People v. Brown*, 107 A.D.3d 1305, __, 968 N.Y.S.2d 224, 226 (3d Dep't 2013), leave to appeal dismissed, 23 N.Y.3d 1018, 992 N.Y.S.2d 801, 16 N.E.3d 1281 (2014); *People v. Myers*, 1 A.D.3d 382, __, 766 N.Y.S.2d 581, 582 (2d Dep't 2003); *People v. Hasenflue*, 252 A.D.2d 829, __, 675 N.Y.S.2d 464, 466 (3d Dep't 1998); *People v. McGreal*, 190 A.D.2d 869, __, 593 N.Y.S.2d 868, 869 (2d Dep't 1993); *People v. Hampe*, 181 A.D.2d 238, __, 585 N.Y.S.2d 861, 863 (3d Dep't 1992); *People v. McAleavey*, 159 A.D.2d 646, __, 553 N.Y.S.2d 38, 38-39 (2d Dep't 1990); *People v. Mason*, 157 A.D.2d 859, __, 550 N.Y.S.2d 432, 433 (2d Dep't 1990); *People v. Fiorello*, 140 A.D.2d 708, __, 529 N.Y.S.2d 27, 28 (2d Dep't 1988); *People v. Mathis*, 136 A.D.2d 746, __, 523 N.Y.S.2d 915, 916 (2d Dep't 1988); *People v. Brown*, 104 A.D.2d 696, __, 480 N.Y.S.2d 578, 579 (3d Dep't 1984); *People v. O'Reilly*, 16 Misc. 3d 775, __, 842 N.Y.S.2d 292, 296 (Suffolk Co. Dist. Ct. 2007). *Cf. People v. Norton*, 135 A.D.2d 984, 522 N.Y.S.2d 958 (3d Dep't 1987); *People v. Benson*, 114 A.D.2d 506, __, 494 N.Y.S.2d 727, 728 (2d Dep't 1985).

§ 27:9 Applicability of *Miranda* to chemical tests/ chemical test refusals

"In the context of an arrest for driving while intoxicated, a police inquiry of whether the suspect will take a blood-alcohol test is not an interrogation within the meaning of *Miranda*." *South Dakota v. Neville*, 459 U.S. 553, 564 n.15, 103 S. Ct. 916, 923 n.15, 74 L. Ed. 2d 748 (1983). *See also id.* at 564, 103 S.Ct. at 923 ("We hold . . . that a refusal to take a blood-alcohol test, after a police officer has lawfully requested it, is not an act coerced by the officer, and thus is not protected by the privilege against self-incrimination"); *People v. Smith*, 18 N.Y.3d 544, 550, 942 N.Y.S.2d 426, 430, 965 N.E.2d 928 (2012); *People v. Berg*, 92 N.Y.2d 701, 703, 685 N.Y.S.2d 906, 907, 708 N.E.2d 979 (1999) ("It is . . . settled that *Miranda* warnings are not required in order to admit the results of chemical analysis tests, or a defendant's refusal to take such tests").

More generally, the 5th Amendment privilege against self-incrimination is not implicated by chemical testing because "the privilege is a bar against compelling 'communications' or 'testimony,' [whereas] compulsion which makes a suspect or accused the source of 'real or physical evidence' does not violate it." *Schmerber v. California*, 384 U.S. 757, 764, 86 S. Ct. 1826, 1832, 16 L. Ed. 2d 908 (1966). *See also People v. Kates*, 53 N.Y.2d 591, 594, 444 N.Y.S.2d 446, 448, 428 N.E.2d 852 (1981) ("Taking a driver's blood for alcohol analysis does not call for testimonial compulsion prohibited by the Fifth Amendment"); *People v. Thomas*, 46 N.Y.2d 100, 103, 412 N.Y.S.2d 845, 846, 385 N.E.2d 584 (1978); *People v. Craft*, 28 N.Y.2d 274, 321 N.Y.S.2d 566, 270 N.E.2d 297 (1971); *People v. Boudreau*, 115 A.D.2d 652, __, 496 N.Y.S.2d 489, 491 (2d Dep't 1985); *Hoffman v. Melton*, 81 A.D.2d 709, __, 439 N.Y.S.2d 449, 450-51 (3d Dep't 1981); *People v. Haitz*, 65 A.D.2d 172, __, 411 N.Y.S.2d 57, 60 (4th Dep't 1978); *People v. Dillin*, 150 Misc. 2d 311, __, 567 N.Y.S.2d 991, 992 (N.Y. City Crim. Ct. 1991).

§ 27:10   Applicability of *Miranda* to questioning by probation/parole officers

As a general rule, a typical meeting between a probationer or parolee and the person's probation/parole officer does not constitute custodial interrogation within the meaning of *Miranda*. *See, e.g., Minnesota v. Murphy*, 465 U.S. 420, 104 S. Ct. 1136, 79 L. Ed. 2d 409 (1984); *People v. English*, 73 N.Y.2d 20, 537 N.Y.S.2d 987, 534 N.E.2d 1195 (1989); *People v. W.*, 24 N.Y.2d 732, 302 N.Y.S.2d 260, 249 N.E.2d 882 (1969). On the other hand:

> A parolee's statements to his parole officer, made while the parolee is in custody and in response to the parole officer's questions about the parolee's suspected involvement in a crime, are considered compelled unless preceded by *Miranda* warnings. Consequently, the parolee's later statements to a police officer, made after *Miranda* warnings but as part of a continuous interrogation, must be suppressed at trial.

English, 73 N.Y.2d at 21, 537 N.Y.S.2d at 987. *See also People v. Parker*, 82 A.D.2d 661, 442 N.Y.S.2d 803 (2d Dep't 1981), order aff'd, 57 N.Y.2d 815, 455 N.Y.S.2d 600, 441 N.E.2d 1118 (1982). *Cf. People ex rel. Maiello by Finkelstein v. New York State Bd. of Parole*, 65 N.Y.2d 145, 490 N.Y.S.2d 742, 480 N.E.2d 356 (1985) (per curiam) (any violation of parolee's right to counsel caused by parole officer's elicitation of admission of parole violation did not bar use of admission in administrative parole revocation hearing).

§ 27:11   Applicability of *Miranda* to juveniles

This issue is discussed at length in *In re Jimmy D.*, 15 N.Y.3d 417, 912 N.Y.S.2d 537, 938 N.E.2d 970 (2010). *See also People v. Stephen J. B.*, 23 N.Y.2d 611, 298 N.Y.S.2d 489, 246 N.E.2d 344 (1969).

§ 27:12 Right to remain silent is a fundamental right

"[T]he right to remain silent [is] a 'fundamental right' under our State Constitution, long protected and recognized under New York law." *People v. Pavone*, 26 N.Y.3d 629, 640, 26 N.Y.S.3d 728, 737, 47 N.E.3d 56 (2015) (citation omitted). "This Court has also recognized that *Miranda* warnings contain an implied promise that a defendant's silence will not be used against the defendant." *Id.* at 640, 26 N.Y.S.3d at 737.

§ 27:13 Use of defendant's pre-arrest silence

In *People v. Pavone*, 26 N.Y.3d 629, 642, 26 N.Y.S.3d 728, 739, 47 N.E.3d 56 (2015), the Court of Appeals made clear that "we reject the People's artificial distinction between defendants who are arrested and remain silent before *Miranda* warnings have been provided, and those who remain silent afterwards. Indeed this Court has even held that *pre-arrest* silence cannot be used against a defendant in the People's case-in-chief"). *See generally People v. Bright*, 71 N.Y.2d 376, 385, 526 N.Y.S.2d 66, 71, 520 N.E.2d 1355 (1988) ("Although a police officer may have the right under appropriate circumstances to stop a person in a public place and make inquiry, a citizen is under no obligation to provide any explanation regarding his conduct. He is permitted to remain silent under the Fifth Amendment to the Federal Constitution and article I, section 6 of the State Constitution") (citation omitted); *Berkemer v. McCarty*, 468 U.S. 420, 439, 104 S. Ct. 3138, 3150, 82 L. Ed. 2d 317 (1984) ("the usual traffic stop is more analogous to a so-called '*Terry* stop' than to a formal arrest. . . . Typically, this means that the officer may ask the detainee a moderate number of questions to determine his identity and to try to obtain information confirming or dispelling the officer's suspicions. But the detainee is not obliged to respond").

§ 27:14 Use of defendant's post-arrest silence

The Court of Appeals has held that "the People could not use defendant's post-arrest silence against the defendant, even absent *Miranda* warnings." *People v. Pavone*, 26 N.Y.3d 629, 640, 26 N.Y.S.3d 728, 737, 47 N.E.3d 56 (2015) (citation omitted). *See also id.* at 642, 26 N.Y.S.3d at 739 ("we reject the People's artificial distinction between defendants who are arrested and remain silent before *Miranda* warnings have been provided, and those who remain silent afterwards"); *People v. Hill*, 24 N.Y.3d 1007, 1008, 998 N.Y.S.2d 753, 753, 23 N.E.3d 1021 (2014) ("Absent 'unusual circumstances,' evidence of a defendant's silence at the time of arrest is generally inadmissible under common-law evidentiary principles").

In *People v. Conyers*, 52 N.Y.2d 454, 458-59, 438 N.Y.S.2d 741,

743-44, 420 N.E.2d 933 (1981), the Court of Appeals explained why it finds silence to be of dubious probative value:

> As is evident from our opinion in *Conyers I,* our decision in that case, although based upon constitutional grounds, was heavily influenced by our conviction that evidence of an individual's pretrial failure to speak when confronted by law enforcement officials is of extremely limited probative worth. As noted in our earlier decision, the individual's silence in such circumstances may simply be attributable to his awareness that he is under no obligation to speak or to the natural caution that arises from his knowledge that anything he says might later be used against him at trial. Alternatively, the individual may refrain from speaking because he believes that efforts to exonerate himself under the circumstances would be futile. Finally, it is a lamentable but undeniable fact of modern society that some of our citizens harbor a mistrust for law enforcement authority which leads them to shun contact with the police even when the avoidance of contact is not in their own best interest. Such individuals may refrain from speaking to law enforcement officials not because they are guilty of some crime, but rather because they are simply fearful of coming into contact with those whom they regard as antagonists. In short, although a defendant's failure to come forward with an exculpatory version of events prior to trial may reflect negatively upon the veracity of his trial testimony, his prior silence also may be attributable to a variety of innocent circumstances that are completely unrelated to the truth or falsity of his testimony. Accordingly, evidence of a defendant's pretrial silence must be regarded as having minimal probative significance and as having a correspondingly low potential for advancing the truth-finding process even when offered solely for purposes of impeachment.
>
> On the other hand, the risk of prejudice is substantial whenever the prosecution attempts to impeach a defendant's trial testimony by questioning him about his prior failure to come forward with an exculpatory version of events. Jurors, who are not necessarily sensitive to the wide variety of alternative explanations for a defendant's pretrial silence, may be prone to construe such silence as an admission and, as a consequence, may draw an unwarranted inference of guilt. Because evidence of a defendant's pretrial silence may have a disproportionate impact upon the minds of the jurors and because the potential for prejudice inherent in such evidence outweighs its marginal probative worth, we conclude that the use of such evidence for impeachment purposes cannot be justified in the absence of unusual circumstances.

(Citations omitted). *See also Pavone,* 26 N.Y.3d at 640-41, 26 N.Y.S.3d at 737-38 (same).

§ 27:15   Use of defendant's selective silence

In *People v. Williams*, 25 N.Y.3d 185, 188, 8 N.Y.S.3d 641, 642, 31 N.E.3d 103 (2015), the Court of Appeals held as follows:

This appeal concerns the People's references in their case-in-chief to defendant's selective silence during custodial interrogation, after defendant had waived his *Miranda* rights and agreed to speak to the police. We hold, as a matter of state evidentiary law, that evidence of a defendant's selective silence generally may not be used by the People as part of their case-in-chief, either to allow the jury to infer the defendant's admission of guilt or to impeach the credibility of the defendant's version of events when the defendant has not testified.

In so holding, the Court reasoned that:

It is a well-established principle of state evidentiary law that evidence of a defendant's pretrial silence is generally inadmissible. In *People v. Conyers,* we extended that principle and held that, absent circumstances not present in that case, "our State rules of evidence preclude the use of a defendant's pretrial silence to impeach his trial testimony." This was so because a defendant's silence is generally ambiguous and "of extremely limited probative worth." We noted that there are many reasons why an individual may choose not to speak to police that are wholly unrelated to the veracity of his or her trial testimony, but that there is a substantial risk that jurors might "construe such silence as an admission and . . . draw an unwarranted inference of guilt."

We subsequently held in *People v. DeGeorge,* that our decision in *Conyers* applied to a defendant's "pretrial" silence and was not limited to "postarrest" silence. We reiterated that, as a matter of state evidentiary law, the People generally may not use evidence of defendant's pretrial silence either on their direct case or to impeach the defendant's trial testimony.

There may be a rare set of circumstances in which it is permissible for the People to refer to a defendant's silence during their case-in-chief. However, the general evidentiary principles established in *Conyers* and *DeGeorge* remain in place today: the People generally may not refer to a defendant's silence during their direct case, and, absent unusual circumstances, the People may not use a defendant's silence to impeach his or her trial testimony.

Id. at 190-91, 8 N.Y.S.3d at 644 (citations omitted). *See also People v. Hill*, 24 N.Y.3d 1007, 1008, 998 N.Y.S.2d 753, 753, 23 N.E.3d 1021 (2014); *People v. DeGeorge*, 73 N.Y.2d 614, 543 N.Y.S.2d 11, 541 N.E.2d 11 (1989); *People v. Conyers*, 52 N.Y.2d 454, 457, 438 N.Y.S.2d 741, 742, 420 N.E.2d 933 (1981) ("Upon reconsideration, we now adhere to our prior ruling and hold that, absent circumstances not here present, our State rules of evidence preclude the use of a defendant's pretrial silence to impeach his trial testimony").

In *People v. Hendricks*, 90 N.Y.2d 956, 957, 665 N.Y.S.2d 45, 46, 687 N.E.2d 1328 (1997), the Court of Appeals held that "the officer's testimony did not constitute an impermissible comment on defendant's invocation of his right to silence" where the defendant validly waived his *Miranda* rights and gave an oral statement, but refused to sign a written statement. In so holding, the Court reasoned as follows:

> Defendant did not invoke his right to silence. On the contrary he waived it, and *after* indicating that he would rather not put his statement in writing, defendant gave an oral statement. Defendant's preference for making his statement orally rather than in writing was not, in this context, an indication that he wanted to cut off further inquiry which would have invoked his right to silence.

Id. at 957, 665 N.Y.S.2d at 45.

§ 27:16   Use of defendant's invocation of *Miranda* rights and/or right to counsel as part of people's case-in-chief

It is well settled that a defendant's invocation of [the right against self-incrimination and the right to counsel] during custodial interrogation may not be used against him as part of the People's case-in-chief. The error was compounded when the People, . . . upon cross-examination, questioned defendant about his prior failure to come forward with an exculpatory version of events, thereby burdening defendant's exercise of his right to remain silent.

People v. Murphy, 51 A.D.3d 1057, __, 856 N.Y.S.2d 713, 714 (3d Dep't 2008) (citations omitted).

In *People v. Johnson*, 70 A.D.3d 1188, 896 N.Y.S.2d 199 (3d Dep't 2010), the Appellate Division, Third Department, reversed the defendant's DWI conviction and granted him a new trial where County Court improperly allowed the People to introduce evidence of the defendant's invocation of his *Miranda* rights and right to counsel as part of their case-in-chief. Specifically:

> It is axiomatic that a defendant's invocation of his [or her] right to counsel during custodial interrogation may not be used against him [or her] by the People as part of their case-in-chief." Here, County Court allowed the People to enter into evidence as part of their direct case a videotape of the booking process pertaining to defendant. At the time of the events portrayed in that videotape, defendant was clearly in custody, having been arrested and given his *Miranda* and DWI warnings. On the videotape, defendant invoked both his right to remain silent and his right to counsel. While County Court gave appropriate curative instructions with respect to defendant's invocation of his right to remain silent, it gave no such instruction as to the invocation of his right to counsel. Under the circumstances here, we are unable to conclude "that there is no reasonable possibility that the evidence of defendant's invocation of his right to counsel contributed to his conviction." Moreover, even though defendant did not object to the admission of the videotape, "we cannot ignore the potential for prejudice.

Id. at __, 896 N.Y.S.2d at 202-03 (citations omitted).

§ 27:17 Use of defendant's silence to impeach

In *People v. Williams*, 25 N.Y.3d 185, 193, 8 N.Y.S.3d 641, 646, 31 N.E.3d 103 (2015), the Court of Appeals reiterated that "[e]vidence of a defendant's selective silence . . . generally may not be used by the People during their case-in-chief and may be used only as 'a device for impeachment' of a defendant's trial testimony in limited and unusual circumstances." (Citation omitted). *See also People v. Pavone*, 26 N.Y.3d 629, 640, 26 N.Y.S.3d 728, 737, 47 N.E.3d 56 (2015); *People v. Hill*, 24 N.Y.3d 1007, 1008, 998 N.Y.S.2d 753, 753, 23 N.E.3d 1021 (2014) ("the use for impeachment purposes of a defendant's silence after receiving *Miranda* warnings has been deemed impermissible as a matter of due process"); *People v. Conyers*, 52 N.Y.2d 454, 457, 438 N.Y.S.2d 741, 742, 420 N.E.2d 933 (1981) ("Upon reconsideration, we now adhere to our prior ruling and hold that, absent circumstances not here present, our State rules of evidence preclude the use of a defendant's pretrial silence to impeach his trial testimony").

§ 27:18 Use of precluded statements to impeach

"[T]he Supreme Court has said that the 'shield provided by *Miranda* cannot be perverted into a license to use perjury by way of a defense, free from the risk of confrontation with prior inconsistent utterances.' " *People v. Fardan*, 82 N.Y.2d 638, 646, 607 N.Y.S.2d 220, 224, 628 N.E.2d 41 (1993) (citation omitted). *See also Harris v. New York*, 401 U.S. 222, 226, 91 S. Ct. 643, 646, 28 L. Ed. 2d 1 (1971); *People v. Reid*, 19 N.Y.3d 382, 388, 948 N.Y.S.2d 223, 227, 971 N.E.2d 353 (2012); *People v. Hults*, 76 N.Y.2d 190, 198, 557 N.Y.S.2d 270, 274, 556 N.E.2d 1077 (1990); *People v. Maerling*, 64 N.Y.2d 134, 485 N.Y.S.2d 23, 474 N.E.2d 231 (1984); *People v. Washington*, 51 N.Y.2d 214, 433 N.Y.S.2d 745, 413 N.E.2d 1159 (1980); *People v. Wise*, 46 N.Y.2d 321, 324, 413 N.Y.S.2d 334, 335, 385 N.E.2d 1262, 14 A.L.R.4th 666 (1978) ("We hold that a statement taken in violation of the *Miranda* rule may properly be used to impeach a defendant's credibility where the statement tends to prove a version of the facts contrary to that given in the defendant's trial testimony") (footnote omitted); *People v. Johnson*, 27 N.Y.2d 119, 313 N.Y.S.2d 728, 261 N.E.2d 644 (1970); *People v. Rahming*, 26 N.Y.2d 411, 418, 311 N.Y.S.2d 292, 298, 259 N.E.2d 727 (1970); *People v. Kulis*, 18 N.Y.2d 318, 274 N.Y.S.2d 873, 221 N.E.2d 541 (1966) (per curiam). *See generally People v. Ricco*, 56 N.Y.2d 320, 323, 452 N.Y.S.2d 340, 342, 437 N.E.2d 1097 (1982) ("We have heretofore held that prior inconsistent statements, though secured in disregard of constitutional safeguards, nevertheless may be admitted to impeach the credibility of a defendant who chooses to take the stand to testify in contradiction of the contents of the flawed statements. We now hold that, without more, such statements may not be used, directly or indirectly, to establish the People's case. Because this standard was not followed, there must be a new trial") (citations omitted).

"Of course, trial courts must exercise care to assure that the precluded evidence is not merely related to the testimony but in fact refutes the testimony given on direct. If the evidence is permitted, the court should issue limiting instructions." *Fardan,* 82 N.Y.2d at 646, 607 N.Y.S.2d at 224 (citation omitted).

In *People v. Sanchez,* 48 Misc. 3d 765, __, 11 N.Y.S.3d 454, 455 (N.Y. City Crim. Ct. 2015):

> After a pretrial *Dunaway / Huntley / Refusal* hearing, the Court suppressed evidence of defendant's refusal to take a breathalyzer test. The Court found that the IDTU officer had not given the defendant adequate warnings as to the consequences of the refusal. However, at trial, after hearing from the parties, the Court granted the People's application to cross-examine the defendant about that refusal in the event he elected to testify, relying on *People v. Harris, aff'd sub nom. Harris v. New York,* which holds that a statement that has been suppressed due to a *Miranda* violation, and is hence inadmissible at trial, can still be used on cross-examination of the defendant for impeachment purposes.

(Citations omitted). In so holding, the Court reasoned as follows:

> It appears that no court in New York has expressly considered the question whether a defendant can be impeached, should he elect to testify at trial, by a refusal to take a breathalyzer test, where that refusal was suppressed under VTL § 1194(2)(f). In this Court's view, however, since it is clear that impeaching a defendant on cross-examination with his refusal is not the same as "admitting" the refusal into evidence, such impeachment is permissible by analogy to *Harris.* If a defendant can be impeached on cross-examination with a statement obtained in violation of *Miranda,* he can also be impeached on cross-examination with a refusal that was obtained in violation of VTL § 11924(2)(f).

Id. at __, 11 N.Y.S.3d at 457-58.

§ 27:19   Statements that are truly involuntary are inadmissible for all purposes

People v. Hults, 76 N.Y.2d 190, 198, 557 N.Y.S.2d 270, 274, 556 N.E.2d 1077 (1990), summarizes the law in this area:

> [A] prior statement which is involuntarily made is inherently unreliable and totally lacking in probative value. Such a statement cannot serve this truthtesting function, even if used only for the limited purpose of impeachment. Thus, a statement actually coerced from a defendant is inadmissible for all purposes. By contrast, a defendant's statement, voluntarily made but obtained in violation of *Miranda v. Arizona,* is inadmissible on the prosecution's direct case

but may nevertheless be used for impeachment where "the trustworthiness of the evidence satisfies legal standards." While these cases arise in the context of protecting a defendant's right to due process and the privilege against self-incrimination, the rule serves the truthtesting function of cross-examination by permitting a statement, which is trustworthy at least to the extent it is voluntary, to be used for impeachment.

(Citations omitted).

§ 27:20 Effect of intoxication on voluntariness of statements

In *People v. Adams*, 26 N.Y.2d 129, 137, 309 N.Y.S.2d 145, 150, 257 N.E.2d 610 (1970), the Court of Appeals made clear that:

> With respect to defendant's argument that her alleged drug intoxication made the statements involuntary, we have held that self-induced intoxication does not *ipso facto* render a confession invalid. It is only when the defendant's will has been overborne by interrogation or the state of intoxication has risen to the degree of mania, or the statements are shown by reference to other evidence to be unreliable, that a confession is rendered inadmissible. The same criteria are applicable to admissions made by a defendant suffering from a mental disease.

(Citations omitted). *See also People v. Schompert*, 19 N.Y.2d 300, 305, 279 N.Y.S.2d 515, 519, 226 N.E.2d 305 (1967) ("The general rule applicable to confessions obtained from persons under intoxication has been well stated to the effect that 'proof that the accused was intoxicated at the time he confessed his guilt of crime will not, without more, bar the reception of the confession in evidence. But if it is shown that the accused was intoxicated to the degree of mania, or of being unable to understand the meaning of his statements, then the confession is inadmissible' ") (citation omitted); *People v. McQueen*, 18 N.Y.2d 337, 346, 274 N.Y.S.2d 886, 892, 221 N.E.2d 550 (1966).

§ 27:21 Effect of injuries/medication on voluntariness of statements

The rule of the previous section applies equally to claims that the defendant's statements were involuntary due to injury and/or medication. *See, e.g., People v. Carbonaro*, 134 A.D.3d 1543, —, 23 N.Y.S.3d 525, 529-30 (4th Dep't 2015), leave to appeal denied, 27 N.Y.3d 994, 2016 WL 2888591 (2016):

> Defendant . . . contends that all of his statements to the police should have been suppressed because, owing to his injuries and the pain medication he was given at the hospital, he was incapable of making voluntary statements. Similarly, defendant contends that he was unable to voluntarily waive his *Miranda* rights and consent

to the blood test at the hospital. We reject those contentions. Even assuming, arguendo, that defendant's thought process was affected by his head injury and the pain he experienced from his fractured leg, we conclude that the record does not support a finding that he was "unable to understand the meaning of his statements." Defendant responded appropriately to questions asked of him by the deputy and the medical personnel who treated him. For instance, when questioned by a nurse at the hospital, defendant was able to state his name, his date of birth, and the reason he was at the hospital. According to the nurse, who testified at the *Huntley* hearing, defendant was aware of his surroundings and did not appear to have difficulty understanding anything that she said. Furthermore, when speaking to the deputy at the hospital, defendant recalled the name of the bar he was at earlier that evening, and accurately stated the name of the road on which the accident occurred. As the court noted in its suppression decision, at no time did defendant "give nonsensical or otherwise inappropriate answers to questions, nor did he ramble or rant on unrelated topics." Under the circumstances, we conclude that defendant's cognitive ability was not so impaired as to render him unable to make voluntary and trustworthy statements, or to waive his *Miranda* rights knowingly and voluntarily.

(Citations omitted). *See also People v. Centerbar*, 80 A.D.3d 1008, __, 914 N.Y.S.2d 784, 786-87 (3d Dep't 2011) ("we perceive no grounds upon which to disagree with County Court's factual determination, after an evidentiary hearing, that, despite his significant injuries, defendant's consent to the blood test was voluntary"); *People v. Mojica*, 62 A.D.3d 100, __, 874 N.Y.S.2d 195, 206 (2d Dep't 2009) ("although the defendant sustained a head wound during the accident, the evidence adduced at the hearing from officers and the defendant's treating physician demonstrate that the defendant was conscious, coherent, and capable of exercising his rights. Further, there was no evidence that in obtaining the defendant's consent, Deputy Sheriff Wyman engaged in coercion, illegality, or deception. As such, the evidence supports the hearing court's determination that the defendant voluntarily consented to the blood draw for testing his BAC"); *People v. John*, 288 A.D.2d 848, __, 732 N.Y.S.2d 505, 506 (4th Dep't 2001). *Cf. People v. Ellis*, 190 Misc. 2d 98, 737 N.Y.S.2d 232 (Cattaraugus County Ct. 2001), aff'd, 309 A.D.2d 1314, 765 N.Y.S.2d 313 (4th Dep't 2003) (defendant's consent to blood test was not voluntary in the circumstances presented).

§ 27:22   Effect of mental disease/defect on voluntariness of statements

In *People v. Howard*, 27 A.D.2d 796, __, 279 N.Y.S.2d 79, 79-80 (4th Dep't 1967), the Appellate Division, Fourth Department, held that:

Evidence adduced at the preliminary hearing by the defendant and

not controverted clearly established that the defendant was insane
and a mental defective at the time he made certain statements to
the police later used on the trial. The failure of the People to sustain
the burden of proving beyond a reasonable doubt that such statements were the product of a rational and meaningful act of volition
required the suppression of such statements by the court.

See also People v. Adams, 26 N.Y.2d 129, 137, 309 N.Y.S.2d 145,
150, 257 N.E.2d 610 (1970) ("It is only when the defendant's will
has been overborne by interrogation or the state of intoxication
has risen to the degree of mania, or the statements are shown by
reference to other evidence to be unreliable, that a confession is
rendered inadmissible. *The same criteria are applicable to admissions made by a defendant suffering from a mental disease*")
(emphasis added).

§ 27:23   5th Amendment only applies to questioning by government agent

The 5th Amendment privilege against compulsory self-
incrimination, which the *Miranda* warnings are designed to protect,
has never been held to apply where a private store detective questions a person without any participation by the government. The
avowed purpose of *Miranda* was to secure the privilege against self-
incrimination from encroachment by governmental action. In the
absence of active governmental participation in a private investigation, no *Miranda* warnings need be administered. Private conduct,
however, may become so pervaded by governmental involvement
that it loses its character as such and invokes the full panoply of
constitutional protections. Relevant indicia of state involvement,
which may transform private conduct into State action, include: a
clear connection between the police and the private investigation,
completion of the private act at the instigation of the police; close
supervision of the private conduct by the police; and a private act
undertaken on behalf of the police to further a police objective.

People v. Ray, 65 N.Y.2d 282, 286, 491 N.Y.S.2d 283, 285, 480
N.E.2d 1065 (1985) (citations omitted). See also People v. Jones,
47 N.Y.2d 528, 419 N.Y.S.2d 447, 393 N.E.2d 443 (1979).

§ 27:24   *Miranda* only applies to "custodial interrogation"

In *People v. Paulman*, 5 N.Y.3d 122, 129, 800 N.Y.S.2d 96,
100-01, 833 N.E.2d 239 (2005), the Court of Appeals reiterated
that:

[B]ecause the privilege applies only when an accused is 'compelled'
to testify, the safeguards required by *Miranda* are not triggered unless a suspect is subject to 'custodial interrogation.' " The standard
for assessing a suspect's custodial status is whether a reasonable
person innocent of any wrongdoing would have believed that he or
she was not free to leave. "The term 'interrogation' under *Miranda*
refers not only to express questioning, but also to any words or ac-

tions on the part of the police (other than those normally attendant
to arrest and custody) that the police should know are reasonably
likely to elicit an incriminating response.

(Citations omitted). *See generally People v. Hawkins*, 55 N.Y.2d
474, 483, 450 N.Y.S.2d 159, 163, 435 N.E.2d 376 (1982) ("the doctrine of *Miranda v. Arizona* is inapplicable in the realm of
corporeal identifications") (citation omitted).

§ 27:25 When is a person "in custody" for purposes of *Miranda*?

In *People v. Yukl*, 25 N.Y.2d 585, 589, 307 N.Y.S.2d 857, 859-60,
256 N.E.2d 172 (1969), the Court of Appeals held that:

> In deciding whether a defendant was in custody prior to receiving
> his warnings, the subjective beliefs of the defendant are not to be
> the determinative factor. The test is not what the defendant
> thought, but rather what a reasonable man, innocent of any crime,
> would have thought had he been in the defendant's position. More-
> over, the fact that a defendant is being interviewed in the police
> station does not necessarily mean that he is to be considered "in
> custody." This is merely one of the factors to be considered in reach-
> ing the ultimate conclusion.

(Citations omitted). *See also People v. Paulman*, 5 N.Y.3d 122,
129, 800 N.Y.S.2d 96, 100, 833 N.E.2d 239 (2005) ("The standard
for assessing a suspect's custodial status is whether a reasonable
person innocent of any wrongdoing would have believed that he
or she was not free to leave"); *People v. Harris*, 48 N.Y.2d 208,
215, 422 N.Y.S.2d 43, 45, 397 N.E.2d 733 (1979) ("The standard
to be applied is whether a reasonable person, innocent of any
crime, would have felt free to leave"); *People v. Pugliese*, 26
N.Y.2d 478, 311 N.Y.S.2d 851, 260 N.E.2d 499 (1970) (per
curiam); *People v. P.*, 21 N.Y.2d 1, 8-9, 286 N.Y.S.2d 225, 232,
233 N.E.2d 255 (1967).

There is at least one bright line, however: a person questioned
at gunpoint is "in custody" for purposes of *Miranda. See People v.
Shivers*, 21 N.Y.2d 118, 121, 286 N.Y.S.2d 827, 830, 233 N.E.2d
836 (1967) ("the primary question for decision is, of course,
whether the defendant was deprived of his freedom in a 'significant' way when he was questioned by the police officer at gun
point. To ask the question is to answer it"). Notably, however,
this does not necessarily mean that any question asked of the
person constitutes an "interrogation" within the meaning of
Miranda. See People v. Huffman, 41 N.Y.2d 29, 34, 390 N.Y.S.2d
843, 846, 359 N.E.2d 353 (1976).

In the context of a routine traffic stop:

It is settled that the safeguards prescribed by *Miranda* become applicable as soon as a suspect's freedom of action is curtailed to a "degree associated with formal arrest." If a motorist who has been detained pursuant to a traffic stop thereafter is subjected to treatment that renders him "in custody" for practical purposes, he will be entitled to the full panoply of protections prescribed by *Miranda*.

Berkemer v. McCarty, 468 U.S. 420, 440, 104 S. Ct. 3138, 3150, 82 L. Ed. 2d 317 (1984).

In *People v. Duncan*, 241 A.D.2d 566, —, 660 N.Y.S.2d 81, 82 (3d Dep't 1997), the Appellate Division, Third Department, held that:

> Inasmuch as [Deputy] Riley advised defendant that he had a warrant for his arrest, defendant was in custody at that moment and any admissions obtained thereafter without the benefit of *Miranda* warnings should have been suppressed.
>
> Moreover, even assuming that Riley had not effected defendant's arrest pursuant to the warrant, defendant's admissions nevertheless would be suppressible. It is axiomatic that a defendant is deemed to be in custody for *Miranda* purposes if a reasonable person, innocent of any wrongdoing, would perceive, under the circumstances, that he or she was in custody. It is unlikely that a reasonable person, having been advised by the police that they had a warrant for his or her arrest, would not deem himself or herself to be in custody.

(Citation omitted).

§ 27:26 Issue of whether defendant was in custody is mixed question of law and fact

In *People v. Cruz*, 90 N.Y.2d 961, 962, 665 N.Y.S.2d 46, 47, 687 N.E.2d 1329 (1997), the Court of Appeals held that:

> [The Appellate Division] specifically affirmed the hearing court's finding that defendant's statements were not the product of custodial interrogation. The court's ruling constitutes a determination on a mixed question of law and fact and, inasmuch as there is support in the record for the determination, it is beyond further review by this Court. Thus, the statements made by defendant in response to the questions of a police officer on the street were admissible despite the lack of prior *Miranda* warnings.

See also People v. Centano, 76 N.Y.2d 837, 560 N.Y.S.2d 121, 559 N.E.2d 1280 (1990); *People v. Paulin*, 25 N.Y.2d 445, 449, 306 N.Y.S.2d 929, 932, 255 N.E.2d 164 (1969).

§ 27:27 What constitutes "interrogation"?

In *Rhode Island v. Innis*, 446 U.S. 291, 300-02, 100 S. Ct. 1682, 1689-90, 64 L. Ed. 2d 297 (1980), the Supreme Court defined what it means to be "interrogated" within the meaning of *Miranda*:

We conclude that the *Miranda* safeguards come into play whenever a person in custody is subjected to either express questioning or its functional equivalent. That is to say, the term "interrogation" under *Miranda* refers not only to express questioning, but also to any words or actions on the part of the police (other than those normally attendant to arrest and custody) that the police should know are reasonably likely to elicit an incriminating response from the suspect. The latter portion of this definition focuses primarily upon the perceptions of the suspect, rather than the intent of the police. This focus reflects the fact that the *Miranda* safeguards were designed to vest a suspect in custody with an added measure of protection against coercive police practices, without regard to objective proof of the underlying intent of the police. A practice that the police should know is reasonably likely to evoke an incriminating response from a suspect thus amounts to interrogation. But, since the police surely cannot be held accountable for the unforeseeable results of their words or actions, the definition of interrogation can extend only to words or actions on the part of police officers that they *should have known* were reasonably likely to elicit an incriminating response.

(Footnotes omitted).

In *People v. Ferro*, 63 N.Y.2d 316, 319, 482 N.Y.S.2d 237, 238, 472 N.E.2d 13 (1984), the Court of Appeals held that:

What constitutes "interrogation" of a suspect who, after *Miranda* warnings, has declined to answer questions is determined not by the subjective intent of the police, but by whether an objective observer with the same knowledge concerning the suspect as the police had would conclude that the remark or conduct of the police was reasonably likely to elicit a response. Because applying that test we conclude that the conduct of the police in placing in front of the cell in which defendant was being detained furs stolen from the murder victim's residence constituted interrogation and because no new *Miranda* warnings were administered to defendant Ferro, his statements made subsequent to viewing the furs should have been suppressed.

(Footnote omitted). *Cf. People v. Huffman*, 61 N.Y.2d 795, 473 N.Y.S.2d 945, 462 N.E.2d 122 (1984) (officer's statement calling defendant a liar—which prompted defendant to confess—not interrogation).

§ 27:28   *Miranda* does not apply to spontaneous utterances

It is well settled that *Miranda* is inapplicable to spontaneous utterances. *See, e.g., People v. Torres*, 21 N.Y.2d 49, 54, 286 N.Y.S.2d 264, 269, 233 N.E.2d 282 (1967). However, "[i]n order for . . . statements to be characterized as spontaneous, it must 'be shown that they were in no way the product of an "interrogation environment," the result of "express questioning or its functional equivalent.'" *People v. Harris*, 57 N.Y.2d 335, 342,

456 N.Y.S.2d 694, 696, 442 N.E.2d 1205, 8 Media L. Rep. (BNA) 2532 (1982) (citation omitted). *See also People v. Lanahan*, 55 N.Y.2d 711, 713, 447 N.Y.S.2d 139, 140, 431 N.E.2d 624 (1981); *People v. Rogers*, 48 N.Y.2d 167, 174, 422 N.Y.S.2d 18, 22, 397 N.E.2d 709 (1979) ("To fit within this narrow exception, the 'spontaneity has to be genuine and not the result of inducement, provocation, encouragement or acquiescence, no matter how subtly employed' ") (citation omitted); *People v. Maerling*, 46 N.Y.2d 289, 302-03, 413 N.Y.S.2d 316, 324, 385 N.E.2d 1245 (1978) ("the spontaneity has to be genuine and not the result of inducement, provocation, encouragement or acquiescence, no matter how subtly employed. For such interrogation tactics often may be more destructive of a defendant's rights than are blatantly coercive techniques"). *See generally People v. Gonzales*, 75 N.Y.2d 938, 555 N.Y.S.2d 681, 554 N.E.2d 1269 (1990); *People v. Ellis*, 58 N.Y.2d 748, 750, 459 N.Y.S.2d 25, 27, 445 N.E.2d 201 (1982).

> The test in such situations cannot be whether, through hindsight, the defendant professes to believe the police intended to provoke an incriminating response. Were that so, virtually any police remark, no matter how innocuous, would constitute an interrogation as long as it was followed by an inculpatory statement. Instead, fully sensitive to the defendant's rights, yet using an objective standard, the Trial Judge must determine whether the defendant's statement can be said to have been triggered by police conduct which should reasonably have been anticipated to evoke a declaration from the defendant.

People v. Lynes, 49 N.Y.2d 286, 295, 425 N.Y.S.2d 295, 299-300, 401 N.E.2d 405 (1980). *See also People v. Howard*, 47 N.Y.2d 988, 419 N.Y.S.2d 974, 393 N.E.2d 1046 (1979).

In *Lanahan, supra,* the defendant's confession was held to be *not* spontaneous as a matter of law under the following circumstances:

> The police arrested defendant at his home pursuant to an arrest warrant and gave him his constitutional preinterrogation warnings. At the time of his arrest, according to the police testimony, defendant stated that he wanted to know what robbery he was charged with and was told that he would be given an explanation when they reached the police barracks. After arriving at the barracks, defendant was again given his preinterrogation warnings, and Investigator Connelly stated to him:

> "I am going to tell you what you are charged with. You are charged with the robbery of the Gasland gas station on Route 7 in the Town of Colonie. You did the job with a kid by the name of Lawless. You used Lawless's car. You parked the car behind the bank, which is about a block behind the Gasland gas station, walked through the fields, stood behind the wooden fence. When the girl came out with the two moneybags, both of you stepped out from behind the fence. You told her to throw the money over and she threw you the money.

"Then you asked—one of you asked her for the car keys, told her not to do anything stupid, got in behind the fence again, ran back to the car and drove to your house and split the money up.

"I said, that is the robbery that you are charged with." Whereupon, defendant responded, "I did it."

55 N.Y.2d at 712-13, 447 N.Y.S.2d at 140 (footnote omitted). *See also People v. Garofolo*, 46 N.Y.2d 592, 603-04, 415 N.Y.S.2d 810, 816, 389 N.E.2d 123, 18 A.L.R.4th 658 (1979) ("While some exchanges between a defendant and his jailers must of necessity occur, there is no excuse for inquiries such as those put here. Queries aimed at the issue of a defendant's guilt or innocence must be proscribed irrespective of their underlying motivation. These hardly masked a form of custodial interrogation no less invidious than that condemned by *Miranda*").

In *People v. Carmine A.*, 53 N.Y.2d 816, 818-19, 439 N.Y.S.2d 915, 916, 422 N.E.2d 575 (1981), the Court of Appeals held as follows:

A statement by a defendant in custody who has invoked his right to counsel must be suppressed unless it is in fact spontaneous. In finding defendant's statement voluntary the Hearing Judge only passed upon whether it was the result of intimidation or coercion, not on whether it was spontaneous. A statement which is the result of interrogation is not spontaneous, for . . . "the spontaneity has to be genuine and not the result of inducement, provocation, encouragement or acquiescence, no matter how subtly employed." Here, that cannot be said. Since defendant's statement was not spontaneous and since it was made after defendant indicated that he wanted an attorney, it must be suppressed.

(Citations omitted).

§ 27:29 "Pedigree question" exception to *Miranda*

"The Supreme Court has recognized that 'routine booking questions' constitute custodial interrogation. Nevertheless, it has held that answers given in response to such questions fall outside the protection of *Miranda* if they are 'reasonably related to the police's administrative concerns.' " *People v. Rodney*, 85 N.Y.2d 289, 292, 624 N.Y.S.2d 95, 97, 648 N.E.2d 471 (1995) (citation omitted). *See also Pennsylvania v. Muniz*, 496 U.S. 582, 600-02, 110 S. Ct. 2638, 2649-50, 110 L. Ed. 2d 528 (1990).

The exception derives from the essential purpose of *Miranda*—to protect defendants from self-incrimination in response to questions posed as part of the investigation of a crime, as distinguished from noninvestigative inquiries. We have also acknowledged the exception.

Because responses to routine booking questions—pedigree questions, as we have referred to them—are not suppressible even when obtained in violation of *Miranda,* defendant lacks a constitutional basis upon which to challenge the voluntariness of his statement and where there is no question of voluntariness, the People are not required to serve defendant with [CPL § 710.30] notice. Because routine administrative questioning by the police presumptively avoids any grounds for challenging the voluntariness of statements given in response to those questions, [CPL § 710.30] notice of such statements is not required.

Rodney, 85 N.Y.2d at 292-93, 624 N.Y.S.2d at 97-98 (citations omitted). *See also People v. Berkowitz*, 50 N.Y.2d 333, 338 n.1, 428 N.Y.S.2d 927, 929 n.1, 406 N.E.2d 783 (1980); *People v. Ryff*, 27 N.Y.2d 707, 314 N.Y.S.2d 17, 262 N.E.2d 222 (1970); *People v. Rivera*, 26 N.Y.2d 304, 309, 310 N.Y.S.2d 287, 290-91, 258 N.E.2d 699 (1970).

The question remains: What is a pedigree question? Questions asking for a person's name, address, height, weight, eye color, date of birth, current age, etc. are pedigree questions. *See Muniz,* 496 U.S. at 601, 110 S.Ct. at 2650. To qualify for the pedigree question exception, questions must be "limited in scope to those necessary for processing a defendant or providing for his physical needs." *People v. Hester*, 161 A.D.2d 665, __, 556 N.Y.S.2d 97, 98 (2d Dep't 1990). In this regard, the *Rodney* Court made clear that:

[T]he People may not rely on the pedigree exception if the questions, though facially appropriate, are likely to elicit incriminating admissions because of the circumstances of the particular case. Such questions fall outside the pedigree exceptions. Thus, the mere claim by the People that an admission was made in response to a question posed solely as an administrative concern does not automatically qualify that admission for the pedigree exception to *Miranda* or exempt the People from the necessity of supplying a CPL 710.30 notice.

85 N.Y.2d at 293, 624 N.Y.S.2d at 98 (citations omitted).

Applying these principles to the case before it, the *Rodney* Court held as follows:

In this case, the inquiry about defendant's employment status comes within the exception. The arresting officer's question was part of a routine booking form and was reasonably related to such administrative concerns as assignment of counsel, setting of bail, and the arraigning court's determination whether to release defendant on his own recognizance. Accordingly, we find no error in the People's failure to give notice of their intent to offer evidence of defendant's statement that he was "in sales." Although the question about defendant's occupation is arguably related to the conduct for which defendant had been arrested, it was not a disguised attempt at investigatory interrogation, and was not reasonably likely to elicit an incriminating response from defendant. Indeed, the incriminating nature of defendant's response arose from his apparent attempt to be humorous, and though the answer was incriminating, preclusion of the evidence is not required because the pedigree exception excuses the absence of CPL 710.30 notice.

Id. at 294, 624 N.Y.S.2d at 98 (citation omitted). *Cf. People v. Antonio*, 86 A.D.2d 614, __, 446 N.Y.S.2d 96, 98 (2d Dep't 1982) ("The questions asked of defendant were clearly not those aimed at ascertaining pedigree since they went to the very heart of the crime charged").

In a DWI case, questions such as where the defendant was coming from, where the defendant was going to, whether the defendant was drinking (and, if so, what and how much), etc., are *not* pedigree questions. In this regard, in *People v. Singh*, 12 Misc. 3d 952, __, 816 N.Y.S.2d 669, 670 (Nassau Co. Dist. Ct. 2006), the defendant stated that he "had, prior to his approximately 11:22 p.m. stop, drunk two or three beers at about 9:30 p.m." Such statement was made post-arrest, pre-*Miranda*, and in response to police questioning. *Id.* at __, 816 N.Y.S.2d at 670. Holding that the defendant's statement did not fall within the pedigree exception to *Miranda*, the Court reasoned that in the context of a DWI arrest, "a post-arrest question regarding recent alcohol consumption would . . . 'go to the very heart of the crime charged,' and therefore be likely to elicit incriminating admissions." *Id.* at __, 816 N.Y.S.2d at 671. *See also People v. Hernandez*, 6 Misc. 3d 572, 790 N.Y.S.2d 356 (Nassau Co. Dist. Ct. 2004); *People v. Lucas*, 161 Misc. 2d 954, __, 615 N.Y.S.2d 838, 839 (Suffolk Co. Dist. Ct. 1994); *People v. Ferrara*, 158 Misc. 2d 671, __, 602 N.Y.S.2d 86, 88 (N.Y. City Crim. Ct. 1993); *People v. Rafferty*, 148 Misc. 2d 494, 560 N.Y.S.2d 741 (Nassau Co. Dist. Ct. 1990).

§ 27:30   "Public safety" exception to *Miranda*

In *New York v. Quarles*, 467 U.S. 649, 104 S. Ct. 2626, 81 L. Ed. 2d 550 (1984), rev'g People v. Quarles, 58 N.Y.2d 664, 458 N.Y.S.2d 520 (1982), the Supreme Court created a "public safety" exception to *Miranda*. Specifically, the Court held that "on these facts there is a 'public safety' exception to the requirement that *Miranda* warnings be given before a suspect's answers may be admitted into evidence." *Id.* at 655, 104 S.Ct. at 2631. "The exception will not be difficult for police officers to apply because in each case it will be circumscribed by the exigency which justifies it. We think police officers can and will distinguish almost instinctively between questions necessary to secure their own safety or the safety of the public and questions designed solely to elicit testimonial evidence from a suspect." *Id.* at 658-59, 104 S.Ct. at 2633.

§ 27:31 "Emergency doctrine" exception to *Miranda*

In *People v. Doll*, 21 N.Y.3d 665, 670-71, 975 N.Y.S.2d 721, 724, 998 N.E.2d 384 (2013), cert. denied, 134 S. Ct. 1552, 188 L. Ed. 2d 568 (2014), the Court of Appeals stated:

> As a general rule, a person who is in custody cannot be questioned without first receiving *Miranda* warnings or after the right to counsel attaches. There are exceptions to these principles, one of which is referred to as the "emergency doctrine." It recognizes that the Constitution "is not a barrier to a police officer seeking to help someone in immediate danger," thereby excusing or justifying otherwise impermissible police conduct that is an objectively reasonable response to an apparently exigent situation. We have explained that the exception is comprised of three elements: (1) the police must have reasonable grounds to believe that there is an emergency at hand and an immediate need for their assistance for the protection of life or property and this belief must be grounded in empirical facts; (2) the search must not be primarily motivated by an intent to arrest and seize evidence; and (3) there must be some reasonable basis, approximating probable cause, to associate the emergency with the area or place to be searched.

(Citations omitted). *See also People v. Krom*, 61 N.Y.2d 187, 473 N.Y.S.2d 139, 461 N.E.2d 276 (1984) (recognizing emergency exception to right to counsel).

§ 27:32 *Miranda* waiver must be knowing, voluntary and intelligent

"A defendant's waiver of his *Miranda* rights must be knowing, voluntary, and intelligent." *People v. Jin Cheng Lin*, 26 N.Y.3d 701, 725, 27 N.Y.S.3d 439, 456, 47 N.E.3d 718 (2016). *See also People v. Rodney*, 85 N.Y.2d 289, 292, 624 N.Y.S.2d 95, 97, 648 N.E.2d 471 (1995). Nonetheless, in appropriate circumstances a waiver can be implicit. *See, e.g., Berghuis v. Thompkins*, 560 U.S. 370, 130 S. Ct. 2250, 176 L. Ed. 2d 1098 (2010); *People v. Sirno*, 76 N.Y.2d 967, 563 N.Y.S.2d 730, 565 N.E.2d 479 (1990); *People v. Davis*, 55 N.Y.2d 731, 447 N.Y.S.2d 149, 431 N.E.2d 634 (1981).

The Court found insufficient proof of a valid *Miranda* waiver in *People v. McAleavey*, 133 Misc. 2d 987, 509 N.Y.S.2d 278 (Suffolk Co. Dist. Ct. 1986).

§ 27:33 "Preamble" can render *Miranda* warnings ineffective

Beginning in 2007, the Queens County District Attorney implemented a central booking prearraignment interview program, launched in conjunction with the initiative to videotape interrogations. The program consisted of a structured, videotaped interview conducted by two members of the District Attorney's staff (an assistant district attorney and a detective investigator [DI]) with a suspect immediately prior to arraignment. During this interview, the DI delivered a scripted preface or "preamble" to the *Miranda* warnings that, among other things, informed the suspect that "this is your opportunity to tell us your story," and "your only opportunity" to do so before going before a judge. After being so cautioned, defendants Jermaine Dunbar (Dunbar) and Collin F. Lloyd-Douglas (Lloyd-Douglas) made statements in their respective interviews, which they later sought to suppress. We hold that the preamble undermined the subsequently-communicated *Miranda* warnings to the extent that Dunbar and Lloyd-Douglas were not " 'adequately and effectively' advised of the choice [the Fifth Amendment] guarantees" against self-incrimination before they agreed to speak with law enforcement authorities. * * *

In sum, the issue in these cases is not whether, under the totality of the circumstances, these defendants' waivers were valid, but rather whether or not they were ever "clearly informed" of their *Miranda* rights in the first place, as is constitutionally required. We agree with the Appellate Division that they were not: the preamble undercut the meaning of all four *Miranda* warnings, depriving Dunbar and Lloyd-Douglas of an effective explanation of their rights. Certainly, if the *Miranda* warnings were preceded by statements that were *directly* contrary to those warnings (*e.g.*, you are required to answer our questions; your statements will be used to help you; you are not entitled to a lawyer) there would be no need to examine the totality of the circumstances to determine if a *Miranda* waiver was knowing, voluntary and intelligent. The preamble did the same thing, albeit in an indirect, more subtle way. While a lawyer would not be fooled, a reasonable person in these defendants' shoes might well have concluded, after having listened to the preamble, that it was in his best interest to get out his side of the story—fast.

People v. Dunbar, 24 N.Y.3d 304, 308, 316, 998 N.Y.S.2d 679, 680-81, 686, 23 N.E.3d 946 (2014), cert. denied, 135 S. Ct. 2051, 191 L. Ed. 2d 971 (2015) and cert. denied, 135 S. Ct. 2052, 191 L. Ed. 2d 971 (2015) (citations omitted).

§ 27:34 Suspect who initially exercises right to remain silent can thereafter waive such right

There is a critical distinction between the right to remain silent and the right to counsel. Specifically, as a general rule "once a suspect in custody requests the assistance of counsel he may not be questioned further in the absence of an attorney." *People v. Cunningham*, 49 N.Y.2d 203, 205, 424 N.Y.S.2d 421, 422, 400 N.E.2d 360 (1980) (per curiam). By contrast, "a suspect, even after exercising his right to remain silent, may change his mind and voluntarily make a statement." *People v. Kinnard*, 62 N.Y.2d 910, 912, 479 N.Y.S.2d 2, 3, 467 N.E.2d 886 (1984).

This rule was discussed in *People v. Gary*, 31 N.Y.2d 68, 69, 69-70, 334 N.Y.S.2d 883, 884, 884-85, 286 N.E.2d 263 (1972):

> The issue presented by this appeal arises upon defendant-appellant's contention that inasmuch as he had once indicated, when first taken into police custody, that he did not wish to make a statement, the authorities were precluded from thereafter seeking to elicit information from him, after again advising him of his *Miranda* rights. * * *
>
> The contention that, having once invoked his right to remain silent, defendant could not again be asked to speak, rests largely upon the general exposition found in *Miranda,* where it was said: "Once warnings have been given, the subsequent procedure is clear. If the individual indicates in any manner, at any time prior to or during questioning, that he wishes to remain silent, the interrogation must cease. At this point he has shown that he intends to exercise his Fifth Amendment privilege; any statement taken after the person invokes his privilege cannot be other than the product of compulsion, subtle or otherwise." There is, however, a clear distinction between the continuation, whether by successive agencies or otherwise, of an "interrogation" thus foreclosed and a subsequent request, upon reiteration of the requisite warnings, for reconsideration of an earlier decision to make no statement. The narrow issue presented by this case, then, is whether the Assistant District Attorney was precluded from inviting the defendant to make a statement because, an hour before, a like request by a police officer had been declined. Neither *Miranda* nor any broader constitutional mandate prohibits a subsequent request, made otherwise than in the course of continued importunity or coercive interrogation in the guise of a request for reconsideration.

(Citations omitted). *See also People v. Buxton*, 44 N.Y.2d 33, 37, 403 N.Y.S.2d 487, 489, 374 N.E.2d 384 (1978) ("that a suspect has once asserted his right to remain silent does not, per se, prohibit his later being asked to speak upon reiteration of the requisite warnings, provided that the subsequent statement is not the product of 'continued importunity or coercive interrogation in the guise of a request for reconsideration.' However, as contrasted with a mere assertion of the right to remain silent, '[i]f the individual states that he wants an attorney, the interrogation must cease until an attorney is present' ") (citations omitted).

§ 27:35 Waiver of *Miranda* rights by person with limited ability to understand English

"Defendant is correct that if his English language comprehension was so deficient that he could not understand the import of his rights, his confession could not have been voluntary. . . .

The People must establish that the defendant 'grasped that he or she did not have to speak to the interrogator; that any statement might be used to the subject's disadvantage; and that an attorney's assistance would be provided upon request, at any time, and before questioning is continued." *People v. Jin Cheng Lin*, 26 N.Y.3d 701, 725-26, 27 N.Y.S.3d 439, 456, 47 N.E.3d 718 (2016) (citation omitted). *See also People v. Alberto*, 22 Misc. 3d 786, __, 877 N.Y.S.2d 628, 633 (Suffolk Co. Dist. Ct. 2008) ("the proof at the hearing did not establish beyond a reasonable doubt that the defendant understood the *Miranda* warnings, whether in English or in Spanish, nor did it establish that the statement was an accurate transcription of his actual words").

§ 27:36   Waiver of *Miranda* rights by person of low intelligence

In *People v. Williams*, 62 N.Y.2d 285, 287, 476 N.Y.S.2d 788, 789, 465 N.E.2d 327 (1984), the Court of Appeals held that:

> An effective waiver of *Miranda* rights may be made by an accused of subnormal intelligence so long as it is established that he or she understood the immediate meaning of the warnings. An inability to comprehend the import of the *Miranda* warnings in the larger context of criminal law generally does not of itself vitiate the validity of the waiver.

Nonetheless, when dealing with a person of subnormal intelligence "close scrutiny must be made of the circumstances of the asserted waiver." *Id.* at 289, 476 N.Y.S.2d at 790.

> Although a suspect must be apprised of his or her rights, providing a general legal education is not the business of the police or the courts. It must be shown that the individual grasped that he or she did not have to speak to the interrogator; that any statement might be used to the subject's disadvantage; and that an attorney's assistance would be provided upon request, at any time, and before questioning is continued. What will suffice to meet this burden will vary from one case to the next. Thus, for example, administering *Miranda* warnings in a language not understood by the suspect would certainly be inadequate. Similarly, to an individual of subnormal intelligence, stating the *Miranda* warnings in sophisticated terms would be as incomprehensible as though they were spoken in a foreign language. As noted above, the detective here was careful to reduce the warnings to simple terms that defendant could understand.

Id. at 289, 476 N.Y.S.2d at 790. *See generally People v. Love*, 57 N.Y.2d 998, 457 N.Y.S.2d 238, 443 N.E.2d 486 (1982) (mental patient capable of waiving *Miranda* rights).

§ 27:37   *Miranda* warnings required to be read at time of arrest

In *People v. Pavone*, 26 N.Y.3d 629, 643, 26 N.Y.S.3d 728, 739,

47 N.E.3d 56 (2015), the Court of Appeals stated that "we consider the post-arrest, pre-*Miranda* situation to be the rarest of events given that *Miranda* warnings are customarily and by law provided upon arrest."

§ 27:38   Effect of late *Miranda* warnings

In *People v. Guilford*, 21 N.Y.3d 205, 208-09, 969 N.Y.S.2d 430, 432, 991 N.E.2d 204 (2013), the Court of Appeals stated:

> Proof of voluntariness compatible with due process, we have said, will depend upon the particular circumstances—"the totality"—of each case. In some situations—where, for example, *Miranda* warnings have been timely given—the requisite inference of voluntariness may be relatively easily drawn. But where there has been official illegality potentially impairing the voluntariness of a subsequent admission, the inference will naturally require a more exacting showing.

> We have recognized this principle most frequently in cases involving late *Miranda* warnings. In *People v. Chapple,* we held that the late interposition of those warnings would be "too late" unless there was a demonstration of a "pronounced break" in interrogation adequate to justify a finding that the defendant was no longer under the sway of the prior questioning when the warnings were given. We have since reaffirmed the need for this more precise showing under our state constitution, notwithstanding federal precedent suggesting that, in the absence of actual coercion, *Miranda* warnings will ordinarily suffice to demonstrate the voluntariness of statements subsequently made. A less demanding rule, we noted, would have little deterrent effect, since the police could then "question a suspect in custody without warning, provided only they thereafter question him or her again after warnings have been given." * * *

> Under the *Chapple-Bethea* doctrine a suspect's course of interrogation is assessed using certain fairly objective criteria to characterize it either as unitary or composed of severable, separately Mirandizable segments. But the inquiry as to whether there has been one interrogatory sequence or several does not address the very stubborn problem posed by actual coercion, which involves the physical, cognitive and emotional depletion of the interrogation subject. In situations where the subject has been interrogated over an extremely lengthy period, the existence of objective indicia of separation may well be inadequate to prove that the defendant has been restored to the status of one no longer under the influence of questioning, so as to render plausible the characterization of a subsequent admission as voluntary beyond a reasonable doubt.

(Citations omitted). *See also People v. Paulman*, 5 N.Y.3d 122, 800 N.Y.S.2d 96, 833 N.E.2d 239 (2005); *People v. Bethea*, 67 N.Y.2d 364, 368, 502 N.Y.S.2d 713, 715, 493 N.E.2d 937 (1986) (per curiam) ("Here, as in *Chapple,* the testimony of the arresting officer establishes the close sequence between the unwarned custodial statement in the van and its repetition soon after defendant arrived at the precinct. There must, therefore, be suppression of the second statement as well as the first"); *People v. Chapple*, 38 N.Y.2d 112, 115, 378 N.Y.S.2d 682, 685-86, 341 N.E.2d 243 (1975) ("Warnings, to be effective under the combined holdings in *Miranda* and *Westover,* must *precede* the subjection of a defendant to questioning. Later is too late, unless there is such a definite, pronounced break in the interrogation that the defendant may be said to have returned, in effect, to the status of one who is not under the influence of questioning").

§ 27:39   Effect of *Miranda* violation on post-*Miranda* statements

In *People v. Malaussena*, 10 N.Y.3d 904, 905, 861 N.Y.S.2d 609, 609-10, 891 N.E.2d 725 (2008), the Court of Appeals held that:

> The trial court did not err in declining to suppress defendant's confessions. Even assuming that he was in custody once a detective observed blood on defendant's shoe, any violation of *Miranda v. Arizona* did not infect his post-*Miranda* admissions. Defendant voluntarily appeared at the police station to speak to detectives, he did not incriminate himself prior to receiving *Miranda* warnings and there was only a brief exchange between the detectives and defendant once the interview arguably became a custodial interrogation. Moreover, although the initial post-*Miranda* interview was conducted by the same detectives and in the same room as the pre-*Miranda* discussions, defendant's decision to disclose the incriminatory information was not the function of a single continuous chain of events since questioning ceased for approximately four hours before he received *Miranda* warnings and confessed for the first time. Consequently, the courts below correctly concluded that the statements were admissible.

(Citations omitted). *See also People v. White*, 10 N.Y.3d 286, 856 N.Y.S.2d 534, 886 N.E.2d 156 (2008); *People v. Paulman*, 5 N.Y.3d 122, 125, 800 N.Y.S.2d 96, 97-98, 833 N.E.2d 239 (2005) ("The primary issue presented in this case is whether two statements defendant made after he was given *Miranda* warnings and waived his right to remain silent should have been suppressed due to the prior, unwarned statement. Under the circumstances of this case, we conclude the subsequent statements were properly received in evidence").

> To determine whether there is a "single continuous chain of events" under *Chapple,* New York courts have considered a number of factors, including the time differential between the *Miranda* violation and the subsequent admission; whether the same police personnel were present and involved in eliciting each statement; whether there was a change in the location or nature of the interrogation; the circumstances surrounding the *Miranda* violation, such as the

extent of the improper questioning; and whether, prior to the *Miranda* violation, defendant had indicated a willingness to speak to police. No one factor is determinative and each case must be viewed on its unique facts. The purpose of the inquiry is to assess where there was a sufficiently "definite, pronounced break in the interrogation" to dissipate the taint from the *Miranda* violation. If so, the Mirandized statement is admissible at trial despite the prior, unwarned statement.

Paulman, 5 N.Y.3d at 130-31, 800 N.Y.S.2d at 102 (citation and footnote omitted).

In *People v. Mayorga*, 64 N.Y.2d 864, 865, 487 N.Y.S.2d 548, 549, 476 N.E.2d 993 (1985), the Court of Appeals held as follows:

Our review of the opinion of the Appellate Division reveals that its conclusion . . . was that defendant's last two statements were the result of such " 'continuous interrogation' that the *Miranda* warnings subsequently administered 'were insufficient to protect his rights' " and that there was no such " 'definite, pronounced break in the interrogation that the defendant may be said to have returned, in effect, to the status of one who is not under the influence of questioning.' "

Whether there has been an attenuating break in an interrogation is, as are most other determinations made in suppression matters which require the drawing of inferences from the facts, a mixed question of law and fact.

(Citation omitted). *See generally People v. Tanner*, 30 N.Y.2d 102, 331 N.Y.S.2d 1, 282 N.E.2d 98 (1972).

In *People v. Moyer*, 292 A.D.2d 793, __, 738 N.Y.S.2d 810, 812-13 (4th Dep't 2002), the Appellate Division, Fourth Department, reversed the defendant's DWI conviction under the following circumstances:

After defendant was taken into custody but before he received *Miranda* warnings, he was questioned by one of two police officers escorting him to a waiting patrol vehicle. Defendant's responses to that questioning were inculpatory. Once defendant was inside the patrol vehicle, the second officer administered *Miranda* warnings. The officers and defendant waited at that location for one hour for a police van to arrive. During that one-hour period, defendant slept in the back of the patrol vehicle. When the van arrived, the second officer re-administered *Miranda* warnings and proceeded to interrogate defendant.

The court properly granted that part of defendant's motion seeking to suppress defendant's pre-*Miranda* statements but erred in failing to grant that part of defendant's motion seeking to suppress the post-*Miranda* statements. . . . Here, defendant was questioned post-*Miranda* in the same location as the pre-*Miranda* questioning and by an officer who was present during the pre-*Miranda* questioning. Thus, despite the one-hour interval between pre-*Miranda* and post-*Miranda* questioning, it cannot be said that there was "such a definite, pronounced break" in the interrogation that defendant was returned to the position of one who was not under the influence of the initial improper questioning.

(Citations omitted).

§ 27:40 Issue of whether police complied with *Miranda* must be submitted to jury if defendant so requests

In *People v. Graham*, 55 N.Y.2d 144, 146, 447 N.Y.S.2d 918, 919, 432 N.E.2d 790 (1982), the Court of Appeals held that the trial court could not:

> [R]efuse defendant's request, made pursuant to CPL 60.45 and 710.70, that it submit the voluntariness of defendant's incriminating statement to the jury when the attack on it was based solely on proof in support of a claim that the police officer to whom it was made failed to advise the defendant of her constitutional rights as required by *Miranda v. Arizona*.

§ 27:41 Officer not necessarily required to read full *Miranda* warnings from card at *Huntley* hearing

In *People v. Gonzalez*, 55 N.Y.2d 720, 722, 447 N.Y.S.2d 145, 146, 431 N.E.2d 630 (1981), the Court of Appeals held that:

> [T]here was sufficient evidence before the suppression court to sustain the factual determination that defendant was duly given his constitutional preinterrogation warnings. Officer Collins testified that he had read defendant his "rights" from a blank police department arrest report form, a copy of which he did not have with him at the suppression hearing. On cross-examination Officer Collins stated that the "rights" to which he was referring were "*Miranda* warnings." In the absence of any proof whatsoever that such reading was or might have been deficient in some particular, the suppression court was warranted in drawing the inference that the constitutional preinterrogation warnings were adequately stated.

See generally People v. Bradway, 285 A.D.2d 831, —, 728 N.Y.S.2d 286, 289 (3d Dep't 2001) ("we reject defendant's assertion that the *Miranda* warnings were inadequate. After the lieutenant advised defendant of his *Miranda* rights he asked, *inter alia,* 'are you willing to answer my questions' rather than the customary 'are you willing to answer my questions *without an attorney.*' As this language did not render the *Miranda* warnings inadequate, we find that defendant was properly apprised of and waived his right to counsel").

§ 27:42 *Miranda* violation subject to harmless error analysis

Miranda violations are subject to harmless error analysis. *See, e.g., People v. Romero*, 27 N.Y.3d 981, 32 N.Y.S.3d 43, 51 N.E.3d 554 (2016); *People v. Pavone*, 26 N.Y.3d 629, 646, 26 N.Y.S.3d 728, 741, 47 N.E.3d 56 (2015); *People v. Paulman*, 5 N.Y.3d 122, 800 N.Y.S.2d 96, 833 N.E.2d 239 (2005); *Matter of Samuel E.L.*, 66 N.Y.2d 984, 499 N.Y.S.2d 377, 489 N.E.2d 1279 (1985); *People v. Rivera*, 57 N.Y.2d 453, 457 N.Y.S.2d 191, 443 N.E.2d 439 (1982).

§ 27:43 When does the right to counsel attach?

In New York, the right to counsel is not merely a Constitutional right—it is both an "indelible right" and a "cherished principle." In this regard, in *People v. Lopez*, 16 N.Y.3d 375, 380, 923 N.Y.S.2d 377, 380, 947 N.E.2d 1155 (2011), the Court stated:

> New York has long viewed the right to counsel as a cherished and valuable protection that must be guarded with the utmost vigilance. Arising from the due process guarantee in our State Constitution, the entitlement to effective assistance of counsel and the privilege against compulsory self-incrimination, the right to counsel is referred to as "indelible" because, once it "attaches," interrogation is prohibited unless the right is waived in the presence of counsel. We have explained that attachment occurs when (1) a person in custody requests the assistance of an attorney or a lawyer enters the case or (2) a criminal proceeding is commenced against the defendant by the filing of an accusatory instrument.

(Citations omitted).

Similarly, in *People v. Ramos*, 99 N.Y.2d 27, 32-33, 750 N.Y.S.2d 821, 824, 780 N.E.2d 506 (2002), the Court stated:

> The State constitutional right to counsel is a "cherished principle" worthy of the "highest degree of [judicial] vigilance." Our decisional law has advanced this principle by holding that the State constitutional right to counsel attaches indelibly in two situations. First, it arises when formal judicial proceedings begin, whether or not the defendant has actually retained or requested a lawyer. Second, the right to counsel attaches when an uncharged individual "has actually retained a lawyer in the matter at issue or, while in custody, has requested a lawyer in that matter." Although these principles are similar to those developed under the Fifth and Sixth Amendments to the Federal Constitution, New York's constitutional right to counsel jurisprudence developed "independent of its Federal counterpart" and offers broader protections.

(Citations and footnote omitted).

§ 27:44 Request for counsel must be unequivocal

When a defendant in custody unequivocally requests the assistance of counsel, any purported waiver of that right obtained in the absence of counsel is ineffective. However, when the defendant's request is not unequivocal, the right to counsel does not attach.

Whether a particular request is or is not unequivocal is a mixed question of law and fact that must be determined with reference to the circumstances surrounding the request including the defendant's demeanor, manner of expression and the particular words found to have been used by the defendant.

People v. Glover, 87 N.Y.2d 838, 839, 637 N.Y.S.2d 683, 684, 661 N.E.2d 155 (1995). *See also People v. Rowell*, 59 N.Y.2d 727, 463 N.Y.S.2d 426, 450 N.E.2d 232 (1983).

Although a request for counsel must be unequivocal, that standard is not difficult to meet. In this regard, the Court of Appeals has made clear that an unequivocal request for counsel has been made where, while being read *Miranda* warnings, the defendant says "no" when asked whether he or she is willing to answer questions without an attorney present. *People v. Carmine A.*, 53 N.Y.2d 816, 818, 439 N.Y.S.2d 915, 916, 422 N.E.2d 575 (1981). *See also People v. Higgins*, 124 A.D.3d 929, —, 1 N.Y.S.3d 424, 428 (3d Dep't 2015) ("defendant's statement at 3:41 a.m., requesting that he be allowed to call his attorney, was sufficiently unequivocal to invoke his right to counsel"); *People v. Harris*, 93 A.D.3d 58, 936 N.Y.S.2d 233 (2d Dep't 2012), order aff'd, 20 N.Y.3d 912, 956 N.Y.S.2d 478, 980 N.E.2d 527 (2012); *People v. Obieke*, 186 Misc. 2d 708, 712 N.Y.S.2d 919 (Monroe Co. Sup. Ct. 2000).

In *People v. Hicks*, 69 N.Y.2d 969, 970, 516 N.Y.S.2d 648, 649, 509 N.E.2d 343 (1987), the Court of Appeals held that the defendant did not unequivocally request counsel under the following circumstances:

[D]efendant and his brother voluntarily came to the police station; defendant was "gratuitously" given *Miranda* warnings; defendant asked the police "should I speak to a lawyer"; the police responded by asking him if he thought he was in trouble; defendant replied "no" and then gave a statement; and defendant was advised that he was not under arrest but was free to leave.

§ 27:45 Custodial interrogation after right to counsel has been invoked—Generally

In *People v. Cunningham*, 49 N.Y.2d 203, 205, 424 N.Y.S.2d 421, 422, 400 N.E.2d 360 (1980) (per curiam), the Court of Appeals very clearly and decisively set forth the law on this issue:

We hold that once a suspect in custody requests the assistance of counsel he may not be questioned further in the absence of an attorney. We intend by our holding to make it clear that an uncounseled waiver of a constitutional right will not be deemed voluntary if it is made after the right to counsel has been invoked.

§ 27:46 Custodial interrogation of person represented by counsel on another matter

In *People v. Rogers*, 48 N.Y.2d 167, 169, 173, 422 N.Y.S.2d 18, 19, 22, 397 N.E.2d 709 (1979), the Court of Appeals held that:

> [O]nce an attorney has entered the proceeding, thereby signifying that the police should cease questioning, a defendant in custody may not be further interrogated in the absence of counsel. We may not blithely override the importance of the attorney's entry by permitting interrogation of an accused with respect to matters which some may perceive to be unrelated. * * *

> We today recognize that the *Taylor* rule is inconsistent with the principles enunciated in *Hobson* and declare that once a defendant is represented by an attorney, the police may not elicit from him any statements, except those necessary for processing or his physical needs. Nor may they seek a waiver of this right, except in the presence of counsel.

> Our acknowledgment of an accused's right to the presence of counsel, even when the interrogation concerns unrelated matters, represents no great quantitative change in the protection we have extended to the individual as a shield against the awesome and sometimes coercive force of the State. An attorney is charged with protecting the rights of his client and it would be to ignore reality to deny the role of counsel when the particular episode of questioning does not concern the pending charge. It cannot be assumed that an attorney would abandon his client merely because the police represent that they seek to question on a matter unrelated to the charge on which the attorney has been retained or assigned. Finally, it is the role of defendant's attorney, not the State, to determine whether a particular matter will or will not touch upon the extant charge. Once a defendant has an attorney as advocate of his rights, the attorney's function cannot be negated by the simple expedient of questioning in his absence.

> The presence of counsel confers no undue advantage to the accused. Rather, the attorney's presence serves to equalize the positions of the accused and sovereign, mitigating the coercive influence of the State and rendering it less overwhelming. That the rule diminishes the likelihood of a waiver of self incriminating statements is immaterial to our system of justice. Although the State has a significant interest in investigating and prosecuting criminal conduct, that interest cannot override the fundamental right to an attorney guaranteed by our State Constitution.

(Citations omitted). *See also People v. Hobson*, 39 N.Y.2d 479, 384 N.Y.S.2d 419, 348 N.E.2d 894 (1976).

In *People v. Burdo*, 91 N.Y.2d 146, 149, 667 N.Y.S.2d 970, 971, 690 N.E.2d 854 (1997), the Court of Appeals reiterated that "[t]he holding of *People v. Rogers* is clear. There we held that 'once an

attorney has entered the proceeding, thereby signifying that the
police should cease questioning, a defendant in custody may not
be further interrogated in the absence of counsel.' " (Citation
omitted). Specifically:

> *Rogers* . . . established the principle that a defendant represented
> by counsel on the charge on which he is held in custody cannot be
> interrogated in the absence of counsel "on any matter." For nearly
> two decades *Rogers* has stood as a workable, comprehensible, bright
> line rule, providing effective guidance to law enforcement while
> ensuring that it is defendant's attorney, not the police, who
> determines which matters are related and unrelated to the subject
> of the representation. We reject the proposal put forth by the dis-
> sent to now modify *Rogers* to "an actual attorney-client relationship
> or an invocation of his right to counsel."

Id. at 150-51, 667 N.Y.S.2d at 972 (citation omitted). *See also
People v. Cohen*, 90 N.Y.2d 632, 665 N.Y.S.2d 30, 687 N.E.2d
1313 (1997); *People v. Grant*, 45 N.Y.2d 366, 408 N.Y.S.2d 429,
380 N.E.2d 257 (1978); *People v. Clark*, 45 N.Y.2d 432, 408
N.Y.S.2d 463, 380 N.E.2d 290 (1978); *People v. Munlin*, 45 N.Y.2d
427, 408 N.Y.S.2d 461, 380 N.E.2d 288 (1978); *People v. Singer*,
44 N.Y.2d 241, 405 N.Y.S.2d 17, 376 N.E.2d 179 (1978).

What about the situation where the defendant is not represented by counsel in connection with the charge for which he or
she is in custody, but is represented by counsel on another matter?

In *People v. Steward*, 88 N.Y.2d 496, 502, 646 N.Y.S.2d 974,
977, 670 N.E.2d 214 (1996), the Court of Appeals held that "in a
subsequent custodial interrogation about matters unrelated to
the charge upon which a defendant was assigned counsel in a
prior separate proceeding, the suspect is competent to waive the
right to counsel in the absence of counsel as to such matters." *See
also People v. Ruff*, 81 N.Y.2d 330, 599 N.Y.S.2d 221, 615 N.E.2d
611 (1993); *People v. Bing*, 76 N.Y.2d 331, 559 N.Y.S.2d 474, 558
N.E.2d 1011 (1990); *People v. Robles*, 72 N.Y.2d 689, 536 N.Y.S.2d
401, 533 N.E.2d 240 (1988); *People v. Colwell*, 65 N.Y.2d 883,
885, 493 N.Y.S.2d 298, 300, 482 N.E.2d 1214 (1985) ("any interest in extending the right to counsel rule articulated in *Rogers*
throughout the often-protracted duration of an appeal is outweighed by the legitimate interest in law enforcement").

In *People v. Alls*, 83 N.Y.2d 94, 608 N.Y.S.2d 139, 629 N.E.2d
1018 (1993), the Court of Appeals analogized a person's status as
a prison inmate to a routine traffic stop or a *Terry* stop (*i.e.,* although the person is clearly not free to leave, the person is not
"in custody" for *Miranda* purposes). In this regard, the Court
held that:

> In the context of a correctional facility environment, despite the

undeniable fact of an inmate's general confinement in the sense of not being free to leave the facility, we can envisage confrontations between correctional officers and prisoners analogous to the relatively brief, generally public, or otherwise on-the-scene investigatory detentions in nonprison settings found not custodial for *Miranda* purposes. On the other hand, to impose a requirement that correctional authorities must administer *Miranda* warnings before even the most casual or spontaneous interchanges with inmates integral to prison life would have an enormous impact upon the ability of correctional authorities to maintain prison order and discipline, in cases where the Fifth Amendment rights of inmates are not seriously implicated. For these reasons, we decline to adopt a per se rule that any questioning of an inmate in a correctional facility is custodial interrogation under *Miranda v. Arizona.*

When, however, the circumstances of the detention and interrogation of a prison inmate are no longer analogous to those kinds of detentions found not custodial in nonprison settings, but instead entail added constraint that would lead a prison inmate reasonably to believe that there has been a restriction on that person's freedom over and above that of ordinary confinement in a correctional facility, *Miranda* warnings are necessary.

Id. at 100, 608 N.Y.S.2d at 142 (citations omitted).

"[W]ith respect to a right to counsel claim, after the People go forward to justify the police interrogation, if the defendant makes a claim that he is represented by counsel on another pending charge of which the police had knowledge, it is the defendant's burden to show that he was, in fact, represented by counsel on the earlier charge at the time of interrogation." *People v. Rosa*, 65 N.Y.2d 380, 387, 492 N.Y.S.2d 542, 547, 482 N.E.2d 21 (1985).

§ 27:47 Noncustodial interrogation of person represented by counsel on another matter

"[E]liciting inculpatory statements from a suspect under noncustodial circumstances 'involves no violation of [the] right to counsel even [where] the police are aware that [the suspect] has counsel on a prior unrelated charge.' " *People v. Bertolo*, 65 N.Y.2d 111, 116, 490 N.Y.S.2d 475, 479, 480 N.E.2d 61 (1985) (citation omitted).

§ 27:48 Request for consent to search after right to counsel has been invoked

In *People v. Johnson*, 48 N.Y.2d 565, 567, 423 N.Y.S.2d 905, 906, 399 N.E.2d 936 (1979), "[t]he question posed [was] whether, after a request for counsel has been made by a suspect in custody, his consent to a warrantless search of his premises may be obtained by a request immediately addressed to him in the absence of counsel. We hold that a consent so obtained is unavailing." In so holding, the Court reasoned as follows:

> We perceive no basis for differentiation with respect to the constraint imposed on the police by a defendant's request for an attorney between their thereafter obtaining a statement from him and their thereafter obtaining his consent to a warrantless search of his premises. As we noted in *People v. Grant,* the Supreme Court in *Miranda v. Arizona* accorded a different significance to an exercise of the constitutional right to counsel than to an election to remain silent in exercise of the constitutional right against self incrimination. "If the individual states that he wants an attorney, the interrogation must cease until an attorney is present. At that time, the individual must have an opportunity to confer with the attorney and to have him present during any subsequent questioning." The defendant's rights are no less at stake and the advice of counsel no less important if the police seek a relinquishment of defendant's constitutional right to be secure against unreasonable searches and seizures than if they seek a waiver of his privilege against self incrimination.

Id. at 568-69, 423 N.Y.S.2d at 907 (citations omitted). *See also People v. Grant,* 45 N.Y.2d 366, 408 N.Y.S.2d 429, 380 N.E.2d 257 (1978).

§ 27:49 Applicability of right to counsel where defendant attempts to bribe arresting officer

In *People v. Middleton,* 54 N.Y.2d 474, 476-77, 446 N.Y.S.2d 211, 212, 430 N.E.2d 1264 (1981), the Court of Appeals held that:

> A defendant who requests counsel after his arrest but then without provocation seeks to buy his way out by offering a bribe to the arresting officer may be questioned by the officer as to anything legitimately related to the bribe offer that would be asked by an officer intending to accept such an offer. Admission in evidence of such a bribe offer, of any repetition of it, of any statements made in answer to such inquiries, or of any contraband of which the officer learns through the answers to such inquiries violates neither defendant's constitutional right to counsel nor his right to be free of unreasonable search and seizure.

§ 27:50 Police procedures that hinder communication between defendant and lawyer retained on defendant's behalf require suppression

"[T]he fundamental rule in this State is that, once the police have been apprised that a lawyer has undertaken to represent a defendant in custody in connection with criminal charges under investigation, the person so held may not validly waive the assistance of counsel except in the presence of the lawyer." *People v. Garofolo,* 46 N.Y.2d 592, 599, 415 N.Y.S.2d 810, 813, 389 N.E.2d 123, 18 A.L.R.4th 658 (1979). In *Garofolo,* the Court of Appeals made clear that the mere fact that:

[G]ood faith efforts are made to locate a defendant who is taken into custody does not absolve the police of their responsibility if their internal procedures are inadequate to keep track of those against whom the restraining hand and the accusing finger of the State have come to rest. In a Nation that prizes individual liberty, it is not asking too much to expect that, in those cases where interference with a person's liberty becomes necessary, no undue delay prevent anyone so circumstanced from securing the protections—here the right to counsel—to which he or she is entitled.
* * *

For these reasons, and because by 9:10 P.M. no significant portion, if any at all, of Garofolo's confession had yet been reduced to writing, we hold as a matter of law that it should have been suppressed.

Id. at 600-01, 601, 415 N.Y.S.2d at 814, 815 (citations omitted). *See also People v. Bevilacqua*, 45 N.Y.2d 508, 514, 410 N.Y.S.2d 549, 552, 382 N.E.2d 1326 (1978) ("Once a lawyer telephones police headquarters with a request that interrogation of his client be stopped, concealment of defendant's whereabouts and failure of intra-police communication, does not permit the police to continue questioning defendant as if no lawyer had entered the proceedings"); *People v. Tompkins*, 45 N.Y.2d 748, 408 N.Y.S.2d 485, 380 N.E.2d 311 (1978). *See generally People v. Washington*, 23 N.Y.3d 228, 233, 989 N.Y.S.2d 670, 674, 12 N.E.3d 1099 (2014) ("the statutory right to legal consultation applies when an attorney contacts the police before a chemical test for alcohol is performed and the police must alert the subject to the presence of counsel, whether the contact is made in person or telephonically").

Chapter 28

Rosario Material

Research References

Westlaw Databases

Handling a Criminal Case in New York (HCCNY)

Treatises and Practice Aids

Muldoon, Handling a Criminal Case in New York §§ 8:34 to 8:42, 8:136 to 8:143

Law Reviews and Other Periodicals

Bandler, The New York Rosario Rule Applied to Computerized Documents: The Rigid and Impractical Duplicative Equivalent Doctrine Requires Modification, 22 Pace L. Rev. 407 (Spring, 2002)

KeyCite®: Cases and other legal materials listed in KeyCite Scope can be researched through the KeyCite service on Westlaw®. Use KeyCite to check citations for form, parallel references, prior and later history, and comprehensive citator information, including citations to other decisions and secondary materials.

---

§ 28:1 In general

Research References

West's Key Number Digest, Criminal Law ⚖627.6(6), 627.7(3), 627.9(4)

In *People v. Rosario*, 9 N.Y.2d 286, 213 N.Y.S.2d 448 (1961), the Court of Appeals held that "a right sense of justice" requires "that the People are obligated to give to the defendant, for use during cross-examination, any nonconfidential written or recorded statements of a prosecution witness that relate to the subject matter of the witness' testimony." *People v. Banch*, 80 N.Y.2d 610, 615, 593 N.Y.S.2d 491, 493 (1992). This rule, the so-called *Rosario* rule, was subsequently extended to apply to pretrial hearings, *see People v. Malinsky*, 15 N.Y.2d 86, 262 N.Y.S.2d 65 (1965), and has been codified by the legislature. *See* CPL §§ 240.44 & 240.45. CPL § 240.75 dramatically limits a defendant's remedy for a *Rosario* violation.

§ 28:2 What is the *Rosario* rule?

Research References

West's Key Number Digest, Criminal Law ⚖627.5(1), 627.7(3)

The *Rosario* rule, which is in actuality a discovery rule, applies to trial and, *upon request*, to pretrial hearings. The "trial" *Rosario* rule is codified at CPL § 240.45(1)(a):

After the jury has been sworn and before the prosecutor's opening address, or in the case of a single judge trial after commencement and before submission of evidence, the prosecutor shall, subject to a protective order, make available to the defendant:

(a) Any written or recorded statement, including any testimony before a grand jury and an examination videotaped pursuant to [CPL § 190.32], made by a person whom the prosecutor intends to call as a witness at trial, and which relates to the subject matter of the witness's testimony.

See also People v. Rosario, 9 N.Y.2d 286, 213 N.Y.S.2d 448 (1961).

The "pretrial hearing" *Rosario* rule is codified at CPL § 240.44(1):

> Subject to a protective order, at a pre-trial hearing held in a criminal court at which a witness is called to testify, each party, at the conclusion of the direct examination of each of its witnesses, shall, upon request of the other party, make available to that party to the extent not previously disclosed:

> 1. Any written or recorded statement, including any testimony before a grand jury, made by such witness other than the defendant which relates to the subject matter of the witness's testimony.

See also People v. Malinsky, 15 N.Y.2d 86, 262 N.Y.S.2d 65 (1965). *See generally People v. McPhee*, 161 Misc. 2d 660, 614 N.Y.S.2d 884 (Queens Co. Sup. Ct. 1994) (CPL § 240.44, by its express and unambiguous terms, applies to *any* pretrial hearing—such as competency hearing); *People v. Diggs*, 140 Misc. 2d 794, 531 N.Y.S.2d 723 (Nassau Co. Dist. Ct. 1988) (CPL § 240.44 applies to CPL § 180.60 preliminary hearing).

As stated by the Court of Appeals, the essence of the *Rosario* rule is that:

> [A] right sense of justice entitles the defense to examine a witness' prior statement, whether or not it varies from his testimony on the stand. As long as the statement relates to the subject matter of the witness' testimony and contains nothing that must be kept confidential, defense counsel should be allowed to determine for themselves the use to be made of it on cross-examination.

> A pretrial statement of a witness for the prosecution is valuable not just as a source of contradictions with which to confront him and discredit his trial testimony. Even statements seemingly in harmony with such testimony may contain matter which will prove helpful on cross-examination. They may reflect a witness' bias, for instance, or otherwise supply the defendant with knowledge essential to the neutralization of the damaging testimony of the witness which might, perhaps, turn the scales in his favor. Shades of meaning, stress, additions or omissions may be found which will place the witness' answers upon direct examination in an entirely different light. As the United States Supreme Court has so well observed, "Flat contradiction between the witness' testimony and the version of the events given (previously) * * * is not the only test of inconsistency. The omission from the reports of facts related at the trial, or a contrast in emphasis upon the same facts, even a different order of treatment, are also relevant to the cross-examining process of testing the credibility of a witness' trial

testimony." *Jencks v. United States*, 353 U.S. 657, 667, 77 S.Ct. 1013, *supra*.

Furthermore, omissions, contrasts and even contradictions, vital perhaps, for discrediting a witness, are certainly not as apparent to the impartial presiding judge as to single-minded counsel for the accused; the latter is in a far better position to appraise the value of a witness' pretrial statements for impeachment purposes.

9 N.Y.2d at 289–90, 213 N.Y.S.2d at 450–51 (citation omitted).

The rule is simple and unequivocal: if the People are in possession of a statement of their own prospective witness relating to the subject matter of that witness' testimony, defense counsel must, in fairness, be given a copy because ordinarily counsel would have no knowledge of it and no other means of obtaining it.

People v. Jones, 70 N.Y.2d 547, 550, 523 N.Y.S.2d 53, 55 (1987) (emphasis added).

It is noteworthy that neither *Rosario* and its progeny, nor CPL §§ 240.44 & 240.45, are "based on State or Federal constitutional principles, but rather on our own balancing of interests." *People v. Machado*, 90 N.Y.2d 187, 192, 659 N.Y.S.2d 242, 245 (1997). *See also People v. Jackson*, 78 N.Y.2d 638, 644, 578 N.Y.S.2d 483, 487 (1991).

§ 28:3   What is *Rosario* material?

Research References

West's Key Number Digest, Criminal Law ☞627.5(1), 627.7(1)

With regard to prosecution witnesses, *Rosario* material consists of:

Any [non-confidential] written or recorded statement, including any testimony before a grand jury and an examination videotaped pursuant to [CPL § 190.32], made by a person whom the prosecutor intends to call as a witness at trial, and which relates to the subject matter of the witness's testimony.

CPL § 240.45(1)(a). *See also* CPL § 240.44(1); *People v. Rosario*, 9 N.Y.2d 286, 213 N.Y.S.2d 448 (1961).

In order to constitute *Rosario* material, a "statement" must (a) be "written or recorded," (b) be "made by a person whom the prosecutor intends to call as a witness," and (c) "relate to the subject matter of the witness's testimony." CPL § 240.45(1)(a); CPL § 240.44(1). In addition, the material must generally be in the "possession or control" of the prosecution. *See People v. Kelly*, 88 N.Y.2d 248, 251 to 52, 644 N.Y.S.2d 475, 476 to 77 (1996).

"The principal consideration for determining whether prosecutors have a fairness obligation under *Rosario* to turn over various materials focuses on whether these items actually are in *or subject to* the possession or control of the particular prosecution office." *Kelly*, 88 N.Y.2d at 252, 644 N.Y.S.2d at 476–77 (emphasis added). *See also People v. Santorelli*, 95 N.Y.2d 412, 422, 718 N.Y.S.2d 696, 701 (2000).

Where *Rosario* material is in the *constructive* possession of the prosecutor's office (which includes tape recordings and documents in the possession of the police), it is irrelevant that the material is not in the *actual* possession of a particular prosecutor (or the case file):

> Where, as here, the existence of a complaint report filed with a police precinct is readily ascertainable by the prosecutor, there is no reason to dilute the *Rosario* obligation by holding that defense counsel should have himself subpoenaed the document. As we observed in *Rosario*, " 'the State has no interest in interposing any obstacle to the disclosure of the facts,' " and **society's interest in maintaining criminal trials as truth-finding processes requires that the burden of locating and producing prior statements of complaining witnesses, filed with police agencies, remain solely with the People**.

People v. Ranghelle, 69 N.Y.2d 56, 64, 511 N.Y.S.2d 580, 585 (1986) (emphasis added) (citation omitted). *See also People v. Giordano*, 274 A.D.2d 748, __, 711 N.Y.S.2d 557, 559–60 (3d Dep't 2000) ("The burden of locating and producing prior statements is on the People; there is no obligation on defense counsel to discover and subpoena documents") (citation omitted).

In this regard, the Court of Appeals has repeatedly made clear that:

> Prosecutors play a distinctive role in the search for truth in criminal cases. As public officers they are charged not simply with seeking convictions but also with ensuring that justice is done. This role gives rise to special responsibilities — constitutional, statutory, ethical, personal — to safeguard the integrity of criminal proceedings and fairness in the criminal process.

Santorelli, 95 N.Y.2d at 420–21, 718 N.Y.S.2d at 700. *See also People v. Steadman*, 82 N.Y.2d 1, 7, 603 N.Y.S.2d 382, 384 (1993). *People v. Pelchat*, 62 N.Y.2d 97, 105, 476 N.Y.S.2d 79, 83 (1984).

Obviously, the written notes and reports of a police officer witness constitute *Rosario* material. *See, e.g., People v. Washington*, 86 N.Y.2d 189, 192, 630 N.Y.S.2d 693, 694 (1995); *People v. Quinones*, 73 N.Y.2d 988, 989, 540 N.Y.S.2d 993, 994 (1989); *People v. Novoa*, 70 N.Y.2d 490, 522 N.Y.S.2d 504 (1987); *Ranghelle*, 69 N.Y.2d at 62, 511 N.Y.S.2d at 584; *People v. Gilligan*, 39 N.Y.2d 769, 384 N.Y.S.2d 778 (1976); *People v. Malinsky*, 15 N.Y.2d 86, 90 to 91, 262 N.Y.S.2d 65, 69 to 70 (1965). "[O]ral testimony by the officers concerning the contents of their memo books does not constitute production of the material. The books themselves ha[ve] to be delivered to defense counsel." *Ranghelle*, 69 N.Y.2d at 65, 511 N.Y.S.2d at 586.

"The character of a statement is not to be determined by the manner in which it is recorded, nor is it changed by the presence or absence of a signature." *People v. Consolazio*, 40 N.Y.2d 446, 453, 387 N.Y.S.2d 62, 65 (1976). Thus, "a witness' statement in narrative form made in preparation for trial by an Assistant District Attorney in his own hand is 'a record of a prior statement by a witness within the compass of the rule in *People v. Rosario* * * * and therefore not exempt from disclosure as a "work product" datum of the prosecutor.' " 40 N.Y.2d at 453, 387 N.Y.S.2d at 65 to 66 (citation omitted).

Memo book notes taken by an investigating officer, consisting of statements made to the officer by a testifying witness, constitute *Rosario* material *regardless of whether the investigating officer testifies*. *Ranghelle*, 69 N.Y.2d at 64 to 65, 511 N.Y.S.2d at 585–86. In other words, the critical issue in determining whether a statement constitutes *Rosario* material is whether the person who uttered the statement is called as a witness—*not* whether the person who wrote down (or recorded or transcribed) the statement is called as a witness.

Police "blotter" entries are classic examples of *Rosario* material. *See, e.g., People v. Giordano*, 274 A.D.2d 748, __, 711 N.Y.S.2d 557, 559 (3d Dep't 2000); *People v. Bowers*, 210 A.D.2d 795, 798, 621 N.Y.S.2d 145, 147 (3d Dep't 1994). As are recorded police radio transmissions. *See People v. Olson*, 126 A.D.3d 1139, __, 6 N.Y.S.3d 160, 162 (3d Dep't 2015), leave to appeal denied, 25 N.Y.3d 1169, 15 N.Y.S.3d 300, 36 N.E.3d 103 (2015) (People conceded that "destruction of the recordings of the radio transmissions made by the trooper during his encounter with defendant" constituted a *Rosario* violation).

"The 'SPRINT' report and the audio tape of the arresting officer's radio communication with the police dispatcher as he followed and apprehended the appellant constitute *Rosario* material." *Matter of Peter C.*, 220 A.D.2d 584, __, 632 N.Y.S.2d 612, 613 (2d Dep't 1995).

A statement made to a private party can constitute *Rosario* material, especially where the statement is (a) prompted by the prosecutor, (b) recorded by law enforcement personnel, and (c) in the prosecution's possession and control. *See People v. Perez*, 65 N.Y.2d 154, 158, 490 N.Y.S.2d 747, 749–50 (1985). *See also People v. Palmer*, 137 A.D.2d 881, 524 N.Y.S.2d 564 (3d Dep't 1988).

Where a key prosecution witness has taken a polygraph examination which contains statements which exculpate the defendant, the polygraph transcript constitutes both *Rosario* and *Brady* material. *People v. Rutter*, 202 A.D.2d 123, __, 616 N.Y.S.2d 598, 603 (1st Dep't 1994), opinion adhered to on reargument, 211 A.D.2d 605, 623 N.Y.S.2d 97 (1st Dep't 1995).

§ 28:4 Assistant District Attorney's notes

Research References

West's Key Number Digest, Criminal Law ⟳627.5(6)

In *People v. Consolazio*, 40 N.Y.2d 446, 453, 387 N.Y.S.2d 62, 65 to 66 (1976), the Court of Appeals held that "a witness' statement in narrative form made in preparation for trial by an Assistant District Attorney in his own hand is 'a record of a prior statement by a witness within the compass of the rule in *People v. Rosario* * * * and therefore not exempt from disclosure as a "work product" datum of the prosecutor.' " 40 N.Y.2d at 453, 387 N.Y.S.2d at 65–66 (citation omitted). *See also People v. Washington*, 86 N.Y.2d 189, 192, 630 N.Y.S.2d 693, 694 (1995); *People v. Barrigar*, 233 A.D.2d 845, __, 649 N.Y.S.2d 756, 757 (4th Dep't 1996); *People v. Callendar*, 227 A.D.2d 499, 643 N.Y.S.2d 142 (2d Dep't 1996), order aff'd, 90 N.Y.2d 831, 660 N.Y.S.2d 710, 683 N.E.2d 332 (1997); *People v. Bell*, 140 A.D.2d 937, __, 529 N.Y.S.2d 617, 618 (4th Dep't 1988) ("The prosecutor's alleged good faith belief that the notes were privileged is irrelevant"); *People v. Cavallerio*, 71 A.D.2d 338, __, 422 N.Y.S.2d 691, 695 (1st Dep't 1979). *See generally People v. Munoz*, 161 A.D.2d 807, __, 556 N.Y.S.2d 136, 137 (2d Dep't 1990) ("the Trial Judge erred in refusing to require the People to disclose the Data Analysis Form prepared by the Assistant District Attorney on duty on the night of the defendant's arrest to the defendant"); *People v. Cubilla*, 181 A.D.2d 788, 581 N.Y.S.2d 90 (2d Dep't 1992) (same); *People v. Nelu*, 157 A.D.2d 864, 550 N.Y.S.2d 905 (2d Dep't 1990) (same).

Nonetheless, prosecutors' notes of conversations with witnesses are frequently improperly withheld from the defense, as ADAs incorrectly (and inexplicably) assert that such notes constitute privileged "attorneys' work product." *See* CPL § 240.10(2), (3).

In *People v. Gourgue*, 239 A.D.2d 357, __, 657 N.Y.S.2d 737, 737 (2d Dep't 1997), the Appellate Division, Second Department, held that "a list of questions prepared by the prosecutor during a pretrial interview with the complaining witness constituted *Rosario* material which should have been disclosed to the defense." (Citation omitted). In so holding, the Court reasoned:

> Here, the prosecutor incorporated factual statements made by the complainant into a list of proposed questions with the admitted intent of circumventing the *Rosario* rule by recording the statements in question form. Since the material prepared by the prosecu-

tor clearly included the complainant's statements and was not merely attorney work product, the court erred in denying the defendant's request for disclosure.

239 A.D.2d at ___, 657 N.Y.S.2d at 738.

Similarly, the Appellate Division, First Department, has made clear that "[i]t has long been the law in this State that the People may not circumvent their disclosure obligations simply by altering the format of the information gleaned from a witness interview, or by recording it after the interview rather than contemporaneously." *People v. Dowling*, 266 A.D.2d 18, ___, 698 N.Y.S.2d 11, 13 (1st Dep't 1999).

"Where a question arises whether portions of the prosecutor's notes fall within the work product exception, the court should conduct an in camera examination of the material." *People v. Barrigar*, 233 A.D.2d 845, ___, 649 N.Y.S.2d 756, 757 (4th Dep't 1996).

§ 28:5 Where existence or relevance of *Rosario* material is in dispute, court should conduct *in camera* inspection of prosecutor's file

Research References

West's Key Number Digest, Criminal Law ⊶627.8(4)

"*Rosario* does not create a right of a defendant to examine the prosecutor's entire file." *People v. Ranghelle*, 69 N.Y.2d 56, 63, 511 N.Y.S.2d 580, 584 (1986). *See also People v. Poole*, 48 N.Y.2d 144, 149, 422 N.Y.S.2d 5, 8 (1979). In this regard, the Court of Appeals has stated:

> In our view, the representation of a prosecutor, as an officer of the court, ought generally to suffice to determine the threshold issue of whether or not any prior statements of a witness exist. However, in cases where either a defendant can articulate a factual basis for the assertion that a prosecutor is improperly denying the existence of prior statements or a prosecutor admits the existence of such statements but contends that they are irrelevant to the testimony of the witness, we believe the better rule would be to place upon the court the responsibility to determine whether or not any relevant statements of the witness exist. In such situations, the trial court ought to inspect, *in camera*, the questioned document, or indeed the entire file if need be, to resolve any dispute on this issue.

Poole, 48 N.Y.2d at 149, 422 N.Y.S.2d at 8 (citations omitted). *See also People v. Adger*, 75 N.Y.2d 723, 551 N.Y.S.2d 190 (1989) (remittal required where trial court refused to examine whether undisclosed material was in fact *Rosario* material); *People v. Dockery*, 278 A.D.2d 427, 717 N.Y.S.2d 657 (2d Dep't 2000); *People v. Gallardo*, 173 A.D.2d 636, 570 N.Y.S.2d 222 (2d Dep't 1991).

§ 28:6   The People cannot be required to "create" *Rosario* material

Research References

West's Key Number Digest, Criminal Law ☜1166(10.10)

"[T]here is absolutely no authority for the imposition of an affirmative duty on the prosecutor to 'create' *Rosario* material." *Matter of Catterson v. Rohl*, 202 A.D.2d 420, —, 608 N.Y.S.2d 696, 699 (2d Dep't 1994). *See also People v. Littles*, 192 A.D.2d 314, 595 N.Y.S.2d 463 (1st Dep't 1993); *People v. Steinberg*, 170 A.D.2d 50, 573 N.Y.S.2d 965 (1st Dep't 1991), *order aff'd*, 79 N.Y.2d 673, 584 N.Y.S.2d 770 (1992).

In *Steinberg*, the Appellate Division, First Department, stated:

> There is no requirement that a prosecutor record in any fashion his interviews with a witness. If the prosecutor chooses to do so, *Rosario* and its progeny require that the recording be furnished to the defense. But nothing in the *Rosario* line of cases in any way imposes an obligation on the prosecutor to create *Rosario* material in interviewing witnesses.

170 A.D.2d at 76, 573 N.Y.S.2d at 981.

§ 28:7   "Duplicative equivalent" exception to *Rosario* rule

Research References

West's Key Number Digest, Criminal Law ☜1166(10.10)

The failure to make timely disclosure of *Rosario* material "will not lead to any sanctions if the undisclosed matter is the 'duplicative equivalent' of material that has previously been disclosed." *People v. Joseph*, 86 N.Y.2d 565, 567, 635 N.Y.S.2d 123, 123 (1995). In determining whether undisclosed *Rosario* material is the "duplicative equivalent" of disclosed material, the Court of Appeals has provided the following guidelines:

> Two documents cannot be "duplicative equivalents" if there are variations or inconsistencies between them. Further, "[s]tatements are not the 'duplicative equivalent' of previously produced statements * * * just because they are 'harmonious' or 'consistent' with them." Indeed, a statement that is consistent with other disclosed material but omits details or facts cannot be considered the "duplicative equivalent" of the disclosed material, since omissions often furnish important subjects for cross-examination. Finally, since the purpose of *Rosario* disclosure is to provide the defense with material for cross-examining specific prosecution witnesses, the fact that withheld information was available through another disclosed document embodying someone else's statements is irrelevant and cannot serve to remedy the harm caused by the prosecution's failure to disclose.

People v. Young, 79 N.Y.2d 365, 370, 582 N.Y.S.2d 977, 980 (1992) (citations omitted). *See also Joseph*, 86 N.Y.2d at 569–70, 635 N.Y.S.2d at 125.

The *Young* court made clear that, in assessing whether undisclosed *Rosario* material is the "duplicative equivalent" of disclosed material, "there continues to be a 'strong presumption of * * * discoverability' and, consequently, the 'exception' has been narrowly circumscribed." 79 N.Y.2d at 369, 582 N.Y.S.2d at 980 (citation omitted). *See also People v. Consolazio*, 40 N.Y.2d 446, 455, 387 N.Y.S.2d 62, 67 (1976) ("[O]nce it is determined that the writings sought by the defendant come within the *Rosario* rule, the better practice would be to direct a turnover forthwith. No sufficiently useful purpose would appear to be served by engaging in a collateral analysis as to whether the defendant would or would not be technically entitled to disclosure").

In addition, the *Young* definition of "duplicative equivalent" presumes that the undisclosed *Rosario* material is still in existence and can be compared to previously disclosed material. In this regard, in *Joseph, supra*, the Court of Appeals expressly held that **"a document that has been lost or destroyed and is therefore no longer available for judicial inspection cannot be deemed the 'duplicative equivalent' of *Rosario* material that has previously been disclosed."** 86 N.Y.2d at 569, 635 N.Y.S.2d at 125 (emphasis added). *See also* 86 N.Y.2d at 567, 635 N.Y.S.2d at 124. In so holding, the *Joseph* Court reasoned that:

> Our holding is based on our practical recognition that a document's unavailability poses an insurmountable barrier to making the detailed comparison and assessment that our decisions in *Ranghelle* and *Young* require.
>
> Contrary to the People's contention, a police officer's testimony regarding the contents of a lost or destroyed police document is not an acceptable substitute for the document itself, nor is it a sufficient basis from which the court could infer the requisite duplicative equivalence. Even where a document has purportedly been transcribed verbatim, inadvertent errors, omissions and deletions can occur, giving rise to precisely the kind of discrepancies that are most useful in cross-examination. Since the transcriber is likely to be unaware of these errors, that individual's testimony cannot provide the necessary assurance that the two documents were alike in all respects.

86 N.Y.2d at 569–70, 635 N.Y.S.2d at 125 (citations omitted). *See also Matter of Rodney B.*, 69 N.Y.2d 687, 512 N.Y.S.2d 17 (1986); *People v. Burch*, 247 A.D.2d 546, __, 669 N.Y.S.2d 299, 300 (2d Dep't 1998) ("Where the 911 tape was destroyed and was thus no longer available for judicial inspection, it cannot be deemed the 'duplicative equivalent' of the so-called 'Sprint report,' the

contents of which were disclosed to the defendant"); *People v. Hagen*, 247 A.D.2d 405, ___, 669 N.Y.S.2d 49, 50 (2d Dep't 1998); *People v. Huynh*, 232 A.D.2d 655, ___, 649 N.Y.S.2d 160, 161 (2d Dep't 1996).

If the People fail to assert their claim of "duplicative equivalence" in the trial court, the claim will be found to have been waived on appeal. *See People v. Quinones*, 73 N.Y.2d 988, 989, 540 N.Y.S.2d 993, 994 (1989), *aff'g* 139 A.D.2d 404, 527 N.Y.S.2d 5 (1st Dep't 1988).

§ 28:8 What is *not Rosario* material?

Research References

West's Key Number Digest, Criminal Law ⬤⬤627.5(1), 627.7(1)

A "statement" does not constitute *Rosario* material if, among other things, the statement (a) is confidential, (b) is not written or recorded, (c) is made by a person that is not called as a witness, (d) does not relate to the subject matter of the witness' testimony, and/or (e) is made by the defendant. *See, e.g.*, CPL § 240.45(1)(a); CPL § 240.45(2)(a); CPL § 240.44(1).

In addition, a statement which would otherwise constitute *Rosario* material will be exempt from disclosure if it is not in, or subject to, the possession or control of the prosecution. *See, e.g.*, *People v. Kelly*, 88 N.Y.2d 248, 251 to 52, 644 N.Y.S.2d 475, 476 to 77 (1996). Examples of items that the Court of Appeals has "removed" from *Rosario* disclosure on this ground are:

1. FBI interview reports pertaining to a *Federal* investigation. *People v. Santorelli*, 95 N.Y.2d 412, 420–22, 718 N.Y.S.2d 696, 700–01 (2000). *See also People v. Marvin*, 258 A.D.2d 964, 685 N.Y.S.2d 499 (4th Dep't 1999); *People v. Kronberg*, 243 A.D.2d 132, ___, 672 N.Y.S.2d 63, 77 (1st Dep't 1998);

2. Interview notes and reports of the State Division of Parole. *People v. Kelly*, 88 N.Y.2d 248, 644 N.Y.S.2d 475 (1996), *overruling* People v. Fields, 146 A.D.2d 505, 537 N.Y.S.2d 157 (1st Dep't 1989);

3. Statements of witnesses, in the possession of the State Department of Correctional Services, made during a prison disciplinary proceeding. *People v. Howard*, 87 N.Y.2d 940, 641 N.Y.S.2d 222 (1996);

4. Audiotape made by Associate Medical Examiner subsequent to autopsy of victim. *People v. Washington*, 86 N.Y.2d 189, 630 N.Y.S.2d 693 (1995);

5. Motor vehicle accident report *filed by civilian complainant* with Department of Motor Vehicles. *People v. Flynn*, 79 N.Y.2d 879, 581 N.Y.S.2d 160 (1992);

6. Untranscribed plea minutes of potential prosecution witness (which had been ordered, but not received, by the prosecution). *People v. Fishman*, 72 N.Y.2d 884, 532 N.Y.S.2d 739 (1988);

7. Personal version of attack by victim, a freelance writer. *People v. Reedy*, 70 N.Y.2d 826, 523 N.Y.S.2d 438 (1987);

8. Report of incident, made by privately employed security guard, to his employer. *People v. Bailey*, 73 N.Y.2d 812, 537 N.Y.S.2d 111 (1988); and

9. Statements of child victims made to a registered social worker during the course of that worker's employment. *People v. Tissois*, 72 N.Y.2d 75, 531 N.Y.S.2d 228 (1988) (in *Tissois*, the privilege against disclosure provided by CPLR § 4508 was invoked). *Cf. People v. DeJesus*, 69 N.Y.2d 855, 514 N.Y.S.2d 708 (1987) (different result where CPLR § 4508 *not* timely invoked). *See also People v. Berkley*, 157 A.D.2d 463, __, 549 N.Y.S.2d 392, 394 (1st Dep't 1990) ("the rape counselor's notes were not *Rosario* material because they were not in the actual or constructive possession of the district attorney's office").

See also Matter of Gina C., 138 A.D.2d 77, 531 N.Y.S.2d 86 (1st Dep't 1988) (newspaper reporter's notes do not constitute *Rosario* material where they were neither gathered at direction of, nor in possession of, any law enforcement agency). *See generally People v. Brock*, 246 A.D.2d 406, 667 N.Y.S.2d 730 (1st Dep't 1998) (bank surveillance photographs [as opposed to videotapes] do not constitute *Rosario* material).

Although a statement may be exempt from *Rosario* disclosure if it is not subject to the control of the People, the same statement constitutes discoverable *Rosario* material if it is in the *actual possession* of the People. *See, e.g., People v. Campbell*, 186 A.D.2d 212, 587 N.Y.S.2d 751 (2d Dep't 1992) (hospital records in possession of District Attorney, containing statements of victim, constituted *Rosario* material); *People v. Wahad*, 204 A.D.2d 156, __, 612 N.Y.S.2d 14, 15 (1st Dep't 1994) (statements to FBI agent).

§ 28:9 "Pretrial hearing" *Rosario* material is only available upon request

Research References

West's Key Number Digest, Criminal Law ☞627.6(6), 627.7(3), 627.9(4)

CPL § 240.44 makes clear that discovery thereunder is only available "*upon request* of the other party." (Emphasis added). *See generally People v. Zephir*, 226 A.D.2d 408, __, 640 N.Y.S.2d 584, 585 (2d Dep't 1996); *People v. Duprey*, 174 A.D.2d 835, __, 571 N.Y.S.2d 137, 138 (3d Dep't 1991). Accordingly, absent a timely request therefor, a party will be found to have waived its right to "pretrial hearing" *Rosario* material.

§ 28:10 Time for disclosure of pretrial hearing *Rosario* material

Research References

West's Key Number Digest, Criminal Law ☞627.5(1)

Although the disclosure of pretrial hearing *Rosario* material typically takes place prior to the commencement of the hearing, CPL § 240.44 states that a party can make such disclosure "at the conclusion of the direct examination of each of its witnesses." Even though such belated disclosure often results in a significant waste of scarce judicial resources (since counsel must be afforded adequate time to review the material), it appears that courts are powerless to order a party to make earlier disclosure. *See, e.g., Matter of Briggs v. Halloran*, 12 A.D.3d 1016, __, 785 N.Y.S.2d 578, 579–80 (3d Dep't 2004); *Matter of Pittari v. Pirro*, 258 A.D.2d 202, __, 696 N.Y.S.2d 167, 171 (2d Dep't 1999); *People v. Zephir*, 226 A.D.2d 408, __, 640 N.Y.S.2d 584, 585 (2d Dep't 1996); *Matter of Catterson v. Rohl*, 202 A.D.2d 420, __, 608 N.Y.S.2d 696, 699 (2d Dep't 1994).

§ 28:11 Remedy for pretrial hearing *Rosario* violation is "re-opened" hearing

Research References

West's Key Number Digest, Criminal Law ☞1166(10.10)

In *People v. Banch*, 80 N.Y.2d 610, 618, 593 N.Y.S.2d 491, 496 (1992), the Court of Appeals held that "a defendant is entitled to a new hearing as a remedy for a pretrial *Rosario* violation, without inquiry into prejudice." In so holding, the *Banch* court made clear that the trial court cannot simply review the *Rosario* material and determine its value to the defense, as " 'a judge's impartial determination as to what portions [of *Rosario* material] may be useful to the defense, is no substitute for the single-minded devotion of counsel for the accused,' " and " 'there is no way, short of speculation, of determining how it might have been used or how its denial to counsel might have damaged defendant's case.' " 80 N.Y.2d at 618, 593 N.Y.S.2d at 496 (citations omitted). In addition, the court noted "that the remedy for a pretrial *Rosario* violation is not automatic reversal of the conviction but a new hearing. Retrial is necessary only if, after that hearing, the motion court concludes that defendant should prevail." 80 N.Y.2d at 619, 593 N.Y.S.2d at 496.

In *People v. Feerick*, 93 N.Y.2d 433, 451, 692 N.Y.S.2d 638, 647

(1999), the Court of Appeals reaffirmed its holding in *Banch*, but held that "[a]lthough *Banch* states a 'new' hearing should be granted," and "[a]lthough some *Rosario* violations may require or lead to . . . a 'full blown' hearing," under the circumstances presented the rationale of *Rosario* only required (a) that the pretrial hearing be "reopened" to the extent necessary to explore the contents of the *Rosario* documents, and (b) that a "new" ruling be issued by the hearing court.

CPL § 240.75 partially affects the *Banch/Feerick* rule. Specifically, CPL § 240.75 provides that:

> The failure of the prosecutor or any agent of the prosecutor to disclose statements that are required to be disclosed under [CPL § 240.44(1)] . . . shall not constitute grounds for any court to order a new pre-trial hearing . . . in the absence of a showing by the defendant that there is a reasonable possibility that the nondisclosure materially contributed to the result of the . . . proceeding; *provided, however, that nothing in this section shall affect or limit any right the defendant may have to a re-opened pre-trial hearing when such statements were disclosed before the close of evidence at trial.*

(Emphasis added).

In other words, if a pretrial hearing *Rosario* violation is disclosed *prior to* the close of evidence at trial, *Banch* and *Feerick* still apply. By contrast, if the disclosure occurs *after* the close of evidence at trial, CPL § 240.75 provides that the pretrial hearing will not be reopened "in the absence of a showing by the defendant that there is a reasonable possibility that the nondisclosure materially contributed to the result of the [hearing]."

§ 28:12   Disclosure of "trial" *Rosario* material is mandatory

Research References

West's Key Number Digest, Criminal Law ⟐1991

CPL § 240.45 makes clear that discovery thereunder is mandatory—*i.e.*, no request by the other side need be made to invoke the right to "trial" *Rosario* material. *See, e.g., People v. King*, 241 A.D.2d 329, __, 659 N.Y.S.2d 469, 470 (1st Dep't 1997).

§ 28:13   Time for disclosure of trial *Rosario* material

Research References

West's Key Number Digest, Criminal Law ⟐627.5(1)

Although the disclosure of trial *Rosario* material typically takes place prior to trial, CPL § 240.45(1) states that the People can make such disclosure "[a]fter the jury has been sworn and before the prosecutor's opening address, or in the case of a single judge trial after commencement and before submission of evidence." CPL § 240.45(2) provides that the defense must make its *Rosario* material available "[a]fter presentation of the people's direct case and before the presentation of the defendant's direct case."

Even though such belated disclosure often results in a significant waste of scarce judicial resources (since counsel must be afforded adequate time to review the material), it appears that courts are powerless to order a party to make earlier disclosure. *See, e.g., Matter of Pittari v. Pirro*, 258 A.D.2d 202, __, 696 N.Y.S.2d 167, 171 (2d Dep't 1999); *Matter of Catterson v. Rohl*, 202 A.D.2d 420, __-__, 608 N.Y.S.2d 696, 698–99 (2d Dep't 1994). In *Rohl*, the Appellate Division, Second Department, held that:

> The statute is clear on its face that a prosecutor is not obligated to provide a defendant with copies of witnesses' statements until such time as trial has commenced, and there is no provision contained in the statute which would give the court authority to vary that statutory time frame. Indeed, CPL 240.40 sets forth the limited circumstances under which the court is authorized to direct discovery.

202 A.D.2d at __, 608 N.Y.S.2d at 698–99.

§ 28:14 Delay in turning over *Rosario* material requires reversal if defendant is substantially prejudiced thereby

Research References

West's Key Number Digest, Criminal Law ⬗1166(10.10)

A delay in turning over *Rosario* material will require reversal if the defendant is substantially prejudiced by the delay. *See People v. Banch*, 80 N.Y.2d 610, 617, 593 N.Y.S.2d 491, 495 (1992); *People v. Martinez*, 71 N.Y.2d 937, 940, 528 N.Y.S.2d 813, 815 (1988); *People v. Ranghelle*, 69 N.Y.2d 56, 63, 511 N.Y.S.2d 580, 585 (1986); *People v. Perez*, 65 N.Y.2d 154, 159, 490 N.Y.S.2d 747, 750 (1985). In this regard, the Court of Appeals has stated:

> Although a delay, particularly an inadvertent one, will generally not adversely affect the defendant's rights, delay in a particular case may cause substantial prejudice to the defense. An attorney preparing for cross-examination must not only decide what questions to ask, but what questions to avoid asking. The fairness concept embodied in the *Rosario* rule cannot be said to have been satisfied when pretrial statements revealing a potential trap for the cross-examiner are furnished to defense counsel only after the trap has sprung.

Perez, 65 N.Y.2d at 160, 490 N.Y.S.2d at 750. *See also People v. Goins*, 73 N.Y.2d 989, 540 N.Y.S.2d 994 (1989) (delayed production of police officer's "daily activity report" required reversal); *People v. Thompson*, 71 N.Y.2d 918, 528 N.Y.S.2d 532 (1988) (delayed production of arresting officer's memo book entry substantially prejudiced defendant).

In *People v. Mackey*, 249 A.D.2d 329, ___, 670 N.Y.S.2d 879, 880 (2d Dep't 1998), the Appellate Division, Second Department, held that:

> The defendant's conviction must be reversed . . . because he was substantially prejudiced by the People's failure to provide certain *Rosario* material related to a critical aspect of the complainant's testimony until after she had been cross-examined. As a result of the People's delay in providing the material — a record book maintained by the complainant which was in the People's control — damaging testimony was unwittingly elicited during her cross-examination. * * *
>
> *Rosario* material must be provided at a time when it meaningfully can be used to prepare cross-examination. "The fairness concept embodied in the *Rosario* rule cannot be said to have been satisfied when pretrial statements revealing a potential trap for the cross-examiner are furnished to defense counsel only after the trap has sprung."

(Citation omitted). *See also People v. Jarrells*, 190 A.D.2d 120, 597 N.Y.S.2d 305 (1st Dep't 1993) (prosecutor's failure to turn over "voucher" prepared by arresting officer substantially prejudiced defendant). *See generally People v. King*, 241 A.D.2d 329, 659 N.Y.S.2d 469 (1st Dep't 1997); *People v. Rutter*, 202 A.D.2d 123, 616 N.Y.S.2d 598 (1st Dep't 1994), opinion adhered to on reargument, 211 A.D.2d 605, 623 N.Y.S.2d 97 (1st Dep't 1995).

§ 28:15   CPL § 240.75 legislatively abrogates "per se" reversal rule of *People v. Ranghelle*

Research References
West's Key Number Digest, Criminal Law ☞627.8(2), 2008

With certain limited exceptions, *People v. Ranghelle*, 69 N.Y.2d 56, 511 N.Y.S.2d 580 (1986), and its progeny had created a "per se" reversal rule where the defendant had been deprived of *Rosario* material at trial. CPL § 240.75 legislatively abrogates the "per se" reversal rule of *Ranghelle*. This statute provides, in pertinent part:

> The failure of the prosecutor or any agent of the prosecutor to disclose statements that are required to be disclosed under . . . [CPL § 240.45(1)(a)] shall not constitute grounds for any court to . . . set aside a conviction, or reverse, modify or vacate a judgment of convic-

tion in the absence of a showing by the defendant that there is a reasonable possibility that the non-disclosure materially contributed to the result of the trial or other proceeding.

See People v. Sorbello, 285 A.D.2d 88, 729 N.Y.S.2d 747 (2d Dep't 2001) (Court analyzes CPL § 240.75, and holds that CPL § 240.75 applies retroactively "to all cases in prosecution or appeal as of its effective date" of February 1, 2001).

The burden of proof placed on the defendant by CPL § 240.75 (*i.e.*, "that there is a reasonable possibility that the nondisclosure materially contributed to the result of the trial or other proceeding"), merely codifies the "prejudice" standard previously established by the Court of Appeals in the *Rosario* context. *See, e.g., People v. Machado*, 90 N.Y.2d 187, 188–89, 193, 659 N.Y.S.2d 242, 243, 245 (1997); *People v. Jackson*, 78 N.Y.2d 638, 649, 578 N.Y.S.2d 483, 490 (1991). In this regard, the Court of Appeals has noted that:

> The "reasonable possibility" test is, after all, "perhaps the most demanding test yet formulated" for harmless error analysis. And we have recognized that the "reasonable possibility" test "properly encourages compliance" with the People's *Brady* obligations. That should be no less true with respect to the People's *Rosario* obligations.

Machado, 90 N.Y.2d at 193, 659 N.Y.S.2d at 245–46 (citations omitted).

Cases applying this standard to *Rosario* violations include *People v. Potter*, 254 A.D.2d 831, __, 681 N.Y.S.2d 704, 705 (4th Dep't 1998); *People v. Wahad*, 204 A.D.2d 156, __, 612 N.Y.S.2d 14, 15 (1st Dep't 1994); *People v. Ramos*, 201 A.D.2d 78, 614 N.Y.S.2d 977 (1st Dep't 1994); *People v. Alvarado*, 201 A.D.2d 486, __, 607 N.Y.S.2d 399, 400 (2d Dep't 1994); *People v. Nikollaj*, 155 Misc. 2d 642, __-__, 589 N.Y.S.2d 1013, 1017–18 (Bronx Co. Sup. Ct. 1992).

§ 28:16 Lost or destroyed *Rosario* material—Sanction generally required

Research References

West's Key Number Digest, Criminal Law ⊙2012

It is well-settled that, in addition to the duty to *produce Rosario* material, the People have an affirmative duty to *preserve Rosario* material as well. *See, e.g., People v. Joseph*, 86 N.Y.2d 565, 570–71, 635 N.Y.S.2d 123, 126 (1995); *People v. Wallace*, 76 N.Y.2d 953, 955, 563 N.Y.S.2d 722, 723 (1990); *People v. Martinez*, 71 N.Y.2d 937, 940, 528 N.Y.S.2d 813, 815 (1988); *People v. Kelly*, 62 N.Y.2d 516, 520, 478 N.Y.S.2d 834, 836 (1984). *See also People v. Watkins*, 189 A.D.2d 623, __, 592 N.Y.S.2d 347, 348 (1st Dep't 1993) (duty to preserve *Rosario* material lasts "until all appeals have been exhausted, and a Police Department policy of destroying evidence does not excuse the People from making *Rosario* material available on retrial"). In *Martinez*, the Court of Appeals held that:

> [I]t is no answer to a demand to produce that the material has been lost or destroyed. If the People fail to exercise care to preserve it and defendant is prejudiced by their mistake, the court must impose an appropriate sanction. The determination of what is appropriate is committed to the trial court's sound discretion, and while the degree of prosecutorial fault may be considered, the court's attention should focus primarily on the overriding need to eliminate prejudice to the defendant.

71 N.Y.2d at 940, 528 N.Y.S.2d at 815. Similarly, in *Wallace*, the court held that:

> Where the People fail to exercise due care in preserving *Rosario* material, and defendant is prejudiced thereby, "the [trial] court *must* impose an appropriate sanction." Although the trial court had discretion to determine the specific sanction to be imposed, it was an abuse of discretion to decline to impose any sanction where, as here, defendant was prejudiced.

76 N.Y.2d at 955, 563 N.Y.S.2d at 723 (citations omitted). *See also People v. Minihan*, 180 Misc. 2d 776, 695 N.Y.S.2d 238 (App. Term, 2d Dep't 1999).

> [I]n such cases the trial court must try to determine the content of the missing material and the circumstances of the loss or destruction. Depending upon the degree of prosecutorial fault and the resulting prejudice to the defendant, the court must then impose an appropriate sanction — preclusion of the witness' testimony or an adverse inference charge, for example. Appellate review is limited to determining whether the trial court acted within the bounds of its discretion in selecting a sanction. Dismissal of the charges is an extreme sanction which "should not be invoked where less severe measures can rectify the harm done by the loss" of the material. On the other hand, where the People have failed to exercise due care in preserving *Rosario* material and the defendant is prejudiced by the loss or destruction, it is an abuse of discretion for the court to impose no sanction.

People v. Banch, 80 N.Y.2d 610, 616, 593 N.Y.S.2d 491, 494 to 95 (1992) (citations omitted). *Cf. People v. Carracedo*, 89 N.Y.2d 1059, 1062, 659 N.Y.S.2d 830, 832 (1997) ("Although the trial court here denied defendant's request to impose a sanction, under the particular facts and circumstances of this case, any risk of prejudice to defendant resulting from the destroyed notes was overcome by the court's instruction to the jury that it was to view the bloodhound evidence 'with utmost caution' and that it was of 'slight probative value' ").

Since some showing of prejudice is essential, we have also stated that "the trial court must try to determine the content of the missing material." However, since a precise replication of a missing document cannot be achieved, the trial court's inquiry must ordinarily be limited to ascertaining the document's subject matter and approximate contents with a view toward determining its relevance.

Joseph, 86 N.Y.2d at 571, 635 N.Y.S.2d at 126 (citation omitted).

§ 28:17   Destroyed audiotape generally requires sanction

Research References

West's Key Number Digest, Criminal Law ⚖2012

Unfortunately, police agencies often engage in the so-called "routine destruction" of *Rosario* material—particularly 911 tape recordings. *See, e.g., People v. Boyd*, 254 A.D.2d 740, __, 679 N.Y.S.2d 768, 769–70 (4th Dep't 1998); *People v. Morris*, 231 A.D.2d 911, __, 647 N.Y.S.2d 893, 893–94 (4th Dep't 1996); *People v. Thomas*, 226 A.D.2d 1071, __, 642 N.Y.S.2d 749, 751 (4th Dep't 1996); *People v. Cortez*, 149 Misc. 2d 886, __-__, 564 N.Y.S.2d 963, 966–68 (N.Y. City Crim. Ct. 1990). Although such a practice would seem to be inexcusable and unacceptable, the courts have been forced to "excuse" such behavior, largely due to the sheer prevalence of the problem.

However, where audiotapes are destroyed despite a timely request therefor by the defense, it is generally an abuse of discretion for the trial court to fail to impose any sanction whatsoever on the People. *See, e.g., People v. Jackson*, 271 A.D.2d 455, __, 707 N.Y.S.2d 128, 129 (2d Dep't 2000) ("Where the tape of a 911 call is not preserved and the defendant is prejudiced thereby, the court must impose an appropriate sanction and the failure to do so requires reversal"); *People v. Burch*, 247 A.D.2d 546, __, 669 N.Y.S.2d 299, 300 (2d Dep't 1998) (same); *People v. Huynh*, 232 A.D.2d 655, __, 649 N.Y.S.2d 160, 161 (2d Dep't 1996) (same); *People v. Parker*, 157 A.D.2d 519, __, 549 N.Y.S.2d 710, 711–12 (1st Dep't 1990) (same); *People v. Nesbitt*, 230 A.D.2d 755, 646 N.Y.S.2d 522 (2d Dep't 1996) (it was abuse of discretion, and prejudicial error, for trial court to deny defendant's request for adverse inference charge where audiotapes unavailable).

Where there is an apparent lack of prejudice to the defendant, and the degree of prosecutorial fault is minimal, a permissive adverse inference charge has been found to be a sufficient sanction for the destruction of a 911 tape. *See, e.g., People v. LaMountain*, 249 A.D.2d 584, 671 N.Y.S.2d 763 (3d Dep't 1998); *People v. Brister*, 239 A.D.2d 513, 658 N.Y.S.2d 362 (2d Dep't 1997). *See also People v. Gillard*, 215 A.D.2d 216, 626 N.Y.S.2d 167 (1st Dep't 1995) (partial preclusion proper sanction for destruction of 911 tape).

§ 28:18 Exception to sanction requirement—Waiver by defense

Research References

West's Key Number Digest, Criminal Law ☞2012

The defense must be careful to request (a) the preservation of *Rosario* material, and (b) a sanction for a *Rosario* violation, or an appellate court will likely find the issue to have been waived.

In *People v. Rogelio*, 79 N.Y.2d 843, 844, 580 N.Y.S.2d 185, 186 (1992), the Court of Appeals held that "[b]y failing to make an unambiguous objection when the *Rosario* violation was first noted and by indicating to the trial court through his equivocal statements that no remedy was desired, defendant has not preserved the issue for appellate review." *See also People v. Graves*, 85 N.Y.2d 1024, 1027, 630 N.Y.S.2d 972, 973 (1995); *People v. Jackson*, 78 N.Y.2d 900, 901, 573 N.Y.S.2d 452, 453 (1991). *Accord People v. Flores*, 84 N.Y.2d 184, 615 N.Y.S.2d 662 (1994) (counsel's decision to "waive" *Rosario* violation did not constitute ineffective assistance).

In *People v. Morris*, 231 A.D.2d 911, __, 647 N.Y.S.2d 893, 893 to 94 (4th Dep't 1996), the Appellate Division, Fourth Department, held that:

> Contrary to defendant's contention, the routine destruction of the 911 tapes did not warrant sanctions. Although those tapes constituted *Rosario* material that the People had an obligation to turn over to defendant upon proper demand, the record does not disclose that any demand was made for discovery of those tapes pursuant to either CPL 240.20 or 240.44. In the absence of a timely demand, the routine destruction of 911 tapes will not be viewed as a lack of due diligence.

(Citation omitted).

Similarly, in *People v. Thomas*, 226 A.D.2d 1071, __, 642 N.Y.S.2d 749, 751 (4th Dep't 1996), the same court held that:

> By failing to request sanctions as a result of the failure of the People to preserve a 911 tape, defendant failed to preserve for review his present contention that the court erred in failing to impose sanctions. In any event, sanctions were not warranted. In Erie County, 911 tapes are preserved for a 90-day period and are then taped over. In the absence of a timely request by a defendant that a 911 tape be preserved, its routine destruction will not be viewed as a lack of due diligence.

(Citation omitted). *See also People v. Hyde*, 172 A.D.2d 305, __, 568 N.Y.S.2d 388, 389 (1st Dep't 1991).

§ 28:19 *Rosario* material and CPL § 30.30

Research References

West's Key Number Digest, Criminal Law ☞577.12(1)

The Court of Appeals has made clear that "prosecutorial delays in producing *Rosario* material and other discovery items [a]re not cognizable under CPL 30.30(3)(b), because there [a]re other specific statutory sanctions available under CPL article 240." *People v. McKenna*, 76 N.Y.2d 59, 64, 556 N.Y.S.2d 514, 516 (1990). In *McKenna*, the court stated that:

> In the leading case, *People v. Anderson*, 66 N.Y.2d 529, 498 N.Y.S.2d 119, 488 N.E.2d 1231, we held that once the People have declared their readiness on the record, their subsequent delays in producing *Rosario* material and complying with certain other discovery obligations do not ordinarily render the indictment subject to dismissal under CPL 30.30, since delays of this nature do not affect the People's readiness to proceed to trial and, in any event, there exist other statutory sanctions for such delays.

76 N.Y.2d at 61, 556 N.Y.S.2d at 514. *See also* CPL § 240.70 (discovery sanctions); *People v. Anderson*, 66 N.Y.2d 529, 537, 498 N.Y.S.2d 119, 124 (1985). In *Anderson*, the court stated that:

> [T]he failure to make *Rosario* material available as required by CPL 240.45 may result under CPL 240.70 in discovery, a continuance, a protective or preclusion order or any other appropriate action . . . Dismissal for lack of *Rosario* material would be appropriate only on motion pursuant to CPL 30.20 and only if preclusion or a short continuance would violate the defendant's constitutional and statutory right to a speedy trial (CPL 30.20) after weighing the factors identified in *People v. Taranovich*, 37 N.Y.2d 442, 445, 373 N.Y.S.2d 79, 335 N.E.2d 303 . . . When no such alternative is provided by the Criminal Procedure Law, however, . . . dismissal is not only permissible but is required if the purpose of the section is to be carried out.

66 N.Y.2d at 537–38, 498 N.Y.S.2d at 124 to 25 (footnote omitted).

§ 28:20 Reciprocal *Rosario*—The defendant's obligations

Research References

West's Key Number Digest, Criminal Law ⊱627.6(6), 627.7(3), 627.9(4)

The CPL places reciprocal *Rosario* obligations on the defendant. At trial, CPL § 240.45(2)(a) provides that:

> 2. After presentation of the people's direct case and before the presentation of the defendant's direct case, the defendant shall, subject to a protective order, make available to the prosecutor:

> (a) any written or recorded statement made by a person *other than the defendant* whom the defendant intends to call as a witness at the trial, and which relates to the subject matter of the witness's testimony.

(Emphasis added). *See People v. Allen*, 104 Misc. 2d 136, 427

N.Y.S.2d 698 (Westchester Co. Sup. Ct. 1980). Notably, written or recorded statements of the defendant are not discoverable.

The pretrial hearing *Rosario* rule codified at CPL § 240.44(1), *see* § 28:2, *supra*, applies equally to both the prosecution and the defense, with the exception that written or recorded statements of the defendant are not discoverable.

§ 28:21   *Rosario* material must be copied and delivered to opposing party

Research References

West's Key Number Digest, Criminal Law ⊂627.6(6), 627.7(3), 627.9(4)

To comply with the obligation to disclose *Rosario* material under CPL §§ 240.44 and 240.45, as well as *People v. Rosario*, 9 N.Y.2d 286, 213 N.Y.S.2d 448 (1961), and *People v. Malinsky*, 15 N.Y.2d 86, 262 N.Y.S.2d 65 (1965), a party must actually "deliver a copy" of such material to the opposing party. *See People v. Caussade*, 162 A.D.2d 4, __, 560 N.Y.S.2d 648, 653 (2d Dep't 1990).

§ 28:22   NYPD procedures for preserving *Rosario* material

Research References

West's Key Number Digest, Criminal Law ⊂2012

In *People v. LaFontaine*, 163 Misc. 2d 83, __, 619 N.Y.S.2d 479, 479 (Bronx Co. Sup. Ct. 1994), the Court, concerned with the "stunning frequency" of *Rosario* violations, "ordered a hearing on the procedures used in the [New York City] Police Department for making and preserving police records prepared after an arrest, the procedures for delivering the documents to the prosecutor, and the procedures used by the prosecutor for delivering the paperwork to the defense." The *LaFontaine* decision details the Court's findings in this regard.

§ 28:23   Applicability of *Rosario* rule to DMV refusal hearings

Research References

West's Key Number Digest, Intoxicating Liquors ⊂108.9

It appears clear that the *Rosario* rule, in sum or substance, is applicable to administrative proceedings where a violation of law is alleged and a "license" is at stake. *See, e.g., Matter of Inner Circle Restaurant, Inc. v. New York State Liquor Auth.*, 30 N.Y.2d 541, __, 330 N.Y.S.2d 389, 390 (1972) ("Upon the new hearing which our reversal mandates the police officer's memorandum book should be made available"); *Matter of Fenimore Circle Corp. v. State Liquor Auth.*, 27 N.Y.2d 716, 314 N.Y.S.2d 180 (1970) ("The State Liquor Authority Hearing Officer should have permitted petitioner's counsel to examine the statements made by Trooper Smith, when that witness took the stand, for purposes of cross-examination, there being no indication that they contained matter that must be kept confidential or that their disclosure would be inimical to the public interest").

In *Matter of Inner Circle Restaurant, Inc.*, the Court of Appeals cited *Matter of Garabendian v. New York State Liquor Auth.*, 33 A.D.2d 980, 307 N.Y.S.2d 270 (4th Dep't 1970), which held that:

> In People v. Rosario, . . . it was held that in a criminal trial a defendant is entitled to examine any pre-trial statement of a witness as long as the statement relates to the subject matter of the witness' testimony and is not confidential. We conclude that a similar rule should be applied in this proceeding which, at least in form, is not of a criminal character but, like a criminal proceeding, is brought to penalize for the commission of an offense against the law.
>
> There should be a new hearing at which the reports of any police officers testifying thereat should be made available to petitioners prior to the commencement of cross-examination.

33 A.D.2d at __, 307 N.Y.S.2d at 271 (citations omitted).

The position of the Department of Motor Vehicles appears to be that the *Rosario* rule is inapplicable to DMV refusal hearings. Nonetheless, 15 NYCRR § 127.6, which governs "discovery" and "evidence" at DMV refusal hearings, provides in pertinent part:

> (a) Prior to a hearing, a respondent may make a request to review nonconfidential information in the hearing file including information which is not protected by law from disclosure . . . The examination will be scheduled for a time at least five days prior to the hearing unless a shorter time is mutually agreed between the hearing officer and the requestor . . . If a request to examine the file is received less than seven days prior to the hearing date, the requestor will be afforded an opportunity to examine the file immediately prior to commencement of the hearing or at an earlier time as may be agreed to in the discretion of the hearing officer.

In addition, most DMV hearing officers will allow defense counsel to review any documents that the police officer(s) have either (a) brought with them and reviewed prior to testifying, and/or (b) used to refresh their recollection while testifying.

Part VIII

CHEMICAL TESTS

Chapter 29

Breath Testing

KeyCite®: Cases and other legal materials listed in KeyCite Scope can be researched through the KeyCite service on Westlaw®. Use KeyCite to check citations for form, parallel references, prior and later history, and comprehensive citator information, including citations to other decisions and secondary materials.

---

§ 29:1 In general

The Court of Appeals has stated that:

Chemical breath tests to determine blood alcohol content (BAC) are an important investigative tool used by law enforcement in the effort to combat driving while intoxicated and related offenses. The administration of these tests is a time-sensitive proposition; to maximize the probative value of BAC evidence, the police endeavor to administer chemical tests as close in time as possible to the motor vehicle infraction, typically within two hours of an arrest.

People v. Smith, 18 N.Y.3d 544, 548, 942 N.Y.S.2d 426, 428, 965 N.E.2d 928 (2012).

In the field of New York DWI law, the phrase "breath test" refers to a preliminary test of a DWI suspect's breath for the presence of alcohol using a preliminary breath screening device such as an Alco-Sensor (commonly referred to as a "PBT"). *See* §§ 7:1 et seq., *supra.* By contrast, the phrase "chemical test" is the term used to describe a test of the alcoholic and/or drug content of a DWI suspect's blood using an instrument other than a PBT. In other words, BAC tests conducted utilizing breath-alcohol analysis machines such as the DataMaster, Intoxilyzer, Alcotest, etc. are referred to as "chemical tests"—*not* "breath tests."

When the phrase "chemical test" came into being, breath-alcohol analysis devices such as the Breathalyzer determined a person's BAC by means of a chemical analysis of the person's breath using actual chemicals. *See* § 29:4, *infra.* By contrast, modern breath test devices utilize infrared absorption spectrometry to determine a person's BAC. Although the modern machines no longer use chemicals, they are still referred to as chemical tests. In this regard, challenges to the use of such machines on the ground that they do not constitute a "chemical test" within the meaning of VTL § 1194 have been unsuccessful. *See, e.g., People v. Summa,* 140 Misc. 2d 763, __, 531 N.Y.S.2d 993, 994–95 (Suffolk Co. Dist. Ct. 1988); *People v. Jones,* 118 Misc. 2d 687, __, 461 N.Y.S.2d 962, 966 (Albany Co. Ct. 1983).

That said, the most common form of chemical test in New York is a chemical test of the suspect's breath. Accordingly, for purposes of this chapter the phrase "chemical test" and the phrase "breath test" are used synonymously.

§ 29:2 Alcohol in the breath does not cause impairment

In *Guthrie v. Jones,* 202 Ariz. 273, 274, 43 P.3d 601, 602 (Ariz. App. Div. 1 2002), the Court pointed out that:

> Alcohol in the breath does not cause impairment; impairment results when alcohol enters the body, is absorbed into the bloodstream, and is transported to the central nervous system and the brain. Although it is thus a blood alcohol reading, not a breath alcohol reading, that establishes whether a person is impaired, breath alcohol readings nonetheless indicate blood alcohol levels, and taking a breath sample is easier and less intrusive than taking a blood sample.

See also State v. Hanks, 172 Vt. 93, 94–95, 772 A.2d 1087, 1089 (Vt. 2001) ("Alcohol in the breath does not cause intoxication. Rather, it is the impact of alcohol on the central nervous system, particularly the brain, that causes the physiological and psychological changes associated with impairment. Alcohol reaches the central nervous system through the blood").

§ 29:3 Is a breath test machine a "device" or an "instrument"?

One of the sillier arguments that arises in DWI cases is the argument over whether a breath test machine should be called a "device" or an "instrument." Prosecutors would like the machine to be called an instrument—which implies a greater degree of accuracy and reliability; whereas defense attorneys prefer the term device—which imputes fallibility.

Of course, neither description is inappropriate. In fact, the Court of Appeals uses such terms interchangeably. *See, e.g., People v. Boscic*, 15 N.Y.3d 494, 912 N.Y.S.2d 556, 938 N.E.2d 989 (2010) (Court referred to BAC DataMaster as "breath-alcohol machine," and used phrases such as "breath-alcohol detection devices," "breath-alcohol detection machines," "breathalyzer machine," "breathalyzer device," "breath-alcohol device," machine, device and instrument); *People v. DeMarasse*, 85 N.Y.2d 842, 623 N.Y.S.2d 845, 647 N.E.2d 1353 (1995) (Court referred to Intoxilyzer 5000 as a machine, a device and an instrument); *People v. Campbell*, 73 N.Y.2d 481, 541 N.Y.S.2d 756, 539 N.E.2d 584 (1989) (Court referred to DuPont Automatic Clinical Analyzer as a machine); *People v. Alvarez*, 70 N.Y.2d 375, 521 N.Y.S.2d 212, 515 N.E.2d 898 (1987) (Court referred to Smith & Wesson Model 900A Breathalyzer as both a machine and a device); *People v. Freeland*, 68 N.Y.2d 699, 506 N.Y.S.2d 306, 497 N.E.2d 673 (1986) (Court referred to Breathalyzer as both a machine and a device); *People v. Mertz*, 68 N.Y.2d 136, 506 N.Y.S.2d 290, 497 N.E.2d 657 (1986) (Court referred to Breathalyzer as an instrument); *People v. Gower*, 42 N.Y.2d 117, 397 N.Y.S.2d 368, 366 N.E.2d 69 (1977) (Court referred to Breathalyzer as a device); *People v. Todd*, 38 N.Y.2d 755, 381 N.Y.S.2d 50, 343 N.E.2d 767 (1975) (Court referred to Breathalyzer as both a machine and an apparatus).

Notably, the Department of Health's list of accepted breath test machines is entitled "Conforming Products List of Evidential Breath Measurement *Devices*." *See* 10 NYCRR § 59.4(b) (emphasis added).

§ 29:4 The Breathalyzer

For decades, the most common type of breath test device used in New York was the Smith & Wesson Breathalyzer Model 900A. The Breathalyzer:

> [I]nvolved chemical oxidation, wherein a breath sample was passed through an ampule containing a chemical mixture (usually potassium dichromate in sulfuric acid). The degree of ethanol content in the breath stimulated changes in the absorption abilities of the solution that could be detected by transmitting light through the sample. Results were then compared with an unreacted sample of the solution to achieve a blood-alcohol concentration reading.

People v. Boscic, 15 N.Y.3d 494, 499, 912 N.Y.S.2d 556, 559, 938 N.E.2d 989 (2010). While the Breathalyzer was state-of-the-art in its day, it is now considered a relic that is no longer in use. Modern breath test devices use a process known as "infrared absorption spectrometry. This technology . . . calculates blood-alcohol concentration by passing infrared light through a chamber holding the breath sample to gauge the absorption rate of 'infrared radiation at specific wavelengths.' " *Id.* at 499, 912 N.Y.S.2d at 559 (citation omitted).

In *People v. Donaldson*, 36 A.D.2d 37, __, 319 N.Y.S.2d 172, 175–76 (4th Dep't 1971), the Appellate Division, Fourth Department, stated that:

> The Breathalyzer has been in public use since 1954 and has been widely accepted and adopted by law enforcement agencies for use in testing blood-alcohol content. It operates on the firmly established principle that at normal body temperature the concentration of alcohol in the blood circulating through the lungs is 2,100 times greater than in the air discharged from the lungs. The apparatus is a semi-automatic analyzer designed to test a blood-alcohol percentage present in any breath sample. Scientifically, the Breathalyzer wastes all but the last portion of a long exhalation, trapping a measured volume which is then forced through a reagent and is ultimately photometrically measured resulting in a calculated reading of the subject's blood-alcohol percentage. Studies have shown that this device is considered to be "fail safe" and that as a general rule its readings are slightly lower than those obtained in a corresponding blood test; and any slight error caused either by mechanical defect or operator fault will usually produce lower rather than higher readings.

(Citation omitted).

A concise description of how a Breathalyzer functioned was set forth in *People v. Tilley*, 120 Misc. 2d 1040, __, 466 N.Y.S.2d 983, 984–85 (Erie Co. Ct. 1983):

THE THEORY AND OPERATION OF THE BREATHALYZER

In order to make a proper determination in the instant matter, it is incumbent upon the Court to fully appreciate the scientific theories and operation of the breathalyzer instrument used by the Town of Tonawanda Police Department. A condensed theory of the instrument has been provided by Smith and Wesson and reads as follows:

The method consists of three principal phases:
  1. Collecting a sample of deep-lung breath.
  2. Passing this sample through a potassium dichromate-sulfuric acid solution.
  3. Measuring the amount of potassium dichromate required to oxidize the alcohol.

The first phase involves having the subject blow, with force, through a mouthpiece into a heated plastic tube. The breath raises a piston in a metal cylinder. When the piston reaches the top of its stroke, it is held in this position by a small magnet aligned with two fixed pole pieces. Two vent holes just below the piston permits the breath to escape so that, when blowing is stopped, the cylinder is full of the last breath. When blowing stops, the piston drops from its supporting iron plate sufficiently to cover the vent holes.

A special valve is incorporated in the top of the sample chamber. It is designed to make leaks virtually impossible. The valve and magnet operate on the same shaft, rotated by the control knob on the panel. When the valve is in the *take* position, the breath passes from the retractable sample tube to the sample chamber. The magnet is aligned with the fixed pole pieces and the piston is supported. When the valve is turned to *analyze*, the magnet is disaligned with the fixed pole pieces, and the piston, by its own weight, forces the measured amount of air through 3 ml. of 50% (by volume) sulfuric acid in water, containing 0.25 mg. of potassium dichromate per ml., and a catalyst.

The sample chamber contains 56.5 ml. This is necessary because the breath is raised from mouth temperature (about 34°C) to 50 3°C. The 52.5 ml. of breath will occupy a larger volume at this higher temperature. Also, the delivery tube from the sample chamber of the test solution is full of room air before the test and full of breath after the test. This volume must be added to the cylinder volume. This adds up to approximately 56.5 ml. The breath bubbles through the test solution in about 30 seconds. One and a half minutes later, the reaction is complete.

Before the test is started, the solution in the "test" [ampoule] is balanced photometrically against a reference [ampoule]. The reading light is moved back and forth between the two [ampoules] until the *null meter* centers. This indicates that each of the two photocells is receiving the same amount of light through the [ampoules]. At this point the blood alcohol pointer is set on the base-line of the scale. After the analysis, the reading light is again turned on. If part of the potassium dichromate has been consumed by alcohol in the test [ampoule], more light will reach the right hand cell and the *null meter* will no longer be centered.

The light is moved by the thumb wheel until the balance is again established as indicated by the centering of the *null meter*. The distance the light was moved is directly proportional to the amount of potassium dichromate used and this is directly related to the amount of alcohol in the breath. The scale is calibrated in per cent blood alcohol.

With this arrangement, when the photometer has been balanced for a reading, line voltage affects each [ampoule] and photocell the same so changes in the voltage make no difference. For the same reason, changes in intensity of the reading light make no difference. The actual output of the photocells makes no difference because they are balanced before each test. The strength of the test solution is unimportant, because only the potassium dichromate used in the test is measured. Thus, the instrument is not dependent on external conditions. The only factor that must be maintained is the accurate volume of the test solution. A special gauge is provided to check this volume in each [ampoule].

§ 29:5 Modern infrared breath test devices—Generally

Modern breath test devices use a process known as "infrared absorption spectrometry. This technology . . . calculates blood-alcohol concentration by passing infrared light through a chamber holding the breath sample to gauge the absorption rate of 'infrared radiation at specific wavelengths.' " *People v. Boscic*, 15 N.Y.3d 494, 499, 912 N.Y.S.2d 556, 559, 938 N.E.2d 989 (2010) (citation omitted). The Department of Health ("DOH") promulgates a "Conforming Products List of Evidential Breath Measurement Devices." *See* 10 NYCRR § 59.4(b). A copy of the DOH Conforming Products List is set forth at Appendix 3. The DOH list, which merely parrots the Conforming Products List promulgated by the National Highway Traffic Safety Administration (NHTSA), *see* 10 NYCRR § 59.4(a), contains literally dozens of different breath test devices.

Breath test devices included on the DOH list allegedly have been tested by NHTSA and found to meet various criteria for accuracy and reliability. *See* 58 Fed. Reg. 48705. Notably, none of the NHTSA testing tests whether so-called "fail-safe" mechanisms allegedly contained within the breath test devices (*e.g.*, mouth-alcohol detectors, radio frequency interference detectors, breath flow monitors, etc.) perform as advertised. Accordingly, inclusion of a particular device on the DOH list does not permit lay witnesses (*e.g.*, breath test operators) to testify as to such matters without a *Frye* hearing. *See, e.g., People v. Burnet*, 25 Misc. 3d 307, 887 N.Y.S.2d 798 (Bronx Co. Sup. Ct. 2009).

The primary breath test machines currently in use in New York are the BAC DataMaster, the DataMaster DMT, the Alcotest 7110 MKIII-C, the Alcotest 9510 and the Intoxilyzer 5000.

§ 29:6 The BAC DataMaster

Although the BAC DataMaster has been in use for more than two decades, the authors have been unable to find a single published decision describing how it works. As a result, the following description is obtained from an undated copy of a BAC DataMaster Operator's Manual:

How the DataMaster Works:

The Optical Path:

Stable, efficient, infrared radiation is provided by the *Grey Body Infrared Energy Source*. The radiation enters and exits the *Sample Cell* through *Quartz Windows* at each end. *Mirrors* provide reflecting surfaces for the precision-folded optical path. The energy exits the sample cell and is directed precisely to the surface of the *Thermo-electrically Cooled Infrared Detector* by the *Quartz Focusing Lens*. On its path to the *Detector*, the energy passes through a spinning *Chopper Wheel* providing the AC signal needed for analysis. The energy further travels through either the *Ethanol Filter* or the *Interference Filters* to select the desired wavelength for analysis. A *Quartz Calibration Plate* of known absorbance is pulled into the energy path for verification of calibration.

The Sample:

Prior to sample delivery, the DataMaster purges the *Sample Cell* and determines a zero ethanol reference. The *Quartz Calibration Plate* is then introduced into the infrared radiation path to verify correct calibration. The subject is prompted visually and audibly to introduce the breath sample. The breath sample passes past the *Flow Thermistor* allowing the DataMaster to monitor both the flow and volume of the sample being delivered. The breath sample then passes through the Inlet into the *Sample Cell* where, sealed from the external environment by the *Quartz Windows* and *Mirrors*, it follows the identical path traveled by the infrared radiation. The breath sample exits the Sample Cell through the *Outlet* and *Check Valve*, preventing the subject from drawing ambient air back into the *Sample Cell*. As the sample passes through the *Sample Cell*, the DataMaster calculates alcohol concentration in real time. The DataMaster utilizes a comprehensive algorithm utilizing flow rate, sample volume, rate of increase in alcohol concentration, and (optionally) sample delivery time, to determine when a valid, alveolar sample has been delivered. Following valid sample delivery, the DataMaster introduces the *Interference Filters* into the radiation path to determine the presence of any interfering compounds in the accepted sample. The final ethanol concentration is then calculated and reported.

(References to accompanying diagram omitted).

The DataMaster utilizes two separate filters, which the Operator's Manual describes as follows:

FILTERS—The filters allow only IR energy of a specific frequency band to strike the photo-detector. There are two such filters, one detecting IR energy at wavelengths of 3.37 microns (u) and one detecting wavelengths of 3.44u.

    1. 3.44u filter, allows to pass through the sample chamber, IR energy that is absorbed specifically by ethanol molecules. As the amount of ethanol from the subject's breath increases in

the chamber, the amount of IR light striking the photo-detector decreases due to the absorption by the ethanol molecules. What is being measured is a drop in electrical output from the photo-detector.

2. 3.37u filter, allows to pass through the sample chamber, IR energy that is absorbed by ethanol and by *acetone*.

The sample chamber has a volume of 50 cubic centimeters, and operates at a temperature of 50? Celsius.

§ 29:7   The Alcotest 7110 MKIII-C

New York Courts have issued no meaningful decisions regarding the functioning of the Alcotest 7110 MKIII-C, instead relying upon the presumption that the device is reliable because it is included on the Department of Health's list of accepted breath test machines. By contrast, the State of New Jersey has conducted meaningful hearings into the accuracy and reliability of this device. *See, e.g., State v. Chun*, 194 N.J. 54, 943 A.2d 114 (2008). In *Chun*, the New Jersey Supreme Court wrote an exhaustive decision analyzing the Alcotest 7110 MKIII-C. With respect to how the device operates, the Court wrote:

B. *Operation of the Alcotest*

In light of the fact that breath testing always relies on the extrapolation of BAC through testing of breath, the precision with which any device evaluates BAC through this method is critical to our consideration of the admissibility of the device's results. We turn then to a description of the manner in which the Alcotest operates.

The Alcotest, which is currently in use in seventeen of our twenty-one counties, as well as in other states, including Alabama and parts of New York, is a device that purports to accurately measure the concentration of alcohol from a human subject through breath testing. The Alcotest is an embedded system, meaning that it is a device with a specific purpose, and it relies on pre-loaded software that the manufacturer refers to as firmware.

The Alcotest uses both infrared (IR) technology and electric chemical (EC) oxidation in a fuel cell to measure breath alcohol concentration. The device therefore produces two test results for each breath sample, one derived from an IR reading and the other, by and large, from an EC reading.

Although the precise mechanism by which these tests are accomplished is not relevant to the issues before us, the IR chamber, also called a cuvette, captures the breath sample and uses infrared energy to calculate absorption of the energy by the alcohol concentrated in the chamber. IR technology has been available since the 1970's or early 1980's and scientists have concluded that it is reliable.

The EC, or fuel cell technology, uses a catalyst to absorb alcohol and provide a second measurement[10] of breath alcohol concentration from a small sample captured from the cuvette. In the EC chamber, voltage is applied to cause the catalytic reaction, which causes any alcohol that is present to oxidize. As that occurs, the oxidation process creates electricity, which is then measured to determine the amount of alcohol interacting with the fuel cell.

10. Draeger has consistently represented that the IR and EC tests are "completely independent" as a basis for its claim that the device is reliable. As our discussion of the fuel cell drift algorithm, *see* Section IX.A., *infra*, explains, however, the reported results of the two tests are not always independent.

C. *Test Administration and the Alcohol Influence Report*

The Alcotest reports the IR and EC readings on a printout from the machine, referred to as the Alcohol Influence Report (AIR). One of the claimed advantages of the Alcotest, as compared to the breathalyzer, is that it is not operator-dependent, but performs its analysis in accordance with a sequence through a computerized program that gives visual prompts to the operator. We turn, then, to a description of the manner in which the device operates in practice in performing these functions.

The actual administration of the test is performed by one of the more than 5000 certified Alcotest operators in New Jersey. When a person has been arrested, based on probable cause that the person has been driving while intoxicated, he or she is transported to the police station to provide a sample for the Alcotest. The Alcotest, consisting of a keyboard, an external printer, and the testing device itself, is positioned on a table near where the test subject is seated.

Operators must wait twenty minutes before collecting a sample to avoid overestimated readings due to residual effects of mouth alcohol. The software is programmed to prohibit operation of the device before the passage of twenty minutes from the time entered as the time of the arrest. Moreover, the operator must observe the test subject for the required twenty-minute period of time to ensure that no alcohol has entered the person's mouth while he or she is awaiting the start of the testing sequence. In addition, if the arrestee swallows anything or regurgitates, or if the operator notices chewing gum or tobacco in the person's mouth, the operator is required to begin counting the twenty-minute period anew.

The Alcotest that is the focus of this matter utilizes software developed in collaboration with the New Jersey State Police and known as New Jersey Firmware version 3.11. This software prompts the operator through a specific testing sequence on each arrestee. Essentially, the process begins when the operator has typed identifying information into the machine through a series of questions and prompts. The device then starts and automatically samples the room air to determine if there are chemical interferents in the room. This is known as a blank air test. Assuming that there are none, the machine then uses its attached wet bath simulator to heat a solution and produce a vapor sample from a control test solution with a known alcohol concentration of 0.10, which is then measured using IR and EC technology. In order to be valid, the control test, in accordance with currently-programmed firmware, must produce results between 0.095 and 0.105. If the results do not identify the known sample within the defined parameters, the device is programmed so that the test cannot proceed. If the machine is working properly as demonstrated by the control test, then the instrument performs a second blank air test, again using room air to purge the test sample out of the chamber.

Assuming that the results of the control test are within the established parameters, the instrument prompts the operator through a message on the LED screen to collect a breath sample. The operator then attaches a new, disposable mouthpiece and removes cell phones and portable electronic devices from the testing area. The operator is required to read the following instruction to the test subject: "I want you to take a deep breath and blow into the mouthpiece with one long, continuous breath. Continue to blow until I tell you to stop. Do you understand these instructions?" The arrestee then provides the first breath sample, which is measured in the IR and EC chambers.

Lights on the LED screen and an audible sound alert the operator when a breath sample which meets the minimum fixed standards, comprised of four criteria, has been provided. The operator then tells the subject to stop and the instrument performs a third blank test to purge the first breath sample. After a two-minute lock-out period during which the device will not permit another test, the instrument prompts the operator to read the instruction again to the arrestee and collect the second breath sample. The second sample is also measured using the IR and EC technology. The second sample is purged from the machine and the device performs a fourth blank test using room air.

If the measurements for the first breath test are out of the accepted range of tolerance with the measurements for the second breath test, the machine prompts the operator to conduct a third breath test. Depending on the relationship among the three tests, the results are reported. The instrument then performs a second control test with the known solution from the simulator. Finally, the air is purged again and a final blank test is performed.

The device gives the operator three minutes to collect each sample. If that time expires without a sample, the device will present the operator with three options. The options are to terminate the test, report that the person refused the test, or continue with the test. If the officer opts to continue the test, the device will purge itself and then prompt the operator to collect another sample. The operator has a maximum of eleven attempts to collect two breath samples. After the eleventh failed test, the only two options permitted by the device are to terminate testing or report refusal.

As currently configured by New Jersey Firmware version 3.11, the software now being utilized, the device will accept a sample only if it meets certain minimum criteria that have been devised by the State. Once the subject has provided an acceptable breath sample, the machine prompts the operator, through a system of lights on the LED screen and an audible beep, to tell the subject that he or she may stop. If any of these minimum test criteria has not been met, the machine will generate an error message and a report of how much air was submitted. The machine then offers the operator the option of giving the person another attempt or asserting refusal.

The results of the test sequence are printed out from the device in a sequentially numbered document referred to as an AIR. The AIR contains the test subject's identifying information, date, time, and test results for each stage of the procedure. Each AIR includes a variety of other information relevant to the test, including the serial number of the device used in the test, dates of and file numbers for calibration and linearity checks, and solution control lot and bottle numbers. The operator must retain a copy of the AIR and give a copy to the arrestee.

In the event that the administration of the test resulted in errors because of, for example, insufficient breath volume or duration, the AIR will report those errors and will not attempt to calculate the BAC from an inadequate sample. Similarly, if the results of the control test do not fall within the acceptable tolerance, the device will produce an AIR that reports that the test could not be accomplished because of an invalid control test.

If the results are within the acceptable tolerance, the AIR shows the BAC values for each IR and EC reading for each of the tests to three decimal places. The AIR then reports the final BAC test result, which will be the lowest of the four acceptable readings, that is, readings within acceptable tolerance, which the device is programmed to truncate to two decimal places. Truncating, as opposed to rounding, involves simply reporting the first and second decimal places and dropping the third. For example, by truncating, a reading of 0.079 percent BAC would be reported as 0.07 and a reading of 0.089 percent BAC would be reported as 0.08. The effect of truncating, as opposed to rounding, is to under-report the concentration, to the benefit of the arrestee.

194 N.J. at 77–83, 943 A.2d at 128–31 (citation and footnotes omitted).

Notably, the *Chun* Court held that "we deem it to be in the interests of justice that some form of training be made available to defense attorneys to enable them to better prepare to represent their clients. However, we agree that the State should not be burdened with this responsibility. We therefore direct that Draeger make Alcotest training, substantially similar to that provided to Alcotest operators and coordinators, available to licensed New Jersey attorneys and their designated experts. The training shall be offered at regular intervals and at locations within the State of New Jersey, at a reasonable cost to those who attend." 194 N.J. at 134, 943 A.2d at 161. *See also* 194 N.J. at 154, 943 A.2d at 174 (same).

The *Chun* Court also ordered, *inter alia*, that:

[T]he State shall forthwith:

A. Commence inspection and recalibration of all Alcotest devices every six months in place of the current annual inspection and recalibration program;

B. Create and maintain a centralized statewide database, comprised of downloaded Alcotest results, and shall make the data, following appropriate redactions of personal identification as needed, available to defendants and counsel; and

C. Produce in discovery the twelve foundation documents identified by the Special Master as follows:

(1) New Standard Solution Report of the most recent control test solution change, and the credentials of the operator who performed that change;

(2) Certificate of Analysis for the 0.10 percent solution used in that New Solution Report;

(3) Draeger Safety Certificate of Accuracy for the Alcotest CU34 Simulator;

(4) Draeger Safety Certificate of Accuracy for the Alcotest 7110 Temperature Probe;

(5) Draeger Safety Certificate of Accuracy for the Alcotest 7110 Instrument;

(6) Calibration Records, including control tests, linearity tests, and the credentials of the coordinator who performed the calibration;

(7) Certificate of Analysis for the 0.10 percent solution used in the calibration control test;

(8) Certificate of Analysis for the 0.04, 0.08, and 0.16 percent solutions used in the calibration linearity test;

(9) New Standard Solution Report, following the most recent calibration;

(10) Draeger Safety Certificates of Accuracy for the Simulators used in calibration;

(11) Draeger Safety Certificate of Accuracy for the Alcotest 7110 Temperature Probe used in calibration; and

(12) Draeger Safety Ertco-Hart Calibration Report.

194 N.J. at 153, 943 A.2d at 173.

§ 29:8   The Intoxilyzer 5000

The Intoxilyzer 5000 is an infrared photometric instrument designed to measure ethyl alcohol in the breath. Its operation is based upon the scientific principle that vaporized alcohol will absorb infrared light of a wavelength of 3.39 microns at a rate different from that of other chemical compounds. The device measures the amount of infrared light absorbed and translates that measurement into a blood alcohol content reading. Although it is a more sophisticated instrument than the breathalyzers used since the early nineteen sixties, its functioning is based, nevertheless, upon the same underlying scientific principle (known as Henry's Law): that . . . the ratio between the concentration of alcohol in one's blood and that in the alveolar air in the lungs is a constant: 2,100:1.

Com. v. Smythe, 23 Mass. App. Ct. 348, 350, 502 N.E.2d 162, 163–64 (Mass. App. Ct. 1987) (footnote omitted).

In *People v. Cialino*, 14 Misc. 3d 999, __, 831 N.Y.S.2d 680, 681 (N.Y. City Crim. Ct. 2007), the Court noted that:

According to "Defense of Drunk Driving Cases, Criminal, Civil" at section 21.06:

The Intoxilyzer 5000 has undergone a number of changes since its introduction in 1983. Accordingly, the so-called "Intoxilyzer 5000" is not a single instrument, but a series of instruments, all called the Intoxilyzer 5000, but with significant differences. Changes have been made to increase stability, increase specificity (reduce potential of effects due to interfering substances), increase accuracy (especially at low breath-alcohol concentrations (BrACs)), and increase data handling capability and remote access.

(2007, Matthew Bender & Company).

In 1986, the Suffolk County District Court held a hearing to determine whether the defendant's Intoxilyzer 5000 test result would be suppressed. *See People v. Gallagher*, 132 Misc. 2d 195, 503 N.Y.S.2d 500 (Suffolk Co. Dist. Ct. 1986), adhered to, 133 Misc. 2d 717, 507 N.Y.S.2d 950 (Dist. Ct. 1986).

At the hearing, the People produced four expert witnesses as to the reliability of the breathalyzer used in this case and the admissibility of the results of tests administered with such instrument. Dr. Leo Dal Cortivo, Chief Toxicologist of the Suffolk County Medical Examiner's Office, testified as to tests performed on solutions of alcohol which corroborated the accuracy of the results found with the Intoxilyzer 5000. Mr. James Witler, Director of Engineering of CMI, Inc., the manufacturer of the Intoxilyzer 5000, explained each of the components of the device and how they worked to produce the test result. Dr. Arthur Flores, Project Director in the Office of Alcohol Countermeasures of the National Highway Traffic Safety Administration, testified that the Intoxilyzer 5000 met the standards developed by the National Bureau of Standards for NHTSA. Finally, P.O. James McCarthy, Supervisor in the Breath-Testing

Unit of the Suffolk County Police Department, stated that he is certified by the New York State Department of Health as a Technical Supervisor, authorized to instruct others as to the operation, calibration and maintenance of the Intoxilyzer 5000.

503 N.Y.S.2d at 501.

Finding that the Intoxilyzer 5000 satisfied the *Frye* test, the Court went on to hold that:

Of course, this acceptance of the results of the Intoxilyzer 5000 is still subject to the People properly introducing a foundation for the admission of said results and that foundation is found in V & TL 1194 or 1194-a, that is:

1. Compliance with V & TL 1194, i.e. that the defendant was under arrest; that the test was administered within two hours of arrest; and that the defendant was properly warned of the significance of taking the test or refusal.

2. That the breath analysis operator has a permit from the New York State Commissioner of Health.

Since the Intoxilyzer 5000 is a qualified evidential breath testing device, it is assumed to meet the criteria of 10 NYCRR 59.4(a):

(1) The quantity of breath analyzed for its alcoholic content shall be established only by direct volumetric measurement or by collection and analysis of a fixed breath volume.

(2) Breath specimens collected for analysis shall be essentially alveolar in composition.

(3) The instrument shall be capable of analyzing a suitable reference standard, the result of which analysis must agree with the reference standard value within the limits of plus or minus 0.01 percent weight per volume, or such limits as set by the State Commissioner of Health.

(4) The specificity of the procedure shall be adequate and appropriate for the analyses of breath specimens for the determination of alcoholic concentration in traffic law enforcement.

Additionally, the Intoxilyzer 5000 is pre-programmed and calibrated, eliminating the need for an operational checklist and the test sequence is predetermined. If the sequence is varied, interrupted or the test malfunctions, the instrument will automatically terminate the test. Finally, V & TL 1194(9) provides that if the test is performed by a person with a permit from the Department of Health, it shall be presumptive evidence that the examination was properly given. This presumption would also indicate that the techniques and methods found in 10 NYCRR 59.5 were followed.

The finding with respect to the admissibility of the results of the Intoxilyzer 5000 will be admissible into evidence as reliable. The defendant's motion to suppress is denied.

503 N.Y.S.2d at 502–03 (citation omitted).

Subsequent to this decision, but prior to the defendant's trial:

Dr. Leo Dal Cortivo of the Suffolk County Medical Examiner's office became aware of a letter to the editors published in the Journal of Analytical Toxicology (Vol. 10, May/June 1986) which he considered to be of sufficient importance to question the accuracy and efficiency of the Intoxilyzer 5000. He notified the authorities in the District Attorney's office. Those officials recognizing their obligations to provide a defendant with exculpatory material notified defense counsel as well as this court. As a result a new hearing was held.

Dr. Dal Cortivo testified that the letter in essence provided the following information and conclusion: A 52-year old cabinet maker with a 20-year history of work-related exposure to paint thinners had been physically examined. A breath alcohol analysis was taken utilizing the Intoxilyzer 5000. The results of two tests on the instrument's digital screen had a readout of the presence of alcohol (.369% and .273%) and an evidence card printout of .312 and the second card of .245 with the notation "interferent subtracted." A blood specimen showed no presence of ethyl alcohol but showed the presence of acetone at a concentration of .026% (w/v). Gas chromatographic headspace analysis for volatile hydrocarbons, 28 days after collection, showed the presence of toluene. (Toluene is a chemical compound found in industrial solvents, paint, plastic and "TNT".) The authors of the letter concluded that since the Intoxilyzer 5000 is capable of correcting for small amounts of acetone in the breath, it was unlikely that a significant portion of the evidence card results of apparent alcohol is attributable to acetone in the subject. (The Intoxilyzer uses an assumed blood-breath ratio for alcohol of 2100 pursuant to the Beer/Lambert Law.) The letter states that because toluene exhibits a blood-breath ratio that is 116 to 300 times less than that of alcohol and because toluene demonstrates significant infrared absorption at the 3.50+.06 micron wave length used by the Intoxilyzer 5000, it was concluded that toluene caused the interference. The Intoxilyzer is an infrared-type instrument in which infrared red light passes through a chamber of room air and a second chamber of the person's breath. Any alcohol present in the subject's breath will absorb the infrared energy at a wave length of 3.39 microns. There are other substances such as acetone that absorb energy at 3.39 microns. The Intoxilyzer 5000 has the ability to detect and eliminate the acetone interference by the utilization of a filter. (The instrument has three filters at various wave lengths, 3.30, 3.48 and 3.80 microns.)

Therefore, since the letter indicates that the Intoxilyzer 5000 may give an incorrect reading by confusing toluene as alcohol, the issue of reliability was raised. Dr. Dal Cortivo testified that he performed various experiments which included a number of combinations of substances in a simulator consisting of acetone, toluene and alcohol. Although he was unaware of any other similar type experiments, he concluded that after his testing, the Intoxilyzer 5000 is a reliable instrument to measure blood alcohol content in an individual.

Defendant's position is that the accuracy of the Intoxilyzer 5000 is questionable. Defendant argues that there have been no tests performed on human subjects and Dr. Dal Cortivo's experiment failed to explain away the results of the test as described within the letter.

People v. Gallagher, 133 Misc. 2d 717, __, 507 N.Y.S.2d 950, 951 (Suffolk Co. Dist. Ct. 1986) (citation omitted). The Court went on to adhere to its prior ruling that the Intoxilyzer 5000 is reliable. 507 N.Y.S.2d at 952.

In 1988, another Judge of the Suffolk County District Court held a hearing regarding the Intoxilyzer 5000. *See People v. Summa*, 140 Misc. 2d 763, __, 531 N.Y.S.2d 993, 994–95 (Suffolk Co. Dist. Ct. 1988). The *Summa* Court held as follows:

Workings of the Intoxilyzer 5000

The Intoxilyzer 5000 uses an infra-red light beam passed through a chamber containing a sample of the subject's breath in order to determine the concentration of ethyl alcohol in that subject's blood. When the machine is turned on, it automatically purges the sample chamber, heats to 45°C, and indicates its readiness. The operator pushes a button and inserts a card. By way of control, fresh air is introduced and analyzed to obtain a reference for the test of the subject's breath. Next, the subject blows into the sample chamber, which holds 81 cubic centimeters of air and is bounded by two lenses. He must blow for four seconds at a sufficient pressure to insure that there is no "mouth alcohol" that could be detected by the machine. The slope of alcohol concentration in the breath is highest at the beginning stages of the test. Thereafter, the slope levels off and approaches zero percent of change.

The breath analysis, which occurs once the slope has leveled off, involves the principle of "infra-red spectroscopy." An infra-red source lamp projects infra-red rays directly through the sample chamber, where they interact with the subject's breath sample. The rays are then channeled through a filter wheel which filters out all hydrocarbons which are not the subject of the test, to wit, everything except ethyl alcohol. An infra-red energy detector then picks up the infra-red rays. A reading of the alcohol concentration appears on a digital display terminal and is printed on the card, and the machine automatically purges itself. As a further control, air from a connected simulator is then introduced into the chamber and tested. Once the result is printed on the card, the machine again purges itself. This entire procedure takes about ninety-five seconds.

531 N.Y.S.2d at 994.

Regarding the reliability of the machine, the *Summa* Court listed the tests that NHTSA performs prior to placing a breath test device on its Conforming Products List, and further stated that:

In addition to the above-described tests, testimony was received demonstrating that the Intoxilyzer 5000 has been constructed with built-in safeguards against an inaccurate reading. If mouth alcohol is being detected, there will be a very rapid rise in the curve on the slope detector, followed by a quick drop-off. In such a case, the machine will reflect "Invalid Test" on the card. Should there be ambient contamination, i.e. if alcohol is present in the room, the machine will indicate the problem. The machine will likewise indicate "Invalid Test" if there is an insufficient breath sample. It also has a built-in detector to determine the presence of radio frequency interference and an internal check to insure that there are no processor errors. If the temperature in the sample chamber is too cool or too warm, or varies during the course of the test, the machine has been programmed to indicate either "Temperature Error" or "Not Ready". There is a central processing unit built into the machine, which monitors the machine's internal functioning. The machine is also equipped with RAM (Random Access Memory), which goes through an operational checklist prior to indicating that the machine is ready for operation.

By reason of the above-described testimony, therefore, evidence has been received as to the nature, function and underlying scientific principles of the Intoxilyzer 5000, enabling this Court to make a finding as to the scientific reliability of the machine and its processes and, hence, to determine the admissibility of the machine's test results in this case.

Conclusion

After hearing and evaluating all of the testimony received at the instant hearing, this Court finds that the infra-red molecular absorption process used in the Intoxilyzer 5000 is generally accepted in its particular scientific field and has achieved general acceptance within the scientific community. As such, this Court is of the opinion that the Intoxilyzer 5000 is a scientifically reliable machine for the testing of BAC. However, the People must still lay the foundation for the introduction of the test results provided by this instrument. As with a Breathalyzer, they must show that the test was given by an authorized individual and that the machine was in good working order. For example, the certificates as to calibration of the machine and its maintenance must be introduced.

531 N.Y.S.2d at 996–97 (footnote omitted).

§ 29:9 The Intoxilyzer 4011AS

The Intoxilyzer 4011AS was a predecessor to the Intoxilyzer 5000. In *People v. Drumm*, 122 Misc. 2d 1051, __, 472 N.Y.S.2d 989, 992–93 (Monroe Co. Ct. 1984), the Monroe County Court found that the Intoxilyzer 4011AS is more reliable than the Breathalyzer, finding that:

[T]here is a second reason why the Court believes that the evidence regarding reliability of the intoxilyzer . . . was legally sufficient.

This involves the nature of the instrument, itself which is a Model 4011AS. This instrument utilizes infrared energy, and is based upon the Beer-Lambert Law of absorption. In this regard, the instrument operates on the same principle as the intoximeter 3000, which is described in detail in *People v. Jones*, 118 Misc. 2d 687, 461 N.Y.S.2d 962 (1983). Simply stated, ethyl alcohol absorbs infrared energy at a wavelength of about 3.39 microns, and the intoxilyzer contains an absorption band, from an infrared energy light source, within this range. Other substances, specifically including acetone, may absorb infrared energy at the same wavelength, and, therefore, unlike the earlier models of the intoxilyzer, as well as the intoximeter 3000, Model 4011AS contains a second absorption band, at 4.48 microns, at which alcohol, but not these other substances, will absorb the infrared energy. Thus, the presence of ethyl alcohol, contained in the breath sample, can be detected, and, furthermore, the alcohol vapor, contained in the sample cell, will absorb the infrared energy in proportion to its concentration. As the concentration of alcohol increases, the amount of infrared energy reaching the detector will proportionately decrease. The result is converted to a blood alcohol content reading, which is displayed, and also printed on a card, which has previously been inserted into the instrument.

The expert witness, who testified at the trial concerning the scientific reliability of the instrument, testified that the instrument contains internal, "fail-safe" mechanisms which assure the proper operation at the time of a test. Thus, if the electronic components are not working properly, for example, an error light would appear and the instrument would not print a ticket. The same would be true if the operator did not follow the proper procedure, the proper temperature was not attained, or any other problem connected with the operation of the instrument, itself.

During cross-examination, the witness stated that the above-described aspects of the instrument, which would be indicative of a malfunction, also have fail-safe mechanisms to assure that they are functioning in a proper manner. Nevertheless, he did acknowledge that he was not claiming that the instrument was infallible, but only that the instrument contained a fail-safe mechanism to detect a problem and prevent a result being printed. Indeed, on a more general level, the intoxilyzer may be subject to some of the same concerns which have been prevalent in regard to the breathalyzer. For instance, breath testing devices, using infrared absorption, like the breathalyzer, are based upon Henry's Law which involves the premise that the percentage of alcohol in the blood is 2100 times the alcohol in the alveolar air of every subject. Recently, questions have been raised about the effect of radio frequency interference, in regard to breath testing devices.

As long as society attempts to deal with the consequences caused by citizens who drive motor vehicles, after the consumption of alcoholic beverages, in terms of degree of intoxication or impairment, as distinguished from an outright prohibition, questions relating to the reliability of breath testing devices will continue to present legal and evidentiary problems. Nevertheless, this Court has concluded that the intoxilyzer Model 4011AS is a more reliable instrument than the breathalyzer, which has been judicially recognized as scientifically reliable. Furthermore, use of this intoxilyzer does not involve some of the problems commonly associated with the wet-chemistry operation of the breathalyzer, such as the qualitative and quantitative content of the chemicals. Also, this Court is convinced that the results are less susceptible to operator error.

Cf. People v. Kester, 130 Misc. 2d 37, __, 494 N.Y.S.2d 823, 825 (Brighton Just. Ct. 1985) (Intoxilyzer 4011AS not judicially accepted in absence of expert witness testimony or statutory or appellate court mandate). *But see People v. Holmes*, 171 Misc. 2d 962, __, 656 N.Y.S.2d 130, 131 (Brighton Just. Ct. 1997) ("Since the *Kester* decision, the Appellate Division decided *Hampe*. That case provides the appellate court mandate missing at the time of *Kester*").

§ 29:10   The Intoximeter 3000

Although the Intoximeter 3000 is no longer used in New York, it is mentioned here because a couple of New York Courts held *Frye* hearings involving this device and issued written decisions describing how it functions. *See People v. Flynn*, 129 Misc. 2d 176, 492 N.Y.S.2d 882 (Queens Co. Sup. Ct. 1985); *People v. Jones*, 118 Misc. 2d 687, 461 N.Y.S.2d 962 (Albany Co. Ct. 1983). The *Jones* decision was particularly thorough:

The issue presented by the motion of the defendant is whether the results of a breath test performed on an Intoximeter 3000, a device employing infrared and electrical analysis of breath vapors, are admissible as evidence in a prosecution for driving while intoxicated.

A suppression hearing was held at which this Court heard testimony from one of the developers of the instrument, from an official of the Bureau of Municipal Police in the New York State Division of Criminal Justice Services, from a Project Director for the breath alcohol program of the U.S. Department of Transportation involved in the evaluation of breath alcohol test devices for the National Highway Traffic Safety Administration and, for the defendant, from a professor of chemistry at the State University of New York at Albany.

This is a case of first impression and may be of broad impact throughout the State of New York; thus a full exposition of the issues and their resolution is required.

FINDINGS OF FACT

The Intoximeter 3000 is a breath-testing device which utilizes infrared energy and electrical current to detect the presence of ethyl alcohol (ethanol) in the breath of a driver. The device, as are all breath-testing devices, is based upon Henry's Law[1] and, unlike the more common breath-testers such as the breathalyzer, upon the Beer-Lambert Law of Absorption.[2]

1. * * * The validity of breath-analysis to determine blood-alcohol content is based on the scientific principle known as Henry's Law which states that at any given temperature, the ratio between the concentration of alcohol in the blood and that in the alveolar air in the lungs is constant. The ratio has been found empirically to be 2100:1 — i.e., for every part of alcohol found in deep lung air, there are 2100 parts of alcohol in the blood stream. This ratio was adopted by the National Highway Safety Council's Committee on Tests for Intoxication in 1952 and has been questioned and reaffirmed since then. In 1972, for example, an Ad Hoc Committee on Blood-Breath Alcohol Relationship sponsored by Indiana University endorsed the continued use of the 2100:1 ratio. (See: 4 Gray, Attorneys' Textbook Medicine, Section 133.73(1))[.]

2. The principle underlying infrared analysis of substances derives from the Beer-Lambert Law of Absorption. This law is the theoretical basis for the operation of devices such as the spectrophotometer as well as the Intoximeter 3000. According to this law, molecules absorb electromagnetic radiation. However, this molecular absorption is selective: only radiation of certain wavelengths will be absorbed by a molecule of any given compound. A compound will absorb radiation of a number of different wavelengths depending upon what elements are present in that compound and how those elements are bonded to each other in the compound. Thus, ethyl alcohol, composed of atoms of carbon, hydrogen and oxygen in a number and array unique to that substance, will absorb radiation at wavelengths of approximately 3.00, 3.39, 7.25, 9.18, 9.50 and 11.5 microns. (These numbers represent the highest levels or "peaks" of absorption. The absorption actually begins and ends at wavelengths surrounding those numbers—e.g. from 9 to 10 microns). No other compound absorbs radiation at those wavelengths and no other wavelength.

It might be said that every chemical compound has "fingerprints" which are unique to it and by which the compound may be identified through infrared spectroscopy. While each chemical compound has its own spectrograph showing all the wavelengths at which it absorbs radiation, more than one compound may absorb energy at any one particular wavelength. Thus, while ethyl alcohol has a major absorption band at 3.39 microns, other compounds such as methyl alcohol, acetic acid, and ketone, including acetone, absorb at that wavelength as well. Thus, the fact that an unknown compound absorbs radiation in the vicinity of 3.39 microns merely narrows down the identity of such compound; in order to specifically identify the compound as ethyl alcohol, an additional process for factoring out other substances which absorb energy at a wavelength of 3.39 microns is necessary. The infrared spectrophotometer can accomplish the entire task by itself by reason of its ability to reverse the entire absorption pattern of a substance through a spectrum ranging from 1 to 100 microns, not just that at a wavelength of 3.39 microns; but it is a much more costly machine than the Intoximeter 3000 and is primarily a sophisticated laboratory instrument not geared to the operational ease required in intoxication testing by law enforcement personnel. However, the same result of factoring out substances other than ethyl alcohol that absorb energy at a wavelength of 3.39 microns is accomplished by the Intoximeter 3000 by the use of a semi-conductor device.

The Intoximeter 3000 is equipped with an infrared energy source of nichrome (an alloy of nickel, chromium and iron) surrounding a ceramic core. An electric current passing through this source causes two beams of infrared energy to be emitted in the direction of a two-chambered gas cell after reflecting off a collimating mirror. After traversing the gas cell, the infrared beams pass through a narrow band interference filter. This filter permits infrared energy with a wavelength ranging from 3.3 to 3.48 microns to pass through and strike a detector while at the same time blocking energy with wavelengths greater or lesser than that range. Thus the beam of energy striking the detector is modified so that it corresponds to one of the major absorption bands of ethyl alcohol.

The cell through which the infrared beams pass has two chambers. One, the reference cell, contains only room air. The other, the sample cell, contains during a test 900 cubic centimeters of the subject's alveolar air. The device gives a reading of the amount of interfering substance[3] in the subject's breath by comparing the amount of infrared energy striking the detector after the two beams pass through the chambers, one through the sample cell, the other through the reference cell. Otherwise stated, the device compares the amount of infrared energy absorbed by the air from the lungs of the subject with the amount absorbed by the air from the room. If the ratio resulting from that reading (energy absorbed by the alveolar air/energy absorbed by the room air) is greater than one, there is present in the subject's breath some substance which absorbs infrared radiation at 3.39 microns. The amount of interfering substance present is determined by the amount of infrared energy it absorbs. At this point it is impossible to conclude that the absorbing substance is ethyl alcohol because in addition to ethyl alcohol there are other substances which absorb radiation at 3.39 microns.

3. By "interfering substance" is meant any substance that absorbs radiation at 3.39 microns, among which are ethyl alcohol and acetone.

In order to enable the Intoximeter 3000 to give a specific reading for ethyl alcohol, another device is necessary. Thus the Intoximeter 3000, in addition to its infrared analysis of breath based on the Beer-Lambert Law of Absorption, also contains a semi-conductor (a Taguci sensor) by which it is able to distinguish ethyl alcohol from

other substances which absorb infrared radiation in the area of
3.39 microns.[4]

4. All known elements generally fall into one of two categories,
insulator or conductor, depending upon their electrical
conductivity. Conductors (also known as metals) will permit
electricity to pass through them; insulators (non-metals) impede
this flow of electrons. This phenomenon occurs across a range of
temperatures. There are, however, two elements which are not so
readily classified. Silicon and germanium are unique among the
elements in that they are insulators at low temperatures and
conductors at high temperatures. This characteristic of "semi-
conductors" makes them useful in electrical devices in which a
variable rate of conductivity is required. The use of semi-
conductors prompted the demise of the vacuum tube as the essential component in such instruments. The semi-conductor itself,
has been succeeded in certain applications by the micro-chip, also
made of silicon, which can perform the same functions, at a faster
rate, while utilizing less space in instruments.

The Taguci sensor is a semi-conductor device the conductivity of
which is influenced by the ambient air in the sample chamber. The
conductivity of the semi-conductor varies when there is present in
that ambient air an oxidizible vapor such as ethyl alcohol or other
hydrocarbon. Programmed into the memory of the computer that is
mated to the Intoximeter 3000 are the specific conductivity readings (in amperes) of the sensor when ethyl alcohol is present in the
sample chamber at varying levels which correspond to the various
blood-alcohol levels. These conductivity readings are predetermined
empirically in the laboratory, and are specific for ethyl alcohol.
Every other substance that absorbs infrared radiation at a
wavelength of 3.39 microns produces a different current in the
semi-conductor. The computer incorporated into the device
compares the outputs from the infrared sensor (amount of infrared
energy absorbed) and the semi-conductor (amperes of electrical
current). If the semi-conductor reading does not correspond to that
stored in the computer's memory for the blood-alcohol level reported
by the infrared sensor, an interferent other than or in addition to
ethyl alcohol is present in the subject's breath. The computer
performs a calculation to determine the difference between the
reading for the blood-alcohol level reported by the infrared sensor
and the reading from the semi-conductor sensor, which difference
automatically reduces the infrared reading by a corresponding
amount. That adjusted amount is reported as the subject's blood-
alcohol level.[5]

5. The Intoximeter 3000 reports all non-ethyl alcohol interfering
substances found by the semi-conductor as "acetone", even though
there may theoretically be some other interferent present.
Acetone not only is the most common interfering substance found
in the human body that, like ethyl alcohol, absorbs infrared radiation at a wavelength of 3.39 microns, but is the only such interferent present in the human body (and mostly in diabetics and
persons on longstanding stringent diets) in sufficient quantity
and with sufficient vapor pressure so as to appear in the breath

and register on the Intoximeter 3000. In the vast multitude of cases, what is reported by the infrared sensor will be ethyl alcohol. * * *

Operation of the Intoximeter 3000 is relatively simple and requires minimal operator intervention compared with more common breath-testing devices.

Each test commences with a twenty minute waiting period during which the subject is observed to insure that he does not ingest any alcohol, regurgitate or vomit. The operator presses a "start" button and then follows the machine's commands to enter his name and identification number and the subject's name. Following the last entry, the machine automatically blanks and purges to remove any residual alcohol fumes and to take a baseline reading, which ought to read ".00." The machine then commands the subject to blow into the breath tube until the machine indicates that a sufficient sample has been entered. The Intoximeter then reports the subject's blood-alcohol content on its display and proceeds to purge and blank itself. The machine then automatically runs a test with a reference solution, the ethyl alcohol content of which has been previously cer-tified by the State Police Laboratory. Following the test with the reference sample, the machine again purges itself. The operator then presses the "print" key, whereupon the information previously entered and the results of the subject's test, the reference sample test and the blank tests, the latter two being control tests to assure that the machine is functioning properly, are printed along with the times that the tests took place. The operator thus is required merely to type certain minimal information on the machine's keyboard; he does not have to handle ampules of chemicals nor turn dials and levers as with more common breath testing devices.

The machine automatically safeguards against any contaminants in the room air and contains fail-safe devices to abort if there are room temperature or electrical or voltage problems, which rarely occur.

118 Misc. 2d at __-__, 461 N.Y.S.2d at 963–65.

§ 29:11   The simulator

10 NYCRR § 59.5(d) provides that a "simulator test" must be run in connection with every breath test:

The result of an analysis of a reference standard with an alcoholic content greater than or equal to 0.08 percent must agree with the reference standard value within the limits of plus or minus 0.01 percent weight per volume, or such limits as set by the commissioner. An analysis of the reference standard shall precede or follow the analysis of the breath of the subject in accordance with the test sequence established by the training agency. Readings for the reference standard, a blank and the subject's breath, shall be recorded.

The "reference standard" referred to in 10 NYCRR § 59.5(d) is commonly known as a "simulator solution." This is a solution that simulates a person with a known BAC (typically .08% or .10%), and is used as a means of ensuring that a breath test device is functioning properly.

The simulator solution is placed inside an enclosed jar that is partially filled with a mixture containing a known percentage of alcohol. Because the jar is a closed container, a certain amount of alcohol will rise into the air above the solution until equilibrium is reached. The higher the temperature of the solution, the more alcohol will rise into the air above it.

This gaseous vapor (which simulates the breath of a drunk person) is blown into the breath test machine via a connecting tube. When the solution is heated to 34° ± .2° Celsius (i.e., the temperature of the average person's breath), the amount of alcohol in the gaseous vapor in the jar will be the amount that the solution is certified to produce. Thus, a .10% simulator solution should produce a reading of .10% when run through a properly functioning breath test device. However, pursuant to 10 NYCRR § 59.5(d), a simulator reading of .09%, .10% or .11% would indicate that the machine is working properly. In other words, breath test machines are only required to be accurate to within .01%.

The Alcotest 9510 breath test device uses a gas reference standard rather than a traditional simulator solution.

In *People v. Dembeck*, 145 Misc. 2d 442, 546 N.Y.S.2d 936 (Suffolk Co. Dist. Ct. 1989), the defendant moved to suppress his breath test result because the simulator test run in conjunction with his breath test produced a reading of .111%—which was more than .01% higher than the solution's certified reading of .10%. The Court held as follows:

> In this case the reference standard value was 0.10 percent at 34° centigrade. Therefore, in order to fall within the above quoted regulation a test of this reference by the Intoxilizer must record a result of 0.09 to 0.11 percent. The test of the reference standard in this case shows a result of .111 percent. Defendant contends that since this value exceeds the upper limit of the regulation by .001 percent, the test is unreliable as a matter of law, and hence, is inadmissible. The court does not agree. In this regard the court notes that 10 NYCRR § 59.5(d) itself requires measurement only to the second decimal place. More importantly, 10 NYCRR § 59.5(e) specifically provides that results of breath tests are to be expressed only to the second decimal place, and that if a reading is given to the third decimal place, the third digit is to be ignored. Therefore, the calibration test in this case is properly expressed as 0.11 percent, and is within the tolerances set by the regulation.

145 Misc. 2d at __, 546 N.Y.S.2d at 937.

Chapter 30

Additional Chemical Test

Research References

Westlaw Databases

Drinking/Driving Litigation (2d ed.) (DRNKDRIVING)
Handling Drunk Driving Cases (2d ed.) (HDRUNKDR)

Treatises and Practice Aids

Nichols and Whited, Drinking/Driving Litigation: Criminal and Civil § 7:8 (2d ed.)
Fiandach, Handling Drunk Driving Cases § 9:8 (2d ed.)

KeyCite®: Cases and other legal materials listed in KeyCite Scope can be researched through the KeyCite service on Westlaw®. Use KeyCite to check citations for form, parallel references, prior and later history, and comprehensive citator information, including citations to other decisions and secondary materials.

---

§ 30:1 Defendant's right to additional chemical test

Research References

West's Key Number Digest, Automobiles ⚖️412, 415

VTL § 1194(2) sets forth the circumstances under which a police officer may request a person to submit to a chemical test for the purpose of determining the alcohol and/or drug content of the person's blood. By contrast, VTL § 1194(4)(b) (formerly VTL § 1194[8]) provides:

> (b) Right to additional test. The person tested shall be permitted to choose a physician to administer a chemical test in addition to the one administered at the direction of the police officer.

This right is statutory (*i.e.*, not constitutional) in nature. *People v. Finnegan*, 85 N.Y.2d 53, 59, 623 N.Y.S.2d 546, 549 (1995). *See also People v. Alvarez*, 70 N.Y.2d 375, 381, 521 N.Y.S.2d 212, 215

(1987); *People v. Cegelski*, 142 Misc. 2d 1023, ___, 539 N.Y.S.2d 639, 641 (Monroe Co. Ct. 1989).

§ 30:2 Scope of the right

Research References

West's Key Number Digest, Automobiles ☜415

In *People v. Finnegan*, 85 N.Y.2d 53, 58, 623 N.Y.S.2d 546, 548–49 (1995), the Court of Appeals ruled that:

> The simple, straightforward declaration of Vehicle and Traffic Law § 1194(4)(b) is that defendants are entitled to their own additional chemical test. The statute is starkly silent as to any implementary duties imposed on the law enforcement personnel as to notice or to direct assistance in obtaining an independent chemical test . . . The statutory right is the defendant's and so is the responsibility to take advantage of it.

> We hold, therefore, that law enforcement personnel are not required to arrange for an independent test or to transport defendant to a place or person where the test may be performed. Of course, the police should not impede arrested individuals from exerting or accomplishing their statutory prerogative. The authorities should even assist persons in custody with appropriate advice and communication means, e.g., a telephone call opportunity. On the other hand, we have settled the general question that the police have no affirmative duty to gather or help gather evidence for an accused.

(Citations omitted). *See also People v. Crandall*, 228 A.D.2d 794, ___, 644 N.Y.S.2d 817, 818 (3d Dep't 1996); *People v. Kirkland*, 157 Misc. 2d 38, ___, 595 N.Y.S.2d 905, 906–07 (Yates Co. Ct. 1993) ("police actions hindering or preventing an independent test may result in a due process violation"). *See generally People v. Miller*, 199 A.D.2d 692, ___, 605 N.Y.S.2d 160, 162–63 (3d Dep't 1993); *People v. Cegelski*, 142 Misc. 2d 1023, ___, 539 N.Y.S.2d 639, 640–41 (Monroe Co. Ct. 1989); *People v. Sauve*, 129 Misc. 2d 666, ___, 493 N.Y.S.2d 689, 691 (Greene Co. Ct. 1985); *People v. Batista*, 128 Misc. 2d 1054, ___, 491 N.Y.S.2d 966, 968 (N.Y. City Crim. Ct. 1985) ("Once the police had made the determination that the defendant would be held, they were obligated, in light of her demand, to assist the defendant in arranging for an independent blood alcohol examination"); *People v. Hoats*, 102 Misc. 2d 386, ___, 423 N.Y.S.2d 425, 426 (Monroe Co. Ct. 1979).

It appears that the police are not required to affirmatively advise the defendant of his/her right to an independent chemical test. *See, e.g., People v. Miller*, 21 A.D.3d 1146, ___, 800 N.Y.S.2d 782, 783 (3d Dep't 2005) ("the statute imposes no burden on the police to advise a defendant of this right"); *Hoats*, 102 Misc. 2d at ___, 423 N.Y.S.2d at 426 ("The police were not required to advise the defendant that he could have his own physician administer the test"); *People v. Wagner*, 127 Misc. 2d 581, __, 486 N.Y.S.2d 610, 611 (Ogden Just. Ct. 1985) (same). *See generally Finnegan*, 85 N.Y.2d at 57, 623 N.Y.S.2d at 548; *Crandall*, 228 A.D.2d at __, 644 N.Y.S.2d at 818.

In *People v. Casimiro*, 308 A.D.2d 456, __, 764 N.Y.S.2d 198, 199 (2d Dep't 2003), the Appellate Division, Second Department, held that "Vehicle and Traffic Law § 1194(4)(b) is not applicable where, as here, the defendant expressly and voluntarily consented to administration of the breathalyzer test and there was no claim or hint of coercion." *See also People v. Ward*, 307 N.Y. 73 (1954).

§ 30:3 Applicability of two-hour rule to additional chemical test

Research References

West's Key Number Digest, Automobiles ⊕415

The two-hour rule, *see* §§ 31:1 et seq., *infra*, does not apply to "the additional test which the driver must be permitted to have administered by a physician of his or her choosing under [VTL] section 1194(4)(b)." *People v. Atkins*, 85 N.Y.2d 1007, 1009, 630 N.Y.S.2d 965, 966 (1995). *See also People v. Smith*, 18 N.Y.3d 544, 548 n.1, 942 N.Y.S.2d 426, 428 n.1, 965 N.E.2d 928 (2012); *People v. Finnegan*, 85 N.Y.2d 53, 59, 623 N.Y.S.2d 546, 549 (1995); *People v. Robinson*, 82 A.D.3d 1269, __, 920 N.Y.S.2d 162, 163 (2d Dep't 2011); *People v. Ward*, 176 Misc. 2d 398, __, 673 N.Y.S.2d 297, 300 (Richmond Co. Sup. Ct. 1998); *People v. Kirkland*, 157 Misc. 2d 38, __, 595 N.Y.S.2d 905, 907 (Yates Co. Ct. 1993); *People v. Cegelski*, 142 Misc. 2d 1023, __, 539 N.Y.S.2d 639, 641 (Monroe Co. Ct. 1989); *People v. Sauve*, 129 Misc. 2d 666, __, 493 N.Y.S.2d 689, 691 (Greene Co. Ct. 1985).

§ 30:4 It is improper for prosecution to suggest that defendant could have obtained additional chemical test

Research References

West's Key Number Digest, Automobiles ⊕415

"[T]he prosecutor impermissibly shift[s] the burden of proof by suggesting that defendant could have the blood sample tested by her own expert." *People v. Dombrowski-Bove*, 300 A.D.2d 1122, __, 753 N.Y.S.2d 259, 261 (4th Dep't 2002). *See also People v. Hall*, 181 A.D.2d 1008, 581 N.Y.S.2d 951 (4th Dep't 1992) (same).

Chapter 31

Two-Hour Rule

Research References

Westlaw Databases
Handling a Criminal Case in New York (HCCNY)

Treatises and Practice Aids
Muldoon, Handling a Criminal Case in New York § 9:73

Law Reviews and Other Periodicals
McCormack and Stone, Clarifying the Admissibility of DWI Chemical Test Refusals in New York: The "Two-Hour Rule" Does Not Apply, 82 St. John's L. Rev. 675 (Spring, 2008)
Shields, Admissibility of DWI Chemical Test Results Obtained After the Two Hour Limit Has Expired, 70-OCT N.Y. St. B.J. 58 (October, 1998)

§ 31:1   In general

Research References

West's Key Number Digest, Automobiles ⊕422.1

"The 'two[-]hour rule' provides that a chemical test must generally be administered within two hours of either the time of arrest for a violation of VTL § 1192 or the time of a positive breath screening test, whichever is later." *People v. Morris*, 8 Misc. 3d 360, —, 793 N.Y.S.2d 754, 758 (N.Y. City Crim. Ct. 2005). Of course, there are exceptions to this general rule. In addition, the continued vitality of the two-hour rule is unclear in light of the Court of Appeals' decision in *People v. Atkins*, 85 N.Y.2d 1007, 630 N.Y.S.2d 965 (1995). *See* § 31:6, *infra*.

§ 31:2   Where does the two-hour rule come from?

Research References

West's Key Number Digest, Automobiles ⊕422.1

The two-hour rule stems from VTL § 1194(2)(a), which provides, in pertinent part:

> 2. Chemical tests. (a) When authorized. Any person who operates a motor vehicle in this state shall be deemed to have given consent to a chemical test of one or more of the following: breath, blood, urine, or saliva, for the purpose of determining the alcoholic and/or drug content of the blood *provided that* such test is administered by or at the direction of a police officer with respect to a chemical test of breath, urine or saliva or, with respect to a chemical test of blood, at the direction of a police officer:
>
> (1) having reasonable grounds to believe such person to have been operating in violation of any subdivision of [VTL § 1192] *and within two hours* after such person has been placed under arrest for any such violation; or . . .
>
> (2) *within two hours* after a breath test, as provided in [VTL § 1194(1)(b)], indicates that alcohol has been consumed by such person and in accordance with the rules and regulations established by the police force of which the officer is a member.

VTL § 1194(2)(a)(1), (2) (emphases added).

§ 31:3 The two-hour rule is an evidentiary rule

Research References

West's Key Number Digest, Automobiles ⟨⟩422.1

In *Matter of Viger v. Passidomo*, 65 N.Y.2d 705, 707, 492 N.Y.S.2d 2, 3 (1985), the Court of Appeals made clear that "[t]he two-hour time period set forth in Vehicle and Traffic Law § 1194(1) [currently VTL § 1194(2)(a)] is an evidentiary rule." *See also Matter of White v. Fisher*, 49 A.D.2d 450, __, 375 N.Y.S.2d 663, 664 (3d Dep't 1975); *People v. Morris*, 8 Misc. 3d 360, __, 793 N.Y.S.2d 754, 758 (N.Y. City Crim. Ct. 2005) (two-hour rule is both evidentiary and procedural).

§ 31:4 Chemical test administered exactly two hours after arrest is "within" two hours for purposes of two-hour rule

Research References

West's Key Number Digest, Automobiles ⟨⟩422.1

In *People v. Zawacki*, 244 A.D.2d 954, 665 N.Y.S.2d 172 (4th Dep't 1997), the Appellate Division, Fourth Department, held that a chemical test administered exactly two hours after arrest is "within" two hours for purposes of VTL § 1194(2)(a)(1).

§ 31:5 Two-hour window begins from later of time of arrest or time of positive breath screening test

Research References

West's Key Number Digest, Automobiles ⟨⟩422.1

In *People v. Zawacki*, 244 A.D.2d 954, 665 N.Y.S.2d 172 (4th Dep't 1997), the Appellate Division, Fourth Department, made clear that the two-hour window begins from either the time of arrest for a violation of VTL § 1192 or the time of a positive breath screening test, whichever is later.

§ 31:6 *People v. Atkins*

Research References

West's Key Number Digest, Automobiles ⟨⟩422.1

The continued vitality of the two-hour rule is unclear in light of *People v. Atkins*, 85 N.Y.2d 1007, 630 N.Y.S.2d 965 (1995). In *Atkins*, the Court of Appeals held that "the two-hour limitation contained in Vehicle and Traffic Law § 1194(2)(a) has no application here where . . . defendant expressly and voluntarily consented to administration of the blood test." 85 N.Y.2d at 1009, 630 N.Y.S.2d at 966. In so holding, the Court reasoned that:

Defendant's contention that the two-hour limitation in section 1194(2)(a) was intended by the Legislature to be an absolute rule of relevance, proscribing admission of the results of any chemical test administered after that period regardless of the nature of the driver's consent, is unpersuasive. This argument is completely undermined by the lack of a corresponding time limit for court-ordered chemical testing under section 1194(3) (*see, People v. McGrath*, 135 A.D.2d 60, 524 N.Y.S.2d 214, *affd. on opn below* 73 N.Y.2d 826, 537 N.Y.S.2d 480, 534 N.E.2d 318) or the additional test which the driver must be permitted to have administered by a physician of his or her choosing under section 1194(4)(b) (*see, People v. Finnegan*, 85 N.Y.2d 53, 59, 623 N.Y.S.2d 546, 647 N.E.2d 758).

85 N.Y.2d at 1009, 630 N.Y.S.2d at 966. *See also People v. Smith*, 18 N.Y.3d 544, 548 n.1, 942 N.Y.S.2d 426, 428 n.1, 965 N.E.2d 928 (2012).

It is noteworthy that (a) the defendant in *Atkins* "expressly and voluntarily" consented to the blood test, 85 N.Y.2d at 1009, 630 N.Y.S.2d at 966, (b) although the test in *Atkins* was not administered until two hours and 28 minutes after the defendant's arrest, the defendant consented to the administration of the test within two hours of his arrest, 85 N.Y.2d at 1008, 630 N.Y.S.2d at 966, and (c) the *Atkins* Court failed to reference the applicable Department of Health rules and regulations, which, at the time that Atkins was decided, clearly imposed a two-hour time limit on sample collection.

§ 31:7　Applying *Atkins*

Research References

West's Key Number Digest, Automobiles ☞422.1

In *People v. Zawacki*, 244 A.D.2d 954, __, 665 N.Y.S.2d 172, 173 (4th Dep't 1997), the Appellate Division, Fourth Department, citing *Atkins*, stated without explanation that "the Court of Appeals has held that the two-hour limit is inapplicable to chemical tests administered pursuant to defendant's actual consent." *See also People v. O'Brien*, 77 A.D.3d 1445, __, 908 N.Y.S.2d 787, 789 (4th Dep't 2010), leave to appeal denied, 15 N.Y.3d 923, 913 N.Y.S.2d 649, 939 N.E.2d 815 (2010); *People v. Marietta*, 61 A.D.3d 997, __, 879 N.Y.S.2d 476, 477 (2d Dep't 2009); *People v. Hoffman*, 283 A.D.2d 928, __, 725 N.Y.S.2d 494, 497 (4th Dep't 2001); *People v. Turner*, 234 A.D.2d 704, __, 651 N.Y.S.2d 655, 657 (3d Dep't 1996); *People v. Abel*, 166 A.D.2d 841, __, 563 N.Y.S.2d 531, 532 (3d Dep't 1990); *People v. Quezada*, __ Misc. 3d __, 876 N.Y.S.2d 600 (Bronx Co. Sup. Ct. 2009); *People v. D.R.*, 23 Misc. 3d 605, __, 872 N.Y.S.2d 911, 913–14 (Bronx Co. Sup. Ct. 2009); *People v. Ward*, 176 Misc. 2d 398, __, 673 N.Y.S.2d 297, 300–01 (Richmond Co. Sup. Ct. 1998). However, even if this is a correct statement of the holding in *Atkins*, the relevance and probative value of a chemical test administered more than two hours from the time of arrest is highly questionable.

Indeed, in *People v. Mertz*, 68 N.Y.2d 136, 146, 506 N.Y.S.2d 290, 295 (1986), the Court of Appeals made clear that "[w]hat the statute proscribes is operation of a motor vehicle '*while* [the operator] has .10 of one per centum or more by weight of alcohol in his blood.'" (Emphasis added). In this regard, "the BAC count shown *within two hours after arrest* is *strong but not conclusive* evidence of the BAC during operation." 68 N.Y.2d at 146, 506 N.Y.S.2d at 295 (emphases added). *See also* §§ 39:1 et seq., Extrapolation, *infra*.

Even if the two-hour rule does not apply to consented-to chemical tests, a test result is nonetheless inadmissible at trial without a proper foundation. *See* §§ 42:1 et seq., Breathalyzer Foundation, *infra*. In this regard, when a chemical test is administered more than two hours after arrest, a proper foundation would appear to require expert witness testimony demonstrating that the belated test result is indicative of the defendant's BAC at the time of operation. *See People v. Victory*, 166 Misc. 2d 549, __, 631 N.Y.S.2d 805, 806 (N.Y. City Crim. Ct. 1995). *See also Smith v. New York*, 191 Misc. 2d 553, __, 742 N.Y.S.2d 792, 797 (Ct. Cl. 2002) ("There has been ample scientific evidence offered to verify that the delay between the time of the arrest and the time a chemical test is given might significantly reduce the reliability of the evidence if that time period is too great").

In *Victory*, *supra*, Judge Joseph J. Maltese provides a virtual treatise on the two-hour rule as it existed prior to *Atkins*, and discusses the various problems associated with attempting to determine what a person's BAC was at the time of operation if a chemical test is not performed until long after operation has ceased. After thoroughly analyzing the law in this area, including *Atkins*, the Court held that in a VTL § 1192 case:

> [U]pon objection of the defense, the prosecution must establish, at a hearing by expert testimony, scientific evidence that a Blood Alcohol Content (BAC) test taken more than two hours after the arrest of the defendant is competent, reliable and probative of the fact that the defendant was impaired or intoxicated when he operated a motor vehicle before such results may be admitted as relevant evidence at the trial.

166 Misc. 2d at __, 631 N.Y.S.2d at 806. In so holding, the Court reasoned that:

> Notwithstanding [case law] which may obviate the issue of consent, BAC tests taken beyond two hours from arrest must still be demonstrated to be scientifically reliable and probative on the issue of intoxication in order to be admitted into evidence. It is inconceivable that the Court of Appeals through *Atkins* intends to com-

municate to the lower courts and the bar that BAC tests administered at any time are admissible in evidence without some limitation or inquiry into their probative value.

166 Misc. 2d at __, 631 N.Y.S.2d at 815.

In addition, the Court ruled that "the People must also establish by clear and convincing evidence that the defendant who consented to take the test more than two hours from arrest, did so in a voluntary manner." 166 Misc. 2d at __, 631 N.Y.S.2d at 815. *See also People v. Capraella*, 165 Misc. 2d 639, __, 629 N.Y.S.2d 965, 970 (N.Y. City Crim. Ct. 1995) ("I hold that to establish express and voluntary consent the burden is upon the prosecutor to establish consent by clear and positive evidence"). *Cf. Atkins*, 85 N.Y.2d at 1009 n.2, 630 N.Y.S.2d at 966 n.2 ("To the extent that defendant argues that his consent to the blood test was not voluntary, that issue was not raised as a basis for suppression before the trial court or otherwise preserved for our review as a matter of law").

In *Capraella*, the Court stated that "[i]t is unclear whether [*Atkins*] will be limited to the facts presented (consent to submit to the test within two hours of arrest-administration of the test after two hours of arrest)," 165 Misc. 2d at __, 629 N.Y.S.2d at 968, and commented that *Atkins* invites litigation in numerous other areas, such as:

a) With respect to [the] sufficiency of misdemeanor pleadings, must express consent be pleaded in a Vehicle and Traffic Law § 1192(2) count where [a] chemical test was administered beyond two hours of arrest?

b) With respect to the suspension of a defendant's license due to an excessive blood alcohol content pending prosecution (Vehicle and Traffic Law § 1193[2][e][7]), should the license be suspended where the chemical test was administered beyond two hours?

c) With respect to the statutory probative values assigned to certain blood alcohol content levels in Vehicle and Traffic Law § 1195, are these values still viable in situations where the chemical test was administered after two hours of the defendant's arrest?

d) With respect to evidence of a defendant's refusal to submit to a chemical test, will such evidence be admissible if the refusal occurs beyond two hours of a defendant's arrest?

e) With respect to the issue presented in this case, what standards should we, as trial level court[s], apply in determining whether an individual expressly and voluntarily consents to submit to a chemical test more than two hours from the point of arrest? 166 Misc. 2d at __, 629 N.Y.S.2d at 969 (citations omitted).

In addressing issue "e)" above, the Court concluded that:

Factors for the court's consideration in determining whether consent was present in relationship of the characteristics of the defendant and details of the interrogation, including the age and intelligence of the defendant, the administration of the *Miranda* warnings, the length of the detention, physical threats, abuse or isolation, reliance upon false promises and the manner itself in which the consent occurred, that is, a reluctant, limited consent or a self prompted spontaneous consent.

166 Misc. 2d at __, 629 N.Y.S.2d at 970.

In *People v. Morris*, 8 Misc. 3d 360, __-__, 793 N.Y.S.2d 754, 756–59 (N.Y. City Crim. Ct. 2005), Judge Matthew A. Sciarrino, Jr. stated, inter alia, that:

The two-hour rule was codified in VTL § 1194(2) and the New York State Department of Health Regulations (10 NYCRR 59.2[c][2]), in 1941 because "the human body rapidly metabolizes alcohol, the two-hour requirement was enacted to ensure that the results of the blood test constituted probative evidence of the defendant's blood alcohol level at the time of the operation of the vehicle." * * *

State legislatures and often courts make an assumption about BAC's that does not properly take the scientific information concerning alcohol absorption into account. Specifically, they presume that the defendant's BAC at the time of the test will be lower than his BAC at the time of the operation of the motor vehicle; this is not always true. * * *

Clearly, VTL § 1194 was not meant to protect incompetent police officers who dally in their effort to bring a defendant to the police station. Such protection would only serve to corrupt the results of a chemical test, and make them scientifically inaccurate. * * *

Waiver or consent will not vitiate the lack of reliability, relevance, and probativeness, and such areas may be challenged by defense counsel. It is only when the test is administered within two hours, does it get a presumption of relevance and reliability.

(Citation and footnote omitted).

In *People v. O'Brien*, 77 A.D.3d 1445, __, 908 N.Y.S.2d 787, 789 (4th Dep't 2010), the Appellate Division, Fourth Department, addressed a situation where a *Victory* hearing was held but the defendant was unhappy with the outcome:

Finally, defendant contends that the court erred in admitting in evidence the results of his blood test inasmuch as those results were unreliable. We reject that contention. Even assuming, arguendo, that the court was required to conduct a hearing pursuant to *People v. Victory* (166 Misc. 2d 549, 631 N.Y.S.2d 805) to determine the admissibility of the blood test results taken more than two hours after defendant's arrest, we conclude that the testimony of the People's expert, a forensic scientist, at that hearing established the reliability of the blood test results and the methods that she used to determine defendant's blood alcohol content (BAC) at the time of the accident. Defendant's contention that the expert made erroneous factual assumptions in estimating defendant's BAC at the time of the accident goes to the weight that the expert's testimony should be accorded, not to the admissibility of the blood test results.

In *People v. Rosa*, 112 A.D.3d 551, 977 N.Y.S.2d 250 (1st Dep't 2013), leave to appeal denied, 22 N.Y.3d 1202, 986 N.Y.S.2d 422, 9 N.E.3d 917 (2014), the Appellate Division, First Department, held that:

> The court properly denied defendant's request for a pretrial hearing to determine whether the test, administered more than two hours after the arrest, was sufficiently reliable to be admissible. Although there are trial court opinions to the contrary, we agree with the analysis set forth in *People v. D.R.*, 23 Misc. 3d 605, 872 N.Y.S.2d 911 [Sup. Ct. Bronx County 2009], which held that such a hearing is not required. While a defendant may challenge the reliability of the test at trial, we see no reason to conduct a pretrial hearing every time testing occurs more than two hours after arrest.

Id. at __, 977 N.Y.S.2d at 251 (citation omitted). *See also People v. Johnson*, 114 A.D.3d 534, __, 980 N.Y.S.2d 447, 448 (1st Dep't 2014), leave to appeal denied (N.Y. June 20, 2014).

§ 31:8   Chemical test administered more than two hours after arrest—Pretrial suppression hearing

Research References

West's Key Number Digest, Automobiles ⚍422.1

CPL § 710.20(5) authorizes a hearing with regard to and the suppression of the results of, "a chemical test of the defendant's blood administered in violation of the provisions of, [VTL § 1194(3)], [Navigation Law § 49-a(8)], [PRHPL § 25.24(7)], or any other applicable law." This section had long been interpreted as being applicable only to compulsory chemical tests, as the statutes enumerated in CPL § 710.20(5)—*i.e.*, VTL § 1194(3), Navigation Law § 49-a(8) and PRHPL § 25.24(7)—deal with the administration of compulsory chemical tests of a defendant's blood.

Indeed, this was the interpretation of CPL § 710.20(5) given by the Appellate Term in *People v. Ayala.* In *Ayala*, the trial court suppressed the results of a consented-to breath test due to the fact that the test was administered more than two hours after the defendant's arrest. The People appealed. The Appellate Term dismissed the People's appeal on the ground that an as-of-right appeal pursuant to CPL § 450.20(8) requires that the order suppressing evidence be entered pursuant to CPL § 710.20. Since *Ayala* involved a consented-to breath test, and thus the order suppressing the test result was not entered pursuant to VTL § 1194(3), Navigation Law § 49-a(8) or PRHPL § 25.24(7), the Appellate Term held that an appeal from the trial court's suppression order was not authorized.

The Court of Appeals reversed, holding that CPL § 710.20(5) "permits suppression not only of court-ordered chemical tests, but also tests administered pursuant to '*any other applicable law*.'" *People v. Ayala*, 89 N.Y.2d 874, 875, 653 N.Y.S.2d 92, 93 (1996) (emphasis added). In so holding, the Court made clear that the "any other applicable law" language in CPL § 710.20(5) encompasses consented-to chemical tests. Accordingly, the inclusion of consent tests within the purview of CPL § 710.20(5) renders these tests subject to pretrial motions to suppress and pretrial suppression hearings.

In *People v. Victory*, 166 Misc. 2d 549, ___, 631 N.Y.S.2d 805, 806 (N.Y. City Crim. Ct. 1995), the Court held that in a VTL § 1192 case:

> [U]pon objection of the defense, the prosecution must establish, *at a hearing* by expert testimony, scientific evidence that a Blood Alcohol Content (BAC) test taken more than two hours after the arrest of the defendant is competent, reliable and probative of the fact that the defendant was impaired or intoxicated when he operated a motor vehicle before such results may be admitted as relevant evidence at the trial.

(Emphasis added).

Two recent cases decided by the Bronx County Supreme Court reached differing conclusions as to the holding and rationale of *Victory*. In the first, *People v. Holbrook*, 20 Misc. 3d 920, 864 N.Y.S.2d 726 (Bronx Co. Sup. Ct. 2008), the Court quoted the above-quoted portion of *Victory*, and held that "[t]his Court agrees with this rationale. Until *Atkins* is clarified, the prosecution must demonstrate through expert testimony at a hearing, the scientific reliability and probative nature of test results obtained more than two hours after the arrest." 20 Misc. 3d at ___, 864 N.Y.S.2d at 730. When the People failed to put forth any such evidence at the *Victory* hearing ordered in *Holbrook*, the Court suppressed the defendant's breath test results. 20 Misc. 3d at ___, 864 N.Y.S.2d at 730.

By contrast, in *People v. D.R.*, 23 Misc. 3d 605, 872 N.Y.S.2d 911 (Bronx Co. Sup. Ct. 2009), the Court, after expressly disagreeing with the rationale of Victory, held that:

> [N]either *Atkins* nor any provision of VTL § 1194 supports the no-

tion that the prosecution must demonstrate either the reliability or the relevance of tests administered more than two hours after arrest.

When properly administered, the reliability of the breathalyzer test is not in question. The *Victory* court's concern with the use a jury may make of the results of a test voluntarily taken more than two hours after arrest is, of course, legitimate, but this issue goes to the weight rather than admissibility of such evidence. While one or both parties can, and in some cases, should call an expert to testify at trial concerning this issue, and, with or without expert testimony, can raise it through cross-examination and argue it to the jury, a pre-trial hearing is simply not mandated. For these reasons, I denied the defendant's motion for such a hearing.

23 Misc. 3d at __, 872 N.Y.S.2d at 916. *See also People v. Quezada*, 24 Misc. 3d 515, __, 876 N.Y.S.2d 600, 603 (Bronx Co. Sup. Ct. 2009) ("What evaporates at the end of two hours is only the implied statutory consent to the taking of the test, and there is nothing to suggest that the Breathalyzer test itself is unreliable merely because a two-hour time frame has elapsed. As to whether the blood-alcohol content in the defendant was measurably higher or lower at the time of arrest three hours earlier—the parties are free to submit evidence on and argue that question to the trier-of-fact at trial, along with the overall matter of the test's reliability").

This issue was likely put to rest by *People v. Rosa*, 112 A.D.3d 551, 977 N.Y.S.2d 250 (1st Dep't 2013), leave to appeal denied, 22 N.Y.3d 1202, 986 N.Y.S.2d 422, 9 N.E.3d 917 (2014). In *Rosa*, the Appellate Division, First Department, held that:

> The court properly denied defendant's request for a pretrial hearing to determine whether the test, administered more than two hours after the arrest, was sufficiently reliable to be admissible. Although there are trial court opinions to the contrary, we agree with the analysis set forth in *People v. D.R.,* 23 Misc. 3d 605, 872 N.Y.S.2d 911 [Sup. Ct. Bronx County 2009], which held that such a hearing is not required. While a defendant may challenge the reliability of the test at trial, we see no reason to conduct a pretrial hearing every time testing occurs more than two hours after arrest.

Id. at __, 977 N.Y.S.2d at 251 (citation omitted).

§ 31:9 Applicability of two-hour rule to compulsory chemical tests

Research References

West's Key Number Digest, Automobiles ⚷422.1

In *People v. Atkins,* 85 N.Y.2d 1007, 1009, 630 N.Y.S.2d 965, 966 (1995), the Court of Appeals stated that there is no two-hour "time limit for court-ordered chemical testing under [VTL] section 1194(3) (*see, People v. McGrath*, 135 A.D.2d 60, 524 N.Y.S.2d 214, *affd. on opn below* 73 N.Y.2d 826, 537 N.Y.S.2d 480, 534 N.E.2d 318)." *See also People v. Smith*, 18 N.Y.3d 544, 548 n.1, 942 N.Y.S.2d 426, 428 n.1, 965 N.E.2d 928 (2012); *People v. Robinson*, 82 A.D.3d 1269, __, 920 N.Y.S.2d 162, 163 (2d Dep't 2011); *People v. Demetsenare*, 243 A.D.2d 777, __, 663 N.Y.S.2d 299, 302 (3d Dep't 1997).

§ 31:10   Applicability of two-hour rule to chemical test refusals

Research References

West's Key Number Digest, Automobiles ☞422.1

In *People v. Brol*, 81 A.D.2d 739, __, 438 N.Y.S.2d 424, 424 (4th Dep't 1981), the Appellate Division, Fourth Department, held that if the defendant "was requested to take the [chemical] test after the two hours had expired, evidence of his refusal was incompetent and should not have been considered by the jury." *See also People v. Walsh*, 139 Misc. 2d 161, __, 527 N.Y.S.2d 349, 350 (Nassau Co. Dist. Ct. 1988).

By contrast, in *People v. Ward*, 176 Misc. 2d 398, __, 673 N.Y.S.2d 297, 300 (Richmond Co. Sup. Ct. 1998), the Court held that "considering the reasoning in *Brol, supra*, in conjunction with several subsequent decisions interpreting the scope of the two hour rule, it seems clear that today the rule has no application in a determination of the admissibility of evidence that a defendant refused a chemical test." *See also People v. Robinson*, 82 A.D.3d 1269, __, 920 N.Y.S.2d 162, 164 (2d Dep't 2011) ("Where, as here, the person is capable, but refuses to consent, evidence of that refusal, as governed by Vehicle and Traffic Law § 1194(2)(f), is admissible into evidence regardless of whether the refusal is made more than two hours after arrest"); *People v. Popko*, 33 Misc. 3d 277, __, 930 N.Y.S.2d 782, 787-88 (N.Y. City Crim. Ct. 2011); *People v. Rodriguez*, 26 Misc. 3d 238, __, 891 N.Y.S.2d 246, 248-49 (Bronx Co. Sup. Ct. 2009); *People v. Coludro*, 166 Misc. 2d 662, __, 634 N.Y.S.2d 964, 967–68 (N.Y. City Crim. Ct. 1995); *People v. Morales*, 161 Misc. 2d 128, __, 611 N.Y.S.2d 980, 984 (N.Y. City Crim. Ct. 1994).

In *People v. Morris*, 8 Misc. 3d 360, __, 793 N.Y.S.2d 754, 757–58 (N.Y. City Crim. Ct. 2005), the Court expressly disagreed with the above-quoted language in *Ward*, and held that the two-hour rule is still applicable to chemical test refusals. *See also* 8 Misc. 3d at __, 793 N.Y.S.2d at 758 ("the evidence of the refusal is suppressed based upon the tolling of the two-hour rule. Two-hours should mean two-hours, absent a knowing waiver and consent to take the test").

Regardless of the admissibility of such evidence at trial, the two-hour rule had always applied to DMV refusal hearings. In this regard, the standardized DMV Report of Refusal to Submit to Chemical Test form expressly stated that "[s]ection 1194 of the Vehicle and Traffic Law requires that the refusal must be within two hours of the arrest." This makes sense in that the "implied consent" provisions of VTL § 1194 only apply *provided that* the chemical test is administered within two hours of either the time of arrest for a violation of VTL § 1192 or the time of a positive breath screening test. *See* VTL § 1194(2)(a)(1), (2); § 31:2, *supra*. Since the civil consequences of a test refusal are imposed on a motorist solely as a penalty for revoking his or her implied consent, and are wholly unrelated to the issue of guilt or innocence, they should not be imposed when the requirements of VTL § 1194(2)(a) are not met.

Nonetheless, in 2012 DMV switched its position on this issue. In other words, DMV no longer applies the two-hour rule to chemical test refusal hearings. A copy of DMV Counsel's Office's letter in this regard is attached hereto as Appendix 68.

In *People v. Harvin*, 40 Misc. 3d 921, 928, 969 N.Y.S.2d 851, 856 (N.Y. City Crim. Ct. 2013), the Court summarized the evolution of the two-hour rule as applied to chemical test refusals, and concluded as follows:

> Jurisprudence like many things can be a continuous journey. The law is not fixed, and even the opinions of a judge can change over the years through discussions with colleagues and by hearing the arguments of advocates. Additionally, the courts that review our decisions, the "policy-making" courts, influence what the law is and what the law should be. Such an evolution has taken place in my decisions on the two-hour rule. While my personal belief may be that the two-hour rule is one of evidence, and that the Legislature designed it as such, clearly that is not a majority opinion, nor does it represent the current state of the law in New York. Likewise, it is clear that if our policy courts consider this rule to be no more than an implied consent rule, then a refusal after two hours should be admitted into evidence as long as it is knowing and persistent, and the People have met their burden as to that knowing and unequivocal refusal in this case. The Legislature, for its part, has had ample opportunity to clearly state a desire to return the two-hour rule to an evidentiary rule if it deemed the courts' positions to be incorrect.

(Citations omitted).

§ 31:11 Applicability of two-hour rule to independent chemical tests

Research References

West's Key Number Digest, Automobiles ⊙─422.1

The two-hour rule does not apply to "the additional test which the driver must be permitted to have administered by a physician of his or her choosing under [VTL] section 1194(4)(b)." *People v. Atkins*, 85 N.Y.2d 1007, 1009, 630 N.Y.S.2d 965, 966 (1995). *See also People v. Finnegan*, 85 N.Y.2d 53, 59, 623 N.Y.S.2d 546, 549 (1995); *People v. Robinson*, 82 A.D.3d 1269, __, 920 N.Y.S.2d 162, 163 (2d Dep't 2011).

§ 31:12 Applicability of two-hour rule to unconscious defendant

Research References

West's Key Number Digest, Automobiles ☞422.1

The two-hour rule clearly applies to "cases where the operator is incapable of giving consent, that is, in the so called 'implied consent' cases." *People v. Ward*, 176 Misc. 2d 398, __, 673 N.Y.S.2d 297, 301 (Richmond Co. Sup. Ct. 1998). *See also People v. Robinson*, 82 A.D.3d 1269, __, 920 N.Y.S.2d 162, 163 (2d Dep't 2011) ("Vehicle and Traffic Law § 1194(2)(a) contains a two-hour time limit within which a chemical test may be performed on a person who is incapable of consenting"); *People v. Mills*, 124 A.D.2d 600, __, 507 N.Y.S.2d 743, 744–45 (2d Dep't 1986); *People v. Victory*, 166 Misc. 2d 549, __, 631 N.Y.S.2d 805, 813–14 (N.Y. City Crim. Ct. 1995); *People v. Morales*, 161 Misc. 2d 128, __, 611 N.Y.S.2d 980, 982 (N.Y. City Crim. Ct. 1994); *People v. Ali*, 151 Misc. 2d 742, __, 573 N.Y.S.2d 575, 576–78 (N.Y. City Crim. Ct. 1991).

§ 31:13 Applicability of two-hour rule to civil cases

Research References

West's Key Number Digest, Automobiles ☞422.1

In *Smith v. New York*, 191 Misc. 2d 553, __, 742 N.Y.S.2d 792, 797 (Ct. Cl. 2002), the Court held that:

> [T]his Court is mindful that the Legislature adopted the two-hour rule to assist prosecutors in prosecuting drunk driving charges by eliminating the requirement of proving the scientific reliability of a BAC test in every prosecution. Thus, this statutorily created mandatory exclusionary rule is, by its terms, limited to criminal prosecutions of violations of this State's Vehicle and Traffic Law. This Court therefore, shall not strictly apply the two-hour exclusionary rule to the case at bar. Rather, the analysis in this civil lawsuit must turn to the issue of whether the chemical test obtained beyond two hours from arrest is scientifically reliable and probative to be admissible.

§ 31:14 What about the Department of Health rules and regulations?

The Department of Health rules and regulations used to

contain a two-hour rule that was separate and distinct from the
two-hour rule contained in VTL § 1194(2)(a). However, such
requirement was deleted when the rules and regulations were
amended in 2010.

Chapter 32

The Blood-Breath Conversion Ratio

Research References

Westlaw Databases

Drinking/Driving Litigation: Criminal and Civil (2d ed.)
    (DRNKDRIVING)
Handling Drunk Driving Cases (2d ed.) (HDRUNKDR)
Intoxication Test Evidence (2d ed.) (INTOX)

Treatises and Practice Aids

Nichols and Whited, Drinking/Driving Litigation: Criminal and Civil
    § 18:1 (2d ed.)
Fiandach, Handling Drunk Driving Cases §§ 13:4 to 13:6 (2d ed.)
Fitzgerald, Intoxication Test Evidence § 19:8 (2d ed.)

KeyCite®: Cases and other legal materials listed in KeyCite Scope can be
researched through the KeyCite service on Westlaw®. Use KeyCite to check
citations for form, parallel references, prior and later history, and comprehensive citator information, including citations to other decisions and secondary
materials.

---

§ 32:1   In general

Research References

West's Key Number Digest, Automobiles ☞422.1

In New York, the DWI statutes make it illegal for a person to
operate a motor vehicle with a proscribed *blood* alcohol concentration (BAC). However, in the vast majority of DWI cases it is the
defendant's *breath—not* his or her *blood*—that is tested to
determine the defendant's purported BAC. It is thus necessary
for a breath test instrument to "convert" a DWI suspect's *breath*
alcohol concentration into a BAC. This is accomplished using
what is commonly referred to as the "blood-breath conversion ratio" (a.k.a. the "blood-breath partition ratio").

"The validity of breath-analysis to determine blood-alcohol
content is based on the scientific principle known as Henry's Law
which states that at any given temperature, the ratio between

the concentration of alcohol in the blood and that in the alveolar air in the lungs is constant. The ratio has been found empirically to be 2100:1—*i.e.*, 2100 parts of deep lung air contain the same amount of alcohol as one part of blood." *People v. Jones*, 118 Misc. 2d 687, __ n.1, 461 N.Y.S.2d 962, 963 n.1 (Albany Co. Ct. 1983). In other words, breath test instruments operate on the "principle that at normal body temperature the concentration of alcohol in the blood circulating through the lungs is 2,100 times greater than in the air discharged from the lungs (4 Gray, Attorney's Textbook of Medicine, § 133.73[1])." *People v. Donaldson*, 36 A.D.2d 37, __, 319 N.Y.S.2d 172, 175 (4th Dep't 1971).

In this regard, breath test instruments are "programmed to convert breath to blood alcohol content by applying a uniform ratio of 2100:1 on the assumption that at normal body temperature the amount of alcohol in 2100 milliliters of breath equals the alcohol in one milliliter of blood." *People v. Nieves*, 143 Misc. 2d 734, __, 541 N.Y.S.2d 1008, 1009 (N.Y. City Crim. Ct. 1989). *See also People v. Singh*, 144 Misc. 2d 402, __, 542 N.Y.S.2d 1018, 1023 (N.Y. City Crim. Ct. 1989) ("when an individual supplies a breath sample for analysis, the breathalyzer automatically converts the figure for concentration of alcohol in the breath into a blood alcohol reading using a fixed 'conversion' ratio of 2100 to 1"); *People v. Brown*, 143 Misc. 2d 270, __, 540 N.Y.S.2d 650, 650–51 (N.Y. City Crim. Ct. 1989) ("The concentration of alcohol in blood is assumed to be 2100 times that in the breath. This calculation is based upon the 1972 National Safety Council's determination that the concentration of alcohol present in 2100 milliliters of lung air at 34° Centigrade will equal the concentration of alcohol present in one milliliter of blood").

Although New York cases addressing the blood-breath conversion ratio tend to deal with the ratio's applicability to Breathalyzer devices, this is solely because the Breathalyzer was the primary breath testing device in use at the time such cases were decided. To the authors' knowledge, *all* breath testing instruments utilize the same, fixed 2,100:1 blood-breath conversion ratio. *See, e.g., People v. Gallagher*, 133 Misc. 2d 717, __, 507 N.Y.S.2d 950, 951 (Suffolk Co. Dist. Ct. 1986) (Intoxilyzer 5000 utilizes 2,100:1 blood-breath conversion ratio); *People v. Flynn*, 129 Misc. 2d 176, __ n.2, 492 N.Y.S.2d 882, 884 n.2 (Queens Co. Sup. Ct. 1985) (Intoximeter 3000 utilizes 2,100:1 blood-breath conversion ratio); *People v. Jones*, 118 Misc. 2d 687, __ n.1, 461 N.Y.S.2d 962, 963 n.1 (Albany Co. Ct. 1983) (same); *People v. Drumm*, 122 Misc. 2d 1051, __, 472 N.Y.S.2d 989, 993 (Monroe Co. Ct. 1984) (Intoxilyzer 4011AS utilizes 2,100:1 blood-breath conversion ratio).

§ 32:2 The inherent flaw in the blood-breath conversion ratio

Research References

West's Key Number Digest, Automobiles ⚷422.1

It was originally believed that the blood-breath partition ratio of 2,100:1 was a fixed, constant ratio applicable to all people. *See, e.g., People v. Donaldson*, 36 A.D.2d 37, __, 319 N.Y.S.2d 172, 175 (4th Dep't 1971); *People v. Flynn*, 129 Misc. 2d 176, __ n.2, 492 N.Y.S.2d 882, 884 n.2 (Queens Co. Sup. Ct. 1985); *People v. Jones*, 118 Misc. 2d 687, __ n.1, 461 N.Y.S.2d 962, 963 n.1 (Albany Co. Ct. 1983).

However, in the late 1980s, a considerable amount of litigation focused on newly discovered evidence establishing both (a) that people do not all have the same blood-breath partition ratio, and (b) that a person's blood-breath partition ratio is not necessarily "fixed" or "constant." *See, e.g., People v. Singh*, 144 Misc. 2d 402, __-__, 542 N.Y.S.2d 1018, 1023–24 (N.Y. City Crim. Ct. 1989); *People v. Nieves*, 143 Misc. 2d 734, __-__, 541 N.Y.S.2d 1008, 1009–11 (N.Y. City Crim. Ct. 1989); *People v. Amores*, 143 Misc. 2d 527, __-__, 541 N.Y.S.2d 695, 696–97 (N.Y. City Crim. Ct. 1989); *People v. Brown*, 143 Misc. 2d 270, 540 N.Y.S.2d 650 (N.Y. City Crim. Ct. 1989). *See generally People v. Serrano*, 142 Misc. 2d 1087, __ n.2, 539 N.Y.S.2d 845, 846–47 n.2 (N.Y. City Crim. Ct. 1989).

In *Singh, supra*, the Court noted that:

As conceded by the People, however, it is also widely accepted among authorities in this field that the ratio of 2100 to 1 is a statistical "mean" and that the actual blood/breath conversion ratio applicable to the population at large, and to any one person, varies depending upon, among other things, the unique body chemistry of each individual.

144 Misc. 2d at __, 542 N.Y.S.2d at 1023. "For those individuals with lower than average ratios, their BAC will be overstated." *Amores*, 143 Misc. 2d at __, 541 N.Y.S.2d at 696.

More specifically:

Leading researchers have . . . learned that in fact partition ratios vary among individuals, that a single individual's ratio is also subject to change, and that the mean population ratio is about 2300:1. Factors which may alter one's ratio include body temperature, hematocrit (red blood cell concentration), state of alcohol absorption, and other conditions.

According to one expert witness, the ratio varies among individuals from 1100:1 to 3400:1. Another researcher has found ratios varying from 1100:1 to 3200:1. Dr. Kurt W. Dubowski, a noted authority, places ratio differences between 1555:1 and 3005:1. He concludes that the breathalyzer with its fixed ratio of 2100:1 understates the blood alcohol of 86% of the population and overstates it for 14% of those tested. Other experts assert that for 95% of the population the breathalyzer ratio of 2100:1 results in a blood alcohol reading that is either accurate or understated.

Nieves, 143 Misc. 2d at __-__, 541 N.Y.S.2d at 1009–10 (citations omitted).

§ 32:3   Accuracy of blood-breath conversion ratio goes to weight, rather than admissibility, of breath test result

Research References

West's Key Number Digest, Automobiles ☞422.1

Although the issue of the inherent flaw in the blood-breath conversion ratio is real and well recognized, *see* previous section, case law makes clear that the issue goes only to the weight to be accorded the defendant's breath test result, not its admissibility. *See People v. Singh*, 144 Misc. 2d 402, __, 542 N.Y.S.2d 1018, 1024 (N.Y. City Crim. Ct. 1989); *People v. Nieves*, 143 Misc. 2d 734, __, 541 N.Y.S.2d 1008, 1011 (N.Y. City Crim. Ct. 1989); *People v. Amores*, 143 Misc. 2d 527, __, 541 N.Y.S.2d 695, 697 (N.Y. City Crim. Ct. 1989); *People v. Brown*, 143 Misc. 2d 270, __, 540 N.Y.S.2d 650, 653 (N.Y. City Crim. Ct. 1989).

In *Nieves, supra*, the Court held that:

Any evidence in general or evidence as to a defendant's individual ratio that would challenge the accuracy of the conversion ratio in a particular case can be tested by the fact finder in the crucible of a trial. Although the reliability in general of the breathalyzer is no longer open to question, its accuracy in any particular case is always open to investigation at the trial (*People v. Alvarez*, 70 N.Y.2d 375, 521 N.Y.S.2d 212, 515 N.E.2d 898 [1987]; *People v. Mertz*, 68 N.Y.2d 136, 506 N.Y.S.2d 290, 497 N.E.2d 657 [1986]). * * *

The trier of fact should consider any relevant general evidence concerning the ratio, including varying ratios of the population, to determine reasonable doubt. Any specific evidence of the defendant's personal ratio would of course be relevant, but general evidence should not be precluded in the absence of such specific evidence. * * *

Like all matters of science, the breathalyzer is subject to miscalculations, therefore requiring openminded inquiry. In the 2nd century A.D., Ptolemy confidently announced that the Sun revolves around the Earth, which remained unquestioned by science until 1543 when Copernicus proved that in fact the Earth revolves around the

Sun. In 1952, seven leading experts agreed in a joint statement that: "The Alcometer, the Intoximeter and [the] Drunkometer . . . will give comparable and reliable results for estimating the concentration of alcohol in the blood." In 1972, several of the original signers adopted a new statement recognizing that all three named devices had been proved to be inaccurate and removed from use.

Because the breathalyzer relies on principles of alleged scientific constancy, all evidence indicating variations or exceptions to these principles should be scrutinized by the fact finder.

143 Misc. 2d at __, 541 N.Y.S.2d at 1011 (citation omitted).

By contrast, in *People v. Lent*, 29 Misc. 3d 14, __, 908 N.Y.S.2d 804, 805-06 (App. Term, 9th & 10th Jud. Dist. 2010), leave to appeal denied, 15 N.Y.3d 806, 908 N.Y.S.2d 166, 934 N.E.2d 900 (2010):

Defendant sought to introduce expert testimony as to the range of individual variation within the general population from the 2,100:1 "conversion" or "partition" ratio used in the Intoxilyzer 5000 EN to derive the concentration of alcohol in a person's blood from the quantity of alcohol vapor detected in a breath sample. Defendant did not challenge the instrument's reliability, but sought to lay the foundation for a jury argument that defendant's individual ratio might differ so significantly from the mean as to diminish the evidentiary weight to be accorded the test results. The District Court precluded the evidence, apparently on relevancy grounds.

On appeal, the Appellate Term affirmed, holding that "evidence of conversion ratio variability within the population should [not] be admissible without proof of defendant's own conversion ratio." 908 N.Y.S.2d at 806. In so holding, the Court cited five out-of-state cases for the proposition that "as a general rule, evidence of [conversion ratio] variability may not be introduced to challenge the reliability of instruments that determine blood alcohol levels from the analysis of breath samples." 908 N.Y.S.2d at 806. The five cases cited by the *Lent* Court in support of this proposition are *People v. McNeal*, 46 Cal. 4th 1183, 96 Cal. Rptr. 3d 261, 210 P.3d 420 (2009); *Guthrie v. Jones*, 202 Ariz. 273, 43 P.3d 601 (Ariz. Ct. App. 2002); *State v. Hanks*, 172 Vt. 93, 772 A.2d 1087 (2001); *Morris v. State, Dept. of Admin., Div. of Motor Vehicles*, 186 P.3d 575 (Alaska 2008), and *State v. Hardesty*, 136 Idaho 707, 39 P.3d 647 (Idaho App. 2002).

The problem is: none of these cases stand for the proposition for which the *Lent* Court cites them. In this regard, unlike New York—which is a *blood* alcohol concentration (BAC) State—all five of the States at issue in the out-of-state cases cited by *Lent* (*i.e.*, California, Arizona, Vermont, Alaska and Idaho) are *breath* alcohol concentration (BrAC) States. The *Hardesty* Court explained why this distinction is critical:

Prior to the adoption of so-called *per se* breath-alcohol statutes, Idaho's DUI statute and statutes of several other states made it illegal for a person to operate a motor vehicle only while having a *blood* alcohol concentration of a certain percent of alcohol, by weight, in the person's blood.

In these states, a person's *blood* alcohol concentration could generally be measured by blood, breath or urine. If measured by breath, it was necessary to convert the breath alcohol concentration to a blood alcohol concentration by utilizing a partition ratio in order to determine whether the person had violated the particular DUI statute. In every jurisdiction where breath testing was employed, the partition ratio was 2100:1—meaning that for every molecule of alcohol in the breath there was presumed to be 2,100 molecules of alcohol in the blood.[1] Evidence regarding the general reliability of breath testing devices and the variability of the standard partition ratio was admissible to challenge whether a defendant's blood alcohol concentration did in fact exceed the statutory limit.

In response to these challenges, several states, including Idaho, amended their DUI statutes to eliminate the need for conversion of a breath alcohol concentration to a blood alcohol concentration by statutorily defining driving under the influence in terms of the concentration of alcohol found in a person's *breath* when breath analysis is used. Idaho's statute was amended in 1987 and now reads:

> It is unlawful for any person who is under the influence of alcohol, drugs or any other intoxicating substances, or who has an alcohol concentration of 0.08, as defined in subsection (4) of this section, or more, as shown by analysis of his blood, urine, or breath, to drive or be in actual physical control of a motor vehicle within this state . . .

Thus, the legislature eliminated the language requiring an analysis of alcohol, by weight, in a person's blood. Driving under the influence is no longer statutorily defined solely in terms of blood alcohol concentration. Driving under the influence is now defined in terms of an alcohol concentration above the statutory limit of .08 percent as found in either a person's blood, breath, or urine. * * *

Under the language of Idaho's amended DUI statute, therefore, a breath alcohol concentration above the proscribed limit of .08 percent is a *per se* violation of the statute regardless of blood alcohol

---

[Section 32:3]

[1]Experts generally agree that the standard 2100:1 partition ratio varies from individual to individual and that an individual's partition ratio can even vary depending on the circumstances present at the time the breath test is administered.

content. . . . Accordingly, conversion from breath alcohol concentration to blood alcohol content is unnecessary, and a person's blood alcohol content is no longer of sole legal consequence. Hardesty's evidence regarding the variability of the standard partition ratio is thus irrelevant. Under I.R.E. 402, evidence that is not relevant is not admissible. Other courts interpreting DUI statutes that, like Idaho's, define driving under the influence in terms of a breath alcohol concentration in excess of the statutory limit have also held that evidence of the variability of the 2100:1 partition ratio is irrelevant and, therefore, inadmissible. * * *

Hardesty's proffered evidence of the variability of the standard 2100:1 partition ratio is irrelevant because a breath alcohol concentration above the prescribed limit of .08 percent is a per se violation of the statute regardless of blood alcohol content.

Hardesty, 136 Idaho at 708-09, 411, 39 P.3d at 648-49, 651 (citations omitted).

Notably, the *Hardesty* Court expressly distinguished several out-of-state conversion ratio cases cited by Hardesty—*including a New York case*—on the ground that the cases were from BAC States as opposed to per se BrAC States. *See id.* at 411 n.3, 39 P.3d at 651 n.3. In other words, the *Hardesty* Court recognized the distinction between BAC States and BrAC States.

In addition, three of the remaining out-of-state cases cited by the *Lent* Court expressly held that although conversion ratio evidence is no longer relevant to a per se BrAC charge, it *is* relevant where the prosecution relies on the breath test result in connection with a common law DUI charge. *See McNeal, supra; Guthrie, supra; Hanks, supra.* In other words, three of the five cases cited by the *Lent* Court for the proposition that "evidence of [conversion ratio] variability may not be introduced to challenge the reliability of instruments that determine blood alcohol levels from the analysis of breath samples" held just the opposite—and the remaining two cases expressly dealt with situations where the BrAC was not being used to determine BAC.

Furthermore, the *McNeal* Court also expressly held that:

Although the Court of Appeal distinguished between "general" and "personal" partition ratio evidence, concluding only the latter is potentially admissible, this distinction does not survive close scrutiny. Both types of evidence challenge the accuracy of a defendant's reported blood-alcohol level, and therefore both can be used to support an inference that, despite a high breath test result, the defendant was not under the influence. Although the inference is less direct when the evidence is not tied to the defendant, and concerns only variability of partition ratios in the population at large, indirectness alone is not a reason to exclude evidence that is logically relevant to a defense.

46 Cal.4th at 1200, 210 P.3d at 431. Thus, *McNeal*—which is

cited with approval by *Lent*, and which was decided in 2009 by California's highest Court—reached the exact opposite conclusion of *Lent*. In fact, the *McNeal* Court expressly held that an attempt to distinguish between "general" and "personal" partition ratio evidence "does not survive close scrutiny." *Id.* at 1200, 210 P.3d at 431.

Notably, the *McNeal* Court went through the history of how California became a BrAC State—including the fact that there were serious issues raised by attempts to preclude a conversion ratio defense in breath test cases prior to enactment of the per se BrAC statute. *See id.* at 1194, 210 P.3d at 426-27. *See also id.* at 1202, 210 P.3d at 432 ("In light of this decision, we need not consider whether a contrary interpretation of section 23610 would raise constitutional concerns").

McNeal also points out that since research has shown that an individual's conversion ratio is variable, *id.* at 1194, 210 P.3d at 426-27, proof of the defendant's individual conversion ratio may not satisfy the *Frye* test. *Id.* at 1202, 210 P.3d at 432. In other words, aside from the *Lent* Court's shifting of the burden of proof to the defendant to prove his or her own conversion ratio, such ratio may not be capable of being proven with any degree of accuracy.

For all of these reasons, it is the authors' position that *Lent* was incorrectly decided.

Chapter 33

Preservation of Breathalyzer Ampoules

Research References

Westlaw Databases

Handling Drunk Driving Cases (2d ed.) (HDRUNKDR)

Treatises and Practice Aids

Fiandach, Handling Drunk Driving Cases § 15:10 (2d ed.)

Law Reviews and Other Periodicals

Gerstenzang, The Breathalyzer, 488 Practising Law Institute Litigation and Administrative Practice Course Handbook Series 69 (December, 1993)

KeyCite®: Cases and other legal materials listed in KeyCite Scope can be researched through the KeyCite service on Westlaw®. Use KeyCite to check citations for form, parallel references, prior and later history, and comprehensive citator information, including citations to other decisions and secondary materials.

---

§ 33:1 Preservation of Breathalyzer ampoules not required

Research References

West's Key Number Digest, Automobiles ⬧424

Unlike newer, infrared breath testing instruments (such as the DataMaster, Intoxilyzer, Alcotest 7110 MK III, etc.), Breathalyzers utilize a chemical solution which comes in vacuum-sealed glass tubes. These tubes, together with the chemical solution contained therein, are commonly referred to as "ampoules." If the chemicals contained in the ampoule solution are not of the proper kind and mixed in the proper proportions, a Breathalyzer test result will not be accurate.

Although fairness would seem to dictate that the defense be provided, upon request, with a sample of the ampoule solution for independent testing, case law makes clear that no such right exists. *See, e.g., People v. Farrell*, 58 N.Y.2d 637, 458 N.Y.S.2d 514 (1982); *People v. DiLorenzo*, 134 Misc. 2d 1000, __, 513 N.Y.S.2d 938, 940 (Nassau Co. Ct. 1987); *People v. Torres*, 125 Misc. 2d 78, __, 478 N.Y.S.2d 771, 776 (N.Y. City Crim. Ct. 1984); *People v. Molina*, 121 Misc. 2d 483, 468 N.Y.S.2d 551 (N.Y. City

Crim. Ct. 1983), *rev'd on other grounds*, 128 Misc. 2d 638, 494 N.Y.S.2d 606 (App. Term, 1st Dep't 1985); *People v. Santiago*, 116 Misc. 2d 340, 455 N.Y.S.2d 511 (N.Y. Co. Sup. Ct. 1982); *People v. LePree*, 105 Misc. 2d 1066, 430 N.Y.S.2d 778 (Rochester City Ct. 1980). *Cf. People v. Richter*, 102 Misc. 2d 285, 423 N.Y.S.2d 610 (Nassau Co. Dist. Ct. 1979).

By contrast, the defendant does have "the option of examining another ampoule from the same batch along with the procedures required to authenticate the test results." *Farrell*, 58 N.Y.2d at 638, 458 N.Y.S.2d at 515. *See also DiLorenzo*, 134 Misc. 2d at __, 513 N.Y.S.2d at 940.

Chapter 34

Duty of Police to Conduct Intoxication-Related Tests and to Preserve Blood/Breath Samples

---

KeyCite®: Cases and other legal materials listed in KeyCite Scope can be researched through the KeyCite service on Westlaw®. Use KeyCite to check citations for form, parallel references, prior and later history, and comprehensive citator information, including citations to other decisions and secondary materials.

---

§ 34:1 In general

Research References

West's Key Number Digest, Automobiles ⬤—425

Absent bad faith, the police are under no constitutional obligation to conduct any particular test(s) to determine whether a DWI suspect is in fact intoxicated, or to preserve evidentiary material which, in theory, might be exculpatory. Nonetheless, if the defendant's blood is withdrawn for BAC or drug testing, the People are required to preserve a sample thereof for independent testing by the defense. By contrast, where a breath test is conducted, preservation of a sample of the defendant's breath for independent testing is not required.

§ 34:2 Duty of police to conduct intoxication-related tests and/or to preserve potentially exculpatory evidentiary material

Research References

West's Key Number Digest, Automobiles ☞425

In *Arizona v. Youngblood*, 488 U.S. 51, 58, 109 S.Ct. 333, 337 (1988), the Supreme Court held that "unless a criminal defendant can show bad faith on the part of the police, failure to preserve potentially useful evidence does not constitute a denial of due process of law." In so holding, the Court reasoned that:

> If the [lower] court meant . . . that the Due Process Clause is violated when the police fail to use a particular investigatory tool, we strongly disagree. *The situation here is no different than a prosecution for drunken driving that rests on police observation alone; the defendant is free to argue to the finder of fact that a breathalyzer test might have been exculpatory, but the police do not have a constitutional duty to perform any particular tests.*

488 U.S. at 58–59, 109 S.Ct. at 338 (emphasis added). *See also People v. Cruz*, 48 N.Y.2d 419, 424–25, 423 N.Y.S.2d 625, 627 (1979) ("whether the defendant is charged with driving while intoxicated or driving while impaired by alcohol, scientific evidence of blood alcohol content, although admissible, is not essential") (citation omitted).

In *People v. Winchell*, 250 A.D.2d 942, __, 673 N.Y.S.2d 474, 476 (3d Dep't 1998), "[d]efendant contend[ed] that police investigators were obligated to preserve evidence which might have been useful to his [intoxication] defense and that their failure to perform an alco-sensor, breathalyzer or blood sample test hindered such efforts, thereby denying him due process of law." In rejecting the defendant's claim, the Appellate Division, Third Department, found it to be:

> Critically important . . . that defendant was not arrested for any intoxication-related offense, thereby relieving any investigative obligation to scientifically determine his blood alcohol content. Under the requisite "bad faith" analysis, no denial of due process can be predicated upon a failure of police agencies to acquire evidence deemed unnecessary to their prosecution.

250 A.D.2d at __, 673 N.Y.S.2d at 476.

Similarly, "probable cause need not always be premised upon the performance of field sobriety tests or any specific number of such tests." *People v. Kowalski*, 291 A.D.2d 669, __, 738 N.Y.S.2d 427, 429 (3d Dep't 2002) (citations omitted). *See also People v. Wallgren*, 94 A.D.3d 1339, __, 943 N.Y.S.2d 639, 643 (3d Dep't 2012) (same); *People v. Herzog*, 75 Misc. 2d 631, __, 348 N.Y.S.2d

510, 513 (Nassau Co. Dist. Ct. 1973) ("To prove intoxication, the law does not require any particular test. Intoxication may be proved by opinion evidence, if believed and provided it is based upon such facts and observations of the defendant as to warrant the conclusion of the opinion").

§ 34:3 Preservation of defendant's blood sample for independent testing *is* required

Research References
West's Key Number Digest, Automobiles ⚖415, 425

CPL § 240.20(1)(f) provides that upon a demand to produce of a defendant, the People must disclose to the defendant, and make available for inspection and testing, any "property" obtained from the defendant. In this regard, CPL § 240.10(3) expressly provides that "blood samples" constitute "property." Thus, if the defendant's blood is withdrawn for chemical testing, the People are required to preserve a sample thereof and to make a portion of such sample available to the defendant for independent testing. *See People v. Karpeles*, 146 Misc. 2d 53, 549 N.Y.S.2d 903 (N.Y. City Crim. Ct. 1989); *People v. North*, 96 Misc. 2d 637, 409 N.Y.S.2d 482 (Amherst Just. Ct. 1978). *See generally People v. White*, 40 N.Y.2d 797, 390 N.Y.S.2d 405 (1976).

In *Karpeles*, the Court stated, inter alia, that:

> Since testimony of blood alcohol content is invariably dispositive in drunk driving cases, independent testing by a defense expert is imperative if the defense is to have a fair opportunity to confront the toxicologist and the findings . . . Finally, as a matter of public policy, it is fundamentally unfair to deny someone reasonable access to fluid specimens taken from one's own body, sought to be used by an adversary and likely to be outcome-determinative.

146 Misc. 2d at __, 549 N.Y.S.2d at 909.

The *inadvertent* failure of the People to preserve the defendant's blood sample for independent testing by the defense does not render the defendant's blood test results inadmissible at trial. *See People v. Briggs*, 81 A.D.2d 1017, __, 440 N.Y.S.2d 143, 144–45 (4th Dep't 1981); *People v. Swanda*, 87 A.D.2d 940, __, 451 N.Y.S.2d 240, 241 (3d Dep't 1982).

However, the trial court must impose a sanction on the People for such failure to preserve. *See People v. Scalzo*, 178 A.D.2d 444, __, 574 N.Y.S.2d 782, 784 (2d Dep't 1991) ("reversal is warranted in this case because of the trial court's failure to impose even the most minimal sanctions on the People for their failure to preserve the defendant's blood sample").

§ 34:4   Preservation of defendant's breath sample for independent testing is *not* required

Research References

West's Key Number Digest, Automobiles ☞415, 425

Both the United States Supreme Court and the New York State Court of Appeals have expressly held that where a breath alcohol test is utilized, preservation of a sample of the defendant's breath for independent testing is *not* required under either the federal or state Constitutions. *See, e.g.*, *California v. Trombetta*, 467 U.S. 479, 104 S.Ct. 2528 (1984); *People v. Alvarez*, 70 N.Y.2d 375, 521 N.Y.S.2d 212 (1987).

In *Trombetta*, the Supreme Court addressed the issue of "whether the Due Process Clause requires law enforcement agencies to preserve breath samples of suspected drunken drivers in order for the results of breath-analysis tests to be admissible in criminal prosecutions," 467 U.S. at 481, 104 S.Ct. at 2530, and concluded that "the Due Process Clause of the Fourteenth Amendment does not require that law enforcement agencies preserve breath samples in order to introduce the results of breath-analysis tests at trial." 467 U.S. at 491, 104 S.Ct. at 2535.

Notably, unlike in New York, DWI suspects in California have the right to choose the type of BAC test that they will submit to (*i.e.*, blood, breath, or urine). *See* 467 U.S. at 482 n.2, 104 S.Ct. at 2530 n.2. In addition, where the suspect chooses a breath test, the test results are inadmissible in court unless, among other things, two separate breath samples are tested and the results register within 0.02 of each other. *See* 467 U.S. at 481, 104 S.Ct. at 2530. *See generally People v. Shepherd*, 130 Misc. 2d 284, __, 496 N.Y.S.2d 205, 207 (Monroe Co. Ct. 1985) ("California's testing methods provide for a safeguard by requiring two samples and, in effect, two tests of a suspect's breath. Since New York has no such statutory or administrative requirement, a suspect is effectively powerless to conduct a cross-check of his own breath"), *rev'd on other grounds*, 68 N.Y.2d 841, 508 N.Y.S.2d 173 (1986).

In a footnote, the *Trombetta* Court stated that "State courts and legislatures, of course, remain free to adopt more rigorous safeguards governing the admissibility of scientific evidence than those imposed by the Federal Constitution." 467 U.S. at 491 n.12, 104 S.Ct. at 2535 n.12. The New York State Court of Appeals addressed this issue in *People v. Alvarez*, 70 N.Y.2d 375, 381, 521 N.Y.S.2d 212, 215 (1987), and held that "as a matter of State constitutional law the police are not required to obtain and preserve a second breath sample for later use by the accused."

In so holding, the Court reasoned that, although "there can be no doubt in New York that the fairness of a criminal proceeding is of particular State concern, and New York historically has provided various protections in this area above the Federal constitutional minimum," 70 N.Y.2d at 379, 521 N.Y.S.2d at 214, "[t]he Supreme Court's analysis and result in *Trombetta* . . . are consonant with New York State law and interests and, we believe, they are analytically correct and provide a fair and proper rule under our State Constitution." 70 N.Y.2d at 379–80, 521 N.Y.S.2d at 214. *See also People v. Merrick*, 188 A.D.2d 764, __, 591 N.Y.S.2d 564, 566–67 (3d Dep't 1992).

The *Alvarez* Court also noted, among other things, that the police are not required "to affirmatively gather evidence for the accused," 70 N.Y.2d at 381, 521 N.Y.S.2d at 215, and that "the Legislature has provided that a defendant has a statutory right to have a personal physician administer an additional chemical test." 70 N.Y.2d at 381, 521 N.Y.S.2d at 215. *See also* VTL § 1194(4)(b) (formerly VTL § 1194(8)); *People v. DiLorenzo*, 134 Misc. 2d 1000, __, 513 N.Y.S.2d 938, 939 (Nassau Co. Ct. 1987); §§ 30:1 et seq., *supra*.

§ 34:5 Failure to administer field sobriety tests to non-English-speaking DWI suspects

In *People v. Salazar*, 112 A.D.3d 5, __, 973 N.Y.S.2d 140, 141-42 (1st Dep't 2013), leave to appeal denied, 22 N.Y.3d 1090, 981 N.Y.S.2d 676, 4 N.E.3d 978 (2014), the Appellate Division, First Department, addressed the following issue: "Does the failure of the police to administer a physical coordination test to a non-English speaking defendant of Hispanic origin arrested for driving while intoxicated violate equal protection and due process, where such tests are routinely administered to English-speaking defendants?" In holding that the failure to administer field sobriety tests to non-English-speaking DWI suspects does not violate Equal Protection or Due Process, the Court noted that "a DWI suspect does not have a due process right to compel the police to administer a coordination test." *Id.* at __, 973 N.Y.S.2d at 146.

§ 34:6 Failure to photograph field sobriety tests

In *People v. Wallgren*, 94 A.D.3d 1339, __, 943 N.Y.S.2d 639, 643 (3d Dep't 2012), the Appellate Division, Third Department, held that:

> County Court found that an officer arbitrarily recorded only certain portions of the encounter with his personal Blackberry cellular device. The nefarious implications of this finding are not supported by the record. The officer testified that he had never previously recorded anything with his Blackberry and was unfamiliar with the process. He realized that the device had stopped recording and

thereafter reengaged it. He later learned that the device automatically stops after a certain time period. This uncontradicted testimony provided a rational explanation for why the recording—which is not required by law—is incomplete, and in no way renders the officer's testimony incredible.

Similarly, no adverse inference or conclusion should be drawn from the officers' choice to take only a few pictures. County Court faulted the officers for not photographing defendant performing the field sobriety tests, but such actions are generally not capable of being captured in still photographs. In any event, the police are not required to take photographs of anything in particular. The presence or absence of pictures may be weighed by the jury, but should not affect the ruling in this suppression motion.

Chapter 35

Radio Frequency Interference

§ 35:1   In general
§ 35:2   Judicial response

Research References

Westlaw Databases

Drinking/Driving Litigation: Criminal and Civil (2d ed.)
  (DRNKDRIVING)
Handling Drunk Driving Cases (2d ed.) (HDRUNKDR)

Treatises and Practice Aids

Nichols and Whited, Drinking/Driving Litigation: Criminal and Civil
  § 12:7 (2d ed.)
Fiandach, Handling Drunk Driving Cases § 14:1 (2d ed.)

KeyCite®: Cases and other legal materials listed in KeyCite Scope can be
researched through the KeyCite service on Westlaw®. Use KeyCite to check
citations for form, parallel references, prior and later history, and comprehensive citator information, including citations to other decisions and secondary
materials.

---

§ 35:1   In general

Research References

West's Key Number Digest, Automobiles ☞424

In 1982, it was discovered that radio frequency interference
(RFI), caused by radio wave or similar transmissions in the vicinity of breath testing instruments, can adversely and unpredictably affect a DWI suspect's breath test result. In September of
1982, Smith & Wesson disseminated a customer advisory both (a)
alerting users of all Smith & Wesson Breathalyzer models of this
issue, and (b) recommending that all evidential breath testing
instruments be tested for RFI. In this regard, the advisory set
forth guidelines for RFI testing. A copy of this document is attached as Appendix 34 [currently reserved]. In January of 1983,
Smith & Wesson prepared and disseminated a summary of the
results of its own RFI testing. A copy of this document is attached as Appendix 35 [currently reserved].

It has subsequently been established that RFI has the potential
to affect most, if not all, breath testing instruments. In an at-

tempt to "cure" this problem, many of the newer, infrared breath testing instruments claim to have built-in RFI detectors that will cause the machine to abort a test if RFI is detected.

§ 35:2 Judicial response

Research References

West's Key Number Digest, Automobiles ⊙—424

In the aftermath of the Smith & Wesson advisory, courts ordered pretrial suppression hearings on the issue of RFI. *See, e.g., People v. Hochheimer*, 119 Misc. 2d 344, 463 N.Y.S.2d 704 (Monroe Co. Sup. Ct. 1983); *People v. Tilley*, 120 Misc. 2d 1040, 466 N.Y.S.2d 983 (Erie Co. Ct. 1983). *See generally People v. Garneau*, 120 A.D.2d 112, __, 507 N.Y.S.2d 931, 933 (4th Dep't 1986) (recognizing existence of suppression hearing on issue of RFI where defendant alleges sufficient facts in support thereof).

Subsequently, however, both the United States Supreme Court and the New York State Court of Appeals have indicated that RFI is an issue to be explored during pretrial discovery and at trial. *See, e.g., California v. Trombetta*, 467 U.S. 479, 104 S.Ct. 2528 (1984); *People v. Alvarez*, 70 N.Y.2d 375, 521 N.Y.S.2d 212 (1987).

Specifically, in *Trombetta*, which involved Intoxilyzer testing devices, the Supreme Court stated that:

> [T]he parties have identified only two sources capable of interfering with test results: *radio waves* and chemicals that appear in the blood of those who are dieting. For defendants whose test results might have been affected by either of these factors, it remains possible to introduce at trial evidence demonstrating that the defendant was dieting at the time of the test *or that the test was conducted near a source of radio waves.*

467 U.S. at 490, 104 S.Ct. at 2534–35 (emphases added).

In *Alvarez*, which involved Breathalyzer Model 900A testing devices, the Court of Appeals, following *Trombetta*, made clear both (a) that "defendant may not be denied discovery which prevents him from challenging the reliability and accuracy of the machine," and (b) "that a defendant *at trial* can adequately explore malfunctions caused by faulty calibration, *radio wave interference*, [etc.] by examining the machine, reviewing calibration and similar records, and questioning the officer who administered the test." 70 N.Y.2d at 380, 521 N.Y.S.2d at 214 (emphases added). *See also People v. Merrick*, 188 A.D.2d 764, __, 591 N.Y.S.2d 564, 566–67 (3d Dep't 1992) (same). *See generally People v. Gower*, 42 N.Y.2d 117, 121, 397 N.Y.S.2d 368, 370 (1977) ("greater dependence can now properly be placed on according full opportunity, through pretrial discovery and other means, to test and challenge the probative worth of [Breathalyzer] evidence"); *People v. English*, 103 A.D.2d 979, ___, 480 N.Y.S.2d 56, 58 (3d Dep't 1984) (same).

In sum, although the issue of RFI is real and well recognized, case law makes clear that the issue goes only to the weight to be accorded the defendant's breath test result, not its admissibility.

Chapter 36 [Reserved]

Chapter 37

Effect of Chemical Test Result

KeyCite®: Cases and other legal materials listed in KeyCite Scope can be researched through the KeyCite service on Westlaw®. Use KeyCite to check citations for form, parallel references, prior and later history, and comprehensive citator information, including citations to other decisions and secondary materials.

---

§ 37:1 In general

Research References

West's Key Number Digest, Automobiles ⊸426

The admissibility and probative value of chemical test evidence has been the subject of voluminous litigation over the years. Although the legislature has provided certain guidance in this regard, *see* VTL § 1195, much of this area is still governed by common law decisions.

On July 1, 2003, New York became a "0.08" state. That is, the threshold BAC currently deemed to constitute legal intoxication was lowered from 0.10% to 0.08%. *See* VTL § 1192(2). In a conforming amendment, VTL § 1195(2) was amended to change the probative values to be accorded various BAC readings under 0.08%. Case law which had interpreted the former versions of VTL §§ 1192(2) and 1195(2) should thus be read with these changes in mind.

§ 37:2   Chemical test results only reported to second decimal place

Research References

West's Key Number Digest, Automobiles ☞426

VTL § 1194(4)(c) provides, in pertinent part:

(c) Rules and regulations. The department of health shall issue and file rules and regulations approving satisfactory techniques or methods of conducting chemical analyses of a person's blood, urine, breath or saliva and to ascertain the qualifications and competence of individuals to conduct and supervise chemical analyses of a person's blood, urine, breath or saliva.

The applicable Department of Health rules and regulations are found at 10 NYCRR Part 59. In this regard, 10 NYCRR § 59.5(e), which pertains to breath testing, expressly provides that "[r]esults of an analysis of breath for alcohol shall be expressed in terms of percent weight per volume, to the second decimal place as found; for example, 0.237 percent found shall be reported as 0.23 percent." Similarly, 10 NYCRR § 59.2(a), which pertains to blood and urine testing, provides that "[a]ll blood and urine alcohol determinations shall be made by quantitative methods and expressed in grams percent or as equivalent to grams of alcohol per 100 milliliters of whole blood to the second decimal place as found; for example, 0.137 percent found shall be reported as 0.13 percent."

Aside from the fact that these rules and regulations are expressly mandated by VTL § 1194(4)(c), the Second, Third and Fourth Departments of the Appellate Division have made clear that the legislature intended for the Department of Health to have "definitive authority" in this area. *See People v. Robinson*, 53 A.D.3d 63, __, 860 N.Y.S.2d 159, 164–65 (2d Dep't 2008), leave to appeal denied, 11 N.Y.3d 857, 872 N.Y.S.2d 80, 900 N.E.2d 563 (2008); *People v. Hampe*, 181 A.D.2d 238, __, 585 N.Y.S.2d 861, 863 (3d Dep't 1992); *People v. McDonough*, 132 A.D.2d 997, __, 518 N.Y.S.2d 524, 525 (4th Dep't 1987). *See also People v. Holmes*, 171 Misc. 2d 962, __, 656 N.Y.S.2d 130, 131 (Brighton Just. Ct. 1997) (same). *See generally People v. Boyst*, 177 A.D.2d 962, 577 N.Y.S.2d 1007 (4th Dep't 1991) (where procedure followed is authorized by 10 NYCRR Part 59, VTL §§ 1194(4)(c) and

1195(1) were not violated, and thus it was not error to admit defendant's blood test results into evidence).

In *People v. Yambo*, 190 Misc. 2d 110, __, 737 N.Y.S.2d 517, 520 (Suffolk Co. Dist. Ct. 2001), the court examined this issue, and held that "[t]his Court is compelled to abide by the rules and regulations of the Department of Health as, the Vehicle and Traffic Law defers to those rules and regulations in establishing the admissibility of breath test results. Wherefore, this court shall not consider evidence of the Breathalyzer reading to the third decimal." *See generally People v. MacDonald*, 89 N.Y.2d 908, 910, 653 N.Y.S.2d 267, 268 (1996) ("error, if any, in permitting the People's forensic scientist to report defendant's blood alcohol level beyond the second decimal point at .089 and .091% was harmless, in view of defendant's conviction for driving while ability impaired"); *People v. Dembeck*, 145 Misc. 2d 442, __, 546 N.Y.S.2d 936, 937 (Suffolk Co. Dist. Ct. 1989) ("10 NYCRR § 59.5(e) specifically provides that results of breath tests are to be expressed only to the second decimal place, and that if a reading is given to the third decimal place, the third digit is to be ignored").

§ 37:3 Probative value of chemical test result less than 0.08%

Research References

West's Key Number Digest, Automobiles ⊙426

VTL § 1195 provides, in pertinent part:

§ 1195. Chemical test evidence.

1. Admissibility. Upon the trial of any action or proceeding arising out of actions alleged to have been committed by any person arrested for a violation of any subdivision of [VTL § 1192], the court shall admit evidence of the amount of alcohol or drugs in the defendant's blood as shown by a test administered pursuant to the provisions of [VTL § 1194].

2. Probative value. The following effect shall be given to evidence of blood-alcohol content, as determined by such tests, of a person arrested for violation of [VTL § 1192]:

(a) Evidence that there was .05 of one per centum or less by weight of alcohol in such person's blood shall be prima facie evidence that the ability of such person to operate a motor vehicle was not impaired by the consumption of alcohol, and that such person was not in an intoxicated condition;

(b) Evidence that there was more than .05 of one per centum but less than .07 of one per centum by weight of alcohol in such person's blood [*i.e.*, .06%] shall be prima facie evidence that such person was not in an intoxicated condition, but such evidence shall be relevant evidence, but shall not be given prima facie effect, in determining whether the ability of such person to operate a motor vehicle was impaired by the consumption of alcohol; and

(c) Evidence that there was .07 of one per centum or more but less than .08 of one per centum by weight of alcohol in such person's blood [*i.e.*, .07%] shall be prima facie evidence that such person was not in an intoxicated condition, but such evidence shall be given prima facie effect in determining whether the ability of such person to operate a motor vehicle was impaired by the consumption of alcohol.

As VTL § 1195(2) makes clear, "[e]vidence that a defendant had less than [.08] of 1% of alcohol in his blood is prima facie evidence that he was not intoxicated." *People v. Cruz*, 48 N.Y.2d 419, 425, 423 N.Y.S.2d 625, 627 (1979). *Cruz* further makes clear that the mere act of "drinking and driving" is not illegal:

> That is not to say, of course, that every person who drinks before driving violates the law. On the contrary the Legislature recognized that the average person can consume a certain amount of alcohol without impairing his ability to operate a motor vehicle as he should. Otherwise the Legislature would not have provided that proof of .05 of 1% or less of blood alcohol content is prima facie evidence that the driver was not impaired or intoxicated (Vehicle and Traffic Law, § 1195, subd. 2, par. [a]) . . . And the Legislature also recognized that some individuals may be able to consume greater amounts of alcohol without being impaired, as would the average driver (Vehicle and Traffic Law, § 1195, subd. 2, par. [c]). Thus the impairment statute, by simply providing prima facie standards, takes into account the "subjective" tolerance of individuals in determining the ability to drive possessed by a defendant at the time of arrest.

48 N.Y.2d at 426, 423 N.Y.S.2d at 628. *See also People v. Hagmann*, 175 A.D.2d 502, __, 572 N.Y.S.2d 952, 954 (3d Dep't 1991); *People v. Koch*, 135 Misc. 2d 352, __, 515 N.Y.S.2d 405, 409 (Rochester City Ct. 1987).

In *People v. Yambo*, 190 Misc. 2d 110, 737 N.Y.S.2d 517 (Suffolk Co. Dist. Ct. 2001), the defendant's Breathalyzer test yielded a BAC of 0.076%. Thus, if considered to two decimal places, the defendant's BAC of .07% only constituted "relevant evidence" of impairment. *See* former VTL § 1195(2)(b); 10 NYCRR § 59.5(e). By contrast, if considered to three decimal places, the defendant's BAC of *more than* 0.07% (but less than .10%) constituted "*prima facie*" evidence of impairment. *See* former VTL § 1195(2)(c).

Correctly concluding that the Department of Health rules and regulations promulgated pursuant to VTL § 1194(4)(c) constitute binding authority on this issue, the court held that "[t]his court is compelled to abide by the rules and regulations of the Department of Health as, the Vehicle and Traffic Law defers to those rules and regulations in establishing the admissibility of breath test results. Wherefore this court shall not consider evidence of the Breathalyzer reading to the third decimal." 190 Misc. 2d at __, 737 N.Y.S.2d at 520.

In *People v. Peacock*, 193 Misc. 2d 672, __, 751 N.Y.S.2d 676, 677 (App. Term, 2d Dep't 2002), the Appellate Term reversed the defendant's conviction of misdemeanor DWAI, and ordered a new trial, where:

> Over defense counsel's objection, the police officer testified to an ultimate issue of fact that the .07 breathalyzer reading indicated that the defendant was impaired. The admission of such testimony was improper. [Former] Vehicle and Traffic Law § 1195(2)(b) expressly provides that a reading of .07 "shall not be given prima facie effect" in determining whether an individual is impaired. The statement, in our view, was not harmless and the remaining evidence was not overwhelming as the case would have otherwise hinged upon the credibility of the witnesses.

§ 37:4 Probative value of chemical test result of 0.08% or more

Research References

West's Key Number Digest, Automobiles ⬢426

While VTL § 1195 assigns probative values to BAC levels *less than* 0.08%, it does not define the probative value to be given to a test result at or above the "legal limit" of 0.08%. In this regard, the Court of Appeals has held that:

> [T]he BAC count shown within two hours after arrest is strong but not conclusive evidence of the BAC during operation . . . We conclude, therefore, that proof of a breathalyzer reading of [.08] or more within two hours after arrest establishes prima facie a violation of Vehicle and Traffic Law § 1192(2) which, together with evidence of one or more of defendant's deportment, speech, stability and the odor of his or her breath, is sufficient to sustain a conviction, absent evidence, expert or other and by whichever party produced, from which the trier of fact could conclude that defendant's BAC at the time of vehicle operation was less than [.08].

People v. Mertz, 68 N.Y.2d 136, 146, 506 N.Y.S.2d 290, 295 (1986). *See also People v. Alvarez*, 70 N.Y.2d 375, 380, 521 N.Y.S.2d 212, 214 (1987) ("in this State a positive breathalyzer test establishes only a prima facie case and is not per se evidence of guilt, thus allowing defendant to argue, for example, that his blood alcohol content was lower when he was driving than when the test was given"); *People v. Knapp*, 272 A.D.2d 637, __, 706 N.Y.S.2d 531, 533 (3d Dep't 2000); *People v. Amores*, 143 Misc. 2d 527, __, 541

N.Y.S.2d 695, 697 (N.Y. City Crim. Ct. 1989) ("proof of a breathalyzer reading of [.08]% or more alone is not enough to establish a prima facie violation of V.T.L. § 1192(2) but must be combined with other indicia of intoxication"); *People v. Brown*, 143 Misc. 2d 270, __, 540 N.Y.S.2d 650, 653 (N.Y. City Crim. Ct. 1989) ("a positive breathalyzer test establishes only a prima facie case and is not a per se evidence of guilt").

§ 37:5 Chemical test result alone insufficient to sustain conviction of violating VTL § 1192

Research References

West's Key Number Digest, Automobiles ⚖426

People v. Mertz, 68 N.Y.2d 136, 146, 506 N.Y.S.2d 290, 295 (1986), makes clear that a chemical test result, without more (such as "evidence of one or more of defendant's deportment, speech, stability and the odor of his or her breath"), is in and of itself insufficient to sustain a conviction of violating VTL § 1192(2). Similarly, where a defendant's chemical test result is at a level constituting "relevant evidence" of impairment (*i.e.*, 0.06%), such test result, without more, is insufficient to establish a prima facie case of DWAI. *See People v. Scallero*, 122 A.D.2d 350, __, 504 N.Y.S.2d 318, 320 (3d Dep't 1986).

In *People v. Koch*, 135 Misc. 2d 352, __, 515 N.Y.S.2d 405, 408 (Rochester City Ct. 1987), the court acquitted the defendant of DWAI, in violation of VTL § 1192(1), where the defendant's BAC was 0.09% but the court (as fact-finder) "rejects as ambiguous at best the other evidence presented by the People, and is left with only the test result."

By contrast, at least one court has held that a defendant can be found guilty of DWAI where she exhibited several indicia of alcohol impairment, even though her "operation of the vehicle during the period of observation by the police officer was not impaired in any way." *People v. Robbins*, 132 Misc. 2d 653, __, 504 N.Y.S.2d 1006, 1008 (Greenburgh Just. Ct. 1986).

§ 37:6 Defense must be allowed to argue that defendant's BAC was less than 0.08% at time of operation

Research References

West's Key Number Digest, Automobiles ⚖426

In *People v. Mertz*, 68 N.Y.2d 136, 139, 506 N.Y.S.2d 290, 291 (1986), the Court of Appeals held that:

A violation of Vehicle and Traffic Law § 1192(2) is not established unless the trier of fact finds that while operating a motor vehicle defendant had a blood alcohol content (BAC) of .[08] of 1% or more

. . . It is . . . error not to permit defendant's attorney to argue on the basis of evidence, whether through cross-examination of the People's witnesses or testimony of defendant's witnesses, expert or other, from which it could be found that defendant's BAC at the time of vehicle operation was less than .[08]%, that if the jury so found defendant was not guilty of violating the subdivision.

See also 68 N.Y.2d at 146 to 47, 506 N.Y.S.2d at 295 to 96 ("When . . . such evidence has been presented, defendant must be permitted to argue its significance to the jury. Because he was foreclosed from doing so and because the court's ruling during defendant's attorney's summation and its instructions at the close of the case were in conflict on this issue, there must be a reversal").

§ 37:7 Required contents of supporting deposition to common law DWI charge where defendant's chemical test result less than 0.08%

Research References

West's Key Number Digest, Automobiles ☞426

Occasionally, the prosecution will charge a defendant with common law DWI (*i.e.*, VTL § 1192[3]) despite the fact that the defendant submitted to a chemical test which produced a BAC reading of less than 0.08%. In such a case, the defendant is charged with driving while *intoxicated* despite the fact that the Legislature has determined that the defendant's BAC constitutes prima facie evidence that he or she was *not* intoxicated. *See* VTL § 1195(2).

Although such a charge is legally possible, *see, e.g., People v. Lawrence*, 53 A.D.2d 705, 384 N.Y.S.2d 37 (3d Dep't 1976), the accusatory instrument in such a situation must do more than follow the "check sheet" format of the standard DWI supporting deposition, as most of the factors on the standard form deposition (*i.e.*, odor of alcoholic beverage, glassy eyes, impaired speech, impaired motor coordination, admission of alcohol consumption, etc.), are consistent not only with intoxication, but also with impairment. *See, e.g., People v. Gingello*, 181 Misc. 2d 163, ―, 694 N.Y.S.2d 579, 582 (Rochester City Ct. 1999), (abrogated on other grounds by, People v. Blair 98 N.Y.2d 722, 749 N.Y.S.2d 809, 779 N.E.2d 748 (2002)).

Accordingly, to be sufficient, the supporting deposition to a common law DWI charge involving a BAC of less than 0.08% must allege *additional* factual allegations, above and beyond the boilerplate on the form, which overcome the statutory presumption that the defendant was *not* intoxicated. *See Gingello*, 181 Misc. 2d at ―, 694 N.Y.S.2d at 582; *People v. Coutard*, 115 Misc.

2d 630, __-__, 454 N.Y.S.2d 639, 643–45 (Nassau Co. Dist. Ct. 1982). *Cf. People v. Gristina*, 186 Misc. 2d 877, 721 N.Y.S.2d 491 (N.Y. City Crim. Ct. 2001).

In *Coutard*, the court held that "[i]n order to overcome the statutory presumption accorded the operator of a motor vehicle by VTL Section 1195, the arresting [officer] must submit a deposition of substantially greater proportion, depth and detail than submitted in [this] case." 115 Misc. 2d at __, 454 N.Y.S.2d at 644. In so holding, the court reasoned that "[i]t would appear to this Court that before a proper charge for the misdemeanor crime of Driving While Intoxicated can be sufficiently laid in [the] face of a blood alcohol content reading of less than .[08]%, a police officer must be able to provide something more than the usual supporting deposition." 186 Misc. 2d 877 at __, 454 N.Y.S.2d at 644–45.

People v. Blair, 98 N.Y.2d 722, 749 N.Y.S.2d 809 (2002), is not to the contrary. In *Blair*, the defendant was charged with violating VTL § 1192(3) despite the fact that, "[45] minutes after he was stopped for a traffic infraction, defendant took a breathalyzer test indicating that he had a .08% blood alcohol level." 98 N.Y.2d at 723, 749 N.Y.S.2d at 810. At the time *Blair* was decided, VTL § 1192(2) prohibited driving with a BAC of 0.10% or more. The Court of Appeals held that:

> The accusatory instrument's supporting documentation contains factual allegations sufficient to establish reasonable cause that defendant violated Vehicle and Traffic Law § 1192(3). Defendant drove without head or tail lights; upon stopping defendant's vehicle, the arresting officer observed defendant had glassy eyes and impaired speech and motor coordination, smelled of alcohol and failed four field sobriety tests, including a "Finger Count Test" in which he was unable to "count his fingers correctly or in order"; and defendant admitted that he drank five to six beers prior to driving and should not have been operating his vehicle. The People were thus entitled to an opportunity to rebut the section 1195(2)(c) presumption at trial.

98 N.Y.2d at 724, 749 N.Y.S.2d at 810. *See also People v. McConnell*, 11 Misc. 3d 57, __-__, 812 N.Y.S.2d 742, 744–45 (App. Term, 9th & 10th Jud. Dist. 2006).

§ 37:8 CJI pattern jury instructions do not sufficiently inform jury of weight to be accorded chemical test result of 0.08% or more

Research References
West's Key Number Digest, Automobiles ⊕426

To avoid the danger of impermissibly shifting the burden of proof to the defendant, "[i]n criminal cases in New York, presumptions are permissive, which means that the jury may, but need not, accept the inference supported by the presumption." Prince, Richardson on Evidence (11th Ed. 1995), at § 3-105. In this regard, "the jury must receive careful instruction on the use it may make of the specific 'presumption.'" Prince, Richardson on Evidence (11th Ed. 1995), at § 3-105.

People v. Mertz, 68 N.Y.2d 136, 506 N.Y.S.2d 290 (1986), makes clear that a chemical test result constitutes "strong but not conclusive evidence," 68 N.Y.2d at 146, 506 N.Y.S.2d at 295, and that "proof of a breathalyzer reading of .[08] or more within two hours after arrest establishes prima facie a violation of Vehicle and Traffic Law § 1192(2)." 68 N.Y.2d at 146, 506 N.Y.S.2d at 295. *Mertz* further states that:

> Presumptive evidence, is . . . like the prima facie evidence to which CPLR 4518(c) refers, evidence which *permits but does not require* the trier of fact to find in accordance with the "presumed" fact, even though no contradictory evidence has been presented. It is, in short, not a presumption which must be rebutted but rather an inference, like the inference of negligence denominated res ipsa loquitur.

68 N.Y.2d at 148, 506 N.Y.S.2d at 297 (emphasis added) (citation omitted).

However, the CJI pattern jury instructions for VTL § 1192(2), citing *Mertz*, merely incorporate the phrase "permits, but does not require," the inference that the defendant's BAC was 0.08 or more at the time of operation. *See* Criminal Jury Instructions New York, 2d Ed., Vol. 2, at VTL 1192–1011. In the absence of an explanation of the type set forth by the Court of Appeals in *Mertz*, the critical significance of the phrase "permits, but does not require," is likely to be lost on a lay jury. As such, the defense should object to this portion of the boilerplate CJI pattern jury instructions, and request that the court's charge, *at a minimum*, include the following language:

> A BREATH TEST RESULT OF .08 OR MORE AFTER ARREST IS STRONG, *BUT NOT CONCLUSIVE*, EVIDENCE OF THE DEFEN-DANT'S BAC DURING OPERATION. IN OTHER WORDS, THE BREATH TEST RESULT IS EVIDENCE WHICH *PERMITS* YOU TO FIND THAT THE DEFENDANT DROVE WITH A BAC OF .08 OR MORE, BUT *DOES NOT REQUIRE* SUCH A FINDING, EVEN IF YOU FIND THAT THE DEFENDANT HAS NOT PRESENTED EVIDENCE CONTRADICTING THE TEST RESULT. IN SHORT, THE TEST RESULT CREATES AN INFERENCE AS TO THE DEFENDANT'S BAC AT THE TIME OF OPERATION, BUT DOES *NOT* CREATE A PRESUMPTION WHICH MUST BE REBUTTED BY THE DEFENDANT.

In *People v. Peart*, 85 A.D.3d 466, ___, 925 N.Y.S.2d 35, 36-37 (1st Dep't 2011), leave to appeal denied, 17 N.Y.3d 861, 932

N.Y.S.2d 26, 956 N.E.2d 807 (2011), the Appellate Division, First Department, appeared to hold that the language in the CJI pattern jury instructions is sufficient.

§ 37:9   Reversal of VTL § 1192(2) conviction generally requires reversal of VTL § 1192(1)/(3) conviction(s)

Research References

West's Key Number Digest, Automobiles ⬥426

In *People v. Gower*, 42 N.Y.2d 117, 122, 397 N.Y.S.2d 368, 371 (1977), the Court of Appeals reversed the defendant's VTL § 1192(2) conviction, and also held that:

> It is not possible . . . to determine that the erroneous admission of the breathalyzer results did not also infect the convictions for violation of subdivisions 1 and 3 of section 1192.

> Accordingly, in each case the order of County Court . . . should be reversed, and the same remitted for a new trial.

Similarly, in *People v. English*, 103 A.D.2d 979, __, 480 N.Y.S.2d 56, 58 (3d Dep't 1984), the Appellate Division, Third Department, held that "[a] chemical test result is highly probative evidence and it is impossible to assess the effect of such evidence on the jury as opposed to the weight given to the other evidence. Therefore, the conviction on the [VTL § 1192(3)] count should also be reversed." (Citation omitted). *See also People v. Corley*, 124 A.D.2d 390, __, 507 N.Y.S.2d 491, 493 (3d Dep't 1986) (same); *People v. Griesbeck*, 17 A.D.3d 717, __, 793 N.Y.S.2d 227, 228 (3d Dep't 2005); *People v. Baker*, 51 A.D.3d 1047, __, 856 N.Y.S.2d 707, 709–10 (3d Dep't 2008); *People v. Borst*, 49 Misc. 3d 63, __, 20 N.Y.S.3d 838, 841 (App. Term, 9th & 10th Jud. Dist. 2015). *Cf. People v. Grune*, 12 A.D.3d 944, 785 N.Y.S.2d 178 (3d Dep't 2004).

§ 37:10   Applicability of VTL § 1195 to civil actions

Research References

West's Key Number Digest, Automobiles ⬥426

In *McCarthy v. Fernandez*, 156 A.D.2d 544, __, 549 N.Y.S.2d 51, 52 (2d Dep't 1989), the Appellate Division, Second Department, held that:

> [T]he trial court acted properly in declining to instruct the jurors as requested. Vehicle and Traffic Law § 1195 and the evidentiary presumptions set forth therein are expressly addressed to cases in which an operator of a vehicle is arrested and prosecuted for a violation of Vehicle and Traffic Law § 1192 (i.e., operation of a motor vehicle while under the influence of alcohol or drugs). No such

situation is present in this case. Moreover, the evidentiary presumptions contained in Vehicle and Traffic Law § 1195(2)(a-c) apply only to evidence of "blood-alcohol content" as determined by the testing of a person's breath, blood, urine or saliva pursuant to Vehicle and Traffic Law § 1194.

By contrast, in *Van Valkenburgh v. Koehler*, 164 A.D.2d 971, __, 559 N.Y.S.2d 766, 767 (4th Dep't 1990), the Appellate Division, Fourth Department, held that:

[T]he court erred in failing to charge Vehicle and Traffic Law § 1195, thereby failing to instruct the jury that the blood alcohol test result of .01 of one percent was prima facie proof that defendant Frederick G. Koehler's ability to drive was not impaired by alcohol and that he was not in an intoxicated condition. Having received evidence of the blood alcohol test result, the court should have instructed the jury with respect to evaluating its significance.

§ 37:11   Applicability of VTL § 1195 to defense expert opinion

In *People v. Fratangelo*, 23 N.Y.3d 506, 2014 WL 2515658 (2014), the Court of Appeals held that:

[I]n a prosecution for drunken driving, the opinion of a defense expert that the defendant's blood alcohol content (BAC) was below the statutory threshold is not "prima facie evidence" that the defendant was not intoxicated. A defendant is nevertheless entitled, upon request, to an instruction that if the jury finds that the BAC was as the expert testified, it may find that the defendant was not intoxicated.

In so holding, the Court reasoned that:

The decisive issue in this case is whether the defense expert's testimony was "[e]vidence" entitled to the "[p]robative value" specified by [VTL] § 1195(2). * * *

A "test administered pursuant to" [VTL] § 1194 is "a chemical test of . . . breath, blood, urine, or saliva." Section 1195(2) is expressly limited to evidence of BAC "as determined by such tests." Since the evidence of her BAC that defendant presented here was not determined by a chemical test but was contained in the opinion of a defense expert, that evidence did not have the "prima facie" effect specified by the statute and defendant was not entitled to the charge she sought.

Id. at __ (citation omitted).

Part IX

BLOOD TESTS

Chapter 38

Blood Tests

Research References

Westlaw Databases

Drinking/Driving Litigation (2d ed.) (DRNKDRIVING)
Handling Drunk Driving Cases (2d ed.) (HDRUNKDR)
Intoxication Test Evidence (2d ed.) (INTOX)

Treatises and Practice Aids

Nichols and Whited, Drinking/Driving Litigation: Criminal and Civil
   §§ 23:1, 23:5, 23:7 to 23:13, 23:17, 23:18, 23:26, 23:27 (2d ed.)
Fiandach, Handling Drunk Driving Cases §§ 12:3 to 12:15, 13:4 to 13:6,
   13:13, 13:19 (2d ed.)
Fitzgerald, Intoxication Test Evidence §§ 18:1, 18:3, 18:4, 18:7 to 18:10,
   18:12, 18:13 to 18:16, 19:1 to 19:7, 20:1 (2d ed.)

KeyCite®: Cases and other legal materials listed in KeyCite Scope can be researched through the KeyCite service on Westlaw®. Use KeyCite to check citations for form, parallel references, prior and later history, and comprehensive citator information, including citations to other decisions and secondary materials.

---

§ 38:1   In general

Research References

West's Key Number Digest, Automobiles ⬤—411

Blood tests are neither as accurate, nor as invulnerable, as is commonly believed. Since blood testing is far less common than breath testing in New York, there has been surprisingly little litigation with regard to the issues that affect the validity of blood testing.

Generally, we see blood tests in the context of prosecutions of vehicular crimes and DWI cases involving serious motor vehicle accidents. Few of these cases go to trial, and the blood test results are accepted at face value. Attorneys are justifiably impressed with the contrast between a police officer with possibly 40 hours of breath test training and the qualifications of a toxicologist or "forensic scientist." In addition, most attorneys are daunted by the prospect of confronting scientific evidence.

Ironically, it is this relative lack of litigation which makes blood testing vulnerable. Contrary to popular belief, the instrumentation is not exact, and results can vary depending upon the procedures followed by the individual laboratory/technician.

While an in-depth discussion of the methodology of blood testing is beyond the scope of this chapter, there is a large volume of literature dealing with intoxication test evidence. Two of the best, insofar as lawyers are concerned, are *Intoxication Test Evidence*, by Edward F. Fitzgerald, Esq. (West Group), and *Drunk Driving Defense*, by Lawrence Taylor, Esq. and Steven Oberman, Esq. (Aspen Law & Business).

We gratefully acknowledge the debt that we owe these three fine attorneys for the information that went into this chapter and for their permission to quote their work as extensively as we did. We would also like to express our appreciation to Michael Snure, Esq., for allowing us to requote him from Lawrence Taylor's book, and for providing additional assistance to us. Finally, our thanks to Fleming Whited, Esq., for his permission to quote from materials that he has prepared; and to Edward Fiandach, Esq., for his permission to quote from his *New York DWI Bulletin*.

§ 38:2 Challenging blood tests—Generally

Research References

West's Key Number Digest, Automobiles ☜411

While this chapter outlines a series of potential challenges that can be used to impeach a blood test result, the fact pattern of a particular case will determine the challenge(s) that would likely be most effective. As with breath tests, no one is likely to believe that blood tests as a whole are completely unreliable. Accordingly, the defense attorney's challenge is to cast doubt on the particular blood test result at issue. The sections that follow address some of the many potential challenges available in blood test cases.

§ 38:3 Who can withdraw the defendant's blood?

Research References

West's Key Number Digest, Automobiles ☜414

In a blood test case, VTL § 1194 places strict limits on who can withdraw the defendant's blood. Effective July 13, 2010, VTL § 1194(4)(a)(1) provides as follows:

4. Testing procedures. (a) Persons authorized to withdraw blood; immunity; testimony. (1) At the request of a police officer, the following persons may withdraw blood for the purpose of determining the alcoholic or drug content therein:

    (i)   a physician, a registered professional nurse, a regis-
tered physician assistant, a certified nurse practitioner, or an advanced emergency medical technician
as certified by the department of health; or

   (ii)   under the supervision and at the direction of a physician, registered physician assistant or certified nurse
practitioner acting within his or her lawful scope of
practice, or upon the express consent of the person
eighteen years of age or older from whom such blood
is to be withdrawn: a clinical laboratory technician or
clinical laboratory technologist licensed pursuant to
article one hundred sixty-five of the education law; a
phlebotomist; or a medical laboratory technician or
medical technologist employed by a clinical laboratory
approved under title five of article five of the public
health law. This limitation shall not apply to the taking of a urine, saliva or breath specimen.

See also Public Health Law § 3702(2). See generally VTL
§ 1194(4)(a)(5) ("The testimony of any person other than a physician, entitled to withdraw blood pursuant to subparagraph one of
this paragraph, in respect to any such withdrawal of blood made
by such person may be received in evidence with the same weight,
force and effect as if such withdrawal of blood were made by a
physician").

Pursuant to the current law, an advanced EMT can now
withdraw blood without being under the direction and supervision of a physician, a physician's assistant, or a certified nurse
practitioner. This has the practical effect of legislatively overruling cases such as *People v. Reynolds*, 307 A.D.2d 391, 762
N.Y.S.2d 683 (3d Dep't 2003), aff'g 193 Misc. 2d 697, 749 N.Y.S.2d
687 (Essex Co. Ct. 2002). In *Reynolds*, the Appellate Division,
Third Department, affirmed the suppression of the defendant's
blood test results on the ground that the defendant's blood was
withdrawn at the direction of a physician's assistant, *not* a physician—in violation of the "wholly unambiguous" language of VTL
§ 1194(4)(a)(1). In so holding, the Court commented that, to the
extent that the procedure utilized in withdrawing the defendant's
blood should be permissible, "the solution is not for this Court to
adopt a strained interpretation of the statute but, rather, for the
Legislature to adopt an appropriate amendment thereto." 762
N.Y.S.2d at 684.

Notably, both VTL § 1194(4)(a)(1) and Public Health Law
§ 3702(2) appear to contradict the Court of Appeals' pronouncement in *Matter of Abe A.*, 56 N.Y.2d 288, 297-98, 452 N.Y.S.2d 6,
11, 437 N.E.2d 265 (1982), that "the method by which the authorized intrusion is to be accomplished must be safe, reliable and

impose no more physical discomfort than is reasonably necessary. *When, as here, the body is to be invaded, the procedure should be carried out by a qualified physician in accordance with accepted medical standards.*" (Emphasis added) (citations omitted). *See generally Schmerber v. California*, 384 U.S. 757, 771-72, 86 S. Ct. 1826, 1836, 16 L. Ed. 2d 908 (1966).

Where the defendant's blood is withdrawn by a person who is not authorized to do so, the remedy is suppression. *See* cases cited in § 38:4, *infra.*

§ 38:4   Supervision of blood withdrawal

Research References

West's Key Number Digest, Automobiles ⚖414

Prior to recent amendments thereto, VTL § 1194(4)(a)(1) provided that unless the defendant's blood was withdrawn by a physician, a registered professional nurse or a registered physician's assistant, the other individuals authorized to withdraw the blood had to do so "under the supervision and at the direction of a physician." In *People v. Moser*, 70 N.Y.2d 476, 522 N.Y.S.2d 497 (1987) (per curiam) the Court of Appeals considered the issue of whether "a physician [must] be actually present, observing the procedure, when a laboratory technician draws a blood sample from a suspect for the purposes of conducting a test to determine its alcoholic or drug content." Concluding that the physician's personal presence was not required, the Court held that:

> Although the personal supervision of a physician is an important safeguard for the health of the suspects to be tested, it would be anomalous in light of the purposes of the amendment to require the physician to put his other duties aside to watch the technician perform the procedure. If that were the requirement, there would be no reason to allow the technician to take the sample in the first place.

> In our view, the concerns addressed by the supervision requirements are adequately served by the physician's authorization of the test, which presumably reflects his medical judgment that it will not put the patient at risk, and his presence to respond to inquiries and emergencies.

70 N.Y.2d at 478, 522 N.Y.S.2d at 498. *See also People v. Butcher*, 38 A.D.3d 942, 830 N.Y.S.2d 844 (3d Dep't 2007).

In *People v. Ebner*, 195 A.D.2d 1006, 600 N.Y.S.2d 569 (4th Dep't 1993), the Appellate Division, Fourth Department, reversed the defendant's DWI conviction on the ground that the procedure used to withdraw the defendant's blood did not comply with the "physician supervision requirement." In *Ebner*, a medical laboratory technician withdrew the defendant's blood pursuant to the authorization of a registered nurse who did not personally observe the taking of the sample. Holding that the test result should have been suppressed, the Court reasoned as follows:

> Although a physician need not be "personally present" when a medical laboratory technician draws blood, the evidence must show that a physician "directed and supervised all activities in the emergency room and that he authorized the taking of the sample." Here, the test was authorized by a registered nurse, who did not personally observe the taking of the sample. That procedure failed to safeguard the health of the patient, which is the purpose behind the supervision requirement. There was no showing that a physician had reached a "medical judgment" that drawing blood would not put defendant, who was seriously injured at risk or that a physician was present "to respond to inquiries and emergencies."

195 A.D.2d at __-__, 600 N.Y.S.2d at 570–71 (quoting *Moser*). *See also People v. Griesbeck*, 17 A.D.3d 717, __, 793 N.Y.S.2d 227, 228 (3d Dep't 2005) ("At trial, the People failed to establish that defendant's blood sample was taken in compliance with Vehicle and Traffic Law § 1194(4)(a)(1)(ii). Specifically, they failed to introduce evidence that the medical technologist who drew defendant's blood was authorized to do so by a physician. Thus, the results of this blood test were improperly admitted into evidence at trial.") (citations omitted); *People v. Reynolds*, 307 A.D.2d 391, 762 N.Y.S.2d 683 (3d Dep't 2003), *aff'g* 193 Misc. 2d 697, 749 N.Y.S.2d 687 (Essex Co. Ct. 2002) (County court's order suppressing defendant's blood test results upheld where defendant's blood was withdrawn at the direction of a physician's assistant, *not* a physician); *People v. Olmstead*, 233 A.D.2d 837, 649 N.Y.S.2d 624 (4th Dep't 1996) (DWI conviction reversed where medical laboratory technician withdrew defendant's blood under supervision of a registered nurse rather than a physician; court expressly rejected the argument that "because the nurse, who could have drawn the blood without the physician's direction, was present and watched the blood being drawn," there was "substantial compliance" with VTL § 1194(4)(a)); *People v. Gertz*, 189 Misc. 2d 315, __, 731 N.Y.S.2d 326, 327 (App. Term, 2d Dep't 2001) (VTL § 1192(2) conviction reversed where "the People did not establish that a physician directed the medical technologist to draw defendant's blood in the emergency room"); *People v. Pickard*, 180 Misc. 2d 942, 691 N.Y.S.2d 884 (Chautauqua Co. Sup. Ct. 1999) (DWI conviction reversed where People failed to prove that medical technologist, who drew defendant's blood, "acted 'under the supervision and at the direction of a physician'"). *See generally People v. Ellis*, 190 Misc. 2d 98, 737 N.Y.S.2d 232 (Cattaraugus Co. Ct. 2001), *aff'd*, 309 A.D.2d 1314, 765 N.Y.S.2d 313 (4th Dep't 2003); *People v. Miller*, 17 A.D.3d

708, 793 N.Y.S.2d 231 (3d Dep't 2005) (appeal held in abeyance and matter remitted for new suppression hearing to determine whether "nurse" who withdrew defendant's blood was "registered professional nurse" as required by VTL § 1194(4)(a)(1)).

In *Miller*, *supra*, the Appellate Division, Third Department, made clear that "Vehicle and Traffic Law § 1194(4)(a)(1) enumerates the persons who, at the request of a police officer, may draw blood from a suspect. If blood is not withdrawn in accordance with this statute, *even if defendant has consented to the withdrawal of his blood*, the results of the blood test must be suppressed." 17 A.D.3d at __, 793 N.Y.S.2d 232 (emphasis added).

In *People v. Steinhilber*, 48 A.D.3d 958, 852 N.Y.S.2d 437 (3d Dep't 2008), leave to appeal denied, 10 N.Y.3d 871, 860 N.Y.S.2d 497, 890 N.E.2d 260 (2008), the Appellate Division, Third Department, held that:

> Contrary to defendant's contention, the surgical resident who drew his blood was qualified to do so since he had received a medical degree in 2003, had passed all of his board examinations and was practicing medicine under the umbrella of an attending physician. He was therefore a "physician" generally (*see Indemini v. Beth Israel Med. Ctr.*, 4 N.Y.3d 63, 67, 790 N.Y.S.2d 625, 823 N.E.2d 1271 [2005] ["(a) medical resident is undoubtedly a physician"]; *compare* Education Law § 6522, *with* Education Law §§ 6525, 6526[1]) and one qualified to draw blood under Vehicle and Traffic Law § 1194(4)(a)(1) (*see People v. Stanton*, 33 Misc. 2d 921, 228 N.Y.S.2d 858 [1962]). Although this resident was not yet licensed at the time, the Legislature has long since dispensed with the requirement that a physician be licensed to qualify as a person authorized to draw blood under this statute (Vehicle and Traffic Law former § 71-a, as amended by L. 1954, ch. 320). Accordingly, we find no error in County Court's denial of defendant's motions to suppress the blood test results.

__ A.D.3d __ at __, 852 N.Y.S.2d at 439.

Notably, VTL § 1194(4)(a)(1)(ii) has been amended both: (a) to permit registered physician's assistants and certified nurse practitioners acting within their lawful scope of practice to supervise blood withdrawals; and (b) to permit blood withdrawals by various individuals without supervision "upon the express consent of the person eighteen years of age or older from whom such blood is to be withdrawn." *See also* previous section. As a result, it is now substantially more difficult to obtain suppression of a blood test result on the ground that the person who withdrew the blood was not properly supervised.

§ 38:5 Alcohol swabs

Research References
West's Key Number Digest, Automobiles ⊙━414

Obviously, if a DWI suspect's arm is sterilized with a swab containing alcohol, this raises the issue of whether the alcohol on the swab contaminated the blood sample taken from the defendant. In this regard, the Department of Health rules and regulations pertaining to blood testing expressly require that:

> If a blood specimen is to be collected for analysis, an aqueous solution of a nonvolatile antiseptic shall be used on the skin. Alcohol or phenol shall not be used as a skin antiseptic.

10 NYCRR § 59.2(d).

Where alcohol has been used as a skin antiseptic, DWI convictions resulting therefrom have been reversed. *See, e.g., People v. Maxwell*, 18 Misc. 2d 1004, 188 N.Y.S.2d 692 (Orange Co. Ct. 1959); *People v. Douglas*, 16 Misc. 2d 181, 183 N.Y.S.2d 945 (Jefferson Co. Ct. 1959); *People v. Ward*, 14 Misc. 2d 518, 178 N.Y.S.2d 708 (Westchester Co. Ct. 1958).

In *Maxwell*, the Court noted that:

> In this case, the minimum procedural safeguards set up by the statute were not complied with, and a procedure for sterilization was adopted which actually ran counter to the procedures established by the police force of which the officer was a member. Such a departure from the direction of the statute renders the result of the blood test thus taken inadmissible, as a matter of law. To hold otherwise would be to render meaningless the language of the statute. * * *

> If the defendant in this case was actually drunk, the failure to administer a proper test has defeated the purpose of the law. Unless convictions thus obtained are struck down, the mandate of the statute will not be carried out, and, what is of more serious consequence, our standard of fairness in the prosecution of criminal cases will gradually disintegrate.

18 Misc. 2d at __, 188 N.Y.S.2d at 694.

In *Douglas*, the Court found as follows:

> The testimony of the physician that extracted the blood from the defendant was to the effect that the defendant's arm was swabbed with alcohol, that the alcohol was cleaned off, but that it would be possible for some of the alcohol to remain on the defendant's arm, and to enter the needle used, and the vial or container in which the substance extracted was placed.

> The testimony of the toxicologist was to the effect that the use of alcohol before the taking of blood was not a recommended State Police procedure; and that a small amount of alcohol used to cleanse the skin, even a fraction of a drop, would "shoot the concentration way up"; or an infinitesimal amount could affect the tests; if such alcohol entered the needle and vial with the blood extracted from

the defendant at the time of the taking of the same; and that a small amount of alcohol taken from outside the blood, and becoming a part of the sample submitted to him, would show a higher concentration than was actually in the blood of the defendant.

The testimony of the physician and of the toxicologist read together causes the conclusion to be reached, that it was possible for some of the alcohol placed on the arm of the defendant to have become mixed with the blood withdrawn from the defendant's arm, and would have affected the result of the test.

16 Misc. 2d at ___, 183 N.Y.S.2d at 946.

In *Ward*, the Court held that:

It appears that at the time of the extraction of the blood specimen, the defendant's arm was swabbed with alcohol as an antiseptic. This procedure is not the practice recommended by the County Department of Laboratories and Research, and it was testified by the chemist who examined the specimen that it was "possible" that alcohol thus used as an antiseptic might have entered the blood withdrawn from the defendant's arm, and affected the result of the test. Sections 71-a and 70, subd. 5 of the Vehicle and Traffic Law must both be construed to permit the admissibility of a chemical test only when conducted in accordance with standard operating procedures. Otherwise, the scientific basis and value of the test are impaired and subject to reasonable doubt, especially where a presumption of intoxication may follow the result.

It was therefore error to admit the result of the test into evidence. This was not a technical error which can be disregarded, for the jury may well have been influenced by the apparent authority of the test.

14 Misc. 2d at ___, 178 N.Y.S.2d at 708-09.

§ 38:6   Plasma, serum, and whole blood

Research References

West's Key Number Digest, Automobiles ☞422.1

In evaluating any blood test result, it is important to know whether the test was performed on plasma, serum, or whole blood. "Human blood is composed of a fluid part (plasma) in which are suspended red and white corpuscles, platelets, and fat globules. If whole blood is centrifuged, the clear liquid which appears in the upper half of the centrifuge tube is serum. The heavier corpuscles sink to the bottom of the tube." *Commonwealth v. Michuck*, 454 Pa. Super. 594, 686 A.2d 403, 405 n.3 (Pa. Super. Ct. 1996).

The distinction between whole blood and blood serum is significant. "Serum is acquired after a whole blood sample is centrifuged," which separates the the blood cells and fibrin, the blood's clotting agent, from the plasma—the clear liquid is the blood serum. When blood serum is tested "the results will show a blood alcohol content which can range from between 10 to 20 percent higher than a test performed on whole blood." The reason for this is because the denser components of whole blood, the fibrin and corpuscles, have been separated and removed from the whole blood, leaving the less dense serum upon which the alcohol level test is performed. The value of the blood alcohol content in the serum is then determined. Because the serum is less dense than whole blood, the weight per volume of the alcohol in the serum will be greater than the weight per volume in the whole blood. Thus, an appropriate conversion factor is required to calculate the corresponding alcohol content in the original whole blood sample.

686 A.2d at 405-06 (citations and footnotes omitted). *See also Melton v. State*, 597 N.E.2d 359, 361 (Ind. App. 1992) ("Stated simply, blood plasma, obtained by centrifuging the blood, is whole blood minus the cells. Blood serum, on the other hand, is whole blood with the clotting elements removed. Plasma or serum samples produce 18% to 20% higher alcohol content values than do whole blood samples. A mathematical calculation is necessary to convert the result of a plasma test into a corresponding blood alcohol content result") (citations omitted).

The Department of Health has recognized the fact that when plasma or serum—as opposed to whole blood—is tested, a conversion factor must be used. In this regard, 10 NYCRR § 59.2(a)(2) provides that:

(a) All blood and urine alcohol determinations shall be made by quantitative methods and reported as whole blood alcohol concentration (BAC) to the second decimal place as found; for example, 0.137 percent found shall be reported as 0.13 percent weight per volume. If specimens other than whole blood are analyzed, the following conversion[] shall apply: * * *

(2) nine tenths of the determined concentration of alcohol in the serum or plasma shall be equivalent to the corresponding BAC.

See also People v. Boyst, 177 A.D.2d 962, 577 N.Y.S.2d 1007 (4th Dep't 1991).

In essence, the Department of Health provides for a 10% conversion factor. Unfortunately, however, physiology is nowhere near that precise. To obtain an accurate reflection of whole blood alcohol concentration through an analysis of plasma or serum, the percentage of the subject's whole blood that is comprised of cellular material as—opposed to plasma—must be known. This percentage is commonly referred to as a person's "hematocrit ratio," which is the ratio of plasma to cellular material. For example, the normal range for males is 42-52, with an average of 47. For females, the normal range is 37-47, with an average of 42. Edward F. Fitzgerald, *Intoxication Test Evidence,* § 18:13, at 18-15 (2d ed. 1995). *See also* Taylor & Oberman, *Drunk Driving Defense*, § 6.04[B], at 440 (6th ed. 2006) (same).

According to Fitzgerald, the blood alcohol concentration determined from plasma or serum will average about 16% higher, and may be 20% to 25% higher or more than whole blood. Consequently, a standard mathematical conversion or reduction to a whole blood value may not be accurate.

> The 16% conversion factor is a reasonable *mean* ratio for persons with a normal hematocrit when blood is drawn in a hospital setting as part of the medical treatment of accident victims (or in that setting at the request of police officers). A full hematological work-up will usually be performed, and one of the results obtained will be the hematocrit ratio of the subject. The higher the actual hematocrit ratio of a subject, the higher the suggested conversion factor which ought to be used to convert plasma to whole-blood alcohol values.

> The hematocrit ratio (*i.e.*, male average 47) describes the proportion of the blood which is made up of the cellular material. The whole blood of a male with a 47 would have approximately 53% plasma. The higher the hematocrit result, the more cellular material present and the less plasma. If a male has an actual hematocrit ratio of 60 instead of 47, we need to make a greater adjustment to convert a plasma alcohol to a whole-blood alcohol. In general, the higher the actual hematocrit value reported, the higher the conversion factor needed to convert the plasma alcohol to whole blood alcohol. If, conversely, prior to the drawing of the sample, the patient's hematocrit had been dropping due to his medical condition or circumstances (let's say to a 30, instead of 47), the plasma value obtained would be more nearly correct for that specimen (less cellular materials is "added back," in effect, when the whole blood value of that sample is considered), so less than the normal correction factor would be required to estimate the whole blood value of the sample delivered to the lab.

Fitzgerald, *Intoxication Test Evidence*, § 18:13, at 18-15-18-16 (footnote omitted).

It should be noted that most hospitals apparently test serum and not whole blood.

§ 38:7 Effect of intravenous transfusions (IVs)

Research References
West's Key Number Digest, Automobiles �®422.1

Contrary to popular belief, the introduction of IV fluids does not reduce the blood alcohol concentration. Rather, the increased water content draws alcohol from the muscle tissue and tends to increase the blood alcohol concentration. The court in *State of North Carolina v. Matthew Thomas Rich, (No. 96-CRS-80158, 80159)* in its decision filed September 19, 1997, at footnote 33, said, in response to the defendant's motion to suppress blood alcohol analysis:

> As such, IV fluids make blood more watery, and, as a result, increased water content of the blood will draw alcohol from the muscle tissue. Such will serve to only increase the alcohol level above and beyond the disparity inherently present. The plasma alcohol concentration (PAC) and whole blood alcohol concentration (BAC) ratio depends on the water content of the plasma and the whole blood. The amount of alcohol in plasma depends on the amount of water present in the blood component chosen for testing.

> Conversion of plasma alcohol test results to an equivalent BAC test result depends upon a conversion factor that varies for individuals and may fluctuate from individual to individual anywhere from 1.10/1 to 1.35/1 or a 10% to 35% variation. Put another way, the plasma blood alcohol content is invariably higher than the blood alcohol content and must be converted if it is to be meaningfully understood by a lay person.

DWI Journal: Law & Science, Vol. 13, No. 8, August 1998, at 8 (citing *North Carolina v. Rich*).

§ 38:8   The blood test kit

Research References

West's Key Number Digest, Automobiles ⚖414

In most cases, the blood sample will be drawn using a kit. One of the most commonly used by law enforcement is sold by NIK Public Safety, Inc., the successor company to Becton Dickinson. This kit purportedly contains:

1) two 10 milliliter vacutainer brand tubes, each containing 100 mg. sodium fluoride and 20 mg. potassium oxalate;
2) one disposable vacutainer holder;
3) one sterile and disposable vacutainer multiple sample needle—20 gauge x 1-1/2";
4) one antiseptic swab (non-alcoholic);
5) one warning label "Discard Needle After Use";
6) two evidence seals for blood vials;
7) two evidence seals for mailer box;
8) two integrity seals for plastic kit box;
9) one white absorbent pad;
10) one instruction sheet—blood collection system;
11) one instruction for police officer;
12) one blood collection report;

13) one consent form;

14) one biohazard label.

There are two sets of instructions in the kit. The first set of instructions are to the police officer who is requesting the blood withdrawal. The second set of instructions are for the person withdrawing the blood. A sample set of instructions to the police officer are as follows:

◆ **CAUTION:** The Needle and Holder should be discarded by the Medical Staff after use.

1. Ask the person withdrawing the blood to use the VACU-TAINER Tube Needle and Holder supplied with this kit. DO NOT REMOVE THE GRAY STOPPER FROM ANY VACUTAINER TUBE.

2. Ask the person withdrawing the blood to cleanse the withdrawal site with aqueous Betadine, Phisohex or other non-alcoholic solution.

3. For DWI Alcohol or DWAI Drugs, get the blood specimen within two hours AFTER the time of arrest.

4. Get approximately **20 ml (2 full gray stopper tubes)**.

5. INVERT tubes immediately after withdrawal of blood to ensure proper mixing with anticoagulant powder. INVERT slowly and completely at least 20 times. DO NOT SHAKE.

6. Write the full name of the person and your initials ON EACH BLOOD TUBE. Then completely fill in all six seals provided with the kit.

7. Seal each VACUTAINER Tube with a completed seal by pressing the center of the seal to the top of the rubber stopper, then firmly press the ends of the seal down on sides of VACUTAINER Tubes.

8. Place sealed tubes with blood specimen back into the original plastic box. The needle, holder and Betadine swab should have been discarded after use by the Medical Staff. Do not place these items back into the kit box.

9. Place the white absorbent pad back on top of sealed tubes with blood specimen. Snap the plastic box lid back on to kit box, tightly closing box. Seal both ends of the plastic kit box with the two red Integrity Seals.

10. Complete the LAB-t form. LIST suspected drugs (if any). PLACE the laboratory copy (original) and Results of Analysis Copy (yellow) around the kit and place back into the cardboard mailer box. Retain the pink Submitting Agency copy on file.

11. Close the cardboard mailer box, locking postal seal. Affix the two remaining seals onto box; one on each side of postal lock seal, taping box closed for security.

12. Deliver specimen to the Laboratory in person OR by Certified OR Registered Mail.

13. The Cardboard box is designed as a mailer. Print on the top of box the LABORATORY ADDRESS and your RETURN ADDRESS. DO NOT insert box into an envelope.

NIK Public Safety, Inc. New York State Police Instructions—Blood Specimen (2/97).

A sample set of instructions to the person withdrawing the blood are as follows:

◆ **IMPORTANT:** Use Only Vacutainer Tubes, Needle, Holder, Swab Pad and Seals provided in this kit.

1. Open needle cartridge. Twist to break the tamper-evident seal. Remove cap, exposing the back portion of the needle and threaded hub. Do not remove front needle cover.

2. Assemble needle to holder. Thread needle into holder until firmly seated.

3. Insert VACUTAINER tube into holder. Push straight onto needle, no further than the guideline on the holder.

4. Apply tourniquet, prepare venipuncture site using only the non-alcoholic antiseptic pad provided in this kit. Position the arm in a downward or lowered altitude.

5. Remove needle cover, perform venipuncture in the usual manner, keeping the tube in an upward position with the stopper uppermost.

6. Push VACUTAINER tube forward to end of holder, piercing the rubber stopper. When blood flows into tube, REMOVE TOURNIQUET AS SOON AS BLOOD BEGINS TO FILL TUBE. DURING THIS PROCEDURE, DO NOT ALLOW CONTENTS OF VACUTAINER TUBE TO CONTACT STOPPER. SPECIAL ATTENTION SHOULD BE GIVEN TO ARM POSITION, TUBE POSITION IN ORDER TO PREVENT POSSIBLE BACKFLOW FROM THE TUBE AND ITS ATTENDANT POSSIBILITY OF ADVERSE REACTION TO THE PATIENT.

7. When the tube fill is complete and blood ceases to flow, remove the tube from the holder. Insert the second VACUTAINER tube straight into the holder until blood flows.

8. When sampling is completed, immediately remove the needle/holder assembly with the last VACUTAINER, then remove the tube from the assembly. Apply and hold a dry sterile compress to the venipuncture site. Elevate the arm.

9. To assure proper mixing with anticoagulant powder, slowly invert the tubes at least five times immediately after blood collection. DO NOT SHAKE VIGOROUSLY!

If this kit is only a blood collection kit, instructions stop here. If kit is for the collection of blood and urine, read step 10.

10. Collect the urine sample in the provided urine collection tube.

NIK Public Safety, Inc. Instructions For Use—Vacutainer Brand Blood Collection System (4/96).

§ 38:9 Out-of-date blood test kit

Research References

West's Key Number Digest, Automobiles ⬤⟿424

It appears that the use of a blood test kit that has "expired" does not, without more, constitute a basis for the suppression of a blood test result. In *People v. Hagin*, 238 A.D.2d 714, 657 N.Y.S.2d 105 (3d Dep't 1997), the Appellate Division, Third Department, stated that it was:

> [U]nconvinced that use of the blood kit beyond its labeled expiration date or defendant's speculation that the blood sample may have been tampered with provide any basis for rejection of the test results. Notably, the People's toxicologist, Donald Loomis, was able to determine that the vials had not malfunctioned and that their seals remained intact because of the existence of a vacuum at the time of his testing. Under the circumstances, we conclude that Loomis' trial testimony provided "reasonable assurance of the identity and unchanged condition of the evidence."

238 A.D.2d at __, 657 N.Y.S.2d at 107 (citation omitted).

However, the above-quoted language does suggest that, in order for such results to be admissible, the People must lay an adequate foundation that the blood test kit was still properly functioning subsequent to its expiration date.

In an article called "How Blood Alcohol Can Be Created *After* Extraction," Dr. Stanley J. Broskey, a forensic chemist and toxicologist in Holland, Pennsylvania, indicates that vacutainers can begin to lose some of their internal vacuum while sitting on a shelf. When this occurs, room air containing microorganisms enters the collection containers. These microorganisms will ultimately cause fermentation which will convert blood sugar to blood alcohol. He suggests inquiring as to whether a bacteriological assay was done of the defendant's blood to rule out production of a "post-collection-forensic-artifact." How Blood Alcohol Can Be Created After Extraction by Stanley J. Broskey, Ph.D., *DWI Journal Law & Science*, Vol. 13, No. 8, at 6 (August 1998).

At a suppression hearing in *People v. Lanfear*, in which the defense had moved for the suppression of the blood test result, the People called Shayna Geller to testify as a representative of Becton Dickinson in regard to an out-of-date blood test kit that had been used to test the blood of the defendant. She indicated that she had worked for Becton Dickinson for 16 years and that she was the assistant manager for medical affairs. She indicated that the expiration date related to the vacuum.

Q   Okay. You testified that the expiration date has to do with the—what did you call it?

A   Vacuum.

Q   Vacuum. What kind of effect does it have on the vacuum?

A   The vacuum in the tube decreases over time from the day it's made, and so that over time the vacuum will be less than that which is stated on the tube.

Q   Okay. Which would cause what?

A   It changes what's called the additive to blood ratio.

Q   Okay. So that if I can understand this properly, it would cause less blood to go into the tube?

A   Correct.

Q   Okay. And that would cause what kind of results as far as the reading?

A   It doesn't change the reading.

Q   It doesn't change at all?

A   No.

> Transcript of *People of the State of New York v. William Lanfear* hearing held in the Lake George Town Court, Warren County, before the Hon. Robert Radloff on November 13, 1992, at pages 40–41.

This testimony is very interesting when juxtaposed with Mr. Snure's observations in regard to the importance of obtaining the proper volume of blood in the tube:

> The expiration dates on blood-alcohol collection kits generally refer to the date beyond which the vacuum will not be warranted by the manufacturer. The vacuum is important for two reasons. First, the vacuum is calculated by design to pull the proper volume of blood into the container when punctured by the vacutainer needle. Second, the vacuum, when properly sealed, maintains the sterile environment. If the vacuum has been compromised, then the proper volume of blood will not be drawn into the vial and the calculated amount of chemicals introduced into the vial as a preservative or anticoagulant will be out of specification with possible effect on the blood test results. Additionally, if the vacuum has been compromised, the tube is no longer sterile and bacteria may have entered the tube, which could cause spoiling or fermentation of the later collected blood alcohol sample.

Lawrence Taylor, Drunk Driving Defense, § 8.3, at S-8:148-149 (Release 3-9/98).

§ 38:10 Blood clotting

Research References

West's Key Number Digest, Automobiles ☞422.1

While clotting of the sample will not affect the amount of alcohol in the blood, it will concentrate the alcohol in the liquid portion of the sample, the part which is tested. Accordingly, this will result in an erroneously high test result. In order to prevent this, an anticoagulant is required to be present in the tube into which the blood is drawn. Part 59.2 of the New York State Department of Health Rules and Regulations, entitled "Methods and Procedures of Determining Blood and Urine Alcohol" requires that blood *shall* be drawn with a:

(i) sterile dry needle into a vacuum container containing a solid anticoagulant; or

(ii) sterile dry needle and syringe and deposited into a clean container containing a solid anticoagulant, which container shall then be capped or stoppered, and identified. 10 NYCRR § 59.2(c)(4)(i) and (ii).

In *Intoxication Test Evidence*, Edward Fitzgerald explained that an anticoagulant combines with calcium ions in the blood to prevent the formation of thrombin. He indicates that that chemical is usually sodium citrate or potassium oxalate. Edward F. Fitzgerald, *Intoxication Test Evidence*, § 19:17, at 19–22 (2d ed. 1995). The NIK Public Safety, Inc. kit indicates that their two 10 milliliter vacutainer tubes contain 20 mg. of potassium oxalate.

While it is clear that the anticoagulant is essential to prevent clotting and an erroneously high test result, there is a real issue as to whether the proper quantity and quality of the anticoagulant is present in the vacutainer. In *People v. Lanfear*, the Becton Dickinson (predecessor company to NIK Public Safety, Inc.) representative testified that her company did not manufacture the chemicals but purchased them from a vendor.

What tests are run to determine whether the anticoagulant contains the correct chemical composition? How do we know that the vacutainer contained the correct amount of anticoagulant? For that matter, how do we know that the particular vacutainer used in our case contained any anticoagulant?

Is it possible to test the blood sample to see if the anticoagulant or preservative is present? Mr. Snure indicates that this can be done after the blood sample has been drawn, but before analysis of the blood. The process is called ion chromatography. In a homicide or vehicular assault case, is it too much to ask that there be some check on the vacutainer to ensure the integrity of the sample? The blood test kits are presumably being purchased in bulk for law enforcement use. Is there any sampling done of "a scientifically acceptable random number for the presence of the preservative and anticoagulant in the proper amounts?" Edward F. Fitzgerald, *Intoxication Test Evidence* at S-8:152.

Generally, the laboratory that analyzes the blood does not test to determine the presence of either the preservative or the anticoagulant. What the prosecution may cite is the absence of any visible clotting and you should anticipate redirect examination that inquires into whether the chemist checked for evidence of clotting. In that regard, Lawrence Taylor, citing Michael J. Snure, Esq. advises that the blood can form microclots which cannot be seen without the aid of a microscope. He quotes Mr. Snure's materials as follows:

> Blood that has been microclotted will not represent a true value because, even with a small degree of clotting, the blood-alcohol concentration in the remaining serum is artificially high. Most analysts only do a naked-eye visual inspection of the blood sample and either do not recognize the phenomenon of microclotting or claim that, if present, it would make such a small difference that it is insignificant, or that the pipettes or syringes they use are so small in diameter that if the blood sample was clotted to any significant degree it would not be testable.

In *People v. McDonagh,* App. Term, 9th & 10th Jud. Dist. (April 3, 1992), the court ruled that a blood alcohol test was inadmissible for failure of proof in regard to the chemicals present in the tubes containing the defendant's blood:

> The only evidence adduced was in the form of testimony by the supervisor of the Suffolk County toxicological laboratory that he had received oral assurances from an unspecified employee of the manufacturer that the requisite chemicals were present in the proper amount. No certification to this effect was introduced into evidence, and the supervisor stated that random testing was not attempted. In view of this deficiency, the results of the test should have been excluded. In the absence of any indication that the requisite foundation cannot be provided, a new trial is required.

People v. McDonagh, Slip Op., at 2.

The same court reached a similar conclusion in *People v. Barker*, 2004 WL 2851451 (App. Term, 9th & 10th Jud. Dists. 2004):

> The results of the blood test, indicating that defendant's blood alcohol level was .24 percent, was improperly admitted at trial. The regulations of the New York State Health Department require that the blood be drawn into, or subsequently deposited into, a container which contains a solid anticoagulant (New York State Department of Health Regulations [10 NYCRR] § 59.2). The court's return fails to establish that the People introduced evidence indicating compli-

ance with said regulations. Due to the lack of competent evidence from which the trier of fact could conclude that the chemicals contained in the tubes into which defendant's blood was drawn were of the proper kind and amount and did not disturb the integrity of the blood sample, a new trial is warranted (*see People v. McDonagh*, NYLJ, Apr. 3, 1992 [App Term, 9th & 10th Jud Dists]).

People v. Boyst, 177 A.D.2d 962, 577 N.Y.S.2d 1007 (4th Dep't 1991), addressed the impact of the complete failure to use an anticoagulant, as opposed to the failure to prove that the chemicals in the vacutainers were of the proper kind and in the proper proportion:

> Defendant's sole contention is that the drawing and testing of a sample of her blood was not in compliance with 10 NYCRR 59.2(c)(4), and that the results were therefore improperly received into evidence pursuant to Vehicle and Traffic Law §§ 1194(4)(c) and 1195(1). Specifically, she contends that, because no anticoagulant was added to her blood sample, the subsequent clotting of that sample and testing of the serum (the unclotted liquid portion of the sample) rendered the results invalid and inadmissible. We disagree. The procedure that was followed is authorized by the regulations (*see*, 10 NYCRR 59.2[a][1]) and thus did not violate the statute. That regulation expressly permits the testing of blood serum, provided that, as was done here, a conversion factor of .9 is used to translate the serum alcohol reading into a blood alcohol reading. Consequently, the court did not err in admitting the test results.

177 A.D.2d at 962, 577 N.Y.S.2d at 1007.

§ 38:11 Fermentation of blood

Research References

West's Key Number Digest, Automobiles ⚬422.1

Blood samples have a tendency to ferment and produce alcohol over a period of time. Accordingly, samples that are preserved for testing for forensic purposes are supposed to contain a preservative to prevent fermentation. In *People v. Scalzi*, 102 A.D.2d 952, 477 N.Y.S.2d 808 (3d Dep't 1984), the court held that the fact that expert testimony established that the blood test tube contained preservatives was sufficient to allow its receipt in evidence. It should be noted that there was no evidence presented which gave rise to a belief that the condition of the blood might have changed:

> In view of the fact that there was no evidence presented giving rise to a reasonable belief that the condition of the blood may have changed, the trial court properly allowed its admission into evidence and left to the jury the weight it was to be accorded.

102 A.D.2d 952 at __, 477 N.Y.S.2d at 810 (citation omitted).

The effects of fermentation can be dramatic. For example, a blood sample with no alcohol can generate a reading of 0.25% or even higher as it decays. Refrigeration is not a substitute for sodium fluoride. While cold will slow the process, it will not prevent it. Lawrence Taylor, Drunk Driving Defense, § 8.3.2, at S-8:154.9 (Release 3-9/98).

As with the anticoagulant, the use of a preservative involves many issues. The quality and the quantity of the preservative should be subject to scrutiny. Michael Snure points out that the chemicals used in the blood test kit are purchased in bulk and mixed in bulk. These mixed chemicals are then dispensed into the test tube vials by weight. Snure indicates that while samples are taken from the bulk mixture to ensure the proper ratio, testing of samples from the vials themselves is not performed. Lawrence Taylor, Drunk Driving Defense, § 8.3, at S-8:147 (Release 3-9/98).

The most common preservative is sodium fluoride which is used in the NIK Public Safety, Inc. kit. The amount of sodium fluoride in the vacutainer can be a fruitful area of inquiry. Larry Taylor points out that most blood alcohol kits contain only 20 mg. of sodium fluoride. He cites A.W. Jones for the proposition that, in order to avoid fermentation, 100 mg. is required. Lawrence Taylor, Drunk Driving Defense, § 8.3.2, at S-8:154.9 (Release 3-9/98) at S-8:154.10.

It is interesting to note that the NIK Public Safety, Inc. kit reflects the presence of 100 mg. of sodium fluoride. While that quantity of sodium fluoride will preserve the blood sample, Larry cites A.W. Jones for the proposition that this preservative may actually increase the amount of alcohol in the sample when headspace gas chromatography is used to analyze it. Citing Dr. Jones' article entitled, "Salting-Out Effect of Sodium Fluoride and Its Influence on the Analysis of Ethanol by Headspace Gas Chromatography, 18 Journal of Analytical Toxicology 292 (September 1994), Larry says:

> Dr. Jones also found that using sodium fluoride to preserve a blood sample actually *increased* the amount of alcohol in the sample when gas chromatography was used to analyze it. According to his research, even 10 mg of sodium fluoride "increased the concentration of ethanol in the equilibrated (34 degrees centigrade) headspace by 8.9% when compared with heparinized blood" (i.e., a blood treated with an anticoagulant). This was due to a "salting-out" effect from the sodium fluoride.

Analysis of Ethanol by Headspace Gas Chromatography, 18 Journal of Analytical Toxicology 292 (September 1994), at 8:154. 10.

For demonstrative purposes, Larry suggests bringing in a fresh vial of blood and allowing the jury to compare it with the evidentiary sample. He indicates that the fresh blood will be bright red while the test sample will be nearly black. Analysis of Ethanol by Headspace Gas Chromatography, 18 Journal of Analytical Toxicology 292 (September 1994), at S-8:154.12.

§ 38:12 Mixing the chemicals in the blood

Research References

West's Key Number Digest, Automobiles ☞425

On a far more mundane level, the mixing of the chemicals with the blood is critical to the integrity of the analysis. The instructions call for the vacutainer to be inverted slowly five times by the person withdrawing the blood and 20 times by the police officer to ensure the proper mixing of the chemicals with the blood sample. It should be understood that blood drawn by nurses in hospitals for hospital analysis does not usually contain any such chemicals. These samples are analyzed immediately and neither require the chemicals, nor the mixing.

In speaking to physicians familiar with emergency room procedures, one of the authors was greeted with laughter and incredulity at the thought of emergency room personnel taking the time to follow this procedure. Larry Taylor cites *State v. Schwalk*, 430 N.W.2d 317 (N.D. 1988), which "reversed a DUI conviction where a foundation had not been laid showing that the collecting officer mixed the blood and chemicals. The court refused to presume "compliance with step four, which requires that immediately upon placing the blood in the glass vial, it must be inverted several times to dissolve the chemicals contained in the vial." Lawrence Taylor, Drunk Driving Defense, § 8.3.2, at S-8:154.10-11 (Release 3-9/98).

§ 38:13 Maintenance of the blood test kit

Research References

West's Key Number Digest, Automobiles ☞414

In addition to attacking the integrity of the components of the blood test kit which are ostensibly there to protect a defendant from an erroneously high test result, Mr. Snure suggests inquiring as to where the kit had been and how it had been maintained prior to the blood draw:

> In conducting discovery, you should learn where the blood kit was kept prior to its being employed in the collection of the blood sample from your client. The most common response is that the kit has been in the trunk of a patrol car for many months. Although the chemicals contained within the vials are relatively inert and are

probably not subject to decomposition or degradation as a result of high temperatures, most juries would view that as an unsatisfactory storage condition for the blood collection kit.

Lawrence Taylor, Drunk Driving Defense, at S-8:150.

§ 38:14   Chain of custody

Research References

West's Key Number Digest, Automobiles ⟳425

The prosecutor must demonstrate a proper chain of custody from the time the blood was drawn until the time that the blood was tested. The chain of custody protects the defendant from the possibility of contamination which may result in an inaccurate blood alcohol reading. This chain should establish who handles the blood sample and for what purpose.

While the People have the burden of establishing that "fungible evidence," such as blood samples, is the identical evidence extracted from the defendant, the failure to establish a chain of custody is excusable where the circumstances reasonably establish the identity and unchanged condition of the evidence in question. *People v. Arthur*, 99 A.D.2d 595, 471 N.Y.S.2d 412 (3d Dep't 1984). *See also People v. Slater*, 166 A.D.2d 828, 562 N.Y.S.2d 985 (3d Dep't 1990).

The Court of Appeals addressed the issue of chain of custody in *People v. Julian*, 41 N.Y.2d 340, 392 N.Y.S.2d 610 (1977). Here, in a drug case, the Court upheld the admission of physical evidence because the proof established that there existed "reasonable assurances of identity and unchanged condition." The identity prong was established by the identification seal attached to the packages at the time the evidence was seized. As for the "unchanged condition" prong, although there was a gap in the chain of evidence, the Court concluded that such gap occurred following the testing of the seized evidence and, thus, there was no possibility that the gap could have permitted any prejudicial alteration of the contents of the drugs.

The general rule is that a break in a chain of custody goes to the weight of the evidence, not its admissibility. Some breaks, however, have resulted in the suppression of the evidence:

> When we consider that the tube was unsealed when given to the nurse and was kept in two households in unlocked refrigerators for two days and the seal had been broken on the cardboard box, together with the fact that there was no testimony as to the sufficiency or identity of the preservative, we conclude that cumulatively such circumstances rendered the evidence inadmissible.

People v. Snyder, 90 A.D.2d 894, 456 N.Y.S.2d 536, 537–38 (3d Dep't 1982). On retrial, the People filled in the gaps of the chain of custody and the court permitted the test result of the blood sample to be admitted. On appeal, the Third Department affirmed, finding that a reversal for failure to establish a chain of custody of the blood sample did not preclude the admission of the blood sample in a subsequent reprosecution where the People cured the chain of custody defect. *People v. Snyder*, 110 A.D.2d 296, 494 N.Y.S.2d 481 (3d Dep't 1985).

While the courts have not been overly impressed with most "breaks" in the chain of custody, juries tend to hold the police and prosecution to a higher standard. Accordingly, painstaking attention should be paid to developing any deviations from standard procedure. In a close case, an otherwise insignificant "break" in the chain of custody may constitute the reasonable doubt the jury needs to acquit your client.

§ 38:15   Gas chromatography

Research References

West's Key Number Digest, Automobiles ⬥422.1

Gas chromatography functions on the principle that different substances will pass through the column used in this process at different rates. Essentially, the gas chromatograph utilizes a steel column filled with a granular substance through which the substances to be tested are passed. The rate at which they pass is monitored and a record made of their passage. This record is called a chromatogram. One of the best descriptions of this process is set forth by Fitzgerald in *Intoxication Test Evidence*:

> The basic principle on which gas chromatography works is fairly simple. The instrument consists of a lengthy piece of tubing (the column), usually made of stainless steel, which has been filled with granular material such as diatomaceous earth (a soft, fine, porous sedimentary deposit) or crushed firebrick. A small amount of nonvolatile liquid is used to coat the particles. A slow stream of inert gas, such as helium or nitrogen, is passed continuously, at a steady rate, through the column, which is kept in an oven at a constant temperature. If a very small amount of a mixture of volatile liquids is injected into the entrance to the hot column, it evaporates immediately, and the components are carried through the column by the gas flow—entering at one end, exiting at the other.

> The various compounds do not pass through the column at the same rate, however. Some go through quickly and others more slowly as they dissolve temporarily in the non-volatile liquid which coats the column particles. As a result, the various components of the mixture are separated from each other, and if the column is a suitable one, they will come out one by one in an order which, by repetition, becomes known and identifiable. A detector attached to the exit of the column is used to monitor the passage of the components of the mixture as they pass out of the column.

Many different devices have been used as detectors. Ideally they should be sensitive enough so that very small amounts can be measured, and they should have linear response so that the signal they generate is directly proportional to the amount of the substance in the sample. The electrical signal from the detector is fed into a recorder which makes a continuous record of the detector output as a function of time. This record is called a chromatogram. When a mixture of volatile compounds is analyzed, the positions of the peaks (*i.e.*, the lengths of time it took the various components of the mixture to come through the column) on the graphs will identify which compounds are present. Both the peak heights, and the areas underneath each peak, are measures of the amounts of each substance that were present in the mixture. (Usually a test sample "run" in the typical forensic lab will have at least two significant peaks: ethanol, and the internal standard).

Blood and other body liquids can be analyzed for alcohol by direct injection of the liquid sample into the chromatograph, but this approach has a number of drawbacks. Repeated injections of blood will result in a buildup of solid residues in the injection port and may eventually plug the column. The volume of blood injected is very small, which means that its exact measurement is uncertain. A necessary part of the G.C. procedure is the use of an internal standard such as n-propyl alcohol or t-butyl alcohol, and in turn, this means that a less exact measurement of the volume of sample "as injected" is required.

Edward F. Fitzgerald, *Intoxication Test Evidence*, § 18:8, at 18-9-10 (2d ed. 1995) (footnotes omitted).

§ 38:16   Headspace gas chromatography

Research References

West's Key Number Digest, Automobiles ⚷⟶422.1

Headspace gas chromatography is significantly different from gas chromatography in that here you are working with an indirect sample. Specifically, in regard to blood alcohol testing,

[A] measured sample of blood is placed in a rubber-capped bottle and held for 20 to 30 minutes in a constant temperature water bath until the alcohol in the blood sample and the vapor are in equilibrium. A sample of the vapor (the "headspace"), usually about 1 ml. is taken by syringe and injected into the chromatograph. The method has the advantage of not fouling the column with the decomposition products of blood. Also, the larger syringe can deliver a more accurate volume of sample and is easier to handle than a microsyringe. The principal disadvantage of the method is that it is not a direct measurement of the alcohol in the blood but an indirect measurement of the vapor *presumably* in equilibrium with the blood. The partition ratio of alcohol between air and blood is not a fixed number but varies with the composition of blood. This results in the same complications which are found in breath testing where the blood: breath ratio in the body varies widely from person to person, and where the use of an average value (2100:1) has been applied to all persons, with at times questionable results.

Edward F. Fitzgerald, *Intoxication Test Evidence*, § 18:9, at 18-12 (2d ed. 1995) (footnote omitted).

The immediate issue that arises is the validity of the sample. With headspace gas chromatography, we are two steps removed from the defendant. Initially, a representative blood sample is drawn from the defendant. Instead of a direct analysis of the sample, we are now dealing with a vapor derived from that blood sample. This is very much akin to breath testing where a representative sample of the alcohol vapor percolating from the defendant's bloodstream is tested for the purpose of determining the blood alcohol concentration. Both are indirect tests and both are subject to the variables inherent to an application of *Henry's Law*. Simply stated, *Henry's Law* states that there is a relationship between volatile chemical substances in liquid and those same volatile chemical substances in vapor. That relationship, whatever it may be, is directly affected by changes in temperature. Accordingly, the validity of the sample that is obtained for introduction into the gas chromatograph is the subject of legitimate inquiry. Did the vapor sample accurately reflect the alcohol concentration in the blood? What factors affect that relationship?

Clearly, temperature will have a dramatic impact upon the concentration of alcohol in the vapor sample trapped in the "headspace." Headspace is simply the space that exists above the level of the liquid. Think of a closed jar that is three-quarters full. The headspace would be the top portion of the jar not filled with liquid.

§ 38:17 Salting out the blood

Research References

West's Key Number Digest, Automobiles ☞422.1

Michael Snure points out that the process by which the alcohol rises from the liquid into the headspace is helped along by chemicals known as "salting agents." The salting agents are part of the standard solution that is mixed with the blood in the preparation of the blood sample for testing. The preservative, sodium fluoride, and the anticoagulant, potassium oxalate, are also salting agents. He suggests a line of inquiry as to the effect of too much salting agent in the blood. Inasmuch as there is no analysis of the sodium fluoride or potassium oxalate, this is a real possibility. He indicates that:

This phenomenon, known as "salting out the blood," results in an artificially high alcohol value in the headspace gas.

Lawrence Taylor, Drunk Driving Defense, § 8.3, at S-8:154.3 (Release 3-9/98).

§ 38:18 Extracting the vapor from the head space

Research References

West's Key Number Digest, Automobiles ☞422.1

Another area of inquiry is the process by which the vapor sample is extracted from the head space and injected into the gas chromatograph. Is there any possibility of contamination of the gas?

§ 38:19 Tracing the sample

Research References

West's Key Number Digest, Automobiles ☞422.1

Once the gas has been extracted from the head space, it is injected into the gas chromatograph. This vapor sample is carried through the column of the gas chromatograph by an inert gas, usually helium, which is injected into the gas chromatograph from another port. The substances, working their way through the column, are defined by the speed at which they progress to the end of the column where they are met by a "flame ionization detector."

> This burns or ionizes the chemicals. The ions then become electrical charges that can be measured by the gas chromatograph computer. The assumption is that the combination of the time it takes the chemical to come off the column combined with the measurement of the flame ionization detector will produce data that identify and quantify the substance. The computer in the gas chromatograph then creates a picture of the chemical.

Michael Snure as quoted by Larry Taylor at S-8:154.4.

§ 38:20 Inherent error

Research References

West's Key Number Digest, Automobiles ☞422.1

The prevalent belief in the criminal justice system is that blood testing is superior to breath testing in that blood testing is far more accurate. Most of us are familiar with the concept of breath testing equipment having a margin of error of 0.01 as being acceptable from the standard solution of 0.10 used to test breath testing equipment. Accordingly, we use the range of 0.09 to 0.11 to argue a 20% deviation in impeaching results obtained on breath testing equipment. Gas chromatography, however, is also subject to an inherent error of 0.02. Succinctly, the identical sample of blood can be tested on two perfectly functioning gas chromatographs and come up with a variation of 0.02 which will be attributed to the idiosyncrasies of two perfectly functioning instruments. It is not uncommon to obtain two different results from the same gas chromatograph testing the same blood sample twice. In those cases, the lower test result is the one reported. In one vehicular homicide case, the defendant's blood was retested by a reputable private laboratory whose director routinely testified for the prosecution. The result obtained was 0.04 lower than that of the state police laboratory.

The common procedure is for the police to draw two vacutainers of blood. One is kept preserved for the defense should a demand be made for defense analysis. While such reanalysis is a risky proposition at best, there are occasions when it is called for. While the retest may produce a result that is higher or lower than the police laboratory, the chances are that the idiosyncrasies of the individual gas chromatograph and the standards used will result in a result that is different.

§ 38:21   Linearity—Challenging the standards

Research References

West's Key Number Digest, Automobiles ⬦422.1

Linearity is the ability of the gas chromatograph to distinguish a 0.10 blood alcohol concentration (BAC) from a 0.18 BAC. A gas chromatograph is an exercise in comparisons. The gas chromatography determines blood alcohol concentrations by comparing the unknown with the known. In order to determine the alcohol concentration of your client's blood, the chromatograph must first be provided with definitions of what a 0.10 versus a 0.05 and a 0.20 are. In other words, known levels of alcohol must be run in order to establish the linearity of the instrument. In this regard, it is critical that the solutions used to calibrate the chromatograph are properly prepared. It is only by the comparison of these known samples with the defendant's sample that a chromatograph is enabled to come up with a result in regard to the unknown. Michael Snure suggests that you should:

> Inquire how the solutions are prepared at those various levels to be used in the calibration process. Are they aqueous (water) solutions containing levels of alcohol? If so, how did the alcohol get into the water? Who measured the alcohol? Was the volume of the alcohol in the aqueous solution measured by some other device before it was used to calibrate the gas chromatograph? How does one know that the mixture was done properly? Another possibility is that the gas chromatograph could be calibrated using whole blood standards,

which are human whole blood samples obtained from a chemical supply house, purportedly containing known levels of alcohol concentration. If so, how were these samples obtained? Who measured the alcohol level in the sample before it was shipped? Has anyone measured the alcohol level in the sample since it was shipped to determine that it contains the level of alcohol that it is purported to contain by the manufacturer?

Taylor, *Drunk Driving Defense*, S-8:154.

It is not uncommon for the quality of a gas chromatograph's performance to vary on the BAC level being tested. For example, the instrument may be centered at 0.10 and the quality of its linearity may deteriorate at higher and significantly lower levels. Accordingly, the laboratory's checks on the linearity of the instrument should be closely examined. Clearly, more than one known value should be run to check the instrument's performance. Edward Fitzgerald suggests:

Linearity checks covering the full range of test results which are regularly observed in-the lab (for example, from 0.01 to 0.35 percent).

§ 38:22 The chromatogram

Research References

West's Key Number Digest, Automobiles ☞422.1

The chromatogram is created by the action of the flame ionization detector which burns the component of the mixture leaving the column. This rather complicated procedure is succinctly set forth by Fleming K. Whited in the materials he prepared for the National Association of Criminal Defense Lawyers "The Ultimate in DUI Defense: Mastering Science, Maximizing Success," September, 1998.

The rate at which various components of the homogeneous mixture exit from the column is monitored by a detector. The most common detector is known as the flame ionization detector, or FID, which functions by burning the individual components which pass through it, thus creating charged particles which are attracted to an electrically charged grid. This transfer of charged particles from the flame to the charged grid gives rise to a flow of current which is detected and displayed on some readout device. The larger the amount of component exiting the column at any single time, the larger the number of charged particles produced and the greater will be the response of the detector. Because each component passes through the column at separate, identifiable rates, the time of response (retention time) of the detector qualitatively identifies the component. That is, a sample of ethyl alcohol will pass through the column at a more rapid rate than a sample of normal -propyl alcohol. Additionally, the size of the response of the detector represents the quantitative measure of the component present in the mixture.

Fleming K. Whited, III, NACDL's The Ultimate in DUI Defense: Mastering Science, Maximizing Success, Cross-Exam of Prosecutor's Expert: Blood—A Non-Mystical Method, § 13.11 (September 1998).

Insofar as reading and understanding the chromatogram is concerned, Edward Fitzgerald provides a comprehensive analysis at Chapter 20 of *Intoxication Test Evidence*. Essentially, the chromatogram consists of a graph reflecting the peaks of the substances that have been burned by the detector. A control or internal standard is run to ensure that the column is functioning properly. This is to be distinguished from the calibrating samples or alcohol standards used to establish the linearity of the chromatograph. The chromatogram may have two peaks representing the internal standard and the other representing the alcohol in that blood sample. Two separate tests of the same blood sample may be run and the chromatogram will then reflect four peaks representing the two alcohol and two internal standard results. Edward F. Fitzgerald, *Intoxication Test Evidence*, § 20.1, at 20-2 (2d ed. 1995).

It is the relationship of the area under the peak of the unknown test sample to the area under the peak of the known ethanol sample which defines the results of the unknown sample. The area under the peak is different from simply the height attained by the particular peak. The height, in and of itself, does not define the concentration of the substance reflected by that peak. It is rather the area under that peak or encompassed by that peak that determines the concentration of the substance. For example, the peak would tend to be taller and skinnier if the substance being tested came out of the column relatively all at once; *i.e.*, the peak would tend to be higher and narrower.

If the substance came out over a relatively longer period of time, the peak would tend to have a wider area under it, but not be as high. Conceivably, the area under both of these peaks could be identical and would reflect identical concentrations of the substance, but would have different heights on the chromatogram.

On a day-to-day basis, the peak height obtained running a 0.10 BAC standard might differ from another day using that same standard. The reason for this is that internal variables will affect the peak obtained, but will not affect the relationship of the substances appearing in the chromatogram. While the peak heights will vary, the proportional relationships between the areas covered by the peaks should remain consistent depending upon the concentrations of the substances being analyzed. Such variables as the volume of the sample being injected and the speed at which the carrier gas proceeds through the column will affect the heights obtained. Fitzgerald, *Intoxication Test Evidence*, at § 20-7.

In evaluating your client's chromatogram, you need to obtain a copy of a quality control (QC) chromatogram produced by a gas chromatograph. It should have been generated at approximately the time of the test of your client and will typically reflect a peak for a known alcohol and the lab's internal standard. Fitzgerald points out that it may not be referred to as a quality control chromatogram, but whatever its designation, it will show a peak for the known ethanol and the peak for the internal standard. The QC chromatogram is used to verify the accuracy of the gas chromatograph. The closer in time to the test run on your client, the more relevant it becomes. Edward F. Fitzgerald, *Intoxication Test Evidence*, § 20:4, at 20-6.

§ 38:23 Multiple samples

Research References

West's Key Number Digest, Automobiles ⚖️422.1

While most of us are not familiar with blood testing, we have a tendency to relate what we know to that which we do not know. Accordingly, we tend to assume that blood testing is akin to breath testing. For example, a breath test device runs only one sample at a time. It may be an air blank, a simulator solution, or the defendant's test. Whichever, there is only one sample being run at one time.

This is not the case with a gas chromatograph. Multiple tests are generally run at the same time. What this means is that the technician is dealing with several vacutainers containing blood from many different defendants. The more samples being tested, the greater the chance for error. This is particularly the case where the common procedure is to take two samples of blood from each defendant's vacutainer. How is the blood extracted from the vacutainer and where does it go from there? How is that sample identified and kept separate from the samples of other defendants being run? What is the effect of the defendant's sample being run following multiple samples from other defendants? Can a buildup of residue in the column contaminate the defendant's sample? Lawrence Taylor, Drunk Driving Defense, § 8.3, at 8:154.2 (Release 3-9/98).

§ 38:24 Proficiency testing

Research References

West's Key Number Digest, Automobiles ⚖️422.1

In addition to the performance of tests and maintenance on the individual gas chromatograph, laboratories are subject to proficiency testing. These proficiency tests consist of the submission of samples to the lab for analysis. The submitting authority knows what the samples contain, but the testing laboratory does not. Records of the results of this proficiency testing are kept and should be the subject of a discovery demand.

§ 38:25 Sample cross-examination

Research References

West's Key Number Digest, Automobiles ☞422.1

The key to the impeachment of a blood test result is to make points that a jury can understand. Too often, the lawyer and the technician are engaging in an incomprehensible dialogue which is completely lost upon the jury. It is the ability to translate complexity into simplicity which determines a lawyer's effectiveness in the courtroom. Many years ago, a lawyer was seeking a hearing on the issue of whether improper testing of the chemicals used in a Breathalyzer required the suppression of his client's blood alcohol concentration.

The lawyer explained how the company supplying the chemicals had failed to provide a representative sample to the state police laboratory for testing. After hearing the People's vigorous opposition to the hearing, the lay judge stated that the defense motion for a pretrial hearing was denied because it was the judge's opinion that such a hearing was completely unnecessary.

Turning from the dismayed defense attorney to the prosecutor, the farmer-judge continued saying that the procedure followed by the chemical supplier would be wholly unacceptable in regard to milk samples. Consequently, no hearing would be required because the court was suppressing the test result based upon the court's own experience and knowledge.

While the judge was a farmer and not a lawyer, his experience with the testing of milk samples rendered the issue clearer to him than to either the prosecutor or defense counsel. In this spirit, Attorney Ed Fiandach produced the following sample cross-examination in his New York DWI Bulletin which he derived from the study of Edward Fitzgerald's *Intoxication Test Evidence*. This sample cross is reproduced with Mr. Fiandach's kind permission:

Q: Would you explain for me the term Hematocrit Ratio?

A: The Hematocrit Ratio is the proportion of blood plasma to cellular material.

Q: The solid to liquid?

A: Roughly.

Q: Now, when alcohol is analyzed in a sample of blood, where is it to be found?

A: Could you explain that further?

Q: Will the alcohol be found in the liquid or solid particles of the blood?

A: Oh, the liquid.

Q: And why is that?

A: Because alcohol is, for the most part, water soluble.

Q: And the results of an alcohol blood analysis are reported how?

A: As a ratio of the weight to volume or w/v.

Q: Now to return to the hematocrit ratio, you said that it is a means of describing the percentage of blood which is composed of cellular material?

A: That's correct.

Q: Then a person who has a ratio of 47 would have blood made up of 47 percent cellular material and 53 percent plasma?

A: That's correct.

Q: And the higher the hematocrit the higher the more non-alcohol absorbing cellular material is present?

A: That's correct.

Q: By the way, do you know what Mr. Hadenough's Hematocrit Ratio was at the time of his arrest and test?

A: I do not.

Q: Then when you calculated your results you assumed a particular Hematocrit Ratio?

A: Correct.

Q: But if the hematocrit value was higher than that which you assumed, to get an accurate result you would have to use a higher conversion factor?

A: That's correct.

Q: Then, without assuming Mr. Hadenough's ratio as it existed on June 11, 1998, you cannot determine what his true blood alcohol content was, can you?

A: I can only do the calculations.

Q: That's not what I asked you. Without assuming Mr. Hadenough's ratio as it existed on June 11, 1998, you cannot determine what his true blood alcohol content was, can you?

A: Well, not without the assumption. No I cannot.

Likewise, it is important to verify whether or not the sample that was tested was clotted or unclotted. In the event that it was clotted, a productive avenue of cross-examination can be as follows:

Q: Tell me, was the sample, at the time you tested it, clotted or unclotted?

A: A little of both.

Q: Now, when you say a little of both, do you know the percentages?

A: I do not.

Q: Now you previously testified that the alcohol will be found in the liquid, non-cellular portion of the blood?

A: That's correct.

Q: How about a clot, will the alcohol go into a clot?

A: Not generally.

Q: And what portion of the blood is heavier, the cellular material or the liquid?

A: The cellular material.

Q: In what percentage?

A: That depends upon the Hematocrit Ratio.

Q: When blood coagulates or clots, what occurs?

A: The cellular material draws together and hardens.

Q: And you tested the liquid portion?

A: I did.

Q: Which was but a portion of the overall weight of the sample?

A: If that's a question, the answer is correct.

Q: But even though it was but a portion of the weight it contained almost all of the alcohol, did it not?

A: That's correct.

Q: Then the concentration of the alcohol in the plasma was higher than that contained in the entire sample of the blood when drawn, was it not?

A: In the plasma, yes. Arguably a non-issue, even the addition of the preservatives can be used to some advantage.

Q: Now, the heparin, why was that added?

A: To prevent clotting.

Q: It did not, did it?

A: No, not completely, it did not.

Q: There was also added some sodium fluoride?

A: Correct.

Q: Why was that?

A: Sodium fluoride is a preservative.

Q: Why is a preservative used?

A: Because an unpreserved alcohol sample can undergo a process of neo-alcohol formation.

Q: Could you explain that for me?

A: Yes, neo-alcohol formation is when bacteria acts upon material naturally present in the blood and causes it to ferment or form alcohol on its own.

Q: Can you, in the course of your testing differentiate between this fermented alcohol and that which may have been present in the sample when drawn?

A: No, I can not.

Q: And theoretically the preservative is supposed to prevent this process from occurring?

A: Not theoretically, it does prevent such formation.

Q: Well, theoretically the heparin was to prevent the formation of clots?

A: That's correct.

Q: All clots?

A: Theoretically.

Q: In this case it did not did it?

A: Well, no.

Q: But you know that because the clot can be visibly verified and we know it was not present in the blood when drawn.

A: That's correct.

Q: But you cannot visibly verify the formation of alcohol through fermentation can you?

A: No, no one can.

Q: For that matter you can't tell whether that occurred at all can you? Finally, if you're confronted with a headspace analysis, don't miss the opportunity to convert the blood test into a less reliable breath test.

Q: Now, this Perkin-Elmer F-45 gas chromatograph, did it directly measure Mr. Hadenough's blood?

A: You mean did I put it directly into the instrument?

Q: Yes.

A: No, it did not.

Q: Could you explain what you did?

A: I withdrew a sample of the vapor which had accumulated above the sample and injected that into the column.

Q: And the amount of alcohol contained in that vapor is the same as the amount of alcohol in the sample of blood, how can that be?

A: It's not, but it bears a relationship to the overall alcoholic content by means of Henry's Law.

Q: Is that the 2100 to one rule?

A: Yes it is.

Q: But that rule relies on certain assumptions such as Mr. Hadenough's Hematocrit Ratio does it not?

A: Yes it does.

Q: And preservatives play a role in altering the ratio, do they not?

A: They might.

Q: And temperature?

A: It might.

Q: Even barometric pressure?

A: Unlikely, but it could.

Q: Just so I understand, you did not utilize the alcohol present in the sample of blood but in the air above it, is that correct?

A: That's correct.

§ 38:26 Defendant's right to test sample

Research References

West's Key Number Digest, Automobiles ☞415

In *People v. Karpeles*, 146 Misc. 2d 53, 549 N.Y.S.2d 903 (N.Y. City Crim. Ct. 1989), the court considered the defendant's right to production and independent testing of a blood sample taken from his person. The People argued that the defendant had not demonstrated the relevancy of retesting the blood sample, a condition precedent to ordering disclosure and testing. In addition, they argued that since the request did not come until seven months after the blood sample had been withdrawn, any tests performed on the blood would not be representative of the defendant's condition at the time of the incident.

The court rejected the People's request that it first determine the integrity and relevancy of the blood sample, holding:

As to all of the broad categories itemized in Section 240.20(1), the defense is entitled to disclosure on demand. Access to such material is a clear statutory right enforceable by court-imposed sanctions, either *sua sponte* or by motion. *See* CPL secs. 240.70, 240.40(1). There is no requirement that the defendant demonstrate materiality and reasonableness. Rather, the burden is placed on the prosecutor, who must demonstrate that the matter sought is either (1) not designated property under section 240.20 or otherwise not subject to disclosure; or (2) for good cause, ought not to be disclosed. Motion practice is therefore limited to applications by the defendant to compel disclosure, enforce prior orders and impose sanctions, and by the prosecution to applications for protective orders to limit, stay or condition disclosure. Only with respect to property not embraced by the broad gambit of section 240.20(1), does there remain a requirement that the defendant first make a showing of materiality and reasonableness. CPL Section 240.40(1)(c).

In light of the broad statutory scheme, the specific inclusion of blood samples in the definition of property makes clear that the Legislature intended that such matter be freely available to the defense. Accordingly, movant is presumptively entitled to the relief sought as a matter of right. The People have the burden of demonstrating that the requested relief should be denied. Given the strong public policy in favor of disclosure and the constitutional considerations discussed *infra*, that burden is a heavy one.

146 Misc. 2d at 56–59, 549 N.Y.S.2d at 906–07 (footnote omitted).

On the admissibility of the test result following a retest by the defendant, the court concluded:

First, a fact-finding hearing must be held before the Court can determine the legal questions of authenticity and admissibility; second, since the passage of time may well be outcome-determinative, any further delay of testing pending investigation, hearing and determination could render the inquiry academic and prejudice the interests of justice.

146 Misc. 2d at 59, 549 N.Y.S.2d at 908.

Insofar as due process is concerned, the court held that:

Since testimony of blood alcohol content is invariably dispositive in drunk driving cases, independent testing by a defense expert is imperative if the defense is to have a fair opportunity to confront the toxicologist and the findings. Indeed, it would be particularly disingenuous to force defendant to first demonstrate authenticity and appropriate storage, since these matters, along with the physical evidence and the expert, are within the exclusive ken and control of the prosecution. *See People v. White*, 40 N.Y.2d 797, 390 N.Y.S.2d 405, 358 N.E.2d 1031 (right of defense to independent testing of narcotics). *See also People v. Evans*, 141 Misc. 2d 781, 783, 534 N.Y.S.2d 640 (Sup. Ct., N.Y. Co. 1988) (defense granted access to prosecution expert "where the government holds a monopoly of expertise"). Finally, as a matter of public policy, it is fundamentally unfair to deny someone reasonable access to fluid specimens taken from one's own body, sought to be used by an adversary and likely to be outcome-determinative.

146 Misc. 2d at 61, 549 N.Y.S.2d at 909 (footnote omitted).

In a postconviction motion for discovery, where the defendant sought to conduct DNA testing of physical evidence presented at trial, the court rejected the district attorney's suggestion that the petitioner should be required to demonstrate the present viability of such testing given the age and condition of the preserved evidence. The court found, in *Matter of Dabbs v. Vergari*, 149 Misc. 2d 844, 570 N.Y.S.2d 765 (Westchester Co. Sup. Ct. 1990), that such a requirement would be an "impossible burden" since it involves expert opinion that could only be had upon examination of the evidence.

In *People v. Scalzo*, 176 A.D.2d 363, 574 N.Y.S.2d 782 (2d Dep't 1991), the court reversed a conviction for criminally negligent homicide, vehicular manslaughter, vehicular assault, and DWI based upon the trial court's refusal to sanction the People for failing to preserve the blood sample, which had yielded a blood alcohol level below the statutory level of intoxication.

> In fashioning an "appropriate" response to the prosecutor's failure to preserve evidence (*see* CPL § 240.70[1]), the overriding concern must be to eliminate any prejudice to the defendant while protecting the interest of society (*see People v. Kelly*, 62 N.Y.2d 516, 520, 478 N.Y.S.2d 834, 467 N.E.2d 498). The fact that the People lose evidence through inadvertence does not excuse the loss (*see, People v. Haupt*, 71 N.Y.2d 929, 528 N.Y.S.2d 808, 524 N.E.2d 129). In the instant case, the court's instruction which suggested that failure to preserve the sample was of "no consequence" clearly did not even attempt to eliminate the prejudice caused the defendant. We consider this failure particularly grave under the instant set of circumstances where the chemical test performed on the sample of the defendant's blood yielded a blood alcohol content that was below the statutory level of intoxication.

176 A.D.2d at __, 574 N.Y.S.2d at 784.

§ 38:27 Defendant's right to independent test

Research References
West's Key Number Digest, Automobiles ⚷415

The police are not required to arrange for an independent test or to transport the defendant to a place where the test may be performed. However, the police should not impede the defendant from obtaining the independent test. In *People v. Finnegan*, 85 N.Y.2d 53, 623 N.Y.S.2d 546 (1995), the defendant was arrested shortly after 2:30 a.m. and brought to the police station where a Breathalyzer test was administered at 3:42 a.m. Two weeks prior to trial, the defendant moved to suppress the Breathalyzer test results, stating that the police failed to assist him in arranging for an independent blood test on the night of his arrest. The trial court denied the defendant's motion. The appellate court affirmed, and held that the police had no affirmative duty to arrange for an independent chemical test. On appeal to the Court of Appeals, the defendant asserted that the police have an affirmative duty to assist the defendant in seeking an independent test. The defendant cited to VTL § 1194(4)(b) which states:

> Right to additional test. The person shall be permitted to choose a physician to administer a chemical test in addition to the one administered at the direction of the police officer.

The defendant argued that the police must give notice of the right to the independent test; the police must transport defendant to the location where the additional test would be performed; and the police must do this within two hours of the defendant's arrest.

The Court of Appeals refused to adopt such a broad interpretation of the statute.

> We hold, therefore, that law enforcement personnel are not required to arrange for an independent test or to transport defendant to a place or person where the test may be performed (see, People v. Miller, 199 A.D.2d 692, 694–695, 605 N.Y.S.2d 160, lv. denied 82 N.Y.2d 928, 610 N.Y.S.2d 180, 632 N.E.2d 490; People v. Cegelski, 142 Misc. 2d 1023, 1024–1025, 539 N.Y.S.2d 639, lv. denied 74 N.Y.2d 846, 546 N.Y.S.2d 1010, 546 N.E.2d 193; People v. Sauve, 129 Misc. 2d 666, 668, 493 N.Y.S.2d 689). Of course, the police should not impede arrested individuals from exerting or accomplishing their statutory prerogative. The authorities should even assist persons in custody with appropriate advice and communication means, e.g., a telephone call opportunity. On the other hand, we have settled the general question that the police have no affirmative duty to gather or help gather evidence for an accused (see, People v. Alvarez, 70 N.Y.2d 375, 521 N.Y.S.2d 212, 515 N.E.2d 898).

> Moreover, we disagree with defendant's assertion that assistance for the independent test must be speedily undertaken so that it, too, is administered within two hours of the arrest.

People v. Finnegan, 623 N.Y.S.2d at 549.

§ 38:28 Options of defendant when asked to provide blood sample

Research References
West's Key Number Digest, Automobiles ☞420

Upon being asked to submit to a blood test, the defendant has three options. First, she can expressly consent to having the blood sample drawn. Second, she can refuse. In appropriate circumstances, the police or prosecutor may then obtain a court order to compel her to provide the sample. Lastly, if the driver is unconscious or so disoriented as to be incapable of giving or refusing consent to the blood test, blood may be drawn pursuant to the implied consent provisions of VTL § 1194(2).

§ 38:29 Unconscious defendant

Research References

West's Key Number Digest, Automobiles ☞420

The taking of a blood sample from an unconscious defendant has passed constitutional muster. In *People v. Kates*, 53 N.Y.2d 591, 444 N.Y.S.2d 446 (1981), although the defendant was conscious, the hearing court found that it was impossible for the police to obtain the defendant's consent in view of his intoxicated and injured condition at the time of the test. On appeal, with regard to the defendant's Fifth Amendment privilege against self-incrimination, the Court of Appeals, citing *Schmerber v. California*, 384 U.S. 757, 86 S.Ct. 1826, found that taking a driver's blood for alcohol analysis does not involve testimonial compulsion. *See also People v. Thomas*, 46 N.Y.2d 100, 412 N.Y.S.2d 845 (1978); *People v. Lerow*, 70 A.D.3d 66, __, 889 N.Y.S.2d 813, 819 (4th Dep't 2009).

The Court also found that the taking of a blood sample from an unconscious driver, without a court order, does not violate the Fourth Amendment when there is probable cause to believe the individual operated the car in an intoxicated condition, exigent circumstances exist, and a reasonable examination procedure is used.

Regarding the Equal Protection Clause the Court stated:

> The distinction drawn between the conscious driver and the unconscious or incapacitated driver does not offend the equal protection clause. It was reasonable for the Legislature, concerned with avoiding potentially violent conflicts between the police and drivers arrested for intoxication, to provide that the police must request the driver's consent, advise him of the consequences of refusal and honor his wishes if he decides to refuse, but to dispense with these requirements when the driver is unconscious or otherwise incapacitated to the point where he poses no threat. Indeed there is a rational basis for distinguishing between the driver who is capable of making a choice and the driver who is unable to do so. Thus, denying the unconscious driver the right to refuse a blood test does not violate his right to equal protection.

People v. Kates, 444 N.Y.S.2d at 448–49. *See also People v. Morrisey*, 21 A.D.3d 597, __, 799 N.Y.S.2d 642, 643–44 (3d Dep't 2005) ("It is irrelevant whether defendant expressly consented or was confused when his driving while intoxicated warnings were read to him . . . Although defendant claims that he did not expressly consent, he never testified that he refused the test. By driving on the roads in this state, defendant gave a statutorily implied consent to submit to a chemical test of his blood"); *People v. Dombrowski-Bove*, 300 A.D.2d 1122, __, 753 N.Y.S.2d 259, 260 (4th Dep't 2002).

Although the taking of a blood sample from an unconscious driver may meet constitutional standards, VTL § 1194(2), governing implied consent, must be addressed. VTL § 1194(2) states:

> Any person who operates a motor vehicle in this state shall be deemed to have given consent to a chemical test of one or more of the following; breath, blood, urine, or saliva, for the purpose of determining the alcoholic and/or drug content of the blood.

For the implied consent provision to apply, VTL § 1194 requires that there be reasonable cause to believe that the driver was in violation of VTL § 1192, and that the test be administered within two hours after the driver's arrest. Thus, if the defendant is unconscious and the foregoing requirements are satisfied, a blood sample may be drawn from the defendant for the purpose of testing his blood alcohol content.

§ 38:30   Unconscious defendant need not be formally arrested for purposes of implied consent law

Research References

West's Key Number Digest, Automobiles ⟜420

New York's implied consent law provides, in pertinent part, that:

> Any person who operates a motor vehicle in this state shall be deemed to have given consent to a chemical test of one or more of the following: breath, blood, urine, or saliva, for the purpose of determining the alcoholic and/or drug content of the blood provided that such test is administered by or at the direction of a police officer with respect to a chemical test of breath, urine or saliva or, with respect to a chemical test of blood, at the direction of a police officer:
>
> (1) having reasonable grounds to believe such person to have been operating in violation of any subdivision of [VTL § 1192] of this article and within two hours *after such person has been placed under arrest* for any such violation.

VTL § 1194(2)(a)(1) (emphasis added).

In *People v. Goodell*, 79 N.Y.2d 869, 581 N.Y.S.2d 157, 589 N.E.2d 380 (1992), the defendant was unconscious at the time the police arrived at the accident scene, and remained so at all relevant times. He claimed that his blood test result should have been suppressed on the ground that VTL § 1194(2)(a)(1) requires an actual, formal arrest—yet he was never formally arrested. In rejecting this claim, the Court of Appeals held as follows:

> [A] formal arrest would have been an empty gesture in defendant's case, since defendant was unconscious when the police first arrived

at the scene of the accident and he remained comatose for approximately two more weeks. Under these circumstances, we decline to hold that the police officer's failure formally to announce defendant's arrest was alone sufficient to vitiate his Vehicle and Traffic Law § 1194(2)(a)(1) authority to direct the administration of a chemical blood alcohol test (cf., People v. Almond, 151 A.D.2d 820, 542 N.Y.S.2d 59 [blood test taken pursuant to Vehicle and Traffic Law § 1194(1) (now § 1194[2][a][1]) suppressed where police found defendant in a conscious state but, without formally placing him under arrest, waited until subsequent medical treatment rendered him unconscious before administering test]).

79 N.Y.2d at 871, 581 N.Y.S.2d at 158. See also People v. Bohacek, 95 A.D.3d 1592, __, 945 N.Y.S.2d 460, 461 (3d Dep't 2012); People v. Lerow, 70 A.D.3d 66, __, 889 N.Y.S.2d 813, 816 (4th Dep't 2009) ("A formal arrest is not required where the suspect is unconscious or is otherwise unable to appreciate the significance of an arrest"); People v. Bradway, 285 A.D.2d 831, __, 728 N.Y.S.2d 286, 288 (3d Dep't 2001); People v. Hart, 266 A.D.2d 698, __, 698 N.Y.S.2d 357, 359-60 (3d Dep't 1999) ("To the extent that defendant argues that he was not technically arrested, a formal arrest was unnecessary because it would have been meaningless due to his unconscious state"); People v. Steel, 265 A.D.2d 586, 697 N.Y.S.2d 649 (2d Dep't 1999); People v. Stuart, 216 A.D.2d 682, 628 N.Y.S.2d 421 (3d Dep't 1995); People v. Carkner, 213 A.D.2d 735, __, 623 N.Y.S.2d 350, 354 (3d Dep't 1995) ("defendant was in a state of semiconsciousness or unconsciousness following the accident so that a formal arrest would have been an empty gesture"); People v. Bagley, 211 A.D.2d 882, __, 621 N.Y.S.2d 166, 167 (3d Dep't 1995); People v. Skinner, 203 A.D.2d 891, __, 611 N.Y.S.2d 720, 721 (4th Dep't 1994).

In People v. Skardinski, 24 A.D.3d 1207, __, 807 N.Y.S.2d 232, 233 (4th Dep't 2005), the Appellate Division, Fourth Department, found that the defendant's blood test results should have been suppressed on the ground that the defendant was not formally arrested prior to the test:

We further reject the contention of the People that there was no need to arrest defendant and to obtain her consent to the blood test because she was in a semiconscious or unconscious state. The State Trooper testified at the suppression hearing that defendant "was talking with people" before he entered the room but that she suddenly closed her eyes when he entered. After the State Trooper spoke to the nurse in the hallway and the nurse entered defendant's room, defendant opened her eyes and responded when the nurse spoke to her. Contrary to the People's contention, the fact that defendant may have feigned unconsciousness for a brief period of time does not obviate the need to arrest defendant and to obtain her consent to the blood test.

§ 38:31 Distinction between Penal Law blood tests and VTL blood tests

Research References

West's Key Number Digest, Automobiles ⊙411

CPL § 60.75 establishes the admissibility of blood tests in vehicular crimes prosecutions. Essentially, if a test result is obtained and is otherwise admissible in a DWI prosecution, its joinder in an indictment with a vehicular crimes charge will render it admissible in evidence in regard to the vehicular crimes counts as well.

CPL § 60.75 states:

In any prosecution where two or more offenses against the same defendant are properly joined in one indictment or charged in two accusatory instruments properly consolidated for trial purposes and where one such offense charges a violation of any subdivision of section eleven hundred ninety-two of the vehicle and traffic law, chemical test evidence properly admissible as evidence of intoxication under subdivision one of section eleven hundred ninety-five of such law, shall also, if relevant, be received in evidence with regard to the remaining charges in the indictments.

In *People v. Grant*, 192 A.D.2d 798, 596 N.Y.S.2d 529 (3d Dep't 1993), the defendant urged that while the blood test results were admissible under the VTL, they were not admissible to prove the penal law offenses. Citing CPL § 60.75, the Third Department concluded that a chemical test admitted in evidence as proof of a violation of VTL § 1192, if relevant, could be received as evidence with regard to the remaining charges in the indictment.

By contrast, *People v. Ladd*, 89 N.Y.2d 893, 653 N.Y.S.2d 259 (1996), presents a situation in which the defendant was not charged with a violation of VTL § 1192, but a blood test result was received in evidence to support the defendant's conviction of criminally negligent homicide and reckless driving. Here, the defendant caused an automobile accident which resulted in the death of both the driver and passenger of the other vehicle. Although the defendant had consumed alcohol on the evening in question, she was not charged with DWI. However, a blood sample was obtained from the defendant and used against her at trial.

On appeal, the defendant claimed, among other things, that since she was not charged with a violation of VTL § 1192, the results of the blood test were inadmissible under CPL § 60.75. The Court of Appeals disagreed, holding that:

CPL 60.75 provides that when Vehicle and Traffic Law charges and Penal Law charges are tried together the evidence obtained pursuant to section 1194 of the Vehicle and Traffic Law is admissible as to both charges . . . . Section 60.75 does not limit the use of blood test results to prosecutions under the Vehicle and Traffic Law or to prosecutions linking Vehicle and Traffic Law and Penal Law offenses. Indeed, section 1195(1) of the Vehicle and Traffic Law provides that blood test results are admissible at the trial of "any action or proceeding" arising out of a factual basis for a driving while intoxicated arrest. The evidence, if legally obtained and relevant, should be admissible in Penal Law prosecutions, notwithstanding the absence of any charge under the Vehicle and Traffic Law.

89 N.Y.2d at 896, 653 N.Y.S.2d at 261.

§ 38:32 Admissibility of compulsory blood test obtained pursuant to search warrant (CPL § 690.10)

Research References

West's Key Number Digest, Automobiles ⬥411

VTL §§ 1192(2) and 1192(2-a)(a) expressly require that the defendant's BAC be proven by a chemical test "made pursuant to the provisions of [VTL § 1194]." In this regard, VTL § 1194(3) contains procedures required to obtain a compulsory chemical test order; and VTL § 1194(4) both (a) provides certain required testing procedures, and (b) requires the Department of Health to promulgate rules and regulations approving satisfactory testing techniques. In a typical DWI case, if the defendant's blood test is not administered in compliance with VTL § 1194, the test result is inadmissible. *See, e.g., People v. Olmstead*, 233 A.D.2d 837, 649 N.Y.S.2d 624 (4th Dep't 1996); *People v. Ebner*, 195 A.D.2d 1006, 600 N.Y.S.2d 569 (4th Dep't 1993).

In *People v. Casadei*, 66 N.Y.2d 846, 498 N.Y.S.2d 357, 489 N.E.2d 244 (1985), the defendant was involved in a DWI-related fatal motor vehicle accident, and was indicted for multiple Penal Law felonies in addition to DWI. County Court granted the defendant's motion to suppress his blood test result on the ground that the test was obtained via a CPL § 690.10 search warrant rather than via a VTL § 1194 compulsory chemical test order. The Court of Appeals affirmed the Appellate Division's reversal of County Court's ruling, reasoning as follows:

> Defendant relies upon *People v. Moselle*, 57 N.Y.2d 97, 454 N.Y.S.2d 292, 439 N.E.2d 1235, for the proposition that the provisions of Vehicle and Traffic Law § 1194, in effect at the time of the accident, constitute the exclusive method of obtaining a blood sample for a violation of Vehicle and Traffic Law § 1192. Although two of the three prosecutions in *Moselle* involved Penal Law violations in addition to Vehicle and Traffic Law violations, there was not in those cases, as there is here, a court order based on probable cause, authorizing the taking of a blood sample. It is clear that a search

warrant may validly be issued to obtain a blood sample, in the event of a violation of the Penal Law, and, in such circumstances, we decline to extend *Moselle* to require separate resort to Vehicle and Traffic Law § 1194 to sustain Vehicle and Traffic Law offenses which are part of the same indictment.

6 N.Y.2d at 847-48, 498 N.Y.S.2d at 358 (citation omitted). *See also People v. Goodell*, 164 A.D.2d 321, __, 565 N.Y.S.2d 929, 932 (4th Dep't 1990), aff'd, 79 N.Y.2d 869, 581 N.Y.S.2d 157, 589 N.E.2d 380 (1992).

§ 38:33   Blood test foundation

Research References

West's Key Number Digest, Automobiles ⊛411

There is surprisingly little case law with regard to the issue of what constitutes a sufficient foundation for the admission of a defendant's blood test results at trial. However, it is clear that the People cannot merely place the test result into evidence with no foundation.

At the outset, an interesting issue is raised by the fact that, unlike in the case of breath testing devices, the Department of Health Rules and Regulations do not recognize the general acceptance of the reliability and accuracy of any specific blood testing instrument(s). *See* 10 NYCRR § 59.4.

In *People v. Campbell*, 73 N.Y.2d 481, 483, 541 N.Y.S.2d 756, 757 (1989), the Court of Appeals addressed the issue of "whether the results of blood alcohol tests performed by hospital technologists using the DuPont Automatic Clinical Analyzer ["DuPont ACA"] are admissible in evidence per se or are subject to the foundation requirements outlined in *People v. Freeland* and *People v. Mertz*." (Citations omitted).

In holding that *Freeland* and *Mertz* apply to blood tests, the *Campbell* Court made certain critical findings:

1. That "State regulations require that a blood alcohol test reading be accurate within .01 grams per 100 milliliters (Chemical Analysis of Blood, Urine, Breath or Saliva for Alcoholic Content, 10 NYCRR 59.2[b][2]). In the cases before us no scientific evidence was presented to establish that the DuPont ACA is reliable for determining blood alcohol content generally or with sufficient accuracy to meet that standard." 73 N.Y.2d at 485, 541 N.Y.S.2d at 758;

2. That the foundational requirements for the admissibility of scientific test evidence are stricter in criminal cases than in civil cases—"In criminal matters the scientific reliability and accuracy of a machine measuring blood alcohol content for forensic purposes must be established before such test results

may be admitted in evidence." 73 N.Y.2d at 485, 541 N.Y.S.2d at 758;

3. That "the State Health Department's permit does not satisfy the accuracy requirement. Although the machine may be accurate to show alcohol toxicity or possible drug interactions for general purposes, there is no proof that it is 'capable of accurately discerning the critical distinction between a legally permissible blood alcohol content and that which is statutorily proscribed.' " 73 N.Y.2d at 485, 541 N.Y.S.2d at 758 (citation omitted); and

4. That, "contrary to the People's claim, the technologist cannot be equated with a chemist or toxicologist who can render an opinion of blood alcohol content based on firsthand knowledge and experience. The technologist, even though granted a permit by the State, does not qualify as an expert on the internal workings of the machine and his or her testimony does not satisfy the distinct foundational requirement that the machine test blood alcohol content accurately within required specifications." 73 N.Y.2d at 485–86, 541 N.Y.S.2d at 758 (citation omitted).

In *People v. Grune*, 12 A.D.3d 944, 785 N.Y.S.2d 178 (3d Dep't 2004), the defendant's blood was tested using a gas chromatograph. The Appellate Division, Third Department, held that:

> [T]here was no proper foundation laid for admission of the results of the BAC test. Specifically, the People failed to elicit testimony from the witness who conducted the test as to whether the testing equipment was properly calibrated and whether the test was properly performed on the particular blood sample taken from defendant. In the absence of this foundation, the BAC test results should not have been admitted.

12 A.D.3d at ___, 785 N.Y.S.2d at 179.

Similarly, in *People v. Baker*, 51 A.D.3d 1047, ___, 856 N.Y.S.2d 707, 709 (3d Dep't 2008), the Court held that:

> It is well settled that a foundation establishing the reliability and accuracy of a machine used to measure blood alcohol content is a prerequisite to admitting the results of a blood alcohol test into evidence. The People failed to set forth proof at trial that the gas chromatograph had been properly calibrated before it was used to test defendant's blood. While the expert who appeared for the People was sufficiently qualified to have rendered an opinion based upon his firsthand testing of the blood, the People did not elicit testimony from him regarding the specific steps he took to ensure the reliability and accuracy of the test that he conducted on defendant's blood sample. General statements about what he typically does with a blood sample are insufficient in the absence of testimony that he actually took such measures with regard to this

blood sample. Here, as in *Grune*, "the People failed to elicit
testimony from the witness who conducted the test as to whether
the testing equipment was properly calibrated and whether the test
was properly performed on the particular blood sample taken from
defendant." Defendant preserved the issue by a timely objection in
which he asserted the lack of a proper foundation. Accordingly, we
conclude that County Court properly reversed these convictions and
directed a new trial as to counts 2 and 4.

(Citations omitted).

§ 38:34 People must establish valid consent to blood test

"To be admissible, the People [a]re required to demonstrate
that defendant consented to the taking of the blood sample
utilized for the test." *People v. Verdile*, 119 A.D.2d 891, __, 500
N.Y.S.2d 846, 848 (3d Dep't 1986). *See also People v. Cole*, 112
A.D.2d 623, __, 492 N.Y.S.2d 486, 486 (3d Dep't 1985) ("the only
significant issue on this appeal is whether defendant voluntarily
gave her consent to a blood sample being taken from her at the
emergency room of a hospital following the accident in question").
In this regard, it is common for this issue to be addressed at a
pretrial suppression hearing. *See, e.g., People v. Centerbar*, 80
A.D.3d 1008, __, 914 N.Y.S.2d 784, 786-87 (3d Dep't 2011) ("we
perceive no grounds upon which to disagree with County Court's
factual determination, after an evidentiary hearing, that, despite
his significant injuries, defendant's consent to the blood test was
voluntary"); *People v. Mojica*, 62 A.D.3d 100, __, 874 N.Y.S.2d
195, 206 (2d Dep't 2009), leave to appeal denied, 12 N.Y.3d 856,
2009 WL 1813878 (2009) ("the evidence supports the hearing
court's determination that the defendant voluntarily consented to
the blood draw for testing his BAC"); *People v. Slater*, 166 A.D.2d
828, __, 562 N.Y.S.2d 985, 987 (3d Dep't 1990) ("We find ample
support for County Court's factual determination that defendant
voluntarily, knowingly and freely gave his consent to the blood
test"); *People v. Skardinski*, 24 A.D.3d 1207, __, 807 N.Y.S.2d
232, 233 (4th Dep't 2005) ("The record does not support the
People's contention that defendant voluntarily consented to the
blood test"); *People v. O'Hanlon*, 5 A.D.3d 1012, __, 773 N.Y.S.2d
633, 634 (4th Dep't 2004); *People v. Atwood*, 2 A.D.3d 1331, __,
768 N.Y.S.2d 918, 919 (4th Dep't 2003); *People v. Ellis*, 190 Misc.
2d 98, __-__, 737 N.Y.S.2d 232, 237–39 (Cattaraugus Co. Ct.
2001), *aff'd*, 309 A.D.2d 1314, 765 N.Y.S.2d 313 (4th Dep't 2003);
People v. Gaffney, 299 A.D.2d 922, __, 750 N.Y.S.2d 383, 383–84
(4th Dep't 2002); *People v. Craig*, 262 A.D.2d 1074, __, 692
N.Y.S.2d 257, 258 (4th Dep't 1999); *People v. Osburn*, 155 A.D.2d
926, __, 547 N.Y.S.2d 749, 751 (4th Dep't 1989).

In *Skardinski*, *supra*, the Appellate Division, Fourth Department, held that:

The record does not support the People's contention that defendant voluntarily consented to the blood test. Defendant had been badly injured in a motor vehicle accident and was receiving morphine at the hospital when the State Trooper spoke with her there. The State Trooper incorrectly informed defendant that her driver's license would be immediately suspended if she did not submit to a chemical test. "Further, although [defendant] had not been arrested, the warnings given to her [by the State Trooper] clearly implied, at least twice, that she had in fact been arrested." When defendant failed to respond to or indicate that she understood the State Trooper's warnings, the State Trooper stepped into the hall to speak with a nurse about the possibility of a court-ordered blood test. The nurse then entered defendant's room and said, "[T]he police are here. They want to take blood for possible, for a DWI, you know. Do you know that's why they're here, we're going to take blood. We need you to consent on this in order to do it." The nurse presented defendant with a clipboard securing the consent form, and defendant signed the consent form at an irregular angle across the title of the document rather than on the designated signature line. Under the circumstances presented herein, we conclude that the People failed to meet their "heavy burden of proving the voluntariness of the purported consent[ ]."

24 A.D.3d at __, 807 N.Y.S.2d at 233 (citations omitted).

§ 38:35 Admissibility of test result where defendant's blood withdrawn outside of New York

In *People v. Lerow*, 70 A.D.3d 66, 889 N.Y.S.2d 813 (4th Dep't 2009), the defendant was injured in a DWI-related motorcycle accident in New York, but was transported to a hospital in Pennsylvania for treatment. The defendant's blood was thereafter withdrawn for alcohol testing in compliance with New York law—but in Pennsylvania. The Appellate Division, Fourth Department, reversed County Court's ruling suppressing the test results, holding as follows:

[T]he specific question of whether a New York State police officer has the authority, under New York's implied consent law, to direct the withdrawal of blood from a suspect who is physically located outside of the state is a case of first impression in New York. "Generally, police officers have no power, including the authority to arrest, outside their geographical jurisdiction." Nonetheless, law enforcement officers may conduct investigations and collect evidence, including by seizure, outside their jurisdictional territory. Thus, courts in various other states have concluded that a police officer may direct the withdrawal of blood from a DWI suspect who has been transported across state lines for medical treatment because "this type of evidence gathering activity by a law enforcement officer is not limited to the officer's territorial jurisdiction."

Here, although Deputy Forsberg was no longer cloaked with state authority once he crossed the border into Pennsylvania, we conclude that he nonetheless remained a "police officer" for purposes of administering New York's implied consent law, even though defendant was physically located in Pennsylvania when the Deputy requested the blood draw. Section 1194 contains no geographic limitation on a police officer's authority to direct medical personnel to draw blood from a suspect motorist for purposes of blood alcohol testing. In our view, where, as here, an accident occurs in New York and the circumstances giving rise to an officer's reasonable grounds to believe that a suspect has violated Vehicle and Traffic Law § 1192 arise in New York, the mere fortuity of the suspect's removal from the state for the purpose of medical treatment should not deprive New York of the ability to enforce its laws proscribing the operation of a motor vehicle on its roadways while under the influence of alcohol. As the Illinois Supreme Court reasoned in confronting analogous facts, "[t]he defendant should not be released from the statutory consequences of his [or her] actions merely because [the defendant] was taken to an adjoining state for treatment of his [or her] injuries."

889 N.Y.S.2d at 817-18 (citations omitted).

§ 38:36   Necessity of formal arrest prior to requesting blood test where defendant is conscious

In *People v. Centerbar*, 80 A.D.3d 1008, __, 914 N.Y.S.2d 784, 786 (3d Dep't 2011), the Appellate Division, Third Department, held that:

[W]here, as here, police possess reasonable grounds to believe that a driver has been driving under the influence, they are authorized to direct that the driver's blood be drawn with the voluntary consent of the driver to submit to a chemical test and are not required to arrest the driver before obtaining such consent. That is, the arrest requirement in the implied consent law, like the two-hour time frame therein, has no application where a driver expressly and voluntarily consents to the administration of a blood alcohol test.

(Citations omitted).

§ 38:37   Testing dried blood

In *People v. Joseph*, 75 A.D.3d 1080, __, 903 N.Y.S.2d 651, 653 (4th Dep't 2010), leave to appeal denied, 15 N.Y.3d 853, 909 N.Y.S.2d 30, 935 N.E.2d 822 (2010), the Appellate Division, Fourth Department, held that:

We reject defendant's contention that Supreme Court erred in admitting in evidence the test results of blood samples taken from the interior of the vehicle driven by defendant on the date of the accident. . . . We also reject the contention of defendant that the court erred in allowing the People's expert to testify that the cocaine found in the blood samples taken from defendant's car was present in defendant's bloodstream prior to the accident. Based upon our review of the transcript of the *Frye* hearing, we conclude that the court properly determined that the techniques employed by the laboratory personnel were generally accepted as reliable within the scientific community. Although the samples tested by the People's expert were unique in the respect that they consisted of dried blood, the techniques employed by the expert, i.e., gas chromatography-mass spectrometry and immunoassay, were routine and generally accepted as reliable to detect the presence of cocaine and its metabolites.

(Citations omitted).

§ 38:38 Blood test results and *Crawford v. Washington*

In *Bullcoming v. New Mexico*, 131 S. Ct. 2705, 2709-10, 180 L. Ed. 2d 610 (2011), the Supreme Court held as follows:

In *Melendez-Diaz v. Massachusetts*, 557 U.S. __, 129 S.Ct. 2527, 174 L.Ed.2d 314 (2009), this Court held that a forensic laboratory report stating that a suspect substance was cocaine ranked as testimonial for purposes of the Sixth Amendment's Confrontation Clause. The report had been created specifically to serve as evidence in a criminal proceeding. Absent stipulation, the Court ruled, the prosecution may not introduce such a report without offering a live witness competent to testify to the truth of the statements made in the report.

In the case before us, petitioner Donald Bullcoming was arrested on charges of driving while intoxicated (DWI). Principal evidence against Bullcoming was a forensic laboratory report certifying that Bullcoming's blood-alcohol concentration was well above the threshold for aggravated DWI. At trial, the prosecution did not call as a witness the analyst who signed the certification. Instead, the State called another analyst who was familiar with the laboratory's testing procedures, but had neither participated in nor observed the test on Bullcoming's blood sample. The New Mexico Supreme Court determined that, although the blood-alcohol analysis was "testimonial," the Confrontation Clause did not require the certifying analyst's in-court testimony. Instead, New Mexico's high court held, live testimony of another analyst satisfied the constitutional requirements.

The question presented is whether the Confrontation Clause permits the prosecution to introduce a forensic laboratory report containing a testimonial certification—made for the purpose of proving a particular fact—through the in-court testimony of a scientist who did not sign the certification or perform or observe the test reported in the certification. We hold that surrogate testimony of that order does not meet the constitutional requirement. The accused's right is to be confronted with the analyst who made the certification, unless that analyst is unavailable at trial, and the accused had an opportunity, pretrial, to cross-examine that particular scientist.

See also People v. Rogers, 8 A.D.3d 888, __, 780 N.Y.S.2d 393, 397

(3d Dep't 2004).

Chapter 39

Extrapolation

Research References

Westlaw Databases

Drinking/Driving Litigation (2d ed.) (DRNKDRIVING)
Handling Drunk Driving Cases (2d ed.) (HDRUNKDR)

Treatises and Practice Aids

Nichols and Whited, Drinking/Driving Litigation: Criminal and Civil
§§ 14:56, 27:6 (2d ed.)
Fiandach, Handling Drunk Driving Cases §§ 10:7, 10:9, 10:12, 10:13 (2d
ed.)

KeyCite®: Cases and other legal materials listed in KeyCite Scope can be
researched through the KeyCite service on Westlaw®. Use KeyCite to check
citations for form, parallel references, prior and later history, and comprehensive citator information, including citations to other decisions and secondary
materials.

---

§ 39:1   Generally

Research References

West's Key Number Digest, Automobiles ⬅355(6), 414

Extrapolation is an attempt to "back-calculate" *from* what a
person's blood alcohol concentration was at the time of testing *to*
what the person's blood alcohol concentration must have been at
the time of operation. This is done by assuming an "average"
elimination rate of alcohol from the person's system. The usual
rate utilized is .015 per hour. Taking the number of hours that
elapse from the time of the operation of the vehicle to the time
that the blood was withdrawn, the alcohol that was presumably

eliminated is added back and the blood-alcohol concentration at the time of operation is determined.

One fairly consistent aspect of DWI cases is that there is almost always a substantial delay between the time of the alleged operation and the time that the blood, breath, or urine sample is drawn from the defendant. Blood tests are usually associated with motor vehicle accidents. There is an inherent delay involved with getting emergency equipment to the scene of an accident, and obtaining a blood sample.

Extrapolation has become an increasingly more common issue as prosecutor's attempt to introduce evidence of what the defendant's blood alcohol content (BAC) might have been at the time of *operation* by working backwards from what the BAC was at the time of *testing*. A defendant's BAC can change dramatically from the time of operation of the motor vehicle to the time of testing. Extrapolation is the biochemical equivalent of astrology. Astrology, however, is less dependent upon assumption and wishful thinking.

§ 39:2   Admission of extrapolation evidence

Research References

West's Key Number Digest, Automobiles ⊸355(6), 414

The legal foundation for extrapolation lies in *People v. Mertz*, 68 N.Y.2d 136, 506 N.Y.S.2d 290 (1986). Here, the court held that it was reversible error for the trial court to deny the *defendant* the right to argue that while the test result may have been inculpatory at the time he was tested, his BAC at the time of operation was less than that required to establish intoxication. In *Mertz*, the defendant was involved in an accident at 2:00 a.m. and taken to the hospital, where a Breathalyzer was administered. The first breath sample, taken at 3:25 a.m., produced a .15 BAC reading. The second sample, taken ten minutes later, yielded a .16 BAC reading. Officer Needleman, who administered the Breathalyzer, testified at trial that the difference between the two readings resulted from the defendant's failure to provide a deep lung air sample the first time. The defense presented expert testimony from a professor of physiology that:

> Alcohol is absorbed into the blood predominantly (ninety percent) through the small intestine and that the time for absorption varies, depending on the presence of food, the type of alcohol, the type of mixer, the physical state of the individual, and the presence of stress or trauma, from fifteen to forty minutes on the one hand to two to three hours on the other. Mixers and the presence of food, he explained, would delay the rate of absorption, fats being digested much more slowly, carbohydrates and proteins more rapidly. He

further identified the food (a bacon cheeseburger with french fries) which defendant had testified he had eaten at about 12:30 a.m., as consisting of protein and carbohydrates but to a large extent fat, the presence of which "dramatically delays the absorption of alcohol," and stated that it was possible that defendant's blood alcohol would be on the increase two to three hours after such a meal and that there was no way to predict from the .15 and .16 readings testified to by Needleman whether defendant's BAC was greater than .10 two hours earlier.

People v. Mertz, 506 N.Y.S.2d at 292.

Defense counsel attempted to argue on summation that it was fair to infer that the defendant's BAC was rising at 3:35 a.m. and that, at the time he was driving, it had been much lower. In response to the prosecutor's objection, the trial judge stated that the issue was whether the breath sample was taken within two hours of arrest and showed a BAC in excess of .10, and that "[t]heir concern would be what was the reading at 3:25 and 3:35, that's all."

The defendant was found guilty of VTL § 1192(2). On appeal, the Appellate Term affirmed, concluding:

> The gravamen of the crime is the operation of a motor vehicle after ingestion of sufficient alcohol to produce the reading condemned by the statute within two hours of arrest.

People v. Mertz, 506 N.Y.S.2d at 292.

On appeal to the Court of Appeals, Judge Meyer explained that in order to be found guilty of VTL § 1192(2), the trier of fact must determine that the defendant had a BAC of .10 or more *while operating a motor vehicle*. Evidence that a chemical test administered within two hours of the arrest produced such a reading is prima facie evidence that the defendant violated VTL § 1192(2). The Court of Appeals concluded that it was error not to allow defense counsel to argue that the defendant's BAC at the time the defendant operated the vehicle was less than .10.

> What this statute prescribes is operation of a motor vehicle "while [the operator] has .10 of one percentum or more by weight of alcohol in his blood." . . . The BAC count shown within two hours after arrest is strong but not conclusive evidence of the BAC during operation. To foreclose a defendant's introduction of evidence seeking to establish that his BAC while operating was less than .10 may raise doubt as to constitutionality (*see, Ulster County Court v. Allen*, 442 U.S. 140, 99 S.Ct. 2213, 60 L.Ed.2d 777) and, as already noted, to construe it as has the Appellate Term is essentially to rewrite the statute. We conclude, therefore, that proof of a Breathalyzer reading of .10 or more within two hours after arrest establishes prima facie a violation of Vehicle and Traffic Law § 1192(2) which, together with evidence of one or more of defendant's deportment, speech, stability, and the odor of his or her breath, is

sufficient to sustain a conviction, absent evidence, expert or other and by whichever party produced, from which the trier of fact could conclude that defendant's BAC at the time of vehicle operation was less than .10. When, however, as here, such evidence has been presented, defendant must be permitted to argue its significance to the jury. Because he was foreclosed from doing so and because the Court's ruling during defendant's attorney's summation and its instructions at the close of the case were in conflict on this issue, there must be a reversal.

People v. Mertz, 506 N.Y.S.2d at 295–96.

In *People v. Ladd*, 89 N.Y.2d 893, 653 N.Y.S.2d 259 (1996), the Court of Appeals considered, but did not decide the issue of the admissibility of extrapolation evidence by the prosecution. Here, the People's expert testified to an estimate of the defendant's blood alcohol concentration at the time of operation by extrapolating backwards from the test result obtained from the subsequent withdrawal of the defendant's blood. Essentially, the expert calculated the rate at which alcohol is eliminated from the body and then added that %age of eliminated alcohol to the test result obtained from the defendant's blood test. Holding that the defendant's objection to the admission of this "relation back" evidence was not preserved, the Court declined to rule on its admissibility.

In *People v. MacDonald*, 227 A.D.2d 672, 641 N.Y.S.2d 749 (3d Dep't), *aff'd*, 89 N.Y.2d 908, 653 N.Y.S.2d 267 (1996), the People used extrapolation to establish the defendant's BAC at the time he had been driving. A forensic toxicologist opined that the defendant's blood alcohol at the time of the accident was between .11% and .13%. The defendant argued on appeal that this "reverse extrapolation" testimony was improper. The Appellate Division, Third Department, disagreed:

[S]ince a proper foundation was laid by the People, the doctor qualified as an expert in his field, and his testimony was properly submitted to the jury for them to accept or reject.

227 A.D.2d at 673, 641 N.Y.S.2d at 751. On appeal, the Court of Appeals refused to address the issue of extrapolation, finding that the defendant failed to make a timely specific objection at trial to the sufficiency of the evidence.

In *People v. Stiffler*, 237 A.D.2d 753, 655 N.Y.S.2d 139 (3d Dep't 1997), the Appellate Division once again upheld the introduction of extrapolation testimony and the qualifications of the People's expert.

Finally, County Court did not abuse its discretion in receiving the expert testimony of David Rockefeller, the technical training supervisor for the Bureau of State (*sic*) Police and, as such, the individual responsible for the New York State Breathalyzer Test Operators Program. In our view, Rockefeller's training, education and experience qualified him to testify concerning the retrograde extrapolation method of determining a subject's blood alcohol level at a specified time interval prior to an established level. We are similarly unpersuaded that defendant's cross-examination of Rockefeller was unduly restricted.

People v. Stiffler, 655 N.Y.S.2d at 140 (citations omitted). *See also People v. Cross*, 273 A.D.2d 702, 711 N.Y.S.2d 533 (3d Dep't 2000); *People v. Hagin*, 238 A.D.2d 714, 657 N.Y.S.2d 105 (3d Dep't 1997) ("nor are we persuaded that the gas chromatograph test or Loomis' method of 'back calculation' to estimate defendant's blood alcohol level to be 0.26% at the time he drove his vehicle were flawed or in any way incompetent or otherwise inadmissible"). 657 N.Y.S.2d at 107.

Absorption of Alcohol

The contention by the defense in *Mertz* was that the driver's BAC was below the statutory limit at the time he was driving, but above the limit when the chemical test was administered. To present, or to respond to, this argument, one must be familiar with the manner in which alcohol is absorbed into and eliminated from the blood.

There are numerous factors which affect the rate of absorption of alcohol into the blood. Upon consuming an alcoholic beverage, the beverage travels to the stomach, where 5% to 20% of the alcohol consumed is absorbed into the blood stream. If the individual's stomach is empty, the alcohol remains in the stomach for a short period of time before entering the small intestine, where the majority of the alcohol is rapidly absorbed through the walls of the small intestine into the blood stream. Fitzgerald and Hume, Erroneous Expert Opinion and the Civil and Criminal Trial of Intoxication Cases: Widmark Revisited, The Champion (December 1983). Once in the blood, the alcohol is carried throughout the body. The characteristic signs of intoxication are exhibited when the alcohol reaches the brain.

§ 39:3 Effect of stomach content

Research References

West's Key Number Digest, Automobiles ⬭355(6), 414

When a person is drinking on an empty stomach, alcohol is absorbed into the blood at a rate greater than it is being eliminated, resulting in a BAC that is rising. It takes approximately 30 to 90 minutes to reach a peak BAC level on an empty stomach. Following a study on individuals who drank alcohol on an empty stomach, it was learned that the peak BAC was reached within 45 minutes for 77% of the subjects and within 75 minutes for 97% of them. As expected, greater quantities of alcohol consumption resulted in a higher peak BAC. However, the time required to reach the peak was not significantly influenced by the quantity of alcohol consumed. Jones, A.W., Jonsson, K.A., and Neri, A., "Peak Blood Ethanol Concentration and the Time of Its Occurrence After Rapid Drinking on an Empty Stomach," *Journal of Forensic Sciences*, JFSCA, vol. 36, no.2, March, 1991, pp. 376–85.

Eventually, the BAC will reach a maximum and begin to decrease as more alcohol is being eliminated than being absorbed. Thus, if a driver is stopped while his BAC is increasing, and a period of time elapses prior to testing, the BAC at the time of testing will be higher than the BAC at the time the individual was driving.

If the person is eating food while drinking alcohol, the alcohol will remain in his stomach with the food for a period of time before it is released into the small intestine through the pyloric valve. While the stomach contents are being broken down, the pyloric valve remains clenched and absorption is delayed. The pyloric valve is a muscle that resembles the clutch portion of a woman's clutch purse. The valve clenches shut when the stomach contains food and liquid being digested. Food is broken down into the stomach into a semi-liquid mass called chyme, which is of a composition and in a form acceptable to the small intestine. The food leaves the stomach and goes into the small intestine. Fitzgerald and Hume, *Intoxication Test Evidence, Criminal and Civil*, § 2:5, p. 13. Thus, the passage of the alcohol into the small intestine, where the alcohol is absorbed more rapidly, is delayed by the presence of food. Bayly and McCallum, *Some Aspects of Alcohol in Body Fluids. Part II: The Change in Blood Alcohol Concentration Following Alcohol Consumption*, 2 Med. J. Austl. 172, 173 (1959); Sedman, et al., *Food Effects on Absorption and Metabolism of Alcohol*, 37 J. Stud. Alcohol 1197 (1976). Studies have shown that it will take up to three hours to reach a maximum BAC level when alcohol is consumed with or after a meal.

However, there is a study that says that most of the alcohol is absorbed through the walls of the stomach into the bloodstream and is not dependent upon getting into the small intestine. This study revealed that the average time required to reach maximum BAC was 41 minutes for both full and empty stomach conditions. The average time required to return to zero BAC was also similar in both conditions. However, this study revealed that the presence of food in the stomach reduced the peak BAC by an average of 21.5%. Watkins and Adler, The Effect of Food on Alcohol Absorption and Elimination Patterns, Journal of Forensic Sciences JFSCA, Vol. 38, No. 2, March 1993, pp. 285–91.

Not only does the *presence* of food affect the rate at which alcohol is absorbed into the blood, the *type* of food present in the stomach will also affect the rate of absorption. Fatty foods, which take longer for the stomach to digest, will increase the period of time the alcohol remains in the stomach. A greasy hamburger is far more of a challenge than a piece of watermelon.

Consider the following scenario:

> An individual enjoys cocktails while consuming a high fat content meal. Assume that upon complete absorption, the individual's blood alcohol level will reach a peak of 0.14 percent. Complete absorption, however, will not occur for three hours due to the large quantity of fat food consumed.

> The individual is involved in a minor accident thirty minutes after his last drink while his blood alcohol level is only 0.04 percent. This low blood alcohol level could be found if an individual were booked immediately. The suspect is taken to police headquarters, however, and waits for testing.

> A test thirty minutes after the accident would show 0.065 percent. Testing at one hour, one and one-half hours and two hours would show 0.088 percent, 0.110 percent, and 0.127 percent, respectively. The individual's .14 percent peak would not be reached until two and one-half hours after the accident.

Fitzgerald and Hume, *The Single Chemical Test for Intoxication: A Challenge to Admissibility*, 66 Mass. L. Rev., 23, 29–30 (1981).

The peak is the highest BAC attained as a result of the absorption of alcohol. Considering these factors (*i.e.*, the amount of alcohol consumed; the amount and type of food ingested; and the amount of time which has elapsed), the determination of an actual BAC by extrapolation is highly dubious.

> Some experts testify that it "can't" take longer than two hours for all of the alcohol to absorb to a peak *after the end of drinking*. That is false. The authors have personal experience with cases where significantly "higher" BACs were obtained on tests 1.5 hours to 2 hours after the driving incident. In one case, a third test was obtained which affirmed the validity of the first two, gave shape to the curve, and confirmed that the BAC was still rising 3 hours after drinking and 2 hours after the "arrest." The values were also consistent with the eating and drinking history. Some studies have also confirmed that alcohol absorption may be continuing, although in small amounts, for even longer periods. Clearly, this area needs considerably more attention than it has been given to date.

Fitzgerald, *Intoxication Test Evidence 2d*, footnote 8, § 2:8.

§ 39:4 Strength of the beverage

Research References

West's Key Number Digest, Automobiles ⊕355(6), 414

The strength of the beverage may also affect the absorption time. The stronger the concentration of alcohol in the stomach or intestine, the greater the driving force pushing it into the blood and the faster it will get into the blood. However, a strong drink is an irritant and may cause the pyloric valve to stay shut. This valve must be open to allow stomach contents to get into the small intestine. If the valve is shut, the absorption of alcohol will be delayed.

§ 39:5   Trauma and shock

Research References

West's Key Number Digest, Automobiles ⊙355(6), 414

In the event there is an accident, blood supply may be preferentially diverted to the heart, lungs and kidneys and away from the digestive system. The body, attempting to cope with the emergency, diverts the blood supply to those places where it is needed most. Thus, the rate of absorption is reduced.

> I will be the first to admit that if any physical or even mental disturbance occurs soon after the food is swallowed, the whole digestive process can be drastically altered. For example, if a person is assaulted or frightened or taken ill, or knocked unconscious half an hour after a meal, the digestive process can either stop entirely or proceed very slowly or irregularly . . .

Fitzgerald, *Intoxication Test Evidence 2d*, § 2:10, quoting *Autopsy* by Dr. Milton Helpern.

§ 39:6   Gastric juices

Research References

West's Key Number Digest, Automobiles ⊙355(6), 414

Gastric juices break down food in the stomach and prepare the stomach contents for absorption into the small intestine. Obviously, the action of these gastric juices has a bearing on the rate at which alcohol is absorbed into the bloodstream. As with virtually every other aspect of physiology, there are significant differences among people. As one individual stated:

> If normal facial features varied as much as gastric juices do, some of our noses would be about the size of navy beans, while others would be the size of 20 lb. watermelons.

Williams, You Are Extraordinary, Pyramid Books, N.Y., 1957, p. 24.

§ 39:7   Sex

Research References

West's Key Number Digest, Automobiles ⊙355(6), 414

Studies have shown that the sex of the individual has an impact on the absorption and elimination of alcohol. One study found that it takes men 1.35% times longer to absorb alcohol than women. Further, the elimination of alcohol by women was 23.6% faster than men. K. M. Dubowski, Human Pharmacokinetics of Ethanol, Alc. Tech. Rep. 5; 55 to 63, 1976.

In an article entitled *High Blood Alcohol Levels in Women*, N. Engl. J. Med., 1990; 322:95-9, Dr. Mario Frezza, *et al.*, discussed the significance of the metabolism of alcohol in the stomach. Essentially, the article reports the fact that alcohol is oxidized in the stomach as the result of "gastroalcohol dehydrogenase activity." Essentially, this activity is far greater in men than it is in women. Further, alcoholism tends to cut this activity in half in men and virtually eliminate it in women.

§ 39:8 Steepling effect

Research References

West's Key Number Digest, Automobiles ☞355(6), 414

Periodic measurements of a person's blood alcohol content over a short period of time reveal a "steepling" effect of breath test results. *See* Rod G. Gullberg, *Employing Simulated Data to Illustrate an Important Cause of the "Steepling" Effect in Breath Alcohol Analysis*, Med. Sci. Law, Vol. 34, No. 4 (1994). In other words, a graphing of the measurements over a short period of time shows various increases and decreases in the blood alcohol content. The graph is not a consistent increase followed by a consistent decrease but, rather, shows "large positive and negative excursions in short intervals over the course of an individual's blood alcohol concentration time curve." The study is summarized in the August 4, 1995, Drinking/Driving Law Letter, at page 242.

The concern is that an arrested individual might provide a breath sample while on a "peak"; as opposed to being tested during a "valley," where the BAC reading would be significantly lower. The author noted that the steepling effect becomes of great concern "at or near the critical per se level." Mr. Goldberg of the Washington State Patrol Breath Test section, measured BACs at intervals of every 0.2 hours. He concluded that the impact of the steepling effect could be reduced through the routine performance of multiple samples for evidentiary purposes.

It is Mr. Goldberg's position that the steepling effect was attributable to both analytical and biological components inherent in breath alcohol sampling and measurement.

§ 39:9 Hyperthermia

Research References

West's Key Number Digest, Automobiles ☞355(6), 414

For each one degree celsius increase in core body temperature, a person's breath alcohol concentration will be falsely elevated approximately 8.62% above her blood alcohol concentration. This conclusion was the result of a study by Glyn R. Fox, Ph.D., and John S. Hayward, Ph.D., entitled, "Effect of Hyperthermia and Breath Alcohol Analysis," published in the Journal of Forensic Science, Vol.34, No.4, July, 1989. According to the authors, the magnitude of this distorting effect is too large to be ignored in breath testing procedures.

A person's core body temperature may be significantly elevated—thereby resulting in an increased breath alcohol concentration—by such factors as fever, consumption of certain drugs (*i.e.*, amphetamines), heavy physical exertion, and exposure to high ambient air or water temperatures as found in saunas or hot tubs. The authors recommend direct monitoring of breath temperature to prevent the increased likelihood of a suspect being unjustly convicted.

§ 39:10   Alcohol elimination

Research References

West's Key Number Digest, Automobiles ☞355(6), 414

In 1932, E. M. P. Widmark, a Swedish chemist, gave a fixed amount of alcohol to 30 individuals on an empty stomach and then tested their BAC at regular intervals. Widmark concluded that the body eliminates alcohol at an average rate of 0.015% per hour. Initially, prosecutors used this 0.015% figure to argue that a suspect's BAC was higher at the time of driving than at the time of testing. However, without knowing whether the BAC was increasing or decreasing at the time of testing, it is impossible to determine whether the BAC at the time the individual was driving was lower or higher than the BAC at the time of the test. If the individual's BAC was increasing (*i.e.*, the rate of absorption of alcohol exceeded the rate of elimination), the BAC at the time of testing would result in a BAC that is higher than the BAC at the time of driving. If the BAC was decreasing (*i.e.*, the 0.015 elimination rate was greater than the absorption rate), the test result would be lower than the BAC at the time the driver operated the vehicle.

While the elimination of alcohol is principally through the liver, some alcohol is eliminated through urine, breath, perspiration, and other routes. Although the average alcohol elimination rate is 0.015% per hour, research has demonstrated that individual elimination rates vary from 0.006% to 0.04% per hour. M. Bogusz, *Comparative Studies on the Rate of Ethanol Elimination*, 22 J. Forensic Science 446 (1977); Kurt M. Dubowski, *Absorption,*

Distribution and Elimination of Alcohol; Highway Safety Aspects, Supp. 10 J. Studies on Alcohol 98 (1985). Just as food affects the rate of absorption, food affects elimination of alcohol as well. Allen J. Sedman, et al., *Food Effects on Absorption and Metabolism of Alcohol*, 37 J. Studies on Alcohol 1197 (1976).

As a person increases in age, there is a significant increase in blood alcohol elimination rates. K. M. Dubowski, *Absorption, Distribution and Elimination of Alcohol: Highway Safety Aspects*, Journal of Studies on Alcohol 10, (July 1985). Further, absorption and elimination rates vary within the same day depending on the time of day. B. M. Jones, *Circadian Variation and the Effects of Alcohol on Cognizant Performance*, U. J. Stud. Alcohol 35: 1212–19 (1974).

In *Missouri v. McNeely*, 133 S. Ct. 1552, 1560-61, 185 L. Ed. 2d 696 (2013), the Supreme Court stated that:

> It is true that as a result of the human body's natural metabolic processes, the alcohol level in a person's blood begins to dissipate once the alcohol is fully absorbed and continues to decline until the alcohol is eliminated. Testimony before the trial court in this case indicated that the percentage of alcohol in an individual's blood typically decreases by approximately 0.015 percent to 0.02 percent per hour once the alcohol has been fully absorbed. More precise calculations of the rate at which alcohol dissipates depend on various individual characteristics (such as weight, gender, and alcohol tolerance) and the circumstances in which the alcohol was consumed. Regardless of the exact elimination rate, it is sufficient for our purposes to note that because an individual's alcohol level gradually declines soon after he stops drinking, a significant delay in testing will negatively affect the probative value of the results.
> * * *
>
> While experts can work backwards from the BAC at the time the sample was taken to determine the BAC at the time of the alleged offense, longer intervals may raise questions about the accuracy of the calculation.

(Citations omitted).

Chapter 40

Compulsory Chemical Test

Research References

Westlaw Databases

Handling a Criminal Case in New York (HCCNY)
Handling Drunk Driving Cases (2d ed.) (HDRUNKDR)
New York Vehicle and Traffic Law 2d (NYVEH)

Treatises and Practice Aids

Muldoon, Handling a Criminal Case in New York § 9:72
Fiandach, Handling Drunk Driving Cases § 9:1 (2d ed.)
Rose, New York Vehicle and Traffic Law 2d § 35:9

§ 40:1 Persons subject to order

Research References

West's Key Number Digest, Automobiles ⊙414

In October 1983, the so-called "bloodsucker" bill became law in New York State. Essentially, this legislation allowed a police officer or a district attorney to make application to specified courts for an order to compel a person to submit to a chemical test to determine the alcohol or drug content of their blood upon a finding of reasonable cause to believe that:

(1) Such person was the operator of a motor vehicle and in the course of such operation a person other than the operator was killed or suffered serious physical injury as defined in section 10.00 of the Penal Law; and

(2) a. either such person operated the vehicle in violation of any subdivision of section 1192 of this article, or

b. a breath test administered by a police officer in accordance with paragraph (b) of subdivision one of this section indicates that alcohol has been consumed by such person; and

(3) such person has been placed under lawful arrest; and

(4) such person has refused to submit to a chemical test or any portion thereof, requested in accordance with the provisions of paragraph (a) of subdivision two of this section, or is unable to give consent to such a test. VTL § 1194(3)(b).

In *People v. Hogue*, 136 A.D.3d 1351, __, 24 N.Y.S.3d 474, 476 (4th Dep't 2016), leave to appeal denied, 27 N.Y.3d 1133, 2016 WL 3767594 (2016), the Appellate Division, Fourth Department, held that:

We reject defendant's . . . contention that the warrant application was insufficient because it failed to provide sufficient facts to support the conclusion that a passenger in defendant's vehicle "suffered serious physical injury" as required by Vehicle and Traffic Law § 1194(3)(b)(1). The warrant application stated that a passenger in the vehicle had been "seriously injured" inasmuch as he had sustained lacerations to the head, was trapped inside the vehicle, and needed to be "[m]ercy [f]lighted" to a hospital. We conclude that those statements are sufficient to meet the requirements of section 1194(3)(b)(1).

§ 40:2 Reasonable cause

Research References

West's Key Number Digest, Automobiles ⊙414

VTL § 1194(3)(c) defines "reasonable cause" as being determined by the totality of the circumstances, which must indicate that the operator was driving in violation of VTL § 1192. Such circumstances may include evidence of operation in violation of VTL § 1100 or any other moving violation; visible indications of alcohol or drug consumption or impairment; the existence of an open container containing an alcoholic beverage in or around the vehicle; or any other evidence indicating that the operator had been impaired by the consumption of alcohol or drugs; or was intoxicated at the time of the incident.

In *People v. Miller*, 50 A.D.3d 1161, 855 N.Y.S.2d 379 (2d Dep't 2008), the Appellate Division, Second Department, held that:

> Contrary to the People's contentions, the blood sample at issue was taken from the defendant in violation of Vehicle and Traffic Law § 1194(2)(a)(1) and § 1194(3), and the results of the test were therefore properly suppressed.

§ 40:3 Local criminal courts excluded

Research References
West's Key Number Digest, Automobiles ☞414

Procedurally, application for a court order may be made to:

> [A]ny supreme court justice, county court judge or district court judge in the judicial district in which the incident occurred, or if the incident occurred in the city of New York before any supreme court justice or judge of the criminal court of the city of New York.

VTL § 1194(3)(d)(1).

The exclusion of the local criminal courts outside of New York City is somewhat anomalous considering their number and accessibility.

§ 40:4 Oral application authorized

Research References
West's Key Number Digest, Automobiles ☞414

The statute provides that the application may be communicated by telephone, radio or other means of electronic communication, or in person. The applicant is required to identify himself by name and title, and the Court must place the applicant under oath as well as any other person providing information in support of the application. VTL § 1194(3)(d)(1) and (2).

§ 40:5 Necessity of oath

Research References
West's Key Number Digest, Automobiles ☞414

Failure to swear the applicant can result in the suppression of any evidence obtained. In *People v. Dunn*, 117 A.D.2d 863, 498 N.Y.S.2d 577 (3d Dep't 1986), the Appellate Division affirmed the suppression of a blood alcohol test result where a state police investigator obtained a search warrant from a local criminal court pursuant to CPL § 690.10. The application was neither subscribed nor sworn to by the investigator. Further, the town judge testified at the hearing that the investigator did not orally swear to the contents of his statement submitted in support of his application for the warrant. Finding a failure to comply with the constitutional and statutory requirements, suppression was mandated. 498 N.Y.S.2d at 577 to 78.

In *People v. Rollins*, 118 A.D.2d 949, 499 N.Y.S.2d 817 (3d Dep't 1986), the trooper was not sworn prior to making the application. The transcript, however, clearly showed that the trooper thought he was sworn. Specifically, the application began with the trooper stating:

William L. Bean, being duly sworn.

Accordingly, the court upheld the oath on the ground that it was clear that the trooper thought he was sworn and did, in fact, swear to the contents of the application retroactively. While a retroactive oath would probably not be sufficient, the fact that the trooper stated he was sworn was sufficient for the court to affirm the validity of the resultant order. 499 N.Y.S.2d at 819.

§ 40:6   Content of application

Research References

West's Key Number Digest, Automobiles ⊕414

The applicant must swear:

(a) that the person from whom the chemical test is requested was the operator of the vehicle;

(b) that in the course of such operation a person, other than the operator, had been killed or seriously injured;

(c) that based upon the totality of the circumstances, there is reasonable cause to believe that such person was operating the motor vehicle in violation of any subdivision of VTL § 1192; and

(d) that after being placed under lawful arrest, such person refused to submit to a chemical test in accordance with the provisions of VTL § 1194, or is otherwise unable to give his consent to such a test.

Additionally, the applicant must make specific allegations of fact to support his statement. Any other person who is properly identified and sworn may present allegations of fact in support of the application. VTL § 1194(3)(d)(2).

In *People v. Hilker*, 133 A.D.2d 986, 521 N.Y.S.2d 136 (3d Dep't 1987), the defendant moved to suppress a compulsory chemical test result on the ground of a conflict between the sworn statement of Officer Barner provided at the time of his application and Barner's testimony at the hearing. Specifically, Officer Barner testified throughout all proceedings that, in his opinion, the defendant was not intoxicated; only impaired. In the application for the order, Barner swore that he believed the defendant was intoxicated.

In rejecting this assertion, the Appellate Division held that the legality of the arrest was not conditioned upon whether the officer specified the correct subdivision of VTL § 1192, or upon his belief as to which subdivision had been violated. The statute required only that Officer Barner had reasonable cause to believe that the defendant had violated any subdivision of VTL § 1192. 521 N.Y.S.2d at 138.

§ 40:7 Hearsay application

Research References

West's Key Number Digest, Automobiles ☞414

In *People v. Whelan,* 165 A.D.2d 313, 567 N.Y.S.2d 817 (2d Dep't 1991), the court held that hearsay was admissible in support of an application for a compulsory chemical test order. The Court held that the *Aguilar-Spinelli* test (*see Aguilar v. Texas*, 378 U.S. 108, 84 S.Ct. 1509 (1964); *Spinelli v. United States*, 393 U.S. 410, 89 S.Ct. 584 (1969)) is as applicable to compulsory chemical test orders as it is to search warrants. Thus, the judge must determine that the informant was reliable and had a basis of knowledge. In this case, the Assistant District Attorney made the application without reference to his sources. While it was clear that the application consisted entirely of hearsay and double hearsay, the court held that that fact, in and of itself, did not render the application defective:

Search warrants based on hearsay information have long been held to be valid where there is "a substantial basis for crediting the hearsay statement" (*People v. Hanlon*, 36 N.Y.2d 549, 557, 369 N.Y.S.2d 677, 330 N.E.2d 631). The procedure for evaluating the hearsay statements of informants involves the two-pronged *Aguilar-Spinelli* test . . ., which remains the controlling test to be applied in New York (*see, People v. Griminger*, 71 N.Y.2d 635, 529 N.Y.S.2d 55, 524 N.E.2d 409). This court has recently held that probable cause to arrest may be established by double hearsay as long as each informant in the chain of narration passes the *Aguilar-Spinelli* test (*see, People v. Greene*, 153 A.D.2d 439, 443–445, 552 N.Y.S.2d 640, *cert. denied* 498 U.S. 947, 111 S.Ct. 363, 112 L.Ed.2d 326). By parity of reasoning, an application under Vehicle and Traffic Law § 1194(3) based on double hearsay would be valid if each informant passes the *Aguilar-Spinelli* test.

567 N.Y.S.2d at 822 (citations omitted).

In this case, the ADA's failure to disclose that his information consisted of hearsay and to state the sources of the hearsay rendered the application fatally defective. *See also People v. Isaac*, 224 A.D.2d 993, 637 N.Y.S.2d 827 (4th Dep't 1996).

Similarly, in *People v. Freeman*, 46 A.D.3d 1375, —, 848 N.Y.S.2d 800, 801-02 (4th Dep't 2007), leave to appeal denied, 10 N.Y.3d 840, 859 N.Y.S.2d 399, 889 N.E.2d 86 (2008), the Appellate Division, Fourth Department, held that:

> We agree with defendant . . . that the court erred in denying his motion to suppress the results of a compulsory blood test performed on him, and we therefore modify the judgment accordingly. . . . [The evidence at the suppression hearing] established that the Trooper who applied for a court-ordered blood test relied upon double hearsay, i.e., statements made by civilian witnesses to a fellow Trooper, to support his belief that the accident in question occurred "in the course of" defendant's operation of a motor vehicle (Vehicle and Traffic Law § 1194[3][b][1]). Although an application for a court-ordered blood test may contain hearsay and double hearsay statements that satisfy the *Aguilar-Spinelli* test, the application must disclose that it is supported by hearsay and identify the source or sources of the hearsay. Here, the application did not disclose that any of its information was based upon statements from civilian witnesses, nor did the application set forth that the Trooper had an independent basis for a finding of reasonable cause to believe that the accident occurred in the course of the operation by defendant of his vehicle. We thus conclude that the application and the ensuing order for a compulsory blood test were defective and that the evidence obtained therefrom should have been suppressed.

(Citations omitted). *See also People v. Earley*, 121 A.D.3d 1192, —, 994 N.Y.S.2d 443, 444-45 (3d Dep't 2014), leave to appeal denied, 25 N.Y.3d 1200, 2015 WL 4875883 (2015) ("the results of the court-ordered blood test should have been suppressed because the investigator who applied for the order failed to advise County Court that he relied on hearsay. . . . Accordingly, the motion to suppress the blood test results should have been granted and, in the absence of those results, the conviction for aggravated driving while intoxicated must be vacated").

In *People v. Walsh*, 137 Misc. 2d 1073, 523 N.Y.S.2d 752 (Monroe Co. Ct. 1988), an Assistant District Attorney applied for a compulsory chemical test order by calling the county court judge at the judge's home. The ADA had been contacted by the police.

> At no time were police officers or others with actual personal knowledge of the facts of the incident put under oath to give sworn testimony prior to the granting of the Court ordered blood test, nor

did the judge have contact with anyone other than the Assistant District Attorney.

523 N.Y.S.2d at 753.

In granting the motion to suppress, the court held that the statute made no provision for a hearsay application and, to the contrary, the statute required that the Court place under oath the applicant as well as any other person providing information in support of the application. 523 N.Y.S.2d at 753.

By contrast, in *People v. Sierra*, 85 A.D.3d 1659, __, 925 N.Y.S.2d 749, 752 (4th Dep't 2011), leave to appeal denied, 17 N.Y.3d 905, 933 N.Y.S.2d 660, 957 N.E.2d 1164 (2011), the Appellate Division, Fourth Department, held that:

> We reject the contention of defendant that the order permitting the chemical test of his blood was not obtained in compliance with Vehicle and Traffic Law § 1194(3). Even assuming, arguendo, that the Assistant District Attorney and County Court . . . failed to comply with the requirements of Vehicle and Traffic Law § 1194(3)(d)(2), we conclude that such noncompliance "was of no moment because there was the requisite substantial compliance with the requirements of the statute." Defendant further contends that the application for the chemical test of his blood was insufficient because the witnesses who offered statements in support thereof were not placed under oath. We reject that contention. "[A]n application for a court-ordered blood test may contain hearsay and double hearsay statements that satisfy the *Aguilar-Spinelli* test [if] the application . . . disclose[s] that it is supported by hearsay and identif[ies] the source or sources of the hearsay." "[T]he two-part *Aguilar-Spinelli* test requir[es] a showing that the informant is reliable and has a basis of knowledge for the information imparted" and, upon our review of the record, we conclude that the *Aguilar-Spinelli* requirements were satisfied here.

(Citations omitted). *See also People v. Licausi*, 122 A.D.3d 771, __, 996 N.Y.S.2d 188, 190 (2d Dep't 2014), leave to appeal denied, 25 N.Y.3d 1166, 15 N.Y.S.3d 298, 36 N.E.3d 101 (2015) ("Under the circumstances here, although the police did not strictly comply with the procedures for obtaining a court order to compel the defendant to submit to a chemical blood test under Vehicle and Traffic Law § 1194(3), there was substantial compliance with the requirements of the statute").

In *People v. Hogue*, 136 A.D.3d 1351, __, 24 N.Y.S.3d 474, 475-76 (4th Dep't 2016), leave to appeal denied, 27 N.Y.3d 1133, 2016 WL 3767594 (2016), the Appellate Division, Fourth Department, held that:

> "[A]n application for a court-ordered blood test may contain hearsay and double hearsay" as long as the application "disclose[s] that it is supported by hearsay and identif[ies] the source or sources of the hearsay." Here, the warrant application and supporting affidavit

both stated that they were based on the observations of the police officer who responded to the scene of the accident.

(Citation omitted).

§ 40:8   Procedure for oral application

Research References
West's Key Number Digest, Automobiles ⬤414

Where the application is being made orally, the judge must place the applicant under oath as well as any other person providing information in support of the application. VTL § 1194(3)(d)(3). The oath and all subsequent communications must be recorded by means of a voice recording device or verbatim stenographic or verbatim long-hand notes. Where a voice recording device is used, or stenographic record is made, the judge is required to have the record transcribed, and must certify its accuracy, and file the original record and transcription with the court within 72 hours of the issuance of the court order. Where longhand notes are taken, the judge is required to subscribe a copy and file it with the court within 24 hours of the issuance of the order. VTL § 1194(3)(d)(3).

Where the application is made orally, the applicant prepares the order in accordance with the judge's instructions. The order must contain the name of the issuing judge, the name of the applicant and the date and time it was issued. If the order is issued in person, the judge must sign it; if it is issued orally by means of electronic communication, the applicant signs it. VTL § 1194(3)(d)(4).

The statute provides that false statements made in support of this application are subject to the penalties of perjury as set forth in Article 210 of the Penal Law. VTL § 1194(3)(d)(5). The statute directs the chief administrator of the courts to establish a schedule to insure that a sufficient number of judges will be available in each judicial district to hear oral applications for court orders authorized by this section. VTL § 1194(3)(d)(6).

§ 40:9   Hospital personnel—Statutory immunity

Research References
West's Key Number Digest, Automobiles ⬤414

Where an order is issued pursuant to this section, the provisions of VTL § 1194(4)(a)(1) specifying those persons authorized to draw blood are applicable. Additionally, the provisions of VTL § 1194(4)(a)(2), (3), (4), and (5) immunizing and indemnifying physicians or other persons drawing blood pursuant to the request of a police officer have been extended to protect other hospital employees and security personnel assisting in the withdrawing of a compulsory blood sample pursuant to VTL § 1194(3).

§ 40:10 Compulsory chemical tests subject to CPL § 710.20 hearing

Research References

West's Key Number Digest, Automobiles ⟜414

This statute also provides for defense motions to suppress results obtained pursuant to this section. CPL § 710.20(5) specifies that compulsory chemical test results are subject to suppression upon the ground that it:

> Consists of a chemical test of the defendant's blood administered in violation of the provisions of subdivision three of section eleven hundred ninety-four of the vehicle and traffic law, subdivision eight of section forty-nine-a of the navigation law or any other applicable law.

§ 40:11 Compulsory test order negates test refusal

Research References

West's Key Number Digest, Automobiles ⟜414

Department of Motor Vehicles' policy deems that a blood sample obtained as a result of a compulsory chemical test order negates the test refusal that gave rise to the application for the order in the first instance. Although the defendant refused a chemical test, the issuance of a compulsory chemical test order removes the case from the purview of the test refusal procedures. Accordingly, a defendant from whom blood has been obtained pursuant to this section is neither subject to a refusal suspension at arraignment, nor subsequent revocation at a test refusal hearing. *See* Department of Motor Vehicle Counsel's letter in Appendix 39.

§ 40:12 Compulsory test order must be in writing

Research References

West's Key Number Digest, Automobiles ⟜414

Although this statute authorizes oral *application* for a compulsory test order, nothing in the law permits blood to be drawn pursuant to an oral order. The applicant is required to reduce the order to writing, fill in the judge's name and sign his own name as well as the time and date that the order is issued.

VTL § 1194(3)(d)(4) states:

> When a judge or justice determines to issue an order to compel

submission to a chemical test based on an oral application, the applicant therefor shall prepare the order in accordance with the instructions of the judge or justice. In all cases the order shall include the name of the issuing judge or justice, the name of the applicant, and the date and time it was issued. It must be signed by the judge or justice if issued in person, or by the applicant if issued orally.

Failure to comply with this procedure can result in the suppression of any evidence obtained. In *People v. Crandall*, 108 A.D.2d 413, 489 N.Y.S.2d 614 (3d Dep't 1985), *aff'd*, 69 N.Y.2d 459, 515 N.Y.S.2d 745 (1987), the state police made oral application for a search warrant for the purpose of searching for drugs on the person of the defendant, his possessions and truck. Although the application passed judicial muster, the police's failure to reduce the order to writing rendered the warrant fatally defective. While the court observed that technical defects might be excused:

> The recording, transcribing, certifying and filing requirements of the statute are designed to insure the regularity of the process of applying for the warrant and to preserve the integrity of the record for review in any ensuing criminal litigation. Mandating the reduction of the warrant to a written instrument and the reading of it to the issuing Judge performs not only these functions, but important others.

489 N.Y.S.2d at 618.

In *People v. White*, 133 Misc. 2d 386, 506 N.Y.S.2d 815 (1986), Judge Fried of the Bronx County Supreme Court was confronted with a motion to suppress a blood test result obtained pursuant to a compulsory chemical test order. The issue was almost identical to that confronted by the appellate division in *People v. Crandall*, 108 A.D.2d 413, 489 N.Y.S.2d 614 (3d Dep't 1985), *aff'd*, 69 N.Y.2d 459, 515 N.Y.S.2d 745 (1987). Citing that decision, Judge Fried rejected arguments of good faith and substantial compliance and granted the motion to suppress.

In *People v. Walsh*, 137 Misc. 2d 1073, 523 N.Y.S.2d 752 (Monroe Co. Ct. 1988), the court held that the failure to reduce the compulsory chemical test order to writing until after the blood had been drawn rendered the procedure fatally defective:

> The statutory language clearly contemplates a written order prepared by the applicant on the other end of the phone line and signed by the applicant at that time because obviously the judge is not present to do it in person. The legislature must have felt that the taking of blood from a person without consent was of sufficient importance to require written documentation.

523 N.Y.S.2d at 753.

It is clear from an examination of the statute as well as these decisions that while the law contemplates an oral application, the order itself must be reduced to writing and failure to do so will constitute a basis for the suppression of any evidence obtained.

§ 40:13   Challenging factual basis of order

Research References

West's Key Number Digest, Automobiles ☞414

Where the defendant makes a preliminary showing that a false statement, made knowingly or with reckless disregard of the truth, was included by the officer in the compulsory order application, the defendant may be entitled to a hearing to determine the validity of the order. In *People v. Putsis*, 217 A.D.2d 670, 630 N.Y.S.2d 86 (2d Dep't 1995), the defendant argued that the results of the compulsory chemical test should have been suppressed because the order directing the test was improperly obtained by false allegations. Here, the defendant was involved in an automobile accident that resulted in fatal injuries. When applying for a compulsory chemical test order, the officer did not advise the court that the defendant's companion had been initially arrested based on the companion's claim that he had been driving. Citing *Franks v. Delaware*, 438 U.S. 154, 165, 98 S.Ct. 2674, 2681 (1978), the court rejected the defendant's argument that the police officer who applied for the order intentionally or recklessly misrepresented the facts.

In *Franks v. Delaware*, the United States Supreme Court articulated the requirements to obtain a hearing where there are allegations of deliberate falsehood or reckless disregard of the truth by the affiant officer.

> To mandate an evidentiary hearing, . . . there must be allegations of deliberate falsehood or of reckless disregard for the truth, and those allegations must be accompanied by an offer of proof. They should point out specifically the portion of the warrant affidavit that is claimed to be false; and they should be accompanied by a statement of supporting reasons . . . . Allegations of negligence or innocent mistake are insufficient . . . . Finally, if these requirements are met and if, when material that is the subject of the alleged falsity or reckless disregard is set to one side, there remains sufficient content in the warrant affidavit to support a finding of probable cause, no hearing is required. On the other hand, if the remaining content is insufficient, the defendant is entitled, under the Fourth and 14th Amendments, to his hearing.

Franks v. Delaware, 438 U.S. at 170–74, 98 S.Ct. at 2684–85. *See also People v. Tambe*, 71 N.Y.2d 492, 527 N.Y.S.2d 372 (1988).

§ 40:14 Presentation of order not required at blood withdrawal

Research References

West's Key Number Digest, Automobiles ⊙414

In *People v. Whelan*, 165 A.D.2d 313, 567 N.Y.S.2d 817 (2d Dep't 1991), the court rejected a motion to suppress on the ground that the compulsory chemical test order had not been made available to the defendant or to medical personnel prior to the drawing of blood. The court held that contrary to the provisions of CPL § 690.50(3) which expressly requires a police officer executing a warrant to give notice of his authority and to show a copy of the warrant if so requested by a person to be searched, VTL § 1194(3) had no such requirement.

Citing *People v. Scalzo*, 139 Misc. 2d 539, 529 N.Y.S.2d 236, the court held:

> Conversely, in *People v. Scalzo*, 139 Misc. 2d 539, 547–548, 529 N.Y.S.2d 236, the same argument was made and rejected on the grounds that (1) former Vehicle and Traffic Law § 1194-a did not require the exhibition of the order, (2) there was no evidence in that case that the defendant or any medical personnel requested to see the order; and (3) the need for promptness in taking blood creates an exigency which excuses the actual production of the order (*see, People v. Mahoney*, 58 N.Y.2d 475, 480–481, 462 N.Y.S.2d 410, 448 N.E.2d 1321). We find the reasoning of *People v. Scalzo* (*supra*), which rejected the argument advanced by the defendant herein, far more persuasive than that in *People v. Armstrong* (*supra*) and hold that there was no requirement in this case to show the court order to the defendant or medical personnel before blood was extracted.

567 N.Y.S.2d at 824.

The *Scalzo* decision was appealed to the Appellate Division, Second Department, where the court held:

> There is no merit to the defendant's contention that suppression was warranted because the court order was not served on him or the medical personnel who performed the blood test. The controlling provision of this statute, Vehicle and Traffic Law § 1194-a, does not contain any such requirement.

People v. Scalzo, 178 A.D.2d 444, 574 N.Y.S.2d 782, 784 (2d Dep't 1991).

In *People v. Elysee*, 12 N.Y.3d 100, 105, 876 N.Y.S.2d 677, 680, 904 N.E.2d 813 (2009), the Court of Appeals made clear that, where the blood sample in question was withdrawn by hospital personnel for treatment purposes, and the People subsequently obtain a properly issued search warrant for the seizure of such sample, it is irrelevant whether the order was obtained subsequent to the withdrawal of the blood:

Here, it is illogical to conclude that a blood sample taken at 5:30 A.M. cannot be seized pursuant to a properly issued court order, merely because the order issued *after* the blood was actually drawn by an authorized person. Furthermore, inasmuch as the Vehicle and Traffic Law authorizes a chemical test under the circumstances of this case, and a court order issued compelling "that the defendant shall submit to a chemical test of the alcohol or drug content of his blood," the seizure of the earlier blood sample was in accord with the statute.

In *People v. Goodell*, 164 A.D.2d 321, 565 N.Y.S.2d 929 (4th Dep't 1990), *aff'd on other grounds*, 79 N.Y.2d 869, 581 N.Y.S.2d 157 (1992), the Appellate Division held that it was unnecessary for the police to exhibit the compulsory chemical test Order prior to the extraction of blood from the defendant. Here, the Genesee County Sheriff's Department had telephoned the hospital and informed them that an Order had been issued. Blood was drawn prior to the delivery of the order to the hospital. In upholding this procedure, the court held:

Considering the exigency of the circumstances, and the fact that the blood sample was not handed over to the Sheriff until the Order had been delivered to the hospital, this procedure can be upheld (*cf., People v. Mahoney*, 58 N.Y.2d 475, 480, 462 N.Y.S.2d 410, 448 N.E.2d 1321).

565 N.Y.S.2d at 932.

Reaching a contrary result, in *People v. Armstrong*, 134 Misc. 2d 800, 512 N.Y.S.2d 323 (Jefferson Co. Ct. 1987), Judge Parker of the Jefferson County Court required that the order not only had to be in existence, it had to be present at the hospital and available to both the defendant and the personnel performing the chemical test prior to the forcible extraction of blood from the defendant. The court stated:

It is incumbent upon the People to show that the order authorizing the chemical test was available to both the defendant and the personnel performing the chemical test. Such action is dictated by the procedure provided in § 1194-a of the Vehicle and Traffic Law. The section specifically provides that the order be prepared in accordance with the instructions of the Judge and, if issued orally, "must be signed . . . by the applicant" (Sec. 1194-a[3][d]). The only possible rationale for this provision is to make available to the defendant, and to the medical personnel, executed and timely authority to compel the chemical test. Anything short of actual delivery of the order would place total reliance upon the applicant's oral representation that such an order exists. Surely, a conflict exists. To insist that the defendant, and more importantly the personnel compelled to administer the test, comply with a verbal authorization, opens the door to possible misrepresentation and potential liability. To avoid these concerns is simply to deliver the executed order. There is no indication that anything less was contemplated by the statute (Sec. 1194-a V & T Law).

People v. Armstrong, 512 N.Y.S.2d at 326.

§ 40:15   Failure to timely file transcript of application does not void order

Research References

West's Key Number Digest, Automobiles ☞414

In *People v. Whelan*, 165 A.D.2d 313, 567 N.Y.S.2d 817 (2d Dep't 1991), the application for the compulsory chemical test order was not filed until more than 72 hours after the issuance of the order; to wit: 74 hours and 31 minutes. Here, the court rejected a motion to suppress the order on the grounds that it was not filed within the 72 hours required by VTL § 1194(3)(d)(3).

> It is obvious that the legislative intent underlying the foregoing statutory provision is two-fold: (1) to ensure that the sworn testimony of the applicant and any supporting witnesses is recorded, thereby assuring the regularity of the application process, and (2) to preserve the application for appellate review . . . It is equally obvious that both of these purposes have been fulfilled in this case, so that substantial rather than literal compliance with the statutory standards herein is sufficient.

567 N.Y.S.2d at 823 (citations omitted). *See also People v. Camarre*, 171 A.D.2d 1003, 569 N.Y.S.2d 224 (4th Dep't 1991) (two-day delay in filing, transcribing, and certifying audio tape not fatal to warrant); *People v. Brinson*, 177 A.D.2d 1019, 578 N.Y.S.2d 38 (4th Dep't 1991) (tape filed within 24 hours satisfactory).

§ 40:16   Inaudible transcription does not void order

Research References

West's Key Number Digest, Automobiles ☞414

In *People v. Stratis*, 137 Misc. 2d 661, 520 N.Y.S.2d 904 (Kings Co. 1987), judgment *aff'd*, 148 A.D.2d 557, 540 N.Y.S.2d 186 (2d Dep't 1989), the tape recording of the oral application for the compulsory chemical test order was inaudible as a result of a mechanical breakdown of the tape recorder. Citing *People v. Crandall*, 108 A.D.2d 413, 489 N.Y.S.2d 614 (3d Dep't 1985), *aff'd*, 69 N.Y.2d 459, 515 N.Y.S.2d 745 (1987); and *People v. Rollins*, 118 A.D.2d 949, 499 N.Y.S.2d 817 (1986), the court held that technical errors such as this were excusable.

In *Crandall*, the officers were sworn, but the administration of the oaths was not recorded or transcribed. There was also some other conversation which was neither recorded nor transcribed. In *Rollins*, the applicant was not sworn prior to making his application; but thought that he was, in fact, so sworn; and did, in fact, swear to the contents of the application retroactively. These omissions were deemed to be technical errors which did not mandate suppression of the chemical test result.

Finding the mechanical breakdown of the tape recorder to be analogous to the situation arising in *Rollins* and *Crandall*, Judge Grajales held that the inability to examine a transcription of the voice recording was not such a defect as would preclude a finding of substantial compliance with the statute. 528 N.Y.S.2d at 910.

§ 40:17 Defendant's refusal entitled People to adverse inference charge

Research References

West's Key Number Digest, Automobiles ⟁413

In *People v. Maddox*, 159 A.D.2d 954, 552 N.Y.S.2d 786 (4th Dep't 1990), the court held that it was proper for the trial court to give an adverse inference charge concerning the defendant's persistent refusal to comply with the court order directing him to give a blood sample. The court, comparing the situation to that in *People v. Paylor*, 70 N.Y.2d 146, 518 N.Y.S.2d 102 (1987), where the defendant failed to call a witness in his control, concluded:

> Where, as here, defendant comes forward with evidence, his failure to produce available evidence within his control creates an adverse inference.

People v. Maddox, 552 N.Y.S.2d at 787.

§ 40:18 Suppressed test may be used to impeach

Research References

West's Key Number Digest, Automobiles ⟁414

Where the blood sample is obtained in the face of a refusal and without a court order, the result of the test cannot be admitted in the People's case in chief. However, in *People v. Donnelly*, 103 A.D.2d 941, 479 N.Y.S.2d 786 (3d Dep't 1984), the court held that if the defendant took the stand and testified concerning his consumption of alcohol prior to the accident, such evidence would be admissible to impeach the defendant's testimony about the quantity of alcohol he consumed, provided the court gave clear limiting instructions as to the proper use of such evidence.

§ 40:19 Applicability of two-hour rule to compulsory chemical tests

In *People v. Atkins*, 85 N.Y.2d 1007, 1009, 630 N.Y.S.2d 965, 966, 654 N.E.2d 1213 (1995), the Court of Appeals stated that there is no two-hour "time limit for court-ordered chemical testing under [VTL] section 1194(3) (*see, People v. McGrath*, 135

A.D.2d 60, 524 N.Y.S.2d 214, *affd. on opn below* 73 N.Y.2d 826, 537 N.Y.S.2d 480, 534 N.E.2d 318)." *See also People v. Smith*, 18 N.Y.3d 544, 548 n.1, 942 N.Y.S.2d 426, 428 n.1, 965 N.E.2d 928 (2012); *People v. Robinson*, 82 A.D.3d 1269, __, 920 N.Y.S.2d 162, 163 (2d Dep't 2011); *People v. Demetsenare*, 243 A.D.2d 777, __, 663 N.Y.S.2d 299, 302 (3d Dep't 1997).

§ 40:20   The body's natural metabolization of alcohol does not constitute a *per se* exigency permitting a warrantless compulsory chemical test

In *Missouri v. McNeely*, 133 S. Ct. 1552, 1556, 185 L. Ed. 2d 696 (2013), the Supreme Court addressed the issue of "whether the natural metabolization of alcohol in the bloodstream presents a *per se* exigency that justifies an exception to the Fourth Amendment's warrant requirement for nonconsensual blood testing in all drunk-driving cases." The Court held both (a) that it does not, and (b) "that exigency must be determined on a case-by-case basis the totality of the circumstances." *Id. See also id.* at 1568 ("We hold that in drunk-driving investigations, the natural dissipation of alcohol in the bloodstream does not constitute an exigency in every case sufficient to justify conducting a blood test without a warrant").

Part X

TEST REFUSALS

Chapter 41

Test Refusals

Research References

Westlaw Databases

Drinking/Driving Litigation: Criminal and Civil (2d ed.) (DRNKDRIVING)

Handling a Criminal Case in New York (HCCNY)

Handling Drunk Driving Cases (2d ed.) (HDRUNKDR)

New York Driving While Intoxicated Defense Forms (NYDWIFM)

New York Vehicle and Traffic Law 2d (NYVEH)

Treatises and Practice Aids

Nichols and Whited, Drinking/Driving Litigation: Criminal and Civil, Chapter 8 (2d ed.)

Nichols and Whited, Drinking/Driving Litigation: Criminal and Civil §§ 8:1 to 8:9, 11:15 (2d ed.)

Muldoon, Handling a Criminal Case in New York §§ 4:18, 4:19

Fiandach, Handling Drunk Driving Cases §§ 6:21, 9:13 (2d ed.)

Rose, New York Vehicle and Traffic Law 2d §§ 10:3, 10:3.50

Forms

Taheri and Orr, NY DWI Defense Forms § 3:5

Law Reviews and Other Periodicals

Crump, The Admission of Chemical Test Refusals After State v. Neville: Drunk Drivers Cannot Take the Fifth, 59 N.D. L. Rev. 349 (1983)

McCormack and Stone, Clarifying the Admissibility of DWI Chemical Test Refusals in New York: The "Two-Hour Rule" Does Not Apply, 82 St. John's L. Rev. 675 (Spring, 2008)

Volk, Automobiles—Refusals of Test, Admissibility: North Dakota's Privilege Against Self-Incrimination As Applied to a Refusal to Submit to a Blood Alcohol Test, 71 N.D. L. Rev. 821 (1995)

KeyCite®: Cases and other legal materials listed in KeyCite Scope can be researched through the KeyCite service on Westlaw®. Use KeyCite to check citations for form, parallel references, prior and later history, and comprehensive citator information, including citations to other decisions and secondary materials.

---

§ 41:1 In general

Research References

West's Key Number Digest, Automobiles ⚷144.1(1.20)

A motorist suspected of violating VTL § 1192 will generally be requested to submit to three separate and distinct types of tests— (1) field sobriety tests, such as the horizontal gaze nystagmus test, the walk-and-turn test, and the one-leg stand test, (2) a breath screening test, such as the Alco-Sensor test, and (3) a chemical test, such as the Breathalyzer, DataMaster, Intoxilyzer, Alcotest, etc., and/or a blood or urine test. This chapter deals with the consequences of refusing to submit to such testing, with the primary focus being on the consequences of a refusal to submit to a chemical test.

§ 41:2 Refusal to communicate with police—Generally

Research References

West's Key Number Digest, Automobiles ☜144.1(1.20)

As a general rule, the People cannot use a defendant's refusal to communicate with the police as part of their direct case, and/or to impeach the defendant's testimony at trial, regardless of whether such conduct takes place prearrest, postarrest, or at the time of arrest. *See, e.g., People v. Basora*, 75 N.Y.2d 992, 993, 557 N.Y.S.2d 263, 264 (1990); *People v. DeGeorge*, 73 N.Y.2d 614, 618–20, 543 N.Y.S.2d 11, 12–14 (1989); *People v. Conyers*, 52 N.Y.2d 454, 438 N.Y.S.2d 741 (1981), and 49 N.Y.2d 174, 424 N.Y.S.2d 402 (1980). *See also Miranda v. Arizona*, 384 U.S. 436, 468 n.37, 86 S.Ct. 1602, 1624 n.37 (1966).

Nonetheless, in *People v. Johnson*, 253 A.D.2d 702, __, 679 N.Y.S.2d 361, 362 (1st Dep't 1998), the Court held that "defendant's refusal to give his name or other pedigree information to the police was properly admitted as evidence of his consciousness of guilt."

§ 41:3 Refusal to submit to field sobriety tests

Research References

West's Key Number Digest, Automobiles ☜144.1(1.20), 413

There is no requirement, statutory or otherwise, that a DWI suspect submit to field sobriety tests. *See Berkemer v. McCarty*, 468 U.S. 420, 439, 104 S.Ct. 3138, 3150 (1984) ("[T]he officer may ask the detainee a moderate number of questions to determine his identity and to try to obtain information confirming or dispelling the officer's suspicions. But the detainee is not obligated to respond"). However, although a DWI suspect has the right to refuse to perform field sobriety tests, the police are not required to inform the suspect of such right, as "[t]here is no statutory or other requirement for the establishment of rules regulating field sobriety tests." *People v. Sheridan*, 192 A.D.2d 1057, __, 596 N.Y.S.2d 245, 245–46 (4th Dep't 1993).

In addition, the refusal to perform field sobriety tests is admissible against the defendant at trial. *See People v. Berg*, 92 N.Y.2d 701, 703, 685 N.Y.S.2d 906, 907 (1999) ("evidence of defendant's refusal to submit to certain field sobriety tests [is] admissible in the absence of *Miranda* warnings . . . because the refusal was not compelled within the meaning of the Self-Incrimination Clause"). The *Berg* Court noted, however, that "the inference of intoxication arising from failure to complete the tests successfully 'is far stronger than that arising from a refusal to take the test.'" 92 N.Y.2d at 706, 685 N.Y.S.2d at 909 (citation omitted).

Similarly, in *People v. Powell*, 95 A.D.2d 783, __, 463 N.Y.S.2d 473, 476 (2d Dep't 1983), the Court held that:

> It is true that the admission into evidence of defendant's refusal to submit to the sobriety test here cannot be deemed a violation of his Federal or State privilege against self-incrimination on the basis that it was coerced . . . There is no constitutional violation in so using defendant's refusal even if defendant was not specifically warned that it could be used against him at trial . . .
>
> [However,] though *admissible*, the defendant's refusal to submit to co-ordination tests in this case on the ground that they would be painful because of his war wounds was nevertheless of *limited probative value* in proving circumstantially that defendant would have failed the tests.

Notably, the *Powell* Court made clear that "[a]s the Court of Appeals has stated in respect to another example of assertive conduct, '[t]his court has always recognized the ambiguity of evidence of flight and insisted that the jury be closely instructed as to its weakness as an indication of guilt of the crime charged' (*People v. Yazum*, 13 N.Y.2d 302, 304, 246 N.Y.S.2d 626, 196 N.E.2d 263)." 95 A.D.2d at __, 463 N.Y.S.2d at 476.

§ 41:4 Refusal to submit to breath screening test

Research References

West's Key Number Digest, Automobiles ⚏144.1(1.20)

VTL § 1194(1)(b) provides that:

> (b) Field testing. Every person operating a motor vehicle which has been involved in an accident or which is operated in violation of any of the provisions of [the VTL] shall, at the request of a police officer, submit to a *breath test* to be administered by the police officer. If such test indicates that such operator has consumed alcohol, the police officer may request such operator to submit to a chemical test in the manner set forth in [VTL § 1194(2)].

(Emphasis added).

The phrase "breath test" in VTL § 1194(1)(b) refers to a preliminary test of a DWI suspect's breath for the presence of alcohol using a preliminary breath screening device such as an Alco-Sensor (commonly referred to as a PBT). The refusal to submit to a breath screening test in violation of VTL § 1194(1)(b) is a traffic infraction. *See* VTL § 1800(a); *People v. Leontiev*, 38 Misc. 3d 716, ___, 956 N.Y.S.2d 832, 837-38 (Nassau Co. Dist. Ct. 2012); *People v. Pecora*, 123 Misc. 2d 259, ___, 473 N.Y.S.2d 320, 323 (Wappinger Just. Ct. 1984); *People v. Steves*, 117 Misc. 2d 841, ___, 459 N.Y.S.2d 402, 403 (Webster Just. Ct. 1983); *People v. Hamza*, 109 Misc. 2d 1055, ___, 441 N.Y.S.2d 579, 581 (Gates Just. Ct. 1981); *People v. Graser*, 90 Misc. 2d 219, ___, 393 N.Y.S.2d 1009, 1014 (Amherst Just. Ct. 1977). *See generally People v. Cunningham*, 95 N.Y.2d 909, 910, 717 N.Y.S.2d 68, 68 (2000).

VTL § 1194(1)(b) makes clear that a motorist is under no obligation to submit to a breath screening test unless he or she has either (a) been involved in an accident, or (b) committed a VTL violation. In addition, since obtaining a breath sample from a motorist for alcohol analysis constitutes a "search" within the meaning of the Fourth Amendment, *see Skinner v. Railway Labor Executives' Ass'n*, 489 U.S. 602, 616–17, 109 S.Ct. 1402, 1413 (1989); *Schmerber v. California*, 384 U.S. 757, 767, 86 S.Ct. 1826, 1834 (1966), submission to such a search cannot lawfully be required in the absence of probable cause. *See People v. Brockum*, 88 A.D.2d 697, ___, 451 N.Y.S.2d 326, 327 (3d Dep't 1982); *Pecora*, 123 Misc. 2d at ___, 473 N.Y.S.2d at 322. *See generally People v. Kates*, 53 N.Y.2d 591, 594–95, 444 N.Y.S.2d 446, 448 (1976). As such, absent a proper factual predicate for a police officer to request that a motorist submit to a breath screening test, a refusal to submit thereto does not violate VTL § 1194(1)(b). *See also* §§ 7:1 et seq., *supra*.

Although the results of an Alco-Sensor test are inadmissible at trial, *see People v. Thomas*, 121 A.D.2d 73, ___, 509 N.Y.S.2d 668, 671 (4th Dep't 1986), *aff'd*, 70 N.Y.2d 823, 523 N.Y.S.2d 437 (1987), in *People v. MacDonald*, 89 N.Y.2d 908, 910, 653 N.Y.S.2d 267, 268 (1996), the Court of Appeals held that "testimony regarding defendant's attempts to avoid giving an adequate breath sample for alco-sensor testing was properly admitted as evidence of consciousness of guilt, particularly in light of the trial court's limiting instructions to the jury on this point."

In perhaps the only published case dealing directly with the issue of the admissibility of an Alco-Sensor test refusal at trial, the court held that an Alco-Sensor test refusal, like an Alco-Sensor test result, is inadmissible. *People v. Ottino*, 178 Misc. 2d 416, 679 N.Y.S.2d 271 (Sullivan Co. Ct. 1998). In so holding, the court reasoned that "to allow the jury to hear the evidence of an alco-sensor test refusal would in effect make admissible that evidence which is clearly inadmissible." 178 Misc. 2d at ___, 679 N.Y.S.2d at 273. Although *MacDonald*, *supra*, appears at first glance to hold otherwise, *MacDonald* is distinguishable from *Ottino* in that the evidence that was permitted in *MacDonald* was not evidence of the defendant's refusal to submit to an Alco-Sensor test, but rather "testimony regarding defendant's [conduct in] attempt[ing] to avoid giving an adequate breath sample for alco-sensor testing." 89 N.Y.2d at 910, 653 N.Y.S.2d at 268.

§ 41:5   Refusal to submit to chemical test

Research References

West's Key Number Digest, Automobiles ⊶144.1(1.20)

The remainder of this chapter deals with the consequences of, and procedures applicable to, a DWI suspect's refusal to submit to a chemical test. In New York, there are two separate and very distinct consequences of refusing to submit to a chemical test. First, the refusal generally can be used against the defendant in a VTL § 1192 prosecution as "consciousness of guilt" evidence. Second, the refusal is a civil violation—wholly independent of the VTL § 1192 charge in criminal court—which results in proceedings before a DMV administrative law judge (ALJ), and generally results in both a significant driver's license revocation and a civil penalty (*i.e.*, fine).

§ 41:6   DMV refusal sanctions civil, not criminal, in nature

Research References

West's Key Number Digest, Automobiles ⊶144.1(1.20)

A DMV refusal hearing is "civil" or "administrative" in nature, as are the consequences resulting therefrom. *See, e.g., Matter of Barnes v. Tofany*, 27 N.Y.2d 74, 77, 313 N.Y.S.2d 690, 693 (1970) ("We hold that the 'double punishment' feature of our Vehicle and Traffic statute—one criminal and the other administrative—is lawful"); *Matter of Brennan v. Kmiotek*, 233 A.D.2d 870, __, 649 N.Y.S.2d 611, 612 (4th Dep't 1996); *Matter of Geary v. Commissioner of Motor Vehicles*, 92 A.D.2d 38, __, 459 N.Y.S.2d 494, 496–97 (4th Dep't), order *aff'd*, 59 N.Y.2d 950, 466 N.Y.S.2d 304 (1983).

§ 41:7   Civil sanctions for chemical test refusal—First offense

Research References

West's Key Number Digest, Automobiles ⊶144.1(1.20)

A chemical test refusal is considered to be a "first offense" if, within the past five years, the person has neither (a) had his or her driving privileges revoked for refusing to submit to a chemical test, nor (b) been convicted of violating any subdivision of VTL § 1192, or been found to have violated VTL § 1192-a, *not arising out of the same incident. See* VTL § 1194(2)(d). The civil sanctions for refusing to submit to a chemical test as a first offense are:

1. Mandatory revocation of the person's driver's license, permit, or nonresident operating privilege for at least one year. VTL § 1194(2)(d)(1)(a);

2. A civil penalty in the amount of $500. VTL § 1194(2)(d)(2); and

3. A driver responsibility assessment of $250 a year for three years. VTL § 1199. *See also* § 46:50, *infra.*

The driver responsibility assessment is also imposed for a conviction of a violation of any subdivision of VTL § 1192. VTL § 1199(1). However, if a person is both convicted of a violation of VTL § 1192 *and* found to have refused a chemical test in accordance with VTL § 1194 in connection with the same incident, only one driver responsibility assessment will be imposed. VTL § 1194.

§ 41:8 Civil sanctions for chemical test refusal—Repeat offenders

Research References

West's Key Number Digest, Automobiles ⊚144.1(1.20)

A chemical test refusal is considered to be a "repeat offense" if, within the past five years, the person has either (a) had his or her driving privileges revoked for refusing to submit to a chemical test, or (b) been convicted of violating any subdivision of VTL § 1192, or been found to have violated VTL § 1192-a, *not arising out of the same incident. See* VTL § 1194(2)(d). In addition, a prior "Zero Tolerance" chemical test refusal, in violation of VTL § 1194-a(3), has the same effect as a prior refusal pursuant to VTL § 1194(2)(c) "solely for the purpose of determining the length of any license suspension or revocation required to be imposed under any provision of [VTL Article 31], provided that the subsequent offense or refusal is committed or occurred prior to the expiration of the retention period for such prior refusal as set forth in [VTL § 201(1)(k)]." VTL § 1194(2)(d)(1)(a).

The civil sanctions for refusing to submit to a chemical test as a repeat offender are:

1. Mandatory revocation of the person's driver's license, permit, or nonresident operating privilege for at least 18 months. VTL § 1194(2)(d)(1)(a);

2. A civil penalty in the amount of $750 (unless the predicate was a violation of VTL § 1192-a or VTL § 1194-a(3), in which case the civil penalty is $500). VTL § 1194(2)(d)(2); and

3. A driver responsibility assessment of $250 a year for three years. VTL § 1199. *See also* § 46:50, *infra*.

The driver responsibility assessment is also imposed for a conviction of a violation of any subdivision of VTL § 1192. VTL § 1199(1). However, if a person is both convicted of a violation of VTL § 1192 *and* found to have refused a chemical test in accordance with VTL § 1194 in connection with the same incident, only one driver responsibility assessment will be imposed. VTL § 1194.

In addition, the DMV will require evidence of alcohol evaluation and/or rehabilitation before it will relicense the person. *See* § 50:15 and Appendix 53, *infra*.

§ 41:9   Civil sanctions for chemical test refusal— Commercial drivers

Research References

West's Key Number Digest, Automobiles ☞144.1(1.20)

Effective November 1, 2006, the holder of a commercial driver's license who refuses to submit to a chemical test as a first offense is subject to the following civil sanctions:

1. Mandatory revocation of the person's commercial driver's license for at least 18 months—*even if the person was operating a personal, noncommercial motor vehicle* (at least three years if the person was operating a commercial motor vehicle transporting hazardous materials). VTL § 1194(2)(d)(1)(c); and

2. A civil penalty in the amount of $500 ($550 if the person was operating a commercial motor vehicle). VTL § 1194(2)(d)(2).

A chemical test refusal by the holder of a commercial driver's license is considered to be a "repeat offense" if the person has *ever* either (a) had a prior finding that he or she refused to submit to a chemical test, or (b) had a prior conviction of any of the following offenses:

1. Any violation of VTL § 1192;

2. Any violation of VTL § 600(1) or (2); or

3. Any felony involving the use of a motor vehicle pursuant to VTL § 510-a(1)(a).

See VTL § 1194(2)(d)(1)(c).

The holder of a commercial driver's license who is found to have refused to submit to a chemical test as a repeat offender is subject to the following civil sanctions:

1. Permanent disqualification from operating a commercial motor vehicle. VTL § 1194(2)(d)(1)(c); and

2. A civil penalty in the amount of $750. VTL § 1194(2)(d)(2).

The DMV Commissioner has the authority to waive such "permanent revocation" from operating a commercial motor vehicle where at least 10 years have elapsed from the commencement of the revocation period, provided:

(i) that during such [10] year period such person has not been found to have refused a chemical test pursuant to [VTL § 1194] and has not been convicted of any one of the following offenses: any violation of [VTL § 1192]; refusal to submit to a chemical test pursuant to [VTL § 1194]; any violation of [VTL § 600(1) or(2)]; or has a prior conviction of any felony involving the use of a motor vehicle pursuant to [VTL § 510-a(1)(a)];

(ii) that such person provides acceptable documentation to the commissioner that such person is not in need of alcohol or drug treatment or has satisfactorily completed a prescribed course of such treatment; and

(iii) after such documentation is accepted, that such person is granted a certificate of relief from disabilities as provided for in [Correction Law § 701] by the court in which such person was last penalized. VTL § 1194(2)(d)(1)(c)(i) to (iii).

However, "[u]pon a third finding of refusal and/or conviction of any of the offenses which require a permanent commercial driver's license revocation, such permanent revocation may not be waived by the commissioner under any circumstances." VTL § 1194(2)(d)(1)(d).

§ 41:10 Chemical test refusal revocation—Underage offenders

Research References

West's Key Number Digest, Automobiles ⚲144.1(1.20)

A person under the age of 21 who is found to have refused to submit to a chemical test, in violation of either VTL § 1194(2)(c) or VTL § 1194-a(3), will have his or her driver's license, permit, or nonresident operating privilege revoked for at least one year. VTL § 1194(2)(d)(1)(b).

A person under the age of 21 who is found to have refused to submit to a chemical test, in violation of either VTL § 1194(2)(c) or VTL § 1194-a(3), and who "has a prior finding, conviction or youthful offender adjudication resulting from a violation of [VTL § 1192] or [VTL § 1192-a], *not arising from the same incident*," will have his or her driver's license, permit, or nonresident operating privilege revoked for at least one year or until the person reaches the age of 21, *whichever is longer*. VTL § 1194(2)(d)(1)(b) (emphasis added).

For further treatment of chemical test refusals by underage offenders, *see* §§ 15:1 et seq., *supra*.

§ 41:11   Chemical test refusal revocation runs separate and apart from VTL § 1192 suspension/revocation

Research References

West's Key Number Digest, Automobiles ⊙⃥144.1(1.20)

The license revocation which results from a chemical test refusal is a "civil" or "administrative" penalty separate and distinct from the license suspension/revocation which results from a VTL § 1192 conviction in criminal court. *See* § 41:6, *supra*. As such, the suspension/revocation periods run separate and apart from each other to the extent that they do not overlap.

In other words, to the extent that a VTL § 1192 suspension/revocation and a chemical test refusal revocation overlap, the DMV runs the suspension/revocation periods *concurrently*; but to the extent that the suspension/revocation periods do *not* overlap, the DMV runs the periods *consecutively*. The following example will illustrate this situation:

A woman over the age of 21 with a New York State driver's license is (a) charged with first offense DWI, and (b) accused of refusing to submit to a chemical test arising out of the same incident.

If the woman pleads guilty to DWAI at arraignment, the 90-day license suspension arising from such conviction will start immediately, and the suspension period will not be credited toward any revocation period imposed by DMV for the chemical test refusal.

If the woman pleads guilty to DWI at arraignment, the six-month license revocation arising from such conviction will start immediately, and the revocation period will not be credited toward any revocation period imposed by DMV for the chemical test refusal.

If the woman pleads not guilty at arraignment, the arraigning judge will suspend her driver's license and provide her with a form entitled "Notice of Temporary Suspension and Notice of Hearing" on one side, and "Waiver of Hearing" on the other side.

This suspension, which lasts the shorter of 15 days or until the DMV refusal hearing, will *not* be credited toward either (a) any revocation period imposed for the chemical test refusal, and/or (b) any suspension/ revocation period imposed for a VTL § 1192 conviction.

If the woman loses her refusal hearing while the criminal case is still pending, her driver's license will be revoked for at least 1 year commencing at the conclusion of the hearing, and the revocation period will not be credited toward any suspension/revocation period imposed for a VTL § 1192 conviction.

If the woman waives her right to a refusal hearing, the DMV will commence the 1 year refusal revocation as of the date it receives the "Waiver of Hearing" form.

Thus, if the woman in the example is not interested in contesting either the DWI charge or the alleged chemical test refusal, her defense counsel should attempt to minimize the amount of time that her driver's license will be suspended/ revoked. In this regard, the best course of action is to negotiate a plea bargain (hopefully to DWAI) which will be entered at the time of arraignment, and to execute the "Waiver of Hearing" form provided by the court and mail it to the DMV immediately.

§ 41:12 DMV refusal sanctions do not apply if chemical test result is obtained

Research References

West's Key Number Digest, Automobiles ⟜144.1(1.20)

Under the circumstances set forth in VTL § 1194(3), a DWI suspect can be subjected to a compulsory (*i.e.*, forcible) court-ordered chemical test despite his or her refusal to consent to such test. If a compulsory chemical test is administered to a DWI suspect, his or her refusal to voluntarily submit to the test is admissible in court as consciousness of guilt evidence. *See People v. Demetsenare*, 243 A.D.2d 777, __, 663 N.Y.S.2d 299, 302 (3d Dep't 1997). *See also* VTL § 1194(2)(f).

By contrast, where a compulsory chemical test is administered, a DWI suspect's refusal to voluntarily submit to the test is *not* a refusal for DMV purposes. In this regard, VTL § 1194(2)(b)(1) provides, in pertinent part:

> (b) Report of refusal. (1) If: (A) such person having been placed under arrest; or (B) after a breath [screening] test indicates the presence of alcohol in the person's system; . . . and having thereafter been requested to submit to such chemical test and having been informed that the person's license or permit to drive and any non-resident operating privilege shall be immediately suspended and subsequently revoked . . . for refusal to submit to such chemical test or any portion thereof, whether or not the person is found guilty of the charge for which such person is arrested . . ., refuses to submit to such chemical test or any portion thereof, *unless a court order has been granted pursuant to [VTL § 1194(3)], the test shall not be given and a written report of such refusal shall be immediately made by the police officer before whom such refusal was made.*

(Emphasis added).

Similarly, VTL § 1194(2)(b)(2) provides that the officer's Report of Refusal must satisfy all of the following requirements:

> The report of the police officer shall set forth reasonable grounds to

believe [1] such arrested person . . . had been driving in violation of any subdivision of [VTL § 1192] . . ., [2] that said person had refused to submit to such chemical test, and [3] *that no chemical test was administered pursuant to the requirements of [VTL § 1194(3)].*

(Emphasis added). *See also* 15 NYCRR § 139.2(a) ("No report [of refusal] shall be made if there was a compulsory test administered pursuant to [VTL § 1194(3)]").

The rationale is that the civil sanctions for a refusal are designed to penalize those who frustrate prosecution under VTL § 1192 by refusing to submit to a chemical test; since prosecution is not frustrated where a compulsory chemical test is obtained pursuant to VTL § 1194(3), DMV refusal sanctions are unnecessary, "and no departmental chemical test refusal hearing should be held in any such case." *See* Appendix 39.

Although both VTL § 1194 and the regulations promulgated thereunder provide that no Report of Refusal should be made where there is a chemical test refusal combined with a compulsory chemical test, no provision is made in either the statute or the regulations for the situation where a DWI suspect refuses a chemical test but is thereafter persuaded by the police to change his or her mind and submit to a test. This is presumably due to the fact that the statute contemplates that once a DWI suspect refuses a chemical test, "unless a court order has been granted pursuant to [VTL § 1194(3)], *the test shall not be given* and a written report of such refusal shall be immediately made by the police officer before whom such refusal was made." VTL § 1194(2)(b)(1) (emphasis added).

In practice, however, the police often persuade a DWI suspect who has refused to submit to a chemical test to change his or her mind and submit to a test. *See, e.g., People v. Cragg,* 71 N.Y.2d 926, 528 N.Y.S.2d 807 (1988); *People v. Stisi,* 93 A.D.2d 951, ___, 463 N.Y.S.2d 73, 75 (3d Dep't 1983). Under such circumstances (*i.e.,* where a chemical test is administered and a test result obtained despite an initial refusal), can the person also be subjected to DMV refusal sanctions? The answer is no.

In this regard, the DMV's position is that the rationale applicable to compulsory chemical tests is equally applicable in this situation. That is, the civil sanctions of refusal are designed to penalize those who frustrate prosecution under VTL § 1192 by refusing to submit to a chemical test; since prosecution is not frustrated where a chemical test is obtained, DMV refusal sanctions are unnecessary and no departmental chemical test refusal hearing should be held in any such case. *See* Appendix 60.

§ 41:13   VTL § 1194 preempts field of chemical testing

Research References

West's Key Number Digest, Automobiles ☞144.1(1.20)

In *People v. Moselle*, 57 N.Y.2d 97, 109, 454 N.Y.S.2d 292, 297 (1982), the Court of Appeals made clear that VTL § "1194 has pre-empted the administration of chemical tests for determining alcoholic blood content with respect to violations under [VTL §] 1192." *See also People v. Prescott*, 95 N.Y.2d 655, 659 & n.3, 722 N.Y.S.2d 778, 780 & n.3 (2001); *People v. Ameigh*, 95 A.D.2d 367, __, 467 N.Y.S.2d 718, 718 (3d Dep't 1983). *See generally People v. Smith*, 18 N.Y.3d 544, 548, 942 N.Y.S.2d 426, 429, 965 N.E.2d 928 (2012) ("The standards governing the administration of chemical tests to ascertain BAC in this circumstance are set forth in Vehicle and Traffic Law § 1194.").

§ 41:14   What is a "chemical test"?

Research References

West's Key Number Digest, Automobiles ☞144.1(1.20)

In the field of New York DWI law, the phrase "breath test" refers to a preliminary test of a DWI suspect's breath for the presence of alcohol using a preliminary breath screening device such as an Alco-Sensor (commonly referred to as a PBT). *See* § 41:4, *supra*. By contrast, the phrase "chemical test" is the term used to describe a test of the alcoholic and/or drug content of a DWI suspect's blood using an instrument other than a PBT.

In other words, BAC tests conducted utilizing breath testing instruments such as the Breathalyzer, DataMaster, Intoxilyzer, Alcotest, etc. are referred to as "chemical tests," *not* "breath tests." Similarly, the phrase "refusal to submit to a chemical test" refers to a DWI suspect's refusal to submit to such a test—*not* to the mere refusal to submit to a breath screening test in violation of VTL § 1194(1)(b).

A chemical test is usually performed both (a) at a police station, and (b) *after* the suspect has been placed under arrest for DWI. By contrast, a breath test is usually performed both (a) at the scene of a traffic stop, and (b) *before* the suspect has been placed under arrest for DWI.

§ 41:15   Who can lawfully be requested to submit to a chemical test?

Research References

West's Key Number Digest, Automobiles ☞144.1(1.20)

VTL § 1194(2)(a) provides, in pertinent part:

2. Chemical tests. (a) When authorized. Any person who operates a motor vehicle in this state shall be deemed to have given consent to a chemical test of one or more of the following: breath, blood, urine, or saliva, for the purpose of determining the alcoholic and/or drug content of the blood provided that such test is administered by or at the direction of a police officer with respect to a chemical test of breath, urine or saliva or, with respect to a chemical test of blood, at the direction of a police officer:

(1) having reasonable grounds to believe such person to have been operating in violation of any subdivision of [VTL § 1192] and within two hours after such person has been placed under arrest for any such violation; or . . .

(2) within two hours after a breath [screening] test, as provided in [VTL § 1194(1)(b)], indicates that alcohol has been consumed by such person and in accordance with the rules and regulations established by the police force of which the officer is a member . . .

For underage offenders being requested to submit to a chemical test pursuant to the Zero Tolerance laws, see § 15:30, supra.

As VTL § 1194(2)(a) makes clear, either a lawful VTL § 1192 arrest or a positive result from a lawfully requested breath screening test is a prerequisite to a valid request that a DWI suspect submit to a chemical test. See, e.g., People v. Moselle, 57 N.Y.2d 97, 107, 454 N.Y.S.2d 292, 296 (1982); Matter of Gagliardi v. Department of Motor Vehicles, 144 A.D.2d 882, __, 535 N.Y.S.2d 203, 204 (3d Dep't 1988) ("In order for the testing strictures of Vehicle and Traffic Law § 1194 to come into play, there must have been a lawful arrest for driving while intoxicated."); People v. Stisi, 93 A.D.2d 951, __, 463 N.Y.S.2d 73, 74 (3d Dep't 1983); Matter of June v. Tofany, 34 A.D.2d 732, __, 311 N.Y.S.2d 782, 783 (4th Dep't 1970); Matter of Burns v. Hults, 20 A.D.2d 752, __, 247 N.Y.S.2d 311, 312 (4th Dep't 1964); Matter of Leonard v. Melton, 58 A.D.2d 669, __, 395 N.Y.S.2d 526, 527 (3d Dep't 1977) (proof that DWI suspect operated vehicle is necessary prerequisite to valid request to submit to chemical test pursuant to VTL § 1194). See also Welsh v. Wisconsin, 466 U.S. 740, 744, 104 S.Ct. 2091, 2095 (1984) ("It is not disputed by the parties that an arrestee's refusal to take a breath test would be reasonable, and therefore operating privileges could not be revoked, if the underlying arrest was not lawful. Indeed, state law has consistently provided that a valid arrest is a necessary prerequisite to the imposition of a breath test.").

§ 41:16   Who can lawfully request that a DWI suspect submit to a chemical test?

Research References

West's Key Number Digest, Automobiles ☞144.1(1.20)

VTL § 1194(2)(a) provides, among other things, that a chemical test must be "administered by or at the direction of a police officer." This requirement "does not preclude the police officer who determines that testing is warranted from administering the test as well . . . [C]orroboration of the results is not required." *People v. Evers*, 68 N.Y.2d 658, 659, 505 N.Y.S.2d 68, 69 (1986).

In *Matter of Murray v. Tofany*, 33 A.D.2d 1080, __, 307 N.Y.S.2d 776, 779 (3d Dep't 1970), the Appellate Division, Third Department, held that a "special policeman" duly appointed by the Mayor of Lake George was a "police officer" authorized to request a chemical test of a DWI suspect. *See also Matter of Giacone v. Jackson*, 267 A.D.2d 673, __, 699 N.Y.S.2d 587, 588 (3d Dep't 1999) (fact that state trooper's "Certificate of Appointment and Acceptance" was not properly filed with Secretary of State does not invalidate his arrests). *See generally Matter of Metzgar v. Tofany*, 78 Misc. 2d 1002, 359 N.Y.S.2d 160 (Nassau Co. Sup. Ct. 1974).

§ 41:17 Should a DWI suspect refuse to submit to a chemical test?

Research References

West's Key Number Digest, Automobiles ⊶144.1(1.20)

There is no simple answer (or even necessarily a correct answer) to the question of whether a DWI suspect should submit to a chemical test in a given situation—a question which usually arises in the middle of the night! The answer depends upon many factors, such as whether there has been an accident involving serious physical injury or death, whether the DWI charge is a felony, whether the person is a repeat/multiple offender, whether the person needs to drive to earn a living, whether the test result is likely to be above the legal limit, whether there is a plea bargaining policy in the county with regard to test refusals and/or BAC limits (*e.g.*, no reduction to DWAI if the defendant's BAC is above 0.15), etc.

The following *general* rules represent the author's current opinions on this issue:

If there has been an accident involving serious physical injury or death—*refuse* the test.

In such a situation, the civil consequences of a refusal are comparatively insignificant and, in any event, the compulsory chemical test that the police will obtain voids the refusal for DMV purposes. *See* § 41:12, *supra*.

If the DWI charge is a felony—*refuse* the test.

In such a situation:

    (a) The civil consequences of a refusal are comparatively insignificant and, in any event, the defendant will generally receive a sentence from the court that will cause his or her driving privileges to be revoked for at least as long as from the refusal.

    (b) Most defendants in this situation accept a negotiated plea bargain prior to being indicted; thus, the DMV refusal hearing is defense counsel's best opportunity to obtain information that would justify a plea bargain outside of a standard, policy-driven offer.

    (c) If the case is litigated, a DWAI verdict is more likely where there is a refusal than where there is a chemical test result of 0.08 or more.

If the DWI charge is a misdemeanor and the person needs to drive to earn a living, take the test.

> In such a situation, a refusal (i) will mandate that the person obtain a VTL § 1192 conviction (in order to obtain a conditional license), and (ii) the person will have to remain on the conditional license longer than if he or she had taken the test. *See* § 41:72, *infra*.

If there is a plea bargaining policy in the county with regard to test refusals and/or BAC limits, take the action that will reduce the likelihood of an unfavorable plea bargain (*e.g.*, some prosecutors tend to offer a better deal where the defendant refuses others tend to punish the defendant for the refusal.

If the person *credibly* claims to have only consumed enough alcohol to produce a chemical test result of less than 0.08 (such a conversation should not be had in a manner likely to be overheard by the police)—take the test.

> The police almost always charge VTL § 1192 suspects who refuse the chemical test with common law DWI, in violation of VTL § 1192(3), and *not* with DWAI; thus, where the person consumed alcohol, but only enough to produce a chemical test result of less than 0.08, the chemical test result may lead to a DWAI charge (or even to no VTL § 1192 charge at all).

In most other situations—refuse the test.

> In light of New York's current DWI laws (e.g., a person who refuses the test cannot be charged with Aggravated DWI (unless there is a child under 16 years of age in the vehicle); everyone convicted of DWI now faces the ignition interlock device requirement; a person whose BAC is .08% or more faces the indefinite suspension of his or her driver's license pending prosecution (with no credit for "time served" upon conviction); etc.), it is increasingly likely that the consequences of taking the test outweigh those of refusing (unless the defendant is sure to pass it).

The authors' previous position was as follows:

If the person is a first offender—take the test.

In such a situation:

(a) If the person needs to drive, a refusal (i) will mandate that he or she obtain a VTL § 1192 conviction (in order to obtain a conditional license), (ii) the person will have to remain on the conditional license longer than if he or she had taken the test, see § 41:72, supra, and (iii) the refusal adds a $500 civil penalty.

(b) If the person does not need to drive, obtains a VTL § 1192 plea, and takes the DDP (but does not obtain a conditional license), a refusal increases the loss of license from approximately two months (i.e., the length of the DDP) to at least 1 year, and adds a $500 civil penalty.

(c) If the person does not need to drive, obtains a DWAI plea, and does not take the DDP, a refusal increases the loss of license from 90 days to at least 1 year, and adds a $500 civil penalty.

(d) If the person does not need to drive, obtains a DWI plea, and does not take the DDP, a refusal adds a $500 civil penalty.

If the person is a second offender within five years and the DWI charge is a misdemeanor—take the test.

In such a situation, most prosecutors require a plea to the DWI charge, and the person is not eligible for either the DDP or a conditional license; a refusal increases the loss of license from at least 6 months to at least 18 months and adds a $750 civil penalty.

If the person is a third offender within 10 years and the DWI charge is a misdemeanor—take the test.

In such a situation, the person may be eligible for the DDP (but will *not* be eligible for a conditional license); if DDP eligible, a refusal increases the minimum loss of license from the length of the DDP to at least 18 months, see §§ 50:1 et seq. and §§ 53:1 et seq., *infra*, and adds a civil penalty of either $500 or $750.

If the person is under the age of 21—the same rules apply as for a person 21 years of age or older.

§ 41:18 There is no constitutional right to refuse to submit to a chemical test

Research References

West's Key Number Digest, Automobiles ⚷144.1(1.20)

It is well settled that "a person suspected of drunk driving has no constitutional right to refuse to take a blood-alcohol test." *South Dakota v. Neville*, 459 U.S. 553, 560 n.10, 103 S.Ct. 916, 921 n.10 (1983). *See also* 459 U.S at 565, 103 S.Ct. at 923 ("Respondent's right to refuse the blood-alcohol test . . . is simply a matter of grace bestowed by the . . . legislature"); *People v. Smith*, 18 N.Y.3d 544, 548, 942 N.Y.S.2d 426, 429, 965 N.E.2d 928 (2012); *People v. Thomas*, 46 N.Y.2d 100, 106, 412 N.Y.S.2d 845, 848

(1978) ("inasmuch as a defendant can constitutionally be compelled to take such a test, he has no constitutional right not to take one"); *People v. Shaw*, 72 N.Y.2d 1032, 1033, 534 N.Y.S.2d 929, 930 (1988); *People v. Mosher*, 93 Misc. 2d 179, __, 402 N.Y.S.2d 735, 736 (Webster Just. Ct. 1978). There are, however, three exceptions to this general rule:

> Taking a driver's blood for alcohol analysis does not . . . involve an unreasonable search under the Fourth Amendment *when there is [1] probable cause, [2] exigent circumstances and [3] a reasonable examination procedure*. So long as these requirements are met . . . the test may be performed absent defendant's consent and indeed over his objection without violating his Fourth Amendment rights.

People v. Kates, 53 N.Y.2d 591, 594–95, 444 N.Y.S.2d 446, 448 (1981) (emphasis added) (citation omitted). *See also Schmerber v. California*, 384 U.S. 757, 86 S.Ct. 1826 (1966); *Missouri v. McNeely*, 133 S. Ct. 1552, 185 L. Ed. 2d 696 (2013).

§ 41:19   There is a *statutory* right to refuse to submit to a chemical test

Research References

West's Key Number Digest, Automobiles ☞144.1(1.20)

Although there is no *constitutional* right to refuse to submit to a chemical test, *see* § 41:18, *supra*, VTL § 1194(2)(b)(1) grants a DWI suspect a qualified "statutory right to refuse the test." *People v. Shaw*, 72 N.Y.2d 1032, 1034, 534 N.Y.S.2d 929, 930 (1988). *See also People v. Smith*, 18 N.Y.3d 544, 548, 942 N.Y.S.2d 426, 429, 965 N.E.2d 928 (2012); *People v. Daniel*, 84 A.D.2d 916, __, 446 N.Y.S.2d 658, 659 (4th Dep't 1981), order aff'd, 57 N.Y.2d 97, 454 N.Y.S.2d 292, 439 N.E.2d 1235 ("The 1953 statute conferred upon the motorist certain rights, the most important of which was the right to refuse to take the test. That statutory right is in excess of the motorist's constitutional rights"), *aff'd sub nom. People v. Moselle*, 57 N.Y.2d 97, 454 N.Y.S.2d 292 (1982); *People v. Wolter*, 83 A.D.2d 187, __, 444 N.Y.S.2d 331, 333 (4th Dep't 1981), *aff'd sub nom.* People v. Moselle, 57 N.Y.2d 97, 454 N.Y.S.2d 292 (1982); *People v. Haitz*, 65 A.D.2d 172, __, 411 N.Y.S.2d 57, 60 (4th Dep't 1978) ("The defendant's right of refusal . . . is a qualified statutory right designed to avoid the unpleasantness connected with administering a chemical test on an unwilling subject"); *People v. Porter*, 46 A.D.2d 307, __, 362 N.Y.S.2d 249, 254 (3d Dep't 1974); *People v. Smith*, 79 Misc. 2d 172, __, 359 N.Y.S.2d 446, 448 (Broome Co. Ct. 1974).

The right of refusal is "qualified" in two ways. First, VTL § 1194(2) penalizes the exercise of the right with a civil penalty, "license revocation and disclosure of [the] refusal in a prosecution for operating a vehicle while under the influence of alcohol or drugs." *People v. Thomas*, 46 N.Y.2d 100, 108, 412 N.Y.S.2d 845, 850 (1978). *See also People v. Smith*, 18 N.Y.3d 544, 548, 942 N.Y.S.2d 426, 429, 965 N.E.2d 928 (2012). Second, under the circumstances set forth in VTL § 1194(3), a DWI suspect can be subjected to a compulsory (*i.e.*, forcible) court-ordered chemical test despite his or her refusal to consent to such test.

In addition, there is no requirement that the defendant be advised of his or her right to refuse, "and the absence of such an advisement does not negate consent otherwise freely given." *People v. Marietta*, 61 A.D.3d 997, __, 879 N.Y.S.2d 476, 477 (2d Dep't 2009).

§ 41:20   Legislative policy for creating statutory right of refusal

Research References

West's Key Number Digest, Automobiles ☞144.1(1.20)

The legislative policy behind the creation of the statutory right of refusal was set forth by the Court of Appeals in *People v. Kates*, 53 N.Y.2d 591, 596, 444 N.Y.S.2d 446, 448 (1981):

> "The only reason the opportunity to revoke is given is to eliminate the need for the use of force by police officers if an individual in a drunken condition should refuse to submit to the test" (Report of Joint Legislative Committee on Motor Vehicle Problems, McKinney's 1953 Session Laws of N.Y., pp. 1912–1928). * * *
>
> It was reasonable for the Legislature, concerned with avoiding potentially violent conflicts between the police and drivers arrested for intoxication, to provide that the police must request the driver's consent, advise him of the consequences of refusal and honor his wishes if he decides to refuse.

See also People v. Paddock, 29 N.Y.2d 504, 506, 323 N.Y.S.2d 976, 977 (1971) (Jasen, J., concurring); *People v. Ameigh*, 95 A.D.2d 367, __, 467 N.Y.S.2d 718, 719 (3d Dep't 1983); *People v. Haitz*, 65 A.D.2d 172, __, 411 N.Y.S.2d 57, 60 (4th Dep't 1978); *People v. Smith*, 79 Misc. 2d 172, __, 359 N.Y.S.2d 446, 448 (Broome Co. Ct. 1974).

§ 41:21   Refusal to submit to a chemical test is not an appropriate criminal charge

Research References

West's Key Number Digest, Automobiles ☞144.1(1.20)

The Court of Appeals has made clear that "the Legislature in the enactment of section 1194 of the Vehicle and Traffic Law [embodied] two penalties or adverse consequences of refusal [to submit to a chemical test]—license revocation and disclosure of [the] refusal in a prosecution for operating a vehicle while under the influence of alcohol or drugs." *People v. Thomas*, 46 N.Y.2d 100, 108, 412 N.Y.S.2d 845, 849–50 (1978). *See also* VTL § 1194(2); *People v. Leontiev*, 38 Misc. 3d 716, __, 956 N.Y.S.2d 832, 837 (Nassau Co. Dist. Ct. 2012). *See generally People v. Ashley*, 15 Misc. 3d 80, __, 836 N.Y.S.2d 758, 761 (App. Term, 9th & 10th Jud. Dist. 2007) ("defendant was also convicted of 'refusal to submit to a breath test.' Though the accusatory instrument refers to Vehicle and Traffic Law § 1194(3), that statute neither compels a person who is arrested for driving while intoxicated to submit to a 'breath test,' nor deems the failure to do so to be a criminal offense. Therefore, the judgment convicting defendant of refusal to take a breath test must be reversed").

Nonetheless, in *People v. Burdick*, 266 A.D.2d 711, __, 699 N.Y.S.2d 173, 175 (3d Dep't 1999), the Appellate Division, Third Department, appears to affirm a defendant's conviction in Delaware county court of, among other things, "refusal to submit to a chemical test (Vehicle and Traffic Law § 1194[2])." In this regard, Delaware County District Attorney Richard D. Northrup, Jr., confirms that this reference in *Burdick* is a typographical error— the defendant was in actuality charged with, and convicted of, refusal to submit to a *breath test* (*i.e.*, Alco-Sensor test), in violation of VTL § 1194(1)(b), which *is* a traffic infraction. *See* VTL § 1800(a); *People v. Pecora*, 123 Misc. 2d 259, __, 473 N.Y.S.2d 320, 323 (Wappinger Just. Ct. 1984); *People v. Hamza*, 109 Misc. 2d 1055, __, 441 N.Y.S.2d 579, 581 (Gates Just. Ct. 1981).

§ 41:22 Refusal warnings—Generally

Research References

West's Key Number Digest, Automobiles ☞144.1(1.20), 421

Various subdivisions of VTL § 1194(2) mandate that a DWI suspect be given adequate "refusal warnings" before an alleged chemical test refusal can be used against him or her at trial and/or at a DMV refusal hearing. *See* VTL § 1194(2)(b)(1); VTL § 1194(2)(c); VTL § 1194(2)(f). To satisfy this requirement, most law enforcement agencies have adopted standardized, boilerplate refusal warnings which track the statutory language of VTL § 1194(2).

In this regard, most police officers carry wallet-size cards which contain *Miranda* warnings on one side, and so-called "DWI warnings" on the other. Model refusal warnings promulgated by DMV read as follows:

   1. You are under arrest for driving while intoxicated.

2. A refusal to submit to a chemical test, or any portion thereof, will result in the immediate suspension and subsequent revocation of your license or operating privilege, whether or not you are convicted of the charge for which you were arrested.

3. If you refuse to submit to a chemical test, or any portion thereof, your refusal can be introduced into evidence against you at any trial, proceeding, or hearing resulting from this arrest.

4. Will you submit to a chemical test of your (breath/blood/urine) for alcohol? or (will you submit to a chemical analysis of your blood/urine for drugs)? *People v. Robles*, 180 Misc. 2d 512, __ n.1, 691 N.Y.S.2d 697, 698–99 n.1 (N.Y. City Crim. Ct. 1999). *See also People v. Smith*, 18 N.Y.3d 544, 546-47, 942 N.Y.S.2d 426, 427, 965 N.E.2d 928 (2012); *People v. Lynch*, 195 Misc. 2d 814, __, 762 N.Y.S.2d 474, 477 (N.Y. City Crim. Ct. 2003).

The statutory refusal warnings, although arguably coercive in nature, do not constitute *impermissible* coercion. *See People v. Dillin*, 150 Misc. 2d 311, __-__, 567 N.Y.S.2d 991, 993–95 (N.Y. City Crim. Ct. 1991). *See also People v. Hochheimer*, 119 Misc. 2d 344, __, 463 N.Y.S.2d 704, 710 (Monroe Co. Sup. Ct. 1983).

§ 41:23 Refusal warnings need not precede request to submit to chemical test

Research References

West's Key Number Digest, Automobiles ☞144.1(1.20), 421

Most police officers, prosecutors, courts, and even defense attorneys are under the incorrect impression that VTL § 1194(2) requires that refusal warnings be read to a DWI suspect before he or she can lawfully be requested to submit to a chemical test. *See, e.g., People v. Whelan*, 165 A.D.2d 313, __ n.1, 567 N.Y.S.2d 817, 819 n.1 (2d Dep't 1991) ("Vehicle and Traffic Law § 1194(2)(b) mandates that prior to requesting an arrested defendant to consent to a chemical test, he must be advised that his license or permit to drive and any non-resident operating privilege shall be immediately suspended and subsequently revoked for refusal to submit to such chemical test whether or not he is found guilty of the charge for which he is arrested").

However, "[o]nly if the driver declines the initial offer to submit to a chemical test, [the driver] having consented to a chemical test by virtue of the operation of a vehicle within the State, VTL § 1194(2)(a), need he or she be informed of the effect of that refusal." *People v. Rosado*, 158 Misc. 2d 50, __ n.1, 600 N.Y.S.2d 624, 625 n.1 (N.Y. City Crim. Ct. 1993). In other words, it is only once a DWI suspect initially refuses to submit to a properly requested chemical test that refusal warnings must be read to him or her in "clear and unequivocal" language, thereby giving the suspect the choice of whether to "persist" in the refusal. *See also People v. Smith*, 18 N.Y.3d 544, 549, 942 N.Y.S.2d 426, 429, 965 N.E.2d 928 (2012) ("To implement the statute, law enforcement authorities have developed a standardized verbal warning of the consequences of refusal to take the test that is given to a motorist suspected of driving under the influence. . . . The duty to give the warning is triggered if the motorist is asked to take a chemical test and declines to do so. If, after being advised of the effect of such a refusal, the motorist nonetheless withholds consent, the motorist may be subjected to the statutory consequences.").

As the Court of Appeals explained in *People v. Thomas*, 46 N.Y.2d 100, 108, 412 N.Y.S.2d 845, 850 (1978), "[u]nder the procedure prescribed by section 1194 of the Vehicle and Traffic Law *a driver who has initially declined to take one of the described chemical tests is to be informed of the consequences of such refusal. If he thereafter persists in a refusal* the test is not to be given (§ 1194, subd. 2); the choice is the driver's." (Emphasis added). *See also Matter of Geary v. Commissioner of Motor Vehicles*, 92 A.D.2d 38, __, 459 N.Y.S.2d 494, 497 (4th Dep't), order *aff'd*, 59 N.Y.2d 950, 466 N.Y.S.2d 304 (1983). *See generally South Dakota v. Neville*, 459 U.S. 553, 565 n.16, 103 S. Ct. 916, 923 n.16 (1983) ("Even though the officers did not specifically advise respondent that the test results could be used against him in court, no one would seriously contend that this failure to warn would make the test results inadmissible, had respondent chosen to submit to the test").

In this regard, the *Rosado* court stated:

> Although the drivers in both *Thomas* and *Geary* were given warnings twice, the statute contains no requirement that warnings precede the initial request to submit to the test. As all drivers consent to submit to the test, VTL § 1194(2)(a), no warnings need precede the first request. It is my belief, having viewed numerous videotaped "refusals," that the practice of reading a legalistic set of warnings to an allegedly intoxicated driver, before the driver is first requested to submit to the test, results in many more refusals to submit than would occur if the driver were first just simply asked. It is my further belief that many police officers mistakenly assume that the refusal warnings are analogous to *Miranda* warnings and must be fully delivered before a chemical test may be administered; I have viewed a number of videotapes in which the officer continued to read the warnings even though the driver agreed to submit to the test.

158 Misc. 2d at __ n.3, 600 N.Y.S.2d at 626 n.3. *See also People v. Coludro*, 166 Misc. 2d 662, 634 N.Y.S.2d 964 (N.Y. City Crim. Ct. 1995). *Cf. People v. Pagan*, 165 Misc. 2d 255, __, 629 N.Y.S.2d

656, 659–60 (N.Y. City Crim. Ct. 1995) (disapproving of procedure set forth in *Thomas* and approved in *Rosado*).

Thus, where a police officer reads the refusal warnings to a DWI suspect prior to requesting that the suspect submit to a chemical test (and the suspect initially refuses), the officer has created a situation in which he or she may be required to read the warnings a second time (in order to allow the suspect to "persist" in the refusal). *See, e.g.*, *Rosado, supra*.

§ 41:24   Refusal warnings must be given in "clear and unequivocal" language

Research References

West's Key Number Digest, Automobiles ☜144.1(1.20), 421

VTL § 1194(2)(f) mandates that refusal warnings be administered to a DWI suspect in "clear and unequivocal" language. *See also* VTL § 1194(2)(b)(1); *People v. Smith*, 18 N.Y.3d 544, 549, 550, 942 N.Y.S.2d 426, 429, 430, 965 N.E.2d 928 (2012); VTL § 1194(2)(c). In this regard, "[t]he determination of the standard for clear and unequivocal language is viewed in the eyes of the person who is being told the warnings, not the person administering them . . . Therefore, the question of whether the warnings were clear and unequivocal [is] decided on the defendant's understanding them, not on the objective standard of whether the police officer read the warnings verbatim from the statute." *People v. Lynch*, 195 Misc. 2d 814, __, 762 N.Y.S.2d 474, 477–78 (N.Y. City Crim. Ct. 2003).

People v. Smith, 18 N.Y.3d 544, 942 N.Y.S.2d 426, 965 N.E.2d 928 (2012), is the seminal case on this issue. In *Smith*, the police read the standardized chemical test refusal warnings to the defendant three times. The defendant's response to the first set of warnings was "that he understood the warnings but wanted to speak to his lawyer before deciding whether to take a chemical test." 18 N.Y.3d at 547, 942 N.Y.S.2d at 427. The defendant's response to the second set of warnings was that he wanted to call his lawyer (which he attempted to do but was unsuccessful). 18 N.Y.3d at 547, 942 N.Y.S.2d at 428. The defendant's response to the third set of warnings was "that he was waiting for his attorney to call him back." 18 N.Y.3d at 547, 942 N.Y.S.2d at 428. "At this juncture, the troopers interpreted defendant's response as a refusal to submit to the test." 18 N.Y.3d at 547, 942 N.Y.S.2d at 428.

The Court of Appeals held that there was no refusal, as (a) the defendant never actually refused to submit to a chemical test, and (b) the police never advised him that his third statement (*i.e.*, that he was waiting for his attorney to call him back) would be construed as a refusal. Critically, the Court found that even though the refusal warnings had been read from the standardized warning card three separate times, "[s]ince a reasonable motorist in defendant's position would not have understood that, unlike the prior encounters, the further request to speak to an attorney would be interpreted by the troopers as a binding refusal to submit to a chemical test, defendant was not adequately warned that his conduct would constitute a refusal. The evidence of that refusal therefore was received in error at trial." 18 N.Y.3d at 551, 942 N.Y.S.2d at 431.

In this regard, the *Smith* Court noted that:

> All that is required for a refusal to be admissible at trial is a record basis to show that, through words or actions, defendant declined to take a chemical test despite having been clearly warned of the consequences of refusal. In this case, such evidence would have been present if, during the third request, troopers had merely alerted defendant that his time for deliberation had expired and if he did not consent to the chemical test at that juncture his response would be deemed a refusal.

18 N.Y.3d at 551-52, 942 N.Y.S.2d at 431.

An issue can (and often does) arise where an individual who is read the refusal warnings does not understand what is meant by the term "chemical test"—especially if the individual has already submitted to one or more breath screening tests. In *People v. Cousar*, 226 A.D.2d 740, __, 641 N.Y.S.2d 695, 695 (2d Dep't 1996), the Appellate Division, Second Department, found that the refusal warnings given to the defendant were sufficiently clear and unequivocal where, when the defendant stated that he did not understand the warning as recited from the police officer's DWI warning card, "the arresting officer explained the warnings to him 'in layman's terms.'" *See also Matter of Cruikshank v. Melton*, 82 A.D.2d 932, 440 N.Y.S.2d 759 (3d Dep't 1981); *Matter of Jason v. Melton*, 60 A.D.2d 707, 400 N.Y.S.2d 878 (3d Dep't 1977); *Matter of Warren v. Melton*, 59 A.D.2d 963, 399 N.Y.S.2d 295 (3d Dep't 1977); *Kowanes v. State Dep't of Motor Vehicles*, 54 A.D.2d 611, 387 N.Y.S.2d 331 (4th Dep't 1976).

On the other hand, where an officer who attempts to explain the refusal warnings in layman's terms does so incorrectly, such warnings do not satisfy the "clear and unequivocal" language requirement. *See Matter of Gargano v. New York State Dep't of Motor Vehicles*, 118 A.D.2d 859, 500 N.Y.S.2d 346 (2d Dep't 1986). *See generally People v. Morris*, 8 Misc. 3d 360, 793 N.Y.S.2d 754 (N.Y. City Crim. Ct. 2005); *Matter of Pucino v. Tofany*, 60 Misc. 2d 778, 304 N.Y.S.2d 81 (Dutchess Co. Sup. Ct. 1969).

Various courts have found that refusal warnings administered to non-English speaking defendants did not satisfy the "clear and unequivocal" language requirement. *See, e.g., People v. Garcia-Cepero*, 22 Misc. 3d 490, __, 874 N.Y.S.2d 689, 692–94 (Bronx Co. Sup. Ct. 2008); *People v. Robles*, 180 Misc. 2d 512, 691 N.Y.S.2d 697 (N.Y. City Crim. Ct. 1999); *People v. Camagos*, 160 Misc. 2d 880, 611 N.Y.S.2d 426 (N.Y. City Crim. Ct. 1993); *People v. Niedzwiecki*, 127 Misc. 2d 919, 487 N.Y.S.2d 694 (N.Y. City Crim. Ct. 1985). *But see People v. Burnet*, 24 Misc. 3d 292, __, 882 N.Y.S.2d 835, 841-42 (Bronx Co. Sup. Ct. 2009); *People v. An*, 193 Misc. 2d 301, 748 N.Y.S.2d 854 (N.Y. City Crim. Ct. 2002).

Refusal warnings read from an outdated warning card (which had not been amended to reflect changes in the law) do not satisfy the "clear and unequivocal" language requirement. *People v. Philbert*, 110 Misc. 2d 1042, 443 N.Y.S.2d 354 (N.Y. City Crim. Ct. 1981).

§ 41:25 Incomplete refusal warnings invalidate chemical test refusal

Research References

West's Key Number Digest, Automobiles ⊙144.1(1.20), 421

VTL § 1194(2)(f) provides that:

(f) Evidence. Evidence of a refusal to submit to such chemical test or any portion thereof shall be admissible in any trial, proceeding or hearing based upon a violation of the provisions of [VTL § 1192] *but only upon a showing that the person was given sufficient warning, in clear and unequivocal language, of the effect of such refusal* and that the person persisted in the refusal.

(Emphasis added).

Where a person has been lawfully arrested for a suspected violation of VTL § 1192, VTL § 1194(2)(b)(1) provides, in pertinent part:

(b) Report of refusal. (1) If: (A) such person having been placed under arrest; or (B) after a breath [screening] test indicates the presence of alcohol in the person's system; . . . *and having thereafter been requested to submit to such chemical test and having been informed that the person's license or permit to drive and any non-resident operating privilege shall be immediately suspended and subsequently revoked for refusal to submit to such chemical test or any portion thereof, whether or not the person is found guilty of the charge for which such person is arrested* . . ., refuses to submit to such chemical test or any portion thereof, unless a court order has been granted pursuant to [VTL § 1194(3)], the test shall not be given and a written report of such refusal shall be immediately made by the police officer before whom such refusal was made.

(Emphasis added).

In the context of a DMV refusal hearing, VTL § 1194(2)(c) provides that:

The hearing shall be limited to the following issues: (1) did the police officer have reasonable grounds to believe that such person had been driving in violation of any subdivision of [VTL § 1192]; (2) did the police officer make a lawful arrest of such person; (3) *was such person given sufficient warning, in clear or unequivocal language, prior to such refusal that such refusal to submit to such chemical test or any portion thereof, would result in the immediate suspension and subsequent revocation of such person's license or operating privilege whether or not such person is found guilty of the charge for which the arrest was made*; and (4) did such person refuse to submit to such chemical test or any portion thereof.

(Emphasis added).

Where the police administer incomplete refusal warnings to a DWI suspect, his or her subsequent refusal to submit to a chemical test is both inadmissible at trial and invalid for DMV purposes. *See, e.g., People v. Boone*, 71 A.D.2d 859, __, 419 N.Y.S.2d 187, 188 (2d Dep't 1979); *Matter of Harrington v. Tofany*, 59 Misc. 2d 197, __, 298 N.Y.S.2d 283, 285–86 (Washington Co. Sup. Ct. 1969).

On the other hand, in *People v. Sanchez*, 48 Misc. 3d 765, __, 11 N.Y.S.3d 454, 455 (N.Y. City Crim. Ct. 2015):

After a pretrial *Dunaway/Huntley/Refusal* hearing, the Court suppressed evidence of defendant's refusal to take a breathalyzer test. The Court found that the IDTU officer had not given the defendant adequate warnings as to the consequences of the refusal. However, at trial, after hearing from the parties, the Court granted the People's application to cross-examine the defendant about that refusal in the event he elected to testify, relying on *People v. Harris*, 25 N.Y.2d 175, 250 N.E.2d 349, 303 N.Y.S.2d 71 (1969), *aff'd sub nom. Harris v. New York*, 401 U.S. 222, 91 S.Ct. 643, 28 L.Ed.2d 1 (1971), which holds that a statement that has been suppressed due to a *Miranda* violation, and is hence inadmissible at trial, can still be used on cross-examination of the defendant for impeachment purposes.

In so holding, the Court reasoned as follows:

It appears that no court in New York has expressly considered the question whether a defendant can be impeached, should he elect to testify at trial, by a refusal to take a breathalyzer test, where that refusal was suppressed under VTL § 1194(2)(f). In this Court's view, however, since it is clear that impeaching a defendant on cross-examination with his refusal is not the same as "admitting" the refusal into evidence, such impeachment is permissible by analogy to *Harris*. If a defendant can be impeached on cross-examination with a statement obtained in violation of *Miranda*, he can also be impeached on cross-examination with a refusal that was obtained in violation of VTL § 11924(2)(f).

Id. at __, 11 N.Y.S.3d at 457-58.

§ 41:26 Informing defendant that chemical test refusal will result in incarceration pending arraignment, whereas submission to test will result in release on appearance ticket, does not constitute impermissible coercion

Research References

West's Key Number Digest, Automobiles ⊕144.1(1.20), 421

Many police departments have a policy pursuant to which, in addition to advising the defendant of the statutory refusal warnings, the defendant is also informed that refusal to submit to a chemical test will result in either (a) incarceration pending arraignment, and/or (b) immediate arraignment at which bail will be set, whereas submission to the test will result in his or her immediate release on an appearance ticket (such as a UTT or DAT). Although such a policy is clearly "coercive" in nature, it apparently does not constitute *impermissible* coercion.

In this regard, in *People v. Cragg*, 71 N.Y.2d 926, 528 N.Y.S.2d 807 (1988), "[d]efendant contend[ed] that the police violated Vehicle and Traffic Law § 1194(2) by administering a breathalyzer test despite defendant's initial refusal to submit to the test, and by informing him of certain consequences—not specifically prescribed by the statute—of such refusal." In rejecting the defendant's claims, the Court of Appeals held:

> Contrary to defendant's assertion, the statute is not violated by an arresting officer informing a person as to the consequences of his choice to take or not take a breathalyzer test. Thus, it cannot be said, in the circumstances of this case, that by informing defendant that his refusal to submit to the test would result in his arraignment before a Magistrate and the posting of bail, the officer violated the provisions of the Vehicle and Traffic Law.

71 N.Y.2d at 927, 528 N.Y.S.2d at 807–08.

Similarly, in *People v. Bracken*, 129 Misc. 2d 1048, __, 494 N.Y.S.2d 1021, 1023 (N.Y. City Crim. Ct. 1985), the court held that:

> "A state plainly has the right to offer incentives for taking a test that provides the most reliable form of evidence of intoxication for use in subsequent proceedings." The issuance of a DAT is such an incentive. * * *

> When the police informed the defendant of the consequences of his failure to submit to a breathalyzer test they were simply providing him a factual recitation of what would happen . . .

> The VTL requires that persons who refuse the test have their licenses "immediately" suspended and sets forth a magistrate as one of

those persons who have the right to effectuate the suspension[.] VTL § 1194(2). The policy to withhold the issuance of the DAT and bring "refusers" to the magistrate is reasonable and not shown to be part of any systemic plan or desire to coerce persons arrested to take the breathalyzer test.

In fact, it would have been unreasonable and unfair not to tell the defendant of the policy to be followed upon his refusal to take the test. Giving the defendant knowledge of his choices concerning his liberty undoubtedly put pressure upon him to take the test. This was not a pressure, however, which rose to the level of impermissible coercion by any constitutional standard.

(Citation omitted). *See also People v. Harrington*, 111 Misc. 2d 648, 444 N.Y.S.2d 848 (Monroe Co. Ct. 1981) (same). *Cf. People v. Stone*, 128 Misc. 2d 1009, __-__, 491 N.Y.S.2d 921, 923–25 (N.Y. City Crim. Ct. 1985) (reaching opposite conclusion).

§ 41:27   What constitutes a chemical test refusal?

Research References
West's Key Number Digest, Automobiles ☞144.1(1.20), 413

"A refusal to submit [to a chemical test] may be evidenced by words or conduct." *People v. Massong*, 105 A.D.2d 1154, __, 482 N.Y.S.2d 601, 602 (4th Dep't 1984). *See also People v. Smith*, 18 N.Y.3d 544, 550, 942 N.Y.S.2d 426, 430, 965 N.E.2d 928 (2012) ("whether a defendant refused in a particular situation may be difficult to ascertain in cases where the accused did not communicate that intent in so many words. To be sure, a defendant need not expressly decline a police officer's request in order to effectuate a refusal that is admissible at trial. A defendant can signal an unwillingness to cooperate that is tantamount to a refusal in any number of ways, including through conduct. For example, where a motorist fails to follow the directions of a police officer prior to or during the test, thereby interfering with the timing of the procedure or its efficacy, this can constitute a constructive refusal."); *People v. Lizaldo*, 124 A.D.3d 432, __, 998 N.Y.S.2d 380, 381 (1st Dep't 2015), leave to appeal denied, 26 N.Y.3d 931 (2015); *People v. Richburg*, 287 A.D.2d 790, __, 731 N.Y.S.2d 256, 258 (3d Dep't 2001); *Matter of Stegman v. Jackson*, 233 A.D.2d 597, __, 649 N.Y.S.2d 529, 530 (3d Dep't 1996); *Matter of McGuirk v. Fisher*, 55 A.D.2d 706, __, 389 N.Y.S.2d 47, 48 (3d Dep't 1976).

"[A] defendant's mere silence cannot be deemed a refusal if the defendant was not *told* any refusal would be introduced into evidence against him." *People v. Niedzwiecki*, 127 Misc. 2d 919, __, 487 N.Y.S.2d 694, 696 (N.Y. City Crim. Ct. 1985). *See also People v. Pagan*, 165 Misc. 2d 255, __, 629 N.Y.S.2d 656, 659 (N.Y. City

Crim. Ct. 1995) (no refusal where the defendant not read full set of refusal warnings until *after* arresting officer deemed her to have refused).

In *Matter of Sullivan v. Melton*, 71 A.D.2d 797, 419 N.Y.S.2d 343 (4th Dep't 1979), the petitioner consented to a chemical test, but placed chewing gum in his mouth at a time and in a manner that the arresting officer took to be a refusal (in light of the requirement in 10 NYCRR § 59.5 that nothing be placed in a DWI suspect's mouth for at least 15 minutes prior to the collection of a breath sample). In reversing the finding of a refusal, the Appellate Division, Fourth Department, found:

> Petitioner consented to submit to the test and was not advised that placing gum in his mouth would constitute a refusal . . . No evidence supports a finding that the test here could not have been given pursuant to this regulation, or that petitioner knowingly thwarted the test . . . No prejudice resulted from petitioner's placing gum in his mouth. This is not the case where an initial consent to submit to the test is vitiated by conduct evidencing a refusal or where the test failed for reasons attributable to petitioner . . . His actions under the circumstances were not the equivalent of a refusal.

71 A.D.2d at __, 419 N.Y.S.2d at 344–45 (citations omitted).

By contrast, in *Matter of White v. Melton*, 60 A.D.2d 1000, __, 401 N.Y.S.2d 664, 665 (4th Dep't 1978), the same court upheld a refusal where:

> [T]he officer warned the petitioner not once but twice of the consequences of refusal and his directive to petitioner that he should not place anything in his mouth was prompted by a rule on a direction sheet from the State Breathalyzer Operator which provides that nothing should be placed in the mouth for twenty minutes prior to taking a test. On the basis of the facts in this record, the referee was justified in finding that petitioner expressed no willingness to take the test and his conduct was the equivalent of a refusal.

See also Matter of Dykeman v. Foschio, 90 A.D.2d 892, __, 456 N.Y.S.2d 514, 515 (3d Dep't 1982) (refusal upheld where the petitioner failed to stop smoking even after being warned that such conduct would be treated as a refusal).

Similarly, in *Matter of Brueck v. Melton*, 58 A.D.2d 1000, __, 397 N.Y.S.2d 271, 272 (4th Dep't 1977), the court upheld a refusal where:

> At the administrative hearing the arresting officer testified that although petitioner initially consented to take a breathalyzer test, she failed to blow any air into the machine as instructed to and only drooled. When advised to sit down and rest before attempting the test again, petitioner responded, "Leave me alone, I'm not going to take any test." Furthermore, petitioner never indicated to the

administrator of the test that she was unable to complete it or that there was any physical reason preventing her from blowing air into the breathalyzer device.

A DWI suspect's refusal/failure to provide an adequate breath (or urine) sample for chemical testing can constitute a refusal. *See, e.g., Craig v. Swarts*, 68 A.D.3d 1407, __, 891 N.Y.S.2d 204, 205 (3d Dep't 2009) ("Although petitioner verbally consented to taking the chemical test, numerous attempts on two separate machines failed to yield a testable sample and petitioner was deemed to have refused the test by his conduct"); *Matter of Johnson v. Adduci*, 198 A.D.2d 352, __, 603 N.Y.S.2d 332, 333 (2d Dep't 1993) (refusal upheld where "petitioner refused to blow into the tube of [a properly functioning] testing machine, thereby preventing his breath from being tested"); *People v. Bratcher*, 165 A.D.2d 906, __, 560 N.Y.S.2d 516, 517 (3d Dep't 1990) ("Defendant's refusal to breathe into the Intoxilyzer after being advised that his first attempt was inadequate to show a reading, together with proof that the machine was in good working order, was sufficient to constitute a refusal"); *Matter of Beaver v. Appeals Bd. of Admin. Adjudication Bureau*, 117 A.D.2d 956, __, 499 N.Y.S.2d 248, 251 (3d Dep't) (dissenting opinion), *rev'd for the reasons stated in the dissenting opinion below*, 68 N.Y.2d 935, 510 N.Y.S.2d 79 (1986); *People v. Adler*, 145 A.D.2d 943, __, 536 N.Y.S.2d 315, 316 (4th Dep't 1988) ("On three separate occasions in the conduct of the test, defendant ostensibly blew into the instrument used to record his blood alcohol content but, in the opinion of the administering officer, did so in such way that the instrument failed to record that a sample was received"); *Matter of Van Sickle v. Melton*, 64 A.D.2d 846, __, 407 N.Y.S.2d 334, 335 (4th Dep't 1978) (petitioner "blew into the mouthpiece of the [properly functioning] apparatus on five occasions without activating the machine"); *Matter of Kennedy v. Melton*, 62 A.D.2d 1152, 404 N.Y.S.2d 174 (4th Dep't 1978); *Matter of DiGirolamo v. Melton*, 60 A.D.2d 960, __, 401 N.Y.S.2d 893, 894 (3d Dep't 1978) ("The consent by the petitioner may be regarded as no consent at all if, as it appears from this record, the test failed for reasons attributable to him"); *People v. Kearney*, 196 Misc. 2d 335, __ n.2, 764 N.Y.S.2d 542, 543 n.2 (Sullivan Co. Ct. 2003).

In this regard, "[t]o establish a refusal, the People must show that the failure to register a sample is the result of defendant's action and not of the machine's inability to register the sample." *People v. Adler*, 145 A.D.2d 943, __, 536 N.Y.S.2d 315, 316 (4th Dep't 1988). *See also People v. Bratcher*, 165 A.D.2d 906, __, 560 N.Y.S.2d 516, 517 (3d Dep't 1990); *Matter of Van Sickle v. Melton*, 64 A.D.2d 846, 407 N.Y.S.2d 334 (4th Dep't 1978). *See generally Matter of Cushman v. Tofany*, 36 A.D.2d 1000, __, 321 N.Y.S.2d 831, 833 (3d Dep't 1971).

By its terms VTL § 1194(2)(f) applies to a persistent *"refusal"* to take the breathalyzer test; it does not apply to a mere "failure" to take or complete the test. The distinction is important. By using the term "refusal" the Legislature made it plain that the statute is directed only at an intentional or willful refusal to take the breathalyzer test. The statute is *not* directed at a mere unintentional failure by the defendant to comply with the requirements of the breathalyzer test.

The requirement that defendant's refusal be intentional grows out of the evidentiary theory underlying the statute. Evidence of a refusal is admissible on the theory that it evinces a defendant's consciousness of guilt. Obviously, an unintentional failure to complete the test does not evidence consciousness of guilt. * * *

The crucial consideration in this regard is whether defendant's conduct was deliberate. Where a defendant does not consciously intend to evade the breathalyzer test, his mere failure to take or complete the test cannot properly be regarded either as a true "refusal" within the meaning of § 1194(2)(f) or as evidence of consciousness of guilt.

People v. Davis, 8 Misc. 3d 158, __, __, 797 N.Y.S.2d 258, 262–63, 263–64 (Bronx Co. Sup. Ct. 2005) (citations omitted).

Where a DWI suspect persistently refuses to submit to a properly requested chemical test, but subsequently changes his or her mind and consents to the test, the subsequent consent does *not* void the prior refusal. *See, e.g., Matter of Viger v. Passidomo*, 65 N.Y.2d 705, 707, 492 N.Y.S.2d 2, 3 (1985) ("Petitioner's willingness to undergo the chemical test to determine the alcohol content of his blood approximately 1 hour and 40 minutes after his arrest does not preclude a determination that he had refused to take such test within the meaning of Vehicle and Traffic Law § 1194(3)(a)"); *Matter of Nicol v. Grant*, 117 A.D.2d 940, __, 499 N.Y.S.2d 247, 248 (3d Dep't 1986); *Matter of O'Brien v. Melton*, 61 A.D.2d 1091, 403 N.Y.S.2d 353 (3d Dep't 1978); *Matter of Reed v. New York State Dep't of Motor Vehicles*, 59 A.D.2d 974, 399 N.Y.S.2d 332 (3d Dep't 1977); *Matter of O'Dea v. Tofany*, 41 A.D.2d 888, 342 N.Y.S.2d 679 (4th Dep't 1973). *See generally Matter of Wilkinson v. Adduci*, 176 A.D.2d 1233, __, 576 N.Y.S.2d 728, 729 (4th Dep't 1991). In *People v. Ferrara*, 158 Misc. 2d 671, __, 602 N.Y.S.2d 86, 89 (N.Y. City Crim. Ct. 1993), the court stated:

The defendant's subsequent willingness to have a blood test performed does not affect the admissibility of the defendant's prior refusal. The fact that the test could have been performed when the defendant agreed does not undermine the admissibility of the refusal. The defendant's later recantation of an earlier refusal doesn't "suffice to undo that refusal." * * *

Thus, the defendant's initial refusal, after having been clearly and unequivocally advised as to the consequences of that refusal, stands as evidence of a consciousness of guilt despite a subsequent change of mind. The defendant may, if he or she chooses, explain to the trier of fact his reasons for refusing to take the test when offered and may, of course, testify to his later willingness to take the blood test in order to soften or obviate the impact of the evidence of the refusal. Plainly, this testimony might convince the trier of fact not to infer a consciousness of guilt from the defendant's refusal to take the test. However, these same facts do not render evidence of the refusal inadmissible at trial.

(Citations omitted).

Where a DWI suspect persistently refuses to submit to a properly requested chemical test but subsequently changes his or her mind and consents, the police can refuse to administer the test to the suspect. *See People v. Adler*, 145 A.D.2d 943, __, 536 N.Y.S.2d 315, 316 (4th Dep't 1988); *Matter of Nicol v. Grant*, 117 A.D.2d 940, 499 N.Y.S.2d 247 (3d Dep't 1986); *Matter of White v. Fisher*, 49 A.D.2d 450, 375 N.Y.S.2d 663 (3d Dep't 1975).

An attempt by a DWI suspect to select the type of chemical test to be administered (*e.g.*, "I consent to a chemical test of my blood, but not of my breath"), to select the location of the test (*e.g.*, "I consent to a test at the hospital, but not at the police station"), to select the person who will draw the blood (*e.g.*, "I consent to a blood test, but only if the blood is drawn by *my* doctor"), and/or to otherwise place conditions on his or her consent to submit to a chemical test generally constitutes a refusal. *See, e.g., People v. Williams*, 68 A.D.3d 414, __, 891 N.Y.S.2d 17, 18 (1st Dep't 2009), leave to appeal denied, 14 N.Y.3d 774, 898 N.Y.S.2d 106, 925 N.E.2d 111 (2010); *Matter of Ehman v. Passidomo*, 118 A.D.2d 707, __, 500 N.Y.S.2d 44, 45 (2d Dep't 1986) ("Vehicle and Traffic Law § 1194 authorizes the police officer to decide the type of test to be administered; it does not provide an option to the petitioner"); *Matter of Gilman v. Passidomo*, 109 A.D.2d 1082, 487 N.Y.S.2d 186 (4th Dep't 1985) (same); *People v. Aia*, 105 A.D.2d 592, __, 482 N.Y.S.2d 56, 57 (3d Dep't 1984) ("The choice of test was the officer's, not defendant's, and there is no showing that the officer was in any way unreasonable in his choice of which test to use"); *Matter of Litts v. Melton*, 57 A.D.2d 1027, 395 N.Y.S.2d 264 (3d Dep't 1977); *Matter of Cushman v. Tofany*, 36 A.D.2d 1000, __, 321 N.Y.S.2d 831, 833 (3d Dep't 1971); *Matter of Shields v. Hults*, 26 A.D.2d 971, 274 N.Y.S.2d 760 (3d Dep't 1966); *Matter of Breslin v. Hults*, 20 A.D.2d 790, 248 N.Y.S.2d 70 (2d Dep't 1964). *See generally Matter of Martin v. Tofany*, 46 A.D.2d 967, __, 362 N.Y.S.2d 57, 58 (3d Dep't 1974) (Petitioner's "explanation that he believed a blood test was required by law, and not chemical test by use of a breathalyzer, as requested by the trooper, lacks merit"); *Matter of Blattner v. Tofany*, 34 A.D.2d 1066, __, 312 N.Y.S.2d 173, 174 (3d Dep't 1970) (Petitioner's "arbitrary insistence that the sample be taken from his hip rather than his arm [together with other conduct] constituted a refusal").

Where a DWI suspect desires to consult with, but is unable to reach, his attorney, "the police officer's statement to him that his insistence on waiting for his attorney constituted a refusal was not misleading or inaccurate." *People v. O'Rama*, 78 N.Y.2d 270, 280, 574 N.Y.S.2d 159, 164 (1991). *See also People v. Smith*, 18 N.Y.3d 544, 551-52, 942 N.Y.S.2d 426, 431, 965 N.E.2d 928 (2012).

In *Matter of Smith v. Commissioner of Motor Vehicles*, 103 A.D.2d 865, __, 478 N.Y.S.2d 103, 104 (3d Dep't 1984), a refusal was found where, after being arrested for DWI and read proper refusal warnings, "petitioner refused to accompany the officer, but instead surrendered the keys to his truck to him and left the scene on foot, announcing that he could be found at a local bar."

§ 41:28 Chemical test refusal must be "persistent"

Research References

West's Key Number Digest, Automobiles ⊙⊸144.1(1.20), 413

VTL § 1194(2)(f) provides that:

(f) Evidence. Evidence of a refusal to submit to such chemical test or any portion thereof shall be admissible in any trial, proceeding or hearing based upon a violation of the provisions of [VTL § 1192] *but only upon a showing* that the person was given sufficient warning, in clear and unequivocal language, of the effect of such refusal and *that the person persisted in the refusal*.

(Emphases added).

The "persistence" requirement, while applicable to Court proceedings based upon a violation of VTL § 1192, is inapplicable to a DMV chemical test refusal hearing—where "the only evidence of refusal necessary [i]s that the petitioner refused at least once to submit to a chemical test." *Matter of Hahne v. New York State Dep't of Motor Vehicles*, 63 A.D.3d 936, 882 N.Y.S.2d 434 (2d Dep't 2009). *See also* VTL § 1194(2)(c) (one of the issues to be determined at a DMV chemical test refusal hearing is "did such person refuse to submit to such chemical test or any portion thereof").

§ 41:29 What constitutes a "persistent" refusal?

Research References

West's Key Number Digest, Automobiles ⊙⊸144.1(1.20), 413

In order for a refusal to be considered "persistent," the motorist must be "offered at least two opportunities to submit to the chemical test, 'at least one of which must take place after being advised of the sanctions for refusal.'" *People v. Pagan*, 165 Misc. 2d 255, __, 629 N.Y.S.2d 656, 660 (N.Y. City Crim. Ct. 1995) (citation omitted). *See also People v. Thomas*, 46 N.Y.2d 100, 108, 412 N.Y.S.2d 845, 850 (1978) ("Under the procedure prescribed by section 1194 of the Vehicle and Traffic Law a driver who has initially declined to take one of the described chemical tests is to be informed of the consequences of such refusal. If he thereafter persists in a refusal the test is not to be given (§ 1194, subd. 2); the choice is the driver's"); *People v. Rosado*, 158 Misc. 2d 50, __ & n.1, __ & n.3, 600 N.Y.S.2d 624, 625 & n.1, 626 & n.3 (N.Y. City Crim. Ct. 1993); *People v. Camagos*, 160 Misc. 2d 880, __, 611 N.Y.S.2d 426, 429 (N.Y. City Crim. Ct. 1993) ("The dictionary defines persistence as to continue steadfastly or often annoyingly, especially in spite of opposition"); *People v. Garcia-Cepero*, 22 Misc. 3d 490, __, 874 N.Y.S.2d 689, 694 (Bronx Co. Sup. Ct. 2008). *See generally People v. O'Reilly*, 16 Misc. 3d 775, __, 842 N.Y.S.2d 292, 297-98 (Suffolk Co. Dist. Ct. 2007); *People v. Davis*, 8 Misc. 3d 158, __, 797 N.Y.S.2d 258, 262–63 (Bronx Co. Sup. Ct. 2005); *People v. Nigohosian*, 138 Misc. 2d 843, __, 525 N.Y.S.2d 556, 559 (Nassau Co. Dist. Ct. 1988).

In *People v. D'Angelo*, 244 A.D.2d 788, __, 665 N.Y.S.2d 713, 713 (3d Dep't 1997), the Appellate Division, Third Department, held that "defendant's words and conduct clearly evince a persistent refusal to submit to a breathalyzer test" where:

> [F]ollowing his arrest, defendant was taken to the City of Glens Falls Police Station, arriving at around 5:00 A.M. on June 1, 1995, where he was immediately provided with the requisite warning. Defendant initially agreed to take the test but, upon learning that he was going to be charged with a felony, changed his mind stating to the officer "What's the point?" The police then reread the warning to him, eliciting an unintelligible mumble from defendant who lay down on a bench and went to sleep. At 5:37 A.M. and 5:47 A.M., the arresting officer unsuccessfully attempted to rouse defendant to ask him to take the test.

See also People v. Richburg, 287 A.D.2d 790, __, 731 N.Y.S.2d 256, 258 (3d Dep't 2001); *People v. O'Reilly*, 16 Misc. 3d 775, __, 842 N.Y.S.2d 292, 297-98 (Suffolk Co. Dist. Ct. 2007).

§ 41:30 VTL § 1194(2)(f) claim is waived by guilty plea

In *People v. Sirico*, 135 A.D.3d 19, 18 N.Y.S.3d 430 (2d Dep't 2015), leave to appeal denied, 27 N.Y.3d 1075, 2016 WL 3402992 (2016), the Appellate Division, Second Department, held that a VTL § 1194(2)(f) claim is waived by guilty plea. Specifically:

> Among the limited group of issues that survive a valid guilty plea

and may be raised on a subsequent appeal are those relating to the denial of a motion to suppress evidence under CPL 710.20. The Legislature has preserved such claims for appellate review through the enactment of CPL 710.70(2). CPL 710.70(2) expressly grants a defendant a statutory right to appellate review of an order denying a motion to suppress evidence "notwithstanding the fact" that the judgment of conviction "is entered upon a plea of guilty." However, the statutory right to appellate review created by CPL 710.70(2) applies to orders which deny a motion to suppress evidence on the grounds enumerated by CPL 710.20. Although CPL 710.20(5) authorizes a defendant to move to suppress evidence of "a chemical test of the defendant's blood administered in violation of the provisions" of Vehicle and Traffic Law § 1194(3) or "any other applicable law," that provision is not implicated here. In this case, the defendant did not move to suppress the results of a chemical test of his blood. Indeed, the police did not perform a chemical test upon the defendant. Rather, he moved to preclude the People from admitting testimony of his refusal to submit to a chemical test. Such a motion cannot be characterized as one seeking suppression under CPL 710.20(5). Accordingly, the defendant does not have a statutory right to appellate review of the County Court's ruling permitting the introduction of evidence of his refusal to submit to a chemical test.

Nor is the defendant's claim that the County Court erred in ruling that the People would be permitted to introduce evidence at trial of his refusal to submit to a chemical test a claim of constitutional dimension, or one that bears upon the integrity of the judicial process. Rather, the court's determination relates to an evidentiary or technical matter. The defendant's motion to preclude evidence of his refusal to submit to a chemical test was predicated upon his claim that the evidence was not admissible pursuant to Vehicle and Traffic Law § 1194(2)(f), rather than upon a claim that evidence was obtained in violation of his constitutional rights. Moreover, the admission of such evidence at trial merely allows a jury to draw an inference of a defendant's consciousness of guilt. The County Court's determination at issue is akin to a *Ventimiglia/Molineux* ruling, a *Sandoval* ruling, and other pretrial rulings that decide motions in limine and which are generally forfeited by virtue of a plea of guilty.

Therefore, we hold that by pleading guilty, the defendant forfeited appellate review of his claim that the County Court erred in ruling that the People would be permitted to introduce evidence at trial that he refused a chemical test pursuant to Vehicle and Traffic Law § 1194(2)(f).

Id. at __, 18 N.Y.S.3d at 435-36 (citations omitted).

§ 41:31 Chemical test refusal need not be "knowing"

Research References
West's Key Number Digest, Automobiles ⚖144.1(1.20), 413

At least two Departments of the Appellate Division have held that, for DMV purposes, a chemical test refusal does not have to be "knowing" in order to be valid. *See, e.g., Matter of Gagliardi v. Department of Motor Vehicles*, 144 A.D.2d 882, __, 535 N.Y.S.2d 203, 204 (3d Dep't 1988); *Matter of Carey v. Melton*, 64 A.D.2d 983, 408 N.Y.S.2d 817 (2d Dep't 1978). The rationale for such a ruling was set forth in *Carey*:

> We note that there is evidence that the petitioner may not have fully comprehended the consequences of his refusal because he was so intoxicated by the consumption of alcohol and/or the inhalation of toxic fumes. Nevertheless, we do not construe the statutory warning contained in [VTL § 1194(2)] as requiring a "knowing" refusal by the petitioner. This interpretation would lead to the absurd result that the greater the degree of intoxication of an automobile driver, the less the degree of his accountability.

64 A.D.2d at __, 408 N.Y.S.2d at 818.

By contrast, in *Matter of Jentzen v. Tofany*, 33 A.D.2d 532, __, 314 N.Y.S.2d 297, 297 (4th Dep't 1969), the Appellate Division, Fourth Department, annulled a DMV refusal revocation where "petitioner did not make an understanding refusal to take the test."

§ 41:32 Refusal on religious grounds does not invalidate chemical test refusal

Research References

West's Key Number Digest, Automobiles ⊙144.1(1.20), 413

In *People v. Thomas*, 46 N.Y.2d 100, 109 n.2, 412 N.Y.S.2d 845, 850 n.2 (1978), the Court of Appeals made clear that:

> Proof . . . that might be explanatory of a particular defendant's refusal to take the test unrelated to any apprehension as to its results (*as, for instance, religious scruples* or individual syncopephobia) should be treated not as tending to establish any form of compulsion but rather as going to the probative worth of the evidence of refusal. Thus, a jury might in such circumstances reject the inference of consciousness of guilt which would otherwise have been available.

(Emphasis added) (citations omitted). *See also People v. Sukram*, 142 Misc. 2d 957, 539 N.Y.S.2d 275 (Nassau Co. Dist. Ct. 1989).

§ 41:33 Suppression of chemical test refusal

Research References

West's Key Number Digest, Automobiles ⊙144.1(1.20), 413

A refusal to submit to a chemical test is potentially suppressible on several grounds. For example, a chemical test refusal, like a chemical test result, can be suppressed:

(a) As the fruit of an illegal stop. *See, e.g., Matter of Byer v. Jackson*, 241 A.D.2d 943, 661 N.Y.S.2d 336 (4th Dep't 1997); *McDonell v. New York State Dept. of Motor Vehicles*, 77 A.D.3d 1379, 908 N.Y.S.2d 507 (4th Dep't 2010);

(b) As the fruit of an illegal arrest. *See, e.g., Dunaway v. New York*, 442 U.S. 200, 99 S.Ct. 2248 (1979); *Brown v. Illinois*, 422 U.S. 590, 95 S.Ct. 2254 (1975); *Mapp v. Ohio*, 367 U.S. 643, 81 S.Ct. 1684 (1961). *See generally Welsh v. Wisconsin*, 466 U.S. 740, 744, 104 S.Ct. 2091, 2095 (1984);

(c) If it is obtained in violation of the right to counsel. *See, e.g., People v. Washington*, 23 N.Y.3d 228, 989 N.Y.S.2d 670, 12 N.E.3d 1099 (2014); *People v. Smith*, 18 N.Y.3d 544, 550, 942 N.Y.S.2d 426, 430, 965 N.E.2d 928 (2012); *People v. Shaw*, 72 N.Y.2d 1032, 534 N.Y.S.2d 929 (1988); *People v. Gursey*, 22 N.Y.2d 224, 292 N.Y.S.2d 416 (1968); and/or

(d) If it is obtained in violation of VTL § 1194. *See, e.g.,* VTL § 1194(2)(f); *People v. Boone*, 71 A.D.2d 859, 419 N.Y.S.2d 187 (2d Dep't 1979).

In this regard, the courts of this state have long recognized the need for a pretrial suppression hearing on the issue of the admissibility of a defendant's alleged refusal to submit to a chemical test. *See, e.g., People v. Boone*, 71 A.D.2d 859, __, 419 N.Y.S.2d 187, 187 (2d Dep't 1979) ("the denial, without a hearing, of defendant's motion to suppress his alleged refusal to submit to a chemical test" constituted reversible error); *People v. Smith*, 18 N.Y.3d 544, 547, 942 N.Y.S.2d 426, 428, 965 N.E.2d 928 (2012) (issue of admissibility of alleged chemical test refusal was addressed at pretrial hearing); 18 N.Y.3d at 551, 942 N.Y.S.2d at 430 ("whether defendant's words or actions amounted to a refusal often constitutes a mixed question of law and fact that requires the court to view defendant's actions in light of all the surrounding circumstances and draw permissible inferences from equivocal words or conduct"); *People v. Williams*, 99 A.D.3d 955, __, 952 N.Y.S.2d 281, 282 (2d Dep't 2012) ("The defendant correctly contends that the hearing court erred in denying his motion to suppress evidence of his refusal to take a breathalyzer test, as the officer administering the test did not advise the defendant that his refusal could be used against him at a trial, proceeding, or hearing resulting from the arrest"); *People v. Guzman*, 247 A.D.2d 552, __, 668 N.Y.S.2d 918, 918 (2d Dep't 1998) (same); *People v. Jones*, 51 Misc. 3d 863, 27 N.Y.S.3d 830 (N.Y. City Crim. Ct. 2016) (Court held "*Dunaway/Johnson/*Refusal hearing"); *People v. Popko*, 33 Misc. 3d 277, __, 930 N.Y.S.2d 782, 784 (N.Y. City Crim. Ct. 2011) (Court held "combined *Ingle* and refusal hearing."); *People v. Brito*, 26 Misc. 3d 1097, 892 N.Y.S.2d 752 (Bronx Co. Sup. Ct. 2010); *People v. Rodriguez*, 26 Misc. 3d 238, 891 N.Y.S.2d 246 (Bronx Co. Sup. Ct. 2009); *People v. O'Reilly,*

16 Misc. 3d 775, —, 842 N.Y.S.2d 292, 294 (Suffolk Co. Dist. Ct. 2007) (Court held "a *Dunaway / Huntley / Mapp* and refusal hearing."); *People v. Davis*, 8 Misc. 3d 158, —, 797 N.Y.S.2d 258, 259 (Bronx Co. Sup. Ct. 2005) ("pre-trial 'refusal hearings' have become common in New York criminal practice"); *People v. Lynch*, 195 Misc. 2d 814, —, 762 N.Y.S.2d 474, 476 (N.Y. City Crim. Ct. 2003) ("the determination of the admissibility of a refusal to submit to a chemical test is best addressed at a hearing held prior to commencement of trial"); *People v. An*, 193 Misc. 2d 301, —, 748 N.Y.S.2d 854, 855 (N.Y. City Crim. Ct. 2002) (Court held *Dunaway*-"Refusal" hearing); *People v. Burtula*, 192 Misc. 2d 597, —, 747 N.Y.S.2d 692, 693 (Nassau Co. Dist. Ct. 2002) ("Whether this request is labeled one for 'suppression' or for a pre-trial determination into the admissibility of evidence, there exists a sufficient body of case law establishing that a defendant is entitled to such a hearing"); *People v. Dejac*, 187 Misc. 2d 287, —, 721 N.Y.S.2d 492, 493 (Monroe Co. Sup. Ct. 2001) (Court held "combined probable cause/*Huntley* and chemical test refusal hearing"); *People v. Robles*, 180 Misc. 2d 512, —, 691 N.Y.S.2d 697, 699 (N.Y. City Crim. Ct. 1999) ("It has become common practice for defendants to request and for the courts to conduct pre-trial hearings on the issue of the admissibility of a defendant's refusal to consent to a chemical test"); *People v. Coludro*, 166 Misc. 2d 662, 634 N.Y.S.2d 964 (N.Y. City Crim. Ct. 1995); *People v. Pagan*, 165 Misc. 2d 255, 629 N.Y.S.2d 656 (N.Y. City Crim. Ct. 1995); *People v. Camagos*, 160 Misc. 2d 880, 611 N.Y.S.2d 426 (N.Y. City Crim. Ct. 1993); *People v. McGorman*, 159 Misc. 2d 736, —, 606 N.Y.S.2d 566, 568 (N.Y. Co. Sup. Ct. 1993); *People v. Ferrara*, 158 Misc. 2d 671, 602 N.Y.S.2d 86 (N.Y. City Crim. Ct. 1993); *People v. Rosado*, 158 Misc. 2d 50, 600 N.Y.S.2d 624 (N.Y. City Crim. Ct. 1993); *People v. Martin*, 143 Misc. 2d 341, —, 540 N.Y.S.2d 412, 416 (Newark Just. Ct. 1989) ("This Court thus holds that a defendant is entitled to a separate pre-trial hearing to determine whether his refusal to take a breathalyzer [sic] test should be submitted to the jury"); *People v. Walsh*, 139 Misc. 2d 161, —, 527 N.Y.S.2d 349, 351 (Nassau Co. Dist. Ct. 1988) ("Where there is a denial by a defendant of a refusal to give his consent to take the test, this Court favors a pre-trial hearing"); *People v. Cruz*, 134 Misc. 2d 115, 509 N.Y.S.2d 1002 (N.Y. City Crim. Ct. 1986); *People v. Delia*, 105 Misc. 2d 483, 432 N.Y.S.2d 321 (Onondaga Co. Ct. 1980); *People v. Hougland*, 79 Misc. 2d 868, 361 N.Y.S.2d 827 (Suffolk Co. Dist. Ct. 1974). *See generally People v. Reynolds*, 133 A.D.2d 499, —, 519 N.Y.S.2d 425, 427 (3d Dep't 1987) ("County Court, following a suppression hearing, did not err in denying defendant's motion to suppress evidence of his refusal to submit to a blood alcohol test after the accident"); *People v. Scaccia*, 4 A.D.3d 808, 771 N.Y.S.2d 772 (4th Dep't 2004)

(same); *People v. Cousar*, 226 A.D.2d 740, 641 N.Y.S.2d 695 (2d Dep't 1996) (same); *People v. Boudreau*, 115 A.D.2d 652, 496 N.Y.S.2d 489 (2d Dep't 1985) (same). *Cf. People v. Carota*, 93 A.D.3d 1072, __, 941 N.Y.S.2d 302, 307 (3d Dep't 2012); *People v. Kinney*, 66 A.D.3d 1238, 888 N.Y.S.2d 260 (3d Dep't 2009) (hearing held after both parties had rested but before case was submitted to jury).

The rationale for such a hearing was concisely set forth by the Court in *Cruz, supra*:

> A hearing held during trial, or a ruling made during the course of the trial, has little practical value to a defendant. Absent pre-trial suppression, the prosecutor is entitled to discuss the refusal to submit to the breathalyzer test with the jury in his opening statement. Once the jury is made aware of this evidence, the damage is done regardless of whether the prosecution is permitted to introduce that evidence at trial. A ruling made during trial excluding that evidence may thus be futile. Nor would curative instructions warning the jury not to consider the evidence eliminate the tremendous prejudicial effect. Therefore the ruling must be made pre-trial. That same conclusion was reached in *People v. Delia*, 105 Misc. 2d 483, 484, 432 N.Y.S.2d 321 (Co. Ct, Onondaga Cty, 1980) and *People v. Houghland* [sic], *supra*, the only reported cases which have dealt with the issue of pre-trial determination of the admissibility of this type of evidence.

134 Misc. 2d at __, 509 N.Y.S.2d at 1004. *See also Burtula*, 192 Misc. 2d at __, 747 N.Y.S.2d at 693–94.

At such a hearing, "the People should assume the burden of demonstrating by a fair preponderance of the evidence . . . that the defendant refused to consent to the test as mandated by V.T.L. 1194(1), (4) [currently VTL § 1194(2)(a), (f)]." *People v. Walsh*, 139 Misc. 2d 161, __, 527 N.Y.S.2d 349, 351 (Nassau Co. Dist. Ct. 1988). *See also People v. Rodriguez*, 26 Misc. 3d 238, __, 891 N.Y.S.2d 246, 248-49 (Bronx Co. Sup. Ct. 2009); *People v. Burnet*, 24 Misc. 3d 292, __, 882 N.Y.S.2d 835, 841 (Bronx Co. Sup. Ct. 2009); *Davis*, 8 Misc. 3d at __, 797 N.Y.S.2d at 260 ("at a refusal hearing (in addition to addressing any special issues that may arise) the People in essence must meet a two part burden. First, they must show by a preponderance of the evidence that clear and proper refusal warnings were delivered to the defendant. Second, they must also show by a preponderance of the evidence that a true and persistent refusal then followed"); 8 Misc. 3d at __, 797 N.Y.S.2d at 267 (same); *Lynch*, 195 Misc. 2d at __, 762 N.Y.S.2d at 478–79; *Burtula*, 192 Misc. 2d at __, 747 N.Y.S.2d at 694; *Robles*, 180 Misc. 2d at __, 691 N.Y.S.2d at 699; *Camagos*, 160 Misc. 2d at __, 611 N.Y.S.2d at 428. *See generally People v. Dejac*, 187 Misc. 2d 287, __, 721 N.Y.S.2d 492, 495–96 (Monroe Co. Sup. Ct. 2001).

In *People v. Annis*, 134 A.D.3d 1433, 21 N.Y.S.3d 795 (4th Dep't 2015), the Appellate Division, Fourth Department, intimated that defense counsel's unreasonable withdrawal of a request for such a hearing can constitute ineffective assistance of counsel.

§ 41:34 Invalid stop voids chemical test refusal

Research References

West's Key Number Digest, Automobiles ⊕144.1(1.20), 413

In *Matter of Byer v. Jackson*, 241 A.D.2d 943, __, 661 N.Y.S.2d 336, 337 (4th Dep't 1997), the petitioner's car was stopped by the police "after he turned right out of a parking lot without using his turn signal," which led to the petitioner being arrested for, among other things, DWI. The petitioner thereafter refused to submit to a chemical test.

A DMV refusal hearing was held, following which the petitioner's driver's license was revoked. On appeal, the respondent conceded "that petitioner did not violate Vehicle and Traffic Law § 1163(a), the underlying predicate for the stop, because the statute does not require a motorist to signal a turn from a private driveway," but nonetheless contended "that the officer's good faith belief that there was a violation of the Vehicle and Traffic Law, coupled with the surrounding circumstances, provided reasonable suspicion of criminality to justify the stop." 241 A.D.2d at __, 661 N.Y.S.2d at 337–38.

The Appellate Division, Fourth Department, disagreed, holding that "[w]here the officer's belief is based on an erroneous interpretation of law, the stop is illegal at the outset and any further actions by the police as a direct result of the stop are illegal." 241 A.D.2d at __, 661 N.Y.S.2d at 338. *See also McDonell v. New York State Dept. of Motor Vehicles*, 77 A.D.3d 1379, __, 908 N.Y.S.2d 507, 508 (4th Dep't 2010) (same).

In *People v. Guthrie*, 25 N.Y.3d 130, 132, 8 N.Y.S.3d 237, 239, 30 N.E.3d 880 (2015), the Court of Appeals partially abrogated the mistake of law doctrine set forth in *Byer*, holding that as long as "the officer's mistake about the law is reasonable, the stop is constitutional." In so holding, the Court reasoned that "the relevant question before us is not whether the officer acted in good faith, but whether his belief that a traffic violation had occurred was objectively reasonable. Recently, in *Heien v. North Carolina*, the Supreme Court of the United States clarified that the Fourth Amendment tolerates objectively reasonable mistakes supporting such a belief, whether they are mistakes of fact or mistakes of law." *Id.* at 134, 8 N.Y.S.3d at 240–41 (citations and footnote omitted).

Critically, in the footnote omitted from the above quote, the *Guthrie* Court stated:

This distinction is significant in that a mistake of law that is merely made in "good faith" will not validate a traffic stop; rather, unless the mistake is objectively reasonable, any evidence gained from the stop—whether based on a mistake of law or a mistake of fact—must be suppressed. Thus, contrary to the dissent's suggestion, our holding in this case does not represent a limitation on the rule set forth in *People v. Bigelow* that there is no good faith exception to the exclusionary rule.

Id. at 134 n.2, 8 N.Y.S.3d at 240 n.2 (citation omitted). *See also id.* at 139, 8 N.Y.S.3d at 244-45 ("As the Supreme Court explained, the requirement that the mistake be objectively reasonable prevents officers from 'gain[ing] [any] Fourth Amendment advantage through a sloppy study of the laws [they are] duty-bound to enforce'") (citation omitted).

Thus, *Guthrie* clearly does not stand for the proposition that all mistake of law stops are now valid. It merely stands for the proposition that "objectively reasonable" mistake of law stops are valid.

§ 41:35 Probable cause to believe motorist violated VTL § 1192 must exist at time of arrest

Research References

West's Key Number Digest, Automobiles ☞144.1(1.20), 413

One of the issues to be determined at a DMV refusal hearing is whether the police officer had reasonable grounds (*i.e.*, probable cause) to believe that the motorist had been driving in violation of VTL § 1192. *See* VTL § 1194(2)(c). In determining whether probable cause existed for the motorist's arrest, observations made, or evidence obtained *subsequent to* the arrest cannot be considered. *See, e.g., People v. Loria*, 10 N.Y.2d 368, 373, 223 N.Y.S.2d 462, 467 (1961), (overruled in part on other grounds by, People v. McQueen, 18 N.Y.2d 337, 274 N.Y.S.2d 886, 221 N.E.2d 550 (1966)); *People v. Oquendo*, 221 A.D.2d 223, __, 633 N.Y.S.2d 492, 493 (1st Dep't 1995); *People v. Feingold*, 106 A.D.2d 583, __, 482 N.Y.S.2d 857, 859 (2d Dep't 1984); *People v. Bruno*, 45 A.D.2d 1025, __, 358 N.Y.S.2d 183, 184 (2d Dep't 1974); *People v. Garafolo*, 44 A.D.2d 86, __, 353 N.Y.S.2d 500, 502 (2d Dep't 1974); *Matter of Obrist v. Commissioner of Motor Vehicles*, 131 Misc. 2d 499, 500 N.Y.S.2d 909 (Onondaga Co. Sup. Ct. 1985).

In *Obrist, supra*, the police, who were waiting at the petitioner's home to arrest him pursuant to a warrant, arrested the petitioner upon his arrival. The police thereafter (a) suspected that the petitioner was intoxicated, (b) requested that the petitioner submit to a chemical test, and (c) upon the petitioner's refusal to submit to such a test, *rearrested* him for DWI. The petitioner ultimately brought an Article 78 proceeding challenging the revocation of his driver's license following a DMV refusal hearing.

In granting the petition, the supreme court held that "[t]he pre-requisite that the arrest must be based upon probable cause of driving while intoxicated has not been met in this case," in that "[a]t the time of the arrest under the warrant, there was no evidence that [petitioner] was intoxicated. He did not stagger. His words were not slurred at the time he was taken into custody. At best, there was an odor of beer on his breath, and his face was slightly flushed." 131 Misc. 2d at __, 500 N.Y.S.2d at 910. More specifically, the court held that:

> The general rule is that there must be probable cause at the time of the arrest. That is, the arresting officer must have "reasonable grounds" for believing that the suspect is or has been under the influence of liquor while operating his vehicle. There was no evidence offered which could establish "reasonable grounds" sufficient to sustain an arrest. The arrest was on other grounds unrelated to a violation under this statute. It is not proper execution of the statutory requirements to make the arrest when the signs of intoxication are not present and then, at some later time decide to request the chemical test.
>
> This is not a case of placing form over substance but rather an insistance [sic] that the statutory requirements of this quasi criminal statute be strictly met.

131 Misc. 2d at __, 500 N.Y.S.2d at 911 (citations omitted).

§ 41:36   Procedure upon arrest—Report of Refusal

Research References

West's Key Number Digest, Automobiles ☞144.1(1.20), 413

Where a person has been lawfully arrested for a suspected violation of VTL § 1192, VTL § 1194(2)(b)(1) provides, in pertinent part:

> (b) Report of refusal. (1) If: (A) such person having been placed under arrest; or (B) after a breath [screening] test indicates the presence of alcohol in the person's system; . . . and having thereafter been requested to submit to such chemical test and having been informed that the person's license or permit to drive and any non-resident operating privilege shall be immediately suspended and subsequently revoked for refusal to submit to such chemical test or any portion thereof, whether or not the person is found guilty of the charge for which such person is arrested . . ., refuses to submit to such chemical test or any portion thereof, unless a court order has been granted pursuant to [VTL § 1194(3)], the test shall not be given and a written report of such refusal shall be immediately made by the police officer before whom such refusal was made.

See also 15 NYCRR § 139.2(a). Similar provisions exist for individuals charged with boating while intoxicated, *see* Navigation Law § 49-a; 15 NYCRR § 139.2(b), and Snowmobiling While Intoxicated. *See* Parks, Recreation & Historic Preservation Law § 25.24; 15 NYCRR § 139.2(c).

In *Matter of Smith v. Commissioner of Motor Vehicles*, 103 A.D.2d 865, —, 478 N.Y.S.2d 103, 104 (3d Dep't 1984), the Appellate Division, Third Department, rejected a claim that the validity of the Report of Refusal was somehow affected by the fact that it was filled out by the chief of police rather than the arresting officer.

§ 41:37 Report of Refusal—Verification

Research References
West's Key Number Digest, Automobiles ⊶144.1(1.20), 413

A Report of Refusal "may be verified by having the report sworn to, or by affixing to such report a form notice that false statements made therein are punishable as a class A misdemeanor pursuant to [PL § 210.45] and such form notice together with the subscription of the deponent shall constitute a verification of the report." VTL § 1194(2)(b)(1). *See also* 15 NYCRR § 139.2(a).

§ 41:38 Report of Refusal—Contents

Research References
West's Key Number Digest, Automobiles ⊶144.1(1.20), 413

The officer's Report of Refusal must "set forth reasonable grounds to believe [1] such arrested person . . . had been driving in violation of any subdivision of [VTL § 1192] . . ., [2] that said person had refused to submit to such chemical test, and [3] that no chemical test was administered pursuant to the requirements of [VTL § 1194(3)]." VTL § 1194(2)(b)(2).

In *Matter of Peeso v. Fiala*, 130 A.D.3d 1442, —, 13 N.Y.S.3d 742, 743 (4th Dep't 2015), the Appellate Division, Fourth Department, held that a Report of Refusal is not required to expressly allege that the motorist's purported intoxication was "voluntary." *Cf. People v. Cruz*, 48 N.Y.2d 419, 428, 423 N.Y.S.2d 625, 629, 399 N.E.2d 513 (1979) ("intoxication is a greater degree of impairment which is reached when the driver has *voluntarily* consumed alcohol to the extent that he is incapable of employing the physical and mental abilities which he is expected to possess in order to operate a vehicle as a reasonable and prudent driver") (emphasis added). In so holding, the Court found that "[p]etitioner's reliance on *People v. Cruz* is misplaced inasmuch as that case involved a criminal conviction for driving while intoxicated." *Id.* at —, 13 N.Y.S.3d at 743-44 (citation omitted).

§ 41:39   Report of Refusal—To whom is it submitted?

Research References

West's Key Number Digest, Automobiles ⊙144.1(1.20), 413

The officer's Report of Refusal "shall be presented to the court upon arraignment of an arrested person." VTL § 1194(2)(b)(2). *See also* 15 NYCRR § 139.2(d) ("Upon the arraignment of the defendant, the police officer shall present to the court copies of the report of refusal to submit to chemical test").

For individuals under the age of 21 charged with a Zero Tolerance law refusal, *see* § 15:54, *supra*.

§ 41:40   Procedure upon arraignment—Temporary suspension of license

Research References

West's Key Number Digest, Automobiles ⊙144.1(1.20), 413

At arraignment in a refusal case, the court is required to temporarily suspend the defendant's driving privileges pending the outcome of a DMV refusal hearing. *See* VTL § 1194(2)(b)(3) ("For persons placed under arrest for a violation of any subdivision of [VTL § 1192], the license or permit to drive and any non-resident operating privilege shall, upon the basis of such written report, be temporarily suspended by the court without notice pending the determination of a hearing as provided in [VTL § 1194(2)(c)]"). *See also* 15 NYCRR § 139.3(a).

Similar provisions exist for individuals charged with boating while intoxicated, *see* Navigation Law § 49-a; 15 NYCRR § 139.3(b), and snowmobiling while intoxicated. *See* Parks, Recreation & Historic Preservation Law § 25.24; 15 NYCRR § 139.3(c). This procedure does not violate the Due Process Clause. *See Matter of Ventura*, 108 Misc. 2d 281, 437 N.Y.S.2d 538 (Monroe Co. Sup. Ct. 1981). *See generally Mackey v. Montrym*, 443 U.S. 1, 99 S.Ct. 2612 (1979).

However, "[i]f the department fails to provide for such hearing [15] days after the date of the arraignment of the arrested person, the license, permit to drive or non-resident operating privilege of such person shall be reinstated pending a hearing pursuant to this section." VTL § 1194(2)(c). In addition, "[i]f the respondent appears for a first scheduled chemical test refusal hearing, and the arresting officer does not appear, the matter will be adjourned and any temporary suspension still in effect shall be terminated." 15 NYCRR § 127.9(c).

In other words, the temporary license suspension imposed at arraignment in a refusal case lasts *the shorter of* 15 days or until the DMV refusal hearing.

§ 41:41 Procedure upon arraignment—Court must provide defendant with waiver form and notice of DMV refusal hearing date

Research References

West's Key Number Digest, Automobiles ⚖=144.1(1.20), 413

VTL § 1194(2)(b)(4) provides that "[t]he court . . . shall provide such person with a scheduled hearing date, a waiver form, and such other information as may be required by the commissioner." 15 NYCRR § 139.3(d) provides more specificity in this regard:

> Upon arraignment . . ., the court shall complete a temporary suspension and notice of hearing form (adding the location and the next available hearing date and time, as provided by the commissioner), and give the appropriate copies to the defendant and the police officer.

See generally 15 NYCRR § 127.1(a) (general requirements of hearing notice); 15 NYCRR § 139.2(d) ("The police officer shall bring his or her own copy of such report to the refusal hearing at the location and on the date and time specified in the temporary suspension and notice of hearing form provided by the court").

The "temporary suspension and notice of hearing form" referenced in 15 NYCRR § 139.3(d) is a two-sided document. The front side is entitled "Notice of Temporary Suspension and Notice of Hearing." The back side is entitled "Waiver of Hearing."

In terms of hearing date availability, 15 NYCRR § 139.4(a) provides that "[t]he commissioner shall provide to all magistrates, in advance, a schedule of hearing dates and locations and forms necessary to carry out the provisions of this Part."

§ 41:42 Effect of failure of court to schedule DMV refusal hearing

Research References

West's Key Number Digest, Automobiles ⚖=144.1(1.20)

The arraigning court will occasionally fail to schedule a DMV refusal hearing, in violation of VTL § 1194(2)(b)(4) and 15 NYCRR § 139.3(d). In this regard, 15 NYCRR § 127.9(a) provides that a chemical test refusal hearing "may be scheduled by the department if the court fails to do so."

§ 41:43 Effect of delay by court in forwarding Report of Refusal to DMV

Research References

West's Key Number Digest, Automobiles ⚖=144.1(1.20)

In *Matter of Mullen v. New York State Dep't of Motor Vehicles*, 144 A.D.2d 886, 535 N.Y.S.2d 206 (3d Dep't 1988), the town court failed to temporarily suspend the petitioner's driver's license at arraignment and/or forward the Report of Refusal to DMV within 48 hours, as is required by VTL § 1194(2). Approximately 10 months later, following a *Huntley*/probable cause hearing, the court finally filed the Report of Refusal. The petitioner sought a writ of prohibition, claiming that, as a result of the town court's delay in forwarding the Report of Refusal to the DMV, "respondents never obtained jurisdiction to review her refusal." 144 A.D.2d at __, 535 N.Y.S.2d at 207. The Appellate Division, Third Department, disagreed. In so holding, the court reasoned that:

> It is well established that mere delay in scheduling a refusal hearing will not oust respondents of jurisdiction . . . [W]e cannot accept petitioner's premise that the 48-hour transfer provision constitutes a jurisdictional prerequisite. In our view, the time schedules specified in Vehicle and Traffic Law § 1194(2) are directory only. By providing for an immediate license suspension procedure in the event of a test refusal, the Legislature was clearly acting "to protect the public, not the impaired driver."

144 A.D.2d at __, 535 N.Y.S.2d at 207 (citation omitted).

§ 41:44　Effect of delay by DMV in scheduling refusal hearing

Research References

West's Key Number Digest, Automobiles ⟿144.1(1.20)

In *Matter of Geary v. Commissioner of Motor Vehicles*, 92 A.D.2d 38, 459 N.Y.S.2d 494 (4th Dep't), order *aff'd*, 59 N.Y.2d 950, 466 N.Y.S.2d 304 (1983), the refusal paperwork was properly forwarded to DMV by the arraigning court. Nonetheless, the DMV did not schedule a refusal hearing until approximately 71/2 months later. Following the refusal hearing, the petitioner's driver's license was revoked. The petitioner filed an Article 78 proceeding, claiming "that he was denied his right to a hearing and determination within a reasonable time under the State Administrative Procedure Act." 92 A.D.2d 38 at __, 459 N.Y.S.2d at 496. The Appellate Division, Fourth Department, disagreed. In so holding, the court reasoned that:

> The statute [VTL § 1194] was designed to enable the authorities to deal promptly and effectively with the scourge of drunken drivers by immediate revocation of their licenses either upon chemical proof of intoxication or upon refusal to submit to the blood test. Time schedules specified in similar legislation for performance of certain acts on the part of an administrative agency have been held to be directory only . . .

No physical characteristic or condition could be more closely related to incompetence to operate a motor vehicle than inebriation, and no aspect of motor vehicle regulation can be more important to the welfare of both operators and the public than keeping inebriated drivers off the public highways . . . [Recent amendments to VTL § 1194] should more effectively accomplish the intent to protect the public, not the impaired driver.

92 A.D.2d 38 at __-__, 459 N.Y.S.2d at 496–97 (citations omitted). *See also Matter of Maxwell v. Commissioner of Motor Vehicles*, 100 A.D.2d 746, 473 N.Y.S.2d 940 (4th Dep't 1984), *rev'g* 109 Misc. 2d 62, 437 N.Y.S.2d 554 (Erie Co. Sup. Ct. 1981); *Matter of Tzetzo v. Commissioner of Motor Vehicles*, 97 A.D.2d 978, 468 N.Y.S.2d 787 (4th Dep't 1983); *Matter of Brown v. Tofany*, 33 A.D.2d 984, 307 N.Y.S.2d 268 (4th Dep't 1970).

In affirming the Appellate Division, the Court of Appeals noted that, although a lengthy delay by the DMV in scheduling a refusal hearing is not *jurisdictional* in nature, in an appropriate case such a delay could result in a finding of an "erroneous exercise of authority" by the *Commissioner. Matter of Geary v. Commissioner of Motor Vehicles*, 59 N.Y.2d 950, 952, 466 N.Y.S.2d 304, 304 (1983). *See also Matter of Correale v. Passidomo*, 120 A.D.2d 525, __, 501 N.Y.S.2d 724, 725 (2d Dep't 1986) ("In order to successfully argue that a delay in scheduling a refusal hearing pursuant to Vehicle and Traffic Law § 1194 constituted a violation of the State Administrative Procedure Act § 301, the petitioner must show that he was substantially prejudiced by such delay"). *See generally Matter of Reed v. New York State Dep't of Motor Vehicles*, 59 A.D.2d 974, __, 399 N.Y.S.2d 332, 333 (3d Dep't 1977) (DMV refusal revocation is "a civil, not criminal, sanction, and, therefore, constitutional speedy trial rights are not in issue"); *Matter of Minnick v. Melton*, 53 A.D.2d 1016, 386 N.Y.S.2d 488 (4th Dep't 1976) (same).

In any event, DMV regulations enacted subsequent to *Geary* expressly provide that a chemical test refusal hearing must be commenced within "[6] months from the date the department receives notice of [the] refusal," 15 NYCRR § 127.2(b)(2), absent (a) "reasonable grounds for postponing the commencement of [the] hearing," and (b) "provided the respondent is given prior notice thereof and an explanation of the grounds for such postponement." 15 NYCRR § 127.2(c). In such a case, "[t]he reasonableness of such postponement shall be reviewable by the Administrative Appeals Board established pursuant to [VTL] article 3-A." 15 NYCRR § 127.2(c).

In *Hildreth v. New York State Dept. of Motor Vehicles Appeals Bd.*, 83 A.D.3d 838, __, 921 N.Y.S.2d 137, 139-40 (2d Dep't 2011), leave to appeal denied, 18 N.Y.3d 804, 938 N.Y.S.2d 862, 962 N.E.2d 287 (2012), the Appellate Division, Second Department, rejected petitioner's claim that his re-scheduled refusal hearing "should have been dismissed for failure to hold a hearing within a reasonable time as required under the State Administrative Procedure Act § 301 or within six months from the date the DMV received notice of his chemical test refusal as required under 15 NYCRR 127.2(b)(2)." In so holding, the Court reasoned that:

> Time limitations imposed on administrative agencies by their own regulations are not mandatory. Absent a showing of substantial prejudice, a petitioner is not entitled to relief for an agency's noncompliance. Accordingly, a petitioner must demonstrate substantial prejudice in order to challenge a delayed chemical test refusal hearing under section 301(1) of the State Administrative Procedure Act. As the petitioner retained his driving privileges while awaiting the hearing, he was not prejudiced by the delay.

83 A.D.3d at ___, 921 N.Y.S.2d at 140 (citations omitted).

§ 41:45   Report of Refusal must be forwarded to DMV within 48 hours of arraignment

Research References
West's Key Number Digest, Automobiles ⟿144.1(1.20)

VTL § 1194(2)(b)(3) provides that "[c]opies of such report must be transmitted by the court to the commissioner . . . Such report shall be forwarded to the commissioner within [48] hours of such arraignment." *See also* 15 NYCRR § 139.3(d) ("Within 48 hours of the arraignment, the court must forward copies of both the refusal report and the temporary suspension and notice of hearing form to the commissioner").

§ 41:46   Forwarding requirement cannot be waived— Even with consent of all parties

Research References
West's Key Number Digest, Automobiles ⟿144.1(1.20), 144.2(1)

VTL § 1194(2)(b)(3) expressly provides that copies of the Report of Refusal "*must be transmitted by the court to the commissioner and such transmittal may not be waived even with the consent of all the parties.*" (Emphasis added). *See also* 15 NYCRR § 139.3(d) ("Timely submission of the refusal report to the Commissioner of Motor Vehicles may not be waived even with consent of all parties"). This section prohibits the parties from negotiating a plea bargain pursuant to which the Report of Refusal is not forwarded to the DMV—which would allow the defendant to avoid the civil consequences of his or her refusal to submit to a chemical test.

§ 41:47 DMV regulations pertaining to chemical test refusals

Research References

West's Key Number Digest, Automobiles ⊸144.1(1.20)

VTL § 1194(2)(e) mandates that DMV enact regulations pertaining to chemical test refusals:

> (e) Regulations. The commissioner shall promulgate such rules and regulations as may be necessary to effectuate the provisions of [VTL § 1194(1) and (2)].

Pertinent DMV regulations are set forth at 15 NYCRR Parts 127, 134, 135, 136, 139, and 155.

§ 41:48 DMV refusal hearings—Generally

Research References

West's Key Number Digest, Automobiles ⊸144.1(1.20), 144.2(.5)

VTL § 1194(2)(c) provides for a due process hearing prior to the imposition of civil sanctions for refusal to submit to a chemical test:

> (c) Hearings. Any person whose license or permit to drive or any non-resident driving privilege has been suspended pursuant to [VTL § 1194(2)(b)] is entitled to a hearing in accordance with a hearing schedule to be promulgated by the commissioner.

§ 41:49 DMV refusal hearings—Waiver of right to hearing

Research References

West's Key Number Digest, Automobiles ⊸144.1(1.20), 144.2(.5)

VTL § 1194(2)(c) provides that "[a]ny person may waive the right to a [DMV refusal] hearing under this section." *See also* 15 NYCRR § 139.4(c) (waiver must be in writing). In this regard, VTL § 1194(2)(b)(4) provides that "[i]f a hearing, as provided for in [VTL § 1194(2)(c)] . . . is waived by such person, the commissioner shall immediately revoke the license, permit, or non-resident operating privilege, *as of the date of receipt of such waiver* in accordance with the provisions of [VTL § 1194(2)(d)]." (Emphasis added). *See also* 15 NYCRR § 139.4(c) ("Any such waiver shall constitute an admission that a chemical test refusal occurred as contemplated by [VTL §] 1194 . . ., and such waiver shall result in administrative sanctions provided by law for the chemical test refusal").

As is noted in § 41:41, *supra*, at arraignment in a refusal case the court is required to provide the defendant with, among other things, a "waiver" form. *See* VTL § 1194(2)(b)(4). The waiver form is located on the reverse side of the form providing the defendant with notice of the date and time of the DMV refusal hearing. However, some courts make (and utilize) photocopies of the "Notice of Temporary Suspension and Notice of Hearing" form—which tend to be blank on the back side. In such a case, if the defendant wishes to waive his or her right to a refusal hearing, defense counsel should specifically request a "Waiver of Hearing" form from the court.

The waiver form allows the defendant to "plead guilty" to, and accept the civil consequences of, refusing to submit to a chemical test. This raises the obvious question—under what circumstances would it be in a defendant's best interest to execute the waiver form?

Since the license revocation which results from a chemical test refusal is a "civil" or "administrative" penalty separate and distinct from the license suspension/revocation which results from a VTL § 1192 conviction in criminal court, the suspension/revocation periods run separate and apart from each other (to the extent that they do not overlap). In other words, to the extent that a VTL § 1192 suspension/revocation and a chemical test refusal revocation overlap, the DMV runs the suspension/revocation periods *concurrently*; but to the extent that the suspension/revocation periods do *not* overlap, the DMV runs the periods *consecutively. See* § 41:11, *supra.*

Thus, if the defendant is not interested in contesting either the DWI charge or the alleged chemical test refusal, defense counsel should attempt to minimize the amount of time that the defendant's driving privileges will be suspended/revoked. In this regard, the best course of action is to negotiate a plea bargain which will be entered at the time of arraignment (or as soon thereafter as possible), and to execute the Waiver of Hearing form and mail it to the DMV immediately.

§ 41:50 DMV refusal hearings—Failure of motorist to appear at hearing

Research References

West's Key Number Digest, Automobiles ☞144.1(1.20), 144.2(.5)

The failure of the motorist to appear at a scheduled DMV refusal hearing "shall constitute a waiver of such hearing, provided, however, that such person may petition the commissioner for a new hearing which shall be held as soon as practicable." VTL § 1194(2)(c). *See also* 15 NYCRR § 127.8; 15 NYCRR § 127.9(b); 15 NYCRR § 139.4(c) (request for new hearing must be in writing).

"However, any action taken at the original hearing, or in effect at that time, may be continued pending such rescheduled hearing." 15 NYCRR § 127.8. In addition, "[a] respondent who has waived a hearing by failing to appear may be suspended pending attendance at an adjourned hearing or a final determination." 15 NYCRR § 127.8. In such a case, the period of license suspension pending the adjourned hearing will *not* be credited toward any license revocation resulting from the hearing.

Even though the respondent's failure to appear at a chemical test refusal hearing constitutes a waiver of the hearing, the DMV hearing officer "may receive the testimony of available witnesses and enter evidence into the record." 15 NYCRR § 127.8. 15 NYCRR § 127.9(b) is more specific in this regard:

> (b) If no adjournment has been granted, and the respondent fails to appear for a scheduled hearing, the hearing officer may take the testimony of the arresting officer and any other witnesses present and consider all relevant evidence in the record. If such testimony and evidence is sufficient to find that respondent refused to submit to a chemical test, the hearing officer shall revoke the respondent's driver's license, permit or privilege of operating a vehicle. If, following such a determination, respondent petitions for a rehearing, pursuant to [15 NYCRR § 127.8] and [VTL § 1194(2)(c)], *it shall be the responsibility of the respondent to insure the presence* [*i.e.*, subpoena] *of any witness he or she wishes to question or cross-examine.*

(Emphasis added).

§ 41:51   DMV refusal hearings—Failure of arresting officer to appear at hearing

Research References

West's Key Number Digest, Automobiles ☞144.1(1.20), 144.2(.5)

Not infrequently, the respondent will appear for the DMV refusal hearing at the date and time set forth in the notice of hearing form, but the arresting officer will fail to appear. Such a situation is governed by 15 NYCRR § 127.9(c) and case law. 15 NYCRR § 127.9(c) provides that:

> (c) If the respondent appears for a first scheduled chemical test refusal hearing, and the arresting officer does not appear, the matter will be adjourned and any temporary suspension still in effect shall be terminated. *At any subsequent hearing, the hearing officer may make findings of fact and conclusions of law based upon the chemical test refusal report and any other relevant evidence in the record, notwithstanding the police officer's nonappearance.*

(Emphasis added).

In other words, even if the arresting officer fails to appear for the DMV refusal hearing not just once, but twice, the respondent can still lose the hearing based solely upon the contents of the officer's written Report of Refusal (assuming that the Report is filled out properly and sets forth a prima facie case). This procedure was condoned in *Matter of Gray v. Adduci*, 73 N.Y.2d 741, 742–43, 536 N.Y.S.2d 40, 41 (1988) (over the persuasive dissent of Judge Kaye):

> Hearsay evidence can be the basis of an administrative determination. Here, the arresting officer's written report of petitioner's refusal is sufficiently relevant and probative to support the findings of the Administrative Law Judge that petitioner refused to submit to the chemical test after being warned of the consequences of such refusal . . .

> Petitioner's additional claim that the Commissioner's determination was made without cross-examination in violation of the State Administrative Procedure Act § 306(3), and of petitioner's right to due process is without merit. Petitioner had the right to call the officer as a witness (*see*, State Administrative Procedure Act § 304[2]). Even though the Administrative Law Judge had adjourned the hearing on prior occasions due to the absence of the police officer, this inconvenience cannot be determinative as a matter of law. Petitioner always had it within his power to subpoena the officer at any time. Even after the Administrative Law Judge decided to introduce the written report on his own motion and proceed with the hearing, petitioner's sole objection voiced was on hearsay grounds. He never claimed on the record before the Administrative Law Judge who was in the best position to afford him a remedy, that he had been misled, prejudiced or biased by the Judge's actions. Indeed, petitioner could have sought an adjournment to subpoena the officer. That he chose not to, was a tactical decision, which is not dispositive of the outcome.

(Citations omitted).

Gray makes clear that before a respondent can lose a DMV refusal hearing based solely upon a nonappearing police officer's Report of Refusal, he or she has both (a) the right to subpoena and cross-examine the arresting officer, and (b) the right to an adjournment for the purpose of subpoenaing the officer. If the respondent requests an adjournment to subpoena the officer (in compliance with *Gray*), and the officer fails to appear in response to such subpoena, due process requires that the refusal charge be dismissed. *See In the Matter of the Administrative Appeal of Thomas A. Deyhle*, Case No. D95-33398, Docket No. 18657 (DMV Appeals Board decision dated August 1, 1997). Our thanks to Glenn Gucciardo, Esq., of Northport, New York, for alerting us to this important decision.

The respondent also has the option of testifying, as well as the right to call "defense" witnesses and to present relevant evidence. In such a case, the officer's Report of Refusal "may be overcome by contrary, substantial evidence of the motorist or others." *See* Memorandum from DMV Administrative Office Director Sidney W. Berke to All Safety Administrative Law Judges, dated June 5, 1986, set forth at Appendix 44. *See also* Appendix 42.

Notably, although the contents of the officer's written Report of Refusal can provide sufficient evidence to sustain a refusal revocation where the officer *fails to appear* for a DMV refusal hearing, where the officer does appear for the hearing and testifies, but fails to demonstrate that complete refusal warnings were administered, the submission into evidence of the Report of Refusal (which contains the complete refusal warnings preprinted thereon) cannot "cure" this defect. *See Matter of Maxfield v. Tofany*, 34 A.D.2d 869, —, 310 N.Y.S.2d 783, 785 (3d Dep't 1970); *Matter of Maines v. Tofany*, 61 Misc. 2d 546, —, 306 N.Y.S.2d 50, 52 (Broome Co. Sup. Ct. 1969). *Cf. Matter of McGowan v. Foschio*, 82 A.D.2d 1015, —, 442 N.Y.S.2d 154, 156 (3d Dep't 1981) (Report of Refusal was properly used to refresh officer's recollection as to content of refusal warnings; *not* as affirmative proof of the contents therein); *Matter of Babcock v. Melton*, 57 A.D.2d 554, —, 393 N.Y.S.2d 76, 77 (2d Dep't 1977) ("Alcohol/Drug Influence Report" form was properly admitted into evidence "since it was admitted only to indicate the exact words of the [refusal] warning").

§ 41:52 DMV refusal hearings—Failure of either party to appear at hearing

Research References

West's Key Number Digest, Automobiles ⬤144.1(1.20), 144.2(.5)

Where neither the arresting officer nor the respondent appear for a scheduled DMV refusal hearing, the respondent will lose the "hearing" based upon either (a) a waiver theory, *see* § 41:50, *supra*, and/or (b) the contents of the officer's written Report of Refusal (assuming that the report is filled out properly and sets forth a prima facie case). *See Matter of Whelan v. Adduci*, 133 A.D.2d 273, 519 N.Y.S.2d 62 (2d Dep't 1987). *See generally Matter of Gray v. Adduci*, 73 N.Y.2d 741, 536 N.Y.S.2d 40 (1988).

§ 41:53 DMV refusal hearings—Should defense counsel bring a stenographer?

Research References

West's Key Number Digest, Automobiles ⬤144.1(1.20), 144.2(.5)

In the past, the authors recommended that defense counsel should bring a stenographer to a DMV chemical test refusal hearing. The reason was primarily based upon the fact that although DMV refusal hearings are tape recorded by the DMV hearing officer, the quality of the recording equipment was generally poor and thus the recordings were often unreliable. This has changed.

Accordingly, it is no longer critical to bring one's own stenographer to a refusal hearing, with one important exception: where time is of the essence in obtaining the hearing transcript. In this regard, it generally takes a long time—sometimes too long—to obtain a refusal hearing transcript via the official transcription service utilized by DMV.

Where counsel chooses to hire a private stenographer at a DMV refusal hearing, it should be kept in mind that the stenographer's minutes are *not* the official record of the hearing. Rather, the DMV tape recording is the official record. While the ALJ will not object to the stenographer's presence, he or she will object if the stenographer unduly impedes the proceedings (*e.g.*, by frequently interrupting, asking witnesses to speak up or slow down, etc.). As such, in order to avoid an unpleasant confrontation with the ALJ, counsel should "prep" the stenographer ahead of time as to his or her role in the proceedings.

§ 41:54   DMV refusal hearings—Fifteen-day rule

Research References
West's Key Number Digest, Automobiles ☞144.1(1.20), 144.2(.5)

At arraignment in a refusal case, the court is required to temporarily suspend the defendant's driving privileges pending the outcome of a DMV refusal hearing. *See* VTL § 1194(2)(b)(3) ("For persons placed under arrest for a violation of any subdivision of [VTL § 1192], the license or permit to drive and any non-resident operating privilege shall, upon the basis of such written report, be temporarily suspended by the court without notice pending the determination of a hearing as provided in [VTL § 1194(2)(c)]"). *See also* 15 NYCRR § 139.3(a).

Similar provisions exist for individuals charged with boating while intoxicated, *see* Navigation Law § 49-a; 15 NYCRR § 139.3(b), and snowmobiling while intoxicated. *See* Parks, Recreation & Historic Preservation Law § 25.24; 15 NYCRR § 139.3(c). This procedure does not violate the Due Process Clause. *See Matter of Ventura*, 108 Misc. 2d 281, 437 N.Y.S.2d 538 (Monroe Co. Sup. Ct. 1981). *See generally Mackey v. Montrym*, 443 U.S. 1, 99 S.Ct. 2612 (1979).

However, "[i]f the department fails to provide for such hearing [15] days after the date of the arraignment of the arrested person, the license, permit to drive or non-resident operating privilege of such person shall be reinstated pending a hearing pursuant to this section." VTL § 1194(2)(c). In addition, "[i]f the respondent appears for a first scheduled chemical test refusal hearing, and the arresting officer does not appear, the matter will be adjourned and any temporary suspension still in effect shall be terminated." 15 NYCRR § 127.9(c).

In other words, the temporary license suspension imposed at arraignment in a refusal case lasts *the shorter of* 15 days or until the DMV refusal hearing.

§ 41:55 DMV refusal hearings—Time and place of hearing

Research References

West's Key Number Digest, Automobiles ⟜144.1(1.20), 144.2(.5)

15 NYCRR § 139.4(b) provides that "[t]he refusal hearing shall commence at the place provided in the notice of hearing form and as close as practicable to the designated time. If the hearing cannot be commenced due to the absence of a hearing officer or the unavailability of the planned hearing site, it will be rescheduled by the department, with notice to the police officer and person accused of the refusal." *See also* 15 NYCRR § 127.2(a).

§ 41:56 DMV refusal hearings—Right to counsel

Research References

West's Key Number Digest, Automobiles ⟜144.1(1.20), 144.2(.5)

"A respondent may be represented by counsel or, in the discretion of the hearing officer, by any other person of his or her choosing." 15 NYCRR § 127.4(a). "Any person representing the respondent must conform to the standards of conduct required of attorneys appearing before courts of this State." 15 NYCRR § 127.4(a). "Failure to conform to such standards shall be grounds for prohibiting the continued appearance of such person on behalf of the respondent." 15 NYCRR § 127.4(a).

§ 41:57 DMV refusal hearings—Adjournment requests

Research References

West's Key Number Digest, Automobiles ⟜144.1(1.20), 144.2(.5)

"Adjournment requests for hearings held pursuant to [VTL § 1194] shall be considered in accordance with [15 NYCRR §§ 127.7 and 127.9]. All other requests for adjournments shall be addressed to the hearing officer, who may order a temporary suspension of the license, permit, [or] nonresident operating privilege . . . pursuant to law and [15 NYCRR] Part 127." 15 NYCRR § 139.4(b). In this regard, 15 NYCRR § 127.7 provides, in pertinent part:

(a) Adjournments of hearings may only be granted by the hearing officer responsible for the particular hearing, or by the Safety Hearing Bureau or the Division of Vehicle Safety, as appropriate.

(b) It is the department's general policy to grant a request for adjournment for good cause if such request is received at least [7] days prior to the scheduled date of hearing and if no prior requests for adjournment have been made. Notwithstanding this policy, requests for adjournments made more than [7] days prior to hearing may be denied by the hearing officer, or supervisor of the hearing officer or by the Safety Hearing Bureau or Division of Vehicle Safety, in their discretion. Grounds for such a denial include, but are not limited to, such a request being a second or subsequent request for adjournment, or where there is reason to believe such request is merely an attempt to delay the holding of a hearing, or where an adjournment will significantly affect the availability of other witnesses scheduled to testify.

(c) Any motorist or designated representative requesting an adjournment should obtain the name and title of the person granting such request. This information will be required in the event of any dispute as to whether an adjournment was in fact granted. Any request which is not specifically granted shall be deemed denied.

(d) Requests for adjournments within [7] days of a scheduled hearing must be made directly to the hearing officer. Such requests will generally not be granted.

(e) (1) Except as provided for in paragraphs (2) and (3) of this subdivision, in any case where an adjournment is granted, any suspension or revocation of a license, permit or privilege already in effect may be continued pending the adjourned hearing. In addition, in the event no such action is in effect, a temporary suspension of such license, permit or privilege may be imposed at the time the adjournment is granted provided that the records of the department or the evidence already admitted furnishes reasonable grounds to believe such suspension is necessary to prevent continuing violations or a substantial traffic safety hazard.

(2) Adjournment of a chemical test refusal hearing held pursuant to Vehicle and Traffic Law, section 1194. Where an adjournment of a chemical test refusal hearing is granted at the request of the respondent, any suspension of a respondent's license, permit or privilege already in effect shall be continued pending the adjourned hearing. In addition, in the event no such suspension is in effect when the adjournment is granted, a temporary suspension of such license, permit or privilege shall be imposed and shall take effect on the date of

the originally scheduled hearing. Such suspension shall not be continued or imposed if the hearing officer affirmatively finds, on the record, that there is no reason to believe that the respondent poses a substantial traffic safety hazard and sets forth the basis for that finding on the record.

(3) Continuance of a chemical test refusal hearing held pursuant to Vehicle and Traffic Law, section 1194. If a chemical test refusal hearing is continued at the discretion of the hearing officer, in order to complete testimony, to subpoena witnesses or for any other reason, and if the respondent's license, permit or privilege was suspended pending such hearing, such suspension shall remain in effect pending the continued hearing unless the hearing officer affirmatively finds on the record that there is no reason to believe that the respondent poses a substantial traffic safety hazard and sets forth the basis for that finding on the record. If respondent's license, permit or privilege was not suspended pending the hearing, the hearing officer may suspend such license, permit or privilege, based upon the testimony provided and evidence submitted at such hearing, if the hearing officer affirmatively finds, on the record, that there is reason to believe that the respondent poses a substantial traffic safety hazard and sets forth the basis for that finding on the record.

(4) In addition to any grounds for suspension authorized pursuant to paragraphs (2) and (3) of this subdivision, a hearing officer must impose a suspension or continue a suspension of a respondent's driver's license, pursuant to paragraphs (2) and (3) of this subdivision, if the respondent's record indicates that:

(i) The person has been convicted of homicide, assault, criminal negligence or criminally negligent homicide arising out of the operation of a motor vehicle.

(ii) The person has [2] or more revocations and/or suspensions of his driver's license within the last [3] years, other than a suspension that may be terminated by performance of an act by the person.

(iii) The person has been convicted more than once of reckless driving within the last [3] years.

(iv) The person has [3] or more alcohol-related incidents within the last 10 years, including any conviction of Vehicle and Traffic Law, section 1192, any finding of a violation of section 1192-a of such law, and a refusal to submit to a chemical test. If a refusal that arises out of the same incident as a section 1192 conviction, this shall count as [1] incident.

The provisions of 15 NYCRR § 127.7 govern requests for

adjournments of chemical test refusal hearings "[n]otwithstanding the fact that such hearings may be held less than [7] days from the date on which the respondent is arraigned in court." 15 NYCRR § 127.9(a).

If an adjournment is granted but the ALJ suspends the motorist's driving privileges during the time period of the adjournment, such suspension period will *not* be credited toward any revocation period ultimately imposed by DMV for the chemical test refusal.

§ 41:58 DMV refusal hearings—Responsive pleadings

Research References

West's Key Number Digest, Automobiles ☞144.1(1.20), 144.2(.5)

DMV regulations provide that "[n]o pre-hearing answers or responsive pleadings are permitted." 15 NYCRR § 127.1(a).

§ 41:59 DMV refusal hearings—Prehearing discovery

Research References

West's Key Number Digest, Automobiles ☞144.1(1.20), 144.2(.5)

Prehearing discovery is governed by 15 NYCRR § 127.6(a):

Prior to a hearing, a respondent may make a request to review nonconfidential information in the hearing file including information which is not protected by law from disclosure. If the file has been sent to the hearing officer or is scheduled to be sent within [7] days of receipt of a request by the Safety Hearing Bureau, examination of the information will be arranged by the hearing officer. The examination will be scheduled for a time at least [5] days prior to the hearing unless a shorter time is mutually agreed between the hearing officer and the requestor. If the file has not been sent to the hearing officer and is not scheduled to be sent within [7] days of receipt of a request by the Safety Hearing Bureau, the file will be made available for examination at the Safety Hearing Bureau before the usual date scheduled for sending the file to the hearing officer. A respondent may elect to examine the file after it is received by the hearing officer rather than while it is in the custody of the Safety Hearing Bureau. If a request to examine the file is received less than [7] days prior to the hearing date, the requestor will be afforded an opportunity to examine the file immediately prior to commencement of the hearing or at an earlier time as may be agreed to in the discretion of the hearing officer.

§ 41:60 DMV refusal hearings—Recusal of ALJ

Research References

West's Key Number Digest, Automobiles ☞144.1(1.20), 144.2(.5)

Requests for recusal of the DMV ALJ are governed by 15 NYCRR § 127.5(a):

A respondent or designated representative may request recusal of an assigned hearing officer. The request and the reason for it must be made to the assigned hearing officer at the beginning of the hearing or as soon thereafter as the requestor receives information which forms the basis for such request. Denial of a request for recusal shall be reviewable by the Administrative Appeals Board . . . under procedures established pursuant to [VTL article] 3-A.

§ 41:61 DMV refusal hearings—Conduct of hearing

Research References

West's Key Number Digest, Automobiles ⚬⟶144.1(1.20), 144.2(.5)

Specific procedures for the conduct of DMV refusal hearings are set forth throughout 15 NYCRR Part 127. Refusal hearings are also governed generally by Article 3 of the State Administrative Procedure Act, by case law, and by the constitutional right to due process. 15 NYCRR § 127.5(c) provides that:

> The order of proof at a hearing shall be determined by the hearing officer. Testimony shall be given under oath or affirmation. The hearing officer, in his or her discretion, may exclude any witnesses, other than a respondent or a representative of the department, if one is present, during other testimony. The hearing officer may also admit any relevant evidence in addition to oral testimony. Any witness may be questioned and/or cross-examined by the hearing officer, by his or her own counsel or representative, and by the party who did not call the witness.

"The privileges set forth in [CPLR article 45] shall be applicable in hearings conducted pursuant to this Part." 15 NYCRR § 127.6(c). "The provisions of [CPLR § 2302], regarding the issuance of subpoenas, are applicable to hearings conducted in accordance with this Part." 15 NYCRR § 127.11(b). *See also* State Administrative Procedure Act § 304(2); *Matter of Gray v. Adduci*, 73 N.Y.2d 741, 743, 536 N.Y.S.2d 40, 41 (1988). In all other respects, "the provisions of the Civil Practice Law and Rules are not binding upon the conduct of administrative hearings." 15 NYCRR § 127.11(a).

"Rules governing the admissibility of evidence in a court of law are not applicable to hearings held by the department." 15 NYCRR § 127.6(b). "Evidence which would not be admissible in a court, such as hearsay, is admissible in a departmental hearing." NYCRR § 127.6(b).

"The provisions of the Criminal Procedure Law are not binding upon the conduct of administrative hearings." 15 NYCRR § 127.11(a). "The provisions of those laws regarding forms of pleading, motion practice, discovery procedures, including demands for bills of particulars, and other matters are not applicable to hearings conducted in accordance with this Part." 15 NYCRR § 127.11(a).

"[U]nder no circumstances shall the respondent be compelled to testify. However, *the hearing officer may draw a negative inference from the failure to testify.*" 15 NYCRR § 127.5(b) (emphasis added). *See also Matter of Peeso v. Fiala*, 130 A.D.3d 1442, __, 13 N.Y.S.3d 742, 744 (4th Dep't 2015).

15 NYCRR § 127.5(c) expressly provides that the ALJ can question, and indeed cross-examine, witnesses at a refusal hearing. This procedure was upheld in *Clark v. New York State Dept. of Motor Vehicles*, 55 A.D.3d 1284, __, 864 N.Y.S.2d 810 (4th Dep't 2008):

> Petitioner . . . contends that he did not receive an impartial hearing because the administrative law judge (ALJ) acted as an advocate for respondent by questioning the witnesses. We reject that contention. The ALJ's questioning concerned whether the officer had reasonable grounds to arrest petitioner for DWI, whether petitioner was given a sufficient warning that his refusal to submit to a chemical test would result in the immediate suspension and subsequent revocation of his license, and whether petitioner refused to submit to a chemical test (see Vehicle and Traffic Law § 1194[2][c]). There is no indication in the record that the ALJ was not impartial.

§ 41:62   DMV refusal hearings—Due process

Research References

West's Key Number Digest, Automobiles ☞144.1(1.20), 144.2(.5)

The imposition of civil sanctions upon a motorist for his or her refusal to submit to a chemical test "is unquestionably legitimate, assuming appropriate procedural protections." *South Dakota v. Neville*, 459 U.S. 553, 560, 103 S.Ct. 916, 920 (1983). In this regard, the Court of Appeals has repeatedly held that:

> It is settled that even where administrative proceedings are at issue, "no essential element of a fair trial can be dispensed with unless waived." In addition, "the party whose rights are being determined must be fully apprised of the claims of the opposing party and of the evidence to be considered, and must be given the opportunity to cross-examine witnesses, to inspect documents and to offer evidence in explanation or rebuttal."

Matter of McBarnette v. Sobol, 83 N.Y.2d 333, 339, 610 N.Y.S.2d 460, 462–63 (1994) (citations omitted). *See also Matter of Simpson v. Wolansky*, 38 N.Y.2d 391, 395, 380 N.Y.S.2d 630, 634 (1975); *Matter of Sowa v. Looney*, 23 N.Y.2d 329, 333, 296 N.Y.S.2d 760, 764 (1968); *Matter of Hecht v. Monaghan*, 307 N.Y. 461, 470 (1954). *See generally Matter of Maxfield v. Tofany*, 34 A.D.2d 869, __, 310 N.Y.S.2d 783, 785 (3d Dep't 1970).

Similarly, the Supreme Court has both (a) made clear that "[t]he rights to confront and cross-examine witnesses and to call witnesses in one's own behalf have long been recognized as essential to due process," and (b) "identified these rights as among the minimum essentials of a fair trial." *Chambers v. Mississippi*, 410 U.S. 284, 294, 93 S.Ct. 1038, 1045 (1973). The *Chambers* Court also made clear that:

> The right of cross-examination is more than a desirable rule of trial procedure. It is implicit in the constitutional right of confrontation, and helps assure the "accuracy of the truth-determining process." It is, indeed, "an essential and fundamental requirement for the kind of fair trial which is this country's constitutional goal." . . . [I]ts denial or significant diminution calls into question the ultimate "integrity of the fact-finding process."

410 U.S. 284 at 295, 93 S.Ct. at 1046 (citations omitted). *See also Davis v. Alaska*, 415 U.S. 308, 315, 316, 94 S.Ct. 1105, 1110 (1974) ("Cross-examination is the principal means by which the believability of a witness and the truth of his testimony are tested . . . [T]he cross-examiner is not only permitted to delve into the witness' story to test the witness' perceptions and memory, but the cross-examiner has traditionally been allowed to impeach, *i.e.*, discredit, the witness").

Also inherent in the right of cross-examination is the ability to "test the witness' recollection [and] to 'sift' his conscience," *Chambers*, 410 U.S. at 295, 93 S.Ct. at 1045; *see also People ex rel. McGee v. Walters*, 62 N.Y.2d 317, 322, 476 N.Y.S.2d 803, 806 (1984), and to "expose intentionally false swearing and also to bring to light circumstances bearing upon inaccuracies of the witnesses in observation, recollection and narration, and to lay the foundation for impeachment of the witnesses." *Hecht*, 307 N.Y. at 474.

The fundamental right of cross-examination is also both (a) codified in State Administrative Procedure Act § 306(3) ("A party shall have the right of cross-examination"), which is applicable to DMV refusal hearings, and (b) contained in DMV's regulations. *See* 15 NYCRR § 127.5(c); 15 NYCRR § 127.9(b). *See generally Matter of Epstein*, 267 A.D. 27, __, 44 N.Y.S.2d 921, 922 (3d Dep't 1943) ("Generally speaking, in quasi judicial proceedings before administrative agencies where the same agency is both the prosecutor and judge, with the resultant tendency to predetermination, practically the only shield left to the accused is his right of cross-examination. Deprived of this, he stands defenseless before a tribunal predisposed to conviction. This right should therefore be preserved in full vigor.").

Finally, where due process is concerned, the underlying merits of the case are irrelevant: " 'To one who protests against the taking of his property without due process of law, it is no answer to say that in this particular case due process of law would have led to the same result because he had no adequate defense upon the merits.' " *Hecht*, 307 N.Y. at 470 (citation omitted).

§ 41:63   DMV refusal hearings—Applicability of the *Rosario* rule

Research References

West's Key Number Digest, Automobiles ☞144.1(1.20), 144.2(.5)

It appears clear that the *Rosario* rule, in sum or substance, is applicable to administrative proceedings where a violation of law is alleged and a "license" is at stake. *See, e.g., Matter of Inner Circle Restaurant, Inc. v. New York State Liquor Auth.*, 30 N.Y.2d 541, —, 330 N.Y.S.2d 389, 390 (1972) ("Upon the new hearing which our reversal mandates the police officer's memorandum book should be made available"); *Matter of Fenimore Circle Corp. v. State Liquor Auth.*, 27 N.Y.2d 716, 314 N.Y.S.2d 180 (1970) ("The State Liquor Authority Hearing Officer should have permitted petitioner's counsel to examine the statements made by Trooper Smith, when that witness took the stand, for purposes of cross-examination, there being no indication that they contained matter that must be kept confidential or that their disclosure would be inimical to the public interest."); *People ex rel. Deyver by Weinstein v. Travis*, 172 Misc. 2d 83, 657 N.Y.S.2d 306, 307 (Erie Co. Sup. Ct.), aff'd, 244 A.D.2d 990, 668 N.Y.S.2d 966 (4th Dep't 1997) ("requiring the production of a witness' notes before an administrative hearing is not so much a grant of a full discovery right to prior written or recorded statements of witnesses . . . but rather, is merely a conformance with the Relator's statutory right to effective cross-examination. Such production, which is neither burdensome nor destructive to the hearing process but which is essential to a knowledgeable examination of the facts to which the witness has just testified, constitutes only fundamental fairness in a quasi-judicial process"), *aff'd for the reasons stated in the opinion below*, 244 A.D.2d 990, 668 N.Y.S.2d 966 (4th Dep't 1997).

In *Matter of Inner Circle Restaurant, Inc., supra*, the Court of Appeals cited *Matter of Garabendian v. New York State Liquor Auth.*, 33 A.D.2d 980, 307 N.Y.S.2d 270 (4th Dep't 1970), which held that:

> In People v. Rosario, . . . it was held that in a criminal trial a defendant is entitled to examine any pre-trial statement of a witness as long as the statement relates to the subject matter of the witness' testimony and is not confidential. We conclude that a similar rule should be applied in this proceeding which, at least in form, is not of a criminal character but, like a criminal proceeding, is brought to penalize for the commission of an offense against the law.

There should be a new hearing at which the reports of any police officers testifying threat should be made available to petitioners prior to the commencement of cross-examination.

33 A.D.2d at __, 307 N.Y.S.2d at 271 (citations omitted).

The position of the Department of Motor Vehicles appears to be that the *Rosario* rule is inapplicable to DMV refusal hearings. Nonetheless, 15 NYCRR § 127.6, which governs "discovery" and "evidence" at DMV refusal hearings, provides in pertinent part:

(a) Prior to a hearing, a respondent may make a request to review nonconfidential information in the hearing file including information which is not protected by law from disclosure . . . The examination will be scheduled for a time at least five days prior to the hearing unless a shorter time is mutually agreed between the hearing officer and the requestor . . . If a request to examine the file is received less than seven days prior to the hearing date, the requestor will be afforded an opportunity to examine the file immediately prior to commencement of the hearing or at an earlier time as may be agreed to in the discretion of the hearing officer.

In addition, most DMV hearing officers will allow defense counsel to review any documents that a testifying police officer has either (a) brought to the hearing and reviewed prior to testifying, and/or (b) used to refresh his or her recollection while testifying.

§ 41:64 DMV refusal hearings—Issues to be determined at hearing

Research References
West's Key Number Digest, Automobiles ⚬‑144.1(1.20), 144.2(.5)

VTL § 1194(2)(c) provides that:

The hearing shall be limited to the following issues: (1) did the police officer have reasonable grounds to believe that such person had been driving in violation of any subdivision of [VTL § 1192]; (2) did the police officer make a lawful arrest of such person; (3) was such person given sufficient warning, in clear or unequivocal language, prior to such refusal that such refusal to submit to such chemical test or any portion thereof, would result in the immediate suspension and subsequent revocation of such person's license or operating privilege whether or not such person is found guilty of the charge for which the arrest was made; and (4) did such person refuse to submit to such chemical test or any portion thereof.

"At a hearing held pursuant to Vehicle and Traffic Law § 1194, the hearing officer is required to determine, inter alia, whether the police lawfully arrested the operator of the motor vehicle for operating such vehicle while under the influence of alcohol or drugs in violation of Vehicle and Traffic Law § 1192. In order for an arrest to be lawful, the initial stop must itself be lawful." *Stewart v. Fiala*, 129 A.D.3d 852, __, 12 N.Y.S.3d 138, 139 (2d Dep't 2015) (citations omitted).

Proof with regard to the chemical test rules and regulations of the arresting officer's police department is not required at a DMV refusal hearing. *Matter of Goebel v. Tofany*, 44 A.D.2d 615, __, 353 N.Y.S.2d 73, 75 (3d Dep't 1974). *See also Matter of Strack v. Tofany*, 46 A.D.2d 712, __, 360 N.Y.S.2d 312, 313 (3d Dep't 1974); *Matter of Manley v. Tofany*, 70 Misc. 2d 910, __, 335 N.Y.S.2d 338, 342–43 (Chenango Co. Sup. Ct. 1972).

§ 41:65 DMV refusal hearings—DMV action where evidence fails to establish all four issues at hearing

Research References

West's Key Number Digest, Automobiles ☞144.1(1.20), 144.2(.5)

"If, after such hearing, the hearing officer, acting on behalf of the commissioner, finds on any one of said issues in the negative, the hearing officer shall immediately terminate any suspension arising from such refusal." VTL § 1194(2)(c). This is referred to as "closing out" the hearing.

§ 41:66 DMV refusal hearings—DMV action where evidence establishes all four issues at hearing

Research References

West's Key Number Digest, Automobiles ☞144.1(1.20), 144.2(.5)

"If, after such hearing, the hearing officer, acting on behalf of the commissioner finds all of the issues in the affirmative, such officer shall immediately revoke the license or permit to drive or any non-resident operating privilege in accordance with the provisions of [VTL § 1194(2)(d)]." VTL § 1194(2)(c). *See generally Matter of Van Woert v. Tofany*, 45 A.D.2d 155, 357 N.Y.S.2d 175 (3d Dep't 1974) (VTL § 1194 applies to motorists operating motor vehicles in New York regardless of whether they possess valid out-of-state driver's licenses).

§ 41:67 DMV refusal hearings—Decision following hearing

Research References

West's Key Number Digest, Automobiles ☞144.1(1.20), 144.2(.5)

"At the conclusion of all proceedings necessary to determine whether the respondent has violated [VTL § 1194(2)], the hearing officer must, as provided in [15 NYCRR § 127.10], either render or reserve decision." 15 NYCRR § 127.5(d). In this regard, 15 NYCRR § 127.10 provides:

(a) The hearing officer may announce his or her decision at the conclusion of the hearing or may reserve decision. A written determination of the case, specifying the findings of fact, conclusions of law and disposition, including any penalty or penalties imposed, shall be sent to the respondent and his or her designated representative by first-class mail.

(b) Except where otherwise specified by statute, the effective date of any penalty or sanction shall be a date established by the hearing officer, which shall in no event be more than 60 days from the date of the determination.

(c) If the hearing officer does not render a decision within 45 days of the conclusion of the hearing, the respondent may serve a demand for decision on the hearing officer. Upon receipt of such demand, the hearing officer must render a decision within 45 days, or the charges shall be deemed dismissed.

"[A] decision by a hearing officer shall be based upon substantial evidence." 15 NYCRR § 127.6(b).

In *Fermin-Perea v. Swarts*, 95 A.D.3d 439, __, 943 N.Y.S.2d 96, 98-99 (1st Dep't 2012):

The arresting officer's refusal report, admitted in evidence at the hearing, indicates that upon stopping petitioner because he was speeding, following too closely, and changing lanes without signaling, the officer observed that petitioner was unsteady on his feet, had bloodshot eyes, slurred speech and "a strong odor of alcoholic beverage on [his] breath." However, the field sobriety test, administered approximately 25 minutes later, a video of which was admitted in evidence at the hearing, establishes that petitioner was not impaired or intoxicated. Specifically, the video demonstrates that over the course of four minutes, petitioner was subjected to standardized field sobriety testing and at all times clearly communicated with the arresting officer, never slurred his speech, never demonstrated an inability to comprehend what he was being asked, and followed all of the officer's commands. Petitioner successfully completed the three tests he was asked to perform; thus never exhibiting any signs of impairment or intoxication.

Certainly, the contents of the arresting officer's refusal report, standing alone, establish reasonable grounds for the arrest under the Vehicle and Traffic Law. However, where, as here, a field sobriety test conducted less than 30 minutes after the officer's initial observations, convincingly establishes that petitioner was not impaired or intoxicated, respondent's determination that there existed reasonable grounds to believe that petitioner was intoxicated has no rational basis and is not inferable from the record. . . . Here, the field sobriety test, conducted shortly after petitioner was operating his motor vehicle, which failed to establish that petitioner was intoxicated or otherwise impaired, leads us to conclude that respondent's determination is not supported by substantial evidence.

The dissent ignores the threshold issue here, namely, that refusal to submit to a chemical test only results in revocation of an operator's driver's license if there are reasonable grounds to believe that the operator was driving while under the influence of drugs or alcohol and more specifically, insofar as relevant here, while intoxicated or impaired. Here, while the officer's initial observations are indeed indicative of intoxication or at the very least, impairment, the results of the field sobriety test administered thereafter—a more objective measure of intoxication—necessarily precludes any conclusion that petitioner was operating his vehicle while intoxicated or impaired. Any conclusion to the contrary simply disregards the applicable burden which, as the dissent points out, requires less than a preponderance of the evidence, demanding only that "a given inference is reasonable and plausible." Even under this diminished standard of proof, it is simply unreasonable and uninferable that petitioner was intoxicated or impaired while operating his motor vehicle and yet, 25 minutes later he successfully and without any difficulty passed a field sobriety test.

(Citations omitted).

Clearly, the majority of the *Fermin-Perea* Court believed that the arresting officer's Report of Refusal was not credible.

In *DeMichele v. Department of Motor Vehicles of New York State*, 136 A.D.3d 629, __, 24 N.Y.S.3d 402, 402-03 (2d Dep't 2016), the Appellate Division, Second Department, annulled a refusal revocation, with costs, under the following circumstances:

In August 2012, while riding his motorcycle in Westchester County, the petitioner lost control and crashed; no other vehicles or individuals were involved in the accident. The petitioner alleges that the accident happened when a coyote struck his motorcycle. As a result of the accident, the petitioner was injured and transferred by ambulance to a nearby hospital. Approximately two hours later, while he was still at the hospital, the petitioner was questioned by a New York State Trooper, who asked if he had consumed alcohol prior to the crash. The petitioner denied such consumption. Nevertheless, according to the Trooper's later filed "Report of Refusal to Submit to Chemical Test" (hereinafter the report), the Trooper detected a "strong odor of alcoholic beverage emanating from [the petitioner's] breath" during their conversation. The petitioner was then arrested for driving while intoxicated in violation of Vehicle and Traffic Law § 1192(3), and subsequently warned that, pursuant to Vehicle and Traffic Law § 1194, a refusal to submit to a chemical test would result in immediate suspension of his driver license. The petitioner declined to submit to the test.

Following an administrative hearing, at which the petitioner testified and the Trooper did not appear, but the report was admitted into evidence, the petitioner was found to have violated Vehicle and

Traffic Law § 1194, and his license was revoked. This determination was affirmed after an administrative appeal to the New York State Department of Motor Vehicles Administrative Appeals Board. The petitioner then commenced this CPLR article 78 proceeding to review the determination, contending that the determination was not supported by substantial evidence. The Supreme Court transferred the matter to this Court pursuant to CPLR 7804(g).

"To annul an administrative determination made after a hearing directed by law at which evidence is taken, a court must conclude that the record lacks substantial evidence to support the determination." Review of the record in this matter demonstrates that the finding of the Administrative Law Judge is not supported by substantial evidence.

As a prerequisite to the chemical test, the Trooper had to have reasonable grounds to believe that the petitioner was operating his motorcycle while under the influence of alcohol. Reasonable grounds are to be determined on the basis of the totality of the circumstances. Here, the Trooper did not witness the circumstances leading to the accident or the accident itself, and his report states that no field sobriety tests were conducted at the scene. Other than the statement in the report that there was a strong odor of alcoholic beverage on the petitioner's breath, there was no evidence that would suggest the petitioner operated his vehicle in an intoxicated state. Accordingly, the totality of circumstances did not warrant the determination that the petitioner violated Vehicle and Traffic Law § 1194 by refusing to submit to a chemical test and to revoke the petitioner's driver license.

(Citations omitted).

§ 41:68 DMV refusal hearings—Appealing adverse decision

Research References

West's Key Number Digest, Automobiles ⚭144.1(1.20), 144.2(.5)

"A person who has had a license or permit to drive or nonresident operating privilege suspended or revoked pursuant to [VTL § 1194(2)(c)] may appeal the findings of the hearing officer in accordance with the provisions of [VTL Article 3-A (*i.e.*, VTL § 260-63)]." VTL § 1194(2)(c). *See also* VTL § 261(1); 15 NYCRR § 127.12. Appeals are filed with the DMV Administrative Appeals Board, *see* VTL § 261(3), using form AA-33A (entitled "New York State Department of Motor Vehicles Appeal Form"), at the following address:

Appeals Processing Unit
PO Box 2935
Albany, NY 12220-0935

Appeals are submitted to the Appeals Board in writing only. "The fact that personal appearances are apparently not permitted before that entity deprive[s] [a petitioner] of no rights." *Matter of Jason v. Melton*, 60 A.D.2d 707, __, 400 N.Y.S.2d 878, 879 (3d Dep't 1977).

The appeal form, together with a nonrefundable $10 filing fee, must be filed within 60 days after *written* notice is given by the DMV of the ALJ's disposition of the refusal hearing. *See* VTL § 261(2); VTL § 261(4). *See also* 15 NYCRR § 155.3(a).

DMV refusal hearings are tape-recorded by the DMV hearing officer, who is provided by the Department with tape recording equipment which is, to be kind, not state of the art. Despite the fact that such tapes (a) frequently contain portions which are inaudible, and (b) are occasionally misplaced or even lost, they nonetheless constitute the "official record" of the hearing, even if the respondent brings his or her own stenographer to the hearing.

In this regard, a timely filed appeal of a DMV refusal hearing disposition is not considered "finally submitted" (and will not be considered by the Appeals Board) until the respondent orders and obtains a transcript of the tape recording of the hearing (*at a nonrefundable cost of $3.19 a page*). *See* VTL § 261(3). *See also* DMV Form AA-33A; *Matter of Nolan v. Adduci*, 166 A.D.2d 277, __, 564 N.Y.S.2d 118, 119 (1st Dep't 1990). Once the transcript is received, the respondent has an additional 30 days within which to submit further argument in support of the appeal.

At the time that the appeal is filed, the respondent can request a "stay" pending the outcome of the appeal. Where such a request is made:

> The appeals board, or chairman thereof, upon the request of any person who has filed an appeal, may, in its discretion, grant a stay pending a determination of the appeal. *Whenever a determination has not been made within [30] days after an appeal has been finally submitted, a stay of execution will be deemed granted by operation of law, and the license, certificate, permit or privilege affected will be automatically restored pending final determination.*

VTL § 262 (emphasis added). *See also* 15 NYCRR § 155.5(b).

If the respondent is dissatisfied with the outcome of the administrative appeal, he or she can seek judicial review via a CPLR Article 78 proceeding. *See* VTL § 263. *See also* 15 NYCRR § 155.6(b). However, "[n]o determination of the commissioner or a member of the department which is appealable under the provisions of this article shall be reviewed in any court unless an appeal has been filed and determined in accordance with this article." VTL § 263. *See also Matter of Winters v. New York State Dep't of Motor Vehicles*, 97 A.D.2d 954, 468 N.Y.S.2d 749 (4th Dep't 1983); *Matter of Giambra v. Commissioner of Motor Vehicles*,

59 A.D.2d 648, __, 398 N.Y.S.2d 301, 302 (4th Dep't 1977), judgment aff'd, 46 N.Y.2d 743, 413 N.Y.S.2d 643, 386 N.E.2d 251 (1978).

There are two exceptions to the requirement that the respondent exhaust administrative remedies prior to filing an Article 78 proceeding challenging the outcome of a DMV refusal hearing. First:

> The requirement of filing an appeal from a determination of the commissioner with the appeals board before a judicial review of such determination may be commenced shall apply only if the appellant is provided with written notification as to the existence of [VTL Article 3-A] and this Part prior to or with the written notice of the determination of the commissioner.

15 NYCRR § 155.7. *See Matter of Laugh & Learn, Inc. v. State of N.Y. Dep't of Motor Vehicles*, 263 A.D.2d 854, 693 N.Y.S.2d 723 (3d Dep't 1999).

Second, VTL § 263 provides that "the refusal of an appeals board to grant a stay pending appeal shall be deemed a final determination for purposes of appeal."

In *Matter of Dean v. Tofany*, 48 A.D.2d 964, 369 N.Y.S.2d 550 (3d Dep't 1975), the petitioner, who was appealing a chemical test refusal revocation to the Appellate Division, died subsequent to oral argument. The court held that, due to the petitioner's death, the proceeding was moot and dismissed the petition.

§ 41:69 Failure to pay civil penalty or driver responsibility assessment

Research References

West's Key Number Digest, Automobiles ☞144.1(1.20)

VTL § 1194(2)(d)(2), which governs the civil penalties imposed for chemical test refusals, provides that "[n]o new driver's license or permit shall be issued, or non-resident operating privilege restored to such person unless such penalty has been paid." *See also* VTL § 1196(5); 15 NYCRR § 139.4(d) ("No new license, permit or privilege (other than a conditional license, permit or privilege issued pursuant to Part 134 of this Title) shall be issued, or restored, until such civil penalty has been paid"); 15 NYCRR § 134.11.

If a person fails to pay the driver responsibility assessment, the DMV will suspend his or her driver's license (or privilege of obtaining a driver's license). VTL § 1199(4). *See also* § 46:50, *infra*. "Such suspension shall remain in effect until any and all outstanding driver responsibility assessments have been paid in full." VTL § 1199(4).

§ 41:70 Chemical test refusals and 20-day Orders

Research References

West's Key Number Digest, Automobiles ⚇144.1(1.20)

Where a license suspension/revocation is required to be imposed for a conviction of DWAI or DWI, *see* VTL § 1193(2)(a), (b), the court is required to suspend/revoke the defendant's driver's license at the time of sentencing, at which time the defendant is required to surrender his or her license to the court. *See* VTL § 1193(2)(d)(1). Similar provisions apply where a license suspension is required to be imposed for DWAI drugs. *See* VTL § 510(2)(b)(v); VTL § 510(2)(b)(vi).

Although the license suspension/revocation takes effect immediately, *see* VTL § 1193(2)(d)(1); VTL § 510(2)(b)(vi), under certain circumstances the sentencing court may issue a so-called "20-day Order," which makes the "license suspension or revocation take effect [20] days after the date of sentencing." VTL § 1193(2)(d)(2). *See also* VTL § 510(2)(b)(vi); §§ 49:1 et seq., *infra*.

In VTL § 1192 cases, a 20-day Order is only appropriately granted to a defendant who is eligible for *both* (a) the DDP, *and* (b) a conditional or restricted use license. This is because the purpose of the 20-day Order is to continue the defendant's driving privileges during the time period that it takes for the court to send, and the DMV to receive and process, the paperwork required for the defendant to sign up for the DDP and obtain a conditional/restricted use license.

In addition, a 20-day Order merely continues the defendant's *existing* driving privileges for 20 days. Thus, if the defendant has any preexisting suspension/revocation on his or her driver's license (other than the suspension/revocation caused by the instant VTL § 1192 conviction), a 20-day Order is useless (as it merely "continues" nonexistent driving privileges).

In the test refusal context, a chemical test refusal does not affect a person's *eligibility* for a 20-day Order, but in many cases a test refusal will render a 20-day Order *ineffective*. For example, if the defendant in a refusal case enters a VTL § 1192 plea at arraignment, the court is required to issue a temporary suspension of the defendant's driving privileges at that time—independent of the VTL § 1192 suspension/revocation—based upon the alleged chemical test refusal. *See* VTL § 1194(2)(b)(3); 15 NYCRR § 139.3(a); § 41:40, *supra*; § 41:54, *supra*. In such a case, a 20-day Order would continue nonexistent driving privileges and would thus be a legal nullity (at least until the temporary suspension is terminated).

Similarly, if the defendant's VTL § 1192 plea is entered subsequent to a DMV chemical test refusal revocation, a 20-day

Order would continue nonexistent driving privileges and would be a legal nullity.

Conversely, a valid 20-day Order would become invalid if the defendant's driving privileges are revoked at a DMV refusal hearing held during the 20-day lifespan of the order.

§ 41:71 Chemical test refusals and the Drinking Driver Program

Research References

West's Key Number Digest, Automobiles ⊕144.1(1.20)

A conditional license allows a person to drive to, from, and during work (among other places) during the time period that the person's driving privileges are suspended or revoked as a result of an alcohol-related traffic offense. *See* VTL § 1196(7). *See also* §§ 50:1 et seq., *infra*. To be eligible for a conditional license, a person must, among other things, participate in the so-called Drinking Driver Program (DDP).

However, eligibility for the DDP requires an alcohol or drug-related *conviction*. In this regard, VTL § 1196(4) provides, in pertinent part, that:

> *Participation in the [DDP] shall be limited to those persons convicted of alcohol or drug-related traffic offenses* or persons who have been adjudicated youthful offenders for alcohol or drug-related traffic offenses, or persons found to have been operating a motor vehicle after having consumed alcohol in violation of [VTL § 1192-a], who choose to participate and who satisfy the criteria and meet the requirements for participation as established by [VTL § 1196] and the regulations promulgated thereunder.

(Emphasis added). *See also* 15 NYCRR § 134.2.

Thus, a person who refuses to submit to a chemical test and whose driving privileges are revoked by the DMV as a result thereof (and who is otherwise eligible for a conditional license), will not be able to obtain a conditional license unless and until the person obtains a VTL § 1192 conviction. As a result, many people who lose their refusal hearings (and who need to drive to earn a living) are virtually forced to accept a DWAI or DWI plea in criminal court in order to obtain a conditional license. This seemingly unfair restriction on conditional license eligibility has been found to be constitutional. *See Matter of Miller v. Tofany*, 88 Misc. 2d 247, __-__, 387 N.Y.S.2d 342, 345–46 (Broome Co. Sup. Ct. 1975).

By contrast, a policy pursuant to which participants in the DDP who had refused to submit to a chemical test were, for that reason alone, automatically referred for additional evaluation and treatment was found to be illegal. *See People v. Ogden*, 117 Misc. 2d 900, __-__, 459 N.Y.S.2d 545, 547–48 (Batavia City Ct. 1983).

§ 41:72 Successful DDP completion does not terminate refusal revocation

Research References
West's Key Number Digest, Automobiles ⬥144.1(1.20)

Ordinarily, upon successful completion of the Drinking Driver Program (DDP), "a participant may apply to the commissioner . . . for the termination of the suspension or revocation order issued as a result of the participant's conviction which caused the participation in such course." VTL § 1196(5). In other words, successful DDP completion generally allows the defendant to apply for reinstatement of his or her full driving privileges.

However, in a further attempt to encourage DWI suspects to submit to properly requested chemical tests, the legislature enacted VTL § 1194(2)(d)(3), which applies where an underlying revocation is for a chemical test refusal:

> (3) Effect of rehabilitation program. No period of revocation arising out of this section may be set aside by the commissioner for the reason that such person was a participant in the alcohol and drug rehabilitation program set forth in [VTL § 1196].

See also VTL § 1196(5); 15 NYCRR § 136.3(a).

§ 41:73 Chemical test refusals and conditional licenses

Research References
West's Key Number Digest, Automobiles ⬥144.1(1.20)

As § 41:71 makes clear, eligibility for a conditional license is contingent upon, among other things, eligibility for the DDP. In addition, even if a person is eligible for the DDP, a conditional license will be denied where, among other things, the person (a) has three or more alcohol-related convictions or incidents within the previous 10 years (in this regard, a chemical test refusal is an alcohol-related incident), *see* 15 NYCRR § 134.7(a)(11), and/or (b) is convicted of DWAI drugs in violation of VTL § 1192(4) (in which case, the person may be eligible for a restricted use license). *See* 15 NYCRR § 134.7(a)(10); 15 NYCRR § 135.5(d); § 41:74, *infra*.

If the person does receive a conditional license, a chemical test refusal revocation has a significant impact on when the DMV will allow the person's full, unrestricted driving privileges to be restored. The reason for this is that successful completion of the

DDP does not terminate a refusal revocation. *See* § 41:72, *supra*. However, the DMV will allow the person to continue to use his or her conditional license pending the expiration of the refusal revocation period (provided that the person does not violate any of the conditions of the conditional license). *See generally* VTL § 1196(7)(e), (f); 15 NYCRR § 134.9(d)(1).

§ 41:74 Chemical test refusals and restricted use licenses

Research References

West's Key Number Digest, Automobiles ☞144.1(1.20)

A restricted use license is very similar to a conditional license, with the exception that to be eligible for a restricted use license the underlying suspension/revocation must be imposed pursuant to VTL § 510 or VTL § 318. *See* VTL § 530; 15 NYCRR § 135.1(a); 15 NYCRR § 135.2; 15 NYCRR § 135.5(b); 15 NYCRR § 135.5(d); 15 NYCRR § 135.9(b).

VTL § 510(2)(b)(v) provides for a mandatory six-month driver's license suspension upon conviction of various drug crimes. Included in the list of such crimes is DWAI drugs, in violation of VTL § 1192(4). The inclusion of DWAI drugs under this provision was redundant in that a conviction of DWAI drugs had already resulted in a license revocation. *See* VTL § 1193(2)(b)(2), (3).

Adding to the confusion, although VTL § 510(6)(i) provides that, where a person's driver's license is suspended pursuant to VTL § 510(2)(b)(v) for a violation of VTL § 1192(4), "the commissioner may issue a restricted use license pursuant to [VTL § 530]," VTL § 530(2) clearly and expressly states that a restricted use license is *not* available (but a conditional license may be available) to a person whose driver's license is revoked for either (a) a conviction of VTL § 1192(4), and/or (b) refusal to submit to a chemical test.

In this regard, the DMV Counsel's Office advises that the DMV interprets VTL § 510(2)(b)(v) and VTL § 510(6)(i) as having (a) shifted the licensing consequences of DWAI drugs from VTL § 1193 to VTL § 510, (b) shifted the license eligibility of a person convicted of DWAI drugs from a conditional license (*see* VTL § 1196) to a restricted use license (*see* VTL § 530), and (c) superseded the language of VTL § 530(2) to the extent that it prohibits the issuance of a restricted use license to a person whose driver's license is revoked for either (i) a conviction of DWAI drugs, and/or (ii) refusal to submit to a chemical test in conjunction with a conviction of DWAI drugs. *See also* 15 NYCRR § 134.7(a)(10); 15 NYCRR § 135.5(d).

In other words, a person whose driver's license is revoked for refusal to submit to a chemical test in conjunction with a conviction of DWAI drugs (who is otherwise eligible for a restricted use license) is eligible for a restricted use license. As with a conditional license, eligibility for a restricted use license requires eligibility for, and participation in, the DDP. *See* 15 NYCRR § 135.5(d). *See also* VTL § 1196(4); 15 NYCRR § 134.2; §§ 50:1 et seq., *infra*.

In addition, as with a conditional license, a chemical test refusal revocation has a significant impact on when the DMV will allow the person's full, unrestricted driving privileges to be restored. The reason for this is that successful completion of the DDP does not terminate a refusal revocation. *See* § 41:72, *supra*. However, the DMV will allow the person to continue to use his or her restricted use license pending the expiration of the refusal revocation period (provided that the person does not violate any of the restrictions of the restricted use license). *See generally* VTL § 530(3).

Our thanks to Ida L. Traschen, Esq. of DMV Counsel's Office, for clarifying this confusing topic.

§ 41:75   Chemical test refusals as consciousness of guilt

Research References

West's Key Number Digest, Automobiles ☞144.1(1.20)

Where a defendant refuses to submit to a chemical test in violation of VTL § 1194(2), evidence of the refusal is admissible against the defendant to show his or her "consciousness of guilt." *See, e.g.*, VTL § 1194(2)(f); *People v. Smith*, 18 N.Y.3d 544, 550, 942 N.Y.S.2d 426, 430, 965 N.E.2d 928 (2012); *People v. Thomas*, 46 N.Y.2d 100, 412 N.Y.S.2d 845 (1978). In *People v. Haitz*, 65 A.D.2d 172, __, 411 N.Y.S.2d 57, 60 (4th Dep't 1978), the Appellate Division, Fourth Department, stated:

> [I]t has long been recognized that the conduct of the accused indicative of a guilty mind has been admissible against him on the theory that an inference of guilt may be drawn from consciousness of guilt. Evidence of the defendant's refusal to blow air into a bag is conduct which may be admitted on the same principle that evidence of an accused's flight or concealment is admissible to show consciousness of guilt. The defendant's refusal to submit to the test constitutes the destruction of incriminating evidence because of the rapid rate at which the body eliminates alcohol from the blood. There is no real difference between a defendant who flees to avoid or escape custody and one who, although in custody, wrongfully withholds his body (the source of incriminating evidence) from examination. The inference of guilt is not illogical or unjustified. As Judge Jasen points out in his concurring opinion in *People v. Paddock*, 29 N.Y.2d 504, 323 N.Y.S.2d 976, 272 N.E.2d 486, "It should be quite obvious that the primary reason for a refusal to submit to a chemical test is that a person fears its results."

(Citations and footnote omitted). *See also Thomas*, 46 N.Y.2d at 106, 412 N.Y.S.2d at 848 ("Realistically analyzed such testimony is relevant only in consequence of the inference it permits that defendant refused to take the test because of his apprehension as to whether he would pass it"); *Smith*, 18 N.Y.3d at 550, 942 N.Y.S.2d at 430 (same); *People v. Beyer*, 21 A.D.3d 592, __, 799 N.Y.S.2d 620, 623 (3d Dep't 2005); *People v. Gallup*, 302 A.D.2d 681, __, 755 N.Y.S.2d 498, 500 (3d Dep't 2003); *Bazza v. Banscher*, 143 A.D.2d 715, __, 533 N.Y.S.2d 285, 286 (2d Dep't 1988) ("Banscher's refusal to submit to a breathalyzer test is admissible as an admission by conduct and serves as circumstantial evidence indicative of a consciousness of guilt"); *People v. Powell*, 95 A.D.2d 783, __, 463 N.Y.S.2d 473, 476 (2d Dep't 1983); *People v. Ferrara*, 158 Misc. 2d 671, __, 602 N.Y.S.2d 86, 89 (N.Y. City Crim. Ct. 1993) ("Evidence of a defendant's refusal to take a chemical test is relevant to demonstrate a defendant's consciousness of guilt").

> Proof . . . that might be explanatory of a particular defendant's refusal to take the test unrelated to any apprehension as to its results (as, for instance, religious scruples or individual syncopephobia) should be treated not as tending to establish any form of compulsion but rather as going to the probative worth of the evidence of refusal. Thus, a jury might in such circumstances reject the inference of consciousness of guilt which would otherwise have been available.

Thomas, 46 N.Y.2d at 109 n.2, 412 N.Y.S.2d at 850 n.2 (citations omitted).

"Needless to say, refusal evidence is probative of a defendant's consciousness of guilt only if the defendant actually declined to take the test." *People v. Smith*, 18 N.Y.3d 544, 550, 942 N.Y.S.2d 426, 430, 965 N.E.2d 928 (2012).

§ 41:76 Test refusals—Jury charge

Research References

West's Key Number Digest, Automobiles ☞144.1(1.20)

The "pattern jury instruction" for a chemical test refusal contained in the Office of Court Administration's Criminal Jury Instructions, *Second Edition* (CJI), provides as follows:

> **Under our law, if a person has been given a clear and unequivocal warning of the consequences of refusing to submit to a chemical test and persists in refusing to submit to such test, and there is no innocent explanation for such refusal, then the jury may, but is not required to, infer that the defendant refused to submit to a chemical test because he or she feared that the test would disclose evidence of the presence of alcohol in violation of law.**

See CJI, at p. VTL 1192-1007 (footnote omitted); CJI, at p. VTL 1192-1021 (footnote omitted). The only cite listed for this instruction is *People v. Thomas*, 46 N.Y.2d 100, 412 N.Y.S.2d 845 (1978). It is safe to say that this instruction is both (a) insufficient as a general matter, and (b) incorrect in at least one important respect.

As a general matter, it is the authors' opinion that the CJI chemical test refusal instruction provides insufficient guidance to the jury as to the probative value of so-called "consciousness of guilt" evidence. In this regard, in *People v. Kurtz*, 92 A.D.2d 962, ___, 460 N.Y.S.2d 642, 642–43 (3d Dep't 1983), the Appellate Division, Third Department, upheld the trial court's charge to the jury "that defendant's refusal to take the test 'raised an inference that * * * he was afraid that he could not pass the test' and this 'raises an inference of consciousness of guilt' which by itself was insufficient to convict, but which could be considered along with all the other evidence in determining whether the prosecution had proven its case beyond a reasonable doubt." The court also cautioned that:

> It is also worth noting that [VTL § 1194] deals only with an inference which can be either accepted or rejected by the jury in light of the other evidence presented and can never be the sole basis for guilt. Here, the trial court made this eminently clear to the jurors and kept the burden of proof . . . squarely upon the prosecution.

92 A.D.2d at ___, 460 N.Y.S.2d at 643. *See also People v. Selsmeyer*, 128 A.D.2d 922, ___, 512 N.Y.S.2d 733, 734 (3d Dep't 1987).

Similarly, both the Court of Appeals and the Appellate Division, Second Department, have made clear that, to be sufficient, a consciousness of guilt jury charge must "closely instruct" the jury as to the comparative weakness of such evidence on the issue of guilt. *See, e.g., People v. Powell*, 95 A.D.2d 783, ___, 463 N.Y.S.2d 473, 476 (2d Dep't 1983) ("As the Court of Appeals has stated in respect to another example of assertive conduct, '[t]his court has always recognized the ambiguity of evidence of flight and insisted that the jury be closely instructed as to its weakness as an indication of guilt of the crime charged' (*People v. Yazum*, 13 N.Y.2d 302, 304, 246 N.Y.S.2d 626, 196 N.E.2d 263)"); *People v. Berg*, 92 N.Y.2d 701, 706, 685 N.Y.S.2d 906, 909 (1999) ("the inference of intoxication arising from failure to complete [certain field sobriety tests] successfully 'is far stronger than that arising from a refusal to take the test' ") (citation omitted); *People v. MacDonald*, 89 N.Y.2d 908, 910, 653 N.Y.S.2d 267, 268 (1996) ("testimony regarding defendant's attempts to avoid giving an adequate breath sample for alco-sensor testing was properly admitted as evidence of consciousness of guilt, particularly in light of the trial court's limiting instructions to the jury on this point").

Since the CJI pattern jury instruction for a chemical test refusal fails to closely instruct the jury as to the comparative weakness of such evidence on the issue of guilt, and/or provide any limiting instructions to the jury on this point, it clearly does not satisfy *MacDonald*, *Yazum*, *Powell*, and/or *Kurtz*.

Aside from a general objection to the CJI chemical test refusal instruction, a specific objection should be made to the inclusion of the phrase "and there is no innocent explanation for such refusal" in the instruction. Not only does this language improperly shift the burden of proof to the defendant, such burden shifting is particularly prejudicial because it comes from the court as opposed to the prosecution.

In addition, the "innocent explanation" language is misleading. In this regard, the CJI pattern instruction appears to instruct the jury that, if the defendant does in fact offer an innocent explanation for his or her refusal, the jury *cannot* infer "that the defendant refused to submit to [the] chemical test because he or she feared that the test would disclose evidence of the presence of alcohol in violation of law." However, *Thomas* clearly states that a defendant's innocent explanation for refusal to submit to a chemical test goes to the weight to be given to the refusal, not its admissibility. *See People v. Thomas*, 46 N.Y.2d 100, 109 n.2, 412 N.Y.S.2d 845, 850 n.2 (1978).

At a minimum, defense counsel should request that the Court also read the generic CJI "consciousness of guilt" pattern jury instruction (*i.e.*, the consciousness of guilt instruction that applies to all consciousness of guilt situations). This charge, which can be found at "http://www.courts.state.ny.us/cji/" under the heading "*GENERAL CHARGES*," provides as follows:

CONSCIOUSNESS OF GUILT

In this case the People contend that (*briefly specify the defendant s conduct; e.g. the defendant fled New York shortly after the crime*), and that such conduct demonstrates a consciousness of guilt.

You must decide first, whether you believe that such conduct took place, and second, if it did take place, whether it demonstrates a consciousness of guilt on the part of the defendant.

In determining whether conduct demonstrates a consciousness of guilt, you must consider whether the conduct has an innocent explanation. Common experience teaches that even an innocent person who finds himself or herself under suspicion may resort to conduct which gives the appearance of guilt.

The weight and importance you give to evidence offered to show consciousness of guilt depends on the facts of the case. Sometimes such evidence is only of slight value, and standing alone, it may never be the basis for a finding of guilt.

(Footnotes omitted).

Unlike the consciousness of guilt portion of the DWI jury instruction, *see* supra, this instruction properly instructs the jury as to the weight to afford consciousness of guilt evidence. It also explains where the "innocent explanation" language in the DWI jury instruction comes from, and places such language in proper context.

Nonetheless, in *People v. Lizaldo*, 124 A.D.3d 432, __, 998 N.Y.S.2d 380, 381 (1st Dep't 2015), leave to appeal denied, 26 N.Y.3d 931 (2015), the Appellate Division, First Department, held as follows:

> The court properly exercised its discretion in declining to expand upon the Criminal Jury Instructions regarding defendant's refusal to take the test. The standard instruction sufficiently instructed the jury to consider all the surrounding facts and circumstances, and the additional language proposed by defendant concerning consciousness of guilt was unnecessary.

> In any event, any error was harmless in view of the overwhelming evidence, independent of the refusal, that defendant [who was only convicted of DWAI] drove while his ability was at least impaired by alcohol.

(Citation omitted).

In *People v. Vinogradov*, 294 A.D.2d 708, __, 742 N.Y.S.2d 698, 700 (3d Dep't 2002), "County Court instructed the jury that asking defendant if he was willing to submit to a breathalyzer test after defendant had declined to speak without an attorney was not a violation of defendant's constitutional right to remain silent." The Appellate Division, Third Department, found that this "instruction was an accurate statement of the law, given the specific facts presented here." 294 A.D.2d 708 at __, 742 N.Y.S.2d at 700.

§ 41:77 Chemical test refusals and the Fifth Amendment

Research References

West's Key Number Digest, Automobiles ☞144.1(1.20)

The Fifth Amendment to the United States Constitution provides that no person "shall be compelled in any criminal case to be a witness against himself." It is well settled that, in the absence of *Miranda* warnings, or an exception thereto, a court must suppress most verbal statements of a defendant that are both (a) communicative or testimonial in nature, and (b) elicited during custodial interrogation. *See Pennsylvania v. Muniz*, 496 U.S. 582, 590, 110 S.Ct. 2638, 2644 (1990). Although test refusals are "communicative or testimonial" in nature, *see, e.g., People v. Thomas*, 46 N.Y.2d 100, 106–07, 412 N.Y.S.2d 845, 849 (1978); *People v. Peeso*, 266 A.D.2d 716, __, 699 N.Y.S.2d 136, 138 (3d Dep't 1999), case law has virtually—but not completely— eliminated the circumstances under which a request that a DWI suspect submit to sobriety and/or chemical testing constitutes a "custodial interrogation."

In *Berkemer v. McCarty*, 468 U.S. 420, 104 S.Ct. 3138 (1984), the Supreme Court held that, although the protections of *Miranda v. Arizona* apply to misdemeanor traffic offenses, persons detained during "ordinary" or "routine" traffic stops are not "in custody" for purposes of *Miranda. See also Pennsylvania v. Bruder*, 488 U.S. 9, 109 S.Ct. 205 (1988). Note, however, that *Berkemer* "did not announce an absolute rule for all motorist detentions, observing that lower courts must be vigilant that police do not 'delay formally arresting detained motorists, and . . . subject them to sustained and intimidating interrogation at the scene of their initial detention.'" *Bruder*, 488 U.S. at 10 n.1, 109 S.Ct. at 207 n.1 (quoting *Berkemer*). In other words, "[i]f a motorist who has been detained pursuant to a traffic stop thereafter is subjected to treatment that renders him 'in custody' for practical purposes, he will be entitled to the full panoply of protections prescribed by *Miranda*." *Berkemer*, 468 U.S. at 440, 104 S.Ct. at 3150.

In *South Dakota v. Neville*, 459 U.S. 553, 564 n.15, 103 S.Ct. 916, 923 n.15 (1983), the Supreme Court held that "[i]n the context of an arrest for driving while intoxicated, a police inquiry of whether the suspect will take a blood-alcohol test is not an interrogation within the meaning of *Miranda*." *See also* 459 U.S. at 564, 103 S.Ct. at 923 ("We hold . . . that a refusal to take a blood-alcohol test, after a police officer has lawfully requested it, is not an act coerced by the officer, and thus is not protected by the privilege against self-incrimination"); *People v. Smith*, 18 N.Y.3d 544, 550, 942 N.Y.S.2d 426, 430, 965 N.E.2d 928 (2012); *People v. Berg*, 92 N.Y.2d 701, 703, 685 N.Y.S.2d 906, 907 (1999) ("It is . . . settled that *Miranda* warnings are not required in order to admit the results of chemical analysis tests, or a defendant's refusal to take such tests"); *People v. Thomas*, 46 N.Y.2d 100, 103, 412 N.Y.S.2d 845, 846 (1978); *People v. Craft*, 28 N.Y.2d 274, 321 N.Y.S.2d 566 (1971); *People v. Boudreau*, 115 A.D.2d 652, __, 496 N.Y.S.2d 489, 491 (2d Dep't 1985); *Matter of Hoffman v. Melton*, 81 A.D.2d 709, __, 439 N.Y.S.2d 449, 450–51 (3d Dep't 1981); *People v. Haitz*, 65 A.D.2d 172, __, 411 N.Y.S.2d 57, 60 (4th Dep't 1978); *People v. Dillin*, 150 Misc. 2d 311, __, 567 N.Y.S.2d 991, 992 (N.Y. City Crim. Ct. 1991).

In *Berg, supra*, the Court of Appeals extended the rationale of *Neville* and *Thomas* to the refusal to submit to field sobriety tests, holding that "evidence of defendant's refusal to submit to certain field sobriety tests [is] admissible in the absence of *Miranda* warnings . . . because the refusal was not compelled within the meaning of the Self-Incrimination Clause." 92 N.Y.2d at 703, 685 N.Y.S.2d at 907. Stated another way, the Court held that "defendant's refusal to perform the field sobriety tests [is] not compelled, and therefore [is] not the product of custodial interrogation." 92 N.Y.2d at 704, 685 N.Y.S.2d at 908. *See also People v. Powell*, 95 A.D.2d 783, __, 463 N.Y.S.2d 473, 476 (2d Dep't 1983).

§ 41:78 Chemical test refusals and the right to counsel

Research References

West's Key Number Digest, Automobiles ⊶144.1(1.20)

In *People v. Smith*, 18 N.Y.3d 544, 549-50, 942 N.Y.S.2d 426, 429-30, 965 N.E.2d 928 (2012), the Court of Appeals summarized the law in this area:

> Vehicle and Traffic Law § 1194 does not address whether a motorist has a right to consult with a lawyer prior to determining whether to consent to chemical testing. However, if the motorist is arrested for driving while intoxicated or a related offense, this Court has recognized a limited right to counsel associated with the criminal proceeding. In *People v. Gursey*, we held that if a defendant arrested for driving while under the influence of alcohol asks to contact an attorney before responding to a request to take a chemical test, the police "may not, without justification, prevent access between the criminal accused and his lawyer, available in person or by immediate telephone communication, if such access does not interfere unduly with the matter at hand." If such a request is made, and it is feasible for the police to allow defendant to attempt to reach counsel without unduly delaying administration of the chemical test, a defendant should be afforded such an opportunity. As we explained in *Gursey*, the right to seek the advice of counsel— typically by telephone—could be accommodated in a matter of minutes and in most circumstances would not substantially interfere with the investigative procedure. That being said, we made clear that there is no absolute right to refuse to take the test until an attorney is actually consulted, nor can a defendant use a request for legal consultation to significantly postpone testing. "If the lawyer is not physically present and cannot be reached promptly by telephone or otherwise," a defendant who has asked to consult with an attorney can be required to make a decision without the benefit of counsel's advice on the question. Where there has been a violation of the limited right to counsel recognized in *Gursey*, any resulting evidence may be suppressed at the subsequent criminal trial.

(Citations omitted). *See also People v. Shaw*, 72 N.Y.2d 1032,

1033-34, 534 N.Y.S.2d 929, 930, 531 N.E.2d 650 (1988); *People v. Gursey*, 22 N.Y.2d 224, 292 N.Y.S.2d 416, 239 N.E.2d 351 (1968); *Matter of Boyce v. Commissioner of N.Y. State Dep't of Motor Vehicles*, 215 A.D.2d 476, __, 626 N.Y.S.2d 537, 538 (2d Dep't 1995) ("an individual may not condition his or her consent to a chemical test to determine blood alcohol content on first consulting with counsel"); *Clark v. New York State Dept. of Motor Vehicles*, 55 A.D.3d 1284, 864 N.Y.S.2d 810 (4th Dep't 2008) (same); *Matter of Cook v. Adduci*, 205 A.D.2d 903, 613 N.Y.S.2d 475 (3d Dep't 1994) (same); *Matter of Wilkinson v. Adduci*, 176 A.D.2d 1233, 576 N.Y.S.2d 728 (4th Dep't 1991) (same); *Matter of Nolan v. Adduci*, 166 A.D.2d 277, 564 N.Y.S.2d 118 (1st Dep't 1990) (same); *Matter of Gagliardi v. Department of Motor Vehicles*, 144 A.D.2d 882, 535 N.Y.S.2d 203 (3d Dep't 1988) (same); *Matter of Smith v. Passidomo*, 120 A.D.2d 599, __, 502 N.Y.S.2d 73, 74 (2d Dep't 1986) (same); *Matter of Brady v. Tofany*, 29 N.Y.2d 680, 325 N.Y.S.2d 415 (1971) (same); *Matter of Finocchairo v. Kelly*, 11 N.Y.2d 58, 226 N.Y.S.2d 403 (1962); *People v. Nigohosian*, 138 Misc. 2d 843, __, 525 N.Y.S.2d 556, 558 (Nassau Co. Dist. Ct. 1988); *Matter of Leopold v. Tofany*, 68 Misc. 2d 3, __, 325 N.Y.S.2d 24, 27 (N.Y. Co. Sup. Ct.), judgment *aff'd*, 38 A.D.2d 550, 327 N.Y.S.2d 999 (1st Dep't 1971). *See generally People v. Wassen*, 150 Misc. 2d 662, 569 N.Y.S.2d 877 (N.Y. City Crim. Ct. 1991) (lawyer under arrest not "available"); *People v. Wilmot-Kay*, 134 Misc. 2d 1081, 514 N.Y.S.2d 313 (Brighton Just. Ct. 1987) (defendant's breath test result suppressed where isolation of in-custody defendant from her sister amounted to a violation of right to counsel).

A request for assistance of counsel must be specific in order to invoke the right to counsel. *See, e.g., People v. Hart*, 191 A.D.2d 991, __, 594 N.Y.S.2d 942, 943 (4th Dep't 1993). *See generally Shaw*, 72 N.Y.2d at 1034, 534 N.Y.S.2d at 930.

Several Courts have held that the right to effective assistance of counsel is violated where the police do not permit the defendant "to conduct a *private* phone conversation with his attorney concerning a breathalyzer test." *People v. Iannopollo*, 131 Misc. 2d 15, __, 502 N.Y.S.2d 574, 577 (Ontario Co. Ct. 1983) (emphasis added). *See also People v. Moffitt*, 50 Misc. 3d 803, __, 19 N.Y.S.3d 713, 715 (N.Y. City Crim. Ct. 2015) (if the "qualified right [to counsel] is to have any meaning, the communication between the defendant and his or her attorney must be private. Because the police prevented that privacy here, the court suppresses the results of the breath test, all statements defendant made while on the phone with his attorney, and that portion of the video showing defendant's breath test and statements to counsel"); *People v. O'Neil*, 43 Misc. 3d 693, __, 986 N.Y.S.2d 302, 312 (Nassau Co. Dist. Ct. 2014) ("if the police are not going to provide a defendant with privacy during a telephone conversation with counsel concerning whether or not to submit to a chemical test, then statements overheard by the police during such consultation with counsel must be suppressed"). In *People v. Youngs*, 2 Misc. 3d 823, __, 771 N.Y.S.2d 282, 284 (Yates Co. Ct. 2003), the court distinguished *Iannopollo*, finding that, in the particular circumstances presented, "private access to the defendant's attorney would have unduly interfered with the matter at hand," and thus was not required under either *Shaw* or *Gursey*.

If the police do not honor a DWI suspect's request to speak with an attorney, and/or fail to take adequate steps to enable the suspect to attempt to reach an attorney, a motion to suppress the suspect's subsequent chemical test refusal (or chemical test result, if the test is taken) will likely be granted. *See, e.g., People v. Washington*, 23 N.Y.3d 228, 989 N.Y.S.2d 670, 12 N.E.3d 1099 (2014); *People v. Green*, 141 A.D.3d 746, 35 N.Y.S.3d 534 (3d Dep't 2016) ("The People further conceded at oral argument that defendant invoked his constitutional and limited statutory right to counsel in response to those warnings and that, under the circumstances of this case, valid grounds existed to suppress his post-invocation statements and evidence related to the DRE, second breathalyzer and blood tests"); *People v. Mora-Hernandez*, 77 A.D.3d 531, 909 N.Y.S.2d 435 (1st Dep't 2010); *People v. Borst*, 49 Misc. 3d 63, __, 20 N.Y.S.3d 838, 840-41 (App. Term, 9th & 10th Jud. Dist. 2015); *People v. Stanciu*, 49 Misc. 3d 430, 11 N.Y.S.3d 836 (N.Y. City Crim. Ct. 2015); *People v. Cole*, 178 Misc. 2d 166, 681 N.Y.S.2d 447 (Brighton Just. Ct. 1998); *People v. Anderson*, 150 Misc. 2d 339, 568 N.Y.S.2d 306 (Nassau Co. Dist. Ct. 1991); *People v. Martin*, 143 Misc. 2d 341, __, 540 N.Y.S.2d 412, 415 (Newark Just. Ct. 1989); *People v. Stone*, 128 Misc. 2d 1009, __, 491 N.Y.S.2d 921, 925 (N.Y. City Crim. Ct. 1985); *People v. Rinaldi*, 107 Misc. 2d 916, 436 N.Y.S.2d 156 (Chili Just. Ct. 1981); *People v. Sweeney*, 55 Misc. 2d 793, 286 N.Y.S.2d 506 (Suffolk Co. Dist. Ct. 1968).

In *Mora-Hernandez*, *supra*, the Appellate Division, First Department, held that:

> The court properly granted defendant's motion to suppress the results of a breathalyzer test and the videotape made of the test on the ground that the officers violated his right to counsel. The police ignored defendant's repeated requests for counsel prior to the administration of the test. A defendant who has been arrested for driving while intoxicated and requests assistance of counsel generally has the right to consult with an attorney before deciding whether to consent to a sobriety test. As in *People v. Gursey*, the officers prevented defendant from contacting his lawyer when there was no indication that granting defendant's request would have substantially interfered with the investigative procedure. The record contradicts the People's contention that defendant voluntarily abandoned his request for counsel when he agreed to take the test.

77 A.D.3d at __, 909 N.Y.S.2d at 435-36 (citations omitted).

In *Borst, supra*, the Appellate Term, 9th & 10th Judicial Districts, held as follows:

Here, notwithstanding the Justice Court's finding to the contrary, the record demonstrates that defendant unequivocally requested the assistance of counsel in connection with making a decision about whether he would take a chemical test. Moreover, since defendant was in police custody at the time that he requested to consult with counsel and he had not memorized the telephone numbers of either of the attorneys he sought to consult, he was reliant on the police to contact the counsel he had requested or to facilitate such contact. As a result, the police were required, but failed, to make reasonable and sufficient efforts to facilitate defendant in contacting counsel, which, under the circumstances presented, could have included either contacting the night operator at the garage where defendant's car was taken to determine whether his cell phones were in his car, and, if so, to retrieve them, or allowing defendant to dial 411 or look in a telephone book for the telephone numbers. Instead, the officers took no affirmative steps to try to help place defendant in contact with either of the requested attorneys. By failing to do so, the police, "without justification, prevent[ed] access between the criminal accused and his lawyer."

49 Misc. 3d at __, 20 N.Y.S.3d at 841 (citations and footnote omitted).

In *Martin, supra*, the court held that:

[T]he denial of access to counsel, after a request for such access is made, is at least as serious a breach of defendant's rights as the failure adequately to advise a defendant of the consequences of his refusal to take the test. I therefore hold that if a defendant is denied access to counsel for the purpose of consulting on the decision of whether or not to submit to a chemical test to determine the alcohol content of his blood, a refusal to submit to such a test may not be used as evidence against the defendant at a subsequent trial. It follows, of course, that the prosecutor may not comment on such refusal, nor shall there be a charge to the jury on such subject.

143 Misc. 2d at __, 540 N.Y.S.2d at 415.

In *Cole, supra*, the defendant stated that he wanted to speak with his attorney prior to deciding whether or not to take a requested breath test. In response to the defendant's request, the police attempted to reach the defendant's attorney, but only at his office phone number (where he was not likely to be, given that it was approximately 3:00 AM). Notably, the attorney's home phone number was also listed in the phone book. Under these circumstances, the court granted the defendant's motion to suppress his breath test result on the ground that the police failed to satisfy their responsibility under *Gursey*. In so holding, the court reasoned that:

The right to consult with counsel cannot be realized if counsel cannot be contacted. Where the defendant is in custody and is reliant on a law enforcement officer to contact the attorney, the officer must make a reasonable attempt to reach defendant's lawyer. If the contact is attempted well outside of normal business hours, efforts to reach the lawyer only at the office when the home phone number is readily available are not reasonable and therefore are insufficient. A reasonable effort in such circumstances requires the officer to locate the lawyer's home phone number if it is listed in either the yellow or the white pages of the phone book. Anything less deprives defendant of his right to access to counsel.

178 Misc. 2d at __, 681 N.Y.S.2d at 449.

In *People v. O'Reilly*, 16 Misc. 3d 775, 842 N.Y.S.2d 292 (Suffolk Co. Dist. Ct. 2007), the Court suppressed the defendant's refusal to submit to a chemical test under the following circumstances:

[T]he defendant invoked his right to counsel when first asked if he would submit to a chemical test of his blood, and again when he was read the *Miranda* warnings, also stating that he did not wish to speak to the officer without his attorney present. A defendant has a qualified right to consult with a lawyer before deciding whether to consent to a chemical test, provided he makes such a request and no danger of delay is posed. Although the defendant received a telephone call at 1:03 a.m., it cannot be determined from the record whether the person he spoke with was an attorney. The record does establish that John Demonico called the precinct at 1:36 a.m. and identified himself as the defendant's attorney.

Officer Talay's two requests that the defendant submit to a chemical test, made before the 1:36 a.m. call by defendant's attorney, were made in violation of the defendant's qualified right to counsel, since the record does not clearly show that the defendant was able to speak with an attorney before the requests were made. After counsel's call at 1:36 a.m., the officer improperly asked the defendant to disclose the content of a privileged communication by asking him if his attorney had advised him to take a chemical test or not, interpreting the defendant's negative response to his question as a refusal.

The defendant's negative response to the officer's improper question was obtained in violation of his Sixth Amendment right to counsel, and the statement itself is subject to suppression on that ground. In addition, it is not clear that this statement was intended to express the defendant's refusal to take the test. The defendant's answer "no" was ambiguous, as the defendant could have meant either that his attorney had not told him whether or not to take the test, or that his attorney had advised him not to take it. Evidence of a defendant's refusal to submit to a chemical test is not admissible at trial unless the People show that the defendant "was given sufficient warning, in clear and unequivocal language, of the effect of such refusal and that [he] persisted in the refusal." The People have not met their burden of demonstrating that the defendant refused to take the chemical test and that he persisted in his refusal, and this evidence shall not be admitted at trial.

16 Misc. 3d at __, 842 N.Y.S.2d at 297-98 (citations omitted).

By contrast, in *People v. O'Rama*, 162 A.D.2d 727, __, 557 N.Y.S.2d 124, 125 (2d Dep't 1990), *rev'd on other grounds*, 78 N.Y.2d 270, 574 N.Y.S.2d 159 (1991), the Appellate Division, Second Department, held that "under the facts of this case, although the defendant requested the assistance of counsel, he was not entitled to wait for an attorney before deciding to take the test since he indicated to the police that he could not get in touch with his attorney because it was too late at night." *See also People v. Dejac*, 187 Misc. 2d 287, 721 N.Y.S.2d 492 (Monroe Co. Sup. Ct. 2001); *People v. Phraner*, 151 Misc. 2d 961, 574 N.Y.S.2d 147 (Suffolk Co. Dist. Ct. 1991). *See generally People v. Vinogradov*, 294 A.D.2d 708, __, 742 N.Y.S.2d 698, 700 (3d Dep't 2002); *People v. DePonceau*, 275 A.D.2d 994, 715 N.Y.S.2d 197 (4th Dep't 2000); *People v. Kearney*, 261 A.D.2d 638, 691 N.Y.S.2d 71 (2d Dep't 1999).

Where counsel has been contacted by phone and advises the motorist to refuse to submit to a chemical test, the motorist can thereafter validly choose to ignore the attorney's advice and consent to the test, and/or waive the limited "right to counsel" without counsel present. *People v. Nigohosian*, 138 Misc. 2d 843, __, 525 N.Y.S.2d 556, 559 (Nassau Co. Dist. Ct. 1988). *See also People v. Harrington*, 111 Misc. 2d 648, 444 N.Y.S.2d 848 (Monroe Co. Ct. 1981). *See generally People v. Phraner*, 151 Misc. 2d 961, 574 N.Y.S.2d 147 (Suffolk Co. Dist. Ct. 1991).

In *People v. Dejac*, 187 Misc. 2d 287, __, 721 N.Y.S.2d 492, 495-96 (Monroe Co. Sup. Ct. 2001), the court addressed the issue of the burden of proof at a hearing dealing with an alleged violation of the qualified right to counsel, and held that:

> [A]fter the People come forward at the hearing to show the legality of police conduct in the first instance, which is required by the statute, Vehicle & Traffic Law § 1194(2)(f) . . ., if defendant makes a claim that he was not "afforded an adequate opportunity to consult with counsel," or that the efforts of the police were not "reasonable and sufficient under the circumstances," it is the defendant's burden to establish such a claim at the hearing.

(Citations omitted).

It has been held that where the defendant persistently refuses to submit to a properly requested chemical test on counsel's advice, such refusal (including the videotape thereof) is admissible at trial. *See People v. McGovern*, 179 Misc. 2d 159, __, 683 N.Y.S.2d 822, 823-24 (Nassau Co. Dist. Ct. 1998).

§ 41:79 Right to counsel more limited at DMV refusal hearing

Research References

West's Key Number Digest, Automobiles ☞144.1(1.20)

The limited "right to counsel" discussed in the previous section is even more limited in the context of a DMV refusal hearing. In this regard, in *Matter of Cook v. Adduci*, 205 A.D.2d 903, __, 613 N.Y.S.2d 475, 476 (3d Dep't 1994), the Appellate Division, Third Department, stated that "[w]hile indeed, in a criminal proceeding, the failure to comply with a defendant's request for assistance of counsel may result in the suppression of evidence obtained, the same consequence does not apply in the context of an administrative license revocation proceeding." (Citations omitted). *See also Matter of Finocchairo v. Kelly*, 11 N.Y.2d 58, 226 N.Y.S.2d 403 (1962); *Clark v. New York State Dep't of Motor Vehicles*, 55 A.D.3d 1284, __, 864 N.Y.S.2d 810, 811–12 (4th Dep't 2008); *Matter of Wilkinson v. Adduci*, 176 A.D.2d 1233, __, 576 N.Y.S.2d 728, 729 (4th Dep't 1991); *Matter of Smith v. Passidomo*, 120 A.D.2d 599, __, 502 N.Y.S.2d 73, 74 (2d Dep't 1986).

By contrast, in *Matter of Leopold v. Tofany*, 68 Misc. 2d 3, __, 325 N.Y.S.2d 24, 27 (N.Y. Co. Sup. Ct.), *aff'd*, 38 A.D.2d 550, 327 N.Y.S.2d 999 (1st Dep't 1971), the court held that:

> [W]here, as here, an attorney seeks to confer with his client, who is then in custody, and such conferring will not improperly delay the timely administering of the chemical examination, that right must be granted, or else a refusal to take such examination or the results of the examination may not be utilized against the alleged drunken driver, either in a criminal proceeding, or in the quasi-criminal proceeding to revoke the driver's license.

In any event, the DMV's position on this issue is set forth in an internal memorandum to "All Safety ALJs" dated May 8, 1990:

> If a respondent is asked to take a chemical test, and responds by requesting the advice of an attorney, the police officer is not required, for Section 1194 purposes, to grant the request. However, if the officer does not inform the respondent that his request is denied and just records a refusal, there has not been a refusal. The respondent should be reasonably informed in some way (words, conduct, circumstances) that he is not going to be given a chance to consult with an attorney before his insistence on speaking to one can be considered a refusal.

A copy of this memorandum is set forth at Appendix 47.

§ 41:80 Chemical test refusals and the right of foreign nationals to consult with consular officials

Research References

West's Key Number Digest, Automobiles ☞144.1(1.20)

"Article 36 of the Vienna Convention on Consular Relations . . . provides for notification of a foreign national's consulate upon the arrest of that foreign national." *People v. Litarov*, 188 Misc. 2d 234, __, 727 N.Y.S.2d 293, 295 (N.Y. City Crim. Ct. 2001) (citation omitted). In *Litarov*, the court held that the Vienna Convention "does not require that a refusal to take a Breathalyzer test should be suppressed because a defendant was denied access to a consular official." 188 Misc. 2d at __, 727 N.Y.S.2d at 295.

§ 41:81 Chemical test refusals and unconscious defendants

Research References

West's Key Number Digest, Automobiles ☞144.1(1.20)

"If a person is unconscious or appears to be unconscious, he is deemed to have impliedly consented to a chemical test." *People v. Feine*, 227 A.D.2d 901, __, 643 N.Y.S.2d 281, 282 (4th Dep't 1996). *See also* VTL § 1194(2)(a); *People v. Massong*, 105 A.D.2d 1154, __, 482 N.Y.S.2d 601, 602 (4th Dep't 1984). As such, blood can properly be drawn from the person for purposes of chemical testing despite the fact that he or she is not afforded an opportunity to refuse the test. *See, e.g., People v. Kates*, 53 N.Y.2d 591, 444 N.Y.S.2d 446 (1981).

By contrast, a DWI suspect who feigns unconsciousness should be treated as a test refusal. *See Massong*, 105 A.D.2d at __, 482 N.Y.S.2d at 602 ("Pretending to be unconscious in our view would be conduct evidencing a refusal to submit to a chemical test"). In such a case, blood cannot properly be drawn from the person for purposes of chemical testing without a court order. *See, e.g.*, VTL § 1194(2)(b)(1); VTL § 1194(3); *People v. Smith*, 18 N.Y.3d 544, 549 n.2, 942 N.Y.S.2d 426, 429 n.2, 965 N.E.2d 928 (2012).

In *Matter of Taney v. Melton*, 89 A.D.2d 1000, 454 N.Y.S.2d 322 (2d Dep't 1982), the Appellate Division, Second Department, held that there was no refusal where (a) the petitioner, who was injured and in the hospital following an automobile accident, agreed to submit to a chemical test but thereafter fell asleep or became unconscious, and (b) there was no competent proof that petitioner was feigning unconsciousness.

The issue thus becomes whether a DWI suspect is actually unconscious, or rather is merely pretending to be. In this regard, courts appear loathe to allow DWI defendants to benefit from feigning unconsciousness. *See, e.g., Feine*, 227 A.D.2d at __, 643 N.Y.S.2d at 282 ("Feigning unconsciousness constitutes a refusal only when it is apparent that defendant is feigning unconsciousness for the purpose of refusing to take the test"); *Massong*, 105

A.D.2d at __, 482 N.Y.S.2d at 602 ("Trooper Hibsch was not qualified to express a medical opinion as to whether the defendant
was unconscious or faking; his opinion [that defendant was fak-
ing] was inapposite and because the defendant appeared unconscious there was no refusal to submit to the chemical test") (citation omitted); *People v. Stuart*, 216 A.D.2d 682, __, 628 N.Y.S.2d
421, 422 (3d Dep't 1995).

In *Kates*, 53 N.Y.2d 591, 444 N.Y.S.2d 446 (N.Y., 1981) the
Court of Appeals held that "denying the unconscious driver the
right to refuse a blood test does not violate his right to equal
protection." 53 N.Y.2d at 596, 444 N.Y.S.2d at 449. In so holding,
the court reasoned:

> The distinction drawn between the conscious driver and the uncon-
> scious or incapacitated driver does not offend the equal protection
> clause. It was reasonable for the Legislature, concerned with avoid-
> ing potentially violent conflicts between the police and drivers ar-
> rested for intoxication, to provide that the police must request the
> driver's consent, advise him of the consequences of refusal and
> honor his wishes if he decides to refuse, but to dispense with these
> requirements when the driver is unconscious or otherwise incapaci-
> tated to the point where he poses no threat. Indeed there is a
> rational basis for distinguishing between the driver who is capable
> of making a choice and the driver who is unable to do so. Thus,
> denying the unconscious driver the right to refuse a blood test does
> not violate his right to equal protection.

53 N.Y.2d at 596, 444 N.Y.S.2d at 448–49.

§ 41:82   Chemical test refusals and CPL § 60.50

Research References

West's Key Number Digest, Automobiles ⌖144.1(1.20)

CPL § 60.50 provides that "[a] person may not be convicted of
any offense solely upon evidence of a confession or admission
made by him without additional proof that the offense charged
has been committed." In the context of DWI cases, CPL § 60.50
can apply where there is a lack of corroboration of a DWI
suspect's admission of operation. *See* §§ 2:1 et seq., *supra*.

In *Matter of Van Tassell v. New York State Comm'r of Motor
Vehicles*, 46 A.D.2d 984, __, 362 N.Y.S.2d 281, 282 (3d Dep't 1974),
the Appellate Division, Third Department, held that the corroboration requirement of CPL § 60.50 does not apply to DMV refusal
hearings, as evidence necessary to sustain a criminal conviction
is not required.

§ 41:83   Chemical test refusals and CPL § 200.60

Research References

West's Key Number Digest, Automobiles ⌖144.1(1.20)

Several crimes are raised from a "lower grade" to a "higher grade" if the defendant commits them while his or her driving privileges are revoked for refusing to submit to a chemical test. *See, e.g.*, PL § 125.13(2)(b) (vehicular manslaughter in the first degree); PL § 120.04(2)(b) (vehicular assault in the first degree); VTL § 511(3)(a)(i); VTL § 511(2)(a)(ii) (AUO 1st). Since an underlying chemical test refusal revocation raises the grade of each of these offenses, proof of such revocation is an element of such offenses. *See* CPL § 200.60(1).

As a result, the People and the court must utilize the procedure set forth in CPL § 200.60. *See People v. Cooper*, 78 N.Y.2d 476, 478, 577 N.Y.S.2d 202, 203 (1991) ("When a defendant's prior conviction raises the grade of an offense, and thus becomes an element of the higher grade offense, the Criminal Procedure Law—reflecting a concern for potential prejudice and unfairness to the defendant in putting earlier convictions before the jury— specifies a procedure for alleging and proving the prior convictions (CPL 200.60)"). This statute provides, in pertinent part, that:

> A previous conviction that "raises an offense of lower grade to one of higher grade and thereby becomes an element of the latter" may not be referred to in the indictment (CPL 200.60[1]). Instead, it must be charged by special information filed at the same time as the indictment (CPL 200.60[2]). An arraignment must be held on the special information outside the jury's presence. If a defendant admits a previous conviction, "that element of the offense * * * is deemed established, no evidence in support thereof may be adduced by the people, and the court must submit the case to the jury without reference thereto and as if the fact of such previous conviction were not an element of the offense." (CPL 200.60[3][a]). If, however, the defendant denies the previous conviction or remains silent, the People may prove that element before the jury as part of their case (CPL 200.60[3][b]).

Cooper, 78 N.Y.2d at 481–82, 577 N.Y.S.2d at 205.

Construed literally, CPL § 200.60 only applies to a defendant's previous *convictions*—*not* to "*conviction-related facts*" such as a chemical test refusal revocation. Faced with this "Catch-22" situation in *Cooper*, the Court of Appeals held that the spirit and purpose of CPL § 200.60 require that the statute be applied not only to previous convictions, but also to relevant "conviction-related facts":

> In a situation such as the one before us—where pleading and proving knowledge of a prior conviction necessarily reveals the conviction—the protection afforded by CPL 200.60 can be effectuated only by reading the statute to require resort to the special information procedure for all of the conviction-related facts that constitute the enhancing element.

Proper application of CPL 200.60 required that defendant be given an opportunity to admit—outside the jury's presence—the element that raised his crime in grade. That opportunity could have been afforded by a special information charging him with the prior conviction, the revocation of his license, and knowledge of the conviction and revocation. If defendant chose to admit those facts, no mention of them was necessary before the jury. If defendant denied all or any of those facts, the People could have proceeded with their proof, as the statute provides.

78 N.Y.2d at 482–83, 577 N.Y.S.2d at 205.

Although *Cooper* involved a charge of vehicular manslaughter in the first degree, its rationale obviously applies to AUO 1st. *See, e.g., People v. Flanagan*, 247 A.D.2d 899, 668 N.Y.S.2d 528 (4th Dep't 1998); *People v. Boyles*, 210 A.D.2d 732, 621 N.Y.S.2d 118 (3d Dep't 1994); *People v. Brockway*, 202 A.D.2d 1015, 609 N.Y.S.2d 481 (4th Dep't 1994); *People v. Sawyer*, 188 A.D.2d 939, 592 N.Y.S.2d 92 (3d Dep't 1992).

In addition, a chemical test refusal revocation is a "conviction-related fact" for purposes of *Cooper*/CPL § 200.60. *See People v. Alshoaibi*, 273 A.D.2d 871, 711 N.Y.S.2d 646 (4th Dep't 2000); *People v. Orlen*, 170 Misc. 2d 737, 651 N.Y.S.2d 860 (Nassau Co. Ct. 1996).

The procedure set forth in CPL § 200.60 and *Cooper* arguably also applies to AUO 2nd. *See generally People ex rel. Paganini v. Jablonsky*, 79 N.Y.2d 586, 590, 584 N.Y.S.2d 415, 416 (1992) ("Appellant reasons that the elements of his [AUO 2nd] conviction included his prior refusal to submit to a chemical test and his prior [DWAI] conviction, both alcohol-related predicates. [W]e may well agree that [appellant's] Vehicle and Traffic Law § 511(2)(a)(ii) conviction had a factual and legal genesis in prior alcohol-related conduct").

§ 41:84   Chemical test refusals and CPL § 710.30 notice

Research References

West's Key Number Digest, Automobiles ⚏144.1(1.20)

A refusal to submit to a chemical test is communicative or testimonial in nature, regardless of the form of the refusal (*e.g.,* oral, written, conduct). *People v. Thomas*, 46 N.Y.2d 100, 106–07, 412 N.Y.S.2d 845, 849 (1978). *See also People v. Peeso*, 266 A.D.2d 716, __, 699 N.Y.S.2d 136, 138 (3d Dep't 1999). In addition, a refusal to submit to a chemical test is potentially suppressible on several grounds. For example, a test refusal, like a chemical test, can be suppressed:

(a) As the fruit of an illegal stop. *See, e.g., Matter of Byer v.*

Jackson, 241 A.D.2d 943, 661 N.Y.S.2d 336 (4th Dep't 1997); *McDonell v. New York State Dept. of Motor Vehicles*, 77 A.D.3d 1379, 908 N.Y.S.2d 507 (4th Dep't 2010);

(b) As the fruit of an illegal arrest. *See, e.g., Dunaway v. New York*, 442 U.S. 200, 99 S.Ct. 2248 (1979); *Brown v. Illinois*, 422 U.S. 590, 95 S.Ct. 2254 (1975); *Mapp v. Ohio*, 367 U.S. 643, 81 S.Ct. 1684 (1961). *See generally Welsh v. Wisconsin*, 466 U.S. 740, 744, 104 S.Ct. 2091, 2095 (1984);

(c) If it is obtained in violation of the right to counsel. *See, e.g., People v. Washington*, 23 N.Y.3d 228, 989 N.Y.S.2d 670, 12 N.E.3d 1099 (2014); *People v. Smith*, 18 N.Y.3d 544, 550, 942 N.Y.S.2d 426, 430, 965 N.E.2d 928 (2012); *People v. Shaw*, 72 N.Y.2d 1032, 534 N.Y.S.2d 929 (1988); *People v. Gursey*, 22 N.Y.2d 224, 292 N.Y.S.2d 416 (1968); and/or

(d) If it is obtained in violation of VTL § 1194. *See, e.g.*, VTL § 1194(2)(f); *People v. Boone*, 71 A.D.2d 859, 419 N.Y.S.2d 187 (2d Dep't 1979).

Nonetheless, in *Peeso, supra*, the Appellate Division, Third Department, stated:

We . . . reject the contention that the absence of notice pursuant to CPL 710.30 precluded the People's offer of evidence concerning defendant's test refusal (*see*, Vehicle and Traffic Law § 1194[2][f]). It is settled law that because there is no compulsion on a defendant to refuse to submit to the chemical test provided for in Vehicle and Traffic Law § 1194(2), the defendant "ha[s] no constitutional privilege or statutory right to refuse to take the test." Therefore, defendant's refusal, although constituting communicative or testimonial evidence, could not "[c]onsist[] of a record or potential testimony reciting or describing a statement of [] defendant involuntarily made, within the meaning of [CPL] 60.45" (CPL 710.20[3]) or thereby implicate the notice requirement of CPL 710.30(1)(a).

266 A.D.2d at __, 699 N.Y.S.2d at 138 (citations omitted). *Cf. People v. Burtula*, 192 Misc. 2d 597, __, 747 N.Y.S.2d 692, 694 (Nassau Co. Dist. Ct. 2002). Notably, since the *Peeso* court found that "the record demonstrates that the People provided adequate notice pursuant to CPL § 710.30(1) of their intent to introduce the refusal at trial," 266 A.D.2d at __, 699 N.Y.S.2d at 138, the above-quoted language is arguably dicta.

In any event, a defendant's refusal to submit to a chemical test is discoverable pursuant to CPL § 240.20(1)(a), which provides for disclosure of "[a]ny written, recorded or oral statement of the defendant . . . made, other than in the course of the criminal transaction, to a public servant engaged in law enforcement activity or to a person then acting under his direction or in cooperation with him."

In this regard, "[i]t is beyond dispute that a defendant's own statements to police are highly material and relevant to a criminal prosecution. It is for this reason that such statements are *always* discoverable, even when the People do not intend to offer them at trial." *People v. Combest*, 4 N.Y.3d 341, 347, 795 N.Y.S.2d 481, 485 (2005) (emphasis added). *See also People v. Fields*, 258 A.D.2d 809, __, 687 N.Y.S.2d 184, 186 (3d Dep't 1999) ("CPL 240.20(1)(a) . . . is not limited to statements intended to be offered by the People 'at trial', i.e., statements offered as part of the People's direct case (*see*, CPL 240.10[4])"); *People v. Crider*, 301 A.D.2d 612, __, 756 N.Y.S.2d 223, 225 (2d Dep't 2003) (pursuant to CPL § 240.20(1)(a), "the People shall provide the defendant with notice of *any* of his statements they are aware of, whether or not they intend to use them for *any* purpose, including but not limited to rebuttal") (emphases added); *People v. Wyssling*, 82 Misc. 2d 708, 372 N.Y.S.2d 142 (Suffolk Co. Ct. 1975); *People v. Bennett*, 75 Misc. 2d 1040, __-__, 349 N.Y.S.2d 506, 519–20 (Erie Co. Sup. Ct. 1973). Thus, any argument by the People that they need only disclose statements to which CPL § 710.30 applies is without merit. *See Combest*, 4 N.Y.3d at 347, 795 N.Y.S.2d at 485; *Fields*, 258 A.D.2d at __, 687 N.Y.S.2d at 185; *People v. Hall*, 181 A.D.2d 1008, 581 N.Y.S.2d 951 (4th Dep't 1992).

§ 41:85   Chemical test refusals and collateral estoppel

Research References

West's Key Number Digest, Automobiles ☞144.1(1.20)

In *People v. Walsh*, 139 Misc. 2d 182, __, 527 N.Y.S.2d 708, 709 (Monroe Co. Ct. 1988), the court held that "the County Court, in criminal proceedings, is not subject to collateral estoppel by decisions resulting from Section 1194 hearings of the Department of Motor Vehicles." *See also People v. Kearney*, 196 Misc. 2d 335, 764 N.Y.S.2d 542 (Sullivan Co. Ct. 2003) (same); *People v. Riola*, 137 Misc. 2d 616, 522 N.Y.S.2d 419 (Nassau Co. Dist. Ct. 1987) (same); *People v. Lalka*, 113 Misc. 2d 474, 449 N.Y.S.2d 579 (Rochester City Ct. 1982) (same). *See generally Matter of Duran v. Melton*, 108 Misc. 2d 120, 437 N.Y.S.2d 49 (Monroe Co. Sup. Ct. 1981).

By contrast, the DMV's position on the issue of collateral estoppel is as follows:

> In adjourned cases, a conviction may already exist on the alcohol charge underlying the refusal on which you are holding the hearing. If there has been a conviction or plea to [VTL § 1192(2,3,4)], then the issues of probable cause and lawful arrest are conclusively decided (collateral estoppel). If there has been a plea to [VTL § 1192(1)], it can be considered an admission against interest on these two issues, but is subject to attac[k] and explanation by the motorist. If there has been an 1192(1) conviction after trial, then all issues must be established without reference to the conviction.

See Memorandum from DMV Administrative Office Director Sidney W. Berke to All Safety Administrative Law Judges, dated June 5, 1986, set forth at Appendix 44. *See also* Appendix 47 (same).

Where a DWI arrest is found to be supported by probable cause both (a) at a DMV refusal hearing, and (b) following a probable cause hearing in town court, the doctrine of collateral estoppel precludes the motorist from relitigating the issue of probable cause in an action for false arrest, false imprisonment, or malicious prosecution, and thus precludes such an action. *Janendo v. Town of New Paltz Police Dep't*, 211 A.D.2d 894, 621 N.Y.S.2d 175 (3d Dep't 1995). *See also Holmes v. City of New Rochelle*, 190 A.D.2d 713, 593 N.Y.S.2d 320 (2d Dep't 1993); *Coffey v. Town of Wheatland*, 135 A.D.2d 1125, 523 N.Y.S.2d 267 (4th Dep't 1987). *Cf. Menio v. Akzo Salt Inc.*, 217 A.D.2d 334, __ n.2, 634 N.Y.S.2d 802, 803 n.2 (3d Dep't 1995) ("To the extent that *Janendo v. Town of New Paltz Police Dept. (supra)* may be interpreted to enable collateral estoppel to be grounded solely upon a probable cause determination of a town justice, we decline to follow it").

§ 41:86   Chemical test refusals and equitable estoppel

Research References

West's Key Number Digest, Automobiles ⇔144.1(1.20)

In *Matter of Ginty*, 74 Misc. 2d 625, 345 N.Y.S.2d 856 (Niagara Co. Sup. Ct. 1973), following his arrest for DWI, the petitioner feigned a heart attack. During the "chaotic" situation which ensued, the petitioner was requested to submit to a chemical test, but the arresting officer failed to administer sufficient refusal warnings to petitioner. Under these unique circumstances, the court held that "the petitioner because of his own actions is estopped" from challenging the sufficiency of the refusal warnings. 74 Misc. 2d at __, 345 N.Y.S.2d at 858.

§ 41:87   Chemical test refusal sanctions as double jeopardy

Research References

West's Key Number Digest, Automobiles ⇔144.1(1.20)

The prosecution of a defendant for a violation of VTL § 1192 following a chemical test refusal revocation does not violate the Double Jeopardy Clause. *Matter of Brennan v. Kmiotek*, 233 A.D.2d 870, 649 N.Y.S.2d 611 (4th Dep't 1996). *See also Matter of Barnes v. Tofany*, 27 N.Y.2d 74, 77, 313 N.Y.S.2d 690, 693 (1970) ("We hold that the 'double punishment' feature of our Vehicle and Traffic statute—one criminal and the other administrative—is lawful"); *People v. Frank*, 166 Misc. 2d 277, 631 N.Y.S.2d 1014 (N.Y. City Crim. Ct. 1995). *See generally People v. Demetsenare*, 243 A.D.2d 777, __, 663 N.Y.S.2d 299, 303 (3d Dep't 1997); *People v. Roach*, 226 A.D.2d 55, 649 N.Y.S.2d 607 (4th Dep't 1996); *Matter of Smith v. County Court of Essex County*, 224 A.D.2d 89, 649 N.Y.S.2d 507 (3d Dep't 1996).

Similarly, the Double Jeopardy Clause is not violated where a DMV license revocation proceeding is commenced despite the motorist's previous acquittal in a criminal case stemming from the same conduct. *Matter of Giudice v. Adduci*, 176 A.D.2d 1175, __, 575 N.Y.S.2d 611, 612 (3d Dep't 1991).

§ 41:88   Admissibility of chemical test result obtained despite refusal

Research References

West's Key Number Digest, Automobiles ⊸144.1(1.20), 413

In the field of chemical testing and chemical test refusals, there is a clear (and critical) distinction between a DWI suspect's constitutional rights and his or her statutory rights. Thus, for example, while a DWI suspect has no *constitutional* right to refuse to submit to a chemical test, *see, e.g.*, *South Dakota v. Neville*, 459 U.S. 553, 560 n.10, 103 S.Ct. 916, 921 n.10 (1983); *Missouri v. McNeely*, 133 S. Ct. 1552, 185 L. Ed. 2d 696 (2013); *Schmerber v. California*, 384 U.S. 757, 86 S.Ct. 1826 (1966); *People v. Shaw*, 72 N.Y.2d 1032, 1033, 534 N.Y.S.2d 929, 930 (1988); *People v. Kates*, 53 N.Y.2d 591, 594–95, 444 N.Y.S.2d 446, 448 (1981); *People v. Thomas*, 46 N.Y.2d 100, 106, 412 N.Y.S.2d 845, 848 (1978), he or she nonetheless has a well recognized *statutory* right to do so. *See, e.g.*, *Shaw*, 72 N.Y.2d at 1034, 534 N.Y.S.2d at 930; *People v. Daniel*, 84 A.D.2d 916, __, 446 N.Y.S.2d 658, 659 (4th Dep't 1981), *aff'd sub nom.* People v. Moselle, 57 N.Y.2d 97, 454 N.Y.S.2d 292 (1982); *People v. Wolter*, 83 A.D.2d 187, __, 444 N.Y.S.2d 331, 333 (4th Dep't 1981), *aff'd sub nom.* People v. Moselle, 57 N.Y.2d 97, 454 N.Y.S.2d 292 (1982); *People v. Haitz*, 65 A.D.2d 172, __, 411 N.Y.S.2d 57, 60 (4th Dep't 1978).

In this regard, VTL § 1194(2)(b)(1) provides that, unless a court order has been granted pursuant to VTL § 1194(3), if a DWI suspect has refused to submit to a chemical test *"the test shall not be given* and a written report of such refusal shall be immediately made by the police officer before whom such refusal was made." (Emphasis added). *See also* VTL § 1194(3)(b) ("Upon refusal by any person to submit to a chemical test or any portion thereof as described above, *the test shall not be given* unless a police officer or a district attorney . . . requests and obtains a court order to compel [the test]") (emphasis added).

In *People v. Moselle*, 57 N.Y.2d 97, 454 N.Y.S.2d 292 (1982), the Court of Appeals:

(a) Made clear that VTL § "1194 has pre-empted the administration of chemical tests for determining alcoholic blood content with respect to violations under [VTL §] 1192." 57 N.Y.2d at 109, 454 N.Y.S.2d at 297; and

(b) Held that "[a]bsent a manifestation of a defendant's consent thereto, blood samples taken without a court order other than in conformity with the provisions of subdivisions 1 and 2 of section 1194 of the Vehicle and Traffic Law are inadmissible in prosecutions for operating a motor vehicle while under the influence of alcohol under section 1192 of that law. Beyond that, blood samples taken without a defendant's consent are inadmissible in prosecutions under the Penal Law unless taken pursuant to an authorizing court order." 57 N.Y.2d at 101, 454 N.Y.S.2d at 293.

See also People v. Smith, 18 N.Y.3d 544, 549 n.2, 942 N.Y.S.2d 426, 429 n.2, 965 N.E.2d 928 (2012) ("If the motorist declines to consent, the police may not administer the test unless authorized to do so by court order (*see* Vehicle and Traffic Law § 1194[3])."); *People v. Kates*, 53 N.Y.2d 591, 596, 444 N.Y.S.2d 446, 448 (1981) ("the Legislature . . . provide[d] that the police must request the driver's consent, advise him of the consequences of refusal *and honor his wishes if he decides to refuse*") (emphasis added); *People v. Thomas*, 46 N.Y.2d 100, 108, 412 N.Y.S.2d 845, 850 (1978) ("Under the procedure prescribed by section 1194 of the Vehicle and Traffic Law a driver who has initially declined to take one of the described chemical tests is to be informed of the consequences of such refusal. If he thereafter persists in a refusal *the test is not to be given* (§ 1194, subd. 2); the choice is the driver's") (emphasis added).

Clearly, according to VTL § 1194(2)(b)(1), VTL § 1194(3)(b), *Moselle*, *Smith*, *Kates*, and *Thomas*, where a DWI suspect is requested to submit to a chemical test, declines, is read refusal warnings, and thereafter persists in his or her refusal, "*the test shall not be given*" (absent a court order pursuant to VTL § 1194(3)). *See also Mackey v. Montrym*, 443 U.S. 1, 5, 99 S.Ct. 2612, 2614 (1979) ("The statute leaves an officer no discretion once a breath-analysis test has been refused: 'If the person arrested refuses to submit to such test or analysis, . . . the police officer before whom such refusal was made *shall immediately* prepare a written report of such refusal' "). Accordingly, a test result obtained under such circumstances should be inadmissible—not because it violates the Constitution—but rather because it violates the statutory scheme of VTL § 1194.

Nonetheless, in *People v. Stisi*, 93 A.D.2d 951, —, 463 N.Y.S.2d 73, 74–75 (3d Dep't 1983), the Appellate Division, Third Department, held:

Defendant interprets section 1194 (subd. 2) of the Vehicle and Traffic Law to mandate that once a defendant refuses to submit to a chemical test after being fully apprised of the consequences of such refusal, all further requests and prompting by the police for defendant to reconsider and submit must immediately cease and the chemical test not be given . . . Defendant's suggested literal interpretation of the subject statutory provision is misplaced and without merit . . .

Section 1194 of the Vehicle and Traffic Law does not, either expressly or by implication, foreclose the police from resuming discussion with a defendant and renewing their request that he submit to a chemical test.

Notably, the *Stisi* court failed to cite *Kates* and/or *Thomas*, each of which appears to support the defendant's "suggested literal interpretation" of VTL § 1194(2).

Although *People v. Cragg*, 71 N.Y.2d 926, 528 N.Y.S.2d 807 (1988), appears at first glance to reach the same conclusion as the *Stisi* court, in actuality it does not. In *Cragg*, "[d]efendant contend[ed] that the police violated Vehicle and Traffic Law § 1194(2) by administering a breathalyzer test despite defendant's initial refusal to submit to the test, and by informing him of certain consequences—not specifically prescribed by the statute—of such refusal." In rejecting the defendant's claims, the Court of Appeals held that:

> Contrary to defendant's assertion, the statute is not violated by an arresting officer informing a person as to the consequences of his choice to take or not take a breathalyzer test. Thus, it cannot be said, *in the circumstances of this case*, that by informing defendant that his refusal to submit to the test would result in his arraignment before a Magistrate and the posting of bail, the officer violated the provisions of the Vehicle and Traffic Law.

71 N.Y.2d at 927, 528 N.Y.S.2d at 807–08 (emphasis added).

However, the wording of the *Cragg* decision indicates that defendant's "initial refusal" to submit to the test preceded the refusal warnings—requiring that the defendant be informed of the consequences of a refusal and given a chance to change his mind. *See Thomas*, 46 N.Y.2d at 108, 412 N.Y.S.2d at 850 ("Under the procedure prescribed by section 1194 of the Vehicle and Traffic Law a driver who has initially declined to take one of the described chemical tests is to be informed of the consequences of such refusal. If he thereafter persists in a refusal the test is not to be given (§ 1194, subd. 2); the choice is the driver's"). Thus, the procedure followed in *Cragg* did not constitute an attempt to persuade the defendant to change his mind after a valid, persistent refusal had occurred. Rather, it is an example of the statute being implemented exactly as envisioned by the legislature and the Court of Appeals. The position that *Cragg* was not intended to change settled law in this area is supported by the fact that *Cragg* (a) is a memorandum decision, (b) did not cite *Stisi*, and (c) did not cite *Moselle*, *Kates*, and/or *Thomas*.

In *People v. Ameigh*, 95 A.D.2d 367, 467 N.Y.S.2d 718 (3d Dep't 1983), the defendant refused to submit to a police-requested chemical test, but his blood was nonetheless drawn and tested by hospital personnel for "diagnostic purposes." In ruling that the test result obtained in this manner was admissible, the Appellate Division, Third Department, reasoned:

> [W]e are not unmindful of the holding by the Court of Appeals in *People v. Moselle*, 57 N.Y.2d 97, 454 N.Y.S.2d 292, 439 N.E.2d 1235 that "[VTL § 1194] has preempted the administration of chemical tests for determining alcoholic blood content with respect to violations under [VTL § 1192]." . . .

> [However], the statutory framework simply does not address itself to evidence of blood-alcohol levels derived as a result of bona fide medical procedures in diagnosing or treating an injured driver. In that context, it is apparent to us that the provision in section 1194 (subd. 2) that the test shall not be given to a person expressly declining the officer's request does not render inadmissible the results of tests not taken at the direction or on behalf of the police. The legislative purpose underlying that provision was "to eliminate the need for the use of force by police officers if an individual in a drunken condition should refuse to submit to the test."

95 A.D.2d at __-__, 467 N.Y.S.2d at 718–19 (citation omitted).

§ 41:89   Admissibility of chemical test refusal evidence in actions arising under Penal Law

Research References

West's Key Number Digest, Automobiles ☞144.1(1.20), 413

In *People v. Loughlin*, 154 A.D.2d 552, __, 546 N.Y.S.2d 392, 393 (2d Dep't 1989), order aff'd, 76 N.Y.2d 804, 559 N.Y.S.2d 962, 559 N.E.2d 656 (1990), the Appellate Division, Second Department, held that "[t]he defendant's contention that evidence of his refusal to take a breathalyzer test should not have been admitted because he was charged with crimes arising under the Penal Law rather than under the Vehicle and Traffic Law . . . is without merit." *See also People v. Stratis*, 137 Misc. 2d 661, __-__, 520 N.Y.S.2d 904, 910–11 (Kings Co. Sup. Ct. 1987), judgment aff'd, 148 A.D.2d 557, 540 N.Y.S.2d 186 (2d Dep't 1989) (VTL § 1194(4) (currently VTL § 1194(2)(f)) applies to penal law violations, and thus evidence of the defendant's refusal to submit to chemical test inadmissible where refusal warnings were not read to the defendant in "clear and unequivocal" language), *aff'd on other grounds*, 148 A.D.2d 557, 54 N.Y.S.2d 186 (2d Dep't 1989).

§ 41:90   Admissibility of chemical test refusal evidence in civil actions

Research References

West's Key Number Digest, Automobiles ☞144.1(1.20), 413

In *Bazza v. Banscher*, 143 A.D.2d 715, __, 533 N.Y.S.2d 285, 286 (2d Dep't 1988), the Appellate Division, Second Department, held that:

> The trial court . . . erred when it prevented the plaintiffs from introducing into evidence Banscher's refusal to submit to a breathalyzer test after the accident. The admission of evidence was not barred by Vehicle and Traffic Law § 1194(4) [currently VTL § 1194(2)(f)]. This provision does not preclude the admission of evidence of a refusal to submit to a blood-alcohol test in proceedings other than criminal prosecutions under Vehicle and Traffic Law § 1192. Instead, with respect to proceedings pursuant to § 1192 only, it establishes prerequisites for the admission of such evidence.

§ 41:91   Applicability of "two-hour rule" to chemical test refusals

Research References

West's Key Number Digest, Automobiles ☞144.1(1.20)

The two-hour rule stems from VTL § 1194(2)(a), which provides, in pertinent part:

> 2. Chemical tests. (a) When authorized. Any person who operates a motor vehicle in this state shall be deemed to have given consent to a chemical test of one or more of the following: breath, blood, urine, or saliva, for the purpose of determining the alcoholic and/or drug content of the blood *provided that* such test is administered by or at the direction of a police officer with respect to a chemical test of breath, urine or saliva or, with respect to a chemical test of blood, at the direction of a police officer:
>
> > (1) having reasonable grounds to believe such person to have been operating in violation of any subdivision of [VTL § 1192] *and within two hours* after such person has been placed under arrest for any such violation; or . . .
>
> > (2) *within two hours* after a breath test, as provided in [VTL § 1194(1)(b)], indicates that alcohol has been consumed by such person and in accordance with the rules and regulations established by the police force of which the officer is a member.

VTL § 1194(2)(a)(1), (2) (emphases added). *See* §§ 31:1 et seq., *supra*.

In *People v. Brol*, 81 A.D.2d 739, __, 438 N.Y.S.2d 424, 424 (4th Dep't 1981), the Appellate Division, Fourth Department, held that if the defendant "was requested to take the [chemical] test after the two hours had expired, evidence of his refusal was incompetent and should not have been considered by the jury." *See also People v. Walsh*, 139 Misc. 2d 161, __, 527 N.Y.S.2d 349, 350 (Nassau Co. Dist. Ct. 1988).

By contrast, in *People v. Ward*, 176 Misc. 2d 398, __, 673 N.Y.S.2d 297, 300 (Richmond Co. Sup. Ct. 1998), the court held that "considering the reasoning in *Brol, supra*, in conjunction with several subsequent decisions interpreting the scope of the two hour rule, it seems clear that today the rule has no application in a determination of the admissibility of evidence that a defendant refused a chemical test." *See also People v. Robinson*, 82 A.D.3d 1269, __, 920 N.Y.S.2d 162, 164 (2d Dep't 2011) ("Where, as here, the person is capable, but refuses to consent, evidence of that refusal, as governed by Vehicle and Traffic Law § 1194(2)(f), is admissible into evidence regardless of whether the refusal is made more than two hours after arrest"); *People v. Rodriguez*, 26 Misc. 3d 238, __, 891 N.Y.S.2d 246, 248-49 (Bronx Co. Sup. Ct. 2009); *People v. Coludro*, 166 Misc. 2d 662, __, 634 N.Y.S.2d 964, 967–68 (N.Y. City Crim. Ct. 1995); *People v. Morales*, 161 Misc. 2d 128, __, 611 N.Y.S.2d 980, 984 (N.Y. City Crim. Ct. 1994).

In *People v. Morris*, 8 Misc. 3d 360, __, 793 N.Y.S.2d 754, 757–58 (N.Y. City Crim. Ct. 2005), the court expressly disagreed with the above-quoted language in *Ward*, and held that the two-hour rule is still applicable to chemical test refusals. *See also* 8 Misc. 3d at __, 793 N.Y.S.2d at 758 ("the evidence of the refusal is suppressed based upon the tolling of the two-hour rule. Two-hours should mean two-hours, absent a knowing waiver and consent to take the test"). In addition, in *People v. Rosa*, 112 A.D.3d 551, __, 977 N.Y.S.2d 250, 250-51 (1st Dep't 2013), leave to appeal denied, 22 N.Y.3d 1202, 986 N.Y.S.2d 422, 9 N.E.3d 917 (2014), the Appellate Division, First Department, stated that "[b]ecause more than two hours had passed since defendant's arrest, the officer who administered the breathalyzer test should not have advised defendant that, if he refused to take the test, his driver's license would be suspended and the refusal could be used against him in court."

Regardless of the admissibility of such evidence at trial, the two-hour rule had always applied to DMV refusal hearings. In this regard, the standardized DMV Report of Refusal to Submit to Chemical Test form expressly stated that "[s]ection 1194 of the Vehicle and Traffic Law requires that the refusal must be within two hours of the arrest." This makes sense in that the "implied consent" provisions of VTL § 1194 only apply *provided that* the chemical test is administered within two hours of either the time of arrest for a violation of VTL § 1192 or the time of a positive breath screening test. *See* VTL § 1194(2)(a)(1), (2); § 31:2, *supra*.

Since the civil sanctions for a chemical test refusal are imposed on a motorist as a penalty for revoking his or her implied consent, and are wholly unrelated to the issue of guilt or innocence, they should not be imposed when the requirements of VTL § 1194(2)(a) are not met.

Nonetheless, in 2012, DMV switched its position on this issue. In other words, DMV no longer applies the two-hour rule to chemical test refusal hearings. A copy of DMV Counsel's Office's letter in this regard is attached hereto as Appendix 68. Critically, however, in *Rosa*, *supra*, the Appellate Division, First Department, stated that "[b]ecause more than two hours had passed since defendant's arrest, the officer who administered the breathalyzer test should not have advised defendant that, if he refused to take the test, his driver's license would be suspended and the refusal could be used against him in court." 112 A.D.3d at __, 977 N.Y.S.2d at 250-51.

In *People v. Harvin*, 40 Misc. 3d 921, 928, 969 N.Y.S.2d 851, 856 (N.Y. City Crim. Ct. 2013), the Court summarized the evolution of the two-hour rule as applied to chemical test refusals, and concluded as follows:

> Jurisprudence like many things can be a continuous journey. The law is not fixed, and even the opinions of a judge can change over the years through discussions with colleagues and by hearing the arguments of advocates. Additionally, the courts that review our decisions, the "policy-making" courts, influence what the law is and what the law should be. Such an evolution has taken place in my decisions on the two-hour rule. While my personal belief may be that the two-hour rule is one of evidence, and that the Legislature designed it as such, clearly that is not a majority opinion, nor does it represent the current state of the law in New York. Likewise, it is clear that if our policy courts consider this rule to be no more than an implied consent rule, then a refusal after two hours should be admitted into evidence as long as it is knowing and persistent, and the People have met their burden as to that knowing and unequivocal refusal in this case. The Legislature, for its part, has had ample opportunity to clearly state a desire to return the two-hour rule to an evidentiary rule if it deemed the courts' positions to be incorrect.

(Citations omitted).

§ 41:92   Loss of videotape containing alleged chemical test refusal requires sanction

Research References

West's Key Number Digest, Automobiles ⌖144.1(1.20)

In *People v. Marr*, 177 A.D.2d 964, 577 N.Y.S.2d 1008 (4th Dep't 1991), the police erased a videotape which had contained discoverable evidence pertaining to, among other things, the defendant's alleged unsuccessful attempts to submit to a breathalyzer test. Following a hearing, the county court "imposed a sanction precluding the People from introducing any evidence of defendant's alleged refusal to submit to the breathalyzer test." 177 A.D.2d at __, 577 N.Y.S.2d at 1009.

On appeal, the Appellate Division, Fourth Department, held that "County Court properly exercised its discretion in fashioning an appropriate sanction. Although an adverse inference charge may also have been appropriate, in our view, the court did not abuse its discretion in precluding the prosecution from introducing evidence at trial of defendant's alleged refusal to submit to the breathalyzer test as its sole sanction for the prosecution's failure to preserve the videotape." 177 A.D.2d at __, 577 N.Y.S.2d at 1009 (citations omitted). *See also People v. Litarov*, 188 Misc. 2d 234, __, 727 N.Y.S.2d 293, 297 (N.Y. City Crim. Ct. 2001) (under circumstances presented, adverse inference charge appropriate sanction for People's loss of videotape of defendant's chemical test refusal).

§ 41:93 Policy of sentencing defendants convicted of DWAI to jail if they refused chemical test is illegal

Research References

West's Key Number Digest, Automobiles ⟊144.1(1.20)

In *People v. McSpirit*, 154 Misc. 2d 784, 595 N.Y.S.2d 660 (App. Term, 9th & 10th Jud. Dist. 1993), the defendant was sentenced to, inter alia, five days in jail upon her conviction of DWAI, in violation of VTL § 1192(1). In this regard, the town court apparently had "a policy of incarcerating those who refuse to take a breathalyzer test and are thereafter convicted of driving while impaired." 154 Misc. 2d at __, 595 N.Y.S.2d at 661.

On appeal, the Appellate Term modified the defendant's sentence by deleting the term of incarceration, holding that "the policy as such is arbitrary, capricious and unauthorized by statute." 154 Misc. 2d at __, 595 N.Y.S.2d at 661.

§ 41:94 Report of refusal to submit to chemical test is discoverable pursuant to CPL § 240.20

Research References

West's Key Number Digest, Automobiles ⟊144.1(1.20)

Where a DWI defendant refuses to submit to a chemical test, or any portion thereof, to determine the alcoholic and/or drug content of his or her blood, "unless a court order has been granted pursuant to [VTL § 1194(3)], the test shall not be given and *a written report of such refusal shall be immediately made by the police officer before whom such refusal was made.*" VTL § 1194(2)(b)(1) (emphasis added). Such a report (a.k.a. a Report of Refusal to Submit to Chemical Test) constitutes a written report or document concerning a physical examination and/or a scientific test or experiment relating to the criminal action. As such, it is discoverable pursuant to CPL §§ 240.20(1)(c) and 240.20(1)(k) (and is not merely *Rosario* material).

A defendant's refusal to submit to a chemical test is also discoverable pursuant to CPL § 240.20(1)(a), which provides for the disclosure of "[a]ny written, recorded or oral statement of the defendant . . . made, other than in the course of the criminal transaction, to a public servant engaged in law enforcement activity or to a person then acting under his direction or in cooperation with him."

§ 41:95   Dentures and test refusals

Research References

West's Key Number Digest, Automobiles ☞144.1(1.20)

There is research indicating that dentures can retain "mouth alcohol" for longer than the 15- to 20-minute continuous observation period which is required to ensure that a breath test is not contaminated by mouth alcohol. *See* 10 NYCRR § 59.5(b). As a result, breath test operators are generally trained to inquire as to whether a DWI suspect wears dentures; and, if the suspect answers affirmatively, to (a) direct the suspect to remove the dentures, (b) direct the suspect to rinse his or her mouth out with water, and (c) conduct a new observation period, prior to the administration of the breath test.

However, a DWI suspect may feel particularly self-conscious in this regard. Thus, the situation can arise where the suspect consents to take a breath test but refuses to remove his or her dentures in connection therewith. Does such conduct constitute a test refusal?

The DMV's position on this issue is that such conduct will constitute a chemical test refusal so long as the police "have advised the individual as to why the dentures must be removed and how such removal is necessary to the validity of the test." *See* Letter from former DMV First Assistant Counsel Joseph R. Donovan to Peter Gerstenzang, set forth at Appendix 45. In this regard, the DMV strongly recommends that police departments incorporate denture removal procedures into their breath test rules and regulations. *See* Letter from former DMV First Assistant Counsel Joseph R. Donovan to Peter Gerstenzang, set forth at Appendix 45. *See also* Letter from former DMV First Assistant Counsel

Joseph R. Donovan to Peter Gerstenzang, set forth at Appendix 46.

§ 41:96 Prosecutor's improper cross-examination and summation in refusal case results in reversal

Research References

West's Key Number Digest, Automobiles ⟂144.1(1.20)

In *People v. Handwerker*, 12 Misc. 3d 19, 816 N.Y.S.2d 824 (App. Term, 9th & 10th Jud. Dist. 2006), the defendant was convicted of DWAI following a jury trial. On appeal, the Appellate Term reversed, finding merit in the defendant's claim "that he was denied a fair trial because, during cross-examination and summation, the prosecution improperly shifted the burden of proof to him by creating a presumption against him that he had to prove his innocence by taking a chemical test." 12 Misc. 3d at __, 816 N.Y.S.2d at 826. Specifically:

> During cross-examination, the prosecutor asked the defendant the following question: "[y]ou didn't say, I want to prove my innocence so give me the test,' right?" The court overruled defense counsel's objection and defendant indicated that he had not made such a request. During summation, the prosecutor remarked, "[w]ell, if he's innocent, then why doesn't he want to take the test to prove that?"

> It is well settled that the People have the unalterable burden of proving beyond a reasonable doubt every element of the crime charged. The prosecutor's inquiry during cross-examination and his remark during summation, in effect, suggested to the jury that it was defendant's burden to prove his innocence by submitting to a chemical test . . . While refusal to take a chemical test is admissible at trial against a defendant as evidence of his consciousness of guilt, the prosecution sought to use defendant's refusal for purposes beyond that allowed by the law. We conclude that the cumulative effect of such misconduct by the prosecution substantially prejudiced defendant's right to a fair trial. Accordingly, the judgment convicting defendant of driving while ability impaired is reversed and a new trial is ordered as to said charge.

12 Misc. 3d at __, 816 N.Y.S.2d at 826 (citations omitted).

In *People v. Anderson*, 89 A.D.3d 1161, __, 932 N.Y.S.2d 561, 563 (3d Dep't 2011):

> No dispute exist[ed] that defendant was adequately warned as to the consequences of his refusal to submit to a chemical test, or that he repeatedly refused to take such a test. Defendant argue[d], nevertheless, that the People's statements and questioning of him at trial regarding his refusal to consent to a chemical blood test deprived him of a fair trial by impermissibly shifting the burden of

proof to him. Specifically, during both cross-examination and summation, the People suggested that, by refusing to take the test, defendant forewent the opportunity to prove his innocence. Supreme Court sustained defendant's objections to these questions and comments, informing the jury that defendant did not bear any burden of proof and that it was entitled, but not required, to infer that defendant refused the test because he feared it would provide evidence of his guilt. *Under these circumstances*, we see no evidence that the burden of proof was improperly shifted to defendant or that he was deprived of a fair trial.

(Emphasis added).

§ 41:97 Improper presentation of refusal evidence to Grand Jury did not require dismissal of indictment

In *People v. Jeffery*, 70 A.D.3d 1512, __, 894 N.Y.S.2d 797, 798 (4th Dep't 2010), "the People failed to comply with the requirements of Vehicle and Traffic Law § 1194(2)(f) and thus improperly presented evidence to the grand jury concerning defendant's refusal to submit to a chemical test." After concluding that the remaining evidence before the Grand Jury was legally insufficient, County Court dismissed the indictment. The Appellate Division, Fourth Department, reversed, concluding that:

Although the court properly concluded that the evidence of defendant's refusal to submit to a chemical test was erroneously presented to the grand jury, we note that " 'dismissal of an indictment under CPL 210.35(5) must meet a high test and is limited to instances of prosecutorial misconduct, fraudulent conduct or errors which potentially prejudice the ultimate decision reached by the [g]rand [j]ury.' " We agree with the People that there were no such instances here. Furthermore, we reject defendant's contention that the grand jury proceedings were impaired by the presentation of the inadmissible evidence. It is well settled that "not every . . . elicitation of inadmissible testimony . . . renders an indictment defective. Typically, the submission of some inadmissible evidence will be deemed fatal only when the remaining evidence is insufficient to sustain the indictment." We also agree with the People that the remaining admissible evidence was legally sufficient to support the indictment.

70 A.D.3d at _, 894 N.Y.S.2d at 798 (citations omitted).

Part XI

EVIDENCE ISSUES

Chapter 42

Breath Test Foundation

§ 42:1 In general

Over the years, what has passed for a sufficient foundation for the admission of a breath test result has become progressively less demanding. This tendency towards oversimplification cuts both ways. On the one hand, it makes the People's life much easier. On the other hand, it has created a situation where no one is required to have any meaningful understanding of how a breath test device actually works. In the authors' experience, many jurors are reluctant to blindly accept the results of a breath test device that has not been adequately explained to them.

This chapter addresses various issues involved in laying a proper foundation for the admission of a breath test result at trial.

§ 42:2 For purposes of this chapter, "breath test" and "chemical test" are used synonymously

In the field of New York DWI law, the phrase "breath test" refers to a preliminary test of a DWI suspect's breath for the presence of alcohol using a preliminary breath screening device such as an Alco-Sensor (a.k.a. a PBT). *See* §§ 7:1 et seq., *supra*. By contrast, the phrase "chemical test" is the term used to describe a test of the alcoholic and/or drug content of a DWI suspect's blood using an instrument other than a PBT.

In other words, BAC tests conducted utilizing breath testing instruments such as the Breathalyzer, DataMaster, Intoxilyzer, Alcotest, etc. are generally referred to as "chemical tests," *not* "breath tests." For purposes of this chapter, however, the terms "breath test" and "chemical test" are used synonymously—as this chapter does not address the admissibility of PBT evidence at trial.

In *People v. Jones*, 118 Misc. 2d 687, __, 461 N.Y.S.2d 962, 966 (Albany Co. Ct. 1983), the Court rejected the defendant's claim that modern infrared breath testing devices do not constitute "chemical tests" because, unlike the old Breathalyzers, no chemical reaction takes place.

§ 42:3 Breath test foundation—Generally

Where the breath test device in question is included on the Department of Health's list of accepted breath test instruments (which is always the case), *see* § 42:12, *infra*, a proper foundation for the admission of a breath test result at trial requires proof:

(a) that the device was properly calibrated and otherwise in proper working order;

(b) that any chemicals used in conducting the test were of the proper kind and mixed in the proper proportions; and

(c) that the test was properly administered.

See, e.g., People v. Boscic, 15 N.Y.3d 494, 497, 912 N.Y.S.2d 556, 558, 938 N.E.2d 989 (2010); *Constantine v. Leto*, 157 A.D.2d 376, __, 557 N.Y.S.2d 611, 613 (3d Dep't 1990), order aff'd, 77 N.Y.2d 975, 571 N.Y.S.2d 906, 575 N.E.2d 392 (1991); *People v. Campbell*, 73 N.Y.2d 481, 484, 541 N.Y.S.2d 756, 757, 539 N.E.2d 584 (1989); *People v. Alvarez*, 70 N.Y.2d 375, 380, 521 N.Y.S.2d 212, 214, 515 N.E.2d 898 (1987); *People v. Freeland*, 68 N.Y.2d 699, 700, 506 N.Y.S.2d 306, 307, 497 N.E.2d 673 (1986); *People v. Mertz*, 68 N.Y.2d 136, 148, 506 N.Y.S.2d 290, 296–97, 497 N.E.2d 657 (1986); *People v. Gower*, 42 N.Y.2d 117, 121–22, 397 N.Y.S.2d 368, 370–71, 366 N.E.2d 69 (1977); *People v. Todd*, 38 N.Y.2d 755, 381 N.Y.S.2d 50, 343 N.E.2d 767 (1975); *People v. Robinson*, 53 A.D.3d 63, __, 860 N.Y.S.2d 159, 165 (2d Dep't 2008); *People v. Hampe*, 181 A.D.2d 238, __ n.1, 585 N.Y.S.2d 861, 862 n.1 (3d Dep't 1992); *People v. Donaldson*, 36 A.D.2d 37, 319 N.Y.S.2d 172 (4th Dep't 1971); *People v. Meikrantz*, 77 Misc. 2d 892, 351 N.Y.S.2d 549 (Broome Co. Ct. 1974).

These issues are discussed in the sections that follow.

§ 42:4 Admissibility of documents used to establish breath test foundation—CPLR § 4518

The documents that are typically used to lay a foundation for the admission of a breath test result have foundational requirements of their own. Such documents generally fall under the so-called "business records" exception to the rule against hearsay. *See* CPLR § 4518. As such, they are generally admissible as long as the requirements of CPLR § 4518 are met. *See People v. Gower*, 42 N.Y.2d 117, 121, 397 N.Y.S.2d 368, 370, 366 N.E.2d 69 (1977) ("It would seem that the requirements of CPLR 4518 could very easily be met and thus its benefits be realized by the prosecution.").

This topic is discussed in detail in §§ 43:1 et seq., *infra. See also* § 42:8, *infra*.

§ 42:5 Effect of *Crawford v. Washington* on admissibility of documents used to establish breath test foundation

In *Crawford v. Washington*, 541 U.S. 36, 124 S. Ct. 1354, 158

L. Ed. 2d 177, 63 Fed. R. Evid. Serv. 1077 (2004), the Supreme Court held that the Confrontation Clause of the 6th Amendment prohibits the use of "testimonial" evidence against the defendant at trial unless both (a) the declarant is unavailable, *and* (b) the defendant had a prior opportunity to cross-examine him or her. 541 U.S. at 68, 124 S.Ct. at 1374. The issue arose as to whether the documents typically used to lay a foundation for the admission of a defendant's breath test results (*e.g.,* Breath Test Instrument Record of Inspection/Maintenance/Calibration, Simulator Solution Certificate of Analysis), fall within the ambit of *Crawford.* In *People v. Pealer,* 20 N.Y.3d 447, 451, 962 N.Y.S.2d 592, 594, 985 N.E.2d 903 (2013), petition for cert. filed (U.S. May 16, 2013), the Court of Appeals settled this issue:

> The question presented in this appeal is whether records pertaining to the routine inspection, maintenance and calibration of breathalyzer machines can be offered as evidence in a criminal trial without producing the persons who created the records. We hold that because such documents are nontestimonial, the records are not subject to the Confrontation Clause requirements set forth in *Crawford v. Washington.*

"At their core, these documents should be viewed as business records (*see* CPLR 4518[a]) which, as a class, are generally deemed nontestimonial." *Id.* at 455, 962 N.Y.S.2d at 597.

Notably, in footnote 1 of its decision in *Melendez-Diaz v. Massachusetts,* 557 U.S. 305, 311 n.1, 129 S. Ct. 2527, 2532 n.1, 174 L. Ed. 2d 314 (2009), the Supreme Court commented that:

> Contrary to the dissent's suggestion, we do not hold, and it is not the case, that anyone whose testimony may be relevant in establishing the chain of custody, authenticity of the sample, or accuracy of the testing device, must appear in person as part of the prosecution's case. While the dissent is correct that "[i]t is the obligation of the prosecution to establish the chain of custody," this does not mean that everyone who laid hands on the evidence must be called. As stated in the dissent's own quotation from *United States v. Lott,* "gaps in the chain [of custody] normally go to the weight of the evidence rather than its admissibility." It is up to the prosecution to decide what steps in the chain of custody are so crucial as to require evidence; but what testimony is introduced must (if the defendant objects) be introduced live. Additionally, documents prepared in the regular course of equipment maintenance may well qualify as nontestimonial records.

(Citations omitted).

By contrast, in *Carreira, supra,* the Watertown City Court provided a persuasive analysis as to why *Crawford* should apply to breath test foundation documents. In this regard, the Court pointed out a "recent and shocking forensic analysis scandal" involving a forensic scientist at the State Police lab, 27 Misc. 3d at —, 893 N.Y.S.2d at 850, and ultimately concluded that "we must beware of putting too much trust in the man behind the curtain. Doing so threatens to undermine one of the fundamental trial protections defendants have enjoyed since this nation's founding." 27 Misc. 3d at —, 893 N.Y.S.2d at 851.

§ 42:6 Proof of calibration

In order for a breath test result to be admissible at trial, the People must establish that the breath test device was properly calibrated and otherwise in proper working order. *See* § 42:3, *supra.* In the field of DWI law, the term "calibration" is a term of art which refers to the actual calibration (or verification thereof) of breath test devices by specially trained technicians at facilities such as the New York State Police lab or the New York State Division of Criminal Justice Services (DCJS) Office of Public Safety. It does *not* refer to so-called "weekly simulator testing" (or similar testing) conducted by police officers at the station. *See, e.g., People v. Boscic*, 15 N.Y.3d 494, 497, 912 N.Y.S.2d 556, 557, 938 N.E.2d 989 (2010) ("As part of the foundation presented in support of the admissibility of the test results, the People offered a police record certifying that the DataMaster had been calibrated (i.e., checked and adjusted by a trained technician) by an employee of the State Division of Criminal Justice Services . . . approximately six months and three weeks before the test was administered to defendant."); *People v. Meikrantz*, 77 Misc. 2d 892, —, 351 N.Y.S.2d 549, 559 (Broome Co. Ct. 1974) ("The term 'calibration' refers to an adjustment of the breathalyzer machine as distinguished from a mere test of the machine. If a weekly test at the station indicates a machine malfunction, it is sent to the laboratory to be calibrated."). *Cf.* 10 NYCRR § 59.1(l) ("Calibration means the activity of verifying that a value generated by the instrument is in acceptable agreement with the assigned value for a traceable and/or certified reference standard, including any adjustment to the instrument to bring it into acceptable agreement.").

The People usually demonstrate that the breath test machine was timely and properly calibrated via a document entitled "Breath Test Instrument Record of Inspection/Maintenance/Calibration" (a.k.a. a "certificate of calibration"). A copy of a certificate of calibration is set forth at Appendix 25. Counsel should carefully scrutinize this document. While, at first glance, a certificate of calibration merely confirms that the machine was in proper working order, the document will occasionally contain notations that significant repairs had recently been made. In addition, where "calibrations" are performed at irregular intervals (for example, in January and then again in April), this is generally an indication that there was a problem and the machine had to be sent back for non-routine maintenance or repairs. In such a case, defense counsel should demand all relevant records documenting the problem. In this regard, where the machine is serviced by DCJS, it is critical that defense counsel obtain the "service authorization form" (which is the form that accompanies a breath test machine when it is sent to DCJS for inspection, maintenance, repair or calibration). Similarly, there are various discoverable documents affiliated with the Alcotest machines utilized by the State Police that are rarely turned over to the defense. *See, e.g., State v. Chun*, 194 N.J. 54, 153, 943 A.2d 114, 173 (N.J. 2008) (setting forth 12 foundation documents that must be provided in discovery in New Jersey in connection with breath tests utilizing the Alcotest 7110 MKIII-C device).

§ 42:7 Timeliness of calibration

In *People v. Todd*, 79 Misc. 2d 630, 631, 360 N.Y.S.2d 754, 759 (Delaware Co. Ct. 1974), the breath test machine used to test the defendant's breath "had not been calibrated for more than six months." County Court found that:

> By analogy in speeding cases, there is a requirement that speedometers of police vehicles be calibrated at least once every six months and it would appear that the same standard should apply to the breathalyzer machine and any similar type of evidence which is used in a criminal prosecution and may deprive a citizen of his right to operate a motor vehicle in this state.

79 Misc. 2d at 634, 360 N.Y.S.2d at 759. On appeal, the Court of Appeals held that "[t]he People failed to establish that the breathalyzer apparatus had been timely calibrated; hence, the results of the breath test were inadmissible. It was incumbent upon the District Attorney to show that the machine was in proper working order." *People v. Todd*, 38 N.Y.2d 755, 756, 381 N.Y.S.2d 50, 50, 343 N.E.2d 767, 767 (1975).

Based upon the above, it had been generally accepted that *Todd* created a "six-month rule" pursuant to which a breath test result obtained from a machine that had not been calibrated for more than six months is inadmissible. In this regard, in *People v. Mickle*, 187 Misc. 2d 718, __, 724 N.Y.S.2d 570, 573 (Canaan Just. Ct. 2001), the Court stated:

> [M]any courts view *People v. Todd* as a clear and controlling authority for support of the proposition of a "six-month rule." This court agrees and finds it to be dispositive here. The rule may be modified at some point by a higher court; however, this court sees no lower court rulings that have been confirmed or overruled by the Court of Appeals. In the absence of such pronouncement, six months is the rule of *Todd*.

(Citation omitted).

The pronouncement that the *Mickle* Court was seeking has come. *See People v. Boscic*, 15 N.Y.3d 494, 912 N.Y.S.2d 556, 938 N.E.2d 989 (2010). In *Boscic*, the Court of Appeals held as follows:

> In this case, we consider whether our decision in *People v. Todd* adopted a standard requiring that breath-alcohol detection devices must be calibrated at least every six months in order for the test results to be admissible at trial. We hold that there is no per se, six-month rule and that the People must instead lay a foundation demonstrating that the particular device used was in proper working order when the test was administered.

15 N.Y.3d at 496, 912 N.Y.S.2d at 557 (citation omitted). In so holding, the Court reasoned as follows:

> Defendant claims that *People v. Todd* established a six-month calibration requirement . . . . Although *Todd* is susceptible to such an interpretation, we do not read it in such a rigid manner. * * *
>
> *Todd* did not explicitly articulate a six-month standard or allude to a specific calibration time frame.
>
> We have not relied on a six-month, bright-line rule in subsequent cases that dealt with the foundation requirements for breath-alcohol evidence. Rather than applying a specific temporal limitation, our post-*Todd* decisions have repeatedly emphasized that the applicable principle is whether the detection instrument was in "proper working order" at the time a test was administered. The Third and Fourth Departments have interpreted our precedent similarly and rejected the notion that it is impossible for a breath-alcohol device to function properly simply because it has not been calibrated for six months. We concur with that view and therefore hold that such evidence is admissible if the People demonstrate that the machine was in proper working order at the time it issued the test results in question.
>
> *Todd* was decided almost 35 years ago and in the ensuing decades, scientific knowledge has advanced dramatically, leading to significant technological changes in breath-alcohol detection devices. The scientific methods incorporated in modern-day breath testing instruments are substantially different from the earlier generations of these devices. . . . More recent technology relies on infrared absorption spectrometry. This technology—which is used in the BAC DataMaster—calculates blood-alcohol concentration by passing infrared light through a chamber holding the breath sample to gauge the absorption rate of "infrared radiation at specific wavelengths." Given the technological advances that have occurred and will continue to evolve, paired with the proliferation of available breath-alcohol detection devices approved for use by the New York State Department of Health (DOH) (*see* 10 NYCRR 59.4), we do not believe that a court-imposed calibration timing rule for all current technologies would be helpful in achieving the primary objective, which is to provide the factfinder a basis to determine

whether the particular instrument used produced reliable results in
a specific instance. Even if we had articulated a bright-line calibration rule more than three decades ago, the changes in scientific
testing methods would have provided reason to revisit it.

It further bears noting that both parties to this litigation recognize
that DOH has been charged by the Legislature to evaluate and approve specific models of breath-alcohol testing machines (*see* Vehicle and Traffic Law § 1194[4][c]). In its regulatory capacity, DOH
has determined that such instruments must be calibrated "at a
frequency as recommended by the device manufacturer" *but not less
than once a year*. The promulgation of these regulations will . . .
provide courts with information regarding recommended calibration
intervals, *not to exceed one year*, when assessing the adequacy of
foundation requirements for the admissibility of breath-alcohol test
results.

15 N.Y.3d at 497–500, 912 N.Y.S.2d at 558–59 (emphases added)
(citations and footnote omitted).

In light of the last portion of this quote from *Boscic*, it can now
be persuasively argued that there exists a "one-year rule" for
breath test instrument calibration.

The *Boscic* Court also noted that:

Our conclusion does not mean that appropriate and adequate
calibration procedures can be disregarded by law enforcement.
Rather, the admissibility of breath-alcohol analysis results remains
premised on the People's ability to demonstrate, among other
requirements, that the device was in "proper working order" when
it was used to test an accused. And nothing prevents an accused
from seeking to introduce relevant evidence that may affect other
foundational issues or the weight that should be given to results
generated by a particular device, as defendant attempted during
his trial.

15 N.Y.3d at 500, 912 N.Y.S.2d at 560 (citation omitted).

Interestingly, while the New York State Court of Appeals
increased the time period between calibrations from 6 months to
one year, *see Boscic, supra*, the New Jersey Supreme Court has
gone in the opposite direction. *See State v. Chun*, 194 N.J. 54,
153, 943 A.2d 114, 173 (N.J. 2008) ("the State shall forthwith:
. . . Commence inspection and recalibration of all Alcotest devices every six months in place of the current annual inspection
and recalibration program").

§ 42:8   Admissibility of calibration records

In *People v. Mertz*, 68 N.Y.2d 136, 147–48, 506 N.Y.S.2d 290,
296, 497 N.E.2d 657 (1986), the Court of Appeals held that:

Admission of the breathalyzer logs over objection that it had not been shown that the entries were made at the time of the acts recorded in them or within a reasonable time thereafter was also error. CPLR 4518(a) expressly requires such foundation evidence. * * *

[In addition,] admissibility under [CPLR § 4518(c)] is governed by the same standards as the general business record exception in subdivision (a). Thus, a certificate made under CPLR 4518(c) which does not set forth that the entries in the certified record were made at the time of the events they record or within a reasonable time thereafter is not admissible under that subdivision. * * *

While the scientific reliability of breathalyzers in general is no longer open to question, there must still be either proper foundation testimony under CPLR 4518(a) or a proper CPLR 4518(c) certificate to establish that the particular instrument used to test a defendant's BAC . . . had been tested within a reasonable period in relation to defendant's test and found to be properly calibrated and in working order.

(Citations omitted).

In *People v. Kinne*, 71 N.Y.2d 879, 880, 527 N.Y.S.2d 754, 755, 522 N.E.2d 1052 (1988), the Court of Appeals clarified this portion of *Mertz*:

County Court held below that the foundation evidence attesting to the proper working order of the breathalyzer was inadmissible because the attached authentication certificate was improperly dated. This conclusion was error. Where a "certification or authentication" replaces the testimony of a live witness, pursuant to CPLR 4518(c), it must state that the documents that it authenticates were produced in the normal course of business at or near the time that the act, transaction, occurrence or event recorded in those documents occurred. The authenticating certificate itself need not be dated or produced at or near the date of the act, transaction, occurrence or event.

Here, the challenged authenticating certificates properly stated that the recordation of the tests performed on the breathalyzer and simulator solution occurred at or near the time these tests were performed. The fact that the authenticating certificates were dated from 8 to 36 days after the tests were performed is irrelevant to a determination regarding the admissibility, under the business records exception to the hearsay rule, of the records of those tests. The recordation of the calibration tests on the breathalyzer occurred seven days after the tests were performed. The recordation of the simulator solution tests occurred on the same day that the tests were performed. This is sufficient to satisfy the dictates of CPLR 4518(a) and *People v. Mertz*.

(Citations omitted).

In *People v. Hernandez*, 31 Misc. 3d 208, —, 915 N.Y.S.2d 824, 825-26 (Rochester City Ct. 2011):

[T]his court was called upon to rule on the admissibility of four breath test foundational documents in separate *per se* DWI cases. One of the documents the Court had before it was essentially the same as that used in New York cases for the past thirty years. The other three documents, however, contained new language not yet validated by our courts in any reported decision. These three documents had neither a "pen & ink" signature nor a raised seal over a stamped inscription. Instead, they bore what looked like a twentieth-generation Xerox copy of a signature. Above the signature was a notation that the document was "Digitally signed under ESRA. . . ." For the reasons which follow, each of the three new documents offered by the People has been found inadmissible by the court.

(Footnote omitted).

This topic is discussed in greater detail in §§ 43:1 et seq., *infra*.

§ 42:9   Proof that chemicals used in conducting test were of proper kind and mixed in proper proportions

In order for a breath test result to be admissible at trial, the People must establish that any chemicals used in conducting the test were of the proper kind and mixed in the proper proportions. *See* § 42:3, *supra*. In the "old" days, Breathalyzer devices utilized a chemical solution which came in vacuum-sealed glass tubes. These tubes, together with the chemical solution contained therein, were commonly referred to as "ampoules." If the chemicals contained in the ampoule solution were not of the proper kind and mixed in the proper proportions, a Breathalyzer test result would not be accurate. *See generally People v. Krebs*, 195 A.D.2d 696, 600 N.Y.S.2d 317 (3d Dep't 1993); *People v. Colon*, 180 A.D.2d 876, 580 N.Y.S.2d 95 (3d Dep't 1992); *People v. Uruburu*, 169 A.D.2d 20, 571 N.Y.S.2d 965 (4th Dep't 1991).

Modern, infrared breath test machines no longer use chemicals in the way that Breathalyzers did. However, as with the old Breathalyzers, so-called "simulator tests" are still required to be run in connection with every breath test. In this regard, 10 NYCRR § 59.5(d) provides that:

The result of an analysis of a reference standard with an alcoholic content greater than or equal to 0.08 percent must agree with the reference standard value within the limits of plus or minus 0.01 percent weight per volume, or such limits as set by the commissioner. An analysis of the reference standard shall precede or follow the analysis of the breath of the subject in accordance with the test sequence established by the training agency. Readings for the reference standard, a blank and the subject's breath, shall be recorded.

The "reference standard" referred to in 10 NYCRR § 59.5(d) is commonly known as a "simulator solution." This is a solution that simulates a person with a known BAC (typically .08% or .10%), and is used as a means of verifying that a breath test device is functioning properly.

The simulator solution is placed inside an enclosed jar that is partially filled with a mixture containing a known percentage of alcohol. *See* Appendix 26. Because the jar is a closed container, a certain amount of alcohol will rise into the air above the solution until equilibrium is reached. The higher the temperature of the solution, the more alcohol will rise into the air above it. This gaseous vapor (which simulates the breath of an intoxicated person) is blown into the breath test machine via a connecting tube. When the solution is heated to 34° ± .2° Celsius (*i.e.*, the temperature of the average person's breath), the amount of alcohol in the gaseous vapor in the jar will be the amount that the solution is certified to produce. Thus, a .10% simulator solution should produce a reading of .10% when run through a properly functioning breath test device. However, pursuant to 10 NYCRR § 59.5(d), a simulator reading of .09%, .10% or .11% would indicate that the machine is working properly. In other words, breath test machines are only required to be accurate to within .01%.

The Alcotest 9510 breath test device uses a gas reference standard rather than a traditional simulator solution.

Simulator solutions are mixed in large quantities known as "lots." Each lot is numbered and has an expiration date. Samples of each lot are sent to a lab for testing (to make sure that they are of the proper kind and mixed in the proper proportions). The lab will generate a document entitled "Simulator Solution Record" or "Simulator Solution Certificate of Analysis." A copy of a simulator solution certificate of analysis is set forth at Appendix 27.

In *People v. Dembeck*, 145 Misc. 2d 442, 546 N.Y.S.2d 936 (Suffolk Co. Dist. Ct. 1989), the defendant moved to suppress his breath test result because the simulator test run in conjunction with his breath test produced a reading of .111%—which was more than .01% higher than the solution's certified reading of .10%. The Court held as follows:

> In this case the reference standard value was 0.10 percent at 34° centigrade. Therefore, in order to fall within the above quoted regulation a test of this reference by the Intoxilizer [sic] must record a result of 0.09 to 0.11 percent. The test of the reference standard in this case shows a result of .111 percent. Defendant contends that since this value exceeds the upper limit of the regulation by .001 percent, the test is unreliable as a matter of law, and hence, is inadmissible. The court does not agree. In this regard the court

notes that 10 NYCRR § 59.5(d) itself requires measurement only to the second decimal place. More importantly, 10 NYCRR § 59.5(e) specifically provides that results of breath tests are to be expressed only to the second decimal place, and that if a reading is given to the third decimal place, the third digit is to be ignored. Therefore, the calibration test in this case is properly expressed as 0.11 percent, and is within the tolerances set by the regulation.

145 Misc. 2d at __, 546 N.Y.S.2d at 937.

§ 42:10 Admissibility of simulator solution certificate of analysis

The same rules that apply to the admissibility of certificates of calibration apply to simulator solution certificates of analysis. *See* §§ 42:4 & 42:8, *supra*. *See also* §§ 43:1 et seq., *infra*.

§ 42:11 Proof that test was properly administered

The third element of a breath test foundation is proof that the test was properly administered. *See* § 42:3, *supra*. In this regard, VTL § 1194(4)(c) (formerly VTL § 1194(9)) provides as follows:

(c) Rules and regulations. The department of health shall issue and file rules and regulations approving satisfactory techniques or methods of conducting chemical analyses of a person's blood, urine, breath or saliva and to ascertain the qualifications and competence of individuals to conduct and supervise chemical analyses of a person's blood, urine, breath or saliva. *If the analyses were made by an individual possessing a permit issued by the department of health, this shall be presumptive evidence that the examination was properly given.* The provisions of this paragraph do not prohibit the introduction as evidence of an analysis made by an individual other than a person possessing a permit issued by the department of health.

(Emphasis added). A copy of a Department of Health permit is set forth at Appendix 50.

In *People v. Mertz*, 68 N.Y.2d 136, 148–49, 506 N.Y.S.2d 290, 296–97, 497 N.E.2d 657 (1986), the Court of Appeals held that:

Vehicle and Traffic Law § 1194(9) provides that proof that the chemical analysis was made by an individual possessing a permit issued by the Department of Health is "presumptive evidence" that the examination was properly given. Presumptive evidence, is, however, like the prima facie evidence to which CPLR 4518(c) refers, evidence which permits but does not require the trier of fact to find in accordance with the "presumed" fact, even though no contradictory evidence has been presented. It is, in short, not a presumption which must be rebutted but rather an inference, like the inference of negligence denominated res ipsa loquitur.

Because the jury may have understood from the charge as given that they were required to accept [the breath] tests as properly given in the absence of testimony that they were not, the effect of the instruction was to shift the burden of proof to defendant. It was, therefore, reversible error.

(Citations omitted). *See also People v. Perez*, 130 A.D.2d 779, 516 N.Y.S.2d 70 (2d Dep't 1987).

In *People v. Sawinski*, 148 A.D.2d 888, 539 N.Y.S.2d 522 (3d Dep't 1989), the defendant challenged the Court's jury charge on this issue. The Appellate Division, Third Department, held as follows:

With respect to County Court's charge that the jury was at liberty to conclude from the fact alone that the officer who administered the chemical test was certified to do so, that the test was therefore properly administered, we note that in addition to giving an instruction that judiciously parrots Vehicle and Traffic Law § 1194(4)(c), the court also charged that the People bore the burden of proof, that defendant was entitled to every favorable inference and that the jury was free to reject the credibility of any evidence, including physical evidence. The case of *People v. Mertz* is unavailing to defendant, for County Court at no point suggested that the jury was required to accept the accuracy of the chemical test in the absence of evidence that it was not properly given. In fact, in view of the extensive testimony and evidence elicited by defendant designed to impeach the accuracy of the chemical test, there was no real danger that the jury would assume that the statutory inference of a properly given test was binding.

148 A.D.2d at __, 539 N.Y.S.2d at 524 (citations omitted).

§ 42:12 Proof that breath test device is scientifically reliable and accurate

"In criminal matters the scientific reliability and accuracy of a machine measuring blood alcohol content for forensic purposes must be established before such test results may be admitted in evidence." *People v. Campbell*, 73 N.Y.2d 481, 485, 541 N.Y.S.2d 756, 758, 539 N.E.2d 584 (1989). That said, the inclusion of a particular breath test machine on the Department of Health's list of accepted breath test devices, *see* 10 NYCRR § 59.4(b) (a copy of which is set forth at Appendix 3), satisfies this requirement. *See, e.g., People v. Robinson*, 53 A.D.3d 63, 860 N.Y.S.2d 159, 165 (2d Dep't 2008) ("the Intoxilyzer, manufactured by CMI, Inc., appears on the list of approved breath-testing instruments compiled by the New York State Department of Health, and the machine is thus presumed reliable"); *People v. Hampe*, 181 A.D.2d 238, __, 585 N.Y.S.2d 861, 862–63 (3d Dep't 1992) ("the general acceptance of the reliability and accuracy of the test results of the BAC Verifier, sufficient to dispense with the foundational evidence thereof through expert testimony, was established by reason of the specific inclusion of the BAC Verifier in the list of breath-testing instruments approved by DOH in regulations promulgated pursuant to Vehicle and Traffic Law § 1194(4)(c)"); *People v. Lent*, 29 Misc. 3d 14, ___, 908 N.Y.S.2d 804, 806 (App. Term, 9th & 10th Jud. Dist. 2010), leave to appeal denied, 15 N.Y.3d 806, 908 N.Y.S.2d 166, 934 N.E.2d 900 (2010) ("the Intoxilyzer 5000 EN is one of those approved instruments. A consequence of the general acceptance in the scientific community of the reliability of the results of blood alcohol testing by such instruments is that it is no longer necessary to establish, through foundational evidence, the reliability of the test results by means of expert testimony.") (citations omitted); *People v. Cialino*, 14 Misc. 3d 999, ___, 831 N.Y.S.2d 680, 680 (N.Y. City Crim. Ct. 2007) ("This court holds that . . . the Intoxilyzer 5000 is a reliable machine, included in the Department of Health schedule, satisfying its criteria for reliability."); *People v. Seide*, 5 Misc. 3d 395, ___, 785 N.Y.S.2d 272, 273–74 (Owego Just. Ct. 2004) (inclusion of Alcotest 7110 MKIII on DOH list of approved breath test devices rendered *Frye* hearing unnecessary); *People v. Holmes*, 171 Misc. 2d 962, 656 N.Y.S.2d 130 (Brighton Just. Ct. 1997) (DataMaster on NHTSA and DOH lists of approved breath test devices; thus, no expert testimony required to establish accuracy and reliability of machine.); *People v. Testa*, 185 Misc. 2d 874, 714 N.Y.S.2d 649 (Auburn City Ct. 2000) (same).

The DOH list, which is entitled "Conforming Products List of Evidential Breath Measurement Devices," *see* 10 NYCRR § 59.4(b), merely parrots the Conforming Products List promulgated by the National Highway Traffic Safety Administration ("NHTSA"). *See* 10 NYCRR § 59.4(a). "DOH currently lists about 100 different models of breath-alcohol testing devices (including the DataMaster) that are approved for use by law enforcement agencies (*see* 10 NYCRR 59.4[b])." *People v. Boscic*, 15 N.Y.3d 494, 499 n.*, 912 N.Y.S.2d 556, 559 n.*, 938 N.E.2d 989 (2010). Breath test devices included on the DOH list allegedly have been tested by NHTSA and found to meet various criteria for accuracy and reliability. *See* 58 Fed. Reg. 48705.

As the above cases demonstrate, New York Courts have consistently relied on the inclusion of a particular breath test device on the DOH list as an adequate substitute for proof that the device actually satisfies the *Frye* standard. By contrast, the NHTSA testing does not test whether so-called "fail-safe" mechanisms allegedly contained within the breath test devices (*e.g.*, mouth-alcohol detectors, radio frequency interference detectors, breath flow monitors, etc.) perform as advertised. Accordingly, inclusion of a particular device on the DOH list does not permit lay witnesses (*e.g.*, breath test operators) to testify as to such matters without a *Frye* hearing. *See, e.g., People v. Burnet*, 25 Misc. 3d 307, 887 N.Y.S.2d 798 (Bronx Co. Sup. Ct. 2009). Notably, since the manufacturers of the devices claim that the internal workings thereof constitute proprietary information, even the police departments who use them and the prosecutors who rely on them have no idea how the devices truly work.

Indeed, in *People v. Robinson*, 53 A.D.3d 63, __-__, 860 N.Y.S.2d 159, 162–64 (2d Dep't 2008), the Appellate Division, Second Department, held that the computer source code governing the operation of an Intoxilyzer 5000EN is discoverable within the meaning of CPL § 240.20(1)(c) and (k), but nonetheless held that:

> [T]he People were not required to make available the Intoxilyzer's source code because the People never possessed it, actually or constructively. The People did not have control over the program simply because it was installed in the EPROM. The Intoxilyzer source code was not the property of the State, since it was owned and copyrighted by its manufacturer, CMI, Inc., a Kentucky corporation, and is a trade secret of CMI, Inc. * * *

> In the matter before this Court, . . . the People do not own or control any portion of the source code, and therefore . . . never possessed it. The People may thus not be compelled to disclose the source code to the defendant.

53 A.D.3d at __, __, 860 N.Y.S.2d at 167, 168 (citations omitted).

As a result, there is disturbingly little case law addressing the very real issue of whether breath test machines can truly be trusted. In this regard, while the Breathalyzer was lauded for decades as being scientifically reliable, it is now viewed as being primitive and susceptible to both operator error and manipulation by dishonest breath test operators.

§ 42:13 Necessity of expert witness testimony as to effect of "ambient air failure"

As is noted in the previous section, breath test devices included on the DOH list allegedly have been tested by NHTSA and found to meet various criteria for accuracy and reliability. However, none of the NHTSA testing tests whether so-called "fail-safe" mechanisms allegedly contained within the breath test devices (*e.g.*, mouth-alcohol detectors, radio frequency interference detectors, breath flow monitors, etc.) perform as advertised. Accordingly, inclusion of a particular device on the DOH list does not permit lay witnesses (*e.g.*, breath test operators) to testify as to such matters without a *Frye* hearing.

In *People v. Burnet*, 25 Misc. 3d 307, __, 887 N.Y.S.2d 798, 799–800 (Bronx Co. Sup. Ct. 2009), the People wanted "to adduce testimony at trial that alcohol vapors emanating from the defendant's body caused the Intoxilyzer 5000 EN to experience an ambient air failure. Because of the apparent uniqueness of the People's theory, this court ordered a hearing 'on both the scientific reliability of ambient air failure as a cause of the intoxilyzer's failure to obtain a reading and whether [the breath test operator] is qualified to testify to it.' " Following the *Frye* hearing, the Court ruled as follows:

> At the hearing, the People called one witness, IDTU Police Officer Edwards, who is affiliated with the New York City Police Department's Highway Patrol. Officer Edwards stated that he received a one-week training course in the use of the Intoxilyzer 5000 EN and during his career as an IDTU officer, he has conducted between five and six hundred chemical breath tests utilizing it. The Defendant called no witnesses. This court finds Officer Edward's testimony credible to the extent indicated herein.

> Officer Edwards testified that on June 1, 2008, he administered an Intoxilyzer 5000 EN breath test to the defendant inside the 45th Precinct. Being unable to obtain a reading, Officer Edwards stated, "ambient failure, what a shock." Officer Edwards testified that an ambient air failure occurs when the intoxilyzer detects the presence of mouth alcohol instead of a deep lung sample. He also stated that if the intoxilyzer detects the presence of alcohol in the room, it may also experience ambient air failure. Should there be ambient contamination, as was the case here, a light on the machine flashes "ambient failure." Officer Edwards then ordered the defendant to step away from the machine and directed him to the other side of the room, opened the door, turned on the fan and re-calibrated the Intoxilyzer 5000 EN. Defendant then appeared to blow into the machine but when he failed to provide a sufficient breath sample, was deemed to have constructively refused.

> *Conclusions of Law*

> As stated, the purpose for which this court ordered a hearing was clearly and unequivocally articulated in its decision of March 2, 2009, which was to determine "the scientific reliability of ambient air failure as a cause of the intoxilyzer's failure to obtain a reading and whether Officer Edwards is qualified to testify to it." Such a hearing, more colloquially referred to as a *Frye* hearing, is intended to determine whether testimony offered by an expert or other skilled witness has been deduced from a well-recognized scientific principle or discovery that it has gained such standing and scientific recognition in the field to which it belongs so as to be scientifically reliable and justified (*Frye v. United States*, 293 F. 1013 [D.C. Cir. 1923]).
> * * *

> While the People correctly state that "the scientific reliability of breathalyzers in general is no longer open to question," their novel theory that the odor of alcohol permeating from the defendant

caused the Intoxilyzer to experience an ambient air failure certainly is. So, although it is no longer necessary to require expert testimony to establish the general reliability of the machine with regards to the nature, function, or scientific principles underlying the Intoxilyzer in every case, here, such testimony is required to determine whether ambient air failure is indeed scientifically recognized and reliable as an accepted theory of an intoxilyzer's operation.

Notwithstanding the clearly stated purpose for which this court ordered a *Frye* hearing, the assistant district attorney inexplicably failed to present any testimony, scientific or otherwise, to establish the scientific reliability of an intoxilyzer's ambient air failure. Instead, he steadfastly reiterated the well-settled principle that the scientific reliability of breathalyzers in general is no longer in question. With this, neither the court nor the defendant disagreed. Obviously, that was not at issue.

Moreover, had the assistant district attorney presented sufficient expert testimony to substantiate the People's ambient air failure theory, which he did not, Officer Edwards would have been entirely incapable of offering such expert testimony . . . . The Court of Appeals has held that a witness who testifies as an expert, "should be possessed of the requisite skill, training, education, knowledge, or experience from which it can be assumed that the information imparted or the opinion rendered is reliable." Here, even though Officer Edwards was trained and qualified to operate the Intoxilyzer 5000 EN, he possessed none of the requisite skill, training, education, knowledge, or experience to testify as to the *scientific* reliability of the prosecution's theory regarding ambient air failure. Thus, while Officer Edwards was certainly competent to testify as to his utilization of the Intoxilyzer 5000 EN, he possessed absolutely no knowledge of the scientific operation of it, nor the science underlying the theory that it may experience an ambient air failure. All he could testify to is that the machine actually experienced an ambient air failure. * * *

Based upon the People's abject failure to establish the scientific reliability of the proposed ambient air failure of the Intoxilyzer 5000 EN, defendant's motion to preclude the People from adducing at trial any testimony or evidence regarding the theory that alcohol vapors caused the Intoxilyzer 5000 EN to experience an ambient air failure is granted. The People are further precluded from offering IDTU Police Officer Edwards either as an expert on, or as being skilled in, the scientific operation of the Intoxilyzer 5000 EN, or its maintenance, functionality, and causes of malfunction. The People are, of course, permitted to elicit testimony from Officer Edwards relative to his operation of the Intoxilyzer 5000 EN and administration of the breath test.

25 Misc. 3d at __-__, 887 N.Y.S.2d at 800–02 (citations and footnotes omitted).

The rationale of *Burnet* applies equally to a variety of claims commonly made by the People regarding the purported capabilities of breath test devices. Simply stated, breath test operators have no knowledge of the scientific operation or internal functioning of breath test devices, and thus cannot properly testify as to the purported internal workings of the machines (*e.g.*, "if mouth alcohol was present, the instrument would detect it and would abort the test"). As an analogy, if a critical issue in a criminal case was whether the defendant's car had skidded, it would obviously be inappropriate for the People to call a car salesman to testify that the car was equipped with anti-lock brakes and was thus incapable of skidding. Rather, such testimony would have to come from an expert witness who has actual knowledge of how anti-lock brakes work—as well as what can go wrong with them.

§ 42:14　Proof of compliance with police department's chemical test rules and regulations

VTL § 1194(2)(a) provides, in pertinent part, that:

Any person who operates a motor vehicle in this state shall be deemed to have given consent to a chemical test of one or more of the following: breath, blood, urine, or saliva, for the purpose of determining the alcoholic and/or drug content of the blood provided that such test is administered by or at the direction of a police officer with respect to a chemical test of breath, urine or saliva or, with respect to a chemical test of blood, at the direction of a police officer: * * *

(2) within two hours after a breath test, as provided in [VTL § 1194(1)(b)], indicates that alcohol has been consumed by such person and *in accordance with the rules and regulations established by the police force of which the officer is a member*.

(Emphasis added).

In response to this statute, many police departments have enacted rules and regulations pertaining to chemical testing. This raises the following issues: (1) is proof of compliance with such rules and regulations required as part of a chemical test foundation; and (2) if not, what is the significance of a failure to comply with the applicable police department rules and regulations?

The Court of Appeals resolved the first issue in *People v. Monahan*, 25 N.Y.2d 378, 306 N.Y.S.2d 453, 254 N.E.2d 758 (1969). In *Monahan*, the defendant was convicted of violating VTL § 1192(2). On appeal, County Court reversed on the ground that "the People had failed to prove by competent evidence the content of, and police compliance with[,] the police 'rules and regulations'" pursuant to VTL § 1194(1) (currently VTL § 1194(2)(a)(2)). 25 N.Y.2d at 380, 306 N.Y.S.2d at 453–54. The Court of Appeals reversed, reasoning as follows:

We have concluded that the evidence was not necessary to the People's case and, in consequence, that the reversal was in error. The intent of the statute seems to be twofold, first, to provide that the police officer, and not the accused, shall determine which of the several permitted forms of test shall be employed, and, second, to assure that the accused, whose implied consent, although revocable, is under the compulsion of the statute, will receive fair treatment in the selection and administering of the testing procedure, this pursuant to rules and regulations and not according to a police officer's *ad hoc* determination in the particular case. It follows that proof of the existent regulations is unnecessary in cases such as this, in which there is presented no substantial question with respect to the validity of the consent or the propriety of the particular form of test selected to be given. The provision for rules and regulations does not bear upon the substantive results of the test, for their reliability is determinable in accordance with medical and scientific standards generally and not according to regulations promulgated by one "police force" or another.

25 N.Y.2d at 380, 306 N.Y.S.2d at 454.

The *Monahan* Court further stated that:

In dealing with medical evidence or scientific proof generally, a foundation does, of course, have to be laid. The blood tested must be identified as that taken from defendant within the prescribed period and it must be shown that the tests were properly and accurately made, pursuant to proper and accepted scientific and technological standards. If, as here, the taking, handling and testing of the blood are items unassailably proven as to reliability, it would then appear irrelevant what the departmental rules contained or whether they were complied with. It could not well be argued that substandard regulations would qualify the report of a scientifically inadequate test or exclude proof of a test meeting otherwise recognized standards.

25 N.Y.2d at 381, 306 N.Y.S.2d at 454–55. *See also People v. Fogerty*, 18 N.Y.2d 664, 666, 273 N.Y.S.2d 343, 344, 219 N.E.2d 801 (1966) ("The failure to file, in a public office, rules governing the [taking of blood] tests does not affect the admissibility in evidence of the results of the tests if found by the court to be intrinsically accurate and reliable.").

* * * * * * * * * *

With regard to the second issue, in *People v. Williams*, 62 N.Y.2d 765, 767, 477 N.Y.S.2d 315, 316, 465 N.E.2d 1251 (1984), the Court of Appeals held that "it was error on the part of the trial court . . . to instruct the jury in effect that they could ignore the failure of the police to have administered the breathalyzer test in accordance with the rules and regulations of the Tioga County Sheriff's Department (Vehicle and Traffic Law, § 1194)."

In sum, *Monahan* makes clear that the failure of the police to follow the applicable police department rules and regulations does not affect the admissibility of the defendant's chemical test result, but *Williams* makes clear that the defense can argue that an officer's failure to follow his or her department's rules and regulations affects the weight to be afforded to such result.

Notably, in *Constantine v. Leto*, 157 A.D.2d 376, __, 557 N.Y.S.2d 611, 613 (3d Dep't 1990), order aff'd, 77 N.Y.2d 975, 571 N.Y.S.2d 906, 575 N.E.2d 392 (1991), the Court, citing *Williams*, made clear that a police agency's chemical test rules and regulations are discoverable. *Cf. Dzialak v. Hults*, 19 N.Y.2d 805, 806, 279 N.Y.S.2d 964, 226 N.E.2d 698 (1967) (rules and regulations not discoverable for purposes of DMV chemical test refusal hearing).

§ 42:15   Proof of proper pretest observation period

The Department of Health (DOH) breath test rules and regulations provide, in pertinent part, that:

> The subject shall be observed for at least 15 minutes prior to the collection of the breath sample, during which period the subject must not have ingested alcoholic beverages or other fluids, regurgitated, vomited, eaten, or smoked, or have placed anything in his/her mouth; if the subject should regurgitate, vomit, smoke or place anything in his/her mouth, an additional 15-minute waiting period shall be required.

10 NYCRR § 59.5(b). *See also People v. Todd*, 79 Misc. 2d 630, __, 360 N.Y.S.2d 754, 758–59 (Delaware Co. Ct. 1974), order rev'd on other grounds, 38 N.Y.2d 755, 381 N.Y.S.2d 50, 343 N.E.2d 767 (1975) (Court adopted the reasoning of *People v. Meikrantz*, 77 Misc. 2d 892, __, 351 N.Y.S.2d 549, 558 (Broome Co. Ct. 1974), and found that "[i]n order to conduct a fair test it is essential . . . that the subject be kept under observation . . . for at least 15 minutes prior to the test.").

The reason why an observation period is required is that if there is alcohol in the defendant's mouth (*i.e.*, "mouth alcohol")—which can be caused by recent consumption of alcohol (including mouthwash containing alcohol), as well as by burping, vomiting, etc.—the defendant's breath test result will be erroneously high. This is because the machine is designed to read the concentration of alcohol in a person's deep lung air, which is far less concentrated than mouth alcohol. Police agencies sometimes demonstrate the effects of mouth alcohol on police recruits using mouthwash and an Alco-Sensor. In this regard, a sober person who has recently consumed mouthwash containing alcohol will generate a breath test result indicating that the person is legally intoxicated. As is set forth in § 42:12, *supra*, breath test devices included on the DOH list allegedly have been tested by NHTSA and found to meet various criteria for accuracy and reliability. *See* 58 Fed. Reg. 48705. Notably, however, the NHTSA testing does not test whether so-called "fail-safe" mechanisms allegedly contained within the breath test devices—such as mouth-alcohol detectors—perform as advertised. Accordingly, inclusion of a particular device on the DOH list does not permit lay witnesses (*e.g.*, breath test operators) to testify as to such matters without a *Frye* hearing. *See, e.g., People v. Burnet*, 25 Misc. 3d 307, 887 N.Y.S.2d 798 (Bronx Co. Sup. Ct. 2009).

Notably, while the Department of Health breath test rules and regulations require an observation period of *at least* 15 minutes, most, if not all, police departments—as well as the breath test devices themselves—require a 20-minute observation period.

What is the significance of a breath test operator's failure to conduct a proper 20-minute observation period? It would seem that the correct answer to this question should be that the test result is inadmissible (on the ground that a test conducted without a proper observation period is not administered properly, *see* § 42:11, *supra*—which issue goes to admissibility and not merely to weight). 25 Misc. 3d 307, 887 N.Y.S.2d 798. *See also* § 42:3, *supra*. However, case law in New York has gone in the opposite direction.

In this regard, there is a body of case law in New York holding that "[f]ailure of the police officer conducting the test to ensure that defendant had nothing in his mouth for 20 minutes before the test was carried out goes only to the weight to be afforded the test result, not its admissibility." *People v. Terrance*, 120 A.D.2d 805, 807, 501 N.Y.S.2d 927, 929 (3d Dep't 1986). *See also People v. McDonough*, 132 A.D.2d 997, __, 518 N.Y.S.2d 524, 526 (4th Dep't 1987); *People v. Williams*, 96 A.D.2d 972, __, 466 N.Y.S.2d 869, 870–71 (3d Dep't 1983), order rev'd on other grounds, 62 N.Y.2d 765, 477 N.Y.S.2d 315, 465 N.E.2d 1251 (1984); *People v. Lent*, 29 Misc. 3d 14, __, 908 N.Y.S.2d 804, 809 (App. Term, 9th & 10th Jud. Dist. 2010), leave to appeal denied, 15 N.Y.3d 806, 908 N.Y.S.2d 166, 934 N.E.2d 900 (2010); *People v. Schuessler*, 14 Misc. 3d 30, __, 829 N.Y.S.2d 808, 809 (App. Term, 9th & 10th Jud. Dist. 2006); *People v. Lebrecht*, 13 Misc. 3d 45, __, 823 N.Y.S.2d 824, 829 (App. Term, 9th & 10th Jud. Dist. 2006). *See generally People v. Kuras*, 236 A.D.2d 873, 653 N.Y.S.2d 888 (4th Dep't 1997).

This rule has undoubtedly led to multiple erroneous DWI convictions in New York. The rule is particularly disturbing in light of the fact that New York only requires that a single breath test be conducted. By contrast, many other States require that two breath tests be conducted (and that the test results must be within .02% of each other). Such a procedure dramatically reduces the likelihood of mouth alcohol contamination.

An Illinois Supreme Court case cogently addressed the significance of a proper observation period. *See People v. Bonutti*, 212 Ill. 2d 182, 288 Ill. Dec. 131, 817 N.E.2d 489 (Ill. Supreme Ct. 2004). The *Bonutti* Court made clear that the critical issue isn't whether the officer *observed* the defendant burp, regurgitate, etc. 212 Ill.2d at 190. Rather, the critical issue is whether the defendant *in fact* did one of these things unbeknownst to the officer. 212 Ill.2d 182. Otherwise, the police could all but ignore the observation period requirement and simply claim that they didn't personally observe the types of conduct that render a breath test result unreliable.

The *Bonutti* Court further reasoned that the purpose of the observation period, and the important public policy at issue, is "to ensure that only accurate breath-alcohol tests are admitted into evidence against a criminal defendant." 212 Ill.2d 182. "The State's reading of [the pertinent administrative regulation] wholly undermines this purpose by virtually ensuring that *inaccurate* test results will be admitted." 212 Ill.2d 182. "The problem, then, is that, while the State's reading of [the pertinent administrative regulation] ensures that breath-alcohol tests are *admissible*, it does nothing to ensure that those results, once admitted, are *reliable*. And reliability, after all, is the paramount concern." 212 Ill.2d at 191. Critically, the *Bonutti* decision made clear that the 20-minute observation period requirement:

> [E]xists because regurgitation within 20 minutes of a breath-alcohol test can render a *false positive*. In other words, a lack of compliance with [the pertinent administrative regulation] has the potential to create criminals out of people who are not. This is not a "technicality," and it is not a contingency that this court will countenance.

212 Ill.2d at 192.

The Court of Criminal Appeals of Tennessee has reached a similar conclusion:

> The officer must be able to show that during the twenty-minute period, nothing happened that would affect the validity of the test. We agree that an unblinking gaze for twenty minutes is not required. However, the officer must be watching the defendant rather than performing other tasks. The state seeks to distinguish *Fields* by pointing to Officer Hostetter's testimony that the defendant did not eat, drink, smoke, vomit, or belch during the observation period. We note, though, that Officer Hostetter admitted that he was not looking at the defendant while he was writing. Despite Officer Hostetter's confidence that he would have heard or smelled any of the listed activities that he did not see, we have previously observed that while "often a belch or regurgitation will produce a noise capable of being heard by another person, this is not always the case." Officer Hostetter's belief that he would have heard or smelled anything he did not see does not satisfy the prerequisite that the defendant must be observed for twenty minutes.

State v. Korsakov, 34 S.W.3d 534, 540–41 (Tenn. Ct. of Crim. App. 2000) (citation omitted).

These cases are certainly persuasive, as New York undoubtedly has the same interest as Illinois and Tennessee in ensuring that only reliable chemical tests are considered in making decisions affecting the important rights of its citizens.

§ 42:16   Proof that operational checklist was followed

The DOH breath test rules and regulations used to require that an "operational checklist" be completed in connection with a breath test. A copy of an operational check list is set forth at Appendix 33. Such requirement has been purged from the rules. In any event, when the State Police switched from using Breathalyzers to using the Alcotest 7110 MKIII, it stopped using an operational checklist—claiming that the Alcotest literally forces the breath test operator (BTO) to go through a series of computerized, electronic checklist prompts that rendered the use of an actual operational checklist irrelevant. Courts seem to agree with this claim. *See generally People v. Gallagher*, 132 Misc. 2d 195, __, 503 N.Y.S.2d 500, 502 (Suffolk Co. Dist. Ct. 1986), adhered to, 133 Misc. 2d 717, 507 N.Y.S.2d 950 (Dist. Ct. 1986) ("the Intoxilyzer 5000 is pre-programmed and calibrated, eliminating the need for an operational checklist").

The current State Police Breath Test Rules, a copy of which is set forth at Appendix 51, require that the BTO "*Operate* the instrument by following the prompts for the electronic operational checklist that appear on the digital display." In other words, the State Police claim that the procedure that the machine forces the BTO to follow constitutes an operational checklist.

Many police departments still utilize an actual operational checklist. When the form is used, it is discoverable. *See, e.g., Constantine v. Leto*, 157 A.D.2d 376, __, 557 N.Y.S.2d 611, 613 (3d Dep't 1990), order aff'd, 77 N.Y.2d 975, 571 N.Y.S.2d 906, 575 N.E.2d 392 (1991) ("records indicating that a machine was not operating properly are discoverable, as are the State Police rules and regulations and the checklist and calibration records") (citations omitted), *aff'd for the reasons stated in the opinion below*, 77 N.Y.2d 975, 571 N.Y.S.2d 906 (1991); *People v. Robinson*, 53 A.D.3d 63, __, 860 N.Y.S.2d 159, 163 (2d Dep't 2008) (same). In addition, when an operational checklist is used the People always seek to introduce it into evidence as part of their breath test foundation (to establish that proper procedures were followed).

§ 42:17   Proof of weekly simulator testing

As with the operational checklist, *see* previous section, when

the State Police switched from using Breathalyzers to using the
Alcotest 7110 MKIII, it stopped regularly conducting so-called
weekly simulator tests. A weekly simulator test occurs when a
BTO—oftentimes a "supervisor"—runs a series of three simulated
breath tests through a breath test machine using a certified .08%
or .10% simulator solution in order to confirm that the machine
is working properly. Where they are conducted, such tests are
traditionally run once a week—which is how they got their name.
Copies of weekly simulator test records are set forth at Appendix
28.

Where such testing has been performed, the People usually
seek to introduce weekly simulator test records into evidence as
proof that the machine was properly calibrated and working
properly. *See, e.g., People v. Tilley*, 120 Misc. 2d 1040, __, 466
N.Y.S.2d 983, 987 (Erie Co. Ct. 1983); *People v. Meikrantz*, 77
Misc. 2d 892, __, 351 N.Y.S.2d 549, 559 (Broome Co. Ct. 1974).
By contrast, there is no rule that such records are required as
part of a breath test foundation.

§ 42:18   Admissibility of breath test result based upon "deficient sample"

In *People v. DeMarasse*, 85 N.Y.2d 842, 623 N.Y.S.2d 845, 647
N.E.2d 1353 (1995), the defendant submitted to two Intoxilyzer
5000 tests. "On the first test the instrument displayed no reading.
A second sample was taken and the Intoxilyzer displayed and
then printed out a reading of .217 and the words 'deficient
sample—value printed was highest obtained.' " 85 N.Y.2d at 844,
623 N.Y.S.2d at 846.

> At trial the officer administering the test and the Technical Supervi-
> sor of Central Testing testified. They explained that the Intoxilyzer
> is an instrument that measures blood alcohol as reflected by the
> alcohol content of the air exhaled from a subject's lungs by passing
> a beam of infrared light through the air sample captured in the
> device's chamber. The Intoxilyzer takes a reading every six tenths
> of a second as the subject breathes into it, thus measuring how the
> alcohol content in the sample changes with the passage of time as
> the air in the chambers comes from progressively deeper parts of
> the subject's lungs. Because the instrument measures the rate of
> change in the alcohol content, and not just the absolute amount,
> the Intoxilyzer can detect "mouth alcohol"—a sudden sharp rise in
> the alcohol content, followed by a sharp decline—and can also detect
> when the alcohol concentration reaches a level state, indicating
> that "deep lung air" is being analyzed. Deep lung air gives the most
> accurate reading because the air at the bottom of the lungs is the
> air nearest to the blood supply, and is in equilibrium with it. If
> mouth alcohol is detected, the test stops, the machine gives no
> reading, and registers "invalid sample". Similarly, if the air flow is
> insufficient or not continuous, no reading is obtained. On the other

hand, a reading is obtained on a "deficient sample". The witnesses explained that in Intoxilyzer terminology a "deficient" sample is not an invalid sample, but merely one in which the subject did not breathe for a long enough period of time to reach sufficient deep lung air to give the most accurate reading obtainable.

The technicians testified that a full sample—which includes a sufficient amount of deep lung air—will invariably give a reading that is equal to, or higher than, the reading obtained from a "deficient" sample or, conversely, the reading for a "deficient" sample will always be lower than or equal to that obtained from a full sample. In other words, any inaccuracy of result will work to the subject's benefit. Moreover, the Intoxilyzer is calibrated to give a result that is always 10% lower than the true reading. Thus, the officers testified that defendant's blood alcohol content was at least .217 on the night he was tested.

85 N.Y.2d at 844–45, 623 N.Y.S.2d at 846.

The Court of Appeals held that this testimony, combined with proof that the machine was in proper working order and that the test was properly administered, constituted a sufficient foundation for the admission of the second test result. In so holding, however, the Court of Appeals noted that the People's proof was uncontradicted. 85 N.Y.2d at 845, 623 N.Y.S.2d at 846. It is also significant that one of the People's witnesses in *DeMarasse* was the Technical Supervisor of Central Testing. In other words, the Court may have reached a different conclusion if the defense had contradicted the People's proof or if the People had relied solely on the testimony of the breath test operator.

In *People v. Nuesi*, 84 A.D.3d 1272, __, 923 N.Y.S.2d 683, 684 (2d Dep't 2011), leave to appeal denied, 17 N.Y.3d 954, 936 N.Y.S.2d 80, 959 N.E.2d 1029 (2011), the Appellate Division, Second Department, held that:

The defendant failed to preserve for appellate review his contention that the results of the Intoxilyzer test should have been suppressed because Officer Mercado lacked the basic knowledge to explain how the Intoxilyzer functioned when reading an insufficient sample. In any event, supporting documents reflected, inter alia, that field tests were performed on the Intoxilyzer before and after Officer Mercado used it on December 16, 2007, which ensured that the device was in good working order and that Officer Mercado followed a 13-step operational checklist when he administered the test to the defendant. Officer Mercado also established that the Intoxilyzer produces a result where a breath sample is "insufficient," or less than the optimal amount, which typically favors the subject and, in this case, was more than twice the permissible amount. Accordingly, contrary to the defendant's contentions, the results of the test were supported by a proper foundation.

(Citations omitted).

§ 42:19   Arresting officer can be breath test operator

In *People v. Evers*, 68 N.Y.2d 658, 659, 505 N.Y.S.2d 68, 69, 496 N.E.2d 227 (1986), the Court of Appeals held that:

Vehicle and Traffic Law § 1194(1) [currently VTL § 1194(2)(a)], which requires chemical testing of a motor vehicle operator's breath, blood, urine or saliva to be administered "at the direction of" a police officer, does not preclude the police officer who determines that testing is warranted from administering the test as well. Where the test is given by an officer trained to administer it and no unusual circumstances have been shown, corroboration of the results is not required.

§ 42:20   Necessity of breath test operator as witness

In *People v. Lin*, 46 Misc. 3d 20, __, 998 N.Y.S.2d 558, 560 (App. Term, 2d, 11th & 13th Jud. Dist. 2014), leave to appeal granted, 25 N.Y.3d 1202, 2015 WL 4876073 (2015), "[p]rior to trial, the People announced that the operator of the Intoxilyzer 5000 instrument used to measure defendant's blood alcohol content had retired out of state and was not presently available to testify, and that, in the operator's place, they would offer the testimony of another officer who was certified to operate the Intoxilyzer 5000 device and who was present at defendant's test, operating a video camera." The trial court permitted this procedure and, following a jury trial, the defendant was convicted of 2 counts of DWI.

On appeal, the Appellate Term, citing, *inter alia*, *Bullcoming v. New Mexico*, 131 S. Ct. 2705, 180 L. Ed. 2d 610 (2011), *Melendez-Diaz v. Massachusetts*, 557 U.S. 305, 129 S. Ct. 2527, 174 L. Ed. 2d 314 (2009), and *Crawford v. Washington*, 541 U.S. 36, 124 S. Ct. 1354, 158 L. Ed. 2d 177, 63 Fed. R. Evid. Serv. 1077 (2004), held that:

The substitute witness, Officer Mercado, a certified and experienced Intoxilyzer 5000 operator, testified as to defendant's condition during the requisite observation period prior to the test. He further testified that he had observed the tester proceed through the steps, from turning on the machine until a test result was produced. Although Officer Mercado did not personally operate the breathalyzer instrument, by observing the operator's actions and listening to the machine, he could determine whether it was successfully self-calibrating. He observed defendant provide three breath samples, two of which the instrument did not analyze as they were inadequate to permit accurate testing, requiring that the testing procedure be recommenced. He heard and saw nothing to indicate that the self-calibration that preceded the third breath analysis was unsuccessful, and there is no indication that Officer Mercado did not see or hear the tester's interactions with defendant in the course of the third test. Officer Mercado personally observed the machine printing the test results, and, at the trial, he identified the printout, from personal knowledge he had acquired at the time the results had been printed, as representing the results of defendant's test. However, Officer Mercado admitted that he had not observed whether the Intoxilyzer 5000 simulator temperature display indicated that the temperature during the test was within a proper range for testing. As such a determination is an essential part of the 13-step operational checklist, and the record does not indicate whether the Intoxilyzer 5000 device shuts itself down and will not perform the test if the temperature is outside the specified range, we are unable to agree that Officer Mercado satisfied the *Bullcoming* standard for the qualifications of a substitute witness, and conclude that defendant's Confrontation Clause rights were violated.

46 Misc. 3d at __, 998 N.Y.S.2d at 561-62.

§ 42:21   Inability of breath test operator to identify defendant as person tested

In *People v. Wilkins*, __ Misc. 3d __, __ N.Y.S.3d __, 2016 WL 3342667, *1 (App. Term, 9th & 10th Jud. Dist. 2016), the trial court set aside the jury's verdict convicting the defendant of Aggravated DWI:

> [O]n the ground that the police officer who had administered the test could not identify defendant as the individual he had tested. The court held that the chemical breath test results were inadmissible and granted the branch of the motion seeking to, in effect, set aside so much of the jury's verdict as found defendant guilty of aggravated driving while intoxicated and to dismiss the count of the accusatory instrument charging that offense.

On appeal, the Appellate Term held that the trial court "erred in failing to [also] set aside that portion of the verdict [convicting the defendant of common law DWI] based on the taint of the improper admission of the chemical breath test results." *Id.* at *2. *See also* § 11:10 & 37:9, *supra*.

Chapter 43

Admissibility of Documents

Research References

Westlaw Databases

Handling a Criminal Case in New York (HCCNY)

Handling Drunk Driving Cases (2d ed.) (HDRUNKDR)

Treatises and Practice Aids

Muldoon, Handling a Criminal Case in New York § 18:203

Fiandach, Handling Drunk Driving Cases §§ 34:11 to 34:11.50 (2d ed.)

Law Reviews and Other Periodicals

Simanoff, Distinctions Between the Public Records Exception to the Hearsay Rule in Federal and New York Practice, 11 Touro L. Rev. 195 (Fall, 1994)

KeyCite®: Cases and other legal materials listed in KeyCite Scope can be researched through the KeyCite service on Westlaw®. Use KeyCite to check citations for form, parallel references, prior and later history, and comprehensive citator information, including citations to other decisions and secondary materials.

---

§ 43:1 Introduction

Research References

West's Key Number Digest, Criminal Law ☞436(2), 444.9

The admissibility of documents is one of the most confusing, complicated, and contradictory areas of law confronting the trial lawyer. Whether in civil or criminal practice, we find ourselves at the bench arguing whether a document, or portions thereof, are admissible. If they are deemed admissible, we then argue as to whether they are admissible to establish the truth of what they contain or to show merely the fact that the statements contained therein were made. The purpose of this chapter is to organize the confusion into distinct parts and attempt to provide some clarification which, hopefully, will be of assistance to you in your practice.

§ 43:2 Business records—Scope of rule generally

Research References

West's Key Number Digest, Criminal Law ☞436(2), 444.9

CPLR § 4518(a) is frequently referred to as the business records rule. It states:

Any writing or record, whether in the form of an entry in a book or otherwise, made as a memorandum or record of any act, transaction, occurrence or event, shall be admissible in evidence in proof of that act, transaction, occurrence or event, if the judge finds that it was made in the regular course of any business and that it was the regular course of such business to make it, at the time of the act, transaction, occurrence or event, or within a reasonable time thereafter. All other circumstances of the making of the memorandum or record, including lack of personal knowledge by the maker, may be proved to affect its weight, but they shall not affect its admissibility. The term business includes a business, profession, occupation and calling of every kind.

All of us are familiar with the litany of a witness reciting that a record was made and kept in the normal course of business. Less familiar are the requisites for the admissibility of a document under this section. Any business or governmental agency can claim that a document is made and kept in the normal course of their business. Any entity can claim that the contents of the document are admissible because the document facially qualifies under CPLR § 4518. Close examination of the admissibility prerequisites reveals that many such records are not admissible and may be excluded from evidence if an objection is properly framed.

After the foundation is laid by opposing counsel, the document is offered in evidence and handed to you for your examination and voir dire. If you have not had an opportunity to examine the document prior to trial via pretrial discovery or otherwise, take the time to examine it carefully before commencing your voir dire of the witness. Subject the document to close scrutiny. On its face, does the document fall within the framework of CPLR § 4518? Is it a document that was made and kept in the normal course of business with which the witness is affiliated? Is the witness a proper custodian of the document? Many times the witness is neither a custodian, nor otherwise in a position to establish the authenticity of the document by testifying that it was made and kept in the normal course of business by the organization he represents.

§ 43:3 Business records—Rule applicable to criminal proceedings

Research References
West's Key Number Digest, Criminal Law ⊙436(2), 444.9

Criminal Procedure Law § 60.10 explains that the business records rule codified at CPLR § 4518 is applicable in criminal proceedings.

> Unless otherwise provided by statute or by judicially established rules of evidence applicable to criminal cases, the rules of evidence applicable to civil cases are, where appropriate, also applicable to criminal proceedings.

CPL § 60.10. *See also People v. Kennedy*, 68 N.Y.2d 569, 510

N.Y.S.2d 853 (1986); *People v. Cratsley*, 86 N.Y.2d 81, 629 N.Y.S.2d 992 (1995). *See generally* Barker & Alexander, *Evidence in New York State and Federal Courts*, § 803(3) (West 1996).

§ 43:4   Business records—The record or document must be prepared by the business or proponent offering it in evidence

Research References

West's Key Number Digest, Criminal Law ⊘436(2), 444.9

The mere filing of papers received from other entities, even if the papers are retained in the regular course of business, is insufficient to qualify the documents as business records. *See People v. Cratsley*, 86 N.Y.2d 81, 629 N.Y.S.2d 992 (1995), *citing*, Standard Textile Company, Inc. v. National Equipment Rental, Ltd., 80 A.D.2d 911, 437 N.Y.S.2d 398 (2d Dep't 1981).

Applying this principle, the Appellate Division, Third Department, in *Colonno v. Executive I Assocs.*, 228 A.D.2d 859, 644 N.Y.S.2d 105 (1996), concluded that a letter prepared by plaintiff's counsel which was received and filed by plaintiff's doctor did not constitute a business record of the doctor because it was prepared by "another business entity."

In *Cratsley*, *supra*, the Court explained the rationale for this rule.

> The reason for this rule is that "[s]uch papers simply are not made in the regular course of business of the recipient, who is in no position to provide the necessary foundation testimony as to the regularity and timeliness of their preparation or the source of information contained in the record" (Alexander, Practice Commentaries, McKinney's Cons. Laws of N.Y., Book 7, CPLR 4518:1, at 105). Nor, generally, would the recipient be aware whether the information was imparted by one under a "business duty" to report to the entrant (*see Johnson v. Lutz*, 253 N.Y. 124, 170 N.E. 517).

People v. Cratsley, 629 N.Y.S.2d at 997.

The party attempting to introduce the document must establish that it was made in the regular course of business. *See, e.g.*, *People v. Ramos*, 13 N.Y.3d 914, 914-15, 895 N.Y.S.2d 294, 294, 922 N.E.2d 880 (2010) ("The trial court erred when it admitted hearsay evidence without a proper foundation (CPLR 4518[a]). Even assuming some documents may be admitted as business records without foundation testimony, the record at issue in this case was not such a document. Nothing on its face indicates that it 'was made in the regular course of business and that it was the regular course of business to make it' ") (citation omitted). To establish such fact, the witness must be familiar with the habits and customary practices for the making of such record. An entity which merely possesses the record but did not make the record generally is not in the position to testify as to the habits and customary practices for the making of such record. Thus, the mere filing of a document received from another entity, even if it is received in the regular course of business, is insufficient to qualify the document for purposes of the Business Records Rule. *See also People v. Pierre*, 157 A.D.2d 750, 550 N.Y.S.2d 44 (2d Dep't 1990).

It is not unusual for the People to offer a document which was made by an entirely different organization from that represented by the witness. For example, in a speeding case you may be confronted with a certification of a radar tuning fork. The certification is done by a private laboratory, and the witness through whom the document is offered is a member of a police organization which is not affiliated with the company that certified the tuning fork. The police department's rules and regulations require it to keep this document, but the certification is not *made* and kept in the normal course of the department's business.

In *People v. Farrell*, 137 Misc. 2d 926, 523 N.Y.S.2d 383 (Dobbs Ferry Just. Ct. 1987), the proposition that the record must be made and kept in the normal course of the proponent agency's business was challenged. Judge Rosenberg considered the admissibility of a Bureau for Municipal Police certificate pertaining to radar. The original certificate, properly authenticated, had been sent to the Dobbs Ferry Police Department. The police department, in turn, copied the documentation provided by the Bureau for Municipal Police, and affixed its own authenticating document to the copy.

Judge Rosenberg reasoned that since the documentation was provided to the Dobbs Ferry Police Department at its request, and since the Bureau for Municipal Police was acting within the scope of its business duty, the Bureau for Municipal Police certificate and the test reports became business records of the Dobbs Ferry Police Department.

> In any event, they are "papers" of the Dobbs Ferry Police Department, which is "a department . . . of a municipal corporation" (*see* CPLR 2307). As such, these records are admissible under CPLR 4518(c) without the necessity of a preliminary showing that they are business records. . . . By virtue of CPLR 2307(b), a certified photostatic copy may be produced in place of the original. (Footnote omitted). The formalities of certification contained in CPLR 4540(b), which apply to the Reynolds Certificate as an official record, are not required by CPLR 4518(c), and therefore the Perilli Affidavit constitutes a satisfactory certification of the annexed photocopies of the Reynolds Certificate and the Test Reports.

Farrell, 523 N.Y.S.2d at 385–86 (citations omitted).

In *People v. Brown*, 128 Misc. 2d 149, 488 N.Y.S.2d 559

(Madison Co. Ct. 1985), the prosecutor attempted to introduce four test reports from the New York State Police Laboratory. The New York State Police received test results from the New York State Police Laboratory. Two reports concerned the calibration of the Breathalyzer, another was an analysis of the Breathalyzer ampoules, and the last was an analysis of the simulator solution. Each report consisted of three pages: the bottom page was the test result and the middle page was a certificate signed by the Director of the New York State Police Crime Laboratory certifying that the annexed copy of the test result was an exact copy of the original record on file in the laboratory (hereinafter "first certificate"). All of the first certificates were photocopies and none contained seals. The top page of each report was a certificate signed by a New York state trooper at the State Police barracks in Oneida, New York (hereinafter "second certificate"). The trooper certified that the copies of the laboratory tests as well as the first certificates were true and accurate, and that the signatory had been designated as the legal custodian of the document. Although the second certificates were originals, they did not contain seals. At trial, defense counsel objected to the introduction of the documents on the ground of improper certification. Initially, the Court noted:

> In the context of the certification of a public document an attestation is the assurance given by the certifier that the copy submitted is accurate and genuine as compared to the original.

488 N.Y.S.2d at 564. Here, although the state trooper's statement on the second certificate indicated that the test result was a true and accurate copy, the state trooper never compared it with the original on file in the New York State Police Laboratory in Albany.

> The touchstone of the certification of a copy of a public document is this attestation and a certification which fails to include it is meaningless. The certification should also describe the documents attested to with some degree of specificity (or incorporate them by reference) and if the signator [sic] has been deputized as the custodian of the original, the certificate should so state. In this case, the state trooper's statement on the second certificate that the test result is a true and accurate copy is a certification to the accuracy of a copy of a copy, he never having compared it with the original on file in Albany. As such, the attestation fails.

488 N.Y.S.2d at 564.

In DWI cases, an ampoule solution may be certified by a private laboratory, rather than a governmental entity. While certified records of state, local, and municipal agencies are admissible pursuant to CPLR § 4518(c), the records of a private company are not admissible unless properly qualified under CPLR § 4518(a) or pursuant to some other section. Such documents are routinely offered and admitted because of the absence of informed objection.

In *People v. Porter*, 46 A.D.2d 307, 362 N.Y.S.2d 249 (3d Dep't 1974), the defendant was involved in a head-on collision with another automobile resulting in the death of the other driver. A blood sample was extracted from the defendant, revealing a BAC of 0.21 of 1% by weight of alcohol. During the trial, the chemist who performed the test died before testifying. The People sought to introduce the records of the chemist pursuant to CPLR § 4518(c). To establish an adequate foundation for the records, the chemist's son, who had been employed in the laboratory for seven years, testified that his father had performed several hundred blood tests in the course of his business, kept a log of every test he performed, and recorded the results of the test immediately upon completion. The chemist's log book was then introduced into evidence. On appeal, the Appellate Division, Third Department, concluded that the son's testimony established an adequate foundation to qualify the log book under the business records exception to the hearsay rule pursuant to CPLR § 4518.

> The chemist's business records were admissible not only to establish that he did perform the test but also to establish the accuracy of said tests.

> In sum, while it is normally advisable, if not necessary, to produce the chemist in cases where a chemical test is arguably an important factor in a jury verdict, there must be some flexibility in the law to accommodate an unusual situation such as this where mindless adherence to rigid rules would ill serve the interests of justice.

362 N.Y.S.2d at 256 (citations omitted).

§ 43:5 Business records—It must be in the ordinary course of business of the proponent to prepare such record or document

Research References

West's Key Number Digest, Criminal Law ⟜436(2), 444.9

The fact that a particular document was prepared by a particular business does not render it a routine document made and kept in the normal course of business of that entity. In *O'Connor v. Incorporated Village of Port Jefferson*, 104 A.D.2d 861, 480 N.Y.S.2d 376 (2d Dep't 1984), an emergency ambulance report was read into evidence. This report was prepared by a member of the volunteer ambulance corps and contained a notation indicating that the plaintiff had taken three Valium and had alcohol on his breath. No testimony was offered to establish that the document was prepared in the ordinary course of business of the ambulance service. Accordingly, its admission into evidence was held to be an error. 480 N.Y.S.2d at 378.

Similarly, an alleged "certified medical report" was inadmissible under CPLR § 4518(a), where the certification of the document failed to state that it was made in the regular course of business, that it was the regular course of business to make the report, and that the report was made contemporaneously with the event recorded. *People v. Cirilo*, 191 A.D.2d 342, 596 N.Y.S.2d 7 (1st Dep't 1993). Although the trial court offered to direct the People to produce the laboratory technician who had prepared the report, the defense declined the offer. Since the technician did not testify, the report was inadmissible as a business record. 596 N.Y.S.2d at 7.

A teletype printout obtained by State Police, showing that the defendant's vehicle was the one bearing the license plate number written down by the victim, was admissible under the business records exception. *People v. Miller*, 150 A.D.2d 910, 541 N.Y.S.2d 257 (3d Dep't 1989). In *Miller*, the printout was properly authenticated by the investigating officer as a document he obtained in the regular course of police business; moreover, the police computers were directly tied into Department of Motor Vehicle computers for that very purpose.

§ 43:6 Business records—The information contained in the record must have come from a source which had an obligation to report the information

Research References

West's Key Number Digest, Criminal Law ☞436(2), 444.9

At trial, we are constantly confronted with admissible records which contain information which may be inadmissible. While the record itself may qualify pursuant to CPLR § 4518, its contents or a portion thereof may not qualify pursuant to this section. In order to be admitted for the *truth* of its contents, the source of the information must be under a business duty to report the information recorded to the person or entity making the record.

In 1930, the New York State Court of Appeals decided the foundation case of *Johnson v. Lutz*, 253 N.Y. 124 (1930). Here, the Court held that the business records statute did not permit the admission in evidence of entries which were based on voluntary hearsay statements made by third parties who were not engaged in that business, or under any duty in relation to that business. From this case, the rule has evolved that there must be an obligation on the part of the person reporting the information to convey such information to the person recording it and creating the record.

In the Matter of Leon R.R., 48 N.Y.2d 117, 421 N.Y.S.2d 863, (1979), the Court of Appeals considered a neglect proceeding arising out of the St. Lawrence County Family Court. Here, the family court had admitted the Department of Social Services' entire record pertaining to the child at issue. The record was admitted pursuant to CPLR § 4518(a) as being made and kept in the normal course of business of the St. Lawrence County Department of Social Services. In reversing both the family court and the Appellate Division, the Court of Appeals held that it was error to admit the entire case file as a business record where many of the entries consisted of statements, reports, and rumors made by persons who had no business duty to report this information to the Department of Social Services. To qualify under CPLR § 4518(a), the proponent of the record must meet a two-part test. First she must:

> [D]emonstrate that it was within the scope of the entrant's business duty to record the act, transaction or occurrence sought to be admitted.

421 N.Y.S.2d at 866. Second, the person providing the information, *i.e.*, the informant, must be:

> [U]nder a contemporaneous business duty to report the occurrence to the entrant as well.

421 N.Y.S.2d at 867. If there are any intervening parties between the person *recording* the information and the person *reporting* the information,

> Each participant in the chain producing the record, from the initial declarant to the final entrant, must be acting within the course of regular business conduct or the declaration must meet the test of some other hearsay exception.

421 N.Y.S.2d at 866–67.

In *Feinstein v. Goebel*, 144 Misc. 2d 462, 544 N.Y.S.2d 968 (Queens Co. Sup. Ct. 1989), at issue was the admissibility of a hospital record in which there were recorded statements made by the patient's son to a resident doctor. The court found that the son had a "duty" to provide information to the doctor regarding the circumstances surrounding the automobile accident.

> His mother was in an agitated and excited state; his father was semi-conscious and on the verge of possible death from excessive internal bleeding. What person under these circumstances would not have a filial duty?

544 N.Y.S.2d at 970.

In *Eggleston v. Richardson*, 88 A.D.2d 750, 451 N.Y.S.2d 470 (4th Dep't 1982), the Appellate Division held that it was error to admit a memorandum made by a case worker under the business records exception where the memorandum related to a conversation had with a parent. The court held that the parent was under no business duty to report the recorded information to the case worker. 451 N.Y.S.2d at 470.

Similarly, the Appellate Division reversed a defense verdict where an accident report was admitted into evidence. *Casey v. Tierno*, 127 A.D.2d 727, 512 N.Y.S.2d 123 (2d Dep't 1987). Here the report contained self-serving statements made by the defendant, and conclusions of the officer adverse to the interests of the plaintiff, which were derived from the defendant's statements. The Court reversed because of the admission of the self-serving hearsay statements, which were made by the defendant, who was under no business duty to report the accident to the police. In addition, the Court observed that the police officer's opinion should not have been admitted absent a foundation establishing his qualifications to conduct a postincident analysis of the physical evidence of the accident. 512 N.Y.S.2d at 124–25.

It is interesting to note that even the unsworn comments of a prosecutor in open court are admissible under CPLR § 4518, where the stenographer, who recorded the comments, and the declarant, who was the prosecutor, were both acting under a business duty. In *Kearney v. City of New York*, 144 Misc. 2d 201, 543 N.Y.S.2d 879 (Kings Co. Sup. Ct. 1989), the court stenographer was under a statutory duty, pursuant to Judiciary Law §§ 290 and 295, to take full stenographic notes of the proceedings of the court. The prosecutor had a duty to disclose evidence favorable to the defendant pursuant to the *Brady* Rule. Therefore, the district attorney's unsworn statements made in open court were held to be admissible as a business record. 543 N.Y.S.2d at 880–81.

§ 43:7 Business records—Record may be admissible to prove only that statement was made

Research References

West's Key Number Digest, Criminal Law ☞436(2), 444.9

While the information contained in a record may not qualify to prove the *truth* of the information contained therein, it may be admitted to establish the *fact that the statement was made*. In *Hayes v. State*, 50 A.D.2d 693, 376 N.Y.S.2d 647 (3d Dep't 1975), order *aff'd* 40 N.Y.2d 1044, 392 N.Y.S.2d 282 (1976), the Court of Appeals affirmed the Appellate Division's reversal and dismissal of a court of claims' judgment in favor of a patient-plaintiff who claimed to have been assaulted by a hospital employee. Here, neither the hospital employee nor the patient-plaintiff testified.

The only evidence that was introduced to prove the alleged assault by the employee upon the patient were hospital and personnel records, which contained hearsay information. Over objection, the trial court received the information contained in these records as proof of the facts of the alleged assault on the grounds that the entries in the record:

> [W]ere the only truly accurate reflection of the events in question, and that they were records kept in the regular course of business.

376 N.Y.S.2d at 648.

In reversing the trial court, the Appellate Division noted that the person reporting the information in regard to the assault was not under a business duty to do so and, therefore, the record was inadmissible to prove the occurrence of the assault. This was true despite the fact that the person who recorded the information *was* under a business duty to obtain and make such a record. Absent some other exception to the hearsay rule, the statements recorded in the record were admissible *merely* to establish the fact that these statements were made.

In *Toll v. State*, 32 A.D.2d 47, 299 N.Y.S.2d 589 (3d Dep't 1969), Judge Cooke explained the law applicable in these circumstances. Here, a New York State trooper investigated, *but did not witness*, an accident involving a state snow plow and a motorist. The trooper's report contained facts, but did not indicate where or from whom the trooper obtained the facts. It also contained conclusions that the trooper drew from those facts.

While the police report was made and kept in the normal course of business of the New York State Police, the entrant (*i.e.*, the trooper) was not a witness to the facts recorded. The person who provided the entrant with the facts of the accident was neither identified nor shown to be under a business duty to relate those facts to the entrant. The court held that where the entrant is not the witness to the facts recorded, and the person giving the entrant the information is *not* under a business duty to relate the facts to the entrant, the record may be admitted *only* to prove that the statement recorded therein was made by the person who reported the facts. *See* 299 N.Y.S.2d at 592. *See also Murray v. Donlan*, 77 A.D.2d 337, 433 N.Y.S.2d 184, 187–90 (2d Dep't 1980).

Insofar as the conclusions drawn by the trooper from the facts which were provided by the unknown source, Judge Cooke observed that the trooper would not have been allowed to testify to such conclusions without establishing the validity of the premises upon which the conclusions were drawn. Accordingly, the written conclusions of the trooper should have been excluded even if the report had been, otherwise, acceptable.

The business entry statute lifts the barrier of the hearsay objection;

it does not overcome any other exclusionary rule which might properly be invoked.

299 N.Y.S.2d at 592 (citations omitted).

The court pointed out, however, that the analysis should not stop there. The statement may still be admitted as proof of the truth of its contents if it qualifies on the basis of another hearsay exception. As an example, Judge Cooke cited *Chemical Leaman Tank Lines, Inc. v. Stevens*, 21 A.D.2d 556, 251 N.Y.S.2d 240 (3d Dep't 1964), where a statement contained in a police report was admitted into evidence as an admission of a defendant driver. 299 N.Y.S.2d at 591.

Practitioners should also be aware of the "recent fabrication rule" *i.e.,*—an otherwise inadmissible statement may be admitted to rebut an inference raised by counsel that a witness' testimony was a recent fabrication. The recent fabrication rule is a dangerous trap for the unwary. It opens the door for the admission of otherwise incompetent, and frequently prejudicial, evidence.

§ 43:8 Business records—Timeliness of record

Research References

West's Key Number Digest, Criminal Law ☞436(2), 444.9

CPLR § 4518(a) requires that the record at issue be made "at the time of the act, transaction, occurrence or event, or within a reasonable time thereafter." Although expressly stated, this requirement is frequently overlooked. The Court of Appeals has held that it is reversible error to admit Breathalyzer test records into evidence where there is no showing that the entries in those records were made at the time of the acts recorded or within a reasonable time thereafter. *People v. Mertz*, 68 N.Y.2d 136, 506 N.Y.S.2d 290 (1986). In *Mertz*, documents had been admitted pursuant to CPLR § 4518(c). In reversing, the Court of Appeals made it clear that the admissibility under CPLR § 4518(c):

[I]s governed by the same standards as the general business record exception in subdivision (a). Thus, a certificate made under CPLR 4518(c) which does not set forth that the entries in the certified record were made at the time of the events they record or within a reasonable time thereafter is not admissible under that subdivision.

506 N.Y.S.2d at 296.

In *People v. Kinne*, 71 N.Y.2d 879, 527 N.Y.S.2d 754 (1988), the Court of Appeals held that recording the results of a calibration test seven days after its occurrence is sufficient to meet the dictates of CPLR § 4518(a).

In *O'Connor v. Incorporated Village of Port Jefferson*, 104 A.D.2d 861, 480 N.Y.S.2d 376 (2d Dep't 1984), the verdict for the defendant was reversed and a new trial ordered where the trial court had admitted a hospital discharge record containing a prejudicial statement made by the plaintiff's girlfriend. The essence of the statement was that the plaintiff-patient was at fault for the occurrence of his injury. The discharge summary containing this statement was prepared some eight months after the occurrence of the injury. The summary reported the girlfriend's statement as having been made to a member of the hospital staff. The Court found that the fact that the statement was made and recorded eight months after the accident rendered it untimely and inadmissible. 480 N.Y.S.2d at 378.

The determination of timeliness thus depends upon the circumstances presented in each individual case. The statute speaks to the information being recorded at the time of the event or "within a reasonable time thereafter." The issue is not so much the number of hours or days that have passed since the occurrence of the event, rather the effect of the passage of time on the memory and, therefore, the accuracy of the person reporting the facts recorded. In *Toll v. State*, 32 A.D.2d 47, 299 N.Y.S.2d 589 (3d Dep't 1969), the Court admitted the accident report of a truck driver which had been made 15 days after the occurrence of the accident. In doing so, the Court stated:

> The statutory requirement that the business record be prepared within a reasonable time after the occurrence, *i.e.*, while the memory of the event was still fresh enough to be fairly reliable, should not be too rigidly applied and did not prevent the introduction of the accident report of the truck driver.

299 N.Y.S.2d at 592 (citations omitted). *See also People ex rel. McGee v. Walters*, 62 N.Y.2d 317, 476 N.Y.S.2d 803 (1984) (report of violation of parole prepared some months after occurrence of alleged violation deemed admissible because of continuing nature of violations); *Standard Textile Co., Inc. v. National Equipment Rental, Ltd.*, 80 A.D.2d 911, 437 N.Y.S.2d 398 (2d Dep't 1981) (letter dated eight months after the event referred to not deemed made within reasonable time).

Where a business routinely copies original records into more permanent form, and then destroys the original, the copy may be made at any time required by the routine of the business, since memory is not being relied upon, vitiating the need for contemporaneous entry. *See People v. Klein*, 105 A.D.2d 805, 481 N.Y.S.2d 743 (2d Dep't), order *aff'd*, 65 N.Y.2d 613, 491 N.Y.S.2d 155 (1985) (entries made in regular course of business in loan and exchange records of Yeshiva admissible where entries were based upon information copied from stolen cash receipt and cash disbursement books).

§ 43:9 Business records—Whether the information contained in the record is relevant to the business of the entity recording the information

Research References

West's Key Number Digest, Criminal Law ☞436(2), 444.9

In examining a record to determine whether it falls within CPLR § 4518(a), you have to look beyond its source and nature and examine its content. While the record may be admissible, its content may be excluded if it is not relevant to the business of the entity recording the information.

Satisfaction of this prerequisite for the admission of information contained in a business record is, perhaps, one of the most difficult to determine. CPLR § 4518(a) requires a judge to determine whether the information contained in the record was made in the regular course of the record keeper's business and whether it was the regular course of that business to record this information.

While it is certainly the business of an emergency room to fill out an emergency room record, the fact that a patient's coat smelled of an alcoholic beverage may or may not be pertinent to the business of the emergency room. If the patient is conscious and is being treated for a broken ankle sustained in an automobile accident, such information would probably not be admitted because it does not relate to the diagnosis and treatment of the patient which is the business of the emergency room.

If the patient is unconscious and this observation was recorded, the statement might be admitted because it relates to diagnosis and treatment in that consumption of alcohol can be a cause or contributing factor to a person being unconscious. Obviously, we are entering the realm of fine distinctions which may be of critical importance to your case.

For example, in *O'Connor v. Incorporated Village of Port Jefferson*, 104 A.D.2d 861, 480 N.Y.S.2d 376 (2d Dep't 1984), the plaintiff-patient's girlfriend made the following statement to the hospital at the time of the plaintiff-patient's discharge:

> The patient, according to his girlfriend Maureen Henderson, said that they were on the beach, whereupon he had a six-pack of beer and four 10 milligram Valium tablets, and following this went over to the life guard stand while the life guards were patrolling the beach and, against his friends advice, moved the life guard stand to the edge of the water at the beach and climbed up on the life guard stand and dove into shallow water at the edge of a lagoon on the Long Island Sound Beach at Port Jefferson.

480 N.Y.S.2d at 377–78. Aside from the other issues already discussed in regard to the admissibility of the girlfriend's state-

ment, do the contents of this statement relate to the diagnosis or treatment of the plaintiff-patient's condition? While it might be argued that the statement as to the consumption of beer and Valium could be relevant to diagnosis and treatment at the time of the plaintiff-patient's admission, it clearly has no relevance to the diagnosis and treatment of the patient insofar as a discharge summary is concerned.

In *Gunn v. New York*, 104 A.D.2d 848, 480 N.Y.S.2d 365 (2d Dep't 1984), the plaintiff brought a suit against the city and transit company based upon an injury she sustained when she stepped off a bus and slipped on a patch of ice which had formed in a hole in the roadway. She sued the city based on its failure to maintain the roadway, and the transit authority because the bus stopped at an unsafe place for her to exit. The Second Department reversed the verdict for the defendants and ordered a new trial on the ground that the trial court had improperly admitted a medical history form which had been filled out at the hospital to which the plaintiff had been taken. 480 N.Y.S.2d at 366.

In the history of present illness portion of the medical history, an entry appeared which indicated that the plaintiff had been walking down the street, slipped on ice, and twisted her ankle. In reversing the defense verdict, the Court stated:

> We find that it was reversible error for the trial court to admit the history portion of plaintiff's medical record into evidence. It was offered to prove the truth of the facts asserted. The entry was not admissible as a business record under CPLR 4518 because it was not germane to plaintiff's diagnosis or treatment.

480 N.Y.S.2d at 367.

The Court further held that this portion of the record was not admissible as an admission because the person who recorded it did not recall whether the information had been reported to him by the plaintiff-patient or someone else. 480 N.Y.S.2d at 367.

Reaching a different result in *People v. Conde*, 16 A.D.2d 327, 228 N.Y.S.2d 69 (3d Dep't 1962), judgment *aff'd*, 13 N.Y.2d 939, 244 N.Y.S.2d 314 (1963), the Third Department admitted a medical report containing a statement by a manslaughter victim asserting that her injury arose from falling from a ladder. In affirming the admission of this record and statement, the Court noted the testimony of the surgeon "that the history of trauma aided his preoperative diagnosis." 228 N.Y.S.2d at 71. *See also People v. Davis*, 95 A.D.2d 837, 463 N.Y.S.2d 876 (2d Dep't 1983) (affirming admission of medical report containing diagnosis "gunshot wound of chest and left upper arm").

However, the admission of a statement contained in a medical report dealing with whether burns had been sustained as a result of an explosion of natural gas or of gasoline vapors was held to be error where such determination was not relevant to diagnosis or treatment of the burns. Such information could not be regarded as having been given in the regular course of business. *Levine v. Shell Oil Company*, 35 A.D.2d 575, 313 N.Y.S.2d 581 (2d Dep't 1970), order modified on other grounds, 28 N.Y.2d 205, 321 N.Y.S.2d 81, 269 N.E.2d 799 (1971). *See also Edelman v. New York*, 81 A.D.2d 904, 435 N.Y.S.2d 603 (1981).

§ 43:10   Business records—Physicians' opinions and hospital records must also be relevant to diagnosis and treatment

Research References

West's Key Number Digest, Criminal Law ☞436(2), 444.9

Physicians' opinions and entries in hospital records are inadmissible if not related to and necessary for a patient's admission or treatment in the hospital. In *Williams v. Alexander*, 309 N.Y. 283 (1955), the Court of Appeals held that it was error for the trial court to admit a statement made by the patient to a hospital physician after the accident. The statement, which described his version of how the accident happened, did not bear upon diagnosis and could not be regarded as having been made in the regular course of hospital business. Judge Fuld reasoned:

> [T]he essential "Guarantee of Trustworthiness" rests upon the fact that "the physicians and nurses . . . themselves rely upon the record" and that the record is designed to be "relied upon in affairs of life and death." Such reasoning, however, will not support the use, or justify the receipt, of a statement detailing the circumstances of the accident where they are immaterial to, and were never intended to be relied upon in, the treatment of the patient. There is no need in that case for the physician to exercise care in obtaining or recording the information or to question the version, whatever it might be, that is given to him. The particulars may be a natural subject of the doctor's curiosity, but neither the inquiry nor the response properly belongs in a record designed to reflect the regular course of the hospital's business.

Williams, 309 N.Y. at 288 (citations omitted). *See also Passino v. DeRosa*, 199 A.D.2d 1017, 606 N.Y.S.2d 107 (4th Dep't 1993) (error to admit portion of plaintiff's medical history recounting her statements as to cause of her injuries, since information not relevant to diagnosis or treatment; statements contradicted plaintiff's trial testimony); *People v. Jackson*, 124 A.D.2d 975, 509 N.Y.S.2d 230 (4th Dep't 1986) (history portion of hospital record as it related to acts and occurrences not relevant to diagnosis or treatment of patient were inadmissible; record included victim's detailed report of incident which improperly bolstered her trial testimony).

In *Boucheron v. Tilley*, 87 A.D.2d 983, 450 N.Y.S.2d 110 (4th Dep't 1982), the plaintiff's malpractice action was predicated upon his having taken a prescription drug resulting in injury to him. The hospital records contained gratuitous opinions by physicians concerning whether the patient's condition was caused by the ingestion of the drug at issue. The Court upheld the lower court's denial of the admission of these opinions on the ground that they were neither necessary for diagnosis nor treatment. 450 N.Y.S.2d at 111.

In *People v. Johnson*, 70 A.D.3d 1188, 896 N.Y.S.2d 199 (3d Dep't 2010), the Appellate Division, Third Department, reversed the defendant's DWI conviction and granted him a new trial where the trial court admitted:

> [D]efendant's emergency room medical records [into evidence] without redacting two notations in the treating physician's report that defendant was intoxicated. Under the facts and circumstances of this case, since the People failed to demonstrate that the question of whether defendant was intoxicated was relevant or germane to the medical diagnosis or treatment of his broken clavicle, the reference to intoxication in the medical records was not admissible pursuant to the business records exception to the hearsay rule. Furthermore, inasmuch as defendant's intoxication was the very issue to be decided by the jury, it cannot be said that the admission of the unredacted record was harmless.

70 A.D.3d at _, 896 N.Y.S.2d at 203 (citations omitted).

Where the opinion or medical history is, however, relevant to diagnosis and treatment, it is admissible to the same extent as if the physician or expert were on the stand. In *People v. Kohlmeyer*, 284 N.Y. 366 (1940), the Court of Appeals upheld the admission of the recorded opinion of a physician in regard to a patient's mental condition.

In *People v. Richardson*, 38 A.D.2d 990, 329 N.Y.S.2d 425 (3d Dep't 1972), the Third Department affirmed the trial court's admission of a medical report containing a diagnosis of a gunshot wound to the right arm, abdomen, and liver. Here, the report was offered by the People as proof of the infliction of serious physical injury in support of a charge of assault in the second degree. *See also Feinstein v. Goebel*, 144 Misc. 2d 462, 544 N.Y.S.2d 968 (Queens Co. Sup. Ct. 1989) (even triple hearsay in hospital record deemed admissible where important to diagnosis).

§ 43:11 Public documents—Scope of rule generally

Research References
West's Key Number Digest, Criminal Law ☞436(2), 444.9

Public documents are admissible pursuant to CPLR § 4520,

under the common law exception, or pursuant to CPLR § 4518(a) or (c). While most records that are admissible pursuant to CPLR § 4520 are also admissible pursuant to CPLR § 4518(a), records admitted pursuant to the business records rule are merely evidence of the fact which they purport to establish. If the record is admitted pursuant to CPLR § 4520 or CPLR § 4518(c), it constitutes prima facie evidence requiring the opposing party against whom the evidence is introduced to come forward with evidence to rebut the presumption arising out of this section.

> Where a public officer is required or authorized, by special provision of law, to make a certificate or an affidavit to a fact ascertained, or an act performed, by him in the course of his official duty, and to file or deposit it in a public office of the state, the certificate or affidavit so filed or deposited is prima facie evidence of the facts stated.

CPLR § 4520.

The admissibility of public documents is based upon the presumption that public officials have no motive to distort the truth in regard to writings made in discharge of their public duties. In addition, requiring the public official to testify constitutes a public inconvenience which might "prove detrimental to efficient public administration." Richardson on Evidence, p. 308 (Prince 11th ed. 1995). Both *Richardson* and the McKinney's Commentaries to CPLR § 4520 point out that the existence of the statute does not preclude a foundation being laid pursuant to the common law which is broader than the statutory provision.

The types of documents that are admissible under this rule are listed in *Richardson on Evidence*. They include such things as:

(a) return of votes made by election inspectors;
(b) report of official toxicologist;
(c) school records admitted on issue of age;
(d) reports of treasurer and reports of department of audit and control; and
(e) weather reports of United States Signal Service. Richardson on Evidence at p.690.

In addition to such documents, other sections of the CPLR provide for the admission of specific documents such as an original certificate of marriage as prima facie evidence of that marriage (CPLR § 4526), a report of the United States Weather Bureau as prima facie evidence of the facts stated (CPLR § 4528), inspection certificates issued by the United States Department of Agriculture on file with the United States Secretary of Agriculture as prima facie evidence of the facts stated (CPLR § 4529).

Insofar as birth and death certificates are concerned, section 4103(3) of the Public Health Law states:

> A certified copy of the record of a birth or death, a certificate of

birth or death, a transcript of a birth or death certificate, a certificate of birth data or certificate of registration of birth, when properly certified by the commissioner or persons authorized to act for him, shall be prima facie evidence in all courts and places of the facts therein stated.

§ 43:12 Public documents—Cause of death

Research References

West's Key Number Digest, Criminal Law ☞436(2), 444.9

While a death certificate and an autopsy report are clearly admissible as public documents, controversy has arisen over the effect of a statement or cause of death contained within such a certificate. In *People v. Hampton*, 38 A.D.2d 772, 327 N.Y.S.2d 961 (3d Dep't 1972), the Appellate Division considered the appeal of a mother who had been convicted of the manslaughter of her daughter. In addition to evidence consisting of photographs of various scars and marks on the deceased child's body, an autopsy report was admitted which stated that death was caused by traumatic shock and battered child syndrome.

In affirming the conviction, the Court held the admission of this opinion contained in the autopsy report to be error. However, because of the other evidence contained in the case, the error was deemed to be harmless. In the Practice Commentaries, Joseph McLaughlin criticizes the Appellate Division's opinion in this regard holding that had the autopsy report been offered as a business record, the opinions contained therein would have been admissible. In *Duffy v. 42nd St. M. & S. N. Av. Ry.*, 266 App. Div. 865, 42 N.Y.S.2d 534 (2d Dep't 1943), the Court held that it was error to limit the evidentiary effect of a death certificate to the time and place of death and exclude from consideration by the jury that portion of the report showing the cause of death.

In line with such reasoning, the Court of Appeals affirmed the reversal of the trial court's refusal to admit the history portion of an autopsy report. *People v. Morris*, 42 A.D.2d 968, 347 N.Y.S.2d 975 (2d Dep't 1973), order *aff'd*, 36 N.Y.2d 877, 372 N.Y.S.2d 210 (1975). *See also People v. Shanis*, 36 N.Y.2d 697, 366 N.Y.S.2d 413, 325 N.E.2d 873 (1975) (error to deny admission of autopsy report on issue of cause of death).

§ 43:13 Public documents—Certified records

Research References

West's Key Number Digest, Criminal Law ☞436(2), 444.9

CPLR § 4518(c) has become the primary means by which the prosecution introduces documentary evidence in regard to scientific tests, hospital records, and materials pertaining to state or local governments. The section is an extension of CPLR § 4518(a) with two key distinctions: 1) documents can be admitted without the necessity of a witness to provide authentication and 2) the prima facie effect of the contents once the document is received.

CPLR § 4518(c) states in pertinent part:

All records, writings and other things referred to in sections 2306 and 2307 are admissible in evidence under this rule and are prima facie evidence of the facts contained, provided they bear a certification or authentication by the head of the hospital, laboratory, department or bureau of a municipal corporation or of the state, or by an employee delegated for that purpose or by a qualified physician. Where a hospital record is in the custody of a warehouse, or "warehouseman" as that term is defined by paragraph (h) of subdivision one of section 7-102 of the uniform commercial code, pursuant to a plan approved in writing by the state commissioner of health, admissibility under this subdivision may be established by a certification made by the manager of the warehouse that sets forth (i) the authority by which the record is held, including but not limited to a court order, order of the commissioner, or order or resolution of the governing body or official of the hospital, and (ii) that the record has been in the exclusive custody of such warehouse or warehousemen since its receipt from the hospital or, if another has had access to it, the name and address of such person and the date on which and the circumstances under which such access was had. Any warehouseman providing a certification as required by this subdivision shall have no liability for acts or omissions relating thereto, except for intentional misconduct, and the warehouseman is authorized to assess and collect a reasonable charge for providing the certification described by this subdivision.

§ 43:14 Public documents—Certified records—Subpoena required?

Research References

West's Key Number Digest, Criminal Law ☞436(2), 444.9

CPLR § 2306 refers to medical records, and CPLR § 2307 pertains to the books, papers, and other things of a library, department, or bureau of a municipal corporation or of the state. Both of these sections refer to the records being produced pursuant to a subpoena duces tecum.

In *Joyce v. Kowalcewski*, 80 A.D.2d 27, 437 N.Y.S.2d 809 (4th Dep't 1981), the trial court sustained an objection to the admission of hospital records on the ground they had not been produced pursuant to a subpoena duces tecum. In reversing the trial court, the Appellate Division cited Professor McLaughlin and held that proper authentication by the custodian of the medical records was all that was required to admit them pursuant to CPLR § 4518(c).

Reaching a contrary result, the Monroe County Court reversed a driving while revoked conviction on the ground that the affidavit of regularity demonstrating the mailing of defendant's notice of revocation was not admissible, and, accordingly, his conviction could not stand. *People v. D'Agostino*, 120 Misc. 2d 437, 465 N.Y.S.2d 834 (Monroe Co. 1983). Judge Mark cited several reasons why the document could not be admitted. Among these was the fact of its not having been produced pursuant to subpoena. *See* 465 N.Y.S.2d at 383. *See also People v. Hoats*, 102 Misc. 2d 1004, 425 N.Y.S.2d 497 (Monroe Co. 1980).

§ 43:15 Public documents—Certified records—Other requirements

Research References

West's Key Number Digest, Criminal Law ⌖436(2), 444.9

While CPLR § 4518(c) is generally viewed as being easier to implement than CPLR § 4520, the provisions of the section must be strictly complied with. For example, CPLR § 2306 addresses itself to transcripts or reproductions of the hospital record, not the originals which are admissible under CPLR § 4518(a). One of the most common errors made by the prosecution introducing certified documents pursuant to CPLR § 4518(c) is to offer a copy of the authenticating certification, rather than an original certification. In essence, they attempt to meet the requirements of the statute by having a copy certify a copy. This is clearly improper and should be objected to.

While CPLR § 4518(c) allows the introduction of certified documents without an authenticating witness, these records are not exempt from the other requirements of CPLR § 4518(a). For example, the document must reflect its source as well as the fact that it was made and kept in the regular course of business of the entity from which it came. *People v. Gower*, 42 N.Y.2d 117, 397 N.Y.S.2d 368 (1977). In *People v. Farrell*, 58 N.Y.2d 637, 458 N.Y.S.2d 514 (1982), the Court of Appeals upheld the admissibility of a certificate of analysis of Breathalyzer ampoules on the ground that a proper CPLR § 4518(a) foundation was laid, and that the record indicated the date the analysis was performed, the individuals who conducted the tests, the materials that were analyzed, and the results that the tests disclosed. *See also People v. Dailey*, 260 A.D.2d 81, __, 700 N.Y.S.2d 307, 309 (4th Dep't 1999).

The most recent pronouncement by the Court of Appeals in this regard is set forth in *People v. Mertz*, 68 N.Y.2d 136, 506 N.Y.S.2d 290 (1986), in which the Court reiterated the applicability of the requirements of CPLR § 4518(a) to documents admitted pursuant to CPLR § 4518(c).

§ 43:16   Public documents—Certified records—Grand jury and preliminary hearing exceptions

Research References

West's Key Number Digest, Criminal Law ⟅436(2), 444.9

Although CPL § 60.10 renders the rules of evidence applicable to civil cases applicable to criminal cases, CPL § 190.30 and CPL § 180.60 statutorily substitute a different standard for the admissibility of certain reports in grand jury proceedings and in preliminary hearings. Specifically, CPL § 190.30(2) states:

> A report or a copy of a report made by a public servant or by a person employed by a public servant or agency who is a physicist, chemist, coroner or medical examiner, firearms identification expert, examiner of questioned documents, fingerprint technician, or an expert or a technician in some comparable scientific or professional field, concerning the results of an examination, comparison or test performed by him in connection with a case which is the subject of a grand jury proceeding, may, when certified by such person as a report made by him or as a true copy thereof, be received in such grand jury proceeding as evidence of the facts stated therein.

CPL § 190.30(3) states:

> A written or oral statement, under oath, by a person attesting to one or more of the following matters may be received in such grand jury proceeding as evidence of the facts stated therein:
>
> (a) that person's ownership or lawful custody of, or license to occupy, premises, as defined in section 140.00 of the penal law, and of the defendant's lack of license or privilege to enter or remain thereupon;
>
> (b) that person's ownership of, or possessory right in, property, the nature and monetary amount of any damage thereto and the defendant's lack of right to damage or tamper with the property;
>
> (c) that person's ownership or lawful custody of, or license to possess property, as defined in section 155.00 of the penal law, including an automobile or other vehicle, its value and the defendant's lack of superior or equal right to possession thereof;
>
> (d) that person's ownership of a vehicle and the absence of his consent to the defendant's taking, operating, exercising control over or using it;
>
> (e) that person's qualifications as a dealer or other expert in appraising or evaluating a particular type of property, his expert opinion as to the value of a certain item or items of property of that type, and the basis for his opinion;

(f) that person's identity as an ostensible maker, drafter, drawer, endorser or other signator of a written instrument and of its falsity within the meaning of section 170.00 of the penal law.

Provided, however, that no such statement shall be admitted when an adversarial examination of such person has been previously ordered pursuant to subdivision 8 of section 180.60, unless a transcript of such examination is admitted.

Similarly, in relation to a preliminary hearing upon felony complaint, CPL § 180.60(8) states:

Upon such a hearing, only non-hearsay evidence is admissible to demonstrate reasonable cause to believe that the defendant committed a felony; except that reports of experts and technicians in professional and scientific fields and sworn statements of the kinds specified in subdivisions two and three of section 190.30 are admissible to the same extent as in a grand jury proceeding, unless the court determines, upon application of the defendant, that such hearsay evidence is, under the particular circumstances of the case, not sufficiently reliable, in which case the court shall require that the witness testify in person and be subject to cross-examination.

In Matter of Rodney J., 83 N.Y.2d 503, 611 N.Y.S.2d 485 (1994), the respondent, a juvenile, was charged with criminal possession of a weapon. Attached to the juvenile delinquency petition was a police laboratory analysis report which stated that the "gun and ammo tested are operable." The report was signed by a Detective Robert Cotter, identified as a "chemist/technician," and contained the following certification:

I hereby certify that the foregoing report is a true and full copy of the original report. False statements made herein are punishable as a Class "A" Misdemeanor pursuant to section 210.45 of the Penal Law.

611 N.Y.S.2d at 486. The respondent moved to dismiss the petition as jurisdictionally defective pursuant to Family Court Act § 311.2, which requires the petition to contain nonhearsay allegations establishing every element of the crime charged. The family court denied the motion after having received assurances from the presentment agency that Detective Cotter was, in fact, the person who had prepared the report. The Appellate Division reversed and dismissed the petition, finding that the accusatory instrument was facially deficient since they lacked a nonhearsay allegation that the weapon was operable. 611 N.Y.S.2d at 486.

The Court of Appeals noted the importance of the juvenile delinquency petition in view of the fact that there is no independent grand jury to review the evidence in a juvenile delinquency proceeding. Justice Levine, writing for the Court, concluded:

The annexed ballistics report, although attesting to the gun's operability, purports only to be a copy of the original report, and gives
no indication that it was signed by the person who tested the gun
and prepared the original report. Although the signature of Detective Cotter appears on the report, he only certified that the report
is an accurate copy of the original report, and did not actually attest to any personal knowledge of the gun's operability. However
likely it may be, as the presentment agency argues, that Detective
Cotter was the technician who tested the gun and prepared the
original report, the fact remains that the nonhearsay nature of the
annexed report is not clear on its face.

611 N.Y.S.2d at 487. *See also Matter of Wesley M.*, 83 N.Y.2d 898,
613 N.Y.S.2d 853 (1994).

Similarly, in *People v. Wheeler*, N.Y.L.J., 10/7/94, p. 27, Col. 2
(Bronx Co. Crim. Ct.), the People filed a copy of a police laboratory analysis report with a certification identical to the one found
in *Matter of Rodney J.* However, here, the body of the report
contained the phrase "by the undersigned." The Court concluded
that a valid ballistics report must state:

> I hereby certify that I tested the gun and ammunition and that the
> foregoing report is a true and full copy of the original report pre-
> pared by me.

In the absence of such certification or any other indication as to
who prepared the original report, the Court found that the accusatory instrument did not meet the requirements for an information set forth in CPL § 100.40(1). *People v. Wheeler, supra.*

In *People v. Dominguez*, N.Y.L.J., 10/7/94, p. 35, Col. 2 (Queens
Co. Sup. Ct.), the defendant contended that the lab reports, which
were submitted to the grand jury pursuant to CPL § 190.30(2),
were hearsay since they failed to indicate that the person who
tested the gun and prepared the report was the same person who
signed the report. Here the certification stated:

> I hereby certify that the foregoing report is a true and full copy of
> the original report made by me. False statements made herein are
> punishable as a Class 'A' misdemeanor, pursuant to Section 210.45
> of the Penal Law.

The Queens County Supreme Court, distinguishing this certification from that in *Matter of Rodney J.*, denied the defendant's
motion to dismiss the indictment, finding that the reports were
prepared by the certifier. Here, the certification acknowledged
that the report was "made by me."

Similarly, in *People v. Young*, 163 Misc. 2d 36, 620 N.Y.S.2d
223 (Queens Ct. Sup. Ct. 1994), a certification containing the
same language used in *Dominguez*, was found sufficient and the
indictment upheld. Here, however, the Court explained that even

if the preparer of the report was not the same person who analyzed the substance at issue, the report would still be admissible evidence for grand jury purposes.

> CPL 190.30(1) provides that general evidentiary rules are applicable to Grand Jury proceedings "where appropriate." Appropriateness should be determined in light of the special functions of a Grand Jury, the possibility of prejudice to the defendant, the availability of post-indictment forums for challenging the evidence (*People v. Thomas*, 160 Misc. 2d 39, 607 N.Y.S.2d 871) and the burdens on police and court resources (*see People v. Brewster*, 100 A.D.2d 134, 473 N.Y.S.2d 984, *aff'd on other grounds*, 63 N.Y.2d 419, 482 N.Y.S.2d 724, 472 N.E.2d 686). A police chemist is unlikely to prepare a report based on the analysis of a stranger or to have no personal knowledge of the test and the person conducting it. There is a sufficient presumption of regularity attached to the report to admit it as competent evidence for the purpose of an indictment.

People v. Young, 620 N.Y.S.2d at 227.

However, the language utilized in the *Dominguez* and *Young* certifications, was found insufficient in *People v. Green, Kings Co. Crim. Ct.*, N.Y.L.J., 10/7/94, p. 34, Col. 6. Here, the court found that the document lacked any assurances that the signer of the document was the person who actually tested the material recovered from the defendant.

Insofar as the admissibility of these documents at a preliminary hearing is concerned, CPL § 180.60(8) provides for an application by the defendant for an order directing the production of the witness on the ground that the documentary evidence in question is not sufficiently reliable. If the court concurs, it must require the witness to testify in person and under go cross-examination.

Insofar as grand jury proceedings are concerned, CPL § 190.30(4) grants the grand jury discretion to require the appearance of the witness in lieu of his statement. Additionally, where the People attempt to offer such a statement into evidence and a preliminary hearing was previously held and a transcript of the examination of the witness generated, such a statement cannot be admitted without submission of that transcript.

§ 43:17 The best evidence rule—Purpose of rule generally

Research References

West's Key Number Digest, Criminal Law ⊙436(2), 444.9

The purpose of the best evidence rule is to prevent fraud and to ensure the authenticity of the document at issue. The application of the rule is limited to written instruments. The nature of those instruments includes everything from official records to memoranda. The general rule is that where it is necessary to prove the contents of a document, that document must be produced or its absence must be accounted for. Richardson on Evidence, p. 578–79 (Prince 10th ed. 1973).

This purpose of the best evidence rule ensures the integrity of the contents of the document which a proponent is attempting to prove. Where the document is evidence of a fact which is independent of the writing and subject to oral proof, the rule is not applicable. For example, proof of payment of a debt is not dependent upon the introduction of a receipt. Richardson on Evidence, p. 581 (Prince 10th ed. 1973).

The best example of this distinction is the difference between proof of a marriage and the proof of a divorce. Marriage is a fact which is documented by a record. Accordingly, marriage could be proven separate and apart from the writing and the rule is not applicable. On the contrary, a divorce comes into existence only by virtue of a judicial decree. Accordingly, the rule would apply and would require that a divorce be proved by such decree. Richardson on Evidence, p. 581–82 (Prince 10th ed. 1973).

For our purposes, the exceptions to the rule are of greater interest than its general application. More often than not, we are confronted with copies of documents being offered under an exception to the best evidence rule. If the document is to be introduced as the record of a private entity, CPLR § 4539 provides a means whereby a copy may be introduced. Insofar as public documents are concerned, CPLR § 4540 provides for their admissibility.

§ 43:18   The best evidence rule—Private documents

Research References

West's Key Number Digest, Criminal Law ☞436(2), 444.9

CPLR § 4539 states:

If any business, institution, or member of a profession or calling in the regular course of business or activity has made, kept or recorded any writing, entry, print or representation and in the regular course of business has recorded, copied, or reproduced it by any process which accurately reproduces or forms a durable medium for reproducing the original, such reproduction, when satisfactorily identified, is as admissible in evidence as the original, whether the original is in existence or not, and an enlargement or facsimile of such reproduction is admissible in evidence if the original reproduction is in existence and available for inspection under direction of the court. The introduction of a reproduction does not preclude admission of the original.

The net effect of CPLR § 4539 is to avoid the application of the best evidence rule to a copy. As with CPLR § 4518, this section does not allow admittance of records whose content would not, otherwise, be received in evidence. To be admitted, the copy must be identified, authenticated, and qualified for admission under the same terms as the original would have been. This section requires that the copy be made in the regular course of business of the entity from which it came. If the copies were prepared for litigation, they do not qualify for admission under CPLR § 4539.

The rationale for CPLR § 4539 is that in today's commercial world, the accuracy of copies is relied on without question. In *People v. Flores*, 138 A.D.2d 512, __, 526 N.Y.S.2d 125, 126 (2d Dep't 1988), the Appellate Division stated:

> This rule recognizes the fact that the modern business practice is to make photograph reproductions in the regular course of business and . . . that photograph reproductions so made are sufficiently trustworthy to be treated as originals for the purpose of a best evidence rule.

People v. Flores, 526 N.Y.S.2d at 126. *See also People v. May*, 162 A.D.2d 977, 557 N.Y.S.2d 203 (4th Dep't 1990).

Note that pursuant to CPLR § 4539, the making, keeping, or recording of the records and the reproduction of the records must be "in the regular course of business or activity" of the particular business, institution or member of a profession.

§ 43:19 The best evidence rule—Copies of public documents

Research References

West's Key Number Digest, Criminal Law ⚖436(2), 444.9

CPLR § 4540 accomplishes for public documents that which CPLR § 4539 does for private documents. This rule provides:

(a) Copies permitted. An official publication, or a copy attested as correct by an officer or a deputy of an officer having legal custody of an official record of the United States or of any state, territory or jurisdiction of the United States, or of any of its courts, legislature, offices, public bodies or boards is prima facie evidence of such record.

(b) Certificate of officer of the state. Where the copy is attested by an officer of the state, it shall be accompanied by a certificate signed by, or with a facsimile of the signature of, the clerk of a court having legal custody of the record, and, except where the copy is used in the same court or before one of its officers, with the seal of the court affixed; or signed by, or with a facsimile of the signature of, the officer having legal custody of the original, or his deputy or clerk, with his official seal affixed; or signed by, or with a facsimile of the signature of, the presiding officer, secretary or clerk of the public body or board and, except where it is certified by the clerk or secretary of either house of the legislature, with the seal of the body or board affixed. If the certificate is made by a county clerk, the county seal shall be affixed.

(c) Certificate of officer of another jurisdiction. Where the copy is attested by an officer of another jurisdiction, it shall be accompanied by a certificate that such officer has legal custody of the record, and that his signature is believed to be genuine, which certificate shall be made by a judge of a court of record of the district or political subdivision in which the record is kept, with the seal of the court affixed; or by any public officer having a seal of office and having official duties in that district or political subdivision with respect to the subject matter of the record, with the seal of his office affixed.

(d) Printed tariff or classification subject to public service commission, commissioner or transportation or interstate commerce commission. A printed copy of a tariff or classification which shows a public service commission or commissioner of transportation number of this state and an effective date, or a printed copy of a tariff or classification which shows an interstate commerce commission number and an effective date, is admissible in evidence, without certification, and is prima facie evidence of the filed original tariff or classification.

In order to admit a copy of a document, certification of the head of a public agency is required along with a seal. If the certification does not bear a seal, the document(s) are inadmissible under CPLR § 4540(b). In *People v. Fiacco*, 146 Misc. 2d 330, 549 N.Y.S.2d 901 (Albany City Ct. 1989), the defendant was charged with DWAI. At trial, four documents were admitted into evidence under the business record rule. Each of the four documents consisted of two pages. One page was a copy of the scientific analysis report. The other page was a copy of the certification by the director of the appropriate state agency which certified the report to be "a true and exact copy of an official record maintained by the Albany Police Department." The certification document also contained the signature of a local police officer. The Albany City Court held that these documents were improperly certified under CPLR § 4540(b) because there were no seals on the documents.

There are no seals on either certificate. Thus, these documents are not properly certified under CPLR 4540(b). *See People v. Brown*, 128 Misc. 2d 149, 153, 488 N.Y.S.2d 559.

More general standards are laid down under CPLR 4518(c) where a seal is not required. However, certification or authentication by the head of the agency or "an employee delegated for that purpose" is required.

The second certificate does not state that the police officer was designated as the legal custodian of the records nor is there any assurance given by the certifier that the copy submitted is accurate and genuine as compared to the original.

Indeed, it is not clear as to exactly which documents have been certified. Is it only the copy of the first certificate or also the underlying copy of the analysis? In any event, it is a copy of a copy and a second certification on all four exhibits must fail. *See People v. Brown, supra.*

For some of the same reasons, a fifth document, a copy of the calibration test record of the Albany Police Department, was erroneously received into evidence. Again, the certification was not done by the head of the agency nor does it state that the officer who signed it had been delegated as the custodian of the records.

549 N.Y.S.2d at 903.

In *People v. Hoats*, 102 Misc. 2d 1004, 425 N.Y.S.2d 497 (Monroe Co. Ct. 1980), the court held that while photocopies of scientific analysis documents accompanied by original certifications are admissible, photocopies of scientific analysis tests which are accompanied by mere photocopied certifications are inadmissible.

As with private documents, copies of public documents are admissible only if the original would have been admitted had it been offered and a proper excuse is offered for the nonproduction of the original certificate. In *People v. Miller*, 199 A.D.2d 692, 605 N.Y.S.2d 160 (3d Dep't 1993), although the police officer who had administered the Breathalyzer test was a certified operator, the officer did not have a current certificate because the Department of Health had yet to issue it. At trial, the officer presented the facsimile copy of a memorandum from the Division of Criminal Justice Services, which indicated that the officer had completed the recertification course and that he had been certified to operate a Breathalyzer device on the date the defendant was arrested. The court admitted the memorandum under the business records exception pursuant to CPLR § 4518(a) as presumptive proof that the examination was properly given. On appeal, the Appellate Division, Third Department held:

> While the document was improperly admitted under CPLR 4518(a), since a proper foundation was not established . . . it was admissible under the best evidence rule since a proper excuse was offered for the nonproduction of the original certificate.

605 N.Y.S.2d at 162 (citations omitted).

While the breadth of CPLR § 4540 seems all-inclusive, it does not include the records of justice courts which are covered by CPLR § 4541, or records of foreign countries, which are dealt with in CPLR § 4542. There must be an attestation to the accuracy of the copy, and the copy must be a verbatim transcription and not a condensation or synopsis of the original.

§ 43:20 Authentication requirement

Research References

West's Key Number Digest, Criminal Law ⊙—436(2), 444.9

The requirement of authentication applies to all writings where the relevancy of the writing is dependent upon the authorship of the instrument. Accordingly, documents such as contracts, deeds, wills, admissions, confessions, and dying declarations require authentication in order to be admitted in evidence. Richardson on Evidence, p. 636 (Prince 10th ed. 1973). As with the best evidence rule, the exceptions to the rule constitute our primary concern. CPLR § 3123(a) provides for the service of a written request for admission, by an opposing party, of the genuineness of any papers, documents, or photographs. CPLR § 3123(c) provides for an application requiring payment for the reasonable expenses incurred in making such proof where your opponent unreasonably refuses to admit the authenticity of the document you are attempting to offer in evidence. Absent a finding by the court that there were good reasons for the denial or the refusal of your opponent to admit, such an order will be made regardless of the result of the action at issue.

CPLR § 4538 provides for authentication by acknowledgment:

Certification of the acknowledgment or proof of a writing, except a will, in the manner prescribed by law for taking and certifying the acknowledgment or proof of a conveyance of real property within the state is prima facie evidence that it was executed by the person who purported to do so. The conveyance of real property, situated within another state, territory or jurisdiction of the United States, which has been duly authenticated, according to the laws of that state, territory or jurisdiction, so as to be read in evidence in the courts thereof, is admissible in evidence in the state.

In addition to acknowledgment, a document may be proven by a comparison of handwriting. CPLR § 4536. Stock market reports are deemed authenticated by virtue of their being published in a newspaper or periodical of general circulation. CPLR § 4533. Newspapers and periodicals in general circulation are deemed self-authenticating absent challenge by the adverse party. CPLR § 4532.

CPLR § 4540 provides for the "self-authentication" of official publications or certified copies of public documents. Certification is permitted by officers having legal custody of the document. The document combined with such certification constitutes prima facie evidence of such record.

The requirement that the copy be attested to by an officer of the state mandates that there be a comparison of the copy with the original. In *People v. Smith*, 258 A.D.2d 245, 697 N.Y.S.2d 783 (4th Dep't 1999), the Appellate Division, Fourth Department, held that a class D felony DWI was properly reduced to a class E felony where the defendant's DMV abstract presented to the grand jury was not properly authenticated. In so holding, the Court reasoned that:

> [D]efendant's DMV abstract qualifies for admission under the common-law public document exception to the hearsay rule.

> The inquiry into the admissibility of the DMV abstract, however, does not end with the determination that it is admissible over a hearsay objection. Following that determination, the question remains whether the document has been properly authenticated. Authentication of official records is governed by CPLR 4540. We reject the People's contention that the DMV abstract is not a copy but an original document that requires no certification of attestation.

> [Regarding the DMV abstract at issue in this case, t]he seal of the State of New York is not embossed on the document in a manner resisting forgery; it is printed on the background of each page. Further, it is clear that the data regarding defendant's driving record was placed on the document after the seal was affixed. Similarly, the certification is in the identical location on each page of the DMV abstract and appears to have been printed prior to the transfer of data regarding defendant's driving record. As a result, the document provides no assurances that any comparison has been made between the copy and the original record, and there is no basis for the assertion of the Commissioner of the Department of Motor Vehicles that it is "a true and complete copy of an electronic record on file" in the Department of Motor Vehicles.

> Because "strict compliance with the rules requiring authentication" of public documents was lacking, the court properly determined that the DMV abstract did not constitute competent and admissible evidence of the alleged [predicate] DWI conviction.

258 A.D.2d 245 at __-__, 697 N.Y.S.2d at 786–87 (citations omitted). *See generally People v. Wray*, 183 Misc. 2d 444, 704 N.Y.S.2d 787 (Kings Co. Sup. Ct. 2000) (DMV computer printouts of defendant's driving record, combined with foundational testimony of DMV ALJ, satisfied CPLR § 4518(a)); *People v. Baker*, 183 Misc. 2d 650, 705 N.Y.S.2d 846 (Oneida Co. Ct. 2000).

In *People v. Sikorski*, 280 A.D.2d 414, 721 N.Y.S.2d 48 (1st Dep't 2001), the Appellate Division, First Department, following *Smith*, held that:

> Contrary to the conclusion reached by Supreme Court, the People failed to establish that defendant committed the crime of aggravated unlicensed operation of a motor vehicle in the first degree, which requires proof that defendant operated a vehicle with 10 or more license suspensions in effect (Vehicle and Traffic Law § 511[3][a][ii]). *In this regard, the abstract of defendant's driving record that was introduced into evidence by the People was not properly certified as required by* CPLR 4540(b).

280 A.D.2d 414 at ___, 721 N.Y.S.2d at 49 (emphasis added).

In *People v. Watson*, 167 Misc. 2d 441, 634 N.Y.S.2d 634 (N.Y. City Crim. Ct. 1995), the People attempted to introduce a DMV abstract into evidence where:

> (1) [T]he official DMV seal and purported attestation of accuracy of the abstract were pre-printed on otherwise blank forms before any data was placed thereon; and (2) neither the DMV Commissioner . . . nor any other employee of that agency compared the copy submitted to the court with the original DMV records.

167 Misc. 2d 441 at ___, 634 N.Y.S.2d at 634. The Court found the abstract inadmissible, noting that "[f]or all that is here known, the DMV clerk who effected the transfer could have retrieved incorrect or incomplete data, or otherwise erred in producing this abstract, with the result that the information [contained therein] might be inaccurate." 167 Misc. 2d 441 at ___, 634 N.Y.S.2d at 638.

In *People v. Garneau*, 120 A.D.2d 112, 507 N.Y.S.2d 931 (4th Dep't 1986), the Appellate Division, Fourth Department, held that:

> It is well settled that to be admissible, any public document must be authenticated as being that which it purports to be. Here, the People made no effort to authenticate the breathalyzer documents, and it was error to receive them in evidence.

> In reaching these conclusions, we recognize the validity of the People's concern that it would prove unmanageable to call as witnesses, for the purpose of authentication, the various public officers who performed the tests and prepared the documents. Surely the various exceptions to the hearsay rule are intended to dispense with that requirement. *What is ultimately at stake here, however, is the right of confrontation, and these exceptions to the hearsay rule are not to be applied absent strict compliance with the rules requiring authentication.*

120 A.D.2d 112 at ___, 507 N.Y.S.2d at 935 (emphasis added) (citations omitted).

In *People v. Brown*, 128 Misc. 2d 149, 488 N.Y.S.2d 559 (Madison Co. Ct. 1985), the court stated that:

> The statutes which permit the copies of public documents in this case to be introduced as an exception to the best evidence rule, CPLR 4518(c) and CPLR 4540, require the documents to be certified or authenticated. Proper authentication or certification depends on the formal execution of the certificate as well as on the content of the attestation itself. * * *

> In the context of the certification of a public document an attestation is the assurance given by the certifier that the copy submitted is accurate and genuine as compared to the original. *The touchstone of the certification of a copy of a public document is [the] attestation and a certification which fails to include it is meaningless.*

128 Misc. 2d 149 at __, __, 488 N.Y.S.2d at 563, 564 (emphasis added).

In *People v. Taveras*, N.Y.L.J., 12/20/96, at p. 33, Col. 3, the defendant was charged with both unlicensed operation and AUO of a motor vehicle. Relying on *Watson, supra*, the defendant moved to dismiss the accusatory instrument on the ground of facial insufficiency in that, among other things, the DMV abstract was not properly certified or attested. The Bronx County Criminal Court distinguished *Watson* on the ground that *Watson* dealt with the admissibility of a DMV abstract into evidence at trial, as opposed to its sufficiency at the pleading stage of the case. In so holding, the court noted that:

> [W]hile this Court does not find *Watson* controlling here, there is some merit to the concern regarding the authenticity of a document offered into evidence which contains a pre-printed signature, certification and seal. As the standard of proof at the pleading stage of a criminal action is more lenient than at the trial stage, defendant's use of the analysis in Watson as to the admissibility of evidence at trial does not apply here. The introduction of these documents at trial is subject to proper foundation testimony.

(Citation omitted).

CPLR § 4541 provides for the authentication of a transcript of a docket book of a justice of the peace and CPLR § 4542 governs the proof of foreign records and documents. Finally, CPLR § 4543 provides for omnibus authentication by methods authorized by any applicable statute or by the rules of evidence of common law.

§ 43:21 Signature or facsimile of authenticating witness's signature must be done with witness's knowledge

Research References

West's Key Number Digest, Criminal Law ☞436(2), 444.9

In *Department of Housing Preservation and Development of the City of New York v. Tiffany General Holding Corp. and Oscar Santangelo*, N.Y.L.J., 7/21/88, p. 20, Col. 2 (Bronx Co. Ct.), Judge Malatzky considered a certified document which bore the stamped signature of an official of the Department of Housing Preservation and Development of the City of New York. Called to the stand, that official testified that he had never reviewed the document in question, and had not affixed the certification stamp with his name, nor did he have knowledge of who had. In disavowing this practice, the court stated:

> The terms certification and authentication are interchangeable. Both mean to attest as being true or as represented. Blacks Law Dictionary 117 [5th Edition 1979] defines attest as "to certify to the verity of a copy of a public document formally by signature; to make a solemn declaration in words or writing to support a fact; to signify by subscription of his name that the signer has witnessed the execution of the particular instrument."
>
> The touchstone of the certification or authentication of a copy of a public document is, thus, the attestation (citation omitted). Hence, a properly certified copy is one which is sworn to and contains an attestation by the official having custody of the original document that it is a true copy. The attestation is the assurance by the certifying officer of the genuineness and correctness of the copy after he has examined and compared it to the original. The power to certify can be delegated to a deputy or clerk or to a person expressly authorized to do so.
>
> In the instant proceeding the testimony of Chief Inspector LaStarza indicates that, although he is the certifying officer with custody of the original document, he did not personally affix his official facsimile stamp nor did he review the documents and compare it to the originals as required. Further, Mr. LaStarza had no knowledge as to who had certified the documents and whether it had been done by a person "expressly authorized" to do so. A certification as we have here, with an undocumented and unproven attestation is therefore meaningless. Therefore, the Court is constrained to giving little evidentiary weight to petitioners 3 and 4 in evidence.

N.Y.L.J., 7/21/88, p. 20, Col. 2 (Bronx Co. Ct.) (citations omitted).

§ 43:22 Documents admissible as past recollection recorded

Research References

West's Key Number Digest, Criminal Law ⚖436(2), 444.9

A document, such as a memorandum prepared by a witness, may be admissible as substantive evidence of the truth of its contents pursuant to the past recollection recorded doctrine. The witness must be unable or unwilling to testify as to its contents, and otherwise competent evidence must establish that: (1) the witness once had knowledge of the contents of the memorandum; (2) the memorandum was prepared by the witness, or at his direction; (3) the memorandum was prepared when the knowledge of the contents was fresh in the mind of the witness; and (4) the witness intended, when the memorandum as made, that it be accurate. *See People v. Briggs*, 190 A.D.2d 995, 593 N.Y.S.2d 622 (4th Dep't 1993). The fact that the witness recalls some of the facts in a memorandum does not operate as a bar to its admissibility where the witness could not recall a number of other facts recited in the memorandum. The memorandum is admissible as a device to augment his memory as past recollection recorded. 190 A.D.2d 995 at __, 593 N.Y.S.2d 622 at 624.

§ 43:23 Use of treatise to cross-examine expert

Research References
West's Key Number Digest, Criminal Law ⟪436(2), 444.9

It is well settled that an expert may be confronted with a treatise on cross-examination for impeachment purposes. *See People v. Feldman*, 299 N.Y. 153 (1949); *Mark v. Colgate University*, 53 A.D.2d 884, 385 N.Y.S.2d 621 (2d Dep't 1976). In order to lay a foundation for the use of the treatise, the witness must concede its authoritativeness. *Ithier v. Solomon*, 59 A.D.2d 935, 399 N.Y.S.2d 450 (2d Dep't 1977); *see also Roveda v. Weiss*, 11 A.D.2d 745, 204 N.Y.S.2d 699 (1960); *Walsh v. Staten Island Obstetrics*, 193 A.D.2d 672, 598 N.Y.S.2d 17 (2d Dep't 1993); *Labate v. Plotkin*, 195 A.D.2d 444, 600 N.Y.S.2d 144 (2d Dep't 1993). However, it is not required that the expert witness has read the treatise. The witness must merely concede that the treatise is an authoritative source. *Mark v. Colgate University*, *supra*.

§ 43:24 Bolstering

Research References
West's Key Number Digest, Criminal Law ⟪436(2), 444.9

In *People v. Borgia*, 263 A.D.2d 553, 692 N.Y.S.2d 780 (3d Dep't 1999), the Appellate Division, Third Department, made clear that:

> It is now axiomatic that the fortification of a witness's testimony and credibility through the use of a prior consistent statement, commonly known as "bolstering," is inadmissible hearsay, except to rebut a claim of recent fabrication. The basis for the rule was made plain in *People v. Katz*, 209 N.Y. 311, 103 N.E. 305, where it was observed that "it is obviously a mistake to suppose that an

untrustworthy story can be made trustworthy by proving numerous
repetitions of it; and equally illogical does it appear to be to attempt to support a credible witness and reliable testimony by any
such broken reed."

263 A.D.2d 553 at __, 692 N.Y.S.2d at 781 (citation omitted).

§ 43:25 Effect of *Crawford v. Washington* on admissibility of documents

Research References

West's Key Number Digest, Criminal Law ⟜436(2), 444.9

The United States Supreme Court's landmark decision in
Crawford v. Washington, 541 U.S. 36, 124 S.Ct. 1354 (2004), will
likely have a substantial impact on the admissibility of documents in criminal cases. In *Crawford*, the Supreme Court held
that the Confrontation Clause of the Sixth Amendment prohibits
the use of "testimonial" evidence against the defendant at trial
unless both (a) the declarant is unavailable, *and* (b) the defendant
had a prior opportunity to cross-examine him or her. 541 U.S. 36
at 68, 124 S.Ct. at 1374.

Admission of the following documents at trial has been found
to violate *Crawford*:

　　1. A blood test result. *See Bullcoming v. New Mexico*, 131 S.
Ct. 2705, 180 L. Ed. 2d 610 (2011); *People v. Rogers*, 8 A.D.3d
888, __, 780 N.Y.S.2d 393, 397 (3d Dep't 2004);

　　2. A VTL § 214 "Affidavit of Regularity/Proof of Mailing" of a
DMV employee. *See People v. Pacer*, 6 N.Y.3d 504, 814 N.Y.S.2d
575 (2006); *People v. Darrisaw*, 66 A.D.3d 1427, 886 N.Y.S.2d
315 (4th Dep't 2009); *People v. Wolters*, 41 A.D.3d 518, 838
N.Y.S.2d 117 (2d Dep't 2007), leave to appeal dismissed, 9
N.Y.3d 884, 842 N.Y.S.2d 796, 874 N.E.2d 763 (2007); *People v.
Capellan*, 6 Misc. 3d 809, __, 791 N.Y.S.2d 315, 316 (N.Y. City
Crim. Ct. 2004);

　　3. DNA reports. *See People v. John*, 27 N.Y.3d 294, 297, 33
N.Y.S.3d 88, 89, 52 N.E.3d 1114 (2016) ("On this appeal, we
address whether defendant's Sixth Amendment right to
confront the witnesses against him was violated when the
People introduced DNA reports into evidence . . . without producing a single witness who conducted, witnessed or supervised
the laboratory's generation of the DNA profile from the gun or
defendant's exemplar. We conclude that, under the circumstances presented here, defendant's right to confrontation was
violated"); and

　　4. A "Latent *Print Report.*" *People v. Hernandez*, 7 Misc. 3d
568, __, 794 N.Y.S.2d 788, 789 (N.Y. Co. Sup. Ct. 2005).

Similarly, in *People v. Umpierre*, 37 Misc. 3d 775, 951 N.Y.S.2d

382 (Bronx Co. Sup. Ct. 2012), the Court applied the rationale of *Bullcoming* to a breath test result, and refused to allow the People to introduce the defendant's test result into evidence at trial unless the breath test operator was available for cross-examination.

Courts had reached differing conclusions as to whether the documents typically used to lay a foundation for the admission of a defendant's breath test results (*e.g.*, Breath Test Instrument Record of Inspection/Maintenance/Calibration, Simulator Solution Certificate of Analysis), fall within the ambit of *Crawford*. *See, e.g., People v. Hulbert*, 93 A.D.3d 953, 939 N.Y.S.2d 661 (3d Dep't 2012); *People v. Damato*, 79 A.D.3d 1060, 913 N.Y.S.2d 740 (2d Dep't 2010); *People v. Lebrecht*, 13 Misc. 3d 45, 823 N.Y.S.2d 824 (App. Term, 9th & 10th Jud. Dist. 2006); *Green v. DeMarco*, 11 Misc. 3d 451, 812 N.Y.S.2d 772 (Monroe Co. Sup. Ct. 2005); *People v. Krueger*, 9 Misc. 3d 950, 804 N.Y.S.2d 908 (Lockport Just. Ct. 2005); *People v. Kanhai*, 8 Misc. 3d 447, 797 N.Y.S.2d 870 (City Crim. Ct. 2005). *Cf. People v. Orpin*, 8 Misc. 3d 768, 796 N.Y.S.2d 512 (Irondequoit Just. Ct. 2005) (calibration and simulator solution certifications inadmissible under *Crawford*); *People v. Carreira*, 27 Misc. 3d 293, 893 N.Y.S.2d 844 (Watertown City Ct. 2010) (abrogated on other grounds by, People v. Pealer, 20 N.Y.3d 447, 962 N.Y.S.2d 592, 985 N.E.2d 903 (2013)); *People v. Heyanka*, 25 Misc. 3d 978, 886 N.Y.S.2d 801 (Suffolk Co. Dist. Ct. 2009) (same). *See generally People v. Deep*, 12 Misc. 3d 1137, __, 821 N.Y.S.2d 381, 383-84 (Ithaca City Ct. 2006) (calibration records for lidar speed detection device not subject to *Crawford*).

The Court of Appeals put this issue to rest in *People v. Pealer*, 20 N.Y.3d 447, 451, 962 N.Y.S.2d 592, 594, 985 N.E.2d 903 (2013), petition for cert. filed (U.S. May 16, 2013):

> The question presented in this appeal is whether records pertaining to the routine inspection, maintenance and calibration of breathalyzer machines can be offered as evidence in a criminal trial without producing the persons who created the records. We hold that because such documents are nontestimonial, the records are not subject to the Confrontation Clause requirements set forth in *Crawford v. Washington*.

Notably, in footnote 1 of its decision in *Melendez-Diaz v. Massachusetts*, 557 U.S. 305, 311 n.1, 129 S. Ct. 2527, 2532 n.1, 174 L. Ed. 2d 314 (2009), the Supreme Court commented that:

> Contrary to the dissent's suggestion, we do not hold, and it is not the case, that anyone whose testimony may be relevant in establishing the chain of custody, authenticity of the sample, or accuracy of the testing device, must appear in person as part of the prosecution's case. While the dissent is correct that "[i]t is the obligation of the prosecution to establish the chain of custody," this does not

mean that everyone who laid hands on the evidence must be called. As stated in the dissent's own quotation from *United States v. Lott*, "gaps in the chain [of custody] normally go to the weight of the evidence rather than its admissibility." It is up to the prosecution to decide what steps in the chain of custody are so crucial as to require evidence; but what testimony is introduced must (if the defendant objects) be introduced live. Additionally, documents prepared in the regular course of equipment maintenance may well qualify as nontestimonial records.

(Citations omitted).

§ 43:26 *Crawford* claim must be preserved to be raised on appeal

Research References

West's Key Number Digest, Criminal Law ☞436(2), 444.9

In *People v. Chambers*, 20 A.D.3d 928, 798 N.Y.S.2d 833 (4th Dep't 2005), the defendant was convicted, following a jury trial, of felony DWI. On appeal, the Appellate Division, Fourth Department, refused to consider the defendant's claim that his constitutional right of confrontation was violated by the admission of certain hospital test results into evidence as business records, holding that such claim was not preserved. 20 A.D.3d at __, 798 N.Y.S.2d at 833.

§ 43:27 Applicability of *Crawford* to proceedings other than trial

Research References

West's Key Number Digest, Criminal Law ☞436(2), 444.9

In applying *Crawford*, courts have made clear that the *Sixth Amendment* right of confrontation is essentially a trial right, and thus that *Crawford* is inapplicable to various pretrial and post-conviction proceedings. *See, e.g., People v. Brink*, 31 A.D.3d 1139, 818 N.Y.S.2d 374 (4th Dep't 2006), leave to appeal denied, 7 N.Y.3d 865, 824 N.Y.S.2d 610, 857 N.E.2d 1141 (2006) (*Crawford* inapplicable to pretrial suppression hearing); *People v. Williams*, 30 A.D.3d 980, 818 N.Y.S.2d 694 (4th Dep't 2006), leave to appeal denied, 7 N.Y.3d 852, 823 N.Y.S.2d 782, 857 N.E.2d 77 (2006) (Sixth Amendment right of confrontation inapplicable to sentencing proceedings).

In *Williams*, however, the Appellate Division, Fourth Department, held that the affidavit of the director of the Criminal History Bureau asserting that the defendant's fingerprint cards "were compared and that 'staff determined' that the fingerprints on those cards were [defendant's]," 30 A.D.3d at __, 818 N.Y.S.2d 694 at 696, were inadmissible at the defendant's persistent violent felony offender hearing, because at such a hearing the People are required to prove the defendant's predicate convictions by " 'proof beyond a reasonable doubt by evidence admissible under the rules applicable to a trial of the issue of guilt.' " 30 A.D.3d at __, 818 N.Y.S.2d 694 at 697 (quoting CPL § 400.15[7][a]).

Chapter 44

Physician-Patient Privilege

Research References

Westlaw Databases

Fiandach, Handling Drunk Driving Cases (2d ed.) (HDRUNKDR)

Treatises and Practice Aids

Fiandach, Handling Drunk Driving Cases §§ 9:21, 34:6 to 34:10 (2d ed.)

Law Reviews and Other Periodicals

Kenny, Physician-Patient Privilege Issues in Article 81 Proceedings, 308 Practising Law Institute Tax Law and Estate Planning Course Handbook Series 89 (August, 2001)

Vilensky, New York Law on Confidentiality of Medical Records-Part I, 66-JAN N.Y. St. B.J. 38 (January, 1994)

KeyCite®: Cases and other legal materials listed in KeyCite Scope can be researched through the KeyCite service on Westlaw®. Use KeyCite to check citations for form, parallel references, prior and later history, and comprehensive citator information, including citations to other decisions and secondary materials.

---

§ 44:1 In general

Research References

West's Key Number Digest, Witnesses ⬅208(1), 209

As a general rule, the physician-patient privilege protects the confidentiality of various information obtained by medical personnel in the course of treating a patient. However, there are a variety of exceptions to the privilege, as well as information not covered by the privilege. In addition, the privilege can be waived. Furthermore, in light of *People v. Greene*, 9 N.Y.3d 277, 849 N.Y.S.2d 461 (2007), evidence obtained as the fruit of a violation of the physician-patient privilege will no longer be suppressible in criminal cases.

§ 44:2 Physician-patient privilege—Defined

Research References

West's Key Number Digest, Witnesses ⬅208(1), 209

The physician-patient privilege is codified in CPLR § 4504(a), which provides, in pertinent part:

Confidential information privileged. Unless the patient waives the privilege, a person authorized to practice medicine, registered professional nursing, licensed practical nursing, dentistry, podiatry or chiropractic shall not be allowed to disclose any information which he acquired in attending a patient in a professional capacity, and which was necessary to enable him to act in that capacity.

§ 44:3 Rationale for physician-patient privilege

Research References

West's Key Number Digest, Witnesses ⬅208(1), 209

At common law, there was no rule prohibiting the disclosure of communications between a physician and patient. In New York in 1828 this rule was changed by statute and the privilege has been so recognized since that time.

The purpose of this rule and the reason motivating the Legislature to establish this physician-patient privilege "is to protect those who are required to consult physicians from the disclosure of secrets imparted to them, to protect the relationship of patient and physician and to prevent physicians from disclosing information which might result in humiliation, embarrassment, or disgrace to patients."

People v. Al Kanani, 33 N.Y.2d 260, 264, 351 N.Y.S.2d 969, 971 (1973) (citations and footnote omitted).

We have previously noted that this State's codification of the physician-patient privilege was based largely "on the belief that fear of embarrassment or disgrace flowing from disclosure of communications made to a physician would deter people from seeking medical help and securing adequate diagnosis and treatment." Additionally, it was feared that physicians would alter or conceal the truth when forced, in the absence of any privilege, to choose between their legal duty to testify and their professional obligation to honor their patients' confidences. A third rationale supporting the privilege that has gained increased currency in recent years is premised on the need to protect the privacy expectations of patients. This court recognized long ago that "[t]he disclosure by a physician, whether voluntary or involuntary, of the secrets acquired by him while attending upon a patient in his professional capacity, naturally shocks our sense of decency and propriety, and this is one reason why the law forbids it." Thus, it has been argued that "the value placed on privacy, manifested both by general concerns for privacy and by the specific concerns for an individual's bodily integrity found in constitutional, statutory, and common law doctrines, suggests a strong policy basis" for the privilege.

Although the physician-patient privilege has been criticized by commentators who maintain that there is little empirical support for the proposition that the privilege promotes public health, that the principle of medical confidentiality is antiquated and no longer regularly observed by physicians, and that protection of patients' privacy is not a sufficiently important interest to justify nondisclosure of legally pertinent medical information, the privilege remains rooted in both the statutory law and public policy of New York State.

Dillenbeck v. Hess, 73 N.Y.2d 278, 285–86, 539 N.Y.S.2d 707, 711–12 (1989) (citations omitted). *See also Matter of Grand Jury Investigation in N.Y. County*, 98 N.Y.2d 525, 529, 749 N.Y.S.2d 462, 464 (2002).

§ 44:4 Physician-patient privilege is given broad and liberal construction

Research References

West's Key Number Digest, Witnesses ⚲208(1), 209

The Court of Appeals has made clear both (a) that "we have frequently stated that the physician-patient privilege is to be given a "'broad and liberal construction to carry out its policy,'" " *People v. Sinski*, 88 N.Y.2d 487, 492, 646 N.Y.S.2d 651, 653 (1996) (citations omitted), and (b) that "we have narrowly construed statutes limiting the privilege and rejected claims that there is a general public interest exception to CPLR 4504." 88 N.Y.2d 487 at 492, 646 N.Y.S.2d at 653. *See also Dillenbeck v. Hess*, 73 N.Y.2d 278, 289, 539 N.Y.S.2d 707, 714 (1989) ("Were we to carve out an exception to the privilege whenever it inhibited the fact-finding process, it would quickly become eviscerated"); *Matter of Grand Jury Investigation of Onondaga County*, 59 N.Y.2d 130, 136, 463 N.Y.S.2d 758, 761 (1983) ("[various] exceptions to the privilege make clear the legislative concept that exceptions to the statutorily enacted physician-patient privilege are for the Legislature to declare").

In this regard, the doctrine of legislative acquiescence provides that "[w]here the practical construction of a statute is well known, the Legislature is charged with knowledge and its failure to interfere indicates acquiescence." *Engle v. Talarico*, 33 N.Y.2d 237, 242, 351 N.Y.S.2d 677, 680–81 (1973). *See also Hammelburger v. Foursome Inn Corp.*, 54 N.Y.2d 580, 588, 446 N.Y.S.2d 917, 922 (1981).

§ 44:5 Physician-patient privilege belongs to patient

Research References

West's Key Number Digest, Witnesses ☞208(1), 209

In Matter of Grand Jury Investigation of Onondaga County, 59 N.Y.2d 130, 135, 463 N.Y.S.2d 758, 760 (1983), the Court of Appeals held that:

> Although the privilege belongs to the patient and may not be asserted by the physician, hospital or anyone else to protect himself with respect to a crime committed against the patient, it may be asserted by the hospital or physician for the protection of a patient who has not waived his or her privilege, even though the patient is suspected of or charged with a crime. Respondent hospital properly asserted the privilege, therefore, and it not being possible to comply with a demand for names and addresses of all persons treated for a knife wound without disclosing privileged information concerning diagnosis and treatment, the subpoena, even as limited, was properly quashed.

(Citations omitted). *See also Dillenbeck v. Hess*, 73 N.Y.2d 278, 290, 539 N.Y.S.2d 707, 714 (1989).

In other words, while the privilege belongs to the patient, "[h]ospitals may assert a physician-patient privilege under CPLR

4504(a) to maintain the confidentiality of patient medical records." *Matter of Grand Jury Investigation in N.Y. County*, 98 N.Y.2d 525, 528, 749 N.Y.S.2d 462, 463 (2002).

§ 44:6 Physician-patient privilege is statutory, not constitutional, in nature

Research References

West's Key Number Digest, Witnesses ⚷208(1), 209

"The privilege, while not one of constitutional magnitude, is a creature of statute now set forth in CPLR 4504 and made applicable to criminal actions by CPL 60.10." *People v. Al Kanani*, 33 N.Y.2d 260, 264 n.*, 351 N.Y.S.2d 969, 971 n.* (1973). *See also People v. Greene*, 9 N.Y.3d 277, 280, 849 N.Y.S.2d 461, 462 (2007) ("The physician-patient privilege is based on statute, not the State or Federal Constitution"); *Dillenbeck v. Hess*, 73 N.Y.2d 278, 283, 539 N.Y.S.2d 707, 710 (1989) ("The physician-patient privilege, presently contained in CPLR 4504, is entirely a creature of statute").

§ 44:7 Physician-patient privilege is applicable to criminal proceedings

Research References

West's Key Number Digest, Witnesses ⚷208(1), 209

Although the physician-patient privilege is codified in the CPLR, it is made applicable to criminal proceedings by CPL § 60.10, which provides that "[u]nless otherwise provided by statute or by judicially established rules of evidence applicable to criminal cases, the rules of evidence applicable to civil cases are, where appropriate, also applicable to criminal proceedings." *See People v. Al Kanani*, 33 N.Y.2d 260, 264 n.*, 351 N.Y.S.2d 969, 971 n.* (1973); *People v. Gonzalez*, 239 A.D.2d 931, __, 659 N.Y.S.2d 591, 592 (4th Dep't 1997); *People v. Carkner*, 213 A.D.2d 735, __, 623 N.Y.S.2d 350, 353 (3d Dep't 1995); *People v. Petro*, 122 A.D.2d 309, __, 504 N.Y.S.2d 67, 68 (3d Dep't 1986).

§ 44:8 Physician's fiduciary duty not to disclose patient confidences is broader than physician-patient privilege

Research References

West's Key Number Digest, Witnesses ⚷208(1), 209

In *Lightman v. Flaum*, 97 N.Y.2d 128, 136, 736 N.Y.S.2d 300, 305 (2001), the Court of Appeals noted that, regardless of the physician-patient privilege, a physician has a fiduciary duty to protect patient confidences:

A . . . dichotomy between professional confidentiality obligations and evidentiary rules designed to preserve confidentiality exists for physicians and other health care professionals. CPLR 4504 prevents the disclosure of information "acquired in attending a patient in a professional capacity, and which was necessary to enable [the physician or other health care professional] to act in that capacity." Nevertheless, information obtained in a professional capacity but not necessary to enable the physician to fulfill his or her medical role is a protected confidence, the disclosure of which constitutes professional misconduct in the absence of patient consent or legal authorization. Thus, although the statutory privileges may in some instances overlap with the applicable fiduciary duties of confidentiality which have been defined elsewhere in the law, those evidentiary rules are not the sources of the underlying duties, and [CPLR] article 45 does not establish the parameters of those fiduciary relationships.

(Citations omitted).

§ 44:9   Types of information to which privilege applies

Research References

West's Key Number Digest, Witnesses ☞208(1), 209, 211(1)

The Court of Appeals has repeatedly made clear that "[t]he privilege applies not only to information communicated orally by the patient, but also to 'information obtained from observation of the patient's appearance and symptoms, unless the facts observed would be obvious to laymen.'" *Dillenbeck v. Hess*, 73 N.Y.2d 278, 284, 539 N.Y.S.2d 707, 711 (1989) (citation omitted). *See also Matter of Grand Jury Investigation in N.Y. County*, 98 N.Y.2d 525, 531, 749 N.Y.S.2d 462, 465–66 (2002); *Matter of Grand Jury Investigation of Onondaga County*, 59 N.Y.2d 130, 135, 463 N.Y.S.2d 758, 760 (1983); *People v. Decina*, 2 N.Y.2d 133, 144–45, 157 N.Y.S.2d 558, 569 (1956).

"Moreover, the form in which the information is sought to be introduced is irrelevant, as the privilege operates whether the information is contained in a patient's medical files or is sought to be introduced at trial in the form of expert testimony." *Dillenbeck*, 73 N.Y.2d at 284, 539 N.Y.S.2d at 711.

Accordingly, the Appellate Division, Second Department's statement that the physician-patient privilege only "seeks to protect evidence of a testimonial or communicative nature" as opposed to "real or physical evidence," *People v. Elysee*, 49 A.D.3d 33, —, 847 N.Y.S.2d 654, 665 (2d Dep't 2007), appears to be erroneous. Notably, the Court of Appeals' subsequent decision in *Elysee*, which affirmed the Appellate Division on other grounds, expressly declined to address this issue. *See People v. Elysee*, 12 N.Y.3d 100, 105, 876 N.Y.S.2d 677, 679, 904 N.E.2d 813 (2009).

§ 44:10 Privilege inapplicable to observations that would be readily apparent to layperson

Research References

West's Key Number Digest, Witnesses ☞208(1), 209, 211(1)

The physician-patient privilege "does not apply to 'such ordinary incidents and facts as are plain to the observation of any one without expert or professional knowledge.'" *People v. Greene*, 9 N.Y.3d 277, 280, 849 N.Y.S.2d 461, 462 (2007) (citation omitted). *See also Matter of Grand Jury Investigation of Onondaga County*, 59 N.Y.2d 130, 134, 463 N.Y.S.2d 758, 760 (1983); *People v. Hedges*, 98 A.D.2d 950, __, 470 N.Y.S.2d 61, 62 (4th Dep't 1983) ("The physician's observations that there was a strong odor of alcohol on defendant's breath, that the defendant's speech was slurred and disjointed and that the defendant was 'extremely intoxicated' could have been made by a lay person and did not depend upon any confidential communication by the defendant. They thus were not privileged"); *People v. Beneway*, 148 Misc. 2d 177, __, 560 N.Y.S.2d 96, 98 (Columbia Co. Ct. 1990) (same).

In Matter of Grand Jury Investigation in N.Y. County, 98 N.Y.2d 525, 530–31, 749 N.Y.S.2d 462, 465 (2002), the Court of Appeals set forth examples of cases where observations made by medical personnel were found to fall outside of the physician-patient privilege:

> The physician-patient privilege generally does not extend to information obtained outside the realms of medical diagnosis and treatment. Indeed, because the policies underlying the physician-patient privilege implicate confidential patient relationships with medical professionals *as* medical professionals, we have generally limited the privilege to information acquired by the medical professional "through the application of professional skill or knowledge." Accordingly, notwithstanding CPLR 4504(a), medical professionals have been authorized to disclose observations of a heroin packet falling from a patient's sock, injuries on a patient's cheek and lip, and a patient's slurred speech and alcohol-laced breath incident to intoxication. Likewise, photographs of methadone-treatment patients taken to prevent unauthorized individuals from obtaining the drug and the names and addresses of a medical professional's patients are outside the ambit of CPLR 4504(a) and must be surrendered pursuant to a valid subpoena.

(Citations omitted).

In *N.Y. County*, the district attorney served broadly worded grand jury subpoenas duces tecum upon 23 hospitals in search of a person who may have been treated for a particular type of wound. Some of the hospitals moved to quash the subpoenas, invoking the physician-patient privilege. The district attorney claimed that the wound in question would have been plainly observable to a layperson. The Court of Appeals disagreed, holding that:

> *Onondaga County* controls this appeal and directs that the challenged subpoenas be quashed. In *Onondaga County*, as in the instant case, the victim was stabbed to death under circumstances that led investigators to conclude that the assailant may have left the scene bleeding. Endeavoring to identify the assailant, the District Attorney of Onondaga County issued a grand jury subpoena on a hospital, seeking "all medical records pertaining to treatment of any person with stab wounds or other wounds caused by a knife." In quashing the subpoena, the Court held that compliance might have "require[d] the hospital to which it is addressed to divulge information protected by the physician-patient privilege." The Court concluded that under those circumstances, it was "not * * * possible to comply with a demand for names and addresses of all persons treated for a knife wound without disclosing privileged information concerning diagnosis and treatment."
>
> We perceive no difference of any actual substance between the subpoena quashed in *Onondaga County* and the ones challenged here. The records potentially responsive to the HHC subpoenas are precisely the same as those sought in *Onondaga County*. Though the District Attorney crafted the instant subpoenas with *Onondaga County* in mind by broadening their scope (to include most bleeding wounds rather than only knife wounds) and narrowing their reach (to include only wounds "plainly observable to a lay person"), the subpoenas still run afoul of *Onondaga County*.
>
> Here, much as in *Onondaga County*, the challenged subpoenas define the class of records sought by the "cause or potential cause" of injury. Thus, the subpoenas inevitably call for a medical determination as to *causation* "through the application of professional skill or knowledge." It is precisely this intrusion into the physician-patient relationship that CPLR 4504(a) seeks to prevent. The inherently medical nature of this judgment is not obviated by attempting to qualify it in terms of what a layperson might plainly observe.

98 N.Y.2d 525 at 531, 749 N.Y.S.2d at 465–66 (citations omitted).

§ 44:11 Applicability of physician-patient privilege to hospital records and blood tests

Research References

West's Key Number Digest, Witnesses ⊙208(1), 209, 211(1)

In *Dillenbeck v. Hess*, 73 N.Y.2d 278, 284 n.4, 539 N.Y.S.2d 707, 711 n.4 (1989), the Court of Appeals held that:

> The suggestion in the dissent that defendant's blood alcohol test results may not qualify as a "communication" protected under CPLR 4504 is clearly erroneous and directly contradicted by the case law and expert authorities. Though a physician is not precluded from

testifying concerning ordinary incidents and facts of a person's medical history that are obvious to those without professional training, it is universally acknowledged that any medical information acquired by the physician through the application of professional skill or knowledge is protected by the statute. Quite clearly, the information obtained by defendant's physician in administering a blood alcohol test to defendant was the product of professional skill and knowledge and would not have been apparent to a layman uninitiated in the medical arts. That information, therefore, is without question a protected communication under CPLR 4504.

(Citations omitted). *See also 73 N.Y.2d 278 at 289*, 539 N.Y.S.2d at 714 ("hospital records relating to defendant's physical condition and blood alcohol content following the accident [] indisputably fall[] within the scope of the physician-patient privilege as information acquired by a physician 'in attending [defendant] in a professional capacity, and which was necessary to enable him to act in that capacity' (CPLR 4504)"); *People v. Petro*, 122 A.D.2d 309, 504 N.Y.S.2d 67 (3d Dep't 1986) (results of hospital blood test performed for diagnostic purposes properly suppressed on physician-patient privilege grounds); *People v. Bashkatov*, 13 Misc. 3d 1101, 827 N.Y.S.2d 594 (N.Y. City Crim. Ct. 2006), appeal dismissed, 18 Misc. 3d 127(A), 856 N.Y.S.2d 25 (App. Term 2007), leave to appeal denied, 10 N.Y.3d 808, 857 N.Y.S.2d 41, 886 N.E.2d 806 (2008).

§ 44:12 Applicability of physician-patient privilege to physical blood sample as opposed to blood test results

There is a critical distinction, for physician-patient privilege purposes, between the *results* of a hospital blood test and the blood sample itself. As the previous section makes clear, hospital blood test results clearly and indisputably fall within the privilege. By contrast, it is unsettled whether a blood sample lawfully withdrawn from the defendant by hospital personnel—but not yet tested—is protected by the privilege.

In this regard, in *People v. Elysee*, 49 A.D.3d 33, 847 N.Y.S.2d 654 (2d Dep't 2007), *aff'd on other grounds*, 12 N.Y.3d 100, 876 N.Y.S.2d 677 (2009), the Appellate Division, Second Department, held that "a physical blood specimen taken from a patient by a medical professional is not 'information' protected by the physician-patient privilege as defined in CPLR 4504(a) and, accordingly, such a blood sample is subject to seizure pursuant to a warrant issued under the authority of CPL 690.10." *10 N.Y.3d 840* at __, 847 N.Y.S.2d at 655. In so holding, the Court reasoned that:

At issue in this case, and what is an issue of first impression in this

Court, is whether the term "information," as used in CPLR 4504(a), should be construed to include a physical blood sample drawn from a patient by a physician or other medical professional defined in the statute. In our view, such an interpretation would constitute an expansion of the privilege neither contemplated nor intended by the Legislature. * * *

[A] medical provider's diagnosis, which involves the professional skill and judgment of the provider, made after evaluating a patient's condition and interpreting certain test results, is privileged. So too, are the actual test results privileged. Viewed in that context, however, a physical blood sample standing alone, prior to being tested by the treating physician or other medical professional, is not similarly protected since it neither communicates nor renders observable any information about a patient upon which treatment can be based or a diagnosis made. * * *

We note in this regard that we continue to recognize that the results of tests performed by a medical professional in the course of diagnosis and treatment and recorded in the defendant's medical records are protected by the physician-patient privilege.

10 N.Y.3d 840 at __, __, __, 847 N.Y.S.2d at 657, 658, 662 (citations omitted). *See also People v. Drayton*, 56 A.D.3d 1278, __, 867 N.Y.S.2d 825, 826 (4th Dep't 2008), leave to appeal granted, 12 N.Y.3d 783, 879 N.Y.S.2d 59, 906 N.E.2d 1093 (2009); *People v. Bolson*, 183 Misc. 2d 155, __-__, 701 N.Y.S.2d 828, 832–33 (Queens Co. Sup. Ct. 1999). *Cf. People v. Muscarnera*, 16 Misc. 3d 622, __-__, 842 N.Y.S.2d 241, 249–51 (Nassau Co. Dist. Ct. 2007); *People v. Bashkatov*, 13 Misc. 3d 1101, 827 N.Y.S.2d 594 (N.Y. City Crim. Ct. 2006).

However, subsequent to all of these decisions, the Court of Appeals left this question undecided in *People v. Elysee*, 12 N.Y.3d 100, 105, 876 N.Y.S.2d 677, 679–80, 904 N.E.2d 813 (2009):

We agree with the lower courts that defendant's motion to suppress the 5:30 A.M. samples was properly denied, though we need not decide whether CPLR 4504 applies to these samples. Pursuant to Vehicle and Traffic Law § 1194(2)(a), "[a]ny person who operates a motor vehicle in this state shall be deemed to have given consent to a chemical test of . . . breath, blood, urine, or saliva, for the purpose of determining the alcoholic and/or drug content of the blood" under certain prescribed conditions. In addition, such chemical tests can also be compelled by court order under Vehicle and Traffic Law § 1194(3) when, among other circumstances,

"a person other than the operator was killed or suffered serious physical injury . . .; and

"such person operated the vehicle in violation of any subdivision of [VTL § 1192] . . . and . . .

"has been placed under lawful arrest; and . . .

"has refused to submit to a chemical test . . . or is unable to give consent to such a test."

Therefore, even if these samples were privileged, under the facts and circumstances of this case, the privilege was overcome when the police officers executed the court order issued pursuant to Vehicle and Traffic Law § 1194(3).

(Citation omitted).

§ 44:13 Exceptions to physician-patient privilege

Research References

West's Key Number Digest, Witnesses ⊶208(1), 209, 211(1)

There are many statutory exceptions to the physician-patient privilege. For example:
    1. CPLR § 4504(b) (respecting disclosure of dental identification data and information concerning a victim of crime under age 16);
    2. CPLR §§ 4504(b), (c) (respecting information as to the mental or physical condition of a deceased patient);
    3. Family Court Act § 1046(a)(vii) (no privilege in proceedings for child abuse or neglect);
    4. Social Services Law § 384-b(3)(h) (providing that the privilege affords no ground for exclusion of evidence in proceedings for guardianship and custody of destitute or dependent children);
    5. Social Services Law §§ 384-b(3)(h), 413, 415 (providing that cases of suspected child abuse or maltreatment must be reported in writing and that such reports are admissible in any proceedings relating to child abuse or maltreatment);
    6. Mental Hygiene Law § 81.09(d) (allowing for inspection of medical records of an alleged incapacitated person);
    7. Public Health Law § 2101(1) (requiring disclosure of communicable disease);
    8. Public Health Law §§ 2101(1), 2785(2) (providing that a court may grant an order for the disclosure of HIV-related information upon an application showing a "compelling need" in judicial proceedings);
    9. Public Health Law § 3373 (abrogating the privilege as to controlled substances);
    10. Penal Law § 265.25 (making it a misdemeanor for a doctor or hospital to fail to report a wound "caused by discharge of a gun or firearm" or "a wound which is likely to or may result in death and is actually or apparently inflicted by a knife, ice pick or other sharp or pointed instrument"); and

11. Penal Law § 265.26 (requiring hospitals and medical professionals to report certain cases of serious burns).

See People v. Sinski, 88 N.Y.2d 487, 491–92, 646 N.Y.S.2d 651, 653 (1996). *See also Matter of Grand Jury Investigation in N.Y. County*, 98 N.Y.2d 525, 532, 749 N.Y.S.2d 462, 466 (2002); *Matter of Grand Jury Investigation of Onondaga County*, 59 N.Y.2d 130, 136, 463 N.Y.S.2d 758, 760 (1983).

§ 44:14   Waiver of physician-patient privilege—Generally

Research References

West's Key Number Digest, Witnesses ☞208(1), 209

As a general rule, where a person affirmatively places his or her medical condition into issue in a case, the person waives the physician-patient privilege. In this regard, in *People v. Al Kanani*, 33 N.Y.2d 260, 264–65, 351 N.Y.S.2d 969, 971 (1973), the Court of Appeals held that:

> [W]here insanity is asserted as a defense and, as here, the defendant offers evidence tending to show his insanity in support of this plea, a complete waiver is effected, and the prosecution is then permitted to call psychiatric experts to testify regarding his sanity even though they may have treated the defendant. When the patient first fully discloses the evidence of his affliction, it is he who has given the public the full details of his case, thereby disclosing the secrets which the statute was designed to protect, thus creating a waiver removing it from the operation of the statute.

(Citation omitted).

In *Koump v. Smith*, 25 N.Y.2d 287, 294, 303 N.Y.S.2d 858, 864 (1969), the Court of Appeals held that:

> [B]y bringing or defending a personal injury action in which mental or physical condition is affirmatively put in issue, a party *waives* the privilege. As a practical matter, a plaintiff or a defendant, who affirmatively asserts a mental or physical condition, must eventually waive the privilege to prove his case or his defense. To uphold the privilege would allow a party to use it as a sword rather than a shield. A party should not be permitted to assert a mental or physical condition in seeking damages or in seeking to absolve himself from liability and at the same time assert the privilege in order to prevent the other party from ascertaining the truth of the claim and the nature and extent of the injury or condition.

> We do not hold that the privilege is waived *whenever* a party defends an action in which his mental or physical condition is in controversy. The rule laid down today is limited to cases in which a defendant affirmatively asserts the condition either by way of counterclaim or to excuse the conduct complained of by the plaintiff. Thus in the instant case where defendant has simply denied the allegation of the complaint, the privilege should be recognized.

The Court of Appeals clarified its decision in *Koump* in *Dillenbeck v. Hess*, 73 N.Y.2d 278, 287–88, 539 N.Y.S.2d 707, 713–14 (1989):

> [A] party does not waive the privilege whenever forced to defend an action in which his or her mental or physical condition is in controversy. In order to effect a waiver, the party must do more than simply deny the allegations in the complaint — he or she must affirmatively assert the condition "either by way of counterclaim or to excuse the conduct complained of by the plaintiff."

(Citation and footnote omitted). *See also* 73 N.Y.2d 278 at 289, 539 N.Y.S.2d at 714 ("Defendant cannot be said to have waived the privilege simply by denying the allegations in the complaint or by testifying that she cannot remember any details of the incident where the fact of her memory loss is not being advanced to excuse her conduct"); *Lopez v. Oquendo*, 262 A.D.2d 24, __, 690 N.Y.S.2d 584, 585 (1st Dep't 1999).

In *People v. Flores*, 40 A.D.3d 876, __, 836 N.Y.S.2d 273, 275 (2d Dep't 2007), leave to appeal denied, 9 N.Y.3d 875, 842 N.Y.S.2d 787, 874 N.E.2d 754 (2007), the Appellate Division, Second Department, held that "the defendant waived his physician-patient privilege by raising an intoxication defense."

§ 44:15 Waiver of physician-patient privilege in DWI cases

Research References

West's Key Number Digest, Witnesses ☞208(1), 209

In *People v. Gonzalez*, 239 A.D.2d 931, __, 659 N.Y.S.2d 591, 592 (4th Dep't 1997), the Appellate Division, Fourth Department, held that:

> [D]efendant waived the privilege by placing his medical condition in issue during cross-examination of a police officer who observed defendant and spoke to him at the hospital. Defendant's reliance on *People v. Osburn*, 155 A.D.2d 926, 547 N.Y.S.2d 749, is misplaced. In that case, the cross-examination of a prosecution witness was undertaken only to show that defendant did not voluntarily consent to a blood test. Here, in contrast, defense counsel attempted to show through cross-examination that the appearance of defendant was the result of his injuries instead of intoxication.

(Citations omitted). *See also People v. Centerbar*, 80 A.D.3d 1008, __, 914 N.Y.S.2d 784, 787 (3d Dep't 2011) ("while defendant's hospital medical records were privileged (*see* CPLR 4504[a]), he placed his physical and mental condition at the time of his consent—as well as his condition before and after—directly in issue by calling the emergency room treating physician to testify regarding his ability to consent, thereby waiving the privilege.

Defendant called upon that physician, and the treating nurse during cross-examination, to testify to their recollection—and based upon the medical records—regarding his condition, treatment and capacity at the hospital and at the time of his consent and, thus, no error occurred").

Similarly, in *People v. Feldmann*, 110 A.D.2d 906, __, 488 N.Y.S.2d 455, 456 (2d Dep't 1985), the Appellate Division, Second Department, held that:

> [T]he trial court properly admitted the hospital records into evidence on the basis that defendant waived his physician-patient privilege through his attorney's cross-examination of Police Officers Smith and Graziose. On his cross-examination of Smith and Graziose, defense counsel questioned the officers about the defendant's subsequent treatment (i.e., the fact that a laceration of defendant's chin required over 200 stitches), in an apparent attempt to elicit evidence that defendant's condition at the scene was due to his injuries and not due to intoxication. Thus, defendant by affirmatively placing his physical condition at issue, waived his physician-patient privilege.

See also People v. O'Connor, 290 A.D.2d 519, __, 738 N.Y.S.2d 55, 56 (2d Dep't 2002) ("Supreme Court correctly advised the defendant that he would waive the physician-patient privilege if he affirmatively placed his medical condition at issue"); *People v. Bolson*, 183 Misc. 2d 155, __, 701 N.Y.S.2d 828, 833 (Queens Co. Sup. Ct. 1999) (same). *See generally People v. Kral*, 198 A.D.2d 670, __, 603 N.Y.S.2d 1004, 1005 (3d Dep't 1993) (although People improperly subpoenaed defendant's hospital records, defendant ultimately waived physician-patient privilege, thereby rendering the violation harmless); *People v. Conklin*, 72 A.D.2d 607, 421 N.Y.S.2d 113 (2d Dep't 1979).

By contrast, in *People v. Osburn*, 155 A.D.2d 926, 547 N.Y.S.2d 749 (4th Dep't 1989), the Fourth Department held that:

> The court erred . . . in concluding that defendant waived the physician-patient privilege by cross-examining certain witnesses about her physical condition and in admitting the hospital's diagnostic test. "[A] party does not waive the privilege whenever forced to defend an action in which his or her mental or physical condition is in controversy." The cross-examination regarding defendant's condition at the hospital was undertaken to show that her consent to the blood test taken at the request of the police was involuntary, and not to excuse her conduct or to show that her appearance was the result of her injuries instead of intoxication.

(Citation omitted).

In addition, in *People v. Carkner*, 213 A.D.2d 735, __-__, 623 N.Y.S.2d 350, 353–54 (3d Dep't 1995), the defendant:

> [R]aised the issue of whether he was the person from whom the

blood sample was drawn by referring to certain discrepancies on a form from his hospital records by which the police requested that the blood sample be taken. The form contained no confidential information, and the question of whether defendant was the person from whom the blood sample was drawn has nothing to do with defendant's physical or mental condition. By raising the identity issue, defendant "opened the door" to permit introduction of evidence relevant to the identity issue. He did not, however, affirmatively put his physical or mental condition in issue so as to waive the physician-patient privilege with regard to all of the confidential information contained in the hospital records. The confidential information should not, therefore, have been admitted into evidence over defendant's objection. We also note that although defendant's medical condition was clearly at issue from the outset insofar as the injuries he sustained in the accident are relevant to his position in the vehicle, defendant's mere denial that he was driving is insufficient to constitute the type of affirmative conduct necessary to waive the physician-patient privilege.

(Citation omitted).

§ 44:16 Violation of physician-patient privilege subject to harmless error analysis

Research References

West's Key Number Digest, Witnesses ⊙⇒208(1), 209

In *People v. Carkner*, 213 A.D.2d 735, __, 623 N.Y.S.2d 350, 354 (3d Dep't 1995), the Appellate Division, Third Department, held that "[t]he violation of defendant's physician-patient privilege is subject to the nonconstitutional harmless error analysis." *See also People v. Feldmann*, 110 A.D.2d 906, __, 488 N.Y.S.2d 455, 456 (2d Dep't 1985).

§ 44:17 Evidence obtained as "fruit" of violation of physician-patient privilege not suppressible

Over the years, it had routinely been held that a violation of the physician-patient privilege would result in the suppression of the evidence obtained as a result of such violation. *See, e.g., People v. Sinski*, 88 N.Y.2d 487, 646 N.Y.S.2d 651 (1996); *People v. Petro*, 122 A.D.2d 309, 504 N.Y.S.2d 67 (3d Dep't 1986); *People v. Bashkatov*, 13 Misc. 3d 1101, 827 N.Y.S.2d 594 (N.Y. City Crim. Ct. 2006), appeal dismissed, 18 Misc. 3d 127(A), 856 N.Y.S.2d 25 (App. Term 2007), leave to appeal denied, 10 N.Y.3d 808, 857 N.Y.S.2d 41, 886 N.E.2d 806 (2008). In *Sinski*, the Court of Appeals held that:

> [T]he disposition of the Legislature since 1972 has been to narrow the statutory exception allowing disclosure of confidential communications, not to expand it. The People's suggestion that the Legislature intended [Public Health Law] section 3373 to generally

abrogate the physician-patient privilege for the purpose of criminal prosecution is not only contrary to the rationale behind the physician-patient privilege—to encourage complete candor in order to secure appropriate treatment—but it is also contradicted by the language of the statute and the Legislature's demonstrated concern over confidentiality in this area.

88 N.Y.2d 494, 646 N.Y.S.2d at 654. The *Sinski* Court went on to hold that "any communications between defendant and his doctors in furtherance of his treatment were obtained in violation of defendant's physician-patient privilege and improperly admitted at trial." 88 N.Y.2d 494 at 495, 646 N.Y.S.2d at 655.

Nonetheless, in *People v. Greene*, 9 N.Y.3d 277, 279, 849 N.Y.S.2d 461, 461 (2007), the Court of Appeals held that "evidence obtained as a result of a violation of the physician-patient privilege need not be suppressed at a criminal trial." The reasoning of *Greene* is as follows:

> [W]e agree with both courts below that, even if there was a violation of the physician-patient privilege, the suppression of the evidence found as a result is not required. The physician-patient privilege is based on statute, not the State or Federal Constitution. Our decisions make clear that a violation of a statute does not, without more, justify suppressing the evidence to which that violation leads.
>
> We have made an exception to this rule only when the principal purpose of a statute is to protect a constitutional right. * * *
>
> There is no constitutional right to privacy in physician-patient communications. The Legislature has created, by statute, several exceptions to the physician-patient privilege. It could, if it chose, make another exception for the disclosure in this case. * * *
>
> The physician-patient privilege . . . does not serve primarily to protect individuals against government conduct; it regulates a private relationship. The primary obligation to comply with CPLR 4504 is the doctor's — or, in this case, the hospital's. To suppress evidence resulting from a violation of section 4504 would be to punish the State for a doctor's or hospital's misconduct — a punishment unlikely to deter doctors and hospitals, who have little interest in whether criminal prosecutions succeed or not.

9 N.Y.3d 277 at 280–81, 849 N.Y.S.2d at 462–63 (citations omitted).

A curious aspect of *Greene* is the court's finding that "[t]o suppress evidence resulting from a violation of section 4504 would be to punish the State for a doctor's or hospital's misconduct." 9 N.Y.3d 277 at 281, 849 N.Y.S.2d at 463. In this regard, wasn't it the State that requested that the doctor or hospital disclose potentially privileged information? Likewise, if the State succeeds in enticing a doctor or hospital to improperly disclose privileged information (*i.e.*, to engage in misconduct)—thereby exposing the doctor or hospital to civil liability and/or to professional discipline—should the State be rewarded for doing so? In fact, it would seem that if a prosecutor were to entice a doctor or hospital to improperly disclose privileged information, such conduct would be unethical.

In addition, although *Greene* appears to overrule *Sinski*, the *Greene* Court did not even mention *Sinski*. However, *Greene* and *Sinski* may be reconcilable. *Sinski* held that "any communications between defendant and his doctors in furtherance of his treatment were obtained in violation of defendant's physician-patient privilege and improperly admitted at trial." 88 N.Y.2d at 495, 646 N.Y.S.2d at 655. *Greene* held that "evidence obtained *as a result* of a violation of the physician-patient privilege need not be suppressed at a criminal trial." 9 N.Y.3d at 279, 849 N.Y.S.2d at 461 (emphasis added). Critically, the evidence at issue in *Greene* was not evidence of a medical nature. Rather, it was evidence that was sought to be suppressed as the "fruit of the poisonous tree." *People v. Greene*, 36 A.D.3d 219, __, 824 N.Y.S.2d 48, 51 (1st Dep't 2006), *aff'd*, 9 N.Y.3d 277, 849 N.Y.S.2d 461 (2007).

In other words, it appears that while the "fruit" of a violation of the physician-patient privilege is admissible at trial—the privileged information itself is still inadmissible. Notably, *Greene* did not expressly overrule any past precedent. Neither does it (a) abrogate the physician-patient privilege, (b) make the privilege inapplicable to criminal cases, and/or (c) encourage medical personnel to violate the privilege. Rather, *Greene* held only that the fruits of a violation of the physician-patient privilege are not suppressible at a criminal trial.

However, in *People v. Drayton*, 56 A.D.3d 1278, __, 867 N.Y.S.2d 825, 826 (4th Dep't 2008), leave to appeal granted, 12 N.Y.3d 783, 879 N.Y.S.2d 59, 906 N.E.2d 1093 (2009), the Appellate Division, Fourth Department, quoting *Greene*, stated:

> Even assuming, arguendo, that the seizure of the blood sample by the police constituted a violation of the physician-patient privilege under CPLR 4504(a), we conclude that the court properly refused to suppress the evidence results from the blood sample inasmuch as "a violation of a statute does not, without more, justify suppressing the evidence to which that violation leads."

See also People v. Bryant, 73 A.D.3d 1442, __, 900 N.Y.S.2d 810, 811 (4th Dep't 2010).

In light of *Greene*, it is especially important that medical personnel and hospitals be reminded of their obligation not to disclose information protected by the physician-patient privilege.

In this regard, a letter to a hospital administrator early on in a case may well prevent the prosecution from improperly gaining access to privileged information.

§ 44:18 Applicability of physician-patient privilege to EMTs

Research References

West's Key Number Digest, Witnesses ⟨⟩208(1), 209

In the spirit of giving the physician-patient privilege a broad and liberal construction, *see* previous section, most courts that have addressed the issue have found that the privilege is applicable to emergency medical technicians (EMTs) (where the information at issue would otherwise be privileged). *See, e.g., People v. Brito*, 26 Misc. 3d 1097, __, 892 N.Y.S.2d 752, 755 (Bronx Co. Sup. Ct. 2010) (Prehospital Care Report (PCR) prepared by EMT protected by physician-patient privilege; observations by EMT that could have been made by layman not protected by privilege); *People v. Muscarnera*, 16 Misc. 3d 622, __-__ & n.4, 842 N.Y.S.2d 241, 248–49 & n.4 (Nassau Co. Dist. Ct. 2007); *People v. Mirque*, 195 Misc. 2d 375, 758 N.Y.S.2d 471 (N.Y. City Crim. Ct. 2003); *People v. Hanf*, 159 Misc. 2d 748, 611 N.Y.S.2d 85 (Monroe Co. Ct. 1994). *Cf. People v. Ackerson*, 149 Misc. 2d 882, 566 N.Y.S.2d 833 (Monroe Co. Ct. 1991). *See generally People v. Bowen*, 229 A.D.2d 954, __, 645 N.Y.S.2d 381, 381–82 (4th Dep't 1996) (Court assumed, without deciding, that person training to be EMT fell within ambit of CPLR § 4504(a)).

§ 44:19 Waiver of physician-patient privilege by presence of third party

Research References

West's Key Number Digest, Witnesses ⟨⟩208(1), 209

In *People v. Decina*, 2 N.Y.2d 133, 141, 157 N.Y.S.2d 558, 566 (1956), the Court of Appeals addressed the issue of "whether the presence of the police guard in the doorway of the room destroys any privilege arising under [the physician-patient privilege] and permits the doctor to testify." More specifically, the Court confronted the issue of "what effect, if any, the presence of the police guard, pursuant to the orders of the district attorney, in or about the doorway of the hospital room, where he could overhear the conversation between Dr. Wechter and defendant, has upon the privilege under section 352. That section does not in so many words require that a communication be confidential or confidentially given in order to be privileged." 2 N.Y.2d 133 at 143, 157 N.Y.S.2d at 568.

After analyzing various case law, the Court held that:

> The true test appears to be whether in the light of all the surrounding circumstances, and particularly the occasion for the presence of the third person, the communication was intended to be confidential and complied with the other provisions of the statute. Applying this test, we hold that under section 352, and the cases construing it, the communication by defendant to Dr. Wechter was privileged, and admission of it by the trial court was error, as correctly stated by the Appellate Division.

2 N.Y.2d 133 at 145, 157 N.Y.S.2d at 569. *See also People v. Jaffarian*, 9 Misc. 3d 455, 799 N.Y.S.2d 733 (Webster Just. Ct. 2005); *People v. Sanders*, 169 Misc. 2d 813, ___-___, 646 N.Y.S.2d 955, 959–61 (Bronx Co. Sup. Ct. 1996).

§ 44:20 Prosecutor's improper comments regarding defendant's medical history results in reversal

In *People v. O'Brien*, 140 A.D.3d 1325, 32 N.Y.S.3d 741 (3d Dep't 2016), the Appellate Division, Third Department, reversed the defendant's conviction of DWI based in part on the prosecutor's improper comments regarding the defendant's medical history. Specifically:

> We are further concerned with the prosecutor's cross-examination of defendant and the personal opinions that she rendered during summation. Defendant concedes in his brief that he failed to preserve his challenge to the prosecutor's cross-examination and summation through objections at trial, but we exercise our interest of justice jurisdiction to take corrective action. Having received the medical records on the morning of April 15, 2014 prior to calling her own first witness, the prosecutor clearly had adequate time to review the three pages before cross-examining defendant the next day. The medical records confirmed that defendant had been exposed to multiple explosions in Afghanistan and had a history of falling from a vehicle and a low back injury. During cross-examination, the prosecutor utilized documentation provided by the defense to question defendant as to his winning an Iron Man award in August 2011 and his being recommended for enrollment in the U.S. Army Ranger School, described as one of the most physically and mentally demanding military programs in the world. Certainly this questioning was an accurate portrayal of defendant's physical fitness prior to being injured during his military service and fair game to a point as to whether defendant was capable of performing the field sobriety tests. The portrayal, however, disregards defendant's actual medical condition as shown in the precluded medical records. This discrepancy came to a head during summation, where the prosecutor stated, "I just didn't really know what to make" of defendant's claimed impairments. She continued, "I'm surprised" given defendant's Iron Man award, and concluded, "I don't understand what happened . . . when he couldn't perform a standardized field sobriety test. It just doesn't make any sense to me."

A prosecutor may not, even during summation, express his or her personal opinion challenging the veracity of the evidence. To express personal surprise as to defendant's claim of incapacity, while in possession of defendant's medical records, was disingenuous and improper. Considering that the jury acquitted defendant of the aggravated driving while intoxicated charge, his ability to perform the field sobriety tests presented a central issue in the case. In our view, the preclusion of the medical records coupled with the prosecutor's summation substantially prejudiced defendant and deprived him of a fair trial.

Id. at __, 32 N.Y.S.3d at 744-45 (citations omitted).

Part XII

PENALTIES AND CONSEQUENCES

Chapter 45

Suspension Pending Prosecution

Research References

Westlaw Databases

Handling a Criminal Case in New York (HCCNY)
Handling Drunk Driving Cases (2d ed.) (HDRUNKDR)

Treatises and Practice Aids

Muldoon, Handling a Criminal Case in New York §§ 4:15 to 4:20
Fiandach, Handling Drunk Driving Cases §§ 33:1 to 33:50 (2d ed.)

Law Reviews and Other Periodicals

Wathen, Transportation and Motor Vehicles; Suspension and Delay of Driver's License for Minors Driving While Intoxicated, 25 Pac. L. J. 842 (January, 1994)

> **KeyCite®:** Cases and other legal materials listed in KeyCite Scope can be researched through the KeyCite service on Westlaw®. Use KeyCite to check citations for form, parallel references, prior and later history, and comprehensive citator information, including citations to other decisions and secondary materials.

---

§ 45:1 In general

Research References

West's Key Number Digest, Automobiles ☞144.1(1.11)

A defendant charged with DWI must be aware of several statutes which, if applicable, call for the mandatory and/or permissive suspension of his or her driver's license pending prosecution. The first statute is Vehicle & Traffic Law § 1193(2)(e)(7)—the so-called "prompt suspension law"—which is generally applicable to a defendant who is charged with DWI *and* who is alleged to have had a BAC of .08% or more at the time of his or her arrest. The second statute, VTL § 1193(2)(e)(1), is applicable to a defendant who is charged with DWI, aggravated DWI, DWAI drugs *or* DWAI combined influence *and* who either (a) has been convicted of any violation of VTL § 1192 within the preceding five years, or (b) is charged with Vehicular Assault or Vehicular Homicide in connection with the current incident. A third statute, VTL § 1194(2)(b)(3), is applicable to a defendant who is charged with a violation of VTL § 1192 *and* who is alleged to have refused to submit to a chemical test.

Prior to the enactment of the prompt suspension law, VTL § 510(3-a) had occasionally been used to suspend DWI defendants' driver's licenses pending prosecution. However, in light of VTL § 1193(2)(e)(1) and (7), as well as the Court of Appeals' decision in *Pringle v. Wolfe*, 88 N.Y.2d 426, 646 N.Y.S.2d 82, 668 N.E.2d 1376 (1996), continued reliance upon VTL § 510(3-a) in this regard would appear to be unwarranted. *See King v. Kay*, 39 Misc. 3d 995, 963 N.Y.S.2d 537 (Suffolk Co. Sup. Ct. 2013).

§ 45:2   VTL § 1193(2)(e)(7)—The prompt suspension law

Research References
West's Key Number Digest, Automobiles ☞144.2(10.2)

A defendant who is charged with DWI, Aggravated DWI or DWAI Combined Influence, *and* who is alleged to have had a Blood Alcohol Content (BAC) of .08% or more at the time of his or her arrest is subject to the prompt suspension law. This law provides, in pertinent part:

> (7) Suspension pending prosecution; excessive blood alcohol content. a. Except as provided in clause a-1 of this subparagraph, a court shall suspend a driver's license, pending prosecution, of any person charged with a violation of [VTL § 1192(2), (2-a), (3) or (4-a)] who, at the time of arrest, is alleged to have had .08 of one percent or more by weight of alcohol in such driver's blood as shown by chemical analysis of blood, breath, urine, or saliva, made pursuant to [VTL § 1194(2) or (3)].

VTL § 1193(2)(e)(7)(a).

Notably, the prompt suspension law, by its express terms, only applies under certain circumstances. For example, the prompt suspension law only applies where the defendant is charged with VTL § 1192(2), (2-a), (3) or (4-a); it does not apply where the defendant is charged with VTL § 1192(1) (*i.e.*, DWAI) or (4) (*i.e.*, DWAI drugs). In addition, the prompt suspension law only applies where a chemical test result is obtained; it does not apply where the defendant is alleged to have refused to submit to a chemical test. *See* Appendix 61.

Furthermore, the prompt suspension law only applies where the defendant's BAC is .08% or more; it does not apply where the defendant's BAC is below .08%, even if he or she is charged with VTL § 1192(3). Moreover, the prompt suspension law only applies where a prosecution is pending. Accordingly, a defendant who enters a plea of guilty *and is sentenced* at arraignment is not subject to the prompt suspension law. On the other hand, a defendant who enters a plea of guilty at arraignment, but whose sentencing is adjourned, is subject to the prompt suspension law (because the prosecution does not terminate until the imposition of sentence).

§ 45:3   VTL § 1193(2)(e)(7)—Suspension procedure

Research References
West's Key Number Digest, Automobiles ☞144.2(10.2)

Pursuant to the express language of the prompt suspension law, in order to impose a suspension thereunder, the court must make two findings. First, the court "must find that the accusatory instrument conforms to the requirements of [CPL §] 100.40." VTL § 1193(2)(e)(7)(b). CPL § 100.40 sets forth the facial sufficiency requirements for local criminal court accusatory instruments. Second, the court must find that "there exists reasonable cause to believe . . . that . . . the holder operated a motor vehicle while such holder had .08 of one percent or more by weight of alcohol in his or her blood as was shown by chemical analysis of such person's blood, breath, urine or saliva, made pursuant to the provisions of [VTL § 1194]." VTL § 1193(2)(e)(7)(b).

If such *tentative* findings are made, the statute provides that "the holder shall be entitled to an opportunity to make a statement regarding these two issues and to present evidence tending to rebut the court's findings." VTL § 1193(2)(e)(7)(b).

The Court of Appeals' decision in *Pringle v. Wolfe*, 88 N.Y.2d 426, 646 N.Y.S.2d 82, 668 N.E.2d 1376 (1996), added in several prerequisites to suspension under the prompt suspension law that do not appear in the statute itself. For example, *Pringle* adds numerous procedural due process requirements into the prompt suspension law which must be complied with before a suspension pending prosecution thereunder can be imposed; and adds the threshold requirements that a *"court may not order suspension of the license unless it has in its possession the results of the chemical test, and, as the Commissioner concedes, these results must be presented to the court in certified, documented form (see, CPLR 4518[c])." Wolfe*, 88 N.Y.2d at 432, 646 N.Y.S.2d at 85–86 (emphasis added). *See also People v. DeRojas*, 180 Misc. 2d 690, 693 N.Y.S.2d 404, 405 (App. Term, 2d Dep't 1999).

In addition, *Pringle* created and granted the defendant an absolute right to a so-called *"Pringle* hearing." In this regard, the *Pringle* court held that "[u]nder the prompt suspension law, the court *must* hold a suspension hearing before the conclusion of the proceedings required for arraignment and before the driver's license may be suspended." 88 N.Y.2d at 432, 646 N.Y.S.2d at 85 (emphasis added). At this hearing, "the court must first determine whether the accusatory instrument is sufficient on its face and next whether there exists reasonable cause to believe that the driver operated a motor vehicle while having a blood alcohol level in excess of [.08] of 1% as shown by a chemical test." *Pringle*, 88 N.Y.2d at 432, 646 N.Y.S.2d at 85. *See also People v. Roach*, 226 A.D.2d 55, 649 N.Y.S.2d 607, 608–09 (4th Dep't 1996).

With regard to the opportunity to rebut, the *Pringle* court held that it would be "meaningless" to allow the defendant "to 'rebut the court's findings' *after* the suspension is ordered." 88 N.Y.2d at 432, 646 N.Y.S.2d at 86. Accordingly, the court interpreted the prompt suspension law to require both (a) that the defendant be "entitled to present evidence to rebut the court's tentative findings *before the court may order the license suspension*," *Pringle*, 88 N.Y.2d at 432, 646 N.Y.S.2d at 86 (emphasis added), and (b) that it is "incumbent on the court to grant a driver's reasonable request for a short adjournment if necessary to marshal evidence to rebut the prima facie showing of 'reasonable cause.' " *Pringle*, 88 N.Y.2d at 433, 646 N.Y.S.2d at 86.

In *People v. Roach*, 226 A.D.2d 55, 649 N.Y.S.2d 607 (4th Dep't 1996), the Appellate Division, Fourth Department, both (a) stated that to invoke the prompt suspension law, the court must find, inter alia, that "there is reasonable cause to believe that the driver failed *a properly administered and reliable chemical sobriety test*," *Roach*, 226 A.D.2d at __, 649 N.Y.S.2d at 609 (emphasis added), and (b) made clear that the defendant's driver's license should not be suspended pending prosecution if the driver rebuts the *prima facie* showing. *Roach*, 226 A.D.2d at __, 649 N.Y.S.2d at 609. *See also People v. Boulton*, 164 Misc. 2d 604, 625 N.Y.S.2d 428, 430 (Troy City Ct. 1995) ("Vehicle and Traffic Law § 1193(2)(e)(7)(b) appears to mandate the return of the license to the defendant whenever evidence is presented tending to rebut the Court's findings. On close analysis this burden is neither onerous nor cumbersome").

Despite the fact that a lawful VTL § 1192 arrest is a prerequisite to a valid request to submit to a chemical test, *see, e.g., Gagliardi v. Department of Motor Vehicles*, 144 A.D.2d 882, 535 N.Y.S.2d 203, 204 (3d Dep't 1988) ("In order for the testing strictures of Vehicle and Traffic Law § 1194 to come into play, there must have been a lawful arrest for driving while intoxicated"), and despite the fact that VTL § 1193(2)(e)(7) requires that the driver fail a chemical test *administered pursuant to* VTL § 1194, neither VTL § 1193(2)(e)(7) nor *Pringle* appear to contemplate that the driver can challenge the lawfulness of his or her arrest at a *Pringle* hearing.

Regardless, the United States Court of Appeals for the Second Circuit recently held, in a similar DWI-related civil forfeiture case, that:

[W]e find that the Due Process Clause requires that claimants be given an early opportunity to test the probable validity of further deprivation, including probable cause for the initial seizure. * * *

As a remedy, we order that claimants be given a prompt post-seizure retention hearing, with adequate notice, for motor vehicles seized as instrumentalities of crime pursuant to N.Y.C.Code § 14-140(b). * * *

Although we decline to dictate a specific form for the prompt retention hearing, we hold that, at a minimum, the hearing must enable claimants to test the probable validity of continued deprivation of their vehicles, including the City's probable cause for the initial warrantless seizure. In the absence of either probable cause for the seizure or post-seizure evidence supporting the probable validity of continued deprivation, an owner's vehicle would have to be released during the pendency of the criminal and civil proceedings. * * *

In conclusion, we hold that promptly after their vehicles are seized under N.Y.C.Code § 14-140 as alleged instrumentalities of crime, plaintiffs must be given an opportunity to test the probable validity of the City's deprivation of their vehicles *pendente lite*, including probable cause for the initial warrantless seizure.

Krimstock v. Kelly, 306 F.3d 40, 68, 68–69, 69, (2d Cir. 2002) (footnote omitted). *See also County of Nassau v. Canavan*, 1 N.Y.3d 134, 144–45, 770 N.Y.S.2d 277, 286, 802 N.E.2d 616 (2003) (same).

The retention of a motor vehicle driven by an alleged drunken driver *pendente lite* pursuant to N.Y.C.Code § 14-140 is analogous to the suspension of the driver's license of an alleged drunken driver *pendente lite* pursuant to VTL § 1193(2)(e)(7). As such, since the *Krimstock* court expressly rejected the New York State courts' assessment of the Constitutional due process requirements associated with the retention of a motor vehicle *pendente lite* pursuant to N.Y.C.Code § 14-140—*Krimstock* expressly rejected, and was critical of, the conclusions of *Grinberg v. Safir*, 181 Misc. 2d 444, 694 N.Y.S.2d 316 (N.Y. Sup 1999), aff'd, 266 A.D.2d 43, 698 N.Y.S.2d 218 (1st Dep't 1999), *see Krimstock*, 306 F.3d at 53—it is reasonable to assume that the Second Circuit would also disagree with the *Pringle* Court's apparent conclusion that the driver need not be given an opportunity to test the lawfulness of his or her warrantless arrest in connection with a suspension *pendente lite* pursuant to VTL § 1193(2)(e)(7).

Nonetheless, in *Vanderminden v. Tarantino*, 60 A.D.3d 55, 871 N.Y.S.2d 760 (3d Dep't 2009), appeal denied, 12 N.Y.3d 708, 879 N.Y.S.2d 55, 906 N.E.2d 1089 (2009), the Appellate Division, Third Department, without addressing *Krimstock* (or other Due Process cases), had the following to say about the scope of a *Pringle* hearing:

As relevant to petitioner's remaining arguments, which pertain to the scope and conduct of his *Pringle* hearing, we begin by noting that the prompt suspension law provides that, in order for the court to issue a suspension order, it must find that (1) the accusatory instrument conforms with CPL 100.40, and (2) reasonable cause exists to believe that the driver operated a motor vehicle with ".08 of one percent or more by weight of alcohol in his or her blood as was shown by chemical analysis of such person's blood, breath, urine or saliva" (Vehicle and Traffic Law § 1193[2][e][7][b]). Where such an initial determination is made, Vehicle and Traffic Law § 1193(2)(e)(7) further provides that the driver "shall be entitled to an opportunity to make a statement regarding these two issues and to present evidence tending to rebut the court's findings" (Vehicle and Traffic Law § 1193[2][e][7][b]). In this case, respondent determined that the simplified information complied with CPL 100.40 and that, based upon the certified breath test results, as well as the arresting officer's supporting deposition, there was reasonable cause to believe that petitioner had a BAC of .08% or more while operating a motor vehicle. Therefore, respondent made the necessary preliminary findings to issue a suspension order.

In rebuttal, petitioner called three police witnesses and attempted to question them regarding the calibration of the breath test device, the administration of the test, and matters relating to probable cause for petitioner's arrest. Respondent precluded any questioning relating to the calibration and maintenance of the breath device as well as to probable cause for the arrest, concluding that such matters were outside the scope of a *Pringle* hearing.

We are not persuaded by petitioner's contention that his due process rights were violated by respondent's rulings. While issues pertaining to the lawfulness of the police stop, probable cause for arrest, and whether the breath test device was working properly at the time of the test are relevant to the admissibility of breath test results at a criminal trial, and may ultimately bear on the determination of criminal culpability, they are beyond the scope of a *Pringle* hearing. Significantly, a *Pringle* hearing is a civil administrative proceeding which runs parallel to the criminal proceedings. It is not a plenary hearing requiring the same level of due process protection as a criminal trial, nor is it "an opportunity for free-wheeling discovery regarding the criminal matter." Indeed, as the Court of Appeals has observed, to "convert the license suspension proceeding into a trial on the merits of the underlying criminal charge . . . would be prohibitively expensive and cumbersome, and would subvert the State's compelling interest in promoting highway safety." For these reasons, we agree with Supreme Court that respondent appropriately limited petitioner's inquiry.

(Citations omitted).

Courts will have to reconcile *Vanderminden* with the Court of Appeals' holding in *Pringle* that "the minimal risk of an erroneous suspension is further diminished by the driver's right to a *meaningful presuspension opportunity to rebut the chemical test results.*" *Pringle v. Wolfe*, 88 N.Y.2d 426, 434, 646 N.Y.S.2d 82, 87, 668 N.E.2d 1376 (1996) (emphasis added).

§ 45:4 VTL § 1193(2)(e)(7)—Applicability to certain underage drivers

Research References

West's Key Number Digest, Automobiles ⊜144.2(10.2)

VTL § 1193(2)(e)(7)(a-1) applies to drivers under 18 years of age who do not yet possess a full class D or class M driver's license. A class D license is a regular, noncommercial driver's license. A class M license is a motorcycle driver's license. VTL § 1193(2)(e)(7)(a-1) provides:

a-1. A court shall suspend a class DJ or MJ learner's permit or a class DJ or MJ driver's license, pending prosecution, of any person who has been charged with a violation of [VTL § 1192(1), (2), (2-a) and/or (3)].

The "J" designation pertains to a junior learner's permit or junior driver's license. A person between 16 and 18 years of age can apply for a junior permit/license. A class DJ or MJ driver's license can be converted to a class D or M driver's license if the holder is at least 17 years of age and has, among other things, successfully completed an approved high school or college driver education course. *See* 15 NYCRR § 2.5. At age 18, a valid class DJ or MJ driver's license automatically converts to a class D or M driver's license.

Notably, unlike the prompt suspension law for class D or M driver's license holders, VTL § 1193(2)(e)(7)(a-1) applies not only where the defendant is charged with VTL § 1192(2), (2-a) and/or (3), but also where he or she is charged with VTL § 1192(1) (*i.e.*, DWAI). In addition, unlike the prompt suspension law for class D or M driver's license holders, no chemical test result is required. Thus, VTL § 1193(2)(e)(7)(a-1) can be applied to chemical test refusal cases and to cases where the chemical test results are not yet available.

VTL § 1193(2)(e)(7)(b) provides that "the suspension occurring under clause a-1 of this subparagraph shall occur immediately after the holder's first appearance before the court on the charge which shall, whenever possible, be the next regularly scheduled session of the court after the arrest or at the conclusion of all proceedings required for the arraignment."

In terms of due process, in order to impose a suspension under VTL § 1193(2)(e)(7)(1-a), the court must make two findings. First, the court "must find that the accusatory instrument conforms to the requirements of [CPL §] 100.40." VTL § 1193(2)(e)(7)(b). CPL § 100.40 sets forth the facial sufficiency requirements for local criminal court accusatory instruments. Second, the court must find that:

[T]here exists reasonable cause to believe either that (a) the holder operated a motor vehicle while such holder had .08 of one percent or more by weight of alcohol in his or her blood as was shown by chemical analysis of such person's blood, breath, urine or saliva, made pursuant to the provisions of [VTL § 1194] or (b) *the person was the holder of a class DJ or MJ learner's permit or a class DJ or*

MJ driver's license and operated a motor vehicle while such holder was in violation of [VTL § 1192(1), (2) and/or (3)].

VTL § 1193(2)(e)(7)(b) (emphasis added).

If such *tentative* findings are made, the statute provides that "the holder shall be entitled to an opportunity to make a statement regarding these two issues and to present evidence tending to rebut the court's findings." VTL § 1193(2)(e)(7)(b). In addition, the additional procedural due process requirements set forth in the Court of Appeals' decision in *Pringle v. Wolfe*, 88 N.Y.2d 426, 646 N.Y.S.2d 82, 668 N.E.2d 1376 (1996), apply. *See* § 45:3, *supra.*

§ 45:5 What if defendant appears for arraignment without counsel?

Research References

West's Key Number Digest, Automobiles ⊙144.2(10.2)

Perhaps the most disturbing aspect of the prompt suspension law is the way in which it is administered by many courts where the defendant appears for arraignment without counsel. In this regard, many defendants who appear for arraignment without counsel in DWI cases have their driver's licenses summarily suspended by the court. No findings are made; no *Pringle* hearing is held; no opportunity to make a statement or present evidence is offered, etc.

Simply stated, such courts are both (a) flagrantly disregarding the requirements of the statute, and (b) flagrantly disobeying the Court of Appeals' decision in *Pringle v. Wolfe*, 88 N.Y.2d 426, 646 N.Y.S.2d 82, 668 N.E.2d 1376 (1996). As such, they are flagrantly disregarding defendants' constitutional right to due process.

However, that is not all. Such courts are also violating one of the most cherished constitutional rights of all—the right to counsel—which right has been zealously protected by the Court of Appeals and has been codified in CPL § 170.10. In this regard, the Court of Appeals has made clear that:

> The State constitutional right to counsel is a "cherished principle" worthy of the "highest degree of [judicial] vigilance." Our decisional law has advanced this principle by holding that the State constitutional right to counsel attaches indelibly in two situations. First, it arises when formal judicial proceedings begin, whether or not the defendant has actually retained or requested a lawyer. . . . Although these principles are similar to those developed under the Fifth and Sixth Amendments to the Federal Constitution, New York's constitutional right to counsel jurisprudence developed "independent of its Federal counterpart" and offers broader protections.

People v. Ramos, 99 N.Y.2d 27, 32–33, 750 N.Y.S.2d 821, 824, 780 N.E.2d 506 (2002) (citations and footnote omitted). *See also*

People v. West, 81 N.Y.2d 370, 373, 599 N.Y.S.2d 484, 486, 615 N.E.2d 968 (1993); *People v. Ross*, 67 N.Y.2d 321, 502 N.Y.S.2d 693, 493 N.E.2d 917 (1986); *People v. Cunningham*, 49 N.Y.2d 203, 207–08, 424 N.Y.S.2d 421, 423–24, 400 N.E.2d 360 (1980).

> This *"indelible" right to counsel . . . attaches* upon defendant's request for an attorney, *at arraignment* or upon the filing of an accusatory instrument. Underlying the rule is the concept that a criminal defendant confronted by the awesome prosecutorial machinery of the State is entitled, at a bare minimum, to the advice of counsel when he is considering surrender of his valuable legal rights.

People v. Grimaldi, 52 N.Y.2d 611, 616, 439 N.Y.S.2d 833, 835, 422 N.E.2d 493 (1981) (emphases added) (citations omitted).

In addition, CPL § 170.10(3) provides:

> 3. *The defendant has the right to the aid of counsel at the arraignment and at every subsequent stage of the action. If he appears upon such arraignment without counsel, he has the following rights*:
>
> (a) *To an adjournment for the purpose of obtaining counsel*; and
>
> (b) To communicate, free of charge, by letter or by telephone, for the purposes of obtaining counsel and informing a relative or friend that he has been charged with an offense; and
>
> (c) To have counsel assigned by the court if he is financially unable to obtain the same; except that this paragraph does not apply where the accusatory instrument charges a traffic infraction or infractions only.

(Emphases added).

Furthermore, CPL § 170.10(4) mandates that the court "must inform the defendant":

> (a) Of his rights as prescribed in subdivision three; *and the court must not only accord him opportunity to exercise such rights but must itself take such affirmative action as is necessary to effectuate them.*

(Emphasis added).

Numerous Court of Appeals decisions clearly establish that, for a waiver of the fundamental constitutional right to counsel to be valid, the court must conduct a *"searching inquiry,"* on the record, into whether the waiver is knowing, voluntary, intelligent, and unequivocal. In *People v. Smith*, 92 N.Y.2d 516, 683 N.Y.S.2d 164, 705 N.E.2d 1205 (1998), the Court of Appeals reiterated that:

> This Court has recognized that defendants may insist on foregoing the benefits associated with the right to counsel and proceeding on

a *pro se* basis. We have consistently also cautioned, however, that the waiver of this fundamental right to counsel requires that a trial court must be satisfied that a defendant's waiver is unequivocal, voluntary and intelligent; otherwise the waiver will not be recognized as effective.

To ascertain whether a waiver meets these appropriately *rigorous requirements*, the trial courts "should undertake a sufficiently 'searching inquiry' " in order to be "reasonably certain" that a defendant appreciates the " '*dangers and disadvantages*' of giving up the *fundamental right to counsel*." Governing principles demand that *appropriate record exploration* between the trial court and defendant be conducted, both to test an accused's understanding of the waiver and to provide a reliable basis for appellate review.

When a record lacks the requisite "searching inquiry" or fails to measure up to the prescribed standards, a waiver of the right to counsel will be deemed ineffective. To pass muster, a "*searching inquiry*" must reflect *record evidence* that defendant's know what they are doing and that choices are exercised "with eyes open."

This Court has also signified that these *record exchanges* should *affirmatively disclose* that a trial court has *delved into a defendant's age, education, occupation, previous exposure to legal procedures and other relevant factors* bearing on a competent, intelligent, voluntary waiver.

Smith, 92 N.Y.2d at 520, 683 N.Y.S.2d at 166–67 (emphases added) (citations omitted). *See also People v. Arroyo*, 98 N.Y.2d 101, 103–04, 745 N.Y.S.2d 796, 798, 772 N.E.2d 1154 (2002) (same); *People v. Slaughter*, 78 N.Y.2d 485, 491–92, 577 N.Y.S.2d 206, 210–11, 583 N.E.2d 919 (1991) (same); *People v. Sawyer*, 57 N.Y.2d 12, 21, 453 N.Y.S.2d 418, 423, 438 N.E.2d 1133 (1982) (same).

In this regard, the United States Supreme Court has made clear that "[p]resuming waiver from a silent record is impermissible. The record must show, or there must be an allegation and evidence which show, that an accused was offered counsel but intelligently and understandingly rejected the offer. Anything less is not a waiver." *Carnley v. Cochran*, 369 U.S. 506, 516, 82 S. Ct. 884, 890, 8 L. Ed. 2d 70 (1962). *See generally People v. Nixon*, 21 N.Y.2d 338, 355, 287 N.Y.S.2d 659, 672, 234 N.E.2d 687 (1967) ("In cases involving defendants without lawyers . . . particular pains must be taken. . . . In such cases inquiry, well beyond the standards thus far propounded, is indicated").

The requirement of a valid waiver of the right to counsel is also codified in CPL § 170.10(6). CPL § 170.10(6) provides, in pertinent part, that except where the only charges are traffic infractions:

If a defendant . . . desires to proceed without the aid of counsel,

. . . the court must permit the defendant to proceed without the aid of counsel if it is satisfied that he made such decision with knowledge of the significance thereof, but if it is not so satisfied it may not proceed until the defendant is provided with counsel, either of his own choosing or by assignment.

Finally, the official Practice Commentaries to CPL § 170.10 provide, in pertinent part, that:

The statutory procedure as outlined, however, omits an essential first step that should be the responsibility of the court whenever the defendant appears without counsel and there has been no warrant of arrest. This is scrutiny of the accusatory instrument for legal sufficiency. The reason for immediate initial appraisal of that instrument is of course that it is the basis of the court's jurisdiction; and, accordingly, if the instrument is not legally sufficient, the court has no authority at all to proceed with the arraignment. It must dismiss the instrument and discharge the defendant.

If the court is satisfied that it has jurisdiction, the next step is to advise the defendant of his or her rights. In this respect the statute reflects New York's long-standing policy that every effort be made for certainty that the defendant is aware, and has reasonable opportunity to avail himself, of the right to representation by counsel. *Thus the court, in addition to advising an unrepresented defendant of the rights set forth in subdivision three, must not only accord the defendant an opportunity to exercise those rights, "but must itself take such affirmative action as is necessary to effectuate them."*

A defendant has the right to the aid of counsel at arraignment and at all subsequent stages of the proceedings, regardless of the gravity of the charge. Under New York statutory law this right is broader than the requirements of the Federal Constitution . . .

Note too, the clear statutory direction that, in cases other than a traffic infraction, the court must not permit defendant to proceed without the aid of counsel unless it is satisfied that the defendant made the choice to do so with knowledge of the value of counsel and risks inherent in self-representation. *This requires a "searching inquiry" as to defendant's appreciation of the "dangers and disadvantages" of attempting to cope with the legal proceedings—e.g.,* various motions, jury selection, introduction of evidence, objections to same, etc.—as distinguished from merely advising as to the seriousness of the charge and of the fact that the defendant could be sentenced to imprisonment. *People v. Kaltenbach*, 1983, 60 N.Y.2d 797, 469 N.Y.S.2d 685, 457 N.E.2d 791.

Preiser, Practice Commentaries, McKinney's Cons. Laws of N.Y., Book 11A, CPL § 170.10, at 12 to 13 (emphases added) (citations omitted).

Simply stated, an unfortunate byproduct of the prompt suspension law is that it puts local criminal courts, who are often under tremendous pressure from groups such as M.A.D.D., S.A.D.D., and R.I.D. in a position where they are forced to balance the fundamental need to impartially protect defendants' constitutional rights with the perceived need to confiscate the driver's licenses of accused drunken drivers at any cost—and, all too often, the latter concern prevails.

In *People v. Rios*, 9 Misc. 3d 1, 801 N.Y.S.2d 113 (App. Term, 9th and 10th Jud. Dist. 2005), the defendant's convictions of various traffic infractions were reversed for failure to properly advise the defendant of his right to counsel.

§ 45:6 Applying *Pringle*

Research References

West's Key Number Digest, Automobiles ☞144.2(10.2)

After years without any appellate guidance in the area, the Appellate Division, Third Department, has recently issued several decisions addressing *Pringle* and the prompt suspension law. The leading case addressing the scope of a *Pringle* hearing is *Matter of Vanderminden v. Tarantino*, 60 A.D.3d 55, 871 N.Y.S.2d 760 (3d Dep't 2009), which is discussed at length in § 45:3, *supra*. *See also Schermerhorn v. Becker*, 64 A.D.3d 843, 883 N.Y.S.2d 325 (3d Dep't 2009); *Matter of Schmitt v. Skovira*, 53 A.D.3d 918, 862 N.Y.S.2d 167 (3d Dep't 2008).

One issue that is now well settled is that "a *Pringle* hearing is a civil administrative proceeding separate and apart from the underlying criminal prosecution, but which runs parallel thereto." *Schermerhorn*, 64 A.D.3d at __, 883 N.Y.S.2d at 328. *See also Vanderminden*, 60 A.D.3d at __, 871 N.Y.S.2d at 764; *Schmitt*, 53 A.D.3d at __, 862 N.Y.S.2d at 170–71. As such, the results of a *Pringle* hearing can be challenged via a CPLR Article 78 proceeding. *Schmitt*, 53 A.D.3d at __, 862 N.Y.S.2d at 172.

In addition, *Schermerhorn* addresses the People's role at a *Pringle* hearing. This issue is addressed in § 45:7, *infra*. Furthermore, *Vanderminden* addresses the applicability of the prompt suspension law to out-of-state licensees. This issue is addressed in § 45:9, *infra*.

§ 45:7 VTL § 1193(2)(e)(7)—What role do the people play at a *Pringle* hearing?

Research References

West's Key Number Digest, Automobiles ☞144.2(10.2)

In *Schermerhorn v. Becker*, 64 A.D.3d 843, 883 N.Y.S.2d 325 (3d Dep't 2009), the Appellate Division, Third Department, squarely addressed the issue of the People's role at a *Pringle* hearing. The Court held that "a district attorney clearly does not hold the status of a party in a *Pringle* hearing." 64 A.D.3d at __, 883 N.Y.S.2d at 329-29. Nonetheless, if they so choose, the People can play a "limited role" at the hearing. 64 A.D.3d at __, 883 N.Y.S.2d at 328. Specifically, the People can remind the Court of the prompt suspension law, offer to provide the Court with the defendant's chemical test result, and "comment in the event that defense counsel attempt[s] to markedly expand the narrow scope and purpose of the *Pringle* hearing." 64 A.D.3d at __ & n.2, 883 N.Y.S.2d at 328 & n.2. *See generally Broome County Dist. Attorney's Office v. Meagher*, 8 A.D.3d 732, 777 N.Y.S.2d 567 (3d Dep't 2004); *Czajka v. Breedlove*, 200 A.D.2d 263, __, 613 N.Y.S.2d 741, 742 (3d Dep't 1994) ("The position of District Attorney is a purely statutory office and, consequently, the only powers and duties which may be exercised by one acting in that post are those conferred by the Legislature, either expressly or by necessary implication.").

Notably, the *Schermerhorn* Court made clear that the People are not required to participate in *Pringle* hearings. 64 A.D.3d at __ n.2, 883 N.Y.S.2d 328 n.2 ("Nor do we suggest that a district attorney's presence at a *Pringle* hearing is required.").

§ 45:8   VTL § 1193(2)(e)(7)—Applicability to chemical test result of exactly .08%

Research References

West's Key Number Digest, Automobiles ⚖144.2(10.2)

The express language of the prompt suspension law states that it applies to a DWI defendant who "is alleged to have had *.08 of one percent or more* by weight of alcohol in such driver's blood as shown by chemical analysis of blood, breath, urine or saliva, made pursuant to [VTL § 1194(2) or (3)]." VTL § 1193(2)(e)(7)(a) (emphasis added). Nonetheless, this state's highest court, in interpreting this law when the proscribed BAC was .10%, clearly and expressly held that:

> The court may not order suspension of the driver's license unless it has in its possession the documented results of a reliable chemical test showing that the driver's blood alcohol level was *in excess of* .10 of 1%.

Pringle v. Wolfe, 88 N.Y.2d 426, 434, 646 N.Y.S.2d 82, 87, 668 N.E.2d 1376 (1996) (emphasis added). In this regard, the *"in excess of* .10 of 1%" language does not appear to be a typographical error; rather, it appears throughout the *Pringle* decision. *See, e.g., Wolfe*, 88 N.Y.2d at 432, 646 N.Y.S.2d at 85 ("At the suspension hearing, the court must first determine whether the accusatory instrument is sufficient on its face and next whether there exists reasonable cause to believe that the driver operated a motor vehicle while having a blood alcohol level *in excess of* .10 of 1% as shown by a chemical test") (emphasis added) (citation omitted); *Wolfe*, 88 N.Y.2d at 430, 646 N.Y.S.2d at 84; *Wolfe*, 88 N.Y.2d at 435, 646 N.Y.S.2d at 88.

This same rationale should apply to a chemical test result of exactly .08% now that the statute has been amended to reflect the change in VTL § 1192(2).

§ 45:9 VTL § 1193(2)(e)(7)—Applicability to out-of-state licensees

Research References

West's Key Number Digest, Automobiles ⊕144.2(10.2)

In *Matter of Vanderminden v. Tarantino*, 60 A.D.3d 55, __, 871 N.Y.S.2d 760, 762–63 (3d Dep't 2009), appeal denied, 12 N.Y.3d 708, 879 N.Y.S.2d 55, 906 N.E.2d 1089 (2009), the Appellate Division, Third Department, held as follows:

> The threshold question is whether petitioner, as the holder of a Vermont license, was subject to the prompt suspension law. Petitioner contends that because the statute authorizes the suspension of a driver's *license* but does not specifically refer to an out-of-state licensee's *driving privileges*, the statute applies only to holders of New York licenses. We do not agree. As noted by the Court of Appeals, Vehicle and Traffic Law article 31, of which section 1193 is a part, is "a tightly and carefully integrated statute the sole purpose of which is to address drunk driving." Within the statutory scheme, section 1193 contains the exclusive criminal penalties and civil sanctions applicable to drunk driving offenses, including the prompt suspension provision that is intended to keep potentially dangerous drivers off New York's roadways while their criminal charges are adjudicated. The role of that provision would be undermined, and its application rendered arbitrary, if it is interpreted to allow the holder of an out-of-state license to continue driving in New York when, under the same circumstances, the holder of a New York license would be prohibited from driving. Given the comprehensive nature and remedial purpose of article 31, we do not believe the Legislature intended such an anomalous result. Accordingly, we construe Vehicle and Traffic Law § 1193(2)(e)(7) as authorizing a court to suspend the driving privileges of an out-of-state licensee under the same circumstances as would justify suspending a New York license.

(Citations and footnote omitted). *See also People v. MacDougall*, 165 Misc. 2d 991, __, 630 N.Y.S.2d 853, 854 (Brighton Just. Ct. 1995) (same). Cf. *People v. Nuchow*, 164 Misc. 2d 24, __, 623 N.Y.S.2d 1006, 1010 (Orangetown Just. Ct. 1995) rejected by, People v. MacDougall, 165 Misc. 2d 991, 630 N.Y.S.2d 853 (Brighton Jus. Ct. 1995) (reaching opposite conclusion).

Where an out-of-state licensee's New York driving privileges are suspended pending prosecution, the Court has the power to issue him or her a hardship privilege. *See People v. Reick*, 33 Misc. 3d 774, 930 N.Y.S.2d 429 (N.Y. City Crim. Ct. 2011). *See also* next section. Similarly, DMV will issue the person a pre-conviction conditional license if he or she is otherwise eligible therefor.

§ 45:10   VTL § 1193(2)(e)(7)—Hardship privilege

Research References

West's Key Number Digest, Automobiles ☞144.2(10.2)

VTL § 1193(2)(e)(7)(e) provides, in pertinent part, that "[i]f the court finds that the suspension imposed pursuant to this subparagraph will result in *extreme hardship*, the court must issue such suspension, but may grant a hardship privilege, which shall be issued on a form prescribed by the commissioner." (Emphasis added). The phrase "extreme hardship" as used in VTL § 1193(2)(e)(7)(e) does not take on its literal meaning. Rather, it is defined as follows:

> "[E]xtreme hardship" shall mean the inability to obtain alternative means of travel to or from the licensee's employment, or to or from necessary medical treatment for the licensee or a member of the licensee's household, or if the licensee is a matriculating student enrolled in an accredited school, college or university travel to or from such licensee's school, college or university if such travel is necessary for the completion of the educational degree or certificate.

VTL § 1193(2)(e)(7)(e).

In *People v. Reick*, 33 Misc. 3d 774, __, 930 N.Y.S.2d 429, 430-31 (N.Y. City Crim. Ct. 2011), the Court held that a hardship privilege can be granted to an out-of-state licensee.

Where the defendant requests a so-called "hardship hearing," the statute makes clear that the hearing must be held within three business days. *See* VTL § 1193(2)(e)(7)(e) ("In no event shall arraignment be adjourned or otherwise delayed more than three business days *solely* for the purpose of allowing the licensee to present evidence of extreme hardship") (emphasis added). Notably, this section merely prohibits the adjournment of the arraignment for more than three business days if the *sole* purpose for the adjournment is to allow the licensee to present evidence of extreme hardship; if an adjournment is granted for reasons other than, or in addition to, this purpose, the three-day limitation does not appear to apply.

In terms of proving extreme hardship, the statute places the burden of proving extreme hardship on the licensee, "who may present material and relevant evidence." VTL § 1193(2)(e)(7)(e).

However, "[a] finding of extreme hardship may not be based *solely upon the testimony of the licensee.*" VTL § 1193(2)(e)(7)(e) (emphasis added). In this regard, the author advises clients to bring proof of where they live and proof of where they work, go to school, etc.; and, if possible, a friend or relative who can corroborate such information. For cases addressing factors to be considered in determining extreme hardship, *see People v. Correa*, 168 Misc. 2d 309, 643 N.Y.S.2d 310 (Richmond City Crim. Ct. 1996), and *People v. Bridgman*, 163 Misc. 2d 818, 622 N.Y.S.2d 431 (Canandaigua City Ct. 1995). "The court shall set forth upon the record, or otherwise set forth in writing, the factual basis for such finding." VTL § 1193(2)(e)(7)(e).

If granted, VTL § 1193(2)(e)(7)(e) provides that a hardship privilege:

[S]hall permit the operation of a vehicle only for travel *to or from the licensee's employment*, or to or from necessary medical treatment for the licensee or a member of the licensee's household, or if the licensee is a matriculating student enrolled in an accredited school, college or university travel to or from such licensee's school, college or university if such travel is necessary for the completion of the educational degree or certificate.

(Emphasis added).

Although the statutory language omits any reference to driving as part of (*i.e.*, during) the licensee's employment, an informal opinion from the DMV Counsel's Office states that a person who needs to drive to and from various job sites may do so, but he or she may *not* drive for purposes such as running errands, picking up work materials, etc. *See* Appendix 62. Notably, however, a more recent informal opinion from DMV Counsel's Office states that DMV has "retreated" from this position. *See* Appendix 67.

§ 45:11   VTL § 1193(2)(e)(7)—Hardship privilege cannot be used to operate commercial motor vehicle

Research References

West's Key Number Digest, Automobiles ⚎144.2(10.2)

"A hardship privilege shall not be valid for the operation of a commercial motor vehicle." VTL § 1193(2)(e)(7)(e).

§ 45:12   VTL § 1193(2)(e)(7)—Preconviction conditional license

Research References

West's Key Number Digest, Automobiles ⚎144.2(10.2)

VTL § 1193(2)(e)(7)(d) provides, in pertinent part:

[I]f any suspension occurring under [VTL § 1193(2)(e)(7)] has been in effect for a period of [30] days, the holder may be issued a conditional license, in accordance with [VTL § 1196], provided the holder of such license is otherwise eligible to receive such conditional license. . . . The commissioner shall prescribe by regulation the procedures for the issuance of such conditional license.

The relevant regulations are set forth at 15 NYCRR § 134.18, which provide as follows:

Section 134.18.   Conditional license issued pending prosecution.

(a) When a driver's license is suspended pending prosecution pursuant to section 1193(2)(e)(7) of the Vehicle and Traffic Law, the holder of such license may be issued a conditional license, 30 days after such suspension takes effect, provided such person is eligible for such a license as set forth in section 134.7 of this Part and section 1196 of the Vehicle and Traffic Law. Such person shall not be required to and may not participate in the alcohol and drug rehabilitation program when issued a conditional license pursuant to this section.

(b) Establishment of conditions. Each conditional license issued under this section shall be subject to the conditions set forth in section 134.9(b) of this Part and section 1196 of the Vehicle and Traffic Law.

(c) Revocation of conditional license. The provisions of section 134.9(c) of this Part shall be applicable to a conditional license issued under this section.

(d) Period of validity. A conditional license issued under this section shall be valid, unless otherwise revoked, suspended or expired, until the prosecution for the pending alcohol-related charge is terminated.

Simply stated, a person whose driver's license is suspended pursuant to the prompt suspension law is eligible for a preconviction conditional license if he or she would be eligible for a conditional license if convicted of the underlying DWI charge, and *vice versa*.

§ 45:13   VTL § 1193(2)(e)(7)—Applicability of preconviction conditional license to commercial and taxicab drivers

Research References

West's Key Number Digest, Automobiles ⟜144.2(10.2)

Prior to September 30, 2005, VTL § 1196(7)(g) provided that "[a]ny conditional license or privilege issued to a person *convicted* of a violation of any subdivision of [VTL § 1192] shall not be valid for the operation of any commercial motor vehicle or taxicab as defined in this chapter." (Emphasis added). Since a person whose driver's license is suspended pending prosecution pursuant to the prompt suspension law is not *convicted* of a VTL § 1192 violation, VTL § 1196(7)(g) was inapplicable to a preconviction conditional license issued to such person. Accordingly, a preconviction conditional license could be used to operate a commercial motor vehicle and/or a taxicab.

A 2007 amendment to VTL § 1193(2)(e)(7)(d) provides that "[a] conditional license issued pursuant to this subparagraph shall not be valid for the operation of a commercial motor vehicle."

On the other hand, DMV will still issue a preconviction conditional license valid for the operation of a taxicab.

§ 45:14 VTL § 1193(2)(e)(7)—Violation of preconviction conditional license is a traffic infraction; violation of hardship privilege constitutes AUO

Research References
West's Key Number Digest, Automobiles ⚖144.2(10.2)

VTL § 1196(7)(f) provides that using a preconviction conditional license "for any use other than those authorized pursuant to [VTL § 1196(7)(a)]" constitutes a traffic infraction. *See also People v. Rivera*, 16 N.Y.3d 654, 655-56, 926 N.Y.S.2d 16, 17, 949 N.E.2d 964 (2011) ("a driver whose license has been revoked, but who has received a conditional license and failed to comply with its conditions, may be prosecuted only for the traffic infraction of driving for a use not authorized by his license, not for the crime of driving while his license is revoked").

By contrast, there is no comparable statute dealing with using a hardship privilege for a use other than those authorized pursuant to VTL § 1193(2)(e)(7)(e). As a result, a person caught violating a hardship privilege can be charged with AUO. *See also* §§ 13:1 et seq., *supra*.

§ 45:15 VTL § 1193(2)(e)(7)—Prompt suspension law does not preclude court from suspending defendant's driver's license under other laws

Research References
West's Key Number Digest, Automobiles ⚖144.2(10.2)

Finally, VTL § 1193(2)(e)(7)(c) expressly states that "[n]othing contained in this subparagraph shall be construed to prohibit or limit a court from imposing any other suspension pending prosecution required or permitted by law." This language presumably refers to suspensions pending prosecution pursuant to VTL § 1193(2)(e)(1), VTL § 1194(2)(b)(3) and VTL § 510(3-a), which are discussed in the sections that follow.

Our thanks to Neal W. Schoen, First Assistant Counsel, and Ida L. Traschen, Associate Counsel, of the DMV Counsel's Office, for their advice and assistance with regard to the prompt suspension law.

§ 45:16   VTL § 1193(2)(e)(1)—Suspension pending prosecution based upon prior conviction or vehicular crime

Research References

West's Key Number Digest, Automobiles ⬥144.2(10.2)

A defendant who is charged with DWI, Aggravated DWI, DWAI Drugs *or* DWAI Combined Influence *and* who either (a) has been convicted of any violation of VTL § 1192 within the preceding five years, or (b) is charged with Vehicular Assault or Vehicular Homicide in connection with the current incident, is also subject to the suspension of his or her driver's license pending prosecution. In this regard, VTL § 1193(2)(e)(1) provides, in pertinent part:

> (1) Suspension pending prosecution; procedure. a. Without notice, pending any prosecution, the court shall suspend such license, where the holder has been charged with a violation of [VTL § 1192(2), (2-a), (3), (4) or (4-a)] and either (i) a violation of a felony under [Penal Law Article 120 or 125] arising out of the same incident, or (ii) has been convicted of any violation under [VTL § 1192] within the preceding [5] years.

VTL § 1193(2)(e)(1)(a).

Notably, VTL § 1193(2)(e)(1), by its express terms, only applies under certain circumstances. For example, it only applies where the defendant is charged with VTL § 1192(2), (2-a), (3), (4) or (4-a); it does not apply where the defendant is charged with VTL § 1192(1) (*i.e.*, DWAI). In addition, VTL § 1193(2)(e)(1) only applies where the defendant either (a) has been convicted of any violation of VTL § 1192 within the preceding five years, or (b) is charged with Vehicular Assault or Vehicular Homicide in connection with the current incident. Furthermore, unlike the prompt suspension law, no chemical test result is required; thus, VTL § 1193(2)(e)(1) can be applied to chemical test refusal cases.

Like the prompt suspension law, VTL § 1193(2)(e)(1) only applies where a prosecution is pending. Accordingly, a defendant who enters a plea of guilty *and is sentenced* at arraignment is not subject to VTL § 1193(2)(e)(1). On the other hand, a defendant who enters a plea of guilty at arraignment, but whose sentencing is adjourned, is subject thereto (because the prosecution does not terminate until the imposition of sentence).

§ 45:17 VTL § 1193(2)(e)(1)—Suspension procedure

Research References

West's Key Number Digest, Automobiles ⊙144.2(10.2)

In order to impose a suspension under VTL § 1193(2)(e)(1), the court must make three findings. First, the court "must find that the accusatory instrument conforms to the requirements of [CPL §] 100.40." VTL § 1193(2)(e)(1)(b). CPL § 100.40 sets forth the facial sufficiency requirements for local criminal court accusatory instruments. Second, the court must find that "there exists reasonable cause to believe that the holder operated a motor vehicle in violation of [VTL § 1192(2), (2-a), (3), (4) or (4-a)]." VTL § 1193(2)(e)(1)(b). Critically, this means that reasonable cause (*i.e.*, probable cause) to believe that the defendant is guilty of DWI, Aggravated DWI, DWAI Drugs or DWAI Combined Influence—and not merely of DWAI Alcohol—is an element of a VTL § 1193(2)(e)(1) suspension. Third, the court must find that "there exists reasonable cause to believe . . . either (i) the person had been convicted of any violation under [VTL § 1192] within the preceding [5] years; or (ii) that the holder committed a violation of a felony under [Penal Law Article 120 or 125]." VTL § 1193(2)(e)(1)(b).

If such *tentative* findings are made, the statute provides that "the holder shall be entitled to an opportunity to make a statement regarding the enumerated issues and to present evidence tending to rebut the court's findings." VTL § 1193(2)(e)(1)(b).

If a suspension is imposed pursuant to VTL § 1193(2)(e)(1) as a result of the defendant being charged with a felony under Penal Law Article 120 or 125:

> [A]nd the holder has requested a hearing pursuant to [CPL Article 180], the court shall conduct such hearing. If upon completion of the hearing, the court fails to find that there is reasonable cause to believe that the holder committed a felony under [Penal Law Article 120 or 125] and the holder has not been previously convicted of any violation of [VTL § 1192] within the preceding [5] years the court shall promptly notify the commissioner and direct restoration of such license to the license holder unless such license is suspended or revoked pursuant to any other provision of this chapter.

VTL § 1193(2)(e)(1)(b).

In light of the Court of Appeals' decision in *Pringle v. Wolfe*, 88 N.Y.2d 426, 646 N.Y.S.2d 82, 668 N.E.2d 1376 (1996), it seems clear both (a) that the procedural due process requirements set forth therein apply equally to both VTL § 1193(2)(e)(1) and (7), and (b) that evidence of a defendant's alleged prior VTL § 1192 conviction must be submitted to the court in "certified, documented form." *See* § 45:3, *supra*. *See also* CPL § 60.60; *People v.*

Van Buren, 82 N.Y.2d 878, 609 N.Y.S.2d 170, 631 N.E.2d 112 (1993); *People v. Smith*, 258 A.D.2d 245, 697 N.Y.S.2d 783 (4th Dep't 1999).

In *People v. Bodendorf*, 52 Misc. 3d 551, 30 N.Y.S.3d 516, 519 (LaGrange J. Ct. 2016), the Court held that "a Breath Alcohol Analysis Record must bear the original signature of the person who certified it for purposes of the prompt suspension law." *See also People v. Sykes*, 167 Misc. 2d 588, __, 638 N.Y.S.2d 1010, 1012 (Monroe Co. Sup 1995), judgment aff'd on other grounds, 225 A.D.2d 1093, 639 N.Y.S.2d 188 (4th Dep't 1996) ("A copy of a certification is tantamount to no certification"); *People v. Brown*, 128 Misc. 2d 149, __, 488 N.Y.S.2d 559, 563 (Madison County Ct. 1985) (same); *People v. Hoats*, 102 Misc. 2d 1004, __, 425 N.Y.S.2d 497, 499 (Monroe County Ct. 1980) (same); *People v. Fiacco*, 146 Misc. 2d 330, __, 549 N.Y.S.2d 901, 903 (Albany N.Y. City Ct. 1989).

In *People v. Osborn*, 193 Misc. 2d 173, 749 N.Y.S.2d 853, 855 (Sullivan County Ct. 2002), the court held that "the principles upon which the Court of Appeals based *Pringle*, *supra*, in regard to V & T § 1193(2)(e)(7) apply equally herein with regard to V & T § 1193(2)(e)(1)." In so holding, the court reasoned that:

> A driver's license is a substantial property right and due process must be followed whether that property right is sought to be taken under V & T § 1193(2)(e)(7) or (2)(e)(1).

> The statutory language of V & T § 1193(2)(e)(7) is almost exactly the same as V & T § 1193(2)(e)(1) with the one exception that one of the criteria for the taking under V & T § 1193(2)(e)(7) is blood alcohol content of [.08] or higher while one of the criteria under V & T § 1193(2)(e)(1) is a prior conviction of any section of V & T § 1192 within the preceding five years. This distinction does not mollify one's Due Process rights under *Pringle*.

Osborn, 193 Misc. 2d at, 749 N.Y.S.2d at 855.

Similarly, in *People v. Giacopelli*, 171 Misc. 2d 844, 655 N.Y.S.2d 835, 839 (Clarkstown J. Ct. 1997), the court held that:

> [B]oth sections 1193(2)(e)(1) and (7), providing for pretrial suspension, have a "deprivational" effect, and as the very same "substantial property interest" is at issue under both statutes, *Pringle v. Wolfe* must apply to both sections equally. Perhaps more importantly, there exists a stronger reason for a hearing under section 1193(2)(e)(1), as there exists no tempering of the suspension with the grant of a "hardship license" as is available in section 1193(2)(e)(7)(e).

§ 45:18 VTL § 1193(2)(e)(1)—Effect of failure to comply with statute

Research References

West's Key Number Digest, Automobiles ⊕144.2(10.2)

In *Plumley v. Leuenberger*, 131 Misc. 2d 543, 500 N.Y.S.2d 911, 913 (Oneida Co. Sup 1985), the court lifted the suspension of the petitioner's driver's license pending prosecution and ordered that the license be returned where the town court failed to follow the requirements of the suspension statute. The court held that the suspension was untimely in that it occurred after the arraignment had been completed. *Leuenberger*, 131 Misc. 2d at __, 500 N.Y.S.2d at 913. In addition, "[n]o findings were made and transmitted to petitioner. Consequently, he was not given an opportunity to rebut them. Thus, there has been no compliance with the statute, and the suspension should be lifted and the license returned." *Leuenberger*, 131 Misc. 2d at __, 500 N.Y.S.2d at 912.

On the other hand, in *Kinney v. Bortle*, 136 Misc. 2d 68, 518 N.Y.S.2d 336, 337 (Oneida Co. Sup 1987), a different judge of the same court held that the town court's failure to comply with the suspension statute "cannot be construed as a waiver of the statutory requirement that petitioner's license be surrendered. A Town Justice simply has no authority to waive the requirements of V & T § 510(2)(b)(vi)(a) and (b). The Town Justice's letter directing surrender of the license which was sent some three week [*sic*] after petitioner's first appearance, is legally effective, and petitioner must immediately comply with that directive."

It should be noted that, since both *Plumley* and *Kinney* were decided long before the Court of Appeals' decision in *Pringle v. Wolfe*, 88 N.Y.2d 426, 646 N.Y.S.2d 82, 668 N.E.2d 1376 (1996), the continued validity of these cases is questionable.

In *People v. Giacopelli*, 171 Misc. 2d 844, 655 N.Y.S.2d 835, 839 (Clarkstown J. Ct. 1997), which was decided subsequent to *Pringle*, the court held both (a) that *Pringle* applies equally to both VTL §§ 1193(2)(e)(1) and (7), and (b) "that having suspended the defendant's driver's license prior to holding a hearing was a violation of the defendant's due process rights to a hearing."

§ 45:19 VTL § 1193(2)(e)(1) & (7)—Suspension time frame

Research References

West's Key Number Digest, Automobiles ⊕144.2(10.2)

The prompt suspension law provides that, with two exceptions, the court must impose a suspension thereunder "no later than at the conclusion of all proceedings required for the arraignment."

VTL § 1193(2)(e)(7)(b). *See also Pringle v. Wolfe*, 88 N.Y.2d 426, 429, 432, 646 N.Y.S.2d 82, 84, 668 N.E.2d 1376 (1996).

The first exception is that if, for some reason, the results of the chemical test are not available prior to the completion of the arraignment (which is only the case where the chemical test is a blood or urine test, as breath test results are available almost instantaneously), "the complainant police officer or other public servant shall transmit such results to the court at the time they become available." VTL § 1193(2)(e)(7)(b). The court is thereafter required to impose a prompt suspension law suspension "as soon as practicable following the receipt of such results and in compliance with the requirements of [VTL § 1193(2)(e)(7)(b)]." *Pringle v. Wolfe*, 88 N.Y.2d 426, 646 N.Y.S.2d 82, 668 N.E.2d 1376 (1996).

The second exception applies to an underage offender with a class DJ or MJ driver's license/learner's permit. In this situation, VTL § 1193(2)(e)(7)(b) provides that "the suspension occurring under clause a-1 of this subparagraph shall occur immediately after the holder's first appearance before the court on the charge which shall, whenever possible, be the next regularly scheduled session of the court after the arrest or at the conclusion of all proceedings required for the arraignment."

VTL § 1193(2)(e)(1)(b) provides that the court must impose a suspension under VTL § 1193(2)(e)(1) "no later than [20] days after the holder's first appearance before the court on the charges or at the conclusion of all proceedings required for the arraignment."

§ 45:20   VTL § 1193(2)(e)(1) & (7)—Length of suspension

Research References

West's Key Number Digest, Automobiles ⊕144.2(10.2)

If imposed, a suspension pending prosecution pursuant to either the prompt suspension law or VTL § 1193(2)(e)(1) will remain in effect for as long as the case is pending. In addition, the time period during which the defendant's driver's license is suspended pending prosecution will *not* be credited toward any postconviction suspension/revocation period if the charges ultimately result in a conviction. *See People v. DeRojas*, 196 Misc. 2d 171, 763 N.Y.S.2d 386, 388–89 (App. Term, 2d Dep't 2003).

Furthermore, it is critical to note that if the defendant's driver's license is suspended pending prosecution pursuant to VTL § 1193(2)(e)(1), the defendant is ineligible for either a hardship privilege and/or a preconviction conditional license (both of which are discussed at length *supra*), as he or she would be ineligible for a conditional license if convicted of the underlying VTL § 1192 or Penal Law charge(s).

Accordingly, if a plea bargain resolution of the case is contemplated, defense counsel should attempt to conclude the case as soon as possible (ideally at arraignment) in order to avoid unnecessarily extending the length of the defendant's loss of license.

§ 45:21   VTL § 1193(2)(e)(1) & (7)—Constitutionality

Research References

West's Key Number Digest, Automobiles ☞144.2(10.2)

In *Pringle v. Wolfe*, 88 N.Y.2d 426, 646 N.Y.S.2d 82, 668 N.E.2d 1376 (1996), the Court of Appeals declared VTL § 1193(2)(e)(7) to be constitutional. In so holding, the court summed up the due process issue as follows:

> In sum, though the private interest affected by the prompt suspension law is substantial, the severity of the license suspension is mitigated by its temporary duration, the availability of a conditional license and hardship relief, and the significant protection of a pre-suspension judicial hearing, which militates heavily in favor of the statute's constitutionality. Further weighing against the driver's interest in maintaining his license are the slight risk of an erroneous deprivation and the overriding State interest in "the prompt removal of a safety hazard" from its streets. Based on the foregoing, we hold that the prompt suspension law affords the driver all the process that is constitutionally due.

Wolfe, 88 N.Y.2d at 435, 646 N.Y.S.2d at 87–88 (citations omitted).

Notably, however, the court left open the possibility that additional constitutional challenges could be raised in the future, stating that, while "various constitutional challenges to the prompt suspension law [are] currently pending in the lower courts, we only have occasion to reach those issues squarely presented on this appeal." *Wolfe*, 88 N.Y.2d at 429 n.1, 646 N.Y.S.2d at 84 n.1.

In addition, a persuasive argument can be made that VTL § 1193(2)(e)(1) is unconstitutional. Ironically, this argument finds its support in *Pringle*, the very case that held VTL § 1193(2)(e)(7) to be constitutional. First of all, unlike a suspension pending prosecution pursuant to VTL § 1193(2)(e)(7), a suspension pending prosecution pursuant to VTL § 1193(2)(e)(1) can theoretically be ordered without notice to the defendant. *See* VTL § 1193(2)(e)(1)(a) ("Without notice, pending any prosecution . . ."). *But see People v. Giacopelli*, 171 Misc. 2d 844, 655 N.Y.S.2d 835, 839 (Clarkstown J. Ct. 1997) (Court held that it is a violation of a defendant's due process rights to suspend his or her driver's license pending prosecution pursuant to VTL § 1193(2)(e)(1) prior to holding a hearing).

Second, unlike under VTL § 1193(2)(e)(7), hardship relief and a preconviction conditional license are not available under VTL § 1193(2)(e)(1). Accordingly, if a presuspension *Pringle*-type hearing is not required with regard to suspensions pending prosecution pursuant to VTL § 1193(2)(e)(1), then two of the three factors that the *Pringle* court found militated in favor of the constitutionality of VTL § 1193(2)(e)(7) are absent from VTL § 1193(2)(e)(1).

§ 45:22   VTL § 1193(2)(e)(1) & (7)—Double Jeopardy and Equal Protection

Research References

West's Key Number Digest, Automobiles ☞144.2(10.2)

It is well settled that the prosecution of a defendant for DWI following the suspension of his or her driver's license pending prosecution does not violate the Double Jeopardy Clause of either the New York State Constitution or the United States Constitution. *See People v. Haishun*, 238 A.D.2d 521, 656 N.Y.S.2d 660 (2d Dep't 1997); *People v. Roach*, 226 A.D.2d 55, 649 N.Y.S.2d 607 (4th Dep't 1996); *Smith v. County Court of Essex County*, 224 A.D.2d 89, 649 N.Y.S.2d 507 (3d Dep't 1996); *People v. Malone*, 175 Misc. 2d 893, 673 N.Y.S.2d 809 (App. Term, 2d Dep't 1997); *People v. Busby*, 175 Misc. 2d 509, 670 N.Y.S.2d 960 (App. Term, 2d Dep't 1997); *People v. Steele*, 172 Misc. 2d 860, 661 N.Y.S.2d 908 (App. Term, 2d Dep't 1997); *People v. Uzquaino*, 172 Misc. 2d 388, 661 N.Y.S.2d 438 (App. Term, 2d Dep't 1997); *People v. Conrad*, 169 Misc. 2d 1066, 654 N.Y.S.2d 226 (App. Term, 2d Dep't 1996).

Similarly, courts have rejected the argument that the prompt suspension law violates the Equal Protection Clause of either the New York State Constitution or the United States Constitution. *See Roach*, 226 A.D.2d at __, 649 N.Y.S.2d at 610; *People v. Condarco*, 166 Misc. 2d 470, 633 N.Y.S.2d 930 (City Crim. Ct. 1995); *People v. Boulton*, 164 Misc. 2d 604, 625 N.Y.S.2d 428 (Troy City Ct. 1995).

§ 45:23   VTL § 1194(2)(b)(3)—Temporary suspension of license at arraignment in chemical test refusal cases

Research References

West's Key Number Digest, Automobiles ☞144.2(10.2)

At arraignment in a chemical test refusal case, the court is required to temporarily suspend the defendant's driving privileges pending the outcome of a DMV refusal hearing. *See* VTL

§ 1194(2)(b)(3) ("For persons placed under arrest for a violation of any subdivision of [VTL § 1192], the license or permit to drive and any non-resident operating privilege shall, upon the basis of such written report, be temporarily suspended by the court without notice pending the determination of a hearing as provided in [VTL § 1194(2)(c)]"). *See also* 15 NYCRR § 139.3(a).

Similar provisions exist for individuals charged with Boating While Intoxicated, *see* Navigation Law § 49-a; 15 NYCRR § 139.3(b), and Snowmobiling While Intoxicated. *See* Parks, Recreation & Historic Preservation Law § 25.24; 15 NYCRR § 139.3(c). This procedure does not violate the Due Process Clause. *See Application of Ventura*, 108 Misc. 2d 281, 437 N.Y.S.2d 538 (Monroe Co. Sup 1981). *See generally Mackey v. Montrym*, 443 U.S. 1, 99 S. Ct. 2612, 61 L. Ed. 2d 321 (1979).

However, "[i]f the department fails to provide for such hearing [15] days after the date of the arraignment of the arrested person, the license, permit to drive or non-resident operating privilege of such person shall be reinstated pending a hearing pursuant to this section." VTL § 1194(2)(c). In addition, "[i]f the respondent appears for a first scheduled chemical test refusal hearing, and the arresting officer does not appear, the matter will be adjourned and any temporary suspension still in effect shall be terminated." 15 NYCRR § 127.9(c).

In other words, the temporary license suspension imposed at arraignment in a refusal case lasts *the shorter of* 15 days or until the DMV refusal hearing.

§ 45:24 VTL § 510(3-a)—Discretionary suspensions

Research References

West's Key Number Digest, Automobiles ☞144.2(10.2)

VTL § 510(3-a), formerly an unlettered paragraph following VTL § 510(3)(i), provides that:

Opportunity to be heard and temporary suspensions. Where revocation or suspension is permissive, the holder, unless he shall waive such right, shall have an opportunity to be heard except where such revocation or suspension is based solely on a court conviction or convictions or on a court commitment to an institution under the jurisdiction of the department of mental hygiene. A license or registration, or the privilege of a non-resident of operating a motor vehicle in this state or of the operation within this state of any motor vehicle owned by him, may, however, be temporarily suspended without notice, pending any prosecution, investigation or hearing.

This section has rarely been used in DWI cases. Rather, it has generally been implemented in cases of reckless and abhorrent driving which demonstrated "a reckless disregard for the life or property of others."

In *Ryan v. Smith*, 139 Misc. 2d 151, 527 N.Y.S.2d 174 (Schenectady Co. Sup 1988), the petitioner brought an Article 78 proceeding challenging the suspension of his driver's license, pursuant to VTL § 510(3-a), pending prosecution of a DWI charge. The suspension appeared to be imposed due to the petitioner's "extraordinarily high" BAC, which was alleged to have been .23%. In upholding the suspension, the court noted that:

> While V & T § 510 in general may be considered a study in ambiguous draftsmanship, it appears from a full reading of the statute, and from reported decisions that both New York State and out of state drivers may have their licenses temporarily suspended pending any prosecution, investigation or hearing.

> Additionally, though the statutory language and structure is at best murky, it indicates that the arraigning court possessed the power to temporarily suspend the license by the force of the last sentence in § 510(3) [currently § 510(3-a)]. It must be firmly kept in mind that the suspension here is of a temporary, discretionary nature pending prosecution, and may not be categorized as a permissive suspension or revocation, or a mandatory suspension without notice . . .

> Moreover, as a temporary, discretionary suspension, the procedural due process safeguards of V & T § 510(2)(b)(vi) [currently VTL § 1193(2)(e)(1)] do not appear to be applicable.

Smith, 139 Misc. 2d at __, 527 N.Y.S.2d at 175 (citations omitted).

In *People v. Forgette*, 141 Misc. 2d 1009, 535 N.Y.S.2d 924, 927 (N.Y. City Crim. Ct. 1988), the court expressly rejected the premise of *Ryan* (*i.e.*, that a suspension pending prosecution pursuant to VTL § 510(3-a) can be based *solely* on an allegedly high BAC).

> Rather, it seems entirely appropriate that a temporary suspension be grounded upon evidence that a driver's *continued* operation of a motor vehicle represents a danger to the public. Part of the criteria should necessarily entail a review of the arraigned charges. . . . Additional evidence demonstrating a threat to the public would normally consist of the defendant's past driving record. . . . Finally, it should be noted that a temporary suspension is indeed just that.

Forgette, 141 Misc. 2d at __, 535 N.Y.S.2d at 927.

In *Buckson v. Harris*, 145 A.D.2d 883, 536 N.Y.S.2d 219, 219–20 (3d Dep't 1988), the petitioner brought an Article 78 proceeding challenging the county court's order "which directed petitioner to refrain from driving a motor vehicle as a condition of bail." The Appellate Division, Third Department, dismissed the petition, citing VTL § 510(3)(i) (currently VTL § 510(3-a)), as well as the fact that the petitioner had numerous prior alcohol-related convictions and was currently charged with felony DWI.

In *King v. Kay*, 39 Misc. 3d 995, 963 N.Y.S.2d 537 (Suffolk Co. Sup. Ct. 2013), the defendant's driver's license was suspended pending prosecution by a Judge of the Suffolk County District Court pursuant to VTL § 1193(2)(e)(7). However, another Judge of the same Court subsequently suspended the defendant's driver's license pursuant to VTL § 510(3-a). The only conceivable reason for doing so would be to deprive the defendant of eligibility for a preconviction conditional license. The defendant challenged the VTL § 510(3-a) suspension via an Article 78 proceeding.

In a very well reasoned decision, the Suffolk County Supreme Court annulled the VTL § 510(3-a) suspension, finding that VTL § 510(3-a) was inapplicable to the case. In so holding, the Court reasoned, in part, as follows:

> Vehicle and Traffic Law § 510(3-a) does not authorize a temporary suspension without a finding that suspension is permissive pursuant to Vehicle and Traffic Law § 510(3). Respondent made no such finding. Further, petitioner is charged solely with violations of Vehicle and Traffic Law § 1192, which without further findings, subjects petitioner to suspension under article 31, not Vehicle and Traffic Law § 510. In fact, at the time of respondent's November 26, 2012 determination, petitioner's license had already been temporarily suspended pursuant to Vehicle and Traffic Law § 1193(2)(e)(7).
>
> The propriety of the respondent's administrative determination must be judged solely on the grounds invoked by respondent. This Court finds no basis in the law to support the temporary suspension of Petitioner's license pursuant to Vehicle and Traffic Law § 510(3-a) on this record.

Id. at __, 963 N.Y.S.2d at 544-45.

Chapter 46

Penalties for VTL § 1192 Offenses

Research References

Westlaw Databases

Charges to the Jury and Requests to Charge in Criminal Case in New York (CTJNY)

Drinking/Driving Litigation: Criminal and Civil (2d ed.) (DRNKDRIVING)

Handling Drunk Driving Cases (2d ed.) (HDRUNKDR)

New York Driving While Intoxicated Defense Forms (NYDWIFM)

New York Vehicle and Traffic Law 2d (NYVEH)

Treatises and Practice Aids

Leventhal, Charges to the Jury and Requests to Charge in a Criminal
Case in New York §§ 47:4, 47:6
Nichols and Whited, Drinking/Driving Litigation: Criminal and Civil
§§ 2:10, 3:12 (2d ed.)
Fiandach, Handling Drunk Driving Cases § 1:30 (2d ed.)
Rose, New York Vehicle and Traffic Law 2d §§ 11:7, 15:1 to 15:4

Forms

Taheri and Orr, NY DWI Defense Forms §§ 1:5, 1:8 to 1:10

Law Reviews and Other Periodicals

Gerstenzang, Defending the DWI Case in New York: The Basics, 4
Practising Law Institute New York Practice Skills Course Handbook
Series 7 (September, 1997)
McIntosh, Illinois' "Zero Tolerance" Law, 84 Ill. B. J. 93 (February,
1996)

KeyCite®: Cases and other legal materials listed in KeyCite Scope can be
researched through the KeyCite service on Westlaw®. Use KeyCite to check
citations for form, parallel references, prior and later history, and comprehensive citator information, including citations to other decisions and secondary
materials.

---

§ 46:1   In general

Research References

West's Key Number Digest, Automobiles ☜359.4

A conviction for any violation of VTL § 1192 will result in various monetary and licensing consequences for the defendant, and
may even result in the defendant's incarceration. In addition,
such a conviction will appear on the defendant's publicly available DMV driving abstract for 10 years, will appear in DMV's
internal records for life, will in most cases appear on the
defendant's DCJS record (*i.e.*, "rap sheet") for life, and will in all
likelihood result in a substantial increase in his or her automobile
insurance premiums for several years. Specific consequences for
common offenses are set forth below.

§ 46:2   New DMV regulations dramatically alter the revocation periods for repeat DWI offenders

Effective September 25, 2012, DMV enacted new regulations
that *dramatically* alter the license revocation periods for repeat
DWI offenders. In this regard, the look-back period for DWI-
related offenses increased from 10 years to a minimum of 25
years (and sometimes lifetime). As a result, a person can have
what appears to be a "clean" DMV driving abstract yet be facing

a lifetime driver's license revocation for (a) a VTL § 1192 offense, (b) a chemical test refusal, or even (c) a traffic infraction carrying 5 or more points. *See, e.g.,* 15 NYCRR § 136.5 and Part 132.

It is absolutely critical that anyone handling a DWI case in New York be familiar with these new regulations, which are discussed at length in §§ 55:1 et seq., *infra*.

§ 46:3 Driving while ability impaired—First offense

Research References

West's Key Number Digest, Automobiles ⚷359.4

Driving while ability impaired (DWAI) in violation of VTL § 1192(1) is a traffic infraction. VTL § 1193(1)(a). A defendant who is convicted of DWAI as a first offense is subject to the following consequences:

    1. A fine of between $300 and $500, up to 15 days in jail, or both. VTL § 1193(1)(a);

    2. Mandatory suspension of his or her driver's license for 90 days. VTL § 1193(2)(a)(1);

    3. Discretionary suspension of his or her registration for 90 days. VTL § 1193(2)(a)(1);

    4. A mandatory surcharge of $250. VTL § 1809(1)(c); VTL § 1809-c(1); VTL § 1809-e(1)(b). If the case is in either a town or village court, the court must add an additional $5 to this surcharge. VTL § 1809(9). *See* §§ 47:1 et seq., *infra*;

    5. A mandatory crime victim assistance fee of $5. VTL § 1809(1)(c);

    6. A mandatory driver responsibility assessment of $250 a year for three years. VTL § 1199. *See* § 46:50, *infra*; and

    7. Discretionary imposition of a requirement that the defendant attend a single session of a victim impact panel. VTL § 1193(1)(f). *See* § 46:30, *infra*.

In addition, the defendant will most likely be eligible for a conditional license. *See* §§ 50:1 et seq., *infra*.

§ 46:4 DWAI—Second offense

Research References

West's Key Number Digest, Automobiles ⚷359.4

Unless 15 NYCRR § 136.5 applies, *see* § 46:2, *supra*, a defendant who is convicted of DWAI after having been convicted of a violation of any subdivision of VTL § 1192 within the preceding five years is subject to the following consequences:

    1. A fine of between $500 and $750, up to 30 days in jail, or both. VTL § 1193(1)(a);

    2. Mandatory revocation of his or her driver's license for at

least six months. VTL § 1193(2)(b)(1). In addition, DMV will require evidence of alcohol evaluation and/or rehabilitation before it will relicense the defendant. *See* §§ 50:1 et seq. and Appendix 53, *infra*;

3. Discretionary revocation of his or her registration for at least six months. VTL § 1193(2)(b)(1);

4. A mandatory surcharge of $250. VTL § 1809(1)(c); VTL § 1809-c(1); VTL § 1809-e(1)(b). If the case is in either a town or village court, the court must add an additional $5 to this surcharge. VTL § 1809(9). *See* §§ 47:1 et seq., *infra*;

5. A mandatory crime victim assistance fee of $5. VTL § 1809(1)(c);

6. A mandatory driver responsibility assessment of $250 a year for three years. VTL § 1199. *See* § 46:50, *infra*; and

7. Discretionary imposition of a requirement that the defendant attend a single session of a victim impact panel. VTL § 1193(1)(f). *See* § 46:30, *infra*.

In addition, the defendant will *not* be eligible for a conditional license. *See* §§ 50:1 et seq., *infra*.

Where the date of the *arrest* for the second offense occurs more than five years after the date of the *conviction* for the first, a defendant convicted of a second DWAI will be penalized as a first offender (unless 15 NYCRR § 136.5 applies). *See* VTL § 1193(1)(a); VTL § 1193(2)(b)(1).

It is critical to note, however, that eligibility for a conditional license is based upon the date of the defendant's prior Drinking Driver Program completion, *not* the date of the prior conviction. *See* §§ 50:1 et seq., *infra*. Thus, a person again charged with a violation of VTL § 1192, more than five years after having been convicted of a violation of VTL § 1192 but less than five years after having completed the Drinking Driver Program, will *not* be eligible for a conditional license.

§ 46:5   DWAI—Third and subsequent offenses

Research References

West's Key Number Digest, Automobiles ⊕359.6

A defendant who is charged with DWAI after having been convicted of two or more violations of any subdivision of VTL § 1192 within the preceding 10 years *can* be charged with a *misdemeanor*, and, if so charged, is subject to the following consequences:

1. A fine of between $750 and $1,500, up to 180 days in jail, or both. VTL § 1193(1)(a);

2. A period of probation of two or three years. PL § 65.00(3)(d);

3. Mandatory revocation of his or her driver's license for at least six months. VTL § 1193(2)(b)(1-a). However, pursuant to 15 NYCRR § 136.5 a person who has 3 DWI-related convictions/incidents within the past 25 years and whose driver's license is revoked for the most recent offense (a) will be ineligible for a conditional license, and (b) will be revoked for at least 5½ years (followed by five more years on a restricted license with an ignition interlock device requirement), and possibly for life. *See* §§ 55:1 et seq., *infra*;

4. Discretionary revocation of his or her registration for at least six months. VTL § 1193(2)(b)(1-a);

5. A mandatory surcharge of $370. VTL § 1809(1)(b)(ii); VTL § 1809-c(1); VTL § 1809-e(1)(b). If the case is in either a town or village court, the court must add an additional $5 to this surcharge. VTL § 1809(9). *See* §§ 47:1 et seq., *infra*;

6. A mandatory crime victim assistance fee of $25. VTL § 1809(1)(b);

7. A mandatory driver responsibility assessment of $250 a year for three years. VTL § 1199. *See* § 46:50, *infra*;

8. Discretionary imposition of a requirement that the defendant attend a single session of a victim impact panel. VTL § 1193(1)(f). *See* § 46:30, *infra*; and

9. A mandatory requirement that the defendant install and maintain a functioning ignition interlock device in any motor vehicle that he or she owns or operates for at least 6 months. VTL § 1198(2)(a); PL § 65.10(2)(k-1). *See* §§ 48:1 et seq., *infra*.

In *People v. Powlowski*, 172 Misc. 2d 240, —, 658 N.Y.S.2d 558, 560 (Rochester City Ct. 1997), the Court held that where the People seek to charge a defendant with DWAI as a misdemeanor under VTL § 1193(1)(a), the defendant's prior convictions "become an element of the higher level offense," and thus "must be pled in the accusatory instrument." *See also People v. Lazzar*, 3 Misc. 3d 328, 771 N.Y.S.2d 863 (Webster Just. Ct. 2004); *People v. Jamison*, 170 Misc. 2d 974, 652 N.Y.S.2d 495 (Rochester City Ct. 1996). *See generally People v. Cooper*, 78 N.Y.2d 476, 478, 577 N.Y.S.2d 202, 203 (1991) ("When a defendant's prior conviction raises the grade of an offense, and thus becomes an element of the higher grade offense, the Criminal Procedure Law—reflecting a concern for potential prejudice and unfairness to the defendant in putting earlier convictions before the jury—specifies a procedure for alleging and proving the prior convictions (CPL 200.60)").

If this was not the case, a defendant could be tried for DWAI as a traffic infraction (which would not entitle him or her to a jury trial), but sentenced for a misdemeanor. As the *Powlowski* Court pointed out, "[t]his interpretation would deny a defendant facing a criminal conviction the right to a jury trial." 172 Misc. 2d at —, 658 N.Y.S.2d at 561.

Insofar as the mechanics of alleging the prior convictions are concerned, the *Powlowski* Court found that the People need only comply with the requirements of CPL § 100.40, and thus need not (and indeed cannot) file a CPL § 200.60 "special information." 172 Misc. 2d at __-__, 658 N.Y.S.2d at 561–62. The Court pointed out that, if the prior convictions are properly alleged, the defendant can avoid the potential prejudice of reference to such convictions in the presence of the jury by admitting to same. 172 Misc. 2d at __, 658 N.Y.S.2d at 562. "However, if the defendant denies the prior conviction[s] or remains mute, the People may prove that element before the jury as part of their case." 172 Misc. 2d at __, 658 N.Y.S.2d at 562.

In *People v. Greer*, 189 Misc. 2d 310, 731 N.Y.S.2d 323 (App. Term, 2d Dep't 2001), the defendant, who had two prior DWAI convictions within the previous 10 years, was charged with DWI but, following a jury trial, was only found guilty of DWAI. Although the People had not taken the appropriate steps to charge the defendant with misdemeanor DWAI prior to trial, the trial court concluded "that it could utilize the procedure prescribed by CPL 400.40 to enhance the grade of [the] offense from [a] traffic infraction to [a] misdemeanor." 189 Misc. 2d at __, 731 N.Y.S.2d at 324.

The Appellate Term, Second Department, held that the elevation of the defendant's DWAI conviction from a traffic infraction to a misdemeanor was improper. In so holding, the Court reasoned that:

> CPL 400.40 provides a "Procedure for determining prior convictions *for the purpose of sentence* in certain cases" (Emphasis added). Said provision does not authorize an elevation of the grade of [the] offense from [a] traffic infraction to [a] crime, irrespective of what was decided by a jury verdict. . . .
>
> [I]f the People had desired a misdemeanor conviction for driving while impaired, it would have been incumbent upon them to establish at trial through legally sufficient evidence that defendant had the prior convictions for driving while impaired. The *jury* would then have been in a position to convict defendant of driving while impaired as a misdemeanor.

189 Misc. 2d at __, 731 N.Y.S.2d at 324 (citations omitted). *See also People v. Harris*, 23 Misc. 3d 250, 870 N.Y.S.2d 859 (Monroe Co. Ct. 2008), rev'g 14 Misc. 3d 497, 828 N.Y.S.2d 832 (Rochester City Ct. 2006). *Cf. People v. Peacock*, 193 Misc. 2d 672, __, 751 N.Y.S.2d 676, 677 (App. Term, 2d Dep't 2002).

It should be noted that misdemeanor DWAI is not a lesser included offense of misdemeanor DWI. *Harris*, 23 Misc. 3d at __, 870 N.Y.S.2d at 865; *Jamison*, 170 Misc. 2d at __, 652 N.Y.S.2d at 496.

§ 46:6 Driving while intoxicated—First offense

Research References

West's Key Number Digest, Automobiles ⌾359.4

Driving while intoxicated (DWI) in violation of VTL § 1192(2) or (3) is a misdemeanor. VTL § 1193(1)(b). Unless 15 NYCRR § 136.5 applies, *see* § 46:2, *supra*, a defendant who is convicted of DWI as a first offense is subject to the following consequences:

1. A fine of between $500 and $1,000, up to one year in jail, or both. VTL § 1193(1)(b);

2. A period of probation of two or three years. PL § 65.00(3)(d);

3. Mandatory revocation of his or her driver's license for at least six months. VTL § 1193(2)(b)(2);

4. Discretionary revocation of his or her registration for at least six months. VTL § 1193(2)(b)(2);

5. A mandatory surcharge of $370. VTL § 1809(1)(b)(ii); VTL § 1809-c(1); VTL § 1809-e(1)(b). If the case is in either a town or village court, the court must add an additional $5 to this surcharge. VTL § 1809(9). *See* §§ 47:1 et seq., *infra*;

6. A mandatory crime victim assistance fee of $25. VTL § 1809(1)(b);

7. A mandatory driver responsibility assessment of $250 a year for three years. VTL § 1199. *See* § 46:50, *infra*;

8. Discretionary imposition of a requirement that the defendant attend a single session of a victim impact panel. VTL § 1193(1)(f). *See* § 46:30, *infra*; and

9. A mandatory requirement that the defendant install and maintain a functioning ignition interlock device in any motor vehicle that he or she owns or operates for at least 6 months. VTL § 1193(1)(b)(ii); VTL § 1198. *See* §§ 48:1 et seq., *infra*.

In addition, the defendant may be eligible for a conditional license. *See* §§ 50:1 et seq., *infra*.

§ 46:7 DWI—Second offense

Research References

West's Key Number Digest, Automobiles ⌾359.4

Unless 15 NYCRR § 136.5 applies, *see* § 46:2, *supra*, a defendant who is convicted of DWI as a misdemeanor after having been convicted of a violation of VTL § 1192(2), (2-a), (3), (4), or (4-a) within the preceding 10 years is subject to the following consequences:

1. A fine of between $500 and $1,000, up to one year in jail, or both. VTL § 1193(1)(b);

2. A period of probation of two or three years. PL § 65.00(3)(d);

3. Mandatory revocation of his or her driver's license for at least one year (at least 18 months where the prior conviction was for aggravated DWI). VTL § 1193(2)(b)(3). In addition, the DMV will require evidence of alcohol evaluation and/or rehabilitation before it will relicense the defendant. *See* §§ 50:1 et seq. and Appendix 53, *infra*;

4. Discretionary revocation of his or her registration for at least one year (at least 18 months where the prior conviction was for aggravated DWI). VTL § 1193(2)(b)(3);

5. A mandatory surcharge of $370. VTL § 1809(1)(b)(ii); VTL § 1809-c(1); VTL § 1809-e(1)(b). If the case is in either a town or village court, the court must add an additional $5 to this surcharge. VTL § 1809(9). *See* §§ 47:1 et seq., *infra*;

6. A mandatory crime victim assistance fee of $25. VTL § 1809(1)(b);

7. A mandatory driver responsibility assessment of $250 a year for three years. VTL § 1199. *See* § 46:50, *infra*;

8. Discretionary imposition of a requirement that the defendant attend a single session of a victim impact panel. VTL § 1193(1)(f). *See* § 46:30, *infra*; and

9. A mandatory requirement that the defendant install and maintain a functioning ignition interlock device in any motor vehicle that he or she owns or operates for at least 6 months. VTL § 1193(1)(b)(ii); VTL § 1198. *See* §§ 48:1 et seq., *infra*.

A defendant who is convicted of DWI as a misdemeanor after having been convicted of a violation of VTL § 1192(2) or (3) within the preceding five years is subject to the following additional mandatory penalties:

1. "[A] term of imprisonment of [5] days or, as an alternative to such imprisonment, . . . [30] days of service for a public or not-for-profit corporation, association, institution or agency as set forth in [PL § 65.10(2)(h)]." VTL § 1193(1-a)(a); and

2. The sentencing court also must:

(i) order the installation of an ignition interlock device approved pursuant to [VTL § 1198] in any motor vehicle owned or operated by the person so sentenced. Such devices shall remain installed during any period of license revocation required to be imposed pursuant to [VTL § 1193(2)(b)], and, upon the termination of such revocation period, for an additional period as determined by the court; and

(ii) order that such person receive an assessment of the degree of their alcohol or substance abuse and dependency pursuant to the provisions of [VTL § 1198-a]. Where such assessment indicates the need for treatment, such court is authorized to impose treatment as a condition of such sentence except that such court shall impose treatment as a condition of a sentence of probation or conditional discharge pursuant to the provisions of [VTL § 1198-a(3)].

Any person ordered to install an ignition interlock device pursuant to [VTL § 1193(1-a)] shall be subject to the provisions of [VTL § 1198(4), (5), (7), (8) and (9)].

VTL § 1193(1-a)(c). *See also* §§ 48:1 et seq., *infra*.

If the defendant is not subject to VTL § 1193(1-a), he or she may be eligible for a conditional license. *See* §§ 50:1 et seq., *infra*.

Where the date of the *arrest* for the second offense occurs more than 10 years after the date of the *conviction* for the first, a defendant convicted of a second DWI will be penalized as a first offender (unless 15 NYCRR § 136.5 applies). *See* VTL § 1193(2)(b)(3).

§ 46:8   Misdemeanor Aggravated DWI—First offense

Research References

West's Key Number Digest, Automobiles ⟠359.4

Aggravated DWI in violation of VTL § 1192(2-a)(a) is a misdemeanor. VTL § 1193(1)(b). Unless 15 NYCRR § 136.5 applies, *see* § 46:2, *supra*, a defendant who is convicted of aggravated DWI as a first offense is subject to the following consequences:

1. A fine of between $1,000 and $2,500, up to one year in jail, or both. VTL § 1193(1)(b);

2. A period of probation of two or three years. PL § 65.00(3)(d);

3. Mandatory revocation of his or her driver's license for at least one year. VTL § 1193(2)(b)(2);

4. Discretionary revocation of his or her registration for at least one year. VTL § 1193(2)(b)(2);

5. A mandatory surcharge of $370. VTL § 1809(1)(b)(ii); VTL § 1809-c(1); VTL § 1809-e(1)(b). If the case is in either a town or village court, the court must add an additional $5 to this surcharge. VTL § 1809(9). *See* §§ 47:1 et seq., *infra*;

6. A mandatory crime victim assistance fee of $25. VTL § 1809(1)(b);

7. A mandatory driver responsibility assessment of $250 a year for three years. VTL § 1199. *See* § 46:50, *infra*;

8. Discretionary imposition of a requirement that the defendant attend a single session of a victim impact panel. VTL § 1193(1)(f). *See* § 46:30, *infra*; and

9. A mandatory requirement that the defendant install and maintain a functioning ignition interlock device in any motor vehicle that he or she owns or operates for at least 6 months. VTL § 1193(1)(b)(ii); VTL § 1198. *See* §§ 48:1 et seq., *infra*.

In addition, the defendant may be eligible for a conditional license. *See* §§ 50:1 et seq., *infra*.

§ 46:9 Misdemeanor Aggravated DWI—Second offense

Research References

West's Key Number Digest, Automobiles ☞359.4

Unless 15 NYCRR § 136.5 applies, *see* § 46:2, *supra*, a defendant who is convicted of aggravated DWI as a misdemeanor after having been convicted of a violation of VTL § 1192(2), (2-a), (3), (4), or (4-a) within the preceding 10 years is subject to the following consequences:

1. A fine of between $1,000 and $2,500, up to one year in jail, or both. VTL § 1193(1)(b);

2. A period of probation of two or three years. PL § 65.00(3)(d);

3. Mandatory revocation of his or her driver's license for at least 18 months. VTL § 1193(2)(b)(3). In addition, DMV will require evidence of alcohol evaluation and/or rehabilitation before it will relicense the defendant. *See* §§ 50:1 et seq. and Appendix 53, *infra*;

4. Discretionary revocation of his or her registration for at least 18 months. VTL § 1193(2)(b)(3);

5. A mandatory surcharge of $370. VTL § 1809(1)(b)(ii); VTL § 1809-c(1); VTL § 1809-e(1)(b). If the case is in either a town or village court, the court must add an additional $5 to this surcharge. VTL § 1809(9). *See* §§ 47:1 et seq., *infra*;

6. A mandatory crime victim assistance fee of $25. VTL § 1809(1)(b);

7. A mandatory driver responsibility assessment of $250 a year for three years. VTL § 1199. *See* § 46:50, *infra*;

8. Discretionary imposition of a requirement that the defendant attend a single session of a victim impact panel. VTL § 1193(1)(f). *See* § 46:30, *infra*; and

9. A mandatory requirement that the defendant install and maintain a functioning ignition interlock device in any motor vehicle that he or she owns or operates for at least 6 months. VTL § 1193(1)(b)(ii); VTL § 1198. *See* §§ 48:1 et seq., *infra*.

In addition, the defendant may be eligible for a conditional license. *See* §§ 50:1 et seq., *infra*.

Where the date of the *arrest* for the second offense occurs more than 10 years after the date of the *conviction* for the first, a defendant convicted of a second aggravated DWI will be penalized as a first offender (unless 15 NYCRR § 136.5 applies). *See* VTL § 1193(2)(b)(3).

§ 46:10 Felony Aggravated DWI—Leandra's Law

Chapter 496 of the Laws of 2009 is called "Leandra's Law"—in memory of a child killed by a drunk driver. One portion of this law made it a class E felony to commit what would otherwise be a misdemeanor violation of VTL § 1192 with a child under the age of 16 in the vehicle. *See* VTL § 1192(2-a)(b).

With one exception, the consequences of a violation of Leandra's Law are the same as the consequences of every other class E felony DWI. *See* VTL § 1193(1)(c)(i)(B); VTL § 1193(2)(b)(2), (3). *See also* § 46:15, *infra*. The exception is that where a Leandra's Law violation is committed by the child's parent, guardian, custodian or other person "legally responsible for" the child, the police are required to report the case to Child Protective Services. *See* VTL § 1192(12)(b).

Where a Leandra's Law violation is charged via simplified traffic information, the ticketing officer is required to make the notation "C.I.V." (*i.e.*, Child In Vehicle) on the ticket. *See* VTL § 1192(12)(a).

§ 46:11 Driving while ability impaired by drugs—First offense

Research References

West's Key Number Digest, Automobiles ⚷359.4

Driving while ability impaired by drugs (DWAI drugs) in violation of VTL § 1192(4) is a misdemeanor. VTL § 1193(1)(b). Unless 15 NYCRR § 136.5 applies, *see* § 46:2, *supra*, a defendant who is convicted of DWAI drugs as a first offense is subject to the following consequences:

1. A fine of between $500 and $1,000, up to one year in jail, or both. VTL § 1193(1)(b);

2. A period of probation of two or three years. PL § 65.00(3)(d);

3. Mandatory revocation of his or her driver's license for at least six months. VTL § 1193(2)(b)(2). *See also* VTL § 510(2)(b)(v) to (vii);

4. Discretionary revocation of his or her registration for at least six months. VTL § 1193(2)(b)(2). *See also* VTL § 510(2)(b)(v) to (vii);

5. A mandatory surcharge of $370. VTL § 1809(1)(b)(ii); VTL § 1809-c(1); VTL § 1809-e(1)(b). If the case is in either a town or village court, the court must add an additional $5 to this surcharge. VTL § 1809(9). *See* §§ 47:1 et seq., *infra*;

6. A mandatory crime victim assistance fee of $25. VTL § 1809(1)(b);

7. A mandatory driver responsibility assessment of $250 a year for three years. VTL § 1199. *See* § 46:50, *infra*; and

8. Discretionary imposition of a requirement that the defendant attend a single session of a victim impact panel. VTL § 1193(1)(f). *See* § 46:30, *infra*.

In addition, the defendant will *not* be eligible for a conditional license, but may be eligible for a restricted use license. *See* 15 NYCRR § 134.7(a)(10); §§ 50:1 et seq., *infra*.

A defendant who is convicted of DWAI Drugs is not subject to the ignition interlock device law (but may nonetheless be subject to an IID requirement if 15 NYCRR § 136.5 applies). *See, e.g.*, § 48:7, *infra*; PL § 65.10(2)(k-1) ("The court may require [the IID] condition only where a person has been convicted of a violation of [VTL § 1192(2), (2-a) or (3)], or any crime defined by the [VTL] or this chapter of which an alcohol-related violation of any provision of [VTL § 1192] is an essential element."); VTL § 1193(1)(b)(ii); VTL § 1198(2)(a); VTL § 1198(3)(d); 9 NYCRR § 358.1; 15 NYCRR § 140.2; *People v. Levy*, 91 A.D.3d 793, __, 938 N.Y.S.2d 315, 316 (2d Dep't 2012), leave to appeal denied, 18 N.Y.3d 995, 945 N.Y.S.2d 650, 968 N.E.2d 1006 (2012) ("We agree with the defendant that the County Court improperly directed, as a condition of probation, that the defendant install an ignition interlock device on her motor vehicle. . . . Here, the defendant's conviction for operating a motor vehicle while under the influence of drugs pursuant to Vehicle and Traffic Law § 1192(4) falls outside the scope of Penal Law § 65.10(2)(k-1).").

§ 46:12   DWAI drugs—Second offense

Research References

West's Key Number Digest, Automobiles ⚷359.4

Unless 15 NYCRR § 136.5 applies, *see* § 46:2, *supra*, a defendant who is convicted of DWAI drugs as a misdemeanor after having been convicted of a violation of VTL § 1192(2), (2-a), (3), (4), or (4-a) within the preceding 10 years is subject to the following consequences:

1. A fine of between $500 and $1,000, up to one year in jail, or both. VTL § 1193(1)(b);

2. A period of probation of two or three years. PL § 65.00(3)(d);

3. Mandatory revocation of his or her driver's license for at least one year (at least 18 months where the prior conviction was for aggravated DWI). VTL § 1193(2)(b)(3). *See also* VTL § 510(2)(b)(v) to (vii). In addition, the DMV will require evidence of alcohol/drug evaluation and/or rehabilitation before it will relicense the defendant. *See* §§ 50:1 et seq. and Appendix 53, *infra*;

4. Discretionary revocation of his or her registration for at least one year (at least 18 months where the prior conviction was for aggravated DWI). VTL § 1193(2)(b)(3). *See also* VTL § 510(2)(b)(v) to (vii);

5. A mandatory surcharge of $370. VTL § 1809(1)(b)(ii); VTL

§ 1809-c(1); VTL § 1809-e(1)(b). If the case is in either a town or village court, the court must add an additional $5 to this surcharge. VTL § 1809(9). *See* §§ 47:1 et seq., *infra*;

6. A mandatory crime victim assistance fee of $25. VTL § 1809(1)(b);

7. A mandatory driver responsibility assessment of $250 a year for three years. VTL § 1199. *See* § 46:50, *infra*; and

8. Discretionary imposition of a requirement that the defendant attend a single session of a victim impact panel. VTL § 1193(1)(f). *See* § 46:30, *infra*.

In addition, the defendant will *not* be eligible for a conditional license, but may be eligible for a restricted use license. *See* 15 NYCRR § 134.7(a)(10); §§ 50:1 et seq., *infra*.

A defendant who is convicted of DWAI Drugs is not subject to the ignition interlock device law (but may nonetheless be subject to an IID requirement if 15 NYCRR § 136.5 applies). *See, e.g.*, § 48:7, *infra*; PL § 65.10(2)(k-1) ("The court may require [the IID] condition only where a person has been convicted of a violation of [VTL § 1192(2), (2-a) or (3)], or any crime defined by the [VTL] or this chapter of which an alcohol-related violation of any provision of [VTL § 1192] is an essential element."); VTL § 1193(1)(b)(ii); VTL § 1198(2)(a); VTL § 1198(3)(d); 9 NYCRR § 358.1; 15 NYCRR § 140.2; *People v. Levy*, 91 A.D.3d 793, __, 938 N.Y.S.2d 315, 316 (2d Dep't 2012), leave to appeal denied, 18 N.Y.3d 995, 945 N.Y.S.2d 650, 968 N.E.2d 1006 (2012) ("We agree with the defendant that the County Court improperly directed, as a condition of probation, that the defendant install an ignition interlock device on her motor vehicle. . . . Here, the defendant's conviction for operating a motor vehicle while under the influence of drugs pursuant to Vehicle and Traffic Law § 1192(4) falls outside the scope of Penal Law § 65.10(2)(k-1).").

Where the date of the *arrest* for the second offense occurs more than 10 years after the date of the *conviction* for the first, a defendant convicted of a second DWAI Drugs will be penalized as a first offender (unless 15 NYCRR § 136.5 applies). *See* VTL § 1193(2)(b)(3).

§ 46:13 DWAI combined influence of drugs or of alcohol and any drug or drugs—First offense

Research References

West's Key Number Digest, Automobiles ☞359.4

DWAI combined influence of drugs or of alcohol and any drug or drugs ("DWAI combined influence") in violation of VTL § 1192(4-a) is a misdemeanor. VTL § 1193(1)(b). Unless 15 NYCRR § 136.5 applies, *see* § 46:2, *supra*, a defendant who is convicted of DWAI combined influence as a first offense is subject to the following consequences:

    1. A fine of between $500 and $1,000, up to one year in jail, or both. VTL § 1193(1)(b);

    2. A period of probation of two or three years. PL § 65.00(3)(d);

    3. Mandatory revocation of his or her driver's license for at least six months. VTL § 1193(2)(b)(2);

    4. Discretionary revocation of his or her registration for at least six months. VTL § 1193(2)(b)(2);

    5. A mandatory surcharge of $370. VTL § 1809(1)(b)(ii); VTL § 1809-c(1); VTL § 1809-e(1)(b). If the case is in either a town or village court, the court must add an additional $5 to this surcharge. VTL § 1809(9). *See* §§ 47:1 et seq., *infra*;

    6. A mandatory crime victim assistance fee of $25. VTL § 1809(1)(b);

    7. A mandatory driver responsibility assessment of $250 a year for three years. VTL § 1199. *See* § 46:50, *infra*; and

    8. Discretionary imposition of a requirement that the defendant attend a single session of a victim impact panel. VTL § 1193(1)(f). *See* § 46:30, *infra*.

In addition, the defendant may be eligible for a conditional license. *See* §§ 50:1 et seq., *infra*.

A defendant who is convicted of DWAI Combined Influence is not subject to the ignition interlock device law (but may nonetheless be subject to an IID requirement if 15 NYCRR § 136.5 applies). *See, e.g.*, § 48:7, *infra*; PL § 65.10(2)(k-1) ("The court may require [the IID] condition only where a person has been convicted of a violation of [VTL § 1192(2), (2-a) or (3)], or any crime defined by the [VTL] or this chapter of which an alcohol-related violation of any provision of [VTL § 1192] is an essential element."); VTL § 1193(1)(b)(ii); VTL § 1198(2)(a); VTL § 1198(3)(d); 9 NYCRR § 358.1; 15 NYCRR § 140.2. *See generally People v. Levy*, 91 A.D.3d 793, __, 938 N.Y.S.2d 315, 316 (2d Dep't 2012), leave to appeal denied, 18 N.Y.3d 995, 945 N.Y.S.2d 650, 968 N.E.2d 1006 (2012) ("We agree with the defendant that the County Court improperly directed, as a condition of probation, that the defendant install an ignition interlock device on her motor vehicle. . . . Here, the defendant's conviction for operating a motor vehicle while under the influence of drugs pursuant to Vehicle and Traffic Law § 1192(4) falls outside the scope of Penal Law § 65.10(2)(k-1).").

§ 46:14 DWAI combined influence—Second offense

Research References

West's Key Number Digest, Automobiles ⊙═359.4

Unless 15 NYCRR § 136.5 applies, *see* § 46:2, *supra,* a defendant who is convicted of DWAI combined influence as a misdemeanor after having been convicted of a violation of VTL § 1192(2), (2-a), (3), (4), or (4-a) within the preceding 10 years is subject to the following consequences:

1. A fine of between $500 and $1,000, up to one year in jail, or both. VTL § 1193(1)(b);

2. A period of probation of two or three years. PL § 65.00(3)(d);

3. Mandatory revocation of his or her driver's license for at least one year (at least 18 months where the prior conviction was for Aggravated DWI). VTL § 1193(2)(b)(3). In addition, DMV will require evidence of alcohol/drug evaluation and/or rehabilitation before it will relicense the defendant. *See* §§ 50:1 et seq. and Appendix 53, *infra;*

4. Discretionary revocation of his or her registration for at least one year (at least 18 months where the prior conviction was for Aggravated DWI). VTL § 1193(2)(b)(3);

5. A mandatory surcharge of $370. VTL § 1809(1)(b)(ii); VTL § 1809-c(1); VTL § 1809-e(1)(b). If the case is in either a town or village court, the court must add an additional $5 to this surcharge. VTL § 1809(9). *See* §§ 47:1 et seq., *infra;*

6. A mandatory crime victim assistance fee of $25. VTL § 1809(1)(b);

7. A mandatory driver responsibility assessment of $250 a year for three years. VTL § 1199. *See* § 46:50, *infra;* and

8. Discretionary imposition of a requirement that the defendant attend a single session of a victim impact panel. VTL § 1193(1)(f). *See* § 46:30, *infra.*

The defendant may be eligible for a conditional license. *See* §§ 50:1 et seq., *infra.*

A defendant who is convicted of DWAI Combined Influence is not subject to the ignition interlock device law (but may nonetheless be subject to an IID requirement if 15 NYCRR § 136.5 applies). *See, e.g.,* § 48:7, *infra;* PL § 65.10(2)(k-1) ("The court may require [the IID] condition only where a person has been convicted of a violation of [VTL § 1192(2), (2-a) or (3)], or any crime defined by the [VTL] or this chapter of which an alcohol-related violation of any provision of [VTL § 1192] is an essential element."); VTL § 1193(1)(b)(ii); VTL § 1198(2)(a); VTL § 1198(3)(d); 9 NYCRR § 358.1; 15 NYCRR § 140.2. *See generally People v. Levy,* 91 A.D.3d 793, __, 938 N.Y.S.2d 315, 316 (2d Dep't 2012), leave to appeal denied, 18 N.Y.3d 995, 945 N.Y.S.2d 650, 968 N.E.2d 1006 (2012) ("We agree with the defendant that the County Court improperly directed, as a condition of probation, that the defendant install an ignition interlock device on her motor vehicle. . . . Here, the defendant's conviction for operating a motor vehicle while under the influence of drugs pursuant to Vehicle and Traffic Law § 1192(4) falls outside the scope of Penal Law § 65.10(2)(k-1).").

Where the date of the *arrest* for the second offense occurs more than 10 years after the date of the *conviction* for the first, a defendant convicted of a second DWAI combined influence will be penalized as a first offender (unless 15 NYCRR § 136.5 applies). *See* VTL § 1193(2)(b)(3).

§ 46:15   DWI, aggravated DWI, DWAI drugs, or DWAI combined influence—Class E felony

Research References

West's Key Number Digest, Automobiles ☞359.4

A defendant who is charged with DWI, aggravated DWI, DWAI drugs, or DWAI combined influence after having been convicted of a violation of VTL § 1192(2), (2-a), (3), (4), or (4-a) (or of vehicular assault in the 1st or 2nd degree, vehicular manslaughter in the 1st or 2nd degree, aggravated vehicular assault, or aggravated vehicular homicide) within the preceding 10 years can be charged with a class E felony, and is subject to the following consequences:

1. A fine of between $1,000 and $5,000, up to four years in state prison, or both. VTL § 1193(1)(c)(i);

2. A period of probation of three, four or five years. PL § 65.00(3)(a)(i);

3. Mandatory revocation of his or her driver's license for at least one year (at least 18 months where either of the convictions was for Aggravated DWI). VTL § 1193(2)(b)(3). *See also* 15 NYCRR § 136.5. In addition, DMV will require evidence of alcohol evaluation and/or rehabilitation before it will relicense the defendant. *See* §§ 50:1 et seq. and Appendix 53, *infra*;

4. Discretionary revocation of his or her registration for at least one year. VTL § 1193(2)(b)(3);

5. A mandatory surcharge of $495. VTL § 1809(1)(b)(i); VTL § 1809-c(1); VTL § 1809-e(1)(b). *See* §§ 47:1 et seq., *infra*;

6. A mandatory crime victim assistance fee of $25. VTL § 1809(1)(b);

7. A mandatory driver responsibility assessment of $250 a year for three years. VTL § 1199. *See* § 46:50, *infra*;

8. Discretionary imposition of a requirement that the defendant attend a single session of a victim impact panel. VTL § 1193(1)(f). *See* § 46:30, *infra*; and

9. If the conviction is for VTL § 1192(2), (2-a) or (3), a mandatory requirement that the defendant install and maintain a functioning ignition interlock device in any motor vehicle that he or she owns or operates for at least 6 months. VTL § 1193(1)(c)(iii); VTL § 1198. *See* §§ 48:1 et seq., *infra*.

A defendant who is convicted of DWI after having been convicted of a violation of VTL § 1192(2) or (3) within the preceding five years is subject to the following additional mandatory penalties:

1. "[A] term of imprisonment of [5] days or, as an alternative to such imprisonment, . . . [30] days of service for a public or not-for-profit corporation, association, institution or agency as set forth in [PL § 65.10(2)(h)]." VTL § 1193(1-a)(a); and

2. The sentencing court also must:

(i) order the installation of an ignition interlock device approved pursuant to [VTL § 1198] in any motor vehicle owned or operated by the person so sentenced. Such devices shall remain installed during any period of license revocation required to be imposed pursuant to [VTL § 1193(2)(b)], and, upon the termination of such revocation period, for an additional period as determined by the court; and

(ii) order that such person receive an assessment of the degree of their alcohol or substance abuse and dependency pursuant to the provisions of [VTL § 1198-a]. Where such assessment indicates the need for treatment, such court is authorized to impose treatment as a condition of such sentence except that such court shall impose treatment as a condition of a sentence of probation or conditional discharge pursuant to the provisions of [VTL § 1198-a(3)].

(iii) Any person ordered to install an ignition interlock device pursuant to [VTL § 1193(1-a)] shall be subject to the provisions of [VTL § 1198(4), (5), (7), (8), and (9)]. VTL § 1193(1-a)(c).

If the defendant is not subject to VTL § 1193(1-a), he or she may be eligible for a conditional license. *See* §§ 50:1 et seq., *infra*.

It should be noted that a prior conviction or convictions of DWAI in violation of VTL § 1192(1), including DWAI as a misdemeanor, cannot serve as a predicate for a felony DWI charge. *See* VTL § 1193(1)(c). In addition, VTL § 1193(1-a) is inapplicable to convictions of VTL §§ 1192(2-a), (4), and/or (4-a).

§ 46:16   DWI, aggravated DWI, DWAI drugs, or DWAI combined influence—Class D felony

Research References

West's Key Number Digest, Automobiles ⚮359.4

A defendant who is charged with DWI, aggravated DWI, DWAI drugs, or DWAI combined influence after having been convicted of a violation of VTL § 1192(2), (2-a), (3), (4), or (4-a) (or of vehicular assault in the 1st or 2nd degree, vehicular manslaughter in the 1st or 2nd degree, aggravated vehicular assault, or aggravated vehicular homicide) twice within the preceding 10—or three or more times within the preceding 15 years—years can be charged with a class D felony, and is subject to the following consequences:

1. A fine of between $2,000 and $10,000, up to seven years in state prison, or both. VTL § 1193(1)(c)(ii); VTL § 1193(1)(c)(ii-a);

2. A period of probation of three, four or five years. PL § 65.00(3)(a)(i);

3. Mandatory revocation of his or her driver's license for at least one year. VTL § 1193(2)(b)(3). However, pursuant to 15 NYCRR § 136.5 a person who has 3 DWI-related convictions/ incidents within the past 25 years and whose driver's license is revoked for a felony DWI offense (a) will be ineligible for a conditional license, and (b) will be revoked for at least six years (followed by five more years on a restricted license with an ignition interlock device requirement), and possibly for life. *See* §§ 55:1 et seq., *infra*;

4. Discretionary revocation of his or her registration for at least one year. VTL § 1193(2)(b)(3);

5. A mandatory surcharge of $495. VTL § 1809(1)(b)(i); VTL § 1809-c(1); VTL § 1809-e(1)(b). *See* §§ 47:1 et seq., *infra*;

6. A mandatory crime victim assistance fee of $25. VTL § 1809(1)(b);

7. A mandatory driver responsibility assessment of $250 a year for three years. VTL § 1199. *See* § 46:50, *infra*;

8. Discretionary imposition of a requirement that the defendant attend a single session of a victim impact panel. VTL § 1193(1)(f). *See* § 46:30, *infra*; and

9. If the conviction is for VTL § 1192(2), (2-a) or (3), a mandatory requirement that the defendant install and maintain a functioning ignition interlock device in any motor vehicle that he or she owns or operates for at least 6 months. VTL § 1193(1)(c)(iii); VTL § 1198. *See* §§ 48:1 et seq., *infra*.

A defendant who is convicted of DWI after having been convicted of a violation of VTL § 1192(2) or (3) two or more times within the preceding five years is subject to the following additional mandatory penalties:

1. "[A] term of imprisonment of [10] days or, as an alternative to such imprisonment, . . . [60] days of service for a public or not-for-profit corporation, association, institution or agency as set forth in [PL § 65.10(2)(h)]." VTL § 1193(1-a)(b); and

2. The sentencing court also must:

(i) order the installation of an ignition interlock device approved pursuant to [VTL § 1198] in any motor vehicle owned or operated by the person so sentenced. Such devices shall remain installed during any period of license revocation required to be imposed pursuant to [VTL § 1193(2)(b)], and, upon the termination of such revocation period, for an additional period as determined by the court; and

(ii) order that such person receive an assessment of the degree of their alcohol or substance abuse and dependency pursuant to the provisions of [VTL § 1198-a]. Where such assessment indicates the need for treatment, such court is authorized to impose treatment as a condition of such sentence except that such court shall impose treatment as a condition of a sentence of probation or conditional discharge pursuant to the provisions of [VTL § 1198-a(3)].

(iii) Any person ordered to install an ignition interlock device pursuant to [VTL § 1193(1-a)] shall be subject to the provisions of [VTL § 1198(4), (5), (7), (8) and (9)]. VTL § 1193(1-a)(c).

In *People v. Smith*, 57 A.D.3d 1410, 870 N.Y.S.2d 209 (4th Dep't 2008), the defendant was convicted, following a jury trial, of DWI as a class D felony. As it turns out, however, one of the defendant's predicate DWI convictions fell outside the 10-year window specified in VTL § 1193(1)(c)(ii) by three days. Although the defendant had failed to preserve this issue, the Appellate Division, Fourth Department, reduced the conviction to DWI as a class E felony, *see* previous section, "as a matter of discretion in the interest of justice." 870 N.Y.S.2d at 210. It should be noted that the unofficial (*i.e.*, West Publishing) version of this case incorrectly states that the date of the *commission* of the predicate DWI charge—as opposed to the date of *conviction*—fell outside the 10-year window. The authors would like to thank Albany County Assistant District Attorney Matthew Peluso for bringing this discrepancy to our attention.

In *People v. Ritter*, 124 A.D.3d 1133, 2 N.Y.S.3d 693 (3d Dep't 2015), the defendant was sentenced to 1½ to six years in prison for a class D felony Aggravated DWI. The defendant challenged the legality of the sentence. The Appellate Division, Third Department, held that:

> [T]here is no merit to defendant's argument that his sentence was unlawful because County Court imposed a minimum term that was less than one third of the maximum on his conviction of aggravated driving while intoxicated, a class D felony. Penal Law § 70.00(3)(b) provides that, for a class D felony, the minimum period "shall not be less than one year *or more than* one-third of the maximum term imposed."

Id. at __, 2 N.Y.S.3d at 694 (citations omitted).

§ 46:17 Commercial drivers and special vehicles

Research References

West's Key Number Digest, Automobiles ⬥359.4

For specific penalties regarding commercial drivers and special vehicles, see §§ 14:1 et seq.

§ 46:18 Underage offenders—First offense

Research References

West's Key Number Digest, Automobiles ⚷359.4

Where a person under the age of 21 is found guilty of a violation of VTL § 1192-a (the so-called "Zero Tolerance" law), his or her driver's license will be suspended, and his or her registration may be suspended, for a period of six months. VTL § 1193(2)(a)(2). He or she will also be liable for a civil penalty in the amount of $125. VTL § 1194-a(2).

In addition, the person will most likely be eligible for a conditional license. *See* §§ 15:1 et seq., *supra*.

Where a defendant under the age of 21 is convicted of, or adjudicated a youthful offender for, a violation of any subdivision of VTL § 1192, his or her driver's license will be revoked, and his or her registration may be revoked, for a period of at least one year. VTL § 1193(2)(b)(6). He or she will otherwise be subject to the same consequences as a person over the age of 21.

In this situation, the defendant will most likely be eligible for the Drinking Driver Program and a conditional license. *See* §§ 50:1 et seq., *infra*. However, successful completion of the Drinking Driver Program will *not* result in full restoration of the defendant's driving privileges prior to the expiration of the minimum revocation period. VTL § 1193(2)(b)(9). *See also* §§ 15:1 et seq., *supra*.

§ 46:19 Underage offenders—Second offense

Research References

West's Key Number Digest, Automobiles ⚷359.4

Where a person under the age of 21 is either (a) found guilty of a violation of VTL § 1192-a, or (b) convicted of, or adjudicated a youthful offender for, a violation of any subdivision of VTL § 1192, and the person has previously been either (a) found guilty of a violation of VTL § 1192-a, or (b) convicted of, or adjudicated a youthful offender for, a violation of any subdivision of VTL § 1192 *not arising out of the same incident*, his or her driver's license will be revoked, and his or her registration may be revoked, for a period of at least one year or until the person reaches the age of 21, *whichever is longer*. VTL § 1193(2)(b)(7).

In addition, the person will *not* be eligible for conditional license. *See* §§ 50:1 et seq., *infra*.

§ 46:20   Effect of prior "Zero Tolerance" adjudication

Research References

West's Key Number Digest, Automobiles ☞359.4

For purposes of determining the length of a license suspension or revocation to be imposed for a subsequent offense committed after a person has been found guilty of a violation of VTL § 1192-a, the effect of the prior Zero Tolerance adjudication is the same as a conviction of DWAI in violation of VTL § 1192(1), *provided that the subsequent offense is committed during the retention period set forth in VTL § 201(1)(k)*. VTL § 1192(8-a). VTL § 201(1)(k) provides, in pertinent part, that the Commissioner may destroy:

> [A]ny records, including any reproductions or electronically created images of such records and including any records received by the commissioner from a court pursuant to [VTL § 1192(10)(c)] or [Navigation Law § 49-b], relating to a finding of a violation of [VTL § 1192-a] or a waiver of the right to a hearing under [VTL § 1194-a] or a finding of a refusal following a hearing conducted pursuant to [VTL § 1194-a(3)] or a finding of a violation of [Navigation Law § 49-b] or a waiver of the right to a hearing or a finding of refusal following a hearing conducted pursuant to [Navigation Law § 49-b], after remaining on file for [3] years after such finding or entry of such waiver or refusal or until the person that is found to have violated such section reaches the age of [21], whichever is the greater period of time.

§ 46:21   Out-of-state convictions

Research References

West's Key Number Digest, Automobiles ☞359.4; Sentencing and Punishment ☞793

Prior to November 1, 2006, VTL § 1192(8) provided that, for purposes of determining the consequences of a violation of VTL § 1192, a prior out-of-state conviction for operating a motor vehicle while under the influence of alcohol or drugs was deemed to be a prior conviction of DWAI in violation of VTL § 1192(1). Effective November 1, 2006, VTL § 1192(8) provides as follows:

> Effect of prior out-of-state conviction. A prior out-of-state conviction for operating a motor vehicle while under the influence of alcohol or drugs shall be deemed to be a prior conviction of a violation of this section for purposes of determining penalties imposed under this section or for purposes of any administrative action required to be taken pursuant to [VTL § 1193(2)]; provided, however, that such conduct, had it occurred in this state, would have constituted a misdemeanor or felony violation of any of the provisions of [VTL § 1192]. Provided, however, that if such conduct, had it occurred in this state, would have constituted a violation of any provisions of

[VTL § 1192] which are not misdemeanor or felony offenses, then such conduct shall be deemed to be a prior conviction of a violation of [VTL § 1192(1)] for purposes of determining penalties imposed under this section or for purposes of any administrative action required to be taken pursuant to [VTL § 1193(2)].

Thus, a prior out-of-state DWI conviction can now potentially be used as a predicate conviction for a felony DWI charge.

Critically, however, the enabling portion of this change to VTL § 1192(8) expressly provides that it only applies to out-of-state convictions that occurred on or after November 1, 2006. *See also People v. Ballman*, 15 N.Y.3d 68, 70, 904 N.Y.S.2d 361, 362, 930 N.E.2d 282, __ (2010) ("This appeal raises the issue whether Vehicle and Traffic Law § 1192(8) allows an out-of-state conviction occurring prior to November 1, 2006 to be considered for purposes of elevating a charge of driving while intoxicated from a misdemeanor to a felony. We hold that it does not").

In addition, where a New York licensee is convicted of operating a motor vehicle while under the influence of alcohol or drugs in another state, his or her driver's license will be revoked, and his or her registration may be revoked, for at least:

(a) ninety days, if the licensee is over 21. VTL § 1193(2)(b)(8);

(b) one year, if the licensee is under 21 and is a "first offender." VTL § 1193(2)(b)(6); VTL § 1193(2)(b)(8); or

(c) one year or until age 21, *whichever is longer*, if the licensee is under 21 and is a "repeat offender." VTL § 1193(2)(b)(7); VTL § 1193(2)(b)(8).

In *Matter of Woods*, 56 A.D.3d 184, 867 N.Y.S.2d 45 (1st Dep't 2008), the Appellate Division, First Department, held that Michigan's felony DWI laws are sufficiently analogous to New York's felony DWI laws to require respondent's disbarment for his conviction of felony DWI in Michigan.

§ 46:22 License suspension or revocation begins at sentencing

Research References

West's Key Number Digest, Automobiles ⟜55, 106, 144.1(1.11), 359.4

Where a license suspension or revocation is required to be imposed pursuant to VTL § 1193(2)(a) or (b), the Court must issue an Order suspending or revoking the defendant's driver's license at the time of sentencing, at which time the defendant must surrender his or her license to the Court. VTL § 1193(2)(d)(1).

The suspension or revocation imposed pursuant to VTL § 1193(2)(d)(1) takes effect immediately. VTL § 1193(2)(d)(1). However, with certain exceptions, the sentencing Court may issue a so-called "20-day Order," which makes the "license suspension or revocation take effect [20] days after the date of sentencing." VTL § 1193(2)(d)(2). *See also* §§ 49:1 et seq., *infra*; VTL § 510(2)(b)(vi).

§ 46:23   Periods of revocation are *minimum* periods

Research References

West's Key Number Digest, Automobiles ☞55, 106, 144.1(1.11), 359.4

Where a driver's license is revoked pursuant to VTL § 1193(2)(b), "no new license shall be issued after the expiration of the minimum period specified in such paragraph, except in the discretion of the commissioner." VTL § 1193(2)(c).

In *People v. Demperio*, 86 N.Y.2d 549, 552, 634 N.Y.S.2d 672, 673 (1995), the Court of Appeals held that this statute provides a defendant with "reason to know that upon revocation of his license, a new license application [is] required."

§ 46:24   Court cannot impose sentence of unconditional discharge

Research References

West's Key Number Digest, Automobiles ☞359.4

Where a defendant is convicted of any violation of VTL § 1192, a court cannot impose a sentence of unconditional discharge. VTL § 1193(1)(e).

§ 46:25   Court must impose fine unless defendant sentenced to incarceration

Research References

West's Key Number Digest, Automobiles ☞359.4

Where a defendant is convicted of any violation of VTL § 1192, a court cannot impose a sentence of conditional discharge or probation "unless such conditional discharge or probation is accompanied by a sentence of a fine as provided in this subdivision." VTL § 1193(1)(e).

On the other hand, where a defendant convicted of any violation of VTL § 1192 is sentenced to incarceration, there is no mandatory fine. In *People v. Moore*, 212 A.D.2d 1062, 623 N.Y.S.2d 42 (4th Dep't 1995), the Appellate Division, Fourth Department, vacated a felony DWI sentence and remitted the case to county court for resentencing on the ground that "County Court's statement that there was a mandatory minimum fine was based upon a misapprehension that the court did not have discretion in sentencing," 212 A.D.2d at __, 623 N.Y.S.2d at 43, and that such misapprehension was "a departure from the "'essential nature" of the right to be sentenced as provided by law.' " 212 A.D.2d at __, 623 N.Y.S.2d at 43 (citation omitted). *See also People v. York*, 123 A.D.3d 1155, 999 N.Y.S.2d 520 (2d Dep't 2014); *People v. Olmstead*, 111 A.D.3d 1063, __, 975 N.Y.S.2d 359, 359-60 (3d Dep't 2013); *People v. Figueroa*, 17 A.D.3d 1130, __, 794 N.Y.S.2d 262, 264 (4th Dep't 2005); *People v. Fehr*, 303 A.D.2d 1039, __, 757 N.Y.S.2d 205, 207 (4th Dep't 2003); *People v. John*, 288 A.D.2d 848, __, 732 N.Y.S.2d 505, 508 (4th Dep't 2001); *People v. Domin*, 284 A.D.2d 731, __, 726 N.Y.S.2d 503, 505 (3d Dep't 2001); *People v. Swan*, 277 A.D.2d 1033, 716 N.Y.S.2d 194 (4th Dep't 2000); *People v. Thomas*, 245 A.D.2d 1136, 667 N.Y.S.2d 536 (4th Dep't 1997). *See generally People v. Gemboys*, 270 A.D.2d 847, 705 N.Y.S.2d 925 (4th Dep't 2000) (even where defendant sentenced to incarceration, fine of $1,000 for class D felony DWI is illegal—although imposition of fine is optional, if fine is imposed the minimum amount is $2,000); *People v. Sudbrink*, 35 A.D.3d 635, __, 825 N.Y.S.2d 762, 763-64 (2d Dep't 2006) (same); *People v. Barber*, 31 A.D.3d 1145, __, 818 N.Y.S.2d 391, 392 (4th Dep't 2006); *People v. Jimerson*, 13 A.D.3d 1140, 788 N.Y.S.2d 526 (4th Dep't 2004); *People v. Castellano*, 6 A.D.3d 278, 774 N.Y.S.2d 703 (1st Dep't 2004); *People v. Smith*, 309 A.D.2d 1282, 764 N.Y.S.2d 732 (4th Dep't 2003).

§ 46:26 DMV required to correct improper license suspension/revocation

Research References

West's Key Number Digest, Automobiles ⬉55, 106, 144.1(1.11), 359.4

Where a court fails to impose, or incorrectly imposes, a license suspension or revocation required pursuant to VTL § 1193(2)(b), the Commissioner is required, upon receipt of a Certificate of Conviction filed pursuant to VTL § 514, to "impose such mandated suspension or revocation, which shall supersede any such order which the court may have imposed." VTL § 1193(2)(b)(10).

This statute, which was enacted in 1990, appears to legislatively overrule *Matter of Sovik v. State of New York Dep't of Motor Vehicles*, 143 Misc. 2d 941, 542 N.Y.S.2d 462 (Onondaga Co. Sup. Ct. 1989). In *Sovik*, the petitioner received a second DWAI conviction arising out of an arrest that occurred within five years of his first conviction. However, the sentencing court improperly imposed a 90-day license *suspension* rather than the six-month *revocation* required by VTL § 1193(2)(b)(1). The Commissioner thereafter imposed the requisite revocation.

The petitioner filed an Article 78 petition seeking to nullify the revocation of his driver's license by the Commissioner. The supreme court agreed that the sentencing court "impermissibly suspended petitioner's license contrary to the express provisions of [VTL] section 1193," but nonetheless held that the Commissioner was not authorized to impose the mandated revocation. 143 Misc. 2d at ___, 542 N.Y.S.2d at 464.

Conversely, a court can "correct" a revocation period improperly imposed by the DMV. *See People v. Eberhardt,* 277 A.D.2d 1044, 715 N.Y.S.2d 349 (4th Dep't 2000).

§ 46:27   Relicensure of defendant sentenced to probation

Research References

West's Key Number Digest, Automobiles ⊙144.3

Where a defendant's driver's license has been revoked pursuant to VTL § 1193(2)(b) and he or she has been sentenced to a period of probation, and a condition of such probation is that the defendant not operate a motor vehicle or apply for a driver's license during the period of probation, "the commissioner may not restore such license until the period of the condition of probation has expired." VTL § 1193(2)(e)(5).

Many standard "Conditions of Probation" forms include one or more provisions prohibiting the defendant from either (a) operating a motor vehicle without the approval of the court, and/or (b) reapplying for a driver's license without permission from the court. In any event, regardless of whether such conditions are in fact a part of the defendant's conditions of probation, the DMV will presume them to be.

As a result, if the defendant's sentence is not intended to include these conditions, the court must strike them from the "Conditions of Probation" form and replace them with language to the effect that "the defendant is not to operate a motor vehicle and/or reapply for a driver's license *unless authorized to do so by the Department of Motor Vehicles. The authorization of the Court and / or the Department of Probation is not required.*"

In order to avoid unnecessary delay at the time of reapplication, the document containing the above-referenced language can be mailed to the DMV ahead of time, at which point the defendant's DMV file will be "coded" to reflect that VTL § 1193(2)(e)(5) does not preclude his or her relicensure.

Modern DMV "Order of Suspension or Revocation" forms (*i.e.,* form MV-1192) contain the following check box questions:

"Is motorist sentenced to ☐ Probation . . . ☐ Conditional Discharge . . ."

[If the motorist is sentenced to probation:]

"Must the motorist obtain permission before applying for a license?
. . . ☐ Yes ☐ No"

"If yes, do they need permission from: ☐ Court ☐ Probation
Department ☐ Both"

This self-explanatory form makes life much easier in cases where
the defendant is sentenced to probation.

§ 46:28 Reapplication after revocation—45-day rule

Research References
West's Key Number Digest, Automobiles ⬞144.3

Where a defendant's driver's license has been revoked pursuant to VTL § 1193(2)(b) or the defendant is subject to a condition
of probation that he or she not operate a motor vehicle or apply
for a driver's license during the period of probation, "application
for a new license may be made within [45] days prior to the
expiration of such minimum period of revocation or condition of
probation, whichever expires last." VTL § 1193(2)(e)(6).

In light of the fact that the DMV is understaffed and handles a
large volume of cases, it is important that defense counsel advise
the defendant to take advantage of this section and reapply for a
driver's license as soon as he or she is eligible to do so. In this
regard, it is the authors' understanding that DMV currently accepts reapplications up to 60 days prior to the expiration of the
minimum revocation period.

§ 46:29 Reinstatement fee

Research References
West's Key Number Digest, Automobiles ⬞144.3

Where a defendant's driver's license has been *suspended* for a
violation of VTL § 1192(1), "such suspension shall remain in effect until a termination of a [sic] suspension fee of [$50] is paid to
the commissioner." VTL § 503(2)(j).

Where a defendant's driver's license has been *revoked* pursuant
to VTL § 510, VTL § 1193, or VTL § 1194, he or she must, "upon
application for issuance of a driver's license, pay to the commissioner a fee of [$100]." VTL § 503(2)(h).

Where a person's driver's license has been either suspended or
revoked for a violation of VTL § 1192-a (the so-called "Zero Tolerance" law), "the fee to be paid to the commissioner shall be
[$100]." VTL § 503(2)(h), (j).

Where a nonresident's driving *privileges* have been revoked pursuant to VTL § 510, VTL § 1193, or VTL § 1194, he or she must, "upon application for reinstatement of such driving privileges, pay to the commissioner of motor vehicles a fee of [$25]." VTL § 503(2)(i).

It is critical that a person pay the applicable reinstatement fee and secure the return of his or her driver's license (or driving privileges) from DMV following an alcohol-or drug-related suspension/revocation, as driving without doing so constitutes AUO. *See* §§ 13:1 et seq., *supra*.

§ 46:30   Victim impact panel

Research References

West's Key Number Digest, Sentencing and Punishment ⚖361

Where a court imposes a sentence for a violation of VTL § 1192, it may require the defendant, as a part of or as a condition of such sentence, to attend a single session of a victim impact panel. VTL § 1193(1)(f). This is a program in which presentations are made concerning the harm caused by, and the impact of, driving while intoxicated. *See* VTL § 1193(1)(f). The presentations are generally made by people who have lost friends and/or family members as a result of alcohol-or drug-related accidents.

§ 46:31   Lifetime revocation—Two convictions of DWI or DWAI drugs involving accidents causing physical injury

Research References

West's Key Number Digest, Automobiles ⚖55, 106, 144.1(1.11), 359.4

Where a driver's license is revoked pursuant to VTL § 1193(2)(b):

> [I]n no event shall a new license be issued where a person has been twice convicted of a violation of [VTL § 1192(3), (4) or (4-a)] or of driving while intoxicated or of driving while ability is impaired by the use of a drug or of driving while ability is impaired by the combined influence of drugs or of alcohol and any drug or drugs where physical injury, as defined in [PL § 10.00], has resulted from such offense in each instance.

VTL § 1193(2)(c).

This section was declared to be constitutional in *Matter of Hauptman v. New York State Dep't of Motor Vehicles*, 158 A.D.2d 600, 551 N.Y.S.2d 572 (2d Dep't 1990). In order to invoke the lifetime revocation set forth in VTL § 1193(2)(c), the DMV must provide the motorist with notice of its intent to permanently revoke his or her driver's license, and the opportunity for a fact-finding hearing. *See Matter of Leader v. Adduci*, 144 Misc. 2d 497, 544 N.Y.S.2d 414 (Westchester Co. Sup. Ct. 1989).

With regard to the "physical injury" requirement, it is clear that the injury can be to anyone, including the person charged with DWI. *See Matter of Quealy v. Passidomo*, 124 A.D.2d 955, 508 N.Y.S.2d 706 (3d Dep't 1986). *See also Hauptman*, 158 A.D.2d at __, 551 N.Y.S.2d at 574; *Leader*, 144 Misc. 2d at __, 544 N.Y.S.2d at 417. In this regard, the *Quealy* Court held that "[t]he fact that petitioner fortuitously did not cause injury to anyone other than himself does not mitigate the fact that he has, on more than one occasion, been involved in an alcohol-related accident of such a magnitude that personal injury resulted." 124 A.D.2d at __, 508 N.Y.S.2d at 708.

In the past, virtually any personal injury, including minor cuts or bruises, could serve as the requisite "*personal* injury." *See, e.g., Matter of Johnston v. Adduci*, 177 A.D.2d 773, 576 N.Y.S.2d 60 (3d Dep't 1991). The statute was amended in 1994, however, to require the injury to be "*physical* injury" as defined in PL § 10.00. Penal Law § 10.00(9) defines physical injury as "impairment of physical condition or substantial pain." The DMV has been applying this amendment retroactively and considering applications for relicensure by motorists revoked for life under the former version of this statute. Essentially, the DMV will review the motorist's file and determine whether the injuries that triggered the lifetime revocation constituted "physical injury" as defined in PL § 10.00.

In *Matter of Rosato v. New York State Dep't of Motor Vehicles*, 7 A.D.3d 718, __, 777 N.Y.S.2d 186, 187 (2d Dep't 2004), the Appellate Division, Second Department, held that:

The appellant's contention that the respondent New York State Department of Motor Vehicles (hereinafter the DMV) should have used the definition of "serious physical injury" under Penal Law § 10.00(10), instead of the lesser standard of "physical injury" contained in Penal Law § 10.00(9), in deciding whether to reissue his driver's license after a prior revocation is without merit. Vehicle and Traffic Law § 1193(2)(c)(3) requires the DMV to use the definition of "physical injury" contained in Penal Law § 10.00. When a statute contains a clear mandate, its plain language must be followed.

§ 46:32 Accidents involving death or serious physical injury

15 NYCRR § 136.4(b-1) provides that:

An application for a driver's license may be denied if the applicant has been convicted of a violation of section 125.10, 125.12, 125.13, 125.14, 125.15, 125.20, 125.22, 125.25, 125.26 or 125.27 of the Penal

Law arising out of the operation of a motor vehicle, or if the applicant has been convicted of a violation of [VTL § 1192] where death or serious physical injury, as defined in section 10.00 of the Penal Law, has resulted from such offense.

§ 46:33 "Permanent" driver's license revocation

Research References

West's Key Number Digest, Automobiles ⚖55, 106, 144.1(1.11), 359.4

VTL § 1193(2)(b)(12) requires "permanent" driver's license revocation for certain repeat offenders. In most cases, however, "permanent" does not actually mean *permanent*. *Cf.* § 46:31, *supra* (a "lifetime" driver's license revocation imposed pursuant to VTL § 1193(2)(c) is truly permanent). Rather, prior to the September 25, 2012 amendments to 15 NYCRR §§ 136.5 and 136.10, *see* §§ 55:1 et seq., *infra*, it meant either five years or eight years (depending on the defendant's prior record). The various subdivisions of VTL § 1193(2)(b)(12) are set forth in the sections that follow.

§ 46:34 Five-year revocation

Research References

West's Key Number Digest, Automobiles ⚖55, 106, 144.1(1.11), 359.4

VTL § 1193(2)(b)(12)(a) provides as follows:

(12) Permanent revocation. (a) Notwithstanding any other provision of this chapter to the contrary, whenever a revocation is imposed upon a person for the refusal to submit to a chemical test pursuant to the provisions of [VTL § 1194] or conviction for any violation of [VTL § 1192] for which a sentence of imprisonment may be imposed, and such person has:

(i) within the previous [4] years been twice convicted of any provisions of [VTL § 1192] or a violation of the penal law for which a violation of [VTL § 1192] is an essential element and at least [1] such conviction was for a crime, or has twice been found to have refused to submit to a chemical test pursuant to [VTL § 1194], or has any combination of [2] such convictions and findings of refusal not arising out of the same incident; or

(ii) within the previous [8] years been convicted [3] times of any provision of [VTL § 1192] for which a sentence of imprisonment may be imposed or a violation of the penal law for which a violation of [VTL § 1192] is an essential element and at least [2] such convictions were for crimes, or has been found, on [3] separate occasions, to have refused to submit to a chemical test pursuant to [VTL § 1194], or has any combination of such convictions and findings of refusal not arising out of the same incident,

such revocation shall be permanent.

Although VTL § 1193(2)(b)(12)(a) provides that a revocation pursuant thereto is "permanent," VTL § 1193(2)(b)(12)(b) provides that DMV *shall* waive such permanency after five years, under the following circumstances:

(b) The permanent driver's license revocation required by [VTL § 1193(2)(b)(12)(a)] shall be waived by the commissioner after a period of [5] years has expired since the imposition of such permanent revocation, provided that during such [5]-year period such person has not been found to have refused a chemical test pursuant to [VTL § 1194] while operating a motor vehicle and has not been convicted of a violation of any subdivision of [VTL § 1192] or [VTL § 511] or a violation of the penal law for which a violation of any subdivision of [VTL § 1192] is an essential element and either:

(i) that such person provides acceptable documentation to the commissioner that such person has voluntarily enrolled in and successfully completed an appropriate rehabilitation program; or

(ii) that such person is granted a certificate of relief from disabilities as provided for in [Correction Law § 701] by the court in which such person was last sentenced.

Provided, however, that the commissioner may, on a case by case basis, refuse to restore a license which otherwise would be restored pursuant to this item, in the interest of the public safety and welfare.

(Emphasis added).

Despite the seemingly mandatory five-year waiver requirement in VTL § 1193(2)(b)(12)(b), new DMV regulation 15 NYCRR § 136.10(b) provides that after five years DMV will either:

(a) impose a non-waivable permanent lifetime license revocation (if the defendant also has one or more "serious driving offenses" within the past 25 years). *See* 15 NYCRR § 136.5(b)(2); §§ 55:1 et seq., *infra*; or

(b) impose *an additional* five-year "waiting period" (with no driving privileges), plus *another 5 years* with restricted driving privileges and a mandatory IID requirement for the entire time. *See* 15 NYCRR § 136.5(b)(3).

In this regard, 15 NYCRR § 136.10(b) irreconcilably conflicts with VTL § 1193(2)(b)(12)(b). 15 NYCRR § 136.10(b) irreconcilably conflicts with VTL § 1193(2)(b)(12)(b) in yet another way. Specifically, although VTL § 1193(2)(b)(12)(b) expressly provides that a five-year "permanent" license revocation generally must be waived as long as the defendant:

(1) has *either* completed treatment *or* obtained a certificate of relief from disabilities (or a certificate of good conduct); *and*

(2) has not been found guilty of violating VTL § 511, VTL § 1192, VTL § 1194 or a VTL § 1192-related Penal Law offense during the revocation period;

new DMV regulation 15 NYCRR § 136.10(b) provides that the revocation will only be waived:

(a) after *another five years*; *and*

(b) only if the defendant:

    (1) has completed treatment; *and*

    (2) has obtained a certificate of relief from disabilities (or a certificate of good conduct); *and*

    (3) isn't denied relicensure pursuant to 15 NYCRR § 136.4 or 15 NYCRR § 136.5; *and*

    (4) hasn't been found guilty of violating VTL § 511, VTL § 1192, VTL § 1194 or a VTL § 1192-related Penal Law offense during the revocation period; *and*

    (5) hasn't driven during the revocation period—as indicated by accidents, convictions or pending tickets.

In the event that these additional requirements are met and *10 years* has elapsed, DMV will then impose *an additional five years* with restricted driving privileges *and* a mandatory IID requirement for the entire time. *See* 15 NYCRR § 136.5(b)(3). Critically, however, if the defendant had a "serious driving offense" within 25 years of the offense that led to "permanent" revocation under VTL § 1193(2)(b)(12), the defendant's driver's license *will* never be restored. *See* 15 NYCRR § 136.5(b)(2). *See also* §§ 55:1 et seq., *infra*.

15 NYCRR § 136.10(b) clearly renders VTL § 1193(2)(b)(12)(b) "superfluous, a result to be avoided in statutory construction." *People v. Litto*, 33 A.D.3d 625, __, 822 N.Y.S.2d 130, 131 (2d Dep't 2006), order aff'd, 8 N.Y.3d 692, 840 N.Y.S.2d 736, 872 N.E.2d 848 (2007).

§ 46:35 Conditional license during period of permanent revocation

Research References

West's Key Number Digest, Automobiles ☞55, 106, 144.1(1.11), 359.4

VTL § 1193(2)(b)(12)(c) provides that:

(c) For revocations imposed pursuant to [VTL § 1193(2)(b)(12)(a)], the commissioner may adopt rules to permit conditional or restricted operation of a motor vehicle by any such person after a mandatory revocation period of not less than [3] years subject to such criteria, terms and conditions as established by the commissioner.

Pursuant to new DMV regulation 15 NYCRR § 134.7(a)(11)(i),

however, a person who has 3 DWI-related convictions/incidents within the past 25 years is ineligible for a conditional license.

§ 46:36 Eight-year revocation

Research References

West's Key Number Digest, Automobiles ⊕55, 106, 144.1(1.11), 359.4

VTL § 1193(2)(b)(12)(d) provides that upon:

(i) a finding of refusal after having been convicted [3] times within [4] years of a violation of any subdivision of [VTL § 1192] or of the penal law for which a violation of any subdivision of [VTL § 1192] is an essential element or any combination of [3] such convictions not arising out of the same incident within [4] years or

(ii) a fourth conviction of any subdivision of [VTL § 1192] after having been convicted of any such subdivision of [VTL § 1192] or of the penal law for which a violation of any of such subdivisions of [VTL § 1192] is an essential element or any combination of [3] such convictions not arising out of the same incident within [4] years or

(iii) a finding of refusal after having been convicted [4] times within [8] years of a violation of any subdivision of [VTL § 1192] or of the penal law for which a violation of any of such subdivisions of [VTL § 1192] is an essential element or any combination of [4] such convictions not arising out of the same incident within [8] years or

(iv) a fifth conviction of any subdivision of [VTL § 1192] after having been convicted of such subdivision or of the penal law for which a violation of any of such subdivisions of [VTL § 1192] is an essential element or any combination of [4] such convictions not arising out of the same incident within [8] years,

such revocation shall be permanent.

As with a revocation pursuant to VTL § 1193(2)(b)(12)(a), although VTL § 1193(2)(b)(12)(d) provides that a revocation pursuant thereto is "permanent," VTL § 1193(2)(b)(12)(e) provides that the DMV can waive such permanency after eight years, under the following circumstances:

(e) The permanent driver's license revocation required by [VTL § 1193(2)(b)(12)(d)] may be waived by the commissioner after a period of [8] years has expired since the imposition of such permanent revocation provided:

(i) that during such [8]-year period such person has not been found to have refused a chemical test pursuant to [VTL § 1194] while operating a motor vehicle and has not been convicted of a violation of any subdivision of [VTL § 1192] or [VTL § 511] or a violation of the penal law for which a violation of any such subdivision[] of [VTL § 1192] is an essential element; and

(ii) that such person provides acceptable documentation to the commissioner that such person has voluntarily enrolled in and successfully completed an appropriate rehabilitation program; and

(iii) after such documentation is accepted, that such person is granted a certificate of relief from disabilities as provided for in [Correction Law § 701] by the court in which such person was last sentenced.

Notwithstanding the provisions of this clause, nothing contained in this clause shall be deemed to require the commissioner to restore a license to an applicant who otherwise has complied with the requirements of this item, in the interest of the public safety and welfare.

However, pursuant to new DMV regulation 15 NYCRR § 136.10(b), DMV will *never* grant a waiver after eight years. Rather, new DMV regulation 15 NYCRR § 136.10(b) provides that the revocation will only be waived:

(a) after *another five years*; *and*
(b) only if the defendant:
    (1) has completed treatment; *and*
    (2) has obtained a certificate of relief from disabilities (or a certificate of good conduct); *and*
    (3) isn't denied relicensure pursuant to 15 NYCRR § 136.4 or 15 NYCRR § 136.5; *and*
    (4) hasn't been found guilty of violating VTL § 511, VTL § 1192, VTL § 1194 or a VTL § 1192-related Penal Law offense during the revocation period; *and*
    (5) hasn't driven during the revocation period—as indicated by accidents, convictions or pending tickets.

In the event that these additional requirements are met and *13 years* has elapsed, DMV will then impose *an additional five years* with restricted driving privileges *and* a mandatory IID requirement for the entire time. *See* 15 NYCRR § 136.5(b)(3). Critically, however, if the defendant had a "serious driving offense" within 25 years of the offense that led to "permanent" revocation under VTL § 1193(2)(b)(12), the defendant's driver's license *will* never be restored. *See* 15 NYCRR § 136.5(b)(2). *See also* §§ 55:1 et seq., *infra*.

A person who is permanently revoked pursuant to VTL

§ 1193(2)(b)(12)(d) is not eligible for any type of conditional or restricted driving privileges during the revocation period. *See* 15 NYCRR § 134.7(a)(11)(i).

§ 46:37 VTL § 1193(2)(b)(12) will not reduce other mandatory revocation

Research References

West's Key Number Digest, Automobiles ☞55, 106, 144.1(1.11), 359.4

VTL § 1193(2)(b)(12)(f) provides that "[n]othing contained in [VTL § 1193(2)(b)(12)] shall be deemed to reduce a license revocation period imposed pursuant to any other provision of law."

Thus, for example, a lifetime driver's license revocation imposed pursuant to VTL § 1193(2)(c), *see* § 46:31, *supra*, will not be reduced by either VTL § 1193(2)(b)(12)(b) or VTL § 1193(2)(b)(12)(e).

§ 46:38 Court cannot impose "scarlet letter" penalty

Research References

West's Key Number Digest, Automobiles ☞359.4

In *People v. Letterlough*, the sentencing court imposed a condition of probation that, if the defendant regained his driving privileges, he would have to affix a fluorescent sign stating "CONVICTED DWI" to the license plates of any vehicle that he operated. The Court of Appeals reversed, holding that "the condition is not reasonably related to defendant's rehabilitation, and, more generally, because, in the absence of more specific legislation, such a condition is outside the authority of the court to impose." 86 N.Y.2d 259, 261, 631 N.Y.S.2d 105, 106 (1995). In addition, the Court noted that "[t]he distraction occasioned by special judicially ordered 'scarlet letter' plates and the reactions of other motorists upon seeing them also poses a potential safety threat." 86 N.Y.2d at 268, 631 N.Y.S.2d at 110. *See also Bursac v. Suozzi*, 22 Misc. 3d 328, 868 N.Y.S.2d 470 (Nassau Co. Sup. Ct. 2008) (Court granted DWI defendant's petition seeking a permanent injunction enjoining and restraining County Executive from posting petitioner's name, picture and identifying information on "Wall of Shame" Internet website and directing the removal of same).

Similarly, a condition of probation that the defendant must attend Alcoholics Anonymous (A.A.) meetings, which are religious in nature, without offering a choice of other alcohol treatment providers, has been held to violate the Establishment Clause of the First Amendment. *See Warner v. Orange County Dep't of Probation*, 115 F.3d 1068 (2d Cir. 1997).

§ 46:39   Sentencing policies

Research References

West's Key Number Digest, Automobiles ⚖️359.4

In general, it is improper for a court to establish sentencing policies with regard to particular categories of defendants. For example, "a policy of incarcerating those who refuse to take a breathalyzer test and are thereafter convicted of driving while impaired . . . is arbitrary, capricious and unauthorized by statute." *People v. McSpirit*, 154 Misc. 2d 784, __, 595 N.Y.S.2d 660, 661 (App. Term, 9th & 10th Jud. Dist. 1993). Such a policy "ignores . . . other criteria warranting an impartial and judicious evaluation, e.g., 'the crime charged, the particular circumstances of the individual before the court, and the purpose of a penal sanction, *i.e.*, societal protection, rehabilitation and deterrence.'" 154 Misc. 2d at __, 595 N.Y.S.2d at 661 (citation omitted). *See also People v. Nicholson*, 237 A.D.2d 973, 654 N.Y.S.2d 906 (4th Dep't 1997).

In *People v. Wilson*, 245 A.D.2d 161, 666 N.Y.S.2d 164 (1st Dep't 1997), the defendant pled guilty to various charges after the Court made the following statement:

> It's my policy that should a defendant who is a predicate felon on a drug case go to trial and if that defendant is found guilty by the jury, that it is my policy to sentence the defendant to the high end of the sentencing chart which would be [121/2] to [25].

> That has been, and barring any unforeseen circumstances, will be my policy, subject, of course, to mitigating circumstances that might develop during the trial or in the probation report. And I think it's important that the defendant be aware of that policy. I'm not making the statement to suggest that a defendant not go to trial and exercise his or her constitutional rights. I'm just talking about sentencing guidelines.

245 A.D.2d at __, 666 N.Y.S.2d at 165. On appeal, the Appellate Division, First Department, held that:

> The inescapable effect of the court's statement, under the circumstances in which the plea was taken, was to coerce defendant into pleading guilty, and we find therefore, that the plea was not a voluntary one. * * *

> In the instant case, the court did not "threaten" to impose a greater sentence—it virtually promised to do so, according to its stated "policy" in such cases. Accordingly, defendant's motion to withdraw his plea should have been granted.

245 A.D.2d at __, 666 N.Y.S.2d at 166. *See also People v. Flinn*, 60 A.D.3d 1304, 875 N.Y.S.2d 364 (4th Dep't 2009).

Similarly, a guilty plea will be vacated where the court incorrectly advises the defendant of the maximum sentence that he or she faces if found guilty after trial. *See People v. Min*, 249 A.D.2d 130, 671 N.Y.S.2d 480 (1st Dep't 1998); *People v. Hurd*, 220 A.D.2d 454, 631 N.Y.S.2d 871 (2d Dep't 1995).

By contrast, it is not coercive for a court to accurately inform the defendant of the possible sentences available. *See People v. Tien*, 228 A.D.2d 280, 643 N.Y.S.2d 345 (1st Dep't 1996); *People v. Crafton*, 159 A.D.2d 271, 552 N.Y.S.2d 273 (1st Dep't 1990).

§ 46:40 Consecutive sentences

Research References

West's Key Number Digest, Automobiles ☞359.4; Sentencing and Punishment ☞545, 631

Penal Law § 70.25(2) provides that:

> When more than one sentence of imprisonment is imposed on a person for two or more offenses committed through a single act or omission, or through an act or omission which in itself constituted one of the offenses and also was a material element of the other, the sentences . . . must run concurrently.

In *People v. Catone*, 65 N.Y.2d 1003, 494 N.Y.S.2d 97 (1985), the defendant drove into and killed a teenage girl as she was crossing the road. After briefly reducing his speed, the defendant sped off. The defendant was subsequently convicted of manslaughter in the second degree and felony leaving the scene of an accident, and sentenced to consecutive terms of imprisonment. On appeal, the Court of Appeals found that "[t]he relevant law and facts of this case demonstrate that the offense of manslaughter in the second degree was a material element of the offense of felony leaving the scene without reporting." 65 N.Y.2d at 1005, 494 N.Y.S.2d at 98. Accordingly, the Court modified the defendant's sentences to run concurrently.

However, the Court noted that "it appears anomalous that the crime of leaving the scene of an accident should be essentially unpunished under these circumstances," and invited the legislature to "reexamine" the language of VTL § 600. 65 N.Y.2d at 1005, 494 N.Y.S.2d at 98. In 1986, the legislature followed this suggestion and amended VTL § 600 to permit consecutive sentences for similar crimes in the future. *See, e.g., People v. Chambers*, 257 A.D.2d 418, 683 N.Y.S.2d 238 (1st Dep't 1999); *People v. Isaac*, 224 A.D.2d 993, ___, 637 N.Y.S.2d 827, 829 (4th Dep't 1996); *People v. Levy*, 157 Misc. 2d 941, 599 N.Y.S.2d 898 (Kings Co. Sup. Ct. 1993).

In People v. Backus, 56 A.D.3d 1119, 867 N.Y.S.2d 290, 291 (4th Dep't 2008), leave to appeal granted, 12 N.Y.3d 764, 876 N.Y.S.2d 715, 904 N.E.2d 852 (2009) and revd in part on other grounds, vacated in part, 14 N.Y.3d 876, 903 N.Y.S.2d 333, 929 N.E.2d 396

(2010), the Appellate Division, Fourth Department, held that "[a]s defendant correctly contends, the offense of driving while intoxicated is a material element of the offense of vehicular assault in the second degree and thus the sentence is illegal insofar as County Court imposed consecutive sentences."

In *People v. Clemens*, 177 A.D.2d 1053, —, 578 N.Y.S.2d 296, 296 (4th Dep't 1991), the Appellate Division, Fourth Department, held that "[t]he trial court erred in ordering that the sentence imposed on defendant's conviction for driving while intoxicated be served consecutively to the sentence of aggravated unlicensed operation of a motor vehicle in the first degree," (citation omitted), and modified defendant's sentences to run concurrently. *See also People v. Milo*, 235 A.D.2d 552, 654 N.Y.S.2d 146 (2d Dep't 1997) (same); *People v. Magistro*, 156 A.D.2d 1029, 550 N.Y.S.2d 875 (4th Dep't 1989) (same).

In *People v. Richburg*, 287 A.D.2d 790, —, 731 N.Y.S.2d 256, 258 (3d Dep't 2001), the Appellate Division, Third Department, stated that sentences imposed for felony DWI and AUO 1st could run consecutively without running afoul of PL § 70.25(2). Critically, however, in *People v. DeMaio*, 304 A.D.2d 988, —, 760 N.Y.S.2d 558, 559 (3d Dep't 2003), the Court clarified its position in *Richburg*:

Although there are numerous factual circumstances that can comprise both the crimes of first degree aggravated unlicensed operation (*see* Vehicle and Traffic Law § 511[3][a][i], [ii]) and felony driving while intoxicated (*see* Vehicle and Traffic Law § 1193[1][c][i], [ii]), *it is apparent that driving while intoxicated can constitute a material element of first degree aggravated unlicensed operation.* It was thus incumbent upon the People to show either that defendant's felony driving while intoxicated was not, in fact, a material element of his first degree aggravated unlicensed operation (*see e.g.* Vehicle and Traffic Law § 511[3][a][ii] [authorizing such charge based upon nonalcohol-related elements]) or that the two offenses were based upon separate and distinct acts. Here, the indictment alleges defendant's driving while under the influence as an element of the charge of first degree aggravated unlicensed operation. Both the offenses to which defendant eventually pleaded guilty are alleged in the indictment to have occurred on the same date, place and time. The plea allocution confirms such facts and, indeed, further reveals that the same prior offenses provided the basis for both the previous revocation of defendant's license and the elevation of the driving while intoxicated to felony status. It is thus clear that defendant's felony driving while intoxicated charge was a material element of his first degree aggravated unlicensed operation and the People failed to show that the two offenses arose from separate and distinct acts.

The People's reliance upon *People v. Richburg*, with no concomitant case-specific factual analysis, is misplaced. *Richburg should not be*

> construed as holding that felony driving while intoxicated and first
> degree aggravated unlicensed operation cannot fall within the
> parameters of Penal Law § 70.25(2). To the contrary, since felony
> driving while intoxicated can constitute a material element of first
> degree aggravated unlicensed operation, the People bear the burden
> when advocating consecutive sentences of showing identifiable sepa-
> rate acts sustaining such sentences. The People failed to make such
> a showing in this case and, therefore, the sentences must be modi-
> fied to run concurrently.

(Emphases added) (citation and footnote omitted). *See also People
v. Khan*, 291 A.D.2d 898, 737 N.Y.S.2d 738 (4th Dep't 2002) (PL
§ 70.25(2) requires concurrent sentences where defendant
convicted of AUO 1st and DWAI); *People v. Fleenor*, 162 A.D.2d
832, 557 N.Y.S.2d 735 (3d Dep't 1990) (concurrent sentences
required where defendant convicted of criminally negligent homicide and DWAI); *People v. Coleman*, 138 A.D.2d 963, 526 N.Y.S.2d
296 (4th Dep't 1988) (concurrent sentences required where
defendant convicted of criminally negligent homicide and DWI).

Shortly after *DeMaio* was decided, the Third Department upheld consecutive sentences in a felony DWAI drugs/AUO 1st case
*where the defendant's only challenge to such sentence was that it
was harsh and excessive. See People v. Clark*, 309 A.D.2d 1076,
766 N.Y.S.2d 710 (3d Dep't 2003). Thus, it is absolutely critical
that defense counsel in a felony DWI/AUO 1st case expressly
object to consecutive sentences on the specific ground that such
sentences violate PL § 70.25(2).

In this regard, where the issue was preserved, the Third
Department invalidated consecutive sentences imposed upon the
defendant for a VOP involving charges of misdemeanor DWI and
AUO 2nd. *See People v. Borush*, 39 A.D.3d 890, 834 N.Y.S.2d 340
(3d Dep't 2007). In so holding, the Court stated that "[b]ecause
the act of driving a motor vehicle while intoxicated and while
suspended was a single act, concurrent sentences should have
been imposed." 39 A.D.3d at __, 834 N.Y.S.2d 341. *Cf. People v.
Skarczewski*, 287 N.Y. 826 (1942) (per curiam).

In *People v. Goldstein*, 12 N.Y.3d 295, 300, 879 N.Y.S.2d 814,
817, 907 N.E.2d 692 (2009), the Court of Appeals stated that "it
is clear . . . that the conduct underlying the count alleging aggravated unlicensed operation of a motor vehicle was distinct
from that involved in the ensuing reckless endangerment offenses and thus permitted a consecutive sentence."

In *People v. Crane*, 129 A.D.3d 741, __, 8 N.Y.S.3d 924, __ (2d
Dep't 2015), the Appellate Division, Second Department, held
that:

> Contrary to the defendant's contention, the imposition of a consecu-
> tive term of imprisonment for his conviction of unauthorized use of

a vehicle in the first degree (Penal Law § 165.08) was not illegal. Although the defendant's conviction of unauthorized use of a vehicle in the first degree, and his convictions of aggravated [DWI] and two counts of [DWI] arose out of a single, extended transaction, the plea colloquy establishes that the convictions of the unauthorized use of a vehicle offense and the above-mentioned driving while intoxicated offenses arose out of separate acts.

(Citations omitted).

§ 46:41   Where fine not part of plea bargain, it may not be imposed without offer to withdraw plea

Research References
West's Key Number Digest, Automobiles ⚖359.4

In *People v. Youngs*, 156 A.D.2d 885, 550 N.Y.S.2d 106 (3d Dep't 1989), the defendant was charged with two counts of felony DWI. At the time, VTL § 1192(5) provided for a mandatory fine. Pursuant to a plea agreement, defendant was to be sentenced to one to three years' imprisonment with no fines. However, the sentencing court imposed the prison sentence, together with the then-mandatory fine.

On appeal, the Appellate Division, Third Department, held (a) that the defendant was entitled to specific performance of his plea bargain, and (b) that the county court should have informed the defendant that the plea bargain could not be kept, and afforded the defendant an opportunity to withdraw his plea. 156 A.D.2d at __, 550 N.Y.S.2d at 107. *See also People v. Rockwell*, 137 A.D.3d 1586, __, 27 N.Y.S.3d 754, 756 (4th Dep't 2016); *People v. Legette*, 131 A.D.3d 546, __, 14 N.Y.S.3d 697, 698 (2d Dep't 2015); *People v. Barber*, 31 A.D.3d 1145, __, 818 N.Y.S.2d 391, 392 (4th Dep't 2006); *People v. Cote*, 265 A.D.2d 681, 697 N.Y.S.2d 184 (3d Dep't 1999) (fine imposed at sentencing vacated where it was not part of plea bargain or plea allocution); *People v. Fulton*, 238 A.D.2d 439, 657 N.Y.S.2d 348 (2d Dep't 1997).

The same rule applies to restitution. *See, e.g., People v. Sirico*, 135 A.D.3d 19, __, 18 N.Y.S.3d 430, 436-37 (2d Dep't 2015), leave to appeal denied, 27 N.Y.3d 1075, 2016 WL 3402992 (2016); *Legette, supra*.

§ 46:42   Court must advise defendant of direct consequences of plea

Research References
West's Key Number Digest, Automobiles ⚖359.4

Prior to accepting a guilty plea from a defendant, the Court is required to advise the defendant of "direct" consequences of the plea—but is *not* required to advise the defendant of "collateral" consequences thereof. *See, e.g., People v. Harnett*, 16 N.Y.3d 200, 205, 920 N.Y.S.2d 246, 248, 945 N.E.2d 439 (2011); *People v. Gravino*, 14 N.Y.3d 546, 553, 902 N.Y.S.2d 851, 855, 928 N.E.2d 1048 (2010); *People v. Catu*, 4 N.Y.3d 242, 244, 792 N.Y.S.2d 887, 888, 825 N.E.2d 1081 (2005); *People v. Ford*, 86 N.Y.2d 397, 403, 633 N.Y.S.2d 270, 272, 657 N.E.2d 265 (1995).

In this regard, a fine is a direct consequence that the defendant must be advised of prior to the entry of a plea. If the defendant is not so advised, then an appellate court will "remit the matter to [the trial court] to impose a sentence that does not include a fine . . . or, in the alternative, afford [the defendant] an opportunity to withdraw his guilty plea." *People v. Stewart*, 92 A.D.3d 1146, __, 940 N.Y.S.2d 178, 180 (3d Dep't 2012). *See also People v. Jones*, 118 A.D.3d 1360, 988 N.Y.S.2d 316 (4th Dep't 2014); *People v. Lafferty*, 60 A.D.3d 1318, 875 N.Y.S.2d 395 (4th Dep't 2009); *People v. McCarthy*, 56 A.D.3d 904, 867 N.Y.S.2d 281 (3d Dep't 2008); *People v. Barber*, 31 A.D.3d 1145, 818 N.Y.S.2d 391 (4th Dep't 2006).

In *Harnett*, the Court of Appeals summarized the law in this area:

> Our cases have drawn a line between the direct and collateral consequences of a plea. The importance of the distinction is that a trial court "*must* advise a defendant of the direct consequences." A court's failure to comply with that obligation "requires reversal" because harmless error analysis is inapposite. * * *
>
> Direct consequences, as we explained in *Ford*, are those that have "a definite, immediate and largely automatic effect on defendant's punishment." Consequences that are "peculiar to the individual's personal circumstances and . . . not within the control of the court system" have been held to be collateral. The direct consequences of a plea—those whose omission from a plea colloquy makes the plea per se invalid—are essentially the core components of a defendant's sentence: a term of probation or imprisonment, a term of post-release supervision, a fine. Our cases have identified no others.

16 N.Y.3d at 205, 920 N.Y.S.2d at 248-49 (citations omitted).

In this regard, the *Harnett* Court held that "failing to warn a defendant who pleads guilty to a sex offense that he may be subject to the Sex Offender Management and Treatment Act (SOMTA)" is a collateral consequence of the plea. 16 N.Y.3d at __, __ N.Y.S.2d at __. *See also People v. Gravino*, 14 N.Y.3d 546, 550, 902 N.Y.S.2d 851, 852, 928 N.E.2d 1048 (2010) ("We hold that because they are collateral rather than direct consequences of a guilty plea, Sex Offender Registration Act (SORA) registration and the terms and conditions of probation are not subjects that a trial court must address at the plea hearing. Put another way, a trial court's neglect to mention SORA or identify potential stipulations of probation during the plea colloquy does not undermine the knowing, voluntary and intelligent nature of a defendant's guilty plea").

In *People v. Catu*, 4 N.Y.3d 242, 244, 792 N.Y.S.2d 887, 887, 825 N.E.2d 1081 (2005), the defendant accepted a plea bargain pursuant to which he would be sentenced to a three-year determinate prison sentence and a $1,000 fine. The Court of Appeals vacated the plea on the ground that the Court failed to advise the defendant that, as a second felony offender, his sentence would include a mandatory period of five years' post-release supervision. 4 N.Y.3d at 244, 792 N.Y.S.2d at 887.

In *People v. Ford*, 86 N.Y.2d 397, 401, 633 N.Y.S.2d 270, 271-72, 657 N.E.2d 265 (1995), the Court of Appeals held that neither Trial Judges nor defense counsel are required to advise a defendant of the possible deportation consequences of his or her plea. Critically, while the *Ford* Court held that defense counsel's failure to advise the defendant of such consequences did not constitute ineffective assistance, 86 N.Y.2d at 404-05, 633 N.Y.S.2d at 273-74, the U.S. Supreme Court reached the opposite conclusion in *Padilla v. Kentucky*, __ U.S. __, __, 130 S. Ct. 1473, 1486, 176 L. Ed. 2d 284 (2010):

> It is our responsibility under the Constitution to ensure that no criminal defendant—whether a citizen or not—is left to the "mercies of incompetent counsel." To satisfy this responsibility, we now hold that counsel must inform her client whether his plea carries a risk of deportation. Our longstanding Sixth Amendment precedents, the seriousness of deportation as a consequence of a criminal plea, and the concomitant impact of deportation on families living lawfully in this country demand no less.

(Citation omitted).

Another aspect of *Ford* has been called into question. Specifically, the *Ford* Court commented in *dicta* that:

> Illustrations of collateral consequences are loss of the right to vote or travel abroad, loss of civil service employment, *loss of a driver's license*, loss of the right to possess firearms or an undesirable discharge from the Armed Services. The failure to warn of such collateral consequences will not warrant vacating a plea because they are peculiar to the individual and generally result from the actions taken by agencies the court does not control.

86 N.Y.2d at 403, 633 N.Y.S.2d at 272-73 (emphasis added) (citations omitted).

In support of its claim that the loss of a driver's license is a collateral consequence, the *Ford* Court cited *Moore v. Hinton*, 513 F.2d 781 (5th Cir. 1975), a federal class action lawsuit challenging the manner in which DWI cases were being handled in Tuscaloosa, Alabama. Critically, however, the *Moore* Court pointed out that:

> *Of crucial importance here . . . is the fact that the Alabama Depart-ment of Public Safety, not the court, deprives the defendant of his license,* acting under authority of 36 Ala.Code § 68. The court merely accepts the defendant's plea, and sentences him to a fine and/or imprisonment. The Department of Public Safety then institutes a separate proceeding for suspension of his license; this suspension is not, therefore, punishment imposed by the court as a result of the guilty plea, but a collateral consequence of the defendant's conviction.

513 F.2d at 782 (emphasis added).

In stark contrast to the situation addressed in *Moore*, a defi-nite, immediate and mandatory component of every DWI-related sentence in New York is that *the Court* suspend or revoke the defendant's driver's license. *See* VTL § 1193(2)(d)(1). In this regard, in *People v. Castellini*, 24 Misc. 3d 66, __, 884 N.Y.S.2d 550, 551 (App. Term, 1st Dep't 2009), the Appellate Term vacated the defendant's guilty plea to DWAI where the trial court misin-formed the defendant with regard to the length of the mandatory driver's license revocation she would receive, reasoning as follows:

> In order for a guilty plea to be entered knowingly, intelligently and voluntarily, a defendant must be advised of the direct consequences of the plea. Although there is no mandatory catechism, a minimum requirement for a valid plea is that the defendant understands the direct penal consequences. Here, the plea minutes show that the court misinformed defendant of the nature and duration of the requisite driver's license sanction, erroneously stating that the sentence would include a 90-day license suspension, when in fact the mandatory sanction was a one-year license revocation. While in some jurisdictions the loss of a driver's license "result[s] from the actions taken by agencies the court does not control," and thus is considered a collateral consequence (*People v. Ford*, 86 N.Y.S.2d at 403, 633 N.Y.S.2d 270, 657 N.E.2d 265, citing *Moore v. Hinton*, 513 F.2d 781 [5th Cir.1975]), the license sanction here involved consti-tuted punishment directly imposed by the court as a result of defendant's guilty plea (*see* Vehicle and Traffic Law § 1193[2][a], [b]), and was thus a direct consequence of the plea. The court's er-ror is not subject to harmless error analysis, and renders the plea invalid.

(Citations omitted). *Cf. People v. Trathen*, 121 A.D.3d 1594, 993 N.Y.S.2d 426 (4th Dep't 2014).

In *People v. Lancaster*, 260 A.D.2d 660, __, 688 N.Y.S.2d 711, 712 (3d Dep't 1999), the Appellate Division, Third Department, held that a Court sentencing a defendant for DWI is not required to advise him or her "that a subsequent conviction of the crime of driving while intoxicated would constitute a felony[, as] [i]t is abundantly clear that the fact that a defendant is subject to enhanced criminal treatment for an offense that he or she may commit in the future is a collateral consequence of the plea, about which a defendant need not be advised." In this regard, "[a] second D.W.I. conviction leading to felony sanctions can be avoided simply by not drinking and driving." *People v. Butler*, 96 A.D.2d 140, __, 468 N.Y.S.2d 274, 277 (4th Dep't 1983).

In *People v. Smith*, 136 A.D.3d 1107, __, 25 N.Y.S.3d 395, 396 (3d Dep't 2016), leave to appeal denied, 27 N.Y.3d 1075, 2016 WL 3403005 (2016), the Appellate Division, Third Department, held that the length of time that the defendant would be required to remain in "alcohol or substance abuse treatment" as part of a judicial diversion program was a collateral consequence of the defendant's plea.

§ 46:43   Prosecutor must honor promise with respect to sentencing recommendation made during plea negotiations

Research References

West's Key Number Digest, Automobiles ⊶359.4

In *People v. Oakes*, 252 A.D.2d 663, 675 N.Y.S.2d 407 (3d Dep't 1998), the defendant pled guilty to felony DWI. As part of the plea, the district attorney agreed to recommend that the county court follow the sentencing recommendation of the presentence investigation report. Nonetheless, at the defendant's sentencing the district attorney made a recommendation of a state prison sentence, and the county court imposed the maximum sentence allowable by law.

On appeal, the Appellate Division, Third Department, vacated the sentence and remitted the matter for resentencing before a different judge. In so holding, the Court reasoned that the district attorney's comments at the defendant's sentencing "violate the clear mandate of the *U.S. Supreme Court in Santobello v. New York (404 U.S. 257*, 92 S.Ct. 495, 30 L.Ed.2d 427), that a prosecutor must honor a promise with respect to a sentencing recommendation made during plea negotiations. 'Such a promise is breached not only by the recommendation of a specific sentence but also by the implicit conveyance of the People's position as to the appropriate punishment.'" 252 A.D.2d at __, 675 N.Y.S.2d at 408–09 (citation omitted). Notably, the Court commented that this was the third time that it had confronted this precise issue involving the same court and district attorney. 252 A.D.2d at __, 675 N.Y.S.2d at 408.

§ 46:44 Appellate Division limits trial court's ability to enhance negotiated sentence based on defendant's conduct between plea and sentencing

Research References

West's Key Number Digest, Automobiles ☞359.4

In *People v. Parker*, 271 A.D.2d 63, 711 N.Y.S.2d 656 (4th Dep't 2000) (per curiam):

> Defendants appeal from judgments of conviction entered upon their negotiated guilty pleas. The plea agreement in each case included a sentencing promise from County Court, conditioned upon the defendant's cooperating with the Probation Department in the preparation of a presentence investigation report and being truthful with the court and the Probation Department. On appeal, defendants challenge the enhancement of their sentences based upon their violation of one or more of those conditions. We conclude in all four cases that the violation of those conditions does not warrant the additional punishment imposed by the court.

271 A.D.2d at __, 711 N.Y.S.2d at 658.

In so holding, the Court reasoned as follows:

> Our analysis is guided by an understanding that plea bargaining plays a vital role in the criminal justice system, and that "an integral part of the plea bargaining process is the negotiated sentence." To say that plea bargaining relieves court congestion and conserves prosecutorial, judicial and penal resources is to understate its significance. Plea bargaining does not merely aid in the administration of criminal justice; it "literally staves off collapse of the law enforcement system." * * *

> Sentencing conditions that are typically imposed and that have been consistently upheld include requirements that the defendant appear for sentencing, complete a drug rehabilitation program and avoid being arrested between the plea and sentencing. Courts have also approved the condition requiring the defendant to meet and cooperate with the Probation Department to enable the preparation of a presentence investigation report. In addition, the Legislature has authorized the imposition of several conditions of probation as presentence conditions (*see*, CPL 400.10[4]).

> The conditions that have been expressly approved by the courts and the Legislature offer a sharp contrast to the conditions imposed upon defendants in these four appeals. A defendant's compliance with conditions requiring no arrests between the plea and sentencing, timely appearance for sentencing, completion of a drug rehabilitation program or attendance at a scheduled Probation Department interview can be objectively determined on the basis of verifiable conduct by the defendant. * * *

The conditions imposed in the four cases before us do not satisfy the requirements of due process because they permit the court to depart from a negotiated sentence based upon its subjective interpretation of a defendant's conduct rather than verifiable factual information. Reasonable minds could reach different conclusions regarding each defendant's compliance with the sentencing conditions imposed by the court. * * *

We conclude, therefore, that the court improperly enhanced defendants' sentences. We further conclude that enforcement of the plea agreement and imposition of the negotiated sentence is the appropriate remedy in each case. * * *

We emphasize that our decision is compelled by the need to safeguard the integrity of the plea bargaining process. Plea bargains are attractive to defendants because of the "reasonable assurance of certainty" provided by the negotiated sentence. "[T]o the extent that the assurance of certainty is diluted the bargaining process becomes less acceptable to defendants, to the detriment of the criminal justice system as a whole." In our view, the sentencing conditions imposed in these four cases dilute the assurance of certainty and transform the plea bargaining process into precisely the type of gamble that a pleading defendant seeks to avoid. We disapprove of the enhancement of these sentences, therefore, not merely to protect the expectations of these defendants but to maintain confidence in the plea bargaining process itself.

271 A.D.2d at __-__, 711 N.Y.S.2d at 660–63 (emphasis added) (citations omitted). *See also People v. Rushlow*, 137 A.D.3d 1482, 28 N.Y.S.3d 476 (3d Dep't 2016); *People v. Denegar*, 130 A.D.3d 1140, 14 N.Y.S.3d 527 (3d Dep't 2015); *People v. Covell*, 276 A.D.2d 824, 714 N.Y.S.2d 370 (3d Dep't 2000). *Cf. People v. Hicks*, 98 N.Y.2d 185, 746 N.Y.S.2d 441 (2002).

The *Parker* Court also "reject[ed] the People's contention that the challenges of defendants to the enhancement of their negotiated sentences are encompassed by their waivers of the right to appeal." 271 A.D.2d at __, 711 N.Y.S.2d at 660.

§ 46:45 Indigent defendants—Inability to pay fine

Research References

West's Key Number Digest, Automobiles ☞359.4

In *Bearden v. Georgia*, 461 U.S. 660, 103 S.Ct. 2064 (1983), the Supreme Court held that:

[I]n revocation proceedings for failure to pay a fine or restitution, *a sentencing court must inquire into the reasons for the failure to pay.* If the probationer willfully refused to pay or failed to make sufficient bona fide efforts legally to acquire the resources to pay, the court may revoke probation and sentence the defendant to imprisonment within the authorized range of its sentencing authority. If the probationer could not pay despite sufficient bona fide efforts to acquire the resources to do so, the court must consider alternative measures of punishment other than imprisonment. *Only if alternative measures are not adequate to meet the State's interests in punishment and deterrence may the court imprison a probationer who has made sufficient bona fide efforts to pay*. To do otherwise would deprive the probationer of his conditional freedom simply because, through no fault of his own, he cannot pay the fine. Such a deprivation would be contrary to the fundamental fairness required by the Fourteenth Amendment.

461 U.S. at 672–73, 103 S.Ct. at 2072–73 (emphases added).

A defendant who cannot afford to pay a court-imposed fine can apply to the court for resentencing. *See* CPL § 420.10(5). CPL § 420.10(5) was formerly designated CPL § 420.10(4). For an excellent discussion of the application of this statute, see *People v. Goddard*, 108 Misc. 2d 742, 439 N.Y.S.2d 71 (N.Y. City Crim. Ct. 1981).

In *People v. Montero*, 124 Misc. 2d 1020, __, 480 N.Y.S.2d 70, 72 (App. Term, 2d Dep't 1984), the Court held that "inasmuch as subdivision 4 of CPL 420.10 permits the court to consider all available sentencing alternatives and does not mandate imprisonment, the section, as construed within the limits set by *Bearden*, cannot be deemed unconstitutional." On the other hand, in *People v. Ingham*, 115 Misc. 2d 64, 453 N.Y.S.2d 325 (Rochester City Ct. 1982), the Court held the mandatory fine excessive and thus unconstitutional as applied to an indigent defendant convicted of DWI in violation of VTL § 1192(3).

A defendant cannot be subjected to a term of incarceration that exceeds the statutory maximum based upon an inability to pay the fine. *See Williams v. Illinois*, 399 U.S. 235, 90 S.Ct. 2018 (1970). *See also People v. Laurino*, 205 A.D.2d 556, __, 613 N.Y.S.2d 206, 207 (2d Dep't 1994); *People v. Levine*, 167 A.D.2d 484, __, 562 N.Y.S.2d 155, 156 (2d Dep't 1990); *People v. Baker*, 130 A.D.2d 582, __, 515 N.Y.S.2d 297, 298 (2d Dep't 1987). *Cf. People v. Alleyne*, 214 A.D.2d 575, __, 625 N.Y.S.2d 77, 78 (2d Dep't 1995). Similarly, a defendant cannot be incarcerated under a "fine only" statute based solely upon an inability to immediately pay the fine in full. *See Tate v. Short*, 401 U.S. 395, 91 S.Ct. 668 (1971).

Unless the issue of a defendant's indigency is raised in the trial court, an appellate court may find that the issue is unpreserved for appellate review. *See, e.g., Baker*, 130 A.D.2d at __, 515 N.Y.S.2d at 298–99; *People v. Aloma*, 92 A.D.2d 572, __, 459 N.Y.S.2d 327, 328–29 (2d Dep't 1983); *People v. Head*, 145 Misc. 2d 984, __, 554 N.Y.S.2d 751, 752 (App. Term, 9th & 10th Jud. Dist. 1990).

In *People v. Pagan*, 176 A.D.2d 472, ___, 574 N.Y.S.2d 518, 518 (1st Dep't 1991), the Appellate Division, First Department, held that "[t]he defendant's application for waiver of the mandatory surcharge due to indigency is premature. If, at the conclusion of his imprisonment, the defendant is unable to pay the surcharge, he may at that time move for a waiver thereof." (Citation omitted). *See also* CPL §§ 420.10(5)(d), 420.35, 420.40; VTL § 1809(5).

By contrast, where "a probationer has willfully refused to pay restitution when he or she can pay, the State is justified in revoking probation and using imprisonment as an appropriate penalty for the offense." *People v. Amorosi*, 96 N.Y.2d 180, 184, 726 N.Y.S.2d 339, 342, 750 N.E.2d 41 (2001).

§ 46:46   Defendant entitled to copy of presentence investigation report

Research References

West's Key Number Digest, Automobiles ⚷359.4

In light of the confidential nature of the material contained in a presentence investigation report (PSIR), many courts will deny the defendant or defense counsel access to a copy of the PSIR. However, CPL § 390.50(2)(a) expressly states that:

Not less than one court day prior to sentencing, unless such time requirement is waived by the parties, the presentence report or memorandum shall be made available by the court for examination and for copying by the defendant's attorney, the defendant himself, if he has no attorney, and the prosecutor.

Although the court may, in its discretion, preclude the disclosure of a part or parts of the PSIR, the court must place on the record that part(s) have been precluded and why. *See* CPL § 390.50(2)(a).

§ 46:47   Service of order commences time period to take appeal

Research References

West's Key Number Digest, Automobiles ⚷359.4

In *People v. Washington*, 86 N.Y.2d 853, 854, 633 N.Y.S.2d 476, 477 (1995), the Court of Appeals held that "service by the prevailing party is necessary under CPL 460.10 in order to commence the time period for the other party to take an appeal."

§ 46:48   DWI "conviction" complete upon plea or verdict of guilty

Research References

West's Key Number Digest, Automobiles ⚷359.4

A prior VTL § 1192 conviction can, depending upon its timing, be used to enhance the level of a new VTL § 1192 charge (*e.g.*, raise the level of a DWI charge from a misdemeanor to a felony), and/or increase the fine and license revocation imposed. As such, the precise date of a prior conviction can be critical. In this regard, CPL § 1.20(13) defines the term "conviction" as:

> [T]he entry of a plea of guilty to, or a verdict of guilty upon, an accusatory instrument other than a felony complaint, or to one or more counts of such instrument.

See also Boykin v. Alabama, 395 U.S. 238, 242, 89 S. Ct. 1709, 1711, 23 L. Ed. 2d 274 (1969) ("A plea of guilty is more than a confession which admits that the accused did various acts; it is itself a conviction"); *id.* at 242, 89 S.Ct. at 1712 ("as we have said, a plea of guilty is more than an admission of conduct; it is a conviction"); *People v. Montilla*, 10 N.Y.3d 663, 668, 862 N.Y.S.2d 11, 14, 891 N.E.2d 1175 (2008) (CPL § 1.20(13) definition of "conviction" applies to Penal Law offenses); *People v. Cunningham*, 182 Misc. 2d 790, 702 N.Y.S.2d 523 (Dutchess Co. Ct. 1999). *See generally Jones v. Kelly*, 9 A.D.2d 395, 194 N.Y.S.2d 585 (4th Dep't 1959) (for purposes of statute requiring revocation of driver's license for 3 speeding and/or misdemeanor convictions within 18 months, "conviction" complete upon plea of guilty).

In *Cunningham*, the defendant was convicted after a bench trial of misdemeanor DWI. He appealed the conviction and obtained a stay of the "judgment of conviction" pending appeal. *See* CPL § 460.50(1). While the appeal was pending, the defendant received another DWI, which the prosecution charged as a felony (using the "stayed" misdemeanor conviction as the predicate). In finding the enhanced charge proper, the Court held that "[a] 'conviction' is complete upon an adjudication of guilt or the entry of a plea of guilty, and cannot be stayed or suspended by operation of CPL 460.50(1)." 182 Misc. 2d at __, 702 N.Y.S.2d at 525 (citations omitted).

Interestingly, the DWI conviction used as the predicate in *Cunningham* was subsequently reversed on appeal! *See People v. Cunningham*, 95 N.Y.2d 909, 717 N.Y.S.2d 68 (2000).

§ 46:49 Mandatory jail or community service in certain cases

Research References
West's Key Number Digest, Automobiles ⊶359.4

Effective September 30, 2003, VTL § 1193(1-a) provides for the following additional DWI penalties:
    (a) Except as provided for in [VTL § 1193(1-a)(b)], a person

who operates a vehicle in violation of [VTL § 1192(2) or (3)] after having been convicted of a violation of [VTL § 1192(2) or (3)] within the preceding [5] years shall, in addition to any other penalties which may be imposed pursuant to [VTL § 1193(1)], be sentenced to a term of imprisonment of [5] days or, as an alternative to such imprisonment, be required to perform [30] days of service for a public or not-for-profit corporation, association, institution or agency as set forth in [PL § 65.10(2)(h)] as a condition of sentencing for such violation. Notwithstanding the provisions of this paragraph, a sentence of a term of imprisonment of [5] days or more pursuant to the provisions of [VTL § 1193(1)] shall be deemed to be in compliance with this subdivision.

(b) A person who operates a vehicle in violation of [VTL § 1192(2) or (3)] after having been convicted on [2] or more occasions of a violation of any of such subdivisions within the preceding [5] years shall, in addition to any other penalties which may be imposed pursuant to [VTL § 1193(1)], be sentenced to a term of imprisonment of [10] days or, as an alternative to such imprisonment, be required to perform [60] days of service for a public or not-for-profit corporation, association, institution or agency as set forth in [PL § 65.10(2)(h)] as a condition of sentencing for such violation. Notwithstanding the provisions of this paragraph, a sentence of a term of imprisonment of [10] days or more pursuant to the provisions of [VTL § 1193(1)] shall be deemed to be in compliance with this subdivision.

VTL § 1193(1-a)(a), (b). *See also* §§ 46:7, 46:15, & 46:16, *supra*.

§ 46:50   Driver responsibility assessment

Research References

West's Key Number Digest, Automobiles ⬸359.4

Effective November 18, 2004, any person who either (a) is convicted of a violation of any subdivision of VTL § 1192, or (b) is found to have refused to submit to a chemical test in accordance with VTL § 1194, is liable to the DMV for payment of a "driver responsibility assessment." VTL § 1199(1). Such driver responsibility assessment applies "[i]n addition to any fines, fees, penalties and surcharges authorized by law." VTL § 1199(1).

The amount of the driver responsibility assessment is $250 a year for three years. VTL § 1199(2). In the event that the person is both convicted of a violation of VTL § 1192 *and* found to have refused a chemical test in accordance with VTL § 1194 in connection with the same incident, only one driver responsibility assessment will be imposed. VTL § 1199(1).

When the DMV receives evidence of the qualifying conviction/
refusal, it will notify the person, by first-class mail, at the person's
address on file with the DMV (or at his or her current address
provided by the U.S. Postal Service), of:
    1. The amount of the driver responsibility assessment;
    2. The time and manner of making required payments; and
    3. That the failure to make such payments will result in the
suspension of his or her driver's license (or privilege of obtaining a driver's license).
VTL § 1199(3).

If the person fails to pay the driver responsibility assessment,
the DMV will suspend his or her driver's license (or privilege of
obtaining a driver's license). VTL § 1199(4). "Such suspension
shall remain in effect until any and all outstanding driver
responsibility assessments have been paid in full." VTL § 1199(4).

The provisions of VTL § 1199 regarding driver responsibility
assessments are also applicable to (a) any person convicted of a
violation of Navigation Law § 49-a, (b) any person convicted of a
violation of PRHPL § 25.24, or (c) any person found to have
refused to submit to a chemical test in accordance with the applicable provisions of either the Navigation Law or the PRHPL
(not arising out of the same incident). VTL § 1199(5).

§ 46:51   Jurisdiction over CPL Article 440 motion

Where a defendant is sentenced to probation, and such probation is transferred to the County in which the defendant resides,
which Court has jurisdiction over a subsequently filed CPL
Article 440 motion to vacate? In this regard, the language of CPL
§ 410.80(2) conflicts with that of CPL §§ 440.10 and 440.20. *See
People v. Mitchell*, 15 N.Y.3d 93, 97–98, 905 N.Y.S.2d 115, 117,
931 N.E.2d 84, __ (2010). In resolving the conflict, the *Mitchell*
Court held that:

> In sum, the amendments to section 410.80(2) were meant to transfer
> from sentencing courts to receiving courts the full range of powers
> and duties necessary for the judiciary to carry out its responsibili-
> ties to enforce the terms and conditions of probationers, and to deal
> with relief from forfeitures and disabilities. There is no suggestion
> in the statute's text or legislative history that the Legislature
> intended, in addition, to divest sentencing courts of their jurisdic-
> tion under article 440 of the Criminal Procedure Law.

15 N.Y.3d at 98-99, 905 N.Y.S.2d at 118.

In other words, jurisdiction to entertain the CPL Article 440
motion rests with the sentencing Court.

§ 46:52   Plea bargain reducing DWI to reckless driving is not improper

In *People v. Crandall*, 39 A.D.3d 1077, 832 N.Y.S.2d 828 (3d Dep't 2007), the defendant was able to negotiate a plea bargain reducing the DWI charges against him to Reckless Driving. He nonetheless appealed, claiming that "his guilty plea was improper because reckless driving is not a lesser included offense of driving while intoxicated." 39 A.D.3d at _, 832 N.Y.S.2d at 828. In rejecting this claim, the Appellate Division, Third Department, held that:

> While defendant is correct in his assertion that the plea entered here does not constitute a lesser included offense as defined by CPL 1.20(37), such error is not jurisdictional in nature. Indeed, conviction of a different offense by plea will only be set aside on jurisdictional grounds if, insofar as is relevant to the instant appeal, "the offense of conviction is not transactionally related to the offense specified in the accusatory instrument." Such clearly is not the case here. Moreover, Vehicle and Traffic Law 1192(10)(a) specifically provides for a plea other than to Vehicle and Traffic Law § 1192(2), (3), (4) or (4-a) where, as here, the prosecutor has determined that the charges laid are not warranted and the basis for the proposed disposition has been set forth on the record.

(Citations omitted).

§ 46:53   "Split" sentences

"Authorized by Penal Law § 60.01(2)(d), a 'split sentence' is one consisting of a term of imprisonment, intermittent or definite, combined with a term of probation or conditional discharge." *Pirro v. Angiolillo*, 89 N.Y.2d 351, 353, 653 N.Y.S.2d 237, 238, 675 N.E.2d 1189 (1996). In this regard, PL § 60.01(2)(d) provides that:

> In any case where the court imposes a sentence of imprisonment not in excess of [60] days, for a misdemeanor or not in excess of [6] months for a felony or in the case of a sentence of intermittent imprisonment not in excess of [4] months, it may also impose a sentence of probation or conditional discharge provided that the term of probation or conditional discharge together with the term of imprisonment shall not exceed the term of probation or conditional discharge authorized by [PL Article 65]. The sentence of imprisonment shall be a condition of and run concurrently with the sentence of probation or conditional discharge.

In *Angiolillo*, the Court of Appeals addressed the issue of "whether a definite sentence that was imposed in conjunction with a term of probation is a condition of or is subsumed within the probationary part of the sentence so that it can be modified, reduced or even eliminated pursuant to the discretionary authority conferred by CPL 410.20," 89 N.Y.2d at 353, 653 N.Y.S.2d at 238, and held that "[h]aving reviewed the statutory language and relevant legislative history, we conclude that the imprisonment part of a split sentence is a penalty that exists separate and apart from the probationary term and that, accordingly, it may not be altered once its service has begun." 89 N.Y.2d at 353, 653 N.Y.S.2d at 238.

As a result of *Angiolillo, People v. Cohen*, 222 A.D.2d 447, 635 N.Y.S.2d 38 (2d Dep't 1995), should no longer be followed.

In *People v. Cerilli*, 80 N.Y.2d 1016, 592 N.Y.S.2d 660, 607 N.E.2d 807 (1992), the Court of Appeals addressed the issue of whether, in a multi-accusatory instrument case, a sentencing court can bypass the requirements of PL § 60.01(2)(d) by, for example, sentencing the defendant to a year in jail on one accusatory instrument and five years' probation on another accusatory instrument in the same case. The Court of Appeals held that such a sentence is impermissible, reasoning as follows:

> That there is no single-accusatory-instrument requirement is confirmed by the legislative history:
>
>> "The proposed subdivision does not permit use of the sentence of probation where the court imposes a sentence of imprisonment for some other crime * * * The use of the sentence would be improper in [this] situation because its basic purpose is to provide a method of supervising offenders without removing them from the community * * * If the court decides to withhold additional imprisonment * * * it can impose a concurrent sentence, or, where authorized, conditional or absolute discharge."
>
> As the Commission indicated, probation is inappropriate for defendants being imprisoned because the "basic purpose" of probation is to provide supervision without removing offenders from the community. This rationale applies with equal force whether defendant is sentenced for related crimes contained in a single accusatory instrument or unrelated crimes charged in separate instruments. So long as defendant is imprisoned for "some other crime" the Legislature did not authorize probation as a sentencing option.

80 N.Y.2d at 1018, 592 N.Y.S.2d 661-62 (citation and footnote omitted). *See also People v. Latzen*, 165 A.D.2d 913, __, 560 N.Y.S.2d 365, 365 (3d Dep't 1990) ("Defendant may not receive at the same sentencing a term of five years' probation on one conviction and more than six months of incarceration on another conviction.").

Where a defendant is sentenced to incarceration in excess of the limits set forth in PL § 60.01(2)(d), the Appellate Division has found the probationary portion of the sentence to be illegal (precluding punishment for an alleged violation of such probation). *See, e.g., People v. Gauthier*, 73 A.D.3d 1229, __, 899 N.Y.S.2d 679, 680 (3d Dep't 2010); *People v. Harris*, 72 A.D.3d 1492, __, 899 N.Y.S.2d 519, 521-22 (4th Dep't 2010), leave to appeal denied, 15 N.Y.3d 774, 907 N.Y.S.2d 462, 933 N.E.2d 1055 (2010); *People v. McClure*, 26 A.D.3d 674, __, 809 N.Y.S.2d 299, 300-01 (3d Dep't 2006); *People v. Antwine*, 299 A.D.2d 151, 753 N.Y.S.2d 355 (1st Dep't 2002); *People v. Maynard*, 295 A.D.2d 805, 743 N.Y.S.2d 912 (3d Dep't 2002); *People v. Wemette*, 285 A.D.2d 729, 728 N.Y.S.2d 805 (3d Dep't 2001); *People v. La Parl*, 276 A.D.2d 814, 718 N.Y.S.2d 889 (3d Dep't 2000); *People v. Furnia*, 223 A.D.2d 887, 636 N.Y.S.2d 488 (3d Dep't 1996); *People v. O'Brien*, 190 A.D.2d 1097, 594 N.Y.S.2d 672 (4th Dep't 1993); *People v. Latzen*, 165 A.D.2d 913, 560 N.Y.S.2d 365 (3d Dep't 1990).

In *People v. Zephrin*, 14 N.Y.3d 296, 899 N.Y.S.2d 739, 926 N.E.2d 246 (2010), the defendant pled guilty to a felony and was sentenced to a split sentence of six months in jail and five years' probation. Critically, the defendant had served the jail portion of the sentence prior to sentencing. As a result, on the date of his sentencing he was sentenced to time served and five years' probation. The defendant violated the terms of his probation. However, while the violation occurred less than five years from the date of sentencing, it occurred more than five years from the date that the defendant had commenced the jail portion of his sentence.

On appeal, the defendant claimed that the five years' probation portion of his sentence should be deemed to have commenced on the date that his jail sentence began (*i.e.*, several months prior to the date of sentencing). In other words, the defendant claimed that the "time served" portion of his sentence was required to include probation as well as jail. The Court of Appeals agreed, reasoning as follows:

> Authorized by Penal Law § 60.01(2)(d), a "split sentence" consists of a term of imprisonment combined with a term of probation or conditional discharge. * * *
>
> Penal Law § 65.00(3)(a) authorizes a five-year term of probation for most felony offenses. Section 65.00(2), however, recognizes that, where a split sentence is imposed, the limitations set forth in Penal Law § 60.01(2)(d) may trump the time period set forth in section 65.00(3)(a). Specifically, section 65.00(2) states: "When a person is sentenced to a period of probation the court shall, *except to the extent authorized by [PL § 60.01(2)(d)]*, impose the period authorized by subdivision three of this section and shall specify . . . the conditions to be complied with" (emphasis added). Taken together, the explicit statutory command of Penal Law § 60.01(2)(d) and Penal Law § 65.00 dictates that, where a court imposes a split sentence, the term of imprisonment and term of probation together

may not exceed, in most cases, five years. In other words, for most felonies, the relevant statutory provisions create a cap of five years that the two components of a split sentence together may not exceed.

Thus, in cases where a defendant has been incarcerated pending sentencing and, as a result, receives credit for time served toward the term of imprisonment of a split sentence (*see* Penal Law § 70.30[3]), that defendant's probationary term is also reduced by the period the defendant was incarcerated prior to sentencing. * * *

Even if Penal Law § 65.15(1) can be read to conflict with the specific directive of Penal Law § 60.01(2)(d), we have held on numerous occasions that a specific statutory provision governs over a more general provision. In this instance, Penal Law § 60.01(2)(d) is not only the more specific statutory command, inasmuch as it was enacted specifically to provide for split sentences, but it is also the later-enacted statute vis-a-vis Penal Law § 65.15(1). We also refuse to read Penal Law § 70.30(3) in isolation to preclude our conclusion. In short, all parts of this sentencing scheme are best harmonized by running the term of probation together with the term of imprisonment, not to exceed five years.

14 N.Y.3d at 299-301, 899 N.Y.S.2d at 741-42 (citations omitted). *See also People v. Teddy W.*, 56 A.D.3d 697, 867 N.Y.S.2d 545 (2d Dep't 2008), leave to appeal denied, 12 N.Y.3d 860, 881 N.Y.S.2d 672, 909 N.E.2d 595 (2009); *People v. Dawson*, 301 A.D.2d 659, 753 N.Y.S.2d 879 (2d Dep't 2003).

As a result of *Zephrin*, *People v. Ellis*, 27 A.D.3d 236, 809 N.Y.S.2d 906 (1st Dep't 2006), and *People v. Feliciano*, 1 A.D.3d 163, 766 N.Y.S.2d 561 (1st Dep't 2003), should no longer be followed.

Conversely to the situation presented in *Zephrin*, it is not uncommon for an in-custody defendant to receive an offer of a split sentence after he or she has already served more jail time than could lawfully be imposed as part of such sentence. For example, the defendant could have been in jail for more than 60 days and then receive an offer of 60 days in jail and three years' probation. Such a sentence is legal. *See, e.g., People v. Conley*, 70 A.D.3d 961, __ 897 N.Y.S.2d 135, 136-37 (2d Dep't 2010); *People v. Marinaccio*, 297 A.D.2d 754, 747 N.Y.S.2d 555 (2d Dep't 2002). In this regard, the appropriate way to impose such a sentence is to "expressly impose[] a sentence of 60 days' imprisonment, which [i]s satisfied by the 'time served' by the defendant" prior to sentencing. *Conley*, 70 A.D.3d at __, 897 N.Y.S.2d at 137. *See also Marinaccio*, 297 A.D.2d at __, 747 N.Y.S.2d at 556.

§ 46:54 Sufficiency of guilty plea

In the past, most local criminal courts had no record of the proceedings beyond the documents in the Court's file and the Judge's notes. As a result, although guilty pleas in such courts are often extremely informal in nature, there was no real means by which to challenge the sufficiency thereof (due to the lack of a sufficient record).

However, now that all proceedings in the local criminal courts are electronically recorded, the People and the Courts should be cognizant of the requirements of *Boykin v. Alabama*, 395 U.S. 238, 89 S. Ct. 1709, 23 L. Ed. 2d 274 (1969). In *Boykin*, the Supreme Court held as follows:

> A plea of guilty is more than a confession which admits that the accused did various acts; it is itself a conviction; nothing remains but to give judgment and determine punishment. Admissibility of a confession must be based on a "reliable determination on the voluntariness issue which satisfies the constitutional rights of the defendant." The requirement that the prosecution spread on the record the prerequisites of a valid waiver is no constitutional innovation. In *Carnley v. Cochran*, we dealt with a problem of waiver of the right to counsel, a Sixth Amendment right. We held: "Presuming waiver from a silent record is impermissible. The record must show, or there must be an allegation and evidence which show, that an accused was offered counsel but intelligently and understandingly rejected the offer. Anything less is not waiver."
>
> We think that the same standard must be applied to determining whether a guilty plea is voluntarily made. For, as we have said, a plea of guilty is more than an admission of conduct; it is a conviction. Ignorance, incomprehension, coercion, terror, inducements, subtle or blatant threats might be a perfect cover-up of unconstitutionality. The question of an effective waiver of a federal constitutional right in a proceeding is of course governed by federal standards.
>
> Several federal constitutional rights are involved in a waiver that takes place when a plea of guilty is entered in a state criminal trial. First, is the privilege against compulsory self-incrimination guaranteed by the Fifth Amendment and applicable to the States by reason of the Fourteenth. Second, is the right to trial by jury. Third, is the right to confront one's accusers. We cannot presume a waiver of these three important federal rights from a silent record.

395 U.S. at 242-43, 89 S.Ct. at 1711-12 (citations and footnote omitted).

In *People v. Harris*, 61 N.Y.2d 9, 19, 471 N.Y.S.2d 61, 66, 459 N.E.2d 170 (1983), the Court of Appeals applied *Boykin* as follows:

> A survey of the decisions of the Federal Courts of Appeals and the State courts . . . reveals a virtual unanimity of opinion that a detailed articulation and waiver of the three rights mentioned in

Boykin is not constitutionally mandated. The clear import of *Boykin* and its progeny is that the Trial Judge has a vital responsibility "to make sure [that the accused] has full understanding of what the plea connotes and of its consequence," not that a new procedural requirement has been imposed, mandating the Trial Judge's ritualistic recitation of the rights waived upon a guilty plea.

(Citations omitted).

In deciding how rigorous a plea allocation should be, factors to be considered include the defendant's prior criminal experience, "the seriousness of the crime, the competency and experience of counsel, the actual intensive participation by counsel, the nature of the crime as clearly understood by laymen, the rationality of the 'plea bargain,' and the speed or slowness of procedure in the particular criminal court." *People v. Nixon*, 21 N.Y.2d 338, 353, 287 N.Y.S.2d 659, 671, 234 N.E.2d 687 (1967). The *Nixon* Court further pointed out that:

> The competency of counsel and the degree of actual participation by counsel, as well as his opportunity for and the fact of consultation with the pleading defendant, are particularly important. Indeed, if independent and good advice in the interest of the defendant is the goal, it is more important that he consult with competent counsel than that a harried, calendar-conscious Judge be the one to perform the function in displacement of the lawyer. Moreover, there are many reasons why a defendant may not wish to be subjected to an inquisition by officials; it may affect him on his prison or parole status; it may be an added pillory for him to experience that he would eschew.

21 N.Y.2d at 354, 287 N.Y.S.2d at 671. By contrast, "[i]n cases involving defendants without lawyers, or those ignorant of the language of the court, particular pains must be taken. . . . In such cases inquiry, well beyond the standards thus far propounded, is indicated." 21 N.Y.2d at 355, 287 N.Y.S.2d at 672.

Thus, the required plea allocation in a case where a speeding ticket is reduced to Parked on Pavement would be less than the required allocation in a case where a defendant charged with Aggravated DWI pleads guilty to the charge and is sentenced to 3 years' probation. Similarly, the required plea allocation in a case where the defendant is represented by experienced defense counsel would be less than the required allocation in a case where the defendant pleads guilty without a lawyer.

In *People v. Tyrell*, 22 N.Y.3d 359, 366, 981 N.Y.S.2d 336, 340, 4 N.E.3d 346 (2013), the Court of Appeals invalidated defendant's guilty pleas in two separate misdemeanor cases on *Boykin* grounds where:

> [T]he records do not affirmatively demonstrate defendant's understanding or waiver of his constitutional rights. In each case,

there is a complete absence of discussion of any of the pertinent
constitutional rights; none are addressed by the court, defense
counsel or defendant. Nor is there any indication that defendant
spoke with his attorney regarding the constitutional consequences
of taking a plea—in fact, these cases were both resolved during arraignment within days of arrest. Put simply, the records in these
cases are inadequate to uphold the judgments of conviction and,
contrary to the dissent's position, the pleas must be vacated.

On the other hand, the Court noted that:

> [C]ontrary to the dissent's assertion, we signal no retreat from the
> principle that trial courts retain broad discretion in the taking of
> pleas and need not follow any kind of rigid catechism. We merely
> apply the well-settled proposition that the record as a whole must
> contain an affirmative demonstration of the defendant's waiver of
> his fundamental constitutional rights—a requirement the dissent
> neglects to mention. And although the dissent suggests that a
> defendant must establish prejudice even where the record is
> completely silent as to his waiver of constitutional rights, *Boykin*
> holds directly to the contrary.

Id. at 366, 981 N.Y.S.2d at 341.

Perhaps realizing the Pandora's box that would be opened if
routine guilty pleas in non-felony cases were required to truly
comply with *Boykin,* the Court of Appeals relaxed the requirements of a valid guilty plea in the trio of cases at issue in *People
v. Conceicao*, 26 N.Y.3d 375, 23 N.Y.S.3d 124, 44 N.E.3d 199
(2015). In this regard, the *Conceicao* Court held as follows:

> The primary issue in these appeals is whether defendants entered
> knowing, intelligent and voluntary guilty pleas when the trial
> courts failed to mention the constitutional rights defendants were
> waiving—the right to a trial by jury, the right to confront one's ac-
> cusers and the privilege against self-incrimination (*see Boykin v.
> Alabama*). We hold that the failure to recite the *Boykin* rights does
> not automatically invalidate an otherwise voluntary and intelligent
> plea. Where the record as a whole affirmatively shows that the
> defendant intentionally relinquished those rights, the plea will be
> upheld.

26 N.Y.3d at 379, 23 N.Y.S.3d at 126-27 (citation omitted).

One of the cases at issue in *Conceicao* was *People v. Sanchez*—a
misdemeanor DWI case. In *Sanchez,* the Appellate Division, First
Department, had held that:

> The record fails to demonstrate that defendant was informed of any
> of the constitutional rights that he was waiving by pleading guilty
> or that he consulted with counsel about the constitutional conse-
> quences of his guilty plea. The only question addressed by the court
> to defendant was whether he wanted to plead guilty. Defense
> counsel then waived "further allocution," and the court imposed
> sentence.

The People's reliance on *People v. Perez,* where this Court upheld a waiver of "formal allocution" regarding a plea to disorderly conduct resulting in a fine, is misplaced. Unlike disorderly conduct, driving while intoxicated is not a petty offense. Such a conviction is a misdemeanor rather than a traffic infraction, it affects a defendant's driving privileges, and it can be the basis for elevating a subsequent similar charge to a felony. Furthermore, in *Perez* there was more in the record than here to show consultation with counsel concerning the plea.

People v. Sanchez, 126 A.D.3d 482, —, 6 N.Y.S.3d 25, 25-26 (1st Dep't 2015), leave to appeal granted, 25 N.Y.3d 1077, 12 N.Y.S.3d 628, 34 N.E.3d 379 (2015) and rev'd, 26 N.Y.3d 375, 23 N.Y.S.3d 124, 44 N.E.3d 199 (2015) (citations omitted). In reversing the Appellate Division, the Court of Appeals stated:

> The record in *Sanchez* . . . reflects a knowing and voluntary plea. Represented by the same attorney that represented the defendant in *Perez,* defendant filed numerous pretrial motions and actively litigated the case for six months. Moreover, defendant was aware of his right to a trial, because his case was on for trial the very same day that defendant pleaded guilty. That his attorney announced at the start of the plea proceeding, without the need for any additional discussion with defendant or the prosecutor, that defendant had decided to plead guilty rather than proceed to the scheduled trial further confirms that defendant made the decision to plead guilty after consulting with counsel prior to the start of the proceeding. And as in *Perez,* defendant, through his attorney, waived a more detailed allocution that might have entailed discussion of the *Boykin* rights.

> We recognize that a DWI is a serious offense that "affects a defendant's driving privileges" and "can be the basis for elevating a subsequent similar charge to a felony." We are also aware that defendant did not affirmatively state on the record, as did the defendant in *Perez,* that he had enough time to speak with his attorney about the plea. Though the plea allocution in *Sanchez* could have been more robust, the record as a whole reveals a knowing and intelligent choice among alternative courses of action.

Conceicao, 26 N.Y.3d at 384, 23 N.Y.S.3d at 130 (citation omitted).

§ 46:55   Pleading client guilty to top charge as ineffective assistance of counsel

In light of *People v. Rivera,* 91 A.D.3d 450, 935 N.Y.S.2d 515 (1st Dep't 2012), leave to appeal denied, 18 N.Y.3d 928, 942 N.Y.S.2d 467, 965 N.E.2d 969 (2012), defense counsel had better think twice before pleading a first offender guilty to DWI without conducting any type of meaningful investigation. In *Rivera,* the Appellate Division, First Department, held that:

> The record supports the court's conclusion, made after a thorough

evidentiary hearing, that defendant did not receive meaningful representation. "In the context of a guilty plea, a defendant has been afforded meaningful representation when he or she receives an advantageous plea and nothing in the record casts doubt on the apparent effectiveness of counsel."

Defense counsel failed to conduct any investigation, make any motions, or even view the video of defendant's breathalyzer test before negotiating a plea bargain whereby defendant would plead guilty to the top count of the accusatory instrument. There were lines of defense that were at least worthy of investigation, including matters that could have affected the accuracy of the breathalyzer results. The attorney's testimony established that there were no strategic reasons for these omissions.

The hearing evidence also established that since defendant had no prior record and no accident occurred, it was extremely unlikely that defendant would receive a jail sentence. Accordingly, defendant received little, if any benefit, by pleading guilty to the top count without ever having received even a minimally accurate assessment of the strength of the People's case.

91 A.D.3d at __, 935 N.Y.S.2d at 515-16 (citation omitted).

Another decision that found defense counsel to be ineffective in a DWI case is *People v. Murray*, 40 Misc. 3d 47, 970 N.Y.S.2d 659 (App. Term, 9th & 10th Jud. Dist. 2013). In *Murray*, "[d]efendant's trial attorney presented no evidence but, rather, argued to the jury that defendant could not be found guilty of the charges because the People could not prove that defendant had operated the motor vehicle within the meaning of the Vehicle and Traffic Law since defendant had no present intent to place the vehicle in motion inasmuch as he was asleep when the police officer found him in the vehicle." *Id.* at __, 970 N.Y.S.2d at 661-62. In this regard, the Court found that "the decision by defendant's trial attorney not to present any evidence, especially evidence regarding defendant's lack of intent to place the vehicle into motion by explaining why the engine was otherwise running, was devoid of any strategic purpose." *Id.* at __, 970 N.Y.S.2d at 662.

In addition, even though defendant's trial attorney focused the defense on the premise that defendant had not operated the vehicle, he did not object, and/or move for preclusion and a mistrial, when the prosecutor repeatedly referred to defendant as the driver of the vehicle, and elicited the police officer's testimony that defendant had told him that "you didn't catch me driving," and that he "had been drinking throughout Port Jervis," which statements were not included in the CPL 710.30 notice. Defendant's trial attorney also did not attempt to impeach the police officer when he testified at trial that defendant had not had identification on him, whereas, at a pretrial hearing, the officer had testified that defendant had provided him with his driver's license.

It is clear that no legitimate trial strategy existed for defendant's trial attorney's actions, which, when considered in the aggregate, deprived defendant of meaningful representation.

Id. at __, 970 N.Y.S.2d at 662. *See also People v. Dollinger*, 128 A.D.3d 1085, __, 9 N.Y.S.3d 635, 637 (2d Dep't 2015) ("the defendant's representation at sentencing by the attorney who had represented the People when he pleaded guilty presented a potential conflict of interest. Moreover, the record establishes that the potential conflict actually operated on or affected the defense. Indeed, the defendant's attorney at sentencing, by characterizing the defendant as a repeat offender, showed that she had not departed from her prosecutorial stance. Accordingly, we vacate the sentence imposed, and remit the matter to the County Court, Putnam County, for resentencing") (citation omitted).

§ 46:56   Jail sentence in DWI case found to be improper

Too often, Courts threaten—either explicitly or implicitly—to sentence DWI defendants to jail if they go to trial and lose. In this regard, in *People v. Rivera*, 91 A.D.3d 450, __, 935 N.Y.S.2d 515, 516 (1st Dep't 2012), leave to appeal denied, 18 N.Y.3d 928, 942 N.Y.S.2d 467, 965 N.E.2d 969 (2012), the Appellate Division, First Department, stated that "since defendant had no prior record and no accident occurred, it was extremely unlikely that defendant would receive a jail sentence."

In *People v. Johnson*, 114 A.D.3d 534, __, 980 N.Y.S.2d 447, 447-48 (1st Dep't 2014), leave to appeal denied (N.Y. June 20, 2014), the same Court held as follows:

Judgment, Supreme Court, Bronx County (Patricia Anne Williams, J.), rendered May 16, 2012, convicting defendant, after a jury trial, of driving while intoxicated (two counts) and operating a motor vehicle without a license, and sentencing her to a term of 30 days of intermittent imprisonment to be served on weekends, a conditional discharge for a period of one year and a $300 fine, unanimously modified, as a matter of discretion in the interest of justice, to the extent of vacating the term of intermittent imprisonment, and otherwise affirmed.

In this regard:

In setting sentence the trial judge should be guided not only by the . . . . objectives of punishment, but also by the criterion that *a minimum amount of confinement* should be imposed "consistent with the protection of the public, the gravity of the offense and the rehabilitative needs of the defendant."

People v. Notey, 72 A.D.2d 279, __, 423 N.Y.S.2d 947, 950 (2d Dep't 1980) (emphasis added) (citation omitted).

§ 46:57 Periods of probation

Prior to February 9, 2014, a person sentenced to probation for a misdemeanor VTL § 1192 offense would be sentenced to three years' probation, and a person sentenced to probation for a felony VTL § 1192 offense would be sentenced to five years' probation. Effective February 9, 2014, the Court now has discretion to impose a period of probation of two or three years for a misdemeanor, *see* Penal Law § 65.00(3)(d), and three, four or five years for a felony. *See* Penal Law § 65.00(3)(a)(i).

Chapter 47

Surcharges and Crime Victim Assistance Fees

Research References

Westlaw Databases

Handling a Criminal Case in New York (HCCNY)
New York Vehicle and Traffic Law 2d (NYVEH)

Treatises and Practice Aids

Muldoon, Handling a Criminal Case in New York §§ 21:72 to 21:80
Rose, New York Vehicle and Traffic Law 2d §§ 12:5, 18:9, 35:36.50

Law Reviews and Other Periodicals

Bamberger, Collateral Consequences of New York Convictions, 30 N.Y.U. Rev. L. & Soc. Change 723 (2006)

KeyCite®: Cases and other legal materials listed in KeyCite Scope can be researched through the KeyCite service on Westlaw®. Use KeyCite to check citations for form, parallel references, prior and later history, and comprehensive citator information, including citations to other decisions and secondary materials.

---

§ 47:1   In general

Research References

West's Key Number Digest, Sentencing and Punishment ⛛2137

Most Vehicle and Traffic Law and Penal Law offenses are subject to a mandatory surcharge and crime victim assistance fee. These fees are levied in addition to any other sentence, fine, or penalty imposed by the court. In recent years, such fees have been steadily increased by the legislature—so much so that the mandatory surcharge/crime victim assistance fee in many minor traffic and criminal matters often exceeds the fine imposed by the court. The primary surcharge statutes are VTL § 1809, PL § 60.35 and CPL § 420.35.

In light of the fact that surcharges are routinely increased, it is critical to note that the amount of a particular surcharge is determined by the law in effect on the date of the *charge*—not the law in effect on the date of the defendant's *conviction*. *See* § 47:4, *infra*.

§ 47:2   Purpose of mandatory surcharges and crime victim assistance fees

Research References

West's Key Number Digest, Sentencing and Punishment ⛛2137

"The mandatory surcharge/crime victim assistance fee is paid to the State to shift costs of providing services to victims of crime from 'law abiding taxpayers and toward those who commit crimes.'" *People v. Quinones*, 95 N.Y.2d 349, 352, 717 N.Y.S.2d 86, 88 (2000) (citation omitted). *See also* State Finance Law § 97-bb.

§ 47:3   Constitutionality of mandatory surcharges and crime victim assistance fees

Research References

West's Key Number Digest, Sentencing and Punishment ⛛2137

Mandatory surcharges and crime victim assistance fees have repeatedly been found to be constitutional. *See, e.g., People v. Barnes*, 62 N.Y.2d 702, 476 N.Y.S.2d 528 (1984); *People v. Dunn*, 254 A.D.2d 511, 680 N.Y.S.2d 125 (3d Dep't 1998); *People v. Arthur*, 234 A.D.2d 792, 651 N.Y.S.2d 672 (3d Dep't 1996); *People v. Ramirez*, 208 A.D.2d 381, 617 N.Y.S.2d 13 (1st Dep't 1994); *People v. Arfman*, 167 A.D.2d 344, 562 N.Y.S.2d 435 (2d Dep't 1990); *People v. Teele*, 157 A.D.2d 592, 550 N.Y.S.2d 339 (1st Dep't 1990); *People v. James*, 144 A.D.2d 717, 535 N.Y.S.2d 452 (3d Dep't 1988); *People v. Burt*, 142 A.D.2d 794, 531 N.Y.S.2d 131 (3d Dep't 1988).

§ 47:4 Amount of surcharge and crime victim assistance fee determined by law in effect on date of *charge*

Research References
West's Key Number Digest, Sentencing and Punishment ⟳2137

Mandatory surcharges and crime victim assistance fees are routinely increased by the legislature. In this regard, an issue arises as to whether the Court should impose (a) the fees in effect on the date of the charge, or rather (b) the fees in effect on the date of the defendant's conviction.

The answer is clear and well settled—the court should impose the mandatory surcharge and crime victim assistance fee in effect on the date of the *charge*; as imposing the fees in effect on the date of the defendant's conviction would "constitute a violation of the U.S. Constitution's ex post facto clause." *People v. Goldwire*, 301 A.D.2d 677, __, 752 N.Y.S.2d 906, 907 (3d Dep't 2003). *See also People v. Pelsey*, 60 A.D.3d 1088, 876 N.Y.S.2d 484 (2d Dep't 2009); *People v. King*, 57 A.D.3d 1495, 869 N.Y.S.2d 832 (4th Dep't 2008); *People v. Johnson*, 57 A.D.3d 323, 869 N.Y.S.2d 84 (1st Dep't 2008); *People v. Caggiano*, 46 A.D.3d 1405, 848 N.Y.S.2d 797 (4th Dep't 2007); *People v. Cruz*, 25 A.D.3d 565, 806 N.Y.S.2d 421 (2d Dep't 2006); *People v. Figueroa*, 17 A.D.3d 1130, 794 N.Y.S.2d 262 (4th Dep't 2005); *People v. McQueen*, 11 A.D.3d 1005, 782 N.Y.S.2d 336 (4th Dep't 2004); *People v. Sullivan*, 6 A.D.3d 1175, 775 N.Y.S.2d 696 (4th Dep't 2004); *People v. Purdue*, 6 A.D.3d 1102, 775 N.Y.S.2d 632 (4th Dep't 2004); *People v. Reeves*, 6 A.D.3d 231, 774 N.Y.S.2d 326 (1st Dep't 2004); *People v. Hager*, 5 A.D.3d 981, 773 N.Y.S.2d 317 (4th Dep't 2004); *People v. Moye*, 4 A.D.3d 488, 772 N.Y.S.2d 352 (2d Dep't 2004); *People v. McIntosh*, 163 A.D.2d 810, 558 N.Y.S.2d 342 (4th Dep't 1990); *People v. Diaz*, 159 A.D.2d 391, 553 N.Y.S.2d 18 (1st Dep't 1990); *People v. Bethea*, 133 A.D.2d 836, 520 N.Y.S.2d 407 (2d Dep't 1987).

§ 47:5 No VTL surcharge or crime victim assistance fee where defendant has paid PL surcharge or crime victim assistance fee

Research References
West's Key Number Digest, Sentencing and Punishment ⟳2137

VTL § 1809(7) provides that "[n]otwithstanding any other provision of [VTL § 1809], where a mandatory surcharge or crime victim assistance fee is imposed pursuant to the provisions of [PL § 60.35], no mandatory surcharge or crime victim assistance fee shall be imposed pursuant to the provisions of [VTL § 1809]."

§ 47:6 No surcharge or crime victim assistance fee for most parking, stopping, and standing violations and/or for violations by pedestrians or bicyclists

Research References

West's Key Number Digest, Automobiles ⊙361; Sentencing and Punishment ⊙2137

The mandatory surcharge provisions of VTL § 1809 do not apply to "traffic infraction[s] involving standing, stopping, or parking or violations by pedestrians or bicyclists." VTL § 1809(1). *See also* VTL § 1809-e(1); *People v. Bey*, 22 Misc. 3d 62, —, 874 N.Y.S.2d 665, 667 (App. Term, 2d & 11th Jud. Dist. 2008).

However, effective July 26, 2013, there is now a $25 surcharge for VTL § 1200, VTL § 1201 and VTL § 1202 convictions. VTL § 1809-aa(1).

In addition, in cities with populations of 100,000 or more (according to the 1980 census), there is a $15 mandatory surcharge for parking, stopping, or standing convictions (involving a motor vehicle). VTL § 1809-a(1). This $15 surcharge is inapplicable, however, if the defendant has paid a mandatory surcharge pursuant to (a) VTL § 1809, (b) VTL § 1809-b (mandatory surcharge for handicapped parking violations), or (c) PL § 60.35. VTL § 1809-a(4).

§ 47:7 New surcharge for parked on pavement convictions

In many parts of the State, a variety of VTL infractions are commonly plea bargained to Parked on Pavement in violation of VTL § 1201(a). Since VTL § 1201(a) is a parking infraction, there was no surcharge attached to this offense. *See* VTL § 1809(1). However, effective July 26, 2013, VTL § 1809-aa(1) provides as follows:

Notwithstanding any other provision of law, whenever proceedings in an administrative tribunal or court result in a conviction for a violation of [VTL § 1200, 1201 or 1202], there shall be levied a mandatory surcharge in addition to any other sentence, fine or penalty otherwise permitted or required, in the amount of [$25].

§ 47:8 No surcharge or crime victim assistance fee where defendant has made restitution or reparation

Research References

West's Key Number Digest, Sentencing and Punishment ⊙2137

VTL § 1809(6) provides that "[n]otwithstanding any other provision of [VTL § 1809], where a person *has made* restitution or reparation pursuant to [PL § 60.27], such person shall not be required to pay a mandatory surcharge or crime victim assistance fee." (Emphasis added).

Similarly, PL § 60.35(6) provides that "[n]otwithstanding any other provision of [PL § 60.35], where a person *has made* restitution or reparation pursuant to [PL § 60.27], such person shall not be required to pay a mandatory surcharge or a crime victim assistance fee." (Emphasis added).

In *People v. Quinones*, 95 N.Y.2d 349, 351, 717 N.Y.S.2d 86, 87 (2000), the Court of Appeals held that "a sentencing court may, under Penal Law § 60.35(6), order a defendant who *has not yet made* restitution to pay both restitution and a mandatory surcharge/crime victim assistance fee." (Emphasis added). *See also People v. Michalski*, 15 A.D.3d 918, 788 N.Y.S.2d 776 (4th Dep't 2005); *People v. Ziolkowski*, 9 A.D.3d 915, 779 N.Y.S.2d 708 (4th Dep't 2004); *People v. Hall*, 303 A.D.2d 601, 756 N.Y.S.2d 494 (2d Dep't 2003); *People v. Cosper*, 248 A.D.2d 397, 669 N.Y.S.2d 637 (2d Dep't 1998); *People v. Cabrera*, 243 A.D.2d 720, 664 N.Y.S.2d 308 (2d Dep't 1997). In such a case, however, once restitution has been made the mandatory surcharge and crime victim assistance fee are no longer required—and the defendant "can seek a refund of those payments." *Quinones*, 95 N.Y.2d at 352, 717 N.Y.S.2d at 88. *See also* PL § 60.35(4); VTL § 1809(4); VTL § 1809-a(3); *Ziolkowski*, 9 A.D.3d at __, 779 N.Y.S.2d at 709; *Cosper*, 248 A.D.2d at __, 669 N.Y.S.2d at 637; *Cabrera*, 243 A.D.2d at __, 664 N.Y.S.2d at 310.

§ 47:9 Surcharge and crime victim assistance fee apply to youthful offenders

Research References

West's Key Number Digest, Sentencing and Punishment ⊕2137

In the past, the mandatory surcharge provisions of the law only applied where the defendant had been "convicted" of a crime or an offense. *See* VTL § 1809(1); VTL § 1809-c(1); VTL § 1809-e(1); PL § 60.35(1). In this regard, since "[a] youthful offender adjudication is not a judgment of conviction for a crime or any other offense," CPL § 720.35(1), a court could not properly impose a surcharge or crime victim assistance fee where a defendant was adjudicated a youth offender. *See, e.g., People v. Floyd J.*, 61 N.Y.2d 895, 474 N.Y.S.2d 476 (1984); *People v. Michael "M"*, 161 A.D.2d 911, 557 N.Y.S.2d 177 (3d Dep't 1990); *People v. Spencer*, 138 A.D.2d 976, 526 N.Y.S.2d 414 (4th Dep't 1988); *People v. Huertas*, 127 A.D.2d 475, 511 N.Y.S.2d 621 (1st Dep't 1987); *People v. Bain*, 126 A.D.2d 985, 511 N.Y.S.2d 801 (4th Dep't 1987).

However, effective February 16, 2005, VTL § 1809(10) and PL § 60.35(10) legislatively overrule these cases by expressly making most mandatory surcharges and crime victim assistance fees applicable to youth offender adjudications. *See also* PL § 60.02(3).

§ 47:10 Unless surcharge/crime victim assistance fee inapplicable, such fees may not be waived

Research References

West's Key Number Digest, Sentencing and Punishment ⚖2137

The previous sections provide for situations in which a defendant is exempt from paying mandatory surcharges and crime victim assistance fees. Where no exemption applies, CPL § 420.35(2) provides that *"[u]nder no circumstances shall the mandatory surcharge . . . or the crime victim assistance fee be waived."* (Emphasis added).

However, where the defendant is indigent, he or she can apply for deferral of the obligation to pay such fees. CPL §§ 420.10, 420.35 and 420.40 set forth the procedures to be followed in this regard. *See also People v. Hopkins*, 185 Misc. 2d 312, 712 N.Y.S.2d 796 (Kings Co. Sup. Ct. 2000); *People v. Brian L.*, 17 Misc. 3d 724, 842 N.Y.S.2d 874 (Watertown City Ct. 2007).

§ 47:11 Surcharge and crime victim assistance fee for VTL Article 9 traffic infractions

Research References

West's Key Number Digest, Automobiles ⚖361; Sentencing and Punishment ⚖2137

VTL Article 9 (*i.e.*, VTL §§ 375 to 384) deals with so-called equipment violations. Where a defendant is convicted of a traffic infraction pursuant to VTL Article 9, he or she is subject to:

1. A mandatory surcharge of $25. VTL § 1809(1)(a);

2. A crime victim assistance fee of $5. VTL § 1809(1)(a);

3. If the case is in either a town or village court, an additional $5 surcharge. VTL § 1809(9); and

4. Effective August 1, 2008, an additional surcharge of $20 (effective July 26, 2013, this amount is $28). VTL § 1809-e(1)(a).

In other words, if the case is in a town or village court, the mandatory surcharge for a VTL Article 9 traffic infraction is $63; otherwise, the mandatory surcharge for a VTL Article 9 traffic infraction is $58.

§ 47:12 Surcharge and crime victim assistance fee for VTL § 1192 traffic infractions

Research References

West's Key Number Digest, Automobiles ⚖361; Sentencing and Punishment ⚖2137

Where a defendant is convicted of DWAI as a traffic infraction, he or she is subject to:

    1. Effective July 1, 2008, a mandatory surcharge of $55. VTL § 1809(1)(c);

    2. A crime victim assistance fee of $5. VTL § 1809(1)(c);

    3. An additional $25 surcharge. VTL § 1809-c(1);

    4. If the case is in either a town or village court, another additional $5 surcharge. VTL § 1809(9); and

    5. Effective August 1, 2008, another additional surcharge of $170. VTL § 1809-e(1)(b).

In other words, if the case is in a town or village Court, the mandatory surcharge for a DWAI traffic infraction is $260; otherwise, the mandatory surcharge for a DWAI traffic infraction is $255.

§ 47:13 Surcharge and crime victim assistance fee for VTL § 1192 misdemeanors

Research References

West's Key Number Digest, Automobiles ☞361; Sentencing and Punishment ☞2137

Where a defendant is convicted of misdemeanor DWAI, DWI, or DWAI Drugs, he or she is subject to:

    1. Effective July 1, 2008, a mandatory surcharge of $175. VTL § 1809(1)(b)(ii);

    2. Effective July 1, 2008, a crime victim assistance fee of $25. VTL § 1809(1)(b);

    3. An additional $25 surcharge. VTL § 1809-c(1);

    4. If the case is in either a town or village court, another additional $5 surcharge. VTL § 1809(9); and

    5. Effective August 1, 2008, another additional surcharge of $170. VTL § 1809-e(1)(b).

In other words, if the case is in a town or village Court, the mandatory surcharge for a VTL § 1192 misdemeanor is $400; otherwise, the mandatory surcharge for a VTL § 1192 misdemeanor is $395.

§ 47:14 Surcharge and crime victim assistance fee for VTL § 1192 felonies

Research References

West's Key Number Digest, Automobiles ☞361; Sentencing and Punishment ☞2137

Where a defendant is convicted of felony DWI or DWAI drugs, he or she is subject to:

    1. Effective July 1, 2008, a mandatory surcharge of $300. VTL § 1809(1)(b)(i);

2. Effective July 1, 2008, a crime victim assistance fee of $25. VTL § 1809(1)(b);

3. An additional $25 surcharge. VTL § 1809-c(1); and

4. Effective August 1, 2008, another additional surcharge of $170. VTL § 1809-e(1)(b).

In other words, the mandatory surcharge for a VTL § 1192 felony is $520.

§ 47:15 Additional surcharges in VTL § 1192 cases

Research References

West's Key Number Digest, Automobiles ☞361; Sentencing and Punishment ☞2137

Although VTL § 1809 already contains enhanced mandatory surcharge provisions applicable to misdemeanor and felony DWI convictions, VTL § 1809-c imposes an additional $25 surcharge in every case resulting in a VTL § 1192 conviction (including DWAI). VTL § 1809-c(1).

In addition, effective August 1, 2008, VTL § 1809-e(1)(b) provides that "[n]otwithstanding any other provision of law, whenever proceedings in a court of this state result in a conviction pursuant to [VTL § 1192], there shall be levied, in addition to any sentence or other surcharge required or permitted by law, an additional surcharge of [$170]."

§ 47:16 Surcharge and crime victim assistance fee for remaining VTL traffic infractions, misdemeanors and felonies

Research References

West's Key Number Digest, Automobiles ☞361; Sentencing and Punishment ☞2137

As § 47:6 demonstrates, the mandatory surcharge provisions of VTL § 1809 do not apply to "traffic infraction[s] involving standing, stopping, or parking or violations by pedestrians or bicyclists." VTL § 1809(1). *See also* VTL § 1809-e(1). *Cf.* VTL § 1809-aa(1). In addition, VTL § 1809(1)(a) addresses surcharges for VTL Article 9 traffic infractions, and VTL § 1809(1)(b) addresses surcharges for VTL § 1192 misdemeanors and felonies. For almost any other VTL conviction, whether it be for:

(a) A traffic infraction;

(b) A misdemeanor (*e.g.*, AUO 2nd or 3rd, reckless driving, misdemeanor leaving the scene of an accident, etc.); or

(c) A felony (*e.g.*, AUO 1st, felony leaving the scene of an accident, etc.), the following fees are applicable:

1. Effective July 1, 2008, a mandatory surcharge of $55. VTL § 1809(1)(c);

2. A crime victim assistance fee of $5. VTL § 1809(1)(c);

3. If the case is in either a town or village court, an additional $5 surcharge. VTL § 1809(9); and

4. Effective August 1,2008, an additional surcharge of $20 (effective July 26, 2013, this amount is $28). VTL § 1809-e(1)(a).

In other words, if the case is in a town or village court, the mandatory surcharge for most VTL offenses is $93; otherwise, the mandatory surcharge for most VTL offenses is $88.

§ 47:17   PL § 60.35 only applies to PL offenses—not to VTL offenses

Research References

West's Key Number Digest, Sentencing and Punishment ☞2137

The mandatory surcharges and crime victim assistance fees contained in PL § 60.35 are only applicable to PL offenses: "Notwithstanding the provisions of [PL § 60.00(1)], the provisions of [PL § 60.35(1)] shall not apply to a violation under any law other than this chapter." PL § 60.35(7). *See also People v. Grant*, 178 A.D.2d 699, __, 577 N.Y.S.2d 162, 162–63 (3d Dep't 1991) (PL § 60.35(1) "expressly exempts from its coverage crimes occurring under the Vehicle and Traffic Law"). In this regard, PL § 60.35(1) begins with the phrase "[e]xcept as provided in [VTL § 1809] . . ."

Thus, the mandatory surcharges and crime victim assistance fees for VTL misdemeanors and felonies (other than VTL § 1192 misdemeanors and felonies) are governed by VTL § 1809(1)(c)—*not* by PL § 60.35(1).

§ 47:18   Surcharge and crime victim assistance fee for PL violations

Research References

West's Key Number Digest, Sentencing and Punishment ☞2137

Where a defendant is convicted of a PL "violation" (as that term is defined in PL § 10.00), he or she is subject to:

1. Effective July 1, 2008, a mandatory surcharge of $95. PL § 60.35(1)(a)(iii);

2. Effective July 1, 2008, a crime victim assistance fee of $25. PL § 60.35(1)(a)(iii); and

3. If the case is in either a town or village court, an additional $5 surcharge. PL § 60.35(9).

In other words, if the case is in a town or village court, the mandatory surcharge for a PL violation is $125; otherwise, the mandatory surcharge for a PL violation is $120.

§ 47:19 Surcharge and crime victim assistance fee for PL misdemeanors

Research References

West's Key Number Digest, Sentencing and Punishment ⟜2137

Where a defendant is convicted of a PL misdemeanor, he or she is subject to:

1. Effective July 1, 2008, a mandatory surcharge of $175. PL § 60.35(1)(a)(ii);

2. Effective July 1, 2008, a crime victim assistance fee of $25. PL § 60.35(1)(a)(ii); and

3. If the case is in either a town or village court, an additional $5 surcharge. PL § 60.35(9).

In other words, if the case is in a town or village court, the mandatory surcharge for a PL misdemeanor is $205; otherwise, the mandatory surcharge for a PL misdemeanor is $200.

§ 47:20 Surcharge and crime victim assistance fee for PL felonies

Research References

West's Key Number Digest, Sentencing and Punishment ⟜2137

Where a defendant is convicted of a PL felony, he or she is subject to:

1. Effective July 1, 2008, a mandatory surcharge of $300. PL § 60.35(1)(a)(i); and

2. Effective July 1, 2008, a crime victim assistance fee of $25. PL § 60.35(1)(a)(i).

In other words, the mandatory surcharge for a PL felony is $325.

§ 47:21 Additional $5 surcharge in town and village court cases

Research References

West's Key Number Digest, Sentencing and Punishment ⟜2137

VTL § 1809(9) provides that "[n]otwithstanding the provisions of [VTL § 1809(1)], in the event a proceeding is in a town or village court, the court shall add an additional [$5] to the surcharges imposed by such [VTL § 1809(1)]."

Similarly, PL § 60.35(9) provides that "[n]otwithstanding the provisions of [PL § 60.35(1)], in the event a proceeding is in a town or village court, such court shall add an additional [$5] to the surcharges imposed by such [PL § 60.35(1)]."

§ 47:22   With certain exceptions, there is a $196 "cap" on surcharges and crime victim assistance fees in VTL cases

Research References

West's Key Number Digest, Sentencing and Punishment ☞2137

Effective July 26, 2013, VTL § 1809(2) provides that:

> Where a person is convicted of [2] or more such crimes or traffic infractions committed through a single act or omission, or through an act or omission which in itself constituted [1] of the crimes or traffic infractions and also was a material element of the other, the court . . . shall impose a crime victim assistance fee and a mandatory surcharge mandated by [VTL § 1809(1)] for each such conviction; provided however, that in no event shall the total amount of such crime victim assistance fees and mandatory surcharges imposed pursuant to [VTL § 1809(1)(a) or (c)] exceed [$196 (for offenses committed prior to July 26, 2013, the amount is $180)].

See generally PL § 80.15.

Note that VTL § 1809(2) applies to mandatory surcharges imposed pursuant to VTL § 1809(1)(a) and (c). By contrast, it does *not* apply to mandatory surcharges imposed pursuant to (a) VTL § 1809(1)(b), (b) VTL § 1809-c(1), (c) VTL § 1809-e(1), (d), VTL § 1809(9), and/or (e) VTL § 1809-aa(1).

Thus, in calculating the $196 cap on mandatory surcharges/ crime victim assistance fees, surcharges for VTL § 1192 *misdemeanors and felonies* are not counted, nor are the additional $25 and $170 surcharges in VTL § 1192 cases, the additional $5 surcharge in town and village court cases or VTL § 1809-aa(1).

On the other hand, the $55 mandatory surcharge and $5 crime victim assistance fee for a DWAI traffic infraction *would* count in calculating the $180 cap (because such fees are imposed pursuant to VTL § 1809(1)(c)—*not* pursuant to VTL § 1809(1)(b), VTL § 1809-c(1), VTL § 1809-e(1), VTL § 1809(9), or VTL § 1809-aa(1)).

§ 47:23   Imposition of multiple surcharges/crime victim assistance fees prohibited in certain PL cases

Research References

West's Key Number Digest, Sentencing and Punishment ☞2137

PL § 60.35(2) provides, in pertinent part, that:

> Where a person is convicted of [2] or more crimes or violations committed through a single act or omission, or through an act or omission which in itself constituted [1] of the crimes or violations and also was a material element of the other, the court shall impose a mandatory surcharge and a crime victim assistance fee in accor-

dance with the provisions of [PL § 60.35] for the crime or violation which carries the highest classification, and no other sentence to pay a mandatory surcharge or a crime victim assistance fee required by [PL § 60.35] shall be imposed.

See generally PL § 70.25(2); PL § 80.15.

Stated another way, "Penal Law § 60.35(2) . . . forbids the imposition of multiple surcharges upon the defendant's conviction of multiple crimes arising from the commission of a single act or through an act which 'in itself constituted one of the crimes and * * * also was a material element of the other.' " *People v. Tarantola*, 187 A.D.2d 546, __, 589 N.Y.S.2d 925, 926 (2d Dep't 1992). *See also People v. Wrotten*, 48 A.D.3d 296, 851 N.Y.S.2d 504 (1st Dep't 2008).

§ 47:24   Surcharge and crime victim assistance fee are paid to the Clerk of the Court

Research References
West's Key Number Digest, Sentencing and Punishment ⚖2137

Mandatory surcharges and crime victim assistance fees are paid to the clerk of the court. VTL § 1809(3); VTL § 1809-a(2); VTL § 1809-c(2); VTL § 1809-e(2); VTL § 1809-aa(2); PL § 60.35(3).

§ 47:25   Person who overpays or erroneously pays surcharge or crime victim assistance fee entitled to refund

Research References
West's Key Number Digest, Sentencing and Punishment ⚖2137

A person who overpays or erroneously pays a mandatory surcharge or crime victim assistance fee (or whose underlying conviction is reversed) is entitled to a refund of such fee(s). VTL § 1809(4); VTL § 1809-a(3); PL § 60.35(4). *See also* § 47:8, *supra*.

§ 47:26   Failure to pay VTL surcharge or crime victim assistance fee can result in scofflaw suspension of defendant's driver's license

Research References
West's Key Number Digest, Sentencing and Punishment ⚖2137

Failure to pay a VTL surcharge or crime victim assistance fee in a timely manner can result in a scofflaw suspension of the defendant's driver's license. *See* VTL § 1809(5-a); VTL § 1809-c(3); VTL § 1809-e(3).

§ 47:27 Defendant cannot be incarcerated for more than 15 days for failure to pay surcharge and/or crime victim assistance fee

Research References

West's Key Number Digest, Sentencing and Punishment ☞2137

Although, under certain circumstances, a defendant can be incarcerated for failure to pay a mandatory surcharge and/or a crime victim assistance fee, the period of incarceration cannot exceed 15 days. CPL § 420.35(1). In addition, such period of incarceration, combined with any other sentence of imprisonment imposed, cannot exceed the maximum term of imprisonment authorized for the offense of which the defendant was convicted. CPL § 420.10(4)(d). *See also People v. Espola*, 238 A.D.2d 281, __, 656 N.Y.S.2d 268, 269 (1st Dep't 1997) (abrogated on other grounds by, People v. Quinones, 95 N.Y.2d 349, 717 N.Y.S.2d 86, 740 N.E.2d 231 (2000)); *People v. Baker*, 130 A.D.2d 582, __, 515 N.Y.S.2d 297, 298 (2d Dep't 1987).

§ 47:28 Collection of surcharge/crime victim assistance fee from incarcerated defendant

Research References

West's Key Number Digest, Sentencing and Punishment ☞2137

VTL § 1809(5) provides, in pertinent part, that:

When a person who is convicted of a crime or traffic infraction and sentenced to a term of imprisonment has failed to pay the mandatory surcharge or crime victim assistance fee required by [VTL § 1809], the clerk of the court . . . that rendered the conviction shall notify the superintendent or the municipal official of the facility where the person is confined. The superintendent or the municipal official shall cause any amount owing to be collected from such person during his term of imprisonment from moneys to the credit of an inmates' fund or such moneys as may be earned by a person in a work release program pursuant to [Correction Law § 860]. * * * For purposes of this subdivision, the term "inmates' fund" shall mean moneys in the possession of an inmate at the time of his admission into such facility, funds earned by him as provided for in [Correction Law § 187] and any other funds received by him or on his behalf and deposited with such superintendent or municipal official.

PL § 60.35(5) provides similar rules for the collection of PL surcharges and crime victim assistance fees from incarcerated defendants.

§ 47:29 Court required to issue summons to defendant at sentencing regarding payment of surcharge in certain PL cases

Research References

West's Key Number Digest, Sentencing and Punishment ⚖2137

PL § 60.35(8) provides, in pertinent part, that:

[A]t the time that the mandatory surcharge . . . is imposed a town or village court may, and all other courts shall, issue and cause to be served upon the person required to pay the mandatory surcharge . . . a summons directing that such person appear before the court regarding the payment of the mandatory surcharge . . . if after [60] days from the date it was imposed it remains unpaid. The designated date of appearance on the summons shall be set for the first day court is in session falling after the [60th] day from the imposition of the mandatory surcharge . . . The summons shall contain the information required by [CPL § 130.10(2)] except that in substitution for the requirement of [CPL § 130.10(2)(c)] the summons shall state that the person served must appear at a date, time and specific location specified in the summons if after [60] days from the date of issuance the mandatory surcharge . . . remains unpaid.

The summons requirement only applies to PL surcharges—*not* to VTL surcharges. In addition, the summons requirement is permissive in town and village courts, whereas it is mandatory in all other courts. Furthermore, "[t]he court shall not issue a summons under [PL § 60.35(8)] to a person who is being sentenced to a term of confinement in excess of 60 days in jail or in the department of correctional services. The mandatory surcharges . . . for those persons shall be governed by the provisions of [PL § 60.30]." PL § 60.35(8).

In *People v. Banks*, 38 A.D.3d 938, __, 830 N.Y.S.2d 839, 841 (3d Dep't 2007), the Appellate Division, Third Department, rejected defendant's claim that a bench warrant issued for failure to pay a mandatory surcharge "was defective because Penal Law § 60.35(8) provides for the issuance of a summons if defendant fails to pay the surcharge. Defendant . . . overlooks the provisions of the CPL which allow the collection of a mandatory surcharge using the same procedures for the collection of a fine and which authorize the issuance of a warrant directing the production of defendant before the court (*see* CPL § 420.35(1); CPL § 420.10(3))."

§ 47:30 Failure to preserve objection to surcharge or crime victim assistance fee can preclude appellate review of claim

Research References

West's Key Number Digest, Sentencing and Punishment ⚖2137

Failure to preserve certain objections with respect to the imposition of a mandatory surcharge or crime victim assistance fee can lead to a waiver of the claim on appeal. *See, e.g., People v. Salmans*, 49 A.D.3d 961, __, 853 N.Y.S.2d 675, 677 (3d Dep't 2008); *People v. Prihett*, 279 A.D.2d 335, 718 N.Y.S.2d 840 (1st Dep't 2001); *People v. Dunn*, 254 A.D.2d 511, 680 N.Y.S.2d 125 (3d Dep't 1998); *People v. Teele*, 157 A.D.2d 592, 550 N.Y.S.2d 339 (1st Dep't 1990); *People v. Burt*, 142 A.D.2d 794, 531 N.Y.S.2d 131 (3d Dep't 1988); *People v. Baker*, 130 A.D.2d 582, 515 N.Y.S.2d 297 (2d Dep't 1987). *Cf. People v. Sullivan*, 6 A.D.3d 1175, 775 N.Y.S.2d 696 (4th Dep't 2004).

§ 47:31 Driver responsibility assessment

Research References

West's Key Number Digest, Sentencing and Punishment ⟜2137

Effective November 18, 2004, any person who either (a) is convicted of a violation of any subdivision of VTL § 1192, or (b) is found to have refused to submit to a chemical test in accordance with VTL § 1194, is liable to DMV for payment of a "driver responsibility assessment." VTL § 1199(1). Such driver responsibility assessment applies "[i]n addition to any fines, fees, penalties and surcharges authorized by law." VTL § 1199(1).

The amount of the driver responsibility assessment is $250 a year for three years. VTL § 1199(2). In the event that the person is both convicted of a violation of VTL § 1192 *and* found to have refused a chemical test in accordance with VTL § 1194 in connection with the same incident, only one driver responsibility assessment will be imposed. VTL § 1199(1).

When DMV receives evidence of the qualifying conviction/refusal, it will notify the person, by first class mail, at the person's address on file with DMV (or at his or her current address provided by the U.S. Postal Service), of:

1. The amount of the driver responsibility assessment;
2. The time and manner of making required payments; and
3. That the failure to make such payments will result in the suspension of his or her driver's license (or privilege of obtaining a driver's license).

VTL § 1199(3).

If the person fails to pay the driver responsibility assessment, DMV will suspend his or her driver's license (or privilege of obtaining a driver's license). VTL § 1199(4). "Such suspension shall remain in effect until any and all outstanding driver responsibility assessments have been paid in full." VTL § 1199(4).

The provisions of VTL § 1199 regarding driver responsibility assessments are also applicable to (a) any person convicted of a violation of Navigation Law § 49-a, (b) any person convicted of a violation of PRHPL § 25.24, or (c) any person found to have refused to submit to a chemical test in accordance with the applicable provisions of either the Navigation Law or the PRHPL (not arising out of the same incident). VTL § 1199(5).

§ 47:32 Court not required to advise defendant of mandatory surcharge prior to plea or at sentencing

"[T]he mandatory surcharge and crime victim assistance fee mandated by Penal Law § 60.35(1) are not a part of a sentence within the meaning of sections 380.20 and 380.40 of the CPL; therefore, a judge need not pronounce them in a defendant's presence during sentencing." *People v. Guerrero*, 12 N.Y.3d 45, 47 876 N.Y.S.2d 687, 688 (2009). *See also People v. Smith*, 57 A.D.3d 1410, __, 870 N.Y.S.2d 209, 210 (4th Dep't 2008).

"[G]iven the mandatory nature of the surcharge, a defendant need not be advised, prior to the entry of his or her plea, that it is part of the sentence." *People v. Neu*, 1 A.D.3d 798, __, 767 N.Y.S.2d 313 (3d Dep't 2003). *See also People v. Fauntleroy*, 57 A.D.3d 1167, 869 N.Y.S.2d 655 (3d Dep't 2008); *People v. Salmans*, 49 A.D.3d 961, __, 853 N.Y.S.2d 675, 677 (3d Dep't 2008); *People v. Swart*, 20 A.D.3d 691, __, 797 N.Y.S.2d 780, 781 (3d Dep't 2005).

Chapter 48

Ignition Interlock Device Program

§ 48:30   VTL § 1198 does not preclude Court from imposing
             any other permissible conditions of probation
§ 48:31   Imposition of IID requirement does not alter length of
             underlying license revocation
§ 48:32   IID requirement runs consecutively to jail sentence
§ 48:33   Applicability of IID requirement to parolees
§ 48:34   IID cannot be removed without "certificate of
             completion" or "letter of deinstallation"
§ 48:35   Constitutionality of VTL § 1198
§ 48:36   Necessity of a *Frye* hearing

KeyCite®: Cases and other legal materials listed in KeyCite Scope can be researched through the KeyCite service on Westlaw®. Use KeyCite to check citations for form, parallel references, prior and later history, and comprehensive citator information, including citations to other decisions and secondary materials.

---

§ 48:1   In general

Effective August 15, 2010, every person who is convicted of common law DWI, per se DWI, or per se Aggravated DWI (*i.e.*, VTL § 1192(2), (2-a) or (3))—committed on or after November 18, 2009—will be required to install an ignition interlock device in any vehicle that the person owns or operates (with the exception of certain employer-owned vehicles) for at least 6 months. *See* VTL § 1193(1)(b)(ii); VTL § 1193(1)(c)(iii). *See also* VTL § 1198; PL § 65.10(2)(k-1). This chapter addresses various issues associated with the ignition interlock device requirement.

§ 48:2   What is an ignition interlock device?

VTL § 119-a defines "ignition interlock device" (a.k.a. "IID") as:

Any blood alcohol concentration equivalence measuring device which connects to a motor vehicle ignition system and prevents a motor vehicle from being started without first determining through a deep lung breath sample that the operator's equivalent breath alcohol level does not exceed the calibrated setting on the device as required by [VTL § 1198].

See also 9 NYCRR § 358.3(k); 10 NYCRR § 59.1(g); 15 NYCRR § 140.1(b)(1).

An ignition interlock device is required to be calibrated to a "set point" of .025% BAC. *See* 9 NYCRR § 358.5(c)(2); 9 NYCRR § 358.5(c)(10)(i); 9 NYCRR § 358.5(d)(6); 10 NYCRR § 59.10(c)(2). The term "set point" means "a preset or predetermined BAC setting at which, or above, the device will prevent the ignition of a motor vehicle from operating." 9 NYCRR § 358.3(x).

§ 48:3 Rules and regulations regarding IIDs

The Department of Health (DOH) is required to publish a list of approved ignition interlock devices. *See* VTL § 1198(6)(a). In addition, both the Division of Probation and Correctional Alternatives (DPCA) and the DOH are required to promulgate regulations regarding ignition interlock devices. *See* VTL § 1193(1)(g); VTL § 1198(6)(b). Such regulations must require, at a minimum, that ignition interlock devices:

(1) have features that make circumventing difficult and that do not interfere with the normal or safe operation of the vehicle;

(2) work accurately and reliably in an unsupervised environment;

(3) resist tampering and give evidence if tampering is attempted;

(4) minimize inconvenience to a sober user;

(5) require a proper, deep, lung breath sample or other accurate measure of blood alcohol content equivalence;

(6) operate reliably over the range of automobile environments;

(7) correlate well with permissible levels of alcohol consumption as may be established by the sentencing court or by any provision of law; and

(8) [be] manufactured by a party covered by product liability insurance.

VTL § 1198(6)(b).

The relevant DOH regulations are contained in 10 NYCRR Part 59 (a copy of which is set forth at Appendix 3). The relevant DPCA regulations are contained in 9 NYCRR Part 358 (a copy of which is set forth at Appendix 63).

§ 48:4 Definitions

Relevant definitions pertaining to the ignition interlock device program are contained in the DPCA regulations, *see* 9 NYCRR § 358.3, and, to a lesser extent, in the DOH regulations. *See* 10 NYCRR § 59.1. In this regard, 9 NYCRR § 358.3 provides as follows:

(a) The term "blood alcohol concentration" or "BAC" shall mean the weight amount of alcohol contained in a unit volume of blood, measured as grams ethanol/100 ml. blood and expressed as %, grams %, % weight/volume (w/v), and % BAC. Blood alcohol concentration in this Part shall be designated as % BAC.

(b) The term "certificate of completion" shall mean a document issued by the monitor after the conclusion of the ignition interlock period, including any extensions or modifications as may have occurred since the date of sentence which shows either completion of the operator's sentence or a change in the conditions of probation or conditional discharge no longer requiring the need for a device.

(c) The term "circumvent" shall mean to request, solicit or allow any other person to blow into an ignition interlock device, or to start a motor vehicle equipped with the device, for the purpose of providing the operator whose driving privileges [are] so restricted with an operable motor vehicle, or to blow into an ignition interlock device or start a motor vehicle equipped with the device for the purpose of providing an operable motor vehicle to a person whose driving privilege is so restricted or to tamper with an operable ignition interlock device.

(d) The term "county" shall mean every county outside of the city of New York, and the City of New York as a whole.

(e) The term "county executive" shall mean a county administrator, county manager, county director or county president and in cities with a population of one million or more, the mayor.

(f) The term "division" shall mean the division of probation and correctional alternatives.

(g) The term "drinking driver program" shall mean an alcohol and drug rehabilitation program established pursuant to [VTL § 1196].

(h) The term "failed tasks" shall mean failure to install the ignition interlock device or failure to comply with a service visit or any requirement resulting therefrom as prescribed by this Part.

(i) The term "failed tests" shall mean a failed start-up retest, failed rolling retest, or missed rolling retest.

(j) The term "failure report recipients" shall mean all persons or entities required to receive a report from the monitor of an operator's failed tasks or failed tests pursuant to a county's plan which may include, but is not limited to[,] the sentencing court, district attorney, operator's alcohol treatment provider, and the drinking driver program, where applicable.

(k) The term "ignition interlock device" shall mean any blood alcohol concentration equivalence measuring device which connects to a motor vehicle ignition system and prevents a motor vehicle from being started without first determining through a deep lung breath sample that the operator's equivalent blood alcohol level does not exceed the calibrated setting on the device as required by standards of the [DOH].

(l) The term "installation/service provider" shall mean an entity approved by a qualified manufacturer that installs, services, and/or removes an ignition interlock device.

(m) The term "lockout mode" shall mean circumstances enumerated in this Part which trigger the ignition interlock device to cause the operator's vehicle to become inoperable if not serviced within [5] calendar days.

(n) The term "monitor" shall mean the local probation department where the operator is under probation supervision or any person(s) or entity(ies) designated in the county's ignition interlock program plan for any operator granted conditional discharge.

(o) The term "operator" shall mean a person who is subject to installation of an ignition interlock device following a conviction of a violation of [VTL § 1192(2), (2-a) or (3),] or any crime defined by the Vehicle and Traffic Law or Penal Law of which an alcohol-related violation of any provision of [VTL § 1192] is an essential element.

(p) The term "qualified manufacturer" shall mean a manufacturer or distributor of an ignition interlock device certified by the [DOH] which has satisfied the specific operational requirements herein and has been approved as an eligible vendor by the [DPCA] in the designated region where the county is located.

(q) The term "region" shall mean counties comprising an area within New York State designated by the [DPCA] where a qualified manufacturer is authorized and has agreed to service.

(r) The term "start-up test" shall mean a breath test taken by the operator to measure the operator's blood alcohol concentration prior to starting the vehicle's ignition.

(s) The term "start-up retest" shall mean a breath test taken by the operator to measure the operator's blood alcohol concentration required within [5] to [15] minutes of a failed start-up test.

(t) The term "rolling test" shall mean a breath test, administered at random intervals, taken by the operator while the vehicle is running.

(u) The term "rolling retest" shall mean a breath test, taken by the operator while the vehicle is running, within [1] to [3] minutes after a failed or missed rolling test.

(1) The term "failed rolling retest" shall mean a rolling retest in which the operator's BAC is at or above the set point.

(2) The term "missed rolling retest" shall mean failure to take the rolling retest within the time period allotted to do so.

(v) The term "service period" shall mean the length of time between service visits.

(w) The term "service visit" shall mean a visit by the operator to[,] or with[,] the installation/service provider for purposes of having the ignition interlock device inspected, monitored, downloaded, recalibrated, or maintained. It shall also mean[,] where applicable, the act by any operator of sending the portion of the interlock device that contains the data log and the breath testing module to the qualified manufacturer for the purposes of downloading the data, reporting to the monitor, and recalibrating the device.

(x) The term "set point" shall mean a preset or predetermined BAC setting at which, or above, the device will prevent the ignition of a motor vehicle from operating.

(y) The term "STOP-DWI" shall mean special traffic options program-driving while intoxicated.

(z) The term "tamper" shall mean to alter, disconnect, physically disable, remove, deface, or destroy an ignition interlock device or any of its component seals in any way not authorized by this Part.

§ 48:5 Scope of IID program

VTL § 1198(1) provides as follows:

Applicability. The provisions of this section shall apply throughout the state to each person required or otherwise ordered by a court as a condition of probation or conditional discharge to install and operate an ignition interlock device in any vehicle which he or she owns or operates.

See also 9 NYCRR § 358.2.

§ 48:6 Who must be required to install and maintain an IID?

Effective August 15, 2010, literally everyone who is convicted of an alcohol-related misdemeanor or felony DWI, or any other crime in either the VTL or the Penal Law of which an alcohol-related violation of VTL § 1192 is an essential element, is required to install and maintain an IID. In this regard, VTL § 1198(2)(a) provides:

In addition to any other penalties prescribed by law, the court shall require that any person who has been convicted of a violation of [VTL § 1192(2), (2-a) or (3)], or any crime defined by this chapter or the penal law of which an alcohol-related violation of any provision of [VTL § 1192] is an essential element, to install and maintain, as a condition of probation or conditional discharge, a functioning ignition interlock device in accordance with the provisions of this section and, as applicable, in accordance with the provisions of [VTL § 1193(1) and (1-a)]; provided, however, the court may not authorize the operation of a motor vehicle by any person whose license or privilege to operate a motor vehicle has been revoked except as provided herein. For any such individual subject to a sentence of probation, installation and maintenance of such ignition interlock device shall be a condition of probation.

In addition, prior to November 1, 2013, VTL § 1193(1)(b)(ii) provided:

In addition to the imposition of any fine or period of imprisonment set forth in this paragraph, the court shall also sentence such person convicted of a violation of [VTL § 1192(2), (2-a) or (3)] to a period of probation or conditional discharge, as a condition of which it shall order such person to install and maintain, in accordance with the provisions of [VTL § 1198], an ignition interlock device in any motor vehicle owned or operated by such person during the term of such probation or conditional discharge imposed for such violation of [VTL § 1192] and in no event for less than [6] months.

Notably, the IID requirement only applied where the defendant was "convicted" of certain DWI offenses. As such, it did not apply to youthful offender adjudications (as such adjudications are not "convictions"). *See* CPL § 720.10.

VTL § 1193(1)(b)(ii) also provided that the duration of a mandatory IID requirement was "during the term of such probation or conditional discharge imposed for such violation of [VTL § 1192] and in no event for a period of less than six months." This language led to considerable confusion in that many people who thought that they had received a six-month IID requirement—and many Judges who thought that they had imposed a six-month IID requirement—were confronted with a situation in which the installer would not remove the IID without a Court order on the ground that the sentence was for *a minimum of* six months as opposed to for *precisely* six months. In addition, defendants who installed the IID prior to sentencing were not given credit for "time served."

The Legislature addressed both of these issues in 2013. In this regard, effective November 1, 2013, VTL § 1193(1)(b)(ii) now provides as follows:

In addition to the imposition of any fine or period of imprisonment set forth in this paragraph, the court shall also sentence such person convicted of, *or adjudicated a youthful offender for*, a violation of [VTL § 1192(2), (2-a) or (3)] to a term of probation or conditional discharge, as a condition of which it shall order such person to install and maintain, in accordance with the provisions of [VTL § 1198], an ignition interlock device in any motor vehicle owned or operated by such person during the term of such probation or conditional discharge imposed for such violation of [VTL § 1192] *and in no event for a period of less than [12] months; provided, however, that such period of interlock restriction shall terminate upon submission of proof that such person installed and maintained an ignition interlock device for at least [6] months, unless the court ordered such person to install and maintain an igni-*

tion interlock device for a longer period as authorized by this subparagraph and specified in such order. The period of interlock restriction shall commence from the earlier of the date of sentencing, or the date that an ignition interlock device was installed in advance of sentencing. Provided, however, the court may not authorize the operation of a motor vehicle by any person whose license or privilege to operate a motor vehicle has been revoked pursuant to the provisions of this section.

(Emphases added).

Similar changes were made to VTL § 1193(1)(c)(iii). Prior to November 1, 2013, VTL § 1193(1)(c)(iii) provided:

In addition to the imposition of any fine or period of imprisonment set forth in this paragraph, the court shall also sentence such person convicted of a violation of [VTL § 1192(2), (2-a) or (3)] to a period of probation or conditional discharge, as a condition of which it shall order such person to install and maintain, in accordance with the provisions of [VTL § 1198], an ignition interlock device in any motor vehicle owned or operated by such person during the term of such probation or conditional discharge imposed for such violation of [VTL § 1192] and in no event for a period of less than [6] months.

Effective November 1, 2013, this section provides:

In addition to the imposition of any fine or period of imprisonment set forth in this paragraph, the court shall also sentence such person convicted of, or adjudicated a youthful offender for, a violation of [VTL § 1192(2), (2-a) or (3)] to a period of probation or conditional discharge, as a condition of which it shall order such person to install and maintain, in accordance with the provisions of [VTL § 1198], an ignition interlock device in any motor vehicle owned or operated by such person during the term of such probation or conditional discharge imposed for such violation of [VTL § 1192] and in no event for a period of less than [12] months; provided, however, that such period of interlock restriction shall terminate upon submission of proof that such person installed and maintained an ignition interlock device for at least [6] months, unless the court ordered such person to install and maintain a[n] ignition interlock device for a longer period as authorized by this subparagraph and specified in such order. The period of interlock restriction shall commence from the earlier of the date of sentencing, or the date that an ignition interlock device was installed in advance of sentencing. Provided, however, the court may not authorize the operation of a motor vehicle by any person whose license or privilege to operate a motor vehicle has been revoked pursuant to the provisions of this section.

See People v. Nunez, 119 A.D.3d 1373, ___, 988 N.Y.S.2d 396, 397 (4th Dep't 2014).

In People v. Vidaurrazaga, 100 A.D.3d 664, 953 N.Y.S.2d 290

(2d Dep't 2012), the Appellate Division, Second Department, made clear that sentencing Courts have discretion in determining how long the IID requirement will remain in effect (*i.e.*, the IID requirement must remain in effect anywhere from a minimum of six months to a maximum of the duration of the period of probation or conditional discharge), and held that:

> Based on the record before us, it is not clear whether the Supreme Court was aware that it had discretion in fixing the duration of the condition requiring the defendant to install and maintain an ignition interlock device in his automobile. We therefore remit the matter to the Supreme Court, Nassau County, for resentencing. We express no opinion as to the appropriate duration of the condition.

Id. at ___, 953 N.Y.S.2d at 293 (citations omitted).

Pursuant to VTL § 1193(1-a), where a defendant is convicted of DWI in violation of VTL § 1192(2) or (3) after having been previously convicted of DWI in violation of VTL § 1192(2) or (3) within the preceding five years, the sentencing Court must, inter alia:

> [O]rder the installation of an ignition interlock device approved pursuant to [VTL § 1198] in any motor vehicle owned or operated by the person so sentenced. Such devices shall remain installed during any period of license revocation required to be imposed pursuant to [VTL § 1193(2)(b)], and, upon the termination of such revocation period, for an additional period as determined by the court.

VTL § 1193(1-a)(c)(i).

Moreover, "[a]ny person ordered to install an ignition interlock device pursuant to [VTL § 1193(1-a)(c)] shall be subject to the provisions of [VTL § 1198(4), (5), (7), (8) and (9)]." VTL § 1193(1-a)(c).

§ 48:7 Who may not be required to install and maintain an IID?

The IID program only applies to people who have been convicted of a violation of VTL § 1192(2), (2-a) or (3), or any other crime in either the VTL or the Penal Law of which an alcohol-related violation of VTL § 1192 is an essential element. *See* PL § 65.10(2)(k-1) ("The court may require [the IID] condition only where a person has been convicted of a violation of [VTL § 1192(2), (2-a) or (3)], or any crime defined by the [VTL] or this chapter of which an alcohol-related violation of any provision of [VTL § 1192] is an essential element"). *See also* VTL § 1198(2)(a); VTL § 1198(3)(d); 9 NYCRR § 358.1; 15 NYCRR § 140.2.

Thus, a defendant who has been convicted of DWAI in violation of VTL § 1192(1), DWAI Drugs in violation of VTL § 1192(4), or DWAI Combined Influence in violation of VTL § 1192(4-a), cannot be ordered to install and maintain an IID. *See People v. Levy*, 91 A.D.3d 793, __, 938 N.Y.S.2d 315, 316 (2d Dep't 2012), leave to appeal denied, 18 N.Y.3d 995, 945 N.Y.S.2d 650, 968 N.E.2d 1006 (2012) ("We agree with the defendant that the County Court improperly directed, as a condition of probation, that the defendant install an ignition interlock device on her motor vehicle. . . . Here, the defendant's conviction for operating a motor vehicle while under the influence of drugs pursuant to Vehicle and Traffic Law § 1192(4) falls outside the scope of Penal Law § 65.10(2)(k-1)."). *See also* VTL § 1198(2)(c) ("Nothing contained in [VTL § 1198] shall authorize a court to sentence any person to a period of probation or conditional discharge for the purpose of subjecting such person to the provisions of [VTL § 1198], unless such person would have otherwise been so eligible for a sentence of probation or conditional discharge").

In *People v. Uribe*, 109 A.D.3d 844, __, 971 N.Y.S.2d 60, 60 (2d Dep't 2013), leave to appeal denied, 23 N.Y.3d 969, 988 N.Y.S.2d 576, 11 N.E.3d 726 (2014), the same Court that decided *Levy, supra*, summarily stated (without explanation) that "[t]he County Court correctly imposed an interlock ignition [sic] requirement as an element of the defendant's sentence (*see* [VTL] §§ 1192[4-a], 1198[2])." However, since a person can violate VTL § 1192(4-a) without consuming alcohol—and thus the consumption of alcohol is not an essential element of a VTL § 1192(4-a) charge—it would appear that VTL § 1198(2) does not authorize the imposition of an IID in VTL § 1192(4-a) cases. *See also* Penal Law § 65.10(2)(k-1) ("The court may require [the IID] condition only where a person has been convicted of a violation of [VTL § 1192(2), (2-a) or (3)], or any crime defined by the [VTL] or this chapter of which an alcohol-related violation of any provision of [VTL § 1192] is an essential element"). *See generally* Penal Law § 60.21 (which is only applicable to VTL §§ 1192(2), (2-a), or (3)).

§ 48:8   Cost, installation and maintenance of IID

The cost of installing and maintaining the ignition interlock device is the responsibility of the defendant:

> [U]nless the court determines such person is financially unable to afford such cost whereupon such cost may be imposed pursuant to a payment plan or waived. In the event of such waiver, the cost of the device shall be borne in accordance with regulations issued under [VTL § 1193(1)(g)] or pursuant to such other agreement as may be entered into for provision of the device.

VTL § 1198(5)(a). *See also* 9 NYCRR § 358.8(a).

In this regard, every qualified IID manufacturer must:

> [A]gree to adhere to a maximum fee/charge schedule with respect to

all operator's costs associated with such devices, offer a payment plan for any operator determined to be financially unable to pay the cost of the ignition interlock device where a payment plan is so ordered, and provide a device free of fee/charge to the operator where the cost is waived by the sentencing court, or pursuant to such other agreement as may be entered into for provision of the device. Any contractual agreement between the operator and the qualified manufacturer or its installation/service providers shall permit an early termination without penalty to the operator when a certificate of completion has been issued, where the sentence has been revoked, and whenever the operator has been transferred to a jurisdiction where the manufacturer does not do business. Nothing shall prevent a qualified manufacturer from lowering the fee/charge schedule during the course of an operator's contract and/or the contractual agreement with the [DPCA].

9 NYCRR § 358.5(c)(3).

Although the cost of an IID is considered a fine for purposes of CPL § 420.10(5), it does not replace, but rather is in addition to, any fines, surcharges or other costs imposed by law. *See* VTL § 1198(5)(a).

The installer/service provider of the ignition interlock device is responsible for the installation, calibration and maintenance of such device. *See* VTL § 1198(5)(b).

§ 48:9   IID installer must provide defendant with fee schedule

An ignition interlock device installer must:

[P]rovide to all operators, at the time of device installation a hardcopy statement of fees/charges clearly specifying warranty details, schedule of lease payments where applicable, any additional costs anticipated for routine recalibration, service visits, and shipping where the device includes the direct exchange method of servicing, and listing any items available without charge if any, along with a list of installation/service providers in their respective county, a toll-free 24 hour telephone number to be called from anywhere in the continental United States to secure up-to-date information as to all installation/service providers located anywhere in the continental United States and for emergency assistance, and a technical support number available during specified business hours to reach a trained staff person to answer questions and to respond to mechanical concerns associated with the ignition interlock device.

9 NYCRR § 358.5(d)(2).

§ 48:10   What if defendant is unable to afford cost of IID?

As is noted in the previous section, the cost of installing and maintaining the ignition interlock device is the responsibility of the defendant "unless the court determines such person is financially unable to afford such cost whereupon such cost may be imposed pursuant to a payment plan or waived." VTL § 1198(5)(a). *See also* 9 NYCRR § 358.5(c)(3); 9 NYCRR § 358.8(a). In this regard, the DPCA has promulgated a form entitled "Financial Disclosure Report" to be used in determining a person's ability to afford the cost of an IID. This form (a copy of which is set forth at Appendix 64) only has to be completed by people seeking a payment plan or a full waiver of the costs of an IID.

Where the defendant claims an inability to afford the costs of an IID, 9 NYCRR § 358.8(b) provides that:

> Any operator who claims financial inability to pay for the device shall submit in advance of sentencing [3] copies of his or her financial disclosure report, on a form prescribed by the [DPCA], to the sentencing court[,] which shall distribute copies to the district attorney and defense counsel. The report shall enumerate factors which may be considered by the sentencing court with respect to financial inability of the operator to pay for the device and shall include, but not be limited to[,] income from all sources, assets, and expenses. This report shall be made available to assist the court in determining whether or not the operator is financially able to afford the cost of the ignition interlock device, and[,] if not[,] whether to impose a payment plan. Where it is determined that a payment plan is not feasible, the court shall determine whether the fee/charge for the device shall be waived.

9 NYCRR § 358.4(d)(3) addresses the issue of how IID manufacturers should divide the costs of providing IIDs to indigent defendants:

> [I]n the event more than one qualified manufacturer does business within its region, the county shall establish an equitable procedure for manufacturers to provide ignition interlock devices without costs where an operator has been determined financially unable to afford the costs and has received a waiver from the sentencing court. The equitable procedure should be based upon proportion of ignition interlock devices paid to each qualified manufacturer by operators in the county.

§ 48:11   Notification of IID requirement

Where a Court imposes the IID condition upon a defendant, the Court must notify DMV of such condition. *See* VTL § 1198(4)(b). In addition, every County must:

> [E]stablish a procedure whereby the probation department and any other monitor will be notified no later than [5] business days from the date an ignition interlock condition is imposed by the sentencing court, any waiver of the cost of the device granted by the sentencing court, and of any intrastate transfer of probation or interstate transfer of any case which either has responsibility to monitor. Such procedure shall also establish a mechanism for advance notification as to date of release where local or state imprisonment is imposed.

9 NYCRR § 358.4(d)(5). *See also* 9 NYCRR § 358.7(a)(1).

Furthermore, IID installers must "notify the monitor and county probation department when an ignition interlock device has been installed on an operator's vehicle(s) within [3] business days of installation." 9 NYCRR § 358.5(d)(16).

§ 48:12 Defendant must install IID within 10 business days of sentencing

Every defendant sentenced to the IID requirement must:

[H]ave installed and maintain a functioning ignition interlock device in any vehicle(s) he or she owns or operates within [10] business days of the condition being imposed by the court or[,] if sentenced to imprisonment[,] upon release from imprisonment, whichever is applicable.

9 NYCRR § 358.7(c)(1).

In this regard, IID installers are required to install an IID within 7 business days of a defendant's request that the device be installed. *See* 9 NYCRR § 358.5(d)(1). Notably, where the defendant's vehicle needs repairs before installation can take place, the seven-day installation period commences when such repairs are completed. *See* 9 NYCRR § 358.5(d)(12).

§ 48:13 Defendant must provide proof of compliance with IID requirement within three business days of installation

Every defendant who has an IID installed must, "within [3] business days of installation, submit proof of installation to the court, county probation department, and any other designated monitor." 9 NYCRR § 358.7(c)(1). *See also* VTL § 1198(4)(a). If the defendant fails to provide proof of installation, the Court may, absent a finding of good cause for the failure which is placed in the record, revoke, modify or terminate the defendant's sentence of probation or conditional discharge. *See* VTL § 1198(4)(a).

An issue had arisen as to how to handle situations in which the defendant failed to install an IID due to the fact that the defendant did not own—and claimed that he or she would not operate—a motor vehicle during the duration of the IID requirement. In this regard, effective November 1, 2013, VTL § 1198(4)(a) defines "good cause" for not installing an IID as follows:

Good cause may include a finding that the person is not the owner of a motor vehicle if such person asserts under oath that such person is not the owner of any motor vehicle and that he or she will not operate any motor vehicle during the period of interlock restriction except as may be otherwise authorized pursuant to law. "Owner" shall have the same meaning as provided in [VTL § 128].

§ 48:14 DMV will note IID condition on defendant's driving record

Where a Court notifies DMV that it has imposed the IID condition upon a defendant, DMV must note such condition on the defendant's driving record. VTL § 1198(4)(b). *See also* VTL § 1198(3)(f).

§ 48:15 How often does defendant have to blow into IID?

The operator of a vehicle equipped with an ignition interlock device is not merely required to blow into the device to start the vehicle. Rather:

> [T]he operator after passing the start-up test allowing the engine to start, [must] submit to an initial rolling test within a randomly variable interval ranging from [5] to [15] minutes. Subsequent rolling tests shall continue to be required at random intervals not to exceed [30] minutes for the duration of the travel. A start-up retest shall be required within [5] to [15] minutes of a failed start-up test. A rolling retest shall be required within [1] to [3] minutes after a failed or missed rolling test.

9 NYCRR § 358.5(c)(2).

§ 48:16 Lockout mode

When an ignition interlock device goes into "lockout mode," it causes the operator's vehicle to become inoperable if not serviced within five calendar days. *See* 9 NYCRR § 358.3(m). "An ignition interlock device shall enter into a lockout mode upon the following events: [1] failed start-up retest, [1] missed start-up retest, [1] failed rolling retest or [1] missed rolling retest within a service period, or [1] missed service visit." 9 NYCRR § 358.5(c)(2).

§ 48:17 Circumvention of IID

It is a class A misdemeanor:

(a) for a defendant subject to the ignition interlock device requirement to request, solicit or allow any other person to either: (i) blow into an ignition interlock device, or (ii) start a motor vehicle equipped with an ignition interlock device, for the purpose of providing the defendant with an operable motor vehicle;

(b) for a person to either (i) blow into an ignition interlock device, or (ii) start a motor vehicle equipped with an ignition interlock device, for the purpose of providing a person sentenced to the ignition interlock device requirement with an operable motor vehicle;

(c) to tamper with or circumvent an otherwise operable ignition interlock device; and/or

(d) for a defendant subject to the ignition interlock device requirement to operate a motor vehicle without such device.
VTL § 1198(9)(a)–(e).

Every ignition interlock device is required to have a label affixed to it "warning that any person tampering, circumventing, or otherwise misusing the device is guilty of a misdemeanor and may be subject to civil liability." VTL § 1198(10). *See also* 10 NYCRR § 59.12(f).

§ 48:18 Duty of IID monitor to report defendant to Court and District Attorney

9 NYCRR § 358.7(d)(1) provides, in pertinent part, that:

Upon learning of the following events:

(i) that the operator has failed to have installed the ignition interlock device on his/her own vehicle(s) or vehicle(s) which he/she operates;

(ii) that the operator has not complied with service visits requirements;

(iii) a report of alleged tampering with or circumventing an ignition interlock device or an attempt thereof;

(iv) a report of a failed start-up retest;

(v) a report of a missed start-up retest;

(vi) a report of a failed rolling retest;

(vii) a report of a missed rolling retest; and/or

(viii) a report of a lockout mode;

the applicable monitor shall take appropriate action consistent with public safety. Where under probation supervision, the county probation department shall adhere to Part 352. With respect to any operator sentenced to conditional discharge, the monitor shall take action in accordance with the provisions of its county ignition interlock program plan.

In this regard:

At a minimum, any monitor shall notify the appropriate court and district attorney, within [3] business days, where an operator has failed to have installed the ignition interlock device on his/her own vehicle(s) or vehicle(s) which he/she operates, where the operator has not complied with a service visit requirement, any report of alleged tampering with or circumventing an ignition interlock device or an attempt thereof, any report of a lock-out mode, and/or any report of a failed test or retest where the BAC is .05 percent or higher.

9 NYCRR § 358.7(d)(1) (emphasis added).

As part of its report to the Court and District Attorney:

The monitor may recommend modification of the operator's condition of his or her sentence or release whichever is applicable as otherwise authorized by law, including extension of his/her ignition interlock period, a requirement that the operator attend alcohol and substance abuse treatment and/or drinking driver program, referral to [DMV] to determine whether [DMV] may suspend or revoke the operator's license, or recommend revocation of his/her sentence or release.

9 NYCRR § 358.7(d)(2).

"Where the operator is under supervision by the division of parole, the monitor shall coordinate monitoring with the division of parole and promptly provide the parole agency with reports of any failed tasks or failed tests." 9 NYCRR § 358.7(d)(3).

§ 48:19 Use of leased, rented or loaned vehicles

Where a defendant is subjected to the ignition interlock device requirement, such requirement applies to every motor vehicle operated by the defendant including, but not limited to, vehicles that are leased, rented or loaned. *See* VTL § 1198(7)(a). In this regard, a defendant who is sentenced to the ignition interlock device requirement must "notify any other person who rents, leases or loans a motor vehicle to him or her of such driving restriction." VTL § 1198(7)(b).

A violation of VTL § 1198(7)(a) or (b) is a misdemeanor. *See* VTL § 1198(7)(c). It is also a misdemeanor for a person to knowingly rent, lease or lend a motor vehicle to a person known to be subject to the ignition interlock device requirement unless such vehicle is equipped with an IID. *See* VTL § 1198(7)(b), (c).

§ 48:20 Use of employer-owned vehicles

Where a defendant who is sentenced to the ignition interlock device requirement is required to operate a motor vehicle owned by the defendant's employer for work-related purposes, the defendant is allowed to operate such vehicle without an ignition interlock device under the following conditions:

1. Only in the course and scope of the defendant's employment;
2. Only if the employer has been notified that the defendant is subject to the ignition interlock device requirement;
3. Only if the defendant has provided the Court and the Probation Department with written proof indicating that the defendant's employer is aware of the ignition interlock device requirement and has granted the defendant permission to operate the employer's vehicle without an ignition interlock device only for business purposes; and
4. The defendant has notified the Court and the Probation

Department of his or her intention to so operate the employer's vehicle.

VTL § 1198(8). *See also* 15 NYCRR § 140.5(c); 9 NYCRR § 358.7(c)(5).

A motor vehicle owned by a business entity that is wholly or partly owned or controlled by a defendant subject to the ignition interlock device requirement does not qualify for the "employer vehicle exemption." *See* VTL § 1198(8); 15 NYCRR § 140.5(c); 9 NYCRR § 358.7(c)(5).

§ 48:21 Preinstallation requirements

Prior to installing an IID, an installer must "obtain and record the following information from every operator":

(i) photo identification;

(ii) the name and policy number of his/her automobile insurance;

(iii) the vehicle identification number (VIN) of all motor vehicles owned or routinely driven by the operator, and a statement disclosing the names of all other individuals who operate the motor vehicle(s) owned or driven by the operator; and

(iv) a notarized affidavit from the registered owner of the vehicle granting permission to install the device if the vehicle is not registered to the operator.

9 NYCRR § 358.5(d)(13). *See also* 9 NYCRR § 358.7(c)(3).

§ 48:22 Mandatory service visit intervals

Every defendant sentenced to the IID requirement must:

[S]ubmit to service visits within [30] calendar days of prior installation or service visits for the collection of data from the ignition interlock device and/or for inspection, maintenance, and recalibration purposes where the device does not automatically transmit data directly to the monitor; and submit to an initial service visit within [30] calendar days of installation and service visits within [60] calendar days of prior service visits where the device either automatically transmits data directly to the monitor for inspection, maintenance, or recalibration purposes or the device head is sent to the qualified manufacturer every [30] calendar days for such purposes, including data download.

9 NYCRR § 358.7(c)(2).

§ 48:23 Accessibility of IID providers

A qualified ignition interlock device manufacturer must:

[A]gree to service every county within [its] region and ensure that there shall be an installation/service provider within 50 miles from the operator's residence or location where the vehicle is parked or

garaged, whichever is closest[,] and ensure repair or replacement of
a defective ignition interlock device shall be made available within
the same 50 mile radius by a fixed or mobile installation/service
provider, or through a qualified manufacturer sending a replacement, within 48 hours of receipt of a complaint, or within 72 hours
where an intervening weekend or holiday. Mobile servicing may be
permissible provided that the above facility requirements are met
and a specific mobile servicing unit with regular hours is indicated.

9 NYCRR § 358.5(c)(4).

§ 48:24 Frequency of reporting by IID providers

A qualified ignition interlock device manufacturer must:

[G]uarantee that an installation/service provider or the manufacturer shall download the usage history of every operator's ignition
interlock device within [30] calendar days between service visits or
if the operator fails to appear for a service visit(s) as soon thereafter as the device can be downloaded, and provide the monitor with
such information and in such format as determined by the [DPCA].

9 NYCRR § 358.5(c)(5).

In addition, the manufacturer must:

Further guarantee that the installation/service provider shall take
appropriate, reasonable and necessary steps to confirm any report
of failed tasks, failed tests, circumvention, or tampering and thereafter notify the appropriate monitor within [3] business days of
knowledge or receipt of data, indicating:

(i) installation of a device on an operator's vehicle(s);

(ii) report of a failed start-up retest;

(iii) report of a missed start-up retest;

(iv) report of a failed rolling retest;

(v) report of a missed rolling retest;

(vi) report of the device entering lockout mode;

(vii) failure of an operator to appear at a scheduled service visit;
or

(viii) report of an alleged circumvention or tampering with the
ignition interlock devices as prohibited by [VTL § 1198(9)(a), (c)
or (d)], or an attempt thereof.

9 NYCRR § 358.7(d)(1).

§ 48:25 Defendant entitled to report of his/her IID usage
history

An ignition interlock device manufacturer must:

[P]rovide, no more than monthly to the operator upon his or her
request, the operator's usage history, including any report of failed
tasks, failed tests, circumvention, or tampering. An operator may

only make [1] request during any month for such information. Such request shall be in writing and provide either an email address or self-addressed stamped envelope.

9 NYCRR § 358.5(c)(6).

§ 48:26 IID providers must safeguard personal information

A qualified ignition interlock device manufacturer must:

[A]gree to safeguard personal information with respect to any operator and any reports and provide access to such records only as authorized herein, by law, or by court order. All records maintained by the manufacturer and any of its installation/service providers with respect to ignition interlock devices in New York State shall be retained in accordance with section 358.9.

9 NYCRR § 358.5(c)(7). *See also* 9 NYCRR § 358.5(c)(10)(vii).

Any monitor may disseminate relevant case records, including failed tasks or failed reports not otherwise sealed or specifically restricted in terms of access by state or federal law[,] to appropriate law enforcement authorities, district attorney, treatment agencies, licensed or certified treatment providers, the judiciary, for law enforcement and/or case management purposes relating to criminal investigations and/or execution of warrants, supervision and/or monitoring of ignition interlock conditions, and treatment and/or counseling. Personal information in any financial disclosure report shall only be accessible to the monitor, court, and district attorney for purposes related to determination of financial affordability. Case record information is not to be used for noncriminal justice purposes and shall otherwise only be available pursuant to a court order. In all such instances, those to whom access has been granted shall not secondarily disclose such information without the express written permission of the monitor that authorized access.

9 NYCRR § 358.7(e).

§ 48:27 Postrevocation conditional license

When the ignition interlock device program first came into effect, it had limited applicability. For example, the program only applied to defendants who were placed on probation for DWI, and thus it generally only applied to recidivist drunk drivers. *See generally People v. Letterlough*, 86 N.Y.2d 259, 268-69, 631 N.Y.S.2d 105, 110, 655 N.E.2d 146 (1995). Such defendants generally were either ineligible for, and/or were in any event prohibited from obtaining, a regular conditional license during the mandatory license revocation period. However, DMV was authorized to grant such defendants a "postrevocation conditional license" for use during the remainder of the term of probation. *See* VTL § 1198(3)(a).

Now that literally everyone who is convicted of an alcohol-

related misdemeanor or felony DWI, or any other crime in either
the VTL or the Penal Law of which an alcohol-related violation of
VTL § 1192 is an essential element, will be required to obtain an
ignition interlock device—regardless of whether they are on
probation and regardless of whether they are repeat offenders—
the concept of the postrevocation conditional license has become
outdated. In this regard, DMV's position is that, for purposes of
determining eligibility for a conditional license, it will treat a
defendant subject to the IID requirement the same as it would
have treated him/her prior to August 15, 2010. *See* §§ 50:1 et
seq., *infra*. In other words, defendants who would be eligible for a
conditional license if they were not subject to the IID requirement (*e.g.*, most first offenders) will still be eligible for a
conditional license after August 15, 2010, notwithstanding the
language of VTL § 1198(3)(a).

To the extent that a "postrevocation conditional license" is still
a relevant concept, such a license is akin to a regular conditional
license. It allows the defendant to drive:

(1) enroute to and from the holder's place of employment,

(2) if the holder's employment requires the operation of a
motor vehicle then during the hours thereof,

(3) enroute to and from a class or course at an accredited
school, college or university or at a state approved institution
of vocational or technical training,

(4) to and from court ordered probation activities,

(5) to and from [DMV] for the transaction of business relating to such license,

(6) for a [3] hour consecutive daytime period, chosen by
[DMV], on a day during which the participant is not engaged
in usual employment or vocation,

(7) enroute to and from a medical examination or treatment
as part of a necessary medical treatment for such participant
or member of the participant's household, as evidenced by a
written statement to that effect from a licensed medical practitioner,

(8) enroute to and from a class or an activity which is an authorized part of the alcohol and drug rehabilitation program
and at which participant's attendance is required, and

(9) enroute to and from a place, including a school, at which
a child or children of the participant are cared for on a regular
basis and which is necessary for the participant to maintain
such participant's employment or enrollment at an accredited
school, college or university or at a state approved institution
of vocational or technical training.

VTL § 1198(3)(b). *See also* 15 NYCRR § 140.5(b).

A person is ineligible for a postrevocation conditional license if he or she has either (a) "been found by a court to have committed a violation of [VTL § 511] during the license revocation period," VTL § 1198(3)(a), or (b) been "deemed by a court to have violated any condition of probation set forth by the court relating to the operation of a motor vehicle or the consumption of alcohol." VTL § 1198(3)(b). *See also* 15 NYCRR § 140.4(a).

DMV cannot deny an application for a postrevocation conditional license "based solely upon the number of convictions for violations of any subdivision of [VTL § 1192] committed by such person within the [10] years prior to application for such license." VTL § 1198(3)(a). *See also* 15 NYCRR § 140.4(b). By contrast:

> A postrevocation conditional license shall be denied to any person if a review of such person's driving record, or additional information secured by [DMV], indicates that any of the following conditions apply:
>
> (1) The person has been convicted of homicide, assault, criminal negligence or criminally negligent homicide arising out of the operation of a motor vehicle.
>
> (2) The conviction upon which eligibility is based involved a fatal accident.
>
> (3) The person has been convicted more than once of reckless driving within the last [3] years.
>
> (4) The person has had a series of convictions, incidents and/or accidents or has a medical or mental condition, which in the judgment of [DMV] tends to establish that the person would be an unusual and immediate risk upon the highway.
>
> (5) The person has been penalized under section [VTL § 1193(1)(d)(1)] for any violation of [VTL § 1192(2), (2-a), (3), (4) or (4-a)].
>
> (6) The person has had a postrevocation conditional license within the last [5] years.
>
> (7) The person has other open suspension or revocation orders on their record, other than for a violation of [VTL § 1192(1), (2), (2-a), (3), (4) or (4-a)].
>
> (8) The person has [2] convictions of a violation of [VTL § 1192(3), (4) or (4-a)] where physical injury has resulted in both instances.
>
> (9) The person has been convicted of an offense arising from the same event which resulted in the current alcohol-related conviction, which conviction, aside from the alcohol-related conviction,

resulted in the mandatory revocation of the person's license for leaving the scene of an accident involving personal injury or death.

(10) The person has had [2] or more revocations and/or suspensions of his driver's license, other than the revocation or suspension upon which his eligibility for the rehabilitation program is based[,] within the last [3] years. This subdivision shall not apply to suspensions which have been terminated by performance of an act by the person, nor to a suspension or revocation resulting from a chemical test refusal, if the person had been convicted of a violation of [VTL § 1192] arising out of the same incident.

(11) The person was the holder of a limited DJ or limited MJ license at the time of the violation which resulted in the revocation.

15 NYCRR § 140.4(c).

A postrevocation conditional license may be revoked by DMV for "sufficient cause," including, but not limited to, "failure to comply with the terms of the condition[s] of probation or conditional discharge set forth by the court, conviction of any traffic offense other than one involving parking, stopping or standing[,] or conviction of any alcohol or drug related offense, misdemeanor or felony[,] or failure to install or maintain a court ordered ignition interlock device." VTL § 1198(3)(c). *See also* 15 NYCRR § 140.5(d).

"Upon the termination of the period of probation or conditional discharge set by the court, the person may apply to [DMV] for restoration of a license or privilege to operate a motor vehicle in accordance with this chapter." VTL § 1198(3)(a). In this regard, 15 NYCRR § 136.10 provides that:

Upon the termination of the period of probation set by the court, the holder of a postrevocation conditional license may apply to the commissioner for restoration of a license or privilege to operate a motor vehicle. An application for licensure shall be approved if the applicant demonstrates that he or she:

(a) has a valid postrevocation conditional license; and

(b) has demonstrated evidence of rehabilitation as required by this Part.

§ 48:28 Intrastate transfer of probation/conditional discharge involving IID requirement

9 NYCRR § 358.7(b) addresses the situation where a defendant subject to the ignition interlock device requirement either (a) resides in another County at the time of sentencing, or (b) desires to move to another County subsequent to sentencing. Where the defendant is on probation:

Where the operator is under probation supervision and resides in another county at the time of sentencing or subsequently desires to reside in another county, upon intrastate transfer of probation, the receiving county probation department selects the specific class and features of the ignition interlock device available from a qualified manufacturer in its region. Thereafter, the operator may select the model of the ignition interlock device meeting the specific class and features selected by the receiving county probation department from a qualified manufacturer in the operator's region of residence. Where intrastate transfer occurs after sentencing and the installation of a different device is required as a result of the transfer, the device shall be installed within [10] business days of relocation. All intrastate transfer of probation shall be in accordance with Part 349.

9 NYCRR § 358.7(b)(1).

Where the defendant is subject to a conditional discharge:

Where an operator has received a sentence of conditional discharge and resides in another county at the time of sentencing or thereafter, the receiving county monitor shall select the class of ignition interlock device available from a qualified manufacturer in its region for any such operator. The operator may select the model of the ignition interlock device from within the class designated by the monitor from a qualified manufacturer in the operator's region of residence. The receiving county monitor shall perform monitor services and the sentencing court retains jurisdiction of the operator. Upon knowledge, the monitor of the sentencing county shall provide necessary operator information in advance to the receiving county monitor. The receiving county monitor shall notify the sentencing court and county district attorney pursuant to paragraph (d) of this section.

9 NYCRR § 358.7(b)(2).

§ 48:29 Interstate transfer of probation/conditional discharge involving IID requirement

9 NYCRR § 358.7(b)(3) and (4) address the situation where a defendant subject to the ignition interlock device requirement either (a) resides in another State at the time of sentencing, or (b) desires to move to another State subsequent to sentencing. In such a situation:

(3) Where an operator, subject to probation supervision or a sentence of conditional discharge, resides or desires to reside out-of-state and is an offender subject to the interstate compact for adult offender supervision pursuant to [Executive Law 259-mm], the governing rules of such compact shall control. Additionally, Part 349 shall apply with respect to transfer of supervision of probationers. Where transfer is permitted, the receiving state retains its authority to accept or deny the transfer in accordance with compact rules. Where an operator is subject to probation supervision and is granted reporting instructions and/or acceptance

by a receiving state, the sending probation department selects the specific class and features of the ignition interlock device available from a qualified manufacturer in the receiving state. Thereafter, the operator may select the model of the ignition interlock device meeting the specific class and features selected by the sending county probation department from a qualified manufacturer in the receiving state region. The device shall be installed prior to relocation or return where feasible. A qualified manufacturer shall make necessary arrangements to ensure the county monitor in New York State and the receiving state receive timely reports from the manufacturer and/or installation/service provider; and

(4) Where an operator resides or desires to reside out-of-state, is not subject to the interstate compact for adult offender supervision and such compact's governing rules, and has been given permission to return or relocate by the sentencing court or monitor, the same provisions with respect to selection specified in paragraph [3] of this subdivision applies and the device shall be installed prior to relocation or return. A qualified manufacturer shall make necessary arrangements to ensure the county monitor receives timely reports from the manufacturer and/or installation/service provider. Pursuant to the compact, an operator convicted of his or her first DWI misdemeanor is not subject to the compact.

(Emphasis added).

§ 48:30   VTL § 1198 does not preclude Court from imposing any other permissible conditions of probation

PL § 60.36 provides that:

Where a court is imposing a sentence for a violation of [VTL § 1192(2), (2-a) or (3)] pursuant to [PL §§ 65.00 or 65.05] and, as a condition of such sentence, orders the installation and maintenance of an ignition interlock device, the court may impose any other penalty authorized pursuant to [VTL § 1193].

See also VTL § 1198(3)(e) ("Nothing contained herein shall prevent the court from applying any other conditions of probation or conditional discharge allowed by law, including treatment for alcohol or drug abuse, restitution and community service").

§ 48:31   Imposition of IID requirement does not alter length of underlying license revocation

"Imposition of an ignition interlock condition shall in no way limit the effect of any period of license suspension or revocation set forth by the commissioner or the court." VTL § 1198(3)(d).

§ 48:32   IID requirement runs consecutively to jail sentence

PL § 60.21 provides that whenever a person is sentenced to

imprisonment for a conviction of VTL § 1192(2), (2-a) or (3), the Court is also required to both: (a) sentence the person to either probation or a conditional discharge, and (b) order the person to install an ignition interlock device. Such period of probation or conditional discharge is required to run consecutively to any period of imprisonment, and to commence immediately upon the person's release from imprisonment. *See, e.g., People v. Sierra*, 126 A.D.3d 1513, __, 4 N.Y.S.3d 565, 566 (4th Dep't 2015), leave to appeal denied, 25 N.Y.3d 1208, 2015 WL 4876249 (2015); *People v. Brainard*, 111 A.D.3d 1162, __, 975 N.Y.S.2d 498, 500 (3d Dep't 2013). Specifically, PL § 60.21 provides that:

> Notwithstanding [PL § 60.01(2)(d)], when a person is to be sentenced upon a conviction for a violation of [VTL § 1192(2), (2-a) or (3)], the court may sentence such person to a period of imprisonment authorized by [PL Article 70] and shall sentence such person to a period of probation or conditional discharge in accordance with the provisions of [PL § 65.00] and shall order the installation and maintenance of a functioning ignition interlock device. Such period of probation or conditional discharge shall run consecutively to any period of imprisonment and shall commence immediately upon such person's release from imprisonment.

It seems clear that this statute, which was enacted as part of a series of statutes and statutory amendments collectively known as "Leandra's Law," *see* Chapter 496 of the Laws of 2009, was intended to be read in conjunction with the ignition interlock device requirement. In other words, it appears clear that the intent of PL § 60.21 is to preclude a person from receiving credit for "time served" on the IID portion of his or her sentence while the person is incarcerated. *See generally People v. Panek*, 104 A.D.3d 1201, 960 N.Y.S.2d 801 (4th Dep't 2013).

This raises the question: If a person has been sentenced to a longer period of incarceration than would otherwise permit a term of probation (or conditional discharge), *see* Penal Law § 60.01(2)(d), what is the potential consequence of violating a condition of such probation (or conditional discharge)?

In *People v. Brown*, 40 Misc. 3d 821, 970 N.Y.S.2d 391 (Erie Co. Sup. Ct. 2013), the Court recognized the inherent conflict between PL § 60.21 and PL § 60.01(2)(d), and held that:

> After review of PL §§ 60.01, 60.21, 65.00, 70.00 and V & T Law §§ 1193, 1198, it is apparent that the legislature has not established a term of imprisonment as a penalty for a violation of probation pursuant to V & T Law § 1193-1(c)(iii) and PL § 60.21. The only penalty set forth for failure to install an ignition interlock device as a condition of probation is a new charge pursuant to V & T Law § 1198-9, a class "A" Misdemeanor.

As the court has no authority to impose a term of imprisonment for this violation of probation the question of Double Jeopardy is moot.

This leaves the question of what sanction the court may impose for a violation of probation in this situation. Since the court cannot impose a term of imprisonment, the choice of remedies is either continued probation or a fine pursuant to PL § 60.01-3(b) or (e).

In *People v. Brainard*, 111 A.D.3d 1162, ___, 975 N.Y.S.2d 498, 500 (3d Dep't 2013), the Appellate Division, Third Department, citing *Brown*, held that:

> County Court has authority to enforce the condition of defendant's conditional discharge. The condition is that defendant install and maintain an ignition interlock device (*see* Penal Law § 65.10[2][k-1]). If the court has reasonable cause to believe that he has violated that condition, the court may file a declaration of delinquency, order defendant to appear and hold a hearing (*see* CPL 410.30, 410.40, 410.70). If the court finds defendant delinquent, it may revoke his conditional discharge and impose another sentence, such as a term of probation or a fine. Thus, the court does have the authority to enforce the terms of the conditional discharge.

(Citations omitted). "Additionally, operation of a vehicle without a court-ordered ignition interlock device is a class A misdemeanor (*see* [VTL] § 1198[9][d], [e]), which would subject defendant to further punishment upon conviction." *Id.* at ___, 975 N.Y.S.2d at 500. The Court also held that Penal Law § 60.21 does not violate Double Jeopardy. *Id.* at ___, 975 N.Y.S.2d at 499-500.

In *People v. Flagg*, 107 A.D.3d 1613, 967 N.Y.S.2d 577 (4th Dep't 2013), the defendant pled guilty to Vehicular Manslaughter 2nd, in violation of PL § 125.12(1), and common law DWI, in violation of VTL § 1192(3). The defendant was resentenced to "a term of probation with respect to each count requiring defendant to equip with an ignition interlock device (IID) any vehicle owned or operated by him." *Id.* at ___, 967 N.Y.S.2d at 578. On appeal, the Appellate Division, Fourth Department, held as follows:

> As the People correctly concede . . ., the resentence is illegal insofar as County Court directed that defendant serve a term of five years of probation following the indeterminate term of imprisonment of 2 to 6 years on the conviction of vehicular manslaughter in the second degree (*see* Penal Law § 60.01[2][d]). Contrary to defendant's contention that the term of imprisonment therefore must be reduced, however, we agree with the People that the proper remedy is to vacate the term of probation imposed on the vehicular manslaughter count. We therefore modify the resentence accordingly. Section 60.21 requires a court to sentence a defendant convicted of a violation of Vehicle and Traffic Law § 1192(2), (2-a), or (3) to a period of probation or conditional discharge and to order the installation and maintenance of a functioning IID. Section 60.21 does not apply, however, to vehicular manslaughter in the second degree.

Id. at ___, 967 N.Y.S.2d at 578. *See also People v. Giacona*, 130
A.D.3d 1565, 14 N.Y.S.3d 850 (4th Dep't 2015).

In *People v. Dexter*, 104 A.D.3d 1184, 960 N.Y.S.2d 773 (4th
Dep't 2013), the defendant, who pled guilty to DWI as a class E
felony, was sentenced to one to three years in prison by a one-
year period of conditional discharge with an IID requirement.
The Appellate Division, Fourth Department, held that the one-
year conditional discharge was illegal—not because PL § 60.21 is
illegal—but rather because PL § 65.05(3)(a) mandates that the
period of conditional discharge "shall be" three years for felony
offenses, and " '[n]either County Court nor this Court possesses
interest of justice jurisdiction to impose a sentence less than the
mandatory statutory minimum.' " *Id.* at ___, 960 N.Y.S.2d at 774
(citation omitted). *See also People v. Barkley*, 113 A.D.3d 1002,
978 N.Y.S.2d 920 (3d Dep't 2014); *People v. O'Brien*, 111 A.D.3d
1028, 975 N.Y.S.2d 219 (3d Dep't 2013); *People v. Marvin*, 108
A.D.3d 1109, 967 N.Y.S.2d 897 (4th Dep't 2013).

In *People v. Bush*, 103 A.D.3d 1248, ___, 959 N.Y.S.2d 361, 362
(4th Dep't 2013), the Appellate Division, Fourth Department,
held that "the portion of [defendant's] sentence imposing a three-
year conditional discharge and an ignition interlock device
requirement is illegal inasmuch as he committed the offense prior
to the effective date of the statute imposing those requirements."

In *People v. Scholz*, 125 A.D.3d 1492, ___, 3 N.Y.S.3d 860, 860-61
(4th Dep't 2015), leave to appeal denied, 25 N.Y.3d 1077, 12
N.Y.S.3d 628, 34 N.E.3d 379 (2015), the Appellate Division,
Fourth Department, held that:

> We reject defendant's contention . . . that the court erred in direct-
> ing that the IID probation commence upon his release from prison.
> Penal Law § 60.21 provides that, when a person is to be sentenced
> for driving while intoxicated, "the court may sentence such person
> to a period of imprisonment authorized by [PL Article 70] and shall
> sentence such person to a period of probation or conditional dis-
> charge in accordance with the provisions of section 65.00 of this
> title and shall order the installation and maintenance of a function-
> ing [IID]." The statute further provides that "[s]uch period of proba-
> tion or conditional discharge shall run consecutively to *any period
> of imprisonment* and shall commence immediately upon such
> person's release from imprisonment" (emphasis added). We
> interpret the phrase "any period of imprisonment" to mean any pe-
> riod of imprisonment imposed on any offense, and not, as defendant
> suggests, any period of imprisonment imposed for driving while
> intoxicated. Thus, we conclude that the court properly directed that
> defendant's term of IID probation for driving while intoxicated run
> consecutively to the sentences imposed for the other counts.

In *People v. Brothers*, 123 A.D.3d 1240, 999 N.Y.S.2d 225 (3d
Dep't 2014), although it was contemplated that the defendant
would plead guilty to both AUO 1st and DWI, the plea colloquy

only addressed the AUO 1st charge. On appeal, the Appellate Division, Third Department, held as follows:

> We . . . agree with defendant that County Court improperly sentenced him to a conditional discharge while apparently under the mistaken belief that defendant had also pleaded guilty to DWI (see Vehicle and Traffic Law § 1192[2]; Penal Law § 60.21). As conceded by the People, conditional discharge is an impermissible sentence for the crime of aggravated unlicensed operation of a motor vehicle in the first degree (see Vehicle and Traffic Law § 511[3][b]) and, accordingly, defendant's sentence must be modified.

Id. at __, 999 N.Y.S.2d at 226.

§ 48:33 Applicability of IID requirement to parolees

Executive Law § 259-c(15-a) requires that everyone who is released from State Prison on parole or conditional release after serving a sentence for felony DWI or Vehicular Assault/Vehicular Manslaughter must install an ignition interlock device in any vehicle that they own or operate during the term of such parole or conditional release. Specifically, Executive Law § 259-c(15-a) provides that:

> Notwithstanding any other provision of law, where a person is serving a sentence for a violation of section 120.03, 120.04, 120.04-a, 125.12, 125.13 or 125.14 of the penal law, or a felony as defined in [VTL § 1193(1)(c)], if such person is released on parole or conditional release the board shall require as a mandatory condition of such release, that such person install and maintain, in accordance with the provisions of [VTL § 1198], an ignition interlock device in any motor vehicle owned or operated by such person during the term of such parole or conditional release for such crime. Provided further, however, the board may not otherwise authorize the operation of a motor vehicle by any person whose license or privilege to operate a motor vehicle has been revoked pursuant to the provisions of the vehicle and traffic law.

§ 48:34 IID cannot be removed without "certificate of completion" or "letter of deinstallation"

An IID installer can "remove an ignition interlock device and return the vehicle to normal operating condition only after having received a certificate of completion or a letter of deinstallation from the monitor as authorized pursuant to section 358.7 of this Part." 9 NYCRR § 358.5(d)(4). In this regard, 9 NYCRR § 358.7(a)(2) provides that "[w]here a monitor learns that the operator no longer owns or operates a motor vehicle in which an ignition interlock device has been installed, the monitor may issue a letter of deinstallation directly to the installation/service provider which authorizes removal of the device."

§ 48:35   Constitutionality of VTL § 1198

Courts have reached differing conclusions with regard to whether VTL § 1198 is Constitutional. *Compare People v. Pedrick*, 32 Misc. 3d 703, 926 N.Y.S.2d 269 (Rochester City Ct. 2011) (statute is Constitutional), *with People v. Walters*, 30 Misc. 3d 737, 913 N.Y.S.2d 893 (Watertown City Ct. 2010) (certain aspects of statute are unconstitutional).

§ 48:36   Necessity of a *Frye* hearing

In *People v. Bohrer*, 37 Misc. 3d 370, 952 N.Y.S.2d 375 (Penfield Just. Ct. 2012), the Court held that evidence of a failed IID test is admissible, without first conducting a *Frye* hearing, at a violation of conditional discharge hearing held pursuant to CPL § 410.70.

Chapter 49

The 20-Day Order

Research References

Westlaw Databases
New York Vehicle and Traffic Law 2d (NYVEH)

Treatises and Practice Aids
Rose, New York Vehicle and Traffic Law 2d § 13:2.60

KeyCite®: Cases and other legal materials listed in KeyCite Scope can be researched through the KeyCite service on Westlaw®. Use KeyCite to check citations for form, parallel references, prior and later history, and comprehensive citator information, including citations to other decisions and secondary materials.

---

§ 49:1   In general

Research References
West's Key Number Digest, Automobiles ☞55, 106, 144.1(1)

When a defendant is sentenced for a violation of VTL § 1192, his or her driver's license will be either suspended or revoked by the court. *See* VTL § 1193(2). *See also* §§ 46:1 et seq., *supra*. At sentencing, the defendant is required to physically surrender his or her driver's license to the court. VTL § 1193(2)(d)(1).

Unless the defendant is granted a so-called "20-Day Order" (also called a "20-Day Stay"), the suspension/revocation of his or her driver's license takes effect immediately upon sentencing. VTL § 1193(2)(d)(1). A certificate of relief from disabilities issued pursuant to Correction Law Article 23 cannot be used to override the provisions of VTL § 1193(2)(d)(1). VTL § 1193(2)(d)(1).

§ 49:2   What is a 20-Day Order?

Research References

West's Key Number Digest, Automobiles ⬤⤳55, 106, 144.1(1)

As is noted in the previous section, when a defendant is sentenced for a violation of VTL § 1192, his or her driver's license will be either suspended or revoked by the court. A 20-Day Order is an order of the court staying the imposition of such suspension/revocation for a period of 20 days from the date of sentencing.

If the defendant is eligible for a 20-Day Order, the court has discretion whether or not to grant it. VTL § 1193(2)(d)(2). However, in the usual case it is difficult to conceive of a reason why a court would not issue a 20-Day Order to an eligible defendant. In the authors' experience, 20-Day Orders are almost always granted to eligible defendants. However, some courts require that the defendant pay the fine and/or surcharge associated with the VTL § 1192 offense before they will issue the order.

§ 49:3   Purpose of a 20-Day Order

Research References

West's Key Number Digest, Automobiles ⬤⤳55, 106, 144.1(1)

The purpose of a 20-Day Order is to allow a defendant who is eligible for both the Drinking Driver Program (DDP) and a conditional or restricted use license to drive during the time period that it takes (a) for the court to complete and file the paperwork regarding the defendant's VTL § 1192 conviction to the DMV, and (b) for the DMV to input the conviction into its computer system. In this regard, a defendant who is eligible for the DDP and a conditional or restricted use license cannot sign up for the DDP and/or obtain a conditional or restricted use license until his or her VTL § 1192 conviction is officially entered into the DMV computer system.

Simply stated, the DMV will not permit a defendant to sign up for the DDP or to obtain a conditional or restricted use license unless and until the defendant's VTL § 1192 conviction triggering eligibility therefor exists in its computer system. Since it often takes approximately seven to 14 days for a VTL § 1192 conviction to make its way into the DMV computer system, the 20-Day Order was created so that defendants who are eligible for the DDP and a conditional or restricted use license will not receive a period of complete license suspension while their VTL § 1192 convictions are being administratively processed by the court and the DMV. The procedure also benefits the courts and the DMV, as they would be deluged by inquiries and complaints by defendants who would check on the status of their convictions on a daily basis until their paperwork had been processed.

§ 49:4   Scope of a 20-Day Order

Research References

West's Key Number Digest, Automobiles ☞55, 106, 144.1(1)

Technically speaking, a 20-Day Order does not *grant* a defendant driving privileges. Rather, it *stays* the imposition of a mandatory suspension/revocation resulting from a VTL § 1192 conviction for a period of 20 days from the date of sentencing. In other words, a 20-Day Order merely continues the defendant's existing driving privileges for 20 days.

Thus, if the defendant had a full, unrestricted driver's license prior to sentencing, the 20-Day Order acts as a full, unrestricted driver's license for a period of 20 days from the date of sentencing. In this regard, even if the defendant obtains a conditional or restricted use license within this 20-day time period, he or she still has full driving privileges for the full 20 days.

By contrast, if the defendant had no driving privileges prior to sentencing (due to, for example, a suspension or revocation for refusing to submit to a chemical test, three speeding violations/misdemeanors within 18 months, too many points, an insurance lapse, failure to answer a ticket, failure to pay child support, etc.), a 20-Day Order would not permit him or her to drive.

There is a notable exception to this rule. Specifically, if the defendant's driver's license is suspended pending prosecution of a VTL § 1192 charge, *see* §§ 45:1 et seq., *supra*, and such suspension is the only suspension that the defendant is currently subject to, a VTL § 1192 conviction (arising out of the same incident) terminates such suspension as a matter of law (as the prosecution is no longer pending). As such, in such a situation the defendant would have a 20-day window during which he or she would have full driving privileges despite the fact that such 20-day period is sandwiched between a preconviction suspension pending prosecution and a postconviction suspension/revocation.

§ 49:5   Eligibility for a 20-Day Order

Research References

West's Key Number Digest, Automobiles ☞55, 106, 144.1(1)

As a general rule, any person who is eligible for the DDP and a conditional or restricted use license following a VTL § 1192 conviction, *see* §§ 50:1 et seq., *infra*, is eligible for a 20-Day Order. Specifically, VTL § 1193(2)(d)(2) provides that:

Except where the license holder has been [1] charged with a violation of [Penal Law Article 120 or 125] arising out of the same incident or [2] convicted of such violation or a violation of any subdivision of [VTL § 1192] within the preceding [5] years, the

[Court] may issue an order making said license suspension or revocation take effect [20] days after the date of sentencing.

Many courts are under the misimpression that a defendant is only eligible for a 20-Day Order if his or her driver's license is *suspended* for a conviction of DWAI, as opposed to *revoked* for a DWI. In this regard, as VTL § 1193(2)(d)(2) makes clear, it is irrelevant whether the defendant's driver's license is revoked as opposed to suspended. Thus, for example, a defendant with no prior VTL § 1192 conviction(s) who pleads guilty to misdemeanor DWI, and whose driver's license is thereby revoked for at least six months, is eligible for a 20-Day Order. In fact, a defendant who is convicted of *felony* DWI is eligible for a 20-Day Order (as long as his or her predicate DWI conviction is more than five years old).

However, as is explained in the previous section, even if the defendant is eligible for (and granted) a 20-Day Order, such order would have no effect if the defendant is precluded from driving for some other reason (*e.g.*, as a condition of probation).

§ 49:6 Chemical test refusals and 20-Day Orders

Research References

West's Key Number Digest, Automobiles ⚬⇒55, 106, 144.1(1)

As is noted previously, a 20-Day Order merely continues the defendant's existing driving privileges for 20 days. Thus, if the defendant had any preexisting suspension/revocation on his or her driver's license, a 20-Day Order is useless (as it merely "continues" nonexistent driving privileges).

In this regard, a chemical test refusal does not affect a defendant's eligibility for a 20-Day Order, but in many cases a test refusal will render a 20-Day Order ineffective. For example, if the defendant in a test refusal case enters a VTL § 1192 plea at arraignment, the court is required to issue a temporary suspension of the defendant's driving privileges at that time—independent of the VTL § 1192 suspension/revocation—based upon the alleged chemical test refusal. *See* VTL § 1194(2)(b)(3); 15 NYCRR § 139.3(a). *See also* § 41:40, *supra*; § 41:54, *supra*. In such a case, a 20-Day Order would continue nonexistent driving privileges, and would thus be a legal nullity (at least until the temporary suspension is terminated).

Similarly, if the defendant's VTL § 1192 plea is entered subsequent to a DMV chemical test refusal revocation, a 20-Day Order would continue nonexistent driving privileges and would be a legal nullity.

Conversely, a valid 20-Day Order would become invalid if the defendant's driving privileges are revoked at a DMV chemical test refusal hearing held during the 20-day life span of the order.

§ 49:7   Court's obligations upon conviction

Research References
West's Key Number Digest, Automobiles ⋘55, 106, 144.1(1)

If a court grants a 20-Day Order, it is required to provide a copy thereof to the defendant. VTL § 1193(2)(d)(2). In this regard, where a defendant's driver's license is suspended/revoked for a violation of VTL § 1192, the court issues the defendant a two-part form entitled:

New York State Department of Motor Vehicles

ORDER OF SUSPENSION OR REVOCATION

The official name of the form is MV-1192. A sample copy of this form is set forth at Appendix 55 [currently reserved]. The top portion of the form is entitled "PART 1-CONTINUATION OF DRIVING PRIVILEGES." This portion of the form is the 20-Day Order. Part 2 of the form is the order suspending or revoking the defendant's driver's license. The 20-Day Order portion of the form provides, in pertinent part:

> According to Section 1193 of the Vehicle and Traffic Law, your driver license will be suspended revoked on *(sentence date plus 20 days)*. This order will allow you to drive, with the same limitations as your driver license, until your suspension/revocation starts. **You must have both parts of this order with you when you drive**. If you do not have both parts of this order with you, you may be charged with a violation of the Vehicle and Traffic Law. When the suspension/revocation starts, you do not have the right to drive unless you receive a conditional license. This order must be turned in before a conditional license can be issued to you.

Implicit in the concept of the 20-Day Order is the premise that the court will forward the paperwork documenting the defendant's VTL § 1192 conviction to DMV in a timely manner. In this regard, VTL § 1193(2)(d)(2) mandates that "[t]he court shall forward to [DMV] the certificates required in [VTL §§ 513 and 514], along with a copy of any order issued pursuant to this paragraph and the license, within [96] hours of sentencing." In order to encourage compliance with the 96-hour rule, the state pays towns and villages $15 for each case in which a town or village court complies with the requirements of VTL § 1193(2)(d)(2). *See* GML § 99-l(1)(i).

§ 49:8   Advice to defendant regarding 20-Day Order

Research References
West's Key Number Digest, Automobiles ⋘55, 106, 144.1(1)

Defense counsel should advise a client to sign up for the DDP and a conditional or restricted use license while the 20-Day Order is still valid; but to wait approximately 16 to 18 days following sentencing before doing so (unless the DMV has notified the client in a more expeditious fashion that his or her VTL § 1192 conviction has been processed). The reason is that if the client goes to DMV too soon (*i.e.*, before his or her VTL § 1192 conviction has "hit" the DMV computer system), such trip will be a waste of time and will have to be repeated.

The client should also be advised that, unless he or she obtains a conditional or restricted use license, continuing to drive after the 20-Day Order has expired constitutes the crime of aggravated unlicensed operation of a motor vehicle in the second degree. *See* VTL § 511(2). *See also* §§ 13:1 et seq., *infra*.

§ 49:9   20-Day Orders in certain drug-related cases

Research References

West's Key Number Digest, Automobiles ☞55, 106, 144.1(1)

VTL § 510(2)(b)(v) provides for the mandatory suspension of a defendant's driver's license where the defendant is convicted of, or adjudicated a youthful offender in connection with, certain crimes involving drugs. In this regard, the court can "issue an order making said license suspension take effect [20] days after the date of sentencing and, if this is done, the license holder shall be given a copy of the order permitting the continuation of driving privileges." VTL § 510(2)(b)(vi).

Chapter 50

The Drinking Driver Program

Research References

Westlaw Databases

Handling a Criminal Case in New York (HCCNY)
New York Driving While Intoxicated Defense Forms (NYDWIFM)

Treatises and Practice Aids

Rose, New York Vehicle and Traffic Law 2d, Chapter 13

Forms

Taheri and Orr, NY DWI Defense Forms § 1:5

Law Reviews and Other Periodicals

Gerstenzang, Defending the DWI Case in New York: The Basics, 4
   Practising Law Institute New York Practice Skills Course Handbook
   Series 7 (September, 1997)

Strahlstrom, Health And Welfare, 24 Pac. L.J. 898 (January, 1993)

KeyCite®: Cases and other legal materials listed in KeyCite Scope can be researched through the KeyCite service on Westlaw®. Use KeyCite to check citations for form, parallel references, prior and later history, and comprehensive citator information, including citations to other decisions and secondary materials.

---

§ 50:1 In general

Research References

West's Key Number Digest, Automobiles ☞359.4

The plea bargain for a first-offense DWI case will usually include the imposition of a conditional discharge, the condition being that the defendant participate in the New York State Drinking Driver Program. This program consists of a series of seven classes totaling a minimum of 15 hours which are designed to deter future violations through the education of the violator. VTL § 1196(1).

§ 50:2 Conditional license

Research References

West's Key Number Digest, Automobiles ☞359.4

The program provides your client with a conditional license which allows him to drive:

(1) enroute to and from the holder's place of employment,

(2) if the holder's employment requires the operation of a motor vehicle then during the hours thereof,

(3) enroute to and from a class or an activity which is an authorized part of the alcohol and drug rehabilitation program and at which his attendance is required,

(4) enroute to and from a class or course at an accredited school, college or university or at a state approved institution of vocational or technical training,

(5) to or from court ordered probation activities,

(6) to and from a motor vehicle office for the transaction of business relating to such license or program,

(7) for a three-hour consecutive day time period, chosen by the administrators of the program, on a day during which the participant is not engaged in usual employment or vocation,

(8) enroute to and from a medical examination or treatment as part of the necessary medical treatment for such participant or member of the participant's household, as evidenced by a written statement to that effect from a licensed medical practitioner, and

(9) enroute to and from a place, including a school, at which a child or children of the holder are cared for on a regular basis and which is necessary for the holder to maintain such holder's employment or enrollment at an accredited school, college or university or at a state approved institution of vocational or technical training.

VTL § 1196(7)(a).

A conditional license cannot be used to drive to or from a high school. The reason why is that high schools are not accredited.

§ 50:3   Five-year eligibility

Research References

West's Key Number Digest, Automobiles ☞359.4

Once a person has participated in the program, she may not do so again for a period of five years. The five years run from the date that the defendant completes the Drinking Driver Program to the date of her commission of a new violation of VTL § 1192.

In *Matter of Clark v. Abrams*, 161 A.D.2d 1208, 555 N.Y.S.2d 995 (4th Dep't 1990), the defendant attended a Drinking Driver Program from November 16, 1983, to May 7, 1984. On August 31, 1988, the defendant was convicted of DWI. Because the defendant had participated in the program within five years immediately preceding his second offense, he was prohibited from participating in the program. The Monroe County Supreme Court ordered the Commissioner of Motor Vehicles to enroll the defendant in the program. The Commissioner appealed. The Appellate Division, Fourth Department, ruled that the supreme court was without authority to order the Commissioner to enroll the defendant in the Drinking Driver Program.

§ 50:4   Prior conviction voids program eligibility

Research References

West's Key Number Digest, Automobiles ☞359.4

It is common for defendants to obtain a reduction of their first DWI offense to DWAI. Since DWAI bears a 90-day suspension, as opposed to a six-month revocation, many defendants ask if they can defer participating in the Drinking Driver Program. Their intention is to "bank" their eligibility for an anticipated future conviction. As admirable as this display of prudence and forethought might, otherwise, be, VTL § 1196(4) precludes such action. A defendant who has a previous conviction for a violation of VTL § 1192 within five years immediately preceding their commission of a new alcohol-or drug-related offense, is ineligible for the Drinking Driver Program, whether they participated initially or not. VTL § 1196(4) is intended to preclude the "banking" of eligibility against future transgressions.

§ 50:5 Vacated conviction voids effect of prior participation

Research References

West's Key Number Digest, Automobiles ⊘359.4

In *Matter of Smith v. Passidomo*, 125 Misc. 2d 942, 480 N.Y.S.2d 973 (Oneida Co. Ct. 1984), the defendant was convicted of DWI in 1980. He enrolled in, and satisfactorily completed, the Drinking Driver Program. In June of 1984, the 1980 conviction was vacated by the Oneida County Court. Based upon a 1983 conviction for DWI, the defendant sought entry into the Drinking Driver Program. He was advised that his prior participation within five years prohibited his being enrolled in the program and given a conditional license. Citing CPL § 160.60 and § 160.50(2)(f), governing termination of criminal actions, the Supreme Court of Oneida County ordered the Department of Motor Vehicles to restore the defendant to his preparticipation status insofar as the Drinking Driver Program was concerned.

§ 50:6 Refusal revocation not terminated by completion of program

Research References

West's Key Number Digest, Automobiles ⊘359.4

Upon successful completion of the program, the individual may apply to the Commissioner for the termination of the suspension or revocation order. The Commissioner may then terminate such order and return the driver's license. VTL § 1196(5).

If the defendant has refused the chemical test, however, she will not be eligible for restoration of full driving privileges until expiration of the revocation period. VTL § 1194(2)(d)(3). The defendant will, however, be allowed to retain her conditional license until the refusal revocation period has expired. A copy of the Department of Motor Vehicles Drinking Driver Program regulations appears at Appendix 56.

§ 50:7 Referral for additional treatment

Research References

West's Key Number Digest, Automobiles ⊘359.4

In advising your client in regard to the Drinking Driver Program, it is imperative that you point out the possibility of referral for additional treatment. Every participant in the program is screened to determine if an alcohol or drug abuse problem exists. Individuals identified as being at risk for alcohol or drug abuse are referred for evaluation. VTL § 1196(1) allows a person to be held for treatment for a period of up to eight months. This period may be extended upon the recommendation of the Department of Mental Hygiene or an appropriate health official administering the program on behalf of a municipality. In practice, defendants identified as problem drinkers are referred for additional treatment to various alcohol treatment facilities. Unsatisfactory participation results in termination of the conditional license and imposition of the original suspension or revocation arising out of the conviction.

§ 50:8 Referral criteria

Research References

West's Key Number Digest, Automobiles ⇌359.4

In preparing these materials, I spoke to Mr. David McGirr, who is a Senior Driver Improvement Analyst with the Department of Motor Vehicles. As cocoordinator of the Alcohol and Drug Rehabilitation Program, he is familiar with referrals and advised me that approximately 25% to 33⅓% of each class were referred upon completion of the initial seven-week program. Individuals so referred were given an evaluation to determine whether they required additional treatment and, if so, what treatment they should receive.

New York State has recently revised the process to determine whether an individual will be referred for additional treatment. The old referral system was based on a matrix, using the score obtained on the Michigan Alcoholism Screening Test (MAST) or Mortimer-Filkins Questionnaire as the primary screening instrument. The old system also considered such factors as the BAC of the individual at the time of arrest, whether the individual was a repeat DWI offender, whether the individual attended a Drinking Driver Program while intoxicated, and self-admissions of a problem. Various combinations of these factors were used to refer individuals for additional treatment.

Significantly, the new referral criteria dropped the use of the BAC as a primary referral criterion. Rather, the Research Institute on Addictions Self Inventory (RIASI) Questionnaire is used as the principal screening instrument for alcohol and drug problems. The evaluator will also consider whether the individual is a repeat DWI offender, whether she attended the Drinking Driver Program while intoxicated, and/or whether the individual admitted to the instructors that he/she has a drinking problem and wants help. *See* Drinking Driver Program Screening Matrix at Appendix 17.

The RIASI Questionnaire has a scoring cutoff point beyond which the individual is likely to be referred.

If an individual has two or more alcohol/drug driving incidents within 10 years, such person may be referred on the basis that research demonstrates that repeat offenders are highly likely to recidivate and to be involved in crashes.

Where an individual provides an unsolicited and direct admission that he/she is currently in treatment, or if the individual requests help for his/her substance abuse problem, the Drinking Driver Program administrator will request that the student sign a statement affirming either of the situations, and refer the individual for additional treatment.

An individual who attends the program while under the influence of alcohol/drugs, or with a detectable odor of alcohol, will be referred.

Also, a student that admits or volunteers that he has been arrested for an alcohol/drug driving violation while enrolled in the program will be required to attend additional alcohol treatment.

§ 50:9   Attorney should advise client of possible referral

Research References

West's Key Number Digest, Automobiles ⚷359.4

One problem faced by attorneys and referral program personnel is that defendants are frequently not aware of their liability in this regard until after a conviction is entered and the proverbial "die is cast." Clients do not generally respond well to a change of rules in midstream. Prior to entering into a plea bargain, the client is aware that she will be going to a Drinking Driver Program for a period of seven weeks. Unless you advise her of a possible referral, she may be taken by surprise after she has committed herself to this course of action. Since the referral is to a private agency which charges your client for its services, her inconvenience is both personal and financial. A referral is much easier to accept when the client is aware of and accepts this possibility prior to the entry of her guilty plea.

§ 50:10   Appealing the referral

Research References

West's Key Number Digest, Automobiles ⚷359.4

If your client wishes to protest her referral and/or the treatment recommended, her first level of appeal is to the Drinking Driver Program Director. After that, the second appeal would be directed towards one of 13 driver improvement analysts located throughout the state. Beyond the Driver Improvement Analysts, the next appellate level is to the Commissioner of the Department of Motor Vehicles. The Commissioner's determination is subject to review via an Article 78 proceeding.

Complaints regarding the treatment ordered can result in a transfer over to the Division of Alcohol and Alcohol Abuse for their review and determination of the appropriate treatment.

§ 50:11 Violation of conditional discharge

Research References

West's Key Number Digest, Automobiles ☞359.4

If your client fails to complete the referral program, she may be brought back to the original court which sentenced her based upon a violation of her conditional discharge. In *People v. Ogden*, 117 Misc. 2d 900, 459 N.Y.S.2d 545 (1983), the defendant was referred for additional treatment based upon the fact that he had refused the Breathalyzer test upon his initial arrest. Upon his failure to comply with the referral, he was brought back to the City Court of Batavia and charged with a violation of his conditional discharge. In dismissing the alleged violation of his conditional discharge, the Court held that the defendant's referral for additional treatment based upon the fact of his test refusal at the time of arrest was arbitrary, illegal and capricious. Additionally, the Court found that the referral of the defendant to a facility some miles distant from his home was similarly improper particularly where adequate facilities were available locally.

§ 50:12 Out-of-state defendants

Research References

West's Key Number Digest, Automobiles ☞359.4

In the past, representation of out-of-state licensees was complicated by the fact of their ineligibility for a conditional license. Essentially, the Department of Motor Vehicles could not place conditions upon a license over which they had no jurisdiction, nor could they issue a conditional license to a person who was not already in possession of a valid New York State driver's license. This situation necessitated legal gymnastics consisting of requesting an adjournment of sufficient duration to allow your client to obtain a valid New York State driver's license. Upon entry of the conviction for a violation of VTL § 1192, this newly acquired license would be suspended and your client issued a conditional license. This situation was particularly painful for truck drivers as well as others who lived in adjoining states, but were employed within the State of New York. In order to remedy this situation, the statute was amended to allow for the issuance of a conditional privilege of "operating a motor vehicle in this state." This conditional privilege is basically identical to the conditional license, but it eliminates the possession of a New York State driver's license as a condition precedent for the conditional operation of a motor vehicle in the State of New York.

§ 50:13   Subsequent arrest upon completion of program

Research References

West's Key Number Digest, Automobiles ⚯359.4

A client with a prior conviction for DWAI, and prior participation in the program within the last five years, is in a most difficult situation. The ADA and the court are loath to grant another reduction to DWAI, and your client is not eligible for the Drinking Driver Program in any event. Whereas, the VTL provides for a 90-day suspension for a first conviction for DWAI, a second conviction for DWAI within five years results in a six-month revocation.

The primary distinction between subsequent convictions for DWI and for DWAI is that a DWI conviction is a predicate for a future felony charge should your client be so unfortunate as to be rearrested within 10 years of his initial conviction for DWI.

§ 50:14   Alcohol rehabilitation required prior to relicensure

Research References

West's Key Number Digest, Automobiles ⚯359.4

Where the defendant has participated in the Drinking Driver Program, and is subsequently convicted of DWI or DWAI within five years of that participation, the Department of Motor Vehicles imposes an additional requirement upon the defendant seeking reinstatement of her license upon expiration of the period of revocation. This requirement mandates her satisfactory participation in an alcohol treatment program approved by the Department of Motor Vehicles. The defendant is obligated to seek out, participate in, and successfully complete an alcohol program prior to her obtaining reinstatement of her driving privileges.

§ 50:15   Third offenders not eligible for conditional license

Research References

West's Key Number Digest, Automobiles ⚯359.4

Under the old rules, a person was generally eligible for a conditional license approximately every five years. In this regard, a person was ineligible for a conditional license if the person, among other things, (a) had a prior VTL § 1192 conviction within the past five years, (b) had participated in the DDP within the past five years, or (c) had two prior DWI-related convictions/incidents within the past 10 years. *See* VTL § 1196(4); 15 NYCRR § 134.7; Chapter 50, *supra*.

Pursuant to the new regulations, a person who has three or more DWI-related convictions/incidents *within the past 25 years* is ineligible for a conditional license. *See* 15 NYCRR § 134.7(a)(11)(i).

§ 50:16 Fees

Research References

West's Key Number Digest, Automobiles ☞359.4

The Drinking Driver Program is "user-funded." There is a $75 administrative fee payable to the Department of Motor Vehicles upon making application for the conditional license and program entry. The fee is non-refundable. In addition, there is a $225 program fee which is paid directly to the agent conducting the program. If your client's license was *suspended*, he/she must pay a $50 suspension termination fee before his/her license will be restored. If your client's license was *revoked*, he/she must apply to the DMV for a new license. Although the application will not be approved before the minimum revocation period has passed, the DMV will accept the application for review up to 60 days before the revocation is to end. To apply for a new license, your client must send a $100 nonrefundable reapplication fee with the application.

§ 50:17 Personnel

Research References

West's Key Number Digest, Automobiles ☞359.4

The people conducting the Drinking Driver Program are not employees of the Department of Motor Vehicles. Rather, they are "program agents" under contract with the Department of Motor Vehicles. The Department of Motor Vehicles oversees the activities of these agents through field staff who check on "program administration, curriculum implementation, and approval and training of instructional staff, as well as in-class program presentations." Drinking Driver Program Director's Guide, pg. 1.3.

§ 50:18 Conditional license disqualifications

Research References

West's Key Number Digest, Automobiles ☞55, 106, 144.1(1.11), 359.4

The fact that a person is eligible for the Drinking Driver Program does not necessarily mean that he or she is eligible for a conditional license. In this regard, N.Y. Comp. Codes R. & Regs. tit. 15, § 134.7 provides:

(a) The issuance of a conditional license shall be denied to any person who enrolls in a program if a review of such person's driving record, or additional information secured by the department, indicates that any of the following conditions apply.

(1) The person has been convicted of homicide, assault, criminal negligence or criminally negligent homicide arising out of operation of a motor vehicle.

(2) The conviction upon which eligibility for a rehabilitation program is based involved a fatal accident.

(3) The person does not have a currently valid New York State driver's license. This paragraph shall not apply to a person whose New York State driver's license has expired, but is still renewable, nor to a person who would have a currently valid New York State driver's license except for the revocation or suspension which resulted from the conviction upon which his eligibility for the rehabilitation program is based, nor to a person who would have a currently valid New York State driver's license except for a suspension or revocation which resulted from a chemical test refusal arising out of the same incident as such conviction.

(4) The person has been convicted of an offense arising from the same event which resulted in the current alcohol-related conviction which conviction would, aside from the alcohol-related conviction, result in mandatory revocation or suspension of the person's driver's license.

(5) The person has had two or more revocations and/or suspensions of his driver's license, other than the revocation or suspension upon which his eligibility for the rehabilitation program is based within the last three years. This subdivision shall not apply to suspensions which have been terminated by performance of an act by the person, nor to a suspension or revocation resulting from a chemical test refusal, if the person had been convicted of a violation of Section 1192 of the Vehicle and Traffic Law arising out of the same incident.

(6) The person has been convicted more than once of reckless driving within the last three years.

(7) The person has had a series of convictions, incidents and/or accidents or has a medical or mental condition, which in the judgment of the commissioner or his designated agent tends to establish that the person would be an unusual and immediate risk upon the highway.

(8) The person has been penalized under section 1193(1)(d)(1) of the Vehicle and Traffic Law for any violation of subdivision 2, 3, or 4 of such section.

(9) The person is reentering the rehabilitation program, as provided in section 134.10(c) of this Part, for a second or subsequent time.

(10) The person has been suspended under section 510(2)(b)(v) of the Vehicle and Traffic Law for a conviction of section 1192(4) of such law. Such person may be eligible for a restricted use license pursuant to Part 135 of this Title.

(11)

(i) The person has three or more alcohol- or drug-related driving convictions or incidents within the last 25 years. For the purposes of this paragraph, a conviction for a violation of section 1192 of the Vehicle and Traffic Law, and/or a finding of a violation of section 1192-a of such law and/or a finding of refusal to submit to a chemical test under section 1194 of such law arising out of the same incident shall only be counted as one conviction or incident. The date of the violation or incident resulting in a conviction or a finding as described herein shall be used to determine whether three or more convictions or incidents occurred within a 25 year period.

(ii) For the purposes of this paragraph, when determining eligibility for a conditional license issued pending prosecution pursuant to section 134.18 of this Part, the term "incident" shall include the arrest that resulted in the issuance of the suspension pending prosecution.

(12) The person was the holder of a limited DJ or limited MJ license at the time of the violation which resulted in the suspension or revocation.

(13) The person, during the five years preceding the commission of the alcohol or drug-related offense or a finding of a violation of section 1192-a of the Vehicle and Traffic Law, participated in the alcohol and drug rehabilitation program or has been convicted of a violation of any subdivision of section 1192 of such law.

(b) If after a person is enrolled in a rehabilitation program and has been issued a conditional license, but, prior to the reissuance of an unconditional license, information is received by the department which indicates that such person was not eligible for a conditional license his conditional license will be revoked.

N.Y. Comp. Codes R. & Regs. tit. 15, § 134.7 is attached hereto as Appendix 56.

§ 50:19 Revocation of conditional license

Research References

West's Key Number Digest, Automobiles ⚖55, 106, 144.1(1.11), 359.4

A conditional license may be revoked for the following reasons:

1. Failure to attend or satisfactorily participate in the program, or for failure to satisfy the requirements for participation in the program.

2. Conviction of any alcohol or drug related traffic offense, misdemeanor or felony.

3. Failure to attempt in good faith to accept rehabilitation. This will be determined by a Department of Motor Vehicle hearing based upon receipt of notification or evidence that an individual is not attempting in good faith to accept rehabilitation.

4. Conviction for speeding, speed contest or racing, reckless driving, following too closely, or conviction for at least one traffic violation other than parking, stopping, standing, equipment, inspection or other non-moving violations where such violation(s) occurred during the period of validity of the conditional license.

5. Upon receipt of a conviction certificate which indicates that an individual has driven in violation of the conditional license.

6. Upon receipt of a conviction certificate which requires mandatory suspension or revocation action.

7. After a Department of Motor Vehicles hearing upon a complaint that an individual is operating or has operated a motor vehicle in violation of the conditional license.

8. Upon receipt of additional information which would make the individual ineligible. Drinking Driver Program Director's Guide, pg. 3.10–3.12. *See also* § 134.9(d) of Part 134 New York State Department of Motor Vehicles' Alcohol and Drug Rehabilitation Program set forth at Appendix 56.

In *People v. Mason*, 10 Misc. 3d 859, 804 N.Y.S.2d 661 (Nassau Co. Dist. Ct. 2005), the defendant, a commercial driver, had been issued a certificate of relief from disabilities (which had allowed him to obtain a conditional commercial driver's license). The defendant's employer asked the Court to revisit the issue of whether the defendant was entitled to a conditional license due to his alleged " 'repeated, brazen disregard with respect to his obligations under the law [including reporting requirements imposed by the Federal Motor Carrier Safety Regulations].' " 10 Misc. 3d at _, 804 N.Y.S.2d at 661. The Court held that "[i]t is the New York State Department of Motor Vehicles which determines eligibility for and issues or declines to issue conditional licenses. All a certificate of relief from disabilities does is eliminate any categoric statutory bar to such issuance. Any questions regarding the conditional license itself must therefore be addressed to the DMV, rather than this Court." 10 Misc. 3d at _, 804 N.Y.S.2d at 662.

§ 50:20   Entry and reentry into program

Research References

West's Key Number Digest, Automobiles ⚖359.4

Initially, a person eligible for the Drinking Driver Program enrolls through the appropriate district Office of the Department of Motor Vehicles. There are 14 district offices situated throughout the state. If an individual leaves the Drinking Driver Program, she may apply for reentry. An application for reentry is made to the district office staff. In order to apply for reentry, the licensee must obtain a letter from the Drinking Driver Program stating that the Director of the program is willing to take the person back into the program. This letter is presented to the district office enforcement section. The enforcement section may:

(a) terminate the conditional license suspension order which is issued as a result of the drop notice.

(b) record the licensee's name and that this is a reentry on the program roster (MV-2028).

(c) instruct the licensee to contact the DDP director to complete program reentry.

(d) call Driver Improvement to have the eligibility date reset.

(e) if the full license was restored prior to the drop out, *i.e.*, based on a DWAI conviction, the license will be reentered in conditional license status. Drinking Driver Manual, pg. 3.12–3. A conditional license may be issued only upon the first reentry. Although second and subsequent reentries may be permitted, a conditional license will not be reissued in such cases. Section 134.10(c) of Part 134, NYS DMV Alcohol and Drug Rehabilitation Program.

§ 50:21   Completion of program documentation

Research References

West's Key Number Digest, Automobiles ⚖359.4

Upon successful completion of the New York State Drinking Driver Program, the motorist will be issued a copy of Form MV-2026 which he/she can use to apply for issuance of an unconditional license. A copy of this form appears as Appendix 57 [currently reserved]. The motorist must present this certificate along with proof of identity, date of birth, and photo license fee.

§ 50:22   Participation as satisfaction of jail sentence

Research References

West's Key Number Digest, Automobiles ⚖359.4

The last sentence of VTL § 1196(4) states:

Notwithstanding any contrary provisions of this chapter, satisfactory participation in and completion of a course in such program shall result in the termination of any sentence of imprisonment that may have been imposed by reason of a conviction therefor; provided, however, that nothing contained in this section shall delay the commencement of such sentence.

While this language would seem to indicate that satisfactory participation in the Drinking Driver Program satisfies any sentence of imprisonment, the Appellate Division, Third Department, held this not to be the case. In *People v. Hilker*, 133 A.D.2d 986, 521 N.Y.S.2d 136 (3d Dep't 1987), the Court affirmed the Tioga County Court's denial of the defendant's CPL § 440.20 motion seeking to set aside his sentence of imprisonment for DWI on the ground that he had satisfactorily completed the Drinking Driver Program. The Court did not, however, explain why § 1196(4) is not applicable, stating:

Finally, under all the circumstances presented, we conclude that the sentence imposed was neither harsh nor excessive, was properly within the discretion of the County Court and, accordingly, not in contravention of the provisions of Vehicle and Traffic Law § 521(1)(c).

521 N.Y.S.2d at 138 [VTL § 521(1)(c) recodified as VTL § 1196(4)].

The Appellate Division, Second Department, in *People v. Sofia*, 201 A.D.2d 685, 608 N.Y.S.2d 254 (1994), ruled that the court must authorize the participation in the Drinking Driver Program for VTL § 1196(4) to apply. Here, the defendant pleaded guilty to two counts of DWI in exchange for two concurrent sentences of six months' incarceration. Following the entry of the pleas, but prior to sentence being imposed, the defendant moved pursuant to VTL § 1196(4) to vacate the jail sentence on the ground that he had already completed the Drinking Driver Program. The supreme court denied the motion. The Appellate Court affirmed, concluding:

As the language of Vehicle and Traffic Law § 1196(4) and 15 NYCRR 134.3 makes clear, whether a defendant may enroll in the alcohol and drug rehabilitation program established by Vehicle and Traffic Law § 1196(4) is a matter to be addressed by the court at sentencing.

People v. Sofia, 608 N.Y.S.2d at 254. It is interesting to note that VTL § 1196(4) provides for a sentencing court to prohibit the entry of a defendant into the Drinking Driver Program. Absent such prohibition, the defendant is eligible for the Program and, logically, successful completion should terminate any sentence of incarceration. This, however, is not the holdings of the cases set forth above.

§ 50:23 DDP does not terminate sentence for AUO

Research References

West's Key Number Digest, Automobiles ⬩359.4

The Court of Appeals has determined that although a conviction for VTL § 511(2) could be traced back to a DWAI conviction, VTL § 511(2) is not an alcohol-related traffic offense encompassed in VTL § 1196(4) such that his prison sentence would be vacated upon completion of the Drinking Driver Program. In People ex rel. *Paganini v. Jablonsky*, 79 N.Y.2d 586, 584 N.Y.S.2d 415 (1992), the defendant was convicted of DWAI in 1986. In 1988, he was again arrested and charged with DWI and AUO 1st. Upon pleading guilty to VTL § 1192(3) and VTL § 511(2), he was sentenced to one-year imprisonment for the VTL § 1192 offense, and 180 days for the VTL § 511 offense.

While his appeal was pending, the defendant enrolled in and completed the Drinking Driver Program. He thereafter petitioned the supreme court for a writ of habeas corpus claiming that both of his jail sentences should have terminated upon completion of the program. The court sustained the writ and directed petitioner's immediate release from custody. The Appellate Division reversed, concluding that VTL § 1196(4) was not applicable to his sentence for VTL § 511(2).

Pursuant to VTL § 1196(4), completion of a Drinking Driver Program results in the termination of any sentence of imprisonment imposed by reason of a conviction for an alcohol or drug-related traffic offense. The defendant argued that an alcohol-related traffic offense is any which have alcohol-related conduct as an essential element. The Court of Appeals disagreed, concluding that the goal of the Drinking Driver Program is to induce drivers with alcohol/drug problems to obtain professional help.

> The statute and the implementing regulation, by targeting and limiting eligibility to participate in the programs, foster that goal. They reflect a rational policy choice not to extend the termination-of-sentence incentive to vehicle and traffic law offenders who knowingly drive without a license—the core element of the Vehicle and Traffic Law § 511(2) offense at issue in this case—because that would not directly foster the particular goals of Vehicle and Traffic Law § 1196 rehabilitation and education programs. That [the defendant's] unlicensed driving conviction may be traced back to a suspension, which was based on his prior refusal to take a chemical test and a prior driving while ability impaired conviction, therefore, does not qualify for the termination-of-sentence remedy.

People v. Jablonsky, 584 N.Y.S.2d at 416.

Our thanks to Thomas J. O'Hern, Esq., for his help with this chapter.

Chapter 51

Certificate of Relief from Disabilities

Research References

Westlaw Databases

Complete Manual of Criminal Forms (3d ed.) (CMCRF)
Handling a Criminal Case in New York (HCCNY)
New York Driving While Intoxicated Defense Forms (NYDWIFM)
New York Vehicle and Traffic Law 2d (NYVEH)

Treatises and Practice Aids

Muldoon, Handling a Criminal Case in New York §§ 21:249, 21:262
Rose, New York Vehicle and Traffic Law 2d § 7:6

Forms

Bailey and Fishman, Complete Manual of Criminal Forms § 111:5 (3d
  ed.)
Taheri and Orr, NY DWI Defense Forms § 1:5

Law Reviews and Other Periodicals

Kamins, 2007 Criminal Law Legislation, 80-FEB N.Y. St. B.J. 35
(February, 2008)

KeyCite®: Cases and other legal materials listed in KeyCite Scope can be
researched through the KeyCite service on Westlaw®. Use KeyCite to check
citations for form, parallel references, prior and later history, and comprehensive citator information, including citations to other decisions and secondary
materials.

---

§ 51:1   In general

Research References

West's Key Number Digest, Automobiles ⊸359.4; Criminal Law
  ⊸1219.5

Correction Law Article 23 governs certificates of relief from
disabilities. "A certificate of relief from disabilities may be
granted as provided in [Correction Law Article 23] to relieve an
eligible offender of any forfeiture or disability, or to remove any
bar to his employment, automatically imposed by law by reason
of his conviction of the crime or of the offense specified therein."

Correction Law § 701(1). A copy of a certificate of relief is set forth at Appendix 13.

This chapter addresses certificates of relief in general, paying particular attention to issues pertinent to DWI cases. In this chapter, the terms "certificate of relief" and "certificate of relief from disabilities" are used synonymously, as are the terms "disabilities" and "forfeitures, disabilities and bars."

§ 51:2   Who is eligible for certificate of relief?

Research References

West's Key Number Digest, Automobiles ⬬359.4; Criminal Law ⬬1219.5

To be eligible for a certificate of relief, a person must be an "eligible offender." Correction Law § 700(1)(a) defines the term "eligible offender" as "a person who has been convicted of a crime or of an offense, but who has not been convicted more than once of a felony."

In *People v. Eastco Bldg. Services*, 23 Misc. 3d 864, __, 873 N.Y.S.2d 874 (N.Y. Co. Sup. Ct. 2009), the Court held that:

> There is no question that in numerous contexts, the term "person" includes a corporation. Indeed the Defendant was convicted here . . . under a Penal Law definition which makes corporate defendants criminally liable under appropriate circumstances. A review of the text of Article 23, however, and a review of the statute's legislative history indicates that the word "person" in Article 23 was not intended to include corporate defendants.

For purposes of Correction Law Article 23, the following additional definitions apply:

1. The term "felony" is defined as "a conviction of a felony in this state, or of an offense in any other jurisdiction for which a sentence to a term of imprisonment in excess of one year, or a sentence of death, was authorized." Correction Law § 700(1)(b); and

2. The term "revocable sentence" is defined as "a suspended sentence or a sentence upon which execution was suspended pursuant to the penal law in effect prior to [September 1, 1967]; or a sentence of probation or of conditional discharge imposed pursuant to the penal law in effect after [September 1, 1967]." Correction Law § 700(1)(c).

In addition, for purposes of Correction Law Article 23, the following rules of construction apply:

(a) [2] or more convictions of felonies charged in separate counts of [1] indictment or information shall be deemed to be [1] conviction;

(b) [2] or more convictions of felonies charged in [2] or more indictments or informations, filed in the same court prior to entry of judgment under any of them, shall be deemed to be [1] conviction; and

(c) A plea or a verdict of guilty upon which sentence or the execution of sentence has been suspended or upon which a sentence of probation, conditional discharge, or unconditional discharge has been imposed shall be deemed to be a conviction.Correction Law § 700(2)(a) to (c).

The supreme court and the county court are not the "same court" for purposes of Correction Law § 700(2)(b). *People v. Ruiz*, 144 Misc. 2d 826, __, 545 N.Y.S.2d 886, 886–87 (Westchester Co. Sup. Ct. 1989).

§ 51:3 Court and/or probation department must advise eligible offender of eligibility for certificate of relief

Research References

West's Key Number Digest, Automobiles ☜359.4; Criminal Law ☜1219.5

The Uniform Rules for Courts Exercising Criminal Jurisdiction provide that:

(a) In all criminal causes, whenever a pre-sentence probation report is submitted to the court, such report shall contain information bearing upon the eligibility of the defendant to obtain a certificate of relief from forfeitures and disabilities under [Correction Law Article 23] and shall further contain a recommendation as to the appropriateness of granting such discretionary relief at the time sentence is pronounced. Whenever a defendant has been sentenced to a period of probation, and has not received such discretionary relief, and if such defendant is apparently eligible for consideration of such discretionary relief, the probation officer supervising such defendant, prior to the termination of the probation period, shall inform the defendant, of his right to make application to the court for a certificate of relief from disabilities, and shall provide such defendant with the required forms in order to enable him or her to make application to the court if he or she should wish to do so.

(b) In all criminal causes, whenever a defendant who is eligible to receive a certificate of relief from disabilities under [Correction Law Article 23] is sentenced, the court, in pronouncing sentence, unless it grants such certificate at that time, shall advise the defendant of his or her eligibility to make application at a later time for such relief.

(c) Failure to comply with the requirements of subdivision

(a) or (b) of this section shall not affect the validity of any sentence.
22 NYCRR § 200.9(a) to (c).

§ 51:4 Certificate of relief not applicable to youthful offender adjudication

Research References
West's Key Number Digest, Automobiles ⊘359.4; Criminal Law ⊘1219.5

In *People v. Doe*, 52 Misc. 2d 656, __, 276 N.Y.S.2d 437, 437–38 (Nassau Co. Dist. Ct. 1967), the Court stated that Correction Law:

> Article 23 is designed to relieve a person who has been *convicted* of a crime or of an offense on only one occasion from disabilities which flow as a result of that conviction. An adjudication as a youthful offender is not deemed to be a conviction nor does it operate as a disqualification to hold public office, public employment or as a forfeiture of any right or privilege or to receive any license granted by public authority.

> It appears, therefore, that Article 23 is not applicable in connection with adjudications as youthful offender and, indeed, is not required.

(Emphasis added) (citation omitted).

§ 51:5 Effect of certificate of relief—Generally

Research References
West's Key Number Digest, Automobiles ⊘359.4; Criminal Law ⊘1219.5

Correction Law § 701(2) provides, with certain exceptions, that:

> Notwithstanding any other provision of law, . . . a conviction of a crime or of an offense specified in a certificate of relief from disabilities shall not cause automatic forfeiture of any license, permit, employment or franchise, including the right to register for or vote at an election, or automatic forfeiture of any other right or privilege, held by the eligible offender and covered by the certificate. Nor shall such conviction be deemed to be a conviction within the meaning of any provision of law that imposes, by reason of a conviction, a bar to any employment, a disability to exercise any right or a disability to apply for or to receive any license, permit or other authority or privilege, covered by the certificate.

Correction Law § 752 prohibits unfair discrimination against persons previously convicted of criminal offenses. In this regard, Correction Law § 753(2) provides that:

In making a determination pursuant to [Correction Law § 752], the

public agency or private employer shall also give consideration to a
certificate of relief from disabilities or a certificate of good conduct
issued to the applicant, which certificate shall create a presumption
of rehabilitation in regard to the offense or offenses specified
therein.

See also Robles v. LiMandri, 107 A.D.3d 592, 967 N.Y.S.2d 722
(1st Dep't 2013); *Dellaporte v. New York City Dept. of Bldgs.*, 106
A.D.3d 446, 965 N.Y.S.2d 44 (1st Dep't 2013). *Cf. DeRaffele v.
State of New York Banking Dept.*, 104 A.D.3d 557, 960 N.Y.S.2d
645 (1st Dep't 2013), leave to appeal denied, 21 N.Y.3d 858, 970
N.Y.S.2d 748, 992 N.E.2d 1093 (2013); *Rampolla v. Banking Dept.
of State*, 93 A.D.3d 526, 940 N.Y.S.2d 257 (1st Dep't 2012); *Wunder-
lich v. New York State Educ. Dept.*, 82 A.D.3d 1345, 918 N.Y.S.2d
257 (3d Dep't 2011), leave to appeal denied, 17 N.Y.3d 715, 933
N.Y.S.2d 656, 957 N.E.2d 1160 (2011).

§ 51:6   Certificate of relief may apply to *all* disabilities, or merely to one or more enumerated disabilities

Research References
West's Key Number Digest, Automobiles ☞359.4; Criminal Law
☞1219.5

A certificate of relief "may be limited to [1] or more enumerated
forfeitures, disabilities or bars, or may relieve the eligible offender of *all* forfeitures, disabilities and bars." Correction Law
§ 701(1) (emphasis added).

§ 51:7   Certificate of relief only removes *automatic* bars to licensing—It does not affect discretionary power of licensing body

Research References
West's Key Number Digest, Automobiles ☞359.4; Criminal Law
☞1219.5

Correction Law § 701(1) provides, in pertinent part, that:

A certificate of relief from disabilities may be granted as provided
in [Correction Law Article 23] to relieve an eligible offender of any
forfeiture or disability, or to remove any bar to his employment,
automatically imposed by law by reason of his conviction of the
crime or of the offense specified therein.

(Emphasis added).

By contrast, Correct. Law § 701(3) provides that:

A certificate of relief from disabilities shall not, however, in any
way prevent any judicial, administrative, licensing or other body,
board or authority from relying upon the conviction specified therein

as the basis for the exercise of its *discretionary power* to suspend, revoke, refuse to issue or refuse to renew any license, permit or other authority or privilege.

(Emphasis added). *See also Matter of Plantone v. State Dep't of State, Div. of Licensing Servs.*, 251 A.D.2d 1049, __, 674 N.Y.S.2d 560, 561 (4th Dep't 1998) ("It is well settled that a certificate of relief from disabilities does not preclude a licensing body from exercising its discretion to revoke a license over which the licensing body has authority").

In *Plantone*, the Appellate Division, Fourth Department, stated that "[c]ontrary to petitioner's contention, that certificate did not prevent respondent from revoking petitioner's license in the exercise of its discretion (*see,* Correction Law § 701[3]); it merely precluded the automatic revocation of petitioner's license to sell real estate (*see,* Correction Law § 701[1])." 251 A.D.2d at __, 674 N.Y.S.2d at 561. *See also Matter of Maneri v. New York State Dep't of State*, 240 A.D.2d 748, __, 660 N.Y.S.2d 26, 27 (2d Dep't 1997); *Matter of Frederick v. Civil Serv. Comm'n of County of Schenectady*, 175 A.D.2d 428, __, 572 N.Y.S.2d 116, 118 (3d Dep't 1991); *Matter of Springer v. Whalen*, 68 A.D.2d 1011, __, 415 N.Y.S.2d 106, 108–09 (3d Dep't 1979); *People v. Adams*, 193 Misc. 2d 78, __, 747 N.Y.S.2d 909, 916 (Kings Co. Sup. Ct. 2002).

§ 51:8 Certificate of relief is not a pardon, nor does it eradicate or expunge the underlying conviction

Research References

West's Key Number Digest, Automobiles ☞359.4; Criminal Law ☞1219.5

Correct. Law § 706 makes clear that "no certificate issued hereunder shall be deemed or construed to be a pardon." *See also Matter of Sugarman*, 64 A.D.2d 166, __, 409 N.Y.S.2d 224, 226 (1st Dep't 1978); *Matter of Glucksman*, 57 A.D.2d 205, __, 394 N.Y.S.2d 191, 193 (1st Dep't 1977).

Neither does a certificate of relief "eradicate or expunge the underlying conviction." *Matter of Morrisette v. Dilworth*, 59 N.Y.2d 449, 451 n.2, 465 N.Y.S.2d 894, 895 n.2 (1983). *See also Mugalli v. Ashcroft*, 258 F.3d 52, 62 (2d Cir. 2001); *United States v. DiNapoli*, 557 F.2d 962, 966 (2d Cir. 1977); *Able Cycle Engines, Inc. v. Allstate Ins. Co.*, 84 A.D.2d 140, __, 445 N.Y.S.2d 469, 472 (2d Dep't 1981); *Matter of Da Grossa v. Goodman*, 72 Misc. 2d 806, __, 339 N.Y.S.2d 502, 505 (N.Y. Co. Sup. Ct. 1972).

§ 51:9 Certificate of relief does not permit holder to retain or to be eligible for public office

Research References

West's Key Number Digest, Automobiles ⟐359.4; Criminal Law ⟐1219.5

Regardless of whether a person is granted a full, unrestricted certificate of relief purportedly relieving him or her of "all disabilities," Correction Law § 701(1) expressly provides that "no such certificate shall apply, or be construed so as to apply, to the right of such person to retain or to be eligible for public office."

The statute does not define the term "public office." However, case law has held that the following positions, among others, constitute a "public office":

1. A firefighter. *Matter of Lang v. Hoberman*, 30 N.Y.2d 829, 335 N.Y.S.2d 76 (1972);

2. A police officer. *Matter of Hodgson v. McGuire*, 75 A.D.2d 763, 427 N.Y.S.2d 820 (1st Dep't 1980); and

3. A notary public. *People v. Olensky*, 91 Misc. 2d 225, 397 N.Y.S.2d 565 (Queens Co. Sup. Ct. 1977).

By contrast, case law has held that the following position does *not* constitute a "public office":

1. A sanitation worker. *Matter of DePaolo v. Bronstein*, 45 A.D.2d 691, 356 N.Y.S.2d 631 (1st Dep't 1974) (per curiam).

§ 51:10 Certificate of relief does not immunize person from immigration consequences of a conviction

Research References

West's Key Number Digest, Automobiles ⟐359.4; Criminal Law ⟐1219.5

A certificate of relief does not immunize a person from the immigration consequences of a conviction. *See Mugalli v. Ashcroft*, 258 F.3d 52, 61–62 (2d Cir. 2001).

§ 51:11 Certificate of relief does not override mandatory driver's license revocation in VTL § 1192 case

Research References

West's Key Number Digest, Automobiles ⟐359.4; Criminal Law ⟐1219.5

Correction Law § 701(2) expressly provides that the provisions thereof (which override the mandatory licensing consequences flowing from certain criminal convictions) do *not* override, inter alia:

1. VTL § 1193(2)(b) (which provides for a mandatory driver's

license revocation following most VTL § 1192 convictions); and/or

2. The VTL where the defendant receives a second or subsequent VTL § 1192 conviction within 10 years.

In this regard, it seems that number "2" above is unnecessary and redundant in light of number "1."

§ 51:12 Certificate of relief does not render prior conviction inadmissible for impeachment purposes

Research References

West's Key Number Digest, Automobiles ☞359.4; Criminal Law ☞1219.5

In *Able Cycle Engines, Inc. v. Allstate Ins. Co.*, 84 A.D.2d 140, __, 445 N.Y.S.2d 469, 473 (2d Dep't 1981), the Appellate Division, Second Department, held that "a certificate of relief from disabilities, since it clearly does not eradicate the underlying conviction, also does not render that conviction inadmissible for impeachment purposes." *See also United States v. DiNapoli*, 557 F.2d 962, 965–66 (2d Cir. 1977).

§ 51:13 Certificate of relief does not relieve person from disclosing prior criminal conviction on employment application

Research References

West's Key Number Digest, Automobiles ☞359.4; Criminal Law ☞1219.5

In Matter of Ghorab v. Sweeney, 219 A.D.2d 793, __, 631 N.Y.S.2d 786, 787 (3d Dep't 1995), the Appellate Division, Third Department, made clear that "[a]lthough a certificate of relief from disabilities serves to remove any bar to an individual's employment automatically imposed by law, it does not relieve an individual from disclosing a prior criminal conviction."

§ 51:14 Certificate of relief does not permit reinstatement of attorney disbarred based upon conviction of a felony

Research References

West's Key Number Digest, Automobiles ☞359.4; Criminal Law ☞1219.5

Judiciary Law § 90(4) provides that an attorney who is convicted of a felony is automatically disbarred. In this regard, a certificate of relief will not result in the reinstatement of such person's license to practice law. *See Matter of Posner*, 80 A.D.3d 238, 914 N.Y.S.2d 24 (1st Dep't 2010), leave to appeal denied, 16 N.Y.3d 709, 922 N.Y.S.2d 271, 947 N.E.2d 163 (2011) (per curiam); *Matter of Sugarman*, 64 A.D.2d 166, 409 N.Y.S.2d 224 (1st Dep't 1978); *Matter of Glucksman*, 57 A.D.2d 205, 394 N.Y.S.2d 191 (1st Dep't 1977).

§ 51:15 Applicability of certificate of relief to commercial drivers

Research References

West's Key Number Digest, Automobiles ⊕359.4; Criminal Law ⊕1219.5

Prior to September 30, 2005, VTL § 1196(7)(g) provided that "[a]ny conditional license or privilege issued to a person convicted of a violation of any subdivision of [VTL § 1192] shall not be valid for the operation of any commercial motor vehicle or taxicab as defined in this chapter." However, if a commercial driver obtained a certificate of relief relieving him or her from the application of VTL § 1196(7)(g), the DMV would issue the driver a conditional license valid for the operation of a commercial motor vehicle.

Effective September 30, 2005, VTL § 1196(7)(g) now provides that the prohibition against using a conditional license for the operation of a commercial motor vehicle applies *"[n]otwithstanding anything to the contrary contained in a certificate of relief from disabilities issued pursuant to [Correction Law Article 23]."* (Emphasis added).

A corresponding amendment was made to VTL § 530(5), which now prohibits the DMV from issuing a restricted use license valid for the operation of a commercial motor vehicle notwithstanding anything to the contrary contained in a certificate of relief.

§ 51:16 Applicability of certificate of relief to taxicab drivers

Research References

West's Key Number Digest, Automobiles ⊕359.4; Criminal Law ⊕1219.5

VTL § 1196(7)(g) provides that:

Notwithstanding anything to the contrary contained in a certificate of relief from disabilities issued pursuant to [Correction Law Article 23], any conditional license or privilege issued to a person convicted of a violation of any subdivision of [VTL § 1192] shall not be valid for the operation of any commercial motor vehicle. *In addition, no such conditional license or privilege shall be valid for the operation of a taxicab as defined in this chapter.*

(Emphasis added).

Critically, when VTL § 1196(7)(g) was amended effective September 30, 2005, the language in the first sentence thereof (which now prohibits the DMV from issuing a conditional license valid for the operation of a commercial motor vehicle notwithstanding anything to the contrary contained in a certificate of relief) was not incorporated into the second sentence (which pertains to taxicabs).

As a result, if a taxicab driver obtains a certificate of relief relieving him or her from the application of VTL § 1196(7)(g), DMV will still issue the driver a conditional license valid for the operation of a taxicab.

Similarly, the corresponding amendment to VTL § 530(5) (which now prohibits the DMV from issuing a restricted use license valid for the operation of a commercial motor vehicle notwithstanding anything to the contrary contained in a certificate of relief) does not apply to taxicabs (or to other non-commercial motor vehicles).

§ 51:17 Applicability of certificate of relief to pistol permit

Research References

West's Key Number Digest, Automobiles ⚷359.4; Criminal Law ⚷1219.5

"[A] person who has been convicted of a felony ordinarily is barred from obtaining a pistol permit." *Matter of Hecht v. Bivona*, 306 A.D.2d 410, __, 761 N.Y.S.2d 485, 485 (2d Dep't 2003). *See also* PL § 400.00(1). However, an unrestricted certificate of relief which relieves the holder of "all disabilities" removes "the automatic bar to an application for, and issuance of, a pistol permit." *Bivona*, 306 A.D.2d at __, 761 N.Y.S.2d at 485. *See also People v. Adams*, 193 Misc. 2d 78, __, 747 N.Y.S.2d 909, 916 (Kings Co. Sup. Ct. 2002); *People v. Flook*, 164 Misc. 2d 284, 625 N.Y.S.2d 405 (Ontario Co. Ct. 1995). In light of *Bivona*, *Matter of Alarie*, 168 Misc. 2d 329, __, 643 N.Y.S.2d 926, 927 (Monroe Co. Ct. 1996), and *Matter of Valhos*, 145 Misc. 2d 657, __, 547 N.Y.S.2d 537, 538 (Schoharie Co. Ct. 1989), should not be followed to the extent that they hold to the contrary.

On the other hand, although in such a case the applicant is not *automatically* barred from obtaining a pistol permit, a court is not precluded "from exercising its discretionary power to deny the application." *Bivona*, 306 A.D.2d at __, 761 N.Y.S.2d at 486. *See also Adams*, 193 Misc. 2d at __, 747 N.Y.S.2d at 916; Correction Law § 701(3).

It should be noted that an issue appears to exist as to whether the possession of a firearm by a person convicted of certain offenses constitutes a *federal* crime regardless of state law and regardless of whether the person has been issued a certificate of relief. *See, e.g., Adams*; *supra, United States v. Craig*, 896 F. Supp. 85 (N.D.N.Y. 1995); 1998 N.Y. Op. Atty. Gen. 23 (Formal Op. No. 98-F8, July 30, 1998).

§ 51:18   Applicability of certificate of relief to "long guns"

Research References

West's Key Number Digest, Automobiles ☞359.4; Criminal Law ☞1219.5

In Matter of Alarie, 168 Misc. 2d 329, __, 643 N.Y.S.2d 926, 927 (Monroe Co. Ct. 1996), the Court held that "the applicants herein, by virtue of their respective Certificates of Relief, may own, possess and use long guns (shot guns and rifles) legally allowed for hunting in the State of New York and are not barred from taking the safety courses and obtaining a New York State hunting license. No special notations are needed on a Certificate of Relief for such activity." *See also People v. Flook*, 164 Misc. 2d 284, 625 N.Y.S.2d 405 (Ontario Co. Ct. 1995). *See generally Matter of Hecht v. Bivona*, 306 A.D.2d 410, 761 N.Y.S.2d 485 (2d Dep't 2003); *People v. Adams*, 193 Misc. 2d 78, __, 747 N.Y.S.2d 909, 912 (Kings Co. Sup. Ct. 2002).

It should be noted that an issue appears to exist as to whether the possession of a firearm by a person convicted of certain offenses constitutes a *federal* crime regardless of state law and regardless of whether the person has been issued a certificate of relief. *See, e.g., Adams*; *supra, United States v. Craig*, 896 F. Supp. 85 (N.D.N.Y. 1995); 1998 N.Y. Op. Atty. Gen. 23 (Formal Op. No. 98-F8, July 30, 1998).

§ 51:19   Applicability of certificate of relief to right to serve on jury

Research References

West's Key Number Digest, Automobiles ☞359.4; Criminal Law ☞1219.5

"[A] felon, whether incarcerated or not, loses the right to serve on a jury." *People v. Adams*, 193 Misc. 2d 78, __, 747 N.Y.S.2d 909, 915 (Kings Co. Sup. Ct. 2002). However:

> Under Corrections [sic] Law § 701, the issuance of a CRD relieves a convicted person of the automatic bar from serving on a jury. It does not, however, restore the right to serve on the jury. The determination whether a defendant is eligible for jury service is made by the Commissioner of Jurors not the Court.

People v. Adams, 193 Misc. 2d 78, —, 747 N.Y.S.2d 909, 915 (Kings Co. Sup. Ct. 2002).

§ 51:20 Criteria for issuance of certificate of relief by Court

Research References

West's Key Number Digest, Automobiles ☞359.4; Criminal Law ☞1219.5

"Any court of this state may, in its discretion, issue a certificate of relief from disabilities to an eligible offender for a conviction that occurred in such court, if the court either (a) imposed a revocable sentence or (b) imposed a sentence other than one executed by commitment to [a state prison]." Correction Law § 702(1). *See also People v. Serrano*, 81 A.D.3d 753, 916 N.Y.S.2d 509 (2d Dep't 2011), leave to appeal denied, 17 N.Y.3d 801, 929 N.Y.S.2d 109, 952 N.E.2d 1104 (2011).

Thus, pursuant to Correction Law § 702(1), a court cannot issue a certificate of relief to a defendant who is sentenced to state prison. *See People v. Dor*, 132 Misc. 2d 568, —, 505 N.Y.S.2d 317, 320 (Kings Co. Sup. Ct. 1986). In such a case, a certificate of relief would have to be issued by the Board of Parole. *See* Correction Law § 703.

In addition, a federal court administering federal criminal law is not a "court of this state" within the meaning of Correction Law § 702(1). *See United States v. Da Grossa*, 446 F.2d 902, 903 (2d Cir. 1971) (per curiam).

Where a defendant is sentenced to probation, and such probation is transferred to the County in which the defendant resides, the new Court having jurisdiction over the case can issue a certificate of relief. *See* CPL § 410.80(2); *People v. Mitchell*, 15 N.Y.3d 93, 96 & n.3, 905 N.Y.S.2d 115, 116 & n.3, 931 N.E.2d 84, _ & n.3 (2010).

Where a court is authorized to issue a certificate of relief, Correction Law § 702(2) provides that:

Such certificate shall not be issued by the court unless the court is satisfied that:

(a) The person to whom it is to be granted is an eligible offender, as defined in [Correction Law § 700];

(b) The relief to be granted by the certificate is consistent with the rehabilitation of the eligible offender; and

(c) The relief to be granted by the certificate is consistent with the public interest.

Furthermore, Correction Law § 701(2) provides that "[a] certificate of relief from a disability imposed pursuant to [VTL § 510(2)(b)(v) and VTL § 510(6)(i) and (j)] may only be issued upon a determination that compelling circumstances warrant such relief." VTL § 510(2)(b)(v) and VTL § 510(6)(i) and (j) provide for various driver's license sanctions where a person is convicted of DWAI drugs or of other state or federal drug charges. In this regard, it should be noted that in a DWAI drugs case the driver's license sanctions set forth in VTL § 510(2)(b)(v) and VTL § 510(6)(i) & (j) overlap with, and in some respects are in conflict with, those set forth in VTL § 1193(2)(b).

§ 51:21   Issuance of certificate of relief in connection with out-of-state or federal conviction

Research References
West's Key Number Digest, Automobiles ☞359.4; Criminal Law ☞1219.5

In *Matter of Application for a Certificate of Relief from Civil Disabilities by C.P. Ward, Inc.*, 184 Misc. 2d 57, __, 707 N.Y.S.2d 605, 605–06 (Monroe Co. Ct. 2000), the Court found that it lacked authority to issue a certificate of relief to "a corporate defendant who sustained a conviction in Federal Court and now seeks relief in State court." In this regard, the *Ward* Court noted that Correction Law § 703(1)(b) provides that "any eligible offender who resides within this state and whose judgment of conviction was rendered by a court in any other jurisdiction" can apply to the Board of Parole for a certificate of relief.

By contrast, one court has reached the opposite conclusion, *see Matter of Da Grossa v. Goodman*, 72 Misc. 2d 806, 339 N.Y.S.2d 502 (N.Y. Co. Sup. Ct. 1972); and another has found that the answer depends upon the sentence imposed upon the defendant by the other jurisdiction. *See Matter of Helmsley*, 152 Misc. 2d 215, 575 N.Y.S.2d 1009 (N.Y. Co. Sup. Ct. 1991).

§ 51:22   Certificate of relief—Time for issuance by court

Research References
West's Key Number Digest, Automobiles ☞359.4; Criminal Law ☞1219.5

A certificate of relief "may be issued (i) at the time sentence is pronounced, in which case it may grant relief from forfeitures as well as from disabilities, or (ii) at any time thereafter, in which case it shall apply only to disabilities." Correct. Law § 702(1).

In addition, "[w]here a certificate of relief from disabilities is not issued at the time sentence is pronounced it shall only be issued thereafter upon verified application to the court." Correct. Law § 702(3).

§ 51:23 Certificate of relief issued by court at any time after sentencing only applies to disabilities—*Not* to forfeitures

Research References

West's Key Number Digest, Automobiles ⬧359.4; Criminal Law ⬧1219.5

Correct. Law § 702(1) provides that a certificate of relief "may be issued (i) at the time sentence is pronounced, in which case it may grant relief from forfeitures as well as from disabilities, or (ii) at any time thereafter, in which case it shall apply only to disabilities."

§ 51:24 Court may request probation department to conduct investigation of applicant for certificate of relief

Research References

West's Key Number Digest, Automobiles ⬧359.4; Criminal Law ⬧1219.5

Correct. Law § 702(3) provides, in pertinent part, that:

The court may, for the purpose of determining whether such certificate shall be issued, request its probation service to conduct an investigation of the applicant, or if the court has no probation service it may request the probation service of the county court for the county in which the court is located to conduct such investigation, or if there be no such probation service the court may request the state director of probation and correctional alternatives to arrange for such investigation. Any probation officer requested to make an investigation pursuant to this section shall prepare and submit to the court a written report in accordance with such request.

§ 51:25 Confidentiality of probation department report of investigation of applicant for certificate of relief

Research References

West's Key Number Digest, Automobiles ⬧359.4; Criminal Law ⬧1219.5

Correct. Law § 702(6) provides that:

Any written report submitted to the court pursuant to [Correction Law § 702] is confidential and may not be made available to any person or public or private agency except where specifically required or permitted by statute or upon specific authorization of the court. However, it shall be made available by the court for examination by the applicant's attorney, or the applicant himself, if he has no attorney. In its discretion, the court may except from disclosure a part or parts of the report which are not relevant to the granting of a certificate, or sources of information which have been obtained on a promise of confidentiality, or any other portion thereof, disclosure of which would not be in the interest of justice. The action of the court excepting information from disclosure shall be subject to appellate review. The court, in its discretion, may hold a conference in open court or in chambers to afford an applicant an opportunity to controvert or to comment upon any portions of the report. The court may also conduct a summary hearing at the conference on any matter relevant to the granting of the application and may take testimony under oath.

§ 51:26   Temporary certificate of relief

Research References
West's Key Number Digest, Automobiles ☞359.4; Criminal Law ☞1219.5

Correct. Law § 702(4) provides, in pertinent part, that:

Where the court has imposed a revocable sentence and the certificate of relief from disabilities is issued prior to the expiration or termination of the time which the court may revoke such sentence, the certificate shall be deemed to be a temporary certificate until such time as the court's authority to revoke the sentence has expired or is terminated.

§ 51:27   Revocation of temporary certificate of relief

Research References
West's Key Number Digest, Automobiles ☞359.4; Criminal Law ☞1219.5

Correct. Law § 702(4) provides, in pertinent part, that:

While temporary, such certificate (a) may be revoked by the court for violation of the conditions of the sentence, and (b) shall be revoked by the court if it revokes the sentence and commits the person to [a state prison]. Any such revocation shall be upon notice and after an opportunity to be heard. If the certificate is not so revoked, it shall become a permanent certificate upon expiration or termination of the court's authority to revoke the sentence.

"Where a certificate of relief from disabilities is deemed to be temporary and such certificate is revoked, disabilities and forfeitures thereby relieved shall be reinstated as of the date upon which the person to whom the certificate was issued receives written notice of such revocation. Any such person shall upon receipt of such notice surrender the certificate to the issuing court or board." Correct. Law § 704(1).

§ 51:28 Use or attempted use of revoked certificate of relief is a misdemeanor

Research References

West's Key Number Digest, Automobiles ⌖359.4; Criminal Law ⌖1219.5

Correct. Law § 704(2) provides that "[a] person who knowingly uses[,] or attempts to use, a revoked certificate of relief from disabilities in order to obtain or to exercise any right or privilege that he would not be entitled to obtain or to exercise without a valid certificate shall be guilty of a misdemeanor."

§ 51:29 Enlargement of certificate of relief

Research References

West's Key Number Digest, Automobiles ⌖359.4; Criminal Law ⌖1219.5

Correct. Law § 702(5) provides that:

Any court that has issued a certificate of relief from disabilities may at any time issue a new certificate to enlarge the relief previously granted, provided, however, that the provisions of [Correction Law § 702(1) to (4)] shall apply to the issuance of any such new certificate.

§ 51:30 Issuance of certificate of relief by Board of Parole

Research References

West's Key Number Digest, Automobiles ⌖359.4; Criminal Law ⌖1219.5

Correct. Law § 703 sets forth the instances in which the Board of Parole can issue, enlarge, and/or revoke a certificate of relief. However, this topic is beyond the scope of this chapter.

§ 51:31 Certificate of relief is filed with NYSIIS

Research References

West's Key Number Digest, Automobiles ⌖359.4; Criminal Law ⌖1219.5

Correct. Law § 705(2) provides that "[a]ny court or board issuing or revoking any certificate [of relief] pursuant to [Correction Law Article 23] shall immediately file a copy of the certificate, or of the order of revocation, with the New York state identification and intelligence system."

Chapter 52

Seal and Return Orders: Clearing the Record

§ 52:1   CPL § 160.50
§ 52:2   CPL § 160.55—Sealing of noncriminal convictions
§ 52:3   Access to and use of sealed records
§ 52:4   Effect of termination of criminal actions in favor of the accused

Research References

Westlaw Databases
Handling a Criminal Case in New York (HCCNY)

Treatises and Practice Aids
Muldoon, Handling a Criminal Case in New York §§ 1:110, 21:80

Law Reviews and Other Periodicals
Raybin, Expungement of Arrest Records: Erasing the Past, 44-MAR Tenn. B.J. 22 (March, 2008)

KeyCite®: Cases and other legal materials listed in KeyCite Scope can be researched through the KeyCite service on Westlaw®. Use KeyCite to check citations for form, parallel references, prior and later history, and comprehensive citator information, including citations to other decisions and secondary materials.

---

§ 52:1   CPL § 160.50

Research References
West's Key Number Digest, Criminal Law ⚖1226(3), 1226(5)

A defendant's prior record is of critical importance in the disposition of any subsequent charges. Since the criminal justice system tends to equate arrests with convictions, it is imperative that the provisions of CPL § 160.50 and § 160.55, the sealing statutes, be implemented whenever possible. These statutes, which contain the operative provisions protecting defendants whose arrests terminate in favorable determinations, serve the goal of ensuring "that one who is charged but not convicted suffers no stigma as a result of his once being the object of an unsustained accusation." *Matter of Hynes v. Karassik*, 47 N.Y.2d 659, 419 N.Y.S.2d 942 (1979). Further, they have a broad thrust and remedial purpose, *Matter of Hynes v. Karassik*, 47 N.Y.2d

659, 662, 419 N.Y.S.2d 942 (1979), and their language is mandatory and has been strictly construed. *Matter of Joseph M.*, 82 N.Y.2d 128, 603 N.Y.S.2d 804 (1993).

CPL § 160.50 provides for the sealing of a defendant's records, and return of his or her fingerprints and photographs, once a criminal action is terminated in the defendant's favor. A favorable termination is defined by the section as a dismissal and/or an adjournment in contemplation of dismissal. CPL § 160.50(1)(a) gives the recipient agency the option of returning or destroying the prints and photos.

> [E]very photograph of such person and photographic plate or proof, and all palmprints and fingerprints taken or made of such person pursuant to the provisions of this article in regard to the action or proceeding terminated . . . and all duplicates and copies thereof, except a digital fingerprint image where authorized pursuant to paragraph (e) *of this subdivision, shall forthwith be, at the discretion of the recipient agency, either destroyed or returned to such person, or to the attorney* who represented such person at the time of the termination of the action or proceeding, at the address given by such person or attorney during the action or proceeding, by the Division of Criminal Justice Services and by any police department, or law enforcement agency having such photograph, photographic plate or proof, palmprint or fingerprints in its possession and under its control.

(Emphasis added). This provision expired on September 1, 1997. Effective September 1, 1997, CPL § 160.50(1)(a) eliminates the discretion to destroy and reinstates the former requirement that these items be returned.

In *Matter of Catterson v. Corso*, 244 A.D.2d 407, 664 N.Y.S.2d 67 (2d Dep't 1997), the Appellate Division, Second Department, held that there is no authority in the CPL for a court to order the destruction of audio and/or video cassette tapes relating to a criminal prosecution upon termination of the action in favor of the defendant. *See* CPL § 160.50(1)(a). However, such tapes would nonetheless be "sealed" pursuant to CPL § 160.50(1)(c).

Once the case has been dismissed and the court record or proceeding sealed, the clerk of the court must immediately notify the Commissioner of the Division of Criminal Justice Services, and the heads of all appropriate police departments and other law enforcement agencies, that the action has terminated in favor of the accused and that the record has been sealed. *See* CPL § 160.50(1). A report of the termination of the action or proceeding in favor of the accused constitutes sufficient notice of sealing, unless the court has determined in the interests of justice that the record not be sealed.

Frequently, a DWI charge will be dismissed, but the record will not be expunged. A subsequently arrested defendant will have this prior arrest considered in the disposition of his case in much the same manner as someone with a prior conviction. Although the report of the dismissal by the court to the Division of Criminal Justice Services should result in the expungement of the record and the return and/or destruction of fingerprints and photographs, it is the defense attorney's obligation to make sure that this occurs. All too often, the fact of the prior arrest shows up in a Division of Criminal Justice Services' record. Even though it later develops that the case was dismissed, the fact of the prior arrest is highly prejudicial and has an impact upon any plea negotiations.

§ 52:2 CPL § 160.55—Sealing of noncriminal convictions

Research References

West's Key Number Digest, Criminal Law ☞1226(3), 1226(5)

CPL § 160.55 provides for the return of fingerprints and photographs where a defendant is convicted of a violation or a traffic infraction. DWAI in violation of VTL § 1192(1) is specifically *exempted* from the application of this statute. *See People v. Alfaro*, 179 Misc. 2d 589, 686 N.Y.S.2d 638 (Greenburgh Just. Ct. 1999).

By virtue of a drafting error, CPL § 160.55 used to provide for the sealing of records for convictions for penal law violations and traffic infractions. While the statute still provides for the sealing of records by the Division of Criminal Justice Services and the return of fingerprints and photographs, there is no provision for the sealing of the criminal court records. Accordingly, a local criminal court will retain a record of such a conviction.

In addition, prosecutors may oppose the entry of a seal and return order where conviction for the offense may serve as a predicate for an enhanced charge or punishment in the future. In *People v. Doles*, 157 Misc. 2d 981, 599 N.Y.S.2d 454 (N.Y. City Crim. Ct. 1993), the People obtained an 18-month delay in the sealing of the records of a defendant who was convicted for what was then a violation of AUO 3rd. The delay was predicated upon the defendant's extensive history of traffic infractions and the fact that the defendant would derive an inequitable benefit if he committed a subsequent offense within 18 months of the entry of his conviction.

§ 52:3 Access to and use of sealed records

Research References

West's Key Number Digest, Criminal Law ☞1226(3.1)

Access to and use of sealed records are continuing subjects of litigation. In *Matter of Hynes v. Karassik*, 47 N.Y.2d 659, 419 N.Y.S.2d 942 (1979), the Grievance Committee was permitted to use evidentiary tape recordings that had been part of a sealed record. The court held that these were not official records and papers protected by the sealing statute. *See also People v. Morris*, 220 A.D.2d 808, 632 N.Y.S.2d 231 (3d Dep't 1995) (photograph taken as part of prior YO adjudication could be used for identification in present crime); *Doe v. District Attorney of County of Nassau*, 166 Misc. 2d 188, 632 N.Y.S.2d 414 (Nassau Co. Sup. Ct. 1995) (District attorney's investigative records are not official records relating to an arrest or prosecution).

In contrast, in *Matter of Dondi*, 63 N.Y.2d 331, 482 N.Y.S.2d 431 (1984), the Court broadened the sealing rule beyond the limited parameters outlined in *Karassik*. Here, the Court held that tapes that had been used as evidence in a criminal trial resulting in acquittal were subject to the sealing rules. The Court held that CPL § 160.50 mandates the sealing of *all* official records and papers relating to the defendant's arrest or prosecution on file with any court, police agency, or prosecutor's office. 482 N.Y.S.2d at 434.

In *Matter of Joseph M.*, 82 N.Y.2d 128, 603 N.Y.S.2d 804 (1993), the Court held that once records are sealed they must remain sealed except in the limited circumstances set forth in CPL § 160.50, which permits unsealing in extraordinary circumstances, in the interests of justice, as well as at the request of the defendant, his designated agent, and various law enforcement personnel acting in a law enforcement capacity. CPL § 160.50(1)(d).

The *Joseph M.* Court construed the exception to the sealing requirement as confined to persons or groups having some association with law enforcement. The Court denied the motion of the New York City Board of Education which sought to unseal a criminal file. *Matter of Joseph M.*, 82 N.Y.2d 128, 603 N.Y.S.2d 804 (1993). *See also People v. Abedi*, 159 Misc. 2d 1010, 607 N.Y.S.2d 862 (N.Y. Co. Sup. Ct. 1994) (prosecutor entitled to unsealing of records of cases formerly pending against criminal defendants, but only where acting as "law enforcement agency"). Each law enforcement agency must separately seek unsealing on their own behalf. *People v. Abedi*, 159 Misc. 2d 1010, 1016, 607 N.Y.S.2d 862 (N.Y. Co. Sup. Ct. 1994).

Unsealing is not limited to criminal justice agencies. For example, a criminal defendant may obtain unsealing of a witness's sealed violation conviction for impeachment purposes. *See People v. Rodriguez*, 152 Misc. 2d 328, 576 N.Y.S.2d 488 (Monroe Co. Sup. Ct. 1991).

Once the cat is out of the bag and a record is unsealed, it may be used as evidence in a criminal or civil proceeding, where no constitutional rights are implicated by its use. *See, e.g., Charles Q. v. Constantine,* 85 N.Y.2d 571, 626 N.Y.S.2d 992 (1995) (improperly unsealed record properly admitted in disciplinary action against state trooper); *People v. Patterson,* 78 N.Y.2d 711, 714–15, 579 N.Y.S.2d 617, 618–19 (1991) (no requirement of suppression of in-court identification, in spite of sealing violation, where no taint attached to identification procedure); *53rd St. Rest. Corp. v. New York State Liquor Auth.,* 220 A.D.2d 588, 632 N.Y.S.2d 815 (2d Dep't 1995).

A word of caution: a protected person's rights to the prophylaxis of the sealing statutes may be waived. For example, a civil suit by a protected person, which affirmatively places in issue elements that are common or related to the prior criminal action, may waive sealing protection. *See Abrams v. Skolnik,* 185 A.D.2d 407, 585 N.Y.S.2d 818 (3d Dep't 1992); *Wright v. Snow,* 175 A.D.2d 451, 572 N.Y.S.2d 503 (3d Dep't 1991).

§ 52:4 Effect of termination of criminal actions in favor of the accused

Research References

West's Key Number Digest, Criminal Law ⊙1226(3.1)

CPL § 160.60 states that the termination of a criminal action in favor of that person, as defined by CPL § 160.50(2), renders the arrest and prosecution a nullity and "the accused shall be restored, in contemplation of law, to the status he occupied before the arrest and prosecution." CPL § 160.60. In *People v. Ellis,* 184 A.D.2d 307, 584 N.Y.S.2d 569 (1st Dep't 1992), the court held that it was not error for the prosecutor to fail to disclose that a complainant had two prior arrests which had been sealed by court order. In addition, it was not error for the complainant to deny the existence of the prior arrests during his testimony, given the fact that the dismissal of the charges renders the arrests a nullity. 584 N.Y.S.2d at 570.

Chapter 53

Timeliness of Prosecutions and Speedy Trial

Research References

Westlaw Databases

Complete Manual of Criminal Forms (3d ed.) (CMCRF)
Constitutional Rights of the Accused (3d ed.) (CONRTACC)
Criminal Procedure (2d ed.) (CRIMPROC)
Drinking/Driving Litigation: Criminal and Civil (2d ed.) (DRNKDRIVING)
Handling a Criminal Case in New York (HCCNY)
New York Driving While Intoxicated Defense Forms (NYDWIFM)

Treatises and Practice Aids

Cook, Constitutional Rights of the Accused, Chapter 17 (3d ed.)
LaFave et al., 6 Criminal Procedure §§ 18.1 to 18.1(e), 18.4(c), 18.5 to 18.5(c) (2d ed.)
Nichols and Whited, Drinking/Driving Litigation: Criminal and Civil § 1:11 (2d ed.)
Muldoon, Handling a Criminal Case in New York §§ 13:12 to 13:125

Forms

Bailey and Fishman, Complete Manual of Criminal Forms §§ 12:39, 12:40 (3d ed.)
Taheri and Orr, NY DWI Defense Forms §§ 3:16, 3:17

Law Reviews and Other Periodicals

Abramovsky and Edelstein, Prosecutorial Readiness, Speedy Trial and the Absent Defendant: Has New York's 25-Year Dilemma Finally Been Resolved?, 15 Touro L. Rev. 25 (Fall, 1998)
Right to a Speedy Trial, 12 Touro L. Rev. 1031 (Spring, 1996)

KeyCite®: Cases and other legal materials listed in KeyCite Scope can be researched through the KeyCite service on Westlaw®. Use KeyCite to check citations for form, parallel references, prior and later history, and comprehensive citator information, including citations to other decisions and secondary materials.

---

§ 53:1   In general

Research References

West's Key Number Digest, Criminal Law ⬥573, 575, 577.4

CPL Article 30 (*i.e.*, CPL §§ 30.10, 30.20, and 30.30) addresses the timeliness of prosecutions (*i.e.*, statutes of limitation), as well as the right to a speedy trial. With regard to the right to a speedy trial, CPL § 30.20(1) in essence codifies the constitutional right to a speedy trial provided by the Sixth Amendment. As such, in this chapter the terms "CPL § 30.20" and "constitutional right to a speedy trial" are used synonymously. CPL § 30.30 provides the defendant with an additional, purely statutory, speedy trial right which both (a) is broader than that provided by the Constitution, and (b) focuses on prosecutorial readiness for trial as opposed to prejudice to the defendant.

§ 53:2 Statutes of limitation—Generally

Research References

West's Key Number Digest, Criminal Law ⚷573, 575, 577.4

Statutes of Limitation serve several purposes—they "protect individuals from having to defend themselves against charges when the basic facts may have become obscured by the passage of time"; they "minimize the danger of official punishment because of acts in the far-distant past"; and they "encourag[e] law enforcement officials promptly to investigate suspected criminal activity."

People v. Seda, 93 N.Y.2d 307, 311, 690 N.Y.S.2d 517, 519 (1999) (citation omitted). On the other hand:

The statute of limitations under CPL 30.10 is not a jurisdictional matter, nor is it a right of constitutional dimension like . . . rights that survive a guilty plea. Clearly, the right to assert this defense can be waived. By pleading guilty, defendant waive[s] the defense.

People v. Parilla, 8 N.Y.3d 654, 659, 838 N.Y.S.2d 824, 827, 870 N.E.2d 142 (2007) (citation omitted).

§ 53:3 CPL § 30.10(2)—Timeliness of prosecutions— Periods of limitation

Research References

West's Key Number Digest, Criminal Law ⚷573, 575, 577.4, 577.7

CPL § 30.10(2) provides that, with certain exceptions, a criminal action must be commenced within the following time periods:

    1. Class A felony—Any time after the commission thereof;

    2. Any other felony—Within five years after the commission thereof;

    3. Misdemeanor—Within two years after the commission thereof; and

    4. Petty offense—Within one year after the commission thereof.

CPL § 30.10(3) provides extensions of the periods of limitation for certain offenses beyond the scope of this book.

§ 53:4 CPL § 30.10(4)—Excludable time

Research References

West's Key Number Digest, Criminal Law ⚷573, 577.4, 577.8 to 577.8(2)

In calculating the period of limitation applicable to a particular case, CPL § 30.10(4) provides exclusions for the following time periods:

(a) Any period following the commission of the offense during which:

(i) the defendant was *continuously outside this state* or

(ii) the *whereabouts* of the defendant were continuously unknown and continuously unascertainable by the exercise of reasonable diligence.

(a) However, in no event shall the period of limitation be extended by more than [5] years beyond the period otherwise applicable under [CPL § 30.10(2)].

(b) When a prosecution for an offense is lawfully commenced within the prescribed period of limitation therefor, and when an accusatory instrument upon which such prosecution is based is subsequently dismissed by an authorized court under directions or circumstances permitting the lodging of another charge for the same offense or an offense based on the same conduct, the period extending from the commencement of the thus defeated prosecution to the dismissal of the accusatory instrument does not constitute a part of the period of limitation applicable to commencement of prosecution by a new charge.

CPL § 30.10(4)(a) to (b) (emphases added).

In *People v. Knobel*, 94 N.Y.2d 226, 701 N.Y.S.2d 695 (1999), the Court of Appeals interpreted the meaning of the phrase *continuously outside this state* for purposes of CPL § 30.10(4)(a)(i):

Our resolution of this case turns on the construction of the statutory phrase "continuously outside this state," as applied to the facts at hand. The Criminal Procedure Law defines neither the term "continuously" nor the phrase "continuously outside this state" for purposes of applying CPL 30.10(4)(a)(i). * * *

For an absence from the State to be "continuous" within the meaning of CPL 30.10(4)(a)(i), the People argue, it need not be a single uninterrupted period of time. We agree. The focus of the tolling provision of CPL 30.10 is "the difficulty of apprehending a defendant who is outside the State." Thus, all periods of a day or more that a nonresident defendant is out-of-State should be totaled and toll the Statute of Limitations.

People v. Knobel, 94 N.Y.2d 229, 230, 701 N.Y.S.2d 697 (citation omitted).

In *People v. Seda*, 93 N.Y.2d 307, 690 N.Y.S.2d 517 (1999), the Court of Appeals interpreted CPL § 30.10(4)(a)(ii), which applies where the defendant's *whereabouts* are unknown, to also apply where the defendant's *identity* is unknown. In so holding, the Court reasoned that:

In its enactment of CPL 30.10(4)(a), the Legislature has carefully balanced the general policy in favor of avoiding prosecution of stale cases against the countervailing policy of ensuring that law enforcement officers have sufficient time to bring suspected criminals to justice by imposing important limitations on the tolling exceptions. The People may benefit from the toll for only those periods during which the defendant's whereabouts remained unknown and were unascertainable through the exercise of reasonable diligence. Furthermore, the limitations period will be extended at most for [5] years. The focus of the tolling exception rests on the difficulty of finding the defendant whether or not the police are aware of his or her identity. The "reasonable diligence" requirement is certainly a deterrent to delaying an investigation, as no automatic toll is contemplated.

People v. Seda, 93 N.Y.2d 307, 311–12, 690 N.Y.S.2d 517 (1999).

§ 53:5   Statute of limitations claim generally must be raised in the defendant's omnibus motion

Research References

West's Key Number Digest, Criminal Law ☞573, 577.4, 577.8(1)

A motion to dismiss on the ground that a prosecution is time-barred by CPL § 30.10 is a "pre-trial motion" which is generally required to be included in the defendant's omnibus motion. *See* CPL §§ 255.10(1)(a), 255.10(1)(b), 255.20, 170.30(1)(d), 170.30(2), 170.45, 210.20(1)(f), 210.20(2), and 210.45.

Prior to the enactment of the CPL, this was an issue to be raised at trial. *See People v. Kohut*, 30 N.Y.2d 183, 186, 331 N.Y.S.2d 416, 419 (1972).

§ 53:6   Accusatory instrument not required to allege facts negating statute of limitations defense

Research References

West's Key Number Digest, Criminal Law ☞573, 577.4, 577.16(5.1)

In *People v. Kohut*, 30 N.Y.2d 183, 186, 331 N.Y.S.2d 416, 419 (1972), the Court of Appeals held that "[l]imitation-tolling facts, saving an otherwise untimely prosecution, need not be alleged in an indictment." In so holding, the Court reasoned that:

Essential allegations are generally determined by the statute defining the crime. If the defining statute contains an exception, the indictment must allege that the crime is not within the exception. But when the exception is found outside the statute, the exception generally is a matter for the defendant to raise in defense, either under the general issue or by affirmative defense.

Limitations are imposed by independent statute. They are neither exceptions nor provisos as categorized in the cases. Hence, in an analogous, if not a stronger sense, they are matters of defense, and avoidance need not be alleged in the indictment.

People v. Kohut, 30 N.Y.2d 183, 187–88, 331 N.Y.S.2d 416(1972) (citations omitted).

§ 53:7   Waiver/forfeiture of statute of limitations claim

Research References

West's Key Number Digest, Criminal Law ☞573, 577.4, 577.10(9)

"New York courts have long recognized that the statute of limitations defense is not jurisdictional and can be forfeited or waived by a defendant." *People v. Mills*, 1 N.Y.3d 269, 274, 772 N.Y.S.2d 228, 230 (2003).

In *Mills*, the defendant was charged with murder in the second degree, in violation of PL § 125.25(2) (depraved indifference murder), which has no statute of limitations. Although the crime took place in 1978, the defendant was not indicted until 2000. As such, while the depraved indifference murder charge was not time-barred, had the defendant been charged with a lesser felony it would have been. In this regard, the defendant believed that he was "overcharged" by the People in an attempt to circumvent the statute of limitations.

At trial, the defendant requested that the court charge the jury with the lesser included offense of criminally negligent homicide, in violation of PL § 125.10 (which has a five-year statute of limitations). The court agreed to do so, but deemed the request a waiver of any statute of limitations defense. The defendant was thereafter convicted of criminally negligent homicide. He appealed. The Court of Appeals held that:

> [W]here an indictment is based on legally sufficient evidence defendant's statute of limitations defense is forfeited or waived by his request to charge the lesser included offense. This rule eliminates the danger of prosecutorial overcharging to circumvent the statute of limitations. Here the evidence before the grand jury was legally sufficient to support the depraved indifference charge.

People v. Mills, 1 N.Y.3d 269, 274, 772 N.Y.S.2d 228, 230 (2003).

§ 53:8   CPL § 30.20—Generally

Research References

West's Key Number Digest, Criminal Law ☞573, 577.4

CPL § 30.20(1) provides that "[a]fter a criminal action is commenced, the defendant is entitled to a speedy trial." This statute, in essence, codifies "the speedy trial guarantee provided by the Sixth Amendment." *People v. Berkowitz*, 50 N.Y.2d 333, 348, 428 N.Y.S.2d 927, 935–36 (1980).

The speedy trial guarantee established by the 6th Amendment to the Federal Constitution and embodied in CPL 30.20 and Civil Rights Law § 12 is intended to ensure fair and humane treatment of an accused person by protecting him or her against prolonged imprisonment while awaiting trial, providing relief from the anxiety and public suspicion that accompanies a criminal accusation which remains untried, and reducing the possibility that through the loss of witnesses or the dulling of memory the means of proving his or her innocence may be lost. It also serves the interests of society in seeing that those accused of crime are swiftly brought to justice.

People v. Anderson, 66 N.Y.2d 529, 534–35, 498 N.Y.S.2d 119, 122–23 (1985) (citations omitted). *See also People v. Watts*, 57 N.Y.2d 299, 302, 456 N.Y.S.2d 677, 679 (1982); *People v. Dean*, 45 N.Y.2d 651, 659, 412 N.Y.S.2d 353, 357 (1978) ("Beyond the requirements of CPL 30.30 there exists a general speedy trial right expressed in CPL 30.20 and section 12 of the Civil Rights Law"); *People v. Johnson*, 38 N.Y.2d 271, 276, 379 N.Y.S.2d 735, 740 (1975); *People v. Johnson*, 38 N.Y.2d 271, 278 n.3, 379 N.Y.S.2d 740 ("the right to a speedy trial does not depend entirely on CPL 30.30 but rests on a broader base (U.S.Const., 6th Amdt.; Civil Rights Law, § 12; CPL 30.20)").

"Although New York does not have a constitutional speedy trial provision, we have long held that in criminal prosecutions an unreasonable delay in prosecuting a defendant following an arrest can constitute a violation of the Due Process Clause of our Constitution." *Matter of Benjamin L.*, 92 N.Y.2d 660, 667, 685 N.Y.S.2d 400, 403 (1999).

§ 53:9   *People v. Taranovich*—Factors to be considered in deciding constitutional speedy trial claim

Research References

West's Key Number Digest, Criminal Law ⚭573, 577.3, 577.4, 577.10(4)

In *People v. Taranovich*, 37 N.Y.2d 442, 445, 373 N.Y.S.2d 79, 81–82 (1975), the Court of Appeals held that:

The following factors should be examined in balancing the merits of an assertion that there has been a denial of defendant's right to a speedy trial:

(1) the extent of the delay;

(2) the reason for the delay;

(3) the nature of the underlying charge;

(4) whether or not there has been an extended period of pretrial incarceration; and

(5) whether or not there is any indication that the defense has been impaired by reason of the delay.

In so holding, the Court reasoned that:

[T]here is no specific temporal duration after which a defendant automatically becomes entitled to release for denial of a speedy trial. Instead, the assertion by the accused of his right to a speedy trial requires the court to examine the claim in light of the particular factors attending the specific case under scrutiny. As this case illustrates, there are no clear cut answers in such an inquiry, and the trial court must engage in a sensitive weighing process of the diversified factors present in the particular case. Moreover, the various factors must be evaluated on an *ad hoc* basis since no rigid precepts may be formulated which apply to each and every instance in which it is averred that there has been a deprivation of the speedy trial right. Additionally, we hasten to add that no one factor or combination of the factors set forth [herein] is necessarily decisive or determinative of the speedy trial claim, but rather the particular case must be considered in light of all the factors as they apply to it.

People v. Taranovich, 37 N.Y.2d 442, 444–45, 373 N.Y.S.2d 79 (1975) (citations omitted).

§ 53:10 *Taranovich* factor (1)—Extent of the delay

Research References

West's Key Number Digest, Criminal Law ⟨⟩573, 577.3, 577.4, 577.15(1)

The first factor, the extent or duration of the delay, is, of course, important inasmuch as it is likely that, all other factors being equal, the greater the delay the more probable it is that the accused will be harmed thereby. However, as crucial as the length of the delay may be, this court has steadfastly refused to set forth a per se period beyond which a criminal prosecution may not be pursued.

People v. Taranovich, 37 N.Y.2d 442, 445, 373 N.Y.S.2d 79, 82 (1975).

§ 53:11 *Taranovich* factor (2)—Reason for the delay

Research References

West's Key Number Digest, Criminal Law ⟨⟩573, 577.3, 577.4, 577.10(4)

The second factor, the reason for the delay, may be in the [defendant's] favor since the District Attorney's failure to indict is attributable to clerical error within his own office. While such inadvertence may seem inexcusable, it will not, in and of itself, be sufficient to warrant the drastic measure of dismissal of the indictment. As far as this factor is concerned, we note also that the delay in handing up the indictment does not appear to have been a deliberate attempt by the prosecution to hamper the [defendant] in the preparation of his defense and, indeed, no such claim is here made.

People v. Taranovich, 37 N.Y.2d 442, 446, 373 N.Y.S.2d 79, 82 (1975).

In *People v. Johnson*, 38 N.Y.2d 271, 277, 379 N.Y.S.2d 735,

741 (1975), the 18-month delay between the defendant's arrest and his guilty plea "was primarily attributable to 'case backlog in the District Attorney's office.'" In other words, the district attorney's office had "a heavy case load, and a shortage of trial attorneys." *People v. Johnson*, 38 N.Y.2d 271, 277, 379 N.Y.S.2d 735 (1975). In this regard, the Court stated that:

> [S]ince the State initiates the action, it is the State's duty to see that the defendant is promptly brought to trial, and whether the delay is an intentional effort to hinder the defense or merely the result of public inattention to the needs of the trial process, the responsibility must ultimately rest on the State. The only consequence of the distinction then is that a delay occasioned by inadequate facilities or personnel *weighs less heavily* against the State—because it furnishes a more neutral reason—than one wholly subject to the prosecutor's control. But the ultimate solution . . . lies with the State and local governments to allocate sufficient public resources to ensure that the ever increasing criminal case load does not overwhelm the courts and prosecutors.

> Thus the fact that the delay here was due to a shortage of personnel in the prosecutor's office, while not exactly a factor in the State's favor, must weigh less heavily than would most other causes. If that were the only factor favoring dismissal, there would be a close question as to whether this particular delay was consistent with the speedy trial requirement, bearing in mind, as we have in the past, that . . . 16 months . . . "seems to have approached the excusable limit of delay attributable to the absence of public trial facilities." What is certain however, is that this factor cannot "outweigh" the fact that the defendant has been incarcerated for 18 months awaiting trial, that he repeatedly sought a speedy trial and that the record indicates that the delay has prejudiced his case.

People v. Johnson, 38 N.Y.2d 271, 279–80, 379 N.Y.S.2d 735, 743 (1975) (citations and footnote omitted).

§ 53:12   *Taranovich* factor (3)—Nature of the charge

Research References

West's Key Number Digest, Criminal Law ☞573, 577.4

The third factor, the nature of the underlying charge, would appear to be in the People's favor. Appellant was arrested for attempted murder, a class B felony, and indicted for assault in the first degree, a class C felony. Upon such a serious charge, the District Attorney may be expected to proceed with far more caution and deliberation than he would expend on a relatively minor offense. Of course, this is not to say that one's right to a speedy trial is dependent upon what one is charged with, but rather that the prosecutor may understandably be more thorough and precise in his preparation for the trial of a class C felony than he would be in prosecuting a misdemeanor.

People v. Taranovich, 37 N.Y.2d 442, 446, 373 N.Y.S.2d 79, 82 (1975).

§ 53:13 *Taranovich* factor (4)—Length of pretrial incarceration

Research References

West's Key Number Digest, Criminal Law ⟷573, 577.4

The fourth factor, whether or not there has been an extended period of pretrial incarceration, is not, in this case, a motivation for dismissal of the indictment on defendant's application since [defendant] was incarcerated for but eight days before he was released on bail. Historically, this factor has been considered significant because the speedy trial guarantee affords the accused a safeguard against prolonged imprisonment prior to the commencement of his trial. Moreover, a defendant confined to jail prior to trial is at an obvious and distinct disadvantage in the sense that he can only assist in the preparation of his defense to a limited degree because he is unable to gather evidence or to contact prospective witnesses.

People v. Taranovich, 37 N.Y.2d 442, 446, 373 N.Y.S.2d 79, 82–83 (1975) (citation omitted).

§ 53:14 *Taranovich* factor (5)—Has the defense been prejudiced by the delay

Research References

West's Key Number Digest, Criminal Law ⟷573, 577.3, 577.4, 577.10(4)

The fifth factor, whether or not there is any indication that the defense has been impaired by reason of the delay, is most critical in view of the facts of this particular case. While, of course, it is not incumbent upon a defendant to show that he has been prejudiced by the delay in the commencement of his trial, a questionable period of delay may or may not be unreasonable depending upon whether or not the likelihood of the defendant's acquittal has been effected thereby. For instance, if the delay precipitated by the prosecution resulted in the defendant's being unable to call certain witnesses, or if the duration of the delay was such that it might be expected that the witnesses would be less able to articulate exactly what had transpired, then the defendant would have a strong argument for dismissal of the indictment. To be sure, we do not depart from the now traditional view in this court that where in the circumstances delay is great enough there need be neither proof nor fact of prejudice to the defendant.

People v. Taranovich, 37 N.Y.2d 442, 446–47, 373 N.Y.S.2d 79, 83 (1975) (citations omitted).

§ 53:15 Applying *Taranovich*

Research References

West's Key Number Digest, Criminal Law ⟷573, 577.3, 577.4, 577.10(4), 577.12(1)

In *People v. Singer*, 44 N.Y.2d 241, 254, 405 N.Y.S.2d 17, 25 (1978), the Court of Appeals held that "[g]enerally when there has been a protracted delay, certainly over a period of years, the burden is on the prosecution to establish good cause."

In *People v. Staley*, 41 N.Y.2d 789, 792, 396 N.Y.S.2d 339, 342 (1977), the Court of Appeals made clear that:

[I]n this State, failure to conduct a prompt prosecution, in a proper case, may require dismissal of an indictment even in the absence of prejudice to the defendant. * * *

[W]hen the delay is long enough, the charges must be dismissed whether or not defendant's ability to present a defense has been shown to have been hampered. Even shorter delays may result in a deprivation of constitutional rights, especially if it is shown that the defendant has been prejudiced by the delay.

See also Singer, 44 N.Y.2d at 253–54, 405 N.Y.S.2d at 25; *People v. Santiago*, 209 A.D.2d 885, __-__, 618 N.Y.S.2d 925, 927–28 (3d Dep't 1994) (67-month delay between arrest and plea denied the defendant the constitutional right to speedy trial, regardless of the defendant's imprisonment on other charges); *People v. Charles*, 180 A.D.2d 868, __-__, 580 N.Y.S.2d 99, 101–03 (3d Dep't 1992) (43-month delay between arrest and trial denied the defendant the constitutional right to speedy trial, regardless of prejudice); *People v. Willis*, 149 A.D.2d 953, 540 N.Y.S.2d 86 (4th Dep't 1989) (four-year delay between commencement of action and the defendant's guilty plea denied the defendant the constitutional right to speedy trial, regardless of prejudice); *People v. DeJesus*, 52 Misc. 3d 138(A), 2016 WL 3766808, *1 (App. Term, 1st Dep't 2016) (per curiam) ("The 42-month delay between defendant's arrest and his plea of guilty was excessive and the People failed to establish good cause therefor. The underlying Vehicle and Traffic Law § 1192 charges, though serious, are relatively simple, and this case did not require any unusual attention or complex preparation to ensure its prompt disposition. In the circumstances, dismissal is the appropriate remedy, despite the absence of any actual prejudice to defendant") (citations omitted). *See generally People v. Johnson*, 38 N.Y.2d 271, 379 N.Y.S.2d 735 (1975) (under facts of case, 18-month delay between arrest and plea denied the defendant the constitutional right to speedy trial and also violated CPL § 30.20); *People v. Moore*, 63 A.D.2d 602, 405 N.Y.S.2d 69 (1st Dep't 1978), *rev'd for the reasons stated in the dissenting opinion of* Justice Sandler, 47 N.Y.2d 872, 419 N.Y.S.2d 74 (1979) (under facts of case, 181/2-month delay between arrest and trial denied the defendant the constitutional right to speedy trial); *People v. Freytes*, 48 N.Y.2d 645, 421 N.Y.S.2d 199 (1979) (same); *People v. Minicone*, 28 N.Y.2d 279, 280, 321 N.Y.S.2d 570, 571 (1971) (in case decided prior to

Taranovich, Court of Appeals held that delay of almost four years between indictment of the defendants and their trial, during which there were long periods of delay that were largely unexplained in the record, deprived the defendants of their constitutional and statutory right to a speedy trial).

In *People v. Watts*, 57 N.Y.2d 299, 303, 456 N.Y.S.2d 677, 680 (1982), the Court of Appeals reiterated that "this court has held that acuity of memory, whether that of a defendant or a nonparty witness, when dulled by a substantial pretrial delay, may sufficiently impair a defense so as to warrant a finding of a denial of a defendant's speedy trial right."

In *People v. Kelly*, 38 N.Y.2d 633, 636, 382 N.Y.S.2d 1, 3 (1976), the Court of Appeals stated:

> This is not to say that a bail case need not be brought to early trial. It should; but some sort of priority should go to jail cases, as must to cases involving serious crimes of great significance to the public interest, a factor present here. In both bail and jail cases priority should be given, among others, to cases where there is a critical issue involving guilt or innocence, or the possible loss of witnesses to the prosecution or the defense.

(Citations omitted). *See also People v. Imbesi*, 38 N.Y.2d 629, 632, 381 N.Y.S.2d 862, 864 (1976).

Similarly, "what may be considered an unreasonable delay in preparing a minor, relatively common street crime for trial may be tolerable when a serious or complex charge is involved." *Johnson*, 38 N.Y.2d at 277, 379 N.Y.S.2d at 741. *See also People v. Taranovich*, 37 N.Y.2d 442, 446, 373 N.Y.S.2d 79, 82 (1975).

In *People v. Thorpe*, 160 Misc. 2d 558, __, 613 N.Y.S.2d 795, 796 (App. Term, 9th & 10th Jud. Dist. 1994), the court concluded that "an unexplained delay of over two years in bringing a simple traffic infraction to trial warrants dismissal."

In *People v. Fisher*, 167 Misc. 2d 850, __, 635 N.Y.S.2d 1002, 1006 (N.Y. City Crim. Ct. 1995), the court stated that "it is reasonable to expect that the People be 'ready for trial' within 60 days from arraignment" on a DWAI charge. *Cf. People v. Polite*, 16 Misc. 3d 18, 842 N.Y.S.2d 670 (App. Term, 1st Dep't 2007) (per curiam) (finding *Fisher* unpersuasive).

In *People v. Attie*, 131 Misc. 2d 921, __, 502 N.Y.S.2d 342, 344 (Long Beach City Ct. 1986), the court found that "the extent of the delay of more than 10 months between the not guilty plea [to 2 traffic infractions] and the date first noticed for trial was excessive thereby depriving the defendant of his right to a speedy trial."

§ 53:16 Applicability of constitutional right to speedy trial to traffic infractions

Research References

West's Key Number Digest, Criminal Law ☞573, 577.4

CPL § 30.20 and the constitutional right to a speedy trial apply to traffic infractions. *See, e.g., People v. Taylor*, 189 Misc. 2d 313, 731 N.Y.S.2d 324 (App. Term, 2d Dep't 2001); *People v. Thorpe*, 160 Misc. 2d 558, __, 613 N.Y.S.2d 795, 796 (App. Term, 9th & 10th Jud. Dist. 1994); *People v. Pilewski*, 173 Misc. 2d 800, __, 660 N.Y.S.2d 525, 528 (Great Neck Just. Ct. 1997); *People v. Fiacco*, 146 Misc. 2d 330, __, 549 N.Y.S.2d 901, 902 (Albany City Ct. 1989); *People v. Attie*, 131 Misc. 2d 921, __, 502 N.Y.S.2d 342, 343 (Long Beach City Ct. 1986); *People v. Zagorsky*, 73 Misc. 2d 420, __, 341 N.Y.S.2d 791, 795 (Broome Co. Ct. 1973). *See also People v. Vancol*, 166 Misc. 2d 93, __, 631 N.Y.S.2d 996, 997 (Westbury Just. Ct. 1995) ("Analogous to the constitutional right, [CPL § 30.20] applies to all offenses, without exception"); Preiser, Practice Commentaries, McKinney's Cons. Laws of NY, Book 11A, CPL § 30.20, at 187 (same). *See generally People v. Fisher*, 167 Misc. 2d 850, __, __-__, 635 N.Y.S.2d 1002, 1003, 1005–06 (N.Y. City Crim. Ct. 1995) (CPL § 30.20 does not apply to traffic infractions, but constitutional right to speedy trial does).

In *People v. Persaud*, 21 Misc. 3d 522, __, 863 N.Y.S.2d 533, 536 (N.Y. City Crim. Ct. 2008), the Court dismissed a DWAI charge on constitutional speedy trial grounds after a delay of 2 1/2 years, in part because the primary consequence faced by the defendant was a 90-day driver's license suspension, yet the defendant's license had been suspended the whole time (rendering "any further suspension . . . a classic example of overkill"). *See also People v. Panagulis*, 49 Misc. 3d 1215(A), 28 N.Y.S.3d 650 (N.Y. City Crim. Ct. 2015).

§ 53:17 Applicability of constitutional right to speedy trial to homicides

Research References

West's Key Number Digest, Criminal Law ☞573, 577.4

Although the statutory right to a speedy trial is inapplicable to certain homicide charges, *see* CPL § 30.30(3)(a); § 53:38, *infra*, the constitutional right to a speedy trial *is* applicable to such charges. *See, e.g., People v. Johnson*, 38 N.Y.2d 271, 272–73, 278 n.3, 379 N.Y.S.2d 735, 737, 742 n.3 (1975); *People v. O'Sullivan*, 121 A.D.2d 658, 504 N.Y.S.2d 49 (2d Dep't 1986); *People v. Rodriguez*, 81 A.D.2d 840, 438 N.Y.S.2d 845 (2d Dep't 1981); *People v. White*, 72 A.D.2d 913, 422 N.Y.S.2d 193 (4th Dep't 1979).

§ 53:18 Applicability of constitutional right to speedy trial to juvenile delinquency proceedings

Research References

West's Key Number Digest, Criminal Law ⊙573, 577.4

In *Matter of Benjamin L.*, 92 N.Y.2d 660, 667, 685 N.Y.S.2d 400, 403 (1999), the Court of Appeals stated that "[a]lthough New York does not have a constitutional speedy trial provision, we have long held that in criminal prosecutions an unreasonable delay in prosecuting a defendant following an arrest can constitute a violation of the Due Process Clause of our Constitution." In this regard, the *Benjamin L.* Court held both (a) that "[i]n light of the need for swift and certain adjudication at all phases of a delinquency proceeding, we conclude that the speedy trial protections afforded under the Due Process Clause are not for criminal proceedings alone and are not at odds with the goals of juvenile proceedings," and (b) "that the *Taranovich* test should be adopted to the juvenile delinquency context." *Matter of Benjamin L.*, 92 N.Y.2d 660, 668, 685 N.Y.S.2d 400 (1999).

§ 53:19 Necessity of hearing

Research References

West's Key Number Digest, Criminal Law ⊙573, 577.4, 577.16(10)

"[W]here a defendant has moved for a [speedy trial] dismissal it may be summarily granted if the answering papers do not present a factual dispute for the court to resolve." *People v. Dean*, 45 N.Y.2d 651, 656, 412 N.Y.S.2d 353, 356 (1978). *See also People v. Gruden*, 42 N.Y.2d 214, 217, 397 N.Y.S.2d 704, 706 (1977) ("Generally hearings are not available merely for the asking. We therefore hold that the court may summarily grant a motion to dismiss unless the papers submitted by the prosecutor show that there is a factual dispute which must be resolved at a hearing").

Similarly, a constitutional speedy trial claim can be denied without a hearing where the defendant's motion papers do not raise any issue of fact on a material point. *See, e.g., People v. Coffaro*, 52 N.Y.2d 932, 934, 437 N.Y.S.2d 666, 667 (1981).

§ 53:20 Waiver/abandonment of constitutional speedy trial claim

Research References

West's Key Number Digest, Criminal Law ⊙573, 577.4, 577.10(9)

The Court of Appeals has repeatedly held that a constitutional speedy trial claim survives a guilty plea and may be raised on appeal, even where the defendant has agreed to waive his or her right to appeal this issue. In this regard, in *People v. Callahan*, 80 N.Y.2d 273, 282, 590 N.Y.S.2d 46, 51 (1992), the Court of Appeals held that:

> [W]e hold, as we held in [*People v. Seaberg*, 74 N.Y.2d 1, 9, 543 N.Y.S.2d 968, 971 (1989)], that a bargained-for waiver of the right to appeal is ineffective to the extent it impairs the defendant's ability to obtain appellate review of a constitutional speedy trial claim. Moreover, this rule applies without regard to whether the facts in the particular case suggest duress arising from the circumstances underlying the speedy trial claim itself.

See also People v. Konieczny, 2 N.Y.3d 569, 573, 780 N.Y.S.2d 546, 548 (2004); *People v. Campbell*, 97 N.Y.2d 532, 535, 743 N.Y.S.2d 396, 397 (2002); *People v. Hansen*, 95 N.Y.2d 227, 230–31 & n.2, 715 N.Y.S.2d 369, 372 & n.2 (2000); *People v. Allen*, 86 N.Y.2d 599, 602, 635 N.Y.S.2d 139, 141 (1995); *People v. Seaberg*, 74 N.Y.2d 1, 9, 543 N.Y.S.2d 968, 971 (1989); *People v. Taylor*, 65 N.Y.2d 1, 5, 6, 489 N.Y.S.2d 152, 154, 155 (1985); *People v. Savage*, 54 N.Y.2d 697, 698, 442 N.Y.S.2d 974, 975 (1981); *People v. Blakley*, 34 N.Y.2d 311, 313–15, 357 N.Y.S.2d 459, 460–62 (1974).

In fact, " 'the nature of the speedy trial guarantee renders [a waiver of such a claim] *inherently* coercive in a plea bargaining situation,' so that a plea conditioned on a waiver 'must be vacated' regardless of the substantive merits of the claim (emphasis supplied)." *Callahan*, 80 N.Y.2d at 282, 590 N.Y.S.2d at 51 (citation omitted). *See generally Matter of Westchester Rockland Newspapers, Inc. v. Leggett*, 48 N.Y.2d 430, 444, 423 N.Y.S.2d 630, 638 (1979) ("The defendant should not be placed in a position where he will have to submit to a continuance at the expense of his right to a speedy trial"); *People v. White*, 32 N.Y.2d 393, 399–400, 345 N.Y.S.2d 513, 519 (1973).

Although *People v. Rodriguez*, 50 N.Y.2d 553, 429 N.Y.S.2d 631 (1980), appears to hold to the contrary, the Court of Appeals made clear, in *Callahan*, that "*Rodriguez* stands only for the limited proposition that a defendant who initially interposes a constitutional speedy trial claim but subsequently *abandons* it before a determination on the claim is made cannot subsequently raise that claim on appeal." 80 N.Y.2d at 282, 590 N.Y.S.2d at 51 (emphasis added). *See also People v. Alexander*, 19 N.Y.3d 203, 947 N.Y.S.2d 386, 970 N.E.2d 409 (2012) (under the unusual facts of the case, the Court of Appeals found a valid waiver of a constitutional speedy trial claim).

§ 53:21 Constitutional speedy trial claim must be properly preserved to be reviewed on appeal

Research References

West's Key Number Digest, Criminal Law ⟐573, 577.4

Although a constitutional speedy trial claim cannot be waived, *see* previous section, the failure to properly raise such claim in the trial court will fail to preserve it for purposes of appellate review, *see People v. Jordan*, 62 N.Y.2d 825, 826, 477 N.Y.S.2d 605, 606 (1984); *People v. Whisby*, 48 N.Y.2d 834, 836, 424 N.Y.S.2d 344, 344 (1979); *People v. Hardy*, 47 N.Y.2d 500, 505, 419 N.Y.S.2d 49, 51–52 (1979); *People v. Primmer*, 46 N.Y.2d 1048, 1049, 416 N.Y.S.2d 548, 549 (1979); *People v. Adams*, 38 N.Y.2d 605, 607, 381 N.Y.S.2d 847, 848 (1976), as will the failure to raise a constitutional speedy trial claim separate and distinct from a CPL § 30.30 claim. *See People v. Lieberman*, 47 N.Y.2d 931, 932, 419 N.Y.S.2d 946, 947 (1979). *See also People v. Cedeno*, 52 N.Y.2d 847, 848, 437 N.Y.S.2d 72, 72 (1981) (same rule applies to a constitutional speedy trial claim characterized as a constitutional due process claim).

In addition, if the defendant properly raises a constitutional speedy trial claim in the trial court but proceeds to trial before the motion is decided, the claim will be deemed abandoned. *See People v. Rodriguez*, 50 N.Y.2d 553, 429 N.Y.S.2d 631 (1980).

§ 53:22   CPL § 30.20(2)—Trial of criminal cases must be given preference over trial of civil cases

Research References

West's Key Number Digest, Criminal Law ☞573, 577.4, 577.8(1)

CPL § 30.20(2) provides that:

Insofar as is practicable, the trial of a criminal action must be given preference over civil cases; and the trial of a criminal action where the defendant has been committed to the custody of the sheriff during the pendency of the criminal action must be given preference over other criminal actions.

§ 53:23   CPL § 30.30—Generally

Research References

West's Key Number Digest, Criminal Law ☞573, 577.4, 577.8(1)

CPL § 30.30, "although inspired by a constitutional right, provide[s] greater protection than the Constitution requires." *People v. Sobotker*, 61 N.Y.2d 44, 48, 471 N.Y.S.2d 78, 80 (1984).

CPL § 30.30 "does not address problems involving speedy trial rights or due process in a constitutional sense. Rather, it is purely a statutory 'readiness rule'. It was enacted to serve the narrow purpose of insuring prompt prosecutorial readiness for trial, and its provisions must be interpreted accordingly." *People v. Sinistaj*, 67 N.Y.2d 236, 239, 501 N.Y.S.2d 793, 794 (1986). *See also People v. Anderson*, 66 N.Y.2d 529, 535, 498 N.Y.S.2d 119, 123 (1985); *People v. Worley*, 66 N.Y.2d 523, 527, 498 N.Y.S.2d 116, 118 (1985).

CPL § 30.30 "was intended only to address delays occasioned by prosecutorial inaction." *People v. McKenna*, 76 N.Y.2d 59, 63, 556 N.Y.S.2d 514, 515 (1990).

§ 53:24   Prejudice to defendant is irrelevant for purposes of CPL § 30.30

Research References
West's Key Number Digest, Criminal Law ☞573, 577.4

In *People v. Hamilton*, 46 N.Y.2d 932, 933–34, 415 N.Y.S.2d 208, 209 (1979) (per curiam), the Court of Appeals stated that "it bears emphasis that the right to a speedy trial guaranteed by CPL 30.30, which relates to prosecutorial readiness, is not dependent in any way on . . . whether the defendant can demonstrate prejudice resulting from the delay."

§ 53:25   CPL § 30.30(1)—Time within which People must be ready for trial

Research References
West's Key Number Digest, Criminal Law ☞573, 577.4, 577.7

CPL § 30.30(1) provides that, except as otherwise provided in CPL § 30.30(3), a speedy trial motion made pursuant to CPL § 170.30(1)(e) or CPL § 210.20(1)(g) *must* be granted where the People are not ready for trial within the following time period:

(a) [6] months of the commencement of a criminal action wherein a defendant is accused of [1] or more offenses, at least [1] of which is a felony;

(b) [90] days of the commencement of a criminal action wherein a defendant is accused of [1] or more offenses, at least [1] of which is a misdemeanor punishable by a sentence of imprisonment of more than [3] months and none of which is a felony;

(c) [60] days of the commencement of a criminal action wherein the defendant is accused of [1] or more offenses, at least [1] of which is a misdemeanor punishable by a sentence of imprisonment of not more than [3] months and none of which is a crime punishable by a sentence of imprisonment of more than [3] months;

(d) [30] days of the commencement of a criminal action wherein the defendant is accused of [1] or more offenses, at least [1] of which is a violation and none of which is a crime.CPL § 30.30(1)(a) to (d).

Note that CPL § 30.30(1)(a) and (b) contain the phrase "a criminal action wherein *a* defendant" (emphasis added), whereas CPL § 30.30(1)(c) and (d) contain the phrase "a criminal action wherein *the* defendant" (emphasis added). In this regard, in a criminal action involving multiple defendants, "CPL § 30.30(1)(a) and (b) require only that 'a' defendant be charged with a felony or a class A misdemeanor, not that all defendants be so charged." *People v. Day*, 139 Misc. 2d 222, 224, 526 N.Y.S.2d 736, 739 (Kings Co. Sup. Ct. 1988). Thus, "[w]hen misdemeanor defendants and felony defendants are joined in one indictment, all must be assigned the same 'speedy trial' time." *People v. Day*, 139 Misc. 2d 222, 225, 526 N.Y.S.2d 736 (Kings Co. Sup. Ct. 1988).

§ 53:26 Six months not necessarily 180 days

Research References
West's Key Number Digest, Criminal Law ⟜573, 577.4, 577.7, 577.8(1)

"The six months that the People have to become ready in felony cases is measured by *calendar* months. Since the number of days in each calendar month may differ, the period in question, which is computed from the date the action was first commenced[,] is not necessarily 180 days." *People v. Cortes*, 80 N.Y.2d 201, 207 n.3, 590 N.Y.S.2d 9, 13 n.3 (1992) (citation omitted).

§ 53:27 What if last day falls on weekend or holiday?

Research References
West's Key Number Digest, Criminal Law ⟜573, 577.4, 577.7, 577.8(1)

Where the last day of the People's time to announce their readiness for trial falls on a weekend or a holiday, "the People's time to announce their readiness [is] extended to the next business day." *People v. Powell*, 179 Misc. 2d 1047, __, 690 N.Y.S.2d 826, 827 (App. Term, 2d Dep't 1999). *See also* Gen. Const. Law § 25-a(1).

§ 53:28 Writ of habeas corpus cannot be used to claim violation of CPL § 30.30(1)

Research References
West's Key Number Digest, Criminal Law ⟜573, 577.4

A writ of habeas corpus cannot be used to claim a violation of CPL § 30.30(1). *See, e.g., People ex rel. Chakwin v. Warden*, 63 N.Y.2d 120, 124–25, 480 N.Y.S.2d 719, 721 (1984); *People ex rel. Harrison v. Greco*, 38 N.Y.2d 1025, 384 N.Y.S.2d 450 (1976); *People ex rel. McDonald v. Warden*, 34 N.Y.2d 554, 354 N.Y.S.2d 939 (1974). The rationale is that a CPL § 30.30(1) "speedy trial claim could be raised at the trial itself and on a direct appeal." *Chakwin*, 63 N.Y.2d at 125, 480 N.Y.S.2d at 721.

§ 53:29 Article 78 proceeding cannot be used to raise speedy trial claim

Research References

West's Key Number Digest, Criminal Law ☞573, 577.4

"A claim of a denial of a speedy trial is not cognizable in an application pursuant to CPLR article 78 for a judgment prohibiting a District Attorney and the Justices of the Supreme Court from proceeding on an indictment." *Matter of Scranton v. Supreme Ct. of State of N.Y.*, 36 N.Y.2d 704, __, 366 N.Y.S.2d 417, 418 (1975). *See also Matter of Lopez v. Justices of Supreme Ct. of N.Y. County*, 36 N.Y.2d 949, __, 373 N.Y.S.2d 552, 553 (1975); *Matter of State of N.Y. v. King*, 36 N.Y.2d 59, 364 N.Y.S.2d 879 (1975); *Matter of Blake v. Hogan*, 25 N.Y.2d 747, __, 303 N.Y.S.2d 505, 506 (1969).

In *King, supra*, the Court of Appeals reasoned that:

> Were allowance of this kind of proceeding to become a precedent, one would have to anticipate innumerable proceedings in all sorts of criminal matters to review allegedly prejudicial errors of law for which there would be no eventual appellate review or only appellate review after final judgments, and then only of conviction. No trial can be conducted while appellate courts by their own protracted proceedings review the alleged errors which may arise preliminary to the trial, during the trial, and before verdict and judgment. Such a system is neither civilized nor even rational. And most certainly it would make speedy trial a legal impossibility.

36 N.Y.2d at 63–64, 364 N.Y.S.2d at 883.

§ 53:30 CPL § 30.30(2)—Time within which jailed defendant must be RORed [released on recognizance] or released on bail if People not ready for trial

Research References

West's Key Number Digest, Criminal Law ☞573, 575, 577.4, 577.7

CPL § 30.30(2) provides that, except as provided in CPL § 30.30(3), "where a defendant has been committed to the custody of the sheriff in a criminal action he must be released on bail or on his own recognizance, upon such conditions as may be just and reasonable, if the people are not ready for trial in that criminal action within" the following time period:

(a) [90] days from the commencement of his commitment to the custody of the sheriff in a criminal action wherein the defendant is accused of [1] or more offenses, at least [1] of which is a felony;

(b) [30] days from the commencement of his commitment to the custody of the sheriff in a criminal action wherein the defendant is accused of [1] or more offenses, at least [1] of which is a misdemeanor punishable by a sentence of imprisonment of more than [3] months and none of which is a felony;

(c) [15] days from the commencement of his commitment to the custody of the sheriff in a criminal action wherein the defendant is accused of [1] or more offenses, at least [1] of which is a misdemeanor punishable by a sentence of imprisonment of not more than [3] months and none of which is a crime punishable by a sentence of imprisonment of more than [3] months;

(d) [5] days from the commencement of his commitment to the custody of the sheriff in a criminal action wherein the defendant is accused of [1] or more offenses, at least [1] of which is a violation and none of which is a crime.CPL § 30.30(2)(a) to (d). *See also* CPL § 170.70 (release of defendant from custody upon failure to replace misdemeanor complaint with information); CPL § 180.80 (release of defendant from custody upon failure to timely dispose of felony complaint or conduct preliminary hearing).

§ 53:31 Situations to which CPL § 30.30(2) does not apply

Research References

West's Key Number Digest, Criminal Law ⊜573, 577.4

CPL § 30.30(3)(c) provides that a motion for release from custody brought pursuant to CPL § 30.30(2) shall not:

(i) apply to any defendant who is serving a term of imprisonment for another offense;

(ii) require the release from custody of any defendant who is also being held in custody pending trial of another criminal charge as to which the applicable period has not yet elapsed; [or]

(iii) prevent the redetention of or otherwise apply to any defendant who, after being released from custody pursuant to [CPL § 30.30] or otherwise, is charged with another crime or violates the conditions on which he has been released, by failing to appear at a judicial proceeding at which his presence is required or otherwise. CPL § 30.30(3)(c)(i) to (iii).

§ 53:32 If bail is set pursuant to CPL § 30.30(2), it must be set in amount that defendant can afford to post

Research References

West's Key Number Digest, Criminal Law ⊜573, 577.4

Where the People are not ready for trial within the time period required by CPL § 30.30(2), the statute provides that the defendant "*must be released* on bail or on his own recognizance, upon such conditions as may be just and reasonable." (Emphasis added). In interpreting this language, the Court of Appeals has made clear that, if the defendant is not RORed, bail must be set in an amount that the defendant can afford to post. In this regard, in *People ex rel. Chakwin v. Warden*, 63 N.Y.2d 120, 125, 480 N.Y.S.2d 719, 721 (1984), the Court held that:

> [T]he plain meaning of CPL 30.30 (subd. 2) is that a defendant's showing of a violation of that section *will* result in the defendant's release, either by a fixing of bail *at an amount which the defendant can post* or by a release of the defendant on his own recognizance. As the People concede, the words "upon such conditions as may be just and reasonable" do not give the trial court the right to maintain bail at an amount which the defendant is unable to meet.

(Emphases added). *See also People ex rel. Zoll v. Warden*, 236 A.D.2d 643, __, 654 N.Y.S.2d 668, 668–69 (2d Dep't 1997) ("CPL 30.30(2)(a) commands that the detainee must be released on bail which he is capable of meeting or upon his own recognizance"); *People ex rel. Ellis v. Koehler*, 165 A.D.2d 848, __, 560 N.Y.S.2d 226, 226 (2d Dep't 1990) (same).

§ 53:33 Writ of habeas corpus can be used to claim violation of CPL § 30.30(2)

Research References

West's Key Number Digest, Criminal Law ⚖573, 577.4

A writ of habeas corpus can be used to claim a violation of CPL § 30.30(2). *See People ex rel. Chakwin v. Warden*, 63 N.Y.2d 120, 125, 480 N.Y.S.2d 719, 721 (1984). The rationale is that:

> While a defendant may bring a pretrial motion to seek release based on a violation of CPL 30.30 (subd. 2), he has no way to effectively appeal an adverse ruling. Obviously, once the defendant's case is tried the legality of his pretrial detention is mooted and the relief guaranteed by CPL 30.30 (subd. 2) would be academic on a direct appeal from a judgment of conviction.

People ex rel. Chakwin v. Warden, 63 N.Y.2d 120, 125, 480 N.Y.S.2d 719 (1984).

§ 53:34 Defendant not required to assert CPL § 30.30(2) rights before People declare readiness for trial

Research References

West's Key Number Digest, Criminal Law ⚖573, 575, 577.4, 577.7

A defendant is not required to assert his or her CPL § 30.30(2) rights before the People declare their readiness for trial in order to be entitled to relief thereunder. Rather, "[o]nce the 90-day period lapses, a defendant is entitled to release in accordance with the provisions of CPL 30.30(2), provided that the provisions of CPL 30.30(3) are not applicable." *People ex rel. Greenstein v. Sheriff of Schenectady County*, 220 A.D.2d 190, __, 645 N.Y.S.2d 339, 341 (3d Dep't 1996).

§ 53:35 CPL § 30.30(2)—Motion procedure

Research References

West's Key Number Digest, Criminal Law ☞573, 577.4, 577.16(10)

CPL § 30.30(6) provides that "[t]he procedural rules prescribed in [CPL § 210.45(1) to (7)] with respect to a motion to dismiss an indictment are also applicable to a motion made pursuant to [CPL § 30.30(2)]." *See generally* § 53:89, *infra*.

§ 53:36 Applicability of CPL § 30.30 to traffic infractions

Research References

West's Key Number Digest, Criminal Law ☞573, 575, 577.4, 577.6

CPL § 30.30 does not apply to traffic infractions. *See, e.g., People v. Taylor*, 189 Misc. 2d 313, 731 N.Y.S.2d 324 (App. Term, 2d Dep't 2001); *People v. Gonzalez*, 168 Misc. 2d 136, 645 N.Y.S.2d 978 (App. Term, 1st Dep't 1996) (per curiam); *People v. Pilewski*, 173 Misc. 2d 800, __, 660 N.Y.S.2d 525, 527 (Great Neck Just. Ct. 1997); *People v. Faison*, 171 Misc. 2d 68, __, 662 N.Y.S.2d 973, 975 (N.Y. City Crim. Ct. 1996); *People v. Fisher*, 167 Misc. 2d 850, __-__, 635 N.Y.S.2d 1002, 1003–04 (N.Y. City Crim. Ct. 1995); *People v. Howell*, 158 Misc. 2d 653, __ n.1, 601 N.Y.S.2d 778, 779 n.1 (N.Y. City Crim. Ct. 1993); *People v. Blake*, 154 Misc. 2d 660, __ n.2, 585 N.Y.S.2d 993, 994 n.2 (N.Y. City Crim. Ct. 1992); *People v. Fiacco*, 146 Misc. 2d 330, __, 549 N.Y.S.2d 901, 902 (Albany City Ct. 1989); *People v. Matute*, 141 Misc. 2d 988, __, 535 N.Y.S.2d 524, 524 (N.Y. City Crim. Ct. 1988); *People v. Wise*, 141 Misc. 2d 409, __-__, 532 N.Y.S.2d 833, 834–35 (Nassau Co. Dist. Ct. 1988); *People v. Michalek*, 138 Misc. 2d 1, __, 521 N.Y.S.2d 609, 610 (N.Y. City Crim. Ct. 1987) (rejected by, People v. Pregent, 142 Misc. 2d 344, 537 N.Y.S.2d 424 (City Ct. 1988)); *People v. Solomon*, 124 Misc. 2d 33, __, 475 N.Y.S.2d 749, 750 (Nassau Co. Dist. Ct. 1984) (rejected by, People v. Pregent, 142 Misc. 2d 344, 537 N.Y.S.2d 424 (City Ct. 1988)); *People v. Zagorsky*, 73 Misc. 2d 420, __-__, 341 N.Y.S.2d 791, 793–95 (Broome Co. Ct. 1973). *See also* Preiser, Practice Commentaries, McKinney's Cons. Laws of NY, Book 11A, CPL § 30.30, at 207-08. *But see People v. Pregent*, 142 Misc. 2d 344, __, 537 N.Y.S.2d 424, 425 (Syracuse City Ct. 1988) (CPL § 30.30 applies to DWAI charge). *See gener-*

ally Matter of Stamos v. Appeals Bd. of N.Y. State Dep't of Motor Vehicles, 309 A.D.2d 572, __, 765 N.Y.S.2d 342, 343 (1st Dep't 2003) (speedy trial provisions of CPL inapplicable to administrative proceedings respecting alleged traffic infractions held pursuant to VTL Article 2-A).

§ 53:37　Applicability of CPL § 30.30 to traffic infractions accompanied by felonies, misdemeanors, or violations

Research References

West's Key Number Digest, Criminal Law ⬩573, 575, 577.4, 577.6

CPL § 30.30(1)(a) provides that the People must be ready for trial within "[6] months of the commencement of a criminal action *wherein* a defendant is accused of [1] or more *offenses*, at least [1] of which is a felony." (Emphases added).

CPL § 30.30(1)(b) provides that the People must be ready for trial within "[90] days of the commencement of a criminal action *wherein* a defendant is accused of [1] or more *offenses*, at least [1] of which is a misdemeanor punishable by a sentence of imprisonment of more than [3] months and none of which is a felony." (Emphases added).

CPL § 30.30(1)(c) provides that the People must be ready for trial within "[60] days of the commencement of a criminal action *wherein* the defendant is accused of [1] or more *offenses*, at least [1] of which is a misdemeanor punishable by a sentence of imprisonment of not more than [3] months and none of which is a crime punishable by a sentence of imprisonment of more than [3] months." (Emphases added).

CPL § 30.30(1)(d) provides that the People must be ready for trial within "[30] days of the commencement of a criminal action *wherein* the defendant is accused of [1] or more *offenses*, at least [1] of which is a violation and none of which is a crime." (Emphases added).

Thus, although CPL § 30.30 does not apply where the defendant is only charged with a traffic infraction or infractions at the outset, *see* previous section, it appears clear that CPL § 30.30 *does* apply to traffic infractions that are part of a larger criminal action "wherein" the defendant is also charged with one or more felonies, misdemeanors or violations. *See* CPL § 30.30(1)(a) to (d).

In this regard, a "traffic infraction" is clearly an "offense" within the meaning of CPL § 30.30(1)(a) to (d). *See, e.g.*, PL § 10.00(1) (" 'Offense' means conduct for which a sentence to a term of imprisonment or to a fine is provided by any law of this state . . . "); PL § 10.00(2) (" 'Traffic infraction' means any *offense* defined as 'traffic infraction' by [VTL § 155]") (emphasis added;

PL § 55.10(4) ("Traffic infraction . . . [A]n *offense* which is defined as a 'traffic infraction' . . .") (emphasis added); CPL § 1.20 (PL § 10.00 definitions are applicable to the CPL); CPL § 1.20(5) (definition of "simplified traffic information" refers to "traffic infractions" as "offenses"); CPL § 100.10(2)(a) (same); CPL § 1.20(37) (DWAI is clearly a "lesser included *offense*" of DWI); CPL § 100.25(2); CPL § 100.25(3); CPL § 100.55; CPL § 170.10(1)(a); CPL § 170.10(4)(b); CPL § 340.20(2)(b); CPL § 710.10(1) (" 'Defendant' means a person who has been charged by an accusatory instrument with the commission of an offense"); CPL § 60.75; CPL § 70.10; CPL § 70.20; VTL § 1196(7)(f). *See also People v. Christensen*, 77 A.D.3d 174, __, 906 N.Y.S.2d 301, 311 (2d Dep't 2010) ("The duty to prosecute 'offenses' necessarily includes 'traffic infraction[s],' which are a type of offense defined by VTL § 155 (Penal Law § 10.00[1], [2])"); *People v. Zapletova*, 191 Misc. 2d 48, __, 742 N.Y.S.2d 773, 775 (Hunter Just. Ct. 2002) ("There can be no legal basis to conclude other than a 'Traffic infraction' is an 'offense' "); *People v. Abajian*, 142 Misc. 2d 250, __, 537 N.Y.S.2d 449, 452 (South Nyack Just. Ct. 1989) ("A traffic infraction is, of course, an 'offense,' albeit it is not a crime"). *See generally People v. Class*, 63 N.Y.2d 491, 496, 483 N.Y.S.2d 181, 184, 472 N.E.2d 1009 (1984), judgment rev'd on other grounds, 475 U.S. 106, 106 S. Ct. 960, 89 L. Ed. 2d 81 (1986) (Court of Appeals refers to "ordinary traffic infraction" as "an offense").

In addition, a "traffic infraction" is a "petty offense," *see* CPL § 1.20(39), and a "petty offense" is clearly a type of "offense." *See, e.g.*, CPL § 10.20(1)(c); CPL § 10.30(1)(a); CPL § 200.20(1) ("An indictment must charge at least one crime and may, in addition, charge in separate counts one or more *other offenses, including petty offenses* . . .") (emphasis added); CPL § 210.20(1-a).

Accordingly, it is the authors' opinion that *People v. Gonzalez*, 168 Misc. 2d 136, 645 N.Y.S.2d 978 (App. Term, 1st Dep't 1996) (per curiam), which both (a) found that a "petty offense" is not an "offense" within the meaning of CPL § 30.30(1)(b), and (b) reasoned that where the most serious charge in a criminal action is dismissed or reduced, the applicable time period for purposes of CPL § 30.30(1) is the period applicable to the most serious *remaining* charge, was incorrectly decided.

In fact, the reasoning of *Gonzalez* was expressly rejected by the Court of Appeals in *People v. Cooper*, 98 N.Y.2d 541, 750 N.Y.S.2d 258 (2002). In *Cooper*, the Court held that:

> [U]nless an event occurs which triggers the specific contingencies of CPL 30.30(5), the general rule articulated in CPL 30.30(1) controls the calculation of the readiness period throughout the criminal action. Under that provision, the readiness time requirement is based on the most serious offense charged in the criminal action, measured from the date of filing of the first accusatory instrument.

People v. Cooper, 98 N.Y.2d 541, 546, 750 N.Y.S.2d 258 (2002). *See also People v. Cooper*, 98 N.Y.2d 541, 546, 750 N.Y.S.2d 258 (2002) ("unless a specific CPL 30.30(5) contingency applies, the general rule set forth in CPL 30.30(1) governs").

Thus, for example, where a charge is reduced from a class A misdemeanor to a class B misdemeanor, the applicable time period for purposes of CPL § 30.30(1) is 90 days—*not* 60 days. *See People v. Cooper*, 98 N.Y.2d 541, 546, 750 N.Y.S.2d 258 (2002). *See also People v. Stateikin*, 163 Misc. 2d 517, 620 N.Y.S.2d 903 (N.Y. City Crim. Ct. 1994); § 53:45, *infra*.

Similarly, pursuant to *Cooper*, where a misdemeanor DWI charge is reduced to the traffic infraction of DWAI, the applicable time period for purposes of CPL § 30.30(1) is 90 days—the action is not removed from the ambit of CPL § 30.30. *See People v. Faison*, 171 Misc. 2d 68, 662 N.Y.S.2d 973 (N.Y. City Crim. Ct. 1996); *People v. Matute*, 141 Misc. 2d 988, 535 N.Y.S.2d 524 (N.Y. City Crim. Ct. 1988). *See also People v. Mahmood*, 10 Misc. 3d 198, 800 N.Y.S.2d 919 (N.Y. City Crim. Ct. 2005). *Cf. People v. Graham*, 39 Misc. 3d 35, 965 N.Y.S.2d 271 (App. Term, 2d, 11th & 13th Jud. Dist. 2013).

§ 53:38 Applicability of CPL § 30.30 to homicides

Research References

West's Key Number Digest, Criminal Law ⟐573, 575, 577.4, 577.6

CPL § 30.30(3)(a) provides that the statutory speedy trial rights granted by CPL § 30.30(1) and (2) "do not apply to a criminal action wherein the defendant is accused of an offense defined in [PL §§] 125.10, 125.15, 125.20, 125.25 and 125.27." In other words, CPL § 30.30(1) and (2) are inapplicable where the defendant is charged with:

1. Criminally negligent homicide (*i.e.*, PL § 125.10);
2. Manslaughter in the second degree (*i.e.*, PL § 125.15);
3. Manslaughter in the first degree (*i.e.*, PL § 125.20);
4. Murder in the second degree (*i.e.*, PL § 125.25); or
5. Murder in the first degree (*i.e.*, PL § 125.27).

See also People v. Johnson, 38 N.Y.2d 271, 278 n.3, 379 N.Y.S.2d 735, 742 n.3 (1975); *People v. O'Sullivan*, 121 A.D.2d 658, 504 N.Y.S.2d 49 (2d Dep't 1986); *People v. Riera*, 99 A.D.2d 972, 472 N.Y.S.2d 663 (1st Dep't 1984); *People v. Rodriguez*, 81 A.D.2d 840, 438 N.Y.S.2d 845 (2d Dep't 1981); *People v. White*, 72 A.D.2d 913, 422 N.Y.S.2d 193 (4th Dep't 1979).

Note that vehicular manslaughter in the second degree (*i.e.*, PL § 125.12), and vehicular manslaughter in the first degree (*i.e.*, PL § 125.13), are *not* included in the clear and unambiguous list of homicides excluded from CPL § 30.30(1) and (2) coverage by CPL

§ 30.30(3)(a). As such, unless a vehicular manslaughter charge is accompanied by a charge listed in CPL § 30.30(3)(a), such charge is subject to the speedy trial requirements of CPL § 30.30(1) and (2). In this regard, "under CPL § 30.30 an indictment is viewed as a single whole unit, and not as separate counts." *People v. Gulston*, 181 Misc. 2d 644, 646, 695 N.Y.S.2d 888, 889 (Kings Co. Sup. Ct. 1999). *See also People v. Gulston*, 181 Misc. 2d 644, 646, 695 N.Y.S.2d 888, 889 (Kings Co. Sup. Ct. 1999). ("By using the word 'wherein' [in CPL § 30.30(3)(a)], the Legislature indicates that the 'criminal action' referred to in this section contains both homicide counts and non-homicide counts").

§ 53:39 Applicability of CPL § 30.30 to *attempted* homicides

Research References

West's Key Number Digest, Criminal Law ⟲573, 575, 577.4, 577.6

It is well settled that CPL § 30.30(3)(a) does not apply to *attempted* homicides. Thus, attempted homicides *are* subject to the provisions of CPL § 30.30(1) and (2). *See, e.g., People v. Williams*, 130 A.D.2d 697, 515 N.Y.S.2d 622 (2d Dep't 1987); *People v. Quinones*, 126 A.D.2d 757, 511 N.Y.S.2d 341 (2d Dep't 1987); *People v. Gordon*, 125 A.D.2d 257, 509 N.Y.S.2d 543 (1st Dep't 1986).

§ 53:40 CPL § 30.30(3)(a)—Constitutionality

Research References

West's Key Number Digest, Criminal Law ⟲573, 574, 577.1, 577.2

CPL § 30.30(3)(a) has been found to be constitutional. *See People v. Colon*, 138 A.D.2d 392, __, 525 N.Y.S.2d 675, 676 (2d Dep't 1988); *People v. Mollete*, 87 Misc. 2d 236, __, 383 N.Y.S.2d 817, 821 (Bronx Co. Sup. Ct. 1976).

§ 53:41 Date on which criminal action is deemed to have commenced—Generally

Research References

West's Key Number Digest, Criminal Law ⟲577.8 to 577.8(2)

CPL § 1.20(17) provides that "[a] criminal action is commenced by the filing of an accusatory instrument against a defendant in a criminal court, and, if more than one accusatory instrument is filed in the course of the action, it commences when the first of such instruments is filed." *See also* CPL § 1.20(16); CPL § 100.05; *People v. Cooper*, 98 N.Y.2d 541, 543, 750 N.Y.S.2d 258, 259 (2002); *People v. Stirrup*, 91 N.Y.2d 434, 438, 671 N.Y.S.2d 433, 435 (1998); *People v. Cousart*, 58 N.Y.2d 62, 66, 458 N.Y.S.2d

507, 509 (1982); *People v. Osgood*, 52 N.Y.2d 37, 43, 436 N.Y.S.2d 213, 216 (1980); *People v. Lomax*, 50 N.Y.2d 351, 356, 428 N.Y.S.2d 937, 939 (1980); *People v. Sturgis*, 38 N.Y.2d 625, 627, 381 N.Y.S.2d 860, 861 (1976). *Cf. People v. Staley*, 41 N.Y.2d 789, 791, 396 N.Y.S.2d 339, 341 (1977) ("Once an arrest has been made, the criminal proceeding is deemed to have started, and defendant is entitled, constitutionally, to a speedy trial").

"Accordingly, each criminal action generally has only one date of commencement for purposes of the CPL 30.30 readiness rule, regardless of how many times the accusatory instrument is amended or replaced." *Cooper*, 98 N.Y.2d at 543, 750 N.Y.S.2d at 259. *See also Lomax*, 50 N.Y.2d at 356, 428 N.Y.S.2d at 939.

By contrast, "[a] criminal action . . . terminates with the imposition of sentence or some other final disposition in a criminal court of the *last* accusatory instrument filed in the case." CPL § 1.20(16)(c) (emphasis added). *People v. Osgood*, 52 N.Y.2d 37, 44–45, 436 N.Y.S.2d 213, 217 (1980). Thus, where a felony action is commenced by the filing of a felony complaint, and this initial accusatory instrument is dismissed due to the prosecutor's "inexcusable failure to prosecute," the People cannot salvage the prosecution by obtaining an indictment and claiming that a "new" criminal action has commenced. *See Osgood, supra.*

In *Osgood*, the Court of Appeals held that:

> [T]he statute states that the criminal action "terminates with the imposition of sentence or some other final disposition in a criminal court of the *last* accusatory instrument filed *in the case*." Here the dismissal of the felony complaint may have finally disposed of the *first* accusatory instrument in the case. But as long as the District Attorney is free to continue the prosecution by obtaining an indictment, dismissal of the felony complaint cannot be said to have disposed of, finally or otherwise, the *last* accusatory instrument "in the case."

> In sum, the six-month ready rule was meant to eliminate unjustified delays and was not intended to provide rewards or incentive for delay. The prosecutor's argument that the return of the indictment, after dismissal of the felony complaint for inexcusable delay in prosecution, commenced a new criminal action and renewed the six-month period, is inconsistent with that purpose and is not commanded by anything the Legislature has said.

52 N.Y.2d at 44–45, 436 N.Y.S.2d at 217 (citation omitted).

Similarly, in *Lomax, supra*, the Court of Appeals held that "a new indictment, returned after the original one had been dismissed, should be *related back* to the commencement of the criminal proceeding for purposes of the six-month readiness period under CPL 30.30(1)(a)." *People v. Sinistaj*, 67 N.Y.2d 236, 239, 501 N.Y.S.2d 793, 794 (1986) (emphasis added).

In *Sinistaj*, the Court of Appeals held that the "relation back" doctrine of *Lomax* and *Osgood* is applicable "for the purpose of computing excludable time under CPL 30.30(4)." *People v. Sinistaj*, 67 N.Y.2d at 237, 501 N.Y.S.2d at 793. In so holding, the Court reasoned that:

> We perceive no logical reason why, when a subsequent indictment is related back to the commencement of the proceeding for purposes of applying the six-month limitation prescribed by CPL 30.30(1)(a), it should not also be related back for the purpose of computing the time to be excluded from that limitation. * * *
>
> [O]ur construction of CPL 30.30 to require that all excludable periods must be deducted from the "total time," starting with the filing of the accusatory instrument (CPL 1.20[16], [17]), is entirely consistent with the purpose of CPL 30.30 as a prosecutorial readiness rule.

People v. Sinistaj, 67 N.Y.2d 236, 239, 240, 501 N.Y.S.2d 793 (1986) (citation omitted).

However, the *Sinistaj* Court made clear that "[o]ur decision here that the new indictment should be related back for purposes of giving effect to the excludable periods under CPL 30.30(4) is dependent on our treatment of the indictment as one that is 'directly derived' from the first accusatory instrument and must therefore be considered under *Osgood* and *Lomax* as part of the original action. Unless the new indictment is 'directly derived' from the first accusatory instrument it is, of course, not related back for purposes of CPL 30.30(1)(a)." *People v. Sinistaj*, 67 N.Y.2d 236, 241 n.4, 501 N.Y.S.2d 793 (1986).

§ 53:42 CPL § 30.30(5)(a) and (b)—Date on which criminal action is deemed to have commenced in certain situations

Research References

West's Key Number Digest, Criminal Law ⟨⟩577.8 to 577.8(2)

"CPL 30.30(5) lists specific situations which require a deviation from the general rule and effectively alters the date a criminal action is deemed to have commenced for purposes of applying the CPL 30.30(1) time frames." *People v. Cooper*, 98 N.Y.2d 541, 544, 750 N.Y.S.2d 258, 259 (2002). In other words:

> [U]nless an event occurs which triggers the specific contingencies of CPL 30.30(5), the general rule articulated in CPL 30.30(1) controls the calculation of the readiness period throughout the criminal action. Under that provision, the readiness time requirement is based on the most serious offense charged in the criminal action, measured from the date of filing of the first accusatory instrument.

People v. Cooper, 98 N.Y.2d 541, 546, 750 N.Y.S.2d 258 (2002).

See also People v. Cooper, 98 N.Y.2d 541, 546, 750 N.Y.S.2d 258 (2002) ("unless a specific CPL 30.30(5) contingency applies, the general rule set forth in CPL 30.30(1) governs").

For example, CPL § 30.30(5)(a) provides that where the defendant is to be (a) tried following the withdrawal of a guilty plea, or (b) retried following:

1. A mistrial;
2. An order for a new trial; or
3. An appeal or collateral attack:

> "the criminal action and the commitment to the custody of the sheriff, if any, must be deemed to have commenced on the date the withdrawal of the plea of guilty or the date the order occasioning a retrial becomes final." CPL § 30.30(5)(a).

In addition, CPL § 30.30(5)(b) provides that "where a defendant has been served with an appearance ticket, the criminal action must be deemed to have commenced on the date the defendant first appears in a local criminal court in response to the ticket." *See also People v. Smietana*, 98 N.Y.2d 336, 340, 746 N.Y.S.2d 678, 680 (2002); *People v. Stirrup*, 91 N.Y.2d 434, 439, 671 N.Y.S.2d 433, 436 (1998) ("Once a defendant appears in response to a DAT, the criminal action is *deemed* commenced for ready-trial purposes"); *People v. Stirrup*, 91 N.Y.2d 434, 438, 671 N.Y.S.2d 433 (1998) (same); *People v. Parris*, 79 N.Y.2d 69, 71, 580 N.Y.S.2d 167, 168 (1992) (per curiam).

In *Parris, supra,* the defendant did not appear in court on the return date of the DAT because he was incarcerated on unrelated charges. 79 N.Y.2d at 70, 580 N.Y.S.2d at 167. Nonetheless, the Court of Appeals held that:

> The statute imposes no obligation upon the People to determine the reason for defendant's absence or to take any action to secure his attendance in order to avoid having the action deemed commenced on the return date of the DAT (*cf.,* CPL 30.30[4][c]). No such obligation should be implied. The Legislature made clear that when a defendant who has received a DAT fails to appear in court on the return date, the speedy trial clock does not begin to run until the defendant actually appears in court, regardless of the reason for defendant's failure to appear.

People v. Parris, 79 N.Y.2d 69, 71–72, 580 N.Y.S.2d 167 (1992) (per curiam).

§ 53:43 Date action commenced is excludable

Research References

West's Key Number Digest, Criminal Law ☞577.8 to 577.8(2)

The date that a criminal action is commenced is excluded for purposes of applying the CPL § 30.30(1) time frames. *See People v. Chavis*, 91 N.Y.2d 500, 504 n.3, 673 N.Y.S.2d 29, 31 n.3 (1998); *People v. Stiles*, 70 N.Y.2d 765, 767, 520 N.Y.S.2d 745, 745 (1987); *People v. DiMeglio*, 294 A.D.2d 239, ___, 743 N.Y.S.2d 83, 84 (1st Dep't 2002) ("when computing a period of days, the first day is excluded but the last day is included").

§ 53:44 Time within which People must be ready for trial where original charges reduced by filing of new accusatory instrument

Research References

West's Key Number Digest, Criminal Law ⊙577.8 to 577.8(2)

CPL § 30.30(5)(c) provides that "where a criminal action is commenced by the filing of a felony complaint, and thereafter, in the course of the same criminal action either":

    1. The felony complaint is, pursuant to CPL Article 180, replaced with or converted to:

      (a) An information;

      (b) A prosecutor's information; or

      (c) A misdemeanor complaint; or

    2. A prosecutor's information is filed pursuant to CPL § 190.70;

the time period applicable for purposes of CPL § 30.30(1) is the period applicable to the charge(s) in the new accusatory instrument, calculated from the date of the filing of such new accusatory instrument. However, "when the aggregate of such period and the period of time, excluding the periods provided in [CPL § 30.30(4)], already elapsed from the date of the filing of the felony complaint to the date of the filing of the new accusatory instrument exceeds *[6] months*, the period applicable to the charges in the felony complaint must remain applicable and continue as if the new accusatory instrument had not been filed." CPL § 30.30(5)(c) (emphasis added).

CPL § 30.30(5)(d) provides that "where a criminal action is commenced by the filing of a felony complaint, and thereafter, in the course of the same criminal action either":

    1. The felony complaint is, pursuant to CPL Article 180, replaced with or converted to:

      (a) An information;

      (b) A prosecutor's information; or

      (c) A misdemeanor complaint; or

    2. A prosecutor's information is filed pursuant to CPL § 190.70;

the time period applicable for purposes of CPL § 30.30(2) is the period applicable to the charge(s) in the new accusatory instrument, calculated from the date of the filing of such new accusatory instrument. However, "when the aggregate of such period and the period of time, excluding the periods provided in [CPL § 30.30(4)], already elapsed from the date of the filing of the felony complaint to the date of the filing of the new accusatory instrument exceeds *[90] days*, the period applicable to the charges in the felony complaint must remain applicable and continue as if the new accusatory instrument had not been filed." CPL § 30.30(5)(d) (emphasis added).

CPL § 30.30(5)(e) provides that where:

1. A count of an indictment is reduced to charge only a misdemeanor or petty offense; and

2. A reduced indictment or a prosecutor's information is filed pursuant to [CPL § 210.20(1-a) and (6)];

the time period applicable for purposes of CPL § 30.30(1) is the period applicable to the charge(s) in the new accusatory instrument, calculated from the date of the filing of such new accusatory instrument. However, "when the aggregate of such period and the period of time, excluding the periods provided in [CPL § 30.30(4)], already elapsed from the date of the filing of the indictment to the date of the filing of the new accusatory instrument exceeds *[6] months*, the period applicable to the charges in the indictment must remain applicable and continue as if the new accusatory instrument had not been filed." CPL § 30.30(5)(e) (emphasis added).

CPL § 30.30(5)(f) provides that where:

1. A count of an indictment is reduced to charge only a misdemeanor or petty offense; and

2. A reduced indictment or a prosecutor's information is filed pursuant to [CPL § 210.20(1-a) and (6)];

the time period applicable for purposes of CPL § 30.30(2) is the period applicable to the charge(s) in the new accusatory instrument, calculated from the date of the filing of such new accusatory instrument. However, "when the aggregate of such period and the period of time, excluding the periods provided in [CPL § 30.30(4)], already elapsed from the date of the filing of the indictment to the date of the filing of the new accusatory instrument exceeds *[90] days*, the period applicable to the charges in the indictment must remain applicable and continue as if the new accusatory instrument had not been filed." CPL § 30.30(5)(f) (emphasis added).

In *People v. Berke*, 66 N.Y.2d 861, 863, 498 N.Y.S.2d 360, 361 (1985), the Court of Appeals held that:

Criminal Court erred in ruling that when a felony charge is dismissed and the judge directs the People to prepare a prosecutor's information as to the misdemeanor charges remaining, CPL

30.30(1)(b) requires dismissal, *without regard to time otherwise excludable*, if the People fail to provide such an information within 90 days of the dismissal order.

(Emphasis added).

§ 53:45 Time within which People must be ready for trial where felony reduced to class A misdemeanor and then further reduced to class B misdemeanor

Research References

West's Key Number Digest, Criminal Law ⚬577.8 to 577.8(2)

In *People v. Cooper*, 98 N.Y.2d 541, 750 N.Y.S.2d 258 (2002), the "[d]efendant was initially arraigned on a complaint charging five felonies and four class A misdemeanors. On the People's motion, the felony charges were subsequently dismissed and defendant was charged by information with the remaining class A misdemeanors." *People v. Cooper*, 98 N.Y.2d 541, 542, 750 N.Y.S.2d 258 (2002).

Pursuant to CPL § 30.30(5)(c), this "resulted in a reduction of the applicable speedy trial time period . . . from six months, measured from the date of filing of the felony complaint, to 90 days, measured from the date of filing of the information." *People v. Cooper*, 98 N.Y.2d 541, 542–43, 750 N.Y.S.2d 258 (2002). "At issue on appeal is what effect the second reduction—from class A to class B misdemeanor charges—had on the trial readiness calculation. This particular reduction in charges is not among the scenarios addressed in CPL 30.30(5)." *People v. Cooper*, 98 N.Y.2d 541, 544–45, 750 N.Y.S.2d 258 (2002).

The Court of Appeals held that "unless a specific CPL 30.30(5) contingency applies, the general rule set forth in CPL 30.30(1) governs." *People v. Cooper*, 98 N.Y.2d 541, 546, 750 N.Y.S.2d 258 (2002). Applying this rule to the facts of the case, the Court held as follows:

Here, because the first reduction fell within the purview of CPL 30.30(5)(c), the action was effectively deemed to have commenced on the filing date of the information, with the readiness period determined by the most serious offense charged in that document—a class A misdemeanor. Thus, the operative period became 90 days measured from the filing date of the information. Because the subsequent reduction to class B misdemeanors is not among the exceptions enumerated in CPL 30.30(5), it had no effect on the readiness equation.

People v. Cooper, 98 N.Y.2d 541, 546, 750 N.Y.S.2d 258 (2002).

In *People v. Sawyer-Plato*, 81 A.D.3d 1444, 916 N.Y.S.2d 722 (4th Dep't 2011), the defendant was erroneously indicted for felony DWI due to the fact that her DMV abstract incorrectly listed her prior DWAI conviction as a DWI. Defendant claimed that the proper speedy trial time period was 90 days rather than six months. Rejecting this claim, the Appellate Division, Fourth Department, held that:

> As the Court of Appeals has written, "unless an event occurs which triggers the specific contingencies of CPL 30.30(5), [which is not the case here,] the general rule articulated in CPL 30.30(1) controls the calculation of the readiness period throughout the criminal action. Under that provision, the readiness time requirement is based on the most serious offense charged in the criminal action, measured from the date of filing of the first accusatory instrument." Here, the most serious offenses charged in this case were the two felony counts of DWI. While the documentation that defendant had a predicate DWI conviction, which formed the basis for the felony charges, was later shown to be erroneous, that does not negate the fact that "the most serious offense charged in the criminal action" was a felony. As a result, the People had six months in which to declare their readiness for trial, and they timely did so on January 4, 2008.

916 N.Y.S.2d at 724 (citations omitted). Notably, had the error been discovered prior to the defendant being indicted, CPL § 30.30(5)(c) likely would have led to a different result.

§ 53:46 Time within which People must be ready for trial where felony complaint replaced with misdemeanor *indictment*

Research References
West's Key Number Digest, Criminal Law ☞577.8 to 577.8(2)

In *People v. Tychanski*, 78 N.Y.2d 909, 573 N.Y.S.2d 454 (1991), the defendant was originally charged by a felony complaint, but the grand jury only indicted her for a misdemeanor. In this regard, "[t]he language of CPL 30.30(5)(c) omits misdemeanor *indictments* from the list of accusatory instruments that will trigger the application of the shorter 90-day speedy trial period." *People v. Tychanski*, 78 N.Y.2d 909, 911, 573 N.Y.S.2d 454 (1991) (emphasis added). As a result, the Court of Appeals held that "because this action was commenced by defendant's arraignment on a felony complaint, and because CPL 30.30(5)(c) is inapplicable, the People had six months in which to be ready for trial"—*not* 90 days. *People v. Tychanski*, 78 N.Y.2d 909, 912, 573 N.Y.S.2d 454 (1991). *See also People v. Tychanski*, 78 N.Y.2d 909, 911, 573 N.Y.S.2d 454 (1991) (same); *People v. Cooper*, 90 N.Y.2d 292, 294–95, 660 N.Y.S.2d 546, 547 (1997).

In a subsequent case involving a defendant also named Cooper, the Court of Appeals further explained its decisions in *Cooper* and *Tychanski*. In *People v. Cooper*, 98 N.Y.2d 541, 546, 750 N.Y.S.2d 258, 261 (2002), the Court stated that:

[U]nless an event occurs which triggers the specific contingencies of CPL 30.30(5), the general rule articulated in CPL 30.30(1) controls the calculation of the readiness period throughout the criminal action. Under that provision, the readiness time requirement is based on the most serious offense charged in the criminal action, measured from the date of filing of the first accusatory instrument.

See also People v. Cooper, 98 N.Y.2d 541, 546, 750 N.Y.S.2d 258 (2002) ("unless a specific CPL 30.30(5) contingency applies, the general rule set forth in CPL 30.30(1) governs").

§ 53:47 Time within which People must be ready for trial where misdemeanor elevated to felony

Research References

West's Key Number Digest, Criminal Law ☞577.8 to 577.8(2)

In *People v. Cooper*, 90 N.Y.2d 292, 660 N.Y.S.2d 546 (1997), the defendant was originally charged with misdemeanor DWI. However, upon learning that the defendant had been convicted of DWI within the preceding 10 years, the People thereafter charged him with felony DWI. The defendant claimed that the People violated CPL § 30.30(1) by failing "to announce their readiness for trial within 90 days of the action's commencement because the action was commenced by the filing of a misdemeanor complaint, notwithstanding the action's subsequent conversion to a felony case." *People v. Cooper*, 90 N.Y.2d 292, 294, 660 N.Y.S.2d 546 (1997).

The Court of Appeals held that, by answering ready within the six-month period applicable to felony prosecutions, the People complied with the speedy trial statute. *People v. Cooper*, 90 N.Y.2d 292, 294, 660 N.Y.S.2d 546 (1997).

In so holding, the Court noted that:

> [T]he speedy trial statute embodies the Legislature's measured determination that the People are entitled to six months to prepare for a felony trial. To accept defendant's argument in this case would penalize the People by reducing their felony trial preparation by three months based simply on the fortuity that the defendant was originally charged with a misdemeanor. We decline to reach such an anomalous result.

People v. Cooper, 90 N.Y.2d 292, 295, 660 N.Y.S.2d 546 (1997).

In a subsequent case involving a defendant also named Cooper, the Court of Appeals further explained its decision in *Cooper*. In *People v. Cooper*, 98 N.Y.2d 541, 546, 750 N.Y.S.2d 258, 261 (2002), the Court stated that:

> [U]nless an event occurs which triggers the specific contingencies of CPL 30.30(5), the general rule articulated in CPL 30.30(1) controls

the calculation of the readiness period throughout the criminal action. Under that provision, the readiness time requirement is based on the most serious offense charged in the criminal action, measured from the date of filing of the first accusatory instrument.

See also People v. Cooper, 98 N.Y.2d 541, 546, 750 N.Y.S.2d 258 (2002) ("unless a specific CPL 30.30(5) contingency applies, the general rule set forth in CPL 30.30(1) governs").

§ 53:48   CPL § 30.30(4)—Excludable time

Research References

West's Key Number Digest, Criminal Law ⬤➡577.8 to 577.8(2)

CPL § 30.30(4) contains a list of time periods that are excludable from the time within which the People must be ready for trial. In this regard, CPL § 30.30(4) provides that, in computing the time within which the People must be ready for trial pursuant to CPL § 30.30(1) and (2), the court must exclude any time period(s) listed in CPL § 30.30(4)(a) to (j).

§ 53:49   Preindictment delay generally *not* excludable

Research References

West's Key Number Digest, Criminal Law ⬤➡577.3, 577.8 to 577.8(2), 577.10(4)

"It is well recognized that preindictment delay is not normally excludable since this phase of criminal prosecution is wholly under the control of the People and there is generally nothing a defendant can do to hinder the People in obtaining an indictment." *People v. Miner*, 162 A.D.2d 767, __, 557 N.Y.S.2d 679, 681 (3d Dep't 1990).

§ 53:50   Time period during which CPL § 180.85 motion pending *not* excludable

Research References

West's Key Number Digest, Criminal Law ⬤➡577.3, 577.8 to 577.8(2)

CPL § 180.85 provides a procedure for a motion to dismiss a felony complaint (other than a felony complaint charging an offense defined in PL § 125.10, 125.15, 125.20, 125.25, or 125.27) "where the count or counts of the felony complaint have not been presented to a grand jury or otherwise disposed of in accordance with this chapter." CPL § 180.85(2). In this regard:

The period from the filing of a motion pursuant to [CPL § 180.85] until entry of an order disposing of such motion shall not, by reason of such motion, be considered a period of delay for purposes of [CPL § 30.30(4)], nor shall such period, by reason of such motion, be excluded in computing the time within which the people must be ready for trial pursuant to [CPL § 30.30].

CPL § 180.85(6).

§ 53:51 Delay in transferring case from arraignment part to IAS part *not* excludable

Research References

West's Key Number Digest, Criminal Law ⚬577.3, 577.8 to 577.8(2), 577.10(4)

In *People v. Collins*, 82 N.Y.2d 177, 181, 604 N.Y.S.2d 11, 13 (1993), the Court of Appeals held that "[a] delay occasioned by a rule-mandated transfer from an Arraignment Part to an IAS Part is not covered by any of the express statutory exclusions set forth in CPL 30.30," and thus is *not* excludable from the time within which the People must be ready for trial. *See also People v. Smith*, 82 N.Y.2d 676, 678, 601 N.Y.S.2d 466, 467 (1993).

§ 53:52 Excludable time—*Reasonable* period of delay resulting from other proceedings concerning defendant

Research References

West's Key Number Digest, Criminal Law ⚬577.3, 577.8 to 577.8(2), 577.10(4), 577.10(8)

CPL § 30.30(4)(a) provides that "a *reasonable* period of delay resulting from other proceedings concerning the defendant" is excludable from the time within which the People must be ready for trial. (Emphasis added). The list of "other proceedings" covered by CPL § 30.30(4)(a) includes, but is not limited to:

1. Proceedings to determine the defendant's competency to stand trial;
2. Any period during which the defendant is incompetent to stand trial;
3. Demand to produce;
4. Request for a bill of particulars;
5. Pretrial motions;
6. Appeals;
7. Trial of other charges; and
8. The time period(s) during which such matters are under consideration by the court.

It is critical to note that CPL § 30.30(4)(a) expressly provides that only a *reasonable* period of delay attributable to the proceedings listed therein is excludable.

§ 53:53   Excludable time—Pretrial motions

Research References

West's Key Number Digest, Criminal Law ☞577.3, 577.8 to 577.8(2), 577.10(4), 577.10(8)

The People do not have an unlimited period of time to respond to a pretrial motion. Rather, they must respond within a "reasonable" period of time—or risk being charged with any undue delay. *See* CPL § 30.30(4)(a). *See also People v. Harris*, 82 N.Y.2d 409, 413, 604 N.Y.S.2d 918, 921 (1993); *People v. Torres*, 60 N.Y.2d 119, 127, 468 N.Y.S.2d 606, 610 (1983); *People v. Gonzalez*, 266 A.D.2d 562, __, 700 N.Y.S.2d 35, 36–37 (2d Dep't 1999); *People v. Owens*, 209 A.D.2d 549, 619 N.Y.S.2d 620 (2d Dep't 1994); *People v. Lloyd*, 202 A.D.2d 1035, __, 610 N.Y.S.2d 111, 112 (4th Dep't 1994); *People v. Commack*, 194 A.D.2d 619, 599 N.Y.S.2d 56 (2d Dep't 1993). In this regard, how much time is "reasonable" must be decided on a case-by-case basis. *Torres, supra*, 60 N.Y.2d at 127–28, 468 N.Y.S.2d at 610.

In *People v. Collins*, 82 N.Y.2d 177, 181, 604 N.Y.S.2d 11, 13 (1993), the Court of Appeals stated that CPL § 30.30(4)(a) "generally refers to delays attributable to responding to and deciding motions actually made." In *People v. Brown*, 99 N.Y.2d 488, 492, 758 N.Y.S.2d 602, 604 (2003), the Court found that the general rule that it announced in *Collins* was inapplicable where the 47-day time period in question "occurred when the trial court adjourned the case after defense counsel announced her intention to file a pretrial motion in a separate, unrelated narcotics case against defendant," but "defendant never actually filed the contemplated motion for which the 47-day adjournment was granted."

§ 53:54   Excludable time—Appeals

Research References

West's Key Number Digest, Criminal Law ☞577.3, 577.8 to 577.8(2), 577.10(4), 577.10(8)

"An appeal that has been 'withdrawn' with the permission of the court is a nullity," as is the People's CPL § 450.50(1) statement. *People v. McIntosh*, 80 N.Y.2d 87, 90, 587 N.Y.S.2d 568, 569 (1992). In *McIntosh*, the Court of Appeals held that:

> [B]ecause a withdrawn appeal by the People is a nullity, it cannot serve as the basis for an exclusion from the time within which the People must be ready for trial pursuant to CPL 30.30 (*see,* CPL 30.30[4][a] [excluding "a reasonable period of delay resulting from other proceedings concerning the defendant, including * * * appeals"]). Thus, as the Appellate Division held, the People's time

to become ready will be deemed to have continued to run notwithstanding their CPL 450.20(8) appeal if, in fact, that appeal is withdrawn before it is determined.

People v. McIntosh, 80 N.Y.2d 87, 90, 587 N.Y.S.2d 568 (1992). *See generally People v. Grafton*, 73 N.Y.2d 779, 536 N.Y.S.2d 738 (1988).

§ 53:55 Excludable time—Period during which defendant is incompetent to stand trial

Research References

West's Key Number Digest, Criminal Law ⟜577.3, 577.8 to 577.8(2), 577.10(4), 577.10(8)

"The speedy trial statute specifically recognizes as a separate factor resulting in delay warranting an exemption from the time limitation 'the period during which *defendant is incompetent to stand trial*' (CPL 30.30[4][a] [emphasis added])." *People v. Santana*, 80 N.Y.2d 92, 102, 587 N.Y.S.2d 570, 575 (1992). In *Santana*, the Court of Appeals held that:

> We hold only, under the unique circumstances of this case where defendant remained an incapacitated person by virtue of the interrelated effect of two orders of New York State Supreme Court, that the period properly exempted under CPL 30.30(4)(a) brought the total time to be counted against the prosecution to less than 180 days.

People v. Santana, 80 N.Y.2d 92, 102–03, 587 N.Y.S.2d 570 (1992).

In *People v. Lebron*, 88 N.Y.2d 891, 644 N.Y.S.2d 915 (1996), the Court of Appeals held that where (a) an order of commitment has been issued, and/or (b) the defendant has been declared incompetent to stand trial, the People are under no obligation to monitor the defendant's competency status.

§ 53:56 Excludable time—Adjournments granted at the request of, or with the consent of, defendant

Research References

West's Key Number Digest, Criminal Law ⟜577.3, 577.8 to 577.8(2), 577.10(4), 577.10(8)

CPL § 30.30(4)(b) provides that "the period of delay resulting from a continuance granted by the court at the request of, or with the consent of, the defendant or his counsel" is excludable from the time within which the People must be ready for trial. In this regard:

> The court must grant such a continuance only if it is satisfied that postponement is in the interest of justice, taking into account the

public interest in the prompt dispositions of criminal charges. A defendant without counsel must not be deemed to have consented to a continuance unless he has been advised by the court of his rights under these rules and the effect of his consent.

CPL § 30.30(4)(b).

In *People v. Dickinson*, 18 N.Y.3d 835, 938 N.Y.S.2d 836, 962 N.E.2d 257 (2011), the People conceded that they were not ready for trial in a timely manner, but argued "that defendant waived his rights under CPL 30.30 by participating in plea negotiations for several months." The Court of Appeals rejected the People's claim, holding that:

> While a defendant may waive rights under CPL 30.30, the record here contains no evidence of any waiver, written or oral. Mere silence is not a waiver. We repeat our observation in *Waldron* that "prosecutors would be well advised to obtain unambiguous written waivers in situations like these."

18 N.Y.3d at 836, 938 N.Y.S.2d at 836 (citation omitted).

In *People v. Waldron*, 6 N.Y.3d 463, 814 N.Y.S.2d 70 (2006), the Court of Appeals held that an informal letter from defense counsel to the district attorney expressly waiving the defendant's speedy trial rights for a period of time was valid and enforceable. In this regard, the Court ruled that:

> CPL 30.30(4)(b) speaks only to the question of when continuances *granted by the court* may be excluded from section 30.30's time limitations. It does not prevent a defendant from making, through a letter from his counsel, a valid waiver of his statutory speedy trial right, and there is no requirement that such a letter be filed contemporaneously at the courthouse.

People v. Waldron, 6 N.Y.3d 463, 468–69, 814 N.Y.S.2d 70 (2006) (emphasis added).

In *People v. Kopciowski*, 68 N.Y.2d 615, 616–17, 505 N.Y.S.2d 52, 53 (1986), the Court of Appeals held that:

> Defendant's requested adjournments in the period between June 2 and October 4 must be excluded in determining the People's compliance with CPL 30.30 (CPL 30.30[4][b], [f]) . . . . Where adjournments are allowed at defendant's request, those periods of delay are expressly waived in calculating the People's trial readiness, without the need for the People to trace their lack of readiness to defendant's actions.

See also People v. Meierdiercks, 68 N.Y.2d 613, 614–15, 505 N.Y.S.2d 51, 52 (1986) (decided the same day as *Kopciowski*) ("the controlling consideration is not whether defendants' actions prevented the People from obtaining accusatory instruments sufficient for trial, but whether defendants waived the delay in the proceedings by requesting or consenting to the adjournments"); *People v. Worley*, 66 N.Y.2d 523, 527, 498 N.Y.S.2d 116, 118 (1985) ("Inasmuch as the Legislature intended CPL 30.30 to address delays caused by the People, the time required for defendant's pretrial motions and his requested adjournments should be excluded").

Critically, however, "a mere failure by defense counsel to object to an adjournment does not constitute 'consent' within the meaning of CPL 30.30(4)(b)." *People v. Cortes*, 80 N.Y.2d 201, 214, 590 N.Y.S.2d 9, 17 (1992). *See also People v. Cortes*, 80 N.Y.2d 201, 216, 590 N.Y.S.2d 9 (1992) ("defense counsel's silence is not sufficient, in itself, to constitute 'consent' "); *People v. Liotta*, 79 N.Y.2d 841, 843, 580 N.Y.S.2d 184, 185 (1992) ("The People's contention that a defendant consents to an adjournment either by failing to object to the adjournment, or by defense counsel's failure to appear is meritless . . . [C]onsent to an adjournment must be clearly expressed by the defendant or defense counsel to relieve the People of the responsibility for that portion of the delay"); *People v. Johnson*, 38 N.Y.2d 271, 273 n.1, 379 N.Y.S.2d 735, 737 n.1 (1975) ("The concurrence with respect to the date fixed by the court should not be considered as an acquiescence with respect to the granting of the adjournment"); *People v. Brown*, 69 A.D.3d 871, —, 895 N.Y.S.2d 127, 129 (2d Dep't 2010) ("Defense counsel's statement 'That's fine' is consistent with an agreement as to the method by which the court would 'notify the parties' of the hearing date. It cannot be seen as a 'clearly expressed' consent to an adjournment of unspecified and unlimited duration").

"The defendant should not be placed in a position where he will have to submit to a continuance at the expense of his right to a speedy trial." *Matter of Westchester Rockland Newspapers, Inc. v. Leggett*, 48 N.Y.2d 430, 444, 423 N.Y.S.2d 630, 638 (1979).

In *People v. Smith*, 82 N.Y.2d 676, 677, 601 N.Y.S.2d 466, 467 (1993), the Court of Appeals held that "the People should be charged with time beyond the dates to which they requested adjournments." In this regard, the Court rejected the People's claim that "an adjournment which is extended because the defense rejects the original date suggested by the People should be, in part, excludable from the time chargeable to them." *People v. Smith*, 82 N.Y.2d 676, 678, 601 N.Y.S.2d 466 (1993). The Court reasoned that:

> The People's contention that defense counsel's unavailability amounted to consent to a longer delay is also unavailing. Adjournments consented to by the defense must be clearly expressed to relieve the People of the responsibility for that portion of the delay. Defense counsel's failure to object to the adjournment or failure to

appear does not constitute consent. The adjournments at issue here were, in the first instance, precipitated by the People's failure to be ready for trial. Other than stating that certain dates were inconvenient, defense counsel never formally consented to the adjournments and did not participate in setting the adjourned dates. Because the actual dates were set either by the court or the prosecution, no justification exists for excluding the additional adjournment time required to accommodate defense counsel's schedule.

People v. Smith, 82 N.Y.2d 676, 678, 601 N.Y.S.2d 466 (1993) (citation omitted). *See generally People v. Conner*, 65 N.Y.2d 852, 493 N.Y.S.2d 307 (1985) ("The courts below found that the delays in question did not arise from the action or with the consent of the defendant or for the defendant's convenience"); *People v. Wallace*, 26 N.Y.2d 371, 374, 310 N.Y.S.2d 484, 486 (1970) ("the fact that appellant's attorney answered 'ready' to calendar calls does not spell out a waiver of the right to a speedy trial. On the contrary, it indicates that appellant wished a trial at the earliest possible date").

In *People v. Clark*, 174 Misc. 2d 324, __, 666 N.Y.S.2d 869, 870 (App. Term, 2d Dep't 1997), the Court held that "the statement by defense counsel, 'Thank you' in response to the clerk's statement, 'Counsel, March 17th?' did not constitute a clear expression of consent, but only an acknowledgment of the specific date of adjournment, as the court below properly determined."

§ 53:57   Excludable time—Delay resulting from absence or unavailability of defendant

Research References

West's Key Number Digest, Criminal Law ☞577.3, 577.8 to 577.8(2), 577.10(4), 577.10(8)

CPL § 30.30(4)(c)(i) provides that "the period of delay *resulting from* the absence or unavailability of the defendant" (emphasis added) is excludable from the time within which the People must be ready for trial. In this regard:

A defendant must be considered absent whenever his location is unknown and he is attempting to avoid apprehension or prosecution, or his location cannot be determined by due diligence. A defendant must be considered unavailable whenever his location is known but his presence for trial cannot be obtained by due diligence.

CPL § 30.30(4)(c)(i).

"[T]he question whether the People have exercised diligence in locating an individual is a mixed question of law and fact." *People v. Luperon*, 85 N.Y.2d 71, 78, 623 N.Y.S.2d 735, 739 (1995). In *Luperon*, the Court of Appeals made clear that, even if "the People acted diligently *overall* in their efforts" to locate the defendant, they are nonetheless liable for time periods—within the "overall" time period—during which they did not act diligently. *People v. Luperon*, 85 N.Y.2d 71, 79–80, 623 N.Y.S.2d 735 (1995) (emphasis added). In addition, the Court refused to create "a blanket exception for 'reasonable administrative delay.' " *People v. Luperon*, 85 N.Y.2d 71, 79, 623 N.Y.S.2d 735 (1995). The *Luperon* Court also emphasized that "the People must establish *as co-equal elements* both that the defendant was missing and that they exercised diligence." *People v. Luperon*, 85 N.Y.2d 71, 81, 623 N.Y.S.2d 735 (1995).

In *People v. Torres*, 88 N.Y.2d 928, 930–31, 646 N.Y.S.2d 790, 791 (1996), the Court of Appeals held that "[t]he People need not exercise due diligence in attempting to locate a defendant who is attempting to avoid apprehension or prosecution." *See generally People v. Sigismundi*, 89 N.Y.2d 587, 657 N.Y.S.2d 381 (1997) (applying former version of CPL § 30.30(4)(c) to unique fact pattern); *People v. Patterson*, 38 N.Y.2d 623, 625, 381 N.Y.S.2d 858, 859 (1976).

A 1984 amendment to CPL § 30.30(4)(c) was enacted to overrule the Court of Appeals' decision in *People v. Sturgis*, 38 N.Y.2d 625, 381 N.Y.S.2d 860 (1976). *See People v. Bolden*, 81 N.Y.2d 146, 151, 597 N.Y.S.2d 270, 272 (1993).

For an analysis of the "checkered and tortured history" of CPL § 30.30(4)(c), see Preiser, Practice Commentaries, McKinney's Cons. Laws of N.Y., Book 11A, CPL § 30.30, at 214–17.

§ 53:58 Excludable time—Delay resulting from defendant's escape from custody or failure to appear in court when required

Research References

West's Key Number Digest, Criminal Law ⊃577.3, 577.8 to 577.8(2), 577.10(4), 577.10(8)

CPL § 30.30(4)(c)(ii) provides that "the period extending from the day the court issues a bench warrant pursuant to [CPL § 530.70] because of the defendant's failure to appear in court when required, to the day the defendant subsequently appears in the court pursuant to a bench warrant or voluntarily or otherwise" is excludable from the time within which the People must be ready for trial where the defendant has either:

1. Escaped from custody; or

2. Failed to appear when required after having previously been released on bail or on his/her own recognizance;

unless the defendant is in custody on another matter.

For an analysis of the "checkered and tortured history" of CPL § 30.30(4)(c), see Preiser, Practice Commentaries, McKinney's Cons. Laws of N.Y., Book 11A, CPL § 30.30, at 214–17.

§ 53:59 Excludable time—Reasonable period of delay when defendant joined for trial with codefendant whose speedy trial time has not expired

Research References

West's Key Number Digest, Criminal Law ⚲577.3, 577.8 to 577.8(2), 577.10(4), 577.10(8)

CPL § 30.30(4)(d) provides that "a reasonable period of delay when the defendant is joined for trial with a co-defendant as to whom the time for trial pursuant to [CPL § 30.30] has not run" is excludable from the time within which the People must be ready for trial. However, this exclusion only applies where "good cause is not shown for granting a severance." CPL § 30.30(4)(d).

§ 53:60 Excludable time—Delay resulting from defendant's detention in another jurisdiction

Research References

West's Key Number Digest, Criminal Law ⚲577.3, 577.8 to 577.8(2), 577.10(4), 577.10(8)

CPL § 30.30(4)(e) provides that "the period of delay resulting from detention of the defendant in another jurisdiction" is excludable from the time within which the People must be ready for trial. However, this exclusion only applies where the district attorney both:

1. Is aware of such detention; and

2. Has been diligent and has made reasonable efforts to obtain the presence of the defendant for trial.

CPL § 30.30(4)(e). *See generally People v. McLaurin*, 38 N.Y.2d 586, 587–88, 381 N.Y.S.2d 835, 835–36 (1976) (per curiam); *People v. McLaurin*, 38 N.Y.2d 123, 126, 378 N.Y.S.2d 692, 694 (1975).

In this regard, "knowledge of the defendant's whereabouts . . . on the part of the police department would, of course, be imputed to the District Attorney's office. A defendant ought not be penalized because of any inadequacy of internal communication within the law enforcement establishment." *McLaurin*, 38 N.Y.2d at 126, 378 N.Y.S.2d at 694.

§ 53:61 Excludable time—Period during which defendant is without counsel through no fault of court

Research References

West's Key Number Digest, Criminal Law ⚲577.3, 577.8 to 577.8(2), 577.10(4), 577.10(8)

CPL § 30.30(4)(f) provides that "the period during which the defendant is without counsel *through no fault of the court*" is excludable from the time within which the People must be ready for trial. (Emphasis added). This exclusion does not apply "when the defendant is proceeding as his own attorney with the permission of the court." CPL § 30.30(4)(f). *See generally People v. Correa*, 77 N.Y.2d 930, 931, 569 N.Y.S.2d 601, 602 (1991).

In *People v. Cortes*, 80 N.Y.2d 201, 209, 590 N.Y.S.2d 9, 14 (1992), the Court of Appeals held that the failure of the 18-B Panel to provide the defendant with assigned counsel for a lengthy period of time was "unquestionably attributable to the 'fault of the court,' and, consequently, the exclusion provided by CPL 30.30(4)(f) is unavailable." However, the delay was nonetheless not chargeable to the People since it (a) "occurred *after* the People had declared themselves ready for trial," *People v. Cortes*, 80 N.Y.2d 201, 210, 590 N.Y.S.2d 9 (1992), and (b) "did not affect the People's ability to present their own case and, consequently, did not affect their 'readiness' as that term is used in CPL 30.30 analysis." 80 N.Y.2d at 210, 590 N.Y.S.2d at 15.

In *People v. Rouse*, 12 N.Y.3d 728, 729, 876 N.Y.S.2d 341, 341–42, 904 N.E.2d 495 (2009) (2009), the Court of Appeals held that "the People did not satisfy their statutory readiness obligation, [and thus]the motion to dismiss the indictment pursuant to CPL 30.30 should have been granted," where:

> The People contend that the 30-day time period from October 5, 2004 to November 4, 2004 was properly chargeable to defendant because his co-defendant was "without counsel." We disagree. Substitute counsel was appointed to co-defendant at the conclusion of the October 5, 2004 calendar call, and thus co-defendant had counsel during the adjournment period requested by the People. Nor does CPL 30.30(4)(f) require the court to determine whether counsel was sufficiently familiar with the case in order for a defendant to be considered with legal representation for purposes of the statute.

In *Vermont v. Brillon*, __ U.S. at __, 129 S. Ct. 1283, 1287, 173 L. Ed. 2d 231 (2009), the Supreme Court held that:

> [T]he Vermont Supreme Court erred in ranking assigned counsel essentially as state actors in the criminal justice system. Assigned counsel, just as retained counsel, act on behalf of their clients, and delays sought by counsel are ordinarily attributable to the defendants they represent. For a total of some six months of the time that elapsed between Brillon's arrest and his trial, Brillon lacked an attorney. The State may be charged with those months if the gaps resulted from the trial court's failure to appoint replacement counsel with dispatch. Similarly, the State may bear responsibility if there is "a breakdown in the public defender system." But, as the Vermont Supreme Court acknowledged, the record does not establish any such institutional breakdown.

(Citations omitted). *See also* __ U.S. at __, 129 S.Ct. at 1291 ("An assigned counsel's failure 'to move the case forward' does not warrant attribution of delay to the State. Contrary to the Vermont Supreme Court's analysis, assigned counsel generally are not state actors for purposes of a speedy-trial claim. While the Vermont Defender General's office is indeed 'part of the criminal justice system,' the individual counsel here acted only on behalf of Brillon, not the State") (citation omitted).

> A contrary conclusion could encourage appointed counsel to delay proceedings by seeking unreasonable continuances, hoping thereby to obtain a dismissal of the indictment on speedy-trial grounds. Trial courts might well respond by viewing continuance requests made by appointed counsel with skepticism, concerned that even an apparently genuine need for more time is in reality a delay tactic. Yet the same considerations would not attend a privately retained counsel's requests for time extensions. We see no justification for treating defendants' speedy-trial claims differently based on whether their counsel is privately retained or publicly assigned.

__ U.S. at __, 129 S.Ct. at 1292. *See also* __ U.S. at __, 129 S.Ct. at 1293 ("In sum, delays caused by defense counsel are properly attributed to the defendant, even where counsel is assigned").

§ 53:62   Excludable time—Periods of delay occasioned by "exceptional circumstances"

Research References

West's Key Number Digest, Criminal Law ☜577.3, 577.8 to 577.8(2), 577.10(4), 577.10(8)

CPL § 30.30(4)(g) provides that "other periods of delay occasioned by exceptional circumstances" are excludable from the time within which the People must be ready for trial. The list of delays occasioned by "exceptional circumstances" covered by CPL § 30.30(4)(g) includes, but is not limited to, the period of delay resulting from a continuance granted at the request of a district attorney if:

1. The continuance is granted because of the unavailability of evidence material to the People's case; *and*

   (a) The district attorney has exercised "due diligence" to obtain such evidence; *and*

   (b) There are reasonable grounds to believe that such evidence will become available in a reasonable period; or

2. The continuance is granted to allow the district attorney additional time to prepare the People's case, *and* additional time is justified by the "exceptional circumstances" of the case.

CPL § 30.30(4)(g). "CPL 30.30 (subd. 4, par. [g]) allows exceptional circumstances to justify periods of delay not expressly covered by the statute, even in the absence of a formal continuance." *People v. Goodman*, 41 N.Y.2d 888, 889, 393 N.Y.S.2d 985, 986 (1977).

"There is no precise definition of what constitutes an exceptional circumstance under CPL 30.30(4)(g)." *People v. Smietana*, 98 N.Y.2d 336, 341, 746 N.Y.S.2d 678, 681 (2002). In *Smietana*, the Court of Appeals held that the 39-day period between the date that the arresting officer filed the accusatory instrument in city court and the date of the defendant's arraignment were excludable as an "exceptional circumstance" under CPL § 30.30(4)(g) where, "through no fault of their own (or of anyone else in the criminal justice system), the People were unaware of the charges prior to arraignment. It is axiomatic that the People cannot prepare for the trial of a case they do not know exists." *People v. Smietana*, 98 N.Y.2d 336, 342, 746 N.Y.S.2d 678 (2002).

The unavailability of a prosecution witness can constitute "exceptional circumstances" for purposes of CPL § 30.30(4)(g). *See, e.g., People v. Zirpola*, 57 N.Y.2d 706, 707, 454 N.Y.S.2d 702, 703 (1982); *Goodman, supra*, 41 N.Y.2d at 889, 393 N.Y.S.2d at 986 (CPL § 30.30(4)(g) applicable where "the victim of the assault was unavailable to testify against the defendant for a substantial period of time following the assault as a result of the injuries that she sustained"). Notably, however, this rule only applies "provided that the People attempted with due diligence to make the witness available." *Zirpola*, 57 N.Y.2d at 707, 454 N.Y.S.2d at 703. *See generally People v. Zimny*, 188 Misc. 2d 600, —-—, 729 N.Y.S.2d 297, 299–300 (Monroe Co. Sup. Ct. 2001) (People failed to demonstrate that they exercised "due diligence" in making arresting State Trooper available for Grand Jury testimony).

Court scheduling problems "do not constitute exceptional circumstances under CPL 30.30(4)(g)." *People v. Chavis*, 91 N.Y.2d 500, 505, 673 N.Y.S.2d 29, 31 (1998). *See also People v. Brothers*, 50 N.Y.2d 413, 417, 429 N.Y.S.2d 558, 560 (1980). *Cf. People v. Castro*, 55 N.Y.2d 972, 973, 449 N.Y.S.2d 184, 184 (1982) ("exceptional circumstances" under CPL § 30.30(4)(g) found where peculiar circumstances of case literally prevented the People from communicating their readiness for trial to the court on the record).

In *People v. Cortes*, 80 N.Y.2d 201, 211–12, 590 N.Y.S.2d 9, 15–16 (1992), the Court of Appeals held that the erroneous dismissal of an indictment is *not* an "exceptional circumstance" for purposes of CPL § 30.30(3)(b) and/or (4)(g). In so holding, the Court reasoned that "[l]egal rulings are routine events in criminal trials. The fact that a particular ruling may be erroneous does not by itself transform that ruling into an 'exceptional circumstance.' " *People v. Cortes*, 80 N.Y.2d 201, 211–12, 590 N.Y.S.2d 9, 15–16 (1992).

In *People v. Washington*, 43 N.Y.2d 772, 401 N.Y.S.2d 1007 (1977), the People claimed that the seven-month delay between the defendant's indictment and his arrest was caused by "exceptional circumstances"—to wit, an ongoing narcotics investigation. However, the proof of such investigation was found to be deficient, as "[n]o activity of any significance was shown but only a variety of unsatisfactory excuses why the investigation did not proceed." *People v. Washington*, 43 N.Y.2d 772, 773–74, 401 N.Y.S.2d 1007 (1977). In this regard, the Court of Appeals made clear that CPL § 30.30(4)(g), "if it is to be given reasonable effect and it is to fulfill the legislative purpose, must be limited to instances in which the prosecution's inability to proceed is justified by the purposes of the investigation and credible, vigorous activity in pursuing it." *People v. Washington*, 43 N.Y.2d 772, 774, 401 N.Y.S.2d 1007 (1977). *See also* § 53:83, *infra*.

§ 53:63 Excludable time—Period during which action ACODed

Research References

West's Key Number Digest, Criminal Law ⬦577.3, 577.8 to 577.8(2), 577.10(4), 577.10(8)

CPL § 30.30(4)(h) provides that "the period during which an action has been adjourned in contemplation of dismissal pursuant to [CPL §§ 170.55], 170.56 and 215.10" is excludable from the time within which the People must be ready for trial.

§ 53:64 Excludable time—Period prior to defendant's actual appearance for arraignment where defendant has been directed to appear pursuant to CPL § 120.20(3) or CPL § 210.10(3)

Research References

West's Key Number Digest, Criminal Law ⬦577.3, 577.8 to 577.8(2), 577.10(4), 577.10(8)

CPL § 30.30(4)(i) provides that "the period prior to the defendant's actual appearance for arraignment in a situation in which the defendant has been directed to appear by the district attorney pursuant to [CPL § 120.20(3)] or [CPL § 210.10(3)]" is excludable from the time within which the People must be ready for trial.

§ 53:65 Excludable time—Period during which "family offense" is before family court

Research References

West's Key Number Digest, Criminal Law ⬦577.3, 577.8 to 577.8(2), 577.10(4), 577.10(8)

CPL § 30.30(4)(j) provides that "the period during which a family offense is before a family court until such time as an accusatory instrument or indictment is filed against the defendant alleging a crime constituting a family offense, as such term is defined in [CPL § 530.11]" is excludable from the time within which the People must be ready for trial.

§ 53:66 Effect of delay in bringing charges against defendant

Research References

West's Key Number Digest, Criminal Law ⊃577.3, 577.8 to 577.8(2), 577.10(4), 577.10(8)

Technically, a delay in bringing charges against a defendant does not implicate "speedy trial" rights, as such rights only attach after a criminal action has been commenced. Nonetheless, the Court of Appeals has made clear that "[i]n this State, 'we have never drawn a fine distinction between due process and speedy trial standards' when dealing with delays in prosecution." *People v. Vernace*, 96 N.Y.2d 886, 887, 730 N.Y.S.2d 778, 779 (2001) (citation omitted). *See also People v. Singer*, 44 N.Y.2d 241, 253, 405 N.Y.S.2d 17, 25 (1978) (same); *People v. Singer*, 44 N.Y.2d 241, 253, 405 N.Y.S.2d 17, 25 (1978) ("We have long held that 'unreasonable delay in prosecuting a defendant constitutes a denial of due process of law' ") (citation omitted); *People v. Staley*, 41 N.Y.2d 789, 791, 396 N.Y.S.2d 339, 341 (1977) (same); *People v. White*, 32 N.Y.2d 393, 397–98, 345 N.Y.S.2d 513, 517 (1973) ("it is only of limited analytical importance whether the right is one of a 'speedy trial' or of 'due process of law' "). In this regard:

> [T]he Supreme Court has drawn a distinction between delays occurring prior to arrest or formal accusation and those occurring afterward. Characterization of the delay as "preindictment" or "postindictment" is often determinative. Delay in bringing the defendant to trial after indictment or arrest is measured against the Sixth Amendment speedy trial requirement which takes into account a number of factors, including actual or potential prejudice to the defendant's case through the loss of witnesses and the dulling of memory. Preindictment delay, on the other hand, is governed by the due process clause which generally requires a showing of actual prejudice before dismissal would be warranted.

Singer, 44 N.Y.2d at 252, 405 N.Y.S.2d at 24 (citation omitted).

"[T]he factors utilized to determine if a defendant's rights have been abridged are the same whether the right asserted is a speedy trial right or the due process right to prompt prosecution" (*i.e.*, the *Taranovich* factors). *Vernace*, 96 N.Y.2d at 887, 730 N.Y.S.2d at 779. *See also Staley*, 41 N.Y.2d at 792, 396 N.Y.S.2d at 342.

In *Staley*, the Court of Appeals dismissed the indictment where, "[a]s a result of the wholly unexplained 31-month delay [between defendant's arrest and his indictment], defendant was denied reasonably prompt prosecution of charges, a denial of due process of law." 41 N.Y.2d at 790, 396 N.Y.S.2d at 341. *See also White*, 32 N.Y.2d at 397–98, 345 N.Y.S.2d at 517 (" 'From a constitutional aspect, it appears that the four and a half years' delay in prosecuting defendant prior to his indictment, but after the initiation of criminal proceedings, deprived him of due process of law' ") (citation omitted).

§ 53:67   Effect of delay in arraigning defendant

Research References

West's Key Number Digest, Criminal Law ⚲577.3, 577.8 to 577.8(2), 577.10(4), 577.10(8)

In *People v. Correa*, 77 N.Y.2d 930, 931, 569 N.Y.S.2d 601, 602 (1991), the Court of Appeals held that "[d]elays between indictment and the arraignment, like other court congestion, do not prevent the People from being ready for trial. Such delays are, therefore, not excludable under CPL 30.30." *See also People v. Cortes*, 80 N.Y.2d 201, 213, 590 N.Y.S.2d 9, 16 (1992); *People v. Wallace*, 26 N.Y.2d 371, 373, 310 N.Y.S.2d 484, 486 (1970) (11-month delay between the defendant's indictment and his arraignment deprived him of his right to a speedy trial).

In *Cortes*, *supra*, the Court of Appeals elaborated that "*Correa* did not go so far as to hold that prearraignment delays are always automatically chargeable to the People. Some prearraignment delays may be excused if they are caused by events recognized as exclusions under CPL 30.30(4)." 80 N.Y.2d at 213, 590 N.Y.S.2d at 16.

In this regard, in *People v. Smietana*, 98 N.Y.2d 336, 342, 746 N.Y.S.2d 678, 682 (2002), the Court of Appeals held that the 39-day period between the date that the arresting officer filed the accusatory instrument in city court and the date of the defendant's arraignment were excludable as an "exceptional circumstance" under CPL § 30.30(4)(g) where, "through no fault of their own (or of anyone else in the criminal justice system), the People were unaware of the charges prior to arraignment. It is axiomatic that the People cannot prepare for the trial of a case they do not know exists."

§ 53:68   Effect of delay in rendering verdict

Research References

West's Key Number Digest, Criminal Law ⚲577.3, 577.8 to 577.8(2), 577.10(4), 577.10(8)

In *People v. South*, 41 N.Y.2d 451, 452, 393 N.Y.S.2d 695, 696

(1977), the Court of Appeals held that "because the verdict in this case, tried in town court before a justice sitting without a jury, was not rendered until 58 days after the close of the trial, the adjudication as a youthful offender must be reversed." In so holding, the Court reasoned that:

> Not unlike a jury which is expected to return its verdict within a reasonable time under CPL article 310 (the provisions of which article are made applicable to local criminal courts, CPL 360.55), so it is under CPL 350.10 (subd. 3, par. [d]) with the Justice in a nonjury trial. His verdict, too, must be rendered within a reasonable time. What will be "reasonable" must, of course, turn largely on the circumstances of the individual case. There will come a point, however, beyond which delay becomes unreasonable as a matter of law. * * *
>
> The Town Justice is not required or expected to write a decision or to make findings of fact or conclusions of law. He is required merely to render a verdict of "guilty" or "not guilty." * * *
>
> Although we base our decision in this case on statutory rather than constitutional grounds, we note that the salutary considerations which undergird a defendant's right to speedy trial extend in part to his right to a prompt verdict while recollection of the evidence is fresh, and argue strongly against dangling delay.
>
> It is our conclusion then, as a matter of law, that the delay of 58 days was unreasonable in this case. (Cf. *People v. O'Brien*, 86 Misc. 2d 139, 381 N.Y.S.2d 972 [conviction of disorderly conduct in Village Court set aside where verdict by Village Justice was returned 35 days after the conclusion of the trial].)

People v. South, 41 N.Y.2d 451, 454–55, 393 N.Y.S.2d 695, 697 (1977). *See also People v. Hryn*, 144 A.D.2d 961, 534 N.Y.S.2d 268 (4th Dep't 1988) ("The court's delay of 7½ months in rendering its verdict was unreasonable as a matter of law"); *People v. Morgan*, 30 Misc. 3d 52, 917 N.Y.S.2d 804 (App. Term, 9th & 10th Jud. Dist. 2010) (72-day delay in rendering verdict following 1-day, 3-witness bench trial unreasonable as a matter of law); *People v. Malone*, 22 Misc. 3d 65, 874 N.Y.S.2d 670 (App. Term, 9th & 10th Jud. Dist. 2009) (42-day delay in rendering verdict following speeding trial unreasonable as a matter of law); *People v. Chapman*, 177 Misc. 2d 551, 679 N.Y.S.2d 496 (App. Term, 2d Dep't 1998) (84-day delay in rendering verdict following one-day bench trial on one-count information involving two prosecution witnesses unreasonable as a matter of law); *People v. Plaza*, 175 Misc. 2d 277, 670 N.Y.S.2d 299 (App. Term, 2d Dep't 1997) (76-day delay in rendering verdict following one-day DWAI bench trial resulted in loss of jurisdiction over defendant); *People v. O'Brien*, 86 Misc. 2d 139, 381 N.Y.S.2d 972 (Wayne Co. Ct. 1976)

(35-day delay in rendering verdict following bench trial constituted reversible error).

§ 53:69   Effect of delay in imposing sentence

Research References

West's Key Number Digest, Criminal Law ☞577.3, 577.8 to 577.8(2), 577.10(4), 577.10(8)

CPL § 380.30(1) provides that, in general, a "[s]entence must be pronounced without unreasonable delay." In this regard, the Court of Appeals has held that "if a long and unexplained sentencing delay is the product of judicial or prosecutorial negligence or mistake—as opposed to defendant's own conduct—the indictment must be dismissed." *People v. Campbell*, 97 N.Y.2d 532, 534, 743 N.Y.S.2d 396, 397 (2002). *See also People v. Drake*, 61 N.Y.2d 359, 367, 474 N.Y.S.2d 276, 280 (1984) ("the New York rule assumes the defendant has been prejudiced by unreasonable delay. He need not prove it. Nor is he required to take affirmative measures and demand that the court sentence him. That burden rests solely with the State and its agents") (citations omitted); *People v. Keller*, 238 A.D.2d 758, __, 656 N.Y.S.2d 484, 486 (3d Dep't 1997) (DWAI conviction reversed where county court failed to impose sentence on that conviction and delay in sentencing exceeded one year).

The *Campbell* Court also held that "[a] meritorious undue delay claim under CPL 380.30(1) affects the legality of sentence where the delay is shown to be unreasonable due to judicial or prosecutorial negligence. Thus, a CPL 380.30(1) claim will survive a defendant's general waiver of the right to appeal." 97 N.Y.2d at 535, 743 N.Y.S.2d at 398.

§ 53:70   Effect of delay between sentence and reversal on appeal

Research References

West's Key Number Digest, Criminal Law ☞577.3, 577.8 to 577.8(2), 577.10(4), 577.10(8)

In *People v. Cousart*, 58 N.Y.2d 62, 64, 458 N.Y.S.2d 507, 508 (1982), the Court of Appeals addressed the issues of whether "a delay of almost five years between defendant's conviction and the Appellate Division's decision reversing that conviction and ordering a new trial constitutes either a violation of the defendant's constitutional right to a speedy trial or his right to due process of law." (Citation omitted). In this regard, the *Cousart* Court held that:

[T]he underlying rationale of the Sixth Amendment's right to a speedy trial extends that right only until the accused is brought to trial. The fact that, on appeal, the defendant may successfully challenge the propriety of that trial does not extend the Sixth Amendment's guarantee of a speedy trial throughout the appellate process. * * *

Similarly, we see no reason to expand the scope of New York's statutory speedy trial right (CPL 30.20, 30.30) into the appellate process. * * *

> [However, a]lthough we have never "drawn a fine distinction between due process and speedy trial standards," we have held that "the State due process requirement of a prompt prosecution is broader than the right to a speedy trial guaranteed by statute (see CPL 30.20; see, also, CPL 30.30) and the Sixth Amendment."

People v. Cousart, 58 N.Y.2d 62, 66–67, 67, 68, 458 N.Y.S.2d 507, 509, 510 (1982) (citation and footnote omitted). Finally, *Cousart* held that:

> [I]n evaluating claims that a defendant's due process rights have been violated by an unreasonable delay in the appellate process, the court must weigh factors similar to those considered in determining whether a defendant's speedy trial rights were violated . . . Thus, a hearing will normally be required to determine whether or not in an individual case there has been a violation of the defendant's due process rights resulting in prejudice which requires dismissal of the charges. At that hearing, it will be the defendant's burden to show that he has been prejudiced by the delay.

People v. Cousart, 58 N.Y.2d 62, 68, 69, 458 N.Y.S.2d 507 (1982).

§ 53:71 People's readiness for trial—Valid accusatory instrument

Research References

West's Key Number Digest, Criminal Law ☞577.3, 577.8 to 577.8(2), 577.10(4), 577.10(8)

It is well settled that the People cannot be ready for trial in the absence of a valid accusatory instrument. *See, e.g.*, *People v. Wilson*, 86 N.Y.2d 753, 754–55, 631 N.Y.S.2d 127, 127 (1995); *People v. Cortes*, 80 N.Y.2d 201, 211, 590 N.Y.S.2d 9, 15 (1992); *People v. Colon*, 110 Misc. 2d 917, __, 443 N.Y.S.2d 305, 307 (N.Y. City Crim. Ct. 1981) ("it is obvious that the People cannot be ready for trial within 90 days or 60 days of commencement of the actions if they have not converted the complaints to jurisdictionally sufficient informations within those periods"), *for the reasons stated in the opinion of Judge Atlas at Crim. Ct. rev'd*, 112 Misc. 2d 790, 450 N.Y.S.2d 136 (App. Term, 1st Dep't 1982), *rev'd for the reasons stated in the opinion of Judge Atlas at Crim. Ct.*, 59 N.Y.2d 921, 466 N.Y.S.2d 319 (1983); *People v. Caussade*, 162

A.D.2d 4, —, 560 N.Y.S.2d 648, 650 (2d Dep't 1990) ("present readiness for trial is established when the People [inter alia] have a valid accusatory instrument upon which the defendant may be brought to trial"); *People v. Rivers*, 184 Misc. 2d 101, —, 707 N.Y.S.2d 297, 298–99 (Clinton Co. Ct. 1999) ("Any statement of readiness with respect to a felony made prior to the filing of the superior court accusatory instrument is an empty declaration").

In this regard, "[i]t is well recognized that preindictment delay is not normally excludable since this phase of criminal prosecution is wholly under the control of the People and there is generally nothing a defendant can do to hinder the People in obtaining an indictment." *People v. Miner*, 162 A.D.2d 767, —, 557 N.Y.S.2d 679, 681 (3d Dep't 1990).

§ 53:72   People's readiness statement—When made

Research References

West's Key Number Digest, Criminal Law ⚷577.3, 577.8 to 577.8(2), 577.10(4), 577.10(8)

In *People v. Kendzia*, 64 N.Y.2d 331, 337, 486 N.Y.S.2d 888, 891 (1985), the Court of Appeals made clear that "the prosecutor must make his statement of readiness when the People are in fact ready to proceed. *The statute contemplates an indication of present readiness, not a prediction or expectation of future readiness.*" (Emphasis added). *See also People v. Carter*, 91 N.Y.2d 795, 798, 676 N.Y.S.2d 523, 526 (1998); *People v. Wilson*, 86 N.Y.2d 753, 754, 631 N.Y.S.2d 127, 127 (1995); *People v. England*, 84 N.Y.2d 1, 4, 613 N.Y.S.2d 854, 856 (1994); *People v. England*, 84 N.Y.2d 1, 5, 613 N.Y.S.2d 854, 856 (1994) ("the statement 'ready for trial' contemplates more than merely mouthing those words"); *People v. Smith*, 82 N.Y.2d 676, 678, 601 N.Y.S.2d 466, 467 (1993); *People v. McKenna*, 76 N.Y.2d 59, 63, 556 N.Y.S.2d 514, 516 (1990); *People v. Brothers*, 50 N.Y.2d 413, 416, 429 N.Y.S.2d 558, 559 (1980); *People v. Hamilton*, 46 N.Y.2d 932, 933, 415 N.Y.S.2d 208, 209 (1979) (per curiam).

Thus, for example, the People cannot claim in a letter sent on May 6 that they will be ready for trial on May 26. *See Kendzia*, 64 N.Y.2d at 338, 486 N.Y.S.2d at 891. *See also People v. Grainger*, 164 Misc. 2d 294, —, 624 N.Y.S.2d 740, 742–43 (N.Y. City Crim. Ct. 1995).

Neither can they validly declare, in response to a motion to dismiss pursuant to CPL § 30.30, "that they had been ready to proceed on a prior date." *People v. Chavis*, 91 N.Y.2d 500, 506, 673 N.Y.S.2d 29, 32 (1998). *See also Kendzia*, 64 N.Y.2d at 336–37, 486 N.Y.S.2d at 890; *Brothers*, 50 N.Y.2d at 416, 429 N.Y.S.2d at 559; *Hamilton*, 46 N.Y.2d at 933, 415 N.Y.S.2d at 209 ("the People must communicate readiness for trial to the court on the record when ready to proceed. It is insufficient, as a matter of law, to inform the court of such a claim for the first time in an affidavit submitted in response to a motion to dismiss the indictment").

§ 53:73 People's readiness statement—How made

Research References

West's Key Number Digest, Criminal Law ⚯577.3, 577.8 to 577.8(2), 577.10(4), 577.10(8)

In *People v. Hamilton*, 46 N.Y.2d 932, 933, 415 N.Y.S.2d 208, 209 (1979) (per curiam), the Court of Appeals held that "the People must communicate readiness for trial to the court on the record when ready to proceed. It is insufficient, as a matter of law, to inform the court of such a claim for the first time in an affidavit submitted in response to a motion to dismiss the indictment." *See also People v. Brothers*, 50 N.Y.2d 413, 416, 429 N.Y.S.2d 558, 559 (1980).

In *People v. Kendzia*, 64 N.Y.2d 331, 337, 486 N.Y.S.2d 888, 890–91 (1985), the Court of Appeals held that an assertion of readiness by the People encompasses two necessary elements:

First, there must be a communication of readiness by the People which appears on the trial court's record. This requires either a statement of readiness by the prosecutor in open court, transcribed by a stenographer, or recorded by the clerk or a written notice of readiness sent by the prosecutor to both defense counsel and the appropriate court clerk, to be placed in the original record. As the prosecutor must make an affirmative representation of readiness, he may not simply rely on the case being placed on a trial calendar.

The second requirement under the statute, as noted in *Hamilton* and *Brothers*, is that the prosecutor must make his statement of readiness when the People are in fact ready to proceed. The statute contemplates an indication of present readiness, not a prediction or expectation of future readiness.

(Citations and footnote omitted). *See also People v. Smith*, 82 N.Y.2d 676, 678, 601 N.Y.S.2d 466, 467 (1993); *People v. McKenna*, 76 N.Y.2d 59, 63, 556 N.Y.S.2d 514, 516 (1990).

In *People v. Chavis*, 91 N.Y.2d 500, 502, 673 N.Y.S.2d 29, 30 (1998), the Court of Appeals held that, for purposes of CPL § 30.30, "a statement of readiness for a [pretrial suppression] hearing is not a substitute for a statement of trial readiness." Thus, subsequent delays due to court congestion were chargeable to the People.

In *People v. Wilson*, 86 N.Y.2d 753, 754, 631 N.Y.S.2d 127, 127 (1995), the People's statement, on the record, "'we have been in contact with the victim. Our intentions are to go forward,'" was found to have "sufficiently indicated the People's readiness for trial."

§ 53:74 People's readiness statement—To whom made

Research References

West's Key Number Digest, Criminal Law ☞577.3, 577.8 to 577.8(2), 577.10(4), 577.10(8)

In *People v. Kendzia*, 64 N.Y.2d 331, 337, 486 N.Y.S.2d 888, 890 (1985), the Court of Appeals held that a communication of readiness by the People:

> [R]equires either a statement of readiness by the prosecutor in open court, transcribed by a stenographer, or recorded by the clerk or a written notice of readiness sent by the prosecutor to both defense counsel and the appropriate court clerk, to be placed in the original record.

(Footnote omitted). In a footnote, the *Kendzia* Court stated that "[i]f the prosecutor's statement of readiness in open court were made without defense counsel present, the prosecutor would have to promptly notify him of the statement of readiness." *People v. Kendzia*, 64 N.Y.2d 331, 337 n.*, 486 N.Y.S.2d 888 (1985).

§ 53:75 People's readiness statement—Illusory statement of readiness is a nullity

Research References

West's Key Number Digest, Criminal Law ☞577.3, 577.8 to 577.8(2), 577.10(4), 577.10(8)

"A statement of readiness at a time when the People are not actually ready is illusory and insufficient to stop the running of the speedy trial clock." *People v. England*, 84 N.Y.2d 1, 4, 613 N.Y.S.2d 854, 856 (1994). *See also People v. England*, 84 N.Y.2d 1, 5, 613 N.Y.S.2d 854, 856 (1994) ("the statement 'ready for trial' contemplates more than merely mouthing those words"); *People v. Cole*, 73 N.Y.2d 957, 958, 540 N.Y.S.2d 984, 985 (1989).

In this regard, the Court of Appeals has made clear that CPL § 30.30 "could become a mockery if an assertion of readiness, without any substantiation, excuses needless delay." *People v. Dean*, 45 N.Y.2d 651, 656, 412 N.Y.S.2d 353, 356 (1978). *See also People v. Greenwaldt*, 103 A.D.2d 933, __, 479 N.Y.S.2d 781, 782 (3d Dep't 1984) ("An assertion of readiness by the People, without substantiation, cannot be used to make a mockery of the speedy trial guarantee embodied in CPL 30.30").

In *People v. Robinson*, 171 A.D.2d 475, __, 567 N.Y.S.2d 401, 403 (1st Dep't 1991), the Appellate Division, First Department, held that:

> An illusory statement of readiness by the People, without the ability to produce their complaining witness, is insufficient to stop the running of time for CPL 30.30 purposes. The test is whether the People are able to present their case and do so immediately. The statement must be made in good faith and reflect an actual, present state of readiness. While subsequent requests for adjournments may indicate a lack of readiness at that time, they do not necessarily invalidate an earlier otherwise proper statement of readiness.

(Citations omitted). *See also People v. Hargro*, 144 A.D.2d 971, __, 534 N.Y.S.2d 274, 275 (4th Dep't 1988) ("The mere announcement of readiness for trial by a prosecutor does not satisfy the People's statutory obligation because the People must be able to substantiate that they are in fact ready to proceed. Only then may the court ascertain whether the People 'effectively' announced their readiness for trial"). *See generally People v. Khachiyan*, 194 Misc. 2d 161, 752 N.Y.S.2d 243 (N.Y. City Crim. Ct. 2002).

§ 53:76 People's readiness statement—Prearraignment statement of readiness

Research References

West's Key Number Digest, Criminal Law ⊕577.3, 577.8 to 577.8(2), 577.10(4), 577.10(8)

In *People v. Carter*, 91 N.Y.2d 795, 796, 676 N.Y.S.2d 523, 524 (1998), the Court of Appeals held that a prearraignment statement of readiness by the People can be effective if it is made "at a point when they had done everything required of them to bring the case to trial." In so holding, the court found that since the People had (a) filed the indictment, (b) announced their readiness on the record, and (c) attempted to notify the defendants by sending letters to their last-known addresses, they had "discharged their duty under CPL 30.30." *People v. Carter*, 91 N.Y.2d 795, 799, 676 N.Y.S.2d 523 (1998). In such a situation, the burden would shift to the defendant to prove that the statement of readiness "did not accurately reflect the People's position or that the mailing was made in bad faith." *People v. Carter*, 91 N.Y.2d 795, 799, 676 N.Y.S.2d 523 (1998).

The court also made clear that, where a defendant has been indicted in a felony case:

> "[T]he Criminal Procedure Law imposes a nondelegable duty on the trial court to arraign the defendant." Responsibility for scheduling an arraignment date and securing a defendant's appearance lies

with the court, not the People. Consequently, the People cannot be charged with the delay between the People's pre-arraignment declaration of readiness and defendants' arraignments.

People v. Carter, 91 N.Y.2d 795, 799, 676 N.Y.S.2d 523, 526 (1998) (citations omitted). *See also People v. Carter*, 91 N.Y.2d 795, 798, 676 N.Y.S.2d 523, 526 (1998) ("a statement of readiness made contemporaneously with the filing of the indictment can be effective to stop the 'speedy trial' clock if the indictment is filed at least two days before the CPL 30.30 period ends"); *People v. Goss*, 87 N.Y.2d 792, 794, 642 N.Y.S.2d 607, 608 (1996) ("where it was possible for the defendant to be arraigned—and the trial to proceed—within the six-month period, a prearraignment statement of readiness was valid").

On the other hand, "a declaration of readiness prior to arraignment is illusory in the 'unusual circumstances' where arraignment within the statutory time period is impossible and that impossibility is attributable solely to the People." *Goss*, 87 N.Y.2d at 796–97, 642 N.Y.S.2d at 610. *See also People v. England*, 84 N.Y.2d 1, 613 N.Y.S.2d 854 (1994); *People v. Leavy*, 204 A.D.2d 898, 612 N.Y.S.2d 488 (3d Dep't 1994).

§ 53:77 People's readiness statement—Court congestion

Research References

West's Key Number Digest, Criminal Law ⊙577.3, 577.8 to 577.8(2), 577.10(4), 577.10(8)

In *People v. Chavis*, 91 N.Y.2d 500, 505, 673 N.Y.S.2d 29, 31 (1998), the Court of Appeals held that "in the absence of a statement of readiness to proceed, any delay due to court congestion is entirely chargeable to the People."

In *People v. Smith*, 82 N.Y.2d 676, 678, 601 N.Y.S.2d 466, 467 (1993), the Court held that "[d]elays caused by the court, such as delays in arraignment or other court congestion, do not excuse the People from timely declaring their readiness for trial." *See also People v. Collins*, 82 N.Y.2d 177, 181, 604 N.Y.S.2d 11, 13 (1993); *People v. McKenna*, 76 N.Y.2d 59, 63, 556 N.Y.S.2d 514, 516 (1990); *People v. Brothers*, 50 N.Y.2d 413, 415, 417, 429 N.Y.S.2d 558, 559, 560 (1980).

By contrast, once the People have validly declared their readiness for trial, delays due to court congestion are *not* chargeable to the People. *See, e.g., McKenna, supra*, 76 N.Y.2d at 63, 556 N.Y.S.2d at 515–16; *Brothers, supra*, 50 N.Y.2d at 417, 429 N.Y.S.2d at 560; *People ex rel. Franklin v. Warden*, 31 N.Y.2d 498, 341 N.Y.S.2d 604 (1973). *See generally People v. Conrad*, 93 Misc. 2d 655, 405 N.Y.S.2d 559 (Monroe Co. Ct. 1976) ("The negligence of the trial court [in scheduling a jury trial] cannot be imputed to the People or prosecutor. The trial court is not 'the people' referred to in the statute"), *aff'd for the reasons stated in the opinion below*, 44 N.Y.2d 863, 407 N.Y.S.2d 694 (1978).

However, if a delay due to court congestion is long enough, a constitutional speedy trial claim may lie. *See Brothers, supra,* 50 N.Y.2d at 417, 429 N.Y.S.2d at 560. *See generally People v. Minicone*, 28 N.Y.2d 279, 281, 321 N.Y.S.2d 570, 572 (1971) (16 months "seems to have approached the excusable limit of delay attributable to the absence of public trial facilities); *People v. Johnson*, 38 N.Y.2d 271, 279–80, 379 N.Y.S.2d 735, 743 (1975) (same).

§ 53:78 People's readiness statement—Dismissal and refiling of indictment requires new assertion of readiness

Research References

West's Key Number Digest, Criminal Law ⌖577.3, 577.8 to 577.8(2), 577.10(4), 577.10(8)

In *People v. Cortes*, 80 N.Y.2d 201, 214, 590 N.Y.S.2d 9, 17 (1992), the Court of Appeals held that:

> While the People are generally not required to declare their readiness repeatedly throughout the pendency of a criminal action, the dismissal of an indictment and the filing of a new one represents such a substantial break in the proceeding that a new communication of readiness is needed to eliminate guesswork and post hoc rationalizations.

§ 53:79 People's readiness statement—People not required to declare readiness repeatedly

Research References

West's Key Number Digest, Criminal Law ⌖577.3, 577.8 to 577.8(2), 577.10(4), 577.10(8)

"[T]he People are generally not required to declare their readiness repeatedly throughout the pendency of a criminal action." *People v. Cortes*, 80 N.Y.2d 201, 214, 590 N.Y.S.2d 9, 17 (1992).

Similarly, "[t]he People are not required on each adjourned date to contact their witness. Aside from its impracticality, such a requirement would be unduly burdensome and vexing to the witnesses." *People v. Robinson*, 171 A.D.2d 475, __, 567 N.Y.S.2d 401, 403 (1st Dep't 1991).

§ 53:80 When People's lack of readiness requires adjournment, does subsequent statement of readiness save them from liability for remainder of adjournment period?

Research References

West's Key Number Digest, Criminal Law ☞577.3, 577.8 to 577.8(2), 577.10(4), 577.10(8)

In *People v. Stirrup*, 91 N.Y.2d 434, 436, 671 N.Y.S.2d 433, 434 (1998), the Court of Appeals held that "when the People's lack of readiness has necessitated an adjournment, a subsequent statement of readiness can save the People from liability for the remainder of the adjournment period." However, the Court made clear that the subsequent statement of readiness must be genuine (as opposed to "a mere empty assertion of readiness"). *People v. Stirrup*, 91 N.Y.2d 434, 440, 671 N.Y.S.2d 433 (1998).

§ 53:81 Postreadiness delay—Generally

Research References

West's Key Number Digest, Criminal Law ☞577.3, 577.8 to 577.8(2), 577.10(4), 577.10(8)

In *People v. Giordano*, 56 N.Y.2d 524, 525, 449 N.Y.S.2d 955, 956 (1982), the Court of Appeals, in a memorandum decision, stated:

> We agree with the Appellate Division that when the District Attorney had announced his readiness on the record he had satisfied his obligation under CPL 30.30. Whatever may in fact have been the reason why the case was not reached for trial thereafter, there is no basis for dismissal pursuant to that statute.

If *Giordano* were to be read literally, there would be no such thing as postreadiness delay. However, the Court of Appeals has made clear that a literal reading of *Giordano* is inappropriate. In this regard, in *People v. Anderson*, 66 N.Y.2d 529, 535, 536, 498 N.Y.S.2d 119, 123 (1985), the Court of Appeals explained that:

> [I]t is clear that our holding in *People v. Giordano* "that when the District Attorney had announced his readiness on the record he had satisfied his obligation under CPL 30.30" is read too broadly if taken to mean that no delay on the part of the People occurring after announcement of readiness is to be counted against them in determining whether the readiness requirements of the section have been met . . . The refusal to read *Giordano* so broadly follows also from CPL 30.30(3)(b), for its wording makes clear beyond dispute that, notwithstanding that the People have answered ready for trial within the statutory time limit, a postreadiness motion to dismiss may be made.

(Citation and footnote omitted). *See also People v. Cortes*, 80 N.Y.2d 201, 210, 590 N.Y.S.2d 9, 15 (1992) ("*Giordano* did not mean that 'no delay on the part of the People * * * after announcement of readiness is to be counted against them' ") (citation omitted).

Thus, even if the People validly declare readiness for trial at some point during a case, such declaration does not mean that CPL § 30.30 is no longer applicable. *See, e.g., People v. Goss*, 87 N.Y.2d 792, 797, 642 N.Y.S.2d 607, 610 (1996) ("Even when the People have validly declared their readiness, they will be charged with periods of 'postreadiness' delay where 'it is the People's dereliction that is preventing the defendant's trial from going forward' ") (citation omitted).

§ 53:82 CPL § 30.30(3)(b)—Speedy trial motion may be denied where People were ready for trial in a timely manner but subsequently were no longer ready due to some "exceptional fact or circumstance"

Research References

West's Key Number Digest, Criminal Law ☞577.3, 577.8 to 577.8(2), 577.10(4), 577.10(8)

CPL § 30.30(3)(b) provides that a speedy trial motion brought pursuant to CPL § 30.30(1) and (2) *may* be denied where the People are not ready for trial if:

(a) The People were ready for trial prior to the expiration of the specified period;

(b) The People's present unreadiness is due to some "exceptional fact or circumstance," including, but not limited to, the "sudden unavailability" of evidence material to their case;

(c) The People have exercised "due diligence" to obtain such evidence; *and*

(d) There are reasonable grounds to believe that such evidence will become available within a "reasonable period of time."

If any of these requirements is not satisfied, CPL § 30.30(3)(b) is inapplicable. *See, e.g., People v. Anderson*, 66 N.Y.2d 529, 538, 498 N.Y.S.2d 119, 125 (1985) ("when despite the sudden unavailability of material evidence and due diligence on the part of the People, there is no basis for belief that the evidence will become available within a reasonable period as contemplated by CPL 30.30(3)(b), dismissal is not only permissible but is required if the purpose of the section is to be carried out").

It is also noteworthy that CPL § 30.30(3)(b) states that even where the requirements thereof are met, a defendant's speedy trial motion "*may* be denied." (Emphasis added). As such, a court has discretion to grant a speedy trial motion *even if the People's present unreadiness for trial is due to some exceptional fact or circumstance that is not their fault.*

§ 53:83   What constitutes an "exceptional fact or circumstance"?

Research References

West's Key Number Digest, Criminal Law ☞577.3, 577.8 to 577.8(2), 577.10(4), 577.10(8)

In *People v. Jones*, 68 N.Y.2d 717, 718–19, 506 N.Y.S.2d 315, 315 (1986), the Court of Appeals held that:

> Lengthy postreadiness delays attributable to defendant do not constitute an "exceptional fact or circumstance" within the meaning of CPL § 30.30(3)(b) sufficient to excuse adjournments resulting from the trial assistant's planned European vacation. Such an adjournment, here amounting to 28 days, is clearly chargeable to the People, especially, as here, where the record suggests that another trial assistant could have been substituted.
>
> Nor do defendant's postreadiness delays, even though totaling some 17 months, constitute an exceptional circumstance within the meaning of CPL § 30.30(3)(b). "[I]t is the People's delay alone that is to be considered, except where that delay directly 'results from' action taken by the defendant."

(Citations omitted). *See also People v. Anderson*, 66 N.Y.2d 529, 536, 498 N.Y.S.2d 119, 124 (1985).

In *People v. Cortes*, 80 N.Y.2d 201, 211–12, 590 N.Y.S.2d 9, 15–16 (1992), the Court of Appeals held that the erroneous dismissal of an indictment is not an "exceptional circumstance" for purposes of CPL § 30.30(3)(b) and/or (4)(g). In so holding, the Court reasoned that "[l]egal rulings are routine events in criminal trials. The fact that a particular ruling may be erroneous does not by itself transform that ruling into an 'exceptional circumstance.' " *People v. Cortes*, 80 N.Y.2d 201, 211–12, 590 N.Y.S.2d 9, 15–16 (1992).

In *People v. DiMeglio*, 294 A.D.2d 239, __, 743 N.Y.S.2d 83, 85 (1st Dep't 2002), the Appellate Division, First Department, found that a seven-day adjournment requested by the People "due to the assigned assistant's family emergency" did not constitute "exceptional circumstances" for purposes of CPL § 30.30(3)(b).

In *People v. Rivera*, 212 A.D.2d 1040, __, 623 N.Y.S.2d 445, 446 (4th Dep't 1995), the Appellate Division, Fourth Department, found that the People's postannouncement lack of readiness "caused by the victim's medical problems"—which medical problems appear to have resulted from a violent assault on the victim by the defendant—constituted an "exceptional circumstance." *See also People v. Hughes*, 136 A.D.2d 916, ___, 525 N.Y.S.2d 88, 89 (4th Dep't 1988); *People v. Walker*, 136 A.D.2d 949, ___, 524 N.Y.S.2d 953, 954 (4th Dep't 1988).

In *People v. Thomas*, 210 A.D.2d 736, ___, 620 N.Y.S.2d 555, 556 (3d Dep't 1994), the Appellate Division, Third Department, held that an adjournment to accommodate a prosecution witness's vacation schedule does not constitute an "exceptional circumstance." *See also People v. Apodoca*, 156 Misc. 2d 133, ___, 591 N.Y.S.2d 726, 729 (N.Y. Co. Sup. Ct. 1992) (same).

In *People v. Buckley*, 188 A.D.2d 1064, ___, 591 N.Y.S.2d 913, 914 (4th Dep't 1992), the Appellate Division, Fourth Department, held that the defendant's unavailability due to the fact that the Governor had signed an order resulting in the defendant's extradition to Pennsylvania to answer a murder charge constituted an "exceptional fact or circumstance."

In *People v. Williams*, 146 Misc. 2d 866, ___, 553 N.Y.S.2d 584, 588 (Bronx Co. Sup. Ct. 1990), the court held that the People's bringing of a CPLR Article 78 proceeding challenging a suppression ruling did not constitute an "exceptional circumstance" where "the People failed to seek a stay of the trial while the Article 78 proceeding was pending."

By contrast, where a delay is caused by the "defendant's having voluntarily absented himself from the proceedings," such delay does not render the People "unready." *People v. Myers*, 171 A.D.2d 148, ___, 575 N.Y.S.2d 152, 154 (2d Dep't 1991).

See also § 53:62, *supra*.

§ 53:84 People must exercise "due diligence" in attempting to bring end to delay caused by "exceptional fact or circumstance"

Research References

West's Key Number Digest, Criminal Law ☞577.3, 577.8 to 577.8(2), 577.10(4)

Even where the People's postreadiness delay is caused by an "exceptional fact or circumstance," CPL § 30.30(3)(b) requires the People to attempt, with "due diligence," to bring an end to such delay. *See, e.g., People v. Robbins*, 223 A.D.2d 735, ___, 637 N.Y.S.2d 208, 211 (2d Dep't 1996); *People v. Thomas*, 210 A.D.2d 736, ___, 620 N.Y.S.2d 555, 556 (3d Dep't 1994); *People v. Williams*, 146 Misc. 2d 866, ___, 553 N.Y.S.2d 584, 586 (Bronx Co. Sup. Ct. 1990) (People failed to exercise due diligence in filing motion to reargue court's suppression ruling).

In this regard, in *People v. Richardson*, 146 Misc. 2d 179, ___,

549 N.Y.S.2d 572, 574 (Bronx Co. Sup. Ct. 1989), the court stated
that:

> [E]ven a circumstance that begins as an exceptional one may lose
> that quality if the People take inadequate action to overcome the
> situation when it is possible to do so. Section 30.30(3)(b), by its
> example that a prosecutor must use due diligence to locate an
> unexpectedly unavailable witness, means that the prosecutor must
> act speedily with appropriate steps to seek to end the exceptional
> circumstance that precludes the People's own readiness. The People
> did not do that here.

See also § 53:62, *supra*.

§ 53:85 In deciding speedy trial motion based in part on postreadiness delay, People receive benefit of portion of readiness period which remained when they originally declared readiness

Research References

West's Key Number Digest, Criminal Law ⚭577.3, 577.7

The Court of Appeals has made clear that "although CPL
30.30(3)(b) recognizes a defendant's right to move for dismissal
after the People have answered ready, '[t]his is not to say that by
answering ready prior to the expiration of the applicable period
stated in subdivision 1 or subdivision 2 the People forfeit their
right to the time remaining.'" *Matter of Hynes v. George*, 76
N.Y.2d 500, 506, 561 N.Y.S.2d 538, 541 (1990) (citation omitted).
See also People v. McKenna, 76 N.Y.2d 59, 66, 556 N.Y.S.2d 514,
517 (1990) ("the People may 'tack' any unexpired prereadiness
days onto the postreadiness period"); *People v. Anderson*, 66
N.Y.2d 529, 534, 536–37, 498 N.Y.S.2d 119, 122, 124 (1985).

Thus, "the People 'are entitled to the full period allowed, either
before or after answering ready.'" *Hynes, supra*, 76 N.Y.2d at
506, 561 N.Y.S.2d at 541 (citation omitted). However, "*Anderson*
cannot be read to support the notion that the People are immune
from a postreadiness order requiring them to go to trial prior to
the expiration of the CPL 30.30(1) readiness period." *Matter of
Hynes v. George*, 76 N.Y.2d 500, 506, 561 N.Y.S.2d 538 (1990).

§ 53:86 Defendant's postreadiness delay generally irrelevant

Research References

West's Key Number Digest, Criminal Law ⚭577.7, 577.10(8)

Postreadiness delay by the defendant is generally irrelevant.
In this regard, in *People v. Jones*, 68 N.Y.2d 717, 718–19, 506
N.Y.S.2d 315, 315 (1986), the Court of Appeals held that:

Nor do defendant's postreadiness delays, even though totaling some 17 months, constitute an exceptional circumstance within the meaning of CPL § 30.30(3)(b). "[I]t is the People's delay alone that is to be considered, except where that delay directly 'results from' action taken by the defendant."

(Citation omitted).

§ 53:87 Defendant need not express readiness for trial

Research References

West's Key Number Digest, Criminal Law ☞577.7, 577.10(8)

It is well settled that "[t]he right to a speedy trial 'is not dependent in any way on whether the defendant has expressed his readiness for trial.'" *People v. Liotta*, 79 N.Y.2d 841, 843, 580 N.Y.S.2d 184, 185 (1992) (citation omitted). *See also People v. Hamilton*, 46 N.Y.2d 932, 933–34, 415 N.Y.S.2d 208, 209 (1979) (per curiam) (same).

§ 53:88 Defendant under no obligation to move case forward

Research References

West's Key Number Digest, Criminal Law ☞577.7, 577.10(8)

In *People v. Staley*, 41 N.Y.2d 789, 793, 396 N.Y.S.2d 339, 343 (1977), the Court of Appeals made clear that "this court has long recognized that a defendant should not be expected to push his own prosecution. The primary responsibility for assuring prompt prosecution rests with the prosecutors. A failure in that responsibility unexplained by acceptable excuse or justification dictates dismissal of the indictment." 41 N.Y.2d at 793, 396 N.Y.S.2d at 343 (citation omitted). *See also People v. Johnson*, 38 N.Y.2d 271, 277, 279, 379 N.Y.S.2d 735, 741, 743 (1975); *People v. White*, 32 N.Y.2d 393, 397 n.4, 345 N.Y.S.2d 513, 517 n.4 (1973); *People v. Minicone*, 28 N.Y.2d 279, 281, 321 N.Y.S.2d 570, 572 (1971) ("The obligation is on the prosecutor to move the trial promptly and no demand by the accused is required to actuate this obligation").

§ 53:89 Speedy trial motion—Procedure

Research References

West's Key Number Digest, Criminal Law ☞573, 577.4, 577.16(6)

In misdemeanor cases, a speedy trial motion must be made in accordance with CPL §§ 170.30(1)(e), 170.30(2), 170.45, 210.45, 255.10(1)(b), and 255.20.

In felony cases, a speedy trial motion must be made in accordance with CPL §§ 210.20(1)(g), 210.20(2), 210.45, 255.10(1)(a), and 255.20.

In *People v. Lawrence*, 64 N.Y.2d 200, 203, 485 N.Y.S.2d 233, 235 (1984), the Court of Appeals held that:

(a) "[A] speedy trial [motion] must be made prior to the commencement of trial or the entry of a plea of guilty";

(b) "The motion must be made in writing and upon reasonable notice to the People";

(c) "An oral application is not sufficient"; and

(d) "Failure to follow the statutory procedure results in a waiver of the claim."

Accordingly, the defendant cannot defer a speedy trial motion until after the entry of a guilty verdict following trial—*even if the court grants him or her permission to do so. People v. Lawrence,* 64 N.Y.2d 200, 203, 207, 485 N.Y.S.2d 233, 235 (1984).

However, *Lawrence* is difficult to reconcile with various other Court of Appeals cases which *have* permitted the parties to "adopt their own rules" by failing to object to informal motion practice. *See, e.g., People v. Mezon*, 80 N.Y.2d 155, 157, 589 N.Y.S.2d 838, 839 (1992) (the People can waive their right to insist that motion to suppress evidence be made "in writing and upon reasonable notice to the people" in conformity with CPL § 710.60(1)); *People v. Jennings*, 69 N.Y.2d 103, 113, 512 N.Y.S.2d 652, 656 (1986) (by failing to insist upon conformity with the procedural requirements of CPL § 210.45(1), the People waived their right to written notice under the statute); *People v. Singleton*, 42 N.Y.2d 466, 470–71, 398 N.Y.S.2d 871, 874 (1977).

In this regard, *Mezon* distinguished *Lawrence* by finding that the procedure at issue in *Lawrence* (*i.e.*, deferring the speedy trial motion until after trial), contravened the "strong public policy" of furthering "orderly trial procedures" and preserving "scarce trial resources." *See Mezon*, 80 N.Y.2d at 160, 589 N.Y.S.2d at 841; *Lawrence*, 64 N.Y.2d at 207, 485 N.Y.S.2d at 238.

§ 53:90   Speedy trial motion—Timeliness of motion

Research References

West's Key Number Digest, Criminal Law ⬥573, 577.4, 577.16(7)

"Motions to dismiss on speedy trial grounds . . . may be made at any time before commencement of trial or entry of a plea of guilty." *People v. Lawrence*, 64 N.Y.2d 200, 205, 485 N.Y.S.2d 233, 236 (1984). *See also* CPL §§ 170.30(1)(e), (2); CPL §§ 210.20(1)(g), (2). In this regard, in *Lawrence* the defendant's trial took place on October 27, and the Court of Appeals stated that "[u]nquestionably, he had an absolute right to make the motion on October 27." 64 N.Y.2d at 206, 485 N.Y.S.2d at 237.

§ 53:91 CPL § 30.30 motion—People's failure to respond to motion

Research References

West's Key Number Digest, Criminal Law ⚷573, 577.4, 577.16(7)

In *People v. Cole*, 73 N.Y.2d 957, 958, 540 N.Y.S.2d 984, 985 (1989), the Court of Appeals held that:

> The court should have granted the defendant's motion to dismiss on speedy trial grounds (CPL 30.30). Defendant's motion challenged the People's assertion of readiness as illusory because they were unable to produce the complainant. The sworn allegations of fact essential to support defendant's motion were conceded by the People when they failed to submit opposition papers contesting these allegations. Under these circumstances the court is required by statute to grant the motion (CPL 210.45[4][c]).

(Citation omitted). *See also People v. Gruden*, 42 N.Y.2d 214, 216, 397 N.Y.S.2d 704, 706 (1977) ("Normally what is not disputed is deemed to be conceded"); *People v. Miner*, 162 A.D.2d 767, —, 557 N.Y.S.2d 679, 681 (3d Dep't 1990).

§ 53:92 CPL § 30.30 motion—Summary granting thereof

Research References

West's Key Number Digest, Criminal Law ⚷573, 577.4, 577.16(6)

"[W]here a defendant has moved for a [speedy trial] dismissal it may be summarily granted if the answering papers do not present a factual dispute for the court to resolve." *People v. Dean*, 45 N.Y.2d 651, 656, 412 N.Y.S.2d 353, 356 (1978). *See also People v. Gruden*, 42 N.Y.2d 214, 217, 397 N.Y.S.2d 704, 706 (1977) ("Generally hearings are not available merely for the asking. We therefore hold that the court may summarily grant a motion to dismiss unless the papers submitted by the prosecutor show that there is a factual dispute which must be resolved at a hearing").

§ 53:93 CPL § 30.30 motion—Burdens of proof; necessity of hearing

Research References

West's Key Number Digest, Criminal Law ⚷573, 577.4, 577.16(8)

In *People v. Goode*, 87 N.Y.2d 1045, 1047, 643 N.Y.S.2d 477, 478 (1996), the Court of Appeals stated that:

> A defendant seeking a speedy trial dismissal pursuant to CPL 30.30 meets his or her initial burden on the motion simply "by alleging only that the prosecution failed to declare readiness within the statutorily prescribed time period." However, once the People

identify the statutory "exclusions on which they intend to rely," the defendant preserves challenges to the People's reliance on those exclusions for appellate review by "identify[ing] any legal or factual impediments to the use of th[o]se exclusions."

(Citations omitted). *See also People v. Luperon*, 85 N.Y.2d 71, 77–78, 623 N.Y.S.2d 735, 738–39 (1995).

In *People v. Santos*, 68 N.Y.2d 859, 861, 508 N.Y.S.2d 411, 413 (1986), the Court of Appeals held that:

Where a defendant moves to dismiss an indictment on the grounds specified in CPL 30.30 and includes in the moving papers sworn allegations that there has been unexcused delay in excess of the statutory maximum, the motion must be granted summarily unless the People controvert the factual basis for the motion. Thus, once a defendant has shown the existence of an unexcused delay greater than three or six months, the burden of showing that time should be excluded falls upon the People. Where the papers submitted by the prosecutor show that there is a factual dispute, there must be a hearing.

(Citations omitted). *See also People v. Lomax*, 50 N.Y.2d 351, 357, 428 N.Y.S.2d 937, 939 (1980); *People v. Berkowitz*, 50 N.Y.2d 333, 349, 428 N.Y.S.2d 927, 936 (1980).

In *Berkowitz, supra*, the Court of Appeals held that:

In this case the court erroneously concluded that [the People's] burden had been met by the calendar notations enscribed by the court officer after each appearance, presumably at the direction of the Presiding Justice. Such notations, however, do not comprise a binding determination as to whether in fact the time span covered by a particular adjournment is to be excluded from the six-month period within which the People must declare their readiness for trial. That determination is one which must be made following an adversarial proceeding at which the defendant has an adequate opportunity to contend that the time is not excludable. It may not be made by the court acting *sua sponte* and in the absence of the parties . . . [T]he calendar notations alone do not suffice to prove that the periods marked "excluded" do in fact come within the ambit of the statutory exclusions. Hence, since the defendant alleged the existence of a delay greater than six months and the People did not provide conclusive proof of sufficient excludable periods, the court erred in denying the motion to dismiss without a full hearing.

50 N.Y.2d at 349, 428 N.Y.S.2d at 936. *See also People v. Nowakowski*, 49 N.Y.2d 723, 724, 426 N.Y.S.2d 261, 261 (1980) ("We conclude that it was error for the court to have disposed of the [CPL 30.30] motion to dismiss in this instance, disclosing on its face an extended delay, on the inadequate, skeletal record before it").

§ 53:94 CPL § 30.30 motion—Burden on People to prove basis for postreadiness adjournment

Research References

West's Key Number Digest, Criminal Law ☞573, 577.4, 577.16(8)

In *People v. Liotta*, 79 N.Y.2d 841, 843, 580 N.Y.S.2d 184, 185 (1992), the Court of Appeals held that:

> [W]here, as here, the court grants adjournments after the People have announced the indictment ready for trial, the burden rests on the People to clarify, on the record, the basis for the adjournment so that on a subsequent CPL 30.30 motion the court can determine to whom the adjournment should be charged. Inasmuch as the People failed to do so in this case, the adjournment must be charged to them.

See also People v. Jamison, 87 N.Y.2d 1048, 1049, 643 N.Y.S.2d 479, 479 (1996); *People v. Collins*, 82 N.Y.2d 177, 182, 604 N.Y.S.2d 11, 13–14 (1993); *People v. Cortes*, 80 N.Y.2d 201, 213, 590 N.Y.S.2d 9, 17 (1992).

§ 53:95 Trial court not required to entertain pro se speedy trial motion of represented defendant

Research References

West's Key Number Digest, Criminal Law ☞573, 577.4, 577.16(6)

In *People v. Rodriguez*, 95 N.Y.2d 497, 500, 719 N.Y.S.2d 208, 209 (2000), the Court of Appeals was "called upon to decide whether a trial court must consider the *pro se* speedy trial motion of a defendant represented by counsel." The Court held that "[b]ecause a criminal defendant is not entitled to hybrid representation, we refuse to prescribe any fixed rule for addressing *pro se* motions and conclude that the decision to entertain such motions lies within the sound discretion of the trial court." *People v. Rodriguez*, 95 N.Y.2d 497, 500, 719 N.Y.S.2d 208 (2000).

§ 53:96 Waiver/forfeiture of statutory speedy trial claim

Research References

West's Key Number Digest, Criminal Law ☞573, 577.4, 577.10(9)

Unlike a constitutional speedy trial claim, a statutory speedy trial claim is waived/forfeited by a guilty plea. *See, e.g., People v. Konieczny*, 2 N.Y.3d 569, 575, 780 N.Y.S.2d 546, 550 (2004); *People v. Hansen*, 95 N.Y.2d 227, 231 n.3, 715 N.Y.S.2d 369, 372 n.3 (2000); *People v. Taylor*, 65 N.Y.2d 1, 6, 489 N.Y.S.2d 152, 155 (1985); *People v. O'Brien*, 56 N.Y.2d 1009, 1010, 453 N.Y.S.2d 638, 639 (1982); *People v. Howe*, 56 N.Y.2d 622, 624, 450 N.Y.S.2d 477, 477 (1982); *People v. Suarez*, 55 N.Y.2d 940, 942, 449

N.Y.S.2d 176, 176 (1982); *People v. Savage*, 54 N.Y.2d 697, 698, 442 N.Y.S.2d 974, 975 (1981); *People v. Thill*, 52 N.Y.2d 1020, 1021, 438 N.Y.S.2d 297, 297–98 (1981); *People v. Clary*, 52 N.Y.2d 1023, 1024, 438 N.Y.S.2d 298, 298 (1981); *People v. Friscia*, 51 N.Y.2d 845, 847, 433 N.Y.S.2d 754, 755 (1980).

This rule applies even if the defendant attempts to "preserve his statutory speedy trial claim for appellate review by obtaining the consent of the prosecutor and the approval of the court at the time the plea is entered." *O'Brien, supra*, 56 N.Y.2d at 1010, 453 N.Y.S.2d at 639. *See also Howe, supra*, 56 N.Y.2d at 624, 450 N.Y.S.2d at 478. In such a situation, however, it appears that the defendant is entitled to withdraw his or her guilty plea. *See People v. Di Raffaele*, 55 N.Y.2d 234, 241, 448 N.Y.S.2d 448, 451 (1982).

§ 53:97 Speedy trial claim must be properly preserved to be reviewed on appeal

Research References

West's Key Number Digest, Criminal Law ⬷573, 577.4, 577.16(5.1)

Like a constitutional speedy trial claim, *see* § 53:21, *supra*, a CPL § 30.30 claim must be properly preserved to be reviewed on appeal. In this regard, it is critical to note:

(a) "[A] speedy trial [motion] must be made prior to the commencement of trial or the entry of a plea of guilty";

(b) "The motion must be made in writing and upon reasonable notice to the People";

(c) "An oral application is not sufficient"; and

(d) "Failure to follow the statutory procedure results in a waiver of the claim."

People v. Lawrence, 64 N.Y.2d 200, 203, 485 N.Y.S.2d 233, 235 (1984).

Accordingly, the defendant cannot defer a speedy trial motion until after the entry of a guilty verdict following trial—*even if the court grants him or her permission to do so. People v. Lawrence*, 64 N.Y.2d 200, 203, 207, 485 N.Y.S.2d 233 (1984).

Similarly, if the defendant properly raises a speedy trial claim in the trial court but proceeds to trial before the motion is decided, the claim will be deemed abandoned. *See People v. Rodriguez*, 50 N.Y.2d 553, 429 N.Y.S.2d 631 (1980).

In *People v. Goode*, 87 N.Y.2d 1045, 1047, 643 N.Y.S.2d 477, 478 (1996), the Court of Appeals stated that:

A defendant seeking a speedy trial dismissal pursuant to CPL 30.30 meets his or her initial burden on the motion simply "by alleging only that the prosecution failed to declare readiness within the statutorily prescribed time period." However, once the People identify the statutory "exclusions on which they intend to rely," the defendant preserves challenges to the People's reliance on those exclusions for appellate review by "identify[ing] any legal or factual impediments to the use of th[o]se exclusions." The purpose of adhering to strict rules of preservation in this context is to provide the court with an "opportunity to remedy the problem and thereby avert reversible error."

(Citations omitted). The *Goode* Court found that the defendant failed to alert the trial court as to which of the statutory exclusions he believed the People were not entitled to, and thus held that the defendant failed to preserve his CPL § 30.30 claim. *See also People v. Beasley*, 16 N.Y.3d 289, 292, 921 N.Y.S.2d 178, 180, 946 N.E.2d 166 (2011); *People v. Luperon*, 85 N.Y.2d 71, 78, 623 N.Y.S.2d 735, 738–39 (1995).

In *Beasley*, the Court of Appeals held that:

Nothing in the People's affirmation would have alerted the trial court that defendant was claiming that the People should be charged with 13 days of postreadiness delay due to the untimely production of the grand jury minutes. It was defendant's duty, either in his initial submission or in a reply, to draw the court's attention to the discrete periods that he now claims should have been chargeable to the People pursuant to CPL 30.30 and to explain why. Not only did defendant fail to highlight the 13-day period, he failed to offer any legal basis for his claim that the entire 42-day period was chargeable as postreadiness delay, or rebut in any way the People's contention that the 42-day period fell within one of the exemptions.

16 N.Y.3d at 292-93, 921 N.Y.S.2d at 180.

§ 53:98 Failure to produce grand jury minutes

Research References

West's Key Number Digest, Criminal Law ⚖573, 577.3, 577.4, 577.10(4), 577.12(1)

In *People v. McKenna*, 76 N.Y.2d 59, 66, 556 N.Y.S.2d 514, 517 (1990), the Court of Appeals held that "the People's five-month failure to provide the Grand Jury minutes in response to defendant's CPL 210.30 dismissal motion is a delay that should be counted against them in determining whether their obligation under CPL 30.30 has been satisfied." In so holding, the Court reasoned that:

[T]he People's concededly negligent failure to provide the Grand Jury minutes for five months after their statement of readiness was made mandates dismissal of the indictment under CPL 30.30. In contrast to the discovery delays considered in *Anderson*, the People's omission did not merely impair defendant's ability to proceed to trial. Rather, because the trial could simply not go forward until the CPL 210.30 motion was decided, the People's dilatory conduct in failing to provide the minutes necessary to that decision was a direct, and virtually insurmountable, impediment to the trial's very commencement. As such, the prosecutorial failure here must be deemed to be one having a direct bearing on the People's readiness, since the People can hardly claim to be "ready" when they have not done all that is required of them to bring the case to the point where it may be tried.

People v. McKenna, 76 N.Y.2d 59, 64, 556 N.Y.S.2d 514 (1990) (citation omitted). *See also People v. England*, 84 N.Y.2d 1, 4, 613 N.Y.S.2d 854, 856 (1994); *People v. Schmadebeck*, 214 A.D.2d 1016, __, 627 N.Y.S.2d 494, 495 (4th Dep't 1995) (delay of more than eight months in filing grand jury minutes resulted in CPL § 30.30 dismissal).

In *People v. Harris*, 82 N.Y.2d 409, 413, 604 N.Y.S.2d 918, 921 (1993), the Court of Appeals held that:

[W]here the People make no objection to the branch of the [defendant's] CPL 210.30 motion seeking inspection of the Grand Jury minutes, the People's obligation to produce the Grand Jury minutes *within a reasonable time* begins to run from the date the defendant's CPL 210.30 motion (to inspect the Grand Jury minutes and to dismiss the indictment) is made.

(Emphasis added). In so holding, the Court reasoned that:

[T]he current—and statutorily mandated—expectation is that a favorable ruling on the motion to inspect will be automatic, except in those exceptional cases in which the prosecution has asserted some "good cause" ground for denial. In other words, the "inspection" aspect of the defendant's CPL 210.30 motion is ordinarily not a litigated matter. * * *

Indeed, in a case such as this, where the People offered no opposition to inspection by the court, it makes little sense to hold that the People may wait for a "ruling" by the court on the "inspection" aspect of the CPL 210.30 motion before coming forward with the Grand Jury minutes, since the decision on that point is inevitable. In these circumstances, waiting for a ruling on the defense's "inspection" request would be pointless.

People v. Harris, 82 N.Y.2d 409, 413–14, 604 N.Y.S.2d 918 (1993) (citations omitted).

Finally, the *Harris* Court found that "36 days was a 'reasonable' period within which the People should have provided the minutes." *People v. Harris*, 82 N.Y.2d 409, 414, 604 N.Y.S.2d 918 (1993). *See also People v. Van Deusen*, 228 A.D.2d 987, 989, 645 N.Y.S.2d 125, 127 (3d Dep't 1996) ("we find that the passage of 47 days from receipt of the motion constitutes a reasonable period within which to assess 'good cause', order the minutes, receive the minutes and provide them to the court"); *People v. Lawrence*, 222 A.D.2d 279, __, 635 N.Y.S.2d 223, 224 (1st Dep't 1995) (period of time in excess of 36 days for production of grand jury minutes chargeable to People); *People v. Edwards*, 215 A.D.2d 498, __, 626 N.Y.S.2d 825, 826 (2d Dep't 1995) (35 days reasonable period of time for production of grand jury minutes); *People v. Roscoe*, 210 A.D.2d 1003, __, 620 N.Y.S.2d 635, 636 (4th Dep't 1994) (following *Harris*, court excluded 36 days as reasonable period of time for production of grand jury minutes); *People v. Lloyd*, 202 A.D.2d 1035, __, 610 N.Y.S.2d 111, 112 (4th Dep't 1994) (same). *See generally People v. Del Valle*, 234 A.D.2d 634, __, 651 N.Y.S.2d 626, 627 (3d Dep't 1996) ("the People concede responsibility for six days of postreadiness delay, occasioned by their failure to deliver the Grand Jury minutes to the court after they were received from the stenographer"); *People v. Sutton*, 199 A.D.2d 878, __, 606 N.Y.S.2d 408, 411 (3d Dep't 1993) ("whether a given period is reasonable will necessarily depend on the District Attorney's . . . ability to exert control over the stenographer"), *following remand*, 209 A.D.2d 878, __, 619 N.Y.S.2d 209, 210 (3d Dep't 1994) (in this particular case "a reasonable time for providing the minutes would be no more than 10 weeks, or 70 days"); *People v. Burwell*, 260 A.D.2d 498, __, 689 N.Y.S.2d 165, 166 (2d Dep't 1999) (charges against defendant dismissed on speedy trial grounds where grand jury minutes taken by stenographer who "worked exclusively for the Westchester County District Attorney's Office" were not transcribed within a reasonable period of time, and record "did not indicate that the prosecutor made any effort to expedite the production of the . . . transcript, nor how long the typing of these minutes would actually have taken").

§ 53:99   Failure to produce incarcerated defendant

Research References

West's Key Number Digest, Criminal Law ⊙573, 577.3, 577.4, 577.10(4), 577.12(1)

"[A]n unexcused, postreadiness delay in producing a defendant in the People's custody could, if sufficiently protracted, result in dismissal under CPL 30.30(3)(b)." *People v. McKenna*, 76 N.Y.2d 59, 64, 556 N.Y.S.2d 514, 516 (1990). *See also People v. England*, 84 N.Y.2d 1, 4, 613 N.Y.S.2d 854, 856 (1994); *People v. Anderson*, 66 N.Y.2d 529, 537–38, 540, 498 N.Y.S.2d 119, 124–25, 126 (1985).

§ 53:100   Failure to produce the discovery material

Research References

West's Key Number Digest, Criminal Law ⊙573, 577.3, 577.4, 577.10(4), 577.12(1)

The Court of Appeals has made clear that "prosecutorial delays in producing *Rosario* material and other discovery items [a]re not cognizable under CPL 30.30(3)(b), because there [a]re other specific statutory sanctions available under CPL article 240." *People v. McKenna*, 76 N.Y.2d 59, 64, 556 N.Y.S.2d 514, 516 (1990). In *McKenna*, the Court stated that:

> In the leading case, *People v. Anderson*, 66 N.Y.2d 529, 498 N.Y.S.2d 119, 488 N.E.2d 1231 [1985], we held that once the People have declared their readiness on the record, their subsequent delays in producing *Rosario* material and complying with certain other discovery obligations do not ordinarily render the indictment subject to dismissal under CPL 30.30, since delays of this nature do not affect the People's readiness to proceed to trial and, in any event, there exist other statutory sanctions for such delays.

76 N.Y.2d at 61, 556 N.Y.S.2d at 514. Examples of the types of "other discovery items" referenced in *McKenna* are laboratory reports, bills of particulars, and drugs (in a drug possession case). *See People v. Anderson*, 66 N.Y.2d 529, 539–40, 542–43, 498 N.Y.S.2d 119, 125–26, 127–28 (1985); *People v. Anderson*, 66 N.Y.2d 529, 543, 498 N.Y.S.2d 119 (1985) ("Essentially what was involved was the People's failure to comply in timely fashion with the demand to produce, for which CPL 240.70(1) provides alternative remedies"). *See also People v. Zale*, 137 A.D.3d 634, —, 28 N.Y.S.3d 360, 361 (1st Dep't 2016), leave to appeal denied, 27 N.Y.3d 1141, 2016 WL 3768212 (2016) ("the People's delay in obtaining and producing the [breath test device] calibration report, ultimately provided to defense counsel just before trial, was at most a failure to comply with a discovery request, which does not render their prior statements of readiness illusory"); *People v. Caussade*, 162 A.D.2d 4, 8, 560 N.Y.S.2d 648, 651 (2d Dep't 1990); *People v. Cole*, 90 A.D.2d 27, —, 457 N.Y.S.2d 589, 590–91 (3d Dep't 1982).

§ 53:101   Failure to produce *Rosario* material

Research References

West's Key Number Digest, Criminal Law ⚖573, 577.3, 577.4, 577.10(4), 577.12(1)

The Court of Appeals has made clear that "prosecutorial delays in producing *Rosario* material and other discovery items [a]re not cognizable under CPL 30.30(3)(b), because there [a]re other specific statutory sanctions available under CPL article 240." *People v. McKenna*, 76 N.Y.2d 59, 64, 556 N.Y.S.2d 514, 516 (1990). In *McKenna*, the Court stated that:

> In the leading case, *People v. Anderson*, 66 N.Y.2d 529, 498 N.Y.S.2d 119, 488 N.E.2d 1231, we held that once the People have declared

their readiness on the record, their subsequent delays in producing *Rosario* material and complying with certain other discovery obligations do not ordinarily render the indictment subject to dismissal under CPL 30.30, since delays of this nature do not affect the People's readiness to proceed to trial and, in any event, there exist other statutory sanctions for such delays.

76 N.Y.2d at 61, 556 N.Y.S.2d at 514. *See also* CPL § 240.70 (discovery sanctions); *People v. Anderson*, 66 N.Y.2d 529, 537, 498 N.Y.S.2d 119, 124 (1985). In *Anderson*, the Court stated that:

[T]he failure to make *Rosario* material available as required by CPL 240.45 may result under CPL 240.70 in discovery, a continuance, a protective or preclusion order or any other appropriate action . . . Dismissal for lack of *Rosario* material would be appropriate only on motion pursuant to CPL 30.20 and only if preclusion or a short continuance would violate the defendant's constitutional and statutory right to a speedy trial (CPL 30.20) after weighing the factors identified in *People v. Taranovich*, 37 N.Y.2d 442, 445, 373 N.Y.S.2d 79, 335 N.E.2d 303 . . . When no such alternative is provided by the Criminal Procedure Law, however, . . . dismissal is not only permissible but is required if the purpose of the section is to be carried out.

66 N.Y.2d at 537–38, 498 N.Y.S.2d at 124–25 (footnote omitted).

§ 53:102 Failure to produce CPL § 710.30 notice

Research References

West's Key Number Digest, Criminal Law ⬤─573, 577.3, 577.4, 577.10(4), 577.12(1)

In *People v. Anderson*, 66 N.Y.2d 529, 537–38, 498 N.Y.S.2d 119, 124–25 (1985), the Court of Appeals stated that:

[T]he failure to give defendant notice of intention to offer evidence of a statement made by him or her prior to trial may, when good cause is shown, result, under CPL 710.30, in permission to give notice during trial and a suppression hearing promptly thereafter . . . [W]hen good cause is shown for the failure to give the notice required by CPL 710.30, dismissal would be appropriate only upon a showing on a 30.20 motion that the time required for a suppression hearing, or the disadvantage to defendant in obtaining necessary witnesses consequent upon the late notice, is violative of defendant's constitutional right to a speedy trial as declared in *Taranovich*. When no such alternative is provided by the Criminal Procedure Law, however, . . . dismissal is not only permissible but is required if the purpose of the section is to be carried out.

§ 53:103 Failure to retain expert on retrograde extrapolation in DWI case

Research References

West's Key Number Digest, Criminal Law ⬤─573, 577.3, 577.4, 577.10(4), 577.12(1)

In *People v. Cross*, 273 A.D.2d 702, —, 711 N.Y.S.2d 533, 534 (3d Dep't 2000), the Appellate Division, Third Department, rejected the defendant's claim that "the People's statement of readiness was illusory inasmuch as the People had not retained an expert on retrograde extrapolation at the time such statement was made."

§ 53:104 Failure to conduct formal lab test of drugs in drug prosecution

Research References

West's Key Number Digest, Criminal Law ⚷573, 577.3, 577.4, 577.10(4), 577.12(1)

In *People v. Van Hoesen*, 12 A.D.3d 5, 7, 783 N.Y.S.2d 89, 90 (3d Dep't 2004), the Appellate Division, Third Department, addressed the following question: "can the People be ready for trial within the meaning of CPL 30.30 in a drug prosecution when the allegedly illegal drugs have not been formally tested?" In answering this question in the affirmative, the court reasoned that:

[N]either [*People v. Swamp*, 84 N.Y.2d 725, 622 N.Y.S.2d 472 (1995)] nor CPL 715.50 compels the prosecution, in order to be ready for trial under CPL 30.30, to have in their possession a formal laboratory analysis concerning alleged drugs . . .

Swamp does not speak to the issue of readiness for trial under CPL 30.30. While it does indeed contemplate that a formal laboratory analysis will be conducted "*prior* to trial," it observes that this analysis will be completed "[b]y the time trial commences." Here, the People did obtain formal laboratory testing prior to trial, albeit only three days beforehand.

Under our interpretation of *Swamp*, the People had legally sufficient evidence to proceed to trial when they indicated their readiness, namely, the testimony of the arresting officer and positive field test results, and the fact that formal laboratory results were not obtained until after the expiration of the CPL 30.30 statutory period does not mandate a finding that their statement of readiness was illusory.

People v. Van Hoesen, 12 A.D.3d 5, 8–9, 783 N.Y.S.2d 89, 91-92 (3d Dep't 2004) (citations omitted). *See also People v. Hunter*, 23 A.D.3d 767, —, 803 N.Y.S.2d 324, 325 (3d Dep't 2005) (same); *People v. McCombs*, 18 A.D.3d 888, —, 795 N.Y.S.2d 108, 109–10 (3d Dep't 2005) (same).

§ 53:105 Failure to raise meritorious speedy trial claim constitutes ineffective assistance of counsel

Research References

West's Key Number Digest, Criminal Law ☞573, 577.3, 577.4, 577.10(4), 577.12(1)

"Failure to raise a meritorious statutory speedy trial claim 'is sufficiently egregious to constitute a denial of meaningful representation.'" *People v. Obert*, 1 A.D.3d 631, __, 766 N.Y.S.2d 264, 265 (3d Dep't 2003) (citation omitted). *See also People v. Johnson*, 288 A.D.2d 501, __, 732 N.Y.S.2d 137, 138 (3d Dep't 2001); *People v. White*, 229 A.D.2d 610, __, 645 N.Y.S.2d 562, 563 (3d Dep't 1996); *People v. Jackson*, 172 A.D.2d 874, __, 568 N.Y.S.2d 177, 179 (3d Dep't 1991); *People v. O'Connell*, 133 A.D.2d 970, __, 521 N.Y.S.2d 121, 122 (3d Dep't 1987).

§ 53:106 "Failure to prosecute"

Research References

West's Key Number Digest, Criminal Law ☞573, 577.3, 577.4, 577.10(4)

In *People v. Douglass*, 60 N.Y.2d 194, 197, 469 N.Y.S.2d 56, 57 (1983), the Court of Appeals held that although a trial judge has the general authority to control his court calendar, "in exercising this authority, he may not dismiss a pending criminal proceeding for 'failure to prosecute.'" In so holding, the Court made clear that:

> [T]rial courts are vested with substantial power to control their calendars and our opinion today should not be read as holding, for example, that a court is obligated to grant every adjournment requested by a prosecutor simply because statutory or constitutional time limitations have not expired. * * *

> Moreover, we do not believe that there is a need to extend to the trial courts the power to dismiss criminal proceedings for "failure to prosecute" in order to protect defendants from unnecessarily protracted prosecution. Indeed, the Legislature has specifically addressed this problem by enacting provisions requiring dismissal of charges when the prosecution is untimely or when the defendant has been denied the right to a speedy trial. Defendants may also avail themselves of constitutional protections. Furthermore, if the court believes that dismissal is warranted in furtherance of justice, CPL 170.30 (subd. 1, par. [g]) and CPL 170.40 specifically authorize the court to so dismiss after considering the 10 factors set forth in the latter statute.

People v. Douglass, 60 N.Y.2d 194, 200, 469 N.Y.S.2d 56 (1983) (citations omitted).

Similarly, "a Judge presiding over a criminal prosecution [does not have] the power to dispose of the matter before him by entering a nonappealable trial order of dismissal on the merits even though no evidence is presented and the merits of the case have not yet been heard." *Matter of Holtzman v. Goldman*, 71 N.Y.2d 564, 566, 528 N.Y.S.2d 21, 23 (1988).

The *Holtzman* Court pointed out several times that "[t]he power of the trial court to deny the People further adjournment is not disputed; the error lies in the corrective action it took after it did so." *Matter of Holtzman v. Goldman*, 71 N.Y.2d 564, 570, 528 N.Y.S.2d 21 (1988). In this regard, the Court made clear that:

> It should be emphasized that the trial court was not helpless here. As suggested in *People v. Douglass*, the court could have denied the adjournment and, if the prosecutor was unable to proceed, placed the case on a reserve calendar to be restored only when ready for trial or dismissed when the speedy trial period had elapsed. Alternatively, petitioner suggests that the court could have exercised its contempt powers if the People failed to use reasonable efforts to produce complainant. It also could have entertained a motion for dismissal in the interest of justice.

Matter of Holtzman v. Goldman, 71 N.Y.2d 564, 574, 528 N.Y.S.2d 21 (1988) (citations and footnote omitted). *See also Matter of Hynes v. George*, 76 N.Y.2d 500, 502, 561 N.Y.S.2d 538, 538 (1990) ("the trial court had the power to deny the People's request for an adjournment and to proceed with jury selection" despite the fact that the People's CPL § 30.30 time had not elapsed).

§ 53:107   Speedy trial and the Interstate Agreement on Detainers

Research References

West's Key Number Digest, Criminal Law ⊸573, 577.4

Pursuant to the Interstate Agreement on Detainers (IAD) (*i.e.*, CPL § 580.20):

> Where a defendant is not brought to trial within the statutory period (*i.e.*, 180 days), the IAD requires that an indictment be dismissed with prejudice. Although the penalty of dismissal is by its terms mandatory, the IAD provides two exceptions: the request for speedy disposition of the charges is void if the prisoner escapes from custody, and the court may grant reasonable and necessary continuances, but only for good cause shown in open court with the prisoner or his attorney present. * * *

> Under the IAD, defendants have a single responsibility: to notify prison officials of their request to be brought to trial on the pending out-of-State charges. Otherwise, the burden of complying with statutory requirements falls upon the respective officials involved. Thus, ensuring that a defendant is brought to trial within the

mandated speedy trial period is the responsibility of prosecutors and courts, not defendants.

People v. Hill, 92 N.Y.2d 406, 410–11, 681 N.Y.S.2d 775, 778 (1998), rev'd, *New York v. Hill*, 528 U.S. 110, 120 S. Ct. 659 (2000) (citations omitted). *See also People v. McBride*, 44 N.Y.2d 1001, 1002, 408 N.Y.S.2d 340, 341 (1978). In *Hill, supra*, the Court of Appeals held that:

> [W]here, as here, the defendant simply concurred in a trial date proposed by the court and accepted by the prosecution, and that date fell outside the 180-day statutory period, no waiver of his speedy trial rights was effected. Defendant's mere concurrence in the suggested date did not constitute an affirmative request for a trial date beyond the speedy trial period. Moreover, it is the burden of the prosecutor and the court to comply with the IAD's speedy trial requirements.

92 N.Y.2d at 412, 681 N.Y.S.2d at 779. The United States Supreme Court reversed, holding that "defense counsel's agreement to a trial date outside the time period required by Article III of the [IAD] bars the defendant from seeking dismissal because trial did not occur within that period." 528 U.S. at 111, 120 S. Ct. at 662.

In *People v. Mungro*, 17 N.Y.3d 785, 786, 929 N.Y.S.2d 85, 85, 952 N.E.2d 1080 (2011), the Court of Appeals held that:

> The People did not violate defendant's right to a speedy trial pursuant to CPL 30.30 by failing to request his presence in New York from federal custody in Ohio until his prosecution there was completed and he began serving his sentence. The People had no statutory authority to request defendant's presence until such time (*see* CPL 580.20 art. IV [a]) and therefore, should not be penalized for the period of time that defendant was unavailable for trial in New York.

See also People v. Vrlaku, 73 N.Y.2d 800, 537 N.Y.S.2d 24, 533 N.E.2d 1053 (1988); *People v. Torres*, 60 N.Y.2d 119, 468 N.Y.S.2d 606, 456 N.E.2d 497 (1983).

§ 53:108 Applicability of speedy trial principles to administrative proceedings

Research References

West's Key Number Digest, Criminal Law ☜573, 577.4

In *Matter of O'Keefe v. Murphy*, 38 N.Y.2d 563, 568, 381 N.Y.S.2d 821, 823 (1976), the Court of Appeals held that:

> Analogizing to speedy trial principles, the appellants urge that the delays here were constitutionally impermissible. However, it must be remembered that we are dealing here with a civil rather than a criminal proceeding so that it is clear that the speedy trial

considerations recently articulated are inapposite. Nevertheless, the due process aspect of delay in the administrative context presents an important issue. The controlling standard is one of "fairness and justice." Thus, whenever a delay in an administrative adjudication significantly or deliberately interferes with a party's capacity to prepare or to present his case, the right to due process has been violated.

(Citations omitted).

§ 53:109   Is CPL § 30.30 dismissal "favorable termination" for purposes of action for malicious prosecution?

Research References

West's Key Number Digest, Criminal Law ⊙─573, 577.4

In *Smith-Hunter v. Harvey*, 95 N.Y.2d 191, 195, 712 N.Y.S.2d 438, 441 (2000), the Court of Appeals held that "a CPL 30.30 dismissal can constitute 'termination of the proceeding in favor of the accused' * * * for purposes of a malicious prosecution action." By contrast:

A termination is not favorable to the accused . . . if the charge is withdrawn or the prosecution abandoned pursuant to a compromise with the accused . . . Accordingly, . . . an adjournment in contemplation of dismissal . . . does not qualify as a favorable termination.

Similarly, if the charge is withdrawn or dismissed out of mercy requested or accepted by the accused, there is no favorable termination . . . Again, applying the exception to the common-law rule, we have held that the dismissal of a prosecution in the interest of justice did not constitute a favorable termination.

Smith-Hunter v. Harvey, 95 N.Y.2d 191, 196–97, 712 N.Y.S.2d 438, 441 (2000) (citation omitted).

Chapter 54

Mandatory Alcohol/Substance Abuse Treatment

KeyCite®: Cases and other legal materials listed in KeyCite Scope can be researched through the KeyCite service on Westlaw®. Use KeyCite to check citations for form, parallel references, prior and later history, and comprehensive citator information, including citations to other decisions and secondary materials.

---

§ 54:1   In general

In 2006, major, sweeping changes were made to New York's DWI laws. In particular, Chapter 732 of the Laws of 2006 was passed. This set of laws amended the VTL, the CPL, the Penal Law and the Mental Hygiene Law, created new DWI offenses, increased the penalties and licensing consequences for certain alcohol- and drug-related offenses, and mandated alcohol/substance abuse screening and/or treatment in virtually every VTL § 1192 case. The new laws took effect on November 1, 2006.

§ 54:2   "Special procedures" regarding mandatory alcohol/substance abuse treatment—VTL § 1198-a

VTL § 1198-a establishes "special procedures" regarding mandatory alcohol/substance abuse screening and treatment that are applicable to most VTL § 1192 cases. VTL § 1198-a contains 7 subsections, which are set forth in the sections that follow.

§ 54:3   Definitions applicable to VTL § 1198-a

VTL § 1198-a(1) sets forth the definitions applicable to VTL § 1198-a. As used herein, the acronym "OASAS" refers to the New York State Office of Alcoholism and Substance Abuse Services. VTL § 1198-a(1) provides that, for purposes of VTL § 1198-a, the following terms have the following meanings:

(a) "Alcohol and substance abuse professional" shall mean persons credentialed by [OASAS] to provide alcohol and substance abuse services pursuant to the mental hygiene law and persons licensed by the state education department in an appropriate health field, including licensed clinical social worker, licensed master social worker, licensed mental health counselor, nurse practitioner, physician, physician's assistant, psychiatrist, psychologist, and registered nurse.

(b) "Licensed agency" shall mean an agency licensed by [OASAS] to provide alcohol and substance abuse services pursuant to the mental hygiene law.

§ 54:4   Who is required to be informally "screened" for alcohol or substance abuse and dependency?

VTL § 1198-a(2)(a) sets forth a list of who is required to be informally screened for alcohol or substance abuse and dependency pursuant to VTL § 1198-a:

Mandatory screening; when authorized. Upon the arraignment of, or at the discretion of the court, prior to the sentencing of any person who:

(i) at arraignment is charged with or prior to sentencing convicted of a first violation of operating a motor vehicle in violation of [VTL § 1192(1), (2), (2-a)(b), or (3)] while such person has less than .15 of one per centum by weight of alcohol in the person's blood as shown by chemical analysis of such person's blood, breath, urine or saliva made pursuant to the provisions of [VTL § 1194], or in violation of [VTL § 1192(4)], or

(ii) has refused to submit to a chemical test pursuant to [VTL § 1194],

the court shall order such person to submit to screening for alcohol or substance abuse and dependency using a standardized written screening instrument developed by [OASAS], to be administered by an alcohol or substance abuse professional.

In layman's terms, the Court must Order the defendant to take a standardized, written screening test developed by OASAS prior to sentencing where the defendant is charged with:

1. DWAI, DWI, or a Leandra's Law violation, and either (a) refused to submit to a chemical test, or (b) took the test and the test result was less than .15%; or

2. DWAI Drugs.

§ 54:5 Who is required to be formally "assessed" for alcohol or substance abuse and dependency?

VTL § 1198-a(2)(b) sets forth a list of who is required to be formally assessed for alcohol or substance abuse and dependency pursuant to VTL § 1198-a:

Mandatory assessment; when authorized. The court shall order a defendant to undergo a formal alcohol or substance abuse and dependency assessment by an alcohol or substance abuse professional or a licensed agency:

(i) when the screening required by [VTL § 1198-a(2)(a)] indicates that a defendant is abusing or dependent upon alcohol or drugs;

(ii) following the arraignment of any person charged with or, at the discretion of the court, prior to the sentencing of any person convicted of a violation of [VTL § 1192(1), (2), (3), (4) or (4-a)] after having been convicted of a violation of any subdivision of [VTL § 1192,] or of [Vehicular Assault 2nd or 1st], as defined, respectively, in [PL §§ 120.03 and 120.04] or of [Aggravated Vehicular Assault], as defined in [PL § 120.04-a,] or of [Vehicular Manslaughter 2nd or 1st], as defined, respectively, in [PL §§ 125.12 and 125.13,] or of [Aggravated Vehicular Homicide], as defined in [PL § 125.14,] within the preceding [5] years[,] or after having been convicted of a violation of any subdivision of [VTL § 1192,] or of [Vehicular Assault 2nd or 1st], as defined, respectively, in [PL §§ 120.03 and 120.04,] or of [Aggravated Vehicular Assault], as defined in [PL § 120.04-a,] or of [Vehicular Manslaughter 2nd or 1st], as defined, respectively, in [PL §§ 125.12 and 125.13,] or of [Aggravated Vehicular Homicide], as defined in [PL § 125.14,] [2] or more times within the preceding [10] years; or

(iii) following the arraignment of any person charged with or, at the discretion of the court, prior to the sentencing of any person convicted of operating a motor vehicle in violation of [VTL §§ 1192(2), (2-a)(b) or (3)] while such person has .15 of one per centum or more by weight of alcohol in the person's blood as shown by a chemical analysis of such person's blood, breath, urine or saliva made pursuant to the provisions of [VTL § 1192(4),] or in violation of [VTL § 1192(2-a)(a)].

In layman's terms, the Court must Order the defendant to obtain a formal alcohol/substance abuse evaluation where the defendant:

(a) "fails" the OASAS screening test described in the previous section;

(b) is charged with DWAI, DWI, DWAI Drugs or DWAI Combined Influence; and either:

(i) has a "prior" within the past five years; or

(ii) has two or more "priors" within the past 10 years; or
(c) is charged with DWI or Aggravated DWI while having a BAC of .15% or more.

§ 54:6 Mandatory assessment procedures

VTL § 1198-a(2)(c) sets forth the procedures applicable to defendants required to obtain a formal assessment (a.k.a. evaluation) for alcohol or substance abuse and dependency pursuant to VTL § 1198-a(2)(b):

> Mandatory assessment; procedure. The assessment ordered by a court pursuant to this section shall be performed by an alcohol or substance abuse professional or a licensed agency which shall forward the results, in writing, to the court and to the defendant or his or her counsel within [30] days of the date of such order.

§ 54:7 Who must enroll in and successfully complete alcohol/substance abuse treatment?

VTL § 1198-a(3) provides that where an assessment pursuant to VTL § 1198-a(2) indicates that the defendant has an alcohol or substance abuse problem, the court must order the defendant to enroll in and successfully complete alcohol/substance abuse treatment:

> Authorized disposition. When a sentence of probation or a conditional discharge is imposed upon a person who has been required to undergo an alcohol or substance abuse and dependency assessment pursuant to [VTL § 1198-a(2)] and where such assessment indicates that such person is in need of treatment for alcohol or substance abuse or dependency, the court shall require, as a condition of such sentence, that such person participate in and successfully complete such treatment. Such treatment shall be provided by an alcohol or substance abuse professional or a licensed agency.

Critically, however, VTL § 1198-a(4) provides that a conditional discharge requiring the successful completion of the Drinking Driver Program (DDP), *see* §§ 50:1 et seq., *supra*, including any assessment and/or treatment required thereby, satisfies the requirements of VTL § 1198-a:

> Any case wherein a court has accepted a plea pursuant to the provisions of [VTL § 1192(10)(a)(ii)] and such plea includes as a condition thereof that the defendant attend and complete the alcohol and drug rehabilitation program established pursuant to [VTL § 1196], including any assessment and treatment required thereby, shall be deemed to be in compliance with the provisions of this section.

Thus, in many (if not most) cases, as long as the Court requires the defendant to attend and complete the DDP (which most Courts have always routinely done), the elaborate scheme set forth in VTL § 1198-a is moot. Similarly, DMV has always required repeat offenders to comply with similar procedures, *see* §§ 50:1 et seq., *supra*; which again indicates that VTL § 1198-a is either moot or redundant.

§ 54:8   OASAS must promulgate a list of authorized treatment providers

The assessment and/or treatment mandated by VTL § 1198-a is required to be provided by an "alcohol or substance abuse professional" or a "licensed agency" as defined by VTL § 1198-a(1). To avoid confusion as to whether particular treatment providers satisfy this requirement, (a) OASAS is required to promulgate a list of authorized treatment providers (and to provide the list to OCA and DMV), and (b) OCA is required to make the list available to every criminal court in the State. In this regard, Mental Hygiene Law § 19.07(g) provides as follows:

> [OASAS] shall develop a list of the names and locations of all licensed agencies and alcohol and substance abuse professionals, as defined in [VTL § 1198-a(1)(a) and (b)], throughout the state which are capable of and available to provide an assessment of, and treatment for, alcohol and substance abuse and dependency. Such list shall be provided to the chief administrator of the office of court administration and the commissioner of motor vehicles.

In addition, VTL § 1198-a(5) provides as follows:

> The chief administrator of the office of court administration shall make available to all courts in this state with jurisdiction in criminal cases a list of alcohol and substance abuse professionals and licensed agencies as provided by [OASAS] pursuant to [Mental Hygiene Law § 19.07(g)].

§ 54:9   Confidentiality of treatment records

VTL § 1198-a(6) addresses the confidentiality of the alcohol/substance abuse treatment records generated as a result of VTL § 1198-a:

> Confidentiality of records. (a) The records and content of all screenings, assessments and treatment conducted pursuant to this section, including the identity, diagnosis and prognosis of each individual who is the subject of such records, and including any statements or admissions of such individual made during the course of such screenings, assessments and treatment, shall be confidential, shall not be disclosed except as authorized by this subdivision, and shall not be entered or received as evidence at any civil, criminal or administrative trial, hearing or proceeding. No person, other than a defendant to whom such records are disclosed, may redisclose such records.
>
> (b) Consistent with [42 U.S.C.A. § 290dd-2], as such law may, from time to time, be amended, such records and content may only be disclosed as follows:

(i) to a court for the sole purpose of requiring a defendant charged with or convicted of a violation of [VTL § 1192(1), (2), (2-a), (3), (4) or (4-a)] to undergo alcohol or substance abuse or dependency assessment or treatment;

(ii) to the defendant or his or her authorized representative; and

(iii) to medical personnel to the extent necessary to meet a bona fide medical emergency.

VTL § 1193(1-a) also incorporates these confidentiality requirements. *See* VTL § 1193(1-a)(d).

§ 54:10 Effect of completion of treatment

VTL § 1198-a(7) addresses the effect of completion of alcohol/substance abuse treatment required by VTL § 1198-a:

> Effect of completion of treatment. Except as provided in [VTL § 1193(2)(b)(9)] or in [VTL § 1194(2)(d)(3)], upon successful completion of treatment ordered pursuant to this section as certified by the alcohol or substance abuse professional or licensed agency which provided such treatment, the defendant may apply to the commissioner on a form provided for that purpose, for the termination of the suspension or revocation order issued as a result of the defendant's conviction. In the exercise of discretion, upon receipt of such application, and upon payment of any civil penalties for which the defendant may be liable, the commissioner is authorized to terminate such order or orders and return the defendant's license or reinstate the privilege of operating a motor vehicle in this state. However, the commissioner shall not issue any new license nor restore any license where said issuance or restoration is prohibited by [VTL § 1193(2)].

In layman's terms, as with successful DDP completion, *see* §§ 50:1 et seq., *supra,* successful completion of treatment ordered pursuant to VTL § 1198-a allows the defendant to apply for reinstatement of his or her full driving privileges, except where the defendant is (a) the holder of a commercial driver's license, *see* §§ 50:1 et seq., *supra,* (b) under 21 years of age (on the date of the offense), *see* §§ 50:1 et seq., *supra,* (c) revoked for refusal to submit to a chemical test, *see* §§ 41:1 et seq., *supra,* and/or (d) subject to a permanent or lifetime license revocation. *See* §§ 41:1 et seq., *supra.* DMV also will not reinstate the defendant's driving privileges if the defendant has a prior VTL § 1192 conviction within the past five years. *See generally* 15 NYCRR § 134.10(b); 15 NYCRR § 136.9.

Chapter 55

New DMV Regulations Affecting Repeat DWI Offenders

KeyCite®: Cases and other legal materials listed in KeyCite Scope can be researched through the KeyCite service on Westlaw®. Use KeyCite to check citations for form, parallel references, prior and later history, and comprehensive citator information, including citations to other decisions and secondary materials.

---

§ 55:1   In general

Starting in approximately 2011, a series of high publicity cases involving repeat DWI offenders led to a campaign to keep these drivers off the road. In this regard, certain politicians attempted to pass legislation that would greatly increase the driver's license revocation periods for repeat DWI offenders. However, the proposed legislation was not enacted.

Dissatisfied with the Legislature's lack of action on this issue, Governor Cuomo directed DMV to enact harsh new administrative regulations that would render the need for legislative action moot. Stated another way, when the Legislature could not agree on how to best address the issue of repeat DWI offenders—and/or could not agree as to whether the existing treatment of repeat DWI offenders was inadequate—the executive branch of government bypassed the Legislature and took matters into its own hands.

The new DMV regulations ordered by Governor Cuomo took effect on September 25, 2012. However, starting in February of 2012, DMV stopped processing the applications for relicensure of thousands of individuals whose driver's licenses were currently revoked and who either (a) had three or more DWI-related convictions/incidents within the new 25-year look-back period, or (b) had five or more DWI-related convictions/incidents within their lifetimes. In this regard, DMV intentionally delayed the applications for relicensure of thousands of individuals who were eligible for immediate relicensure under existing laws, existing regulations, and the DMV policy that had been in effect since at least January of 1986. The purpose of the delay was to prevent repeat DWI offenders from being relicensed prior to the enactment of the harsh new regulations ordered by the Governor—so that the (as yet nonexistent) regulations could subsequently be retroactively applied to their applications for relicensure.

This Chapter discusses the new DMV regulations, as well as various potential challenges thereto.

§ 55:2   Summary of preexisting DMV policy

Prior to the enactment of its new regulations, DMV had a policy regarding repeat DWI offenders that had been in effect since at least January of 1986. *See* Appendix 53 ("Letter from Department of Motor Vehicles Regarding Multiple Offenders"). Unless the person (a) was underage, (b) had refused to submit to a chemical test, or (c) was a commercial driver—and as long as the person provided proof of alcohol/drug treatment—the policy was as follows:

1. *2nd offenders*—if the person was eligible for the Drinking Driver Program (DDP), the license would be restored upon successful completion thereof. Otherwise, license restored at the conclusion of the minimum statutory revocation period.

2. *3rd offenders*—if eligible for the DDP, license restored upon successful completion thereof. Otherwise, license restored after 18 months.

3. *4th offenders*—if eligible for the DDP, license restored upon successful completion thereof. Otherwise, license restored after 24 months.

4. *5th offenders*—if eligible for the DDP, license restored upon successful completion thereof. Otherwise, license restored after 30 months.

5. *6th and subsequent offenders*—license only restored upon Court order.

Pursuant to this policy, DWI-related convictions/incidents were only taken into account if they occurred within a 10-year period. In this regard, prior to the enactment of the new regulations, 15 NYCRR § 136.1(b)(3), provided as follows:

> History of abuse of alcohol or drugs. A history of abuse of alcohol or drugs shall consist of a record of *[2] or more incidents, within a 10 year period*, of operating a motor vehicle while under the influence of alcoholic beverages and/or drugs or of refusing to submit to a chemical test not arising out of the same incident, whether such incident was committed within or outside of this state.

(Emphasis added).

Thus, for example, if a person was convicted of his or her 6th DWI, but had no DWI-related convictions/incidents within the past 10 years, the person was treated as a 1st offender for purposes of the above policy—and is still treated as a first offender for purposes of all existing DWI statutes. *See, e.g.*, VTL §§ 1193(1)(a), 1193(1)(c)(i), 1193(1)(c)(ii), 1193(1)(d) (2), 1193(1)(d) (4)(i), 1193(1)(d)(4)(ii), 1193(2)(b)(12)(a), 1193(2)(b)(12)(d), 1194(2)(d) (1) & 1198(3)(a). *See also* PL §§ 120.04(3), 120.04-a(3), 125.13(3) & 125.14(3). *See generally* VTL § 201(1)(k); CPL § 160.55(5)(c) (records pertaining to a VTL § 1192-a finding are required to be sealed after three years or when the person turns 21, whichever is longer).

§ 55:3 Effective date of new regulations

The effective date of the new DMV regulations is September 25, 2012. Critically, unlike new laws—which generally only apply to offenses committed on or after the effective date thereof—the new regulations are being applied retroactively. In fact, the new regulations were applied to applications for relicensure that were received in February of 2012 (as these applications were intentionally not decided until after the new regulations took effect).

§ 55:4 Summary of new regulations—Key definitions

The new DMV regulations contain the following key definitions:

1. *"Dangerous repeat alcohol or drug offender"*—
    (a) any driver who, within his or her lifetime, has [5] or more alcohol- or drug-related driving convictions or incidents in any combination; or
    (b) any driver who, during the 25 year look back period, has [3] or [4] alcohol- or drug-related driving convictions or incidents in any combination and, in addition, has [1] or more serious driving offenses during the 25 year look back period.
    See 15 NYCRR § 132.1(b).

2. *"Alcohol- or drug-related driving conviction or incident"* (hereinafter "DWI")—any of the following, not arising out of the same incident:

   (a) a conviction of a violation of VTL § 1192 (or an out-of-state conviction for operating a motor vehicle while under the influence of alcohol or drugs);

   (b) a finding of a violation of VTL § 1192-a (*i.e.*, the Zero Tolerance law);

   (c) a conviction of a Penal Law offense for which a violation of VTL § 1192 is an essential element; or

   (d) a finding of a refusal to submit to a chemical test pursuant to VTL § 1194.

   See 15 NYCRR §§ 132.1(a) & 136.5(a)(1).

3. *"High-point driving violation"*—any violation for which 5 or more points are assessed on a person's driving record.

   See 15 NYCRR §§ 132.1(c) & 136.5(a)(2)(iii).

4. *"Serious driving offense"* (hereinafter "SDO")—any of the following, within the 25-year look-back period:

   (a) a fatal accident;

   (b) a driving-related Penal Law conviction;

   (c) conviction of 2 or more high-point driving violations; or

   (d) 20 or more total points from any violations.

   See 15 NYCRR §§ 132.1(d) & 136.5(a)(2).

   The new regulations do not define what would constitute a "driving-related Penal Law conviction." In this regard, however, DMV Counsel's Office advises that a driving-related Penal Law offense is one in which the operation of a motor vehicle is an essential element. Thus, for example, a DWI that is plea bargained to Reckless Endangerment would not constitute a driving-related Penal Law conviction.

5. *"25-year look-back period"*—the time period 25 years prior to, and including, the date of the revocable offense.

   See 15 NYCRR §§ 132.1(e), 136.1(b)(3) & 136.5(a)(3).

6. *"Revocable offense"*—the violation, incident or accident that results in the revocation of a person's driver's license and which is the basis of the application for relicensure.

   See 15 NYCRR § 136.5(a)(4).

Upon reviewing an application for relicensure, DMV will review the applicant's entire driving record and evaluate any offense committed between the date of the revocable offense and the date of application as if the offense had been committed immediately prior to the date of the revocable offense.

See id.

For purposes of this definition, "date of the revocable offense" means the date of the *earliest* revocable offense that resulted in a license revocation that has not been terminated by DMV.

See id.

7. *License with "A2 problem driver restriction"*—a driver's license that is treated like a restricted use license, *see* VTL § 530; 15 NYCRR § 135.9(b), and which will be revoked for the reasons that would lead to the revocation of a probationary license (*i.e.*, (a) following too closely, (b) speeding, (c) speed contest, (d) operating out of restriction, (e) reckless driving, or (f) any two other moving violations).

See 15 NYCRR §§ 3.2(c)(4) & 136.4(b)(3); VTL § 510-b(1); DMV website.

If the revocable offense leading to the issuance of a license with an A2 problem driver restriction was DWI-related, an ignition interlock device ("IID") requirement will be imposed. *See* 15 NYCRR §§ 3.2(c)(4), 136.4(b)(1) to (3) & 136.5(b)(3) to (4).

§ 55:5 Summary of new regulations—Key provisions

The sections that follow summarize the key provisions of the new DMV regulations.

§ 55:6 New regulations only apply to repeat DWI offenders

The new regulations only affect repeat DWI offenders. There are no changes to the rules applicable to first offenders.

§ 55:7 New regulations generally only apply where person's license is revoked

A critical aspect of the new regulations is that they generally only apply where the defendant's driver's license is revoked (as opposed to suspended). This is because license suspensions do not trigger either a full record review or the need to submit an application for relicensure, whereas license revocations trigger both.

Thus, a conviction of DWAI (as opposed to DWI) can now mean the difference between a 90-day license suspension and a lifetime license revocation. In this regard, however, it must not be forgotten that there are several circumstances in which a DWAI conviction results in a license revocation. *See* §§ 46:1 et seq., *supra. See also* §§ 14:1 et seq. and 15:1 et seq., *supra.*

In addition, 15 NYCRR Part 132 is the primary exception to the rule that the new regulations only apply where the defendant's driver's license is revoked. Part 132 applies to "dangerous repeat alcohol or drug offenders" who are convicted of high-point driving violations (which violations generally do not, in and of themselves, even lead to a license suspension—let alone a revocation). *See* §§ 55:14 & 55:15, *infra*.

§ 55:8 DMV's definition of "history of abuse of alcohol or drugs" now utilizes 25-year look-back period

Prior to September 25, 2012, DMV defined "history of abuse of alcohol or drugs" as:

A history of abuse of alcohol or drugs shall consist of a record of *[2] or more incidents, within a 10 year period,* of operating a motor vehicle while under the influence of alcoholic beverages and/or drugs or of refusing to submit to a chemical test not arising out of the same incident, whether such incident was committed within or outside of this state.

15 NYCRR former § 136.1(b)(3) (emphasis added).

Pursuant to the new regulations, the look-back period in 15 NYCRR § 136.1(b)(3) is now 25 years.

§ 55:9 Second offenders

Under the old rules, unless a person (a) was underage, (b) had refused to submit to a chemical test, or (c) was a commercial driver, successful completion of the DDP would terminate any outstanding license suspension/revocation period. *See* VTL § 1196(5). In other words, successful DDP completion generally allowed the person to apply for reinstatement of his or her full driving privileges. In this regard, it was possible for second or third offenders to re-obtain their full licenses back in as little as seven to eight weeks.

Pursuant to the new regulations, a person who has a second DWI-related conviction/incident within the past 25 years can still obtain a conditional license (if eligible under the old rules), but can no longer reobtain his or her full license back prior to the expiration of the minimum suspension/revocation period (*i.e.*, successful DDP completion no longer terminates a license suspension/revocation for second offenders). *See* 15 NYCRR §§ 134.10(b), 134.11, & 136.5(b)(5).

§ 55:10 Third offenders no longer eligible for conditional license

Under the old rules, a person was generally eligible for a conditional license approximately every five years. In this regard, a person was ineligible for a conditional license if the person, among other things, (a) had a prior VTL § 1192 conviction within the past five years, (b) had participated in the DDP within the past five years, or (c) had two prior DWI-related convictions/incidents within the past 10 years. *See* VTL § 1196(4); 15 NYCRR § 134.7; §§ 50:1 et seq., *supra.*

Pursuant to the new regulations, a person who has three or more DWI-related convictions/incidents *within the past 25 years* is ineligible for a conditional license. *See* 15 NYCRR § 134.7(a)(11)(i).

§ 55:11   It is often now necessary to obtain person's lifetime driving record

A person's publicly available DMV driving abstract only goes back 10 years; and non-DWI-related convictions/incidents do not even remain on an abstract for nearly that long. However, the new DMV regulations apply to offenses/incidents going back a minimum of 25 years—and sometimes forever.

As a result, it is now often necessary to obtain a person's full, lifetime driving record before giving the person advice on how to proceed in a pending matter. At the present time, it appears that the only way to obtain such records is to file a FOIL request with DMV. *See* Form MV-15F.

§ 55:12   New lifetime revocation #1—Person has five or more lifetime DWIs and is currently revoked

15 NYCRR § 136.5(b)(1) provides that:

(b) Upon receipt of a person's application for relicensing, the Commissioner shall conduct a lifetime review of such person's driving record. If the record review shows that:

(1) the person has [5] or more alcohol- or drug-related driving convictions or incidents in any combination within his or her lifetime, then the Commissioner shall deny the application.

In other words, pursuant to the new regulations a person with five or more lifetime DWI-related convictions/incidents whose driver's license is currently revoked for any reason will *never* be relicensed.

§ 55:13   New lifetime revocation #2—Person has three or four DWIs and one or more SDOs within the 25-year look-back period and is currently revoked

15 NYCRR § 136.5(b)(2) provides that:

(b) Upon receipt of a person's application for relicensing, the Commissioner shall conduct a lifetime review of such person's driving record. If the record review shows that: * * *

(2) the person has [3] or [4] alcohol- or drug-related driving convictions or incidents in any combination within the 25 year look back

period and, in addition, has [1] or more serious driving offenses within the 25 year look back period, then the Commissioner shall deny the application.

In other words, pursuant to the new regulations a person with three or four DWI-related convictions/incidents and one or more SDOs within the 25-year look-back period whose driver's license is currently revoked for any reason will *never* be relicensed.

§ 55:14 New lifetime revocation #3—Person has five or more lifetime DWIs and is convicted of a high-point driving violation

15 NYCRR § 132.1(b) provides, in pertinent part, that:

"Dangerous repeat alcohol or drug offender" means:

(1) any driver who, within his or her lifetime, has [5] or more alcohol- or drug-related driving convictions or incidents in any combination.

15 NYCRR § 132.2 provides that:

Upon receipt of notice of a driver's conviction for a high-point driving violation, the Commissioner shall conduct a review of the lifetime driving record of the person convicted. If such review indicates that the person convicted is a dangerous repeat alcohol or drug offender, the Commissioner shall issue a proposed revocation of such person's driver license. Such person shall be advised of the right to request a hearing before an [ALJ], prior to such proposed revocation taking effect. The provisions of Part 127 of this Chapter shall be applicable to any such hearing.

15 NYCRR § 132.3 provides that:

The sole purpose of a hearing scheduled pursuant to this Part is to determine whether there exist unusual, extenuating and compelling circumstances to warrant a finding that the revocation proposed by the Commissioner should not take effect. In making such a determination, the [ALJ] shall take into account a driver's entire driving record. Unless the [ALJ] finds that such unusual, extenuating and compelling circumstances exist, the judge shall issue an order confirming the revocation proposed by the Commissioner.

In other words, pursuant to the new regulations a person with five or more lifetime DWI-related convictions/incidents who is convicted of a traffic infraction carrying five or more points will be *permanently* revoked unless the person requests a hearing at which he or she establishes that "there exist unusual, extenuating and compelling circumstances to warrant a finding that the revocation proposed by the Commissioner should not take effect."

The reason why a license revocation pursuant to 15 NYCRR Part 132 is a lifetime revocation is that, once revoked, the person is subject to 15 NYCRR § 136.5(b)(1). *See* § 55:12, *supra*.

Notably, not long after Part 132 was enacted cell phone and texting infractions were added to the list of high-point driving violations. *See* 15 NYCRR § 131.3(b)(4)(iii). Thus, under the new regulations a cell phone ticket can lead to a permanent, lifetime driver's license revocation.

§ 55:15   New lifetime revocation #4—Person has three or four DWIs and one or more SDOs within the 25-year look-back period and is convicted of a high-point driving violation

15 NYCRR § 132.1(b) provides, in pertinent part, that:

"Dangerous repeat alcohol or drug offender" means: * * *

(2) any driver who, during the 25 year look back period, has [3] or [4] alcohol- or drug-related driving convictions or incidents in any combination and, in addition, has [1] or more serious driving offenses during the 25 year look back period.

15 NYCRR § 132.2 provides that:

Upon receipt of notice of a driver's conviction for a high-point driving violation, the Commissioner shall conduct a review of the lifetime driving record of the person convicted. If such review indicates that the person convicted is a dangerous repeat alcohol or drug offender, the Commissioner shall issue a proposed revocation of such person's driver license. Such person shall be advised of the right to request a hearing before an [ALJ], prior to such proposed revocation taking effect. The provisions of Part 127 of this Chapter shall be applicable to any such hearing.

15 NYCRR § 132.3 provides that:

The sole purpose of a hearing scheduled pursuant to this Part is to determine whether there exist unusual, extenuating and compelling circumstances to warrant a finding that the revocation proposed by the Commissioner should not take effect. In making such a determination, the [ALJ] shall take into account a driver's entire driving record. Unless the [ALJ] finds that such unusual, extenuating and compelling circumstances exist, the judge shall issue an order confirming the revocation proposed by the Commissioner.

In other words, pursuant to the new regulations a person with three or four DWI-related convictions/incidents and one or more SDOs within the 25-year look-back period who is convicted of a traffic infraction carrying five or more points will be *permanently* revoked unless the person requests a hearing at which he or she establishes that "there exist unusual, extenuating and compelling circumstances to warrant a finding that the revocation proposed by the Commissioner should not take effect."

The reason why a license revocation pursuant to 15 NYCRR Part 132 is a lifetime revocation is that, once revoked, the person is subject to 15 NYCRR § 136.5(b)(2). *See* § 55:13, *supra*.

Notably, not long after Part 132 was enacted cell phone and texting infractions were added to the list of high-point driving violations. *See* 15 NYCRR § 131.3(b)(4)(iii). Thus, under the new regulations a cell phone ticket can lead to a permanent, lifetime driver's license revocation.

§ 55:16   New lifetime revocation #5—Person revoked for new DWI-related conviction/incident while on license with A2 problem driver restriction

Pursuant to the new regulations, a person who has three or four DWI-related convictions/incidents—but no SDOs—within the 25-year look-back period may be eligible for a restricted use license containing a so-called "A2 problem driver restriction." In this regard, 15 NYCRR § 3.2(c)(4) provides:

A2-Problem driver restriction. The operation of a motor vehicle shall be subject to the driving restrictions set forth in section 135.9(b) and the conditions set forth in section 136.4(b) of this Title. As part of this restriction, the commissioner may require a person assigned the problem driver restriction to install an ignition interlock device in any motor vehicle that may be operated with a Class D license or permit and that is owned or operated by such person. The ignition interlock requirement will be noted on an attachment to the driver's license or permit held by such person. Such attachment must be carried at all times with the driver license or permit.

Both 15 NYCRR § 136.5(b)(3) and 15 NYCRR § 136.5(b)(4) provide that:

If such license with an A2 restriction is later revoked for a subsequent alcohol- or drug-related driving conviction or incident, such person shall thereafter be ineligible for any kind of license to operate a motor vehicle.

§ 55:17   Person has three or four DWIs, no SDOs, and is currently revoked for a DWI-related conviction/incident—Statutory revocation + five more years + five more years on an A2 restricted use license with an IID

Pursuant to the new regulations, a person who has three or four DWI-related convictions/incidents—but no SDOs—within the 25-year look-back period, and whose license is currently revoked for a DWI-related offense, will serve out the minimum statutory revocation period *plus* five more years, after which the person may be granted a license with an A2 problem driver restriction (with an IID requirement) for an additional five years.

Specifically, 15 NYCRR § 136.5(b)(3) provides, in pertinent part:

(b) Upon receipt of a person's application for relicensing, the Commissioner shall conduct a lifetime review of such person's driving record. If the record review shows that: * * *

(3)(i) the person has [3] or [4] alcohol- or drug-related driving convictions or incidents in any combination within the 25 year look back period but no serious driving offenses within the 25 year look back period and (ii) the person is currently revoked for an alcohol- or drug-related driving conviction or incident, then the Commissioner shall deny the application for at least [5] years after which time the person may submit an application for relicensing. *Such waiting period shall be in addition to the revocation period imposed pursuant to the Vehicle and Traffic Law.* After such waiting period, the Commissioner may in his or her discretion approve the application, provided that upon such approval, the Commissioner shall impose the A2 restriction on such person's license for a period of [5] years and shall require the installation of an [IID] in any motor vehicle owned or operated by such person for such [5]-year period.

(Emphasis added).

§ 55:18   Person has three or four DWIs, no SDOs, and is currently revoked for a non-DWI-related conviction/incident—Statutory revocation + two more years + two more years on an A2 restricted use license with no IID

Pursuant to the new regulations, a person who has three or four DWI-related convictions/incidents—but no SDOs—within the 25-year look-back period, and whose license is currently revoked for a *non*-DWI-related offense, will serve out the minimum statutory revocation period *plus* two more years, after which the person may be granted a license with an A2 problem driver restriction (with no IID requirement) for an additional two years.

Specifically, 15 NYCRR § 136.5(b)(4) provides, in pertinent part:

(b) Upon receipt of a person's application for relicensing, the Commissioner shall conduct a lifetime review of such person's driving record. If the record review shows that: * * *

(4)(i) the person has [3] or [4] alcohol- or drug-related driving convictions or incidents in any combination within the 25 year look back period but no serious driving offenses within the 25 year look back period and (ii) the person is not currently revoked as the result of an alcohol- or drug-related driving conviction or incident, then the Commissioner shall deny the application for at least [2] years, after which time the person may submit an application for relicensing. *Such waiting period shall be in addition to the revocation period imposed pursuant to the Vehicle and Traffic Law.* After such waiting period, the Commissioner may in his or her discretion approve the application, provided that upon such approval, the Commissioner shall impose an A2 restriction, with no ignition interlock requirement, for a period of [2] years.

(Emphasis added).

§ 55:19 Applicability of new regulations to person who is "permanently" revoked pursuant to VTL § 1193(2)(b)(12)

Prior to the enactment of the new DMV regulations, VTL § 1193(2)(b) (12) already provided for five- and eight-year permanent license revocations for repeat DWI offenders. *See* §§ 46:1 et seq., *supra*. The new regulations consider these revocation periods to be the minimum statutory revocation periods for purposes of 15 NYCRR § 136.5(b)(3).

Thus, under the new regulations, where a person is subject to a five- or eight-year waivable "permanent" revocation pursuant to VTL §§ 1193(2)(b) (12), at the end of the five- or eight-year minimum statutory period DMV will now either:

(a) impose a *lifetime license revocation*; or

(b) pursuant to 15 NYCRR § 136.5(b)(3), add five more years to the revocation (for a total of 10 or 13 years with no driving privileges whatsoever), after which the person may be granted an A2 restricted use license with an IID requirement for an additional five years.

See 15 NYCRR §§ 136.10(b), 136.5(b)(1), 136.5(b)(2) & 136.5(b)(3).

In this regard, 15 NYCRR § 136.10(b) provides as follows:

(b) Application after permanent revocation. The Commissioner may waive the permanent revocation of a driver's license, pursuant to [VTL §] 1193(2)(b)(12)(b) and (e), only if the statutorily required waiting period of either [5] or [8] years has expired since the imposition of the permanent revocation and, during such period, the applicant has not been found to have refused to submit to a chemical test pursuant to [VTL §] 1194 and has not been convicted of any violation of section 1192 or section 511 of such law or a violation of the Penal Law for which a violation of any subdivision of [VTL §] 1192 is an essential element. In addition, the waiver shall be granted only if:

(1) The applicant presents proof of successful completion of a rehabilitation program approved by the Commissioner within [1] year prior to the date of the application for the waiver; provided, however, if the applicant completed such program before such time, the applicant must present proof of completion of an alcohol and drug dependency assessment within [1] year of the date of application for the waiver; and

(2) The applicant submits to the Commissioner a certificate of relief from civil disabilities or a certificate of good conduct pursuant to Article 23 of the Correction Law; and

(3) The application is not denied pursuant to section 136.4 or section 136.5 of this Part; and

(4) There are no incidents of driving during the period prior to the application for the waiver, as indicated by accidents, convictions or pending tickets. The consideration of an ap-

plication for a waiver when the applicant has a pending ticket shall be held in abeyance until such ticket is disposed of by the court or tribunal.

§ 55:20   Legal challenges to the new DMV regulations

At the present time, the new DMV regulations are being vigorously challenged on numerous grounds. Some of the issues being raised are set forth below.

§ 55:21   The Legislature has preempted the field of DWI law in a manner that limits the discretion of other branches of government to expand the scope of the DWI laws

The issue of whether the new DMV regulations are a good idea is arguably irrelevant. Rather, the issue is whether, under the Constitution, the executive branch of government can engage in inherently legislative activity on an issue that the Legislature has been unable to reach agreement upon.

The Court of Appeals has *repeatedly* made clear both (a) that the Legislature has given significant thought to the topic of DWI-related offenses, and has enacted "tightly and carefully integrated" statutes covering these offenses, *see People v. Prescott*, 95 N.Y.2d 655, 659 (2001), and (b) that, as a result, creative attempts to expand the scope of the relevant statutes are inappropriate—*even if such interpretation of the laws would otherwise be valid. See, e.g.*:

1. *People v. Rivera*, 16 N.Y.3d 654 (2011) (defendant whose driver's license is revoked for DWI and who commits a new DWI while on a conditional license cannot be prosecuted for the felony of AUO 1st, in violation of VTL § 511(3), but rather can only be prosecuted for the traffic infraction of VTL § 1196(7)(f));
2. *People v. Ballman*, 15 N.Y.3d 68 (2010) (VTL § 1192(8) does not allow an out-of-State DWI conviction occurring prior to November 1, 2006, to be considered for purposes of elevating a new DWI charge from a misdemeanor to a felony);
3. *People v. Litto*, 8 N.Y.3d 692 (2007) (the term "intoxicated" in VTL § 1192(3) only applies to intoxication caused by alcohol—not, as the People claimed, to intoxication caused by *any* substance);
4. *People v. Prescott*, *supra* (a person cannot be charged with *attempted* DWI); and
5. *People v. Letterlough*, 86 N.Y.2d 259 (1995) (condition of probation that defendant would have to affix a fluorescent sign stating "CONVICTED DWI" to the license plates of any vehicle that he operated is illegal).

In *Prescott*, the Court of Appeals specifically stated, *inter alia*, that:

> In addition to criminal penalties, [VTL §] 1193 further imposes mandatory minimum periods for license suspension or revocation. These sanctions, like the criminal penalties, are correlated to the specific nature and degree of the section 1192 violation.
>
> The Legislature placed great significance on the enforcement of specific statutory penalties for drunk driving. . . . Thus, *the Legislature has made it clear that the courts must look to section 1193 for the appropriate penalties and sentencing options for drunk driving offenses.*

95 N.Y.2d at 660–61 (emphasis added) (citations omitted). *See also Letterlough*, 86 N.Y.2d at 269 ("While innovative ideas to address the serious problem of recidivist drunk driving are not to be discouraged, the courts must act within the limits of their authority and cannot overreach by using their probationary powers to accomplish what only the legislative branch can do"); VTL § 510(3)(a) (DMV's discretionary authority to suspend or revoke a driver's license—*or to deny a license to an unlicensed person*—pursuant to VTL § 510 does not apply to violations of VTL § 1192).

§ 55:22   The new DMV regulations conflict with existing statutes—Generally

It is axiomatic that an administrative regulation that conflicts with a statute is illegal. *See, e.g.*, *Matter of Broidrick v. Lindsay*, 39 N.Y.2d 641, 649 (1976) ("In conclusion, the . . . regulations are invalid for lack of legislative authorization, [as well as] for inconsistency with applicable State statutes"); *Sciara v. Surgical Assocs. of Western New York, P.C.*, 104 A.D.3d 1256, 1257 (4th Dep't 2013) ("it is well established that, in the event of a conflict between a statute and a regulation, the statute controls"). The new DMV regulations conflict with existing statutes—both directly and implicitly—in multiple key respects.

§ 55:23   The new regulations conflict with VTL § 1193(2)(b)(12)

Perhaps the most direct conflict between the new DMV regulations and existing law is the conflict between VTL § 1193(2)(b)(12)(b) and 15 NYCRR Part 132, 15 NYCRR § 136.5(b) and 15 NYCRR § 136.10(b). Several existing statutes directly address the issue of repeat DWI offenders. Specifically, there are three "permanent" driver's license revocations: (a) one that is truly *permanent*; *see* VTL § 1193(2)(c) (3), (b) one that is waivable after 5 years; *see* VTL §§ 1193(2)(b)(12)(a)/(b), and (c) one that is waivable after 8 years. *See* VTL §§ 1193(2)(b)(12)(d)/(e).

VTL §§ 1193(2)(b)(12)(a)/(b) provide for a five-year "permanent" driver's license revocation where a person either:

(a) has 3 DWI-related convictions (and/or chemical test refusal findings) within 4 years; or

(b) has 4 DWI-related convictions (and/or chemical test refusal findings) within 8 years.

VTL §§ 1193(2)(b)(12)(a)/(b) make clear that a driver's license cannot be "permanently" revoked—even for five years—unless the person has at least three DWI-related convictions (and/or chemical test refusal findings) within four years, or at least four DWI-related convictions (and/or chemical test refusal findings) within eight years. Since 15 NYCRR Part 132 and 15 NYCRR § 136.5(b) contain multiple greater-than-five-year license revocations that are triggered by as few as three DWI-related convictions/incidents *over a period of 25 years*, they appear to irreconcilably conflict with VTL §§ 1193(2)(b)(12)(a)/(b).

Simply stated, where a person's DWI-related driving record would not result in a five-year license revocation under the "permanent" revocation statute targeting repeat DWI offenders, it would seem that DMV cannot lawfully enact administrative regulations that trump the statute and impose a greater-than-five-year license revocation on the person. Yet the new DMV regulations do exactly that. Thus, if the new DMV regulations are legal, then VTL §§ 1193(2)(b)(12)(a)/(b) are "superfluous, a result to be avoided in statutory construction." *People v. Litto*, 33 A.D.3d 625, 626 (2d Dep't 2006), *aff'd*, 8 N.Y.3d 692 (2007).

In addition, VTL § 1193(2)(b)(12)(b) provides that:

(b) *The permanent driver's license revocation required by clause (a) of this subparagraph shall be waived by the commissioner after a period of [5] years has expired since the imposition of such permanent revocation*, provided that during such [5]-year period such person has not been found to have refused a chemical test pursuant to [VTL § 1194] while operating a motor vehicle and has not been convicted of a violation of any subdivision of [VTL § 1192] or section [VTL § 511] or a violation of the penal law for which a violation of any subdivision of [VTL § 1192] is an essential element *and either*:

(i) that such person provides acceptable documentation to the commissioner that such person has voluntarily enrolled in and successfully completed an appropriate rehabilitation program; *or*

(ii) that such person is granted a certificate of relief from disabilities or a certificate of good conduct pursuant to [Correction Law Article 23].

Provided, however, that the commissioner may, on a case by case basis, refuse to restore a license which otherwise would be restored pursuant to this item, in the interest of the public safety and welfare.

(Emphases added).

VTL § 1193(2)(b)(12)(b) clearly provides that even where a person has three DWI-related convictions (and/or chemical test refusal findings) within four years (or four DWI-related convictions (and/or chemical test refusal findings) within eight years), DMV is generally *required* to immediately waive the "permanent" revocation after five years. Nonetheless, under the new DMV regulations everyone who has three or more DWI-related convictions/incidents within the past 25 years will receive a greater-than-five-year—and in some cases *lifetime*—driver's license revocation (unless the current revocation is not DWI-related and the person does not have an SDO on his or her driving record).

Thus, the new DMV regulations impose a greater-than-five-year license revocation on both:

(a) people who are ineligible for a five-year revocation under VTL § 1193(2)(b) (12); and

(b) people who fall within VTL § 1193(2)(b) (12) but are statutorily entitled to a waiver after five years.

With regard to the latter group, despite the five-year waiver requirement in VTL § 1193(2)(b)(12)(b), new regulation 15 NYCRR § 136.10(b) provides that after five years DMV will either:

(a) impose a non-waivable *permanent* lifetime license revocation (if the motorist also has one or more SDOs within the past 25 years). *See* 15 NYCRR § 136.5(b)(2); or

(b) impose *an additional* five-year "waiting period" (with no driving privileges), *plus* another five years with restricted driving privileges *and* a mandatory IID requirement for the entire time. *See* 15 NYCRR § 136.5(b)(3).

15 NYCRR § 136.10(b) irreconcilably conflicts with VTL § 1193(2)(b)(12)(b) in yet another way. Specifically, although VTL § 1193(2)(b)(12)(b) expressly provides that a five-year "permanent" license revocation generally must be waived as long as the motorist:

(1) has *either* completed treatment *or* obtained a certificate of relief from disabilities (or a certificate of good conduct); *and*

(2) has not been found guilty of violating VTL § 511, VTL § 1192, VTL § 1194 or a VTL § 1192-related Penal Law offense during the revocation period;

new DMV regulation 15 NYCRR § 136.10(b) provides that the revocation will only be waived:

(a) after *another five years*; *and*

(b) only if the motorist:

(1) has completed treatment; *and*

    (2) has obtained a certificate of relief from disabilities (or a certificate of good conduct); *and*

    (3) isn't denied relicensure pursuant to 15 NYCRR § 136.4 or 15 NYCRR § 136.5; *and*

    (4) hasn't been found guilty of violating VTL § 511, VTL § 1192, VTL § 1194 or a VTL § 1192-related Penal Law offense during the revocation period; *and*

    (5) hasn't driven during the revocation period—as indicated by accidents, convictions or pending tickets.

In the event that these additional requirements are met and *10 years* has elapsed, DMV will then impose *an additional five years* with restricted driving privileges *and* a mandatory IID requirement for the entire time. *See* 15 NYCRR § 136.5(b)(3).

The new DMV regulations appear to illegally conflict with VTL § 1193(2)(b) (12) in still more ways. For example, VTL §§ 1193(2)(b)(12)(d)/(e) provide for an eight-year, waivable "permanent" driver's license revocation where a person has five DWI-related convictions (and/or chemical test refusal findings) within eight years. This statute provides a clear legislative determination that five DWI-related convictions (and/or chemical test refusal findings) should generally result in an eight-year driver's license revocation—and should only result in such a lengthy license revocation if the convictions occur within a time frame of eight years.

Simply stated, where a person's DWI-related driving record would not result in an eight-year license revocation under the "permanent" revocation statute targeting repeat DWI offenders, it would seem that DMV cannot lawfully enact administrative regulations that trump the statute and impose a greater-than-8-year license revocation on the person. Yet the new DMV regulations impose a permanent lifetime license revocation where a person has 5 DWI-related convictions/incidents over the course of his or her entire lifetime. *See* 15 NYCRR § 136.5(b)(1). *See also* 15 NYCRR Part 132. Thus, if DMV's new regulations are legal, then VTL §§ 1193(2)(b)(12)(d)/(e) are also "superfluous, a result to be avoided in statutory construction." *Litto*, 33 A.D.3d at 626.

Notably, in order for a person to be subject to a five-year license revocation pursuant to VTL § 1193(2)(b)(12)(a)(i), at least one of the person's DWI-related convictions must be for a crime; and in order for a person to be subject to a five-year license revocation pursuant to VTL § 1193(2)(b)(12)(a)(ii), *at least two* of the person's DWI-related convictions must be for crimes. In other words, under the statute it is not enough to merely have four DWI-related convictions within eight years. Rather, at least two of the convictions must be for crimes.

By contrast, the new DMV regulations contain no requirement

that *any* of the person's DWI-related convictions be for a crime. In addition, Zero Tolerance law (*i.e.*, VTL § 1192-a) findings do not count as DWI-related offenses for purposes of VTL § 1193(2)(b) (12), but they do count for purposes of the new DMV regulations. *See* 15 NYCRR §§ 132.1(a) & 136.5(a)(1).

In sum, VTL § 1193(2)(b) (12) provides clear statutory limits regarding (a) when a driver's license can be "permanently" revoked, (b) what offenses can be counted for purposes of "permanent" revocation, and (c) for how long a "permanent" revocation can continue. The new DMV regulations appear to directly and irreconcilably conflict with this statute.

§ 55:24   The five-year IID portion of the new regulations conflicts with VTL § 1198, PL § 65.10(2)(k-1) and case law

The five-year IID portion of 15 NYCRR §§ 3.2(c)(4), 136.4(b)(2) and 136.5(b)(3) conflicts with existing statutes and case law. In this regard, PL § 65.10(2)(k-1) makes clear that an IID can be mandated:

> *[O]nly* where a person has been convicted of a violation of [VTL § 1192(2), (2-a) or (3)], or any crime defined by the [VTL] or [the PL] of which an alcohol-related violation of any provision of [VTL § 1192] is an essential element. The offender shall be required to install and operate the [IID] *only* in accordance with [VTL § 1198].

(Emphases added).

In *People v. Levy*, 91 A.D.3d 793, 794 (2d Dep't 2012), the Appellate Division, Second Department, held that "County Court improperly directed . . . that the defendant install an [IID] on her motor vehicle. . . . Here, the defendant's conviction for operating a motor vehicle while under the influence of drugs pursuant to Vehicle and Traffic Law § 1192(4) falls outside the scope of Penal Law § 65.10(2)(k-1)."

In addition, in *People v. Letterlough*, 86 N.Y.2d 259, 268 (1995), the Court of Appeals made clear that:

> A recent enactment authorizes courts to order a defendant, as a condition of probation, to install an "ignition interlock device" that attaches to the vehicle's steering mechanism and ignition (Vehicle and Traffic Law § 1198) . . . . Clearly, no such legislative initiative would have been necessary if this type of condition could have been imposed by the courts on a case-by-case basis under Penal Law § 65.10's existing catch-all provision.

Levy makes clear that an IID requirement can only be imposed where there is express statutory authorization therefor; and *Letterlough* makes clear that such a requirement cannot be imposed under a generic, "catch-all" provision simply because a Court or an administrative agency thinks it is a good idea.

To make matters worse, 15 NYCRR § 136.5(b)(3) mandates the imposition of a five-year IID requirement on individuals who could not lawfully be subjected to an IID pursuant to either PL § 65.10(2)(k-1) or VTL § 1198 (e.g., individuals who have only been convicted of violating VTL § 1192(1) or VTL § 1192(4), or who have only been found guilty of refusing to submit to a chemical test in violation of VTL § 1194 or of underage drinking and driving in violation of VTL § 1192-a).

In addition, the Legislature has declared that the cost of an IID is a fine. See VTL § 1198(5)(a). It is axiomatic that DMV has no authority to impose—as opposed to collect—fines or fees. See *Matter of Redfield v. Melton*, 57 A.D.2d 491, 495 (3d Dep't 1977). Thus, it appears that the IID portion of the new DMV regulations also constitutes an illegal fine.

§ 55:25 The 25-year look-back portion of the new regulations conflicts with numerous statutes

The Legislature has repeatedly made clear that (unless there was physical injury or the motorist is a commercial driver) the relevant look-back period for DWI-related offenses is never more than 10 years. *See, e.g.*, VTL §§ 1193(1)(a), 1193(1)(c)(i), 1193(1)(c)(ii), 1193(1)(d)(2), 1193(1)(d)(4)(i), 1193(1)(d)(4)(ii), 1193(2)(b)(12)(a), 1193(2)(b)(12)(d), 1194(2)(d)(1), & 1198(3)(a). *See also* PL §§ 120.04(3), 120.04-a(3), 125.13(3), & 125.14(3).

For example, a prior DWI conviction can only be used to elevate the level of a new DWI charge from a misdemeanor to a felony if the prior conviction was within 10 years of the new offense. *See, e.g.*, VTL §§ 1193(1)(c)(i) & 1193(1)(c)(ii). Thus, a person who is charged with DWI 10 years and one day after being convicted of a previous DWI is treated as a first offender. *See, e.g., People v. Smith*, 57 A.D.3d 1410 (4th Dep't 2008) (class D felony DWI reduced to class E felony DWI because one of defendant's two predicate DWI convictions was 10 years and three days old, and it thus could not be counted).

Similarly, a prior DWI conviction can only be used to elevate the level of a Vehicular Assault/Vehicular Manslaughter charge if the prior conviction was within 10 years of the current offense. *See, e.g.*, PL §§ 120.04(3), 120.04-a(3), 125.13(3), & 125.14(3).

A DWAI charge is only a misdemeanor—as opposed to a traffic infraction—if the defendant has two prior VTL § 1192 convictions within the past 10 years. *See* VTL § 1193(1)(a).

A chemical test refusal is only treated as a repeat offense if the motorist has a prior refusal or DWI-related conviction within the previous five years. *See* VTL § 1194(2)(d)(1).

For purposes of issuing a postrevocation conditional license, "the commissioner shall not deny such issuance based solely upon the number of convictions for violations of any subdivision of [VTL § 1192] committed by such person within the ten years prior to application for such license." VTL § 1198(3)(a).

Records pertaining to a VTL § 1192-a finding are required to be sealed after three years or when the motorist turns 21, whichever is longer. *See* CPL § 160.55(5)(c). *See also* VTL § 201(1)(k) ("Upon the expiration of the period for destruction of records pursuant to this paragraph, the entirety of the proceedings concerning the violation or alleged violation of [VTL § 1192-a] . . . from the initial stop and detention of the operator to the entering of a finding and imposition of sanctions . . . shall be deemed a nullity, and the operator shall be restored, in contemplation of law, to the status he occupied before the initial stop and prosecution").

Finally, for purposes of "permanent" driver's license revocation, DWI-related convictions are only relevant for, at most, eight years. *See* VTL § 1193(2)(b) (12).

Simply stated, the Legislature has repeatedly and unequivocally made clear, over a period of decades, that (unless there was physical injury or the motorist is a commercial driver) DWI-related convictions/incidents that are more than 10 years old are too remote in time to be relevant—even in vehicular homicide cases. In changing from a 10-year to a 25-year (and in some cases lifetime) look-back period, the new DMV regulations would appear to conflict with well over a dozen statutes.

§ 55:26 The new regulations violate the separation of powers doctrine

Article III, § 1 of the New York State Constitution provides that "[t]he legislative power of this state shall be vested in the senate and assembly." *See also Matter of Medical Soc'y of State v. Serio*, 100 N.Y.2d 854, 864 (2003). The new DMV regulations are clearly legislative in nature. Indeed, the Governor's press release that accompanied the announcement of the new regulations expressly states that "[u]nder current law, drivers who are convicted of multiple alcohol or drug related driving offenses cannot permanently lose their licenses." The Governor's press release also states that " '[w]e are saying "enough is enough" to those who have chronically abused their driving privileges and threatened the safety of other drivers, passengers and pedestrians.' " *See id.* In the release, DMV Commissioner Fiala is quoted as saying " '[t]he Department of Motor Vehicles is proud to be *working with Governor Cuomo* in a concerted effort to address the problems caused by the most dangerous drivers with a history of repeat alcohol- or drug-related driving offenses.' " *Id.* (emphasis added). These comments make clear that DMV bypassed the Legislature in addressing the issue of repeat DWI offenders.

It is axiomatic that an administrative agency cannot set social policy. Rather, it can only implement social policy enacted by the Legislature. *See Serio*, 100 N.Y.2d at 865 (" '[e]ven under the broadest and most open-ended of statutory mandates, an administrative agency may not use its authority as a license to correct whatever societal evils it perceives' ") (quoting *Boreali v. Axelrod*, 71 N.Y.2d 1, 9 (1987)). In *Boreali*, the Court of Appeals held that:

> Here, we cannot say that the broad enabling statute in issue is itself an unconstitutional delegation of legislative authority. However, we do conclude that the agency stretched that statute beyond its constitutionally valid reach when it used the statute as a basis for drafting a code embodying its own assessment of what public policy ought to be.

71 N.Y.2d at 9. More specifically:

> [T]he Public Health Council overstepped the boundaries of its lawfully delegated authority when it promulgated a comprehensive code to govern tobacco smoking in areas that are open to the public. While the Legislature has given the Council broad authority to promulgate regulations on matters concerning the public health, the scope of the Council's authority under its enabling statute must be deemed limited by its role as an administrative, rather than a legislative, body. In this instance, the Council usurped the latter role and thereby exceeded its legislative mandate, when, following the Legislature's inability to reach an acceptable balance, the Council weighed the concerns of nonsmokers, smokers, affected businesses and the general public and, without any legislative guidance, reached its own conclusions about the proper accommodation among those competing interests. In view of the political, social and economic, rather than technical, focus of the resulting regulatory scheme, we conclude that the Council's actions were ultra vires and that the order and judgment of the courts below, which declared the Council's regulations invalid, should be affirmed.

Id. at 6.

Boreali would appear to compel the conclusion that the new DMV regulations are illegal and ultra vires. While DMV undoubtedly has a certain amount of discretion to decide, on a case-by-case basis, whether a particular individual poses a unique and immediate threat to the motoring public and should be revoked for a longer-than-normal period of time, it is quite another thing for an administrative agency to declare, *with no legislative guidance*, that entire groups—consisting of thousands of individuals—can be generically characterized as "persistently dangerous drivers" and punished far more severely than has ever been thought possible.

This is particularly true where, as here, (a) the groups in question have always existed, (b) the motorists in question had always been permitted to get their licenses back in a well-known time frame, and (c) there has been no legislative determination that a change in circumstances has taken place and/or that a change in policy was necessary (or even welcome). In this regard, the doctrine of legislative acquiescence provides that "[w]here the practical construction of a statute is well known, the Legislature is charged with knowledge and its failure to interfere indicates acquiescence." *Engle v. Talarico*, 33 N.Y.2d 237, 242 (1973).

Simply stated, the Legislature's failure to enact any new legislation addressing the issue of repeat DWI offenders is a tacit acknowledgment that the status quo should not be disturbed. While the executive branch of government may be frustrated by the Legislature's lack of action, taking matters into its own hands violates the separation of powers doctrine and is illegal and ultra vires. *See also People v. Letterlough*, 86 N.Y.2d 259, 269 (1995) ("While innovative ideas to address the serious problem of recidivist drunk driving are not to be discouraged, the courts must act within the limits of their authority and cannot overreach by using their probationary powers to accomplish what only the legislative branch can do"); *id.* ("Since . . . the creation of such a penalty out of whole cloth usurps the legislative prerogative, the condition, however well-intended, cannot be upheld").

Notably, the Appellate Division, First Department, recently struck down New York City's "large soda ban" based upon the separation of powers doctrine as delineated in *Boreali*. *See New York Statewide Coalition of Hispanic Chambers of Commerce v. New York City Dep't of Health and Mental Hygiene*, __ A.D.3d __, 2013 WL 3880139 (1st Dep't 2013).

§ 55:27 The new regulations are being applied retroactively

One of the more disturbing aspects of the new DMV regulations is that DMV is applying them to offenses that were committed—and to license revocations that had commenced—prior to the date that the regulations were enacted. In this regard, it is axiomatic that "[t]he States are prohibited from enacting an *ex post facto* law." *Garner v. Jones*, 529 U.S. 244, 249 (2000). *See also Peugh v. United States*, 133 S.Ct. 2072, 2081 (2013). "One function of the *Ex Post Facto* Clause is to bar enactments which, by retroactive operation, increase the punishment for a crime after its commission." *Garner*, 529 U.S. at 249. *See also Peugh*, 133 S.Ct. at 2081.

In *Garner*, *supra*, the United States Supreme Court made clear that retroactive changes to the rules governing the parole of inmates can violate the *Ex Post Facto* Clause. 529 U.S. at 250.

See also Peugh, 133 S.Ct. at 2085. *Peugh*, which was decided by the Supreme Court on June 10, 2013, held that "there is an *ex post facto* violation when a defendant is sentenced under Guidelines promulgated after he committed his criminal acts and the new version provides a higher applicable Guidelines sentencing range than the version in place at the time of the offense." 133 S.Ct. at 2078. In so holding, the Court reasoned as follows:

> A retrospective increase in the Guidelines range applicable to a defendant creates a sufficient risk of a higher sentence to constitute an *ex post facto* violation. . . .
>
> Our holding today is consistent with basic principles of fairness that animate the *Ex Post Facto* Clause. The Framers considered *ex post facto* laws to be "contrary to the first principles of the social compact and to every principle of sound legislation." The Clause ensures that individuals have fair warning of applicable laws and guards against vindictive legislative action. * * *
>
> [T]he *Ex Post Facto* Clause does not merely protect reliance interests. It also reflects principles of "fundamental justice." * * *
>
> "[T]he *Ex Post Facto* Clause forbids the [government] to enhance the measure of punishment by altering the substantive 'formula' used to calculate the applicable sentencing range." That is precisely what the amended Guidelines did here. Doing so created a "significant risk" of a higher sentence for Peugh, and offended "one of the principal interests that the *Ex Post Facto* Clause was designed to serve, fundamental justice."

Id. at 2084–85, 2088 (citations omitted).

Critically, the *Peugh* Court—citing *Garner*—stated that "our precedents make clear that the coverage of the *Ex Post Facto* Clause is not limited to legislative acts." *Id.* at 2085. Numerous federal Circuit Courts of Appeals have also made clear that administrative regulations are subject to the *Ex Post Facto* Clause where they have "the force and effect of law." *See, e.g., Metheny v. Hammonds*, 216 F.3d 1307, 1310 (11th Cir. 2000); *Shabazz v. Gabry*, 123 F.3d 909, 915 n.12 (6th Cir. 1997); *Hamm v. Latessa*, 72 F.3d 947, 957 (1st Cir. 1995); *Dehainaut v. Pena*, 32 F.3d 1066, 1073 (7th Cir. 1994); *Flemming v. Oregon Bd. of Parole*, 998 F.2d 721, 726 (9th Cir. 1993); *U.S. ex rel. Forman v. McCall*, 709 F.2d 852, 559 (3d Cir. 1983) ("We note at the outset that the fact that the guidelines are administrative regulations rather than statutes does not preclude their being 'laws' for ex post facto purposes, for it is a fundamental principle of administrative law that '[v]alidly promulgated regulations have the force and effect of law' ") (citation omitted).

Regardless of whether the *Ex Post Facto* Clause technically applies to the new regulations, in *Bowen v. Georgetown Univ. Hosp.*, 488 U.S. 204, 208–09 (1988), the Supreme Court held as follows:

> Retroactivity is not favored in the law. Thus, congressional enact-

ments *and administrative rules* will not be construed to have retroactive effect unless their language requires this result. By the same principle, a statutory grant of legislative rulemaking authority will not, as a general matter, be understood to encompass the power to promulgate retroactive rules unless that power is conveyed by Congress in express terms. *Even where some substantial justification for retroactive rulemaking is presented, courts should be reluctant to find such authority absent an express statutory grant.*

(Emphases added) (citations omitted).

In this regard, New York Courts—including the Third Department—have also recognized a presumption that new administrative regulations, like new laws, apply prospectively. *See, e.g., Matter of Montgomerie v. Tax Appeals Tribunal*, 291 A.D.2d 129, 132 (3d Dep't 2002); *Matter of Rudin Mgmt. Co. v. Commissioner, Dep't of Consumer Affairs*, 213 A.D.2d 185, 185 (1st Dep't 1995); *Matter of Good Samaritan Hosp. v. Axelrod*, 150 A.D.2d 775, 777 (2d Dep't 1989); *Matter of Linsley v. Gallman*, 38 A.D.2d 367, 369 (3d Dep't 1972), *aff'd on opinion below*, 33 N.Y.2d 863 (1973).

Retroactively changing the rules applicable to the length of a driver's license revocation after a person has pled guilty to a VTL § 1192 offense (and/or after the person has applied for relicensure) is analogous to retroactively changing the rules applicable to how long the person will remain in prison for the offense. In both situations the person has a legitimate—indeed Constitutional—expectation at the time of sentencing/application that the rules then in effect will not change after the fact. Faith in our legal system would literally evaporate if sentences can validly be changed, long after a plea bargain is entered, at the whim of an administrative agency. Notably, the *Peugh* Court repeatedly made clear that one of the principal interests that the *Ex Post Facto* Clause was designed to serve is "fundamental justice."

In *People v. Luther*, 41 Misc. 3d 185, __, 970 N.Y.S.2d 674, 681 (East Rochester Just. Ct. 2013), aff'd, 48 Misc. 3d 699, 12 N.Y.S.3d 491 (Monroe Co. Ct. 2014), the Court held that:

The fundamental concept of the prohibition of ex post fact laws is putting a defendant on notice that certain conduct may lead to specified violations and consequences. In this case, at the time of the violation and the plea, the defendant was not on notice that a third violation of V & T § 1192(3) would or could lead to a suspension of driving privileges for two (2) years [sic five (5) years] beyond the mandatory six (6) month revocation. While DWI was illegal before and after the regulatory change, the punishment/consequences as to driving privileges were [more than] quadrupled. While this may or may not constitute an ex post facto law, it certainly violates basic[ ] principals of justice.

The defendant's motion to vacate the plea of guilty is granted. The matter is restored to the trial calendar on all pending charges.

(Citations omitted). *Cf. People v. Wheaton*, __ Misc. 3d __, __ N.Y.S.3d __, 2015 WL 3751408 (Seneca County Ct. 2015) (Court disagrees with *Luther*'s conclusion that CPL § 440.10 is applicable to this type of situation).

§ 55:28   Although DMV can theoretically deviate from the new regulations in "unusual, extenuating and compelling circumstances," in reality this standard cannot be met

15 NYCRR § 136.5(d) provides that:

> While it is the Commissioner's *general policy* to act on applications in accordance with this section, the Commissioner shall not be foreclosed from consideration of unusual, extenuating and compelling circumstances that may be presented for review and which may form a valid basis to deviate from the *general policy*, as set forth above, in the exercise of discretionary authority granted under sections 510 and 1193 of the Vehicle and Traffic Law. If an application is approved based upon the exercise of such discretionary authority, the reasons for approval shall be set forth in writing and recorded.

(Emphases added). *See also* 15 NYCRR § 132.3.

According to 15 NYCRR § 136.5(d), the new DMV regulations are merely a "general policy" that DMV is free to deviate from in its discretion upon a showing of "unusual, extenuating and compelling circumstances." It is the authors' understanding, however, that the DMV employees at the Driver Improvement Bureau who review "compelling circumstances" claims are instructed to never grant them. As such, the employees who review such claims in reality have no discretion whatsoever. They simply deny them all.

In this regard, it appears that DMV's so-called "general policy" is not a general policy at all. Rather, it is a hard-and-fast rule that (a) has no exceptions, and (b) has the force and effect of law. Notably, the DMV regulations do not define what would constitute "unusual, extenuating and compelling circumstances"; nor are there any guidelines to assist a DMV employee in rendering such a determination. Accordingly, even if it is theoretically possible to meet this standard, there is no policy in effect to ensure that similarly situated individuals are treated similarly. Thus, even if "compelling circumstances" claims are actually judged on their merits (which they aren't), the claims are reviewed in an arbitrary and capricious manner.

§ 55:29   Court of Appeals to decide the lawfulness of the new regulations

There are currently three cases pending before the Court of

Appeals that are challenging the lawfulness of the new regulations on a variety of grounds. The relevant Appellate Division decisions are *Matsen v. New York State Dept. of Motor Vehicles*, 134 A.D.3d 1283, 21 N.Y.S.3d 441 (3d Dep't 2015); *Carney v. New York State Dept. of Motor Vehicles*, 133 A.D.3d 1150, 20 N.Y.S.3d 467 (3d Dep't 2015); and *Acevedo v. New York State Dept. of Motor Vehicles*, 132 A.D.3d 112, 14 N.Y.S.3d 790 (3d Dep't 2015).

APPENDICES

Department of Motor Vehicles Regulations

APPENDIX 1 *[Reserved]*

APPENDIX 2

New York City Police Intoxicated Driver Testing Unit Evaluation

---

REQUEST TO PERFORM COORDINATION TESTS   (2)

M_____, I would like you to do some simple
tests to see if your physical coordination is impaired. Each test
will be explained to you. That camera will photograph your actions
and anything you say will be recorded. You have a right to refuse
to take these tests or stop at any time without penalty.

Now M _____ ARE YOU WILLING TO TAKE THIS TEST

****

***** If prisoner "REFUSES"- Then say ********

Let it be a matter of record that the prisoner has refused to submit
to a filmed and recorded coordination test. Video-Tape coverage is
hereby ended.

(E36842)

- PREFACE -   (1)

This is Police Officer _____ Sh.#_____ I.D.T.U.
about to offer a Breathalyzer test to:

_____ Arrest #____, _____ Pct.

Time is now_____ _____ 196___

Arresting Officer is Police Officer_____

Shield #_____ of the _____Precinct.

Camera Technician is Police Officer _____

Shield #_____of the I.D.T.U.

(E36842)   **BM 225 (10-84)**

HIGHWAY DISTRICT INTOXICATED DRIVER EVALUATION   (1)

Mr./Ms. _____ you have been arrested for driving
while intoxicated. I am here to conduct a CHEMICAL BREATH TEST to determine
the presence or absence of alcohol in your blood. You may take this test or
refuse to do so. A refusal to submit to a chemical test will result in the
immediate suspension and subsequent revocation of your license or operating
privilege , whether or not you are found guilty of the charge for which you
were arrested.

Your refusal to submit to a chemical test can be introduced in evidence
against you at any trial, proceeding, or hearing resulting from this arrest.
If you take this test, the results may be used against you in a court of law.
"WILL YOU SUBMIT TO A CHEMICAL TEST OF YOUR BREATH?"

If the defendant states that he will submit to the test, the IDTU
Technician will announce that "VIDEO TAPE WILL BE SUSPENDED UNTIL COMPLETION
OF THE BREATHALYZER TEST."

If the defendant states that he will not submit to the test, the IDTU
Technician shall proceed and offer the coordination test to the defendant.

(E36843)

SPEECH TEST   (3)

M _____ _____

   for the purpose of identification ....

- Will you please tell me your name ?

- Where do you live ?

- How old are you ?

   ....THANK YOU..............

CLEAR   SLURRED   INCOHERENT   OTHER   REFUSED

[ ]   [ ]   [ ]   [ ]   [ ]

                                                        (E3685)

BALANCE TEST   (4)

M _____, I want to see if you can stand up straight.
Let me show you what I want you to do before you start.

Stand up straight, face me, like this'
Put your feet together, like this'
Put your head back, like this' look at the ceiling'
Now close your eyes,
Stay like that until I count to ten'

Allright M _____ *(repeat).

Allright M _____ Open your eyes, Thank you

STEADY   SWAYING   SAGGING   FALLING   REFUSED

[ ]   [ ]   [ ]   [ ]   [ ]

                                                        (E3686)

FINGER TO NOSE TEST   (5)

Now, M _____, I would like you to touch the tip of
your nose with the tip of the index finger of each hand. This is the
index finger.
Let me show you what to do before you start;

Stand up straight like this'
Lift your arms up like this'
Close your eyes'
Now, touch the tip of your nose with the tip of the right index finger
Now, touch the tip of your nose with the tip of the left index finger
Put your arms down'

Allright M _____, let's begin.......*(repeat).

HAND   ACCURATE   INACCURATE   REFUSED
R
[ ]   [ ]   [ ]   [ ]
L
[ ]   [ ]   [ ]   [ ]

                                                        (E3687)

WALKING AND TURNING TEST   (7)

M _____, Please turn around, I would like you to
walk back and forth on this line. Let me explain to you what I
want you to do before you start walking.

NOW. Walk along this line in your normal walking manner, <u>Stop</u>
      on my command, turn around and walk back along the line, <u>Stop</u>
      on my command, turn around and walk back along the line and
      <u>Stop</u> on my command

Allright M _____, #(repeat).

TEST WALKING TURNING	STEADY	UNSTEADY	FALLING	OTHER	REFUSED
	☐	☐	☐	☐	☐

(E3689)

COIN TEST   (6)

Now, M _____, Will you please step back ?
I am going to place three coins (Quarters) on the floor right in
front of you. I would like you to pick them up and give them back
to me.

        (place coins along the tape, at least three feet apart)

Allright M _____, take your time, pick up those coins
          and give them back to me!

        Thank you!

STEADY	UNSTEADY	UNABLE	OTHER	REFUSED
☐	☐	☐	☐	☐

(E3688)

HANDWRITING SPECIMEN   (8)

M _____, will you sit in that chair ?

M _____, for the purpose of identification,
will you please write your name next to the X on this line.

                (if the prisoner refuses)

Since you won't write your name, will you write your address ?
NOTE: (only request the prisoner to write his name or address)

Prisoner wrote:	NAME	ADDRESS	REFUSED
	☐	☐	☐

For the record--- M _____, has written,

(E3690)

CONCLUSION   (9)

Thank you M _____

The coordination test is finished.........

Video-Tape coverage is hereby ended.

****

(LJ691)

APPENDIX 3

New York State Department of Health Rules and Regulations for Chemical Tests (Breath, Blood, Urine and Saliva)

PART 59 CHEMICAL ANALYSIS OF BLOOD, URINE, BREATH OR SALIVA FOR ALCOHOLIC CONTENT

(Statutory authority: Environmental Conservation Law, § 11-1205(6); Vehicle and Traffic Law, §§ 1194(4)(c), 1198(6))

[Current with amendments included in the New York State Register, Volume XXXVIII, Issue 34, dated August 24, 2016.]

Sec.

Section 59.1. Definitions

(a) **Techniques and methods** means the collection, processing and determination of the alcoholic content of body fluids such as human blood, saliva or urine, and of breath or alveolar air by protocols and/or instruments determined by the commissioner to be acceptable.

(b) **Per centum by weight of alcohol** as used in the Vehicle and Traffic Law and the Environmental Conservation Law means percent weight per volume, that is, grams of alcohol per 100 milliliters of whole blood.

(c) **Chemical tests/analyses** include breath tests conducted

1671

on breath analysis instruments approved by the commissioner in accordance with section 59.4 of this Part.

(d) **Training agency or agencies** means the Office of Public Safety of the Division of Criminal Justice Services, the Division of State Police, the Nassau County Police Department, the Suffolk County Police Department, and/or the New York City Police Department.

(e) **Commissioner** means the New York State Commissioner of Health.

(f) **Department** means the New York State Department of Health.

(g) **Ignition interlock device** means any blood alcohol concentration equivalence measuring device which connects to a motor vehicle ignition system and prevents a motor vehicle from being started without first determining through a deep lung breath sample that the operator's equivalent breath alcohol level does not exceed the calibrated setting on the device as required by standards in this Part.

(h) **Blood alcohol concentration (BAC)** means the weight amount of alcohol contained in a unit volume of blood, measured as grams ethanol/100 ml blood and expressed as %, grams %, % weight/volume (w/v), and % BAC. Blood alcohol concentration in this Part shall be designated as % BAC.

(i) **Testing laboratory** means a nationally recognized, independent materials testing laboratory that is not affiliated with, and operates autonomously from, any ignition interlock device manufacturer, is properly equipped and staffed to carry out test procedures required by this Part, and is independently accredited in accordance with requirements for the competence of testing and calibration laboratories promulgated as a standard by the International Organization for Standardization (ISO), or other commensurate standard acceptable to the department.

(j) **Breath analysis instrument** means a device that complies with section 59.4 of this Part.

(k) **Saliva** means oral fluid.

(l) **Calibration** means the activity of verifying that a value generated by the instrument is in acceptable agreement with the assigned value for a traceable and/or certified reference standard, including any adjustment to the instrument to bring it into acceptable agreement.

[Current with amendments included in the New York State Register, Volume XXXVIII, Issue 34, dated August 24, 2016.]

Section 59.2. Techniques and methods for determining blood and urine alcohol

(a) All blood and urine alcohol determinations shall be made by quantitative methods and reported as whole blood alcohol concentration (BAC) to the second decimal place as found; for example, 0.137 percent found shall be reported as 0.13 percent weight per volume. If specimens other than whole blood are analyzed, the following conversions shall apply:

(1) three fourths of the determined concentration of alcohol in the urine shall be equivalent to the corresponding BAC; and

(2) nine tenths of the determined concentration of alcohol in the serum or plasma shall be equivalent to the corresponding BAC.

(b) Analytical procedures for blood and urine alcohol analysis shall include the following controls in conjunction with any sample or series of 10 samples analyzed sequentially or simultaneously:

(1) a blank analysis as appropriate; and

(2) analysis of a suitable reference sample of known alcoholic content greater than or equal to 0.08 percent weight per volume, the result of which analysis shall agree with the reference sample value within the limits of plus or minus 0.01 percent weight per volume or such limits as specified by the commissioner.

(c) An analysis of urine shall be made upon two specimens collected at least 30 minutes apart.

(d) If a blood specimen is to be collected for analysis, an aqueous solution of a nonvolatile antiseptic shall be used on the skin. Alcohol or phenol shall not be used as a skin antiseptic.

(e) Specimens shall be clearly identified at the time of collection.

[Current with amendments included in the New York State Register, Volume XXXVIII, Issue 34, dated August 24, 2016.]

Section 59.3. Blood, urine and saliva alcohol analysis; permits

(a) Individuals performing chemical analyses for blood, urine and saliva alcohol content may apply to the commissioner for a permit.

(b) A permit for the performance of chemical analyses for blood, urine and saliva alcohol content shall be issued by the commissioner to an applicant who:

(1) is a high school graduate and has one year of laboratory experience acceptable to the commissioner; or

(2) has satisfactorily completed two years of college study and has six months of laboratory experience acceptable to the commissioner; and

(3) demonstrates to the satisfaction of the commissioner proficiency in the chemical analyses of the alcoholic content of blood and any other sample type that the commissioner requires; and

(4) has access to appropriate laboratory facilities for the performance of such analyses.

(c) The applicant shall demonstrate proficiency in the techniques and methods of analysis by correctly analyzing and reporting results, within limits of accuracy established by the commissioner, for 75 percent of the samples for each set of proficiency tests issued by the commissioner.

(d) A permit shall be issued for a period of one year and may be renewed annually thereafter. A permit shall not be issued or renewed if, for two consecutive sets of proficiency tests, the applicant or permit holder:

(1) does not meet the proficiency requirements of this section; or

(2) fails to report proficiency test results; or

(3) reports results after three weeks from the date of distribution of proficiency test samples, except that the commissioner, for good cause, may extend such time on request made during such three-week period.

[Current with amendments included in the New York State Register, Volume XXXVIII, Issue 34, dated August 24, 2016.]

Section 59.4. Breath analysis instruments

(a) The commissioner approves, for use in New York State, breath analysis instruments found on the Conforming Products List of Evidential Breath Alcohol Measurement Devices as established by the U.S. Department of Transportation/National Highway Traffic Safety Administration (NHTSA), published in the Federal Register on March 11, 2010 (75 Fed. Reg. 11624-11627, available for public inspection and copying at the Department of Health Records Access Office, Corning Tower, Empire State Plaza, Albany, NY 12237). A facsimile of that list is set forth in subdivision (b) of this section. At the request of a training agency, the commissioner may approve a breath analysis instrument that has been accepted by NHTSA but is not on the Conforming Products List published in the Federal Register on March 11, 2010, if the commissioner determines that approval of such instrument is appropriate.

(b) Conforming Products List of Evidential Breath Measurement Devices

Federal Register / Vol. 75, No. 47 / Thursday, March 11, 2010 / Notices

CONFORMING PRODUCTS LIST OF EVIDENTIAL BREATH MEASUREMENT DEVICES		
Manufacturer and model	Mobile	Nonmobile
Alcohol Countermeasure Systems Corp., Mississauga, Ontario, Canada:		

CONFORMING PRODUCTS LIST OF EVIDENTIAL BREATH MEASUREMENT DEVICES		
Manufacturer and model	Mobile	Nonmo-bile
Alert J3AD*	X	X
Alert J4X.ec	X	X
PBA3000C	X	X
BAC Systems, Inc., Ontario, Canada:		
Breath Analysis Computer*	X	X
CAMEC Ltd., North Shields, Tyne and Ware, England:		
IR Breath Analyzer*	X	X
CMI, Inc., Owensboro, Kentucky:		
Intoxilyzer Model:		
200	X	X
200D	X	X
240 (aka: Lion Alcolmeter 400+ outside the U.S.)	X	X
300	X	X
400	X	X
400PA	X	X
1400	X	X
4011*	X	X
4011A*	X	X
4011AS*	X	X
4011AS -A*	X	X
4011AS -AQ*	X	X
4011 AW*	X	X
4011A27 -10100*	X	X
4011A27 -10100 with filter*	X	X
5000	X	X
5000 (w/Cal. Vapor Re-Circ.)	X	X
5000 (w/3/8″ ID Hose option)	X	X
5000CD	X	X
5000CD/FG5	X	X
5000EN	X	X
5000 (CAL DOJ)	X	X
5000VA	X	X
8000	X	X
PAC 1200*	X	X
S -D2	X	X

CONFORMING PRODUCTS LIST OF EVIDENTIAL BREATH MEASUREMENT DEVICES		
Manufacturer and model	Mobile	Nonmobile
S -D5 (aka: Lion Alcolmeter SD -5 outside the U.S.)	X	X
Draeger Safety, Inc. (aka: National Draeger) Irving, Texas: Alcotest Model:		
6510	X	X
6810	X	X
7010*	X	X
7110*	X	X
7110 MKIII	X	X
7110 MKIII -C	X	X
7410	X	X
7410 Plus	X	X
7510	X	X
9510	X	X
Breathalyzer Model:		
900	X	X
900A*	X	X
900BG*	X	X
7410	X	X
7410 -II	X	X
EnviteC by Honeywell GmbH, Fond du Lac, Wisconsin:		
AlcoQuant 6020	X	X
Gall's Inc., Lexington, Kentucky:		
Alcohol Detection System-A.D.S. 500	X	X
Guth Laboratories, Inc., Harrisburg, Pennsylvania:		
Alcotector BAC -100	X	X
Alcotector C2H5OH	X	X
Intoximeters, Inc., St. Louis, Missouri:		
Photo Electric Intoximeter*		X
GC Intoximeter MK II*	X	X
GC Intoximeter MK IV*	X	X
Auto Intoximeter*	X	X
Intoximeter Model:		
3000	X	X
3000 (rev B1)*	X	X

CONFORMING PRODUCTS LIST OF EVIDENTIAL BREATH MEASUREMENT DEVICES		
Manufacturer and model	Mobile	Nonmobile
3000 (rev B2)*	X	X
3000 (rev B2A)*	X	X
3000 (rev B2A) w/FM option*	X	X
3000 (Fuel Cell)*	X	X
3000 D*	X	X
3000 DFC*	X	X
Alcomonitor		X
Alcomonitor CC	X	X
Alco-Sensor III	X	X
Alco-Sensor III (Enhanced with Serial Numbers above 1,200,000)	X	X
Alco-Sensor IV	X	X
Alco-Sensor IV XL	X	X
Alco-Sensor V	X	X
Alco-Sensor AZ	X	X
Alco-Sensor FST	X	X
Intox EC/IR	X	X
Intox EC/IR II	X	X
Intox EC/IR II (Enhanced with serial number 10,000 or higher)X		
Portable Intox EC/IR	X	X
RBT -AZ	X	X
RBT -III	X	X
RBT III -A	X	X
RBT IV	X	X
RBT IV with CEM (cell enhancement module)	X	X
Komyo Kitagawa, Kogyo, K.K., Japan:		
Alcolyzer DPA -2*	X	X
Breath Alcohol Meter PAM 101B*	X	X
Lifeloc Technologies, Inc., (formerly Lifeloc, Inc.), Wheat Ridge, Colorado:		
PBA 3000B	X	X
PBA 3000-P*	X	X
PBA 3000C	X	X
Alcohol Data Sensor	X	X
Phoenix	X	X

CONFORMING PRODUCTS LIST OF EVIDENTIAL BREATH MEASUREMENT DEVICES		
Manufacturer and model	Mobile	Nonmo-bile
Phoenix 6.0	X	X
EV 30	X	X
FC 10	X	X
FC 20	X	X
Lion Laboratories, Ltd., Cardiff, Wales, United Kingdom:		
Alcolmeter Model:		
300	X	X
400	X	X
400+ (aka: Intoxilyzer 240 in the U.S.)	X	X
SD -2*	X	X
SD -5 (aka: S -D5 in the U.S.)	X	X
EBA*	X	X
Intoxilyzer Model:		
200	X	X
200D	X	X
1400	X	X
5000 CD/FG5	X	X
5000 EN	X	X
Luckey Laboratories, San Bernardino, California:		
Alco-Analyzer Model:		
1000*		X
2000*		X
Nanopuls AB, Uppsala, Sweden:		
Evidenzer	X	X
National Patent Analytical Systems, Inc., Mansfield, Ohio:		
BAC DataMaster (with or without the Delta-1 accessory):		
BAC Verifier DataMaster (w/or without the Delta-1 accessory)	X	X
DataMaster cdm (w/or without the Delta-1 accessory)	X	X
DataMaster DMT	X	X
Omicron Systems, Palo Alto, California:		
Intoxilyzer Model:		

CONFORMING PRODUCTS LIST OF EVIDENTIAL BREATH MEASUREMENT DEVICES		
Manufacturer and model	Mobile	Nonmo- bile
4011*	X	X
4011AW*	X	X
PAS International, Fredericksburg, Virginia:		
Mark V Alcovisor	X	X
Plus 4 Engineering, Minturn, Colorado:		
5000 Plus 4*	X	X
Seres, Paris, France:		
Alco Master	X	X
Alcopro	X	X
Siemans-Allis, Cherry Hill, New Jersey:		
Alcomat*	X	X
Alcomat F*	X	X
Smith and Wesson Electronics, Springfield, Massachusetts:		
Breathalyzer Model:		
900*	X	X
900A*	X	X
1000*	X	X
2000*	X	X
2000 (non-Humidity Sensor)*	X	X
Sound-Off, Inc., Hudsonville, Michigan:		
AlcoData	X	X
Seres Alco Master	X	X
Seres Alcopro	X	X
Stephenson Corp.:		
Breathalyzer 900*	X	X
Tokai-Denshi Inc., Tokyo, Japan:		
ALC -PRO II (US)	X	X
U.S. Alcohol Testing, Inc./Protection Devices, Inc., Rancho Cucamonga, California:		
Alco-Analyzer 1000		X
Alco-Analyzer 2000		X
Alco-Analyzer 2100	X	X
Verax Systems, Inc., Fairport, New York:		
BAC Verifier*	X	X
BAC Verifier Datamaster	X	X

CONFORMING PRODUCTS LIST OF EVIDENTIAL BREATH MEASUREMENT DEVICES		
Manufacturer and model	Mobile	Nonmobile
BAC Verifier Datamaster II*	X	X

* Instruments marked with an asterisk (*) meet the Model Specifications detailed in 49 FR 48854 (December 14, 1984) (i.e., instruments tested at 0.000, 0.050, 0.101, and 0.151 BAC.) Instruments not marked with an asterisk meet the Model Specifications detailed in 58 FR 48705 (September 17, 1993), and were tested at BACs = 0.000, 0.020, 0.040, 0.080, and 0.160. All instruments that meet the Model Specifications currently in effect (dated September 17, 1993) also meet the Model Specifications for Screening Devices to Measure Alcohol in Bodily Fluids.

(c) No law enforcement agency shall use a breath analysis instrument unless the training agency has verified that representative samples of the specific make and model perform properly. Maintenance shall be conducted as specified by the training agency, and shall include, but shall not be limited to, calibration at a frequency as recommended by the device manufacturer or, minimally, annually.

(d) Training agencies shall be responsible for maintaining records pertaining to verification and maintenance (including calibration) of breath analysis instruments and standards; provided, however, that record keeping maintenance may be delegated, in whole or in part, to the law enforcement agency using the breath analysis instrument(s).

[Current with amendments included in the New York State Register, Volume XXXVIII, Issue 34, dated August 24, 2016.]

Section 59.5. Breath analysis; techniques and methods

The following breath analysis techniques and methods shall be a component of breath analysis instrument operator training provided by training agencies and shall be used by operators performing breath analysis for evidentiary purposes:

(a) A breath sample shall be collected at the direction and to the satisfaction of a police officer and shall be analyzed with breath analysis instruments meeting the criteria set forth in section 59.4 of this Part.

(b) The subject shall be observed for at least 15 minutes prior to the collection of the breath sample, during which period the subject must not have ingested alcoholic beverages or other fluids, regurgitated, vomited, eaten, or smoked, or have placed anything in his/her mouth; if the subject should regurgitate, vomit, smoke or place anything in his/her mouth, an additional 15-minute waiting period shall be required.

(c) A system purge shall precede both the testing of each subject and the analysis of the reference standard.

(d) The result of an analysis of a reference standard with an alcoholic content greater than or equal to 0.08 percent must agree with the reference standard value within the limits of plus or minus 0.01 percent weight per volume, or such limits as set by the commissioner. An analysis of the reference standard shall precede or follow the analysis of the breath of the subject in accordance with the test sequence established by the training agency. Readings for the reference standard, a blank and the subject's breath, shall be recorded.

(e) Results of an analysis of breath for alcohol shall be expressed in terms of percent weight per volume, to the second decimal place as found; for example, 0.237 percent found shall be reported as 0.23 percent.

[Current with amendments included in the New York State Register, Volume XXXVIII, Issue 34, dated August 24, 2016.]

Section 59.6. Breath analysis permit program

Training agencies shall submit an application for approval of a breath analysis permit program or a training program for breath analysis to the commissioner. Other agencies seeking approval of such programs shall submit an application to the commissioner through the Office of Public Safety of the Division of Criminal Justice Services. The application shall include:

(a) a description of the techniques and methods to be utilized;

(b) the make and model of the breath analysis instruments used;

(c) an outline of the material presented in the breath analysis instrument operator and technical supervisor training program;

(d) the name of the individual primarily responsible for each training program and for the breath analysis program;

(e) the name and qualifications of one or more individuals meeting the requirements for technical supervisor under section 59.9 of this Part; and

(f) such other information as the commissioner shall require.

[Current with amendments included in the New York State Register, Volume XXXVIII, Issue 34, dated August 24, 2016.]

Section 59.7. Breath analyzer operator permits

(a) A permit valid for two years shall be issued by the commissioner to breath analysis instrument operators who have completed an approved program based upon standards acceptable to the training agency and certified by the commissioner. Such program shall consist of a minimum of 24 hours of instruction and training with identified learning objectives, supervised by one or more individuals certified as technical supervisors, and shall include:

(1) three hours of instruction on the effects of alcohol on the human body;

(2) five hours of instruction on operational principles of the selected techniques and methods, including a functional description and a detailed operational description of the breath analysis instrument(s) with a demonstration;

(3) five hours of instruction on the legal aspects of chemical tests generally, and of the particular techniques and methods to be employed;

(4) three hours of instruction on supplemental information to include nomenclature appropriate to the field of chemical tests for alcohol;

(5) six hours of laboratory participation using approved breath analysis instruments and simulators, or other reference standards;

(6) a passing score on a one-hour formal examination designed to evaluate whether the operator has met the course learning objectives; and

(7) a demonstration of analytical proficiency on each breath analysis instrument for which the operator is seeking certification.

(b) A permit as a breath analysis instrument operator shall be renewed for a two-year period, provided that, within the 120 calendar days preceding the permit's expiration date, the operator: completes a retraining program that minimally includes an instructional course in breath analysis designed to refresh and update the operator's knowledge in areas described in subdivision (a) of this section; satisfactorily meets the course's learning objectives as determined by a technical supervisor; demonstrates analytical proficiency on each breath analysis instrument for which the operator is seeking permit renewal; and attains a passing score on a formal examination; or, in lieu of such formal retraining, with the concurrence of the responsible training agency, provided that the operator and his/her superior officer submits to the training agency, a written declaration that the operator has performed six or more breath analyses on subjects in accordance with this Part on each breath analysis instrument for which the operator is seeking permit renewal during the 24 months preceding permit expiration. Notwithstanding such a submission, every four years all operators shall participate successfully in the retraining course described in this subdivision.

(c) (1) Whenever a breath analysis instrument operator's

permit is not renewed prior to the expiration date, the commissioner may extend such expiration date for 30 calendar days, provided that the training agency and operator jointly submit a written request for such extension, describing the reasons for the failure to renew in a timely manner. The operator's permit shall remain valid during the 30-day extension period.

(2) If the operator fails to meet the conditions for permit renewal pursuant to subdivision (b) of this section within the extension period authorized pursuant to paragraph (1) of this subdivision, the permit shall become void and not renewable; an operator whose permit becomes void may apply for a new permit by repeating the requirements of subdivision (a) of this section; and the effective date of any such new permit shall be the date of commissioner approval, without back dating to the date on which the prior permit became void.

(d) A training agency shall submit to the commissioner documentation of breath analysis instrument operator training for initial issuance and renewal of a permit in a format designated by the commissioner.

[Current with amendments included in the New York State Register, Volume XXXVIII, Issue 34, dated August 24, 2016.]

Section 59.8.   Revocation or suspension of permits

(a) The commissioner or the training agencies may at any time and from time to time require breath analysis instrument operators or technical supervisors to demonstrate their ability to operate properly the breath analysis instrument(s) for which they hold a permit.

(b) The operator's permit may be revoked by the commissioner based on information acquired by the commissioner, or a training agency, that the operator does not conduct breath tests in accordance with techniques and methods as instructed by the training agency, that the operator's performance is unreliable, or the operator is incompetent. Upon revocation, the operator shall return any and all permits to the commissioner.

(c) The training agency may suspend the permit of any operator under its supervision when, in its judgment, the operator does not conduct breath tests in accordance with techniques and methods as established by the training agency, the operator's performance is unreliable or the operator is incompetent. The training agency shall immediately notify the commissioner in writing of any such suspension and furnish a copy of such notice to the suspended operator, who shall not be permitted to operate the breath analysis instrument until such time as the suspension is removed.

(d) An operator whose permit has been suspended by the training agency may appeal to the commissioner who shall decide whether suspension shall be affirmed or set aside. The commissioner may reinstate the permit of the operator making such appeal under such conditions as the commissioner deems necessary.

(e) An operator whose permit has been revoked shall not be eligible for a new permit within 12 months from the date of revocation or at such other time as may be determined by the commissioner.

[Current with amendments included in the New York State Register, Volume XXXVIII, Issue 34, dated August 24, 2016.]

Section 59.9. Technical supervisor; qualifications and certification

(a) The commissioner may authorize certification of an applicant as technical supervisor for a period of four years, provided such applicant submits satisfactory evidence through the training agency that he/she meets the following qualifications:

(1) thirty semester hours of college credits, including eight semester hours of chemistry;

(2) certification as an operator of the breath analysis instrument(s) to be supervised, or possession of equivalent experience or training to qualify as an operator; and

(3) satisfactory completion of a technical supervisor's course, the content of which shall include:

(i) advanced survey of current information concerning alcohol and its effect on the human body (one hour);

(ii) operational principles and theories applicable to the program (two hours);

(iii) breath analysis instrument maintenance and calibration (two hours);

(iv) legal aspects of chemical testing (one hour); and

(v) principles of instruction (two hours); or

(4) training and experience equivalent to a technical supervisor's course and acceptable to the commissioner.

(c) A technical supervisor shall have responsibility for:

(1) breath analysis instrument operator training, competency evaluation, and periodic examination to ensure maintenance of technical knowledge and proficiency;

(2) maintenance, including calibration of breath analysis instruments and equipment under his/her supervision and preparation and standardization of chemicals used for testing and/or evaluation of such chemicals, by direct performance of such tasks or by delegating performance to another person with demonstrated competency, but who need not be qualified as a technical supervisor; provided, however, when-

ever such tasks are so delegated, the technical supervisor shall review the work product to ensure that the assigned designee's performance meets expectations; and

(3) periodic inspection of breath analysis instrument performance.

(d) A technical supervisor's certificate may be renewed for a period of four years upon submission of a written application and statement that he/she has carried out his/her duties in accordance with this Part. Suspension or revocation pursuant to section 59.8 of this Part of a breath analysis instrument operator's permit held by a technical supervisor shall result in suspension or revocation, respectively, of the individual's certification as a technical supervisor.

[Current with amendments included in the New York State Register, Volume XXXVIII, Issue 34, dated August 24, 2016.]

Section 59.10.   Certification criteria for ignition interlock devices

(a) A manufacturer of ignition interlock devices shall apply to the department to certify a device for use in New York State. The application shall be on a form or format specified by the department with documents appended as necessary to provide the requisite information, and shall include, but not be limited to:

(1) name and address of the manufacturer, and contact information, including identification of a person to respond to department inquiries;

(2) name and model of the ignition interlock device;

(3) a detailed description of the ignition interlock device, including: instructions for its installation and operation; technical specifications, including, but not limited to, accuracy; calibration stability; data security; and capability for data collection and recording, tamper detection, and retesting; and unsupervised operation in a range of environmental conditions;

(4) the manufacturer's statement that all ignition interlock devices of the same make and model sold or offered for sale or lease, for which certification is sought, meet the requirements of this Part; and

(5) a certificate or other document from an insurance carrier licensed in New York State demonstrating that the manufacturer holds product liability insurance with minimum liability limits of one million dollars per occurrence and three million dollars aggregate. The documentation shall include the issuing company's statement that at least thirty (30) days notice will be provided to the department whenever the issuing company intends to cancel the insurance before

the policy's expiration date. Liability coverage shall include defects in product design and materials, as well as in manufacture, calibration, installation and removal of devices.

(b) The manufacturer shall provide the testing laboratory with:

(1) six representative instruments of each ignition interlock device model for which certification is sought, from which the testing laboratory shall select at least two for testing;

(2) instructions for device installation and operation; and

(3) a description of the device's capabilities, including, but not limited to: security; data collection and recording; tamper detection; circumvention prevention; retesting; and unsupervised operation in a range of environmental conditions.

(c) At the request of a manufacturer of ignition interlock devices, the commissioner shall certify the ignition interlock device for use in New York State, provided the manufacturer:

(1) demonstrates, through arrangements with a testing laboratory, that the model meets or exceeds the model specifications for breath alcohol ignition interlock devices adopted by NHTSA and published in the Federal Register on April 7, 1992 (57 Fed. Reg. 11772–11787, available for public inspection and copying at the Department of Health Records Access Office, Corning Tower, Empire State Plaza, Albany, NY 12237);

(2) demonstrates, through arrangements with a testing laboratory, that the device meets the model specifications specified in paragraph (1) of this subdivision when calibrated to a set point of 0.025% BAC;

(3) has requested certification for a device that employs fuel cell technology or another technology with demonstrated comparable accuracy and specificity;

(4) has demonstrated that the certified device can and would be installed to allow normal operation of the vehicle after it is started, except as specifically approved by the department; and

(5) has demonstrated compliance with all the requirements of this Part.

(d) Certification shall be effective as of the date of its issuance.

(e) Certified ignition interlock devices installed in vehicles shall be uniquely serial-numbered.

(f) Each certification shall cover only one model of ignition interlock device. Modifications to a model of a device, without regard to the manufacturer's assigning a new model number, shall be reported to the department as required in section 59.12 of this Part.

(g) The department may deny, suspend or revoke the certification of an ignition interlock device for reasons including:

(1) the device does not meet the requirements for certification specified in this Part, including but not limited to, the commissioner's determination that the testing laboratory misrepresented a device's meeting such requirements;

(2) the manufacturer has failed to comply with any requirement of this Part or of Part 358 of Title 9 of the Official Compilation of Codes, Rules and Regulations of the State of New York;

(3) substantial evidence exists that devices manufactured, sold, leased, offered for sale or leased, or installed in vehicles do not function in accordance with the specifications in this Part or are easily circumvented or tampered with;

(4) substantial evidence exists that the manufacturer has not made adequate provision for effective and timely maintenance, inspection, calibration and repair of installed devices;

(5) the manufacturer is no longer in the business of manufacturing devices;

(6) the manufacturer fails to retain the required product liability insurance, including through cancellation or non-renewal;

(7) the manufacturer has been convicted of a crime or offense related to fraud; or

(8) the ignition interlock device does not meet federal model specifications for breath alcohol ignition interlock devices adopted by NHTSA after the specifications referred to in paragraph (1) of subdivision (c) of this section are adopted.

(h) Notice of an ignition interlock device's certification, discontinuation, suspension and revocation shall be published in the State Register, and shall be provided promptly to the Division of Probation and Correctional Alternatives. The commissioner shall make available a list of certified ignition interlock devices upon request.

[Current with amendments included in the New York State Register, Volume XXXVIII, Issue 34, dated August 24, 2016.]

Section 59.11. Testing of ignition interlock devices

(a) The department may require a testing laboratory, as defined in section 59.1 of this part, to submit its credentials for department review prior to accepting any report submitted by the testing laboratory in support of an ignition interlock device manufacturer's application for certification.

(b) The testing laboratory shall provide, directly to the

department, a detailed report of test data and findings of the ignition interlock device's performance on each standard, generated by the testing laboratory, documenting that at least two representative instruments of an ignition interlock device model have successfully met the requirements of subdivision (c) of section 59.10 of this Part.

(c) The testing laboratory's report shall minimally include: a description of tests performed; data and findings for each test conducted, with numerical readouts as appropriate; a description of the effectiveness of the ignition interlock device's security provisions, if any, for detection and recording of attempted tampering and preventing circumvention; the reliability of the device's data recording features; and a description of the effectiveness of the device over a range of environmental conditions. The report shall include a dated and signed attestation by the person supervising such testing that identifies the ignition interlock device model and manufacturer, and states that all tests on the named device model were conducted in accordance with NHTSA specifications.

[Current with amendments included in the New York State Register, Volume XXXVIII, Issue 34, dated August 24, 2016.]

Section 59.12. Continued ignition interlock device certification

(a) An ignition interlock device certification shall remain in effect until:

(1) the manufacturer files a written request for discontinuance;

(2) the department issues to the manufacturer a written notice of suspension or revocation of approval; or

(3) the manufacturer modifies the device so that it does not meet the federal model specifications for breath alcohol ignition interlock devices in effect when it was certified.

(b) No manufacturer who makes an operational modification to a model of an ignition interlock device that has been certified pursuant to this Part shall release the modified device for use pursuant to Vehicle and Traffic Law Section 1198 without having obtained the express approval of the department. Manufacturers shall submit to the department a description of the intended operational modification(s), and the commissioner shall determine either that the existing certification shall continue in effect for the ignition interlock device as modified or that the manufacturer must apply for separate certification for the modified device. For purposes of this section, "operational modification" means any change to product design or function that would or could affect the device's anti-circumvention, anti-tampering or analytical features, as determined by the department.

(c) A manufacturer shall ensure that the department is provided with documentation of current insurance by notifying the department in writing of each renewal of coverage, each change of issuing company, and each change in liability limits.

(d) The department may require manufacturers whose devices are certified pursuant to this Part to periodically renew the certifications. Information required for renewal of certification shall minimally include:

(1) verification that information on file with the department, including, but not limited to, manufacturer's address and contact person, is current;

(2) an attestation that the department has been notified of any operational modification made to the certified model, or that no modification was made; and

(3) documentation of current insurance coverage.

(e) Each device shall be provided with a supply of disposable spit-trap mouthpieces, and the manufacturer shall ensure availability of additional mouthpieces.

(f) A manufacturer shall provide to installation/service providers that install its certified device(s) a sufficient number of labels to label each device installed and replace labels as needed. The label shall contain a notice printed in at least 10-point boldface type, reading as follows: "WARNING—ANY PERSON TAMPERING, CIRCUMVENTING OR OTHERWISE MISUSING THE DEVICE IS GUILTY OF A MISDEMEANOR AND MAY BE SUBJECT TO CIVIL LIABILITY."

[Current with amendments included in the New York State Register, Volume XXXVIII, Issue 34, dated August 24, 2016.]

APPENDIX 4

Letter from Department of Motor Vehicles Regarding Relicensure of Probationers

JOHN A. PASSIDOMO
Commissioner

STATE OF NEW YORK
DEPARTMENT OF MOTOR VEHICLES
THE GOVERNOR NELSON A. ROCKFELLER EMPIRE STATE PLAZA, ALBANY, NEW YORK 12228

June 10, 1985

Peter Gerstenzang, Esq.
41 State Street
Albany, New York 12207

Dear Mr. Gerstenzang:

This is in response to your recent telephone inquiry.

Our present policy concerning probationers is to code them ineligible for the drinking driver program and conditional licenses. We require permission from the individual's probation officer before we will allow these people into the program.

This policy was a result of complaints from several probation departments. We had permitted probationers to obtain conditional licenses when the terms of probation forbade driving. Unfortunately, we had not been advised of the prohibitions.

At the request of Suffolk County probation, we are attempting to make all their probationers eligible. If we have problems from the existence of two policies, we shall drop the exception in Suffolk cases.

Very truly yours,

Alfred J. Frakes, Director
Driving Licensing Services

AJF:maf

APPENDIX 5

Drug Influence Evaluation Form

NEW YORK STATE DRUG INFLUENCE EVALUATION

Evaluator		DRE #	Rolling Log #	Evaluator's Agency

Recorder/Witness	Crash: ☐ None ☐ Fatal ☐ Injury ☐ Property	Arresting Officer (Name, ID#)

Arrestee's Name (Last, First, Middle)	Date of Birth	Sex	Race	Arresting Officer Agency

Date Examined / Time /Location	Breath Results: Test Refused ☐ Results Instrument #:	Chemical Test: Urine ☐ Blood ☐ Test or tests refused ☐

Miranda Warning ☐ Yes ☐ No Given By:	What have you eaten today? When?	What have you been drinking?	How much?	Time of last drink?

Time now/ Actual	When did you last sleep?	How long?	Are you sick or injured? ☐ Yes ☐ No	Are you diabetic or epileptic? ☐ Yes ☐ No

Do you take insulin? ☐ Yes ☐ No	Do you have any physical defects? ☐ Yes ☐ No	Are you under the care of a doctor or dentist? ☐ Yes ☐ No

Are you taking any medication or drugs? ☐ Yes ☐ No	Attitude:	Coordination:

Speech:	Breath Odor:	Face:

Corrective Lenses: ☐ None ☐ Glasses ☐ Contacts, if so ☐ Hard ☐ Soft	Eyes: ☐ Reddened Conjunctiva ☐ Normal ☐ Bloodshot ☐ Watery	Blindness: ☐ None ☐ Left ☐ Right	Tracking: ☐ Equal ☐ Unequal
Pupil Size: ☐ Equal ☐ Unequal (explain)	Vertical Nystagmus ☐ Yes ☐ No	Able to follow stimulus ☐ Yes ☐ No	Eyelids ☐ Normal ☐ Droopy

Pulse and time	HGN	Left Eye	Right Eye	Convergence	ONE LEG STAND
1 ___ / ___	Lack of Smooth Pursuit				
2 ___ / ___	Maximum Deviation				
3 ___ / ___	Angle of Onset				

Modified Romberg Balance	Walk and Turn Test					ONE LEG STAND

Modified Romberg Balance — approx / approx

Walk and Turn Test:
- Cannot keep balance
- Starts too soon
- Stops walking
- Misses heel-toe
- Steps off line
- Raises arms
- Actual steps taken

1st Nine / 2nd Nine

	L	R
Sways while balancing	☐	☐
Uses arms to balance	☐	☐
Hopping	☐	☐
Puts foot down	☐	☐

Internal clock estimated as 30 seconds	Describe turn	Cannot do test (explain)	Type of footwear:

Draw lines to spots touched

R / L

2 4 5 / 1 3 6

PUPIL SIZE	Room Light (2.5 – 5.0)	Darkness (5.0 – 8.5)	Direct (2.0 – 4.5)	Nasal area:
Left Eye				
Right Eye				Oral cavity:

Rebound Dilation: ☐ Yes ☐ No	Pupillary Unrest: ☐ Yes ☐ No	Reaction to Light:

RIGHT ARM **LEFT ARM**

Blood pressure	Temperature
Muscle tone: ☐ Normal ☐ Flaccid ☐ Rigid Comments:	

What drugs or medications have you been using?	How much?	Time of use?	Where were the drugs used? (Location)

Date / Time of arrest:	Time DRE was notified:	Evaluation start time:	Evaluation completion time:	Precinct/Station:

Officer's Signature:	DRE #	Reviewed/approved by / date:

Opinion of Evaluator:	☐ Rule Out ☐ Medical	☐ Alcohol ☐ CNS Depressant	☐ CNS Stimulant ☐ Hallucinogen	☐ Dissociative Anesthetic ☐ Narcotic Analgesic	☐ Inhalant ☐ Cannabis

Revised 5/2013

APPENDIX 6

Drug Symptom Chart

DRUG ABUSE RECOGNITION PROGRAM: SYMPTOMOLOGY CHART

	HGN	VERT NYST	NON-CONV	PULSE	PUPIL SIZE	REACTION	POSSIBLE EFFECTS	DURATION OF EFFECTS	METHODS OF INGESTION	OVERDOSE SYMPTOMS
ALCOHOL	YES	POSS WITH HIGH B.A.	YES	POSS UP	NEAR NORMAL	SLOW	BLOODSHOT/WATERY EYES, ALCOHOL BEV. ODOR, UNCOORDINATED, SLURRED SPEECH, ELEV. B.P.	RAPID ABSORPTION RATE OF METABOLIZATION: .02 B.A. REDUCTION PER HOUR	ORAL	COMA, COLD CLAMMY SKIN, RAPID AND WEAK PULSE, TOTAL LOSS OF CONTACT W/WORLD, DEAD DRUNK
DEPRESSANTS	YES	POSS WITH HIGH DOSE	YES	DOWN	NEAR NORMAL	SLOWED	BLOODSHOT/WATERY EYES, NO ALCOHOL ODOR, UNCOORDINATED, SLURRED SPEECH, DROWSY	BARBITURATE: 1-16 HR METHAQUALONE: 4-8 HR TRANQUILIZERS: 4-8 HR CHLORAL HYDRATE: 5-8 HR	ORAL INJECTED	COMA, COLD CLAMMY SKIN, RAPID AND WEAK PULSE, TOTAL LOSS OF CONTACT W/WORLD, DEATH
INHALANTS	GENERALLY PRESENT BUT DEPENDS ON SUBSTANCE			UP	DEPENDS ON SUBSTANCE	NEAR NORMAL	ODOR OF SUBSTANCE, CONFUSED, REDDENED NASAL PASSAGES, WATERY EYES, SNEEZING / COUGHING	VARIABLE (DEPENDS ON SUBSTANCE)	INHALATION	UNCONSCIOUS COMA DEATH
PHENCYCLIDINE	YES	YES	YES	UP	NEAR NORMAL	NEAR NORMAL	SLOW SPEECH, MEMORY LOSS, AGITATION, BLANK STARE, NON-COMMUNICATIVE, RIGIDITY, CYCLIC BEHAVIOR, GAIT ATAXIA	ONSET: 1-5 MIN PEAK: 15-30 MINS HALF-LIFE: 4-5 HRS NORMALCY: 24-48 HRS	ORAL SMOKED INJECTION ABSORBED INHALATION	VIOLENT BEHAVIOR, PARANOIA, SEIZURES, PSYCHOSIS, HEART FAILURE, DEATH
CANNABIS	NO	NO	YES	UP	NEAR NORMAL OR SLIGHT DILATION	NEAR NORMAL	REDDENING OF CONJUNCTIVAE, LACK OF INHIBITIONS, BODY TREMORS, DISORIENTED, LACK OF DIVIDED ATTENTION	ONSET: MINUTES PEAK: 20-30 MINS HALF-LIFE: 1-3 HRS NORMALCY: VARIED DUE TO FAT SOLUBILITY	SMOKING ORAL	FATIGUE PARANOIA PSYCHOSIS
HALLUCINOGENS	GENERALLY NOT PRESENT DEPENDS ON SUBSTANCE			UP	DILATION	SLOWED	TREMORS, HALLUCINATIONS, POOR TIME DISTANCE PERCEPT., SYNESTHESIA, FLASHBACKS, PILOERECTION (LSD)	VARIABLE (DEPENDS ON SUBSTANCE)	ORAL SMOKED INHALED INJECTION ABSORBED	LONGER, MORE INTENSE TRIPS, PSYCHOSIS, DEATH
NARCOTIC ANALGESICS	NO	NO	NO	DOWN	CONSTRICTION	LITTLE OR NO VISIBLE REACTION	PTOSIS, MUSCLE RELAXATION, COOL TO TOUCH, ITCHING, DRY MOUTH, EUPHORIA, FEW OVER VEIN, CONSTIPATION	HEROIN: 4-6 HRS DEMEROL: 3-4 HRS CODEINE: 3-4 HRS DARVON: 6-12 HRS FENTANYL: 5-2? MINS METHADONE: 22-25 HRS	INJECTION ORAL SNORTING SMOKING	SHALLOW BREATHING, COLD/CLAMMY SKIN, RAPID/WEAK PULSE, RESPIRATORY DEPRESSION, DEATH
STIMULANTS	NO	NO	NO	UP	DILATION	SLOWED	RESTLESS, TALKATIVE, HYPERFLEXIA, DRY MOUTH, BRUXISM, BODY TREMORS, LOSS OF APPETITE, PARANOIA	COCAINE: 15-90 MINS (DEPENDS ON INGESTION METHOD) METHAMPHETAMINE: 4-8 HRS	ORAL SMOKING SNORTING INJECTION	AGITATION, PARANOIA, CONVULSIONS, PSYCHOSIS

APPENDIX 7

A Guide to Direct Examination of a Drug Recognition Expert

A GUIDE TO THE DIRECT EXAMINATION OF A DRUG
RECOGNITION EXPERT*

By Peter Gerstenzang, Esq.

41 State Street

Albany, New York 12207

Copyright ©1995

Peter Gerstenzang, Esq.

All Rights Reserved

Table of Contents

---

*GERSTENZANG, O'HERN, HICKEY & GERSTENZANG, 41 State
Street, Albany, New York 12207.

A GUIDE TO THE DIRECT EXAMINATION OF A DRUG RECOGNITION EXPERT

Introduction

In October of 1989, the New York City Department of Transportation STOP-DWI Program sponsored and funded a two-day workshop, the purpose of which was to design a prosecution for the crime of driving while under the influence of drugs. Dr. Ilona Lubman and Linda Irengreene, Esq. of the Department of Transportation organized this program. The workshop was held under the supervision of the Kings County District Attorney's Office and was conducted by six senior prosecutors: Barry Aaron, Esq., Criminal Court, Bureau Chief; Dana Paisinelli, Esq., Supervising Assistant District Attorney, Criminal Court Bureau; Don Berke, Esq., Supervising Assistant District Attorney, Criminal Court Bureau; Mark Schindelheim, Esq., Transit and Auto Crimes Bureau Chief, Joe Petrosino, Esq., Transit and Auto Crimes Deputy Bureau Chief, and Jane Meyers, Esq., Director of Training.

Judge Cliff J. Vanell, who was then an Assistant District Attorney with the City of Phoenix, Arizona's Prosecutor's Office, was invited to attend as a consultant. Judge Vanell is a national expert on the prosecution of driving while under the influence of drugs and has completed the NHTSA curriculum for the Drug

Evaluation and Classification Program. He wrote a programmed workbook to guide prosecutors through the Drug Influence Evaluation used by drug recognition experts. In addition to his contributions to the workshop, Judge Vanell designed the format of this trial guide and assisted in the development of its content.

Former Inspector Terrence Randell and Lieutenant Ernest Gormley of the New York City Police Department contributed time, personnel and expertise to this project. Both Inspector Randell and Lieutenant Gormley had been involved with the drug recognition program since its inception and were directly responsible for the development of this program in New York City.

Six drug recognition experts from the New York City Police Department provided technical advice and assistance. My thanks to Sergeant Joseph Ficarola, Officer John Itzhaki, Officer Michael Pisano, Officer Steve Placido, Officer Steven Stasinski, and Officer Eugene Venezia.

I would also like to acknowledge the contributions of Dr. William J. Closson, Director of Clinical Chemistry and Toxicology, the Brunswick Hospital Center, Inc.; and Henry Boland of the New York State Bureau for Municipal Police who reviewed the guide prior to its publication.

The trial guide that follows is designed to elicit detailed testimony from a drug recognition expert regarding the procedure followed in evaluating a defendant. The guide does not attempt to establish a foundation for obtaining the expert's opinion as to the category of drug the expert concludes has been used by the defendant. Until both the evaluation process and the training given the DREs has been granted judicial recognition in New York State, it is going to be very difficult to qualify a DRE as an expert for the purpose of obtaining his or her opinion. Absent such recognition, a physiologist or some other recognized expert should be called for the purpose of providing an opinion as to the classification of drugs which would produce the symptoms observed by the DRE. The observations of the arresting officer and the Drug Recognition Expert combined with the opinion of an expert witness, and the testimony of the toxicologist as to the specific drug found in the defendant's blood, constitute the People's case.

DIRECT EXAMINATION OF A DRUG RECOGNITION EXPERT

By PETER GERSTENZANG, ESQ.

Copyright ©1995

Peter Gerstenzang, Esq.

Q. Would you state your name, rank, shield number and command for the record?

A.

Q. How long have you been employed as a police officer?

A.

Q. I direct your attention to (date of arrest) and ask you if you were working on that date?

A.

Q. What hours were you working?

A.

Q. Who, if anyone, were you working with?

A.

Q. What were the nature of your duties that date?

A.

Q. I direct your attention to the hour of (time officer arrived at the Intoxicated Driver Testing Unit) and ask you to tell the Court where you were?

A. I was at the Intoxicated Driver Testing Unit.

Q. What was your purpose for being there?

A. I am a drug recognition expert and I was there for the purpose of conducting an evaluation.

Q. Who was the subject of that evaluation?

A. (Defendant's name.)

Q. Do you see the individual that was the subject of this evaluation in the courtroom?

A. Yes.

Q. Would you point him out please?

Let the record reflect that the witness has identified the defendant (name).

DRE DEFINED

Q. What is a Drug Recognition Expert?

A. A DRE is a person who has been trained in a standardized
    method of determining whether observable physical impair-
    ment and behavior is the result of the use of drugs. If drug
    use is suspected, the method provides procedures for
    determining whether the observable impairment is the result
    of alcohol alone, or whether it is a result of other drugs. The
    method also provides procedures for determining the cate-
    gory of drugs which is causing the impairment. (Obtained
    and modified from Phoenix, Arizona Prosecutor's Guide, page
    5.)

DRE TRAINING

Q. What did the training consist of?

A. The training consisted of 56 hours of classroom training and
    hands on evaluation of defendants. This was followed by 40
    hours of supervised certification training. I was required to
    conduct and write 15 evaluations under the supervision of a
    certified drug recognition instructor and I had to correctly
    evaluate a minimum of four categories of drugs, which were
    verified by Toxicology. (Phoenix, Arizona Prosecutor's Guide,
    page 6)*

Q. What was covered in your classroom training?

A. We were trained to distinguish between seven broad catego-
    ries of drug groups based on shared symptomatology. We
    were also trained to do a standard evaluation sequence and
    to record and document the results of our evaluation on a
    standardized form which also serves as a checklist for the
    procedure. Finally, we were trained in how to interpret the
    results obtained from the evaluation.

Q. What is the basis for grouping drugs into seven categories?

A. We were trained that drugs could be grouped based upon
    common or shared symptoms.

Q. What are these seven groups?

A.

1) Central nervous system depressants.
2) Central nervous system stimulants.
3) Hallucinogens.
4) Phencyclidine.
5) Narcotic Analgesics.
6) Inhalants.

---

*Current minimum requirements are in flux. These were the NYPD stan-
dards as of June 1989. The International Association of Chiefs of Police (IACP),
the National Certifiers of DRE's have adopted minimum standards which
require 12 evaluations in three categories. Each police agency is encouraged to
exceed the minimum standards.

7) Cannabis.

Q. Were you tested in regard to your qualifications?

A. Yes. I was given a qualifying exam as well as oral and written certification tests. Finally, I was observed by (number of instructors, must be at least 2) instructors who recommended me for certification.

Q. What was the result of that testing?

A. I qualified as a DRE.

Q. Upon being qualified, were you issued any form of certification?

A. Yes.

Q. I show you People's _____ for identification and ask you to tell the court what it is.

A. This is my certification as a Drug Recognition Expert issued by the International Association of Chiefs of Police.

   (At this time, I offer People's _____ for identification into evidence.)

Q. How long have you been a Drug Recognition Expert?

A. (Number of years as DRE.)

Q. How many people have you tested using these techniques?

A. (Number of people tested.)

Q. Did you perform a drug evaluation of the defendant?

A. Yes I did.

Q. How many different parts are there to the evaluation of a person to determine whether they are under the influence of a drug?

A. There are 8 basic parts of the examination.

Q. What are the evaluation procedures?

A.

   (1) Breath alcohol test.

   (2) Interview of the arresting officer.

   (3) Preliminary assessment of a person's speech, breath, appearance, demeanor, behavior.

   (4) A two part eye examination, the first part consisting of examining the subject's eyes for jerking movement, tracking ability, and ability to converge; the second part consisting of examining the subject's eyes for pupil size and the effect of light on the pupils.

   (5) Psycho-physical evaluation of the subject based on divided attention tests.

   (6) Examination of the subject's vital signs (blood pressure, pulse rate and temperature).

(7) Examination of the subject for drug administration sites. This consists of an inspection of the subject's nose and mouth for signs of drug ingestion; and examination of the subject's arms and neck for signs of drug ingestion and muscle tension.

(8) Obtaining urine sample.

DRUG EVALUATION PROCEDURE

1. Breath Alcohol Test

Q. What was the first part of that evaluation?

A. The first is a breath alcohol test to determine whether alcohol is the cause or contributing factor for the physical impairment of the defendant.

Q. What type of breath alcohol test was performed?

A. (Possible answers: Alco-Sensor, Breathalyzer, Intoxilyzer or Intoximeter 3000) [Foundation may or may not be required where evidence indicates that alcohol was not a cause or contributing factor to the impairment of the defendant]. Before eliciting testimony as to negative Alco-Sensor test *at trial*, see *People v. Thomas*, 121 A.D.2d 73, 509 N.Y.S.2d 668 (4th Dept. 1986), aff'd 70 N.Y.2d 823, 523 N.Y.S.2d 437, 517 N.E.2d 1323 (1987); also see *People v. Salino*, 139 Misc.2d 386, 527 N.Y.S.2d 169 (1988) where New York City Criminal Court holds that negative breath alcohol test neither relevant nor admissible.

Q. What if anything did the breath alcohol test indicate as to whether alcohol was the cause or contributing factor to the physical impairment of the defendant?

A. The test indicated that alcohol was/was not a cause or contributing factor to the physical impairment of the defendant.

2. Interview of Arresting Officer

Q. What was the second component of the test you performed on the defendant?

A. The second component was an interview of the arresting officer as to his observations of the defendant.

Q. Was this done?

A. Yes.

Q. Did you obtain the officer's observations?

A. Yes. (Elicit fact that you obtained his observations, i.e., something that you did; not something that the arresting officer said which is hearsay. Alternatively, argue that you are not offering the contents of the officer's observations, merely proof that the officer's observations were obtained as part of the procedures. Hopefully, arresting officer will have already testified as to his observations.)

3. Preliminary Questioning

Q. What was the third part of the test?

A. The third part consists of preliminary questioning. These are questions asked of the defendant and observations made of the defendant as he answers these questions.

Q. What questions did you ask him?

A. I don't recall them verbatim as I sit here. I followed our drug evaluation form which contains the questions.

Q. Would it refresh your recollection of the questions to refer to the drug evaluation form?

A. Yes it would.

    (Your Honor, I request that the witness be allowed to refresh his recollection by referring to the drug evaluation form. Mark form for identification.)

Q. I show you People's _____ for identification and ask if this is the drug evaluation form you are referring to?

A. Yes.

Q. Officer, would you please refer to People's _____ for identification and tell us the questions you asked the defendant and the defendant's answers.

A.

(1) What time is it now?
Defendant's answer: _____

(2) When did you sleep last?
Defendant's answer: _____

(3) How long?
Defendant's answer: _____

(4) Do you take insulin?
Defendant's answer: _____

(5) Are you taking any medication or drugs?
Defendant's answer: _____

(6) What have you eaten today?
Defendant's answer: _____

(7) When did you eat?
Defendant's answer: _____

(8) Are you sick or injured?
Defendant's answer: _____

(9) Do you have any physical defects?
Defendant's answer: _____

(10)   What have you been drinking?

Defendant's answer: _____

(11)   How much have you been drinking?

Defendant's answer: _____

(12)   Are you a diabetic or epileptic?

Defendant's answer: _____

(13)   Are you under the care of a doctor or dentist?

Defendant's answer: _____

Q. What if any observations did you make of the defendant while he was speaking?

    (1)   Speech?

    (2)   Breath odor?

    (3)   Face?

4. Eye Examinations

A. Eye Movements

Q. What was the fourth test that you performed?

A. The next portion of the test is observing how the defendant's eyes move. (Avoid use of technical terminology such as "horizontal gaze nystagmus.")

Q. How is this performed?

A. This test is performed by having the defendant follow a moving object with his eyes for the purpose of seeing whether the eyes move smoothly or with a jerking motion?

i. Smooth Pursuit

Q. How is this test performed?

A. There are five parts to this test. The first part is simply moving an object, usually a pen, from a point near the person's nose outwards towards the side of his face so that the eyeball follows it from one side of the eye to the other. (Have witness demonstrate various motions with pen throughout testimony.)

Q. Did you perform this part of the test on the defendant?

A. Yes I did.

Q. Which eye did you do first?

A. I did the left eye.

Q. What if any observations did you make of the left eye in the performance of this test?

A. As I moved the pen from one side of his left eye to the other, his eye moved in a jerky (or smooth motion).

Q. Did you perform this part of the test on the defendant's right eye?

A. Yes I did.

Q. What if any observations did you make of the right eye?

A. As I moved the pen from one side of his right eye to the other, his eye moved in a jerky (or smooth motion).

ii. Maximum Deviation

Q. What is the second part of this test?

A. The second part of this test is to get the defendant to follow the pen so that his left eyeball moves to the outer corner of his eye. You hold the pen steady and see if the left eye jerks while it is at that position.

Q. Did you perform this portion of the test on the defendant?

A. Yes I did.

Q. How long did you have him hold his eye at the outer corner?

A. About four seconds.

Q. What did you observe?

A.

Q. Did you perform this part of the test on the defendant's right eye?

A. Yes I did.

Q. What did you observe?

A.

iii. Onset of Jerking

Q. What is the third part of this test?

A. The third part is checking to see *if* and at what angle with the nose the eye starts to jerk.

Q. How is this portion of the test performed?

A. This is done by placing the pen about 15 inches from the defendant's nose and slowly moving the pen toward the outer corner of his eye. I start with the left eye and watch it closely for the first sign of jerking. If I see any jerking, I stop moving the pen and hold it steady. I make sure that the eye really is jerking. If it is not, the procedure is to start moving the pen further towards the outer portion of the eye and watch for jerking. If there is jerking, I locate the point at which the jerking begins and estimate the angle of this point with the defendant's nose.

Q. Did you perform this portion of the test in regard to the defendant's left eye?

A. Yes I did.

Q. What did you observe?

A.

Q. Did you perform this portion of the test in regard to the defendant's right eye?

A. Yes I did.

Q. What did you observe?

A.

iv. Vertical Movement

Q. What was the fourth eye test you performed?

A. This test involves having the defendant move his eyes up and down while holding his head still. Instead of holding the pen up and down in front of his eyes, I held the pen sideways and asked him to look at the middle ring that divides the top of the pen from the bottom of the pen. I then moved the pen straight up and then down and watched how his eyes followed the pen. I looked to see if there was any jerkiness in his eyes as he followed the pen.

Q. Did you perform this test upon the defendant?

A. Yes I did.

Q. What did you observe?

A.

B. Eye Convergence

Q. What is the fifth part of the eye test?

A. The fifth part of the eye test was done by holding the pen about 15 inches in front of the defendant's face with the tip of it pointing at his nose. The defendant was asked to hold his head still and follow the pen with his eyes. Keeping the pen about 15 inches from the defendant's nose, I moved the pen in a slow circle. Once I determined that the defendant was following the pen as I moved it, I brought it slowly and steadily in towards the bridge of his nose. I did this to see whether or not both eyes would move together and converge at the bridge of his nose.

Q. What were the results of this test?

A. (Answer).

C. Pupil Size*

Q. What was the next part of the test?

A. Observing whether the defendant's pupils were of equal size.

---

*Usually performed during the preliminary examination.

Q. How did you determine this?

A. I estimated the defendant's pupil size using an eye gauge that has different sizes of pupils. (Identify and offer the gauge into evidence.)

Q. How does the eye gauge work?

A. The eye gauge has a series of dark circles, with diameters ranging from 1.0 mm to 9.0 mm, in half millimeter increments. The eye gauge is held up along side the defendant's eye and the gauge is moved up or down until I located the circle closest in size to the defendant's pupil.

Q. What was the result of this test?

A. (Result of this test.)

D. Pupil Reaction

Q. What was the next part of the examination?

A. The next part is called the dark room examination.

Q. What is the dark room examination?

A. These are observations of the size of the defendant's pupils at various levels of light.

Q. What were the different levels of light that you used?

A. We estimated the pupil size at room light, near total dark, indirect light, and direct light.

i. Room Light

Q. How was the room light portion of this test performed?

A. The test was performed by determining the size of the defendant's pupils in room light.

Q. What were the results of the room light portion of the evaluation?

A. (Detail results.)

ii. Darkness

Q. How was the near total darkness portion of the evaluation conducted?

A. The defendant was taken into a room which was almost completely dark. There was a waiting period of 90 seconds to allow both the defendant's and my eyes to adapt to the dark. Then the defendant's eyes were examined by use of a penlight. I covered the tip of the penlight with my finger and thumb so that only a reddish glow and no white light emerged. Holding the glowing tip of the penlight, I moved the light up towards the defendant's left eye until I could see the pupil, separate and apart, from the colored portion of the eye or the iris. I held the tip of the penlight, brought the eye gauge up alongside the defendant's left eye and located the circle that was closest in size to the pupil as it appeared in the dark room. I then repeated this procedure on the defendant's right eye.

Q. What were the results of this portion of the examination?

A. (Detail results of evaluation.)

iii. Indirect

Q. How was the indirect light portion of the evaluation conducted.

A. Upon completion of the near total darkness portion of the exam, I uncovered the tip of the penlight and shone it across the defendant's left eye so that the light just barely eliminated the shadow from the ridge of his nose. I made sure that the light did not shine directly into the defendant's eye, but rather across it. I held the penlight in that position and brought the eye gauge up alongside the defendant's left eye. I located the circle that came closest to the size of the defendant's pupil and repeated the process on the defendant's right eye.

Q. What were the results of this portion of the evaluation?

A. (Detail results of evaluation.)

iv. Direct

Q. How was the direct light portion of the evaluation conducted?

A. For the direct light portion of the examination, I left the tip of the penlight uncovered and brought it from the side of the defendant's face and shone it directly into the defendant's left eye. I held the penlight in that position and brought the eye gauge up alongside the left eye and found the circle closest in size to the pupil. I then repeated that procedure for the defendant's right eye. The results of all four examinations were recorded.

Q. What were the results of this portion of the evaluation?

A. (Detail results of evaluation.)

5. Psycho-physical Tests

Q. What is the fifth part of the DRE examination?

A. The fifth part is the divided attention or psycho-physical tests.

Q. How many parts are there to this part of the examination?

A. There are four psycho-physical tests.

Q.   Are these psycho-physical tests used exclusively for drug rec-
     ognition evaluations?

A.   No.

Q.   Under what other circumstances are they used?

A.   They are standardized field sobriety tests which are used in
     cases involving alcohol as well as drugs.

Q.   In addition to the drug recognition evaluation and training,
     have you received any other training concerning these
     psycho-physical tests?

A.   Yes, (detail training you received.)

A. Romberg Balance Test

Q.   What was the first psycho-physical test that was performed
     upon the defendant?

A.   The first was the Romberg Balance test.

Q.   Prior to asking the defendant to perform this test, did you
     explain and demonstrate the test to him?

A.   Yes.

Q.   Would you explain and demonstrate this test for the court
     and jury in the same manner that you explained and demon-
     strated it for the defendant on the date of arrest?

A.   The defendant was asked to stand straight with his feet
     together and his arms down at his sides. He was told to stay
     in this position while he was being given the instructions.
     Part of the test is to see if he would follow that instruction
     and not try to start the test until told to begin. The defendant
     was then asked if he understood the instructions. The
     defendant was then instructed that when told to "begin" he
     was to tilt his head back slightly and close his eyes. Once he
     had done this, he was told that he must keep his head tilted
     back with his eyes closed until *he thought* 30 seconds had
     gone by.

Q.   What is the purpose of this?

A.   The purpose is to observe his balance and his perception of
     time. The defendant was told that when he thought 30
     seconds had gone by, he was to immediately put his head
     forward and open his eyes. The defendant was once again
     asked if he understood and then he was told to begin.

ROMBERG BALANCE TEST CRITERIA

Q.   What did you look for when the defendant was performing
     this test?

A.   I looked to see if he was standing still with his feet together.

—I looked for body tremors.

—I looked to see if there were eyelid tremors.

—I looked for swaying and whether the swaying was from front to back, side to side, and how many inches from the center he was swaying.

—I looked for muscle tension, whether his muscles were rigid or relaxed.

—I also looked for any statements or sounds that he made while he was performing this test.

—Finally, I recorded the number of seconds that he stood with his head tilted back and his eyes closed and compared that with the 30 seconds that he was told to stand there.

Q. How did the defendant perform this test?

A. (Answer).

B. Walk and Turn Test

Q. What was the next psycho-physical test?

A. The next psycho-physical test was the walk and turn test.

Q. Prior to asking the defendant to perform this test, did you explain and demonstrate the test for the defendant?

A. Yes.

Q. Would you please explain and demonstrate the test for the court and jury in the same manner that you did for the defendant on the date of arrest?

A. This test was performed by the defendant being first given specific instructions in regard to walking a line. He was told to place his right foot on the line ahead of his left foot with the heel of the right foot against the toe of the left foot.

   — He was told to put his arms down against his sides and keep them there throughout the test.

   — He was told to hold this position until he was given the instructions for the performance of the test. I emphasized to the defendant that he should not start walking until I told him to "*begin.*"

   — At this time, I asked the defendant if he understood my instructions.

   — He indicated that he did.

WALK — I instructed him that when I told him to "*begin,*" he was to take nine heel to toe steps down the line and turn around and take nine heel to toe steps back on the line.

   — He was told that every time he took a step, he was to place his heel against the toe of the other foot. (Have witness demonstrate this test.)

TURN —   He was told that when the ninth step had been
            taken, he was to leave his front foot on the line and
            turn around taking a series of small steps with the
            other foot. (Have witness demonstrate a proper
            turn.)

WALK —   He was reminded that after turning, he was to take
            another nine heel to toe steps back up the line.

COUNT—   Finally, he was told to watch his feet as he walked
            and to count off the steps out loud: 1-9.

        —   His final instruction was that once he started walk-
            ing, he was to keep walking until the test had been
            completed.

        —   Again, before I told him to begin, I asked him if he
            understood these instructions and he indicated that
            he did.

Q. Did he perform this test?

A. Yes he did.

WALK AND TURN TEST CRITERIA

Q. As he performed this test, what did you look for?

A. There were eleven basic things that I looked for:
   (1) Whether he kept his balance during the instructions.
   (2) Whether he started walking too soon.
   (3) Whether he stepped off the line while he was walking.
   (4) Whether he raised his arms while he was walking.
   (5) Whether he missed walking heel-to-toe.
   (6) Whether he stopped walking.
   (7) Whether he took the wrong number of steps.
   (8) Whether he turned improperly.
   (9) Whether he had body tremors.
   (10) Whether his muscle tension was rigid, relaxed, or normal.
   (11) Any statements or sounds he made while he performed
         the test.

Q. What were your observations of the defendant in the perfor-
    mance of this test?

A. (Answer).

C. One Leg Stand Test

Q. What was the third psycho-physical test that you performed?

A. The third test was the one-leg stand.

Q. Prior to asking the defendant to perform this test, did you
    explain and demonstrate the test to him?

A. Yes.

Q. Would you explain and demonstrate this test for the court and jury in the same manner that you explained and demonstrated for the defendant on the date of arrest?

A. In this test, the defendant was asked to stand straight with his feet together and his arms down at his sides. Again, he was told to maintain this position while he was given the instructions and it was emphasized that he was not to start the test until he was told to *"begin."*

—At this point, he was asked if he understood?

—Then he was told that when he was instructed to *"begin,"* he was to raise his right foot in a stiff leg manner and hold the foot about six inches off the ground with the toes pointed out. (Have witness demonstrate proper stance.)

—The defendant was told that he must keep his arms at his sides and must keep looking directly at his elevated foot while counting out 30 seconds as follows:

"one-thousand-and-one, one-thousand-and-two, etc.

—He was again asked if he understood and was told to *"begin."*

—After he completed the test, he was told to perform it again while standing on his right foot.

ONE LEG STAND TEST CRITERIA

Q. What did you look for when the defendant performed this test?

A. There were eight things I looked for:

1) The first was whether or not he raised his arms.

2) Whether he swayed.

3) Whether there was any hopping on one foot.

4) Whether he put the foot that he had raised down.

5) I looked to see if he was standing still and straight during the instructions.

6) I looked to see if there were any body tremors.

7) Whether the defendant's muscles were more rigid or more relaxed.

8) Finally I noted any statements or sounds that the defendant made while performing the test.

DEFENDANT'S PERFORMANCE

Q. What observations did you make of the defendant as he performed this test?

A.

D. Finger to Nose Test

Q. What was the fourth psycho-physical test that was performed?

A. The fourth psycho-physical test performed was the finger to nose test.

Q. Prior to asking the defendant to perform this test, did you explain and demonstrate the test to him?

A. Yes.

Q. Would you explain and demonstrate this test for the court and jury in the same manner that you explained and demonstrated it for the defendant on the date of arrest?

A.

—In this test, the defendant was told to place his feet together and stand straight.

—He was then told to extend his arms straight towards me and to make a fist with each hand. (Officer should be on his feet demonstrating this.)

—The defendant was then told to extend the index finger from each hand. He was then told to put his arms down at his sides with the index fingers extended.

—The defendant was then told that when he was told to *"begin,"* he was to tilt his head back slightly and close his eyes.

—He was then told that when he was instructed to *"begin,"* he was to bring the tip of the index finger up to the tip of his nose. (Demonstrate it while it is being explained.)

—The defendant was further told that as soon as he touched the tip of his nose, he was to return his arm to his side.

—The defendant was told that when he was told *"RIGHT,"* he was to move the right-hand index finger to his nose; when he was told *"LEFT,"* he was to move the left-hand index finger to his nose.

—At this point, the defendant was asked if he understood the instructions.

—The defendant was then told to tilt his head back and close his eyes and to keep them closed until he was told to open them.

—The defendant was then told the following sequence:
"LEFT . . . RIGHT . . . LEFT . . . RIGHT . . . RIGHT . . . LEFT."

FINGER TO NOSE TEST CRITERIA

Q. What did you look for when the defendant performed this test?

A.

—Whether the defendant's fingertips touched his nose or other parts of his face.

—Whether his body swayed.

—Whether there were any body tremors.

—Whether there were eyelid tremors.

—The defendant's muscle tension.

—Any statements or sounds made by the defendant while performing the test.

Q. Did you make a record of the defendant's performance of this test?

A. Yes. I noted on the evaluation form exactly where each fingertip touched the defendant's face. I also indicated on the form which finger was actually used by the defendant each time.

Q. What were your observations of the defendant in the performance of this test?

A. Detail to the jury the manner in which the defendant performed the test.

E. Videotape

The New York City Police Department as well as some other law enforcement agencies videotape the performance of the psycho-physical tests. If a videotape exists, it may be offered into evidence as a fair and accurate representation of the defendant's performance at the time and date in issue.

Q. Officer, was the defendant's performance of the four physical tests recorded on videotape.

A. Yes.

Q. I show you People's _____ for identification and ask you to tell the Court what it is.

A. This is the videotape of the defendant's performance of the physical tests.

Q. Prior to your taking the stand, did you view this videotape?

A. Yes.

Q. Does the videotape fairly and accurately depict the defendant's performance of the physical tests on (date of arrest)?

A. Yes.

At this time, I offer People's _____ for identification into evidence and request that the jury be allowed to view the videotape.

6. Vital Signs

Q. What is the sixth part of the examination?

A. The sixth part of the examination is called the vital signs.

Q. What were the vital signs that you checked?

A. I checked pulse rate, blood pressure and temperature.

A. Pulse

Q. How did you check the pulse rate?

A. I checked the pulse by placing my fingers on the defendant's skin next to an artery, pressed down, and felt the artery expand as the blood surged through. Each surge was a pulse and I counted the pulses that occurred in one minute and that gave me the pulse rate.

Q. How did you know that you were feeling an artery rather than a vein?

A. I knew because we were trained that you can't feel the surge or pulse in the vein.

Q. How often did you take the defendant's pulse?

A. I took his pulse three times. I took it during the preliminary examination. I took it following the finger to nose test, and I took it at the time that I checked the blood pressure and temperature.

B. Blood Pressure

Q. What was the next test?

A. The next test was blood pressure.

Q. What is blood pressure?

A. Blood pressure is the force that the circulating blood exerts on the walls of the arteries.

Q. What, if anything, did you use to measure blood pressure?

A. I used an instrument called a sphygmomanometer.

Q. What, if any, training have you had in the use of this instrument?

A. (Detail training.)

Q. How did you use this device to determine the defendant's blood pressure?

A. This device has a special cuff that was wrapped around the defendant's arm and inflated with air. As the air was pumped in, the cuff squeezed tightly on the arm. When the pressure got high enough, it squeezed the artery completely shut so that no blood flowed through it.

The next thing I did was to slowly release the air in the cuff so that the pressure on the arm and on the artery started to drop. The pressure continued to drop until blood once again started to flow through the artery. Blood starts to flow once the pressure inside the artery overcomes the pressure outside the artery.

At this point, blood will spurt through the artery each time the heart contracts. This is called the systolic level and the pressure at which this occurs is called systolic pressure. I continued to relax the air pressure in the cuff until it dropped down to the point where the blood started to flow continuously through the artery. This level is called the diastolic level and the pressure reading at this point is called diastolic pressure.

Q. How did you know when the blood started to spurt, as opposed to when it was flowing?

A. I listened to the spurting blood using a stethoscope. When there is no blood flowing, you hear nothing through the stethoscope. When you release the air from the cuff slowly, you will hear a spurting sound when the blood starts to spurt through the artery. As you continue to allow the air pressure to drop, the surges of blood become steadily longer. When you reach the diastolic pressure, the blood flows steadily and all sounds cease.

Q. What did you determine the defendant's blood pressure to be when you performed this test?

A. Defendant's blood pressure was _____.

C. Temperature

Q. What was the final test?

A. The final test was temperature. I took the defendant's temperature using an electronic thermometer. Each time we test someone, we use a fresh disposable mouthpiece.

Q. What did you determine the defendant's temperature to be?

A.

7. Drug Administration Sites

A. Nasal and Oral Examination

Q. Prior to leaving the dark room, what if any other examination did you do?

A. I checked the defendant's nose and mouth.

Q. What did you look for?

A. I looked for signs that the defendant had been using drugs.

Q. What kinds of things did you look for?

A. Different categories of drugs will have different effects. For example, certain kinds of drugs will irritate the inside of the nose and/or leave residue around, and in the mouth and nose. Some drugs will cause the nose to run and some substances will leave a distinctive odor on the defendant's breath and around the nasal area. On the other hand, the absence of any such signs can, also, be helpful in doing an evaluation.

Q. What if any observations did you make of the defendant's mouth and nose?

A.   (Answer.)

B. Arm and Neck Examination

Q.   What is the next part of the examination?

A.   This was a check of the defendant's arms and neck to see if
     he had needle marks and to determine whether his muscles
     were rigid, normal or relaxed.

Q.   Did you do that in this case?

A.   Yes I did.

Q.   What did you do?

A.   I ran my hands over the defendant's arms and neck feeling
     for bumps which would indicate needle marks. I have an
     instrument which is basically a lighted magnifying glass
     which I use to examine any bumps that I find. The instru-
     ment helps me to determine whether or not the bump is a
     needle mark.

Q.   How do you tell whether bumps are the results of the use of
     a needle or the result of some other cause?

A.   (Detail training in this regard.)

Q.   What were the results of this part of the examination?

A.

8. Urine Sample

Q.   What is the tenth part of the evaluation?

A.   The tenth part of the evaluation consists of obtaining a urine
     sample from the defendant for submission to a laboratory.

Q.   Did you obtain a urine sample from the defendant?

A.   Yes I did.

Q.   How was this done?

A.   The defendant was taken into the bathroom and a urine
     sample was obtained by having the defendant urinate into a
     container which is used for this purpose.

Q.   Did you witness the taking of the sample?

A.   Yes I did.

Q.   What did you do with the urine sample after you obtained it?

A.   The plastic containers of urine were sealed with tape and my
     initials as well as the job number were placed on it. The
     containers were placed in an envelope and taken to head-
     quarters where they were placed in a refrigerator.

Q.   What happened to the urine sample after it was logged in at
     your headquarters?

A. It was transported to the laboratory for analysis.

Q. Who transported it?

A. Officer Jones, bonded courier, etc.

Q. Did this complete your evaluation of the defendant?

A. Yes it did.

Q. During the course of this evaluation, did you have any conversation with the defendant?

A. Yes I did.

Q. Would you detail for the court and jury the contents of that conversation?

A. Admissions made by the defendant. (*Miranda* warnings are usually read by the arresting officer and evidence in that regard would normally be established prior to the DRE's testimony).

APPENDIX 8

New York State Department of Motor Vehicles' Affidavit of Regularity/Proof of Mailing

---

AFFIDAVIT OF REGULARITY/PROOF OF MAILING

_____ Court   County_____

People vs. _____   (DOB _____)

State of New York, County of Albany SS:

Marcus P. Salm, being duly sworn deposes and says:

1. That he is the department's Records Manager in the Public Services Bureau, and has been designated as the employee responsible for the issuance of suspension/revocation orders for the Department of Motor Vehicles, Empire State Plaza, Albany, New York.

2. That he is familiar with the procedures for the preparation and mailing of orders of suspension and revocation of driver licenses and/or vehicle registrations.

3. That those procedures provide that department personnel must determine from department records that a suspension/revocation order affecting a driver license or registration must be issued.

4. That the actual order of suspension or revocation is either produced electronically through the department computer system or that it must be produced through manual operations.

5. That if the order is produced electronically, it is reviewed by department personnel to compare the address on the license file with the address supplied by the court. If the addresses differ, the address supplied by the court is the address to which the order is sent.

6. That if the order is produced through manual operations, a work copy (form MV-111 or DS-110) of the order is first prepared by personnel to include the latest recorded address. Upon completion of the work order, the department case record is referred to a typist in the Driver Improvement Bureau for preparation of a typed order of suspension or revocation (form MV-110).

7. That when the order has been reviewed and accepted by department personnel, the case record is referred to a Control Unit in the Driver Improvement Bureau for bursting of the multiple copy order of suspension or revocation and distribution of the various copies as follows:

   a) copy 1 to licensee or registrant;

   b) copy 2 to case file;

   c) copy 3 to Driver Improvement stop desk for entry on the department computer (except those orders which have been electronically produced and recorded);

   d) copies 4, 5, and 6 to appropriate District Offices of the Department of Motor Vehicles to effect voluntary compliance or police enforcement.

8. That copy 1, addressed to the licensee and/or registrant at the address verified by personnel, is placed in a window envelope.

9. That the various copies of the formal notice of suspension/revocation are placed in a designated basket in the Control Unit.

10. That two times daily the contents of the basket are removed and delivered to the department's mail room.

11. That upon information and belief, these boxes are emptied by mail room personnel and their contents sorted and packed into mail sacks which are collected daily by the U.S. Postal Service for delivery to the motorists.

12. That when delivery of a formal notice of suspension cannot be effected by the U.S. Postal Service as addressed, such notices are routinely returned to the Department of Motor Vehicles.

13. That upon information and belief, the orders referenced were processed, distributed and/or mailed from this department in the manner and form described.

_____
(Signature)

Sworn to and signed before me this

_____ day of _____, 19 _____

_____
(Notary Public)

MV 94.4 (8/92)

1721

APPENDIX 9

New York State Police Associate Counsel's Letter Regarding Towing Vehicles Pursuant to VTL § 511-B

STATE OF NEW YORK

DONALD O. CHESWORTH
SUPERINTENDENT

NEW YORK STATE POLICE

BUILDING NO. 22
GOVERNOR W. AVERELL HARRIMAN
STATE OFFICE BUILDING CAMPUS
ALBANY, NEW YORK 12226

June 16, 1986

Peter Gerstenzang, Esq.
Gerstenzang, Weiner & Gerstenzang
41 State Street
Albany, New York   12207

RE: Vehicle & Traffic Law § 511-b

Dear Mr. Gerstenzang:

We have advised our members to arrange for towing of all
vehicles governed by Vehicle and Traffic Law §511-b. The statute's language is directory rather than discretionary--officers
"shall" have the cars towed.

While the State Police or a municipal police department may
have defenses to a lawsuit where a vehicle is not towed as
required by statute, (e.g. special duty, proximate cause), a suit
alleging the failure to tow a vehicle in circumstances set forth
in §511-b could nonetheless require expenditures of time and
money to defend it. I would expect, in such a suit, to see an
allegation of negligence based on violation of statute.

Very truly yours,

Robert A. Jones
Associate Counsel
(E1666)

APPENDIX 10

Department of Motor Vehicles' Mock Abstract of Driving Record

(SAMPLE)

```
Document # ALI  001
PRINT DATE: 11/28/2011 TIME: 12:34:98  OPERATOR: I  OFFICE: DAB


                                        CLIENT ID#: 522367836
   MOTORIST,MICHELLE                 DOB: 01/25/1983  SEX: F
   6 EMPIRE STATE PLAZA              HEIGHT: 5-6  EYE COLOR: BLUE
   ALBANY          NY 12228          COUNTY: ALBA
                                     MI #: M15752 74568 811149-83


   RESTRICTIONS: CORRECTIVE LENSES,INTERLOCK DEVICE
        Record Summary Line

   LICENSE CLASS: *D*                STATUS:REVOKED     EXPIRATION: 01/25/2018

   SUSP/REV SUMMARY: TOTAL   6 (SCOFFS  1 ON  1 DATES) JUDGEMENT 9     0

   ********************          ACTIVITY          ********************
   CLASS CHANGE: 06/17/1999     NEW: *DJ*   OLD: PERMIT

   ACCIDENT PREVENTION COURSE COMPLETED ON: 11/22/2008
      UP TO 4 POINTS CAN BE REDUCED FROM TOTAL POINTS FROM  05/22/2007 - 11/22/2008
   N/A - NON 19-A DRIVER OR COURSE PRIOR TO 01/01/94

   ******************      SUSPENSIONS/REVOCATIONS      ******************
      SUSPENSION: 02/04/2011 PEND PROSECUTION-CT   ORDER #: A1102090000
         CLEAR ON: 03/07/2011 REQUIREMENTS MET

      SUSPENSION: 10/20/2011 FLD PAY DRIV ASSESS   ORDER #: A110820D000

      SUSPENSION: 03/14/2011 INS. NOT IN EFFECT    ORDER #: C1103010000

      REVOCATION: 03/09/2011 DR INTOX & .08% ALCH  ORDER #: D1105180000
    COMPLIED ON: 03/09/2011

      REVOCATION: 05/02/2011 AGG DWI CHILD IN VEH  ORDER #: D1106020000
    COMPLIED ON: 05/02/2011

      SUSPENSION: 12/17/2010 TEMP - PDG C/T HRG    ORDER #: H110128
    COMPLIED ON: 12/17/2010
         CLEAR ON: 01/02/2011 TIME SERVED
```

Continued Page 2

[SIGNATURE]
COMMISSIONER OF MOTOR VEHICLES

DS-242.1 (2/12)

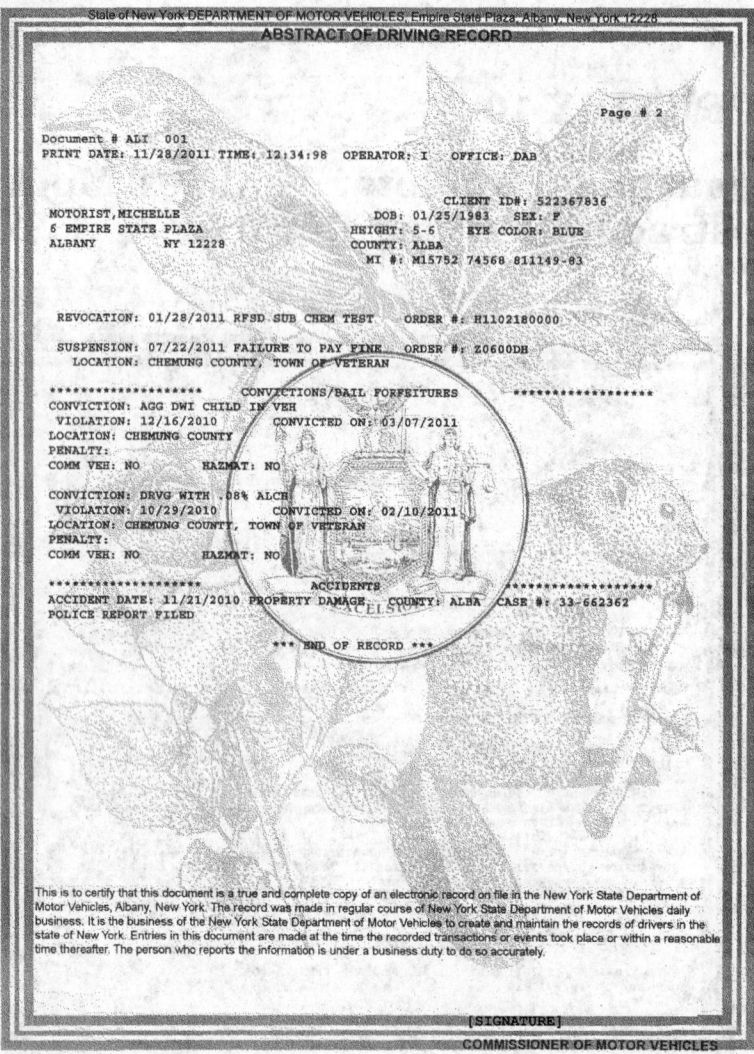

State of New York DEPARTMENT OF MOTOR VEHICLES, Empire State Plaza, Albany, New York 12228

ABSTRACT OF DRIVING RECORD

Page # 2

Document # ALI 001
PRINT DATE: 11/28/2011 TIME: 12:34:98 OPERATOR: I   OFFICE: DAB

CLIENT ID#: 522367836
MOTORIST, MICHELLE   DOB: 01/25/1983   SEX: F
6 EMPIRE STATE PLAZA   HEIGHT: 5-6   EYE COLOR: BLUE
ALBANY   NY 12228   COUNTY: ALBA
                                      MI #: M15752 74568 811149-83

REVOCATION: 01/28/2011 RFSD SUB CHEM TEST   ORDER #: H1102180000

SUSPENSION: 07/22/2011 FAILURE TO PAY FINE   ORDER #: Z0600DB
   LOCATION: CHEMUNG COUNTY, TOWN OF VETERAN

******************* CONVICTIONS/BAIL FORFEITURES *****************
CONVICTION: AGG DWI CHILD IN VEH
   VIOLATION: 12/16/2010   CONVICTED ON: 03/07/2011
LOCATION: CHEMUNG COUNTY
PENALTY:
COMM VEH: NO   HAZMAT: NO

CONVICTION: DRVG WITH .08% ALCH
   VIOLATION: 10/29/2010   CONVICTED ON: 02/10/2011
LOCATION: CHEMUNG COUNTY, TOWN OF VETERAN
PENALTY:
COMM VEH: NO   HAZMAT: NO

*******************   ACCIDENTS   *****************
ACCIDENT DATE: 11/21/2010 PROPERTY DAMAGE COUNTY: ALBA CASE #: 33-662362
POLICE REPORT FILED

*** END OF RECORD ***

DS-242.1 (2/12)   PAGE 2 OF 5

DESCRIPTION OF ABSTRACT OF DRIVING RECORD

Form DS-242 (Abstract of Driving Record) shows basic licensing information. Most suspensions and revocations are displayed on an abstract while they are open and an additional four years from the date they are cleared. Suspensions for refusal to submit to a chemical test are displayed for five years from the date of suspension. Accidents are displayed for the remainder of the calendar year of the accident date, plus three years. Most traffic convictions will display for the remainder of the calendar year of the conviction date, plus three years. Convictions for operating a motor vehicle under the influence of alcohol or drugs are displayed for ten years from the conviction date. Some serious violations, such as vehicular homicide, are displayed permanently.

Each abstract identifies the motorist, gives the class of license, the current license status, the license expiration date and any restrictions and/or endorsements that limit or expand the driving privilege.

THE RECORD SUMMARY LINE SHOULD ALWAYS BE USED TO DETERMINE THE CURRENT STATUS OF THE DRIVER'S LICENSE OR DRIVING PRIVILEGE.

The **Record Summary Line** is printed just above the "Activity" section. It shows the class of license or permit that is held, and whether the status is Valid, Revoked, Suspended, Cancelled, Surrendered or Approved (for future license privileges after a revocation). It will also show the type of document the motorist has (a permit, a license, a conditional or restricted use license, or a non-driver ID card) and when the license/permit/ID card expires. If the individual has not had a NY driver license or non-driver ID, that information appears on the Record Summary Line as NO NY LICENSE. There will be more than one Record Summary Line if the motorist has a valid license in one class and a valid permit in another class. It is also possible to have a valid non-commercial license while the commercial privilege (CDL) is revoked or suspended (this is shown on more than one Record Summary Line).

Other license information is grouped in separate sections by action type. Each section is separated by a line of asterisks and a heading that identifies the information that is in each section. The **ACTIVITY** section is first, followed by **SUSPENSIONS/REVOCATIONS, CONVICTIONS/BAIL FORFEITURES** and **ACCIDENTS**.

The **ACTIVITY** section of the record shows: accident prevention course completion and the period of time for which the point reduction applies; "prohibits" (which prevent transactions from taking place until requirements are met); CDL history information; reciprocity information (a NY license issued on the basis of a valid license presented from another jurisdiction); information that the NY license was surrendered to another jurisdiction; special licenses or privileges (such as conditional or restricted use); and various notes such as stolen license information.

The **SUSPENSIONS/REVOCATIONS** section shows the type of action imposed (suspension or revocation) and the date it took effect, the reason for the suspension or revocation, and the Order number of the suspension or revocation. Suspensions/revocations for moving violations and all reasons other than scofflaws (failure to answer a traffic ticket or to pay a fine) are grouped together and listed in Order number sequence, so they are not always in chronological order. Suspensions for scofflaws are shown after the moving violations and are listed by the effective date of the suspension; the most recent appears first. Two additional fields may be shown: "Complied On" and "Clear On". "Complied On" refers to the date on which all license documents were surrendered. "Clear On" refers to the date on which the suspension/revocation was terminated; the date will be followed by the reason for the termination.

The **CONVICTIONS/BAIL FORFEITURES** section shows: the type of violation the driver was convicted of; the date of the violation; the date of the conviction; the location where the violation occurred; and the amount of the fine ("Penalty"). Additional information that may be shown includes sentence length in days, whether a commercial vehicle was involved and, depending on the violation, the number of points that accompany the violation.

The **ACCIDENTS** section shows: the date of the accident; whether there was a fatality, personal injury and/or property damage; the county where the accident occurred; whether a police and/or motorist report was filed; and, when appropriate, that the accident is excluded from DMV's program requiring a re-examination after a series of three accidents.

EXPLANATION OF LICENSE STATUS ON "RECORD SUMMARY LINE"

VALID:	Unless expired, full driving privileges are in effect for the class of license shown.
SUSPENDED:	Driving privilege is temporarily withdrawn for class of license shown.
REVOKED:	Driving privilege is withdrawn for class of license shown.
CANCELLED:	Driving privilege in all classes has been cancelled.
SURRENDERED:	The driver has voluntarily given up his/her driving privilege in all classes.
APPROVED:	Driver is authorized to have driving privileges returned after revocation, but has not yet obtained a license or learner permit.

A license with any status shown above may also be expired.

DS-242.1 (2/12)

PAGE 3 OF 5

NEW YORK STATE DRIVER LICENSE CLASSES

License class codes are used by every state as a national standard. Commercial driver licenses (CDLs) will appear on the Record Summary Line as license class CDL A, B or C. A driver who has one class of license, and who obtains a motorcycle license or a learner permit for another class, will have more than one Record Summary Line to show the status of each license class. A driver with only a Class M or MJ license is limited to motorcycle operation.

CLASS CDL A

Valid for operation of a tractor-trailer combination, truck-trailer combination, tractor, truck, taxicab, passenger vehicle, Class B or Class C Limited Use Motorcycle, or Limited Use Automobile.

CLASS CDL B

Valid for operation of a heavy single-unit vehicle (such as a truck or bus) with a Gross Vehicle Weight Rating (GVWR) of more than 26,000 pounds, or for the tractor portion of a tractor-trailer. Also valid for the operation of a taxicab, passenger vehicle, Class B or Class C Limited Use Motorcycle, or Limited Use Automobile.

CLASS CDL C

Valid for operation of a single-unit vehicle (such as a truck or bus) with a GVWR of 26,000 pounds or less that transports 15 or more passengers, or that transports passengers under Article 19-A of the Vehicle & Traffic Law, or that carries hazardous materials. Also valid for the operation of a taxicab, passenger vehicle, Class B or Class C Limited Use Motorcycle, or Limited Use Automobile.

CLASS Non-CDL C

This class is in the process of being eliminated and is only issued when a Farm (F)(G) and/or Tow Truck (W) endorsement is applied for. Valid for operation of a single-unit vehicle (such as medium trucks, farm vehicles and some heavy recreational vehicles) with a GVWR of 26,000 pounds or less that does not require a CDL endorsement. Also valid for the operation of a passenger vehicle, Class B or Class C Limited Use Motorcycle, or Limited Use Automobile.

CLASS D

Valid for operation of a single-unit vehicle or recreational vehicle with a GVWR of 26,000 pounds or less, a passenger vehicle, Class B or Class C Limited Use Motorcycle, a Limited Use Automobile.

CLASS DJ

Valid for operation of a single-unit vehicle with a GVWR of 10,000 pounds or less, a passenger vehicle, Class B or Class C Limited Use Motorcycle, or Limited Use Automobile. Issued only to drivers younger than 18 years of age; automatically becomes a Class D license on the individual's 18th birthday.

CLASS E

Valid for operation of a single-unit vehicle with a GVWR of 26,000 pounds or less used to transport up to 14 passengers for hire, that does not fall under Article 19-A. Also valid for the operation of a taxicab, passenger vehicle, Class B or Class C Limited Use Motorcycle, or Limited Use Automobile.

CLASS M

Valid for operation of a motorcycle (including Limited Use Motorcycle).

CLASS MJ

Valid for operation of a motorcycle (including Limited Use Motorcycle). Issued only to drivers younger than 18 years of age; automatically becomes a Class M license on the individual's 18th birthday.

NOTE: If the motorist does not have a NY license or learner permit, the Record Summary Line will read NO NY LICENSE. If the motorist has only a non-driver identification card, the Record Summary Line will read ID ONLY.

NEW YORK STATE LIMITED DRIVING PRIVILEGES
When appropriate, the type of limited driving privilege will follow the license class on the Record Summary Line.

CONDITIONAL: A limited driving privilege granted to NYS licensed drivers who are suspended/revoked for alcohol or drug-related convictions.

CONDITIONAL PRIVILEGE: A limited driving privilege granted to drivers licensed in other states who are suspended/revoked in NYS for alcohol or drug-related convictions.

PRE-CONVICTION CONDITIONAL LICENSE: A limited driving privilege granted to NYS licensed drivers who have been suspended in NYS for alcohol or drug-related violations (not yet convicted).

PRE-CONVICTION CONDITIONAL PRIVILEGE: A limited driving privilege granted to drivers licensed in other states who are suspended in NYS for alcohol or drug-related violations (not yet convicted).

RESTRICTED USE: A limited driving privilege granted to NYS licensed drivers who are suspended/revoked for reasons other than alcohol/drug-related convictions.

RESTRICTED USE PRIVILEGE: A limited driving privilege granted to drivers licensed in other states who are suspended/revoked in NYS for reasons other than alcohol/drug-related convictions.

POST REVOCATION CONDITIONAL LICENSE: A limited driving privilege granted to NYS licensed drivers who have ignition interlock devices as a probation condition, and who have completed the minimum revocation period required after an alcohol or drug-related conviction.

LIMITED USE ENDING DATE MM/DD/YYYY: A limited driving privilege granted to junior drivers who pass their road test within 6 months of receiving a learner permit. After the ending date, full driving privileges are granted.

EXAMPLES OF VIOLATION MESSAGES

AGG UNL OP MISD	Aggravated unlicensed operation, a second degree misdemeanor
CL/RL-CONV TRAF INF	Traffic infraction occurring during conditional/restricted license program
CONSUME ALC UNDER 21	Operation of a motor vehicle after consuming alcohol while under 21 years of age
DISOBEYED TRAF DEV	Disobeyed traffic device
DRIVING WHILE INTOX	Driving while intoxicated
DRVG WHILE IMPAIRED	Driving while ability impaired by alcohol
FAC AGG UNL OP INF	Facilitating aggravated unlicensed operation of a motor vehicle
FLD ANSWER SUMMONS	Failed to answer a traffic ticket
FLD PAY CHILD SUPP	Failed to pay child support
FLD PAY DRIV ASSESS	Failed to pay driver responsibility assessment
LEAV SCENE INC - PD	Leaving the scene of a property damage incident without reporting
NO INSP OVER 60 DAYS	No inspection - Over 60 days
OP MV - MOBILE PHONE	Operation of a motor vehicle while using a hand held mobile phone
OPER OUT OF REST-INF	Operating in violation of a driver license restriction – an infraction
OPER W/O INS – INF	Operating without insurance – an infraction
PEND PROS-CT BAC	Pending prosecution by court for blood alcohol content
PEND PROSECUTION-CT	Pending prosecution by court
PNG SUBMSN TO CRT-OS	Pending submission to out-of-state court
RFSD SUB CHEM TEST	Refused to submit to a chemical test
SPD NOT REAS/PRUDENT	Speed not reasonable and prudent
SUSP BY COURT 510	Suspended by court under Section 510 of the Vehicle and Traffic Law
TEMP - PDG C/T HRG	Suspension pending chemical test hearing
UNREG MOT VEH - INF	Unregistered motor vehicle – an infraction
3 SPEED/MISDEM 18 MO	Three speeding violations or misdemeanors within 18 months

APPENDIX 11

Simplified Traffic Information

SGT100PXNK

New York State - Department of Motor Vehicles
SIMPLIFIED INFORMATION/CERTIFICATE CONCERNING VIOLATION OF LAW RELATING TO VEHICLES

The people of the State of New York
VS.

Local Police Code		Date of Arraignment	
Last Name(Defendant)	First Name	M.I.	Court Adjournment Record	Docket Number

Number and Street		Apt. No.	Photo Lic Shown ☒	Date From	Code	Date To	Requested By
City	State	Zip Code	Owner is Oper. ○	Lic. Class			
Client ID Number		Sex	Date Expires				
Lic State	Date of Birth	Veh. Type	Year	Make	Color		
Plate Number		Reg State	Registration Expires				

THE PERSON DESCRIBED ABOVE IS CHARGED AS FOLLOWS

			Amount	Date	Receipt No.
		Bail			
Time	Date of Offense	IN VIOLATION OF	Refund		
			Fine		
Violation Section		Traffic Infraction ○ Misd ○ Felony ○	Surcharge		
Description of Violation		MPH MPH ZONE			
		US DOT#			
		Comm Veh ○ Bus ○ HazMat ○			
C/T/V/Name	County	Hwy.No Loc.Code			
Street Name		Hwy Type NCIC/ORI			

AFFIRMED UNDER PENALTY OF PERJURY

(Officer's Signature)

Officer operating radar

Date of Affirmation	Arrest Type	Badge/Shield	Officer's Com./Div./Stat.

Officer's Last Name

First Name		M.I.

THIS MATTER IS SCHEDULED TO BE HANDLED ON THE APPEARANCE DATE BELOW IN:

Address

City	State	Zip

○ Return by mail before or in person on: Date   Time
○ Must appear in person on:

SECTION 1807 OF THE VEHICLE AND TRAFFIC LAW PROVIDES THAT DEFENDANT, IN CERTAIN CASES, MUST BE INFORMED IN SUBSTANCE AS FOLLOWS:

"A plea of guilty to this charge is equivalent to a conviction after trial. If you are convicted, not only will you be liable to a penalty, but in addition your license to drive a motor vehicle or motorcycle, and your certificate of registration, if any, are subject to suspension and revocation as prescribed by law."

To Judge or Clerk of Court: Checkmark the appropriate box or boxes below.

I HEREBY CERTIFY THAT:

☐ Upon arraignment, that the above instruction was given orally to the defendant.

☐ The defendant appeared in response to a ticket upon which the above instructions were printed in bold type, in accordance with Section 1807 of the Vehicle and Traffic Law.

☐ Defendant entered a plea of guilty in writing pursuant to Section 1805 of the Vehicle and Traffic Law.

FOR COURT USE ONLY

Court Code	Justice Code	Date Adjudicated	Date Sentence Imposed
Charge Convicted of ○ AS ABOVE ○ VTL ○ Other	Disposition/Sentence	Fine $ Surcharge $	
Bail Forfeiture Date ○ LIC ○ REG	Amount $ ○ Rev ○ Susp ○ Mand. ○ Perm DAYS/MONTHS/YEAR		
DWI Test Type	DWI Test Results		

I hereby certify that the information given on this certificate is a true abstract from the records of this court.

Signature of Judge or Clerk of Court   Date

Name of Judge

Supporting Deposition Issued: None ☒   Speeding(Gen101) ○   Non - Speeding(Gen101a) ○

UTO-1.7(4/02)

1731

APPENDIX 12

Supporting Deposition to Support Simplified Traffic Information

SUPPORTING DEPOSITION / CPL 710.30 NOTICE TO SUPPORT SIMPLIFIED TRAFFIC INFORMATION
LOCAL CRIMINAL COURT

COUNTY OF

STATE OF NEW YORK
THE PEOPLE OF THE STATE OF NEW YORK
VS

UTT NUMBER

Officer   of the

a Police Officer and the Complainant alleges that the Defendant committed a violation of
1. (Law/Section/Subsection)
2. Description of Violation
3. Date   Time   C/T/V of
4. Vehicle Year   Make   Color   License Plate No.   State
5. General Direction of Travel by Defendant
6. Highway (Type/Name)
7. Defendant's Speed
8. Charge based on Officer's
9. Speed Verified by   Model
10. Additional Information

TO THE ABOVE NAMED DEFENDANT:

PLEASE TAKE NOTICE THAT PURSUANT TO SECTION 710.30(1)(A) OF THE CRIMINAL PROCEDURE LAW, THE PEOPLE INTEND TO OFFER AT A TRIAL OF THE ABOVE ENTITLED ACTION EVIDENCE OF A STATEMENT MADE BY YOU ON ▮▮▮▮▮▮▮ AT ▮▮▮▮▮ P AT ▮▮▮▮▮▮RD, To Officer Name ▮▮▮▮▮▮▮ a public servant

IN WHICH YOU SUBSTANTIALLY STATED AS FOLLOWS:

FALSE STATEMENTS MADE HEREIN ARE PUNISHABLE AS A CLASS A
MISDEMEANOR PURSUANT TO SECTION 210.45 OF THE PENAL LAW OF THE
STATE OF NEW YORK

Affirmed Under Penalty of Perjury

APPENDIX 13

Certificate of Relief from Disabilities

F-OR **COURT OR BOARD OF PAROLE**
Docket, File, or other Identifying No.

STATE OF NEW YORK

CERTIFICATE OF RELIEF FROM DISABILITIES

This certificate is issued to the holder to grant relief from all or certain enumerated disabilities, forfeitures, or bars to his employment automatically imposed by law by reason of his conviction of the crime or of the offense specified herein.

This certificate shall NOT be deemed nor construed to be a pardon.

SEE REVERSE SIDE FOR EXPLANATION OF THE LAW GOVERNING THIS CERTIFICATE.

This Original Certificate is to be presented to the person to whom awarded. One copy is to be retained by the issuing agency, and one copy is to be filed with the N.Y.S. D |v. Of Criminal Justice Services, Executive Park, Stuyvesant Plaza, Albany, N.Y. 12203

1 For use by DCJS	HOLDER OF CERTIFICATE			3. NYSID Number (if not known supply fingerprints to DCJS If fingerprints are unobtainable, complete items 15-1 8 below.)
	2. Last Name	First Name	Middle Initial	
4. Crime or offense for which con~cted		5. Date of arrest		6 Date of sentence
7 Court of disposition (Court. Part Term_ Venue)		8 Certificate issued by: ☐ COURT INDICATED IN NO. 7 ☐ STATE BOARD OF PAROLE		
9 Date this certificate issued		1 0. If this Certificate replaces Certificate of Relief From Disabilities previously Issued, give date of previous Certificate. Date: ☐ Not Applicable		

I 1. CHECK ONE BOX ONLY
This certificate shall:

a ☐ Relieve the holder of all forfeitures, and of all disabilities and bars to employment, excluding the right to retain or to be eligible for public office, by virtue of the fact that this certificate is issued at the time of sentence. The Date of Sentence in this case must agree with the Date Certificate Issued.

b ☐ Relieve the holder of all disabilities and bars to employment, excluding the right to be eligible for public office.

c ☐ Relieve the holder of the forfeitures, disabilities or bars hereinafter enumerated _____

12. ☐ This certificate shall be considered permanent.

☐ This certificate shall be considered temporary until _____ After this date, unless revoked earlier by the Issuing court or parole board, this certificate shall be considered permanent. A person who knowingly uses or attempts to use a revoked certificate in order to obtain or exercise any right or privilege that he would not be entitled to obtain or to exercise without valid certificate shall be guilty of a misdemeanor.

13 Signature of issuing official(s)	Print or type name(s)	14 Title(s)

Complete the following for DCJS only if fingerprints are not available

15. Sex ☐ Male ☐ Female	16. Color	17. Height Ft in.	18. Date of Birth (Month, Day, Year)

Form DP-53 (Rev. 9172)

1735

APPENDIX 14

Fill in the Blank Deposition

Arrest #	DA #	Court #	Misc. #

COURT: _____ OF _____

☐ SUPPORTING DEPOSITION
☐ DWI BILL OF PARTICULARS

STATE OF NEW YORK: COUNTY OF _____

THE PEOPLE OF THE STATE OF NEW YORK

against

_____ _____ _____ DEFENDANT
(Last)   (First)   (Middle)

The above "DEFENDANT" is charged by Simplified Traffic Information ("SLED") Number(s): _____ (or attached accusatory instrument) with OPERATING A MOTOR VEHICLE UNDER THE INFLUENCE OF ALCOHOL contrary to Section 1192 of the Vehicle and Traffic Law. A Supporting Deposition and/or Bill of Particulars pursuant to Sections 100.25 & 200.95, respectively, of the Criminal Procedure Law are hereby provided, as follows. THE UNDERSIGNED COMPLAINANT, upon direct knowledge unless otherwise specified, avers that the defendant, on or about the ____ of _____ 19___, at or about ____ AM/PM, operated a (color) _____ 19___ (make) _____ motor vehicle, bearing State of _____ registration number _____ in a _____ erly direction on _____ a public highway/parking lot in the City/Town/Village of _____ County of _____, State of New York while in an intoxicated condition and/or having a ____ % blood alcohol content

1. GENERAL INFORMATION

Arrest Date: __/__/__ Arrest Time ____ AM/PM

Date of Birth __/__/__ Sex ☐ M ☐ F ☐ U

License State _____ Motorist I.D. No. _____

Defendant's Address/Phone No. _____

Vehicle: ☐ Impounded ☐ Towed ☐ Left

Road Conditions _____

Traffic _____ Weather _____

☐ PRIOR CONVICTIONS

Sections	How Many	Date(s)	As a Felony
1192.1			
1192.2			☐
1192.3			☐
1192.4			☐
1192.5			
Out of State			☐

7. MANNER/DESCRIPTION OF VIOLATION

☐ Erratic Operation: _____ explain

☐ VTL Violation of Section(s): _____

☐ Accident: ☐ Property Damage ☐ Injury
   ☐ Injury Other than Driver
   ☐ "SPI" (Serious Physical Injury)
   ☐ "D" (Fatality)

☐ Civilian Complaint

☐ Roadblock

☐ Other _____

Time of Stop _____ AM/PM

8. VEHICLE OPERATION SHOWN BY

☐ Complainant's Observations

☐ Civilian Witness(es) Identification

☐ Admissions (see Number 9)

☐ Further Observations as follows:
   ☐ Defendant at the Wheel
   ☐ Defendant near the Vehicle
   ☐ Keys in the Ignition
   ☐ Motor Running
   ☐ Defendant Injured in Crash

☐ Other: _____

3. PROBABLE CAUSE FOR ARREST

A. Observation of the Defendant's:
☐ Driving
☐ Odor of Alcoholic Beverage
☐ Glassy Eyes
☐ Impaired Speech
☐ Impaired Motor Coordination
☐ Other: _____
☐ Performance of Field Test(s) ☐ Refused

	Fail	Pass
☐ Gaze Nystagmus	☐	☐
☐ Walk and Turn	☐	☐
☐ One Leg Stand	☐	☐
☐ Finger to Nose	☐	☐
☐ Rhomberg Test	☐	☐
☐ Finger Count	☐	☐
☐ Reciting the Alphabet	☐	☐
☐ Other: _____	☐	☐
specify		

☐ Defendant Disabled _____ specify

B. Admissions By The Defendant:
☐ Oral (See Number 9)
☐ Conduct:
   ☐ Screening Test Refusal
   ☐ Chemical Test Refusal
   ☐ Resisted Apprehension
☐ Other _____

C. Other Evidence as Follows:
☐ Open Container of an Alcoholic Beverage in or near Vehicle
☐ Positive Breath Screening Test: TIME ____ AM/PM
☐ Civilian Witness(es)
☐ Other _____

5. NO ALCOHOL ALTER TEST SHOWN BY

☐ Continual Police Observation
☐ Admissions (See Number 9)
☐ Civilian Witnesses
☐ Video
☐ Other _____

6. CHEMICAL TEST INFORMATION

Time of Test _____ AM/PM

Location of Test _____

Witness to Test _____

☐ Blood (Results to be delivered later)

☐ BREATH TEST B.A.C. 0 ____ %

Breath Test Operator

☐ Other Test _____ B.A.C. 0 ____ %
    (specify)

Inst # _____ Model # _____

Amp # _____ Sim Lot # _____

Blood Test Drawn By _____

☐ Nurse ☐ Physician ☐ EMT ☐ Lab Tech

☐ Court ordered blood test

Judge _____

Location of lab for analysis _____

☐ Refusal

4. PRESENT CHARGES

☐ DWAI	1192.1
☐ DWI 0.10% BAC or Greater	1192.2
☐ DWI Intox	1192.3
☐ Felony 0.10% BAC or Greater	
(1192.2 and 1193.1(c))	
☐ Felony DWI	(1192.3 and 1193.1(c))
☐ Other VTL Violation(s) _____	
☐ Other Offense(s) _____	
☐ Current Susp/Revoc (Sec 511)	

VERIFICATION

False Statements made herein are punishable as a Class "A" misdemeanor pursuant to Section 210.45 of the Penal Law

Police Agency _____

Arresting Officer (Signature) _____

Arresting Officer (Print Name) _____

Shield # _____ Precinct/Troop/Station _____

☐ Supporting Deposition Served on Defendant

Date	Officer's Initials	Defendant's Initials

DCJS-3204 (10/92)

COURT COPY

9.

PEOPLE V _____ COURT _____ OF _____

         Last   First   Middle

Arrest # _____

710.30 NOTICE

PLEASE TAKE NOTICE THAT THE PEOPLE, PURSUANT TO SECTION 710.30 OF THE CRIMINAL PROCEDURE LAW, INTEND TO USE ALL STATEMENTS OR ADMISSIONS REFLECTED HEREIN MADE BY THE DEFENDANT TO A LAW ENFORCEMENT OFFICIAL

A CONVERSATION AT ARREST SCENE

Time ____ AM/PM Date __/__/__
To Whom: _____

DEFENDANT SAID THAT HE/SHE
☐ Had been drinking
   How Many ____ Type ____
   Where _____
☐ Operated the Vehicle
☐ Did Not Drink since Operation of Vehicle Ceased
☐ Was Driving to _____
☐ Was Driving from _____
☐ Had Prior Alcohol Convictions
☐ Is Currently DWI Susp/Revoc
☐ Would Not Take a Screening Test
☐ Would Not Take a Chemical Test
☐ AS IN ATTACHMENT HERETO
☐ Other _____

B CONVERSATION

Time ____ AM/PM Date __/__/__ specify location
To Whom: _____

DEFENDANT SAID THAT HE/SHE
☐ Had been drinking
   How Many ____ Type ____
   Where _____
☐ Operated the Vehicle
☐ Did Not Drink since Operation of Vehicle Ceased
☐ Was Driving to _____
☐ Was Driving from _____
☐ Had Prior Alcohol Convictions
☐ Is Currently DWI Susp/Revoc
☐ Would Not Take a Screening Test
☐ Would Not Take a Chemical Test
☐ AS IN ATTACHMENT HERETO
☐ Other _____

C IDENTIFICATION OF DEFENDANT
☐ Confirmation (at or near scene)
☐ Observation (of operation or upon other occasion)

D VIDEO
☐ Yes ☐ No

E WARNINGS GIVEN
☐ Refusal Time _____ AM/PM
   Given by _____
   Location _____
☐ Miranda Time _____ AM/PM
   Given by _____
   Location _____
☐ 710.30 Notice served on Defendant

Date	Officer's Initials	Defendant's Initials

DCJS-3204 (10/92)

COURT COPY

APPENDIX 15

New York Department of Motor Vehicles' Licensing or Relicensing After Revocation Action (15 NYCRR PART 136)

Part 136 LICENSING OR RELICENSING AFTER REVOCATION ACTION

Sec.

Section 136.1. Introduction

(a) *Intent.* Section 510 of the Vehicle and Traffic Law provides that a license may be issued after revocation in the discretion of the commissioner. In exercising such discretion and in keeping with his responsibility to provide meaningful safeguards for the general public who are users of the highways, it is the purpose of the commissioner to utilize departmental driver improvement programs in order to rehabilitate problem drivers through the use of education and explanation. It is the further purpose of the commissioner to take disciplinary action in order to force a change in the attitude and driving habits of problem drivers, where the Department's review indicates that such action is necessary for the protection of the applicant and the public alike. This Part is intended to implement such purposes by establishing criteria to identify individual problem drivers, the application of which shall result in a presumption, in certain cases, that the involved driver would present a potential danger to himself or other users of the highway if allowed to be licensed or relicensed.

(b) *Definitions.*

(1) Problem driver. A *problem driver* is an applicant for a driver's license or privilege who has had a series of convictions, incidents and/or accidents or has a medical or mental condition, which in the judgment of the commissioner or his or her designated agent, upon review of the applicant's entire driving history, establishes that the person would be an unusual and immediate risk upon the highways. The commissioner or his or her designated agent shall set forth in writing the basis for the determination that an applicant is a problem driver.

(2) Disability. A *disability* is any condition, whether mental, emotional or physiological, which is likely to diminish the ability of an individual to safely control or operate a motor vehicle.

(3) History of abuse of alcohol or drugs. A *history of abuse of alcohol or drugs* shall consist of a record of two or more incidents, within a 25 year period, of operating a motor vehicle while under the influence of alcoholic beverages and/or drugs or of refusing to submit to a chemical test not arising out of the same incident, whether such incident was committed within or outside of this state.

(4) Rehabilitative effort. *Rehabilitative effort* shall consist of referral of an individual with a history of abuse of alcohol or drugs to any agency certified by the Office of Alcoholism and Substance Abuse and/or agents authorized by professional license or professional certification, such as that granted by a board of examiners of the State Education Department, for evaluation of the extent of alcohol and/or drug use and satisfactory participation in any treatment recommended by such agency, and/or evidence of abstinence from, or controlled use of, alcohol and/ or drugs for a period of time sufficient to indicate that such person no longer constitutes a danger to other users of the highway.

(5) Safety factor. A *safety factor* is a conviction for, or a finding by a departmental hearing officer of, any violation of the Vehicle and Traffic Law or of any local law, ordinance, order, rule or regulation relating to traffic, except violations relating to parking, standing or stopping; an accident with conviction involvement; an accident where a finding of gross negligence in the operation of a motor vehicle or operating a motor vehicle in a manner showing a reckless disregard for the life or property of others is made by a departmental hearing officer; and a finding of a chemical test refusal. A bail for-

feiture shall be considered a conviction for purposes of this Part.

(c) The provisions of this Part shall apply to an application for restoration of a driver's license or driving privilege.

Historical Note

Sec. filed Jan. 15, 1980; amds. filed: Nov. 12, 1982; Feb. 17, 1983; April 25, 1984 eff. April 25, 1984; amds. filed Feb. 8, 2011 eff. Feb. 23, 2011; emergency rulemaking eff. Feb. 22, 2013, expired; amd. filed Apr. 15, 2013 eff. May 1, 2013; amd. filed Jan. 21, 2015 eff. Feb. 11, 2015.

Section 136.2. Approval of application.

Except as provided in sections 136.3, 136.4 and 136.5 of this Part, an application for a driver's license shall be approved.

In addition, an application for re-licensure shall be waived under the following circumstances:

(a) If the licensee holds a commercial driver's license and a conviction results in the revocation of both the commercial and non-commercial portion of his or her driver's license, the commercial portion of the driver's license shall be automatically restored after the minimum one-year revocation period is served, if the non-commercial portion of the license has been restored as the result of either completion of the alcohol and drug rehabilitation program or approval for re-licensure pursuant to this Part.

(b) If the licensee holds a commercial driver's license and such license is revoked as the result of a conviction that results solely in the revocation of the commercial portion of such license, then such license shall be automatically restored after the one-year minimum revocation period is served.

(c) Subdivisions (a) and (b) shall not be applicable to a person whose license is suspended or revoked for an independent violation or violations at the time at which such person would be eligible for restoration of the commercial portion of his or her license pursuant to such subdivisions.

Historical Note

Sec. filed Jan. 15, 1980; amd. filed Aug. 25, 2006 eff. Sept. 13, 2006.

Section 136.3. Grounds for immediate denial of application.

An application for a driver's license shall be denied without further review if:

(a) the minimum waiting period provided by statute has not expired; and/or

(b) there is evidence of an open suspension or suspensions which have not been fully complied with; and/or

(c) the applicant fails to furnish any requested document or information required by the commissioner as part of the record review.

Historical Note

Sec. filed Jan. 15, 1980 eff. March 1, 1980.

Section 136.4. Denial of application following record review

(a) An application for a driver's license shall be denied if:

(1) a disability, as defined in section 136.1(b)(2) of this Part, is found, unless evidence shall be presented to satisfy the commissioner, that such individual may safely operate a motor vehicle; and/or

(2) there is a history of abuse of alcohol or drugs, as defined in section 136.1(b)(3) of this Part, with insufficient evidence of rehabilitative effort; and/or

(3) There is a combination of safety factors, as defined in section 136.1(b)(5) of this part, resulting in 25 or more negative units, as set forth in section 136.6(a) of this Part.

(b)

(1) An application for a driver's license may be denied if a review of the entire driving history provides evidence that the applicant constitutes a problem driver, as defined in section 136.1(b)(1) of this Part. If an application is denied pursuant to this paragraph, no application shall be considered for a minimum of one year from the date of denial. In lieu of such denial, the applicant may be issued a license or permit with a problem driver restriction, as set forth in section 3.2(c)(4) of this Title and paragraph (2) of this subdivision.

(2) Upon the approval of an application for relicensing of a person who is deemed a problem driver under this subdivision, the Commissioner may impose a problem driver restriction on such person's license or permit, as set forth in section 3.2(c)(4) of this Title. As a component of this restriction, the Commissioner may require such person to install an ignition interlock device in any motor vehicle owned or operated by such person. The ignition interlock requirement will be noted on the attachment to the driver license or permit held by such person. Such attachment must be carried at all times with the driver license or permit.

(3)

(i) Revocation of license or permit with problem driver restriction. A license or permit that contains a problem driver restriction shall be revoked:

(*a*) upon the holder's conviction of a traffic violation

or combination of violations, committed while such restriction is in effect, which the Commissioner deems serious in nature; or

(b) for the holder's failure to install and maintain an ignition interlock device in motor vehicles owned or operated by the holder, when required to do so under such restriction.

The attachment, provided for in paragraph (2) of this subdivision, shall set forth the violation or violations that will result in such a revocation. A revocation for any of the above reasons shall be issued without a hearing based upon receipt of a certificate or certificates of conviction. The Commissioner may also revoke a license or permit with a problem driver restriction, without a hearing, upon receipt of a certificate of conviction that indicates that the applicant has driven in violation of the conditions of such restriction.

(ii) Application for relicensure after revocation of license or permit with problem driver restriction.

(a) Except as provided in section 136.5(b)(3)(i) of this Part, if the applicant held a license or permit with a problem driver restriction and such restriction was for a period of five years, and such person's license or permit is revoked pursuant to this paragraph, the Commissioner shall deny the application for at least five years, in addition to any revocation period imposed pursuant to the Vehicle and Traffic Law. After such waiting period, the Commissioner may approve the application, provided that upon such approval the Commissioner shall impose the problem driver restriction on such person's license for a period of five years and may require the installation of an ignition interlock device in any motor vehicle owned or operated by such person for a period of no less than two but no more than five years. Such period shall be based, in part, on the period of time the applicant had installed an ignition interlock device pursuant to section 136.5(b)(3)(i) of this Part. Notwithstanding any other provision of this subdivision, if such applicant's license or permit with a problem driver restriction was previously revoked pursuant to the provisions of this paragraph, no new license or permit shall be issued, except that the Commissioner shall not be foreclosed from consideration of unusual, extenuating and compelling circumstances that may be presented for review and which may form a valid basis to deviate from the general policy, as set forth above, in the exercise of discretionary authority granted under section 510 of the Vehicle and Traffic Law. If an application is approved based upon the exercise of such discretionary authority, the reasons for approval shall be set forth in writing and recorded.

(b) Except as provided in section 136.5(b)(4)(i) of this Part, if the applicant held a license or permit with a problem driver restriction and such restriction was for a period of two years, and such person's license or permit is revoked pursuant to this paragraph, the Commissioner shall deny the application for at least two years, in addition to any minimum revocation period imposed pursuant to the Vehicle and Traffic Law. After such waiting period, the Commissioner may approve the application, provided that upon such approval the Commissioner shall impose the problem driver restriction on such person's license for a period of two years. Notwithstanding any other provision of this subdivision, if such applicant's license or permit with a problem driver restriction was previously revoked pursuant to the provisions of this paragraph, no new license or permit shall be issued, except that the Commissioner shall not be foreclosed from consideration of unusual, extenuating and compelling circumstances that may be presented for review and which may form a valid basis to deviate from the general policy, as set forth above, in the exercise of discretionary authority granted under section 510 of the Vehicle and Traffic Law. If an application is approved based upon the exercise of such discretionary authority, the reasons for approval shall be set forth in writing and recorded.

(4) Employer vehicle. A person required to operate a motor vehicle owned by such person's employer in the course and scope of his or her employment may operate that vehicle without installation of an ignition interlock device only in the course and scope of such employment and only if such person carries in the motor vehicle written documentation indicating the employer has knowledge of the restriction imposed and has granted permission for the person to operate the employer's vehicle without the device only for business purposes. Such documentation shall display the employer's letterhead and have an authorized signature of the employer. A motor vehicle owned by a business entity that is wholly or partly owned or controlled by a person subject to the problem driver restriction is not a motor vehicle owned by the employer for purposes of the exemption provided in this paragraph and shall be deemed to be owned by the person subject to the problem driver restriction.

(c) An application for a driver's license may be denied if the applicant has been convicted of a violation of section 125.10, 125.12, 125.13, 125.14, 125.15, 125.20, 125.22, 125.25, 125.26

or 125.27 of the Penal Law arising out of the operation of a motor vehicle, or if the applicant has been convicted of a violation of section 1192 of the Vehicle and Traffic Law where death or serious physical injury, as defined in section 10.00 of the Penal Law, has resulted from such offense.

(d) An application for a driver's license may be denied if the applicant is currently revoked pursuant to:

(1) a determination of a department of motor vehicles' administrative law judge following a hearing:

(i) to investigate a fatal accident; or

(ii) held under Article 2-A of the vehicle and traffic law where the applicant was convicted of a violation and such violation resulted in the death of, or serious physical injury to, a person other than the applicant.

(2) a judgment of conviction certified by a court of competent jurisdiction, where the violation resulted in the death of, or serious injury to, a person other than the applicant.

(e) In any situation in which the commissioner would propose to deny an application pursuant to the provisions of this section, the grounds for the proposed denial shall be sent to the applicant, who shall be provided with an opportunity to respond. The applicant's response shall be considered before a determination is made. Failure to respond within the period specified by the commissioner shall result in denial of the application.

(f) While it is the Commissioner's general policy to deny an application based on those elements cited in subdivisions (a), (b), (c) and (d) of this section, the commissioner shall not be foreclosed from consideration of unusual, extenuating or compelling circumstances which may be presented for review, which form a valid basis to deviate from the general policy, as set forth above, in the exercise of the discretionary authority granted undersection 510 of the Vehicle and Traffic Law. If an application is approved based upon the exercise of such discretionary authority, the reasons for approval shall be stated in writing and recorded. If an application is approved under such circumstances, the Commissioner may impose a problem driver restriction on such person's license or permit for a period of three years, as set forth in section 3.2(c)(4) of this Title, and may require the installation of an ignition interlock device in any motor vehicle owned or operated by such person for such three-year period.

Historical Note

Sec. filed Jan. 15, 1980; amd. filed April 25, 1984 eff. April 25, 1984. Amended (a)(1) and (b); amds. filed Feb. 8, 2011 eff. Feb. 23, 2011; emergency rulemaking eff. Sept. 25, 2012, expired Dec. 23, 2012; emergency rulemaking eff. Dec. 24, 2012, expired Feb. 21, 2013; emergency rulemaking eff. Feb. 22, 2013, expired; amd. filed Apr. 15, 2013 eff. May 1, 2013; amd. filed Jan. 21, 2015 eff. Feb. 11, 2015; amd. filed June 21, 2016 eff. July 6, 2016. Current with amendments included in the New York State Register, XXXVIII, Issue 34 dated August 24, 2016.

Section 136.5.   Special rules for applicants with multiple alcohol- or drug-related driving convictions or incidents and for applicants with an alcohol-related conviction related to a fatal accident

(a) For the purposes of this section:

(1) **Alcohol- or drug-related driving conviction or incident** means any of the following, not arising out of the same incident:

(i)   a conviction of a violation of section 1192 of the Vehicle and Traffic Law or an out-of-state conviction for operating a motor vehicle while under the influence of alcohol or drugs;

(ii)   a finding of a violation of section 1192-a of the Vehicle and Traffic Law or a finding of a refusal to submit to a chemical test under section 1194-a of the Vehicle and Traffic Law; provided, however, that no such findings shall be considered after the expiration of the retention period contained in paragraph (k) of subdivision 1 of section 201 of the Vehicle and Traffic Law;

(iii)   a conviction of an offense under the Penal Law for which a violation of section 1192 of the Vehicle and Traffic Law is an essential element; or

(iv)   a finding of refusal to submit to a chemical test under section 1194 of the Vehicle and Traffic Law, where such finding does not arise out of an incident that resulted in a conviction of a violation of section 1192 of the Vehicle and Traffic Law.

(2) **Serious driving offense** means:

(i)   a fatal accident;

(ii)   a driving-related Penal Law conviction;

(iii)   conviction of two or more violations for which five or more points are assessed on a violator's driving record pursuant to Section 131.3 of this Title; or

(iv)   20 or more points from any violations.

(3) **25 year look back period** means the period commencing upon the date that is 25 years before the date of the revocable offense and ending on and including the date of the revocable offense.

(4) **Revocable offense** means the violation, incident or accident that results in the revocation of the person's drivers

license and which is the basis of the application for relicensing. Upon reviewing an application for relicensing, the Commissioner shall review the applicant's entire driving record and evaluate any offense committed between the date of the revocable offense and the date the application is reviewed by the Commissioner as if it had been committed immediately prior to the date of the revocable offense. For purposes of this section, **date of the revocable offense** means the date of the earliest revocable offense that resulted in a license revocation for which the revocation has not been terminated by the Commissioner's subsequent approval of an application for relicensing.

(b) Upon receipt of a person's application for relicensing, the Commissioner shall conduct a lifetime review of such person's driving record. If the record review shows that:

(1) the person has five or more alcohol- or drug-related driving convictions or incidents in any combination within his or her lifetime, then the Commissioner shall deny the application.

(2) the person has three or four alcohol- or drug-related driving convictions or incidents in any combination within the 25 year look back period and, in addition, has one or more serious driving offenses within the 25 year look back period, then the Commissioner shall deny the application.

(3)

(i) the person has three or four alcohol- or drug-related driving convictions or incidents in any combination within the 25 year look back period but no serious driving offenses within the 25 year look back period; and

(ii) the person is currently revoked for an alcohol- or drug-related driving conviction or incident, then the Commissioner shall deny the application for at least five years after which time the person may submit an application for relicensing. Such waiting period shall be in addition to the revocation period imposed pursuant to the Vehicle and Traffic Law. After such waiting period, the Commissioner may in his or her discretion approve the application, provided that upon such approval, the Commissioner shall impose the A2 restriction on such person's license for a period of five years and shall require the installation of an ignition interlock device in any motor vehicle owned or operated by such person for such five-year period. Such waiting period shall be extended for an additional five years if the Commissioner finds that the person has any incidents of driving during the waiting period, as indicated by accidents, convictions or pending tickets or adjudications. If such license with an A2 restriction is later revoked for a subsequent alcohol- or drug-related driving conviction or incident or for a conviction which arises out of a fatal accident, such person shall thereafter be ineligible for any kind of license to operate a motor vehicle.

(4)

(i)   the person has three or four alcohol- or drug-related driving convictions or incidents in any combination within the 25 year look back period but no serious driving offenses within the 25 year look back period; and

(ii)   the person is not currently revoked as the result of an alcohol- or drug-related driving conviction or incident, then the Commissioner shall deny the application for at least two years, after which time the person may submit an application for relicensing. Such waiting period shall be in addition to the revocation period imposed pursuant to the Vehicle and Traffic Law.

After such waiting period, the Commissioner may in his or her discretion approve the application, provided that upon such approval, the Commissioner shall impose an A2 restriction, with no ignition interlock requirement, for a period of two years. Such waiting period shall be extended for an additional two years if the Commissioner finds that the person has any incidents of driving during the waiting period, as indicated by accidents, convictions or pending tickets or adjudications. If such license with an A2 restriction is later revoked for a subsequent alcohol- or drug-related driving conviction or incident or for a conviction which arises out of a fatal accident, such person shall thereafter be ineligible for any kind of license to operate a motor vehicle;

(5) the person has two alcohol- or drug-related driving convictions or incidents in any combination within the 25 year look back period, then the Commissioner may in his or her discretion approve the application after the minimum statutory revocation period is served.

(6) the person has been twice convicted of a violation of subdivision 3, 4 or 4-a of section 1192 of the Vehicle and Traffic Law or of driving while intoxicated or of driving while ability is impaired by the use of a drug or of driving while ability is impaired by the combined influence of drugs or of alcohol and any drug or drugs where physical injury, as defined in section 10.00 of the Penal law, has resulted from such offense in each instance, then the commissioner shall deny the application;

(7) the person is otherwise eligible for relicensing under this section, but is applying for relicensing due to revocation

arising out of an alcohol-related conviction involving a fatal accident, the Commissioner may approve the application after the minimum revocation period is served, provided that upon such approval, the Commissioner shall impose the A2 restriction on such person's license for a period of three years and shall require the installation of an ignition interlock device in any motor vehicle owned or operated by such person for such period. For the purpose of this paragraph, **alcohol-related conviction** shall mean:

(i)   a conviction of a violation of section 1192 of the Vehicle and Traffic Law; or

(ii)   a conviction of an offense under the Penal Law for which a violation of section 1192 of the Vehicle and Traffic Law is an essential element.

(c) The grounds for any denial shall be set forth in writing and a copy shall be made available to the person making the application for relicensing.

(d) While it is the Commissioner's general policy to act on applications in accordance with this section, the Commissioner shall not be foreclosed from consideration of unusual, extenuating and compelling circumstances that may be presented for review and which may form a valid basis to deviate from the general policy, as set forth above, in the exercise of discretionary authority granted under sections 510 and 1193 of the Vehicle and Traffic Law. If an application is approved based upon the exercise of such discretionary authority, the reasons for approval shall be set forth in writing and recorded. If an approval is granted based upon unusual, extenuating and compelling circumstances, the applicant may be issued a license or permit with a problem driver restriction, as set forth in section 3.2(c)(4) of this Title, and may be required to install an ignition interlock device in any motor vehicle owned or operated by such person for a period of five years. The provisions of this subdivision shall not apply to denials under paragraph (6) of subdivision (b) of this section.

(e) If there are two alcohol- or drug-related driving convictions or incidents on an applicant's driving record, the consideration of an application for relicensing shall be held in abeyance if the applicant has at least one ticket pending for alcohol- or drug-related driving offenses where the pending ticket or tickets, if disposed of as a conviction of the original charge, would result in the denial of the application. In addition, if, after an application for relicensing is approved, the Commissioner receives information that indicates that such application should have been denied or that the applicant operated a motor vehicle prior to approval or after approval of such application but prior to obtaining a valid permit or license, the Commissioner shall rescind such approval and the license or privilege granted shall be revoked.

Historical Note

Sec. filed Jan. 15, 1980; amds. filed: Feb. 2, 1983; April 25, 1984 eff. April 25, 1984; amds. filed Feb. 8, 2011 eff. Feb. 23, 2011; emergency rulemaking eff. Sept. 25, 2012, expired Dec. 23, 2012; emergency rulemaking eff. Dec. 24, 2012, expired Feb. 21, 2013; emergency rulemaking eff. Feb. 22, 2013, expired; amd. filed Apr. 15, 2013 eff. May 1, 2013; amd. filed Jan. 21, 2015 eff. Feb. 11, 2015; amd. filed June 21, 2016 eff. July 6, 2016. Current with amendments included in the New York State Register, XXXVIII, Issue 34 dated August 24, 2016.

Section 136.6. Weighing of safety factors.

(a) There shall be assigned to each safety factor a negative unit as follows:

Safety Factor	Assigned Negative Units	
	Over one year to three years of application	Within one year of application
(1) for each reportable accident of record with a finding by the referee of gross negligence in the operation of a motor vehicle in a manner showing a reckless disregard for the life and property of others.	-5	-8
(2) for each reportable accident of record with conviction involvement or with a finding by the referee of a violation of the Vehicle and Traffic Law	-3	-4
(3) for the first and second speeding conviction of record*	-3	-4
(4) for the third and subsequent speeding conviction*	-5	-8
(5) for reckless driving, speed contest or passing a stopped school bus	-5	-8
(6) for each conviction of record for leaving the scene of a personal injury accident of record	-8	-11

(7) for each alcohol related offense of record as follows:		
(i) conviction for violation of subdivision (1) of Section 1192 of the Vehicle and Traffic Law: first offense second offense third offense	-5 -8 -11	-8 -11 -14
(ii) conviction for violation of subdivision (2), (2-a), (3), (4), or (4-a) of section 1192 of the Vehicle and Traffic Law: first offense second or subsequent offense	-8 -11	-11 -14
(iii) chemical test refusal	-6	-11
(8) for each conviction of homicide, criminally negligent homicide, or assault arising out of the operation of a motor vehicle	-11	-14
(9)(i) for each incident of driving during a period of alcohol-related license suspension or revocation	-10	-12
(ii) for each other incident of driving during a period of license suspension or revocation	-8	-10
(10) for each conviction or finding by the Commissioner's referee of a violation of section 392 of the Vehicle and Traffic Law	-3	-4
(11) for each other conviction of record for a moving violation	-2	-3
*For each speeding violation of 25 miles per hour or more over the posted speed limit, add one point.		

(b) The point reduction program shall not apply to any of the negative units listed in subdivision (a) of this section.

(c) For the purpose of this Part, the time periods for the computation of safety factors shall commence as of the date on which the incident occurred.

(d) In any case where two or more safety factors which are not independent of each other arise out of a single incident, only one of these safety factors shall be taken into consideration. The safety factor which shall be taken into consideration in these cases shall be the safety factor having the greater weight, except that where two safety factors are of equal weight, either one may be taken into consideration.

Examples:

(1) Where an accident and a conviction for reckless driving arise out of the same incident, only the reckless driving conviction, which is the safety factor having the greater weight, is considered, because these safety factors are not independent of each other.

(2) Where a conviction of any subdivision of Section 1192 of the Vehicle and Traffic Law and a finding of a chemical test refusal arise out of the same incident, only one of these two safety factors having equal weight is considered, because these safety factors are not independent of each other.

(3) Where a person is convicted of reckless driving and the incident occurred during a period of license revocation, both of these safety factors shall be taken into consideration because these safety factors are independent of each other.

(e) Where a person is convicted of or adjudicated for an offense committed outside of this state, and where such offense has been made part of the person's New York State driving record, such offense shall carry the equivalent safety factor assigned under subdivision (a) of this section, as if the offense was committed in this state.

Historical Note

Sec. filed Jan. 15, 1980; amds. filed: Feb. 2, 1983; May 21, 2002; Nov. 1, 2006 as emergency measure; Jan. 30, 2007 as emergency measure; April 30, 2007 as emergency measure; June 19, 2007 eff. July 3, 2007. Amended (a), (d); amds. filed Feb. 8, 2011 eff. Feb. 23, 2011.

Section 136.7. Licenses from other jurisdictions.

Notwithstanding any other provision of this Part, whenever a license has been revoked after a determination that such license was irregularly obtained based upon submission of a driver's license from another jurisdiction, which license was not valid at the time of submission, such revocation shall not be terminated, and no new license issued:

(a) if the license from the other jurisdiction was revoked at the time of submission, until at least one year has elapsed from the date of the revocation issued by the other jurisdiction, or until such revocation is no longer in effect in the other jurisdiction, whichever occurs sooner; or

(b) if the license from the other jurisdiction was suspended at the time of submission, until such suspension period is terminated.

Historical Note

Sec. filed Jan. 15, 1980; renum. 136.8, new filed June 14, 1990 eff. July 3, 1990.

Section 136.8.   Effect of application denial.

Denial of a application for license shall be appealable to the Administrative Appeals Board, except that the appeals board shall not consider any material which had not been previously submitted. In such a case, the applicant shall be required to submit any additional material in a new application.

Historical Note

Sec. filed Jan. 15, 1980; amd. filed April 25, 1984; renum. 136.9, new added by renum. 136.7, filed June 14, 1990 eff. July 3, 1990.

Section 136.9.   Effect of completion of the alcohol and drug rehabilitation program.

The successful completion of the article 21 alcohol and drug rehabilitation program, where no intervening safety factors occurred between the date such person entered the program and the date the application for a license is made and with no subsequent incidents of operating a motor vehicle while under the influence of alcoholic beverages or drugs, shall be considered evidence of rehabilitative effort satisfactory for the purposes of this Part. Provided, however, if enrollment in the program based upon the plea bargaining provisions of Vehicle and Traffic Law, section 1192(10)(a)(ii) and (10)(d), and if such person would not otherwise have been eligible for enrollment in the program pursuant to section 1196(4) of such law, then completion of the program, may not, in the commissioner's discretion, be deemed evidence of rehabilitative effort.

Historical Note

Sec. added by renum. 136.8, filed June 14, 1990; amd. filed Nov. 1, 2006 as emergency measure; Jan. 30, 2007 as emergency measure eff. Jan. 30, 2007.

Section 136.10.   Application for relicensing

(a) Application by the holder of a post-revocation conditional license. Upon the termination of the period of probation set by the court, the holder of a post-revocation conditional license may apply to the Commissioner for restoration of a license or privilege to operate a motor vehicle. An application for licensure may be approved if the applicant demonstrates that he or she:

(1) has a valid post-revocation conditional license; and

(2) has demonstrated evidence of rehabilitation as required by this Part.

(b) Application after permanent revocation. The Commissioner may waive the permanent revocation of a driver's license, pursuant to Vehicle and Traffic Law section 1193(2)(b)(12)(b) and (e), only if the statutorily required waiting period of either five or eight years has expired since the imposition of the permanent revocation and, during such period, the applicant has not been found to have refused to submit to a chemical test pursuant to Vehicle and Traffic Law section 1194 and has not been convicted of any violation of section 1192 or section 511 of such law or a violation of the Penal Law for which a violation of any subdivision of such section 1192 is an essential element. In addition, the waiver shall be granted only if:

(1) The applicant presents proof of successful completion of a rehabilitation program approved by the Commissioner within one year prior to the date of the application for the waiver; provided, however, if the applicant completed such program before such time, the applicant must present proof of completion of an alcohol and drug dependency assessment within one year of the date of application for the waiver; and

(2) The applicant submits to the Commissioner a certificate of relief from civil disabilities or a certificate of good conduct pursuant to Article 23 of the Correction Law; and

(3) The application is not denied pursuant to section 136.4 or section 136.5 of this Part; and

(4) There are no incidents of driving during the period prior to the application for the waiver, as indicated by accidents, convictions or pending tickets. The consideration of an application for a waiver when the applicant has a pending ticket shall be held in abeyance until such ticket is disposed of by the court or tribunal.

Historical Note

Sec. filed Aug. 27, 1996 eff. Sept. 11, 1996; emergency rulemaking eff. Sept. 25, 2012, expired Dec. 23, 2012; amd. filed Apr. 15, 2013 eff. May 1, 2013.

APPENDIX 16

New York State Department of Motor Vehicles' Alcohol & Drug Abuse Rehabilitative Program Summary

New York State Department of Motor Vehicles

ALCOHOL & DRUG ABUSE REHABILITATIVE PROGRAM SUMMARY

PART I — COMPREHENSIVE EVALUATION — *(If the evaluation and treatment is conducted by different persons or agencies, the evaluation summary must be forwarded to the treatment provider.)*

Last Name	First		M.I.	Date of Birth *(Month/Day/Year)*

Mailing Address *(Street & No.)*	City	State	Zip Code	Date(s) of Evaluation

REFERRAL INFORMATION — *Indicate which of the following items formed the basis for referral to you for a treatment evaluation.*

☐ Referred by Drinking Driver Program *(Identify)* _____
☐ Referred directly by DMV
☐ DWI/DWAI conviction(s); Number of conviction(s) _____ ; Date(s) of conviction _____
☐ Blood Alcohol Content (BAC) at time of arrest _____
☐ Chemical Test Refused
☐ Driver's License revoked/suspended;   ☐ Conditional License Issued

COMPREHENSIVE EVALUATION — *Indicate which of the following items were addressed during the evaluation process.*

A. Alcohol/Drug Abuse History	Personal	Family/Friends
1. Substances used..........	☐	☐
2. Alcohol usage and pattern of abuse..........	☐	☐
3. Drug usage and pattern of abuse..........	☐	☐
4. Attempts to stop use/abuse of alcohol/drugs..........	☐	☐
5. Other (specify)..........	☐	☐
6. Prior treatment completed date: _____		
Name of provider _____		

B. Psychosocial Assessment
1. ☐ Marital history
2. ☐ Family background
3. ☐ Employment history
4. ☐ Legal history
5. ☐ Personal relationships
6. ☐ Other

C. Health History
1. ☐ General health
2. ☐ Health problems
3. ☐ Nutritional assessment
4. ☐ Date of last physical exam
5. ☐ Referred for physical exam
6. ☐ Referred for blood tests
7. ☐ Other

DIAGNOSIS

A. Problem(s)
1. ☐ Alcoholism
2. ☐ Alcohol Abuse
3. ☐ Drug Abuse *(specify)* _____
4. ☐ Other Problem *(specify)* _____
5. ☐ None

B. Primary Diagnosis _____

C. Secondary Diagnosis *(if applicable)* _____

TREATMENT RECOMMENDATION

1. Treatment for ☐ alcoholism ☐ alcohol abuse ☐ drug abuse   is ☐ Recommended;   ☐ NOT recommended;   at this time.

2. Motorist is referred for:
☐ Detoxification (NOT Treatment)
☐ Residential treatment
☐ Inpatient treatment
☐ Outpatient treatment

☐ Support Services *(check one)*:
☐ Maintenance   ☐ AA   ☐ Other
☐ Other *(specify)* _____

3. Anticipated length of treatment: _____

EVALUATOR—PART I *(To be completed by person conducting the evaluation.)*

Name *(Print/Type)* _____

Agency _____   Phone Number ( )

Signature _____   Date _____

1755

APPENDIX 17

Screening Matrix Used by Drinking Driver Program

DRINKING DRIVER PROGRAM
Screening Matrix

	CRITERION	OBJECTIVE STANDARD	RATIONALE
1.	RIASI Score	10 or higher score	Targets largest number of dependent people with smallest percentage of false +/−'s. Research on cutoff points.
2.	Two or more alcohol/drug driving incidents within 10 years	2 or more unrelated incidents within 10 years on NYS-DMV file. Incidents are NOT: * info from class activities; * hearsay from other sources; * more than 10 years from current violation date.	Research shows repeaters are highly likely to recidivate, to be involved in crashes/fatal accidents and be diagnosed in need of treatment. Consistent with Part 136 of DMV regulations.
3.	Self-disclosure	A. An unsolicited and direct admission by student that "I'm currently in treatment for alcohol/drug abuse or dependency." B. A direct request from student to get help for his/her own substance abuse problem. NOTE: The DDP must get a signed statement from student affirming either of these situations.	A. No person can be legally kept in treatment without an abuse or dependency diagnosis being made. B. When people ask for help, they should get it.
4.	Attending class under influence of alcohol/drugs	A. Detectable odor of alcohol and confirmation of drinking after discussion with DDP staff.	A. DDP attendance rules inform students that drinking alcohol on class days will cause referral.

CRITERION	OBJECTIVE STANDARD	RATIONALE
	B. Aberrant, disruptive behavior during class and confirmation of substance abuse after discussions with DDP staff.	B. This act is likely to yield abuse/dependence diagnosis.
	NOTE: The instructor must document standards in accord with DMV's policy on page 6.5, B.3.a. of the DDP Director's Guide.	C. People who drink, then go to class show lack of control and poor judgment.
5. Arrest for an alcohol/drug driving violation while enrolled in DDP	A. Student admits or volunteers this information. B. Arrest reported in newspaper. NOTE: DDP must get copy of ticket or of Court's Suspension Pending Prosecution order.	Supports Section 1193 of V & T Law: Suspension Pending Prosecution.

APPENDIX 18
Photo of Alcotest

APPENDIX 19
Photo of Datamaster

Data Preservation

APPENDIX 20   [Reserved]

APPENDIX 21   *[Reserved]*

APPENDIX 22 *[Reserved]*

APPENDIX 23   *[Reserved]*

APPENDIX 24   *[Reserved]*

APPENDIX 25

Datamaster Certification

STATE OF NEW YORK
DIVISION OF CRIMINAL JUSTICE SERVICES
Four Tower Place
Albany, New York 12203-3764
http://criminaljustice.state.ny.us

CERTIFICATION PURSUANT TO CPLR 4518
OF RECORDS MAINTAINED
IN THE REGULAR COURSE OF BUSINESS

I, John R. Digman, Assistant Director, Office of Public Safety, New York State Division of Criminal Justice Services, 4 Tower Place, Albany, New York 12203, having been duly designated and authorized by the Commissioner of the Division of Criminal Justice Services, do hereby certify and authenticate, as provided by subdivision c of rule 4518 of the Civil Practice Law and Rules, that the copies annexed hereto are exact photocopies of the original record of the Office of Public Safety which are in my possession, custody and control.

I further certify that the original records of inspection/maintenance/calibration of NATIONAL PATENT ANALYTICAL SYS. DATAMASTER DMT breath test instrument, serial number 111806 performed on March 4, 2010 Office of Public Safety employee FRANK SGARLATA of which the annexed are photocopies, were made in the regular course of business of the New York State Division of Criminal Justice Services, Office of Public Safety, that such records were made at the time such inspection/maintenance/calibration was performed or within a reasonable time thereafter, and further that it was the regular course of the Office of Public Safety's business to make such records at the time such inspection/maintenance/calibration was performed, or within a reasonable time thereafter, and to provide such instrument's records to the agency that requested them.

John R. Digman
Assistant Director
Office of Public Safety

State of New York
County of Albany
Sworn to before me
On the 4th day of October, 2010

Notary Public, State of New York
Commission Expires April 26, 2011

LISA MARIE COPPOLO
Notary Public, State of New York
No. 02CO5076818
Qualified in Schenectady County
Commission Expires April 28, 2011

An Equal Opportunity/Affirmative Action Agency

BREATH TEST INSTRUMENT
RECORD OF INSPECTION / MAINTENANCE / CALIBRATION

Name of Submitting Agency: Watervliet Police Police Department
Manufacturer: NAT'L PATENT ANALYTICAL SYS
Model: DATAMASTER DMT   Serial Number: 111806
Date: March 04, 2010

Reference Solution Lot Number: 09070
Reference Solution Standard: 0.100 % at 34.0 degrees centigrade

Test No	Test Result	Simulator Temperature
1	0.099 %	34.02 degrees centigrade
2	0.099 %	34.02 degrees centigrade
3	0.098 %	34.02 degrees centigrade
4	0.099 %	34.00 degrees centigrade

Reference Solution Lot Number: 09100
Reference Solution Standard: 0.080 % at 34.0 degrees centigrade

Test No	Test Result	Simulator Temperature
1	0.077 %	34.01 degrees centigrade
2	0.076 %	34.01 degrees centigrade
3	0.077 %	34.02 degrees centigrade
4	0.077 %	34.03 degrees centigrade

I hereby certify that I have performed any necessary maintenance procedures and calibrated NAT'L PATENT ANALYTICAL SYS breath test instrument model DATAMASTER DMT, serial number 111806, and have determined that it is accurate and reliable for the determination of ethyl alcohol in the blood by analysis of the breath. The instrument's test results are recorded above and this instrument satisfies all limits and standards established by the New York State Commissioner of Health as enumerated in Part 59, Subchapter D of Chapter II, TITLE 10(Health) of the Official Compilation of Codes, Rules and Regulations of the State of New York, (10 NYCRR Part 59) as amended.

I further certify that the entries made in these records of inspection /maintenance /calibration were made at the time that such inspection /maintenance /calibration of the above identified breath test instrument was performed, or within a reasonable time thereafter.

FRANK SGARLATA
Technician

BREATH TEST INSTRUMENT
RECORD OF INSPECTION / MAINTENANCE / CALIBRATION

Manufacturer: NAT'L PATENT ANALYTICAL SYS
Model: DATAMASTER DMT
Serial Number: 111806
Date: March 04, 2010

1. General Appearance and condition of this device ——————:
   OK

2. Check controls and indicators ————————————: **OK**

3. Check breath flow indicator ————————————: **OK**

4. Check printer operation ————————————: **OK**

5. System cycles through all modes ————————: **OK**

6. Record any repairs made to this instrument and list services provided:
   REPLACED DMT PCB, DETECTOR, AND FILTER BLOCK. CALIBRATED INSTRUMENT. RAN SUBJECT, TECHNICIAN AND DIAGNOSTIC TESTS. CHECKED SETUP VOLTAGES, PRINT AND REMOTE OPERATION. VERIFIED CALIBRATION, OK

FRANK SGARLATA
Technician
Office of Public Safety

APPENDIX 26

Photo of Simulator

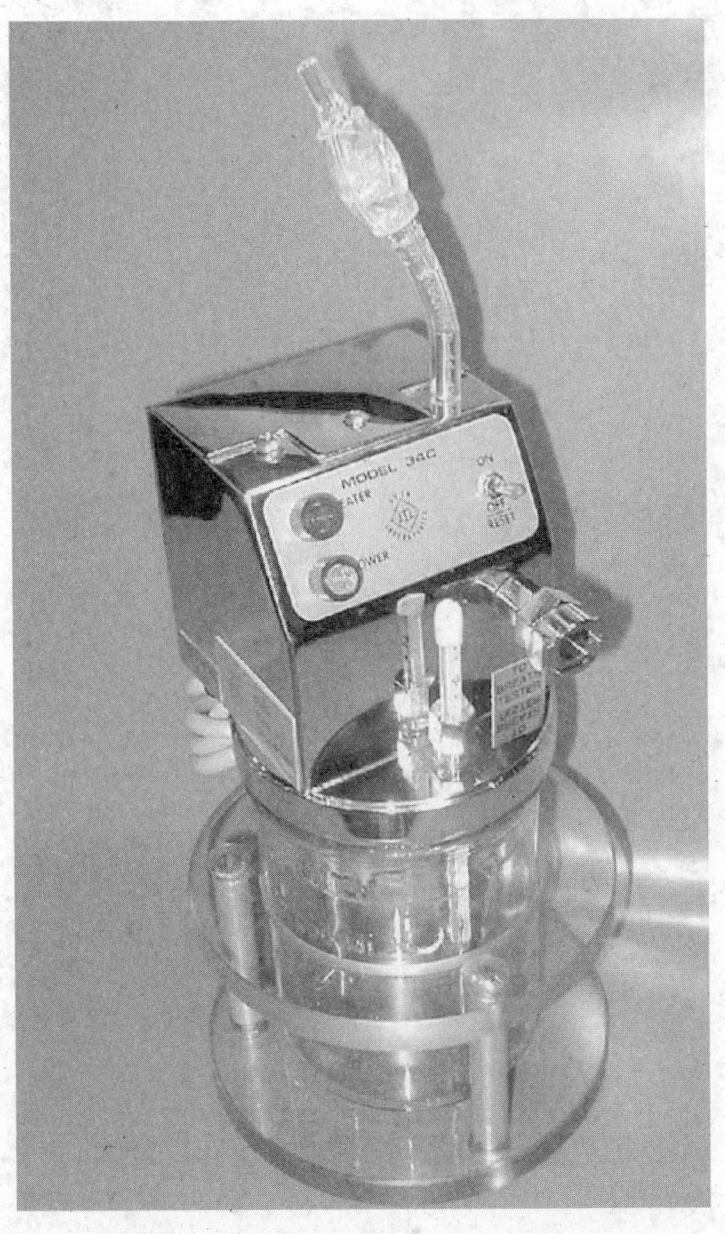

APPENDIX 27

Certificate of Analysis of Simulator Solution

CERTIFIED COPY (CPLR RULE 4518)

0.10% SIMULATOR SOLUTION RECORD

Lot Number 10110, dated May 25, 2010

I, Jennifer F Limoges, Supervisor of Forensic Services, Forensic Investigation Center, do hereby certify and authenticate, as provided by Rule 4518, subdivision c, Civil Practice Law and Rules, that the document annexed hereto is an exact copy of an electronic record of the New York State Police Forensic Investigation Center which has been delegated to my possession, custody and control by the Superintendent of the New York State Police. This record was made in the regular course of business of the New York State Police Forensic Investigation Center, it is the regular course of the Forensic Investigation Center business to make such record, and such record was made at the time of each event recorded in it or within a reasonable time thereafter.

Digitally signed under
ESRA by Jennifer F
Limoges on
2010.06.01 07:32:04 -04'00'

Jennifer F Limoges

Supervisor of Forensic Services

Forensic Investigation Center

JOHN P. MELVILLE
ACTING SUPERINTENDENT

NEW YORK STATE POLICE
FORENSIC INVESTIGATION CENTER
BUILDING 30
1220 WASHINGTON AVE.
ALBANY, NY 12226-3000

0.10% SIMULATOR SOLUTION RECORD

Report Date: May 25, 2010

Manufacturer: Guth Laboratories, Inc.

Lot Number: 10110

Expiration Date: 11/5/2010

Analysis Results: 0.120 g/dL

Simulator solution lot number 10110 has been tested by headspace gas chromatography to contain the appropriate concentration of ethyl alcohol and is hereby approved for use.

When this simulator solution is used with a properly operating breath testing instrument, it will provide a value of 0.10% within acceptable limits.

Carrie A. Kirkton	*Jennifer F Limoges*
Digitally signed under ESRA by Carrie A Kirkton on 2010.05.25 13:44:37 -04'00'	Digitally signed under ESRA by Jennifer F Limoges on 2010.06.01 07:31:01 -04'00'

Carrie A Kirkton   Jennifer F Limoges

Forensic Scientist III   Supervisor of Forensic Services
Breath Analysis Technical Supervisor   Breath Analysis Technical Supervisor

Page 1 of 1

1780

APPENDIX 28

Weekly Simulator Test Record

March 2011

Infrared Instrument
Weekly Calibration Verification Test Record

Department: _____   Instrument Serial #: 117 806

Test Date	Simulator Solution Lot #	Simulator Temperature			Sim. Serial#	Test Results			Breath Analysis Supervisor	Sim. Sol. Change *
		1	2	3		1	2	3		
3/1/11	10270	33.98	34.00	34.01	117 806	.09	.09	.09		
3/1/11	10270	34.03	34.00	34.02	117806	.09	.09	.09		✓
3/7/11	10270	34.01	34.01	33.99	117 806	.09	09	.09		
3/14/11	10270	34.01	34.01	34.01	117806	05	.05	09		
3/22/11	10270	34.07	34.02	34.00	117806	.09	.09	09		
3/29/11	10270	34.00	33.98	34.01	117806	.09	.09	.09		

* - Please enter a √ to denote simulator solution change taking place

Version 8/7/2006

1781

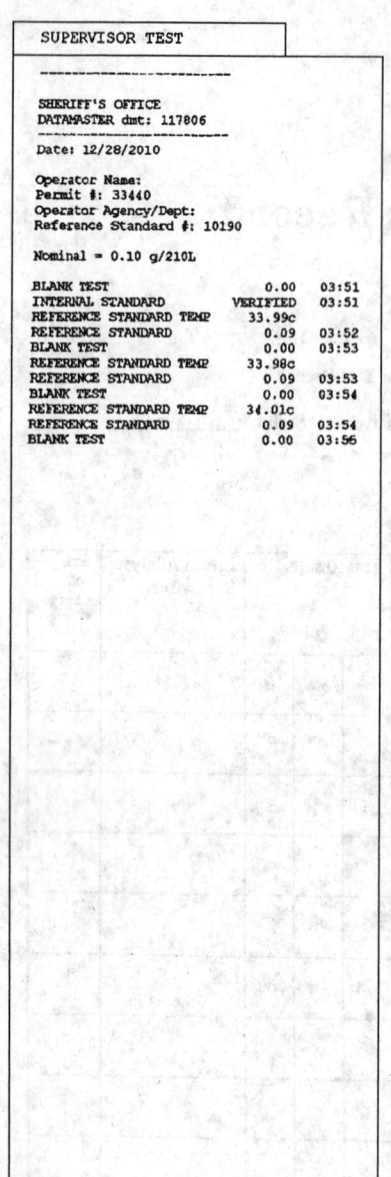

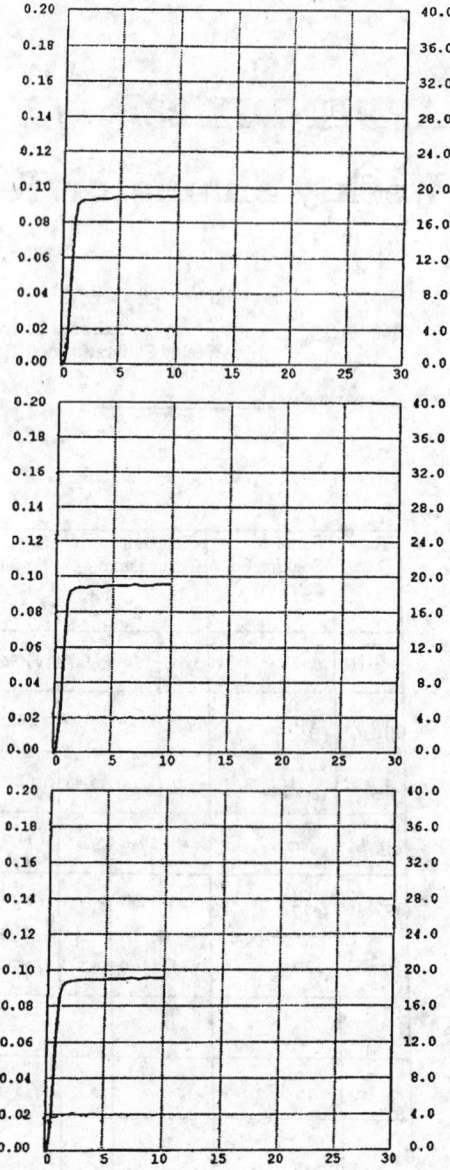

APPENDIX 29   *[Reserved]*

APPENDIX 30 *[Reserved]*

APPENDIX 31 *[Reserved]*

APPENDIX 32 *[Reserved]*

APPENDIX 33

Operational Checklist

STATE OF NEW YORK DIVISION OF CRIMINAL JUSTICE SERVICES			DataMaster DMT Operational CheckList	
New York DataMaster DMT Operational CheckList	Case/Ticket Number:	Date:	Arresting Agency /Department:	
Subject Name:	Blood Alcohol: 0. 11 %	Time of Subject Sample: 2231	Instrument Serial Number: 117806	
Reference Standard Lot Number: 10270	Reference Standard Test Results 0. 09 % Reference Standard Temperature 34.01 °C	Time of Reference Standard Test: 2232	Simulator Serial Number: 1006	

PREPARATION: Check defendant's mouth for any foreign matter.

1. ☑ Nothing taken orally, e.g. smoking, regurgitation, or vomit by defendant for 20 minutes immediately prior to test. Start time of observation period, 2207 .

2. ☑ Turn power switch to "ON" position(if applicable).

3. ☑ Wait for ready indicator as display will read: "READY PUSH RUN"

4. ☑ Check simulator temperature and connections. Record Reference Standard Lot Number.

5. ☑ Press "RUN" button to initiate test.

6. ☑ Answer user questions, instrument automatically initiates test sequence.

7. ☑ When prompted, secure breath sample from subject.

8. ☑ Upon completion of the subject's test and reference standard test, record information from the printout on the check list.

9. ☑ Attach one copy of the subject's test printout to check list.

10. ☑ Complete prompt suspension provision certification on the print ticket.

Operator Name, Rank and Department:	Permit Number:

Rev October 2006

APPENDIX 34 *[Reserved]*

APPENDIX 35 [Reserved]

APPENDIX 36

Intoxilyzer Functional Diagram

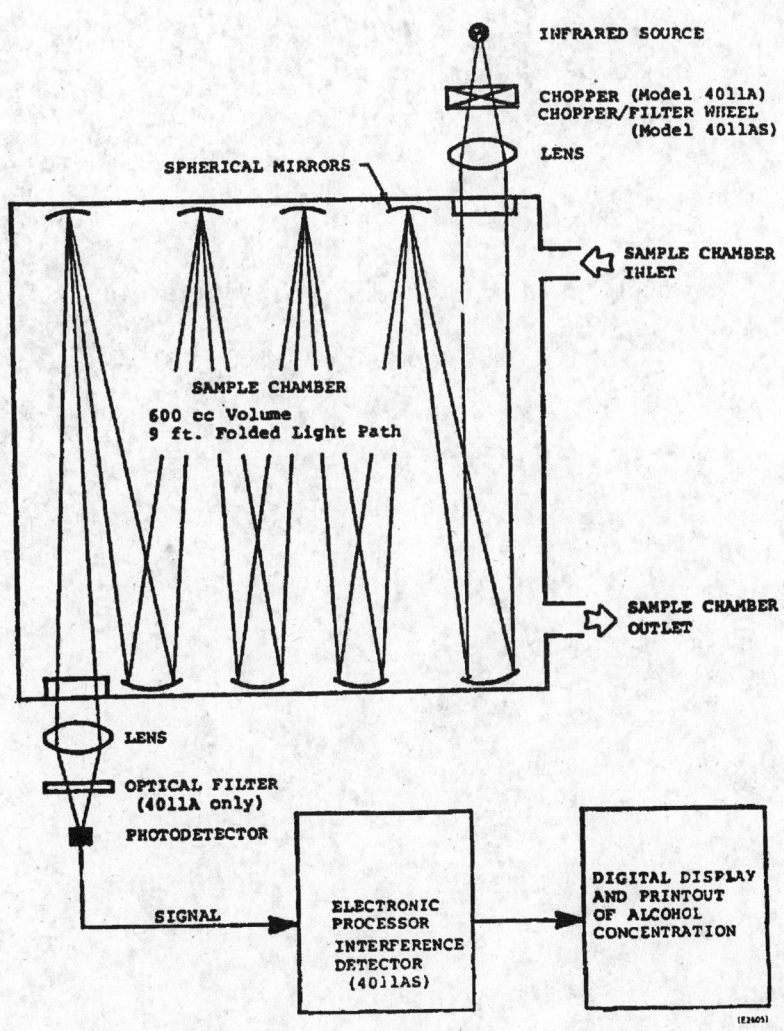

INFRARED SOURCE

CHOPPER (Model 4011A)
CHOPPER/FILTER WHEEL
(Model 4011AS)

LENS

SPHERICAL MIRRORS

SAMPLE CHAMBER
INLET

SAMPLE CHAMBER
600 cc Volume
9 ft. Folded Light Path

SAMPLE CHAMBER
OUTLET

LENS

OPTICAL FILTER
(4011A only)

PHOTODETECTOR

SIGNAL

ELECTRONIC
PROCESSOR
INTERFERENCE
DETECTOR
(4011AS)

DIGITAL DISPLAY
AND PRINTOUT
OF ALCOHOL
CONCENTRATION

(E2605)

1797

APPENDIX 37

Functional Diagram of Intoximeter 3000

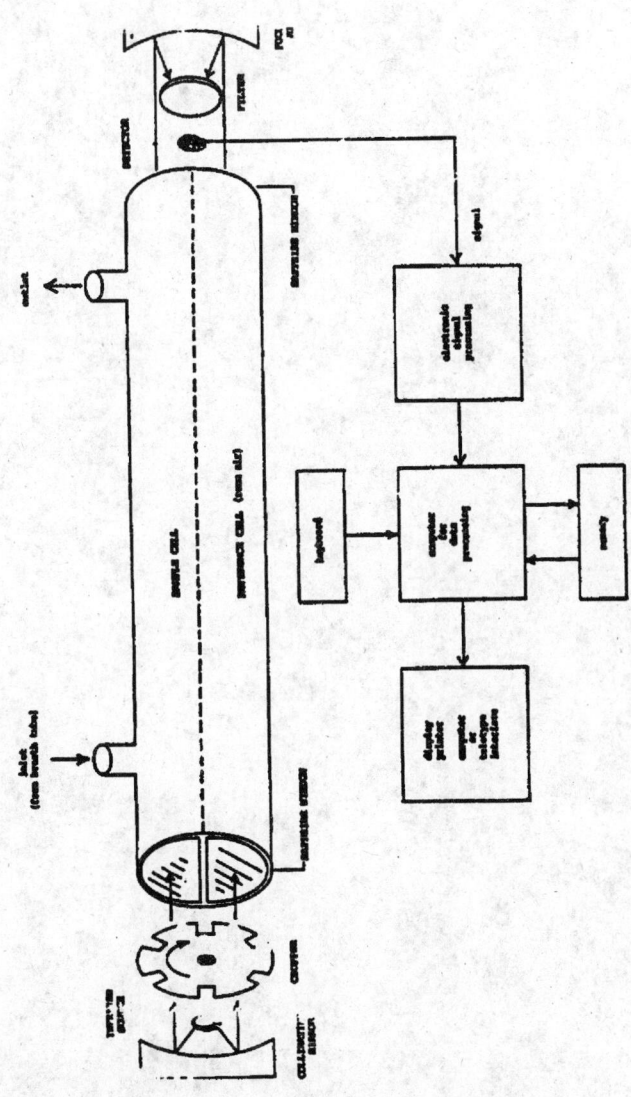

APPENDIX 38   *[Reserved]*

APPENDIX 39

Department of Motor Vehicles' Counsel's Opinion Regarding VTL § 1194(A) Orders' Effect on Test Refusal

STATE OF NEW YORK

DEPARTMENT OF MOTOR VEHICLES

THE GOVERNOR NELSON A. ROCKEFELLER

JOHN A. PASSIDOMO   EMPIRE STATE PLAZA
  COMMISSIONER

                   ALBANY, NEW YORK 12228

STANLEY M. GRUSS
  DEPUTY COMMISSIONER AND COUNSEL

May 15, 1985

Peter Gerstenzang, Esq.
Gerstenzang, Weiner & Gerstenzang
41 State Street
Albany, New York 12207

Dear Mr. Gerstenzang:

You have requested an opinion regarding the ramifications of a chemical test of blood, ordered pursuant to Section 1194-a of the Vehicle and Traffic Law, on a prior refusal to submit to a breath test, resulting in the issuance of such order.

The procedure which ultimately results in a Department of Motor Vehicles' chemical test refusal hearing is set forth in Section 1194-2 of the Vehicle and Traffic Law. That procedure is initiated by the police officer's submission to the court of a written report of refusal. Section 1194-2 provides that such report must state that no chemical test was administered pursuant to Section 1194-a of the Vehicle and Traffic Law.

This is consistent with the intent of Section 1194, which is designed to provide an equivalent penalty for those who frustrate prosecution under Section 1192 of the Vehicle and Traffic Law by virtue of refusal. Where evidence of blood alcohol content is obtained under Section 1194-a, prosecution is not frustrated.

It is, therefore, this Department's opinion that a test ordered pursuant to Section 1194-a vitiates a prior chemical test refusal, and no departmental chemical test refusal hearing should be held in any such case.

If I may be of any further assistance, please do not hesitate to contact me.

Sincerely,

STANLEY M. GRUSS
Deputy Commissioner and Counsel

SMG/dc

1803

APPENDIX 40

New York Department of Motor Vehicles' Chemical Test Refusals (15 NYCRR Part 139)

Part 139 CHEMICAL TEST REFUSALS

Section 139.1.   Introduction

[Current with amendments included in the New York State Register, Volume XXXVI, Issue 35, dated September 3, 2014.]

Section 1194 of the Vehicle and Traffic Law provides for the temporary suspension and subsequent revocation of a license or operating privilege when a person refuses to submit to a chemical test. Section 49-a of the Navigation Law provides for the temporary suspension and subsequent suspension of the privilege of operating a vessel when a person refuses to submit to a chemical test. Section 25.24 of the Parks, Recreation and Historic Preservation Law contains a similar provision regarding refusing a chemical test when operating a snowmobile. In order to facilitate the orderly taking and recording of such actions, and to insure that hearings are held in timely fashion, these regulations are promulgated pursuant to the authority contained in section 1194 of the Vehicle and Traffic Law, section 25.24 of the Parks, Recreation and Historic Preservation Law and section 49-a of the Navigation Law. Unless otherwise noted, *commissioner* shall refer to the Commissioner of Motor Vehicles, and *department* shall refer to the Department of Motor Vehicles.

Sec. filed Jan. 2, 1981; amds. filed: Aug. 10, 1993; June 13, 2000 eff. June 28, 2000.

Section 139.2.   Police officer procedure upon arrest and arraignment

[Current with amendments included in the New York State Register, Volume XXXVI, Issue 35, dated September 3, 2014.]

(a) If any person who has been placed under arrest for any

violation of section 1192 of the Vehicle and Traffic Law (or who has taken a breath test, pursuant to section 1194[1] of such law, which indicates that the person has consumed alcohol) is requested to submit to a chemical test, the police officer shall inform the person that the license or permit to drive and any nonresident operating privilege shall be immediately suspended and subsequently revoked for refusal to submit to such chemical test or any portion thereof, whether or not the person is found guilty of the charge for which he or she was arrested. If the person thereafter refuses to submit, the test shall not be given unless a court order has been granted pursuant to section 1194(3) of the Vehicle and Traffic Law. The arresting police officer shall cause to be made a written report of such refusal on a form provided by or acceptable to the commissioner, verified as provided by law (Report of Refusal to Submit to Chemical Test). No report shall be made if there was a compulsory test administered pursuant to section 1194(3) of the Vehicle and Traffic Law.

(b) If any person who has been placed under arrest for any violation of section 49-a of the Navigation Law (or who has taken a breath test, pursuant to section 49-a[6] of such law, which indicates the person has consumed alcohol) is requested to submit to a chemical test, the police officer shall inform the person that the privilege to operate a vessel shall be immediately suspended for refusal to submit to such chemical test, whether or not the person is found guilty of the charge for which he or she was arrested. If the person thereafter refuses to submit, the test shall not be given unless a court order has been granted pursuant to section 49-a(8) of the Navigation Law. The arresting police officer shall cause to be made a written report of such refusal on a form provided by or acceptable to the commissioner, verified as provided by law (Report of Refusal to Submit to Chemical Test—Vessel). No report shall be made if there was a compulsory test administered pursuant to section 49-a(8) of the Navigation Law.

(c) If any person who has been placed under arrest for any violation of section 25.24 of the Parks, Recreation and Historic Preservation Law (or who has taken a breath test, pursuant to section 25.24[5][b] of such law, which indicates the person has consumed alcohol) is requested to submit to a chemical test, the police officer shall inform the person that the privilege to operate a snowmobile shall be immediately suspended for refusal to submit to such chemical test, whether or not the person is found guilty of the charge for which he or she was arrested. If the person thereafter refuses to submit, the test shall not be given unless a court order has been granted pursuant to section 25.24(7)(d)(4) of such law. The arresting police officer shall cause to be made a written report of such refusal on a form provided by or acceptable to the commissioner, verified as provided by law (Report of Refusal to Submit to Chemical Test—Snowmobile). No report shall be made if there was a compulsory test administered pursuant to section 25.24(7)(d)(4) of such law.

(d) *Upon arraignment.* Upon the arraignment of the defendant, the police officer shall present to the court copies of the report of refusal to submit to chemical test. The police officer shall bring his or her own copy of such report to the refusal hearing at the location and on the date and time specified in the temporary suspension and notice of hearing form provided by the court.

Sec. filed Jan. 2, 1981; amds. filed: Aug. 10, 1993; June 13, 2000 eff. June 28, 2000.

Section 139.3. Court procedure upon arraignment

[Current with amendments included in the New York State Register, Volume XXXVI, Issue 35, dated September 3, 2014.]

(a) Upon arraignment of a defendant under arrest for any violation of section 1192 of the Vehicle and Traffic Law the court shall, upon the basis of the police officer's report of refusal, temporarily suspend without notice the license or permit to drive and any nonresident operating privilege of the defendant.

(b) Upon arraignment of a defendant under arrest for any violation of section 49-a of the Navigation Law, the court shall, upon the basis of the police officer's report of refusal, temporarily suspend without notice the defendant's privilege to operate a vessel.

(c) Upon arraignment of a defendant under arrest for any violation of section 25.24 of the Parks, Recreation and Historic Preservation Law, the court shall, upon the basis of the police officer's report of refusal, temporarily suspend without notice the defendant's privilege to operate a snowmobile.

(d) Upon arraignment under either subdivision (a), (b) or (c) of this section, the court shall complete a temporary suspension and notice of hearing form (adding the location and the next available hearing date and time, as provided by the commissioner), and give the appropriate copies to the defendant and the police officer. Within 48 hours of the arraignment, the court must forward copies of both the refusal report and the temporary suspension and notice of hearing form to the commissioner, and in the case of an arraignment for violation of Navigation Law, section 49-a or Parks, Recreation and Historic Preservation Law, section 25.24, the court must forward an additional copy of the report of refusal to the Commissioner of Parks, Recreation and Historic Preservation. Timely submission of the refusal report to the Commissioner of Motor Vehicles may not be waived even with consent of all parties.

Sec. filed Jan. 2, 1981; amds. filed: Aug. 10, 1993; June 13, 2000 eff. June 28, 2000.

Section 139.4. Provisions applicable to the Department of Motor Vehicles

[Current with amendments included in the New York State Register, Volume XXXVI, Issue 35, dated September 3, 2014.]

(a) The commissioner shall provide to all magistrates, in advance, a schedule of hearing dates and locations and forms necessary to carry out the provisions of this Part.

(b) Time of hearing. The refusal hearing shall commence at the place provided in the notice of hearing form and as close as practicable to the designated time. If the hearing cannot be commenced due to the absence of a hearing officer or the unavailability of the planned hearing site, it will be rescheduled by the department, with notice to the police officer and person accused of the refusal. Adjournment requests for hearings held pursuant to section 1194 of the Vehicle and Traffic Law shall be considered in accordance with sections 127.7 and 127.9 of this Title. All other requests for adjournments shall be addressed to the hearing officer, who may order a temporary suspension of the license, permit, nonresident operating privilege, or privilege of operating a vessel or snowmobile pursuant to law and Part 127 of this Title.

(c) Waiver of hearing. A person may waive, in writing, the right to a chemical test refusal hearing. Any such waiver shall constitute an admission that a chemical test refusal occurred as contemplated by section 1194 of the Vehicle and Traffic Law, section 25.24 of the Parks, Recreation and Historic Preservation Law, or section 49-a of the Navigation Law, as the case may be, and such waiver shall result in administrative sanctions provided by law for the chemical test refusal. Failure to appear at a scheduled hearing shall also constitute a waiver; however, the person who failed to appear may make a written request to the commissioner for a rescheduled hearing to be held as soon as practicable in accordance with section 127.8 of this Title.

(d) Civil penalty. Any person whose license, permit, nonresident operating privilege has been revoked, or whose privilege to operate a vessel or snowmobile has been suspended, for refusal to submit to a chemical test shall be liable for payment of a civil penalty as provided by law. No new license, permit or privilege (other than a conditional license, permit or privilege issued pursuant to Part 134 of this Title) shall be issued, or restored, until such civil penalty has been paid.

(e) Notice to the Commissioner of Parks, Recreation and Historic Preservation. The commissioner shall notify the Commissioner of Parks, Recreation and Historic Preservation of any suspension of a person's vessel or snowmobile operating privilege as the result of a hearing or waiver of hearing, and of any restoration of the privilege following such suspension, and of a reversal on appeal of any such suspension.

Sec. filed Jan. 2, 1981; amd. filed Aug. 10, 1993 eff. Aug. 25, 1993. Amended (a)—(d); added (e); amd. filed June 13, 2000 eff. June 28, 2000; amd. filed Nov. 19, 2007 eff. Dec. 5, 2007.

APPENDIX 41

New York State Department of Motor Vehicles' Procedures for Safety Hearings (Part 127)

Section 127.1. Notice of hearing; answers

(a) **Generally.** All parties shall be given reasonable notice of a hearing. The notice shall include (1) a statement of the time, place and nature of the hearing, (2) a statement of the legal authority and jurisdiction under which the hearing is to be held, (3) a reference to the particular sections of the statutes and regulations involved, where possible, (4) a short and plain statement of the matters asserted, (5) a statement that interpreter services will be made available, upon request of a deaf respondent, at no charge, (6) a statement that a party may be represented by counsel and (7) a statement of other rules and rights contained in the Department's Administrative Adjudication Plan pursuant to Executive Order 131, section III(B)(11). No pre-hearing answers or responsive pleadings are permitted.

(b) In a hearing initiated through a complaint or investigation of the Division of Vehicle Safety, notice shall be mailed at least 30 days prior to the scheduled date of the hearing, unless a hearing is required by law to be held at an earlier time. Notices of vehicle safety hearings shall be mailed by certified mail to the respondent at his or her last-known address on file with the department.

(c) Except for hearings scheduled by a court or hearings governed by subdivision (b) of this section, it is the department's policy to mail notices of hearings at least 14 days prior to the scheduled date of the hearing, unless a hearing is required by law to be held at an earlier time. A notice of hearing shall be mailed by first class mail to the respondent at his or her last-known address on file with the department unless a different method of service is required by law. Any notice not returned by the post office for non-delivery shall be presumed received by the respondent.

Historical Note

Sec. filed Nov. 25, 1986; amd. filed Feb. 7, 1991 eff. Feb. 27, 1991; amd. filed Dec. 7, 2009 eff. Dec. 23, 2009. Current with amendments included in the New York State Register, XXXVIII, Issue 34 dated August 24, 2016.

Section 127.2.   Time and place of hearing

(a) All hearings, whether scheduled by the department or by a court, shall be commenced at the time and place specified in the notice of hearing, or as soon thereafter as is practicable.

(b) Except as provided in subdivision (c) of this section, hearings shall be commenced within the following time limitations:

(1) for a vehicle safety hearing, 12 months from the filing of a complaint or, where no complaint is filed, from the initiation of the department's investigation;

(2) for a chemical test refusal hearing, six months from the date the department receives notice of refusal;

(3) for a hearing to investigate a fatal accident, 12 months from the date of death;

(4) for any other hearing not required by law, one year form the department's receipt of the facts which give rise to the hearing; and

(5) notwithstanding any of the above provisions, for any hearing, other than a chemical test refusal hearing or a temporary suspension pending hearing imposed pursuant to section 415(9-a) of the Vehicle and Traffic Law, where a temporary suspension pending such hearing is in effect, 30 days from the effective date of such suspension.

(c) If the department has reasonable grounds for postponing the commencement of a hearing in excess of the time limitations specified in subdivision (b) of this section, such hearing may be commenced as soon thereafter as is practicable, provided the respondent is given prior notice thereof and an explanation of the grounds for such postponement. The reasonableness of such postponement shall be reviewable by the Administrative Appeals Board established pursuant to article 3-A of the Vehicle and Traffic Law or the Repair Shop Review Board established pursuant to article 12-A of such law, provided an appealable determination is subsequently made.

(d) Any time during which the department has offered a respondent a waiver of hearing contingent on the respondent's acceptance of a penalty specified by the department shall not be considered in calculating the time limitations set forth in subdivision (b) of this section.

(e) Any time following a general audit of a facility, during which a facility is given an opportunity to correct deficiencies noted in such audit, shall not be considered in calculating the time limitations set forth in subdivision (b) of this section.

Historical Note

Sec. filed Nov. 25, 1986; amds. filed: May 16, 1990; Feb. 7, 1991; July 19,

2001 eff. Aug. 8, 2001. Amended (b)(3), (5). Current with amendments included in the New York State Register, XXXVIII, Issue 34 dated August 24, 2016.

Section 127.3. Suspensions pending hearing

(a) Whenever the department suspends a license, privilege or permit pending a hearing, the respondent shall be provided with a notice of suspension, mailed to the respondent's last known address on file with the department. Such suspension shall specify the time and place at which the hearing is scheduled to be held.

(b) Except as otherwise provided in subdivision (d) of this section, no suspension pending a hearing shall be issued unless:

(1) the scheduled hearing date is no later than 30 days from the date of such suspension, or no later than 10 days if such suspension is imposed pursuant to section 415(9-a) of the Vehicle and Traffic Law and either:

(2) for a vehicle safety hearing or other hearing involving a business licensed or regulated by the commissioner, the commissioner has reasonable grounds to believe that such suspension is necessary to prevent continuing violations; or

(3) for hearings involving a driver's license or privilege, the commissioner has reasonable grounds to believe that the respondent, if allowed to continue to drive, would pose an unusual or immediate risk upon the highways.

(c) A statement specifying the basis for the commissioner's determination that such suspension satisfies the criteria set forth in subdivision (b) of this section shall be provided to the respondent.

(d) This subdivision shall not apply to the following: temporary suspension pending chemical test refusal hearings mandated by section 1194 of the Vehicle and Traffic Law; suspensions issued pursuant to section 127.7(e) of this Part upon adjournment of a hearing; suspensions issued pursuant to section 127.8 of this Part following a respondent's failure to appear at a hearing.

Historical Note

Sec. filed Nov. 25, 1986; amd. filed Feb. 7, 1991; renum. 127.4, new filed April 28, 1992; amd. filed July 19, 2001 eff. Aug. 8, 2001. Amended (b)(1). Current with amendments included in the New York State Register, XXXVIII, Issue 34 dated August 24, 2016.

Section 127.4. Appearances

(a) A respondent may be represented by counsel or, in the discretion of the hearing officer, by any other person of his or her choosing. Any person representing the respondent must conform to the standards of conduct required of attorneys appearing before courts of this State. Failure to conform to such standards shall be grounds for prohibiting the continued appearance of such person on behalf of the respondent.

(b) A complainant or witness may be represented by counsel or other representative. However, the ability of the complainant, witness or such counsel or representative to question and/or cross-examine witnesses may be limited or prohibited by the hearing officer if, in his or her discretion, the hearing officer feels that such questioning or cross-examination is irrelevant or unduly repetitious.

Historical Note

Sec. filed Nov. 25, 1986; amd. filed Feb. 7, 1991; renum. 127.5, new added by renum. 127.3, filed April 28, 1992 eff. May 13, 1992. Current with amendments included in the New York State Register, XXXVIII, Issue 34 dated August 24, 2016.

Section 127.5. Conduct of hearings; recusal

(a) A respondent or designated representative may request recusal of an assigned hearing officer. The request and the reason for it must be made to the assigned hearing officer at the beginning of the hearing or as soon thereafter as the requestor receives information which forms the basis for such request. Denial of a request for recusal shall be reviewable by the Administrative Appeals Board or Repair Shop Review Board under procedures established pursuant to articles 3-A and 12-A of the Vehicle and Traffic Law, provided a final, adverse determination is subsequently made which is appealable by the requestor to the appropriate board.

(b) At the hearing, the respondent or his or her designated representative may admit or deny any allegation made in the notice of hearing. Any matter which has been stipulated to or admitted on the open record by the respondent shall be deemed proven. Failure to respond to any allegation shall be deemed a denial of such allegation, and under no circumstances shall the respondent be compelled to testify. However, the hearing officer may draw a negative inference from the failure to testify.

(c) The order of proof at a hearing shall be determined by the hearing officer. Testimony shall be given under oath or affirmation. The hearing officer, in his or her discretion, may exclude any witnesses, other than a respondent or a representative of the department, if one is present, during other testimony. The hearing officer may also admit any relevant evidence in addition to oral testimony. Any witness may be questioned and/or cross-examined by the hearing officer, by his or her own counsel or representative, and by the party who did not call the witness.

(d) At the conclusion of all proceedings necessary to determine whether the respondent has violated any of the provisions of the Vehicle and Traffic Law or these regulations, the hearing officer must, as provided in section 127.10 of this Part, either render or reserve decision. At such time, the hearing officer shall advise the respondent that, for the sole purposes of establishing an appropriate penalty, the respondent may offer any relevant comments or testimony regarding respondent's prior record as provided by or revealed to the hearing officer.

(e) The provisions of sections 124.1(b), 124.2(b) and 124.4(a) through (e) of this Title shall be applicable to hearings held under section 1194-a of the Vehicle and Traffic Law relating to a charge of a violation of section 1192-a of such law.

Historical Note

Sec. filed Nov. 25, 1986; amd. filed Feb. 7, 1991; renum. 127.6, new added by renum. and amd. 127.4, filed April 28, 1992; amds. filed: Nov. 1, 1996 as emergency measure; Jan. 7, 1997 eff. Jan. 22, 1997. Added (e). Current with amendments included in the New York State Register, XXXVIII, Issue 34 dated August 24, 2016.

Section 127.6. Evidence; discovery

(a) Prior to a hearing, a respondent may make a request to review nonconfidential information in the hearing file including information which is not protected by law from disclosure. If the file has been sent to the hearing officer or is scheduled to be sent within seven days of receipt of a request by the Safety Hearing Bureau, examination of the information will be arranged by the hearing officer. The examination will be scheduled for a time at least five days prior to the hearing unless a shorter time is mutually agreed between the hearing officer and the requestor. If the file has not been sent to the hearing officer and is not scheduled to be sent within seven days of receipt of a request by the Safety Hearing Bureau, the file will be made available for examination at the Safety Hearing Bureau before the usual date scheduled for sending the file to the hearing officer. A respondent may elect to examine the file after it is received by the hearing officer rather than while it is in the custody of the Safety Hearing Bureau. If a request to examine the file is received less than seven days prior to the hearing date, the requestor will be afforded an opportunity to examine the file immediately prior to commencement of the hearing or at an earlier time as may be agreed to in the discretion of the hearing officer.

(b) Rules governing the admissibility of evidence in a court of law are not applicable to hearings held by the department. Evidence which would not be admissible in a court, such as hearsay, is admissible in a departmental hearing. The standard of proof at a hearing shall be the preponderance of the evidence.

(c) The privileges set forth in article 45 of the Civil Practice Law and Rules shall be applicable in hearings conducted pursuant to this Part.

Historical Note

Sec. filed Nov. 25, 1986; amd. filed Feb. 7, 1991; renum. 127.7, new added by renum. 127.5, filed April 28, 1992 eff. May 13, 1992; amd. filed Mar. 15, 2016 eff. Mar. 30, 2016. Current with amendments included in the New York State Register, XXXVIII, Issue 34 dated August 24, 2016.

Section 127.7. Adjournments

(a) Adjournments of hearings may only be granted by the hearing officer responsible for the particular hearing, or by the Safety Hearing Bureau or the Division of Vehicle Safety, as appropriate.

(b) It is the department's general policy to grant a request for adjournment for good cause if such request is received at least seven days prior to the scheduled date of hearing and if no prior requests for adjournment have been made. Notwithstanding this policy, requests for adjournments made more than seven days prior to hearing may be denied by the hearing officer, or supervisor of the hearing officer or by the Safety Hearing Bureau or Division of Vehicle Safety, in their discretion. Grounds for such a denial include, but are not limited to, such a request being a second or subsequent request for adjournment, or where there is reason to believe such request is merely an attempt to delay the holding of a hearing, or where an adjournment will significantly affect the availability of other witnesses scheduled to testify.

(c) Any motorist or designated representative requesting an adjournment should obtain the name and title of the person granting such request. This information will be required in the event of any dispute as to whether an adjournment was in fact granted. Any request which is not specifically granted shall be deemed denied.

(d) Requests for adjournments within seven days of a scheduled hearing must be made directly to the hearing officer. Such requests will generally not be granted.

(e) (1) Except as provided for in paragraphs (2) and (3) of this subdivision, in any case where an adjournment is granted, any suspension or revocation of a license, permit or privilege already in effect may be continued pending the adjourned hearing. In addition, in the event no such action is in effect, a temporary suspension of such license, permit or privilege may be imposed at the time the adjournment is granted provided that the records of the department or the evidence already admitted furnishes reasonable grounds to believe such suspension is necessary to prevent continuing violations or a substantial traffic safety hazard.

(2) Adjournment of a chemical test refusal hearings held pursuant to Vehicle and Traffic Law, section 1194. Where an adjournment of a chemical test refusal hearing is granted at

the request of the respondent, any suspension of a respondent's license, permit or privilege already in effect shall be continued pending the adjourned hearing. In addition, in the event no such suspension is in effect when the adjournment is granted, a temporary suspension of such license, permit or privilege shall be imposed and shall take effect on the date of the originally scheduled hearing. Such suspension shall not be continued or imposed if the hearing officer affirmatively finds, on the record, that there is no reason to believe that the respondent poses a substantial traffic safety hazard and sets forth the basis for that finding on the record.

(3) Continuance of a chemical test refusal hearing held pursuant to Vehicle and Traffic Law, section 1194. If a chemical test refusal hearing is continued at the discretion of the hearing officer, in order to complete testimony, to subpoena witnesses or for any other reason, and if the respondent's license, permit or privilege was suspended pending such hearing, such suspension shall remain in effect pending the continued hearing unless the hearing officer affirmatively finds, on the record, that there is no reason to believe that the respondent poses a substantial traffic safety hazard and sets forth the basis for that finding on the record. If respondent's license, permit or privilege was not suspended pending the hearing, the hearing officer may suspend such license, permit or privilege, based upon the testimony provided and evidence submitted at such hearing, if the hearing officer affirmatively finds, on the record, that there is reason to believe that the respondent poses a substantial traffic safety hazard and sets forth the basis for that finding on the record.

(4) In addition to any grounds for suspension authorized pursuant to paragraphs (2) and (3) of this subdivision, a hearing officer must impose a suspension or continue a suspension of a respondent's driver's license, pursuant to paragraphs (2) and (3) of this subdivision, if the respondent's record indicates that:

(i) The person has been convicted of homicide, assault, criminal negligence or criminally negligent homicide arising out of the operation of a motor vehicle.

(ii) The person has two or more revocations and/or suspensions of his driver's license within the last three years, other than a suspension that may be terminated by performance of an act by the person.

(iii) The person has been convicted more than once of reckless driving within the last three years.

(iv) The person has three or more alcohol-related incidents within the last 10 years, including any conviction of Vehicle and Traffic Law, section 1192, any finding of a violation of section 1192-a of such law, and a refusal to submit to a chemical test. If a refusal that arises out of the same incident as a section 1192 conviction, this shall count as one incident.

(f) *Adjournments of hearings held under section 1194-a of the Vehicle and Traffic Law.*

(1) Adjournments of hearings may only be granted by the hearing officer responsible for the particular hearing, by a supervisor of such hearing officer or by the Safety Hearing Bureau.

(2) It is the department's general policy to grant a request for adjournment for good cause if such request is received at least seven days prior to the scheduled date of hearing and if no prior requests for adjournment have been made. Notwithstanding this policy, requests for adjournments made more than seven days prior to hearing may be denied by the hearing officer, or supervisor of the hearing office or by the Safety Hearing Bureau. Grounds for such a denial include, but are not limited to, such a request being a second or subsequent request for adjournment, or where there is reason to believe such request is merely an attempt to delay the holding of a hearing, or where an adjournment will significantly affect the availability of other witnesses scheduled to testify.

(3) Any motorist or designated representative requesting an adjournment should obtain the name and title of the person granting such request. This information will be required in the event of any dispute as to whether an adjournment was in fact granted. Any request which is not specifically granted shall be deemed denied.

(4) Requests for adjournments within seven days of a scheduled hearing must be made directly to the hearing officer. Such requests will generally not be granted, unless the initial hearing was scheduled less than seven days from the date on which respondent was first notified of the hearing by the police officer.

(5) A temporary suspension of a license, permit or privilege may be imposed at the time a second or subsequent adjournment requested by the respondent is granted provided that the records of the department or the evidence already admitted furnishes reasonable grounds to believe such suspension is necessary to prevent continuing violations or a substantial traffic safety hazard.

(6) Unless an adjournment has been granted, upon the respondent's failure to appear for a scheduled hearing, the commissioner shall suspend the license or permit to drive or

nonresident operating privilege until the respondent petitions and a rescheduled hearing is conducted. If the rescheduled hearing is adjourned at the request of a person other
than the respondent, the respondent's license or privilege
shall be restored by the commissioner.

(7) If a police officer does not appear for a hearing, the
hearing officer shall have the authority to dismiss the charge.
A respondent shall have the right to waive a hearing.

(8) If the respondent fails to appear at a hearing, the hearing shall be rescheduled and no testimony shall be taken in
the respondent's absence.

Historical Note

Sec. filed Nov. 25, 1986; renum. 127.8, new added by renum. and amd. 127.6,
filed April 28, 1992; amds. filed: Nov. 1, 1996 as emergency measure; Jan. 7,
1997 eff. Jan. 22, 1997. Added (f); amd. filed Nov. 19, 2007 eff. Dec. 5, 2007.
Current with amendments included in the New York State Register, XXXVIII,
Issue 34 dated August 24, 2016.

Section 127.8.   Failure to appear; waiver

Except as provided in section 127.9 of this Part, in any case
where no adjournment is requested or, if requested, is not
granted, the respondent's failure to appear shall be deemed to
be a waiver of hearing. Any person who is deemed to have
waived a hearing under these circumstances may request a
rehearing within a reasonable time, which shall, if such request
is granted, be held as soon as is practicable. However, any action taken at the original hearing, or in effect at that time,
may be continued pending such rescheduled hearing. No
rehearing will be scheduled as a substitute for an appeal pursuant to section 127.12 of this Part. Upon a respondent's failure to appear, the referee may receive the testimony of available witnesses and enter evidence into the record. A respondent
who has waived a hearing by failing to appear may be
suspended pending attendance at an adjourned hearing or a
final determination; provided, however, when a respondent is
suspended pending hearing pursuant to section 398-f(1)(b) of
the Vehicle and Traffic Law, such suspension shall be terminated upon the respondent's attendance at such hearing.

Historical Note

Sec. filed Nov. 25, 1986; amd. filed Feb. 7, 1991; renum. 127.9, new added by
renum. and amd. 127.7, filed April 28, 1992; amd. filed July 19, 2001 eff.
Aug. 8, 2001. Current with amendments included in the New York State
Register, XXXVIII, Issue 34 dated August 24, 2016.

Section 127.9.   Chemical test refusal hearings

(a) Chemical test refusal hearings are required to be
scheduled by the court which arraigns the respondent on a related charge of a violation of section 1192 of the Vehicle and
Traffic Law, but may be scheduled by the department if the

court fails to do so. Notwithstanding the fact that such hearings may be held less than seven days from the date on which the respondent is arraigned in court, requests for adjournments of chemical test refusal hearings are governed by section 127.7 of this Part.

(b) If no adjournment has been granted, and the respondent fails to appear for a scheduled hearing, the respondent's failure to appear shall be deemed to be a waiver of hearing. Respondent may petition for a rehearing, pursuant to section 127.8 of this Part and section 1194-2(c) of the Vehicle and Traffic Law. If such a rehearing is granted, it shall be the responsibility of the respondent to insure the presence of any witness he or she wishes to question or cross-examine.

(c) If the respondent appears for a first scheduled chemical test refusal hearing, and the arresting officer does not appear, the matter will be adjourned and any temporary suspension still in effect shall be terminated. At any subsequent hearing, the hearing officer may make findings of fact and conclusions of law based upon the chemical test refusal report and any other relevant evidence in the record, notwithstanding the police officer' s nonappearance.

Historical Note

Sec. filed Nov. 25, 1986; amd. filed Feb. 7, 1991; renum. 127.10, new added by renum. and amd. 127.8, filed April 28, 1992 eff. May 13, 1992; amd. filed Nov. 19, 2007 eff. Dec. 5, 2007. Current with amendments included in the New York State Register, XXXVIII, Issue 34 dated August 24, 2016.

Section 127.10. Decisions

(a) The hearing officer may announce his or her decision at the conclusion of the hearing or may reserve decision. A written determination of the case, specifying the findings of fact, conclusions of law and disposition, including any penalty or penalties imposed, shall be sent to the respondent and his or her designated representative by first-class mail.

(b) Except where otherwise specified by statute, the effective date of any penalty or sanction shall be a date established by the hearing officer, which shall in no event be more than 60 days from the date of the determination.

(c) If the hearing officer does not render a decision within 45 days of the conclusion of the hearing, the respondent may serve a demand for decision on the hearing officer. Upon receipt of such demand, the hearing officer must render a decision within 45 days, or the charges shall be deemed dismissed.

Historical Note

Sec. filed Nov. 25, 1986; amd. filed Feb. 7, 1991; renum. 127.11, new added by renum. 127.9, filed April 28, 1992 eff. May 13, 1992. Current with amendments included in the New York State Register, XXXVIII, Issue 34 dated August 24, 2016.

Section 127.11.   Effect of other laws

(a) The provisions of the Criminal Procedure Law are not binding upon the conduct of administrative hearings. Except as provided in subdivision (b) of this section and section 127.6(b) of this Part, the provisions of the Civil Practice Law and Rules are not binding upon the conduct of administrative hearings. The provisions of those laws regarding forms of pleading, motion practice, discovery procedures, including demands for bills of particulars, and other matters are not applicable to hearings conducted in accordance with this Part.

(b) The provisions of section 2302 of the Civil Practice Law and Rules, regarding the issuance of subpoenas, are applicable to hearings conducted in accordance with this Part.

Historical Note

Sec. filed Nov. 25, 1986; renum. 127.12, new added by renum. and amd. 127.10, filed April 28, 1992 eff. May 13, 1992. Current with amendments included in the New York State Register, XXXVIII, Issue 34 dated August 24, 2016.

Section 127.12.   Appeals

Any posthearing application to review a finding or a sanction imposed is an appeal and shall be governed by article 3-A or 12-A of the Vehicle and Traffic Law, as appropriate, and Parts 155 and 82 of this Title.

Historical Note

Sec. added by renum. 127.11, filed April 28, 1992 eff. May 13, 1992. Current with amendments included in the New York State Register, XXXVIII, Issue 34 dated August 24, 2016.

Section 127.13.   Adjudicatory proceedings

(a) This section applies to adjudicatory proceedings conducted pursuant to section 471-a of the Vehicle and Traffic Law.

(b) Request for a hearing. A request for a hearing shall be in writing and made on a form and in a manner prescribed by the commissioner. The request shall contain a short and plain statement of the facts relied upon by the dealer to support a claim that the franchiser has violated one or more specific provisions of article 17-a of the Vehicle and Traffic Law together with a request for a specific remedy other than damages. The request shall be accompanied by copies of all correspondence between the dealer and the franchiser and other documents relevant to the claims made in the request.

(c) Notice of hearing. The dealer and franchiser shall be given reasonable notice of a hearing. The notice shall include:

(1) a statement of the time, place and nature of the hearing;

(2) the addresses of the dealer and franchiser;

(3) the name and address of the presiding officer assigned to the matter;

(4) a statement of the legal authority and jurisdiction under which the hearing is to be held;

(5) a reference to the particular section of the statutes and rules involved, where possible;

(6) a short and plain statement of the matters asserted by the dealer;

(7) a statement advising the franchiser of the right to submit, within 20 days of receipt of such hearing notice, a short and plain statement of answers to the allegations of the request and of facts on which the franchiser relies in defense of such allegations;

(8) a statement advising the dealer of the right to submit, within 20 days of receipt of the franchiser's answering statement an additional statement of facts and documentary material only to the extent of answering new matter raised by the franchiser;

(9) a statement that the dealer or franchiser may be represented by counsel; and

(10) a statement that interpreter services will be made available upon request of a deaf person, at no charge.

(d) Time and place of hearing. All hearings shall be commenced at the time and place specified in the notice of hearing, or as soon thereafter as practicable, but in no event sooner than 60 days from the date of the notice.

(e) Disclosure. At least 15 days prior to the commencement of a hearing, each party shall disclose to the other party all documents or other materials, including those that may have been maintained in electronic form, that the party intends to introduce at the hearing. Each party shall submit a copy of such disclosure to the presiding officer when disclosure to the other party is made.

(f) Recusal.

(1) A party may request recusal of a presiding officer. The request and the reason for it must be made in writing to the assigned presiding officer at the beginning of the hearing or as soon thereafter as the requestor receives information which forms the basis for such request, whichever occurs first. Denial of a request for recusal shall be reviewable by the Administrative Appeals Board under procedures established pursuant to articles 3-A of the Vehicle and Traffic Law, provided that a final, adverse determination is subsequently made which is appealable by the requestor to the Administrative Appeals Board.

(g) Conduct of hearings; evidence.

(1) The order of proof at a hearing shall be determined by the presiding officer. Testimony shall be given under oath or affirmation. The presiding officer, in his or her discretion, may exclude witnesses. The presiding officer may admit any relevant evidence in addition to oral testimony. Any witness may be questioned and/or cross-examined by the presiding officer, by the witness's counsel or representative, and by the party who did not call the witness.

(2) Rules governing the admissibility of evidence in a court of law are not applicable to hearings held by the department. Evidence which would not be admissible in court, such as hearsay, is admissible in a departmental hearing. The decision of the presiding officer shall be based upon a preponderance of the evidence.

(3) The privileges set forth in article 45 of the Civil Practice Law and Rules shall be applicable to adjudicatory proceedings conducted pursuant to this section.

(h) Adjournments. Adjournments of hearings may only be granted by the presiding officer responsible for the particular hearing, by a supervisor of such presiding officer. It is the department's policy to grant a request for adjournment for good cause if such request is made in writing and received at least seven days prior to the scheduled hearing and if no prior requests for adjournment have been made. Notwithstanding this policy, requests for adjournments made more than seven days prior to hearing may be denied by the presiding officer, or supervisor of the presiding officer, in their discretion. Grounds for such a denial include, but are not limited to, such a request being a second or subsequent request for adjournment, where there is reason to believe such request is merely an attempt to delay the holding of a hearing, or where an adjournment will significantly affect the availability of other witnesses scheduled to testify. Requests for adjournments within seven days of a scheduled hearing must be made in writing directly to the presiding officer. Such requests will generally not be granted. Such requests may be granted in the discretion of the presiding officer for good cause shown.

(i) Failure to appear; waiver. In any proceeding where no adjournment is requested or, if requested, is not granted, the failure of any party to appear shall be deemed to be a waiver of hearing. Upon any party's failure to appear, the presiding officer may receive testimony of available witnesses and enter evidence into the record.

(j) Resolution without a hearing. Either party may request a resolution of the dispute without a hearing. The request must be made in writing and must be received by the presiding officer at least 15 days prior to the scheduled hearing. The request must be accompanied by sufficient information to permit a determination of whether any unresolved material issue of fact exists and may be accompanied by a legal memorandum. A copy of such request and all supporting documentation must be served upon the other party when the request is submitted to the presiding officer. Proof of service upon the other party shall accompany the request to the presiding officer. The other party shall have the opportunity to respond to such request. Such response must be received by the presiding officer within 15 days of receipt of the request for resolution without a hearing. The response may be accompanied by a legal memorandum. A copy of any response must be served upon the requesting party when the response is submitted to the presiding officer. Proof of service upon the requesting party shall accompany the response to the presiding officer. If necessary, in order to allow the presiding officer to evaluate the request for a resolution without a hearing, the presiding officer may adjourn the scheduled hearing, with notice to all parties of the adjournment.

(k) The presiding officer shall render a decision not later than 90 days after the close of the hearing, or, if appropriate, the granting of a request for resolution without a hearing. The decision of the presiding officer shall be based upon the preponderance of the evidence. The presiding officer shall prepare a decision which shall include findings of fact, a determination on each charge, and, in the event of a determination of a violation, the remedy to be ordered.

Historical Note

Sec. filed June 3, 2008 eff. June 18, 2008. Current with amendments included in the New York State Register, XXXVIII, Issue 34 dated August 24, 2016.

APPENDIX 42

New York State Department of Motor Vehicles' Commissioner's Memorandum Regarding the Introduction of Report of Refusal in Evidence Pursuant to CPLR § 4520

Re: Peter D. Perucki
Administrative Appeals Board
Docket No. 9492

COMMISSIONER'S MEMORANDUM

Appellant appeals from a determination, after a hearing, revoking his driver's license for refusal to submit to a chemical test of blood alcohol content.

The arresting police officer did not testify at the chemical test refusal hearing, but the officer's Report of Refusal was admitted into evidence by the Administrative Law Judge. In accordance with the statute (Vehicle and Traffic Law, Section 1194(2)), the report was duly verified, contained the Penal Law warning that false statements therin were punishable as a Class A misdemeanor, and was subscribed by the arresting officer.

Appellant objected to the introduciton of the Report of Refusal upon the gound that it denied him the opportunity to confront and cross-examine the arresting police officer. The objection was overruled and the report was admitted into evidence. Appellant did not testify nor offer any witnesses or evidence in his behalf.

The Report of Refusal indicated that appellant had been involved in an automobile accident and that he was arrested for driving while intoxicated after the responding officer observed a strong odor of alcoholic beverage on his breath. It also noted that appellant admitted he had been drinking beer. The Report of Refusal also contains the printed form statutory chemical test warning (Vehicle and Traffic Law, Section 1194(2))* which was checked to indicate that it had been recited to the appellant and further indicated that the time of arrest was 7:20 p.m. and the refusal occurred at 7:25 p.m.

*Section 1194(2) provides in pertinent part:
"2. If such person having been placed under arrest. . .and having therafter been requested to submit to such chemical test and having been informed that his license or permit to drive and any non-resident operating privilege shall be immediately suspended and subsequently revoked for refusal to submit to such chemical test, whether or not he is found guilty of the charge for which he is arrested, refuses to submit to such test,. . .the test shall not be given and a written report of such refusal shall be immediately made by the police officer before whom such refusal was made."

Under CPLR 4520, the Report of Refusal is an official record admissible into evidence and constitutes prima facie evidence of the facts stated therein. (See People v. Hisonoff, 293 NY 597 [medical examiner's autopsy report]; Borselin v. Wickham Brothers, Inc., 6 AD 2d 784 [police accident report]; People v Hoats, 102 Misc. 2d 1004 [breathalyzer test results].) In conformity with the statute, it is made in the course of a police officer's official duty, is duly sworn to or certified and filed in a public office as required by statute (Vehicle and Traffic Law, Section 1194(2)).

Absent substantial evidence to the contrary, a properly admitted Report of Refusal may constitute substantial evidence of a refusal to submit to a chemical test of blood alcohol content. (CPLR 7803(4); see Richardson v. Perales, 402 US 389, 402; People ex rel. Vega v. Smith, 66 NY 2d 130, 139-140; See Richardson on Evidence, Section 58 [10th ed.].

Also, where a motorist has not exercised his or her right to sub-poena the arresting officer, (State Administrative Procedure Act, Section 304(2)) there is no denial of due process where a refusal report is admitted into evidence prusuant to CPLR 4520 and findings are made thereon, despite the report's hearsay character and the absence of cross-examination. (See Richardson v. Perales, supra at 402).

In this case, based upon the contents of the Report of Refusal and absent any evidence to the contrary, the Administrative Law Judge was entitled to find as he did that (1) the police officer had resonable grounds to believe that appellant was driving while under the influence of alcohol; (2) that a lawful arrest was made; (3) that appellant was sufficiently warned of the consequences of a test refu-sal; and (4) that appellant refused to submit to a chemical test.

Accordingly, the determination is affirmed.

Patricia B. Adduci
Commissioner
(E1a6*)

Dated:

APPENDIX 43

Letter From Dr. Kurt Dubowski Regarding Effect of Dentures on Breath Test Result

The
University of Oklahoma

Oklahoma City Campus-Health Sciences Center

TOXICOLOGY LABORATORIES
College of Medicine

Kurt M. Dubowski, Ph.D.
  George Lynn Cross Research
  Professor of Medicine and Director

March 4, 1983

Peter Gerstenzang, Esq.
New York State Police Academy
State Campus
Albany, New York 12226

Dear Mr. Gerstenzang:

This is in response to your letter of 21 February 1983 requesting information on the effect, if any, of dentures on the results of breath-alcohol
analyses by means of a Breathalyzer. That question has been raised
periodically, and substantial information exists on the subject, including
experimental findings obtained in my own laboratories, published by others
in the open scientific literature, and obtained in additional but so far
unpublished experiments with which I have been associated.

In responding, I am limiting my comments to breath-alcohol anaylses which
have been properly conducted in every respect, including a documented preceding "deprivation" period of at least 15 minutes prior to administration
of the breath test, during which interval the subject was continuously
observed and had not ingested alcohol or alcoholic beverages, regurgitated,
vomited, eaten, or smoked. Also predicated are qualified breath-alcohol
test operators and properly calibrated and operative analysis devices.

Under those circumstances, a breath-alcohol anaylsis and its results will
not be affected by presence of dentures in the tested subject.

The usual implication in inquiries concerning the effect of dentures is
that they may serve as a reservoir of retained "mouth-alcohol" from prior
ingestion of alcoholic beverages and may falsely elevate the existing
breath-alcohol concentration, if any, beyond the normal deprivation period.
That is not the case. Alcohol is rapidly absorbed from the mucous membra-
nes of the oral cavity and disappears from the mouth in exponential fashion
once alcohol contact or ingestion is terminated. The standard 15-minute
deprivation period is more than ample to eliminate reportable concentrations
of alcohol in expired breath (i.e., concentrations greater than 0.009
g/210L) arising from residual alcohol in the mouth.

*Documentation of the above subject is to be found in the following sour-
ces, among others:

1827

Peter Gerstenzang, Esq.   March 4, 1983
                                                     Page Two

    1) Begg, T. B. et al.: "Breathalyzer and Kitagawa-Wright
       Methods of Measuring Breath Alcohol," Brit. Med. J. 1:
       9-15 (1964)

    2) Kempe, C. R.: "Study of the Dissipation Rate of Ethanol
       from the Oral Cavity," Law & Order 20 (No. 9): 94
       (1972)

    3) Dubowski, K.M.: "Studies in Breath-Alcohol Analysis:
       Biological Factors," Z. Rechtsmedizin 76: 93-117
       (1975).

I hope this information is useful.

                  Sincerely yours,

                  Kurt M. Dubowski, Ph.D.
            Distinguished Professor of Medicine

KMD/ps

APPENDIX 44

Memorandum of Sidney W. Berke, DMV Administrative Adjudication Office Director, Regarding Introduction of Report of Refusal into Evidence

State of New York - Department of Motor Vehicles

MEMORANDUM

TO: All Safety Administrative Law Judges   DATE: June 5, 1986

FROM: Sidney W. Berke   OFFICE: Administrative Adjudication

SUBJECT: C.T. Refusal Report: Police Officer Absent Implementation Commissioner's memorandum # 9492

As previously discussed in Sid Firestone's memorandum of July 8, 1985, when a police officer has failed to appear on more than one occasion, the refusal report should be admitted into evidence. It can constitute substantial evidence of refusal.

Attached is a commissioner's memorandum approving its use as substantial evidence to support a finding of refusal in the face of an argument that cross-examination was denied (the motorist did not testify). The police officer is to be considered a public officer, thereby invoking CPLR 4520 (and the common law rule; copies attached).

As noted in both memoranda, the report may be overcome by contrary, substantial evidence of the motorist or others. This is primarily a credibility determination for the A.L.J. The motorist's demeanor and the content of his testimony may show his testimony to be incomplete, contradictory, evasive, or incredible, and therefore insufficient to overcome the refusal report.

The finding of contrary substantial evidence is to be supported by the testimony of the motorist and any other evidence. It is your obligation to obtain the facts. Please also bear in mind that the evidence offered by the respondent affects the weight to be given the Report of Refusal, not its admissibility.

In adjourned cases, a conviction may already exist on the alcohol charge underlying the refusal on which you are holding the hearing. If there has been a conviction or plea to 1192(2,3,4), then the issues of probable cause and lawful arrest are conclusively decided (collateral estoppel). If there has been a plea to 1192(1), it can be considered an admission against interest on these two issues, but is subject to attach and explanation by the motorist. If there has been an 1192(1) conviction after trial, then all issues must be established without reference to the conviction.

SIDNEY W. BERKE
Director

SWB:smb
Enc.

11/26/86

Particularly in this type of situation, where the officer is not present to testify, it is essential that the report state a valid reason for the initial stop. e.g. stopped for speeding, disobeying sign, crossing double yellow line etc.

APPENDIX 45

Letter from Joseph R. Donovan, DMV First Assistant Counsel, Regarding Removal of Dentures Prior to Breath Test

STATE OF NEW YORK

DEPARTMENT OF MOTOR VEHICLES

THE GOVERNOR NELSON A. ROCKEFELLER

PATRICIA B. ADDUCI
COMMISSIONER

EDWARD A. SHERIDAN
DEPUTY COMMISSIONER AND COUNSEL

EMPIRE STATE PLAZA

ALBANY, NEW YORK 12228

LEGAL DIVISION
JOSEPH R. DONOVAN
FIRST ASSISTANT COUNSEL

Peter Gerstenzang, Esq.
41 State Street
Albany, New York 12207

Dear Mr. Gerstenzang:

In your telephone conversation of March 12, 1986, with Mrs. Scrodanus of this office, you requested the departmental position on the requirement of police enforcement agencies to remove dentures prior to the administration of a breathalyzer exam.

The Department of Motor Vehicles will hold that a valid chemical test refusal finding has been made if an individual has refused to remove dentures prior to submitting to the breathalyzer examination. The finding of a chemical test refusal will be upheld by the deapartment so long as:

1) the police enforcement personnel have advised the individual as to why the dentures must be removed and how such removal is necessary to the validity of the test, and

2) the police enforcement agency has incorporated the requirement for denture removal into its regulations for the administration of a breathalyzer exam.

I trust the above explanation shall prove both informative and helpful.

Very truly yours,

JOSEPH R. DONOVAN
First Assistant Counsel

JRD/pr

APPENDIX 46

Letter from Joseph R. Donovan, DMV First Assistant Counsel, Regarding Police Department Procedures on Test Refusals and Removal of Dentures

STATE OF NEW YORK

DEPARTMENT OF MOTOR VEHICLES

THE GOVERNOR NELSON A. ROCKEFELLER

PATRICIA B. ADDUCI
COMMISSIONER

EDWARD A. SHERIDAN
DEPUTY COMMISSIONER AND COUNSEL

EMPIRE STATE PLAZA

ALBANY, NEW YORK 12228

LEGAL DIVISION
JOSEPH R. DONOVAN
FIRST ASSISTANT COUNSEL

January 13, 1987

Peter Gerstenzang
Gerstenzang, Weiner & Gerstenzang
Attorneys at Law
41 State Street
Albany, NY 12207-2835

Dear Peter:

Please excuse the delay in responding to your letter (and enclosures) of December 11, 1986, regarding police department regulations and procedures concerning denture removal and breath test administration.

If the procedures which you sent to me were followed, I am (virtually) certain that a chemical test refusal, based upon the failure to remove dentures, would be found. While I am not convinced that it is absolutely necessary that the requirement be incorporated into the police department regulations, it is clearly the safer course of action.

My opinion is that the procedure clearly overcomes the problem which gave rise to the reversal of the chemical test refusal finding in the Greenlee case.

Please do not hesitate to contace me if I may be of any further assistance.

Very truly yours,

JOSEPH R. DONOVAN
First Assistant Counsel

JRD/NWS/ms

APPENDIX 47

DMV Commissioner's Memorandum Regarding Test Refusals and the Right to Counsel

State of New York—Department of Motor Vehicles

MEMORANDUM

TO: All Safety ALJs   DATE: May 8, 1990
FROM: George Christian   OF-FICE: Admin. Adjudication

SUB-JECT: Chemical Test Refusal

(1) effect of DWI conviction
(2) refusal conduct—request for attorney

Questions regarding the above subjects were raised at regional peer review meetings.

(1) Sometimes a refusal hearing will follow a judgment of conviction for DWI. The judgment should be treated as conclusive proof of the underlying facts, and the respondent cannot contest probable cause or arrest legality at the hearing. (See *People v. Thomas*, 74 A.D.2d 317, 428 N.Y.S.2d 20, affd. 53 N.Y.2d 338, 441 N.Y.S.2d 650, 424 N.E.2d 537; *Matter of Levy*, 37 N.Y.2d 279, 372 N.Y.S.2d 41, 333 N.E.2d 350; *S.T. Grand Inc. v. City of New York*, 32 N.Y.2d 300, 344 N.Y.S.2d 938, 298 N.E.2d 105; *Matter of Arancia v. Ambach*, 76 A.D.2d 967, 429 N.Y.S.2d 67.)

If there has been a judgment of conviction of DWAI, a traffic infraction, as the result of a plea, it is an admission against interest but respondent may contest all issues (*Ando v. Woodberry*, 8 N.Y.2d 165, 203 N.Y.S.2d 74, 168 N.E.2d 520.) If the DWAI judgment was by verdict after trial, there is no admission against interest and all issues may be contested. (See *Montalvo v. Morales*, 18 A.D.2d 20, 239 N.Y.S.2d 72; *Augustine v. Village of Interlaken*, 68 A.D.2d 705, 418 N.Y.S.2d 683 (4th Dep't 1979).)

(2) If a respondent is asked to take a chemical test, and responds by requesting the advice of an attorney, the police officer is not required, for Section 1194 purposes, to grant the

1835

request. However, if the officer does not inform the respondent that his request is denied and just records a refusal, there has not been a refusal. The respondent should be reasonably informed in some way (words, conduct, circumstances) that he is not going to be given a chance to consult with an attorney before his insistence on speaking to one can be considered a refusal.

GC: pa

APPENDIX 48

Refusal Warning Card

DWI WARNING

1. You are under arrest for driving while intoxicated.
2. A refusal to submit to a chemical test or any portion thereof, will result in the immediate suspension and subsequent revocation of your license or operating privilege, whether or not you are found guilty of the charge for which you were arrested.
3. Your refusal to submit to a chemical test, or any portion thereof, can be introduced into evidence against you at any trial, proceeding or hearing resulting from this arrest.
4. Will you submit to a chemical test to determine the alcohol or drug content of your blood?

DWAI DRUGS WARNING

1. You are under arrest for driving while ability impaired by the use of drugs.
2. A refusal to submit to a chemical test or any portion thereof, will result in the immediate suspension and subsequent revocation of your license or operating privilege, whether or not you are found guilty of the charge for which you were arrested.
3. Your refusal to submit to a chemical test or any portion thereof, can be introduced into evidence against you at any trial, proceeding or hearing resulting from this arrest.
4. Will you submit to a chemical test to determine the alcohol or drug content of your blood?

1837

APPENDIX 49

DWI Investigative Notes

New York State Police
DWI Investigative Notes

NAME: _____

LAST   FIRST

DOB: _____ TIME: _____ DATE: _____

LOCATION: _____

INITIAL OBSERVATIONS:	OBSERVATIONS OF DRIVER:
OBSERVATIONS OF STOP:	OBSERVATION OF THE EXIT:
SPEECH:	COORDINATION:
ATTITUDE:	FACE:
BREATH:	FOOTWEAR:
ODORS:	OTHER:
CHEMICAL TEST/MIRANDA WARNINGS: GIVEN BY:	WHAT HAVE YOU EATEN TODAY? WHEN?
TIME NOW?	WHEN DID YOU LAST SLEEP? HOW LONG?
ARE YOU SICK OR INJURED?	DO YOU TAKE INSULIN?
DO YOU HAVE ANY PHYSICAL DEFECTS?	ARE YOU TAKING ANY MEDICATION OR DRUGS?
ARE YOU DIABETIC OR EPILEPTIC?	ARE YOU UNDER THE CARE OF A DOCTOR OR DENTIST?

WHAT HAVE YOU BEEN DRINKING?

HOW MUCH?   TIME OF LAST DRINK?

STATEMENTS: _____

HAVE YOU EVER BEEN ARRESTED FOR DRIVING WHILE INTOXICATED?   YES   NO

HAVE YOU EVER BEEN CONVICTED OF DRIVING WHILE INTOXICATED?   YES   NO

IF YES: WHERE, WHEN _____

WHAT AGENCY: _____

- OVER -   TB - 36 (12/94)

BLINDNESS: NONE LEFT EYE RIGHT EYE	TRACKING: EQUAL UNEQUAL	EYES: NORMAL
ABLE TO FOLLOW STIMULUS: YES NO	EYELIDS: NORMAL DROOPY	BLOODSHOT WATERY

HORIZONTAL GAZE NYSTAGMUS			
LACK OF SMOOTH PURSUIT	LEFT EYE	RIGHT EYE	VERTICAL NYSTAGMUS YES NO
NYSTAGMUS AT MAXIMUM DEVIATION			CORRECTIVE LENS: NONE GLASSES CONTACTS: HARD SOFT
NYSTAGMUS PRIOR TO 45°			PUPIL SIZE: EQUAL UNEQUAL (EXPLAIN)

WALK AND TURN TEST

CANNOT KEEP BALANCE _____

STARTS TOO SOON _____

STOPS WALKING		
MISSES HEEL-TOE		
STEPS OFF LINE		
RAISES ARMS		
ACTUAL STEPS TAKEN		

DESCRIBE TURN	CANNOT DO TEST (EXPLAIN)

ONE LEG STAND

ROMBERG BALANCE

( ) SWAYS WHILE BALANCING ( )
( ) USES ARMS TO BALANCE ( )
( ) HOPPING ( )
( ) PUTS FOOT DOWN ( )

INTERNAL CLOCK

ESTIMATED AT 30 SEC.

◯ RIGHT   △ LEFT

OTHER FIELD SOBRIETY TESTS

NAME OF TEST:

DRAW LINES FROM SPOTS TOUCHED

DESCRIBE PERFORMANCE:

BREATH RESULTS: REFUSED   RESULTS   %
INSTRUMENT #:

TICKET NUMBER:

OTHER CHEMICAL TESTS: URINE   BLOOD

INDICATE ANY TESTS REFUSED:

APPENDIX 50

Department of Health Permit

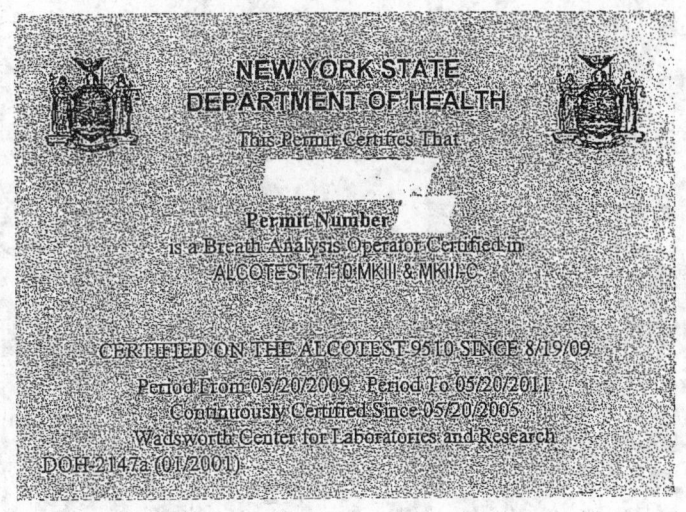

New York State Department of Health permit card reading:

NEW YORK STATE
DEPARTMENT OF HEALTH
This Permit Certifies That

Permit Number
is a Breath Analysis Operator Certified in
ALCOTEST 7110 MKIII & MKIII-C

CERTIFIED ON THE ALCOTEST 9510 SINCE 8/19/09

Period From 05/20/2009   Period To 05/20/2011
Continuously Certified Since 05/20/2005
Wadsworth Center for Laboratories and Research
DOH-2147a (01/2001)

APPENDIX 51

New York State Police Breath Test Rules

TB-4 (06/03)

John P. Melville
SUPERINTENDENT

STATE OF NEW YORK
NEW YORK STATE POLICE
BUILDING 22
1220 WASHINGTON AVE.
ALBANY, NEW YORK 12226-2252

NEW YORK STATE POLICE
BREATH TEST RULES

1. Only a Breath Test Instrument for which a Member possesses a valid Breath Analysis Operator's Certificate (DOH2147a), issued by the Department of Health shall be used for breath tests given in connection with arrests under any law or ordinance that permits the taking of a breath test to determine the blood alcohol content, particularly the following laws:

    The Vehicle And Traffic Law;

    The Parks, Recreation And Historic Preservation Law;

    The Environmental Conservation Law;

    The Navigation Law; and

    The General Business Law (in conjunction with Federal Aviation Regulations).

2. When you administer a breath test utilizing the Alcotest 7110 (MK III or MK IIIC) and Alcotest 9510

    ● Operate the instrument by following the prompts for the electronic operational checklist that appear on the digital display.

APPENDIX 52

BMP Model Police Rules and Regulations

PROPOSED RULES AND REGULATIONS GOVERNING THE ARREST FOR DWI AND PROCEDURES FOR ADMINISTERING CHEMICAL BREATH TEST FOR POSSIBLE ADOPTION BY POLICE DEPARTMENTS

An arresting officer must have reasonable grounds that a driver of a motor vehicle is intoxicated before he can lawfully arrest for driving while intoxicated. He must first be placed under arrest for driving while intoxicated (for positive screening tests, see Section 1193A of these regulations) before the arresting officer can request him to submit to a chemical test to determine the amount of alcohol in his blood. It will be the policy of this department that the definition of a chemical test for alcohol content shall be a breathalyzer test on all driving while intoxicated or impaired arrests; except when health indicates the use of a blood or urine test, or when the breath test instrument is not available.

Following arrest, the officer must request the driver to submit to a chemical test, by using the following language:

1. You are under arrest for driving while intoxicated.
2. A refusal to submit to a chemical test will result in the immediate suspension and subsequent revocation of your license or operating privilege, whether or not you are found guilty of the charge for which you were arrested.
3. Your refusal to submit to a chemical test, can be introduced into evidence against you at any trial, proceeding or hearing resulting from this arrest.
4. Will you submit to a chemical test of your breath for alcohol? (Will you submit to a chemical analysis of your urine/blood for drugs?)

The answer must be either "YES" or "NO." The arresting officer should if possible, witness the testing of the person arrested, whether it be blood, urine, or breath. The test must be given no later than two hours after the time of arrest or after a positive breath screening test.

When the arresting officer requests the defendant to submit to a breath test to determine the alcohol content in his blood, the test must be conducted by a duly trained operator, who has been certified as a breath test operator and possesses a valid permit issued by the New York State Department of Health. The arresting officer should avoid, if possible, administering the breath test. The certified operator who performs the test must record the information on the breathalyzer operational checklist, recording the results of the test, the ampoule number, instrument serial number, name of the person tested, the date, time of test, arresting officer's name and badge number, signature of witness, time, results and lot number of known value solution. Prepared by the Bureau for Municipal Police, State of New York.

Breath analysis; techniques or methods. Breath testing techniques and methods must meet the following criteria:

a.   Breath samples shall be collected within two hours of the time of the arrest or a positive screening test and shall be analyzed with instruments meeting the criteria set forth in Section 59.4 and outlined in Part 59.5 of Chapter 897 of the Laws of the State of New York (1972) and promulgated in Part 59 of the Administrative Rules and Regulations, Subchapter D of Chapter 2, Title 10 (Health) of the Official Compilation of Codes, Rules, and Regulations of the State of New York.

b.   Examine mouth and remove any foreign substance. Continuous observation of the subject shall be maintained for 20 minutes prior to the collection of the breath specimen, during which period the subject must not have ingested alcoholic beverages or other fluids, regurgitated, vomited, eaten, or smoked or be allowed to place anything in his mouth; if the subject should regurgitate or vomit, an additional 15 minute waiting period is required.

c.   A system purge must *immediately* precede *both* the testing of each subject *and the analysis of the reference sample.*

d.   The result of an analysis of a suitable reference sample, such as air equilibrated with a reference solution of alcoholic content of greater than 0.08 percent weight per volume at a known temperature, must agree with the reference sample value within the limits of plus or minus 0.01 percent weight per volume, or such limits as set by the State Commissioner of Health. This analysis shall (immediately) follow the analysis of the breath of the subject and shall be recorded.

e.   Results of an analysis of breath for alcohol shall be expressed in terms of percent weight per volume, to the second decimal place as found; for example, 0.237 percent shall be reported as 0.23 percent.

   f.   Proper and adequate records of operations, certificates of
        analysis for the ampoule and known value solution shall be
        maintained by this agency.

Once each week, calibration tests will be conducted on Breathalyzer Model 900/900A in accordance with the following
procedures:

   1.   Three consecutive tests will be conducted using the same
        ampoule and a known value solution/reference sample.
   2.   The calibration test record form indicating the three test
        results will be filled in following each test.
   3.   The breath test instrument will in addition be calibrated
        on a semiannual basis by the New York State Bureau for
        Municipal Police. It will be the responsibility of the rank-
        ing breath test operator to forward the letter of request to
        the Bureau for Municipal Police.

If the officer requests a blood test, a proper evidence tag must
be affixed to the test tube with the following information:

   a.   Name and address of person arrested.
   b.   Place, time, and date test taken.
   c.   Doctor's name and address.

Prepared by the Bureau for Municipal Police, State of New York.

   The test tube shall be sealed and initialed by the doctor in the
presence of the officer. The arresting officer will be responsible
for maintaining the continuity of the blood, for evidence to be
used in court. The blood sample test tube will be delivered to the
State Police or any other authorized lab, (by the arresting officer)
and if possible should remain with the arresting officer until it is
delivered. If sample is mailed send certified with receipt
requested. Be sure the doctor does not use alcohol to swab skin.
Only test tubes supplied by the New York State Health Department or Lab used by the department, will be used to contain
blood test samples. Evidence forms will be complete in detail and
will accompany the blood test sample to the lab.

   If the arresting officer requests a urine test, there must be two
samples secured. The second test must be one half hour after the
first test is taken, and both tests must be taken within the two
hour limit after the driver of the vehicle has been arrested or after a positive screening test.

   The arresting officer should witness the defendant give the
sample of urine, the first and second time. Both specimens of
urine must be placed in clean jars containing no preservative.
Both urine tests must then be labeled with the defendant's name,
address, date, time sample obtained, and the officer's name, rank,
and badge number. Each vial must be sealed and initialed. The
arresting officer will be responsible for the continuity of the evidence, and will be transported to the authorized lab, by the ar-

resting officer or sent by certified mail with return receipt requested.

If after submitting to a chemical test designated by the officer, the defendant states that he wishes to have his own doctor withdraw blood, or take a urine sample, inform him that he may call his own doctor who may withdraw an additional specimen of blood or urine. This will be at the defendant's expense.

If the defendant desires to discuss with his attorney whether or not to submit to a blood, urine or breathalyzer test, find out the name of his attorney and either let the defendant talk to the attorney on the telephone or tell the attorney that the defendant wishes to see him regarding submitting to the requested test, keeping in mind that the test must be conducted within the two hour time limit. Should the defendant or his attorney prolong it beyond the two hour limit, it becomes a refusal. (All parties concerned should be notified of expiration time of two hour period.)

If the defendant refuses to submit to any of the above mentioned chemical alcohol tests and there is reasonable grounds for arrest, he is to be booked for DWI, Section 1192-3, V & T Law, and a State refusal form must be filled out in quadruplicate by the arresting officer and two copies submitted to the court. The refusal form will be forwarded to the Department of Motor Vehicles, Albany, New York by the court within 48 hours.

Under no circumstances will the defendant be allowed to drive his vehicle, after being placed under arrest for violation of Section 1192, Subdivision 1, 2, 3, or 4. It will be impounded, stored in a safe place (unless there is another person present, who has a driver's license, and is not in an intoxicated condition, and is willing to assume the responsibility of removing the vehicle, and with owner's permission, the vehicle may be released to him). If the vehicle is impounded, the owner or any one designated by him, must come to our headquarters, and sign a release before it can be turned over to him. The vehicle is impounded at no expense to the Department.

In the case of a person suspected of driving while their ability is impaired by the use of drugs, the same procedure will be followed as prescribed for driving while intoxicated, and ability impaired by the use of intoxicating beverages, with the exception that any driver suspected of driving while their ability is impaired by the use of drugs, shall be requested to submit to a urine test. (To be conducted in the same manner as for intoxication). The urine test specimens will be placed in a clean jar, as previously outlined, containing no preservatives. It will be sealed with the date, name, time, time of arrest, what the specimen is, officer's name and badge number. It will be the arresting officer's responsibility to maintain the continuity of the evidence, and deliver or mail the test specimen to the authorized lab along with the evidence form completely filled out.

The fingerprinting and photographing of persons arrested for driving while intoxicated, driving while ability is impaired by drugs, will be guided by Article 160, Section 160.10 Sub 1 (c) and Sub 2 and 3 of the Criminal Procedure Laws of the State of New York.

The Alcohol Influence Report Form will be completed on all arrests for violation of Section 1192, (All Subdivisions) of the Vehicle and Traffic Law, a copy of which must be maintained in the case file.

When making an arrest for any of the Subdivisions of Section 1192, the following procedures in order will be followed:

a. Reasonable grounds for arrest (observations or screening device).

b. Advise subject he is under arrest (for violation Section 1192, Subdivision 3 of the Vehicle and Traffic Law, if observations warrant. Section 1192 Subdivision 1 or 2 if screening device is used).

c. Refusal to submit warning given verbatim to defendant.

d. Miranda Warning.

e. Check defendant's mouth for any foreign substance.

f. Observe defendant for 20 minutes:
  1. Nothing taken orally by mouth.
  2. No smoking.
  3. Does not regurgitate or vomit.

If any of the previously mentioned occur, the waiting period must be started again.

g. Test administered by certified breath test operator (for blood, by doctor, registered nurse or laboratory technician, registered physician's assistant).

h. Operational checklist form completed.

i. Physical condition report form completed.

j. Record of arrest/disposition form completed.

k. Booking/arraignment—follow Department Rules & Regulations.

l. When making a court appearance for a DWI trial, the following forms/certificates will be needed:
  1. Information(s)-UTT(s).
  2. DWI refusal form, if any.
  3. Miranda Warning Card.
  4. Physical condition report.
  5. Operational checklist form.
  6. Record of arrest disposition form.
  7. Calibration test record.

8. Ampoule certificate of analysis.

9. Known value solution certificate of analysis.

10. Department R & R's governing administration of chemical tests.

11. Breath test operator certification.

12. Department of Health permit card.

Pre-arrest Screening Device, Vehicle and Traffic Law Section 1193A. This device, if available, will be used at a motor vehicle accident and following every hazardous moving violation arrest or ticket. It may also be used in connection with any vehicle and traffic violation during the hours of the most frequent occurrence of the offense of Driving While Intoxicated in accordance with Section 1193-A, V & T Law.

The prearrest screening device is not to be used to reinforce probable cause, if arrest was made on officer's observations.

Before administering the breath test, the subject's mouth should be checked for any foreign substances that might contaminate the test. An observation period of 20 minutes is required following the same procedures for an evidential test.

If the subject refuses to take the screening test, the officer will issue a Uniform Traffic Ticket for violation of Section 1193-A Vehicle and Traffic Law.

Following a positive screening test:

1. The officer should arrest the motor vehicle operator for a violation of NYS Vehicle and Traffic Law, Section 1192-1 or 1192-2.

2. Once the arrest is affected for 1192-1 or 1192-2, the motor vehicle operator will be advised of the refusal to submit and miranda warnings as previously described.

3. The arresting officer will request the motor vehicle operator to submit to an evidential test which will be administered pursuant to these Rules and Regulations.

APPENDIX 53

Letter from Department of Motor Vehicles Regarding Multiple Offenders

PATRICIA B. ADDUCI
Commissioner

STATE OF NEW YORK
DEPARTMENT OF MOTOR VEHICLES
THE GOVERNOR NELSON A. ROCKFELLER EMPIRE STATE PLAZA, ALBANY, NEW YORK 12228

January 7, 1986

Peter Gerstenzang
c/o Gerstenzang, Weiner & Gerstenzang
41 State Street
Albany, New York 12207-2835

Dear Mr. Gerstenzang:

This will confirm our telephone conversation concerning the Commissioner's policy on repeat drinking/driving offenders.

1. Second Conviction
   A. If ineligible for the drinking driver program we will approve at the end of the statutory revocation period.

   B. Evidence of alcohol evaluation and/or rehabilitation will be required.

2. Third Conviction
   A. Allowed to enroll in the drinking driver program if eligible but will not be granted a conditional license.

   B. If not eligible for the D.D.P., a minimum revocation period of eighteen months will be imposed.

   C. See 1B.

3. Fourth Conviction
   A. See 2A.

   B. If not eligible for the drinking driver program a minimum revocation period of twenty-four months will be imposed.

   C. See 1B.

Peter Gerstenzang   -2-   January 7, 1986

    4. Fifth Conviction
        A. See 2A.

        B. If not eligible for the drinking driver program a mini-
           mum revocation period of thirty months will be imposed.

        C. See 1B.

    5. Sixth and Subsequent Convictions
        At the present time we will deny based on a history of
        alcohol related offenses. We will continue to deny until
        some Court tells us that we must approve. (Denials are,
        of course, appealable through the Administrative Appeals
        Board.)

        If we have a change in policy in the future, I will advise
you.

                                Very truly yours,

                                Alfred J. Frakes, Director
                                Driver Licensing Services
                                                    (E1663)

AJF:mj

APPENDIX 54

Penalty Chart

GLENN EDWARD MURRAY
ATTORNEY AT LAW
The Cornell Mansion
484 Delaware Avenue
Buffalo, New York 14202-1304
(716) 884-0139
gemesq@mac.com
www.glennmurraylaw.com

September 29, 2011
NOTE: Effective 2011, for permanent revocation, DMV policy is to deny conditional license applications.

MURRAY'S DUI CHARTS & CHECKLISTS

Legend

ADWI	Aggravated DWI
ARI	Alcohol Related Incident
AUO	Aggravated Unlicensed Operation
BAC	Blood Alcohol Content
AUO	Aggravated Unlicensed Operation
CDL	Commercial Drivers License
CL	Conditional License
CMV	Commercial Motor Vehicle
CRD	Certificate of Relief from Civil Disabilities
DDP	Drinking Driver Program
DWAI	Driving While Ability Impaired
DWAID	Driving While Ability Impaired by Drugs/Alcohol
DWI	Driving While Intoxicated
DRA	Driver Responsibility Assessment
F/DWI	Felony DWI
GVWR	Gross Vehicle Weight Rating
HM	Hazardous Material
HP	Hardship Privilege
IID	Interlock Ignition Device
M/DWAI	Misdemeanor DWI
MPR	Minimum Period of Revocation
MSC	Mandatory Surcharge
OP	Operator
PCCL	Pre-Conviction Conditional License
PDO	Property Damage Only (accident)
PI	Physical Injury
PL	Penal Law
PV	Private Vehicle
Rev.	Revocation
SPP	Suspension Pending Prosecution
Susp.	Suspension
SV	Special Vehicle
VA	Vehicular Assault
VM	Vehicular Manslaughter
VAF	Victim Assistance Fee
YOA	Youthful Offender Adjudication
ZT	Zero Tolerance (aka "Baby DWI")

> **Caution:** The attached charts and checklists are designed as a partial finding tool.
> They are not a substitute for research of statutes and case law on a case-by-case basis.

1

GLENN EDWARD MURRAY, ESQ.   CHARTS & CHECKLISTS

MURRAY'S DUI CHARTS & CHECKLISTS

COURT CONVICTION PENALTIES

OFFENSE	FINE	MSC/VAF +$5 Town/Village	JAIL	LICENSE SANCTION
Infraction - Driving While Ability Impaired				
• 1st	$300-500[1]	$260	up to 15 dys[2]	susp. 90-days[3]
• 2d - any 1192 w/in 5 yrs.	$500-750[4]	$260	up to 30 dys[5]	rev. 6-mo.[6]
Misdemeanor - Driving While Ability Impaired				
• 3d - any 1192 w/in 10 yrs.	$750-1,500[7]	$400	up to 180 days[8]	rev. 6-mo.[9]
Misdemeanor - Driving While Intoxicated				
1192-2,3	$500-1,000[10]	$400	up to 1-yr.[11]	rev. 6-mo.[12]
Misdemeanor - Aggravated Driving While Intoxicated				
1192-2(a) .18 BAC, or above	$1,000-2,500[13]	$400	up to 1-yr.[14]	Rev 1 yr.[15]
Misdemeanor - Driving While Ability Impaired by Drugs				
1192-4	$1,000-2,500	$400	up to 1-yr.[16]	rev. 6 mo.[17]
Misdemeanor - Driving While Ability Impaired by Drugs & Alcohol (combined)				
1192-2-4-a	$500-1,000[18]	$400	up to 1-yr.[19]	rev. 6-mo.[20]
E Felony - Driving While Intoxicated (prior YOA not predicate)				
2d 1192-2,-2(a) -3,-4,-4(a) or PL 120.03.04 or 125.12,13 w/in 10 years; CIV w/ 1192-2, 1192-3, 1192-4, 1192-4-a	$1,000-5,000[21]	$520	up to 4-yrs.[22]	rev. 1 yr. or 18 mo.[23]
D Felony - Driving While Intoxicated (prior YOA not predicate)				
3d 1192-2,-2(a) -3,-4,-4(a) or PL 120.03, 04 or 125.12,13 w/in 10 years	$2,000-10,000[24]	$520	up to 7-yrs.[25]	rev. 1 yr. or 18 mo.[26]
2d §1192-3,-4,-4-a DWI conviction, both with "physical injury"				
No time limitation	see above		see above	rev. lifetime[27]
DMV REFUSAL PENALTIES				
NON CDL	1st		1 yr.	$500 + $750 DRA
NON CDL	2d w/in 5 yrs. (prior refusal or 1192 or 1192-a)		18 mo.	$750 + $750 DRA
CMV Operation CDL			18 mo.	$550 + $750 DRA

PERMANENT REVOCATION FOR REPEAT CONVICTIONS/REFUSALS (See *infra*)

INTERLOCK IGNITION & MANDATORY COMMUNITY SERVICE / JAIL

1192 (2-a) and for post-8/15/10 convictions: 1192-2, 1192-3 require IID. (§ 1193-1(b)). If 2d § 1192 or -3 w/in 5 yrs, also requires 5 days jail or 30 days community service (§ 1193 (1-a)(a); if 3d § 1192-2 or -3 w/in 10 yrs, requires 10 days jail or 60 days community service. (§ 1193-1a(c)).

PLEA REDUCTION POLICY (ERIE COUNTY)

No reduction to DWAI if • accident, •.14 % BAC or above, • under age 21 • prior DUI conviction, • refusals are discretionary if otherwise eligible.

2

GLENN EDWARD MURRAY, ESQ.   CHARTS & CHECKLISTS

DUI CONSEQUENCES - SANCTIONS AND ENHANCERS

SUSPENSION PENDING PROSECUTION	SUSPENSION & REV. UPON REFUSAL
If charged with 1192-2,-2(a)-3,-4, or 4(a): • prior 1192 conviction w/in 5-yrs.[28], or • charged with felony under PL Art. 120 or 125 [same incident]. • May only be imposed w/in 20 days after, or at conclusion of arraignment.[29] Re: Refusal, BAC see *infra*.	• suspension (pending hearing) at arraignment for 15 days or until hearing, whichever earlier.[30] • if DMV finds refusal or waiver ($500 or $750 civil penalty[31]) rev. for 1-yr., or 18 mo.[32] Not eligible for HSP! 1st and 2d offenders eligible for PCCL and CL only if DDP eligible.

SUSPENSION: BAC .08 % OR MORE	
Predicates: • reasonable cause: operated motor vehicle with BAC of .08% or more • accusatory instrument complies with CPL .100.40. *Suspension imposed by court:* • at arraignment-HSP hearing may be adjourned for 3 days (for HSP proof) or at conclusion of arraignment. • until disposition, whichever longer. • no Pre-conviction CL (PCCL) available 30 days after SPP, and only if eligible for post-conviction CL. CRD is no relief for CDL privilege.[33] • DJ or MJ license may be suspended on less than .08.[34]	*Extreme Hardship License:* • burden of proof on motorist. • factual finding by court required. • requires more than motorist testimony. *Driving Limitations:* • to and from (not during) employment; necessary medical treatment for the licensee or member of licensee's household; or re: educ. degree or cert. • CL eligible after 30 days, only if Post-Conv. CL elig.[35] Some work-related driving to/from worksites permitted.

PRE-CONVICTION CL (PCCL) /POST-CONVICTION CL	OPERATORS UNDER 21
Eligible: Criteria includes: • BAC SPP (Pre-conviction)(or 1192 conviction (or YOA) (30-Days after SPP); • enrolled in ADRP(if post-conviction); • license holder (not learners permit); • no prior ADRP participation or eligibility during 5-yrs. prior to offense; and • ADRP not prohibited by judge (if post-conviction).[36] If on probation, letter from probation officer "not prohibited" required.	• 1- year rev. upon any 1192 conviction, YOA or refusal. • 1-year rev. or until 21, whichever greater, upon any 2d 1192 conviction or YOA (not same incident).[37]
	ZERO TOLERANCE
	BAC > .02-.07% = "consume alcohol" • No suspension pending prosecution "Detention" (not an "arrest") CL eligible "Guilty finding" (not a "conviction") Suspension (not revocation)[38] Discretionary 20-day order.

TWENTY(20)-DAY ORDERS	INTERSTATE/UNLICENSED
Eligible: • no prior 1192 conviction w/in 5-yrs prior to arrest, and • no incidental conviction for PL Art. 120 or 125 crime.[39] • requires valid license • not otherwise rev. or susp.	• *NY driver/out of state offense: NY sanctions based on out-of state equivalent based classification if committed in NY. (post 11/1/07).* • *NY offense/nonresident or unlicensed[40]:* Privilege (not license) sanction same as if NY home state license.[41]

DRUG CONVICTIONS/YOA/JUVENILE DELINQUENCY	MISCELLANEOUS
Re: Penal Law drug offense: 6-month suspension if conviction, YOA, or juvenile delinquency finding for drug crime. 20-day order, CRD (Corr. L. 701-2), and restricted use license (VTL 530) available.[42] If prior 1192 w/in 5 yrs, 1 yr. rev.[43]	Boating While Intoxicated (BWI): Navigation L. 49-a and Snowmobiling While Intoxicated (SWI), Parks & Rec L. 25.24, do not affect driver's license, but may affect insurance.

---

[1] 1193-1(a).
[2] 1193-1(a).
[3] 1193-2(a).
[4] 1193-5. CMV per se Level I: .04 or more and not more than .06% BAC.
[5] 1193-6. CMV per se Level II: more than .06 and less than .08% BAC, but DWAI may be charged.
[6] 1193-2(b)(1).
[7] 1193-1(a),(c),(d). Chap. 652, laws of 1996 increased penalties eff. 11/1/96.
[8] 1193-1(a). Prior to 11/1/94 this was an infraction with 90-day maximum jail term.
[9] 1193-2(b)(3)(1)(a).
[10] 1193-1(b).
[11] 1193-1(b).
[12] 1193-2(b).
[13] 1193-1(b).
[14] 1193-1(b).
[15] 1193-2(b)(3).
[16] 1193-1(b).

[17] 1193-2(b).
[18] 1193-1(b).
[19] 1193-1(b).
[20] 1193-2(b)(3).
[21] 1193-4(c).
[22] 1193-1(c).
[23] 1193-2(b)(3).
[24] 1193-4(c),(d)(4).
[25] 1193-1(c); PL 70.00-2(d).
[26] 1193-2(b)(3); 1192(2-a).
[27] 1194-2(d)(2). *See Rosato v. Department of Motor Vehicles*, 7 AD3d 718, 777 NYS2d 186 (2d Dept, 2004).
[28] Ch. 312 (§ 3) L. 1994 deleted the word "such" in 1193-2(e)(1)(a).
[29] 1193-2(e)(1).
[30] 1194-2(b).
[31] 1194-2(d)(2).
[32] 1194-2(d)(1)(a).
[33] 1193-2(e)(7); (effective 11/1/94).
[34] 1193-2(e)(7)(a-1).
[35] 1193-2(2)(e)(7)(d). Expires on termination of prosecution.
[36] 1196-4; *See* 15 NYCRR 134.7.
[37] 1193-2(b)(6);1194-2(d)(1)(b).
[38] 1192-a, 1194-a.
[39] 1193-2(d)(2).
[40] 1192-8.
[41] 510-2(c).
[42] 510-2(b).
[43] 1192-4.

4

GLENN EDWARD MURRAY, ESQ.   CHARTS & CHECKLISTS

CHECKLIST OF COMMON DUI CONSEQUENCES

COURT

ARRAIGNMENT

Susp. pending prosecution; • Prior w/in 5 years (until disposition - no HP, no PCCL and no CL); • Incidental PL charge (until disposition - no CL or Hardship if fatality); or • BAC of .08% or more (30 days or until disposition, whichever is longer: unless extreme hardship obtained P CCL eligible after 30 days, only if BAC only basis for suspension and CL eligible); Eligible for post -conviction conditional license (see eligibility above)?
Susp. pending refusal hearing [until hearing or 15 days]. • Not eligible for HP or PCCL.

DMV

REFUSAL HEARING

Minimum period if revoked: 1-yr. or 18 months (if prior refusal or 1192 conviction w/in 5 years).
Civil penalty for chemical test refusal: • $500.00, or • $750.00 (if prior 1192 conviction or YOA or refusal w/in 5 yrs).
May be eligible for post-conviction conditional license? (only if convicted of § 1192 - same incident)

COURT

CONVICTION

Suspension (90 days) or Rev. (___ 6 months, or ___ 1 year) minimum.
Probation (IID, abstain/relicen./testing/$30 monthly fee (Exec. L. 257-c), etc.)
Eligible for 20-day order (only if valid license; not eligible if refusal rev. in effect)
Eligible for conditional license (only if, *inter alia*, convicted).
Court conditions (*i.e.* victim impact panel).
ADRP (eligibility, cost & referral danger).

RELICENSURE

Minimum period of revocation "MPR" : ___ months.
Early application (45 days before expiration of MPR).
DRA & refusal civil penalty must be paid prior to relicensure

ENHANCED CHARGES (Repeat offenders)

Repeat offenders (YOA not prior for enhanced charges but is prior for revocation predicate)

COLLATERAL CONSEQUENCES

CDL holder, accident (PI or PDO), professional licenses, etc.

5

CHECKLIST OF COMMON PENALTIES - REPEAT OFFENDERS			
Prior(s):	**Event:**	**Penalty:**	**Comments:**
Within 4 years			
2 §1192 convictions or refusals, or 2 prior VA or VM w/in 4 yrs. or combo	1192 Conviction or refusal finding	Permanent rev.	Eligible for relicensure after 5 yrs. **Per DMV discretionary policy, CL will not be granted.**
3 §1192 convictions or refusals or 2 prior VA or VM w/in 4 yrs. or combo	1192 Conviction or refusal finding	Permanent rev.	Eligible for relicensure after 8 yrs. **Per DMV discretionary policy, CL will not be granted.**
Within 5 Years:			
Any §1192 conviction w/in 5 yrs.	Arraignment	SPP[1]	No hardship privilege available (cf. BAC SPP)
(computed from prior offense/refusal date to pending offense/refusal date)	Refusal Finding	Rev. 1-yr. & $750 civil penalty[2]	1-yr. computed from date of refusal finding
Prior DWAI conviction w/in 5 yrs.	2d DWAI conviction w/in 5 yrs.	> fine/jail max. & Rev. 1-yr.[3]	6 mo. computed from date of conviction. YOA usually has same effect as conviction.
Prior 1192 conviction w/in 5 yrs.	2d 1192 conviction w/in 5 yrs.	Min. 5 days jail or 30 days CS and ignition interlock[4]	Min. 10 days jail or 60 days CS if 3d § 1192 w/in 5 yrs. and ignition interlock[5]
Prior 1192 conviction w/in 5 yrs.	Rev./Susp.	Ineligible for 20-Day order[6]	Also ineligible if PL Art. 120 or 125 conviction
DDP participation w/in 5 yrs. (from DDP completion to offense date)	BAC SPP CL Ineligibility	Ineligible for CL or PCCL[7]	5 yrs. computed from date of DDP discharge.[8]
Refusal finding (computed from prior refusal to offense date)	Refusal	Rev. 1-yr. & $750 civil penalty[9]	1-yr. computed from date of refusal hearing/finding
	Under 21 conviction (1192) or refusal	Any §1192 conviction	Rev. 1-yr., or until age 21,[10]
Within 8 Years:			
4 prior §1192 w/in 8 yrs or 2 prior VA or VM.	1192 Conviction or refusal finding	Permanent revocation	Eligible for relicensure after 8 yrs., no CL.
Within 10 Years:			
Any §1192 conviction	Any §1192 charge	No plea reduction	Erie County DA policy[11]
One (1) DWI conviction	DWI conviction	E/Felony[12]	Rev. 1-yr.[13]
Two (2) or more DWIs	DWI conviction	D/Felony[14]	Rev. 1-yr.[15]
Two (2) or more alcohol-related incidents (ARIs)	Rev./Susp.	Cert. of Rehab. (DS-449) required.	ARIs include convictions or refusals.[16]
Three (3) or more ARIs.	1192 conviction	Extended waiting period for relicensure	6 mo. for each ARI, computed from most recent conviction unless DDP Cert. of Rehab.
Ten (10) or > susp. for fail to appear or pay	AUO conviction	E/Felony[17]	Suspensions must be from separate dates
No Time Limit:			
Any §1192 conviction or current §1192 rev.	VM 2d	VM 1st[18]	Defendant's admission precludes proof of predicate[19]
§ 1192-3,4,4(a) accident with physical injury (PI)	Same as prior	Lifetime rev.[20]	PI as defined by Penal Law. Not avoided by CRD.

---

[1] 1193-2(e)(7). Defendant entitled to *Pringle* hearing (*See Pringle*, 88 NY2d 426, 646 NYS2d 82 (1996); *Giacopelli*, 665 Misc.2d 835, 655 NYS2d 845 (Clarkston Town Ct., 1997).
[2] 1194-2(d)(2).
[3] 1193-2(b)(1).
[4] 1193 (1)(d)(1-a) - eff 9/30/2003.
[5] 1193 (1)(d)(1-b) - eff 9/30/2003.
[6] 1193-2(d)(2).
[7] 1192-2(2)(e)(7)(D).

6

[8] 1196-4; *See* 15 NYCRR 134.7.

[9] 1194-2(d)(1)(a).

[10] 1194-2(d)(1)(b).

[11] Erie County policy also prohibits plea reduction if BAC >.13%, accident, under age 21, or combative toward arresting officer.

[12] Note that a certificate of conviction, by itself, is insufficient to establish predicate. *Van Buren*, 82 N.Y.2d 878, 609 N.Y.S.2d 170 (1993). Note: Prior F/DWI not a predicate to 2d Felony Offender; but is a predicate for Persistent Felony Offender. *See* NY Driving While Intoxicated, by Fiandach § 35.4 (LCP 1996).

[13] *Clearwater*, 98 AD2d 912, 470 N.Y.S.2d 934 (3d Dep't., 1983).

[14] 1193-4(c),(d)(4).

[15] *Homero*, 172 Misc.2d 99, 656 N.Y.S.2d 843 (Sup. Ct Nassau Co., 1997).

[16] Refusal incidental to conviction is not counted. Certificate of Rehabilitation (DS-449) within 1-yr prior to appl. for relic. required with appl for relicensure.

[17] 511-3(b).

[18] PL § 125.13.

[19] See CPL § 200.60; *Cooper*, 78 NY2d 476, 577 N.Y.S.2d 202 (1991).

[20] 1193-c(3).

7

| Glenn Edward Murray, Esq. | ©2011 | Buffalo, New York |

BAC % LIMITS

	.01	.02	.03	.04	.05	.06	.07	.08	.10+	
ANY VEHICLE										
Motorists under age 21 (for "Zero Tolerance" purposes only)				Consumed alcohol[1]						
Any motorist						DWAI[2]		MDWI[3] ADWI If .18 BAC, or above		
COMMERCIAL MOTOR VEHICLE				DWAI[4]	MDWI[5]					

BLOOD ALCOHOL CONTENT PRESUMPTIONS (§ 1195-2)

Presumed not impaired (less than .05%) If under age 21, see zero tolerance	Presumed DWAI (>.05 and < .08)	Presumed MDWI (.08 or above) Presumed. ADWI If .18 BAC, or above

LEGEND
Consumed alcohol: Basis for administrative detention, guilty finding, and suspension; **DWAI:** Driving while ability impaired (traffic infraction)
MDWI: Misdemeanor driving while intoxicated **FDWI:** Felony driving while intoxicated

* CAUTION
Repeat offenders are subject to enhanced penalties not referenced in this chart; designed as a finding tool and not a substitute for case-by-case legal research and analysis.

---

[1] 1192-a.
[2] 1195-2, 1192-1
[3] 1192-2-a.
[4] 1192-5 (CMV level I).
[5] 1192-6(CMV level II).

8

Glenn Edward Murray, Esq.   ©2011   Buffalo, New York

DUI Contact addresses & phone numbers

Buffalo DMV ALJ:

NYS DMV
Ellicott Square Building
295 Main Street
Buffalo, New York 14203
Fax: 716-851-8267

ALJ Glenn Murray: 716-851-8207
ALJ Paul Crapsi: 716-851-8237
ALJ Dan Dillon: 716-851-8245

Safety Hearing Bureau:

New York State Department of Motor Vehicles
Safety Hearing Bureau
The Governor Nelson A. Rockefeller
Empire State Plaza
Albany, New York 12228-0240

Phone: 518-474-0875
Fax to: 518-473-8575

Refusal Waiver address:

Date waiver received or postmarked (whichever earlier) will commence revocation period.
Best to mail to Albany Safety Hearing Bureau and cc by mail or fax to local Safety Hearing Bureau
New York State Department of Motor Vehicles   Phone: 518-474-0875
6 Empire State Plaza, Room 312   Fax to: 518-473-8575
Albany, New York 12228-0240

DMV Website:

DMV has as a web site with valuable information and printable forms, regarding DMV application procedures and fees:

http://www.nydmv.state.ny.us

Driver Improvement Adjudication Unit:

New York State Department of Motor Vehicles   Phone: 518-474-0774
Driver Improvement Adjudication Unit:

9

APPENDIX 55

20-Day Order and Order of Suspension and Revocation

- Always give Part 2 to the motorist.
- Give Part 1 to the motorist ONLY if you are granting continuation of driving privileges.

New York State Department of Motor Vehicles
ORDER OF SUSPENSION OR REVOCATION

PART 1 - CONTINUATION OF DRIVING PRIVILEGES

Motorist Name (Last, First, MI)	Date of Birth	Year License Expires	License class	Restrictions
Sample, Joe	01	01	60		

According to Section 1193 of the Vehicle and Traffic Law, your driver license will be ☐ suspended ☐ revoked on _____. This order will allow you to drive, with the same limitations as your driver license, until your suspension/
(sentence date plus 20 days)
revocation starts. **You must have both parts of this order with you when you drive.** If you do not have both parts of this order with you, you may be charged with a violation of the Vehicle and Traffic Law. When the suspension/revocation starts, you do not have the right to drive unless you receive a conditional license. This order must be turned in before a conditional license can be issued to you.

MV-1192 (4/11)

☒ _____
(Signature of Judge or Clerk of Court)

New York State Department of Motor Vehicles
ORDER OF SUSPENSION OR REVOCATION

PART 2

Motorist Name (Last, First, MI)	Date of Birth	Sex
Sample, Joe	01 01 60	☐ Male ☐ Female

Number and Street Address	Apt #	Ticket Number (if unavailable, enter Docket Number)
123 Main Street		2G123456SP

City	State	Zip Code	Driver License #
Somewhere	NY	12345	123-456-789

COURT/VIOLATION (Certificate of Conviction must be attached)

Judge Name	Violation Date	Conviction Date	
	01 01 01		☐ Check if Youthful Offender

Court Code	Vehicle Class		
	☐ Commercial Motor Vehicle (CMV)	☐ Special Vehicle	☐ All Others

SUSPENSION/REVOCATION

According to Section 1193-2 of the Vehicle and Traffic Law, your driver license/privilege is:
☐ Suspended for 90 days (conviction of 1192-1 first offense only if not operating a CMV or Special Vehicle).
☐ Revoked for at least _____
Duration (Enter ONLY one of the options listed on the back of this form)

Sentence date ___ / ___ / ___ . This order will be effective on _____ because of your conviction of a
(sentence date or sentence date plus 20 days)
violation of Subdivision___ of section 1192 of the Vehicle and Traffic Law.

PROBATION/CONDITIONAL DISCHARGE

A person convicted of a violation of VTL 1192(2-a)(a) or (b) **committed on or after 12/18/09** must be sentenced to a conditional discharge or probation and the installation and use of the interlock device.

A person convicted of a violation of VTL 1192(2) or (3) **committed on or after 11/18/09 and who is sentenced on or after 8/15/10** must be sentenced to a conditional discharge or probation and the installation and use of the interlock device.

Is motorist sentenced to ☐ Probation - If sentenced to probation, how long is the sentence? ☐ 3 Years ☐ 5 Years
☐ Conditional Discharge - If sentenced to conditional discharge, how long is the sentence? ☐ 1 year ☐ 3 years
Must the motorist obtain permission before applying for a license? Only applies if motorist is sentenced to probation. ☐ Yes ☐ No
   If yes, do they need permission from: ☐ Court ☐ Probation Department ☐ Both
Has the motorist been ordered to install an ignition interlock device? ☐ Yes ☐ No

LICENSE SURRENDER — Has the motorist surrendered his/her license?

☐ Yes ☐ No If you have not turned in your driver license to the court, you must turn it in to the Department of Motor Vehicles
              If you turn in a temporary license, you must also turn in your photo license when you receive it.

Motorist Signature	Signature of Judge or Clerk of Court
☒	☒

MV-1192 (4/11)

☐ Copy 1: Motorist   ☐ Copy 2: DMV   ☐ Copy 3: Court

APPENDIX 56

Department of Motor Vehicles' Alcohol and Drug Rehabilitation Program (Part 134)

Part 134 ALCOHOL AND DRUG REHABILITATION PROGRAMS

(Statutory authority: VTL Sections 215, 521)

Section 134.1. Introduction

(a) *Intent.* Article 21 of the Vehicle and Traffic Law as added by chapter 291 of the Laws of 1975, and recodified in article 31 by chapter 47 of the Laws of 1988, provides for the establishment of an alcohol and drug rehabilitation program for the purpose of providing rehabilitation to drivers convicted of alcohol or drug-related driving offenses or persons who have been adjudicated youthful offenders for alcohol or drug-related traffic offenses or persons found to have been operating a motor vehicle after having consumed alcohol in violation of section 1192-a of the Vehicle and Traffic Law to alleviate the threat to the lives and well-being of the citizens of this State posed by alcohol and drug-related driving. Although this article provides for the issuance of conditional licenses to persons enrolled in such program, this provision is incidental to the primary purpose of the legislation, highway safety. This Part is intended to implement the legislative intent by establishing criteria for eligibility of persons for entrance into such programs, issuance and use of conditional licenses, procedures to be followed by the courts, the Department of Motor Vehicles and motorists in conjunction with such programs, as well as the curricula to be used in such programs and the qualifications of persons who will be conducting such programs.

(b) *Definitions.*

(1) Program. As hereinafter used in this Part, the terms *program, alcohol* and *drug rehabilitation program, rehabilitation program,* or *course* shall mean a specific curriculum which must include training in a classroom setting, and may include instruction, discussion, testing, interviewing, counseling, referral for extended alcohol or drug rehabilitative activities and such rehabilitative activities, all of which have been

approved by the commissioner and are administered by program administrators designated as such by the commissioner. Any extended alcohol or drug rehabilitative activities which occur after eight months following enrollment in the program must be recommended licensed providers of such services.

(2) Full period of suspension or revocation effectively served. A person will be deemed to have effectively served the full period of a suspension if he has received a suspension order, has surrendered his driver's license in response to such suspension order, has not been issued an unconditional license and has not operated a motor vehicle for the period of time for which his license has been suspended. A person will be deemed to have effectively served the full period of a revocation if he has received a revocation order, has surrendered his driver's license in response to such revocation order, has not been issued an unconditional license and has not operated a motor vehicle for a period of at least six months.

Sec. filed Sept. 26, 1975; amds. filed: May 27, 1997; June 21, 2005 eff. July 6, 2005. Amended (a).

Section 134.2. Persons eligible for program

Any person who is convicted of a violation of any subdivision of section 1192 of the Vehicle and Traffic Law, or is found to have been operating a motor vehicle after having consumed alcohol in violation of section 1192-a of this article, or of an alcohol or drug-related traffic offense in another state, shall be eligible for enrollment in an alcohol and drug rehabilitation program unless: such person has participated in a program established pursuant to article 31 of the Vehicle and Traffic Law within the five years immediately preceding the date of commission of the alcohol or drug-related offense or such person has been convicted of a violation of any subdivision of section 1192 of such law during the five years immediately preceding commission of an alcohol or drug-related offense; with respect to persons convicted of a violation of section 1192 of the Vehicle and Traffic Law, is prohibited from enrolling in a program by the judge who imposes sentence upon the conviction; or the commissioner is prohibited from issuing such new license to a person because of two convictions of a violation of section 1192 of the Vehicle and Traffic Law where physical injury, as defined in section 10 of the Penal Law, has resulted in both instances. Notwithstanding the provisions of this section, a person shall be eligible for enrollment in the alcohol and drug rehabilitation program if such person is sentenced pursuant to the plea bargaining provisions set forth in Vehicle and Traffic Law, section 1192(10)(a)(ii) and (10)(d).

Sec. filed Sept. 26, 1975; amds. filed: Feb. 4, 1980; Feb. 22, 1996; May 27,

1997; Nov. 1, 2006 as emergency measure; Jan. 30, 2007 as emergency measure; April 30, 2007 as emergency measure; June 19, 2007 eff. July 3, 2007.

Section 134.3. Court action upon conviction of a violation of section 1192 of the Vehicle and Traffic Law

Article 21 of the Vehicle and Traffic Law permits a judge who imposes sentence upon a conviction of a violation of any subdivision of section 1192 of the Vehicle and Traffic Law to prohibit a defendant from enrolling in a rehabilitation program under article 21. It is recommended that the following procedures be followed:

(a) *Prohibition from enrollment by a judge.* If a judge wishes to prohibit the defendant from enrolling in a rehabilitation program, upon conviction the judge may impose any penalty provided by law and he should suspend or revoke the defendant's driver's license, whichever is appropriate, pick up such defendant's driver's license, and forward the driver's license and a certificate of conviction to the commissioner within 48 hours of conviction. A statement indicating that the judge is prohibiting the defendant from enrolling in a rehabilitation program must be prominently placed on the certificate of conviction or on an accompanying letter on court stationery.

(b) *No prohibition from enrollment by the judge.* If a judge does not wish to prohibit the defendant from enrolling in a rehabilitation program, upon conviction, it is recommended that the judge impose, in addition to any other sentence required or permitted by law, a sentence of conditional discharge or probation, the conditions of such discharge or probation being that the defendant enroll in and satisfactorily complete a rehabilitation program established pursuant to article 21 of the Vehicle and Traffic Law. The judge should suspend or revoke the defendant's driver's license as required by section 1193 of the Vehicle and Traffic Law. A certificate of conviction indicating the sentence of conditional discharge should be forwarded to the commissioner within 48 hours of conviction. All additional action in relation to enrollment in a rehabilitation program will be taken by the Department of Motor Vehicles.

Sec. filed Sept. 26, 1975; amd. filed May 27, 1997 eff. June 11, 1997. Amended (b).

Section 134.4. Initial procedures by the Department of Motor Vehicles upon receipt of a certificate of conviction for a violation of section 1192 of the Vehicle and Traffic Law

(a) *Certificate of conviction indicates prohibition from enrollment by the judge.* Upon receipt of a certificate of conviction for a violation of section 1192 of the Vehicle and Traffic Law when such certificate or an accompanying letter indicates that the convicting judge has prohibited the defendant from entering a rehabilitation program, the department will issue a confirming revocation or suspension order when a revocation or suspension has been imposed by the court, or, will issue an appropriate suspension or revocation order when such action has not been taken by the court. No further action with respect to rehabilitation programs will be taken by the department.

(b) *Certificate of conviction does not indicate prohibition from enrollment by the judge.* Upon receipt of a certificate of conviction for a violation of section 1192 of the Vehicle and Traffic Law when such certificate or an accompanying letter does not indicate a prohibition from enrollment by the judge, the department will make a review of the defendant's driving record.

(1) Unless such review indicates that the defendant is ineligible to enroll in a rehabilitation program based upon criteria set forth in section 134.2 of this Part, the department will issue the appropriate suspension or revocation order against the defendant's driver's license, if the court has not already done so and will notify the defendant that he is eligible for enrollment in a rehabilitation program. Such notification will include instructions for enrollment in a rehabilitation program. The suspension or revocation order will indicate the effective date of the order. Unless such review indicates that the defendant is ineligible to enroll in a rehabilitation program in accordance with the provisions set forth in section 134.2 of this Part, the department will also apply the criteria established in section 134.7 of this Part to determine whether the defendant is eligible for the issuance of a conditional license. Unless such review indicates that the defendant is ineligible for the issuance of a conditional license, the department will also notify the defendant that he may be eligible for such license. Such notification will include instructions for making application for the conditional license.

(2) If a review of the defendant's driving record indicates that the defendant is ineligible for enrollment in a rehabilitation program as set forth in section 134.2 of this Part, only the appropriate revocation or suspension order will be issued to the defendant. No further action with respect to rehabilitation programs will be taken by the department.

Sec. filed Sept. 26, 1975; amd. filed May 27, 1997 eff. June 11, 1997. Amended (b)(1).

Section 134.5. Procedures to be followed by defendant who receives notification of eligibility for enrollment in a rehabilitation program

Upon receipt of notification from the department of eligibility for enrollment in a rehabilitation program, the defendant may apply for enrollment in such a program. To make application, the defendant shall submit a completed waiver form and other necessary forms, as directed on the notice. The commissioner or designated person shall apply the criteria set forth in section 134.2 of this Part to determine the applicant's final eligibility for enrollment in a program. If the applicant is found to be eligible for enrollment, and he has met all requirements for enrollment established by statute and this Part, the applicant shall be enrolled in a rehabilitation program. In addition, if the applicant is eligible for the issuance of a conditional license, in accordance with criteria established in section 134.7 of this Part, a conditional license will be issued to the applicant in accordance with this Part.

Sec. filed Sept. 26, 1975; amds. filed: June 24, 1980; May 27, 1997 eff. June 11, 1997.

Section 134.6. Waiver required

(a) Included in an application for enrollment in a rehabilitation program shall be a waiver by the applicant. Such waiver shall provide that the applicant agrees:

(1) to accept and abide by all conditions contained on the conditional license, if such a license is issued to him;

(2) to complete the rehabilitation program, including referrals for evaluation and treatment;

(3) to pay all fees required for the rehabilitation program;

(4) except as provided for in section 134.9(d)(2) of this Part, if for any reason any conditional license which is issued to him is revoked, or if he fails to satisfactorily complete the rehabilitation program, the suspension or revocation of his license resulting from the conviction for which he was enrolled in the program shall be reimposed for the full period of such suspension or revocation, unless such full period has already been effectively served; and

(5) before the issuance of a conditional license, if such a license is issued to him, and before the reinstatement or return of an unconditional driver's license is made to him, he must satisfy any outstanding administrative suspensions, notices or bars, such as suspensions or bars for failure to answer traffic summonses.

(b) No person shall be permitted to enroll in a rehabilitation program unless a waiver signed by the applicant is filed with the department.

Sec. filed Sept. 26, 1975; amds. filed: May 27, 1997; Dec. 23, 1999 eff. Jan. 12, 2000. Amended (a)(4).

Section 134.7. Criteria for issuance of a conditional license

(a) The issuance of a conditional license shall be denied to any person who enrolls in a program if a review of such person's driving record, or additional information secured by the department, indicates that any of the following conditions apply.

(1) The person has been convicted of homicide, assault, criminal negligence or criminally negligent homicide arising out of operation of a motor vehicle.

(2) The conviction, adjudication or finding upon which eligibility for a rehabilitation program is based involved a fatal accident.

(3) The person does not have a currently valid New York State driver's license. This paragraph shall not apply to a person whose New York State driver's license has expired, but is still renewable, nor to a person who would have a currently valid New York State driver's license except for the revocation or suspension which resulted from the conviction, adjudication or finding upon which his eligibility for the rehabilitation program is based, nor to a person who would have a currently valid New York State driver's license except for a suspension or revocation which resulted from a chemical test refusal arising out of the same incident as such conviction, adjudication or finding of a violation of section 1192-a of the Vehicle and Traffic Law section.

(4) The person has been convicted of an offense arising from the same event which resulted in the current alcohol-related conviction, adjudication or finding which conviction would, aside from the alcohol-related conviction, adjudication or finding result in mandatory revocation or suspension of the person's driver's license.

(5) The person has had two or more revocations and/or suspensions of his driver's license, other than the revocation or suspension upon which his eligibility for the rehabilitation program is based within the last three years. This subdivision shall not apply to suspensions which have been terminated by performance of an act by the person, nor to a suspension or revocation resulting from a chemical test refusal, if the person had been convicted of a violation of section 1192 of the Vehicle and Traffic Law or found to be in violation of section 1192-a of such law arising out of the same incident.

(6) The person has been convicted more than once of reckless driving within the last three years.

(7) The person has had a series of convictions, incidents and/or accidents or has a medical or mental condition, which in the judgment of the commissioner or his designated agent tends to establish that the person would be an unusual and immediate risk upon the highway.

(8) The person has been penalized under section 1193(1)(d) of the Vehicle and Traffic Law for any violation of subdivision 2, 2-a, 3, 4, or 4-a of section 1192 of such law.

(9) The person is reentering the rehabilitation program, as provided in section 134.10(c) of this Part, for a second or subsequent time.

(10) The person has been suspended under section 510(2)(b)(v) of the Vehicle and Traffic Law for a conviction of section 1192(4) of such law. Such person may be eligible for a restricted use license pursuant to Part 135 of this Title.

(11)

(i) The person has three or more alcohol- or drug-related driving convictions or incidents within the last 25 years. For the purposes of this paragraph, a conviction for a violation of section 1192 of the Vehicle and Traffic Law, and/or a finding of a violation of section 1192-a of such law and/or a finding of refusal to submit to a chemical test under section 1194 of such law arising out of the same incident shall only be counted as one conviction or incident. The date of the violation or incident resulting in a conviction or a finding as described herein shall be used to determine whether three or more convictions or incidents occurred within a 25 year period.

(ii) For the purposes of this paragraph, when determining eligibility for a conditional license issued pending prosecution pursuant to section 134.18 of this Part, the term "incident" shall include the arrest that resulted in the issuance of the suspension pending prosecution.

(12) The person was the holder of a limited DJ or limited MJ license at the time of the violation which resulted in the suspension or revocation.

(13) The person, during the five years preceding the commission of the alcohol or drug-related offense or a finding of a violation of section 1192-a of the Vehicle and Traffic Law, participated in the alcohol and drug rehabilitation program or has been convicted of a violation of any subdivision of section 1192 of such law.

(b) If after a person is enrolled in a rehabilitation program and has been issued a conditional license, but, prior to the reissuance of an unconditional license, information is received by the department which indicates that such person was not eligible for a conditional license his conditional license will be revoked.

Sec. filed Sept. 26, 1975; amds. filed: Jan. 2, 1981; July 13, 1987; Dec. 11, 1989; June 13, 1994; May 27, 1997; Dec. 23, 1999; May 18, 2004; June 21, 2005; Nov. 1, 2006 as emergency measure; Jan. 30, 2007 as emergency measure; April 30, 2007 as emergency measure; June 19, 2007 eff. July 3, 2007. Amended (a)(8), added (a)(13); amd. filed Aug. 2, 2011 eff. Aug. 17, 2011; emergency rulemaking eff. Sept. 25, 2012, expired Dec. 23, 2012; emergency rulemaking eff. Dec. 24, 2012, expired Feb. 21, 2013; emergency rulemaking eff. Feb. 22, 2013, expired; amd. filed Apr. 15, 2013 eff. May 1, 2013.

Section 134.8. [Repealed]

Sec. filed Sept. 26, 1975; repealed, filed Jan. 2, 1981 eff. Jan. 2, 1981.

Section 134.9. Conditional license

A conditional license will be issued only by the department which will establish the conditions applicable to each individual license based upon information submitted by the applicant.

(a) *Form of conditional license.* The conditional license will be a two-part form. One part shall be computer generated and will bear a notation indicating that it is a conditional license. The other part will be manually generated and will contain the specific conditions applicable to that particular conditional license. The holder of a conditional license, when required to display such license, must display both parts of such license.

(b) *Establishment of conditions.* Each conditional license shall contain the condition that such license shall be subject to revocation for operation outside of the limitations appearing on such license. Each conditional license will contain the limitations or use of such license as prescribed by the department, and as accepted by the holder. Such conditions shall be limited to operation: to and from the holder's place of employment; during the course of employment, when required; to and from a class or an activity which is an authorized part of the rehabilitation program and at which the holder's attendance is required; enroute to and from a class or course at an accredited school or approved institute of vocational or technical training; enroute to and from a medical examination or treatment as part of a necessary medical treatment for such participant or member of his household, as evidenced by a written statement to that effect from a licensed medical practitioner; during a three-hour consecutive daytime period as specified by the department on a day during which the holder is not engaged in his usual employment or vocation; to and from court-ordered probation activities; to and from a motor vehicle office for the transaction of business relating to such license or program; or enroute to and from a place, including a school, at which a child or children of the holder are cared for on a regular basis and which is necessary for the holder to maintain such holder's employment or enrollment at an accredited school, college or university or at a State-approved institution of vocational or technical training;

(c) A conditional license issued to a person convicted of, or adjudicated a youthful offender for, a violation of any subdivision of section 1192 of the Vehicle and Traffic Law or found to have violated section 1192-a of such law shall not be valid for the operation of commercial motor vehicles as defined in section 501-a of such law or taxicabs as defined in section 148-a of such law.

(d) *Revocation of conditional license.*

(1) A conditional license which has been issued shall be revoked upon: the holder's conviction of any traffic violation, other than parking, stopping, standing, equipment, inspection or other nonmoving violations where such violation occurred during the period of validity of the conditional license; or for the holder's failure to attend any portion or portions of the rehabilitation program in accordance with attendance rules established for the program. A revocation for any of the above reasons shall be issued without a hearing based upon receipt of a certificate of conviction, or in the case of failure to attend any portion or portions of the rehabilitation program upon certification of the person administering such program. In addition, the commissioner may revoke a conditional license after a hearing, based upon a finding that the holder has not satisfactorily participated in the rehabilitation program, or that the holder is not attempting in good faith to accept rehabilitation, or upon a complaint that the holder is operating or has operated a motor vehicle in violation of the conditions imposed on his conditional license. The commissioner may also revoke a conditional license without a hearing upon receipt of a certificate of conviction which indicates that the applicant has driven in violation of the conditions of such license.

(2) Persons under 21 years of age. The provisions of this subdivision shall apply to any person under the age of 21 who enters a rehabilitation program and is issued a conditional license as a result of a conviction for a violation of any subdivision of section 1192 of the Vehicle and Traffic Law, committed when such person was under the age of 21. Notwithstanding any other provisions of this Part, if any such person's conditional license is revoked and such person has completed a rehabilitation program as provided for in section 134.10 of this Part, time served shall be credited toward the remaining portion of the revocation pe-

riod, calculated from the effective date of the order of revocation which resulted in the issuance of the conditional license, to the date of the violation which resulted in the revocation of the conditional license.

(e) *Extra-territorial effect of conditional license.* Whether a conditional license will be honored by other states will be dependent upon the laws of each such other state. This state will honor a similar type license issued by another state to a resident of the issuing state to the extent of the conditions imposed. The holder of a conditional license issued pursuant to article 31 should check with the appropriate motor vehicle authorities of any other state in such other state.

(f) *Period of validity of conditional license.* Unless otherwise revoked by the commissioner, a conditional license will be valid from the date of its issuance until the expiration date contained thereon or until the holder's unconditional license is returned to him, whichever occurs first.

Sec. filed Sept. 26, 1975; amds. filed: July 13, 1987; Feb. 15, 1991 as emergency measure; May 15, 1991 as emergency measure; July 9, 1991; July 12, 1991 as emergency measure; May 27, 1997; Dec. 23, 1999; June 21, 2005 eff. July 6, 2005. Amended (c).

Section 134.10.   Completion of a rehabilitation program

(a) *Requirements for satisfactory completion of a rehabilitation program.* In order for a person to satisfactorily complete a rehabilitation program, he must have paid all necessary fees and have attended and actively participated in all segments of such rehabilitation program as required by the department, including completion of extended participation upon the recommendation of the appropriate officials.

(b) *Results of satisfactory completion of a rehabilitation program.* Upon satisfactory completion of a program, any unexpired suspension or revocation which was issued as a result of the conviction for which the person was eligible for enrollment in the program may be terminated by the commissioner unless the termination is prohibited under section 1193 of the Vehicle and Traffic Law or this Subchapter, or if the termination is based upon enrollment in the program pursuant to the plea bargaining provisions of Vehicle and Traffic Law section 1192(10)(a)(ii) and 1192(10)(d), or if such person would not otherwise be eligible for enrollment in the program pursuant to section 1196(4) of such law, or if the person has two or more alcohol- or drug-related driving convictions or incidents within 25 years from the date of enrollment in the program.

(c) *Failure to satisfactorily complete a rehabilitation program.* If a person fails to satisfactorily complete a rehabilitation program, in addition to revocation of any conditional license which may be held by such person, the suspension or revocation of such person's unconditional driver's license will be reinstated for the full period of such suspension or revocation, unless such full period has already been effectively served. Such person may apply for reentry into the rehabilitation program. A conditional license may only be issued upon the first such reentry. Although second and subsequent reentries may be permitted, a conditional license will not be reissued in such cases.

(d) *Appeals.* Appeals from decisions of treatment or program personnel regarding an individual's participation or treatment shall be directed to the program director. If said director is unable to resolve the matter, such appeals shall be directed to the Division of Driver Licensing. If said division is unable to resolve the matter, such appeals shall be sent to the commissioner who shall make a determination. Prior to making a determination the commissioner may consult with experts in the field of alcoholism and rehabilitation and any other appropriate agencies.

Sec. filed Sept. 26, 1975; amds. filed: Feb. 4, 1980; Jan. 2, 1981; Dec. 9, 1982; Dec. 11, 1989; Aug. 27, 1996; May 27, 1997; Jan. 30, 2007 as emergency measure; April 30, 2007 as emergency measure; June 19, 2007 eff. July 3, 2007. Amended (b); emergency rulemaking eff. Sept. 25, 2012, expired Dec. 23, 2012; emergency rulemaking eff. Dec. 24, 2012, expired Feb. 21, 2013; emergency rulemaking eff. Feb. 22, 2013, expired; amd. filed Apr. 15, 2013 eff. May 1, 2013.

Section 134.11.   Issuance of unconditional driver's license

Satisfactory completion of a rehabilitation program or expiration of the term of suspension, whichever occurs first, will initiate the necessary action to provide for the termination of the suspension or revocation which was the basis for entry into the rehabilitation program, provided however, no such suspension or revocation shall be terminated prior to the expiration of the term of suspension or revocation if the applicant for the unconditional license has two or more alcohol- or drug-related driving convictions or incidents within the preceding 25 years. Upon a determination of satisfactory completion of the rehabilitation program or the term of suspension, and unless otherwise determined by the commissioner, as provided for in subdivision (b) of section 134.10 of this Part, a notice of termination of the suspension or revocation and an unconditional license will be issued. However, no such license will be issued until all civil penalties due the department are paid or if there are any outstanding suspensions, revocations, or bars against such license until such suspensions, revocations, or bars are satisfactorily disposed of by the applicant. Any conditional license which is still valid will be terminated concurrently with the return of the unconditional driver's license and must be returned to the department. A conditional license shall not be

renewed more than one year after the issuance of the conditional license if a revocation is issued for a chemical test refusal and the holder of the conditional license has not paid the civil penalty required by section 1194 of the Vehicle and Traffic Law.
Sec. filed Sept. 26, 1975; amds. filed: Jan. 2, 1981; May 27, 1997; Nov. 1, 2006 as emergency measure; Jan. 30, 2007 as emergency measure; April 30, 2007 as emergency measure; June 19, 2007 eff. July 3, 2007; emergency rulemaking eff. Sept. 25, 2012, expired Dec. 23, 2012; emergency rulemaking eff. Dec. 24, 2012, expired Feb. 21, 2013; emergency rulemaking eff. Feb. 22, 2013, expired; amd. filed Apr. 15, 2013 eff. May 1, 2013.

Section 134.12.   Notification to the court

In any case where the sentence upon conviction consists of a conditional discharge, the department will notify the convicting court of the final disposition of any action relating to any person who has not been prohibited from enrolling in a rehabilitation program by a judge. Notification of ineligibility for a rehabilitation program and failure to enroll in the program if eligible or failure to satisfactorily complete such a program will be sent to the court as expeditiously as possible, so that where appropriate the court may take the necessary steps to resentence the defendant for a failure to meet the conditions of any conditional discharge. Notification of satisfactory completion of a rehabilitation program will be sent to the appropriate court. Such notification will indicate compliance of the defendant with the conditions of the conditional discharge which may have been imposed by the court relating to enrollment and satisfactory completion of a rehabilitation program.
Sec. filed Sept. 26, 1975; amds. filed: April 1, 1976; May 27, 1997 eff. June 11, 1997.

Section 134.13.   Out-of-state convictions

All of the provisions of this Part shall be applicable to the holder of a New York State driver's license who has been convicted of an alcohol-or drug-related traffic offense in another state except that those provisions which relate to the actions of the convicting judge, the effect of satisfactory completion of a rehabilitation program upon a sentence of fine or imprisonment and notification to the court by the department shall not be applicable. In addition, if the driving privileges of a New York licensee convicted in another state are suspended or revoked by such other state, the conditional license issued by the commissioner will not permit the holder to operate in such other state during the term of suspension or revocation of his driving privileges within that state, unless specifically permitted by that state.
Sec. filed Sept. 26, 1975; amd. filed Feb. 4, 1980 eff. Feb. 4, 1980.

Section 134.14.   Fees

Article 21 provides for the establishment of a schedule of fees to be paid by or on behalf of each participant in the program, which fees shall defray the ongoing expenses of the program.

(a) This fee shall consist of two parts:

(1) that portion of the fee necessary to defray the administrative costs of the Department of Motor Vehicles in administering the program, which shall be paid by the applicant to the department at the time he makes application for acceptance in a rehabilitation program; and

(2) that portion of the fee required for enrollment in a program which shall be paid by the applicant prior to entry into the program to the entity authorized by the department to conduct a rehabilitation program. Such fee shall not be refundable unless the person is denied enrollment in the program upon his application. Moreover, no portion of the fee shall be refundable by reason of the participant's withdrawal or expulsion from the program.

(b) Except as provided in subdivisions (c) and (d) of this section, the total fee for a rehabilitation program shall not exceed $300. Seventy-five dollars of any such total fee shall represent the reimbursement of costs for administrative expenses incurred by the Department of Motor Vehicles and sentencing courts. A participant in the program shall not be required to pay the $75 fee to the department if such participant held a conditional license pending prosecution under section 134.18 of this Part, if such conditional license was not revoked, and such conditional license was issued as the result of the same violation on which participation in such program is based. The commissioner may require that up to $5 of the total fee for a rehabilitation program shall be used for reimbursement of costs for curriculum enhancements to be developed by the Department of Motor Vehicles and/or a third party authorized by the department. If the commissioner so requires, written notification of such requirement shall be sent to all rehabilitation programs, and such portion of the fee shall be paid by the program directly to such authorized third party.

(c) A participant in a program who transfers to another program shall pay to the new program a fee of $25, plus $10 for each session remaining to be completed in the new program.

(d) A participant who has previously withdrawn from a program and subsequently reenters such program shall pay a reenrollment fee of $50 to the program.

(e) Each program shall submit an annual fiscal report and an annual statistical report, on a form prescribed by the commissioner. Such reports shall be filed with the department no later than April 30th in the year following the calendar year to which it pertains.

(f) In addition to the fees established in the preceding subdivisions of this section, there may be an additional charge for extended alcohol or drug rehabilitative activities to which any defendant is referred by the program administrator as part of the rehabilitation program.

Sec. filed Sept. 26, 1975; amds. filed: Nov. 18, 1977; Sept. 25, 1980; June 1, 1987; July 13, 1989; March 27, 1990; Dec. 4, 1991; Oct. 28, 1993; Feb. 22, 1996; Nov. 14, 1996; May 11, 2004 eff. May 26, 2004. Amended (b).

Section 134.15. Establishment of alcohol and drug rehabilitation programs

The department may enter into an agreement with a municipality, a department of a municipality, or other agency to provide that such municipality, department thereof, or other agency shall conduct a rehabilitation program. Any agreement shall provide that any such party shall conduct the program in accordance with a curriculum approved by the department, in a facility acceptable to the department, administered by and given by persons who are approved by and who meet qualifications established by the commissioner. Such party shall agree to abide by any class size limitation established by the department, to charge not more than the fee prescribed by the department and to cooperate fully with the department in the conduct and administration of any such program including the monitoring and evaluation of any phases of the program or its administration by persons designated by the commissioner. No program will be approved if any referral for extended rehabilitative activities is connected in any manner with the person making such referral so that financial or other benefits will result to such person as a result of such referral.

Sec. filed Sept. 26, 1975 eff. Sept. 29, 1975.

Section 134.16. Confidentiality of records

Any record relating to a person enrolled in such a program generated by the agency which is conducting a rehabilitation program shall be confidential and shall not be disclosed other than in conjunction with the rehabilitation program to any person other than the person himself and, where appropriate, the Department of Motor Vehicles. This provision shall not apply to any notification of satisfactory completion of a program or notification that the person has failed or is failing to satisfactorily complete a program.

Sec. filed Sept. 26, 1975 eff. Sept. 29, 1975.

Section 134.17. [Repealed]

Sec. filed Sept. 26, 1975; repealed, filed May 27, 1997 eff. June 11, 1997.

Section 134.18. Conditional license issued pending prosecution

(a) When a driver's license is suspended pending prosecution pursuant to section 1193(2)(e)(7) of the Vehicle and Traffic Law, the holder of such license may be issued a conditional license, 30 days after such suspension takes effect, provided such person is eligible for such a license as set forth in section 134.7 of this Part and section 1196 of the Vehicle and Traffic Law. Such license shall not be valid for the operation of a commercial motor vehicle or a taxicab. The holder of such license shall not be required to and may not participate in the alcohol and drug rehabilitation program when issued a conditional license pursuant to this section.

(b) *Establishment of conditions.* Each conditional license issued under this section shall be subject to the conditions set forth in section 134.9(b) of this Part and section 1196 of the Vehicle and Traffic Law.

(c) *Revocation of conditional license.* The provisions of section 134.9(d) of this Part shall be applicable to a conditional license issued under this section.

(d) *Period of validity.* A conditional license issued under this section shall be valid, unless otherwise revoked, suspended or expired, until the prosecution for the pending alcohol-related charge is terminated.

Sec. filed Feb. 22, 1996 eff. March 13, 1996; amd. filed June 3, 2008 eff. June 18, 2008.

APPENDIX 57

Notice of Completition of New York State Drinking Driver Program

MV 2026 (9/87)   New York State - Department of Motor Vehicles
NOTICE OF COMPLETION OF NEW YORK STATE
DRINKING DRIVER PROGRAM

Name of Motorist _____
                    Last   First   M.I.

No. & Street _____

City _____ State _____ ZIP _____

Date of Birth _____ Sex _____ Completion Date _____

Entrance Date _____

Conviction was related to ☐ Alcohol - **CODE 0** or ☐ Drugs - **CODE 1**
Name of Drinking   Location
Driver Program _____ Code _____

No. & Street _____

City _____ State _____ ZIP _____

If motorist was transferred from another Drinking Driver Program, check box ☐
Location code of program from which the motorist transferred _____
I certify that the individual named has successfully completed all aspects of the Drinking Driver Program as designated by the Commissioner of Motor Vehicles.

Authorized Signature _____ CODE 0 _____

1. TO MOTORIST - USE THIS COPY TO APPLY FOR UNCONDITIONAL LICENSE

APPENDIX 58 *[Reserved]*

APPENDIX 59 *[Reserved]*

APPENDIX 60

Letter from Department of Motor Vehicles Regarding Chemical Test Refusal

STATE OF NEW YORK
DEPARTMENT OF MOTOR VEHICLES

6 EMPIRE STATE PLAZA, ALBANY, NY 12228

RAYMOND P. MARTINEZ
Commissioner

JILL A. DUNN
Deputy Commissioner and Counsel

JAN

Legal Division
NEAL W. SCHOEN
Chief Counsel

January 4, 2002

Eric H. Sills, Esq.
Gerstenzang, O'Hern, Hickey & Gerstenzang
210 Great Oaks Boulevard
Albany, NY 12203

Re: Chemical Test Refusal

Dear Mr. Sills:

Neal Schoen has asked that I respond to your letter of December 26, 2001 regarding
chemical test refusals.

You pose the following scenario: a motorist persistently refuses to submit to a properly
requested chemical test. The motorist changes her mind and consents to take the test.
The police allow her to take the test and a test result is obtained. Is this deemed a
refusal?

Sanctions are imposed for those who refuse a chemical test because such refusal may
frustrate the prosecution's case related to the underlying DWI charge. However, in the
case you describe, the prosecution's case is not impaired because a test result is obtained.
Thus, the Department would not deem this scenario to constitute a refusal.

Please do not hesitate to contact me if I can be of further assistance.

Very truly yours,

Ida L. Traschen
Associate Counsel

ILT/mw
cc: Lucia Ferrara
Sandy Sussman

APPENDIX 61

Letter from Department of Motor Vehicles Regarding Suspension Pending Prosecution

 **STATE OF NEW YORK**
DEPARTMENT OF MOTOR VEHICLES
6 EMPIRE STATE PLAZA, ALBANY, NY 12228

RAYMOND P. MARTINEZ
Commissioner

JILL A. DUNN
Deputy Commissioner and Counsel

Legal Division
NEAL W. SCHOEN
Chief Counsel

APR – 9

April 4, 2002

Eric H. Sills, Esq.
Gerstenzang, O'Hern, Hickey & Gerstenzang
210 Great Oaks Boulevard
Albany, NY 12203

Re: Suspension Pending Prosecution

Dear Mr. Sills:

Neal Schoen has requested that I respond to your recent letter regarding suspension pending prosecution.

You ask whether a defendant's driver's license can lawfully be suspended pending prosecution pursuant to either Vehicle and Traffic Law §1193(2)(e)(1) and/or §1193(2)(e)(7) under the following circumstances:

1. The defendant is charged with common law DWI, in violation of VTL §1192(3);

2. The defendant refused to submit to a chemical test (and no test result was obtained); and

3. The defendant has no prior VTL §1192 convictions within the past five years (and there is no Penal Law Article 120 or 125 charges).

Under this set of facts, there is no statutory basis for a mandatory suspension pending prosecution. VTL §1193(2)(e)(1) provides that a driver's license must be suspended pending prosecution if the driver is charged with a violation of §1192(2), (3) or (4) <u>and</u> has any §1192 convictions within the preceding five years (or if there is an accompanying charge of vehicular assault or vehicular manslaughter). VTL §1193(2)(e)(7) provides that a driver's license must be suspended pending prosecution if the driver is charge with a violation of §1192(2) or (3) <u>and</u> has a BAC reading of .10 or more at the time of arrest. In the situation described above, there is no BAC reading and no prior alcohol conviction. Thus, a mandatory suspension would not be appropriate under these circumstances.

I trust this information will assist you.

Very truly yours,

Ida L. Traschen
Associate Counsel

ILT/mw

APPENDIX 62

Letter from Department of Motor Vehicles Regarding Hardship Privilege

RICHARD E. JACKSON, JR.
COMMISSIONER

WILLIAM J. FLORENCE, JR.
DEPUTY COMMISSIONER & COUNSEL

STATE OF NEW YORK
DEPARTMENT OF MOTOR VEHICLES
EMPIRE STATE PLAZA
ALBANY NEW YORK 12228

LEGAL DIVISION
NEAL W. SCHOEN
FIRST ASSISTANT COUNSEL

June 24, 1998

Timothy P. Donaher, Esq.
Doyle & Donaher
1501 East Avenue, Suite 201
Rochester, New York 14610

Dear Mr. Donaher:

I have received your letter of June 23, 1998 regarding <u>People v.</u>
<u>Raymond Speranza</u>.

You ask for an informal opinion from the Department regarding the
breadth of the hardship privilege. Section 1193(2)(e)(7) of the
Vehicle and Traffic Law provides that the hardship privilege may
be used "to travel to and from the licensee's employment." This
is distinguished from the conditional license which may be used
during the course of the licensee's employment.

In Mr. Speranza's case, he is the manager of various job sites
which his company has been hired to clean. It is the
Department's position that the hardship privilege may be used to
travel to and from each job site since each site is a separate
base of employment. However, Mr. Speranza may not travel during
the course of his employment, i.e., he may not run errands or
pick up materials for his work, for example.

I trust this information assists you.

Very truly yours,

Ida L. Traschen

IDA L. TRASCHEN
Assistant Counsel

ILT/hb

APPENDIX 63

DPCA Regulations for Ignition Interlock Devices

Section 358.1. Objective

This Part's objective is to promote public/traffic safety, offender accountability, and quality assurance through the establishment of minimum standards for the usage and monitoring of ignition interlock devices imposed by a criminal court for a felony or misdemeanor under the Vehicle and Traffic Law or Penal Law.

Historical Note

Emergency rulemaking eff. Apr. 23, 2010, expired July 21, 2010; emergency rulemaking eff. July 21, 2010, expired; emergency rulemaking eff. Sept. 7, 2010, expired Nov. 5, 2010; amds. filed Oct. 19, 2010 eff. Nov. 3, 2010. Current with amendments included in the New York State Register, XXXVIII, Issue 34 dated August 24, 2016.

Section 358.2. Applicability

This Part shall be applicable to every county, monitor, and operator, and shall govern qualified manufacturers and installation/service providers as to use, installation, and reporting with respect to ignition interlock devices imposed upon the aforementioned criminal court population within New York State and be effective immediately except sections 358.6 through 358.10 of this Part which shall be effective August 15, 2010.

Historical Note

Emergency rulemaking eff. Apr. 23, 2010, expired July 21, 2010; emergency rulemaking eff. July 21, 2010, expired; emergency rulemaking eff. Sept. 7, 2010, expired Nov. 5, 2010; amds. filed Oct. 19, 2010 eff. Nov. 3, 2010. Current with amendments included in the New York State Register, XXXVIII, Issue 34 dated August 24, 2016.

Section 358.3. Definitions

When used in this Part:

(a) The term **blood alcohol concentration** or **BAC** shall mean the weight amount of alcohol contained in a unit volume of blood, measured as grams ethanol/ 100 ml. blood and expressed as %, grams %, % weight/volume (w/v), and % BAC. Blood alcohol concentration in this Part shall be designated as % BAC.

(b) The term **certificate of completion** shall mean a document issued by the monitor after the conclusion of the ignition interlock period, including any extensions or modifications as may have occurred since the date of sentence which shows either completion of the operator's sentence or a change in the conditions of probation or conditional discharge no longer requiring the need for a device.

(c) The term **circumvent** shall mean to request, solicit or allow any other person to blow into an ignition interlock device, or to start a motor vehicle equipped with the device, for the purpose of providing the operator whose driving privileges is so restricted with an operable motor vehicle, or to blow into an ignition interlock device or start a motor vehicle equipped with the device for the purpose of providing an operable motor vehicle to a person whose driving privilege is so restricted or to tamper with an operable ignition interlock device.

(d) The term **county** shall mean every county outside of the city of New York, and the City of New York as a whole.

(e) The term **county executive** shall mean a county administrator, county manager, county director or county president and in cities with a population of one million or more, the mayor.

(f) The term **division** shall mean the division of criminal justice services.

(g) The term **drinking driver program** shall mean an alcohol and drug rehabilitation program established pursuant to section 1196 of the Vehicle and Traffic Law.

(h) The term **failed tasks** shall mean failure to install the ignition interlock device or failure to comply with a service visit or any requirement resulting therefrom as prescribed by this Part.

(i) The term **failed tests** shall mean a failed start-up re-test, failed rolling re-test, or missed rolling re-test.

(j) The term **failure report recipients** shall mean all persons or entities required to receive a report from the monitor of an operator's failed tasks or failed tests pursuant to a county's plan which may include, but is not limited to the sentencing court, district attorney, operator's alcohol treatment provider, and the drinking driver program, where applicable.

(k) The term **ignition interlock device** shall mean any blood alcohol concentration equivalence measuring device which connects to a motor vehicle ignition system and prevents a motor vehicle from being started without first determining through a deep lung breath sample that the operator's equivalent blood alcohol level does not exceed the calibrated setting on the device as required by standards of the Department of Health.

(l) The term **installation/service provider** shall mean an entity approved by a qualified manufacturer that installs, services, and/or removes an ignition interlock device.

(m) The term **lockout mode** shall mean circumstances enumerated in this Part which trigger the ignition interlock device to cause the operator's vehicle to become inoperable if not serviced within five calendar days.

(n) The term **monitor** shall mean the local probation department where the operator is under probation supervision or any person(s) or entity (ies) designated in the county's ignition interlock program plan for any operator granted conditional discharge.

(o) The term **operator** shall mean a person who is subject to installation of an ignition interlock device for a felony or misdemeanor under the Vehicle and Traffic Law or the Penal Law.

(p) The term **qualified manufacturer** shall mean a manufacturer or distributor of an ignition interlock device certified by the New York State Department of Health which has satisfied the specific operational requirements herein and has been approved as an eligible vendor by the division in the designated region where the county is located.

(q) The term **region** shall mean counties comprising an area within New York State designated by the division where a qualified manufacturer is authorized and has agreed to service.

(r) The term **start-up test** shall mean a breath test taken by the operator to measure the operator's blood alcohol concentration prior to starting the vehicle's ignition.

(s) The term **start-up re-test** shall mean a breath test taken by the operator to measure the operator's blood alcohol concentration required within five (5) to fifteen (15) minutes of a failed start-up test.

(t) The term **rolling test** shall mean a breath test, administered at random intervals, taken by the operator while the vehicle is running.

(u) The term **rolling re-test** shall mean a breath test, taken by the operator while the vehicle is running, within one to three minutes after a failed or missed rolling test.

(1) The term **failed rolling re-test** shall mean a rolling re-test in which the operator's BAC is at or above the set point.

(2) The term **missed rolling re-test** shall mean failure to take the rolling re-test within the time period allotted to do so.

(v) The term **service period** shall mean the length of time between service visits.

(w) The term **service visit** shall mean a visit by the operator or another driver of the subject vehicle to or with the
installation/service provider for purposes of having the ignition
interlock device inspected, monitored, downloaded, recalibrated,
or maintained. It shall also mean where applicable, the act by
any operator of sending the portion of the interlock device that
contains the data log and the breath testing module to the
qualified manufacturer for the purposes of downloading the
data, reporting to the monitor, and recalibrating the device.

(x) The term **set point** shall mean a pre-set or predetermined BAC setting at which, or above, the device will
prevent the ignition of a motor vehicle from operating.

(y) The term **STOP-DWI** shall mean special traffic options
program-driving while intoxicated.

(z) The term **tamper** shall mean to alter, disconnect, physically disable, remove, deface, or destroy an ignition interlock
device or any of its component seals in any way not authorized
by this Part.

Historical Note

Emergency rulemaking eff. Apr. 23, 2010, expired July 21, 2010; emergency
rulemaking eff. July 21, 2010, expired; emergency rulemaking eff. Sept. 7,
2010, expired Nov. 5, 2010; amds. filed Oct. 19, 2010 eff. Nov. 3, 2010. Current with amendments included in the New York State Register, XXXVIII,
Issue 34 dated August 24, 2016.

Section 358.4. County ignition interlock program plan

(a) Every county shall establish a county ignition interlock
program plan with respect to usage of ignition interlock devices
and monitoring the compliance of an operator subject to installation of an ignition interlock device as directed by a sentencing court. Such plan shall be approved by the county executive
and become effective on or before August 15, 2010, and shall be
filed with the division no later than June 15, 2010. Where a
plan has been amended by the county, it shall be promptly filed
with the division in advance of its effective date.

(b) Every county shall develop a plan in consultation with
the county's probation director, district attorney, and in New
York City the district attorney from each of the five boroughs,
sheriff or Police Commissioner where applicable, STOP-DWI
Coordinator, a representative of its drinking driver program
where applicable and where more than one program exists in
the county, a representative designated by the county executive, a superior and local criminal court judge designated by
the administrative judge for the county, and in New York City
a superior and local criminal court judge designated by the
deputy chief administrative judge, a representative of an
agency providing legal services to those unable to afford counsel

in criminal cases designated by the county executive. Nothing herein shall prohibit a county from consulting with other persons or entities as the county executive deems appropriate with respect to development of its plan.

(c) Every plan shall specify monitoring by the probation department where the operator is subject to a period of probation supervision and may designate one or more alternative persons or entities, in lieu of the probation department, responsible for monitoring where an ignition interlock device has been imposed pursuant to a conditional discharge. An alternative person or entity may include but is not limited to the sheriff, police commissioner, district attorney, STOP-DWI coordinator, traffic safety board representative, drinking driver program, treatment alternative for safer communities program, or any other similar individual, agency, or organization. Nothing shall preclude a county from sharing monitoring resources, including equipment, with another county to effectuate the provisions of this Part.

(d) Every plan at a minimum shall:

(1) designate the persons or entities, or combination thereof, responsible for monitoring an operator's compliance with an ignition interlock requirement in cases where an operator does not receive a period of probation supervision; establish that where an operator is under probation supervision, the probation department selects the specific class and features of the ignition interlock device available from a qualified manufacturer in its region. The operator may select the model of the ignition interlock device, meeting the specific class and features selected by the probation department from a qualified manufacturer in the operator's region of residence;

(2) establish that where an operator has received a sentence of conditional discharge, the monitor shall select the class of ignition interlock device available from a qualified manufacturer in its region for any such operator. The operator may select the model of the ignition interlock device from within the class designated by the monitor from a qualified manufacturer in the operator's region of residence;

(3) in the event more than one qualified manufacturer does business within its region, the county shall establish an equitable procedure for manufacturers to provide ignition interlock devices without costs where an operator has been determined financially unable to afford the costs and has received a waiver from the sentencing court. The equitable procedure should be based upon proportion of ignition interlock devices paid to each qualified manufacturer by operators in the county;

(4) through any available funding earmarked for such purpose, establish a distribution formula for probation supervision and/or monitoring purposes associated with this Part;

(5) establish a procedure whereby the probation department and any other monitor will be notified no later than five business days from the date an ignition interlock condition is imposed by the sentencing court, any waiver of the cost of the device granted by the sentencing court, and of any intrastate transfer of probation or interstate transfer of any case which either has responsibility to monitor. Such procedure shall also establish a mechanism for advance notification as to date of release where local or State imprisonment is imposed; and

(6) establish a procedure governing failure report recipients, including method and timeframe with respect to specific notification and circumstances. At a minimum the procedure shall be consistent with the provisions of section 358.7(d) of this Part with respect to sentencing court and district attorney notification of specific failed tasks and failed tests reports.

Historical Note

Emergency rulemaking eff. Apr. 23, 2010, expired July 21, 2010; emergency rulemaking eff. July 21, 2010, expired; emergency rulemaking eff. Sept. 7, 2010, expired Nov. 5, 2010; amds. filed Oct. 19, 2010 eff. Nov. 3, 2010. Current with amendments included in the New York State Register, XXXVIII, Issue 34 dated August 24, 2016.

Section 358.5. Approval process and responsibilities of qualified manufacturers

(a) (1) On or after August 15, 2010, only a qualified manufacturer may conduct business in New York State with respect to any operator. An interested manufacturer of a certified ignition interlock device seeking to conduct business within New York State shall apply to the division to become a qualified manufacturer in one or more designated regions of New York State.

(2) The four regions of the State by counties for purposes of this Part are as follows:

(i) Region 1: Allegany, Cattaraugus, Cayuga, Chautauqua, Chemung, Erie, Genesee, Livingston, Monroe, Niagara, Ontario, Orleans, Schuyler, Seneca, Steuben, Wayne, Wyoming, and Yates;

(ii) Region 2: Broome, Chenango, Clinton, Cortland, Essex, Franklin, Fulton, Hamilton, Herkimer, Jefferson, Lewis, Madison, Oneida, Onondaga, Oswego, St. Lawrence, Tioga, and Tompkins;

(iii) Region 3: Albany, Columbia, Delaware, Dutchess,

Greene, Montgomery, Orange, Otsego, Putnam, Rensselaer, Rockland, Saratoga, Schenectady, Schoharie, Sullivan, Ulster, Warren, and Washington; and

(iv) Region 4: Bronx, Kings, Nassau, New York, Queens, Richmond, Suffolk, and Westchester.

(b) (1) The format and content of any application shall be established by the division. The application deadline for any manufacturer seeking approval of the division as a qualified manufacturer to conduct business by August 15, 2010 shall be on or before May 12, 2010. Thereafter, applications may be filed at any time for division approval by manufacturers seeking to conduct business after August 15, 2010. The application shall require at a minimum that the manufacturer submit relevant information, reports, and other documents requested by the division with respect to competitive pricing, service performance, select one or more regions in which it shall agree to conduct business, and certify that it will comply with all applicable provisions specified in this Part with respect to service delivery. In addition, the manufacturer or its representative shall provide a signed statement that the manufacturer or its representative will indemnify and hold harmless the State of New York, the division, the Department of Health, every county where it does business, and their officers, employees and agents from all claims, demands and actions as a result of property damage and/or injury or death to persons which arise, directly or indirectly, out of any act or omission by the manufacturer, its representative, or installation/service providers relating to the installation, service, inspection, maintenance, repair, use and/or removal of the ignition interlock device.

(2) Every manufacturer who applies shall provide a thorough description of each device intended for use in New York State, provide proof of such certification by the Department of Health for each device intended for use in New York State, and the fee structure associated with that specific device. Descriptive information about the device shall include but not be limited to: make and model of device, special features of the device such as camera, reporting capabilities, removable head, global positioning satellite, and real-time or next day reporting. Fee structure information shall include any and all fees charged to the operator, including but not limited to installation fee, monthly fee, any special service fees, shipping fee, and de-installation fee. The proposed fee structure shall take into consideration and be based upon an anticipated 10 percent waiver of the fees by sentencing courts due to operator unaffordability. On or about February 15, 2011 and annually thereafter, the division shall review requests by qualified manufacturers for rate adjustments which shall include information submitted by qualified manufacturers

involving unaffordability waivers granted by courts. At its discretion, the division shall approve rate adjustments where appropriate.

(3) The division shall classify all certified ignition interlock devices into categories based upon features and provide such list to every county. This classification system and subsequent device classification is subject to change by the division as new information becomes available. Upon review of a manufacturer's application, the division shall make a determination whether the manufacturer satisfies all requirements to be designated a qualified manufacturer and provide notification to the applicant and every county within the region that the qualified manufacturer may conduct business. Every qualified manufacturer shall enter into a contractual agreement for a minimum period of three years with the division setting forth the requirements of the qualified manufacturer and all of its installation/service providers consistent with this Part and the application submission approved by the division.

(c) Every qualified manufacturer shall:

(1) adhere to all regulatory provisions of the Department of Health with respect to certification, testing, labeling, reporting and any additional requirements, and shall also specifically adhere to its responsibilities contained in this Part;

(2) agree that an ignition interlock device shall conform to National Highway Traffic Safety Administration standards and Department of Health specifications, be calibrated at a set point of .025 BAC percent, and also require the operator after passing the start-up test allowing the engine to start, to submit to an initial rolling test within a randomly variable interval ranging from 5 to 15 minutes. Subsequent rolling tests shall continue to be required at random intervals not to exceed thirty (30) minutes for the duration of the travel. A start-up re-test shall be required within 5 to 15 minutes of a failed start-up test. A rolling re-test shall be required within one to three minutes after a failed or missed rolling test. An ignition interlock device shall enter into a lockout mode upon the following events: one failed start-up retest, one missed start-up re-test, one failed rolling re-test or one missed rolling re-test within a service period, or one missed service visit;

(3) agree to adhere to a maximum fee/charge schedule with respect to all operator's costs associated with such devices, offer a payment plan for any operator determined to be financially unable to pay the cost of the ignition interlock de-

vice where a payment plan is so ordered, and provide a device free of fee/charge to the operator where the cost is waived by the sentencing court, or pursuant to such other agreement as may be entered into for provision of the device. Any contractual agreement between the operator and the qualified manufacturer or its installation/service providers shall permit an early termination without penalty to the operator when a certificate of completion has been issued, where the sentence has been revoked, and whenever the operator has been transferred to a jurisdiction where the manufacturer does not do business. Nothing shall prevent a qualified manufacturer from lowering the fee/charge schedule during the course of an operator's contract and/or the contractual agreement with the division;

(4) agree to service every county within a region and ensure that there shall be an installation/service provider within 50 miles from the operator's residence or location where the vehicle is parked or garaged, whichever is closest and ensure repair or replacement of a defective ignition interlock device shall be made available within the same 50 mile radius by a fixed or mobile installation/service provider, or through a qualified manufacturer sending a replacement, within 48 hours of receipt of a complaint, or within 72 hours where an intervening weekend or holiday. Mobile servicing may be permissible provided that the above facility requirements are met and a specific mobile servicing unit with regular hours is indicated;

(5) guarantee that an installation/service provider or the manufacturer shall download the usage history of every operator's ignition interlock device within 30 calendar days between service visits or if the operator fails to appear for a service visit(s) as soon thereafter as the device can be downloaded, and provide the monitor with such information and in such format as determined by the division. Further guarantee that the installation/service provider shall take appropriate, reasonable and necessary steps to confirm any report of failed tasks, failed tests, circumvention, or tampering and thereafter notify the appropriate monitor within three business days of knowledge or receipt of data, indicating:

(i)   installation of a device on an operator's vehicle(s);

(ii) report of a failed start-up re-test;

(iii) report of a missed start-up re-test;

(iv) report of a failed rolling re-test;

(v)   report of a missed rolling re-test;

(vi) report of the device entering lockout mode;

(vii) failure of an operator to appear at a scheduled service visit; or

(viii) report of an alleged circumvention or tampering with the ignition interlock devices as prohibited by paragraph (a), (c) or (d) of subdivision (9) of section 1198 of the Vehicle and Traffic Law, or an attempt thereof;

(6) provide, no more than monthly to the operator upon his or her request, the operator's usage history, including any report of failed tasks, failed tests, circumvention, or tampering. An operator may only make one request during any month for such information. Such request shall be in writing and provide either an email address or self-addressed stamped envelope;

(7) agree to safeguard personal information with respect to any operator and any reports and provide access to such records only as authorized herein, by law, or by court order. All records maintained by the manufacturer and any of its installation/service providers with respect to ignition interlock devices in New York State shall be retained in accordance with section 358.9 of this Part;

(8) ensure that the installation/service provider complies with division and county reporting requirements in providing information and reports as may be necessary with respect to an operator's use of the ignition interlock device;

(9) establish and distribute to the division, its installation/service providers, and any county where it does business prior to August 15, 2010, or if subsequently approved as a qualified manufacturer prior to doing business in the State, a current list of all installation/service providers in the county, including business name, address and telephone number and maintain a toll-free 24 hour telephone number to be called from anywhere in the continental United States for an up-to-date listing of installation/service providers in the continental United States and for emergency assistance. Distribute an up-to-date listing of New York State installation/service providers to the division;

(10) provide written certification to the division in a format prescribed by the division that all installation/service providers:

(i) have been trained in advance as to installation, maintenance, troubleshooting, set point requirement of .025 BAC percent, and recalibration of such manufacturer's devices;

(ii) have instructions as to installation and usage of such manufacturer's devices;

(iii) have agreed to comply with their manufacturer's service agreements;

(iv) have agreed to comply with the provisions of this subdivision and subdivision (d) of this section;

(v) have agreed to provide hands-on training to the operator, any member of the same family or household, or any owner of a motor vehicle in which an ignition interlock device is being installed, with a valid driver's license who appears with the operator at installation to receive training as to the operation of an installed device on the vehicle, and to provide written or video instructional material to the operator;

(vi) have been informed of New York State law governing circumvention of ignition interlock devices and penalties associated therewith;

(vii) have agreed to safeguard personal information with respect to any operator and any reports and provide access to such records only as authorized herein, by law, or court order; and

(viii) have been made aware that non-compliance will result in immediate removal and updating the listing of installation/service providers identified in paragraph (9) of this subdivision. An installation/service provider may be reinstated by the division, at its discretion, upon satisfactory proof from the qualified manufacturer of corrective action;

(11) conduct annual quality assurance audits or reviews of installation/service providers to ensure compliance with applicable laws, regulations and any contractual agreements and provide the division with yearly sworn statements that such audits have been conducted. Failure to conduct quality assurance audits may result in removal of the qualified manufacturer from doing business in the State of New York. Nothing shall preclude the division and/or its representative from conducting random audits and quality assurance audits or reviews;

(12) take all reasonable steps necessary to prevent tampering or circumvention of the ignition interlock device and promptly notify the division, the applicable county's monitor and district attorney of any reasonable belief that an employee of an installation/service provider has attempted to alter or has altered ignition interlock data or has been otherwise involved in tampering or circumventing an ignition interlock device of any operator or any attempt thereof. Failure to notify the monitor and the district attorney may result in removal of the qualified manufacturer from doing business in the State of New York;

(13) provide immediate notice to the division and the applicable county monitor(s) of any removal of any installation/ service provider and the reasons for such;

(14) provide immediate notice to the division and the Department of Health whenever the manufacturer's device has been disapproved, suspended, revoked, or otherwise cancelled by another state or jurisdiction;

(15) submit reports, as requested and in such format as determined by the division, for each model or type of certified device, including, but not limited to:

(i) operator and other vehicular user operation error;

(ii) faulty automotive equipment that directly impacts successful implementation and use of the device;

(iii) apparent misuse or attempts to circumvent or tamper/bypass a device;

(iv) device malfunctions, including action taken by the manufacturer to correct such malfunctions;

(v) deficiencies in device calibration stability; and

(vi) operator, vehicular user, and installation/service provider complaints;

(16) provide documentation and verification of insurance (to be submitted upon each policy issuance or renewal) covering product liability, including coverage in New York State, with a minimum policy limit of $1 million per occurrence, and $3 million aggregate total. The manufacturer shall provide a signed statement holding harmless the State of New York, the division, every county, and their employees and agents from all claims, demands, and actions, as a result of damage or injury to persons or property that may arise, directly or indirectly, out of any act or omission by the manufacturer or their installation/service provider relating to the installation, service, repair, use and/or removal of an ignition interlock device;

(17) submit any other information determined by the division to be relevant to the effectiveness, reliability and value of ignition interlock devices as a sentencing sanction; and

(18) agree that the consequences of a failure to adhere to any manufacturer requirements specified in this Part may result in removal of the qualified manufacturer from doing business in the State of New York.

(d) Every qualified manufacturer shall ensure that its installation/service providers comply with the following additional requirements:

(1) the ignition interlock device shall be installed in any

vehicle(s) owned or operated by the operator within seven business days of the operator's request for installation of the device;

(2) provide to all operators, at the time of device installation a hardcopy statement of fees/charges clearly specifying warranty details, schedule of lease payments where applicable, any additional costs anticipated for routine recalibration, service visits, and shipping where the device includes the direct exchange method of servicing, and listing any items available without charge if any, along with a list of installation/service providers in their respective county, a toll-free 24 hour telephone number to be called from anywhere in the continental United States to secure up-to-date information as to all installation/service providers located anywhere in the continental United States and for emergency assistance, and a technical support number available during specified business hours to reach a trained staff person to answer questions and to respond to mechanical concerns associated with the ignition interlock device;

(3) record the odometer reading of the motor vehicle in which the ignition interlock device is installed and during all service visits;

(4) remove an ignition interlock device and return the vehicle to normal operating condition only after having received a certificate of completion or a letter of de-installation from the monitor as authorized pursuant to section 358.7 of this Part. Where at the time of removal the installation/service provider notices any failed tests that have not been backed up by a successful re-test, the monitor shall be notified for approval before the removal is made. Where the device includes direct exchange method of servicing, the qualified manufacturer shall report to the monitor before removal is made. If a device is removed for repair and cannot be reinstalled immediately, a substitute device shall be provided;

(5) installation shall be performed in a professional manner by persons trained and authorized by the manufacturer pursuant to section paragraph (c)(10) of this section;

(6) installation shall be performed according to the manufacturer's detailed written instructions, with calibration to the required set point of.025 BAC percent and in a manner so as to ensure proper vehicular operation;

(7) at the time of installation permanently affix the warning label notice prescribed by the Department of Health in a highly visible location on the installed ignition interlock device;

(8) be equipped with the necessary tools and equipment to

ensure proper ignition interlock device installation and removal;

(9) perform installations and maintenance, including recalibrations, within a secure area of the installation/service provider's or qualified manufacturer's business establishment or at a location serviced by a mobile unit to prevent unauthorized persons from observing or accessing secured items such as tamper seals and installation, data download, transmission, or recalibration instructions;

(10) maintain records of installation and maintenance work performed on the devices;

(11) screen vehicles for mechanical and electrical conditions that would interfere with the functioning of the device, such as low battery or alternator voltage, defective horn, untuned engine, and frequent stalling;

(12) prior to installation, require that the operator complete mechanical repairs or adjustments where necessary for the proper functioning of the device. In such event, the seven day installation period in paragraph (1) of this subdivision shall commence when repairs or adjustments are completed;

(13) prior to installation of the ignition interlock device, obtain and record the following information from every operator:

(i) photo identification;

(ii) the name and policy number of his/her automobile insurance;

(iii) the vehicle identification number (VIN) of all motor vehicles owned or routinely driven by the operator, and a statement disclosing the names of all other individuals who operate the motor vehicle(s) owned or driven by the operator; and

(iv) a notarized affidavit from the registered owner of the vehicle granting permission to install the device if the vehicle is not registered to the operator;

(14) if, during the installation, the operator fails to pass the initial breath test, the installation will be halted and the monitor notified;

(15) after installation during any service visit, recalibrate as necessary or required in this Part and check the device and vehicle to ensure proper operation;

(16) notify the monitor and county probation department when an ignition interlock device has been installed on an operator's vehicle(s) within three business days of installation;

(17) complete the following with respect to service visits:

(i) document photo identification from the operator during all required in-person services;

(ii) provide service/monitoring of the ignition interlock device as required herein;

(iii) recalibrate as necessary the ignition interlock device at each service visit;

(iv) check for signs of circumvention or tampering; and

(18) adhere to any other applicable State or Federal requirement.

Historical Note

Emergency rulemaking eff. Apr. 23, 2010, expired July 21, 2010; emergency rulemaking eff. July 21, 2010, expired; emergency rulemaking eff. Sept. 7, 2010, expired Nov. 5, 2010; amds. filed Oct. 19, 2010 eff. Nov. 3, 2010. Current with amendments included in the New York State Register, XXXVIII, Issue 34 dated August 24, 2016.

Section 358.6. Cancellation, suspension, and revocation of qualified manufacturers, installation/service providers, and certified ignition interlock devices

(a) Any of the following reasons may result in revocation of a certified ignition interlock device or removal of a qualified manufacturer or installation/service provider:

(1) when there is a voluntary request by a manufacturer to cancel certification of a device;

(2) when notified by the Department of Health that a device no longer meets their regulatory standards;

(3) when a device is discontinued by the manufacturer;

(4) when the manufacturer's liability insurance is terminated or cancelled;

(5) when the manufacturer or installation/service provider conceals or attempts to conceal its true ownership;

(6) when materially false or inaccurate information is provided relating to a device's performance standards;

(7) when there are defects in design, materials, or workmanship causing repeated failures of a device;

(8) when the manufacturer or installation/service provider knowingly permits nonqualified service technicians to perform work;

(9) when a manufacturer or installation/service provider assists users with circumventing or tampering with a device;

(10) when service or the submission of required reports is not provided in a timely manner as required by this Part;

(11) when the manufacturer or installation/service provider refuses to provide an ignition interlock device free of charge to an operator who has received a judicial waiver;

(12) when there is a pattern of substandard customer service;

(13) when a manufacturer or installation/service provider interferes with or obstructs a review or investigation by the division or any designee;

(14) when there are any other violations of the provisions contained in this Part, including division and Department of Health regulations, or any ignition interlock contractual agreement;

(15) upon notification of disapproval, suspension, revocation, or cancellation of a manufacturer's device by another state or jurisdiction;

(16) when a manufacturer or installation/service provider provides gratuities or any other personal incentives to a State or local official or any monitor for purposes of soliciting business; and

(17) when a manufacturer or installation/service provider conducts business in New York State outside of the designated region or regions of operation approved by the division.

Historical Note

Emergency rulemaking eff. Apr. 23, 2010, expired July 21, 2010; emergency rulemaking eff. July 21, 2010, expired; emergency rulemaking eff. Sept. 7, 2010, expired Nov. 5, 2010; amds. filed Oct. 19, 2010 eff. Nov. 3, 2010. Current with amendments included in the New York State Register, XXXVIII, Issue 34 dated August 24, 2016.

Section 358.7. Monitoring

(a) (1) Any monitor shall receive notification pursuant to its county plan of all operators which it has responsibility to monitor within five (5) business days of the sentencing court's order imposing the condition of an ignition interlock device and of an operator's release from imprisonment, in accordance with section 358.4(d)(3) of this Part. Such monitor shall obtain proof of installation by the operator and installation/service provider. The installation/service provider shall provide notification of installation of an ignition interlock device to the appropriate monitor and probation department in accordance with section 358.5 (d)(16) of this Part and the operator in accordance with subdivision (c) of this section.

(2) Where a monitor learns that the operator no longer owns or operates a motor vehicle in which an ignition interlock device has been installed, the monitor may issue a letter of de-installation directly to the installation/service provider which authorizes removal of the device.

(b) (1) Where the operator is under probation supervision and resides in another county at the time of sentencing or subsequently desires to reside in another county, upon intrastate transfer of probation, the receiving county probation department selects the specific class and features of the ignition interlock device available from a qualified manufacturer in its region. Thereafter, the operator may select the model of the ignition interlock device meeting the specific class and features selected by the receiving county probation department from a qualified manufacturer in the operator's region of residence. Where intrastate transfer occurs after sentencing and the installation of a different device is required as a result of the transfer, the device shall be installed within 10 business days of relocation. All intrastate transfer of probation shall be in accordance with Part 349 of this Title.

(2) Where an operator has received a sentence of conditional discharge and resides in another county at the time of sentencing or thereafter, the receiving county monitor shall select the class of ignition interlock device available from a qualified manufacturer in its region for any such operator. The operator may select the model of the ignition interlock device from within the class designated by the monitor from a qualified manufacturer in the operator's region of residence. The receiving county monitor shall perform monitor services and the sentencing court retains jurisdiction of the operator. Upon knowledge, the monitor of the sentencing county shall provide necessary operator information in advance to the receiving county monitor. The receiving county monitor shall notify the sentencing court and county district attorney pursuant to subdivision (d) of this section.

(3) Where an operator, subject to probation supervision or a sentence of conditional discharge, resides or desires to reside out-of-state and is an offender subject to the interstate compact for adult offender supervision pursuant to section 259-mm of the Executive Law, the governing rules of such compact shall control. Additionally, Part 349 of this Title shall apply with respect to transfer of supervision of probationers. Where transfer is permitted, the receiving state retains its authority to accept or deny the transfer in accordance with compact rules. Where an operator is subject to probation supervision and is granted reporting instructions and/or acceptance by a receiving state, the sending probation department selects the specific class and features of the ignition interlock device available from a qualified manufacturer in the receiving state. Thereafter, the operator may select the model of the ignition interlock device meeting the specific class and features selected by the sending county probation department from a qualified manufacturer in the receiving

state region. The device shall be installed prior to relocation or return where feasible. A qualified manufacturer shall make necessary arrangements to ensure the county monitor in New York State and the receiving state receive timely reports from the manufacturer and/or installation/service provider.

(4) Where an operator resides or desires to reside out-of-state, is not subject to the interstate compact for adult offender supervision and such compact's governing rules, and has been given permission to return or relocate by the sentencing court or monitor, the same provisions with respect to selection specified in paragraph (3) of this subdivision applies and the device shall be installed prior to relocation or return. A qualified manufacturer shall make necessary arrangements to ensure the county monitor receives timely reports from the manufacturer and/or installation/service provider. Pursuant to the compact, an operator convicted of his or her first DWI misdemeanor is not subject to the compact.

(c) Every operator shall:

(1) have installed and maintain a functioning ignition interlock device in any vehicle(s) he or she owns or operates within 10 business days of the condition being imposed by the court or if sentenced to imprisonment upon release from imprisonment, whichever is applicable and to have the device installed in accordance with this Part and, within three business days of installation, submit proof of installation to the court, county probation department, and any other designated monitor. Nothing in this Part shall preclude an operator from having installed a certified ignition interlock device in excess of the class and/or features authorized herein;

(2) submit to service visits within 30 calendar days of prior installation or service visits for the collection of data from the ignition interlock device and/or for inspection, maintenance, and recalibration purposes where the device does not automatically transmit data directly to the monitor; and submit to an initial service visit within 30 calendar days of installation and service visits within 60 calendar days of prior service visits where the device either automatically transmits data directly to the monitor for inspection, maintenance, or recalibration purposes or the device head is sent to the qualified manufacturer every 30 calendar days for such purposes, including data download. However, an operator shall only remove the device head upon receipt of a new device head;

(3) provide the installation/service provider and the monitor prior to installation of the ignition interlock device, the following information:

(i) his/her photo identification/license for examination purposes;

(ii) the name and policy number of his/her motor vehicle insurance;

(iii) the vehicle identification number (VIN) of all motor vehicles owned or routinely driven by the operator, and a statement disclosing the names of all other individuals who operate the motor vehicle(s) owned or driven by the operator; and

(iv) a notarized affidavit from the registered owner of the vehicle granting permission to install the device if the vehicle is not registered to the operator;

(4) present photo identification/license for examination purposes during any in-person service visit; and

(5) provide the monitor with documentation requested by the monitor as to vehicle(s) owned or driven by the operator. Prior to an operator legally driving an employer's vehicle within the scope of his or her employment, the operator must provide satisfactory proof to the monitor that the employer has been notified of the operator's driving privilege is restricted and necessitates installation and maintenance of a functioning ignition interlock device and such employer grants permission for the operator to drive the employer's vehicle without the device only for business purposes. Such exemption for business purposes shall not apply to any vehicle owned by a business entity all or partly owned or controlled by the operator. Any operator shall provide satisfactory proof to the monitor that any other person who rents, leases, or loans a motor vehicle to him or her has been notified that the operator's driving privilege is restricted and necessitates installation of the ignition interlock device on any vehicle he or she owns or operates and that the person grants permission for the operator to install the device on such vehicle(s) and operate the vehicle(s). Further, prior to return of any vehicle which is leased, rented, or loaned, the operator shall comply with service visit requirements of this Part.

(d) (1) Upon learning of the following events:

(i) that the operator has failed to have installed the ignition interlock device on his/her own vehicle(s) or vehicle(s) which he/she operates;

(ii) that the operator has not complied with service visits requirements;

(iii)   a report of alleged tampering with or circumventing an ignition interlock device or an attempt thereof;

(iv)   a report of a failed start-up re-test;

(v)   a report of a missed start-up re-test;

(vi)   a report of a failed rolling re-test;

(vii)   a report of a missed rolling re-test; and/or

(viii)   a report of a lockout mode;

the applicable monitor shall take appropriate action consistent with public safety. Where under probation supervision, the county probation department shall adhere to Part 352 of this Title. With respect to any operator sentenced to conditional discharge, the monitor shall take action in accordance with the provisions of its county ignition interlock program plan. At a minimum, any monitor shall notify the appropriate court and District Attorney, within three business days, where an operator has failed to have installed the ignition interlock device on his/her own vehicle(s) or vehicle(s) which he/she operates, where the operator has not complied with a service visit requirement, any report of alleged tampering with or circumventing an ignition interlock device or an attempt thereof, any report of a lock-out mode, and/or any report of a failed test or re-test where the BAC is .05 percent or higher.

(2) The monitor may recommend modification of the operator's condition of his or her sentence or release whichever is applicable as otherwise authorized by law, including extension of his/her ignition interlock period, a requirement that the operator attend alcohol and substance abuse treatment and/or drinking driver program, referral to the Department of Motor Vehicles to determine whether the department may suspend or revoke the operator's license, or recommend revocation of his/her sentence or release.

(3) Where the operator is under supervision by the Division of Parole, the monitor shall coordinate monitoring with the Division of Parole and promptly provide the parole agency with reports of any failed tasks or failed tests.

(e) Any monitor may disseminate relevant case records, including failed tasks or failed reports not otherwise sealed or specifically restricted in terms of access by State or Federal law to appropriate law enforcement authorities, District Attorney, treatment agencies, licensed or certified treatment providers, the judiciary, for law enforcement and/or case management purposes relating to criminal investigations and/or execution of warrants, supervision and/or monitoring of ignition interlock conditions, and treatment and/or counseling. Personal information in any financial disclosure report shall only be accessible to the monitor, court, and District Attorney for purposes related to determination of financial affordability. Case record information is not to be used for noncriminal justice purposes and shall otherwise only be available pursuant to a court order. In all such instances, those to whom access has been granted shall not secondarily disclose such information without the express written permission of the monitor that authorized access.

Historical Note

Emergency rulemaking eff. Apr. 23, 2010, expired July 21, 2010; emergency rulemaking eff. July 21, 2010, expired; emergency rulemaking eff. Sept. 7, 2010, expired Nov. 5, 2010; amds. filed Oct. 19, 2010 eff. Nov. 3, 2010. Current with amendments included in the New York State Register, XXXVIII, Issue 34 dated August 24, 2016.

Section 358.8. Costs and maintenance

(a) Any operator shall pay the cost of installing and maintaining the ignition interlock device unless the operator has been determined to be financially unable to afford the cost of the ignition interlock device by the sentencing court whereupon such cost may be imposed pursuant to a payment plan or waived.

(b) Any operator who claims financial inability to pay for the device shall submit in advance of sentencing three copies of his or her financial disclosure report, on a form prescribed by the division, to the sentencing court which shall distribute copies to the District Attorney and defense counsel. The report shall enumerate factors which may be considered by the sentencing court with respect to financial inability of the operator to pay for the device and shall include, but not be limited to income from all sources, assets, and expenses. This report shall be made available to assist the court in determining whether or not the operator is financially able to afford the cost of the ignition interlock device, and if not whether to impose a payment plan. Where it is determined that a payment plan is not feasible, the court shall determine whether the fee/charge for the device shall be waived.

Historical Note

Emergency rulemaking eff. Apr. 23, 2010, expired July 21, 2010; emergency rulemaking eff. July 21, 2010, expired; emergency rulemaking eff. Sept. 7, 2010, expired Nov. 5, 2010; amds. filed Oct. 19, 2010 eff. Nov. 3, 2010. Current with amendments included in the New York State Register, XXXVIII, Issue 34 dated August 24, 2016.

Section 358.9. Record retention and disposition

Record retention and disposition of all records of the county, any qualified manufacturer, and installation/service provider with respect to this Part shall be in accordance with the applicable Records Retention and Disposition Schedule promulgated by the State Education Department.

Historical Note

Emergency rulemaking eff. Apr. 23, 2010, expired July 21, 2010; emergency rulemaking eff. July 21, 2010, expired; emergency rulemaking eff. Sept. 7, 2010, expired Nov. 5, 2010; amds. filed Oct. 19, 2010 eff. Nov. 3, 2010. Current with amendments included in the New York State Register, XXXVIII, Issue 34 dated August 24, 2016.

Section 358.10.   Liability

Nothing contained in the Part shall impose liability upon the division, the State of New York, or any county, for any damages related to the installation, monitoring or maintenance of an ignition interlock device or an operator's use or failure to use such devices.

Historical Note

Emergency rulemaking eff. Apr. 23, 2010, expired July 21, 2010; emergency rulemaking eff. July 21, 2010, expired; emergency rulemaking eff. Sept. 7, 2010, expired Nov. 5, 2010; amds. filed Oct. 19, 2010 eff. Nov. 3, 2010. Current with amendments included in the New York State Register, XXXVIII, Issue 34 dated August 24, 2016.

APPENDIX 64

DPCA Financial Disclosure Report

NEW YORK STATE
IGNITION INTERLOCK DEVICE PROGRAM - FINANCIAL DISCLOSURE REPORT
CONFIDENTIAL

FINANCIAL DISCLOSURE INSTRUCTIONS

IN ORDER TO BE PROCESSED AS AN APPLICATION FOR JUDICIAL CONSIDERATION OF FINANCIAL AFFORDABILITY, ALL
INFORMATION REQUESTED ON THIS REPORT MUST BE COMPLETELY, PROPERLY AND ACCURATELY PROVIDED. DATED
SIGNATURE OF THE DEFENDANT IS ALSO REQUIRED.

QUALIFYING INFORMATION SECTION *

DEFENDANT'S NAME LAST, FIRST, MI (MIDDLE INITIAL): ENTER DEFENDANT'S NAME.

ADDRESS: ENTER DEFENDANT'S MAILING ADDRESS

DEFENDANT'S LICENSE NUMBER: ENTER DEFENDANT'S DRIVER LICENSE NUMBER.

DATE OF BIRTH: ENTER DEFENDANT'S BIRTHDATE

LIVING ARRANGEMENTS AND LENGTH OF TIME IN CURRENT ARRANGEMENT: DESCRIBE THE DEFENDANT'S PRESENT LIVING
ARRANGEMENT AND THE LENGTH OF TIME IN THIS LIVING ARRANGEMENT (E.G. HOMELESS, MARRIED LIVING WITH SPOUSE
AND/OR CHILD(REN), SINGLE/DIVORCED/WIDOWED LIVING ALONE, SINGLE/DIVORCED/WIDOWED LIVING WITH CHILD(REN),
SINGLE/DIVORCED/WIDOWED LIVING WITH PARENTS WITH OR WITHOUT CHILD(REN), CO-HABITATING, LIVING WITH
RELATIVE(S) OTHER THAN SPOUSE OR PARENT).

LIST OTHER PEOPLE IN HOUSEHOLD: LIST ANY OTHER PEOPLE WHO LIVE IN THE SAME HOUSEHOLD WITH THE DEFENDANT,
INCLUDING SPOUSE AND ANY DEPENDENTS.

EMPLOYMENT STATUS: CHECK THE APPROPRIATE RESPONSE. IF EMPLOYED, PROVIDE ALL INFORMATION REQUESTED IN
THE "EMPLOYED" SECTION ONLY AND PROCEED TO THE "FINANCIAL REPORTING SECTION". DOCUMENTS THAT CAN BE USED
AS VERIFICATION OF EMPLOYMENT INCLUDE A RECENT PAY STUB OR A COMPANY OR EMPLOYER LETTER. IF UNEMPLOYED,
PROVIDE ALL INFORMATION REQUESTED IN THE "UNEMPLOYED" SECTION AND PROCEED TO THE "FINANCIAL REPORTING
SECTION". DOCUMENTS THAT CAN BE USED AS VERIFICATION OF UNEMPLOYMENT INCLUDE BENEFITS STATEMENT/CHECK
STUB FOR UNEMPLOYMENT BENEFITS, EMPLOYER LETTER, OR DISABILITY VERIFICATION.

FINANCIAL REPORTING SECTION **

DO NOT LEAVE ANY SPACES BLANK. PLACE A ZERO IN THE APPROPRIATE SPACE
IF THE DEFENDANT HAS NO SUCH INCOME OR EXPENSES.

A - MONTHLY INCOME FROM WAGES: ENTER **TOTAL GROSS** FOR **ALL** WAGES. THE FOLLOWING DOCUMENTS CAN BE USED AS
VERIFICATION: PAY CHECK STUB, W-2 FORM OR EMPLOYER STATEMENT.

B - MONTHLY INCOME FROM OTHER SOURCES: ENTER ALL INCOME RECEIVED FROM SOURCES OTHER THAN EMPLOYMENT.
("RENTAL INCOME" REFERS TO INCOME RECEIVED FROM RENTAL PROPERTY THAT IS OWNED BY THE DEFENDANT.) THE
FOLLOWING DOCUMENTS CAN BE USED AS VERIFICATION: PAYMENT STUB, MOST RECENT STATE OR FEDERAL TAX RETURN,
BANK STATEMENT, COURT RECORDS, LETTERS FROM THE BENEFIT OFFICE REGARDING MONTHLY BENEFIT AMOUNT, ETC.

C - MISCELLANEOUS INCOME DURING PAST 12 MONTHS: SPECIFY **ALL** OTHER INCOME, REGARDLESS OF SOURCE.

D - CURRENT BALANCES: SPECIFY **ALL** TYPES AND AMOUNTS.

E - PERSONAL PROPERTY: LIST THE MARKET VALUE OF **ALL** PERSONAL PROPERTY OWNED.

F - MONTHLY EXPENSES: ENTER **ALL** MONTHLY EXPENSES AS APPROPRIATE. THE FOLLOWING DOCUMENTS CAN BE USED AS
VERIFICATION: EXPENSE RECEIPTS, PAYMENT BOOK, MOST RECENT BILL.

SUBMIT 3 COPIES OF THIS COMPLETED REPORT TO THE SENTENCING COURT

DPCA-500IID-FDR Available at http://www.dpca.state.ny.us   *1 OF 5*

NEW YORK STATE
IGNITION INTERLOCK DEVICE PROGRAM - FINANCIAL DISCLOSURE REPORT
CONFIDENTIAL

QUALIFYING INFORMATION SECTION *

DEFENDANT'S LAST NAME _____ FIRST NAME _____ MI ____

DEFENDANT'S LICENSE NUMBER _____ DATE OF BIRTH _____

HOME ADDRESS _____

CITY _____ STATE _____ ZIP _____

MAILING ADDRESS
IF DIFFERENT _____

CITY _____ STATE _____ ZIP _____

PROVIDE INFORMATION FOR EACH VEHICLE OWNED

IF MORE THAN 3 VEHICLES PLEASE ATTACH ADDITIONAL SHEET WITH REQUIRED INFORMATION

	YEAR	MAKE	MODEL	VALUE
VEHICLE ONE				
VEHICLE TWO				
VEHICLE THREE				

DESCRIBE LIVING ARRANGEMENTS _____

LENGTH OF TIME IN CURRENT ARRANGEMENT _____

OTHER PEOPLE LIVING IN HOUSEHOLD:

NAME	AGE	RELATIONSHIP	NAME	AGE	RELATIONSHIP

EMPLOYMENT STATUS (CHECK ONE)

EMPLOYED ☐   UNEMPLOYED ☐

PLACE OF EMPLOYMENT _____   LENGTH OF UNEMPLOYMENT _____

ADDRESS _____   LAST PLACE OF EMPLOYMENT _____

POSITION _____   LAST EMPLOYMENT FROM _____

LENGTH OF TIME _____   TO _____

VERIFICATION DOCUMENT (SPECIFY & ATTACH) _____   VERIFICATION DOCUMENT (SPECIFY & ATTACH) _____

NEW YORK STATE
IGNITION INTERLOCK DEVICE PROGRAM - FINANCIAL DISCLOSURE REPORT
CONFIDENTIAL

FINANCIAL REPORTING SECTION **

A: MONTHLY INCOME FROM WAGES

SELF $ _____

SPOUSE $ _____

OTHER HOUSEHOLD MEMBERS $ _____

$ _____

HOW OFTEN IS DEFENDANT PAID? _____
(WKLY, BI-WKLY, MNTHLY, BI-MNTHLY)

B: MONTHLY INCOME FROM OTHER SOURCES

PENSION INCOME $ _____

RENTAL INCOME $ _____

CERTIFICATES OF DEPOSIT $ _____

TRUSTS/STOCKS/BONDS $ _____

CHILD SUPPORT $ _____

SPOUSAL MAINTENANCE/ALIMONY $ _____

LEGAL SETTLEMENTS/AWARD $ _____

AFDC/FOOD STAMPS/RENTAL ASSISTANCE $ _____

WORKERS COMP $ _____

UNEMPLOYMENT COMP $ _____

COUNTY/CITY WELFARE $ _____

OTHER: $ _____

$ _____

$ _____

C: MISCELLANEOUS INCOME DURING PAST 12 MONTHS

LOTTERY $ _____

SWEEPSTAKE(S) $ _____

DISABILITY INSURANCE $ _____

BONUS $ _____

WAGERING $ _____

LEGAL SETTLEMENT/AWARD $ _____

ANNUITY $ _____

SPECIFY | AMOUNTS

OTHER _____ $ _____

$ _____

$ _____

D: CURRENT ACCOUNT BALANCES

SAVINGS ACCOUNT $ _____

CHECKING ACCOUNT $ _____

INDIVIDUAL RETIREMENT ACCOUNT $ _____

DEFERRED COMPENSATION ACCOUNT $ _____

TRUST ACCOUNT $ _____

OTHER ACCOUNTS (SPECIFY & AMOUNT) $ _____

DPCA-500IID-FDR Available at http://www.dpca.state.ny.us   *3 OF 5*

NEW YORK STATE
IGNITION INTERLOCK DEVICE PROGRAM - FINANCIAL DISCLOSURE REPORT
CONFIDENTIAL

E: PERSONAL PROPERTY

DO YOU OWN:

REAL ESTATE

LOCATION _____   VALUE $ _____

LOCATION _____   VALUE $ _____

LOCATION _____   VALUE $ _____

REC VEHICLE/CAMPER

MAKE _____   VALUE $ _____

ATV 3/4 WHEEL

MAKE _____   VALUE $ _____

MOTORCYCLE

MAKE _____   VALUE $ _____

BOAT

MAKE _____   VALUE $ _____

MAKE _____   VALUE $ _____

PERSONAL PROPERTY   (ELECTRONICS, ART, JEWELRY, FURNITURE, ETC.)

APPROXIMATE VALUE _____

F: MONTHLY EXPENSES

RENT/MORTGAGE $ _____	WATER/SEWER $ _____
HOME ELECTRIC/GAS $ _____	FOOD $ _____
TELEPHONE (LANDLINE) $ _____	TELEPHONE (CELL) $ _____
HEALTH/LIFE INSURANCE $ _____	CHILD CARE $ _____
AUTOMOBILE INSURANCE(S) $ _____ SPECIFY NUMBER _____	AUTOMOBILE FUEL/GAS $ _____
	ALCOHOL $ _____
AUTOMOBILE LOAN(S) $ _____ SPECIFY NUMBER _____	CIGARETTES/OTHER TOBACCO PRODUCTS $ _____
SPOUSAL MAINTENANCE/ALIMONY $ _____	CABLE TELEVISION $ _____
INTERNET SERVICE $ _____	SATELLITE TV/RADIO $ _____
BEEPERS/PAGERS $ _____ SPECIFY NUMBER _____	MEDICAL PRESCRIPTIONS $ _____

NEW YORK STATE
IGNITION INTERLOCK DEVICE PROGRAM - FINANCIAL DISCLOSURE REPORT
CONFIDENTIAL

F: MONTHLY EXPENSES CONTINUED *

SPECIFY BELOW: AMOUNTS

CREDIT CARD CHARGE(S)/OTHER _____ $ _____
           LOAN AMOUNT(S)
                           _____ $ _____

                           _____ $ _____

                           _____ $ _____

                           _____ $ _____

WORK RELATED TRAVEL _____ $ _____

       RECREATION _____ $ _____

                           _____ $ _____

                           _____ $ _____

   OTHER EXPENSES _____ $ _____

                           _____ $ _____

                           _____ $ _____

* ATTACH ADDITIONAL SHEET WITH REQUIRED INFORMATION IF MORE SPACE IS NECESSARY.

THE INFORMATION PRESENTED HEREIN IS TRUTHFUL AND ACCURATE TO THE BEST OF MY KNOWLEDGE.

_____   _____
      DEFENDANT SIGNATURE   DATE

_____
        PRINT NAME

APPENDIX 65

Order of Suspension Pending Prosecution Hardship Privilege and Order of Suspension

New York- State Department of Motor Vehicles

ORDER OF SUSPENSION PENDING PROSECUTION
HARDSHIP PRIVILEGE

Please Print

PART 1 - HARDSHIP PRIVILEGE

Motorist Name	Date of Birth	Yr. Lic. Expires	Lic. Class	Restrictions
	/ /			

YOUR EMPLOYER AND/OR SCHOOL YOU ATTEND

Name	Address (No. and Street, City or Town, State and ZIP Code)
Name	Address (No. and Street, City or Town, State and ZIP Code)
Name	Address (No. and Street, City or Town, State and ZIP Code)

Under the authority of Section 1193 of the Vehicle and Traffic Law, your license is suspended immediately. This order will allow you to drive to or from work, to or from medical treatment (for yourself or a member of your immediate household), or if you are a student enrolled in a school, college or university, you may drive to and from school if such travel is necessary for the completion of your degree or certificate. **You must have both parts of this order with you when you drive.**

REASON FOR GRANTING HARDSHIP PRIVILEGE (this privilege is not valid unless this part is completed by the Court):

This hardship privilege is not valid: if you are convicted; if you do not have a valid driver license; if your license is revoked or suspended after this order is issued; or if your license is expired more than two years.

Date _____   _____
                                              (Judge's Signature)

MV-1193 (10/02)

New York State Department of Motor Vehicles

ORDER OF SUSPENSION PENDING PROSECUTION.

Please Print

PART 2

Motorist Name		Date of Birth		☐ Male ☐ Female
Address (Number & Street)	Apt. No.	TSLE&D Ticket Number (or Docket Number)		Violation Date
City		State	Zip Code	Police NCIC/ORI Number

Under the authority of Section 1193 of the Vehicle and Traffic Law, your license is suspended immediately, pending prosecution for a charge of violating Section: ☐ II92-1   ☐ 1192-2   ☐ 1192-3   ☐ 1192-4 of the New York State Vehicle and Traffic Law.

☐ You have been convicted of violating a subdivision of Section 1192 of the V&T Law within the past five years, or you are charged with a felony under Article 120 or 125 of the New York State Penal Law. **(You are not eligible for a hardship privilege or conditional license under these circumstances.)**

☐ You are alleged to have had .08 of one percent or more by weight of alcohol in your blood, as shown by chemical analysis of blood, breath, urine or saliva according to Section 1194 of the V&T Law. **(If this box is checked, you may be eligible for a conditional license after 30 days. The Department of Motor Vehicles will notify you of your eligibility.)**

☐ You have a DJ/MJ license/permit and are charged with violating subdivisions 1, 2 or 3 of Section 11 92 of the Vehicle and Traffic Law. You may be eligible for a conditional license after 30 days. The Department of Motor Vehicles will notify you of your eligibility

Court	Court Code	Effective Date of Suspension / /
Judge's Name		Justice Code

COMPLIANCE - Has motorist turned in photo license and any permits to the court?
☐ Yes - photo license attached   ☐ No
☐ Yes - permit(s) attached

Motorist Signature ➡   Signature of Judge or Clerk of Court ➡

Note to Court Clerk: Send the "DMV" copy of this MV-1193 to your designated data entry site.

DMV OFFICE USE ONLY			
LICENSE: ☐ Suspended	EFFECTIVE DATE: / /	HARDSHIP PRIVILEGE: ☐ Yes ☐ No	COMPLIANCE: ☐ Yes ☐ No

MV-1193 (10102)   CUSTOMER

APPENDIX 66

Notice of Temporary Suspension Notice of Hearing and Waiver of Hearing

New York State Department of Motor Vehicles

NOTICE OF TEMPORARY SUSPENSION AND NOTICE OF HEARING

(Section 1194 of Vehicle & Traffic Law)

Read Both Sides, Please!

DISTRIBUTION

Complete four (4) copies of this form (please print). Distribute as follows: One (1) copy to Motorist, one (1) copy for court records, one (1) copy to the arresting officer, and mail one (1) copy, with a copy of the Police Chemical Test Refusal Report (AA-134), to the Department of Motor Vehicles, SAFETY HEARING BUREAU, 6 Empire State Plaza, Room 312, Albany, New York 12228-0312.

Motorist's Last Name	First	M.I.	Date of Birth (MM/DD/YYYY) / /	☐ Male ☐ Female

Motorist's Street Address (include Street Number and Name, Rural Delivery Box and (or Apartment Number).	Ticket Number

City	State	Zip Code

Date of Alleged Refusal / /	Location of Refusal	Arresting officer

Police Agency	Telephone Number (Area Code) ( )	Tax Registry Number (NYC Only)	Command #	Precinct No.

Arraignment Date / /	Court Name	Street	City/Town	Zip Code	County

Docket No.	License Turned In? ☐ Yes ☐ No

ATTENTION: MOTORIST

Your driver license (or driving privilege if you don't live in New York State) has been temporarily suspended by the court for your alleged refusal to submit to a chemical test (Section 1194-2 of the Vehicle and Traffic Law). The suspension is effective on the arraignment date shown above. This court suspension will end m 15 days or on the date of hearing, whichever comes first. However, further action concerning your license will be taken by the Department of Motor Vehicles on the date of the hearing.

Bring this notice with you to the hearing. You may have an attorney or other representative with you at the hearing, and you should be prepared to present all evidence and witnesses in your behalf at the hearing.

If you need special accommodations (such as a handicap-accessible hearing site, or if you are hearing-impaired), please contact the Safety Hearing Bureau at (518) 474-1509 as soon as possible before the hearing. If you are hearing-impaired, we will provide an interpreter at no charge. It is your responsibility to being an English translator to the hearing, if you need one.
This chemical test hearing is independent of the criminal court case charging you with DWI. Do not assume that a criminal plea or dismissal in court will affect this hearing.

If you do not come to the hearing, your absence will be considered your agreement to waive the hearing. This will result in immediate revocation of your license or driving privilege.

VOLUNTARY WAIVER OF HEARING

You may waive the hearing by sending a written waiver to the Safety Hearing Bureau of the Department of Motor Vehicles. To request a waiver see the other side of this notice.

ATTENTION: MOTORIST AND ARRESTING OFFICER

You are required to appear in person for a hearing (Section 1194-2 of the Vehicle and Traffic Law) based on the written report of the police officer that the motorist named above refused to submit to a chemical test for the purpose of determining the alcohol or drug content of his/her blood, after being properly warned of the consequences of refusing. The hearing will also determine if the motorist's license should be revoked. The officer should bring this notice and a copy of the refusal report (AA-134) to the hearing.

Date of Hearing (or Waiver) / /	Time of Hearing _____ ☐ A.M.	_____ ☐ P.M.

Hearing Location

Judge or Clerk of the Court: sign above to indicate that motorist was handed this Notice of Temporary Suspension.

AA-137 (10/10)

New York State Department of Motor Vehicles
Safety Hearing Bureau
6 Empire State Plaza, Room 312
Albany New York 12228-0312
Telephone No: (518) 474-1509

WAIVER OF HEARING
CONSENT TO REVOCATION OF DRIVER LICENSE
BASED ON REFUSAL TO SUBMIT TO CHEMICAL TEST
(Section 1194 of Vehicle & Traffic Law)

If you want to voluntarily waive the hearing, complete this form and send it to the above address.

TO: **COMMISSIONER OF MOTOR VEHICLES**

Motorists Last Name	First	M.I.	Date of Birth (MM/DD/YYYY) / /	☐ Male ☐ Female
Motorists Street Address (include Street Number and Name, Rural Delivery Box, and/or Apartment Number)			Ticket Number	
City	State	Zip Code	Daytime Telephone No. (Area Code) ( )	

On ____ / ____ / ____, I was arrested in the ☐City ☐Town ☐Village, of _____
(Date)

in the County of _____, New York by a member of _____
(Police Agency)

on a charge of operating a motor vehicle while under the influence of alcohol or drugs, in violation of Section 1192 of the Vehicle and Traffic Law of the State of New York. It is alleged that I refused to submit to a chemical test as described in section 1194 of the Vehicle and Traffic Law. I was driving a motor vehicle with license plate number _____

By signing this document, I waive my right to an administrative hearing by the Department of Motor Vehicles to decide if my license should be revoked for my refusal to submit to a chemical test as described above. Because of such refusal, I agree to have my license (or driving privilege in New York State) revoked.

I agree that, if presented, the testimony of the arresting officer would establish all required elements to prove a refusal to submit to a chemical test, as described in Section 1194 of the Vehicle and Traffic Law.

I understand that this means my license (or privilege of driving a motor vehicle in New York State) will be revoked. Before I may be issued a new license or have my driving privilege restored, I must pay a $500 civil penalty required by law ($550 if I hold a commercial driver license or was operating a commercial motor vehicle at the time of the offense).

I understand that a chemical test refusal will result in a driver responsibility assessment of $750, payable to DMV in three (3) annual installments of $250. If I do not pay the assessment DMV will suspend my driver license, learner permit, and/or driving privileges.

If this is my second chemical test refusal in five years, or if I have been convicted of a violation of any subdivision of Section 1192 of the Vehicle and Traffic Law within the past five years, I must pay a $750 civil penalty before I may be issued a new license or have my driving privilege restored. Multiple alcohol/drug incidents (3 or more) may result in permanent driver license/driving privilege revocation.

Signature of Driver _____   Date ____ / ____ / ____
(Sign Name in Full)

(Enclose your New York State license, if it was not previously surrendered.)
www.dmv.ny.gov

AA-137 (10/10)

APPENDIX 67

Letters from Department of Motor Vehicles Revising Opinion Regarding Hardship Privilege

 **STATE OF NEW YORK**
DEPARTMENT OF MOTOR VEHICLES

6 EMPIRE STATE PLAZA, ALBANY, NY 12228

DAVID J. SWARTS
Commissioner

NEAL W. SCHOEN
Deputy Commissioner and Counsel

IDA L. TRASCHEN
First Assistant Counsel
Legal Bureau

May 12, 2010

Steven B. Epstein, Esq.
215 Hilton Avenue
Hempstead, New York 11551-1200

Re: Hardship Privilege

Dear Mr. Epstein:

I have received your letter of May 11, 2010, regarding the scope of the hardship privilege, as set forth in Vehicle and Traffic Law §1193(2)(e)(7)(e), which provides in part:

> For the purposes of this clause, "extreme hardship" shall mean the inability to obtain alternative means of travel **to or from** the licensee's employment, or to or from necessary medical treatment for the licensee or a member of the licensee's household, or if the licensee is a matriculating student enrolled in an accredited school, college or university travel to or from such licensee's school, college or university if such travel is necessary for the completion of the educational degree or certificate.

The Department has retreated from the opinion expressed in the "Speranza letter", which you enclosed. First, we defer to the court hearing the case because it is the court that grants the hardship privilege and has all of the facts about a particular defendant before it for consideration. Second, we believe that the opinion in the "Speranza letter" was too broad; i.e., the hardship privilege was not intended for travel to several job sites. Such travel falls within the scope of the conditional license, which may be used during the course of one's employment. Thus, in our opinion, it would not be appropriate for an attorney to use the hardship privilege to travel to and from various courts to represent his clients. He could travel to and from his office where he has his base of operation.

I trust this information assists you.

Very truly yours,

Ida L. Traschen

Ida L. Traschen
First Assistant Counsel

ILT/mjs

STATE OF NEW YORK
DEPARTMENT OF MOTOR VEHICLES

6 EMPIRE STATE PLAZA, ALBANY, NY 12228

BARBARA J. FIALA
Commissioner

NEAL W. SCHOEN
Deputy Commissioner and Counsel

IDA L. TRASCHEN
First Assistant Counsel
Legal Bureau

June 13, 2012

JUN 15 2012

Peter Gerstenzang, Esq.
Gerstenzang, O'Hern, Hickey, Sills & Gerstenzang
210 Great Oaks Boulevard
Albany, New York 12203

Re: Hardship Privilege

Dear Mr. Gerstenzang:

On June 24, 1998, I wrote a letter, which commented on the scope of the hardship privilege in relation to the case People v. Speranza. The letter is published as Appendix 62 in your book Handling the DWI Case in New York. Upon further review, Counsel's Office has modified the position expressed in the 1998 letter and requests that this letter be published in the next edition of your book.

Vehicle and Traffic Law §1193(2)(e)(7) provides that a court may grant a hardship privilege if the suspension pending prosecution results in extreme hardship. Extreme hardship is defined as:

> "[T]he inability to obtain alternative means of travel to or from the licensee's employment, or to or from necessary medical treatment for the licensee or a member of the licensee's household, or if the licensee is a matriculating student enrolled in an accredited school, college or university travel to or from such licensee's school, college or university if such travel is necessary for the completion of the educational degree or certificate."

The scope of the hardship privilege arises most often in the context of traveling to and from the licensee's place of employment. Since the privilege is limited to travel *to and from* one's place of employment, the Department believes that the opinion in the "Speranza letter" was too broad; i.e., the hardship privilege is not intended for travel to and from several job sites. Such travel falls within the scope of the conditional license, which may be used *during the course* of one's employment.

The essential question to be answered is whether travel is intrinsic to the defendant's job. If it is essential, then the hardship privilege is most likely not appropriate. For example, in our opinion, the privilege should not be issued to an attorney who travels to and from various courts to represent clients, nor should the privilege be issued to a doctor who makes house calls. The Department, of course, defers to the court that must decide whether to issue the privilege. This letter only expresses the opinion of the Department.

Very truly yours,

Ida L. Traschen

Ida L. Traschen
First Assistant Counsel

ILT/dmv

APPENDIX 68

Department of Motor Vehicles' Counsel's Opinion Regarding Time Limitations for Chemical Test Refusals

DEPARTMENT OF MOTOR VEHICLES
COUNSEL'S OFFICE

OPINION OF COUNSEL
(#1-12)

Subject: Time Limitations for Chemical Test Refusals

Date: June 29, 2012

Question

Is a motorist deemed to have refused a chemical test when the refusal occurs more than two hours after the arrest?

Discussion

It has been the long-standing position of the Department of Motor Vehicles that a motorist is deemed to have refused to submit to a chemical if the refusal occurs within two hours of the motorist's arrest. As you are aware, that position was based solely on statutory interpretation, since there are no Court of Appeals decisions that directly speak to the issue. Those Court of Appeals opinions that do exist speak only to the admissibility of evidence of a refusal, or blood alcohol content evidence obtained more than two hours after arrest, at a criminal trial.

However, evolving case law on the issue clearly indicates that the courts have taken a more expansive view. In People v. Atkins, 85 N.Y.2d 1007 (1995), the motorist consented to a blood test within two hours of his arrest, but it was not administered until after the two hours had expired. The Court of Appeals admitted the results of the test, holding that the two-hour rule has no application where the defendant expressly consents to the test. Relying on the holding in Atkins, the court in People v. Ward, 176 Misc. 2d 398 (Sup. Ct. Richmond Co. 1998), deciding whether to admit evidence of a refusal obtained more than two hours after arrest, held that

> if evidence of the results of a chemical test expressly consented to by a defendant and administered beyond the two-hour limit is competent, then evidence of a refusal to take such a test, obtained beyond the two-hour limit, must similarly be competent (see, People v. Morales, 161 Misc. 2d 128; contra, People v. Walsh, 139 Misc. 2d 161). A contrary conclusion would not only seem to defy reason, but would permit an operator of a motor vehicle to refuse a properly requested chemical test without consequence. 176 Misc. 2d at 403.

2

The <u>Ward</u> decision has been followed in several other cases, including <u>People v. Elfe</u>, 33 Misc. 3d 1221A (Sup. Ct. Bronx Co. 2011) and <u>People v. Popko</u>, 33 Misc. 3d 277 (Crim. Ct. Kings Co. 2011).

In light of these recent and well-reasoned holdings that the two-hour rule is inapplicable to refusals, it is the Department's view that a motorist who refuses to submit to a chemical test more than two hours after the time of arrest is deemed to have refused, assuming that the other statutory elements of a refusal (i.e., reasonable grounds, arrest, warning and refusal) are established at the hearing.

APPENDIX 69

2012 Proposed Amendments to New York Department of Motor Vehicles Regulations

PROPOSED   **PROPOSED**

STATE OF NEW YORK

DEPARTMENT OF MOTOR VEHICLES

Pursuant to the authority contained in Sections 215(a) and 501(2)(c) of the Vehicle and Traffic Law, the

Commissioner of Motor Vehicles hereby amends the Regulations of the Commissioner of Motor Vehicles as

follows:

* * * * * * * * * *

Subdivision (c) of section 3.2 is amended by adding a new paragraph (4) to read as follows:

(4) A2-Problem driver restriction. The operation of a motor vehicle shall be subject to the driving restrictions set forth in section 135.9(b) and the conditions set forth in section 136.4(b) of this Title. As part of this restriction, the commissioner may require a person assigned the problem driver restriction to install an ignition interlock device in any motor vehicle that may be operated with a Class D license or permit and that is owned or operated by such person. The ignition interlock requirement will be noted on an attachment to the driver's license or permit held by such person. Such attachment must be carried at all times with the driver license or permit.

* * * * * * * * * *

STATE OF NEW YORK

DEPARTMENT OF MOTOR VEHICLES

Pursuant to the authority contained in Sections 215(a), 510(3)(a) and 510(3)(d) of the

Vehicle and Traffic Law, the Commissioner of Motor Vehicles hereby amends the Regulations

of the Commissioner of Motor Vehicles by adding a new section to read as follows:

* * * * * * * * * *

PART 132
Dangerous Repeat Alcohol or Drug Offenders

132.1. Definitions. For the purposes of this Part:

(a) Alcohol- or drug-related driving conviction or incident means a conviction of a
violation of section 1192 of the Vehicle and Traffic Law, a finding of a violation of section
1192-a of the Vehicle and Traffic Law, a conviction of an offense under the Penal Law for which
a violation of section 1192 of the Vehicle and Traffic Law is an essential element, or a finding of
refusal to submit to a chemical test under section 1194 of the Vehicle and Traffic Law, not
arising out of the same incident.

(b) Dangerous repeat alcohol or drug offender means:

(1) any driver who, within his or her lifetime, has five or more alcohol- or drug-
related driving convictions or incidents in any combination; or

(2) any driver who, within the 25 years preceding the date of commission of a
high-point driving violation, has three or four alcohol- or drug-related driving convictions or
incidents in any combination and, in addition, has one or more serious driving offenses within
the 25 years preceding the date of the commission of a high-point driving violation.

(c) High-point driving violation means any violation for which five or more points are
assessed on a violator's driving record pursuant to Section 131.3 of this subchapter.

(d) Serious driving offense means (i) a fatal accident; (ii) a driving-related Penal Law
conviction; (iii) conviction of two or more high-point driving violations, other than the violation
that forms the basis for the record review under Section 132.2 of this Part; or (iv) 20 or more
points from any violations, other than the violation that forms the basis for the record review
under Section 132.2 of this Part.

* * * * * * * * *

132.2. Lifetime record review.

Upon receipt of notice of a driver's conviction for a high-point driving violation, the Commissioner shall conduct a review of the lifetime driving record of the person convicted. If such review indicates that the person convicted is a dangerous repeat alcohol or drug offender, the Commissioner shall issue a proposed revocation of such person's driver license. Such person shall be advised of the right to request a hearing before an administrative law judge, prior to such proposed revocation taking effect. The provisions of Part 127 of this Chapter shall be applicable to any such hearing.

* * * * * * * * * *

132.3. Hearings.

The sole purpose of a hearing scheduled pursuant to this Part is to determine whether there exist unusual, extenuating and compelling circumstances to warrant a finding that the revocation proposed by the Commissioner should not take effect. In making such a determination, the administrative law judge shall take into account a driver's entire driving record. Unless the administrative law judge finds that such unusual, extenuating and compelling circumstances exist, the judge shall issue an order confirming the revocation proposed by the Commissioner.

* * * * * * * *

PROPOSED   **PROPOSED**

STATE OF NEW YORK

DEPARTMENT OF MOTOR VEHICLES

Pursuant to the authority contained in Sections 215(a), 1196(5) and 1196(7)(a) of the

Vehicle and Traffic Law, the Commissioner of Motor Vehicles hereby amends the Regulations

of the Commissioner of Motor Vehicles as follows:

* * * * * * * * * *

Paragraph (8) of subdivision (a) of section 134.7 is amended to read as follows:

(8) The person has been penalized under section 1193(1)(d)[(1)] of the Vehicle
and Traffic Law for any violation of subdivision 2, 2-a, 3, 4, or 4-a of section 1192 of such law.

* * * * * * * * * *

Subparagraph (i) of paragraph (11) of subdivision (a) of section 134.7 is amended to read

as follows:

(i) The person has three or more alcohol- or drug-related driving
convictions or incidents within the last [ten] twenty-five years. For the purposes of this
paragraph, a conviction for a violation of section 1192 of the Vehicle and Traffic Law, and/or a
finding of a violation of section 1192-a of such law and/or a finding of refusal to submit to a
chemical test under section 1194 of such law arising out of the same incident shall only be
counted as one conviction or incident. The date of the violation or incident resulting in a
conviction or a finding as described herein shall be used to determine whether three or more
convictions or incidents occurred within a [10] 25 year period.

* * * * * * * * * *

Subdivision (b) of section 134.10 is amended to read as follows:

(b) Results of satisfactory completion of a rehabilitation program. Upon satisfactory
completion of a program, any unexpired suspension or revocation which was issued as a result of
the conviction for which the person was eligible for enrollment in the program may be
terminated by the commissioner unless the termination is prohibited under section 1193 of the
Vehicle and Traffic Law or this Subchapter, or if the termination is based upon enrollment in the
program pursuant to the plea bargaining provisions of Vehicle and Traffic Law section
1192(10)(a)(ii) and 1192(10)(d), or if such person would not otherwise be eligible for enrollment
in the program pursuant to section 1196(4) of such law, or if the person has two or more alcohol-

or drug-related driving convictions or incidents within 25 years from the date of enrollment in the program.

* * * * * * * * * *

Section 134.11 is amended to read as follows:

134.11 Issuance of unconditional driver's license.

Satisfactory completion of a rehabilitation program or expiration of the term of suspension, whichever occurs first, will initiate the necessary action to provide for the termination of the suspension or revocation which was the basis for entry into the rehabilitation program, provided however, no such suspension or revocation shall be terminated prior to the expiration of the term of suspension or revocation if the applicant for the unconditional license has two or more alcohol- or drug-related driving convictions or incidents within the preceding 25 years. Upon a determination of satisfactory completion of the rehabilitation program or the term of suspension , and unless otherwise determined by the commissioner, as provided for in subdivision (b) of section 134.10 of this Part, a notice of termination of the suspension or revocation and an unconditional license will be issued. However, no such license will be issued until all civil penalties due the department are paid or if there are any outstanding suspensions, revocations, or bars against such license until such suspensions, revocations, or bars are satisfactorily disposed of by the applicant. Any conditional license which is still valid will be terminated concurrently with the return of the unconditional driver's license and must be returned to the department. A conditional license shall not be renewed more than one year after the issuance of the conditional license if a revocation is issued for a chemical test refusal and the holder of the conditional license has not paid the civil penalty required by section 1194 of the Vehicle and Traffic Law.

* * * * * * * * * *

PROPOSED   **PROPOSED**

STATE OF NEW YORK

DEPARTMENT OF MOTOR VEHICLES

Pursuant to the authority contained in Sections 215(a), 501(2)(c), 510(6), 1193(2)(b)(12), 1193(2)(c)(1)

and 1194(2)(d)(1) of the Vehicle and Traffic Law, the Commissioner of Motor Vehicles hereby amends the

Regulations of the Commissioner of Motor Vehicles as follows:

* * * * * * * * * *

Subdivision (b) of section 136.4 is amended to read as follows:

(b)(1) An [applicant] application for a driver's license [shall] may be denied if a review of the entire driving history provides evidence that the applicant constitutes a problem driver, as defined in section 136.1(b)(1) of this Part. If an application is denied pursuant to this paragraph, no application shall be considered for a minimum of one year from the date of denial. In lieu of such denial, the applicant may be issued a license or permit with a problem driver restriction, as set forth in section 3.2(c)(4) of this Chapter and paragraph (2) of this subdivision.

(2) Upon the approval of an application for relicensing of a person who is deemed a problem driver under this subdivision, the commissioner may impose a problem driver restriction on such person's license or permit, as set forth in section 3.2(c)(4) of this Title. As a component of this restriction, the commissioner may require such person to install an ignition interlock device in any motor vehicle owned or operated by such person. The ignition interlock requirement will be noted on the attachment to the driver license or permit held by such person. Such attachment must be carried at all times with the driver license or permit.

(3) Revocation of license or permit with problem driver restriction. A license or permit that contains a problem driver restriction shall be revoked (i) upon the holder's conviction of a traffic violation or combination of violations, committed while such restriction is in effect, which the Commissioner deems serious in nature; or (ii) for the holder's failure to install and maintain an ignition interlock device in motor vehicles owned or operated by the holder, when required to do so under such restriction. The attachment, provided for in paragraph (2) of this subdivision, shall set forth the violation or violations that will result in such a revocation. A revocation for any of the above reasons shall be issued without a hearing based upon receipt of a certificate or certificates of conviction. The commissioner may also revoke a license or permit with a problem driver restriction, without a hearing, upon receipt of a certificate of conviction that indicates that the applicant has driven in violation of the conditions of such restriction.

(4) Employer vehicle. A person required to operate a motor vehicle owned by such person's employer in the course and scope of his or her employment may operate that vehicle without installation of an ignition interlock device only in the course and scope of such employment and only if such person carries in the motor vehicle written documentation indicating the employer has knowledge of the restriction imposed and has

granted permission for the person to operate the employer's vehicle without the device only for business purposes. Such documentation shall display the employer's letterhead and have an authorized signature of the employer. A motor vehicle owned by a business entity that is wholly or partly owned or controlled by a person subject to the problem driver restriction is not a motor vehicle owned by the employer for purposes of the exemption provided in this paragraph and shall be deemed to be owned by the person subject to the problem driver restriction.

* * * * * * * * * *

Section 136.5 is amended to read as follows:

136.5 [Miscellaneous grounds for denial.] Special rules for applicants with multiple alcohol- or drug-related driving convictions or incidents.

[(a) Notwithstanding any other provision of this Part, two convictions for driving while intoxicated, with personal injury involvement in each, regardless of the extent of such injury, shall result in a denial of an application.

(b) Notwithstanding any other provision of this Part, the Commissioner may deny an application where the revocation sought to be terminated was imposed as a result of a conviction for a violation of section 125.10, 125.12, 125.13, 125.14, 125.15, 125.20, 125.22, 125.25, 125.26 or 125.27 of the Penal Law arising out of the operation of a motor vehicle, or a conviction for a violation of section 1192 of the Vehicle and Traffic Law which resulted in a death or serious injury, as defined in section 10.00 of the Penal Law. The ground for such denial shall be set forth in writing and a copy shall be made available to the applicant.]

(a) For the purposes of this section:

(1) "Alcohol- or drug-related driving conviction or incident" means a conviction of a violation of section 1192 of the Vehicle and Traffic Law, a finding of a violation of section 1192-a of the Vehicle and Traffic Law, a conviction of an offense under the Penal Law for which a violation of section 1192 of the Vehicle and Traffic Law is an essential element, or a finding of refusal to submit to a chemical test under section 1194 of the Vehicle and Traffic Law, not arising out of the same incident.

(2) "Serious driving offense" means (i) a fatal accident; (ii) a driving-related Penal Law conviction; (iii) conviction of two or more violations for which five or more points are assessed on a violator's driving record pursuant to Section 131.3 of this subchapter; or (iv) 20 or more points from any violations.

(3) "Revocable offense" means the violation, incident or accident that results in the revocation of the person's drivers license and which is the basis of the application for relicensing. Upon reviewing an application for relicensing, the Commissioner shall review the applicant's entire driving record and evaluate any offense committed between the date of the revocable offense and the date of application as if it had been committed immediately prior to the date of the revocable offense. For purposes of this section, "date of the revocable offense" means the date of the earliest revocable offense that resulted in a license revocation for which the revocation has not been terminated by the Commissioner's subsequent approval of an application for relicensing.

(b) Upon receipt of a person's application for relicensing, the Commissioner shall conduct a lifetime review of such person's driving record. If the record review shows that:

(1) the person has five or more alcohol- or drug-related driving convictions or incidents in any combination within his or her lifetime, then the Commissioner shall deny the application.

(2) the person has three or four alcohol- or drug-related driving convictions or incidents in any combination within the 25 years preceding the date of the revocable offense and, in addition, has one or more serious driving offenses within the 25 years preceding the date of the revocable offense, then the Commissioner shall deny the application.

(3) (i) the person has three or four alcohol- or drug-related driving convictions or incidents in any combination within the 25 years preceding the date of the revocable offense but no serious driving offenses within the 25 years preceding the date of the revocable offense and (ii) the person is currently revoked for an alcohol- or drug-related driving conviction or incident, then the Commissioner shall deny the application for at least five years, after which time the person may submit an application for relicensing. After such waiting period, the Commissioner may in his or her discretion approve such application, provided that upon such approval, the Commissioner shall impose the A2 restriction on such person's license for a period of five years and shall require the installation of an ignition interlock device in any motor vehicle owned or operated by such person for such five-year period. If such license with an A2 restriction is later revoked for a subsequent alcohol- or drug-related driving conviction or incident, such person shall thereafter be ineligible for any kind of license to operate a motor vehicle.

(4) (i) the person has three or four alcohol- or drug-related driving convictions or incidents in any combination within the 25 years preceding the date of the revocable offense but no serious driving offenses within the 25 years preceding the date of the revocable offense and (ii) the person is not currently revoked as the result of an alcohol- or drug-related driving conviction or incident, then the Commissioner shall deny the application for at least two years, after which time the person may submit an application for relicensing. After such waiting period, the Commissioner may in his or her discretion approve the application after the minimum statutory revocation period is served, provided that upon such approval, the Commissioner shall impose an A2 restriction, with no ignition interlock requirement, for a period of two years. If such license with an A2 restriction is later revoked for a subsequent alcohol- or drug-related driving conviction or incident, such person shall thereafter be ineligible for any kind of license to operate a motor vehicle.

(5) the person has two alcohol- or drug-related driving convictions or incidents in any combination within the 25 years preceding the date of the revocable offense, then the Commissioner may in his or her discretion approve the application after the minimum statutory revocation period is served.

(6) the person has been twice convicted of a violation of subdivision three, four or four-a of section 1192 of the Vehicle and Traffic Law or of driving while intoxicated or of driving while ability is impaired by the use of a drug or of driving while ability is impaired by the combined influence of drugs or of alcohol and any drug or drugs where physical injury, as defined in section 10.00 of the Penal Law, has resulted from such offense in each instance, then the Commissioner shall deny the application.

(c) The grounds for any denial shall be set forth in writing and a copy shall be made available to the person making the application for relicensing.

(d) While it is the Commissioner's general policy to act on applications in accordance with this section, the Commissioner shall not be foreclosed from consideration of unusual, extenuating and compelling circumstances that may be presented for review and which may form a valid basis to deviate from the general policy, as set forth above, in the exercise of discretionary authority granted under section 510 of the Vehicle and Traffic Law. If an application is approved based upon the exercise of such discretionary authority, the reasons for approval shall be set forth in writing and recorded.

* * * * * * * * * *

Section 136.10 is amended to read as follows:

136.10 Application for relicensing.

(a) Application by the holder of a post-revocation conditional license. Upon the termination of the period of probation set by the court, the holder of a post-revocation conditional license may apply to the Commissioner for restoration of a license or privilege to operate a motor vehicle. An application for licensure [shall] may be approved if the applicant demonstrates that he or she:

[(a)](1) has a valid post-revocation conditional license; and
[(b)](2) has demonstrated evidence of rehabilitation as required by this Part.

(b) Application after permanent revocation. The commissioner may waive the permanent revocation of a driver's license, pursuant to Vehicle and Traffic Law section 1193(2)(b)(12)(b), only if the statutorily required waiting period of either five or eight years has expired since the imposition of the permanent revocation and, during such period, the applicant has not been found to have refused to submit to a chemical test pursuant to Vehicle and Traffic Law section 1194 and has not been convicted of any violation of section 1192 or section 511 of such law or a violation of the Penal Law for which a violation of any subdivision of such section 1192 is an essential element. In addition, the waiver shall be granted only if:

(1) The applicant presents proof of successful completion of a rehabilitation program approved by the commissioner within one year prior to the date of the application for the waiver; provided, however, if the applicant completed such program before such time, the applicant must present proof of completion of an alcohol and drug dependency assessment within one year of the date of application for the waiver; and

(2) The applicant submits to the commissioner a certificate of relief from civil disabilities or a certificate of good conduct pursuant to Article 23 of the Correction Law; and

(3) The application is not denied pursuant to section 136.4(b) or section 136.5 of this Part; and

(4) There are no incidents of driving during the period prior to the application for the waiver, as indicated by accidents, convictions or pending tickets. The consideration of an application for a waiver when the applicant has a pending ticket shall be held in abeyance until such ticket is disposed of by the court or tribunal.

* * * * * * * * * *

New York ★ State ☰ State Agencies   ✚ Search all of NY.gov

Department of Motor Vehicles
Changes That Affect Multiple Alcohol/Drugged-Driving Offenders

New regulations that take effect on September 25, 2012 affect drivers with multiple alcohol/drugged-driving related convictions or incidents. The highlights of the regulatory changes are provided below.

- Applicants with two or more alcohol/drugged-driving related convictions or incidents within the preceding 25 years will be required to serve their entire sanction period (suspension or revocation) even if they complete the Drinking Driver Program (DDP).

- Applicants with three or four alcohol/drugged-driving related convictions or incidents within the preceding 25 years, without a serious driving offense and whose revocation does NOT result from an alcohol or drugged driving conviction or incident, will be denied relicensing for two years in addition to the statutory revocation period, and then will be relicensed with a problem driver restriction for two years. A serious driving offense means a fatal accident; a driving-related penal law conviction; conviction of two or more violations for which five or more points are assessed; or 20 or more points from any violations. (See below for information about the problem driver restriction.)

- Applicants with three or four alcohol/drugged-driving related convictions or incidents within the preceding 25 years, without a serious driving offense and whose revocation DOES result from an alcohol or drugged driving conviction or incident, will be denied relicensing for five years in addition to the statutory revocation period, and then will be relicensed with a problem driver restriction for 5 years with an ignition interlock.

- Applicants with three or four alcohol/drugged-driving related convictions or incidents within the preceding 25 years, with a serious driving offense will be permanently denied relicensure, subject to compelling or extenuating circumstances.

- Applicants with five or more alcohol/drugged-driving related convictions or incidents on their lifetime driving record will be permanently denied relicensing, subject to compelling or extenuating circumstances.

Offense History	DMV Action
Five or more DWIs lifetime = "Persistently Dangerous Driver"	Permanent denial (subject to compelling or extenuating circumstances)
In last 25 years, three or four DWIs + one Serious Driving Offense (SDO) = "Persistently Dangerous Driver"	Permanent denial (subject to compelling or extenuating circumstances)
If revocation for alcohol-related offense, three or four DWIs without any SDO in last 25 years	Deny for five years in addition to statutory revocation period, then relicense with restricted license and interlock for five years.
If revocation for non-alcohol-related offense, three or four DWIs without any SDO in last 25 years	Deny for two years in addition to statutory revocation period, then relicense with restricted license for two years, but no interlock.
Two DWIs	No full relicensing until end of statutory minimum revocation period, even if DDP

You can also read the Governor's press release about these changes.

The Regulations and FAQs

You can read the new regulations and read the frequently asked questions below to help you better understand the regulations.

What happens if I am not eligible for a conditional or restricted license?

You must serve the entire term of your suspension or revocation and then reapply to the DMV for a new driver license.

What is required to apply for a new license after revocation?

You must submit a completed form MV-44 (Application for Driver License or Non-Driver ID Card) and a non-refundable $100 fee to:

Driver Improvement Unit (DIU)
6 Empire State Plaza
Albany, New York 12228

http://www.dmv.ny.gov/problem.htm

9/25/2012

The DIU will make a determination based on your driving record, and a response will be mailed to you. The response will include instructions about your next steps.

Can some drivers have their full privileges restored at their local DMV office?

Yes, the following drivers who hold a conditional license can continue to visit a DMV office for restoration of their driving privileges:

- A driver with two alcohol/drugged-driving convictions or incidents within the previous 25 years who has completed the DDP and has served the entire suspension or revocation period, or
- A driver with one alcohol/drugged-driving conviction or incident within the previous 25 years who has completed the DDP.

If I have a conditional license based on one alcohol/drugged-driving conviction or incident, must I serve the minimum suspension or revocation period?

If there is only one alcohol/drugged-driving conviction or incident on your record, you can receive or apply for a new driver license without the need to serve the full revocation period if you first complete the DDP.

What happens if I have a conditional or restricted license and I drop out of the DDP?

Your conditional or restricted license will be revoked. After a review of your driving record, you may be eligible to re-enroll in the DDP and have your conditional or restricted license re-issued.

What happens if my driver license application is denied at the local DMV office?

You can submit a completed form MV-44 (Application for Driver License or Non-Driver ID Card) and a non-refundable $100 fee to:

> Driver Improvement Unit (DIU)
> 6 Empire State Plaza
> Albany, New York 12228

The DIU will make a determination based on your driving record, and a response will be mailed to you. The response will include instructions about your next steps.

What happens if my application is denied by the DIU?

Follow the instructions in the denial letter from the DIU.

What happens if my application is approved by the DIU?

Follow the instructions in the approval packet response from the DIU

How can I get a copy of my full lifetime driving record?

To get a copy of your full lifetime driving record, submit a Freedom of Information Law request using form MV-15F (Freedom of Information Law Request Form).

Problem Driver Restriction

What is a problem driver?

Part 136.1 of the Regulations of the Commissioner of Motor Vehicles [15 NYCRR 136.1(b)(1)] defines a problem driver as "an applicant for a driver license or privilege who has had a series of convictions, incidents and/or accidents or has a medical or mental condition, which in the judgment of the commissioner or his/her designated agent, upon review of the applicant's entire driving history, establishes that the person would be an unusual and immediate risk upon the highways."

http://www.dmv.ny.gov/problem.htm

9/25/2012

What is a problem driver restriction?

This restriction will control and restrict your driving. The restriction allows you to drive only:

- To and from your place of employment.
- During the hours of your employment, if your occupation requires the operation of a motor vehicle.
- To and from a medical appointment which is part of a necessary medical treatment for you or a member of your household. You may be required to provide a written statement from your licensed medical provider that verifies the travel is necessary.
- To and from a Motor Vehicle office to transact business related to the license/permit/privilege that contains a problem driver restriction.
- To and from a child's school/day-care if the child's attendance at the school/day-care is necessary for you to maintain employment or to maintain enrollment at an accredited school, college or university or a state-approved institution of vocational or technical training.
- To and from an accredited school, college or university or a State-approved institution of vocational or technical training in which you are enrolled.

These restrictions are outlined on an attachment issued to you by the DMV. You must carry the attachment whenever you operate a motor vehicle.

To which classes of license can a problem driver restriction be applied?

The problem driver restriction can only be applied to a class D license. It cannot be applied to any commercial driver license (CDL) Class A,B or C, junior operator license Class DJ, motorcycle operator license Class M or MJ or a class E driver license.

Can I drive through New York State with my out-of-state CDL license if my New York State record has the problem driver restriction?

No. A driver with a CDL issued in another state cannot operate a commercial motor vehicle in New York State with a problem driver restriction on their New York State record.

Can I drive through New York State with my out-of-state license with the problem driver restriction?

Yes. You must carry your completed, signed and dated problem driver restriction attachment and abide by the problem driver restrictions listed on the attachment.

Is there a cost for this restriction?

No, you will pay the required driver licens fees at the DMV office, but there is no additional fee for the problem driver restriction.

Where will the problem driver restriction be displayed?

Your photo driver license or permit will have an A2 restriction displayed on the front of the document, and the words "PROBLEM DRIVER RESTRICTION" will be displayed on the back of the document.

How long will the restriction be in effect? Is there any way I can have the restriction removed early?

If your revocation was due to an alcohol-related incident, the restriction remains in effect for five years from the date you receive your driver license or permit. If your revocation was not due to an alcohol related incident, the restriction remains in effect for two years from the date you receive your driver license or permit.

The restriction cannot be removed earlier.

What happens if I have a moving violation conviction before I obtain my driver license or permit with the problem driver restriction?

The approval for a driver license or permit with the problem driver restriction will be withdrawn.

http://www.dmv.ny.gov/problem.htm   9/25/2012

What if I receive a traffic ticket while I have a problem driver restriction?

If you are convicted of any one of the following violations, your driver license with the problem driver restriction will be revoked:

- Following too closely (tailgating),
- Speeding, speed contest,
- Operating out of restriction,
- Reckless driving, or
- Any two other traffic violations. This includes a seat belt or cell phone violation by the vehicle operator, but does not include parking, stopping, standing, equipment, inspection or other non-moving violations.

Your driver license will be revoked for a minimum of 30 days. You may then apply for to the DIU for a new license and must pay a non-refundable $100 application fee.

Problem Driver Restriction with DMV Mandated Ignition Interlock Device

What is a problem driver restriction with a DMV mandated ignition interlock device?

If your driving history includes alcohol-related violations, you may be required to install an ignition interlock device on any and all vehicles you own and operate. You are also subject to the problem driving restrictions. In addition, your problem driver restriction attachment will indicate that you are required to have an ignition interlock device.

Is the DMV mandated ignition interlock device different from a device ordered by a court under Leandra's Law?

Yes. The DMV mandated ignition interlock is imposed and removed administratively by DMV. An interlock restriction imposed by a court under Leandra's Law is imposed and removed by DMV under the orders of the court and is monitored by the court and designated monitors.

Which ignition interlock device do I need?

Any device that is approved by the New York State Division of Criminal Justice Services. For information see the Ignition Interlock page, click on Interlock Devices tab.

Where can I go to have an ignition interlock device installed?

Visit the Ignition Interlock page at the Web site of the NYS Division of Criminal Justice Services. See Manufacturer/ Vendor tab and click on Service Center locations.

What does the interlock device cost?

For information about installation fees, visit the Ignition Interlock page at the Web site of the NYS Division of Criminal Justice Services. Click on Interlock Device Tab.

Do I have to install the device in just my vehicle?

No, devices must be installed in any and all vehicles you own or operate.

For how long must the device be installed?

The device must be installed for five years from the date you receive your driver license or permit.

Can I have the interlock device removed early?

No, you must have the device installed for five years while you have the problem driver restriction.

http://www.dmv.ny.gov/problem.htm

9/25/2012

What happens if I operate a vehicle with no interlock device installed?

You can be issued a traffic ticket for driving out of restriction. If you are convicted, your driver license will be revoked.

Table of Laws and Rules

UNITED STATES CONSTITUTION

UNITED STATES PUBLIC LAWS

FEDERAL RULES OF EVIDENCE

FEDERAL REGISTER

CALIFORNIA VEHICLE CODE

NEW YORK CONSTITUTION

NEW YORK CIVIL PRACTICE LAW AND RULES

Sec.	Sec.	Sec.	Sec.
Art. 45	41:61		43:6; 43:18
Art. 78	41:68; 45:6; 53:29; 53:83	4518[a]	42:5; 43:2; 43:4; 43:5; 43:6; 43:8; 43:9; 43:11; 43:13; 43:15; 43:19; 43:20
207	24:9		
1310(4)	9:13	4518[c]	17:19; 43:4; 43:8; 43:11; 43:13; 43:14; 43:15; 45:3
1310(5)	9:13		
1311	9:13; 9:14	4520	43:11; 43:15
2214	24:9	4526	43:11
2214(b)	24:9	4528	43:11
2302	41:61	4529	43:11
2306	43:14; 43:15	4532	43:20
2307	20:41; 20:50; 20:99; 43:14	4533	43:20
3123(a)	43:20	4536	43:20
3123(c)	43:20	4538	43:20
4504	44:4; 44:6; 44:11; 44:17	4539	43:17; 43:18; 43:19
4504(a)	44:2; 44:5; 44:12; 44:15; 44:18	4540	43:17; 43:19; 43:20
4504(b)	44:13	4540(b)	43:19
4504(c)	44:13	4541	43:19; 43:20
4508	28:8	4542	43:19; 43:20
4518	11:49; 42:4; 43:2; 43:3; 43:4;	4543	43:20

NEW YORK CIVIL RIGHTS LAW

Sec.	Sec.
12	53:8

NEW YORK CORRECTION LAW

Sec.	Sec.	Sec.	Sec.
Art. 23	14:5; 14:29; 49:1; 51:1; 51:2; 51:3; 51:15; 51:31	702(2)	51:20
700(1)(a)	51:2	702(3)	51:22; 51:24
700(1)(b)	51:2	702(4)	51:26; 51:27
700(1)(c)	51:2	702(5)	51:29
700(2)(a) to (c)	51:2	702(6)	51:25
700(2)(b)	51:2	703	51:20; 51:30
701	14:12; 14:31; 14:48; 41:9	703(1)(b)	51:21
701(1)	51:1; 51:6; 51:7; 51:9	704(1)	51:27
701(2)	51:5; 51:11; 51:20	704(2)	51:28
701(3)	51:7; 51:17	705(2)	51:31
701[1]	51:7	706	51:8
701[3]	51:7	752	51:5
702(1)	51:20; 51:22; 51:23	753(2)	51:5

NEW YORK CRIMINAL PROCEDURE LAW

NEW YORK CRIMINAL PROCEDURE LAW—Continued

NEW YORK CRIMINAL PROCEDURE LAW—Continued

NEW YORK CRIMINAL PROCEDURE LAW—Continued

NEW YORK CRIMINAL PROCEDURE LAW—Continued

NEW YORK EXECUTIVE LAW

NEW YORK FAMILY COURT ACT

NEW YORK GENERAL CONSTRUCTION LAW

NEW YORK GENERAL MUNICIPAL LAW

NEW YORK INSURANCE LAW

NEW YORK JUDICIARY LAW

NEW YORK MENTAL HYGIENE LAW

NEW YORK NAVIGATION LAW

NEW YORK PENAL LAW—Continued

NEW YORK PUBLIC OFFICERS LAW

NEW YORK SOCIAL SERVICES LAW

NEW YORK STATE LAW

NEW YORK STATE ADMINISTRATIVE PROCEDURE ACT

NEW YORK STATE FINANCE LAW

NEW YORK VEHICLE AND TRAFFIC LAW

NEW YORK VEHICLE AND TRAFFIC LAW—Continued

NEW YORK VEHICLE AND TRAFFIC LAW—Continued

NEW YORK VEHICLE AND TRAFFIC LAW—Continued

NEW YORK VEHICLE AND TRAFFIC LAW—Continued

NEW YORK VEHICLE AND TRAFFIC LAW—Continued

NEW YORK VEHICLE AND TRAFFIC LAW—Continued

NEW YORK VEHICLE AND TRAFFIC LAW—Continued

NEW YORK VEHICLE AND TRAFFIC LAW—Continued

NEW YORK VEHICLE AND TRAFFIC LAW—Continued

NEW YORK UNIFORM JUSTICE COURT ACT

NEW YORK SESSION LAWS

NEW YORK CODE RULES AND REGULATIONS—STATE SANITARY CODE

OFFICIAL COMPILATION OF CODES, RULES AND REGULATIONS FOR THE STATE OF NEW YORK

OFFICIAL COMPILATION OF CODES, RULES AND REGULATIONS FOR THE STATE OF NEW YORK—Continued

9 N.Y.C.R.R. Sec.	Sec.
358.5(c)(10)(vii)	48:26
358.5(d)(1)	48:12
358.5(d)(2)	48:9
358.5(d)(4)	48:34
358.5(d)(6)	48:2
358.5(d)(12)	48:12
358.5(d)(13)	48:21
358.5(d)(16)	48:11
358.7(a)(1)	48:11
358.7(a)(2)	48:34
358.7(b)	48:28
358.7(b)(1)	48:28
358.7(b)(2)	48:28
358.7(b)(3)	48:29
358.7(b)(4)	48:29
358.7(c)(1)	48:12; 48:13
358.7(c)(2)	48:22
358.7(c)(3)	48:21
358.7(c)(5)	48:20
358.7(d)(1)	48:18; 48:24
358.7(d)(2)	48:18
358.7(d)(3)	48:18
358.7(e)	48:26
358.8(a)	48:8; 48:10
358.8(b)	48:10

10 N.Y.C.R.R. Sec.	Sec.
Part 59	11:4; 37:2; 48:3
59.1	48:4
59.1(g)	48:2
59.1(l)	42:6
59.2(a)	37:2
59.2(a)(2)	38:6
59.2[b][2]	38:33
59.2(c)(4)(i) and (ii)	38:10
59.2(d)	38:5
59.4	11:51; 38:33
59.4(a)	29:5; 42:12
59.4(b)	7:8; 29:3; 29:5; 42:12
59.5	7:8; 41:27
59.5(b)	7:8; 7:14; 41:95; 42:15
59.5(c)	7:8
59.5(d)	7:8; 29:11; 42:9
59.5(e)	37:2; 37:3
59.5(f)	20:40
59.10(c)(2)	48:2

10 N.Y.C.R.R. Sec.	Sec.
59.12(f)	48:17

15 N.Y.C.R.R. Sec.	Sec.
Part 91	13:46; 16:4
Part 124	15:43
Part 127	41:47; 41:61
Part 132	55:7; 55:14; 55:15; 55:23
Part 134	41:47
Part 135	41:47
Part 136	41:47
Part 139	41:47
Part 155	41:47
2.5	15:3; 15:27; 45:4
3.2(c)(4)	55:4; 55:16; 55:24
6.27(b)	14:57; 14:59
6.28(b)	14:57; 14:59
50:18	10:25
91.4(b)	16:7
91.7(a)	17:9; 20:44
91.7(b)	17:9; 20:44
91.11(a)	17:9; 20:44
122.2	13:46; 16:18
124.1(b)	15:43
124.2(b)	15:43
124.4	15:43
124.4(a) to (e)	15:43
124.5	15:44
127.1(a)	41:41; 41:58
127.2(a)	41:55
127.2(b)(2)	41:44
127.2(c)	41:44
127.4(a)	41:56
127.5(a)	41:60
127.5(b)	41:61
127.5(c)	41:61; 41:62
127.5(d)	41:67
127.5(e)	15:43
127.6	28:23; 41:63
127.6(a)	41:59
127.6(b)	41:61; 41:67
127.6(c)	41:61
127.7	41:57
127.7(f)(1) to (5)	15:41; 15:62
127.7(f)(6)	15:39; 15:60
127.7(f)(7)	15:35; 15:40; 15:57; 15:61
127.7(f)(8)	15:39; 15:60

OFFICIAL COMPILATION OF CODES, RULES AND REGULATIONS FOR THE STATE OF NEW YORK—Continued

NEW YORK ATTORNEY GENERAL OPINIONS

NEW YORK CITY ADMINISTRATIVE CODE

Table of Cases

County, 172 Misc. 2d 402, 656 N.Y.S.2d 839 (Sup 1997)—§ 14:3

Barnes v. Tofany, 27 N.Y.2d 74, 313 N.Y.S.2d 690, 261 N.E.2d 617 (1970)—§ 11:79

Barnes v. Tofany, 27 N.Y.2d 74, 313 N.Y.S.2d 690, 261 N.E.2d 617 (1970)—§§ 23:71; 41:6; 41:87

Barry, In re, 129 A.D.3d 57, 6 N.Y.S.3d 528 (4th Dep't 2015)—§ 11:96

Baxter, Matter of, 231 A.D.2d 964, 647 N.Y.S.2d 592 (4th Dep't 1996)—§§ 9:26; 11:96

Bazza v. Banscher, 143 A.D.2d 715, 533 N.Y.S.2d 285 (2d Dep't 1988)—§§ 41:75; 41:90

Bearden v. Georgia, 461 U.S. 660, 103 S. Ct. 2064, 76 L. Ed. 2d 221 (1983)—§ 46:45

Beaver v. Appeals Bd. of Administrative Adjudication Bureau, State Dept. of Motor Vehicles, 117 A.D.2d 956, 499 N.Y.S.2d 248 (3d Dep't 1986)—§ 41:27

Begay v. U.S., 553 U.S. 137, 128 S. Ct. 1581, 170 L. Ed. 2d 490 (2008)—§ 12:28

Benjamin L., In re, 92 N.Y.2d 660, 685 N.Y.S.2d 400, 708 N.E.2d 156 (1999)—§§ 53:8; 53:18

Benjamin S. v. Kuriansky, 55 N.Y.2d 116, 447 N.Y.S.2d 905, 432 N.E.2d 777 (1982)—§ 19:19

Berghuis v. Thompkins, 560 U.S. 370, 130 S. Ct. 2250, 176 L. Ed. 2d 1098 (2010)—§ 27:32

Berkemer v. McCarty, 468 U.S. 420, 104 S. Ct. 3138, 82 L. Ed. 2d 317 (1984)—§§ 5:6; 6:16; 11:58; 27:4; 27:5; 27:7; 27:8; 27:13; 27:25; 41:3; 41:77

Biggerstaff v. Drago, 65 A.D.3d 728, 883 N.Y.S.2d 657 (3d Dep't 2009)—§ 11:95

Birchfield v. North Dakota, 136 S. Ct. 2160, 195 L. Ed. 2d 560 (2016)—§ 11:56

Blackburn v. State of Ala., 361 U.S. 199, 80 S. Ct. 274, 4 L. Ed. 2d 242 (1960)—§ 25:1

Blake v. Hogan, 25 N.Y.2d 747, 303 N.Y.S.2d 505, 250 N.E.2d 568 (1969)—§ 53:29

Blanchfield v. State, 104 Misc. 2d 21, 427 N.Y.S.2d 682 (Ct. Cl. 1980)—§ 1:14

Blattner v. Tofany, 34 A.D.2d 1066, 312 N.Y.S.2d 173 (3d Dep't 1970)—§ 41:27

Blumberg v. Lennon, 44 A.D.2d 769, 354 N.Y.S.2d 261 (4th Dep't 1974)—§ 11:43

Boersma v. Erie County Pistol Permit Dept., 233 A.D.2d 938, 649 N.Y.S.2d 879 (4th Dep't 1996)—§ 11:95

Booth v. Clary, 83 N.Y.2d 675, 613 N.Y.S.2d 110, 635 N.E.2d 279 (1994)—§ 23:10

Boreali v. Axelrod, 71 N.Y.2d 1, 523 N.Y.S.2d 464, 517 N.E.2d 1350, 2 I.E.R. Cas. (BNA) 1213, 13 O.S.H. Cas. (BNA) 1498, 108 Lab. Cas. (CCH) ¶ 55850, 1988 O.S.H. Dec. (CCH) ¶ 28132 (1987)—§ 55:26

Born, 166 Misc. 2d—§ 17:14

Boucheron v. Tilley, 87 A.D.2d 983, 450 N.Y.S.2d 110 (4th Dep't 1982)—§ 43:10

Bowen v. Georgetown University Hosp., 488 U.S. 204, 109 S. Ct. 468, 102 L. Ed. 2d 493, 23 Soc. Sec. Rep. Serv. 511 (1988)—§ 55:27

Boyce v. Commissioner of New York State Dept. of Motor Vehicles, 215 A.D.2d 476, 626 N.Y.S.2d 537 (2d Dep't 1995)—§ 41:78

Boykin v. Alabama, 395 U.S. 238, 89 S. Ct. 1709, 23 L. Ed. 2d 274 (1969)—§§ 46:48; 46:54

Brady v. Department of Motor Vehicles, 98 N.Y.2d 625, 748 N.Y.S.2d 889, 778 N.E.2d 539 (2002)—§ 14:43

468 N.Y.S.2d 865, 456 N.E.2d 806 (1983)—§ 23:38

Carey v. Melton, 64 A.D.2d 983, 408 N.Y.S.2d 817 (2d Dep't 1978)—§ 41:31

Carney v. New York State Dept. of Motor Vehicles, 133 A.D.3d 1150, 20 N.Y.S.3d 467 (3d Dep't 2015)—§ 55:29

Carnley v. Cochran, 369 U.S. 506, 82 S. Ct. 884, 8 L. Ed. 2d 70 (1962)—§ 45:5

Casalino Interior Demolition Corp. v. Martinez, 29 A.D.3d 691, 814 N.Y.S.2d 720 (2d Dep't 2006)—§ 5:8

Case v. Sedita, 128 A.D.3d 1328, 8 N.Y.S.3d 744 (4th Dep't 2015)—§ 23:20

Casey v. Tierno, 127 A.D.2d 727, 512 N.Y.S.2d 123 (2d Dep't 1987)—§ 43:6

Catterson v. Corso, 244 A.D.2d 407, 664 N.Y.S.2d 67 (2d Dep't 1997)—§ 52:1

Catterson v. Rohl, 202 A.D.2d 420, 608 N.Y.S.2d 696 (2d Dep't 1994)—§§ 20:81; 20:86; 28:6; 28:10; 28:13

Catti v. W.E. Bryant's, Inc., 107 A.D.2d 865, 484 N.Y.S.2d 307 (3d Dep't 1985)—§ 11:76

Chakwin on Behalf of Ford, People ex rel. v. Warden, New York City Correctional Facility, Rikers Island, 63 N.Y.2d 120, 480 N.Y.S.2d 719, 470 N.E.2d 146 (1984)—§§ 53:28; 53:32; 53:33

Chambers v. Mississippi, 410 U.S. 284, 93 S. Ct. 1038, 35 L. Ed. 2d 297 (1973)—§ 41:62

Charles Q. v. Constantine, 85 N.Y.2d 571, 626 N.Y.S.2d 992, 650 N.E.2d 839 (1995)—§ 52:3

Chemical Leaman Tank Lines, Inc. v. Stevens, 21 A.D.2d 556, 251 N.Y.S.2d 240 (3d Dep't 1964)—§ 43:7

Chimel v. California, 395 U.S. 752, 89 S. Ct. 2034, 23 L. Ed. 2d 685 (1969)—§ 1:44

Christopher S., 126 Misc. 2d—§ 5:6

Clark v. New York State Dept. of Motor Vehicles, 55 A.D.3d 1284, 864 N.Y.S.2d 810 (4th Dep't 2008)—§§ 41:61; 41:78; 41:79

Clark v. Abrams, 161 A.D.2d 1208, 555 N.Y.S.2d 995 (4th Dep't 1990)—§ 50:3

Clute v. McGill, 229 A.D.2d 70, 655 N.Y.S.2d 201 (3d Dep't 1997)—§ 11:89

Clute v. McGill, 229 A.D.2d 70, 655 N.Y.S.2d 201 (3d Dep't 1997)—§ 9:8

Coffey v. Town of Wheatland, 135 A.D.2d 1125, 523 N.Y.S.2d 267 (4th Dep't 1987)—§ 41:85

Coleman v. New York City Transit Authority, 37 N.Y.2d 137, 371 N.Y.S.2d 663, 332 N.E.2d 850 (1975)—§ 11:27

Collins v. AA Trucking Renting Corp., 209 A.D.2d 363, 618 N.Y.S.2d 801 (1st Dep't 1994)—§ 25:16

Collura, 160 Misc. 2d—§ 5:3

Colonno v. Executive I Associates, 228 A.D.2d 859, 644 N.Y.S.2d 105 (3d Dep't 1996)—§ 43:4

Colorado v. Bertine, 479 U.S. 367, 107 S. Ct. 738, 93 L. Ed. 2d 739 (1987)—§ 1:44

Colorado v. Connelly, 479 U.S. 157, 107 S. Ct. 515, 93 L. Ed. 2d 473 (1986)—§ 25:2

Com. v. Michuck, 454 Pa. Super. 594, 686 A.2d 403 (1996)—§ 38:6

Com. v. Smythe, 23 Mass. App. Ct. 348, 502 N.E.2d 162 (1987)—§ 29:8

Constantine v. Leto, 157 A.D.2d 376, 557 N.Y.S.2d 611 (3d Dep't 1990)—§§ 11:47; 11:52; 42:3

Constantine v. Leto, 157 A.D.2d 376, 557 N.Y.S.2d 611 (3d Dep't 1990)—§§ 7:8; 7:14; 20:4; 20:24; 20:40; 20:99

Constantine v. Solomon, 194

38, 459 N.Y.S.2d 494 (4th Dep't 1983)—§§ 41:6; 41:23; 41:44

Geer, Claim of, 255 A.D.2d 676, 679 N.Y.S.2d 457 (3d Dep't 1998)—§ 14:39

Giacone v. Jackson, 267 A.D.2d 673, 699 N.Y.S.2d 587 (3d Dep't 1999)—§ 41:16

Giambra v. Commissioner of Motor Vehicles, 59 A.D.2d 648, 398 N.Y.S.2d 301 (4th Dep't 1977)—§ 41:68

Giglio v. U.S., 405 U.S. 150, 92 S. Ct. 763, 31 L. Ed. 2d 104 (1972)—§ 21:9

Giles v. State of Md., 386 U.S. 66, 87 S. Ct. 793, 17 L. Ed. 2d 737 (1967)—§§ 21:1; 21:9

Gilman v. Passidomo, 109 A.D.2d 1082, 487 N.Y.S.2d 186 (4th Dep't 1985)—§ 41:27

Gina C., Matter of, 138 A.D.2d 77, 531 N.Y.S.2d 86, 15 Media L. Rep. (BNA) 2113 (1st Dep't 1988)—§ 28:8

Gingello, 181 Misc. 2d—§§ 17:14; 17:17; 37:7

Ginty, Application of, 74 Misc. 2d 625, 345 N.Y.S.2d 856 (Sup 1973)—§ 41:86

Giudice v. Adduci, 176 A.D.2d 1175, 575 N.Y.S.2d 611 (3d Dep't 1991)—§§ 23:73; 41:87

Glucksman, Matter of, 57 A.D.2d 205, 394 N.Y.S.2d 191 (1st Dep't 1977)—§§ 51:8; 51:14

Goebel v. Tofany, 44 A.D.2d 615, 353 N.Y.S.2d 73 (3d Dep't 1974)—§ 41:64

Goldstein, In re, 285 A.D.2d 187, 728 N.Y.S.2d 758 (2d Dep't 2001)—§§ 11:96; 13:19

Good Samaritan Hosp. v. Axelrod, 150 A.D.2d 775, 542 N.Y.S.2d 28 (2d Dep't 1989)—§ 55:27

Gorghan v. DeAngelis, 7 N.Y.3d 470, 824 N.Y.S.2d 202, 857 N.E.2d 523 (2006)—§ 23:31

Gorman v. Rice, 24 N.Y.3d 1032,

998 N.Y.S.2d 141, 22 N.E.3d 1009 (2014)—§ 23:33

Gould v. New York City Police Dept., 89 N.Y.2d 267, 653 N.Y.S.2d 54, 675 N.E.2d 808, 25 Media L. Rep. (BNA) 1104 (1996)—§ 20:100

Grady v. Corbin, 495 U.S. 508, 110 S. Ct. 2084, 109 L. Ed. 2d 548 (1990)—§ 23:6

Grand Jury Investigation in New York County, In re, 98 N.Y.2d 525, 749 N.Y.S.2d 462, 779 N.E.2d 173 (2002)—§§ 44:3; 44:5; 44:9; 44:10; 44:13

Grand Jury Investigation of Onondaga County, Matter of, 59 N.Y.2d 130, 463 N.Y.S.2d 758, 450 N.E.2d 678 (1983)— §§ 44:4; 44:5; 44:9; 44:10; 44:13

Gray v. Adduci, 73 N.Y.2d 741, 536 N.Y.S.2d 40, 532 N.E.2d 1268 (1988)—§ 11:69

Gray v. Adduci, 73 N.Y.2d 741, 536 N.Y.S.2d 40, 532 N.E.2d 1268 (1988)—§§ 41:51; 41:52; 41:61

Green v. DeMarco, 11 Misc. 3d 451, 812 N.Y.S.2d 772 (Sup 2005)—§ 43:25

Green v. County Court of Tompkins County, 61 A.D.2d 1098, 403 N.Y.S.2d 560 (3d Dep't 1978)—§ 23:29

Greene v. Melton, 54 A.D.2d 1060, 388 N.Y.S.2d 714 (3d Dep't 1976)—§ 12:24

Greenstein on Behalf of Lewis, People ex rel. v. Sheriff of Schenectady County, 220 A.D.2d 190, 645 N.Y.S.2d 339 (3d Dep't 1996)—§ 53:34

Griffin v. Wisconsin, 483 U.S. 868, 107 S. Ct. 3164, 97 L. Ed. 2d 709 (1987)—§ 4:10

Grinberg v. Safir, 266 A.D.2d 43, 698 N.Y.S.2d 218 (1st Dep't 1999)—§ 9:23

Grinberg v. Safir, 181 Misc. 2d 444, 694 N.Y.S.2d 316 (Sup 1999)—§ 45:3

136, 700 N.Y.S.2d 77, 722 N.E.2d 45 (1999)—§§ 5:2; 5:4; 5:7; 5:9

Mullen v. New York State Dept. of Motor Vehicles, 144 A.D.2d 886, 535 N.Y.S.2d 206 (3d Dep't 1988)—§ 41:43

Murray v. Donlan, 77 A.D.2d 337, 433 N.Y.S.2d 184 (2d Dep't 1980)—§ 43:7

Murray v. Tofany, 33 A.D.2d 1080, 307 N.Y.S.2d 776 (3d Dep't 1970)—§ 41:16

N

Nassau, County of v. Canavan, 1 N.Y.3d 134, 770 N.Y.S.2d 277, 802 N.E.2d 616 (2003)—§§ 9:23; 9:24; 11:76; 45:3

Nassau County v. Bigler, 1 Misc. 3d 910(A), 781 N.Y.S.2d 626 (Sup 2001)—§ 23:70

Nassau Police Dept., County of v. Judge, 237 A.D.2d 354, 654 N.Y.S.2d 174 (2d Dep't 1997)—§ 20:99

Navarette v. California, 134 S. Ct. 1683, 188 L. Ed. 2d 680 (2014)—§ 1:16

New York v. Belton, 453 U.S. 454, 101 S. Ct. 2860, 69 L. Ed. 2d 768 (1981)—§ 1:44

New York v. Class, 475 U.S. 106, 106 S. Ct. 960, 89 L. Ed. 2d 81 (1986)—§ 1:41

New York v. Harris, 495 U.S. 14, 110 S. Ct. 1640, 109 L. Ed. 2d 13 (1990)—§§ 4:1; 4:6

New York v. Quarles, 467 U.S. 649, 104 S. Ct. 2626, 81 L. Ed. 2d 550 (1984)—§ 27:30

New York, City of v. Tiffany General Holding Corp. and Oscar Santangelo, N.Y.L.J., 7/21/88—§ 43:21

New York Statewide Coalition of Hispanic Chambers of Commerce v. New York City Dept. of Health and Mental Hygiene, 110 A.D.3d 1, 970 N.Y.S.2d 200 (1st Dep't 2013)—§ 55:26

Nichols v. U.S., 511 U.S. 738, 114 S. Ct. 1921, 128 L. Ed. 2d 745 (1994)—§§ 9:5; 11:16; 11:66; 23:50

Nicol v. Grant, 117 A.D.2d 940, 499 N.Y.S.2d 247 (3d Dep't 1986)—§ 41:27

Nieves, 143 Misc. 2d—§ 32:2

Noblett, 172 Misc. 2d—§ 17:14

Nolan v. Adduci, 166 A.D.2d 277, 564 N.Y.S.2d 118 (1st Dep't 1990)—§§ 41:68; 41:78

North Carolina v. Pearce, 395 U.S. 711, 89 S. Ct. 2072, 23 L. Ed. 2d 656 (1969)—§ 23:51

Northland Transp. Inc. v. Jackson, 271 A.D.2d 846, 706 N.Y.S.2d 501 (3d Dep't 2000)—§ 14:50

O

O'Brien, In re, 309 A.D.2d 184, 765 N.Y.S.2d 71 (2d Dep't 2003)—§§ 9:26; 11:96

O'Brien v. Melton, 61 A.D.2d 1091, 403 N.Y.S.2d 353 (3d Dep't 1978)—§ 41:27

Obrist v. Commissioner of Motor Vehicles, 131 Misc. 2d 499, 500 N.Y.S.2d 909 (Sup 1985)—§ 41:35

Ocean-Clear, Inc. v. Continental Cas. Co., 94 A.D.2d 717, 462 N.Y.S.2d 251 (2d Dep't 1983)—§ 20:99

O'Connor v. Incorporated Village of Port-Jefferson, 104 A.D.2d 861, 480 N.Y.S.2d 376 (2d Dep't 1984)—§§ 43:5; 43:8; 43:9

O'Dea v. Tofany, 41 A.D.2d 888, 342 N.Y.S.2d 679 (4th Dep't 1973)—§ 41:27

O'Keefe v. Murphy, 38 N.Y.2d 563, 381 N.Y.S.2d 821, 345 N.E.2d 292 (1976)—§ 53:108

Osborn, 193 Misc. 2d—§ 45:17

Owen v. Stroebel, 65 N.Y.2d 658, 491 N.Y.S.2d 611, 481 N.E.2d 243 (1985)—§ 23:29

P

Padilla v. Kentucky, 559 U.S. 356, 130 S. Ct. 1473, 176 L. Ed. 2d 284 (2010)—§§ 11:87; 46:42

Paganini, People ex rel. v. Jablonsky, 79 N.Y.2d 586, 584 N.Y.S.2d 415, 594 N.E.2d 909 (1992)—§§ 13:17; 41:83; 50:23

Pantaleo, 141 Misc. 2d—§ 24:16

Papaioannou v. Kelly, 14 A.D.3d 459, 788 N.Y.S.2d 378 (1st Dep't 2005)—§ 11:95

Passino v. DeRosa, 199 A.D.2d 1017, 606 N.Y.S.2d 107 (4th Dep't 1993)—§ 43:10

Pastrana v. Baker, 55 N.Y.2d 315, 449 N.Y.S.2d 461, 434 N.E.2d 697 (1982)—§ 23:21

Payton v. New York, 445 U.S. 573, 100 S. Ct. 1371, 63 L. Ed. 2d 639 (1980)—§§ 4:1; 4:3; 4:9

Pecora, 123 Misc. 2d—§ 41:4

Peeso v. Fiala, 130 A.D.3d 1442, 13 N.Y.S.3d 742 (4th Dep't 2015)—§§ 41:38; 41:61

Pennsylvania v. Bruder, 488 U.S. 9, 109 S. Ct. 205, 102 L. Ed. 2d 172 (1988)—§§ 6:16; 6:18; 11:58; 27:5; 27:8; 41:77

Pennsylvania v. Muniz, 496 U.S. 582, 110 S. Ct. 2638, 110 L. Ed. 2d 528 (1990)—§§ 6:15; 6:18; 11:58; 20:12; 26:23; 27:1; 27:8; 27:29; 41:77

People v. Abajian, 142 Misc. 2d 250, 537 N.Y.S.2d 449 (J. Ct. 1989)—§ 53:37

People v. Abbamonte, 43 N.Y.2d 74, 400 N.Y.S.2d 766, 371 N.E.2d 485 (1977)—§ 23:10

People v. Abdul-Akim, 27 Misc. 3d 1220(A), 910 N.Y.S.2d 764 (Sup 2010)—§ 1:14

People v. Abdul, 279 A.D.2d 298, 720 N.Y.S.2d 5 (1st Dep't 2001)—§ 26:20

People v. Abdul Karim Al-Kanani, 33 N.Y.2d 260, 351 N.Y.S.2d 969, 307 N.E.2d 43 (1973)— §§ 44:3; 44:6; 44:7; 44:14

People v. Abedi, 159 Misc. 2d 1010, 607 N.Y.S.2d 862 (Sup 1994)—§ 52:3

People v. Abel, 166 A.D.2d 841, 563 N.Y.S.2d 531 (3d Dep't 1990)—§§ 11:38; 11:94; 31:7

People v. Abelo, 79 A.D.3d 668, 914 N.Y.S.2d 54 (1st Dep't 2010)— §§ 13:4; 13:21

People v. Abrucci-Kohan, 52 Misc. 3d 919, 2016 WL 1174766 (N.Y. J. Ct. 2016)—§ 1:15

People v. Acevedo, 27 Misc. 3d 889, 897 N.Y.S.2d 899 (N.Y. City Crim. Ct. 2010)—§ 13:47

People v. Acevedo, 69 N.Y.2d 478, 515 N.Y.S.2d 753, 508 N.E.2d 665 (1987)—§ 23:58

People v. Ackerson, 149 Misc. 2d 882, 566 N.Y.S.2d 833 (County Ct. 1991)—§ 44:18

People v. Ackroyd, 144 Misc. 2d 149, 543 N.Y.S.2d 848 (Sup 1989)—§ 12:26

People v. Acosta, 66 A.D.3d 792, 887 N.Y.S.2d 187 (2d Dep't 2009)—§ 1:36

People v. Adames, 83 N.Y.2d 89, 607 N.Y.S.2d 919, 629 N.E.2d 391 (1993)—§ 23:31

People v. Adams, 193 Misc. 2d 78, 747 N.Y.S.2d 909 (Sup 2002)—§§ 51:7; 51:17; 51:18; 51:19

People v. Adams, 57 N.Y.2d 1035, 457 N.Y.S.2d 783, 444 N.E.2d 33 (1982)—§§ 10:26; 19:20

People v. Adams, 38 N.Y.2d 605, 381 N.Y.S.2d 847, 345 N.E.2d 318 (1976)—§ 53:21

People v. Adams, 32 N.Y.2d 451, 346 N.Y.S.2d 229, 299 N.E.2d 653 (1973)—§ 1:42

People v. Adams, 26 N.Y.2d 129, 309 N.Y.S.2d 145, 257 N.E.2d 610 (1970)—§§ 25:2; 27:20; 27:22

People v. Adger, 75 N.Y.2d 723, 551 N.Y.S.2d 190, 550 N.E.2d 443 (1989)—§ 28:5

People v. Adler, 145 A.D.2d 943, 536 N.Y.S.2d 315 (4th Dep't 1988)—§ 41:27

People v. Afrika, 13 A.D.3d 1218, 787 N.Y.S.2d 774 (4th Dep't 2004)—§ 20:56

People v. Ahmed, 66 N.Y.2d 307, 496 N.Y.S.2d 984, 487 N.E.2d 894 (1985)—§ 23:42

People v. Aia, 105 A.D.2d 592, 482 N.Y.S.2d 56 (3d Dep't 1984)—§§ 27:6; 41:27

People v. Akwa, 151 Misc. 2d 106, 573 N.Y.S.2d 216 (Sup 1991)—§ 1:14

People v. Alamo, 34 N.Y.2d 453, 358 N.Y.S.2d 375, 315 N.E.2d 446, 70 A.L.R.3d 1193 (1974)—§§ 2:3; 11:29

People v. Alberto, 22 Misc. 3d 786, 877 N.Y.S.2d 628 (Dist. Ct. 2008)—§§ 11:27; 27:35

People v. Alcindor, 157 Misc. 2d 725, 598 N.Y.S.2d 449 (N.Y. City Crim. Ct. 1993)—§§ 26:8; 26:9

People v. Aldrich-O'Shea, 6 Misc. 3d 35, 789 N.Y.S.2d 804 (App. Term 2004)—§ 26:28

People v. Alejandro, 70 N.Y.2d 133, 517 N.Y.S.2d 927, 511 N.E.2d 71 (1987)—§§ 16:9; 16:10; 16:16; 16:24; 16:27; 16:30; 20:63; 20:70; 24:12

People v. Alexander, 19 N.Y.3d 203, 947 N.Y.S.2d 386, 970 N.E.2d 409 (2012)—§ 53:20

People v. Alfaro, 179 Misc. 2d 589, 686 N.Y.S.2d 638 (J. Ct. 1999)—§§ 11:27; 52:2

People v. Ali, 151 Misc. 2d 742, 573 N.Y.S.2d 575 (N.Y. City Crim. Ct. 1991)—§ 31:12

People v. Aliaj, 36 Misc. 3d 682, 946 N.Y.S.2d 430 (Sup 2012)—§ 7:8

People v. Allen, 89 A.D.3d 742, 932 N.Y.S.2d 142 (2d Dep't 2011)—§ 1:14

People v. Allen, 86 N.Y.2d 599, 635 N.Y.S.2d 139, 658 N.E.2d 1012 (1995)—§§ 23:46; 53:20

People v. Allen, 158 A.D.2d 932, 551 N.Y.S.2d 96 (4th Dep't 1990)—§ 13:51

People v. Allen, 104 Misc. 2d 136, 427 N.Y.S.2d 698 (Sup 1980)—§ 28:20

People v. Allende, 39 N.Y.2d 474, 384 N.Y.S.2d 416, 348 N.E.2d 891 (1976)—§ 1:5

People v. Alleyne, 214 A.D.2d 575, 625 N.Y.S.2d 77 (2d Dep't 1995)—§ 46:45

People v. Alls, 83 N.Y.2d 94, 608 N.Y.S.2d 139, 629 N.E.2d 1018 (1993)—§ 27:46

People v. All State Properties, LLC, 29 Misc. 3d 201, 907 N.Y.S.2d 549 (J. Ct. 2010)—§§ 16:23; 20:50; 20:59; 20:62

People v. Almendarez, 24 Misc. 3d 649, 876 N.Y.S.2d 861 (Dist. Ct. 2009)—§ 16:22

People v. Aloma, 92 A.D.2d 572, 459 N.Y.S.2d 327 (2d Dep't 1983)—§ 46:45

People v. Alonzo, 16 N.Y.3d 267, 920 N.Y.S.2d 302, 945 N.E.2d 495 (2011)—§ 23:19

People v. Alshoaibi, 273 A.D.2d 871, 711 N.Y.S.2d 646 (4th Dep't 2000)—§§ 13:10; 13:25; 41:83

People v. Alston, 9 Misc. 3d 1046, 805 N.Y.S.2d 258 (N.Y. City Crim. Ct. 2005)—§ 1:27

People v. Altruz, 198 A.D.2d 423, 604 N.Y.S.2d 134 (2d Dep't 1993)—§ 1:36

People v. Alvarado, 201 A.D.2d 486, 607 N.Y.S.2d 399 (2d Dep't 1994)—§§ 20:87; 28:15

People v. Alvarez, 151 A.D.2d 684, 543 N.Y.S.2d 935 (2d Dep't 1989)—§ 1:36

People v. Alvarez, 141 Misc. 2d 686, 534 N.Y.S.2d 90 (N.Y. City Crim. Ct. 1988)—§§ 2:9; 16:37; 25:12

People v. Brister, 239 A.D.2d 513, 658 N.Y.S.2d 362 (2d Dep't 1997)—§ 28:17

People v. Brito, 26 Misc. 3d 1097, 892 N.Y.S.2d 752 (Sup 2010)—§§ 24:18; 41:33; 44:18

People v. Brock, 246 A.D.2d 406, 667 N.Y.S.2d 730 (1st Dep't 1998)—§ 28:8

People v. Brockenshire, 197 A.D.2d 921, 602 N.Y.S.2d 459 (4th Dep't 1993)—§ 22:14

People v. Brockum, 88 A.D.2d 697, 451 N.Y.S.2d 326 (3d Dep't 1982)—§§ 7:5; 7:6; 7:9; 7:11; 41:4

People v. Brockway, 202 A.D.2d 1015, 609 N.Y.S.2d 481 (4th Dep't 1994)—§§ 9:4; 13:25; 41:83

People v. Brol, 81 A.D.2d 739, 438 N.Y.S.2d 424 (4th Dep't 1981)—§§ 31:10; 41:91

People v. Brooks, 38 Misc. 3d 946, 957 N.Y.S.2d 626 (J. Ct. 2013)—§ 17:14

People v. Brooks, 266 A.D.2d 864, 697 N.Y.S.2d 804 (4th Dep't 1999)—§ 1:14

People v. Brothers, 123 A.D.3d 1240, 999 N.Y.S.2d 225 (3d Dep't 2014)—§§ 13:45; 48:32

People v. Brothers, 50 N.Y.2d 413, 429 N.Y.S.2d 558, 407 N.E.2d 405 (1980)—§§ 53:62; 53:72; 53:73; 53:77

People v. Brown, 48 Misc. 3d 582, 9 N.Y.S.3d 830 (N.Y. City Crim. Ct. 2015)—§ 20:40

People v. Brown, 107 A.D.3d 1305, 968 N.Y.S.2d 224 (3d Dep't 2013)—§ 27:8

People v. Brown, 40 Misc. 3d 821, 970 N.Y.S.2d 391 (Sup 2013)—§ 48:32

People v. Brown, 31 Misc. 3d 794, 919 N.Y.S.2d 324 (N.Y. City Ct. 2011)—§§ 13:4; 13:47

People v. Brown, 69 A.D.3d 871, 895 N.Y.S.2d 127 (2d Dep't 2010)—§ 53:56

People v. Brown, 99 N.Y.2d 488, 758 N.Y.S.2d 602, 788 N.E.2d 1030 (2003)—§ 53:53

People v. Brown, 168 Misc. 2d 923, 646 N.Y.S.2d 241 (N.Y. City Ct. 1996)—§§ 26:10; 26:12

People v. Brown, 160 A.D.2d 1037, 553 N.Y.S.2d 875 (3d Dep't 1990)—§§ 9:5; 11:16; 24:21

People v. Brown, 157 A.D.2d 790, 550 N.Y.S.2d 389 (2d Dep't 1990)—§ 19:11

People v. Brown, 143 Misc. 2d 270, 540 N.Y.S.2d 650 (N.Y. City Crim. Ct. 1989)—§§ 32:1; 32:2; 32:3; 37:4

People v. Brown, 140 A.D.2d 266, 528 N.Y.S.2d 565 (1st Dep't 1988)—§§ 26:19; 27:2

People v. Brown, 128 Misc. 2d 149, 488 N.Y.S.2d 559 (County Ct. 1985)—§§ 43:4; 43:20; 45:17

People v. Brown, 112 A.D.2d 945, 492 N.Y.S.2d 625 (2d Dep't 1985)—§ 1:14

People v. Brown, 104 A.D.2d 696, 480 N.Y.S.2d 578 (3d Dep't 1984)—§§ 11:58; 27:6; 27:8

People v. Brown, 53 N.Y.2d 979, 441 N.Y.S.2d 662, 424 N.E.2d 549 (1981)—§§ 9:18; 11:23; 11:37; 11:38; 11:39

People v. Brown, 104 Misc. 2d 157, 427 N.Y.S.2d 722 (N.Y. City Crim. Ct. 1980)—§§ 20:29; 20:36

People v. Brown, 73 A.D.2d 112, 426 N.Y.S.2d 128 (3d Dep't 1980)—§ 11:39

People v. Brown, 40 N.Y.2d 381, 386 N.Y.S.2d 848, 353 N.E.2d 811 (1976)—§ 23:25

People v. Brown, 24 N.Y.2d 168, 299 N.Y.S.2d 190, 247 N.E.2d 153 (1969)—§ 22:7

People v. Bruno, 45 A.D.2d 1025, 358 N.Y.S.2d 183 (2d Dep't 1974)—§§ 1:35; 41:35

People v. Bryant, 73 A.D.3d 1442, 900 N.Y.S.2d 810 (4th Dep't 2010)—§ 44:17

N.Y.S.2d 24, 215 N.E.2d 345 (1966)—§ 20:98

People v. Caban, 14 N.Y.3d 369, 901 N.Y.S.2d 566, 927 N.E.2d 1050 (2010)—§ 12:15

People v. Cabrera, 10 N.Y.3d 370, 858 N.Y.S.2d 74, 887 N.E.2d 1132 (2008)—§ 12:15

People v. Cabrera, 13 Misc. 3d 1205(A), 824 N.Y.S.2d 756 (N.Y. City Crim. Ct. 2006)—§ 5:8

People v. Cabrera, 243 A.D.2d 720, 664 N.Y.S.2d 308 (2d Dep't 1997)—§ 47:8

People v. Caggiano, 46 A.D.3d 1405, 848 N.Y.S.2d 797 (4th Dep't 2007)—§ 47:4

People v. Cagle, 158 A.D.2d 931, 551 N.Y.S.2d 95 (4th Dep't 1990)—§ 9:4

People v. Calcasola, 80 Misc. 2d 429, 364 N.Y.S.2d 301 (App. Term 1975)—§ 10:6

People v. Calhoun, 73 A.D.2d 972, 424 N.Y.S.2d 247 (2d Dep't 1980)—§ 1:36

People v. Calise, 167 Misc. 2d 277, 639 N.Y.S.2d 671 (N.Y. City Crim. Ct. 1996)—§§ 13:6; 26:12; 26:22

People v. Callahan, 80 N.Y.2d 273, 590 N.Y.S.2d 46, 604 N.E.2d 108 (1992)—§ 53:20

People v. Callendar, 227 A.D.2d 499, 643 N.Y.S.2d 142 (2d Dep't 1996)—§ 28:4

People v. Camagos, 160 Misc. 2d 880, 611 N.Y.S.2d 426 (N.Y. City Crim. Ct. 1993)—§§ 24:18; 41:24; 41:29; 41:33

People v. Camarre, 171 A.D.2d 1003, 569 N.Y.S.2d 224 (4th Dep't 1991)—§ 40:15

People v. Cammarata, 216 A.D.2d 965, 629 N.Y.S.2d 716 (4th Dep't 1995)—§§ 9:11; 13:36

People v. Campbell, 36 A.D.3d 1016, 827 N.Y.S.2d 768 (3d Dep't 2007)—§§ 13:7; 13:30

People v. Campbell, 97 N.Y.2d 532, 743 N.Y.S.2d 396, 769 N.E.2d 1288 (2002)—§§ 53:20; 53:69

People v. Campbell, 186 A.D.2d 212, 587 N.Y.S.2d 751 (2d Dep't 1992)—§ 28:8

People v. Campbell, 73 N.Y.2d 481, 541 N.Y.S.2d 756, 539 N.E.2d 584 (1989)—§§ 7:8; 7:14; 11:47; 11:51; 29:3; 38:33; 42:3; 42:12

People v. Campbell, 141 Misc. 2d 470, 533 N.Y.S.2d 666 (N.Y. City Crim. Ct. 1988)—§ 16:10

People v. Cannella, N.Y.L.J., 4/12/94—§ 7:9

People v. Cannon, 191 Misc. 2d 136, 743 N.Y.S.2d 224 (Sup 2002)—§ 20:25

People v. Cantor, 36 N.Y.2d 106, 365 N.Y.S.2d 509, 324 N.E.2d 872 (1975)—§§ 1:2; 1:5

People v. Cantre, 65 N.Y.2d 790, 493 N.Y.S.2d 127, 482 N.E.2d 923 (1985)—§ 1:17

People v. Canute, 8 A.D.3d 1125, 778 N.Y.S.2d 247 (4th Dep't 2004)—§§ 2:2; 13:38

People v. Capellan, 6 Misc. 3d 809, 791 N.Y.S.2d 315 (N.Y. City Crim. Ct. 2004)—§§ 13:4; 43:25

People v. Capraella, 165 Misc. 2d 639, 629 N.Y.S.2d 965 (N.Y. City Crim. Ct. 1995)—§ 31:7

People v. Carbonaro, 134 A.D.3d 1543, 23 N.Y.S.3d 525 (4th Dep't 2015)—§§ 27:6; 27:21

People v. Cardenas, 165 Misc. 2d 587, 632 N.Y.S.2d 937 (App. Term 1995)—§ 24:15

People v. Carkner, 213 A.D.2d 735, 623 N.Y.S.2d 350 (3d Dep't 1995)—§§ 38:30; 44:7; 44:15; 44:16

People v. Carley, 248 A.D.2d 548, 669 N.Y.S.2d 870 (2d Dep't 1998)—§ 12:12

People v. Carlsons, 171 Misc. 2d 943, 656 N.Y.S.2d 116 (Sup 1997)—§ 13:48

People v. Carmine A., 53 N.Y.2d

903, 695 N.Y.S.2d 625 (3d Dep't 1999)—§ 4:5

People v. Cedeno, 52 N.Y.2d 847, 437 N.Y.S.2d 72, 418 N.E.2d 665 (1981)—§ 53:21

People v. Cegelski, 142 Misc. 2d 1023, 539 N.Y.S.2d 639 (County Ct. 1989)—§§ 30:1; 30:2; 30:3

People v. Centano, 76 N.Y.2d 837, 560 N.Y.S.2d 121, 559 N.E.2d 1280 (1990)—§ 27:26

People v. Centeno, 168 Misc. 2d 172, 637 N.Y.S.2d 254 (Sup 1995)—§§ 26:4; 26:12; 26:15; 26:22; 26:30

People v. Centerbar, 80 A.D.3d 1008, 914 N.Y.S.2d 784 (3d Dep't 2011)—§§ 27:21; 38:34; 38:36; 44:15

People v. Cerilli, 80 N.Y.2d 1016, 592 N.Y.S.2d 660, 607 N.E.2d 807 (1992)—§ 46:53

People v. Chaffee, 183 A.D.2d 208, 590 N.Y.S.2d 625 (4th Dep't 1992)—§§ 1:14; 5:5

People v. Chahine, 150 Misc. 2d 242, 568 N.Y.S.2d 526 (N.Y. City Crim. Ct. 1991)—§ 20:36

People v. Chamberlain, 221 A.D.2d 869, 634 N.Y.S.2d 249 (3d Dep't 1995)—§§ 9:10; 16:42

People v. Chambers, 20 A.D.3d 928, 798 N.Y.S.2d 833 (4th Dep't 2005)—§ 43:26

People v. Chambers, 257 A.D.2d 418, 683 N.Y.S.2d 238 (1st Dep't 1999)—§§ 12:24; 23:47

People v. Chambers, 184 A.D.2d 716, 585 N.Y.S.2d 84 (2d Dep't 1992)—§ 22:9

People v. Chaney, 253 A.D.2d 562, 686 N.Y.S.2d 871 (3d Dep't 1998)—§§ 1:36; 26:34

People v. Chann, 221 A.D.2d 155, 633 N.Y.S.2d 150 (1st Dep't 1995)—§ 1:25

People v. Chapman, 177 Misc. 2d 551, 679 N.Y.S.2d 496 (App. Term 1998)—§ 53:68

People v. Chapple, 38 N.Y.2d 112, 378 N.Y.S.2d 682, 341 N.E.2d 243 (1975)—§ 27:38

People v. Charles, 180 A.D.2d 868, 580 N.Y.S.2d 99 (3d Dep't 1992)—§ 53:15

People v. Charles, 78 N.Y.2d 1044, 576 N.Y.S.2d 81, 581 N.E.2d 1336 (1991)—§§ 23:23; 26:32

People v. Charles, 61 N.Y.2d 321, 473 N.Y.S.2d 941, 462 N.E.2d 118 (1984)—§ 23:18

People v. Chase, 186 Misc. 2d 487, 720 N.Y.S.2d 707 (App. Term 2000)—§ 12:22

People v. Chase, 85 N.Y.2d 493, 626 N.Y.S.2d 721, 650 N.E.2d 379 (1995)—§§ 26:7; 26:11; 26:19; 27:2

People v. Chavis, 91 N.Y.2d 500, 673 N.Y.S.2d 29, 695 N.E.2d 1110 (1998)—§§ 53:43; 53:62; 53:72; 53:73; 53:77

People v. Chennault, 20 N.Y.2d 518, 285 N.Y.S.2d 289, 232 N.E.2d 324 (1967)—§ 25:1

People v. Cheperuk, 64 Misc. 2d 498, 315 N.Y.S.2d 203 (County Ct. 1970)—§ 10:1

People v. Chess, 149 Misc. 2d 430, 565 N.Y.S.2d 416 (J. Ct. 1991)—§§ 17:14; 20:41; 20:50

People v. Chestnut, 43 A.D.2d 260, 351 N.Y.S.2d 26 (3d Dep't 1974)—§ 10:33

People v. Chilton, 69 N.Y.2d 928, 516 N.Y.S.2d 633, 509 N.E.2d 327 (1987)—§ 1:14

People v. Chism, 194 A.D.2d 351, 598 N.Y.S.2d 481 (1st Dep't 1993)—§ 1:2

People v. Chittaranjans, 185 Misc. 2d 871, 714 N.Y.S.2d 650 (Dist. Ct. 2000)—§§ 17:14; 17:15

People v. Christensen, 77 A.D.3d 174, 906 N.Y.S.2d 301 (2d Dep't 2010)—§§ 19:23; 53:37

People v. Christopher S., 126 Misc. 2d 594, 483 N.Y.S.2d 609 (N.Y.

People v. Cohen, 131 Misc. 2d 898, 502 N.Y.S.2d 123 (N.Y. City Ct. 1986)—§§ 16:23; 17:14; 20:41; 20:50; 20:59; 20:62

People v. Coker, 121 A.D.3d 1305, 995 N.Y.S.2d 288 (3d Dep't 2014)—§§ 11:94; 26:35

People v. Colavito, 87 N.Y.2d 423, 639 N.Y.S.2d 996, 663 N.E.2d 308 (1996)—§§ 20:1; 20:50; 20:55

People v. Colburn, 48 Misc. 3d 971, 8 N.Y.S.3d 898 (J. Ct. 2015)— § 17:14

People v. Coldiron, 79 Misc. 2d 338, 360 N.Y.S.2d 788 (App. Term 1974)—§ 16:19

People v. Coldiron, 77 Misc. 2d 102, 355 N.Y.S.2d 518 (Spec. Sess. 1974)—§ 16:19

People v. Cole, 24 A.D.3d 1021, 807 N.Y.S.2d 166 (3d Dep't 2005)—§ 26:25

People v. Cole, 178 Misc. 2d 166, 681 N.Y.S.2d 447 (J. Ct. 1998)—§ 41:78

People v. Cole, 187 A.D.2d 873, 590 N.Y.S.2d 542 (3d Dep't 1992)—§ 1:36

People v. Cole, 73 N.Y.2d 957, 540 N.Y.S.2d 984, 538 N.E.2d 336 (1989)—§§ 53:75; 53:91

People v. Cole, 112 A.D.2d 623, 492 N.Y.S.2d 486 (3d Dep't 1985)—§ 38:34

People v. Cole, 90 A.D.2d 27, 457 N.Y.S.2d 589 (3d Dep't 1982)—§§ 20:52; 20:71; 20:94; 53:100

People v. Coleman, 12 Misc. 3d 712, 819 N.Y.S.2d 407 (Sup 2006)—§ 26:14

People v. Coleman, 199 A.D.2d 330, 605 N.Y.S.2d 105 (2d Dep't 1993)—§ 25:15

People v. Coleman, 138 A.D.2d 963, 526 N.Y.S.2d 296 (4th Dep't 1988)—§§ 23:47; 46:40

People v. Collins, 288 A.D.2d 860, 732 N.Y.S.2d 188 (4th Dep't 2001)—§ 20:25

People v. Collins, 82 N.Y.2d 177, 604 N.Y.S.2d 11, 624 N.E.2d 139 (1993)—§§ 53:51; 53:53; 53:77; 53:94

People v. Collins, 92 A.D.2d 740, 461 N.Y.S.2d 90 (4th Dep't 1983)—§ 11:23

People v. Collins, 70 A.D.2d 986, 417 N.Y.S.2d 819 (3d Dep't 1979)—§§ 2:3; 2:10; 3:2; 11:94

People v. Collura, 160 Misc. 2d 831, 610 N.Y.S.2d 1018 (N.Y. City Crim. Ct. 1994)—§§ 5:3; 5:4

People v. Colombo, 31 N.Y.2d 947, 341 N.Y.S.2d 97, 293 N.E.2d 247 (1972)—§ 23:53

People v. Colon, 180 A.D.2d 876, 580 N.Y.S.2d 95 (3d Dep't 1992)—§§ 24:15; 24:16; 42:9

People v. Colon, 138 A.D.2d 392, 525 N.Y.S.2d 675 (2d Dep't 1988)—§ 53:40

People v. Colon, 110 Misc. 2d 917, 443 N.Y.S.2d 305 (N.Y. City Crim. Ct. 1981)—§ 53:71

People v. Coludro, 166 Misc. 2d 662, 634 N.Y.S.2d 964 (N.Y. City Crim. Ct. 1995)—§§ 24:18; 31:10; 41:23; 41:33; 41:91

People v. Colwell, 65 N.Y.2d 883, 493 N.Y.S.2d 298, 482 N.E.2d 1214 (1985)—§ 27:46

People v. Combest, 4 N.Y.3d 341, 795 N.Y.S.2d 481, 828 N.E.2d 583, 33 Media L. Rep. (BNA) 1666 (2005)—§§ 20:11; 20:12; 26:21; 41:84

People v. Commack, 194 A.D.2d 619, 599 N.Y.S.2d 56 (2d Dep't 1993)—§ 53:53

People v. Compton, 157 A.D.2d 903, 550 N.Y.S.2d 148 (3d Dep't 1990)—§ 19:14

People v. Conceicao, 26 N.Y.3d 375, 23 N.Y.S.3d 124, 44 N.E.3d 199 (2015)—§ 46:54

People v. Condarco, 166 Misc. 2d 470, 633 N.Y.S.2d 930 (N.Y. City Crim. Ct. 1995)—§§ 11:80; 45:22

People v. Corley, 124 A.D.2d 390, 507 N.Y.S.2d 491 (3d Dep't 1986)—§§ 11:10; 20:40; 20:49; 20:93; 37:9

People v. Cornell, 16 N.Y.3d 801, 921 N.Y.S.2d 641, 946 N.E.2d 740 (2011)—§ 11:87

People v. Coronado, 139 A.D.3d 452, 30 N.Y.S.3d 628 (1st Dep't 2016)—§ 1:7

People v. Correa, 168 Misc. 2d 309, 643 N.Y.S.2d 310 (N.Y. City Crim. Ct. 1996)—§ 45:10

People v. Correa, 77 N.Y.2d 930, 569 N.Y.S.2d 601, 572 N.E.2d 42 (1991)—§§ 53:61; 53:67

People v. Correia, 140 Misc. 2d 813, 531 N.Y.S.2d 998 (J. Ct. 1988)—§ 20:41

People v. Cortes, 80 N.Y.2d 201, 590 N.Y.S.2d 9, 604 N.E.2d 71 (1992)—§§ 53:26; 53:56; 53:61; 53:62; 53:67; 53:71; 53:78; 53:79; 53:81; 53:83; 53:94

People v. Cortese, 136 A.D.2d 724, 524 N.Y.S.2d 62 (2d Dep't 1988)—§ 22:7

People v. Cortez, 149 Misc. 2d 886, 564 N.Y.S.2d 963 (N.Y. City Civ. Ct. 1990)—§§ 20:5; 20:57; 28:17

People v. Cosper, 248 A.D.2d 397, 669 N.Y.S.2d 637 (2d Dep't 1998)—§ 47:8

People v. Cote, 265 A.D.2d 681, 697 N.Y.S.2d 184 (3d Dep't 1999)—§§ 19:18; 46:41

People v. Couluris, 148 Misc. 2d 984, 562 N.Y.S.2d 345 (Dist. Ct. 1990)—§§ 4:2; 4:5

People v. Cousar, 226 A.D.2d 740, 641 N.Y.S.2d 695 (2d Dep't 1996)—§§ 41:24; 41:33

People v. Cousart, 58 N.Y.2d 62, 458 N.Y.S.2d 507, 444 N.E.2d 971 (1982)—§§ 53:41; 53:70

People v. Coutard, 115 Misc. 2d 630, 454 N.Y.S.2d 639 (Dist. Ct. 1982)—§§ 17:17; 37:7

People v. Covell, 276 A.D.2d 824,

714 N.Y.S.2d 370 (3d Dep't 2000)—§ 46:44

People v. Craft, 28 N.Y.2d 274, 321 N.Y.S.2d 566, 270 N.E.2d 297 (1971)—§§ 7:5; 11:57; 27:9; 41:77

People v. Crafton, 159 A.D.2d 271, 552 N.Y.S.2d 273 (1st Dep't 1990)—§ 46:39

People v. Cragg, 71 N.Y.2d 926, 528 N.Y.S.2d 807, 524 N.E.2d 128 (1988)—§§ 11:46; 41:12; 41:26; 41:88

People v. Craig, 262 A.D.2d 1074, 692 N.Y.S.2d 257 (4th Dep't 1999)—§ 38:34

People v. Crandall, 39 A.D.3d 1077, 832 N.Y.S.2d 828 (3d Dep't 2007)—§§ 11:42; 46:52

People v. Crandall, 287 A.D.2d 881, 731 N.Y.S.2d 553 (3d Dep't 2001)—§ 11:94

People v. Crandall, 255 A.D.2d 617, 681 N.Y.S.2d 99 (3d Dep't 1998)—§ 10:2

People v. Crandall, 228 A.D.2d 794, 644 N.Y.S.2d 817 (3d Dep't 1996)—§§ 20:40; 20:93; 30:2

People v. Crandall, 199 A.D.2d 867, 606 N.Y.S.2d 357 (3d Dep't 1993)—§§ 11:65; 13:3; 13:51

People v. Crandall, 69 N.Y.2d 459, 515 N.Y.S.2d 745, 508 N.E.2d 657 (1987)—§ 1:39

People v. Crandall, 108 A.D.2d 413, 489 N.Y.S.2d 614 (3d Dep't 1985)—§§ 40:12; 40:16

People v. Crane, 129 A.D.3d 741, 8 N.Y.S.3d 924 (2d Dep't 2015)—§§ 23:47; 46:40

People v. Cratsley, 86 N.Y.2d 81, 629 N.Y.S.2d 992, 653 N.E.2d 1162 (1995)—§§ 43:3; 43:4

People v. Crider, 301 A.D.2d 612, 756 N.Y.S.2d 223 (2d Dep't 2003)—§§ 20:11; 26:21; 41:84

People v. Crisp, 268 A.D.2d 247, 700 N.Y.S.2d 693 (1st Dep't 2000)—§ 24:9

446 N.Y.S.2d 658 (4th Dep't 1981)—§§ 41:19; 41:88

People v. Daniels, 97 A.D.3d 845, 948 N.Y.S.2d 431 (3d Dep't 2012)—§ 12:4

People v. Daniels, 254 A.D.2d 54, 681 N.Y.S.2d 483 (1st Dep't 1998)—§ 20:12

People v. Daniger, 227 A.D.2d 846, 642 N.Y.S.2d 732 (3d Dep't 1996)—§ 11:56

People v. Darling, 50 A.D.2d 1038, 377 N.Y.S.2d 718 (3d Dep't 1975)—§ 11:42

People v. Darrisaw, 66 A.D.3d 1427, 886 N.Y.S.2d 315 (4th Dep't 2009)—§§ 13:4; 43:25

People v. Davenport, 173 A.D.2d 633, 570 N.Y.S.2d 219 (2d Dep't 1991)—§ 22:7

People v. Davidson, 98 N.Y.2d 738, 751 N.Y.S.2d 161, 780 N.E.2d 972 (2002)—§§ 24:4; 24:12

People v. David W, 83 A.D.2d 690, 442 N.Y.S.2d 278 (3d Dep't 1981)—§ 2:3

People v. Davila, 27 Misc. 3d 921, 901 N.Y.S.2d 787 (Sup 2010)—§ 1:47

People v. Davis, 112 A.D.3d 959, 977 N.Y.S.2d 87 (2d Dep't 2013)—§ 12:20

People v. Davis, 58 A.D.3d 896, 870 N.Y.S.2d 602 (3d Dep't 2009)—§ 1:14

People v. Davis, 23 Misc. 3d 30, 879 N.Y.S.2d 268 (App. Term 2009)—§ 10:28

People v. Davis, 8 Misc. 3d 158, 797 N.Y.S.2d 258 (Sup 2005)—§§ 24:18; 41:27; 41:29; 41:33

People v. Davis, 163 Misc. 2d 947, 623 N.Y.S.2d 92 (N.Y. City Ct. 1995)—§ 26:8

People v. Davis, 81 N.Y.2d 281, 598 N.Y.S.2d 156, 614 N.E.2d 719 (1993)—§§ 21:12; 21:15

People v. Davis, 169 A.D.2d 379, 564 N.Y.S.2d 320 (1st Dep't 1991)—§ 1:36

People v. Davis, 72 N.Y.2d 32, 530 N.Y.S.2d 529, 526 N.E.2d 20 (1988)—§§ 23:18; 23:19

People v. Davis, 61 N.Y.2d 202, 473 N.Y.S.2d 146, 461 N.E.2d 283 (1984)—§ 25:8

People v. Davis, 95 A.D.2d 837, 463 N.Y.S.2d 876 (2d Dep't 1983)—§ 43:9

People v. Davis, 55 N.Y.2d 731, 447 N.Y.S.2d 149, 431 N.E.2d 634 (1981)—§ 27:32

People v. Davis, 41 N.Y.2d 678, 394 N.Y.S.2d 865, 363 N.E.2d 572 (1977)—§ 20:61

People v. Dawson, 301 A.D.2d 659, 753 N.Y.S.2d 879 (2d Dep't 2003)—§ 46:53

People v. Dawson, 50 N.Y.2d 311, 428 N.Y.S.2d 914, 406 N.E.2d 771, 20 A.L.R.4th 232 (1980)—§ 25:8

People v. Day, 150 A.D.2d 595, 541 N.Y.S.2d 463 (2d Dep't 1989)—§ 21:16

People v. Day, 139 Misc. 2d 222, 526 N.Y.S.2d 736 (Sup 1988)—§ 53:25

People v. Deacy, 140 Misc. 2d 232, 530 N.Y.S.2d 753 (Dist. Ct. 1988)—§ 1:14

People v. Dean, 74 N.Y.2d 643, 542 N.Y.S.2d 512, 540 N.E.2d 707 (1989)—§§ 11:51; 16:27; 17:13; 24:10; 24:12

People v. Dean, 80 A.D.2d 695, 436 N.Y.S.2d 455 (3d Dep't 1981)—§ 11:90

People v. Dean, 45 N.Y.2d 651, 412 N.Y.S.2d 353, 384 N.E.2d 1277 (1978)—§§ 53:8; 53:19; 53:75; 53:92

People v. Dean, 56 A.D.2d 242, 392 N.Y.S.2d 134 (4th Dep't 1977)—§ 23:15

People v. DeBlase, 142 A.D.2d 926, 530 N.Y.S.2d 352 (4th Dep't 1988)—§ 27:6

People v. De Bour, 40 N.Y.2d 210, 386 N.Y.S.2d 375, 352 N.E.2d

People v. Duquette, 100 A.D.3d 1105, 952 N.Y.S.2d 909 (3d Dep't 2012)—§ 13:34

People v. Durden, 211 A.D.2d 568, 621 N.Y.S.2d 611 (1st Dep't 1995)—§ 25:8

People v. Dusing, 5 N.Y.2d 126, 181 N.Y.S.2d 493, 155 N.E.2d 393 (1959)—§ 20:41

People v. Dymond, 158 Misc. 2d 677, 601 N.Y.S.2d 1001 (County Ct. 1993)—§§ 2:4; 2:5

People v. Earley, 121 A.D.3d 1192, 994 N.Y.S.2d 443 (3d Dep't 2014)—§§ 12:26; 40:7

People v. Eason, 283 A.D.2d 655, 725 N.Y.S.2d 84 (2d Dep't 2001)—§ 13:39

People v. Eastco Bldg. Services, 23 Misc. 3d 864, 873 N.Y.S.2d 874 (Sup 2009)—§ 51:2

People v. Eastman, 181 A.D.2d 1050, 582 N.Y.S.2d 586 (4th Dep't 1992)—§ 9:11

People v. Easton, 307 N.Y. 336, 121 N.E.2d 357 (1954)—§ 16:21

People v. Eberhardt, 277 A.D.2d 1044, 715 N.Y.S.2d 349 (4th Dep't 2000)—§ 46:26

People v. Ebner, 195 A.D.2d 1006, 600 N.Y.S.2d 569 (4th Dep't 1993)—§§ 11:65; 24:17; 38:4; 38:32

People v. Eccleston, 161 A.D.2d 1184, 556 N.Y.S.2d 182 (4th Dep't 1990)—§ 12:20

People v. Echevarria, 6 N.Y.3d 89, 809 N.Y.S.2d 509, 843 N.E.2d 149 (2005)—§§ 23:22; 23:34

People v. Eckert, 2 N.Y.2d 126, 157 N.Y.S.2d 551, 138 N.E.2d 794 (1956)—§ 11:94

People v. Edenholm, 9 A.D.3d 892, 779 N.Y.S.2d 688 (4th Dep't 2004)—§ 13:14

People v. Edmonds, 157 Misc. 2d 966, 599 N.Y.S.2d 441 (County Ct. 1993)—§ 1:4

People v. Edwards, 95 N.Y.2d 486, 719 N.Y.S.2d 202, 741 N.E.2d 876 (2000)—§§ 1:17; 5:9

People v. Edwards, 215 A.D.2d 498, 626 N.Y.S.2d 825 (2d Dep't 1995)—§ 53:98

People v. Edwards, 158 Misc. 2d 615, 601 N.Y.S.2d 539 (N.Y. City Ct. 1993)—§ 2:4

People v. Elam, 179 A.D.2d 229, 584 N.Y.S.2d 780 (1st Dep't 1992)—§ 1:14

People v. Eleby, 137 A.D.2d 708, 525 N.Y.S.2d 51 (2d Dep't 1988)—§ 20:21

People v. Elithorpe, 50 Misc. 3d 1077, 21 N.Y.S.3d 848 (County Ct. 2015)—§ 11:98

People v. Ellis, 53 Misc. 3d 225, 34 N.Y.S.3d 880 (N.Y. City Ct. 2016)—§ 17:14

People v. Ellis, 27 A.D.3d 236, 809 N.Y.S.2d 906 (1st Dep't 2006)—§ 46:53

People v. Ellis, 190 Misc. 2d 98, 737 N.Y.S.2d 232 (County Ct. 2001)—§§ 24:17; 27:21; 38:4; 38:34

People v. Ellis, 184 A.D.2d 307, 584 N.Y.S.2d 569 (1st Dep't 1992)—§ 52:4

People v. Ellis, 62 N.Y.2d 393, 477 N.Y.S.2d 106, 465 N.E.2d 826 (1984)—§§ 1:26; 1:27

People v. Ellis, 58 N.Y.2d 748, 459 N.Y.S.2d 25, 445 N.E.2d 201 (1982)—§ 27:28

People v. Elpenord, 24 A.D.3d 465, 806 N.Y.S.2d 675 (2d Dep't 2005)—§§ 1:44; 5:4

People v. Elwell, 50 N.Y.2d 231, 428 N.Y.S.2d 655, 406 N.E.2d 471 (1980)—§ 1:16

People v. Elysee, 12 N.Y.3d 100, 876 N.Y.S.2d 677, 904 N.E.2d 813 (2009)—§§ 11:73; 40:14; 44:9; 44:12

People v. Elysee, 49 A.D.3d 33, 847 N.Y.S.2d 654 (2d Dep't 2007)—§§ 44:9; 44:12

People v. Engeman, 135 Misc. 2d 228, 514 N.Y.S.2d 588 (N.Y. City Ct. 1987)—§ 16:22

People v. Feerick, 93 N.Y.2d 433, 692 N.Y.S.2d 638, 714 N.E.2d 851 (1999)—§§ 20:82; 28:11

People v. Fehr, 303 A.D.2d 1039, 757 N.Y.S.2d 205 (4th Dep't 2003)—§ 46:25

People v. Feine, 227 A.D.2d 901, 643 N.Y.S.2d 281 (4th Dep't 1996)—§ 41:81

People v. Feingold, 106 A.D.2d 583, 482 N.Y.S.2d 857 (2d Dep't 1984)—§§ 1:35; 41:35

People v. Feldman, 299 N.Y. 153, 85 N.E.2d 913 (1949)—§ 43:23

People v. Feldmann, 110 A.D.2d 906, 488 N.Y.S.2d 455 (2d Dep't 1985)—§§ 44:15; 44:16

People v. Felicia, 52 Misc. 3d 212, 27 N.Y.S.3d 841 (N.Y. City Crim. Ct. 2016)—§§ 10:2; 10:27

People v. Feliciano, 1 A.D.3d 163, 766 N.Y.S.2d 561 (1st Dep't 2003)—§ 46:53

People v. Feliciano, 139 Misc. 2d 247, 527 N.Y.S.2d 964 (N.Y. City Crim. Ct. 1988)—§ 26:15

People v. Felipe, 79 A.D.3d 1454, 913 N.Y.S.2d 398 (3d Dep't 2010)—§ 12:4

People v. Fenti, 106 A.D.2d 912, 483 N.Y.S.2d 495 (4th Dep't 1984)—§ 22:11

People v. Ferguson, 162 Misc. 2d 187, 616 N.Y.S.2d 440 (J. Ct. 1994)—§ 23:60

People v. Ferguson, 67 N.Y.2d 383, 502 N.Y.S.2d 972, 494 N.E.2d 77 (1986)—§§ 23:17; 23:29; 23:33

People v. Fernandez, 20 N.Y.3d 44, 956 N.Y.S.2d 443, 980 N.E.2d 491 (2012)—§§ 13:46; 16:4; 16:18

People v. Ferrara, 158 Misc. 2d 671, 602 N.Y.S.2d 86 (N.Y. City Crim. Ct. 1993)—§§ 24:18; 27:3; 27:29; 41:27; 41:33; 41:75

People v. Ferro, 22 Misc. 3d 7, 871 N.Y.S.2d 814 (App. Term 2008)—§ 16:18

People v. Ferro, 63 N.Y.2d 316, 482 N.Y.S.2d 237, 472 N.E.2d 13 (1984)—§§ 27:3; 27:27

People v. Fevziekinici, 191 Misc. 2d 510, 743 N.Y.S.2d 651 (Sup 2002)—§ 24:9

People v. Fiacco, 146 Misc. 2d 330, 549 N.Y.S.2d 901 (N.Y. City Ct. 1989)—§§ 16:40; 43:19; 45:17; 53:16; 53:36

People v. Fields, 258 A.D.2d 809, 687 N.Y.S.2d 184 (3d Dep't 1999)—§§ 20:11; 20:12; 20:57; 26:21; 26:38; 41:84

People v. Figueroa, 17 A.D.3d 1130, 794 N.Y.S.2d 262 (4th Dep't 2005)—§§ 46:25; 47:4

People v. Figueroa, 6 A.D.3d 720, 776 N.Y.S.2d 574 (2d Dep't 2004)—§ 13:54

People v. Figueroa, 164 Misc. 2d 814, 625 N.Y.S.2d 839 (N.Y. City Crim. Ct. 1995)—§ 16:34

People v. Finch, 19 Misc. 3d 840, 854 N.Y.S.2d 885 (Dist. Ct. 2008)—§ 16:26

People v. Finnegan, 85 N.Y.2d 53, 623 N.Y.S.2d 546, 647 N.E.2d 758 (1995)—§§ 11:60; 11:62; 30:1; 30:2; 30:3; 31:11; 38:27

People v. Fiorello, 140 A.D.2d 708, 529 N.Y.S.2d 27 (2d Dep't 1988)—§ 27:8

People v. Firth, 3 N.Y.2d 472, 168 N.Y.S.2d 949, 146 N.E.2d 682 (1957)—§ 20:98

People v. Fisher, 70 A.D.3d 114, 890 N.Y.S.2d 477 (1st Dep't 2009)—§ 19:13

People v. Fisher, 20 Misc. 3d 1136(A), 867 N.Y.S.2d 377 (J. Ct. 2008)—§ 1:14

People v. Fisher, 9 Misc. 3d 1121(A), 862 N.Y.S.2d 809 (N.Y. City Ct. 2005)—§ 11:94

People v. Fisher, 167 Misc. 2d 850, 635 N.Y.S.2d 1002 (N.Y. City Crim. Ct. 1995)—§§ 16:40; 53:15; 53:16; 53:36

People v. Fisher, 165 Misc. 2d 650,

People v. Freeland, 68 N.Y.2d 699, 506 N.Y.S.2d 306, 497 N.E.2d 673 (1986)—§§ 7:8; 11:47; 11:49; 29:3; 42:3

People v. Freeman, 46 A.D.3d 1375, 848 N.Y.S.2d 800 (4th Dep't 2007)—§§ 11:39; 40:7

People v. Freytes, 48 N.Y.2d 645, 421 N.Y.S.2d 199, 396 N.E.2d 481 (1979)—§ 53:15

People v. Frieary, 144 A.D.2d 382, 533 N.Y.S.2d 935 (2d Dep't 1988)—§ 9:6

People v. Friscia, 51 N.Y.2d 845, 433 N.Y.S.2d 754, 413 N.E.2d 1168 (1980)—§ 53:96

People v. Fuller, 96 N.Y.2d 881, 730 N.Y.S.2d 773, 756 N.E.2d 61 (2001)—§§ 23:22; 23:42

People v. Fulton, 238 A.D.2d 439, 657 N.Y.S.2d 348 (2d Dep't 1997)—§§ 19:18; 46:41

People v. Fulton, 162 Misc. 2d 360, 616 N.Y.S.2d 881 (Sup 1994)—§ 24:9

People v. Furber, 169 A.D.2d 841, 565 N.Y.S.2d 210 (2d Dep't 1991)—§ 13:35

People v. Furnia, 223 A.D.2d 887, 636 N.Y.S.2d 488 (3d Dep't 1996)—§ 46:53

People v. Furst, 1 Misc. 3d 654, 765 N.Y.S.2d 753 (N.Y. City Ct. 2003)—§§ 17:8; 17:10; 17:11; 17:13

People v. Fyffe, 249 A.D.2d 938, 672 N.Y.S.2d 552 (4th Dep't 1998)—§ 20:83

People v. Fysekis, 164 Misc. 2d 627, 625 N.Y.S.2d 861 (N.Y. City Crim. Ct. 1995)—§ 16:40

People v. G., 158 Misc. 2d 893, 602 N.Y.S.2d 512 (Sup 1993)—§ 26:14

People v. Gabbay, 175 Misc. 2d 421, 670 N.Y.S.2d 962 (App. Term 1997)—§§ 16:19; 16:39; 16:40

People v. Gabriel, 164 Misc. 2d 473, 625 N.Y.S.2d 433 (N.Y. City Crim. Ct. 1995)—§ 13:45

People v. Gaffney, 299 A.D.2d 922, 750 N.Y.S.2d 383 (4th Dep't 2002)—§ 38:34

People v. Gagne, 127 Misc. 2d 327, 485 N.Y.S.2d 938 (County Ct. 1985)—§ 11:14

People v. Galak, 80 N.Y.2d 715, 594 N.Y.S.2d 689, 610 N.E.2d 362 (1993)—§§ 1:44; 5:4

People v. Gallagher, 69 N.Y.2d 525, 516 N.Y.S.2d 174, 508 N.E.2d 909 (1987)—§ 12:19

People v. Gallagher, 133 Misc. 2d 717, 507 N.Y.S.2d 950 (Dist. Ct. 1986)—§§ 29:8; 32:1

People v. Gallagher, 132 Misc. 2d 195, 503 N.Y.S.2d 500 (Dist. Ct. 1986)—§ 29:8

People v. Gallardo, 173 A.D.2d 636, 570 N.Y.S.2d 222 (2d Dep't 1991)—§ 28:5

People v. Gallup, 302 A.D.2d 681, 755 N.Y.S.2d 498 (3d Dep't 2003)—§§ 8:4; 20:17; 41:75

People v. Gammon, 19 N.Y.3d 893, 950 N.Y.S.2d 65, 973 N.E.2d 160 (2012)—§ 23:40

People v. Garafolo, 44 A.D.2d 86, 353 N.Y.S.2d 500 (2d Dep't 1974)—§§ 1:35; 41:35

People v. Garcia-Cepero, 22 Misc. 3d 490, 874 N.Y.S.2d 689 (Sup 2008)—§§ 6:19; 41:24; 41:29

People v. Garcia, 20 N.Y.3d 317, 959 N.Y.S.2d 464, 983 N.E.2d 259 (2012)—§§ 1:8; 1:28; 1:29

People v. Garlock, 29 Misc. 3d 1223(A), 920 N.Y.S.2d 243 (J. Ct. 2010)—§§ 1:14; 1:15

People v. Garneau, 120 A.D.2d 112, 507 N.Y.S.2d 931 (4th Dep't 1986)—§§ 35:2; 43:20

People v. Garofolo, 46 N.Y.2d 592, 415 N.Y.S.2d 810, 389 N.E.2d 123, 18 A.L.R.4th 658 (1979)—§§ 27:28; 27:50

People v. Garriga, 189 A.D.2d 236, 596 N.Y.S.2d 25 (1st Dep't 1993)—§ 1:36

People v. Gary, 31 N.Y.2d 68, 334

People v. Goldstein, 12 N.Y.3d 295, 879 N.Y.S.2d 814, 907 N.E.2d 692 (2009)—§§ 13:35; 23:47; 46:40

People v. Goldwire, 301 A.D.2d 677, 752 N.Y.S.2d 906 (3d Dep't 2003)—§ 47:4

People v. Golley, 195 A.D.2d 713, 601 N.Y.S.2d 871 (3d Dep't 1993)—§ 11:63

People v. Gomez-Kadawid, 66 A.D.3d 1124, 888 N.Y.S.2d 621 (3d Dep't 2009)—§ 20:91

People v. Gomez, 13 N.Y.3d 6, 884 N.Y.S.2d 339, 912 N.E.2d 555 (2009)—§§ 1:44; 5:4

People v. Gonzales, 75 N.Y.2d 938, 555 N.Y.S.2d 681, 554 N.E.2d 1269 (1990)—§ 27:28

People v. Gonzalez, 90 A.D.3d 1668, 935 N.Y.S.2d 826 (4th Dep't 2011)—§ 10:30

People v. Gonzalez, 99 N.Y.2d 76, 751 N.Y.S.2d 830, 781 N.E.2d 894 (2002)—§§ 23:2; 23:42; 23:43

People v. Gonzalez, 266 A.D.2d 562, 700 N.Y.S.2d 35 (2d Dep't 1999)—§ 53:53

People v. Gonzalez, 239 A.D.2d 931, 659 N.Y.S.2d 591 (4th Dep't 1997)—§§ 44:7; 44:15

People v. Gonzalez, 168 Misc. 2d 136, 645 N.Y.S.2d 978 (App. Term 1996)—§§ 16:40; 53:36; 53:37

People v. Gonzalez, 88 N.Y.2d 289, 644 N.Y.S.2d 673, 667 N.E.2d 323 (1996)—§ 4:8

People v. Gonzalez, 80 N.Y.2d 883, 587 N.Y.S.2d 607, 600 N.E.2d 238 (1992)—§ 1:33

People v. Gonzalez, 61 N.Y.2d 633, 471 N.Y.S.2d 847, 459 N.E.2d 1285 (1983)—§ 23:20

People v. Gonzalez, 55 N.Y.2d 720, 447 N.Y.S.2d 145, 431 N.E.2d 630 (1981)—§ 27:41

People v. Gonzalez, 71 A.D.2d 775, 419 N.Y.S.2d 322 (3d Dep't 1979)—§§ 1:36; 26:34

People v. Gonzalez, 39 N.Y.2d 122, 383 N.Y.S.2d 215, 347 N.E.2d 575 (1976)—§ 4:7

People v. Goode, 87 N.Y.2d 1045, 643 N.Y.S.2d 477, 666 N.E.2d 182 (1996)—§§ 53:93; 53:97

People v. Goodell, 79 N.Y.2d 869, 581 N.Y.S.2d 157, 589 N.E.2d 380 (1992)—§§ 11:61; 38:30

People v. Goodell, 164 A.D.2d 321, 565 N.Y.S.2d 929 (4th Dep't 1990)—§§ 38:32; 40:14

People v. Goodman, 69 N.Y.2d 32, 511 N.Y.S.2d 565, 503 N.E.2d 996 (1986)—§§ 23:5; 23:58

People v. Goodman, 41 N.Y.2d 888, 393 N.Y.S.2d 985, 362 N.E.2d 615 (1977)—§ 53:62

People v. Goodson, 57 N.Y.2d 828, 455 N.Y.S.2d 757, 442 N.E.2d 54 (1982)—§§ 26:38; 26:39

People v. Gordon, 125 A.D.2d 257, 509 N.Y.S.2d 543 (1st Dep't 1986)—§ 53:39

People v. Goss, 87 N.Y.2d 792, 642 N.Y.S.2d 607, 665 N.E.2d 177 (1996)—§§ 53:76; 53:81

People v. Gourgue, 239 A.D.2d 357, 657 N.Y.S.2d 737 (2d Dep't 1997)—§ 28:4

People v. Gower, 42 N.Y.2d 117, 397 N.Y.S.2d 368, 366 N.E.2d 69 (1977)—§§ 11:10; 11:47; 11:49; 29:3; 35:2; 37:9; 42:3; 42:4; 43:15

People v. Grady, 272 A.D.2d 952, 708 N.Y.S.2d 765 (4th Dep't 2000)—§ 1:3

People v. Grafton, 73 N.Y.2d 779, 536 N.Y.S.2d 738, 533 N.E.2d 668 (1988)—§ 53:54

People v. Graham, 39 Misc. 3d 35, 965 N.Y.S.2d 271 (App. Term 2013)—§ 53:37

People v. Graham, 54 A.D.3d 1056, 865 N.Y.S.2d 259 (2d Dep't 2008)—§ 1:26

People v. Graham, 192 Misc. 2d 528, 748 N.Y.S.2d 203 (Sup 2002)—§ 1:4

People v. Hyde, 172 A.D.2d 305, 568 N.Y.S.2d 388 (1st Dep't 1991)—§§ 20:5; 28:18

People v. Hyndman, 194 Misc. 2d 335, 753 N.Y.S.2d 811 (County Ct. 2002)—§ 20:94

People v. Iannelli, 69 N.Y.2d 684, 512 N.Y.S.2d 16, 504 N.E.2d 383 (1986)—§ 24:12

People v. Iannone, 45 N.Y.2d 589, 412 N.Y.S.2d 110, 384 N.E.2d 656 (1978)—§§ 20:61; 23:18; 24:12

People v. Iannopollo, 131 Misc. 2d 15, 502 N.Y.S.2d 574 (County Ct. 1983)—§ 41:78

People v. Imbesi, 38 N.Y.2d 629, 381 N.Y.S.2d 862, 345 N.E.2d 333 (1976)—§ 53:15

People v. Ingham, 115 Misc. 2d 64, 453 N.Y.S.2d 325 (N.Y. City Ct. 1982)—§ 46:45

People v. Ingle, 36 N.Y.2d 413, 369 N.Y.S.2d 67, 330 N.E.2d 39 (1975)—§§ 1:5; 1:9; 1:14

People v. Ingraham, 274 A.D.2d 828, 711 N.Y.S.2d 863 (3d Dep't 2000)—§ 20:83

People v. Inserra, 4 N.Y.3d 30, 790 N.Y.S.2d 72, 823 N.E.2d 437 (2004)—§§ 16:25; 16:30

People v. Iqbal, 31 Misc. 3d 94, 926 N.Y.S.2d 256 (App. Term 2011)—§ 16:22

People v. Ireland, 175 A.D.2d 139, 572 N.Y.S.2d 29 (2d Dep't 1991)—§ 11:97

People v. Irizarry, 79 N.Y.2d 890, 581 N.Y.S.2d 649, 590 N.E.2d 234 (1992)—§ 1:2

People v. Isaac, 224 A.D.2d 993, 637 N.Y.S.2d 827 (4th Dep't 1996)—§§ 12:24; 23:47; 40:7

People v. Iwasiw, 167 Misc. 2d 1013, 641 N.Y.S.2d 521 (J. Ct. 1996)—§ 24:16

People v. Izquierdo, 292 A.D.2d 247, 739 N.Y.S.2d 78 (1st Dep't 2002)—§ 20:47

People v. Jackson, 32 Misc. 3d

139(A), 936 N.Y.S.2d 60 (App. Term 2011)—§ 10:27

People v. Jackson, 99 N.Y.2d 125, 752 N.Y.S.2d 271, 782 N.E.2d 67 (2002)—§§ 5:7; 5:8; 5:9

People v. Jackson, 271 A.D.2d 455, 707 N.Y.S.2d 128 (2d Dep't 2000)—§§ 20:5; 28:17

People v. Jackson, 202 A.D.2d 689, 609 N.Y.S.2d 320 (2d Dep't 1994)—§ 25:23

People v. Jackson, 154 Misc. 2d 718, 593 N.Y.S.2d 410 (Sup 1992)—§§ 21:5; 21:6

People v. Jackson, 172 A.D.2d 874, 568 N.Y.S.2d 177 (3d Dep't 1991)—§ 53:105

People v. Jackson, 78 N.Y.2d 900, 573 N.Y.S.2d 452, 577 N.E.2d 1044 (1991)—§ 28:18

People v. Jackson, 78 N.Y.2d 638, 578 N.Y.S.2d 483, 585 N.E.2d 795 (1991)—§§ 20:87; 28:2; 28:15

People v. Jackson, 124 A.D.2d 975, 509 N.Y.S.2d 230 (4th Dep't 1986)—§ 43:10

People v. Jacob, 161 Misc. 2d 768, 615 N.Y.S.2d 601 (Sup 1994)—§ 23:12

People v. Jacquin, 71 N.Y.2d 825, 527 N.Y.S.2d 728, 522 N.E.2d 1026 (1988)—§§ 6:18; 11:58; 19:12; 27:8

People v. Jaffarian, 9 Misc. 3d 455, 799 N.Y.S.2d 733 (J. Ct. 2005)—§ 44:19

People v. Jakobson, 119 A.D.3d 815, 990 N.Y.S.2d 88 (2d Dep't 2014)—§ 12:2

People v. James, 17 Misc. 3d 623, 842 N.Y.S.2d 859 (N.Y. City Crim. Ct. 2007)—§ 1:14

People v. James, 144 A.D.2d 717, 535 N.Y.S.2d 452 (3d Dep't 1988)—§ 47:3

People v. James, 4 N.Y.2d 482, 176 N.Y.S.2d 323, 151 N.E.2d 877 (1958)—§ 16:28

People v. Jamison, 170 Misc. 2d

City Crim. Ct. 1987)—§§ 7:5; 7:6; 7:11; 11:45; 24:13

People v. Johnson, 107 A.D.2d 763, 107 A.D.2d 1093, 484 N.Y.S.2d 129 (2d Dep't 1985)—§ 9:12

People v. Johnson, 66 N.Y.2d 398, 497 N.Y.S.2d 618, 488 N.E.2d 439 (1985)—§§ 1:17; 1:30; 1:31; 11:28

People v. Johnson, 48 N.Y.2d 565, 423 N.Y.S.2d 905, 399 N.E.2d 936 (1979)—§ 27:48

People v. Johnson, 38 N.Y.2d 271, 379 N.Y.S.2d 735, 342 N.E.2d 525 (1975)—§§ 53:8; 53:11; 53:15; 53:17; 53:38; 53:56; 53:77; 53:88

People v. Johnson, 27 N.Y.2d 119, 313 N.Y.S.2d 728, 261 N.E.2d 644 (1970)—§ 27:18

People v. Jones, 51 Misc. 3d 863, 27 N.Y.S.3d 830 (N.Y. City Crim. Ct. 2016)—§ 41:33

People v. Jones, 118 A.D.3d 1360, 988 N.Y.S.2d 316 (4th Dep't 2014)—§ 46:42

People v. Jones, 33 Misc. 3d 181, 927 N.Y.S.2d 586 (N.Y. City Crim. Ct. 2011)—§ 7:8

People v. Jones, 73 A.D.3d 662, 901 N.Y.S.2d 274 (1st Dep't 2010)—§ 1:36

People v. Jones, 9 N.Y.3d 259, 848 N.Y.S.2d 600, 878 N.E.2d 1016 (2007)—§§ 16:9; 16:30

People v. Jones, 10 Misc. 3d 413, 805 N.Y.S.2d 807 (County Ct. 2005)—§§ 7:1; 7:15

People v. Jones, 292 A.D.2d 792, 738 N.Y.S.2d 790 (4th Dep't 2002)—§ 26:20

People v. Jones, 95 N.Y.2d 721, 723 N.Y.S.2d 761, 746 N.E.2d 1053 (2001)—§§ 1:36; 26:33

People v. Jones, 177 A.D.2d 1000, 578 N.Y.S.2d 20 (4th Dep't 1991)—§ 9:4

People v. Jones, 169 A.D.2d 986, 565 N.Y.S.2d 262 (3d Dep't 1991)—§§ 25:22; 25:23

People v. Jones, 151 Misc. 2d 582, 582 N.Y.S.2d 325 (App. Term 1991)—§ 9:20

People v. Jones, 158 A.D.2d 911, 551 N.Y.S.2d 78 (4th Dep't 1990)—§ 11:97

People v. Jones, 70 N.Y.2d 547, 523 N.Y.S.2d 53, 517 N.E.2d 865 (1987)—§ 28:2

People v. Jones, 68 N.Y.2d 717, 506 N.Y.S.2d 315, 497 N.E.2d 682 (1986)—§§ 53:83; 53:86

People v. Jones, 125 Misc. 2d 91, 477 N.Y.S.2d 975 (Sup 1984)—§ 1:14

People v. Jones, 118 Misc. 2d 687, 461 N.Y.S.2d 962 (County Ct. 1983)—§§ 11:44; 29:1; 29:10; 32:1; 32:2; 42:2

People v. Jones, 47 N.Y.2d 528, 419 N.Y.S.2d 447, 393 N.E.2d 443 (1979)—§§ 27:3; 27:23

People v. Jones, 44 N.Y.2d 76, 404 N.Y.S.2d 85, 375 N.E.2d 41 (1978)—§ 21:18

People v. Jordan, 15 N.Y.3d 727, 905 N.Y.S.2d 797, 931 N.E.2d 1053 (2010)—§ 23:41

People v. Jordan, 62 N.Y.2d 825, 477 N.Y.S.2d 605, 466 N.E.2d 145 (1984)—§ 53:21

People v. Jorgensen, 26 N.Y.3d 85, 19 N.Y.S.3d 814, 41 N.E.3d 778 (2015)—§ 12:29

People v. Jornov, 65 A.D.3d 363, 881 N.Y.S.2d 776 (4th Dep't 2009)—§ 12:4

People v. Joseph, 75 A.D.3d 1080, 903 N.Y.S.2d 651 (4th Dep't 2010)—§§ 12:20; 38:37

People v. Joseph, 86 N.Y.2d 565, 635 N.Y.S.2d 123, 658 N.E.2d 996 (1995)—§§ 20:5; 28:7; 28:16

People v. Joyner, 46 A.D.3d 473, 848 N.Y.S.2d 146 (1st Dep't 2007)—§ 1:36

People v. J.T., 13 Misc. 3d 1212(A), 824 N.Y.S.2d 757 (N.Y. City Crim. Ct. 2006)—§ 13:47

People v. Judware, 252 A.D.2d 663,

People v. Kester, 130 Misc. 2d 37, 494 N.Y.S.2d 823 (J. Ct. 1985)—§ 29:9

People v. Kestler, 201 A.D.2d 955, 607 N.Y.S.2d 823 (4th Dep't 1994)—§§ 2:8; 11:34

People v. Ketcham, 93 N.Y.2d 416, 690 N.Y.S.2d 874, 712 N.E.2d 1238 (1999)—§§ 1:17; 1:34

People v. Kevin W., 22 N.Y.3d 287, 980 N.Y.S.2d 873, 3 N.E.3d 1121 (2013)—§ 1:39

People v. Key, 45 N.Y.2d 111, 408 N.Y.S.2d 16, 379 N.E.2d 1147 (1978)—§§ 2:7; 16:4; 16:5; 16:10; 16:27; 16:30; 16:31; 17:12; 17:13; 17:14; 17:15; 17:16; 23:49; 24:10; 24:12

People v. Key, 87 Misc. 2d 262, 391 N.Y.S.2d 781 (App. Term 1976)—§§ 2:7; 16:31; 17:14; 17:15; 17:16

People v. Khachiyan, 194 Misc. 2d 161, 752 N.Y.S.2d 243 (N.Y. City Crim. Ct. 2002)—§ 53:75

People v. Khalek, 91 N.Y.2d 838, 666 N.Y.S.2d 1020, 689 N.E.2d 914 (1997)—§ 23:24

People v. Khan, 291 A.D.2d 898, 737 N.Y.S.2d 738 (4th Dep't 2002)—§§ 11:63; 13:32; 13:35; 23:47; 23:68; 46:40

People v. Khan, 182 Misc. 2d 83, 697 N.Y.S.2d 457 (App. Term 1997)—§§ 2:3; 2:4

People v. Khan, 168 Misc. 2d 192, 638 N.Y.S.2d 858 (N.Y. City Crim. Ct. 1995)—§ 2:3

People v. Khuns, 191 Misc. 2d 655, 746 N.Y.S.2d 230 (J. Ct. 2001)—§ 11:27

People v. Kibbe, 35 N.Y.2d 407, 362 N.Y.S.2d 848, 321 N.E.2d 773 (1974)—§ 12:12

People v. King, 57 A.D.3d 1495, 869 N.Y.S.2d 832 (4th Dep't 2008)—§ 47:4

People v. King, 241 A.D.2d 329, 659 N.Y.S.2d 469 (1st Dep't 1997)—§§ 20:85; 20:97; 28:12; 28:14

People v. King, 79 A.D.2d 1033, 437 N.Y.S.2d 931 (2d Dep't 1981)—§§ 1:36; 26:34

People v. King Solomon, 113 Misc. 2d 790, 449 N.Y.S.2d 875 (Sup 1982)—§§ 9:5; 11:16; 24:21

People v. Kinnard, 62 N.Y.2d 910, 479 N.Y.S.2d 2, 467 N.E.2d 886 (1984)—§ 27:34

People v. Kinne, 71 N.Y.2d 879, 527 N.Y.S.2d 754, 522 N.E.2d 1052 (1988)—§§ 42:8; 43:8

People v. Kinney, 66 A.D.3d 1238, 888 N.Y.S.2d 260 (3d Dep't 2009)—§§ 24:18; 41:33

People v. Kirkey, 17 A.D.3d 1149, 793 N.Y.S.2d 856 (4th Dep't 2005)—§ 1:17

People v. Kirkland, 89 N.Y.2d 903, 653 N.Y.S.2d 256, 675 N.E.2d 1208 (1996)—§ 26:37

People v. Kirkland, 157 Misc. 2d 38, 595 N.Y.S.2d 905 (County Ct. 1993)—§§ 30:2; 30:3

People v. Kirkland, 188 A.D.2d 1083, 592 N.Y.S.2d 188 (4th Dep't 1992)—§ 22:13

People v. Kirksey, 186 Misc. 2d 514, 718 N.Y.S.2d 583 (N.Y. City Ct. 2000)—§ 13:5

People v. Klein, 105 A.D.2d 805, 481 N.Y.S.2d 743 (2d Dep't 1984)—§ 43:8

People v. Knack, 72 N.Y.2d 825, 530 N.Y.S.2d 541, 526 N.E.2d 32 (1988)—§§ 9:5; 11:16; 24:21

People v. Knapp, 272 A.D.2d 637, 706 N.Y.S.2d 531 (3d Dep't 2000)—§ 37:4

People v. Knapp, 113 A.D.2d 154, 495 N.Y.S.2d 985 (3d Dep't 1985)—§ 9:12

People v. Knapp, 57 N.Y.2d 161, 455 N.Y.S.2d 539, 441 N.E.2d 1057 (1982)—§ 1:39

People v. Knapp, 52 N.Y.2d 689, 439 N.Y.S.2d 871, 422 N.E.2d 531 (1981)—§ 4:1

People v. Knickerbocker, 136 A.D.2d 769, 523 N.Y.S.2d 227

People v. Kurtz, 129 Misc. 2d 1098, 495 N.Y.S.2d 608 (County Ct. 1985)—§ 23:59

People v. Kurtz, 92 A.D.2d 962, 460 N.Y.S.2d 642 (3d Dep't 1983)—§ 41:76

People v. Kurtz, 51 N.Y.2d 380, 434 N.Y.S.2d 200, 414 N.E.2d 699 (1980)—§§ 11:81; 23:26; 23:63

People v. Kyriazas, 2002 WL 31972172 (N.Y. Sup 2002)—§ 24:9

People v. La Borde, 66 A.D.2d 803, 410 N.Y.S.2d 886 (2d Dep't 1978)—§ 1:14

People v. Ladd, 89 N.Y.2d 893, 653 N.Y.S.2d 259, 675 N.E.2d 1211 (1996)—§§ 11:84; 38:31; 39:2

People v. Lafferty, 60 A.D.3d 1318, 875 N.Y.S.2d 395 (4th Dep't 2009)—§ 46:42

People v. LaFontaine, 92 N.Y.2d 470, 682 N.Y.S.2d 671, 705 N.E.2d 663 (1998)—§ 1:23

People v. LaFontaine, 163 Misc. 2d 83, 619 N.Y.S.2d 479 (Sup 1994)—§ 28:22

People v. Laing, 79 N.Y.2d 166, 581 N.Y.S.2d 149, 589 N.E.2d 372 (1992)—§§ 24:15; 26:3; 26:7; 26:42

People v. Lalka, 113 Misc. 2d 474, 449 N.Y.S.2d 579 (N.Y. City Ct. 1982)—§ 41:85

People v. La Mountain, 249 A.D.2d 584, 671 N.Y.S.2d 763 (3d Dep't 1998)—§ 28:17

People v. Lamour, 189 A.D.2d 825, 592 N.Y.S.2d 451 (2d Dep't 1993)—§ 22:13

People v. Lamphear, 35 A.D.2d 305, 316 N.Y.S.2d 113 (3d Dep't 1970)—§ 12:26

People v. Lanahan, 55 N.Y.2d 711, 447 N.Y.S.2d 139, 431 N.E.2d 624 (1981)—§ 27:28

People v. Lancaster, 260 A.D.2d 660, 688 N.Y.S.2d 711 (3d Dep't 1999)—§§ 9:3; 11:87; 46:42

People v. Lancaster, 69 N.Y.2d 20, 511 N.Y.S.2d 559, 503 N.E.2d 990 (1986)—§§ 9:21; 21:17

People v. Landy, 59 N.Y.2d 369, 465 N.Y.S.2d 857, 452 N.E.2d 1185 (1983)—§ 1:34

People v. Lane, 144 Misc. 2d 953, 550 N.Y.S.2d 529 (App. Term 1989)—§ 1:22

People v. Lane, 60 N.Y.2d 748, 469 N.Y.S.2d 663, 457 N.E.2d 769 (1983)—§ 15:70

People v. Lang, 30 Misc. 3d 1224(A), 926 N.Y.S.2d 346 (J. Ct. 2011)—§ 1:14

People v. Langhorn, 141 Misc. 2d 612, 533 N.Y.S.2d 820 (N.Y. City Crim. Ct. 1988)—§ 20:95

People v. La Parl, 276 A.D.2d 814, 718 N.Y.S.2d 889 (3d Dep't 2000)—§ 46:53

People v. Latham, 90 N.Y.2d 795, 666 N.Y.S.2d 557, 689 N.E.2d 527 (1997)—§ 25:9

People v. Latham, 83 N.Y.2d 233, 609 N.Y.S.2d 141, 631 N.E.2d 83 (1994)—§§ 23:4; 23:12; 23:28

People v. Latzen, 165 A.D.2d 913, 560 N.Y.S.2d 365 (3d Dep't 1990)—§ 46:53

People v. Laurino, 205 A.D.2d 556, 613 N.Y.S.2d 206 (2d Dep't 1994)—§§ 13:14; 46:45

People v. Lawrence, 222 A.D.2d 279, 635 N.Y.S.2d 223 (1st Dep't 1995)—§ 53:98

People v. Lawrence, 64 N.Y.2d 200, 485 N.Y.S.2d 233, 474 N.E.2d 593 (1984)—§§ 24:3; 24:7; 53:89; 53:90; 53:97

People v. Lawrence, 53 A.D.2d 705, 384 N.Y.S.2d 37 (3d Dep't 1976)—§§ 11:23; 17:17; 37:7

People v. Lawrence, 74 Misc. 2d 1019, 346 N.Y.S.2d 330 (Dist. Ct. 1973)—§ 20:17

People v. Lawson, 191 A.D.2d 514, 594 N.Y.S.2d 346 (2d Dep't 1993)—§ 11:23

People v. Layou, 71 A.D.3d 1382, 897 N.Y.S.2d 325 (4th Dep't 2010)—§ 1:14

People v. Lin, 46 Misc. 3d 20, 998 N.Y.S.2d 558 (App. Term 2014)—§ 42:20

People v. Lindsey, 13 A.D.3d 651, 787 N.Y.S.2d 385 (2d Dep't 2004)—§ 1:14

People v. Lindsly, 99 A.D.2d 99, 472 N.Y.S.2d 115 (2d Dep't 1984)—§ 23:60

People v. Lingle, 16 N.Y.3d 621, 926 N.Y.S.2d 4, 949 N.E.2d 952 (2011)—§ 23:41

People v. Liotta, 79 N.Y.2d 841, 580 N.Y.S.2d 184, 588 N.E.2d 82 (1992)—§§ 53:56; 53:87; 53:94

People v. Litarov, 188 Misc. 2d 234, 727 N.Y.S.2d 293 (N.Y. City Crim. Ct. 2001)—§§ 20:27; 41:80; 41:92

People v. Littlejohn, 184 A.D.2d 790, 585 N.Y.S.2d 495 (2d Dep't 1992)—§ 26:8

People v. Littles, 192 A.D.2d 314, 595 N.Y.S.2d 463 (1st Dep't 1993)—§ 28:6

People v. Litto, 8 N.Y.3d 692, 840 N.Y.S.2d 736, 872 N.E.2d 848 (2007)—§§ 10:29; 11:3; 11:6; 11:37; 11:38; 11:39; 12:2; 55:21

People v. Litto, 33 A.D.3d 625, 822 N.Y.S.2d 130 (2d Dep't 2006)—§§ 46:34; 55:23

People v. Livigni, 88 A.D.2d 386, 453 N.Y.S.2d 708 (2d Dep't 1982)—§§ 1:28; 1:29

People v. Livingston, 175 Misc. 2d 322, 668 N.Y.S.2d 443 (County Ct. 1997)—§§ 9:21; 21:17

People v. Lizaldo, 124 A.D.3d 432, 998 N.Y.S.2d 380 (1st Dep't 2015)—§§ 41:27; 41:76

People v. Lizzio, 178 A.D.2d 741, 577 N.Y.S.2d 178 (3d Dep't 1991)—§ 9:17

People v. Lloyd, 202 A.D.2d 1035, 610 N.Y.S.2d 111 (4th Dep't 1994)—§§ 53:53; 53:98

People v. Lloyd, 167 A.D.2d 856, 562 N.Y.S.2d 257 (4th Dep't 1990)—§ 13:54

People v. Lochan, 23 Misc. 3d 1106(A), 885 N.Y.S.2d 712 (N.Y. City Crim. Ct. 2009)— § 1:14

People v. Lomax, 50 N.Y.2d 351, 428 N.Y.S.2d 937, 406 N.E.2d 793 (1980)—§§ 53:41; 53:93

People v. Lopez, 16 N.Y.3d 375, 923 N.Y.S.2d 377, 947 N.E.2d 1155 (2011)—§ 27:43

People v. Lopez, 75 A.D.3d 610, 905 N.Y.S.2d 647 (2d Dep't 2010)—§ 1:14

People v. Lopez, 56 A.D.3d 280, 867 N.Y.S.2d 83 (1st Dep't 2008)—§§ 1:36; 26:34

People v. Lopez, 263 A.D.2d 434, 695 N.Y.S.2d 76 (1st Dep't 1999)—§ 1:36

People v. Lopez, 170 Misc. 2d 278, 648 N.Y.S.2d 231 (N.Y. City Crim. Ct. 1996)—§§ 16:19; 16:32

People v. Lopez, 84 N.Y.2d 425, 618 N.Y.S.2d 879, 643 N.E.2d 501 (1994)—§§ 20:13; 26:7; 26:15; 26:16; 26:17; 26:22; 26:37

People v. Lopez, 159 Misc. 2d 264, 603 N.Y.S.2d 948 (N.Y. City Crim. Ct. 1993)—§ 26:8

People v. Lopez, 144 Misc. 2d 325, 544 N.Y.S.2d 410 (Sup 1989)—§ 2:2

People v. Lopez, 71 N.Y.2d 662, 529 N.Y.S.2d 465, 525 N.E.2d 5 (1988)—§§ 9:5; 24:21

People v. Loria, 10 N.Y.2d 368, 223 N.Y.S.2d 462, 179 N.E.2d 478 (1961)—§§ 1:35; 41:35

People v. Loughlin, 76 N.Y.2d 804, 559 N.Y.S.2d 962, 559 N.E.2d 656 (1990)—§ 11:23

People v. Loughlin, 154 A.D.2d 552, 546 N.Y.S.2d 392 (2d Dep't 1989)—§ 41:89

People v. Louree, 8 N.Y.3d 541, 838 N.Y.S.2d 18, 869 N.E.2d 18 (2007)—§ 23:41

People v. Lourido, 70 N.Y.2d 428, 522 N.Y.S.2d 98, 516 N.E.2d 1212 (1987)—§ 25:7

487 N.Y.S.2d 548, 476 N.E.2d 993 (1985)—§ 27:39

People v. Mazzola, 12 Misc. 3d 1165(A), 819 N.Y.S.2d 212 (Dist. Ct. 2006)—§§ 1:14; 1:15

People v. McAleavey, 159 A.D.2d 646, 553 N.Y.S.2d 38 (2d Dep't 1990)—§§ 11:58; 27:8

People v. McAleavey, 133 Misc. 2d 987, 509 N.Y.S.2d 278 (County Ct. 1986)—§§ 22:3; 27:32

People v. McBride, 14 N.Y.3d 440, 902 N.Y.S.2d 830, 928 N.E.2d 1027 (2010)—§§ 4:1; 4:3

People v. McBride, 44 N.Y.2d 1001, 408 N.Y.S.2d 340, 380 N.E.2d 172 (1978)—§ 53:107

People v. McCarthy, 56 A.D.3d 904, 867 N.Y.S.2d 281 (3d Dep't 2008)—§ 46:42

People v. McCarthy, 135 A.D.2d 1113, 523 N.Y.S.2d 291 (4th Dep't 1987)—§ 1:28

People v. McCarthy, 14 N.Y.2d 206, 250 N.Y.S.2d 290, 199 N.E.2d 382 (1964)—§ 1:35

People v. McCaskell, 217 A.D.2d 527, 630 N.Y.S.2d 66 (1st Dep't 1995)—§§ 20:11; 26:19

People v. McClure, 26 A.D.3d 674, 809 N.Y.S.2d 299 (3d Dep't 2006)—§ 46:53

People v. McCombs, 18 A.D.3d 888, 795 N.Y.S.2d 108 (3d Dep't 2005)—§ 53:104

People v. McConnell, 11 Misc. 3d 57, 812 N.Y.S.2d 742 (App. Term 2006)—§§ 17:17; 37:7

People v. McDonagh, Slip Op.— § 38:10

People v. McDonald, 179 Misc. 2d 479, 689 N.Y.S.2d 600 (N.Y. City Crim. Ct. 1999)—§§ 16:22; 16:25

People v. McDonnell, 27 Misc. 3d 56, 901 N.Y.S.2d 451 (App. Term 2010)—§§ 3:2; 11:32

People v. McDonough, 132 A.D.2d 997, 518 N.Y.S.2d 524 (4th Dep't 1987)—§§ 37:2; 42:15

People v. McDonough, 39 A.D.2d 188, 333 N.Y.S.2d 128 (3d Dep't 1972)—§§ 11:78; 23:67

People v. McDowell, 28 N.Y.2d 373, 321 N.Y.S.2d 894, 270 N.E.2d 716 (1971)—§ 12:4

People v. McFadden, 20 N.Y.3d 260, 959 N.Y.S.2d 108, 982 N.E.2d 1241 (2012)—§§ 23:22; 23:34

People v. McFadden, 126 A.D.2d 970, 511 N.Y.S.2d 745 (4th Dep't 1987)—§ 26:19

People v. McGee, 68 N.Y.2d 328, 508 N.Y.S.2d 927, 501 N.E.2d 576 (1986)—§ 22:15

People v. McGettrick, 139 Misc. 2d 403, 528 N.Y.S.2d 758 (N.Y. City Ct. 1988)—§§ 16:23; 20:41; 20:50; 20:59; 20:62

People v. McGorman, 159 Misc. 2d 736, 606 N.Y.S.2d 566 (Sup 1993)—§§ 24:18; 41:33

People v. McGovern, 179 Misc. 2d 159, 683 N.Y.S.2d 822 (Dist. Ct. 1998)—§ 41:78

People v. McGrantham, 12 N.Y.3d 892, 885 N.Y.S.2d 244, 913 N.E.2d 936 (2009)—§§ 12:15; 12:26

People v. McGrath, 135 A.D.2d 60, 524 N.Y.S.2d 214 (2d Dep't 1988)—§§ 11:62; 31:9

People v. McGreal, 190 A.D.2d 869, 593 N.Y.S.2d 868 (2d Dep't 1993)—§§ 11:58; 27:8

People v. McIntosh, 96 N.Y.2d 521, 730 N.Y.S.2d 265, 755 N.E.2d 329 (2001)—§ 1:2

People v. McIntosh, 80 N.Y.2d 87, 587 N.Y.S.2d 568, 600 N.E.2d 199 (1992)—§ 53:54

People v. McIntosh, 163 A.D.2d 810, 558 N.Y.S.2d 342 (4th Dep't 1990)—§ 47:4

People v. McKay, 101 A.D.2d 960, 479 N.Y.S.2d 87 (3d Dep't 1984)—§ 20:29

People v. McKenna, 76 N.Y.2d 59, 556 N.Y.S.2d 514, 555 N.E.2d

11:3; 11:9; 11:30; 11:31; 11:47; 11:49; 16:31; 16:32; 17:16; 29:3; 31:7; 37:4; 37:5; 37:6; 37:8; 39:2; 42:3; 42:8; 42:11; 43:8; 43:15

People v. Mestey, 61 A.D.2d 447, 402 N.Y.S.2d 577 (1st Dep't 1978)—§ 1:14

People v. Mezon, 228 A.D.2d 621, 644 N.Y.S.2d 763 (2d Dep't 1996)—§ 1:27

People v. Mezon, 80 N.Y.2d 155, 589 N.Y.S.2d 838, 603 N.E.2d 943 (1992)—§§ 17:13; 24:10; 24:11; 53:89

People v. Michael, 48 N.Y.2d 1, 420 N.Y.S.2d 371, 394 N.E.2d 1134 (1979)—§§ 23:1; 23:6; 23:29; 23:32; 23:42

People v. Michael M, 161 A.D.2d 911, 557 N.Y.S.2d 177 (3d Dep't 1990)—§§ 15:69; 47:9

People v. Michaels, 174 Misc. 2d 982, 667 N.Y.S.2d 646 (N.Y. City Crim. Ct. 1997)—§ 13:4

People v. Michalek, 82 N.Y.2d 906, 609 N.Y.S.2d 172, 631 N.E.2d 114 (1994)—§ 22:13

People v. Michalek, 138 Misc. 2d 1, 521 N.Y.S.2d 609 (N.Y. City Crim. Ct. 1987)—§§ 16:40; 53:36

People v. Michalski, 15 A.D.3d 918, 788 N.Y.S.2d 776 (4th Dep't 2005)—§ 47:8

People v. Michel, 56 N.Y.2d 1014, 453 N.Y.S.2d 639, 439 N.E.2d 355 (1982)—§ 26:12

People v. Michtavy, 32 Misc. 3d 133(A), 936 N.Y.S.2d 60 (App. Term 2011)—§ 13:45

People v. Mickle, 187 Misc. 2d 718, 724 N.Y.S.2d 570 (Town Ct. 2001)—§§ 11:48; 24:16; 42:7

People v. Middleton, 54 N.Y.2d 474, 446 N.Y.S.2d 211, 430 N.E.2d 1264 (1981)—§ 27:49

People v. Middleton, 54 N.Y.2d 42, 444 N.Y.S.2d 581, 429 N.E.2d 100 (1981)—§§ 8:4; 10:8

People v. Miedema, 24 Misc. 3d 132(A), 899 N.Y.S.2d 62 (App. Term 2009)—§§ 2:9; 16:37; 25:12

People v. Milaski, 62 N.Y.2d 147, 476 N.Y.S.2d 104, 464 N.E.2d 472 (1984)—§ 1:25

People v. Miles, 82 A.D.3d 1010, 918 N.Y.S.2d 594 (2d Dep't 2011)—§ 1:2

People v. Miles, 3 Misc. 3d 566, 774 N.Y.S.2d 647 (N.Y. City Ct. 2003)—§ 13:55

People v. Miles, 64 N.Y.2d 731, 485 N.Y.S.2d 747, 475 N.E.2d 118 (1984)—§ 16:30

People v. Miley, 12/6/2002 NYLJ 30, col. 6 (Nassau Co. Ct. 2002)—§ 8:4

People v. Miller, 50 A.D.3d 1161, 855 N.Y.S.2d 379 (2d Dep't 2008)—§ 40:2

People v. Miller, 21 A.D.3d 1146, 800 N.Y.S.2d 782 (3d Dep't 2005)—§§ 27:6; 30:2

People v. Miller, 17 A.D.3d 708, 793 N.Y.S.2d 231 (3d Dep't 2005)—§§ 24:17; 38:4

People v. Miller, 196 Misc. 2d 591, 764 N.Y.S.2d 498 (J. Ct. 2003)—§ 3:5

People v. Miller, 217 A.D.2d 810, 630 N.Y.S.2d 99 (3d Dep't 1995)—§ 22:3

People v. Miller, 199 A.D.2d 692, 605 N.Y.S.2d 160 (3d Dep't 1993)—§§ 11:9; 11:23; 30:2; 43:19

People v. Miller, 194 A.D.2d 230, 607 N.Y.S.2d 507 (4th Dep't 1993)—§ 11:94

People v. Miller, 156 Misc. 2d 824, 594 N.Y.S.2d 978 (Sup 1993)—§ 20:91

People v. Miller, 163 A.D.2d 627, 558 N.Y.S.2d 269 (3d Dep't 1990)—§§ 11:35; 13:12; 23:11

People v. Miller, 162 A.D.2d 248, 556 N.Y.S.2d 607 (1st Dep't 1990)—§ 1:36

People v. Miller, 150 A.D.2d 910, 541 N.Y.S.2d 257 (3d Dep't 1989)—§ 43:5

People v. Miller, 149 A.D.2d 538, 539 N.Y.S.2d 809 (2d Dep't 1989)—§ 1:27

People v. Moore, 5 N.Y.3d 725, 800 N.Y.S.2d 49, 833 N.E.2d 192 (2005)—§ 16:30

People v. Moore, 196 Misc. 2d 340, 765 N.Y.S.2d 218 (J. Ct. 2003)—§ 3:5

People v. Moore, 196 Misc. 2d 120, 761 N.Y.S.2d 431 (App. Term 2002)—§ 2:3

People v. Moore, 186 Misc. 2d 614, 720 N.Y.S.2d 898 (Dist. Ct. 2000)—§§ 2:4; 24:20

People v. Moore, 178 Misc. 2d 163, 682 N.Y.S.2d 798 (County Ct. 1998)—§ 26:30

People v. Moore, 212 A.D.2d 1062, 623 N.Y.S.2d 42 (4th Dep't 1995)—§§ 9:19; 46:25

People v. Moore, 186 A.D.2d 591, 588 N.Y.S.2d 388 (2d Dep't 1992)—§§ 1:36; 1:37

People v. Moore, 66 N.Y.2d 1028, 499 N.Y.S.2d 393, 489 N.E.2d 1295 (1985)—§ 25:9

People v. Moore, 63 A.D.2d 602, 405 N.Y.S.2d 69 (1st Dep't 1978)—§ 53:15

People v. Moore, 32 N.Y.2d 67, 343 N.Y.S.2d 107, 295 N.E.2d 780 (1973)—§ 1:9

People v. Moquin, 77 N.Y.2d 449, 568 N.Y.S.2d 710, 570 N.E.2d 1059 (1991)—§ 23:27

People v. Mora-Hernandez, 77 A.D.3d 531, 909 N.Y.S.2d 435 (1st Dep't 2010)—§ 41:78

People v. Morales, 35 Misc. 3d 558, 939 N.Y.S.2d 824 (N.Y. City Crim. Ct. 2012)—§§ 2:9; 16:37; 25:12

People v. Morales, 273 A.D.2d 102, 709 N.Y.S.2d 544 (1st Dep't 2000)—§ 13:4

People v. Morales, 248 A.D.2d 731, 670 N.Y.S.2d 591 (2d Dep't 1998)—§ 26:27

People v. Morales, 161 Misc. 2d 128, 611 N.Y.S.2d 980 (N.Y. City Crim. Ct. 1994)—§§ 31:10; 31:12; 41:91

People v. Morales, 159 Misc. 2d 745, 610 N.Y.S.2d 720 (N.Y. City Crim. Ct. 1994)—§ 26:8

People v. Morales, 65 N.Y.2d 997, 494 N.Y.S.2d 95, 484 N.E.2d 124 (1985)—§ 27:4

People v. Morales, 42 N.Y.2d 129, 397 N.Y.S.2d 587, 366 N.E.2d 248 (1977)—§ 1:36

People v. Moreno, 70 N.Y.2d 403, 521 N.Y.S.2d 663, 516 N.E.2d 200 (1987)—§ 22:7

People v. Moretti, 142 Misc. 2d 331, 537 N.Y.S.2d 735 (N.Y. City Ct. 1988)—§§ 16:10; 16:28; 17:14

People v. Morgan, 30 Misc. 3d 52, 917 N.Y.S.2d 804 (App. Term 2010)—§ 53:68

People v. Morgan, 178 Misc. 2d 595, 682 N.Y.S.2d 533 (County Ct. 1998)—§ 20:35

People v. Morgan, 219 A.D.2d 759, 631 N.Y.S.2d 449 (3d Dep't 1995)—§ 13:50

People v. Morgan, 90 Misc. 2d 416, 395 N.Y.S.2d 363 (Sup 1977)—§ 23:49

People v. Morris, 8 Misc. 3d 360, 793 N.Y.S.2d 754 (N.Y. City Crim. Ct. 2005)—§§ 11:62; 31:1; 31:3; 31:7; 31:10; 41:24; 41:91

People v. Morris, 231 A.D.2d 911, 647 N.Y.S.2d 893 (4th Dep't 1996)—§§ 20:5; 28:17; 28:18

People v. Morris, 220 A.D.2d 808, 632 N.Y.S.2d 231 (3d Dep't 1995)—§ 52:3

People v. Morris, 61 N.Y.2d 290, 473 N.Y.S.2d 769, 461 N.E.2d 1256 (1984)—§ 23:18

People v. Morris, 86 A.D.2d 763, 448 N.Y.S.2d 82 (4th Dep't 1982)—§ 9:11

People v. Morris, 42 A.D.2d 968, 347 N.Y.S.2d 975 (2d Dep't 1973)—§ 43:12

People v. Morrisey, 21 A.D.3d 597, 799 N.Y.S.2d 642 (3d Dep't 2005)—§ 38:29

550 N.Y.S.2d 905 (2d Dep't
1990)—§ 28:4

People v. Nenni, 269 A.D.2d 785,
704 N.Y.S.2d 405 (4th Dep't
2000)—§ 1:4

People v. Nenni, 261 A.D.2d 900,
689 N.Y.S.2d 912 (4th Dep't
1999)—§ 1:36

People v. Nesbitt, 1 A.D.3d 889,
767 N.Y.S.2d 187 (4th Dep't
2003)—§ 1:4

People v. Nesbitt, 230 A.D.2d 755,
646 N.Y.S.2d 522 (2d Dep't
1996)—§§ 20:5; 28:17

People v. Nesci, 178 Misc. 2d 685,
683 N.Y.S.2d 375 (App. Term
1998)—§ 20:99

People v. Nester, 275 N.Y. 628, 11
N.E.2d 790 (1937)—§ 11:85

People v. Neu, 1 A.D.3d 798, 767
N.Y.S.2d 313 (3d Dep't
2003)—§ 47:32

People v. Newball, 76 N.Y.2d 587,
561 N.Y.S.2d 898, 563 N.E.2d
269 (1990)—§§ 26:3; 26:35;
26:37

People v. Ney, 191 Misc. 2d 185,
742 N.Y.S.2d 506 (N.Y. City
Ct. 2002)—§ 17:6

People v. Nicholson, 237 A.D.2d
973, 654 N.Y.S.2d 906 (4th
Dep't 1997)—§ 46:39

People v. Nicodemus, 247 A.D.2d
833, 669 N.Y.S.2d 98 (4th
Dep't 1998)—§ 1:14

People v. Niedzwiecki, 127 Misc.
2d 919, 487 N.Y.S.2d 694 (N.Y.
City Crim. Ct. 1985)—§§ 25:7;
41:24; 41:27

People v. Nieves, 143 Misc. 2d 734,
541 N.Y.S.2d 1008 (N.Y. City
Crim. Ct. 1989)—§§ 24:15; 32:1;
32:2; 32:3

People v. Nigohosian, 138 Misc. 2d
843, 525 N.Y.S.2d 556 (Dist.
Ct. 1988)—§§ 41:29; 41:78

People v. Nikollaj, 155 Misc. 2d
642, 589 N.Y.S.2d 1013 (Sup
1992)—§§ 20:87; 28:15

People v. Nimmons, 95 A.D.3d

1360, 945 N.Y.S.2d 358 (2d
Dep't 2012)—§ 12:4

People v. Nixon, 21 N.Y.2d 338,
287 N.Y.S.2d 659, 234 N.E.2d
687 (1967)—§§ 45:5; 46:54

People v. Noblett, 172 Misc. 2d
826, 660 N.Y.S.2d 517 (County
Ct. 1997)—§§ 16:10; 16:27;
16:28; 17:14; 24:12

People v. North, 96 Misc. 2d 637,
409 N.Y.S.2d 482 (Town Ct.
1978)—§§ 20:30; 34:3

People v. Norton, 135 A.D.2d 984,
522 N.Y.S.2d 958 (3d Dep't
1987)—§§ 11:58; 27:8

People v. Notey, 72 A.D.2d 279, 423
N.Y.S.2d 947 (2d Dep't
1980)—§ 46:56

People v. Novoa, 70 N.Y.2d 490,
522 N.Y.S.2d 504, 517 N.E.2d
219 (1987)—§§ 21:10; 28:3

People v. Nowakowski, 49 N.Y.2d
723, 426 N.Y.S.2d 261, 402
N.E.2d 1162 (1980)—§ 53:93

People v. Nuccio, 78 N.Y.2d 102,
571 N.Y.S.2d 693, 575 N.E.2d
111 (1991)—§§ 16:4; 16:5; 16:10;
16:26; 16:27; 17:4; 17:5; 17:10;
17:12; 17:13; 17:24; 23:49

People v. Nuchow, 164 Misc. 2d 24,
623 N.Y.S.2d 1006 (J. Ct.
1995)—§ 45:9

People v. Nunez, 119 A.D.3d 1373,
988 N.Y.S.2d 396 (4th Dep't
2014)—§ 48:6

People v. O'Bannard, N.Y.L.J.,
5/20/94—§ 9:4

People v. Obert, 1 A.D.3d 631, 766
N.Y.S.2d 264 (3d Dep't
2003)—§ 53:105

People v. Obieke, 186 Misc. 2d 708,
712 N.Y.S.2d 919 (Sup
2000)—§ 27:44

People v. O'Brien, 140 A.D.3d 1325,
32 N.Y.S.3d 741 (3d Dep't
2016)—§§ 20:51; 44:20

People v. O'Brien, 111 A.D.3d 1028,
975 N.Y.S.2d 219 (3d Dep't
2013)—§ 48:32

People v. O'Brien, 77 A.D.3d 1445,

796 N.Y.S.2d 512 (J. Ct. 2005)—§ 43:25

People v. Ortiz, 83 N.Y.2d 840, 611 N.Y.S.2d 500, 633 N.E.2d 1104 (1994)—§ 4:2

People v. Osborn, 193 Misc. 2d 173, 749 N.Y.S.2d 853 (County Ct. 2002)—§ 45:17

People v. Osborne, 60 A.D.3d 1310, 875 N.Y.S.2d 396 (4th Dep't 2009)—§§ 12:20; 13:10

People v. Osborne, 91 N.Y.2d 827, 666 N.Y.S.2d 556, 689 N.E.2d 526 (1997)—§ 20:83

People v. Osburn, 155 A.D.2d 926, 547 N.Y.S.2d 749 (4th Dep't 1989)—§§ 38:34; 44:15

People v. Osgood, 52 N.Y.2d 37, 436 N.Y.S.2d 213, 417 N.E.2d 507 (1980)—§ 53:41

People v. Osorio, 75 N.Y.2d 80, 550 N.Y.S.2d 612, 549 N.E.2d 1183 (1989)—§ 25:17

People v. O'Sullivan, 121 A.D.2d 658, 504 N.Y.S.2d 49 (2d Dep't 1986)—§§ 53:17; 53:38

People v. Otero, 51 A.D.3d 553, 858 N.Y.S.2d 157 (1st Dep't 2008)—§ 1:36

People v. Ottino, 178 Misc. 2d 416, 679 N.Y.S.2d 271 (County Ct. 1998)—§§ 7:8; 7:13; 7:14; 41:4

People v. Ottomanelli, 107 A.D.2d 212, 486 N.Y.S.2d 748 (2d Dep't 1985)—§ 11:20

People v. Outram, 22 Misc. 3d 131(A), 880 N.Y.S.2d 875 (App. Term 2009)—§ 13:49

People v. Owens, 209 A.D.2d 549, 619 N.Y.S.2d 620 (2d Dep't 1994)—§ 53:53

People v. Owens, 203 A.D.2d 106, 610 N.Y.S.2d 485 (1st Dep't 1994)—§ 22:8

People v. P., 21 N.Y.2d 1, 286 N.Y.S.2d 225, 233 N.E.2d 255 (1967)—§ 27:25

People v. Pabon, 167 Misc. 2d 214, 640 N.Y.S.2d 421 (N.Y. City Crim. Ct. 1995)—§ 13:21

People v. Pacer, 6 N.Y.3d 504, 814 N.Y.S.2d 575, 847 N.E.2d 1149 (2006)—§§ 13:3; 13:4; 13:10; 43:25

People v. Paddock, 29 N.Y.2d 504, 323 N.Y.S.2d 976, 272 N.E.2d 486 (1971)—§ 41:20

People v. Padilla, 21 N.Y.3d 268, 970 N.Y.S.2d 486, 992 N.E.2d 414 (2013)—§ 5:4

People v. Padro, 132 A.D.3d 485, 17 N.Y.S.3d 641 (1st Dep't 2015)—§ 14:51

People v. Pagan, 211 A.D.2d 532, 622 N.Y.S.2d 9 (1st Dep't 1995)—§§ 25:1; 25:3

People v. Pagan, 165 Misc. 2d 255, 629 N.Y.S.2d 656 (N.Y. City Crim. Ct. 1995)—§§ 24:18; 41:23; 41:27; 41:29; 41:33

People v. Pagan, 176 A.D.2d 472, 574 N.Y.S.2d 518 (1st Dep't 1991)—§ 46:45

People v. Page, 266 A.D.2d 733, 698 N.Y.S.2d 774 (3d Dep't 1999)—§ 2:3

People v. Palencia, 130 A.D.3d 1072, 15 N.Y.S.3d 89 (2d Dep't 2015)—§ 7:8

People v. Palmer, 137 A.D.2d 881, 524 N.Y.S.2d 564 (3d Dep't 1988)—§ 28:3

People v. Palmiere, 124 A.D.2d 1016, 508 N.Y.S.2d 775 (4th Dep't 1986)—§ 27:6

People v. Palumbo, 162 Misc. 2d 650, 618 N.Y.S.2d 197 (Sup 1994)—§ 20:15

People v. Panagulis, 49 Misc. 3d 1215(A), 28 N.Y.S.3d 650 (N.Y. City Crim. Ct. 2015)—§ 53:16

People v. Panek, 104 A.D.3d 1201, 960 N.Y.S.2d 801 (4th Dep't 2013)—§ 48:32

People v. Pannell, 287 A.D.2d 659, 731 N.Y.S.2d 750 (2d Dep't 2001)—§ 26:30

People v. Pantaleo, 141 Misc. 2d 251, 536 N.Y.S.2d 369 (N.Y. City Crim. Ct. 1988)—§§ 24:15; 24:16

People v. Percz, 100 Misc. 2d 1018, 420 N.Y.S.2d 477 (Dist. Ct. 1979)—§§ 10:5; 11:64

People v. Perez-Correoso, 48 Misc. 3d 839, 11 N.Y.S.3d 405 (N.Y. City Crim. Ct. 2015)—§ 5:8

People v. Perez, 27 Misc. 3d 880, 898 N.Y.S.2d 402 (Sup 2010)—§ 6:19

People v. Perez, 193 Misc. 2d 169, 749 N.Y.S.2d 850 (J. Ct. 2002)—§ 21:18

People v. Perez, 130 A.D.2d 779, 516 N.Y.S.2d 70 (2d Dep't 1987)—§ 42:11

People v. Perez, 65 N.Y.2d 154, 490 N.Y.S.2d 747, 480 N.E.2d 361 (1985)—§§ 20:97; 28:3; 28:14

People v. Perez, 73 A.D.2d 677, 423 N.Y.S.2d 220 (2d Dep't 1979)—§ 11:63

People v. Perrilla, 240 A.D.2d 313, 660 N.Y.S.2d 113 (1st Dep't 1997)—§ 1:36

People v. Perry, 87 N.Y.2d 353, 639 N.Y.S.2d 307, 662 N.E.2d 787 (1996)—§§ 17:1; 17:6

People v. Perry, 221 A.D.2d 736, 633 N.Y.S.2d 848 (3d Dep't 1995)—§ 22:3

People v. Persaud, 21 Misc. 3d 522, 863 N.Y.S.2d 533 (N.Y. City Crim. Ct. 2008)—§ 53:16

People v. Peryea, 68 A.D.3d 1144, 889 N.Y.S.2d 741 (3d Dep't 2009)—§ 12:20

People v. Pesantes, 10 Misc. 3d 676, 809 N.Y.S.2d 859 (N.Y. City Crim. Ct. 2005)—§§ 15:9; 15:10

People v. Peters, 188 A.D.2d 1037, 592 N.Y.S.2d 1004 (4th Dep't 1992)—§ 13:10

People v. Peters, 135 A.D.2d 841, 522 N.Y.S.2d 944 (2d Dep't 1987)—§ 20:26

People v. Peters, 43 A.D.2d 599, 348 N.Y.S.2d 786 (3d Dep't 1973)—§ 26:27

People v. Petersen, 4 N.Y.2d 992,

177 N.Y.S.2d 510, 152 N.E.2d 532 (1958)—§ 11:88

People v. Peterson, 266 A.D.2d 738, 698 N.Y.S.2d 777 (3d Dep't 1999)—§ 1:14

People v. Peterson, 151 A.D.2d 512, 542 N.Y.S.2d 301 (2d Dep't 1989)—§ 22:14

People v. Petro, 122 A.D.2d 309, 504 N.Y.S.2d 67 (3d Dep't 1986)—§§ 44:7; 44:11; 44:17

People v. Petterson, 103 A.D.2d 811, 477 N.Y.S.2d 691 (2d Dep't 1984)—§ 12:24

People v. Philbert, 110 Misc. 2d 1042, 443 N.Y.S.2d 354 (N.Y. City Crim. Ct. 1981)—§ 41:24

People v. Phillip, 279 A.D.2d 802, 718 N.Y.S.2d 727 (3d Dep't 2001)—§ 12:4

People v. Phillips, 4 A.D.3d 233, 771 N.Y.S.2d 658 (1st Dep't 2004)—§ 1:36

People v. Phillips, 183 A.D.2d 856, 584 N.Y.S.2d 83 (2d Dep't 1992)—§§ 20:13; 26:4; 26:12; 26:16; 26:22

People v. Phinney, 22 N.Y.2d 288, 292 N.Y.S.2d 632, 239 N.E.2d 515 (1968)—§§ 20:98; 27:7

People v. Phippen, 232 A.D.2d 790, 649 N.Y.S.2d 191 (3d Dep't 1996)—§ 12:12

People v. Phraner, 151 Misc. 2d 961, 574 N.Y.S.2d 147 (Dist. Ct. 1991)—§ 41:78

People v. Pickard, 180 Misc. 2d 942, 691 N.Y.S.2d 884 (Sup 1999)—§§ 24:17; 38:4

People v. Pierre, 157 Misc. 2d 812, 599 N.Y.S.2d 412 (N.Y. City Crim. Ct. 1993)—§ 13:47

People v. Pierre, 157 A.D.2d 750, 550 N.Y.S.2d 44 (2d Dep't 1990)—§ 43:4

People v. Pilewski, 173 Misc. 2d 800, 660 N.Y.S.2d 525 (J. Ct. 1997)—§§ 16:40; 17:23; 53:16; 53:36

People v. Pilotti, 127 A.D.2d 23,

People v. Prowse, 60 A.D.3d 703, 875 N.Y.S.2d 121 (2d Dep't 2009)—§ 10:4

People v. Prue, 2001 WL 1729710 (N.Y. County Ct. 2001)—§ 8:4

People v. Pugliese, 26 N.Y.2d 478, 311 N.Y.S.2d 851, 260 N.E.2d 499 (1970)—§ 27:25

People v. Purdue, 6 A.D.3d 1102, 775 N.Y.S.2d 632 (4th Dep't 2004)—§ 47:4

People v. Putsis, 217 A.D.2d 670, 630 N.Y.S.2d 86 (2d Dep't 1995)—§ 40:13

People v. Quarles, 168 Misc. 2d 638, 639 N.Y.S.2d 661 (N.Y. City Ct. 1996)—§§ 13:45; 16:10; 16:26; 16:28; 17:14

People v. Quezada, 24 Misc. 3d 515, 876 N.Y.S.2d 600 (Sup 2009)—§§ 31:7; 31:8

People v. Quinn, 153 Misc. 2d 139, 580 N.Y.S.2d 818 (Dist. Ct. 1991)—§§ 8:4; 10:8

People v. Quinn, 100 Misc. 2d 582, 419 N.Y.S.2d 811 (Police Ct. 1979)—§ 17:2

People v. Quinn, N.Y.L.J., 2/11/92—§ 10:8

People v. Quinones, 95 N.Y.2d 349, 717 N.Y.S.2d 86, 740 N.E.2d 231 (2000)—§§ 47:2; 47:8

People v. Quinones, 73 N.Y.2d 988, 540 N.Y.S.2d 993, 538 N.E.2d 345 (1989)—§§ 28:3; 28:7

People v. Quinones, 126 A.D.2d 757, 511 N.Y.S.2d 341 (2d Dep't 1987)—§ 53:39

People v. Quinto, 245 A.D.2d 121, 666 N.Y.S.2d 146 (1st Dep't 1997)—§ 26:20

People v. Radcliffe, 204 A.D.2d 1035, 612 N.Y.S.2d 534 (4th Dep't 1994)—§ 9:12

People v. Rafferty, 148 Misc. 2d 494, 560 N.Y.S.2d 741 (Dist. Ct. 1990)—§ 27:29

People v. Rahming, 26 N.Y.2d 411, 311 N.Y.S.2d 292, 259 N.E.2d 727 (1970)—§ 27:18

People v. Ramirez, 89 N.Y.2d 444, 654 N.Y.S.2d 998, 677 N.E.2d 722 (1996)—§ 23:47

People v. Ramirez, 208 A.D.2d 381, 617 N.Y.S.2d 13 (1st Dep't 1994)—§ 47:3

People v. Ramos, 13 N.Y.3d 914, 895 N.Y.S.2d 294, 922 N.E.2d 880 (2010)—§ 43:4

People v. Ramos, 99 N.Y.2d 27, 750 N.Y.S.2d 821, 780 N.E.2d 506 (2002)—§§ 27:3; 27:43; 45:5

People v. Ramos, 201 A.D.2d 78, 614 N.Y.S.2d 977 (1st Dep't 1994)—§§ 20:87; 28:15

People v. Ramos, N.Y.L.J., 1/29/90—§ 21:4

People v. Ramroop, 50 Misc. 3d 1090, 27 N.Y.S.3d 811 (N.Y. City Crim. Ct. 2016)—§§ 9:23; 11:76

People v. Ramrup, 51 Misc. 3d 393, 26 N.Y.S.3d 417 (Sup 2016)—§ 20:40

People v. Ramrup, 47 Misc. 3d 1223(A), 17 N.Y.S.3d 385 (Sup 2015)—§ 20:40

People v. Rance, 227 A.D.2d 936, 644 N.Y.S.2d 447 (4th Dep't 1996)—§ 1:16

People v. Randall, 135 A.D.2d 915, 522 N.Y.S.2d 314 (3d Dep't 1987)—§ 1:33

People v. Ranghelle, 69 N.Y.2d 56, 511 N.Y.S.2d 580, 503 N.E.2d 1011 (1986)—§§ 20:87; 20:97; 28:3; 28:5; 28:14; 28:15

People v. Rattelade, 226 A.D.2d 1107, 642 N.Y.S.2d 1 (4th Dep't 1996)—§ 9:4

People v. Ray, 65 N.Y.2d 282, 491 N.Y.S.2d 283, 480 N.E.2d 1065 (1985)—§ 27:23

People v. Rayford, 80 A.D.3d 780, 916 N.Y.S.2d 603 (2d Dep't 2011)—§ 13:4

People v. Reding, 167 A.D.2d 716, 564 N.Y.S.2d 489 (3d Dep't 1990)—§ 7:9

People v. Reed, 45 A.D.3d 1333,

People v. Rivera, 9 N.Y.3d 904, 843 N.Y.S.2d 532, 875 N.E.2d 24 (2007)—§ 26:41
People v. Rivera, 212 A.D.2d 1040, 623 N.Y.S.2d 445 (4th Dep't 1995)—§ 53:83
People v. Rivera, 210 A.D.2d 178, 620 N.Y.S.2d 365 (1st Dep't 1994)—§ 20:11
People v. Rivera, 173 A.D.2d 360, 570 N.Y.S.2d 5 (1st Dep't 1991)—§ 26:20
People v. Rivera, 119 A.D.2d 517, 501 N.Y.S.2d 38 (1st Dep't 1986)—§ 21:9
People v. Rivera, 60 N.Y.2d 110, 468 N.Y.S.2d 601, 456 N.E.2d 492 (1983)—§§ 23:10; 23:12
People v. Rivera, 57 N.Y.2d 453, 457 N.Y.S.2d 191, 443 N.E.2d 439 (1982)—§ 27:42
People v. Rivera, 58 A.D.2d 147, 396 N.Y.S.2d 26 (1st Dep't 1977)—§ 25:10
People v. Rivera, 26 N.Y.2d 304, 310 N.Y.S.2d 287, 258 N.E.2d 699 (1970)—§ 27:29
People v. Rivers, 184 Misc. 2d 101, 707 N.Y.S.2d 297 (County Ct. 1999)—§ 53:71
People v. Roach, 226 A.D.2d 55, 649 N.Y.S.2d 607 (4th Dep't 1996)—§§ 11:80; 23:72; 41:87; 45:3; 45:22
People v. Robbins, 223 A.D.2d 735, 637 N.Y.S.2d 208 (2d Dep't 1996)—§ 53:84
People v. Robbins, 132 Misc. 2d 653, 504 N.Y.S.2d 1006 (J. Ct. 1986)—§ 37:5
People v. Roberto H. (Anonymous), 67 A.D.2d 549, 416 N.Y.S.2d 305 (2d Dep't 1979)—§ 1:36
People v. Roberts, 203 A.D.2d 600, 611 N.Y.S.2d 214 (2d Dep't 1994)—§ 21:14
People v. Roberts, 81 A.D.2d 674, 441 N.Y.S.2d 408 (2d Dep't 1981)—§§ 1:36; 26:34
People v. Robertson, 149 A.D.2d 442, 539 N.Y.S.2d 785 (2d Dep't 1989)—§ 25:23
People v. Robillard, 2002 WL 377027 (N.Y. County Ct. 2002)—§ 13:11
People v. Robinson, 82 A.D.3d 1269, 920 N.Y.S.2d 162 (2d Dep't 2011)—§§ 30:3; 31:9; 31:10; 31:11; 31:12; 40:19; 41:91
People v. Robinson, 53 A.D.3d 63, 860 N.Y.S.2d 159 (2d Dep't 2008)—§§ 7:8; 11:47; 11:51; 20:40; 37:2; 42:3; 42:12; 42:16
People v. Robinson, 97 N.Y.2d 341, 741 N.Y.S.2d 147, 767 N.E.2d 638 (2001)—§§ 1:5; 1:18; 1:38; 5:4; 11:74
People v. Robinson, 171 A.D.2d 475, 567 N.Y.S.2d 401 (1st Dep't 1991)—§§ 53:75; 53:79
People v. Robinson, 74 N.Y.2d 773, 545 N.Y.S.2d 90, 543 N.E.2d 733 (1989)—§§ 1:28; 1:29
People v. Robinson, 133 A.D.2d 859, 520 N.Y.S.2d 415 (2d Dep't 1987)—§ 21:8
People v. Robles, 180 Misc. 2d 512, 691 N.Y.S.2d 697 (N.Y. City Crim. Ct. 1999)—§§ 24:18; 41:22; 41:24; 41:33
People v. Robles, 173 A.D.2d 337, 569 N.Y.S.2d 704 (1st Dep't 1991)—§ 12:4
People v. Robles, 72 N.Y.2d 689, 536 N.Y.S.2d 401, 533 N.E.2d 240 (1988)—§ 27:46
People v. Rocket, 156 Misc. 2d 641, 594 N.Y.S.2d 568 (J. Ct. 1992)—§§ 1:14; 5:5
People v. Rockwell, 137 A.D.3d 1586, 27 N.Y.S.3d 754 (4th Dep't 2016)—§§ 19:18; 46:41
People v. Rodgers, 205 Misc. 1106, 131 N.Y.S.2d 622 (County Ct. 1954)—§ 18:9
People v. Rodney, 85 N.Y.2d 289, 624 N.Y.S.2d 95, 648 N.E.2d 471 (1995)—§§ 20:12; 26:3; 26:23; 27:2; 27:29; 27:32
People v. Rodriguez, 16 N.Y.3d 341, 921 N.Y.S.2d 628, 946 N.E.2d 726 (2011)—§ 2:12

People v. Sierra, 126 A.D.3d 1513, 4 N.Y.S.3d 565 (4th Dep't 2015)—§ 48:32

People v. Sierra, 85 A.D.3d 1659, 925 N.Y.S.2d 749 (4th Dep't 2011)—§ 40:7

People v. Sigismundi, 89 N.Y.2d 587, 657 N.Y.S.2d 381, 679 N.E.2d 620 (1997)—§ 53:57

People v. Sikorski, 280 A.D.2d 414, 721 N.Y.S.2d 48 (1st Dep't 2001)—§§ 13:27; 43:20

People v. Silva, 122 A.D.2d 750, 506 N.Y.S.2d 55 (1st Dep't 1986)—§ 24:9

People v. Silvers, 195 Misc. 2d 739, 761 N.Y.S.2d 472 (N.Y. City Ct. 2003)—§§ 1:14; 1:15

People v. Simmons, 31 A.D.3d 1143, 817 N.Y.S.2d 817 (4th Dep't 2006)—§ 12:15

People v. Simmons, 173 A.D.2d 875, 571 N.Y.S.2d 80 (2d Dep't 1991)—§ 20:11

People v. Simmons, 58 A.D.2d 524, 395 N.Y.S.2d 188 (1st Dep't 1977)—§ 1:14

People v. Simone, 39 N.Y.2d 818, 385 N.Y.S.2d 765, 351 N.E.2d 432 (1976)—§ 1:14

People v. Singer, 44 N.Y.2d 241, 405 N.Y.S.2d 17, 376 N.E.2d 179 (1978)—§§ 27:46; 53:15; 53:66

People v. Singh, 12 Misc. 3d 952, 816 N.Y.S.2d 669 (Dist. Ct. 2006)—§ 27:29

People v. Singh, 144 Misc. 2d 402, 542 N.Y.S.2d 1018 (N.Y. City Crim. Ct. 1989)—§§ 24:15; 32:1; 32:2; 32:3

People v. Singleton, 42 N.Y.2d 466, 398 N.Y.S.2d 871, 368 N.E.2d 1237 (1977)—§§ 17:13; 24:10; 24:11; 53:89

People v. Sinistaj, 67 N.Y.2d 236, 501 N.Y.S.2d 793, 492 N.E.2d 1209 (1986)—§§ 53:23; 53:41

People v. Sinski, 88 N.Y.2d 487, 646 N.Y.S.2d 651, 669 N.E.2d 809 (1996)—§§ 44:4; 44:13; 44:17

People v. Sirianni, 109 Misc. 2d 781, 440 N.Y.S.2d 988 (County Ct. 1981)—§§ 9:5; 24:21

People v. Sirico, 135 A.D.3d 19, 18 N.Y.S.3d 430 (2d Dep't 2015)—§§ 19:18; 41:30; 46:41

People v. Sirkin, 146 Misc. 2d 1030, 553 N.Y.S.2d 593 (J. Ct. 1990)—§§ 16:27; 17:13; 24:10

People v. Sirno, 76 N.Y.2d 967, 563 N.Y.S.2d 730, 565 N.E.2d 479 (1990)—§ 27:32

People v. Skarczewski, 287 N.Y. 826, 41 N.E.2d 99 (1942)—§§ 13:35; 23:47; 46:40

People v. Skardinski, 24 A.D.3d 1207, 807 N.Y.S.2d 232 (4th Dep't 2005)—§§ 38:30; 38:34

People v. Skinner, 284 A.D.2d 906, 726 N.Y.S.2d 193 (4th Dep't 2001)—§ 4:9

People v. Skinner, 203 A.D.2d 891, 611 N.Y.S.2d 720 (4th Dep't 1994)—§ 38:30

People v. Slater, 166 A.D.2d 828, 562 N.Y.S.2d 985 (3d Dep't 1990)—§§ 38:14; 38:34

People v. Slaughter, 78 N.Y.2d 485, 577 N.Y.S.2d 206, 583 N.E.2d 919 (1991)—§ 45:5

People v. Sleasman, 24 A.D.3d 1041, 805 N.Y.S.2d 736 (3d Dep't 2005)—§ 12:4

People v. Slochowsky, 116 Misc. 2d 1069, 456 N.Y.S.2d 1018 (Sup 1982)—§ 20:99

People v. Slocum, 112 A.D.2d 641, 492 N.Y.S.2d 159 (3d Dep't 1985)—§ 12:24

People v. Slowe, 125 Misc. 2d 591, 479 N.Y.S.2d 962 (County Ct. 1984)—§ 20:15

People v. Smietana, 98 N.Y.2d 336, 746 N.Y.S.2d 678, 774 N.E.2d 743 (2002)—§§ 53:42; 53:62; 53:67

People v. Smith, 136 A.D.3d 1107, 25 N.Y.S.3d 395 (3d Dep't 2016)—§§ 11:87; 46:42

People v. Solomon, 160 Misc. 2d 945, 612 N.Y.S.2d 779 (Sup 1994)—§ 20:19

People v. Solomon, 124 Misc. 2d 33, 475 N.Y.S.2d 749 (Dist. Ct. 1984)—§§ 16:38; 16:40; 53:36

People v. Sorbello, 285 A.D.2d 88, 729 N.Y.S.2d 747 (2d Dep't 2001)—§§ 20:87; 28:15

People v. Sorbo, 170 Misc. 2d 390, 649 N.Y.S.2d 318 (Sup 1996)—§ 25:3

People v. Sorhaindo, 42 Misc. 3d 140(A), 986 N.Y.S.2d 867 (App. Term 2014)—§ 7:12

People v. Soto, 26 N.Y.3d 455, 23 N.Y.S.3d 632, 44 N.E.3d 930 (2015)—§ 2:15

People v. South, 29 Misc. 3d 92, 912 N.Y.S.2d 837 (App. Term 2010)—§ 16:30

People v. South, 41 N.Y.2d 451, 393 N.Y.S.2d 695, 362 N.E.2d 246 (1977)—§ 53:68

People v. Spann, 56 N.Y.2d 469, 452 N.Y.S.2d 869, 438 N.E.2d 402 (1982)—§ 23:18

People v. Sparber, 10 N.Y.3d 457, 859 N.Y.S.2d 582, 889 N.E.2d 459 (2008)—§ 23:41

People v. Specks, 77 A.D.2d 669, 430 N.Y.S.2d 157 (2d Dep't 1980)—§§ 1:36; 26:34

People v. Spencer, 289 A.D.2d 877, 736 N.Y.S.2d 428 (3d Dep't 2001)—§§ 2:6; 2:10; 7:16; 11:30; 16:31; 17:16

People v. Spencer, 84 N.Y.2d 749, 622 N.Y.S.2d 483, 646 N.E.2d 785 (1995)—§§ 1:5; 1:14; 1:16

People v. Spencer, 138 A.D.2d 976, 526 N.Y.S.2d 414 (4th Dep't 1988)—§§ 15:69; 47:9

People v. Sperber, N.Y.L.J., 3/23/89—§ 21:13

People v. Sperling, 165 Misc. 2d 1024, 631 N.Y.S.2d 221 (Dist. Ct. 1995)—§ 17:5

People v. Spicer, 105 A.D.2d 1100, 482 N.Y.S.2d 169 (4th Dep't 1984)—§ 1:14

People v. Spiegelman, 142 Misc. 2d 617, 537 N.Y.S.2d 964 (J. Ct. 1989)—§ 17:12

People v. Spinelli, 214 A.D.2d 135, 631 N.Y.S.2d 863 (2d Dep't 1995)—§ 25:8

People v. Spitaleri, 9 N.Y.2d 168, 212 N.Y.S.2d 53, 173 N.E.2d 35, 86 A.L.R.2d 322 (1961)—§ 25:9

People v. Spruill, 47 N.Y.2d 869, 419 N.Y.S.2d 69, 392 N.E.2d 1252 (1979)—§ 26:13

People v. Spurling, 199 A.D.2d 624, 604 N.Y.S.2d 997 (3d Dep't 1993)—§ 12:19

People v. Stack, 140 A.D.2d 389, 527 N.Y.S.2d 569 (2d Dep't 1988)—§§ 9:16; 11:20; 11:63

People v. Staley, 41 N.Y.2d 789, 396 N.Y.S.2d 339, 364 N.E.2d 1111 (1977)—§§ 53:15; 53:41; 53:66; 53:88

People v. Stanciu, 49 Misc. 3d 430, 11 N.Y.S.3d 836 (N.Y. City Crim. Ct. 2015)—§ 41:78

People v. Stanton, 241 A.D.2d 687, 660 N.Y.S.2d 169 (3d Dep't 1997)—§ 9:21

People v. Starowicz, 207 A.D.2d 994, 617 N.Y.S.2d 100 (4th Dep't 1994)—§§ 11:22; 11:42

People v. State, 233 A.D.2d 837, 649 N.Y.S.2d 624 (4th Dep't 1996)—§§ 24:17; 38:4; 38:32

People v. Stateikin, 163 Misc. 2d 517, 620 N.Y.S.2d 903 (N.Y. City Crim. Ct. 1994)—§ 53:37

People v. Steadman, 82 N.Y.2d 1, 603 N.Y.S.2d 382, 623 N.E.2d 509 (1993)—§§ 9:21; 21:10; 28:3

People v. Steel, 265 A.D.2d 586, 697 N.Y.S.2d 649 (2d Dep't 1999)—§ 38:30

People v. Steele, 172 Misc. 2d 860, 661 N.Y.S.2d 908 (App. Term 1997)—§§ 11:80; 23:72; 45:22

People v. Steg, 51 A.D.2d 810, 380 N.Y.S.2d 270 (2d Dep't 1976)—§ 1:14

1998)—§§ 17:4; 17:10; 17:13; 24:10

People v. Todd, 38 N.Y.2d 755, 381 N.Y.S.2d 50, 343 N.E.2d 767 (1975)—§§ 7:8; 11:47; 11:48; 29:3; 42:3; 42:7

People v. Todd, 79 Misc. 2d 630, 360 N.Y.S.2d 754 (County Ct. 1974)—§§ 11:48; 42:7

People v. Tolentino, 14 N.Y.3d 382, 900 N.Y.S.2d 708, 926 N.E.2d 1212 (2010)—§ 13:40

People v. Tomlin, 130 A.D.3d 1455, 12 N.Y.S.3d 740 (4th Dep't 2015)—§ 25:20

People v. Tompkins, 45 N.Y.2d 748, 408 N.Y.S.2d 485, 380 N.E.2d 311 (1978)—§ 27:50

People v. Tornatore, 125 Misc. 2d 400, 479 N.Y.S.2d 462 (Dist. Ct. 1984)—§ 3:2

People v. Torre, 48 Misc. 3d 745, 11 N.Y.S.3d 445 (Dist. Ct. 2015)—§ 20:40

People v. Torres, 125 A.D.3d 1481, 3 N.Y.S.3d 851 (4th Dep't 2015)—§ 2:12

People v. Torres, 88 N.Y.2d 928, 646 N.Y.S.2d 790, 669 N.E.2d 1112 (1996)—§ 53:57

People v. Torres, 190 A.D.2d 52, 597 N.Y.S.2d 492 (3d Dep't 1993)—§ 20:91

People v. Torres, 151 Misc. 2d 682, 573 N.Y.S.2d 255 (N.Y. City Crim. Ct. 1991)—§ 16:25

People v. Torres, 74 N.Y.2d 224, 544 N.Y.S.2d 796, 543 N.E.2d 61 (1989)—§ 1:41

People v. Torres, 125 Misc. 2d 78, 478 N.Y.S.2d 771 (N.Y. City Crim. Ct. 1984)—§§ 20:48; 33:1

People v. Torres, 60 N.Y.2d 119, 468 N.Y.S.2d 606, 456 N.E.2d 497 (1983)—§§ 53:53; 53:107

People v. Torres, 21 N.Y.2d 49, 286 N.Y.S.2d 264, 233 N.E.2d 282 (1967)—§ 27:28

People v. Torrey, 144 A.D.2d 865, 534 N.Y.S.2d 807 (3d Dep't 1988)—§§ 8:4; 20:17

People v. Totman, 208 A.D.2d 970, 617 N.Y.S.2d 234 (3d Dep't 1994)—§ 2:3

People v. Tousley, 86 Misc. 2d 1059, 383 N.Y.S.2d 996 (County Ct. 1976)—§ 13:37

People v. Toussaint, 40 A.D.3d 1017, 837 N.Y.S.2d 218 (2d Dep't 2007)—§ 12:24

People v. Towey, 52 Misc. 3d 471, 28 N.Y.S.3d 838 (Dist. Ct. 2016)—§ 16:18

People v. Tracey, 25 Misc. 3d 849, 885 N.Y.S.2d 559 (County Ct. 2009)—§ 11:6

People v. Tracey, 6 Misc. 2d 681, 167 N.Y.S.2d 320 (County Ct. 1957)—§ 3:5

People v. Trathen, 121 A.D.3d 1594, 993 N.Y.S.2d 426 (4th Dep't 2014)—§§ 11:87; 46:42

People v. Travis, 67 A.D.3d 1034, 890 N.Y.S.2d 552 (2d Dep't 2009)—§ 9:12

People v. Troiano, 35 N.Y.2d 476, 363 N.Y.S.2d 943, 323 N.E.2d 183 (1974)—§§ 1:11; 1:42

People v. Trotter, 54 A.D.3d 1065, 863 N.Y.S.2d 924 (2d Dep't 2008)—§ 1:36

People v. Trotter, 28 A.D.3d 165, 810 N.Y.S.2d 610 (4th Dep't 2006)—§ 5:8

People v. Tucker, 91 A.D.3d 1030, 936 N.Y.S.2d 386 (3d Dep't 2012)—§ 12:4

People v. Turck, 178 Misc. 2d 892, 681 N.Y.S.2d 454 (J. Ct. 1998)—§§ 16:23; 20:50; 20:59; 20:62

People v. Turkenich, 137 A.D.2d 363, 529 N.Y.S.2d 385 (2d Dep't 1988)—§ 25:1

People v. Turner, 47 Misc. 3d 100, 10 N.Y.S.3d 794 (App. Term 2015)—§ 7:8

People v. Turner, 234 A.D.2d 704, 651 N.Y.S.2d 655 (3d Dep't 1996)—§§ 6:18; 9:12; 31:7

People v. Turriago, 219 A.D.2d 383,

People v. Vedder, 43 Misc. 3d
1234(A), 993 N.Y.S.2d 645
(N.Y. City Ct. 2014)—§ 11:27

People v. Vega, 178 A.D.2d 1018,
578 N.Y.S.2d 342 (4th Dep't
1991)—§ 1:16

People v. Velez, 19 N.Y.3d 642, 951
N.Y.S.2d 461, 975 N.E.2d 907
(2012)—§ 23:41

People v. Velez, 168 A.D.2d 207,
562 N.Y.S.2d 91 (1st Dep't
1990)—§ 26:20

People v. Velez, 147 Misc. 2d 865,
556 N.Y.S.2d 818 (Sup
1990)—§ 20:36

People v. Velez, 118 A.D.2d 116,
504 N.Y.S.2d 404 (1st Dep't
1986)—§ 21:9

People v. Velit, 2002 WL 334690
(N.Y. City Crim. Ct. 2002)—
§ 5:4

People v. Ventimiglia, 52 N.Y.2d
350, 438 N.Y.S.2d 261, 420
N.E.2d 59 (1981)—§§ 20:6;
20:76; 22:2; 24:16

People v. Vera, 47 N.Y.2d 825, 418
N.Y.S.2d 575, 392 N.E.2d 562
(1979)—§ 23:10

People v. Verdile, 119 A.D.2d 891,
500 N.Y.S.2d 846 (3d Dep't
1986)—§ 38:34

People v. Vernace, 96 N.Y.2d 886,
730 N.Y.S.2d 778, 756 N.E.2d
66 (2001)—§ 53:66

People v. Victory, 166 Misc. 2d 549,
631 N.Y.S.2d 805 (N.Y. City
Crim. Ct. 1995)—§§ 31:7; 31:8;
31:12

People v. Vidaurrazaga, 100 A.D.3d
664, 953 N.Y.S.2d 290 (2d
Dep't 2012)—§ 48:6

People v. Vielman, 31 A.D.3d 674,
818 N.Y.S.2d 291 (2d Dep't
2006)—§ 25:21

People v. Vierno, 159 Misc. 2d 770,
606 N.Y.S.2d 557 (N.Y. City
Crim. Ct. 1993)—§ 16:4

People v. Vilardi, 76 N.Y.2d 67, 556
N.Y.S.2d 518, 555 N.E.2d 915
(1990)—§§ 20:4; 20:5; 21:2;
21:11; 21:15

People v. Vilardi, 150 A.D.2d 819,
542 N.Y.S.2d 238 (2d Dep't
1989)—§ 21:2

People v. Villani, 59 N.Y.2d 781,
464 N.Y.S.2d 726, 451 N.E.2d
473 (1983)—§ 20:60

People v. Villeneuve, 232 A.D.2d
892, 649 N.Y.S.2d 80 (3d Dep't
1996)—§§ 6:18; 10:8

People v. Vines, 51 A.D.3d 827, 859
N.Y.S.2d 661 (2d Dep't
2008)—§ 7:8

People v. Vinogradov, 294 A.D.2d
708, 742 N.Y.S.2d 698 (3d
Dep't 2002)—§§ 41:76; 41:78

People v. Vollick, 148 A.D.2d 950,
539 N.Y.S.2d 187 (4th Dep't
1989)—§ 9:4

People v. Vrlaku, 73 N.Y.2d 800,
537 N.Y.S.2d 24, 533 N.E.2d
1053 (1988)—§ 53:107

People v. W., 24 N.Y.2d 732, 302
N.Y.S.2d 260, 249 N.E.2d 882
(1969)—§ 27:10

People v. Wagner, 127 Misc. 2d
581, 486 N.Y.S.2d 610 (J. Ct.
1985)—§ 30:2

People v. Wahad, 204 A.D.2d 156,
612 N.Y.S.2d 14 (1st Dep't
1994)—§§ 20:87; 28:8; 28:15

People v. Waldron, 6 N.Y.3d 463,
814 N.Y.S.2d 70, 847 N.E.2d
367 (2006)—§ 53:56

People v. Walker, 20 N.Y.3d 122,
957 N.Y.S.2d 272, 980 N.E.2d
937 (2012)—§§ 1:44; 5:4; 20:46

People v. Walker, 21 Misc. 3d 748,
865 N.Y.S.2d 530 (N.Y. City
Crim. Ct. 2008)—§§ 2:9; 16:37;
25:12

People v. Walker, 83 N.Y.2d 455,
611 N.Y.S.2d 118, 633 N.E.2d
472 (1994)—§ 22:3

People v. Walker, 136 A.D.2d 949,
524 N.Y.S.2d 953 (4th Dep't
1988)—§ 53:83

People v. Wallace, 76 N.Y.2d 953,
563 N.Y.S.2d 722, 565 N.E.2d
471 (1990)—§§ 20:5; 28:16

People v. Wallace, 26 N.Y.2d 371,

People v. Weinberg, 146 Misc. 2d
441, 558 N.Y.S.2d 439 (App.
Term 1990)—§ 16:39

People v. Weinberg, 34 N.Y.2d 429,
358 N.Y.S.2d 357, 315 N.E.2d
434 (1974)—§§ 16:14; 16:16

People v. Weinert, 178 Misc. 2d
675, 683 N.Y.S.2d 690 (App.
Term 1998)—§§ 9:18; 11:40

People v. Wells, 21 N.Y.3d 716, 977
N.Y.S.2d 712, 999 N.E.2d 1157
(2013)—§ 1:44

People v. Wells, 53 A.D.3d 181, 862
N.Y.S.2d 20 (1st Dep't 2008)—
§§ 11:22; 12:18

People v. Wells, 7 N.Y.3d 51, 817
N.Y.S.2d 590, 850 N.E.2d 637
(2006)—§ 23:19

People v. Wells, 186 A.D.2d 867,
588 N.Y.S.2d 938 (3d Dep't
1992)—§ 11:94

People v. Wells, 133 A.D.2d 385,
519 N.Y.S.2d 553 (2d Dep't
1987)—§§ 20:11; 26:19

People v. Wemette, 285 A.D.2d
729, 728 N.Y.S.2d 805 (3d
Dep't 2001)—§ 46:53

People v. Wenceslao, 69 Misc. 2d
160, 329 N.Y.S.2d 391 (N.Y.
City Crim. Ct. 1972)—§ 12:23

People v. Wenstley, 152 A.D.2d
1000, 544 N.Y.S.2d 96 (4th
Dep't 1989)—§ 9:4

People v. Wenz, 12 Misc. 3d 134(A),
820 N.Y.S.2d 845 (App. Term
2006)—§ 11:98

People v. Werner, 55 A.D.2d 317,
390 N.Y.S.2d 711 (4th Dep't
1977)—§ 1:36

People v. Wernick, 89 N.Y.2d 111,
651 N.Y.S.2d 392, 674 N.E.2d
322 (1996)—§ 8:4

People v. Wesley, 83 N.Y.2d 417,
611 N.Y.S.2d 97, 633 N.E.2d
451 (1994)—§ 8:4

People v. Wesley, 73 N.Y.2d 351,
540 N.Y.S.2d 757, 538 N.E.2d
76 (1989)—§ 1:37

People v. West, 81 N.Y.2d 370, 599
N.Y.S.2d 484, 615 N.E.2d 968
(1993)—§ 45:5

People v. West, 80 A.D.2d 680, 436
N.Y.S.2d 424 (3d Dep't
1981)—§ 19:16

People v. Wheaton, 49 Misc. 3d
378, 17 N.Y.S.3d 586 (County
Ct. 2015)—§ 55:27

People v. Wheeler, N.Y.L.J.,
10/7/94—§ 43:16

People v. Whelan, 165 A.D.2d 313,
567 N.Y.S.2d 817 (2d Dep't
1991)—§§ 40:7; 40:14; 40:15;
41:23

People v. Whipple, 97 N.Y.2d 1,
734 N.Y.S.2d 549, 760 N.E.2d
337 (2001)—§§ 3:3; 11:32

People v. Whipple, 276 A.D.2d 827,
714 N.Y.S.2d 374 (3d Dep't
2000)—§§ 13:27; 13:50

People v. Whisby, 48 N.Y.2d 834,
424 N.Y.S.2d 344, 400 N.E.2d
286 (1979)—§ 53:21

People v. Whitaker, 79 A.D.2d 668,
433 N.Y.S.2d 849 (2d Dep't
1980)—§§ 1:36; 26:34

People v. White, 45 Misc. 3d 694,
990 N.Y.S.2d 403 (N.Y. City
Crim. Ct. 2014)—§ 20:40

People v. White, 10 N.Y.3d 286,
856 N.Y.S.2d 534, 886 N.E.2d
156 (2008)—§ 27:39

People v. White, 283 A.D.2d 964,
725 N.Y.S.2d 499 (4th Dep't
2001)—§ 12:4

People v. White, 229 A.D.2d 610,
645 N.Y.S.2d 562 (3d Dep't
1996)—§ 53:105

People v. White, 173 A.D.2d 897,
569 N.Y.S.2d 816 (3d Dep't
1991)—§ 11:94

People v. White, 73 N.Y.2d 468,
541 N.Y.S.2d 749, 539 N.E.2d
577 (1989)—§§ 26:3; 26:33;
26:35

People v. White, 133 Misc. 2d 386,
506 N.Y.S.2d 815 (Sup
1986)—§ 40:12

People v. White, 72 A.D.2d 913,
422 N.Y.S.2d 193 (4th Dep't
1979)—§§ 53:17; 53:38

People v. White, 40 N.Y.2d 797,

646 N.Y.S.2d 866 (2d Dep't 1996)—§§ 20:58; 20:99

Pittari v. Pirro, 258 A.D.2d 202, 696 N.Y.S.2d 167 (2d Dep't 1999)—§§ 20:58; 20:81; 20:86; 20:101; 28:10; 28:13

Plante, In re, 7 A.D.3d 98, 776 N.Y.S.2d 817 (2d Dep't 2004)—§ 13:19

Plantone v. State Dept. of State, Div. of Licensing Services, 251 A.D.2d 1049, 674 N.Y.S.2d 560 (4th Dep't 1998)—§ 51:7

Plumley v. Leuenberger, 131 Misc. 2d 543, 500 N.Y.S.2d 911 (Sup 1985)—§ 45:18

Plummer v. Rothwax, 63 N.Y.2d 243, 481 N.Y.S.2d 657, 471 N.E.2d 429 (1984)—§§ 23:29; 23:30

Polito v. Walsh, 8 N.Y.3d 683, 840 N.Y.S.2d 1, 871 N.E.2d 537 (2007)—§§ 23:8; 23:10

Posner, In re, 80 A.D.3d 238, 914 N.Y.S.2d 24 (1st Dep't 2010)—§ 51:14

Powell v. Wiman, 287 F.2d 275 (5th Cir. 1961)—§ 21:9

Powlowski, 172 Misc. 2d—§ 17:18

Pringle v. Wolfe, 88 N.Y.2d 426, 646 N.Y.S.2d 82, 668 N.E.2d 1376 (1996)—§§ 11:72; 15:27; 17:19; 45:1; 45:3; 45:4; 45:5; 45:8; 45:17; 45:18; 45:19; 45:21

Property Clerk, New York City Police Dept. v. Duck Jae Lee, 183 Misc. 2d 360, 702 N.Y.S.2d 792 (Sup 2000)—§ 9:23

Property Clerk of New York City Police Dept. v. Ferris, 77 N.Y.2d 428, 568 N.Y.S.2d 577, 570 N.E.2d 225 (1991)—§ 9:14

Property Clerk of Police Dept. of City of New York v. Harris, 9 N.Y.3d 237, 848 N.Y.S.2d 588, 878 N.E.2d 1004 (2007)—§§ 9:23; 11:76

Prudhomme v. Hults, 27 A.D.2d 234, 278 N.Y.S.2d 67 (3d Dep't 1967)—§§ 2:3; 2:4

Przybylowicz v. White, 115 A.D.2d

939, 496 N.Y.S.2d 832 (3d Dep't 1985)—§ 11:95

Pucino v. Tofany, 60 Misc. 2d 778, 304 N.Y.S.2d 81 (Sup 1969)—§ 41:24

Q

Quealy v. Passidomo, 124 A.D.2d 955, 508 N.Y.S.2d 706 (3d Dep't 1986)—§ 46:31

R

Rampolla v. Banking Dept. of State, 93 A.D.3d 526, 940 N.Y.S.2d 257 (1st Dep't 2012)—§ 51:5

Randall v. Rothwax, 78 N.Y.2d 494, 577 N.Y.S.2d 211, 583 N.E.2d 924 (1991)—§§ 23:6; 23:29

Redfield v. Melton, 57 A.D.2d 491, 395 N.Y.S.2d 725 (3d Dep't 1977)—§ 55:24

Reed v. New York State Dept. of Motor Vehicles, 59 A.D.2d 974, 399 N.Y.S.2d 332 (3d Dep't 1977)—§§ 41:27; 41:44

Rhode Island v. Innis, 446 U.S. 291, 100 S. Ct. 1682, 64 L. Ed. 2d 297 (1980)—§ 27:27

Richmond, 174 Misc. 2d—§ 5:3

Rivera v. Firetog, 11 N.Y.3d 501, 872 N.Y.S.2d 401, 900 N.E.2d 952 (2008)—§§ 23:17; 23:29

Robles, 180 Misc. 2d—§ 41:33

Robles v. LiMandri, 107 A.D.3d 592, 967 N.Y.S.2d 722 (1st Dep't 2013)—§ 51:5

Rocket, 156 Misc. 2d—§ 5:5

Rodney B., Matter of, 69 N.Y.2d 687, 512 N.Y.S.2d 17, 504 N.E.2d 384 (1986)—§ 28:7

Rodney J., Matter of, 83 N.Y.2d 503, 611 N.Y.S.2d 485, 633 N.E.2d 1089 (1994)—§§ 16:28; 16:30; 43:16

Romano v. Stanley, 90 N.Y.2d 444, 661 N.Y.S.2d 589, 684 N.E.2d 19 (1997)—§§ 8:4; 11:12; 11:21

Rosato v. New York State Dept. of

915, 573 N.Y.S.2d 456, 577 N.E.2d 1048 (1991)—§ 16:19

Shmaruk, In re, 29 A.D.3d 138, 812 N.Y.S.2d 623 (2d Dep't 2006)—§§ 9:26; 11:96

Sills v. New York State Div. of State Police, 248 A.D.2d 920, 669 N.Y.S.2d 990 (3d Dep't 1998)—§ 20:100

Simpson v. Wolansky, 38 N.Y.2d 391, 380 N.Y.S.2d 630, 343 N.E.2d 274 (1975)—§ 41:62

Skinner v. Railway Labor Executives' Ass'n, 489 U.S. 602, 109 S. Ct. 1402, 103 L. Ed. 2d 639, 4 I.E.R. Cas. (BNA) 224, 130 L.R.R.M. (BNA) 2857, 13 O.S.H. Cas. (BNA) 2065, 49 Empl. Prac. Dec. (CCH) ¶ 38791, 111 Lab. Cas. (CCH) ¶ 11001, 1989 O.S.H. Dec. (CCH) ¶ 28476 (1989)—§§ 1:36; 7:6; 7:11; 11:45; 11:56; 24:13; 41:4

Smith-Hunter v. Harvey, 95 N.Y.2d 191, 712 N.Y.S.2d 438, 734 N.E.2d 750 (2000)—§ 53:109

Smith, 170 Misc. 2d—§ 5:3

Smith, 139 Misc. 2d—§ 45:24

Smith v. County Court of Essex County, 224 A.D.2d 89, 649 N.Y.S.2d 507 (3d Dep't 1996)—§§ 11:80; 45:22

Smith v. State, 191 Misc. 2d 553, 742 N.Y.S.2d 792 (Ct. Cl. 2002)—§§ 31:7; 31:13

Smith v. Commissioner of Motor Vehicles, 103 A.D.2d 865, 478 N.Y.S.2d 103 (3d Dep't 1984)—§§ 7:14; 41:27; 41:36

Smith v. County Court of Essex County, 224 A.D.2d 89, 649 N.Y.S.2d 507 (3d Dep't 1996)—§§ 23:71; 23:72; 41:87

Smith v. Passidomo, 120 A.D.2d 599, 502 N.Y.S.2d 73 (2d Dep't 1986)—§§ 41:78; 41:79

Smith v. Passidomo, 125 Misc. 2d 942, 480 N.Y.S.2d 973 (Sup 1984)—§ 50:5

South Dakota v. Neville, 459 U.S. 553, 103 S. Ct. 916, 74 L. Ed. 2d 748 (1983)—§§ 11:46; 11:55; 11:57; 27:9; 41:18; 41:23; 41:62; 41:77; 41:88

Sovik v. State of N.Y. Dept. of Motor Vehicles, 143 Misc. 2d 941, 542 N.Y.S.2d 462 (Sup 1989)—§ 46:26

Sowa v. Looney, 23 N.Y.2d 329, 296 N.Y.S.2d 760, 244 N.E.2d 243 (1968)—§ 41:62

Spinelli v. U.S., 393 U.S. 410, 89 S. Ct. 584, 21 L. Ed. 2d 637 (1969)—§ 40:7

Springer v. Whalen, 68 A.D.2d 1011, 415 N.Y.S.2d 106 (3d Dep't 1979)—§ 51:7

Squadrito v. Griebsch, 1 N.Y.2d 471, 154 N.Y.S.2d 37, 136 N.E.2d 504 (1956)—§ 20:98

Stamos v. Appeals Bd. of New York State Dept. of Motor Vehicles, 309 A.D.2d 572, 765 N.Y.S.2d 342 (1st Dep't 2003)—§§ 17:22; 53:36

Standard Textile Co., Inc. v. National Equipment Rental, Ltd., 80 A.D.2d 911, 437 N.Y.S.2d 398 (2d Dep't 1981)—§ 43:8

Stark v. New York State Dept. of Motor Vehicles, 104 A.D.2d 194, 483 N.Y.S.2d 824 (3d Dep't 1984)—§ 4:5

State v. Chun, 194 N.J. 54, 943 A.2d 114 (2008)—§§ 29:7; 42:6; 42:7

State v. Doriguzzi, 334 N.J. Super. 530, 760 A.2d 336 (App. Div. 2000)—§ 8:4

State v. Hanks, 172 Vt. 93, 772 A.2d 1087 (2001)—§§ 29:2; 32:3

State v. Hardesty, 136 Idaho 707, 39 P.3d 647 (Ct. App. 2002)—§ 32:3

State v. Korsakov, 34 S.W.3d 534 (Tenn. Crim. App. 2000)—§ 42:15

State v. Schwalk, 430 N.W.2d 317 (N.D. 1988)—§ 38:12

State v. Stowers, 136 Or. App. 448, 902 P.2d 117 (1995)—§ 10:19

Index

CONVICTIONS—Cont'd
Forfeiture of motor vehicle, post-conviction, **9:13**
Higher level offense conviction mandates dismissal of lesser included offenses, **12:20**
Immigration consequences, **51:10**
Moral certainty conviction standard in circumstantial evidence cases, **11:94**
Moral certainty standard, VTL Section 1192 violations, **11:94**
Moral certainty standard in circumstantial evidence cases, **11:94**
Out of State Convictions, this index
Pistol permit denial after VTL Section 1192 convictions, **11:95**
Predicate conviction in felony DWI case, suppressing, **24:21**
Prior Convictions, this index
Sandoval issues, generally. Prior Convictions, this index
Suppression of evidence of predicate conviction in felony DWI case, **9:3, 24:21**
Twenty day orders, **49:5, 49:7**

COPIES
Authentication, **43:20**
Best evidence rule, **43:18-43:19**
Discovery documents, making copies and delivering to opposing party, **20:88**
Presentence investigation report, defendant entitled to copy, **46:46**

CORRECTION OFFICERS' PERSONAL RESIDENCE ADDRESSES
Discovery, protective order, **20:75**

CORROBORATION
Admission, **2:8, 25:11, 25:12**
Confessions, **2:8, 25:11, 25:12**
Informations, **25:12**
Misdemeanor informations, **25:12**
Operation, **2:8**
Operation admissions, **11:34**

COSTS
Fines, this index
Ignition interlock device, installation and maintenance, **48:8, 48:10**
Sanctions, this index
Surcharges, this index

COUNSEL
Attorneys, this index

COURT PERSONNEL
Defense attorney's interaction with, **18:6**

CRAWFORD V. WASHINGTON
Aggravated unlicensed operation, applicability to, **13:4**

CRIMES AND OFFENSES
Aggravated Unlicensed Operation, this index
Assault, this index
Driving While Ability Impaired, this index

DISCOVERY—Cont'd

MIRANDA WARNINGS—Cont'd

MISDEMEANOR COMPLAINTS

PROBATION—Cont'd
Driving while intoxicated—Cont'd
Drivers' licenses—Cont'd
Revocation, **9:1**
Periods, **46:57**
Ignition Interlock Device Program, this index
Jurisdiction over CPL Article 440 motion, **46:51**
Plea bargaining, **19:8**
Split sentences, **46:53**
Underage offenders, probationary license, **15:5, 15:6**
Warrantless search of probationer's home, **4:10**

PROOF
Aggravated Unlicensed Operation, this index
Burden of Proof, this index
Ignition interlock device program, Proof of compliance, **48:13**
Intent to move vehicle, **2:4**
Moral certainty standard in circumstantial evidence cases, **11:94**
Prior convictions, **9:4**
Supporting depositions, proof of service, **17:10, 17:19**

PROPERTY DAMAGE
Vehicular crimes, leaving the scene of accident without reporting, **12:23**

PROSECUTORS
Criteria for prosecution, **19:4**
Defense attorney's interaction with, Generally, **18:1**
Discovery, **18:3**
Exculpatory evidence. Discovery, this index
Fabrication of testimony charges by prosecution, **25:21**
Improper comments resulting in reversal, **44:20**
Information, accusatory instruments
Form and content, **16:12**
Waiver of right to be prosecuted by information, **16:16**
Plea bargaining
See also Plea Bargaining, this index
Off-the record agreements, **19:19**
Perspective of prosecutor, **19:3**
Public policy considerations, **19:9, 19:10**
Pre-sentence investigation report, honoring promise with respect to sentencing
recommendation, **46:43**
Rosario material, assistant district attorney's notes, **28:4**
Seal and Return, this index
Seizure and retention of vehicles involved in DWI felonies, **9:22**
Speedy trial, generally, **24:6-24:7**

PROTECTIVE ORDERS
Generally, **20:72**
Personal residence addresses of police and correction officers, **20:75**
Requiring exclusive possession in discovering party's attorney, **20:73**